Contemporary Authors

Contemporary Authors

A BIO-BIBLIOGRAPHICAL GUIDE TO
CURRENT AUTHORS AND THEIR WORKS

ANN EVORY

Editor

volumes **33-36**

first revision

GALE RESEARCH COMPANY • BOOK TOWER • DETROIT, MICHIGAN 48226

CONTEMPORARY AUTHORS

Published by
Gale Research Company, Book Tower, Detroit, Michigan 48226
Each Year's Volumes Are Revised About Five Years Later

Frederick G. Ruffner, *Publisher*   James M. Ethridge, *Editorial Director*

Christine Nasso, *General Editor, Contemporary Authors*

Ann Evory, *Editor*
Linda Metzger, *Associate Editor*
Peter M. Gareffa, Penelope S. Gordon, Victoria France Hutchinson,
Margaret Mazurkiewicz, Douglas A. Riley, Nancy M. Rusin,
and Catherine Stadelman, *Assistant Editors*
Ellen Koral, *Editorial Assistant*
Michaeline Nowinski, *Production Manager*

Preface

This volume represents a complete revision of bio-bibliographical material which originally appeared in *Contemporary Authors,* Volumes 33-36, published in 1973. The material is up-to-date, in most cases, through mid-1978.

Questions and Answers About Revised Volumes
of
Contemporary Authors

How much change is undertaken when past volumes of *Contemporary Authors* are revised? Every part of every sketch is changed, if necessary. Present production techniques provide for fast, economical typesetting of all material used in revised volumes, and no attempt is made to minimize changes.

About 80-85% of all sketches in revised volumes have one or more changes from the original volume. The nature and extent of the revisions can be seen by comparing the original listings for Heywood (Woody) Allen, Daniel Berrigan, Nathaniel Branden, Clayton Eshleman, Michael S. Harper, Edward Heath, Alger Hiss, June Jordan, Yousuf Karsh, Bil Keane, Lila Perl, Paul Theroux, and Joseph Wambaugh with the revised sketches in this volume.

How are revised volumes prepared? Clippings of previously published sketches are sent to authors at their last-known addresses. Authors mark material to be deleted or changed, and insert any new personal data, new affiliations, new books, new work in progress, new sidelights, and new biographical/critical sources. Gale makes great efforts to encourage responses from all authors, and has a toll-free telephone number so authors can conveniently reply by phone without personal expense.

How do you revise previously published sketches if the authors do not return marked clippings? First, every attempt is made to reach authors through previous home addresses, business affiliations, publishers, organizations, or other practicable means either by mail or telephone. When necessary, searches are made to determine whether the authors have died. A number of sources are checked for obituaries, including newspaper and magazine indexes.

If living authors fail to reply, or if authors are now deceased, work proceeds on verifying and updating the previously published information. Biographical dictionaries are checked (a task made easier through the use of Gale's *Biographical Dictionaries Master Index* and new *Author Biographies Master Index*), as are bibliographical sources, such as *Cumulative Book Index, The National Union Catalog,* etc. In other words, all steps are taken which can reasonably be expected to confirm or invalidate previous information, or to provide additional information. Sketches not personally verified by the authors are marked as follows:

> † Research has yielded new information which has been added to the sketch
> † † Research has yielded no new information

Do all sketches in a revised volume undergo some change? No, they do not. In a sense, however, *all* sketches in a revised volume are "revised" sketches, in that the authors have examined them and indicated that the information they furnished for the previous edition is currently correct, or a revision editor has checked as many facts as possible and made the same determination. Obviously, previously published information which is verified as still accurate is just as helpful to the reference user as information newly added.

How much revision takes place in an average volume? It is difficult to measure. Revised Volumes 1-4, for example, showed a net increase of about 70 pages, and Revised Volumes 5-8 an increase of

200 pages. These increases represented only the *net* change in the number of pages, however; they did not measure the total amount of change, since things like new addresses do not affect sketch length, and deletions of memberships or transfers of items from "Work in Progress" to the bibliography of published works usually result in decreases in space used.

Sketches of deceased and inactive authors have been removed from recent revision volumes and listed separately in the two volumes of *Contemporary Authors—Permanent Series*. Even with the substantial number of sketches which were transferred, however, recent revision volumes have been larger than the corresponding original volumes.

What is the rationale behind the *Permanent Series?* The purpose of the *Permanent Series* was to remove from the revision cycle entries for deceased authors and authors past normal retirement age who were presumed to be no longer actively writing. Since revised volumes of *Contemporary Authors* were consistently larger than original volumes, and since Gale knew that future revised volumes would continue to grow, it seemed reasonable to list separately in the *Permanent Series* those entries which would not require future revision. This procedure was both logical in itself and comparable to the practices of other biographical reference-book publishers. For example, sketches removed from *Who's Who in America* are published periodically in *Who Was Who in America*.

Will the *Permanent Series* be continued? No. Experience has proved that a cumulative series devoted entirely to authors cannot effectively be treated in the same way as a repetitive series devoted to noteworthy persons in general. The *Permanent Series* has, therefore, been discontinued with the publication of Volume 2. The two *Permanent Series* volumes are an integral part of the entire *Contemporary Authors* series and will be kept in print along with all other volumes in the series because they contain sketches of deceased and inactive authors drawn from volumes 9-36. In the future, all entries appearing in a given volume of *Contemporary Authors* will be retained in that volume when it is revised, whether the subjects of the sketches are active or inactive, living or dead.

Can any volumes of *Contemporary Authors* safely be discarded because they are obsolete? Users who have all the revised volumes published to date *and* the two *Permanent Series* volumes can discard the superseded volumes. Subsequently, all unrevised volumes may be discarded each time corresponding revised volumes are published.

An unusual number of biographical publications have been appearing recently, and the question is now often asked whether a charge is made for listings in such publications. Do authors listed in *Contemporary Authors* make any payment or incur any other obligation for their listings? Some publishers charge for listings or require purchase of a book by biographees. There is, however, absolutely no charge or obligation of any kind attached to being included in *CA*. Copies of the volumes in which their sketches appear are offered at courtesy discounts to persons listed, but less than five percent of the biographees purchase copies.

Cumulative Index Should Always Be Consulted

Since *CA* is a multi-volume series which does not repeat author entries from volume to volume, the cumulative index published in alternate new volumes of *CA* will continue to be the user's guide to the location of an individual author's listing. Authors not included in this revision will be indicated in the cumulative index as having appeared in specific original volumes of *CA* (for the benefit of those who do not hold *Permanent Series* volumes), *and* as having their finally revised sketches listed in a specific *Permanent Series* volume.

As always, suggestions from users concerning revision or any other aspect of *CA* will be welcomed.

CONTEMPORARY AUTHORS

† Research has yielded new information which has been added to the sketch, but the author has not personally verified the entry in this edition.

† † Research has yielded no new information, but the author has not personally verified the entry in this edition.

ABBAGNANO, Nicola   1901-

PERSONAL: Born July 15, 1901, in Salerno, Italy; son of Ulisse Abbagnano. *Education:* Attended University of Naples. *Home:* Via Morosini 22, 20135 Milan, Italy. *Office:* Faculty of Letters and Philosophy, University of Turin, Turin, Italy.

CAREER: University of Turin, Turin, Italy, member of Faculty of Letters and Philosophy, 1936-39, professor of history of philosophy, Faculty of Letters and Philosophy, 1939—. *Member:* Accademia Nazionale dei Lincei (Rome), Accademia delle Scienze (Turin).

WRITINGS: Le Sorgenti irrazionali del pensiero, Perrella, 1923; *Il Problema dell'arte,* Perrella, 1925; *Il Nuovo idealismo inglese ed americano,* Perrella, 1927; *La Filosofia di E. Meyerson e la logica dell'identita,* Perrella, 1929; *Guglielmo di Ockham,* Carabba, 1931; *La Nozione del tempo secondo Aristotele,* Carabba, 1933; *La Fisica nuova,* Guida, 1934; (translator, and author of introduction and commentary) Saint Augustine, *Confessioni,* Paravia, 1939, 2nd edition, 1945; *La Struttura dell'esistenza,* Paravia, 1939; *Bernardino Telesio,* Fratelli Bocca, 1941; *Introduzione all'esistenzialismo,* Bompiani, 1942, 7th edition, Il Sagiattore (Milan), 1971; *Storia della filosofia,* Unione Tipografico-Editrice Torinese, Volume I: *Filosofia antica e medievale,* 1946, Volume II: *Filosofia moderna fino a Kant,* 1948, Volume III: *Filosofia del XIX e XX Secolo,* 1950, 2nd edition of the three volumes, 1963; *Filosofia, religione, scienza,* Taylor, 1947, 3rd edition, 1967; *Esistenzialismo positivo: Due saggi,* Taylor, 1948 (selections appear in translation, see below); *Storia del pensiero scientifico,* Paravia, 1951; *Corso di pedagogia, anno 1951-52,* Faculty of Letters and Philosophy, University of Turin, 1952, and similarly titled volumes, *1952-53,* 1953, and, *1954-55,* 1955; *Possibilita e liberta* (includes articles reprinted from various journals and collections), Taylor, 1956 (selections appear in translation, see below); (with Aldo Visalberghi) *Linee di storia della pedagogia,* two volumes, Paravia, 1957-58; *Problemi di sociologia,* Taylor, 1959, 2nd edition, enlarged, 1967; *La Religione* (booklet), Cooperativa Libraria Universitaria Torinese, 1961; *Dizionario de filosofia,* Unione Tipografico-Editrice Torinese, 1961, revised and enlarged 2nd edition, 1971; *Scritti scelti* (selected works), edited by Giovanni De Crescenzo and Pietro Laveglia, [Salerno], 1967; *Per o contro l'uomo* (articles published between 1964-1967 in *La Stampa*),

Rizzoli, 1968; *Critical Existentialism* (contains selections from *Esistenzialismo positivo* and *Possibilita e liberta*), translated by Nino Langiulli, Doubleday-Anchor, 1969; *Fro il Futto e il Mille,* Rizzoli, 1973.

With others: *Il Problema della storia,* [Milan], 1944; *Fondamenti logici della scienza,* De Silva, 1947; *Saggi di critica delle scienze,* De Silva, 1950; *La Mia prospettiva filosofica,* Editrice Liviana, 1950; Mario dal Pra, editor, *Il Pensiero di John Dewey,* Fratelli Bocca, 1952; *Verita e storia: Un Dibattito sul metodo della storia della filosofia,* Arethusa, 1956; Cornelio Fabro, editor, *Studi Kierkegaardiani,* Morcelliana, 1957; *Studi sulla dialettica,* Taylor, 1958.

Editor: Giovanni Battista Vico, *La Scienza nuova, e opere scelte,* Unione Tipografico-Editrice Torinese, 1952, 2nd edition, 1976; (general editor, and editor with others of Volume I) *Storia delle scienze,* three volumes, Unione Tipografico-Editrice Torinese, 1962; *La Filosofia antica* (anthology), Laterza, 1963; *La Filosofia medievale* (anthology), Laterza, 1963; (and translator with Marian Abbagnano), John Locke, *Saggi Sull' intelletto umano,* Unione Tipografico Editrice Torinese, 1971.

Contributor of regular columns to *La Stampa* (newspaper). Editor of two quarterly journals, *Rivista di Filosofia* and *Quaderni de Sociologia.*

SIDELIGHTS: Nicola Abbagnano's major works have been translated into Spanish for publication in Buenos Aires or Barcelona.

BIOGRAPHICAL/CRITICAL SOURCES: Filosofia perenne e personalita filosofiche, Cedam, 1942; Giorgio Giannini, *L'Esistenzialismo positivo di Nicola Abbagnano,* Morcelliana, 1956; Antonio Santucci, *Esistenzialismo e filosofia italiana,* Il Mulino, 1959; Pietro Chiodi, *Il Pensiero esistenzialista,* Garzanti, 1960; Maria A. Simona, *La Notion de liberte dans l'existenzialisme positif de Nicola Abbagnano,* University of Fribourg, 1962; Sandro Travaglia, *La Nozione di possibilita nel pensiero di Nicola Abbagnano,* Cedam, 1969; Adriana Dentone, *La "Possibilita" in Nicola Abbagnano,* Marzurati, 1971; Antonio Quarta, *Esistenza, scienza societa, nella filosafia di Nicola Abbagnano,* Glaux, 1971.

*   *   *

ABBOTT, Martin   1922-1977

PERSONAL: Born August 14, 1922, in Seneca, S.C.; son of

Willis W. and Mae (Graham) Abbott; married first wife, Helen L., June 22, 1946; married second wife, Edithgene B. Sparks (a college teacher), January 16, 1971; children: (first marriage) Gary, Judith. *Education:* Presbyterian College, A.B., 1944; Emory University, M.A., 1948, Ph.D., 1954. *Politics:* Independent. *Religion:* Presbyterian. *Home:* 1679 Pine Valley Rd., Milledgeville, Ga. 31061.

CAREER: Delta State College, Cleveland, Miss., instructor in history, 1948-50; Oglethorpe College (now University), Atlanta, Ga., associate professor, 1952-56, professor of history, 1956-68; University of South Florida, Tampa, professor of history and chairman of department, 1968-69; Georgia College, Milledgeville, Callaway Professor of Southern History, 1969-72; Georgia Military College, Milledgeville, chairman of department of social studies, 1972-74. Fulbright lecturer, University of Mainz, 1960-61. *Military service:* U.S. Army, 1943. *Member:* Organization of American Historians, Southern Historical Association, Old Capital Historical Society. *Awards, honors:* American Philosophical Society research grant, 1972-73.

WRITINGS: The Freedman's Bureau in South Carolina, 1865-1872, University of North Carolina Press, 1967. Contributor of about thirty articles and more than one hundred reviews to journals and newspapers.

WORK IN PROGRESS: A history of southern Negroes during Reconstruction.†

(Died May 26, 1977)

*   *   *

ABBOTT, Richard H(enry)   1936-

PERSONAL: Born August 18, 1936, in Springfield, Ill.; son of Richard H. II and Anne (Marbold) Abbott; married Nancy Winfree (an artist), September 4, 1964 (divorced, 1974); married Marie LaLiberte Richmond (a sociologist), 1976; children: (first marriage) Robert Miller, Louisa Elizabeth. *Education:* Grinnell College, B.A., 1958; University of Missouri, M.A., 1959; University of Wisconsin, Ph.D., 1963. *Home:* 1070 Green Hills Dr., Ann Arbor, Mich. 48105. *Office:* Department of History, Eastern Michigan University, 1718 Whittier, Ypsilanti, Mich. 48197.

CAREER: Old Dominion University, Norfolk, Va., assistant professor of history, 1963-66; Eastern Michigan University, Ypsilanti, Mich., assistant professor, 1966-68, associate professor, 1968-73, professor of history, 1973—. Visiting professor, University of Iowa, 1970. *Member:* Organization of American Historians.

WRITINGS: Ohio's War Governors, Ohio State University Press, 1962; *Cobbler in Congress: Life of Henry Wilson, 1812-1875,* University Press of Kentucky, 1972; (contributor) James Mohr, editor *Radical Republicans in the North,* Johns Hopkins Press, 1976. Contributor of articles to *Civil War History, Agricultural History, Virginia Magazine of History and Biography,* and of book reviews to *Journal of American History, Journal of Southern History, Michigan History, Civil War History,* and *Journal of Negro History.*

WORK IN PROGRESS: Research on the Republican Party's political aims during Reconstruction, troop recruitment in the North during the Civil War, and Massachusetts politics during Reconstruction, 1865-74.

*   *   *

ABCARIAN, Richard   1929-

PERSONAL: Born January 29, 1929, in Reedley, Calif.; son

of Manoog and Annie (Hallaian) Abcarian; married Janet Lee Blodgett (a teacher), September 22, 1951; children: Jennifer, Robin, Sara, Peter. *Education:* Attended Fresno State College (now California State University, Fresno), 1947-49; University of California, Berkeley, B.A., 1952, M.A., 1955, Ph.D., 1961; University of San Fernando Valley College of Law, J.D., 1976. *Home:* 18030 Acre St., Northridge, Calif. 91325. *Office:* Department of English, California State University, Northridge, Calif. 91330.

CAREER: California State University, Northridge, assistant professor, 1959-64, associate professor, 1964-68, professor of English, 1968—. Senior Fulbright lecturer in American literature, College Litteraire, Universite de Pau, France, 1967-68. *Member:* National Council of Teachers of English, Philological Association of the Pacific Coast.

WRITINGS: (Editor) *Richard Wright's Native Son: A Critical Handbook,* Wadsworth, 1970; (editor) *Words in Flight: An Introduction to Poetry,* Wadsworth, 1972; (editor with Marvin Klotz) *Literature: The Human Experience,* St. Martin's, 1973; (editor with Klotz) *The Experience of Fiction,* St. Martin's, 1975. Contributor to literature journals.

WORK IN PROGRESS: Critical studies of Richard Wright.

*   *   *

ABEND, Norman A(nchel)   1931-

PERSONAL: Born November 20, 1931, in Boston, Mass.; son of Harry and Violet (Spitaler) Abend; married Sydney Rose, March 24, 1953; children: Aaron, Michael, David, Peter. *Education:* Georgia Institute of Technology, B.S.C.E., 1953; Yale Bureau of Highway Traffic, certificate, 1957; Cornell University, M.S., 1967; Boston University, graduate study, 1970—. *Politics:* Independent. *Religion:* Jewish. *Home and office:* 304 Concord Rd., Wayland, Mass. 01778.

CAREER: Partner, Planning Services Group, 1960-63; independent consultant, full time, 1963-66, part-time, 1966—; Boston University, Boston, Mass., assistant director of research, 1966—. President and director, North East Development Corp. Lecturer, Boston University Urban Affairs Program, Harvard University, 1965, 1966, and St. Anselm's College, 1965. Assistant project director, Boston Regional Survey; project director, Portland Area Comprehensive Transportation Study; co-director, Manchester Metropolitan Planning Study. Consultant to Central Merrimack Valley, Redwood Shores Traffic Analysis, Massachusetts Board of Regional Community Colleges, Massachusetts Department of Public Health, New Hampshire State Planning Project, Cape Cod Planning and Economic Development Commission, Haverhill Industrial Council, Greater Lowell Area Planning Commission, and Mississippi Governors Emergency Council. *Member:* American Society of Civil Engineers, Institute of Traffic Engineers.

WRITINGS: (With Melvin R. Levin) *University Impact on Housing Supply and Rental Levels in the City of Boston,* Urban Institute, 1970; (with Levin) *Bureaucrats in Collision: Intergovernmental Relations in Area Transportation Planning,* M.I.T. Press, 1971. Also contributor to *Transportation and Environment,* Shenkman Press, edited by Barbara Woods. Contributor to *Traffic Quarterly* and *Traffic Engineering.*

WORK IN PROGRESS: Two chapters on environment, one for an urban affairs primer, the other for a book on conservation.

ABRAMS, Peter D(avid) 1936-

PERSONAL: Born August 6, 1936, in Chicago, Ill.; son of Jack H. (a credit and collection clerk) and Beatrice (Greilsheim) Abrams; married Barbara Carole Abrams, December 26, 1965; children: Lizabeth Ann, Jason Lewis. *Education:* University of Chicago, B.A., 1957; DePaul University, M.A., 1960; Illinois Institute of Technology, Ph.D., 1963. *Home:* 116 Stoney Creek Rd., DeKalb, Ill. 60115. *Office:* Bureau of University Research, Northern Illinois University, DeKalb, Ill. 60115.

CAREER: Illinois Teachers College Chicago-North (now Northeastern Illinois University), Chicago, assistant professor of psychology and coordinator of research and development, 1962-65; Northern Illinois University, DeKalb, associate professor of education, 1966-69, professor of educational administration and services, and director of Bureau of University Research, 1969—. *Member:* Association of Educational Data Systems, DeKalb Planning Commision, Phi Delta Kappa.

WRITINGS: (With Walter Corvine) *Basic Data Processing,* Holt, 1966, 2nd edition, 1971; (with Corvine) *Teaching Basic Data Processing,* Holt, 1967.

WORK IN PROGRESS: Essentials of Data Processing.†

*   *   *

ABT, Lawrence Edwin 1915-

PERSONAL: Born January 5, 1915, in Canton, Ohio; son of Edwin I. (a businessman) and Edna S. (Goldstandt) Abt; married Virginia Ripner, June 17, 1947; children: Janet Ellen. *Education:* New York University, B.S., 1936, Ph.D., 1947; Columbia University, M.A., 1939. *Home:* 151 Rockland Ave., Larchmont, N.Y. 10538. *Office:* 147 East 50th St., New York, N.Y. 10022.

CAREER: Private practice of psychotherapy, Larchmont, N.Y. and New York, N.Y., 1939—. Consultant, Veterans Administration, 1949-64. *Military service:* U.S. Naval Reserve, 1942-46; became lieutenant commander. *Member:* American Psychological Association (fellow), American Orthopsychiatric Association (fellow), Sigma Xi.

*WRITINGS—*Editor: (With Leopold Bellak) *Projective Psychology: Clinical Approaches to the Total Personality,* Knopf, 1950; *Progress in Clinical Psychology,* Grune, Volumes I-III (with Daniel Brower), 1952-58, Volumes IV-IX (with B. F. Riess), 1960-70; (with S. L. Weissman) *Acting Out: Theoretical and Clinical Aspects,* Grune, 1965; (with Stanley Rosner) *The Creative Experience,* Grossman, 1970; (with Irving R. Stuart) *Children of Separation and Divorce,* Grossman, 1972; (with Stuart) *Interracial Marriage,* Grossman, 1973; (with Rosner) *Essays in Creativity,* North River Press, 1975; (with Rosner) *The Creative Expression,* North River Press, 1976.

AVOCATIONAL INTERESTS: Photography and sound recording.

*   *   *

ACHESON, Dean (Gooderham) 1893-1971

April 11, 1893—October 12, 1971; American lawyer, statesman, and author of books on U.S. domestic and foreign affairs. Obituaries: *New York Times,* October 13, 1971; *Washington Post,* October 13, 1971; *Newsweek,* October 25, 1971; *Time,* October 25, 1971; *Current Biography,* November, 1971; *National Review,* November 5, 1971. (See index for *CA* sketch)

ACKER, Duane Calvin 1931-

PERSONAL: Born March 13, 1931, in Atlantic, Iowa; son of Clayton and Ruth (Kimball) Acker; married Shirley Hansen, March 23, 1952; children: Diane, LuAnn. *Education:* Iowa State University, B.S., 1952, M.S., 1953; Oklahoma State University, Ph.D., 1957. *Religion:* Protestant. *Office:* President's Office, Kansas State University, 106 Anderson Hall, Manhattan, Kan. 66506.

CAREER: Oklahoma State University, Stillwater, instructor in animal husbandry, 1953-55; Iowa State University, Ames, instructor, 1955-56, assistant professor, 1956-58, associate professor of animal science, 1958-62; Kansas State University, Manhattan, associate dean of animal science and assistant director of agricultural experimental station, 1962-66; South Dakota State University, Brookings, dean of College of Agriculture and Biological Sciences and director of agricultural experimental station, 1966-74; University of Nebraska at Lincoln, vice-chancellor for agriculture and national resources, 1974-75; Kansas State University, president, 1975—. Member of International Conference on Agricultural Curriculums, Paris, 1970. Consultant to U.S. Agency for International Development, Argentina, 1961. Director, Northwestern National Bank of Sioux Falls, 1972-74, and Northwestern National Bank of Omaha, 1975. *Member:* National Association of State Universities and Land Grant Colleges (chairman of Division of Agriculture, 1970-71), American Association for the Advancement of Science, U.S. Deans of Agriculture (chairman, 1969-70), American Society of Animal Science, Sigma Xi, Gamma Sigma Delta, Alpha Zeta, Phi Kappa Phi.

WRITINGS: Animal Science Laboratory Manual, Iowa State University, 1958; *Animal Science and Industry,* Prentice-Hall, 1963, 2nd edition, 1971. Contributor to agriculture and education journals.

*   *   *

ACKERSON, Duane (Wright, Jr.) 1942-

PERSONAL: Born October 17, 1942, in New York, N.Y.; son of Duane Wright (a civil engineer) and Virginia Gale (Rabe) Ackerson; married Catherine McFarland, August 19, 1967; children: Elizabeth Margaret. *Education:* Attended George Washington University, 1960-63; University of Oregon, B.A., 1964, M.F.A., 1967. *Home:* 1272 Elm N.W., Salem, Ore. 97304. *Office:* Eaton Hall, Willamette University, Salem, Ore. 97301.

CAREER: Salem College, Winston-Salem, N.C., instructor in English, 1967-68; Idaho State University, Pocatello, instructor, 1968-71, assistant professor of English and director of creative writing department, 1971-74; Willamette University, Salem, Ore., writer-in-residence, 1976—. Arts administration internship, National Endowment for the Arts, 1975. Participant, Idaho Council of Teachers of English Poetry Workshops, 1968-69; coordinator, Poetry in the High Schools for Idaho, 1970-71. *Member:* Science Fiction Writers of America, Pacific Northwest College English Association (member of board of directors, 1971—). *Awards, honors:* Neuberger Award for playwriting, University of Oregon, 1965; National Endowment for the Arts, creative writing fellowship, 1974-75.

WRITINGS: (Editor) *A Prose Poem Anthology* (pamphlet), Dragonfly Press, 1970; (editor) *Recycle This Poem* (pamphlet), Dragonfly Press, 1970; *UA Flight to Chicago* (poetry pamphlet), Best Cellar Press, 1971; *Inventory* (poetry pamphlet), Hermes Free Press, 1971; *Poems about Hard Times* (pamphlet), Dragonfly Press, 1971; (with Russell Edson and

Michael Benedikt) *Works: Edson Benedikt Ackerson,* Dragonfly Press, 1972; *Old Movie House,* Dragonfly Press, 1972; *The Lost Refrigerator,* Dragonfly Press, 1974; (co-editor) *54 Prose Poems,* Best Cellar Press, 1974; *The Eggplant,* Confluence Press, 1977. Works anthologized in *Quixote's Northwest Poets,* edited by Jim Bertolino, Quixote Press, 1968, *Our Only Hope Is Humor: Some Public Poems,* Ashland Poetry Press, 1972, *The Land on the Tip of a Hair,* edited by Wang Hui Ming, Barre, 1972, *Hearse's Prose Poem Anthology* edited by E. V. Griffith, Hearse, 1972, *Poems One Line and Longer,* Grossman, 1973, *Year's Best Science Fiction, 1974,* Bobbs-Merrill, 1975, *Imperial Messages,* Avon, 1976, and *Future Pastimes,* Aurora, 1977. Also author of several plays including radio dramas. Contributor to *Northwest Review, Tennessee Poetry Journal, Transpacific, Colorado Quarterly, December, Lillabulero, Phylon, Pebble, Apple, The Seventies* and other publications. Assistant editor, *Northwest Review,* 1966-67; editor, *Dragonfly,* 1969—.

WORK IN PROGRESS: Selected Stones, prose poems.

AVOCATIONAL INTERESTS: Duane Ackerson told *CA* that he is "interested in: science fiction, musical comedy (would like to write one someday), movies, and drama."

*   *   *

ADAMS, A. John 1931-

PERSONAL: Born November 22, 1931, in Liverpool, England; son of Wilfrid and Francine (Bertrand) Adams; married Vibeke Dinsen, June 3, 1963. *Education:* Studied at Alliance Francaise in Paris, 1955, and University of Munich, 1956-57. *Home:* 1406 30th St. N.W., Washington, D.C. 20007. *Office:* John Adams Associates, Inc., 1825 K St. N.W., Washington, D.C. 20006.

CAREER: Daily Telegraph, London, England, reporter, 1952-56; Radio Free Europe, news executive in Munich, Germany, 1956-60, bureau chief in Bonn, Germany, 1960-62; American Broadcasting Co. News, New York City, writer, 1964; Columbia Broadcasting System News, New York City, writer, 1965-70; Investment Company Institute, Washington, D.C., associate director, public relations, 1970-71; director, Office of Public Affairs, U.S. Price Commission, 1972-73; John Adams Associates, Inc., Washington, D.C., president, 1973—. *Military service:* British Army, King's Shropshire Light Infantry, 1951-52; served in Korea; became second lieutenant. Territorial Army, 1956; became captain. *Member:* Overseas Press Club, Institute of Journalists, Writers Guild, English-Speaking Union, Georgetown Citizens Association.

WRITINGS: (With Joan Martin Burke) *Civil Rights: A Current Guide to the People, Organizations, and Events,* Bowker, 1970; (editor) *Energy Policy: Industry Perspectives,* Ballinger, 1975. Writer of television documentaries. Contributor to *Spectator* and other journals in Europe and United States.

WORK IN PROGRESS: Biography of Albert Szent-Gyoergyi, discoverer of Vitamin C.

*   *   *

ADAMS, Clinton 1918-

PERSONAL: Born December 11, 1918, in Glendale, Calif.; son of Merritt Cooley and Effie (Mackenzie) Adams; married Mary Elizabeth Atchison (a research editor), January 9, 1943; children: Michael Gerald. *Education:* University of California, Los Angeles, B.Ed., 1940, M.A., 1942. *Home:*

1917 Morningside Dr. N.E., Albuquerque, N.M. 87110. *Office:* University of New Mexico, Albuquerque, N.M. 87131.

CAREER: University of California, Los Angeles, instructor, 1946-48, assistant professor of art, 1948-54; University of Kentucky, Lexington, professor of art, head of department, and director of Art Gallery, 1954-57; University of Florida, Gainesville, professor of art and head of department, 1957-60; Tamarind Lithography Workshop, Los Angeles, Calif., associate director, 1960-61, program consultant, 1961—; University of New Mexico, Albuquerque, dean of College of Fine Arts, 1961-76, director of Tamarind Institute (formerly Tamarind Lithography Workshop, now a division of University of New Mexico), 1970—, associate provost and dean of Faculties, 1976—. Painter and lithographer; work is included in collections of Museum of Modern Art, Brooklyn Museum, Art Institute of Chicago, Pasadena Art Museum, Los Angeles County Art Museum, Dallas Museum of Fine Arts, and other museums; exhibitor in major shows around the country. Chairman of the board of directors, Santa Monica Municipal Art Gallery, 1953; member of board of directors, Santa Fe Opera, 1964-70. *Military service:* U.S. Army Air Forces, 1942-46; became warrant officer. *Member:* Mid-America College Art Association (president, 1972-73). *Awards, honors:* More than forty awards for paintings and lithographs in museum and gallery shows.

WRITINGS: Cubism: Its Impact on the United States, 1910-1930, University of New Mexico Art Museum, 1967; (with Garo Z. Antreasian) *The Tamarind Book of Lithography: Art and Techniques,* Abrams, 1971; *Fritz Scholder: Lithographs,* New York Graphic Society, 1975. Contributor to art journals. Editor, *Tamarind Technical Papers,* 1974—.

BIOGRAPHICAL/CRITICAL SOURCES: Wilhelm Weber, *History of Lithography,* McGraw, 1966; Emil Weddige, *Lithography,* International Textbook, 1966; *Tamarind: Homage to Lithography,* Museum of Modern Art, 1969.

*   *   *

ADAMS, Don(ald Kendrick) 1925-

PERSONAL: Born February 21, 1925, in North Berwick, Me.; son of Howard Franklin and Amy (Welsh) Adams; married Janet Cabe, June 1, 1960; children: Lance Howard, Amy Louise. *Education:* University of New Hampshire, B.S., 1949; University of Connecticut, M.A., 1954, Ph.D., 1956. *Home:* 1106 Gilchrest Dr., Pittsburgh, Pa. 15235. *Office:* School of Education, University of Pittsburgh, Pittsburgh, Pa. 15213.

CAREER: Norwich Free Academy, Norwich, Conn., teacher, 1948-51; University of Massachusetts, Amherst, assistant professor of comparative education, 1956-57; U.S. State Department, educational consultant in Seoul, Korea, 1957-58; George Peabody College for Teachers, Nashville, Tenn., associate professor of education, 1958-61; Syracuse University, Syracuse, N.Y., professor of comparative education and chairman of cultural foundations department, 1961-69; University of Pittsburgh, Pittsburgh, Pa., professor of education and economic and social development, 1969—, chairman of International and Development Education Program. Scholar-in-residence, East-West Center, University of Hawaii, 1965-66. Consultant to United Nations, U.S. Office of Education, Peace Corps, David McKay Co., Inc. (publisher), and other organizations. *Military service:* U.S. Army Air Forces, 1943-45, U.S. Air Force, 1951-55; became first lieutenant.

MEMBER: International Society for Educational Planners (president, 1972-73), International Studies Association (council member), Comparative Education Society (president, 1965-66; member of board of directors, 1966-69), National Education Association, Society for International Development, John Dewey Society, National Society for the Study of Education, Phi Delta Kappa.

WRITINGS: (With I. N. Thut) *Educational Patterns in Contemporary Society,* McGraw, 1964; (editor) *Educational Planning,* Center for Development Education, Syracuse University, 1964; *Higher Educational Reforms in the Republic of Korea,* U.S. Office of Education, 1965; (editor) *Introduction to Education: A Comparative Analysis,* Wadsworth, 1966; (with Robert M. Bjork) *Education in Developing Areas,* McKay, 1969; *Education and Modernization in Asia: A Systems Analysis,* Addison-Wesley, 1970; (editor) *Education and National Development,* Routledge & Kegan Paul, 1971; *Schooling and Social Change in Modern America,* McKay, 1972. Editor, "Planning, Policy and Theory in Education" series, McKay. Contributor of over forty articles to American and foreign professional journals.

WORK IN PROGRESS: Educational Planning and Policy Making, for McKay.

* * *

ADAMS, John F(estus)   1930-

PERSONAL: Born June 30, 1930, in Zillah, Wash.; son of L. Spencer and Pearl (Utter) Adams; married Emily Stanton, January 2, 1965; children: Erika Barkley, Cora Stephanie. *Education:* University of Washington, Seattle, B.A., 1952, M.A., 1957, Ph.D., 1960. *Home address:* Route 1, Box 171, Colfax, Wash. 99111. *Agent:* Curtis Brown Ltd., 575 Madison Ave., New York, N.Y. 10022. *Office:* Department of English, Washington State University, Pullman, Wash. 99163.

CAREER: University of Washington, Seattle, acting instructor in English, 1959-60; University of Denver, Denver, Colo., assistant professor, 1960-64, associate professor of English, 1964-65; University of California, Irvine, associate professor of English, 1965-69; Washington State University, Pullman, professor of English, 1969—. *Military service:* U.S. Army, Transportation Corps, 1952-54; became captain. *Member:* Modern Language Association of America, Rocky Mountain Modern Language Association.

WRITINGS: Two Plus Two Equals Minus Seven, Macmillan, 1969; *An Essay on Brewing, Vintage and Distillation together with Selected Remedies for Hangover Melancholia; or, How to Make Booze,* Doubleday, 1970; *Beekeeping: The Gentle Craft,* Doubleday, 1972; (self-illustrated) *Backyard Poultry Raising: The Chicken Growing, Egg Laying, Feather Plucking, Incubating, Caponizing, Finger Licking Handbook,* Doubleday, 1977. Contributor to literature journals and to *Field and Stream.*

WORK IN PROGRESS: Research and field work on Western history, early mining towns, and western bad men.

* * *

ADAMS, Michael (Evelyn)   1920-

PERSONAL: Born May 31, 1920, in Addis Ababa, Ethiopia; son of Reginald (a banker) and Florence (Spenser) Adams; married Celia Pridham, July 23, 1957; children: Rosalind, David, Paul. *Education:* Oxford University, M.A., 1947. *Home:* Brook House, High St., Westerham, Kent, England. *Office: Middle East International,* 21 Collingham Rd., London SW5 ONU, England.

CAREER: British Broadcasting Corp. (BBC), scriptwriter on European service, 1948-53; *Guardian,* London, England, Middle East correspondent, 1956-62; Council for the Advancement of Arab-British Understanding, London, director of information, 1968—; *Middle East International,* London, editor, 1971—. *Military service:* Royal Air Force, 1939-45. *Awards, honors:* Harkness fellow in the United States, 1954-55.

WRITINGS: Suez and After: Year of Crisis, Beacon Press, 1958; *Umbria,* Faber, 1964; *Voluntary Service Overseas: The Story of the First Ten Years,* Faber, 1968; *Chaos or Rebirth: The Arab Outlook,* BBC Publications, 1968, International Publications Service, 1970; (editor) *Middle East: A Handbook,* Praeger, 1971 (published in England as *Handbook to the Middle East,* Anthony Blond, 1971; (with Christopher Mayhew), *Publish It Not ... The Middle East Cover-Up,* Longman, 1975. Also author of a number of historical documentaries for BBC television. Editor, *Middle East International,* 1971—.

BIOGRAPHICAL/CRITICAL SOURCES: Spectator, April 19, 1968.

* * *

ADAMS, Terrence Dean   1935-

PERSONAL: Born June 5, 1935, in Milwaukee, Wis.; son of Dean C. and Kathleen Adams; married Janete Perinovic, June 29, 1957; children: Beth Ann, Teri Lynn. *Education:* Carroll College, Waukesha, Wis., B.S., 1966; Marquette University, M.A., 1968. *Home:* 2420 South 88th St., West Allis, Wis. 53227. *Office:* Milwaukee Area Technical College, 1015 North Sixth St., Milwaukee, Wis. 53203.

CAREER: U.S. Air Force, 1957-62; Milwaukee Area Technical College, Milwaukee, Wis., associate dean, 1968—, and director of TV College program. *Member:* American Association of University Professors, Pi Kappa Delta.

WRITINGS: Problem Solving Discussion: A Practitioner's Handbook, McCutchan, 1970. Also author of *Dial-a-Motion: Introduction to Parliamentary Procedure,* Milwaukee Area Technical College Press. Contributor to *Wisconsin Business News, National Engineer,* and *Industrial and Educational Television.*

* * *

ADDINGTON, Larry H(olbrook)   1932-

PERSONAL: Born November 16, 1932, in Charlotte, N.C.; son of Laurence Eugene (a banker) and Gertrude (Willson) Addington; married Amanda Adams, June 29, 1963; children: Catherine. *Education:* University of North Carolina at Chapel Hill, B.A., 1955, M.A., 1956; Duke University, Ph.D., 1962. *Religion:* Methodist. *Home:* 1341 New Castle St., Charleston, S.C. 29407. *Office:* Department of History, The Citadel, Charleston, S.C. 29407.

CAREER: San Jose State College (now University), San Jose, Calif., assistant professor of history, 1962-64; The Citadel, Charleston, S.C., assistant professor, 1964-66, associate professor, 1966-70, professor of history, 1970—. Visiting professor, Duke University, 1976-77. Historical consultant to U.S. Army Institute of Advanced Studies, Operations Research, Inc., 1968-69. *Military service:* U.S. Air Force, 1956-59; became lieutenant. U.S. Air Force Reserve, 1959-68; became captain. *Member:* American Historical Association, American Association of University Professors, American Military Institute, Association of the United States Army, Phi Beta Kappa. *Awards, honors:*

Moncado Award, American Military Institute, 1967, for best article in *Military Affairs;* Outstanding Service Award, Operations Research, Inc., 1969.

WRITINGS: From Moltke to Hitler: The Evolution of German Military Doctrine, 1865-1939 (booklet), The Citadel, 1966; (editor) *Firepower and Maneuver: Selected Historical Studies,* Institute of Advanced Studies, U.S. Army, 1969; *The Blitzkrieg Era and the German General Staff: 1865-1941,* Rutgers University Press, 1971. Contributor to *World Book Encyclopedia* and military journals.

WORK IN PROGRESS: U.S. Coast Artillery: A History; History of Modern Warfare, a textbook.

* * *

ADELMAN, Gary 1935-

PERSONAL: Born July 1, 1935, in Brooklyn, N.Y.; son of Malcolm George (a businessman) and Estelle (Storch) Adelman; married Jane Saltzman; married second wife, Bette Orovan Josefsberg (an assistant in English), August 17, 1965; children: (stepchildren) Katherine, John, Carrie, James, Madeline. *Education:* University of Michigan, B.A., 1957; Columbia University, M.A., 1958, Ph.D., 1962. *Politics:* New Left. *Home:* 910 West White, Champaign, Ill. 61820. *Office:* Department of English, University of Illinois, Urbana, Ill. 61801.

CAREER: Brooklyn College of the City University of New York, Brooklyn, N.Y., instructor in English, 1959-63; University of Illinois at Urbana-Champaign, assistant professor, 1963-70, associate professor of English, 1970—.

WRITINGS: Political Poems, Midwest Monographs, Depot Press, 1968; *Honey Out of Stone* (novel in poetry and prose), Doubleday, 1970. Contributor to literary journals.

WORK IN PROGRESS: The Devourer, a novel.

* * *

ADELSBERGER, Lucie 1895-1971

April 12, 1895—November 2, 1971; German-born American physician, scientist, and cancer researcher. Obituaries: *New York Times,* November 4, 1971.

* * *

ADELSTEIN, Michael E. 1922-

PERSONAL: Born November 21, 1922, in New York, N.Y.; son of Samuel (a manufacturer) and Lillian (Gittler) Adelstein; married Carol Simon, December 27, 1945; children: Janet, Jay. *Education:* University of Pennsylvania, B.S., 1943; University of Michigan, M.A., 1947, Ph.D., 1958. *Politics:* "Generally Democratic." *Religion:* Jewish. *Home:* 1883 Manassas Dr., Lexington, Ky. 40504. *Office:* Department of English, University of Kentucky, Lexington, Ky. 40506.

CAREER: College of William and Mary, Williamsburg, Va., instructor in English, 1947-49; Little White House, Warm Springs, Ga., administrative assistant, 1951-52; University of Michigan, Ann Arbor, instructor in English, 1955-57; University of Kentucky, Lexington, assistant professor, 1958-66, associate professor, 1966-73, professor of English, 1973—. Vice-president, Better Schools, Inc., 1959-60. *Military service:* U.S. Army, 1943-45; became technical sergeant; received five campaign stars. *Member:* Modern Language Association of America, National Council of Teachers of English, American Association of University Professors, American Business Communication Associa-

tion, Society of Technical Communicators, Omicron Delta Kappa.

WRITINGS: Fanny Burney, Twayne, 1968; (editor with Jean C. Pival) *Ecocide and Population,* St. Martin's, 1971; *Contemporary Business Writing,* Random House, 1971; (editor with Pival) *Women's Liberation,* St. Martin's, 1972; (editor with Pival) *Drugs,* St. Martin's, 1972; (with Pival) *The Writing Commitment,* Harcourt, 1976; (editor with Pival) *The Reading Commitment,* Harcourt, 1978. Writer (and teacher) of taped course used in freshman English at University of Kentucky and its community colleges, and "Business of Writing," a television course used by government, industry, and educational television stations.

* * *

ADIZES, Ichak 1937-

PERSONAL: Born October 22, 1937, in Skoplje, Yugoslavia; son of Salamon (a businessman) and Diamanta (Kalderon) Adizes. *Education:* Hebrew University of Jerusalem, B.A., 1963; Columbia University, M.B.A., 1965, Ph.D., 1968. *Religion:* Jewish. *Office:* 6336 Graduate School of Management, University of California, Los Angeles, Calif. 90024.

CAREER: Economist for Government of Israel, 1961-62; University of California, Los Angeles, associate professor of managerial studies and international business, 1967—. Visiting professor, University of Tel Aviv and Hebrew University of Jerusalem, 1970, and Standford University, 1977. Lecturer in Yugoslavia, Brazil, Peru, Mexico, Chile, Sweden, and other countries, as well as in the United States, 1967—. President and senior associate, M DOR Institute, Los Angeles, 1976—. Consultant to governments, business and other groups, including government of Israel and Ghana, Dun & Bradstreet, Los Angeles Music Center Performing Arts Council, Northrop Aviation, and others. *Member:* American Economic Association, Academy of Management, American Academy of Political and Social Science. *Awards, honors:* National Endowment for the Arts grant, 1968-69; Ford Foundation travel and study grant, 1969.

WRITINGS: Industrial Democracy: Yugoslav Style, Free Press, 1971; (with E. Mann-Bovgese) *Self-Management: New Dimensions to Democracy,* American Bibliographic Center-Clio Press, 1976. Contributor to business and economics journals in the United States, Europe, and Latin America.

WORK IN PROGRESS: Performing Arts: Managerial Practices; Management Styles.

SIDELIGHTS: Ichak Adizes speaks Serbo-Croatian, Spanish, French, Italian, and Bulgarian, as well as English and Hebrew.

* * *

ADKINS, Jan 1944-

PERSONAL: Born November 7, 1944, in Gallipolis, Ohio; son of Alban B. (a contractor) and Dixie (Ellis) Adkins; married Deborah Kiernan, September 14, 1968 (died, 1976); married Dorcas Peirce, December, 1977; children: Sally, Samuel Ulysses. *Education:* Ohio State University, B.A., 1969. *Home:* 591 Front St., Marion, Mass. 02738. *Agent:* Perry Knowlton, Curtis Brown Ltd., 575 Madison Ave., New York, N.Y. 10022.

CAREER: Ireland & Associates Architects, Columbus, Ohio, designer, 1963-66, 1969; writer, graphic designer, and illustrator, 1969—; Buzzard Inc. (advertising agency), Marion, Mass., vice-president and art director, 1974-76. *Awards, honors:* Jacobsen Short Story Award, Ohio State University, 1969, for "One, Two"; Bojklyn Museum Art Citation, 1972, 1973, 1974; *The Art and Industry of Sandcastles* was nominated for National Book Award, 1972; Lewis Carroll Shelf Award, 1973; Children's Book Showcase Awards, 1974, for *Toolchest,* 1976, for *Inside.*

WRITINGS—All published by Walker & Co., except as indicated: *The Art and Industry of Sandcastles,* 1970; *The Craft of Making Wine,* 1971; *How a House Happens,* 1972; *The Craft of Sail,* 1973; *Toolchest: A Primer of Woodcraft,* 1973; *Small Gardener: Big Surprise,* Ginn, 1974; *The Bakers: On Making Bread,* Scribner, 1975; *Inside: Seeing beneath the Surface,* 1975; *Luther Tarbox,* Scribner, 1977; *Moving On,* Scribner, 1978; *Symbols: A Silent Language,* 1978; *Wooden Ship,* Houghton, 1978. Contributor to *Harper's, Smithsonian, Cricket,* and *Woodenboat.*

WORK IN PROGRESS: The Art and Ingenuity of the Wood Stove, for Everest House; *Moving Heavy Things,* for Houghton; *Letter Box,* for Walker & Co.; *Wood Works,* for Little, Brown, completion expected 1979.

* * *

ADLER, Helmut E(rnest) 1920-

PERSONAL: Born November 25, 1920, in Nuremberg, Germany; came to United States in 1940, naturalized in 1943; son of Paul (an engineer) and Lola (Offenbacher) Adler; married Leonore Loeb, May 22, 1943; children: Barry Peter, Beverly Sharmaine, Evelyn Renee. *Education:* Columbia University, B.S., 1948, A.M., 1949, Ph.D., 1952. *Religion:* Jewish. *Home:* 162-14 86th Ave., Jamaica, N.Y. 11432. *Office:* Department of Psychology, Yeshiva University, New York, N.Y. 10033.

CAREER: Yeshiva University, New York City, instructor, 1950-53, assistant professor, 1953-57, associate professor, 1957-64, professor of psychology, 1964—; Columbia University, New York City, member of scientific staff, 1952-55, lecturer in psychology, 1955-60. American Museum of Natural History, New York City, fellow, 1955-69, research associate, 1969—. *Military service:* U.S. Army, 1942-46. *Member:* American Psychological Association (fellow), American Meteorological Society, Animal Behavior Society, Eastern Psychological Association (fellow), New York Academy of Sciences.

WRITINGS: (With J. D. Macdonald and D. Goodwin) *Bird Behavior,* Sterling, 1962, published as *Curiosities of Bird Life,* Castle, 1967; (translator) Gustav Theodor Fechner, *Elements of Psychophysics,* Volume I, edited by Davis H. Howes and Edwin G. Boring, Holt, 1966; (with Macdonald and Goodwin) *Bird Life: For Young People,* Sterling, 1969; (editor) *Orientation: Sensory Basis,* New York Academy of Sciences, 1971; (editor with wife, Leonore Loeb Adler, and Ethel Tobach) *Comparative Psychology at Issue,* New York Academy of Sciences, 1973; *Fish Behavior: Why Fishes Do What They Do,* T.F.H. Publications, 1975; (contributor) R. W. Rieber and K. Salzinger, editors, *The Roots of American Psychology: Historical Influences and Implications for the Future,* New York Academy of Sciences, 1977. Contributor to professional journals; department editor and contributor to *Encyclopedia Judaica,* 1971.

WORK IN PROGRESS: Sensory Basis of Animal Orientation; editing *Animal Migration, Orientation, and Navigation,* for Academic Press.

AVOCATIONAL INTERESTS: Breeding miniature Dachshunds, tropical fish.

* * *

AGAN, Raymond J(ohn) 1919-

PERSONAL: Born July 8, 1919, in Knoxville, Iowa; son of Charles Raymond and Clara May (Vannatta) Agan; married Mary Lou Boyce, December 26, 1949; children: Charla Joanne (Mrs. William J. Schapfel), John Raymond. *Education:* Iowa State University, B.S., 1940, M.S., 1950; University of Missouri, Columbia, Ed.D., 1955; Swiss International Institute, certificate, 1968. *Religion:* Presbyterian. *Home:* 2309 Avenue S, Huntsville, Tex. 77340. *Office:* Sam Houston State University, Huntsville, Tex. 77340.

CAREER: Teacher of agriculture in public schools in Iowa, 1940-45; Carnation Co., Fresh Milk Division, Los Angeles, Calif., technician, 1945-50; Wayne State College, Wayne, Neb., head of department of agriculture, 1950-53; Oregon State University, Corvallis, instructor, 1953-55, assistant professor of agricultural education, 1955-57; Kansas State University, Manhattan, associate professor, 1958-62, professor of agricultural education, 1963-68, professor of vocational education, 1968-71; Sam Houston State University, Huntsville, Tex., professor of vocational education, 1971—. Consultant to University of Costa Rica, 1963-64, to United Nations Development Fund, 1965, Peace Corps program in Paraguay, 1968, and UNESCO program in Colombia, 1969-70. *Member:* American Vocational Association (member of international committee), Phi Delta Kappa.

WRITINGS: (With V. R. Cardozier) *Teacher Education in Agriculture,* Interstate, 1967; *Interdisciplinary Vocational Education,* Kansas State University, 1968; *Curriculum for Man in an International World,* Kansas State University, 1971. Contributor to professional journals. International editor, *Agricultural Education Journal.*

WORK IN PROGRESS: A book; work on curriculum guides; professional articles in the area of career education.

* * *

AGGERTT, Otis J. 1916-1973

PERSONAL: Born May 31, 1916, in Ashland, Ill.; son of Otis (a building contractor) and Maude (Bentley) Aggertt; married Harriet Lucile Larson (a teacher), August 14, 1938; children: Kristine Lucile, Kathryn Maude (Mrs. Hans Taeubert), Gretchen Aline (Mrs. Michael Lee Weber), Otis Jon. *Education:* Western Illinois University, B.Ed., 1938; University of Illinois, M.A., 1947; Michigan State University, Ed.D., 1960. *Politics:* Democratic Party. *Home:* 4310 Park Ave., Terre Haute, Ind. 47805. *Office:* Department of Speech, Indiana State University, Terre Haute, Ind. 47809.

CAREER: Ordained Universalist minister, 1963; teacher in public high schools in Kewanee, Springfield, and Little York, Ill., 1938-44, 1946-49; Albion College, Albion, Mich., associate professor of speech, 1946-56; Indiana State University, Terre Haute, professor of speech and head of speech communication area, 1956-73. Minister in Universalist Churches of Horton, Mich., 1952-56, and Hutsonville, Ill., beginning 1958. *Wartime service:* Conscientious objector, drafted into civilian public service, 1944-46. *Member:* Speech Communication Association, Indiana Speech Association, American Forensic Association, American Association of University Professors, American Civil Liberties Union, Rhetoric Association of America, American Association of Parliamentarians, Theta Alpha Phi, Pi Kappa Delta, Delta Sigma Rho, Tau Kappa Alpha.

WRITINGS: (With Elbert R. Bowen) *Communicative Reading,* Macmillan, 1956, 4th edition (with Bowen and William Rickert), 1978; *A Student Speaks,* Burgess, 1971. Contributor to *Quarterly Journal of Speech, Contemporary Education, Speech Notes,* and other journals.

WORK IN PROGRESS: A Preaching Professor, a book of sermons; *Letters from a Religious Objector;* research in oral interpretation of literature, general semantics, teaching the basic college course, and liberal religion.

SIDELIGHTS: Otis J. Aggertt once told *CA* that his "philosophy is oriented primarily to pragmatism, general semantics, and Unitarian Universalism." He was "profoundly influenced by the Sermon on the Mount, John Dewey, and Alfred Korzybski." Aggertt added: "[I am] obsessed by the idea of the significance of persons!" *Avocational interests:* Poetry, gardening, and tropical fish.†

(Died October, 1973)

* * *

AGOSTINELLI, Maria Enrica 1929-

PERSONAL: Born January 8, 1929, in Milan, Italy; daughter of Piero (an engineer) and Anita (Dell'Oro) Agostinelli. *Education:* Attended Liceo Classico e Accademia di Belle Arti di Brera, Milan, Italy.

CAREER: Illustrator and author of children's books. *Member:* Sindacato Nazionale Scrittori, Sindacato Pittori e Scultori. *Awards, honors:* Premio Diomira Editori, Milan, 1959.

WRITINGS: (Self-illustrated) *I Know Something You Don't Know* (juvenile), F. Watts, 1970; (self-illustrated) *Der eine gross der andere klein,* Verlag Heinrich Ellermann, 1970.

Illustrator of juvenile books: Italo Calvino, *Il Barone rampante,* Einaudi, 1959; Lina Schwarz, *Ancora . . . e poi basta!,* Mursia, 1961; Mariella Linder, *Il 7 agosto di mago mollica,* Mursia, 1962; Gianni Rodari, compiler, *Enciclopedia della favola,* three volumes, Editori Riuniti, 1963; Rodari, *La Freccia azzurra,* Editori Riuniti, 1964; Antonio Gramsci, *L'Albero del riccio,* Editori Riuniti, 1965; Luigi Santucci, *Poesie con le gambe corte,* Mursia, 1966; D. Ziliotto, *Tea Patata,* Vallecchi, 1968; Ginevra Bompiani, *Piazza pulita,* Bompiani, 1968; Gyorgy Vegh, *La Volpe gialla,* Editrice Morano, 1968.

WORK IN PROGRESS: A self-illustrated juvenile, "*Hallo, Tina? Ich bin Tano.*" "*Hallo, Tano? Ich bin Tina,*" for Verlag Heinrich Ellermann; illustrating *Gli affari del signor Gatto* by Gianni Rodari, to be published by Einaudi.

BIOGRAPHICAL/CRITICAL SOURCES: Casabella, November, 1960; *Syllabic Tornbole,* Number 97, 1961; *Children's Books in Italy,* Number 131, 1967.††

* * *

AIKEN, John R(obert) 1927-

PERSONAL: Born August 3, 1927, in Boston, Mass.; son of John William and Florence (Messier) Aiken; married Lois M. Mitchell, December 22, 1949; children: Lisa Ann, Emily Ann. *Education:* Attended Worcester Junior College, 1947-48; Iowa Wesleyan College, B.A. (summa cum laude), 1950; University of Iowa, M.A., 1951; University of Rochester, Ph.D., 1966. *Home:* 3856 Wruck Rd., Harland, N.Y. 14067.

CAREER: Teacher of history in Marshalltown, Iowa, 1951-54; Niagara Falls School System, Niagara Falls, N.Y.,

teacher of history, 1954-62; State University of New York at Buffalo, instructor, 1964-65, assistant professor, 1965-66, associate professor, 1966-68, professor of history, beginning 1968. Consultant, World Wide Wax Museums and Seneca Indian Nation. *Military service:* U.S. Navy, 1945-46. *Member:* Institute for Early American History and Culture, American Historical Association, American Society of Legal History. *Awards, honors:* Fulbright fellowship, 1961; New York State University research awards, 1966, 1968, 1970; National Endowment for the Humanities grant, 1967.

WRITINGS: (With Eric Brunger, J. Wilhelms, and Richard Aiken) *Outpost of Empires: The Story of Niagara Falls,* Frank E. Richards, 1960; (with Richard Aiken) *Power: Gift of Niagara,* Buffalo and Erie County Historical Society, 1962; (with Brunger) *Historical Land Valuation of Big Tree Cession, 1797-1842,* Indian Claims Commission, 1970. Also author of *The Emergence of a Legal Profession in Colonial New York,* Academic Press. Author of scripts of two educational television programs on Brazil. Contributor to *Social Studies, Pennsylvania Magazine of History and Biography, Church History,* and *Labor History.*

WORK IN PROGRESS: Utopianism and Law in Early America; Indian Affairs and Government Land Policies; Arbitration in Early New York.††

* * *

AKASHI, Yoji 1928-

PERSONAL: Born September 25, 1928, in Tokyo, Japan; came to United States in 1951; married Muneko Sato, August 20, 1968. *Education:* Eastern Nazarene College, A.B., 1955; Georgetown University, Washington, D.C., M.A., 1958, Ph.D., 1963. *Office:* Center for Japanese Studies, Nanzan University, 18 Yamazato-cho, Showa Ku, Nagoya 466, Japan.

CAREER: Geneva College, Beaver Falls, Pa., associate professor of Asian history, 1963-74; Nanzan University, Nagoya, Japan, professor of Asian history, 1974—, Center for Japanese Studies, director. Visiting professor, University of Malaya, 1975-76. *Member:* International House of Japan, American Political Science Association, National Political Science Honor Society, American Historical Association, Association for Asian Studies, Japan International Relations Association, Japan Southeast Asian Studies Association. *Awards, honors:* Outstanding Scholar of America, 1971; Cleland Award for Advanced Research and Publication, 1971.

WRITINGS: The Nanyang Chinese National Salvation Movement, 1937-1947, University of Kansas, Center for East Asia, 1970; *The Japanese Military Administration in Southeast Asia, 1941-1945,* Sydney University Press, 1972. Contributor of articles in Japanese and English to *Kokusai Seiji, Journal of South Seas Society, Asian Studies, In Depth* (Geneva College periodical), *Asian Forum,* and *Southeast Asia History and Culture;* contributor of reviews to *Ajia Keizai, Toyo Gakuho, Asian Economies, Journal of Modern History, Journal of Asian Studies,* and other periodicals.

WORK IN PROGRESS: Japan's Maneuvers for Peace with China, 1941-1945; The Greater East Asian Co-Prosperity Sphere, 1940-1945; The Japanese Military Administration in Malaya-Singapore, 1941-45.

AVOCATIONAL INTERESTS: Gardening, antique collecting, traveling.

ALAILIMA, Fay C. 1921-
(Fay Calkins)

PERSONAL: Born September 24, 1921, in Auburn, N.Y.; daughter of J. Birdsall and Gladys (Gilkey) Calkins; married Valao J. Alailima (a teacher), January 25, 1952; children: Gladys, Birdsall, Charles, Marie, Fay Jr., Cecilia. *Education:* Oberlin College, B.A., 1943; Haverford College, M.A., 1945; University of Chicago, Ph.D., 1951. *Religion:* Protestant. *Home:* 5609 Pia St., Honolulu, Hawaii 96821. *Office:* Leeward Community College, Pearl City, Hawaii 96782.

CAREER: Samoa College, Apia, Western Samoa, instructor, 1960-64; East West Center, Honolulu, Hawaii, senior specialist, 1964-65; teacher in Kamehameha Schools in Honolulu, 1965-68; Hawaii Lea College, Kailua, assistant professor of social science, 1968-70; Leeward Community College, Pearl City, Hawaii, coordinator of urban studies, 1970—.

WRITINGS—Under name Fay Calkins: *The CIO and the Democratic Party,* University of Chicago Press, 1952, reprinted, 1975; *My Samoan Chief,* Doubleday, 1962. Also author with husband, Valao J. Alailima, under name Fay C. Alailima, *Samoan Values and Economic Development,* 1964.

* * *

ALAYA, Flavia (M.) 1935-

PERSONAL: Surname is pronounced Ah-*lah*-ya; born May 16, 1935, in New Rochelle, N.Y.; daughter of Mario Salvatore (a teacher) and Maria (a teacher; maiden name, Spagnola) Alaya; married; children: Harry Mario, Christopher Robert, Nina Maria Browne. *Education:* Barnard College, B.A., 1956; University of Padua, graduate study, 1957-58; Columbia University, M.A., 1960, Ph.D., 1965. *Home:* 520 East 28th St., Paterson, N.J. 07514. *Office:* Department of English, Ramapo College of New Jersey, Mahwah, N.J. 07430.

CAREER: University of North Carolina at Greensboro, instructor in English, 1959-60; Barnard College, New York City, lecturer and assistant in English, 1960-62; Hunter College of the City University of New York, New York City, lecturer in English, 1962-66; New York University, New York City, instructor, 1966-67, assistant professor of English, 1967-71; Ramapo College of New Jersey, Mahwah, associate professor, 1971-73, professor of English and comparative literature, 1973—, founding director of School of Intercultural Studies, 1971-73. *Member:* Modern Language Association of America, Victorian Society in America, American Association of University Professors, English Institute, Research Society for Victorian Periodicals, Northeast Victorian Studies Association, Passaic County Historical Society (vice-president and trustee). *Awards, honors:* Fulbright and Italian Government scholar in Italy, 1957-58; Guggenheim Foundation fellowship, 1974-75.

WRITINGS: William Sharp-"Fiona Macleod," 1855-1905, Harvard University Press 1970. Contributor to *Victorian Poetry, Journal of the History of Ideas,* and other journals.

WORK IN PROGRESS: A Poetics of Place, a theoretical study of literary environments; *The Darkened Garden,* Italy in the Victorian literary imagination; research on Olive Schreiner, Nadine Gordimer, and women within the South African literary tradition.

ALAZRAKI, Jaime 1934-

PERSONAL: Born January 26, 1934, in La Rioja, Argentina; came to United States, 1962, naturalized in 1971; son of Leon (a businessman) and Clara Antonia (Bolomo) Alazraki; married Naomi Parver (a physician), April 29, 1962; children: Daphne G., Adina Lynn. *Education:* Hebrew University of Jerusalem, B.A., 1962; Columbia University, M.A., 1964, Ph.D. (with honors), 1967. *Home:* 2037 Soledad Ave., La Jolla, Calif. 92037. *Office:* Department of Literature, University of California, San Diego, La Jolla, Calif. 92037.

CAREER: Columbia University, New York, N.Y., instructor in Spanish, 1964-67; University of California, San Diego, La Jolla, assistant professor, 1967-68, associate professor, 1968-71, professor of Spanish, 1971—, head of Spanish section, Department of Literature, 1970-74. Visiting professor at University of Wisconsin—Madison, summer, 1974, and University of California, Los Angeles. *Member:* Modern Language Association of America, International Institute of Ibero-American Literature, American Association of Teachers of Spanish and Portuguese, Argentine Society of Writers. *Awards, honors:* Domingo R. Nieto gold medal, Junta de Historia y Letras (La Rioja, Argentina), 1968, for *La Prosa narrative de Jorge Luis Borges;* Guggenheim fellowship, 1971-72; National Endowment for Humanities fellow, 1975-76.

WRITINGS: Poetica y poesia de Pablo Neruda, Las Americas, 1965; *La Prosa narrativa de Jorge Luis Borges,* Gredos (Madrid), 1968, 2nd revised edition, 1974; *Jorge Luis Borges,* Columbia University Press, 1971; *El Escritor y la critica: Borges,* Taurus (Madrid), 1976; (editor with R. Grass and R. Salmon) *Homenaje a Andres Jduarte,* American Hispanist, 1976; (editor with J. Jvask) *The Final Island: The Fiction of Julio Cortazar,* University of Oklahoma Press, 1977; *Versiones/Inversiones/Reversiones: El espejo como mode lo estructural del relato en los cuentos de Borges,* Gredos (Madrid), in press. Contributor to *Romanic Review, Symposium, Revista Iberoamericana, Cuadernos Americanos, Studies in Short Fiction, Books Abroad, Hispanic Review, Tri-Quarterly, Hispania, Revista Hispanica Moderna, Modern Language Journal, Dada/Surrealism, El Vrogallo, Iberoromania, Style,* and other journals and newspapers. Member of editorial board, *Journal of Spanish Studies,* 1974-77, *Latin American Literary Review,* 1975—, *Hispanic Review,* 1977—, and *Revista Iberoamericana,* 1977.

WORK IN PROGRESS: Borges and the Kabbalah; Form and Meaning in the Short Stories of Julio Cortazar, expected completion in 1977.

SIDELIGHTS: Jaime Alazraki told *CA:* "In my approach to literature I place major emphasis on form. I understand the latter as the true realization of theme. My scholarship on Borges has enabled me to bring together my interests in contemporary Latin American fiction and in the mystical side of religion, particularly the Kabbalah, whose texts I studied with Gershom Scholem at the Hebrew University of Jerusalem."

BIOGRAPHICAL/CRITICAL SOURCES: Times Literary Supplement, April 16, 1970; *Bulletin of Hispanic Studies,* April, 1970; *Hispanic Review,* July, 1970; *Modern Language Review,* July, 1970; *Books Abroad,* winter, 1970; *Modern Language Journal,* February, 1972; *America Latina en su literatura,* 1972.

ALBERTS, Robert C(arman)   1907-

PERSONAL: Born July 15, 1907, in Pittsburgh, Pa.; son of William Edward (a building contractor) and Leonora (Carman) Alberts; married Zita Doberneck. *Education:* University of Pittsburgh, A.B., 1930, M.A., 1931. *Politics:* "Member of the extreme center." *Religion:* Protestant. *Home:* 99 Gladstone Rd., Pittsburgh, Pa. 15217.

CAREER: Pittsburgh Coal Co., Pittsburgh, Pa., sales manager in retail department, 1930-38; *Pittsburgh Bulletin-Index Magazine,* Pittsburgh, member of editorial staff, 1938-42, editor, 1940-42; Ketchum, MacLeod & Grove, Inc. (advertising agency), Pittsburgh, account executive, 1942-43, 1948-69, vice-president, 1956-69. *Military service:* U.S. Army, 1943-46. *Member:* Early American Industries Association, Authors Guild, Authors League of America, Pennsylvania Historical Association, Western Pennsylvania Historical Society (secretary and member of executive committee), Pittsburgh Bibliophiles. *Awards, honors:* Book Award of Society of Colonial Wars, 1966, for *The Most Extraordinary Adventures of Major Robert Stobo.*

WRITINGS: The Most Extraordinary Adventures of Major Robert Stobo (History Book Club selection), Houghton, 1965; *The Golden Voyage: The Life and Times of William Bingham, 1752-1804,* Houghton, 1969; (editor) *North American Big Game,* Boone and Crockett Club, 1971; *The Good Provider: H. J. Heinz and His 57 Varieties,* Houghton, 1969; (editor) *North American Big Game,* Boone and Crockett Club, 1971; *George Rogers Clark and the Winning of the Old Northwest,* National Park Service, 1976; *Mount Washington Tavern: The Story of a Famous Inn, a Great Road, and the People Who Used Them,* National Park Service, 1976. Also author of *"A Charming Field for an Encounter": George Washington's Fort Necessity,* National Park Service. Contributor to *New York Times Book Review, New York Times Magazine,* and to *Dictionary of Canadian Biography.* Civilian editor in Germany for *U.S. Army Information and Education Bulletin,* 1946-48; contributing editor, *American Heritage,* 1971—.

BIOGRAPHICAL/CRITICAL SOURCES: Chicago Tribune, August 8, 1965; *New York Times Book Review,* August 15, 1965, February 8, 1970; *Saturday Review,* October 23, 1965; *New York Times,* December 20, 1966; *Best Sellers,* November 1, 1969; *Book World,* January 11, 1970; *American Historical Review,* June, 1970; *Wall Street Journal,* January 8, 1974; *New York Times Magazine,* November 17, 1974.

*   *   *

ALBRECHT, C(harles) Milton   1904-

PERSONAL: Born September 17, 1904, in Dundee, Ill.; son of Charles J. and Mary (Wendt) Albrecht; married Evelyn Thoman, January 3, 1929. *Education:* Antioch College, A.B., 1929; University of California, Berkeley, M.A., 1931, Ph.D., 1937. *Politics:* Democrat. *Home:* Stratford Hill Apartments, No. 420, Chapel Hill, N.C. 27514.

CAREER: University of Idaho, Moscow, instructor, 1937-42, assistant professor of English, 1943-46; State University of New York at Buffalo, assistant professor, 1946-48, associate professor, 1948-55, professor of sociology, 1965-75, professor emeritus, 1975—, College of Arts and Sciences, assistant dean, 1956-58, associate dean, 1957-58, dean, 1958-65. Member of board of directors, Buffalo Urban League, 1952-61, Western New York Research Center, 1960-66, and Buffalo Chamber Music Society, 1961-76. Member of research advisory committee, Community Welfare Council, 1952-60.

MEMBER: American Sociological Association (emeritus member), National Council on Family Relations, National Society for the Study of Education, American Association of University Professors, Eastern Sociological Society, Phi Beta Kappa. *Awards, honors:* State University of New York Research Division faculty research fellowships, summers, 1966, 1968, 1971.

WRITINGS: (Editor) *Studies in Sociology,* State University of New York at Buffalo, 1967; (senior editor, with James H. Barnett and Mason Griff) *The Sociology of Art and Literature,* Praeger, 1970. Contributor to psychology, sociology, and education journals.

WORK IN PROGRESS: A book on theories of the arts in relation to society; further research on sociology of art and literature.

SIDELIGHTS: C. Milton Albrecht's travels throughout the world include many visits to Central America to study Mayan civilization, art, and artifacts.

*   *   *

ALBRIGHT, Bliss (James F.)   1903-

PERSONAL: Born September 27, 1903, in Leonard, Tex.; son of Jacob D. (a merchant) and Mollie (Jordan) Albright; married Rogene Hoard, December 24, 1924; children: James Lucien. *Education:* Attended Columbia University, 1930. *Politics:* Democrat. *Religion:* Methodist. *Home:* 3832 Hanover, Dallas, Tex. 75225.

CAREER: Methodist Publishing House, Dallas, Tex., shipping clerk, 1925, order filler, 1926; Cokesbury Book Store, Dallas, buyer, 1929, general manager, 1940-59, regional manager, 1959-70. *Member:* American Booksellers Association (vice-president and member of board of directors, 1928-68; honorary life member), Dallas Booksellers Association, Press Club of Dallas.

WRITINGS: Selling Books, Bowker, 1944; *What to Tell the Neophyte: Bookselling Is a Good Career,* American Booksellers Association, 1964, revised edition, 1970; (editor) *Treasury of Inspirational Classics,* Revell, 1966; (editor) *The Eternal Things: The Best of Grace Noll Crowell,* Harper, 1977. Contributor to Dallas newspapers.

WORK IN PROGRESS: A Treasury of Inspirational Prayers.

BIOGRAPHICAL/CRITICAL SOURCES: Time, September 26, 1949.

*   *   *

ALBRIGHT, William F(oxwell)   1891-1971

May 24, 1891—September 19, 1971; American biblical scholar and author. Obituaries: *New York Times,* September 20, 1971; *Washington Post,* September 21, 1971; *Time,* October 4, 1971; *L'Express,* October 4-10, 1971; *Publishers Weekly,* October 11, 1971.

*   *   *

ALBROW, Martin   1937-

PERSONAL: Born June 24, 1937, in Norwich, England; son of Cyril and Alice (Woods) Albrow; married Isabella Carver, September 1, 1962; children: Nicholas, John, Stephen. *Education:* Peterhouse, Cambridge, B.A., 1958, Ph.D., 1974. *Home:* 98 Pen-y-lan Rd., Cardiff, Wales. *Office:* University College, P.O.B. 78, Cardiff, CF1 1XL Wales.

CAREER: University of Reading, Reading, England, lecturer in sociology, 1963-66; University College, Cardiff, Wales, senior lecturer in sociology, 1967-76, professor of sociology and head of department, 1976—, dean of Faculty of Economic and Social Studies, 1976—, Levahulme Faculty Fellow in European studies, 1973. Lister Lecturer of British Association, 1970. *Member:* British Sociological Association, Association of University Teachers.

WRITINGS: Bureaucracy, Praeger, 1970.

WORK IN PROGRESS: Research on the sociology of Max Weber.

*   *   *

ALDOUBY, Zwy H(erbert) 1931-

PERSONAL: Original name, Herbert Dubensky; name legally changed in 1952; born July 16, 1931, in Cernowitz, Russia; son of Paul and Ann (Bochkis) Dubensky; married Yedida Saad, 1952; married second wife, Sofia Gilert, 1957; children: (second marriage) Ilan (son). *Education:* Attended Sorbonne, University of Paris, 1952-54; Tel-Aviv University, B.A., 1956; Columbia University, M.A., 1959. *Religion:* Jewish. *Home:* 210 West 101st St., New York, N.Y. 10025. *Agent:* Sterling Lord Agency, 660 Madison Ave., New York, N.Y. 10021.

CAREER: Israeli government service, Ministry of Foreign Affairs, 1952-54, Ministry of Defense, 1954-56; journalist and correspondent for *Habokes, Gale: Zahal,* and *Bamahane,* Tel-Aviv, Israel; editor for *Women's Wear Daily,* New York City; freelance writer for *Look, Stern, Sie Und Er,* and other periodicals. President, Dan Leeds Productions, New York City, 1970—. *Military service:* Haganah, Palmach, and Israel Defence Forces, 1946-50.

WRITINGS: Havered, [Tel-Aviv], 1955; *Lipanda,* Editions de Paris, 1959; (with Quentin Reynolds and others) *Minister of Death: The Adolph Eichmann Story,* Viking, 1960; (with Jerrold Ballinger) *The Shattered Silence: The Eli Cohen Affair,* Coward, 1971.

Television documentaries: "Francisco Franco, Caudillo of Spain," 1964; "An Appointment with Death," 1969; "Sheysasakeiley," 1970; "And So Ends," 1970; "The Non-Smoking Cruise," 1971. Author of pamphlets on the Spanish Blue Division, the Council of Europe, and NATO. Also has written scripts for "Sounds of New York" radio show.

WORK IN PROGRESS: The Reichsleader (the Martin Bormann story), for Viking; *The Selector,* for Coward; *The Franco Era,* for Editions de Paris; a group of television documentaries dealing with emerging countries around the world; several pilot television films for an espionage series and a museum and history series.

SIDELIGHTS: The Shattered Silence, about Israeli master spy Eli Cohen, was filmed in Israel and Argentina. Albert Malz and the author did the screen adaptation for producer William L. Snyder.

BIOGRAPHICAL/CRITICAL SOURCES: Michael Bar-Zohar, *The Avengers,* Hawthorne, 1970; *Variety,* November 11, 1970, December 16, 1970, April 28, 1971; *Show,* August, 1971; *Jewish Press,* September 3, 1971.†

*   *   *

ALEXANDER, Edward P(orter) 1907-

PERSONAL: Born January 11, 1907, in Keokuk, Iowa; son of Walter Sheron (a trainmaster) and Anna Moody (Carter) Alexander; married Alice Wagner Bolton, November 27, 1929; children: Alice Anne (Mrs. John Davidson), John

Thorndike, Mary Sheron. *Education:* Drake University, A.B., 1928; State University of Iowa, M.A., 1931; Columbia University, Ph.D., 1938. *Religion:* Presbyterian. *Home:* 111 Country Club Dr., Newark, Del. 19711.

CAREER: Teacher of social studies in secondary schools, Iowa and Minn., 1928-32; New York State Historical Association, Ticonderoga and Cooperstown, N.Y., director, 1934-41; supervisor of Historical Records Survey, N.Y. State, 1936-38; State Historical Society of Wisconsin, Madison, director, 1941-46; Colonial Williamsburg Foundation, Williamsburg, Va., Director of Interpretation, 1946-72, vice-president, 1947-72; University of Delaware, Newark, director of museum studies, 1972-77. Chairman, Virginia Historical Landmarks Commission, 1966-71. *Member:* American Association of Museums (president, 1957-60), American Association for State and Local History (president, 1942-44), American Historical Association, Rochester Museum of Arts and Sciences (fellow), Phi Beta Kappa.

WRITINGS: A Revolutionary Conservative: James Duane of New York, Columbia University Press, 1938; (editor) *The Journal of John Fontaine: An Irish Huguenot Son in Spain and Virginia, 1710-1719,* Colonial Williamsburg Foundation, 1972. Editor, *New York History,* 1939-41, *Wisconsin Magazine of History,* 1941-46.

WORK IN PROGRESS: Museums in Motion: An Introduction to the History and Functions of Museums.

*   *   *

ALEXANDER, Floyce 1938-

PERSONAL: Born December 31, 1938, in Fort Smith, Ark.; son of Manuel Romain and Velma Lorene (Brown) Alexander; married Elizabeth Ludington, September 18, 1965 (divorced July 26, 1968); married Paula Thornton, May 7, 1969 (divorced, 1971); married Karen Lee Clarke, May 26, 1972. *Education:* Yakima Valley Junior College, A.A., 1958; University of Washington, Seattle, B.A., 1962; Washington State University, M.A., 1971; University of Massachusetts—Amherst, M.F.A., 1974. *Home:* 10430 Gravelly Lake Dr. S.W., Apt. 45, Tacoma, Wash. 98499.

CAREER: Washington State University Press, Pullman, editorial assistant, 1963-70; free-lance author, especially of poetry; teacher.

WRITINGS: Ravines (poems), Stone Marrow Press, 1971; (contributor) Robert Bly, editor, *Forty Poems Touching on Recent American History,* Beacon Press, 1970; *Machete* (poems), Lillabulero Press, 1972. Also author of *Bottom Falling Out of the Dream* (poems), 1976. Co-editor, with Juliana Mutti, *Agape.* Contributor of short stories, reviews, and essays, to many different periodicals, including *Kayak, Sumac, New: American and Canadian Poetry, Nation, Poetry Northwest, Minnesota Review, Western Humanities Review, Spectrum, Lynx, Fronwood, Granite,* and *Voyages.*

WORK IN PROGRESS: A novel, a collection of short stories, a book of essays, and a new book of poetry.

AVOCATIONAL INTERESTS: Trying to help the poor and the otherwise disadvantaged within my reach.

*   *   *

ALEXANDER, John T(horndike) 1940-

PERSONAL: Born January 18, 1940, in Cooperstown, N.Y.; son of Edward Porter (a historical administrator) and Alice (Bolton) Alexander; married Maria Kovalak Hreha, June 13, 1964; children: Michal, Darya. *Education:* Wesleyan University, Middletown, Conn., B.A., 1961; Indiana University, M.A., 1963, Ph.D., 1966. *Home:* 2216 Orchard Lane, Lawrence, Kan. 66044. *Office:* Department of History, University of Kansas, Lawrence, Kan. 66045.

CAREER: University of Kansas, Lawrence, assistant professor, 1966-70, associate professor, 1970-74, professor of history, 1974—. *Member:* American Historical Association, American Association for the Advancement of Slavic Studies, Central States Slavic Conference, Rocky Mountain Association for the Advancement of Slavic Studies.

WRITINGS: Autocratic Politics in a National Crisis: The Imperial Russian Government and Pugachev's Revolt, 1773-1775, Indiana University Press, 1969; (editor and translator) S. F. Platonov, *The Time of Troubles: A Historical Study of the Internal Crisis and Social Struggle in Sixteenth and Seventeenth Century Muscovy,* University Press of Kansas, 1970; *Emperor of the Cossacks: Pugachev and the Rural Revolution of 1773-1774* (monograph), Coronado Press, 1973; (author of introduction) Charles de Mertens, *An Account of the Plague that Raged at Moscow,* Oriental Research Partners, 1977. Contributor to journals in his field.

WORK IN PROGRESS: The Moscow Plague of 1771: A Social History; a survey of the reign of Catherine the Great, 1762-1796.

*   *   *

ALEXANDER, Jon   1940-

PERSONAL: Born January 2, 1940, in Carbondale, Ill.; son of Orville Burris (a political scientist) and Ola (Anderson) Alexander; married Linda Marie Tripp (chairman of Ottawa New School), September 5, 1962; children: Jon, Jr., Gern. *Education:* Southern Illinois University, B.A., 1961, M.A., 1962; University of Kansas, Ph.D., 1965. *Home:* R.R. 1, Osgoode, Ontario, Canada. *Office:* Department of Political Science, Carleton University, Ottawa, Ontario, Canada.

CAREER: Carleton University, Ottawa, Ontario, assistant professor of political science, 1967—. Visiting scholar, Center for the Study of Democratic Institutions, Santa Barbara, Calif., 1965-66; visiting assistant professor, Emory University, 1966-67, and Columbia University, 1967. Founding member and secretary of board of directors, Pestalozzi College, 1970-71. Member of committee of experts, Liberal Party of Canada, 1970—. Project proposal evaluation consultant, Canada Council, Government of Canada, 1970-71. Research associate and science advisor, Science Council of Canada, 1973-74. *Member:* American Political Science Association, Caucus for a New Political Science (founder), Canadian Political Science Association, International Studies Association, Midwest Political Science Association, Pi Sigma Alpha (chapter secretary, 1959-60).

WRITINGS: The Educational Crisis, Pestalozzi College Press, 1970; *Ruminations on Education,* Pestalozzi College Press, 1971; (contributor) M. Donald Hancock and Gideon Sjoberg, editors, *Politics in the Post-Welfare State: Responses to the New Individualism,* Columbia University Press, 1972. Also author with Patrick Esmonde-White, *Report 1970: National Hostel Task Force,* Canadian Welfare Council, 1971. Contributor to *Change, Graduate Front, Public Administration Review, Saturday Night, Octopus, Contexte,* and other publications. Member of editorial board, *Survival,* 1974—.

WORK IN PROGRESS: The use of political propaganda by the U.S. Central Intelligence Agency for cold warfare at home and abroad.

ALEXANDER, William M(arvin)   1912-

PERSONAL: Born February 19, 1912, in McKenzie, Tenn.; son of E. Marvin (a physician) and Lillis (McElroy) Alexander; married Nell McLeod, June 6, 1935; children: William M., Jr., Philip M. *Education:* Bethel College, McKenzie, Tenn., B.A., 1934; George Peabody College for Teachers, M.A., 1936; Columbia University, Ph.D., 1940. *Politics:* Democrat. *Religion:* Presbyterian. *Home:* 610 Northwest 89th St., Gainesville, Fla. 32601. *Office:* College of Education, Norman Hall, University of Florida, Gainesville, Fla. 32601.

CAREER: Teacher in public schools in McKenzie, Tenn., 1934-36; Cincinnati Public Schools, Cincinnati, Ohio, assistant director of curriculum, 1939-41; University of Tennessee, Knoxville, associate professor of education, 1941-43; Battle Creek Schools, Battle Creek, Mich., assistant superintendent of schools, 1946-49; Winnetka Schools, Winnetka, Ill., superintendent of schools, 1949-50; University of Miami, Coral Gables, Fla., professor of education, 1950-58; George Peabody College for Teachers, Nashville, Tenn., professor of education and chairman of department, 1958-63; University of Florida, Gainesville, professor of education, 1963—, chairman of Division of Curriculum and Instruction, 1963-66, director of Institute for Curriculum Improvement, 1966-69, chairman, Department of Instructional Leadership and Support, 1975—. Visiting summer professor at University of California, Columbia University, University of Illinois, and University of Hawaii. Fulbright scholar, University of Tehran, 1974-75. Member of board of directors, Joint Council on Economic Education, 1961-64, and George Peabody College for Teachers, 1969-73. *Military service:* U.S. Naval Reserve, active duty, 1943-46; became lieutenant.

MEMBER: Association for Supervision and Curriculum Development (president, 1959-60), National Education Association, American Educational Research Association, National Association of Secondary School Principals, American Association of University Professors, John Dewey Society, Phi Delta Kappa, Kappa Delta Pi.

WRITINGS: (With John Galen Saylor) *Secondary Education: Basic Principles and Practices,* Rinehart, 1950, 2nd edition (with Saylor) published as *Modern Secondary Education: Basic Principles and Practices,* Holt, 1959, 3rd edition (with Saylor and E. L. Williams) published as *The High School: Today and Tomorrow,* 1971; (with Saylor) *Curriculum Planning for Better Teaching and Learning,* Rinehart, 1954, 2nd edition (with Saylor) published as *Curriculum Planning for Modern Schools,* Holt, 1966, 3rd edition (with Saylor) published as *Planning Curriculum for Schools,* 1974; (with Paul M. Halverson) *Effective Teaching in Secondary Schools,* Rinehart, 1956; *Are You a Good Teacher,* Holt, 1959; (with Vynce A. Hines, Ernest L. Bentley, R. J. Moriconi, and James D. Wells) *Independent Study in Secondary Schools,* Holt, 1967; *The Changing Secondary School Curriculum: Readings,* Holt, 1967, 2nd edition published as *The Changing High School Curriculum: Readings,* 1972; (with Williams, Hines, Mary Compton, Dan Prescott, and Ronald Kealy) *The Emergent Middle School,* Holt, 1968, 2nd edition, 1969; (editor) *The High School of the Future: Memorial to Kimball Wiles,* C. E. Merrill, 1969; (with Glenys Unruh) *Innovations in Secondary Education,* Holt, 1970, 2nd edition (with Unruh), 1974; (editor) *The Changing High School Curriculum: Readings,* Holt, 1972. Contributor of more than a hundred articles to education journals. Editor, "Rinehart Education Pamphlets," 1957-62; editor, special issue of *National Elementary Principal* on middle schools,

November, 1971; advisory editor, *Americana Encyclopedia,* 1965—.

WORK IN PROGRESS: Articles for educational journals.

SIDELIGHTS: Many of William Alexander's books have been translated into several languages including Spanish, Dutch, and Serbo-Croatian.

* * *

ALLARDYCE, Gilbert Daniel 1932-

PERSONAL: Born Feburary 5, 1932; in Newton, Mass.; son of James B. (a machinist) and Jane (McCallam) Allardyce; married Elizabeth Wilson, May 23, 1957; children: Thomas Bruce, Gil Daniel. *Education:* Boston University, B.A., 1957, M.A., 1958; University of Iowa, Ph.D., 1966. *Home:* 15 Michener Ct., Fredericton, New Brunswick, Canada. *Office:* Department of History, University of New Brunswick, Fredericton, New Brunswick, Canada.

CAREER: Stanford University, Stanford, Calif., instructor in history, 1963-66; University of New Brunswick, Fredericton, professor of history, 1966—. *Military service:* U.S. Air Force, 1950-53; became staff sergeant. *Member:* American Historical Association.

WRITINGS: (Editor) *The Place of Fascism in European History,* Prentice-Hall, 1971.

WORK IN PROGRESS: Research on French fascism.

* * *

ALLEGER, Daniel E(ugene) 1903-

PERSONAL: Surname is accented on first syllable; born October 18, 1903, in East Stroudsburg, Pa.; son of Frank H. (a machinist) and Lena (Ruff) Alleger; married M. Carolyn Breckenridge, May 6, 1933 (died, 1974); children: Martha Alice (Mrs. C. K. Henley). *Education:* Pennsylvania State University, B.A., 1926, M.S., 1943; also attended Syracuse University, 1941. *Home:* 1710 Southwest 49th Pl., Gainesville, Fla. 32601. *Office:* University of Florida, 309 GSIS, Gainesville, Fla. 32601.

CAREER: United Fruit Co., Honduras and Guatemala, banana production and researcher, 1926-31; Metropolitan Life Insurance Co., Stroudsburg, Pa., agent, 1931-41; Bethlehem Steel Co., Bethlehem, Pa., product supervisor, 1942-45; University of Florida, Gainesville, associate professor of economic development, 1945-73, associate professor emeritus, 1973—. *Member:* International Association of Agricultural Economists, Rural Sociology Society, Gamma Sigma Delta.

WRITINGS: (Editor) *Fertile Lands of Friendship,* University of Florida Press, 1962; (editor and contributor) *Social Change and Aging in the Twentieth Century,* University of Florida Press, 1964; (editor) Samuel Bard, *Waikna, or Adventures on the Mosquito Shore,* University of Florida Press, 1965; *The Genesis of the Allegers,* privately printed, 1970.

Research bulletins, published by Florida Agricultural Experiment Station, University of Florida, Gainesville: (With Max M. Tharp) *Rural Land Ownership in Florida,* 1949; (with Tharp) *Current Farm Leasing Practices in Florida,* 1951; *Rental Arrangements on Crop-Share Farms,* 1952; *Agricultural Activities of Industrial Workers and Retirees,* 1953; *Rural Farm Retirement,* 1957; *Rural Areas in Transition,* 1964; *Retirement Income Expectations of Rural Southerners,* 1969; *Anomia and Differential Success,* 1971; *Florida's Rural Land,* 1974.

Experiment station circulars, with Charles M. Hampson and Harold M. Ellis, published by Florida Agricultural Experiment Station, 1955: *Field Lease Guide, Cash Rent Farm Lease Guide, Share-Tenant Lease Guide, Sharecropping Agreement Guide.*

Other published reports: (With Charles M. Hampson) *Indicators of Florida Farm Prosperity,* Florida State Department of Agriculture, 1948; (with Francisco Montoya) *Organizacion y operacion de fincas de cana,* Ministry of Agriculture (Costa Rica), 1957; *Problems in Agricultural Resource Adjustment,* University of Florida Mission to Costa Rica, 1957; (with Paulino Gutierrez) *Selling Cattle in Costa Rica by Direct Bargaining,* University of Florida Mission to Costa Rica, 1958; *The Cattle Situation in Costa Rica,* University of Florida Mission to Costa Rica, 1958; *Agricultural Policy Planning for Guatemala,* University of Florida Mission to Costa Rica, 1958; (with Betty W. Bailey, Alice C. Stubbs, and James C. Fortson) *Economic Provisions for Old Age of Rural Families in Five Southern States,* University of Georgia Agricultural Experiment Station, 1968.

Contributor: T. Lynn Smith, editor, *Living in the Later Years,* University of Florida Press, 1952; Irving T. Webber, editor, *Aging: A Current Appraisal,* University of Florida Press, 1956; *Retirement Income of the Aging,* U.S. Senate, 1961; *A Place to Live,* U.S. Department of Agriculture, 1963; *The Stream of History,* Jackson County Historical Society of Arkansas, 1974. Contributor to *Rural Sociology, Florida Cattlemen, Florida Grower and Rancher, Agricultural Science Review,* and other publications.

WORK IN PROGRESS: The Early Breckenridges of the Deep South.

* * *

ALLEN, David 1925-

PERSONAL: Born March 6, 1925, in New Haven, Conn.; son of David and Mary Ann (Ptansky) Allen; married Tula Prauner (a portrait painter and sculptor), January, 1961. *Education:* Attended Yale University, 1945-46; University of Chicago, M.A., 1951. *Home:* 178 Pascack Rd., Park Ridge, N.J. 07656. *Agent:* (Lectures) Richard Fulton, Inc., 200 West 57th St., New York, N.Y.

CAREER: Writer. Has worked as a road builder, textbook salesman, and book advertising and publicity man; was associated with a management consulting firm as writer and account executive; had his own business as an importer and manufacturer of fashion wigs. *Military service:* U.S. Army Air Forces, navigator, 1943-45; became second lieutenant; received Air Medal and cluster, Bronze Star Medal, three battle stars.

WRITINGS: The Nature of Gambling, Coward, 1952; *The Price of Women,* Jarrow Press, 1971. Contributor to *New York Times Magazine.*

WORK IN PROGRESS: Two books, one tentatively titled *When Raleigh Was Tried for Treason;* and *The New Case for Gun Control.*

AVOCATIONAL INTERESTS: Camping, travel to places of historical, geological, and anthropological interest.††

* * *

ALLEN, Dick 1939-

PERSONAL: Born August 8, 1939, in Troy, N.Y.; son of Richard Sanders (a historian and writer) and Doris (Bishop)

Allen; married Lori Negridge (a high school teacher), August 13, 1960; children: Richard Negridge, Tanya Angell. *Education:* Syracuse University, A.B., 1961; Brown University, M.A., 1963, additional graduate study, 1963-64. *Politics:* Republican. *Religion:* Unitarian Universalist. *Home:* 74 Fern Cir., Trumbull, Conn. 06611. *Office:* Division of Creative Writing, Department of English, University of Bridgeport, Bridgeport, Conn. 06602.

CAREER: Syracuse University, Syracuse, N.Y., manager of community relations, 1961; Wright State University, Dayton, Ohio, instructor in creative writing and American literature, 1964-68; University of Bridgeport, Bridgeport, Conn., assistant professor, 1968-71, associate professor, 1971-75, professor of American literature and creative writing, 1975—, director of creative writing, 1968—. Director, Mad River Writers' Conference, 1967; staff writer and teacher of short story writing, Indiana Writers' Conference, 1967, 1968; judge for belles lettres, Van Wyck Brooks Awards, 1971. *Member:* Modern Language Association of America, Science Fiction Research Association, Common Cause, World Future Society, Poets and Writers. *Awards, honors:* Academy of American Poets poetry prize, 1962; Hart Crane memorial fellowship for poetry, 1965; *Poetry* magazine's Union League Civic and Arts Foundation prize for poetry, 1970; Robert Frost Fellowship in Poetry, Bread Loaf Writer's Conference, 1972; San Jose National Bicentennial Poetry Prize, 1976.

WRITINGS: Anon and Various Time Machine Poems, Delacorte, 1971; (editor) *Science Fiction: The Future,* Harcourt, 1971; (co-editor) *Detective Fiction: Crime and Compromise,* Harcourt, 1974; *Regions with No Proper Names,* St. Martin's, 1975; *Looking Ahead: The Vision of Science Fiction,* Harcourt, 1975. Contributor to poetry and science fiction anthologies, including Dell's *SF-12,* Random House's *Contemporary American Poetry,* and Scribner's *The Modern Age.* Contributor of more than three hundred poems, articles, essays, and reviews to *Antioch Review, Poetry, New York Herald Tribune, Prairie Schooner, Prism International, Cimarron Review, West Coast Review, North American Review, Western Humanities Review, Paris Review, Beloit Poetry Journal,* and other publications. Editor-in-chief, *Mad River Review,* 1966-68. Co-editor, *Looking Ahead.* Contributing editor, *American Poetry Review,* 1972—; contributing editor and member of advisory board, *Dictics,* 1973—.

WORK IN PROGRESS: Two books of poetry, *The Space Sonnets,* completion expected in 1979, and *The People through the Train Window;* a creative writing textbook and numerous anthologies.

SIDELIGHTS: Dick Allen told *CA:* "I describe myself as perhaps the only American 'science fiction' poet in captivity, working heavily with SF subjects, future-casting, surrealistic satire, war and ecology politics. One of my main concerns in poetry, in addition to attempting to extend the human vision beyond Rilke, is to bring back to American poetry the story-telling quality, the dramatic poem, in order to explore the myth and wonder of the *average* American's experience. I tirelessly maintain . . . that it is possible for contemporary American poets to reach the same audience which has responded so tremendously to the folk rock poets, even *sans* electric guitar. I have been strongly influenced by both Christian and Far Eastern religions (especially Zen Buddhism); I am somewhat of a "mystic." I believe deeply in human freedom, dignity, and in our last ditch fight to save the race from self-destruction. The writings of Ralph Waldo

Emerson and Henry David Thoreau have been the major influences of my life."

Allen continues: "In the late 1970's I have found myself increasingly drawn to traditional forms of poetry as well as to poetry of meditation and sexuality. There is a 'beyond' which is arriving, perhaps through a wall such as in Doris Lessing's *Memoirs of a Survivor.*"

*   *   *

ALLEN, Heywood 1935-
(Woody Allen)

PERSONAL: Born Allen Stewart Konigsberg, December 1, 1935, in Brooklyn, N.Y.; name legally changed to Heywood Allen; son of Martin (a waiter and jewelry engraver) and Nettie (Cherry) Konigsberg; married Harlene Rosen, 1954 (divorced, 1960); married Louise Lasser (an actress), February 2, 1966 (divorced). *Education:* Attended New York University and City College (now City College of the City University of New York), 1953. *Politics:* Democrat. *Agent:* Mike Hutner, United Artists Corp., 729 Seventh Ave., New York, N.Y. 10019.

CAREER: Comedian, actor, director, and writer for television, films, and the stage. Began writing jokes for columnists and celebrities while in high school; regular staff writer for National Broadcasting Corp., 1952, writing for such personalities as Herb Shriner, Sid Caesar, Art Carney, Kaye Ballard, Buddy Hackett, Carol Channing, Pat Boone, Jack Paar and Garry Moore. Performer in nightclubs, on television, in films, and on the stage, 1961—. *Awards, honors:* Sylvania award, 1957, for script of a "Sid Caesar Show"; Academy Awards for best director and best original screenplay, from Academy of Motion Picture Arts and Sciences, National Society of Film Critics award, and New York Film Critics Circle award, all 1977, for film, "Annie Hall."

WRITINGS—Under name Woody Allen: *Getting Even,* Random House, 1971; *Without Feathers,* Random House, 1975.

Screenplays: "What's New, Pussycat?," United Artists, 1965; (with Frank Buxton, Len Maxwell, Louise Lasser, Mickey Rose, Julie Bennett, and Bryna Wilson) "What's Up, Tiger Lily?," American International, 1966; (with Rose) "Take the Money and Run," Cinerama, 1969; (with Rose) *Bananas* (produced by United Artists, 1970), Random House, 1978; "Play It Again, Sam" (adaptation of his play; also see below), Paramount, 1972; "Everything You Always Wanted to Know about Sex But Were Afraid to Ask" (adaptation of book of the same title by David Ruben), United Artists, 1972; (with Marshall Brickman) *Sleeper* (produced by United Artists, 1973), Random House, 1978; *Love and Death* (produced by United Artists, 1975), Random House, 1978; (with Brickman) *Annie Hall* (produced by United Artists, 1977), Random House, 1978; "Interiors," United Artists, 1978.

Plays: *Don't Drink the Water* (two-act comedy; first produced on Broadway at Morosco Theatre, November 17, 1966), Random House, 1967; *Play It Again, Sam* (three-act comedy; first produced on Broadway at Broadhurst Theatre, February 12, 1969), Random House, 1969.

Author of recordings, "Woody Allen," 1964, and "Woody Allen, Volume 2," 1965, both produced by Colpix Records. Also author of "Woody's First Special," networked by Columbia Broadcasting System, September 21, 1969. Contributor to *New Yorker, Saturday Review, Playboy, Esquire,* and numerous other publications.

SIDELIGHTS: Even though Woody Allen has been responsible for amassing over ''$60 million in movie grosses,'' writes Al Cohn, ''the one-time $35-a-week nightclub comic still regards himself as a *schlemiel*. Certainly, he looks the part: the thick glasses exaggerating a worried stare, the slight stature showing not a trace of paunch. And judging from his self-description, he apparently still lives the part. If it's all true, then Allen surely ranks as the world's funniest and most versatile schlemiel. His movies are well-received by critics and audiences alike. He has written for Broadway and his short stories appear regularly. Jazz musicians rate him a talented clarinetist.'' Stuart Rosenthal says that ''Woody Allen has the distinction of being one of the American cinema's few original, fully-developed comic personalities since the days of the Marx Brothers, Mae West, and W. C. Fields. His work reflects the neuroses and insecurities of modern life while mimicking the forces that create them. Thus, his style is an eclectic bombardment of literary, television, movie and Madison Avenue techniques, and his target is the ordinary mortal's inadequacy in the face of the *cliches* that these sources promote.''

Allen has become almost as famous for his attitudes, personality, and life style as for his work. Richard Pienciak writes: ''It is no secret that Woody Allen almost never surfaces early in the day, loves lightly browned chocolate malts, owns a white Rolls-Royce despite hating automobiles, rarely attends parties and hates everything Hollywood stands for.'' Discussing his reclusive nature, Woody Allen says that he ''always had difficulty with people, men and women, on a social level. Before, when I was shy and unknown, I thought that if I could only make it in some way, it would really help relieve me socially and I could relax and go to parties and do things. But then as soon as I did become known, I thought 'My God, I'm well known, I can't go out.' '' He is content to ''sit in the movies all day, to go for walks. I don't mind going to the beach for a weekend, but it's not uppermost in my mind. I'm Mr. New York City. I like to hang out with the fight mob at Madison Square Garden. If I was good enough, I could sit and play jazz all day. I think I have the type of public image where if I was caught with twelve teen-age girls in bed, or God knows what else, it would not hurt me. I think I'm a publicly avowed pervert and general scrounge.''

Woody Allen is sometimes looked upon as a comic genius whose references to literature and parodies of the classics are indicative of a ''deeper'' meaning in his work. Allen responds: ''People have always thought of me as an intellectual comedian, and I'm not. I'm a one-liner comic like Bob Hope and Henny Youngman. I do wife jokes. I make faces. I'm a comedian in the classic style.'' To those who dissect his comedy searching for hidden messages, he says: ''I do what I think is funny and it's one hundred percent instinctive. . . . I can only describe it in terms of what I've heard: contemporary, neurotic, more intellectually oriented, loser, little man, doesn't get along with machines, out of place with the world—all that crap. . . . I just want to be funny. I'm not moralizing or didactic in any way. And if in addition to being funny a point can be made, an inference from it, then that's all fine.'' As if to emphasize his non-intellectual nature, Allen lists as influences many of the great comedians of film, radio, and television, including the Marx Brothers, Buster Keaton, Charlie Chaplin, W. C. Fields, and Jack Benny; but the two comics who most affected his style were Bob Hope and Mort Sahl. He calls them ''two stand-up monologists who talk as themselves; they have these slick individual personalities; they're bright and sharp; they both have political

jokes, although Sahl's are much deeper; they have this great monologue style, great phrasing.''

A film producer named Charles K. Feldman saw Allen's nightclub act at the ''Blue Angel'' in 1964, and shortly thereafter hired him to rewrite a script for a comedy film. The motion picture was released as ''What's New, Pussycat?'' and Woody Allen became the writer of the highest grossing comedy in history. According to Eric Lax, ''Feldman made millions of dollars on it, and Woody had instant, if moderate, credibility as a screenwriter and actor, even though his script was massacred by Feldman and the experience was not very enjoyable for Woody. . . . There were many differences between Woody and Feldman, but the most important was philosophical: Woody wanted funny, artistic successes; Feldman wanted commercial successes.'' As Allen would say after making three films on his own, ''If they had let me make it, I could have made it twice as funny and half as successful.'' Perhaps as a reflection of the conflict surrounding its script, or as an indication of the error in hindering Allen's creativity, ''What's New, Pussycat?'' opened to rather unenthusiastic reviews. Particularly hostile was the *New York Times* critic who wrote: ''Woody Allen, the nightclub comedian, is formally charged with the minor offense of having written what is alleged to be the screenplay of 'What's New, Pussycat?' But Mr. Allen can deny it, if he wants to, and he is bound to be believed. He can simply state that no one in his right mind could have written this excuse for a script. . . . The idea is neurotic and unwholesome, it lacks wit, and the actors slamming through it are not true humorists.''

In ''What's Up, Tiger Lily?'' Woody Allen added a dubbed sound-track to a Japanese mystery-spy-thriller with absolutely no concern for the original plot; the result was a film which created a cult following among some dedicated fans. Stuart Rosenthal writes: ''Although gimmicky, 'What's Up, Tiger Lily?' still makes audiences sick with laughter and demonstrates Allen's flair for turning cliches back against the media that propagate them. It also suggests the way in which he would later exploit structural discontinuity in developing his own filmmaking style.'' Penelope Gilliatt believes that ''daily life for this brilliant, courteous man seems to be a matter of endlessly fending off guilt, which settles on the balconies of his intellect like the pigeons on the terraces of his apartment. . . . In 'What's Up, Tiger Lily?' through the use of soberly inappropriate English dialogue, he dubs his own worries and crevices of self-doubt onto a Japanese melodrama. The film speaks for the lack of confidence that he knows so precisely how to use without begging for pity. . . .''

After the success of ''What's New, Pussycat?'' and **''What's Up, Tiger Lily?,''** Allen was able to obtain the financing to write his own film, direct it, and star in it. ''Take the Money and Run'' became the first in a long line of films over which he had almost complete artistic control. In a review, Vincent Canby states that ''Allen's major accomplishment is in his successful translation of the nightclub comedian into screen terms. 'Take the Money and Run' is as funny to look at as it is to listen to.'' Judith Crist calls Woody Allen ''a gifted and sophisticated young satirist [who] has sustained his comic vein remarkably well. . . . Beautifully compact, 'Take the Money and Run' is simply rib-cracking fun; retrospectively, there's the joy of remembered laughter at something that isn't smut, doesn't involve those four-letter illiteracies, and isn't dumb.'' Allen says: ''Naturally for my first movie I stayed with my safest stuff, which is stuff I know: abject humility. I was very timid in that picture. But there was no way I could have been anything else. I had never made a film, I was never the star of a picture before.''

In 1969, Dr. David Reuben published *Everything You Always Wanted to Know about Sex But Were Afraid to Ask,* a self-help sex manual which was to become a best seller. Woody Allen bought film rights to the book, kept the title, and proceeded to make a motion picture which was not even loosely based on the original; other than the title, the only thing the two have in common is the central theme: sex. The film consists of seven separate, unrelated sketches dealing with the subject. Thomas Meehan writes: ''While all of the sketches have their funny moments, only three of the seven really come off. Three for seven, .429, is a terrific batting average in baseball, but it's not all that terrific in moviemaking.'' He goes on to call Allen ''the most talented comic writer and actor working these days in the American movie business. I thought, for example, that two of his earlier pictures, 'Take the Money and Run,' and 'Bananas,' were among the funniest movies made in this country since the days of W. C. Fields and the Marx Brothers. If you didn't like 'Take the Money and Run' and 'Bananas,' however, you'd better stay away from this one because, when compared to Allen's previous pictures, 'Everything You Always Wanted to Know about Sex' is a decided disappointment.'' Stuart Rosenthal agrees that this film does not represent Allen at his best; he calls it ''extremely uneven, with long laughterless intervals between its audacious high points. The major problem seems to be one of development within episodes. By dividing the film into seven short sketches, Allen forces himself to follow through on an initial idea in each case. He no longer has licence to move erratically from one point to another entirely unrelated point as he could in 'Bananas.' But in at least four of the segments, he exhausts his premise simply by stating it. Everything beyond that constitutes over-elaboration of a single gag.''

Apparently Allen agreed that ''Everything You Always Wanted to Know about Sex'' lacked a certain amount of discipline; his next film, ''Sleeper,'' according to Rosenthal, ''has a stylistic homogeneity not to be found in his earlier efforts. It consistently draws upon incongruities of shape, size and motion for its wit, and its spoken gags, for the most part, branch logically from the germinal concept of a man awakening in a totalitarian society two hundred years after being frozen by scientists. Allen's surprisingly accomplished jazz/ragtime score further unifies the film.'' Before beginning production on the film, Woody Allen said: ''I feel less secure with 'Sleeper' than I have with any of my films going into it. . . . This is a physically hard and dangerous film, but it's necessary; and I think if a person's funny, he can be funny verbally as well as physically. I've tried to make a marriage here of good verbal gags and plenty of jokes.''

''Love and Death'' has been called Woody Allen's answer to *War and Peace.* In this film, set in Czarist Russia, he boldly takes on all of Russian literature. Judith Crist writes: ''Allen continues the giant strides he began with 'Sleeper' toward truly original filmmaking and away from the stand-up character-cum-shtik restrictions that separate the comic from the comedian as a performer, and the comedy-writer from the humorist as a creative artist. Not to worry: the quintessential Woody is still on hand, the gentle-rationalist fumbler in a society always a bit beyond his coping. . . .'' Stefan Kanfer feels that ''it is as if one of Isaac Bashevis Singer's Hasidic schoolboys were managing Tolstoy's estate and Dostoevsky's psychoses. *The Brothers Karamazov* meet the Brothers Marx; the epic of *War and Peace* is re-

duced to a battle of church and shtetl.'' David Sterritt says that ''Love and Death'' is ''very much a Woody Allen picture—which makes sense since he directed and wrote it, besides starring. It has Allen's usual comic consistency and sense of detail. It showcases Allen's performing talents in a smoothly assembled setting that pulses to the beat of a racing Prokofiev score. And it swims in a sea of Allenesque irony—irony that might be very sad if it weren't laced with chuckles several times per minute. . . .''

Woody Allen recalls taking the idea for ''Love and Death'' to the executives at United Artists: ''Imagine their delighted surprise when I read them the script . . . with its plot that went from war to political assassination, ending with the death of its hero caused by a cruel trick of God. Never having witnessed eight film executives go into cardiac arrest simultaneously, I was quite amused. Regaining their breath, they proceeded to assure me that while they respected the seriousness of the premise, they thought my basic talent lay more in the direction of some of the simpler Three Stooges shorts. Though they agreed that death and atheism were indeed provocative subjects for farce, they said they would call the police if I didn't leave their office and never come back. Invoking the artistic-prerogative clause in my contract, a clause which gives me total control over what necktie I can wear while rewriting, I insisted that I go forward with the project. The U.A. moguls shrewdly asked for some kind of collateral and, placing my right arm in escrow, we came to an agreement.'' Allen believes that from the beginning the film ''was cursed by mysterious, cosmic shenanigans. Probably because the movie is highly critical of God. It implies He doesn't exist, or, if He does, He really can't be trusted. (Since coming to this conclusion I have twice been nearly struck by lightning and once forced to engage in a long conversation with a theatrical agent).''

''Annie Hall,'' if critics, movie-goers, and the Academy Awards selection committee are to be believed, is unquestionably Allen's finest artistic accomplishment. The film is a rather thinly-veiled autobiographical treatment of his real-life relationship with actress Diane Keaton, and has been the cause of much speculation on how much is revealed about Allen's closely-guarded personal life. He maintains that the film is fiction, saying: ''If people go out and say 'Yes, it was based on his life,' or 'Gee, isn't that amazing, a man makes up such a wild story,' that's fine with me either way.'' In a review of ''Annie Hall,'' Richard Schickel writes: ''Comedians are supposed to shtik to their lasts: Harpo could never speak and Groucho could never be at a loss for words; Fields could never seem to draw a sober breath or a sunny moral. What then, is Woody Allen doing starring in, writing and directing a ruefully romantic comedy that is at least as poignant as it is funny and may be the most autobiographical film ever made by a major comic? . . . What he is doing is growing, right before our eyes, and it is a fine sight to behold.'' Janet Maslin says that for the first time Allen ''seems capable of inviting genuine identification from his viewers, of channeling his comic gifts into material of real substance, of exerting a palpable emotional tug. 'Annie Hall' is bracingly adventuresome and unexpectedly successful, with laughs as satisfying as those in any of Allen's other movies and a whole new staying power.'' Vincent Canby concludes, ''['Annie Hall'] at last, puts Woody in the league with the best directors we have.''

Obviously the Academy of Motion Picture Arts and Sciences agreed with Canby's assessment of Woody Allen's work on ''Annie Hall.'' The film won the award for best picture in 1977, with Allen taking honors for best director and, with Marshall Brickman, best original screenplay; in addition, Diane Keaton was awarded an Oscar for best actress. The awards ceremony was held on Monday, April 3, 1978, and as he promised when the nominations were announced, Woody Allen was not present. He was in New York at Michael's Pub playing clarinet with the New Orleans Funeral and Ragtime Orchestra, a group he plays with every Monday night. When Allen was questioned, several years earlier, about the failure of one of his films to gain an Academy Award nomination, he said: "[The awards are] political and bought and negotiated for, and the whole concept of awards is silly. I cannot abide by the judgment of other people, because if you accept them when they say you deserve an award, then you have to accept them when they say you don't. . . . You put yourself in their hands as you're judged, and you're flattered, and the next year they say, 'No, you don't get it, Steve McQueen gets it'—and you know you were fantastic. The whole thing goes against everything you've worked for in your life. . . . I wish it was different. I think it would be wonderful if the Academy Awards were truly a spectacular occasion and the awards meant something and glamorous people did them and it was really a step-out night." Charles Joffe, producer of ''Annie Hall'' and an associate of Allen's for eighteen years, accepted the awards in his name; he told the audience: ''It's very hard for Woody to accept laurels for his work. He's interested in how well his work comes out and not in prizes.''

Woody Allen's books, *Getting Even* and *Without Feathers,* consist mainly of essays previously published in the *New Yorker.* According to Robert Lasson in a review of *Getting Even:* ''Allen doesn't hit every time. Some of the pieces are little underdeveloped buds. Others depend too much on technique rather than content and the result is more pyrotechnic wheel-spinning. But what sour ingrate would argue with a collection that contains five or six pieces of contemporary humor which are bound to last forever. . . . Anyone who has been bewailing the dearth of written humor will be cheered by this dizzy and dizzying collection.'' The title of *Without Feathers* comes from Emily Dickinson who, in one of her poems, called hope ''the thing with feathers.'' Allen's pessimism naturally prompted him to select a more appropriate name for his book. He says: ''How wrong Emily Dickinson was! Hope is not 'the thing with feathers.' The thing with feathers has turned out to be my nephew. I must take him to a specialist in Zurich.'' Arthur Cooper feels that Allen ''manages to make us laugh out loud until we make fools of ourselves. Except for two or three pieces that flirt dangerously with self-parody, his new collection . . . is the funniest book since *Getting Even,* which also had Allen's name on it.'' Cooper calls Woody Allen ''an intelligent, serious man who derives his funniest material from his darkest obsessions—God, sex, and particularly, death. . . .''

The films of Woody Allen are a diverse group ranging from the pandemonium of ''Bananas'' to the segmented ''Everything You Always Wanted to Know about Sex'' to the relatively disciplined ''Annie Hall.'' Throughout all of his work, however, there are several recurring themes which have become unmistakable Allen trademarks; the most significant, and most prevalent, of these is the subject of death. Eric Gerber writes: ''If Allen's humor, no matter what shape it takes, can be said to have a unifying theme it is the comedian's concern with his death. References to such abound. He jokes, 'I keep wondering if there is an afterlife, and if there is will they be able to break a twenty?' and we all laugh. But his concern is very real. You wonder just how serious he is when he says, 'I don't want to achieve immor-

tality through my work. I want to achieve it through not dying.''' Allen admits, ''there *is* a preponderance of death jokes in what I write. There are a lot of sex jokes too. But I don't do them consciously. They just appear.'' Eric Lax says that ''one reason the death jokes appear is that [Allen] is preoccupied with death. To him it is an irrational, hostile act on the part of the universe. He cites Tolstoy when he says that 'any man over thirty-five with whom death is not the main consideration is a fool.''' Allen concludes, ''what is it about death that bothers me so much? Probably the hours.''

''Many people think it is fun to make a comedy film,'' Allen writes, ''fun to dress up in amusing costumes, to speak bright lines, to play scenes with beautiful women in which one gets to fondle and kiss them, every day, take after take. Well, sir, let me be the first to kill that dream. Just because one deals in comedy doesn't mean the set is aflame with hilarity, or that everyone in the cast and crew is doubled over in laughter. Making a funny film provides all the enjoyment of getting your leg caught in the blades of a threshing machine. As a matter of fact, it's not even that funny.'' In his opinion, ''there's no question that comedy is harder to do than serious stuff. There's no question in my mind that comedy is less valuable than serious stuff. It has less of an impact, and I think for a good reason. When comedy approaches a problem, it kids it but it doesn't resolve it. Drama works it through in a more emotionally fulfilling way. I don't want to sound brutal, but there's something immature, something second-rate in terms of satisfaction when it is compared to drama. And it will always be that way.'' To the question of ''redeeming social value'' in his work, Allen replies: ''To me, all art—comedy, opera, painting, anything—is a diversion, an entertainment. So I view my own work in that same way. I don't think that it needs to be redeemed, I think it's strictly a pleasure item. If you have a certain set of values and a certain mentality, you get pleasure out of watching a situation comedy on television, and that's fine, then someone else who has a more complex or, to me, deeper grasp on life gets pleasure out of seeing a fine play or listening to a symphony. But in the end, it's all entertainment. I don't believe in art as a social force.''

Allen has stated that if he had his life to live over, ''I would do the exact same things I've done, with the possible exception of seeing 'The Magus.''' When asked if he believes in God, he replied: ''I believe there is an all powerful old gentleman with a white beard, in the heavens, who does not find me amusing.'' His favorite character in fiction is ''J. Edgar Hoover in *The Warren Report,*'' and he adds that he has been ''influenced by Kafka, Rilke, *The Bible, A Boy's Guide to Forestry,* and *Advanced Sexual Positions—How to Achieve Them without Laughing.*'' ''[Robert] Benchley has become a new idol for me,'' Allen once told a *Time* reporter, ''perhaps because everybody else also imitates Perelman's complicated style, I've tried to get simpler, like Benchley, and to write about subjects that really concern me.'' The aim of his life's work is ''to forge in the smithy of my soul the uncreated conscience of my race. Then to see if they can be turned out in plastic.''

In addition to those films which he directed, Woody Allen's acting credits include parts in ''Casino Royale,'' ''The Front,'' and the film version of his play, ''Don't Drink the Water.''

AVOCATIONAL INTERESTS: Tennis, spectator sports (especially basketball), jazz (plays clarinet in a band; practices daily while working on films).

BIOGRAPHICAL/CRITICAL SOURCES: New York Times, June 23, 1965, August 24, 1969, May 2, 1971; *Time,* November 25, 1966, April 14, 1967, February 21, 1967, July 3, 1972, October 27, 1975, April 25, 1977; *New Yorker,* December 3, 1966, February 22, 1969, December 27, 1969, July 15, 1972, November 5, 1973, February 4, 1974, April 25, 1977; *Saturday Review,* December 3, 1966, March 1, 1969, May 14, 1977; *Nation,* December 12, 1966, March 3, 1969; *Commonweal,* December 23, 1966, July 11, 1969, November 12, 1971; *America,* January 7, 1967, April 5, 1969; *Life,* April 28, 1967, August 23, 1969, October 6, 1972; *Harper's Bazaar,* December, 1968, December, 1971; *Playbill,* March, 1969; *New York,* March 10, 1969, September 22, 1969; *Holiday,* May, 1969; *McCalls,* June, 1969; *Cue,* August 23, 1969, September 13, 1969.

Book World, October 17, 1971; *New York Times Book Review,* October 24, 1971; *Seventeen,* May, 1972, November, 1975; *Vogue,* December, 1972; Bill Adler and Jeffrey Feinman, *Woody Allen: Crown Prince of American Humor,* Pinnacle Books, 1975; Eric Lax, *On Being Funny: Woody Allen and Comedy,* Charterhouse, 1975; *Miami Herald,* June 15, 1975; *Houston Post,* June 29, 1975; *Esquire,* July, 1975, May, 1977; *Films in Review,* August-September, 1975; *Newsweek,* June 7, 1976, May 2, 1977, March 18, 1978; *Redbook,* October, 1976; Richard Anobile, *Woody Allen's "Play It Again, Sam,"* Grosset, 1977; *Christian Century,* June 22, 1977; *Ms,* November, 1977; Lee Guthrie, *Woody Allen: A Biography,* Drake, 1978; *Detroit Free Press,* April 9, 1978.†

*   *   *

ALLEN, Howard W. 1931-

PERSONAL: Born May 17, 1931, in Dahlgren, Ill.; son of Omar E. (a businessman) and Helen (Wilson) Allen; married Loreta Kay Warren (a secretary), December 27, 1956; children: Mark Wilson, Robin Warren, Laura Susan. *Education:* Attended Southern Illinois University, 1949-51; University of Chicago, B.A., 1954, M.A., 1955; University of Washington, Seattle, Ph.D., 1960. *Politics:* Democratic. *Religion:* None. *Home Address:* R.R. 4, Carbondale, Ill. 62901. *Office:* Department of History, Southern Illinois University, Carbondale, Ill. 62901.

CAREER: University of Akron, Akron, Ohio, instructor, 1959-61, assistant professor of history, 1961-62; Southern Illinois University, Carbondale, assistant professor, 1962-67, associate professor, 1967-73, professor of history, 1973—. University of Michigan, research associate, Inter-University Consortium for Political Research, 1964-66, visiting scholar, 1976-77. *Military service:* U.S. Air Force, 1951-52. *Member:* American Historical Association, Organization of American Historians, Social Science History Association. *Awards, honors:* American Council of Learned Societies grants-in-aid, 1966-67; National Science Foundation grants, 1971-73.

WRITINGS: (Editor with Jerome M. Clubb) *Electoral Change and Stability in American Political History,* Free Press, 1971. Contributor to history and politics journals. Member of board of editors, *Social Science History.*

WORK IN PROGRESS: Progressive Reform and the Political System, with Jerome M. Clubb.

*   *   *

ALLEN, James Lovic 1929-
(Jim Allen, Allen James)

PERSONAL: Born January 2, 1929, in Atlanta, Ga.; son of James L. (a civil servant) and Effie (Schell) Allen; married Barbara Foster, June 13, 1953 (divorced September, 1976); children: Melinda Sue, Algernon Foster. *Education:* Tulane University, B.A., 1953, M.A., 1954; University of Florida, Ph.D., 1959. *Politics:* Democrat. *Religion:* Unitarian. *Home:* 42 Wainaku St., Apt. 103-A, Hilo, Hawaii 96720. *Office:* Department of English, University of Hawaii at Hilo, Hilo, Hawaii 96720.

CAREER: University of Tennessee, Knoxville, instructor in English, 1954-56; Stephen F. Austin State College (now Stephen F. Austin State University), Nacogdoches, Tex., assistant professor of English, 1959-60; University of Southern Mississippi, Hattiesburg, associate professor of English, 1960-63; University of Hawaii at Hilo, professor of English, 1963—. Visiting professor at Western Washington State College, summer, 1968, Hartwick College, summer, 1969, Stephen F. Austin State University, 1970-71, and University of Tennessee, Knoxville, 1976—. Research consultant, *Modern British Literature. Military service:* U.S. Navy, 1946-49. *Member:* Modern Language Association of America, American Association of University Professors, Phi Beta Kappa.

WRITINGS: (Under name Jim Allen) *Locked In: Surfing for Life,* A. S. Barnes, 1970. Also author of poems under pseudonym Allen James. Contributor of scholarly articles, largely about W. B. Yeats, and poems to *Explicator, Modern Drama, English Studies, Journal of Aesthetics and Art Criticism, Journal of Modern Literature, Sewanee Review, Twentieth Century Literature,* and other journals. First managing editor, *Southern Quarterly,* 1962-63. Member of editorial board, *Twentieth Century Literature.*

WORK IN PROGRESS: Yeat's Epitaph: A Key to Symbolic Unity in His Life and Work; Familial Relationships in the Cultural Achievements of W. B. Yeats and His Siblings.

SIDELIGHTS: James Allen told *CA:* "My entire career as a Yeats scholar has been and will continue to be [a] commitment to the proposition that historical and biographical criticism, rather than 'the new criticism,' are fundamental to an understanding of this poet's work and that such a critical approach leads to the inescapable conclusion that Yeats literally and fervently believed in the basic tenets of his personal cosmology and 'religion.' I believe that the extensive publication of previously unpublished materials by the poet will validate beyond question this position with the late 1970's and the 1980's."

AVOCATIONAL INTERESTS: Surfing, jazz and folk music, playing mandolin, banjo, and saxophone.

*   *   *

ALLEN, John Jay 1932-

PERSONAL: Born May 20, 1932, in Wichita, Kan.; son of Charles M. (a realtor) and Helen (McKee) Allen; married Tulia Rodriguez, July 4, 1956; children: Tulia R., Leticia H. *Education:* Duke University, A.B., 1954; Middlebury College, M.A., 1957; University of Wisconsin, Ph.D., 1960. *Home:* 1020 Northwest 61st Ter., Gainesville, Fla. 32605. *Office:* Department of Romance Languages and Literature, University of Florida, Gainesville, Fla. 32611.

CAREER: University of Florida, Gainesville, assistant professor, 1960-65, associate professor, 1966-68, professor of Spanish, 1969—. *Military service:* U.S. Army, 1954-56. *Member:* Modern Language Association of America, American Association of Teachers of Spanish and Portuguese, American Association of University Professors, Southern Atlantic Modern Language Association.

WRITINGS: Don Quixote: Hero or Fool?, University of Florida Press, 1969; *Don Quijote de la Mancha*, Editorial Catedra (Madrid), 1977. Contributor to *Hispania, Modern Language Notes, Romance Notes, Symposium, Revista Hispanica Moderna*, and *Hispano-Italic Studies*.

WORK IN PROGRESS: Research on Petrarchan imagery in Spanish Golden Age poetry; irony in *Don Quixote*.

* * *

ALLEN, Reginald E. 1931-

PERSONAL: Born March 13, 1931, in Philadelphia, Pa.; son of Amos Samuel and Alice (Bodine) Allen; married Ann Branin Usilton, 1960; children: Alice, Elizabeth, Ruth, William. *Education:* Haverford College, A.B., 1953; University of St. Andrews, B.Phil., 1957; Yale University, Ph.D., 1958. *Office:* Department of Philosophy, Northwestern University, Evanston, Ill. 60201.

CAREER: University of Minnesota, Minneapolis, lecturer, 1957-58, instructor, 1958-60, assistant professor of philosophy, 1960-62; Indiana University at Bloomington, associate professor, 1962-64, professor of philosophy, 1964-68; Purdue University, Lafayette, Ind., professor of philosophy, 1968-69; University of Toronto, Toronto, Ontario, professor of philosophy, 1969-78, special lecturer in law, 1973-78; Northwestern University, Evanston, Ill., professor of philosophy, 1978—. Visiting professor, Yale University, 1971-72; Cowling Professor, Carleton College, 1977. Member, Institute for Advanced Study, Princeton, N.J., 1966-67, 1974-75. *Member:* American Philosophical Association, Society for the Promotion of Hellenic Studies.

WRITINGS: Greek Philosophy: Thales to Aristotle, Free Press, 1965; (editor) *Studies in Plato's Metaphysics*, Routledge & Kegan Paul, 1966; *Plato's Euthyphro and the Earlier Theory of Forms*, Humanities, 1970; (editor with D. J. Furley) *Studies in Presocratic Philosophy*, Humanities, 1970. Contributor to philosophical and philological journals, and other publications.

* * *

ALLEN, Robert F(rances) 1928-

PERSONAL: Born December 26, 1928, in New York, N.Y.; son of Edwin E. and Mary (Thompson) Allen; married Elaine J. Bender, November 21, 1956; children: Judd, Peter. *Education:* State Teachers College, Plattsburgh (now State University of New York College at Plattsburgh), B.S., 1949; New York University, M.A., 1951, Ph.D., 1957; Columbia University, additional study, 1957-59. *Home and office:* SRI Human Resources Institute, Tempe Wick Rd., Morristown, N.J. 07960.

CAREER: Kean College of New Jersey, Union, professor of psychology, 1957—; SRI Human Resources Institute, Morristown, N.J., president, 1970—. Director, Metropolitan Area Consultation Center, 1957—. President, Scientific Resources, Inc., 1964—. Consultant to universities, government agencies, and business organizations. U.S. congressional candidate, 1968, 1970. *Military service:* U.S. Marine Corps, 1950-53; became sergeant. *Member:* American Academy of Political and Social Science, American Psychological Association, American Association of Behavioral Scientists, New York Society of Clinical Psychologists. *Awards, honors:* Founders' Day award, New York University, 1957.

WRITINGS: Social Integration and the English Language: Development of Puerto Rican Children, Ford Foundation,

1956; *College Fields Study*, U.S. Department of Health, Education and Welfare, 1966; *Teacher Aide System*, Macmillan, 1968; *From Delinquency to Freedom*, S.C. Publications, 1969; *The Quiet Revolution*, Grosset, 1977. Contributor of articles to *Journal of Applied Behavioral Science, Psychiatric Outpatient Journal, Journal of Criminal Law, Criminology and Police Science*, and *Sloan Management Review*.

SIDELIGHTS: Robert F. Allen told *CA:* "I am convinced that people are too often the victims of the cultures in which they happen to find themselves. I am interested in seeing that my writing, research, and political and social activities contribute to our ability to create our own environments rather than merely being the products of what happens to exist. My experience in a variety of settings indicated to me that it is quite possible for us to do this. The Normative Systems approach to change which I have been working on for the last fifteen years and which will be the subject of a book now being readied for publication, is an approach by which this can be accomplished."

* * *

ALLEN, Ross R(oundy) 1928-

PERSONAL: Born January 21, 1928, in Salt Lake City, Utah; son of William B. (a contractor) and Rebecca (Roundy) Allen; married Maurine Neilson, September 20, 1949; children: Raquel (Mrs. Stephen Teuscher), Connie V., Kim, Ross R., Jr., Trent, Heather Lei. *Education:* University of Utah, B.S., 1952, M.S., 1955, Ed.D., 1962. *Religion:* Church of Jesus Christ of Latter-day Saints. *Home:* 1110 North Rose St., Logan, Utah 84321. *Office:* College of Education, Utah State University, Logan, Utah 84321.

CAREER: High school mathematics teacher in Meeker, Colo., 1952-55, in Salt Lake City, Utah, 1956-57; Church College of Hawaii, Laie, Oahu, registrar and director of admissions, 1957-60, assistant professor of secondary education, 1960-63, head of department of secondary education, 1963-66; teacher of mathematics in Essex, England, 1963-64; Utah State University, Logan, associate professor of secondary education, 1966-70, professor of mathematics education, 1970—, acting head of department of secondary education, 1967-68, director of admissions and teacher education, 1967-69. Bishop of Mormon Church. Fulbright lecturer in Laos, 1973-74. *Military service:* U.S. Air Force, 1946-49; served in Japan. *Member:* Association for Supervision and Curriculum Development, National Education Association, Phi Delta Kappa, Phi Kappa Phi.

WRITINGS: (Editor) *Issues in School Measurement and Evaluation*, Simon & Schuster, 1970; (editor) *Seminar Topics in Secondary Education*, Simon & Schuster, 1970. Contributor to *Salt Lake Tribune* and to education journals in the United States and abroad.

WORK IN PROGRESS: Children's travel stories.

* * *

ALLEN, William A(ustin) 1916-

PERSONAL: Born July 23, 1916, in Minneapolis, Minn.; son of Guy Delos and Harriett (Schreyer) Allen; married Ruth Marie Nelson (a teacher), August 19, 1949; children: Craig, Carol Jane, William II, Laura Beth. *Education:* University of Minnesota, B.A., 1947, M.P.H., 1952. *Religion:* Protestant. *Residence:* Philadelphia, Pa.

CAREER: Philadelphia Department of Public Health, Philadelphia, Pa., coordinator of information and education,

1955—. Visiting instructor, Temple University, University of Pennsylvania, and Philadelphia Community College; adjunct instructor, University of Minnesota. Co-chairman, Philadelphia Health Fair, 1957; member of regional council, President's Committee on Health Education; former member of regional planning council, North East Philadelphia. *Military service:* U.S. Naval Reserves, 1942-45. *Member:* American Public Health Association (fellow), Pennsylvania Public Health Association (former president), Philadelphia Inter-agency Council on Smoking and Health (former chairman), Philadelphia Cancer Education and Service Program (coordinator), Philadelphia Stop Obesity Sensibly Program. *Awards, honors:* Chapel of Four Chaplains Award for community service.

WRITINGS: (With William A. Fackler and Gerhard Angermann) *Learning to Live without Cigarettes,* Doubleday, 1968. Editor, *Air Pollution Control Progress.*

WORK IN PROGRESS: Health materials for the general public; working on a guidebook for physically handicapped teenagers.

SIDELIGHTS: William Allen is concerned with cigarette smoking, obesity, and lack of exercise as dangers to good health, and is interested in the preventive aspects of medicine. He has traveled to South America and Europe.

*   *   *

ALLENTUCK, Marcia Epstein   1928-

PERSONAL: Born June 8, 1928, in New York, N.Y.; married Jack Allentuck (an engineer and economist), August 5, 1949; children: Isa. *Education:* New York University, B.A. (summa cum laude), 1948; Columbia University, Ph.D. (with first class honors), 1964. *Religion:* Jewish. *Home:* 5 West 86th St., Apt. 12B, New York, N.Y. 10024. *Office:* Department of English, City College of the City University of New York, New York, N.Y. 10031; and Department of Art History, Graduate School and University Center of the City University of New York, 33 West 42nd St., New York, N.Y. 10036.

CAREER: Lecturer in English at Columbia University, New York City, 1955-57, New York University, New York City, fall, 1956, and Hunter College (now Hunter College of the City University of New York), New York City, spring, 1957; Sarah Lawrence College, Bronxville, N.Y., instructor in English, 1962-63; City University of New York, New York City, 1959—, began as lecturer, currently professor of English, City College, and professor of art history, Graduate School and University Center.

MEMBER: Modern Language Association of America, William Morris Society and Kelmscott Fellowship (member of executive council, 1965-67), Society of Architectural Historians, Royal Society of Arts (fellow), Modern Humanities Research Association, Lessing Society of America, Milton Society of America, British Society for the Philosophy of Science, British Society for Aesthetics, American Society for Aesthetics, Society for the Philosophy of Science (British), Conference on British Studies, Bibliographical Society of America, Scottish History Society, International Comparative Literature Association, American Comparative Literature Association, Renaissance Society of America, College Art Association, International Council on Museums, Augustan Reprint Society, Keats-Shelley Association of America, Keats-Shelley Association (British), Manuscript Society, American Society of Eighteenth-Century Studies, Association for Scottish Literary Studies, P.E.N., Phi Beta Kappa.

AWARDS, HONORS: Howard postdoctoral fellowship at Brown University, 1966-67; Chapelbrook postdoctoral fellowship, 1969-70; grants from, New York State Department of Education, 1965-66, American Philosophical Society, 1966, American Council of Learned Societies, 1967, Henry E. Huntington Library, 1968, National Translation Center, University of Texas, 1968-69, Harvard University, 1972-73, and National Endowment for the Humanities, 1973-74.

WRITINGS: The Works of Henry Needler, Augustan Reprint Society, 1961; *The Achievement of Isaac Bashevis Singer,* Southern Illinois University Press, 1969; *John Graham's System and Dialectics of Art,* Johns Hopkins Press, 1971. Contributor of more than one hundred articles to literature and art journals. Has written and read more than fifty learned papers at academic meetings in the United States and Europe.

BIOGRAPHICAL/CRITICAL SOURCES: New York Times, November 1, 1969.

*   *   *

ALLEY, Robert S.   1932-

PERSONAL: Born January 5, 1932, in Richmond, Va.; son of Reuben E. (an editor) and Mary (Sutherland) Alley; married Norma Crane (an elementary school teacher), August 17, 1957; children: Robert S., Jr., John R. *Education:* University of Richmond, B.A., 1953; Southern Baptist Theological Seminary, B.D., 1956; Princeton University, M.A., 1960, Ph.D., 1962. *Politics:* Democrat. *Home:* 7009 Bandy Rd., Richmond, Va. 23229. *Office:* Department of Religion, University of Richmond, Richmond, Va. 23173.

CAREER: William Jewell College, Liberty, Mo., assistant professor of religion, 1961-63; University of Richmond, Richmond, Va., assistant professor, 1963-66, associate professor, 1966-73, professor of religion, 1973—. Treasurer of McCarthy for President campaign in Virginia, 1968. *Member:* American Academy of Religion, American Association of University Professors, American Civil Liberties Union (president, Richmond chapter, 1967).

WRITINGS: Revolt Against the Faithful: A Biblical Case for Inspiration as Encounter, Lippincott, 1970; *So Help Me God: Religion and the Presidency, Wilson to Nixon,* John Knox, 1972; (contributor) *As a Cultural Force,* Praeger, 1976; *Television: Ethics for Hire?,* Abingdon, 1976. Also author of filmscripts, "Television, For Better or Worse," and "How Dare These Little Half Hour Shows . . . ?," both produced on Public Broadcasting Service, 1977.

*   *   *

AL-MARAYATI, Abid A(min)   1931-

PERSONAL: Born October 14, 1931; son of Amin Hussein and Badria Haj (Ghazi) Al-Marayati; married Ayda Cheik, March 18, 1977; children: (previous marriage) Ghazi Daniel. *Education:* Attended college in Tripoli, Lebanon, 1948-49; Bradley University, B.A., 1952, M.A., 1954; New York University, Ph.D., 1959. *Home:* 2109 Terrace View W., Toledo, Ohio 43606. *Office:* Department of Political Science, University of Toledo, Toledo, Ohio 43606.

CAREER: United Nations, New York, N.Y., intern, 1954, secretary of Iraq delegation to U.N. General Assembly, 1955, secretary of Yemen delegation to U.N. General Assembly, 1956-60; University of Massachusetts, Amherst, instructor in department of government, 1960; International Atomic Energy Agency, Vienna, Austria, technical assistance officer, Division of Economic and Technical Assistance, 1960-62; State University of New York College at Plattsburgh, associate professor of political science, 1962-64; Harvard University, Cambridge, Mass., research fellow, 1964-65; Arizona State University, Tempe, associate professor of political science, 1965-68; University of Toledo, Toledo, Ohio, professor of political science, 1968—, formerly chairman of department, currently director of the Center for International Studies. Part-time lecturer and consultant, American Institute for Foreign Trade, 1965-68; research associate, Graduate School of International Studies, University of Denver, 1965-67.

WRITINGS: A Diplomatic History of Modern Iraq, Speller, 1961; *Middle Eastern Constitutions and Electoral Laws,* Praeger, 1968; (with others) *The Middle East: Its Governments and Politics,* Duxbury Press, 1972. Contributor *to Middle East Forum, Foreign Affairs Reports, Pakistan Horizon,* and other journals.

WORK IN PROGRESS: International Relations of the Middle East and North Africa, for Schenkman.

*   *   *

ALMARAZ, Felix D(iaz), Jr. 1933-

PERSONAL: Born December 2, 1933, in San Antonio, Tex.; son of Felix Diaz, Sr. (a carpenter) and Antonia (Rodriguez) Almaraz; married Maria Guadalupe Olivares (a teacher and writer), August 12, 1961; children: Antonio Olivares. *Education:* St. Mary's University, San Antonio, Tex., B.A. (magna cum laude), 1959, M.A., 1962; University of New Mexico, Ph.D., 1968. *Politics:* Democrat. *Religion:* Roman Catholic. *Home:* 5907 Forest Cove, San Antonio, Tex. 78240. *Office:* Division of Social Science, University of Texas, San Antonio, Tex.

CAREER: Harlandale Independent School District, San Antonio, Tex., teacher in public schools, 1960-64; U.S. Atomic Energy Commission, Los Alamos, N.M., historical information analyst, Office of the Project Historian, 1966; St. Mary's University, San Antonio, Tex., assistant professor of history, 1967-70; Pan American University, Edinburg, Tex., associate professor of history, 1970; South San Antonio Independent School District, San Antonio, director, Bilingual Education Center, 1971-73; University of Texas at San Antonio, associate professor of history, 1973—. Visiting associate professor of history, University of Texas at Austin, 1971. Consultant, lecturer, or participant in various Mexican-American, educational, and historical organizations, institutes, and workshops, 1967—. Member of humanities panel, Texas Commission on the Arts and Humanities, 1972—. *Member:* American Historical Association, American Association of University Professors, Western History Association, Texas State Historical Association (life), Historical Society of New Mexico.

AWARDS, HONORS: Excellence in Forensics Award, Express Publishing Co., 1957; Teacher's Medal, Freedoms Foundation of Valley Forge, 1966; Presidio La Bahia Award, Sons of the Republic of Texas, Goliad, Tex., 1969; research fellowship, National Endowment for the Humanities, St. Mary's University, 1969-70; American Association for State and Local History award of merit, 1975, for *Tragic Cavalier.*

WRITINGS: Standing Room Only: A History of the San Antonio Little Theatre, 1912-1962, Texian Press, 1964; (contributor) *Conference on the Role of the Mexican American in the History of the Southwest,* Inter-American Institute of Pan American College, 1969; *Tragic Cavalier: Governor Manuel Salcedo of Texas, 1808-1813,* University of Texas

Press, 1971; (contributor with wife, Maria Olivares Almaraz) Peter I. Rose, editor, *Many Peoples, One Nation,* Random House, 1971. Contributor of articles and reviews to *Texana, Journal of the West, Arizona and the West, Southwestern Historical Quarterly, West Texas Historical Association Yearbook, Pacific Historical Review, Red River Valley Historical Review, Social Science Journal,* and *New Mexico Historical Review.* Regional editor, *Journal of the West,* 1968—; member of editorial advisory board, *Southwestern Historical Quarterly,* 1971-74.

WORK IN PROGRESS: With wife, Maria Olivares Almaraz, *Reading Exercises on Mexican Americans,* for Continental Press; research on Franciscan missions of the middle Rio Grande of Coahuila, Texas in the eighteenth century; a book tentatively titled *A Knight Without Armor: A Biography of Carlos E. Castaneda, Mexican American Historian, 1896-1958;* research on the Mexican American historical heritage in nineteenth-century Texas.

BIOGRAPHICAL/CRITICAL SOURCES: American-Statesman (Austin, Tex.), June 6, 1971; *Light* (San Antonio, Tex.), September 12, 1971.

*   *   *

ALSTON, Mary Niven 1918-
(Marian Niven)

PERSONAL: Born November 5, 1918, in Morganton, N.C.; daughter of Louis Watson (a dentist) and Charlotte Niven (a painter; maiden name McKinney) Alston. *Education:* Bryn Mawr College, A.B., 1941; Columbia University, M.A., 1944; graduate study at Union Theological Seminary, New York, N.Y. *Politics:* "Independent (Usually vote Democrat or Republican)." *Religion:* Episcopalian. *Agent:* Raines & Raines, 475 Fifth Ave., New York, N.Y. 10017.

CAREER: History teacher in Tappahannock, Va., and Newark, N.J., 1944-47; various paid choir positions. Vestrywoman, Church of the Resurrection.

WRITINGS: (Under pseudonym, Marian Niven) *Altar and the Crown,* Sewanee Press, 1972. Contributor (under Mary Niven Alston) to *Journal of the History of Medicine.*

WORK IN PROGRESS: Three novels, one in the Victorian period; a sequel to *Altar and the Crown.*

AVOCATIONAL INTERESTS: Sewing, animals.†

*   *   *

ALTHOFF, Phillip 1941-

PERSONAL: Born August 30, 1941, in Centralia, Ill.; son of Emil E. S. and Mary Emma (Stearns) Althoff; married second wife, Candace Kay Ruth, December 23, 1971; children: (first marriage) Sarah Elisabeth. *Education:* Illinois State University, B.A., 1963; University of Iowa, M.A., 1966, Ph.D., 1970. *Politics:* None. *Religion:* None. *Office:* Department of Political Science, Kansas State University, Manhattan, Kan. 66502.

CAREER: Western Michigan University, Kalamazoo, instructor in political science, 1966-67; University of Western Ontario, London, lecturer, 1967-68, assistant professor of political science, 1968-69; Cornell College, Mount Vernon, Iowa, visiting assistant professor, 1969-70; Kansas State University, Manhattan, assistant professor, 1970-75, associate professor of political science, 1975—. *Awards, honors:* Woodrow Wilson fellow, 1963-64.

WRITINGS: (With Michael Rush) *An Introduction to Political Sociology,* Thomas Nelson, 1971, Bobbs-Merrill, 1972;

(editor with Robert B. Leachman) *Preventing Nuclear Theft: Guidelines for Industry and Government,* Praeger, 1972.

WORK IN PROGRESS: Research on nationalism, internationalism, fascism, and communism in Latin America; research on revolutionary ideology and revolutionary leaders and leadership in Latin America.

*   *   *

ALTMAN, Dennis 1943-

PERSONAL: Born August 16, 1943, in Sydney, Australia; son of Andrew (an engineer) and Assia (Patkin) Altman. *Education:* University of Tasmania, B.A. (honors), 1964; Cornell University, M.A., 1966. *Politics:* "Libertarian Socialist." *Religion:* None. *Home:* 8 D/8 Hampden St., Paddington, New South Wales, Australia 2021. *Office:* Government Department, University of Sydney, Sydney, New South Wales, Australia 2006.

CAREER: Monash University, Melbourne, Victoria, Australia, lecturer in politics, 1966-68; University of Sydney, Sydney, New South Wales, Australia, lecturer, 1969-75, senior lectuer in American politics, 1975—. News commentator and drama critic, Australian Broadcasting Commission. *Member:* Australasian Political Science Association, National Union of Australian University Students (member of executive board, 1964), Council for Civil Liberties, Gay Liberation Front (Sydney).

WRITINGS: (Contributor) H. Mayer, editor, *Australian Politics: A Reader,* F. W. Cheshire, 1969; (contributor) R. Gordon, editor, *The Australian New Left,* Heinemann, 1970; *Homosexual: Oppression and Liberation,* Outerbridge & Dienstfrey, 1971. Also contributor of chapters to many books including *The Way Out,* 1975, *Studies In E. M. Forster,* 1977, *Australian Society,* 1977. Contributor of book reviews to *Bulletin, National Times, Washington Post,* and *The Review;* contributor of articles to *Politics, Australian Outlook, Australian Quarterly, Arena, Other Voices, Masque,* and other publications.

WORK IN PROGRESS: Research on the inter-relationship between cultural and political change for a book; a comparative study of gay movements; a collection of writings.

SIDELIGHTS: Dennis Altman has traveled in the U.S. and Europe. He told *CA:* "My involvement with Gay Liberation both in the States and in Australia, has made me conscious of the complex nature of repression in contemporary liberal societies, and will undoubtedly continue to influence my writings." He adds: "It is difficult to summarise one's politics in one line. I have been involved in various activities that are generally considered radical—anti-war, anti-apartheid and gay liberation demonstrations, for example. I am committed to a loose form of marxism, but one need also bear in mind that any genuine radical position is one that allows both for error and for constant development."

*   *   *

ALVAREZ, Joseph A. 1930-

PERSONAL: Born October 2, 1930, in New York, N.Y.; son of Raul (an electric company supervisor) and Helen (Woehl) Alvarez; married Marianne Besser, December 17, 1955 (died November 14, 1971); married Margaret Hoehn, June 20, 1977; children: (first marriage) Krista. *Education:* City College (now City College of the City University of New York), B.A., 1955; Sonoma State College (now California State College, Sonoma), M.A. *Residence:* Santa

Rosa, Calif. *Agent:* Curtis Brown Ltd., 575 Madison Ave., New York, N.Y. 10022.

CAREER: Writer's Digest, Cincinnati, Ohio, circulation director, 1955-58; Book-of-the-Month Club, New York, N.Y., advertising executive, 1958-61; professional writer, 1961—. *Member:* Author's Guild.

WRITINGS: (With C. W. Mattison) *Man and His Resources in Today's World,* Creative Education Press, 1967; *Vice Presidents of Destiny,* Putnam, 1969; *Politics in America,* Creative Education Press, 1971; *From Reconstruction to Revolution,* Atheneum, 1971. Educational film strips: "Streets, Prairies and Valleys: The Life of Carl Sandburg"; "The World of Mark Twain"; "The Regulatory Agencies"; "Mass Media"; "The Puritan Legacy"; "From Colony to Country: Early American Literature"; "We Are Indians: American Indian Literature"; "Do We Really Have Freedom of the Press?"

WORK IN PROGRESS: Textbook on technical writing.

AVOCATIONAL INTERESTS: Tennis, guitar.

*   *   *

ALVAREZ-ALTMAN, Grace (DeJesus) 1926-

PERSONAL: Born April 9, 1926, in Dominican Republic; came to United States in 1928; naturalized in 1947; daughter of Antonio Baul (a barber) and Consuelo (Burgos) Cerda; married Pedro Alvarez (a minister), June 23, 1945 (died, 1967); married Robert Lee Altman (a teacher), April 20, 1970; children: (first marriage) Anthony, Consuelo, Martha, Stevie. *Education:* Hunter College (now Hunter College of the City University of New York), B.A., 1945; Columbia University, M.A., 1947; University of Southern California, Ph.D., 1964. *Home:* 19 Lancet Way, Brockport, N.Y. 14420. *Agent:* Editorial Castalia, Zurbana 39, Madrid 10, Spain. *Office:* Department of Modern Languages, State University of New York College, Brockport, N.Y. 14420.

CAREER: History and Spanish teacher in secondary schools in New York and New Hampshire, 1945-49; La Sierra Prep School, Loma Linda, Calif., instructor in Spanish and history, 1949-60; La Sierra College (now Loma Linda University), Loma Linda, assistant professor of Spanish, 1960-62, associate professor of modern languages, 1963-66; Loma Linda University, Loma Linda, associate professor of modern languages, 1966-67; State University of New York College at Brockport, associate professor of modern languages and supervisor of teacher training in languages, 1967—. U.S. delegate to International Congress of Onomastic Sciences in Vienna, Austria, 1969, Sophia, Bulgaria, 1972; delegate to XIIIe Congres International de Linguistique et Philologie Romanes, Universite Laval, Quebec, Canada, 1971. Professional violinist, pianist, and choir director.

MEMBER: Modern Language Association of America, American Name Society, American Association of University Professors, American Association of Teachers of Spanish and Portuguese, American Council of Teachers of Foreign Languages, Canadian Onomastic Institute, Northeastern Modern Language Association, New York State Association of Foreign Language Teachers, Name Institute (New York).

WRITINGS: Toponimos en apellidos hispanos, Editorial Castalia (Madrid), 1968; *The Cuba of New York State: Hispanic Toponymy of the Empire State,* Straight Publishing Co., 1971. Contributor of poems and articles to journals in her field. Editor of *Garcia Lorca Review* and *Literary Onomastics Studies.*

WORK IN PROGRESS: Patronymicos en Apellidos Hispanos and a dictionary of Spanish names in the United States.

SIDELIGHTS: Grace Alvarez-Altman told *CA* her main interest in writing is to produce ''a comprehensive study of all pertinent facts of Spanish onomastics and reevaluate all of Garcia Lorca's works. I am also very interested in improving methods of teaching languages in the face of the present crisis of the profession.''

*　　*　　*

AMABILE, George 1936-
(George Los)

PERSONAL: Surname is pronounced A-*mah*-be-lay; born May 29, 1936, in Jersey City, N.J.; son of Anthony Thomas (a civil engineer) and Josephine Mary (Masi) Amabile; married Delia Deane Wilson, September 6, 1960 (divorced, 1972); children: Natasha, Tamara. *Education:* Amherst College, A.B., 1957; University of Minnesota, M.A., 1961; University of Connecticut, Ph.D., 1969. *Politics:* Independent. *Religion:* ''I believe in the sun.'' *Home:* 17-75 Young St., Winnipeg, Manitoba, Canada. *Office:* Department of English, University of Manitoba, Winnipeg 19, Manitoba, Canada.

CAREER: During his early years Amabile worked as a folk singer, short order cook, house painter, waiter on the Great Northern Railroad, carpenter's apprentice, encyclopedia salesman, and farm laborer; University of Manitoba, Winnipeg, instructor, 1963-65, assistant professor, 1966-68, and 1969-71, associate professor of English and creative writing, 1971—. Writer in residence, University of British Columbia, 1968-69. Has also read his poetry at colleges, on television, on Canadian network radio, and at the 1976 Olympic Games in Montreal; formerly taught in a Schenectady, N.Y. high school and at Stony Mountain Penitentiary. *Member:* Modern Language Association of America, Association of Canadian University Teachers of English, League of Canadian Poets, American Civil Liberties Union. *Awards, honors:* Canada Council grants, 1968, 1969.

*WRITINGS—*Poems: *Blood Ties,* Sono Nis Press, 1972; *Open Country,* Turnstone Press, 1976; *Flower and Song,* Borealis Press, 1977.

Contributor to poetry anthologies, including *Young American Poets,* 1968, *''New Yorker'' Book of Poems,* 1970, *Made in Canada,* 1970, and *Canadian Poems for Children,* 1972. Contributor of more than fifty poems to *Prairie Schooner, Fiddlehead, Signet, Minnesota Review, Critic, New Yorker, Harper's, Carolina Quarterly,* and other periodicals. Former editor of *Ivory Tower,* and *Penny Paper;* co-founder and co-editor, *Par Point;* founder and editor, *Northern Light.*

WORK IN PROGRESS: A film script, ''The Survivor''; a novel, *Fire and Salt;* new poems; selected poems; a number of songs.

SIDELIGHTS: George Amabile told *CA:* ''I write for many reasons, for pleasure, because I believe that creative work is necessary to psychic and spiritual health, and to communicate meaningful experiences to others who may be interested in them. . . . I write because I am alive, and because when I do I'm most awake, most real. Writing is something I've chosen, it is not a vocation or a destiny. But I might have chosen anything: Any work can become an art form, and I've seen hot dog salesmen that had more style than Dick Cavett.

''I believe people should do whatever turns them on. As long as it doesn't screw up others. I think everyone in North America should be guaranteed a living income at birth, and thus freed from the slavery of corporations. I believe that all the Space Agency machinery and money should now be used to find a new power source, a way of developing Deuterium reactors. I believe in sexual freedom. I believe that big business is bad business. I believe in clean air and drinkable lakes. I don't think there should be a draft. I don't do drugs any more, but think they should be legalized.''

AVOCATIONAL INTERESTS: Carpentry, baseball, music (voice, guitar, and piano), tennis, swimming, photography, camping, fishing, hunting.

*　　*　　*

AMBROSINI, Maria Luisa

PERSONAL: Born in Pavia, Italy; daughter of Oreste and Cornelia (Bergamaschi) Boggeri; married Mario Ambrosini (a specialist in international law), 1941 (died, 1956). *Education:* Attended University of Lausanne and University of Paris; University of Padua, Doctorate in economics, 1934; additional study at University of Vienna, 1934-37, and Columbia University. *Religion:* Roman Catholic. *Home:* Via della Lungarina 65, Rome, Italy 00153; and Casal Rosso Borghese, Anzio (Rome), Italy. *Agent:* Harold Ober Associates, 40 East 49th St., New York, N.Y. 10017; Gabriela Baldner, 8 Muenchen 23, Lowithstrasse 8, Germany; Eric Linder, Corso Mattiotti, 3 Milan, Italy; and Hughes Massie Ltd., 69 Great Russell St., London, England.

CAREER: Columbia University, Teachers College, New York, N.Y., assistant to Professor Edward L. Thorndike; member of staff of International Secretariat, Institute of Pacific Relations, 1937-39; returned to Italy at outbreak of World War II; directed the press service of the Italian Department of Finance; worked with displaced children and other war victims. Delegate of the International Association of Women Lawyers in their dealings with the United Nations. Has made postwar social and economic surveys for Italian government.

WRITINGS: (With Mary Willis) *The Secret Archives of the Vatican* (Book-of-the-Month Club alternate), Little, Brown, 1969, 3rd edition, 1972. Contributor to *Harper's.*

WORK IN PROGRESS: With Mary Willis, *Forget about Ceramics,* a book on retirement, and *You Call Them Children,* juvenile science fiction.

SIDELIGHTS: Maria Luisa Ambrosini told *CA* that she took up writing seriously after her husband's death in 1956, shifting from social and economic to literary and historical subjects.

BIOGRAPHICAL/CRITICAL SOURCES: Books in the News, January 19, 1970; *Washington Star,* Feburary 1, 1970; *Christian Century,* February 4, 1970; *New York Times Book Review,* February 15, 1970; *Saturday Review,* February 28, 1970; *Book Currents,* March 11, 1970; *National Review,* April 7, 1970; *Theology Digest Book Survey,* June 26, 1970; *Book-of-the-Month Club News,* July, 1970; *Il Giornale d'Italia* (Rome), August 4-5, 1970; *Sunday Press,* December 20, 1970; *Irish Times,* February 4, 1971; *Australian,* March 1, 1971; *Sydney Morning Herald,* March 15, 1971; *Times Literary Supplement,* March 26, 1971; *Catholic Weekly* (Sydney), April 1, 1971; *Cape Argus* (Capetown), October 2, 1971; *Telegraph* (London), November 22, 1971.†

AMEND, Victor E(arl) 1916-

PERSONAL: Born October 14, 1916, in Kansas; son of Victor E. (a farmer) and Ada (Beatley) Amend; married Elizabeth Petrock (a teacher), June 22, 1946; children: Robert Harper, Charles Allen. *Education:* University of Kansas, B.A., 1939, M.A., 1941; University of Michigan, Ph.D., 1953. *Politics:* Democrat. *Religion:* Unitarian Universalist. *Home:* 7535 North Gale St., Indianapolis, Ind. 46240. *Office:* Department of English, Butler University, Indianapolis, Ind. 46208.

CAREER: Teacher in public schools of Kansas, 1940-41; Knox College, Galesburg, Ill., instructor in English, 1952-53; Butler University, Indianapolis, Ind., assistant professor, 1953-57, associate professor, 1957-69, professor of English, 1969—. *Military service:* U.S. Army, 1942-46. *Member:* Modern Language Association of America, National Council of Teachers of English, American Association of University Professors, American Civil Liberties Union.

WRITINGS: (Editor with L. T. Hendrick) *Ten Contemporary Thinkers,* Free Press, 1964; (editor with Hendrick) *Readings from Left and Right,* Free Press, 1969. Contributor to literature journals.

*   *   *

AMICK, Robert Gene 1933-

PERSONAL: Surname is pronounced *Ay*-mick; born June 6, 1933, in Detroit, Mich.; son of Jack (a tap dancer in vaudeville) and Susanna (Deleau) Amick; married Stephanie Jones (an elementary school teacher), August 11, 1959; children: Victoria II. *Education:* San Francisco State College (now University), B.A., 1959, M.A., 1962. *Politics:* Independent. *Religion:* None. *Residence:* Claremont, Calif. *Office:* Department of Psychology, Mount San Antonio College, Walnut, Calif. 91789.

CAREER: Mount San Antonio College, Walnut, Calif., professor of psychology, 1962—. Staff psychologist, Pomona Valley Mental Health Authority, Pomona, Calif., 1964—. *Military service:* U.S. Navy, 1950-54; received Korean ribbon with three battle stars. *Member:* American Association of Family Counselors, American Academy of Social Sciences, Phi Delta Kappa.

WRITINGS—With J. H. Brennecke; all published by Glencoe Press: *Struggle for Significance,* 1971, 2nd edition, 1975; *Significance: The Struggle We Share,* 1971, 2nd edition, 1975; *Psychology and Human Experience,* 1974; *Readings in Psychology and Human Experience,* 1974.

WORK IN PROGRESS: Second editions of *Psychology and Human Experience* and *Readings in Psychology and Human Experience.*

*   *   *

AMMERMAN, Leila T(remaine) 1912-

PERSONAL: Born February 3, 1912, in Buffalo, N.Y.; daughter of DeWitt Charles (a minister) and Alice (Dowd) Tremaine; married Roy E. Ammerman (a minister), July 14, 1934; children: Earle T., Dorothy (deceased), Alice (deceased), Garnette Mae. *Education:* Studied under tutors ("due to childhood heart condition"). *Politics:* Democratic. *Religion:* Christian Church (Disciples of Christ). *Home:* 5091 Starfish Dr. S.E., St. Petersburg, Fla. 33705. *Office:* Beach Memorial Chapel, 301 Corey Ave., St. Petersburg Beach, Fla. 33706.

CAREER: Girl's Club of Portsmouth, Portsmouth, Va., director, 1963-65; Little Library (a reading room for all philosophies), St. Petersburg, Fla., director, 1965-73; Beach Memorial Chapel, St. Petersburg Beach, Fla., secretary, 1975—. Member of curriculum and planning council, Christian Church; former member of board of directors, Christian Churches of Pennsylvania.

WRITINGS—All published by Abingdon, except as indicated: (Editor) *Of Such Is the Kingdom* (anthology), 1954; *Abingdon Promotion-Rally Day Book,* 1955; *Abingdon Easter Programs,* 1960; *Abingdon Mother's Day Book,* 1960; *Abingdon Christmas Programs,* 1960; *Inspiring Devotional Programs for Women's Groups,* W. A. Wilde, 1960, new edition, Baker Book, 1971; *Programs for Special Days,* W. A. Wilde, 1961; *The Golden Ladder of Stewardship,* W. A. Wilde, 1962, new edition, Baker Book, 1971. Also author of *Be Still and Know: First Steps in the Art of Meditation,* privately printed. Contributor of stories, articles, and poems to periodicals.

WORK IN PROGRESS: Research project, *God in the Silence–Guidance in Meditation.*

*   *   *

ANDELSON, Robert V(ernon) 1931-

PERSONAL: Born February 19, 1931, in Los Angeles, Calif.; son of Abraham (a merchant) and Ada (Markson) Andelson; married Geraldine Rippetoe, July 1, 1959; married second wife, Bonny Johnson (a junior college English teacher), June 7, 1964. *Education:* Los Angeles City College, A.A., 1950; University of Chicago, A.B. (equivalent), 1952; University of Southern California, A.M., 1954, Ph.D., 1960. *Politics:* Republican. *Religion:* Congregationalist. *Home:* 534 Cary Dr., Auburn, Ala. 36830. *Office:* Department of Philosophy, Auburn University, Auburn, Ala. 36830.

CAREER: Arlington College, Arlington, Calif., professor of philosophy and social sciences, 1954-58; ordained minister of Congregationalist Church, 1959; Henry George School of Social Sciences, San Diego, Calif., executive director, 1959-62; Northland College, Ashland, Wis., professor of philosophy and religion, 1962-63; Northwestern State University, Natchitoches, La., assistant professor of philosophy and government, 1963-65; Auburn University, Auburn, Ala., assistant professor, 1965-69, associate professor, 1969-73, professor of philosophy, 1973—. Visiting lecturer, California Baptist Theological Seminary, 1956-59; member of academic advisory council, Henry George School of Social Sciences, 1970—; trustee, Henry George Foundation of America, 1971—. *Member:* American Philosophical Association, American Association of University Professors (chapter president, 1975-76), Southern Society for Philosophy and Psychology, Alabama Philosophical Society (president, 1968-69). *Awards, honors:* Foundation for Social Research grant, 1959; Relm Foundation grant, 1967; George Washington Honor Medal from Freedoms Foundation, 1971.

WRITINGS: Imputed Rights: An Essay in Christian Social Theory, foreword by Russell Kirk, University of Georgia Press, 1971. Contributor to *New Review, Personalist, Discourse, Southern Journal of Philosophy,* and other journals. Member of editorial board, *American Journal of Economics and Sociology* and *Personalist.*

WORK IN PROGRESS: Editing and contributing to *The Gospel of George: A Century of Criticism Summarized and Evaluated.*

ANDERSCH, Alfred 1914-

PERSONAL: Born February 4, 1914, in Munich, Germany; son of Alfred A. and Hedwig (Watzek) Andersch; married Gisela Dichgans (a painter), 1950; children: Michael, Martin, Annette. *Education:* Attended Wittelsbacher Gymnasium, Munich. *Home:* 6611 Berzona, Ticino, Switzerland.

CAREER: Worked in a Munich publishing house as a young man to learn book trade; because of his Communist activities was held in Dachau Concentration Camp for six months, 1933; after release worked in industry; following World War II was a newspaper editor, working on *Der Ruf* and later on *Texte und Zeichen;* radio broadcaster, 1948-60; leader of an Artic expedition for German television, 1965. *Member:* Duetsche Akademie fuer Sprache und Dichtkunst, Bayerische Akademie der Schoenen Kuenste, P.E.N. *Awards, honors:* Deutscher Kritiker-Preis, 1958, for *Sansibar;* Nelly Sachs-Preis, 1968; Prix Charles Veillon, 1968, for *Efraim;* Literaturpris der Bayerisken Academic der Schoeuen Knuste.

WRITINGS: Deutsche Literatur in der Entscheidung (essays), Volk & Zeit, 1948; (editor) *Europaeische Avantgarde* (anthology), Verlag der Frankfurter Hefte, 1949; *Kirschen der Freiheit: Ein Bericht* (autobiographical), Frankfurter Verlagsanstalt, 1952; *Piazza San Gaetano: Suite* (narrative), Walter-Verlag, 1957; *Sansibar: Oder, der letzte Grund* (novel), Walter-Verlag, 1957, translation by Michael Bullock published as *Flight to Afar,* Coward, 1958, edition in German with introduction and notes by Walter G. Hesse published in England under original title, Harrap, 1964; *Geister und Leute,* Walter-Verlag, 1958, translation by Christa Armstrong published as *The Night of the Giraffe and Other Stories,* Random House, 1964; *Fahrerflucht* (radio play), Hans Bredow-Institut, 1958, published with three other radio plays under same title, Deutcher Taschenbuch Verlag, 1956, and singly in *Deutsche Lektuere,* edited by Paul G. Krauss, Holt, 1969.

Die Rote (novel), Walter-Verlag, 1960, translation by Bullock published as *The Redhead,* Pantheon, 1961; *Der Tod des James Dean* (radio play; text adapted from John Dos Passos and others), Tschudy, 1960; *Paris ist eine ernste Stadt* (narrative), Olten, 1961; *Wanderungen im Norden* (travel narrative; illustrated with color pictures by his wife, Gisela Andersch), Walter-Verlag, 1962; *Ein Liebhaber des Halbschattens* (stories), Walter-Verlag, 1963; *Die Blindheit des Kunstwerks und andere Aufsaetze* (essays and other writings), Suhrkamp, 1965; *Bericht, Roman, Erzaehlungen* (collection with bibliography of Andersch's works), Walter-Verlag, 1965; *Aus Einem roemischen Winter* (travel narrative), Walter-Verlag, 1966; *Efraim* (novel), Diogenes Verlag, 1967, translation by Ralph Manheim published as *Efraim's Book,* Doubleday, 1970; (contributor) Wolfgang Tschechne, editor, *Geliebte Staedte,* Fackeltraeger-Verlag, 1967; *Ein Auftrag fuer Lord Glouster* (collection), Signal-Verlag, 1968; *Hohe Breitengrade* (travel narrative on Arctic expedition), Diogenes Verlag, 1968; *Mein Verschwinden in Providence* (nine stories), Diogenes Verlag, 1971; *Norden, Sueden, rechis und links* (essays), Diogenes Verlag, 1972. Also author of *Winterspelt,* 1975.

Other radio scripts include: ''Strahlende Melancholie,'' 1953; ''Die Buerde des weissen Mannes, Brennpunkt Indochina,'' 1953; ''Die Feuerinsel oder die Heimkehr des Kapitaen Tizzoni,'' 1955; ''Synnoeves Halsband,'' 1958; ''Aktion ohne Fahnen'' (adaptation from *Sansibar),* 1958; (with Helmuth Krapp) ''Biologie und Tennis,'' 1958; ''Der Albino,'' 1960; ''Von Ratten und Evangelisten,'' 1960; ''Russisches Roulette,'' 1961.

SIDELIGHTS: Reviewing Alfred Andersch's *Efraim's Book,* Charles Markmann writes: ''It is not always easy to follow, but it is an impressively convincing synthesis of the simultaneous levels of his narrator so that past and present and even future and potential, desired and hated and feared, are elements that in every successful work of art strikes one as inevitable.''

Andersch's novels, *Sansibar* and *Die Rote,* are the most widely reprinted of his works. *Die Rote* was made into a film in Germany.

BIOGRAPHICAL/CRITICAL SOURCES: Nation, December 13, 1971.

* * *

ANDERSEN, R(udolph) Clifton 1933-

PERSONAL: Born April 8, 1933, in Chicago, Ill.; son of Rudolph T. (a rollturner) and Myrtle (Lloyd) Andersen; married Carolyn Johnstone, December 28, 1955; children: Lynn Elizabeth, Kathleen Mary. *Education:* Indiana University, B.S., 1955, M.B.A., 1958, D.B.A., 1960. *Politics:* Independent. *Religion:* Episcopal. *Home:* 1604 Taylor Dr., Carbondale, Ill. 62901. *Office:* Department of Marketing, College of Business and Administration, Southern Illinois University, Carbondale, Ill. 62901.

CAREER: University of Texas at Austin, assistant professor, 1960-63, associate professor of marketing, 1963-67; Southern Illinois University at Carbondale, College of Business and Administration, professor of marketing, 1967—, chairman of department, 1967-72, associate dean, 1976—. Consultant to Gulf Oil Co., Texas Oil Jobbers Association, Tracor, Inc., and Foley's of Houston. Member of board of directors, United Fund of Carbondale, 1971—. *Military Service:* U.S. Army, 1955-57. *Member:* American Marketing Association, Midwest Business Administration Association, Southern Marketing Association, Beta Gamma Sigma, Pi Sigma Epsilon, Rotary International. *Awards, honors:* Ford Foundation doctoral fellowship, 1958-59, 1959-60.

WRITINGS: (Editor with Philip R. Cateora) *Marketing Insights: Selected Readings,* Appleton, 1963, 3rd edition, 1974; (with William P. Dommermuth) *Distribution Systems: Firms, Functions and Efficiencies,* Appleton, 1972. Contributor to *Journal of Marketing, Journal of Retailing,* and *Business Topics.*

WORK IN PROGRESS: Research on efficiency and productivity in marketing channels.

* * *

ANDERSON, Camilla M(ay) 1904-

PERSONAL: Born June 21, 1904, in Sidney, Mont.; daughter of Peter and Bertha (Josephsen) Anderson; married Leonard Friendly (an organist), July 5, 1941 (died, 1960); children: Janet Carol. *Education:* University of Oregon, B.A., 1925; University of Oregon Medical School, M.D., 1929. *Politics:* Republican. *Religion:* Protestant. *Home and office:* 405 West Main St., Sidney, Mont. 59270.

CAREER: Binghamton State Hospital (psychiatric), Binghamton, N.Y., assistant physician, 1931-32; Broome County (N.Y.) Tuberculosis Hospital, physician in charge of Women's Service, 1933-34; Pittsburgh City Hospitals, Pittsburgh, Pa., psychiatrist in charge of Women's Psychiatric Service, 1934-36; Allegheny County (Pa.) Hospital, psychiatrist in charge of Women's Receiving Service, 1936; Public Charities Association of Pennsylvania, Philadelphia, Pa., director of Mental Hygiene Division, 1937-40; Philadelphia General Hospital, Philadelphia, part-time psychiatrist, assistant to chief visiting psychiatrist, 1939-41; Washington Institute of Mental Hygiene, Washington, D.C., psychiatrist, assistant to director, 1941-45; Veterans Administration Mental Hygiene Clinic, Salt Lake City, Utah, chief psychiatrist, 1948-52; University of Utah, College of Medicine, Salt Lake City, assistant clinical professor of psychiatry, 1948-57; Veterans Administration Mental Hygiene Clinic, Seattle, Wash., senior psychiatrist, 1957-58; Oregon State Hospital, Salem, director, Outpatient Department, 1958-64; California Institution for Women, Frontera, chief psychiatrist, 1964-69. Private practice of psychiatry, Philadelphia, Pa., 1939-41, Washington, D.C., 1942-48, Salt Lake City, Utah, 1952-57. Part-time assistant professor of mental hygiene, Duquesne University, 1935-38; lecturer in mental hygiene and/or psychiatry at numerous universities, medical schools, foundations, and clubs throughout the United States, 1924—; deputy health officer, Richland County, Mont., 1974—. Psychiatric consultant to various organizations and government committees, 1942-64.

MEMBER: American Medical Women's Association, American Psychiatric Association (fellow, 1944, life fellow, 1967—), Academy of Religion and Mental Health (charter member), Montana Psychiatric Association. *Awards, honors:* Oregon Woman of Achievement, 1962; Montana Woman of Achievement, 1974.

WRITINGS: Emotional Hygiene, Lippincott, 1937, 4th edition, 1948; *Saints, Sinners and Psychiatry,* Lippincott, 1950; *Beyond Freud: A Creative Approach to Mental Health,* Harper, 1957; *Jan, My Brain Damaged Daughter,* Durham Press, 1963; *Society Pays,* Walker & Co., 1972; (contributor) Ratibor-Ray M. Jurjevich, editor, *Direct Psychotherapy: 28 American Originals,* University of Miami Press, 1973; (contributor) R. Weber, editor, *Handbook on Learning Disabilities: A Prognosis for the Child, the Adolescent, and the Adult,* Prentice-Hall, 1974. Contributor of articles to various scientific and educational journals, including *International Clinics, Mental Hygiene, American Practitioner and Digest of Treatment, Journal of the American Medical Women's Association, American Journal of Psychoanalysis, Journal of Institute for Rational Living,* and *American Journal of Corrections.*

WORK IN PROGRESS: A book presenting a new (newer than Freud) system of psychodynamics, and a correlation between this system and the essential elements of the Judeo-Christian religion; a handbook of psychiatry for the legal profession.

SIDELIGHTS: While attending courses in the Washington School of Psychiatry in the late 1940's Camilla Anderson "became disenchanted with Freudian psychoanalysis. I left Washington . . . and began presenting my own concepts of psychodynamics in a series of publications . . . from 1950 to the present." Dr. Anderson has been especially active in the application of psychiatric techniques to the examination of criminals and juvenile offenders. She was instrumental in the establishment of a Behavior Clinic in connection with the Criminal Court of Allegheny County, Pa., in the late 1930's. She told *CA* that "getting into psychiatry was purely accidental—the result of the 1929 stock market crash and few openings for women in medicine, combined with the totally irrelevant and gratuitous advice of a cowboy brother to take the [Binghamton position] . . . because he had sold a load of horses in the Finger Lakes region only recently; it was beautiful country and he believed I would like it. So—I got into my field on a load of horses! My involvement and expertise

in the area of minimal brain damage derives from my personal experience with my daughter, now 35, who has taught me much and has opened many vistas that would otherwise be hidden. Without the help of my daughter and [late] husband, I would be no doubt still be a run-of-the-mill psychiatrist."

Emotional Hygiene was designated an official text in mental hygiene for Army nurses by the Surgeon General of the U.S. Army in 1944. Another of Camilla Anderson's books, *Saints, Sinners and Psychiatry,* is used extensively in colleges and universities as a mental hygiene text.

*   *   *

ANDERSON, Carl Dicmann 1912-

PERSONAL: Born April 2, 1912, in Baltimore, Md.; son of Nels Dicmann (a salesman) and Jennie (Freund) Anderson; married Bessie Crane, August 30, 1936; children: Don Dicmann, Jean (Mrs. David White). *Education:* Pacific Union College, B.Th., 1934, B.A., 1936; Andrews University, M.A., 1957; American University, Ph.D., 1960. *Politics:* Republican. *Religion:* Seventh-day Adventist. *Home address:* Route 3, Box 217C, Dayton, Tenn. 37321. *Office:* Advanced Training Program, Laurelbrook School, Route 3, Dayton, Tenn. 37321.

CAREER: Teacher of history in Seventh-day Adventist schools in Texas, California, Maryland, Michigan, Indiana, Alabama, Tennessee, and Canada, 1936-68; Oakwood College, Huntsville, Ala., associate professor, 1968-70, professor of history and chairman of department, 1970-75; Laurelbrook School, Dayton, Tenn., educational coordinator, advance training program, 1975—. *Member:* American Historical Association, Organization of American Historians, National Council for the Social Studies, National Historical Society, International Oceanographic Association.

WRITINGS: Ancient World, Andrews University, 1966, revised edition, 1975; *Modern World,* privately published, 1976; *Crises in Seventh-day Adventist Education,* privately published, 1976.

WORK IN PROGRESS: College textbooks on ancient, European, and American history; a history of Oakwood College, with James Dykes and Otis B. Edwards.

AVOCATIONAL INTERESTS: Philately.

*   *   *

ANDERSON, Edgar 1920-
(Edgars Andersons)

PERSONAL: Born June 17, 1920, in Tukums, Latvia; naturalized U.S. citizen; son of Voldemar (a civil servant) and Emilija Alma (Kaneps) Anderson; married Velta Peterson, 1950 (divorced, 1958); married Ligita Apinis (an actress), June 19, 1958; children: (first marriage) Raymond Edgar; (second marriage) Philip Rudolf. *Education:* University of Riga, M.A., 1944; graduate study at University of Wuerzburg, 1945-49, University of Leiden, 1948, and University of Pennsylvania, 1950-53; University of Chicago, Ph.D., 1956. *Religion:* Lutheran. *Home:* 2571 Booksin Ave., San Jose, Calif. 95125. *Office:* Department of History, School of Humanities and the Arts, San Jose State University, San Jose, Calif. 95114.

CAREER: University of Wuerzburg, extension division, Wuerzburg, Germany, instructor in history, 1945-49; Lake Forest College, Lake Forest, Ill., instructor in history, 1953-57; San Jose State University, San Jose, Calif., assistant professor, 1957-59, associate professor, 1959-63, professor of history, 1963—. Distinguished professor of history, Livingston University, 1969. Has been visiting professor and made lecture tours in North America, West Indies, Australia, New Zealand, and Europe; led historical and archaeological expedition to Trinidad and Tobago, 1960. General chairman, second International Conference on Baltic Studies, 1970; session chairman, International Conference on East European and Slavic Studies, 1974. Regular broadcaster for Voice of America, 1970—.

MEMBER: Academy of Political Science, American Association for the Advancement of Slavic Studies, American Historical Association, Association for the Advancement of Baltic Studies (vice-president, 1969-70, president, 1972-73), Society for the Advancement of Scandinavian Study, Conference on British Studies, Conference on Slavic Studies, Institute of Caribbean Studies, Baltisches Forschungsinstitut, Baltische Historische Kommission, Naval Records Club. *Awards, honors:* American Council of Learned Societies fellow, 1956-57; Outstanding Educator of America, 1972; Outstanding Professor, San Jose State University, 1973; research grants from American Philosophical Society, Baltiska Humanistiska Institutet, and a number of other groups.

WRITINGS: Western World, Castle of Light (Hanau), 1949; *Western Horizon,* Castle of Light, 1949; (editor) *Cross-Road Country, Latvia,* Latvju Gramata (Waverly, Iowa), 1953; *Tobago,* Harro von Hirschheydt Verlag (Hanover), 1962; (editor) Adolfs Kaktins, *Dzives Opera,* Daugava Foerlag (Stockholm), 1965; *History of Latvia: Foreign Policy, 1914-1920,* Daugava Foerlag, 1967; *Die Militaerische Situation der baltischen Staaten,* Institutum Balticum, 1969; *The Ancient Couronians in Africa,* Gramatu Draugs (New York), 1970; *The Ancient Couronians in America and the Colonization of Tobago,* Daugava Foerlag, 1970.

Contributor: *The American Historical Association's Guide to Historical Literature,* Macmillan, 1961; Janis Silins, editor, *Rakstu Krajums,* Volume II, Latvian Association for Humanities and Arts, 1963; Jueri G. Poska, editor, *Pro Baltica: Melanges dedies a Kaarel R. Pusta,* Publications du comite des amis de K. R. Pusta, 1965; Hans von Rimscha, Arved F. von Taube, and Juergen von Hehn, editors, *Beitraege zur Geschichte der Losloesung der baltischen Provinzen von Russland und zur Entstehung der baltischen Staaten,* Johann Gottfried Herder-Institut, Volume I, 1971, Volume II, 1977; *Handbook for Graduate Students in East Central European Studies,* Institute on East Central Europe, Columbia University, 1971; Witold S. Sworakowski, editor, *World Communism: A Handbook, 1918-1965,* Hoover Institution, 1971; Arvids Ziedonis, Mardi Valgemae, and William L. Winter, editors, *Baltic History,* Ohio State University Press, 1974; Daniel H. Thomas and Lynn Case, editors, *The Guide to the Diplomatic Archives of Western Europe,* University of Pennsylvania Press, 1975.

Editor of supplementary volumes of *Latvju Enciklopedija,* 1962 and 1978; editor and contributor to volumes of proceedings of Conference on Baltic Studies, 1969, 1971. Contributor of more than sixty articles to *Caribbean Quarterly, Illustrated Word,* and to journals of Slavic studies in the United States and Europe.

WORK IN PROGRESS: A three-volume work, *The Baltic Area in World Affairs, 1914-1920, 1920-1940,* and *1940-1945; The Crimean War in Northern Europe;* a two-volume *History of Latvia, 1920-1940,* and *1940-1945; Latvia and the Latvians.*

SIDELIGHTS: Edgar Anderson speaks German, Russian. French, and Swedish, as well as English and Latvian.

ANDERSON, Henry P.   1927-

PERSONAL: Born December 14, 1927, in Mexia, Tex.; son of Oscar A. (a teacher) and Ethel (Pope) Anderson; divorced; children: Stephen, David, Rachel, Eugene, Dorothy. *Education:* Pomona College, B.A. (cum laude), 1949; University of Hawaii, M.A., 1951; Stanford University, graduate study, 1951-52; University of California, Berkeley, M.P.H., 1956. *Politics:* Democrat. *Religion:* Humanist. *Address:* P.O. Box 1173, Berkeley, Calif. 94701.

CAREER: University of California, Berkeley, research assistant, 1956-59; AFL-CIO Agricultural Workers Organizing Committee, Stockton, Calif., research director, 1959-62; California Department of Public Health, Berkeley, research specialist, 1962-74. *Military service:* U.S. Army, 1945-46. *Member:* Citizens for Farm Labor (chairman, 1963—), Phi Beta Kappa.

WRITINGS: (With Joan London) *So Shall Ye Reap,* Crowell, 1970; (contributor) *The Manas Reader,* Grossman, 1971. Contributor to *The Freeman, New America, Catholic Worker, Liberation, Peace News,* and other periodicals.

WORK IN PROGRESS: A collection of essays, tentatively entitled *To Render the World a More Human Place;* research and writing on pesticides and their effects on human health.

BIOGRAPHICAL/CRITICAL SOURCES: Christian Century, April 21, 1971.

*   *   *

ANDERSON, Jack   1935-

PERSONAL: Born June 15, 1935, in Milwaukee, Wis.; son of George William (a motion picture projectionist) and Eleanore (Forse) Anderson. *Education:* Northwestern University, B.S., 1957; Indiana University, M.A., 1958; University of California, Berkeley, additional graduate study, 1958-59. *Home:* Apt. 1C, 110 Thompson St., New York, N.Y. 10012. *Office: Dance* Magazine, 10 Columbus Cir., New York, N.Y. 10019.

CAREER: Oakland Tribune, Oakland, Calif., assistant drama critic, 1960-62; City of Berkeley, Calif., delivery truck driver, 1963; *Dance* (magazine), New York, N.Y., editorial assistant, 1964-69, associate critic, 1970—. Poet-in-residence, University of Kansas, 1970; New York correspondent, *Dancing Times,* London, England, 1971—; program editor, Brooklyn Academy of Music, 1971-72; assistant dance critic, *New York Times,* 1978—. *Awards, honors:* National Endowment for the Arts grant, 1968, for manuscript of *The Invention of New Jersey;* National Endowment for the Arts fellowship, 1973-74.

WRITINGS—Poetry, except as indicated: *The Hurricane Lamp,* New/Books, 1969; *The Invention of New Jersey,* University of Pittsburgh Press, 1969; *Dance* (prose), Newsweek, 1974; *City Joys,* Release Press, 1975; *The Dust Dancers,* Bookmark, 1977; *Toward the Liberation of the Left Hand,* University of Pittsburgh Press, 1977. Contributor of poems to *Nation, Transatlantic Review, Antioch Review, Prairie Schooner, Carleton Miscellany, Poetry,* and other journals, and of ballet and modern dance criticism to *Ramparts, London Daily Mail, New York Times, Nation,* and other publications.

WORK IN PROGRESS: Poetry and dance history.

SIDELIGHTS: Jack Anderson spent the major part of 1970-71 and 1975 living in Europe.

ANDERSON, James M(axwell) 1933-

PERSONAL: Born April 9, 1933, in Seattle, Wash.; son of Maxwell Frank and Virginia (Thompson) Anderson; married Margery Sheridan Lea (an English teacher), August 7, 1957; children: Kristin Siwan, Corri James. *Education:* University of Washington, B.A., 1958, M.A., 1961, Ph.D., 1963. *Home:* 3024 Underhill Dr. N.W., Calgary, Alberta, Canada. *Office:* Department of Linguistics, University of Calgary, 2920 24th Ave., Calgary, Alberta, Canada T2N 1N4.

CAREER: Georgetown University, Washington, D.C., assistant professor of linguistics, 1963-68; University of Alberta, Edmonton, associate professor of linguistics, 1968-70; University of Calgary, Calgary, Alberta, associate professor, 1970-76, professor of linguistics, 1976—. Fulbright lecturer at University of Valladolid, 1964-65, University of Barcelona, 1965-66, and University of Deusto, 1966. *Military service:* U.S. Army, 1951-54. *Member:* International Linguistic Association, Linguistic Society of America, Modern Language Association of America, Canadian Linguistic Association, American Association of University Professors, Canadian Association of University Teachers, Philological Association of the Pacific Coast, Alberta Linguistic Association (vice-president, 1970-71, president, 1971-72). *Awards, honors:* University of Alberta research grant, 1969-70; University of Calgary research grant, 1971-72; Canada Council research grant, 1972-73, 1976-77.

WRITINGS: (Editor with J. A. Creore) *Readings in Romance Linguistics,* Mouton, 1972; *Structural Aspects of Language Change,* Longman, 1973. Contributor to *Lingua, Orbis, Romance Notes, Word,* and other publications.

WORK IN PROGRESS: A study of epigraphic remains of ancient Iberia.

*   *   *

ANDERSON, John Bayard 1922-

PERSONAL: Born February 15, 1922, in Rockford, Ill.; son of Albin (a grocer) and Mabel Edna (Ring) Anderson; married Keke Machakos, January 4, 1953; children: Eleanora, John Bayard, Jr., Diane, Karen Beth, Susan Kimberly. *Education:* University of Illinois, B.A. (magna cum laude), 1942, J.D., 1946; Harvard University, LL.M., 1949. *Politics:* Republican. *Religion:* Evangelical Free Church. *Home:* 2520 35th Place N.W., Washington, D.C. 20001. *Office:* 1101 Longworth Building, U.S. House of Representatives, Washington, D.C. 20515.

CAREER: Admitted to Illinois Bar, 1946; Northeastern University, Boston, Mass., instructor in law, 1947-49; private practice of law in Rockford, Ill., 1949-52; U.S. Department of State, foreign service officer assigned to East Berlin, 1952-55; private practice of law in Rockford, Ill., 1955-56; state's attorney for Winnebago County, Ill., 1956-60; U.S. House of Representatives, Washington, D.C., congressman from Illinois 16th District, 1960—, chairman of House Republican Conference, 1969—. *Military service:* U.S. Army, Field Artillery, World War II; became staff sergeant; received four battle stars. *Member:* Phi Beta Kappa. *Awards, honors:* Named outstanding layman of the year by National Association of Evangelicals, 1964.

WRITINGS: (Contributor) Mary McInnis, editor, *We Propose: A Modern Congress,* McGraw, 1966; (contributor) Melvin R. Laird, editor, *Republican Papers,* Doubleday, 1968; *Between Two Worlds: A Congressman's Choice,* Zondervan, 1970; (editor and contributor) *Congress and*

Conscience, Lippincott, 1970; *Vision and Betrayal in America,* World Books, 1975. Contributor to journals.

*   *   *

ANDERSON, Malcolm 1934-

PERSONAL: Born May 13, 1934, in Knutsford, England; son of James Armstrong and Helen (Potts) Anderson; married Eileen Calan, September 14, 1957; children: Denis Ian, Keith James, Helen Catharine. *Education:* Oxford University, B.A., 1957, M.A. and D.Phil., 1961. *Home:* 6 Binswood Ave., Leamington Spa, Warwickshire, England. *Office:* School of Politics, University of Warwick, Coventry CV4 7AL, England.

CAREER: University of Manchester, Manchester, England, lecturer in government, 1960-64; Fondation Nationale des Sciences Politiques, Paris, France, research fellow, 1964-65; University of Warwick, Coventry, England, senior lecturer, 1965-73, professor of politics, 1973—. Visiting professor, University of British Columbia, 1969.

WRITINGS: (Contributor) David M. Shapiro, editor, *The Right in France, 1880-1919: Three Studies,* Southern Illinois University Press, 1962; (translator) Maurice Duverger, *An Introduction to the Social Sciences: With Special Reference to Their Methods,* Allen & Unwin, 1964; *Government in France,* Pergamon, 1970; *Conservative Politics in France,* Allen & Unwin, 1974. Editor, Allen & Unwin's "Studies in Political Science" series. Regular contributor to *Report on World Affairs;* contributor to learned journals.

WORK IN PROGRESS: The Politics of Frontier Regions in Europe.

*   *   *

ANDERSON, Norman Dean 1928-

PERSONAL: Born January 29, 1928, in Dickens, Iowa; son of Eddie (a farmer) and Effie (Condra) Anderson; married Mary Martha Breuer, November 23, 1952; children: Brent, Beth, Jeffrey, Todd, Jonathan, Julie. *Education:* University of Iowa, B.A., 1951, M.A., 1956; Ohio State University, Ph.D., 1965. *Religion:* Presbyterian. *Home:* 1000 Lake Boone Trail, Raleigh, N.C. 27607. *Office:* Department of Science Education, 326 Poe Hall, North Carolina State University, Raleigh, N.C. 27607.

CAREER: High school science teacher in Burlington, Iowa, 1952-57, 1958-59, and Bettendorf, Iowa, 1959-61; Ohio State University, Columbus, instructor in science education, 1961-63; North Carolina State University, Raleigh, assistant professor, 1963-66, associate professor, 1966-71, professor of science education, 1971—. Summer master teacher in science, Harvard University, 1964; visiting lecturer, Ohio State University, summers, 1967, 1968, 1969, University of Maryland, 1970, and East Carolina University, 1970; director of National Science Foundation summer institutes in earth science, 1966, 1967, 1968, in marine environments, 1971. Chairman, North Carolina State Advisory Council on Elementary and Secondary Education, 1968-70. Trustee, Peace College, 1970-75. *Military service:* U.S. Army, Engineers, 1946-47.

MEMBER: American Association for the Advancement of Science (fellow), National Education Association (life member), National Science Teachers Association (life member), National Association for Research in Science Teaching, Association for Education of Teachers of Science, National Association of Geology Teachers, Central Association of Science and Mathematics Teachers, North Carolina Academy of Science, Phi Delta Kappa, Phi Kappa Phi.

Awards, honors: North Carolina State University Outstanding Teaching Awards, 1965, 1970.

WRITINGS: (With J. Allen Hynek) *Challenge of the Universe,* Scholastic Book Services, 1962; (contributing editor in astronomy and astronautics) *Compton's Illustrated Science Dictionary,* David-Stewart, 1963; *Investing Science Using Your Whole Body,* McGraw-Hill, 1975.

With Walter R. Brown: *Life Science: A Search for Understanding,* Lippincott, 1971, revised edition, 1977; *Physical Science: A Search for Understanding,* Lippincott, 1972, revised edition, 1977; *Earth Science: A Search for Understanding,* Lippincott, 1973, revised edition, 1977; *Fires,* Addison-Wesley, 1976; *Famines,* Addison-Wesley, 1976; *Snowstorms and Avalanches,* Addison-Wesley, 1976. Contributor to journals of science education.

WORK IN PROGRESS: A book on investigating science in the swimming pool and surf, for McGraw-Hill.

* * *

ANDERSON, O(rvil) Roger 1937-

PERSONAL: Born August 4, 1937, in East St. Louis, Ill.; son of Orvil Noel (a life insurance underwriter) and Marie (Diekemper) Anderson. *Education:* Washington University, St. Louis, Mo., A.B., 1959, M.A., 1961, Ed.D., 1964. *Religion:* Reorganized Church of Jesus Christ of Latter-day Saints. *Home:* 501 West 120th St., New York, N.Y. 10027. *Office:* Department of Natural Sciences, Teachers College, Columbia University, 525 West 120th St., New York, N.Y. 10027.

CAREER: Columbia University, Teachers College, New York, N.Y., assistant professor, 1964-67, associate professor, 1968-70, professor of natural sciences, 1970—, Lamont-Doherty Geological Observatory, Palisades, N.Y., research associate, 1967-71, senior research associate in biology, 1971—. *Member:* American Association for the Advancement of Science (fellow), American Institute of Biological Sciences, National Association for Research in Science Teaching, National Association of Biology Teachers, New York Academy of Sciences, Sigma Xi.

WRITINGS: Structure in Teaching: Theory and Analysis, Teachers College Press, 1969; *Quantitative Analysis of Structure in Teaching,* Teachers College Press, 1971; *Teaching Modern Ideas of Biology,* edited by Willard Jacobson, Teachers College Press, 1972. Contributor to scientific and educational research journals. Editor, *Journal of Research in Science Teaching,* 1970-75.

WORK IN PROGRESS: Further studies on the analysis of structure in communication, and scientific research in cell biology.

* * *

ANDERSON, Patrick 1936-

PERSONAL: Born July 11, 1936, in Fort Worth, Tex.; married Ann Michael, March 31, 1962; children: Laura, Michael. *Education:* University of the South, B.A., 1957. *Politics:* Democrat. *Residence:* Waterford, Va.

CAREER: Worked for three years as a reporter and columnist for the Nashville *Tennessean;* served on the White House staff, 1962-64, with the Kennedy and Johnson administrations.

WRITINGS: The Presidents' Men (nonfiction), Doubleday, 1968; *The Approach to Kings* (novel), Doubleday, 1970; *Actions and Passions* (novel), Doubleday, 1974; *The President's Mistress* (novel), Simon & Schuster, 1976. Contributor of articles and reviews to magazines, including *Esquire, New Republic, Reader's Digest,* and *New York Times Book Review.*

WORK IN PROGRESS: A novel.

SIDELIGHTS: Anthony West calls *The President's Men* "an incomplete and sketchily researched study of some of the men who have been Presidential aides since F.D.R. took office. . . . It is a very characteristic piece of modern journalism. That is to say that it is the work of an outsider pretending to be an insider, and that it is couched in a twaddlingly vulgar language that its author supposes to be forceful and direct." Robert G. Sherrill does not see Anderson as an "outsider," but he feels that "when you consider Anderson's access, his opportunities for pilfering and eavesdropping, it is hard not to damn him as a gentlemanly bungler. He served on both Kennedy and Johnson committees, and still wallows in the privilege of an appointee. Very few Washington reporters have the time or the carte blanche that Anderson had for wandering down White House corridors and I can think of very few of the best ones who, given his opportunities, would not have come up with a fuller or more fleshly portrait of the President's men."

Ronnie Dugger writes: "Anderson's information seems reliable enough, but usually he does not make clear where it comes from. We are struggling these days in such a miasma of information, misinformation, pot-plant reports, propaganda and rumors palmed off as the hot stuff, that serious political writers are going to have to tie their information to their sources as much as possible, otherwise, we may as well give ourselves over to a madhouse mix of reality, fantasy, exhortation and confusion—a house of mirrors, with Mark Land selling tickets and *Ramparts* covers on the marquee. An amiable, chatty writer, Anderson does not go deeply into the sources of these assistants' values, but his sketches are pointed and fun to read, and since he has interviewed many of the men he writes about, he makes a contribution to the literature on the Presidency. Had he proceeded with more skepticism about the assumptions of the cold war and the sufficiency of the goals of the New and ensuing Deals to social reality in America, we might have received from him more pertinent assessments. . . .''

BIOGRAPHICAL/CRITICAL SOURCES: Vogue, September 15, 1968; *New York Times Book Review,* September 29, 1968; *Nation,* November 25, 1968; *Christian Science Monitor,* November 27, 1968; *Commentary,* April, 1969; *New York Times,* October 28, 1970.

* * *

ANDERSON, Paul E. 1925-

PERSONAL: Born March 5, 1925, in Iron River, Mich.; son of A. J. T. and Karen Marie (Henriksen) Anderson; children: Sheryl Jean, Pamela Dee, Brien Paul. *Education:* University of Michigan, A.B., 1948, J.D., 1950. *Politics:* "Open." *Religion:* "Open." *Home:* 1730 Kearny St., San Francisco, Calif. 94133. *Office:* 235 Montgomery St., Suite 1301, San Francisco, Calif. 94111.

CAREER: Kent, Brookes & Anderson (law firm), San Francisco, Calif., partner, 1952-69; Hastings College of Law, San Francisco, professor of law, 1959-75; private practice of law, San Francisco, 1969—. Special assistant to chief counsel, Internal Revenue Service, 1951-52; chairman of committee on taxation, State Bar of California, 1963-64. Mayor, City of San Mateo, 1957-59. *Military service:* U.S. Army, Corps of Engineers, 1943-46. *Member:* International Bar Association,

American Bar Association (chairman, section of Taxation Committee on Limitations, 1959), State Bar of California, Lawyers' Club of San Francisco, Phi Beta Kappa. *Awards, honors:* San Mateo, California, Man of the Year, 1958; delegate to 9th Circuit Court of Appeals, 1971.

WRITINGS: Tax Planning of Real Estate, American Bar Association and American Law Institute, 1957, 7th edition, 1977; *Tax Factors in Real Estate Operations,* Prentice-Hall, 1960, 5th edition, 1977. Contributor to journals. Real estate editor, *Journal of Taxation,* 1961-76.

WORK IN PROGRESS: The Marital Deduction: History, Current Application and Evaluation.

AVOCATIONAL INTERESTS: Archaeology.

* * *

ANDERSON, William Davis 1938-

PERSONAL: Born September 25, 1938, in Dallas, Tex.; son of William D. (an investment broker) and Katherine (Watts) Anderson. *Education:* University of Texas, B.A., 1960, M.A., 1962, Ph.D., 1966. *Politics:* Democrat. *Home:* 7137-28 Shoup Ave., Canoga Park, Calif. 91307. *Office:* Department of English, California State University, 18111 Nordhoff St., Northridge, Calif. 91324.

CAREER: King College, Bristol, Tenn., assistant professor of English, 1962-63; University of Texas at Arlington, instructor in foreign languages, 1963-65; California State University, Northridge, assistant professor, 1966-69, associate professor, 1969-70, professor of English, 1970—. *Member:* Modern Language Association of America, National Council of Teachers of English, Phi Beta Kappa. *Awards, honors:* U.S. Office of Education fellow, University of Nebraska, 1967-68.

WRITINGS: A New Look at Children's Literature, Wadsworth, 1972.

WORK IN PROGRESS: Bodies, a novel.

AVOCATIONAL INTERESTS: Theater improvisations.

* * *

ANDREACH, Robert J. 1930-

PERSONAL: Born August 19, 1930, in Newark, N.J.; son of Anthony J. (a manager in industry) and Gertrude (Foran) Andreach; married Constance Tallagnon, December 21, 1958; children: Kevin, Jason. *Education:* Rutgers University, A.B., 1953; New York University, M.A., 1958, Ph.D., 1963. *Office:* Department of English, Monmouth College, West Long Branch, N.J. 07764.

CAREER: University of Toledo, Toledo, Ohio, instructor in English, 1961-63; University of Rhode Island, Kingston, instructor in English, 1963-65; State University of New York at Binghamton, assistant professor of English, 1965-69; manager of restaurant in Irvington, N.J., 1969-71; Monmouth College, West Long Branch, N.J., associate professor of English, 1971—. *Military service:* U.S. Army, 1953-55; served in Germany. *Member:* Modern Language Association of America, American Association of University Professors.

WRITINGS: Studies in Structure: The Stages of the Spiritual Life in Four Modern Authors, Fordham University Press, 1964; *The Slain and Resurrected God: Conrad, Ford, and the Christian Myth,* New York University Press, 1970.

WORK IN PROGRESS: A novel.†

ANDREWS, Claire 1940-
(Keith Claire, a joint pseudonym)

PERSONAL: Born November 22, 1940, in London, England; married Keith Andrews. *Home:* 14 Beechwood Ave., Kew, Surrey, England. *Agent:* John Farquharson Ltd., 15 Red Lion Sq., London WC1R 4QW, England.

WRITINGS—With husband, Keith Andrews, under joint pseudonym Keith Claire: *Duringwitch* (novel), Eyre & Spottiswoode, 1968; *The Tree-Wakers* (novel), Methuen, 1970; *The Otherwise Girl* (novella), Holt, 1976.

BIOGRAPHICAL/CRITICAL SOURCES: Punch, October 16, 1968; *Times Literary Supplement,* April 16, 1970.

* * *

ANDREWS, Clarence A(delbert) 1912-
(Steven Randall)

PERSONAL: Born October 24, 1912, in Waterloo, Iowa; son of Harry Leon (a chauffeur) and June Jennie (Jones) Andrews; married Ollie Mae Easley, June 12, 1937; children: Linda (Mrs. Richard Thompson), Terry Kathleen (Mrs. Leonardo Lasansky), Steven Randall. *Education:* Attended Sheldon Junior College, Sheldon, Iowa, 1950-51; University of Iowa, B.A., 1954, M.A., 1960, Ph.D., 1963. *Politics:* Independent. *Religion:* Unitarian-Universalist. *Home:* 108 Pearl St., Iowa City, Iowa 52240. *Office:* School of Journalism, University of Iowa, Iowa City, Iowa 52242.

CAREER: Chamberlain Corp., Waterloo, Iowa, writer, editor, and publisher, 1953-58; University of Iowa, Iowa City, instructor in English, 1958-60; Colorado State University, Fort Collins, assistant professor of technical journalism, 1960-61; University of Iowa, instructor, 1961-63, assistant professor, 1963-67, associate professor of English, 1967-69; Michigan Technological University, Houghton, professor of humanities, and director of technical and scientific communications, 1971-75; University of Iowa, adjunct professor of English and visiting professor of journalism, 1975—. Summer visiting professor, Naval Ordinance Test Station, China Lake, Calif., 1959. *Military service:* U.S. Army Air Forces, 1944-46. Iowa National Guard, 1947-53; became first sergeant. *Member:* National Council of Teachers of English, Conference on College Composition and Communication, Authors League of America, Society for the Study of Midwest Literature, Midwest Modern Language Association, Phi Beta Kappa, Kappa Tau Alpha. *Awards, honors:* National University Extension award for distinguished independent study course, 1976.

WRITINGS: (With Richard Lloyd-Jones) *Technical and Scientific Writing,* University of Iowa, 1963; *Writing: Growth through Structure,* Glencoe Press, 1972; *A Literary History of Iowa,* University of Iowa Press, 1972; *Technical and Business Writing,* Houghton, 1975; (editor) *Growing Up in Iowa,* Iowa State University Press, 1977. Also author of *First Presbyterian Church: 125th Anniversary (1840-1965) History,* published by the church, 1966. Author of introductions to seventeen paperbacks. Contributor to magazines and newspapers. Editor, *The Personnel Administrator,* 1960-61.

WORK IN PROGRESS: A History of Chicago Literature; Writing Business Reports.

SIDELIGHTS: Clarence Andrews writes: "I regard teaching and writing as parallel activities, the one conducted mostly through personal contact (I also teach by correspondence and soon will be teaching by radio and television), the other conducted through the print medium. Thus I do not see the conflicts many see as existing between research and publication, and classroom teaching.

"It also seems obvious to me that in the future we will depend more and more on the audiovisual medium for both teaching and publication. I am not depressed by this possibility; I see a great potential in wise and skillful use of radio, television, closed-circuit television and sound recordings. This does not mean that the book or magazine will disappear, however."

AVOCATIONAL INTERESTS: Stamp collecting and model railroading.

* * *

ANDREWS, Keith 1930-
(Keith Claire, a joint pseudonym)

PERSONAL: Born September 2, 1930, in London, England; married; wife's name Claire. *Home:* 14 Beechwood Ave., Kew, Surrey, England. *Agent:* John Farquharson Ltd., 15 Red Lion Sq., London WC1R 4QW, England.

WRITINGS—With wife, Claire Andrews, under joint pseudonym Keith Claire: *Duringwitch* (novel), Eyre & Spottiswoode, 1968; *The Tree-Wakers* (novel), Methuen, 1970; *The Otherwise Girl* (novella), Holt, 1976.

BIOGRAPHICAL/CRITICAL SOURCES: Punch, October 16, 1968; *Times Literary Supplement,* April 16, 1970.

* * *

ANDREWS, Margaret E(lizabeth)

PERSONAL: Born in Minneapolis, Minn.; daughter of James (an engineer) and Eugenia (Goff) Andrews. *Education:* University of Minnesota, B.S., 1931, M.A., 1936; attended Stanford University, 1940-41; University of Colorado, Ed.D., 1954. *Home:* 7220 Monardo Lane, Minneapolis, Minn. 55435. *Office:* Department of Education, College of St. Catherine, St. Paul, Minn. 55116.

CAREER: High school business teacher in Buffalo, Minn., 1931-34; Northwestern National Bank, Minneapolis, Minn., secretary to vice-president, 1934-36; Virginia Junior College, Virginia, Minn., instructor in business, 1936-37; high school business teacher in Minneapolis, 1937-40; post-high-school office coordinator in Minneapolis, 1941-43; public schools of Minneapolis, consultant in business education and placement, 1943-69; College of St. Catherine, St. Paul, Minn., 1969—, began as assistant professor, currently professor of education. Member, President's Advisory Commission on Young Workers; member, Minnesota Governor's commissions on status of women, youth employment, and juvenile delinquency; member, Youth Development Project Planning Committee. Visiting summer professor at University of Illinois, 1955, and at University of North Dakota, 1965; summer lecturer, Hunter College of the City University of New York, 1968.

MEMBER: American Personnel and Guidance Association (emeritus member), American Vocational Association (past vice-president for business education), National Association of Supervisors of Business Education, National Vocational Guidance Association, National Business Education Association, American School Counselors Association, Administrative Management Society (honorary member), National Secretaries Association (honorary member), American Association of University Women (member of board, Minneapolis branch), North-Central Business Education Association (past vice-president), Minnesota Education Association, Minnesota Business Education Association, Minnesota

Coordinators Association, Minnesota Psychological Association, Minnesota Vocational Association, Twin City Vocational Guidance Association (past president; member of board of directors, 1942-60), Twin City Personnel Managers Association, Delta Pi Epsilon, Pi Lambda Theta, Zonta International.

WRITINGS: Providing School Placement Services, Science Research Associates, 1957; (with Donald J. Mulkerne) *Civil Service Tests for Typists,* McGraw, 1968; (consulting editor) *Office Job Training,* McGraw, 1973.

"Opportunity Knocks" series; published by McGraw: *About Him,* 1968; *The Job You Want,* 1968; *You Said It,* 1969; *It's Up to You,* 1970; *You Pay for It,* 1970. Consulting editor to McGraw business books. Contributor to education yearbooks and journals. Former member of editorial board, *Vocational Guidance Quarterly;* business education editor, *American Vocational Journal.*

* * *

ANGEL, Daniel D. 1939-

PERSONAL: Born December 23, 1939, in Detroit, Mich.; son of Ernest Almond and Hallie (Lancaster) Angel; married Patricia Schuster (a register of deeds in Calhoun County, Mich.), July 10, 1965; children: Scott. *Education:* Attended Taft Junior College, 1957-58; Wayne State University, B.A., 1961, M.A., 1963; Northwestern University, additional study, 1964; Purdue University, Ph.D., 1965. *Politics:* Republican. *Religion:* Methodist. *Home:* 501 Brighton, El Centro, Calif. 92243. *Office:* Office of the President, Imperial Valley College, Imperial, Calif. 92251.

CAREER: University of Delaware, Newark, assistant professor of communication, 1965-66; Albion College, Albion, Mich., assistant professor of communication, 1966-69, director of continuing education, 1969-72; elected representative of 49th District to Michigan State legislature, 1973-77; Imperial Valley College, Imperial, Calif., president, 1978—. Visiting lecturer, Queens College of the City University of New York, Flushing, N.Y., summer, 1969. Special assistant to U.S. Senator Robert P. Griffin, Washington, D.C., summer, 1969; chairman of platform committee, Michigan State Republican Convention, 1971. *Member:* Michigan Intercollegiate Speech League (president), Michigan Community Action Program Chairman's Association (president), California Community and Junior College Association, Calhoun County Community Action Agency (chairman), Marshall Jaycees.

WRITINGS: George Romney: A Political Biography, Exposition, 1967; *William G. Milliken: A Touch of Steel,* Public Affairs Press, 1970; *Critical Issues Facing Michigan Higher Education 1978,* Michigan House of Representatives, 1978.

* * *

ANGELES, Jose 1930-

PERSONAL: Born August 13, 1930, in Valencia, Spain; son of Pascual (an insurance salesman) and Castello (Amparo) Angeles; married Maria del Socorro Blasco, August 6, 1955; children: Cesar, Fernando, Laura, Jose, Jr. *Education:* University of Valencia, Licenciado en Letras, 1953, Ph.D. (with highest honors), 1959; University of Madrid, graduate research, 1953-55. *Office:* Modern Languages Department, Florida State University, Tallahassee, Fla. 32306.

CAREER: University of Valencia, Valencia, Spain, professor of Spanish literature and history, 1955-59; Alvern

College, Milwaukee, Wis., assistant professor of Spanish, 1959-63; Florida State University, Tallahassee, assistant professor, 1963-66, associate professor, 1966-72, professor of Spanish, 1972—. *Member:* Modern Language Association of America, American Association of Teachers of Spanish and Portuguese, South Atlantic Modern Language Association, Instituto de Estudios Ibericos (Spain), Sigma Delta Pi (national board member and director, State of Florida). *Awards, honors:* San Isidoro de Sevilla prize for research in the humanities, Spain, 1959.

WRITINGS: (With Carmen Rivera) *Galdos,* University Press of Virginia, 1969; (contributor) J. Schraibman, editor, *Homenaje a Sherman H. Eoff,* Castalia (Madrid), 1970; *Introduccion a la literatura espanola,* McGraw, 1970; (contributor) *Victor R. B. Oelschaeger Festschrift,* University of North Carolina Press, 1976; *Estudios sobre Antonio Machado,* Ariel (Barcelona), 1977. Contributor to *Hispania, Revista de Literatura, Duquesne Hispanic Review, Kentucky Foreign Language Quarterly, Hispanic Review, Revista de Estudios Hispanicos, Atenea, Insula,* and *Books Abroad.*

WORK IN PROGRESS: A book on Jorge Guillen's *Cantico, Myth and Poetry;* essays on Antonio Machado, expected completion in 1978; several articles on contemporary Spanish poetry and Galdos.

AVOCATIONAL INTERESTS: Late nineteenth- and twentieth-century literature, modern art, poetry, travel, and chess.

*   *   *

ANGELES, Peter A.   1931-

PERSONAL: Spelling of surname legally changed; born February 21, 1931, in Ambridge, Pa.; son of Adam Peter and Kalliope (Moschos) Angelos; married Elizabeth McConnaughy (a medical research assistant), June 7, 1951; children: Beth, Jane, Adam. *Education:* Columbia University, B.A., 1952, M.A., 1954, Ph.D., 1956. *Politics:* Independent. *Religion:* Unitarian-Universalist. *Home:* 974 Cocopah Dr., Santa Barbara, Calif. 93110. *Agent:* Richard Hagle, Editorial Services, 243 East North Ave., Elmhurst, Ill. 60126. *Office:* Department of Philosophy, Santa Barbara City College, Santa Barbara, Calif.

CAREER: University of Western Ontario, London, assistant professor, 1956-63, associate professor, 1963-70; Santa Barbara City College, Santa Barbara, Calif., professor of philosophy, 1970—. Visiting professor, Albert Schweitzer College, Vaud, Switzerland, 1966. *Awards, honors:* Canada Council fellowship, 1968-69; National Endowment for the Humanities fellowship, 1973.

WRITINGS: The Possible Dream: Toward Understanding the Black Experience, Friendship, 1970; *The Problem of God,* C. E. Merrill, 1974; *Introduction to Sentential Logic,* C. E. Merrill, 1976; (editor) *Critiques of God,* Prometheus Books, 1976; *A Moth/Une Mite,* Tundra Books, 1976; (contributor) James L. Christian, editor, *Extra Terrestial Intelligence: The First Encounter,* Prometheus Books, 1976; *Dictionary of Philosophy,* Barnes & Noble, 1977. Contributor of technical articles, children's stories, poetry, and one-act avant-garde plays to journals and literary magazines.

WORK IN PROGRESS: A reader in bioethics; a textbook on bioethics; a Greek cookbook, *Yiayia and Pappou's Fifty Greek Recipes.*

SIDELIGHTS: Peter Angeles told *CA:* "Writing children's stories and plays is my first love, but it is difficult getting them published and I can't make a living at it, thus I spend my time on textbooks—not that I make a living on them but they contribute somewhat to my academic reputation and survival. I keep living in the dream that someday publishers will see how good my children's stories really are and buy a bundle of them."

*   *   *

ANSBERRY, William F.   1926-

PERSONAL: Born July 18, 1926, in Logansport, Ind.; son of Michael C. (a railroad employee) and Mary E. (Freking) Ansberry; married Ruth Baynes, April 17, 1954; children: Michael, Elizabeth Ann, William, Patti. *Education:* Attended University of Notre Dame, 1944; Ball State University, B.S., 1951, M.A., 1955; Miami University, Oxford, Ohio, graduate study, 1959-60; University of Cincinnati, Ph.D., 1968. *Politics:* Independent. *Religion:* Roman Catholic. *Home:* 2032 Steven Dr., Cape Girardeau, Mo. 63701. *Office:* Department of Political Science, Southeast Missouri State University, Cape Girardeau, Mo. 63701.

CAREER: Teacher in North Vernon and Lowell, Ind., schools, 1951-57; teacher in North College Hill, Ohio, schools, 1957-67; University of Cincinnati, Cincinnati, Ohio, member of faculty, 1963-67; Southeast Missouri State University, Cape Girardeau, associate professor of political science, 1967—. President, St. Vincent School Board; member of board of directors, Cape Girardeau County Association for the Retarded. *Military service:* U.S. Army, 1944-46. *Member:* American Political Science Association, Missouri Academy of Science.

WRITINGS: Arms Control and Disarmament: Success or Failure?, McCutchan, 1969.

WORK IN PROGRESS: The politics of international Communism.

*   *   *

ANTHONY, Edward   1895-1971

August 4, 1895—August 16, 1971; American publisher, biographer, and author of personal reminiscences. Obituaries: *New York Times,* August 18, 1971; *Washington Post,* August 20, 1971; *Publishers Weekly,* September 13, 1971.

*   *   *

ANTILL, James Macquarie   1912-

PERSONAL: Born June 10, 1912, in Sydney, Australia; son of Horace Sutherland (a business agent) and May A. V. (Brook) Antill; married Hilda D. Whitty, March 17, 1942; married second wife, Audrey V. Mockett, July 29, 1966. *Education:* University of Sydney, B.E. (civil), 1932; University of New South Wales, M.E. (civil), 1968. *Religion:* Protestant. *Home:* 79 Muston St., Mosman 2088, New South Wales, Australia. *Office address:* Consulting Construction Engineer, P.O. Box 100, Cremorne Junction 2090, New South Wales, Australia.

CAREER: New South Wales, Australia, Local Government Engineer's Certificate, 1939; Metropolitan Water Board, Sydney, New South Wales, supervising engineer, 1933-38; Sir Robert McAlpine Ltd., London, England, supervising engineer, 1936; Shire Councils of Berrigan and Bingara, New South Wales, shire engineer, 1939-42; Julius, Poole & Gibson, Consulting Engineers, Sydney, resident engineer, 1943-44; McDonald Constructions Proprietary Ltd., Sydney and Canberra, chief construction engineer, 1945-52; Stresscrete Constructions Proprietary Ltd., Sydney and Melbourne, managing director and chief engineer, 1952-58; James M. Antill, Consulting Engineer, Sydney, principal, 1958—. Examiner and visiting lecturer in construction, University of Sydney and University of New South Wales, 1956—. Has made study tours in Europe, North and South America, and Asia.

MEMBER: Institution of Engineers (fellow, 1968; chairman of Sydney Division, 1969; councillor, 1970—), Institute of Arbitrators (fellow, 1975), American Concrete Institute, Australasian Institute of Mining and Metallurgy (associate member), Concrete Institute of Australia (honorary life member), Royal Australian Historical Society (vice-president, 1963-75). *Awards, honors:* Warren Prize, 1951, George A. Taylor Medal, 1957, and Institution Award, 1969, all from Institution of Engineers, Australia, for notable contributions to the literature of the engineering profession.

WRITINGS: (With Watson Steele) *History of All Saints College, Bathurst,* Angus & Robertson, 1952, revised edition, 1964; (with Paul Ryan) *Civil Engineering Construction,* Angus & Robertson, 1957, 4th edition, 1974; (with Ronald Woodhead) *Critical Path Methods in Construction Practice,* Wiley, 1965, 2nd edition, 1970; *Civil Engineering Management,* American Elsevier, 1970, 2nd edition, Angus & Robertson, 1973; *Construction Contracts Administration,* A.F.C.C. (Sydney), 1975. Also author of historical monographs and contributor to historical journals and to technical journals in the United States, England, Australia, and India.

WORK IN PROGRESS: Application of critical path methods to the evaluation of work changes and delays in construction contracts.

* * *

ANTRIM, Harry T(homas) 1936-

PERSONAL: Born February 17, 1936, in Richmond, Va.; son of Robert Emmett (a farmer) and Eliza (Eldridge) Antrim; married Louanne Self (a college professor), March 23, 1957; children: Donald Eldridge, Terry Carter (daughter). *Education:* Davidson College, A.B., 1957; University of Florida, M.A., 1962, Ph.D., 1967. *Politics:* Democrat. *Religion:* Episcopalian. *Home:* 4302 Ingraham Hwy., Miami, Fla. 33133. *Office:* Department of English, Florida International University, Tamiami Trail, Miami, Fla. 33154.

CAREER: John and Mable Ringling Museum of Art, Sarasota, Fla., assistant curator, 1957-59; University of Florida, Gainesville, instructor in English, 1962-65; University of Virginia, Charlottesville, assistant professor, 1965-71; Florida International University, Miami, associate professor, 1971-73, professor of English, 1973—, assistant dean of College of Arts and Sciences, 1971-73, vice-president of associated writing programs. Chairman of selection committee, First Novel Award, William Faulkner Foundation. *Military service:* U.S. Army, 1959-61; became first lieutenant. *Member:* Modern Language Association of America, American Association of University Professors.

WRITINGS: T. S. Eliot's Concept of Language, University of Florida Press, 1971. Contributor to literature journals.

WORK IN PROGRESS: A biography of T. S. Eliot.

* * *

ANTTILA, Raimo (Aulis) 1935-

PERSONAL: Born April 21, 1935, in Lieto, Finland; son of Lauri Nikolai (a metalworker) and Tyyne (Alikirri) Anttila; married Seija Gerdt (an artist), July 25, 1959; children: Se-

lene (daughter), Matti (son). *Education:* University of Turku, Humanististen Tieteiden Kandidaatti, 1959, Filosofian Kandidaatti, 1961; University of Toronto, graduate study, 1961-62; Yale University, Ph.D., 1966. *Home:* 1022 Cedar St., Santa Monica, Calif. 90405. *Office:* Department of Linguistics, University of California, 405 Hilgard Ave., Los Angeles, Calif. 90024.

CAREER: University of California, Los Angeles, assistant professor, 1965-70, associate professor, 1970-74, professor of linguistics, 1974—. Professor of general linguistics, University of Helsinki, 1972-74. *Military service:* Finnish Army, Infantry, 1955-56; became second lieutenant. *Member:* International Linguistics Association, Linguistic Society of America, Societe Neophilologique de Helsinki, Linguistic Association of Great Britain, International Committee on Historical Linguistics.

WRITINGS: Uusimman aannehistorian suunnasta ja luonteesta, Phonetics Department, University of Turku, 1969; *Proto-Indo-European Schwebeablaut,* University of California Press, 1969; *An Introduction to Historical and Comparative Linguistics,* Macmillan, 1972; *The Indexical Element in Morphology,* Institut fuer Sprachwissenschaft, 1975; *Analogy,* Mouton, 1977. Contributor of more than sixty articles and reviews to *Language, Ural-Altaische Jahrbuecher, Die Sprache, Kratylos, Statistical Methods in Linguistics, Glossa, General Linguistics,* and other publications. Editor for comparative linguistics, *Journal of Indo-European Studies;* member of editorial board, *Language, Vinttaja,* and *Historiographia Linguistica.*

WORK IN PROGRESS: Research in the processes of language patterning and change from the semiotic point of view, with J. Peter Maher and Uhlan V. Slagle.

SIDELIGHTS: Raimo Anttila told *CA:* "Today's scientific writers about language seem to shun the essay style, but I find it more accurate and permanent than the current pseudoformalism as an alleged mirror of innately given concepts like 'chair.' These formalists have also a vested interest in not knowing the humanistic tradition, which would take the patents from their marketable 'wisdom.'"

AVOCATIONAL INTERESTS: Camping, girl watching, and the wild west.

* * *

APPEL, John J. 1921-

PERSONAL: Born August 11, 1921, in Germany; naturalized U.S. citizen; son of Jacob and Susanna (Ortweiler) Appel; married Selma Dubin (an author and researcher), 1956; children: Michael. *Education:* University of Miami, B.A., 1949, M.A., 1951; University of Pennsylvania, Ph.D., 1960. *Home:* 219 Oakland Dr., East Lansing, Mich. 48823. *Office:* Department of American Thought and Language, Michigan State University, East Lansing, Mich. 48823.

CAREER: University of Miami, Coral Gables, Fla., instructor in basic skills and English, 1951-56, lecturer in evening college, 1952-56; Dade County Schools, Fla., special education teacher, 1952-54; Jewish Community Center, Baltimore, Md., director of adult education, 1959-60; Essex Community College, Essex, Md., instructor in history and social science, 1960-62; Michigan State University, East Lansing, assistant professor of American thought and language, 1962-67, associate professor of history and American thought and language, 1967-70, associate professor, James Madison College, 1967-69, 1971, professor of American thought and language, 1971—. Faculty member, New York

State Historical Association Adult Education Seminar, 1969; visiting scholar, Smithsonian Institution, 1969-70; lecturer at Carnegie-Mellon University, University of Pennsylvania, and Lakehead University. *Military service:* U.S. Army, 1942-45.

MEMBER: American Historical Association, Organization of American Historians, American Studies Association, American Association of University Professors, Immigration History Group (executive secretary, 1971-74), American Committee for Irish Studies, American Jewish Historical Society.

WRITINGS: (Contributor) M. Fishwick, editor, *American Studies: Methods, Models, Prospects,* University of Pennsylvania Press, 1964; (contributor) Leonard Dinnerstein and F. C. Jaher, editors, *Aliens: A History of Ethnic Minorities in America,* Appleton, 1970; *The New Immigration,* Pitman, 1971. Advisory editor, "The American Immigration Collection" series, Arno Press, 1969-70; editor with wife, Selma Appel, *Reader's Digest* Books "Destination America" series, 1975-76. Writer, with Selma Appel, of audio visual materials, "The Distorted Image: Immigrant and Ethnic Stereotypes in American Popular Graphics," 1973. Contributor to *Encyclopedia Judaica* and to literature and history journals.

WORK IN PROGRESS: The Jews in American Caricature, Jews in Christian Iconography, The Evolution of St. Patrick's Day in American Cartoons, all slide, sound and text projects for educational use.

AVOCATIONAL INTERESTS: Collecting cartoons, caricatures, and photographs depicting immigrant experience.

*   *   *

APPLEBY, Jon 1948-

PERSONAL: Born March 19, 1948, in Washington, D.C.; married Jill Hastings (an elementary school teacher), November, 1970. *Education:* Wesleyan University, Middletown, Conn., B.A., 1970. *Religion:* Humanism.

CAREER: Has worked as a bookstore clerk, bank computer operator, and short order cook; Architects for Elementary Education (designers of furniture for classrooms), carpenter, beginning 1971.

WRITINGS: Skate (novel), Farrar, Straus, 1972.

WORK IN PROGRESS: A second novel; a set of parodies.

SIDELIGHTS: Jon Appleby told *CA:* "I try to value my life by the number of things I have yet to say and accomplish, [not by] . . . what has gone by. I try not to be my own historian."††

*   *   *

APPLEGATE, James (Earl) 1923-

PERSONAL: Born September 16, 1923, in Mount Ayr, Ind.; son of Earl H. (a teacher) and Lena (Bender) Applegate; married Joan Strait (a musicologist), January 25, 1953; children: John Strait, Mary Sinclair, Celia Stewart, James David Robert. *Education:* Johns Hopkins University, B.A., 1943, Ph.D., 1954. *Politics:* Democrat. *Religion:* Episcopalian. *Home:* 666 Philadelphia Ave., Chambersburg, Pa. 17201. *Office:* Division of Humanities, Wilson College, Chambersburg, Pa. 17201.

CAREER: University of Rochester, Rochester, N.Y., instructor in English, 1950-54; University of Maryland, Overseas Program, lecturer in English in England, 1954-55; University of Rochester, assistant professor of English, 1955-56;

Elmira College, Elmira, N.Y., 1956-65, began as assistant professor, became associate professor of English; Wilson College, Chambersburg, Pa., professor of English and chairman of department, 1965-76, coordinator of humanities division, 1976—. *Military service:* U.S. Army, 1943-46; became staff sergeant. *Member:* Modern Language Association of America, Renaissance Society of America, Pennsylvania College English Association (vice-president).

WRITINGS: (With Gordon Browne and Gretchen C. Hankins) *Adventures in World Literature,* Harcourt, 1970. Also editor, with wife, Joan Strait Applegate, of *The Complete Songs of Henry Lawes.*

*   *   *

ARBIB, Robert (Simeon, Jr.) 1915-

PERSONAL: Surname is pronounced *Ar*-bib; born March 17, 1915, in Gloversville, N.Y.; son of Robert Simeon (an importer) and Edna (Henry) Arbib; married Renee Johnson, August 25, 1946; children: Robert B. *Education:* Yale University, B.S., 1937. *Politics:* Liberal Democrat. *Religion:* Unitarian Universalist. *Home:* 226 Guion Dr., Mamaroneck, N.Y. 10543. *Agent:* Wendy Weil, Julian Bach Literary Agency, Inc., 3 East 48th St., New York, N.Y. 10017. *Office:* National Audubon Society, 950 Third Ave., New York, N.Y. 10022.

CAREER: Grey Advertising Co., New York City, copy supervisor, 1939-49; Cecil & Presbrey Advertising Co., New York City, copy supervisor, 1949-51; Kenyon & Eckhardt, Inc., creative supervisor in New York City, Los Angeles, Calif., and San Francisco, Calif., 1951-61; D'Arcy Advertising Co., New York City, associate creative director, 1961-68; National Audubon Society, New York City, editor, *American Birds* (magazine), 1970—. Trustee, Mamaroneck Free Library, 1965-74; chairman, Mamaroneck Park Commission, 1966—. *Military service:* U.S. Army, 1941-46; became chief warrant officer.

MEMBER: American Ornithologists' Union, Cooper Ornithological Society, Wilson Ornithological Society, Federation of New York State Bird Clubs (past president), Linnaean Society of New York (fellow; past president). *Awards, honors:* John Burroughs Medal of American Museum of Natural History, 1972, for *The Lord's Woods.*

WRITINGS: Here We Are Together: The Notebook of an American Soldier in Britain, Longmans, Green, 1946; (with O. Sewall Pettingill and S. H. Spofford) *Enjoying Birds around New York City,* Houghton, 1966; (with Tony Soper) *The Hungry Bird Book: How to Make Your Garden Their Haven on Earth,* Taplinger, 1971; *The Lord's Woods,* Norton, 1971. Has done editorial work on McGraw's "Our Living World of Nature" series. Contributor to magazines.

WORK IN PROGRESS: Two children's books on nature subjects; a novel; a book about bird-watching; book reviews and forewords.

SIDELIGHTS: Robert Arbib wrote to *CA:* "Am trying to seriously settle down and finish a book now perhaps two-thirds completed, on the subject of the annual Christmas Bird Count, an insane event now participated in by better than 30,000 people each year. The work is going terribly slowly, and constantly interrupted by such trivia as sleeping, eating, earning a living, reading, conversing, travel, speechifying, gardening, bird-watching, and other distractions. Concentrating on all these pursuits, at the expense of serious writing, gives one a delicious sense of guilt, without which life would be meaningless and happy."

ARD, Ben N(eal), Jr. 1922-

PERSONAL: Born December 6, 1922, in Dallas, Tex.; son of Ben Neal (a physician) and Maudie Lou (Yeattes) Ard; *Education:* University of California, Los Angeles, B.A., 1947; Oregon State University, M.S., 1954; University of Michigan, Ph.D., 1962. *Home:* 52 Cambon Dr., San Francisco, Calif. 94132. *Office:* Department of Counseling, San Francisco State University, San Francisco, Calif. 94132.

CAREER: Merrill-Palmer Institute, Detroit, Mich., fellow in marriage counseling and family life education, 1953-54; Volunteers of America, Los Angeles, Calif., counselor, 1954-55; California Tuberculosis and Health Association, San Francisco, counselor, 1955-56; Michigan State University, East Lansing, assistant professor of family life, 1956-59; University of Michigan, Ann Arbor, teaching fellow, 1959-60; Central Michigan University, Mount Pleasant, associate professor, 1960-61, professor of psychology, 1961-63; San Francisco State University, San Francisco, professor of counseling, 1963—. Psychologist in private practice, San Francisco, 1964—. *Member:* American Psychological Association, American Personnel and Guidance Association, American Association of Marriage and Family Counselors (fellow; former member of board of directors), Society for the Scientific Study of Sex, California State Marriage Counseling Association (fellow; past president).

WRITINGS: (Editor) *Counseling and Psychotherapy,* Science & Behavior Books, 1966, revised edition, 1975; (co-editor) *Handbook of Marriage Counseling,* Science & Behavior Books, 1969, 2nd edition, 1976; (contributor) H. A. Otto, editor, *The New Sexuality,* Science & Behavior Books, 1971; (contributor) Albert Ellis, editor, *Growth through Reason,* Science & Behavior Books, 1971; *Treating Psychosexual Dysfunction,* Jason Aronson, 1974. Contributor to journals of counseling and family life. Associate editor, *Family Coordinator: Journal of Education, Counseling, and Services.*

*   *   *

ARDIES, Tom 1931-

PERSONAL: Born August 5, 1931, in Seattle, Wash.; son of John (a salesman) and Irene (Nutt) McIntyre; married Sharon Bernard, April 27, 1963; children: Robyn, Sarita. *Education:* Attended Daniel McIntyre Collegiate Institute, Winnepeg, Canada. *Home:* 1543 Beverly Dr., Palm Springs, Calif. 92262.

CAREER: Vancouver Sun, Vancouver, British Columbia, reporter, columnist, and editorial writer, 1950-64; *Honolulu Star Bulletin,* Honolulu, Hawaii, telegraph editor, 1964-65; special assistant to governor of Guam, 1965-67; writer. *Military service:* U.S. Air Force; received Commendation ribbon.

WRITINGS—All published by Doubleday: *Their Man in the White House,* 1971; *This Suitcase Is Going to Explode,* 1972; *Pandemic,* 1973; *Kosygin Is Coming,* 1974. Writer of screenplay "Russian Roulette," based on novel, *Kosygin Is Coming.*

WORK IN PROGRESS: A novel.

AVOCATIONAL INTERESTS: Travel.

*   *   *

ARDREY, Robert 1908-

PERSONAL: Born October 16, 1908, in Chicago, Ill.; son of Robert Leslie (an editor and publisher) and Marie (Haswell) Ardrey; married Helen Johnson, June 12, 1938 (divorced, 1960); married Berdine Grunewald (an artist and actress), August 11, 1960; children: (first marriage) Ross, Daniel; stepchildren: Vanessa (Mrs. Norman Jenkins). *Education:* University of Chicago, Ph.B., 1930; also studied playwriting with Thronton Wilder, 1930-35. *Home:* Mornington, 7 Dalebrook Rd., Kalk Bay, Cape Town, South Africa. *Agent:* Brandt & Brandt, 101 Park Ave., New York, N.Y. 10017; and Margery Vosper Ltd., 26 Charing Cross Rd., Suite 8, London WC2H ODG, England.

CAREER: Playwright, screenwriter, and author of books on anthropology. *Member:* Royal Society of Literature (fellow), Authors Guild, Dramatists Guild, Writers Guild of America, West, Phi Beta Kappa. *Awards, honors:* Guggenheim fellow, 1937-38; Sidney Howard Memorial Award, Playwrights Company, 1940, for "Thunder Rock"; Theresa Helburn Memorial Award, Theater Guild, 1961, for "Shadow of Heroes"; Wilkie Brothers Foundation grant, 1963; Academy Award nomination for best screenplay, 1966, for "Khartoum"; International Forum for Neurological Organization award, 1970; University of Chicago award for professional achievement, 1972.

WRITINGS: Worlds Beginning (novel), Duell, Sloan & Pearce, 1944; *The Brotherhood of Fear* (novel), Random House, 1952; *African Genesis: A Personal Investigation into the Animal Origins and Nature of Man,* Atheneum, 1961; *The Territorial Imperative: A Personal Inquiry into the Animal Origins of Property and Nations,* Atheneum, 1966; *The Social Contract: A Personal Inquiry into the Evolutionary Sources of Order and Disorder,* Atheneum, 1970; *The Hunting Hypothesis: A Personal Inquiry Concerning the Evolutionary Nature of Man,* Atheneum, 1976.

Plays: *Star Spangled* (three-act comedy; first produced on Broadway at John Golden Theatre, March 10, 1936), Samuel French, 1937; "How to Get Tough about It," first produced on Broadway at Martin Beck Theatre, February 8, 1938; "Casey Jones," first produced on Broadway at Fulton Theatre (now Helen Hayes Theatre), February 19, 1938; *Thunder Rock* (also see below; three-act; first produced on Broadway at Mansfield Theatre [now Brooks Atkinson Theatre], November 14, 1939), Hamish Hamilton, 1940, Dramatists Play Service, 1941, revised acting edition, Dramatists Play Service, 1950; "Jeb" (also see below), first produced on Broadway at Martin Beck Theatre, February 21, 1946; *Sing Me No Lullaby* (three-act; first produced Off-Broadway at Phoenix Theatre, October 14, 1954), Dramatists Play Service, 1955; *Shadow of Heroes: A Play in Five Acts from the Hungarian Passion* (also see below; first produced on West End at Piccadilly Theatre, October 7, 1959; produced Off-Braodway at York Playhouse, December 5, 1961), Collins, 1958; *Plays of Three Decades* (contains "Thunder Rock," "Jeb," and "Shadows of Heroes"), Atheneum, 1968.

Screenplays: "They Knew What They Wanted" (based on the play by Sidney Howard), RKO, 1940; "A Lady Takes a Chance," RKO, 1943; "The Green Years" (based on the novel by A. J. Cronin), M-G-M, 1946; "The Three Musketeers" (based on the novel by Alexander Dumas), M-G-M, 1948; "The Secret Garden" (based on the novel by Frances Hodgson Burnett), M-G-M, 1949; "Madame Bovary" (based on the novel by Gustave Flaubert), M-G-M, 1949; "Quentin Durward" (based on the novel by Sir Walter Scott), M-G-M, 1955; "The Power and the Prize" (based on the novel by Howard Swiggett), M-G-M, 1956; "The Wonderful Country" (based on the novel by Tom Lea), United Artists, 1959; (with John Gay) "The Four Horsemen of the

Apocalypse'' (based on the novel by Vicente Blasco Ibanez), M-G-M, 1962; "Khartoum," United Artists, 1966; "Out of Africa" (based on a collection of sketches by Isak Dinesen), United Artists, 1969. Also author of documentary, "The Animal Within," 1975.

SIDELIGHTS: A former playwright and screenwriter, Robert Ardrey turned to anthropology when his theatre experiences gave him "a growing dissatisfaction with contemporary understanding of human motivations." In his books Ardrey draws conclusions about the nature of human beings from observations of the behavior of lower animals and from studies on prehominid life forms. According to Geoffrey Gorer, Ardrey "believes that the basic truths about man's present and future can be described by studying the bones of *australopithecus,* prehominids which may possibly be in man's ancestral line. From these handfuls of bones he constructs ... prehominid heirarchical [*sic*] societies of co-operative hunters, already possessing language and ritual, and setting the inevitable behavior patterns of their human descendants, which we can flout only to our peril."

Although most critics find his descriptions of animal behavior and anthropological studies accurate and colorfully explicated, many take exception to the conclusions Ardrey draws from his material. A *Times Literary Supplement* reviewer states in an article on *The Territorial Imperative:* "It is a pity that so many reckless statements blemish a book that contains much information, vigorously presented and imparting to the reader some of the author's patent enthusiasm and wonder. Mr. Ardrey is a successful playwright and has had some training as an anthropologist; unfortunately the outlook and mode of expression appropriate to a dramatist have too often overwhelmed the caution, critical spirit and precision of language necessary in the scientist."

Other critics find Ardrey's former vocation no handicap to his later works. In a review of *African Genesis,* Eric Sevareid describes Ardrey's book as "an intellectual exercise and literary work of no mean order.... [It] is solid enough to stand or fall by its own weight, as measured by time and further debate. So much that Mr. Ardrey's scientific credentials, or lack thereof, ought not be a part of the fierce argument the book should arouse.... [It is] a dramatist's illumination and interpretation of the drama of the Animal Man—stark, frightening in its implications, yet somehow also inspiring and satisfying to the human ego."

BIOGRAPHICAL/CRITICAL SOURCES: New York Herald Tribune, November 12, 1961; *New York Times Book Review,* November 19, 1961, May 23, 1976; *Nation,* February 24, 1962; *Time,* September 16, 1966, March 15, 1976; *Christian Century,* April 19, 1967; *Times Literary Supplement,* June 8, 1967; *National Observer,* October 14, 1968; *Book World,* October 4, 1970; *Best Sellers,* October 15, 1970; *Saturday Review,* October 24, 1970, April 3, 1976; *New Republic,* October 31, 1970; *Observer,* November 1, 1970; *Smithsonian Magazine,* December, 1970; *Washington Post,* January 2, 1971; *Nouvelle Ecole,* winter, 1971-72; *Chicago Daily News,* May 29, 1974.

*   *   *

ARELLANES, Audrey Spencer 1920-

PERSONAL: Born February 23, 1920, in Lance Creek, Wyo.; daughter of William Sidney and Edith Catherine (Hall) Spencer; married Lester Glenn Arellanes (an author-historian), September 28, 1946; children: Denetia Ynez. *Education:* Attended University of California at Los Angeles. *Home:* 1206 North Stoneman Ave., No. 15, Alham-

bra, Calif. 91801. *Office:* Avery International, San Marino, Calif. 91108.

CAREER: California Physicians Service, Los Angeles, Calif., secretary to claims manager, 1946-54; Calcor (manufacturer of pre-fabricated buildings), Whittier, Calif., secretary to vice-president, and assistant editor of house organ, 1954-58; California College of Medicine (now part of University of California at Los Angeles), Los Angeles, research assistant in biokinetics laboratory, 1958-62; Avery International (manufacturer of pressure-sensitive adhesives), San Marino, Calif., administrative assistant, 1963—. Owner and operator, Bookworm Press, Calif., 1965—. *Member:* American Society of Bookplate Collectors and Designers (sole officer; editor-treasurer, 1970—), Manuscript Society (secretary-treasurer, Southern California chapter; member of board of directors, 1975-77; executive secretary, 1975—), Society of California Archivists, Rounce and Coffin Club.

WRITINGS: Bookplates: A Selected Annotated Bibliography of the Periodical Literature, Gale, 1971; *Thomas Bird Mosher: Excerpts from His Correspondence with Washington Irving Way,* Bookworm Press, 1972. Editor of *Bookplates in the News,* and the *Year Book* of the American Society of Bookplate Collectors and Designers.

WORK IN PROGRESS: A book about the Cord, a classic automobile of the 1930's far ahead of the time in its design, and the man for whom it was named, E. L. Cord.

SIDELIGHTS: In 1965, Audrey Arellanes purchased sufficient type to set up a single poem, and Bookworm Press was born. This first effort, printed on a friend's proof press, was *Beauregard,* Lester Glenn Arellanes' tribute to a pet cat. Arellanes has since handset such items as a uniquely and carefully designed reprinting of *The Elephant Cutlet,* from Ludwig Bemelmans' *My War with the United States,* and a miniature book, *Fireflies: Selections from Rabindranath Tagore.*

BIOGRAPHICAL/CRITICAL SOURCES: American Book Collector, November-December, 1969; Lois Rather, *Women as Printers,* Rather Press, 1970.

*   *   *

ARENT, Arthur 1904-1972

September 29, 1904—May 18, 1972; American editor, playwright, novelist, and screenwriter. Obituaries: *New York Times,* May 20, 1972. (See index for *CA* sketch)

*   *   *

ARIAN, Edward 1921-

PERSONAL: Born July 20, 1921, in Cleveland, Ohio; son of George (a house painter) and Fannie (Hart) Arian; married Yvette Bardon (a teacher and librarian), September 13, 1942; children: Carol (Mrs. Daniel Coope), Anne Lesley. *Education:* Curtis Institute of Music, diploma, 1942; Coombs College, B.M., 1960; Bryn Mawr College, Ph.D., 1970. *Home:* 116 Boulder Rd., Plymouth Meeting, Pa. 19462. *Office:* Department of Political Science, Drexel University, Philadelphia, Pa. 19104.

CAREER: Philadelphia Musical Academy, Philadelphia, Pa., instructor in double bass, 1960—; Temple University, Philadelphia, instructor in double bass, 1960—; Drexel University, Philadelphia, assistant professor, 1970-71, associate professor, 1971-75, professor of political science, 1975—, chairman of department of history and politics, 1977—, director of Graduate Program in Arts Administration. Bass violin player, Philadelphia Orchestra, 1947-67. Vice-chairman, Commonwealth of Pennsylvania Council on the Arts. *Military service:* U.S. Navy, 1942-45. *Member:* American Political Science Association, American Society for Public Administration, American Civil Liberties Union (member of state board of Pennsylvania). *Awards, honors:* Samuel S. Fels Fund grant, 1971; grants from Southeastern Pennsylvania Regional Council and Pennsylvania Department of Community Affairs, for internship programs in public administration.

WRITINGS: Bach, Beethoven, and Bureaucracy: The Case of the Philadelphia Orchestra, University of Alabama Press, 1971.

WORK IN PROGRESS: Research on a curriculum for training in arts administration at Drexel University.

*   *   *

ARLOTTO, Anthony (Thomas) 1939-

PERSONAL: Born November 1, 1939, in Jersey City, N.J.; son of Thomas (a plumber) and Mary (Colaneri) Arlotto. *Education:* Boston College, A.B., 1961; graduate study at University of Leiden, 1961-62, and University of Washington, Seattle, 1962-64; Harvard University, Ph.D., 1966; Stanford University, M.B.A., 1977. *Politics:* Liberal Republican. *Religion:* Catholic. *Office:* Controller's Division, Wells Fargo Bank, 475 Sansome St., San Francisco, Calif. 94111.

CAREER: Harvard University, Cambridge, Mass., instructor, 1966-69, assistant professor of linguistics, 1969-75, senior tutor at John Winthrop House, 1973-75; Wells Fargo Bank, San Francisco, Calif., financial analyst, 1977—.

WRITINGS: Introduction to Historical Linguistics, Houghton, 1972. Contributor to learned journals. Consultant on etymologies, *American Heritage Dictionary.*

SIDELIGHTS: Anthony Arlotto writes: "In 1975, I gave up my academic career and entered Stanford Business School. After settling into life in the business world, I hope to return to writing, both fiction and non-fiction."

*   *   *

ARMAND, Louis 1905-1971

January 17, 1905—August 30, 1971; French civil servant, engineer, industrialist, and author of books on contemporary Europe. Obituaries: *New York Times,* August 31, 1971; *Washington Post,* September 2, 1971; *L'Express,* September 6-12, 1971; *Newsweek,* September 13, 1971; *Current Biography,* October, 1971. (See index for *CA* sketch)

*   *   *

ARMBRUSTER, Carl J. 1929-

PERSONAL: Born June 25, 1929, in Cincinnati, Ohio; son of Harry (a meat cutter) and Mary E. (Kempker) Armbruster. *Education:* Loyola University of Chicago, A.B., 1952, M.A., 1958; West Baden College, Ph.L., 1954, S.T.L., 1961; Haus Sentmaring, Muenster, Germany, pastoral studies, 1961-62; Institut Catholique de Paris, S.T.D. (with highest distinction), 1966.

CAREER: Former Roman Catholic priest, entered Society of Jesus (Jesuits), 1947, ordained, 1960; instructor in Latin and speech at Jesuit high school in Chicago, Ill., 1954-57; Loyola University of Chicago, Bellarmine School of Theology, Chicago, assistant professor of theology, 1966-72, assistant academic dean, 1967-68, director of field education, 1967-70; Boston College, Boston, Mass., visiting professor

of systematic and historical theology, Weston College of Theology, Cambridge, Mass., 1971-72, visiting professor of systematic theology at main campus, 1972. Guest professor, Bethany Theological Seminary (Church of the Brethren seminary), spring, 1968; director, Regis Hall Retreat House, 1969-70; associate chaplain, Harvard-Radcliffe Catholic Student Center, 1970-72; visiting research fellow, Cambridge Center for Social Studies, 1971. *Member:* American Academy of Religion, Catholic Theological Society of America (member of board of directors, 1971-73). *Awards, honors:* American Association of Theological Schools faculty fellowship, 1970-71.

WRITINGS: (With E. McMahon, J. O'Malley, R. Cahill) *Challenge* (prayerbook), Loyola University Press, 1958; *The Vision of Paul Tillich,* Sheed, 1967. Contributor of articles and reviews to *America, Commonweal, Social Order, Christus* (Paris), and other journals.

WORK IN PROGRESS: The Emerging Ministry.†

*   *   *

ARMENTROUT, William W(infield) 1918-

PERSONAL: Born December 8, 1918, in Pittsburg, Kan.; son of Winfield Dockery (a college educator) and Dora (Sauer) Armentrout; married Berda Elkjer, June 24, 1944; children: Barbara, Robert, Beth. *Education:* University of Missouri, B.J., 1939; Northern Colorado University, A.B., 1940; Columbia University, M.A., 1940; Stanford University, Ed.D., 1953. *Office:* Department of Education, California State Polytechnic University, San Luis Obispo, Calif. 93407.

CAREER: Guidance counselor in Menlo Park, Calif., 1940-41; Stanford University, Palo Alto, Calif., associate registrar, 1946-49; California State Polytechnic University, San Luis Obispo, Calif., assistant professor, 1953-59, associate professor, 1960-66, professor of education, 1967—, assistant to dean of Arts and Sciences Division, 1960-61, coordinator of secondary education, 1961-73, coordinator of credential advisement and teacher candidate selection, 1973—. *Military service:* U.S. Army Air Forces, 1941-46; served in the Caribbean; became captain. *Member:* Phi Delta Kappa.

WRITINGS: What Should the Purpose(s) of American Education Be?, Kendall/Hunt, 1971. Contributor to education and psychology journals.

*   *   *

ARMOUR, Rollin Stely 1929-

PERSONAL: Born December 5, 1929; son of Thomas (a general contractor) and Frankie (Calhoun) Armour; married Mary Anne Crum, May 30, 1957; children: Ellen True, Rollin Stely, Jr., Stephen Frank. *Education:* Baylor University, B.A., 1950; Southern Baptist Theological Seminary, B.D., 1953; Harvard University, S.T.M., 1956, Th.D., 1963. *Home:* 913 Cherokee Rd., Auburn, Ala. 36830. *Office:* Department of Religion, Auburn University, Auburn, Ala. 36830.

CAREER: Clergyman of Southern Baptist Convention; Statson University, DeLand, Fla., assistant professor, 1960-65, associate professor, 1965-67, professor of religion, 1967-73; Auburn University, Auburn, Ala., professor of religion and head of department, 1973—. *Military service:* U.S. Army, chaplain, 1953-55; became first lieutenant. *Member:* American Academy of Religion (vice-president of Southern section, 1971-72; president of Southern section, 1972-73), American Society of Church History, Southern Baptist Historical Society (vice-president, 1971-72; president, 1972-73), Florida Baptist Historical Society, Omicron Delta Kappa, Phi Alpha Theta, Lambda Chi Alpha. *Awards, honors:* Frank S. and Elizabeth Brewer Award of American Society of Church History, 1966, for manuscript of *Anabaptist Baptism: A Representative Study;* Society for Religion in Higher Education fellowship for the study of Asian religion, 1968-69.

WRITINGS: Anabaptist Baptism: A Representative Study, Herald Press, 1966.

WORK IN PROGRESS: Study of Asian religions and of the Christian apologetic.

SIDELIGHTS: Rollin Armour traveled and studied in Europe, 1958-59, and in North Africa and Asia, 1969.

*   *   *

ARMSTRONG, Frederick H(enry)   1926-

PERSONAL: Born March 27, 1926, in Toronto, Ontario, Canada; son of Silas H. (superintendent of Toronto playgrounds) and Dorothy L. (Goode) Armstrong; married Joan Biberovich, August 6, 1960; children: Dale H., Irene E. *Education:* University of Toronto, B.A., 1949, M.A., 1951, Ph.D., 1965. *Religion:* Presbyterian. *Home:* 1 Franklin Ave., London, Ontario, Canada. *Office:* Department of History, University of Western Ontario, London, Ontario, Canada.

CAREER: Royal Ontario Museum, Toronto, assistant in numismatics, 1948-51; in general insurance business, Toronto, 1951-60; University of Toronto, Toronto, instructor in history, 1960-63; University of Western Ontario, London, lecturer, 1963-65, assistant professor, 1965-68, associate professor, 1968-75, professor of history, 1975—. Architectural and Historical Advisory Committee, City of London, member, 1973—, vice-chairman, 1977—. Consultant, National Heritage Ltd., 1970-75. *Member:* Canadian Historical Association, Royal Historical Society, Champlain Society (member of council, 1974—), American Numismatic Society, Institut d'Histoire de l'Amerique Francaise, Ontario Historical Society (member of executive committee, 1963-65, 1972—; second vice-president, 1975-76, first vice-president, 1976—). *Awards, honors:* Newell scholarships from American Numismatic Society, 1947-48; grants from Centennial Commission, 1966, and Canada Council, 1968, 1969, 1971, 1973, 1974.

WRITINGS: (Editor, and author of introduction and appendices) Henry Scadding, *Toronto of Old,* Oxford University Press, 1966; *Handbook of Upper Canadian Chronology and Territorial Legislation,* Lawson Library Centennial Publication, University of Western Ontario, 1967; (co-editor, author of introduction, and contributor) *Approaches to Teaching Local History: Using Upper Canadian and Ontario Examples,* Oxford University Press, 1969; (co-editor and contributor) *Aspects of Nineteenth Century Ontario: Essays Presented to James J. Talman,* University of Toronto Press, 1974; (co-author) *Reflections on London's Past,* Corp. of the City of London, 1975. Contributor to *Dictionary of Canadian Biography* and *Americana Annual;* contributor of about 130 articles and reviews to historical journals and newspapers. Consulting editor, Patricia W. Hart, *Pioneering in North York: A History of the Borough,* General Publishing, 1968. Assistant editor, *Ontario History,* 1961-62.

WORK IN PROGRESS: Writing a book on early Toronto business, for University of Toronto Press; a book on early

Toronto, for National Museum of Man, Ottawa; research on officials in Ontario and Quebec prior to 1841.

AVOCATIONAL INTERESTS: Photography, gardening, music.

*   *   *

ARMSTRONG, John Borden   1926-

PERSONAL: Born December 20, 1926, in Lower Merion, Pa.; son of Arthur Tibbits (a mill representative) and Anna (Harris) Armstrong; married Bonnie Barton, September 2, 1962; children: John Borden, Jr., Andrew Barton. *Education:* Dickinson College, A.B., 1949; Boston University, A.M., 1951, Ph.D., 1962. *Politics:* Democrat. *Religion:* Episcopalian. *Home:* 214 South St., Hingham, Mass. 02043. *Office:* Department of History, Boston University, Boston, Mass. 02215.

CAREER: Budd Co., Philadelphia, Pa., metallurgical technician, 1949-50; Bethlehem Steel Co., Philadelphia, 1951-53; Boston University, Boston, Mass., instructor, 1962-66, assistant professor, 1966-69, associate professor, 1969-77, professor of history, 1977—. Chairman, Committee for a New England Bibliography; member of national committee, Citizens' League Against the Sonic Boom, 1967-71. *Member:* American Historical Association, Organization of American Historians, American Studies Association, American Association for State and Local History, Colonial Society of Massachusetts (member of council, 1969-71), Society for the Preservation of New England Antiquities (member of board of trustees, 1970-73). *Awards, honors:* National Endowment for the Humanities research grant, 1971.

WRITINGS: Factory under the Elms: A History of Harrisville, New Hampshire, 1774-1969, M.I.T. Press, 1969.

WORK IN PROGRESS: Research for a book tentatively entitled *Corporation Wives in the Gilded Age.*

BIOGRAPHICAL/CRITICAL SOURCES: Historical New Hampshire, spring, 1970; *Boston Globe,* May 13, 1970; *Yale Review,* autumn, 1970; *Journal of Economic History,* June, 1971.

*   *   *

ARNADE, Charles W(olfgang)   1927-
(Julius Giersch)

PERSONAL: Born May 11, 1927, in Goerlitz, Germany; son of Kurt Conrad (in the military) and Johanna (Giersch) Arnade; married Marjorie J. McLain (a medical technologist), December 18, 1948; children: Frank, Carlos, Stephen, Timothy, Jeanette, Peter, Christopher. *Education:* University of Michigan, A.B., 1950, M.A., 1952; University of Florida, Ph.D., 1955. *Politics:* Democrat. *Religion:* Catholic. *Home:* 219 North Main St., San Antonio, Fla. 33576. *Office:* Social Science Building, University of South Florida, Tampa, Fla. 33620.

CAREER: Worked as a supply clerk, Corporacion Boliviana de Fomento, Bolivia, 1944-46, and at odd jobs, 1946-49; University of Michigan, Ann Arbor, clerk in International Center, 1949-50, assistant foreign student adviser, 1950-51, researcher, William Clements Library, 1951-52; University of Florida, Gainesville, instructor in history and American institutions, 1952-56, assistant professor of history, 1958-60; Florida State University, Tallahassee, assistant professor of history and political science, 1956-58; University of South Florida, Tampa, associate professor of history and social studies, 1960-63, professor of history, director of international studies, and acting chairman of history department, 1963-66, professor of social science and American civilization, 1966-69, professor of international studies, 1969—, professor of American ideas (American institutions) and chairman of department, 1969-72. Visiting associate professor of history, University of Iowa, 1960-61; Fulbright professor, University of Madrid, 1965-66; visiting professor of history, University of Ile-Ife, Nigeria, 1969-70; visiting professor at local universities in India and Nepal, 1972; lecturer at universities in East Germany, Poland, Bulgaria, and Yugoslavia, 1975. Lecturer on U.S. State Department International Educational Exchange Service tour in Latin America, 1957, 1958, 1976, and in Nigeria, 1969-70; Peace Corps, consultant to Latin American Division, 1960-66, campus liaison officer, 1962-66. Consultant and historical research director, St. Augustine Historical Restoration and Preservation Commission, 1960-66; member of Florida State Antiquity Commission, 1964-66; technical advisor, Ministry of Tourism, Spain, 1965-68; chairman, Selection Board of Historical Sites for Florida Board of Parks, 1966-68; educational consultant, Office of the Governor of Florida, 1967-68. Director and moderator of International Radio Roundtable, University of Michigan, 1949-52.

MEMBER: Southern Historical Association (Latin American section; member of program committee, 1958-62; program chairman, 1964), Florida Historical Society (member of program committee, 1957-61; member of executive board, 1962-64), Florida Anthropological Society (member of executive board, 1962-63; vice-president, 1963-64; president, 1964-65; executive secretary, 1965-68), St. Augustine Historical Society (member of research committee, 1958-59), American Association of University Professors (University of South Florida chapter; president, 1966-68), Phi Beta Kappa, Phi Kappa Phi, Phi Alpha Theta, Alpha Kappa Delta. *Awards, honors:* Woodrow Wilson fellow, University of San Francisco Xavier, Sucre, Bolivia, and National Archive of Bolivia, 1952-53; Social Science Research Council grant for Latin America, 1963; Ford Foundation grant to Biafra, 1969-70.

WRITINGS: The Emergence of the Republic of Bolivia, University of Florida Press, 1957, revised edition, Russell, 1970; *Florida on Trial, 1593-1602,* University of Miami Press, 1959; *The Siege of St. Augustine in 1702,* University of Florida Press, 1959; (with Josef Kuehnel) *El Problema del humanista Tadeo Haenke: Nuevas perspectivas en la investigacion haenkeana,* Instituto Cultural Boliviano-Aleman, Universidad de San Francisco Xavier, 1960; *The Failure of Spanish Florida* (pamphlet; originally published in *Americas,* January, 1960), Academy of American Franciscan History, 1960; *La Historia de Bolivia y la de los Estados Unidos de America: Una Comparacion,* Universidad Tomas Frias, 1962; *La Dramatica Insurgencia de Bolivia,* [La Paz, Argentina], 1964; *Cattle Raising in Spanish Florida, 1513-1763* (pamphlet; originally published in *Agricultural History,* number 3, 1961), St. Augustine Historical Society, 1965; (editor and author of introduction) *Vilute pazos Kaukis: Compendio de la historia de los Estados Unidos de Norte America publicado en 1825,* [La Paz], 1976.

Contributor: (Author of foreword) David Hartzler Zook, Jr., *The Conduct of the Chaco War,* Bookman Associates, 1961; James Covington, editor, *Pirates, Indians and Spaniards: Father Escobedo's La Florida,* Great Outdoors, 1963; Jose B. Balseiro, editor, *Presencia Hispanica en la Florida,* [Miami], 1976. Contributor to *Encyclopaedia Britannica,* 1961, *Britannica Book of the Year,* 1962-64, *New Catholic Encyclopedia,* 1967, *Reader's Digest Almanac,* 1968, *World Mark Encyclopedia of Nations* (London), 1971;

contributor of numerous essays, articles in German, Spanish, and English, and over 300 book reviews and abstracts to *William and Mary Quarterly, Journal of Inter-American Studies, Nuevo Mundo* (La Paz), *South Atlantic Quarterly, Revista Chilena de Historia Y Geografia, Vital Speeches of the Day, Americas, Florida Historical Quarterly, Problemas Internacionales, Florida Anthropologist, Tequesta, Jahrbuch des Museums fuer Volkerkunde* (Leipzig), and other professional journals. *Hispanic American Historical Review* (Duke University Press quarterly), member of bibliographic committee, 1957-65, book review editor, 1961-65; editor, *ALAS* (Association for Latin American Studies) *Bulletin,* 1959-60; associate editor, *Florida Historical Quarterly,* 1959-61; member of editorial board, *Historical Abstracts,* 1963-68.

WORK IN PROGRESS: A History of Bolivia; An Outline History of Spanish Florida.

SIDELIGHTS: Charles Arnade was born in Germany, has lived in China, Italy, Spain, Switzerland, Bolivia, Chile, Argentina, Jamaica, Nigeria, Yugoslavia, India, Nepal, and the United States. He has been associated with the training program of the Peace Corps since its inception, and was the first foreign professor to enter Biafra at the end of the civil war, in 1969.

BIOGRAPHICAL/CRITICAL SOURCES: Aufbau: 25 Years (New York), April 29, 1960; Fernando Diez de Medina, *El Alfarero desvelado,* Gisbert (La Paz), 1964; *Florida Accent* (Tampa), June 18, 1967.

*   *   *

ARNOLD, Adlai F(ranklin) 1914-
(A. Franklin)

PERSONAL: Born May 24, 1914, in Cash, Ark.; son of James Columbus and Gertrude (Linn) Arnold; married Delilah Pickartz, October 7, 1939. *Education:* Arkansas Polytechnic College, student, 1948; University of Arkansas, B.S., 1950, M.S., 1951; Oklahoma State University, Ph.D., 1962. *Politics:* Independent. *Religion:* Church of Christ. *Home and office:* 929 Skyline Dr., Van Buren, Ark. 72956.

CAREER: Civilian Conservation Corps, Ouachita National Forest, Ark., senior leader, 1933-37; U.S. Department of Agriculture, timber management assistant at Ozark National Forest, Russellville, Ark., 1937-51, county supervisor for Farmer's Home Administration, 1951-56, agricultural economist for Economic Research Service in Asuncion, Paraguay, 1965-70 and in Monrovia, Liberia, 1970-75; independent consultant on agricultural economics, 1975—. Agricultural economist, University of Arkansas, Fayetteville, 1956-65. Advisor, Institute of Rural Welfare and Ministry of Agriculture, Planning and Policy, Paraguay; advisor, Ministry of Agriculture on Planning and Economic Management, Liberia. Former president, Ozark (Ark.) Chamber of Commerce. *Member:* American Agricultural Economics Association, Rotary International (former president, Ozark chapter).

WRITINGS—All published by Agricultural Experiment Station, University of Arkansas, except as indicated: *Economics of Growing Turkeys from Poult to Market Bird, 1957 and 1958,* 1959; (with D. G. Lafferty) *Inputs and Outputs of Major Forage Crops on Livestock Farms in the Arkansas Ozark Area,* 1960; (with W. B. Back) *Potential Increases in Farm Income from Upstream Watershed Development: A Case Study of Boggy Creek Watershed in Washita County of Oklahoma,* Oklahoma Experiment Station, 1962; *Costs and Returns from Feeder Pigs,* 1963; (with J. Bruce Hottel)

Economic Study of Land Use Adjustment Potentials of Areas Adjacent to the Ozark National Forest, 1963; (with Hottel) *Crops, Pasture, Timber, and Livestock Enterprises for the Boston Mountain and Ozark Highland Areas of Arkansas,* 1965; *Foundations of an Agricultural Policy in Paraguay,* Praeger, 1971. Author, under pseudonym A. Franklin, of "Field and Pasture," column in county newspaper, 1954-56. Contributor to *Arkansas Agricultural Economist, Oklahoma Current Economics,* and *Arkansas Farm Research.* Co-editor, *Arkansas Agricultural Economist,* 1964-65.

WORK IN PROGRESS: Agricultural Sector Analysis in Liberia, West Africa.

SIDELIGHTS: Adlai Arnold told *CA:* "For several years as I have worked with people in developing countries I have observed the close relationship of their values to their material prosperity—the relationship of their spiritual welfare to their material and physical welfare. In this manner I have come to understand that the welfare of a people is determined by their root values—by their evolving institutions and arrangements for resolving conflicts over the scarce resources of nature. It now seems clear to me why all nations—including the rich and powerful—have made so little headway in improving the welfare of the poor: our efforts are yet too weak to overcome the greed and selfishness which breed corrupt governments and perpetuate the 'inhumanity of man to man.'

"It is true that material resources are scarce but this is not the greatest problem; if we could eradicate ignorance, fear, distrust and hatred, we could then cooperate to produce the things needed for the good life. Life could be so much easier for multiplied millions if we could be producing goods and services to uplift man in the place of the great masses of military hardware we are now turning out for his destruction. If we ever achieve our goal of a peaceful world we must somehow find a way to eliminate our greed for power and the corresponding fear of being attacked."

*   *   *

ARONSON, Elliot 1932-

PERSONAL: Born January 9, 1932, in Chelsea, Mass.; son of Harry and Dorothy Aronson; married Vera Rabinek, September 8, 1954; children: Hal, Neal, Julie, Joshua. *Education:* Brandeis University, B.A., 1954; Wesleyan University, Middletown, Conn., M.A., 1956; Stanford University, Ph.D., 1959. *Politics:* Radical. *Religion:* Jewish. *Home:* 1525 Laurent St., Santa Cruz, Calif. *Office:* Kresge College, University of California, Santa Cruz, Calif. 95064.

CAREER: Harvard University, Cambridge, Mass., lecturer in social psychology, 1959-62; University of Minnesota, Minneapolis, associate professor and director of research, Laboratory for Research in Social Relations, 1962-64, professor of social psychology, 1964-65; University of Texas at Austin, professor of social psychology and director of social psychology program, 1965-74; University of California, Kresge College, Santa Cruz, member of faculty, 1974—. Center for Advanced Study in the Behavioral Sciences, Stanford, Calif., visiting fellow, 1965-66, fellow, 1970-71; National Training Laboratories, intern in applied behavioral sciences, summer, 1970, professional member, 1970—. Licensed psychologist, state of Texas, 1970.

MEMBER: American Association for the Advancement of Science, American Psychological Association (fellow). *Awards, honors:* National Institute of Mental Health grants, 1966-71, 1968-75, 1970-71; Socio-Psychological Prize of

American Association for the Advancement of Science, 1970; National Media Award from American Psychological Association.

WRITINGS: (Editor with Gardner Lindzey and contributor) *The Handbook of Social Psychology,* 2nd edition (Aronson was not associated with earlier edition), Addison-Wesley, Volume I: *Theories,* 1968, Volume II: *Research Methods,* 1969, Volume III: *The Individual in a Social Context,* 1969, Volume IV: *Group Psychology and Phenomena of Interaction,* 1969, Volume V: *Applied Social Psychology,* 1969; (editor with R. P. Abelson, W. J. McGuire, T. M. Newcomb, and P. H. Tannenbaum, and contributor) *Theories of Cognitive Consistency: A Sourcebook,* Rand McNally, 1968; (editor) *Voices of Modern Psychology,* Addison-Wesley, 1969; *The Social Animal,* W. H. Freeman, 1972, 2nd edition, 1976; *Readings about the Social Animal,* W. H. Freeman, 1973, 2nd edition, 1976; (with Robert Helmreich) *Social Psychology,* Van Nostrand, 1973.

Contributor: J. W. Atkinson, editor, *Motives in Fantasy, Action, and Society,* Van Nostrand, 1958; Shel Feldman, editor, *Cognitive Consistency,* Academic Press, 1966; Dorwin Cartwright and A. F. Zander, editors, *Group Dynamics,* 3rd edition, Harper, 1968; Leonard Berkowitz, editor, *Advances in Experimental Social Psychology,* Volume IV, Academic Press, 1969; W. J. Arnold and David Levine, editors, *Nebraska Symposium on Motivation: 1969,* University of Nebraska Press, 1969; C. G. McClintock, editor, *Experimental Social Psychology,* Holt, 1971.

Contributor of more than sixty articles to psychology journals. Co-editor, "Bobbs-Merrill Reprint Series in Psychology," 1960—; consulting editor, *Journal of Personality and Social Psychology,* 1963—, *Journal of Experimental Social Psychology,* 1964—, and *Personality: An International Journal,* 1970—.

WORK IN PROGRESS: With J. M. Carlsmith and Phoebe Ellsworth, *How to Do Experiments in Social Psychology,* for Addison-Wesley; with David Mettee, *The Psychology of Interpersonal Attraction;* five chapters for *Principles of Psychology,* edited by Paul Mussen and Mark Rosenzweig, for Heath.

*   *   *

ASANTE, Molefi K. 1942-
(Arthur L. Smith)

PERSONAL: Original name, Arthur L. Smith; name legally changed in 1975; born August 14, 1942, in Valdosta, Ga.; son of Arthur L. and Lillie (Wilkson) Smith; married Jean Scarber, July 22, 1966; children: Kasina Eka. *Education:* Oklahoma Christian College, B.A. (cum laude), 1964; Pepperdine College (now University), M.A., 1965; University of California, Los Angeles, Ph.D., 1968. *Religion:* Christian. *Home:* 190 Chaumont Dr., Williamsville, N.Y. 14221. *Office:* Department of Communication, State University of New York at Buffalo, Buffalo, N.Y. 14226.

CAREER: Instructor at California State Polytechnic College (now University), Pomona, 1966-67, and San Fernando Valley State College (now California State University, Northridge), 1967; Purdue University, Lafayette, Ind., assistant professor of communication, 1968-69; University of California, Los Angeles, assistant professor, 1969-70, associate professor of speech, 1971-73, director of Center for Afro-American Studies, 1970-73; State University of New York at Buffalo, professor of communication and chairman of department, 1973—. Chairman, Indiana State Civil Rights Commission on Higher Education and the Afro-American,

1968-69. Member of selection committee, Martin Luther King and Woodrow Wilson fellowships, 1970-72.

MEMBER: International Communication Association, Speech Communication Association (member of legislative assembly, 1971-73), National Association of Dramatic and Speech Arts, American Academy of Political and Social Science, Western Speech Association, Pacific Speech Association. *Awards, honors:* Christian Education Guild Writer's Award, 1965.

WRITINGS—Under name Arthur L. Smith: *Break of Dawn* (poems), Dorrance, 1964; *Rhetoric of Black Revolution,* Allyn & Bacon, 1969; (with Andrea Rich) *Rhetoric of Revolution,* Moore Publishing, 1970; (contributor) Donn Parsons and Wil Linkugel, editors, *Television and the New Persuasion,* Usher, 1970; (editor with Stephen Robb) *The Voice of Black Rhetoric,* Allyn & Bacon, 1971; (contributor) Larry Barker and Robert Kobler, editors, *Speech Communication Behavior,* Prentice-Hall, 1971; (with Anne Allen and Hernandez Deluvina) *How to Talk with People of Other Races,* Trans-Ethnic Foundation, 1971; (editor) *Language, Communication and Rhetoric in Black America,* Harper, 1972; *Transracial Communication,* Prentice-Hall, 1973.

Under name Molefi K. Asante: *Social Uses of Mass Communication,* State University of New York at Buffalo, 1976; (with Jerry K. Frye) *Contemporary Public Communication,* Harper, 1977. Contributor to speech journals. Member of board of editors "Black Men in America" reprint series, 1969-70; editor, *Journal of Black Studies,* 1969—; editorial associate, *Speech Teacher,* 1970-73; contributing editor, *Encore,* 1970-72; book reviewer, *Journal of Communication,* 1970-72; member of advisory board, *Black Law Journal,* 1971-73, *Race Relations Abstract,* 1973-77.

WORK IN PROGRESS: The nature of the black communicative experience as expressed in language styles; principal symbols and their value for a multi-ethnic society; and other research projects in ethno-rhetoric and interracial communication.

*   *   *

ASHBY, (Darrel) LeRoy   1938-

PERSONAL: Born November 19, 1938, in Grand Junction, Colo.; son of Samuel Franklin (a janitor) and Mildred (Hooker) Ashby; married Mary Elizabeth Gross (a teacher), July 3, 1958; children: Steven Eugene, Eric Lee. *Education:* Adams State College, B.A., 1960; University of Wyoming, M.A., 1961; University of Maryland, Ph.D., 1966. *Politics:* Democrat. *Religion:* Unitarian Universalist. *Home:* 1280 Northeast Hillside Cir., Pullman, Wash. 99163. *Office:* Department of History, Washington State University, Pullman, Wash. 99163.

CAREER: University of Bridgeport, Bridgeport, Conn., assistant professor of history, 1966-70; Illinois State University, Normal, assistant professor of history, 1970-72; Washington State University, Pullman, associate professor, 1972-76, professor of history, 1976—. *Military service:* National Guard, 1956-64; became staff sergeant. *Member:* American Studies Association, Organization of American Historians.

WRITINGS: The Spearless Leader: Senator Borah and the Progressive Movement in the 1920's, University of Illinois, 1972; (editor with Bruce Martin Stave) *The Discontented Society: Interpretations of Twentieth Century American Protest,* Rand McNally, 1972.

ASHFORD, Margaret Mary   1881-1972
(Daisy Ashford)

1881—January 15, 1972; English author of the best-selling *The Young Visiters,* written at the age of five. Obituaries: *Sunday Times* (London), January 16, 1972; *New York Times,* January 18, 1972; *Washington Post,* January 21, 1972; *Publishers Weekly,* February 28, 1972.

*   *   *

ASTLEY, Joan Bright   1910-

PERSONAL: Born September 27, 1910, in Argentina; daughter of Trevor Percy and Mary Lindsay (Harper) Bright; married Philip Reginald Astley, July 4, 1949 (deceased); children: Richard Jacob. *Education:* Educated privately. *Politics:* Conservative. *Religion:* Protestant. *Home:* 11 Crescent Pl., London SW3 2EA, England. *Agent:* Mark Hamilton, A. M. Heath & Co., 40-42 William IV St., London WC2N 4DD, England.

CAREER: British Government, secretary with British legation in Mexico City, Mexico, 1931-36; Royal Institute of International Affairs, London, England, secretary, 1936-38; with War Office, London, 1938-41; served on Sir Winston Churchill's staff at War Cabinet Office, London, 1941-46; free-lance writer and researcher, 1946-49. *Awards, honors:* Order of the British Empire.

WRITINGS: History of the Northumberland Hussars, 1924-1949, Mawson, Swann & Morgan, 1950; *History of the Ninth Queen's Royal Lancers, 1936-1945,* Gale & Polden, 1950; *Inner Circle: A View of War at the Top,* Little, Brown, 1971. Contributor to *Atlantic* and *Economist.*

WORK IN PROGRESS: A biography of Major-General Sir Colin McVeign Gubbins.

*   *   *

ATHANASSIADIS, Nikos   1904-

PERSONAL: Born July 14, 1904, in Mytilene, Island of Lesbos, Greece; son of Apostolos (an industrial worker) and Irena (Michailidi) Athanassiadis; married Vanna Lambropoulou, June 6, 1944; children: Apostolos. *Education:* Educated at Lyceum of Mytilene on the Island of Lesbos, Greece. *Home:* Spefsippou No. 39, Athens, Greece.

CAREER: Director of Agricultural Bank of Greece, Athens, Greece, 1935-58; author, 1958—. *Military service:* Greek Navy, 1925-27. *Member:* Greek National Authors Society (member of administrative board), Greek International Council on Social Welfare. *Awards, honors:* "Ourani" literary award (Greece), 1957, for *Pera apo to anthropino;* first government prize, 1972, for *Theos archaios.*

WRITINGS—Novels, except as indicated: *To vivlio tou nissiou mou* (title means "The Book of My Island"), Xenos (Athens), 1950; *Pera apo to anthropino* (title means "Beyond the Human"), Stegi tou Vivliou (Athens), 1956, 3rd edition, Dorikos (Athens), 1972; *Stavrossi choris anastassi* (title means "Crucifixion without Resurrection"), Fexis (Athens), 1963, 2nd edition, Dorikos, 1972; *To gymno koritsi,* Alvin Redman-Hellas (Athens), 1964, 2nd edition, Dorikos, 1968, translation by Stefanos Zotos published as *A Naked Girl,* Orion Press, 1968; *Psilafitos kosmos* (title means "The Vague World"), Dorikos, 1970; *Theos archaios* (title means "Ancient God"; collection of fourteen short stories), Sideris (Athens), 1971; *Thyella ke Galini,* Dorikos, 1975.

Plays: "Protomi" (title means "The Bust"), first produced

in 1933; "Triti praxi" (title means "The Third Act"), first produced in 1934.

Also author of eight other plays for theatre. Translation of short novel, "Dyo syntrophi" (title means "The Two Companions"), by Alex Steinmetz anthologized in *Der Tod des Grossen Ochsen,* Paul Neff Verlag (Vienna), 1962. Contributor of articles, critiques, and short novels to literary journals and periodicals in various countries.

WORK IN PROGRESS: Two novels, *To karo me ta scoupidia* (title means "The Rublish Card"), and *Den tha xanagyrisso spiti* (title means "I Won't Come Back Home").

SIDELIGHTS: Nikos Athanassiadis' novels have been translated into several languages, including French, German, Spanish, Danish, and Japanese.

BIOGRAPHICAL/CRITICAL SOURCES: Apostolos Sachinis, *Nei pezographi,* J. D. Kollaros, 1965; *Les Nouvelles Litteraires,* March 4, 1965, August 18, 1966; G. Valetas, *Epitomi istoria tis neoellinikis logotechnias,* Petros K. Ranos, 1966; *Le Figaro,* June 20, 1966; *Le Monde,* August 20, 1966; *New York Times,* October 9, 1966; *National Herald,* November 20, 1966; *Best Sellers,* November 1, 1968; *New York Times Book Review,* November 17, 1968; *Sunday Advocate,* January 26, 1969.

*   *   *

ATHAY, R(obert) E.   1925-

PERSONAL: Born November 23, 1925, in Smithfield, Utah; son of Henry E. (a businessman) and Mabel (Jacques) Athay; married Helen Welch, April 2, 1948; children: Robert N., Lawrence D., Alice L. *Education:* Utah State University, B.A., 1949; Vanderbilt University, M.A., 1950; American University, Ph.D., 1969. *Religion:* Church of Jesus Christ of Latter-day Saints (Mormon).

CAREER: U.S. Government, Washington, D.C., economist, 1951-66; Center for Naval Analyses, Arlington, Va., economist, 1966-72. *Military service:* U.S. Army Air Forces, 1944-46. *Member:* American Economic Association, Association for Comparative Economics.

WRITINGS: The Economics of Soviet Merchant Shipping Policy, University of North Cerolina Press, 1971.†

*   *   *

ATKINS, G(eorge) Pope   1934-

PERSONAL: Born March 4, 1934, in Austin, Tex.; son of George Taylor (in advertising, printing, and publishing business) and Louise (Long) Atkins; married Joan Jorns, August 27, 1960; children: Forrest Taylor, Virginia Louise, Kristen Audra. *Education:* University of Texas, Main University (now University of Texas at Austin), B.A., 1955, graduate student, 1959-60; American University, Washington, D.C., M.A., 1962, Ph.D., 1966. *Home:* 34 Decatur Ave., Annapolis, Md. 21403. *Office:* Department of Political Science, U.S. Naval Academy, Annapolis, Md. 21401.

CAREER: First National City Bank (of New York), bank officer in New York, N.Y., Cordoba and Buenos Aires, Argentina, and Guayaquil, Ecuador, 1962-66; U.S. Naval Academy, Annapolis, Md., assistant professor, 1966-70, associate professor, 1970-77, professor of political science, 1977—. Guest scholar, Brookings Institution, 1972; visiting professor, Institute of Latin American Studies, University of London, 1977. *Military service:* U.S. Navy, 1955-59; served as aviator. *Member:* American Political Science

Association, American Association of University Professors (president of Naval Academy chapter, 1976-78), International Studies Association, Latin American Studies Association, Inter-American Council of Washington, D.C. (president, 1970-71).

WRITINGS: (Contributor) Paolo E. Coletta, editor, *Threshold to American Internationalism,* Exposition Press, 1970; (with Larman C. Wilson) *The United States and the Trujillo Regime,* Rutgers University Press, 1972; (contributor) Charles Cochran, editor, *Civil-Military Relations,* Free Press, 1974; (contributor) Harold E. Davis and Wilson, editors, *Latin American Foreign Policies,* Johns Hopkins University Press, 1975; *Latin America in the International Political System,* Free Press, 1977.

WORK IN PROGRESS: Research on civil-military relations and foreign military influences in Latin America, beginning with a book-length case study of Argentina.

*   *   *

AUGSBURGER, David W.   1938-

PERSONAL: Born August 14, 1938, in Delphos, Ohio; son of Clarence (a painter) and Estella R. (Shenk) Augsburger; married Nancy Louise Wert, August 13, 1960; children: Deborah Jean, Judith Anne. *Education:* Eastern Mennonite College, A.B., 1960; Eastern Mennonite Seminary, B.D., 1963; School of Theology at Claremont, Ph.D., 1974. *Office:* Associated Mennonite Biblical Seminaries, 3003 Benham Ave., Elkhart, Ind. 46514.

CAREER: Clergyman of Mennonite Church, 1963—. Mennonite Broadcasts, Inc., Harrisonburg, Va., program director, 1961-65, writer and speaker, 1966-74; Northern Baptist Theological Seminary, Lombard, Ill., associate professor of pastoral counseling, 1974-78; Associated Mennonite Biblical Seminaries, Elkhart, Ind., associate professor of pastoral counseling, 1978—. Has scripted more than 300 "Mennonite Hour" and three thirteen week series of "Choice" radio programs. *Awards, honors:* Award of Merit for distinctive broadcasting from National Religious Broadcasters, 1970; Gabriel Award for distinctive broadcasting from Catholic Broadcasters Association of Los Angeles, 1971.

WRITINGS: So What? Everybody's Doing It!, Moody, 1969; *Man Uptight,* Moody, 1970; *Be All You Can Be,* Creation House, 1970; *Seventy Times Seven,* Moody, 1970; *Witness Is Withness,* Moody, 1971; *Cherishable: Love and Marriage,* Herald Press, 1971; *The Love Fight: Caring Enough to Confront,* Herald Press, 1973. Also author of *Communicating Good News,* Herald Press. Writer of radio and television scripts.

*   *   *

AUKERMAN, Robert C.   1910-

PERSONAL: Born April 22, 1910, in Merrittstown, Pa.; son of Robert C. (a minister) and Bertha M. (Tarr) Aukerman; married Louise Agnes Rose (a kindergarten specialist), June 25, 1938; children: Robert III, William George, James Vance. *Education:* Wayne University (now Wayne State University), A.B., 1935, A.M., 1936; University of Michigan, Ph.D., 1945. *Religion:* Protestant. *Home:* 33 Clarke Lane, Kingston, R.I. 02881. *Office:* Department of Education, University of Rhode Island, Kingston, R.I. 02881.

CAREER: Social studies teacher in public schools in Detroit, Mich., 1936-48; University of Michigan, Ann Arbor, lecturer in economics, 1946-48; Wayne University (now Wayne State University), Detroit, Mich., lecturer in secondary education, 1947-48; Northeast Missouri State Teachers College (now Northeast Missouri State University), Kirksville, professor of education and dean of instruction, 1948-54; University of Rhode Island, Kingston, professor of education, 1954-76, professor emeritus, 1976—. Visiting lecturer in education at University of Oklahoma, summer, 1952, Pennsylvania State University, summer, 1953, Bowling Green State University, summer, 1967, and Yeshiva University, summer, 1972. Lecturer in reading workshops at Morehead State University, Ohio University, Mount Mercy College, California State University, Sacramento, Western Washington State College (now Western Washington University), Eastern Kentucky University, and Massey University.

MEMBER: International Reading Association, American Psychological Association, College Reading Association (president, 1963-64), National Council for the Social Studies, New England Reading Association, Phi Delta Kappa.

WRITINGS: Approaches to Beginning Reading, Wiley, 1971; *Reading in the Secondary School Classroom,* McGraw, 1972; (editor) *Some Persistent Questions on Beginning Reading,* International Reading Association, 1972; *How Do I Teach Reading?,* Wiley, 1978. Editor, *New England Reading Association Journal,* 1964-71.

WORK IN PROGRESS: The Basal Reader Approach to Reading, for Wiley.

AVOCATIONAL INTERESTS: Music, photograhy, travel.

*   *   *

AUSTIN, Allen 1922-

PERSONAL: Born May 24, 1922, in Mayfield, Ky.; son of George C. (an insurance salesman) and Ella (Owsley) Austin; married Susan Matzka, March 12, 1949; children: Wendy, Sandra. *Education:* Wayne University (now Wayne State University), A.B., 1944; Columbia University, M.A., 1950; New York University, Ph.D., 1956. *Home:* 5462 South Blackstone, Chicago, Ill. 60615. *Office:* Department of English, Indiana University Northwest, 3400 Broadway, Gary, Ind. 46408.

CAREER: Long Island University, Greenvale, N.Y., instructor in English, 1949; Indiana University, East Chicago Extension, assistant professor, 1959-63; Indiana University Northwest, Gary, associate professor, 1964-68, professor of English, 1968—, chairman of department, 1970—. *Military service:* U.S. Navy, 1943-46; became lieutenant junior grade. *Member:* Modern Language Association of America.

WRITINGS: T. S. Eliot: The Literary and Social Criticism, Indiana University Press, 1971. Contributor to literature journals.

WORK IN PROGRESS: A book interpreting Herman Melville's *Moby Dick.*

*   *   *

AUSTIN, Anthony 1919-

PERSONAL: Born June 21, 1919, in Harbin, China; son of Theodore M. (a musician) and Lydia (Lebedeff) Austin; married Betty Jane Roncovieri, December 31, 1952; children: Andrea. *Education:* Attended schools in Shanghai, China. *Politics:* Democrat. *Religion:* Lutheran. *Office: New York Times,* 229 West 43rd St., New York, N.Y. 10036.

CAREER: China Press, Shanghai, China, reporter, 1937-40; *Shanghai Evening Post and Mercury,* Shanghai, reporter,

1940-41; United Press, Peking correspondent, 1945-49, Washington correspondent, 1950-58; United Press International (UPI), correspondent from Moscow and Paris, 1958-61; *New York Times,* New York, N.Y., writer and editor, 1961—. *Member:* American Newspaper Guild. *Awards, honors:* Overseas Press Club award for best book on foreign affairs, 1971, for *The President's War; Playboy* award for best short story, 1973, for "When the American Came."

WRITINGS: (Editor with Robert Clurman) *The China Watchers* (anthology), Pyramid Publications, 1969; *The President's War,* Lippincott, 1971; (co-author) *You and Election '72,* Prentice-Hall, 1972.

WORK IN PROGRESS: Research on U.S. Chinese relations.

BIOGRAPHICAL/CRITICAL SOURCES: Book World, October 17, 1971.

*   *   *

AVALLE-ARCE, Juan Bautista 1927-
(Luis Galvez de Montalvo, Gabriel Goyeneche)

PERSONAL: Surname is pronounced Ah-*vah*-yay Ar-say; born May 13, 1927, in Buenos Aires, Argentina; son of Juan Bautista (a senator) and Maria (Martina) Avalle-Arce; married Constance M. Marginot, August 20, 1956 (died, 1969); married Diane Janet Pamp (a college professor), August 29, 1969; children: (first marriage) Juan Bautista Alejandro Guadalupe III, Maria Martina, Alejandro Alcantara; (second marriage) Maria la Real Alejandra. *Education:* Attended Colegio Nacional de Buenos Aires, 1941-47, and Universidad de Buenos Aires, 1942-47; Harvard University, A.B., 1951, M.A., 1952, Ph.D., 1955. *Politics:* Carlist. *Religion:* Catholic. *Home:* "Euskaletxea," Garret Rd., Durham, N.C. 27707. *Office:* Department of Romance Languages and Literature, University of North Carolina, Chapel Hill, N.C. 27514.

CAREER: Ohio State University, Columbus, assistant professor, 1955-57, associate professor of Romance languages, 1957-61, acting chairman of department, 1960, postdoctoral fellow, 1958-59; Smith College, Northampton, Mass., professor of Spanish, 1961-65, Sophia Smith Professor of Hispanic Studies, 1965-69, chairman of department, 1966-69, director of graduate studies, 1961-69; University of North Carolina, Chapel Hill, William Rand Kenan, Jr. Professor of Spanish, 1969—. Visiting scholar in the humanities at University of Bridgeport, 1968, University of Georgia, 1972, and University of Virginia, 1976; lecturer at various universities in the U.S. and Europe. Consultant for several university presses, including those of Princeton University, University of Texas, and University of California. Member of national board of advisors, Instituto Cultural Hispanico, Spain; member of advisory board, Bryn Mawr College.

MEMBER: Modern Language Association of America (former secretary and chairman, Spanish Golden Age), Hispanic Society of America, Modern Humanities Research Association, Renaissance Society of America, Council of Graduate Schools, Academy of Literary Stories (founding member), Real Sociedad Vascongada de Amigos del Pais, Asociacion Internacional de Hispanistas (founding member), Sociedad de Bibliofilos Espanoles, Centro de Estudios Jacobeos (Santiago), Centre d'Etudes Superieures de Civilisation Medievale (Universite de Poitiers), Instituto Internacional de Literatura Iberoamericana. *Awards, honors:* Premio Literario del Centro Gallego, 1948, for "Rosalia de Castro: A Critical Study"; Susan Anthony Potter Literary

Prize, Harvard University, 1951, for "The Poetry of Jorge de Montemayor"; grants from American Philosophical Society, 1958 and 1963, American Council of Learned Societies, 1962 and 1967-68, and National Endowment for the Humanities, 1967-68; Guggenheim fellow, 1960-61; Bonsoms Medal, Government of Spain, 1962, for critical works on Cervantes.

WRITINGS: Conocimiento y vida en Cervantes, Imprenta Universitaria (Buenos Aires), 1959; *La Novela pastoril española,* Revista de Occidente (Madrid), 1959; *Deslindes cervantinos,* Edhigar (Madrid), 1961; (author of prologue and notes) Miguel de Cervantes Saavedra, *La Galatea,* two volumes, Espasa-Calpe (Madrid), 1961, 2nd edition, 1968; (author of prologue and notes) Gonzalo Fernandez de Oviedo, *El Sumario de Historia Natural,* Anaya (Madrid), 1962; *El Inca Garcilaso en sus Comentarios,* Gredos (Madrid), 1963, 2nd edition, 1970; (author of introduction and notes) Miguel de Cervantes Saavedra, *Three Exemplary Novels: El Licenciado vidriera, El Casamiento enganoso, El Coloquio de los perros,* Dell, 1964; *Bernal Frances y su romance,* Imprenta Universitaria (Barcelona), 1966; (editor and author of introduction and notes) Miguel de Cervantes Saavedra, *Los Trabajos de Persiles y Sigismunda,* Castalia (Madrid), 1969; (editor) Miguel de Cervantes Saavedra, *Ocho entremeses,* Prentice-Hall, 1970; *Don Juan Valera: Morsamor,* Labor (Barcelona), 1970; *Temas Hispanicos Medievales,* Gredos, 1972; (author of prologue and notes) Lope de Vega, *El Peregrino,* Castalia, 1972; *El Cronista Pedro de Escavias: Una vida del siglo XV,* University of North Carolina Press, 1974; (with E. C. Riley) *Summa Cervantina,* Tamesis Books, 1974; *Neuvos deslinoes cervantinos,* [Barcelona], 1975; *Las Memorias de Gonzalo Fernandez de Ouieda,* two volumes, University of North Carolina Press, 1975; *Don Quijote como forma de vida,* [Madrid], 1976. Also author, under pseudonym Luis Galvez de Montalvo, of "The Poetry of Jorge de Montemayor"; author, under pseudonym Gabriel Goyeneche, of several lyric poems.

Contributor: German Bleiberg and E. L. Fox, editors, *Spanish Thought and Letters in the Twentieth Century,* Vanderbilt University Press, 1966; A. N. Zahareas, editor, *Ramon del Valle-Inclan: A Critical Appraisal of His Life and Works,* Las Americas, 1968. Contributor of more than 150 articles, essays, and poems to numerous periodicals and journals, including *Hispanic Review, Romance Philology, Texas Quarterly, Bulletin of Hispanic Studies, Hispanofila, Publication of the Modern Language Association (PMLA), Insula, Modern Language Notes, Boletin de la Real Academia Espanola, Cuadernos Hispanoamericanos, Romance Notes, Filologia,* and *American Philosophical Society Yearbook.* Editor, *Studies in the Romance Languages and Literatures;* contributing editor, *McGraw-Hill Encyclopedia of World Biography* and *Diccionario Enciclopedico Salvat Universal.* Member of editorial board, *Hispanic Review, Anales Galdosianos, Romance Monographs* (University of Kentucky), Tamesis Books (London), *Romance Notes.*

WORK IN PROGRESS: Don Fadrique Enriquez: Vida y obras, expected completion in 1978.

SIDELIGHTS: Juan Avalle-Arce told *CA* he "cannot remember having had an interest other than books (except horses); probably reading *Don Quixote* at age 7-8 got me as affected by literature as he was. . . . The traditional values and way of life are vital to me. Being Barlitt Grand Cross of the Sovereign Military Teutonic Order of the Levant is proof." Avalle-Arce has traveled extensively in the Americas, Europe, and Africa, and knows Basque, French, Ital-

ian, Portuguese, German, Guarani, Latin, Greek, and Arabic in addition to his native Spanish.

AVOCATIONAL INTERESTS: Fox-hunting, polo, breaking and training hunting horses, cooking, wine-tasting.

*   *   *

AVERY, Laurence G(reen) 1934-

PERSONAL: Born December 7, 1934, in Birmingham, Ala.; son of Julius Hilliar (a minister) and Martha (Green) Avery; married Rachel Reid, August 31, 1957; children: Jonathan Reid, Laura Rebecca. *Education:* Baylor University, B.A., 1957; University of Michigan, M.A., 1958; University of Texas, Ph.D., 1966. *Home:* 612 Churchill Dr., Chapel Hill, N.C. 27514. *Office:* Department of English, University of North Carolina, Chapel Hill, N.C. 27514.

CAREER: University of North Carolina at Chapel Hill, assistant professor, 1966-71, associate professor, 1971-77, professor of English, 1977—. *Member:* Modern Language Association of America, Southeastern Modern Language Association. *Awards, honors:* Post-doctoral fellowship, University of Texas, 1966; National Endowment for the Humanities fellowship, 1971-72.

WRITINGS: A Catalogue of the Maxwell Anderson Collection, University of Texas Press, 1969; (editor) Maxwell Anderson, *Notes on a Dream,* University of Texas Press, 1971; (editor) *Dramatist in America: Letters of Maxwell Anderson, 1912-1958,* University of North Carolina Press, 1977. Contributor to *Modern Drama, North Dakota Quarterly, Papers of the Bibliographical Society of America,* and *American Literature.*

WORK IN PROGRESS: An intellectual history of American drama.

*   *   *

AVNI, Abraham Albert 1921-

PERSONAL: Original name, Steiner; name legally changed in 1950; born September 6, 1921, in Brno, Czechoslovakia; came to United States in 1958, naturalized in 1970; son of Arthur (an engineer) and Paula (Grosser) Steiner; married Judith Glaser, May 28, 1948; children: Nurit. *Education:* Hebrew University of Jerusalem, M.A., 1949; University of Wisconsin—Madison, Ph.D., 1963. *Religion:* Jewish. *Home:* 7121 Carita, Long Beach, Calif. 90808. *Office:* Department of English, California State University, Long Beach, Calif. 90840.

CAREER: Minister of Education, Jerusalem, Israel, private secretary, 1952-54; University of Wisconsin—Madison, instructor in Hebrew and Bible, 1958-64; California State University, Long Beach, assistant professor, 1964-67, associate professor, 1967-72, professor of English and comparative literature, 1972—. *Military service:* British Army, 1941-46. *Member:* Modern Language Association of America, Byron Society, Conference on Christianity and Literature. *Awards, honors:* National Foundation for Jewish Culture fellowship, 1963; California State College (now University), Long Beach summer research grant, 1967 and 1974.

WRITINGS: The Bible and Romanticism, Mouton, 1969; (contributor) Roger Johnson and others, editors, *Moliere and the Commonwealth of Letters: Patrimony and Posterity,* University Press of Mississippi, 1975. Contributor to *French Review, Publications of the Modern Language Association, Comparative Literature,* and other publications.

WORK IN PROGRESS: Research in the influence of the

Bible on different French and English writers; a more comprehensive book on the Bible's influence on European literatures, completion expected in 1979.

AVOCATIONAL INTERESTS: Playing the piano, tennis, and ice skating.

* * *

AWE, Chulho 1927-

PERSONAL: Born January 27, 1927, in Soonchun, Korea; son of Kwanyoung (a gold mine owner) and Yongsoon (Lee) Awe; married Aesun Kim (a blood-gas specialist in open heart surgery), October 10, 1958; children: Moses, Joseph. *Education:* Sunghueng Mining Technical College, B.S., 1948; Central Theological Seminary, B.D., 1956; McCormick Theological Seminary, additional study, 1963. *Politics:* None. *Religion:* Christianity (Protestant). *Home and office:* 60-07 43rd Ave., Woodside, N.Y. 11377.

CAREER: Holdong Gold Mining Co., Hwanghae, Korea, mining technical engineer, 1948-49; Presbyterian Church of Korea, Seoul, staff member, industrial evangelism committee and program director, 1957-66; New York Bible Society International, New York City, marine chaplain, 1966-73. Member of chaplain service, City of New York Emergency Control Board, 1970-73. Member of board of directors, Central Theological Seminary, 1962—. *Awards, honors:* Outstanding achievement award, Central Theological Seminary, 1956.

WRITINGS: Guidebook of Industrial Evangelism (in Korean), Presbyterian Church of Korea, 1958; *Handbook of Industrial Evangelism* (in Korean), Presbyterian Church of Korea, 1962; *Decision at Dawn: The Underground Christian Witness in Red Korea,* Harper, 1965. Contributor to *Christian Weekly* and *Christian Thoughts.*

WORK IN PROGRESS: Second part of autobiography, *Rainbows at Night; Bridge to Unknown Land,* research on Korean seamen.

* * *

AXELROD, Joseph 1918-

PERSONAL: Born January 15, 1918, in Kingston, Mass. *Education:* University of Chicago, B.A., 1937, M.A., 1938, Ph.D., 1945. *Office:* School of Humanities, San Francisco State University, San Francisco, Calif. 94132.

CAREER: Chicago City College, Chicago, Ill., instructor in humanities, 1943-45; University of Chicago, Chicago, assistant professor of humanities, 1945-50; San Francisco State College (now University), San Francisco, Calif., associate professor, 1950-55, professor of humanities, 1955-62; California State College, Dominguez Hills, dean of School of Humanities and Fine Arts, 1962-65; San Francisco State University, dean of undergraduate studies, 1965-66, professor of humanities and comparative literature, 1966—. Fulbright lecturer, Berlin Teachers College, 1955-56; visiting professor at colleges and universities, including University of the Americas and Northwestern University. University of California, Berkeley, visiting research specialist, 1967-69, lecturer in higher education, 1969—. Director of project on language and area studies, American Council on Education, 1960-61. *Awards, honors:* Ford Foundation faculty fellowship, 1952-53.

WRITINGS: (Editor) *Graduate Study for Future College Teachers,* American Council on Education, 1959; (with D.N. Bigelow) *Resources for Language and Area Studies in the United States,* American Council on Education, 1962;

(with M. B. Freedman, W. R. Hatch, Joseph Katz, and Nevitt Sanford) *Search for Relevance: Campus in Crisis,* Jossey-Bass, 1969; *The University Teacher As Artist,* Jossey-Bass, 1973. Contributor to professional journals. Consulting editor, Jossey-Bass series in higher education, 1967—.

WORK IN PROGRESS: Research on styles of teaching at the college level.

* * *

AXELROD, Robert 1943-

PERSONAL: Born May 27, 1943, in Chicago, Ill.; son of James (an artist) and Rose (Alter) Axelrod. *Education:* University of Chicago, B.A., 1964; Yale University, M.A., 1966, Ph.D., 1969. *Home:* 770 Peninsula Ct., Ann Arbor, Mich. 48105. *Office:* Department of Political Science, University of Michigan, Ann Arbor, Mich. 48109.

CAREER: University of California, Berkeley, assistant professor of political science, 1968-74; University of Michigan, Ann Arbor, associate professor of political science, 1974—.

WRITINGS: Conflict of Interest: A Theory of Divergent Goals with Applications to Politics, Markham, 1970; (editor) *Structure of Decision: The Cognitive Maps of Political Elites,* Princeton University Press, 1976. Contributor to professional journals.

WORK IN PROGRESS: Research on cognition in decision making.

* * *

AXFORD, Lavonne B(rady) 1928-

PERSONAL: Born June 30, 1928, in Fort Collins, Colo.; daughter of Cornelius Joseph and Alice (Dondelinger) Brady; married H. William Axford (a librarian), November 11, 1956. *Education:* University of Colorado, B.A., 1952; University of Denver, M.A., 1956; Florida State University, additional graduate study, 1968-69. *Politics:* Liberal. *Religion:* None. *Home:* 2250 Lawrence, Eugene, Ore. 97405.

CAREER: University of Denver, Denver, Colo., reference librarian in Business Library, 1957-58; St. Thomas Seminary, Denver, head librarian, 1958-64; Jefferson County Public Library, Golden, Colo., head librarian, 1964-65; Arapahoe Junior College, Littleton, Colo., head librarian, 1965-67; Florida Atlantic University, Dade Center, Miami Beach, head librarian, 1968; Scottsdale Community College, Scottsdale, Ariz., director of library services, 1970-73; full-time writer in Eugene, Ore., 1973—. Lecturer in library science, University of the Punjab, Lahore, West Pakistan, 1962-63; occasional visiting professor, School of Librarianship, University of Oregon, 1973—.

WRITINGS: A Directory of Educational Programs for the Gifted, Scarecrow, 1971; *An Index to the Poems of Ogden Nash,* Scarecrow, 1972; *Weaving, Spinning, and Dyeing,* Libraries Unlimited, 1972; (editor) *English Language Cookbooks, 1600-1973,* Gale, 1976.

* * *

AXFORD, Roger W(illiam) 1920-

PERSONAL: Born July 22, 1920, in Grand Island, Neb.; married Geraldine E. Lukes (a free-lance writer), August 27, 1949; children: Naida, Scott, Vickie. *Education:* Nebraska Wesleyan University, A.B., 1942; University of Chicago, M.A., 1949, Ph.D., 1961. *Office:* Center for Higher and

Adult Education, Arizona State University, Tempe, Ariz. 85281.

CAREER: Chicago (Ill.) Board of Education, teacher in adult Americanization program, 1949; Bacone College, Muskogee, Okla., dean, 1949-50; Roosevelt University, Chicago, assistant to vice-president, 1950-54; Shimer College, Mount Carroll, Ill., vice-president, 1955-56; University of Wisconsin, assistant director of Racine Center, 1956-61, assistant professor of adult education and associate director of instructional services for Milwaukee Extension Division, 1961-65; Northern Illinois University, De Kalb, associate professor of education and director of adult education, 1965-66; University of Maine, Orono, associate professor and coordinator of adult education, 1968-70; Indiana University of Pennsylvania, Indiana, professor of adult education and dean of School of Continuing and Non-Resident Education, 1970-75; Arizona State University, Center for Higher and Adult Education, Tempe, associate professor of adult education, 1975—. Visiting professor, Florida State University, 1964; education consultant in Venezuela and Puerto Rico, summer, 1964.

MEMBER: International Congress of University Adult Education, Adult Education Association of the U.S.A. (chairman of professional training and development section, 1963-67; New England representative on executive committee, 1969-70), National Seminar on Adult Education Research, National University Extension Association, National Education Association, Association for Latin American Studies, Wisconsin Academy of Arts, Sciences and Letters.

WRITINGS: (Contributor) *Speaking about Adults,* Adult Education Department, Northern Illinois University, 1966; (editor) *College-Community Consultation,* Enlightenment Press, 1967; (editor with Weldon Bradtmueller and Neil Dortch) *Adult Basic Education: Administrator, Community, Clientele,* Northern Illinois University, 1968; *Adult Education: The Open Door,* International Textbook Co., 1969; (contributor) *Handbook of Adult Education,* Macmillan, 1970; *Spanish Speaking Heroes: 23 Biographies,* Pendell, 1973; *Fundamentos y propositos de la Educacion de Adultos,* Editorial Troquel, 1977. Contributor of more than eighty articles and reviews to *Milwaukee Journal, Christian Home, Better Camping,* and other education publications. Writer of Associated Press series, "Never Too Old to Learn," reprinted in booklet form by Florida Institute for Continuing Education, 1965.

AVOCATIONAL INTERESTS: Tennis, swimming, house building (Axford built his own home, 1952-54), art collecting.

*   *   *

AZNEER, J. Leonard 1921-

PERSONAL: Born May 26, 1921, in Lublin, Rumania; brought to United States in 1922; son of Morris (a presser) and Ida (Stein) Azneershansky; married second wife, Patricia A. Cottrille (a pediatrician), December 5, 1974; children: (first marriage) Jay Barry, Reva (Mrs. Leslie Pearlstein), Ira Brant. *Education:* Attended Rabbi Isaac Elchanan Theological Seminary, 1938-41; Yeshiva University, B.A., 1941; Jewish Theological Seminary of America, Rabbi, 1945, M.H.L., 1949; University of Pittsburgh, Ph.D., 1959. *Home:* 3511 Southwest 27th St., Des Moines, Iowa 50321. *Office:* College of Osteopathic Medicine and Surgery, 3200 Grand Ave., Des Moines, Iowa 50312.

CAREER: Rabbi in Allentown, Pa., 1944-45, Bay City, Mich., 1945-47, and Schenectady, N.Y., 1947-50; Temple

Anshe Emeth, Youngstown, Ohio, rabbi, 1950-67; Youngstown State University, Youngstown, Ohio, adjunct professor of philosophy, 1950-65, associate professor of education, 1965-71, head of department of Hebrew, 1952-62; College of Osteopathic Medicine and Surgery, Des Moines, Iowa, president, 1971—. Visiting lecturer, Albion College, 1945-47; lecturer, Union College, 1948-49; member of faculty of Conference on Self-Instructional Material, University of Rochester, 1967. Educational consultant, Nahari Foundation and Library on Penology and Criminology, 1956-58; director of research, Association for Educational Motivation, 1965-66; Edlen Research, director of research, 1966-70, executive vice-president, 1967-70; president, Relaxabed. *Member:* Society for Professional Education, Rabbinical Assembly of America, American Association of Osteopathic Medical Colleges (member of board of governors), Society for the Scientific Study of Religion, American Association of University Professors, Phi Kappa Delta, Kappa Delta Pi.

WRITINGS: Diabetic Acidosis: A Programmed Text, F. A. Davis, 1968; *Passover: A Programmed Text,* Hebrew Publishing, 1969; *Sukkot: A Programmed Text,* Hebrew Publishing, 1969; *Resuscitation: A Programmed Text,* F. A. Davis, 1970. Contributor to religious, education, and medical journals.

WORK IN PROGRESS: A study in educational sociology regarding college faculty attitudes to new morality; a programmed text in bedside diagnosis and treatment of arthritis; writing on medical curricula for the 70's and on changes in applicants and admissions procedures in osteopathic schools.

AVOCATIONAL INTERESTS: Painting, writing fiction.

*   *   *

BACKER, John H. 1902-

PERSONAL: Born October 18, 1902, in Vienna, Austria; son of Arthur and Frieda (Brand) Backer; married Evelyn K. Crawford (a consumer consultant), May 7, 1946. *Education:* Columbia University, B.S., 1954, M.A., 1955, Ph.D., 1972. *Home:* 3069 Cleveland Ave. N.W., Washington, D.C. 20008.

CAREER: U.S. Office for Military Government, military government officer in Germany, 1945-48; U.S. Foreign Service officer, 1955-70; U.S. Senate, Washington, D.C., special counsel and legislative assistant, 1973—. *Military service:* U.S. Army, 1942-46; became lieutenant colonel; received Bronze Star Medal.

WRITINGS: Priming the German Economy: American Occupational Policies, 1945-48, Duke University Press, 1971; *The Decision to Divide Germany: American Foreign Policy in Transition,* Duke University Press, 1978.

WORK IN PROGRESS: Various research papers on the occupation of Germany.

*   *   *

BACKMAN, Milton V., Jr. 1927-

PERSONAL: Born June 11, 1927, in Salt Lake City, Utah; son of Milton V. and Florence (Peterson) Backman; married Kathleen McLatchy, June 11, 1953; children: Kristine, Karl, Karen. *Education:* University of Utah, B.S., 1954, M.A., 1955; University of Pennsylvania, Ph.D., 1959. *Politics:* Republican. *Religion:* Church of Jesus Christ of Latter-day Saints. *Home:* 291 East 4075 North, Provo, Utah 84601. *Office:* 156 Joseph Smith Memorial Bldg., Brigham Young University, Provo, Utah 84602.

CAREER: West Texas State University, Canyon, assistant professor of history, 1958-60; Brigham Young University, Provo, Utah, professor of church history and American history, 1960—. *Military service:* U.S. Merchant Marine, 1945-47; served in the Pacific. U.S. Air Force, 1951-52; became technical sergeant.

WRITINGS: American Religions and the Rise of Mormonism, Deseret, 1965, 2nd edition, 1970; *Joseph Smith's First Vision: The First Vision in Its Historical Context,* Bookcraft, 1971; *Christian Churches of America: Origins and Beliefs,* Brigham Young University Press, 1976. Writer of pamphlets on the Mormon Church; contributor of about a dozen articles and reviews to journals.

WORK IN PROGRESS: Editing, volume II of *Comprehensive History of the Latter-day Saints.*

* * *

BACKUS, Jean L(ouise) 1914-
(David Montross)

PERSONAL: Born February 24, 1914, in Pasadena, Calif.; daughter of Charles Shepard (a businessman) and Cora Montross (Pope) Backus. *Education:* University of California, Berkeley, B.A., 1937. *Home:* 265 Purdue Ave., Kensington, Calif. 94708.

MEMBER: Mystery Writers of America (vice-president, northern California chapter, 1973-74).

WRITINGS—Under pseudonym David Montross, except as indicated: *Traitor's Wife,* Crime Club, 1962; *Troika,* Crime Club, 1963; *Fellow Traveler,* Crime Club, 1965; (under name Jean L. Backus) *Dusha,* Walker & Co., 1971. Contributor of short stories and articles to periodicals. Associate editor, *California Monthly,* 1943-46.

WORK IN PROGRESS: A northern California family saga.

* * *

BAER, Daniel J(oseph) 1929-

PERSONAL: Born September 28, 1929, in Philadelphia, Pa.; son of Edmund Joseph (a hotel manager) and Rosemary (Laverty) Baer; married Elizabeth Carter, August 30, 1957; children: Christopher, Elizabeth, Theresa. *Education:* La Salle College, B.A., 1955; Fordham University, M.A., 1958, Ph.D., 1961. *Politics:* "Liberal—Independent." *Religion:* Catholic. *Home:* 76 Templewood Dr., Duxbury, Mass. 02332. *Office:* Department of Psychology, Boston College, Chestnut Hill, Mass. 02167.

CAREER: Boston College, Chestnut Hill, Mass., assistant professor, 1962-66, associate professor, 1966—. Member of board of directors, Project Breakthrough. *Military service:* U.S. Air Force, 1951-54; became lieutenant. *Member:* American Psychological Association, American Statistical Association, American Public Health Association (fellow), American Association for the Advancement of Science (fellow), New York Academy of Science (fellow).

WRITINGS: (With F. J. Kelly) *Outward Bound Schools As an Alternative to Institutionalization for Adolescent Delinquent Boys,* Fandel Press, 1968. Contributor to *Journal of Psychology, Perceptual and Motor Skills, Journal of Social Psychology, Journal of Genetic Psychology,* and other publications.

WORK IN PROGRESS: Delinquency and Outward Bound.

AVOCATIONAL INTERESTS: Amateur radio (call letters KIYTX), sailing, cross-country skiing.

BAERWALD, Hans H(erman) 1927-

PERSONAL: Born June 18, 1927, in Tokyo, Japan; son of Ernst D. (a business executive) and Otti (Forell) Baerwald; married Diane Aamoth (a research associate), August 26, 1950; children: Andrea, Jan, David. *Education:* University of California, Berkeley, B.A., 1950, M.A., 1952, Ph.D., 1956. *Politics:* Democrat. *Home:* 914 Bluegrass Lane, Los Angeles, Calif. 90049. *Office:* Department of Political Science, University of California, Los Angeles, Calif. 90024.

CAREER: University of California, Berkeley, teaching assistant in political science, 1952-54; Miami University, Oxford, Ohio, assistant professor, 1956-61, associate professor of political science, 1961-62; University of California, Los Angeles, lecturer, 1962-65, associate professor, 1965-69, professor of political science, 1969—. Visiting lecturer, University of California, Berkeley, 1961. *Military service:* U.S. Army, 1945-49. *Member:* American Political Science Association, Association for Asian Studies, Phi Beta Kappa. *Awards, honors:* Ford Foundation fellowship, 1954-56.

WRITINGS: The Purge of Japanese Leaders Under the Occupation, University of California Press, 1959; (with Dan Jacobs) *Chinese Communism,* Harper, 1963; (with Peter Odegard) *The American Republic,* Harper, 1964, 2nd edition, 1969; (contributor) Wayne Wilcox and others, editors, *Asia and the International System,* Winthrop Publishing, 1972; *Japan's Parliament: An Introduction,* Cambridge University Press, 1974; (contributor) James W. Morley, editor, *Deterrent Diplomacy,* Columbia University Press, 1976; (contributor) James Rosenau and others, editors, *World Politics,* Free Press, 1976. Contributor to *Asian Survey, Pacific Affairs, Japan Interpreter.*

WORK IN PROGRESS: Contributing a chapter to a book on Japanese foreign policy, edited by R. A. Saclapino, for University of California Press.

AVOCATIONAL INTERESTS: Music.

* * *

BAGWELL, Philip S(idney) 1914-

PERSONAL: Born February 16, 1914, in Ventnor, Isle of Wight; son of Philip William (a bookseller) and Nellie (Aldrich) Bagwell; married Rosemary Burnley Olney (a social worker), July 16, 1953; children: Susan, Alison Jane, Richard Philip. *Education:* University of Southampton, B.Sc. (second class honors) and Cambridge Teacher's Certificate, 1936; London School of Economics and Political Science, Ph.D., 1950. *Politics:* Christian Socialist. *Home:* 14 Brent Way, Finchley, London N3 IAL, England. *Office:* Department of History, Polytechnic of Central London, 309 Regent St., London W.1, England.

CAREER: University of London, London, England, lecturer, College of Estate Management, 1949-51; Polytechnic of Central London, London, 1951—, currently professor of history, 1972—. Treasurer of house committee, Rehabilitation Centre for Alcoholics, London. *Military service:* British Army, Royal Corps of Signals, 1940-45; became sergeant; mentioned in dispatches. *Member:* Economic History Society, Society for the Study of Labour History (secretary, 1965-70).

WRITINGS: The Railwaymen: A History of the National Union of Railwaymen, Fernhill, 1963; *The Railway Clearing House in the British Economy: 1842-1922,* Augustus M. Kelley, 1968; (with G. E. Mingay) *Britain and America: A Study of Economic Change: 1850-1939,* Praeger, 1970; (contributor) Asa Briggs, editor, *Essays in Labour*

History: 1886-1923, Macmillan, 1971; *The Transport Revolution from 1770,* Batsford, 1974; *Industrial Relations in Nineteenth-Century Britain,* Irish University Press, 1974.

WORK IN PROGRESS: Preparation of a book on British shipping since 1820; *The Railwaymen,* Volume II: *The Beeching Era and After,* for Allen & Unwin.

*   *   *

BAGWELL, William Francis, Jr.   1923-

PERSONAL: Born January 19, 1923, in Donalds, S.C.; son of William Francis and Eula (Dodson) Bagwell; married Maude Magill. *Education:* Furman University, B.A., 1947; Columbia University, M.S., 1950; Emory University, graduate study, 1951-52; New York University, Ph.D., 1968. *Religion:* Society of Friends. *Home address:* P.O. Box 175, Cheyney, Pa. 19319. *Office:* Cheyney State College, Cheyney, Pa. 19319.

CAREER: Church World Service, New York City, news bureau director, 1947-49; George Washington University, Washington, D.C., special writer and public relations representative, 1952-55; Furman University, Greenville, S.C., director of news service and editor of alumni magazine, 1955-58; American Friends Service Committee, High Point, N.C., community relations regional director, 1958-65; Quaker Program at the United Nations, New York City, program associate, 1965-67; Cheyney State College, Cheyney, Pa., professor of social science and director of college-community services, 1967—. Founder and first president, Greenville, S.C. Human Relations Council, 1956-58; member, North Carolina Advisory Committee to the U.S. Civil Rights Commission, 1959-62. *Military service:* U.S. Army, Medical Corps, 1943-46. *Member:* Adult Education Association, National Association of Human Rights Workers, United Nations Association (board member of Manhattan chapter, 1966-67), Sigma Delta Chi. *Awards, honors:* Kappa Delta Pi human relations award, 1965.

WRITINGS: School Desegregation in the Carolinas, University of South Carolina Press, 1972. Contributor to *Friends Journal, Christian Century, Town and County Church, Highroad,* and other publications.

WORK IN PROGRESS: Research in human relations, black studies, and social history of the South.

*   *   *

BAHR, Erhard   1932-

PERSONAL: Born August 21, 1932, in Kiel, Germany; son of Klaus and Gisela (Badenhausen) Bahr. *Education:* Studied at University of Heidelberg, 1952-53, and University of Freiburg, 1953-56; University of Kansas, M.S.Ed., 1958; University of Cologne, additional study, 1958-62; University of California, Berkeley, Ph.D., 1968. *Home:* 2364 Nalin Dr., Los Angeles, Calif. 90024. *Office:* Department of Germanic Languages, University of California, Los Angeles, Calif. 90024.

CAREER: University of California, Los Angeles, acting assistant professor, 1966-68, assistant professor, 1968-70, associate professor, 1970-72, professor of German, 1972—. *Member:* Modern Language Association of America, American Association of Teachers of German, American Lessing Society, Goethe-Society, Heinrich-Heine Society, International Association of German Writers. *Awards, honors:* Distinguished Teaching Award, University of California, Los Angeles, 1970.

WRITINGS: Georg Lukacs, Colloquium (Berlin), 1970;

Die Ironie im Spaetwerk Goethes, E. Schmidt (Berlin), 1972; (with Ruth G. Kunzer) *George Lukacs,* Ungar, 1972; *Ernst Bloch,* Colloquium, 1974.

WORK IN PROGRESS: Goethe Scholarship 1952-1972; a history of German literature; *Love and Money in German Literature;* a biography of Nelly Sachs, completion expected in 1979.

*   *   *

BAHR, Jerome   1909-

PERSONAL: Surname is pronounced Barr; born October 26, 1909, in Arcadia, Wis.; son of Joseph and Eda (Bouska) Felsheim; married Metta Smith, 1928 (deceased); married Becky Boehm, 1933 (deceased); married Jean Blaney (a teacher), February 11, 1955; children: (second marriage) Tonia (Mrs. Daniel O'Shea); (third marriage) Nicholas, Antony; Robert Sloan (stepson). *Education:* Attended University of Minnesota, 1928-29, 1931-33. *Religion:* "Nonpracticing Catholic." *Home:* 800 Hillcrest Dr., Santa Fe, N.M. 87501.

CAREER: Started writing for newspapers at age sixteen; reporter for *Louisville Courier-Journal,* Louisville, Ky., 1929-30, and *Minneapolis Star,* Minneapolis, Minn., 1931-33; headed for New York to write, 1933, and lived there and worked at odd jobs, 1933-42; officer in U.S. Army Air Forces and U.S. Air Force, 1942-50, leaving active duty as major; civilian writer with U.S. Department of Defense in Washington, D.C., and vicinity, 1951-58, 1964-68, and civilian press officer in Germany, 1958-64; writer with U.S. Office of Education, Washington, D.C., 1968-71; retired from government service, 1971, to live and write in Santa Fe, N.M.

WRITINGS—"All Good Americans" (fictional cycle of short stories, sketches, and novellas): Volume I: *All Good Americans,* foreword by Ernest Hemingway, Scribner, 1937; Volume II: *Wisconsin Tales,* Trempealeau Press, 1964; Volume III: *The Linen Suit and Other Stories,* Trempealeau Press, 1957; Volume IV: *Holes in the Wall: Portraits of the Cold War,* Luce, 1970; Volume V: *The Pershing Republic,* Trempealeau Press, 1971; Volume VI: *The Lonely Scoundrels,* Trempealeau Press, 1974; Volume VII: *Five Novellas,* Trempealeau Press, 1977.

Other: *The Platinum Tower* (novel), Scribner, 1939. Contributor of short stories to national magazines and articles to education magazines. Former reviewer for *Baltimore Sun.*

WORK IN PROGRESS: Farrago, a play; short stories, sketches, and critical reviews.

SIDELIGHTS: Jerome Bahr told *CA:* "A short-story writer, if he's worth anything, always tries to expand his medium and stoutly resists any crippling limitations that might relegate it to the status of minor art. He fights against confining it to a certain length, refuses to concede that it must have a preordained form, and jumps at the chance to poach on the domain of the novel, play, essay or any other fair game. . . . This eclectic approach has given the modern story an elasticity and vitality that makes it admirably suited to cope with our variegated contemporary life." Bahr goes on to say "As my published works indicate, I have always had a preference for short fiction over the novel. I not only possess great confidence in the short story as a true art vehicle, but I feel its partisans should be more aggressive about it."

BIOGRAPHICAL/CRITICAL SOURCES: New York Times Book Review, March 28, 1937, June 2, 1957, September 27, 1970; *Herald Tribune,* April 4, 1937; *Saturday Review,* July 18, 1964, May 30, 1970, May 1, 1971; *Chicago Tribune,* August 2, 1964; *Army Times,* June 24, 1970, March 24, 1971; *Publishers Weekly,* January 18, 1971, March 21, 1977.

* * *

BAILEY, Eric 1933-

PERSONAL: Born April 15, 1933, in Manchester, England; son of George (a gardener) and Gladys (Waddington) Bailey; married Doris Joan Johnson (a teacher), February 23, 1957. *Education:* Attended college part-time in London. *Politics:* "Near-anarchist." *Religion:* "Near-Christian." *Home:* 43 Lullington Rd., London S.E.20, England. *Agent:* Campbell Thomson & McLaughlin Ltd., 31 Newington Green, London N16 9PU, England.

CAREER: Journalist, 1954—; Southern Television, Dover, England, free-lance reporter, 1959-61; *Yorkshire Post,* Leeds, England, sub-editor, 1961-63; *Ottawa Citizen,* Ottawa, Ontario, editor, 1966-67; Central Office of Information, London, England, information officer, 1968-69; Zambia News Agency, Lusaka, Zambia, advisory sub-editor, 1969-71. *Military service:* Royal Air Force, 1951-54; served in Singapore. *Member:* Crime Writers' Association (London).

WRITINGS: Leave of Absence (crime novel), John Long, 1968; *Cradle's Revenge* (crime novel), John Long, 1969.

WORK IN PROGRESS: A novel dealing with the expatriate situation in independent Africa.

AVOCATIONAL INTERESTS: Travel ("which provides background and gratifies a personal feeling that since I can't take it with me I must use it up"), photography, attempting to master foreign languages.

BIOGRAPHICAL/CRITICAL SOURCES: Books and Bookmen, October, 1968.†

* * *

BAILKEY, Nels M(artin) 1911-

PERSONAL: Born March 6, 1911, in Barron, Wis.; son of Julius W. (a railroad terminal superintendent) and Jennie (Thompson) Bailkey; married Therese Zuzok, March 8, 1955; children: Martin, Jennifer. *Education:* Attended Antioch College, 1930-32; University of Wisconsin—Madison, B.A., 1934, M.A., 1935, Ph.D., 1938. *Politics:* Independent. *Home:* 621 Honore Dr., New Orleans, La. 70121. *Office:* History Department, Tulane University, New Orleans, La. 70118.

CAREER: University of Wisconsin—Madison, instructor in history, 1938-39; University of Tulsa, Tulsa, Okla., assistant professor of history and head of history and political science department, 1939-46; University of Oklahoma, Norman, associate professor of history, 1946-47; Tulane University, New Orleans, La., associate professor, 1947-61, professor of history, 1961—. Fulbright exchange professor, University of Birmingham, Birmingham, England, 1953. *Member:* American Historical Association, American Association of University Professors, Southern Historical Association.

WRITINGS: Understanding "A History of Civilization", Volume I, Prentice-Hall, 1958; *History of Civilization I: A Study Guide to be Used with USAFI College Course D457,* published for U.S. Armed Forces Institute by Prentice-Hall, 1962; (with T. Walter Wallbank and Alastair M. Taylor) *Civilization Past and Present,* Scott, Foresman, 1962, 5th edition, 1977; (editor) *Readings in Ancient History from Gilgamesh to Charlemagne,* Heath, 1969, 2nd edition published as *Readings in Ancient History: From Gilgamesh to Diocletian,* 1976; (with Wallbank) *Western Perspectives: A Concise History of Civilization,* Scott, Foresman, 1973; (editor with Wallbank and others) *Western Civilization: People and Progress,* Scott, Foresman, 1977. Contributor of articles to *American Historical Review* and *Osiris.*

* * *

BAIN, Joe S. 1912-

PERSONAL: Born July 4, 1912, in Spokane, Wash.; son of Joe S. (a business executive) and Frances (Snow) Bain; married Beatrice Metcalf (an educator), September 7, 1937; children: Jennifer (Mrs. David Malone), Joe S. III. *Education:* University of California, Los Angeles, A.B., 1935; Stanford University, additional study, 1935-36; Harvard University, M.A., 1939, Ph.D., 1940. *Home:* 916 Peralta Ave., Albany, Calif. 94706. *Office:* Department of Economics, University of California, Berkeley, Calif. 94720.

CAREER: Harvard University, Cambridge, Mass., instructor, 1936-39; University of California, Berkeley, assistant professor, 1939-45, associate professor, 1945-49, professor of economics, 1949—. *Member:* American Economic Association (vice-president, 1969-70).

WRITINGS: War and Postwar Developments in the Southern California Petroleum Industry, Haynes Foundation, 1944; *The Economics of the Pacific Coast Petroleum Industry,* University of California Press, Part I: *Market Structure,* 1944, Part II: *Price Behavior and Competition,* 1945, Part III: *Public Policy toward Pricing and Competition,* 1947; (with Frederick T. Moore) *Literature on Price Policy and Related Topics, 1933-1947: A Selective Bibliography,* University of California Press, 1947; *Pricing, Distribution, and Employment: Economics of an Enterprise System,* Holt, 1948, revised edition, 1953; *Price Theory,* Holt, 1952; *Barriers to New Competition: Their Character and Consequences in Manufacturing Industries,* Harvard University Press, 1956; *Industrial Organization,* Wiley, 1959, 2nd edition, 1968; *International Differences in Industrial Structure: Eight Nations in the 1950s,* Yale University Press, 1966; (with R. E. Caves and Julius Margolis) *Northern California's Water Industry: The Comparative Efficiency of Public Enterprise in Developing a Scarce Natural Resource,* Johns Hopkins Press, 1966; (editor) *Essays on Economic Development,* Institute of Business and Economic Research, University of California, 1970; *Essays on Price Theory and Industrial Organization,* Little, Brown, 1972; *Environmental Decay: Economic Cases and Remedies,* Little, Brown, 1973. Contributor to academic journals.

* * *

BAIRD, Joseph Armstrong (Jr.) 1922-

PERSONAL: Born November 22, 1922, in Pittsburgh, Pa.; son of Joseph A. (a physician) and L. C. Baird. *Education:* Oberlin College, B.A. (magna cum laude), 1944; Harvard University, M.A., 1947, Ph.D., 1951. *Home:* 1830 Mountain View Dr., Tiburon, Calif. 94920. *Office:* Department of Art History, University of California, Davis, Calif. 95616.

CAREER: University of Toronto, Toronto, Ontario, 1949-53, began as lecturer, became instructor in art history; University of California, Davis, 1953—, began as instructor, currently professor of art history. Curator and consultant, California Historical Society, 1961-62, 1967-70; cataloger of Robert B. Honeyman, Jr. Collection in Bancroft Library, University of California, Berkeley, 1964-65. Lecturer in

United States and Mexico. *Member:* Society of Architectural Historians, National Trust for Historic Preservation, Victorian Society in America. *Awards, honors:* Award of Merit, California Historical Society.

WRITINGS: Time's Wondrous Changes: San Francisco Architecture, 1776-1915, California Historical Society, 1962; *The Churches of Mexico,* University of California Press, 1962; *California's Pictorial Letter Sheets, 1849-1896,* David Magee, 1967; *Historic Lithographs of San Francisco,* Burger & Evans, 1972; *The West Remembered,* California Historical Society, 1973; *Theodore Wares, the Japanese Years,* Oakland Museum, 1976. Contributor of articles and reviews to journals in his field.

*   *   *

BAJEMA, Carl Jay 1937-

PERSONAL: Born May 25, 1937, in Plainwell, Mich.; son of John A. (a grocer) and Jennie (Geukes) Bajema; married Ann Bos (a registered nurse), 1959; children: Mark Alan, Christopher Marshall. *Education:* Grand Rapids Junior College, A.A., 1957; Western Michigan University, B.S., 1959, M.A., 1961; Michigan State University, Ph.D., 1963. *Religion:* Agnostic. *Office:* Department of Biology, Grand Valley State College, Allendale, Mich. 49428.

CAREER: Teacher of science in public schools of Grand Rapids, Mich., 1959-60; Mankata State College, Mankato, Minn., assistant professor of biology, 1963-64; Grand Valley State College, Allendale, Mich., assistant professor, 1964-68, associate professor, 1968-72, professor of biology, 1972—. Harvard University, research associate in population studies, School of Public Health, 1967-71, visiting professor of anthropology, 1974-75. Vice-president, Planned Parenthood Association of Kent County, 1965-66; member of board of directors, National Association for Repeal of Abortion Laws, 1969-72. *Member:* American Institute of Biological Sciences, American Society of Human Genetics, Ecological Society of America, American Association for the Advancement of Science. *Awards, honors:* Population Council senior fellow at University of Chicago, 1966-67.

WRITINGS: (Editor) *Natural Selection in Human Populations,* Wiley, 1971; (editor) *Eugenics Then and Now,* Dowden, 1976; (with Garrett Hardin) *Biology: Its Principles and Implications,* W. H. Freeman, 1978.

WORK IN PROGRESS: Research in the Ongoing Evolution of Human Behavior, and history of evolutionary thought.

*   *   *

BAKER, Alton Wesley 1912-

PERSONAL: Born May 28, 1912, in Chickasha, Okla.; son of Charles Wesley and Frances Cornelia (Hennington) Baker; married Mary Elizabeth Dill (an author), June 4, 1938; children: Don Wesley, Viki Joan. *Education:* University of Texas, B.B.A., 1936; George Washington University, A.M., 1947; Ohio State University, Ph.D., 1952. *Address:* Box 250, Blanco, Tex. 78606. *Office:* Department of Management, Southern Methodist University, Dallas, Tex. 75222.

CAREER: Dill Manufacturing Corp., Austin, Tex., owner and president, 1937-40; Fairchild Corp., Hagerstown, Md., division head, 1943-47; Ohio State University, Columbus, research associate and associate professor of management, 1947-54; Southern Methodist University, Dallas, Tex., professor of management, 1954—, chairman of department,

1950—, also member of faculty of Legal Institute, Graduate School of Banking, and Supervisory Institute. Consultant to U.S. Postmaster General, and director of research on reorganization, 1966-69; expert consultant, 1969—. Former research consultant, Human Resources Research Institute, Air University.

MEMBER: Society for the Advancement of Management, Academy of Management, Industrial Relations Research Association, National Vocational Guidance Association, American Association of University Professors, Delta Sigma Pi, Delta Chi, Rotary International.

WRITINGS: (With Aaron Sartain) *The Supervisor and His Job,* McGraw, 1965, 3rd edition, in press.

Book-length monographs published by Bureau of Business Research, Ohio State University, include: *Provisions of Collective Bargaining Contracts in the Ohio Retail Lumber Trade,* 1949; (with James C. Yokum) *Wages, Hours, and Fringe Benefits in Ohio Hardware Stores,* 1950; *Wages, Hours, and Fringe Benefits in the Ohio Retail Lumber Trade,* 1950; *Sources of Information on Personnel Management and Labor Relations,* 1951; (with Ralph Currier Davis) *Labor-Management Arbitration,* 1951; (with Davis) *Ratios of Staff to Line Employees and Stages of Differentiation of Staff Functions,* 1954; *Personnel Management in Small Plants,* 1955.

WORK IN PROGRESS: Principles of Middle Management, for McGraw.

*   *   *

BAKER, Donald G(ene) 1932-

PERSONAL: Born February 16, 1932, in Elgin, Ill.; son of Glenn O. (an insurance salesman) and Helen (Splitgerber) Baker. *Education:* Elgin Community College, A.A., 1951; University of Denver, B.A., 1953; Syracuse University, M.A., 1958, Ph.D., 1961. *Home:* Wild Duck Lane, Hampton Bays, N.Y. 11946. *Office:* Department of Political Science, Southampton College of Long Island University, Southampton, N.Y. 11968.

CAREER: Skidmore College, Saratoga Springs, N.Y., instructor, 1959-61, assistant professor, 1961-64, director of American studies program, 1959-64; Long Island University, Southampton College, Southampton, N.Y., associate professor, 1964-68, professor of political science, 1968—, director of Social Science Division, 1964-71. Senior research fellow, University of Rhodesia, 1975-76. Director, New York State Graduate Legislative Internship Program, 1961-65; consultant to Peace Corps, 1964-65, and to various bodies on school desegregation, civil rights, and other social issues. *Military service:* U.S. Army, 1954-56. *Member:* American Political Science Association, American Studies Association, American Association of University Professors.

WRITINGS: (With C. Sheldon) *Postwar America: The Search for Identity,* Glencoe Press, 1969; (co-author and editor) *Politics of Race: Comparative Studies,* Heath, 1975. Contributor of articles and reviews to *American Political Science Review, Polity, South Atlantic Quarterly, Canadian Review of American Studies, Midwest Quarterly, State Government, Journal of Ethnic Studies, Social Dynamics, International Review of Modern Sociology,* and other journals.

WORK IN PROGRESS: Comparative studies of racism in U.S., Canada, New Zealand, Australia, South Africa, and Rhodesia; relationships between politics and literature.

BAKER, John H(enry) 1936-

PERSONAL: Born November 23, 1936, in Akron, Ohio; son of Duane Russell and Margaret (Harter) Baker; married Dorothy Wekall, August 9, 1959; children: Carolyn Louise, Craig Russell. *Education:* Claremont Men's College, B.A., 1958; Princeton University, Ph.D., 1961. *Religion:* Presbyterian. *Home:* 1100 West Carter, Carbondale, Ill. 62901. *Office:* Department of Political Science, Southern Illinois University, Carbondale, Ill. 62901.

CAREER: Claremont Men's College, Claremont, Calif., assistant professor of political science, 1963-66; Southern Illinois University, Carbondale, associate professor of political science, 1966—, assistant to president, 1971-72, assistant provost, 1972-75, chairman of department of political science, 1976—. Member of Carbondale Zoning Board of Appeals, 1969—. *Military service:* U.S. Army, 1961-63; became first lieutenant. U.S. Army Reserve, 1958—; present rank, major. *Member:* American Political Science Association, American Association of University Professors, Midwest Political Science Association.

WRITINGS: Urban Politics in America, Scribner, 1971.

WORK IN PROGRESS: Studying urban politics and American intergovernmental relations; *The Modern Presidency.*

*   *   *

BAKER, Joseph E(llis) 1905-

PERSONAL: Born August 24, 1905, in Sullivan, Ill.; son of Zion Frost (a farmer) and Estella (Ellis) Baker; married Matilda Janes, July 23, 1932; children: Ann (Mrs. John Tate), Mary Jane (Mrs. Ray Shoultz), John A. *Education:* University of Illinois, B.A., 1927, M.A., 1928; Princeton University, Ph.D., 1931. *Politics:* Democrat. *Religion:* Presbyterian. *Home:* 30 South Governor, Iowa City, Iowa 52240. *Office:* Department of English, University of Iowa, Iowa City, Iowa 52240.

CAREER: Princeton University, Princeton, N.J., instructor in English, 1929; Northwestern University, Evanston, Ill., instructor in English, 1931-35; University of Iowa, Iowa City, instructor, 1935-38, assistant professor, 1938-46, associate professor, 1946-52, professor of English, 1952-73, professor emeritus, 1973—. Visiting professor at University of Alabama, Michigan State University, City College of the City University of New York, and Clemson University. *Member:* American Association of University Professors (local chapter president), Modern Language Association of America, Phi Beta Kappa. *Awards, honors:* Fulbright professor, 1954-55.

WRITINGS: The Novel and the Oxford Movement, Princeton University Press, 1932; (editor) Robert Browning, *Pippa Passes and Shorter Poems,* Odyssey, 1947; (editor) *Reinterpretation of Victorian Literature,* Princeton University Press, 1950; *Shelley's Platonic Answer to a Platonic Attack on Poetry,* University of Iowa Press, 1965. Contributor to critical and professional journals. Member of editorial board, *Philological Quarterly* and *Victorian Poetry.*

WORK IN PROGRESS: Church Vandalism through High Level Conspiracy.

SIDELIGHTS: Joseph Baker told *CA,* "Scholarly work should be pursued boldly, in the spirit of investigative journalism."

BAKER, Letha Elizabeth (Mitts) 1913-

PERSONAL: Born June 26, 1913, in Capron, Okla.; daughter of Olie Elmer (a farmer) and Bessie (Roberson) Mitts; married Elton M. Baker (a college professor), May 19, 1935; children: Ronald Murray, David Scott. *Education:* Northwestern State College, Alva, Okla., B.A., 1933; Oklahoma State University, M.A., 1937; Oregon State University, additional study, 1939-41. *Religion:* Protestant. *Residence:* Indianola, Wash.; and Carmel, Calif.

CAREER: High school teacher of Spanish, English, and music in Forgan, Okla., 1933-35; Southwestern State College, Weatherford, Okla., instructor in Spanish, 1938-39; Oregon State University, Corvallis, instructor in Spanish, 1941-42; Fresno State College (now California State University, Fresno), instructor in Spanish, 1946-47; Olympic and Rainier (Wash.) Telephone Companies, co-owner and secretary of board of directors, 1952-67. Member of board of directors, Warren Reading Foundation, 1965-71. *Member:* National Writers Club, Cherokee Historical Society, Indianola Community Club.

WRITINGS: Cherokee Country (novel), Binfords & Mort, 1968. Also author of *Seven Trails* and *Bring My People Home.* Contributor of travel articles to newspapers.

WORK IN PROGRESS: A nutrition book in progress.

SIDELIGHTS: Letha Baker has lived in Mexico, South America, and Asia. She told *CA:* "If I live to be a hundred I'll still have things to write about, and I may well live that long for through a recent thorough study of nutrition, I've found the way to excellent health after a lifetime of illnesses." *Avocational interests:* Travel, painting, piano and guitar, gemology (especially collecting antique jewelery), theater, comparative religion, nutrition.

*   *   *

BAKER, Paul T(hornell) 1927-

PERSONAL: Born February 28, 1927, in Burlington, Iowa; son of Palmer Ward and Viola (Thornell) Baker; married Thelma M. Shoher (an instructor in anthropology), February 21, 1949; children: Deborah C., Amy L., Joshua S., Felicia B. *Education:* Attended University of Miami, Coral Gables, Fla., 1947-49; University of New Mexico, B.A., 1951; Harvard University, Ph.D., 1956. *Home address:* R.D. 1, Box 115E, Bellefonte, Pa. 16823. *Office:* Department of Anthropology, Pennsylvania State University, University Park, Pa. 16802.

CAREER: Quarter Master Corp, Natick, Mass., physical anthropologist at Research Development Center, 1952-57; Pennsylvania State University, University Park, assistant professor, 1958-61, associate professor, 1961-64, professor of anthropology, 1964—, acting head of department of sociology and anthropology, 1964-65, and of department of anthropology, 1968-70, director of Andean biocultural studies, 1964-74. Member of fellowship review board, National Institute of Mental Health, 1966-70; president of board of directors, Benner Township School Board, 1961-62. *Military service:* U.S. Army, 1945-47; served in European theater of operations.

MEMBER: American Association of Physical Anthropologists (president, 1969-71), American Anthropological Association (fellow), American Association for the Advancement of Science (fellow), U.S. Executive Committee for the International Biological Program, U.S. National Committee for Man and th Biosphere, Committee on Biological Bases of Social Behavior, Oxford Sailing Association. *Awards, honors:* Fulbright research scholar, Peru, 1962; Fulbright lecturer, Brazil, 1962; NATO senior science fellow, Oxford University, 1968; Guggenheim Memorial fellowship, 1974-75.

WRITINGS: (Editor with J. S. Weiner) *Biology of Human Adaptability,* Oxford University Press, 1966; (contributor) Francisco Salzano, editor, *The Ongoing Evolution of Latin American Populations,* C. C Thomas, 1971; (contributor) G. A. Harrison and A. J. Boyce, editors, *The Structure of Human Populations,* Clarendon Press, 1972; (contributor) N. B. Slonim, editor, *Environmental Physiology,* Mosby, 1975; (editor with M. A. Little, and contributor) *Man in the Andes: A Multidisciplinary Study of High Altitude Quechua,* Dowden, 1976; (editor and contributor) *Human Population Problems in the Biosphere: Some Research Strategies and Designs,* UNESCO, 1977; (editor) *The Biology of High Altitude Peoples,* Cambridge University Press, in press. Editor, "Anthropological modules" series for Addison-Wesley. Contributor of more than fifty articles to professional journals. Associate editor, *Human Biology;* former associate editor, *American Journal of Physical Anthropology;* former contributing editor, *Handbook of Latin American Studies;* editor of physical anthropology, *American Anthropologist,* 1973-76.

WORK IN PROGRESS: Research on biological effects of migration of human populations; researching the peoples of Samoa.

SIDELIGHTS: Paul Baker's research has been conducted in the desert, the Artic, and in the Himalayas and mountainous regions of Peru. *Avocational interests:* Sailing.

*   *   *

BAKER, R(onald) J(ames)   1924-

PERSONAL: Born August 24, 1924, in London, England; became Canadian citizen, 1951; son of James Herbert Walter (a printer) and Ethel Frances (Miller) Baker; married former wife, Helen Gillespie Elder, 1949; married Frances Marilyn Frazer, 1976; children: (previous marriage) Ann, Lyn, Ian, Sarah, Katherine. *Education:* University of British Columbia, B.A., 1951, M.A., 1953. *Office:* Office of the President, University of Prince Edward Island, Charlottetown, Prince Edward Island, Canada.

CAREER: University of British Columbia, Vancouver, lecturer, 1951-53, instructor, 1953-54, 1956-57, assistant professor, 1957-62, associate professor of English, 1962-63, secretary of Senate Committee on Academic Organization, 1961-62; Simon Fraser University, Burnaby, British Columbia, professor of English, 1964-69, director of Academic Planning, 1964-65, head, department of English, 1964-68; University of Prince Edward Island, Charlottetown, president, 1969—. Member of board of governors, Holland College, 1969—, Nova Scotia Technical College, 1970—; Canada Council, member, 1970-76, executive, 1971-76. Lecturer, University of Alberta, 1960 and University of Victoria, 1962. *Military service:* Royal Air Force, 1943-47; served as navigator/flying controller, and liaison officer on disarmament in Germany; became flight lieutenant.

MEMBER: Royal Society of Arts (fellow, 1971—), Modern Language Association of America, National Council of Teachers of English, Association of Canadian University Teachers of English (president, 1967-68), International Association of Professors of English, Canadian Linguistic Association (executive, 1958-60), Linguistic Society of America, Conference on College Composition and Communication (member of committee; executive, 1967-69), Cana-

dian Association of University Teachers, Canadian Council of Teachers of English (member of program committee, 1968; director, 1969—), Philological Society (London), Canadian Civil Liberties Association, Canadian Club (Charlottetown; president, 1975), Chamber of Commerce, Charlottetown (council member, 1970-72). *Awards, honors:* Humanities Research Council of Canada fellowships, 1954 and 1955, and travel grant, 1968; Royal Society of Canada fellowship, 1954-56; Canadian Centennial Medal, 1967; Canada Council research grant, 1969; LL.D., University of New Brunswick, 1970.

WRITINGS: (Editor) *The Faculty Handbook,* University of British Columbia, 1960; (with W. G. Hardwick) *North Shore Regional College Study,* Tantalus Research (Vancouver), 1965; (with Hardwick) *Regional College Study: Delta, Langley, Richmond, Surrey,* Tantalus Research, 1966.

Contributor: J. B. MacDonald, editor, *Higher Education in British Columbia,* University of British Columbia, 1962; H. B. Allen, editor, *Readings in Applied English Linguistics,* Appleton, 1963; *Looking at Language,* Gage (Toronto), 1966, Scott, Foresman, 1969; *College-University Articulation,* Academic Board for Higher Education in British Columbia, 1969. Editor and co-author, President's Report, University of British Columbia, 1955-59. Contributor of articles and reviews to *Queen's Quarterly, Canadian Literature, Journal of the Canadian Linguistic Association, Times Literary Supplement, Education, Vancouver Sun, Dalhousie Review,* and other literary journals and newspapers. Contributor to Canadian Broadcasting Corp. radio and television.

*   *   *

BAKER, Thomas Harrison   1933-

PERSONAL: Born October 14, 1933, in Houston, Tex.; son of Thomas Harrison, Jr. and Lily Bess (Kyle) Baker; married Carolyn Pierce, 1955; children: Catherine, Jana Bess. *Education:* Texas A & M University, B.A., 1955; University of Texas at Austin, M.A., 1963, Ph.D., 1965. *Politics:* Democrat. *Home:* 2 Arrow Brook Ct., Little Rock, Ark. 72207. *Office:* Department of History, University of Arkansas at Little Rock, 33rd St. and University Ave., Little Rock, Ark. 72204.

CAREER: Daily News, Garland, Tex., city editor, 1957-59; Mississippi State College for Women, Columbus, assistant professor of history, 1963-68; research associate on Lyndon B. Johnson Oral History Project, Tex., 1968-69; University of Arkansas at Little Rock, professor of history, 1969—, associate vice-chancellor for academic affairs, 1973—. *Military service:* U.S. Air Force, active duty, 1955-57; reserve duty, 1957-69; became major. *Member:* Organization of American Historians, Southern Historical Association, West Tennessee Historical Society, Arkansas Historical Association. *Awards, honors:* First place in column writing competition, Texas Press Association, 1958.

WRITINGS: The Memphis Commercial Appeal: The History of a Southern Newspaper, Louisiana State University Press, 1972.

WORK IN PROGRESS: General work in the history of the South.

*   *   *

BAKLANOFF, Eric N.   1925-

PERSONAL: Born December 9, 1925, in Graz, Austria; son of Nicholas W. and Lucile (King) Baklanoff; married H.

Christina Janes (an art professor), May 1, 1956 (divorced June, 1972); children: Nicholas, Tanya. *Education:* Attended Antioch College, 1943-44; Ohio State University, B.A., 1949, M.A., 1950, Ph.D., 1958. *Politics:* Republican. *Religion:* Episcopalian. *Home:* 12-A Indian Lake, Northport, Ala. 35476. *Office:* Economics Department, University of Alabama, Box J, University, Ala. 35486.

CAREER: Chase National Bank, New York, N.Y., member of International Division in Puerto Rico, 1950-54; Louisiana State University, Baton Rouge, assistant professor of economics, 1958-61; Vanderbilt University, Nashville, Tenn., associate professor of economics and director of Graduate Center for Latin American Studies, 1962-65; Louisiana State University, professor of economics and director of Latin American Studies Institute, 1965-68; University of Alabama, University, professor of economics and dean of International Studies and Programs, 1969-73, Board of Visitors Research Professor of Economics, 1974—. *Military service:* U.S. Navy, 1944-46.

MEMBER: Latin American Studies Association, Southeastern Conference on Latin American Studies (president, 1963-64), Southern Economic Association, Omicron Delta Epsilon, Sigma Delta Pi, Beta Gamma Sigma. *Awards, honors:* Fulbright fellowship, University of Chile, 1957; Vanderbilt University fellowship to Brazil, summer, 1963; Center for Advanced Studies in the Behavioral Sciences fellowship, 1964-65; Louisiana State University grants, University of the Americas, summer, 1966, Spain, summer, 1968; Wenner-Gren Foundation grant, 1966; U.S. State Department travel grant to Spain, 1974; University of Alabama Research Grants Committee summer fellowship, 1975-76.

WRITINGS: (Editor and contributor) *New Perspectives of Brazil,* Vanderbilt University Press, 1966; (editor and contributor) *The Shaping of Modern Brazil,* Louisiana State University Press, 1969; (contributor) Carmelo Mesa-Lago, editor, *Revolutionary Change in Cuba,* University of Pittsburgh Press, 1971; (contributor) John Saunders, editor, *Modern Brazil: New Patterns and Development,* University of Florida Press, 1971; (contributor) Robert B. Williamson, William P. Glade, Jr., and Karl M. Schmitt, editors, *Latin American-U.S. Economic Interactions,* American Enterprise Institute for Public Policy Research, 1974; *Expropriation of U.S. Investments in Cuba, Mexico, and Chile,* Praeger, 1975; (editor and contributor) *Mediterranean Europe and the Common Market,* University of Alabama Press, 1976; *The Economic Transformation of Spain and Portugal,* Praeger, 1978.

WORK IN PROGRESS: Contributions to *Yucatan: A World Apart,* edited by Edward Moseley and Edward Terry, for University of Alabama Press.

*   *   *

BALAS, David L(aszlo) 1929-

PERSONAL: Born August 6, 1929, in Kispest, Hungary; came to United States in 1959, naturalized in 1965; son of Laszlo and Maria (Borbely) Balas. *Education:* Pontificium Athenaeum Anselmianum, Rome, Italy, Ph.B., 1951, S.T.B., 1954, S.T.L., 1956, Ph.L., 1958, S.T.D., 1963. *Home address:* Rt. 2, Box 1, Irving, Tex. 75062. *Office:* Department of Theology, University of Dallas, Irving, Tex. 75060.

CAREER: Entered Cistercian Order (Catholic religious order) in Hungary, 1948—; ordained a priest in 1954. Fled to Western Europe in 1950, when Communist government suppressed Cistercian Order in Hungary; moved to United States, 1959; University of Dallas, Irving, Tex., instructor, 1959-62, assistant professor, 1962-66, associate professor, 1966-71, professor of philosophy and theology, 1971—, chairman of department, 1967—. Visiting professor, Pontificium Anthenaeum Anselmianum, Rome, Italy, 1970, 1972. *Member:* American Academy of Religion, American Catholic Philosophical Association, American Society of Church History, Association for Symbolic Logic, Catholic Theological Society of America, College Theology Society, Association Internationale pour l'Etude de la Philosophie Medievale, Association Internationale pour l'Etudes Patristiques, Council of Southwestern Theological Schools (member of executive committee; president, 1972-73), Catholic Interracial Council (Dallas; member of advisory board).

WRITINGS: Metousia Theou: Man's Participation in God's Perfections According to St. Gregory of Nyssa, Herder (Rome), 1966. Contributor of articles and reviews to *Merleg, Anglican Theological Review, Modern Schoolman, Thomist,* and *Proceedings* of the American Catholic Philosophical Association, 1966, and of the Sixth International Conference on Patristic Studies, 1971.

WORK IN PROGRESS: A paper, "Eternity and Time in the Thought of Gregory of Nyssa," which will eventually be expanded into a book; further articles and books on Gregory of Nyssa; extensive research on the early Greek Christian notion of salvation as communion with God and participation in God's life.

SIDELIGHTS: David Balas told *CA:* "Both my religious and scholarly vocations ripened during the years of the second world war (which I lived through first in my native country Hungary, and then as a refugee in Germany): the radical crisis of all established political orders and social conventions forced me to reflect on the ultimate foundations of the meaning of individual and social life.... Very early in the course of my studies I became interested in the encounter between Hellenistic (Greek-Roman) culture and the Jewish-Christian tradition. Thus much of my research has concerned the early Christian transformation of Greek philosophy.... Connected with [this] is my interest in the contemporary problem of 'Hermenuetics' (i.e. general theory of interpretation).... These two main fields of interest are connected in a vision of the intellectual history of the West as a history of reinterpretations of two interacting traditions: the 'Logos' (reason) of Greek philosophy and the 'Logos' ('Word of God') of Jewish-Christian religion."

BIOGRAPHICAL/CRITICAL SOURCES: Cistercian Studies, Volume II, number 2, 1967; *Journal of Theological Studies,* Volume XIX, 1968.

*   *   *

BALDUCCI, Carolyn (Feleppa) 1946-

PERSONAL: Born February 13, 1946, in Pelham, N.Y.; daughter of Ernest J., Sr. (a certified public accountant) and Rosaria (Pignone) Feleppa; married Gioacchino Balducci (a professor of Italian film and literature), December 28, 1968; children: Sirad (daughter). *Education:* Manhattanville College, B.A., 1967. *Politics:* Democrat. *Religion:* Roman Catholic. *Home:* 602 Oswego St., Ann Arbor, Mich. 48104. *Office:* Residential College, University of Michigan, Ann Arbor, Mich. 48108.

CAREER: Ingenue, New York City, "Lively Arts" editor and assistant to fiction editor, 1967-68; National Student Travel Association, New York City, editor, 1968; Popular Culture Press, Bowling Green, Ohio, associate editor, 1968-

70; University of Michigan, Residential College, Ann Arbor, Mich., writer in residence, 1976-77, currently lecturer in creative writing. *Member:* Authors Guild, Women in Communication, Society of Children's Book Writers. *Awards, honors:* Notable Book for Young People, American Library Association, 1971, for *Is There a Life After Graduation, Henry Birnbaum?;* Ohio Program in the Humanities grants, 1975, 1977.

WRITINGS: Is There Life after Graduation, Henry Birnbaum?, Houghton, 1971; *Earwax,* Houghton, 1972; *A Self-Made Woman: The Biography of Nobel Prize Winner Grazia Deledda,* Houghton, 1975. Also author of play, "Alcuin: A Fierce and Eloquent Plea for the Rights of Women," 1975, and screenplay, "Summer on the Lakes," 1977. Poetry anthologized in *Poets and Michigan,* 1977. Contributor to *Harvard Advocate, New York Times Book Review, Review,* and *New York Magazine.* Guest editor, *Mademoiselle,* 1966; editor, *Student Traveller Abroad,* 1969-70.

WORK IN PROGRESS: A novel, *Wife of the Anonymous Man; The Old Rat's Tale;* biographical studies of Margaret Fuller and Eleanora Duse; translation of *Wirrwarr* by Sanguinetti; translations of various Italian folk tales.

SIDELIGHTS: Carolyn Balducci told *CA:* "By teaching and continuing with my writing I am trying to find a new language. Listen to people, read billboards, dream. But don't imagine it's purely a matter of semiotics or morphology or literary criticism. Writing is the struggle to see things as they really are. Sounds artistic. It's not: the body suffers as much as the mind. I can't explain why I'm a writer. Can you explain why you are not?"

BIOGRAPHICAL/CRITICAL SOURCES: Mademoiselle, June, 1966; *Kirkus Review,* October 1, 1975; *Milwaukee Journal,* January 18, 1976; *Puget Sound Chronicle,* March, 1976; *Bulletin for Center for Children's Books,* May, 1976; *Liberty Cap,* May, 1976; *Jackson Sun,* June 6, 1976; *Young Miss,* October, 1976; *Commonweal,* November 19, 1976.

*   *   *

BALL, Brian N(eville)   1932-
(B. N. Ball, Brian Kinsey-Jones)

PERSONAL: Born June 19, 1932, in Cheshire, England; son of Walter Hope and Elsie (Booth) Ball; married Margaret Snead, August 7, 1953; children: Jane Nicola, Kathryn Amanda. *Education:* Attended Chester College, 1953-55; London University, B.A., 1960; Sheffield University, M.A., 1968.

CAREER: Doncaster College of Education, Doncaster, England, beginning 1965, became senior lecturer in English. *Military service:* British Army, 1950-52. *Member:* Doncaster Prose and Poetry Society (chairman, 1968-70), Rotherham Golf Club.

WRITINGS—All novels, except as indicated: (Editor) *Tales of Science Fiction* (short stories), Hamish Hamilton, 1964; *Sundog,* Dobson, 1965, Avon, 1969; *Timepiece,* Dobson, 1969, Ballantine, 1970; *Timepivot,* Ballantine, 1970; *Timepit,* Dobson, 1971; *Lesson for the Damned,* New English Library, 1971; *Night of the Robots,* Sidgwick & Jackson, 1972; *The Probability Man,* Daw Books, 1972; *The Regiments of Night,* Daw Books, 1972; *Planet Probability,* Daw Books, 1972; *The Singularity Station,* Daw Books, 1973; *Death of a Low-Handicap Man,* Arthur Barker, 1974; *Montenegrin Gold,* Arthur Barker, 1974; *The Space Guardians,* Sidgwick & Jackson, 1974, Aeonian, 1975; *Keegan,*

the No-Option Contract, Arthur Barker, 1975; *Keegan, the One-Way Deal,* Mayflower, 1976; *Witchfinder, the Mark of the Beast,* Mayflower, 1976.

Under pseudonym Brian Kinsey-Jones: *Lay Down Your Wife for Another,* New English Library, 1971.

Children's books, under name B. N. Ball: *Mr. Tofat's Term,* Holmes McDougall, 1964; *The Paris Adventure,* Holmes McDougall, 1966; *Focus on Space,* Holmes McDougall, 1966; *Princess Priscilla,* illustrations by Lisa James, Abelard, 1975; *Jackson's Friend,* illustrations by Carolyn Harrison, Hamish Hamilton, 1975; *Jackson's House,* Hamish Hamilton, 1975; *Jackson's Holiday,* illustrations by Harrison, Hamish Hamilton, 1977.

Also author of an educational book, *Basic Linguistics for Secondary Schools,* Methuen, 1966-67. Contributor of short stories and reviews to periodicals, including *Guardian* and *Times Educational Supplement.*

WORK IN PROGRESS: A long historical novel, to be the first of a series; a science fiction novel, *The Far Shores of Time.*

SIDELIGHTS: Brian Ball told *CA:* "I like action that's spasmodic—golf, writing, playing with my kids; I believe books should be the same—spasmodic, totally involving. I *hate* analysing literature though I have to do it for a living: it's almost totally destructive of energy. In my own writing I follow advice from an old hand, Mack Reynolds, who I met just once: 'write the sort of thing you'd like to read.'"†

*   *   *

BALL, Howard   1937-

PERSONAL: Born August 13, 1937, in New York, N.Y.; son of Abe (a businessman) and Fay (Kintish) Ball; married Carol Neidell, July 7, 1963; children: Susan Gabrielle, Sheryl Lisa, Melissa Paige. *Education:* Hunter College (now Hunter College of the City University of New York), B.A., 1960; Rutgers University, M.A., 1963, Ph.D., 1970. *Office:* Department of Political Science, Mississippi State University, Starkville, Miss. 39762.

CAREER: Rutgers University, New Brunswick, N.J., instructor in political science, 1960-65; Hofstra University, Hempstead, N.Y., assistant professor of political science, beginning 1965; Mississippi State University, Starkville, professor of political science, 1976—. *Military service:* U.S. Air Force National Guard, 1958-66; became staff sergeant. *Member:* American Political Science Association, Pi Sigma Alpha.

WRITINGS: (Editor with Thomas P. Lauth, Jr.) *Changing Perspectives in Contemporary Political Analysis,* Prentice-Hall, 1971; *The Warren Court's Conceptions of Democracy,* Fairleigh Dickenson University Press, 1971; *The Vision and the Dream of Justice Hugo L. Black: An Examination of a Judicial Philosophy,* University of Alabama Press, 1975; *No Pledge of Privacy: The Watergate Tapes Litigation, 1973-1974,* Kennikat, 1977; *Judicial Craftsmanship or Fiat?: Direct Overturn by the United States Supreme Court,* Greenwood Press, 1978. Contributor to *Hofstra Review* and *Annals.*

WORK IN PROGRESS: Administration of Justice in a Local Community.†

*   *   *

BALL, Jane Eklund   1921-
(Jane Mary Eklund)

PERSONAL: Born October 4, 1921, in Los Angeles, Calif.;

daughter of Emil Julius (a mining engineer) and Hallie (a teacher; maiden name, Pettibone) Eklund; married Everett Loran Ball, Jr. (an artist), October 21, 1951; children: Everett Holman, Francesca, Jocelyn. *Education:* University of California, Los Angeles, B.A., 1943; Stanford University, M.A., 1950. *Religion:* Episcopalian. *Office:* Department of English, William Howard Taft High School, Ventura Blvd. and Winnetka, Woodland Hills, Calif.

CAREER: William Howard Taft High School, Woodland Hills, Calif., English teacher, 1964—.

WRITINGS: (Under name Jane Mary Eklund) *The Only Gift* (novel), Houghton, 1949; *Philippa* (novel), Houghton, 1953; *Designs for Reading: Short Stories* (textbook), Houghton, 1969; *The Range of Literature: Fiction* (textbook), Houghton, 1969.

WORK IN PROGRESS: A novel.

SIDELIGHTS: Jane Ball wrote to *CA:* "I write because it is a necessary part of the life experience for me. What comes of the writing later does not interest me as much as what I am working on next."

*   *   *

BALL, John M(iller) 1923-

PERSONAL: Born January 7, 1923, in Highland Park, Mich.; son of John Rathbone (a laborer) and Helen (Miller) Ball; children: John Scott, James Scott, Judith Susan. *Education:* Central Michigan College of Education (now Central Michigan University), A.B., 1948; University of Michigan, M.A., 1950; University of Chicago, S.M., 1952; Michigan State College of Agriculture and Applied Science (now Michigan State University), Ph.D., 1961. *Politics:* Democrat. *Religion:* Unitarian Universalist. *Home:* 108 Elizabeth St. N.E., Atlanta, Ga. 30307. *Office:* Department of Geography, Georgia State University, Atlanta, Ga. 30303.

CAREER: High school teacher of social studies in Artesia, Calif., 1954-57; Central Michigan University, Mount Pleasant, instructor in geography, 1957-61; Slippery Rock State College, Slippery Rock, Pa., professor of geography and head of department, 1961-65; University of Georgia, Athens, associate professor of geography, 1965-70; Georgia State University, Atlanta, professor of geography, 1970—. *Military service:* U.S. Army Air Forces, 1942-46; became sergeant.

MEMBER: American Geographical Society, National Council for Geographic Education (vice-president, 1972; president, 1973), Latin American Studies Association, American Association of University Professors, Association of American Geographers, National Council for the Social Studies, American Civil Liberties Union.

WRITINGS: Introducing New Concepts of Geography in the Social Studies Curriculum, Geography Curriculum Project, University of Georgia, 1970; *A Bibliography of Geographic Education,* Geography Curriculum Project, University of Georgia, 1970; (editor with John Steinbrink and Joseph Stoltman) *The Social Sciences and Geographic Education: A Reader,* Wiley, 1971; *Migration and the Rural Municipio of Mexico,* Bureau of Business and Economic Research, Georgia State University, 1971; (editor with Merrill Ridd, Robert Sawyer, and Fred Dohrs) *Metropolitan America: Concepts and Teaching Strategies,* National Council for Geographic Education, 1972. Contributor to geography and education journals. Associate editor, *Journal of Geography.*

BALLARD, Edward Goodwin 1910-

PERSONAL: Born January 3, 1910, in Fairfax, Va.; son of James W. (a lawyer) and Margaret Lewis (Goodwin) Ballard; married Lucy McIver Watson, November 22, 1938; children: Susanne (Mrs. M. Dowouis), Lucy (Mrs. David Armentrout), Edward Marshall. *Education:* College of William and Mary, A.B., 1931; Harvard University, graduate study, 1931-32; University of Virginia, M.A., 1934, Ph.D., 1946. *Religion:* Episcopalian. *Home:* 2320 Calhoun St., New Orleans, La. 70118. *Office:* Department of Philosophy, Tulane University, 6823 St. Charles Ave., New Orleans, La. 70118.

CAREER: Ecole Internationale, Palma, Majorca, instructor in mathematics, 1932; Virginia Military Institute, Lexington, instructor in English, 1939-41; Tulane University, New Orleans, La., assistant professor, 1946-53, associate professor, 1953-58, professor of philosophy, 1958—. Visiting professor at Yale University, 1963-64, and Louisiana State University, 1969. *Military service:* U.S. Naval Reserve, active duty, 1942-46; became commander; received three battle stars for service in Pacific theater. *Member:* American Philosophical Association, Metaphysical Society of America, Society for Phenomenology and Existential Philosophy, Southern Society for Philosophy and Psychology (president, 1967), Husserl Circle (chairman, 1970).

WRITINGS: Art and Analysis, Nijhoff, 1957; *Socratic Ignorance: An Essay on Platonic Self-Knowledge,* Nijhoff, 1960; *Philosophy at the Crossroads,* Louisiana State University Press, 1971; (editor with C. E. Scott, and contributor) *Heidegger in Europe and America,* Nijhoff, 1973.

Contributor: George A. Schrader, Jr., editor, *Existential Philosophers,* McGraw, 1967; John Sallis, editor, *Heidegger and the Path of Thinking,* Duquesne University Press, 1970; F. J. Smith, editor, *Phenomenology in Perspective,* Nijhoff, 1970; Lester E. Embree, editor, *Life-World and Consciousness: Essays for Aaron Gurwitsch,* Northwestern University Press, 1972; P. J. Bossert, editor, *Phenomenological Perspectives: Historical and Systematic Essays in Honor of Herbert Spiegelberg,* Nijhoff, 1973; C. Bigger and D. Cornay, editors, *Eros and Nihilism,* Kendall/Hunt, 1976.

Translator: (And author of introduction) *The Philosophy of Jules Lachelier,* Nijhoff, 1960; (with L. E. Embree) *Husserl: An Analysis of His Phenomenology,* Northwestern University Press, 1967.

Contributor to *American Encyclopedia of Philosophy* and *Dictionary of the History of Ideas.* More than fifty articles, three critical reviews, and about twenty-five short reviews have been published in professional journals. Member of editorial board, *Southern Journal of Philosophy, Research in Phenomenology,* and *Tulane Studies in Philosophy.*

WORK IN PROGRESS: Two book-length essays, *A Humanistic Measure of Technological Culture* and *Toward An Ontology of Experience.*

SIDELIGHTS: Edward Ballard lived in France for about five years. *Avocational interests:* Gardening, boating, judo, travel.

*   *   *

BALTZELL, E(dward) Digby 1915-

PERSONAL: Born November 14, 1915, in Philadelphia, Pa.; son of E. Digby (an insurance broker) and Caroline (Duhring) Baltzell; married Jane Piper (an artist), February 26, 1943; children: Eve, Jan. *Education:* University of Pennsylvania, B.S., 1939; Columbia University, Ph.D., 1952.

Politics: Democrat. *Religion:* Episcopalian. *Home:* 1724 DeLancey Pl., Philadelphia, Pa. 19103. *Office:* Department of Sociology, University of Pennsylvania, Philadelphia, Pa. 19104.

CAREER: University of Pennsylvania, Philadelphia, instructor, 1948-55, assistant professor, 1955-58, associate professor, 1958-65, professor of sociology, 1965—. *Military service:* U.S. Naval Reserve, active duty, 1942-45; became lieutenant junior grade; received Air Medal. *Member:* American Sociological Association, Pennsylvania Historical Society.

WRITINGS: (Contributor) Richard Bendix and Seymour M. Lipset, editors, *Class, Status and Power,* Free Press, 1953, revised edition, 1966; *Philadelphia Gentleman,* Quadrangle, 1958; *Protestant Establishment,* Random House, 1964.

BIOGRAPHICAL/CRITICAL SOURCES: Nation, April 3, 1967.

*   *   *

BANANI, Amin 1926-

PERSONAL: Born September 23, 1926, in Tehran, Iran; came to United States in 1944, naturalized in 1954; son of Musa (a businessman) and Samihe (Rafi'i) Banani; married Sheila Wolcott, February 11, 1951; children: Susanne, Laila. *Education:* Stanford University, B.A., 1947, Ph.D., 1959; Columbia University, M.A., 1949. *Office:* Department of Near Eastern Languages and Cultures, University of California, Los Angeles, 405 Hilgard, Los Angeles, Calif. 90024.

CAREER: Stanford University, Palo Alto, Calif., instructor in history, 1958-59; Reed College, Portland, Ore., assistant professor of humanities, 1959-61; Harvard University, Cambridge, Mass., research fellow and assistant professor, 1961-63; University of California, Los Angeles, associate professor, 1964-69, professor of history and Persian literature, 1969—, chairman of department of Near Eastern languages and cultures, 1976—, acting director of Von Grunebaum Center for Near Eastern Studies, 1974-76. *Member:* Middle East Studies Association of North America (member of board of directors, 1972-75), American Institute for Iranian Studies (vice-president, 1969-71), Society for Iranian Studies (member of executive council, 1969—), Royal Asiatic Society.

WRITINGS: The Modernization of Iran, 1921-1941, Stanford University Press, 1961; (contributor) Girdhari L. Tikku, editor, *Islam and Its Cultural Divergence,* University of Illinois Press, 1971; (contributor) Ehsan Yar-Shater, editor, *Iran Faces the Seventies,* Praeger, 1971; (editor) *Individualism and Conformity in Classical Islam,* Harassowitz, 1977; (editor) *State and Society in Iran,* Society for Iranian Studies, 1977; (contributor) M. Tehranian, editor, *Communication Policy for Development,* Routledge & Kegan Paul, 1977.

WORK IN PROGRESS: A book, tentatively entitled *A Quest for Persian Identity;* Persian ritual drama.

*   *   *

BANDERA, V(ladimir) N(icholas) 1932-

PERSONAL: Born December 11, 1932, in Stry, Ukraine; came to United States in 1949, naturalized in 1954; son of Joseph (an economist) and Maria Bandera; married Sophie Zayachkivsky, September 22, 1956; children: Mark, Peter, Christina. *Education:* University of Connecticut, B.A. (cum laude), 1954; University of California, Berkeley, Ph.D.,

1960. *Religion:* Ukrainian Catholic. *Home:* 148 Trent Rd., Philadelphia, Pa. 19151. *Office:* Department of Economics, Temple University, Philadelphia, Pa. 19122.

CAREER: Boston College, Chestnut Hill, Mass., assistant professor, 1960-64, associate professor of economics, 1964-72, director of Slavic and East European Center, beginning 1971; Temple University, Philadelphia, Pa., professor of economics, 1972—. Fulbright professor, Universita degli Studi, Pavia, Italy, 1966; visiting professor of economics and associate at Institute of International Studies, University of California, Berkeley, 1968-69. *Military service:* U.S. Army, 1954-56. *Member:* American Economic Association, American Association for the Advancement of Slavic Studies. *Awards, honors:* William Holcomb Memorial Award, 1953; Ford Foundation doctoral fellow, 1959; Eliot Jones Award, Western Economic Association, 1959.

WRITINGS: Foreign Capital as an Instrument of National Economic Policy, Nijhoff, 1964, 2nd edition, 1968; (editor with Z. L. Meynyk) *The Soviet Economy in Regional Perspective,* Praeger, 1973. Contributor to *Journal of Political Economy, Kyklos, Oxford Economic Papers, Soviet Studies,* and *Incomonia Internazionale.*

WORK IN PROGRESS: Research on international finance, foreign investment, and economic imperialism.

SIDELIGHTS: V. N. Bandera has lectured on international economic policies at universities in Canada, Yugoslavia, Germany, and Turkey, as well as the United States and Italy. He is fluent in Italian, German, and Ukrainian. Some of his works have been translated into German, Ukrainian, Turkish, and Yugoslavian.†

*   *   *

BANDY, Eugene Franklin (Jr.) 1914-
(Eugene Franklin)

PERSONAL: Born December 15, 1914, in Atlanta, Ga.; son of Eugene Franklin (a professional fund raiser) and Marjorie (Champion) Bandy; married Beth E. Lawson, August 27, 1948; children: Eugene F. III, John Champion. *Education:* University of Illinois, A.B., 1938. *Home:* 11 Lincoln Ave., Port Chester, N.Y. 10573. *Agent:* Oliver Swan, Oscar Collier Associates, 280 Madison Ave., New York, N.Y. 10016; and Meredith Bernstein, Henry Morrison, Inc., 58 West 10th St., New York, N.Y. 10011.

CAREER: Caples Co., New York City, vice-president, 1946-60; Geyer, Morey, Ballard, New York City, vice-president, 1960-63; Buchen Advertising, Inc., New York City, vice-president, 1963-70; Wyman Associates, Inc., New York City, executive vice-president, 1970-73; Pavilion Advertising Agency, New York City, president, 1974—. *Military service:* U.S. Army, Signal Corps, 1942-46; became captain. *Member:* Mystery Writers of America, Authors Guild, Overseas Press Club.

WRITINGS—Under name Eugene Franklin: *Murder Trapp,* Stein & Day, 1971; *The Money Murders,* Stein & Day, 1972; *The Bold House Murders,* Stein & Day, 1973. Former staff editor, *World Book Encyclopedia* and Consolidated Book Publishers. Contributor to *Alfred Hitchcock Mystery Magazine.*

WORK IN PROGRESS: A suspense novel, *The Shannonese Hustle.*

SIDELIGHTS: Eugene Bandy's books have been translated into Italian and German.

BANKS, Arthur S. 1926-

PERSONAL: Born May 30, 1926, in Quincy, Mass.; son of Gordan T. (a dealer in rare manuscripts) and Miriam (Goodspeed) Banks. *Education:* Cornell University, A.B., 1951; George Washington University, A.M., 1954, Ph.D., 1967. *Home:* Center Rd., Shirley, Mass. 01464. *Office:* Center for Social Analysis, State University of New York, Binghamton, N.Y. 13901.

CAREER: George Washington University, Washington, D.C., lecturer, 1958-59, assistant professor of political science and research associate, Sino-Soviet Institute, 1966-68; University of New Hampshire, Durham, instructor in department of government, 1959-60; Indiana University, Bloomington, research associate in International Development Research Center, 1963-65; State University of New York at Binghamton, associate professor of political science and director of Center for Comparative Political Research, 1968-76, professor of political science and senior fellow of Center for Social Analysis, 1976—. *Military service:* U.S. Marine Corps, 1943-46. *Member:* American Political Science Association, Pi Gamma Mu, Pi Sigma Alpha. *Awards, honors:* National Science Foundation research grant, 1969-71.

WRITINGS: (With Robert B. Textor) *A Cross-Polity Survey,* M.I.T. Press, 1963; *Cross-Polity Time-Series Data,* M.I.T. Press, 1971; (editor) *Political Handbook of the World: 1975,* McGraw, 1975; (editor) *Political Handbook of the World: 1976,* McGraw, 1976; (editor) *Political Handbook of the World: 1977,* McGraw, 1977. Contributor to political science and social science journals.

* * *

BANKS, J(ohn) Houston 1911-

PERSONAL: Born February 9, 1911, in Ripley, Tenn.; son of Roderick Stanton (a lawyer) and Ella Celestine (Sinclair) Banks; married Mary Rhea Fowler (a teacher), March 11, 1933; children: John Fowler, Betty Rhea (Mrs. Sam Stephenson). *Education:* Tennessee Polytechnical Institute (now Tennessee Technological University), B.S., 1935; George Peabody College for Teachers, M.A., 1938, Ph.D., 1949. *Home:* 3708 Lealand Lane, Nashville, Tenn. 37204. *Office:* Department of Mathematics, George Peabody College for Teachers, Nashville, Tenn. 37203.

CAREER: Teacher and principal in Tennessee public schools, 1934-42; mathematics instructor for U.S. Army Air Forces, 1942-44; East Central Junior College, Decatur, Miss., instructor in mathematics and dean, 1944-46; Florence State College (now University), Florence, Ala., professor of mathematics, 1946-49; George Peabody College for Teachers, Nashville, Tenn., associate professor, 1949-57, professor of mathematics, 1958—, chairman of department, 1960-75. Visiting professor at Auburn University, 1956, and University of New Brunswick, 1960. Consultant on textbook project in Central America, U.S. Agency for International Development, 1964-70.

MEMBER: National Council of Teachers of Mathematics (member of board of directors, 1963), National Education Association, Mathematical Association of America, Tennessee Mathematics Teachers Association (president, 1954), Tennessee Academy of Sciences, Tennessee Education Association, Sigma Xi, Kappa Delta Pi, Phi Delta Kappa, Pi Mu Epsilon.

WRITINGS: Elements of Mathematics, Allyn & Bacon, 1956, 3rd edition, 1969; *Learning and Teaching Arithmetic,* Allyn & Bacon, 1959, 2nd edition, 1964; (with Arville Wheeler) *Question and Answer Book in Arithmetic,* Arthur C. Crofts, 1960; (with F. L. Wren) *Elements of Algebra,* Allyn & Bacon, 1962; (with Max A. Sobel) *Algebra: Its Elements and Structure,* two volumes, McGraw, 1965, 3rd edition, 1977; *Elementary School Mathematics: A Modern Approach for Teachers,* Allyn & Bacon, 1966; (with Herbert F. Spitzer, Paul C. Burns, Mary V. Kahrs, and Mary O. Folsom) *Elementary School Mathematics Concepts, Properties, Operations,* four books, McGraw, 1967; (with Spitzer, Burns, Kahrs, and Folsom) *Mathematics Concepts, Properties, Operations,* two books, McGraw, 1968; (with Charles H. Butler and F. Lynwood Wren) *Teaching of Secondary Mathematics,* 5th edition (Banks was not associated with earlier editions), McGraw, 1970; (with Alfred S. Pasamentier and Robert L. Bannister) *Geometry: Its Elements and Structure,* McGraw, 1972, 2nd edition, 1977. Contributor to education journals.

* * *

BANKS, James A(lbert) 1941-

PERSONAL: Born September 24, 1941, in Marianna, Ark.; son of Matthew (a farmer) and Lula (Holt) Banks; married Cherry A. McGee (a counselor), February 15, 1969; children: Angela Marie, Patricia Ann. *Education:* Chicago City Junior College, A.A., 1963; Chicago State College (now University), B.Ed., 1964; Michigan State University, M.A., 1967, Ph.D., 1969. *Religion:* Methodist. *Home:* 1333 Northwest 200th St., Seattle, Wash. 98177. *Office:* 122 Miller Hall-DQ-12, University of Washington, Seattle, Wash. 98195.

CAREER: Teacher in Joliet, Ill., 1965, in Chicago, Ill., 1965-66; University of Washington, Seattle, assistant professor, 1969-71, associate professor, 1971-73, professor of education, 1973—. Visiting professor of education, University of Michigan, summer, 1975. Member of the national advisory council on ethnic heritage studies, U.S. Office of Education. *Member:* Association for Supervision and Curriculum Development (member of board of directors), Social Science Education Consortium (member of board of directors), National Council for the Social Studies (member of board of directors, 1973-74; chairperson of Task Force on Ethnic Studies Curriculum Guidelines, 1975-76). *Awards, honors:* National Defense Education Act fellowship, U.S. Office of Education, 1966; Spencer fellowship, National Academy of Education, 1973; named "Outstanding Young Man" by Washington State Jaycees, 1975.

WRITINGS: (With wife, Cherry A. Banks) *March toward Freedom: A History of Black Americans,* Fearon, 1970, 2nd edition, 1974; *Teaching the Black Experience: Methods and Materials,* Fearon, 1970; (editor with William W. Joyce) *Teaching the Language Arts to Culturally Different Children,* Addison-Wesley, 1971; (editor with Joyce) *Teaching Social Studies to Culturally Different Children,* Addison-Wesley, 1971; (author of foreword) Thomas T. Lyons, *Black Leadership in American History,* Addison-Wesley, 1971; (editor with Jean D. Grambs) *Black Self-Concept: Implications for Education and Social Science,* McGraw, 1972; *Ethnic Studies in the Social Context* (monograph), National Urban League, 1972; (editor) *Teaching Ethnic Studies: Concepts and Strategies,* National Council for the Social Studies, 1973; *Teaching Strategies for the Social Studies,* Addison-Wesley, 1973, 2nd edition, 1977; *Teaching Strategies for Ethnic Studies,* Allyn & Bacon, 1975; (with Carlos E. Cortes, Geneva Gay, Ricardo L. Garcia and Anna S. Ochoa) *Curriculum Guidelines for Multiethnic Education,*

National Council for the Social Studies, 1976; (author of foreword) Francis P. Hunkins, *Involving Students in Questioning,* Allyn & Bacon, 1976; *Multiethnic Education: Practices and Promises,* Phi Delta Kappa Educational Foundation, 1977.

Contributor: Robert L. Green, editor, *Racial Crisis in American Education,* Follett, 1969; Jean D. Grambs and John C. Carr, editors, *Black Image: Education Copes with Color,* W. C. Brown, 1972; V. R. Rogers and T. P. Weinland, editors, *Teaching Social Studies in the Urban Classroom,* Addison-Wesley, 1972; Richard Wisniewski, editor, *Teaching about Life in the City,* National Council for the Social Studies, 1972; Jonathon C. McLendon, editor, *Guide to Reading for Social Studies Teachers,* National Council for the Social Studies, 1973; Delmo Della-Dora and James E. House, editors, *Education for an Open Society,* Association for Supervision and Curriculum Development, 1974; *The Final Report and Recommendations of the Summer Institute on the Improvement of American Education,* U.S. Government Printing Office, 1974; Roosevelt Johnson, editor, *Black Scholars on Higher Education in the 70s,* ECCA Publications, 1974; Norene Harris, Nathaniel Jackson, and Carl E. Rydingsword, editors, *The Integration of American Schools: Problems, Experiences, Solutions,* Allyn & Bacon, 1975; Raymond H. Muessig, editor, *Controversial Issues in the Social Studies: A Contemporary Perspective,* National Council for the Social Studies, 1975; B. Othanel Smith and Donald E. Orlosky, editors, *Socialization and Schooling,* Phi Delta Kappa, 1975; M. Patricia Golden, editor, *The Research Experience,* Peacock Publishers, 1976; Melvin M. Tumin and Walter Plotch, editors, *Pluralism in a Democratic Society,* Praeger, 1977; Frank Klassen and Donna M. Gollnick, editors, *Pluralism and the American Teacher: Issues and Case Studies,* American Association of Colleges for Teacher Education, 1977; Donald R. Wentworth and W. Lee Hansen, editors, *Perspectives in Economic Education,* Social Science Education Consortium, 1977.

Contributor of over forty articles to professional journals, including *Educational Leadership, Social Education, School Review, Social Studies, Journal of Afro-American Issues,* and *Integrated Education.* Guest editor, *Phi Delta Kappan,* January, 1972. Member of editorial boards, *Journal of Afro-American Issues, Interracial Books for Children Bulletin,* and *Review of Education.*

WORK IN PROGRESS: A second edition of *Teaching Strategies for Ethnic Studies;* an American history book for junior high school grades, for Allyn & Bacon; research related to the emerging stages of ethnicity and their curricular implications; research related to ethnicity and educational policy in selected nations, including England, Mexico, Puerto Rico, France, United States, and Canada.

BIOGRAPHICAL/CRITICAL SOURCES: Chicago Sun-Times, April 27, 1966.

*   *   *

BANKWITZ, Philip Charles Farwell 1924-

PERSONAL: Born February 17, 1924, in Greenfield, Mass.; son of Charles Edward (a businessman) and Elizabeth (Russell) Bankwitz. *Education:* Harvard University, A.B. (magna cum laude), 1947, A.M., 1948, Ph.D., 1952. *Politics:* Democrat. *Religion:* Congregationalist. *Home:* 36 Colton St., Farmington, Conn. 06032. *Office:* Department of History, Trinity College, Summit St., Hartford, Conn. 06106.

CAREER: Trinity College, Hartford, Conn., instructor,

1954-57, assistant professor, 1957-60, associate professor, 1960-68, professor of history, 1968—. Visiting professor of history, Pierson College, Yale University, 1974. *Military service:* U.S. Army, Intelligence, 1943-45; served in Europe; became staff sergeant; received Croix de Guerre. *Member:* Society for French Historical Studies (secretary-general, 1973—), American Historical Association, Societe d'Histoire Moderne, Foreign Policy Association of Greater Hartford, Hasty Pudding-Institute of 1770 and D.U. Club (both Harvard). *Awards, honors:* Fulbright scholar in Paris, France, 1950-51; William Koren, Jr. Prize of Society for French Historical Studies, 1961, for best article in French history; American Council of Learned Societies research fellow, 1970-71; Camargo Foundation fellow, Cassis, France, 1974-75.

WRITINGS: Maxime Weygand and Civil-Military Relations in Modern France, Harvard University Press, 1967; (contributor) Brison Gooch, editor, *Interpreting European History,* Dorsey, 1967; *Alsatian Autonomist Leaders, 1919-1947,* Regents Press, 1978. Twentieth-century editor, *French Historical Studies,* 1970-73; reviewer for *Journal of Modern History, American Historical Review,* and other journals.

WORK IN PROGRESS: A social and political analysis of the careers of Pierre-Etienne Flandin and Edouard Daladier, 1930-1947.

BIOGRAPHICAL/CRITICAL SOURCES: Virginia Quarterly Review, summer, 1968; *American Historical Review,* October, 1968.

*   *   *

BANNOCK, Graham 1932-

PERSONAL: Surname is pronounced *Ban-*knock; born July 10, 1932, in London, England; son of Eric Burton and Winifred (Sargent) Bannock; married Francoise Vranckx, February 26, 1971. *Education:* London School of Economics and Political Science, B.Sc., 1955. *Agent:* A. D. Peters, 10 Buckingham St., Adelphi, London WC2N 6BU, England. *Office:* Economists Advisory Group Ltd., 54B Tottenham Ct. Rd., London W.1, England.

CAREER: Economist Intelligence Unit, London, England, economist, 1956-58; Rover Co., Solihull, England, economic adviser, 1958-60; Organization for Economic Co-operation and Development, Paris, France, principal administrator, Economics Division, 1960-62; Rover Co., economic adviser, 1962-67; Ford (Britain), Warley, England, manager of market research, 1967-68; manager of advanced programs, Ford of Europe, Inc., Dunton, 1968-69; Committee of Inquiry on Small Firms, Department of Trade and Industry, London, England, director of research, 1970—. Managing director, Economists Advisory Group. *Military service:* British Army, Royal Army Service Corps, 1950-52; became sergeant. *Member:* Royal Economic Society, Society of Business Economists.

WRITINGS: (With A. J. Merrett) *Business Economics and Statistics,* Hutchinson, 1962; *The Juggernauts,* Bobbs-Merrill, 1971; (with Ray Rees and R. E. Baxter) *The Penguin Dictionary of Economics,* Penguin, 1973; *How to Survive the Slump,* Penguin, 1976; *Smaller Business in Britain and Germany,* Wilton House, 1976. Contributor of articles and reviews to learned journals and newspapers.

WORK IN PROGRESS: A major revision of *The Penguin Dictionary of Economics;* two long-term projects, an official history of the Rover Company, and a book on converting a barn into a house.

BANTOCK, Gavin (Marcus August) 1939-

PERSONAL: Born July 4, 1939, in Barnt Green, Worcestershire, England; son of Raymond (an examination coach) and Margaret (a composer; maiden name, More) Bantock. *Education:* Oxford University, B.A. (honors), 1963, Diploma of Education, 1964, M.A., 1968. *Agent:* Helen McGowan, Parwich Vicarage, Ashbourne, Derbyshire DE6 1QD, England. *Office:* Department of English, Reitaku University, Kashiwa-shi, Chiba-ken, Japan.

CAREER: Head of English department at independent secondary schools in England, 1964-69, at Barcote School, Faringdon, 1964-66, Birmingham Tutorial School, Birmingham, 1966-67, and Hydesville Tower School, Walsall, 1967-69; Reitaku University, Chiba-ken, Japan, lecturer in English, 1969—. *Member:* Society of Authors. *Awards, honors:* Richard Hillary Memorial Prize, 1964, for *Christ;* Alice Hunt-Bartlett, 1966, for *Christ;* Eric Gregory Award, 1969, for *Poems.*

WRITINGS—Poetry: *Christ: A Poem in Twenty-Six Parts,* Donald Parsons, 1965; *Juggernaut: Selected Poems,* Anvil Press Poetry, 1968; *A New Thing Breathing,* Anvil Press Poetry, 1969; *Poems: Contemporary British Poetry,* Swallow Press, 1971; *Eirenikou: A Peace Poem,* Anvil Press Poetry, 1972.

Collections of essays; all published by Kinseido (Tokyo): *Land of the Setting Sun,* 1973; *Disunited Kingdom,* 1974; *Twenty Eggs in One Basket,* 1975; *Nobler in the Mind,* 1976; *United Chaos of America,* 1977.

Poetry represented in anthologies including: *The Oxford Book of Twentieth-Century English Verse,* 1973, *The Faber Book of Twentieth-Century Verse,* 1975, *New Poems,* 1977. Also author of a play, "Frederick the Great: The Last of the Kings," performed by University of Keele players at Edinburgh Festival, 1968. Contributor of poems to periodicals in the United States and Great Britain.

WORK IN PROGRESS: Translating Anglo-Saxon and Middle English works; a novel, plays, and poems.

AVOCATIONAL INTERESTS: Travel (has traveled throughout all parts of the world), building stone walls, Japanese archery, gardening, mountain climbing, theater and film direction, music, playing pipe organ, badminton, reading poetry, drinking sake, Japanese festival dancing, dragons, Zen, the sea.

*   *   *

BARBER, Richard (William) 1941-

PERSONAL: Born October 30, 1941, in Dunmow, Essex, England; married Helen Tolson, 1970. *Education:* Corpus Christi College, Cambridge, M.A., 1967. *Home:* Stangrove Hall, Alderton, Woodbridge, England.

CAREER: Writer and publisher. Founder, Boydell Press, 1969. *Member:* Royal Society of Literature (fellow). *Awards, honors:* Somerset Maugham Award of Society of Authors, 1971, for *The Knight and Chivalry.*

WRITINGS: Arthur of Albion: An Introduction to the Arthurian Literature and Legends of England, Barnes & Noble, 1961; *Henry Plantagenet: A Biography,* Barrie & Rockliff, 1964, Roy, 1967; (with Francis E. Camps) *The Investigation of Murder,* M. Joseph, 1966.

Knighthood and Chivalry, Scribner, 1970, revised edition, Cardinal Publications, 1974 (published in England as *The Knight and Chivalry,* Longmans, Green, 1970, revised edition, Boydell Press, 1974); *Samuel Pepys Esq.,* G. Bell,

1970, University of California Press, 1971; (with Anne Riches) *Dictionary of Fabulous Beasts,* Macmillan, 1971, Walker & Co., 1972; *The Figure of Arthur,* Longman, 1973; *King Arthur,* Cardinal Publications, 1973 (published in England as *King Arthur in Legend and History,* Boydell Press, 1973); *Cookery and Recipes from Rome to the Renaissance,* Lane, 1974; *Aubrey's "Brief Lives,"* Foho Society, 1975; *A Strong Land and a Sturdy,* Seabury, 1976; *Companion Guide to Southern France,* Collins, 1977; *Tournaments,* Kestrel, 1978; *Edward Prince of Wales and Aquitaine,* Scribner, 1978; *Campaigns of the Black Prince,* Foho Society, 1978; *Circle of Gold,* BBC Publications, 1978; *Dictionary of Mythology,* Kestrel, in press.

WORK IN PROGRESS: Penguin Guide to Medieval Europe.

*   *   *

BARD, Harry 1906-1976

PERSONAL: Born December 24, 1906, in Baltimore, Md.; son of Rubin and Fannye (Rothenberg) Bard; married Eleanor Ruth Blumberg, August 19, 1934; children: Fane Bard Brenner, Robert. *Education:* Attended Baltimore City College and Towson State College; Johns Hopkins University, B.S., 1929; Columbia University, M.A., 1939; University of Maryland, Ed.D., 1951. *Home:* 5705 Rubin Ave., Baltimore, Md. 21215. *Office:* Community College of Baltimore, 2901 Liberty Heights Ave., Baltimore, Md. 21215.

CAREER: Public schools of Baltimore, Md., elementary and secondary school teacher, 1926-34, secondary school supervisor of social studies, 1934-45, assistant director of curriculum, 1945-55, director, 1955-59; Baltimore Junior College, Baltimore, dean, 1959-61; Community College of Baltimore, Baltimore, president, 1961-76. Guest professor at University of Nebraska, Syracuse University, New York University, and other colleges and universities. U.S. delegate to international UNESCO seminar, Lake Success, N.Y., 1948. Maryland Constitutional Convention Commission, chairman of legislative committee, 1966-67, convention delegate, 1967; member of board, Maryland Hospital Education and Research Foundation; chairman, Baltimore Mayor's Task Advisory Committee on Councilmanic Redistricting, 1970; trustee, Middle States Association of Colleges and Secondary Schools, 1972.

MEMBER: National Council for the Social Studies, Association for Supervision and Curriculum Development, American Association of Junior Colleges, American Council on Education, Maryland Council of Community College Presidents (chairman, 1968-70), Maryland Association of Junior Colleges (president, 1966), Maryland Association for Supervision and Curriculum Development (founder; past president), Maryland History Teachers Association (past president), Maryland Historical Society, United Nations Association of Maryland (president, 1957-59), Phi Delta Kappa. *Awards, honors:* Maryland State Senate citation, 1957, for writings on Maryland government; annual alumni award from Maryland State Teachers College, 1959; annual Service to Youth Award, and Youth and Government Medal, both from Baltimore Y.M.C.A., 1960; distinguished merit citation from National Conference of Christians and Jews, 1965; Afro-American Newspaper Award, 1968; Bard Library dedicated in his honor, 1970; Professor Harry Carman Award from Middle States Council for Social Studies, 1974. LL.D., Morgan State College, 1959, Loyola College, Baltimore, Md., 1965.

WRITINGS: Maryland: The State and Its Government,

Oxford Book Co., 1943; (with Harold R. Manakee) *Active Citizenship,* Winston, 1951; *Maryland Today,* Oxford Book Co., 1962; (with Willis D. Moreland and Thelma N. Cline) *Citizenship and Government in Modern America,* Holt, 1966; *Maryland State and Government: It's New Dynamics,* Cornell Maritime, 1974. Also author of *Maryland Government in Action.* Contributor of more than two hundred articles to magazines and professional journals.†

(Died October, 1976)

*   *   *

BARNABY, (Charles) Frank 1927-

PERSONAL: Born September 27, 1927, in Hampshire, England; son of Charles Hector (in Royal Air Force) and Lilian (Sainsbury) Barnaby; married Sandra Ann McKee (a graphic artist), November 2, 1963 (divorced); married Wendy Elizabeth Fields, December 19, 1972. *Education:* University of London, B.Sc., 1950, M.Sc., 1953, Ph.D., 1960, Diploma in International Relations, 1967. *Politics:* British Liberal Party. *Religion:* Agnostic. *Home and office:* San Kuai, Chilbolton, Stockbridge, Hampshire, England.

CAREER: United Kingdom Atomic Energy Authority, Aldermaston, England, member of scientific staff, 1951-57; Medical Research Council, London, England, member of senior scientific staff, 1959-68; Pugwash Conferences on Science and World Affairs, London, England, executive secretary, 1968-70; Stockholm International Peace Research Institute, Stockholm, Sweden, director, 1971—. *Member:* Institute of Strategic Studies, National Union of Journalists, Fabian Society.

WRITINGS: The Nuclear Future, Fabian Society, 1969; (editor) *Preventing the Spread of Nuclear Weapons,* Humanities, 1969; (editor with Anders Boserup) *Implications of Anti-Ballistic Missile Systems,* Humanities, 1969; *Radionuclides in Medicine,* Souvenir Press, 1970; *Man and the Atom: The Uses of Nuclear Energy,* Thames & Hudson, 1971, Funk, 1972. Contributor to scientific journals. Military technology correspondent, *New Scientist.*

WORK IN PROGRESS: Editing Geoffrey Chapman's "Science Series"; further writing on disarmament, arms control, military technology, and social consequences of science and technology.

*   *   *

BARNARD, (Virgil) John 1932-

PERSONAL: Born November 5, 1932, in Wichita, Kan.; son of Hugh B. and Ora (Burford) Barnard; married Joan Pennock (a college administrator), August 25, 1953; children: Bruce, Elizabeth, Stephen. *Education:* Oberlin College, B.A., 1955; University of Chicago, M.A., 1957, Ph.D., 1964. *Home:* 3248 Woodside Ct., Bloomfield Hills, Mich. 48013. *Office:* Department of History, Oakland University, Rochester, Mich. 48063.

CAREER: University of Chicago, Chicago, Ill., lecturer in history, 1957-58; Ohio State University, Columbus, instructor in American history, 1960-64; Oakland University, Rochester, Mich., assistant professor, 1964-67, associate professor, 1967-71, professor of American history, 1971—. Research fellow at Charles Warren Center for Studies in American History, Harvard University, 1967-69. *Member:* American Historical Association, Organization of American Historians.

WRITINGS: From Evangelicalism to Progressivism at Oberlin College: 1866-1917, Ohio State University Press,

1969; (associate editor; Robert H. Bremner and others, editors) *Children and Youth in America: A Documentary History,* Harvard University Press, Volume I, 1970, Volume II, 1971, Volume III, 1974. Contributor to *Dictionary of American Biography;* contributor of reviews to professional journals.

*   *   *

BARNES, John B(ertram) 1924-

PERSONAL: Born February 14, 1924, in Texarkana, Tex.; son of Ed C. and Gladys (Hamilton) Barnes; married Shirley Payne, July 23, 1948; children: Brandee, Becky. *Education:* University of Denver, B.A., 1949, M.A., 1950; University of Wyoming, Ed.D., 1955. *Home:* 414 Summit Ridge Rd., Boise, Idaho 83702. *Office:* Office of the President, Boise State University, Boise, Idaho. 83707.

CAREER: Northern Wyoming Community College, dean of adult education and community services, 1953-55; Southern Illinois University at Carbondale, assistant director of community development, 1955-57; Arizona State University, Tempe, professor of administration and director of educational research and school planning, 1957-62; Arizona Western College, Yuma, first president, 1962-67; Boise State University, Boise, Idaho, president, 1967—. Visiting summer professor at University of Michigan, 1963, Michigan State University, 1964, Northern Arizona University, 1965, and University of Arizona, 1966. Chairman of advisory council, Idaho State Department of Employment.

MEMBER: American Educational Research Association, Society for College and University Planning, American Association of University Professors, International Platform Association, Phi Delta Kappa, Rotary Club. *Awards, honors:* Distinguished Alumni Award, University of Denver, 1964.

WRITINGS: The Dynamics of Educational Research, Bureau of Educational Research, Arizona State University, 1958; *Educational Research for Classroom Teachers,* Putnam, 1960; (editor with Gerald R. Reed) *The Emerging State College: Seminar Dialogue,* Boise State College Press, 1970. Contributor of about forty articles to professional journals.†

*   *   *

BARNES, R(ichard) G(ordon) 1932-

PERSONAL: Born November 5, 1932, in San Bernardino, Calif.; son of Harold Maxwell and Kathleen (Hatcher) Barnes; married Catherine Maurice Beston, August 17, 1953; married second wife, Mary Recor Twiss (a teacher), May 23, 1972; children: (first marriage) Elizabeth, Harold, Henry, Jean Isabella; (second marriage) Sarah, Richard. *Education:* Pomona College, B.A. (magna cum laude), 1954; Harvard University Graduate School, A.M., 1955; Claremont Graduate School, Ph.D., 1958. *Politics:* "Enlightened left." *Religion:* "Orientalized Episcopal." *Home:* 434 West Seventh St., Claremont, Calif. 91711. *Office:* Department of English, Pomona College, Claremont, Calif. 91711.

CAREER: University of California, Riverside, instructor in English, 1958-59; Pomona College, Claremont, Calif., assistant professor, 1961-62, associate professor, 1962-66, professor of English and theater arts, 1966—. *Military service:* U.S. Naval Reserve, 1951-55. *Member:* Modern Language Association of America, Renaissance Society of America, Mediaeval Association of the Pacific, Canyon Cinema Cooperative, Phi Beta Kappa.

WRITINGS: Plays and Fugitive Essays 1963-1966, privately printed, 1966; *An Anglo-Saxon Gnomic Poem,* Grabhorn-Hoyem, 1968; (translator) *Three Spanish Sacramental Plays,* Chandler Publishing, 1969; *Episodes in Five Poetic Traditions,* Chandler Publishing, 1972; *The Complete Poems of R. G. Barnes,* Grabhorn-Hoyem, 1972; *Thirty-One Views of San Bernardino* (poems), Spectator Press, 1975; (editor) *The Psalms of David and Others,* translated by Arthur Golding, Arion, 1977. Also author of *A Lake on the Earth,* 1977. Author of plays, "Eighth Avatar," first produced in fall, 1967, "The Death of Buster Quinine," 1972, "Purple," 1973, "The Bradford and Barnes Poverty Circus," 1976, and "Melchizedek on Live," 1977.

Films: "Xing," Canyon, 1968; "Another Movie," Canyon, 1968; "Any Time at All," Claremont, 1970; "Two Poems of the T'ang Dynasty," Claremont, 1970.

WORK IN PROGRESS: Ninth Avatar; The House of the Rising Moon; Sacramental Fun House, with Stanley Crouch; *Music and Poetry of the Ars Nova.*

SIDELIGHTS: R. G. Barnes is competent in Spanish, French, Latin, Italian, Portuguese, and Quenki.

* * *

BARNETT, Richard C(hambers) 1932-

PERSONAL: Born April 27, 1932, in Davenport, Fla.; son of Jones Richard and Helen June (Chambers) Barnett; married Betty May Tribble (a teacher), October 18, 1957; children: Amy, Colin. *Education:* Wake Forest University, B.A., 1953; University of North Carolina at Chapel Hill, M.Ed., 1954, Ph.D., 1962; attended University of London, 1960-61. *Politics:* Democrat. *Religion:* Baptist. *Home:* 2130 Royall Dr., Winston-Salem, N.C. 27106. *Office:* Department of History, Wake Forest University, Winston-Salem, N.C. 27109.

CAREER: Gardner-Webb College, Boiling Springs, N.C., instructor in history, 1956-58; Wake Forest University, Winston-Salem, N.C., instructor, 1961-62, assistant professor, 1962-67, associate professor, 1967-76, professor of history, 1976—, chairman of department, 1968-75. President, Winston-Salem P.T.A. council, 1969-71; member of board of managers, North Carolina P.T.A., 1971—. *Military service:* U.S. Army, Counter Intelligence Corps, 1954-56. *Member:* American Historical Association, American Association of University Professors, Conference on British Studies, Carolinas Symposium on British Studies, Northamptonshire Record Society, Past and Present Society, Wachovia Historical Society.

WRITINGS: Place, Profit, and Power, University of North Carolina Press, 1969; (contributor) B. G. Gokhale, editor, *Images of India,* Popular Prakashan (India), 1971.

WORK IN PROGRESS: A biography of Thomas Cecil, first Earl of Exeter: 1542-1623.

* * *

BARNEY, LeRoy 1930-

PERSONAL: Born April 17, 1930, in Blackfoot, Idaho; son of Bryan Lee (a farmer) and Lillian Gertrude (Dixon) Barney; married Arla Marie Worlton, June 5, 1953; children: Vicki Marie, Sharyn Lee, Kevin LeRoy, Ronald Allen, Paula Sue. *Education:* Utah State University, B.S., 1956, M.S., 1959; University of Northern Colorado, Ed.D., 1965. *Religion:* Church of Jesus Christ of Latter-day Saints. *Home:* 240 Tilton Park Dr., DeKalb, Ill. 60115. *Office:* Department of Education, Northern Illinois University, DeKalb, Ill. 60115.

CAREER: Elementary teacher in Portland, Ore., 1956-57, and in Logan, Utah, 1957-64; Northern Illinois University, DeKalb, assistant professor, 1965-68, associate professor, 1968-72, professor of reading, 1972—. Visiting summer professor, Colorado State College, 1967. *Military service:* U.S. Air Force, 1948-53; served in Pacific; became staff sergeant; received five campaign ribbons. *Member:* International Reading Association, National Education Association (life member), National Council of Teachers of English, Phi Delta Kappa (life member).

WRITINGS: (Contributor and editorial assistant) *Building Reading Power,* Kendall/Hunt, 1969; (with Weldon Bradtmueller and Roberta Starkey) *Social Studies Education for Young Americans,* Kendall/Hunt, 1969; *The Process of Teaching Reading: Psychological, Sociological, Semantic,* Kendall/Hunt, 1971; *The Teaching Act Applied to Science,* Kendall/Hunt, 1971; (contributor) *Encyclopedia of Common Diseases,* Rodale Press, 1976; *Phonics: The F.I.R.S.T. Approach to Reading,* Weber Costello, 1977. Also author of film, "Dictionary for Beginners," Coronet Films, 1971. Contributor of eighty-four articles to education journals, and to *Salt Lake Tribune, Parents' Magazine,* and other publications.

WORK IN PROGRESS: Language Backgrounds for the Teacher of Reading (tentative title).

AVOCATIONAL INTERESTS: Mystery stories, adventure stories, and juveniles.

* * *

BARNEY, Natalie (Clifford) 1878(?)-1972

1878(?)—February 3, 1972; American translator, essayist, and part of the Paris literary circle which included Hemingway, Proust, and Joyce. Obituaries: *New York Times,* February 3, 1972; *Washington Post,* February 7, 1972.

* * *

BARR, (Chester) Alwyn (Jr.) 1938-

PERSONAL: Given name is pronounced All-win; born January 18, 1938, in Austin, Tex.; son of Chester Alwyn (a businessman) and Wilma (Matlock) Barr; married Nancy Dement, November 18, 1961; children: Juliana, Alicia. *Education:* University of Texas, B.A., 1959, M.A., 1961, Ph.D., 1966. *Politics:* Democrat. *Religion:* Methodist. *Home:* 2707 53rd St., Lubbock, Tex. 79413. *Office:* Department of History, Texas Tech University, Lubbock, Tex. 79409.

CAREER: Texas State Historical Association, Austin, Tex., editorial assistant, 1961-66; Purdue University, Lafayette, Ind., assistant professor of history, 1966-69; Texas Tech University, Lubbock, associate professor, 1969-75, professor of history, 1975—, director of ethnic studies program, 1970-75. *Military service:* National Guard, 1959-65; became staff sergeant. *Member:* American Historical Association, Organization of American Historians, Southern Historical Association, Texas State Historical Association (fellow), Phi Alpha Theta. *Awards, honors:* L. R. Bryan, Jr. Award from Texas Gulf Coast Historical Association, 1964, for *Polignac's Texas Brigade;* summer grants from American Association for State and Local History, 1967 and National Foundation on the Arts and the Humanities, 1969; Coral Horton Tullis Memorial Prize from Texas State Historical Association, 1971; American Council of Learned Societies grant, 1971-72.

WRITINGS: Polignac's Texas Brigade, Texas Gulf Coast

Historical Association, 1964; (editor) *Charles Porter's Account of the Confederate Attempt to Seize Arizona and New Mexico,* Pemberton, 1964; (author of introduction) J. P. Blessington, *The Campaigns of Walker's Texas Division,* Pemberton, 1968; (author of introduction) J. Mason Brewer, *Negro Legislators of Texas,* Pemberton, 1970; *Reconstruction to Reform: Texas Politics, 1876-1906,* University of Texas Press, 1971; *Black Texans,* Jenkins Publishing, 1974. Contributor to *Encyclopedia of World Biography, Handbook of Texas,* and *Encyclopedia of Southern History;* contributor of more than sixty articles and reviews to historical journals. Editorial assistant, *Southwestern Historical Quarterly,* 1961-66.

WORK IN PROGRESS: A biography of Roger Q. Mills; a study of black ghettoes in the Southwest.

SIDELIGHTS: Alwyn Barr told *CA:* "As my publications indicate, my academic career has progressed from a somewhat narrow interest in the Civil War to a broader interest in the South and then to the related field of Black history, especially in the period from 1850 to 1900. At this stage I am particularly interested in the history of lower class or 'anonymous Americans,' especially minority groups."

*   *   *

BARR, Doris W(ilson) 1923-

PERSONAL: Born July 31, 1923, in Vincennes, Ind.; daughter of Guy H. (a physician) and Mary (Ecker) Wilson; married John H. Barr (a real estate agent), January 9, 1950; children: David W., John Vance. *Education:* Indiana University, A.B., 1945; Northwestern University, M.S., 1949; University of Illinois, M.A., 1952, Ph.D., 1958. *Home:* 1209 Waverly, Champaign, Ill. *Office:* 2 Main St., Champaign, Ill.

CAREER: Parkland College, Champaign, Ill., instructor in English, 1967—.

WRITINGS: Effective English for the Career Student, Wadsworth, 1971; *Writing, Listening, Speaking for Business and Professional Students,* Wadsworth, 1972.

*   *   *

BARRAL, Mary-Rose 1925-

PERSONAL: Surname is pronounced bar-*rall;* born June 30, 1925, in Orbassano, Italy; came to United States in 1941, naturalized in 1954; daughter of Romuald J. (an entrepreneur) and Dossolina (Trossi) Barral. *Education:* Fordham University, B.S., 1956, M.A., 1958, Ph.D., 1963. *Politics:* Independent. *Religion:* Roman Catholic. *Residence:* East Orange, N.J. *Office:* Department of Philosophy, Seton Hall University, South Orange, N.J. 07079.

CAREER: Seton Hall University, South Orange, N.J., instructor, 1960-62, assistant professor, 1962-64, associate professor, 1964-67, professor of philosophy, 1967—, assistant chairman of department, 1963-68. *Member:* International Husserl Society, International Metaphysical Society, Metaphysical Society of America, American Catholic Philosophical Association, American Philosophical Association, American Association of University Professors, Research Society, Hegel Society of America (founding member).

WRITINGS: Merleau-Ponty: The Role of the Body-Subject, Duquesne University Press, 1965; *Progressive Neutralism: A Philosophical Aspect of American Education,* Nauwelaerts, 1970. Contributor to *Acts of the International Congress of Vienna, Journal* of the Interamerican Congress of Brazil, *Southern Journal of Philosophy, International*

Philosophical Quarterly, Arezzo Giornale de Metafisica (Italy), and *Review of Metaphysics.*

WORK IN PROGRESS: A book, tentatively entitled *Sartre on Love; Husserl's Phenomenology; Another Aspect of Anselm's Thought; Values in American Higher Education.*

SIDELIGHTS: Mary-Rose Barral told *CA:* "In writing I strive for clarity and directness; to be understood and to enlighten is the aim, usually achieved, as acknowledged by students and colleagues. To arrive at intersubjective relations with students and colleagues is the most satisfying experience sought. Cultivation of moral and aesthetic values is reflected in lectures and writings.... Extensive travel at home and abroad is usually rich in human exchanges at philosophy gatherings as well as at fortuitous meetings."

AVOCATIONAL INTERESTS: Ecology, youth, music, art, and dance.

*   *   *

BARRETT, Clifford L(eslie) 1894-1971

December 3, 1894—October 29, 1971; American educator and author of books on philosophy. Obituaries: *New York Times,* October 31, 1971.

*   *   *

BARRETT, James H(enry) 1906-

PERSONAL: Born September 12, 1906, in Fredonia, Kan.; son of William W. (a printer) and Anna (Dodd) Barrett; married Louise Miller, September 30, 1928; children: Beverly Ann Moore, Coralee Joyce (Mrs. Al Carter). *Education:* Municipal University of Wichita (now Wichita State University), B.Mus., 1938; Colorado State College of Education (now University of Northern Colorado), A.M., 1948, Ed.D., 1952. *Religion:* Congregationalist. *Home:* 1638 Lexington Ave., Pueblo, Colo. 81001.

CAREER: Municipal University of Wichita (now Wichita State University), Wichita, Kan., head of department of music education, 1938-42; Edinburgh (Tex.) public schools, vice-principal, 1942-45; Hutchinson (Kan.) public schools, head of music department, 1945-62; University of Southern Colorado, Pueblo, chairman of Division of Behavioral Sciences, beginning 1962. Member of advisory board, Colorado State Fair; member of senior citizens task force, Pueblo Chamber of Commerce; chairman of advisory committee, Salvation Army, Pueblo. *Member:* American Gerontological Society, American Geriatrics Society, Phi Delta Kappa, Phi Mu Alpha.

WRITINGS: Music in General Education, Foster Publishing, 1958; *Gerontological Psychology,* text edition, C. C Thomas, 1972. Also author of *Women and Their Banking,* Republic National Bank (Pueblo, Colorado).

WORK IN PROGRESS: Psychology of Music, and *The Retirement Syndrome.*

AVOCATIONAL INTERESTS: Philately, growing roses, fishing.

*   *   *

BARRETTO, Laurence Brevoort 1890-1971
(Larry Barretto)

May 30, 1890—December 30, 1971; American novelist, correspondent, and critic. Obituaries: *New York Times,* January 2, 1972.

BARRICK, Mac E(ugene) 1933-

PERSONAL: Born July 5, 1933, near Carlisle, Pa.; son of John Russell (a cabinetmaker) and Ella (Stover) Barrick; married Jean Moffitt, June 5, 1954; children: Melodi, Michele. *Education:* Dickinson College, A.B., 1955; University of Illinois, M.A., 1957; University of Pennsylvania, Ph.D., 1965. *Politics:* Republican. *Religion:* "Unorthodox." *Residence:* Carlisle, Pa. *Office:* Department of Spanish, Shippensburg State College, Shippensburg, Pa. 17257.

CAREER: Lycoming College, Williamsport, Pa., instructor, 1961-62, assistant professor of Spanish, 1962-64; Dickinson College, Carlisle, Pa., assistant professor of Spanish, 1964-68; Shippensburg State College, Shippensburg, Pa., associate professor of Spanish, 1968—. Visiting lecturer, University of Delaware, 1961, Villanova University, 1967, 1969. *Member:* Modern Language Association of America, Mediaeval Academy of America, Renaissance Society of America, American Folklore Society, American Association of Teachers of Spanish and Portuguese, Pennsylvania Folklore Society (president, 1967-68), Pennsylvania State Modern Language Association (business manager, 1964-67).

WRITINGS: (Editor) Gaspar Gomez de Toledo, *Tercera Parte de Celestina: A Critical Edition,* University of Pennsylvania Press, 1973. Contributor to *Keystone Folklore Quarterly, Pennsylvania Folklife, Romance Notes, Modern Language Notes,* and other publications. Associate editor, *Abstracts of Folklore Studies,* 1968-73.

WORK IN PROGRESS: What the Old Folks Said: An Anthology of Cumberland County Folklore; Lewis the Robber: A Pennsylvania Folk Hero in Life and Legend; An Index of Pennsylvania Folk Beliefs and Superstitions.

* * *

BARRY, James Donald 1926-

PERSONAL: Born February 28, 1926, in Oak Park, Ill.; son of Frank J. (employee of an electrical company) and Irene (Carrigan) Barry; married Mary Anne Byrne (a social worker), March 31, 1951; children: John, Anne, Patrick, Brian, Michael. *Education:* Loyola University, Chicago, Ill., student, 1943-44, 1946-48, Ph.B., 1948, M.A., 1951; Northwestern University, Ph.D., 1955. *Religion:* Roman Catholic. *Home:* 6739 Newgard Ave., Chicago, Ill. 60626. *Office:* Department of English, Loyola University, 820 North Michigan Ave., Chicago, Ill. 60611.

CAREER: Loyola University, Chicago, Ill., instructor, 1953-55, assistant professor, 1955-61, associate professor, 1961-66, professor of English, 1966—, chairman of department, 1973-76, associate vice-president for academic programs, 1976—. Rogers Park Community Council, president, 1966-68, member of board of directors, 1970-75; Allied North Side Community Organizations, chairman, 1971-73, member of governing body, 1973—. *Military service:* U.S. Army, Infantry, 1944-46; served in European theater; received Combat Infantryman's Badge. *Member:* College English Association, Conference on English Education, Modern Language Association of America, National Council of Teachers of English, American Association for Higher Education, Society for College and University Planning, Conference on College Composition and Communication (associate chairman, 1971-72; chairman, 1972-73), American Association of University Professors, Dickens Society.

WRITINGS: (Contributor) Lionel Stevenson, editor, *Victorian Fiction: A Guide to Research,* Harvard University Press, 1964; (editor with William McDonald, Jr., and contributor) *Language into Literature,* Science Research Associates, 1965; (editor) *The Future of the English Curriculum,* Modern Language Association, 1967; (contributor) George H. Furd, editor, *Victorian Fiction: A Second Guide to Research,* Modern Language Association, 1977. Contributor to professional journals.

WORK IN PROGRESS: Studies on Charles Dickens.

* * *

BARTELL, Ernest 1932-

PERSONAL: Born January 22, 1932, in Chicago, Ill.; son of Joseph L. and Anna M. (Arturi) Bartell. *Education:* University of Notre Dame, Ph.D., 1953; University of Chicago, A.M., 1954; Holy Cross College, Washington, D.C., M.A., 1961; Princeton University, Ph.D., 1966. *Office:* Fund for the Improvement of Postsecondary Education, U.S. Department of Health, Education and Welfare, Washington, D.C. 20202.

CAREER: Entered Order of Congregatio a Sancta Cruce (Fathers and Brothers of Holy Cross), 1955; ordained Roman Catholic priest, 1961. University of Notre Dame, Notre Dame, Ind., instructor, 1961-62, assistant professor, 1966-68, associate professor of economics and chairman of department, 1968-71, Center for the Study of Man in Contemporary Society, associate director, 1968-69, director, 1969-71; Princeton University, Princeton, N.J., instructor in economics, 1965-66; Stonehill College, North Easton, Mass., president, 1971-77; U.S. Department of Health, Education and Welfare, Washington, D.C., director of Fund for the Improvement of Postsecondary Education, 1977—. Director, Economic Analysis of Nonpublic Education in the United States, President's Commission on School Finance, 1971; participant in other projects sponsored by foreign, federal, state, and local agencies. Visiting lecturer and consultant, Peace Corps Training Program, Arecibo, Puerto Rico, 1965-69. Economic consultant, Notre Dame Office for Education Research, 1969-71, Massachusetts Legislative Committee for Nonpublic Schools, 1970, and New York Governor's Commission for Elementary and Secondary Education, 1970-71. Member of federal and state educational committees. Participant in various professional and educational conferences. Member of board of directors, King's College; member of board of trustees, Emmanuel College; member of board of trustees and board of fellows, University of Notre Dame; member of board and mentor, Association of Governing Boards of Universities and Colleges. *Member:* American Economic Association, Association for Social Economics, Society for Values in Higher Education, Catholic Economic Association, American Association for Higher Education, Midwest Council of the Association for Latin American Studies.

WRITINGS: National Income Statistics: Dominica, 1961-64, University of the West Indies, 1965; (contributor) S. Shapiro, editor, *Man and Integration in Latin America,* University of Notre Dame Press, 1967; *Mutual Aid,* American Institute for Free Labor Development, 1967; *Economy and the People,* American Institute for Free Labor Development, 1967; *Costs and Benefits of Catholic Elementary and Secondary Schools,* University of Notre Dame, 1969; (with A. Corazzini and others) *Higher Education in the Boston Metropolitan Area,* Board of Higher Education (Boston), 1969; (with K. Brown and others) *Catholic Education in St. Louis: Allocation and Distribution of Financial and Human Resources,* University of Notre Dame, 1970; *Metropolitan*

II: An Econometric Study of Potential and Realized Demand for Higher Education in the Boston Metropolitan Area, State of Massachusetts, 1970; (with others) *Economic Problems of Nonpublic Schools,* Office for Education Research, University of Notre Dame, 1971. Contributor to *Assignment Children* (a UNICEF publication), *Current History, America, Notre Dame Journal of Education, Review of Social Economy,* and other publications.

* * *

BARTEN, Harvey H(arold) 1933-

PERSONAL: Born July 7, 1933, in Newark, N.J.; son of Alexander (a businessman) and Tanya (Rich) Barten; married Sybil Speier (a psychologist), August 28, 1960; children: Rebecca Ann, Julie Karina. *Education:* Harvard University, A.B., 1955, M.D., 1959. *Office:* 12 Overhill Rd., Scarsdale, N.Y. 10583.

CAREER: Private practice of psychiatry in Scarsdale, N.Y., 1966—; Guidance Center of New Rochelle, New Rochelle, N.Y., medical director, 1969-77; Cornell University, Medical College, New York, N.Y., clinical associate professor of psychiatry, 1972—. Chairman, New Rochelle Mental Health Council. *Military service:* U.S. Air Force, 1963-65; served as captain. *Member:* American Psychiatric Association (fellow), Westchester Medical Society.

WRITINGS: (Editor with Leopold Bellak) *Progress in Community Mental Health,* Grune & Stratton, Volume I, 1969, Volume II, 1972, Volume III, 1975; (editor) *Brief Therapies,* Behavioral Publications, 1971; (with wife, Sybil Barten) *Children and Their Parents in Brief Therapy,* Behavioral Publications, 1972.

* * *

BARTLETT, Elsa Jaffe 1935-
(Elsa Jaffe)

PERSONAL: Born July 20, 1935, in Pittsburgh, Pa.; daughter of Aaron M. (a businessman) and Hortense (Greenberg) Jaffe; married Jonathan Bartlett (a book editor), June 26, 1968; children: Noah Michael. *Education:* Attended Smith College, 1953-55; Columbia University, B.F.A., 1957; Bank Street College of Education, M.S., 1966; Harvard University, Ed.D., 1974. *Office:* Bartlett Associates, 131 East 19th St., New York, N.Y. 10003.

CAREER: Teacher in New York City public schools, 1961-63; Bank Street College of Education, New York City, writer in publications department, 1963-65, and in Educational Resources Center, 1965-66; Bartlett Associates (educational consultants), New York City, director, 1967—. Psychologist, Rockefeller University, 1972—. *Member:* International Reading Association, American Educational Research Association, Society for Research in Child Development, Pi Lambda Theta.

WRITINGS: Adventures in Living: A Preschool Learning Program, Western Publishing, 1970; *Encounters: Reality in Reading and Language Series,* Cambridge Book Co., 1971; *Sesame Street/Electric Company Reading Program,* Addison-Wesley, 1973.

Under name Elsa Jaffe: (With Virginia Brown and others) *Skyline Series,* Books A-C, Webster, 1965. Also author of teacher's guides to *Bank Street Readers,* Macmillan, 1965-66.

* * *

BASKETTE, Floyd K(enneth) 1910-

PERSONAL: Born July 2, 1910, in Chama, N.M.; son of Alexander H. (an engineer) and Pella (Persson) Baskette; married Carol G. Albright (a teacher), June 7, 1934; children: Kathleen Karen (Mrs. Kent Mollohan), Floyd Kenneth, Jr. *Education:* University of Missouri, B.J., 1932, M.A., 1936; attended University of Wisconsin, 1938-39, 1944-45. *Politics:* Democrat. *Religion:* Protestant. *Home:* 2735 Seventh St., Boulder, Colo. 80302. *Office:* School of Journalism, University of Colorado, Boulder, Colo. 80302.

CAREER: Adams State College, Alamosa, Colo., assistant professor of social studies, 1932-38; University of Wisconsin—Madison, assistant professor of journalism, 1938-39; Syracuse University, Syracuse, N.Y., assistant professor of journalism, 1940-41; Emory University, Atlanta, Ga., associate professor of journalism, 1941-50; University of Colorado, Boulder, associate professor, 1950-52, professor of journalism, 1952-77, professor emeritus, 1977—. Lecturer, University of Wisconsin, 1944-45; director of journalism training program (under Fulbright grants) at Hislop College, Nagpur, 1954-55, and University of Rangoon, 1955-56. Part-time copywriter, *Atlanta Constitution,* 1941-50, and *Denver Post,* summers, 1952-53; copy editor, *Honolulu Advertiser,* summers, 1956-58. Director of Methodist Writers' Workshop. *Member:* Association for Education in Journalism, Sigma Delta Chi, Kappa Tau Alpha.

WRITINGS: Colorado Pronunciation Guide, Pruett, 1943; (with George C. Bastien and Leland D. Case) *Editing the Day's News,* 4th edition (Baskette was not associated with earlier editions), Macmillan, 1956; (with Jack Z. Sissors) *The Art of Editing,* Macmillan, 1971, 2nd edition, 1977. Also author of materials for Methodist Publishing House; contributor to journalism and literary periodicals. Associate editor, *Journalism Quarterly,* 1945-50.

* * *

BASSETT, Edward Eryl 1940-

PERSONAL: Born September 16, 1940, in Ruabon, Denbigh, Wales; son of Alun Charles (an educational administrator) and Ada (Prince) Bassett; married Kathleen Mary Rait Brown, September 4, 1966; children: Ian Gareth, Rachel Mary. *Education:* Oxford University, B.A., 1962; University of Wales, M.Sc., 1964, Ph.D., 1969. *Home:* 7 Dameham Close, Canterbury, Kent, England. *Office:* Mathematical Institute, University of Kent, Canterbury, Kent, England.

CAREER: University College of Wales, Aberystwyth, assistant lecturer in statistics, 1965-66; Imperial College, London, England, lecturer in statistics, 1966-70; University of Kent, Canterbury, England, lecturer in statistics, 1970—. *Member:* Royal Statistical Society (fellow).

WRITINGS: (With D. J. Bartholomew) *Let's Look at the Figures,* Penguin, 1971.

WORK IN PROGRESS: Research on statistical inference and on applications of statistics to the social sciences.

* * *

BATEY, Richard (Alexander) 1933-

PERSONAL: Born January 19, 1933, in Johnson City, Tenn.; son of Jackson Smith, Jr. and Jessie (Alexander) Batey; married Carolyn Kay Turrentine (a high school teacher), August 21, 1953; children: Evelyn Evon, Richard Edgar, Helen Kay. *Education:* David Lipscomb College, B.A., 1955; Vanderbilt University, B.D., 1958, Ph.D., 1961. *Home:* 4327 Rhodes Ave., Memphis, Tenn. 38111. *Office:* Department of Religion, Southwestern at Memphis, 2000 North Pkwy., Memphis, Tenn. 38112.

CAREER: Harding Graduate School of Religion, Memphis, Tenn., assistant professor of New Testament, 1960-65; Southwestern at Memphis, Memphis, Tenn., assistant professor, 1965-68, associate professor, 1968-72, W. J. Millard Professor of Religion, 1972—. *Member:* Society of Biblical Literature, American Academy of Religion, Studiorum Novi Testamenti Societas. *Awards, honors:* Fulbright research scholar at University of Tuebingen, 1963-64.

WRITINGS: Paul's Letter to the Romans, R. B. Sweet, 1969; (editor) *New Testament Issues,* Harper, 1970; *New Testament Nuptial Imagery,* E. J. Brill, 1971; *Jesus and the Poor,* Harper, 1972; *Thank God, I'm O.K.,* Abingdon, 1976.

AVOCATIONAL INTERESTS: Racquetball.

*   *   *

BATSON, George (Donald)   1918-1977

PERSONAL: Born February 13, 1918, in Brooklyn, N.Y.; son of Donald A. and Vera Melvin (Freystadt) Batson. *Education:* Attended high schools in Brooklyn, N.Y. and Summit, N.J. *Home:* 245 East 21st St., New York, N.Y. 10010; and Saltare, Fire Island, N.Y. 11782.

CAREER: Writer for stage and television. *Military service:* U.S. Army, Signal Corps, 1942-46. *Member:* Dramatists Guild.

WRITINGS—Plays; all published by Samuel French (New York), except as indicated: *Every Family Has One* (three-act comedy), 1942; *The Doctor Has a Daughter* (three-act comedy), 1943; *Ramshackle Inn* (three-act comedy; first produced on Broadway at Royale Theatre, January 4, 1944), Dramatists Play Service, 1944; *Hangman's Noose* (three-act mystery), 1947; (with John Kirkland) *Strange Boarders* (three-act comedy; first produced as "A Dangerous Woman" in Detroit at Lafayette Theatre, 1947), Dramatists Play Service, 1947; *A Broom for the Bride* (three-act comedy), 1948; *Dangerous Nan McGrew* (three-act comedy), 1949; *Rehearsal for Death* (three-act comedy), 1949; *Terrible Turners* (three-act comedy), 1950; *Miss Private Eye* (three-act comedy), 1951; *I Found April* (three-act comedy; first produced as "A Date with April" on Broadway at Royale Theatre, April 15, 1953), 1957; (with Donn Harman) *Her Majesty, Miss Jones* (three-act comedy), Dramatists Play Service, 1959; *Murder on Arrival* (three-act mystery; first produced on West End at Westminster Theatre, June 19, 1954), 1960; *Design for Murder* (three-act mystery; first produced as "Celia" in New Hope, Pa. at Bucks County Playhouse, 1954; produced as "House on the Rocks" in Harrisburg, Pa. at Festival Theatre, June, 1958), 1960; *Two Faces of Murder* (first produced in Bournemouth, England at Lea's Pavillion Theatre, 1961), Samuel French (London), 1961; *The House on the Cliff: A Mystery Comedy* (three-act comedy), 1967.

Unpublished plays: "Treat Her Gently," first produced in Dallas at Majestic Theatre, 1941, produced as "Punch and Julia" in Washington, D.C. at National Theatre, May, 1942; "Magnolia Alley," first produced in Skowhegan, Me., 1948, produced on Broadway at Mansfield Theatre (now Brooks Atkinson Theatre), April 18, 1949; "Murder at Midnight," first produced in Frinton, England at By the Sea Theatre, 1961; "By Whose Hand," first produced in Bournemouth, England at Lea's Pavillion Theatre, 1962; "Woman on the Moor," first produced in England in repertory, 1971. Also author of scripts for television dramas.

AVOCATIONAL INTERESTS: Travel, reading.†

(Died July 25, 1977)

BATTEN, James William   1919-

PERSONAL: Born August 5, 1919, in Goldsboro, N.C.; son of Albert LeMay and Lydia Annie (Davis) Batten; married Sara Magdalene Storey, June 1, 1945. *Education:* University of North Carolina, A.B., 1940, M.A., 1947, Ed.D., 1960; additional graduate study at Columbia University, 1942, and University of California, Berkeley. *Politics:* Democrat. *Religion:* Baptist. *Office:* School of Education, East Carolina University, Greenville, N.C. 27834.

CAREER: High school science teacher in Kenly, N.C., 1940-41, and in Princeton, N.C., 1947-50; high school principal in Micro, N.C., 1950-58; Morehead Planetarium, Chapel Hill, N.C., narrator in celestial mechanics, 1958-60; East Carolina University, Greenville, N.C., associate professor, 1960-62, professor of education, 1962—, assistant dean of School of Education, 1965—, chairman of department of secondary education, 1967—. Teacher of science, Wilmington Junior College, 1946-47. Trainer of seven Mercury astronauts in celestial recognition, National Aeronautics and Space Administration, 1960; lecturer on earth and space science, 1960-68. Consulting editor, Macmillan Publishing Co. *Military service:* U.S. Navy, 1941-46. U.S. Naval Reserve, 1946-61; became lieutenant commander.

MEMBER: National Education Association, National Society for the Study of Education, Association for Supervision and Curriculum Development, National Association of Secondary School Principals, National Science Teachers Association, American Association of Teachers of French, American Educational Research Association, American Association of University Professors, Horace Mann League, North Carolina Association of Educators, North Carolina Literary and Historical Association, Phi Delta Kappa, Kappa Delta Pi.

WRITINGS: Our Neighbors in Space, Morehead Planetarium, 1962, revised edition, 1969; *Research as a Tool for Understanding,* W. C. Brown, 1965; *Stars, Atoms, God,* Colonial Press (Chapel Hill), 1968; *Soils: Their Nature, Classification, and Uses,* University of Alabama Press, 1970, revised edition, 1977; *Understanding Research,* Educational Publications, 1971; *Rumblings of a Rolling Stone,* Morgan Printers, 1974; *Human Procedures in Educational Research,* Morgan Printers, 1976. Contributor to scholarly journals and to magazines. Consulting editor, *New Standard Encyclopedia.*

SIDELIGHTS: James Batten has traveled in Canada, Central America, Europe, Africa, the South Pacific, Japan, and the Philippines. *Avocational interests:* Small boat sailing, gardening.

*   *   *

BAUDY, Nicolas   1904(?)-1971

1904(?)—September 26, 1971; Hungarian-born French novelist and journalist. Obituaries: *L'Express,* October 4-10, 1971.

*   *   *

BAUER, Royal D(aniel) M(ichael)   1889-

PERSONAL: Born October 25, 1889, in Union, Mo.; son of Michael William (a clerk) and Rebecca Hannah (Witthaus) Bauer; married Helen Elizabeth Clark, June 30, 1921; children: Elizabeth Acheson (Mrs. Edward W. Kaminski, Jr.), Edward Clark, Mary Jocelyn (Mrs. James M. Kyle III). *Education:* University of Missouri, B.S., 1923; Northwestern University, M.B.A., 1935. *Politics:* Republican.

Religion: Methodist. *Home:* 3848 Duncan Pl., Palo Alto, Calif. 94306.

CAREER: Certified public accountant; employed as clerk, bookkeeper, and staff accountant, 1906-17, 1920-29; University of Missouri, Columbia, instructor, 1929, assistant professor, 1929-31, associate professor, 1931-41, professor of accounting, 1941-60, professor emeritus, 1960—, chairman of department of accounting and statistics, 1941-56, auditor of the university, 1944-45. Member, Missouri State Board of Accountancy, 1939-42. Member of church board of stewards, intermittently, 1924-45, church financial secretary, 1924-49; member of board of directors, Y.M.C.A., Columbia, Mo., 1932-40. *Military service:* U.S. Navy, 1917-19. *Member:* American Institute of Certified Public Accountants, American Accounting Association, Missouri Society of Certified Public Accountants, California Society of Certified Public Accountants, State Historical Society of Missoui, Missouri Historical Society, Beta Gamma Sigma (president of local chapter, 1931-60), Phi Chi Theta (honorary), Delta Sigma Pi (member of Nation grand council, 1945-57). *Awards, honors:* Citation of merit, University of Missouri Alumni Association, 1962.

WRITINGS: (With Paul H. Darby) *Elementary Accounting,* Barnes & Noble, 1942, 4th edition, 1972; (with Roy T. Culey) *Auditing,* South-Western, 1953, 2nd edition (with Joseph A. Silvoso), 1965. Author and co-author of pamphlets on individual income taxes, published by University of Missouri, 1945-56.

*   *   *

BAUGHMAN, Ernest W(arren) 1916-

PERSONAL: Surname is pronounced *bauff*-min; born September 10, 1916, in Manson, Iowa; son of Alpha E. and Martha (Zook) Baughman; married Frances Jensen, June 23, 1940. *Education:* Ball State Teachers College (now Ball State University), A.B., 1938; University of Chicago, M.A., 1939; Indiana University, Ph.D., 1953. *Politics:* Democrat. *Home:* 616 Vassar Drive N.E., Albuquerque, N.M. 87106. *Office:* Department of English, University of New Mexico, Albuquerque, N.M. 87106.

CAREER: Wilson Junior High School, Muncie, Ind., English teacher, 1939-42; Indiana University, Bloomington, instructor in English, 1946-48; University of New Mexico, Albuquerque, instructor, 1949-51, assistant professor, 1951-56, associate professor, 1956-64, professor of English, 1964—. Panelist, New York History Association seminars, 1953; special lecturer, Folklore Institute of America, 1958. Democratic party precinct official, 1963-70. *Member:* Modern Language Association of America, American Folklore Society (fellow; member of executive board, 1968-71), American Association of University Professors, New Mexico Folklore Society (vice-president, 1971-72; president, 1972-73).

WRITINGS: (Contributor) B. A. Botkin, editor, *A Treasury of American Folklore,* Crown, 1944; (author of notes) Vance Randolph, editor, *Sticks in the Knapsack,* Columbia University Press, 1958; *Type and Motif-Index of the Folktales of England and North America,* Mouton, 1966. Contributor to *New England Quarterly, Hoosier Folklore Bulletin, English Journal, New Mexico Folklore Record,* and other publications. Editor, *Hoosier Folklore Bulletin,* 1945, *Hoosier Folklore,* 1946-48, and *New Mexico Folklore Record,* 1952-56, 1974-77.

WORK IN PROGRESS: Hawthorne's literary devices; characteristics of American folklore; interrelation of church and civil authority in the Massachusetts Bay Colony.

BAUMANN, Carol Edler 1932-

PERSONAL: Born August 11, 1932, in Plymouth, Wis.; daughter of Clarence Henry (a salesman) and Beulah (Weinhold) Edler; married Richard J. Baumann (a store owner), February 28, 1959; children: Dawn, Wendy. *Education:* University of Wisconsin, B.A., 1954; University of London, Ph.D., 1957. *Politics:* Democrat. *Religion:* Lutheran. *Home:* 5109 North Woodburn St., Milwaukee, Wis. 53217. *Office:* Institute of World Affairs, University of Wisconsin, Milwaukee, Wis. 53201.

CAREER: University of Wisconsin—Madison, instructor in political science, 1957-61, project associate, National Security Studies Group, 1958-61; University of Wisconsin—Milwaukee, lecturer, 1961-62, assistant professor, 1962-67, associate professor, 1967-72, professor of political science, 1972—, director, Institute of World Affairs, University Extension, 1964—. United Nations Association of the U.S.A., Wisconsin Division vice-chairman, 1971—, member of national board of directors, 1977—. Member of board of directors, World Affairs Council of Milwaukee, 1964-74, and International Institute of Milwaukee County, 1964—; Democratic candidate for Congress, Ninth Congressional District, 1968. *Member:* American Political Science Association, International Studies Association, National Council of Community World Affairs Organizations (vice-president), Society for Citizen Education in World Affairs (vice-president), Midwest Conference of Political Scientists, Wisconsin Political Science Association, Phi Beta Kappa, Phi Kappa Phi, Phi Eta Sigma. *Awards, honors:* Fulbright fellowship, 1954-55; Honorary Woodrow Wilson fellow, 1954-55; Marshall Scholar, 1954-57.

WRITINGS: Political Co-operation in NATO (monograph), National Security Studies Group, University of Wisconsin, 1960; *Western Europe: What Path to Integration?,* Heath, 1967; (with Kay Wahner) *Great Decisions-1968,* Institute of World Affairs (Milwaukee), 1969; *The Diplomatic Kidnappings: A Revolutionary Tactic of Urban Terrorism,* Nijhoff (The Hague), 1973. Also author of study guides for political science courses. Contributor of articles and reviews to *Political Science Quarterly, Transactions* of Wisconsin Academy of Sciences, Arts and Letters, *Wiscouncilor, Adult Leadership,* and *Milwaukee Journal.*

WORK IN PROGRESS: A book on U.S.-West European relations, with Jean Rey.

*   *   *

BAXTER, Batsell Barrett 1916-

PERSONAL: Born September 23, 1916, in Cordell, Okla.; son of Batsell (a college president) and Fay (Scott) Baxter; married Wanda Roberts, December 22, 1938; children: Scott, Alan, John. *Education:* Abilene Christian College, B.A., 1937; University of Southern California, M.A., 1938, Ph.D., 1944; Vanderbilt University, B.D., 1957. *Home:* 3703 Mayfair Ave., Nashville, Tenn. 37215. *Office:* Department of Religion, David Lipscomb College, Nashville, Tenn. 37203.

CAREER: Minister of Church of Christ, 1936; Pepperdine College (now University), Los Angeles, Calif., instructor, 1938-43, professor of speech, 1944-45; David Lipscomb College, Nashville, Tenn., professor of speech and head of department, 1945-56, chairman of Bible department, 1956—. Speaker, "Herald of Truth" radio and television program, 1961—. Lecturer and preacher in Japan, Hawaii, and Korea, 1957; headed workers establishing new Church of Christ congregations in London, England, 1961, 1963. *Member:*

Speech Association of America (member of executive council), Southern Speech Association (former president), Tennessee Speech Association (former president), Pi Delta Kappa, Pi Kappa Delta. *Awards, honors:* Named Alumnus of the Year by Alumni Association of Abilene Christian College, 1961.

WRITINGS: Heart of Yale Lectures, Macmillan, 1947; (with Norvel Young) *Preachers of Today,* Gospel Advocate, Volume I, 1952, Volume II, 1959, Volume III, 1964, Volume IV, 1970; *Speaking for the Master,* Macmillan, 1954; *If I Be Lifted Up,* Gospel Advocate, 1956; *Great Preachers of Today,* Volume I, Biblical Research Society, 1960; (with Young) *Churches of Today,* Gospel Advocate, Volume I, 1960, Volume II, 1969; *Making God's Way Our Way,* Gospel Advocate, 1964; *As a Man Thinketh in His Heart,* Washington Industries, 1966; *I Believe Because. . .,* Baker Book, 1971; *America, It's Not Too Late,* Baker Book, 1974; *When Life Tumbles In,* Baker Book, 1974.

* * *

BAY, Christian 1921-

PERSONAL: Born April 19, 1921, in Oslo, Norway; son of Jens and Ruth (Amneus) Bay; married Juanita Evelyn Boozer (a health services administrator), April 17, 1959; children: Marit, Mia, Helge. *Education:* University of Oslo, LL.B., 1943, Ph.D., 1959. *Politics:* Radical. *Religion:* Agnostic. *Home:* 3 Austin Crescent, Toronto, Ontario, Canada. *Office:* Department of Political Economy, University of Toronto, Toronto, Ontario, Canada.

CAREER: Michigan State University, East Lansing, Mich., assistant professor of political science, 1957; University of California, Berkeley, assistant professor of speech, 1957-62; Stanford University, Stanford, Calif, research associate and lecturer, 1961-66; University of Alberta, Edmonton, professor of political science, 1966-72; University of Toronto, Toronto, Ontario, professor of political economy, 1972—. *Member:* American Political Science Association (member of council, 1971-73), Caucus for a New Political Science (chairman, 1971-72). *Awards, honors:* Center for Advanced Studies, Stanford University, fellow, 1954-55; Woodrow Wilson Award of American Political Science Association, 1959, for *Structure of Freedom.*

WRITINGS: Structure of Freedom, Stanford University Press, 1958, with new preface, Atheneum, 1965; *Naar lov maa brytes,* Pax (Oslo), 1968.

* * *

BAYER, William 1939-
(Leonie St. John, a joint pseudonym)

PERSONAL: Surname is pronounced *buy*-er; born February 20, 1939, in Cleveland, Ohio; son of Lee G. (a lawyer) and Eleanor (a writer; maiden name, Perry) Bayer. *Education:* Harvard University, B.A. (cum laude), 1960. *Agent:* Arlene Donovan, International Creative Management, 40 West 57th St., New York, N.Y. 10019.

CAREER: United States Information Agency, Washington, D.C. and New York, N.Y., staff film maker, 1963-68; freelance writer and film maker, 1968—. *Awards, honors:* American Film Institute, grant for screenplay, 1968, grant for film production, 1969; Golden Hugo Award, Chicago International Film Festival, 1970, for ''Mississippi Summer''; National Endowment for the Arts research grant, 1973.

WRITINGS: (With Nancy Harmon, under joint pseudonym Leonie St. John) *Love with a Harvard Accent* (novel), Ace

Books, 1962; *In Search of a Hero* (novel), World Publishing, 1966; *Breaking Through, Selling Out, Dropping Dead* (nonfiction), Macmillan, 1971; *The Great Movies* (nonfiction), Grosset, 1973; *Stardust* (novel), Dell, 1974; *Visions of Isabelle* (novel), Delacorte, 1976; *Tangier* (novel), Dutton, 1978.

Screenplays: ''Rice,'' U.S. Information Agency, 1967; ''Processions,'' U.S. Information Agency, 1968; ''In Touch,'' United Artists, 1970; (with Brian de Palma) ''Red Ice,'' Filmways, 1970; ''Mississippi Summer,'' Limited Partnership Co., 1970. Contributor to *New York Times, New York,* and other publications.

WORK IN PROGRESS: A novel of erotic terror set in New York.

SIDELIGHTS: William Bayer writes: ''From 1972 through 1976 I lived in North Africa where I wrote two books: a fictionalized biography of the Saharan adventuress, Isabelle Eberhardt (*Visions of Isabelle*), and my latest novel, *Tangier,* which deals with expatriate decadence in a politically enflamed milieu. Now I am done writing about bizarre personages in exotic locales, and with living an expatriate author's life. Recently I moved back to the United States with the intention of devoting myself to the craft of the commercial novel—having told myself for years that I could write a best-seller if I put my mind to it, I've decided, finally, to find out if that's true.''

* * *

BAYLEY, Charles C(alvert) 1907-

PERSONAL: Born March 5, 1907, in Congleton, England; son of Harry (a foreman) and Hannah (Calvert) Bayley; married Ethel Mary Wooliscroft, September 11, 1936; children: Ann, Susan. *Education:* University of Manchester, B.A., 1928, M.A., 1929; University of Chicago, Ph.D., 1937. *Religion:* Anglican. *Home:* 3425 Stanley, Apt. 303, Montreal, Quebec, Canada. *Office:* Department of History, McGill University, Montreal, Quebec, Canada.

CAREER: University of Toronto, Toronto, Ontario, lecturer in history, 1931-32; Colorado College, Colorado Springs, assistant professor of history, 1933-34; McGill University, Montreal, Quebec, lecturer, 1935-40, assistant professor, 1940-48, associate professor, 1949-58, professor of history, 1958—, chairman of the department, 1961—. *Member:* Royal Society of Canada (elected fellow, 1961), American Historical Association. *Awards, honors:* Guggenheim fellowship, 1948-49; Senior Canada Council fellowship, 1954-55; Killam fellowship, 1971-72.

WRITINGS: (With F. Chambers and C. Grant) *This Age of Conflict: A Contemporary World History, 1914-1943,* Harcourt, 1949; *The Formation of the German College of Electors in the Mid-Thirteenth Century,* University of Toronto Press, 1949; *War and Society in Renaissance Florence: The De Militia of Leonardo Bruni,* University of Toronto Press, 1961; *Mercenaries for the Crimea: The German, Swiss and Italian Legions in British Service, 1854-1856,* McGill-Queen's University Press, 1976.

WORK IN PROGRESS: The Condottieri of the Early Renaissance.

SIDELIGHTS: Charles Bayley's main vocational interest is the impact of war on society and the inter-relationship between the two.

* * *

BEACH, Vincent W(oodrow) 1917-

PERSONAL: Born November 22, 1917, in Greenwood,

Ark.; son of R. H. and Elizabeth (Thames) Beach; married Virginia Hereford, September 5, 1947; children: Vincent, Jr., John, Charles. *Education:* University of Arkansas, B.S.E., 1939, M.A., 1947; University of Illinois, Ph.D., 1950. *Politics:* Democrat. *Religion:* Baptist. *Home:* 280 Abbey Pl., Boulder, Colo. 80302. *Office:* Department of History, University of Colorado, Boulder, Colo. 80302.

CAREER: University of Arkansas, Fayetteville, instructor in history, 1946-47; East Tennessee State University, Johnson City, assistant professor of history, 1950-51; University of Colorado, Boulder, assistant professor, 1951-56, associate professor, 1956-61, professor of history, 1961—. *Military service:* U.S. Navy, gunnery officer, 1942-46; became lieutenant. *Member:* Rotary International. *Awards, honors:* Fellowships from University of Colorado and American Philosophical Society.

WRITINGS: 1825: The Decisive Year of Charles X's Reign (monograph), University of Colorado Press, 1967; (contributor) James Frigulietti and Emmet Kennedy, editors, *The Shaping of Modern France,* Macmillan, 1969; *Charles X of France: His Life and Times,* Pruett, 1971. Contributor to *Western Humanities Review, University of Colorado Studies, Journal of Modern History, Social Science, Historian, Queen's Quarterly, Colorado Quarterly,* and *Denver Post.*

WORK IN PROGRESS: A book on the Assembly of Notables, 1787.

SIDELIGHTS: Vincent Beach traveled to Europe in 1953, 1960-61, and 1966-67.

*   *   *

BEAGLEHOLE, J(ohn) C(awte)   1901-1971

June 13, 1901—October 10, 1971; New Zealand scholar and historian. Obituaries: *New York Times,* October 16, 1971. (See index for *CA* sketch)

*   *   *

BEARDSLEY, Theodore S(terling), Jr.   1930-

PERSONAL: Born August 26, 1930, in East St. Louis, Ill.; son of Theodore Sterling (an attorney and executive) and Margaret A. (Kienzle) Beardsley; married Lenora J. Fierke, May 21, 1955; children: Theodore Sterling III, Mark A., Mary Elizabeth. *Education:* Southern Illinois University, B.S., 1952; Washington University, M.A., 1954; University of Heidelberg, graduate study, 1955-56; University of Pennsylvania, Ph.D., 1961. *Politics:* Republican. *Religion:* Roman Catholic. *Office:* Hispanic Society of America, 613 West 155th St., New York, N.Y. 10032.

CAREER: Rider College, Trenton, N.J., instructor, 1957-59, assistant professor of modern languages and chairman of the department, 1959-61; Southern Illinois University, Carbondale, assistant professor of Spanish, 1961-62; University of Wisconsin—Madison, assistant professor of Spanish, 1962-65; Hispanic Society of America, New York, N.Y., director, 1965—. Visiting professor, New York University, 1967-69, Columbia University, 1969. Chairman, Museums Council of New York, 1972-73; member of board of directors, Spanish Institute, Inc. Consultant to Library of Congress, 1973. *Military service:* U.S. Army, 1954-56. *Member:* Hispanic Society of America, Renaissance Society of America, Grolier Club. *Awards, honors:* Fulbright travel grant, 1952; French Government Teaching Award, 1952-53; Max Bryant fellowship, 1953-54; Jusserand Traveling fellowship from University of Pennsylvania, 1963; American Council of Learned Societies grant, 1964; Premio Bibliofilia, Barce-

lona, 1973; Corresponding member award from Academia Espanol, 1973; Fulbright lecturer, Ecuador, 1974.

WRITINGS: Hispano-Classical Translations Printed between 1480 and 1699, Duquesne University Press, 1970; *Tomas Navarro Tomas: A Tentative Bibliography, 1908-1970,* Centro de Estudios Hispanicos, Syracuse University, 1971; *Elogio de la Bibliofilia,* Porter-Libros, 1974. Also author of libretto, "Ponce de Leon," 1973. Contributor to *Hispanic Review, Renaissance and Reformation, Estafeta Literaria, Papeles de Son Armadans,* and other publications. Member of advisory board, *Hispanic Review.* General editor of "El hispanismo en Estados Unidos" which appeared serially in *Estafeta Literaria* (Madrid), 1972-73.

WORK IN PROGRESS: Articles for professional journals; essays.

*   *   *

BEAVER, (Jack) Patrick   1923-
(John Billington)

PERSONAL: Born February 5, 1923, in Croydon, England; son of Jack (a composer) and Rose Violet Beaver; married Pamela Stewart; married second wife, Ame Dilworth-Parr (in public relations), 1969; children: (first marriage) Anthony Patrick, Sally Ann. *Education:* Largely self-educated (schooling was frequently interrupted by ill health). *Politics:* Conservative. *Home:* 2 Museum Chambers, Bury Pl., London W.C.1, England. *Agent:* A. M. Heath & Co., 40-42 William IV St., London WC2N 4DD, England.

CAREER: Traveled widely in the merchant marine; a self-taught musician who earned a living as a composer for twenty years; has also produced and directed documentary films, worked as a professional photographer, lectured, and done research for American scholars; writer. *Military service:* Served in Royal Engineers and later in Royal Air Force. *Member:* Performing Rights Society.

WRITINGS: The Big Ship: Brunel's Great Eastern, Evelyn, 1969; *The Crystal Palace 1851-1936: A Portrait of Victorian Enterprise,* International Publications Service, 1970; *A History of Lighthouses,* P. Davies, 1971, Citadel, 1973; *A History of Tunnels,* diagrams by wife, Ame Beaver, P. Davies, 1972, Citadel, 1973; (author of introduction, notes, and glossary) *The Wipers Times,* P. Davies, 1973; (compiler) *Victorian Parlour Games for Today,* P. Davies, 1974; *Yes! We Have Some: The Story of Fyffes,* Publications for Companies, 1976. Contributor of articles of an antiquarian nature and, under pseudonym John Billington, of semihumourous articles on food and drink to magazines.

WORK IN PROGRESS: Two books for Hugh Evelyn, one on the history of luxury hotels and one on the Grand Union Canal.

SIDELIGHTS: Patrick Beaver told *CA* he "writes to make a living.... [I] have tried many ways of earning [a] living.... When I turn to something it is generally a success but when I *do* succeed I get fed up and look for something new. [I] have now tired of writing but can think of nothing else."†

*   *   *

BECK, Earl R(ay)   1916-

PERSONAL: Born September 8, 1916, in Junction City, Ohio; son of Ernest R. (a school superintendent) and Mary Frances (Helser) Beck; married Marjorie L. Culbertson, November 7, 1944; children: Ann M., Mary Sue. *Education:* Capital University, A.B., 1937; Ohio State University,

M.A., 1939, Ph. D., 1942. *Politics:* Democrat. *Religion:* Presbyterian. *Home:* 2514 Killarney Way, Tallahassee, Fla. 32303. *Office:* Department of History, Florida State University, Tallahassee, Fla. 32306.

CAREER: Capital University, Columbus, Ohio, instructor in history, 1942-43; Ohio State University, Columbus, instructor in history, 1946-49; Florida State University, Tallahassee, assistant professor, 1949-52, associate professor, 1952-60, professor of history, 1960—, chairman of department, 1967-72. Visiting summer professor, University of Kentucky, 1948, Louisiana State University, 1955, Tulane University, 1959, Duke University, 1966. *Military service:* U.S. Army, 1943-46. *Member:* American Historical Association, Conference Group for Central European History, Spanish Historical Society, Southern Historical Association.

WRITINGS: Verdict on Schacht: A Study in the Problem of Political "Guilt," Florida State University Press, 1956; *The Death of the Prussian Republic: A Study in Reich-Prussian Relations, 1932-1934,* Florida State University Press, 1959; (contributor) *Contemporary Civilization,* Volume I, Scott, Foresman, 1959; *On Teaching History in Colleges and Universities,* Florida State University Press, 1966; *Germany Rediscovers America,* Florida State University Press, 1968. Also author of *A Time of Triumph and of Sorrow: Spain under Alphonso XII, 1874-1885,* 1977. Contributor to historical and education journals.

WORK IN PROGRESS: Gregorio Maranon: Humanist Historian, completion expected in 1979.

* * *

BECK, Evelyn Torton   1933-

PERSONAL: Born January 18, 1933, in Vienna, Austria; U.S. citizen; daughter of Max (in fur business) and Irma (Lichtman) Torton; married Anatole Beck (a professor of mathematics), 1954 (divorced, 1974); children: Nina Rachel, Micah Daniel. *Education:* Brooklyn College (now Brooklyn College of the City University of New York), B.A., 1954; Yale University, M.A., 1955; University of Wisconsin, Ph.D., 1969. *Home:* 2602 Arbor Dr., Madison, Wis. 53711. *Office:* Department of Comparative Literature, University of Wisconsin, Madison, Wis. 53706.

CAREER: University of Maryland, College Park, lecturer in comparative literature, 1971-72; University of Wisconsin—Madison, 1972—, began as assistant professor, currently associate professor of comparative literature, German, and women's studies. Guest lecturer, Edgewood College, 1970. *Member:* American Comparative Literature Association, Modern Language Association of America, National Women's Studies Association. *Awards, honors:* American Council of Learned Societies grant, 1971-72.

WRITINGS: (Contributor) Isaac Bashevis Singer, *A Friend of Kafka,* Farrar, 1970; *Kafka and the Yiddish Theater,* University of Wisconsin Press, 1971; (with Jost Hermand) *Interpretive Synthesis: The Task of Literary Scholarship,* Ungar, 1976. Contributor of translations of Isaac Bashevis Singer's works to *New Yorker, Commentary,* and *Southern Review.*

WORK IN PROGRESS: Editing with Julia Sherman, *The Prism of Sex;* interviews with Alice Schwazer and May Sarton; writing on contemporary feminist culture.

* * *

BECKER, Abraham S(amuel)   1927-

PERSONAL: Born February 7, 1927, in New York, N.Y.; son of Morris (a teacher) and Bella (Newman) Becker; married Tamar Shfiron (a professor of sociology), June 7, 1950; children: Doron (son), Ornah (daughter). *Education:* Harvard University, A.B. (with honors), 1949; Columbia University, M.A. and Certificate of Russian Institute, 1952, Ph.D., 1959. *Residence:* Los Angeles, Calif. *Office:* RAND Corp., 1700 Main St., Santa Monica, Calif. 90406.

CAREER: Mid-European Studies Center of the Free Europe Committee, New York, N.Y., research supervisor, 1953-54; Corporation for Economic and Industrial Research, Washington, D.C., economist, 1955-57; RAND Corp., Santa Monica, Calif., economist and senior economist, 1957—. Lecturer, University of California, Los Angeles, 1963, 1967-68, 1970. Visiting professor of economics and Russian studies, Hebrew University, 1972-73. U.S. representative, United Nations expert group on the redirection of military budgets, 1974, 1976. *Member:* American Economic Association, Association for Comparative Economic Studies Association for the Study of Soviet-Type Economies (now merged with Association for Comparative Economic Studies; member of executive committee, 1968-69).

WRITINGS: Prices of Producers Durables in the United States and the USSR in 1955, RAND Corp., 1959; *Soviet National Income 1958-1964: National Accounts of the USSR in the Seven Year Plan Period,* University of California Press, 1969; *Israel and the Palestinian Occupied Territories: Military-Political Issues in the Debate,* RAND Corp., 1971; (with B. Hansen and M. Kerr) *The Economics and Politics of the Middle East,* American Elsevier, 1975; *Military Expenditure Limitation for Arms Control: Problems and Projects,* Ballinger, 1977.

Contributor: Edmund S. Phelps, editor, *The Goal of Economic Growth: Sources, Costs, Benefits,* Norton, 1962; J. P. Hardt and others, *Mathematics and Computers in Soviet Economic Planning,* Yale University Press, 1967; *Sowjetsystem und demokratische Gesellschaft: eine vergleichende Enziklopaedie,* Verlag Herder, 1968; V. G. Treml and J. P. Hardt, editors, *Soviet Economic Statistics,* Duke University Press, 1972; S. S. Alexander and P. Y. Hammond, editors, *Political Dynamics in the Middle East,* American Elsevier, 1972; M. Confino and S. Shamir, editors, *The USSR and the Middle East,* Israel University Press, 1973; J. S. Szyliowicz and B. O'Neill, editors, *The Energy Crisis and U.S. Foreign Policy,* Praeger, 1975; *Military Aspects of the Israeli-Arab Conflict,* University Publishing Projects (Tel Aviv), 1975.

WORK IN PROGRESS: Soviet Defense Economics.

* * *

BECKER, Ruby Wirt   1915-

PERSONAL: Born October 20, 1915, in Jamaica, Iowa; daughter of Alva Clarence (a farmer) and Angie (Dickey) Wirt; married Elmer M. P. Becker (a filtration plant operator), June 4, 1939; children: Terry Phillip, James Allen. *Education:* Attended Simpson College, Indianola, Iowa, 1936-37; San Diego State College (now University), B.E., 1958. *Religion:* Protestant. *Home:* 9304 Crest Dr., Spring Valley, Calif. 92077.

CAREER: Teacher in public schools in Iowa, 1934-39; La Mesa-Spring Valley School District, La Mesa, Calif., kindergarten teacher, 1955—. *Member:* National Education Association, California Teachers Association.

WRITINGS: Through My Window (rhymes for children), illustrations by Celeste K. Foster, Denison, 1969.

WORK IN PROGRESS: Books for primary children.†

BECKER, Wesley C(lemence) 1928-

PERSONAL: Born March 17, 1928, in Rochester, N.Y.; son of William Henry (a baker) and Alcey (Cole) Becker; married Barbara Ann Beckel, June 15, 1950 (divorced, 1968); married Janis Wetherell, October 14, 1968 (divorced, 1972); married Julia M. Green, July 20, 1972; children: (first marriage) Jill, Jeffrey, Linda, James; (second marriage) Karen; (third marriage) David, Brandin. *Education:* Stanford University, A.B., 1951, M.A., 1953, Ph.D., 1955. *Office:* Follow Through Project, University of Oregon, Eugene, Ore. 97403.

CAREER: University of Illinois, Urbana, visiting lecturer, summer, 1955, instructor, 1955-56, assistant professor, 1956-60, associate professor, 1960-63, professor of psychology, 1963-67, professor of psychology and educational psychology, Bureau of Educational Research, 1967-70; University of Oregon, Eugene, professor of special education and codirector of Follow Through Project, 1970—. Member, Children's Center Research Advisory Committee, 1965-68. Consultant to Kankakee State Hospital, 1958-67, Illinois Institute for Juvenile Research, 1966-68, Task Force on the Mental Health of Youth, 1968, and primary consultant to twenty Follow Through programs, 1968-70; consultant to Academic Press, Prentice-Hall, and Holt, 1964—. *Military service:* U.S. Army, Ordnance, 1946-49; became staff sergeant. *Member:* American Psychological Association (fellow), American Educational Research Association, Phi Beta Kappa, Sigma Xi.

WRITINGS: (With S. Kirk) *Conference on Children with Minimal Brain Impairment,* Easter Seal Research Foundation, 1963; (contributor) M. Hoffman and Hoffman, editors, *Review of Child Development Research,* Volume I, Russell Sage, 1964; (contributor with D. R. Peterson) H. C. Quay, editor, *Theory and Research in Juvenile Delinquency,* Van Nostrand, 1965; (contributor with others) Henry Dupont, editor, *Educating Emotionally Disturbed Children Readings,* Holt, 1969; (contributor with others) R. K. Parker, editor, *Readings in Educational Psychology,* Allyn & Bacon, 1969.

Concepts and Operation, or How to Make Kids Smart, University of Calgary, 1970; *Parents Are Teachers: A Child Management Program,* Research Press, 1971; (with Engelmann, and Thomas) *Teaching: A Course in Applied Psychology,* Science Research Associates, 1971; (editor) *Empirical Bases for Change in Education,* Science Research Associates, 1971; (with K. Daniel O'Leary) Mary B. Harris, editor, *Classroom Uses of Behavior Modification,* C. E. Merrill, 1972; (contributor with others) K. Daniel O'Leary and Susan G. O'Leary, editors, *Classroom Management,* Pergamon, 1972; (with Janis Becker) *Successful Parenthood,* Follett, 1974.

(With Engelmann and Thomas) *Teaching 1: Classroom Management,* Science Research Associates, 1975; *Teaching 2: Cognitive Learning and Instruction,* Science Research Associates, 1975; *Teaching 3: Evaluation of Instruction,* Science Research Associates, 1976. Contributor of about forty research papers to psychology journals; contributor of articles and reviews to professional journals.

*   *   *

BECKETT, John A(ngus) 1916-

PERSONAL: Born April 27, 1916, in Portland, Ore.; son of John Wallace and Agnes (Scott) Beckett; married Elizabeth Debusk (a teacher), June 15, 1940; children: Ann Meredith (Mrs. Jerrold Immel), Kathleen Scott (Mrs. Kenneth P.

Day), John Thomas. *Education:* University of Oregon, B.S., 1939; Harvard University, M.B.A., 1946. *Politics:* Republican. *Religion:* Protestant. *Home:* 55 Mill Pond Rd., Durham, N.H. 03824. *Office:* Whittemore School of Business and Economics, University of New Hampshire, Durham, N.H. 03824.

CAREER: Massachusetts Institute of Technology, Cambridge, assistant professor of accounting, 1946-52; McKinsey & Co., San Francisco, Calif., senior consultant, 1952-54; Spreckels Sugar Co., San Francisco, treasurer, 1954-56; Arthur Young & Co., Chicago, Ill., principal, 1956-58; Executive Office of the President, Washington, D.C., assistant director of U.S. Bureau of Budget, 1958-60; Smith Barney & Co. (stockbrokers), New York, N.Y., administrative manager, 1960-61; University of New Hampshire, Durham, professor of management, 1961—. Member, New Hampshire Legislature, 1971-72. *Military service:* U.S. Army, 1943-46; became first lieutenant. *Member:* American Institute of Certified Public Accountants, Beta Gamma Sigma (honorary member).

WRITINGS: (With R. H. Robnett and Thomas M. Hill) *Accounting: A Management Approach,* Irwin, 1951; (editor) *Industrial Accountant's Handbook,* Prentice-Hall, 1953; *Management Dynamics: The New Synthesis,* McGraw, 1971. Contributor to professional journals.

WORK IN PROGRESS: General systems theory applied to the study of management; *The Thinking Process.*

*   *   *

BECKMAN, Gunnel 1910-

PERSONAL: Born April 16, 1910, in Falkoeping, Sweden; daughter of John K. (a company director) and Villy (Wiedesheim-Paul) Torulf; married Birger Beckman (a publisher), June 23, 1933; children: Staffan, Bjorn, Ingar (Mrs. Johan Hirschfeldt), Svante, Suzanne. *Education:* University of Lund, B.M., 1932. *Home:* Alnaesvaegen 8, Solna, Sweden.

CAREER: Writer for young people. Member (layman) of court of Judicial District of Solan for six years. *Member:* Swedish Authors Association, K.R.U.M., Amnesty (Association for humanizing the treatment of criminals). *Awards, honors:* Bonnier's Prize for best book for young people, 1969, for *Tilltraede till festen;* prize of 3,000 kronor from The Fund for Furtherance of Good Literature, 1969 and 1973; Nils Holgusson prize, 1975; Authors Fund prize, 1976.

WRITINGS: (Reviser) *Swedish for Tourists* (booklet), 12th edition, Svenska Bokfoerlaget, 1955; *Medan katten var borta* (title means "When the Cat Was Away"), Bonnier, 1960; *Unga froeken Tova* (title means "Young Miss Tova"), Bonnier, 1961; *Visst goer det ont* (title means "It Hurts—No Doubt"), Bonnier, 1963; *Misstaenkt* (title means "Suspect"), Bonnier, 1965; *Flickan utan namn,* Bonnier, 1967, translation by Anne Parker published as *The Girl without a Name,* Harcourt, 1970; *Pa galej med farmor* (title means "Out on the Spree with Grandma"), Bonnier, 1968.

Tilltraede till festen, translation by Joan Tate published as *Admission to the Feast,* and in paperback as *Nineteen Is Too Young to Die,* Macmillan, 1971; *Foersoek att foerstaa* (title means "Try to Understand"), Bonnier, 1971, translation by Joan Tate published as *A Room of His Own,* Bodley Head, 1973, Viking, 1974; *Tre veckor oever tiden,* Bonnier, 1973, translation by Joan Tate published as *Mia Alone,* Viking, 1975; *Varen da allting haende,* Bonnier, 1974, translation by Joan Tate published in England as *The Loneliness of*

Mia, Bodley Head, 1975, published as *That Early Spring,* Viking, 1977; *M som i Maggan* (title means "M. as in Maggan"), Bonnier, 1975; *Ett slag i ansiktet* (title means "A Blow in Your Face"), Bonnier, 1976; *Varfoer just Eva* (title means "Why Eve?"), Cavefors, 1977.

SIDELIGHTS: An adaptation of *Nineteen Is Too Young to Die* was presented in four parts on Swedish radio, 1970; an adaptation of *A Room of His Own* was presented on Norwegian radio; an adaptation of *Mia* was presented on Swedish, Danish, and Norwegian radios. Most of Gunnel Beckman's books have been translated into the Scandanavian languages; some have been translated into German, Dutch, and Japanese.

*   *   *

BECKNER, Weldon (Earnest) 1933-

PERSONAL: Born January 14, 1933, in Clayton, N.M.; son of E. H. (a businessman) and Ursula (Brown) Beckner; married Betty Farr (a teacher), May 10, 1952; children: Brenda, Marilyn, Gayla, Jan. *Education:* Wayland Baptist College, B.S., 1955; Texas Technological University (now Texas Tech University), M.Ed., 1959; University of Colorado, Ed.D., 1966. *Religion:* Baptist. *Home:* 3424 62nd St., Lubbock, Tex. 79413. *Office:* College of Education, Texas Tech University, Lubbock, Tex. 79409.

CAREER: Teacher in elementary and high schools of Texas, 1955-59; principal of elementary and high schools in Colorado, 1959-63, and assistant principal of high school in Boulder, Colo., 1964-65; Texas Tech University, Lubbock, 1965—, currently professor of secondary education and school administration. Visiting summer professor, University of Virginia, 1969, Pan American University, 1972, and Texas Woman's University, 1975. *Member:* American Educational Studies Association, National Association of Secondary School Principals, National Education Association, Association for Supervision and Curriculum Development, Phi Delta Kappa.

WRITINGS—All published by International Textbook Co., except as indicated: (With Wayne Dumas) *Introduction to Secondary Education,* 1968; (editor with Dumas) *Readings in Secondary Education,* 1968; (editor with Dumas) *American Education: Foundations and Superstructure,* 1970; (with Joe D. Cornett) *Secondary School Curriculum: Content and Structure,* 1972; (with Cornett) *Introductory Statistics for the Behavioral Sciences,* C. E. Merrill, 1975. Contributor to education journals.

WORK IN PROGRESS: An introductory textbook for teacher education; a high school history text.

SIDELIGHTS: Weldon Beckner told *CA:* "In my writing, as in my teaching, I am trying to make teachers and teaching materials more flexible, more human, and more creative. Failure to strengthen these elements in our schools and in our society will mean failure to adequately meet the opportunities and challenges of contemporary and future life."

*   *   *

BECKOVIC, Matija 1939-

PERSONAL: Born November 29, 1939, in Senta, Yugoslavia; son of Vuk (a military man) and Zorka (Tausan) Beckovic; married Vera Pavladoljska; children: Olja and Ljudmila (twins). *Education:* Attended University of Belgrade, 1958-59. *Religion:* Serbian Orthodox Church. *Home:* Vladimira Tomonovica 19, Belgrade, Yugoslavia 11000.

CAREER: Journalist in Belgrade, Yugoslavia, 1962—;

writer and producer for the stage, radio, and television, 1965—. *Member:* Serbian Writers Guild. *Awards, honors:* Awards for both prose and poetry, including award of Serbian Writers Guild and award of City of Belgrade, 1971, for *Rece mi je dan coek.*

WRITINGS: Vera Pavladoljska, Radomir Ras, 1962; *Metak lutalica* (poems), Prosveta, 1963; *Tako je govorio Matija,* Prosveta, 1965; *Dr. Janez Pacuka o meduvremenu,* Matica Srpsks, 1970, translation by Drenka Willem published as *Random Targets* (see below); (with Dusko Radovic) *Ce: Tragedija koja traje,* privately printed, 1970, translation by Willem published as *Che: A Permanent Tradegy* with *Random Targets,* Harcourt, 1970; *Rece mi je dan coek,* Prosveta, 1971; *Metja Vuka Uanitoga* (poems), Srpska kujizevna Zadruga, 1976.

WORK IN PROGRESS: Poetry and nonfiction.

*   *   *

BECKWITH, Burnham Putnam 1904-
(John Burnham, John Putnam)

PERSONAL: Born September 2, 1904, in Carthage, Mo.; son of Herbert Henry (a capitalist) and Louise (Taylor) Beckwith. *Education:* Stanford University, B.A., 1926; attended Harvard University, 1926-28; University of Southern California, M.A., 1930, Ph.D., 1932; Columbia University, postdoctoral research, 1935-37; attended New School for Social Research, 1936-37. *Politics:* Socialist. *Religion:* Positivist. *Home:* 656 Lytton Ave., No. C430, Palo Alto, Calif. 94301.

CAREER: University of Kansas, Lawrence, instructor in economics, 1934-35; Queens College (now Queens College of the City University of New York), Flushing, N.Y., instructor in economics, 1937-38; University of Georgia, Athens, associate professor of economics, 1938-40; War Production Board, Washington, D.C., economist and statistician, 1941-45; Biarritz American University, Biarritz, France, instructor, 1945-46; U.S. Office of Military Government, Berlin, Germany, economist and statistician, 1946-49; private study, travel, and writing, 1949—.

WRITINGS: Contemporary English and American Theories Concerning the Effect of Commercial Banking upon the Supply of Physical Capital, University of Southern California Press, 1935; (under pseudonym John Burnham) *Total War,* Meador Publishing, 1943; (under pseudonym John Putnam) *The Modern Case for Socialism,* Meador Publishing, 1943, 3rd edition published as *The Case for Liberal Socialism,* Exposition Press, 1976; *The Economic Theory of a Socialist Economy,* Stanford University Press, 1949, 2nd revised edition published as *Liberal Socialism: The Pure Welfare Economics of a Liberal Socialist Economy,* Exposition Press, 1974; *Marginal-Cost Price-Output Control,* Columbia University Press, 1955; *Religion, Philosophy, and Science,* Philosophical Library, 1957; *The Next 500 Years,* Exposition Press, 1968; *Government by Experts,* Exposition Press, 1972; *Free Goods,* privately printed, 1977; *Liberal Socialism Applied,* privately printed, 1978. Editor, *Statistical Annex to the Monthly Report of the Military Governor,* OMGUS (Berlin), 1947-48.

WORK IN PROGRESS: Research on ideal income determination and ideal society.

*   *   *

BEDDALL, Barbara G(ould) 1919-

PERSONAL: Born October 28, 1919, in Tarrytown, N.Y.;

daughter of Gerald Blenkiron (a fuel engineer) and Anna (Curtiss) Gould; married Edward A. Beddall (a corporation vice-president), October 29, 1949; children: Thomas Gould. *Education:* Swarthmore College, B.A., 1941; Columbia University, B.S., 1942; Yale University, M.S., 1962. *Home:* 2502 Bronson Rd., Fairfield, Conn. 06430.

CAREER: Time, Inc., New York, N.Y., research librarian, 1944-52. *Member:* American Association for the Advancement of Science, History of Science Society, American Ornithologists' Union, Association for Tropical Biology, Society for the Bibliography of Natural History, Society of Systematic Zoology, British Ornithologists' Union, International Society for Tropical Ecology, Northeastern Bird-Banding Association, Wilson Ornithological Society.

WRITINGS: (Editor) *Wallace and Bates in the Tropics: An Introduction to the Theory of Natural Selection,* Macmillan, 1969; (author of introduction, appendix, and anthology) Jose de Acosta, *Historia Natural y Moral de las Indias,* revised edition (Beddall was not associated with earlier editions), Valencia Cultural (Spain), 1977. Contributor to *Diccionario Historico de la Ciencia Moderna en Espana.* Contributor to *Journal of the History of Biology, Wilson Bulletin,* and *Systematic Zoology.*

WORK IN PROGRESS: The work of Spanish naturalists, particularly in Latin America.

AVOCATIONAL INTERESTS: Bird watching.

BIOGRAPHICAL/CRITICAL SOURCES: Scientific American, October, 1969.

*   *   *

BEDINI, Silvio A.   1917-

PERSONAL: Born January 17, 1917, in Ridgefield, Conn.; son of Vincent L. S. (a businessman) and Cesira (Stefanelli) Bedini; married Gerda Hintz, October 20, 1951; children: Leandra Anne, Peter David. *Education:* Attended Columbia University, 1935-36, 1937-42. *Religion:* Roman Catholic. *Home:* 4303 47th St. N.W., Washington, D.C. 20016. *Office:* National Museum of History and Technology, Smithsonian Institution, Washington, D.C. 20560.

CAREER: Self-employed in Ridgefield, Conn., 1945-61; Smithsonian Institution, Washington, D.C., curator of Division of Mechanical and Civil Engineering, U.S. National Museum, 1961-65, assistant director of Museum of History and Technology, 1965-71, deputy director, 1971—. *Military service:* U.S. Army, 1942-45. *Member:* Society of American Historians, History of Science Society, Society for the History of Technology (member of advisory council), American Historical Association, American Philosophical Society, American Antiquarian Society, Washington Academy of Sciences (fellow). *Awards, honors:* Abbott Payson Usher Award of Society for the History of Technology, 1962; Outstanding Performance Award of Smithsonian Institution, 1965; LL.D., University of Bridgeport, 1970.

WRITINGS: Ridgefield in Review, Walker-Rackliffe Co., 1958; *The Scent of Time,* American Philosophical Society, 1963; *Early American Scientific Instruments and Their Makers,* Smithsonian Institution, 1964; (with Francis R. Maddison) *Mechanical Universe,* American Philosophical Society, 1966; (contributor) *Saggi su Galileo Galilei,* G. Barbera (Florence), 1967; (contributor) Ernan McMullin, editor, *Galileo: Man of Science,* Basic Books, 1968; (with Wernher von Braun and Fred L. Whipple) *Moon: Man's Greatest Adventure,* edited by C. Davis Thomas, Abrams, 1970; *The Life of Benjamin Banneker,* Scribner, 1972;

Thinkers and Tinkers: Early American Men of Science, Scribner, 1975; *Adventures in Time,* Abrams, in press.

WORK IN PROGRESS: Thomas Jefferson: Man of Science.

*   *   *

BEEBE, Ralph K(enneth)   1932-

PERSONAL: Born February 14, 1932, in Caldwell, Idaho; son of Glen S. (a farmer) and Fannie M. (Nutting) Beebe; married Wanda L. Pierson, June 8, 1953; children: Diane, Lori, Kenneth. *Education:* George Fox College, A.B., 1954; Linfield College, M.Ed., 1955; University of Oregon, M.A., 1969, Ph.D., 1972. *Religion:* Friends Church (Quaker). *Home:* 212 Carlton Way, Newberg, Ore. 97132. *Office:* Department of History, George Fox College, Newberg, Ore. 97132.

CAREER: George Fox College, Newberg, Ore., instructor in physical education, dean of men, and director of athletics, 1955-57; history teacher at Willamette High School, Eugene, Ore., 1957-66, and at Winston Churchill High School, Eugene, 1966-74; George Fox College, associate professor of history, 1974—. *Member:* National Education Association, American Historical Association, Organization of American Historians, Oregon Historical Society, Oregon Education Association.

WRITINGS: A Garden of the Lord: A History of Oregon Yearly Meeting of Friends Church, Barclay Press, 1968; *The Worker and Social Change: The Pullman Strike of 1894,* Heath, 1970; *Thomas Jefferson: The Embargo, and the Decision for Peace,* Addison-Wesley, 1972. Contributor to education and religion journals.

*   *   *

BEECH, Keyes   1913-

PERSONAL: Born August 13, 1913, in Pulaski, Tenn.; son of Walter and Leona (Carden) Beech; married Linda Corley Mangelsdorf (a writer), June 15, 1951 (divorced, 1969); married Yuko Horiguchi, July 11, 1973; children: (first marriage) Walter, Keyes, Jr., Barnaby; (second marriage) Hannah. *Education:* Attended Harvard University, 1952-53. *Office:* Foreign Correspondents Club, No. 142 Chome Marunouchi Chiyoda-Ku, Tokyo, Japan.

CAREER: Evening Independent, St. Petersburg, Fla., copyboy, 1931-36, reporter, 1936-37; reporter for *Akron Beacon Journal,* Akron, Ohio, 1937-42, and *Honolulu Star-Bulletin,* Honolulu, Hawaii, 1945-47; *Chicago Daily News,* Chicago, Ill., Far East correspondent, 1947—. *Military service:* U.S. Marine Corps, combat correspondent, 1942-45. *Member:* Foreign Correspondents Club, American Club, and Tokyo Lawn Tennis Club (all Tokyo). *Awards, honors:* Pulitzer Prize for international reporting and Sigma Delta Chi Award, both for coverage of the Korean War, 1951; Harvard University Neiman fellow, 1952-53.

WRITINGS: (With Raymond Henri and other Marine combat correspondents) *U.S. Marines on Iwo Jima,* Dial, 1945; (with George McMilan and other Marine combat correspondents) *Uncommon Valor: Marine Divisions in Action,* Infantry Journal Press, 1946; *Tokyo and Points East,* introduction by James A. Michener, Doubleday, 1954; *Not without the Americans: A Personal History,* Doubleday, 1971. Contributor to *Saturday Evening Post, McCall's,* and other magazines.

BIOGRAPHICAL/CRITICAL SOURCES: Best Sellers, March 1, 1971.†

BEECH, Robert (Paul) 1940-

PERSONAL: Born December 31, 1940, in Denver, Colo.; son of Kenneth and Ruth (Paulson) Beech; married Mary Jane Higdon, June 12, 1962; children: Robert David, Richard Alan. *Education:* University of Colorado, B.A. (cum laude), 1962; Michigan State University, M.A., 1964, Ph.D., 1967.

CAREER: American Institute of Indian Studies, Calcutta, India, research fellow, 1967-68; New York University, School of Education, New York, N.Y., assistant professor of educational psychology, beginning 1968, evaluation director, Dial-a-Drill (computer-assisted instruction program), Center for Field Research and School Services, 1969-70. Certified psychologist, State of Michigan, 1969. Chairman of four symposiums held in the United States, 1970. *Member:* American Psychological Association, American Educational Research Association, Society for the Psychological Study of Social Issues, Asian Studies Association, Eastern Psychological Association, Educational Research Association of New York State, Psi Chi, Phi Kappa Phi.

WRITINGS: (Editor with James G. Ramsay) *Psychological Foundations of Education: Selected Academic Readings,* Associated Educational Services, 1969; *An Evaluation of the Dial-a-Drill Program,* two volumes, Center for Field Research and School Services, New York University, 1969-70; (editor with wife, M. J. Beech, and contributor) *Bengal: Change and Continuity,* Michigan State University Press, 1971. Also contributor to *Educational Psychology Text,* edited by New York University Associates.

WORK IN PROGRESS: Cross-cultural studies of values and value systems, particularly as related to Bengal.†

* * *

BEECHHOLD, Henry F(rank) 1928-
(Annraoi O'Doire)

PERSONAL: Name legally changed in 1932; born July 25, 1928, in Miami, Fla.; son of Irvin Mitchell (a real estate broker) and Dorothy (Stone) Mitchell Beechhold; married Irene Pollack, January 31, 1954; children: Adrienne, Matthew. *Education:* Oklahoma State University, B.S., 1951, M.A., 1952; Pennsylvania State University, Ph.D., 1956. *Politics:* Democrat. *Home:* 13 Perry Dr., West Trenton, N.J. 08628. *Office:* Department of English, Trenton State College, Trenton, N.J. 08625.

CAREER: Oklahoma Military Academy, Claremore, instructor, 1952-53; University of Maine, Orono, instructor, 1956-59, associate professor of English, 1959-62; Trenton State College, Trenton, N.J., associate professor, 1963-68, professor of English, 1968—, chairman of linguistics program. Adjunct professor, Hunter College of the City University of New York, 1969-72. *Military service:* U.S. Army, 1945-47. Oklahoma National Guard, 1952-53; became first lieutenant. *Member:* International Linguistic Association, Linguistic Society of America, Neurolinguistic Society, National Council of Teachers of English, College English Association, Irish-American Culture Institute (member of national council), Linguistic Association of Great Britain, American Radio Relay League (life member), Aircraft Owners and Pilots Association, National Pilots Association, New Jersey Association of Teachers of English, New Jersey Universities Association (co-founder and president). *Awards, honors:* Named "New Jersey Education Writer of the Year" by New Jersey Association of teachers of English, 1972, for *The Creative Classroom;* shared an Emmy from National Academy of Television Arts and Sciences, 1976, for work on network series "Grammar Rock"; named "Literary Luminary of New Jersey" by New Jersey Writers Conference, 1977.

WRITINGS: Early Irish History and Mythology in "Finnegans Wake," [Ann Arbor], 1956; *The Creative Classroom,* Scribner, 1971; (with J. L. Behling) *The Science of Language and the Art of Teaching,* Scribner, 1972.

Plays: "Tohu Bohu," first performed in Trenton, N.J. at Trenton State College, 1968; "The Waiting Room," first produced in Trenton at New Jersey State Cultural Center, 1969; "Third Act," first produced in Yardley, Pa. at Yardley Playhouse, 1970. Also author of "The Message," "The Interview," and "The Labyrinth," all unpublished and unproduced.

Libretti: "Between the Shadow and the Dream," first produced in Trenton, N.J. at Artist's Showcase Theatre, 1970. Author of "When Flowers Fail." commissioned, but not yet produced.

Contributor to *College English, Poet-Lore, Literary Review, Pivot, Bitterroot, Eire-Ireland,* and other publications. Associate editor, *Eire-Ireland;* executive editor, *Bitterroot.*

WORK IN PROGRESS: A novel; a pilot teleplay for a new TV series.

AVOCATIONAL INTERESTS: Music, photography, astronomy, Ireland and Gaelic language, electronics (licensed amateur radio operator), aviation (licensed private pilot).

* * *

BEEKMAN, Allan 1913-

PERSONAL: Born January 16, 1913, in Utica, N.Y.; son of I. Earl (a building contractor) and Anna (Hayes) Beekman; married Take Okawa (a translator), December 20, 1948. *Education:* Attended public schools in New York. *Politics:* Democrat. *Home:* 1279-203 Ala Kapuna St., Honolulu, Hawaii 96819.

CAREER: Pacific Citizen, Los Angeles, Calif., political reporter and commentator, 1966, book editor, 1967; *The East* (magazine), Tokyo, Japan, Hawaiian correspondent, 1968—; Pacific Book Distributor, Honolulu, Hawaii, owner, 1971. Freelance writer, 1942—. *Member:* Japanese American Citizens League.

WRITINGS: Hawaiian Tales, Harlo, 1970. Contributor to *Saint Detective Magazine, Pacific Sports and Features,* and other periodicals.

WORK IN PROGRESS: The Pearl Harbor Attack; The Niihau Incident; editing *Japanese Immigrant Tales,* translated with wife, Take Okawa Beekman.

* * *

BEEKMAN, E(ric) M(ontague) 1939-

PERSONAL: Born September 25, 1939, in Amsterdam, Netherlands; son of Anton Albert (an engineer) and Geertrui Johanna (van As) Beekman; married Faith L. Foss; children: (previous marriage) Dylan. *Education:* Received secondary education in the Netherlands; attended Hope College, 1958-60; University of California, Berkeley, B.A., 1963; University of Ghent, graduate study, 1965-66; Harvard University, Ph.D., 1968. *Politics:* None. *Religion:* None. *Home:* 15 Franklin St., Northampton, Mass. 01060. *Agent:* David Otte, The Otte Co., 9 Park St., Boston, Mass. 02108. *Office:* Department of Germanic Languages, University of Massachusetts, Amherst, Mass. 01002.

CAREER: University of Massachusetts, Amherst, assistant professor, 1968-71, associate professor of Germanic languages and comparative literature, 1971—. Visiting scholar at the invitation of the Dutch and Belgian governments, 1976. Military service: U.S. Army, 1957-58. Awards, honors: Woodrow Wilson fellowship, 1963-64; Fulbright fellowship in Belgium, 1965-66; National Translation Center grant, 1969-70; John Anson Kittredge Fund grant for the arts, 1971.

WRITINGS: (Contributor) L. S. Dembo, editor, Criticism: Speculative and Analytical Essays, University of Wisconsin Press, 1968; Homeopathy of the Absurd: The Grotesque in Paul van Ostaijen's Creative Prose, Nijhoff, 1970; Lame Duck (novel), Houghton, 1971; (translator, editor, and author of notes) Patriotism Incorporated and Other Tales by Paul van Ostaijen, University of Massachusetts Press, 1971; (contributor) Richard Kostelanetz, editor In Youth, Ballantine, 1972; (editor, translator, and author of notes) The Oyster and the Eagle: Selected Aphorisms and Parables of Multatuli, University of Massachusetts Press, 1974; (contributor) Philip Rahv, editor, Modern Occasions 2, Kennikat, 1974; Carnal Lent (poems), Pennyroyal Press, 1975; (contributor) Marc Hanrez, editor, Les ecrivains et la guerre d'Espagne, Pantheon (Paris), 1975; The Killing Jar (novel), Houghton, 1976; (contributor of translations) Howard Schwartz, editor, Imperial Messages: One Hundred Modern Parables, Avon, 1976.

Contributor to Nez Directions 21 and 24, 1969, New Directions 30, 1975, and to Encyclopedia of World Literature in the 20th Century, 1971. Contributor of poems, stories, and articles to periodicals, including Boston Spectator, John O'London's, Chicago Review, London Magazine, Modern Occasions, Massachusetts Review, TDR, Panache, and Dark Horse.

WORK IN PROGRESS: Translating from the Dutch, Life on Earth, a novel by J. J. Slauerhoff; The Kindness of Strangers, a novel.

SIDELIGHTS: E. M. Beekman lived in Indonesia for two years. Some of his works have been translated into French, Italian, Dutch, and Japanese.

*   *   *

BEGGS, Donald L(ee) 1941-

PERSONAL: Born September 16, 1941, in Harrisburg, Ill.; son of C. J. and Mary (Fitzgerald) Beggs; married Shirley Malone, March 19, 1963; children: Brent Alan, Pamela Ann. Education: Southern Illinois University, B.S., 1963, M.S., 1964; University of Iowa, Ph.D., 1966. Office: Department of Guidance and Educational Psychology, College of Education, Southern Illinois University, Carbondale, Ill. 62901.

CAREER: University of Iowa, Iowa City, instructor in educational psychology, 1966; Southern Illinois University, Carbondale, assistant professor, 1966-69, associate professor of educational psychology, 1969—, associate dean of graduate studies and research, 1970—. Member: American Educational Research Association, American Psychological Association, National Council on Measurement in Education, Phi Delta Kappa, Phi Kappa Phi.

WRITINGS: (With others) Research Design in the Behavioral Sciences: Multiple Regression Approach, Southern Illinois University Press, 1969; (with Keith A. McNeil) Readings in Educational Testing, Simon & Schuster, 1969; (with John W. Wick) Evaluation for Decision-Making in the Schools, Houghton, 1971; (contributor) Glenn Bracht, edi-

tor, Perspectives in Educational and Psychological Measurement, Prentice-Hall, 1972. Contributor of more than twenty articles to education journals.

*   *   *

BEHNKE, Frances L.

PERSONAL: Born in Fayette, Ala.; daughter of James Thomas and Lizzie (Newton) Berry; married John Alden Behnke (a science editor), December 30, 1957. Education: University of Arkansas, B.S., 1934; Emory University, M.S., 1940; Columbia University, Ed.D., 1959. Politics: Independent. Religion: Methodist. Home: 106 Morningside Dr., New York, N.Y. 10027.

CAREER: Columbia University, Barnard College, New York City, lecturer in chemistry, 1956-59; Hunter College of the City University of New York, New York City, lecturer in science education, 1960-61; Columbia University, Teachers College, New York City, lecturer in science education, 1961-76. Director, Out-of-School Science Program. Consultant, Thomas Alva Edison Foundation. Member: American Association for the Advancement of Science (fellow), National Science Teachers Association, National Association of Biology Teachers (national vice-president, 1957), Association for the Education of Teachers of Science, Ornithology Society, Georgia Botanical Club, Iota Sigma Pi (president), Sigma Delta Epsilon, Pen and Brush Club.

WRITINGS: The Golden Adventure Book of Magnetism, Golden Press, 1962; What We Find When We Look under Rocks, McGraw, 1969; The Natural History of Termites, Scribner, 1977. Series editor, "Golden Adventures" series, Golden Press; series editor, "What We Find When . . . " series, McGraw. Also editor of series of photomicrographic books, published by Coward, 1976. Contributor to School and Society, School Science and Mathematics, American Biology Teacher, American Physics Teacher, Chemical and Engineering News. Editor, Science World Teaching Guides (high school edition). Editor of television scripts and school booklets.

WORK IN PROGRESS: The Changing World of Living Things, for Holt; Ants and Their Trades; technical editor of three "Changing World" books on birds, the weather, and the decomposers.

SIDELIGHTS: Frances Behnke lived and studied in Marburg, Germany for two years.

*   *   *

BEHRENS, Herman D(aniel) 1901-

PERSONAL: Born August 6, 1901, in El Dorado, Kan.; son of Nichols J. and Elizabeth (Dahlke) Behrens; married Ivalee Mae Atkins, May 29, 1926. Education: Kansas State Teachers College of Emporia, B.Sc., 1925; Ohio State University, M.A., 1930, Ph.D., 1932. Politics: Republican. Religion: United Church. Home: 10812 Mission Lane, Sun City, Ariz. 85351.

CAREER: Elementary teacher in Florence, Kan., 1920-22; high school chairman of social studies in Pratt, Kan., 1925-29; Ohio State University, Columbus, instructor in psychology, 1932-33; Minot State Teachers College (now Minot State College), Minot, N.D., professor of education, 1933-35; Geneseo Normal and Training School (now State University of New York College at Geneseo), Geneseo, N.Y., instructor, 1935-39, professor of education and chairman of department, 1939-52; State University Teachers College (now State University of New York College at Oneonta),

Oneonta, N.Y., professor of education, 1952-53, director of Division of Elementary Education, 1953-61; Ohio Northern University, Ada, professor of education, 1961-68. Summer lecturer, Indiana University, 1967. *Member:* Phi Delta Kappa, Kappa Delta Pi, Kiwanis Club.

WRITINGS: (With Hazel Hicks) *A Handbook for Student Teaching,* W. C. Brown, 1954; (with Glenn Maynard) *The Changing Child: Readings in Child Development,* Scott, Foresman, 1972. Contributor to *Encyclopedia of Psychology* and to education journals.

* * *

BEICHNER, Paul E(dward) 1912-

PERSONAL: Surname is pronounced *Beek-ner;* born July 23, 1912, in Franklin, Pa.; son of Edward Louis and Mabel (Piper) Beichner. *Education:* University of Notre Dame, A.B., 1935, M.A., 1941; Holy Cross College, Washington, D.C., theological studies, 1935-39; Yale University, Ph.D., 1944. *Home:* University of Notre Dame, Notre Dame, Ind. 46556. *Office:* Mediaeval Institute, University of Notre Dame, Notre Dame, Ind. 46556.

CAREER: Ordained Roman Catholic priest, member of Congregation of the Holy Cross, 1939; Yale University, New Haven, Conn., research fellow, 1944-45; University of Notre Dame, Notre Dame, Ind., instructor, 1945-48, assistant professor, 1948-52, associate professor, 1952-57, professor of English, 1957—, professor at Mediaeval Institute, 1971—, assistant dean of College of Arts and Letters, 1949-50, assistant to academic vice-president, 1950-52, dean of Graduate School, 1952-71. Member of national selection committee for Fulbright awards to United Kingdom, 1955, and Woodrow Wilson fellowship program, 1958-67. Midwest Conference on Graduate Study and Research, member of executive committee, 1965-68, chairman, 1966-67; member of executive committee, Council of Graduate Schools in the United States, 1966-69; member of advisory council on graduate education, U.S. Office of Education, 1969-72. *Member:* Mediaeval Academy of America, Modern Language Association of America.

WRITINGS: The Medieval Representative of Music, Jubal or Tubalcain? (booklet), Mediaeval Institute, University of Notre Dame, 1954; (editor) *Aurora: Petri Rigae Biblia Versificata: A Verse Commentary on the Bible,* two volumes, University of Notre Dame Press, 1965; *Once upon a Parable: Fables for the Present,* University of Notre Dame Press, 1974. Contributor to *New Catholic Encyclopedia, Dictionnaire des Lettres Francais, Lexikon fuer Theologie und Kirche,* and to journals, including *Marianum* (Rome), *Le Moyen Age,* and *Mediaeval Studies* (Toronto).

WORK IN PROGRESS: Chaucer studies; further study on medieval verse Bibles.

AVOCATIONAL INTERESTS: Making woodcuts and prints.

* * *

BEILHARZ, Edwin Alanson 1907-

PERSONAL: Born June 18, 1907, in Phillipsburg, Kan.; son of William Tobias (a carpenter) and Lavara (Lowe) Beilharz; married Frances Marian Fuller, June 19, 1937; children: Frieda M. Beilharz Rosenberg, Ann Beilharz Pflager, Alan F., Claire G. *Education:* Creighton University, A.B., 1931; University of Nebraska, M.A., 1934; University of California, Berkeley, Ph.D., 1951. *Politics:* Democrat. *Religion:* Roman Catholic. *Home:* 16021 Wood Acres Rd., Los Ga-

tos, Calif. 95030. *Office:* Department of History, University of Santa Clara, Santa Clara, Calif. 95053.

CAREER: University of Santa Clara, Santa Clara, Calif., instructor, 1936-41, assistant professor, 1941-45, associate professor, 1945-51, professor of history, 1951-72, professor emeritus, 1972—. *Member:* American Historical Association, Catholic Historical Association, Pacific Coast Council of Latin American Studies (secretary-treasurer, 1964), California Historical Society. *Awards, honors:* Doctor of Humane Letters, University of Santa Clara, 1972.

WRITINGS: The New Frontiers and the Old, University of Santa Clara, 1961; *Felipe de Neve: First Governor of California,* California Historical Society, 1971; *We Were '49ers: Chilean Accounts of the California Gold Rush,* Ritchie, 1976. Contributor to history journals.

WORK IN PROGRESS: A book, tentatively entitled *Institutions in Conflict.*

* * *

BELDING, Robert E(dward) 1911-

PERSONAL: Born July 29, 1911, in Claremont, N.H.; son of Anson Wood (an editor and publisher) and Mary Alice (Miller) Belding; married Marjorie Terbeek (a secretary), August 20, 1946; children: Jacqueline Louise, Nancy Alison. *Education:* Hiram College, B.A., 1939; Boston University, M.Ed., 1948; Western Reserve University (now Case Western Reserve University), Ph.D., 1953. *Home:* 5A-Quail Creek Condominium, North Liberty, Iowa 52317. *Office:* 224 L.C.M., College of Education, University of Iowa, Iowa City, Iowa 52240.

CAREER: Instructor in French at Kents Hill School, Readfield, Me., 1939-41, and Chicago Latin School for Boys, Chicago, Ill., 1946-48; Muskingum College, New Concord, Ohio, assistant professor of foundations of education, 1948-49; Cedar Crest College, Allentown, Pa., associate professor of psychology and head of department, 1950-53; Parsons College, Fairfield, Iowa, professor of education and psychology and head of departments, 1953-59; University of Iowa, Iowa City, associate professor, 1959-64, professor of social foundations of education and chairman of department, 1964—. Visiting professor at Colorado State University, summers, 1952-59, University of Nottingham, 1962-63, Cambridge University, summer, 1966, and University of Oslo, summer, 1967. *Military service:* U.S. Army, 1942-45.

MEMBER: Comparative Education Society (member of board of directors, 1975—), History of Education Society (member of board of directors, 1969—), Midwest Regional History of Education Society (past president), American-Scandinavian Foundation, Phi Delta Kappa.

WRITINGS: Students Speak around the World, University of Iowa Press, 1960; *Personal School Reports from the Past,* University of Iowa Press, 1961; *European Classrooms: Schools of Four Nations,* Sernoll, 1966; (contributor) Harold Full, editor, *Controversy in American Education,* Macmillan, 1967; *Worker Education in Selected European Countries,* Center for Labor and Management, University of Iowa, 1973. Contributor of about 100 articles to education journals, *Norseman,* and *American-Swedish Monthly.*

WORK IN PROGRESS: Charted Links in America's Educational History; researching a book on Scandinavian schools.

SIDELIGHTS: Robert Belding's main interest is in Scandinavian schools, but he has visited schools or consulted on education in sixteen countries of Europe and South America and in Australia, India, and Iran. His current historical interest is in the American academies and in Midwestern school innovations.

*   *   *

BELEW, M. Wendell 1922-

PERSONAL: Born May 4, 1922, in Keefer, Ky.; son of Marion J. and Pet (Barker) Belew; married Edna Mae Record (a school teacher), December 14, 1946; children: Wendell, Jr., Cathy, Belle. *Education:* Attended University of Kentucky, 1939-40; Georgetown College, Georgetown, Ky., A.B., 1943; Southern Baptist Theological Seminary, B.D., 1949. *Home:* 3187 Mangum Lane S.W., Atlanta, Ga. 30311. *Office:* Home Mission Board, Southern Baptist Convention, 1350 Spring St. N.W., Atlanta, Ga. 30309.

CAREER: First Baptist Church, Mt. Vernon, Ky., pastor, 1947-52; General Association of Kentucky Baptists, director of Kentucky mountain missions, 1953-56; Southern Baptist Convention, Home Mission Board, Atlanta, Ga., director of church-centered missions, 1956-58, secretary of department of associational missions, 1959-64, secretary of associational administration services and church extension department, 1964-66, program secretary of department of pioneer missions, 1966, secretary of department of pioneer missions, 1967-70, director of division of missions, 1971—. Southern Baptist Theological Seminary, W. W. Brookes Visiting Professor of Missions, 1969-70, visiting professor of missions, 1976; lecturer, Fuller Theological Seminary, 1977; visiting professor of church growth studies, Midwestern Baptist Theological Seminary. *Military service:* U.S. Navy, 1943-46; became lieutenant. *Awards, honors:* D.D., Georgetown College, 1966.

WRITINGS: The Dark's A-Creepin', Home Mission Board, Southern Baptist Convention, 1964; *Song of Hawaii*, Home Mission Board, Southern Baptist Convention, 1968; *Churches, and How They Grow*, Broadman, 1971; *Missions in the Mosaic*, Home Mission Board, Southern Baptist Convention, 1974; *Tomorrow's Land: A Story of Baptists in Kentucky's Mountains, 1776-1976*, Kentucky Woman's Missionary Union (Middletown, Ky.), 1976; *The Leaven and the Salt*, Home Mission Board, Southern Baptist Convention, 1977; *Concepts of Baptist Brotherhood*, Brotherhood Commission (Memphis, Tenn.), in press. Contributor to Southern Baptist periodicals.

WORK IN PROGRESS: Children in the Marketplace; Creative Discipleship; Church Mission Strategy.

AVOCATIONAL INTERESTS: Other cultures, art, and horticulture.

*   *   *

BELITSKY, A(braham) Harvey 1929-

PERSONAL: Born August 27, 1929, in Brockton, Mass.; son of Aaron and Bertha (Yarmalowsky) Belitsky; married Helen Mintz (an editor), March 10, 1968; children: Bryna Sara, Aaron Asher. *Education:* University of Wisconsin, B.A., 1952; Syracuse University, M.A., 1953; Harvard University, Ph.D., 1960. *Politics:* Independent. *Religion:* Jewish. *Home:* 7821 Morningside Dr. N.W., Washington, D.C. 20012. *Office:* National Center for Productivity and Quality of Working Life, 2000 M St. N.W., Washington, D.C. 20036.

CAREER: Rutgers University, New Brunswick, N.J., instructor, 1959-60, assistant professor of economics, 1961-62; Lawrence College, Appleton, Wis., assistant professor of economics, 1962-64; W. E. Upjohn Institute for Employment Research, Washington, D.C., research economist, senior staff, 1964-75; currently affiliated with National Center for Productivity and Quality of Working Life, Washington, D.C. *Military service:* U.S. Navy, 1954-57; became lieutenant. *Member:* American Economic Association, Industrial Relations Research Association (board of governors, Washington chapter, 1971-74).

WRITINGS: (Contributor) S. A. Levitan and I. H. Siegel, editors, *Dimensions of Manpower Policy: Programs and Research*, Johns Hopkins Press, 1966; (with Harold L. Sheppard) *The Job Hunt*, Johns Hopkins Press, 1966; *Private Vocational Schools and Their Students: Limited Objectives, Unlimited Opportunities*, Schenkman, 1969; *Productivity and Job Security: Retraining to Adapt to Technological Change*, U.S. Government Printing Office, 1977. Contributor to *Encyclopedia of Education* and *Journal of Economic Issues*.

*   *   *

BELKNAP, Robert L(amont) 1929-

PERSONAL: Born December 23, 1929, in New York, N.Y.; son of Chauncey (a lawyer) and Dorothy (Lamont) Belknap; married Josephine Hornor (a teacher), August 20, 1955; children: Lydia, Ellen, Abigail. *Education:* Princeton University, A.B., 1951; School of Living Oriental Languages, Paris, further study, 1951-52; Columbia University, M.A., 1954, Ph.D., 1960. *Politics:* Republican. *Religion:* Dutch Reformed. *Home:* 440 Riverside Dr., New York, N.Y. 10027. *Office:* Department of Slavic Languages, Columbia University, 718 Hamilton Hall, New York, N.Y. 10025.

CAREER: Columbia University, New York, N.Y., 1957—, began as instructor, currently professor of Russian, and director of the Russian Institute. *Military service:* U.S. Army, 1953-55. *Awards, honors:* Woodrow Wilson fellow, 1951-52; Ford Foundation fellow, 1955-57; Inter-University Committee travel grant for study in Leningrad, 1963.

WRITINGS: The Structure of "The Brothers Karamazov," Mouton, 1966; (with Richard Kuhns) *Tradition and Innovation: General Education and the Reintegration of the University*, Columbia University Press, 1977.

*   *   *

BELL, Alan P(aul) 1932-

PERSONAL: Born January 18, 1932, in Newark, N.J.; son of George Alexander (an insurance broker) and Edna (Hoburg) Bell; married Lundie Lenoir, August 15, 1955; married second wife, Shirley Levine, June 25, 1964; children: (first marriage) Terry; (second marriage) Toby, Joshua, Rachel. *Education:* University of the South, A.B., 1952; General Theological Seminary, M.Div., 1955; Columbia University, M.A., 1964, Ph.D., 1967. *Home:* Sare Rd., Bloomington, Ind. 47401. *Office:* Institute for Sex Research, Bloomington, Ind. 47401.

CAREER: Indiana University, Bloomington, assistant professor, 1967-70, associate professor, 1970-74, professor of education, 1974—; Institute for Sex Research, Bloomington, senior research psychologist, 1967—, member of executive committee and board of trustees. Director, Center for Human Growth, Bloomington; member of advisory board, Community Sex Information and Educational Service. *Member:* American Psychological Association, National Sex and Drug Forum (member of board of directors), Sex

Information and Education Council of the United States (chairperson), Indiana Psychological Association, Sigma Xi, Psi Chi.

WRITINGS: (With Calvin S. Hall) *The Personality of a Child Molester: An Analysis of Dreams,* Aldine-Atherton, 1971; (with Martin S. Weinberg) *Homosexuality: An Annotated Bibliography,* Harper, 1972; *Homosexualities: A Study of Diversity among Men and Women,* Simon & Schuster, 1978. Contributor to professional journals, including *Journal of Counseling Psychology, Developmental Psychology, Journal of Sex Research,* and *Medical Aspects of Human Sexuality.*

WORK IN PROGRESS: A second volume on the development of sexual orientation; *Life Portraits: A Study of Men and Their Careers;* a primer for beginning counseling students, *One with One.*

* * *

BELL, Eileen 1907-

PERSONAL: Born October 28, 1907, in Clifton, Bristol, England; daughter of Edward John and Catherine (Jefferd) Bowerbank; married Randal Mulcaster Bell, 1937; children: Giles Sebastian. *Education:* Howard Jones School of Music, L.R.A.M. (Licentiate of Royal Academy of Music), 1925. *Home:* 1 Willow Cottages, Kew Green, Richmond on Thames, Surrey, England. *Agent:* David Higham Associates Ltd., 5-8 Lower John St., Golden Sq., London WIR 3PE, England.

CAREER: Teacher of music, textile designer, and consultant interior designer.

WRITINGS—Juvenile: Tales from the End Cottage, illustrations by Prudence Seward, Penguin, 1970; *More Tales from the End Cottage,* Penguin, 1972; (with others) "Lift-off Number Series" (set of twenty-seven cards), Davis & Moughton, 1972, three books, 1975.

WORK IN PROGRESS: Summer Tales; The Wicked Cats of Saltbox Farm; Oxford Child; Ten Years to Grow Up.

SIDELIGHTS: A reviewer writes of *Tales from the End Cottage* in the *Times Literary Supplement:* "Those well-contrived and unaffected stories describe the easy-going, companionable life of Mrs. Apple, her two cats, two Pekinese dogs, seven hens, and their various friends, both animal and human. . . . The stories give an appealing picture of country life through all the seasons of the year, even though the rural scene may sometimes seem a little too rosily painted."

Eileen Bell wrote *CA* that she believes strongly in the preservation of ancient buildings, both in the country and cities. She also believes in the protection of the countryside from chemical and other types of pollution.

AVOCATIONAL INTERESTS: Country crafts and lore, gardening, pottery-making.

BIOGRAPHICAL/CRITICAL SOURCES: Times Literary Supplement, August 14, 1970.†

* * *

BELL, James Edward 1941-

PERSONAL: Born May 12, 1941, in Chicago, Ill; son of Codie Dee (a business consultant) and Clara (Reynolds) Bell; married Ruth Wilder (a nurse), September 5, 1964; children: Carl Douglas, Sara Wilder. *Education:* University of Minnesota, B.A., 1963, Ph.D., 1967. *Home:* 5033 Round Tower Pl., Columbia, Md. 21044. *Office:* Department of

Psychology, Howard Community College, Columbia, Md. 21044.

CAREER: University of Minnesota, Minneapolis, Minn., instructor, 1965-66; Hanover College, Hanover, Ind., assistant professor of psychology, 1966-68; Elmira College, Elmira, N.Y., assistant professor of psychology, 1968-71; Howard Community College, Columbia, Md., associate professor of psychology, 1971—. *Member:* American Association of University Professors, American Psychological Association, Maryland Association of Junior Colleges.

WRITINGS: A Guide to Library Research in Psychology, W. C. Brown, 1971. Contributor to *Journal of Experimental Social Psychology, Improving College and University Teaching,* and to *Psychological Reports.*

WORK IN PROGRESS: Booklet to help psychology students critically evaluate secondary sources in psychology.

* * *

BELLAMY, Francis Rufus 1886-1972

December 24, 1886—February 2, 1972; American editor, publisher, and author of popular histories. Obituaries: *New York Times,* February 4, 1972; *Washington Post,* February 4, 1972; *Publishers Weekly,* February 28, 1972.

* * *

BELOK, Michael V(ictor) 1923-

PERSONAL: Born June 22, 1923, in Whiting, Ind.; son of Michael (a fireman) and Helen (Dobos) Belok; married Georgina Pilkington, July 31, 1965. *Education:* Attended Harvard University, 1943-44; Indiana University, B.S., 1948; Arizona State University, M.A., 1953; University of Southern California, Ph.D., 1958. *Home:* 1015 West Fairway Dr., Mesa, Ariz. 85201. *Office:* College of Education, Arizona State University, Tempe, Ariz. 85281.

CAREER: University of Southern California, Los Angeles, lecturer in education, 1958-59; Arizona State University, Tempe, assistant professor, 1959-69, professor of education, 1969—. Visiting lecturer, University of Southern California, summers, 1959-60. *Military service:* U.S. Army, 1943-46. *Member:* History of Education Society, American Educational Studies Association, Far Western Philosophy of Education Society, Kappa Delta Pi, Phi Delta Kappa, Delta Tau Kappa (chancellor of Southwest region).

WRITINGS: (With Thomas M. Weiss) *Psychological Foundations of Education,* W. C. Brown, 1963; (contributor) Clifton L. Hall, editor, *Readings in American Education,* Scott, Foresman, 1966; (contributor) J. S. Roucek, editor, *The Teaching of History,* Philosophical Library, 1967; (contributor) Jean Grambs, editor, *School and Society: A Book of Readings,* Prentice-Hall, 1967; (with O. R. Bontrager) *Approaches to Values in Education,* W. C. Brown, 1967; (contributor) Roucek, editor, *The Slow Learner,* Philosophical Library, 1969; (contributor) G. C. Hallen and Rajeshwar Prasad, editors, *Sorokin and Sociology,* Satish Book Enterprise, 1970; (contributor) James C. Stone and Frederick W. Schneider, editors, *Readings in Foundations of Education,* Crowell, 1971; (with R. F. Ryberg) *Explorations in the History and Sociology of American Indian Education,* Sadna Prakashan, 1973; *Noah Webster Revisited,* Bureau of Educational Research, Arizona State University, 1973; *Forming the American Minds: Early Schoolbooks and Their Compilers, 1783-1837,* Satish Book Enterprise, 1973; *Conflict, Permanency, Change and Education,* Satish Book Enterprise, 1976; *Sex, Race, Ethnicity and Education,* Anu Prakashan, 1977.

Contributor of more than fifty articles and reviews to professional journals in the fields of education, sociology, history, semantics, and law, and to *American Book Collector.* Contributing editor, *International Review of History and Political Science;* American book review editor, *V.O.C. Journal of Education;* consulting editor, *Indian Sociological Bulletin;* honorary editor, *International Journal of Legal Research;* member of editorial board, *Indian Journal of Social Research, Journal of Thought,* and *International Behavioural Scientist.*

WORK IN PROGRESS: A textbook, *Explorations in the History of American Education;* continuing research on the subject of old schoolbooks.

AVOCATIONAL INTERESTS: Book collecting (especially early schoolbooks and periodicals).

* * *

BELOTE, James H(ine) 1922-

PERSONAL: Surname is pronounced Bah-*loat;* born October 4, 1922, in Bellevue, Wash.; son of William M. and Adelaide (Hine) Belote; married Edith Wunderlin, August 27, 1953; children: John Arthur, Nancy Gayle. *Education:* University of Washington, Seattle, B.A., 1948, M.A., 1949; University of California, Berkeley, Ph.D., 1954. *Politics:* Republican. *Religion:* Church of Christ Scientist. *Home:* 16 La Salle St., Elsah, Ill. 62028. *Office:* Department of History, Principia College, Elsah, Ill. 62028.

CAREER: U.S. Government, Washington, D.C., intelligence specialist, 1954-60; University of Virginia, George Mason College, Fairfax, instructor in history, 1957-60; Principia College, Elsah, Ill., assistant professor, 1960-67, associate professor, 1967-70, professor of history, 1970—, chairman of department, 1970-76. *Military service:* U.S. Army Air Forces, 1942-46; served in North Africa, Italy, Germany, France, and Belgium, 1944-46. *Member:* American Historical Association, American Military Institute, U.S. Naval Institute, American Aviation Historical Society, Phi Beta Kappa.

WRITINGS: (With brother, William M. Belote) *Corregidor: The Saga of a Fortress,* Harper, 1967; (with William M. Belote) *Typhoon of Steel: The Battle for Okinawa,* Harper, 1970; *Titans of the Seas: The Development and Operations of Japanese and American Carrier Task Forces during World War II,* Harper, 1975.

* * *

BELTRAN, Miriam 1914-

PERSONAL: Surname is pronounced Bel-*tran;* born May 9, 1914, in San Francisco, Calif.; daughter of Walter E. and Mary (Foley) Kropp; married Pedro Beltran (a publisher), August 30, 1950. *Education:* Stanford University, B.A., 1935. *Religion:* Roman Catholic. *Address:* c/o Kropp, 35 Florence St., San Francisco, Calif. 94133.

CAREER: International Business Machines Corp., San Francisco, Calif., employed in systems service, 1939-43; U.S. Department of State, junior economic analyst in Washington, D.C., and then in Lima, Peru, 1943-45; *La Prensa* (daily newspaper), Lima, chairman of board of directors, 1959-70. Member of freedom of the press committee, Inter-American Press Association, 1959-63. Member of board of directors, Lima Art Museum. *Member:* Cosmopolitan Club (New York), Town and Country Club (San Francisco). *Awards, honors:* Order of Isabel the Catholic (Spain), 1958; Arts and Letters Award bestowed by Andre Malraux, French Minister of Cultural Affairs, 1961.

WRITINGS: Cuzco: Window on Peru, Crowell Collier, 1956, revised edition, Knopf, 1970.

* * *

BELY, Jeanette L(obach) 1916-

PERSONAL: Born January 15, 1916, in Brooklyn, N.Y.; daughter of John Michael (a manufacturer) and Anna M. (Kalechitz) Lobach; married Joseph Bely, May 11, 1946 (divorced, 1950); children: Jeanette, Leona. *Education:* St. John's University, B.B.A., 1938, Ph.D., 1961; Columbia University, M.A., 1939; also attended New York University, 1954-56. *Office:* Department of Education, Bernard M. Baruch College of the City University of New York, 17 Lexington Ave., New York, N.Y. 10010.

CAREER: Miller Schools, Inc., New York City, teacher of secretarial studies and accounting, 1940-42, administrative assistant, 1942-48; Pace College (now University), New York City, instructor in stenography, 1951-53; Hunter College (now Hunter College of the City University of New York), New York City, lecturer in business education, 1954; Bernard M. Baruch College of the City University of New York, New York City, associate professor of business education, 1954—, faculty member of Graduate School, 1975-76, deputy chairman of department of education, 1972-73. Technical editor, consultant, and reviewer for Simon & Schuster, Prentice-Hall, and Houghton Mifflin. Consultant, lecturer, and speaker at business seminars, workshops, and conventions. *Member:* International Society for Business Education, National Education Association, National Business Education Association, Administrative Management Society (chairman, speakers' bureau, 1966—), Eastern Business Teachers Association, Eastern Business Education Association, Business Education Association of Metropolitan New York (executive board member; executive board member of Pitman Teachers Association), Business Teachers Association of New York State, New York State Teachers Association, American Museum of Natural History, Smithsonian Institution, Delta Pi Epsilon. *Awards, honors:* Merit award, Administrative Management Socieity, 1969.

WRITINGS: (Contributor) Abraham Klein, editor, *The World Secretarial Handbook,* World Publishing, 1968; *The Implications of Open Admissions at City University of New York and Its Impact On the 4-Year Colleges* (monograph), Business Education Association, 1972; *Pitman Secretarial Shorthand for Colleges,* with teachers manual, Pitman, 1976. Editor and contributor to *Business Education Association Yearbook;* also contributor to *Balance Sheet.*

* * *

BENANTE, Joseph P(hilip) 1936-

PERSONAL: Born December 31, 1936, in Garfield, N.J.; son of Henry A. (an accountant) and Jeanette (Azzolino) Benante. *Education:* Seton Hall University, B.A., 1959; attended Immaculate Conception Seminary, New York, N.Y., 1959-63. *Home:* 11 Monroe St., Garfield, N.J. 07026. *Agent:* Knox Burger, 39½ Washington Sq. S., New York, N.Y. 10012. *Office:* 46 East Broadway, New York, N.Y. 10002.

CAREER: Roman Catholic priest, Long Island, N.Y., 1963-69; *Paterson News,* Paterson, N.J., editorial staff member, 1969-70; Lower Eastside Service Center, New York, N.Y., drug abuse rehabilitation counselor, 1970—.

WRITINGS: A Fragile Bark, Simon & Schuster, 1971.

WORK IN PROGRESS: Research on the pagan roots of Judeo-Christianity.

SIDELIGHTS: A former priest, Benante is also now a tatoo artist and considers human freedom paramount in future writing efforts which will no longer be in fictional form.

* * *

BENDER, Coleman C. 1921-

PERSONAL: Born March 30, 1921, in Coalport, Pa.; son of Harry and Annie Bender; married Pauline Rexford (a researcher), 1947; children: Sue Ann, David. *Education:* Pennsylvania State University, B.A., 1946, M.A., 1948; University of Illinois, Ph.D., 1955. *Home:* 81 Bromfield St., Watertown, Mass. 02172. *Office:* Department of Speech, Emerson College, Boston, Mass. 02116.

CAREER: Pennsylvania State University, State College, instructor in speech, 1946-48; University of Illinois at Urbana-Champaign, Urbana, instructor in speech, 1948-50; Chanute Air Force Base, Illinois, educational specialist, 1951; Emerson College, Boston, Mass., professor of speech, chairman of department of speech, and chairman of graduate studies, 1951—. Works with both police and prisoners in training programs. *Military service:* U.S. Army Air Forces, 1942-46. *Member:* International Communication Association, Municipal Police Science Institute, Massachusetts Speech Association.

WRITINGS: (With B. P. McCabe) *Speaking Is a Practical Matter,* Holbrook, 1968, 3rd edition, 1976; *Guidebook to Speech Communication,* Holbrook, 1969; (editor with John W. Zorn) *The Word in Context,* Holbrook, 1970; (editor with Zorn) *Problems and Issues in Relevance,* Holbrook, 1970; (with John Zacitaris) *Speech Communication: A Rational Approach,* Wiley, 1976.

* * *

BENDER, Henry E(dwin), Jr. 1937-

PERSONAL: Born March 6, 1937, in Evanston, Ill.; son of Henry Edwin (a broker of animal by-products) and Nancy (Barry) Bender; married Barbara E. Caven, November 25, 1967; children: Phillip M. *Education:* Purdue University, B.S., 1958; University of New Mexico, graduate study, 1958-64, University of Denver, M.A., 1965. *Politics:* Independent. *Religion:* Protestant. *Home:* 6257 Solano Dr., San Jose, Calif. 95119. *Office:* General Products Division, International Business Machines Corp., P.O. Box 50020, 555 Bailey Ave., San Jose, Calif. 95150.

CAREER: ACF Industries, Inc. (designers of nuclear rocket pressure vessels), Albuquerque, N.M., associate design engineer, 1958-64; Kaman Nuclear, Colorado Springs, Colo., part-time library consultant, 1965; International Business Machines Corp. (IBM), San Jose, Calif., librarian, 1965-72, programmer trainee, 1972, editor, 1973-74, programming publications writer, 1974—. *Member:* American Society of Mechanical Engineers, U.S.-China Peoples Friendship Association, National Railway Historical Society (president of Central Coast chapter, 1971-73), Railway and Locomotive Historical Society, Railroadians of America, Railroad Station Historical Society, Zero Population Growth, Pacific Locomotive Association, Rocky Mountain Railroad Club, Railroad Club of New Mexico (president, 1958-60).

WRITINGS: Uintah Railway: The Gilsonite Route, Howell-North Books, 1970. Editor, *New Mexico Railroader,* 1958-64.

WORK IN PROGRESS: Research on locomotives and railways of China.

* * *

BENDER, Louis W. 1927-

PERSONAL: Born February 8, 1927, in Graceham, Md.; son of Elmer D. (a minister) and Mildred L. (Walters) Bender; married; wife's name, Elizabeth; children: James Perry, Paul Douglas. *Education:* Moravian College, B.A., 1950; Lehigh University, M.A., 1952, Ed.D., 1965; additional graduate study at Temple University and New York University, 1953-56. *Religion:* Presbyterian. *Home:* 4325 Jackson View Dr., Tallahassee, Fla. 32303. *Office:* Department of Higher Education, Florida State University, Tallahassee, Fla. 32306.

CAREER: English teacher and counselor in Quakertown, Pa., 1951-54; director of guidance in Westwood, N.J., 1954-57; high school dean of boys in Scarsdale, N.Y., 1957-61; high school principal in Tarrytown, N.Y., 1961-62; Bucks County (Pa.) public schools, assistant county superintendent, 1962-65; Pennsylvania Department of Education, Harrisburg, Pa., director of bureau of community colleges, 1965-68, acting assistant commissioner for higher education, 1968-69, assistant commissioner, 1969-70; Florida State University, Tallahassee, professor of higher education, 1970—, and director of State and Regional Higher Education Center. Evening and summer session instructor, Fairleigh Dickinson University, 1954-60; visiting professor at Lehigh University, 1964, Syracuse University, 1969, and North Carolina State University at Raleigh, 1976; national lecturer, Nova University, 1972-78. Member of advisory board, E.R.I.C. Clearing House for Higher Education, 1975-78; consultant for media systems, Harcourt, Brace, Jovanovich, Inc., 1976—. *Military service:* U.S. Army, 1945-47.

MEMBER: National Council of State Directors of Community Junior Colleges (life member; chairman, 1968-69), Council of Colleges and Universities (president, 1975-76), American Association of School Administrators, National Education Association, Council of Educational Facility Planners, American Association of Junior Colleges, Phi Delta Kappa. *Awards, honors:* Pennsylvania governor's awards for excellence, 1967, 1968.

WRITINGS: (With James L. Wattenbarger and Norman C. Harris) *A Plan for Community College Education in West Virginia,* West Virginia Board of Regents, 1971; (with Richard C. Richardson, Jr. and Clyde E. Blocker) *Governance of the Two-Year College,* Prentice-Hall, 1972; *Improving Statewide Planning,* Jossey-Bass, 1974; (with Blocker and S. V. Martorana) *The Political Terrain of American Post-Secondary Education,* Nova University Press, 1975; *Federal Regulation and Higher Education,* American Association for Higher Education, 1977; (with Benjamin Wygal) *Relating to the Public: Challenge of the Community College,* Jossey-Bass, 1978. Contributor to educational journals.

WORK IN PROGRESS: A study of field-based doctoral programs operating in other than home state of sponsoring institution.

* * *

BENDER, Robert M. 1936-

PERSONAL: Born March 15, 1936, in Chicago, Ill.; son of Alex (a businessman) and Edith (Neimark) Bender; married Eleanor M. Shufelt (an editor and teacher), October 5, 1963;

children: Alyssa Juliet, Gillian Penelope, Jessica Ariadne. *Education:* Illinois Institute of Technology, B.S., 1957; University of Michigan, M.A., 1958, Ph.D., 1963. *Home:* 107 Westwood Ave., Columbia, Mo. 65201. *Office:* Department of English, University of Missouri, Columbia, Mo. 65201.

CAREER: University of Michigan, Ann Arbor, instructor in English, 1962-63; Brooklyn College of the City University of New York, Brooklyn, N.Y., instructor, 1963-64, 1965-66, assistant professor of English, 1966-68; University of Missouri—Columbia, assistant professor, 1968-69, associate professor of English, 1969—. *Member:* International Shakespeare Association, Modern Language Association of America, National Education Association. *Awards, honors:* American Council of Learned Societies fellow, 1964-65.

WRITINGS: (With Charles L. Squier) *The Sonnet: A Comprehensive Anthology of British and American Sonnets from the Renaissance to the Present,* Washington Square Press, 1965; *Five Courtier Poets,* Washington Square Press, 1968; *The Shaping of Fiction,* Washington Square Press, 1970.

WORK IN PROGRESS: A study of characterization in Shakespeare's plays; two novels.

*   *   *

BENELL, Florence B(elle)   1912-

PERSONAL: Born October 10, 1912, in San Francisco, Calif.; daughter of Charles (an artist) and Anna (Slifkin) Benell. *Education:* University of Michigan, A.B., 1931, M.S.P.H., 1933; University of Chicago, Ph.D., 1951. *Home address:* P.O. Box 19183, Sacramento, Calif. 95819. *Office:* Department of Health Science, California State University, 6000 J St., Sacramento, Calif. 95819.

CAREER: Milwaukee State College, Milwaukee, Wis., instructor in health education, 1939-44; Tuberculosis Institute, Chicago, Ill., director of health education, 1944-47; Eastern Illinois University, Charleston, health coordinator, 1948-49; Florida State University, Tallahassee, associate professor of health, 1950-51; Illinois Social Hygiene League, Chicago, associate director, 1953-63; Chicago Board of Health, Chicago, chief health educator, 1958-63; California State University, Sacramento, assistant professor, 1964-69, associate professor, 1969-70, professor of health, 1971—.

WRITINGS: An Educational Approach to VD Control, National Press Books, 1965; *Behavioral Dynamics of Sex Education,* Kendall-Hunt, 1967. Contributor to health and education journals.

*   *   *

BENELLO, C. George   1926-

PERSONAL: Born November 10, 1926, in New York, N.Y.; son of Giacomo (an engineer) and Katherine (Lytton) Benello; married Lestra Carpe (a physician); children: Julian, Allen. *Education:* Harvard University, A.B., 1949; attended Universite Laval, 1949-50, and Brown University, 1951; San Francisco State College (now University), M.A., 1962.

CAREER: Goddard College, Plainfield, Vt., professor of sociology, 1968-71; McGill University, Montreal, Quebec, assistant professor of sociology, beginning 1971. Parallel Institute, fellow, 1970—, member of board of directors, 1971—, president, 1972—; member of board of directors, University Settlement, 1972—. *Member:* American Academy of Social and Political Science.

WRITINGS: (Editor with Dimitrios Roussopoulos) *The Case for Participatory Democracy,* Grossman, 1971; (contributor) H. P. Drietzel, editor, *Recent Sociology,* Number 1, Macmillan, 1969; (contributor) Patricia Long, editor, *The New Left: A Collection of Essays,* Sargent, 1970. Contributor to popular magazines, including *Our Generation* and *Canadian Dimension.* Editor, *Our Generation* and *Current.*

WORK IN PROGRESS: The Commission on the Year One, with Michael Miles.

SIDELIGHTS: C. George Benello made the first Atlantic crossing by trimaran in 1960.†

*   *   *

BENGTSSON, Arvid   1916-

PERSONAL: Born May 7, 1916, in Loensboda, Sweden; married Gunilla Persson, July 15, 1944; children: Ingemar, Cecilia, Gertrude, Kerstin. *Education:* Horticultural College of Alnarp, graduate in landscape architecture, 1945. *Home:* Ungmaestaregatan 54, Gothenburg, Sweden.

CAREER: Director of parks, Gothenburg, Sweden. *Member:* International Playground Association (past president).

WRITINGS: Environmental Planning for Children's Play, Praeger, 1970; *Adventure Playgrounds,* Crosby Lockwood, 1971, Praeger, 1972; *The Child's Right to Play,* International Playground Association, 1974; *Vom Schulhof Zum Spielhof,* Bauverlag, 1978.

BIOGRAPHICAL/CRITICAL SOURCES: Times Literary Supplement, May 28, 1970.

*   *   *

BEN-ISRAEL-KIDRON, Hedva

PERSONAL: Born in Jerusalem, Israel; daughter of Izhak (an author and bookseller) and Friedericke (Tretter) Ben-Israel; married Micha A. Kidron (an electronics engineer), 1964; children: Oren, Dan, Irad. *Education:* Hebrew University of Jerusalem, M.A. (cum laude), 1949; Girton College, Cambridge, Ph.D., 1955. *Religion:* Jewish. *Home:* 19 Balfour St., Jerusalem, Israel. *Office:* Department of History, Hebrew University of Jerusalem, Jerusalem, Israel.

CAREER: Hebrew University of Jerusalem, Jerusalem, Israel, instructor, 1957-60, lecturer, 1960-65, senior lecturer in history, 1965—. *Military service:* Israeli Army, company commander during War of Independence, 1948-49. *Awards, honors:* Betty Miller Literary Award, Union of Jewish Women (England), 1969, for *English Historians on the French Revolution.*

WRITINGS: English Historians on the French Revolution, Cambridge University Press, 1968. Writer of scripts for Israeli Broadcasting Service and for television. Contributor to *Hebrew Encyclopaedia, Encyclopaedia of Education, Jerusalem Post, English Historical Review, Journal of the History of Ideas,* and other periodicals.

WORK IN PROGRESS: Research centered on the eve of the second World War and on the process of colonization and decolonization, especially in Africa.

*   *   *

BENNE, Kenneth D(ean)   1908-

PERSONAL: Born May 11, 1908, in Morrowville, Kan.; son of Henry (a farmer) and Bertha (Thrun) Benne. *Education:* Kansas State University of Agricultural and Applied Science, B.S., 1930; University of Michigan, M.A., 1936;

Columbia University, Ph.D., 1941. *Politics:* Independent. *Religion:* Methodist. *Home:* 8 Kilsyth Ter., Brookline, Mass. 02146; and Center Lovell, Me. 04016.

CAREER: Rural school teacher in Washington County, Kan., 1925-27; high school science teacher in Concordia, Kan., 1930-35, in Manhattan, Kan., 1935-36; University of Illinois at Urbana-Champaign, Urbana, 1941-46, assistant professor, later associate professor of philosophy of education; Columbia University, New York, N.Y., associate professor of philosophy of education, 1946-48; University of Illinois at Urbana-Champaign, professor of philosophy of education, 1948-53; Boston University, Boston, Mass., professor of human relations and philosophy, 1953-73, professor emeritus, 1973—. Centennial Professor, University of Kentucky, 1965. Co-inventor of the "training group"; co-founder of National Training Laboratories. *Military service:* U.S. Naval Reserve, 1942-46.

MEMBER: Philosophy of Education Society (past president), American Philosophical Association, American Sociological Association, Adult Education Association (president, 1956), Society for the Study of Social Issues, International Association of Applied Social Scientists (co-founder; chairman of board, 1971-74), Authors Guild. *Awards, honors:* Kilpatrick Award for outstanding contribution to American philosophy of education, 1943; D.H.L., Lesley College, 1969, Morris Brown College, 1971.

WRITINGS: A Conception of Authority, Teachers College Press, 1943, reprinted, Russell, 1971; (with R. Bruce Raup, Bunnie Smith, and George Axtelle) *The Improvement of Practical Intelligence,* Harper, 1951; (with Warren Bennis and Robert Chin) *The Planning of Change,* Holt, 1961; (with Leland Bradford and Jack Gibb) *T-Group Theory and Laboratory Method,* Wiley, 1964; *Education for Tragedy,* University of Kentucky Press, 1967; *The Soul of Post-Contemporary Man,* Boston University Human Relations Center, 1970; (with others) *The Laboratory Method of Changing and Learning,* Science & Behavior Books, 1975. Contributor of poems, articles, and reviews to forty journals; contributing editor of six periodicals.

WORK IN PROGRESS: A book of verse; research on ethics of training and consultation in human relations; a study of the self, *I, You and We.*

AVOCATIONAL INTERESTS: Book collecting.

* * *

BENNER, Ralph Eugene (Jr.) 1932-

PERSONAL: Born January 4, 1932, in Lansing, Mich.; son of Ralph Eugene (a doctor) and Mary (Chamberlin) Benner; married Shirley Nelson, September 16, 1955; married second wife, Judith Bartlett, November 25, 1967; children: (first marriage) Valerie, (second marriage) Katherine, Jamie. *Education:* University of California, Los Angeles, M.A., 1955. *Politics:* Republican. *Religion:* Religious Science. *Residence:* Sherman Oaks, Calif. *Agent:* Donald MacCampbell, Inc., 12 East 41st St., New York, N.Y. 10017.

CAREER: Laufer Publishing Co., Hollywood, Calif., editorial director, 1965—. Teacher of magazine journalism at University of California, Los Angeles. *Military service:* U.S. Army Reserve, 1956-62; retired as captain.

WRITINGS: (With Mary Jo Clements) *Young Actors' Guide to Hollywood,* Coward, 1962; (with Shirley Benner) *Sex and the Teenager,* Macfadden, 1964; *Songbird,* Macfadden, 1970.

BENNETT, Edward M(oore) 1927-

PERSONAL: Born September 28, 1927, in Dixon, Ill.; son of John Francis and Marguerite (Moore) Bennett; married Margery Harder, September 3, 1950; children: Michael Dana. *Education:* Butler University, B.A., 1952; University of Illinois, M.A., 1956, Ph.D., 1961. *Home:* 1315 Orchard Dr. N.E., Pullman, Wash. 99163. *Office:* 323 Wilson Hall, Washington State University, Pullman, Wash. 99163.

CAREER: Texas A & M University, College Station, instructor in American history, 1960-61; Washington State University, Pullman, assistant professor, 1961-66, associate professor, 1966-71, professor of U.S. diplomatic history, 1971—, representative to Pacific-Eight Conference, 1965—, and to National Collegiate Athletic Association, 1966—, president of Pacific-Eight Conference, 1972—. Member of advisory council, Washington State Council on Higher Education. *Military service:* U.S. Army, 1946-47; served in Korea. U.S. Air Force, intelligence officer, 1952-54.

MEMBER: Organization of American Historians, American Historical Association (member of executive committee, Pacific Coast branch), Society of Historians of American Foreign Relations, American Association of University Professors, Phi Alpha Theta.

WRITINGS: (Editor) *Polycentrism: Growing Dissidence in the Communist Bloc?,* Washington State University Press, 1967; *Recognition of Russia: An American Foreign Policy Dilemma,* Ginn, 1970; (editor with Richard D. Burns, and contributor) *Diplomats in Crisis: United States-Chinese-Japanese Relations, 1919-1941,* ABC-Clio, 1974; (with Howard C. Payne and Raymond Callahan) *As the Storm Clouds Gathered: European Perceptions of American Foreign Policy in the 1930's,* Schenkman, in press. Contributor to academic journals.

WORK IN PROGRESS: A two-volume study on Franklin D. Roosevelt and Soviet-American relations, 1933-1945.

* * *

BENNETT, Gordon C. 1935-

PERSONAL: Born September 1, 1935, in Philadelphia, Pa.; son of Harold Walter and Agnes (Raff) Bennett; married Ruth Packer, June 8, 1957; children: Brad Alan, Cherry Lynn. *Education:* Dickinson College, A.B., 1957; Temple University, M.A., 1967; Berkeley Baptist Divinity School, B.D., 1960. *Home:* 1743 Russell Rd., Paoli, Pa. 19301. *Office:* Department of Speech and Drama, Eastern College, St. Davids, Pa. 19087.

CAREER: Clergyman of American Baptist Convention; minister of churches in Fredericktown, Ohio, 1960-65, and Narberth, Pa., 1965-68; Eastern College, St. Davids, Pa., instructor, 1968-70, assistant professor of speech and drama, 1970—. Actor in and director of church and campus plays; co-founder of King's Players, chancel drama team playing in Philadelphia area. *Member:* Speech Communication Association, Religious Speech Communication Association (chairman, religious drama committee), Speech Association of the Eastern States, Fellowship of Reconciliation. *Awards, honors:* Book award, Religious Commonwealth Association, 1976, for *Happy Tales, Fables, and Plays.*

WRITINGS: (With William D. Thompson) *Dialogue Preaching: The Shared Sermon,* Judson, 1969; *God Is My Fuehrer: A Dramatic Interpretation of the Life of Martin Niemoeller,* Friendship, 1970; *Readers Theatre Comes to Church,* John Knox, 1972; *From Nineveh to Now,* Bethany Press, 1973; *Happy Tales, Fables, and Plays,* John Knox, 1975. Contributor to religion publications.

WORK IN PROGRESS: Stories and articles on religious communication; two plays.

AVOCATIONAL INTERESTS: Playing tennis and softball, camping, writing, and amateur acting.

*   *   *

BENNETT, James R(ichard)   1932-

PERSONAL: Born March 15, 1932, in Harrison, Ark.; son of Joseph Volney (a pharmacist) and Mildred (Dickinson) Bennett; married Jo Ann Keenan (a librarian), February 25, 1951; children: John Volney, Michelle Katherine. *Education:* University of Arkansas, B.A., 1953, M.A., 1954; Stanford University, Ph.D., 1961. *Politics:* Democrat. *Religion:* Humanist. *Home:* 833 East Ash, Fayetteville, Ark. 72701. *Office:* Department of English, University of Arkansas, Fayetteville, Ark. 72701.

CAREER: University of Montana, Missoula, instructor, 1960-61, assistant professor of English, 1961-62; Western Washington State College (now Western Washington University), Bellingham, assistant professor, 1962-65; University of Arkansas, Fayetteville, assistant professor, 1965-66, associate professor, 1966-71, professor of English, 1971—, chairman of humanities program. Fulbright lecturer in Yugoslavia, 1968-69. *Military service:* U.S. Air Force, 1954-56; became first lieutenant. *Member:* Modern Language Association of America, American Association of University Professors, National Council of Teachers of English, College English Association, American Civil Liberties Union (state board member), South Central Modern Language Association, Arkansas Council of Teachers of English (president, 1972-73).

WRITINGS: (Editor) *Prose Style: A Historical Approach through Studies,* Chandler Publishing, 1972. Contributor of articles to *Victorian Poetry, D. H. Lawrence Review, Crane Review, Mill News Letter,* and other publications. Editor, *Style,* 1966—.

WORK IN PROGRESS: Criticism of American business in American literature; a book on World War II European anti-Nazi resistance movements.

AVOCATIONAL INTERESTS: Canoeing, hiking, camping, swimming.

*   *   *

BENNETT, Joseph D.   1922-1972

January 26, 1922—March 29, 1972; American banker, editor, critic, novelist, and short story writer. Obituaries: *New York Times,* April 8, 1972. (See index for *CA* sketch)

*   *   *

BENNETT, Scott (Boyce)   1939-

PERSONAL: Born July 22, 1939, in Kansas City, Mo.; son of Preston Theodore and Louise (Scott) Bennett; married Carol Glass, June 20, 1960; children: Beth, Theodore, Myron. *Education:* Oberlin College, A.B., 1960; Indiana University, M.A., 1966, Ph.D., 1967; University of Illinois, M.S., 1976. *Home:* 711 South Race, Urbana, Ill. 61801. *Office:* 230 Library, University of Illinois at Urbana-Champaign, Urbana, Ill. 61801.

CAREER: St. Paul's College, Lawrenceville, Va., instructor in English, 1964-65; University of Illinois at Urbana-Champaign, Urbana, assistant professor of English, 1967-74, assistant professor of library science, 1974—. *Member:* American Library Association, Association of

College and Research Libraries, Research Society for Victorian Periodicals, American Association of University Professors, American Civil Liberties Union. *Awards, honors:* Woodrow Wilson fellow, 1960-61.

WRITINGS: (Editor with Clara Kirk and Rudolf Kirk) W. D. Howells, *The Altrurian Romances,* Indiana University Press, 1968; (editor with Ronald Gottesman) *Art and Error: Modern Textual Editing,* Indiana University Press, 1970; (editor) W. D. Howells, *Indian Summer,* Indiana University Press, 1972; *The Clarence Comet: Henry Earnest Searle, 1866-1889,* Sydney University Press, 1974. Contributor to literary journals.

WORK IN PROGRESS: Revolutions in Thought, on the effort to use literacy to control social tension in early nineteenth-century Britain.

*   *   *

BENOIT, Leroy James   1913-

PERSONAL: Born August 23, 1913, in Newton, Mass.; son of Alexander James (an electrical engineer) and Phoebe (White) Benoit; married Edith Doris Meyer (a nutritionist), May 29, 1939; children: Peter Allan, Diane (Mrs. J. John Ryan). *Education:* Tufts University, A.B., 1936; University of Paris, Licence-es-Lettres, 1937; Harvard University, A.M., 1938, Ph.D., 1942. *Politics:* Independent. *Religion:* Methodist. *Office:* Department of Foreign Languages, Georgia State University, Atlanta, Ga. 30303.

CAREER: Harvard University, Cambridge, Mass., assistant professor of French, 1939-42; Amherst College, Amherst, Mass., associate professor of Romance languages, 1945-47; Johns Hopkins University, Baltimore, Md., associate professor of Romance languages, 1947-51; U.S. State Department, Washington, D.C. and abroad, cultural attache, 1951-58; Cornell University, Ithaca, N.Y., professor of French, 1966-72; Georgia State University, Atlanta, professor of French and Portuguese, 1972—, chairman of department of foreign languages, 1972—, director of summer program abroad, 1972—. Visiting professor at University of Lisbon, 1951-52, and University of Sao Paulo, 1954-55; Ford Foundation specialist in English teaching, Japan, 1964-68, and Algeria, 1968—. Consultant to Ford Foundation, U.S. State Department, and U.S. Office of Education. *Military service:* U.S. Army Air Forces, 1942-45; became major; received Distinguished Flying Cross, Purple Heart, Air Medal, and French Legion of Honor. *Member:* Linguistic Society of America, Modern Language Association of America, American Association of Teachers of French, Phi Beta Kappa. *Awards, honors:* Member, Order of the British Empire; LL.D., University of Coimbra, 1954.

WRITINGS: Appreciations du Francais moderne, Holt, 1972. Contributor to *Studies in Philology* and *Modern Language Journal.*

WORK IN PROGRESS: History of French Language.

SIDELIGHTS: Leroy Benoit has traveled extensively in Europe and in Brazil. *Avocational interests:* Collecting antique clocks, celestial navigation, deep water sailing.

*   *   *

BENSON, Frederick R.   1934-

PERSONAL: Born June 26, 1934, in New York, N.Y.; son of Louis and Emma Benson; married Diana G. Fung (a registered nurse and teacher), January, 1959 (divorced); children: Michele Nicole, Laurence Scott. *Education:* Southern Methodist University, B.A., 1955; New York University,

M.A., 1962, Ph.D., 1966. *Agent:* Leda Hanson, 440 East 79th St., New York, N.Y. 10021. *Office:* African Sculpture Unlimited, 145 Spring St., New York, N.Y. 10012.

CAREER: High school teacher in Pearl River, N.Y., 1959-62; Rider College, Trenton, N.J., instructor in English, 1962-66; City College of the City University of New York, New York City, assistant professor of English, 1966-70; Briarcliff College, Briarcliff Manor, N.Y., associate professor of English, 1970-75; African Sculpture Gallery, New York City, director, 1975—. Lecturer at other colleges and universities, including Rutgers University, Hunter College of the City University of New York, and New Jersey Institute of Technology. Active in little theater and Off-Broadway productions, 1955-65. *Military service:* U.S. Army, Special Services officer, 1955-58; served in France. *Member:* Modern Language Association of America, American Comparative Literature Association, Asia Society, National Council of Teachers of English, American Association of University Professors, New York Comparative Literature Colloquium (charter member). *Awards, honors:* National Science Foundation research fellowship at Columbia University, 1962.

WRITINGS: Writers in Arms: The Literary Impact of the Spanish Civil War, New York University Press, 1967; *Ernest Hemingway,* [Paris], 1975. Contributor of articles on sixteen modern writers to *World Biography,* McGraw, 1972.

WORK IN PROGRESS: Editing *Western Literature: A Historical Approach,* a textbook, completion expected in 1978; *The Still, Sad Music,* a novel, completion expected in 1978.

*   *   *

BENSON, Robert S(later) 1942-

PERSONAL: Born June 6, 1942, in Culver City, Ind.; son of Ernest B. (an educator) and Ruth (an educator; maiden name, Kenney) Benson. *Education:* Harvard University, B.A. (magna cum laude), 1964, M.B.A. (with high distinction), 1966. *Home:* 5645 North Glenwood Ave., Chicago, Ill. 60660.

CAREER: U.S. Department of Defense, Washington, D.C., assistant to assistant secretary of defense, 1966-68; National Urban Coalition, Washington, D.C., western regional director and director of national priorities project, 1968-71; Childrens World (early education centers), Chicago, Ill., vice-president, 1971—. Lecturer in various cities of the United States.

WRITINGS: (Editor with Harold Wolman) *Counterbudget: A Blueprint for Changing National Priorities, 1971-1976,* foreword by Sol M. Linowitz, Praeger, 1970; *The Cost of Security: National Defense and Military Assistance Requirements for the Seventies,* [Washington, D.C.], 1971. Contributor to *Washington Monthly* and *Fortune.*

SIDELIGHTS: Walter Pincus, reviewing *Counterbudget,* writes: "... The guts of the book—and they are substantial indeed—are in the impassioned chapter-by-chapter recitation of where this country is domestically—from its troubled schools, hospitals and homes to its failing transportation systems to its farms to its aging system of laws and administration of justice.... There are limitations—or gaps—in some analyses.... The weaknesses in presentation are, however, minimal and the overall effect of a concentrated reading is either depression at the state we are in or determination to help make it better—or both."

AVOCATIONAL INTERESTS: Politics, ballet, classical and folk music, tennis, and golf.†

BENTHUL, Herman F(orrest) 1911-

PERSONAL: Born December 22, 1911, in Celeste, Tex.; married Irene Bellomy (an elementary school teacher); children: Joyce (Mrs. Barney Terrell), Barbara (Mrs. George Taylor). *Education:* East Texas State Teachers College (now East Texas State University), B.A., 1935; Southern Methodist University, M.A., 1942; University of Texas at Austin, Ph.D., 1954; postdoctoral study at Columbia University, 1963. *Religion:* Methodist. *Home address:* Box 433, Golden, Tex. 75444. *Office:* East Texas State University, Commerce, Tex. 75428.

CAREER: Principal in school districts in Bellefonte and Lindale, Tex., 1933-40; superintendent of schools in Covington, Tex., 1940-42; principal of schools in Hillsboro and Tyler, Tex., 1942-47; Dallas Independent School District, Dallas, Tex., principal, 1947-50, consultant and coordinator, 1950-68, deputy assistant superintendent in elementary education, 1968-69, assistant superintendent in curriculum development, 1969-73; East Texas State University, Commerce, adjunct professor, 1973—. Member of executive board, Dallas Health and Science Museum. *Member:* Texas Association of Supervision and Curriculum Development (president), Reading Association (president), Phi Delta Kappa (president, 1959-60).

WRITINGS: (Editor with Mayna Fain Bode) *Holiday Reader,* Noble, 1957; (editor) *Literature of the Old Southwest,* Noble, 1958; (with Clara Jo Bridges) *Texas Roundup,* Noble, 1965; (with Orrel T. Baldwin) *American Heroes All,* Noble, 1965; (co-author) *Spell Correctly,* Silver Burdett, 1965; (with E. Anderson and A. M. Utech) *From Sounds to Words: The Silver Burdett Spelling Readiness Program,* with teachers manual, Silver Burdett, 1966; (co-author) "Oral Reading and Linguistic" series, Benefic Press, 1973; (co-author) "Career Education Readers" series, Benefic Press, 1975. Writer of column, "Wording Your Way through Texas," *Houston Chronicle,* 1976-77. Contributor to education journals and *Red Cross Magazine.*

AVOCATIONAL INTERESTS: Word history, study of outdoor life.

*   *   *

BERBEROVA, Nina (Nikolaevna) 1901-

PERSONAL: Born August 8, 1901, in St. Petersburg, Russia; came to United States in 1951, naturalized in 1959; daughter of Nikolai and Natalia (Karaulova) Berberova; married Vladislav Khodasevich (a poet); married second husband, Nikolai Makeev (a painter); married third husband, George Kochevitsky (a pianist), September 24, 1954. *Education:* Studied at Institute of Art History in Russia, and at Sorbonne, University of Paris. *Home:* 44 Stanworth Lane, Princeton, N.J. 08540.

CAREER: Left Russia in 1922, lived in Germany, Czechoslovakia, and Italy; went to live in France in 1925; writer, journalist, translator, and editor in Paris, 1925-50; worked as a language instructor at the Berlitz School, radio announcer for the "Voice of America," office machine operator, and as editor of a Russian language periodical, 1951-58; Yale University, New Haven, Conn., lecturer, 1958-63; Princeton University, Princeton, N.J., professor of literature, 1963-71. Instructor at Indiana University, summers, 1962, 1963, Columbia University, 1970-71, University of Pennsylvania, fall, 1973, and Princeton University, 1976-77; Katherine McBride Visiting Lecturer, Bryn Mawr College, spring, 1976. Guest at Yaddo, Saratoga Springs, New York, 1964-66.

WRITINGS: (Translator into Russian from the French) Romain Rolland, *Mahatma Ghandi,* Beseda (Berlin), 1924; *Posledenye i pervye* (novel), Povolotzky (Paris), 1929; (with Andre Fontainas) *Le Symbolisme en France* [and] *Le Symbolisme russe* (the former by Fontainas, the latter by Berberova), Cahiers de la Quinzaine (Paris), 1931; *Povelitelnitsa* (novel), Parabola (Berlin), 1932; *Alexandre Blok et son temps,* Editions du Chene, 1935; *Chaikovskii* (biography), Petropolis (Berlin), 1936; *Borodin* (in Russian), Petropolis, 1937; *Bez zakata* (novel), Dom Knigi (Paris), 1938; "Madame" (play), first produced in Paris, 1938; *Oblegchenie uchasti* (stories), YMCA Press, 1949; *Protsess V. A. Kravchenko,* [Paris], 1949; (translator into French with Mina Journot) Jules Margoline, *La Condition inhumaine: Cinq ans dans les camps de concentration sovietiques,* [Paris], 1949; (translator into French) Fiodor Dostoevsky, *Eternel mari,* Editions du Chene, 1949.

(Editor) Vladislav Khodasevich, *Literaturnye stat'i i vospominaniia,* Chekhov Publishing House (New York), 1954; (editor) *Sobranie stikhov Vladislava Khodasevicha,* [Munich], 1959; (contributing editor with L. J. Kent) Nikolai Gogol, *Tales and Plays,* translation by Constance Garnett, revised edition, Pantheon, 1964; (editor and author of introduction with Kent) Leo Tolstoy, *Anna Karenina,* translation by Garnett, revised edition, Modern Library, 1965; *The Italics Are Mine* (autobiography), authorized translation by Philippe Radley, Harcourt, 1969, original Russian version published with letters of Kerensky, Gorky, and Bunin as *Kursiv Moi,* Fink Verlag, 1972; (contributor) Alfred Appel, Jr. and Charles Newman, editors, *Nabokov: Criticisms, Reminiscences, Translations, and Tributes,* Northwestern University Press, 1970; (author of notes and commentary) Andrey Bely, *The First Encounter,* translation by G. Janacek, Princeton University Press, 1978. Also author of short stories and verse, and translator into Russian of works of T. S. Eliot and Constantine Cavafy. Contributor to Russian language emigre newspapers and magazines in Germany, France, and the United States. Editor of literary sections of several emigre periodicals.

SIDELIGHTS: Nina Berberova's biography, *Chaikovskii,* was filmed as "Life of Peter Chaikovsky," in a joint venture by Warner Brothers and Sovkino.

BIOGRAPHICAL/CRITICAL SOURCES: Marc Slonim, *Modern Russian Literature,* Oxford University Press, 1953; Gleb Struve, *Russkaya literature za rubezhom,* Chekhov Publishing House, 1956; *New York Times Book Review,* May 25, 1969; *New Yorker,* August 16, 1969; *Spectator,* November 29, 1969; Nina Berberova, *The Italics Are Mine* (autobiography), Harcourt, 1969.

*   *   *

BERENDSOHN, Walter A(rthur) 1884-

PERSONAL: Born September 10, 1884, in Hamburg, Germany; son of Bernhard Salomon (a merchant) and Florette (Sonn) Berendsohn; married Dorothea Margaretha Eggert, June 26, 1918; children: Anne Elisabeth (Mrs. Gerhard Romm), Karin Ilse (Mrs. Walter Braun). *Education:* Attended Matthias Claudius Gymnasium, Wandbek, and Abiturium Realgymnasium, Berlin; Germanistic studies at University of Berlin, University of Freiburg, University of Munich; University of Kiel, Dr. phil., 1911. *Politics:* Social Democrat. *Religion:* Jewish. *Office:* German Institute, University of Stockholm, Stockholm, Sweden.

CAREER: Germanistic Seminary, Hamburg, Germany, assistant, 1914-20; University of Hamburg, Hamburg, pri-

vatdocent, 1920-26, professor specializing in Scandinavian literature, 1926-33; lecturer and writer in Denmark, 1933-43; fled to Sweden in September, 1943; Swedish Academy, Stockholm, researcher, 1943—; University of Stockholm, Stockholm, Sweden, guest professor of the history of literature, 1947—, director of research in refugee literature at German Institute, 1966—. Lecturer at Cambridge University, University of London, and other universities. *Military service:* German Army, 1914-18; served on Western Front; became lieutenant. *Member:* Sonntagskreis, Strindberg-Lagerloef Society, and other Swedish societies; Freemason. *Awards, honors:* Awards from the city of Stockholm and from various foundations.

WRITINGS: Stil und Form der Apborismen Lichtenberg, Muehlau, 1912.

Der Impressionismus Hofmannsthals, Genthe, 1920; *Die Ethik studentischen Lebens,* Genthe, 1920; *Grundformen volkstuemlicher Erzaehlerkunst in den Kinder- und Hausmaerchen der Brueder Grimm,* Genthe, 1921, 2nd edition, M. Saendig, 1968; (translator) Rudolf Kjellen, *Die Grossmaechte und die Weltkrise,* Teubner Verlagsgeschaeft, 1921; *Goethes Knabendichtung* (i.e. "Joseph"), Genthe, 1922; *Erdgebundene Sittlichkeit,* Oldenburg, 1923; *Der Stil Carl Spittelers,* Grethlein, 1923; *Politische Fuehrerschaft,* Oldenburg, 1924; *Selma Lagerloef: Heimat und Leben, Kuenstlerschaft, Werke, Wirkung und Wert,* Albert Langen, 1927, translation and abridged edition by George F. Timpson published as *Selma Lagerloef: Her Life and Work,* preface by V. Sackville-West, Nicholson & Watson, 1931, Doubleday, 1932, reprinted, Kennikat, 1968; *Knut Hamsun,* Albert Langen, 1929.

Zur Vorgeschichte des "Beowulf," Levin & Munksgaard, 1935; *Der lebendige Heine im germanischen Norden,* Schoenberg, 1935.

Nordisk digtning af verdensry (lectures), Schoenberg, 1942; *Strindbergsproblem: Essaer och studier,* Kooperativa Foerbundets Bokfoerlag, 1946; *Die humanistiche Front,* Volume I, Europa Verlag, 1946; *Strindbergs sista levnadsaar,* Saxon & Lindstroem, 1948; *Martin Andersen Nexoe,* Gyldendal, 1948.

Aufbauarbeit in Israel: Erlebnisse, Studien, Betrachtungen, Bernard & Graefe, 1953; *Fantasi og virkelighed i H.C. Andersens "Eventyr og historier,"* Jydsk Centraltrykkeri's Forlag, 1955; *August Strindberg: Ein geborener Dramatiker,* Langen & Mueller, 1956.

Die Idee der Humanitaet in Vergangenheit und Gegenwart: Essays, Akazien-Verlag A. Buss, 1961; *Das Volk der Bibel im Land der Vaeter: Der junge Staat Israel,* Seewald Verlag, 1962; *August Strindbergs Skaergaards- och Stockholmsskildringar,* Raben & Sjoegren, 1962; *Dag Hammarskjoeld und sein Werk,* Bokfoerlaget Fabel, 1965, abridged edition, Kulturamt der Stadt Dortmund, 1967; *Thomas Mann: Kuenstler und Kaempfer in bewegter Zeit,* Schmidt-Roemhild, 1965, translation by George C. Buck published as *Thomas Mann: Artist and Partisan in Troubled Times,* University of Alabama Press, 1973; *Humane Tendenzen im Atomzeitalter,* Agis-Verlag, 1965; (editor) Thomas Mann, *Sieben Manifeste zur juedischen Frage 1936-1948,* Melzer, 1966; (compiler and author of commentary) *Briefe an Strindberg,* Kupferberg, 1967; *Deutsche Literatur der Fluechtlinge aus dem Dritten Reich,* four volumes, Tyska Institutionen, 1967-69; (translator and author of introduction) August Strindberg, *Das Kloster, Einsam, mit Nachwort; August Strindbergs autobiographische Schriften,* Claassen Verlag, 1968.

Die kuenstlerische Entwicklung Heines im "Buch der Lieder," University of Stockholm Press, 1970; (translator) August Strindberg, *Die Stadtreise und andere Gedichte,* Claassen Verlag, 1970; *Thomas Mann und die Seinen,* Francke Verlag, 1973; (translator from the Danish) Hans Christian Andersen, *Phantasie und Wirklichkert in den "Marchen und Geschichten,"* M. Sandig, 1973; *Nelly Sachs: Einfuchrung in das werk der Dechterin juidischen Schicksals,* Agora Verlag, 1974; *Meine Sammlungen in der Deutschen Bibliothek, Frankfurt M.sect 1952: Rezensionen,* Stockholmer Koordinations-stelle zur Erforschung der deutschsprachigen Exil-Literatur, 1974; *August Strindberg: Der Mensch und seine Umwelt-Das Werk-Der schoepferische Kuenstler,* Rodopi, 1974.

Booklets and other short works: *Der neuendtdeckte "Joseph" als Knabendichtung Goethes: Stilkritische Untersuchungen,* [Hamburg], 1921; *Noch ein Stueck Knabendichtung Goethes,* [Hamburg], 1924; *Zur Methode der Reimuntersuchung im Streit um Goethes "Joseph,"* [Hamburg], 1926; *Schillers Wilhelm Tell als Kunstwerk,* University of Stockholm Press, 1960; *Das Wort als geistige Waffe: Heines politische Dichtung "Deutschland, ein Wintermaerchen,"* Kulturamt der Stadt Dortmund, 1960; *August Strindbergs Parisschilderungen,* Kulturamt der Stadt Dortmund, 1962; *Struktur- och stilanalysen: Ett noedvaendigt komplement till den svenska Strindbergforskningen,* Horisont, 1964; *Thomas Manns Goethe-fernstes Werk "Doktor Faustus,"* Saltsjoe-Duvnaes, 1964; *Thomas Manns "Bekenntnisse des Hochstaplers Felix Krull,"* Stockholm Studies in Modern Philology, 1964; *August Strindberg und die Frauen,* Kulturamt der Stadt Dortmund, 1968; *Nelly Sachs: Mysterienspiel vom Leiden Israels "Eli,"* Kulturamt der Stadt Dortmund, 1969; *Aufsaetze und Rezensionen,* Stockholmer Koordinations-stelle zur Erforschung der deutschsprachigen Exil-Literatur, 1974; *Rezensionen,* Deutsches Institut, Stockholms Universitat, 1974; *Vom Lebensweg und Lebenswerk Frank Zwillingers,* [Stockholm], 1975.

Author of other studies and of journal articles (his bibliography runs to 750 items).

SIDELIGHTS: Berendsohn's books and booklets have been published in Denmark, Switzerland, and United States in addition to Germany, and his articles in many other countries. English is the third language he speaks, and he reads French, Danish, and Norwegian. He has visited the United States and made eleven trips to Israel.

* * *

BERG, Paul Conrad 1921-

PERSONAL: Born July 12, 1921, in Hallstead, Pa.; son of Conrad Diedrich (a farmer) and Etta (Luce) Berg; married Rosalie Helm, January 26, 1945; children: Mary Lucetta, Doris Roxanna, Ruth Elizabeth. *Education:* Syracuse University, B.A. (magna cum laude), 1949; Cornell University, M.S., 1950, Ph.D., 1953. *Politics:* Republican. *Religion:* Protestant. *Home:* 6033 Poplar Ridge Rd., Columbia, S.C. 29206. *Office:* College of Education, University of South Carolina, Columbia, S.C. 29208.

CAREER: University of Florida, Gainesville, assistant professor of English and associate director of reading laboratory and clinic, 1952-56; State University College of Education at Fredonia (now State University of New York College at Fredonia), associate professor of education, 1956-57; University of South Carolina, College of Education, Columbia, professor of education, 1957—, director of reading clinic,

1957-75, Alumni Chair Professor of Education, 1970—. Certified psychologist in New York and South Carolina. Ford Foundation consultant in reading to Government of India, New Delhi, 1971. *Military service:* U.S. Army Air Forces, 1942-46; became staff sergeant. *Member:* American Psychological Association, International Reading Association (member of board of directors, 1964-66), National Reading Conference (president, 1967-68).

WRITINGS: (With George Spache) *The Art of Efficient Reading,* Macmillan, 1955, revised edition, 1978; (with Spache) *Faster Reading for Business,* Crowell, 1958; (contributor) Oscar S. Causey, editor, *The Reading Teacher's Reader,* Ronald, 1958; *Skimming and Scanning Workbook,* Educational Development Laboratories, 1962; *Teaching Efficient Reading,* Manasagangotri (Mysore), 1971. Writer of script for "Fun With Words—Word Twins," Coronet Films, 1969. Contributor to *Seventh Mental Measurements Yearbook,* Gryphon, 1971, and to a number of yearbooks of International Reading Conference. Contributor of more than thirty articles to education journals. Member of editorial board, *Journal of Reading Behavior,* 1969—.

WORK IN PROGRESS: Reading improvement materials at the middle school level; test of perception for beginning readers.

SIDELIGHTS: Paul Berg told *CA:* "Perhaps nothing can set the stage for writing better than having a way with words, but, unfortunately, no one is born with this innate capacity. It helps, of course, to be born to a literate family, but whether or not such is the case, the mastery of language is ours alone to accomplish. Perhaps there is no better way to internalize the graces of a language than to read widely and deeply, to have read the masters and the clowns, the hacks and the scholars. I honestly believe that if one is not an avid reader he can never become an accomplished writer, although he may search out and map the outline dimensions of a topic. When I say write, I mean the ability to handle, as a potter does his clay, a shapeless, formless mass of words, and from the sensitive fingers of the mind fashion an object of art, even though it may be utilitarian, as a description of an object or thing. One cannot really be taught this art of word-forming and molding; it must be grasped and pulled from the depths of accumulated experience and reflections on these experiences, with reading being an important part of the exercise. In response to the question of how he knew where to chisel, Michaelangelo answered that it was an easy matter to chip away and bring the inner figure into view. Michaelangelo had so filled his inner vision with the forms and structures of art that he saw them clearly in the unhewn marble, and he firmly believed that the sculptor's stone held captive the literal forms of beauty, awaiting only the releasing by the chisel. Such, at least partially, is writing. We hear, and we see with an inward eye our own private story, explanation, or description, and we simply strike out all the words that do not belong." His *Teaching Efficient Reading* has been translated into several Indian languages.

* * *

BERGENDOFF, Conrad J(ohn) I(mmanuel) 1895-

PERSONAL: Born December 3, 1895, in Shickley, Neb.; son of Carl August (a clergyman) and Emma Mathilda (Fahlberg) Bergendoff; married Gertrude E. Carlson, June 28, 1922; children: Conrad Luther, Beatrice Gertrude (Mrs. Richard Wilson), Elizabeth Ann (Mrs. Richard Thulin). *Education:* Augustana College, Rock Island, Ill., A.B., 1915, B.D., 1921; University of Pennsylvania, A.M., 1916;

Columbia University, graduate study, 1917-18; University of Chicago, graduate courses, 1921-28, Ph.D., 1928; also studied at University of Uppsala and University of Berlin, 1925-26. *Home:* 10 Hawthorne Rd., Rock Island, Ill. 61201.

CAREER: Augustana College, Rock Island, Ill., professor of education and assistant professor of English, 1916-17; assistant pastor in New York, N.Y., 1917-19; ordained in Augustana Synod of Lutheran Church, 1921; pastor in Chicago, Ill., 1921-31; Augustana College, Rock Island, Ill., professor of systematic theology and dean of Theological Seminary, 1931-35, president of seminary, 1935-48, president of college, 1935-62, president emeritus, 1962—. Member of board of directors, Association of American Colleges, 1940-41; president, American Association of Theological Schools, 1946-48; executive secretary of Board of Theological Education, Lutheran Church in America, 1962-64. Member of Illinois State Board of Higher Education, 1962-69, and Illinois Arts Council, 1965-69. President, Augustana Swedish Institute, 1940-67; trustee, American Scandinavian Foundation, 1943-70.

MEMBER: Swedish Pioneer Historical Society, Augustana Historical Society, Phi Beta Kappa, Contemporary Club (Davenport, Iowa), Black Hawk Hiking Club, Rock Island Rotary Club. *Awards, honors:* Th.D., University of Uppsala (Sweden), 1938; LL.D., Upsala College, 1943; Litt.D., Rockford College, 1958, National College of Education, 1968; D.D., Concordia Theological Seminary (St. Louis), 1967; L.H.D., Marycrest College, 1968. Order of the North Star from the King of Sweden, second class, 1944, first class, 1976; B'nai B'rith Man of the Year Award, 1961.

WRITINGS: Olavus Petri and Ecclesiastical Transformation in Sweden, Macmillan, 1929; *One, Holy, Catholic, Apostolic Church,* Augustana Book Concern, 1954; *The Doctrine of the Church in American Lutheranism,* Muhlenberg, 1956; (editor and translator) Martin Luther, *Works,* Volume XL, Concordia, 1958; *The Church of the Lutheran Reformation,* Concordia, 1967; *Augustana: Profession of Faith* (history of Augustana College, 1860-1935), Augustana College Library, 1969. Contributor to history, education, and denominational journals. Editor, *Augustana Quarterly,* 1929-48, and *Lutheran Quarterly,* 1949-52.

WORK IN PROGRESS: Biographical Register of Pastors of the Augustana Synod.

BIOGRAPHICAL/CRITICAL SOURCES: The Swedish Immigrant Community in Transition: Essays in Honor of Conrad J. I. Bergendoff, Augustana Historical Society, 1963.

*   *   *

BERGER, Josef   1903-1971
(Jeremiah Digges)

May 12, 1903—November 11, 1971; American journalist, speech writer, editor, short story writer, and author of children's books. Obituaries: *New York Times,* November 12, 1971. (See index for *CA* sketch)

*   *   *

BERINGAUSE, Arthur F.   1919-

PERSONAL: Born January 15, 1919, in New York, N.Y.; son of Herman (a patternmaker) and Sally (Fayer) Beringause; married Thelma Schwartz (a registered nurse), June 27, 1948; children: Kurt, Eric. *Education:* City College (now City College of the City University of New York), New York, N.Y., B.A., 1939, M.S. in Ed., 1946; New York Uni-

versity, M.A., 1952, Ph.D., 1954. *Religion:* Jewish. *Home:* 74 Brown Rd., Scarsdale, N.Y. 10583.

CAREER: Teacher of English in public schools of New York, N.Y., 1946-54; Childs High School, Bronx, N.Y., chairman of English, 1954-61; Queens College of the City University of New York, Flushing, N.Y., assistant professor of English and supervisor of department in School of General Studies, 1961-64; Bronx Community College of the City University of New York, Bronx, N.Y., professor of English and chairman of department, 1964-68. Instructor in English at New York University, 1953-56, and Yeshiva University, 1957-59; lecturer at Brooklyn College, 1946-53, Hunter College, 1956 (now both of the City University of New York), and Queens College of the City University of New York, 1959-61. *Military service:* U.S. Army, 1942-45; became first lieutenant. *Member:* Modern Language Association of America, National Council of Teachers of English, American Name Society.

WRITINGS: Brooks Adams, Knopf, 1955; *James Joyce's Philosophy,* Cresset, 1963; (with Daniel K. Lowenthal) *The Range of College Reading,* Houghton, 1968; *English Literature since 1945,* McCormick-Mathers, 1969. Also editor of ''Modern Grammar'' series, seven books, published by American Book Company. Book reviewer, *Jewish Press,* 1975—. Contributor to *Bucknell Review* and other journals. Guest editor, *Names,* 1970.

WORK IN PROGRESS: A Hebrew onomatology.

*   *   *

BERKOWITZ, David Sandler   1913-

PERSONAL: Born August 20, 1913, in Pittsburgh, Pa.; son of Abraham Jacob and Nellie (Sandler) Berkowitz; married Jessie Cohen, September 8, 1940; children: Carl Sandler, Naomi Judith. *Education:* Harvard University, A.B. (magna cum laude), 1938, A.M., 1940, Ph.D., 1946. *Home:* 93 Beaumont Ave., Newtonville, Mass. 02160. *Office:* Department of History, Brandeis University, Waltham, Mass. 02154.

CAREER: Connecticut College for Women (now Connecticut College), New London, lecturer in history, 1946; Emerson College, Boston, Mass., associate professor of history and chairman of department of social science, 1946-47; Brandeis University, Waltham, Mass., associate professor, 1948-49, professor of political science, 1949-57, professor of history, 1949—, assistant to president and director of university planning, 1948-52. Visiting lecturer at Harvard University, 1957-58, and Folger Institute of Renaissance and Eighteenth Century Studies, 1972-73. Member of advisory board, Yale Center for Parliamentary History; consultant to Armed Forces Representative, Harvard University, 1942-44, and Temporary Commission on Need for a State University, state of New York, 1946-48; member, Anonymous Board of Selection for Naval Aviation, 1942-44. Assistant secretary and assistant treasurer of board of trustees, Brandeis University, 1948-52; Waltham Family Service Association, director, 1949-71, president, 1959-61; incorporator, Waltham Savings Bank and Waltham Hospital, 1952—; director of New England Transportation Company, 1956-62, and Region West Family Counseling Service, Inc., 1962—; Berkshire Associates, Inc., director, 1959—, president, 1959-65, treasurer, 1966—; director and president, Waltham Community Foundation, Inc., 1971—. Member, Committee for the Bromsen Memorial Lecture in Humanistic Bibliography, Boston Public Library, 1971—.

MEMBER: American Association of University Professors, American Historical Association, Conference on British Studies, Society for the History of Discoveries, Renaissance Society of America (member of council), American Society of Legal History, American Printing History Association, Oxford Bibliographical Society, Phi Beta Kappa. *Awards, honors:* Rogers traveling fellowship, 1941-42; Folger Shakespeare Library Senior fellowship, 1971-72; American Bar Legal History research fellowship, 1972-73.

WRITINGS: Inequality of Opportunity in Higher Education, State University of New York (Albany), 1948; (with others) *Matching Needs and Facilities in Higher Education,* State of New York, 1948; *Bibliotheca Bibliographica Britannica; or, Bibliographies in British History,* privately printed, Book I: *Resources Bibliography,* two volumes, 1963, Book II: *Subject Bibliography,* five volumes, 1964-69; *A Descriptive Catalogue of the Incunabula of the Brandeis University Library,* Society of Bibliophiles at Brandeis University, 1963; *Brandeis University Library, Guide to Research Materials in the Library: The Renaissance Period,* Brandeis University Library, 1963; (contributor) Louis Kronenberger, editor, *The Scholarly Uses of Rare Books,* Society of Bibliophiles at Brandeis University, 1964; *From Ptolemy to the Moon: Progress in the Art of Exploration and Navigation,* Brandeis University Library, 1965; *Documentation in Second and Later Citations by Shortened Forms of Reference,* privately printed, 1965; *Bibliotheca Bibliographica Incunabula,* privately printed, 1967; *In Rememberence of Creation,* Brandeis University Press, 1968; *Bibliographies for Historical Researchers,* privately printed, 1969; (editor) *The Work of Six Days,* Society of Bibliophiles at Brandeis University, 1970; (contributor) Roman Schnur, editor, *Studien zur Geschichte eines politischen Begriffs,* [Berlin], 1975. Contributor to *Justice, History and Theory, Renaissance News, Brandeis University Bibliophiles, Renaissance Quarterly, American Journal of Legal History,* and *Octavo.* Editor, *Octavo,* 1971—.

WORK IN PROGRESS: Scholar in Politics: Life and Times of John Selden; Stuart England, 1603-1660; A Bibliographical Manual, for Cambridge University Press; *Humanist Scholarship and Public Order; Two Tracts by Richard Morison against the Pilgrimage of Grace,* for University Press of Virginia; Book III of *Bibliotheca Bibliographica Britannica; Bibliotheca Bibliographica Incunabula: A Manual of Incunabulistics;* editing with S. E. Hawthorne, *Classics of English Legal History,* for Garland Publishing; editing a book entitled *The Legacy of Humanism.*

*   *   *

BERKOWITZ, Luci 1938-

PERSONAL: Born February 23, 1938, in Ogdensburg, N.Y.; daughter of Harold H. (a psychiatrist) and Catherine (Halperin) Berman; divorced. *Education:* Ohio State University, B.A., 1960, M.A., 1961, Ph.D., 1965. *Politics:* Democrat. *Religion:* None. *Home:* 28791 Top of the World Dr., Laguna Beach, Calif. 92651. *Office:* Department of Classics, University of California, Irvine, Calif. 92717.

CAREER: Ohio State University, Columbus, assistant professor of classics, 1965-66; University of Wisconsin—Milwaukee, assistant professor of classics, 1966-67; University of California, Irvine, assistant professor, 1967-70, associate professor of classics, 1970—. Resident scholar, Thesaurus Linguae Graecae. *Member:* American Philological Association, American Classical League, Philological Association of the Pacific Coast, Eta Sigma Phi. *Awards, honors:* University of California fellowship at Humanities Institute, 1967-68.

WRITINGS: Index Arnobianus, Georg Olms Verlagsbuchhandlung, 1967; (with Theodore F. Brunner) *The Elements of Scientific and Specialized Terminology,* Burgess, 1967; (with Brunner) *Index Verborum Quae in Saturis Auli Persi Flacci Reperiuntur,* Georg Olms Verlagsbuchhandlung, 1968; (with Brunner) *Index Lucilianus,* Georg Olms Verlagsbuchhandlung, 1969; (translator and editor with Brunner) Sophocles, *Oedipus Tyrannus* (critical edition), Norton, 1970. Also author of *A Canon of Greek Authors and Works from Homer to A.D. 200.* Contributor of articles to journals.

WORK IN PROGRESS: A book or a book-length monograph on Vergil's "Fourth Eclogue" as a metapoem; research in ancient pastoral poetry.

AVOCATIONAL INTERESTS: Rock music, the theater, water sports.

*   *   *

BERLAK, Harold 1932-

PERSONAL: Born July 31, 1932, in Somerville, Mass.; son of William and Dora (Davis) Berlak; married Ann Abramson (an associate professor), September, 1962; children: Mariam Lea, Rachel Louise, Lev Herschel. *Education:* Boston University, B.A., 1954; Harvard University, A.M., 1957, Ed. D., 1964. *Home:* 7133 Washington Ave., University City, Mo. 63130. *Office:* Graduate Institute of Education, Washington University, St. Louis, Mo. 63105.

CAREER: History teacher in Wenham, Mass., 1957-59, in Concord, Mass., 1959-61; special supervisor of social studies in Concord, Mass., 1962-63; University of California, Santa Barbara, assistant professor of education, 1963-64; Washington University, St. Louis, Mo., associate professor in Graduate Institute of Education, 1964—, director of Metropolitan St. Louis Social Studies Center, 1968—. Master teacher, Harvard-Newton Summer School, 1961, 1962, 1964. *Member:* Social Science Education Consortium (member of board of directors, 1967-69), Phi Delta Kappa.

WRITINGS: (With James P. Shaver) *Democracy, Pluralism, and the Social Studies,* Houghton, 1968; (with T. R. Tomlinson) *People, Choices, Decisions,* Random House, 1973. Former book review editor, *Harvard Education Review.* Contributor to education journals.

WORK IN PROGRESS: With wife, Ann C. Berlak, *The Dilemmas of Schooling: A Dialectical Behaviorist Perspective.*

*   *   *

BERLIND, Bruce 1926-

PERSONAL: Surname is pronounced Ber-*lind;* born July 17, 1926, in New York, N.Y.; son of Peter Sydney (an administrator) and Mae (Miller) Berlind; married Doris Lidz, June 15, 1947 (divorced, 1951); married Mary Dirlam, September 11, 1954; children: (second marriage) Lise, Anne, John, Paul, Alexandra. *Education:* Princeton University, A.B., 1947; Johns Hopkins University, M.A., 1950, Ph. D., 1958. *Home:* 62 Broad St., Hamilton, N.Y. 13346. *Office:* Department of English, Colgate University, Hamilton, N.Y. 13346.

CAREER: Colgate University, Hamilton, N.Y., instructor, 1954-58, assistant professor, 1958-63, associate professor, 1963-66, professor of English, 1966—, chairman of department, 1967-72. U.S. Information Service lecturer in Germany, 1963; poet-in-residence, University of Rochester, 1966. *Military service:* U.S. Army, 1945-46, 1950-52; became first lieutenant. *Member:* Modern Language Association of America, Poetry Society of America, American Association of University Professors (president of New York state conference, 1964-65; member of council, 1967-70).

WRITINGS: (Editor with Henry Fischer) *Bred in the Bone: An Anthology of Verse,* Ampersand Press, 1945; *Three Larks for a Loony* (poems), Chenango Editions, 1957; *Ways of Happening* (poems), Chenango Editions, 1959; *Companion Pieces* (poems), Penyeach Press, 1971. Contributor of poetry to *Chicago Review, Poetry, Poetry Northwest, Epoch, Mill Mountain Review, Shenandoah, Transatlantic Review, Honest Ulsterman, Perspectives,* and other journals. Associate editor, *Hopkins Review,* 1949-53.

WORK IN PROGRESS: The Day Nobody Died; Life Annuity, a translation of Thoby-Marcelin's poems, *A fond perdu,* for Adam Poets; translating works by Hungarian poet Agnes Nemes Nagy; a collection of poems.

SIDELIGHTS: Bruce Berlind told *CA:* "I am increasingly interested in the matter of 'voice' in poetry, but in what I fear is an unfashionable way. Current attitudes toward 'voice' (and I have used such language myself) view it as the distinctive and identifying element of a poet's personality—as if the entire direction of a poet's apprenticeship were to discover, and 'give voice to,' an essential pre-verbal self that would ultimately define his concerns and be his style. My growing conviction is that the voice of a poem proceeds not from the personality of the poet, but from the special circumstances of the poem's materials; that the voice of a poem is as much a product of its creation as any of its other effects. Such a view is of course discomfiting to readers who expect poetry to be 'self-expression,' as is the view (which I also hold) that the 'feeling' of a poem is similarly a product of its making."

AVOCATIONAL INTERESTS: Flying (Bruce Berlind is a private pilot).

*   *   *

BERNAL, J(ohn) D(esmond)   1901-1971

May 10, 1901—September 15, 1971; British physicist and educator. Obituaries: *New York Times,* September 16, 1971; *Washington Post,* September 16, 1971; *Newsweek,* September 27, 1971.

*   *   *

BERNSTEIN, Lewis   1915-

PERSONAL: Born January 28, 1915, in Stanhope, N.J.; son of Philip (a merchant) and Dora (Kaplan) Bernstein; married Rosalyn Samuel (a social worker), June 18, 1940; children: Paul Alan, Ellen. *Education:* Wayne State University, B.S., 1939, M.A., 1941; University of Colorado, Ph.D., 1951. *Politics:* Independent. *Religion:* None. *Home:* 3355 Carminito Gandara, La Jolla, Calif. 92037.

CAREER: Veterans Administration Hospital, Albuquerque, N.M., clinical psychologist, 1946-48; Veterans Administration Hospital, Denver, Colo., assistant chief clinical psychologist, 1951-57, chief clinical psychologist, 1957-59; Jewish National Home for Asthmatic Children and Children's Asthma Research Institute and Hospital, Denver, director of psychological services and research psychologist, 1959-62; Veterans Administration Hospital, Wood, Wis., chief of psychology service, 1962-65; Milwaukee Psychiatric Hospital, Milwaukee, Wis., director of psychology, beginning 1962. Assistant clinical professor of psychology at School of Medicine and lecturer in psychology at Graduate

School, University of Colorado, Boulder, 1957-62; professor of psychology, Medical College of Wisconsin, Milwaukee, beginning 1962; University of Wisconsin—Milwaukee, lecturer, 1965-70, clinical associate professor of psychology, 1970-73. Examiner, American Board of Professional Psychology, 1964—. Member, Committee on Mental Health for Greater Milwaukee, 1964-68. *Military service:* U.S. Army, 1942-46; became first lieutenant.

MEMBER: American Psychological Association (fellow), American Association for the Advancement of Science (fellow), Interamerican Psychological Society, Midwestern Psychological Association, Colorado Psychological Association (president, 1957-58; member of board of directors, 1959-62), Sigma Xi, Psi Chi.

WRITINGS: (Editor with B. C. Burris) *Contribution of the Social Sciences to Psychotherapy,* C. C Thomas, 1967; (with Richard H. Dana) *Interviewing and the Health Professions,* Appleton, 1970, 2nd edition, published as *Interviewing: A Guide for Health Professionals,* 1974. Contributor of about fifty articles to professional journals. Associate editor, *Journal of Asthma Research.*

WORK IN PROGRESS: Perspectives in Psychosocial Medicine; research on medical education and on the effects of early experience on later behavior.

*   *   *

BERNSTEIN, Norman R.   1927-

PERSONAL: Born October 12, 1927, in New York, N.Y.; son of Aaron Moses (a watch importer) and Rachel (Hochberg) Bernstein; married Marilyn Gabe (a law student), August 30, 1953; children: Michael, Genya. *Education:* Cornell University, B.A., 1949; New York Medical College, M.D., 1951. *Politics:* "Cynically liberal." *Religion:* Jewish. *Home:* 87 Garden St., Cambridge, Mass. 02138. *Office:* Massachusetts General Hospital, Boston, Mass. 02114.

CAREER: Fifth Avenue Hospital, New York, N.Y., intern, 1952; Kings County Hospital, Brooklyn, N.Y., resident, 1952-54; Commonwealth Fund fellow at Massachusetts Institute of Technology, 1954-56; Boston College, Chestnut Hill, Mass., lecturer in School of Social Work, 1957-65; Massachusetts General Hospital, Boston, 1965—, began as assistant psychiatrist and associate director of child psychiatry, currently director of child psychiatry; Harvard University, Medical School, Boston, Mass., instructor, 1965-70, assistant professor of psychiatry, 1970—. Member of teaching staff, National Neurological Hospital, Mexico, 1962—; director of psychiatric training, Fernald School, 1966—; director of psychiatry, Shriners Burns Institute, 1968—. *Military service:* U.S. Army, 1946-47.

MEMBER: American Psychiatric Association, American College of Psychiatrists, American Board of Psychiatry and Neurology (member of committee on certification), Group for the Advancement of Psychiatry, American Academy of Child Psychiatry (councillor), Royal Society for Health, International Burn Society, Massachusetts Medical Association. *Awards, honors:* Certificate of Merit from Society for Clinical and Experimental Hypnosis, 1965.

WRITINGS: Diminished People, Little, Brown, 1971.

WORK IN PROGRESS: Bearing Disfigurement, a book on the later adaptations of burn-disfigured people, for Little, Brown.

AVOCATIONAL INTERESTS: Sculpture (he has executed a series of busts of men of medicine).

BERRIGAN, Daniel 1921-

PERSONAL: Born May 9, 1921, in Two Harbors, Minn.; son of Thomas William (a railraod engineer) and Frida (Fromhart) Berrigan. *Education:* St. Andrew on Hudson, B.A., 1946; Woodstock College, Baltimore, Md., M.A., 1952. *Agent:* Elizabeth Bartelme, 227 East 25th St., New York, N.Y. 10010. *Office:* Woodstock College, 475 Riverside Dr., New York, N.Y. 10027.

CAREER: Entered Order of Society of Jesus (Jesuits), 1939, ordained Roman Catholic priest, 1952; St. Peter's Preparatory School, Jersey City, N.J., teacher of French, English, and Latin, 1945-49; ministerial work in Europe, 1953-54; Brooklyn Preparatory School, Brooklyn, N.Y., instructor in French and theology, 1954-57; Lemoyne College, Syracuse, N.Y., associate professor of theology, 1957-62; sabbatical in Europe, 1962-63; *Jesuit Missions,* New York City, assistant editor, 1963-65; Cornell University, Ithaca, N.Y., associate director of United Religious Work, 1966-69; convicted of conspiracy and destruction of government property, October, 1968; sentenced to three-year term in federal prison; began serving sentence, August, 1970; paroled, February 24, 1972; Woodstock College, New York City, professor of theology, 1972—. Served as auxiliary military chaplain in Germany, 1954; religious director, Walter Farrell Guild, 1954-57; staff worker, Office of Economic Opportunity, Pueblo, Colo., summer, 1967; co-founder, Catholic Peace Fellowship. Visiting lecturer at various colleges and universities. *Awards, honors:* Lamont Poetry Award, and National Book Award nomination, 1957, for *Time without Number;* National Book Award nomination, 1967, for *No One Walks Waters;* Frederick G. Melcher Book Award, Unitarian Universalist Association, 1970, for *The Trial of the Catonsville Nine, No Bars to Manhood,* and *Trial Poems: A Poet, a Painter;* National Book Award nomination, 1970, for *No Bars to Manhood;* Thomas More Award, 1971, for *The Dark Night of Resistance.*

WRITINGS: The Bride: Essays in the Church, Macmillan, 1959; *The Bow in the Cloud: Man's Covenant with God,* Coward, 1961; *They Call Us Dead Men: Reflections on Life and Conscience,* Macmillan, 1966; *Consequences: Truth and . . .,* Macmillan, 1967; *Go from Here: A Prison Diary,* Open Space Action Committee, 1968; *The Trial of the Catonsville Nine* (one-act play; first produced in Los Angeles at Mark Taper Forum; produced Off-Broadway at Good Shepherd-Faith Church, February 4, 1971; produced on Broadway at Lyceum Theatre, June, 1971), Beacon Press, 1970; *No Bars to Manhood,* Doubleday, 1970; *The Dark Night of Resistance,* Doubleday, 1971; (with Robert Coles) *The Geography of Faith: Conversations between Daniel Berrigan, When Underground, and Robert Coles,* Beacon Press, 1971; *America Is Hard to Find* (contains letters from Danbury Prison and writings from underground), Doubleday, 1972; (with Lee Lockwood) *Absurd Convictions, Modest Hopes: Conversations after Prison with Lee Lockwood,* Random House, 1972; *Jesus Christ,* illustrations by Gregory Harris and Deborah Harris, Doubleday, 1973; *Lights On in the House of the Dead: A Prison Dairy,* Doubleday, 1974; (with Thich Nhat Hanh) *The Raft Is Not the Shore: Conversations toward a Buddhist/Christian Awareness,* Beacon Press, 1975; *A Book of Parables,* Seabury, 1977; *The Uncommon Book of Prayer,* Fellowship of Reconciliation, 1977; *The Prayer of the Lamb,* Seabury, 1977.

Poetry: *Time without Number,* Macmillan, 1957; *Encounters,* World Publishing, 1960, new edition, Associated Artists, 1965; *The World for Wedding Ring,* Macmillan, 1962;

No One Walks Waters, Macmillan, 1966; *Love, Love at the End: Parables, Prayers, and Meditations,* Macmillan, 1968; *Night Flight to Hanoi: War Diary with 11 Poems,* Macmillan, 1968; *False Gods, Real Men: New Poems,* Macmillan, 1969; *Crime Trial,* Impressions Workshop, 1970; (with Tom Lewis) *Trial Poems: A Poet, a Painter,* Beacon Press, 1970; *Selected Poetry of Daniel Berrigan S.J.,* Anchor-Doubleday, 1970; *Selected and New Poems,* Doubleday, 1973; *Prison Poems,* Unicorn Press, 1973; *Prison Poems,* Viking, 1974.

Poems anthologized in several volumes, including *From One Word,* Devin, 1950, *Anthology of Catholic Poets,* edited by Joyce Kilmer, with a new supplement by James Edward Tobin, Doubleday, 1955, *Sealed unto the Day,* Catholic Poetry Society of America, 1955, and *Twentieth-Century American Poetry,* edited by Conrad Aiken, Modern Library, 1963. Contributor to numerous periodicals.

SIDELIGHTS: In February, 1968, Daniel Berrigan and Howard Zinn of Boston University went to Hanoi, North Vietnam to assist in obtaining the release of three captured American fliers. The diary which Berrigan kept on the trip as well as eleven poems recording his feelings about the experience are included in *Night Flight to Hanoi.* A writer for the *Virginia Quarterly Review* calls the book "a manifestation of the moral hysteria which has swept the minds of so many good men over the past few years. Father Berrigan, motivated by love and moral anguish, condemns the United States for its behavior in an 'immoral' war, but then he goes on to exalt Lenin and Ho Chi Minh to the status of modern saints. He condemns the fliers he rescued because they still believed in America after their confinement, because they did not succumb to the Communist teachings of their captors. What began as a book of love ends as a book of hate. Father Berrigan becomes the merciless accuser of a God of revenge and violence. The book is a frightening document, for in it poet becomes mouthpiece for propaganda and priest becomes prosecutor. It is a flight into a night of moral rage; there is no dawn of new love and understanding at the end of that flight."

On May 17, 1968, Daniel and Philip Berrigan and seven other Roman Catholics entered Draft Board 33 in Catonsville, Md., seized files concerning potential draftees, took the folders outside in wire baskets, and burned the documents with homemade napalm. They then waited, praying, for fifteen minutes, until federal authorities came to arrest them. A portion of the note given reporters shortly before the raid read: "We destroy these draft records not only because they exploit our young men but because they represent misplaced power concentrated in the ruling class of America. . . . We confront the Catholic Church, other Christian bodies, and the synagogues of America with their silence and cowardice in face of our country's crimes. . . . Now this injustice must be faced, and this we intend to do, with whatever strength of mind, body, and grace that God will give us. May God have mercy on our nation." Later, at the trial at which he was sentenced to three years in prison, Daniel Berrigan stated, "I burned some paper because I was trying to say that the burning of children was unhuman and unbearable, and . . . a cry is the only response."

Although he was supposed to begin his three year sentence on April 9, 1970, Berrigan, his brother and two other defendants decided to go underground. In an interview given while he was evading federal agents, Berrigan gave his reasons for refusing to voluntarily submit to imprisonment: "There is a mythology abroad in our country, sedulously fostered by liberals . . . [that] has to do with the moral necessity of joining illegal action to legal consequences. . . . The principle is obviously of interest to those in power. . . . It aims with vigor at . . . bring[ing] even the most passionate conscience under the control of unchangeable, presumably beneficent, public authority. Ethical men may, in such a way, become a powerful support to an evil regime." On August 11, 1970, Berrigan was captured by federal agents on Block Island, R.I., at the home of two friends and fellow writers, William Stringfellow and Anthony Towne. Stringfellow remarked after the arrest: "Daniel Berrigan is our friend and is always welcome in our home. Any visit from him is an honor for us because he is a priest of uncommon conscience, he is a citizen of urgent moral purpose and a human being of exemplary courage." After serving half of his sentence, Berrigan was paroled on February 24, 1972.

The Trial of the Catonsville Nine, a "prose report" produced on the stage in Los Angeles, and on and Off-Broadway, received generally favorable critical notices. Clive Barnes called the play "a wonderfully moving testament to nine consciences. It is radical, but not at all chic, and the sincerity of its sentiments reveals the simplicity of men with many fears but no doubts." Many critics hesitated to call the work a play. Ned O'Gorman described it as "a moral guide, a warming, a radiant explication of the Gospels." Berrigan explained some of his thoughts about the relationship between theatre and protest in a taped message recorded while he was still underground. Berrigan told the cast of his play: "But it does seem to me that actors, with their moral passions and their bodily gestures, are in a certain place with regard to the spirit. They are exerting pressure against the outer darkness. They are creating and communicating light around their bodies, the light of the spirit of man. They are saying something that others are saying in prison, and in the underground, and in exile, and, indeed, in death."

In a review of *Jesus Christ* Cornelia Holbert writes: "Interleaved with Father Berrigan's prose-poem are powerful pages of Christian symbols in rich color, sometimes inscrutable, but endlessly scrutable, witness to the Word. . . . There is a great and beautiful book for those already committed to peace." However, M. J. Rush feels that "Father Berrigan's text, brief as it is, suggests little, if any, connection with the illustrations. As a result, there is almost no continuity in the book. . . . Apart from a few welcome exceptions, the illustrations, which take up most of the book, are dull, obvious and uninviting. . . . The feeble attempt to make the cross the unifying factor seems more like an afterthought."

In *The Raft Is Not the Shore* Berrigan and Thich Nhat Hanh, a Buddhist monk, record their conversations about Jesus and Buddha, government, economics, war, prison, self-immolation, and death. Both men participated in active resistance to the war in Indo-China and they share a disenchantment with "the system" as well as a disillusionment with the "communities of resistance" in which they placed their hopes for the future. D. J. O'Hanlon says that Berrigan and Hanh "challenge us to create communities, countercultural islands of sanity, in which humanness can happen." According to Sister Gregory Duffy ". . . the thinking of the two men can be summed up in a quotation from Buddha: 'My doctrine is only a raft helping to bring you to the other shore, not ultimate reality; you shouldn't worship it.'"

Berrigan is acknowledged by most critics as a skillful and profound poet; one who blends art and protest without diluting either ingredient. Miller Williams writes: "Daniel Berrigan shows us in *False Gods, Real Men* that a poem *can,* of course, make a point; that a poet can be partisan as a

poet. But he demonstrates also how important compassion and a sense of irony are to the partisan poet, how especially redeeming they are when anger and bitterness exist. Berrigan's protest comes out of no hate and is not inflated. His is the agony of seeing a wrong world, without the smugness of the righteous that has been the hallmark of almost all protest poetry." Edward B. Fiske believes that Berrigan's poems "tend to move on ideas rather than feelings. Their beauty lies more in the finely-honed line than the strong image. At his best, however, he has a superb capacity for planting high thoughts firmly in the soil of the present." Edward Duff describes Berrigan as "a person of imaginative insight, a master of metaphor, a stylist of shining affirmation but, most significant, he is an artist of acute and resonant sensibility."

A reviewer for *Choice* feels that *Selected and New Poems* "shows that Berrigan has developed as a poet over the passage of years. His earliest verse is closely allied to, and sometimes directly imitative of, such older poets as Emily Dickinson, G. M. Hopkins, and even Robert Frost, except for Berrigan's characteristically erratic punctuation and line and stanza arrangement, which seem to obscure needlessly the directness of his statement. In his later poetry he is much more open to experimentation in the use of alliteration, internal rhyme, and typography. . . . Much more than . . . many present-day poets, Berrigan is highly topical."

Prison Poems contains verse written during the author's eighteen month prison term. Anthony Towne calls the book "a delight not only to read but to look at. . . . Even if you loathe poetry, you can from time to time merely look at this volume and rejoice. . . . There is a touch of the politician about Daniel Berrigan (not enough to corrupt, but enough to suggest charisma), but his politics of outrage, and his phrases in that context are outrageous, or as has been noted, foul-mouthed. . . . The language of prisons, like the language of armies, is obscenity. That is because prisons, like armies, are obscenities." A *Publisher's Weekly* reviewer feels that "in style, tone, imagery, idiom and insight, these three-score poems convey a toughened singleness of vision that is no less religious, even mystical, for all its resort to a blunt, sardonic vernacular. . . . Berrigan moves in close to 'whiff the cup' of prison life; his glimpses of brother prisoners are moving, his message is *hang on.*"

Berrigan believes that his roles as priest and radical are naturally linked. He once wrote that he became a Jesuit because "they had a revolutionary history." At a lecture/discussion he stated: "For a priest to speak out on war ought to be no surprise. For him to be silent should be a surprise." In her book, *Divine Disobedience,* Francine Du Plessix Gray emphasizes the theological motivation in those acts of protest in which both Berrigan brothers have participated. "Like the early Christians, the Berrigans look upon the Second Coming, bringing either man's perfectability or his destruction, as imminent in their own lives. There is no time to atone, to improve, to do penance. Like the Old Testament prophets, who wrote in moments of historical crisis, the Berrigans demand that society be made perfect in our lifetime to avoid an apocalyptic destruction. 'Redeem the times,' Daniel wrote. . . . 'The times are inexpressibly evil.'"

Berrigan told an interviewer: "I'm very privileged in that I'm in a position to do exactly what I want, which is electrifying humanity. I've no stomach to come on as some sort of moral figure. I would really just like to awaken a bit of hope in people, because I have some. At least, I try to be a guy who has tried to be faithful to his conscience and life. . . . And, well, maybe we can all do it." To Daniel Berrigan, his mission is very clear. "Peace is something that has to be *done,''* he once remarked, "with your heart and your hands, like love.''

BIOGRAPHICAL/CRITICAL SOURCES—Books: Daniel Berrigan, *Go from Here: A Prison Diary,* Open Space Action Committee, 1968; Francine Du Plessix Gray, *Divine Disobedience,* Knopf, 1970; D. Berrigan and Robert Coles, *The Geography of Faith: Conversations between Daniel Berrigan, When Underground, and Robert Coles,* Beacon Press, 1971; William V. Casey and Philip Nobile, editors, *The Berrigans,* Praeger, 1971; William Stringfellow and Anthony Towne, *Suspect Tenderness: The Witness of the Berrigans,* Holt, 1971; D. Berrigan and Lee Lockwood, *Absurd Convictions, Modest Hopes: Conversations after Prison with Lee Lockwood,* Random House, 1972; D. Berrigan, *Lights On in the House of the Dead: A Prison Diary,* Doubleday, 1974; Richard Curtis, *The Berrigan Brothers,* Hawthorn, 1974; *Contemporary Literary Criticism,* Volume IV, Gale, 1975.

Periodicals: *New Yorker,* April 9, 1966, March 14, 1970; *Poetry,* November, 1966, autumn, 1968; *New York Times Book Review,* July 28, 1968; *Newsweek,* October 14, 1968, February 22, 1971, February 7, 1972; *Nation,* November 18, 1968, May 4, 1970; *Carleton Miscellany,* fall, 1968; *Saturday Review,* June 14, 1969; *Virginia Quarterly Review,* winter, 1969; *Christian Century,* May 20, 1970, June 24, 1970, April 7, 1971, December 19, 1973; *New Republic,* June 20, 1970, December 12, 1970, March 6, 1971, April 13, 1974; *New York Times,* August 12, 1970, January 31, 1971, February 8, 1971, May 30, 1971, June 16, 1971; *New York Review of Books,* November 7, 1970; *Washington Post,* December 18, 1970, August 18, 1971; *New York,* February 22, 1971; *Christian Science Monitor,* March 2, 1971; *Commonweal,* February 18, 1972; *Best Sellers,* October 1, 1972, September 15, 1973, October 1, 1973, March, 1976; *Publisher's Weekly,* July 23, 1973; *America,* September 15, 1973, December 13, 1975; *National Review,* November 9, 1973, March 1, 1974; *Choice,* February, 1974; *Detroit,* April 6, 1975.

* * *

BERRY, Barbara J. 1937-
(B. J. Berry)

PERSONAL: Born February 17, 1937, in Westfield, N.Y.; married Warren J. Berry (a purchasing manager), July 13, 1957. *Education:* Jamestown Community College, A.A., 1957. *Address:* Box 231, Ashville, N.Y.

CAREER: Journal Press, Inc., Jamestown, N.Y., proof reader, 1958-61. *Member:* Authors Guild.

WRITINGS—Youth books: *Shannon,* Follett, 1968; (under name B. J. Berry) *Just Don't Bug Me,* Follett, 1971; *Let 'er Buck: The Rodeo,* Bobbs-Merrill, 1971; *A Look of Eagles,* Bobbs-Merrill, 1973; *The Thoroughbreds,* Bobbs-Merrill, 1974; *His Majesty's Mark,* Bobbs-Merrill, 1976. Author of a series of stories for *Sports Afield.*

WORK IN PROGRESS: The Standardbreds.

AVOCATIONAL INTERESTS: Horses, especially American Saddle Horses, and dogs, especially Chesapeake Bay Retrievers.

BIOGRAPHICAL/CRITICAL SOURCES: New York Times Book Review, May 2, 1971.

* * *

BERRY, Mary Frances 1938-

PERSONAL: Born February 17, 1938, in Nashville, Tenn.; daughter of George F. and Frances (Southall) Berry. *Education:* Howard University, B.A., 1961, M.A., 1962; University of Michigan, Ph.D., 1966, J.D., 1970. *Office:* Department of History, University of Colorado, Boulder, Colo. 80309.

CAREER: Central Michigan University, Mount Pleasant, assistant professor of history, 1966-68; Eastern Michigan University, Ypsilanti, assistant professor, 1968-70, associate professor of history, 1970; University of Maryland, College Park, associate professor of history, beginning 1969; currently faculty member at University of Colorado, Boulder. Adjunct associate professor, University of Michigan, 1970-71. *Member:* American Historical Association, Organization of American Historians, American Society for the Study of Legal History.

WRITINGS: Black Resistance/White Law: A History of Constitutional Racism in America, Appleton, 1971; *Military Necessity and Civil Rights Policy: Black Citizenship and the Constitution, 1861-1868,* Kennikat, 1977. Contributor of articles and reviews to history and law journals.

WORK IN PROGRESS: A judicial biography of Supreme Court Justice Harold H. Burton; an interpretative history of the United States.

* * *

BERRY, Thomas Elliott 1917-

PERSONAL: Born August 25, 1917, in Philadelphia, Pa.; son of Samson (a businessman) and Elizabeth (McCorkle) Berry; married Helen Walker, May 25, 1940; children: Thomas Laurence, Ruth Ann, Janet Elaine, Suzanne Walker, David Walker, Timothy Alan, William Philip. *Education:* University of Pennsylvania, A.B., 1939, A.M., 1940; University of Pittsburgh, Ph.D., 1949. *Politics:* Republican. *Religion:* Episcopalian. *Home:* 510 Spring Grove Lane, West Chester, Pa. 19380. *Office:* Department of English, West Chester State College, West Chester, Pa. 19380.

CAREER: West Chester State College, West Chester, Pa., instructor, 1946-48, assistant professor, 1948-49, associate professor, 1949-51, professor of English, 1951—. Lecturer at Pennsylvania State University, Drexel University, Penn Morton College, and Widener College.

WRITINGS: Journalism Today, Chilton, 1958; *Most Common Mistakes in English Usage,* Chilton, 1961, 2nd edition, revised, McGraw, 1971; (editor) *Values in American Culture,* Odyssey, 1966; (editor) *The Biographer's Craft,* Odyssey, 1967; (editor) *Readings in American Criticism,* Odyssey, 1970; *The Study of Language: An Introduction,* Dickenson, 1970; *The Twentieth Century American Newspaper in the American Novel,* Scarecrow, 1970; *The Craft of Writing,* McGraw, 1974; *Journalism in America,* Hastings House, 1976. Contributor of more than forty articles to magazines and scholarly journals.

WORK IN PROGRESS: A History of American Literature.

* * *

BERRYMAN, John 1914-1972

October 25, 1914—January 7, 1972; American poet, biographer, and editor. Obituaries: *New York Times,* January 8, 1972; *Washington Post,* January 8, 1972; *Sunday Times* (London), January 9, 1972; *Newsweek,* January 17, 1972; *Time,* January 17, 1972; *Publishers Weekly,* January 24, 1972. (See index for *CA* sketch)

BERSON, Harold 1926-

PERSONAL: Born November 23, 1926, in Los Angeles, Calif.; married; wife's name, Paula (an artist). *Education:* University of California, Los Angeles, B.A., 1953. *Home:* 172 Stanton St., New York, N. Y. 10002.

CAREER: Worked briefly for Bureau of Public Assistance, Los Angeles, Calif., before becoming a full-time illustrator; began illustrating books in the late 1950's, mainly working in brush and ink and in watercolor.

WRITINGS—Self-illustrated adaptations of folktales; all published by Crown, except as indicated: *Raminagrobis and the Mice*, Seabury, 1965; *Pop! Goes the Turnip*, Grosset, 1966; *Why the Jackal Won't Speak to the Hedge-Hog: A Tunisian Folk Tale* (Junior Literary Guild selection), Seabury, 1969; *How the Devil Gets His Due*, 1972; *The Thief Who Hugged a Moonbeam*, Seabury, 1972; *Balarin's Goat*, 1972; *Henry Possum*, 1973; *The Boy, the Baker, the Miller and More*, 1974; *Mouse Is Not a Mouse*, 1975; *I'm Bored, Ma*, 1976; *The Rats Who Lived in the Delicatessen*, 1976; *Kassum's Shoes*, 1977.

Illustrator: Mary Coyle Chase, *Loretta Mason Potts*, Lippincott, 1958; Rutherford G. Montgomery, *In Happy Hollow*, Doubleday, 1958; Helen Diehl Olds, *Silver Button*, Knopf, 1958; William Rose Littlefield, *Seventh Son of a Seventh Son*, Lothrop, 1959; Daniel Walden, *Nutcracker*, Lippincott, 1959.

Elizabeth Reeve Morrow, *A Pint of Judgment*, Knopf, 1960; Leland B. Jacobs, *Belling the Cat, and Other Stories*, Golden Press, 1960; Ilo Orleans, *The Zoo That Grew*, Walck, 1960; Frances Hodgson Burnett, *Racketty-Packetty House, and Other Stories*, Scribner, 1961; Phyllis McGinley, *Mince Pie and Mistletoe* (poems), Lippincott, 1961; Hans Christian Andersen, *The Nightingale*, Lippincott, 1962; Dana Faralla, *Swanhilda-of-the-Swans*, Lippincott, 1964; Odille Ousley, *Mr. Bear's Bow Ties*, Ginn, 1964; Betsy Cromer Byars, *The Dancing Camel*, Viking, 1965; Faralla, *The Wonderful Flying-Go-Round*, World Publishing, 1965; Beman Lord, *The Perfect Pitch*, Walck, 1965; Hilaire Belloc, *The Bad Child's Book of Beasts, and More Beasts for Worse Children*, Grosset, 1966; Mary McBurney Green, *When Will I Whistle?*, F. Watts, 1967; Edward Lear, *The Pelican Chorus*, Parents' Magazine Press, 1967; Lord, *The Day the Spaceship Landed*, Walck, 1967; Barbara K. Walker, *Watermelons, Walnuts, and the Wisdom of Allah*, Parents' Magazine Press, 1967; Nikolai Semenovich Leskov, *The Wild Beast*, Funk, 1968; Lord, *Shot-Put Challenge*, Walck, 1969; Walker, *Pigs and Pirates: A Greek Tale*, David White, 1969; Al Perkins, *King Midas and the Golden Touch*, Beginner Books, 1969; Mabel Watts, *The King and the Whirly-Bird*, Parents' Magazine Press, 1969; Miriam B. Young, *A Bear Named George*, Crown, 1969.

Edmund W. Hildick, *The Dragon That Lived under Manhattan*, Crown, 1970; Harry Behn, *What a Beautiful Noise*, World Publishing, 1970; Lord, *Shrimp's Soccer Goal*, Walck, 1970; Lord, *The Spaceship Returns*, Walck, 1970; Miriam Chaikin, *Ittki Pittki*, Parents' Magazine Press, 1971; Ivana Brlic-Mazuranic, *The Brave Adventures of Zapitch*, Walck, 1972; Walker, *New Patches for Old*, Parents' Magazine Press, 1974; Dorothy Van Woerkum, *Abu Ali*, Macmillan, 1976; Van Woerkum, *Abu Ali and His Friends*, Macmillan, 1977.

Also contributes illustrations almost monthly to *Humpty Dumpty's Magazine*, in which his work first appeared.

AVOCATIONAL INTERESTS: Travel (most recently to France, Sicily, and Tunisia), music, ballet.

BERTHOFF, Rowland (Tappan) 1921-

PERSONAL: Born September 20, 1921, in Toledo, Ohio; son of Nathaniel and Helen (Tappan) Berthoff; married Tirzah Margaret Park, August 5, 1954; children: Thomas Arthur, Margaret Olivia, Andrew Warner, Clarissa Helen. *Education:* Oberlin College, A.B., 1942; Harvard University, A.M., 1947, Ph.D., 1952. *Politics:* Democrat. *Religion:* Presbyterian. *Home:* 7195 Washington Ave., St. Louis, Mo. 63130. *Office:* Department of History, Washington University, St. Louis, Mo. 63130.

CAREER: Princeton University, Princeton, N.J., instructor, 1952-57, assistant professor of history, 1957-62; Washington University, St. Louis, Mo., associate professor, 1962-65, professor of history, 1965—, William Eliot Smith Professor, 1974—, chairman of department, 1968-74. Fulbright lecturer, University of Edinburgh, 1965-66. *Military service:* U.S. Army, Infantry, 1942-46; became first lieutenant. *Member:* Organization of American Historians, Southern Historical Association. *Awards, honors:* Fulbright scholar at University of Wales, 1952-53; American Council of Learned Societies fellow, 1960-61.

WRITINGS: British Immigrants in Industrial America, 1790-1950, Harvard University Press, 1953; *An Unsettled People: Social Order and Disorder in American History*, Harper, 1971. Contributor to history journals.

WORK IN PROGRESS: Research on republican liberty and social equality in America, 1776-1976; a book on the social ideology of small business; an article on the Welsh in America, for *Harvard Encyclopedia of Ethnic Groups*.

*   *   *

BERWICK, Keith (Bennet) 1928-

PERSONAL: Born October 15, 1928, in Montreal, Quebec, Canada; son of Hugh Bennet and Freda (Wilson) Berwick; married Jean Shepherd, May 3, 1952 (divorced, 1965); married Vera Servi (a newspaper columnist), July 2, 1965 (divorced, 1972); children: (first marriage) Rebecca, Sarah, Jeffrey, Rachel. *Education:* Syracuse University, A.B., 1953; University of Chicago, M.A., 1957, Ph.D., 1959. *Politics:* Peace and Freedom Party. *Religion:* Baha'i. *Address:* P.O. Box 24140, Los Angeles, Calif. 90024.

CAREER: University of California, Los Angeles, instructor, 1959-61, assistant professor, 1961-65, lecturer in history, 1965-71; Claremont Men's College and Claremont Graduate School, Claremont, Calif., visiting professor, 1969-70, associate professor of history, 1971-74; Pepperdine University, Malibu, Calif., distinguished visiting professor of American studies, 1975—. Fellow, International College, Los Angeles, 1972—; academic humanist, Western Humanities Center, University of California, Los Angeles, 1974-76; visiting professor of history, California State University, Los Angeles, 1976-77. Moderator of nationally syndicated television program, "Speculation," for Public Broadcasting Service, 1965-71; host of "At One With . . ." (a one-hour interview program), 1975—; producer of television programs for KNBC-TV (Los Angeles) and National Broadcasting Co. Consultant, California Bill of Rights Project, 1964-66. *Military service:* U.S. Air Force, 1951-55; became staff sergeant. *Member:* American Historical Association, Organization of American Historians, Southern Historical Association, Sigma Delta Chi. *Awards, honors:* Grants from Colonial Williamsburg, 1957-61, Social Science Research Council, 1960-61, Huntington Library, 1962, and American Philosophical Society, 1962-63.

WRITINGS: The Federal Age, 1789-1829, America in the Process of Becoming, American Historical Association, Service Center for Teachers of History, 1961; *To Be Free: The Coming of the Revolution in Virginia,* Holt, 1975; *The American Revolutionary Experience, 1776-1976,* Western Humanities Center, 1975; *American Heroes: Classic, Romantic and Modern,* Oxford University Press, 1976. Contributor to *Frontier, Los Angeles Times Calendar, Center, Gerontology, American Scholar, William and Mary Quarterly,* and other history journals. Associate editor and book review editor, *Pacific Historical Review,* 1960-65.

*   *   *

BEST, Gary A(llen)   1939-

PERSONAL: Born July 27, 1939, in Oceanside, Calif.; son of Charles Richard and Vivian (Misner) Best; married Shirley Seelhammer (an occupational therapist), December 18, 1962; children: Joanna E. *Education:* Los Angeles State College of Applied Arts and Sciences (now California State University), B.A., 1961; California State College (now University), Los Angeles, M.A.,1965; University of Minnesota, Ph.D., 1968. *Home:* 515 North Ranch Lane, Glendora, Calif. 91740. *Office:* Department of Special Education, California State University, 5151 State University Dr., Los Angeles, Calif. 90032.

CAREER: Special education classroom teacher in public schools of Los Angeles, Calif., 1961-65; California State University, Los Angeles, assistant professor, 1968-70, associate professor, 1970-75, professor of special education, 1975—. Summer instructor in special education, University of Minnesota, 1966, 1967, 1968; visiting summer professor at University of Victoria, 1970 and Western Michigan University, 1972. *Member:* Council for Exceptional Children, American Association of Sex Educators, Counselors and Therapists. *Awards, honors:* United Cerebral Palsy Association research grant, summer, 1971.

WRITINGS: (Contributor) G. Orville Johnson and Harriet D. Blank, editors, *Exceptional Children Research Review,* Council for Exceptional Children, 1968; (editor with Barbara Dunn and others) *Selected Readings in Special Education,* Simon & Schuster, 1970; *Individuals with Physical Disabilities: An Introduction for Educators,* Mosby, 1978. Contributor to *Exceptional Children, Cerebral Palsy Journal, Journal of Home Economics,* and other journals. Associate editor, *Exceptional Children.*

*   *   *

BETTIS, Joseph Dabney   1936-

PERSONAL: Born September 19, 1936, in Graham, Tex.; son of Jack and Jo (Dabney) Bettis; married second wife, Lynne Shangraw Masland, December 21, 1975; children: David, Mark, Daniel, Mary, Molly. *Education:* Southern Methodist University, B.A., 1958; Drew University, B.D. (cum laude), 1961; Princeton University, M.A., 1963, Ph.D., 1964. *Home:* 616 North Forest, Bellingham, Wash. 98225. *Office:* Fairhaven College, Western Washington University, Bellingham, Wash. 98225.

CAREER: Rutgers University, Douglass College, New Brunswick, N.J., instructor in religion, 1962-64; University of Alabama, University, assistant professor, 1964-66, associate professor of religious studies and chairman of the department, 1966-72, Thompson Lecturer, 1967; University of Nebraska at Omaha, Distinguished Professor of Humanities, 1972-73, College of Public Affairs and Community Service, scholar in residence, 1972-73, associate dean and pro-

fessor in residence, 1973-75; Western Washington University, Fairhaven College, Bellingham, professor and dean, 1975—. Education Program specialist, U.S. Office of Education, 1966; consultant, Community Action Program, Office of Economic Opportunity, 1966—; chairman, Head Start Advisory Board, 1967. Member of regional selection committee, Danforth Associate Program, 1968-70. College of Arts and Sciences representative, University Senate, University of Alabama, 1966-67, 1968-69. Research associate, Institute for the Study of Contemporary Social Problems, 1975—. *Member:* American Academy of Religion, Alabama Council of Human Relations (member of executive board, 1966-67), Tuscaloosa Council of Human Relations (chairman, 1966-67), Omicron Delta Kappa. *Awards, honors:* University of Alabama research grants, 1965-66, 1968; Danforth associate, 1966—; University of Alabama International Studies grant, 1970; National Endowment for the Humanities fellowship, 1970-71; Metropolitan Life Insurance Co. educational grant, 1977; National Endowment for the Humanities consultants program grant, 1977.

WRITINGS: (Editor) *Phenomenology of Religion,* Harper, 1969; (contributor) George Hunsinger, editor, *Karl Barth and Radical Politics,* Westminster, 1976. Contributor to *Scottish Journal of Theology, Pulpit, Religious Studies, Christian Century, Interpretation, Journal of the American Academy of Religion,* and other publications.

WORK IN PROGRESS: Karl Barth and Radical Social Ethics.

*   *   *

BETTS, Emmett Albert   1903-

PERSONAL: Born February 1, 1903, in Elkhart, Iowa; son of Albert Henry (a businessman) and Grace L. (Greenwood) Betts. *Education:* Des Moines University, B.S., 1925; University of Iowa, M.S., 1928, Ph.D., 1931. *Home:* 144 Lake Mariam Rd. S.E., Lakewood Estates, Winter Haven, Fla. 33880. *Office:* P.O. Box 8065, University of Miami, Coral Gables, Fla. 33124.

CAREER: School vocational director in Orient, Iowa, 1922-24; superintendent of schools in Northboro, Iowa, 1925-29; school psychologist and elementary principal in Shaker Heights, Ohio, 1931-34; State Teachers College (now State University of New York College at Oswego), Oswego, N.Y., director of teacher education, summer sessions, and reading clinic, 1934-37; Pennsylvania State College (now University), State College, research professor of education and director of reading clinic, 1937-45; Temple University, Philadelphia, Pa., professor of psychology and director of reading clinic, 1945-54; Betts Reading Clinic, Haverford, Pa., director, 1954-61; University of Miami, Coral Gables, Fla., research professor of education, lecturer in psychology, and director of Reading Research Laboratory, 1961—. Member of summer faculty or participant in vision and reading institutes at more than forty other colleges and universities, 1930—. Consultant to Air University, Maxwell Field, Ala., to Academic Dimensions Systems, Inc., and other educational groups. Staff officer of Pennsylvania Wing, Civil Air Patrol, 1946-61. Trustee, Lake Placid Club Education Foundation, 1968—.

MEMBER: International Reading Association (formerly International Council for the Improvement of Reading Instruction [founder]), National Council on Aviation Education (member of board of directors; vice-president), National Conference on Research in English, Simpler Spelling Association (member of board, 1966-71; president, 1967-71),

Phonemic Spelling Council (president, 1971—), National Aerospace Educational Council (vice-president; honorary director, 1972—), American Association for the Advancement of Science, American Association of Applied Psychology, American Association of School Administrators (life member), American Psychological Association (fellow), American Educational Research Association, Progressive Education Association, Association for Childhood Education International, National Education Association, Linguistic Society of America, National Council for the Social Studies, National Society for the Study of Education, American Association of University Professors, Society for the Advancement of Education, New York Academy of Sciences, Southeastern Psychological Association, Aircraft Owners and Pilots Association, National Aeronautics Association, LuLu Flying Squadron, Greater Miami Aviation Association, Phi Delta Kappa, Psi Chi, Shriner.

AWARDS, HONORS: Apollo Award, American Optometric Association, 1962; Citation of Merit and Founders Award, International Reading Association, 1971; Gold Medal Award, *Education,* 1971; certificate of Meritorious Achievement in Clinical Psychology, 1971; Certificate for Aerospace Education Leadership, National Aerospace Education Council, 1971; L.L.D., Sioux Falls College, 1972; Melvil Dewey Centennial Gold Medal, Phonemic Spelling Council, 1977; and other awards for education leadership and achievement.

WRITINGS: Prevention and Correction of Reading Difficulties, Row, Peterson, 1936; (with Mabel O'Donnell) *Here We Go: A Diagnostic Reading Readiness Book,* Row, Peterson, 1938, 3rd revised edition, 1955; *The Initial Stages of Reading Readiness,* Row, Peterson, 1939; *Spelling Vocabulary Study: Grade Placement of Words in Seventeen Spellers,* American Book Co., 1940; (with Thelma M. Betts) *An Index to Professional Literature on Reading and Related Topics,* American Book Co., 1945; *Foundations of Reading Instruction,* American Book Co., 1946, 4th revised edition, 1957; *Second Spelling Vocabulary Study: Grade Placement of Words in Eight Recent Spellers,* American Book Co., 1949.

Series: (Editor and contributor) A. M. Anderson and others, "American Adventure" series, twenty-one books with teacher's guides, Harper, 1941-67 (some titles in the series were published originally by Wheeler Publishing); (with Mabel-Louise Arey) "Betts-Arey Directed Spelling Activities," seven books, American Book Co., 1941, revised edition, 1948; (with Harry A. Greene and others) "Basic Language" series, six books, 1943-47, revised edition, 1958; (with Carolyn M. Welch and others) "Betts Basic Reading-Study Program: The Language Arts Series," thirteen readers with teacher's guides, study aids, and tests, American Book Co., 1948-52, subsequent editions with additional readers and aids, 4th edition published as "Betts New Reading-Study Program," American Book Co., 1970; (with P. A. Killgallon and Mary Louise Friebele) "Language Arts Spellers," fourteen books with teacher's guides and workbooks, American Book Co., 1953-54, revised edition, 1957.

Contributor: Jerome E. Leavitt, editor, *Readings in Elementary Education,* W. C. Brown, 1961; Lester D. Crow, Alice Crow, and Walter Murray, editors, *Teaching in the Elementary School,* Longmans, Green, 1961; Albert J. Harris, editor, *Readings on Reading Instruction,* McKay, 1964; Verna Dieckman Anderson and others, editors, *Readings in the Language Arts,* Macmillan, 1964; Lawrence E. Hafner, editor, *Improved Reading in Secondary Schools,* Macmillan, 1967; Virgil M. Howes and Helen Fisher Darrow, edi-

tors, *Reading and the Elementary School Child,* Macmillan, 1968; M. A. Dawson, compiler, *Developing Comprehension,* International Reading Association, 1968; (author of foreword) Harry Baker, *Biographical Sagas of Will Power,* Vantage, 1970; Godfrey Dewey, *Relative Frequency of English Spellings,* Teachers College Press, 1970.

Other publications include bibliographies, evaluation materials, tests and test reviews, and charts. Contributor to *Compton's Pictured Encyclopedia,* to yearbooks and conference proceedings, and more than two hundred articles to *Visual Digest, Optometic Weekly,* and educational journals.

Chairman of editorial board, National Conference on Research in English, 1934-54; editor and contributor, *My Weekly Reader,* 1938-69; *Education,* reading editor, 1948-69, member of editorial board, 1948-57, 1969—, editor-in-chief, 1955-69; associate editor, *Journal of Experimental Education,* 1938—; advisory editor, *Highlights for Children,* 1945—; member of editorial advisory committee, *Annual Progress in Reading,* 1945—; member of editorial advisory board, *Compton's Illustrated Science Dictionary,* 1963, and *Compton's Dictionary of Natural Science,* 1965; contributing editor, *Reading Teacher,* 1971—; member of editorial board, *Reading Improvement,* 1973—.

WORK IN PROGRESS: An experimental study of the motivated, perceptual, and cognitive processing of graphic symbols at the phoneme-grapheme and higher levels of linguistic and cognitive structures.

AVOCATIONAL INTERESTS: Flying, parachute jumping, soaring, amateur radio.

BIOGRAPHICAL/CRITICAL SOURCES: Elementary English, Volume XXXV, number 4, April, 1958; *Chicago Tribune Magazine,* November 5, 1969, November 12, 1969, November 19, 1969; *Education,* Volume XCI, number 3, February-March, 1971; *Reading Teacher,* October, 1971.

*   *   *

BETTS, William W(ilson), Jr. 1926-

PERSONAL: Born July 25, 1926, in Clearfield, Pa.; son of William Wilson (a philatelist) and Bernyce (Anderson) Betts; married Jane Jackson, June 29, 1951; children: Michael Jackson, Thomas Anderson. *Education:* Dickinson College, A.B., 1949; University of Minnesota, graduate student, 1949; Pennsylvania State University, A.M., 1950, Ph.D., 1954. *Politics:* Republican. *Religion:* United Methodist. *Home:* R. D. 2, Indiana, Pa. 15701. *Office:* Department of English, Indiana University of Pennsylvania, Indiana, Pa. 15701.

CAREER: High school teacher of English in Greenwood, Del., 1950-52; Ohio University, Athens, instructor in English, 1954-55; Indiana University of Pennsylvania, Indiana, associate professor, 1955-57, professor of English, 1957—, assistant basketball coach, 1955-68, 1971—, associate dean of Graduate School, 1968-71. *Military service:* U.S. Navy, 1944-46; served in Pacific theater. *Member:* Association of State College and University Faculties, Modern Language Association of America (chairman of Anglo-German literary relations section, 1954), Wildlife Federation, National Audubon Society, Trout Unlimited. *Awards, honors:* Distinguished Scholar Award, Indiana University of Pennsylvania, 1971.

WRITINGS: (Editor with Philip A. Shelley and Arthur O. Lewis) *Anglo-German and American-German Crosscurrents,* Volume I, University of North Carolina Press, 1957; *Lincoln and the Poets,* University of Pittsburgh Press, 1965;

A Docketful of Wry, Park Press, 1970. Contributor of numerous articles on education and literature to scholarly journals, and of nature essays and short stories to conservation and outdoors magazines, including *National Wildlife, Defenders, New England Galaxy, Pennsylvania Game News,* and *Pennsylvania Angler*.

WORK IN PROGRESS: The Painter and the Poet, an anthology of poems inspired by paintings.

SIDELIGHTS: William W. Betts told *CA:* "My writing inclines to nostalgia. For the most part it is inspired by memories of a time which was more agrarian than the present, of a time when an identity with the land was possible.

"I write largely of western Pennsylvania, out of affection for the wild creatures to be found in that region, particularly for the raptors and the game birds, which I know best.

"I write always for the natural environment and against those forces which threaten it. In these times I never want for inspiration."

AVOCATIONAL INTERESTS: Outdoor life and conservation (he is presently a deputy waterways patrolman).

*   *   *

BEVAN, E. Dean 1938-

PERSONAL: Born January 13, 1938, in Independence, Kan.; son of Earl R. (a public school administrator) and Josephine (Weage) Bevan; married Judith Ware, January 30, 1960; children: John Hayden. *Education:* University of Kansas, A.B., 1960, M.A., 1965, M.Phil., 1968, Ph.D., 1971. *Religion:* Episcopalian. *Home:* 908 Holiday Dr., Lawrence, Kan. 66044. *Office:* Department of English, Baker University, Baldwin, Kan. 66006.

CAREER: Center for Research, Inc., Lawrence, Kan., research publications editor, 1964-68; Baker University, Baldwin, Kan., 1969—, began as assistant professor, currently associate professor of English. Editorial director, Interpretation Systems, Inc., Lawrence. *Military service:* U.S. Army Reserve, 1960—; present rank, colonel. *Member:* Modern Language Association of America, American Association of University Professors.

WRITINGS: (Editor) *Concordance to the Plays and Prefaces of Bernard Shaw,* Gale, 1971.

WORK IN PROGRESS: A Samuel Johnson concordance.

*   *   *

BHATTACHARJI, Sukumari 1921-

PERSONAL: Born July 12, 1921, in Midnapore, West Bengal, India; daughter of Sarasi Kumar (a teacher) and Santabala (Ray) Datta; married Amal Bhattacharji (a professor), June 1, 1948 (deceased); children: Tanika (daughter). *Education:* Victoria College, B.A., 1942; University of Calcutta, M.A. (English), 1944, M.A. (Sanskrit), 1954; Jadavpur University, Ph.D., 1964. *Politics:* Marxist. *Religion:* Atheist. *Home:* P489 Keyatola Rd., Calcutta 29, West Bengal, India. *Office:* Jadavpur University, Calcutta 32, West Bengal, India.

CAREER: Lady Brabourne College, Calcutta, West Bengal, India, lecturer in English, 1945-56; Jadavpur University, Calcutta, lecturer in comparative literature, 1956-57, lecturer in Sanskrit, 1957-64, reader in Sanskrit, 1964—. Visiting fellow, Clare College, Cambridge University, 1966-67; visiting professor, Wilson College, Chambersburg, Pa., fall, 1974, and Carleton College, Northfield, Minn., spring, 1976. Participated in the International Oriental Congress in Michi-

gan, 1967, and in Canberra, Australia, 1971; also participated in the International Congress on Religion and the Humanizing of Man, Los Angeles, 1972, the UNESCO Conference in Sanskrit, New Delhi, 1972, and the International Ramayana Conference, New Delhi, 1976. *Member:* Asiatic Society (West Bengal).

WRITINGS: Indian Theogony, Cambridge University Press, 1970. Contributor of about twenty articles to journals in India.

WORK IN PROGRESS: A history of Vedic Sanskrit literature; a history of Buddhist Sanskrit literature; a history of the Indian epic-Puranic literature.

AVOCATIONAL INTERESTS: Music, painting, drama, and literature.

*   *   *

BIBERMAN, Herbert 1900-1971

March 4, 1900—June 30, 1971; American screenwriter, film director and producer. Obituaries: *New York Times,* July 1, 1971. (See index for *CA* sketch)

*   *   *

BIER, William C(hristian) 1911-

PERSONAL: Born May 1, 1911, in Brooklyn, N.Y.; son of Christian J. (a credit manager) and Adelaide (Kraus) Bier. *Education:* Woodstock College, A.B., 1934, S.T.L., 1941; Fordham University, M.A., 1939; Catholic University of America, Ph.D., 1948. *Office:* Department of Psychology, Fordham University, Bronx, N.Y. 10458.

CAREER: Roman Catholic priest of Society of Jesus (Jesuits); Fordham University, Bronx, N.Y., instructor, 1948-51, assistant professor, 1951-55, associate professor, 1955-66, professor of psychology, 1966—, chairman of department, 1958-68, organizer of Pastoral Psychology Institutes, 1955—, associate vice-president for academic affairs, 1973—. Certified psychologist in state of New York. *Member:* American Psychological Association (fellow), Academy of Religion and Mental Health (member of professional board). *Awards, honors:* American Catholic Psychological Association award, 1962; Academy of Religion and Mental Health award, 1967.

WRITINGS—All published by Fordham University Press: (Editor) *Problems in Addiction: Alcoholism and Narcotics,* 1962; *The Adolescent: His Search of Understanding,* 1963; *Personality and Sexual Problems in Pastoral Psychology,* 1964; *Marriage: A Psychological and Moral Approach,* 1965; (editor) *Woman in Modern Life,* 1968; *Psychological Testing for Ministerial Selection,* 1970; (editor) *Conscience: Its Freedom and Limitations,* 1971; *Alienation: Plight of Modern Man?,* 1972; *Aging: Its Challenge to the Individual and to Society,* 1974; *Human Life: Problems of Birth, of Living and of Dying,* 1977. Editor, "Pastoral Psychology Series," Fordham University Press, 1955—.

BIOGRAPHICAL/CRITICAL SOURCES: Commonweal, September 27, 1968; *Christian Century,* February 24, 1971.

*   *   *

BIERBAUM, Margaret 1916-

PERSONAL: Born January 19, 1916, in Fairfield, Conn.; daughter of John V. (an engineer) and Margaret (Stepler) McNally; married Robert Bierbaum (a supervisor at White Co.), 1944; children: Richard and Linda (twins). *Education:* University of Bridgeport, B.S., 1956, M.S., 1958. *Religion:*

Roman Catholic. *Home:* 25 Margemere Dr., Fairfield, Conn. 06430.

CAREER: Teacher in elementary school in Fairfield, Conn., 1936-37; Burr Farms School, Westport, Conn., teacher of language arts, 1937—. University of Bridgeport, field associate and guest lecturer, 1960—, member of Reading Research Council. *Member:* National Education Association, International Reading Association, Connecticut Education Association.

WRITINGS: (With Paul McKee) *English for Meaning,* Books 5-6, Houghton, 1968; (contributor) Paul C. Burns, editor, *Elementary School Language Arts,* Rand McNally, 1969. Contributor to education journals.

WORK IN PROGRESS: Forty Lessons in Creative Writing.

*   *   *

BIERHORST, John (William) 1936-

PERSONAL: Born September 2, 1936, in Boston, Mass.; son of John William and Sadie Belle (Knott) Bierhorst; married Jane Elizabeth Byers (a graphic designer), June 25, 1965; children: Alice Byers. *Education:* Cornell University, B.A., 1958. *Address:* Box 566, West Shokan, N.Y. 12494.

CAREER: Former concert pianist; became attracted to the study of native American cultures during a botanical field trip to Peru in 1964; subsequently visited pre-Columbian sites in Yucatan and Mexico. *Member:* American Folklore Society, American Anthropological Association. *Awards, honors: In the Trail of the Wind* was a Children's Book Council Showcase Title, 1972.

WRITINGS—Published by Farrar, Strauss, except as indicated: (Editor) *The Fire Plume: Legends of the American Indians,* Dial, 1969; (editor) *The Ring in the Prairie: A Shawnee Legend,* Dial, 1970; (editor) *In the Trail of the Wind: American Indian Poems and Ritual Orations,* 1971; (editor) *Four Masterworks of American Indian Literature:* "Quetzalcoatl," "The Ritual of Condolence," "Cuceb," "The Night Chant," 1974; (editor) *Songs of the Chippewa,* 1974; (editor) *The Red Swan: Myths and Tales of the American Indians,* 1976; (editor and translator) *Black Rainbow: Legends of the Incas and Myths of Ancient Peru,* 1976; *The Girl Who Married a Ghost and Other Tales from the North American Indian,* Four Winds, 1978.

WORK IN PROGRESS: An English translation of the codex, *Cantares Mexicanos* (a sixteenth-century compilation of poetry and drama in the Aztec language); a book about American Indian music.

*   *   *

BIESANZ, Mavis Hiltunen 1919-

PERSONAL: Surname is pronounced Bih-*sahnz;* born July 27, 1919, in Minn.; daughter of Peter (a farmer) and Hilja (Lempia) Hiltunen; married John Biesanz (a professor), August 31, 1940; children: Richard, Barry, Kathryn. *Education:* Attended Winona State College, 1936-38; University of Iowa, B.A. (summa cum laude), 1940; Wayne State University, graduate study, 1956-60. *Politics:* "Liberal Democrat with increasingly radical leanings." *Religion:* Unitarian. *Home:* Apartado 8-3880, San Jose, Costa Rica.

CAREER: Urban Area Traffic Study, Detroit, Mich., editor, 1959-60. *Member:* American Sociological Association (life member), Costa Rican Association of University Women, Phi Beta Kappa.

WRITINGS: (With husband, John Biesanz) *Costa Rican Life,* Columbia University Press, 1944; (with John Biesanz) *Modern Society: An Introduction to Social Science,* Prentice-Hall, 1954, 3rd edition, 1964; (with John Biesanz) *The People of Panama,* Columbia University Press, 1955; (with John Biesanz) *Introduction to Sociology,* Prentice-Hall, 1969, 3rd edition, 1978; (with son, Richard Biesanz, and daughter-in-law, Karen Zubris Biesanz) *The Costa Ricans,* Prentice-Hall, 1978. Also editor of and contributor to *Land of Lace and Legend: An Informal Guide to Paraguay,* 3rd edition, 1965.

SIDELIGHTS: Mavis Biesanz told *CA* that she plans to turn to writing novels and short stories. She has written a 103-page family history, which is in the Immigrant Archives of the University of Minnesota. Biesanz has traveled through most of Europe and Latin America; she has lived in Germany, Paraguay, Guatemala, Panama, and Costa Rica. *Avocational interests:* Fiction, poetry, humanist psychology, needlework, and photography.

*   *   *

BIGART, Robert James 1947-

PERSONAL: Born March 13, 1947, in Honesdale, Pa.; son of John Norman (a meat cutter) and Jeane (Hance) Bigart. *Education:* Harvard University, B.A. (cum laude), 1969; University of Chicago, graduate student, 1971-72. *Home:* 739 Minnesota Ave., Missoula, Mont. 59801.

WRITINGS: (Editor) *Environmental Pollution in Montana,* Mountain Press, 1972. Contributor to *Human Organization, Montana Business Quarterly, American Anthropologist, Plains Anthropologist, Elementary School Journal,* and *Montana Magazine of Western History.*

WORK IN PROGRESS: With Clarence Woodcock, writing historical materials about the Salish and Kootenai Indians of Montana.

SIDELIGHTS: Robert Bigart told *CA:* "My home is in Western Montana and I am very interested in the social and economic problems in the area. I am not very ideologically oriented but am very attached to Western Montana and the people who live there."

*   *   *

BIGGS, Anselm G. 1914-

PERSONAL: Born January 11, 1914, in Pocahontas, Va.; son of John Gordon and Mary (Heatherman) Biggs. *Education:* Belmont Abbey College, A.B., 1936; Catholic University of America, M.A., 1946, Ph.D., 1949. *Home and office:* Belmont Abbey College, Belmont, N.C. 28012.

CAREER: Roman Catholic priest; Belmont Abbey College, Belmont, N.C., instructor in Latin, 1940-48, professor of history, 1948—. dean of students, 1954-56, academic dean, 1961-64. *Member:* American Historical Association, American Catholic Historical Association, Mediaeval Academy of America, American Benedictine Academy.

WRITINGS: Diego Gelmirez: First Archbishop of Compostela, Catholic University of America Press, 1949; (translator) Ludwig Hertling, *History of the Catholic Church,* Westminster, 1957; (translator) Hubert Jedin, editor, *Handbook of Church History,* Herder & Herder, Volume III, 1969, Volume IV, 1970.

*   *   *

BILLINGTON, Rachel 1942-

PERSONAL: Born May 11, 1942, in Oxford, England;

daughter of Francis Aungier Pakenham, 7th Earl of Longford (former leader of House of Lords and writer) and Elizabeth Packenham, Countess of Longford (a writer; maiden name, Harman); married Kevin Billington (a film director and theatre director), December 6, 1967; children: Nathaniel, Catherine Rose, Chloe Margaret. *Education:* University of London, B.A. (honors), 1963. *Religion:* Roman Catholic. *Residence:* London, England. *Agent:* Carol Smith Literary Agency, 2 John St., London, England.

CAREER: Novelist.

WRITINGS—Novels; published by Heinemann, except as indicated: *All Things Nice,* 1969; *The Big Dipper,* 1970; *Lilacs Out of the Dead Land,* 1971, McCall Books, 1972; *Cock Robin,* 1972; *Beautiful,* 1974, Pinnacle Books, 1976; *A Painted Devil,* 1975. Also author of two radio plays for BBC, "Mrs. Bleasdale's Lodger," and "Mary, Mary."

WORK IN PROGRESS: A new novel and a play.

SIDELIGHTS: Rachel Billington is the only novelist in a family frequently referred to in print as the "writing Pakenhams." Her father, Lord Longford, has produced six books on such topics as politics, banking, and philosophy, and her mother, writing as Elizabeth Longford, has done biographies of Queen Victoria and the Duke of Wellington among other books. A sister, Lady Antonia Fraser wrote *Mary, Queen of Scots,* and a brother, Thomas Pakenham also deals with historical subjects. In 1969 each of the five had a book published. Another sister, Mrs. Judith Kanzantzis, writes poetry.

BIOGRAPHICAL/CRITICAL SOURCES: Times Literary Supplement, May 28, 1970.

*　　*　　*

BINGER, Norman H(enry) 1914-

PERSONAL: Born June 20, 1914, in Milwaukee, Wis.; son of Harry F. (a naturalist) and Hermine (Reif) Binger; married Jane Fuller (a teacher), June 15, 1949; children: Charles. *Education:* University of Wisconsin, B.S., 1937; Miami University, Oxford, Ohio, M.A., 1939; Ohio State University, Ph.D., 1942. *Home:* 629 Beth Lane, Lexington, Ky. 40503. *Office:* Department of German, University of Kentucky, Lexington, Ky. 40506.

CAREER: University of Michigan, Ann Arbor, instructor in German, 1946-47; Virginia Military Institute, Lexington, Va., assistant professor of German, 1947-49; University of Kentucky, Lexington, instructor, 1949-51, assistant professor, 1951-57, associate professor, 1957-72, professor of German, 1972—. Fulbright research fellow, University of Vienna, 1957-58. *Military service:* U.S. Army, 1942-46; became first sergeant. *Member:* American Association of Teachers of German (president of South Atlantic chapter, 1967-69), South Atlantic Modern Language Association.

WRITINGS: (Compiler) *Bibliography of German Plays,* Shoe String, 1970; (translator and editor) Moritz Busch, *Travels between the Hudson and the Mississippi, 1851-1852,* University Press of Kentucky, 1971.

*　　*　　*

BINGHAM, Jonathan Brewster 1914-

PERSONAL: Born April 24, 1914, in New Haven, Conn.; son of Hiram (a U.S. senator) and Alfreda (Mitchell) Bingham; married June R. Rossbach (a writer), September 20, 1939; children: Sherrell (Mrs. Richard Downes), June Mitchell (Mrs. Erik Esselstyn), Timothy Woodbridge, Claudia Rossbach (Mrs. Bhajan). *Education:* Yale University, B.A., 1936, LL.B., 1939, M.A., 1949. *Home:* 5000 Independence Ave., Riverdale, N.Y. 10471. *Office:* House Office Building, Washington, D.C. 20515.

CAREER: Practiced law in New York City, 1939-41, 1946-51, 1953-54; U.S. Government, Washington, D.C., attorney with Office of Price Administration, 1941-42, chief of Alien Enemy Control Section, Department of State, 1945-46, and deputy administrator, Technical Cooperation Administration (Point Four), 1951-53; secretary to Governor of New York State, 1955-58; Goldwater & Flynn (law firm), New York City, member of firm, 1959-61; United Nations, New York City, U.S. representative on Trusteeship Council, 1961-62, president of Trusteeship Council, 1962, U.S. representative on Economic and Social Council, 1962-63, member of U.S. Mission, 1961-64; elected to U.S. House of Representatives, 1964, served as congressman from 23rd New York District, 1965-72, and as congressman from 22nd New York District, 1973—. Fellow, Yale University Corp., 1949-51. Trustee, Twentieth Century Fund. President, Bronx County Society for Mental Health, 1960-62. *Military service:* U.S. Army, Military Intelligence, 1942-45; became captain.

MEMBER: American Bar Association, Bronx County Bar Association, Bar Association of the City of New York; Century Association and Coffee House (both New York). *Awards, honors:* L.H.D., Bard College, 1957.

WRITINGS: Shirt-Sleeve Diplomacy: Point 4 in Action, John Day, 1954; (with brother, Alfred M. Bingham) *Violence and Democracy,* World Publishing, 1970. Contributor to *New York Times Magazine, Atlantic, Bulletin of the Atomic Scientists,* and other publications.

SIDELIGHTS: Jonathan Bingham told *CA:* "My main interest has been politics and government service. However, I have always enjoyed writing. I was editor-in-chief of two publications at Groton School, board chairman of the *Yale Daily News,* and note editor of the *Yale Law Journal.* My war job was principally as editor of a super-secret daily publication which went to the President and other top officials. In the late 1940's I edited a publication for the New York State Democratic Committee as a volunteer.

"My first book was based directly on my experience in the Technical Cooperation Administration. My second book, written in collaboration with my brother, was written at the suggestion of the editor of a series of books for young people; at that time (late 1960s), many young people were persuaded that violence was the only way to achieve justice and social change. Our book was essentially an argument to the contrary, and an argument *for* greater participation, especially at the community level."

*　　*　　*

BIRCH, Leo Bedrich 1902-

PERSONAL: Original surname, Bischitzky; born February 7, 1902, in Prague, Czechoslovakia; son of Adolphe (a doctor) and Antoinette (Heller) Bischitzky; married Mimi Anna Piroutek, October 11, 1930. *Education:* Staatsrealgymnasium, Prague, B.A., 1920; also attended University of Vienna, University of Heidelberg, and University of Paris. *Politics:* "For regime under responsible elite; friends call me theocratic in a sense." *Religion:* Roman Catholic. *Home:* 1487 Teller Ave., Bronx, N.Y. 10457.

CAREER: Professor of French and German at several gymnasiums in Vienna, Austria, 1930-38; held various positions in industry, New York, N.Y., 1939-64. *Member:* World Poetry Society Intercontinental, Avalon World Art Academy.

WRITINGS: The Old and the New Adam (verse), Guild Quarterly Press, 1969; *Poems and Translations: Mallarme, Valery, Peguy,* Guild Quarterly Press, 1971; (translator) La Fontaine, *Seventy-one Fables and One Epilogue,* Copyshop (New York), 1974, revised edition, Fermaprint (New York), 1977; *Cities in Green Flames* (verse), Copyshop, 1975. Contributor to *Cyclo-Flame, Guild, Hoosier Challenger, Poet Intercontinental, Moon Age Poets.*

WORK IN PROGRESS: Aphorisms.

SIDELIGHTS: Leo Birch lists as his "most important formative influences": Rilke, Claudel, Valery, Stefan George, and Goethe. He told *CA:* "Religiously I have compared Protestantism, Catholicism, Judaism, Nietzsche. My conclusion: I believe in free will as a must for the relationship between God and man, and hope for the emergence of a purer form of m-a-n as against the superman of Nietzsche. Man is not yet. Man is a caret."

* * *

BIRNBAUM, Milton 1919-

PERSONAL: Born June 6, 1919, in Przemysl, Poland; brought to United States in 1927, naturalized citizen; son of Hyman and Theresa (Kleinhaus) Birnbaum; married Ruth Kushner (a teacher), June 23, 1946; children: Ellen Barbara. *Education:* City College (now City College of the City University of New York), B.A., 1942; New York University, M.A., 1948, Ph.D., 1956. *Politics:* Independent. *Religion:* Jewish. *Home:* 132 Groveland St., Springfield, Mass. 01108. *Office:* Office of the Dean, School of Arts and Sciences, American International College, Springfield, Mass. 01109.

CAREER: American International College, Springfield, Mass., instructor, 1948-50, assistant professor, 1950-56, associate professor, 1956-62, professor of English and chairman of the department, 1962-73, dean of School of Arts and Sciences, 1973—. *Military service:* U.S. Army, 1942-45; became sergeant. *Member:* Modern Language Association of America, National Council of Teachers of English, College English Association, Phi Beta Kappa. *Awards, honors:* Founders Day award, New York University, 1956.

WRITINGS: (Contributor) G. A. Panichas, editor, *Mansions of the Spirit: Essays in Religion and Literature,* Hawthorn, 1967; *Aldous Huxley's Quest for Values,* University of Tennessee Press, 1971; (contributor) Panichas, editor, *The Politics of Twentieth Century Novelists,* Hawthorn, 1971; (author of introduction) Aldous Huxley, *Encyclopaedia of Pacifism,* Garland Publishing, 1972; (contributor) Robert E. Kuehn, editor, *Aldous Huxley: A Collection of Critical Essays,* Prentice-Hall, 1974. Contributor to *Texas Studies in Literature and Language, Comparative Studies in Literature, Personalist, College English Association Forum, Hibbert Journal, Chronicle of Higher Education, College English,* and other publications.

WORK IN PROGRESS: Research on the connections between religion and literature, with special emphasis on Hawthorne, Hemingway, and Shakespeare; satirical and serious essays on "higher" education.

SIDELIGHTS: Milton Birnbaum's special areas of interest are the British novel between the World Wars, the American renaissance, and religion and literature. He has traveled to England, Italy, Switzerland, Holland, and Israel. Birnbaum told *CA:* "Aldous Huxley has been my special interest because of his classical temper, his encyclopedic interests, and because his writing has always been concerned with trying to infuse life with greater meaning." He added: "The most important advice I have to give to aspiring writers is not to get discouraged by the inevitable number of rejections submitted manuscripts may receive. One acceptance will change the entire picture."

* * *

BIRNEY, Alice L(otvin) 1938-

PERSONAL: Born March 6, 1938, in New York, N.Y.; daughter of Hyman and Esther (Cooperman) Lotvin; married G. Adrian Birney (a college teacher), June 4, 1964; children: Hannah Sophia. *Education:* Barnard College, A.B., 1959; Ohio State University, M.A., 1962; University of California, San Diego, Ph.D., 1968. *Home:* 612 G St. S.E., Washington, D.C. 20003. *Office:* Library of Congress, Washington, D.C.

CAREER: Mansfield State College, Mansfield, Pa., associate professor of English, 1968-69; University of California, San Diego, La Jolla, lecturer in literature, 1971-72; Library of Congress, Washington, D.C., English literature specialist, 1973—. Member of bibliographic committee, World Shakespeare Bibliography, 1977—. *Member:* Modern Language Association of America, Renaissance Society of America, Shakespeare Society of America. *Awards, honors:* Amy Loveman Poetry Award, Barnard College, 1959; *Lyric Magazine* Poetry Award, 1959; University of California, San Diego Dissertation fellowship, 1967-68.

WRITINGS: Satiric Catharsis in Shakespeare: A Theory of Dramatic Structure, University of California Press, 1972. Contributor of poetry and articles to *Cresset, Et. Al., Falcon,* and other journals. Assistant editor, *Italian Quarterly,* 1964-66.

WORK IN PROGRESS: A book of poetry; a biography of Sir John Hayward, the Elizabethan historian; and transcribing and editing on unpublished Hayward manuscript from Folger Library.

* * *

BISHAI, Wilson B. 1923-

PERSONAL: Born May 18, 1923, in Minia, Egypt; came to United States in 1951, naturalized in 1962; married Elizabeth Ann Gutman (a librarian), August 28, 1958; children: William, David, Linda. *Education:* Columbia Union College, B.A., 1953; Andrews University, M.A., 1954; Johns Hopkins University, Ph.D., 1959. *Home:* 434 William St., Stoneham, Mass. 02180. *Office:* Center for Middle Eastern States, Harvard University, Cambridge, Mass. 02138.

CAREER: Johns Hopkins University, Baltimore, Md., assistant professor of Arabic, 1960-66; Harvard University, Cambridge, Mass., senior lecturer in Arabic, 1966—. *Member:* American Historical Association, Middle East Studies Association, American Oriental Society, American Linguistic Society. *Awards, honors:* Fulbright summer research grant, 1963.

WRITINGS: Islamic History of the Middle East, Allyn & Bacon, 1968; *Concise Grammar of Literary Arabic: A New Approach,* Kendall/Hunt, 1971; *Humanities in the Arabic Islamic World,* W. C. Brown, 1972.

WORK IN PROGRESS: A Reader in Islamic History; Advanced Arabic Syntax; and a computerized program for teaching Arabic.

SIDELIGHTS: Wilson Bishai speaks Arabic, Hebrew, Coptic, Egyptian, French, and German.

* * *

BISHOP, Joseph W(arren), Jr. 1915-

PERSONAL: Born April 15, 1915, in New York, N.Y.; son of Joseph Warren (an editor) and Edna (Dashiell) Bishop; married Susan Carroll Oulahan (a teacher), May 6, 1950; children: Joseph Warren III. *Education:* Dartmouth College, A.B., 1936; Harvard University, LL.B., 1940. *Politics:* Independent. *Religion:* Agnostic. *Home:* 83 East Rock Rd., New Haven, Conn. 06511. *Office:* Law School, Yale University, New Haven, Conn. 06520.

CAREER: Admitted to Bar of District of Columbia, 1941, Bar of New York State, 1954, Bar of Connecticut, 1963; U.S. War Department, Washington, D.C., law clerk and special assistant to under secretary of war, 1940-43; Cleary, Gottlieb, Friendly & Cox (law firm), Washington, D.C., associate, 1946-47; U.S. Department of Justice, Office of Solicitor General, Washington, D.C., special assistant to attorney general, 1947-50; United States High Commission in Germany, assistant to general counsel, 1950-52; U.S. Department of the Army, Washington, D.C., deputy general counsel and acting general counsel, 1952-53; Milbank, Tweed, Hope & Hadley (law firm), New York, N.Y., staff lawyer, 1953-57; Yale University, Law School, New Haven, Conn., associate professor, 1957-59, professor of law, 1959—, Richard Ely Professor of Law, 1967—. Visiting professor of law, University of Muenster, 1965; member of faculty, Salzburg Seminar in American Law, 1967; visiting fellow, Clare Hall, Cambridge University, 1974. Special counsel, New York, New Haven & Hartford Railroad, 1961-74. Expert consultant, Securities and Exchange Commission, 1959. *Military service:* U.S. Army, 1943-46; became major; received Bronze Star. U.S. Army Reserve, 1946-64, retired as colonel. *Member:* New Haven Lawn Club. *Awards, honors:* Decoration for exceptional civilian service, Department of the Army, 1953.

WRITINGS: (With George T. Washington) *Indemnifying the Corporate Executive,* Ronald, 1963; (contributor) Roland J. Stanger, editor, *West Berlin: The Legal Context,* Ohio State University Press, 1966; *Obiter Dicta,* Atheneum, 1971; *Justice under Fire: A Study of Military Law,* Charterhouse, 1974. Contributor to *Commentary, Harper's, Yale Law Journal, Business Lawyer, Harvard Law Review, University of Pennsylvania Law Review, Columbia Law Review, American Journal of International Law, New Republic, New York Times Magazine,* and *Esquire.*

WORK IN PROGRESS: A book on the legal problems of controlling terrorism, particularly in Northern Ireland.

SIDELIGHTS: Joseph Bishop told *CA* that he is "interested in skinning pompous frauds, in recent years especially new left frauds."

* * *

BISSET, Donald 1910-

PERSONAL: Born August 30, 1910, in London, England; divorced; children: one son. *Education:* Attended Warehousemen, Clerks, and Drapers School, Surrey, England. *Home:* 33 Andrews House, Barbican, London EC2Y 8AB, England. *Agent:* A. M. Heath & Co. Ltd., 40-42 William IV St., London WC2N 4DD, England.

CAREER: Actor; appeared with the National Theatre and Royal Shakespeare Theatre companies, in the television film

"Henry VIII," in New York, N.Y., 1971, and later that year played in "The Great Waltz" at Drury Lane Theatre, London, England. Writer of children's books. *Military service:* British Army, 1940-46; became lieutenant.

WRITINGS: Anytime Stories, Faber, 1954, Transatlantic, 1955; *Sometime Stories,* Methuen, 1957; *Next Time Stories,* Methuen, 1959; *This Time Stories,* Methuen, 1961; *Another Time Stories,* Methuen, 1963; *Little Bear's Pony,* Benn, 1966; *Hello Lucy,* Benn, 1967; *Talks with a Tiger,* Methuen, 1967; *Kangaroo Tennis,* Benn, 1968; *Nothing,* Benn, 1969; *Upside Down Land,* Progress Publishing House (Moscow), 1969.

Time and Again Stories, Methuen, 1970; *Benjie the Circus Dog,* Benn, 1970; *Barcha the Tiger,* Benn, 1971; *Tiger Wants More,* Methuen, 1971; *Yak and the Sea Shell,* Methuen, 1971; *Yak and the Painted Cave,* Methuen, 1971; *Yak Goes Home,* Methuen, 1971; *Yak and the Buried Treasure,* Methuen, 1972; *Yak and the Ice Cream,* Methuen, 1972; *Father Tingtang's Journey,* Methuen, 1973; *Jenny Hopalong,* Benn, 1973; *The Happy Horse,* Benn, 1974; *The Adventures of Mandy Duck,* Methuen, 1974; *Hazy Mountain,* Penguin, 1975; *"Oh Dear!" Said Tiger,* Methuen, 1975; *Paws with Shapes,* Intercontinental Books, 1976; (with Michael Morris) *Paws with Numbers,* Intercontinental Books, 1976; *The Story of Smokey the Horse,* Methuen, 1977; *Baby Crow Learns to Fly,* Benn, 1977; *This Is Ridiculous,* Benn, 1977; *Yak,* Methuen, 1978. Also author of *The Lost Birthday,* published in English in Russia. Author of television serial, "Yak," produced in color cartoons, 1971.

WORK IN PROGRESS: Sound cassettes and video cassettes of his stories.

SIDELIGHTS: Donald Bisset told *CA:* "My conception of the world is animistic. Things, ideas, stones, flowers, animals, people, rain and sunshine in a sense are equally alive. I believe that writing (and all art) is doing better than you know. It is transcending limitations." Bisset's books have been translated into sixteen European languages.

AVOCATIONAL INTERESTS: Horseback riding, tennis.

BIOGRAPHICAL/CRITICAL SOURCES: Times Literary Supplement, April 16, 1970.

* * *

BITTERMANN, Henry J(ohn) 1904-

PERSONAL: Born November 9, 1904, in New York, N.Y.; son of Peter John (a businessman) and Veronica (Popp) Bittermann; married, 1928; married second wife, Kathleen Studdart (an economist), May 22, 1948; children: Jane (Mrs. Courtney Chapman). *Education:* Amherst College, B.A., 1925; University of Chicago, Ph.D., 1932. *Home:* 6931 33rd St. N.W., Washington, D.C. 20015.

CAREER: Ohio State University, Columbus, instructor, 1929-32, assistant professor, 1932-37, associate professor of economics, 1937-47; U.S. Treasury Department, Washington, D.C., economist in Division of Monetary Research, 1943-48, financial adviser, Office of International Finance Coordination, 1948-62, director, Office of International Financial Policy Coordination, 1962-64. Technical secretary, United Nations Monetary and Financial Conference, 1944; adviser, U.S. delegation, board of governors of International Monetary Fund and International Bank. *Member:* American Economic Association, American Association of University Professors, Royal Economic Society, International Club (Washington), Phi Beta Kappa.

WRITINGS: State and Federal Grants-in-Aid, Mentzer,

Bush & Co., 1938, reprinted, Johnson Reprint, 1971; *The Refunding of International Debt,* Duke University Press, 1973. Contributor to economics, philosophy, and law journals.

WORK IN PROGRESS: Research on international financial problems.

*   *   *

BITTON, Davis 1930-

PERSONAL: Born February 22, 1930, in Blackfoot, Idaho; son of Ronald Wayne and Lola (Davis) Bitton; married Peggy Carnell, June 1, 1955; children: Ronald, Kelly, Timothy, Jill, Stephanie. *Education:* Brigham Young University, B.A., 1956; Princeton University, M.A., 1958, Ph.D., 1961. *Religion:* Church of Jesus Christ of Latter-day Saints. *Home:* 534 Perry's Hollow Rd., Salt Lake City, Utah 84103. *Office:* Department of History, University of Utah, Salt Lake City, Utah 84112.

CAREER: University of Texas at Austin, instructor, 1959-62, assistant professor of history, 1962-64; University of California, Santa Barbara, assistant professor of history, 1964-66; University of Utah, Salt Lake City, associate professor, 1966-71, professor of history, 1971—. *Military service:* U.S. Army, 1953-55. *Member:* American Historical Association, Mormon History Association (president, 1970-71), Utah State Historical Society.

WRITINGS: The French Nobility in Crisis, 1560-1640, Stanford University Press, 1969; (editor) *The Reminiscences and Civil War Letters of Levi Lamoni Wight: Life in a Mormon Splinter Colony on the Texas Frontier,* University of Utah Press, 1970; *Wit and Whimsy in Mormon History,* Deseret, 1974; *A Guide to Mormon Diaries,* Brigham Young University Press, 1977.

WORK IN PROGRESS: Early Modern French Demography; A Social History of the Mormons.

*   *   *

BJORNARD, Reidar B(ernhard) 1917-

PERSONAL: Surname is pronounced *By*-ear-nard; surname originally Kallestad, name legally changed in 1940; born November 29, 1917, in Trondheim, Norway; came to United States in 1950, naturalized in 1961; son of Jonas G. (a pastor) and Anna (Hansen) Kallestad; married Karin H. Ohrn (a saleswoman), March 30, 1946; children: Trond A., Liv Anne, Erik Jon. *Education:* University of Oslo, Candidate in Theology, 1937-43, 1948-49; Southern Baptist Theological Seminary, Th.D., 1954; attended Uppsala University, 1962, and American School of Oriental Research, 1962. *Religion:* Christian. *Home:* 22 West 756 Hackberry Dr., Glen Ellyn, Ill. 60137. *Office:* Northern Baptist Theological Seminary, Lombard, Ill. 60148.

CAREER: First Baptist Church, Tromsoe, Norway, pastor, 1946-48; Berkeley Baptist Divinity School, Berkeley, Calif., professor of Old Testament, 1954-65; Baptist Theological Seminary, Rueschlikon, Switzerland, professor of Old Testament, 1965-68; Northern Baptist Theological Seminary, Lombard, Ill., professor of Old Testament, 1968—. *Military service:* Norwegian Liberation Army, 1943-46; became captain. *Member:* Society of Biblical Literature, American Association of University Professors, American Baptist Ministers Association, Society for Old Testament Studies (Great Britain). *Awards, honors:* Fulbright travel grant, 1950.

WRITINGS: (Translator) S. Mowinckel, *Old Testament as Word of God,* Abingdon, 1959; *Toward Man's Redemption,* Judson, 1964; *Broadman Bible Commentary,* Volume IV: *Esther,* Broadman, 1971. Contributor to *Tyndale Family Bible Encyclopedia, Foundations* and *Review and Expositor.*

WORK IN PROGRESS: A study of Old Testament prophetic movement; a book on Isaiah.

SIDELIGHTS: Reidar Bjornard is fluent in the Scandinavian languages and in German; he reads French, Hebrew, Greek, and Latin. *Avocational interests:* Church music (organ and choir).

*   *   *

BLACK, Hugo Lafayette 1886-1971

February 27, 1886—September 25, 1971; American jurist. Obituaries: *New York Times,* September 25, 1971; *Washington Post,* September 26, 1971; *Newsweek,* October 4, 1971; *Time,* October 4, 1971; *L'Express,* October 4-10, 1971; *New Republic,* October 9, 1971.

*   *   *

BLACK, John N(icholson) 1922-

PERSONAL: Born June 28, 1922, in Birmingham, England; son of Harold and Margaret (Nicholson) Black; married Mary Webb, February 23, 1952 (deceased); married Wendy Waterston, August 8, 1967; children: (first marriage) Linda, Adrian; (second marriage) Nicholas, Julian. *Education:* Oxford University, M.A., 1952, D.Phil., 1952; University of Adelaide, D.Sc., 1964. *Politics:* Liberal-humanitarian. *Religion:* None. *Home:* Westholm, Orchehill Ave., Gerrards Cross, Buckinghamshire, England. *Office:* Bedford College, University of London, Regents Park, London NW1 4NS, England.

CAREER: University of Adelaide, Adelaide, South Australia, reader in agronomy, 1952-63; University of Edinburgh, Edinburgh, Scotland, professor of forestry and natural resources and head of department, 1964-71; University of London, Bedford College, London, England, principal, 1971—. *Military service:* Royal Air Force, 1942-46; became squadron leader. *Member:* Royal Society of Edinburgh (fellow).

WRITINGS: The Dominion of Man, Edinburgh University Press, 1970. Contributor of papers on ecological subjects to scientific journals.

WORK IN PROGRESS: A study of the dramatic craftsmanship of the librettist, Salvatore Cammarano.

SIDELIGHTS: John Black was trained originally as a musician, especially as a conductor of opera, but changed his field following war service.

*   *   *

BLACK, Martha E(llen) 1901-

PERSONAL: Born January 4, 1901, in Shawano County, Wis.; daughter of David S. (a lumberman) and Catherine (Sechrist) Black. *Education:* University of Wisconsin, Ph.B., 1928; Northwestern University, M.A., 1939; graduate study at University of Chicago, University of Colorado, and Bradley University. *Religion:* Congregational. *Home:* 401 East Chicago St., Elgin, Ill. 60120.

CAREER: Elgin Public Schools, Elgin, Ill., teacher, 1929-46; Office of Public Instruction, Springfield, Ill., state director of speech correction, 1946-66; conductor of workshops and lecturer, 1967—. Founding president, Kane

County Teachers' Credit Union, 1936-44. *Member:* American Speech and Hearing Association (fellow), State Directors of Speech and Hearing (president, 1965-66), Chicago Speech and Hearing Association (president, 1955-57), Elgin Teachers' Association (president, 1934-35).

WRITINGS: Speech Correction in the Schools, Prentice-Hall, 1964; *School Speech Therapy: A Source Book,* Stanwix, 1970; *Speech Therapy in the Public Schools,* Bobbs-Merrill, 1972. Contributor of various articles to professional journals. Former editorial consultant, *Journal of Speech and Hearing Disorders.*

* * *

BLACK, Percy 1922-

PERSONAL: Born January 6, 1922, in Montreal, Quebec, Canada; son of Ovido (a merchant) and Rose (Vasilevsky) Black; married Virginia Anne (a philosopher), June 21, 1951; children: Deborah, David, Elizabeth, Ben-Jon. *Education:* Sir George Williams College, B.Sc, 1944; McGill University, M.Sc., 1946; Harvard University, Ph.D., 1953. *Politics:* Independent. *Religion:* "Love." *Office:* Department of Psychology, Pace University, Pleasantville, N.Y. 10570.

CAREER: University of Kentucky, Lexington, instructor in social sciences, 1948-49; University of Chicago, Chicago, Ill., fellow in race relations, 1949-50; University of Minnesota, Minneapolis, fellow in child psychology, 1950-51; University of New Brunswick, Fredericton, assistant professor of psychology, 1951-53; University of London, London, England, visiting scholar, 1953-54; Social Attitude Survey, Yonkers, N.Y., principal in motivational research, 1955-67; Pace University, Pleasantville, N.Y., 1967—, began as associate professor, currently professor of psychology. *Military service:* Canadian Officers Training Corps, 1941-43. *Member:* American Psychological Association, American Association for the Advancement of Science (fellow), Southern Society for Philosophy and Psychology, New York Academy of Sciences. *Awards, honors:* Psi Chi award for research on effect of affects on interpersonal behavior, 1953.

WRITINGS: The Mystique of Modern Monarchy, C. A. Watts, 1953; (contributor) I. T. Sanders, editor, *Societies Around the World,* Dryden, 1953, revised edition, Holt, 1956.

WORK IN PROGRESS: The Violation of Conscience; The Search for Self and Other.

* * *

BLACKBURN, Paul 1926-1971

November 24, 1926—September 13, 1971; American poet, translator, and educator. Obituaries: *New York Times,* September 15, 1971.

* * *

BLACKHAM, Garth J. 1926-

PERSONAL: Born November 13, 1926, in Moroni, Utah; son of Merrill E. and Erma (Hardy) Blackham; married Sharon Galbraith, September 9, 1952; children: two. *Education:* Attended Brigham Young University, 1946-48; Utah State University of Agriculture and Applied Science, B.S., 1950, M.S., 1952; Cornell University, Ph.D., 1954. *Home:* 131 East La Jolla Dr., Tempe, Ariz. 85282. *Office:* College of Education, Arizona State University, Tempe, Ariz. 85281.

CAREER: State Hospital South, Blackfoot, Idaho, assistant psychologist, 1952; Child Study and Consultation Service, Phoenix, Ariz., psychologist, 1954-62; Arizona State University, Tempe, associate professor, 1962-65, professor of counseling and educational psychology, 1965—. *Member:* American Psychological Association, American Personnel and Guidance Association, Arizona State Psychological Association (executive secretary of board of examiners, 1962-63; member of executive council, 1971; president, 1976-77).

*WRITINGS—*All published by Wadsworth: *The Deviant Child in the Classroom,* 1967; (senior author with Adolph Silberman) *Modification of Child Behavior: Principles and Procedures,* 1971; *Modification of Child and Adolescent Behavior,* 1975; (co-author) *Counseling: Theory, Process and Practice,* 1977. Contributor to education journals.

WORK IN PROGRESS: Psychotherapy with Children.

* * *

BLACKMAN, Sheldon 1935-

PERSONAL: Born April 20, 1935, in Brooklyn, N.Y.; son of Charles and Rose (Wagner) Blackman; married Sherry Kunda (a college teacher), September 15, 1957; children: Susan, Michael. *Education:* Princeton University, A.B., 1956; Ohio State University, M.A., 1958, Ph.D., 1960. *Residence:* Staten Island, N.Y. *Office:* North Richmond Community Mental Health Center, 55 Austin Pl., Staten Island, N.Y.

CAREER: Veterans Administration Hospital, Chillicothe, Ohio, clinical psychology trainee, 1956-58; Veterans Administration Mental Hygiene Clinic, Columbus, Ohio, clinical psychology intern, 1958; Staten Island Mental Health Society, Staten Island, N.Y., research psychologist, 1963-64, assistant director of research, 1965-68, director of research, 1968-70. Certified psychologist in State of New York. Visiting research associate, Princeton University, 1964; clinical assistant professor, State University of New York, Downstate Medical Center, 1965-67; clinical associate professor, New York Hospital, Cornell University Medical College, 1969-75; adjunct associate professor, Richmond College of the City University of New York, 1970-72. Lecturer, Notre Dame College of St. John's University, 1968-70; director of research and program development, North Richmond Community Mental Health Center, 1970—. *Military service:* U.S. Army, 1959-63; became captain. *Member:* American Psychological Association, Eastern Psychological Association, Phi Beta Kappa, Sigma Xi.

WRITINGS: (With Kenneth M. Goldstein) *An Introduction to Data Management in the Behavioral and Social Sciences,* Wiley, 1971. Contributor of about forty articles to professional journals.

WORK IN PROGRESS: A book with Kenneth M. Goldstein, *Five Approaches to the Study of Cognitive Style,* for Wiley.

* * *

BLACKMER, Donald L. M. 1929-

PERSONAL: Born July 6, 1929, in Boston, Mass.; son of Alan Rogers and Josephine (Bedford) Blackmer; married Joan Dexter, August 25, 1951; children: Stephen, Alexander, Katherine. *Education:* Harvard University, A.B. (magna cum laude), 1952, A.M., 1956, Ph.D., 1967. *Home:* 2 King's Lane, Concord, Mass. *Office:* School of Humanities and Social Science, 20 D-204, Massachusetts Institute of Technology, Cambridge, Mass. 02139.

CAREER: Massachusetts Institute of Technology, Cambridge, executive assistant to director of Center for International Studies, 1956-61, lecturer, 1960-61, assistant professor, 1961-67, associate professor, 1967-73, professor of political science, 1973—, assistant director, Center for International Studies, 1961-68, associate dean, School of Humanities and Social Science, 1973—. Research associate in west European studies, Harvard University, 1973—. American Council of Learned Societies, member of planning group on comparative communist studies. Military service: U.S. Army, Army Security Agency, 1953-55. Member: Council for European Studies (chairman, 1972-73). Awards, honors: Sheldon traveling fellow of Harvard University, 1952-53.

WRITINGS: (Editor with Max F. Millikan, and contributor) The Emerging Nations: Their Growth and United States Policy, Little, Brown, 1961; Unity in Diversity: Italian Communism and the Communist World, M.I.T. Press, 1967; (editor with Sidney Tarrow, and contributor) Communism in Italy and France, Princeton University Press, 1975.

WORK IN PROGRESS: Further research on Italian communism.

*　　*　　*

BLACKMON, C(harles) Robert 1925-

PERSONAL: Born February 17, 1925, in Bee Ridge, Fla.; son of Nelson Samuel and Oma Grace (Walker) Blackmon; married D. Evelyn Hendry (an elementary school teacher), September 25, 1955; children: Janet Lynn. Education: Attended University of Tampa, 1946-47; Emory University, B.A., 1949, M.Ed., 1950; University of Florida, Ed.Sp., 1960, Ed.D., 1962. Politics: "Usually Democrat." Religion: Baptist. Home: 2633 June St., Baton Rouge, La. 70808. Agent: Scott Meredith Literary Agency, Inc., 845 Third Ave., New York, N.Y. 10022. Office: Bureau of Educational Research, College of Education, Louisiana State University, Baton Rouge, La. 70803.

CAREER: Decatur News, Decatur, Ga., associate editor, 1949-50; teacher of social studies, English, and science in junior high schools in Palmetto, Fla., 1950-55, and Tampa, Fla., 1955-58; administrative dean of junior high school in Tampa, Fla., 1958-59; Florida State University, Tallahassee, instructor, 1959-61, assistant professor of education, 1961-64; principal of high school in Stone Mountain, Ga., 1964-65; University of Southwestern Louisiana, Lafayette, associate professor, 1965-69, professor of education, 1969-71, coordinator of research in education, 1969-71; Louisiana State University, Baton Rouge, associate professor of education, 1971—, director, Bureau of Educational Research, 1973—. Instructor in evening division, University of Tampa, fall, 1958; interim instructor in education, University of Florida, spring, 1961. Military service: U.S. Naval Reserve, active duty, 1943-46. Civil Air Patrol, 1960-64; became major.

MEMBER: American Educational Research Association, Society of Research Administrators, National Conference of Professors of Educational Administration, International Society of Educational Consultants (founder and chairman), Louisiana Education Research Association, Louisiana Teachers Association, Phi Society, Phi Delta Kappa.

WRITINGS: (Editor and contributor) Selected Papers on Value, National Conference of Professors of Educational Administration and University of Southwestern Louisiana, 1968; (editor and contributor) Procedures in Educational Research, University of Southwestern Louisiana Books-

tore, 1968, 5th edition, 1971; (contributor) Richard I. Miller, editor, The Nongraded School, Harper, 1968; (editor and contributor) Changing Behaviors and Values, Anderson Center, Bowling Green State University, 1969; (editor and contributor) Laboratory Schools: U.S.A., Faculty Publications Committee, University of Southwestern Louisiana, 1971. Contributor of articles on education and aerospace to professional journals and of poetry to literary journals. Book review editor, Florida Education, 1961-64; editor, Laboratory School Administration Association Newsletter, 1967-69; editor of publications, Values Group of National Conference of Professors of Educational Administration, 1968-70.

WORK IN PROGRESS: A book on the supervising teacher; research on the visiting teacher and on educational futurism.

SIDELIGHTS: C. Robert Blackmon told CA: "I am indebted to a remarkable sucession of elementary and high school teachers for the motivation to achieve.... Much of my writing is technical or professional in relation to education; therefore, I regard the writing of short stories and poetry as pleasant therapy." Avocational interests: Writing short stories and poems, travel, swimming, fishing, playing clarinet.

*　　*　　*

BLACKWELL, Richard Joseph 1929-

PERSONAL: Born July 31, 1929, in Cleveland, Ohio; son of Edward and Cecelia (Koch) Blackwell; married Rosemary Gallagher (a social worker), January 16, 1954; children: Richard, Thomas. Education: Attended Massachusetts Institute of Technology, 1947-48; John Carroll University, A.B., 1950; St. Louis University, M.A., 1952, Ph.D., 1954. Religion: Roman Catholic. Home: 7700 Missy Ct., St. Louis, Mo. 63123. Office: Department of Philosophy, St. Louis University, 221 North Grand Blvd., St. Louis, Mo. 63103.

CAREER: John Carroll University, Cleveland, Ohio, instructor, 1954-57, assistant professor of philosophy, 1957-61; St. Louis University, St. Louis, Mo., associate professor, 1961-66, professor of philosophy, 1966—. Military service: U.S. Army, 1954-56. Member: American Association for the Advancement of Science, Philosophy of Science Association, American Catholic Philosophical Association, American Philosophical Association (Western division).

WRITINGS: (Translator with R. J. Spath and W. E. Thirlkel) St. Thomas Aquinas, Commentary on Aristotle's Physics, Yale University Press, 1963; (translator and author of introduction) Christian Wolff, Preliminary Discourse on Philosophy in General, Bobbs-Merrill, 1963; Discovery in the Physical Sciences, University of Notre Dame Press, 1969; (contributor) A. L. Fisher and G. B. Murray, editors, Philosophy and Science as Modes of Knowing, Appleton, 1969. Contributor to New Catholic Encyclopedia and to professional journals. Associate editor, Modern Schoolman.

WORK IN PROGRESS: A section for The Concept of Matter in Modern Philosophy, edited by Ernan McMullin, for University of Notre Dame Press; further studies on the history and epistemology of scientific discovery; a book of translations with notes of the scientific and philosophical writings of Christian Huygens (1629-1695).

*　　*　　*

BLAIKIE, Robert J. 1923-

PERSONAL: Born October 8, 1923, in Kenya, Africa; son

of New Zealand missionary parents, William and Laura (Peterson) Blaikie; married Patricia A. Stephenson, June 25, 1955; children: Ian, Cheryl, Graham. *Education:* University of Edinburgh, M.A., 1951; University of St. Andrews, B.D., 1954. *Politics:* "Slightly left of centre." *Home:* 69 St. Leonard's Rd., Mount Eden, Auckland 4, New Zealand.

CAREER: Ordained in Presbyterian ministry, 1954; Church of Scotland Mission, missionary in Northern Rhodesia (now Zambia), 1954-58; Presbyterian Church of New Zealand, parish minister, 1959—, presently at Mt. Eden Presbyterian Church, Auckland. *Military service:* Royal Navy, 1942-46; became sub-lieutenant.

WRITINGS: *'Secular Christianity' and God Who Acts,* Eerdmans, 1970. Contributor to theology journals in Scotland and New Zealand.

AVOCATIONAL INTERESTS: Gardening, reading, and music.†

*   *   *

BLAIR, Kay Reynolds 1942-

PERSONAL: Born October 25, 1942, in Franklin, Tenn.; daughter of William Edward (a meat inspector) and Louise (Kimery) Reynolds; married Edward Humphrey Blair (a college professor and curator), February 24, 1966; children: Darrell Edward, Kimery Kay. *Education:* Attended Southwestern at Memphis, 1960-62, and George Peabody College for Teachers, 1962-63; Memphis State University, B.S., 1964; also studied at Western State College of Colorado, 1967-68, and Colorado Mountain College, 1971-72. *Home:* 912 Harrison Ave., Leadville, Colo. 80461.

CAREER: WHER-Radio, Memphis, Tenn., disc jockey, 1964-65; Abingdon Press, Nashville, Tenn., copy editor, 1965-66; KBRR-Radio, Leadville, Colo., disc jockey, 1966-70. Member of board of directors, Lake County Civic Center Association, 1971. *Member:* Kappa Pi. *Awards, honors:* Colorado Broadcasters woman of the year, 1970.

WRITINGS: (With E. Richard Churchill, Linda R. Churchill, and husband, Edward H. Blair) *Fun with American Literature,* Abingdon, 1968; *Ladies of the Lamplight,* Timberline Books, 1971.

WORK IN PROGRESS: Research on western history.

*   *   *

BLAKE, Robert W(illiam) 1930-

PERSONAL: Born January 25, 1930, in Springfield, Vt.; son of Kenneth D. (a salesman) and Erma Rhoda (Curtis) Blake; married Carol Ann Clark (a teacher), October 30, 1953; children: David, Brett, Robert W. *Education:* American International College, A.B., 1952; Boston University, A.M., 1954; University of Rochester, Ed.D., 1964. *Politics:* Registered Republican. *Religion:* Episcopalian. *Home:* 66 Lynnwood Dr., Brockport, N.Y. 14420. *Office:* Department of Curriculum and Instruction, State University of New York College at Brockport, Brockport, N.Y. 14420.

CAREER: Canandaigua Academy, Canandaigua, N.Y., English teacher, 1959-61, chairman of department of English, 1960-61, and vice-principal, 1961-62; State University of New York College at Brockport, associate professor, 1963, professor of education, 1963—, chairman of department of curriculum and instruction, 1970—. Vestryman, lay reader, and usher, Episcopalian Church. *Military service:* U.S. Army, 1955-56. *Member:* National Council of Teachers of English, New York State English Council (president, 1971-72; fellow, 1972).

WRITINGS: (With Paul McKee, Arno Jewett, and Corinne Watson) *English for Meaning,* Houghton, 1966; *The Effect of Special Instruction on the Ability of Seventh and Eighth Graders,* U.S. Office of Education, 1966. Editor, *English Record,* 1967-70.

WORK IN PROGRESS: *Talking to Writers: A Handbook for Teachers; Living with Language: Teaching the Language Arts.*

SIDELIGHTS: Robert Blake wrote *CA:* "I see all of my writing coming from a wish to explain to myself and others the pleasures of teaching English. All I ever wanted to be was an English teacher. Much of my early writing was about teaching the English language, but now I am spending most of my time on the composing process in writing and in teaching writing at all levels of schooling. I've even begun to publish poems in order to learn from the inside how best to teach others to write poetry. I probably originally started writing as part of the academic 'publish or perish' syndrome, but I write regularly now, of course, to get the business of the world done, to think, to learn about myself and others, and because, finally, I'm most truly happy when I am writing."

*   *   *

BLANFORD, James T. 1917-

PERSONAL: Born January 25, 1917, in Shelbyville, Ill.; son of Edward James (a poultry broker) and Myrtle (Tracy) Blanford; married Mary Evelyn Nay (a college professor), June 9, 1940; children: Bruce, Thomas, William, Tracy (daughter). *Education:* Central Normal College, B.S., 1938; Indiana University, M.S., 1942, Ed.D., 1951. *Home:* 1113 Walnut St., Cedar Falls, Iowa 50613. *Office:* Department of Business, University of Northern Iowa, Cedar Falls, Iowa.

CAREER: University of Northern Iowa, Cedar Falls, assistant professor, 1949-53, associate professor, 1953-56, professor of accounting, 1956—, chairman of department of business, 1972-73. *Military service:* U.S. Navy, 1943-46; became lieutenant. *Member:* American Accounting Association, American Association of University Professors.

WRITINGS: (With Lloyd Virgil Douglas and Ruth I. Anderson) *Teaching Business Subjects,* Prentice-Hall, 1958, 3rd edition, 1973; (with Cletus A. Clow and others) *Gregg Accounting: Advanced Course,* McGraw, 1958, 2nd edition, 1969.

*   *   *

BLANK, Leonard 1927-

PERSONAL: Born May 10, 1927, in New York, N.Y.; son of Samuel and Mildred (Bernstein) Blank; married Bernice Bukaretsky, November 14, 1953; children: Jordan, Rona, Lyda. *Education:* Brooklyn College (now Brooklyn College of the City University of New York), B.A., 1949, M.A., 1952; New York University, Ph.D., 1955, additional study, 1961-67; Stanford University, additional study, 1955-57. *Home:* 4 Rumson Rd., Kendall Park, N.J. 08824. *Office:* Medical School, Rutgers University, New Brunswick, N.J. 08903.

CAREER: Diplomate in clinical psychology. Princeton Associates for Human Resources, Inc. (behavioral service firm), Princeton, N.J., president, 1968—; Rutgers University, Graduate School, New Brunswick, N.J., adjunct associate professor of psychology, 1969-75, adjunct professor at Medical School, 1975—. *Member:* American Psychological Association (fellow). *Awards, honors:* Distinguished Alumnus award, New York University, 1956.

WRITINGS: (Editor with Henry P. David) *Manpower and Psychology* (monograph), U.S. Government Printing Office, 1963; (editor with David) *Sourcebook for Training in Clinical Psychology,* Springer Publishing, 1964; *Psychological Evaluations in Psychotherapy,* Aldine, 1964; (editor with G. Gottsegen and M. Gottsegen) *Confrontation: Encounters in Self and Interpersonal Awareness,* Macmillan, 1971.

WORK IN PROGRESS: Age of Shrinks.

*   *   *

BLANKENSHIP, William D(ouglas) 1934-

PERSONAL: Born June 25, 1934, in San Jose, Calif.; son of Douglas N. and Iva (Maxwold) Blankenship; married Linda Rushworth, January 7, 1961; children: Lisa, Douglas, Kristen, Adam, Beth. *Education:* University of Southern California, B.A., 1957. *Agent:* Bill Berger Associates, Inc., 444 East 58th St., New York, N.Y. 10022.

CAREER: Arcadia Tribune, Arcadia, Calif., reporter, 1959-60; Seward Covert & Associates, Cleveland, Ohio, advertising account executive, 1960-62; Chamber of Commerce, Pasadena, Calif., communications manager, 1962-67; International Business Machines Corp., Armonk, N.Y., senior editor of *Think* Magazine, beginning 1967. *Military service:* U.S. Army, 1957-59.

WRITINGS: The Helix File, Walker, 1972; *The Programmed Man* (novel), Walker, 1973; *The Leavenworth Irregulars,* Bobbs-Merrill, 1974; *Tiger Ten,* Putnam, 1976; *Yukon Gold,* Dutton, 1977.†

*   *   *

BLASE, Melvin G(eorge) 1933-

PERSONAL: Born May 15, 1933, in St. Charles, Mo.; son of Edwin L. and Amanda (Westerfeld) Blase; married Betty Lee Weiser, September 5, 1954; children: Lawrence, Louis, Ann. *Education:* University of Missouri, B.S., 1955, M.S., 1956; Iowa State University, Ph.D., 1960; additional study, Michigan State University, 1972. *Home address:* R.R. 2, Columbia, Mo. 65201. *Office:* Department of Economics, University of Missouri, Columbia, Mo. 65201.

CAREER: U.S. Department of Agriculture at Iowa State University, Ames, research economist, 1956-60; Air Force Institute of Technology, Wright-Patterson Air Force Base, Ohio, assistant to dean of School of Systems and Logistics, 1960-61, assistant professor of logistics and engineering, 1961-63; Iowa State University, Technical Assistance Team, Lima, Peru, assistant professor and advisor to Peruvian government, 1963-65; University of Missouri—Columbia, associate professor, 1965-73, professor of economics, 1973—, director, Center for International Programs and Studies, 1977—. Evening school instructor, Wittenberg University, 1961-62, Miami University, Oxford, Ohio, 1961-63. Director, Midamerica International Agricultural Consortium, 1976-77. Consultant to Brown & Root, 1965-66, National Council of Churches, 1967—, U.S. Department of State, 1970—, U.S. Department of Agriculture, 1975—, U.S. Department of Commerce, 1975—, and Rockefeller Foundation, 1977—. Lay delegate of United Church of Christ to National Council of Churches conference, 1962; lay delegate of Ohio Conference of Congregational Christian Churches to General Synod of United Church of Christ, 1963; member of board of directors, Union Church, Lima, Peru, 1964-65. *Member:* American Economics Association, American Agricultural Economic Association, American

Association for the Advancement of Science, Society for International Development, Latin American Studies Association, Association for Evolutionary Economics, Southern Agricultural Economic Association, Gamma Sigma Delta, Gamma Alpha.

WRITINGS: (With John F. Timmons) *Soil Erosion Control in Western Iowa: Progress and Problems,* Agricultural and Home Economics Experiment Station, Iowa State University, 1961; (with Timmons and R. Burnell Held) *Soil Erosion and Some Means for Its Control,* Agricultural and Home Economics Experiment Station, 1962; (with others) *An Annotated Bibliography on Economic and Social Development in Missouri: 1960-67,* Agricultural Experiment Station, University of Missouri, 1968; (with Edwin D. Welliver and William J. Staub) *An Investigation of the Effects of Urban Expansion on the Taxation of Real Property in West Central Missouri,* Agricultural Experiment Station, University of Missouri, 1968; (with Coy G. McNabb) *Public Water for Rural Areas and Small Towns,* Extension Division, University of Missouri, 1969; (editor with Joseph B. Goodwin) *Readings in International Agricultural Economic Development,* M.S.S. Educational Publishing, 1970; (editor) *Institutions in Agricultural Development,* Iowa State University Press, 1971; *Institution Building: A Source Book,* Sage Publications, 1973.

Contributor: Ian Burton and Robert W. Kates, editors, *Readings in Resource Management and Conservation,* University of Chicago Press, 1965; W. Johnson and David R. Kamerschen, editors, *Macro-Economics: Selected Readings,* Houghton, 1970; John R. Brake, editor, *Emerging and Projected Trends Likely to Influence the Structure of Midwest Agriculture, 1970-1985,* College of Law, University of Iowa, 1970; E. R. Duncan, editor, *Dimensions of World Food Problems,* Iowa State University Press, 1977. Contributor of many articles to *Land Economics, Growth and Change, Science, American Journal of Agricultural Economics, Business and Government Review, Indian Journal of Agricultural Economics, Journal of Developing Areas, Sloan Management Review,* and other publications.

*   *   *

BLEDSOE, Joseph C(ullie) 1918-

PERSONAL: Born September 16, 1918, in Carrollton, Ga.; son of James Arthur (a retail sales manager) and Elizabeth (Denney) Bledsoe; married Adele Berryman, June 5, 1948; children: Joseph Christian, Gisela Adele. *Education:* University of Georgia, A.B.Ed., 1939, M.S.Ed., 1940; George Peabody College for Teachers, Ph.D., 1952. *Politics:* Independent. *Religion:* Baptist. *Home:* 260 Burnett St., Athens, Ga. 30601. *Office:* Department of Educational Psychology, 325 Aderhold Hall, University of Georgia, Athens, Ga. 30601.

CAREER: U.S. Civil Service Commission, Atlanta, Ga., rating examiner and administrative aide, 1940-42; Veterans Administration Regional Office, Atlanta, Ga., vocational adviser, 1945-46; Air University, Maxwell Air Force Base, Montgomery, Ala., educational psychologist, 1946-47; University of Georgia, Athens, assistant professor, 1948-56, associate professor, 1956-60, professor of educational psychology, 1960—. University of Wisconsin—Madison, visiting lecturer in education, 1958. *Military service:* U.S. Army, 1942-45; personnel consultant, Asiatic-Pacific Theatre; became captain. *Member:* American Psychological Association (fellow), American Educational Research Association, Psi Chi, Kappa Delta Pi, Phi Delta Kappa, Pi Mu Epsilon, Xi Phi Xi, Phi Kappa Phi.

WRITINGS: (With Ira Edward Aaron and Karl Claudius Garrison) *Workbook in Educational Psychology,* Appleton, 1955; *Essentials of Educational Research,* Edwards Bros., 1963, 2nd edition, Optima House, 1972; *A Study Guide in Statistical Inference,* Optima House, 1971. Contributor to psychology and education journals.

*   *   *

BLEGEN, Carl (William)   1887-1971

January 27, 1887—August 24, 1971; American archaeologist. Obituaries: *New York Times,* August 26, 1971.

*   *   *

BLEVINS, William L.   1937-

PERSONAL: Born September 17, 1937, in Benham, Ky.; son of William Arthur and Margaret M. (Doll) Blevins; married Carolyn DeArmond, June 26, 1959; children: Suzanne Cara, William Arthur II, Alan Ray. *Education:* Carson-Newman College, A.B., 1959; Southern Baptist Theological Seminary, B.D., 1962; New Orleans Baptist Theological Seminary, Th.D., 1967; University of Tennessee, additional study. *Politics:* Democrat. *Residence:* Jefferson City, Tenn. *Office:* Department of Religion, Carson-Newman College, Jefferson City, Tenn. 37760.

CAREER: Carson-Newman College, Jefferson City, Tenn., professor of religion and chairman of department, 1967—. *Member:* American Academy of Religion, Society of Biblical Literature, Association of Baptist Professors of Religion, Kiwanis Club (vice-president, 1970; president, 1971).

WRITINGS: Context: Christian Calling, Convention Press, 1971; *Birth of a New Testament,* J-K Publishers, 1975. Contributor to *Faculty Studies, Collegiate Teacher, Review and Expositor, Theological Educator, Context,* and *Now.*

WORK IN PROGRESS: A textbook entitled *Grace and Demand: A Study of Jesus' Soteriology.*

AVOCATIONAL INTERESTS: Tennis, music, travel.

*   *   *

BLICQ, Anthony   1926-

PERSONAL: Surname rhymes with "stick"; born November 15, 1926, in England; son of Sanford (a newspaper editor) and Marjorie (Steele) Blicq; married Laura Engelbach, October 9, 1958; children: Sarah Louise, Justine Emma. *Education:* Attended Kelvin High School, Winnipeg, Manitoba, and Elizabeth College in England. *Politics:* Liberal. *Religion:* Anglican. *Home:* 2675 West 41st Ave., Vancouver, British Columbia, Canada. *Agent:* Carl Brandt, Brandt & Brandt, 101 Park Ave., New York, N.Y. 10017. *Office:* University of British Columbia Press, Vancouver 8, British Columbia, Canada.

CAREER: Free-lance writer under a pseudonym, 1963-65; Oxford University Press, Oxford, England, staff member, 1965-69; University of British Columbia Press, Vancouver, director, 1969—. *Awards, honors:* Canada Council bursary award for *The Rise and Fall of Married Charlie.*

WRITINGS: The Rise and Fall of Married Charlie (novel), Deutsch, 1970. Contributor of fiction to magazines.

WORK IN PROGRESS: A novel.

SIDELIGHTS: Anthony Blicq has lived in London, Athens, Rome, and various places in Spain.

BIOGRAPHICAL/CRITICAL SOURCES: Times Literary Supplement, May 28, 1970.

BLIVEN, Naomi   1925-

PERSONAL: Surname rhymes with "given"; born December 28, 1925, in New York, N.Y.; daughter of Frederic and Minnie (Goodfriend) Horowitz; married Bruce Bliven, Jr. (a writer), May 26, 1950; children: Frederic B. *Education:* Hunter College (now Hunter College of the City University of New York), A.B. (with honors), 1945. *Politics:* Democrat. *Office:* c/o *New Yorker,* 25 West 43rd St., New York, N.Y. 10036.

CAREER: New Republic, New York City, member of editorial staff, 1945-47; Random House, New York City, an editor, 1949-54; *New Yorker,* New York City, book reviewer, 1958—. *Member:* Phi Beta Kappa.

WRITINGS: (With husband, Bruce Bliven, Jr.) *New York: The Story of the World's Most Exciting City,* Random House, 1969.

BIOGRAPHICAL/CRITICAL SOURCES: New York Times Book Review, January 4, 1970.

*   *   *

BLOCK, Jack   1921-

PERSONAL: Born October 5, 1921, in Chicago, Ill.; son of Louis I. (a journalist) and Dorothy (Dolnick) Block; married Adele Teschion (a psychiatric social worker), December 26, 1947 (divorced, 1976); children: Jerome, Margaret. *Education:* University of Minnesota, B.A., 1948; University of Iowa, M.A., 1951. *Politics:* Democrat. *Office:* San Diego Mesa College, 7250 Mesa College Dr., San Diego, Calif. 92111.

CAREER: University of Iowa, Iowa City, instructor in English, 1948-53; U.S.A.F. Air University, Maxwell Air Force Base, Ala., associate professor of communication skills, 1954-55; Convair-Astronautics (aerospace company), San Diego, Calif., management training specialist, 1956-59; Non-Linear Systems (electronics company), Del Mar, Calif., publications director, 1959-65; General Atomic (research laboratory), San Diego, proposal editor, 1965-67; San Diego Mesa College, San Diego, instructor in English, 1968—. Part-time instructor in scientific and technical writing, University of California Extension, San Diego, 1956-67. *Military service:* U.S. Army Air Force, 1941-43. *Member:* American Federation of Teachers, Delta Phi Lambda. *Awards, honors:* Honorary creative writing society award, 1947, for several short stories.

WRITINGS: (With Joseph Labonville) *English Skills for Technicians,* McGraw, 1971, 2nd edition, in press. Also author of a handbook on solid-state component connectors, for use in electronics courses. Contributor of numerous technical articles to trade magazines, and of satirical essays to *San Diego Magazine.*

WORK IN PROGRESS: A textbook tentatively entitled *Elements of Business Style;* a text-workbook with Joseph Witzman on hotel-motel management, for Prentice-Hall; other texts.

AVOCATIONAL INTERESTS: Broad interest in music, plays piano, flute and piccolo in community and college orchestras; also electronics, photography; exploring remote regions of Baja California.

*   *   *

BLOCK, Libbie   1910(?)-1972

1910(?)—March 30, 1972; American novelist and short story writer. Obituaries: *New York Times,* April 1, 1972.

BLOCKER, Clyde (Edward) 1918-

PERSONAL: Born October 31, 1918, in Huntington, Ind.; son of Loyd Sherman (a shop foreman) and Fern (Rarrick) Blocker; married Janne Steele (a teacher), December 25, 1941; children: Vincent, David, Ann. *Education:* Indiana University, B.S., 1941, M.S., 1946; Columbia University, Ed.D., 1951.

CAREER: Testing technician for public schools of Dallas, Tex., 1942; University of Tulsa, Tulsa, Okla., dean of men, 1946-51; General American Life Insurance Co., St. Louis, Mo., personnel manager, 1951-54; Flint Community Junior College, Flint, Mich., dean of men, 1954-55, dean of college, 1955-61; University of Texas at Austin, associate professor of educational administration, 1961-64; Harrisburg Area Community College, Harrisburg, Pa., president, 1964-74. Lecturer at Washington University, St. Louis, Mo., 1954, and Shippensburg State College, 1969; summer lecturer at Michigan State University, 1957, 1960, University of California, Berkeley, 1961, 1967, and George Peabody College for Teachers, 1968, 1969. Secretary of board of trustees, American College Testing Program, 1968—; trustee, Dr. C.E.L. Keen Foundation. *Military service:* U.S. Army Air Forces, 1942-46.

MEMBER: American Psychological Association, American Educational Research Association, American Association of Higher Education, American Association of Junior Colleges, American Association of University Professors, Pennsylvania Association of Colleges and Universities, Pennsylvania Community College Presidents Council.

WRITINGS: (With Robert H. McCabe) *Relationships between the Informal Organization and the Curriculum in Six Junior Colleges,* [Austin, Texas], 1964; (with Robert H. Plummer and R. C. Richardson) *The Two-Year College: A Social Synthesis,* Prentice-Hall, 1965; (with Richardson) *Student's Guide to the Two-Year College,* Prentice-Hall, 1968; *Vocational Education in the Area Schools* (research report), Institute for Educational Development (New York), 1970; (with Richardson and L. W. Bender) *Governance of the Two-Year College,* Prentice-Hall, 1972; (with James W. Selgas and John C. Saussy) *The Impact of the College on the Local Economy,* Harrisburg Area Community College, 1973; *Student Services: An Evaluation,* Harrisburg Area Community College, 1974; (editor) *Humanizing Student Services,* Jossey-Bass, 1974. Also author of other research reports on education. Contributor of many articles to education journals. Member of editorial board, *Educational Administration Quarterly,* 1964-67.

WORK IN PROGRESS: Writing on college administration.†

* * *

BLODGETT, Harriet Eleanor 1919-

PERSONAL: Born September 28, 1919, in Lyndonville, Vt.; daughter of Floyd Kidder and Clara Inez (Goss) Blodgett. *Education:* Tufts University, B.S., 1940; University of Minnesota, M.A., 1943, Ph.D., 1953. *Home:* 2401 34th Ave. S., Minneapolis, Minn. 55406. *Office:* 4330 West River Rd., Minneapolis, Minn. 55406.

CAREER: State of Minnesota, St. Paul, psychologist, 1943-46; University of Minnesota, Minneapolis, instructor, 1946-53, assistant professor of child welfare, 1953-54; Rochester State Hospital, Rochester, Minn., research psychologist, 1954-55; Sheltering Arms (day school), Minneapolis, program director, 1955—. Member of Minnesota Governor's

Advisory Board on Handicapped, Gifted and Exceptional Children, 1959-66, and State Board of Examiners of Psychologists, 1968-74. *Member:* American Psychological Association, American Association on Mental Deficiency (fellow), Council on Exceptional Children, Minnesota Psychological Association, Minnesota Human Genetics League.

WRITINGS: (With Grace J. Warfield) *Understanding Mentally Retarded Children,* Appleton, 1959; *Mentally Retarded Children: What Parents and Others Should Know,* University of Minnesota Press, 1971.

* * *

BLUM, Shirley Neilsen 1932-

PERSONAL: Born October 14, 1932, in Petaluma, Calif.; daughter of Melvin Louis (a physician) and Anna (Keyes) Neilsen; married Walter C. Hopps, 1955; married second husband, Irving Blum (a gallery dealer), September 12, 1967; children: (second marriage) Jason Ferus. *Education:* Stockton College, A.A., 1952; University of Chicago, M.A., 1955; Radcliffe College, further graduate study, 1955-56; University of California, Los Angeles, Ph.D., 1964. *Home:* 78 Briary Rd., Dobbs Ferry, N.Y. 10522. *Office:* Humanities Division, State University of New York College, Purchase, N.Y. 10577.

CAREER: University of Chicago, Chicago, Ill., instructor in humanities and art history, 1961-62; University of California, Riverside, 1962-73, began as assistant professor, became associate professor of art history; Colgate University, Hamilton, N.Y., Dana Professor of Fine Arts, 1973-74; State University of New York College at Purchase, professor of art history, 1977—. *Member:* College Art Association of America (member of board of directors), American Association of University Professors, Phi Beta Kappa. *Awards, honors:* Woodrow Wilson fellow; Belgian American fellow; National Endowment for the Humanities senior fellow.

WRITINGS: (With John Coplans) *Jawlensky and the Serial Image* (catalogue), University of California, 1966; *Early Netherlandish Triptychs: A Study in Patronage,* University of California Press, 1969. Contributor to *New Catholic Encyclopedia.*

* * *

BLUMBERG, Arnold 1925-

PERSONAL: Born May 9, 1925, in Philadelphia, Pa.; son of Louis (a dentist) and Rose (Bleecher) Blumberg; married Thelma Lillian Alpert, December 26, 1954; children: Raphael D., Eva R., Michael S. *Education:* University of Pennsylvania, B.S., 1947, M.S., 1948, Ph.D., 1952. *Religion:* Jewish. *Home:* 3901 Glen Ave., Baltimore, Md. 21215. *Office:* Linthicum Hall 119C, Towson State University, Baltimore, Md. 21204.

CAREER: Philadelphia Public High Schools, Philadelphia, Pa., teacher of social studies, 1950-58; Towson State University, Baltimore, Md., associate professor, 1958-64, professor of history, 1964—. Visiting lecturer, Mohawk Valley Community College; lecturer in history, University of Rhode Island, summer, 1967. *Military service:* U.S. Army, 1943-45. *Member:* American Historical Association (life member), Society for French Historical Studies, American Association of University Professors, Phi Alpha Theta. *Awards, honors:* Danforth research grant, 1961; American Philosophical Society grant, 1966; Towson State University research committee research grants, 1967-76.

WRITINGS: A History of Congregation Shearith Israel, Sherwood Press, 1970; *A Manual for Undergraduate Term Papers,* Kendall-Hunt, 1970; *The Diplomacy of the Mexican Empire: 1863-1867,* American Philosophical Society, 1971. Contributor to twenty history journals. Abstractor, *Historical Abstracts,* 1963—.

WORK IN PROGRESS: A View of Jerusalem, 1849-1858; The Consular Diary of James and Elizabeth Anne Finn.

SIDELIGHTS: Arnold Blumberg told *CA:* "I am essentially a diplomatic historian, primarily interested in the period 1848-1871, though some of my work concerns the late nineteenth and twentieth centuries. In the writing of diplomatic history, the scholar has the special obligation of obtaining access to as many archival collections as possible, simply because diplomats take more pains than most people to ensure the secrecy of their true opinions. It is the historian's duty to transcribe or summarize every document which survives, which may conceivably cast light on past events. Very often, a document which appeared at first glance to be inconsequential, has proven to provide the key to otherwise hidden meanings in other documents. In the long run, the historian enjoys the wonderful moment of insight only when he can place side by side, vast masses of documentation, apparently unrelated, but seen as a united whole when brought together. Eventually, the diplomatic historian's task is easiest if he resolves from the first, to avoid 'short cuts.' If to save a few minutes, he neglects to take notes on apparently inconsequential documents, he may find himself wasting hours of time, months or years later, trying to find documents which he remembers having seen, but which he can no longer locate."

*   *   *

BODENHEIMER, Edgar   1908-

PERSONAL: Born March 14, 1908, in Berlin, Germany; son of Siegmund and Rosi (Maass) Bodenheimer; married Brigitte M. Levy (a professor of law), June 6, 1935; children: Peter, Thomas, Rosemarie. *Education:* University of Heidelberg, Doctor Juris, 1933; University of Washington, Seattle, LL.B., 1937. *Home:* 542 Miller Dr., Davis, Calif. 95616. *Office:* School of Law, University of California, Davis, Calif. 95616.

CAREER: Attorney, U.S. Department of Labor, 1940-42; principal attorney, Office of Alien Property Custodian, 1942-46; University of Utah, Salt Lake City, associate professor, 1946-51, professor of law, 1951-66; University of California, Davis, professor of law, 1966—. *Member:* American Association for Political and Legal Philosophy (vice-president, 1969-70). *Awards, honors:* National Endowment for the Humanities senior fellowship, 1970-71.

WRITINGS: Jurisprudence: The Philosophy and Method of Law, Harvard University Press, 1962, revised edition, 1974; *Treatise on Justice,* Philosophical Library, 1967; *Power, Law and Society,* Crane, Russak, 1973. Member of editorial board, *American Journal of Comparative Law.*

BIOGRAPHICAL/CRITICAL SOURCES: Luis Recasens Siches, *Panorama del Pensamiento Juridico* (title means "Panorama of Legal Thought"), [Mexico City], 1963.

*   *   *

BODKIN, Ronald G(eorge)   1936-

PERSONAL: Born May 29, 1936, in Philadelphia, Pa.; son of Ernest Aaron (a chemical engineer) and Marjory (Bickel) Bodkin; married (Winona) Susann Roberts, July 15, 1961;

children: Christie Lynn, Amy, Ronald J. *Education:* Swarthmore College, B.A. (with highest honors), 1957; University of Pennsylvania, M.A., 1959, Ph.D., 1962. *Religion:* United Church of Canada. *Home:* 2087 Knightsbridge Rd., Ottawa, Ontario, Canada K2A OR1. *Office:* Department of Economics, University of Ottawa, Ottawa, Ontario, Canada K7N 6N5.

CAREER: Penn Mutual Life Insurance Co., Philadelphia, Pa., actuarial assistant, summers, 1956-68; University of Pennsylvania, Philadelphia, instructor, 1957-60, lecturer in economics, 1961-62; Yale University, New Haven, Conn., lecturer, 1962-63, assistant professor of economics, 1963-65, member of research staff of Cowles Foundation for Research in Economics, 1962-65, and visiting research associate, 1971-72; University of Western Ontario, London, associate professor, 1965-67, professor of economics, 1967-75, on leave as project manager of CANDIDE econometric model project, Economic Council of Canada, 1972-74; University of Ottawa, Ottawa, Ontario, professor of economics, 1975—. Visiting summer lecturer, University of Colorado, 1964. Consultant to government and private groups, including National Bureau of Economic Research, 1961-64, Economic Council of Canada, 1965-66, U.S. Bureau of Labor Statistics, 1967, Department of Manpower and Immigration of Government of Canada, 1969-71, and Canadian Radio and Television Commission, 1977. *Member:* American Economic Association, Econometric Society, Canadian Economics Association, Canadian Association of University Teachers, Eastern Economic Association, Phi Beta Kappa, Pi Gamma Mu, Beta Gamma Sigma, Delta Sigma Rho. *Awards, honors:* Canada Council leave fellowship, 1971-72.

WRITINGS: (Contributor) Irwin Friend and Robert Jones, editors, *Consumption and Saving,* Volume II, University of Pennsylvania Press, 1960; (contributor) *Inflation, Growth, and Employment,* Prentice-Hall, 1964; *The Wage-Price-Productivity Nexus,* University of Pennsylvania Press, 1966; (contributor) S. F. Kaliski, editor, *Canadian Economic Policy since the War,* Private Planning Association, 1966; (with E. P. Bond, G. L. Reuber, and T. R. Robinson) *Price Stability and High Employment: The Options for Canadian Economic Policy, An Econometric Study,* Economic Council of Canada, 1967; (contributor) Ball and Doyle, editors, *Inflation: Selected Readings,* Penguin, 1969. Also co-editor of a report on a CANDIDE econometric model project, published by Economic Council of Canada, 1975. Contributor of about thirty articles and reviews to economics journals in North America and Europe. Member of editorial board, *Canadian Journal of Economics,* 1968-70, *International Economic Review,* 1969—, *Eastern Economic Journal,* 1974-76.

WORK IN PROGRESS: The operation and estimation of a variable lag in the orders-shipments mechanism for investment goods in a simple business cycle model; evaluation of economic models.

SIDELIGHTS: Ronald Bodkin writes: "As a research social scientist, I have become more and more convinced of the importance of competent writing as the final—and most crucial—stage of any research project."

*   *   *

BODLE, Yvonne Gallegos   1939-

PERSONAL: Surname rhymes with "yodel"; born December 5, 1939, in Tucumcari, N.M.; daughter of Joseph M. and Ruby (Bates) Gallegos; married Michael Eugene Bodle (a rancher), December 18, 1965; children: Robert Joseph, Michelle Yvonne. *Education:* San Jose State College (now University), B.A., 1963; Columbia University, M.A., 1964. *Religion:* Roman Catholic. *Home:* 2936 Salimar Beach Dr., Ventura, Calif. 93001. *Office:* Ventura College, Ventura, Calif. 93003.

CAREER: High school teacher of business subjects in Oxnard, Calif., 1964-65; Ventura College, Ventura, Calif., instructor in business, 1965—, distributive education and medical secretarial program coordinator. *Member:* American Association of University Women, California Business Education Association (district coordinator and vice-president, 1965-67), Ventura County Business Educators Association (founder and president, 1967-68), Kappa Delta Pi, Pi Lambda Theta, Forty Leaguers of Ventura County.

WRITINGS: (With Ruth Anderson and others) *The Administrative Secretary: Practicum,* McGraw, 1970; (with Joe Corey) *Retail Selling* (high school text with workbook), McGraw, 1972, revised edition, 1977; *McGrath Story,* privately printed, 1972; *Villanova,* privately printed, 1974. Contributor to business and education journals.

*   *   *

BOHAN, Peter

PERSONAL: Born in New York, N.Y.; son of Daniel Joseph (a builder) and Mary Ellen (Sheridan) Bohan; married Frances Fall, July 2, 1960. *Education:* Attended University of Bristol, 1947-48; Rensselaer Polytechnic Institute, B.Eng., 1950; graduate study at Columbia University, 1954-55, and Courtauld Institute of Art, London, 1958-59; Yale University, M.A., 1957, Ph.D., 1961. *Office:* History of Art Department, State University of New York College, New Paltz, N.Y. 12561.

CAREER: Grumman Co., and Republic Aircraft Co., Long Island, N.Y., guided missiles engineer, 1950-55; Yale University, Art Gallery, New Haven, Conn., assistant curator of Garvan Collection, 1959-63; Southern Connecticut State College, New Haven, assistant professor of art history, 1962-63; State University of New York College at New Paltz, director of College Art Gallery, 1963-68, professor of art history, 1963—. President, Ninety Miles Off Broadway (theater group), 1964-65; member of board of directors, Colonial Arts Foundation; consultant in urban historic preservation and restoration. Has participated in various art exhibitions, 1967-69. *Military service:* U.S. Army, 1945-46; served in European theater. *Member:* Society of Architectural Historians, College Art Association, Amerscot Highland Bagpipe Band (pipe sergeant, 1968—). *Awards, honors:* Several awards for paintings; Fulbright award for research in England, 1958-59; State University of New York fellowship for research abroad, 1970-71; Award of Merit from Connecticut League of Historical Societies, 1972, for *Early Connecticut Silver: 1700-1840.*

WRITINGS: American Gold: 1700-1860, Yale University Art Gallery, 1963; *Arts of Japan, from the Munsterberg Collection,* State University of New York College at New Paltz Art Gallery, 1964; (with Artine Artinian) *From Victor Hugo to Jean Cocteau* (French portraits), State University of New York College at New Paltz Art Gallery, 1965; *First New Paltz Intercollegiate Student Exhibition,* State University of New York College at New Paltz Art Gallery, 1966; (with Philip Hammerslough) *Early Connecticut Silver: 1700-1840,* Wesleyan University Press, 1970. Contributor to *Antiques.*

WORK IN PROGRESS: The Architecture of James and Decimus Burton: 1780-1850.

SIDELIGHTS: Peter Bohan writes: "I am primarily an architectural historian with most experience in 19th and 20th century European and American architecture. My early background is English, but in recent years I have spent much time in France and Spain, which I know very well. As a result, I have done considerable field work in medieval art and built a considerable personal slide collection especially of Romanesque and Gothic architecture, sculpture and stained glass. My particular interest is in the *design* aspects of historical art and architecture."

AVOCATIONAL INTERESTS: Travel, photography.†

*   *   *

BOHNSTEDT, John W(olfgang) 1927-

PERSONAL: Born February 22, 1927, in Berlin, Germany; naturalized U.S. citizen; son of Werner August (a professor) and Bertha (Norden) Bohnstedt; married Frieda Pfenning, September 18, 1948; children: Stephen, Mary. *Education:* Michigan State University, B.A., 1950; University of Minnesota, M.A., 1952, Ph.D., 1959. *Politics:* Democrat. *Religion:* Episcopalian. *Home:* 5543 North Bond St., Fresno, Calif. 93710. *Office:* Department of History, California State University, Fresno, Calif. 93740.

CAREER: University of South Dakota, Vermillion, instructor in history, 1955-56; California State University, Fresno, instructor, 1956-59, assistant professor, 1959-64, associate professor, 1964-68, professor of history, 1968—. *Military service:* U.S. Army, 1945-47; served in Germany. *Member:* American Historical Association, Conference Group on Central European History, Phi Alpha Theta. *Awards, honors:* Fulbright research fellow in Austria, 1953-54; American Philosophical Society research grant, 1965; Fresno State College (now California State University, Fresno) Distinguished Teaching Award, 1966.

WRITINGS: The Infidel Scourge of God: The Turkish Menace as Seen by German Pamphleteers of the Reformation Era, American Philosophical Society, 1968. Contributor to journals.

WORK IN PROGRESS: A History of the World in the Nineteenth Century.

SIDELIGHTS: John Bohnstedt writes: "I am fascinated by the study, teaching, and writing of history because history is the drama of mankind. It tells us much about man's tragic inadequacies, but also about his superb potentialities. Since time immemorial man has been engaged in a revolt against his own shortcomings—in an unending quest for truth, beauty, justice, and happiness." *Avocational interests:* Gardening.

*   *   *

BOHRNSTEDT, George W(illiam) 1938-

PERSONAL: Born September 28, 1938, in Arcadia, Wis.; son of Russell Gail (a businessman) and Agnes (Brecht) Bohrnstedt; married Josephine Brunory, November 8, 1962 (divorced); married Ilene Nagel Bernstein, June 30, 1973; children: (first marriage) Elizabeth Ann, Brian Russell, Matthew Montgomery. *Education:* University of Wisconsin, B.S., 1960, M.S., 1963, Ph.D., 1966. *Office:* Institute of Social Research, 1022 East Third, Indiana University, Bloomington, Ind. 47401.

CAREER: University of Wisconsin—Madison, assistant to dean of men, 1962-64, instructor, 1967-69, lecturer in sociology, 1968-69, associate study director of Social Behaviour Research Center, 1967-70; University of Minnesota, Minneapolis, associate professor of sociology and chairman of department, 1970-73; Indiana University at Bloomington, professor of sociology, 1973—, director of Institute of Social Research, 1974—. Visiting fellow, Yale University, 1976-77. Member of Small Grants Committee, National Institute of Mental Health. Consultant to State of Wisconsin Alcoholism Services, 1968. *Military service:* U.S. Army, 1962.

MEMBER: American Sociological Association (member of Stouffer Award selection committee, 1973-74; chairman of methodology section, 1977-79), American Statistical Association, Sociological Research Association, Society of Experimental Social Psychologists, Society of Multivariate Experimental Psychologists, Psychometric Society, American Association for Public Opinion Research (member of program committee, 1977). *Awards, honors:* National Science Foundation summer fellow, 1960; Belding Scholar, Foundation for Child Development, 1976-77.

WRITINGS: (Editor with E. F. Borgatta) *Sociological Methodology: 1969,* Jossey-Bass, 1969; (editor with Borgatta) *Sociological Methodology: 1970,* Jossey-Bass, 1970; (contributor) Gene Summers, editor, *Attitude Measurement,* Rand McNally, 1970. Also contributor, R. E. Schell, editor, *Readings in Developmental Psychology Today,* 2nd edition, Random House. Contributor of numerous articles to professional journals, including *American Sociological Review, Social Science, Psychology Today, Journal of Vocational Behaviour,* and *Journal of Experimental Education.* Co-editor, *Sociological Methods and Research,* 1971—.

WORK IN PROGRESS: Several papers on how children come to make self-attributions of characteristics such as physical attractiveness, intelligence, athletic ability, etc.

* * *

BOIS, J(oseph) Samuel 1892-

PERSONAL: Surname is pronounced bwa; born April 21, 1892, in Stratford, Quebec, Canada; came to United States in 1956, naturalized in 1963; son of Samuel (a carpenter) and Alice (Deslongchamps) Bois; married Caroline Hill, June 24, 1941 (divorced, 1969); married Eva Ducharme, June 13, 1969; children: (first marriage) Leonard, Johannna. *Education:* Laval University, B.A., 1910; McGill University, M.A., 1934, Ph.D., 1936. *Home:* 26124 Anawood Pl., Hemet, Calif. 92343.

CAREER: Roman Catholic priest, 1915-36; Psychological Institute, Montreal, Quebec, president, 1936-41; Stevenson & Kellogg (management consultants), Montreal, staff psychologist, 1945-47; Bois & Howard, Montreal, senior partner, 1947-53; Bois & Mahoney, Montreal, senior partner, 1953-56; Bois, McCay & Associates Ltd. (management consultants), Montreal, president, 1953-57; Viewpoints Institute, Los Angeles, Calif., director of research and education, 1963—. Creator of "Executive Methods," a management development program in use in United States and Canada since 1948. Vice-president, Opinion Surveys Ltd., 1937-41. Extension lecturer. University of California, Riverside, San Diego, and Los Angeles, 1961—; lecturer, School of Public Administration, University of Southern California, 1968—. Has given radio lectures in Montreal, Los Angeles, and San Francisco, Calif. Consultant, Dominion-Provincial Youth Training Plan, 1937-40; consultant in management development research, 1956-62. *Military service:* Canadian Army, 1941-45; became lieutenant colonel. *Member:* International Society for General Semantics (former board member), American Psychological Association (life fellow), Canadian Psychological Association

(life fellow; president, 1949-50), American Association for the Advancement of Science (fellow), Institute of General Semantics (fellow).

WRITINGS: La Decouverte de soi-meme, Psychological Institute (Montreal), 1937, revised edition published as *Psychologie pour tous,* 1945; *Le Bonheur s'apprend,* Psychological Institute, 1941; *Psychologie et medecine,* Psychological Institute, 1944; *Explorations in Awareness,* Harper, 1957; *The Art of Awareness,* W. C. Brown, 1966, 2nd edition, 1973; *Communication as Creative Experience,* Viewpoints Institute, 1968; *Breeds of Men: Post-Korzybskian General Semantics,* School of Public Administration, University of Southern California, 1969, revised edition published as *Breeds of Men: Toward the Adulthood of Humankind,* Harper, 1970; *Epistemics: The Science-Art of Innovating,* International Society for General Semantics, 1972. Author of columns in *Le Jour* and *L'Action Medicale,* 1937-41. Contributor to professional journals in psychology, management science, and general semantics. Editor, *Khaki,* 1942-45.

BIOGRAPHICAL/CRITICAL SOURCES: History of American Psychology, A. A. Roback, 1952; *ETC: A Review of General Semantics,* December, 1969.

* * *

BOLIAN, Polly 1925-

PERSONAL: Surname is pronounced *Bol*-yun; born September 20, 1925, in Mississippi. *Education:* Studied at Corcoran Gallery of Art and George Washington University, 1943-45; Rhode Island School of Design, B.F.A., 1947. *Residence:* Easthampton, N.Y.

CAREER: Free-lance artist and writer, New York, N.Y., and vicinity, 1948—. As artist, works in variety of mediums—painting, drawing, lithographs, silk screens, photography, plastics, wood, clay, and papier-mache. Consultant to Head Start, Job Corps, private companies and voluntary organizations.

WRITINGS—All self-illustrated youth books: (With Marilyn Schima) *I Know a House Builder,* Putnam, 1968; (with Schima) *I Know a Nurse,* Putnam, 1969; (with Schima) *Something Grows,* Prentice-Hall, 1969; (with Schima) *Magic of Life,* Prentice-Hall, 1970; (with Shirley Hinds) *First Book of Safety,* F. Watts, 1970; *Growing Up Slim,* American Heritage Press, 1971; *Symbols: The Language of Communication,* F. Watts, 1975. Consulting editor, *Advances in Voluntary Sterilization,* 1973, and *New Advances in Sterilization,* 1976. Contributor of health education materials to periodicals.

WORK IN PROGRESS: A novel.

SIDELIGHTS: Polly Bolian told *CA:* "I am a multi-media person and work in whatever medium best suits the job (or whatever mixed media)—from planar (flat) images of all types (photography, silk screens, litho, paintings, drawings, etc.) to three-dimensional (plastics, wood, mache, clay, etc.). Most of my writing pertains to health area materials."

* * *

BONGAR, Emmet W(ald) 1919-

PERSONAL: Surname is pronounced *Bahn*-gahr; born November 26, 1919, in Brooklyn, N.Y.; son of Irving John (in insurance) and Etta (Wald) Bongar; married Audrey Miller (a teacher), September 2, 1949; children: Michael, Mary. *Education:* Danbury State Teachers College (now Western Connecticut State College), B.S., 1941; Columbia University, M.A., 1947, additional graduate study, 1947-48.

Politics: Independent. *Religion:* Presbyterian. *Home:* 1055 Marseille Dr., Marion, Ohio 43302.

CAREER: Connecticut State Highway Department, New Milford, transitman and draftsman, 1941-42, senior engineer's aide, 1946; Columbia University, New York, N.Y., admissions counselor, 1947-48, technical assistant in drama and stagecraft, 1948-49; Youngstown Playhouse, Youngstown, Ohio, technical director, 1949-50; Community Playhouse, Oak Ridge, Tenn., director, 1950-52; Union Carbide & Carbon, Oak Ridge, electronic and instrument buyer, 1952-55; Hazeltine Corp., Little Neck, N.Y., expeditor, 1955-56; Westinghouse Electric Co., Pittsburgh, Pa., contract administrator and buyer, 1956-66; General Electric Co., Cincinnati, Ohio, buyer, 1966-67; Thiel College, Greenville, Pa., assistant professor of theater arts and director of Thiel Players, 1967-74; Marion Power Shovel Co., Marion, Ohio, purchasing agent, 1974—. Director or technical director of summer theaters at Rocky Hill, Conn., 1948, Kennebunkport, Me., 1949, and Long Island, N.Y., 1950. *Military service:* U.S. Navy, 1942-46. *Member:* American Educational Theatre Association, American Association of University Professors, Theatre Association of Pennsylvania, Phi Kappa Delta, Alpha Psi Omega.

WRITINGS: The Theatre Student: Practical Stage Lighting, Rosen Press, 1971.

*   *   *

BOONE, Daniel R. 1927-

PERSONAL: Born October 30, 1927, in Chicago, Ill.; son of Claude B. (a salesman) and Pearl L. (Richardson) Boone; married Mary M. Mosenthal, December 28, 1954; children: Penny, James, Robbie, Rebecca. *Education:* University of Redlands, B.A., 1951; Western Reserve University (now Case Western Reserve University), M.A., 1954, Ph.D., 1958. *Politics:* Democrat. *Religion:* Christian. *Home:* 5715 North Genematas Dr., Tucson, Ariz. 85704. *Agent:* Jane Jourdan Browne Multimedia Product Development, Inc., 170 South Beverly Dr., Suite 314, Beverly Hills, Calif. 90212. *Office:* Department of Speech and Hearing Science, University of Arizona, Tucson, Ariz. 85721.

CAREER: Highland View Hospital, Cleveland, Ohio, chief of audiology and pathology, 1956-60; Western Reserve University (now Case Western Reserve University), Cleveland, assistant professor of speech pathology, 1960-63; University of Kansas, Kansas City, associate professor of speech pathology, 1963-66; University of Denver, Denver, Colo., professor of speech pathology, 1966-73; currently professor and director of speech pathology, University of Arizona, Tucson. Member of Denver Board Professional Services, American Cancer Society; member of board of directors, Palos Verdes Civic Association. *Military service:* U.S. Army, 1945-47. *Member:* American Speech and Hearing Association (fellow; vice-president, 1969; president, 1976), Academy of Aphasia, Colorado Speech and Hearing Association (president, 1972), Sigma Xi.

WRITINGS: An Adult Has Aphasia, Interstate, 1965; *The Voice and Voice Therapy,* Prentice-Hall, 1971, 2nd edition, 1977; *Cerebral Palsy,* Bobbs-Merrill, 1972. Contributor of about thirty articles to professional journals.

WORK IN PROGRESS: Ripe Tomatoes, fiction; *The Scoring of Speech and Hearing Therapy,* a manual for self-accountability of speech and hearing clinicians.

BOOTHROYD, (John) Basil 1910-

PERSONAL: Born March 4, 1910, in Worksop, England; son of James (a secretary) and Sarah Jane (Binch) Boothroyd; married Phyllis Barbara Youngman (a reader, recorded books for the blind), June 10, 1939; children: Toby James Franklin. *Education:* Educated in England. *Home:* 56 Oathall Rd., Haywards Heath, West Sussex RH16 3EN, England. *Agent:* A. P. Watt & Son, 26/28 Bedford Row, London WC1R 4HL, England; and (lectures) Associated Speakers, 24A Park Rd., Hayes, Middlesex VB4 8JN, England. *Office: Punch,* 23/27 Tudor St., London EC4Y 0HR, England.

CAREER: Bank clerk, 1927-52; *Punch,* London, England, regular contributor, 1938—, assistant editor, 1952-70. Broadcaster, chiefly as a humorist. *Military service:* Royal Air Force, 1941-46; became flight lieutenant. *Member:* Savage Club, B.B.C. Club. *Awards, honors:* Made a Freeman of the City of London, 1974; Imperial Tobacco Award, 1976, for best radio comedy script.

WRITINGS—Published by Allen & Unwin, except as indicated: *Home Guard Goings-on from "Punch," or the London Charivari, 1940-41,* 1941; *Adastral Bodies from "Punch,"* 1942; *Are Sergeants Human?,* 1945; *Are Officers Necessary?,* 1946; *Lost, a Double-Fronted Shop,* 1947; *The House about a Man,* 1959; *Motor If You Must* (collection from *Punch*), 1960, 2nd enlarged edition, 1966; *To My Embarrassment,* 1961; *The Whole Thing's Laughable,* 1964; *You Can't Be Serious,* 1967; *Let's Stay Married,* 1967, Simon & Schuster, 1968; *Stay Married Abroad,* 1968; *Boothroyd at Bay: Some Radio Talks,* 1970; *Prince Philip: An Informal Biography,* McCall Books, 1971 (published in England as *Philip: An Informal Biography,* Longman, 1971); *Accustomed as I Am: The Loneliness of the Long Distance Speaker; or, All You'd Never Guess about Public Speaking,* 1975; *Let's Move House,* 1977.

Contributor to *Homage to P. G. Wodehouse,* 1973, and *Fodor's Guide to Great Britain,* 1977. Author of historical booklets for Ford Motor Co., 1973, and for Phillips, Son & Neale (London art dealers), 1974.

WORK IN PROGRESS: America, I Love You, reminiscences of his 1971 visit to the United States.

SIDELIGHTS: "Apart from the approved life of Prince Philip," Basil Boothroyd notes, "my choice of subjects is governed by comic possibilities." While writing the biography, undertaken at Prince Philip's request, Boothroyd was given a room at Buckingham Palace for a year. *Motor If You Must* and *The House about a Man* have been translated into German. *The House about a Man* has also been translated into Italian.

BIOGRAPHICAL/CRITICAL SOURCES: Punch, December 13, 1967, December 11, 1968; *Books and Bookmen,* January, 1968; *Best Sellers,* August 1, 1968; *Detroit News,* October 3, 1971.

*   *   *

BORAAS, Roger S(tuart) 1926-

PERSONAL: Surname is accented on first syllable; born February 4, 1926, in Stillwater, Minn.; son of Justin N. (a farmer) and Esther (Johnson) Boraas; married Aina Anderson, June 22, 1948; children: Miriam Ruth, Marcia Christine, Roger Scott. *Education:* Gustavus Augustus College, B.A., 1948; Augustana Theological Seminary, B.D., 1952; further study at Union Theological Seminary, New York, N.Y., 1953-54, and Oberlin Graduate School of Theology,

1955-58; Drew University, Ph.D., 1965. *Home:* 50 Fernwood Rd., East Orange, N.J. 07017. *Office:* Department of Religion, Upsala College, East Orange, N.J. 07019.

CAREER: Ordained Lutheran clergyman, 1952; Upsala College, East Orange, N.J., instructor, 1958-61, assistant professor, 1962-66, associate professor, 1966-70, professor of religion, 1970—, director of Ancient Near East study program, 1968—. Member of Drew-McCormick archaeological expeditions to Balatah, 1962, 1964, 1966, 1968; chief archaeologist, Andrews University expedition to Heshbon, 1968, 1971, 1973, 1974, 1976; secretary-treasurer American Center of Oriental Research in Amman, Inc., 1969—. *Military service:* U.S. Navy, 1944-46. *Member:* Society of Biblical Literature, American Academy of Religion, American Association of University Professors, American Schools of Oriental Research.

WRITINGS—All published by Andrews University Press: (With S. H. Horn and others) *Heshbon 1968*, 1969; (with Horn and others) *Heshbon 1971*, 1973; (with Horn and others) *Heshbon 1973*, 1975; (with L. Geraty and others) *Heshbon 1974*, 1976.

WORK IN PROGRESS: Schechem: The Early Iron Age, findings of the joint archaeological expeditions at Tell Balatah, Jordan, 1957-69.

SIDELIGHTS: On his various expeditions Roger Boraas has visited European museum centers and traveled in Greece, Turkey, Israel, Syria, Jordan, Iraq, Lebanon, and Egypt.

*   *   *

BORCHARDT, Frank L(ouis) 1938-

PERSONAL: Born November 16, 1938, in New York, N.Y.; son of Hermann (an author) and Dorothea (Redmer) Borchardt. *Education:* Saint Peter's College, A.B., 1960; University of Berlin, further study, 1960-61; Johns Hopkins University, M.A., 1962, Ph.D., 1965. *Religion:* Roman Catholic. *Home:* 100 East Forest Hills Blvd., Durham, N.C. 27707. *Office:* Department of German, Duke University, Durham, N.C. 27706.

CAREER: Northwestern University, Evanston, Ill., assistant professor of German, 1965-68; Queens College of the City University of New York, Flushing, N.Y., assistant professor of German and comparative literature, 1968-71; Duke University, Durham, N.C., associate professor of German, 1971—. *Member:* American Association of Teachers of German, Modern Language Association of America, Renaissance Society of America, Association d'humanisme et Renaissance. *Awards, honors:* Woodrow Wilson fellow, 1960; Fulbright research fellow, University of Wuerzburg, 1971-72.

WRITINGS: German Antiquity in Renaissance Myth, Johns Hopkins Press, 1971. Contributor to language journals.

WORK IN PROGRESS: Typology of Apocalyptic Thought.

*   *   *

BOREL, Jacques 1925-

PERSONAL: Born December 17, 1925, in Paris, France; son of Pierre (a civil servant) and Lucie (Dubee) Borel; married Christiane Idrac (a school headmistress), September 25, 1948; children: Denis, Anne, Helene, Claude, Claire. *Education:* Lycee Henri-IV, Paris, Baccalaureat, 1944, Li-

cence, 1948; Sorbonne, University of Paris, Diplome d'etudes superieures, 1949. *Home:* 22 rue Charles de Gaulle, Bures-sur-Yvette 91440, Essonne, France.

CAREER: English teacher at Lycee Blaise-Pascal, Clermont-Ferrand, 1952-54, Lycee Paul Lapie, Courbevoie, 1954-56, and Lycee Rodin, Paris, 1956-67, all in France. Visiting professor at Middlebury College, 1966, Portland State College (now University), 1967, University of Hawaii, 1968, and University of California, Irvine, 1969. *Awards, honors:* Prix Goncourt (France), 1965, for *L'Adoration;* Chevalier Ordre des Arts et Lettres, 1971.

WRITINGS: (Editor and author of notes) Paul Marie Verlaine, *Ouevres completes,* two volumes, Club du Meilleur Livre, Volume I, 1959, Volume II, 1960; (editor and author of introduction) Verlaine, *Oeuvres poetiques completes,* Gallimard, 1962; *L'Adoration* (novel), Gallimard, 1965, translation by Norman Denny published as *The Bond,* Doubleday, 1968; (translator into French) James Joyce, *Le Chat et le diable,* Gallimard, 1966; (editor and author of notes) Verlaine, *La Bonne chanson, Romances sans paroles* [and] *Sagesse,* Librairie Generale Francaise, 1966; (translator into French and author of prefaces) James Joyce, *Poemes: Chamber Music and Pomes penyeach,* bilingual edition, Gallimard, 1967; *Tata ou de l'education: Piece morale et didactique en 2 actes et 3 tableaux,* Gallimard, 1967; (author of preface) *Romanciers au travail: Faulkner, Pasternak, Mauriac, E. M. Forster,* translation from the English by Jean Rene Major, Gallimard, 1967; (author of preface) Joachim Du Bellay, *Les Regrets, Antiquities de Rome* [and] *La Defense et illustration de la langue francaise,* edited by Samuel Silvestre de Sacy, Librairie Generale Francaise, 1967; (author of preface) Eugene Guillevic, *Terraque* [and] *Executoire,* Gallimard, 1968.

Le Retour (novel; sequel to *L'Adoration*), Gallimard, 1970; (contributor) *Les Critiques de notre temps et Camus,* Garnier, 1970; (contributor) *Positions et oppositions sur le Roman contemporain,* Editions Klincksieck, 1971; (author of preface) Leon-Paul Fargue, *Epaisseurs* [and] *Vulturne,* Gallimard, 1971; (author of preface) Francis Jammes, *De L'Angelus de l'aube a l'angelus du soir,* Gallimard, 1971; *Marcel Proust* (essay), Seghers, 1972; (editor and author of introduction) Verlaine, *Oeuvres en prose completes,* Gallimard, 1972; (author of preface and notes) Verlaine, *Fetes galantes, Romances sans paroles* [and] *Poems saturniens,* Gallimard, 1973; *La depossession, journal de Ligenere,* Gallimard, 1973; *Commentaires: Rousseau, Stendhal, Proust,* Gallimard, 1974; (contributor) *Tableau de la litterature Francaise, III,* Gallimard, 1974; *Un Voyage ordinaire,* La Table Ronde, 1975. Contributor of poems and essays to *Nouvelle Revue Francaise, Critique, Mercure de France, Cahiers du Sud, Figaro Litteraire, Botteghe Oscure, Europe, Cahiers Du Chemin,* and other journals.

WORK IN PROGRESS: A novel; a book of essays, *Lecture des poetes.*

SIDELIGHTS: Winner of the Prix Goncourt in 1965, *The Bond* is a semi-autobiographical account of an only son and his relationship to his widowed mother. Claire Tomalin calls the book "a huge, ironical slab of total recall.... Its piling up of detail is of the kind a patient might offer his analyst or a self-absorbed lover his very enraptured mistress.... Borel does, however, provide a perceptive comment of his own early in the story, in which he speaks of his consciousness at the age of 10, of himself as a figure from literature rather than life; his tantrums, runnings away, suicide attempt, erotic initiations—the implication, well sustained throughout, is that all were undergone to make raw material for the supreme experience of turning it into *la litterature.*"

Paul A. Doyle of the State University of New York believes "a curious unevenness possesses the book.... Too much space is given to trivial matters . . . the author has no sense of Joycean selection.... One of the novel's difficulties is that the hero is not at all likable, and it becomes difficult for the reader to identify with him or to show much sympathy." This may be because, as Vivian Mercier of *New York Times Book Review* points out, *The Bond* "is a profoundly French book." She cites the strength of the "bond" between mother and son, the leisurely pace of narration, and "the narrator's Proustian fascination with his own portrait as well as his mother's" as characteristic of its Frenchness. She adds that Borel, being conventionally religious, has "substituted the journal for the confession box," and in the future "might well turn to issuing installments of his *journal* instead of 'thinly disguised' autobiographies."

BIOGRAPHICAL/CRITICAL SOURCES: Observer Review, April 28, 1968; *Best Sellers,* August 1, 1968; *New York Times Book Review,* September 8, 1968; *L'Express,* May 25-31, 1970; Pierre-Henri Simon, *Parier pour l'homme,* Editions du Seuil, 1973; Bettina Knapp, *Off-Stage Voices,* Whitson Publishing, 1975; Knapp, *French Novelists Speak Out,* Whitson Publishing, 1976.

*   *   *

BORG, Walter R(aymond)   1921-

PERSONAL: Born June 24, 1921, in Chicago, Ill.; son of Walter Raymond (an engineer) and Mary (Martie) Borg; married Marie Ramazzotti, July 11, 1948; children: Adrienne, John, Robert, Cheryl. *Education:* San Diego State College (now University), B.A., 1943; University of California, Berkeley, M.A., 1947, Ph.D., 1948. *Home:* 410 Spring Creek Rd., Providence, Utah 84332. *Office:* Department of Psychology, Utah State University, Logan, Utah 84321.

· *CAREER:* University of Texas, Main University (now University of Texas at Austin), assistant professor of educational psychology, 1948-51; U.S. Air Force Officer Military Schools, San Antonio, Tex., director of training analysis and development, 1951-55; Air University, Maxwell Air Force Base, Air Force Personnel and Training Research Center, Montgomery, Ala., director of officer education research laboratory, 1955-57; Utah State University, Logan, director of Educational Research Bureau, 1957-66; Far West Laboratory for Educational Research and Development, Berkeley, Calif., program director, 1961-71; Utah State University, professor of psychology, 1971—. Consultant to U.S. Department of Health, Education, and Welfare, U.S. Army, University of Kentucky, University of Minnesota, University of Virginia, the states of California and Utah, and other educational and governmental groups. *Military service:* U.S. Navy, 1943-46; became lieutenant junior grade. *Member:* American Psychological Association, American Educational Research Association, American Association for the Advancement of Science, National Society for the Study of Education.

WRITINGS: Educational Research: An Introduction, McKay, 1963, revised edition (with Meredith Gall), 1971; *An Evaluation of Ability Grouping,* Utah State University, 1964; *Ability Grouping in the Public Schools,* Dembar Educational Research Services, 1965; (with Marjorie L. Kelley, Philip Langer, and Gall) *The Minicourse: A Microteaching Approach to Teacher Education,* Macmillan, 1970; *Classroom Management,* National Resource and Dissemination

Center, University of South Florida, 1974; *Improving Pupil Achievement through Teacher Language,* National Resource and Dissemination Center, University of South Florida, 1974; *Self-Concept,* National Resource and Dissemination Center, University of South Florida, 1975. Contributor of more than fifty articles to psychology and education journals.

WORK IN PROGRESS: Research related to training of elementary school teachers; studying research and development related to teacher education; research and development on mainstreaming in elementary schools.

*   *   *

BORTNER, Doyle M(cClean)   1915-

PERSONAL: Born April 4, 1915, in Gettysburg, Pa.; son of Homer (an educator) and Mary Agnes (McClean) Bortner; married Alba Pignatiello (a librarian), April 24, 1943. *Education:* Gettysburg College, B.A., 1936; Pennsylvania State University, M.A., 1937; Temple University, Ed.D., 1950. *Politics:* Democrat. *Religion:* Unitarian Universalist. *Home:* 66 Clinton Ave., Montclair, N.J. 07042. *Office:* School of Education, City College of the City University of New York, Convent Ave. and 138th St., New York, N.Y. 10031.

CAREER: Perkiomen Preparatory School, Pennsburg, Pa., teacher of social studies, 1937-41; high school teacher of English and social studies in Bernardsville, N.J., 1945-46; Temple University, Philadelphia, Pa., instructor in secondary education, 1946-48; Bates College, Lewiston, Me., associate professor, 1948-51, professor of education, 1951-52, chairman of department of education and psychology, 1948-52; Hofstra College (now University), Hempstead, N.Y., professor of education and chairman of Division of Education, 1952-61; Jersey City State College, Jersey City, N.J., dean of college, 1961-64; City College of the City University of New York, School of Education, New York, N.Y., professor of education, 1964—, associate dean, 1964-66, dean, 1966—. Visiting professor at University of Maine, summers, 1950-52, University of Puerto Rico, summer, 1959, and New York University, summers, 1959, 1960. Member of New York State Council for Administrative Leadership, 1960-61. *Military service:* U.S. Army, 1941-45; became captain.

MEMBER: American Association of School Administrators, National School Public Relations Association, American Association of University Professors, Association for Higher Education, Phi Beta Kappa, Phi Delta Kappa, Kappa Delta Pi, Kappa Phi Kappa.

WRITINGS: Public Relations for Teachers, Simmons-Boardman, 1959; *Public Relations for Public Schools,* Schenkman, 1972. Contributor to education journals.

*   *   *

BORTNER, Morton   1925-

PERSONAL: Born June 11, 1925, in Philadelphia, Pa.; son of David (a merchant) and Anna (Chernicoff) Bortner; married Juliet Zimmerman (a psychologist), February 24, 1952; children: Kathy, Judd. *Education:* University of Pennsylvania, A.B., 1947; Columbia University, M.A., 1950, Ph.D., 1956. *Home:* 28-28 211th St., Bayside, N.Y. 11360. *Office:* Psychology Department, Ferkauf Graduate School of Humanities and Social Sciences, Yeshiva University, 55 Fifth Ave., New York, N.Y. 10003.

CAREER: New York Medical College and Flower and

Fifth Avenue Hospitals, New York City, assistant professor of psychology and chief psychologist in department of physical medicine and rehabilitation, 1956-65; Yeshiva University, Ferkauf Graduate School of Humanities and Social Sciences, New York City, professor of psychology, 1965—. Kennedy Foundation scholar, 1965-73. *Member:* American Psychological Association (fellow).

WRITINGS: (Editor and contributor) *Evaluation and Education of Children with Brain Damage,* C. C Thomas, 1968; (contributor) E. F. Waldon, editor, *Differential Diagnosis of Speech and Hearing Problems of Mental Retardates,* Catholic University of America Press, 1968; (contributor) Stella Chess and Alexander Thomas, editors, *Annual Progress in Child Psychiatry and Child Development,* Brunner, 1968; (contributor) F. Warner and R. Thrapp, editors, *Readings in Controversial Issues in Education of the Mentally Retarded,* MSS Information Corp., 1971; (contributor) Judy Rosenblith, W. Allinsmith, and Joana Williams, editors, *The Causes of Behavior: Readings in Child Development and Educational Psychology,* 3rd edition, Allyn & Bacon, 1972. Contributor of more than twenty articles to professional journals.

*　　*　　*

BORTSTEIN, Larry 1942-

PERSONAL: Surname is pronounced Bort-*stine;* born November 25, 1942, in Bronx, N.Y.; son of William and Shirley (Ecker) Bortstein; married Veronica Weber, June 28, 1969; children: Steven. *Education:* City College of the City University of New York, B.A., 1963. *Politics:* Democrat. *Religion:* Hebrew. *Home:* 10025 East Girard Ave., No. 349, Denver, Colo. 80231.

CAREER: Sports writer for *New York Mirror,* 1962-63, Associated Press, 1964, National Collegiate Athletic Bureau, 1964-66, and Madison Square Garden Basketball Publicity, 1966-67; Pyramid Publications, New York, N.Y., sports editor, 1967-69; full-time free-lance writer, 1969—. Publicity writer on auto racing and tennis, Ruder & Finn Public Relations Agency. Covered Maccabiah Games in Israel, 1965, Pan-American Games in Winnipeg, 1967, and Olympic Games in Mexico City, 1968, and Munich, 1972. *Member:* American Society of Journalists and Authors, Authors League, Football Writers Association of America, U.S. Basketball Writers Association, American Auto Racing Writers and Broadcasters Association, International Motor Press Association, U.S. Tennis Writers Association, U.S. Track and Field Writers Association, Sigma Delta Chi.

WRITINGS: Football Stars of 1969, Pyramid Publications, 1969; *Super Joe: The Joe Namath Story,* Grosset, 1969; *Len Dawson: Super Bowl Quarterback,* Grosset, 1970; *Football Stars of 1970,* Pyramid Publications, 1970; *Football Stars of 1971,* Pyramid Publications, 1971; (with Henry Berkowitz) *Scuba, Spear and Snorkel,* Cowles, 1971; *Ali: An Intimate Biography,* Tower, 1971; *Who's Who in Auto Racing,* Sports, Inc., 1972; *Who's Who in Golf,* Sports, Inc., 1972; *Who's Who in Pro Hockey,* Sports, Inc., 1972; *UCLA's Fabulous Bruins: The Story of a Basketball Dynasty,* St. Martin's, 1972; *ABC's Wide World of Sports Quiz Book,* Stadia Sports Publishing, 1973; *Great Moments of Baseball,* Tempo Books, 1973; *The Indianapolis 500: Speedway to Fame,* Troll Associates, 1974; *Dr. J—Dave Cowens,* Tempo Books, 1974; *Great Tennis Players: King, Evert, Court, Goolagong,* Tempo Books, 1974; *Great Racing Drivers,* Tempo Books, 1974; *My Greatest Day in Hockey,* Tempo Books, 1974; *The Big Ones,* Tempo Books, 1975;

(with Phil Berger) *The Boys of Indy,* Pinnacle, 1977; *After Olympic Glory,* Warne, 1977; *Dave Kingman,* Putnam, 1977. Editor, *Auto Racing Sports Stars of 1972* (magazine); co-editor, *Motorcycle Sports Stars of 1972* (magazine).

WORK IN PROGRESS: MPH: Cars at Speed, for Stadia Sports Publishing.

*　　*　　*

BOSSONE, Richard M. 1924-

PERSONAL: Surname is pronounced Boss-*own;* born August 8, 1924, in Philadelphia, Pa. *Education:* University of California, Berkeley, B.A., 1948; San Francisco State College (now University), M.A., 1951; University of Southern California, Ph.D., 1958. *Residence:* New York, N.Y. *Office:* Graduate School and University Center, City University of New York, 33 West 42nd St., New York, N.Y. 10036.

CAREER: Junior high school English and reading teacher in El Cerrito, Calif., 1951-53; high school English teacher in Whittier, Calif., 1953-54; El Camino College, Torrance, Calif., instructor in English, 1954-59; University of California, Riverside, associate professor of English education, 1961-67; City University of New York, New York, N.Y., associate professor of English education at Richmond College, 1967-70, professor of English at Bernard Baruch College, 1970-74, professor of English at Graduate School and University Center, 1974—. Editorial consultant, Holt, Rinehart & Winston, 1959-61. *Military service:* U.S. Army Air Forces, 1942-45. *Member:* Modern Language Association of America, National Council of Teachers of English, National Society for the Study of Education, Conference on College Composition and Communication, American Association of Junior Colleges, New York State English Association.

WRITINGS: (Contributor) *Promising Practices in the Teaching of English,* National Council of Teachers of English, 1963; (contributor) *Classroom Practices in Teaching English, 1965-66,* National Council of Teachers of English, 1965; *Remedial English Instruction in California Public Junior Colleges: An Analysis and Evaluation of Current Practices,* California State Department of Education and Addison-Wesley, 1966; *Reading Problems of Community College Students,* City University of New York, 1970; (co-author) *Basic English: Computer Assisted Instruction,* Computer Curriculum Corp., 1970; *Teaching Basic English Courses: Readings and Comments,* Van Nostrand, 1971; *Handbook of Basic English Skills,* Ginn, 1971, revised edition, Wiley, 1978; *Three Modes of Teaching Remedial English,* City University of New York, 1973; *A Strategy for Coping with High School and College Remedial English Problems,* City University of New York, 1976; *English Proficiency,* McGraw, 1978. Contributor of more than thirty-five articles and studies to various journals. Editor, Addison-Wesley junior college English textbooks, 1964-67.

*　　*　　*

BOTTOM, Raymond 1927-

PERSONAL: Born May 23, 1927, in Cincinnati, Ohio; son of Bert and Tressie (Anderson) Bottom; married Linda Loveland (a teacher), July 2, 1971; children: Elaine (Mrs. Wendell Miller). *Education:* Western Kentucky State College (now Western Kentucky University), B.A., 1951; Eastern Michigan University, M.A., 1960; Wayne State University, Educational Specialist, 1966. *Politics:* Independent. *Religion:* Protestant. *Home:* 120 Ruff Dr., Monroe, Mich.

CAREER: Teacher in the schools of Trenton, Ky., 1951-55, and Botkins, Ohio, 1955-58; City of Monroe, Michigan, teacher at Custer School, 1958-62, school principal, 1962-69, director of compensatory education, 1969-71, administration assistant, 1971-73, assistant superintendent, 1974—. Military service: U.S. Army, 1945-47; became sergeant. Awards, honors: Awards for innovative programs from Scholastic and Instructor.

WRITINGS: The Education of Disadvantaged Children, Parker Publishing, 1970; (with O. J. Robertson) Hardwood Hero (juvenile), Abingdon, 1971. Contributor of short stories, poems, and articles to periodicals, including Ideals, Progressive Farmer, Outdoor Life, National Motorist, Furrow, and Classmate.

WORK IN PROGRESS: A series of articles on adult basic education.

* * *

BOTTOME, Edgar M. 1937-

PERSONAL: Born March 9, 1937, in Logan, W. Va.; son of Paul Bottome; married, 1972; two children. Education: Vanderbilt University, B.A. (magna cum laude), 1959; Tufts University, M.A., 1960, M.A. in Law and Diplomacy, 1963, Ph.D., 1967. Home: 5 Andrews Lane, Amesbury, Mass. 01913. Office: Goddard College, Plainfield, Vt. 05667.

CAREER: Tufts University, Medford, Mass., instructor in government, 1961-63; Boston University, Boston, Mass., member of faculty, 1963-71, instructor in M.A. program in Heidelberg, Germany, 1967-68; University of Maryland, College Park, instructor in government, 1961-62; Goddard College, Plainfield, Vt., 1970—, currently regional director of graduate program, Boston region. Military service: U.S. Army, 1960-62; became first lieutenant.

WRITINGS: The Missile Gap: A Study of the Formulation of Military and Political Policy, Fairleigh Dickinson University Press, 1971; The Balance of Terror: A Guide to the Arms Race, Beacon Press, 1971. Contributor to Commonweal, Current, Annals of the Academy of Political and Social Sciences, and other periodicals.

* * *

BOUDREAUX, Patricia Duncan 1941-

PERSONAL: Born December 26, 1941, in Baton Rouge, La.; daughter of Thomas M., Jr. (a laboratory technician) and Dorothy (Norman) Duncan; married John Pierre Boudreaux (a teacher and coach), August 28, 1965; children: John Pierre, Jr., Denise Marie, Debbie Ann. Education: Louisiana State University, B.S., 1963, M.S., 1965. Religion: Roman Catholic. Home: 1246 Perkins Rd., Baton Rouge, La. 70806.

CAREER: Teacher of dance in a private school in Baton Rouge, La., 1954-62; Louisiana State University, Baton Rouge, instructor in dance and gymnastics, 1965-67.

WRITINGS: (With Barry L. Johnson) Basic Gymnastics for Girls and Women, Appleton, 1971.†

* * *

BOURDEAUX, Michael 1934-

PERSONAL: Born March 19, 1934, in Praze, Cornwall, England; son of Richard Edward (a master baker) and Lillian (Blair) Bourdeaux; married Gillian Davies, August 27, 1960; children: Karen Jane, Mark David. Education: Attended Truro School, Cornwall; St. Edmund Hall, Oxford, B.A.

(honors in Russian and theology), 1959; studied at Moscow State University, 1959-60; Oxford University, M.A., 1961, B.D., 1968. Religion: Church of England (Episcopalian). Home: 34 Lubbock Rd., Chislehurst, Kent BR7 5JJ, England. Agent: Jonathan Clowes Ltd., 19 Jeffrey's Pl., London NW1 9PP, England. Office: Centre for the Study of Religion and Communism, Keston College, Heathfield Rd., Keston, Kent BR2 6BA, England.

CAREER: Ordained priest in Episcopalian Church, 1960; Centre de Recherches, Geneva, Switzerland, research associate, 1965-68; University of London, London School of Economics and Political Science, London, England, research fellow, 1968-70; Keston College, Keston, England, founder and director, 1969—. Visiting professor, St. Bernard's Seminary, Rochester, N.Y., 1969; research fellow, Royal Institute of International Affairs, 1970-77. Committee member, New Philharmonia Chorus, 1966-76. Military service: Royal Air Force, 1952-54; became flight lieutenant. Member: American Association for the Advancement of Slavic Studies.

WRITINGS: Opium of the People: The Christian Religion in the U.S.S.R., Faber, 1965, Bobbs-Merrill, 1966, 2nd edition, Mowbray, 1977; Religious Ferment in Russia: Protestant Opposition to Soviet Religious Policy, St. Martin's, 1968; (contributor) URSS: Dibattito nella communita cristiana, Jaca Book (Milan), 1968; (contributor) Donald R. Cutler, editor, The Religious Situation in 1969, Beacon Press, 1969; (author of introduction) Rosemary Harris and Xenia Howard-Johnston, editors, Christian Appeals from Russia, Hodder & Stoughton, 1969; (contributor with Peter Reddaway) Max Hayward and W.C. Fletcher, editors, Religion and the Soviet State, Pall Mall, 1969; Patriarch and Prophets: Persecution of the Russian Orthodox Church Today, Praeger, 1970; (editor) Religious Minorities in the Soviet Union, 1960-70, Minority Rights Group, 1970; (contributor) George Schoepflin, editor, The Soviet Union and Eastern Europe: A Handbook, Anthony Blond, 1970; (editor with Howard-Johnston) The Evidence That Convicted Aida Skripnikove, David Cook, 1971. Contributor to Church Times, Christian Century, Tablet, Church of England Newspaper, Problems of Communism, Survey, and Russian Review. Editor, Keston News Service (information service on religion in Communist countries), 1975—, and The Right to Believe (news sheet), 1976—. Founder, Religion in Communist Lands (journal), 1973.

WORK IN PROGRESS: Land of Crosses: The Catholic Church in Lithuania Today; The Unknown Fatherland; general editor of series, "Keston Books" (grouping all new titles and new editions of all old books published in association with Keston College).

SIDELIGHTS: Michael Bourdeaux' books have been translated into Portuguese, Norwegian, Swedish, Dutch, and other languages. He told CA: "The main aim of my work and of Keston College [and] the Centre for the Study of Religion and Communism is to provide factual data on major religious developments in the communist world. We wish to inform churches and universities objectively and thus to build up a sympathetic world public opinion in favour of religious freedom under communism. My 'motivation'—learning at first hand about the persecution of religion in Russia. . . ."

BIOGRAPHICAL/CRITICAL SOURCES: Times Literary Supplement, March 7, 1968; Christian Century, May 29, 1968, July 8, 1970.

BOURNE, Geoffrey Howard 1909-

PERSONAL: Born November 17, 1909, in Perth, Western Australia; came to United States in 1957, naturalized in 1962; son of Walter Howard (a printer) and Mary Anne (Mellon) Bourne; married Gwenllian Myfanwy Jones (a psychologist), December 26, 1935 (divorced, 1964); married Maria Nelly Golarz (a research scientist), October 31, 1966; children: (first marriage) Peter Geoffrey, Merfyn Howard. *Education:* University of Western Australia, B.Sch., 1930, B.Sc. (honors), 1931, M.Sc., 1932; D.Sc., 1935; Oxford University, D.Phil., 1943. *Politics:* None. *Religion:* Episcopalian. *Home:* 849 Lullwater Pkwy., Atlanta, Ga. 30307. *Office:* Yerkes Regional Primate Research Center, Emory University, Atlanta, Ga. 30322.

CAREER: Australian Institute of Anatomy, Canberra, biologist, 1933-35; Commonwealth of Australia Advisory Council on Nutrition, Canberra, biochemist, 1935-37; Oxford University, Oxford, England, Beit Memorial Fellow in Medical Research, 1938-41, demonstrator in physiology, 1941-44, 1946-47; Mackenzie-Mackinnon Research Fellow of Royal College of Physicians, London, England, and Royal College of Surgeons of England, 1941-44; University of London, London, reader in histology at London Hospital Medical College, 1947-57; Emory University, Atlanta, Ga., professor of anatomy and chairman of department, 1957-62, director of Yerkes Regional Primate Research Center, 1962—. *Military service:* British Army, in charge of research and development for Special Forces in South-East Asia, 1944-45, nutritional adviser to Military Administration of Malaya, 1945-46; became lieutenant colonel.

MEMBER: Society for Experimental Biology and Medicine, American Association of Anatomists, Royal Society of Medicine (fellow), Zoological Society (fellow), Nutrition Society, Anatomical Society of Great Britain and Northern Ireland, Gerontological Society (fellow), British Institute of Biology (fellow), International Society for Cell Biology, British Interplanetary Society, Aerospace Medical Association, and more than fifteen other national and international scientific societies; Zoological Society of Atlanta (president).

WRITINGS: Nutrition and the War (based on his series of articles published under a pseudonym in *Discovery,* 1938-39), Cambridge Press, 1940, revised and enlarged edition, Cambridge University Press, 1942, Macmillan (New York), 1943; *War-Time Food for Mother and Child,* Oxford University Press, 1942; *Starvation in Europe,* Allen & Unwin, 1943; *The Mammalian Adrenal Gland,* Clarendon Press, 1949; *How Your Body Works,* Sigma Books, 1949; *Aids to Histology,* 5th edition (Bourne was not associated with earlier editions), Williams & Wilkins, 1950, 7th edition, 1960; *An Introduction to Functional Histology,* Little, Brown, 1953, 2nd edition, 1960; *Vitamin C in the Animal Cell,* Springer-Verlag, 1957; *Division of Labor in Cells,* Academic Press, 1962, 2nd edition, 1970; (with Totada R. Shantha and Sohan L. Manocha) *A Stereotaxic Atlas of the Java Monkey Brain,* Williams & Wilkins, 1968; *The Ape People,* Putnam, 1971; *Primate Odyssey,* Putnam, 1974; *Non-Human Primates and Medical Research,* Academic Press, 1974; (with Maury Cohen) *The Gentle Giants: The Gorilla Story,* Putnam, 1975.

Editor: (And contributor) *Cytology and Cell Physiology,* Clarendon Press, 1942, 3rd edition, Academic Press, 1964; (with George W. Kidder) *Biochemistry and Physiology of Nutrition,* two volumes, Academic Press, 1953; *The Biochemistry and Physiology of Bone,* Academic Press, 1956,

2nd edition, three volumes, 1972; (with William B. Yapp) *The Biology of Ageing,* Hafner, 1957; *The Structure and Function of Muscle,* three volumes, Academic Press, 1960, 2nd edition, four volumes, 1972-73; Vladimir Korenchevsky, *Physiological and Pathological Ageing,* Hafner, 1961; (with Eileen M. H. Wilson as assistant editor) *Structural Aspects of Ageing,* Pitman Medical Publishing, 1961, Hafner, 1962; (with Maurice Sandler) *Atherosclerosis and Its Origin,* Academic Press, 1963; *Medical and Biological Problems of Space Flight* (proceedings of conference held in Nassau, 1961), Academic Press, 1963; (with M. Nelly Golarz) *Muscular Dystrophy in Man and Animals,* Hafner, 1963; *In Vivo Techniques in Histology,* Williams & Wilkins, 1967; *The Structure and Function of Nervous Tissue,* Academic Press, Volume I, 1968, Volumes II-III, 1969, Volumes IV-VI, 1972; *The Chimpanzee,* Volumes I-V, Albert J. Phiebig, 1969-71, Volume VI, S. Karger, 1973.

Editor with J. F. Danielli, *International Review of Cytology* (annual), Academic Press, 1952—; editor, *World Review of Nutrition and Dietetics* (annual), S. Karger, 1959—. Contributor to *Encyclopaedia Britannica* and to medical and scientific journals.

SIDELIGHTS: As director of the institute housing the largest collection of apes in the world, Geoffrey H. Bourne is "intimately concerned with the life, intelligence, relationships of great apes." *Avocational interests:* Gem cutting and polishing, running (held the mile championship in Australia), water skiing, boating.

*   *   *

BOURNE, L(arry) S(tuart) 1939-

PERSONAL: Born December 24, 1939, in London, Ontario, Canada; son of Stuart Howard (a mechanic) and Florence (Adams) Bourne; married Paula O'Neill (an educational researcher), August 14, 1967; children: David Stuart Alexander, Alexandra Lucy Elisabeth. *Education:* University of Western Ontario, B.A. (honors), 1961; University of Alberta, M.A., 1963; University of Chicago, Ph.D., 1966. *Home:* 26 Anderson Ave., Toronto, Ontario, Canada M5P 1H4. *Office:* Centre for Urban and Community Studies, University of Toronto, 159 St. George St., Toronto, Ontario, Canada M5S 1A1.

CAREER: University of Toronto, Toronto, Ontario, assistant professor, 1966-69, associate professor, 1969-73, professor of geography, 1973—, Centre for Urban and Community Studies, associate director, 1969-72, director, 1972—. *Member:* Association of American Geographers, Canadian Association of Geographers, Canadian Association of University Teachers, Urban Studies Association, Regional Science Association, Land Economics Fraternity.

WRITINGS: Private Redevelopment of the Central City, University of Chicago, 1967; (editor) *Internal Structure of the City,* Oxford University Press, 1971; (editor) *Urban Systems Development in Central Canada: Selected Papers,* University of Toronto Press, 1972; (editor) *The Form of Cities in Central Canada,* University of Toronto Press, 1973; (editor) *Urban Futures for Central Canada,* University of Toronto Press, 1974; *Urban Systems: Strategies for Regulation,* Oxford University Press, 1975; (editor) *Systems of Cities,* Oxford University Press, in press.

*   *   *

BOURNE, Ruth M.

PERSONAL: Born in Wheeling, W. Va.; daughter of

Charles L. (a potter) and Grace (Wood) Bourne. *Education:* Indiana University, A.B., 1922, M.A., 1925; Yale University, Ph.D., 1931. *Politics:* Non-partisan. *Religion:* Methodist. *Home:* 4041 Ibis St., Apt. 802, San Diego, Calif. 92103.

CAREER: High school teacher, 1922-29; Bowling Green State University, Bowling Green, Ohio, assistant professor of history, 1931-40; Winthrop College, Rock Hill, S.C., assistant professor of history, 1939-44; California Western University, San Diego, associate professor of history, 1953-64, head of department, 1958-63; American Bibliographical Center, Santa Barbara, Calif., assistant editor of *America: History and Life,* 1964-67. *Awards, honors:* American Association of University Women fellowship, 1929; Fulbright fellowship for research in British West Indies and England, 1952-63; American Philosophical Society grant, 1967.

WRITINGS: Queen Anne's Navy in the West Indies, Yale University Press, 1938, new edition, 1972; (contributor) John Joseph Murray, editor, *Essays in Modern European History,* Indiana University Press, 1951. Contributor of articles to history journals.

WORK IN PROGRESS: A biography of Daniel Parke II, governor of the English Leeward Islands, 1706-1710, *Daniel Parke II and the Virginia Scene, 1669-1710.*

*   *   *

BOWEN, Croswell 1905-1971

February 12, 1905—July 15, 1971; American journalist and author of books on crime. Obituaries: *New York Times,* July 16, 1971.

*   *   *

BOWEN, Desmond 1921-

PERSONAL: Born July 25, 1921, in Ottawa, Ontario, Canada; son of Gordon Titus and Victoria (Reilly) Bowen; married Jean D. Fraser, December 25, 1942; children: Kurt, Deirdre, Patricia, Paul, Caitlin. *Education:* Carleton University, Ottawa, Ontario, B.A. (with honors), 1950; Queen's University, Kingston, Ontario, M.A., 1951, Ph.D., 1955; Repon Hall, Oxford, postdoctoral study, 1955-56. *Home:* 28 Melgund Ave., Ottawa, Ontario, Canada.

CAREER: Ordained minister of Anglican Church of Canada, 1956. Directorate of Naval Intelligence, Ottawa, Ontario, technical officer, 1951-53; Colombo Plan Administration, Ottawa, Ontario, training officer, 1953-54; pastor of Anglican churches in Canada, England, and Ireland, 1956-60; Carleton University, Ottawa, Ontario, assistant professor, 1961-63, associate professor, 1963-68, professor of history, 1968-71; Trinity College, Dublin, Ireland, visiting professor of Irish history, 1971-72. Has done broadcasts over Radio Telefis Eireann, Dublin, and British Broadcasting Corp., Belfast. *Military service:* Royal Air Force, 1941. Royal Canadian Air Force, 1941-45. *Member:* Royal Society of Antiquaries of Ireland.

WRITINGS: The Idea of the Victorian Church: A Study of the Church of England, 1833-1889, McGill University Press, 1968; *Souperism: Myth or Reality,* Mercier Press, 1971; *Protestant Crusade in Ireland,* Gill & Macmillan (Dublin), 1977.

WORK IN PROGRESS: Paul Cullen and Irish Protestantism; Catholics and Protestants in Northern Ireland, 1800-1870.

BOWERS, John 1928-

PERSONAL: Born March 12, 1928, in Lenoir City, Tenn.; son of Tip Richard and Stella (Swafford) Bowers. *Education:* University of Tennessee, B.A., 1951. *Residence:* New York, N.Y. *Agent:* Georges Borchardt, Inc., 145 East 52nd St., New York, N.Y. 10022.

CAREER: U.S. Department of State, Washington, D.C., personnel officer, 1955-62; free-lance writer, New York, N.Y., 1962—. *Military service:* U.S. Army, 1946-47; served in Korea.

WRITINGS—Novels, except as indicated: *The Colony,* Dutton, 1971; *The Golden Bowers* (collection of essays and articles), Tower, 1971; *No More Reunions,* Dutton, 1973; *Helene,* Ballantine, 1976.

WORK IN PROGRESS: A novel.

SIDELIGHTS: John Bowers told *CA:* "Most of my education, in the positive sense, came outside of standard ways. Coming across a contraband copy of Henry Miller's work in Tennessee in the early 1950's had a most liberating effect upon me. I found out about the 'real' world in the Army, in holding menial jobs while bumming around on the West Coast, and while working, miraculously, for a few years as a Personnel Officer in the State Department."

*   *   *

BOWIE, Norman E. 1942-

PERSONAL: Born June 6, 1942, in Biddeford, Me.; son of Lawrence Walker (a retail manager) and Helen (Jacobsen) Bowie; married Bonnie Bankert, June 11, 1966; children: Brian, Peter. *Education:* Bates College, A.B., 1964; Union Theological Seminary, New York, N.Y., additional study, 1964; University of Rochester, Ph.D., 1968. *Politics:* Democrat. *Home:* 3 Woodsman Dr., Newark, Del. 19711. *Office:* Department of Philosophy, University of Delaware, Newark, Del. 19711.

CAREER: Lycoming College, Williamsport, Pa., assistant professor of philosophy, 1968-69; Hamilton College, Clinton, N.Y., assistant professor 1969-74, associate professor of philosophy, 1974-77; University of Delaware, Newark, director of Center for the Study of Values, 1977—. *Member:* American Philosophical Association (executive secretary, 1972-77), American Association of University Professors, American Association for the Advancement of Science, Society for Political and Legal Philosophy, Canadian Philosophical Association, Phi Beta Kappa.

WRITINGS: Towards a New Theory of Distributive Justice, University of Massachusetts, 1971; (with Robert L. Simon) *The Individual and the Political Order,* Prentice-Hall, 1977. Contributor of articles and reviews to professional journals.

WORK IN PROGRESS: An anthology on business ethics, with Thomas Beauchamp.

*   *   *

BOWLES, D(elbert) Richard 1910-

PERSONAL: Born August 15, 1910, in Miami, Okla.; son of George Richard (a farmer) and Lyda (Allen) Bowles; married Willie D. Worley (a school librarian), April 9, 1939; children: David R., Barbara Allen (Mrs. David Michael O'-Connell). *Education:* Sam Houston State College (now University), student, 1927-29; Southern Methodist University, B.S., 1931; University of Texas at Austin, M.Ed., 1938, Ph.D., 1952. *Politics:* Democrat. *Religion:* United

Methodist. *Home address:* P.O. Box 347, San Marcos, Tex. 78666.

CAREER: Teacher of social studies and mathematics in public schools of Flomot, Tex., 1933-34, and Humble, Tex., 1934-36; teacher and administrator in elementary schools of Beeville, Tex., 1936-39, and Austin, Tex., 1939-67; Southwest Texas State University, San Marcos, associate professor of education, 1967-75. Visiting summer lecturer at Texas A&M University, 1946, 1947, Sam Houston State College (now University), 1951, West Virginia University, 1953, University of California, Berkeley, 1955, Louisiana State University, 1957, and University of Texas at Austin, 1952, 1966-68. Member of Texas board of governors, Educators Security Insurance Co., 1965-71. Consultant, Character Education Project, Columbia University. *Military service:* U.S. Army Air Forces, 1942-45.

MEMBER: National Education Association, Association for Childhood Education International, United States Metric Association, Inc., Texas State Teachers Association (president, 1960-61), Texas Committee for Public Education (vice-president, 1964-66), Sigma Delta Chi, Phi Delta Kappa.

WRITINGS: (Contributor) M. E. DeVault, editor, *Improving Mathematics Programs,* C. E. Merrill, 1961; (contributor) T. R. Porter, compiler, *Physical Science Teaching Tips from The Science Teacher,* National Science Teachers Association, 1967; *Effective Elementary School Administration,* Parker Publishing, 1968; *Make Way for Metrication,* Lerner, 1975. Also author of two sound-filmstrip series, "Early Texas Homes," 1970, and "The Metric System," 1974. Contributor of articles and reviews to education journals. Member of editorial board, *Journal of Educational Trends.*

* * *

BOWLES, Edmund A(ddison)   1925-

PERSONAL: Born March 24, 1925, in Cambridge, Mass.; son of Edward L. (a consulting engineer) and Lois (Wuerpel) Bowles; married Marianne von Recklinghausen (an artist), June 4, 1952; children: Margaret Anne, David Addison. *Education:* Swarthmore College, B.A., 1949; Berkshire Music Center, Diploma, 1949; Yale University, Ph.D., 1966. *Politics:* None. *Religion:* None. *Home:* 3234 Valley Lane, Falls Church, Va. 22044.

CAREER: Massachusetts Institute of Technology, Cambridge, instructor in humanities department, 1951-55; Bell Telephone Laboratories, Murray Hill, N.J., staff member of publications department, 1955-59; IBM Corp., New York, N.Y., assistant manager of department of arts and sciences, 1959-66, manager of professional activities in department of university relations, Armonk, N.Y., 1964-67, senior program administrator in humanities, libraries, museums, public sector industry marketing, Washington, D.C., 1968—. Orchestral musician (timpanist). Lectured in Europe on library automation, 1970, 1971. Vice-president, Westchester Symphony Orchestra, 1963-64; member of board of directors, Clarion Concerts and Music for Westchester, 1964-65; associate director, Dupont Circle Consortium, 1971-75; president, Northern Virginia Youth Symphony, 1974-76. Consultant to Lincoln Center Library-Museum of the Performing Arts, 1964-65. *Military service:* U.S. Army, 1943-46; became staff sergeant. U.S. Army Reserve, 1950-70; became major.

MEMBER: American Association of Museums, American Musicological Society (council member, 1966-70), American

Musical Instrument Society, American Association for Information Science (liaison representative from Music Library Association, 1970-75), International Musicological Society, Mediaeval Academy of America, Fellowship of Makers and Restorers of Ancient Instruments (London; fellow). *Awards, honors:* Grant from American Council of Learned Societies, 1964-65, and from National Endowment for the Humanities, 1971-72.

WRITINGS: (Contributor) Jan LaRue, editor, *Aspects of Medieval and Renaissance Music,* Norton, 1966; (editor) *Computers in Humanistic Research: Readings and Perspectives,* Prentice-Hall, 1967; (contributor) Harry B. Lincoln, editor, *Music and the Computer: Composition and Research,* Cornell University Press, 1968. Also author of *Musical Life and Performance Practices in the Fifteenth Century,* 1977. Contributor of about forty articles and reviews to computer journals and to music journals in the United States and Europe.

WORK IN PROGRESS: Musical Instruments in Late Medieval Festivities; Technological Innovations in Nineteenth-Century Timpani.

* * *

BOWMAN, Frank Paul   1927-

PERSONAL: Born June 12, 1927, in Portland, Ore.; son of Frank George and Mary (Pahl) Bowman. *Education:* Reed College, B.A., 1949; Yale University, M.A., 1952, Ph.D., 1955. *Politics:* Democrat. *Religion:* Episcopal. *Home:* 1810 South Rittenhouse Sq., Philadelphia, Pa. 19103. *Office:* Williams Hall, University of Pennsylvania, Philadelphia, Pa. 19174.

CAREER: University of California, Berkeley, assistant professor of French, 1954-62; Reed College, Portland, Ore., associate professor of French, 1962-63; University of Pennsylvania, Philadelphia, associate professor, 1963-67, professor of French, 1967—. *Military service:* U.S. Army, 1944-45. *Member:* Association Internationale des Etudes Francaises, Modern Language Association of America, Modern Humanities Research Association, Societe des Etudes Romantiques (director), Phi Beta Kappa. *Awards, honors:* Guggenheim fellow, 1968-69.

WRITINGS: Prosper Merimee: Heroism, Pessimism, and Irony, University of California Press, 1962; *Montaigne: Essays* (critical analysis), Edward Arnold, 1965; *Eliphas Levi: Visionnaire romantique,* Presses Universitaires de France, 1969; *Le Christ romantique,* Droz, 1972.

* * *

BOWMAN, LeRoy   1887-1971

November 21, 1887—September 30, 1971; American educator and sociologist. Obituaries: *New York Times,* October 1, 1971.

* * *

BOWMAN, Mary Jean   1908-

PERSONAL: Born October 17, 1908, in New York, N.Y.; daughter of Harold Martin (a professor) and Mary (Kauffman) Bowman; married C. Arnold Anderson (a professor), July 18, 1943; children: Lloyd Barr. *Education:* Vassar College, B.A., 1930; Radcliffe College, M.A., 1932; Harvard University, Ph.D., 1938. *Politics:* Independent. *Religion:* Protestant. *Home:* 5650 Dorchester Ave., Chicago, Ill. 60637. *Office:* Department of Economics, University of Chicago, Chicago, Ill. 60637.

CAREER: Massachusetts Women's State Prison, social case worker and researcher, 1932-34; U.S., Department of Agriculture, Northwest Central Region, director of consumer purchases studies, 1935-36; Iowa State College (now University), Ames, member of Economics Department faculty, 1936-43; U.S. Department of Labor, Washington, D.C., senior economist, 1945-46; University of California, Berkeley, member of Economics Department faculty, 1948-49; Resources for the Future, New York, N.Y., writer and researcher, 1957-60; University of Chicago, Chicago, Ill., professor of economics and education, 1958—. Teacher, University of Minnesota, summer, 1941; visiting professor at Upsala University, Sweden, 1974, and London School of Economics and Political Science, University of London, 1975. Trustee, Teachers Insurance and Annuity Association, 1972-76. Consultant to UNESCO, U.S. Bureau of the Census, National Institute of Education, Greek Ministry of Education, and Ford Foundation.

MEMBER: American Economic Association (member of executive committee), Econometric Society, National Bureau of Economic Research (member of conference on income and wealth), Social Science Research Council (member of committee for business enterprise research, 1954-58; member of committee on graduate record examinations in economics, 1956-58), International Association for Research in Income and Wealth, Southern Economic Association, Phi Beta Kappa. *Awards, honors:* Fulbright research scholar, Sweden, 1955-56; Fulbright visiting distinguished professor, University of Zagreb, Yugoslavia, 1973; Guggenheim fellow, Sweden, 1974.

WRITINGS: (With Lee Bach) *Economic Analysis and Public Policy,* Prentice-Hall, 1943, 2nd edition, 1949; (editor) *Expectations, Uncertainty and Business Behavior,* Social Science Research Council, 1958; (with W. Warren Haynes) *Resources and People in East Kentucky,* Johns Hopkins University, 1963; (editor with husband, C. A. Anderson) *Education and Economic Development,* Aldine, 1965; (with H. Dudley Plunkett) *Elites and Change in the Kentucky Mountains,* University Press of Kentucky, 1972; (with C. A. Anderson and Vincent Tinto) *Where Colleges Are and Who Attends,* McGraw, 1972; *School and the Future in Japan,* Tokyo University Press, 1977. Contributor of articles on economics of education, regional development, poverty, and income distribution to professional journals.

WORK IN PROGRESS: Research on schooling and labor markets in Japan; *Economics of Education in a World of Change.*

* * *

BOWMAN, Paul Hoover 1914-

PERSONAL: Born June 20, 1914, in Philadelphia, Pa.; son of Paul Haynes (an edcuator) and Flora (Hoover) Bowman; married Evelyn Stouffer, April 11, 1942; children: Richard, Marilyn, Douglas, Debora. *Education:* Bridgewater College, A.B., 1934; University of Pennsylvania, A.M., 1938; Crozer Theological Seminary, B.D., 1938; University of Chicago, Ph.D., 1951. *Religion:* Church of the Brethren. *Home:* 8724 West 67th St., Shawnee Mission, Kan. 66202. *Office:* Institute for Community Studies, University of Missouri, 2 West 40th, Kansas City, Mo. 64111.

CAREER: American Friends Service Committee, administrator of war relief in Spain and France, 1938-40; Brethren Service Committee, international representative in South America, 1940-44; University of Louisville, Louisville, Ky., assistant professor of psychology, 1948-52; University of

Chicago, Chicago, Ill., research associate in human development, 1952-62; Mental Health Foundation, Kansas City, Mo., director of department of prevention, 1962-64; University of Missouri—Kansas City, professor of psychology and executive director of Institute for Community Studies, 1964—. Member of advisory committee on youth employment, U.S. Department of Labor, 1962-63, and of review panel, National Institute of Mental Health, 1963-65. Member of national board, Church of the Brethren. Member of board of Park College, McPherson College, and of Urban Coalition, Metropolitan Kansas City. Consultant to Department of Health, Puerto Rico, 1960, and to Ministry of Education, Brazil, 1961, 1963, 1965.

MEMBER: American Psychological Association, American Educational Research Association. *Awards, honors:* Research grants from National Institute of Mental Health and U.S. Office of Education, at intervals, 1957-65; LL.D., Bridgewater College, 1962.

WRITINGS: (With Harold S. Guetzkow) *Men and Hunger,* Elgin Press, 1946; (with others) *Studying Children and Training Counselors* (monograph), University of Chicago Press, 1953; (with others) *Mobilizing Community Resources for Youth* (monograph), University of Chicago Press, 1956; (with Robert J. Havighurst and others) *Growing Up in River City,* Wiley, 1962.

Contributor: Alexander Frazier, editor, *New Insights and the Curriculum,* National Education Association, 1963; Milton Kornrich, editor, *Underachievement,* C. C Thomas, 1965; Robert Strom, editor, *Inner City Classroom,* C. E. Merrill, 1966. Contributor to sociology and education journals.

* * *

BOWSER, Pearl 1931-
(Joan Bowser)

PERSONAL: Born June 25, 1931, in New York, N.Y.; daughter of William (a postal clerk) and Pearl (Bradley) Johnson; married Leroy Bowser (an urban planner), October 15, 1955; children: Jora, Gillian. *Education:* Attended Brooklyn College (now Brooklyn College of the City University of New York), 1949-51; also attended Brooklyn Museum Art School and New School for Social Research; New York University, Motion Picture Specialist, 1977. *Home:* 71 Joralemon St., Brooklyn, N.Y. 11201. *Office:* Tuesday Publications, 437 Madison Ave., New York, N.Y. 10022.

CAREER: Columbia Broadcasting System, New York City, television and radio researcher, 1956-59; Filmakers, New York City, production assistant, researcher, and unit manager, 1959-61; Tuesday Publications, New York City, food editor of *Tuesday* magazine under name Joan Bowser, 1966—. Administrator, Southern Christian Leadership Conference art show honoring Martin Luther King, Jr. at Museum of Modern Art, 1968-69; executive director, Chamba Educational Film Services, 1970—. Assistant manager of audience development, Brooklyn Academy of Music, 1970-71; teacher of Black film history, Rutgers University, 1972; lecturer to numerous colleges, universities, and community groups throughout the United States and Canada. Co-host of weekly television program, "Up South News," on the Brooklyn College Network; panelist and guest on various television and radio shows, primarily in the area of Black films and filmaking. Judge, Film Workshop, Philadelphia, and Black Film Festival. Consultant, WETA-TV, Washington, D.C., and Oscar Micheaux Awards presentations, Oakland, Calif., 1974-76.

MEMBER: National Association of Media Women (treasurer, New York City chapter), Association of Black Artists (founding member), Experimental Intermedia Foundation, Brooklyn Cultural League, Willowtown Association (president).

WRITINGS: (Editor) *Tuesday's Soul Food Cookbook,* Bantam, 1969; (with Joan Eckstein) *A Pinch of Soul,* Avon, 1970.

WORK IN PROGRESS: A biography of Oscar Micheaux, black film-maker, 1918-1940.

* * *

BOYD, James M(oore) 1919-

PERSONAL: Born April 15, 1919, in San Francisco, Calif.; son of James (a business executive) and Elizabeth (Dundas) Boyd; married Vera L. Miller, January 28, 1944; children: James Moore, Jr. *Education:* University of California, Berkeley, B.A., 1940, M.A., 1951; Columbia University, Ph.D., 1968. *Home:* 1312 East Shore Dr., Alameda, Calif. 94501. *Office:* Department of Political Science, University of California, Berkeley, Calif. 94720.

CAREER: U.S. Air Force, 1940-69; commissioned 2nd lieutenant, 1940; served in European Theater on War Department General Staff, as chief of military personnel in Germany, and later as commandant of cadets at Advanced Flying School, 1940-51; served at Pentagon Hq. USAF, as deputy assistant director of plans, chief of policy division, and chief of foreign agreements division, as air attache at U.S. Embassy in Cairo, and as U.S. Air Force representative to the Department of State, 1951-65; military advisor, chief of staff of military staff committee and member of U.S. delegation to United Nations, 1965-69; retired as colonel; University of California at Berkeley and University of California Extension, lecturer, 1970-71; affiliated with department of political science, University of California, Berkeley, 1972—. *Member:* American Political Science Association, Air Force Association, Commonwealth Club of California, Pi Sigma Alpha. *Awards, honors*—Military: Silver Star, Legion of Merit with oak leaf cluster, Bronze Star Medal with oak leaf cluster, Commendation Medal, Purple Heart.

WRITINGS: United Nations Peace-Keeping Operations: A Military and political Appraisal, Praeger, 1971. Contributor to *International Organization.*

* * *

BOYUM, Joy Gould 1934-
(Joy Gould)

PERSONAL: Born December 8, 1934, in New York, N.Y.; daughter of David (a businessman) and Beatrice (Levine) Gould; married Asmund Andersen Boyum (a chemical engineer), September 5, 1960; children: David, Ingrid. *Education:* Barnard College, Columbia University, B.A., 1955; New York University, M.A., 1957, Ph.D., 1962. *Home:* 45 Remsen St., Brooklyn, N.Y. 11201. *Office:* Department of English, New York University, Washington Square, New York, N.Y. 10003.

CAREER: New York University, New York, N.Y., 1960—, began as associate professor, currently professor of English. *Member:* Modern Language Association of America, National Council of Teachers of English, National Society of Film Critics, New York Film Critics Circle (vice-chairman, 1976; chairman, 1977).

WRITINGS: (With Adrienne Scott) *Film as Film,* Allyn & Bacon, 1971; (contributor) *Movie Comedy,* Grossman, 1977.

Contributor to *Encyclopedia Brittanica* and *World Book Encyclopedia Yearbook.* Regular contributor to columns ''On Film'' and ''On Television'' in *Wall Street Journal;* contributor of articles to *Television Quarterly, English Journal, Teachers College Record,* and *Scholastic Teacher;* contributor of poetry under name Joy Gould to *Folder.*

* * *

BRACEWELL-MILNES, (John) Barry 1931-

PERSONAL: Born December 29, 1931, in Wallington, Surrey, England; son of Henry (an actuary) and Kathleen (Hill) Bracewell-Milnes. *Education:* New College, Oxford, B.A., 1956, M.A., 1958; King's College, Cambridge, Ph.D., 1959. *Religion:* Church of England. *Home:* 26 Lancaster Ct., Banstead, Surrey, England.

CAREER: Iron and Steel Board, London, England, economist, 1960-63; Federation of British Industries, London, economist, 1964-65; Confederation of British Industry, London, assistant economic director, 1965-67, deputy economic director, 1967-68, economic director, 1968-73; author and consultant, 1973—. *Military service:* British Army, 1950-51; became lieutenant. *Member:* Royal Statistical Society (fellow), Institute of Statisticians (fellow), International Fiscal Association, Montpelerin Society, Society of Business Economists, Society of Authors.

WRITINGS: The Cost of Cutting Taxes, Manchester Statistical Society, 1969; (contributor) Vito Tanzi and others, editors, *Taxation: A Radical Approach,* Transatlantic, 1970; *The Measurement of Fiscal Policy: An Analysis of Tax Systems in Terms of the Political Distinction between ''Right'' and ''Left,''* Confederation of British Industry, 1971; (contributor) Peter Ady, editor, *Private Foreign Investment and the Developing World,* Praeger, 1971; *Pay and Price Control Guide,* Butterworth & Co., 1973; *The Counter-Inflation Act, 1973,* Butterworth & Co., 1973; *Is Capital Taxation Fair?,* Institute of Directors, 1974; *Eastern and Western Economic Integration,* St. Martin's, 1976 (published in England as *Economic Integration in East and West,* Croom Helm, 1976); *The Camel's Back: An International Comparison of Tax Burdens,* Centre for Policy Studies, 1976. Also author of numerous pamphlets on economics and taxes. Contributor to proceedings and other publications of economic organizations; contributor of articles to journals.

WORK IN PROGRESS: Three books, *Investment Incentives, Industry Under Attack: How Taxes Frustrate the Creation of Wealth,* for Centre for Policy Studies, and *Tax Avoidance and Evasion: Political Power versus Economic Law.*

SIDELIGHTS: Barry Bracewell-Milnes explained to *CA:* ''My professional interest is market economics in general and fiscal economics, especially the economics of personal taxation, in particular. The core of my published work has been concerned with the politics, logic and mathematics of personal taxation, and I have a substantial programme in mind to take this work further.'' *Avocational interests:* Music, travel.

* * *

BRADFORD, Patience Andrewes 1918-
(Patience Andrewes)

PERSONAL: Born April 21, 1918, in Plymouth, Devonshire, England; daughter of Hugh and Edith (Tapson) Andrewes; married John Bradford (an archaeologist), December 11, 1948 (deceased). *Education:* Attended Queen

Anne's School, Caversham, England and Courtauld Institute of Art; Sorbonne, University of Paris, Diplome. *Politics:* Conservative. *Religion:* Church of England. *Home:* 12 Winchester Rd., Oxford OX2 6NA, Oxfordshire, England.

CAREER: During World War II was an education officer, and worked at the War Office; also has taught for Oxford Extramural Delegacy; Oxford University Press, London, England, illustrations editor in education department, 1960-63.

WRITINGS—All under name Patience Andrewes: *A Thirteenth Century Villein,* Oxford University Press, 1962; *Frederick II of Hohenstaufen,* Oxford University Press, 1970.

WORK IN PROGRESS: An illustrated book on the history and development of English agriculture Norman to nineteenth century, for G. Bell.

SIDELIGHTS: Patience Bradford used to travel about the Mediterranean with her archeologist husband, but now she is confined to a wheelchair.

*   *   *

BRADLEY, Harold Whitman 1903-

PERSONAL: Born July 9, 1903, in Greenwood, R.I.; son of Harold E. and Lillian (Whitman) Bradley; married Elizabeth Forbes, August 28, 1940; married second wife, Pearle E. Quinn (a university professor), December 5, 1947; children: (first marriage) Anne Elizabeth; (second marriage) David Whitman. *Education:* Pomona College, B.A., 1925, M.A., 1926; Stanford University, Ph.D., 1932. *Politics:* Democrat. *Religion:* Methodist. *Home:* 212 Craighead Ave., Nashville, Tenn. 37205. *Office:* Department of History, University of Tennessee, Nashville, Tenn.

CAREER: High school teacher in Burbank, Calif., 1926-27; Santa Barbara State Teachers College (now University of California, Santa Barbara), instructor in history, 1929-30; Stanford University, Stanford, Calif., instructor in history, 1930-36, assistant professor of history, 1936-42, associate professor of history, 1942-45; University of Washington, Seattle, assistant professor of history, 1938-39; Claremont Graduate School, Claremont, Calif., dean, 1945-53, professor of history, 1953-54; Vanderbilt University, Nashville, Tenn., professor of history, 1954-72, professor emeritus, 1972—, chairman of department, 1954-62; University of Tennessee at Nashville, lecturer in history, 1973—. Member of Tennessee House of Representatives, 1964-72; alternate delegate to Democratic National Convention, 1952.

MEMBER: American Historical Association, Organization of American Historians, American Studies Association (president of Kentucky-Tennessee chapter, 1956-57; member of national council, 1972-75), Southern Historical Association, Phi Beta Kappa. *Awards, honors:* Albert J. Beveridge Prize, American Historical Association, 1943, for *American Frontier in Hawaii: 1789-1843.*

WRITINGS: American Frontier in Hawaii: 1789-1843, Stanford University, 1942; *The United States: 1492-1877,* Scribner, 1972; *The United States from 1865,* Scribner, 1973. Contributor to *Encyclopaedia Britannica* and *Collier's Encyclopedia Yearbook.* Member of board of editors, *Pacific Historical Review,* 1940-54, and *Mississippi Valley Historical Review,* 1946-49.

*   *   *

BRADLEY, R. C. 1929-

PERSONAL: Born August 29, 1929, in Windsor, Mo.; son

of Beecher Floyd and Zella Fern (Morgan) Bradley; married Marilyn Elizabeth Brown, June 3, 1962; children: R. C., Jr., Danny Ray. *Education:* Central Missouri State College (now University), B.S., 1950, M.S., 1955, Educational Specialist Degree, 1962; University of Missouri, Ed.D., 1963. *Religion:* Baptist. *Home:* 2032 Houston Pl., Denton, Tex. 76201. *Office:* Elementary Division, Education Building, North Texas State University, Denton, Tex. 76203.

CAREER: Public schools of Clinton, Mo., elementary teacher, 1950-57, principal, 1957-59; University of Missouri, Columbia, instructor in Laboratory School, 1959-63; North Texas State University, Denton, professor of elementary education, 1963—. Conducts lecturers and presentations on education throughout the U.S. Member of board of directors, Reading and Adult Literacy Council, Denton, 1964—. *Member:* National Education Association (life member), International Reading Association, Association for Supervision and Curriculum Development, American Association of University Professors, Texas Association for Supervision and Curriculum Development (member of board of directors, 1969—), Texas Elementary Principals and Supervision Association. Aero-Space Educational Council, Phi Delta Kappa.

WRITINGS—Published by University Press (Wolf City, Tex.), except as noted: *The Education of Exceptional Children,* 1970, revised edition, 1975; *Parent-Teacher Interviews: A Modern Concept of Oral Reporting,* 1971; *Improving Instruction of the Experienced Teacher,* 1974; *The Beginning Elementary School Teacher in Action,* 1974; *Jesus: The Greatest Master Teacher of Us All,* 1976; *The Role of the School in Driving Little Boys Sane,* Bassi Association, 1976; *Instructional Design and Strategies for Increasing Teaching Power,* 1977. Writer of monographs; contributor of more than one hundred articles to education journals. Editor of *Journal* of Texas Elementary Principals and Supervisors Association, 1970—, and *Journal* of Texas Association for Supervision and Curriculum Development, 1970—.

WORK IN PROGRESS: Motivating Secondary School Students: How to Perform the Miracle, for Bassi Association.

SIDELIGHTS: R. C. Bradley told *CA:* "What prompts my delving into educational issues? The belief that schools can be better than they are. No teacher gets up in the morning and goes to school with the intent of harming anybody. But even well-meaning persons unwittingly, unconsciously, and unknowingly can affect people in negative ways. Consequently, I believe that my work invites the teacher to look at the positive side of teaching, and by so doing, simply knowing certain data and information causes her/him to change because he is moved to really want to. What education needs is more teachers who do what they ought rather than what they want. Educators must change."

*   *   *

BRADY, Irene 1943-

PERSONAL: Born December 29, 1943, in Oregon; daughter of Dave (a farmer) and Gwynne (Cumberland) Brady; married Larry Kistler (a phlebotonist), April 4, 1969. *Education:* Oregon College of Art, B.P.A., 1975. *Residence:* Medford, Ore.

CAREER: Writer and illustrator, 1964—; botanical illustrator, Botanical Museum, Harvard University, 1968-70; illustrator and writer for *Audubon* and *Ranger Ricks Nature Magazine,* 1969-77; college instructor in book illustration,

Ashland, Ore., 1974—. Member of board of directors, Oregon College of Art. *Member:* National Audubon Society, National Wildlife Foundation, Zero Population Growth. *Awards, honors:* Outstanding Science Books for Children award, National Science Teachers Assocaition and Children's Book Council, 1974, for *Owlet, the Great Horned Owl.*

WRITINGS—Self-illustrated juveniles: *America's Horses and Ponies,* Houghton, 1969; *A Mouse Named Mus,* Houghton, 1972; *Owlet, the Great Horned Owl,* Houghton, 1974; *Wild Mouse,* Scribner, 1976; *Doodlebug,* Houghton, 1977.

WORK IN PROGRESS: Books about animals for younger children.

SIDELIGHTS: Irene Brady writes: "My main goal in writing is to impart important information about the fantastic world we live in to children in an interesting manner, and to also hold the attention and interest of any adult who may get stuck reading the book to a youngster. Several things are fundamental to me in communicating to others what I want to share about nature. One item is accuracy, another is detail, and yet another is the beauty, perfection and rightness of nearly all things in their natural state.... My illustrations, which take more time and involvement than the writing, attempt to do the same things in an artistic fashion, closely meshing the story with reality and detail in the overall picture of wilderness habitat.... One of my less agreeable habits (in a social sense) is stopping suddenly on highways to pick up dead animals (road casualties), then storing them in my freezer for later sketching. I enjoy improvising on the piano, traveling, and reading."

* * *

BRAINERD, Barron 1928-

PERSONAL: Born April 13, 1928, in New York, N.Y.; Canadian citizen; son of John Bliss and June (Wilson) Brainerd; married Marilyn Alger Crowe, 1975. *Education:* Attended University of Chicago, 1943-45; Massachusetts Institute of Technology, S.B., 1949; University of Michigan, M.S., 1951, Ph.D., 1954. *Home:* 53 Wolfrey Ave., Toronto, Ontario, Canada. *Office:* Department of Mathematics, University of Toronto, Toronto, Ontario, Canada.

CAREER: New Bedford Textile Institute, New Bedford, Mass., instructor in mathematics, 1949-50; University of British Columbia, Vancouver, instructor in mathematics, 1954-57; University of Western Ontario, London, assistant professor of mathematics, 1957-59; University of Toronto, Toronto, Ontario, assistant professor, 1959-62, associate professor, 1962-67, professor of mathematics 1967—, professor of linguistics, 1973—. Visiting senior research fellow, Australian National University, 1962-63. *Member:* Canadian Linguistic Association, Canadian Mathematical Congress, Linguistic Society of America, Australian Mathematical Society, American Association for the Advancement of Science, Classification Society, London Mathematical Society. *Awards, honors:* Summer Research Institute fellowships, Canadian Mathematical Congress, 1956-59; Nuffield fellowship, 1960.

WRITINGS: (With others) *Topics in Mathematics,* four volumes, Ryserson, 1966; (contributor) H. Brandt Corstius, editor, *Grammars for Number Names,* Dordrecht, 1968; (with others) *Foundations of Analysis,* Appleton, 1971; *Introduction to the Mathematics of Language Study,* American Elsevier, 1971; *Weighing Evidence in Language and Literature: A Statistical Approach,* University of Toronto

Press, 1974. Contributor to *Canadian Journal of Mathematics, Canadian Mathematical Bulletin, Journal of Mathematical Analysis and Applications, Foundations of Language, Information and Control,* and other journals in Canada, Europe, Japan, Australia, and the United States.

* * *

BRAKEL, Samuel J(ohannes) 1943-

PERSONAL: Born November 10, 1943, in Lisse, Netherlands; son of Willem (an economist) and Henriette (de Hoest) Brakel; married Linda F. Stowell, November 2, 1968; children: Lia, Christian. *Education:* Davidson College, A.B., 1965; University of Chicago Law School, J.D., 1968. *Politics:* Independent. *Religion:* Atheist. *Home:* 3502 Golfview Dr., Hazel Crest, Ill. 60429. *Office:* American Bar Foundation, 115 East 60th St., Chicago, Ill. 60637.

CAREER: American Bar Foundation, Chicago, Ill., research attorney, 1969—.

WRITINGS—Published by American Bar Foundation, except as indicated: (Editor with Ronald S. Rock) *The Mentally Disabled and the Law,* revised edition (Brakel was not associated with earlier edition), University of Chicago Press, 1971; *Wisconsin Judicare: A Preliminary Appraisal,* 1972; *Free Legal Services for the Poor: Staffed Office Vs. Judicare,* 1973; *Judicare: Public Funds, Private Lawyers, and Poor People,* 1974; *Presumption, Bias, and Incompetency in the Criminal Process,* 1975; (with Wallace Loh) *Regulating the Multistate Practice of Law,* 1975. Contributor to *Denver Law Journal, American Criminal Law Quarterly,* and *American Bar Association Journal.*

WORK IN PROGRESS: Legal Problems of the Institutionalized; Mental Disability and the Law.

* * *

BRANDEN, Nathaniel 1930-

PERSONAL: Surname legally changed to Branden in early 1950's; born April 9, 1930, in Brampton, Ontario, Canada; came to United States, 1949, naturalized, 1965; son of Joseph and Dinah (Copp) Blumenthal; married Barbara Weidman (a writer), January, 1953 (divorced, 1968); married Patrecia Gullison (an actress under name Patrecia Wynand), November 7, 1969 (died March 31, 1977). *Education:* Attended University of California, Los Angeles, 1949-51; New York University, B.A., 1954, M.A., 1956; California Graduate Institute, Ph.D., 1973. *Politics:* Libertarian. *Religion:* Atheist. *Agent:* Gerard McCauley, P.O. Box 456, Cranbury, N.J. 08512. *Office:* Biocentric Institute, 9255 Sunset Blvd., Los Angeles, Calif. 90069.

CAREER: Psychologist, licensed in New Jersey, Pennsylvania, and the District of Columbia; marriage, family, and child counselor, licensed in California; private practice of psychotherapy, 1956—. Nathaniel Branden Institute (adult education in philosophy and psychology), New York, N.Y., founder and president, 1958-68; Biocentric Institute (research, teaching, therapy), Los Angeles, Calif., executive director, 1968—, conductor of workshop/intensive, "Self-Esteem and the Art of Being." Lecturer in biology and psychology at University of Southern California, 1969; guest lecturer at universities in United States and Canada. *Member:* American Psychological Association, American Association for the Advancement of Science, American Association of Marriage and Family Counselors, American Association of Group Psychotherapy, Academy of Psychologists in Marital Therapy, California State Marriage Counseling Association, California Psychology Association.

WRITINGS: Who Is Ayn Rand?: An Analysis of the Novels of Ayn Rand (includes biographical essay by former wife, Barbara Branden), Random House, 1962; (contributor) Ayn Rand, *The Virtue of Selfishness: A New Concept of Egoism,* New American Library, 1964; (contributor) Ayn Rand, *Capitalism: The Unknown Ideal,* New American Library, 1966; *The Psychology of Self-Esteem: A New Concept of Man's Psychological Nature,* Nash Publishing, 1969; *Breaking Free: Introducing a New Technique of Psychological Self-Exploration,* Nash Publishing, 1970; *The Disowned Self,* Nash Publishing, 1972. Co-founder, with Ayn Rand and contributor, *Objectivist Newsletter,* 1962-65, and its successor, *Objectivist,* 1966-68. Contributor of articles to anthologies and professional journals.

SIDELIGHTS: One of the most frequent associations made when discussing Nathaniel Branden and the psychology of self-esteem involves the name of Ayn Rand. A colleague of Miss Rand for many years until their disassociation in 1968, Branden was responsible for the popularization of Objectivist philosophy as it appeared in such Rand novels as *The Fountainhead* and *Atlas Shrugged.* It follows then that Branden's first book would be about Rand and her Objectivist teachings. A *Kirkus Review* critic writes that Branden, in his book *Who Is Ayn Rand?,* "has supplied precisely what her admirers will appreciate: a subtle but utterly explicit refutation of almost every direct attack and every indirect argument raised since *Atlas Shrugged* touched off a modern crusade more than four years ago. To his credit, however, Branden does not merely stand on the defensive. Deftly, he illuminates the cardinal principles at the base of Ayn Rand's ethical system." A *San Francisco Chronicle* reporter, however, does not agree: "The essays are indecently biased toward the philosophies which Ayn Rand has unfolded via her four novels about heroic individuals 'as people might or should be.' ... As literary analysis, it does clear up some of the mysteries of the woman's writings, but as informative literature, it is too slanted to be very valuable."

In an interview with the staff of *Reason* magazine, Branden discussed his former alliance with Ayn Rand and stated that in spite of his personal alienation from her, he still regards Rand as "one of the greatest minds in history—and the greatest novelist that I have ever read." Branden added some personal insights into the character of Ayn Rand when he stated that: "to attack a person's mental processes, or their motives, in the case of disagreements, was one of her favorite strategies. She taught her whole circle to do it. ... All of her friends, all of the circle of which I was a member, were in terror of her. ... What makes the story so tragic is that there is a whole other side of Ayn Rand which is benevolent, generous, innocent, magnanimous."

Although no longer involved with the teaching of Objectivism as a philosophy, some of its basic principles are contained in his current psychological theories, first introduced in 1969 with the publication of *The Psychology of Self-Esteem.* According to the publisher of this book the central theme is "the role of self-esteem in man's life: the need of self-esteem, the nature of that need, the conditions of its fulfillment, the consequences of its frustration, and the impact of man's self-esteem (or lack of it) on his values, responses, and goals." Addressing the 1970 Annual Convention of the American Psychological Association, Branden said: "We are living in an age and in a culture increasingly antagonistic to individualism and to the ideal of personal autonomy. Many psychologists and psychiatrists share this antagonism and express their hostility through therapeutic practices that are subversive not only of the patient's autonomy but also of his self-esteem and mental health."

Recently the Biocentric Institute began offering an intensive, "Self-Esteem and the Art of Being," with Nathaniel Branden as the conductor of the workshop. In an interview with a reporter from the *Detroit Free Press,* Branden discussed his own role in the workshop: "I'm not a psychologist who preaches adjustment—people may want you to adjust to things that are crazy. I say be true to your own experience, your own unique and distinct powers. Be confident that if you do so, you will find people with whom you can have good relationships. ... The purpose is not to teach clients that as a therapist, I am brilliant, but to teach them what they are."

BIOGRAPHICAL/CRITICAL SOURCES: Kirkus Review, April 15, 1962; *Life,* April 7, 1967; *New York Times Book Review,* May 5, 1968; *Los Angeles Times,* March 19, 1970; *Choice,* October, 1970; *Detroit News,* November 22, 1970; *Reason,* October, 1971; *Detroit Free Press,* May 29, 1977.

*　　　*　　　*

BRANDT, Richard M(artin) 1922-

PERSONAL: Born September 13, 1922, in Cleveland, Ohio; son of Arthur (an engineer) and Lucile (Martin) Brandt; married Mattice Fritz, 1946; children: Mattice F. (Mrs. Michael Ranney), Richard M., Jr., William F., Mark A. *Education:* University of Virginia, B.M.E., 1943; University of Michigan, M.A., 1949; University of Maryland, Ed.D., 1954. *Office:* School of Education, University of Virginia, Charlottesville, Va. 22903.

CAREER: Gar Wood Industries, Detroit, Mich., industrial engineer, 1946-47; high school teacher in Willow Run, Mich., 1948-49; University of Delaware, Newark, instructor in human development, 1950-52; University of Maryland, College Park, assistant professor, 1954-57, associate professor, 1957-65; University of Virginia, Charlottesville, associate professor, 1965-68, professor of educational psychology, 1968—, chairman of department of foundations of education, 1968-74, dean of School of Education, 1974—. State executive secretary, Delaware Congress of Parents and Teachers, 1950-52. *Military service:* U.S. Naval Reserve, 1944-46; became lieutenant junior grade.

MEMBER: American Psychological Association, American Educational Research Association, Society for Research in Child Development, National Education Association, Association for Supervision and Curriculum Development, Kappa Delta Pi, Phi Delta Kappa.

WRITINGS: (With Hugh V. Perkins, Jr.) *Research Evaluating a Child Study Program* (monograph), Society for Research in Child Development, 1956; *Studying Behavior in Natural Settings,* Holt, 1972; (editor with Charles W. Beegle) *Observational Methods in the Classroom,* Association for Supervision & Curriculum Development, 1973. Contributor to education journals.

*　　　*　　　*

BRANLEY, Franklyn M(ansfield) 1915-

PERSONAL: Born June 5, 1915, in New Rochelle, N.Y.; son of George Percy and Louise (Lockwood) Branley; married Margaret Genevieve Lemon (an elementary school teacher), June 26, 1938; children: Sandra Kay (Mrs. Edward C. Bridges), Mary Jane (Mrs. Robert Day). *Education:* State Normal School (now State University of New York

College at New Paltz), lifetime license, 1936; New York University, B.S., 1942; Columbia University, M.A., 1948, Ed.D., 1957. *Religion:* Unitarian. *Home:* 4 London Ct., Woodcliff Lake, N.J. 07680. *Office:* American Museum-Hayden Planetarium, 81st St. and Central Park W., New York, N.Y. 10024.

CAREER: Elementary, junior, and senior high school teacher in Spring Valley, N.Y., 1936-42, Nyack, N.Y., 1942-44, and New York City, 1944-54; Jersey State Teachers College (now Jersey City State College), Jersey City, N.J., associate professor of science, 1954-56; American Museum of Natural History, Hayden Planetarium, New York City, director of educational services, 1956—, associate astronomer, 1956-63, astronomer, 1963—, chairman, 1968—. Part-time instructor at Columbia University, 1945, Alabama State Teachers College (now Alabama State University), 1947, Southwest Louisiana College, 1949, New York University, 1962. National Science Foundation, referee, 1960—, advisor to Teacher Education Project, 1961; advisor to U.S. Science Exhibit of Century 21 Exposition, World's Fair, Seattle, Wash., 1962; advisor or director of various conferences and institutes sponsored by National Science Foundation and other scientific organizations.

MEMBER: American Astronomical Society (director, Program of Visiting Professors in Astronomy, 1958—; Committee on Education in Astronomy, 1958—), National Science Teachers Association, American Association for the Advancement of Science (fellow), Royal Astronomical Society (fellow), Authors Guild. *Awards, honors:* Edison Award for outstanding children's science book of 1961, for *Experiments in Sky Watching;* named Outstanding Citizen, Newburgh, N.Y., 1965.

WRITINGS—All juveniles; published by Crowell, except as indicated: *Lodestar, Rocket Ship to Mars: The Record of the First Operation Sponsored by the Federal Commission for Interplanetary Exploration, June 1, 1971* (science fiction), 1951; *Experiments in the Principles of Space Travel,* 1955, revised edition, 1973; *Mars,* 1955, revised edition published as *Mars: Planet Number Four,* 1966; *Exploring by Satellite: The Story of Project Vanguard,* 1957; *Solar Energy,* 1957; *A Book of Satellites for You,* 1958, 2nd edition, 1971; *Man Moves toward Outer Space,* Saga Press, 1958; (contributor) Lawrence M. Levin, editor, *The Book of Popular Science, 1958 Edition,* Grolier Society, 1958; (contributor) Clarence W. Sorenson, *A World View* (social studies text), Silver Burdett, 1958; *A Book of Moon Rockets for You,* 1959, 3rd edition, 1970; *Experiments in Sky Watching,* 1959, revised edition, 1967.

A Guide to Outer Space, Home Library Press, 1960; *The Planets and Their Satellites,* Science Materials Center, 1960; *A Book of Planets for You,* 1961, revised edition, 1966; *Exploring by Astronaut: The Story of Project Mercury,* 1961; (editor) *"Reader's Digest" Science Reader* (stories and articles), three books, Reader's Digest Services, 1962-64; (author of preface) *The Natural History Library,* American Museum of Natural History and Doubleday, 1962; *A Book of Astronauts for You,* 1963; *Exploration of the Moon,* published for American Museum of Natural History by Natural History Press, 1963, revised edition, 1966; *Apollo and the Moon,* published for American Museum-Hayden Planetarium by Natural History Press, 1964; (with Milton O. Pella and John Urban) *Science Horizons,* two volumes, Ginn, Grade 7: *The World of Life,* 1965, Grade 8: *The Physical World,* 1965; *A Book of the Milky Way Galaxy for You,* 1965; *The Christmas Sky,* 1966; *A Book of Stars for*

You, 1967; *A Book of Mars for You,* 1968; *The Mystery of Stonehenge,* 1969; *A Book of Venus for You,* 1969.

A Book of Outer Space for You, 1970; *Man in Space to the Moon,* 1970; (editor with Roma Gans) Philip Balestrino, *The Skeleton Inside You,* 1971; *Pieces of Another World: The Story of Moon Rocks,* 1972; *Think Metric!,* 1973; *A Book of Flying Saucers for You,* 1973; *The End of the World,* 1974; *Shakes, Quakes, and Shifts: Earth Tectonics,* 1974; *A Book of Planet Earth for You,* 1975; *Energy for the Twenty-first Century,* 1975; *From Rainbows to Lasers,* 1977.

Juvenile books with Nelson Frederick Beeler; all published by Crowell: *Experiments in Science,* 1947, revised and enlarged edition, 1955; *Experiments with Electricity,* 1949; *More Experiments in Science,* 1950; *Experiments in Optical Illusion,* 1951; *Experiments in Chemistry,* 1952; *Experiments with Airplane Instruments,* 1953; *Experiments with Atomics,* 1954; *Experiments with Light,* 1957; *Experiments with a Microscope,* 1957.

Juvenile books with Eleanor K. Vaughan; all published by Crowell: *Mickey's Magnet,* 1956; *Rusty Rings a Bell,* 1957; *Timmy and the Tin Can Telephone,* 1959.

"Exploring Our Universe" series; all published by Crowell: *The Nine Planets,* 1958, revised edition, 1971; *The Moon, Earth's Natural Satellite,* 1960, revised edition, 1971; *Mars, Planet Number Four,* 1962, revised edition, 1966; *The Sun, Star Number One,* 1964; *The Earth: Planet Number Three,* 1966; *The Milky Way: Galaxy Number One,* 1969; *Comets, Meteoroids and Asteroids: Mavericks of the Solar System,* 1974; *Black Holes, White Dwarfs and Superstars,* 1975.

"Let's Read and Find Out" series (for young children); all published by Crowell: *The Moon Seems to Change,* 1960; *Big Tracks, Little Tracks,* 1960; *What Makes Day and Night,* 1961; *Rockets and Satellites,* 1961, revised edition, 1970; *Sun; Our Nearest Star,* 1961; *The Air Is All Around You,* 1962; *The Big Dipper,* 1962; *What the Moon Is Like,* 1963; *Rain and Hail,* 1963; *Snow Is Falling,* 1963; *Flash, Crash, Rumble, and Roll,* 1964, published as *Flash, Crash, Rumble, and Roll: Alphabet Teaching Book,* 1966; *North, South, East and West,* 1966; *High Sounds, Low Sounds,* 1967; *Floating and Sinking,* 1967; R. Gans, editor, *Gravity Is a Mystery,* 1970; *Oxygen Keeps You Alive,* 1971; *Weight and Weightlessness,* 1972; *The Beginning of the Earth,* 1972; *Eclipse: Darkness in Daytime,* 1973; *Sunshine Makes the Seasons,* 1974; *Light and Darkness,* 1975; *Roots Are Food Finders,* 1975.

"Young Math" series (for children); all published by Crowell: *Measure with Metric,* 1975; *How Little and How Much: A Book about Scales,* 1976.

Adult books: *Science, Seven and Eight* (textbook), Saga Press, 1945; (editor) *Scientist's Choice: A Portfolio of Photographs in Science,* Basic Books, 1958; (editor) *Earth, Air and Space* (symposium on International Geophysical Year, September 12, 1957); American Museum-Hayden Planetarium, 1958; *Astronomy* (college textbook), Crowell, 1975. Also author of introduction to *Astro-Murals,* Astro-Murals (Washington, D.C.), 1960. Contributor of weekly article to *Young America,* 1942-46 (now defunct); contributor to *Grade Teacher Magazine, Curator, New York Times Magazine, Natural History, Elementary School Science Bulletin, Nature and Science,* and other periodicals. First chairman of editorial board, Natural History Press, 1962—; advisor, *Science and Children,* 1963, *Nature and Science,* 1963-69.

SIDELIGHTS: Franklyn Branley told *CA* there is a "need

for accurate, readable material for young people. They are the nation's most important resource, and any investment in them will be repaid many fold." He first noticed the tremendous dearth of science education books for children while teaching grade school in New York, and has been helping to fill the gap ever since. S. V. Keenan writes that Branley's own education began after his mother's death in 1918, when he was boarded with his brothers and sister at Plattekill, N.Y., "listening to the recitations of the other classes in a country school which had a 'woodshed, outhouse, water pail and dipper, double desks, pot-belly stove.'" Keenan also notes that Branley believes "children's ability to understand, study, and persevere is terribly underrated by adults. . . . We throw away a tremendous potential when we delay the exposure of young people to the excitement of science until they have become cynical sophisticates—say twelve years old."

In *Books Are By People*, Lee Bennett Hopkins calls Branley a man with "tremendous foresight," mentioning that *Exploring by Satellite* was published the day after Russia launched Sputnik (October 4, 1957). He quotes the scientist as saying: "'To write is to accept a challenge. You have to find out what children really want to know, assess yourself, and determine what skills you have to give them. Each book should be important, interesting, contain an element of surprise for *every* reader, whether it is about the sonic boom or honeybees or how a baby is conceived. Actually, a good book for children is also a good book for adults.'"

AVOCATIONAL INTERESTS: Oil painting, scuba diving, fishing, gardening, boating.

BIOGRAPHICAL/CRITICAL SOURCES: Wilson Library Bulletin, September, 1961; *Young Reader's Review*, December, 1966; Lee Bennett Hopkins, *Books Are By People*, Citation, 1969; *New York Times Book Review*, September 7, 1969; *Natural History*, December, 1970.

* * *

BRAUDE, William Gordon 1907-

PERSONAL: Born April 25, 1907, in Telsiai, Lithuania; came to United States in 1920; son of Isaac and Rachel (Halperin) Braude; married Pearl Finkelstein, June, 1938; children: Joel Isaac, Benjamin Meir, Daniel. *Education:* University of Cincinnati, B.A. (summa cum laude), 1929; Hebrew Union College-Jewish Institute of Religion, Rabbi, 1931; Brown University, M.A., 1934, Ph.D., 1937. *Home:* 93 Arlington Ave., Providence, R.I. 02906. *Office:* 70 Orchard Ave., Providence, R.I. 02906.

CAREER: Rabbi of congregation in Rockford, Ill., 1931-32; Congregation Sons of Israel and David (Temple Beth-El), Providence, R.I., rabbi, 1932—. Lecturer, Brown University, 1935-37, 1969; visiting professor, Yale University, 1968; guest lecturer, Providence College, 1970; resident scholar at Hebrew Union College, Jerusalem, and visiting lecturer at Hebrew University of Jerusalem, 1971-72; special visiting fellow, University of Connecticut, spring, 1976. *Member:* Phi Beta Kappa. *Awards, honors:* D.D., Brown University, 1955; D.H.L., Hebrew Union College-Jewish Institute of Religion (New York), 1959, and University of Rhode Island, 1960; Litt. D., Providence College, 1969.

WRITINGS: Jewish Proselyting in the First Five Centuries of the Common Era: The Age of the Tannaim and Amoraim, Brown University, 1940; (translator) *The Midrash on Psalms,* Yale University Press, 1959; (translator) *Pesikta Rabbati: Discourses for Feasts, and Special Sabbaths,* two volumes, Yale University Press, 1968; (translator) Israel J.

Kapstein, *Pesikta De Rab,* Jewish Publication Society, 1975. Contributor of articles and reviews to religious journals.

WORK IN PROGRESS: An essay for inclusion in *Kiev Festschrift,* for KTAV Publishing.

BIOGRAPHICAL/CRITICAL SOURCES: Times Literary Supplement, June 12, 1969.

* * *

BRAUER, Jerald C(arl) 1921-

PERSONAL: Born September 16, 1921, in Fond du Lac, Wis.; son of Carl L. (a railroad engineer) and Anna Mae (Linde) Brauer; married Muriel N. Nelson, March 18, 1945; children: Christopher, Marian Ruth, Thomas Carl. *Education:* Carthage College, A.B., 1943; Northwestern Lutheran Theological Seminary, B.D., 1945; University of Chicago, Ph.D., 1948. *Home:* 5620 South Blackstone Ave., Chicago, Ill. 60637. *Office:* Divinity School, University of Chicago, 207 Swift Hall, Chicago, Ill. 60637.

CAREER: Ordained minister, United Lutheran Church of America, 1951. Union Theological Seminary, New York, N.Y., instructor in church history and history of Christian thought, 1948-50; University of Chicago, Chicago, Ill., assistant professor, 1950-54, associate professor, 1954-59, professor of history of Christianity, 1959-69, Naomi Shenstone Donnelley Professor, 1969—, dean of federated theological faculty, 1955-60, dean of Divinity School, 1960-70, International House, member of board of governors, president, 1973—. Visiting professor, University of Frankfurt, summer, 1961; visiting lecturer at eight Japanese universities, including University of Tokyo and University of Kokugakuin, 1966. President, Board of Theological Education of Lutheran Church in America, 1962-69; member of board of theological education, Rockefeller Brothers Fund for Theological Education, Inc.; member of board of trustees, Carthage College and Augustana College. Delegate, Lutheran World Federation Assembly, Helsinki, 1963; official delegate, Vatican II Council, Rome, 3rd session, 1964, 4th session, 1965.

MEMBER: American Society of Church History (president, 1960), Institute for Advanced Pastoral Studies (member of board of directors), Council on Religion and International Affairs (member of board of trustees). *Awards, honors:* D.D., Miami University, Oxford, Ohio, 1956; LL.D., Carthage College, 1957; S.T.D., Ripon College, 1961; D.H.L., Gettysburg College, 1963; National Endowment for the Humanities fellow, 1977-78.

WRITINGS: Protestantism in America, Westminster, 1953, revised edition, 1965; (with Jaroslav Pelikan) *Luther and the Reformation,* National Lutheran Council, 1953; *Basic Questions for the Christian Scholar* (brochure), National Lutheran Council, 1954; (editor) Paul Tillich, *The Future of Religions,* Harper, 1966; *Images of Religion in America,* Fortress, 1967; (editor) *Essays in Divinity,* Volume II: *The Impact of the Church on Its Culture,* University of Chicago Press, 1967, Volume V: *Reinterpretation in American Church History,* University of Chicago Press, 1968; (editor) Tillich, *My Travel Diary: 1936,* Harper, 1970; (editor) *Religion and the American Revolution,* Fortress, 1976. Series editor, "Essays in Divinity," University of Chicago Press, 1967-69; editor, *Westminster Dictionary of Church History,* Westminster, 1971. Contributor to *American People Encyclopedia* and *Encyclopaedia Britannica;* contributor of articles to religion and theology journals. Co-editor, *Church History,* 1962; editor, *Criterion.*

WORK IN PROGRESS: Research on the nature of Puritanism, Puritanism and politics, and Revivalism in American culture.

BIOGRAPHICAL/CRITICAL SOURCES: Christian Century, October 2, 1968.

* * *

BRAUN, John R(ichard) 1928-

PERSONAL: Born December 24, 1928, in Brooklyn, N.Y.; son of John and Nellie (Thompson) Braun; married Jo-Ann Homan, May 21, 1960; children: John Richard, Jr. *Education:* Long Island University, A.B., 1950; University of Nebraska, graduate study, 1950-51; University of California, Berkeley, Ph.D., 1957. *Home:* 254 Fairfield Woods Rd., Fairfield, Conn. 06430. *Office:* Department of Psychology, University of Bridgeport, Bridgeport, Conn. 06602.

CAREER: Carleton College, Northfield, Minn., instructor, 1956-57, assistant professor of psychology, 1957-59; Bucknell University, Lewisburg, Pa., assistant professor of psychology, 1959-60; Texas Christian University, Fort Worth, associate professor of psychology, 1960-61; University of Bridgeport, Bridgeport, Conn., associate professor, 1961-62, professor of psychology, 1962—, chairman of department, 1961-72. Licensed in clinical psychology by State of Connecticut. Research psychologist, U.S. Public Health Service, summer, 1957; summer visiting professor at University of Nebraska, 1958, and Long Island University, 1959. *Military service:* U.S. Army, 1946-47. *Member:* American Psychological Association, Eastern Psychological Association, Sigma Xi, Psi Chi.

WRITINGS: Clinical Psychology in Transition, World Publishing, 1961, revised edition, 1965; *Contemporary Research in Learning,* Van Nostrand, 1963. Contributor to scientific journals.

* * *

BREED, Paul F. 1916-

PERSONAL: Born October 20, 1916, in Norwich, N.Y.; son of Floyd Randall (a pattern-maker) and Anna (Martin) Breed. *Education:* University of Chicago, Ph.B., 1950, M.A.L.S., 1955. *Home address:* Route 7, Box 1123, Asheville, N.C. 28803.

CAREER: University of Chicago Library, Chicago, Ill., assistant reference librarian, 1952-55; University of Detroit Library, Detroit, Mich., head of reference department, 1955-59; Wayne State University Library, Detroit, music librarian, 1959-60, reference librarian, 1960-65, bibliographer, 1965-77, former part-time instructor in department of library science. *Military service:* U.S. Army, 1941-45; became technical sergeant.

WRITINGS: (With Desiree DeCharms) *Songs in Collections: An Index,* Information Coordinators, 1966; (with Florence Sniderman) *Dramatic Criticism Index: A Bibliography of Commentaries on Playwrights from Ibsen to the Avant-Garde,* Gale, 1971; (with Fernande Bassan) *An Annotated Bibliography of French Language and Literature,* Garland Publishing, 1976.

AVOCATIONAL INTERESTS: Art history, music, gardening.

* * *

BREESKIN, Adelyn Dohme 1896-

PERSONAL: Born July 19, 1896, in Baltimore, Md.; daughter of Alfred R. L. (a manufacturing chemist) and Emmie (Blumner) Dohme; married Elias Breeskin (a concert pianist), April 12, 1920 (deceased); children: Jean (Mrs. Clayton Timbrell), Dorothy (Mrs. Samuel E. Brown, Jr.), Gloria (Mrs. Cornelius Peck). *Education:* Studied at Bryn Mawr College and Radcliffe College; School of Fine Arts, Crafts and Decorative Design, Boston, graduate, 1918. *Home:* 1254 31st St. N.W., Washington, D.C. 20007. *Office:* National Collection of Fine Arts, Smithsonian Institution, Washington, D.C. 20560.

CAREER: Metropolitan Museum, New York, N.Y., assistant in print department, 1918-20; Baltimore Museum of Art, Baltimore, Md., curator of prints and drawings, 1930-62, general curator, 1938-42, acting director, 1942-47, director, 1947-62; Washington Gallery of Modern Art, Washington, D.C., director, 1962-64; Smithsonian Institution, Washington, D.C., consultant, 1962-68, 1974—, curator of contemporary art, National Collection of Fine Arts, 1968-74. U.S. commissioner, American Pavilion, Venice Exhibition, 1960. Lecturer in United States and abroad. Trustee, American Federation of Arts. *Member:* Association of Art Museum Directors (president, 1956-57), International Graphic Arts Society (member of American jury of selection, 1955-65), Print Council of America (secretary, 1956). *Awards, honors:* L.D., Goucher College, 1953; Star of Solidarity from Government of Italy, 1954; D.F.A. from Washington College, 1961, Wheaton College, 1961, Hood College, 1966, Morgan State College, 1966, and Maryland Institute, 1975; Distinguished Service Award, University of Maryland, 1962.

WRITINGS: The Graphic Works of Mary Cassatt: A Catalogue Raisonne, H. Bittner & Co., 1948; *Mary Cassatt: A Catalogue Raisonne of the Oils, Pastels, Watercolors, and Drawings,* Smithsonian Institution Press, 1970; (compiler) *Two American Painters: Fritz Scholder and T. C. Cannon,* Smithsonian Institution Press, 1972. Author of introductions to art and exhibition catalogues.

* * *

BREILLAT, Catherine 1950-

PERSONAL: Born July 13, 1950, in Bordeaux, France; daughter of Marcel (a doctor) and Marie-Jeanne (Meillan) Breillat. *Education:* Lycee de Jeunes Filles de Niort, Deux Seures, France, Bachelor's degree, 1967. *Religion:* Catholic ("no observances").

*WRITINGS—*All novels: *L'Homme facile,* Bourgois, 1968, translation by Harold J. Salemson published as *A Man for the Asking,* Morrow, 1969; *Les Vetements de Mer,* F. Wimille, 1971; *Le Silence, apres . . . ,* F. Wimille, 1971; *Le Soupirail,* Authier, 1974.

WORK IN PROGRESS: Tragedie in Alexandrine, a novel.

SIDELIGHTS: Written at the age of sixteen and published in Europe two years later, Catherine Breillat's first novel, according to *National Review,* was called "the most indecent book of the year" by *Der Stern.*

Breillat told *CA* that writing allows her leisure time for other pursuits, such as making films, publishing poems, and being alone.

BIOGRAPHICAL/CRITICAL SOURCES: National Review, August 12, 1969.†

* * *

BREIT, William (Leo) 1933-
(Marshall Jevons, a joint pseudonym)

PERSONAL: Surname rhymes with "light"; born February

13, 1933, in New Orleans, La.; son of Murray (a store manager) and Sylvia (Shor) Breit. *Education:* University of Texas, B.A., 1955, M.A., 1956; Michigan State University, Ph.D., 1961. *Home:* 18 Deer Path Rd., Charlottesville, Va. 22901. *Office:* Department of Economics, University of Virginia, Charlottesville, Va. 22903.

CAREER: Michigan State University, East Lansing, instructor, 1957-60, lecturer in economics, 1961; Louisiana State University, Baton Rouge, assistant professor, 1961-64, associate professor of economics, 1964-65; University of Virginia, Charlottesville, associate professor, 1965-70, professor of economics, 1970—. Visiting professor at University of Colorado, summer, 1966, University of California, Berkeley, summer, 1968, and University of Texas at Austin, spring, 1975. *Member:* American Economics Association, Mont Pelerin Society, Mystery Writers of America, Greencroft Club.

WRITINGS: (Editor with H. M. Hochman) *Readings in Microeconomics,* Holt, 1968, 2nd edition, 1971; (with R. L. Ransom) *The Academic Scribblers: American Economists in Collision,* Holt, 1971; (editor with W. P. Culbertson) *Science and Ceremony: The Institutional Economics of C. E. Ayres,* University of Texas Press, 1976; (with K. G. Elzinga) *The Antitrust Penalties: A Study in Law and Economics,* Yale University Press, 1976; (with K. G. Elzinga, under joint pseudonym Marshall Jevons) *Murder at the Margin* (mystery), Thomas Horton, 1978. Contributor to Canadian and American journals. Associate editor, *Social Science Quarterly;* member of editorial board, *Journal of Economic Issues.*

AVOCATIONAL INTERESTS: Philately (especially in connection with former French colonies in Africa), Burmese and Abyssinian cats.

*   *   *

BRENT, Harold Patrick   1943-
(Harry Brent)

PERSONAL: Born December 24, 1943, in Holyoke, Mass.; son of Harold Francis (a postal clerk) and Anna (McCarthy) Brent; divorced; children: Elizabeth Ann, James Patrick, Miranda. *Education:* Providence College, Providence, R.I., A.B., 1965; University of Nevada, M.A., 1967; University of Wisconsin, Ph.D., 1973. *Politics:* Socialist. *Home:* 3612 Hamilton St., Philadelphia, Pa. 19104. *Office:* Department of English, College of Arts and Sciences, Rutgers University, Camden, N.J.

CAREER: Bradley University, Peoria, Ill., instructor, 1967-69; Rutgers University, College of Arts and Sciences, Camden, N.J., assistant professor of medieval literature and linguistics, 1972—, director of freshman English, 1976—. *Member:* Modern Language Association of America, National Council of Teachers of English (member of board of directors, 1976-77), Conference on College Composition and Communication.

WRITINGS—Under name Harry Brent: (With William Lutz) *On Revolution,* Winthrop, 1971; (with Lutz) *Rhetorical Considerations,* Winthrop, 1974, 2nd edition, 1977. Reviewer, conducting "Brent on Books," for WSTO-TV, Stoughton, Wis. Contributor of articles and reviews to professional journals.

WORK IN PROGRESS: The Social Criticism of the Wakefield Master; The Winthrop Rhetoric Handbook.

BRESLIN, James E.   1935-

PERSONAL: Born December 12, 1935, in New York, N.Y.; son of James Thomas (an accountant) and Marion (Clancy) Breslin; married Glenna Fink, November 23, 1963; children: Jennifer, Susannah. *Education:* Brooklyn College (now Brooklyn College of the City University of New York), B.A., 1957; University of North Carolina, M.A., 1959; University of Minnesota, Ph.D., 1964. *Politics:* Independent. *Religion:* Independent. *Home:* 21 Avis Rd., Berkeley, Calif. 94707. *Office:* Department of English, University of California, Berkeley, Calif. 94720.

CAREER: University of Minnesota, Minneapolis, instructor in English, 1961-64; University of California, Berkeley, assistant professor, 1964-70, associate professor of American and modern literature, 1970—. *Member:* Modern Language Association of America. *Awards, honors:* Research fellow, National Endowment for the Arts, 1977.

WRITINGS: (Contributor) Phillip Damon, editor, *Literary Criticism and Historical Understanding: Selected Papers from the English Institute,* Columbia University Press, 1967; *William Carlos Williams: An American Artist,* Oxford University Press, 1970; "American Voices" (selection of readings from American autobiographies), produced in Washington, D.C. at the John F. Kennedy Center for the Performing Arts, 1976. Contributor to literature journals and *New Physician.*

WORK IN PROGRESS: The Transformation of Contemporary American Poetry, a study of the radical shift in American poetry that took place in the late 1950's, including studies of Allen Ginsberg, Robert Lowell, Denise Levertov, James Wright, Frank O'Hara, and Adrienne Rich.

SIDELIGHTS: James Breslin's *William Carlos Williams* is "not only better than usual" writes a *New Republic* reviewer, it is "certainly the best short introduction" to Williams.

BIOGRAPHICAL/CRITICAL SOURCES: Sewanee Review, November 14, 1970; *New Republic,* December 12, 1970; *Virginia Quarterly Review,* spring, 1971; *Times Literary Supplement,* May 28, 1971; *American Literature,* November, 1971.

*   *   *

BRETTSCHNEIDER, Bertram D(onald)   1924-

PERSONAL: Born May 7, 1924, in Brooklyn, N.Y.; son of Joseph (a pharmacist) and Fannie (Cohn) Brettschneider; married Rita Roberta Fischman (an attorney), June 25, 1950; children: Jane Ann, Joseph Michael. *Education:* Tulane University, B.A., 1947, M.A., 1948; Yale University, graduate study, 1948-50; Columbia University, M.A., 1951; New York University, Ph.D., 1956. *Religion:* Jewish. *Home:* 2 Crosby Pl., Huntington, N.Y. 11743. *Agent:* Shirley Collier Agency, 1127 Stradella Rd., Los Angeles, Calif. 90024. *Office:* Department of Philosophy, Hofstra University, Hempstead, N.Y. 11550.

CAREER: University of Connecticut, Fort Trumbull Branch, New London, instructor in philosophy, 1949-50; elementary school teacher in Valley Stream, N.Y., 1951-54; Hofstra University, Hempstead, N.Y., associate professor, 1954-63, associate dean of faculty, 1959-64, professor of philosophy in New College, 1963—, chairperson of department, 1974—. Visiting associate professor, New York University, 1959-62. *Military service:* U.S. Army, 1943-46. *Member:* American Philosophical Association, Society for Phenomenology and Existential Philosophy, American Society for

Aesthetics, College Art Association. *Awards, honors:* Selected Outstanding Teacher of the Year, Hofstra University, 1968.

WRITINGS: The Philosphy of Samuel Alexander: Idealism in "Space, Time, and Deity," Humanities, 1964; (with Charles J. Calitri) *The Goliath Head* (novel), Crown, 1972.

WORK IN PROGRESS: The Art and Ideas of Jacques Callot.

SIDELIGHTS: Bertram Brettschneider has traveled extensively in France, Italy, Spain, U.S.S.R., Greece, and Great Britain.

* * *

BREWER, Edward S(amuel) 1933-

PERSONAL: Born January 15, 1933, in Hamilton, Ontario, Canada; son of Edward James and Doris Irene (Farrell) Brewer; married Marilyn Louise Follows, July 2, 1956 (divorced, 1975); married Barbara Hewitt Swan, December, 1975. *Education:* Westlawn School of Yacht Design, yacht designer, 1960. *Politics:* Conservative. *Religion:* Anglican. *Residence:* Brooklin, Me. 04616.

CAREER: Luders Marine Construction Co., Stamford, Conn., naval architect, 1960-67; Edward S. Brewer & Associates, Inc., Brooklin, Me., naval architect, 1967—; Yacht Design Institute, Brooklin, instructor, 1969—. *Military service:* Canadian Army, 1952-57; became lieutenant. *Member:* Society of Naval Architects and Marine Engineers, Society of Small Craft Designers, American Boat and Yacht Council, Royal Kenebbecasis Yacht Club.

WRITINGS: Understanding Boat Design, International Marine Publishing Co., 1970; *Cruising Yacht Designs,* Seven-Seas Press, 1976. Also author of textbooks for Yacht Design Institute. Contributor to *Touring Bike, Sail,* and *Cruising World.* Technical editor, *Motor Boating and Sailing* (magazine), 1974-76.

WORK IN PROGRESS: Yacht Designing.

AVOCATIONAL INTERESTS: Sailing, canoeing, mountain climbing, back-packing, motorcycling.

* * *

BREWER, Garry Dwight 1941-

PERSONAL: Born October 2, 1941, in San Francisco, Calif.; son of Dwight C. and Querida (Colson) Brewer; married Saundra Tonsager (a special education teacher), December 3, 1962 (divorced, 1975); married Shelley Marshall, May 11, 1976; children: (first marriage) Gabrielle, Gregory. *Education:* Attended U.S. Naval Academy, 1959-61; University of California, Berkeley, A.B., 1963; San Diego State College (now University), M.S., 1966; Yale University, M.Phil., 1968, Ph.D., 1970. *Politics:* Independent. *Religion:* Presbyterian. *Home:* Wingate Rd., Guilford, Conn. 06437. *Office:* School of Organization and Management, Yale University, New Haven, Conn. 06520.

CAREER: Rand Corp., Santa Monica, Calif., staff member, 1970-72, senior staff member, 1972-74; University of California, Berkeley, assistant professor of political science, 1970-71; University of California, Los Angeles, lecturer in political science, 1971; University of Southern California, Los Angeles, lecturer in public administration, 1972-73; Rand Graduate Institute of Policy Studies, Santa Monica, faculty member, 1973-75; Yale University, New Haven, Conn., associate professor of organization and management, 1975—. Consultant to Rand Corp., 1969-70, 1974—, Na-

tional Science Foundation, 1972—, Ford Foundation, 1972—, Russell Sage Foundation, 1974-76, and other institutions. Member of board of directors of Children's Research Institute of California, 1974—, and National Advisory Committee on Children, 1975—. Summer research fellow, Office of Secretary of Defense, Advanced Research Projects Agency, 1967; fellow, Center for Advanced Study in the Behavioral Sciences, 1974-75. Research director and associate producer of a television documentary, "What Do We Do Now?," 1976. *Military service:* U.S. Navy, 1963-66; became lieutenant. U.S. Naval Reserve, 1966-70.

MEMBER: American Society for Public Administration, American Political Science Association, American Association for the Advancement of Science, American Education Research Association, Society for Values in Higher Education, Association for Computing Machinery, Association for Asian Studies, Council on Applied Social Science Research, Pi Sigma Alpha. *Awards, honors:* Research grants from Rand Corp., 1974-75, Fleischman Foundation, 1973-75, Russell Sage Foundation, 1975-76, and Bureau of Education for the Handicapped, 1976-77.

WRITINGS: (With R. Brunner) *Organized Complexity: Empirical Theories of Political Development,* Free Press, 1971; (with M. Shubik and E. Savage) *Gaming Literature Review: A Critical Survey of Literature on Gaming and Allied Topics,* Rand Corp., 1971; *Politicians, Bureaucrats and the Consultant: A Critique of Urban Problem Solving,* Basic Books, 1973; (with Shubik and Savage) *A Partially Annotated Bibliography of Urban Models,* Datum, 1973; (with Brunner) *Political Development and Change: A Policy Approach,* Free Press, 1975.

Contributor: Joseph La Palombara, editor, *Bureaucracy and Political Development,* Princeton University Press, 1967; Robert O. Tilman, editor, *International Biographical Directory of Southeast Asian Specialists,* Interuniversity Southeast Asia Committee of the Association of Asian Studies, 1969; Arthur I. Siegel, editor, *Symposium on Computer Simulation as Related to Manpower and Personnel Planning,* Bureau of Naval Personnel, 1971; T. R. LaPorte, editor, *Organized Social Complexity: Challenge to Politics and Policy,* Princeton University Press, 1974; H. D. Lasswell and D. Lerner, editors, *Values and Development: Appraising Asian Experience,* MIT Press, 1974; W. D. Hawley and D. Rogers, editors, *Improving the Quality of Urban Management,* Sage Publications, 1974; C. E. Sherrick, editor, *1980 Is Now,* John Tracy Clinic, 1974; B. Famighetti and others, editors, *Education Yearbook 1974-1975,* Macmillan Educational, 1975; T. Robinson and N. Choucri, editors, *Forecasting in International Relations,* W. H. Freeman, 1977.

Author of numerous papers and research reports. Contributor to *U.S. Naval Institute Proceedings,* 1967, and proceedings of American Political Science Association, 1971, and Military Operations Research Society, 1973. Contributor of reviews and articles to *Air University Review, Military Review, Yale Alumni Magazine, Policy Sciences, Public Policy, Science, Journal of Conflict Resolution,* and other periodicals. Editorial associate, *Public Policy,* 1973—; editor of *Policy Sciences,* 1974-76, and *Simulation and Games,* 1977—; member of editorial board of Redaktion *TRANSFER,* 1975—, *Policy Sciences,* 1977—, *Policy & Politics,* 1977—, and *Policy Studies Annual Review,* 1977—.

WORK IN PROGRESS: Three books: *The War Game: A Critique of Military Problem Solving, The Scope of the Policy Sciences,* and *Handicapped Children: Policy and Practice.*

AVOCATIONAL INTERESTS: Handicrafts (neckties and skirts), golf.

*   *   *

BRIDGES, William   1933-

PERSONAL: Born November 24, 1933, in Boston, Mass.; son of Ronald and Helen (Emery) Bridges; married Mondi Kump (a psychiatric social worker), December 27, 1959; children: Anne, Sarah, Margaret. *Education:* Harvard University, A.B., 1955; Columbia University, A.M., 1956; Brown University, Ph.D., 1963. *Home:* 6773 Giovanetti Rd., Forestville, Calif. 95436. *Office:* Passage-Ways, 818 Cherry St., Santa Rosa, Calif. 95404.

CAREER: Pine Manor Junior College, Chestnut Hill, Mass., director of admissions, 1958-60, chairman of department of English, 1962-66; Mills College, Oakland, Calif., Aurelia Henry Reinhardt Associate Professor of American Literature, 1966-74; Passage-Ways, Santa Rosa, Calif., director, 1974—. Member of governing board, Humanistic Psychology Institute. Lecturer and consultant on adult development. *Military service:* U.S. Army, 1956-58; served in Germany. *Member:* Association for Humanistic Psychology (educational coordinator, 1971—).

WRITINGS: Spokesmen of the Self: Emerson, Thoreau, and Whitman, Chandler Publishing, 1971; *The Seasons of Our Lives,* Wayfarer Press, 1977. Contributor to popular and academic journals.

WORK IN PROGRESS: A study of the archaic concept of passage and the dynamics of personal change, with particular reference to the so-called "mid-life transition."

SIDELIGHTS: William Bridges told *CA:* "I continue to draw on my background in the humanities (as in a recent reinterpretation of the Oedipus myth), but in the last four years my focus has shifted from literary and educational subjects per se toward the process of transition and transformation that we encounter in our middle years. I am particularly concerned to see how many of our 'personal problems' are not so much the sign of breakdowns as of breakthroughs—or what could be breakthroughs, if we were not so unaware of the developmental phases of adult life. Having had my theoretical say on this subject in *The Seasons of Our Lives,* I am currently writing on its more personal aspects—on the *experience* of profound transition. We have so few guidelines and signposts to the adult years in our culture, and so many people withdraw (for lack of them) into old and outlived patterns. It is this tendency that gives aging its bad name in America."

*   *   *

BRIDGES, William (Andrew)   1901-

PERSONAL: Born January 27, 1901, in Franklin, Ind.; son of Harry (a banker) and Katherine (Vaught) Bridges; married Lynn Vandivier, July 31, 1924 (died, 1949); married Lucille Hedges, July 20, 1962 (died, 1968); married Nana Hedges Marts, May 3, 1969. *Education:* Franklin College of Indiana, A.B., 1923. *Politics:* Democrat. *Religion:* Baptist. *Home:* 85 Brook Manor, Pleasantville, N.Y. 10570. *Office:* New York Zoological Park, New York, N.Y. 10460.

CAREER: Chicago Tribune, Chicago, Ill., reporter for European Edition in Paris, France, 1923-25, for Riviera Edition in Nice, France, 1924; *Franklin Star,* Franklin, Ind., reporter, 1925; *Paris Times,* Paris, rewrite desk, 1926-28; *New York Sun,* New York City, rewrite desk, 1929-34; New York Zoological Society, New York City, editor and cu-

rator of publications, 1935-66, curator emeritus, 1966—. Has made collecting trips for New York Bronx Zoo to Trinidad, British Guiana, Mexico, and the Belgian Congo. *Member:* Phi Delta Theta. *Awards, honors:* Litt. D., Franklin College of Indiana, 1952.

WRITINGS: (With Raymond L. Ditmars) *Snake-Hunters' Holiday,* Appleton, 1936; (with Ditmars) *Wild Animal World,* Appleton, 1938; (with Roger Conant) *What Snake Is That?,* Appleton, 1939; *Toco Toucan,* Harper, 1940; *Big Zoo,* Viking, 1941; *True Zoo Stories,* Sloane, 1948; *The Illustrated Book of Wild Animals of the World,* Garden City Publishing, 1948; *Zoo Babies,* Morrow, 1953; *Zoo Expeditions,* Morrow, 1954; *Zoo Pets,* Morrow, 1955; *Zoo Doctor,* Morrow, 1957; *Zoo Celebrities,* Morrow, 1959; *The Golden Book of Zoo Animals,* Golden Press, 1962; *Ookie,* Morrow, 1962; *Walt Disney's Animal Adventures in Lands of Ice and Snow,* Whitman Publishing, 1963; *Lion Island,* Morrow, 1965; (with Lee Saunders Crandall) *A Zoo Man's Notebook,* University of Chicago Press, 1966; *The Bronx Zoo Book of Wild Animals,* Golden Press, 1968; *The New York Aquarium Book of the Water World,* American Heritage Press, 1970; *Zoo Careers,* Morrow, 1971; *Gathering of Animals: An Unconventional History of the New York Zoological Society,* Harper, 1974. Contributor of articles on animal subjects to magazines and journals.

AVOCATIONAL INTERESTS: Collecting books on natural history, the 1890's, and medieval life.

*   *   *

BRIEGEL, Ann C(arrick)   1915-

PERSONAL: Born February 23, 1915, in Westerville, Ohio; daughter of Samuel H. and Sarah M. (Stewart) Carrick; married D. L. Briegel (a consulting engineer), June 19, 1938; children: Samuel, Kristina. *Education:* Ohio Wesleyan University, B.A., 1936; Ohio State University, M.A., 1937. *Religion:* Protestant. *Home:* 5116 Vernon Springs Dr., Atlanta, Ga. 30338. *Office:* Department of English, DeKalb Community College, 555 North Indian Creek Dr., Clarkston, Ga. 30021.

CAREER: DeKalb Community College, Clarkston, Ga., instructor in English, 1966—. *Member:* American Association of University Professors, National Council of Teachers of English, Conference on College Composition and Communication (member of executive committee, 1972-74).

WRITINGS: Conceive and Compose, Holbrook, 1971. Editor, Southeastern Regional Newsletter, Conference on College Composition and Communication, 1971-72.†

*   *   *

BRIGGS, F(red) Allen   1916-

PERSONAL: Born April 23, 1916, in Superior, Neb.; son of James D. (a Baptist minister) and Sadie D. (Reavis) Briggs; married Mary Ruth Garrett (a teacher), December 22, 1941; children: Janet (Mrs. Garrett Welch), Allen Garrett, Marylyn Briggs Donaldson, James. *Education:* Central Missouri State College (now University), B.S., 1937; Baylor University, M.A., 1941; Indiana University, Ph.D., 1954. *Home:* 409 Surrey, Laredo, Tex. 78041. *Office:* Department of English, Laredo State University, Box 537, Laredo, Tex. 78040.

CAREER: High school English teacher in Conroe, Tex., 1939-42; Hardin-Simmons University, Abilene, Tex., associate professor of English, 1947-54; Sul Ross State University, Alpine, Tex., professor of English, 1954-67; University of South Florida, Tampa, professor of English and education, and coordinator of English education, 1967-69; Laredo State University, Laredo, Tex., professor of English, 1970—. Fulbright professor of English, National Polytechnic University and Graduate School of Economics, Athens, Greece, 1957-58. Director, National Defense Education Act (NDEA) Institute in Linguistics, Alpine, Tex., 1965. *Member:* National Council of Teachers of English, National Reading Conference, Conference on English Education, Conference on College Composition and Communication, American Association of University Professors, Texas Council of Teachers of English (president, 1965-67, member of executive board, 1970—).

WRITINGS: Tricks of the Trade in Teaching Language Arts, Cathedral Press, 1961; *The Play of Words,* Harcourt, 1972. Contributor of articles to many journals. Editor, *English in Texas,* 1966-67.

WORK IN PROGRESS: A book on general language; *Por Ninos from Two Cultures.*

* * *

BRIGGS, George M(cSpadden) 1919-

PERSONAL: Born February 21, 1919, in Grantsburg, Wis.; son of George McSpadden and Mary Etta (McNelly) Briggs; married Eleanor Reese, June 21, 1941; children: Catherine, Marilyn, Nancy. *Education:* University of Wisconsin, B.S., 1940, M.S., 1941, Ph.D., 1944. *Home:* 877 Revere Rd., Lafayette, Calif. 94549. *Office:* Department of Nutritional Sciences, University of California, Berkeley, Calif. 94720.

CAREER: University of Maryland, College Park, associate professor, 1945-46, professor of poultry nutrition, 1946-47; University of Minnesota, Minneapolis, associate professor of poultry nutrition, 1947-51; National Institutes of Health, Bethesda, Md., chief of nutrition unit of National Institute of Arthritis and Metabolic Diseases, 1951-58, executive secretary of biochemistry and pharmacology training committees, Division of General Medical Sciences, 1958-60; University of California, Berkeley, professor of nutrition and biochemist in Agricultural Experiment Station, 1960—, chairman of department of nutritional sciences and lecturer in School of Public Health, 1960-70.

MEMBER: American Association for the Advancement of Science (fellow), American Chemical Society, American Dietetic Association, American Institute of Biological Sciences, American Institute of Nutrition (president, 1967-68), American Public Health Association (fellow), American Society of Animal Science, American Society of Biological Chemists, Animal Nutrition Research Council, Institute of Food Technologists, Nutrition Society of Great Britain, Poultry Science Association, Society for Experimental Biology and Medicine, Society for Nutrition Education (president, 1968-69), Federation of American Societies for Experimental Biology (member of board, 1957-58, 1966-69), International Union of Nutritional Sciences (chairman of committee on graduate degrees in nutrition, 1967-72), Sigma Xi, Phi Kappa Phi. *Awards, honors:* Borden Award of Poultry Science Association, 1958, for basic research in the area of nutritional interrelationships.

WRITINGS: (With L. Jean Bogert and Doris Howes Calloway) *Nutrition and Physical Fitness,* 8th edition (Briggs was not associated with earlier editions), Saunders, 1966, 9th edition, 1973. Contributor of about one hundred articles to science journals. Associate editor, *Nutrition Reviews,* 1954-58; member of editorial board, *Journal of Nutrition,* 1962-67, and *American Journal of Clinical Nutrition,* 1975-77; executive editor, *Journal of Nutrition Education,* 1968-76.

BRIGGS, Kenneth R. 1934-

PERSONAL: Born November 25, 1934, in Fort Worth, Tex.; son of Clinton Gibson and Lenora (Field) Briggs; married Faye Matthews, March 2, 1954; children: Pamela, Russell Scott, Janet Elayne. *Education:* North Texas State University, B.S., 1959, M.Ed., 1963, Ed.D., 1966. *Home:* 197 Stratton Lane, Beaumont, Tex. 77707. *Office:* Box 10034, Lamar University, Beaumont, Tex. 77710.

CAREER: High school mathematics teacher and coach in Dallas, Tex., 1959-61, in Seagoville, Tex., 1961-64; North Texas State University, Denton, instructor in psychology and education, 1964-66; Lamar University, Beaumont, Tex., assistant professor, 1966-69, associate professor, 1969-72, professor of secondary education, 1973—. *Military service:* U.S. Air Force, 1953-57; became staff sergeant. *Member:* National Education Association (life member), American Association for Higher Education, Association of Teacher Educators, Association for Research in Growth Relationships, Texas Association of College Teachers, Texas Society of College Teachers of Education, Texas Association of Teacher Educators, Texas State Teachers Association (life member), Phi Delta Kappa (life member).

WRITINGS: Teaching in the 70's, Kendall/Hunt, 1971. Contributor to education journals.

AVOCATIONAL INTERESTS: Tennis, coin collecting.

* * *

BRIGHT, William 1928-

PERSONAL: Born August 13, 1928, in Oxnard, Calif.; son of Oliver E. (a farmer) and Ethel (Ruggles) Bright; married Elizabeth Halloran, 1952 (divorced); married second wife, Jane Orstan, 1962 (deceased); married third wife, Marcia Kinnamon, 1964 (deceased); married fourth wife, Debra Levy, 1975; children: (first marriage) Susannah. *Education:* University of California, Berkeley, A.B., 1949, Ph.D., 1955. *Office:* Department of Linguistics, University of California, Los Angeles, Calif. 90024.

CAREER: Deccan College, Poona, India, linguistic scholar, 1955-57; U.S. State Department, Washington, D.C., linguist, 1957-58; University of California, Berkeley, assistant professor of speech, 1958-59; University of California, Los Angeles, assistant professor, 1959-62, associate professor, 1962-66, professor of linguistics and anthropology, 1966—. *Military service:* U.S. Army, 1952-54. *Member:* Linguistic Society of America. *Awards, honors:* American Council of Learned Societies fellowship, 1964-65; Guggenheim fellowship, 1972.

WRITINGS: The Karok Language, University of California Press, 1957; *An Outline of Colloquial Kannada,* Deccan College, 1958; (with S. A. Khan) *The Urdu Writing System,* American Council of Learned Societies, 1958; *Spelling for Foreign Students of English,* College Book Store, 1959; (with S. Rau and M. Narvekar) *Spoken Kannada,* University of California (Berkeley), 1960; *Animals of Acculturation in the California Indian Languages,* University of California Press, 1960; (editor) *Studies in California Linguistics,* University of California Press, 1964; (editor) *Sociolinguistics,* Mouton, 1965; *A Luiseno Dictionary,* University of California Press, 1968; *Variation and Change in Language,* Stanford University Press, 1976. Contributor to over twenty-five books. Editor, *Language.*

WORK IN PROGRESS: American Indian languages; sociolinguistics of South Asia.

BRILLIANT, Richard 1929-

PERSONAL: Born November 20, 1929, in Boston, Mass.; son of Frank (a businessman) and Pauline (Apt) Brilliant; married Eleanor Luria (a doctor of social work), June 24, 1951; children: Stephanie, Livia, Franca, Myron. *Education:* Yale University, B.A., 1951, M.A., 1956, Ph.D., 1960; Harvard University, LL.B., 1954. *Home:* 10 Wayside Lane, Scarsdale, N.Y. 10583. *Office:* Department of Art History, Columbia University, New York, N.Y. 10027.

CAREER: Admitted to the Bar of the State of Massachusetts, 1954; University of Pennsylvania, Philadelphia, assistant professor, 1962-64, associate professor, 1964-69, professor of art history, 1969-70; Columbia University, New York, N.Y., professor of art history and archaeology, 1970—. Mellon Visiting Professor of Fine Arts, University of Pittsburgh, 1971. *Member:* College Art Association, Society for Biblical Literature, American Academy in Rome (fellow), Society for the Promotion of Hellenic and Roman Studies, American Numismatic Society, Archaeological Institute of America, German Archaeological Institute (corresponding member), Connecticut Academy of Arts and Sciences, Massachusetts Bar Association, Phi Beta Kappa. *Awards, honors:* Fulbright scholar in Italy, 1957-59; Rome Prize from American Academy in Rome, 1960-62; Guggenheim fellow, 1967-68; National Endowment for the Humanities grant, 1972-73.

WRITINGS: Gesture and Rank in Roman Art, Connecticut Academy of Arts and Sciences, 1963; *The Arch of Septimus Severus in Rome,* American Academy in Rome, 1967; *Arts of the Ancient Greeks,* McGraw, 1973; *Roman Art,* Phaidon, 1974. Contributor of articles and reviews to journals.

WORK IN PROGRESS: Provincial Art; The Concept of the Primitive: Captain Cook to Surrealism; Essays in Roman Art.

SIDELIGHTS: Brilliant told *CA:* "I have lived in Rome more than six years and travelled widely looking at works of art—I like to read, write, and teach—I enjoy very much doing what I am doing."

*   *   *

BRISBANE, Holly E. 1927-

PERSONAL: Born September 15, 1927, in Lakefield, Minn.; daughter of Charles H. (a farmer) and Rose (Seydel) Wagner; married Robert C. Brisbane (sales manager of an insurance company), December 1, 1951; children: James Guydon. *Education:* South Dakota State College (now South Dakota State University), B.S., 1949; Mankato State College, M.A. (with honors), 1952. *Politics:* Republican. *Religion:* Lutheran. *Home:* 521 Day St., Fairmont, Minn. 56031.

CAREER: High school teacher of home economics and English in Sioux Valley, Minn., 1952-53, Welcome, Minn., 1953-55, and Fairmont, Minn., 1955-61. *Member:* American Home Economics Association, Minnesota Home Economics Association, American Association of University Women (chapter president, 1964-65), Interlaken Golf Club (Fairmont).

*WRITINGS—*With Audrey Riker; textbooks: *The Developing Child,* Charles A. Bennett, 1965, 3rd edition, 1978; *Married Life,* Charles A. Bennett, 1970, revised edition, 1976. Contributor of articles to *Parents' Magazine, Ladies' Home Journal, Snow Sports,* and to home economics journals and travel magazines.

AVOCATIONAL INTERESTS: Travel (has visited more

than twenty countries in Africa, U.S.S.R., Southeast Asia, Australia, Europe, and Central America), golf, skiing, interior decorating, fashion designing, sewing.

*   *   *

BRODY, Baruch A(lter) 1943-

PERSONAL: Born April 21, 1943, in Brooklyn, N.Y.; son of Lester and Gussie (Glass) Brody; married Dena Grosser, August, 1965; children: Todd Daniel, Jeremy Keith. *Education:* Brooklyn College of the City University of New York, B.A., 1962; Princeton University, M.A., 1965, Ph.D., 1967. *Religion:* Jewish. *Home:* 4315 Breakwood, Houston, Tex. 77096. *Office:* 304 Lovett Hall, Rice University, Houston, Tex. 77001.

CAREER: Massachusetts Institute of Technology, Cambridge, assistant professor, 1967-73, associate professor of philosophy, 1973-75; Rice University, Houston, Tex., associate professor, 1975-77, professor of philosophy, 1977—, chairman of department, 1975—, chairman of legal studies program, 1976—. Member of Jewish Community Council of Boston, 1971-73; former member of Town Meeting, Brookline, Mass. *Member:* American Philosophical Association.

WRITINGS: (Editor with Nicholas Capaldi) *Science: Men, Methods, and Goals,* W. A. Benjamin, 1968; (editor) *Thomas Reidy Essays,* M.I.T. Press, 1969; (editor) *Moral Rules and Particular Circumstances,* Prentice-Hall, 1970; (editor) *Readings in the Philosophy of Science,* Prentice-Hall, 1970; (editor) *Readings in the Philosophy of Religion,* Prentice-Hall, 1973; *Logic: Theoretical and Applied,* Prentice-Hall, 1973; *Abortion and the Sanctity of Human Life,* M.I.T. Press, 1975; *Beginning Philosophy,* Prentice-Hall, 1976; (editor) *Mental Health,* Reidel, 1978. Contributor to *Journal of Philosophy, Monist, Philosophy of Science, American Philosophical Quarterly,* and other publications.

WORK IN PROGRESS: Identity and Essence; Sir William Hamilton's Philosophical Writings.

*   *   *

BRODY, David 1930-

PERSONAL: Born June 5, 1930, in Elizabeth, N.J.; son of Barnet (a fruit peddler) and Ida (Gulker) Brody; married Susan Schapiro, October 20, 1955; children: Sara, Pamela, Jonathan. *Education:* Harvard University, A.B., 1952, M.A., 1953, Ph.D., 1958. *Home:* 62 Richardson Rd., Kensington, Calif. 94707. *Office:* Department of History, University of California, Davis, Calif. 95616.

CAREER: Columbia University, New York, N.Y., assistant professor of history, 1961-65; Ohio State University, Columbus, associate professor of history, 1965-67; University of California, Davis, professor of history, 1967—. *Member:* American Historical Association, Organization of American Historians, Labor History Association. *Awards, honors:* Social Science Research Council fellow, 1966-67.

WRITINGS: Steelworkers in America, Harvard University Press, 1960; *The Butcher Workmen,* Harvard University Press, 1964; *Labor in Crisis,* Lippincott, 1965; (editor) *Industrial America in the Twentieth Century,* Crowell, 1967; (with J. Braeman and R. H. Bremner) *Change and Continuity in Twentieth-Century America,* Ohio State University Press, 1968; (editor, with I. Unger and P. Goodman) *The American Past,* Xerox College Publishing, 1971; (editor, with Unger and Goodman) *The Course of American History,* Xerox College Publishing, 1971; (editor, with Unger and Goodman) *The Record of American History,* Xerox College Publishing, 1971; (editor, with Braeman and Bremner) *Twentieth-Century American Foreign Policy,* Ohio State University Press, 1971; (editor) *The American Labor Movement,* Harper, 1971; (editor) *Essays on the Age of Enterprise, 1870-1900,* Dryden, 1974.

WORK IN PROGRESS: A book on labor and the New Deal; an interpretative history of American labor.

* * *

BROMLEY, John Carter 1937-

PERSONAL: Born October 5, 1937, in Denver, Colo.; son of Charles Dunham (a lawyer) and Sarah (Wendelken) Bromley; children: Lauren Coles. *Education:* Attended University of Michigan, 1958-59; University of Colorado, A.B., 1961, M.A., 1963; graduate study at University of Copenhagen, 1964-65, and University of Denver, 1965-69. *Home:* 522 Humboldt St., Denver, Colo. 80203. *Office:* Office of the Senate Majority Leader, Suite 222, State Capital, Denver, Colo. 80220.

CAREER: Wayne State College, Wayne, Neb., instructor in English, 1961-63; Copenhagen International High School, Copenhagen, Denmark, headmaster, 1964-65; University of Colorado, Boulder, instructor in English, 1965-70; State of Colorado, Office of the Governor, Denver, director of research, 1970-74; newspaper columnist, 1974—. *Military service:* U.S. Army, 1958. *Member:* Modern Language Association of America, Royal Modern Language Association, Shakespeare Research Opportunities (contributing member), Chi Psi.

WRITINGS: The Shakespearean Kings, Colorado Associated University Press, 1971.

WORK IN PROGRESS: Shakespeare's Ancient World, a study of Shakespeare's artistry as a political dramatist and social theorist; *1974: The Year of the Rat,* a study of the national and international events of that year, with emphasis upon the Middle East, Ireland, Cyprus, and the Nixon resignation.

* * *

BRONWELL, Arthur B. 1909-

PERSONAL: Born August 18, 1909, in Chicago, Ill.; son of Arthur F. and Lulu M. Bronwell; married Virginia R. White, August 2, 1941; children: James Arthur, Susan Virginia Bronwell Carter. *Education:* Illinois Institute of Technology, B.S., 1933, M.S., 1936; Northwestern University, M.B.A., 1945. *Home:* Hillyndale Rd., Storrs, Conn. 06268. *Office:* School of Engineering, University of Connecticut, Storrs, Conn. 06268.

CAREER: Northwestern University, Evanston, Ill., instructor, 1937-40, assistant professor, 1940-43, associate professor, 1943-47, professor of electrical engineering, 1947-54; American Society for Engineering Education, Evanston, Ill., executive secretary, 1947-55; Worcester Polytechnic Institute, Worcester, Mass., president, 1955-62; University of Connecticut, Storrs, professor of electrical engineering, 1962—, dean of School of Engineering, 1970—. Holder of patents connected with color television. Member of advisory committee, National Science Foundation.

MEMBER: Institute of Electrical and Electronics Engineers (fellow), American Society for Engineering Education, Council on Foreign Relations. *Awards, honors:* Distinguished Alumni Citation, Illinois Institute of Technology, 1957; LL.D., Northeastern University, 1955; D.Sc., Wayne State University, 1958.

WRITINGS: (With Robert Beam) *Theory and Applications of Microwaves,* McGraw, 1947; *Advanced Mathematics in Physics and Engineering,* McGraw, 1955; *Science and Technology in the World of the Future,* Wiley, 1970. Editor, *Journal of Engineering Education* (publication of American Society for Engineering Education), 1945-48.

WORK IN PROGRESS: Freedom and the Creative Society.

* * *

BROOKOVER, Wilbur B(one) 1911-

PERSONAL: Born March 30, 1911, in Huntington County, Ind.; son of Guy L. (a museum director) and Erma (Bone) Brookover; married Edna M. Eberhart (a teacher), June 21, 1937; children: Linda Brookover Bourque, Thomas, George. *Education:* Manchester College, A.B., 1933; University of Wisconsin, M.A., 1939, Ph.D., 1943. *Politics:* Democrat. *Religion:* Protestant. *Home:* 930 Huntington Rd., East Lansing, Mich. 48823. *Office:* Michigan State University, 142 West Owen 'Hall, East Lansing, Mich. 48823.

CAREER: High school social studies teacher and athletic coach in Indiana, 1933-38; Butler University, Indianapolis, Ind., instructor in sociology, 1940-41; Indiana State Teachers College (now Indiana State University), Terre Haute, instructor, 1941-43; University of Wisconsin—Madison, lecturer in sociology, 1946; Michigan State University, East Lansing, assistant professor, 1946-48, associate professor, 1948-53, professor of social science, sociology and anthropology, 1953-57, professor of sociology and education, 1957—, and of urban and metropolitan studies, 1973—, director, Bureau of Educational Research, and coordinator, Ford Foundation Pakistan Project, 1957-60, assistant dean, Research and Publications, College of Education, 1960-63, chairman, Foundations of Education, College of Education, 1963, and director, Social Science Teaching Institute, 1964-67, associate director, Center for Urban Affairs, 1970-73. Member, East Lansing City Council, 1967-75; Mayor of East Lansing, Mich., 1971-75. Visiting professor, Western Michigan University, 1966-68; research consultant, U.S. Office of Education, Department of Health, Education and Welfare. *Military service:* U.S. Navy, 1943-46; U.S. Naval Reserve, retired as lieutenant.

MEMBER: American Sociological Association (former visiting scientist; president, Sociology of Education Section, 1966, 1978), American Educational Research Association, Ohio Valley Sociological Society (president, 1961-62), Torch Club (local president, 1971).

WRITINGS: (Co-author) *Youth and the World at Work,* Social Research Service, Michigan State College, 1949; (editor with Edgar Schuler, Duane Gibson, and others) *Readings in Sociology,* Crowell, 1952, 5th edition, 1975; (with Orden C. Smucker and John Fred Thaden) *A Sociology of Education,* American Book Co., 1955, 2nd edition (with David Gottlieb), 1964, 3rd edition (with Edsel L. Erickson), Dorsey, 1975; (co-editor) *Readings in Social Science,* three volumes, Michigan State University Press, 1955; (with Ann Paterson and Shailer Thomas) *Self-Concept of Ability and School Achievement,* Report I, Office of Research and Publications, Michigan State University, 1962, Report II (with Jean LePere, Don Hamachek, Thomas, and Erickson), School for Advanced Study, Research Services, Michigan State University, 1965, Report III (with Erickson and Lee Joiner), Human Learning Research Institute, Michigan State University, 1967; (with others) *The College Student,*

Library of Education, Center for Applied Research in Education, 1965; (with Kenton Schurr) *The Effect of Special Class Placement on the Self-Concept of Ability of the Educable Mentally Retarded Child*, Educational Publication Services, Michigan State University, 1967; (with Erickson) *Society, Schools, and Learning* (Education Book List selection as outstanding book in education, 1969-70), Allyn & Bacon, 1969.

Contributor: M. H. and John Berry Biesanz, *Modern Society: An Introduction to Social Science,* Prentice-Hall, 1954; *The Conference on Education and Student Life in the United States,* Northwestern University and Hazen Foundation, 1957; *Education for a Changing World of Work,* U.S. Government Printing Office, 1963. Contributor to *National Council of Social Studies Yearbook, Education for Citizenship,* 1952, *Personnel and Guidance Journal,* 1969, and *Encyclopedia of Education,* 1971; contributor of articles to *Journal of Educational Research, Teachers College Journal, American Sociological Review, Journal of Experimental Education, Social Science, Education Digest, Educational Leadership, Sociology and Social Research, School and Society, Kolner Zeitschrift fuer Sociologie and Sozialpsychologie, Phi Delta Kappan, Journal of Human Resources, Medicine and Science in Sports,* and other periodicals and educational journals. Author of monographs and research reports. Associate editor, *Sociology of Education,* 1965-71.

WORK IN PROGRESS: A research project entitled "Identification and Analysis of Elementary School Social Environment with Social Economic Status and Racial Composition of the Selected School Population."

* * *

BROOKS, George E(dward), Jr. 1933-

PERSONAL: Born April 20, 1933, in Lynn, Mass.; son of George Edward and Bessie H. (Critzer) Brooks; married Mary C. Crowley (an artist), June 15, 1957; children: George E. III, Douglas J. *Education:* Dartmouth College, A.B., 1957; Boston University, M.A., 1958, Ph.D., 1962. *Home:* 1701 Longwood W., Bloomington, Ind. 47401. *Office:* Department of History, Indiana University, Bloomington, Ind. 47401.

CAREER: Boston University, Boston, Mass., instructor in history, spring, 1960, summer, 1962; Indiana University, Bloomington, assistant professor, 1962-68, associate professor, 1968-75, professor of history, 1975—. Visiting associate professor, Tufts University, summer, 1969. *Military service:* U.S. Army, Military Police, 1954-55. *Member:* African Studies Association (fellow). *Awards, honors:* Herman Frederic Lieber Memorial Award for distinguished teaching, 1970; Social Science Research Council grant for research in Portugal, 1971-72; National Endowment for the Humanities grant for research in Portugal and West Africa, 1976-77.

WRITINGS: (Editor with Norman R. Bennett) *New England Merchants in Africa: A History through Documents, 1802-1865,* Boston University Press, 1965; (contributor) Bennett, Daniel McCall, and Jeffrey Butler, editors, *Western African History,* Praeger, 1969; *Yankee Traders, Old Coasters and African Middlemen: A History of American Legitimate Trade with West Africa in the Nineteenth Century,* Boston University Press, 1970; *The Kru Mariner in the Nineteenth Century: An Historical Compendium* (monograph), Liberian Studies Association, 1972. Contributor of articles to *Sierra Leone Studies, American Neptune,* and other journals; contributor of reviews to *Choice* and

American Historical Review. Member of editorial advisory board, *African Historical Studies,* 1968—, and *Liberian Studies Journal,* 1968—.

WORK IN PROGRESS: Two monographs, *Guinea-Bissau in the Nineteenth Century: Evolution of a Luso-African,* and *Commerce on the Windward Coast of West Africa in the Nineteenth Century;* editing a volume of the journals, letters, and business correspondence of Enoch Richmond Ware, African trader and founder of an American firm trading with West Africa.

* * *

BROOKS, Lester 1924-

PERSONAL: Born November 8, 1924, in Des Moines, Iowa; son of Lester James (a regional manager for Prudential Insurance) and Dorothy (Boldrick) Brooks; married Patricia Kersten (a writer), September 10, 1950; children: Lester James III, Jonathan, Christopher. *Education:* University of Iowa, A.B., 1948; Columbia University, A.M., 1949; University of London, further graduate study, 1949. *Politics:* Democrat. *Home:* 43 Marshall Ridge Rd., New Canaan, Conn. 06840. *Agent:* Paul R. Reynolds, Inc., 12 East 41st St., New York, N.Y. 10017.

CAREER: National Urban League, New York City, assistant public relations director, 1950-51; U.S. Foreign Service, information officer in Manila, Philippines, 1951-53; Chase Manhattan Bank, New York City, community relations director, 1958-64; writer specializing in Black and contemporary Japanese history. Director, Art Originals Ltd.; vice-president, National Council on Philanthropy, 1964; member of communication committee, National Urban League. *Military service:* U.S. Army, 1943-46; served in Pacific theater.

MEMBER: Association for Asian Studies, Committee of Concerned Asian Scholars, Public Relations Society of America, National Association for the Advancement of Colored People, National Urban League, Authors Guild, Museum of Black History, Connecticut Civil Liberties Union. *Awards, honors: Great Civilizations of Ancient Africa* was included among the best books of 1971 by Children's Book Council, *School Library Journal,* American Library Association's *Booklist,* and the Library of Congress; *How to Buy Property Abroad* was selected for one hundred best business books of 1974 by *Library Journal.*

WRITINGS: (Ghost-writer) Whitney M. Young, Jr., *To Be Equal,* McGraw, 1964; *Behind Japan's Surrender,* McGraw, 1968; (ghost-writer) Henry Steeger, *You Can Remake America,* Doubleday, 1970; *Great Civilizations of Ancient Africa* (teen book), Four Winds, 1971; (with Guichard Parris) *Blacks in the City: A History of the Urban League,* Little, Brown, 1971; *Great American Autos* (juvenile), Scholastic Book Services, 1972; (with wife, Patricia Brooks) *How to Buy Property Abroad,* Doubleday, 1974; (with P. Brooks) *How to Buy a Condominium,* Stein & Day, 1975, condensed edition, U.S. News & World Report, 1976.

BIOGRAPHICAL/CRITICAL SOURCES: Village Voice, November 6, 1969; *Journal of Economic Literature,* December, 1974.

* * *

BROOKS, William D(ean) 1929-

PERSONAL: Born September 10, 1929, in Bucklin, Kan.; son of William Lloyd (a cattleman) and Fonzie (Smith) Brooks; married Grace Margaret Andrews (a university teacher), August 22, 1948; children: Susan Jean, William

Steven, Randy Mark, Debra Dee. *Education:* Southwestern College, Winfield, Kan., A.B., 1950; University of Colorado, M.A., 1960; Ohio University, Ph.D., 1965. *Home:* 911 Mockingbird Lane, Norman, Okla. 73091. *Office:* Kaufman Hall, University of Oklahoma, Norman, Okla. 73069.

CAREER: Haven High School, Haven, Kan., teacher, 1950-54; Garden City Junior College, Garden City, Kan., instructor in speech, 1954-61; McPherson College, McPherson, Kan., associate professor of speech and chairman of the department, 1961-63; Ohio University, Athens, instructor in speech, 1964; University of Kansas, Lawrence, assistant professor of communications and associate chairman of the department, 1965-67; Purdue University, Lafayette, Ind., associate professor, 1967-71, director of teacher training in speech, 1967-77; University of Oklahoma, Norman, professor of communication and chairman of department, 1977—.

WRITINGS: Introduction to Debate, Exposition, 1966; *Methods of Research in Communication,* Houghton, 1970; *Speech Communication,* W. C. Brown, 1971; *Instructional Strategies for Speech Communication,* W. C. Brown, 1971; *Teaching Speech Communication in the Secondary School,* Houghton, 1972; *Public Communication,* Harper, 1974; *Interpersonal Communication,* W. C. Brown, 1976; *Business Communication,* Cummings, 1977.

AVOCATIONAL INTERESTS: Collecting antique and classic cars.

*　　*　　*

BROWER, Linda A. 1945-
(Linda A. Meeks)

PERSONAL: Born June 9, 1945, in Toledo, Ohio; daughter of James Calvin (an advertising executive) and Elsie (Day) Brower; married Jack Meeks, Jr., December 19, 1970. *Education:* University of Toledo, B.A., 1968; University of Wisconsin, M.S. in Ed., 1969. *Religion:* Congregationalist. *Home:* 2473 Danvers Ct., Columbus, Ohio 43220. *Office:* Ohio State University, 1760 Neil Ave., Columbus, Ohio 43210.

CAREER: Ohio State University, Columbus, instructor in health education, 1969—. *Member:* American Association for Health, Physical Education and Recreation, American School Health Association, Ohio Council of Family Relations, Family Life and Sex Education Council, Pi Beta Phi, Alpha Kappa Delta.

WRITINGS: (Editor with John J. Burt) *Education for Sexuality: Concepts and Programs for Teaching,* Saunders, 1970.

WORK IN PROGRESS: Health Science: Concepts and Behavioral Objectives for the Elementary School, with John J. Burt.†

*　　*　　*

BROWN, Duane 1937-

PERSONAL: Born July 10, 1937, in Owensville, Ind.; son of Lester W. (a farmer) and Mary R. (Wilson) Brown; married Sandra Dee Thompson (a school counselor), July 24, 1968; children: Cassandra, Kindra, Jeffry, Tamara. *Education:* Purdue University, B.S., 1959, M.S., 1962, Ph.D., 1965. *Politics:* Republican. *Home:* 619 Long Leaf Dr., Chapel Hill, N.C. 27514. *Office:* School of Education, University of North Carolina, Chapel Hill, N.C. 27514.

CAREER: High school teacher of biology and agriculture in

Spiceland, Ind., 1959-62; Indiana Department of Public Instruction, Indianapolis, field supervisor of guidance, 1963-65; Iowa State University, Ames, assistant professor of guidance and counseling, 1965-68; West Virginia University, Morgantown, associate professor of counseling and guidance and chairman of department, 1968-73; University of North Carolina at Chapel Hill, professor of guidance and counseling, 1973—, coordinator of counseling psychology program, 1973—. Visiting summer instructor, Purdue University, 1965; visiting summer professor at Gannon College, 1966, 1968, 1973, and Drake University, 1967, 1969. *Member:* American Personnel and Guidance Association, Association of Counselor Educators and Supervisors, National Vocational Guidance Association, American School Counselors Association, American Psychological Association, Phi Delta Kappa.

WRITINGS: Vocational Choice: A Review and Critique, Houghton, 1970; *Changing Student Behavior: A New Approach to Discipline,* W. C. Brown, 1971; (with David J. Srebalus) *Guidance Concepts and Practices: An Introduction,* W. C. Brown, 1972; (editor with Srebalus) *Guidance Concepts and Practices: Selected Readings,* W. C. Brown, 1973; (with G. D. Brown) *Survey of Social Science,* McGraw, 1975; (with wife, Sandra Dee Brown) *Consulting with Elementary School Teachers,* Houghton, 1975; *Consultation: Strategy for Improving Education,* Allyn & Bacon, 1978. Contributor of more than twenty articles to journals in his field.

WORK IN PROGRESS: Second edition of *Survey of Social Science.*

AVOCATIONAL INTERESTS: Hunting, fishing, camping.

*　　*　　*

BROWN, Frederic 1906-1972

October 29, 1906—March 13(?), 1972; American mystery and science fiction writer and author of film and television scripts. Obituaries: *New York Times,* March 14, 1972; *Washington Post,* March 14, 1972.

*　　*　　*

BROWN, Gerald W(illiam) 1916-

PERSONAL: Born February 16, 1916, Emmet, Neb.; son of Matt A. (a farmer) and Nellie (Manson) Brown; married Barbara Howland (a teacher), May 18, 1945; children: Bruce Henry, Andrew William. *Education:* Attended Westmar College, 1934-36; University of Nebraska, B.S., 1939; attended U.S. Naval Academy, 1941; University of California, Berkeley, M.A., 1951; Stanford University, Ed.D., 1954. *Politics:* Republican. *Home address:* Box 307, Danville, Calif. 94526. *Office:* Department of Education, California State University, Hayward, 25800 Hillary St., Hayward, Calif. 94542.

CAREER: Teacher in high schools in Pierce, Neb. and Carlisle, Iowa, 1939-42, and in Farmington, N.M. and Lafayette, Calif., 1945-52; Los Angeles State College of Applied Arts and Sciences (now California State University, Los Angeles), assistant chairman of division of education, 1954-60; University of California, Riverside, associate professor of secondary education, 1960-64; University of Hawaii, Honolulu, associate professor of elementary education, 1964-65; California State University, Hayward, director of teacher education, 1965-68, professor of education, 1967—. Curriculum coordinator, U.S. Agency of International Development project in Jamaica, 1968-69. International teaching fellow, University of Melbourne, 1971-73. Mathematics textbook advisor and consultant, Curriculum Advisor's Service. *Military service:* U.S. Navy, engineering officer, 1942-45. *Member:* National Education Association (life), National Council of Teachers of Mathematics, National Commission of Teacher Education and Professional Standards, National Society for the Study of Education, California Teachers Association, California State Mathematics Council, Commonwealth Club of San Francisco.

WRITINGS: (With Edwin Wandt) *The Essentials of Educational Evaluation,* Holt, 1957; (with Lucien Kinney and Russell Blythe) "Holt Arithmetic" series, Holt, *Book I,* with workbook, 1961, *Book II,* with workbook, 1961; (with Kinney and Vincent Ruble) "Holt General Mathematics" series, Holt, *Book I,* 1966, revised edition published as *Problem Solving Mathematics,* 1972, *Book II,* 1968. Contributor to *California Mathematics Council Bulletin, Mathematics Teacher, Arithmetic Teacher, Updating Mathematics, California Journal of Secondary Education, Christian Science Monitor,* and other publications. Editor, *California Mathematics Council Bulletin,* 1955-60; mathematics editor, *California Journal of Secondary Education,* 1957-60.

*   *   *

BROWN, John Pairman 1923-

PERSONAL: Born May 16, 1923, in Hanover, N.H.; son of Bancroft Huntington (a professor) and Eleanor (Pairman) Brown; married Dorothy Emily Waymouth, June 26, 1954; children: George, Felicity, Maryam, David. *Education:* Dartmouth College, A.B. (summa cum laude), 1944; Harvard University, additional study, 1946-49; General Theological Seminary, New York, N.Y., S.T.B., 1952; Union Theological Seminary, New York, N.Y., Th.D., 1956. *Politics:* "Peace-oriented." *Home:* 1630 Arch St., Berkeley, Calif. 94709.

CAREER: Ordained Episcopal priest, 1953; Hobart College, Geneva, N.Y., instructor in classics, 1956-58; American University of Beirut, Beirut, Lebanon, associate professor of ancient history, 1958-65; Church Divinity School of the Pacific, Berkeley, Calif., professor of New Testament and Christian ethics, 1965-67; South Campus Community Ministry, Berkeley, Calif., theologian, 1967-72; Ecumenical Peace Institute of Northern California, member of staff, 1972—; interim executive director, Northern California Ecumenical Council, 1977—. *Military service:* U.S. Army Air Forces, 1944-46; became sergeant. *Member:* Society of Biblical Literature, American Philological Association.

WRITINGS: The Displaced Person's Almanac, privately printed, 1961, Beacon Press, 1962; *The Liberated Zone: A Guide to Christian Resistance,* John Knox, 1969; *The Lebanon and Phoenicia: Ancient Texts Illustrating Their Physical Geography and Native Industries,* Volume I: *The Physical Setting and the Forest,* American University of Beirut, 1969; *Planet on Strike,* Seabury, 1970; *To a Sister on Laurel Drive,* Seabury, 1971; (with Richard L. York) *The Covenant of Peace: A Liberation Prayer Book,* Morehouse, 1971.

Contributor to Malcolm Boyd, editor, *The Underground Church,* Sheed, 1968 and Paul A. Crow, Jr. and William Jerry Boney, editors, *Church Union at Mid-Point,* Association Press. Also contributor to *Journal of Biblical Literature, New Testament Studies, Christian Century, Journal of Semitic Studies,* and other publications.

WORK IN PROGRESS: A reconstruction of the *Book of Jesus,* three volumes, for Judson; a book on survival; a nov-

elistic history of the early church against the Roman empire, first volume titled *The Census of Quirinius.*

*   *   *

BROWN, Les(ter L.) 1928-

PERSONAL: Born December 20, 1928, in Indiana Harbor, Ind.; son of Irving H. (a retailer) and Helen (Feigenbaum) Brown; married Jean Rosalie Slaymaker, June 12, 1959; children: Jessica, Joshua, Rebecca. *Education:* Roosevelt University, B.A., 1950. *Politics:* Democrat. *Religion:* Jewish. *Home:* 131 North Chatsworth Ave., Larchmont, N.Y. 10538. *Office:* New York Times, 229 West 43rd St., New York, N.Y. 10036.

CAREER: Downbeat magazine, Chicago, Ill., associate editor, 1955-56; Gate of Horn (cabaret), Chicago, operator and owner, 1956-57; *Variety,* Inc., Chicago, bureau chief, 1957-65, New York City, television and radio editor, 1965-73; *New York Times,* New York City, television-radio correspondent, 1973—. Instructor, Columbia College of Chicago, 1959-62. Adjunct professor in mass communications, Hunter College of the City University of New York, 1972-75; faculty member, New School for Social Research, 1977—. *Military service:* U.S. Army, 1951-53.

WRITINGS: Television: The Business Behind the Box, Harcourt, 1971; *Electric Media,* Harcourt, 1973; *The New York Times Encyclopedia of Television,* Quadrangle, 1977. Contributor to *Britannica Book of the Year* and to periodicals.

SIDELIGHTS: Les Brown told *CA:* "I write books because of my intense interest in the subject I have covered for newspapers most of my professional life. The books catch the overflow of the material I gather in my daily work, but more importantly they allow me to organize and interpret my own reporting and to make a tapestry of the thousands of strands of information that appear without much intertwining in the scattered, seemingly unconnected and often brief newspaper pieces. To state it another way, in newspaper work one covers aspects of the system (in my case, television) according to their topicality; in a book the writer takes on the system whole. My books have all been written without sabbaticals from my job, on the weekends and in the evenings after the children have gone to bed; it is not a regimen I would recommend."

Les Brown wrote the lyrics to the song "Abilene."

*   *   *

BROWN, Michael 1931-

PERSONAL: Born March 7, 1931; son of Raymond (a naval officer) and Gwendolyn (Salisbury) Brown; married Sybil Frances Thompson (a senior information officer in civil service), July 24, 1959. *Education:* Birkbeck College, London, B.A. (honors), 1958. *Politics:* Socialist. *Religion:* None. *Home:* 33 Rugby Chambers, Rugby St., London W.C.1, England. *Office:* Hamish Hamilton Children's Books Ltd., 34 Bloomsbury Way, London W.C.1, England.

CAREER: Hamish Hamilton Children's Books Ltd., London, England, production director.

WRITINGS—All juvenile: (Editor) *Small Boat Adventures,* illustrations by Gareth Floyd, David White, 1968; *Shackleton's Epic Voyage,* illustrations by Raymond Briggs, Coward, 1969; (editor) *The Hamish Hamilton Book of Sea Legends,* illustrations by Krystyna Turska, Hamish Hamilton, 1971, published as *A Cavalcade of Sea Legends,* Walck, 1972; *All at Sea: Adventures and Misadventures Afloat,*

Hamish Hamilton, 1975; *Sailing Ships,* Hamish Hamilton, 1975.

BIOGRAPHICAL/CRITICAL SOURCES: Books and Bookmen, November, 1968; *Times Literary Supplement,* October 16, 1969.†

* * *

BROWN, Ralph Adams 1908-

PERSONAL: Born June 13, 1908, in Vershire, Vt.; son of Evarts Philbrook (a merchant) and Alma F. (Adams) Brown; married Marian A. Rayburn (a psychologist), February 8, 1947; children: Richard Adams, Linda Viola (Mrs. James N. Kerr). *Education:* University of New Hampshire, B.A., 1929; Columbia University, M.A., 1933, Ed.D., 1950. *Politics:* Democrat. *Religion:* Presbyterian. *Home:* 44 West Court St., Cortland, N.Y. 13045. *Office:* Department of History, State University of New York College at Cortland, Graham Ave., Cortland, N.Y. 13045.

CAREER: Montpelier Seminary, Montpelier, Vt., assistant headmaster, 1930-32; teacher in high schools in New Jersey, 1933-34, 1938-42; radio announcer and newspaper reporter in Cornish, N.H., 1934-37; National Council for the Social Studies, New York, N.Y., assistant editor, 1946-47; State University of New York College at Cortland, professor of American history, 1947-58, 1961—, chairman of department, 1947-58, dean of college, 1958-61. Chairman, New York State Council on Economic Education, 1962-64. Trustee, Cortland Free Library, 1956-61; director, Dime Federal Savings & Loan Association, Cortland, 1964—; chairman, Cortland County Liberal Party, 1966-68. *Military service:* U.S. Coast Guard, 1942-45; became chief petty officer.

MEMBER: National Council for the Social Studies (member of board of directors, 1960-63), National Education Association, American Historical Association, Organization of American Historians, New Hampshire Historical Society, Cortland Rotary Club (president, 1963-64).

WRITINGS: (Editor with wife, Marian R. Brown) *Impressions of America,* two volumes, Harcourt, 1966; (with James Frost, David Ellis, and William B. Fink) *An American History: Evolution of a Free People,* Follett, 1967; (general editor) Dorothy Nilsen, *Exploring with American Heroes,* teacher's edition, Follett, 1967; (editor with Marian R. Brown) *Reading List in American History for High Schools,* National Council for the Social Studies, 1970; *The Presidency of John Adams,* University Press of Kansas, 1975; (with Marian R. Brown) *Europeans Observe the American Revolution,* Messner, 1976. Consultant for ten biographical films and twelve biographical filmstrips produced by McGraw. Contributor of several thousand reviews to more than a hundred magazines and newspapers. Book review editor, *Sea Power,* 1944-45, *American Heritage,* 1947-54, *History News,* 1955-59, *Social Education,* 1960-63, and *American History Illustrated,* 1967-70. General editor, McGraw's "Cluster Series in Biography," 1969; senior editor, Kennikat's "Scholarly Reprint" series, 1969—.

WORK IN PROGRESS: The Lumber Industry in the State of New York, 1790-1830, and *The New Hampshire Press to 1790.*

* * *

BROWN, Robert Goodell 1923-

PERSONAL: Born April 14, 1923, in Evanston, Ill., son of William Goodell (a telegrapher) and Clarine (Todd) Brown; married Inge J. E. Richert (executive vice-president of

American Production and Inventory Control Society), May 20, 1967; children: Jeffrey, Shirley Jane. *Education:* Yale University, B.E., 1944, M.A., 1948. *Address:* P.O. Box 332, Norwich, Vt. 05055.

CAREER: Operations Evaluation Group, Washington, D.C., member of staff, 1948-50; Willow Run Research Center, Willow Run, Mich., head of department of operations research, 1950-53; Arthur D. Little, Inc., Cambridge, Mass., senior member of operations research staff, 1951-67; Curtiss Wright Corp., Wood Bridge, N.J., vice-president, 1967-68; International Business Machines, Inc. (IBM), White Plains, N.Y., industrial consultant, 1968-71; Materials Management Systems, Norwich, Vt., president, 1971—. Visiting lecturer, Amos Tuck School of Business Administration, Dartmouth College, 1964; professor of production operations, Boston University, 1966-67; ALCOA Visiting Professor of Industrial Engineering, Lehigh University, 1971-72. Treasurer, International Federation of Operations Research Societies, 1962-65. *Military service:* U.S. Navy, 1944-46.

MEMBER: American Society of Mechanical Engineers, American Mathematical Society, Operations Research Society of America, Institute of Management Sciences, American Production and Inventory Control Society. *Awards, honors:* American Production and Inventory Control Society Communications Award, 1971.

WRITINGS: Statistical Forecasting for Inventory Control, McGraw, 1959; *Smoothing Forecasting and Prediction,* Prentice-Hall, 1963; *Decision Rules for Inventory Management,* Holt, 1967; *Management Decisions for Production Operations,* Dryden, 1971; *Source Book in Production Management,* Dryden, 1971; *Material Management Systems,* Wiley, 1977. Contributor of more than one hundred articles to professional journals.

WORK IN PROGRESS: A book on the professional practice of consulting, tentatively entitled, *A Consultant's Guide to Management; A Manager's Guide to Production Control.*

AVOCATIONAL INTERESTS: Swimming, skiing, sports car rallies, and music.

* * *

BROWN, Sidney DeVere 1925-

PERSONAL: Born January 29, 1925, in Douglass, Kan.; son of Leonard Reeves (a farmer) and Jessie Maybelle (Berger) Brown; married Ruth Esther Murray (a sociologist), January 24, 1948; children: Margaret, Nancy, Russell Frederick. *Education:* Southwestern College, Winfield, Kan., B.A., 1947; University of Wisconsin, M.A., 1950, Ph.D., 1953. *Politics:* Democrat. *Religion:* United Methodist Church. *Home:* 700 Nancy Lynn Ter., Norman, Okla. 73069. *Office:* Department of History, University of Oklahoma, Norman, Okla. 73019.

CAREER: High school teacher in Protection, Kan., 1947-48; Oklahoma State University, Stillwater, instructor, 1952-53, assistant professor, 1953-59, associate professor, 1959-66, professor of history, 1966-71; University of Oklahoma, Norman, professor of history, 1971—. Visiting professor, University of Illinois, 1968-69; visiting summer professor at University of Kansas, 1958, University of Wisconsin, 1960, University of Colorado, 1964, and University of Nebraska, 1963. *Military service:* U.S. Naval Reserve, active duty, 1943-46; became lieutenant junior grade.

MEMBER: American Historical Association, Association

for Asian Studies, Japan Society, International House of Japan, Midwest Conference on Asian Affairs (president, 1959-60), Southwest Conference on Asian Studies (president, 1977-78). *Awards, honors:* Ford Foundation fellowship in Tokyo, 1956-57; American Philosophical Society grant for travel in Japan, 1971; Japan Foundation fellow in Tokyo, 1977-78.

WRITINGS: (Editor) *Studies on Asia 1962,* University of Nebraska Press, 1962; (contributor) Bernard S. Silberman and H. D. Harootunlan, editors, *Japan's Modern Leadership,* University of Arizona Press, 1966; (editor) *Studies on Asia 1967,* University of Nebraska Press, 1967; (contributor) David Wurfel, editor, *Meiji Japan's Centennial,* University Press of Kansas, 1971; (contributor) Rochard E. Burns and Edward W. Bennett, editors, *Diplomats in Crisis,* American Bibliographic Center—Clio Press, 1974. Contributor to history journals.

WORK IN PROGRESS: The Political Diary in Meiji Japan: A Translation of the Diary of Kido Takayoshi, 1868-1877.

AVOCATIONAL INTERESTS: Jazz music, collegiate sports, photography, politics.

*   *   *

BROWN, Stephen W. 1940-

PERSONAL: Born December 16, 1940, in Asheville, N.C.; son of Newton Webb and Launia (Cole) Brown; married Anna Louise Williamson, December 18, 1960; children: Anna Maria, Jennifer Lee. *Education:* Brevard College, A.A., 1959; High Point College, B.A., 1961; Boston University, S.T.B., 1967. *Home:* 231 Island Dr., Key Biscayne, Fla. 33149. *Office:* 160 Harbor Dr., Key Biscayne, Fla. 33149.

CAREER: Announcer, disc jockey, and newscaster during college years with radio stations in Brevard, Greensboro, and Winston Salem, N.C., and Boston, Mass.; First United Presbyterian Church, Quincy, Mass., senior minister, 1968-73; Key Biscayne Presbyterian Church, Key Biscayne, Fla., senior pastor, 1973—. Member of board of directors of Woodward School for Girls, Trinity School of Cape Cod, and Survival, Inc. (drug rehabilitation center). Chairman of board of trustees, Boston Presbytery of United Presbyterian Church.

WRITINGS: Where the Action Is, Revell, 1971; *So Now You Are a Christian . . . ,* Revell, 1972.

*   *   *

BROWN, Theodore L(awrence) 1928-

PERSONAL: Born October 15, 1928, in Green Bay, Wis.; son of Lawrence A. and Martha (Kedinger) Brown; married Audrey Catherine Brockman, January 6, 1951; children: Mary Margaret, Karen Anne, Jennifer, Philip, Andrew. *Education:* Illinois Institute of Technology, B.S., 1950; Michigan State University, Ph.D., 1956. *Office:* School of Chemical Sciences, University of Illinois at Urbana-Champaign, Urbana, Ill. 61801.

CAREER: University of Illinois at Urbana-Champaign, instructor, 1956-58, assistant professor, 1958-61, associate professor, 1961-65, professor of chemistry, 1965—, A. P. Sloan fellow, 1962-66. Member of board of directors, Champaign County (Ill.) Opportunities Industrialization Center, 1969—. Visiting scientist, International Meteorological Institute, Stockholm, Sweden, 1972. *Military service:* U.S. Navy, 1950-53; became lieutenant. *Member:* American

Chemical Society, American Association for the Advancement of Science, Chemical Society of London (fellow), Sigma Xi, Alpha Chi Sigma. *Awards, honors:* Du Pont fellow, Michigan State University, 1955-56; National Science Foundation senior postdoctoral fellow, 1964-65; American Chemical Society award in inorganic chemistry, 1972.

WRITINGS: (With Russell S. Drago) *Experiments in General Chemistry,* Allyn & Bacon, 1960, 3rd edition, 1970; *General Chemistry,* C. E. Merrill, 1964, 2nd edition, 1968; *Energy and the Environment,* C. E. Merrill, 1971; (with H. E. LeMay, Jr.) *Chemistry: The Central Science,* Prentice-Hall, 1977. Contributor of about 130 articles to scientific journals. Associate editor, *Inorganic Chemistry.*

WORK IN PROGRESS: Several scientific projects.

SIDELIGHTS: Theodore Brown told *CA* he is working on literature and text materials for the non-scientist. "I am especially interested in developing readable material which expounds the relevance of scientific work to society. To this end I have studied extensively in other areas of science."

*   *   *

BROWN, Theodore M(orey) 1925-

PERSONAL: Born November 11, 1925, in Winthrop, Mass.; married Barbara M. Rome (a children's librarian), May 29, 1951; children: Lisa N., David O. *Education:* Massachusetts Institute of Technology, B.Arch., 1953; Harvard University, M.A., 1956; State University of Utrecht, Ph.D., 1958. *Home:* 92 Ithaca Rd., Ithaca, N.Y. 14850. *Office:* History of Art Department, 35 Goldwin Smith Hall, Cornell University, Ithaca, N.Y. 14850.

CAREER: University of Louisville, Louisville, Ky., assistant professor, 1958-62, associate professor of art history, 1962-67; Cornell University, Ithaca, N.Y., associate professor, 1967-71, professor of art history, 1971—. *Military service:* U.S. Navy, 1943-46. *Member:* College Art Association of America, Society of Architectural Historians, American Studies Association.

WRITINGS: The Work of G. Rietveld, Architect, Bruna & Zoon (Utrecht), 1958; *Introduction to Louisville Architecture,* Louisville Free Public Library, 1960; (with Margaret M. Bridwell) *Old Louisville,* University of Louisville, 1961; *Margaret Bourke-White: Photojournalist,* A. D. White Museum of Art (Ithaca), 1972. Contributor to art, architecture, and photographic journals.

WORK IN PROGRESS: The Pursuit of Truth, Goodness and Beauty.

AVOCATIONAL INTERESTS: Photography, designing and making furniture.

*   *   *

BROWN, Walter Lee 1924-

PERSONAL: Born June 13, 1924, in Gatesville, Tex.; son of Franklin Jeremiah (a farmer) and Alice Belle (Berry) Brown; married Jane Richart, August 11, 1950; children: Michael Morgan, Phillip Richont, Janet Lee (deceased). *Education:* Texas Agricultural & Mechanical College (now Texas A & M University), B.A., 1949; University of Texas, M.A., 1950, Ph.D., 1955. *Politics:* Democrat. *Religion:* Episcopalian. *Home:* 1138 North Vandeventer, Fayetteville, Ark. 72701. *Office:* Department of History, University of Arkansas, Fayetteville, Ark. 72701.

CAREER: University of Arkansas, Fayetteville, instructor, 1954-57, assistant professor, 1957-61, associate professor,

1961-67, professor of history, 1967—. *Military service:* U.S. Army Air Forces, 1943-46. *Member:* American Historical Association, Organization of American Historians, Arkansas Historical Association (secretary-treasurer). *Awards, honors:* Stebbins Prize of Arkansas Historical Association, 1956.

WRITINGS: (Editor) *Our Arkansas,* Steck, 1958, revised edition, 1964. Editor, *Arkansas Historical Quarterly,* 1958—.

WORK IN PROGRESS: Biographies of Albert Pike and Jefferson Davis; a history of Arkansas.

* * *

BROWN, William F(rank) 1920-

PERSONAL: Born September 13, 1920, in San Antonio, Tex.; son of Frank James (an auto dealer) and Jewell Elizabeth (Hodge) Brown; married Mary Falbo, June 29, 1947; children: Nancy Marie (Mrs. Martin Everett Cherry), Billie Jeanne, Elizabeth Anne, Mary Louise. *Education:* Trinity University, B.S., 1950; University of Texas at Austin, M.A., 1952, Ed.D., 1955. *Politics:* Republican. *Religion:* Presbyterian. *Home address:* Route 1, Box 100, Wimberley, Tex. 78676. *Office:* Southwest Texas State University, San Marcos, Tex. 78666.

CAREER: School of Aviation Medicine, Randolph Air Force Base, Tex., research associate in psychology, 1955-56; George Washington University, Washington, D.C., research scientist with Human Resources Research Office, 1956-58; Southwest Texas State University, San Marcos, associate professor, 1958-67, professor of education, 1967—, director of Testing and Guidance Center, 1958-68, director of counselor education, 1975—. Publisher, Effective Study Materials, San Marcos, 1964—; director of Upward Bound project, 1965-68, and Educational Psychology Research Services, 1969—; consultant, Division of Drug Education and Crime Prevention, Texas Education Agency, beginning 1970. *Military service:* U.S. Army Air Forces, 1942-48; became captain. *Member:* American Psychological Association, American Personnel and Guidance Association, Interamerican Society of Psychology, American Association for the Advancement of Science, American Association of University Professors. *Awards, honors:* Nancy Wimmer Award, American Personnel and Guidance Association, 1967, for developing student-to-student counseling program.

WRITINGS: (With Wayne H. Holtzman) *A Guide to College Survival,* Prentice-Hall, 1972; *Student-to-Student Counseling,* University of Texas Press, 1972, revised edition, in press. Author of "Student's Guides to Effective Study" (twelve booklets), Effective Study Materials, 1968-72, and of other booklets, tests, and filmstrips on effective study. Contributor of more than thirty articles to psychology and education journals.

WORK IN PROGRESS: Research projects in Mexican and U.S. universities to determine the cross-cultural adaptability of student-to-student study skills counseling; the translation and adaptation of guides, manuals, and tests for Spanish-speaking populations.

AVOCATIONAL INTERESTS: Photography, philately, cactus cultivation.

* * *

BROWN, William F(erdinand) 1928-

PERSONAL: Born April 16, 1928, in Jersey City, N.J.; son of Douglas (in ethical drug business) and Dorothy (Ferrett) Brown; married Ann Distler (in direct sales for Doncaster, Inc.), June 21, 1950; children: Debra Susan, William Todd. *Education:* Princeton University, A.B. (cum laude), 1950. *Politics:* Independent. *Religion:* None. *Home:* 44 Grahampton Lane, Greenwich, Conn. 06830. *Agent:* Charles Hunt, Fifi Oscard Associates, 19 West 44th St., New York, N.Y. 10036. *Office:* 22A Stoneboat Rd., Westport, Conn. 06880.

CAREER: Look, New York City, writer, 1950-51; Music Corporation of America, Los Angeles, Calif., agent, 1952-54; Batten, Barton, Durstine & Osborne (advertising agency), New York City, television producer, 1954-61; freelance author, illustrator, cartoonist, and writer for network television. *Military service:* U.S. Army, 1951-52; became first lieutenant. *Member:* American Society of Composers, Authors and Publishers, National Cartoonists Society, Dramatists Guild, Writers Guild of America, East. *Awards, honors:* Antoinette Perry Memorial Award (Tony) nomination for best musical book, American Theatre Wing, 1975, for "The Wiz"; Drama Desk Award for best musical book, The Drama Desk, 1975, for "The Wiz."

WRITINGS: Tiger, Tiger, Coward, 1950; *Beat Beat Beat,* New American Library, 1959; *The Girl in the Freudian Slip* (cartoons), New American Library, 1960; *The Abominable Showmen,* New American Library, 1960; *The World Is My Yo-Yo,* Pocket Books, 1963; "The Girl in the Freudian Slip" (play; no relation to earlier book), first produced on Broadway, 1967; (author of sketches, continuity and additional dialogue) "New Faces of 1968," produced on Broadway, 1968; (author of book) "How to Steal an Election" (musical revue), produced Off-Broadway, 1968; (author of book) "The Wiz" (musical), first produced on Broadway at Majestic Theatre, January 5, 1975.

Illustrator: Juliet Lowell, *Dear Folks,* Putnam, 1960; Lowell, *Dear Mr. Congressman,* Duell, 1960; Lowell, *Dear Man of Affairs,* Putnam, 1961; Frederic A. Birmingham, *The Complete Cookbook for Men,* Harper, 1961; Harold Dunn, *Those Crazy Mixed-up Kids,* New American Library, 1962.

Writer for network television, including "David Frost Review," "That Was the Week That Was," "Ed Sullivan Show," "Dean Martin Show," "Jackie Gleason Show," "Johnny Carson Show," "Merv Griffin Show," "Love American Style," and "Silents Please"; writer for television specials and pilot shows. Writer of night club acts, cabaret revues, comedy commercials, and live and film industrial shows. Co-author and co-artist, with Mel Casson, of comic strip "Boomer" (formerly "Mixed Singles"), United Features Syndicate, 1972—. Contributor of short stories and articles to *Vogue, Pageant, Argosy, Show,* and other magazines; cartoons have been published in *Saturday Evening Post, Collier's, Esquire,* and other periodicals.

WORK IN PROGRESS: Two musicals, a play, and a television series.

SIDELIGHTS: "William F. Brown's book absorbs L. Frank Baum's classic [*The Wizard of Oz*] into the black experience with good-humored cleverness. Some will say 'The Wiz' exploits that experience with its flip references to drugs, sex and such matters, but in our culture of interlocking exploitations how refreshing to see it done with warmth and flair," writes Jack Kroll.

Brown told *CA:* "'The Wiz' opened on Broadway on January 5, 1975 and is still running. How long it will continue to run is anybody's guess. I would think through 1978 anyway. There is a national company which opened in Los Angeles in June of 1975, and is still running. It's booked well into 1979.

Another company, a bus and truck company, will open in the fall of 1978 and tour for about a year at least. There was an Australian company that ran for about six months in 1976, and a Japanese company that same year that had a limited engagement of about six weeks.

"'The Wiz' is being made into a movie by Universal. It will star Diana Ross, Lena Horne, Richard Pryor, Nipsey Russell, Michael Jackson, Ted Ross, and Mabel King. It is scheduled for release around Christmas, 1978.

"My working habits when I write are usually that I will create new material in the morning, work from nine till one, take a break for lunch, rewrite my morning's work in the afternoon. That's the ideal arrangement. It doesn't always work out that way. My favorite times to write are morning and late afternoon.

"I began writing professionally when I was in college, but I have always written (and drawn) since I can remember.... The two people who got me started writing for theatre and for TV, and who encouraged me to try it, were Julius Monk and Max Liebman. I began writing full-time in 1962, and did so because I'd always wanted to. And still do.''

BIOGRAPHICAL/CRITICAL SOURCES: New York Times, May 19, 1967, May 3, 1968, October 14, 1968; *Newsweek,* November 11, 1968, January 20, 1975; *New Yorker,* January 13, 1975.

* * *

BROWN-AZAROWICZ, Marjory F. 1922-

PERSONAL: Born November 10, 1922, in Calgary, Alberta, Canada; daughter of Charles and Isobella (Glenday) Brown; married; children: Eddie, Diane, Calvin. *Education:* University of British Columbia, B.A., 1950; University of Alberta, B.Ed., 1953, A.Mus., 1954; University of Toronto, A.R.C.T., 1953; University of Washington, M.A., 1956, Ph.D., 1961. *Office:* Department of Education, George Mason University, Fairfax, Va. 22030.

CAREER: Teacher in public schools of Alberta, 1940-56; State University of New York College at Buffalo, associate professor of education, 1960-66; Fairfax County Schools, Fairfax, Va., reading teacher, 1967-68; George Mason University, Fairfax, associate professor of education, 1968—. Teaches piano privately and occasionally gives recitals. *Member:* Virginia Education Association, Pi Lambda Theta, Kappa Delta Pi.

WRITINGS: A Handbook of Creative Choral Speaking, Burgess, 1970. Also author of *Best Books for Your Baby.* Contributor to education journals. Former editor, *George Mason College Quarterly of Education.*

WORK IN PROGRESS: Methodology in Spelling.

* * *

BROWNING, Robert 1914-

PERSONAL: Born January 15, 1914, in Glasgow, Scotland; son of Alexander Martin (a box manufacturer) and Jean (Miller) Browning; children: Tamara Helen, Anna Margaret. *Education:* University of Glasgow, M.A., 1935; Balliol College, Oxford, B.A., 1939, M.A., 1945. *Home:* 17 Belsize Park Gardens, London N.W.3, England. *Office:* Birkbeck College, University of London, Malet St., London W.C.1, England.

CAREER: University of London, London, England, lecturer, 1947-55, reader, 1955-65, professor of classics and ancient history, 1965—. Secretary, Classical Journals Board.

Military service: British Army, 1939-46; became major. *Member:* Society for Hellenic Studies (member of council, 1965—; president, 1974-78), Society for Roman Studies, Association of University Teachers.

WRITINGS: Medieval and Modern Greek, Hutchinson, 1969; *Justinian and Theodora,* Praeger, 1971; *Byzantium and Bulgaria: A Comparative Study across the Early Medieval Frontier,* University of California Press, 1975; *The Emperor Julian,* University of California Press, 1976; *Studies in Byzantine History, Literature and Education,* Variorum, 1977. Contributor to encyclopedias; contributor to learned journals in England, France, Belgium, Germany, Greece, United States, and the Soviet Union. Member of editorial board, *Past and Present.*

WORK IN PROGRESS: Further studies in language and literature of medieval Greek world.

SIDELIGHTS: Robert Browning is fluent in French, German, Italian, Russian, Bulgarian, modern Greek, and Serbo-Croat. Translations of Browning's books have been published in Greek, Italian, German, and Polish.

* * *

BROWNSTEIN, Michael 1943-

PERSONAL: Born August 25, 1943, in Philadelphia, Pa. *Education:* Attended Antioch College, 1961-64; New School of Social Research, B.A., 1966.

CAREER: Poet and novelist; free-lance writer. Instructor, University of Colorado and Naropu Institute. *Awards, honors:* Poet's Foundation grant, 1966; Fulbright fellow, Paris, 1967-68; Frank O'Hara Award, 1969, for *Highway to the Sky.*

WRITINGS: Highway to the Sky, Columbia University Press, 1969; *Brainstorms,* Bobbs-Merrill, 1971; *30 Pictures,* Grape Press, 1972; *Country Cousins,* Braziller, 1974; *Strange Days Ahead,* Z Press, 1976. Also author of *Behind the Wheel.*

WORK IN PROGRESS: Poetry and prose.

AVOCATIONAL INTERESTS: Travel.

* * *

BRUCE, Lennart 1919-

PERSONAL: Born February 21, 1919, in Stockholm, Sweden; came to United States in 1964; son of Johan Gottfrid (a businessman) and Agda (Paulson) Bruce; married Harriet Gernandt, May 25, 1944 (divorced, 1959); married Sonja Ericson (an executive secretary), July 22, 1960; children: (first marriage) Johan, Gunilla. *Education:* Attended University of Stockholm and University of Uppsala. *Home:* 1815 Jones St., San Francisco, Calif. 94109.

CAREER: Owned and operated a transport company, cold storage plants and supermarkets in West Africa, a fruit export firm in South America, food marketing, movie distribution and electronics companies in Sweden; free-lance writer, 1964—. Lecturer on poetry, San Francisco Conservatory of Music, 1968. Has given many public readings of his own work in California and Oregon. Has also broadcast on radio programs in San Francisco and New York City.

*WRITINGS—*All poetry, except as indicated: *Making the Rounds,* Kayak, 1967; (translator with Matthew Zion) Fernando Alegria, *Instructions for Undressing the Human Race,* Kayak, 1968; *Observations,* Kayak, 1968; *Moments of Doubt,* Cloud Marauder Press, 1969; *The Mullioned Window,* Kayak, 1970; *The Robot Failure* (prose), Cloud,

Marauder Press, 1971; *Letter of Credit*, Kayak, 1973; *Sub-poemas*, Panjandrum, 1974; *Exposure*, Cloud Marauder Press, 1975; (translator) Vilhelm Ekelund, *Agenda* (prose), Cloud Marauder Press, 1976. Contributor of more than one hundred poems to *Nation, Saturday Review, New American Review, Choice, Sumac, Massachusetts Review, Tennessee Poetry Journal, New Mexico Quarterly, Chelsea, Green Flag, City Lights,* and other publications.

* * *

BRUCE, Sylvia (Valerie) 1936-

PERSONAL: Born February 25, 1936, in Ilford, Essex, England; daughter of Henry Hope (a consulting central heating engineer) and Iris (Goymer) Bruce; married, 1972 (separated, 1975); children: Devi. *Education:* Attended Somerville College, Oxford, 1955-59; University of London, B.A. (honours in English), 1960, Birkbeck College, graduate study, 1976—. *Politics:* "Churchillian Tory." *Religion:* Agnostic. *Residence:* London, England. *Agent:* Richard Scott Simon Ltd., 32 College Cross, London N1, England.

CAREER: University of London, Imperial College of Science and Technology, London, England, clerk at registry, 1960-62; Penguin Books Ltd., Harmondsworth, Middlesex, England, editor, specializing in Shakespeare, 1964-68; Allen Lane, Penguin Press, London, managing editor, 1968; freelance copy editor, 1969—; teacher of verse reading, 1971-75. *Member:* University of London Convocation, Howard League for Penal Reform. *Awards, honors:* Arts Council of Great Britain grant, 1974.

WRITINGS: The Powers on High (novel), Hutchinson, 1964; *The Wonderful Garden* (novel), Hutchinson, 1969. Also author of *The Love of a Woman*, in press. Contributor of poems to *Isis, Altash, New Measure,* and *Antigonish Review,* and articles and reviews to *Aylesford Review, Books and Bookmen,* and other periodicals.

WORK IN PROGRESS: Research on Henry Harland; novels about El Dorado and about two women pirates; verse translations of Lorca; research on T. S. Eliot's *Four Quartets.*

SIDELIGHTS: Sylvia Bruce spent the years 1962-64 in Guatemala City. Although she is not ("emphatically not") a member of "women's lib," she "regards war, marriage, and prisons as institutions of which she disapproves, despite any lapses indicating the contrary."

* * *

BRUCHAC, Joseph III 1942-

PERSONAL: Surname is pronounced Brew-shack; born October 16, 1942, in Saratoga Springs, N.Y.; son of Joseph E. (a taxidermist) and Flora (Bowman) Bruchac; married Carol Worthen, June 13, 1964; children: James Edward, Jesse Bowman. *Education:* Cornell University, A.B., 1965; Syracuse University, M.A., 1966; State University of New York at Albany, graduate study, 1971-73; Union Graduate School, Ph.D., 1975. *Religion:* Animist. *Home address:* R.F.D., Greenfield Center, N.Y. 12833. *Agent:* Julie Fallowfield, McIntosh & Otis, Inc., 475 Fifth Ave., New York, N.Y. 10017. *Office:* Greenfield Review Press, Greenfield Center, N.Y. 12833.

CAREER: Worked as laborer, surveyor, and tree surgeon during his school years; Keta Secondary School, Ghana, West Africa, teacher of English and literature, 1966-69; Skidmore College, Saratoga Springs, N.Y., instructor in creative writing and in African and black literatures, 1969-

73, teacher of creative writing at Great Meadows Institute, Comstock Prison, 1972—. Publisher, editor of *Greenfield Review*, Greenfield Review Press, Greenfield Center, N.Y., 1969—. *Member:* Poetry Society of America, College Language Association, Northeastern Modern Language Association, National Wildlife Federation. *Awards, honors:* Coordinating Council of Literary Magazines grants, 1971, 1972; New York State Arts Council grant, 1972; Vermont Arts Council grant, 1972; monthly poetry prize from Poetry Society of America, February, 1972.

WRITINGS—Poetry, except as indicated: *Indian Mountain and Other Poems*, Ithaca House, 1971; (editor with William Witherup) *Words from the House of the Dead: An Anthology of Prison Writings from Soledad*, Greenfield Review Press, 1971; *The Buffalo in the Syracuse Zoo*, Greenfield Review Press, 1972; *The Poetry of Pop*, Dustbooks, 1973; *Flow*, Cold Mountain Press, 1975; *Turkey Brother and Other Iroquois Folk Tales*, Crossing Press, 1976; *The Road to Black Mountain*, Thorp Springs Press, 1976; *This Earth Is a Drum*, Cold Mountain Press, 1977; *The Dreams of Jesse Brown* (novel), Cold Mountain Press, 1977.

Poems included in numerous anthologies, including: *New Campus Writing*, edited by Nolan Miller, McGraw, 1966; *Syracuse Poems, 1963-1969*, edited by George P. Elliott, Syracuse University Press, 1970; *The Young American Poets*, edited by Paull Carroll, Follett, 1972; *Our Only Hope Is Humor: Some Public Poems*, edited by Robert McGovern and Richard Snyder, Ashland Poetry Press, 1972; *From the Belly of the Shark: An Anthology of Native American Writing*, edited by Walter Lowenfels, 1973; *The Shadow of the Savage*, edited by Robert McGill, 1973.

Also author of "Peter Davis," an album of songs which has been recorded. Contributor of poetry to over two-hundred periodicals, including *Nickel Review, Kite, Black Academy Review, The Legon Observer,* and *New Era*. Assistant editor, *Epoch,* 1964-65; contributing editor, *Nickel Review,* 1967-71; editor, *Greenfield Review,* 1970—; contemporary music editor, *Kite,* 1971—.

WORK IN PROGRESS: Entering Onandaga and *There Are No Trees in Prison,* both poetry; *Border Crossing,* poems and translations from West Africa; two collections of Iroquois folk tales; *Shaman Song* and *Foxy,* both novels.

SIDELIGHTS: "Much of my writing and my life relates to the problem of being an American," Joseph Bruchac writes. "While in college I was active in Civil Rights work and in the anti-war movement. . . . I went to Africa to teach—but more than that to be taught. It showed me many things. How much we have as Americans and take for granted. How much our eyes refuse to see because they are blinded to everything in a man's face except his color. And most importantly, how human people are everywhere—which may be the one grace that can save us all.

"My writing is informed by several key sources. One of these is nature, another is the native American experience. (I'm part Indian). . . . I like to work outside, in the earth-mother's soil, with my hands . . . but maintain my life as an academic for a couple of reasons: it gives me time to write (sometimes) and it gives me a chance to share my insights into the beautiful and all too fragile world of men and living things we have been granted. Which is one of the reasons I write—not to be a man apart, but to share."

BRUCHEY, Stuart (Weems) 1917-

PERSONAL: Surname is pronounced Bru-*shay;* born August 6, 1917, in Washington, D.C.; son of Walter Latrobe (a teletype expert) and Nellie (Richardson) Bruchey; married Eleanor Small (a professor), June 16, 1956; children: Andrew, Samuel. *Education:* Johns Hopkins University, A.B., 1943, M.A., 1946, Ph.D., 1956. *Politics:* Democrat. *Religion:* Unitarian Universalist. *Home:* 460 Riverside Dr., New York, N.Y. 10027. *Office:* Department of History, Columbia University, New York, N.Y. 10027.

CAREER: U.S. Department of the Army, Washington, D.C., historian, 1945-49; Dickinson College, Carlisle, Pa., instructor in history, 1956-57; Northwestern University, Evanston, Ill., assistant professor of history, 1957-59; Michigan State University, East Lansing, assistant professor, 1959-60, associate professor, 1960-64, professor of history, 1964-67; Columbia University, New York, N.Y., professor of history, 1967-68, Allan Nevins Professor of American Economic History, 1968—. Fellow of Center for Studies of Recent American History, Johns Hopkins University, 1965-66; member of Institute for Advanced Study, Princeton University, 1973-74; fellow of Center for Advanced Study in Behavioral Sciences, Stanford University, 1975-76. *Member:* American Historical Association, Organization of American Historians, Economic History Association (vice-president, 1975-76). *Awards, honors:* Social Science Research Council faculty fellowship, 1963-64; Guggenheim fellow, 1973-74; National Endowment for the Humanities fellow, 1975-76.

WRITINGS: Robert Oliver: Merchant of Baltimore, 1783-1819, Johns Hopkins Press, 1956; *Roots of American Economic Growth: 1607-1861,* Harper, 1965; (editor) *The Colonial Merchant,* Harcourt, 1967; (editor) *Cotton and the Growth of the American Economy,* Harcourt, 1968; (editor with A. D. Chandler and Louis Galambos) *The Changing Economic Order,* Harcourt, 1969; *Growth of the Modern American Economy,* Harper, 1975. General editor: "Allan Nevins Reprints in American Economic History," Harper, 1969; "Columbia Economic History of the Modern World," 1972—; "Uses and Abuses of America's Natural Resources," Arno, 1972; "American Business Abroad," Arno, 1976; "Dissertations in American Economic History," Arno, 1975-76; "Dissertations in European Economic History," Arno, 1977.

WORK IN PROGRESS: A volume on American economic history from 1607 to the present, for Oxford University Press.

AVOCATIONAL INTERESTS: Theater, music.

*   *   *

BRUESS, Clint E. 1941-

PERSONAL: Surname is pronounced Bruce; born September 7, 1941, in Duluth, Minn.; married Patricia Carey, June 4, 1963; children: Carey Ray, Todd Allen. *Education:* Macalester College, B.S., 1963; University of Maryland, M.A., 1965; Temple University, Ed.D., 1968. *Religion:* Presbyterian. *Home:* 608 Worcester Rd., Towson, Md. 21204. *Office:* Department of Health Science, Towson State University, Towson, Md. 21204.

CAREER: Towson State University, Towson, Md., professor and chairman of department of health science, 1969—. *Member:* American School Health Association, American Association of Sex Educators and Counselors, Sex Information and Education Council of the United States, National

Council on Family Relations, Association for the Advancement of Health Education, Maryland Public Health Association, Phi Delta Kappa. *Awards, honors:* Honor award for slide-tape program, National Council on Family Relations, 1975, for "Sex Is Not a Dirty Word."

WRITINGS: (Editor with J. T. Fisher) *Selected Readings in Health,* Macmillan, 1971; *Education for Human Sexuality,* Towson State University, 1976; (with John E. Gay) *Implementing Comprehensive School Health,* Macmillan, 1978. Also author with Neil E. Gallagher, of a slide-tape series, "How the Health Are You?," Harper, 1974. Contributor to health and medical journals.

WORK IN PROGRESS: A college-level health text, for Wiley; a text on human sexuality, for Saunders.

*   *   *

BRUNE, Lester H(ugo) 1926-

PERSONAL: Born January 14, 1926, in Reading, Ohio; son of Frederick Gustave (a minister) and Marie (Bueker) Brune; married Joan L. Herzfeld (a teacher), October 21, 1950. *Education:* Elmhurst College, A.B., 1948; Bradley University, M.A., 1950; University of Rochester, Ph.D., 1959. *Home:* 2704 North Lehman Rd., Peoria, Ill. 61604. *Office:* Department of History, Bradley University, Peoria, Ill. 61625.

CAREER: Elmhurst College, Elmhurst, Ill., admissions counselor, 1950-51; Morris Harvey College, Charleston, W. Va., instructor in history, 1951-53; Bradley University, Peoria, Ill., assistant professor, 1956-62, associate professor, 1962-67, professor of history, 1968—, chairman of department, 1970—, assistant dean of College of Liberal Arts, 1962-65. Adjunct professor of history, Moorhead State College, 1971. *Member:* American Historical Association, Foreign Policy Association, Society for Historians of American Foreign Relations, Organization of American Historians, Phi Kappa Phi (secretary), Phi Alpha Theta, Pi Sigma Phi. *Awards, honors:* Association for Middle-Eastern Studies fellow at University of Illinois, summer, 1961.

*WRITINGS—*Programmed instruction texts; all published by Media Masters, except as indicated: *Ancient History to the Fall of Rome,* 1968; *China and Japan to 1600 A.D.,* 1968; *India and Southeast Asia to 1600 A.D.,* 1968; *The Middle East to 1600 A.D.,* 1968; *The Middle Ages and Early Modern Europe to 1700 A.D.,* 1968; (with Charles E. P. Simmons) *Mexico and South America,* 1969; *The United States,* 1969; *Europe Since 1500 A.D.,* 1969; *The Mid-East Since 1500 A.D.,* 1969; *China and Japan Since 1600 A.D.,* 1969; *India and Southeast Asia Since 1600 A.D.,* 1969; (editor) *Origins of Tomorrow,* two volumes, Holbrook, 1973. Contributor to history journals.

WORK IN PROGRESS: A study on Franklin D. Roosevelt as a leader who integrated military and diplomatic decision before Pearl Harbor.

SIDELIGHTS: Lester Brune wrote *CA:* "My publications resulted from efforts to experiment with better methods for teaching history. The present generation of historians need more than ever to discover a better means for nourishing the vitality of the study of history as a means for continuing to provide humanistic insights in a technically oriented world." He has traveled through Europe, Japan, China, the United Arab Republic, Lebanon, Greece, and the Aegean.

*   *   *

BRUNNER, Theodore F(riederich) 1934-

PERSONAL: Born July 3, 1934, in Nuremberg, Germany;

son of John (a lithographer) and Margaret (Klaussner) Brunner; married Judith Mesching, July 5, 1957 (divorced, 1973); children: Christine, Catherine. *Education:* University of Wisconsin—Milwaukee, B.A., 1960; Stanford University, M.A., 1963, Ph.D., 1965. *Home:* 28791 Top of the World Dr., Laguna Beach, Calif. 92651. *Office:* Thesaurus Linguae Graecae Project, University of California, Irvine, Calif. 92717.

CAREER: Ohio State University, Columbus, assistant professor of classics, 1964-66; University of California, Irvine, assistant professor, 1966-69, associate professor of classics, 1969-75, chairman of department, 1968-72, associate dean of humanities, 1969-72, director of Thesaurus Linguae Graecae, 1972—. *Military service:* U.S. Marine Corps, 1953-56; became sergeant. *Member:* American Philological Association, Archaeological Institute of America, Association Internationale de Papyrologues, Philological Association of the Pacific Coast, Classical Association of the Pacific States, Classical Alliance of the Western States, California Classical Association. *Awards, honors:* University of California fellowship at Humanities Institute, 1967; grants from Mellon Foundation, National Endowment for the Humanities, and other organizations.

WRITINGS: (With Luci Berkowitz) *The Elements of Scientific and Specialized Terminology*, Burgess, 1967; (with Berkowitz) *Index Verborum Quae in Saturis Auli Persi Flacci Reperiuntur*, Georg Olms Verlagsbuchhandlung, 1967; (with Berkowitz) *Index Lucilianus*, Georg Olms Verlagsbuchhandlung, 1968; (translator and editor with Berkowitz) Sophocles, *Oedipus Tyrannus* (critical edition), Norton, 1970. Author of numerous articles on Greek and Roman literature and philology.

WORK IN PROGRESS: Research on Roman poetry of the Augustan period, Roman satire, Greek tragedy, and the history of science.

AVOCATIONAL INTERESTS: Flying (holds private and commercial pilot's licenses).

*   *   *

BRUNO, Michael 1921-

PERSONAL: Born April 4, 1921, in New York, N.Y.; son of C. (a grocer and realtor) and Eva Bruno. *Education:* Attended Cummington School (experimental school for authors and artists), Cummington, Mass., 1941; University of Pittsburgh, B.A., 1942.

CAREER: Editor on various magazines and writer and account executive in public relations for almost twenty years; now free-lance writer.

WRITINGS: Venus in Hollywood: The Continental Enchantress from Garbo to Loren, Lyle Stuart, 1970. In earlier years had verse published in *New York Times, New York Herald Tribune,* and literary quarterlies; more recently contributor to *Cue, Variety,* and *Signature.*

WORK IN PROGRESS: A history of early talking movies; a biography of architect Stanford White.††

*   *   *

BRUSH, John E(dwin) 1919-

PERSONAL: Born September 2, 1919, in Jefferson, Pa.; son of Edwin Charles (a clergyman) and Helen (Humphrey) Brush; married Miriam Kelly (a college professor), August 21, 1942; children: Jonathan, Kamala Brush Truscott, Steven, Timothy. *Education:* Attended Bucknell University,

1938-41; University of Chicago, B.A., 1942; University of Wisconsin, M.A., 1947, Ph.D., 1952. *Politics:* Unaffiliated. *Religion:* Society of Friends. *Home:* 101 Overbrook Rd., Piscataway, N.J. 08854. *Office:* Department of Geography, Rutgers University, New Brunswick, N.J. 08903.

CAREER: St. Louis University, St. Louis, Mo., instructor in geography, 1950-51; Rutgers University, New Brunswick, N.J., lecturer, 1951-52, assistant professor, 1952-56, associate professor, 1956-58, professor of geography, 1958—, chairman of department, 1967-73, 1977—. *Wartime service:* Conscientious Objector; assigned alternative service, 1943-46. *Member:* Association of American Geographers, American Geographical Society, Association for Asian Studies. *Awards, honors:* Guggenheim fellow, 1957-58.

WRITINGS: Population of New Jersey, Rutgers University Press, 1956, revised edition, 1958; (contributor) Norton Sydney Ginsburg, editor, *The Pattern of Asia,* Prentice-Hall, 1958; (with Howard L. Gauthier, Jr.) *Service Centers and Consumer Trips: Studies on the Philadelphia Metropolitan Fringe,* Department of Geography, University of Chicago, 1968; (contributor) Wilbur Zelinsky and others, editors, *Geography and a Crowding World,* Oxford University Press, 1970; (contributor) R. L. Singh, editor, *Urban Geography in Developing Countries,* National Geographic Society of India, 1973. Contributor of articles to *Annals* of Association of American Geographers and *Geographical Review.*

WORK IN PROGRESS: Field studies on growth, spatial patterns of population, and socio-economic structure of Indian cities, sponsored by American Institute of Indian Studies, University of Chicago.

SIDELIGHTS: John Brush spent most of his childhood, 1923-30 and 1931-38, in India, where his parents were missionaries in Bengal for the American Baptist Foreign Mission Society. He told *CA* that the focus of his interest is analysis of the spatial distribution of settlement, population growth and characteristics, and land use, especially in India and the United States.

*   *   *

BRY, Adelaide 1920-

PERSONAL: Surname rhymes with tree; born November 6, 1920, in Rochester, N.Y.; daughter of Adolph (a businessman) and Elsie (Milhalovitch) Friedman; children: Barbara, Douglas. *Education:* Attended Connecticut College; Simmons College, B.S., 1942; Temple University, M.Ed., 1972. *Religion:* Transcendental Meditation. *Home:* 110 Penarth Rd., Cynwyd, Pa. 19004. *Agent:* Sterling Lord Agency, 660 Madison Ave., New York, N.Y. 10021.

CAREER: Writer; consultant on communications problems; leader of communications workshops for business and industry. *Member:* International Transactional Analysis Association, Philadelphia Public Relations Association.

WRITINGS: Inside Psychotherapy, Basic Books, 1972; *The TA Primer,* Harper, 1973; *TA Games,* Harper, 1975; *A Primer of Behavioral Psychology,* New American Library, 1975; *The Sexually Aggressive Woman,* Peter H. Wyden, 1975; *TA for Families,* Harper, 1976; *est: 60 Hours That Transform Your Life,* Harper, 1976; *How to Get Angry without Feeling Guilty,* New American Library, 1977. Contributor of articles to national periodicals, including *Ladies Home Journal, Vogue,* and *New Woman,* and newspapers.

WORK IN PROGRESS: Directing the Movies of Your Mind, for Harper.

BRYAN, Carter R(oyston) 1911-

PERSONAL: Born June 17, 1911, in Peoria, Ill.; son of James Yeaman (an insurance executive) and Anna R. (Gibson) Bryan; married Madeleine Patricia Cummins, June 17, 1939 (divorced, 1948); married Anna Marie Schneider (a physician), July 6, 1950; children: (second marriage) Caroline Elizabeth, Carter Royston II, Anna Regena, Hugh Hunter. Education: Attended University of Arizona, 1934-35; University of California, Berkeley, B.A., 1937; University of Vienna, Rer.Pol.D., 1940. Politics: Democrat. Religion: Episcopalian. Home: "Tor Bryan," Rt. 1, Box 217 D., Kearneysville, W.Va. 25430.

CAREER: Correspondent in Vienna, Austria, and southeast Europe for International News Service, Times (London), and New York Times, 1938-40; Foreign Commerce Weekly, Washington, D.C., editor, 1940-42; U.S. Department of Commerce, Washington, D.C., chief economist, American Republics Unit, 1942-43; U.S. Office of War Information, Washington, D.C., information specialist, 1943, chief of Italian Section, 1943-44, chief of Balkans Division, 1944-45; World Report, Washington, D.C., economics editor, 1946; U.S. Army, civilian posts as foreign trade adviser, Military Government of Korea, Seoul, 1946-47, chief of printing and publishing unit, Supreme Command, Allied Powers in Japan, Tokyo, 1947-48, chief of political and economic intelligence, Commander-in-Chief, Europe, and European Command, Berlin and Heidelberg, Germany, 1948-50; National Production Authority, Washington, D.C., member of planning and review staff, 1951-52; Tor Bryan Estates (subdivision), Oxon Hill, Md., developer, 1952-55; University of Maryland, College Park, 1955-76, began as instructor, professor of journalism, 1965-76, acting head of department, 1966-68. Executive secretary, National Committee of Educators for Lyndon Johnson for President, 1960.

MEMBER: American Economic Association, Association for Education in Journalism, Overseas Writers, White House Correspondents Association, American Association of University Professors, Phi Delta Theta, Sigma Delta Chi, Pi Delta Epsilon, Kappa Tau Alpha. Awards, honors: Institute of International Education exchange scholar, 1937-38; invitational research scholar of South African and Spanish governments to study press systems, 1967.

WRITINGS: A Survey of the American Press, U.S. Office of War Information, 1943; (with John Merrill and Marvin Alisky) The Foreign Press, Louisiana State University Press, 1964, revised edition, 1970; Negro Journalism Before Emancipation, Association for Education in Journalism, 1970. Also author of A Time to Die. Contributor to magazines and newspapers. Editor, International Reference Service.

*   *   *

BRYANT, Jerry H(olt) 1928-

PERSONAL: Born July 5, 1928, in Dinuba, Calif.; son of Byrle Arden and Adele (Holt) Bryant; married Carol Siddens, November 25, 1968; children: Melaine, Craig. Education: Attended Fresno State College (now California State University, Fresno), 1948-51; University of California, Los Angeles, B.A., 1953, M.A., 1955, Ph.D., 1959. Politics: Democrat. Home: 5630 Greenridge Rd., Castro Valley, Calif. 94546. Office: Department of English, California State University, Hayward, Calif. 94542.

CAREER: Arizona State University, Tempe, assistant professor of English literature, 1958-63; California State University, Hayward, assistant professor, 1964-65, associate

professor, 1965-69, professor of English literature, 1969—. Military service: U.S. Marine Corps, 1946-48. Awards, honors: Folger Shakespeare Library summer fellowship, 1960.

WRITINGS: The Open Decision: The Contemporary American Novel and Its Intellectual Background, Free Press, 1970. Contributor of articles and reviews to Library, Shakespeare Quarterly, South Atlantic Quarterly, Arizona Quarterly, Studies in Black Literature, Nation, Saturday Review, Life, and other periodicals.

WORK IN PROGRESS: A study of violence in Black American fiction.

SIDELIGHTS: Reviewing The Open Decision in American Literature, Maurice Beebe writes: "In this wide-ranging and useful book, Jerry Bryant demonstrates that American fiction since the Second World War is largely existentialist in its philosophy. By the 'open decision' he means that contemporary writers assume without guilt or doubt the primacy of self-consciousness in a world bereft of God, but that instead of despairing like their predecessors of the modernist period, they insist on the worth and glory of the responsible individual who reserves to himself the right to choose among the widest possible range of contingencies, including awareness that freedom is ultimately limited."

AVOCATIONAL INTERESTS: Motoring in the San Francisco Bay area and the Sierras, tennis, baseball, football.

BIOGRAPHICAL/CRITICAL SOURCES: American Literature, November, 1971.

*   *   *

BRYDE, John F(rancis) 1920-

PERSONAL: Born August 4, 1920, in Augusta, Kan.; son of John Francis (owner of a storage garage) and Mary (Laughlin) Bryde; married Melanie Hondel, August 2, 1968; children: Melanie Marie, Bonnie Lee, John, Jr. Education: St. Louis University, A.B., 1943, M.A., 1944, Ph.L., 1945, S.T.B., 1952; University of Denver, Ph.D., 1965. Home: 618 Catalina, Vermillion, S.D. 57069. Office: Department of Educational Psychology, University of South Dakota, Vermillion, S.D. 57069.

CAREER: Roman Catholic priest; Holy Rosary Mission, Pine Ridge, S.D., high school teacher, 1945-48, missionary, 1948-55, researcher in Indian education, 1953-55, superintendent of school, 1955-68; University of South Dakota, Vermillion, associate professor of Indian psychology, 1968—. Director, National Defense Education Act-Office for Economic Opportunity Institutes for Teachers of Indians, 1966-68; researcher and writer, U.S. Bureau of Indian Affairs, 1968-70.

WRITINGS: The Indian Student, University of South Dakota Press, 1970; Modern Indian Psychology, Institute of Indian Studies, University of South Dakota, 1971; Indian Students and Guidance, Houghton, 1971. Contributor to education journals. Chairman of editorial board, University of South Dakota Educational Journal.

WORK IN PROGRESS: A bilingual first reader for Sioux Indian children.

*   *   *

BRYDEN, John R(ennie) 1913-

PERSONAL: Born August 22, 1913, in Detroit, Mich.; son of William W. (a carpenter) and Kate (Schaefer) Bryden; married Helen Elaine Hume (a librarian), September 6,

1947; children: Lynn Elaine, John Reed. *Education:* Transylvania College (now Transylvania University), A.B., 1937; Fontainebleau Conservatory, France, student, 1938; Harvard University, A.M., 1942; University of Michigan, Ph.D., 1951. *Religion:* Christian Church (Disciples of Christ). *Home:* 760 Malabu Dr., Lexington, Ky. 40502. *Office:* Transylvania University, Lexington, Ky. 40508.

CAREER: Transylvania University, Lexington, Ky., professor of music and chairman of department, 1937-51; University of Illinois at Urbana-Champaign, assistant professor of music, 1951-53; Wayne State University, Detroit, Mich., assistant professor of music, 1953-58, director of humanities program, 1956-58, chairman of department of humanities, 1958-64; Transylvania University, professor of humanities and academic dean, 1964-75, professor of music, 1975—, vice-president for academic affairs, 1965-71, provost, 1971-74. *Military service:* U.S. Army, 1941-45; became captain. U.S. Army Reserve, 1945-68, retiring as lieutenant colonel. *Member:* American Musicological Society, Society for Ethnomusicology, American Association of University Professors, Southern Humanities Association, Masonic Lodge, Rotary International, Phi Mu Alpha. *Awards, honors:* Wayne State University, faculty research fellowship, 1958; Transylvania University faculty research grants, 1966, 1968.

WRITINGS: String Duos, American String Teachers Association, 1957; (with David G. Hughes) *An Index of Gregorian Chant,* Harvard University Press, 1969. Contributor to music journals.

WORK IN PROGRESS: A critical examination of art works concerning "The Last Supper."

* * *

BUCHANAN, James J(unkin) 1925-

PERSONAL: Born March 7, 1925, in Pittsburgh, Pa.; son of John Grier (an attorney) and Charity (Packer) Buchanan; married Joanne Cherrington, March 31, 1951; children: Susan G., Edison C., Constance P., James J., Jr., Charles S. *Education:* Princeton University, A.B., 1946, M.A., 1951, Ph.D., 1954; Harvard University, M.B.A., 1948. *Politics:* Democrat. *Religion:* Episcopal. *Home:* 1721 Joseph St., New Orleans, La. 70115. *Office:* Department of Classics, 437 Newcomb Hall, Tulane University, New Orleans, La. 70118.

CAREER: First Boston Corporation, member of staff of advisory department, 1948-51; Princeton University, Princeton, N.J., instructor, 1953-56, assistant professor of classics, 1956-60; Southern Methodist University, Dallas, Tex., professor of classics and chairman of department, 1960-62, dean of College of Arts and Sciences, 1962-64; Tulane University, New Orleans, La., professor of classics, 1964—.

WRITINGS: Boethius: Consolation of Philosophy, Ungar, 1956; *Theorika,* J. J. Augustin, 1962; *Zosimus: Historia Nova,* Trinity University Press (San Antonio), 1967.

* * *

BUCHARD, Robert 1931-

PERSONAL: Born December 24, 1931, in Lausanne, Switzerland; son of Maurice and Sidonie (Decaillet) Buchard; married Agnes Ollivier, March 3, 1961; children: Christophe, Eric, Hugues. *Education:* Attended University of Paris. *Religion:* Roman Catholic. *Office:* French TV, 15 Cognac-Jay, Paris, France.

CAREER: Paris-Presse, Paris, France, reporter, 1959-64; French Television, Paris, reporter, 1964—. *Newsweek,* correspondent in Algiers, 1961-62.

WRITINGS: Trente secondes sur New York (novel), A. Michel, 1969, translation by June P. Wilson and Walter B. Michaels published as *Thirty Seconds over New York,* Morrow, 1970; *Organisation armee secrete, fevrier 1961-juillet 1962,* J'ai lu, 1972.

SIDELIGHTS: Robert J. McCarthy writes in *Best Sellers:* "Surely 'Thirty Seconds Over New York' is a comic novel, whether intentionally or unintentionally. Buchard, in my opinion, has given us a novel of sound social satire and has written a delightful parody of cliched western attitudes, as embodied in the whole spy-novel genre.... If this is not a spoof in which Buchard implicitly says that the whole matter is a question of rival paranoias, then I must be much mistaken. Taken as a comedy, this is funny and instinctive, too."

BIOGRAPHICAL/CRITICAL SOURCES: Best Sellers, March 15, 1970.†

* * *

BUCK, Charles (Henry, Jr.) 1915-

PERSONAL: Born July 1, 1915, in Baltimore, Md.; son of Charles Henry (a lawyer) and Adele (Strauss) Buck; married Elizabeth Richards, August 30, 1944; married second wife, Elizabeth Greenleaf (a school principal), August 1, 1957; children: (first marriage) Charles, William, Richard. *Education:* Johns Hopkins University, B.A., 1935; Ph.D., 1938; Episcopal Theological School, B.D., 1941. *Home:* 53 Powell St., Brookline, Mass. 02146. *Office:* St. Paul's Cathedral, 138 Tremont St., Boston, Mass. 02111.

CAREER: Episcopal Theological School, Cambridge, Mass., 1945-53, began as instructor, became professor of New Testament; St. Paul's Cathedral, Boston, Mass., dean, 1953—. *Military service:* U.S. Naval Reserve, chaplain, 1942-45; became lieutenant commander.

WRITINGS: A Chronology of the Plays of Plautus, privately printed, 1941; (with Greer Taylor) *Saint Paul: A Study in the Development of His Thought,* Scribner, 1969.

BIOGRAPHICAL/CRITICAL SOURCES: New York Times Book Review, March 15, 1970.

* * *

BUCK, Harry M(erwyn, Jr.) 1921-

PERSONAL: Born November 18, 1921, in Enola, Pa.; son of Harry Merwyn (a minister) and Edith (Ackerly) Buck; married Esther Gingrich (a teacher), June 5, 1943; children: David, L. Paul. *Education:* Albright College, A.B., 1942; attended Lutheran Theological Seminary at Gettysburg, 1944-46; Evangelical School of Theology, Reading, Pa., M.Div., 1945; Pennsylvania State College (now University), graduate study, 1946-48; University of Chicago, Ph.D., 1954; University of Pennsylvania, postdoctoral study, 1965. *Home:* 1053 Wilson Ave., Chambersburg, Pa. 17201. *Office:* Department of Religion, Wilson College, Chambersburg, Pa. 17201.

CAREER: Wellesley College, Wellesley, Mass., instructor, 1951-56, assistant professor of biblical history, literature, and interpretation, 1956-59; Wilson College, Chambersburg, Pa., associate professor, 1959-68, professor of religion studies, 1968—. Visiting professor, University of Pennsylvania, 1967. Chairman, American Textual Criticism Seminar, 1960-62; member, lectionary commission, International Greek New Testament Project; delegate, Council on the Study of Religion. Executive director, Wilson Books, 1973—. Consultant, American Bible Society Greek New Testament Project.

MEMBER: American Academy of Religion (executive director and treasurer, 1958-73), Society of Biblical Literature, Association of Asian Studies, American Association of University Professors, Studiorum Novi Testamentum Societas. *Awards, honors:* East-West Philosophers' Conference fellowship, 1959; U.S. Educational Foundation in India grant, 1961; faculty training fellowship, American Institute of Indian Studies and Society for Religion in Higher Education, 1965-66; participating fellowship, International Conference, University of Malaya, 1966; Christian and Mary Linback Award for distinguished teaching, 1967; Ford-Wilson Fund grants, 1969, 1970.

WRITINGS: The Johannine Lessons in the Greek Gospel Lectionary, University of Chicago Press, 1958; *People of the Lord: The History, Scriptures, and Faith of Ancient Israel,* Macmillan, 1966; (contributor) J. M. Myers and others, editors, *Search the Scriptures,* E. J. Brill, 1969; (contributor) *Professor K. A. Nilakanta Sastri: Felicitation Volume,* Rathnam Press (Madras), 1971; (contributor) Eugene Barth and others, editors, *Festschrift in Honor of F. W. Gingrich,* E. J. Brill, 1972; (contributor) David Edward Aune, editor, *Studies in New Testament and Early Christian Literature: Essays in Honor of Alan P. Wikgren,* E. J. Brill, 1972. Also author of *The Sandals of Lord Rama,* and contributor to *Festschrift in Honor of Jacob Myers.* Contributor to *Journal of the American Academy of Religion, Journal of Bible and Religion, Bible Translator, Liberal Education,* and other publications. Managing editor, *Journal of the American Academy of Religion,* 1961-73; editor, *Anima,* 1974—; editor, *Religion and Human Experience.*

WORK IN PROGRESS: In the Footsteps of Lord Rama, a Phenomenological Study of the Ramayana.

*   *   *

BUCKLEY, Francis J(oseph) 1928-

PERSONAL: Born August 31, 1928, in Los Angeles, Calif.; son of Francis J. (a realtor) and Elizabeth Agnes (Haiss) Buckley. *Education:* Attended University of Notre Dame, 1944-45, University of Santa Clara, 1945-49; Gonzaga University, B.A., 1951, M.A., 1952; Alma College, Los Gatos, Calif., S.T.L., 1959; University of Santa Clara, S.T.M., 1959; Gregorian University, Rome, Italy, S.T.D., 1964; University of Michigan, postdoctoral study, 1973-74. *Home and office:* University of San Francisco, San Francisco, Calif. 94117.

CAREER: Ordained Roman Catholic priest; member of Society of Jesus (Jesuits); Bellarmine College Preparatory, San Jose, Calif., instructor in religion and Latin, 1952-55; University of San Francisco, San Francisco, Calif., instructor, 1960-61, assistant professor, 1963-68, associate professor, 1968-72, professor of dogmatic theology, 1972—, acting chairman of department of religion, 1971-73, director of graduate programs in religious education, 1974-75, associate director, 1975—. Chaplain, St. Elizabeth Infant Hospital, San Francisco, 1964-72. Official delegate to Asian Catechetical and Liturgical Conference, 1967, Latin American Catechetical Conference, 1968, and International Catechetical Congress in Rome, 1971. Member of board of directors of Stanford-Santa Clara Ecumenical Colloquium, 1967-69; member of board of trustees, Jesuit community at University of San Francisco, 1969-76; member of board of directors, Council on the Study of Religion, 1972-75; member of board of trustees, Loyola Marymount University, 1974—. Adviser to U.S. Bishops at Roman Synod on Catechesis, 1977.

MEMBER: American Society of Church History, Catholic Biblical Association, Catholic Theological Society of America, College Theology Society (regional chairman, 1966-72; member of board of directors, 1969-76; president, 1972-74), Religious Education Association, International Society of Jesuit Ecumenists, Association of Professors and Researchers in Religious Education.

WRITINGS: Christ and the Church According to Gregory of Elvira, Gregorian University Press, 1964; (with Johannes Hofinger) *The Good News and Its Proclamation,* University of Notre Dame Press, 1968; *Children and God: Communion, Confession, Confirmation,* Corpus Publications, 1970; *"I Confess"—The Sacrament of Penance Today,* Ave Maria Press, 1972.

"On Our Way" series, with Sister Maria de la Cruz Aymes; published by Sadlier: *With Christ to the Father,* 1966; *Christ's Life in Us,* 1967; *Jesus,* 1968; *Spirit,* 1968; *Jesus in the Gospels and the Eucharist,* 1969; *In the Spirit of Jesus,* 1969; *One in Christ,* 1970; *God's People,* 1970.

"New Life" series, with Aymes; published by Sadlier: *Our Father,* 1971; *Christ Our Life,* 1971; *Jesus Our Lord,* 1971; *Spirit of God,* 1972; *One in the Lord,* 1973; *God among Us,* 1973; *Jesus Forgives,* 1974.

Editor with Cyr Miller: "Faith and Life" series, eighteen books, Bruce, 1970-72. Contributor to *New Catholic Encyclopedia* and to more than twenty theological and religious journals.

WORK IN PROGRESS: Christian Formation, in light of theology, psychology, sociology, history, and comparative religion; and *Theological Method.*

SIDELIGHTS: Francis J. Buckley reads in nine languages—Latin, Greek, Hebrew, German, French, Italian, Spanish, Portuguese, and Dutch. His catechetical works with Sister Maria de la Cruz Aymes have been translated into several foreign languages.

*   *   *

BUCKNALL, Barbara J(ane) 1933-

PERSONAL: Surname is pronounced *Buck*-nall; born June 8, 1933, in Teddington, England; daughter of Eric Herbert (a metallurgist) and Mary (Macaulay) Bucknall. *Education:* Lady Margaret Hall, Oxford, B.A., 1955, M.A., 1958, University of London, Diploma of Librarianship, 1958; Northwestern University, graduate study, 1960-62, Ph.D., 1966. *Politics:* "Vague and uninformed but democratic." *Religion:* Religious Society of Friends. *Home:* 160 Highland Ave., St. Catharines, Ontario, Canada. *Office:* Department of French, Brock University, St. Catharines, Ontario, Canada.

CAREER: University of Illinois, Champaign, instructor, 1962-66, assistant professor of French, 1966-69; Brock University, St. Catharines, Ontario, assistant professor, 1969-71, associate professor of French, 1971—. *Member:* Modern Language Association of America, American Association of Teachers of French. *Awards, honors:* Canada Council fellow, 1974-75.

WRITINGS: The Religion of Art in Proust, University of Illinois Press, 1969. Also author of a novel. Contributor to *Encyclopedia of World Literature in the Twentieth Century.* Contributor of articles to *Humanities Association Review* and other scholarly journals.

WORK IN PROGRESS: The Realism and Relevance of Fairy Stories; revision of a manuscript on Proust and three of his literary friends; a study on Rabelais and the comic strip; a study on Rimbaud and science fiction; a book of children's stories.

SIDELIGHTS: Barbara Bucknall has "decided to write fantasy rather [than] studying its psychology."

* * *

BUDICK, Sanford 1942-

PERSONAL: First syllable of surname rhymes with "view"; born July 5, 1942, in New York, N.Y.; son of Harry N. (an optometrist) and Sylvia (Schreiber) Budick; married Emily Miller, July 4, 1968; children: three. *Education:* Harvard University, A.B., 1963; Yale University, M.A., 1964, Ph.D., 1966. *Religion:* Jewish. *Office:* Department of English, Cornell University, Ithaca, N.Y. 14850.

CAREER: Cornell University, Ithaca, N.Y., instructor, 1966-67, assistant professor, 1967-70, associate professor of English, 1971—. Hebrew University of Jerusalem, visiting senior lecturer in English, 1970-71, associate professor, 1972—. *Member:* Modern Language Association of America. *Awards, honors:* Research fellowships from American Council of Learned Societies, 1970, and American Philosophical Society, 1971.

WRITINGS: Dryden and the Abyss of Light: A Study of "Religio Laici" and "The Hind and the Panther," Yale University Press, 1970; *Poetry of Civilization: Mythopoeic Displacement in the Verse of Milton, Dryden, Pope, and Johnson,* Yale University Press, 1974. Contributor to English journals and *Times Literary Supplement* (London).

WORK IN PROGRESS: A book on *Paradise Lost.*

* * *

BUEHR, Walter Franklin 1897-1971

May 14, 1897—January 2, 1971; American artist, illustrator, and author of children's books. Obituaries: *Publishers' Weekly,* September 20, 1971. (See index for *CA* sketch)

* * *

BUELL, Frederick H(enderson) 1942-

PERSONAL: Born November 17, 1942, in Bryn Mawr, Pa.; son of Clarence Addison (a business executive) and Marjorie (a cartoonist; maiden name, Henderson) Buell. *Education:* Yale University, B.A., 1964, law student, 1964-65; Free University of Berlin, graduate study, 1968-69; Cornell University, Ph.D., 1970. *Home:* 290 Riverside Dr., Apt. 10-D, New York, N.Y. 10025. *Office:* Department of English, Queens College of the City University of New York, Flushing, N.Y. 11367.

CAREER: Queens College of the City University of New York, Flushing, N.Y., instructor, 1970-71, assistant professor, 1971-73, associate professor of English, 1973—. *Awards, honors:* Award from Academy of American Poets, 1970; National Endowment for the Arts fellowship, 1972; American Philosophical Society fellowship, 1977.

WRITINGS: Theseus and Other Poems, Ithaca House, 1971; *W. H. Auden as a Social Poet,* Cornell University Press, 1973. Poetry editor, *A Shout in the Street* (magazine).

WORK IN PROGRESS: A book of poems, *A Voice Came Out of the Stars,* for Collection Generation; a book on contemporary American poetry.

SIDELIGHTS: Frederick Buell told *CA:* "I am a compulsive reader and traveler; my reading is not limited to literature, but extends to biology, astronomy, layman's physics,

ancient history, and comparative religion; my travels have included most of Europe, North Africa, Southeast Asia, and South America."

BIOGRAPHICAL/CRITICAL SOURCES: Hudson Review, October, 1971.

* * *

BUFFINGTON, Albert F(ranklin) 1905-

PERSONAL: Born July 11, 1905, in Pillow, Pa.; son of John N. and Lizzie (Hepler) Buffington; married Dorothy Lorine Harris, June 20, 1932; children: Albert Franklin, Jr., Lorine Harris. *Education:* Attended University of Berlin, 1926; Bucknell University, A.B., 1928; Harvard University, A.M., 1932, Ph.D., 1937. *Home:* 7960 East Camelback Rd., Scottsdale, Ariz. 85251. *Office:* Department of Foreign Languages, Arizona State University, Tempe, Ariz. 85281.

CAREER: Central High School, Scranton, Pa., head of German department, 1928-30; Harvard University, Cambridge, Mass., instructor in German, 1930-37; University of New Hampshire, Durham, instructor, 1937-39, assistant professor, 1939-44, associate professor of German, 1944-45; Pennsylvania State University, University Park, associate professor, 1945-48, professor of German, 1948-65, professor emeritus, 1965—, head of the department, 1963-65; Arizona State University, Tempe, professor of German, 1965-75, professor emeritus, 1975—. Lecturer, United States Information Service, Rheinpfalz, Germany, 1961. *Member:* Modern Language Association of America, American Association of Teachers of German, Rocky Mountain Modern Language Association, Pennsylvania German Society, Pennsylvania German Folklore Society, Arizona Foreign Language Association, Arizona College Association, Delta Phi Alpha. *Awards, honors:* Citations from Carl Schurz Memorial Foundation, 1955, Society for German-American Studies, 1973, and Pennsylvania German Society, 1974.

WRITINGS: (Contributor) *Studies in Honor of John Albrecht Walz,* Lancaster Press, 1941; (editor with Walter E. Boyer and Don Yoder) *Songs Along the Mahantongo,* Dutch Folklore Center, Franklin and Marshall College, 1951, 2nd edition Folklore Associates, 1964; (with Preston A. Barba) *A Pennsylvania German Grammar,* Schlecter's, 1954, revised edition, Pennsylvania German Folklore Society, 1965; (editor) Harry Hess Reichard and I. R. Reichard, *The Reichard Collection of Early Pennsylvania German Plays,* Pennsylvania German Society, Fackenthal Library, Franklin and Marshall College, 1962; *Dutchified German Spirituals,* Pennsylvania German Society, 1966; (contributor) S. Z. Buehne and others, editors, *Helen Adolf Festschrift,* Ungar, 1968; *Pennsylvania German Secular Folksongs,* Pennsylvania German Society, 1974. Contributor to *Morning Call, American Speech, American German Review, Commonwealth,* and other publications.

* * *

BUKTENICA, Norman A(ugust) 1930-

PERSONAL: Born May 27, 1930, in Chicago, Ill.; son of August and Theresa (Ruick) Buktenica; married Dena Jaffe (an adult-education teacher), October 30, 1955; children: Julie, Laurie. *Education:* Wabash College, B.A., 1952; Roosevelt University, M.A., 1956; University of Chicago, Ph.D., 1966. *Office:* Department of Psychology, George Peabody College for Teachers, Nashville, Tenn. 37203.

CAREER: Dr. Julian D. Levinson Research Foundation, Chicago, Ill., psychologist, 1955-57; Highland Park, Ill., public schools, school psychologist, 1956-57; Illinois Department of Public Instruction, Galesburg and Elgin, Ill., clinical assistant and psychologist, 1958-59; Proviso Township (Ill.) Department of Education for Exceptional Children, school psychologist, 1959-66; Woodlawn Mental Health Center, Chicago, psychologist, 1964-67; George Peabody College for Teachers, Nashville, Tenn., associate professor, 1967-71, professor of psychology, 1971—, director of school psychology training program, 1967-72, director of transactional–ecological psychology training program, 1972—, chairman of school of psychology program committee. Assistant assessment officer, University of Chicago, Peace Corps Training Program, Pakistan, 1963; superintendent of public instruction, State of Illinois, 1964-65; psychologist, Project Head Start, 1965-67; coordinating psychologist, Hawaii State Department of Education, 1966; instructor in psychology, Stritch School of Medicine, Loyola University of Chicago, 1966-67; co-director of John J. Madden Zone Center, Illinois Department of Health, 1966-67. *Military service:* U.S. Army, 1952-54. *Member:* American Educational Research Association, American Association of Mental Deficiency, American Psychological Association, Tennessee Association for Psychology in the Schools (president elect, 1971-72), Tennessee Psychological Association (chairman of school psychology committee, 1970—), Psi Chi.

WRITINGS: (With Keith E. Beery) *Beery-Buktenica Visual-Motor Integration Test,* Follett, 1967; *Visual Learning,* Dimensions Publishing, 1968. Also contributor to *The Estate of Childhood,* edited by S. K. Schiff, for C. C Thomas. Contributor of about a dozen articles to psychology and education journals. Editorial consultant, *Journal of School Psychology,* 1967-72, *School Psychology Digest,* 1972—.

WORK IN PROGRESS: Developing an experimental edition of *Test of Non-Verbal Auditory Discrimination.†*

*   *   *

BULATKIN, Eleanor Webster 1913-

PERSONAL: Born September 2, 1913, in Baltimore, Md.; daughter of Silas Rodney (a marine engineer) and Anna May (Rich) Webster; married Iliya Fomich Bulatkin (a research chemist), September 27, 1946 (died October, 1974). *Education:* Maryland Institute of Fine and Applied Arts, Certificate, 1934; Johns Hopkins University, M.A., 1951, Ph.D., 1952. *Religion:* Episcopalian. *Home:* 167 West Winter St., Delaware, Ohio 43015. *Office:* Department of Romance Languages, Ohio State University, Columbus, Ohio 43210.

CAREER: University of Maryland, College Park, instructor, 1952-57, assistant professor of French and Spanish, 1957-61, Office of International Programs, member of steering committee, member of committee for Latin American studies; Ohio State University, Columbus, associate professor, 1961-64, professor of Romance languages, 1964—, chairman of department, 1966-72. Fulbright lecturer in Spanish linguistics, Caro y Cuervo Institute, Bogota, Colombia, 1960-61. *Member:* Modern Language Association of America, Association of Departments of Foreign Languages (member of executive committee, 1970-72), Linguistic Society of America, Modern Humanities Research Association, Medieval Academy of America, American Association of University Professors, Midwest Modern Language Association.

WRITINGS: (Contributor) Urban T. Holmes and Kenneth R. Scholberg, editors, *French and Provencal Lexicography:*

Essays Presented to Honor Alexander Herman Schutz, Ohio State University Press, 1964; *Structural Arithmetic Metaphor in the Oxford "Roland,"* Ohio State University Press, 1972. Contributor to language journals.†

*   *   *

BULLARD, E(dgar) John III 1942-

PERSONAL: Born September 15, 1942, in Los Angeles, Calif.; son of Edgar J. and Katherine (Dreisbach) Bullard. *Education:* University of California, Los Angeles, B.A., 1965, M.A., 1968. *Home:* 1031 Peniston St., New Orleans, La. 70115. *Office address:* New Orleans Museum of Art, P.O. Box 19123, New Orleans, La. 70179.

CAREER: National Gallery of Art, Washington, D.C., curator of special projects, 1968-73; New Orleans Museum of Art, New Orleans, La., director, 1973—. Member of museum advisory panel, National Endowment for the Arts, 1974—. Member of board of advisors, Georgia Museum of Art. *Member:* American Association of Museums, College Art Association of America, Association of Art Museum Directors.

WRITINGS: Edgar Degas, McGraw, 1971; (with David W. Scott) *John Sloan: 1871-1951,* Boston Book & Art Inc., 1971; *Mary Cassatt: Oils and Pastels,* Watson-Guptill, 1972; *A Panorama of American Painting,* New Orleans Museum of Art, 1975. Contributor to art and museum magazines.

*   *   *

BULLARD, Roger A(ubrey) 1937-

PERSONAL: Born August 1, 1937, in Memphis, Tenn.; son of Roger Maurice (an electrician) and Mable (Bennett) Bullard; married Carol Hawthorne, May 21, 1961; children: Kenneth Maurice, Floyd Andrew. *Education:* Union University, Jackson, Tenn., B.A., 1958; University of Kentucky, M.A.,1959; Southwestern Baptist Theological Seminary, B.D., 1962; Vanderbilt University, Ph.D., 1965. *Politics:* Democrat. *Religion:* Baptist. *Residence:* Wilson, N.C. *Office:* Department of Religion, Atlantic Christian College, Wilson, N.C. 27893.

CAREER: Atlantic Christian College, Wilson, N.C., associate professor, 1965-68, professor of religion and philosophy, 1968—. *Member:* Society of Biblical Literature, Association of Baptist Professors of Religion, Institute for Antiquity and Christianity (corresponding member), American Association of University Professors, Southern Baptist Historical Society. *Awards, honors:* Christian Research Foundation Award for translation, 1964; American Council of Learned Societies grant, 1968; National Foundation for the Humanities grant, 1969.

WRITINGS: The Hypostasis of the Archons: The Coptic Text with Translation and Commentary, de Gruyter, 1970; (contributor of Old Testament translations) *Today's English Version of the Bible,* American Bible Society, 1976. Contributor of reviews to professional journals.

WORK IN PROGRESS: Member of committee translating deuterocanonical texts.

SIDELIGHTS: Among the ancient languages, Roger Bullard is competent in Greek, Latin, Hebrew, and Coptic. He also has a reading knowledge of several modern languages. *Avocational interests:* Music.

BULLITT, Orville H(orwitz) 1894-

PERSONAL: Born July 30, 1894, in Cape May, N.J.; son of William C. and Louisa G. (Horwitz) Bullitt; married Susan B. Ingersoll, November 15, 1916; children: Orville H., Jr., Rita S., John C., Louisa H. *Education:* University of Pennsylvania, B.S., 1915. *Politics:* Democrat. *Religion:* Episcopalian. *Residence:* Fort Washington, Pa. *Office:* 1500 Walnut St., Philadelphia, Pa. 19102.

CAREER: Newbold's Son & Co., partner, 1926-43; president, Beaver Coal Co., Philadelphia, Pa., beginning 1931; currently president, Beaver Management Corp., Philadelphia. Former director of Westmoreland Coal Co., Virginia Coal & Iron Co., Central Pennsylvania National Bank, Fidelity Bank, and other organizations; former trustee, Philadelphia Saving Fund Society. Regional director, War Production Board, 1941-45. University of Pennsylvania Hospital, president, 1931-59, chairman of the board, 1960-62; Philadelphia Orchestra Association, director, 1933—, president and chairman of the board, 1938-61; life trustee, University of Pennsylvania; trustee, Philadelphia Museum of Art; chairman, University of Pennsylvania Press. *Military service:* U.S. Army, 1917-19. *Awards, honors:* L.H.D., University of Pennsylvania, 1970.

WRITINGS: Search for Sybaris, Lippincott, 1969; (editor) *For The President—Personal and Secret: Correspondence between Franklin D. Roosevelt and William C. Bullitt,* Houghton, 1972.

WORK IN PROGRESS: A history of Phoenicians.

SIDELIGHTS: Bullitt's book is the record of eight years of search for the ancient Greek city of Sybaris, lost without a trace in 510 B.C. when it was conquered by a rival city, Croton. Bullitt instigated and supported the work of the team headed by Froelich G. Rainey, director of the Museum of the University of Pennsylvania, that found the buried city in 1968.

BIOGRAPHICAL/CRITICAL SOURCES: Book World, September 21, 1969, December 17, 1972; *Best Sellers,* October 1, 1969, February 1, 1973; *New York Times Book Review,* October 5, 1969, December 17, 1972; *Christian Science Monitor,* December 20, 1972; *New Yorker,* January 6, 1973; *American Historical Review,* October 3, 1973.

* * *

BULLOCK, Charles S(pencer) III 1942-

PERSONAL: Born July 22, 1942, in Nashville, Tenn.; son of Charles Spencer, Jr. (a statistician) and Elenor (Davis) Bullock; married Frances Lee Mann, September 10, 1965; children: Georgia Beth, Judith Rebecca Lee. *Education:* William Jewell College, B.A., 1964; Emory University, law student, 1964-65; Washington University, St. Louis, Mo., M.A., 1967, Ph.D., 1968. *Politics:* Democrat. *Religion:* Episcopalian. *Home:* 160 Williamsburg Lane, Athens, Ga. 30605. *Office:* Department of Political Science, University of Georgia, Athens, Ga. 30601.

CAREER: University of Georgia, Athens, assistant professor, 1968-72, associate professor, 1972-75, professor of political science, 1977—; University of Houston, Houston, Tex., professor of political science, 1975-77. *Member:* American Political Science Association, Southern Political Science Association, Midwest Political Science Association, Southwest Political Science Association.

WRITINGS: (Compiler with R. T. Golembiewski and Harrell R. Rodgers) *The New Politics: Polarization or Utopia?,* McGraw, 1970; (with Rodgers) *Law and Social Change,* McGraw, 1972; (editor, with Rodgers) *Black Political Attitudes,* Markham, 1972; (with Rodgers) *Racial Equality in America,* Goodyear Publishing, 1975; (with Rodgers) *Coercion to Compliance,* Lexington, 1976; (with J. E. Anderson and D. W. Brady) *Public Policy and Politics in America,* in press. Contributor to political science, education, and black journals.

WORK IN PROGRESS: Studies on educational discrimination and congressional politics.

* * *

BUNCHE, Ralph Johnson 1904-1971

August 7, 1904—December 9, 1971; American diplomat; recipient of the Nobel Peace Prize for his arbitration of the 1949 Arab-Israeli truce. Obituaries: *New York Times,* December 10, 1971; *Washington Post,* December 10, 1971; *L'Express,* December 13-19, 1971; *Newsweek,* December 20, 1971; *Time,* December 20, 1971; *Nation,* December 27, 1971.

* * *

BUNNELL, Peter C(urtis) 1937-

PERSONAL: Born October 25, 1937, in Poughkeepsie, N.Y.; son of Harold C. (an engineer) and Ruth (Buckhout) Bunnell. *Education:* Rochester Institute of Technology, B.F.A., 1959; Ohio University, M.F.A., 1961; Yale University, M.A., 1965. *Home:* 40 McCosh Cir., Princeton, N.J. 08540. *Office:* Department of Art and Archaeology, Princeton University, Princeton, N.J. 08540.

CAREER: Museum of Modern Art, New York City, curator of photography, 1966-72; Princeton University, Princeton, N.J., visiting lecturer in department of art and archaeology, 1970-72, McAlpin Professor of the History of Photography and Modern Art, 1972—, faculty curator of photography, 1972—, director of art museum, 1973—. Visiting lecturer at Institute of Film and Television, New York University, 1968-70, department of art, Dartmouth College, 1968, and college seminar program, Yale University, 1973. Television host of special seventy-five-minute program, "Time, Light and Vision: The Art of Photography," for WNET-TV, New York City.

MEMBER: Society for Photographic Education (member of board of directors, 1968—; secretary, 1970-73; chairman, 1973-77), College Art Association (member of board of directors, 1975—), Association of Art Museum Directors, Friends of Photography (member of board of trustees, 1974—; vice-president, 1977), American Federation of Arts (member of international exhibitions committee), Photographic Historical Society of America. *Awards, honors:* Robert Chapman Bates fellow, Yale University, 1963-65; fellowship for studies in the history of photography, Polaroid Corp., 1965-66.

WRITINGS: (Assistant to Egbert Haverkamp-Begeman, senior editor) *Color in Prints: European and American Color Prints, 1500 to the Present,* Art Gallery, Yale University, 1962; (translator with F. Bunnell) Y. Ziswiler, *Extinct and Vanishing Animals: A Biology of Extinction and Survival,* Springer, 1967; (with Russell Edson) *Jerry N. Uelsmann,* Aperture, 1970, revised and enlarged edition, 1973; *Eight Photographs/Edward Weston,* Doubleday, 1971; (editor with Alan Trachtenberg and Peter Neill) *The City: American Experience,* Oxford University Press, 1971; (author of introduction) Max Waldman, *Waldman on Theater,* Doubleday, 1971; *Barbara Morgan,* Morgan & Morgan,

1972; (author of introduction) Dianne Vanderlip, editor, *Photographic Portraits*, Moore College of Art, 1972; (editor with Robert Sobieszek) *The Literature of Photography*, sixty-two volumes, Arno, 1973; (author of introduction) *A Portfolio of Ten Photographs by Elliott Erwitt*, Witkin-Berley, 1974; *Jerry N. Uelsmann: Silver Meditations*, Morgan & Morgan, 1975; (author of introduction) *Helen Gee and the Limelight*, Carlton Gallery, 1977; (contributor) *Conversations with Wright Morris: Critical Views and Responses*, University of Nebraska Press, 1977. Also author of *Nonsilver Printing Processes: Four Selections, 1886-1927*, Arno.

Publications include bibliographies and chronologies for *Paul Caponigro*, Grossman, 1967, 2nd edition, Aperture, 1972, *Mirrors Messages Manifestations*, Aperture, 1969, *W. Eugene Smith*, Aperture, 1969, *Paul Strand: A Retrospective Monograph*, Aperture, 1971, and other bibliographies, exhibition brochures, and checklists. Editor with Nathan Lyons, *Photography 63* and *Photography 64*, George Eastman House. Contributor of articles and reviews to *Aperture, Arts in Virginia, Artscanada, Camera, Art in America, Afterimage, Creative Camera, Print Collector's Newsletter, Choice, New York Times Book Review*, and other periodicals.

WORK IN PROGRESS: A two-volume anthology of nineteenth- and twentieth-century writings on photography; co-editing a reprint series of photographic literature; historical dictionary of photography; a critical history of twentieth-century photography; monographs on photographers Alfred Stieglitz and Clarence H. White.

SIDELIGHTS: Peter C. Bunnell is the first McAlpin Professor of the History of Photography at Princeton University. He wrote *CA*: "The principal motivation in my writing is to expand the understanding of photography as a creative medium. In this endeavor I hope to speak both to the viewer of photographs and to the photographer. In each case the challenge is to broaden the conceptual and intellectual orientation through which photographs are usually made and interpreted. Photography has existed in something of an intellectual and critical vacuum for too long." He has traveled through England, France, Belgium, Holland, Germany, Austria, Switzerland, and Italy.

BIOGRAPHICAL/CRITICAL SOURCES: *Time*, April 13, 1970; *New York Times*, June 6, 1971, April 18, 1972; *Newsweek*, October 21, 1974; *Village Voice*, July 19, 1976.

* * *

BUNUAN, Josefina S(antiago) 1935-

PERSONAL: Surname is accented on second syllable; born September 11, 1935, in Cabanatuan City, Philippines; came to United States in 1963, naturalized in 1970; daughter of Jose Villanueva and Ignacia Payumo (Santiago) Bunuan. *Education*: University of the Philippines, A.B. (cum laude), 1958; Kindergarten Training College, Melbourne, Australia, diploma in early childhood education, 1960; Boston College, M.Ed., 1965; Boston University, Ed.D., 1969. *Religion*: Roman Catholic. *Home*: 27 Hodgdon Ter., West Roxbury, Mass. 02132. *Office*: Department of Elementary Education, Worcester State College, 486 Chandler St., Worcester, Mass. 01602.

CAREER: University of the Philippines, Dilman, Quezon City, instructor in preschool education, 1958-60; Newport Pre-school Center, Melbourne, Australia, director, 1960; University of the Philippines, instructor in child development, 1961-64; Boston University, Boston, Mass., resident director, 1965-67; Worcester State College, Worcester,

Mass., associate professor of educational psychology, 1969—. Vice-president, United Nations and Colombo Plan Students Association, Melbourne, Australia, 1958-60; consultant, Pinck & Leodas Educational Enterprise, Cambridge, Mass., 1969. *Member*: Pi Lambda Theta. *Awards, honors*: University of the Philippines fellowship to the United States, 1963-67.

WRITINGS: (With David Hilton and David Quist) *Educational Measurement and Evaluation Workbook*, Kendall-Hunt, 1971. Contributor to *Education Quarterly*.

WORK IN PROGRESS: Editing *Readings in Educational Psychology*.

AVOCATIONAL INTERESTS: Swimming, fencing, reading, writing, playing piano.

BIOGRAPHICAL/CRITICAL SOURCES: *Manila Times*, January 26, 1960; John St. Vianey, editor, *A Longitudinal Assessment of Pre-School Children in Haptic Learning*, U.S. Office of Education, 1968.†

* * *

BURCHARD, Rachael C(aroline) 1921-

PERSONAL: Born August 27, 1921, in Hendersonville, N.C.; daughter of Henry Homer and Olive (Gowan) Ballenger; married Waldo Wadsworth Burchard (a sociology professor), May 24, 1945; children: Gina Michel, Petrea Celeste, Stuart Gregory, Margot Theresa. *Education*: Linfield College, B.A., 1945; University of California, Berkeley, further study, 1946-47; Northern Illinois University, M.A., 1966, doctoral candidate, 1969-71. *Religion*: "Contemporary Christian." *Home*: 907 Sharon Dr., DeKalb, Ill. 60115.

CAREER: English and drama teacher in high schools in Berkeley, El Cerrito, and Lafayette, Calif., 1947-53; Northern Illinois University, DeKalb, instructor in English and drama at Laboratory School, 1958-70, instructor in English at the university, 1970-72; Rock Valley College, Rockford, Ill., instructor on rhetoric and literature, 1974-76. Children's Community Theatre, DeKalb, writer and director, 1958-67, president, 1963-65. *Member*: National Council of Teachers of English, American English Association, American Association of University Professors, National Children's Theatre Association, Modern Language Association of America, Midwest Modern Language Association, Illinois Education Association.

WRITINGS: *John Updike: Yea Sayings*, Southern Illinois University Press, 1971. Contributor of poetry and articles to *English Journal, Synopsis, American Bard*, and numerous local and college publications.

WORK IN PROGRESS: Research on the contemporary novel.

SIDELIGHTS: Rachael Burchard's book is "a valuable contribution to our understanding of a complex writer," writes John Hill. Norris Yates, while feeling that the book "hardly justifies the implication of her title that Updike is predominately a 'yea-sayer,'" calls the book "useful and largely valid."

BIOGRAPHICAL/CRITICAL SOURCES: *Christian Century*, March 31, 1971; *Cresset*, October, 1971; *American Literature*, November, 1971; *CEA Critic*, May, 1972.

* * *

BURGESS, Charles (Orville) 1932-

PERSONAL: Born January 18, 1932, in Portland, Ore.; son

of Rex Orville and Glendora (Sundrud) Burgess; married Patricia Mae Stewart, April 22, 1976; children: (prior marriage) Donna Claire, Jo Dell, Robert Charles. *Education:* University of Oregon, B.A., 1957; University of Wisconsin, M.A., 1958, Ph.D., 1962. *Home:* 5528 30th Ave. N.E., Seattle, Wash. 98105. *Office:* 202 Miller Hall, University of Washington, Seattle, Wash. 98195.

CAREER: University of California, Riverside, assistant professor of history of education, 1962-64; University of Washington, Seattle, assistant professor, 1964-66, associate professor, 1966-70, professor of history of education, 1970—. National post-doctoral fellow, Harvard University, 1967-68. *Military service:* U.S. Air Force, 1950-54; became staff sergeant. *Member:* History of Education Society (president, 1971-72), American Historical Association, American Educational Research Association (vice-president, 1976-78), Organization of American Historians, Phi Beta Kappa. *Awards, honors:* Danforth Foundation fellow, 1957-62.

WRITINGS: Nettie Fowler McCormick, Wisconsin State Historical Society, 1962; (editor with Charles Strickland) *Health, Growth, and Heredity,* Teachers College Press, 1965; (with Merle L. Borrowman) *What Doctrines to Embrace,* Scott, Foresman, 1969. Contributor to education and history journals. Consulting editor, *Educational Studies.*

WORK IN PROGRESS: A book, tentatively entitled, *The State versus the Family: Compulsory Education in the American Experience.*

* * *

BURGESS, John H(enry) 1923-

PERSONAL: Born August 9, 1923, in Niagara Falls, N.Y.; son of John H. and Mary Ann (Crandell) Burgess; married Sylvia Marie Johnson (a teacher), June 30, 1965. *Education:* Attended Ripon College, 1943-45; Kent State University, B.S., 1948; University of Miami, Coral Gables, Fla., M.A., 1950. *Office:* 3412 Midland Ave., Syracuse, N.Y. 13205.

CAREER: Western College for Women (now Western College), Oxford, Ohio, instructor in psychology, 1950-51; Speedways Conveyors, Inc., Buffalo, N.Y., sales correspondent, 1952-53; Bell Aerospace Corp., Buffalo, member of engineering psychology staff, 1953-66; Illinois Department of Mental Health, Adolph Meyer Center, Decatur, Ill., member of Operations Research staff, 1966-67, regional director of research and evaulation, 1967-74; Army Corps of Engineers, Champaign, Ill., psychologist, 1973-76; freelance writer, 1976—. Member of Community Services Group of Decatur, 1969; participant in White House Children's Conference, 1970; member of South Central Illinois Health Council, 1971—. *Military service:* U.S. Army, 1943-46; became staff sergeant. *Member:* American Psychological Association, International Society of Semantics.

WRITINGS: The Christian Pagan: A Naturalistic Survey of Christian History, Mimir Publishers, 1969; *The Time Dimension in Science and Psychology,* Adams Press, 1971; *System Approaches to the Design and Evaluation of Public Services,* Associated University Presses, 1977. Contributor to *Human Factors Journal, Journal for the Scientific Study of Religion, American Rationalist, ETC: A Review of General Semantics, Social Psychiatry, Administration in Mental Health,* and other journals in his field.

WORK IN PROGRESS: Two textbooks, one on the human engineering of business and engineering forms, and one on psychological health and mental health studies in self-help and control therapies; long-range research in the application

of various operations and systems research methods for investigation, analysis, and evaluation of domestic control systems in transportation, housing, pollution, and rehabilitation services; research on bureaucratic impediments to goal accomplishment.

* * *

BURIAN, Jarka M(arsano) 1927-

PERSONAL: Given name originally Jaroslav; born March 10, 1927, in Passaic, N.J.; son of Jaroslav Valerian (a skilled worker) and Olga (a teacher; maiden name, Marsano) Burian; married Grayce Susan DeLeo (a college teacher), June 15, 1951. *Education:* Rutgers University, B.A., 1949; Columbia University, M.A., 1950; Cornell University, Ph.D., 1955. *Home:* 7 MacPherson Ter., Albany, N.Y. 12206. *Office:* Department of Theatre, State University of New York, 1400 Washington Ave., Albany, N.Y. 12222.

CAREER: Cornell University, Ithaca, N.Y., instructor in English, 1951-55; State University of New York at Albany, assistant professor, 1955-59, associate professor, 1959-63, professor of theatre, 1963—, chairman of department, 1971-74, acting head of University Theatre, 1962-64. Visiting professor of dramatic art, University of California, Berkeley, 1961-62. Producer-director, Arena Summer Theatre, Albany, N.Y., 1959, 1963-64, 1966-68, 1972-73. *Military service:* U.S. Army, 1946-47, 1950-51; became staff sergeant. *Member:* American Educational Theatre Association, United States Institute for Theatre Technology, American Association of University Professors, American Society for Theatre Research, Phi Beta Kappa. *Awards, honors:* Special award from United States Institute for Theatre Technology for *The Scenography of Josef Svoboda.*

WRITINGS: Central Staging: New Force in the Theatre, privately printed, 1950; (translator) Karel Capek, "The Insect Comedy," first produced in Albany at State University of New York University Theatre, March, 1957; *O Americkem dramatu a divadelnictvi* (title means "American Drama and Theatre"), Universita J. E. Purkyne (Brno, Czechoslovakia), 1966; *The Scenography of Josef Svoboda,* Wesleyan University Press, 1971. Also author of an adaptation of Jaroslav Hasek's *Good Soldier Schweik,* as yet unpublished. Contributor to *Plays and Players, Educational Theatre Journal, Drama Survey, Theatre Annual, Drama Review,* and *Theatre Design and Technology.*

WORK IN PROGRESS: A book-length study of post-war Czech theatre.

* * *

BURKE, Russell 1946-

PERSONAL: Born August 23, 1946, in Plainfield, N.J.; son of Russell Ely II and Theo (Welles) Burke. *Education:* University of Maryland, B.A., 1972.

CAREER: University of Maryland, McKeldin Library, College Park, library assistant, 1971-72.

WRITINGS: (With William H. Gerdts) *History of American Still-Life Painting,* Praeger, 1971.

WORK IN PROGRESS: Editing and annotating the diary of American painter Jervis McEntee, for Archives of American Art; *History of American Miniature Painting.*†

* * *

BURKETT, Eva M(ae) 1903-

PERSONAL: Born April 9, 1903, in Culleoka, Tenn.;

daughter of Absalom Daniel (a farmer) and Nancy C. (McNeill) Burkett. *Education:* Middle Tennessee State College (now University), B.S., 1927; George Peabody College for Teachers, M.A., 1930, Ph.D., 1936; also attended University of Chicago, 1948, Columbia University, 1955, University of Michigan, 1956, University of Indiana, Georgetown University, 1960, Harvard University, 1965, University of Southern California, 1967. *Politics:* Democrat. *Religion:* Presbyterian. *Home:* 206 Experiment Lane, Columbia, Tenn. 38401.

CAREER: State Teachers College, Murfreesboro (now Middle Tennessee State University), associate professor of English, 1935-47; Drake University, Des Moines, Iowa, assistant professor of English, 1947-51; McKendree College, Lebanon, Ill., instructor in English, 1951-52; Army Education Program, Otsu, Japan, education advisor, 1952-54; Tennessee Polytechnic Institute (now Tennessee Technological University), Cookeville, assistant professor of English, 1954-56; Anatolia College, Thessaloniki, Greece, teacher of English as a foreign language, 1956-57; Southern State College, Magnolia, Ark., professor of English and chairman of humanities division, 1957-63; State College of Arkansas, Conway, professor of English, 1963-71. Director, N.D.E.A. Institute for Advanced Study in English, State College of Arkansas, 1967. *Member:* Modern Language Association of America, National Council of Teachers of English, College English Association.

WRITINGS: (Editor with Joyce S. Steward) *Introductory Readings in Literary Criticism,* Addison-Wesley, 1968; *Prose: A Systematic Approach to Writing,* Cummings, 1970; *Writing in Subject-Matter Fields: A Bibliographic Guide, with Annotations and Writing Assignments,* Scarecrow, 1977. Contributor to *Philological Quarterly, Arkansas Education Journal,* and *College Composition and Communication.*

WORK IN PROGRESS: American English Dialects in Literature.

* * *

BURKILL, T(om) A(lec)   1912-

PERSONAL: Born April 18, 1912, in Thorne, Yorkshire, England; son of Tom Stephenson and Sarah Anne (Drinkall) Burkill; married Bella Moorhouse (a private secretary), September 16, 1952. *Education:* University of Manchester, B.A. (with first class honors), 1936, B.D. (with distinction), 1938, M.A., 1940, Ph.D., 1942; Oxford University, D.Phil., 1947; Harvard University, S.T.M., 1949; University of Rhodesia, D.Litt., 1974. *Politics:* Liberal. *Office:* Department of Theology and Philosophy, University of Rhodesia, P.O. Box MP 167, Mount Pleasant, Salisbury, Rhodesia.

CAREER: Minister of the Congregational Church in England and the United States, and of the United Church of Canada; minister of the Presbyterian Church of Southern Africa; Liverpool Regional Committee for Adult Education in His Majesty's Forces, Liverpool, England, minister and lecturer, 1942-44; University of Mainz, Mainz, Germany, lecturer in English language and philosophy, 1947-48; Institute for Adult Education, Benghazi, North Africa, director, 1949-51; Le Service International, East London, England, volunteer work, 1952-53; University of London, London, England, minister and extension lecturer in philosophy and theology, 1953-60; researcher and writer in England, 1967-69; University of Rhodesia, Salisbury, head of department of theology and philosophy, 1969—. Visiting professor at Cornell University, 1960-62, University of Chicago, 1963-

64, and University of Alberta, 1964-67; visiting lecturer, University of Bonn, 1976; visiting research fellow, Wolfson College, Oxford University, 1976. Executive secretary for World Congress of Faiths, 1959-60. Theological consultant for Rhodesian Committee on Church Unity, 1972—.

AWARDS, HONORS: Dr. Williams Divinity Scholar and Prizeman, London, 1937; Certificat d'Assiduite, College de France, 1939; Faulkner fellow, University of Manchester, 1940; Daniel Jones research fellow, Oxford University, 1944.

WRITINGS: Mysterious Revelation: An Examination of the Philosophy of St. Mark's Gospel, Cornell University Press, 1963; *God and Reality in Modern Thought,* Prentice-Hall, 1963; (contributor) *Classical Studies in Honor of Harry Caplan,* Cornell University Press, 1966; *The Evolution of Christian Thought,* Cornell University Press, 1971; *New Light on the Earliest Gospel: Seven Markan Studies,* Cornell University Press, 1972; (editor and reviser with G. Vermes) Paul Winter, *On the Trial of Jesus,* de Gruyter & Co., 1974. Contributor to *Festschrift for Morton Smith: Christianity, Judaism and Other Greco-Roman Cults,* E. J. Brill. Contributor to *The Interpreter's Dictionary of the Bible,* Abingdon, 1962. Contributor to *Nature, Philosophy, Theologische Zeitschrift, Numen, Hibbert Journal, Studia Theologica, La Revue de l'Histoire des Religions, Die Zeitschrift fuer die Neutestamentliche Wissenschaft, La Revue Philosophique, Vigiliae Christianae, Journal of Biblical Literature, Dialogue, Philosophical Review,* and *La Revue Internationale de Philosophie.*

WORK IN PROGRESS: Myth and the Scientific Mind; member of international team engaged on the translation and updating of Emil Schurer's *Die Geschichte des juedischen Volkes im Zeitalter Jesu Christi,* for T. & T. Clark, Edinburgh.

* * *

BURKS, David D.   1924-

PERSONAL: Born January 21, 1924, in Duluth, Minn.; son of Walter D. (a teacher) and Cora (Voyles) Burks; children: Stephen, Maria, Ramona. *Education:* Earlham College, A.B., 1945; University of Chicago, Ph.D., 1952. *Residence:* Yonkers, N.Y. *Office:* Department of History, Hunter College of the City University of New York, 695 Park Ave., New York, N.Y. 10021.

CAREER: Muskingum College, New Concord, Ohio, member of history department faculty, 1949-53; Otterbein College, Westerville, Ohio, member of history department faculty, 1953-56; U.S. Department of State, Washington, D.C., Latin American research specialist, 1956-60; University of Michigan, Dearborn Extension, professor of Latin American history, 1960-64, Horace Rackham faculty fellow, 1961-63; Indiana University, Bloomington, professor of Latin American history, 1964-71; Hunter College of the City University of New York, New York, N.Y., professor of Latin American history, 1971—, chairman of Inter-American Affairs, 1972-73, 1975-77. Research fellow, Council on Foreign Relations, New York, N.Y., 1962-63. Lecturer at Foreign Service Institute. Consultant to U.S. State Department. *Member:* American Historical Association, Conference on Latin American History, Latin American Studies Association, National Council of Associations for International Studies.

WRITINGS: (With Karl Michael Schmitt) *Evolution or Chaos: Dynamics of Latin American Government and Politics,* Praeger, 1963; *Cuba Under Castro,* Foreign Policy

Association, 1964; (contributor) A. Curtis Wilgus, editor, *The Caribbean: Its Hemispheric Role,* University of Florida Press, 1967; *Survey of the Alliance for Progress: Insurgency in Latin America,* U.S. Government Printing Office, 1968. Contributor to *Encyclopedia Americana;* contributing editor, *Handbook of Latin American Studies.* Contributor of articles to *American Historical Review, Current History,* and *Hispanic American Historical Review.*

WORK IN PROGRESS: A monograph on Fidel Castro; a book on the impact of Castroism on Latin America, with stress on implications for U.S. policy; book reviews of publications relating to Latin American history.

AVOCATIONAL INTERESTS: Gardening, hiking, camping.

* * *

BURLEY, W(illiam) J(ohn) 1914-

PERSONAL: Born August 1, 1914, in Falmouth, England; son of William John (a builder) and Annie (Curnow) Burley; married Muriel Wolsey (a school secretary), April 10, 1938; children: Alan John, Nigel Philip. *Education:* Oxford University, degree in zoology (with honors), 1953. *Politics:* Labour. *Religion:* ''None (Humanist).'' *Home:* St. Patrick's, Holywell, Newquay, Cornwall, England.

CAREER: Gas engineer, 1933-49, served as assistant manager and manager of gas undertakings in southwest England; Newquay School, Newquay, Cornwall, England, head of biology department and sixth form tutor, 1953-74; full-time writer, 1974—. *Member:* Royal Entomological Society, Crime Writers' Association.

WRITINGS—All published by Gollancz, except as indicated: *A Taste of Power,* 1966; *Three Toed Pussy,* 1968; *Death in Willow Pattern,* Walker & Co., 1969; *To Kill a Cat,* Walker & Co., 1970; *Guilt Edged,* 1971, Walker & Co., 1972; *Death in a Salubrious Place,* 1972; *Death in Stanley Street,* 1974, Walker & Co., 1975; *Wycliffe and the Pea-green Boat,* Walker & Co., 1975; *Wycliffe and the Schoolgirls,* Walker & Co., 1976; *The Schoolmaster,* Walker & Co., 1977.

WORK IN PROGRESS: Wycliffe and the Scapegoat; Charles and Elizabeth; The Balancing Act; research on a comparison of organic and social evolution.

SIDELIGHTS: W. J. Burley's books have been published in Germany, Switzerland, Denmark, Sweden, France, Holland, Spain, and Italy.

* * *

BURNETT, Calvin 1921-

PERSONAL: Born July 18, 1921, in Cambridge, Mass.; son of Nathan Lowe (a physician and surgeon) and Addie (Waller) Burnett; married Torrey Milligan, August 20, 1960; children: Elizabeth Tobey. *Education:* Massachusetts School of Art (now Massachusetts College of Art), B.F.A., 1942; Massachusetts College of Art, B.S., 1951; Boston University, M.F.A., 1960. *Office:* Massachusetts College of Art, Boston, Mass. 20115.

CAREER: Graphic artist; communications and education illustrator and advertising artist for several firms; deCordova and Dana Museum, Lincoln, Mass., instructor in graphic art, 1953-56; Massachusetts College of Art, Boston, associate professor, 1956-71, professor of art, 1971—. Has exhibited his work in more than twenty-five institutions, 1943—, including Boston Institute of Contemporary Art, Oakland

Museum of Art, Taller de Graphico (Mexico), Museum of Fine Arts, Boston, and Children's Art Center, Boston. *Awards, honors:* More than twenty awards for art, 1947—, including those of Association of American Artists, New England Print Competition, Cambridge Art Association, Atlanta University.

WRITINGS: Objective Drawing Techniques (designed and illustrated by author), Reinhold, 1966.

* * *

BURNETT, David (Benjamin Foley) 1931-1971
(Terrave Bernarn, Peter Pace)

November 5, 1931—November 21, 1971; American editor. Obituaries: *New York Times,* November 22, 1971; *Publishers Weekly,* December 6, 1971. (See index for *CA* sketch)

* * *

BURNETTE, O(llen) Lawrence, Jr. 1927-

PERSONAL: Born September 30, 1927, in Bethel, N.C.; son of Ollen L. (an engineer) and Eva E. (Highsmith) Burnette; married Elizabeth Tull, August 25, 1951; children: Elizabeth A., O. Lawrence III, Graham T., John H., William N. *Education:* University of Richmond, B.A., 1945; University of Virginia, M.A., 1948, Ph.D., 1952. *Religion:* Presbyterian. *Residence:* Danville, Va. *Office address:* West Piedmont Planning District Commission, P.O. Box 1191, Martinsville, Va.

CAREER: History teacher in high school in Petersburg, Va., 1948-49; Virginia Military Institute, Lexington, instructor in history, 1951-53; Charles Scribner's Sons, Charlottesville, Va., field editor, 1953-57; State Historical Society of Wisconsin, Madison, book editor, 1957-63; Birmingham-Southern College, Birmingham, Ala., research professor of history, 1963-72; Stratford College, Danville, Va., dean of faculty and research professor of history, 1972-74; West Piedmont Planning District Commission, Martinsville, Va., executive director, 1975—. President and editor-in-chief, Rockbridge Press, Lexington, Va. *Military service:* U.S. Navy, 1945-47. U.S. Naval Reserve, 1954—; present rank, captain. *Member:* Organization of American Historians, American Association of University Professors (president of Alabama conference, 1969-71), Southern Historical Association, Alabama Coalition for Better Education (director), Phi Beta Kappa, Omicron Delta Kappa.

WRITINGS: (Editor and author of introduction with W. C. Haygood) *A Soviet View of the American Past,* translation by Ann E. Yanko and Peter A. Kersten of American history section of Soviet Encyclopedia, with preface by Adlai Stevenson, State Historical Society of Wisconsin, 1960, Peter Smith, 1960; *A Syllabus of American History,* University of Wisconsin, 1960; (editor) *Wisconsin Witness to Frederick Jackson Turner,* State Historical Society of Wisconsin, 1961; *Life in America,* Harper, 1964; *Beneath the Footnote: A Guide to the Use and Preservation of American Historical Documentation,* State Historical Society of Wisconsin, 1970.

WORK IN PROGRESS: Origins of American Imperialism.

* * *

BURNHAM, John C(hynoweth) 1929-

PERSONAL: Born July 14, 1929, in Boulder, Colo.; son of William A. (a civil engineer) and Florence (Hasbrouck) Burnham; married Marjorie A. Spencer, August 31, 1957;

children: Leonard, Abigail, Peter, Melissa. *Education:* Stanford University, B.A., 1951, Ph.D., 1958; University of Wisconsin, M.A., 1952. *Politics:* None. *Home:* 4158 Kendale Rd., Columbus, Ohio 43220. *Office:* Department of History, Ohio State University, Columbus, Ohio 43210.

CAREER: Claremont Men's College, Claremont, Calif., lecturer in history, 1956-57; Stanford University, Stanford, Calif., instructor in history, 1957-58; Foundations' Fund for Research in Psychiatry, postdoctoral fellow in New Haven, Conn., 1958-61; San Francisco State College (now University), San Francisco, Calif., assistant professor of history, 1961-63; Ohio State University, Columbus, assistant professor, 1963-66, associate professor, 1966-69, professor of history, 1969—. Senior Fulbright lecturer at University of Melbourne, 1967, University of New England, and University of Tasmania, 1973.

WRITINGS: Lester Frank Ward in American Thought, Public Affairs Press, 1956; *Psychoanalysis and American Medicine, 1894-1917: Medicine, Science, and Culture,* International Universities Press, 1967; (editor) *Science in America: Historical Selections,* Holt, 1971; (editor with Dorothy Kempf) *Edward J. Kempf: Selected Papers,* Indiana University Press, 1974; (co-author) *Progressivism,* Schenkman, 1977. Contributor to history and medical journals.

WORK IN PROGRESS: History of the Cultural Impact of American Physiology and Psychology.

* * *

BURNS, James W(illiam) 1937-

PERSONAL: Born January 24, 1937, in New Haven, Conn.; son of James W. and Helen W. Burns; married Marjorie Harris, August 11, 1962 (divorced); children: Amy Lois, Kristin Helen, Katharine Mary. *Education:* Central Connecticut State College, B.S., 1958; Pennsylvania State University, M.Ed., 1964, Ed.D., 1969. *Home:* 4513 West Main, D-3, Kalamazoo, Mich. 49007. *Office:* Department of Education, Western Michigan University, Kalamazoo, Mich. 49001.

CAREER: Elementary school teacher in Greenwich, Conn., 1958-62; Pennsylvania State University, University Park, director of Curriculum Center, 1962-68; Western Michigan University, Kalamazoo, associate professor of teacher education, 1968—. *Member:* International Reading Association, National Education Association, National Council of Teachers of English, American Association for Kindergarten, Nursery-Elementary Education, National Association for the Education of Young Children, Phi Delta Kappa, Kappa Delta Pi.

WRITINGS: (With J. D. McAulay, Anthony Conte, and Dorothy Skeel) *Who Am I?* Sadlier, 1971; (with McAulay, Conte, and Skeel) *My Family and My Community,* Sadlier, 1971; (with McAulay, Conte, and Skeel) *My Community and Other Communities,* Sadlier, 1971; (with J. J. Bosa, R. A. Crowell, and L. R. Harning) *The Development and Evaluation of an Inservice Education Model to Develop Informal, Individualized Learning and Teaching Practices* (monograph), Center for Educational Research, Western Michigan University, 1975; (contributor with Harning and Crowell) Leo C. Stine, editor, *The New Campus,* Association for Field Services in Teacher Education, 1975. Contributor to education journals. Member of board of consultants, *Learning* magazine, 1975-76.

BURNS, Zed H(ouston) 1903-

PERSONAL: Born November 3, 1903, in St. Paul, Minn.; son of John Gamble (a railroad executive) and Lois (Barncard) Burns; married Rubye McBride (a school teacher), January 26, 1935; children: Cassandra Joyce. *Education:* Alabama Polytechnic Institute (now Auburn University), B.S., 1927, M.S., 1929; University of Cincinnati, Ed.D., 1937; University of Southern Mississippi, M.A., 1970; postdoctoral study at Columbia University and University of Alabama. *Religion:* Baptist. *Office:* 1208 Marie St., Hattiesburg, Miss. 39401.

CAREER: Has worked as a salesman, draftsman, and architect; State Teachers College (now Jacksonville State University), Jacksonville, Ala., assistant professor of biology, 1930-34; teacher of special classes and safe driving in public schools in Birmingham, Ala., 1935-38; Appalachian State Teachers College (now Appalachian State University), Boone, N.C., associate professor of education, 1938-41; Clemson College (now University), Clemson, S.C., assistant professor of industrial education, 1941-46; Alabama Polytechnic Institute (now Auburn University), Auburn, appraiser and counselor at Veterans Guidance Center, 1946-48; Mississippi State College for Women, Columbus, professor of education, 1948-49; Shorter College, Rome, Ga., academic dean, 1949-50; University of Southern Mississippi, Hattiesburg, professor of educational psychology, 1950—, counselor in Guidance Center, 1950-51, chairman of department of psychology, 1951-56, chairman of department of industrial arts, 1956-68. Vocational consultant, U.S. Department of Health, Education and Welfare, 1962-71. *Military service:* U.S. Army, 1943-45; entered as lieutenant. U.S. Army Adjutant Generals Corps, 1943-63; retired as major.

MEMBER: American Psychological Association (fellow), Southeastern Psychological Association, Southern Society for Philosophy and Psychology, Southern Historical Society, Mississippi Historical Society, Sons of Confederate Veterans, Sons of the American Revolution (president of local chapter), Phi Delta Kappa, Phi Alpha Theta, Pi Kappa Alpha.

WRITINGS: Ship Island and the Confederacy, University and College Press of Mississippi, 1971; *Confederate Forts,* Southern Historical Publications, 1977. Contributor of articles and reviews to history and education journals.

* * *

BURRELL, Berkeley G. 1919-

PERSONAL: Born June 12, 1919, in Washington, D.C.; married A. Parthenia Robinson (owner of drycleaning business), 1951; children: Berkeley G., Jr. *Education:* Attended Howard University. *Home:* 1346 Jackson St. N.E., Washington, D.C. 20017. *Office:* National Business League, 4324 Georgia Ave. N.W., Washington, D.C. 20011.

CAREER: Burrell's Superb Cleaners, Washington, D.C., owner, 1946—; National Business League, Washington, D.C., president, 1962—. President, Burrell Industries; partner, Graham Associates. Lecturer in College of Urban Studies, Howard University, Fisk University, Vanderbilt University, Morgan State College, and American University. Member of board of trustees of research foundation of Doctor's Hospital, Joint Council on Economic Education, Robert R. Moton Institute, and Daniel H. Williams University; member of advisory board, Council for Financial Aid to Education; board member, Corporation for Blacks in Public Broadcasting. Advisor to five U.S. presidents. Senior warden, St. Mary's Episcopal Church; president, St. Mary's

Court Housing Development Center. *Military service:* U.S. Army, 1945-46; became staff sergeant. Korean War, 1951; became sergeant first class. *Awards, honors:* Virginia College, honorary Doctor of Arts degree.

WRITINGS: (With John Seder) *Getting It Together: Black Businessmen in America,* Harcourt, 1971. Writer of syndicated column, "Down to Business." Member of editorial board, *Black Forum.*

*   *   *

BURRELL, David B(akewell) 1933-

PERSONAL: Born March 1, 1933, in Akron, Ohio; son of Roger Allen and Nancy (Bakewell) Burrell. *Education:* University of Notre Dame, B.A. (magna cum laude), 1954; Gregorian University, S.T.L., 1960; Yale University, Ph.D., 1965. *Office:* Department of Philosophy, University of Notre Dame, Notre Dame, Ind. 46556.

CAREER: Entered Order of Congregatio a Sancta Cruce (Fathers and Brothers of the Holy Cross), 1954, ordained Roman Catholic priest, 1959; University of Notre Dame, Notre Dame, Ind., instructor, 1964-66, assistant professor, 1966-70, associate professor of philosophy, 1970—. *Member:* Society for Religion in Higher Education, American Philosophical Association.

WRITINGS: (Editor) B. J. Lonergan, *Verbum: World and Idea in Aquinas,* University of Notre Dame Press, 1967; *Analogy and Philosophical Language,* Yale University Press, 1973; *Exercises in Religious Understanding,* University of Notre Dame Press, 1974; *Aquinas: God and Action,* University of Notre Dame Press, in press.

Contributor: Frederick Crowe, editor, *Spirit as Inquiry,* St. Xavier College, 1964; Frederick J. Crosson and K. Sayre, editors, *Philosophy and Cybernetics,* University of Notre Dame Press, 1967; Michael Novak, editor, *American Philosophy and the Future,* Scribner, 1968; Maryellen Muckenhirn, editor, *The Future as the Presence of Shared Hope,* Sheed, 1968; Robert A. Evans, editor, *Future of Philosophical Theology,* Westminster, 1971; Aidan Kavanaugh, editor, *Roots of Ritual,* Eerdmans, 1971. Contributor to *New Scholasticism, Theological Studies, International Philosophical Quarterly, Philosophical Studies,* and other publications.

*   *   *

BURRELL, Roy E(ric) C(harles) 1923-

PERSONAL: Born July 25, 1923, in Ilford, Essex, England; son of Percival Charles (a laborer) and Ellen (Parmenter) Burrell; married Joyce Riche (a teacher), April 16, 1949; children: Gillian. *Education:* Borough Road College, Isleworth, England, Teaching Diploma, 1949. *Home:* 21 Manor Rd., Ashford, Middlesex, England. *Agent:* Howard Moorepark, 444 East 82nd St., New York, N.Y. 10028. *Office:* Department of History, Longford Comprehensive School, Feltham, Middlesex, England.

CAREER: Longford Comprehensive School, Feltham, Middlesex, England, head of department of history, 1959—. *Military service:* Royal Navy, Fleet Air Arm and General Service, 1942-46; became leading aircraftsman; received France and Germany star and Atlantic star.

WRITINGS: The Early Days of Man (juvenile), illustrations by Tony Dyson and Burrell, Wheaton, 1965, McGraw, 1968; *The Romans and Their World,* illustrations by Dyson, Pergamon, 1970; *The Romans in Britain,* illustrations by Dyson, Wheaton, 1971, Pergamon, 1972. Writer of com-

puter history courses used by National Physical Laboratory in experiments.

WORK IN PROGRESS: A book on the industrial revolution.

AVOCATIONAL INTERESTS: Archeology, inventions, ecology, astronomy.†

*   *   *

BURT, Cyril (Lodowic) 1883-1971

March 3, 1883—October 10, 1971; English psychologist and educator. Obituaries: *New York Times,* October 13, 1971. (See index for *CA* sketch)

*   *   *

BURTON, Genevieve 1912-

PERSONAL: Born June 29, 1912, in Philadelphia, Pa.; daughter of George (a rose grower) and Edith May (Bryant) Burton; married W. Laurence Casebeer, April 2, 1956 (deceased). *Education:* Germantown Hospital School of Nursing, R.N., 1933; University of Pennsylvania, Public Health Nursing Certificate, 1939, B.S., 1947; University of North Carolina, M.P.H., 1948; Columbia University, Ed.D., 1953. *Religion:* Episcopalian. *Home and office:* 2705 Woodleigh Rd., Havertown, Pa. 19083.

CAREER: Private duty nurse in Philadelphia, Pa., 1933-38; Community Health and Civic Association, Ardmore, Pa., public health nurse, 1939-41; public health nurse, U.S. Public Health Service, 1941-43; field secretary, North Carolina Congress of Parents and Teachers, 1948-51; University of Pennsylvania, Philadelphia, assistant professor in School of Nursing, 1952-62, lecturer at University Hospital, 1953-60, associate in research and director of alcoholic research project in department of psychiatry, School of Medicine, 1953-67; Institute for Alcoholism and Narcotic Addiction, Philadelphia, director of research and marriage and family life consultant, 1967-74; director, Bryn Mawr Treatment Center for Alcoholism, 1974-76; currently a marriage and family counselor in private practice. Lecturer at Germantown Hospital School of Nursing, 1956-62, and Lankenau Hospital School of Nursing, 1961-71; instructor in Summer School of Alcohol Studies, Rutgers University, 1966—. *Military service:* U.S. Navy, Nurse Corps, 1943-46. U.S. Naval Reserve, 1946-72; became lieutenant commander. *Member:* American Association of Marriage and Family Counselors, National Council on Family Relations, Alcohol and Drug Problems Association of North America.

WRITINGS: (Contributor) *Marriage Counseling: A Casebook,* Association Press, 1958; *Personal, Impersonal and Interpersonal Relations: A Guide for Nurses,* Springer Publishing, 1958, revised edition, 1964 (revised edition published in England as *Nurse and Patient: The Influence of Human Relationships,* edited by Michael Belint, Tavistock Publications, 1965), 4th edition, 1977. Contributor of about twenty articles to public health, alcoholism, and nursing journals.

SIDELIGHTS: Nurse and Patient: The Influence of Human Relationships has been translated into Japanese, Swedish, and German.

*   *   *

BUSCH, Frederick 1941-

PERSONAL: Born August 1, 1941, in Brooklyn, N.Y.; son of Benjamin (a lawyer) and Phyllis (Schnell) Busch; married Judith Burroughs (a teacher), November 29, 1963; children:

Benjamin, Nicholas. *Education:* Muhlenberg College, B.A., 1962; Columbia University, M.A., 1967. *Agent:* John Cushman Associates, Inc., 25 West 43rd St., New York, N.Y. 10036. *Office:* Department of English, Colgate University, Hamilton, N.Y. 13346.

CAREER: North American Precis Syndicate, New York, N.Y., editor-writer, 1964-65; Management Magazines, Greenwich, Conn., editor-writer, 1965-66; Colgate University, Hamilton, N.Y., 1966—, began as assistant professor, currently associate professor of English. *Member:* American Association of University Professors. *Awards, honors:* Woodrow Wilson fellowship, 1962-63; National Education Association fellow, 1976-77.

WRITINGS: I Wanted a Year without Fall (novel), Calder & Boyars, 1971; *Hawkes: A Guide to His Fiction,* Syracuse University Press, 1973; *Breathing Trouble and Other Stories,* Calder & Boyars, 1974; *Manual Labor* (novel), New Directions, 1974; *Domestic Particulars* (short stories), New Directions, 1976; *The Mutual Friend* (novel), Harper, 1978. Contributor of short stories to *Esquire, Harper's, New American Review,* and other journals.

WORK IN PROGRESS: A novel; a collection of short stories.

SIDELIGHTS: In a review of *Breathing Trouble and Other Stories,* Susan Knight says that "Busch's message is at times gloomily convincing. A metaphoric, rhythmed prose provides an often powerful back-up to the plot, conveying states of heart and broken mind more adequately than any long, authorial explanation." A writer for the *Times Literary Supplement* calls Frederick Busch "a spiky and demanding talent. A highly self-conscious writer, his style draws attention to itself like the raised sinews of a poised hand, and the act of writing and the difficulties a writer has in relating to others are recurrent themes."

Joyce Carol Oates, reviewing the novel *Manual Labor,* writes: "[This book] is something of a tour de force. Stylistically, it is very 'contemporary,' that is, its sentences are terse, cautious, precise, at times mildly ironic, but never do they veer into abstraction. . . . It is as if the deliberately underplayed technique of the French *nouveau roman* were utilized for humanistic purposes, with the intention of charting not the helpless disintegration of two people but, boldly enough, their difficult, minimal survival and the subsequent strengthening of their marriage. . . . Frederick Busch is to be congratulated for having so beautifully combined the rigorous discipline of one kind of novel with the genuinely compelling concerns of another." However, in a review of this same novel, Saul Maloff says: "Everything is given, nothing revealed. Everything has its source in literary conceit smuggled in from the presumed American romantic tradition. . . . In college workshops across the land this sort of thing sometimes goes by the name of 'creative writing'; there still exist undergraduates who are moved by it."

BIOGRAPHICAL/CRITICAL SOURCES: New Statesman, February 15, 1974; *Times Literary Supplement,* February 22, 1974; *New York Times Book Review,* November 3, 1974; *New Republic,* December 7, 1974; *Commonweal,* April 25, 1975; *Contemporary Literary Criticism,* Volume VII, Gale, 1977.

*   *   *

BUSH, Clifford L(ewis) 1915-

PERSONAL: Born December 20, 1915, in Groton, N.Y.; son of Lewis E. and Ruth (Hall) Bush; married Alison

Howard (a teacher), March 28, 1941 (died April 11, 1972); children: Becky (Mrs. Clinton M. Boxwell III), Bonnie. *Education:* Cortland State Teachers College (now State University of New York College at Cortland), B.Ed., 1939; Alfred University, M.Ed., 1947, Syracuse University, Ed.D., 1950. *Politics:* Republican. *Religion:* Protestant. *Home:* 50 Parker Ave., Maplewood, N.J. 07040. *Office:* Kean College of New Jersey, Morris Ave., Union, N.J. 07083.

CAREER: Teacher and principal in elementary and secondary schools of New York State, 1936-47; Syracuse University, Syracuse, N.Y., instructor in education, 1947-49; Western Reserve University (now Case Western Reserve University), Cleveland, Ohio, associate professor of education and chairman of department, 1949-58; Kean College of New Jersey, Union, professor of education and chairman of department, 1958-64, professor of communication sciences, 1964—. *Member:* International Reading Association, National Education Association, College Reading Association, American Association of School Administrators, New Jersey Education Association, New Jersey State College Faculty Association, Phi Delta Kappa.

WRITINGS: (With Mary C. Austin and Mildred H. Huebner) *Reading Evaluation,* Ronald, 1961; (with Huebner) *Strategies for Reading in the Elementary School,* Macmillan, 1970, revised edition, 1978; (with Robert C. Andrews) *Dictionary of Reading and Learning Disabilities,* Educational and Psychological Associates Press, 1973, revised edition, Western Psychological Association Press, 1977. Contributor to education journals.

*   *   *

BUSH, Robert (Ray) 1920-1972

American psychologist and educator. Obituaries: *New York Times,* January 7, 1972.

*   *   *

BUSS, Martin J(ohn) 1930-

PERSONAL: Born November 4, 1930, in Paoking, Hunan, China; son of Rudolph (a clergyman) and Julie (Schmidt) Buss; married Nancy Macpherson, June 19, 1954; children: Samuel, Jonathan, Mary, Jeanne. *Education:* Bloomfield College, B.A., 1951; Princeton Theological Seminary, B.D., 1954, Th.M., 1955; Yale University, Ph.D., 1958. *Home:* 1779 Ridgewood Dr. N.E., Atlanta, Ga. 30307. *Office:* Department of Religion, Emory University, Atlanta, Ga. 30322.

CAREER: Macalester College, St. Paul, Minn., assistant professor of religion, 1957-58; Coe College, Cedar Rapids, Iowa, visiting lecturer in religion, 1958-59; Emory University, Atlanta, Ga., assistant professor, 1959-66, associate professor, 1966-77, professor of religion, 1977—.

WRITINGS: (Contributor) James M. Robinson and John B. Cobb, Jr., editors, *Theology as History,* Harper, 1967; *The Prophetic Word of Hosea: A Morphological Study,* Walter de Gruyter, 1969; (contributor) John H. Hayes, editor, *Old Testament Form Criticism,* Trinity University Press, 1974.

WORK IN PROGRESS: Writing on the theory of interpretation and on law.

*   *   *

BUSTAMANTE, A(gustin) Jorge 1938-

PERSONAL: Born April 23, 1938; son of Agustin Figueroa

and Eloisa (Fernandez) Bustamante; married Yolanda de la Mora (a psychologist); children: Jorge, Mariana. *Education:* Centro Universitario Mexico, Bachiller en Leyes, 1954; Universidad Nacional Autonoma de Mexico, lawyer, 1965; University of Notre Dame, M.A., 1970, Ph.D., 1975. *Home:* Cerro de la Estrella 123, Campestre-Churnbusco, Mexico 21, D.F., Mexico. *Office:* El Colegio de Mexico, Centro de Estudios Sociologicos, Camino al Ajusco 20, Pedregal de Sta Teresa, Mexico 20, D.F., Mexico.

CAREER: Universidad Nacional Autonoma de Mexico, Mexico City, Mexico, assistant professor of political and social sciences, 1965-68; Union de Universidades de America Latina, Mexico City, research associate, 1966-67; Universidad Nacional Autonoma de Mexico, Mexico City, associate professor, Instituto de Investigaciones Sociales, 1972-73; University of Texas at Austin, assistant professor of sociology, 1973-75; El Colegio de Mexico, Centro de Estudios Sociologicos, Mexico City, professor of sociology, 1975—. Mexican delegate to United States-Mexico talks on undocumented immigration from Mexico, 1976. *Member:* International Sociological Association, American Sociological Association, Association of Border Scholars. *Awards, honors:* Award for research paper, Ohio Valley Sociological Association, 1970.

WRITINGS: (With Francisco Villagran Kramer) *Legislacion universitaria latino-americana,* Union de Universidades de America Latina, 1967; (with Julian Samora and Gilbert Cardenas) *Los Mojados: The Wetback Story,* University of Notre Dame Press, 1971; *Espaldas Mojadas: Materia Prima para la Expansion del Capital Nortamericano,* El Colegio de Mexico Press, 1975; (with Rodolfo Stavenhagen and others) *El Ingenio del Hombre* (high school text), Editorial Continental, 1976. Contributing editor, *Aztlan,* 1977.

WORK IN PROGRESS: With Julian Samora, a book on the salient issues related to the United States-Mexico border region; a research project on Mexican outmigration to the United States.

AVOCATIONAL INTERESTS: The socio-economic and cultural phenomena of the United States-Mexico border region.

* * *

BUTCHER, James Neal 1933-

PERSONAL: Born November 20, 1933, in Bergoo, W.Va.; son of Lionel Glenn (a coal miner) and Georgia (Neal) Butcher; married Nancy Oakley, May 30, 1954; children: Sherry, Jay, Neal. *Education:* Guilford College, B.A., 1960; University of North Carolina at Chapel Hill, M.A., 1962, Ph.D., 1964. *Home:* 6880 Brookview Dr. N.E., Minneapolis, Minn. 55432. *Office:* Department of Psychology, University of Minnesota, Minneapolis, Minn. 55455.

CAREER: University of North Carolina at Chapel Hill, instructor in psychology, 1960-61; Raleigh Mental Health Center, Raleigh, N.C., psychology trainee, 1961-62; Veterans Administration Hospital, Durham, N.C., psychology intern, 1962-63; University of North Carolina at Chapel Hill, instructor in psychology, 1963-64; University of Minnesota, Minneapolis, assistant professor, 1964-67, associate professor, 1967-70, professor of psychology, 1970—. Visiting instructor in psychology, North Carolina College, 1963-64. *Military service:* U.S. Army, Airborne Infantry, 1951-54; served in Korea, 1952-53. *Member:* American Psychological Association, Midwestern Psychological Association, Minnesota Psychological Association, Guilford Scholarship Society.

WRITINGS: (Editor) *MMPI: Research Developments and Clinical Applications,* McGraw, 1969; *Abnormal Psychology,* Brooks-Cole, 1971; *Objective Personality Assessment,* General Learning Press, 1971; (editor) *Objective Personality Assessments: Changing Perspectives,* Academic Press, 1972. Also author, with Paolo Pancheri, of *Handbook of Cross-National MMPI Research.*

WORK IN PROGRESS: Research on cross-cultural objective personality assessment; personality characteristics associated with college adjustment; crisis intervention therapy; psychotherapy.

* * *

BUTCHVAROV, Panayot K. 1933-

PERSONAL: Born April 2, 1933, in Sofia, Bulgaria; married, 1954; children: two. *Education:* Robert College, Turkey, B.A., 1952; University of Virginia, M.A., 1954, Ph.D., 1955. *Home:* 2507 Princeton Rd., Iowa City, Iowa 52240. *Office:* Department of Philosophy, University of Iowa, Iowa City, Iowa 52240.

CAREER: University of Baltimore, Baltimore, Md., instructor in philosophy, 1955-57; University of South Carolina, Columbia, assistant professor of philosophy, 1957-59; Syracuse University, Syracuse, N.Y., assistant professor, 1959-61, associate professor, 1961-66, professor of philosophy, 1966-68; University of Iowa, Iowa City, professor of philosophy, 1968—, chairman of department, 1970—. *Member:* American Philosophical Association, Phi Beta Kappa.

WRITINGS: Resemblance and Identity: An Examination of the Problem of Universals, Indiana University Press, 1966; *The Concept of Knowledge,* Northwestern University Press, 1970. Contributor of articles to journals, including *Analysis, Philosophical Quarterly, Review of Metaphysics, Philosophy, Philosophy and Phenomenological Research.*

* * *

BUTLER, Annie L(ouise) 1920-

PERSONAL: Born September 21, 1920, in Huntsville, Ala.; daughter of George B. (a postmaster) and Marilee (Dilworth) Butler. *Education:* Alabama College (now University of Montevallo), B.S., 1943; University of Iowa, M.A., 1944; Columbia University, Ed.D., 1958. *Home:* 1014 Greenwood Ave., Bloomington, Ind. 47401. *Office:* Department of Elementary Education, Indiana University, Bloomington, Ind. 47401.

CAREER: St. Cloud Teachers College (now St. Cloud State College), St. Cloud, Minn., supervisor of nursery school, 1944-46; University of Alabama, Tuscaloosa, director of nursery school, 1946-51; Columbia University, Teachers College, New York, N.Y., teacher of preschool children, Agnes Russell Center, 1951-53, supervisor of student teaching and part-time instructor, 1953-54; Newark State Teachers College (now Kean College of New Jersey), Union, N.J., assistant professor of early childhood education, 1954-57; New York State Education Department, Albany, N.Y., associate in child development, 1957-60; Indiana University at Bloomington, assistant professor, 1960-66, associate professor, 1966-72, professor of childhood education, 1972—, curriculum coordinator, Project Head Start Staff Orientation Program, 1965-67. Consultant, Project Head Start, 1965-69; chairman of board of directors, Child Development Associate Consortium, 1975-76.

MEMBER: Association for Childhood Education International (vice-president representing nursery school, 1967-69; president, 1973-75), International Reading Association (member of Committee on Day Care and Reading, 1971), U.S. National Committee on Early Childhood Education (secretary, 1971-73), National Association for the Education of Young Children (member of Commission on Mass Media, 1970-72), American Association of Elementary-Nursery-Kindergarten Educators, American Association of University Women (Bloomington, Ind. chapter; secretary, 1963-65; first vice-president, 1965-67), Midwest Association for the Education of Young Children, Indiana Association for the Education of Young Children (vice-president, 1966-67; president, 1967-68), Association for Supervision and Curriculum Development, Indiana University Women's Faculty Club (vice-president, 1965-66; president, 1966-67), Pi Lambda Theta, Delta Kappa Gamma. *Awards, honors:* Holder of grants totaling over $200,000 from U.S. Office of Education and U.S. Office of Economic Opportunity.

WRITINGS: (With Lorene Kimball Fox) *All Children Want to Learn,* Grolier Society, 1954; (contributor) *Reading in the Kindergarten,* Association for Childhood Education International, 1962; (contributor) *Social Studies for Young Americans,* Kendall-Hunt Co., 1970; (editor) *Current Research in Early Childhood Education: A Compilation and Analysis for Program Planners,* American Association of Elementary-Kindergarten-Nursery Educators, 1970; (with Edward Gotts, Nancy Quisenberry, and Robert Thompson) *Literature Search and Development of an Evaluation System in Early Childhood Education* (series of reports), U.S. Office of Education, 1971; *Early Childhood Education: Planning and Administering Programs,* Van Nostrand, 1974; (with Gotts and Quisenberry) *Early Childhood Programs: Developmental Objectives and Their Uses,* C. E. Merrill, 1975. Contributor to *Hoosier School Board Journal, Childhood Education, Indiana Principal, Nursery School Portfolio, Theory into Practice, Early Years, Current Concerns in Early Childhood Education Viewpoints,* and other professional journals. Also author of a series of ten articles for the Associated Press, 1972. Chairman of publications committee, *Childhood Education,* 1970-72.

WORK IN PROGRESS: A book, tentatively entitled *Play as Development,* with E. Gotts and N. Quisenberry.

* * *

BUTLER, Ernest Alton 1926-
(Bill Butler)

PERSONAL: Born September 27, 1926, in Greenville, N.C.; son of Walter Braxton and Mabel C. (Corrin) Butler; married Ann D. Davis, September 20, 1958; children: David, Susan, Michael, Polly. *Education:* Attended Columbia University, 1946-49. *Politics:* Republican. *Religion:* Methodist. *Home:* 6 Ft. Amherst Rd., Glens Falls, N.Y. 12801. *Agent:* Paul R. Reynolds, Inc., 12 East 41st St., New York, N.Y. 10017.

CAREER: McCormick & Co., Baltimore, Md., sales executive, 1949-50; E. A. Butler Associates, Inc., New York City, president and chairman of board of directors, 1950—; Garnet Mountain Ski Area & Lodge, North River, N.Y., owner, 1960—; Panel-Ad, Inc., New York City, vice-president and chairman of board of directors, 1965—; Little One Shops, Philadelphia, Pa., owner, 1965—; Garnet Mountain Construction Co., North River, president and chairman of board of directors, 1965—; Butler Management Services, Inc., New York City, president and chairman of board of directors, 1969—. *Military service:* U.S. Marine Corps,

1942-45. *Member:* Society of Professional Management Consultants, New York Athletic Club, Campfire Club (Chappaqua, N.Y.), Miami Yacht Club, Dutch Treat Club (New York), Lake George Club.

WRITINGS: The Right Approach, Follett, 1961; *Move In and Move Up,* Macmillan, 1970. Also author of *The Answer to the Profit Crisis in American Business.* Writer of "On the Job," a syndicated column in the *Chicago Tribune.*

* * *

BUTTRESS, Frederick Arthur 1908-

PERSONAL: Born December 11, 1908, in Cambridge, England; son of Arthur William (a railway worker) and Emily (Holmes) Buttress; married Doris Kathleen May Peck, June 8, 1933; children: Kay Elizabeth. *Education:* Attended Central School, Cambridge, 1920-24. *Religion:* Church of England. *Home:* 26 Langham Rd., Cambridge, England.

CAREER: Cambridge University, Cambridge, England, librarian in School of Agriculture, 1924-72. *Military service:* National Fire Service (in England and overseas), 1939-46. *Member:* International Association of Agricultural Librarians and Documentalists, Association of Cambridge University Assistants (former president), Cambridge Cricket Association (vice-president). *Awards, honors:* M.A., Cambridge University, 1972.

WRITINGS: Agricultural Periodicals of the British Isles, 1681-1900, and Their Locations, privately printed, 1950; *World List of Abbreviations of Scientific, Technological and Commercial Organizations,* Leonard Hill, 1954, 4th edition published as *World Guide to Abbreviations of Organizations,* Barnes & Noble, 1971, 5th edition, Gale, 1974. Contributor to *Quarterly Bulletin of International Association of Librarians and Documentalists, Agricultural History,* and other periodicals.

WORK IN PROGRESS: Abbreviations of Organizations.

* * *

BUZZATI, Dino 1906-1972

1906—January 28, 1972; Italian journalist, science fiction writer, and author of books on Italian culture. Obituaries: *New York Times,* January 29, 1972; *Washington Post,* January 31, 1972; *Publishers Weekly,* February 28, 1972.

* * *

BYARS, Betsy 1928-

PERSONAL: Born August 7, 1928, in Charlotte, N.C.; daughter of George Guy and Nan (Rugheimer) Cromer; married Edward Ford Byars (a professor of engineering at West Virginia University), June 24, 1950; children: Laurie, Betsy Ann, Nan, Guy. *Education:* Attended Furman University, 1946-48; Queens College, Charlotte, N.C., B.A., 1950. *Home:* 641 Vista Pl., Morgantown, W.Va. 26505.

CAREER: Writer of books for children. *Awards, honors:* John Newbery Medal, American Library Association, 1971, for *The Summer of the Swans;* Dorothy Canfield Fisher Memorial Book Award, Vermont State Congress of Parents and Teachers, 1975, for *The 18th Emergency.*

WRITINGS—Published by Viking, except as indicated: *Clementine,* Houghton, 1962; *The Dancing Camel,* 1965; *Rama the Gypsy Cat,* 1966; *The Groober,* Harper, 1967; *The Midnight Fox,* 1968; *Trouble River,* 1969; *The Summer of the Swans* (Junior Literary Guild selection; A.L.A. Notable Book), 1970; *Go and Hush the Baby,* 1971; *The House of Wings,* 1972; *The 18th Emergency,* 1973; *The Winged Colt of Casa Mia,* 1973; *After the Goat Man,* 1974; *The Lace Snail,* 1975; *The TV Kid,* 1976; *The Pinballs,* Harper, 1977; *Cartoons,* 1978. Contributor of articles to *Saturday Evening Post, TV Guide, Look,* and other magazines.

SIDELIGHTS: "The hallmark of a Betsy Byars book," writes a *New York Times Book Review* critic, "is its sensitive and subtle telling that echoes the spoken and unspoken thoughts of young people. In a succession of psychologically sound stories . . . she has developed her theme: that the extreme inward pain of adolescence lessens as a person reaches outward." Alice Bach notes that Byars "raises thundering questions, but, lacking the egotist's compulsion to provide pat answers, she challenges us to respond to her characters, to react to their situation—to reach toward our own conclusions rather than to swallow the novel passively. And of course she succeeds."

Betsy Byars finds most of her book ideas in real-life incidents. Her writing is done during the winter because her summers are spent as an essential adjunct to her husband's gliding hobby—assembling the glider, taking it apart, and driving the sailplane trailer around the country to retrieve the pilot and craft.

BIOGRAPHICAL/CRITICAL SOURCES: Young Readers' Review, January, 1967; *Commonweal,* November 22, 1968; *New York Times Book Review,* September 14, 1969, April 23, 1972, June 4, 1972, November 5, 1972, June 10, 1973, August 19, 1973, November 4, 1973, October 13, 1974, December 15, 1974, May 2, 1976; *Times Literary Supplement,* July 20, 1970, April 6, 1973, September 19, 1975, July 16, 1976; *Publishers' Weekly,* September 6, 1971; *Saturday Review,* May 20, 1972; *Center for Children's Books Bulletin,* November, 1972, September, 1973, March, 1974, March, 1975, September, 1976, April, 1977; *New York Review of Books,* December 14, 1972; *Christian Science Monitor,* October 3, 1973, November 7, 1973, June 10, 1975; *Psychology Today,* January 10, 1974; *Children's Literature Review,* Volume I, Gale, 1976.

* * *

BYCHOWSKI, Gustav 1895-1972

August 21, 1895—April 3, 1972; Polish-born psychoanalyst. Obituaries: *New York Times,* April 5, 1972.

* * *

CAIRNS, Trevor 1922-

PERSONAL: Born April 17, 1922; son of John Thomas and Emily (Wisbach) Cairns; married Heather Mary Bowman, April 2, 1956; children: Conrad, Edmund. *Education:* Balliol College, Oxford, B.A., 1943, M.A., 1947; King's College, Newcastle upon Tyne, M.Ed., 1953. *Politics:* "Convinced floating voter." *Religion:* "Unconvinced." *Home:* 4 Ashmore Ter., Sunderland, Tyne and Wear, England. *Office:* Polytechnic, Sunderland, Tyne and Wear, England.

CAREER: History master at secondary schools in Bristol, England, 1944-45, Midhurst, England, 1945-49, and Newcastle upon Tyne, England, 1950-54; Training College, Bedford, England, lecturer in history, 1955-60; Polytechnic, Sunderland, England, lecturer in history and head of department, 1960—. *Member:* Historical Association (president of Sunderland branch, 1963-66), Association of Teachers in Colleges and Departments of Education, Society for Nautical Research. *Awards, honors: Men Become Civilized* and *The Romans and Their Empire* received bronze medals at International Book Fair in Leipzig, 1971.

WRITINGS: (General editor) "Cambridge Introduction to the History of Mankind" (series of secondary school texts; contains course books, topic books, and slides), Cambridge University Press, 1969—, author of the following course books in the series: Volume I: *Men Become Civilized,* 1969, published as *People Become Civilized,* Lerner, 1975, Volume II: *The Romans and Their Empire,* 1970, Lerner, 1975, Volume III: *Barbarians, Christians and Muslims,* 1971, Lerner, 1975, Volume IV: *The Middle Ages,* 1972, Lerner, 1975, Volume V: *Europe Finds the World,* 1973, revised edition published as *Europe and the World,* Lerner, 1975, Volume VI: *The Birth of Modern Europe,* 1975, Lerner, 1975, Volume VII: *The Old Regime and the Revolution,* 1976, Volume VIII: *Power for the People,* 1978.

WORK IN PROGRESS: Europe Rules the World, Volume IX of "Cambridge Introduction to the History of Mankind."

SIDELIGHTS: Cairns believes that "history is *the* liberal education." He told *CA:* "I have come to view the history of the human race as one great continuing story, with civilizations, nations and individuals making their contributions in sub-plots and episodes. There is no saga to equal it. In the books I write and edit I am always aware that each one, even when it seems complete in itself, is a piece of this greater story."

His specialized interests are in the sixteenth-century, in Spain and Spanish America, in naval and nautical history, and in military architecture. He collects weapons and used to make models ("not enough time nowadays").

* * *

CALDWELL, Gaylon L(oray) 1920-

PERSONAL: Born September 11, 1920, in Hyrum, Utah; son of Morris S. (a Union Pacific agent) and Marie (Christensen) Caldwell; married Victoria Mae Bigler, August 1, 1947; children: Thomas, Camden, Melissa, Kimberly. *Education:* Utah State University, B.S., 1947; University of Nebraska, M.A., 1948; Stanford University, Ph.D., 1951. *Home:* 2904 Bonnie Lane, Stockton, Calif. 95204. *Office:* Department of Political Science, University of the Pacific, Stockton, Calif. 95204.

CAREER: Brigham Young University, Provo, Utah, associate professor of political science, 1951-60; U.S. Information Agency, Washington, D.C., coordinator of Binational Center programs, 1960-70; University of the Pacific, Stockton, Calif., provost and professor of political science, 1970—. Director, Binational Cultural Centers, Guatemala and Peru; U.S. cultural attache, Peru and Mexico. Member of board of directors, American School of Mexico City. *Military service:* U.S. Army Air Corps, 1942-46. U.S. Air Force Reserves, 1946—; present rank, captain. *Member:* American Association of University Professors, American Political Science Association, Western Political Science Association, Sigma Alpha Epsilon, Commonwealth Club. *Awards, honors:* Lilly scholarship, 1957.

WRITINGS: American Government Today, Norton, 1963, revised edition (with Robert M. Lawrence), 1969. Also author of *La teoria y la practica del gobierno estadounidense actual,* 1972. Contributor to professional journals in English and Spanish.

WORK IN PROGRESS: A political novel; works on experimental college-level education.

CALHOUN, Richard James 1926-

PERSONAL: Born September 5, 1926, in Jackson, Tenn.; son of Richard James and Grace (Bray) Calhoun; married Doris Somerville (a teacher), June 5, 1954; children: Carolyn Bray, Martin Lewis, Rebecca Ellen. *Education:* George Peabody College for Teachers, B.A., 1948; Johns Hopkins University, M.A., 1950; University of North Carolina at Chapel Hill, Ph.D., 1959. *Politics:* Democrat. *Religion:* Episcopalian. *Home:* 107 Strawberry Lane, Clemson, S.C. 29631. *Office:* Department of English, Clemson University, 107 Strode Tower, Clemson, S.C. 29631.

CAREER: Jacksonville State College (now University), Jacksonville, Ala., instructor in English, 1950-51; Davidson College, Davidson, N.C., assistant professor of English, 1958-61; Clemson University, Clemson, S.C., assistant professor, 1961-63, associate professor, 1963-66, professor of English, 1966-68, alumni professor of English, 1968—. Senior Fulbright lecturer at University of Ljubljana and University of Sarajevo, both Yugoslavia, 1969-70 and at Aarhus University and Odense University, both Denmark, 1975-76. *Military service:* U.S. Army, 1945. *Member:* Modern Language Association of America, Society for the Study of Southern Literature (member of executive committee, 1970-72), Southern Atlantic Modern Language Association. *Awards, honors:* Postdoctoral fellowship from Duke University and University of North Carolina, 1964-65.

WRITINGS: (Editor with John C. Guilds) *A Tricentennial Anthology of South Carolina Literature,* University of South Carolina Press, 1971; *James Dickey: The Expansive Imagination, 1957-72,* Everett Edwards, 1972; (editor with Ernest M. Lander) *Two Decades of Change: The South Since the Supreme Court Desegregation Decision,* University of South Carolina Press, 1975. Editor, "Cassette Lecture Series on Modern American Poetry," Everett Edwards, 1972—. Contributor of articles on literary criticism of modern poetry to anthologies and literature journals. Co-editor, *South Carolina Review.*

WORK IN PROGRESS: American Poetry: Post-Modernism in the 1970s.

AVOCATIONAL INTERESTS: Music, art, collecting art prints.

* * *

CALITRI, Princine

PERSONAL: Daughter of Blaise (a lawyer) and Cira (an opera singer; maiden name, Bivona) Merendino; married Henry Calitri (a dentist); children: Sharyl, Henry, Michael, Steven, Kenneth, Vincent. *Education:* Attended Feagin School of Speech, New York, N.Y., American Academy of Dramatic Art, and New York University. *Politics:* Independent. *Religion:* Episcopalian. *Agent:* Anita Diamant, 51 East 42nd St., New York, N.Y. 10017.

CAREER: Has worked as a public relations director, and as writer, commentator, and director for a National Broadcasting Corp. (NBC) station in West Virginia. *Member:* Authors Guild, Authors League of America, Advertising Club (New York), American Legion Auxiliary, Pascack Valley Players, Service Wives Club.

WRITINGS: Harry A. Bruno, Public Relations Pioneer, Denison, 1968; *Come Along to Puerto Rico,* Denison, 1971.

Plays; all published by Baker's Plays: *One Love Had Mary,* 1958; *Four in Hand* (one-act), 1969; *Year In, Year Out* (one-act), 1970; *No Lullabye for Me* (one-act), 1971.

Author of "Parent's Corner," a column appearing regularly in *Hackensack Record.* Features editor, *Dental Management.*

WORK IN PROGRESS: Come Along to Spain and *Come Along to Venezuela,* for Denison; a biography.

AVOCATIONAL INTERESTS: Theater, ballet, travel.†

* * *

CALLAGHAN, Catherine A. 1931-

PERSONAL: Born October 30, 1931, in Berkeley, Calif.; daughter of Bernard Joseph (a high school principal) and Catherine (Regan) Callaghan. *Education:* University of California, Berkeley, B.A., 1954, Ph.D., 1963. *Address:* P.O. Box 512, Brentwood, Calif. 94513. *Office:* Department of Linguistics, Ohio State University, Columbus, Ohio 43210.

CAREER: Ohio State University, Columbus, assistant professor, 1965-68, associate professor of linguistics and anthropology, 1968—. *Member:* American Association for the Advancement of Science, Linguistic Society of America, American Anthropoligical Association, Phi Beta Kappa, Sigma Xi. *Awards, honors:* Woodrow Wilson fellow, 1960-61; National Science Foundation fellowships, 1966—.

WRITINGS: Lake Miwok Dictionary, University of California Press, 1965; *Bodega Miwok Dictionary,* University of California Press, 1970. Contributor of about a dozen articles and reviews to language and linguistics journals.

WORK IN PROGRESS: Reconstruction of Proto Miwok and field work on Miwok languages.

SIDELIGHTS: Catherine Callaghan told *CA,* "Let us stop arrogantly despoiling other cultures." *Avocational interests:* The occult, judo, karate, poetry, science fiction.

* * *

CALLAHAN, John F(rancis) 1912-

PERSONAL: Born May 13, 1912, in Chicago, Ill.; son of Cornelius J. and Della (Lynch) Callahan. *Education:* Loyola University, Chicago, Ill., A.B., 1933, M.A., 1934; University of Chicago, Ph.D., 1940. *Residence:* Bethesda, Md. *Office:* Department of Classics, Georgetown University, Washington, D.C. 20057.

CAREER: Loyola University, Chicago, Ill., instructor, 1937-40, assistant professor of classics, 1941-43; Georgetown University, Washington, D.C., associate professor, 1946-50, professor of classics and ancient philosophy, 1950—. Visiting instructor, Harvard University, 1940-41; visiting scholar, Dumbarton Oaks, Harvard University, 1977-78. *Military service:* U.S. Navy, 1943-46; became lieutenant.

MEMBER: International Institute of Arts and Letters, American Philological Association, American Philosophical Association, Archaeological Institute of America, Metaphysical Society of America, American Association of University Professors. *Awards, honors:* Rockefeller Foundation fellowship, 1947; Fund for the Advancement of Education fellowship, 1953-54; Fulbright research fellowship, 1953-54, 1955; J. S. Guggenheim Foundation fellowship, 1958-59; National Endowment for the Humanities fellowship, 1967; research grants from American Council of Learned Societies and American Philosophical Society, 1970, American Research Center in Egypt, 1971-72, and National Endowment for the Humanities, 1972-73.

WRITINGS: Four Views of Time in Ancient Philosophy, Harvard University Press, 1948, 2nd edition, Greenwood

Press, 1968; *Augustine and the Greek Philosophers,* Villanova University Press, 1967; (editor) *Gregorii Nysseni opera: De oratione dominica, De beatitudinibus,* E. J. Brill (Leiden), in press; (co-author) *Interpretations of Plato,* E. J. Brill, in press. Contributor of articles and reviews to various philological and philosophical journals. Member of board of editors, *Journal of the History of Ideas.*

* * *

CALLAHAN, Nelson J. 1927-

PERSONAL: Born August 30, 1927, in Cleveland, Ohio; son of Nelson James (a banker) and Mary (Mulholland) Callahan. *Education:* St. Mary's Seminary, Cleveland, Ohio, M.Div., 1953. *Home and office:* 525 Dover Rd., Bay Village, Ohio 44140.

CAREER: Roman Catholic priest; assistant pastor of churches in Cleveland, Ohio, 1953-65; St. Peter High School, Cleveland, director of guidance, 1965-67; St. John College of Cleveland, Cleveland, chaplain and assistant professor of theology, 1967-74; currently pastor of St. Raphael Parish, Bay Village, Ohio. Prosynodal judge, Diocesan Tribunal; historian and archivist, Diocese of Cleveland. Member of planning board, national conference of ethnicity, Cleveland State University. *Member:* American Catholic Historical Society, Catholic Theological Society, Canon Law Society of America, Great Lakes Historical Society, First Friday Club.

WRITINGS: A Case for Due Process in the Church, Alba, 1971; (editor) *A Catholic Journey through Ohio,* St. Meinrad Press, 1976; (with William Hickey) *The History of the Irish in Cleveland,* Cleveland State University Press, 1977; (editor) *The Diary of Richard Burtsell, 1865-1868,* Arno, 1978.

WORK IN PROGRESS: Further publication of portions of Richard Burtsell's diary.

* * *

CAMERON, Allan W(illiams) 1938-

PERSONAL: Born June 21, 1938, in Racine, Wis.; son of Angus Ewan and Jane (Williams) Cameron. *Education:* Dartmouth College, A.B. (magna cum laude), 1960; Fletcher School of Law and Diplomacy, Tufts University, A.M., 1964, M.A.L.D., 1965. *Politics:* Independent. *Religion:* Episcopalian. *Home:* 32 Hamilton Rd., Apt. 208, Arlington, Mass. 02174. *Office:* Fletcher School of Law and Diplomacy, Tufts University, Medford, Mass. 02155.

CAREER: Bates College, Lewiston, Me., instructor in government, 1965-68; Abt Associates, Inc. (consulting firm), Cambridge, Mass., senior political analyst, 1968-70; Tufts University, Fletcher School of Law and Diplomacy, Medford, Mass., assistant professor of international politics, 1970—, assistant dean, 1970-76, associate dean, 1976—. *Military service:* U.S. Navy, 1960-63; became lieutenant. *Member:* American Political Science Association, Association of Asian Studies, American Association of University Professors, New England Political Science Association, Phi Beta Kappa.

WRITINGS: (Contributor) W. Raymond Duncan, editor, *Soviet Policy in Developing Countries,* Ginn-Blaisdell, 1970; *Viet-Nam Crisis: A Documentary History, 1940-1956,* Volume I, Cornell University Press, 1971; *Indochina: Prospects after "The End",* American Enterprise Institute for Public Policy Research, 1976. Contributor of articles to periodicals and professional journals.

WORK IN PROGRESS: Two books, *Viet-Nam Crisis: A*

Documentary History, Volume II: *1956-1965,* and *The Soviet Union and Vietnam: 1954-1964;* research on Soviet foreign policy, low-level violence, and Vietnam.

SIDELIGHTS: Allan Cameron has travelled widely in Europe and Asia.

* * *

CAMERON, James R(eese) 1929-

PERSONAL: Born August 27, 1929, in Columbus, Ohio; son of James Francis (a minister) and Mildred (Preble) Cameron; married Ruth Allen (a professor), August 26, 1950; children: James Allen, Laura Jean. *Education:* Eastern Nazarene College, A.B., 1951; Boston University, M.A., 1952, Ph.D., 1959. *Religion:* Nazarene. *Home:* 64 Davis St., Wollaston, Mass. 02170. *Office:* Department of History, Eastern Nazarene College, Quincy, Mass. 02170.

CAREER: Eastern Nazarene Academy, Wollaston, Mass., history instructor, 1951-55; Eastern Nazarene College, Quincy, Mass., assistant professor, 1955-59, associate professor, 1959-64, professor of history, 1964—. Vice-president, South Shore Council of Churches, 1976—; president, Inter-Church Council, 1977—; member, Quincy Historic District Commission. *Member:* American Historical Association, Mediaeval Academy of America, Conference on British Studies, Quincy Historical Society (historian).

WRITINGS: Frederick William Maitland and the History of English Law, Oklahoma University Press, 1961; *New Beginnings: Quincy and Norfolk County,* Quincy Historical Society, 1966; *Eastern Nazarene College: The First Fifty Years, 1900-1950,* Beacon Hill Press, 1968; *Church on the Campus,* Wollaston Church of the Nazarene, 1972; (contributor) H. Hobart Halley, editor, *Quincy, 350 Years,* [Quincy, Mass.], 1974.

WORK IN PROGRESS: General Joseph Palmer.

* * *

CAMP, James 1923-

PERSONAL: Born April 29, 1923, in Alexandria, La.; son of Andrew Frank and Susannah (Barrett) Camp; married Jocelyn Agnew (a college professor of English), June 18, 1969. *Education:* Louisiana State University, B.A., 1949; Columbia University, M.A., 1950; University of Michigan, Ph.D., 1965. *Home:* 365 West End Ave., No. 7C, New York, N.Y. 10024. *Office:* Department of Humanities, New Jersey Institute of Technology, Newark, N.J. 07102.

CAREER: Olivet College, Olivet, Mich., instructor in English, 1950-54; University of Michigan, Ann Arbor, instructor in English, 1962-63; New Jersey Institute of Technology, Newark, N.J., 1963—, began as instructor, professor of English, 1974—. *Military service:* U.S. Army Air Forces, 1942-45; served in the Pacific. *Member:* Modern Language Association of America, University Film Association. *Awards, honors:* Avery Hopwood award in poetry, 1955.

WRITINGS: (Editor with X. J. Kennedy) *Mark Twain's Frontier,* Holt, 1964; *Edict from the Emperor* (poetry), Burning Deck Press, 1969; (editor with Kennedy and Keith Waldrop) *Pegasus Descending: A Treasury of the Best Bad Poems in English,* Macmillan, 1971; (with Kennedy and Waldrop) *Three Tenors, One Vehicle* (poetry), Open Places, 1975; *Carnal Refreshment* (poetry), Burning Deck Press, 1975.

Contributor: D. C. Hope, editor, *The Wolgamot Interstice,*

Burning Deck Press, 1961; Robert M. Bender and Charles L. Squier, editors, *The Sonnet,* Washington Square Press, 1965; *Best Poems of 1968: Borestone Mountain Poetry Awards,* Pacific Books, 1969; X. J. Kennedy, editor, *Introduction to Poetry,* Little, Brown, 1971. Contributor of poetry to *Paris Review, Prism International, Open Places,* and other periodicals. Co-editor, *Burning Deck,* 1963-65.

* * *

CAMPBELL, Colin Dearborn 1917-

PERSONAL: Born February 10, 1917, in Cooperstown, N.Y.; son of James Samuel and Marion A. (Jennings) Campbell; married Rosemary Garst, June 18, 1949; children: William Garst, Janet Adele. *Education:* Harvard University, B.A., 1938; University of Iowa, M.A., 1941; University of Chicago, Ph.D., 1950; Dartmouth College, M.A., 1965. *Home:* 9 North Park St., Hanover, N.H. 03755. *Office:* Department of Economics, Dartmouth College, Hanover, N.H. 03755.

CAREER: Rensselaer Polytechnic Institute, Troy, N.Y., instructor in economics, 1946-47; Drake University, Des Moines, Iowa, assistant professor of economics, 1949-51; Central Intelligence Agency (CIA), Washington, D.C., economist, 1952-54; Federal Reserve System, Washington, D.C., economist, 1954-56; Dartmouth College, Hanover, N.H., assistant professor, 1956-59, associate professor, 1959-64, professor of economics, 1964—, chairman of department, 1965-66. Adjunct scholar, American Enterprise Institute for Public Policy Research. Member of U.S. Tax Advisory Group to Republic of Korea, 1959-60, Presidential Task Force on Aging, 1969-70, and Census Advisory Committee on Privacy and Confidentiality, 1972—. Member of board of directors, Dartmouth National Bank of Hanover, 1961—; former member of board of directors, Howe Library (Hanover); director, Thomas Jefferson Center Foundation, 1972—. *Military service:* U.S. Army, Ordnance Corps, 1941-46, 1951-53; became captain. *Member:* American Economic Association, Mont Pelerin Society.

WRITINGS: (With wife, Rosemary G. Campbell) *An Introduction to Money and Banking,* Holt, 1972, 2nd edition, Dryden, 1975. Contributor to economics journals.

* * *

CAMPBELL, John Franklin 1940(?)-1971

1940(?)—November 6, 1971; American editor, essayist, short story writer, and foreign policy critic. Obituaries: *New York Times,* November 7, 1971; *Washington Post,* November 8, 1971; *Newsweek,* November 22, 1971.

* * *

CAMPBELL, Penelope 1935-

PERSONAL: Born December 18, 1935, in Bishop, Md.; daughter of Welford Shepard and Marie (Ewers) Campbell; married Seaborn Phillips Jones (an engineer), May 29, 1971. *Education:* Baylor University, B.A., 1957; Ohio State University, M.A., 1959, Ph.D., 1967. *Home:* 912 West Ponce de Leon Ave., Decatur, Ga. 30030. *Office:* Department of History and Political Science, Agnes Scott College, Decatur, Ga. 30030.

CAREER: Agnes Scott College, Decatur, Ga., assistant professor, 1965-70, associate professor of history and political science, 1970—. *Member:* American Historical Association, American Association of University Professors, African Studies Association. *Awards, honors:* Fulbright grant to India, 1968.

WRITINGS: Maryland in Africa, University of Illinois, 1971.

WORK IN PROGRESS: Research on American activity in Africa.

AVOCATIONAL INTERESTS: Travel (has traveled through India and Africa), and sailing.

* * *

CANNON, Garland (Hampton) 1924-

PERSONAL: Born December 5, 1924, in Fort Worth, Tex.; son of Garland Hampton (a fireworks wholesaler) and Myrtle (Goss) Cannon; married Patricia Richardson, February 14, 1947; children: Margaret, India, Jennifer, William. *Education:* University of Texas, B.A., 1947, Ph.D., 1954; Stanford University, M.A., 1952. *Religion:* Methodist. *Home:* 805 Hawthorn, College Station, Tex. 77840. *Office:* Department of English, Texas A&M University, College Station, Tex. 77843.

CAREER: Instructor in English at University of Hawaii, Honolulu, 1949-52, University of Texas, Main University (now University of Texas at Austin), 1952-54, and University of Michigan, Ann Arbor, 1954-55; University of California, Berkeley, assistant professor of speech, 1955-56; American University Language Center, Bangkok, Thailand, academic director, 1956-57; University of Florida, Gainesville, assistant professor of English, 1957-58; University of Puerto Rico, Rio Piedras, visiting professor of linguistics, 1958-59; Columbia University, Teachers College, New York, N.Y., assistant professor of linguistics, 1959-62, director of English Language Program in Afghanistan, 1960-62; Northeastern Illinois State College (now Northeastern Illinois University), Chicago, associate professor of linguistics, 1962-63; Queens College of the City University of New York, Flushing, N.Y., associate professor of English, 1963-66; Texas A&M University, College Station, associate professor, 1966-67, professor of English, 1967—. Visiting professor of humanities, University of Michigan, 1970-71. *Military service:* U.S. Marine Corps, 1943-46.

MEMBER: Conference on College Composition and Communication, American Dialect Society, International Linguistic Association, Linguistic Society of America, Modern Language Association of America, National Council of Teachers of English. *Awards, honors:* American Philosophical Society grants to England, 1964, 1966, 1974; *The Letters of Sir William Jones* was selected by *Sunday Telegraph* (London) as one of the Best Books of the Year, 1970.

WRITINGS: Sir William Jones, Orientalist: A Bibliography, University of Hawaii Press, 1952; *Oriental Jones: A Biography,* Asia Publishing House, 1964; (editor) *The Letters of Sir William Jones,* two volumes, Clarendon Press, 1970; *A History of the English Language,* Harcourt, 1972. Contributor to about twenty language and Asian studies journals.

WORK IN PROGRESS: A Transformational Grammar of the English Language; a revision of *Oriental Jones.*

SIDELIGHTS: "What Professor Cannon has succeeded in doing," writes Frederick Hilles of *The Letters of Sir William Jones,* "is to add one more name to the great English letter-writers of the golden age of letter-writing." *Avocational interests:* Stamp collecting.

BIOGRAPHICAL/CRITICAL SOURCES: Spectator, August 1, 1970; *Yale Review,* winter, 1971; *Times Literary Supplement,* January 1, 1971; *Journal of English and Germanic Philology,* April, 1971; *American Historical Review,* December, 1971; *English Historical Review,* October, 1972.

CANTOR, Muriel G. 1923-

PERSONAL: Born March 2, 1923, in Minneapolis, Minn.; daughter of Leo and Bess (Willis) Goldsman; married Joel M. Cantor (a psychologist), August 6, 1944; children: Murray R., Jane O., James L. *Education:* University of California, Los Angeles, B.A., 1964, M.A., 1966, Ph.D., 1969. *Home:* 8408 Whitman Dr., Bethesda, Md. 20034. *Office:* Department of Sociology, American University, Washington, D.C. 20016.

CAREER: Immaculate Heart College, Los Angeles, Calif., instructor in sociology, 1966-68; American University, Washington, D.C., instructor, 1968-69, assistant professor, 1969-72, associate professor, 1972-76, professor of sociology, 1976—, chairman of department, 1973-75, 1977—. *Member:* American Sociological Association, Sociologists for Women in Society, Southern Sociological Society, Eastern Sociological Association, District of Columbia Sociological Society, Society for Study of Social Problems.

WRITINGS: Hollywood TV Producer, Basic Books, 1971; (with Phyllis L. Stewart) *Varieties of Work Experience,* Schenkman, 1974; (contributor) Jack Goldsmith and Sharon S. Goldsmith, editors, *The Police Community: Dimensions of an Occupational Subculture,* Palisades, 1974. Contributor of articles and reviews to public opinion and sociology journals. Editor, *SWS Newsletter* (national newsletter for Sociologists for Women in Society), 1977—.

WORK IN PROGRESS: Social Organization of Mass Media; A Social History of Hollywood.

*   *   *

CAPLAN, Lionel

PERSONAL: Born in Montreal, Canada; married Ann Patricia Bailey (an anthropologist), 1967; children: Emma, Mark. *Education:* University of London, Ph.D., 1965. *Office:* Department of Anthropology, School of Oriental and African Studies, University of London, London WC1E 7HU, England.

CAREER: University of London, London, England, lecturer, 1965-76, reader in anthropology, 1976—.

WRITINGS: Land and Social Change in East Nepal: A Study of Hindu-Tribal Relations, University of California Press, 1970; *Administration and Politics in a Nepalese Town: The Study of a District Capital and Its Environs,* Oxford University Press, 1975.

*   *   *

CARBALLIDO, Emilio 1925-

PERSONAL: Born May 22, 1925, in Cordoba, Veracruz, Mexico; son of Francisco and Blanca Rosa (Fentanes) Carballido; children: Juan de Dios. *Education:* Universidad Nacional Autonoma de Mexico, student in Facultat de Derecho, 1945-46, Facultad de Filosofia y Letras, 1946-49, majoring in dramatic art and English letters. *Politics:* 3rd positionist. *Religion:* Catholic. *Home:* Avenida Constituyentes 207, Mexico D.F. 18, Mexico. *Office:* Instituto Nacional de Bellas Artes, Palacio de Bellas Artes, Mexico D.F. 1, Mexico.

CAREER: Universidad Veracruzana, Xalapa, Mexico, subdirector of Escuela de Teatro, 1954, member of Editorial Council, 1959—, professor in Faculty of Philosophy and Letters, 1960-61; Instituto Nacional de Bellas Artes, Mexico City, Mexico, professor in Escuela de Arte Teatral, 1955—. Ballet Nacional A.C., Mexico, literary advisor, 1957—,

public relations representative on tour with dance company in Europe and Asia, 1957-58; Instituto Politecnico Nacional, Mexico, employed with Departamento de Difusion Cultural, 1960-74, director, Taller de Composicion Dramatica, 1969-74; professor of dramatic theory and composition and head of Seminario de Teatro Mexicano, Universidad Nacional Autonoma de Mexico, Mexico City, 1965-68. Guest of Minister of the Interior of Japan, 1960, and of Minister of the Exterior of the Federal Republic of Germany, 1966. Visiting professor, Rutgers University, 1965-66, University of Pittsburgh, 1970-71.

MEMBER: Sindicato de Trabajadores de la Produccion Cinematografica (secretario, Seccion de Autores y Adaptadores). *Awards, honors:* Second prize, Concurso Nacional de Teatro, 1950, for *La Zona intermedia;* Rockefeller fellowship, New York, N.Y., 1950; Centro Mexicano de Escritores fellowship, 1951-52, 1955-56; second prize, libretto contest, Opera Nacional, 1953, for "El Pozo"; first prize, Universidad Nacional Autonoma de Mexico contest, 1954, for *La Hebra de oro; El Nacional* prize, 1954, for *La Danza que suena la tortuga;* first prize in theatre, Festival Regional, Instituto Nacional de Bellas Artes, 1955, and Ruiz de Alarcon critics' prize for the best work of 1957, both for *Felicidad; El Nacional* prize, 1958, for *El Dia que se soltaron los leones;* Premio de los Criticos No-asociados for the best work of 1960, for *El Relojero de Cordoba;* Menorah de Oro prize for best film continuity of 1961, for "Macario"; Instituto Internacional de Teatro prize, Mexican branch, 1962, and honorable mention, Paris, 1963, both for *Medusa; Casa de las Americas* prize, 1962, for *Un Pequeno dia de ira;* Ruiz de Alarcon prize for best play of the year, 1966, for *Yo tambien hablo de la rosa,* and 1968, for *Medusa; El Heraldo* prize, 1967, for *Te juro, Juana, que tengo ganas,* 1968, for *Medusa,* and 1975, for "Las cartas de Mozart"; Asociacion de Criticos y Cronistas prize, 1976, for *Un Pequeno dia de ira.*

WRITINGS—Plays: La Zona intermedia: Auto sacramental [and] *Escribir, por ejemplo* ("La Zona intermedia: Auto sacramental" first produced in Mexico City at Teatro Latino, 1950, published in English in *The Golden Thread and Other Plays* [see below]; "Escribir, por ejemplo" [monologue; also see below] first produced in Mexico City at Teatro del Caracol, 1950), Coleccion Teatro Mexicano, 1951.

"Felicidad" (three-act; first produced at Festival Dramatico del Distrito Federal, Mexico, at Teatro Reforma del Seguro Social, 1955; produced in Mexico City at Teatro Rodano, 1957), published in *Concurso Mexicano de Teatro, obras premiadas,* Instituto Nacional de Bellas Artes, 1956; *La Hebra de oro* (contains "La Hebra de oro" [three-act "dance of death"; first produced in Mexico City at Teatro Reforma, 1959] and "El Lugar y la boro" [trilogy]), Imprenta Universitaria, Universidad Nacional Autonoma de Mexico, 1957, both plays published in English in *The Golden Thread and Other Plays* (see below); *La Danza que suena la tortuga* (three-act comedy; first produced as "Palabras cruzadas" in Mexico City at Teatro de la Comedia, 1955), Fonda de Cultura Economica, 1957; *D.F.* (nine one-act pieces; contains "Misa primera," "Selaginela" [monologue; first produced in Mexico City at Teatro de la Feria del Libro, 1959], "El Censo" [comedy; first produced in Mexico City at Teatro de la Feria del Libra, 1959; produced in New York by Spanish Repertory Theatre, 1977], "Escribir, por ejemplo," "El Espejo" [published in English in *The Golden Thread and Other Plays* (see below)], "Hipolito," "Tangentes," "Parasitas" [monologue; first produced in

German as "Die Parasiten" in Kiel, Germany at Theatre of the State Capital, 1963], and "La Medalla"), Coleccion Teatro Mexicano, 1957, 2nd edition published with preamble and five additional plays ("La Perfecta casado" [one-act; first produced in Xalapa, Mexico, at Teatro del Estado, 1963], "Paso de madrugado," "El Solitario en octubre," "Un Cuento de Navidad," and "Pastores de la ciudad" [pastoral; written with Luisa Josefina Hernandez; music by R. Sanz; first produced in Mexico City at Teatro Universitario de Puebla]), Universidad Veracruzana, 1962.

Teatro (contains "El Relojero de Cordoba" [two-act comedy; first produced in Mexico City at Teatro del Bosque, 1960; published in English in *The Golden Thread and Other Plays* (see below)], "Medusa" [five-act tragicomedy; translation by Mary Madiraca first produced under same title in Ithaca, N.Y. at Cornell University, 1966], "Rosalba y los llaveros" [three-act comedy; first produced in Mexico City at Palacio de Bellas Artes, 1950], and "El Dia que se soltaron los leones" [three-act farce; first produced in Havana at Teatro del Sotano, 1963; translation by William T. Oliver published as "The Day They Let the Lions Loose" in *New Voices in Latin American Theatre*, University of Texas Press, 1971]), Fondo de cultura Economic, 1960, French & European Publications, 1969; *Las Estatuas de marfil* (three-act; first produced in Mexico City at Teatro Ofelia, 1960), Universidad Veracruzana, 1960; "Teseo" (tragicomedy; first produced in Mexico City at Teatro Xola, 1962), published in *La Palabra y el hombre*, Number 24, 1962, published in English in *The Golden Thread and Other Plays* (see below); *Un Pequeno dia de ira* (first produced in Havana on Cuban television, 1969; produced in Mexico City at Teatro il de Julio, 1976; translation by Margaret Sayers Peden produced as "A Short Day's Anger" in Pittsburgh, Pa. at University of Pittsburgh, 1970), Casa de las Americas (Havana), 1962; "Silencio, pollos pelones, ya les van a echar su maiz . . .!" (farce; first produced in Ciudad Juarez, Mexico, at Teatro del Seguro Social, 1963; produced in Mexico City at Teatro Urueta, 1964; translation by Ruth S. Lamb produced as "Shut Up, You Plucked Chickens, You're Going to Be Fed!" in Claremont, Calif. at Scripps College, 1969), Aguilar, 1963.

"Te juro, Juana, que tengo ganas" (farce; first produced in Mexico City at Teatro del Granero, 1967), published in *La palabra y el hombre*, Number 35, 1965; *Yo tambien hablo de la rosa* (first produced in Mexico City at Teatro Jiminez Rueda, 1966; translation by Myrna Winer produced as "I Also Speak about the Rose" in Northridge, Calif. at San Fernando Valley State College, 1972), Departamento de Teatro, Instituto Nacional de Bellas Artes, 1966, 2nd edition, 1970, translation by William I. Oliver published as "I Too Speak to the Rose" in *Drama and Theatre*, Number 1, 1970; *Las Noticas del dia* (dialogue), Coleccion Teatro de Bolsillo, 1968; *Acapulco, los lunes* (farce; first produced in Mexico City at Teatro Antonio Caso, 1970), Ediciones Sierra Madre, 1969.

The Golden Thread and Other Plays (contains "The Mirror," "The Time and the Place: Dead Love," "The Glacier," "The Wine Cellar," "The Golden Thread," "The Intermediate Zone," "The Clockmaker from Cordoba," and "Theseus"), translation and introduction by Margaret Sayers Peden, University of Texas Press, 1970; (compiler) *Teatro Joven de Mexico* (anthology), Editorial Novaro, 1973; (compiler and contributor) *El arca de noe* (anthology), Secretaria de Educacion Publica, 1974.

Unpublished plays; all produced in Mexico City, Mexico, unless otherwise noted: "La Triple porfia" (one-act farce),

first produced at the theatre of Escuela de Arte Teatral, Instituto Nacional de Bellas Artes, 1949; "El Triangulo sutil" (one-act farce), privately produced, 1949; "El Invisible" and "Ermesinda" (two ballets; the former with music by Ignacio Longares; the latter with music by Eduardo Hernandez Moncada), first produced at Palacio de Bellas Artes, 1952; "La Sinfonia domestica" (three-act comedy), first produced at Teatro Ideal, 1953; (with Sergio Magana) "El Viaje de Nocresida" (three-act juvenile comedy), first produced at Palacio de Bellas Artes, 1953; (with Luisa Bauer and Fernando Wagner) "Cinco pasos al cielo" (three-act juvenile comedy), first produced at Palacio de Bellas Artes, 1959.

"La Lente maravillosa," "El Jardinero y los pajaros," [and] "Guillermo y el nahual" (three short plays for young children, written for Recreo Infantil del Bosque), first produced at Teatro Orientacion, 1960; "Homenaje a Hidalgo" (pageant with actors, dance company, chorus, soloists, and symphony orchestra), music by Rafael Elizondo, first produced, under direction of Anna Sokolow, at Palacio de Bellas Artes, 1960, produced in a greatly enlarged version under direction of Guillermina Bravo at Plaza de la Alhondiga, 1965 and 1966; "Misa de seis" (opera), music by Carlos Jimenez Mabarak, first produced at Palacio de Bellas Artes, 1962; "Los Hijos del capitan Grant" (three-act melodrama for children, based on the novel by Jules Verne), first produced by Compania Estudiantil de la Preparatoria No. 5 at their theatre, 1964, produced at Palacio de Bellas Artes, 1966; "Almanque de Juarez" (dramatic collage-spectacle), first produced at Teatro del Bosque, 1968; "Tianguis!" (spectacle), first produced at Auditorio Nacional, 1968; "Un Vals sin fin por el planeta" (comedy), directed by Carballido, first produced at Teatro Orientacion, 1970; "La Fonda de las siete cabrillas" (farce based on "Don Bonifacio" by Manuel Eduardo de Gorostiza), first produced by Compania Popular de la Ciudad de Mexico in their portable theatre at various locations in the city, 1970-71; "Conversacion entre las ruinas," translation by Myra Gann produced as "Conversation among the Ruins" in Kalamazoo, Mich. at Kalamazoo College, 1971; "Las cartas de Mozart," first produced at Teatro Jimenez Rueda, 1975; "Nahui Ollin" (commissioned by Consejo Nacional de Cultura, Venezuela), first produced in Caracas, Venezuela, 1977.

Novels; except as otherwise noted: *La Veleta oxidada*, Los Presentes (Mexico), 1956; *El Norte*, Universidad Veracruzana, 1958, translation by Margaret Sayers Peden published as *The Norther*, introduction by Peden, University of Texas Press, 1968; *La Caja vacia* (short stories), Fondo de Cultura Economica, 1962; *Las Visitaciones del diablo: Folletin romantico en XV partes*, J. Mortiz (Mexico), 1965, 2nd edition, 1969; *El Sol*, J. Mortiz, 1970; *Las zapatos de fierro*, illustrations by Leticia Tarrago, J. Mortiz, 1977.

Also author of filmscripts, "Felicidad," "Los Novios," "Macario" (produced by Azteca, 1968), "Las Visitaciones des diablo," "Rosa blanca," "El Aguila descalza," "La Torre de marfil," and approximately twenty others.

Plays anthologized in: *Antologia de obras en un acto*, Coleccion Teatro Mexicano, 1958; *Spiele in einem Akt*, Suhrkamp Verlag, 1961; *Tres novelas, tres dramas*, Holt, 1970; *Three Contemporary Latin American Plays*, edited by Ruth S. Lamb, Xerox College Publishing, 1971. Novel included in *Dos novelas mexicanas*, Editorial Arca (Montevideo), 1968. Short stories anthologized in *Mexico, llano grande*, Horst Erdmann Verlag (Stuttgart), 1962, *Le Piu belle novelle de tutti i paesi*, [Milan], 1966, and *El Cuento mexicano*, Barralt (Barcelona), 1970.

Contributor of plays to *Revista de Bellas Artes, Revista de la Universidad de Mexico, Novedades, El Nacional,* and *America, Revista Antologica;* contributor of stories to *Texas Quarterly* and *Izvestia* (Moscow). Founder and director of *Tramoya,* theatre quarterly published by Universidad Veracruzuna, 1975—.

WORK IN PROGRESS: Editing two anthologies of young Mexican dramatists, *Nueve autores jovenes de Mexico,* and *Teatro de para Jovenes.*

SIDELIGHTS: Emilio Carballido told *CA,* "My points of view are *in* my work." He lists as specifically important plays "Yo tambien hablo de la rosa" ("clearest personal statement"), "El Relojero de Cordoba" (a "piece of satisfying craft"), and "La Hebra de oro" ("work of transition, where something very important got through"). Recipient of over a dozen drama awards in his own country and abroad, Carballido is, as *Stage* notes, "one of the outstanding creators of the new Latin American Theatre."

Several of Carballido's plays have been produced on Mexican television, notably "Felicidad," "La Danza que suena la tortuga," and "El Relojero de Cordoba." "El Censo" was produced on Spanish television, 1970, and "Yo tambien Hablo de la rosa" was produced on French television as "Et moi aussi, je parle de la rose," 1973 and 1974.

BIOGRAPHICAL/CRITICAL SOURCES: Stage, December 23, 1970; *Choice,* March, 1971; *Texto Critico* (Xalapa, Mexico), Number 3, 1976.

* * *

CARDOZO, Michael H. 1910-

PERSONAL: Born September 15, 1910, in New York, N.Y.; married in 1937; children: three. *Education:* Dartmouth College, A.B., 1932; Yale University, LL.B., 1935. *Residence:* Washington, D.C.

CAREER: Admitted to the Bar of New York State, 1936, and the Bar of U.S. Supreme Court, 1940; Parker & Duryee (law firm), New York, N.Y., staff lawyer, 1935-38; U.S. Government, Washington, D.C., attorney with U.S. Securities and Exchange Commission, 1938-40, special assistant to attorney general, tax division, 1940-42, with Lend-Lease and Foreign Economic Administrations, 1942-45, Department of State, staff member of Office of the Legal Adviser, 1945-52, assistant legal adviser for economic affairs, 1951-52; Cornell University, Ithaca, N.Y., associate professor of law, 1952-56, professor of law, 1956-63; Association of American Law Schools, Washington, D.C., executive director, 1963-73. Visiting professor of law, Northwestern University, 1961-62, University of Pennsylvania, 1964-65, Howard University, 1965-66, and Georgetown University, 1966-67. Consultant, U.S. Economic Cooperation Administration, 1952, U.S. House of Representatives, 1956, U.S. Department of State, 1958, U.S. Senate, 1960-61, Naval War College, 1959-62, 1971, U.S. Department of Health, Education and Welfare, 1965-70, and Salzburg Seminar in American Studies, 1968. *Awards, honors:* Fulbright and Guggenheim fellowships to Europe, 1958-59.

WRITINGS: (With others) *Report of Committee on Department of State and United Nations Publications,* [Lancaster, Pa.], 1956; *Exchange of Patent Rights and Technical Information under Mutual Aid Programs,* U.S. Government Printing Office, 1958; *Diplomats in International Cooperation: Stepchildren of the Foreign Service,* Cornell University Press, 1962; *The Association Process: Decision Making in the Association of American Law Schools,* Association of American Law Schools, 1975. Contributor of articles to legal journals and other publications.

* * *

CARGILL, Oscar 1898-1972

March 19, 1898—April 18, 1972; American educator, editor, and author of books on English and American literature. Obituaries: *New York Times,* April 20, 1972. (See index for *CA* sketch)

* * *

CARLETON, Mark T. 1935-

PERSONAL: Born February 7, 1935, in Baton Rouge, La.; son of Roderick Lewis and Helen (Parker) Carleton; married Maureen O'Hearn, July 6, 1963; children: Roderick Lewis, Michael Owen, Mark Albert. *Education:* Yale University, A.B., 1957; Stanford University, M.A., 1964, Ph.D., 1970. *Office address:* Box 3118, Baton Rouge, La. 70821.

CAREER: Foothill Junior College, Los Altos Hills, Calif., instructor in history, 1962-64; San Francisco State College (now University), San Francisco, Calif., instructor in history, 1964-65; Louisiana State University, Baton Rouge, lecturer, 1965-68, assistant professor, 1968-73, associate professor of history, 1973-76; Public Affairs Research Council of Louisiana, Inc., Baton Rouge, La., director of research, 1976—. *Military service:* U.S. Marine Corps, 1957-60. U.S. Marine Corps Reserve, 1960-64. *Member:* Phi Beta Kappa. *Awards, honors:* Certificate of Commendation, American Association for State and Local History, 1973, for *Politics and Punishment.*

WRITINGS: Politics and Punishment: The History of the Louisiana State Penal System, Louisiana State University Press, 1971; (co-editor) *Readings in Louisiana Politics,* Claitors, 1975. Author of study guide to *The Democratic Experience,* Scott, Foresman, 1966, 2nd edition, 1968. Contributor to *Dictionary of American History* and *Encyclopedia of Southern History;* contributor of articles and reviews to *Louisiana History, Louisiana Studies, American Historical Review,* and *Journal of Southern History.* Managing editor, *Louisiana History,* 1968-69.

* * *

CARLILE, Henry 1934-

PERSONAL: Born May 6, 1934, in San Francisco, Calif.; son of Aurelio Prieto and Grace (Harris) Carlile; married Sandra McPherson (a poet), July 22, 1966; children: Phoebe. *Education:* Grays Harbor College, A.A., 1960; University of Washington, Seattle, B.A., 1962, M.A., 1967. *Home:* 7349 Southeast 30th Ave., Portland, Ore. 97202. *Office:* Department of English, Portland State University, Portland, Ore. 97201.

CAREER: Portland State University, Portland, Ore., associate professor of English, 1967—. *Military service:* U.S. Army, 1953-56. *Awards, honors:* Academy of American Poets, University of Washington, second prize in poetry, 1967; National Endowment for the Arts discovery grant, 1970, fellowship in poetry, 1976; Devins Award, Kansas City Poetry Contest, 1971, for *The Rough-Hewn Table.*

WRITINGS: The Rough-Hewn Table (poems), University of Missouri Press, 1971. Guest co-editor, *Poetry Northwest,* summer, 1972.

WORK IN PROGRESS: A second book of poems.

CARLOCK, John R(obert) 1921-

PERSONAL: Born July 30, 1921, in Bloomington, Ill.; son of Claud B. (a government employee) and Myrtle E. (Skelton) Carlock; children: John M., Claud M., Kevin E. R. *Education:* Illinois State University, B.Ed., 1943, M.S., 1951; attended University of Illinois, 1940-41, Harvard University, 1943-44, Massachusetts Institute of Technology, 1944, University of Wisconsin, 1956-57, and University of Michigan, 1975. *Politics:* Republican. *Office:* U-213, Illinois State University, Normal, Ill. 61761.

CAREER: Science teacher at high schools in Tonica, Ill., 1942-43, and Petersburg, Ill., 1946-48; Libby, McNeill, Libby (food processors), Chicago, Ill., consultant, 1947, 1949-55, product head, quality control and research, 1948-49; Alpha Cellulose Corp., Bloomington, Ill., control chemist, 1949-51; Illinois State University, Normal, instructor, 1951-58, assistant professor, 1958-70, associate professor of biological science, 1970—. Has presented a series of multimedia programs of nature photography and music in New York, Chicago, St. Louis, Denver, Indianapolis, and various other cities. Consultant, Educational Testing Service. *Military service:* U.S. Naval Reserve, active duty, 1942-46; became lieutenant.

MEMBER: National Association of Biology Teachers, National Science Teachers Association, Association for Higher Education, National Education Association, American Association of University Professors, Association for Teacher Education, Association of Midwestern College Biology Teachers (president, 1968; executive secretary and editor, 1968—; honorary life member, 1976), Illinois Education Association (president of Central Division, 1966-67), Illinois Association for Teacher Education, Illinois Association for Higher Education (charter board member), Illinois State Academy of Science (co-chairman of science teaching section, 1961-63), Illinois Chemistry Teachers Association, Illinois Science Teachers Association, Northern Illinois Association of Biology Teachers, Phi Delta Kappa, Kappa Phi Kappa, Kappa Delta Pi, Gamma Theta Upsilon.

WRITINGS: (With Harold A. Moore) *The Spectrum of Life,* published with laboratory manual, Harper, 1970; *Hypothesis: A Simulation of Science,* Tecolote Press, 1975.

WORK IN PROGRESS: Research on simulation gaming in science and on innovation in laboratory exercises.

AVOCATIONAL INTERESTS: Nature and scientific photography (many of his photographs have been published in books and periodicals).

*   *   *

CARLSON, Ronald L. 1934-

PERSONAL: Born December 10, 1934, in Iowa City, Iowa; son of Arthur A. (owner of an industrial pattern company) and Louise Carlson; married Mary Murphy, 1965; children: Michael, Andrew. *Education:* Augustana College, Rock Island, Ill., B.A., 1956; Northwestern University, J.D., 1959; Georgetown University, LL.M., 1961. *Politics:* Republican. *Religion:* Methodist. *Home:* 401 Oakley, Clayton, Mo. 63105. *Office:* School of Law, Washington University, St. Louis, Mo. 63130.

CAREER: Practicing attorney in Washington, D.C., and Iowa, 1961-65; U.S. commissioner, Southern District of Iowa, 1964-65; University of Iowa, Iowa City, assistant professor, 1965-67, associate professor, 1967-69, professor of law, 1969-73; Washington University, St. Louis, Mo., professor of law, 1973—. Consultant to criminal code review

study committee, Iowa Legislature, 1969-73. *Member:* American Bar Association, American Judicature Society, American Association of University Professors, Iowa State Bar Association. *Awards, honors:* Distinguished teaching award, Washington University, 1976.

WRITINGS: Criminal Justice Procedure for Police, W. H. Anderson, 1970; (with Ladd) *Ladd and Carlson on Evidence,* Callaghan, 1972, supplement, 1976. Contributor to professional journals and to *Parade.*

BIOGRAPHICAL/CRITICAL SOURCES: Iowa Law Review, October, 1971.

*   *   *

CARMICHAEL, D(ouglas) R(oy) 1941-

PERSONAL: Born October 23, 1941, in Harvey, Ill.; son of Roy S. and Thelma (Fontechia) Carmichael. *Education:* University of Illinois, B.S., 1963, M.A.S., 1964, Ph.D., 1968. *Residence:* New York, N.Y. *Office:* American Institute of Certified Public Accountants, 1211 Ave. of the Americas, New York, N.Y. 10036.

CAREER: University of Texas at Austin, associate professor of accounting, 1967-69; American Institute of Certified Public Accountants, New York, N.Y., vice-president of technical services, 1969—. Adjunct associate professor, Columbia University, summer, 1970; adjunct professor, New York University, 1970—. *Member:* American Institute of Certified Public Accountants, American Accounting Association, Illinois Society of Certified Public Accountants, Beta Alpha Psi, Beta Gamma Sigma, Delta Sigma Pi, Sigma Iota Epsilon. *Awards, honors:* Harry J. Loman Foundation research grant, 1966.

WRITINGS: (With John J. Willingham) *Auditing Concepts and Methods,* McGraw, 1971, 2nd edition, 1975; (with Willingham) *Perspectives in Auditing,* McGraw, 1971, 2nd edition, 1975; *The Auditor's Reporting Obligation,* American Institute of Certified Public Accountants, 1972; (with B. Makela) *Corporate Financial Reporting: The Benefits and Problems of Disclosure,* American Institute of Certified Public Accountants, 1977. Contributor of more than fifty articles to journals.

WORK IN PROGRESS: Research on the auditor's role and responsibilities.

AVOCATIONAL INTERESTS: Theater, movies, sailing, water skiing, magic (worked as a semiprofessional magician for several years).

*   *   *

CARNES, Ralph L(ee) 1931-

PERSONAL: Born May 28, 1931, in Tallapoosa, Ga.; son of Randal Julian (a writer) and Lettie (Buttram) Carnes; married Valerie Bohanan (an associate dean at Roosevelt University), April 28, 1967. *Education:* Emory University, B.A., 1959, M.A., 1960, Ph.D., 1965. *Home and office:* 11906 Leafy Arbor, Houston, Tex. 77070.

CAREER: Quartermaster Data Processing Section, machine records department, Atlanta General Depot, Atlanta, Ga., civilian-in-charge, 1953-54; Trust Company of Georgia, Atlanta, assistant manager of IBM data processing department, 1954-55; Oglethorpe College, Atlanta, assistant professor of philosophy, 1961-64, chairman of department, 1962-64; University of South Alabama, Mobile, assistant professor of philosophy and head of department, 1964-65; University of North Dakota, Grand Forks, assistant professor of philosophy, 1966-69; Roosevelt University, Chicago, Ill., associate professor 1969-71, professor of philosophy, 1971-77, associate dean of College of Arts and Sciences, 1971-72, dean of the college, 1972-77; I * Med, Inc., Houston, Tex., vice-president for development, 1977—. Danforth Foundation associate, 1972. *Member:* American Association of University Professors, Modern Language Association of America, American Philosophical Association (Western division), North Dakota-Manitoba Linguistics Association, Georgia Philosophical Association. *Awards, honors:* Hill Foundation grant, 1966; University of North Dakota research grants, 1966-67, 1967-68, 1968-69.

WRITINGS: (Editor and contributor with wife, Valerie Carnes) *The New Humanities: Culture, Crisis, Change,* Holt, 1972; (with V. Carnes and Kelly Freas) *The Officers of the Bridge,* privately printed, 1976; (with V. Carnes) *Bodysculpture: Weight Training for Women,* Simon & Schuster, 1978. Contributor to *University of North Dakota Quarterly, ETC: The Journal of General Semantics,* and *Proceedings* of the North Dakota-Manitoba Linguistics Circle.

WORK IN PROGRESS—With wife, Valerie Carnes: *The Third Generation,* a novel; *The Great Youth Hustle: A Social History of the Sixties; Essays on Linguistic Relativity; The Michael St. James Model's Book; Guide to Health and Recreation: Houston, Texas; Renaissance: The Complete Makeover Book for Women.* "Beyond the New Critics," an article examining the post-New Criticism with a logical analysis of the Beardslean metacriticism.

SIDELIGHTS: Ralph Carnes told *CA:* "My prevailing intellectual condition is that I must learn as much about as many things as it is possible for me to learn about within the lifespan that I will enjoy. I have and I have always had an insatiable compulsion to learn. I am not so much interested in the accumulation of facts as I am in discerning patterns, causes, and underlying philosophies."

AVOCATIONAL INTERESTS: Flamenco guitar, building electronics equipment, oil painting, karate, racing motorcycles.

*   *   *

CARNES, Valerie Folts-Bohanan 1945-

PERSONAL: Born November 19, 1945, in Chattanooga, Tenn.; daughter of Ross W. (a county superintendent) and Valerie Fairfax (Folts) Bohanan; married Ralph L. Carnes (a college dean), April 28, 1967. *Education:* University of Tennessee at Chattanooga, B.A. (summa cum laude), 1962; Emory University, M.A., 1963, Ph.D., 1967. *Residence:* Houston, Tex. *Office:* Nova Industries, 11211 Katy Freeway, Houston, Tex. 77079.

CAREER: University of North Dakota, Grand Forks, assistant professor of English, 1966-69, director of humanities program in New School of Behavioral Studies, 1968-69; Roosevelt University, Chicago, Ill., assistant professor, 1969-74, associate professor of English, 1974-77, associate dean in College of Continuing Education, 1972-75; Nova Industries, Houston, Tex., director of communications and public relations, 1977—. Visiting lecturer in English, Indiana University Northwest, 1970. Member of board of directors, Urban Life Center, Roosevelt University, 1971-72. Danforth Foundation associate, 1972.

MEMBER: International Society for General Semantics, Modern Language Association of America, American Association of University Professors, Renaissance Society of

America, Milton Society of America, Chicago Area College English Association (member of board directors, 1971-77), North Dakota-Manitoba Linguistics Circle, Alpha Lambda Delta, Chi Delta Phi. *Awards, honors:* Hill Foundation grant, 1966; University of North Dakota research grants, 1966-67, 1967-68, 1968-69; Illinois Humanities Council grant, 1975.

WRITINGS: (Contributor) R. B. Browne and M. Fishwick, editors, *Icons of Popular Culture,* Bowling Green University, 1970; (editor and contributor with husband, Ralph L. Carnes) *The New Humanities: Culture, Crisis, Change,* Holt, 1972; (with R. L. Carnes and Kelly Freas) *The Officers of the Bridge,* privately printed, 1976; (with R. L. Carnes) *Bodysculpture,* Simon & Schuster, 1978; (contributor) *Renaissance East and West,* University Press of America, in press. Columnist, *Chicago Elite Magazine,* 1976-77. Contributor to *University of North Dakota Quarterly, English Literary History, Scopcraeft, Lost Generation Journal, World Literature Written in English,* and *Proceedings* of the North Dakota-Manitoba Linguistics Circle.

WORK IN PROGRESS: With husband, Ralph L. Carnes, *The Great Youth Hustle: A Social History of the Sixties; Image and Structure in the Poems of George Herbert,* for Johns Hopkins Press; *The Expatriate Vision: The Little Magazines of the 1920's,* for Ungar; *Improv'd by Tract of Time: Human History in Milton's "Paradise Lost"; Sathanas,* a novel.

SIDELIGHTS: Valerie Carnes reads Spanish, German, medieval Italian, French, and Latin. *Avocational interests:* Piano, guitar, autoharp, karate, ballet, tropical plants, French cooking, fashion and interior design, refinishing antique furniture, collage, and painting.

*   *   *

CARNOCHAN, W(alter) B(liss) 1930-

PERSONAL: Born December 20, 1930, in New York, N.Y.; son of Gouverneur Morris (a businessman) and Sibyll (Bliss) Carnochan; married Nancy Carter, June 25, 1955; children: Lisa, Sarah, Gouverneur, Sibyll. *Education:* Harvard University, A.B., 1953, Ph.D., 1960. *Home:* 555 Manzanita Way, Woodside, Calif. 94062. *Office:* Graduate Division, Stanford University, Stanford, Calif. 94305.

CAREER: Stanford University, Stanford, Calif., instructor, 1960-62, assistant professor, 1962-68, associate professor, 1968-73, professor of English, 1973—, dean of graduate studies, 1975—, vice-provost, 1976—.

WRITINGS: (Editor) George Etherege, *The Man of Mode,* University of Nebraska Press, 1966; *Lemuel Gulliver's Mirror for Man,* University of California Press, 1968; *Confinement and Flight: An Essay on English Literature of the Eighteenth Century,* University of California Press, 1977.

WORK IN PROGRESS: A book, tentatively entitled *Fiction, Pleasure, and Pain.*

BIOGRAPHICAL/CRITICAL SOURCES: Yale Review, autumn, 1969; *Journal of English and Germanic Philology,* April, 1970; *Review of English Studies,* May, 1970.

*   *   *

CARPENTER, Charles A. (Jr.) 1929-

PERSONAL: Born June 8, 1929, in Hazleton, Pa.; son of Charles A. (an engineering executive) and Frances (Kenyon) Carpenter; married Randi Rothrock, November 4, 1950; children: Carol, Linda (Mrs. Montgomery Northrup),

Janet, Diane. *Education:* Allegheny College, B.A., 1951; Kent State University, M.A.L.S., 1952; Cornell University, M.A., 1960, Ph.D., 1963. *Politics:* Liberal. *Religion:* None. *Home:* 908 Lehigh Ave., Binghamton, N.Y. 13903. *Office:* Department of English, State University of New York, Binghamton, N.Y. 13901.

CAREER: Dickinson College, Carlisle, Pa., assistant librarian, 1952-54; Muskingum College, New Concord, Ohio, head librarian, 1954-55; Cornell University, Goldwin Smith Humanities Library, Ithaca, N.Y., librarian, 1955-61; University of Delaware, Newark, assistant professor of English, 1962-67; State University of New York at Binghamton, assistant professor, 1967-70, associate professor of English, 1970—.

WRITINGS: Bernard Shaw and the Art of Destroying Ideals: The Early Plays, University of Wisconsin Press, 1969; *Modern British Drama: A Goldentree Bibliography,* AHM Publishing, 1977. Contributor to literature journals. Member of editorial board, *Modern Drama,* 1974—.

WORK IN PROGRESS: International Bibliography of Modern Drama Studies, 1966-1980; further studies of absurdist plays.

AVOCATIONAL INTERESTS: Playing tournament bridge, ping-pong.

*   *   *

CARPENTER, Joyce Frances

PERSONAL: Born in Chelmsford, Essex, England; daughter of William Harold (a Church of England clergyman) and Elsie (a musician, orchestra director, and playwright; maiden name, Varley) Carpenter. *Education:* Educated privately at home. *Politics:* Conservative. *Religion:* "Reared in Church of England; recent convert to Roman Catholic faith." *Home:* Flat 1, 44 Lansdowne Rd., London W11 2LU, England.

CAREER: Professional actress, appearing in plays and musicals in London, England, in motion pictures, television, and radio, including seven years on British Broadcasting Corp. radio series, "Mrs. Dale's Diary." Gives recitals of her work at theatres, concert halls, churches, and colleges. Read her poems nightly on Thames Television, December 27, 1976—January 4, 1977.

WRITINGS: Attitude (poems), Etcetera Press, 1976; *Away in a Manger* (Nativity play; first produced by a professional company in London at West End churches, December, 1976), Hub Publications, 1976; *Reflection* (poems), Etcetera Press, 1977; *Tales of Genkuji,* C. Allen, in press.

Contributor of stories to collections edited by Dorothy Mildred Prescott and published by Blandford: *More Stories for Junior Assembly,* 1971; *More Readings for the Senior Assembly: Meaning in Life,* 1973; *Further Stories for the Junior Assembly,* 1974; *More Stories for Infants at Home and at School,* 1975; *Stories for Middle School Assembly,* 1976. Contributor of poems to anthologies, including: *Swing Back,* Orbis Publishing, 1971; *New Bond Anthology,* Bond Street Publishers, 1971; *Poets Year Book,* Arts Council of Great Britain, 1975; *Christian Poetry* (annual), edited by Frances Horovitz, Fellowship of Christians in the Arts, 1975, 1976; *Poets Forum,* National Poetry Centre, in press. Also author of children's stories broadcast on "Listen with Mother" program, BBC radio, 1976-77. Has had more than one hundred poems and three hundred short stories published in magazines; contributor of inspirational articles to religious press.

WORK IN PROGRESS: Short stories, poems, and articles for women's and general magazines, and for children's publications; a novel.

BIOGRAPHICAL/CRITICAL SOURCES: Stage, May 20, 1971.

*   *   *

CARR, Albert Z(olotkoff)   1902-1971
(A. H. Z. Carr)

January 15, 1902—October 28, 1971; American economist, government official, short story writer, essayist, biographer, and historian. Obituaries: *New York Times,* October 29, 1971; *Washington Post,* October 29, 1971. (See index for *CA* sketch)

*   *   *

CARRIER, Constance   1908-

PERSONAL: Born July 29, 1908, in New Britain, Conn.; daughter of Lucius (an accountant) and Lilian (Jost) Carrier. *Education:* Smith College, B.A., 1929; Trinity College, Hartford, Conn., M.A., 1940. *Religion:* Congregationalist. *Residence:* New Britain, Conn. *Office:* Tufts University, Medford, Mass. 02155.

CAREER: High school teacher of Latin in New Britain and West Hartford, Conn., 1931-69; Tufts University, Medford, Mass., conductor of workshop courses in Latin for teachers, 1966—. *Awards, honors: The Middle Voice* was Lamont Poetry Selection of American Academy of Poets, 1954; Poetry Society of America annual prize, 1954; other awards for individual poems; several fellowships at MacDowell Colony, Peterborough, N.H., and at Yaddo, Saratoga, N.Y.

WRITINGS: The Middle Voice (poems), A. Swallow, 1955; (translator) Sextus Aurelius Propertius, *The Poems of Propertius,* introduction and notes by Palmer Bovie, Indiana University Press, 1963; (translator) Albius Tibullus, *The Poems of Tibullus,* introduction and notes by Edward M. Michael, Indiana University Press, 1968; *The Angled Road* (poems), Swallow Press, 1973; (contributor of translations) Publius Terentius Afer, *The Complete Comedies of Terence,* edited by Bovie, Rutgers University Press, 1974. Contributor to *Harper's, Atlantic, New Yorker, Nation, Poetry* (Chicago), *American Scholar,* and other periodicals and newspapers.

AVOCATIONAL INTERESTS: Domestic architecture, reading biography and history; "people, places, things."

*   *   *

CARTER, Alan   1936-

PERSONAL: Born July 31, 1936, in London, England; son of Frederick John and Florence (Pope) Carter; married Liliane Engelborghs (a translator), August 21, 1971. *Education:* London School of Economics and Political Science, B.Sc., 1958. *Home:* 100 Ave. Charles Quint, Brussels 1080, Belgium; and 12 Green End, Granborough, Buckinghamshire, England.

CAREER: University of Antwerp, Antwerp, Belgium, faculty of languages, lecturer in political, economic, and social institutions of English speaking countries, 1963—. *Military service:* British Army, 1958-60; became second lieutenant.

WRITINGS: John Osborne: Biography and Criticism, Oliver & Boyd, 1969, Barnes & Noble, 1970. Contributor to *The Reader's Encyclopedia of English Literature* and to periodicals.

WORK IN PROGRESS: Co-author of a book of advanced English grammar for foreign students; a study of isolation and silence as themes in the theater.

AVOCATIONAL INTERESTS: Travel, antiques (especially porcelain), period architecture (he owns a 1724 cottage).

* * *

CARTER, Alfred Edward 1914-

PERSONAL: Born September 29, 1914, in Victoria, British Columbia, Canada; son of Alfred Edward (an engineer) and Irene Beatrice (Nason) Carter. *Education:* Attended University of British Columbia, McGill University, and University of London. *Home:* 4B, 329 Dearing, Athens, Ga. 30601; and 13 rue Saint-Antoine, 75004, Paris, France. *Office:* Department of Romance Languages, University of Georgia, Athens, Ga. 30601.

CAREER: Department of State, Ottawa, Ontario, translator, 1959-61; University of South Carolina, Columbia, associate professor of romance languages, 1961-64; University of Georgia, Athens, professor of romance languages, 1964—.

WRITINGS: The Idea of Decadence in French Literature: 1830-1900, University of Toronto Press, 1958; *Beaudelaire et la critique francaise: 1868-1917,* University of South Carolina Press, 1962; *Verlaine: A Study in Parallels,* University of Toronto Press, 1969; *Verlaine,* Twayne, 1972; *Charles Baudelaire,* Twayne, 1977.

WORK IN PROGRESS: Decadence: The Western Neurosis.

BIOGRAPHICAL/CRITICAL SOURCES: Books Abroad, summer, 1970; *Times Literary Supplement,* September 25, 1970.

* * *

CARTER, Harold 1925-

PERSONAL: Born April 14, 1925, in Neath, Glamorganshire, Wales. *Education:* University College of Wales, B.A., M.A. *Office:* Department of Geography, Llandinam Building, University College of Wales, University of Wales, Aberystwyth, Wales.

CAREER: University of Wales, University College of Wales, Aberystwyth, Gregynog Professor of Human Geography, 1968—. *Military service:* Royal Air Force, 1944-47.

WRITINGS: The Towns of Wales, University of Wales Press, 1965; *The Growth of the Welsh City System,* University of Wales Press, 1969; (with W.K.D. Davies) *Urban Essays: Studies in the Geography of Wales,* Longmans, Green, 1970; *The Study of Urban Geography,* E. J. Arnold, 1972, 2nd edition, 1975; (editor) *Geography, Culture and Habitat: Selected Essays of E. G. Bowen,* Gomer Press, 1976.

* * *

CARTER, (William) Hodding, Jr. 1907-1972

February 3, 1907—April 4, 1972; American publisher, editor, novelist, historian, author of children's books, and books on the contemporary South. Obituaries: *New York Times,* April 5, 1972; *Washington Post,* April 6, 1972; *Newsweek,* April 17, 1972; *Time,* April 17, 1972; *Current Biography,* May, 1972. (See index for *CA* sketch)

* * *

CARTER, James Puckette 1933-

PERSONAL: Born October 7, 1933, in Chicago, Ill.; son of Morris R. (a physician) and Ruth (Puckette) Carter; married Gena Marie Hunter, April 29, 1961 (divorced, 1976); children: James, Jr., Rebecca, Geoffrey. *Education:* Northwestern University, B.S., 1954, M.D., 1957; Columbia University, M.S. (parasitology), 1962, Dr.P.H., 1966. *Home:* 2318 Burgundy St., New Orleans, La. 70117. *Office:* Department of Nutrition and Nursing, School of Public Health and Tropical Medicine, Tulane University, 1430 Tulane Ave., New Orleans, La. 70112.

CAREER: Minneapolis General Hospital, Minneapolis, Minn., intern, 1957-58; University of Minnesota Hospitals, Minneapolis, resident in pediatrics, 1958-59, 1961-62; Vanderbilt University, School of Medicine, Nashville, Tenn., staff pediatrician and nutritionist, 1965-76, assistant professor, 1965-72, associate professor of pediatrics and of nutrition, 1972-76, member of Vanderbilt nutrition group at U.S. Naval Medical Research Unit, Cairo, Egypt, 1965-67; Tulane University, School of Public Health and Tropical Medicine, New Orleans, La., professor of nutrition and chairman of department, 1976—, School of Medicine, clinical professor of pediatrics, 1976—. Meharry Medical College, associate clinical professor in department of family and community health, 1971-76, project director, maternal and child health, 1971-76. Guest lecturer at University of Tampa, Florida Southern College, and other universities; participated in National Academy of Sciences workshops in Ghana and Zaire, 1971, 1976. Member, National Council on Hunger and Malnutrition, 1969—; panel chairman, White House Conference on Food, Nutrition, and Health, 1969; member of research advisory committee, Agency for International Development. *Military service:* U.S. Naval Reserve, 1959-61; became lieutenant.

MEMBER: American Institute of Nutrition, American Board of Pediatrics, American Society for Clinical Nutrition. *Awards, honors:* U.S. Public Health Service fellow in tropical medicine at Columbia University and University of Ibadan, 1964-66; Milbank Memorial Fund faculty fellowship, 1968-73.

WRITINGS: (With E. A. West) *Keeping Your Family Healthy Overseas,* Delacorte, 1971. Contributor of about fifteen articles to medical and nutrition journals.

WORK IN PROGRESS: Research on the relationship between nutrition and school performance, and on nutrition and parasitism.

* * *

CARTER, James Richard 1940-

PERSONAL: Born December 22, 1940, in Urbana, Ill.; son of Vern Lemuel (an engineer) and Vera (Lawrence) Carter; married Dorothy Kay Conner, March 25, 1964; children: Susan Kathleen, Richard James. *Education:* Attended Massachusetts Institute of Technology, 1958-59; Whitman College, B.A., 1963; University of Oregon, M.A., 1967, Ph.D., 1969. *Politics:* Republican. *Religion:* Christian Church (Disciples of Christ). *Home:* 1122 North Ohio, Caldwell, Idaho 83605. *Office:* Department of Economics, College of Idaho, Caldwell, Idaho 83605.

CAREER: U.S. Government, Washington, D.C., economic analyst, 1966-68; Oregon College of Education, Monmouth, assistant professor of economics, 1968-70; College of Idaho, Caldwell, assistant professor, 1970-73, associate professor of economics, 1973—. *Member:* American Economic Association, Association for the Study of Grants Economies.

WRITINGS: The Net Cost of Soviet Foreign Aid, Praeger, 1971.

CARTER, John T(homas) 1921-

PERSONAL: Born December 16, 1921, in Mantee, Miss.; son of John F. (a professor and clergyman) and Mattie (George) Carter; married Frances Tunnell (a professor), March 16, 1946; children: John W., Frankye Nell. *Education:* Attended Clarke Memorial College, 1940-42; Mississippi State College (now University), B.S., 1947; University of Tennessee, M.S., 1948; University of Illinois, Ed.D., 1954; University of Dayton, postdoctoral study, 1963. *Politics:* Republican. *Religion:* Baptist. *Home:* 2561 Rocky Ridge Rd., Birmingham, Ala. 35243. *Office:* School of Education, Samford University, 800 Lakeshore Dr., Birmingham, Ala. 35209.

CAREER: Elementary school principal and teacher in Maben, Miss., 1946-47; Wood Junior College, Mathiston, Miss., professor of agriculture, 1947-48; Clarke Memorial College, Newton, Miss., professor of agriculture, 1948-56; Samford University, Birmingham, Ala., professor of education, 1956—, associate dean of education. Guest professor, Hong Kong Baptist College, 1965-66; instructor and consultant for industrial firms, including Stockham Valve and Fitting Co., 1960-69, Thomas Foundries, 1968—, and Caldwell Foundries, 1969—. Became lieutenant colonel in Civil Air Patrol. *Military service:* U.S. Army, paratrooper, 1942-45; became sergeant. *Member:* National Education Association, National Aerospace Education Association (former member of board of directors), International Council on Education for Teachers, Alabama Association of Teacher Educators (past president), Kiwanis Club (past local president), Kappa Delta Pi, Kappa Phi Kappa, Phi Delta Kappa. *Awards, honors:* Brewer Award, Civil Air Patrol, 1973.

WRITINGS—For young people: *Mike and His Four-Star Goal,* Convention Press, 1960; *East Is West,* Convention Press, 1966; *Witness in Israel,* Broadman, 1969; (with wife, Frances T. Carter) *Sharing Times Seven,* Convention Press, 1971. Also author of Sunday School lessons for Southern Baptist Convention. Author of "Guidelines for Daily Living" column, *Ambassador Life,* 1964-70. Contributor to education journals.

*   *   *

CARTER, M(argaret) L(ouise) 1948-

PERSONAL: Born April 29, 1948, in Norfolk, Va.; daughter of John Ervin (a certified public accountant) and Margaret (Townsend) Greunke; married Leslie Roy Carter (a U.S. naval ensign), September 21, 1966; children: Brian David, Richard Alan, Leonard James IV. *Education:* Attended Old Dominion College, 1968; College of William and Mary, B.A., 1972; University of Hawaii, M.A., 1974. *Politics:* Liberal—no party affiliation. *Religion:* Baptist. *Home:* 1339 Spruance Rd., Monterey, Calif. 93940. *Agent:* Michael O'Neill, P.O. Box 461, Birmingham, Mich. 48012.

MEMBER: Count Dracula Society (Los Angeles; governor, 1970—), Dame of Noble Order of Count Dracula, Christopher Lee International Club, Mythopoeic Society. *Awards, honors:* Count Dracula Society award, 1976, for *Shadow of a Shade.*

WRITINGS: (Editor) *Curse of the Undead* (vampire stories), Fawcett, 1970; (author of preface) T. P. Prest, *Varney the Vampyre,* edited by D. P. Varma, McGrath, 1970; (editor) *Demon Lovers and Strange Seductions,* Fawcett, 1972; *Shadow of a Shade: A Survey of Vampirism in Literature,* Gordon Press, 1975. Contributor to *Daily Press,* Newport News, Va., and *Monterey Peninsula Herald,* Monterey, Calif.

WORK IN PROGRESS: A Dracula Casebook (anthology of criticism of *Dracula*); two Gothic novels, *Lair of the Life-drinkers* and *Gate of Shadows;* a film adaptation of Prest's *Varney the Vampyre,* "with hope of eventually getting it produced."

SIDELIGHTS: M. L. Carter told *CA:* "I owe my literary interests and career to Bram Stoker. Reading *Dracula* at the age of 13 caused me to become interested in horror, fantasy, and science fiction, as well as to write my first story shortly thereafter. . . . My interest in Stoker led me to join the Count Dracula Society (devoted to the serious study of Gothic fiction and horror films) in 1969; through the Society, I met Dr. D. P. Varma (author of *The Gothic Flame*) . . . [who] helped to expand my awareness of the philosophical and psychological significance of vampirism."

M. L. Carter added: "In the last couple of years I have developed a fervent admiration for C. S. Lewis. I am collaborating with a friend on a novel of the supernatural that will be my first attempt at combining explicit Christianity with horror. The novels I am presently marketing have pronounced Lovecraftian elements; I try to present the lure of that world-view while making it clear that the heroine ought to resist the lure."

Carter is especially interested in "adapting obscure Gothic novels of the late 18th and early 19th centuries, with their peculiar compulsion of subliminal horror, to the medium of the cinema."

*   *   *

CARTER, Paul A(llen) 1926-

PERSONAL: Born September 3, 1926, in New Bedford, Mass.; son of Manfred Amos (a clergyman and poet) and Ina R. (Fisk) Carter; married Julienne Kay Raffety, August 26, 1962; children: Christina Julia, Brian Allen, Bruce Douglas, Robert Kennedy. *Education:* Wesleyan University, Middletown, Conn., B.A. (magna cum laude), 1950; Columbia University, M.A., 1951, Ph.D., 1954; also attended Union Theological Seminary, New York, N.Y. *Office:* Department of History, University of Arizona, Tucson, Ariz. 85721.

CAREER: Columbia University, School of General Studies, New York, N.Y., lecturer in history, 1954-55; Cornell University, Ithaca, N.Y., acting assistant professor of history, 1955; University of Maryland, College Park, assistant professor of history, 1955-56; University of Montana, Missoula, assistant professor, 1956-59, associate professor of history, 1959-62; Northern Illinois University, De Kalb, associate professor, 1966-69, professor of history, 1969-73; University of Arizona, Tucson, professor of history, 1973—. Summer instructor at University of Alberta, 1956, Wesleyan University, 1958, 1959, and College of Wooster, 1966; visiting associate professor, Smith College, 1962-63, University of Massachusetts, 1964-65, and Amherst College, 1965-66; visiting lecturer, University of California, Berkeley, 1963-64. Lecturer; free-lance manuscript critic for publishers. Member, Citizens for McGovern, 1971-72. *Military service:* U.S. Navy, 1944-46. *Member:* Organization of American Historians (member of Turner Prize committee, 1973-75; member of nominating board, 1976-77, chairman, 1977), American Society of Church History, Phi Beta Kappa.

WRITINGS: The Decline and Revival of the Social Gospel: Social and Political Liberalism in American Protestant Churches, 1920-1940, Cornell University Press, 1956, revised edition, Archon Books, 1971; *The Twenties in America,* Crowell, 1968, revised edition, 1975; (editor) *The*

Uncertain World of Normalcy: The 1920s, Pitman, 1971; *The Spiritual Crisis of the Gilded Age*, Northern Illinois University Press, 1971; *Another Part of the Twenties*, Columbia University Press, 1977; *The Creation of Tomorrow: Fifty Years of Magazine Science Fiction*, Columbia University Press, 1977. Contributor of articles to *Church History, Wisconsin Magazine of History, Pacific Northwest Quarterly, Historical Magazine of the Protestant Episcopal Church, Theology Today, Journal of Popular Culture, American Studies,* and *American Scholar;* contributor of science fiction short stories to *Astounding Science Fiction,* and *Magazine of Fantasy and Science Fiction.*

SIDELIGHTS: Paul A. Carter told *CA* that his purpose in writing is "to work out an understanding of part of the past, including part of my own past." Reviewing *Another Part of the Twenties,* Robert Kirsch praises the way Carter "lights up parts of the age which have been in obscurity too long." Kirsch characterizes the book as "a relaxed and informal study" in which Carter is "trying to examine the unexplored territory between the polar opposites of the period. . . . By asking what we in the late '70s *need* from the '20s (apart from what we *seek*), he has found some bracing material."

One of Carter's science fiction stories has been translated and published in French, and one was used on NBC radio's "Dimension X" program.

BIOGRAPHICAL/CRITICAL SOURCES: Critic, November, 1971; *Christian Century,* November 24, 1971, May 11, 1977; *New England Quarterly,* September, 1972; *Los Angeles Times,* March 25, 1977; *New York Times Book Review,* May 8, 1977; *Yale Review,* June, 1977; *Journalism Quarterly,* summer, 1977; *Times Literary Supplement,* August 26, 1977; *History: Reviews of New Books,* September, 1977.

* * *

CARTER, Robert A(yres) 1923-
(Alison Ayres)

PERSONAL: Born September 16, 1923, in Omaha, Neb.; son of George W. and Zeta (Hart) Carter; married Marjorie Marker (divorced); married Winifred Allen Scott, April 21, 1973; children: (first marriage) Jonathan Barlow, Randall Ayres. *Education:* Attended University of Chicago, 1941-43; New School for Social Research, A.B., 1949. *Politics:* "American citizen." *Religion:* Christian. *Home address:* c/o The Players, 16 Gramercy Park, New York, N.Y. 10003.

CAREER: Stephens College, Columbia, Mo., instructor in French, 1951-53; Doubleday & Co., New York City, director of advertising and publicity, 1960-66, director of books for young readers, 1966-68; Museum of Modern Art, New York City, director of publications, 1968-70; Franklin Spier, Inc. (advertising firm), New York City, account executive, 1971-74, vice-president, 1974—. Member, New Dramatists Committee, 1959-62. *Military service:* U.S. Army Air Forces, 1944-46. *Member:* Authors Guild, Publishers Ad Club (president, 1963-65), The Players. *Awards, honors:* Fulbright scholar at University of Paris, 1949-50; Russell L. Reynolds Award, National Association of College Stores, 1967.

WRITINGS: Manhattan Primitive, Stein & Day, 1971. Also author of plays: "Guests of Summer," "Tandem," and "Bughouse Square."

WORK IN PROGRESS: A novel entitled *Rainbow Territory;* a novel, *The Fevered Heart,* under the pseudonym Alison Ayres.

SIDELIGHTS: "The greatest satisfactions I have had at my typewriter," notes Robert Carter, "have come from writing poetry." He goes on to describe poetry as "a completely gratuitous art, and the most glorious, incorporating . . . dance in its rhythms, music, visual imagery, thought, feeling, and that indescribable element we call soul."

AVOCATIONAL INTERESTS: Travel, tennis, swimming, fishing.

BIOGRAPHICAL/CRITICAL SOURCES: Christian Science Monitor, July 8, 1971; *New York Times Book Review,* July 25, 1971; *Best Sellers,* August 1, 1971.

* * *

CARTER, Robert M(ack) 1925-

PERSONAL: Born September 7, 1925, in Kennett, Mo.; son of Louis J. (a justice of the peace) and Jennie (Moore) Carter; married Phyllis Anne Bumke (a registered nurse), September 25, 1948; children: Kathrine, Richard, Christopher, John. *Education:* University of Michigan, B.A., 1950, M.A., 1951; Michigan State University, Ph.D., 1966. *Religion:* United Methodist. *Home:* 1061 Woodview Dr., Flint, Mich. 48507. *Office:* Department of Industrial Administration, General Motors Institute, 1700 West Third Ave., Flint, Mich. 48502.

CAREER: General Motors Institute, Flint, Mich., member of faculty, 1951—, currently professor in department of industrial administration. *Military service:* U.S. Coast Guard, 1943-46; served in the Pacific. *Member:* International Communication Association, International Transactional Analysis Association, American Business Communication Association, Michigan Speech Association.

WRITINGS: (Editor) *Communication in Organizations,* Gale, 1972; (editor with S. Tubbs) *Shared Experiences: Readings in Human Communication,* Hayden, 1977. Contributor to *Organizational Communication Abstracts* and to speech and religious journals.

WORK IN PROGRESS: Organizational communication problems.

SIDELIGHTS: Robert Carter told *CA,* "I enjoy achieving brevity with clarity in writing, and I find it challenging to avoid using the verb 'to be.'"

* * *

CARTER, William 1934-

PERSONAL: Born December 25, 1934, in Los Angeles, Calif.; son of Edward William and Christine (Dailey) Carter; married Deirdre Clairmont, 1958 (divorced); married Barbara Newcomb, 1965 (divorced); married Betty Southern, February, 1970 (divorced). *Education:* Stanford University, B.A., 1957. *Politics:* Independent. *Religion:* Siddha Yoga. *Home:* 535 Everett Ave., Palo Alto, Calif. 94301.

CAREER: Has worked as clarinet player with Turk Murphy's Jazz Band, and as free-lance jazz clarinetist; free-lance photographer, 1960—. Member of editorial staff, Harper & Row Publishers, Inc., New York City, 1962-63; Photographer, Camera Press Ltd., London, England, and Photo Researchers, New York City. *Military service:* National Guard Reserve, 1957-58, 1959-62. U.S. Army, 1958; served in Medical Corps. *Member:* Bohemian Club (San Francisco). *Awards, honors:* Publications award, Chicago Geographical Society, 1975, for *Middle West Country.*

WRITINGS: Ghost Towns of the West, photographs by author, Sunset Books, 1971; *Middle West Country,* Houghton, 1975. Contributor of articles and photographs to *Life, Geographical Magazine* (London), *Oceans, Women's Wear Daily,* and other periodicals.

SIDELIGHTS: William Carter has traveled widely, worked in more than thirty countries, especially the Middle East and Europe, and lived in Beirut for two years and London for three. His "most interesting expedition was to the Kurds in the mountains of northern Iraq, . . . [and] greatest photo inspiration was the work of Cartier-Bresson and Edward Weston." He is a devotee of Swami Muktananda of Ganesh-puri, India.

AVOCATIONAL INTERESTS: Classical and jazz music, literature, and the arts.

* * *

CARUSO, John Anthony 1907-

PERSONAL: Born June 11, 1907, near Uniontown, Pa.; son of Domenico (a farmer) and Concetta (Muraca) Caruso; married Marie Camille Collart, December 27, 1948; children: Johanna Marie, Camille Annette. *Education:* University of Pittsburgh, A.B., 1946; West Virginia University, M.A., 1947, Ph.D., 1949. *Home:* 888 Riverview Dr., Morgantown, W.Va. 26505. *Office:* Department of History, West Virginia University, Morgantown, W.Va. 26506.

CAREER: West Virginia University, Morgantown, assistant professor, 1950-61, associate professor, 1961-62, professor of history, 1962-72, professor emeritus, 1974—. Visiting lecturer in comparative literature in Spain, 1975.

WRITINGS: The Liberators of Mexico, Pageant, 1954, Peter Smith, 1967; *The Appalachian Frontier,* Bobbs-Merrill, 1959; *The Great Lakes Frontier,* Bobbs-Merrill, 1961; (contributor) *America's Historylands,* National Geographic Society, 1962; *The Southern Frontier,* Bobbs-Merrill, 1963; *The Mississippi Valley Frontier,* Bobbs-Merrill, 1966; (contributor) *Le Sud au Temps de Scarlett,* Hachette, 1966; (co-author) *Illustrated Bi-Centennial History of the United States,* two volumes, U.S. News and World Report, 1973. Also author of *Jefferson's Empire: The Golden Age of the American West,* 1977.

* * *

CARVER, Raymond 1938-

PERSONAL: Born May 25, 1938, in Clatskanie, Ore.; son of Clevie Raymond (a laborer) and Ella (Casey) Carver; married Maryann Burk (a teacher), June 7, 1957; children: Christine L., Vance L. *Education:* Humboldt State College (now California State University, Humboldt), A.B., 1963; University of Iowa, further study, 1963-64. *Politics:* Democrat. *Home:* 1131 Henry Lane, McKinleyville, Calif. 95521. *Agent:* Paul R. Reynolds, Inc., 12 East 41st St., New York, N.Y. 10017. *Office:* University of California, Santa Cruz, Calif. 95060.

CAREER: Science Research Associates, Inc., Palo Alto, Calif., editor, 1967-70; University of California, Santa Cruz, lecturer in creative writing, 1971—; University of California, Berkeley, lecturer in fiction writing, 1972—. Visiting lecturer, Writers Workshop, University of Iowa, 1973-74. *Awards, honors:* National Endowment for the Arts Discovery Award for poetry, 1970; Joseph Henry Jackson Award for fiction, 1971; Wallace Stegner Creative Writing Fellowship, Stanford University, 1972-73; National Book Award nomination in fiction, 1977.

WRITINGS: Near Klamath (poems), Sacramento State College, 1968; *Winter Insomnia* (poems), Kayak, 1970; *Will*

You Please Be Quiet, Please? (short stories), McGraw, 1976; *At Night the Salmon Move* (poems), Capra, 1976; *Furious Seasons* (short stories), Capra, 1977. Work is represented in many anthologies, including *Best American Short Stories: 1967, Short Stories from the Literary Magazines, Best Little Magazine Fiction, 1970 and 1971, Prize Stories: The O. Henry Awards,* 1973, 1974, 1975, *Pushcart Prize Anthology,* 1976, and *New Voices in American Poetry.* Contributor of poems and stories to national periodicals, including *Esquire* and *Harper's,* and to literary journals. Editor, *Quarry* (magazine), 1971—.

WORK IN PROGRESS: Stories, poems, and a novel.

AVOCATIONAL INTERESTS: Travel.

* * *

CARY, Lucian 1886-1971

January 1, 1886—September 7, 1971; American novelist, short story writer, editor, and authority on guns. Obituaries: *New York Times,* September 9, 1971.

* * *

CASMIER, Adam A(nthony) 1934-

PERSONAL: Surname is pronounced *Kaz*-meer; born July 16, 1934, in New Orleans, La.; son of Marcel (a porter) and Ida (Theodore) Casmier; married Amelia Fields, November 30, 1957 (divorced, 1968); married Susan Bobrow (an associate professor of English), August 24, 1968; children: (first marriage) Michael, Brenda, Lynn, Stephen, Gail, John, Elizabeth; (second marriage) Elizabeth. *Education:* Xavier University of Louisiana, B.A., 1956; University of Notre Dame, M.A., 1957; St. Louis University, graduate student, 1960-64. *Home:* 7426 Stanford, St. Louis, Mo. 63130. *Office:* Department of English, Forest Park Community College, 5600 Oakland Ave., St. Louis, Mo. 63110.

CAREER: Forest Park Community College, St. Louis, Mo., instructor, 1964-66, assistant professor, 1966-68, associate professor of English, 1968—. *Member:* National Council of Teachers of English.

WRITINGS: (With Robert Bobrow) *Focus: Photographs for Composition,* Dickenson, 1970; (editor with Sally Souder) *Coming Together: Modern Stories by Black and White Americans,* Dickenson, 1972.

WORK IN PROGRESS: Editing *To Dispel Our Ignorance: Essays on Black Literature.*

SIDELIGHTS: Adam Casmier told *CA* that *Coming Together* "is the answer to racist short story anthologies. I believe that black material has to be incorporated into the entire college curriculum. I believe students have to be made aware of the nature of our racist society. *Coming Together* is a step in those directions."†

* * *

CASSELL, Frank A(llan) 1941-

PERSONAL: Surname sounds like "castle"; born February 23, 1941, in Hammond, Ind.; son of Frank Hyde (a professor) and Marguerite (Fletcher) Cassell; married Elizabeth Weber (a research analyst), April 1, 1961; children: David, Jonathan. *Education:* Wabash College, Crawfordsville, Ind., B.A., 1963; Northwestern University, M.A., 1966, Ph.D., 1968. *Home:* 4139 North Stowell, Shorewood, Wis. 53211. *Office:* Chapman Hall, University of Wisconsin, Milwaukee, Wis. 53201.

CAREER: University of Wisconsin—Milwaukee, assistant

professor, 1967-72, associate professor of history, 1972—, assistant chancellor, 1975—. *Member:* American Historical Association, Organization of American Historians, Southern Historical Association, Maryland Historical Society, Wisconsin Civil Liberties Union (chairman, Wisconsin affiliate, 1973). *Awards, honors:* Woodrow Wilson fellowship, 1963; William Henry Kiekhofer Memorial Teaching Award, University of Wisconsin, 1971; American Philosophical Society grant-in-aid, 1972; Fulbright lecturer in Japan, 1973-74.

WRITINGS: Merchant Congressman in the Young Republic: Samuel Smith of Maryland, 1752-1839, University of Wisconsin Press, 1972. Contributor of articles to *Maryland Historical Magazine, Military Affairs,* and *Journal of Negro History.*

WORK IN PROGRESS: Research for a political history of Baltimore from the Revolution to the War of 1812.

* * *

CASSELS, Alan 1929-

PERSONAL: Born February 20, 1929, in Liverpool, England; son of Alexander Grant and Emily M. (Parry) Cassels; married Nancy E. Gardner (a university lecturer), June 19, 1961; children: Celia P., Jennifer L. *Education:* Oxford University, B.A. (honors), 1952, M.A., 1956; University of Michigan, Ph.D., 1961. *Office:* Department of History, McMaster University, Hamilton, Ontario, Canada.

CAREER: Trinity College, Hartford, Conn., instructor in history, 1959-62; University of Pennsylvania, Philadelphia, assistant professor of history, 1962-67; McMaster University, Hamilton, Ontario, associate professor, 1967-71, professor of history, 1971—. Visiting lecturer, Sweet Briar College, 1956-57; visiting assistant professor, Haverford College, 1963-64. *Military service:* British Army, 1947-49. *Member:* American Historical Association, Society for Italian Historical Studies, Phi Beta Kappa. *Awards, honors:* Danforth summer research grant, 1961; essay prize from Society for Italian Historical Studies for article published in *Journal of Modern History,* 1962; Canada Council Leave fellowship, 1973-74.

WRITINGS: Fascist Italy, Crowell, 1968; *Mussolini's Early Diplomacy,* Princeton University Press, 1970; *Fascism,* Crowell, 1975; (contributor) *Reappraisals of Fascism,* Watts, 1975. Contributor to history journals. Contributing editor, *Handbook of World History,* Philosophical Library, 1968, and *Foreign Affairs 50-Year Bibliography,* Council on Foreign Relations, 1972.

WORK IN PROGRESS: Research on Britain and France between the two world wars.

* * *

CASSIDY, John A(lbert) 1908-

PERSONAL: Born April 5, 1908, in Sharon, Pa.; son of William Thomas (a locomotive engineer) and Mary A. (Broderick) Cassidy; married Margaret Byrd Shaw (a high school counselor), June 10, 1944; children: John Shaw. *Education:* Westminster College, New Wilmington, Pa., A.B., 1930; Western Reserve University (now Case Western Reserve University), M.A., 1947, Ph.D., 1950. *Politics:* Liberal. *Religion:* Episcopalian. *Home:* 1322 Longfellow Ave., South Bend, Ind. 46615. *Office:* Department of English, Indiana University at South Bend, 1825 Northside Blvd., South Bend, Ind. 46615.

CAREER: High school teacher of English in Sharon, Pa.,

1933-39; University of Notre Dame, South Bend, Ind., assistant professor of English, 1950-54; English teacher at South Bend (Ind.) community schools, 1954-57; Indiana University at South Bend, associate professor, 1957-64, professor of English, 1964—. Professional musician (has performed in major roles in numerous operas). *Military service:* U.S. Army Air Forces, 1942-46; became captain. *Member:* Modern Language Association of America, American Council of Learned Societies, College English Association, American Association of University Professors, Midwest Modern Language Association. *Awards, honors:* Summer research grant, Indiana University, 1963—.

WRITINGS: Algernon C. Swinburne, Twayne, 1964; *Robert W. Buchanan,* Twayne, 1972. Contributor to *Encyclopedia Americana;* contributor to literature journals.

WORK IN PROGRESS: A book on "fleshly controversy," between Buchanan and Swinburne; research on musical backgrounds of English literature.

SIDELIGHTS: John Cassidy told *CA:* "Biography has always fascinated me, especially as it is reflected in the writings of literary artists. I agree with Charles Sainte-Beuve that the more one knows of an artist's life, the better does he understand the artist's work." While in the military, Cassidy traveled through North and West Africa, Italy, Spain, Portugal, France, and Germany.

AVOCATIONAL INTERESTS: Golf, farming, travel.

* * *

CASTLE, Charles 1939-

PERSONAL: Born May 26, 1939; son of Alfred Howard and Rebecca (Rossouw) Castle. *Education:* Attended Witwatersrand Technical College, South Africa. *Religion:* Methodist. *Agent:* London Management, 235-241 Regent St., London W1A 2JT, England.

CAREER: Television director, producer; fashion and theatre designer; professional dancer on stage, in films, and on television. *Member:* Film Production Association of Great Britain, British Actors Equity, Writers Guild of Great Britain. *Awards, honors:* Received honorary degree in designing; Monte Carlo Festival award, and Hollywood TV Festival award.

WRITINGS: (With Diana Napier Tauber) *This Was Richard Tauber,* W. H. Allen, 1971; *Noel: Biography of Noel Coward,* W. H. Allen, 1977. Also author of scripts for radio series, "Boy Meets Girl."

WORK IN PROGRESS: A biography of Joan Crawford.

SIDELIGHTS: Charles Castle has traveled in Europe, Africa, Asia, and the Americas. He told *CA* that he has a "preference for art and music subjects—biographies on figures from those worlds. . . . I like the short stories of H. H. Munro (Saki) and Somerset Maugham, and the wit of Noel Coward. . . . " Castle's book, *This Was Richard Tauber* was produced on television by the British Broadcasting Corp.

AVOCATIONAL INTERESTS: Breeding Welsh mountain ponies, opera, ballet.

* * *

CASWELL, Helen (Rayburn) 1923-

PERSONAL: Born March 16, 1923, in Long Beach, Calif.; daughter of Odis Claude (a carpenter) and Helen (Kepner) Rayburn; married Dwight Allan Caswell (a research engineer), December 27, 1942; children: Dwight Allan, Jr.,

Philip Rayburn, Mary Helen, Christopher Edwards, John Albert. *Education:* Attended University of Oregon, 1940-42. *Religion:* Episcopalian. *Home:* 15095 Fruitvale Ave., Saratoga, Calif. 95070. *Agent:* Miss Norma Fryatt, Box 213, Manchester, Mass. 01944.

CAREER: Portrait painter, specializing in studies of children. *Member:* Society of Western Artists, Saratoga Contemporary Artists. *Awards, honors:* James D. Phelen Award for Narrative Poetry; San Francisco Browning Club award for dramatic monologue.

WRITINGS: Jesus, My Son, John Knox, 1962; *A Wind on the Road,* Van Nostrand, 1964; *A New Song for Christmas,* Van Nostrand, 1966; *Shadows from the Singing House,* Tuttle, 1968; *You Are More Wonderful,* C. R. Gibson, 1970; *Never Wed an Old Man,* Doubleday, 1975.

*   *   *

CAUDILL, Harry M(onroe)   1922-

PERSONAL: Born May 3, 1922, in Whitesburg, Ky.; son of Cro Carr and Martha V. (Blair) Caudill; married Anne Frye, December 15, 1949; children: James, Diane, Harry Frye. *Education:* University of Kentucky, B.L., 1948. *Politics:* Democrat. *Home address:* Box 727, Whitesburg, Ky. 41858. *Office:* Department of History, University of Kentucky, Lexington, Ky. 40506.

CAREER: Admitted to Bar of State of Kentucky, 1948; lawyer in private practice, 1948-76; University of Kentucky, Lexington, professor of Appalachian studies, 1977—. Member of Kentucky State legislature, 1954-60. Has presented lectures to numerous universities and colleges, and served on many conferences on public affairs throughout the U.S. *Military service:* U.S. Army, Infantry, World War II. *Member:* American Bar Association, Soil Conservation Society of America, Sierra Club, Audubon Society, Kentucky State Historical Society, Omicron Delta Kappa, Phi Delta Phi. *Awards, honors:* Friends of American Writers award of merit, 1963, for *Night Comes to the Cumberlands;* Kentucky Statesman award, 1968; Tom Wallace Forestry award, 1976, and others. Honorary degrees from Tusculum College, 1966, Berea College, 1971, and University of Kentucky, 1971.

WRITINGS: Night Comes to the Cumberlands: A Biography of a Depressed Area (American Library Association notable book selection), Atlantic-Little, Brown, 1963; *Dark Hills to Westward: The Saga of Jennie Wiley,* Atlantic-Little, Brown, 1969; *My Land Is Dying* (American Library Association notable book selection), Dutton, 1971; *The Senator from Slaughter County,* Atlantic, 1974; *A Darkness at Dawn,* University Press of Kentucky, 1976; *Watches of the Night* (American Library Association notable book selection), Atlantic, 1976. Contributor of articles to periodicals including *Senior Citizen, Reader's Digest, Inter-play, Intellectual Digest, Defenders of Wildlife,* and others.

SIDELIGHTS: In a review of *Dark Hills to Westward,* Madison Jones states: "Caudill has been at pains to present all the facts that can be ascertained. The potential for sheer narrative excitement implicit in the material is, of course, a built-in advantage; but, with a novelist's eye for detail and timing and proportion, he makes the most of his moments . . . [and] brings to the job not only considerable research but also the imagination able to animate his facts."

BIOGRAPHICAL/CRITICAL SOURCES: America, July 20, 1963; *New Republic,* July 20, 1963; *New York Herald Tribune Book Review,* July 21, 1963; *Saturday Review,*

August 31, 1963; *Book World,* July 13, 1969; *New York Times Book Review,* July 13, 1969.

*   *   *

CAWOOD, John W.   1931-

PERSONAL: Born April 8, 1931, in Tampa, Fla.; son of James Benson (a salesman) and Inez (Brewer) Cawood; married Patsy Lee Jernigan, September 2, 1951; children: Laura Lee, Jeffrey Scott. *Education:* Attended University of Miami, Coral Gables, Fla., 1949-51; King's College, Briarcliff Manor, N.Y., B.A., 1954; Dallas Theological Seminary, Th.M., 1957, Th.D., 1959. *Politics:* Republican. *Home:* 45 East Marthart Ave., Havertown, Pa. 19083. *Office:* Philadelphia College of Bible, Arch St., Philadelphia, Pa. 19103.

CAREER: Ordained independent minister, 1959; Miami Bible College, Miami, Fla., teacher and registrar, 1959-63; Calvary Church, Miami, youth director, 1959-63; Philadelphia College of Bible, Philadelphia, Pa., professor of Bible doctrine, 1963—. *Member:* Evangelical Theological Society, Association for Higher Education.

WRITINGS: The New Tongues Movement, Philadelphia College of Bible, 1965; *Let's Know the Bible,* Revell, 1971.

WORK IN PROGRESS: What God Says about Marriage.

*   *   *

CAZDEN, Robert E.   1930-

PERSONAL: Legally adopted original family name, 1948; born August 29, 1930, in New York, N.Y.; son of Paul (a physician) and Gertrude (Feldman) Cohen; married Joann Louise Cohn, January 16, 1958; children: David, Roger, Eugene. *Education:* University of California, Los Angeles, A.B., 1952; University of Southern California, M.A., 1954; University of California, Berkeley, M.L.S., 1955; University of Chicago, Ph.D., 1965. *Home:* 1245 Eldermere Rd., Lexington, Ky. 40502. *Office:* Department of Library Science, University of Kentucky, Lexington, Ky. 40506.

CAREER: Musician and musicologist in earlier years; librarian at University of California, Berkeley, 1955-57, and Oregon State University, Corvallis, 1959-65; University of Kentucky, Lexington, assistant professor, 1965-69, associate professor of library science, 1969—. *Member:* Printing Historical Society, Immigration History Society, Gutenberg Gesellschaft, Wolfenbuetteler Arbeitskreis fuer Geschichte des Buchwesens.

WRITINGS: German Exile Literature in America, 1933-50: A History of the Free German Press and Book Trade, American Library Association, 1970. Contributor of essays to *The German Contribution to the Building of the Americas: Studies in Honor of Karl J. R. Arndt,* Clark University Press, 1977 and *German-American Literature: An Introduction,* Scarecrow, 1977. Contributor to library and history journals.

WORK IN PROGRESS: A social history of the German book trade in America from the colonial period to the twentieth century.

*   *   *

CHAFFIN, Lillie D(orton)   1925-

PERSONAL: Surname is pronounced *Chay*-fin; born February 1, 1925, in Varney, Ky.; daughter of Kenis Roscoe and Fairy Belle (Kelley) Dorton; married Thomas W. Chaffin (self-employed in trucking), August 6, 1942; children:

Thomas Randall. *Education:* Attended University of Akron, 1951-52; Pikeville College, B.S., 1958; Eastern Kentucky University, M.A., 1971, additional study, 1971—. *Religion:* Baptist. *Address:* Box 42, Meta Station, Pikeville, Ky. 41501.

CAREER: Elementary teacher in Barberton, Ohio, 1957-52, and Pikeville, Ky., 1954-68; Kimper School, Kimper, Ky., librarian, 1968-72; Johns Creek High School, Pikeville, librarian, 1973-77; Pikeville College, Pikeville, writer-in-residence, 1973-77. Publisher and editor, Poetry Press, 1976-77. *Member:* National Federation of State Poetry Societies, Kentucky State Poetry Society, Kentucky State Pen Women (vice-president). *Awards, honors:* First prizes from National League of American Pen Women for *A Garden Is Good,* 1965, and *I Have a Tree,* 1972; International Poetry Prize, 1967, for *A Stone for Sisyphus;* Child Study Association award, 1971, for *John Henry McCoy;* named poet of the year, Alice Lloyd College, 1968; named outstanding alumna of year, Pikeville College, 1971.

WRITINGS: A Garden Is Good (juvenile nonfiction), Rand McNally, 1963; *Tommy's Big Problem* (juvenile fiction), Lantern Press, 1965; *Lines and Points* (poetry), Pikeville College, 1966; *A Stone for Sisyphus* (poetry), South and West, 1967; (with Marion Butwin) *America's First Ladies* (biography), two volumes, Lerner, 1969; *Bear Weather* (juvenile poetry), Macmillan, 1969; *I Have a Tree* (juvenile non-fiction), David White, 1969; *First Notes* (poetry), Golden Horseshoe, 1969; *In My Backyard* (juvenile poetry), Golden Horseshoe, 1970; (with R. Conrad Stein) *A World of Books* (autobiography), Childrens Press, 1970; *John Henry McCoy* (juvenile fiction), Macmillan, 1971; *Freeman* (juvenile fiction), Macmillan, 1972; *Coal: Energy and Crisis,* Harvey House, 1974; *Eighth Day Thirteenth Moon,* Pikeville College Press, 1975. Contributor of short stories, poems, and articles to *Child Life, Jack and Jill, Prairie Schooner, Lyric,* and more than two hundred other magazines and newspapers, adult and juvenile. Fiction editor, *Pen Woman,* 1970—. Poetry editor, *Twigs,* 1976-77.

WORK IN PROGRESS: Several projects, including an adult novel.

SIDELIGHTS: Lillie Chaffin told *CA:* "I am vitally concerned about stripmining and pollution of the air and water, about so many people's lack of concern for their fellowmen, about the involvement of children who are physically and mentally deprived by the inequities in our society, and by the failure among all of us in communicating our real needs and our emotions. I have tried to probe these feelings in my stories and poems."

AVOCATIONAL INTERESTS: Reading, drama and dramatic programs, art and music.

* * *

CHAKOUR, Charles M. 1929-

PERSONAL: Born September 10, 1929, in Worcester, Mass.; son of Mitchell G. (a machinist) and Adele (Kaffroonie) Chakour; married Genevieve Louise King (a teacher), March 23, 1951; children: Catherine, Deborah, James. *Education:* Union College, Barbourville, Ky., A.B., 1951; Garrett Theological Seminary, B.D., 1953; Northwestern University, additional study, 1953-55. *Home:* 854 Cherry Blossom Lane, Naperville, Ill. 60540.

CAREER: Pastor of United Methodist churches, 1954-70; Wesley United Methodist Church, Naperville, Ill., pastor, 1970—. Instructor in speech at Kendall College, 1954-55,

and Elmhurst College, 1955-56. Moderator of "Drumbeats" program, WJVM Radio, Sterling, Ill., 1966-70. Chairman of Joliet Commission on Human Rights, 1965-66; president of Whiteside County Mental Health Association, 1970.

WRITINGS: Brief Funeral Meditations, Abingdon, 1971. Contributor to religious journals. Religion editor and columnist, *Funeral Service Journal,* 1964-69.

* * *

CHALMERS, Harvey II 1890-1971

September 11, 1890—October 6, 1971; American industrialist and novelist. Obituaries: *New York Times,* October 8, 1971.

* * *

CHAMBERLAIN, Betty 1908-

PERSONAL: Born February 10, 1908, in East Orange, N.J.; daughter of John Payson and Elizabeth Jennings (Webster) Chamberlain; divorced. *Education:* Attended Columbia University, 1927-28; Smith College, A.B., 1929; Sorbonne, University of Paris, L. es lettres, 1934. *Politics:* "Democrat mostly." *Religion:* None. *Home:* Cornwall Bridge, Cornwall, Conn. 06754; and 342 East 65th St., New York, N.Y. 10021. *Office:* Art Information Center, Inc., 189 Lexington Ave., New York, N.Y. 10016.

CAREER: Librarian in public libraries in Mt. Vernon, N.Y., and New York City, 1924-28; Metropolitan Museum of Art, New York City, member of information staff and translator, 1929-32; translator, hostess for foreign guests, American Cyanamid Co., 1934-37; Works Project Administration (WPA), Philadelphia, Pa., editor, Historical Records Survey, 1938-39; Philadelphia Museum of Art, Philadelphia, librarian, 1939-40; Museum of Modern Art, New York City, assistant to the director and editor, 1940-42; *Time* (magazine), New York City, researcher and writer of art section, 1940-42, reporter on war labor, 1943-44; Office of War Information, Washington, D.C. and New York City, member of Domestic Graphics staff, 1942-43; U.S. Maritime Commission, Washington, D.C., liaison work in shipyard labor relations, 1944-45; an editor and head of production, *Magazine of Art,* 1945-48; Museum of Modern Art, director of publicity, 1948-54; *Art News* (published monthly), New York City, managing editor, 1954-56; Brooklyn Museum, Brooklyn, N.Y., director of publicity and community development, 1956-59; Betty Chamberlain Associates, New York City, president, 1959—. Director, Art Information Center, Inc. (non-profit organization), New York City, 1959—; R. R. Bowker Company, New York City, editor, *Who's Who in American Art,* 1969; Museum of American Folk Arts, New York City, member of advisory board; member of Mayor's Committee for New York Shakespeare Festival. Justice of the Peace, Cornwall, Conn. Member of Cornwall, Conn. Democratic Town Committee. *Member:* American Civil Liberties Union, Eastern Co-operative Association, American Museum Association. *Awards, honors:* National Endowment for the Arts grant, for Art Information Center, Inc., 1971 and 1973.

WRITINGS: The Artist's Guide to His Market, Watson-Guptill, 1970, enlarged and revised edition, 1975. Contributor to *American Artist;* author of art columns in Carnegie Hall and Lincoln Center programs. Former writer and editor for *Physicians' Forum.*

CHAMETZKY, Jules 1928-

PERSONAL: Born May 24, 1928, in Brooklyn, N.Y.; son of Benjamin and Anna (Zweig) Chametzky; married Anne Halley (a teacher and writer), February 21, 1953; children: Matthew, Robert, Peter. *Education:* Brooklyn College (now Brooklyn College of the City University of New York), B.A., 1950; University of Minnesota, M.A., 1952, Ph.D., 1958. *Home:* 244 Amity St., Amherst, Mass. 01002. *Office:* Department of English, University of Massachusetts, Amherst, Mass. 01002.

CAREER: University of Minnesota, Minneapolis, instructor in English, 1954-56; Boston University, Boston, Mass., instructor in humanities, 1956-58; University of Massachusetts, Amherst, assistant professor, 1959-64, associate professor, 1964-69, professor of English, 1969—, director, Study Center and Exchange Program in Freiburg, 1976-77. Visiting lecturer, University of Massachusetts, 1958-59; visiting professor, Free University of Berlin, 1970-71, Yale University, spring, 1976. *Member:* Modern Language Association of America, American Association of University Professors, American Studies Association, Coordinating Council of Literary Magazines (secretary of executive committee, 1967-72). *Awards, honors:* Fulbright professor, 1961-62, 1966-67; distinguished teacher, University of Massachusetts, 1969.

WRITINGS: (Editor with Sidney Kaplan) *Black and White in American Culture,* University of Massachusetts Press, 1969; *From the Ghetto: The Fiction of Abraham Cahan,* University of Massachusetts Press, 1977. Editor, *Faulkner Studies,* 1953-54; co-editor, *Massachusetts Review,* 1963-69, 1971-74.

*   *   *

CHAMPIGNY, Robert J(ean) 1922-

PERSONAL: Born September 30, 1922, in Chatellerault, France; son of Fernand (an accountant) and Albertine (Poussard) Champigny; married Myriam Cohen, October 25, 1948. *Education:* University of Poitiers, Lic. es Let., 1943; Ecole Normale Superieure, further study, 1943-47, Agrege, 1947; Sorbonne, University of Paris, D. es Let., 1956. *Office:* Department of French, Indiana University, Bloomington, Ind. 47401.

CAREER: Indiana University, Bloomington, instructor, 1950-53, assistant professor, 1953-56, associate professor, 1956-60, professor, 1960-64, research professor of French, 1964—. *Member:* Modern Language Association of America, American Association of Teachers of French. *Awards, honors:* Ford Foundation fellow, 1955-56; American Council of Learned Societies fellow, 1964-65; Palmes Academiques from Academie Francaise.

WRITINGS—Poetry: *Depot,* Seghers, 1952; *L'Intermonde,* Seghers, 1953; *Bruler,* Seghers, 1955; *Monde,* Seghers, 1960; *La Piste,* Regain (Monaco), 1964; *Horizon,* Regain, 1969; *Les Passes,* Saint-Germain-des-Pres, 1972; *L'Analyse,* Saint-Germain-des-Pres, 1974.

Other: *Portrait of a Symbolist Hero,* Indiana University Press, 1954; *Prose et Poesie,* Seghers, 1957; *Stages on Sartre's Way,* Indiana University Press, 1959; *Sur un heros paien,* Gallimard, 1959, translation by Rowe Portis published as *A Pagan Hero: An Interpretation of Meursault in Camus' "The Stranger,"* University of Pennsylvania Press, 1970; *Le Genre romanesque,* Regain, 1963; *Le Genre poetique,* Regain, 1963; *Le Genre dramatique,* Regain, 1965; *Pour une esthetique de l'essai,* Lettres Modernes, 1967; *La*

Mission, La Demeure, La Roue (epics), Saint-Germain-des-Pres, 1969; *Humanism and Human Racism,* Mouton, 1972; *Ontology of the Narrative,* Mouton, 1972; *Le Jeu philosophique,* Saint-Germain-des-Pres, 1976; *What Will Have Happened,* Indiana University Press, 1977.

BIOGRAPHICAL/CRITICAL SOURCES: Modern Language Journal, March, 1974; *Journal of Aesthetics and Art Criticism,* summer, 1975.

*   *   *

CHANEY, Otto Preston, Jr. 1931-

PERSONAL: Born February 16, 1931, in Concord, N.C.; son of Otto Preston and Anna (Soltis) Chaney; married Bridget Gillespie; children: David, Melissa. *Education:* Davidson College, B.S., 1953; Georgetown University, M.A., 1963; American University, Ph.D., 1969. *Religion:* Methodist. *Home and office:* American Embassy, Prague, Czechoslovakia.

CAREER: U.S. Army, regular officer, 1953—, with current rank of colonel; has served with U.S. Military Liaison Mission to Soviet Forces in East Germany, as intelligence estimates officer in Vietnam, and as Military Assistance Command Vietnam representative to Paris peace talks; intelligence analyst in the Department of the Army, Defense Intelligence Agency, and the Office of National Estimates, all Washington, D.C.; presently U.S. Army attache in Prague, Czechoslovakia. *Member:* American Military Institute, Pi Sigma Alpha, Pi Kappa Alpha. *Awards, honors*—Military: Bronze Star Medal, Meritorious Service Medal, Joint Service Commendation Medal with oak-leaf cluster. Other: Award from *Military Review,* 1969, for article, "Was It Surprise?"

WRITINGS: Zhukov, University of Oklahoma Press, 1971; *Marshal Georgi K. Zhukov,* Ballantine, 1974. Contributor to military journals.

SIDELIGHTS: Otto Chaney's books have been published in several languages including Dutch, Spanish, and Croatian.

*   *   *

CHANEY, William A(lbert) 1922-

PERSONAL: Born December 23, 1922, in Arcadia, Calif.; son of Horace Pierce and Esther (Bowen) Chaney. *Education:* University of California, Berkeley, A.B., 1943, Ph.D., 1961. *Religion:* Episcopalian. *Home:* 215 East Kimball St., Appleton, Wis. 54911. *Office:* Department of History, Lawrence University, Appleton, Wis. 54911.

CAREER: Harvard University, Cambridge, Mass., junior fellow of Society of Fellows, 1949-52; Lawrence University, Appleton, Wis., assistant professor, 1952-58, associate professor, 1958-62, George McKendree Steele Associate Professor of Western Culture, 1962-66, George McKendree Steele Professor of Western Culture, 1966—, chairman of department of history, 1967-71. Lecturer, Michigan State University, summer, 1958. *Member:* American Historical Association, Mediaeval Academy of America, American Society of Church History, Modern Language Association of America, Conference on British Studies, Archaeological Institute of America, American Association of University Professors. *Awards, honors:* American Council of Learned Societies grant, 1966-67.

WRITINGS: (Contributor) S. Thrupp, editor, *Early Medieval Society,* Appleton, 1967; *The Cult of Kingship in Anglo-Saxon England: The Transition from Paganism to*

Christianity, University of California Press, 1970. Contributor to encyclopedias and historical journals.

WORK IN PROGRESS: Medieval Kingship.

*   *   *

CHANNING, Steven A. 1940-

PERSONAL: Born December 18, 1940, in Brooklyn, N.Y.; married Rhoda Kramer (a librarian), August 31, 1963; children: Laura Hope. *Education:* Brooklyn College of the City University of New York, B.A., 1962; New York University, M.A., 1965; University of North Carolina at Chapel Hill, Ph.D., 1968. *Home:* 118 Dundee Dr., Lexington, Ky. 40503. *Office:* Department of History, University of Kentucky, Lexington, Ky.

CAREER: University of Kentucky, Lexington, assistant professor, 1968-71, associate professor of American history, 1972—. Senior postdoctoral research fellow, Institute of Southern History, Johns Hopkins University, 1971-72; visiting associate professor, Stanford University, 1972-73; Fulbright senior lecturer, University of Genova, Italy, 1977-78. *Member:* American Historical Association, Organizaton of American Historians, American Civil Liberties Union, Southern Historical Association. *Awards, honors:* Allen Nevins Award of Society of American Historians, 1968, for *Crisis of Fear;* research grants from American Philosophical Society and American Council of Learned Societies, 1971; research fellowships from American Council of Learned Societies, 1973-74 and Guggenheim Foundation, 1977.

WRITINGS: Crisis of Fear: Secession in South Carolina, Simon & Schuster, 1970; *Kentucky: A Bicentennial History,* Norton, 1977. Also author of *The Five Faces of Kentucky.* Contributor to *Biographical Encyclopedia of American History, Encyclopedia of Southern History, Biographical Directory of the Governors of the United States,* and *Reviews in American History.*

WORK IN PROGRESS: The Divided South: Race, Class, and Nation, 1860-1865, completion expected in 1979.

SIDELIGHTS: Steven Channing told *CA:* "I find my career as an historian deeply satisfying both as a teacher, a research scholar, and writer. As a college student I had hoped to write fiction, but chose American history instead because it seemed to fulfill my intellectual and artistic impulses better. I have also become interested in using television as a medium for historical expression . . . the study of history and its presentation to a concerned audience is a vital aspect of our cultural life."

*   *   *

CHAO, Kang 1929-

PERSONAL: Born March 23, 1929, in Harbin, China; son of Hsi-meng and Tie-lan (Chang) Chao; married Jessica Chung-yee Chen, February 18, 1956; children: Tonia, Constance. *Education:* Attended National Tsing Hua University, 1947-49; National Taiwan University, B.A., 1951; University of Michigan, M.A., 1957, Ph.D., 1962. *Home:* 6318 Woodington Way, Madison, Wis. 53711. *Office:* Department of Economics, University of Wisconsin, Madison, Wis. 53706.

CAREER: University of Rochester, Rochester, N.Y., assistant professor of economics, 1960-62; University of Michigan, Ann Arbor, assistant professor of economics, 1962-65; University of Wisconsin—Madison, assistant professor, 1966-67, associate professor, 1967-69, professor of economics, 1969—. Visiting assistant professor of economics, Uni-

versity of California, Berkeley, 1965-66. *Member:* American Economic Association, Association for Asian Studies.

WRITINGS: The Rate and Pattern of Industrial Growth in Communist China, University of Michigan Press, 1965; *The Construction Industry in Communist China,* Aldine, 1967; *Agricultural Production in Communist China, 1949-1965,* University of Wisconsin Press, 1970; *Capital Formation in Mainland China, 1952-1965,* University of California Press, 1974; *The Development of Cotton Textile Production in China,* Harvard University Press, 1977.

*   *   *

CHAPMAN, John 1900-1972

June 25, 1900—January 19, 1972; American drama critic and editor. Obituaries: *New York Times,* January 20, 1972; *Washington Post,* January 21, 1972; *Newsweek,* January 31, 1972; *Time,* January 31, 1972.

*   *   *

CHARD, Leslie F. II 1934-

PERSONAL: Born September 2, 1934, in Dunkirk, N.Y.; son of Leslie Frank and Sarah (Higham) Chard; married Anne Smith (a teacher), April 5, 1961 (divorced); children: Leslie F. III, Kathleen Mègan, Sarah Ellen. *Education:* Trinity College, Hartford, Conn., B.A., 1956, M.A., 1958; Duke University, Ph.D., 1962. *Home:* 3380 Bishop St., Cincinnati, Ohio 45220. *Office:* Department of English, University of Cincinnati, Cincinnati, Ohio 45221.

CAREER: Emory University, Atlanta, Ga., instructor, 1961-64, assistant professor of English, 1964-66; University of Cincinnati, Cincinnati, Ohio, associate professor, 1966-75, professor of English, 1975—. *Member:* American Society for Eighteenth-Century Studies, Modern Language Association of America, American Association of University Professors, Midwest Modern Language Association. *Awards, honors:* Frank Weil fellowship for research in religion and the humanities, 1967; Society for Health and Human Values fellowship, 1974.

WRITINGS: Dissenting Republican, Mouton, 1972. Contributor to professional journals.

WORK IN PROGRESS: An intellectual biography of publisher Joseph Johnson; an anthology of criticism of English, German, and French Romantic periods; *The City in Literature, 1770-1850.*

AVOCATIONAL INTERESTS: Tennis, gardening, travel, and studying England.

*   *   *

CHARLIP, Remy 1929-

PERSONAL: Surname is pronounced Shar-lip; born January 10, 1929, in Brooklyn, N.Y.; son of Max (a house painter) and Sarah (Fogel) Charlip. *Education:* Cooper Union, B.F.A.; studied at various times at Black Mountain College, Reed College, Juilliard School of Music, Merce Cunningham Studio, Connecticut College, and Art Students' League of New York. *Home:* 60 East Seventh St., New York, N.Y. 10003.

CAREER: Actor, dancer, choreographer, producer, stage director and designer; author and illustrator of children's books; also involved in experimental theater, conductor of drama workshops, stager of "happenings," and film maker. Choreographer and actor with original Living Theatre Company; member of Merce Cunningham Dance Company for eleven years; director, designer, actor, and dancer at American Place Theatre, Cafe La Mama, Open Theatre, Pocket Theatre, and other playhouses; founding member of children's theatre group, the Paper Bag Players and actor in first four original productions; director with Shirley Kaplan of children's theater at Sarah Lawrence College, 1967-71, and co-conductor of classes called "Workshop in Making Things Up" and "Inlets and Outlets"; toured with his own company in the series "Intermedia 68," sponsored by National Endowment for the Arts; director of "Biography," opening piece presented by National Theatre of the Deaf on tour, 1971-72; lecturer, workshop director, or consultant at School of Visual Arts, Penland School of Crafts, Radcliffe College, Washington State University, New School for Social Research, and other schools. Staged the opening of the Pepsi-Cola/EAT Pavilion at Expo '70 in Japan, using five hundred yards of China silk in a spectacle called "Hommage a Loie Fuller"; taught thirty librarians and staged the "Book Event: The Book Is Dead! Long Live the Book!" for a cultural festival in Caen, Normandy, 1972. Choreographer and director, London Contemporary Dance Theatre, 1972—; choreographer, Scottish Theatre Ballet, 1973, and Welsh Dance Theatre, 1974. Designer and developer with four other artists of a Black and Puerto Rican heritage museum in the Bronx, under grant from New York State Council of the Arts; member of advisory panel for Connecticut Commission on the Arts "Project Create," the Brooklyn Children's Museum "Muse," and Judson Poets' Theatre and Dance Theatre.

AWARDS, HONORS: Village Voice Obie Award for direction of "A Beautiful Day" at Judson Poets' Theatre, 1966; Boys' Clubs of America Gold Medal, jointly with Burton Supree, 1967, for *Mother, Mother, I Feel Sick, Send for the Doctor, Quick, Quick, Quick;* Yale University grant for work on "Writing with the Camera," 1968-69; *Arm in Arm* was selected by the *New York Times* as one of the ten best books of 1969 and received first prize at the Bologna Book Fair, 1971; two Gulbenkian Awards, 1972, for Scottish Theatre Ballet and London Contemporary Dance Theatre.

WRITINGS—Author and illustrator: *Dress Up and Let's Have a Party,* W. R. Scott, 1956; *Where Is Everybody?,* W. R. Scott, 1957; *It Looks Like Snow,* W. R. Scott, 1962; *Fortunately* (play), Parents' Magazine Press, 1964; *I Love You,* McGraw, 1967; *Arm in Arm: A Collection of Connections, Endless Tales, Reiterations, and Other Echolalia,* Parents' Magazine Press, 1969.

Author with Judith Martin, and illustrator: *The Tree Angel* (story and play), Knopf, 1961; *Jumping Beans,* Knopf, 1962.

Author with Burton Supree, and illustrator: *Mother, Mother, I Feel Sick, Send for the Doctor, Quick, Quick, Quick,* Parents' Magazine Press, 1966; *Harlequin and the Gift of Many Colors,* Parents' Magazine Press, 1973.

Author: (With George Ancona and Mary Beth) *Handtalk: An ABC of Finger Spelling and Sign Language,* Parents' Magazine Press, 1974; (with Jerry Joyner) *Thirteen,* Parents' Magazine Press, 1975; (with Lilian Moore) *Hooray for Me!,* Parents' Magazine Press, 1975; *What Good Luck, What Bad Luck,* Scholastic Book Services, 1977. Also author of four hour-long plays for Paper Bag Players, "Scraps," "Cut-Ups," "Group-Soup," and "Fortunately."

Illustrator: Margaret Wise Brown, *David's Little Indian,* W. R. Scott, 1956; Bernadine Cook, *The Curious Little Kitten,* W. R. Scott, 1956; Brown, *The Dead Bird,* W. R. Scott, 1958; Betty Miles, *What Is the World?,* Knopf, 1958; Ruth

Krauss, *A Moon or a Button,* Harper, 1959; Miles, *A Day of Summer,* Knopf, 1960; Miles, *A Day of Winter,* Knopf, 1961; Brown, *Four Fur Feet,* W. R. Scott, 1961; Sandol Stoddard Warburg, *My Very Own Special Particular Private and Personal Cat,* Houghton, 1963; Krauss, *What a Fine Day for . . . ,* Parents' Magazine Press, 1967; (with Demetra Maraslis) Jane Hyatt Yolen, *The Seeing Stick,* Crowell, 1977.

WORK IN PROGRESS: Making Things Up, based on teaching the use of personal material (things unique to the person) for the creation of original work, whether it be a play, book, dance, painting, or film.

SIDELIGHTS: "Remy Charlip has designed *Handtalk* with the same clarity, humor and refreshing good sense found in his other books," writes *New York Times Book Review* critic Cynthia Feldman. *Thirteen,* a picture book with short captions, was termed "a disappointment" by C. A. Cote, but a *Horn Book* reviewer writes: "*Thirteen* is not only original in its use of imagery, but it also suggests an entirely different approach to picture books. . . . The pictures do not illustrate a story, nor are they simply drawn as works of art; the images respond to each other—not to any verbal concept."

BIOGRAPHICAL/CRITICAL SOURCES: New York Times Book Review, November 9, 1969, May 5, 1974, May 4, 1975, October 5, 1975, November 16, 1975; *New York Times,* December 8, 1969, December 5, 1975; *Times Literary Supplement,* December 6, 1974; *School Library Journal,* May, 1975, December, 1975, September, 1977; *Christian Science Monitor,* May 7, 1975; *Horn Book,* April, 1976; *Language Arts,* May, 1976.†

*   *   *

CHASTEEN, Edgar R(ay) 1935-

PERSONAL: Born November 16, 1935, in Cleburne, Tex.; son of Marvin E. (a salesman) and Cora (Revier) Chasteen; married Bobbie Amos, April 19, 1957; children: Deborah, David, Brian. *Education:* Sam Houston State University, B.S., 1957, M.A., 1959; University of Missouri—Columbia, Ph.D., 1966. *Politics:* Independent. *Religion:* Baptist. *Home:* 1702 Magnolia, Liberty, Mo. 64068. *Office:* Department of Sociology, William Jewell College, Liberty, Mo. 64068.

CAREER: Southwestern State College, Weatherford, Okla., instructor in sociology, 1961-63; University of Missouri—Columbia, instructor in sociology, 1963-64; Institute for Community Studies, Kansas City, Mo., research associate, 1964-69; William Jewell College, Liberty, Mo., associate professor, 1965-71, professor of sociology, 1971—. Director, Ethnic Activities Center of Mid-America. Consultant to Co-operative Social Welfare Action Program, Kansas City, 1969-71, and Regional Educational Laboratory, Kansas City, 1972. *Member:* American Sociological Association, American Association for the Advancement of Science, Midwest Sociological Society, Missouri Society for Sociology and Anthropology (vice-president, 1970), Missouri Academy of Science (chairman for anthropology-sociology, 1973).

WRITINGS: The Case for Compulsory Birth Control, Prentice-Hall, 1971. Contributor of more than twenty articles to professional journals and national magazines.

WORK IN PROGRESS: Runner, an inspirational and motivational book; research on the church as an agent of ethnic cohesion; an introductory sociology text.

AVOCATIONAL INTERESTS: Touring North America in a camper-trailer.

* * *

CHATFIELD, Hale 1936-

PERSONAL: Born March 26, 1936, in Passaic, N.J.; son of Wilson Fritcher (in sales promotion) and Anne (Webster) Chatfield; married Denise Zadeik (an organist and music instructor), June 22, 1957; children: Stephen, Jennifer, Peter, Alexander. *Education:* Wesleyan University, Middletown, Conn., B.A., 1957; Rutgers University, A.M., 1963. *Home:* 13560 Old State Rd., Huntsburg, Ohio 44046. *Office:* Hiram College, Hiram, Ohio 44234.

CAREER: Olivetti-Underwood Corp., New York, N.Y., sales supervisor, 1963-64; Hiram College, Hiram, Ohio, instructor, 1964-66, assistant professor, 1967-72, associate professor, 1972—, dean of students, 1971-74. Co-chairman of literary advisory panel, Ohio Arts Council, 1968-72. *Military service:* U.S. Naval Reserve, 1957-60; became lieutenant. *Member:* American Association of University Professors. *Awards, honors:* National Endowment for the Humanities fellowship, 1975.

WRITINGS: The Young Country and Other Poems, privately printed, 1959; *Teeth* (poems), New/Books, 1968; (contributor) *Higher Education for the Disadvantaged,* Southern Illinois University Press, 1968; (editor with Eugene Redmond) Henry Dumas, *Poetry for My People,* Southern Illinois University Press, 1970; (editor with Redmond) Henry Dumas, *Ark of Bones and Other Stories,* Southern Illinois University Press, 1970; *At Home* (poems), Ashland Poetry Press, 1971; (with William Kloefkorn) *Voyages to the Land Sea VII,* University of Wisconsin—La Crosse, 1977; *Water Colors* (poems), Konglomerati Press, 1977; *What Color Are Your Eyes?* (poems), Juniper Press, in press. Work included in many anthologies, and published in *Antioch Review, Kenyon Review, Trace, Poetry Northwest, University Review, Mediterranean Review, Beloit Poetry Journal, San Francisco Review, Audit, Epos, Laurel Review,* and other journals. *Hiram Poetry Review,* founder and editor, 1967-75, contributing editor, 1975—.

WORK IN PROGRESS: Little Fictions, Loving Lies (stories and prose-poems), for Konglomerati Press; two novels and a book of poems.

BIOGRAPHICAL/CRITICAL SOURCES: Antioch Review, winter, 1962-63.

* * *

CHATHAM, James R(ay) 1931-

PERSONAL: Born November 11, 1931, in Caryville, Fla.; son of Clifton Lee and Sadie (McMinn) Chatham; married Nina McCoy, May 27, 1961; children: Nina Stephanie. *Education:* Florida State University, B.A., 1953, M.A., 1955, Ph.D., 1960; University of Madrid, graduate study, 1956-57. *Religion:* Episcopalian. *Home:* 605 Lakeview Dr., Starkville, Miss. 39759. *Office address:* Department of Foreign Languages, Mississippi State University, P.O. Drawer FL, State College, Miss. 39762.

CAREER: Mississippi State University, State College, instructor, 1957-59, associate professor of foreign languages, 1960-63; University of Alabama, University, associate professor of Romance languages, 1963-64; Mississippi State University, professor of foreign languages and head of the department, 1964—. *Military service:* U.S. Army, 1953-55. *Member:* Modern Language Association of America, Mediaeval Academy of America, American Association of Teachers of Spanish and Portuguese, American Council on the Teaching of Foreign Languages (member of board of directors, 1967-68), South Atlantic Modern Language Association, South Central Modern Language Association, Mississippi Modern Language Association (president, 1968-70), Phi Kappa Phi (president of Mississippi State University chapter).

WRITINGS: (With Enrique Ruiz-Fornells) *Dissertations in Hispanic Languages and Literatures: An Index of Dissertations Completed in the United States and Canada, 1876-1966,* University Press of Kentucky, 1970. Contributor to *Oelschlaeger Festschrift,* 1976; also contributor to *Hispania, Modern Language Journal, Romance Notes,* and *Revista de Estudios Hispanicos.*

* * *

CHAZANOF, William 1915-

PERSONAL: Surname is accented on first syllable; born August 23, 1915, in New York, N.Y.; son of Morris and Sara (Gold) Chazanof; married Helen Wohl (a teacher and reading specialist), June 22, 1941; children: Esther Chazanof Retish, Jansen Allen. *Education:* New York College for Teachers (now State University of New York at Albany), B.S., 1938; Columbia University, M.A., 1942; Syracuse University, Ph.D., 1956. *Politics:* Democrat. *Religion:* Jewish. *Home:* 41 Cottage St., Fredonia, N.Y. 14063. *Office:* Department of History, State University of New York College, 99 Washington Ave., Fredonia, N.Y. 14063.

CAREER: Teacher of social studies in junior high school in Kingston, N.Y., 1938-42; State University of New York College at Fredonia, associate professor, 1948-63, professor of social studies, 1963—, professor of history, 1966—. *Military service:* U.S. Army Air Forces, 1942-45; became sergeant; received five Bronze Star medals. *Member:* American Historical Association, Organization of American Historians, National Council for the Social Studies, American Association of University Professors, Senate Professional Association. *Awards, honors:* Named Distinguished Teaching Professor, State University of New York College at Fredonia.

WRITINGS: Joseph Ellicott and the Holland Land Company: The Opening of Western New York, Syracuse University Press, 1970; *Welch's Grape Juice: From Corporation to Co-operative,* Syracuse University Press, 1977.

* * *

CHEAVENS, (Sam) Frank 1905-

PERSONAL: Born June 15, 1905, in Torreon, Mexico; son of John Self (a minister) and Katherine (Herndon) Cheavens; married Lula Lee Fountain, September 3, 1929; children: John M. *Education:* Baylor University, B.A., 1927; University of Texas, Main University (now University of Texas at Austin), M.A., 1947, Ph.D., 1957. *Politics:* Democrat. *Home:* 2108 Miriam Lane, Arlington, Tex. 76010. *Office:* Psychology Department, University of Texas at Arlington, Arlington, Tex. 76010.

CAREER: Austin State School, Austin, Tex., psychologist, 1946-51; counselor in public schools in Austin, 1951-54; Austin Child Guidance Clinic, Austin, psychologist, 1954-57; University of Texas at Arlington, assistant professor, 1957-59, associate professor, 1959-61, professor of psychology and head of department, 1961—. Consultant to Hogg Foundation of Mental Health, University of Texas,

1950-60, U.S. Office of Economic Opportunity, and to numerous state and local mental health associations. *Member:* American Psychological Association, Texas Psychological Association, Texas Mental Health Association.

WRITINGS: Arrow Lie Still (novel), Story Book Press, 1951; *Leading Group Discussions,* Hogg Foundation of Mental Health, 1958; *Developing Discussion Leaders in Brief Workshops* (booklet), Hogg Foundation of Mental Health, 1963; *How to Stop Feeling Blue,* Fell, 1971; *Creative Parenthood: Advantages You Can Give Your Child,* Word Books, 1971; *They Were Better Parents after Group Discussion,* Sable Press, 1974; *Dandelion and Devil-Horse* (poems), Baylor University Press, 1975. Contributor of articles, stories, and poems to numerous magazines; outdoor editor, *Texas Parade Magazine,* 1950-55.

WORK IN PROGRESS: An historical novel on Alvar Nunez Cabeza de Vaca, first European to cross the North American continent.

AVOCATIONAL INTERESTS: Boating, swimming, and fishing.

*   *   *

CHENEY, Frances Neel   1906-

PERSONAL: Surname rhymes with "rainy"; born August 19, 1906, in Washington, D.C.; daughter of Thomas Meeks (a mechanical engineer) and Carrie (Tucker) Neel; married Brainard Cheney (a writer), June 21, 1928. *Education:* Vanderbilt University, B.A., 1928, graduate courses, 1930-36; George Peabody College for Teachers, B.S.L.S., 1934; University of Chicago, further graduate study, summer, 1937; Columbia University, M.S.L.S., 1940. *Religion:* Roman Catholic. *Home:* 112 Oak St., Smyrna, Tenn. 37167. *Office:* School of Library Science, George Peabody College for Teachers, Nashville, Tenn. 37203.

CAREER: Vanderbilt University, Nashville, Tenn., librarian in chemistry department, 1928-29, head of circulation department, 1929-30, head of reference department, 1930-37; Joint University Libraries, Nashville, head of reference department, 1937-43, 1945-46; Library of Congress, Washington, D.C., assistant to Chair of Poetry, 1943-44, bibliographer in General Reference and Bibliography Division, 1944-45; George Peabody College for Teachers, Nashville, part-time instructor, 1941-43, 1945, assistant professor, 1946-49, associate professor, 1949-67, professor of library science, 1967-75, professor emeritus, 1975—, acting director of Peabody Library School, 1956-58, associate director, 1960-75. Visiting professor, Japan Library School, Keio University, Tokyo, 1951-52.

MEMBER: American Library Association (member of council, 1954-68; member of executive board, 1956-61), American Society of Indexers, Association of American Library Schools (president, 1956-57), Bibliographical Society of America, Catholic Library Association (past chairman of Mid-South unit), Southeastern Library Association (president, 1960-62), Tennessee Library Association (president, 1946-47), Beta Phi Mu (past president). *Awards, honors:* Beta Phi Mu Good Teaching Award, 1959; Isadore Gilbert Mudge Citation, American Library Association, 1962, for distinguished contribution to reference librarianship; D. Litt., Marquette University, 1966; Outstanding Reference Librarian Award, Southeastern Library Association, 1970; Henry H. Hill Award, George Peabody College for Teachers, 1971, for excellence in teaching; Constance Lindsay Skinner Award, 1976.

WRITINGS: (Editor) *Sixty American Poets, 1886-1944,* preface and critical notes by Allan Tate, Library of Congress, 1944; (compiler) *Cartels, Combines and Trusts: A Selected and Annotated List of References,* Library of Congress, 1945; (co-editor) *The Classified List of Reference Books and Periodicals for College Libraries,* revised edition (Cheney not associated with earlier editions), Southern Association of Colleges and Secondary Schools, 1947; (contributor) *Great Human Issues of Our Times,* George Peabody College for Teachers, 1954; *Fundamental Reference Sources,* American Library Association, 1971.

Contributor to *Encyclopedia Americana* and *New International Yearbook;* contributor of about thirty articles and reviews to library journals. Editor of monthly review column, "Current Reference Books," in *Wilson Library Bulletin,* 1942-73; editor, *Tennessee Librarian,* 1949-51, 1953-56.

WORK IN PROGRESS: A new edition of *Fundamental Reference Sources.*

*   *   *

CHERNOFF, Goldie Taub   1909-

PERSONAL: Born May 8, 1909, in Austria; daughter of Morris and Pauline (Mahler) Taub; married David Chernoff; children: Richard Steinfeld. *Education:* Attended Pratt Institute, Cooper Union College, and Columbia University. *Politics:* "Humane." *Residence:* San Diego, Calif. *Mailing address:* c/o Scholastic Book Services, 50 West 44th St., New York, N.Y. 10036.

CAREER: Montefiore Hospital, Brooklyn, N.Y., occupational therapist, 1931-42; Jewish Sanitarium and Hospital, Brooklyn, director of occupational therapy and recreation, 1946-50; Sephardic Home for the Aged, Brooklyn, director of occupational therapy and recreation, 1951-56; Camp Fire Girls, Inc., New York, N.Y., arts and crafts specialist, 1956-71. Arts and crafts counselor at summer camps, 1929-33, 1955. Director, Children's Camp Program, Pine Park Hotel and Camp, 1946. *Member:* National Council of Jewish Women (group leader in recreation, Brooklyn section).

WRITINGS—All juveniles: Just a Box?, Scholastic Book Services, 1971, hardcover edition, Walker & Co., 1973; *Puppet Party,* Scholastic Book Services, 1971, hardcover edition, Walker & Co., 1972; *Pebbles and Pods: A Book of Nature Crafts,* Walker & Co., 1973; *Clay-Dough, Play-Dough,* Walker & Co., 1974; *Easy Costumes You Don't Have to Sew,* Scholastic Book Services, 1977. Member of editorial staff, *Sephardic News, Camp Fire Girl,* and *Program Headlights.*

SIDELIGHTS: Goldie Taub Chernoff has organized public transportation and anti-pollution action programs and has testified at public hearings in New York City, Charlotte, North Carolina, and San Diego, California.

*   *   *

CHERRINGTON, Ernest H(urst), Jr.   1909-

PERSONAL: Born September 10, 1909, in Westerville, Ohio; son of Ernest Hurst (a writer and editor) and Betty Clifford (Denny) Cherrington; married Ann McAfee Naylor, June 25, 1933; children: Robert Naylor, Ernest Hurst III (died, 1971). *Education:* Ohio Wesleyan University, B.A. (magna cum laude), 1931, M.S., 1932; University of California, Berkeley, Ph.D., 1935. *Religion:* Presbyterian. *Home:* Jefferson Blvd., Braddock Heights, Md. 21714.

CAREER: University of California, Lick Observatory, Mount Hamilton, research fellow, 1933-35, Alexander F.

Morrison research fellow, 1935; Syracuse University, Syracuse, N.Y., instructor in mathematics and astronomy, 1935-36; Perkins Observatory, Delaware, Ohio, assistant astronomer, 1935-46; Ohio State University, Columbus, and Ohio Wesleyan University, Delaware, instructor, 1936-40, assistant professor of astronomy, 1940-46; Centenary College of Louisiana, Shreveport, associate professor of physics and astronomy, 1946-47, professor of physics and astronomy, 1947-48, assistant dean of college, 1946-47, dean, 1947-48, head of department of physics and astronomy, 1946-48; University of Akron, Akron, Ohio, professor of astronomy, 1948-67, dean of Buchtel College of Arts and Sciences, 1948-60, director of graduate studies, 1955-60, dean of Graduate Division, 1960-67; Hood College, Williams Observatory, Frederick, Md., professor of astronomy, 1967-75. Member of advisory board for *Handbook of Tables for Mathematics* and *Standard Mathematical Tables*, 1965—. *Military service:* U.S. Army Air Forces, 1942-46; became major.

MEMBER: American Astronomical Society, American Institute of Physics, Royal Astronomical Society of Canada, Astronomical Society of the Pacific, Phi Beta Kappa, Sigma Xi, Omicron Delta Kappa, Sigma Pi Sigma, Pi Mu Epsilon, Pi Kappa Delta.

WRITINGS: Exploring the Moon through Binoculars (Book-of-the-Month Club selection), McGraw, 1969. Contributor of more than a hundred monographs, technical papers, and popular articles on astronomy and higher education to professional and popular journals.

WORK IN PROGRESS: Exploring the Heavens through Binoculars and Telescopes, an extensive guide to stellar objects which can be explored through binoculars or a small telescope.

* * *

CHERRINGTON, Leon G.   1926-

PERSONAL: Born June 29, 1926, in Vinita, Okla.; son of Leon Harold (a restaurant owner) and Bessie (Chanton) Cherrington; married Joan Tilbury, June 13, 1945; children: Jodie, Chris Ann, Grant, Todd. *Education:* Oklahoma Baptist University, B.A., 1958; University of Oklahoma, M.A., 1962; further graduate study at University of Kansas, summer, 1963, and University of North Carolina, summer, 1969. *Politics:* Democrat. *Religion:* Christian. *Home address:* Box 874, Fayetteville, W.Va. 25840.

CAREER: Federal Civil Service employee in Vinita and Oklahoma City, Okla., 1946-54; teacher of history and Latin at public schools in Kermit, Tex., 1960-64; Oklahoma College of Liberal Arts (now University of Science and Arts of Oklahoma), Chickasha, teacher of history and interdisciplinary studies, beginning 1966. *Military service:* U.S. Army Air Forces, 1944-46. *Member:* National Education Association, Oklahoma Education Association. *Awards, honors:* Education Professions Development Act scholarship, 1969.

WRITINGS: (Author with Richard W. Massa and others) *Contemporary Man in World Society: A Syllabus and Introductory Reader,* McCutchan, 1969; (editor with Massa) *Philosophical Man: Selected Readings,* McCutchan, 1969; (editor with Massa) *Aesthetic Man: His Contemporary Values,* McCutchan, 1969; (editor with Massa) *Inquisitive Man: His Quest for Freedom and Identity,* McCutchan, 1969.†

* * *

CHESTER, Alfred   1929(?)-1971

1929(?)—July 27(?), 1971; American novelist, short story writer, and reviewer. Obituaries: *New York Times,* August 2, 1971.

* * *

CHEVALIER, Maurice   1888-1972

September 12, 1888—January 1, 1972; French showman and actor. Obituaries: *New York Times,* January 2, 1972; *Washington Post,* January 2, 1972; *Sunday News* (Detroit), January 2, 1972; *Newsweek,* January 10, 1972; *Time,* January 10, 1972.

* * *

CHEW, Allen F.   1924-

PERSONAL: Born August 8, 1924, in McKeesport, Pa.; son of Joseph Thompson and Charlotte Mary (Kline) Chew; married Irene Hans, July 12, 1950; children: Cynthia, Cathlene, Clifford. *Education:* Attended College of William and Mary, 1946-47; George Washington University, B.A., 1949, M.A., 1950; Georgetown University, Ph.D., 1960. *Home:* 2102 Essex Lane, Colorado Springs, Colo. 80909. *Office:* Department of History, University of Colorado, Colorado Springs, Colo.

CAREER: U.S. Army enlisted service, 1943-45, served in European Theatre; U.S. Air Force Reserve, career officer, 1950-69, served as intelligence officer in the United States and Europe, 1950-64, served as associate professor of Russian history at U.S. Air Force Academy, Colorado Springs, Colo., 1964-69, retired as lieutenant colonel; University of Wisconsin—Oshkosh, professor of history and chairman of department, 1971-74. Part-time teacher of Russian history in University of Maryland Overseas Program, 1961-64, and University of Colorado at Colorado Springs, 1976—. *Member:* American Association for the Advancement of Slavic Studies, Phi Beta Kappa, National Association for Retarded Citizens. *Awards, honors*—Military: ETO Service Medal with five bronze stars and one bronze arrowhead. Other: Freedoms Foundation award, 1956.

WRITINGS: An Atlas of Russian History, Yale University Press, 1967, revised edition, 1970; *The White Death: The Epic of the Soviet-Finnish Winter War,* Michigan State University Press, 1971.

SIDELIGHTS: Allen F. Chew told *CA:* "Although I received advance royalties and a formal contract from a Finnish publisher for *The White Death* in 1972, political considerations make it unlikely that the Finnish language edition will ever be published. This is indicative of the unfortunate position of Finland."

* * *

CHIN, Frank (Chew, Jr.)   1940-
(Francisco de Menton)

PERSONAL: Born February 25, 1940, in Berkeley, Calif.; son of Frank Chew and Lilac Bowe Yoke (Quan) Chin; divorced; children: Elizabeth, Gabriel Jackson. *Education:* Attended University of California, Berkeley, 1958-61, and State University of Iowa, 1961-63; University of California, Santa Barbara, B.A., 1965. *Home:* 330 Union St., San Francisco, Calif. 94133. *Agent:* Dorothea Oppenheimer, 866 United Nations Plaza, New York, N.Y. 10017.

CAREER: Western Pacific Railroad Co., Oakland, Calif., clerk, 1962-65; Southern Pacific Railroad, Oakland, brakeman, 1966; King Broadcasting Co., Seattle, Wash., production writer, story editor and writer, 1966-69; free-lance consultant and lecturer on Chinese-America and racism, 1969-

70. Part-time lecturer in Asian-American studies, University of California, Davis, and San Francisco State College (now University), 1969-70; lecturer in creative writing, University of California, Berkeley, 1972. Film consultant, Western Washington State College (now Western Washington University), 1969-70. Artistic director, Asian American Theater workshop, 1976—. *Awards, honors:* Joseph Henry Jackson Award, 1965, for unpublished novel "A Chinese Lady Dies"; James T. Phelan Award in short fiction, 1966; East-West Players Playwriting award, 1971, for "The Chickencoop Chinaman"; Rockefeller playwrights grant, 1974; National Endowment for the Arts creative writing grant, 1974.

WRITINGS: (Editor with others) *Aiiieeeee! an Anthology of Asian-American Writers,* Howard University Press, 1974.

Film scripts: "S.R.T. Act Two," produced in Seattle, by KING-TV, December, 1966; "The Bel Canto Carols," Crown Station Productions, 1966; "A Man and His Music," Crown Station Productions, 1967; "Ed Sierer's New Zealand," Crown Station Productions, 1967; "Searfair Preview," Crown Station Productions, 1967; "The Year of the Ram," Crown Station Productions, 1967; "And Still Champion . . . !," Crown Station Productions, 1967; "The Report," Crown Station Productions, 1967; "Mary," King Screen Productions, 1969; "Rainlight Rainvision," King Screen Productions, 1969; "Chinaman's Chance," produced by WNET-TV in New York, N.Y., November 16, 1971.

Plays: "The Chickencoop Chinaman," first staged in New York at American Place Theatre, June, 1972; "The Year of the Dragon," first produced in New York at American Place Theatre, 1974, televised on "Theatre in America" series, PBS-TV, 1975. Also author of play "Gee, Pop! . . . A Real Cartoon."

Work represented in anthologies, including: *The Young American Writers,* edited by Richard Kostelanetz, Funk, 1967; *19 Necromancers from Now,* edited by Ishmael Reed, Doubleday, 1970; *The Urban Reader,* edited by Susan Cahill and Michele Cooper, Prentice-Hall, 1971; *Asian-American Authors,* edited by Kaiyu Hsu, Houghton, 1972. Contributor of articles and reviews to *Seattle, Ramparts, Intellectual Digest,* and *New York Times.* Editor, *Yardbird Reader,* Volume III.

WORK IN PROGRESS: A Chinese-American resources project; *Charlie Chan on Main,* a novel; *El Chino,* a novel; "Shopping Bags," an opera.

SIDELIGHTS: Reviewing *Aiiieeeee!,* Robert Coles praises the selections' tone of "wry, thoughtful detachment, even in the face of hardship and misery."

Chin told *CA:* "America is illiterate in, hostile to, deadset against the Chinese-American sensibility. I don't like that. Nothing but racist polemics have been written about us, from the 19th century missionaries to Tom Wolfe. Nothing but lies that have, through long acceptance, become the sick racist truths of America's collective unconscious coocoo. I don't like that. . . . And all my writing . . . is Chinaman backtalk. Unlike the white creation Charlie Chan, I say 'I' and 'we'."

BIOGRAPHICAL/CRITICAL SOURCES: Cue, June 17, 1972; *New York,* June 26, 1972; *Variety,* June 28, 1972; *New Yorker,* June 2, 1975; *Pacific Historical Review,* November, 1975.

*   *   *

CHINN, William G.   1919-

PERSONAL: Born May 26, 1919, in San Francisco, Calif.; son of Chong Dung and Helen (Leong) Chinn; married Grace Q. Wong, December 20, 1947; children: Lenore, Kevin. *Education:* University of California, Berkeley, A.B., 1941, M.A., 1956. *Home:* 539 29th Ave., San Francisco, Calif. 94121. *Office:* Department of Mathematics, City College of San Francisco, 50 Phelan Ave., San Francisco, Calif. 94112.

CAREER: San Francisco Unified Schools, San Francisco, Calif., teacher of mathematics, 1947-61, supervisor, 1961-65; Stanford University, Stanford, Calif., project coordinator of School Mathematics Study Group, 1965-67; City College of San Francisco, San Francisco, teacher of mathematics, 1967—. Member, United States Commission on Mathematical Instruction, 1973-77. *Military service:* U.S. Army Air Forces, 1942-46, became first lieutenant. *Member:* American Mathematical Society, Mathematical Association of America, National Council of Teachers of Mathematics, California Mathematics Council. *Awards, honors:* Fellowships from Crown-Zellerbach Foundation, 1955, National Science Foundation and American Association for the Advancement of Science, 1958 and 1959.

WRITINGS: (With others) *Intermediate Mathematics,* School Mathematics Study Group, 1961; (with others) *First Course in Algebra,* School Mathematics Study Group, 1963, revised edition, 1965; (with others) *A Brief Course in Mathematics for Elementary School Teachers,* School Mathematics Study Group, 1963; *Mathematics for the Elementary Schools,* Book K, School Mathematics Study Group, 1965, revised edition, 1966; (with others) *Mathematics for the Elementary Schools,* Book L, School Mathematics Study Group, 1965, revised edition, 1966; (with Norman E. Steenrod) *First Concepts of Topology,* Random House, 1966; (with Dolciani, Wooton, and Beckenbach) *Modern School Mathematics, 7,* Houghton, 1967; (with others) *Developing Mathematics Readiness in Preschool Programs,* School Mathematics Study Group, 1967; (with others) *Secondary School Mathematics,* three volumes, School Mathematics Study Group, 1968-71; (with Florence D. Jacobson) *Elementary Functions,* Silver Burdett, 1968; (with Philip J. Davis) *3.1416 and All That,* Simon & Schuster, 1969; (with Dolciani, Wooton, and Beckenbach) *Modern School Mathematics, 1, Pre-Algebra,* Houghton, 1970; (with David W. Blakeslee) *Introductory Statistics and Probability: A Basis for Decision Making,* Houghton, 1971; (with Tracewell and Dean) *Arithmetic and Calculators,* W. H. Freeman, 1978. Contributor to *Radiology Journal, Nation's Schools, American Scientist, Bulletin of the California Mathematics Council,* and other publications. Member of editorial panel, "New Mathematical Library," 1961-67, 1976—. Contributing editor, Scholastic Magazines, 1963-65; member of national board, *TYC Math Journal.*

*   *   *

CHISHOLM, Roger K.   1937-

PERSONAL: Born November 17, 1937, in Oak Park, Ill.; son of Alexander R. (a consultant) and Myrtle (Hahn) Chisholm; married Jean Clifford, July 15, 1961; children: Margaret Jean, Janet Elaine, Elizabeth Ann. *Education:* University of Illinois, B.S., 1959; Iowa State University, M.S., 1960; University of Chicago, Ph.D., 1967. *Religion:* Presbyterian. *Office:* Department of Economics, Memphis State University, Memphis, Tenn. 38152.

CAREER: University of Kansas, Lawrence, assistant professor of economics, 1964-65; Northwestern University, Evanston, Ill., assistant professor of managerial economics,

1965-71; Memphis State University, Memphis, Tenn., associate professor of economics, 1971—. *Member:* American Economic Association, American Agricultural Economic Association, American Society for the Study of the Grants Economy, Public Choice Society, Midwest Economic Association, Western Economic Association, Midsouth Academy of Economists.

WRITINGS: (With G. R. Whitaker, Jr.) *Forecasting Methods,* Irwin, 1971; (editor with M. F. Tuite and Michael Radnor) *Interorganizational Decision Making,* Aldine, 1972; (with M. H. McCarthy) *Economics,* Scott, Foresman, 1978.

* * *

CHOATE, J(ulian) E(rnest, Jr.) 1916-

PERSONAL: Born February 27, 1916, in Wingo, Ky.; son of Julian Ernest and Emily Margaret (Creed) Choate; married Florence Marie Jones, March 2, 1934; children: Jerry Jones, Emily Teresa. *Education:* Attended Freed-Hardeman College, 1938-40; Murray State University, B.S., 1942; George Peabody College, M.A., 1948; Vanderbilt University, Ph.D., 1954, B.D., 1958. *Politics:* Democrat. *Home:* 3714 Belmont Blvd., Nashville, Tenn. 37215. *Office:* Department of Philosophy, David Lipscomb College, Nashville, Tenn. 37203.

CAREER: Ordained minister of Church of Christ, 1938; Water Valley Junior High School, Water Valley, Ky., principal, 1942-43; Wingo High School, Wingo, Ky., teacher, 1943-44; Gleason High School, Gleason, Tenn., principal, 1944-46; David Lipscomb College, Nashville, Tenn., 1946—, began as instructor, professor of philosophy, 1954—.

WRITINGS: The American Cowboy: The Myth and the Reality, University of Oklahoma Press, 1954; *I'll Stand on the Rock: A Biography of H. Leo Boles,* Gospel Advocate, 1965; *Roll Jordan Roll: A Biography of Marshall Keeble,* Gospel Advocate, 1968; *The Anchor That Holds: A Biography of Benton Cordell Goodpasture,* Gospel Advocate, 1972. Staff writer, *Gospel Advocate.*

WORK IN PROGRESS: A sequel to *The American Cowboy.*

* * *

CHORON, Jacques 1904-1972

January 8, 1904—March 30, 1972; Russian-born American philosopher, educator, and authority on suicide. Obituaries: *New York Times,* March 31, 1972; *Washington Post,* April 1, 1972. (See index for *CA* sketch)

* * *

CHRISTENSEN, Otto H(enry) 1898-

PERSONAL: Born March 25, 1898, in Mahtowa, Minn.; son of Christ (a farmer) and Dorothy Christensen; married Dorothy Kocher (a dietitian consultant), June 30, 1925; children: Bruce Vincent, Ilene Louise (Mrs. Donald Caster). *Education:* Union College and University, Lincoln, Neb., B.A., 1938; Seventh-day Adventist Theological Seminary, M.A., 1945; University of Chicago, Ph.D., 1951. *Religion:* Seventh-day Adventist. *Home and office address:* R.R. 2, Spring City, Tenn. 37381.

CAREER: Pioneer missionary to Mongolia, 1931-38; Cha-Sui Mission, China, director, 1938-40; pastoral worker for conferences in Michigan and Illinois, 1941-47; Emmanuel

Missionary College (now Andrews University), Berrien Springs, Mich., professor of biblical languages, 1947-55, 1963-64; Southern Missionary College, Collegedale, Tenn., chairman of division of religion, 1955-63; Oakwood College, Huntsville, Ala., professor of biblical languages, 1964-65; Andrews University, Berrien Springs, seminary librarian, 1966-67. *Member:* National Society of Biblical Literature, American Schools of Oriental Research, National Association of Professors of Hebrew (former member of advisory board).

WRITINGS—All published by Review & Herald: (Editor with F. D. Nichols) *Seventh-day Adventist Bible Commentary,* Volume II: *Joshua,* 1954; (with others) *Problems in Translation,* 1954; *Getting Acquainted with God,* 1970; *Mission Mongolia,* 1974. Contributor to *Youth's Instructor, Advent Review and Sabbath Herald, Ministry,* and *Still Waters.*

SIDELIGHTS: Otto Christensen has traveled widely in Asia, Europe, Middle East, South America, and Australia. He speaks Chinese, Mongolian, Swedish, Danish, and Norwegian, and has reading competence in Greek, Hebrew, Syriac, Aramaic, German, French, and Spanish.

* * *

CHRISTIAN, Henry A(rthur) 1931-

PERSONAL: Born August 22, 1931, in Jersey City, N.J.; son of Henry Arthur (a physician) and Anne V. (Kotyuka) Christian; married Ann L. Quinn, 1951; children: Carolyn, Judith, Peter. *Education:* Yale University, B.A., 1953, M.A., 1954; Brown University, Ph.D., 1967. *Home:* 435 Wyoming Ave., Millburn, N.J. 07041. *Office:* Department of English, Rutgers University, Newark, N.J. 07102.

CAREER: Hopkins Grammar School, New Haven, Conn., instructor in English, 1954-58; Yale University, New Haven, assistant director, American studies for foreign students, 1955; Fulbright lecturer in Denmark, 1958-59; Rutgers University, Newark, N.J., instructor, 1962-67, assistant professor, 1967-72, associate professor of English, 1972—, chairman of department, 1975-78, director of Program in American Studies, 1974-77. Member of Fulbright Regional Interviewing Committee, State of Connecticut, 1959-61, State of New Jersey, 1962—. Millburn Short Hills Volunteer First Aid Squad, trustee, 1968-71, crew chief, 1968-76, president, 1975—. *Member:* Modern Language Association of America, American Studies Association, Immigration History Group of American Historical Association, British-American Alumni Association of English Speaking Union (founding committee). *Awards, honors:* Citation from U.S. Department of State, 1959, and U.S. Department of Health, Education, and Welfare, Teacher Exchange Section, 1971.

WRITINGS: (Editor) *Louis Adamic: A Checklist,* Kent State University Press, 1971. Contributor of articles to *Fulbright Monitor, Twentieth Century Literature, Fitzgerald Newsletter, Princeton University Library Chronicle, Menckeniana, Journal of General Education, Papers in Slovene Studies, Modern Language Studies, Zbornik Obcine Grosuplje,* and *Nasi razgledi* (Slovenia, Yugoslavia).

WORK IN PROGRESS: A biography of Louis Adamic, expected completion date, 1978; research on Upton Sinclair, Frank Lloyd Wright, and other American figures in literature, art, and architecture.

SIDELIGHTS: Henry A. Christian told *CA* that his primary field is American civilization and he is "interested in literary style and artistic design and the interrelationships therein. I believe in publishing research that is primarily new and otherwise untouched. I believe biography is the key to the truth of the twentieth century in America, about which we have said much but really know little decade by decade, especially in respect to the 1930's. I received my early research and writing training from the late Hemingway scholar, Charles A. Fenton; my faith in scholars from Hyatt H. Waggoner.''

*   *   *

CHRISTINE, Charles T(hornton) 1936-

PERSONAL: Born February 21, 1936, in Philadelphia, Pa.; son of Charles L. (an auto mechanic) and Mildred (Thornton) Christine; married Dorothy W. Weaver, August 22, 1961; children: Charles Weaver. *Education:* Temple University, B.S. (cum laude), 1962; Ohio University, M.Ed., 1964; Ohio State University, Ph.D., 1971. *Politics:* Republican. *Religion:* Lutheran. *Home:* 1071 Laurence Dr., Blue Bell, Pa. 19422. *Office:* Montgomery County Intermediate Unit, Blue Bell, Pa. 19422.

CAREER: School teacher in Ardsley, N.Y., 1964-67; school principal in Newark, Ohio, 1967-70; Old Mill Lane School, Wilmington, Del., principal, 1971-76; Montgomery County School District, Intermediate Unit, Blue Bell, Pa., assistant director of non-public school services, 1976—. Lecturer, Ohio State University, 1969. *Military service:* U.S. Air Force, 1953-58; became lieutenant. U.S. Air Force Reserve, 1958—; present rank, lieutenant colonel. *Member:* National Association of Elementary School Principals, International Reading Association, Delaware Association of School Administrators, Phi Delta Kappa, Psi Chi, Sword Society.

WRITINGS: (Contributor) James A. Banks and William Joyce, editors, *Teaching Social Studies to Culturally Different Children*, Addison-Wesley, 1970; (with wife, Dorothy Weaver Christine) *A Practical Guide to Curriculum and Instruction*, Parker Publishing, 1971. Contributor to *Journal of Psychological Studies, Elementary School Journal, Grade Teacher, National Elementary Principal*, and other publications.

WORK IN PROGRESS: Research in educational theory, philosophical analysis of major statements on educational practice; research in learning disabilities.

*   *   *

CHRISTINE, Dorothy Weaver 1934-

PERSONAL: Born May 12, 1934, in Philadelphia, Pa.; daughter of Francis (an insurance clerk) and Gladys (Shreiner) Weaver; married Charles T. Christine (a school principal), August 22, 1961; children: Charles Weaver. *Education:* West Chester State College, B.S., 1956; Ohio University, M.Ed., 1964; Ohio State University, graduate study, 1969-71. *Politics:* Republican. *Religion:* Lutheran. *Home:* 1071 Laurence Dr., Blue Bell, Pa. 19422.

CAREER: Formerly employed as school teacher and school psychologist. *Member:* Kappa Delta Pi.

WRITINGS: (Contributor) James A. Banks and William Joyce, editors, *Teaching Social Studies to Culturally Different Children*, Addison-Wesley, 1970; (with husband, Charles T. Christine) *A Practical Guide to Curriculum and Instruction*, Parker Publishing, 1971. Contributor to *Journal of Psychological Studies, Elementary School Journal*, and *Grade Teacher.*

WORK IN PROGRESS: Physiological-psychological study of learning disabled children.

*   *   *

CHUBB, Thomas Caldecot 1899-1972

November 1, 1899—March 22, 1972; American reviewer, journalist, poet, and biographer. Obituaries: *New York Times,* March 22, 1972; *Washington Post,* March 23, 1972. (See index for *CA* sketch)

*   *   *

CHUNG, Kyung Cho 1921-
(Kyong-Jo Chong)

PERSONAL: Born November 13, 1921, in Seoul, Korea; son of Yang Soon (a businessman) and Byung Ok (Peng) Chung; married Yo K. Sa, October 10, 1958. *Education:* Waseda University, B.A., 1944; Seoul National University, A.B., 1947; New York University, M.A., 1951. *Home:* 2023 South Carmel Hills Dr., Carmel, Calif. 93921. *Office address:* P.O. Box 834, Presidio of Monterey, Calif. 93940.

CAREER: U.S. Defense Language Institute, Monterey, Calif., professor of foreign languages, 1951—. Honorary professor, Kunkuk University; advisor, Korean-American Foundation. *Member:* Korean Research Council (director), American Association of University Professors, American Association for Asian Studies, South Carmel Hills Home-Owners Association (president). *Awards, honors:* D.L., Pusan National University, 1965; D.Litt., Sungkyunkwan University, 1968.

WRITINGS: Korea Tomorrow: Land of Morning Calm, Macmillan, 1957; *New Korea: New Land of the Morning Calm*, Macmillan, 1962; *Naeil Hankuk* (title means ''Korea Tomorrow''), Yulu Culture Co., 1965; *Sae Hankuk* (title means ''New Korea''), Samjungdang Co., 1968; *Korea: The Third Republic*, Macmillan, 1971. Editor, *Korean Research Bulletin.*

WORK IN PROGRESS: A book on Korean unification, *One Korea*, completion expected in 1978.

*   *   *

CHURCH, Richard 1893-1972

March 26, 1893—March 4, 1972; English poet, novelist, editor, and literary critic. Obituaries: *New York Times,* March 5, 1972; *Time,* March 20, 1972. (See index for *CA* sketch)

*   *   *

CHYET, Stanley F. 1931-

PERSONAL: Surname rhymes with *buy*-it; born April 2, 1931, in Boston, Mass.; son of Jacob M. (a telegrapher) and Beatrice L. (Miller) Chyet; married Geraldine A. Hyman, June 17, 1956; children: Michael Lewisohn, Susan Elise. *Education:* Brandeis University, B.A., 1952; Hebrew Union College—Jewish Institute of Religion, B.H.L., 1954, M.A.H.L. and Rabbi, 1957, Ph.D., 1960. *Office:* Hebrew Union College—Jewish Institute of Religion, 3077 University Mall, Los Angeles, Calif. 90007.

CAREER: Hebrew Union College—Jewish Institute of Religion, Cincinnati, Ohio, assistant professor, 1962-65, associate professor, 1965-69, professor of American Jewish history, 1969-76; staff member, American Jewish Archives, 1960-66, associate director, 1966-76; Hebrew Union College—Jewish Institute of Religion, Los Angeles, Calif., professor of Jewish history, 1976—. *Military service:* U.S.

Army Reserve, chaplain, 1957-60; became first lieutenant. *Member:* American Jewish Historical Society, Central Conference of American Rabbis, Jewish Publication Society of America, Labor Zionist Organization of America.

WRITINGS: Lopez of Newport, Wayne State University Press, 1970; *Lives and Voices,* Jewish Publication Society, 1972; (with J. R. Marcus) *Historical Essay on the Colony of Surinam, 1788,* American Jewish Archives-Ktav, 1974; (with J. Gutmann) *Moses Jacob Ezekiel: Memoirs from the Baths of Diocletian,* Wayne State University, 1975. Associate editor, *American Jewish Archives,* 1966-76.

*   *   *

CLARDY, J(esse) V. 1929-

PERSONAL: Born February 15, 1929, in Olney, Tex.; son of Jesse Ellis and Tiny Clardy. *Education:* Texas College of Arts and Industries (now Texas A & I University), B.S. and M.S., 1951; University of Michigan, Ph.D., 1961. *Politics:* Republican. *Home:* 1004 Broad St., Warrensburg, Mo. 64093. *Office:* University of Missouri, Kansas City, Mo.

CAREER: University of Missouri, Kansas City, professor of Slavic studies, 1964—. *Military service:* U.S. Army. *Member:* Association for the Advancement of Slavic Studies.

WRITINGS: Philosophical Ideas of Alexander Radishchev, Twayne, 1964; *G. R. Derzavin: A Political Biography,* Mouton, 1967, Humanities, 1968. Contributor to journals, including *Slavonic Review.*

WORK IN PROGRESS: The Superfluous Man in Russian Letters.

SIDELIGHTS: J. V. Clardy has traveled in the Soviet Union several times, and has made a study of the schools there. He is especially interested in "how the Russians detect and handle bright students . . . [and] in their using older students to teach younger ones."

*   *   *

CLARIZIO, Harvey F(rank) 1934-

PERSONAL: Born July 23, 1934, in St. Paul, Minn.; son of Edward and Agnes (Pothen) Clarizio; married Donna Ekdahl, August 21, 1959; children: Michael, Suzanne, Mark, Julie. *Education:* College of St. Thomas, B.A., 1956; University of Minnesota, M.A., 1958, S.Ed., 1959; University of Illinois, Ed.D., 1966. *Home:* 236 Maplewood Dr., East Lansing, Mich. 48823. *Office:* Department of Educational Psychology, Michigan State University, East Lansing, Mich. 48823.

CAREER: Department of Parks and Recreation, St. Paul, Minn., director of recreation center, 1956-58; Cambridge State Hospital, Cambridge, Minn., clinical psychologist, 1958; Loyola Child Guidance Center, Chicago, Ill., psychologist, 1959; Champaign Public Schools, Champaign, Ill., school psychologist, 1960-63; University of Illinois at Urbana–Champaign, assistant professor of special education, 1964-66; Michigan State University, East Lansing, assistant professor, 1966-69, associate professor, 1969-73, professor of educational psychology, 1973—. *Member:* American Psychological Association, Society for Research in Child Development.

WRITINGS: (Compiler and editor) *Mental Health and the Educative Process: Selected Readings,* Rand McNally, 1969; (with George F. McCoy) *Behavior Disorders in School-Aged Children,* Chandler Publishing, 1970, 2nd edi-

tion published as *Behavior Disorders in Children,* Crowell, 1976; (with others) *Contemporary Issues in Educational Psychology,* Allyn & Bacon, 1970, 3rd edition, 1977; *Toward Positive Classroom Discipline,* Wiley, 1971, 2nd edition, 1976; *Educational Psychology,* Wiley, 1972; (with Robert Craig and William Mehrens) *Contemporary Educational Psychology: Concepts, Issues, Applications,* Wiley, 1975. Contributor to education journals.

*   *   *

CLARK, C. E. Frazer, Jr. 1925-

PERSONAL: Born August 26, 1925, in Detroit, Mich.; son of C. E. Frazer (an educator) and Lucy (Huffman) Clark; married Margaret Swanson, August 7, 1953; children: C. E. Frazer III, Douglass Alexander. *Education:* Kenyon College, B.A., 1951; Wayne State University, M.A., 1956. *Home:* 1700 Lone Pine Rd., Bloomfield Hills, Mich. 48013. *Office:* Paramarketing, Inc., 1565 Woodward Ave., Bloomfield Hills, Mich. 48013.

CAREER: Florez, Inc., Detroit, Mich., account executive, 1952-63; Jam Handy Organization, Detroit, account executive, 1964-66; Paramarketing, Inc., Bloomfield Hills, Mich., founder, partner, and president, 1967—; Bruccoli Clark Publishers, Bloomfield Hills and Columbia, S.C., co-founder and partner, 1969—. Director of Parasciences, Bloomfield Hills, and John Henderson, Inc., Detroit. Member of board of governors, Clements Library. *Member:* American Antiquarian Society, Modern Language Association of America, Society for Applied Anthropology (fellow), National Hawthorne Society (co-founder and president), Bibliographical Society of America, Sons of the Whiskey Rebellion, Grolier Club, Pittsburgh Bibliophiles, Friends of Leland Township Public Library, Friends of Detroit Public Library (president), Prismatic Club, Book Club of Detroit.

WRITINGS—All published by Gale, except as indicated: (Compiler) *Checklist of Nathaniel Hawthorne,* C. E. Merrill, 1969; (editor) *Love Letters of Nathaniel Hawthorne,* Information Handling Service, 1972; (compiler) *Hawthorne at Auction, 1894-1971,* 1972; (compiler with Matthew J. Bruccoli) *Hemingway at Auction, 1930-1973,* 1973; (managing editor) *Pages,* 1976; (editor) *Nathaniel Hawthorne: A Descriptive Bibliography,* University of Pittsburgh Press, 1977.

Series: (Managing editor) "Conversations" series, Volume I: *Conversations with Writers,* 1977, Volume II: *Conversations with Jazz Musicians,* 1977, Volume III: *Conversations with Writers II,* 1978; (editor with Bruccoli, Richard Layman, and Benjamin Franklin V) "First Printings of American Authors" series, four volumes, 1978; (managing editor) "Dictionary of Literary Biography" series, Volume I: *American Renaissance in New England,* edited by Joel Myerson, 1978, Volume II: *American Novelists since World War II,* edited by Jeffrey Helterman, 1978. Editor with Bruccoli, *Fitzgerald/Hemingway Annual,* 1969—; editor, *Nathaniel Hawthorne Journal,* 1971—.

WORK IN PROGRESS: Volume V of "First Printings of American Authors" series.

SIDELIGHTS: "Clark owns the most valuable private library in Detroit and, according to prestigious bookworld sources, one of the most notable single-author collections put together in this country in recent years," explains Patricia Chargot of the *Detroit Free Press.* For years C. E. Frazer Clark has been collecting works by and about Nathaniel Hawthorne. Totaling some 30,000 pieces, his collection includes first printings and reprints of books and articles, letters, manuscripts, critical studies, and books, including 289 different printings of *The Scarlet Letter.* Clark first became interested in collecting rare books in his graduate school days at Wayne State University. In an old book store near the campus he found a first edition of *The Scarlet Letter* signed by Hawthorne. He paid for it by giving the owner of the book store a dollar a week for forty-five weeks. Clark explains his further involvement in book collecting: "Then I worked as [the book store owner's] apprentice and became an instant, collector. I started small, buying ephemera. Eventually, I was faced with going back and filling in holes. When Hawthorne material became scarce, I chose Hemingway as a second interest, and collected his works seriously for seven years. But the material became so expensive, I just couldn't do it." In 1975 Clark sold his Hemingway collection to the University of Maryland so that he could invest even more in Hawthorne material. During his search for works authored by Hawthorne, Clark came across a letter which revealed that Hawthorne wanted to start a newspaper with his college classmate Henry Wadsworth Longfellow, a fact not known at the time. This find resulted in Clark publishing his first book. He reports, "I then began to discover I have a responsibility, as a collector, first to scholarship."

Clark has mounted exhibits from his collection in Liverpool, England, where he was the guest of the Lord Mayor of Liverpool, in Paris, France, at the Grolier Club in New York, Kent State University and various other colleges, universities, and organizations.

BIOGRAPHICAL/CRITICAL SOURCES: Detroit Free Press, June 1, 1975; *Detroit News,* November 28, 1976, April 4, 1977; *New York Times,* May 22, 1977.

* * *

CLARK, Kenneth B(ancroft)   1914-

PERSONAL: Born July 24, 1914, in Panama Canal Zone; son of Arthur Bancroft and Miriam (Hanson) Clark; married Mamie Phipps (a psychologist), April 14, 1938; children: Kate Miriam (Mrs. Donald Harris), Hilton Bancroft. *Education:* Howard University, B.A., 1935, M.A., 1936; Columbia University, Ph.D., 1940. *Religion:* Episcopalian. *Residence:* Hastings-on-Hudson, N.Y. *Office:* Clark, Phipps, Clark & Harris, Inc., 60 East 86th St., New York, N.Y. 10028.

CAREER: Hampton Institute, Hampton, Va., assistant professor of psychology, 1940-41; U.S. Office of War Information, Washington, D.C., assistant social science analyst, 1941-42; City College of the City University of New York, New York, N.Y., instructor, 1942-49, assistant professor, beginning 1949, professor, 1960-70, distinguished professor of psychology, 1970-75, professor emeritus, 1975—. Visiting professor at Columbia University, summer, 1955, University of California, Berkeley, summer, 1958, and Harvard University, summer, 1965. Research director, Northside Center for Child Development, 1946-66; founder and chairman of board of directors, Harlem Youth Opportunities Unlimited (HARYOU), 1962-64; president, Metropolitan Applied Research Center, Inc. (MARC Corp.), 1967-75; president, Clark, Phipps, Clark & Harris, 1975—. Social science consultant, National Association for the Advancement of Colored People, 1950—; member of Committee on Foreign Affairs Personnel, U.S. Department of State, 1961-62. Member of board of directors of Harper & Row, Lincoln Savings Bank, and Presidential Life Insurance; former member of board of directors, New York State Urban De-

velopment Corp. Member, New York State Board of Regents, 1966—; trustee, University of Chicago.

MEMBER: American Psychological Association (fellow; president, 1970-71), American Association for the Advancement of Science (president, 1970-71), Society for the Psychological Study of Social Issues (president, 1949-50), Phi Beta Kappa, Sigma Xi. *Awards, honors:* Rosenwald fellow, 1940-41; Spingarn Medal, National Association for the Advancement of Colored People, 1961; Kurt Lewin Memorial Award, Society for the Psychological Study of Social Issues, 1966. Honorary degrees from Amherst College, Columbia University, Haverford College, Yeshiva University, Oberlin College, Johns Hopkins University, New York University, Princeton University, University of Massachusetts, Lincoln University, Morgan State University, Carnegie-Mellon University, and others.

WRITINGS: Prejudice and Your Child, Beacon Press, 1955, 2nd edition enlarged, 1963; (with Lawrence Plotkin) *The Negro Student at Integrated Colleges,* National Scholarship Service and Fund for Negro Students, 1963; *The Negro Protest: James Baldwin, Malcolm X, Martin Luther King Talk with Kenneth B. Clark,* Beacon Press, 1963; *Dark Ghetto: Dilemmas of Social Power,* foreword by Gunnar Myrdal, Harper, 1965; *Social and Economic Implications of Integration in the Public Schools* (pamphlet condensed from seminar on manpower policy and program), U.S. Department of Labor, 1965; (editor with Talcott Parsons) *The Negro American,* foreword by President Lyndon B. Johnson, Houghton, 1966; (with Jeannette Hopkins) *A Relevant War against Poverty: A Study of Community Action Programs and Observable Change,* Metropolitan Applied Research Center, 1968, Harper, 1969; (with Harold Howe) *Racism and American Education: A Dialogue and Agenda for Action,* Harper, 1970; (editor with Meyer Weinberg) *W. E. B. Du Bois: A Reader,* Harper, 1970; (editor) Allen W. Trelease, *White Terror: The Ku Klux Klan Conspiracy and Southern Reconstruction,* Harper, 1971; *Pathos of Power,* Harper, 1974; *Beyond the Ghetto,* Harper, in press. Contributor to journals.

SIDELIGHTS: Kenneth B. Clark's studies on the psychological effects of racism were cited by the U.S. Supreme Court in its landmark school desegregation decision of 1954. As a founder of HARYOU, Clark developed several concepts which became important measures in the national anti-poverty program of the 1960's. His book *Dark Ghetto* is regarded by many as a classic.

Although Maurice Carroll found *Pathos of Power* "murky" and "pretentious," *Newsweek*'s Margo Jefferson hailed it as "a reasoned and angry meditation" on the ill uses of power. She goes on to say that "Clark is a master at deflating bureaucratic and intellectual sophistries."

BIOGRAPHICAL/CRITICAL SOURCES: Best Sellers, July 1, 1974; *Wall Street Journal,* July 11, 1974; *Newsweek,* July 29, 1974; *America,* August 24, 1974; *New York Times,* September 28, 1974; *Virginia Quarterly Review,* fall, 1974.

* * *

CLARK, Marjorie A.   1911-

PERSONAL: Born July 15, 1911, in Poole, Dorsetshire, England; daughter of A. Walter and Agnes Rigler; married J.A.G. Clark, December 29, 1943 (deceased); children: James D. *Education:* Attended high school and commercial school in Courtenay, British Columbia, Canada and Multnomah School of Bible, one year. *Religion:* Evangelical. *Home:* R.R. 1, Comox, British Columbia, Canada V9N 5N1.

CAREER: Stenographer for Royal Bank of Canada, Courtenay, British Columbia, for seven years; Christian Missions in Many Lands, missionary in Portugal and Africa, 1939-42; British Consulate, Angola, Portuguese West Africa, clerk, 1943-44; Courtenay-Comox Argus, Courtenay, clerk and writer, 1947-52; Moody Institute of Science, Los Angeles, Calif., writer, 1956-65; Success with Youth, Inc., Phoenix, Ariz., free-lance writer, 1958-77. Sunday School teacher and counselor and cook in Christian camps for many years.

WRITINGS: African Holiday, Pickering & Inglis, 1954; (with Edith Holden) *Seaview Adventures,* Pickering & Inglis, 1956; *The Link,* Augustana Press, 1956; *The Silent Search,* Moody, 1971; *Captive on the Ho Chi Minh Trail,* Moody, 1974; *Party Fun for Junior,* Moody, 1976. Writer of films and filmstrips; contributor of serials, short stories, and articles to magazines, mostly evangelical.

* * *

CLARK, Walter Van Tilburg 1909-1971

August 3, 1909—November 10, 1971; American novelist, short story writer, and educator. Obituaries: *New York Times,* November 12, 1971; *Washington Post,* November 12, 1971; *Newsweek,* November 22, 1971; *Time,* November 22, 1971; *Publishers Weekly,* November 29, 1971. (See index for *CA* sketch)

* * *

CLARK, William A(rthur) 1931-
(Bill Clark)

PERSONAL: Born August 14, 1931, in Geneva, N.Y.; son of Henry George and Ella (Steward) Clark; married Charlotte Ann Jobe (a free-lance photographer), April 30, 1966; children: Cynthia Lynn, Catherine Suzanne, Leonard Jobe. *Education:* Syracuse University, B.A., 1953. *Politics:* Independent. *Religion:* Episcopalian. *Residence:* Waterford Township, Mich. *Office: Detroit News,* 615 Lafayette Blvd., Detroit, Mich. 48231.

CAREER: Geneva Times, Geneva, N.Y., sports editor, 1954-56; *Syracuse Herald Journal,* Syracuse, N.Y., sports writer, 1956-64; reporter for *Winston-Salem Journal,* Winston-Salem, N.C., 1964-65, and *Dayton Daily News,* Dayton, Ohio, 1965-69; D. J. Edelman, Inc., New York, N.Y., public relations account executive, 1970; *Harrisburg Patriot News,* Harrisburg, Pa., writer and copy editor, 1970-72; *Palm Beach Post,* West Palm Beach, Fla., feature writer, 1972-73; *Detroit News,* Detroit, Mich., writer, 1973-75, assistant city editor, 1975—. *Awards, honors:* Award for best feature on bowling, *Bowling* (magazine), 1958; Dutton Sports Story Award for best news feature story, 1961, for "It Ended in Silence"; American Auto Racing Writers and Broadcasters Association Award for best feature on auto racing, 1967; second place for best general news feature, Ohio Associated Press, 1967; Edgar Allan Poe Special Award, true crime category, Mystery Writers of America, 1971, for *The Girl on the Volkswagen Floor;* Michigan Associated Press Editorial Association award for newswriting, 1973.

WRITINGS: The Girl on the Volkswagen Floor, Harper, 1971. "It Ended in Silence," written under name Bill Clark, was included in Dutton's *Best Sports Stories of 1961* and *Best Sports Stories 1945-65.*

WORK IN PROGRESS: Researching another book.

AVOCATIONAL INTERESTS: History (especially modern European), religion, politics, and transportation.

CLAYTON, John 1892-

PERSONAL: Born December 1, 1892, in Tosten, Mont.; son of Heber and Rebecca (Keener) Clayton; married Helena Mullart, February 19, 1920; children: Evan Dale (deceased), Rodrick K. *Education:* Attended Occidental College. *Home:* 1844 Lincoln Ave., Chicago, Ill. 60614.

CAREER: Chicago Tribune, Chicago, Ill., foreign correspondent, 1919-28; public relations director and publisher, 1928-39; Edward H. Weiss & Co., Chicago, advertising executive and writer, 1939-63. *Military service:* U.S. Army Air Service, 1917-19. U.S. Army Air Forces, 1942-46. U.S. Air Force, 1951-52.

WRITINGS: (Compiler and contributor) *Illinois Fact Book and Historical Almanac 1763-1968,* Southern Illinois University Press, 1970. Also composer of an opera, "Soldiers in the Underworld."

WORK IN PROGRESS: Working on a collection of over fifty songs; composing a sonata.

* * *

CLEAVES, Emery N(udd) 1902-

PERSONAL: Born May 16, 1902, in North Scituate, Mass.; son of Arthur W. (a clergyman) and Mary E. (Nudd) Cleaves; married Ione Marie Page, August 17, 1924; children: Nancy W. (Mrs. C. Meriweather Blaydes). *Education:* Harvard University, B.S., 1923. *Politics:* Independent Republican. *Religion:* Baptist. *Home:* 1123 Round Hill Rd., Fairfield, Conn. 06430. *Office:* Farley Manning Associates, 342 Madison Ave., New York, N.Y. 10017.

CAREER: Worked for New York Life Insurance Co., Boston, Mass., 1922-25, and John Price Jones Corp., New York City, 1925-29; Interstate Button Co., New York City, president, 1929-38; Robert Heller & Associates (management engineers), Cleveland, Ohio, staff member, 1940-42; Celanese Corp. of America, New York City, vice-president in charge of public relations, 1946-59, vice-president of Celanese Development Co. of New York City, 1959-64; Farley Manning Associates (formerly P.R. Counsel), New York City, financial and corporate public relations, 1964—. *Military service:* U.S. Naval Reserve, active duty, 1942-46; became commander. *Member:* Harvard Club of New York.

WRITINGS: Plenty of Searoom: A Yankee Boyhood, Houghton, 1970; *Sea Fever: The Making of a Sailor,* Houghton, 1972.

* * *

CLINEBELL, Howard J., Jr. 1922-

PERSONAL: Born June 3, 1922, in Springfield, Ill.; son of Howard J. and Clem (Whittenberg) Clinebell; married Charlotte Holt (a social worker and psychotherapist); children: John H., Donald R., Susan E. *Education:* DePauw University, B.A. (cum laude), 1944; Garrett Theological Seminary, B.D. (summa cum laude), 1947; William A. White Institute of Psychiatry, Certificate in Applied Psychiatry for the Ministry, 1949; Columbia University, Ph.D., 1954; University of Pennsylvania, additional study, 1967-68. *Home:* 1408 Ashland Ave., Claremont, Calif. 91711. *Office:* School of Theology at Claremont, 1325 North College Ave., Claremont, Calif. 91711.

CAREER: Received clinical pastoral training in New York State hospitals, 1947-48, 1956-57; pastor of Method st churches in Indiana, Illinois, and New York, 1943-57; minister of counseling at church in Pasadena, Calif., 1957-59;

Methodist Hospital, Arcadia, Calif., chaplain, 1958-59; New York University, New York, N.Y., lecturer in religious education, 1955-57; School of Theology at Claremont, Calif., professor of pastoral counseling, 1959—; Claremont Graduate School, Claremont, faculty member in departments of psychology and religion, 1968—. Director of Pasadena Area Pastoral Counseling Center, 1959-63, and Claremont Area Pastoral Counseling Center, 1963-65; clinical director, Pomona Valley Pastoral Counseling and Growth Centers, 1976-78. Member, National Task Force on Religious Support Systems for Commission on Mental Health, 1977—.

MEMBER: International Association of Group Psychotherapy, American Association of Pastoral Counselors (diplomate president, 1964-65), American Association of Marriage Counselors (fellow), American Orthopsychiatric Association (fellow), American Society of Group Psychotherapy and Psychodrama, National Council on Family Relations, Society for the Scientific Study of Religion, Association for Humanistic Psychology, Phi Beta Kappa. *Awards, honors:* National Institute of Mental Health and American Association of Theological Schools grant, 1966-67; Outstanding Educators of America award, 1974; American Association of Pastoral Counselors distinguished contribution award, 1974.

WRITINGS: Understanding and Counseling the Alcoholic through Religion and Psychology, Abingdon, 1956, revised edition, 1968; *Mental Health through Christian Community,* Abingdon, 1965; *Understanding Alcoholism* (booklet), General Board of Christian Social Concern, Methodist Church, 1965; *Basic Types of Pastoral Counseling,* Abingdon, 1966; *The Pastor and Drug Dependency* (booklet), National Council of Churches, 1968; (with Harvey Seifiert) *Personal Growth and Social Change,* Westminster, 1969.

(With wife, Charlotte H. Clinebell) *The Intimate Marriage,* Harper, 1970; (editor) *Community Mental Health: The Role of Churches and Temples,* Abingdon, 1970; (with wife, Charlotte H. Clinebell) *Crisis and Growth: Helping Your Troubled Child,* Fortress, 1971; *The People Dynamic: Changing Self and Society through Growth Groups,* Harper, 1972; *The Mental Health Ministry of the Local Church,* Abingdon, 1972; *Growth Counseling for Marriage Enrichment, Pre-Marriage and the Early Years,* Fortress, 1975; *Growth Counseling for Mid-Years Couples,* Fortress, 1977; *Growth Groups,* Abingdon, 1977.

Contributor: Raymond G. McCarthy, editor, *Drinking and Intoxication,* Free Press, 1959; R. J. Catanzaro, editor, *Alcoholism: The Total Treatment Approach,* C. C Thomas, 1967; Raban Hathorn, William Genne, and Mordecai Brill, editors, *Marriage: An Interfaith Guide for All Couples,* Association Press, 1970; R. C. Leslie and E. H. Mudd, editors, *Professional Growth for Clergymen,* Abingdon, 1970; H. A. Otto, editor, *Marriage and Family Enrichment,* Abingdon, 1976; E. V. Stein, editor *Fathering: Fact or Fable?,* Abingdon, 1977. Editor, "Creative Pastoral Care and Counseling" series, ten volumes, Fortress, 1975—. Contributor of about forty articles to professional journals. Member of editorial advisory board, *Journal of Pastoral Care,* 1966—, *Pastoral Psychology,* 1968—.

WORK IN PROGRESS: Research on growth counseling; seven more volumes for "Creative Pastoral Care and Counseling" series.

SIDELIGHTS: Howard Clinebell told *CA,* "Through my writings on growth counseling, I hope to help counselors and psychotherapists to move away from pathology-centered methods and toward hope-centered human potentials approaches." Clinebell has lectured and conducted workshops in Alaska, Japan, Singapore, India, England, the Philippines, Sweden, Fiji, New Zealand, Tonga, Iceland, Norway, Panama, Finland, and Australia. His books have been translated into German, Spanish, Dutch, Finnish, Korean, and Chinese.

AVOCATIONAL INTERESTS: Mountains, backpacking, hiking.

BIOGRAPHICAL/CRITICAL SOURCES: Pastoral Psychology, April, 1962.

* * *

CLIVE, Geoffrey 1927-1976

PERSONAL: Born September 22, 1927, in Berlin, Germany; came to United States in 1940, naturalized in 1945; son of Bruno (a lawyer) and Rose (Rosenfeld) Clive. *Education:* Colgate University, B.A., 1948; Harvard University, M.A., 1950, Ph.D., 1953. *Religion:* Jewish. *Residence:* Cambridge, Mass. *Office:* Department of Philosophy, University of Massachusetts, 100 Arlington St., Boston, Mass. 02116.

CAREER: University of Delaware, Newark, instructor in philosophy, 1953-54; University of Connecticut, Storrs, instructor in philosophy, 1954-56; University of Arkansas, Fayetteville, assistant professor of philosophy, 1956-57; Clark University, Worcester, Mass., assistant professor of philosophy, 1957-61; University of Florida, Gainesville, associate professor of philosophy, 1966-67; University of Massachusetts, Boston, associate professor, 1967-72, professor of philosophy, 1972-76. Visiting associate professor of philosophy, Washington University, 1961-62, Vanderbilt University, 1963-66; Fulbright lecturer, University of Saarland, Germany, 1962-63. *Member:* American Philosophical Association (Eastern division). *Awards, honors:* George Santayana fellowship, Harvard University, 1969-70; American Philosophical Society grant, 1970.

WRITINGS: The Romantic Enlightenment, Meridian, 1960; (editor) *Nietzsche: An Anthology,* New American Library, 1965; *The Broken Icon: Intuitive Existentialism in Classical Russian Fiction,* Macmillan, 1972.

WORK IN PROGRESS: A study of dialectical reasoning.

AVOCATIONAL INTERESTS: Music.†

(Died, 1976)

* * *

CLOGAN, Paul M(aurice) 1934-

PERSONAL: Born July 9, 1934, in Milton, Mass.; son of Michael J. (a salesman) and Agnes J. (Murphy) Clogan; married Julie S. Davis, June, 1972; children: Michael Rodger. *Education:* Boston College, B.A., 1956, M.A., 1957; University of Illinois, Ph.D., 1961; American Academy in Rome, F.A.A.R., 1967. *Office:* Department of English, North Texas State University, Denton, Tex. 76203.

CAREER: Duke University, Durham, N.C., instructor, 1961-62, assistant professor of English, 1962-65; Case Western Reserve University, Cleveland, Ohio, associate professor of English, 1965-71; Cleveland State University, Cleveland, adjunct professor of English, 1971-72; North Texas State University, Denton, professor of English, 1972—. Visiting lecturer at University of Keele, 1965, University of Pisa, 1966, and University of Tours, 1977. Consultant to Educational Testing Service, Association of Centers for Medieval and Renaissance Studies, Library of Congress, Harvard University Press, Rutgers University Press, and Duke University Press. Has lectured at various seminars, congresses, and educational institutions in U.S. and Europe.

MEMBER: International Arthurian Society, Modern Language Association of America (life member; member of program committee, 1970), Mediaeval Academy of America (life member; member of nominating committee, 1975-76), Modern Humanities Research Association, Renaissance Society of America, Dante Society of America, Early English Text Society, Society for the Study of Medieval Language and Literature, American Philological Association. *Awards, honors:* Duke Endowment grant, 1961-62; American Council of Learned Societies fellow, 1963-64; American Philosophical Society grants, 1964-69; Prix de Rome fellow, 1966-67; senior Fulbright-Hays postdoctoral research fellow, 1966-67; Bollingen Foundation grant, 1966-67; National Endowment for the Humanities grant, 1969-70; American Council of Learned Societies grant, 1970-71; North Texas State University faculty research grants, 1972-75.

WRITINGS: (Editor and author of introduction) Publius Papinius Statius, *Medieval Achilleid of Statius,* E. J. Brill, 1968; (editor) *Medieval and Renaissance Studies in Review,* Press of Case Western Reserve University, 1971; *Social Dimension in Medieval and Renaissance Studies,* Press of Case Western Reserve University, 1972.

Editor and contributor: *Medievalia et Humanistica: In Honor of S. Harrison Thomson,* Press of Case Western Reserve University, 1970; *Medieval and Renaissance Spirituality,* North Texas State University Press, 1973; *Medieval Historiography,* North Texas State University Press, 1974; *Medieval Hagiography and Romance,* Cambridge University Press, 1975; *Medieval Poetics,* Cambridge University Press, 1976; *Transformation and Continuity,* Cambridge University Press, 1977. Editor, *Medievalia et Humanistica: Studies in Medieval and Renaissance Culture,* 1968—. Contributor to professional journals, magazines, and newspapers.

WORK IN PROGRESS: The Legend of Thebes: From Myth to Romance; Chaucer and the Italian Tradition.

*   *   *

COBB, Vicki   1938-

PERSONAL: Born August 19, 1938, in New York, N.Y.; daughter of Benjamin Harold (a labor arbitrator) and Paula (Davis) Wolf; married Edward S. Cobb (a psychology professor), January 31, 1960; children: Theodore Davis, Joshua Monroe. *Education:* Attended University of Wisconsin, 1954-57; Barnard College, B.A., 1958; Columbia University, M.A., 1960. *Home:* 410 Riverside Dr., New York, N.Y. 10025.

CAREER: Scientific researcher in Rye, N.Y., at Sloan-Kettering Institute and Pfizer & Co., 1958-61; science teacher in high school in Rye, 1961-64; Teleprompter Corp., New York City, hostess and principal writer of television series, "The Science Game," 1972—; American Broadcasting Co., New York City, writer for "Good Morning America," 1976. Owner and creator of television programs, Creative Televisions for Children, Inc., 1972—. *Member:* Authors Guild, Authors League, Writers Guild. *Awards, honors:* Cable television award for best educational television show, 1973, for "The Science Game."

WRITINGS—All juvenile: *Logic,* F. Watts, 1969; *Cells,* F.

Watts, 1970; *Gases,* F. Watts, 1970; *Making Sense of Money,* Parents' Magazine Press, 1971; *Sense of Direction: Up, Down, and All Around,* Parents' Magazine Press, 1972; *Science Experiments You Can Eat,* Lippincott, 1972; *How the Doctor Knows You're Fine,* Lippincott, 1973; *The Long and Short of Measurement,* Parents' Magazine Press, 1973; *Heat,* F. Watts, 1973; *Arts and Crafts You Can Eat,* Lippincott, 1974; *Supersuits,* Lippincott, 1975; *Magic ... Naturally,* Lippincott, 1977. Editor, "McGraw-Hill Text Films," Elementary Science Study Prints section, 1970.

BIOGRAPHICAL/CRITICAL SOURCES: Science Books, December, 1972, March, 1974, May, 1977; *Childhood Education,* January, 1975; *School Library Journal,* November, 1975, November, 1976, March, 1977; *Teacher,* January, 1976; *Children's Literature Review,* Volume II, Gale, 1976.

*   *   *

COCHRANE, James L.   1942-

PERSONAL: Born August 31, 1942, in Nyack, N.Y.; son of Thomas and Anna Cochrane. *Education:* Wittenberg University, A.B., 1964; Tulane University, Ph.D., 1968. *Office:* Department of Economics, University of South Carolina, Columbia, S.C. 29208.

CAREER: Tulane University, New Orleans, La., instructor in economics, 1967-68; University of South Carolina, Columbia, assistant professor, 1968-71, associate professor, 1971-76, professor of economics, 1976—. *Member:* American Economic Association, Royal Economic Society, Canadian Economic Association, Econometric Society, American Association of University Professors, Southern Economic Association, Western Economic Association.

WRITINGS: Macroeconomics before Keynes, Scott, Foresman, 1970; *Macroeconomics: Analysis and Policy,* Scott, Foresman, 1974. Contributor to economics journals in the United States and other countries. Member of editorial board, *History of Political Economy,* 1971—, and *Southern Economics Journal,* 1971—.

*   *   *

CODDING, George A(rthur), Jr.   1923-

PERSONAL: Born June 23, 1923, in Salem, Ore.; son of George Arthur (an attorney) and Maude Fern (Corlies) Codding; married Yolands Cleste Legini, June 17, 1961; children: Christine, George III, William Henry, Jennifer. *Education:* University of Washington, B.A., 1943, M.A., 1948; University of Geneva, Dr.Sc.Pol., 1952. *Politics:* Democrat. *Home:* 6086 Simmons, Boulder, Colo. 80303. *Office:* Department of Political Science, University of Colorado, Boulder, Colo. 80302.

CAREER: International Telecommunication Union, Geneva, Switzerland, administrative assistant, 1949; University of Pennsylvania, Philadelphia, lecturer, 1953-55, assistant professor of political science, 1955-61; University of Colorado, Boulder, associate professor, 1961-65, professor of political science, 1965—, chairman of department, 1971—, chairman of B.A. in international affairs committee. Member of study group on international organization of the European Center of the Carnegie Foundation of International Peace, 1965-66; member of General Electric Satellite Broadcast Advisory Board, 1967-70, National Commission on the Causes and Prevention of Violence, 1968-69, and behavioral sciences evaluation panel on the National Science Foundation graduate fellowships, 1969—. Member of board of directors, Radio Colorado Corp. Consultant to UNESCO, 1957-59, secretary-general of International Telecommunication Union, 1964-65, U.S. Department of Commerce, 1969, and Office of Telecommunications, Department of Commerce, 1976. Project referee, Canada Council, National Science Foundation. *Military service:* U.S. Navy, communications and deck officer, 1943-46; became lieutenant junior grade.

MEMBER: International Political Science Association, American Political Science Association, American Society of International Law, American Academy of Political and Social Science, Western Political Science Association, Rocky Mountain Social Science Association, Boulder Flycasters Chapter of Trout Unlimited (president, 1976). *Awards, honors:* Social Science Research Council grant-in-aid, 1955; Guggenheim fellowship, 1958-59; University of Colorado faculty fellowship, 1965-66, 1973-74; faculty award, Social Science Foundation, University of Denver, 1966.

WRITINGS: The International Telecommunication Union: An Experiment in International Cooperation, E. J. Brill (Leiden), 1952; *Broadcasting without Barriers,* UNESCO (Paris), 1959; *The Federal Government of Switzerland,* Houghton, 1961, revised edition, 1965; *The Universal Postal Union: Coordinator of the International Mails,* New York University Press, 1964; *Governing the Commune of Veyrier: Politics in Swiss Local Government,* Bureau of Governmental Research, University of Colorado, 1967.

Contributor: Edward Collins, Jr., editor, *International Law in a Changing World,* Random House, 1970; C. D. Kernig, editor, *The Soviet System and Democratic Society,* Verlag Herder, 1971. Contributor to *Journal of the Federal Communications Bar Association, American Journal of International Law, Current History, Nation, Orbis, Foreign Affairs,* and other publications. Member of editorial board, "Monograph Series in World Affairs," Social Science Foundation, University of Denver, and *Journal of International Law and Policy,* 1971—. Manuscript referee, Stanford University Press, *American Political Science Review, Western Political Quarterly,* and *Studies in Race Relations.*

WORK IN PROGRESS: Telecommunications and the Political System: National and International; The Specialized Agencies of the United Nations: Change and Development in International Organizations; Comparative International Organization and International Organization Administration; The Decline of Ideology in French Politics: The Socialist Party of France.

*   *   *

CODRESCU, Andrei   1946-
(Tristan Tzara, Urmuz, Betty Laredo)

PERSONAL: Born December 20, 1946, in Sibiu, Romania; became United States citizen, 1971; son of Vlad Julius (an ambassador) and Eva (Brancoveanu) Codrescu; married Alice Henderson (a painter), September 19, 1969; children: Lucian. *Education:* University of Rome, M.A., 1966. *Politics:* "Monarco-Anarchist." *Religion:* Hindu. *Home address:* P.O. Box 341, Monte Rio, Calif. 95462. *Agent:* Curtis Brown Ltd., 575 Madison Ave., New York, N.Y. 10022. *Office:* Transylvanian Liberation Front, 150 A. Sanchez, San Francisco, Calif. 94114.

CAREER: Writer. Codrescu also characterizes himself as "revolutionary," "sexual reformer," and "priest." *Military service:* "Guerrilla Army." *Member:* Authors League of

America, P.E.N. American Center, Transylvanian Liberation Front, Dada Council for World Revolution, Restore the Monarchy Now. *Awards, honors:* Big Table Younger Poets award, 1970, for *License to Carry a Gun;* National Endowment for the Arts fellowship, 1973.

WRITINGS—Poetry: *License to Carry a Gun,* Follett, 1970; *History of the Growth of Heaven,* Grape Press, 1971, enlarged edition, Braziller, 1973; *The, Here, What, Where,* Isthmus Press, 1972; *Secret Training,* Grape Press, 1973; *A Serious Morning,* Capra, 1973; *Grammar & Money,* Arif, 1973; *The Marriage of Insult and Injury,* Cymric Press, 1977; *Au Bout Du Monde,* Four Zoas, 1977; *The Lady Painter,* Four Zoas, 1977.

Other: *Why I Can't Talk on the Telephone,* Kingdom Kum Press, 1971; *How I Became Howard Johnson,* Parnassus, 1972; (with others) *The Questionable Hell,* Parnassus, 1972; *The Life and Times of an Involuntary Genius* (novel), Braziller, 1975; *For Max Jacob,* Tree Books, 1975; *The Repentence of Lorraine* (novel), Pocket Books, 1977. Also author of *Meat from the Goldrush;* author of a pamphlet, "36 Poems by Betty Laredo." Contributor of poetry to magazines under pseudonyms Tristan Tzara and Urmuz.

WORK IN PROGRESS: Mad Tall Napoleon, a biography and anthology; *Lasting the Ascension,* poems; three novellas; a new novel; an epic musical about Amtrack for the American Ballet Theater; a cabaret in collaboration with Lynn Swanson and Jim Gustafson.

*   *   *

COFFEY, Alan R.   1931-

PERSONAL: Born April 14, 1931, in Washington, D.C.; son of Homer and Margaret (Denny) Coffey; married Beverly Austen (a school teacher), November 22, 1953; children: Alison, Annette, Alana. *Education:* San Jose State College (now University), B.A., 1961, M.A., 1963. *Religion:* Protestant. *Home:* 22420 Old Logging Rd., Los Gatos, Calif. 95030. *Office:* Santa Clara County Probation Department, San Jose, Calif.

CAREER: U.S. Air Force, 1947-56, leaving service as technical sergeant; police dispatcher in Santa Clara County, Calif., 1956-60; Santa Clara County Probation Department, San Jose, Calif., probation officer and supervisor of probation officers, 1960-64, director of staff development, 1964—. Part-time teacher of sociology, psychology, and criminology at University of California, Santa Cruz, San Jose State University, De Anza College, and Foothill College, 1964—. Systems consultant, Stanford Research Institute; consultant, National College of District Attorneys.

WRITINGS: (Co-author) *Principles of Law Enforcement,* Wiley, 1968, 2nd edition, 1974; *Human Relations,* Prentice-Hall, 1971, 2nd edition, 1975; *Police Community Relations,* Prentice-Hall, 1972; (co-author) *Police and the Criminal Law,* Goodyear Publishing, 1972; (co-author) *Corrections: A Component of the Criminal Justice System,* Goodyear Publishing, 1973; *An Introduction to the Criminal Justice System and Process,* Prentice-Hall, 1975; *Criminal Justice as a System: Readings,* Prentice-Hall, 1975; *Process and Impact of Justice,* Glencoe Press, 1975; *Police Intervention into Family Crisis,* Davis Publishing, 1975; *Juvenile Corrections: Treatment and Rehabilitation,* Prentice-Hall, 1975; *Prevention of Crime and Delinquency,* Prentice-Hall, 1975; *Correctional Administration: The Management of Probation and Parole,* Prentice-Hall, 1975; (co-author) *Process and Impact of Juvenile Justice,* Glencoe Press, 1976; *Juvenile Justice as a System: Law Enforcement to Rehabilita-*

tion, Prentice-Hall, 1977; *Administration of Criminal Justice: A Management Systems Approach,* Prentice-Hall, 1977.

SIDELIGHTS: Alan Coffey told *CA:* "Crime has not yielded to justice—common knowledge to most. Of course certain facts and theories must be married if justice is to improve—the usual motive for criminal justice authors, myself included. But that's only part of my writing motive. I get a great deal of satisfaction from the expanded teaching and consulting experiences that seem to accompany successful books—even a short consulting job that pays practically nothing can move me to write an entire volume."

* * *

COFFIN, Dean 1911-

PERSONAL: Born January 26, 1911, in Flushing, N.Y.; son of Howard Aldridge (a businessman and U.S. congressman) and Abbey (Ghodey) Coffin; married Winifred DeForest (an actress), April 7, 1934; children: Cella De-Forest (Mrs. William Morey), Howard Aldridge II, Tristram DeForest, Fred DeForest, William Vail. *Education:* Brown University, A.B., 1933. *Politics:* Republican. *Religion:* Episcopalian. *Home and office:* 125 South Glenhurst, Birmingham, Mich. 48009. *Agent:* Collins-Knowlton-Wing, Inc., 60 East 56th St., New York, N.Y. 10022.

CAREER: Jam Handy Organization, Detroit, Mich., writer, 1934-44, editor and account executive, 1944-49; freelance writer and producer of stage plays, 1949-54; Wilding, Inc., Cleveland, Ohio, writer, 1954, manager, 1955-57, vice-president, 1957-58; Jam Handy Organization, vice-president, 1959-65; Dean Coffin & Associates (writing, consulting services), principal, in Hollywood, Calif., and in Birmingham, Mich., 1965—. Affiliated with College of Lifelong Learning, Wayne State University, Detroit, Mich. Administrative manager of *Show* and administrative vice-president of *Entertainment World* (both magazines), 1969-70. *Member:* Phi Delta Theta, Players (New York), Players Club (Detroit), St. Dunstan's Guild (Bloomfield Hills, Mich.).

WRITINGS: Under the Robe (novel), Whitmore, 1970. Also author of a documentary film, "The Jury"; author of other films for government and industry.

Plays produced: "The High Cost of Loving" (musical drama), produced, 1965, by Bloomfield Art Association, Bloomfield Hills, Mich. Editor, *Communicator.*

* * *

COFFMAN, Edward M. 1929-

PERSONAL: Born January 27, 1929, in Hopkinsville, Ky.; son of Howard B. (a salesman) and Mada (Wright) Coffman; married Anne Rouse, June 30, 1955; children: Anne, Lucia, Edward M., Jr. *Education:* University of Kentucky, A.B.J., 1951, M.A., 1955, Ph.D., 1959. *Politics:* Democrat. *Religion:* Protestant. *Office:* Department of History, University of Wisconsin, Madison, Wis. 53706.

CAREER: Memphis State University, Memphis, Tenn., instructor, 1957-58, assistant professor of history, 1959-60; G. C. Marshall Research Association, Arlington, Va., research associate, 1960-61; University of Wisconsin—Madison, assistant professor, 1961-66, associate professor, 1966-68, professor of history, 1968—. Visiting Eisenhower Professor, Kansas State University, 1969-70. Member of advisory committee, U.S. Army Historical Program; member, National Historical Publications and Re-

search Commission, 1972-76. *Military service:* U.S. Army, 1951-53; became lieutenant. *Member:* Organization of American Historians, American Military Institute, Southern Historical Society. *Awards, honors:* Guggenheim fellowship, 1973-74.

WRITINGS: The Hilt of the Sword: The Career of Peyton C. March, University of Wisconsin Press, 1966; *The War to End All Wars: The American Military Experience in World War I,* Oxford University Press, 1968.

WORK IN PROGRESS: A social history of the American Army in peacetime, 1784-1940, for Oxford University Press.

BIOGRAPHICAL/CRITICAL SOURCES: Virginia Quarterly Review, spring, 1969.

* * *

COGSWELL, James A(rthur) 1922-

PERSONAL: Born November 29, 1922, in Houston, Tex.; son of Prentiss Arthur (a businessman) and Germaine (Giroud) Cogswell; married Margaret E. Griffin, June 11, 1945; children: Margaret Ann, James Arthur, Jr., Sara Linda, Daniel Herbert. *Education:* Southwestern at Memphis, B.A., 1942; Union Theological Seminary, Richmond, Va., B.D., 1945, Th.D., 1961; Princeton Theological Seminary, Th.M., 1948. *Home:* 1347 Talcott Pl., Decatur, Ga. 30033.

CAREER: Pastor of Presbyterian church in Pascagoula, Miss., 1945-46; instructor in Bible at Davidson College, Davidson, N.C. and Southwestern at Memphis, Memphis, Tenn., 1947; Presbyterian missionary to Japan, 1948-61; Shikoku Christian College, Zentsuji, Japan, professor of Bible and Greek, 1950-53; Kinjo University, Nagoya, Japan, professor of Bible and English, 1957-60; Board of World Missions of Presbyterian Church of the United States, Nashville, Tenn., secretary for Asia, 1961-67; pastor of Presbyterian church in Franklin, Tenn., 1967-71; Presbyterian Church of the United States, Atlanta, Ga., director of Task Force on World Hunger, 1971—. Representative of Church World Service to U.N. World Food Conference, Rome, 1974. Chairman, Task Force on World Hunger, National Council of Churches, 1974-75, and Agricultural Missions, Inc., 1976—. Executive producer of film "Kwacha: A New Day in Africa," 1976. *Awards, honors:* D.D., Southwestern at Memphis, 1961.

WRITINGS: Until the Day Dawn: A History of the Work of the Japan Mission of the Presbyterian Church in the United States, Board of World Missions, Presbyterian Church, 1957, revised edition, 1967; *Response: The Church in Mission to a World in Crisis,* published with teacher's book (with Sue Nichols), CLC Press, 1971; *The Promise of the New: Studies in Matthew,* Presbyterian Church, 1974; (editor) *The Church and the Rural Poor: The Role of the Church in Rural Economic Development,* John Knox, 1975.

* * *

COHEN, Allan Y. 1939-

PERSONAL: Born November 1, 1939, in Leroy, N.Y.; son of Eli H. (a business executive) and Blanche (Speiller) Cohen. *Education:* Harvard University, A.B. (summa cum laude), 1961, M.A., 1965, Ph.D., 1966. *Religion:* Sufi. *Home:* 3703 Mosswood Dr., Lafayette, Calif. 94549. *Office:* Department of General Studies, John F. Kennedy University, 12 Altarinda Way, Orinda, Calif. 94563.

CAREER: Potentials, Inc., director of research, 1964-66; U.S. Peace Corps, field assessment officer, 1966; University of California, Berkeley, therapist and counselor at

Counseling Center, and instructor in psychology in extension courses, 1967-69; John F. Kennedy University, Orinda, Calif., assistant professor, 1967-68, associate professor, 1968-72, professor of psychology, 1975—, dean of students, 1970-74, director, Institute for Drug Abuse Education and Research, 1970—. Visiting professor, Pacific Schools of Religion, 1972; executive director, Pacific Institute for Research and Evaluation, 1973—. Consulting psychologist in drug abuse prevention and education; lecturer at high schools, colleges, and professional organizations in the United States and abroad. *Member:* American Psychological Association, Association for Humanistic Psychology.

WRITINGS: (With Peter Marin) *Understanding Drug Use: An Adult's Guide to Drugs and the Young,* Harper, 1971; *Alternatives to Drug Abuse: Steps toward Prevention* (monograph), National Clearing House for Drug Abuse Information, 1973; (with E. Schaps and H. Resnik) *Balancing Head and Heart: Sensible Ideas on the Prevention of Drug and Alcohol Abuse,* Prevention Materials Institute, 1975; (editor) Meher Baba, *The Mastery of Consciousness: An Introduction and Guide to Practical Mysticism and Methods of Spiritual Development,* Harper, 1977. Contributor to health and student journals.

WORK IN PROGRESS: A book tentatively entitled *Invisible Door: Implications of Psychic Experience,* for Harper.

SIDELIGHTS: As a graduate student and assistant to Professors Timothy Leary and Richard Alpert, Allan Cohen was involved in the early research with psychedelic drugs. He took LSD and related drugs some thirty times before splitting with the "psychedelic utopians" and rejecting the use of chemicals as a means of personal growth. Cohen told *CA:* "A Commonwealth edition of *The Mastery of Consciousness* has been released in England. . . . Of it, Pete Townshend, composer and musician (The Who) said, 'I feel very passionately about this book; . . . it has been needed a long time and is finally here.'"

AVOCATIONAL INTERESTS: Flying, athletics, travel, especially to India and the East.

BIOGRAPHICAL/CRITICAL SOURCES: Saturday Review, April 17, 1971.

*   *   *

COHEN, Arthur M.   1927-

PERSONAL: Born June 14, 1927, in Caldwell, N.J.; son of Harry (a merchant) and Rae (Berke) Cohen; married Barbara Harris, August 24, 1952 (divorced, 1976); children: William, Wendy, Andrew, Nancy. *Education:* University of Miami, A.B., 1949, M.A., 1955; Florida State University, Ph.D., 1964. *Politics:* Democratic. *Religion:* Jewish. *Home:* 1749 Mandeville Lane, Los Angeles, Calif. 90049. *Office:* Graduate School of Education, University of California, Los Angeles, Calif. 90024.

CAREER: Previously employed as a bricklayer and general contractor; University of California, Los Angeles, assistant professor, 1964-70, associate professor, 1970-75, professor of higher education, 1975—. Director, Educational Resources Information Center Clearinghouse for Junior Colleges, 1966—; president, Center for the Study of Community Colleges, 1974—. *Military service:* U.S. Coast Guard, 1945-46. *Member:* American Association of Junior Colleges, American Association for Higher Education, California Educational Research Association (secretary, 1972; president, 1975).

WRITINGS: (With Florence B. Brawer) *Focus on*

Learning: Preparing Teachers for the Two-Year College (monograph), School of Education, University of California, 1968; (editor with John Prihoda) *The Junior College Curriculum* (anthology), Associated Educational Services Corp., 1968; *Dateline '79: Heretical Concepts for the Community College,* Glencoe Press, 1969; (with John E. Roueche) *Institutional Administrator or Educational Leader? The Junior College President* (monograph), ERIC Clearinghouse for Junior College Information, 1969; (with Brawer) *Measuring Faculty Performance* (monograph), American Association of Junior Colleges, 1969; (with Brawer) *Student Characteristics: Personality and Dropout Propensity* (monograph), ERIC Clearinghouse for Junior Colleges, 1970; *Objectives for College Courses,* Glencoe Press, 1970; (with Brawer and John Lombardi) *A Constant Variable,* Jossey-Bass, 1971; (editor with Leslie Purdy) *College Curriculum and Instruction* (anthology), Simon & Schuster, 1971; (with Brawer) *Confronting Identity: The Community College Instructor,* Prentice-Hall, 1972; *Toward a Professional Faculty,* Jossey-Bass, 1973; (with others) *College Responses to Community Demands,* Jossey-Bass, 1975; (with Brawer) *The Two-Year College Instructor Today,* Praeger, 1977.

WORK IN PROGRESS: Research on the humanities and the sciences in two-year colleges.

SIDELIGHTS: Arthur M. Cohen told *CA,* "My writing focuses on the community college as a special form of post-secondary education—what it is, what it could be, how it should be managed, what it means to its students and faculty members—with particular emphasis on college curriculum and instruction."

*   *   *

COHEN, Henry   1933-

PERSONAL: Born September 23, 1933, in Brooklyn, N.Y.; son of Sam and Lily Cohen. *Education:* Columbia University, B.A., 1955; Cornell University, Ph.D., 1965. *Office:* History Department, Loyola University, Chicago, Ill. 60626.

CAREER: Ohio State University, Columbus, instructor in history, 1962-64; California State College at Long Beach (now California State University, Long Beach), assistant professor of history, 1964-69; Loyola University, Chicago, Ill., assistant professor, 1969-71, associate professor of history, 1971—. *Member:* American Historical Association, Economic History Association, Organization of American Historians. *Awards, honors:* Social Science Research Council fellowship, 1960-62.

WRITINGS: (Contributor) David M. Ellis and others, editors, *The Frontier in American Development: Essays in Honor of Paul Wallace Gates,* Cornell University Press, 1969; *Business and Politics in America from the Age of Jackson to the Civil War,* Greenwood Press, 1971.

WORK IN PROGRESS: A history of the American political economy; research on crime and police in the United States.

SIDELIGHTS: Henry Cohen wrote *CA:* "I am interested in American civilization as a whole. Its cohesion and fragmentation, and their consequences, are among my central preoccupations."

*   *   *

COHEN, Peter Zachary   1931-

PERSONAL: Born October 27, 1931; married; wife's name, Suzanne; children: Jay, Todd. *Education:* University of

Wyoming, B.S., 1953, M.A., 1961. *Home:* Route 1, Alta Vista, Kan. 66834. *Office:* Department of English, Kansas State University, Manhattan, Kan. 66502.

CAREER: Kansas State University, Manhattan, instructor in English, 1961—. Member of Wabaunsee County (Kan.) Planning Commission, 1969—. *Military service:* U.S. Army, 1954-56. *Member:* American Association of University Professors, Authors Guild, and several wildlife organizations.

WRITINGS—All juveniles; all published by Atheneum, except as indicated: *The Muskie Hook,* 1969; *The Bull in the Forest* (Junior Literary Guild selection), 1969; *Morena* (Junior Literary Guild selection), 1970; *The Authorized Autumn Charts of the Upper Red Canoe River Country,* 1972; *Foal Creek,* 1972; *Bee,* 1975; *The Cannon in the Park* (children's play; first produced in Hoxie, Kan. at Continental Theatre, September, 1975), Modern Theatre for Youth, 1975. Author of two movie scripts for Xerox Educational Films.

WORK IN PROGRESS: Fiction and non-fiction for adults and children.

SIDELIGHTS: Peter Cohen lives on a small farm "raising sheep, horses and chickens under fence, [and] coyotes, rabbits, owls, and the evening stars, too, I guess, by letting them run loose." He says that he returns from contacts with the field-and-stream-out-of-doors "with a renewed sense of wonder at the world," and writes "to try to discover more about the 'whys' and 'what ifs' of the attitudes and situations I feel and observe."

BIOGRAPHICAL/CRITICAL SOURCES: PTA Magazine, September, 1969; *Book World,* November 9, 1969, May 7, 1972; *Publishers Weekly,* March 20, 1972.

* * *

COHEN, Ronald 1930-

PERSONAL: Born January 22, 1930, in Canada; came to United States in 1963; son of Maxwell B. and Pauline (Golant) Cohen; married Diana Barbara Williams, June 21, 1955; children: Paul Yerima, Stephen Benjamin. *Education:* University of Toronto, B.A., 1951; University of Wisconsin, M.Sc., 1954, Ph.D., 1960. *Home:* 1040 Michigan Ave., Evanston, Ill. 60202. *Office:* Department of Anthropology, Northwestern University, Evanston, Ill. 60201.

CAREER: University of Toronto, Toronto, Ontario, lecturer in anthropology, 1958-61; McGill University, Montreal, Quebec, assistant professor of anthropology, 1961-63; Northwestern University, Evanston, Ill., associate professor, 1963-68, professor of anthropology and political science, 1968—, chairman of the department of anthropology, 1971-72; Ahmadu Bello University, Zaria, Nigeria, professor of sociology and head of department (on leave from Northwestern University), 1972-74. Founder and first chairman, International African Institute, London. Member of review board, National Institute of Mental Health research grants, 1968. Consulting director, Canadian Centre for Research in Anthropology, 1962—. Chairman, Committee on African Studies in Canada, 1962-63. Has done field work in Nigeria and Canada.

MEMBER: Association of Social Anthropologists, Committee on African Studies, African Studies Association (fellow), African Studies Association of Canada, American Anthropological Association (fellow), American Sociological Association, International African Institute of London, African Students Foundation of Canada (chairman, 1961-63), American Political Science Association, Society of So-

cial Anthropologists of Great Britain, Rhodes-Livingston Institute of Zambia, Central States Anthropological Association.

WRITINGS: An Anthropological Survey of Communities of the Mackenzie-Slave Lake Region of Canada, Department of Northern Affairs and Natural Resources (Ottawa), 1962; (with Helgi Osterreich) *Good Hope Tales,* National Museum of Canada, 1965; *The Kanuri of Bornu,* Holt, 1967; (with John Middleton) *Comparative Political Systems: Studies in the Politics of Pre-Industrial Societies,* Natural History Press, 1967; (editor and contributor with R. Naroll) *Handbook of Methodology in Cultural Anthropology,* Natural History Press, 1970; (editor with Middleton, and contributor) *Tribe to Nation in Africa,* Chandler Publishing, 1970; *Dominance and Defiance,* American Anthropological Association, 1971; (editor) *The Origins of the State: A Symposium,* Institute for the Study of Human Issues, 1977.

Contributor: G. Zollschan and D. Hirsch, editors, *Explorations in Social Change,* Houghton, 1964; J. Butler, editor, *Boston University Publications in Africa History,* Volume II, Boston University Press, 1966; M. Swartz, V. Turner, and A. Tuden, editors, *Political Anthropology,* Aldine, 1966; S. M. Lipset, editor, *Politics and the Social Sciences,* Oxford University Press, 1967; (with A. Schlegel) J. Helm, editor, *American Ethnological Society, Essays on the Problem of the Tribe,* University of Washington Press, 1968; Tuden and L. Plotnicov, editors, *Class and Status in Sub-Saharan Africa,* Free Press, 1970; P. J. Bohannan, editor, *Divorce and After,* Natural History Press, 1970; M. Crowder, editor, *West African Chiefs,* Faber, 1970; J. Paden and E. Soja, editors, *The African Experience,* Northwestern University Press, 1970; (with L. Brenner) A. Ajayi and Crowder, editors, *The History of West Africa,* Volume I, Clarendon Press, 1971, Volume II, Longman, 1973; Turner, editor, *The Impact of Colonialism,* Hoover Institution, 1971; H. Volpe and R. Melson, editors, *Communalism in Nigeria,* Michigan State University Press, 1971; Tessler, Spain, and O'Barr, editors, *Research Techniques in Africa,* 1971. Also contributor to *Sociology in Africa,* edited by P. Wilmot, 1973, *Power Structure and Social Transformation,* edited by T. R. Burns and W. Buckley, 1976, and *The Early States,* edited by H. J. H. Claessen and P. Skalnik, 1977

Contributor to *Anthropologica, Canadian Journal of Corrections, International Journal, American Anthropologist, Man, Canadian Journal of African Studies, Journal of Social Issues, Current Anthropology, Savanna, Africa,* and other professional journals. Assistant editor, *Anthropologica,* 1962—; abstractor in charge of anthropology and related fields, *African Abstracts,* 1966-70; member of editorial board, *Journal of Social History,* 1967—; assistant editor, *American Anthropologist,* 1970-72.

* * *

COHEN, Stephen S. 1941-

PERSONAL: Born May 11, 1941, in New York, N.Y.; son of Benjamin and Ann Cohen. *Education:* Williams College, B.A., 1962; attended Institute of Political Studies, Paris, 1960-61; London School of Economics, Ph.D. *Office:* Department of City Planning, University of California, Berkeley, Calif. 94720.

CAREER: Williams College, Williamstown, Mass., instructor in political science, 1964-65; Brandeis University, Waltham, Mass., assistant professor of economics, 1965-68; University of California, Berkeley, associate professor of city and regional planning, 1968—.

WRITINGS: *Modern Capitalist Planning: The French Model,* Harvard University Press, 1969, 2nd revised edition, University of California Press, 1977. Contributor of articles to journals in his field.

WORK IN PROGRESS: A book on the political economy of advanced capitalist nations.

*   *   *

COHN, Jules 1930-

PERSONAL: Born June 18, 1930, in New Brunswick, N.J.; son of Edward Abraham and Mae (Rose) Cohn; married Barbara Schwartzman, December, 1964 (divorced, 1970). *Education:* Rutgers University, A.B., 1951, A.M., 1954, Ph.D., 1958. *Religion:* Jewish. *Home:* 4 Washington Square Village, Apt. 3P, New York, N.Y. 10012. *Office:* Department of Political Science, City University of New York, 135 West 51st St., New York, N.Y. 10020.

CAREER: Bard College, Annandale-on-Hudson, N.Y., instructor in humanities, 1954-58; Brooklyn College (now Brooklyn College of the City University of New York), New York City, instructor in political science, 1958-61; Turku University, Turku, Finland, and Abo Akademi, Abo, Finland, Fulbright professor of American civilization, 1960-61; City of New York, N.Y., deputy to the executive coordinator of program and policy development in Office of Mayor, and director of Division of Research, Planning, and Training in Neighborhood Conservation Bureau, 1962-64; Harvard University-Massachusetts Institute of Technology Joint Center for Urban Studies, Cambridge, Mass., member, 1964-65; New York University, New York City, associate professor of politics, 1965-68; City University of New York, New York City, professor of political science and coordinator of urban planning for Manhattan Community College, 1969—. Member of national executive council, American Jewish Committee, 1970—. Consultant to government and industrial organizations.

MEMBER: American Political Science Association, National Association of Housing and Redevelopment Officials, American Society for Public Administration, International Political Science Association, American Sociological Association, New York Academy of Sciences, New York Historical Society, Phi Alpha Theta, Pi Sigma Alpha, Harvard Club of New York City, City Club of New York. *Awards, honors:* U.S. Department of Labor manpower research grant, 1972-73.

WRITINGS: (Editor with Charles Lawrence and Carl Nordstrom) *Man, Culture, and Society,* Brooklyn College Press, 1961; *Municipal Politics,* American Education Publications, 1967; (contributor) J. A. Scott, editor, *Economic Development in Central Cities,* Urban Social Science Research Center, Rutgers University, 1970; *The Conscience of the Corporations: Business and Urban Affairs,* Johns Hopkins Press, 1971; (contributor) David M. Gordon, editor, *Problems in Political Economy: An Urban Perspective,* Heath, 1971; (contributor) Jeffrey K. Hadden, L. H. Masotti, and C. J. Larson, editors, *Metropolis in Crisis,* F. E. Peacock, 1971; (contributor) Harold Lazarus, Jerome E. Schnee, and E. Kirby Warren, editors, *The Progress of Management: Process, Behavior, and Operations Research,* Prentice-Hall, 1972. Contributor of about fifteen articles to sociology and political science journals.

WORK IN PROGRESS: *Memoirs of an Organization Man.*

COLBOURN, H(arold) Trevor 1927-

PERSONAL: Born February 24, 1927, in Armidale, New South Wales, Australia; son of Harold Arthur (an engineer) and Ella Mary (Henderson) Colbourn; married Beryl Richards Evans, January 10, 1949; children: Katherine Elizabeth, Lisa Sian Elinor. *Education:* University College, Exeter, B.A. (honors), 1948; College of William and Mary, M.A., 1949; Johns Hopkins University, A.M., 1951, Ph.D., 1953. *Religion:* Episcopalian. *Office:* Office of the President, Florida Technological University, Orlando, Fla. 32816.

CAREER: Pennsylvania State University, State College, instructor, 1952-54, assistant professor of history, 1954-59; Indiana University at Bloomington, assistant professor, 1959-63, associate professor, 1963-67, professor of history, 1967; University of New Hampshire, Durham, dean of Graduate School, 1967-73; San Diego State University, San Diego, Calif., vice president for academic affairs, 1973-77, acting president, 1977-78; Florida Technological University, Orlando, president, 1978—. *Member:* American Historical Association, Organization of American Historians.

WRITINGS: *The Lamp of Experience: Whig History and the Intellectual Origins of the American Revolution,* University of North Carolina Press, for Institute of Early American History, 1965; (editor) *The Colonial Experience,* Houghton, 1966; (editor with James T. Patterson) *The American Past in Perspective,* two volumes, Allyn & Bacon, 1970; (with Henry F. Bedford) *The Americans: A Brief History,* Harcourt, 1972, 2nd edition, 1976; (editor) *Fame and the Founding Fathers: Essays by Douglass Adair,* Norton, 1974. Contributor of articles and reviews to *Saturday Review* and to professional journals.

WORK IN PROGRESS: *History of Colonial America,* for Prentice-Hall.

BIOGRAPHICAL/CRITICAL SOURCES: *South Atlantic Quarterly,* spring, 1967.

*   *   *

COLE, Robert H. 1918-

PERSONAL: Born April 27, 1918, in Kansas City, Mo.; son of Roy L. (a banker) and Meta (Hartzell) Cole; married Mary Rose Craycroft, November 30, 1942; children: Robert H., Jr., Richard L. *Education:* University of Illinois, B.S., 1939, M.S., 1940; University of North Carolina, Ph.D., 1952. *Religion:* Presbyterian. *Home:* 920 Robert Rd., Lincoln, Neb. 68510. *Office:* 315 College of Business Administration Building, University of Nebraska, Lincoln, Neb. 68508.

CAREER: Westinghouse Electric Corp., Pittsburgh, Pa., member of marketing research staff, 1940-41; Federal Reserve Bank, Kansas City, Mo., assistant industrial economist, 1946-48; University of Illinois at Urbana-Champaign, instructor, 1950-52, assistant professor of marketing, 1952-57; University of Nebraska at Lincoln, associate professor, 1957-60, professor of marketing, 1960—. Part-time instructor, William Jewell College, 1946-48. *Military service:* U.S. Army, 1941-46; became captain. U.S. Army Reserve, 1946-61; retired as major. *Member:* American Marketing Association, Beta Gamma Sigma, Phi Kappa Phi, Alpha Kappa Psi, Sigma Alpha Epsilon.

WRITINGS: (With others) *Manufacturer and Distributor Brands,* Bureau of Economic and Business Research, University of Illinois, 1955; *Revolving Credit,* Bureau of Business Management, University of Illinois, 1957; (with Phillip McVey) *Radiation Processing: The Potential Market,* Nuclear Industries Corp., 1958; (with R. S. Hancock) *Consumer and Commercial Credit Management*, Irwin, 1960, 5th edition (as sole author), 1976. Author of other booklets and bulletins on credit banking and retailing. Contributor to *Journal of Marketing, Yearbook of Agriculture, Television Digest*, and other marketing journals.

* * *

COLE, (Andrew) Thomas (Jr.)   1933-

PERSONAL: Born August 22, 1933, in Chilhowie, Va.; son of Andrew Thomas (a physician) and Katharine (Tilly) Cole; married Katherine Stein, December 31, 1965; children: Helena Elizabeth. *Education:* Harvard University, A.B., 1954, Ph.D., 1960. *Home:* 194 Conner, New Haven, Conn. 06511. *Office:* Department of Classics, Yale University, New Haven, Conn. 06520.

CAREER: Harvard University, Cambridge, Mass., instructor in Latin and Greek, 1959-62; Stanford University, Palo Alto, Calif., assistant professor of Latin and Greek, 1962-65; Yale University, New Haven, Conn., associate professor, 1965-71; professor of Latin and Greek, 1971—. *Military service:* U.S. Army, 1956-57. *Awards, honors:* Fulbright fellowship to Italy, 1954-55.

WRITINGS: Democritus and the Sources of Greek Anthropology, Press of Case Western Reserve University, 1967; (editor with C. M. Dawson) *Studies in Latin Poetry*, Cambridge University Press, 1969; (editor with David Ross) *Studies in Latin Language and Literature*, Cambridge University Press, 1973.

WORK IN PROGRESS: Greek and Latin metrics; Greek political and social thought.

BIOGRAPHICAL/CRITICAL SOURCES: Times Literary Supplement, July 9, 1970.†

* * *

COLEMAN, Richard Patrick   1927-

PERSONAL: Born July 21, 1927, in Great Bend, Kan.; son of Russell Patrick (an accountant) and Fern (Wallace) Coleman. *Education:* University of Tulsa, B.A., 1948; University of Iowa, M.A., 1949; University of Chicago, Ph.D., 1959. *Politics:* 'Unpredictable.'' *Religion:* Presbyterian. *Home:* 246 Brattle, Cambridge, Mass. 02138. *Office:* Joint Center for Urban Studies, 53 Church, Cambridge, Mass. 02138.

CAREER: University of Chicago, Committee on Human Development, Chicago, Ill., research associate, 1952-56; Social Research, Inc., Chicago, research associate, 1957-63, vice-president, 1964-69; Joint Center for Urban Studies of the Massachusetts Institute of Technology and Harvard University, Cambridge, Mass., senior research associate, 1969—. *Member:* Quadrangle Club (Chicago).

WRITINGS: (With Lee Rainwater and Gerald Handel) *Workingman's Wife: Her Personality, World and Life Style*, Oceana, 1959; (with Bernice L. Neugarten) *Social Status in the City*, Jossey-Bass, 1971; *Social Standing in America*, Basic Books, in press.

Monographs; published by Joint Center for Urban Studies of the Massachusetts Institute of Technology and Harvard University: *Index of Urban Status*, 1973; *Seven Levels of Housing: An Exploration in Public Imagery*, 1973; (with David Birch) *America's Housing Needs: 1970-1980*, 1974.

WORK IN PROGRESS: The Collegiate Social Ladder, a book about status symbolism; *The Geography of Social Class*, a study of metropolitan residential distribution; *A Midwestern Elite*, a study on continuity and circulation of leadership in Kansas City.

* * *

COLES, William Allan   1930-

PERSONAL: Born October 15, 1930, in Boston, Mass.; son of Philip and Sonia (Young) Coles. *Education:* Harvard University, A.B., 1951, M.A., 1952, Ph.D., 1956. *Home:* 1050 Wall St., Ann Arbor, Mich. 48105. *Office:* Department of English, University of Michigan, Ann Arbor, Mich. 48104.

CAREER: University of Virginia, Charlottesville, instructor in English, 1956-58; University of North Carolina at Chapel Hill, assistant professor of English, 1958-62; University of Michigan, Ann Arbor, assistant professor, 1962-67, associate professor, 1967-72, professor of English, 1972—. Member of board of visitors, Codman House Museum, Lincoln, Mass. *Member:* Modern Language Association of America, Keats-Shelley Association, Victorian Society, Society of Architectural Historians of Great Britain, Browning Institute.

WRITINGS: (With Henry Hope Reed) *Architecture in America: A Battle of Styles*, Appleton, 1961; (editor) *Architecture and Society: Selected Essays of Henry Van Brunt*, Belknap Press, 1969; (author of introduction) Edith Wharton and Ogden Codman, Jr., *The Decoration of Houses*, Norton, 1977. Contributor to learned journals. Editor and member of board of directors, *Classical America*.

WORK IN PROGRESS: Editing the correspondence of Mary Russell Mitford and Thomas Noon Talfourd; a study of the writings of artists on art in late nineteenth-century Europe and America.

* * *

COLFORD, William E(dward)   1908-1971

May 9, 1908—August 12, 1971; American educator, editor, and translator. Obituaries: *New York Times*, August 14, 1971. (See index for *CA* sketch)

* * *

COLLIER, Christopher   1930-

PERSONAL: Born January 29, 1930, in New York, N.Y.; son of Edmund (a writer) and Katharine (Brown) Collier; married Virginia Wright (a teacher), August 21, 1954; married second wife, Bonnie Bromberger (a librarian), December 6, 1969; children: (first marriage) Edmund Quincy, Sally McQueen; (second marriage) Christopher Zwissler. *Education:* Clark University, Worcester, Mass., B.A., 1951; Columbia University, M.A., 1955, Ph.D., 1964. *Home:* 876 Orange Center Rd., Orange, Conn. 06477. *Office:* Department of History, University of Bridgeport, Bridgeport, Conn. 06602.

CAREER: Teacher in public schools in Greenwich, Conn., 1955-58, and New Canaan, Conn., 1959-61; Columbia University, Teachers College, New York, N.Y., instructor in history, 1958-59; University of Bridgeport, Bridgeport, Conn., instructor, 1961-64, assistant professor, 1964-67, associate professor, 1967-71, professor of history, 1971—, chairman of department, 1978—. *Military service:* U.S. Army, 1952-54. *Member:* American Historical Association, Organization of American Historians, Connecticut Historical Society. *Awards, honors:* Newberry Honor, Jane Addams Peace Price, and American Book Award nomination, all 1975.

WRITINGS: (Editor) *Public Records of the State of Connecticut 1965-1967*, State Library of Connecticut, 1967; *Roger Sherman's Connecticut: Yankee Politics and the American Revolution*, Wesleyan University Press, 1971; *Connecticut in the Continental Congress*, Pequot Press, 1973.

With James L. Collier; all juveniles; published by Scholastic Book Service: *My Brother Sam Is Dead*, 1974; *The Bloody Country*, 1976; *The Winter Hero*, 1978. Editor, Monographs in British History and Culture, 1967-72. Contributor to history journals.

WORK IN PROGRESS: Historical Geography of Connecticut; Beginnings of Political Parties in Connecticut; juvenile fiction.

* * *

COLLINS, Douglas 1912-1972

August 31, 1912—March 4, 1972; English businessman and author of children's books. Obituaries: *Variety*, March 15, 1972.

* * *

COLMAN, Arthur D. 1937-

PERSONAL: Born September 29, 1937, in New York, N.Y.; son of Jack Kelley (a lawyer) and Miriam (Greenblatt) Colman; married Libby Lee (a writer), October 26, 1963; children: Shoshana, Jonah, Ariel. *Education:* Harvard University, A.B. (magna cum laude), 1958, M.D., 1962; summer study and research at Peter Bent Brigham Hospital, 1959, and National Institute of Neurology, London, England, 1960. *Religion:* Jewish. *Home and office:* 412 Napa St., Sausalito, Calif. 94965.

CAREER: Beth Israel Hospital, Boston, Mass., intern, 1962-63; University of California Medical Center, Langely Porter Neuropsychiatric Institute, San Francisco, resident, 1963-66; Washington School of Psychiatry, Washington, D.C., graduate of Associated Faculties Program in Community Psychiatry, 1966-68; Etonim Hospital, Jerusalem, Israel, staff psychiatrist and head of research, 1969-70; University of California, San Francisco, assistant clinical professor, 1970-71, associate clinical professor of psychiatry, 1971—. In private practice of psychiatry in Sausalito, Calif., 1971—. Lecturer in department of architecture, University of California, Berkeley, 1971—; visiting professor of U.S. Surgeon General, 1972. Member of advisory committee, Planned Parenthood. *Military service:* U.S. Army, Medical Corps, 1966-69; became major. *Member:* American Psychiatric Association (fellow), International Association for Applied Social Sciences (charter member). *Awards, honors:* American Group Psychotherapy Association prize for writing; California Department of Mental Hygiene research grant, 1965-66; U.S. Army Research and Development Command grant, 1967-69.

WRITINGS: *The Planned Environment in Psychiatric Treatment*, C. C Thomas, 1971; (with wife, Libby Colman) *Pregnancy: The Psychological Experience*, McGraw, 1971; (contributor) E. J. Thomas, editor, *Behavior Modification Procedures*, Aldine, 1973; (contributor) *International Symposium of Behavior Modification*, Appleton-Century-Crofts, 1973; (contributor with L. Colman) *Towards a Better Beginning*, International Childbirth Education Association, 1973; (contributor) V. A. Christopherson, editor, *Man in Rehabilitation Nursing*, McGraw, 1974; (contributor) E. Miller, editor, *Task and Organization*, Tavistock

Publications, 1974; (editor with H. Bexton and contributor) *Group Relations Reader*, Grex, 1975; (with L. Colman) *Love and Ecstasy*, Seabury, 1975; (contributor) Sheldon Kopp, *The Naked Therapist*, Knapp, 1976. Contributor to *Proceedings* of the Human Factor Society. Contributor of more than thirty articles to professional journals.

WORK IN PROGRESS: With wife, Libby Colman, *Earth Father, Sky Father*, a study of images for male parents.

SIDELIGHTS: Pregnancy has been published in French and Spanish.

* * *

COLMAN, Libby Lee 1940-

PERSONAL: Born March 26, 1940, in Brooklyn, N.Y.; daughter of Theodore R. (a lawyer) and Josephine (Chandler) Lee; married Arthur D. Colman (a psychiatrist and author), October 26, 1963; children: Shoshana, Jonah, Ariel. *Education:* Wellesley College, B.A., 1962; San Francisco State College (now University), M.A., 1965; George Washington University, Ph.D., 1972. *Home:* 412 Napa St., Sausalito, Calif. 94965. *Office:* Department of Humanities, New College of California, San Francisco, Calif.

CAREER: High school English and journalism teacher in Boiceville, N.Y., 1962-63; San Francisco State College (now University), San Francisco, Calif., instructor in English, 1965-66; George Washington University, Washington, D.C., instructor in English, 1967-68; New College of California, San Francisco, instructor in humanities, 1971—.

WRITINGS: (With husband, Arthur D. Colman) *Pregnancy: The Psychological Experience*, McGraw, 1971; (contributor with A. D. Colman) *Towards A Better Beginning*, International Childbirth Education Association, 1973; (with A. D. Colman) *Love and Ecstasy*, Seabury, 1975; (with Elisabeth Bing) *Making Love during Pregnancy*, Bantam, 1977. Contributor to *California Health*. Associate editor, *Birth and the Family Journal*.

WORK IN PROGRESS: With husband, Arthur D. Colman, *Earth Father, Sky Father*, a study of images for male parents.

SIDELIGHTS: Pregnancy has been published in translation in France and Spain.

BIOGRAPHICAL/CRITICAL SOURCES: San Francisco Examiner & Chronicle, April 9, 1972; *Contemporary Psychology*, December, 1975.

* * *

COLUM, Padraic 1881-1972

December 8, 1881—January 12, 1972; Irish-born American poet, essayist, novelist, playwright, biographer, folklorist, and author of children's books. Obituaries: *Detroit News*, January 12, 1972; *New York Times*, January 12, 1972; *Washington Post*, January 13, 1972; *Newsweek*, January 24, 1972; *Time*, January 24, 1972; *Publishers Weekly*, February 21, 1972.

* * *

COLWELL, Robert 1931-

PERSONAL: Born June 5, 1931, in Montreal, Quebec, Canada; son of Charles L. (an architect) and Evelyn (Ott) Colwell; married Jo Ann Ray, May 20, 1951; children: Garrick C., Roxann L. *Residence:* Madeira Beach, Fla.

WRITINGS—All published by Stackpole: *Introduction to Backpacking*, 1970; *Introduction to Foot Trails in America*,

1972; *Introduction to Water Trails in America,* 1973; *Guide to Snow Trails,* 1974; *Guide to Bicycle Trails,* 1975. Contributor of poems and short stories to several dozen literary magazines.

WORK IN PROGRESS: Going It Alone; Into a Darker Age.

* * *

COMBS, Richard Earl 1934-

PERSONAL: Born January 10, 1934, in Clinton, Ind.; son of Jesse Truman and Iona (Elmore) Combs; married Adele Westgate (an academic librarian), April 20, 1957. *Education:* Indiana University, A.B., 1961; Columbia University, M.S.L.S., 1965. *Home:* 1100 Church St., Evanston, Ill. 60201. *Office:* Northbrook Public Library, 1201 Cedar Lane, Northbrook, Ill. 60062.

CAREER: Indiana University Press, Bloomington, copy editor of monographs, 1962-64; Brooklyn Public Library, Brooklyn, N.Y., librarian, 1964-66; Newport Public Library, Newport, R.I., head librarian, 1966-68; Northbrook Public Library, Northbrook, Ill., head librarian, 1968—. Part-time instructor, University of Rhode Island, 1966-68, Chicago City College, 1973. Member of board of directors, Newport Community Center, 1967-68; member of board, Northfield Township Drug Education Association, 1970—. *Military service:* U.S. Navy, photographer's mate, 1952-56. *Member:* American Library Association, New England Library Association (director II, 1968), Rhode Island Library Association (president, 1968), Illinois Library Association. *Awards, honors:* Colorado Writers' Conference fellowship, 1961; Council on Library Resources fellowship, 1972-73.

WRITINGS: Authors: Critical and Biographical References, Scarecrow, 1971. Contributor of articles to *American Libraries, Cosmopolitan, Road and Track,* and other publications. Editor, *Rhode Island Library Association Bulletin,* 1966-68.

WORK IN PROGRESS: A book entitled *The City and the Library in Transition;* researching for book entitled *Library Architecture: Solutions and Innovations.*†

* * *

CONAWAY, James (Alley) 1941-

PERSONAL: Born April 15, 1941, in Memphis, Tenn.; son of Frank Elmer (an engineer) and Kathryn (Alley) Conaway; married Penelope Brennan, September 26, 1964; children: Brennan James, Deborah Jessica, Susanna Lane. *Education:* Attended University of North Carolina, 1959-61; Southwestern at Memphis, B.A., 1963; Stanford University, graduate study, 1963-64. *Residence:* Bucks County, Pa.

CAREER: Times-Picayune, New Orleans, La., reporter, 1965-66; *Daily American,* Rome, Italy, reporter, 1967; freelance journalist. *Awards, honors:* Wallace Stegner Creative Writing fellowship at Stanford University, 1963-64; Alicia Patterson fellowship, 1974.

WRITINGS: The Big Easy (novel), Houghton, 1970; *Judge: The Life and Times of Leander Perez* (biography), Knopf, 1973; *The Texans* (nonfiction), Knopf, 1976. Contributor to *Atlantic, New York Times Magazine,* and literary journals.

BIOGRAPHICAL/CRITICAL SOURCES: Washington Post, January 18, 1974.

CONE, James H. 1938-

PERSONAL: Born August 5, 1938, in Fordyce, Ark.; son of Charlie and Lucille Cone; married Rose Hampton (a college lecturer), December 25, 1958; children: Michael Lawrence, Charles Pierson. *Education:* Attended Shorter College, two years; Philander Smith College, B.A., 1958; Garrett Theological Seminary, B.D., 1961; Northwestern University, M.A., 1963, Ph.D., 1965. *Home:* 99 Claremont Ave., New York, N.Y. 10027. *Office:* Department of Theology, Union Theological Seminary, New York, N.Y. 10027.

CAREER: Clergyman of Methodist Church; Philander Smith College, Little Rock, Ark., assistant professor of religion and philosophy, 1964-66; Adrian College, Adrian, Mich., assistant professor of religion, 1966-69; Union Theological Seminary, New York, N.Y., assistant professor, 1969-70, associate professor, 1970-73, professor of theology, 1973-77, Charles A. Briggs Professor of Systematic Theology, 1977—. Visiting professor of theology, University of the Pacific, summer, 1969, Drew University, 1971-73, Princeton Theological Seminary, 1976-77; visiting associate professor of religion, Barnard College, 1969-71, 1974; Harris Franklin Hall Lecturer, Garrett Theological Seminary, 1970; Edgar Godspeed Lecturer, Denison University, 1971; lecturer in systematic theology, Woodstock College, 1971-73. Lecturer at over fifty other colleges and universities and at churches and institutes. *Member:* National Committee of Black Churchmen (member of board of directors), American Academy of Religion, Congress of African Peoples, Black Methodists for Church Renewal, Alpha Kappa Mu.

WRITINGS: (Contributor) C. Eric Lincoln, editor, *Is Anybody Listening to Black America,* Seabury, 1968; *Black Theology and Black Power,* Seabury, 1969; *A Black Theology of Liberation,* Lippincott, 1970; *The Spirituals and the Blues: An Interpretation,* Seabury, 1972; *The God of the Oppressed,* Seabury, 1975. Contributor to *Encyclopaedia Britannica;* contributor of about twenty articles and reviews to *Ladies' Home Journal, Ebony, Christian Century,* and other publications. Contributing editor, *Christianity and Crisis.*

SIDELIGHTS: Black Theology and Black Power has been published in translation in Germany; French, Spanish, and Japanese translations are in preparation.

BIOGRAPHICAL/CRITICAL SOURCES: Christian Century, December 17, 1969, October 21, 1970; *Washington Post,* February 21, 1970, February 6, 1971; *New York Times,* January 30, 1971.

* * *

CONFORD, Ellen 1942-

PERSONAL: Born March 20, 1942, in New York, N.Y.; daughter of Harry and Lillian (Pfeffer) Schaffer; married David Conford (an English professor), November 23, 1960; children: Michael. *Education:* Attended Hofstra College (now Hofstra University), 1959-62. *Home:* 70 Roy Ave., Massapequa, N.Y. 11758.

CAREER: Writer of books for children and young adults. Consultant, Nassau County Cultural Arts Division of Board of Cooperative Educational Services. *Awards, honors: The Alfred G. Graebner Memorial High School Handbook of Rules and Regulations* was chosen Notable Young Adult Book of 1976 by the American Library Association.

WRITINGS—For young people; all published by Little, Brown: Impossible, Possum (Junior Literary Guild selection), 1971; *Why Can't I Be William?,* 1972; *Dreams of Vic-*

tory (Junior Literary Guild selection), 1973; *Felicia the Critic* (Junior Literary Guild selection), 1973; *Just the Thing for Geraldine*, 1974; *Me and the Terrible Two*, 1974; *The Luck of Pokey Bloom*, 1975; *Dear Lovey Hart, I Am Desperate*, 1975; *The Alfred G. Graebner Memorial High School Handbook of Rules and Regulations*, 1976; *And This Is Laura*, 1977; *Eugene the Brave*, in press. Contributor of stories and poems to national periodicals, including *Teen, Reader's Digest,* and *Modern Bride;* contributor of reviews to *New York Times* and *American Record Guide.*

* * *

CONKIN, Paul K(eith) 1929-

PERSONAL: Born October 25, 1929, in Chuckey, Tenn.; son of Harry T. and Dorothy (Staten) Conkin; married Dorothy L. Tharp, August 14, 1954; children: Keith Tharp, Claudia Sue, Lydia Kathleen. *Education:* Milligan College, B.A., 1951; Vanderbilt University, M.A., 1953, Ph.D., 1957. *Home:* 4625 Ames St., Madison, Wis. 53711. *Office:* Department of History, University of Wisconsin, Madison, Wis. 53706.

CAREER: University of Southwestern Louisiana, Lafayette, assistant professor of philosphy and history, 1957-59; University of Maryland, College Park, assistant professor, 1959-61, associate professor, 1961-66, professor of history, 1966-67; University of Wisconsin—Madison, professor of history, 1967-76, Merle Curti Professor of History, 1976—. *Military service:* U.S. Army, 1953-55. *Member:* American Historical Association, Organization of American Historians. *Awards, honors:* Albert J. Beveridge Award in American history, 1958; Guggenheim fellow, 1966-67; National Endowment for the Humanities senior fellow, 1972-73.

WRITINGS: Tomorrow a New World: The New Deal Community Program, Cornell University Press, 1959; *Two Paths to Utopia: The Hutterites and the Llano Colony,* University of Nebraska Press, 1964; *F.D.R. and the Origins of the Welfare State,* Crowell, 1967, published as *The New Deal,* Crowell, 1967; *Puritans and Pragmatists: Eight Eminent American Thinkers,* Dodd, 1968; (with Roland Stromberg) *The Heritage and Challenge of History,* Dodd, 1971; *Self-Evident Truths,* Indiana University Press, 1974; (with David Burner) *A History of Recent America,* Crowell, 1974. Contributor to journals.

WORK IN PROGRESS: Two books.

SIDELIGHTS: Reviewer Gary Houston praises Paul Conkin's *Puritans and Pragmatists,* while disagreeing with the author's concept of an intellectual tradition which encompasses both. "These essays," adds Houston, "exhibit a warm, perceptive, and thorough appreciation of the interplay between biography and philosophy."

BIOGRAPHICAL/CRITICAL SOURCES: Christian Science Monitor, August 23, 1969; *American Historical Review,* December, 1972; *Journal of Southern History,* February, 1975; *William and Mary Quarterly,* April, 1975; *Journal of American History,* September, 1975.

* * *

CONN, Frances G. 1925-

PERSONAL: Born January 28, 1925, in Oil City, Pa.; daughter of Simon B. (a businessman) and Dorothy (Phillips) Goldberg; married Robert H. Conn, January 1, 1948; children: Paul Michael, Lois Marie. *Education:* University of Michigan, B.A., 1946; Temple University and Pennsylvania State University, graduate study, 1960-61; American

University, M.Ed., 1972, Ph.D., 1977. *Home:* 8320 Woodhaven Blvd., Bethesda, Md. 20034. *Agent:* Ann Elmo Agency, Inc., 52 Vanderbilt Ave., New York, N.Y. 10017. *Office:* Northern Virginia Community College, Alexandria, Va.

CAREER: Self-employed sociological and educational consultant, researcher, and writer, Washington, D.C., 1961-71; National Retired Teachers' Association-American Association of Retired Persons, Washington, D.C., national coordinator of health education programs, 1971-73; George Washington University Medical Center, Washington, D.C., deputy director of population information program, 1973-77; Northern Virginia Community College, Alexandria, instructor, 1978—.

WRITINGS: (With S. S. Rosenberg) *The First Oil Rush,* Meredith, 1967; (contributor) E. L. Wenzel and M. H. Arbuthnot, *Time for Discovery,* Scott, Foresman, 1971; *Ida Tarbell: Muckraker* (juvenile), Thomas Nelson, 1972. Contributor of articles to *Parents' Magazine, Catholic Digest, Grit,* and other magazines.

SIDELIGHTS: The First Oil Rush has been published in German translation.

* * *

CONN, Peter J. 1942-

PERSONAL: Born September 27, 1942, in Rockville Centre, N.Y.; son of Ira Francis and Alice (St. Onge) Conn; married Therese Farrington, August 29, 1964; children: Steven, David, Alison. *Education:* Providence College, A.B., 1964; Yale University, M.A., 1966, M.Phil., 1967, Ph.D., 1969. *Office:* Department of English, University of Pennsylvania, 3304 Walnut, Philadelphia, Pa. 19104.

CAREER: University of Pennsylvania, Philadelphia, instructor, 1967-69, assistant professor, 1969-73, associate professor of English, 1973—, associate dean of College of Arts and Sciences, 1970-74. Master, Robert C. Hill College House, 1973-76. *Awards, honors:* Woodrow Wilson fellowship, 1964; National Endowment for the Humanities summer fellowship, 1976.

WRITINGS: (Editor with William Adams and Barry Slepian) *Afro-American Literature,* Houghton, 1970; (editor with R. W. Lewis) Graham Greene, *The Power and the Glory* (critical edition), Viking, 1970. Contributor to literature journals.

WORK IN PROGRESS: Research on the American 1900's.

* * *

CONSOLO, Dominick P(eter) 1923-

PERSONAL: Born February 5, 1923, in Ridgway, Pa.; son of Nick and Marietta (Viglione) Consolo; married Jeanne Kaufman (a mathematics teacher), July 2, 1948; children: Kitty, Nancy. *Education:* Miami University, Oxford, Ohio, B.A., 1948, M.A., 1950; University of Iowa, Ph.D., 1958. *Office:* Department of English, Denison University, Granville, Ohio 43023.

CAREER: University of Iowa, Iowa City, instructor in English, 1957-58; Denison University, Granville, Ohio, assistant professor, 1958-63, associate professor, 1963-67, professor of medieval and contemporary literature, 1967—. Fulbright lecturer on Shakespeare, Tel-Aviv University, 1964-65. *Military service:* U.S. Army Air Forces, 1943-46; became staff sergeant. *Member:* Modern Language Association of America, American Association of University Professors, Johnson Society (secretary), Pi Delta Epsilon, Delta Tau Delta.

WRITINGS: (Contributor) R. O. Evans, editor, *Graham Greene: Some Critical Considerations,* University of Kentucky Press, 1963; (editor) D. H. Lawrence, *The Rocking-Horse Winner,* C. E. Merrill, 1969; (editor with W. O. Brasmer) *Black Drama,* C. E. Merrill, 1970; (editor) Walt Whitman, *Out of the Cradle,* C. E. Merrill, 1971. Contributor to *World Book Encyclopedia,* 1975.

WORK IN PROGRESS: Style in contemporary American fiction.

SIDELIGHTS: Dominick Consolo spent 1971 in Italy, studying Italian writers' views of contemporary American fiction.

* * *

COOK, Bruce 1932-

PERSONAL: Born April 7, 1932, in Chicago, Ill.; son of Robert Neal (a train dispatcher) and Gladys (Moon) Cook; married Catherine Coghlan, December 5, 1956; children: Robert Neal, Catherine Marie, Cecilia Mary. *Education:* Loyola University, Chicago, B.S., 1955. *Religion:* Roman Catholic. *Home:* 9809 Culver St., Kensington, Md. 20795. *Agent:* Mary Yost Associates, 141 East 55th St., New York, N.Y. 10022.

CAREER: Worked in various editorial and public relations posts in Chicago, Ill., 1958-65; free-lance writer, 1965-67; *National Observer,* Silver Spring, Md., book review editor, 1967-71, movie critic, 1971-75. *Military service:* U.S. Army, German translator, 1955-58.

WRITINGS: The Beat Generation, Scribner, 1971; *Listen to the Blues,* Scribner, 1973; *Dalton Trumbo,* Scribner, 1977. Writer of articles, and of industrial, business, and documentary films.

WORK IN PROGRESS: A novel.

BIOGRAPHICAL/CRITICAL SOURCES: New York Times, August 26, 1971; *Detroit News,* September 5, 1971.

* * *

COOK, Daniel 1914-

PERSONAL: Born August 21, 1914, in Bismarck, N.D.; son of Sylvanus Daniel (an insurance agent) and Lavinia (Hedger) Cook; married Jane McElwain, June, 1941; married second wife, Jean-Marie McKenna (an English instructor), September 24, 1966; children: (first marriage) John, Thomas, Samuel. *Education:* University of Wisconsin, B.A., 1940, M.A., 1941; University of California, Berkeley, Ph.D., 1954. *Office:* Department of English, American University of Beirut, Beirut, Lebanon.

CAREER: Duke University, Durham, N.C., instructor in English, 1950-52; G. & C. Merriam Co., Springfield, Mass., associate editor of Merriam-Webster dictionaries, 1952-57; Southern Illinois University, Carbondale, associate professor of English, 1957-65; American University of Beirut, Beirut, Lebanon, visiting professor, 1963-64, professor of English and linguistics, 1965—. Fulbright lecturer in linguistics, Damascus University, 1961-62; Fulbright lecturer in applied linguistics, University of Silesia. Consultant on language textbooks to McGraw-Hill Publishing Co., 1959-60, and Doubleday & Co., on school dictionaries to Fawcett Publications, 1961-62, and Harcourt, Brace & World, 1963, on lexicography to Grolier Society, 1961-62. Consultant on

program development, teaching English as a foreign language, to Raytheon Service Corp., Saudi Arabia; consultant to Ministry of Health, Bahrain, Ministry of Planning, Kuwait, and Centre for the Teaching of Arabic, Khartoum University, Sudan. *Military service:* U.S. Naval Reserve, 1942-46; became lieutenant.

MEMBER: Modern Language Association of America, Linguistic Society of America, American Dialect Society, Mediaeval Academy of America, Association of University Teachers of English in the Arab World.

WRITINGS: (Editor and author of introduction and notes) *The "Canterbury Tales" of Geoffrey Chaucer,* abridged bilingual edition, Doubleday-Anchor, 1961; (associate editor) *Webster's New International Dictionary,* 3rd edition, Merriam, 1961; (editor and author of introduction and notes) Geoffrey Chaucer, *Troilus and Criseyde,* Doubleday-Anchor, 1966; (editor and author of notes) William Shakespeare, *Julius Caesar, Macbeth* [and] *Hamlet* (textbook series), Holt, 1969-70. Author of various papers and reviews on scholarly subjects; contributor of numerous articles to encyclopedias, including *Grolier Society Encyclopaedia.*

WORK IN PROGRESS: Translating, with notes and introduction, *Beowulf;* a series of essays on selected *Canterbury Tales.*

SIDELIGHTS: Daniel Cook teaches and lives in the Arab world, and has "an elementary command" of Arabic. For amusement, he skis in Lebanon in the winter and cruises the eastern Mediterranean in a small sailing yacht in the summer. Whenever possible, he also lives in a 110-year-old house on his farm in Virginia, alternating between desk work and farming.

* * *

COOK, Gladys Moon 1907-

PERSONAL: Born April 8, 1907, in Columbia, Iowa; daughter of Elmer Homer (a laborer) and Bertha (Miller) Moon; married Robert Cook, May 5, 1928 (deceased); children: Bruce A. *Education:* Attended Des Moines University, 1925-27, and Northwestern University, 1959-64; Columbia College, Chicago, Ill., B.A., 1967. *Religion:* Congregationalist. *Home:* 1628 West Touhy Ave., Chicago, Ill. 60626.

CAREER: Perrin & Associates (advertising agency), Chicago, Ill., head bookkeeper, 1956-69. *Member:* Poets and Patrons, Inc. (former workshop chairman), National League of American Pen Women (secretary of Chicago chapter), Poets of Chicago (former president), Midland Authors Society, Iota Sigma Epsilon (former secretary and treasurer). *Awards, honors:* Friends of Literature award, 1976, for *Vashti and the Strange God.*

WRITINGS—Juvenile novels: Escape, Moody, 1971; *Vashti and the Strange God,* David Cook, 1975. Work is represented in collections, including *Yearbook of Modern Poetry,* Young Publications, 1971, and *Outstanding Contemporary Poetry,* Pied Piper, 1972. Contributor to numerous little magazines and newspapers.

WORK IN PROGRESS: Pestilence in the Land, a Civil War story; *Things Happen in Montana,* a boy's novel about Montana as it was in 1913.

SIDELIGHTS: Gladys Cook told *CA:* "I feel a great concern about India's impoverished masses. I believe ignorance keeps them where they are and education is the best answer to their plight. With this in mind, I wrote *Vashti and the Strange God.*

"I think every writer feels himself under a compulsion to put down in readable words what he considers the truth. We have great literature from ages past because the truth, as those authors saw it, is as applicable today as it was when it was written. We are an emotional, imaginative, loving, hating, beautiful, horrific and frustrated people."

AVOCATIONAL INTERESTS: Travel.

*   *   *

COOK, Robert I. 1920-

PERSONAL: Born March 28, 1920, in Traverse City, Mich.; married Barbara Johnson, July 17, 1943; children: Cynthia, James, Carolyn. *Education:* Michigan State University, B.A., 1949, M.A., 1954, Ph.D., 1974. *Politics:* Democrat. *Religion:* Roman Catholic. *Home:* 204 West Felicity, Angola, Ind. 46703. *Office:* Department of Business Administration, Tri-State University, Angola, Ind. 46703.

CAREER: Tri-State University, Angola, Ind., assistant professor, 1950-54, associate professor, 1955-68, professor of management, 1968—. *Military service:* U.S. Army Air Forces, 1942-45; became technical sergeant. *Member:* National Association of Purchasing Management (Fourth District professional development chairman, 1967), Academy of Management.

WRITINGS: (Editor with Paul T. McElhiney) *Logistics of Materials Management: Readings in Modern Purchasing,* Houghton, 1969. Contributor to management and purchasing journals.

*   *   *

COOKE, William 1942-

PERSONAL: Born December 27, 1942, in Stoke-on-Trent, Staffordshire, England; son of William (a builder) and Ann Maria (Docksey) Cooke. *Education:* University of Leeds, B.A., 1964, M.A., 1966, Ph.D., 1969. *Home:* 17, Stuart Ave., Trentham, Stoke-on-Trent, Staffordshire ST4 8BG, England.

CAREER: Thistley Hough School, Stoke-on-Trent, England, teacher, 1968-70; City of Stoke-on-Trent Sixth Form College, Stoke-on-Trent, tutor of English literature, 1970—.

WRITINGS: Edward Thomas: A Critical Biography, 1878-1917, Faber, 1970; (contributor) Peter Porter and Charles Osborne, editors, *New Poetry I,* Arts Council of Great Britain, 1975; (contributor) Norman Hidden, editor, *Over to You,* English Speaking Board, 1975; (contributor) Patricia Beer and Kevin Crossley-Holland, editors, *New Poetry II,* Arts Council of Great Britain, 1976.

WORK IN PROGRESS: Editing the letters of Edward Thomas to Harold Monro for publication under the title, "A Writing Animal," in a special issue of *Poetry Wales* commemorating the centenary of Edward Thomas's birth; a first book of poetry.

BIOGRAPHICAL/CRITICAL SOURCES: Spectator, February 14, 1970; *Observer,* February 15, 1970; *Times Literary Supplement,* April 30, 1970; *London Magazine,* June, 1970.

*   *   *

COOLIDGE, Clark 1939-

PERSONAL: Born February 26, 1939, in Providence, R.I.; son of Arlan Ralph (a teacher) and Sylvia (Clark) Coolidge; married Susan Hopkins, December 17, 1967; children: Celia Elizabeth. *Education:* Attended Brown University, 1956-58. *Residence:* New Lebanon, N.Y.; Hancock, Mass.

CAREER: Musician since his high school days and former drummer with the Serpent Power, a San Francisco rock group; WPFM-FM, Providence, R.I., disc jockey, 1958; Brown University, Providence, searcher at Rockefeller Library, 1964-65; KPFA-FM, Berkeley, Calif., producer of "Words" (weekly hour of new poetry), 1969-70; writer. Member of board of directors, Shaker Heights Association, Inc., Hancock, Mass., 1971—. *Awards, honors:* American Literary Anthology Award, 1968, for poem, "Soda Gong"; Poets Foundation Award, 1968.

WRITINGS—Poetry, except as indicated: *Flag Flutter & U.S. Electric,* Lines Press, 1966; *Clark Coolidge,* Lines Press, 1967; *Ing,* Angel Hair Books, 1969; (with Tom Veitch) *To Obtain the Value of the Cake Measure from Zero* (play), Grape Press, 1970; *Space,* Harper, 1970; *The So,* Adventures in Poetry Editions, 1971; *Suite V.,* Adventures in Poetry Editions, 1973; *The Maintains,* This Press, 1974; *Polaroid,* Adventures in Poetry Editions, 1975. An issue of *Big Sky* was devoted to Coolidge's poetry, 1972. Co-editor, *Joglars,* 1964-66.

WORK IN PROGRESS: A book of writings and drawings, with Philip Guston; *The Cave Work,* with Bernadette Mayer; a long poem.

AVOCATIONAL INTERESTS: Spelunking, collecting minerals.

BIOGRAPHICAL/CRITICAL SOURCES: Poetry, March, 1967, January, 1972; *Newsweek,* March 3, 1969.

*   *   *

COOPER, Edmund 1926-
(Richard Avery)

PERSONAL: Born April 30, 1926, in Marple, Cheshire, England; son of Joseph (a shopkeeper) and Harriet (Fletcher) Cooper; married Joyce Plant (a teacher), April 13, 1946; married second wife, Valerie Makin, October 19, 1963; children: (first marriage) Glynis (Mrs. David Reeve), Daryl, Troy, Guy; (second marriage) Shaun, Justine, Regan, Jason. *Education:* Educated at Manchester Grammar School, 1937-41. *Religion:* Atheist. *Home and office:* "Stammers," Madehurst, near Arundel, Sussex, England.

CAREER: After leaving school, worked as warehouse labourer, then as a British civil servant; joined Merchant Navy as radio officer at age of 17, spent two years at sea, 1944-46; became a teacher and began writing, 1947-51, retreated to country to write full time; journalist, 1961-66; full-time writer, 1966—. *Member:* P.E.N.

WRITINGS—All science fiction: *Deadly Image* (novel), Ballantine, 1958 (published in England as *The Uncertain Midnight,* Hutchinson, 1958); *Tomorrow's Gift* (short stories), Ballantine, 1958; *Seed of Light* (novel), Ballantine, 1959; *Wish Goes to Slumber Land,* Hutchinson, 1960; *Voices in the Dark* (short stories), Digit Books, 1960; *Tomorrow Came* (short stories), Panther Books, 1963; *Transit* (novel), Lancer Books, 1964; *All Fools' Day* (novel), Walker, 1966; *A Far Sunset,* Walker, 1967; *News from Elsewhere* (short stories), Mayflower Books, 1968, Berkley Publishing, 1969; *The Last Continent,* Dell, 1969; *The Square Root of Tomorrow* (short stories), R. Hale, 1970; *Unborn Tomorrow* (short stories), R. Hale, 1971; (with Roger L. Green) *Double Phoenix,* Ballantine, 1971; *Who Needs Men?,* Ace Books, 1972.

All published by Hodder & Stoughton: *Five to Twelve* (Science Fiction Book Club selection), 1968, Putnam, 1969; *Sea-Horse in the Sky* (Science Fiction Book Club selection),

1969, Putnam, 1970; *Son of Kronk,* 1970, published as *Kronk,* Putnam, 1971; *The Overman Culture,* 1971, Putnam, 1972; *The Cloud Walker,* 1973; *The Tenth Planet,* 1973; *The Slaves of Heaven,* 1974; *Prisoner of Fire,* 1974.

Under pseudonym Richard Avery; "The Expendables" series (novels); published by Fawcett: *The Deathworms of Kratos,* 1975; *The Rings of Tantalus,* 1975; *The Wargames of Zelos,* 1975; *The Venom of Argus,* 1976. Science fiction book reviewer for *Sunday Times* (London), 1967—. Contributor of short stories to numerous magazines in various countries, including *American Mercury, B.B.C., Courier, Everybody's, John Bull, London Mystery Magazine, Mirror Pocket Book,* and *Saturday Evening Post.*

WORK IN PROGRESS: A novella, tentatively entitled *The Games,* to be included in a collection of stories tentatively entitled *Jupiter Laughs;* another science fiction novel, tentatively entitled *Adversane.*

SIDELIGHTS: Edmund Cooper's style has been summed up as "one part Edgar Rice Burroughs, two parts Sir James Frazer, and three parts of his own science fantasy" by a *Books and Bookmen* reviewer.

Cooper told *CA* that he "has recently become very disillusioned with technology and politics. No civilization is immortal . . . Western civilization will disintegrate in the early 21st century." He has "not lost faith in humanity but believes that there will be a new dark age before another and possibly, more viable civilization emerges."

Cooper's books have been translated into several languages, including French, Italian, German, Portuguese, Japanese, and Dutch. *The Uncertain Midnight* was made into a ten-part serial and shown on television in Switzerland and other countries in the 1960's. Film rights to *Transit* have been sold to Twentieth Century-Fox.

AVOCATIONAL INTERESTS: Chess, music, "trying to discover what people are really like."

BIOGRAPHICAL/CRITICAL SOURCES: New Statesman, July 14, 1967; *Books and Bookmen,* September, 1967, May, 1968, November, 1973; *Books,* April, 1970; *Observer,* January 10, 1971, September 3, 1972, December 23, 1973; *Times Literary Supplement,* February 15, 1974.

* * *

COOPER, Gladys 1888-1971

December 18, 1888—November 17, 1971; English actress. Obituaries: *New York Times,* November 18, 1971; *Washington Post,* November 18, 1971; *Newsweek,* November 29, 1971; *Time,* November 29, 1971.

* * *

COOPER, Philip (Jr.) 1926-

PERSONAL: Born January 5, 1926, in Jackson, Miss.; son of Philip (a chemical engineer) and Mildred (Macgowan) Cooper; married Margaret Lindabury, September 8, 1956; children: Marian, Paul, Barbara, Cynthia, Robin. *Education:* Tulane University, B.A., 1947; Columbia University, M.A., 1956; University of Rochester, Ph.D., 1967. *Home:* 429 Drury Lane, Baltimore, Md. 21229. *Office:* Department of English, University of Maryland Baltimore County, Baltimore, Md. 21228.

CAREER: Dartmouth College, Hanover, N.H., instructor in English, 1956-57; University of Rochester, Rochester, N.Y., instructor in the humanities at Eastman School of Music, 1957-63, graduate associate in English in the univer-

sity, 1963-65; Hollins College, Hollins College, Va., assistant professor of English, 1965-68; University of Maryland Baltimore County, Baltimore, assistant professor, 1968-71, associate professor of English, 1971—. *Military service:* U.S. Naval Reserve, active duty, 1943-46; became lieutenant. *Member:* Modern Language Association of America, American Association of University Professors, English Institute.

WRITINGS: The Autobiographical Myth of Robert Lowell, University of North Carolina Press, 1970.

WORK IN PROGRESS: Further studies in autobiographical form and poetic motion.

BIOGRAPHICAL/CRITICAL SOURCES: Times Literary Supplement, June 11, 1971; *Roanoke Times,* July 18, 1971; *American Literature,* November, 1971.

* * *

COPE, David 1941-

PERSONAL: Born May 17, 1941, in San Francisco, Calif.; son of Howell N. (a businessman) and Evlyn (Schleicher) Cope; married Mary Jane Stluka, August 12, 1967; children: Timothy, Stephen. *Education:* Arizona State University, B.Music, 1963; University of Southern California, M.Music, 1965. *Residence:* Oxford, Ohio. *Office:* Department of Music, Miami University, Oxford, Ohio 45056.

CAREER: Kansas State College of Pittsburg (now Pittsburg State University), instructor in music, 1966-68; California Lutheran College, Thousand Oaks, instructor in music, 1968-69; Prairie View Agricultural and Mechanical College (now Prairie View A & M University), Prairie View, Tex., associate professor of music, 1969-70; Cleveland Institute of Music, Cleveland, Ohio, teacher of composition, 1970-73; Miami University, Oxford, Ohio, associate professor of music, 1973—. Composer of more than fifty musical works. President, Composers Autograph Publications; co-director, Portfolio Concerts of New Music; director, Performance Group. *Member:* American Society of Composers, Authors and Publishers, Association of Independent Composers and Performers, Phi Mu Alpha.

WRITINGS: New Directions in Music, W. C. Brown, 1971; *New Music Notation,* Kendall/Hunt, 1976; *New Music Composition,* Macmillan, 1977. Music has been published by Media Press, Seesaw Music Corp., Carl Fischer, and Discant. Editor, *Composer* (magazine), 1968—.

WORK IN PROGRESS: Editing an anthology of writings on new music.

* * *

COPPA, Frank John 1937-

PERSONAL: Born July 18, 1937, in New York, N.Y.; son of Peter Paul and Fanny Coppa; married Rosina Genovese (an educator), August 7, 1965; children: Francesca, Melina. *Education:* Brooklyn College (now Brooklyn College of the City University of New York), B.A., 1960; Catholic University of America, M.A., 1962, Ph.D., 1966. *Religion:* Roman Catholic. *Office:* Department of History, St. John's University, Jamaica, N.Y. 11432.

CAREER: St. John's University, Jamaica, N.Y., instructor, 1965-66, assistant professor, 1966-70, associate professor of history, 1970—. Member of Columbia University Seminar on Modern Italy. *Member:* American Historical Association, Catholic Historical Association, Society for Italian Historical Studies, Inter-university Center for European Studies, New York State Association of European Historians. *Awards, honors:* Fulbright grant to Italy, 1964-65; U.S. Educational Foundation grant, 1965; various university grants, 1967, 1969, 1974; National Endowment for the Humanities grant, summer, 1977.

WRITINGS: (Contributor) Gaetano L. Vincitorio, editor, *Studies in Modern History,* St. John's University Press, 1968; (co-editor and contributor) *From Vienna to Vietnam: War and Peace in the Modern World,* W. C. Brown, 1969; *Planning, Protectionism and Politics in Liberal Italy: Economics and Politics in Liberal Italy,* Catholic University Press, 1971; *Camillo di Cavour,* Twayne, 1973; *Cities in Transition: From the Ancient World to Urban America,* Nelson-Hall, 1974; *Religion in the Making of Western Man,* St. John's University Press, 1974; *The Immigrant Experience in America,* [Boston], 1976; (contributor) Philip C. Dolce and George Skau, editors, *Power and the Presidency,* Scribner, 1976; (contributor) Dolce, editor, *Suburbia,* Doubleday, 1976. Contributor to *Catholic Historical Review, Journal of Modern History, Journal of Economic History, American Historical Review, Clio, La Parola del Popolo,* and other publications.

WORK IN PROGRESS: A work on the impact of television, *Television and the Transformation of the West.*

*   *   *

COPPEL, Alec   1909(?)-1972

1909(?)—January 22, 1972; Australian playwright and screenwriter. Obituaries: *Stage,* January 27, 1972.

*   *   *

CORBIN, Donald A(lvin)   1920-

PERSONAL: Born September 23, 1920, in Medford, Ore.; son of Charles Alvin and Florence Ruth (Sparks) Corbin; married Dorothy J. Hohman, June 6, 1943; children: Robert Donald, Gail Louise. *Education:* University of California, Berkeley, B.S., 1942, M.B.A., 1943, Ph.D., 1954. *Home:* 44-055 Aumoana Pl., Kaneohe, Hawaii 96744. *Office:* College of Business Administration, University of Hawaii, Honolulu, Hawaii 96822.

CAREER: Accounting and auditing positions in San Francisco and Oakland, Calif., 1942-46; American Institute of Banking, Oakland, lecturer in business administration, 1946-54; private C.P.A. practice, 1947—; U.S. Civil Service Commission, San Francisco, expert examiner, 1947-50; University of California, Berkeley, lecturer in accounting, 1947-54; University of California, Riverside, assistant professor, 1954-59, associate professor of economics, 1959-60; University of Hawaii, Honolulu, professor of accounting and business economics, 1961—. Visiting lecturer, Massachusetts Institute of Technology, 1956-57; professor-in-residence, M.B.A. Tachikawa Air Force Base, 1967; visiting professor, University of Washington, 1968. Consultant to businesses, tourism industries, and manufacturers in California, Massachusetts, and Hawaii. *Member:* American Accounting Association, National Association of Accountants, Hawaii Society of C.P.A.'s, Hawaiian Government Employees Association (member of statewide board of directors, 1968-70), Kaneohe Yacht Club, Beta Gamma Sigma.

WRITINGS: Accounting and Economic Decisions, Dodd, 1964; (with Russell Taussig) *Workbook to Accompany Accounting and Economic Decisions,* Dodd, 1964; (contributor) Louis Geller, editor, *New Perspectives in Business*

Economics, Heath, 1966; (contributor) S. Davidson, editor, *Handbook of Modern Accounting,* McGraw, 1970; (with Eugene Richman) *Principles of Real Estate Investment Analysis* (syllabus), General Hawaii Development Corp., 1970. Also author of other syllabi for University of California Extension Division. Contributor to *Accounting Review, Journal of Accountancy, Financial Analysts Journal, Journal of Political Economy, Management Accounting,* and other publications.

*   *   *

CORD, Robert L.   1935-

PERSONAL: Born April 21, 1935, in New York, N.Y.; son of Edward H. (an attorney) and Evelyn (Lewis) Cord. *Education:* City College (now City College of the City University of New York), B.B.A., 1956; Syracuse University, M.A., 1958, Ph.D., 1967. *Home:* 160 Commonwealth Ave., Boston, Mass. 02115. *Office:* Department of Political Science, College of Liberal Arts, Northeastern University, Boston, Mass. 02115.

CAREER: High school teacher in Camillus, N.Y., 1958-60; Northeastern University, Boston, Mass., assistant professor of social studies in education, 1962-66, assistant professor of political science, 1966-70, associate professor, 1970-76, professor of political science, 1976—. Assistant city planner in urban renewal, Syracuse, N.Y., summer, 1959; liberal arts fellow in law and political science, Harvard Law School, Harvard University, 1970-71. Consultant, University of Wisconsin-U.S. State Department African Educators Program, summer, 1969. *Member:* American Political Science Association, American Association of Political and Social Scientists, American Association of University Professors, Pi Sigma Alpha, Phi Kappa Phi.

WRITINGS: Protest, Dissent, and the Supreme Court, Winthrop, 1971; *Political Science: An Introduction,* Prentice-Hall, 1974; (contributor) Peter Lewis and Kenneth Peoples, editors, *The Supreme Court and the Criminal Process,* Saunders, 1977.

*   *   *

CORDEN, W(arner) M(ax)   1927-

PERSONAL: Born August 13, 1927, in Breslau, Germany; son of Ralph Simon and Katherine (Levy) Corden; married Dorothy Grace Martin, June 1, 1957; children: Jane Margaret. *Education:* University of Melbourne, B.Comm., 1949, M.Comm., 1953; London School of Economics, Ph.D., 1956. *Residence:* Canberra, Australia. *Office:* Department of Economics, Australian National University, Canberra 2600, Australia.

CAREER: University of Melbourne, Melbourne, Australia, lecturer in economics, 1958-61; Australian National University, Canberra, fellow in economics, 1962-67; Oxford University, Nuffield College, Oxford, England, fellow and reader in international economics, 1967-76; Australian National University, professor of economics, 1976—.

WRITINGS: (Editor with H. W. Arndt) *The Australian Economy: A Volume of Readings,* F. W. Cheshire, 1963; *The Theory of Protection,* Clarendon Press, 1971; *Trade Policy and Economic Welfare,* Clarendon Press, 1974; *Inflation, Exchange Rates, and the World Economy,* Clarendon Press, 1977.

*   *   *

CORREIA-AFONSO, John   1924-

PERSONAL: Born July 15, 1924, in Benaulim, Goa, India;

son of Francisco and Luzia (De Heredia) Correia-Afonso. *Education:* St. Xavier's College, Bombay, India, B.A., 1943; University of Bombay, M.A., 1945, Ph.D., 1953; Weston College, Weston, Mass., S.T.L., 1958. *Home and office:* St. Xavier's College, Bombay 400 001, India.

CAREER: Entered Society of Jesus (Jesuits), 1946, ordained Roman Catholic priest, 1957; St. Xavier's College, Bombay, India, professor of history, 1960-65, president, 1963-65; Society of Jesus, provincial superior in Bombay, 1965-67, secretary-general in Rome, Italy, 1967-70, assistant to superior general, Rome, 1970-75; St. Xavier's College, professor of history, 1975—. *Member:* Royal Asiatic Society (fellow), Association for Asian Studies. *Awards, honors:* Sir Pherozeshah Mehta research scholarship, 1945-48.

WRITINGS: Jesuit Letters and Indian History, Indian Historical Research Institute, 1955, 2nd edition, Oxford University Press, 1969; *Even unto the Indies,* Messenger (Bombay), 1956; *The Soul of Modern India,* Heras Institute, 1960.

WORK IN PROGRESS: Essays in Historical Method; research on the traveler as historian.

SIDELIGHTS: John Correia-Afonso speaks seven languages—English, French, Italian, Portuguese, Spanish, Konkani, and Marathi.

* * *

CORRIGAN, Ralph L(awrence), Jr. 1937-

PERSONAL: Born June 24, 1937, in New Rochelle, N.Y.; son of Ralph Lawrence and Eleanor (Farrell) Corrigan; married Judith Ann Miller (an artist), August 12, 1961; children: Jennifer Lenore, Ralph Lawrence III, Brenna Terese. *Education:* Iona College, B.A., 1959; Fordham University, M.A., 1962, Ph.D., 1973. *Home:* 22 Ruth St., Trumbull, Conn. 06611. *Office:* Department of English, Sacred Heart University, Bridgeport, Conn. 06604.

CAREER: Siena College, Loudonville, N.Y., instructor, 1962-66, assistant professor of English, 1966-67; Sacred Heart University, Bridgeport, Conn., 1967—, began as assistant professor, currently associate professor of English, chairman of department, 1972-76. *Member:* National Council of Teachers of English, Conference on College Composition and Communication, Connecticut Council of Teachers of English.

WRITINGS: Themes for Study, Holt, 1966; (editor) *Preparation of the English Teacher,* Connecticut Council of Teachers of English, 1970; *The Function of the Green World in Selected Plays of Eugene O'Neill,* University Microfilms, 1973; (editor) *New England Bike Tour,* Sacred Heart University, 1974. Editor, *Connecticut English Journal,* 1968-73.

WORK IN PROGRESS: A collection of short stories about a small town in the Catskills; *Developing a Writer,* a textbook for writing courses; *Here's Dickie: The Biography of an Ex-Heroin Addict.*

AVOCATIONAL INTERESTS: Movies, bicycling.

* * *

COSGRAVE, Patrick 1941-

PERSONAL: Born September 28, 1941, in Dublin, Ireland; son of Patrick John and Margaret (Fitzgerald) Cosgrave; married Ruth Edwards (a business executive), July 31, 1965 (divorced); married Norma Cooper; children: (second marriage) Rebecca. *Education:* University College, Dublin,

B.A., 1964, M.A., 1965; Peterhouse, Cambridge, Ph.D., 1968. *Politics:* Conservative. *Religion:* Church of England. *Home:* 118 Kyrle Rd., London SW11, England. *Agent:* Carol Smith, 2 John St., London WC1, England. *Office:* Spectator, 99 Gower St., London WC1E GAE, England.

CAREER: Spectator, London, England, associate editor, 1971—. Special adviser to Leader of the Opposition.

WRITINGS: The Public Poetry of Robert Lowell, Gollancz, 1970, Taplinger, 1972; *Churchill at War,* Volume I: *Alone, 1939-40,* Collins, 1974; *Cheyney's Law* (novel), Macmillan (London), 1977; *Margaret Thatcher: A Tory and Her Party,* Hutchinson, 1978. Also author of numerous pamphlets. Contributor of articles and reviews to *Daily Telegraph, Spectator, Round Table, Encounter, Times,* and *Alternative.*

WORK IN PROGRESS: Churchill at War, Volume II, *1940-1945; The Defence of the Realm: British Defence Policy since 1945;* two sequels to *Cheyney's Law, The Three Colonels* and *Adventure of State; Israel: For Gentiles Only.*

AVOCATIONAL INTERESTS: Dogs, cats, birds, and animals generally; roses, China, horse-riding, cricket, classical languages.

BIOGRAPHICAL/CRITICAL SOURCES: Listener, November 26, 1970; *Times Literary Supplement,* July 28, 1974, July 29, 1977.

* * *

COSTELLO, David F(rancis) 1904-

PERSONAL: Born September 1, 1904, in Nebraska; son of Thomas (manager of a grain elevator business) and Mary L. (Mallory) Costello; married Cecilia C. Waldkirch, June 12, 1929; children: Barbara M. (Mrs. Virgil McDougle), David K., Donald R. *Education:* Peru State Teachers College (now Peru State College), Peru, Neb., A.B., 1925; University of Chicago, M.S., 1926, Ph.D., 1934. *Home and office:* 4965 Hogan Dr., Fort Collins, Colo. 80521.

CAREER: Marquette University, Milwaukee, Wis., instructor in botany, 1926-32; U.S. Forest Service, Rocky Mountain Forest and Range Experimental Station, Fort Collins, Colo., forest ecologist, 1934-37, chief of Division of Range Research, 1937-53; U.S. Forest Service, Pacific North West Forest and Range Experimental Station, Portland, Ore., chief of Division of Range, Wildlife Habitat, and Recreation Research, 1953-64. Special lecturer, Colorado Agricultural and Mechanical College (now Colorado State University), 1942-53; guest professor, State College of Washington (now Washington State University), 1957; guest speaker, University College of North Wales, 1962; consultant on environmental preservation and management, 1975—. President, Welfare Bureau, Inc., Fort Collins, 1938-48.

MEMBER: American Association for the Advancement of Science (fellow), Ecological Society of America, Outdoor Photographers League (life member), Authors League of America, American Institute of Biological Sciences, Sigma Xi. *Awards, honors:* Citation of American Society of Range Management for distinguished service in range research and ecology, 1970.

WRITINGS: Range Ecology, U.S. Department of Agriculture Forest Service, 1939; *The World of the Porcupine,* Lippincott, 1966; *The World of the Ant,* Lippincott, 1968; *The Prairie World,* Crowell, 1969; *The World of the Prairie Dog,* Lippincott, 1970; *The World of the Gull,* Lippincott, 1971; *The Desert World,* Crowell, 1972; *The Mountain World,*

Crowell, 1975. Contributor of more than 150 articles to popular periodicals, including *True, Sports Illustrated, Outdoor Life,* and *Farm Journal,* and about the same number of technical articles on ecology, range management, and recreation research to professional journals.

WORK IN PROGRESS: The Seashore World, for Crowell.

* * *

COSTIGAN, Daniel M. 1929-

PERSONAL: Born February 13, 1929, in Orangeburg, N.Y.; son of John E. (an artist) and Ida (Blessin) Costigan; married Dorothy Knopczyk, September 15, 1956; children: Drew, Christopher. *Education:* R.C.A. Institutes, graduate, 1950; New York University, B.S., 1964. *Religion:* Protestant. *Home:* 8 Wyndmoor Way, Edison, N.J. 08817. *Agent:* Patricia Lewis, 450 Seventh Ave., Room 602, New York, N.Y. 10001. *Office:* Bell Laboratories, Holmdel, N.J. 07733.

CAREER: Worked as a radio technician, 1948-61; free-lance writer, 1955—; Bell Laboratories, Holmdel, N.J., engineer in micrographic and electronic information systems development, 1961—. Chairman, National Microfilm/Electronic Industries Association Microfilm-Facsimile Standards Committee, 1971—. *Military service:* U.S. Army, 1951-53. *Member:* Institute of Electrical and Electronic Engineers, National Micrographics Association (member, publications committee), Telephone Pioneers of America, Kappa Tau Alpha. *Awards, honors:* Certificate of appreciation, National Microfilm Association, 1972.

WRITINGS: FAX: The Principles and Practice of Facsimile Communication, Chilton, 1971; *Micrographic Systems,* National Micrographics Association, 1971. Contributor to *Radio Electronics, Popular Electronics, Medical Times, Journal of Micrographics, World Car Guide, Road & Track,* and other journals and periodicals.

WORK IN PROGRESS: Trials and Triumphs of an American Artist, a book-length biography of J. E. Costigan; *Sending Documents and Graphics Electronically,* a technical textbook.

SIDELIGHTS: Daniel Costigan told *CA:* "As an aspiring writer of both fiction and fact, my principal idol had been the late Nevil Shute, the noted British romantic engineer/iting has taken something less than a literary direction, it is nevertheless gratifying to know that I have created something of value to someone."

AVOCATIONAL INTERESTS: Amateur stereo photography, music.

* * *

COTTER, James Finn 1929-

PERSONAL: Born July 5, 1929, in Boston, Mass.; son of James B. (a customs inspector) and Catherine (Finn) Cotter; married Emily Kay Kerrick (a college teacher), December 26, 1960; children: Anne, James, John. *Education:* Boston College, B.A., 1954, M.A., 1955; Fordham University, M.A., 1957, Ph.D., 1963; University of Louvain, graduate study, 1957-60. *Politics:* Democrat. *Religion:* Roman Catholic. *Home:* 372 Grand St., Newburgh, N.Y. 12550. *Office:* Department of English, Mount Saint Mary College, Newburgh, N.Y. 12550.

CAREER: Fordham University, New York, N.Y., instructor, 1960-63, assistant professor of English, 1963; Mount

Saint Mary College, Newburgh, N.Y., associate professor, 1963-67, professor of English, 1967—. Fulbright lecturer, University of Oran, Oran, Algeria, 1970-71. Chairman, Newburgh Human Relations Commission; member of board of directors, Orange County Council of Community Services, 1967-69. *Member:* Modern Language Association of America, Hudson Valley Philharmonic Society, Newburgh Historical Society. *Awards, honors:* National Endowment for the Humanities grant, 1968.

WRITINGS: Inscape: The Christology and Poetry of Gerard Manley Hopkins, University of Pittsburgh Press, 1972. Contributor of poetry to *America, Commonweal, Spirit, Nation, New York Times,* and *Thought,* and of articles to *Explicator, English Language Notes, Studies in Philology,* and other periodicals; poetry reviewer, *America.*

WORK IN PROGRESS: Learning the Way: A Guide for the Imagination, a book of poetry and prose.

SIDELIGHTS: James Cotter told *CA:* "Faced with the choice of spending a day in the library or in a museum, I would not hesitate to visit the museum. I love the visual in literature. My single effort is to see and teach others to see. Living in the Hudson Highlands gives me wonderful chances for walking and looking."

* * *

COTTLE, Thomas J. 1937-

PERSONAL: Born January 22, 1937, in Chicago, Ill.; son of Maurice H. (a physician) and Gitta (a pianist; maiden name, Gradova) Cottle; married Kay Mikkelsen, June 28, 1964; children: Claudia Mari, Jason Edwin, Sonya Ruth. *Education:* Harvard University, B.A., 1959; University of Chicago, M.A., 1964, Ph.D., 1968. *Religion:* Jewish. *Agent:* William Morris Agency, 1350 Avenue of the Americas, New York, N.Y. 10019. *Office:* 12 Beaconsfield Rd., Brookline, Mass. 02146.

CAREER: Harvard University, Cambridge, Mass., assistant professor of social relations, 1965-70; Massachusetts Institute of Technology, Cambridge, research sociologist, Medical Department and Education Research Center, 1970-73; Children's Defense Fund, Cambridge, researcher-writer, 1973-75; Tavistock Clinic, London, England, attached staff member, 1975-77; Harvard University, Medical School, Cambridge, lecturer in psychology, 1977-78. Visiting distinguished professor of psychology, Amherst College, 1977-78. *Member:* American Sociological Association, American Psychological Association.

WRITINGS: Time's Children: Impressions of Youth, Little, Brown, 1971; *The Prospect of Youth,* Little, Brown, 1972; (with Craig Eisendrath and Laurence Fink) *Lighting a Fire in the University,* Schenkman, 1972; *The Abandoners,* Little, Brown, 1973; *The Voices of School,* Little, Brown, 1973; (with Stephen L. Klineberg) *The Present of Things Future,* Free Press, 1973; *Black Children, White Dreams,* foreward by Walter F. Mondale, Houghton, 1974; *A Family Album: Portraits of Intimacy and Kinship,* Harper, 1974; *Perceiving Time: A Psychological Investigation with Men and Women,* Wiley, 1976; *Busing,* Beacon Press, 1976; *Barred from School: 2 Million Children!,* New Republic, 1976; *Readings in Adolescent Psychology: Current Perspectives,* Harper, 1977; *Children in Jail,* Beacon Press, 1977; *College: Reward and Betrayal,* University of Chicago Press, 1977; *Private Lives and Public Accounts,* University of Massachusetts Press, 1977.

WORK IN PROGRESS: A book, *Youth and a Sensuous God.*

SIDELIGHTS: Thomas Cottle is a specialist in children's rights, with a reputation for compassion. Even the occasional dissonant voice concedes this. Critic Sara Blackburn, discussing *Black Children, White Dreams*, writes: "We don't need more studies by experts, no matter how caring, of how bright, sensitive and thus worthy of salvation are the victims of our political and social crimes. Whether Cottle intends it or not, that is the undeniable thrust of this work." But others praise his "noble and passionate approach," "sensitive portraits," and "perceptive" observations.

BIOGRAPHICAL/CRITICAL SOURCES: New Republic, February 17, 1973, September 7, 1974, April 19, 1975; *New York Times Book Review*, March 4, 1973, March 3, 1974, November 21, 1976; *Book World*, April 15, 1973, February 3, 1974, October 24, 1976; *America*, February 9, 1974, April 26, 1975, February 26, 1977, April 9, 1977; *Atlantic*, March, 1974; *Christian Science Monitor*, March 13, 1974; *New Yorker*, April 7, 1975; *Social Science Quarterly*, September, 1975; *American Journal of Sociology*, March, 1976; *Contemporary Psychology*, April, 1976, March, 1976, June, 1977; *Social Forces*, June, 1976; *Contemporary Sociology*, September, 1976; *Nation*, January 15, 1977; *Review of Metaphysics*, March, 1977; *Progressive*, March, 1977; *Books West*, April, 1977; *Commonweal*, April 15, 1977.

* * *

COTTON, John W(healdon) 1925-

PERSONAL: Born October 8, 1925, in McMinnville, Ore.; son of Earl B. and Ruth (Whealdon) Cotton; married Corliss Clark, August 23, 1947; children: one daughter, one son. *Education:* Willamette University, A.B. (cum laude), 1947; Indiana University, A.M., 1950, Ph.D., 1952. *Politics:* Democrat. *Religion:* Methodist. *Office:* Graduate School of Education, University of California, Santa Barbara, Calif. 93106.

CAREER: Northwestern University, Evanston, Ill., instructor, 1951-53, assistant professor, 1953-59, associate professor of psychology, 1959-60; University of California, Santa Barbara, associate professor, 1960-63, professor of psychology, 1963-66, professor of education and psychology, 1966—, chairman of department of psychology, 1961-64, associate dean of Graduate Division, 1963-65. *Member:* American Association for the Advancement of Science, American Educational Research Association, American Psychological Association (fellow), American Statistical Association, Psychometric Society, Psychonomic Society, American Association of University Professors, Western Psychological Association, Phi Delta Kappa. *Awards, honors:* National Science Foundation research grants, 1954-56, 1956-59, 1959-62; U.S. Public Health Service research grants, 1959-61, 1963-64, 1966-70; University of Chicago, post-doctoral fellow, 1957-58; research grant from U.S. Navy Research and Development Center, 1976.

WRITINGS: (With B. J. Underwood, C. P. Duncan, and J. A. Taylor) *Elementary Statistics* and *Workbook*, Appleton, 1954, 2nd edition (with Underwood, Duncan, and J. T. Spence), 1968, 3rd edition, Prentice-Hall, 1976; (contributor) M. H. Marx, editor, *Theories in Contemporary Psychology*, Macmillan, 1963; *Elementary Statistical Theory for Behavior Scientists*, Addison-Wesley, 1967; (with B. C. Mathis and Lee Sechrest) *Psychological Foundations of Education: Learning and Teaching*, Academic Press, 1970; (contributor) M. R. Rosenzweig and L. W. Porter, editors, *Annual Review of Psychology*, Annual Reviews, 1976; (editor with R. L. Klatzky) *Semantic Factors in Cognition*,

Erlbaum, in press. Also author of *Par for the Corps: A Review of the Literature on Selection, Training, and Performance of Peace Corps Volunteers*, 1975. Contributor of more than fifty articles and reviews to psychology journals. Consulting editor, *Journal of Experimental Psychology*, 1963-71; member of editorial board, *Review of Educational Research*, 1966-69; consulting editor, Academic Press, 1971-73; advisory editor, *Contemporary Psychology*, 1974—.

* * *

COURANT, Richard 1888-1972

January 8, 1888—January 27, 1972; Silesian-born American mathematician and educator. Obituaries: *New York Times*, January 29, 1972; *Washington Post*, January 30, 1972; *Newsweek*, February 7, 1972; *Current Biography*, March, 1972.

* * *

COUSTEAU, Philippe Pierre 1940-

PERSONAL: Surname is pronounced Coo-*stow;* born December 30, 1940, in Toulon, Var, France; son of Jacques-Yves (oceanographer and co-inventor of the aqualung) and Simone (Melchior) Cousteau; married Janice O. Sullivan, February 10, 1967. *Education:* Formal education began at a boarding school in Normandy; at seventeen began study of aerodynamics in Paris, receiving licenses as glider pilot, airplane pilot, and private pilot; continued his education in Monaco, 1960; received degree in science from College of Normandy, 1963; studied electronic engineering at Worcester Polytechnic Institute and Massachusetts Institute of Technology, 1964, and also was licensed as a commercial pilot that same year. *Home:* 4314 Marina City Dr., Marina Del Rey, Calif. 90291. *Office:* The Cousteau Society, 8150 Beverly Blvd., Los Angeles, Calif. 90048.

CAREER: Made his first trip on his father's ship, *Calypso*, in 1951 (aged eleven), sailed aboard the *Calypso* to the Red Sea in 1952, and subsequently on expeditions to Greece, Turkey, Africa, the North Sea, Italy, and Tunisia; on a second trip to the Red Sea in 1963 worked with his father on the filming of "World without Sun" (winner of Academy of Motion Picture Arts and Sciences award as best documentary feature, 1964); filmed the Conshelf III experiment for a National Geographic Society television special in 1965, when he spent twenty-eight days below the sea with five other divers; became director of Jacques Cousteau's film production firm in Paris, Les Requins Associes, 1966, and then vice-president of the firm; director of photography for television film series, "The Undersea World of Jacques Cousteau," on numerous expeditions, 1968-69, overall director for the series, produced for Metromedia Producers Corp., 1970-75; photographer and producer of motion pictures and television projects as partner in Thalassa, Inc., Los Angeles, 1969-74; vice-president, The Cousteau Society, Los Angeles, conducting research and education on environmental quality, 1974—, director of television films, including "Oasis in Space" series, and "Cousteau Odyssey" series. Also has participated in U.S. Navy scientific experiments with deep diving. *Military service:* French Navy, 1961-62 (during Algerian war). *Awards, honors:* "Truk," which he filmed, was nominated for Emmy Award of National Academy of Television Arts and Sciences, 1971; more than a dozen cinematography awards.

WRITINGS: (With father, Jacques-Yves Cousteau) *Les Requins*, Flammarion, 1970, translation by Francis Price published as *The Shark: Splendid Savage of the Sea*, Doubleday, 1970. Contributor to *Sea, Oceans, Skin Diver,* and other magazines and newspapers.

WORK IN PROGRESS: A survey of the Mediterranean Sea and its tributaries for "Cousteau Odyssey."

BIOGRAPHICAL/CRITICAL SOURCES: Los Angeles Times, November 10, 1968, June 26, 1977; *Los Angeles Herald Examiner,* August 24, 1969; *Gentlemen's Quarterly,* March, 1971; *Star-Phoenix* (Saskatoon, B.C.), November 21, 1973; *Kansas City Times* (Missouri), October 8, 1975; *Ft. Lauderdale News,* October 27, 1975; *Miami Herald,* October 28, 1975; *Signature* (Diners Club magazine), November, 1975; *Ft. Worth Star Telegram,* December 8, 1975; *Hollywood Independent,* January 29, 1976; *Newsday,* October 20, 1976; *Hommes Vogues* (Paris), June-July, 1977; *El Mercurio* (Santiago, Chile), July 20, 1976; *Le Point* (Paris), August 8, 1977.†

*   *   *

COVEY, Stephen R.   1932-

PERSONAL: Born October 24, 1932, in Salt Lake City, Utah; son of Stephen Glenn and Louise (Richards) Covey; married Sandra Merrill, August 14, 1956; children: Cynthia, Maria, Stephen, Michael Sean, David, Catherine, Colleen, Jenny. *Education:* University of Utah, B.S., 1952; Harvard University, M.B.A., 1957; Brigham Young University, D.R.E., 1976. *Religion:* Church of Jesus Christ of Latter-day Saints. *Home:* 2160 North Oakcrest Lane, Provo, Utah 84601. *Office:* Brigham Young University, 302 JKB, Provo, Utah 84601.

CAREER: Church of Jesus Christ of Latter-day Saints, president of mission in Ireland, 1962-65; Brigham Young University, Provo, Utah, administrative posts, 1965-69, associate professor of organizational behavior, 1970—. Guest lecturer, Brookings Institution, Washington, D.C., 1961—.

WRITINGS: The Spiritual Roots of Human Relations, Deseret, 1970; *How to Succeed with People,* Deseret, 1971.

*   *   *

COVINGTON, James W.   1917-

PERSONAL: Born August 29, 1917, in Fulton, Mo.; son of Warren S. and Louise (Middleton) Covington; married Sofia Hernandez, June 5, 1954; children: Virginia Maria. *Education:* St. Louis University, B.S., 1941, M.A., 1943; University of Oklahoma, Ph.D., 1950. *Religion:* Roman Catholic. *Home:* 2901 South Beach Dr., Tampa, Fla. 33609. *Office:* Department of History, University of Tampa, Tampa, Fla.

CAREER: University of Tampa, Tampa, Fla., associate professor, 1950-53, professor of history, 1954—, Dana Professor of History, 1975—, dean of evening division, 1961-64. Senior historian, Apollo History, National Aeronautics and Space Administration (NASA), 1968-69. *Military service:* U.S. Army Air Forces, 1942-43. *Member:* Society of American Ethnology, Florida Anthropological Society (past president), Florida Historical Society (member of board of directors, 1962-65), Tampa Historical Society. *Awards, honors:* Florida History Award, Peace River Historical Society, 1970; Truman Hunter award, 1970.

WRITINGS: Story of the University of Tampa, University of Tampa Press, 1955; *Story of Southwestern Florida,* Lewis Historical Publishing Co., 1958; (editor) *Pirates, Indians and Spaniards,* Great Outdoors Publishing, 1965; (editor) *British Meet the Seminoles,* University of Florida State Museum, 1967.

WORK IN PROGRESS: Third Seminole War; Indians of Florida.

AVOCATIONAL INTERESTS: Travel.

*   *   *

COWEN, Roy C(hadwell)   1930-

PERSONAL: Born August 2, 1930, in Kansas City, Mo.; son of Roy Chadwell (a businessman) and Mildred F. (Schuetz) Cowen; married Hildegard Bredemeier, October 6, 1956. *Education:* Yale University, B.A., 1952; University of Goettingen, Dr.Phil., 1961. *Religion:* Methodist. *Home:* 2874 Baylis Dr. N., Ann Arbor, Mich. 48104. *Office:* Department of German, University of Michigan, Ann Arbor, Mich. 48109.

CAREER: University of Michigan, Ann Arbor, instructor, 1960-64, assistant professor, 1964-67, associate professor, 1967-71, professor of German, 1971—. *Military service:* U.S. Navy, 1952-56. *Member:* Modern Language Association of America, Internationale Vereinigung fuer Germanische Sprach-und Literaturwissenschaft. *Awards, honors:* Senior fellowship, National Endowment for the Humanities, 1972-73.

WRITINGS: (Editor) Christian Dietrich Grabbe, *Scherz, Satire, Ironie und tiefere Bedeutung,* Blaisdell, 1969; (editor) Franz Grillparzer, *Des Meeres und der Liebe Wellen,* Blaisdell, 1969; (editor) Georg Buechner, *Dantons Tod,* Blaisdell, 1969; *Neunzehntes Jahrhundert (1830-1880),* Francke-Verlag, 1970; *Christian Dietrich Grabbe,* Twayne 1972; *Naturalismus: Kommentar zu einer Epoche,* Winkler-Verlag, 1973; (editor and contributor) Grabbe, *Werke in zwei Baenden mit cinem Vommentarbande,* Hanser Verlag, 1975-77. Contributor to journals in United States and Germany.

*   *   *

COWIE, Alexander   1896-

PERSONAL: Born March 8, 1896, in St. Paul, Minn.; son of George Grey (a statistician) and Mary (Hanrahan) Cowie; married Elspeth Nicholson, September 3, 1926; children: Alan, Gwendolen. *Education:* University of Minnesota, A.B., 1919, A.M., 1920; Yale University, Ph.D., 1930; Wesleyan University, M.A., 1949. *Home:* 118 Pine St., Middletown, Conn. 06457.

CAREER: University of Illinois, Urbana, instructor in English, 1920-22; University of Minnesota, Minneapolis, instructor in English, 1922-23; Wesleyan University, Middletown, Conn., instructor, 1924-27, assistant professor, 1927-45, associate professor, 1945-49, professor of English, 1949-64, professor emeritus, 1964—. Visiting lecturer in American literature at Trinity College, Hartford, Conn., 1941, Ohio State University, 1941, University of Minnesota, 1945, University of Pennsylvania, 1949, and Boston College, 1961; guest lecturer for U.S. Department of State, University of Lund and Gothenburg University, Sweden, 1951-52; visiting lecturer on American fiction at Salzburg Seminar in American Studies, Austria, 1960; American specialist lecturer on American literature in Denmark, Sweden, Iceland, 1960—; Fulbright lecturer on American literature, University of Coimbra, Portugal, 1964-65; Distinguished Visiting Scholar, Kent State University, 1967-68. *Military service:* U.S. Army, 1918. *Member:* College English Association, Modern Language Association of America, New England College English Association (vice-president, 1963).

WRITINGS: Educational Problems at Yale College in the

18th Century, Yale University Press, 1936; *John Trumbull, Connecticut Wit,* University of North Carolina Press, 1936, reprinted, Greenwood Press, 1972; (editor and author of chronology and bibliography) William Gilmore Simms, *The Yemassee,* American Book Co., 1937; (contributor) R. E. Spiller and others, editors, *Literary History of the United States,* three volumes, Macmillan, 1948; *Rise of the American Novel,* American Book Co., 1948, revised edition, Van Nostrand, 1951; *American Writers Today,* Radiotjaenst (Stockholm), 1956; (contributor) C.L.F. Gohdes, editor, *Essays on American Literature in Honor of Jay B. Hubbell,* Duke University Press, 1967; (author of introduction) Karl Pomeroy Harrington, *Richard Alsop, a Hartford Wit,* Wesleyan University Press, 1969; (editor) Simms, *Yemassee,* Hafner, 1971; (editor with Sydney J. Krause and S. W. Reid) *The Novels and Related Works of Charles Brockden Brown: Weiland and Memoirs of Carwin,* Volume I, Kent State University Press, 1977. Author of twenty radio scripts and introductions for Swedish Broadcasting Corp., 1956. Contributor of articles and reviews to *Saturday Review, New York Times, American Literature, New England Quarterly, American Scholar, CEA Critic,* and other journals, and to *Encyclopaedia Britannica, World Book Encyclopedia,* and *Dictionary of American Biography.*

WORK IN PROGRESS: An introduction to Charles Brockden Brown's *Wieland,* for the Modern Language Association's "Critical Editions of American Authors" series; research in contemporary American fiction.

* * *

COX, Edward Franklin 1925-

PERSONAL: Born February 24, 1925, in Fort Myers, Fla.; son of James Bryant (a realtor) and Bess (Tollette) Cox; married Martha Ann Lieb (a piano teacher), June 19, 1954; children: Martha Elizabeth, Jeanne Ella, Ruth Rebecca, Edward Franklin, Jr., Jacqueline Judith, Rachel Abigail. *Education:* Indiana University, A.B. (with high honors), 1949, A.M., 1950, Ph.D., 1957; Institute on History and Philosophy of Science and Mathematics, postdoctoral study, 1967. *Home:* 3809 Robertann Dr., Kettering, Ohio 45420. *Office:* Department of History, Wright State University, 7751 Colonel Glenn Hwy., Dayton, Ohio 45431.

CAREER: Albright College, Reading, Pa., instructor in history, 1952; Indiana University, Southeastern Extension Center, Jeffersonville, instructor in history, 1954; Alpena Community College, Alpena, Mich., instructor in history, 1954-55; Pikeville College, Pikeville, Ky., instructor in history, 1955-56; Bethel College, McKenzie, Tenn., professor of history, 1956-60; Eastern Illinois University, Charleston, assistant professor, 1960-65, associate professor of history, 1965; Miami University, Dayton, Ohio, associate professor of history and acting chairman of department, 1965-66; Wright State University, Dayton, associate professor, 1966-68, professor of history, 1968—, acting chairman of department, 1966-67. *Military service:* U.S. Navy, 1944-46.

MEMBER: American Historical Association, National Council for the Social Studies, Organization of American Historians, Southern Historical Association, Phi Beta Kappa, Phi Alpha Theta. *Awards, honors:* Grants from *Congressional Quarterly,* 1961, American Philosophical Society, 1965, and National Science Foundation, 1967.

WRITINGS: (Co-author) *Syllabus of the History of Western European Civilization,* Indiana University Press, 1951, revised edition, 1953; *Voting in Postwar Federal Elections: A Statistical Analysis of Party Strengths since 1945,* Wright State University Press, 1968; *State and National Voting in Federal Elections, 1910-1970,* Archon Books, 1972. Contributor to yearbooks, *Historical Abstracts,* and historical journals.

WORK IN PROGRESS: History of campaigns for adoption of the metric system of weights and measures, completion expected in 1978.

* * *

COX, James W(illiam) 1923-

PERSONAL: Born January 18, 1923, in Kingston, Tenn.; son of Isham Monroe (a grocer) and Carrie (Driskill) Cox; married Patricia Parrent, August 4, 1951; children: David Allan, Kenneth Mitchell. *Education:* Carson-Newman College, A.B., 1944; Southern Baptist Theological Seminary, B.D., 1947, Th.D., 1953; postdoctoral study at Union Theological Seminary, 1963, Princeton Theological Seminary, 1964-65, and University of Zurich, 1965, 1971-72. *Home:* 516 Dover Rd., Louisville, Ky. 40206. *Office:* Southern Baptist Theological Seminary, 2825 Lexington Rd., Louisville, Ky. 40206.

CAREER: Pastor of Baptist churches in New Market, Tenn., 1943-44, Frankfort, Ky., 1945-53, and Johnson City, Tenn., 1954-59; Southern Baptist Theological Seminary, Louisville, Ky., professor of homiletics, 1959—. Interim pastor at Baptist churches in New York, N.Y., 1964-65, Columbus, Ga., 1966-67, and Alexandria, Va., 1970. Visiting lecturer at Princeton Theological Seminary, 1964-65, and Protestant Episcopal Theological Seminary, 1977. Trustee of Carson-Newman College, 1954-59, and East Tennessee Baptist Hospital, 1956-59. *Member:* Association of Seminary Professors in the Practical Fields, American Academy of Homiletics. *Awards, honors:* American Association of Theological Schools faculty fellowship award, 1971.

WRITINGS: (Contributor) *Professor in the Pulpit,* Broadman, 1963; (contributor) *Baptist Advance,* Broadman, 1964; *Learning to Speak Effectively,* Hodder & Stoughton, 1966; (translator) Hans Windisch, *Spirit-Paraclete in the Fourth Gospel,* Fortress, 1968; (compiler with Ernest A. Payne and Stephen F. Winward) *Minister's Worship Manual,* World Publishing, 1969; (translator and editor) Eduard Schweizer, *God's Inescapable Nearness,* Word Books, 1972; *A Guide to Biblical Preaching,* Abingdon, 1977; *The Twentieth-Century Pulpit,* Abingdon, 1978. Contributor to *Encyclopedia of Southern Baptists;* contributor to religious periodicals. Author of weekly newspaper column, "A Meditation," in *Roane County Banner,* 1940-42. Member of editorial board, *Review and Expositor,* 1965-69, 1972—; contributing editor, *New Pulpit Digest.*

SIDELIGHTS: James Cox told *CA:* "My experience as a pastor has convinced me of the need for vital communal worship and of the indispensability of preaching in that context. My books are designed to undergird and improve worship and preaching. French and German have been useful in my research and in my interviews in 1972 of liturgical specialists (Catholic, Orthodox, and Protestant) in Switzerland, Germany, and Austria."

* * *

COX, R(alph) Merritt 1939-

PERSONAL: Born June 29, 1939, in Richmond, Va.; son of Ralph O. and Elizabeth (Merritt) Cox. *Education:* University of Richmond, B.A., 1961; University of Wisconsin,

M.A., 1962, Ph.D., 1967. *Office:* Department of Modern Languages, College of William and Mary, Williamsburg, Va. 23185.

CAREER: University of Wisconsin—Madison, instructor in Spanish, 1965-66; Duke University, Durham, N.C., instructor, 1966-67, assistant professor of Spanish, 1967-72; College of William and Mary, Williamsburg, Va., associate professor, 1972-77, professor of Spanish, 1977—. Chairman of awards committee for foreign languages, Star-News Newspapers, Wilmington, N.C., 1970. *Member:* Modern Language Association of America, American Association of Teachers of Spanish and Portuguese, American Society for Eighteenth-Century Studies, Hispanic Society of America (corresponding member), South Atlantic Modern Language Association, Phi Beta Kappa, Phi Alpha Theta, Sigma Delta Pi. *Awards, honors:* American Philosophical Society grant, 1972; Phi Beta Kappa award for scholarship, 1976.

WRITINGS: The Reverend John Bowle: The Genesis of Cervantean Criticism, University of North Carolina Press, 1971; *Tomas de Iriarte,* Twayne, 1972; *Juan Melendez Valdes,* Twayne, 1974. Also author of *An English Ilustrado: The Reverend John Bowle,* 1977. Contributor to romance language journals.

WORK IN PROGRESS: Eighteenth-Century Spanish Literature, for Twayne.

*   *   *

COX, Rachel Dunaway 1904-

PERSONAL: Born January 20, 1904, in Murray, Ky.; daughter of Enoch T. (a physician) and Khadra (Fergeson) Dunaway; married Reavis Cox (a college professor), February 18, 1928; children: David Jackson, Rosemary (Mrs. Jon J. Masters). *Education:* University of Texas, A.B., 1925; Columbia University, A.M., 1930; University of Pennsylvania, Ph.D., 1943. *Politics:* Republican. *Religion:* Presbyterian. *Home:* 219 Sykes Lane, Wallingford, Pa. 19086.

CAREER: New York Herald Tribune, New York City, reporter, 1926-28; Young Women's Christian Association (YWCA), New York City, teacher of adult education courses, 1928-30, director of education at West Side branch, 1930-35; American Red Cross, caseworker at Walter Reed Army Hospital, Washington, D.C., 1944; Bryn Mawr College, Bryn Mawr, Pa., lecturer, 1944-45, assistant professor, 1945-48, associate professor, 1948-56, professor of psychology and education, 1956-71, professor emeritus, 1971—, director of Child Study Institute, 1944-70, chairman of department of education and child development, 1944-71; clinical psychologist in private practice at Gaskell House, Manchester Royal Infirmary, Manchester, England, 1972; clinical psychologist in private practice, Wallingford, Pa., 1973—. Member of board of directors of Sleighton School for Girls, beginning 1946, Woods School, 1960-62, and Developmental Center for Autistic Children, beginning 1960.

MEMBER: American Psychological Association, American Personnel and Guidance Association, National Association of Social Workers, Society for Personality Assessment (fellow), Eastern Psychological Association, Pennsylvania Psychological Association, Phi Beta Kappa, Sigma Xi, Theta Sigma Phi. *Awards, honors:* B'nai B'rith of Philadelphia Award for service to youth, c. 1960; Bryn Mawr College distinguished teaching award, 1971; distinguished service award, Pennsylvania Psychological Association, 1975.

WRITINGS: Counselors and Their Work, Archive Press, 1945; *Youth into Maturity: A Study of Men and Women in the First Ten Years after College,* Mental Health Materials Center, 1970. Contributor to psychology journals.

WORK IN PROGRESS: Research on personality development in middle age.

SIDELIGHTS: Rachel Cox spent 1971-72 in Europe, observing mental health programs in England and on the continent.

BIOGRAPHICAL/CRITICAL SOURCES: British Journal of Medical Education, June, 1971.

*   *   *

CRACKEL, Theodore J(oseph) 1938-

PERSONAL: Born September 10, 1938, in Urbana, Ill.; son of Orville L. (a businessman) and Aleta (Smith) Crackel; married Kay Knight, September 2, 1961 (divorced); married Mai Thi Nguyen, October 14, 1972; children: (first marriage) Todd, Dana (daughter); (second marriage) John, Robert. *Education:* University of Illinois, B.A., 1962; Rutgers University, M.A., 1971. *Home address:* P.O. Box 551, Olney, Ill. 62450.

CAREER: U.S. Army, officer, 1962—, currently teaching history at U.S. Army colleges, with present rank of major. *Member:* American Historical Association, Organization of American Historians, Association of the United States Army.

WRITINGS: The Army Additional Duty Guide, Stackpole, 1970, 2nd edition, 1973. Contributor of numerous articles and reviews to state and national history journals.

WORK IN PROGRESS: Mobility in early America; a study of the Army and society in the early nineteenth century.

SIDELIGHTS: Theodore Crackel told *CA,* "Since 1970 I have turned almost exclusively to history—teaching and writing."

*   *   *

CRAIG, Bill 1930-

PERSONAL: Born February 28, 1930, in Glasgow, Scotland; son of William McMurtrie (an engineer) and Christina (Baird) Craig; married Alro Dorrill, May 25, 1956. *Education:* Attended secondary school in Glasgow, Scotland. *Home and office:* 62 Kenneth Crescent, London N.W.2, England. *Agent:* Harvey Unna and Stephen Durbridge, Ltd., 14 Beaumont Mews, Marylebone High St., London W1N 4HE, England.

CAREER: Industrial chemist; journalist. *Member:* Writers Guild of Great Britain (past councillor).

WRITINGS: September Can Be Dangerous in Edinburgh, Walker & Co., 1971 (published in England as *Scobie in September,* Hutchinson, 1971). Also author of about two hundred plays, comedies, dramatizations, and series episodes for television, including a six-part serial adaptation of Lewis Grassic Gibbon's *Sunset Song.*

WORK IN PROGRESS: Research on sixteenth-century European history for a projected television series.

SIDELIGHTS: Robert Ray, in his review of *Scobie in September,* describes it as "a thriller.... Every few pages provide another surprise, a turn, a red herring, until one wishes that there *was* a butler to suspect.... There is no time for characterization, for narrative, because there is this constant, feverish attempt to change the scene and change it *visually*."

BIOGRAPHICAL/CRITICAL SOURCES: Bookseller, March 20, 1971; *Books and Bookmen,* April, 1971.†

* * *

CRAINE, Eugene R(ichard) 1917-1977

PERSONAL: Born June 4, 1917, in Altoona, Pa.; son of L. Frank and May G. (Cooney) Craine; married Carol Ward, October 27, 1942; children: Eric, Brian. *Education:* Maryville College, Maryville, Tenn., B.A., 1940; University of Tennessee, M.A., 1946; University of Oklahoma, Ph.D., 1954. *Home:* 4940 North Camono de la Codorniz, Tucson, Ariz. 85705.

CAREER: Fort Hays Kansas State College, Hays, instructor, 1946-49, assistant professor, 1949-53, associate professor, 1954-56, professor of history and advisor, Foreign Service Program, 1946-67, chairman of history department, 1958-67; University of Oklahoma, Norman, visiting professor of history, 1962-63, 1966-67; Wright State University, Dayton, Ohio, professor of history, 1967-75, chairman of department, 1967-72. *Military service:* U.S. Army, 1942-45; became lieutenant.

MEMBER: American Historical Association, Organization of American Historians, Archaeological Institute of America, Society for American Archaeologists, Conference on Latin America, Kansas Historical Association, Kansas Association of Teachers of History (president, 1965), Kansas Anthropological Association (president, 1956-58), Ohio Historical Society, Ohio Academy of History, Phi Kappa Phi, Phi Alpha Theta, Pi Gamma Mu, Phi Eta Sigma. *Awards, honors:* Kansas Institutional research grant, Yucatan, Mexico, 1966; Wright State University research grants, Yucatan, Mexico, 1968, 1969, 1970, 1971.

WRITINGS: The Story of Fort Roberdeau (pamphlet), [Altoona, Pa.], 1940; (editor) *Coal-Oil Canyon: A Preliminary Report* (pamphlet), Kansas Anthropological Association, 1960; *The United States and the Independence of Buenos Aires,* Kansas State Printing Press, 1961; (contributor) *Kansas: The First Century,* Lewis Historical Publishing Co., 1965; *The Chronicles of Michoacan,* University of Oklahoma Press, 1970. Editor, publications of Kansas Anthropological Association; contributor of numerous articles and reviews to *Journal of Western Folklore* and other periodicals.

WORK IN PROGRESS: Translating and editing, with notes, the *Codex Perez,* to be published posthumously by the University of Oklahoma Press.†

(Died October 20, 1977)

* * *

CRAMTON, Roger C. 1929-

PERSONAL: Born May 18, 1929, in Pittsfield, Mass.; son of Edward Allen (a physician) and Dorothy (Conant) Cramton; married Harriet Haseltine, June 29, 1952; children: Ann, Charles, Peter, Cutter. *Education:* Harvard University, A.B., 1950; University of Chicago, J.D., 1955. *Politics:* Republican. *Religion:* Congregationalist. *Home:* 49 Highgate Cir., Ithaca, N.Y. 14850. *Office:* Law School, Cornell University, Ithaca, N.Y. 14850.

CAREER: University of Chicago, Chicago, Ill., assistant professor of law, 1957-61; University of Michigan, Ann Arbor, professor of law, 1961-70; Administrative Confer-

ence of the United States, Washington, D.C., chairman, 1970-72; assistant attorney general, U.S. Department of Justice, 1972-73; Cornell University, Law School, Ithaca, N.Y., professor and dean, 1973—. *Member:* American Bar Association, American Law Institute, Federal Bar Association, American Association of University Professors, Michigan State Bar Association, Phi Beta Kappa.

WRITINGS: (With David P. Currie and Herma Kay) *Conflict of Laws,* West Publishing, 1969, 2nd edition, 1975.

* * *

CRANE, Sylvia E(ngel) 1918-

PERSONAL: Born February 23, 1918, in Portsmouth, Va.; daughter of Aaron (a businessman) and Freida (Drimmer) Engel; married John O. Crane (a writer and foundation trustee), July 7, 1945; children: Charles M., Thomas S. *Education:* Brooklyn College (now Brooklyn College of the City University of New York), B.A., 1938; Columbia University, additional study, 1940-41, 1954-58. *Home:* 315 West 106th St., New York, N.Y. 10025.

CAREER: Free-lance historian, journalist, and political analyst, 1968—. *Member:* Organization of American Historians, American Historical Society, Academy of Political Science, Americans for Democratic Action (civil liberties chairman).

WRITINGS: White Silence: Greenough, Powers, and Crawford, American Sculptors in 19th Century Italy, University of Miami Press, 1972. Contributor of essays to *Journal of Aesthetics and Art Criticism, Bulletin of the Archaeological Association of Rome,* and *La Revue Liberale.* Contributor to *La Voce Repubblicana* (Rome), *Astrolabio* (Rome), and *Esprit* (Paris).

WORK IN PROGRESS: A sequel to *White Silence,* on the Italian influences in 19th-century American culture (literature, painting, sculpture); research on the political economy of John Taylor of Caroline.

SIDELIGHTS: Sylvia Crane and her husband have lived in Rome, where they own property, for several months at a time since 1947. She believes that "Italy had a rich influence on our culture, hitherto unmarked or little noted; a possible corrective to the low self and public image of Italo-Americans. As for studies of Jefferson and John Taylor of Caroline, they founded a democratic tradition and ideology in the American South, that was adumbrated by the slavery controversy and should be retrieved."

* * *

CRAYDER, Dorothy

PERSONAL: Born in New York, N.Y.; daughter of Harris (a manufacturer) and Sarah (Kinsberg) Crayder; married Robert Newman (a writer); children: Hila (Mrs. Gerald Feil). *Education:* Attended New York University; also studied journalism at Columbia University. *Home and office:* 7 School St., Stonington, Conn. 06378. *Agent:* Harold Ober Associates, Inc., 40 East 49th St., New York, N.Y. 10017.

CAREER: Has worked as secretary, salesgirl, manager of an art gallery, and model. *Member:* Authors Guild. *Awards, honors:* Children's Spring Book Festival Award, *Book World,* 1973, for *She, the Adventuress.*

WRITINGS—Children's books; published by Atheneum, except as noted: (With Helen McCully) *The Christmas Pony,* Bobbs-Merrill, 1967; *The Pluperfect of Love,* 1971;

She, the Adventuress, 1973; *She and the Dubious Three*, 1974; *Ishkabibble!*, 1976; *The Riddles of Mermaid House*, 1977. Also author of short stories and radio and television plays.

WORK IN PROGRESS: A children's book, *Joker, Who Are You?*, for Harper.

BIOGRAPHICAL/CRITICAL SOURCES: Kirkus Reviews, February 15, 1973, November 15, 1974, April 15, 1976; *Center for Children's Books Bulletin*, July, 1973, January, 1975, September, 1976; *Teacher*, December, 1973; *Publishers Weekly*, July 22, 1974; *Language Arts*, September, 1976.

*   *   *

CREIGHTON, Helen (Evelyn) 1914-

PERSONAL: Born March 7, 1914, in Unity, Pa.; daughter of Lawrence Crawford (a physician) and Maude M. (McCutcheon) Creighton. *Education:* Waynesburg College, A.B., 1933; Slippery Rock State College, additional study, 1933; University of Pittsburgh, graduate study, 1934-36; University of Michigan, M.A., 1936; George Washington University, J.D., 1942; Georgetown University, Nursing Diploma, 1953, B.S.N., 1956; Catholic University of America, graduate study, 1954-56; St. Louis University, M.S.N., 1969. *Home:* 2614 North Bartlett, Milwaukee, Wis. 53211. *Office:* School of Nursing, University of Wisconsin, Milwaukee, Wis. 53201.

CAREER: Public school teacher in Verona, Pa., 1933-37; Arlington Hall Junior College, Washington, D.C., professor of mathematics, 1937-42; U.S. War Department, Transportation Corps, Washington, D.C., administrative assistant (legal), 1942-45; private practice of law in Washington, D.C., 1945-50; Visiting Nurse Association, Washington, D.C., public health staff nurse, 1953-54; Georgetown University, School of Nursing, Washington, D.C., instructor, 1954-56, assistant professor of nursing, 1956-59; University of Southwestern Louisiana, Lafayette, associate professor of nursing, 1956-69; University of Wisconsin—Milwaukee, professor of nursing, 1969—. South Dakota State University, visiting summer professor, 1960, 1961, visiting professor, 1963.

MEMBER: American Nurses Association (representative on National Mal-Practice Commission, 1971—), American Academy of Nursing (fellow), American Bar Association, National League for Nursing, Wisconsin Nurses Association, Wisconsin League for Nursing, Milwaukee Professional Nurses Association, Tau Kappa Alpha, Theta Sigma Pi, Kappa Beta Pi, Order of the Coif, Altrusa Club, Newman Club. *Awards, honors:* Mary Roberts Writer's Award, 1964; travel grant from Ethicon, 1966; honorary doctorate from Georgetown University, 1978.

WRITINGS: Law Every Nurse Should Know, Saunders, 1957, 3rd edition, 1975; (with Sister Catherine Armington) *Nursing of People with Cardiovascular Problems* (1st edition privately printed), 2nd edition, Little, Brown, 1971. Contributor of about one hundred articles to nursing journals in the United States and abroad. Regular monthly columnist, *Law for the Nurse;* editorial supervisor, *Supervisor Nurse*, 1971—; member of editorial board, *Nursing*, 1971—.

*   *   *

CREMIN, Lawrence A(rthur) 1925-

PERSONAL: Born October 31, 1925, in New York, N.Y.; son of Arthur T. and Theresa (Borowick) Cremin; married Charlotte Raup (a teacher), September 19, 1956; children: Joanne Laura, David Lawrence. *Education:* City College (now City College of the City University of New York), B.S.S., 1946; Columbia University, A.M., 1947, Ph.D., 1949. *Home:* 35 East 85th St., New York, N.Y. 10028. *Office:* Department of Philosophy, Social Sciences, and Education, Teachers College, Columbia University, New York, N.Y. 10027.

CAREER: Columbia University, Teachers College, New York, N.Y., instructor, 1949-51, assistant professor, 1951-54, associate professor, 1954-57, professor, 1957, chairman of department of philosophy, social sciences, and education, 1958—, Frederick A. P. Barnard Professor of Education, 1961—. Visiting associate professor of education, University of California, Los Angeles, 1956, Harvard University, 1957; visiting professor of education, Salzburg Seminar in American Studies, 1956, Harvard University, 1961; fellow, Center for Advanced Study in the Behavioral Sciences, 1964-65, 1971-72. U.S. Office of Education, chairman of Curriculum Improvement Panel, 1963-65, chairman of Regional Laboratories Panel, 1965-66; chairman, Carnegie Commission on the Education of Educators, 1966-70. Member of educational advisory board, John Simon Guggenheim Memorial Foundation. Trustee, Dalton Schools, Children's Television Workshop, and Spencer Foundation. *Military service:* U.S. Army Air Forces, 1944-45. *Member:* National Academy of Education (president, 1969—), Phi Beta Kappa. *Awards, honors:* Guggenheim fellowship, 1957-58; Bancroft Prize in American history, 1962, for *The Transformation of the School;* American Educational Research Association award for distinguished contributions to education research, 1969; Creative Educational Leadership award, New York University, 1971; Butler Medal, Columbia University, 1972; Townsend Harris Medal, 1974; Litt.D., Columbia University, 1975; L.H.D., Ohio State University, 1975; LL.D., University of Bridgeport, 1975.

WRITINGS: The American Common School: An Historic Conception, Teachers College Press, 1951; (with Robert Freeman Butts) *A History of Education in American Culture*, Holt, 1953; (with D. A. Shannon and M. E. Townsend) *A History of Teachers College, Columbia University*, Columbia University Press, 1954; *Public Education and the Future of America*, National Education Association, 1955; (with M. L. Borrowman) *Public Schools in Our Democracy*, Macmillan, 1956; (editor) *The Republic and the School: Horace Mann on the Education of Free Men*, Teachers College Press, 1957; *The Transformation of the School*, Knopf, 1961; *The Genius of American Education*, University of Pittsburgh Press, 1965; *The Wonderful World of Ellwood Patterson Cubberley*, Teachers College Press, 1965; (with Lee J. Cronbach, Patrick Suppes, and others) *Research for Tomorrow's Schools: Disciplined Inquiry for Education*, Macmillan, 1969; *American Education: The Colonial Experience, 1607-1789*, Harper, 1970; *Public Education*, Basic Books, 1976; *Traditions of American Education*, Basic Books, 1977. Editor, "Classics in Education" series, Teachers College Press. Associate editor, *Teachers College Record*, 1952-59; member of editorial board, *History of Education Journal, Sociology of Education, History of Education, International Review of Education*, and *Year Book of Education*.

WORK IN PROGRESS: A three-volume comprehensive history of American education.

BIOGRAPHICAL/CRITICAL SOURCES: Saturday Review, March 20, 1971, October 19, 1974; *National Elementary Principal*, January/February, 1975.

CRESSEY, William W. 1939-

PERSONAL: Born June 6, 1939, in Hartford, Conn.; son of Wolcott Hale (a teacher) and Beatrice (a teacher; maiden name, Whitney) Cressey; married Virginia Mullen (a teacher), June 6, 1964; children: Sally MacFarlin, James Mullen. *Education:* Attended University of Madrid, 1959-60; Trinity College, Hartford, Conn., B.A., 1961; University of Illinois, M.A., 1962, Ph.D., 1966. *Home:* 4425 Stanford St., Chevy Chase, Md. 20015. *Office:* Department of Spanish, Georgetown University, Washington, D.C. 20057.

CAREER: University of Michigan, Ann Arbor, assistant professor of Spanish, 1965-71; Georgetown University, Washington, D.C., associate professor of Spanish, 1970—. Visiting professor of Spanish, University of Hawaii, 1969-70. Workshop director, Michigan Department of Education, 1969. *Member:* Linguistic Society of America, American Association of Teachers of Spanish and Portuguese, American Association of University Professors.

WRITINGS: (With E. E. Borsoi) *Tertulia*, Appleton, 1972. Contributor to linguistics journals.

WORK IN PROGRESS: Research on the sound system of Spanish, with a book expected to result.

* * *

CRIGHTON, John C(lark) 1903-

PERSONAL: Born December 4, 1903, in Richmond, Va.; son of John Clark (a milliner) and Florence (Hope) Crighton; married Rebecca Wright, May 1, 1943; children: Nancy Hope (Mrs. Dabney Doty, Jr.), Florence Elizabeth (Mrs. Rodney Olsen). *Education:* Lynchburg College, B.A., 1925; Columbia University, M.A., 1930, Ph.D., 1948; London School of Economics, additional study, 1932-33. *Politics:* Democrat. *Religion:* Episcopalian. *Home and office:* 601 Manor Dr., Columbia, Mo. 65201.

CAREER: New York Telephone Co., New York, N.Y., accountant, 1927-29; Lynchburg College, Lynchburg, Va., instructor in history, 1930-32; U.S. Office of Education, Washington, D.C., research assistant, 1934; Stephens College, Columbia, Mo., professor of social studies, 1935-42, 1946-70. Member, Columbia (Mo.) Board of Health, 1949-53; chairman of Columbia Personnel Advisory Board, 1955-58, and Boone County Human Development Corp., 1965-68; vice-chairman of Columbia Land Clearance for Redevelopment Authority and Columbia Housing Authority, 1956-62. *Military service:* U.S. Army, 1942-46; became captain; received Bronze Star. U.S. Army Reserve, 1946-63; became lieutenant colonel. *Member:* Missouri Writers Guild, Missouri State Historical Society, Boone County Historical Society. *Awards, honors:* American Association for State and Local History merit award, 1975, for series of feature articles.

WRITINGS: (With Joseph H. Senturia) *Business and Government*, University of Chicago Press, 1935; *Missouri and the World War, 1914-17*, University of Missouri Press, 1947; *Stephens: A Story of Educational Innovation*, American Press, 1970. Contributor to *Encyclopaedia Britannica, Missouri Historical Review, American Journal of International Law*, and other publications; feature writer, *Lynchburg (Va.) News;* book reviewer, *Zeitschrift fuer Sozialforschung.*

WORK IN PROGRESS: A History of Medical Services in Missouri; The Trade in Horses and Mules in Missouri for Belligerent Armies.

SIDELIGHTS: John C. Crighton has traveled in England, France, Belgium, Germany, Switzerland, and Denmark. He is competent in Latin, Greek, Anglo-Saxon, French, and German.

* * *

CROCKETT, James Underwood 1915-

PERSONAL: Born October 9, 1915, in Haverhill, Mass.; son of Earle Royce and Inez (Underwood) Crockett; married Margaret Williams, July 28, 1943; children: Carol Ellen (Mrs. Joseph E. Ward), Robert Bryan, Jean Elizabeth, Mary Margaret. *Education:* Attended University of Massachusetts—Amherst and Agricultural and Mechanical College of Texas (now Texas A&M University). *Religion:* Congregationalist. *Address:* P.O. Box 307, Concord, Mass. 01742.

CAREER: Employed by Oak Park Nurseries, East Patchogue, N.Y., 1935-39; Japanese Nursery Co., Houston, Tex., superintendent, 1939-40; Crockett's Flower Shop, Lexington, Mass., owner, 1946-48; *Flowery Talks* (a florist's bulletin), Concord, Mass., owner, 1947—; host of "Crockett's Victory Garden" (a weekly television program), Public Broadcasting Service, 1975—. Member of board of trustees, Bangor Theological Seminary; moderator, Trinitarian Congregational Church, 1958-60; member of forestry and historic district commissions, Town of Concord. *Military service:* U.S. Navy, 1941-45; became lieutenant. *Member:* American Orchid Society, Garden Writers of America, American Rose Society, Royal Horticultural Society, Massachusetts Horticultural Society, Massachusetts Flower Growers Association, Horticultural Club of Boston, Rotary Club of Concord (president, 1965-66). *Awards, honors:* Alpha Tau Gamma Alumnus of the Year award, 1972; honorary Doctor of Science, University of Massachusetts, 1976.

WRITINGS: Window Sill Gardening, Doubleday, 1958; *Greenhouse Gardening as a Hobby*, Doubleday, 1961; (editor) *Greenhouse Handbook for the Amateur*, Brooklyn Botanic Garden, 1963; *Foliage Plants for Indoor Gardening*, Doubleday, 1967; *Encyclopedia of Gardening*, Time-Life, Volume I: *Annuals*, 1971, Volume II: *Roses*, illustrations by Allianora Rosse, 1971, Volume III: *Landscape Gardening*, illustrations by Rebecca A. Merrilees and Barbara Wolff, 1971, Volume IV: *Lawns and Ground Covers*, illustrations by Rosse, 1971, Volume V: *Flowering House Plants*, illustrations by Rosse, 1971, Volume VI: *Bulbs*, illustrations by Rosse, 1971, Volume VII: *Evergreens*, illustrations by Merrilees and John Murphy, 1971, Volume VIII: *Perennials*, illustrations by Rosse, 1972, Volume IX: *Flowering Shrubs*, illustrations by Rosse, 1972, Volume X: *Trees*, 1972, Volume XI: *Foliage House Plants*, 1972, Volume XII: *Vegetables and Fruits*, 1972, Volume XIII: *Herbs*, 1977, Volume XIV: *Wildflower Gardening*, 1977, Volume XV: *Greenhouse Gardening*, 1977; *Crockett's Victory Garden*, Little, Brown, 1977; *Crockett's Indoor Garden*, Little, Brown, 1978.

SIDELIGHTS: James Underwood Crockett has made several extensive trips to Europe, Latin America, the Caribbean, Canada, and Hawaii in search of specimens.

* * *

CROMPTON, Anne Eliot 1930-

PERSONAL: Born April 6, 1930, in Northampton, Mass.; daughter of Samuel A. (a professor) and Ethel (a writer; maiden name, Cook) Eliot; married Willard Crompton (a woodworker), November 24, 1951; children: Carrie, Joseph, Nancy, Catherine, Samuel. *Education:* Attended Newton

College, 1948-49. *Politics:* "Quite liberal most of the time." *Religion:* "Informal."

WRITINGS: The Sorcerer, Little, Brown, 1971; *Deer Country,* Little, Brown, 1973; *The Winter Wife,* Little, Brown, 1975; *The Rain-Cloud Pony,* Holiday House, 1977; *The Lifting Stone,* Holiday House, 1978.

SIDELIGHTS: Anne Crompton told *CA:* "In my writing I try to put the beautiful, fantastic real world of nature before the reader and say: 'Look at this! This is to love!'" *Avocational interests:* Ecology.

*   *   *

CROMPTON, Louis (William) 1925-

PERSONAL: Born April 5, 1925, in Port Colborne, Ontario, Canada; son of Clarence Lee (a master mariner) and Mabel (Weber) Crompton. *Education:* University of Toronto, B.A., 1947, M.A., 1948; University of Chicago, A.M., 1950, Ph.D., 1955. *Home:* 1806 D, Lincoln, Neb. 68502. *Office:* Department of English, University of Nebraska, Lincoln, Neb. 68508.

CAREER: University of British Columbia, Vancouver, lecturer in mathematics, 1948-49; University of Toronto, Toronto, Ontario, lecturer in English, 1953-55; University of Nebraska at Lincoln, assistant professor, 1955-60, associate professor, 1960-64, professor of English, 1964—. *Member:* Modern Language Association of America, American Association of University Professors. *Awards, honors:* Christian Gauss Award, Phi Beta Kappa Senate, 1969, for *Shaw the Dramatist.*

WRITINGS: (Editor) Charles Dickens, *Great Expectations,* Bobbs-Merrill, 1964; (editor) George Bernard Shaw, *Arms and the Man,* Bobbs-Merrill, 1969; *Shaw the Dramatist,* University of Nebraska Press, 1969; (editor) Shaw, *The Road to Equality: Ten Unpublished Lectures and Essays, 1884-1918,* Beacon Press, 1971; (contributor) L. Crew, editor, *The Gay Academic,* ETC Publications, 1977; (editor) Shaw, *The Great Composers,* University of California Press, 1978. Editor with J. H. Raleigh of Bobbs-Merrill "Shaw" series; member of editorial board, Arno Press "Homosexuality in Society, History and Literature" series, 1975. Member of editorial board, *Shaw Review.*

WORK IN PROGRESS: A history of moral, legal, and literary attitudes towards homosexuality since the Greeks.

BIOGRAPHICAL/CRITICAL SOURCES: Saturday Review, June 21, 1969; *Virginia Quarterly Review,* autumn, 1969; *Books and Bookmen,* April, 1972; *Times Literary Supplement,* August 4, 1972.

*   *   *

CRONE, (Hans-) Rainer 1942-

PERSONAL: Born July 6, 1942, in Hamburg, Germany; son of Arnold (a doctor of medicine) and Erica (Schottmueller) Crone. *Education:* Studied at Universities of Hamburg, Berlin, Freiburg, Bonn, and Paris; Free University of Berlin, Ph.D., 1974. *Home:* Loehrsweg 2, Hamburg 20, West Germany. *Office:* Department of Art, Yale University, New Haven, Conn. 06520.

CAREER: Has held several positions in the field of art including, assistant to director, Werner Haftmann, National galerie, Berlin, Germany, 1968, assistant film director to Rosa Von Praunheim on the movie "Berliner Bettwurst," released in West Germany, 1973; guest curator of the Stedelijk Museum, Amsterdam, for the first continental retrospective of British painter Peter Blake, 1973; curator of the first retrospective show of drawings by Andy Warhol, 1976; University of Washington, Seattle, Wash., visiting professor, 1975-77; Yale University, New Haven, Conn., assistant professor of the history of art, 1976—. *Awards, honors:* Federal Republic of Germany film award, for "The Art of Michael Heizer"; *A Golden Picture Show by the Artist Andy Warhol* was judged as one of the most beautiful books of 1976 in the Federal Republic of Germany.

WRITINGS: Andy Warhol, Hatje Verlag, 1970, translation by John William Gabriel published under same title, Praeger, 1970; *Die revolutionaere Aesthetik Andy Warhols,* Melzer Verlag, 1971. Author and producer, "The Art of Michael Heizer" (monographical film), shown on German television, 1972; author of "Orange Monument: Christo's Valley Curtain," shown on German television, 1974. Also author of catalogue to the Warhol exhibition, *A Golden Picture Show by the Artist Andy Warhol,* 1976. Also contributor of several articles to periodicals.

WORK IN PROGRESS: A book on Kazirmir Malevich and non-objective art; studies on the meaning of abstract art.

*   *   *

CROOKALL, Robert 1890-

PERSONAL: Born July 31, 1890, in Lancaster, England; son of Robert (a clerk of works) and Margaret (Hastings) Crookall; married Gladys Kate Stoneham, April 10, 1928 (deceased, 1969); children: John Roland. *Education:* Westminster College, Diploma in Education, 1911; Bristol University, B.Sc. (first class honors), 1922, Ph.D., 1926, D.Sc., 1930. *Home:* 9 Lansdown Rd. Mansions, Bath BA1 5ST, England.

CAREER: University of Aberdeen, Aberdeen, Scotland, lecturer in botany, 1925-26; Her Majesty's Geological Survey, Institute of Geological Studies, London, England, geologist, 1926-52.

WRITINGS—Geological publications: *Coal Measure Plants,* Edward Arnold, 1929; (with Francis B. A. Welch) *British Regional Geology: Bristol and Gloucester District,* H.M.S.O., 1935, 2nd edition, edited by G. A. Kellaway and Welch, 1948; *The Kidston Collection of Fossil Plants, with an Account of the Life and Work of Robert Kidston* (catalogue), H.M.S.O., 1938; (contributor) George Hoole Mitchell, *The Geology of the Warwickshire Coalfield,* Geological Survey & Museum, 1942; (contributor) Mitchell, *The Geology of the Northern Part of the South Staffordshire Coalfield, Cannock Chase Region,* Geological Survey & Museum, 1945; (contributor) Benjamin Hilton Barrett and W. E. Graham, *Economic Geology of Canonbie Coalfield, Dumfriesshire and Cumberland,* Geological Survey & Museum, 1945; *Fossil Plants of the Carboniferous Rocks of Great Britain* (monograph), H.M.S.O., Part 1, 1955, Part 2, 1959, Part 3, 1964, Part 4, 1966, Part 5, 1968, Part 6, 1969, Part 7, 1977. Contributor of articles to *Geological Magazine, Memoirs* of the Geological Survey of Great Britain, *Naturalist,* and other scientific publications.

Books on astral projection: *The Study and Practice of Astral Projection,* Wehman, 1961 (published in England as *The Study and Practice of Astral Projection: Analyses of Case Histories,* Aquarian Press, 1961); *The Supreme Adventure: Analyses of Psychic Communications,* Fernhill, 1961; *The Techniques of Astral Projection: Denouement after Fifty Years,* Wehman, 1964; *More Astral Projections: Analyses of Case Histories,* Wehman, 1964; *During Sleep: The Possibility of "Co-operation,"* Theosophical Publishing, 1964;

Intimations of Immortality: "Seeing" That Led to "Believing," published for Churches' Fellowship for Psychical and Spiritual Studies by James Clarke, 1965; *The Next World—and the Next: Ghostly Garments,* Theosophical Publishing, 1966; *The Mechanism of Astral Projection,* Darshzna International, 1968; *The Interpretation of Cosmic and Mystical Experiences,* James Clarke, 1969; *Out-of-the-Body Experiences: A Fourth Analysis,* University Books, 1970; *The Jung-Jaffe View of Out-of-the-Body Experiences,* published for Churches' Fellowship for Psychical and Spiritual Studies by World Fellowship Press, 1970; (contributor) *Case Book of Astral Projection,* University Books, 1972. Also author of *Events on the Threshold of the After Life,* 1969, *Ecstasy: The Release of the Soul from the Body,* 1973, and *"Dreams" of High Significance,* 1974. Contributor to *Light Magazine.*

SIDELIGHTS: After more than forty years in the field of geology and coal technology as a respected government scientist, Robert Crookall became an authority on astral projection. This phenomenon is ascribed by theosophists to the existence of a second, "astral" body belonging to each individual, sometimes able to carry the spirit away from the material body during sleep, and surviving it in death. Contained in the folklore and literature of primitive cultures, and in those of ancient Egypt, India, Ghana, Tibet, and Polynesia, among others, "out-of-body" experiences are typically viewed by many contemporary scientists and psychologists as subjective feats of human imagination. Crookall, however, belongs to the school of parapsychologists which considers these experiences based on non-("semi-" or "super-" physical) reality. With Swiss scientists Jung and Jaffe, he documents and classifies thousands of cases of astral projection, a process described in *The Jung-Jaffe View of Out-of-the-Body Experiences,* in a thoroughly scientific fashion. In a review for *Books and Bookmen,* Laura Bartlett calls it a "deeply argued, fascinating" account of an intriguing phenomenon which, incidentally, reinforces "the old Christian idea of survival after death."

Considering himself "a deeply religious man," Crookall "believes that concepts of the soul are not unscientific, and hopes to reconcile religious faith and scientific integrity in matters relating to the human soul." Crookall goes on to write: "Out-of-the-body experiences are taking the foremost place in the study of survival, the earlier, mediumistic, phenomena having failed to clinch the question. The present result, though not absolute 'proof,' is practical certainty."

BIOGRAPHICAL/CRITICAL SOURCES: Dennis Barden, *Mysterious Worlds,* W. H. Allen, 1970; *Books and Bookmen,* August, 1970.

* * *

CROPP, Ben(jamin) 1936-

PERSONAL: Born January 19, 1936, in Solomon Islands; son of Allan Herbert (a missionary) and Louise (Taylor) Cropp; married Van Laman, April, 1964; married second wife, Eva Elizabeth Papp (a secretary and film model), January 27, 1968. *Education:* Brisbane Teachers College, teaching certificate, 1954. *Politics:* "None really." *Religion:* Methodist. *Home and office:* 74 Admiralty Dr., Paradise Waters, Surfers Paradise, Queensland 4217, Australia.

CAREER: General teacher in schools in Queensland and New South Wales, Australia, 1954-61; Ben Cropp Productions, Queensland, managing director, film producer, photographer, and author, 1961—. Director, Ben Cropp Theatre and Marineland of Australia. *Member:* Australian Cinema-

tographers Society, World Skindiving Federation (chairman, photographic committee), Australian Skindiving Federation (chairman, photographic committee), American Littoral Society (honorary member); honorary member of several skindiving organizations around the world. *Awards, honors:* World Underwater Photographer of the Year award, 1964.

WRITINGS: Handbook for Skindivers, Afco Printery, 1963, 4th edition, Pollard, 1972; *Shark Hunters,* Rigby, 1964, Macmillan, 1971; *Sammy the Seal,* Rigby, 1966, Tri-Ocean, 1967; *Cheeky the Dolphin,* Rigby, 1968; *Whale of a Shark,* Rigby, 1969. Contributor of numerous articles and photo features to magazines and newspapers in various countries.

WORK IN PROGRESS: Television series of ten specials entitled "This Rugged Coast."

SIDELIGHTS: Ben Cropp's television series "This Rugged Coast" is being filmed on an adventurous eighteen-month circumnavigation of Australia in his own cruiser. He expects the series to be seen on Australian, Japanese, and American television.

Cropp told *CA* that skindiving has been his main hobby for twenty-eight years, the production of underwater television films his profession for the past sixteen.

AVOCATIONAL INTERESTS: Wreck-hunting, fishing, surfing, snow skiing, marine and wild life conservation.

BIOGRAPHICAL/CRITICAL SOURCES: Oceans, Number 2, 1970, Number 5, 1971, Number 1, 1972; *National Geographic,* April, 1972.

* * *

CROSS, K(athryn) Patricia 1926-

PERSONAL: Born March 17, 1926, in Normal, Ill.; daughter of Clarence L. (a professor) and Katherine (Dague) Cross. *Education:* Illinois State University, B.S., 1948; University of Illinois, A.M., 1951, Ph.D., 1958. *Home:* 904 Oxford St., Berkeley, Calif. 94707. *Office:* Educational Testing Service, 1947 Center St., Berkeley, Calif. 94704.

CAREER: Harvard Community High School, Harvard, Ill., mathematics teacher, 1948-49; University of Illinois, Urbana, research assistant, department of psychology, 1949-53, assistant dean of women, 1953-59; Cornell University, Ithaca, N.Y., dean of women, 1959-60, dean of students, 1960-63; Educational Testing Service, Princeton, N.J., and Berkeley, Calif., senior research psychologist, 1963—. Research educator, Center for Research and Development in Higher Education, University of California, Berkeley, 1966—. *Member:* American Association of Higher Education (member of board of directors, 1972-75; vice-president, 1973-74; president, 1974-75). *Awards, honors:* Foundation for Economic Education fellowship in industry, 1962; Best Books award, Pi Lambda Theta, 1968, for *The Junior College Student: A Research Description;* School and Society Outstanding Books in Education award, 1971, for *Beyond the Open Door;* American Council on Education Book Award, 1976, for *Accent on Learning.* Honorary doctorates from Illinois State University, 1970, Grand Valley State College, 1975, and Northeastern University, 1975.

WRITINGS: (With R. Linn and J. Davis) *A Guide to Research Design: Institutional Research Program for Higher Education,* Educational Testing Service, 1965; *The Junior College Student: A Research Description,* Educational Testing Service, 1968; *Beyond the Open Door: New Students to Higher Education,* Jossey-Bass, 1971; *New Students and New Needs in Higher Education,* Center for Research and Development in Higher Education, University of California, 1972; (editor with S. B. Gould, and contributor) *Explorations in Non-Traditional Studies,* Jossey-Bass, 1972; (with J. R. Valley and others) *Planning Non-Traditional Programs: An Analysis of the Issues for Postsecondary Education,* Jossey-Bass, 1974; *Accent on Learning: Improving Instruction and Reshaping the Curriculum,* Jossey-Bass, 1976.

Contributor: *Trends in Postsecondary Education,* U.S. Government Printing Office, 1970; T. O'Banion and A. Thurston, editors, *Junior College Student Personnel Work: Practice and Potential,* Prentice-Hall, 1971; *White House Conference on Youth,* Center for Research and Development in Higher Education, University of California, 1971; *Invitational Papers for the Select Education Subcommittee of the Education and Labor Committee of the House of Representatives,* Educational Testing Service, 1971; O'-Banion and Thurston, editors, *Student Development Programs in the Community Junior College,* Prentice-Hall, 1972; M. L. McBee and K. A. Blake, editors, *The American Woman: Who Will She Be?,* Glencoe Press, 1974; D. W. Vermilye, editor, *Lifelong Learners: A New Clientele for Higher Education,* Jossey-Bass, 1974; W. T. Furniss and P. A. Graham, editors, *Women in Higher Education,* American Council on Education, 1974; J. F. Hughes, editor, *The Search for Alternatives,* American Council on Education, 1975; Vermilye, editor, *Individualizing the System,* Jossey-Bass, 1976. Contributor to *Journal of Personality, Journal of the National Association of Women Deans and Counselors, Research Reporter,* and other publications. Editor, *Research Reporter,* 1966-73, and *Findings,* 1974-75; consulting editor, *Journal of Higher Education,* 1974; member of editorial board, *Community/Junior College Research Quarterly,* and *Journal of Personalized Instruction.*

WORK IN PROGRESS: Research on women and on non-traditional study.

*   *   *

CROSS, Richard K(eith) 1940-

PERSONAL: Born May 19, 1940, in Hackensack, N.J.; son of Gordon Keith and Marguerite (Grossmann) Cross; married Christa Maria Wolf, December 18, 1970; children: Catherine. *Education:* Princeton University, A.B. (magna cum laude), 1962; Stanford University, M.A., 1966, Ph.D., 1967. *Office:* Department of English, University of California, Los Angeles, Calif. 90024.

CAREER: Dartmouth College, Hanover, N.H., instructor in English, 1966-68; University of California, Los Angeles, assistant professor, 1968-74, associate professor of English, 1974—, vice-chairman of department, 1976-77. Fulbright lecturer, University of Wuerzburg, 1971-72. *Awards, honors:* Humanities Institute fellow, 1970, 1974; American Council of Learned Societies grant-in-aid, 1973.

WRITINGS: Flaubert and Joyce: The Rite of Fiction, Princeton University Press, 1971. Also author of *Malcolm Lowry: A Preface to His Fiction.* Contributor to *Twentieth Century Literature, Contemporary Literature, Modern Fiction Studies,* and *Modern Philology.*

*   *   *

CROTHERS, J(essie) Frances 1913-
(Jessie F. Crothers, Frances J. Wright)

PERSONAL: Born June 24, 1913, in Ravenna, Ohio; daughter of W. J. (a mechanical engineer) and Ethel D.

(Soper) Hinds; married Thomas E. Crothers (a music educator), June 4, 1938; children: Jerome Thomas. *Education:* Kent State University, B.S., 1935; attended Otis Art Institute, Los Angeles, Calif., 1935-36; Northwestern University, M.A., 1949; also studied art at University of Hartford and Willimantic School of Art. *Religion:* Lutheran. *Home:* 81 Flagg Rd., West Hartford, Conn. 06117.

CAREER: Ferdinand Perret Research Library, Los Angeles, Calif., assistant to director during 1930's; art director in southern Ohio, 1938-41; assistant to director, children's theatre of Northwestern University and City of Evanston, Ill., 1943-44; Cain Park Public Theatre, Cleveland Heights, Ohio, head of children's theatre puppet work, 1943-44; Evanston (Ill.) Public Schools, head of research project, working with handicapped children, 1943; Gary (Ind.) Public Schools, special drama teacher in auditorium department, 1944-46; Salem (Conn.) Public Schools, speech re-education work, using puppets, 1946, director, Salem Drama Group and Salem Puppeteers, 1946-51; arts and crafts instructor, adult education teacher, and public speaker in New England, 1952-66; Hartford (Conn.) Public Schools, art department instructor, 1957-72; full-time writer and researcher on puppetry, 1972—. Lecturer on art research topics and all aspects of puppetry to schools and organizations, 1944—. *Wartime service:* Head of Women's Division Civil Defense, Washingtonville, Ohio, 1941-43.

MEMBER: International Marionette Group of the World, Puppeteers of America, British Puppet and Model Theatre Guild (London), British Educational Puppet Association (London), Canadian Puppet Association, Nederlandse Vereniging voor het Poppenspelaanwezig (Holland), New England Guild of Puppetry, New York Guild of Puppetry, Los Angeles Guild of Puppetry, Long Island Guild of Puppetry, Catholic Fine Arts Group (New England Division), Eastern Star Organization (former officer, Salem and West Hartford, Conn.), Quota Club International (Salem and Hartford; former president), Business and Professional Women's Club of Hartford, Amaranth (a Masonic branch; former Royal Matron and Warder), Phi Beta, Lambda Chi, Cardinal Key, Alpha Psi Omega, Alpha Gamma Delta. *Awards, honors:* Best actress award, Kent State University, 1933; state medal for second place in college and university acting, Ohio, 1933.

WRITINGS: The Puppeteer's Library Guide: A Bibliographic Index to the Literature of the World Puppet Theatre, Volume I: *The Historical Background of Puppetry and Its Related Fields,* Scarecrow, 1971.

Privately printed books of poetry: *Moon Glow,* 1932, *Star Chippings,* 1934, *Rain Smoke,* 1936, *Sun Pennies,* 1940, *Blue Winds in the Poplars,* 1965. Also author of the following privately printed books: *Folklore and Legend Puppet Plays, School Puppet Plays,* and *Educational, Therapeutic and Religious Use of Puppetry.* Author of a pageant, "Patriot's Dream Come True." Contributor of poems to various periodicals; poetry anthologized in four collections, including *America Singing,* National Poetry Society, 1933, 1934, 1935.

WORK IN PROGRESS: Five more volumes of *The Puppeteer's Library Guide.*

SIDELIGHTS: J. Frances Crothers began *The Puppeteer's Library Guide* in an effort to demonstrate the educational, therapeutic, religious, and political value of puppetry. The series, which will consist of six volumes when completed, is the only bibliography of its kind in the world. Organizations from numerous countries are sending small bibliographies in their native languages to be incorporated into this voluminous work. Crothers is a professional actress, director, and dramatic producer, as well as an authority on puppetry. While working in the Cain Park Public Theatre in Ohio during the 1940's, she designed and directed in the first and largest open-air, "permanent-park-puppet theatre" in America. One of her projects for the public playground program of Evanston, Ill., involved the writing, directing, and producing of a pageant, "Patriot's Dream Come True," for 1,000 people, including music and dance.

BIOGRAPHICAL/CRITICAL SOURCES: Evanston (Ill.) *News,* June 29, 1950.

* * *

CROWTHER, Geoffrey 1907-1972

May 13, 1907—February 5, 1972; English editor and economist. Obituaries: *New York Times,* February 7, 1972; *Washington Post,* February 9, 1972; *Publishers Weekly,* February 14, 1972.

* * *

CRUDEN, Robert 1910-

PERSONAL: Born April 21, 1910, in Scotland; son of Robert (an autoworker and hairdresser) and Elizabeth (Ironside) Cruden; married Janet Metzger, July 14, 1930; children: Robert W., Janet E. (Mrs. C. A. Christensen). *Education:* Hiram College, B.A., 1951; Western Reserve University (now Case Western Reserve University), M.A., 1952, Ph.D., 1959. *Home:* 14344 Northwest Springville Rd., Portland, Ore. 97229. *Office:* Department of History, Lewis and Clark College, Portland, Ore. 97219.

CAREER: Writer in publicity and public relations for labor and community organizations in Cleveland and Akron, Ohio, 1931-49; Baldwin-Wallace College, Berea, Ohio, instructor, 1954-56, assistant professor, 1956-62, associate professor of history, 1962-63; Lewis and Clark College, Portland, Ore., associate professor, 1963-66, professor of history, 1966—. Lecturer in history, Case Western Reserve University, 1952-63. *Military service:* U.S. Army, 1944-46; served in Pacific theater; became technical sergeant. *Member:* American Historical Association, Organization of American Historians, Southern Historical Association.

WRITINGS: James Ford Rhodes: The Man, the Historian and His Work, Press of Case Western Reserve University, 1961; *The Negro in Reconstruction,* Prentice-Hall, 1969; *The War That Never Ended: The American Civil War,* Prentice-Hall, 1972.

WORK IN PROGRESS: A social history of the various American peoples, tentatively entitled *One and Many,* for Prentice-Hall.

* * *

CUDLIPP, Edythe 1929-
(Julia Alcott, Jane Horatio, Rinalda Roberts, E. F. Van Zandt)

PERSONAL: Born September 4, 1929, in Jamestown, N.Y.; daughter of Edwin F. and Edna (Van Zandt) Cudlipp; married Bruce Stewart Lachlan, Jr., October 1, 1970 (divorced, 1974). *Education:* Mount Holyoke College, B.A., 1951; University of Heidelberg, further study, 1955. *Home:* 82 Horatio St., New York, N.Y. 10014. *Agent:* Balkin Agency, 403 West 115th St., New York, N.Y. 10025.

CAREER: U.S. Army, civilian editor in Heidelberg, Germany, 1957-62; *American Businessman,* Washington, D.C.,

writer, 1963-65; *This Week,* New York City, associate editor, 1965-67; *Coronet,* New York City, senior editor, 1967-70; free-lance writer, 1970—.

WRITINGS: Understanding Women's Liberation, Paperback Library, 1971; (under pseudonym Jane Horatio) *A Matter of Life and Death,* Award Books, 1971; (with Jane Sorensen) *The New Way to Become the Person You'd Like to Be,* McKay, 1973; (under pseudonym Rinalda Roberts) *The Four Marys,* Popular Library, 1976.

Under pseudonym Julia Alcott; all published by Signet: *A Long Lost Love,* 1976; *The Key to Her Heart,* 1976; *Island of Love,* 1977.

WORK IN PROGRESS: Research for an historical romance and a nonfiction book.

* * *

CULLEY, Thomas R(obert) 1931-

PERSONAL: Born July 17, 1931, in Wilmington, Calif.; married Judy J. Duckworth, April 12, 1952; children: Timothy Paul. *Education:* Attended Diablo Valley College, 1959, College of San Mateo, 1963-69, University of California, San Francisco, 1969-71, and Humboldt State College (now Humboldt State University), 1971. *Home:* 46 Pacifico Ave., Daly City, Calif. 94015.

CAREER: Police Department, Daly City, Calif., lieutenant, 1959—. Instructor, College of San Mateo, 1966—. *Military service:* U.S. Coast Guard, 1950-53.

WRITINGS: (With David A. Hansen) *The Police Leader,* C. C Thomas, 1971; (with Hansen) *The Police Training Officer,* C. C Thomas, 1972.

WORK IN PROGRESS: With David A. Hansen and John Bogohsian, a children's book entitled *My Dad the Policeman; American Justice: The Role of Law Enforcement; Models of Police Communications.*

SIDELIGHTS: Thomas Culley told *CA:* "Police are consistently under observation by the public, the news media, and their leaders. I submit that they must have professional bearing and the ability to communicate their role in society to all. Communication is the key to such things as establishing areas of trust and understanding with minorities and with the community at large. For this reason I stress the importance of training and supervision in this important area of law enforcement. Without the support of the people, the police are helpless. With the support of the public, the department becomes viable and a significant force for the benefit of all."

* * *

CULROSS, Michael (Gerard) 1942-

PERSONAL: Surname is accented on first syllable; born July 31, 1942, in Rochester, N.Y.; son of Raymond William (a photographer) and Jeanette (Thompson) Culross; married Betty Ann Henderson (a singer and teacher), May 6, 1965; children: Kathy, Tom, Patti, Peter, Michael, Jr., Melissa. *Education:* University of Iowa, B.A., 1967; Syracuse University, M.A., 1968. *Politics:* None. *Religion:* None.

CAREER: Operation Area Arts, Green Bay, Wis., instructor in creative writing, 1968-69; University of Wisconsin—Green Bay, lecturer in creative writing, 1969-71; Antioch College/West, Los Angeles, Calif., teacher of creative writing, 1972-75. Has given poetry readings at colleges and universities, including Bowling Green State University, Viterbo College, and Lawrence University. *Member:*

Modern Language Association of America. *Awards, honors:* Finalist, United States Award, University of Pittsburgh Press, 1969, 1970, 1971; finalist, Devins Award, Kansas City Poetry Contest, 1970.

WRITINGS: The Bushleaguers (chapbook), Libman Press, 1970; *The Lost Heroes* (poems), University of Pittsburgh Press, 1974. Contributor to poetry anthologies, including *From Out of the Salt Mound,* Salt Mound Press, 1968, and *Syracuse Poems 1963-1969,* Syracuse University Press, 1970. Wrote, produced, and co-directed film ''The Bushleaguers,'' based on and using the poems from his chapbook. Contributor of poems to more than twenty little magazines, including *Black Swamp Review, Carolina Quarterly, Counterpoint, Iowa Review, North American Review,* and *Transpacific.*

AVOCATIONAL INTERESTS: Jazz, photography, filmmaking.†

*   *   *

CUMMING, Primrose Amy 1915-

PERSONAL: Born April 7, 1915, in Isle of Thanet, England; daughter of Arthur Somerville and Emily Christin (Heath) Cumming. *Education:* Educated privately. *Politics:* Liberal. *Religion:* ''Christian in the broadest sense.'' *Home:* Wynberg, Sandhurst, Hawkhurst, Kent, England.

CAREER: Writer. *Military service:* Auxiliary Territorial Service, 1940-45.

WRITINGS—Juveniles: *Doney,* Country Life, 1934; *Spider Dog,* Country Life, 1936; *Silver Snaffles,* Blackie & Son, 1937; *The Silver Eagle Riding School,* A. & C. Black, 1938; *Rachel of Romney,* Country Life, 1939; *The Wednesday Pony,* Blackie & Son, 1939; *Ben,* Dent, 1939; *Silver Eagle Carries On,* A. & C. Black, 1940; *The Chestnut Filly,* Blackie & Son, 1940; *Owls Castle Farm,* A. & C. Black, 1942; *The Great Horses,* Dent, 1946; *Trouble at Trimbles,* Country Life, 1949; *Four Rode Home,* Dent, 1951; *Rivals to Silver Eagle,* A. & C. Black, 1954; *No Place for Ponies,* Dent, 1954, published as *The Mystery Pony,* Criterion, 1957; *The Deep Sea Horse,* Dent, 1956; *The Flying Horseman,* Dent, 1959; *The Mystery Trek,* Dent, 1964; *Foal of the Fjords,* Dent, 1966; *Penny and Pegasus,* Dent, 1969. Regular contributor of scripts to pictorial magazines and annuals.

WORK IN PROGRESS: Seven stories for pictorial section of a horse book to be published by Intercontinental Book Productions.

SIDELIGHTS: Primrose Cumming told *CA:* ''I write for children to try to interest them in the country things that enthralled me as a child—and still does. After over forty years it is very rewarding to find one's books are being passed down the generations as family heirlooms.'' Four of Miss Cumming's books have been translated into Swedish.

AVOCATIONAL INTERESTS: Countryside, horses (riding, breeding, and schooling), gardening, flower arranging, music, handiwork.

BIOGRAPHICAL/CRITICAL SOURCES: Books and Bookmen, January, 1970.

*   *   *

CUMMING, William P(atterson) 1900-

PERSONAL: Born October 31, 1900, in Nagoya, Japan; son of Calvin Knox (a missionary) and Ona (Patterson) Cumming; married Elizabeth Lathrop Chandler, December 22,

1931; children: Edward Chandler (deceased), Robert Patterson. *Education:* Davidson College, A.B., 1921; Princeton University, M.A., 1922, Ph.D. 1925. *Politics:* Democratic. *Religion:* Presbyterian (U.S.). *Home:* 313 Woodland St., Davidson, N.C. 28036. *Office:* Department of English, Davidson College, Davidson, N.C. 28036.

CAREER: Williams College, Wiliamstown, Mass., instructor in English, 1926-27; Davidson College, Davidson, N.C., 1927-68, professor of English, 1937-68, Irvin Professor of English, 1961-68, professor emeritus, 1968—, chairman of the department, 1964-68. Visiting professor of English and Fulbright lecturer, Annamalai University, India, 1963-64, Shikoku College, Zentsuji, Japan, 1964; Nebenzahl Lecturer in the history of cartography, Newberry Library, Chicago, 1970. Attache, U.S. State Department, Germany, 1945-46. Chairman, North Mecklenburg Chapter, American Red Cross, 1941-43. *Member:* Modern Language Association of America (president, 1956-57), American Association of University Professors, South Atlantic Modern Language Association, Historical Society of North Carolina (president, 1955-56), Phi Beta Kappa, Omicron Delta Kappa, Lions International. *Awards, honors:* Guggenheim fellow, 1958-59; R. W. Connor Award, Historical Society of North Carolina, 1969, for *Captain James Wimble: His Maps, and the Colonial Cartography of the North Carolina Coast.*

WRITINGS: (Editor) *The Revelations of St. Birgitta,* Oxford University Press, 1929; (editor) *The Discoveries of John Lederer,* University Press of Virginia, 1958; *The Southeast in Early Maps,* Princeton University Press, 1958, 2nd edition, University of North Carolina Press, 1962; *Cartography of Colonial Carolina,* University of South Carolina Press, 1961; *North Carolina in Maps,* North Carolina Department of Archives and History, 1966; *Captain James Wimble: His Maps, and the Colonial Cartography of the North Carolina Coast,* North Carolina Department of Archives and History, 1969; (with R. A. Skelton and D. B. Quinn) *The Discovery of North America* (Book-of-the-Month Club selection), American Heritage Press, 1972; (editor with H. Wallis) Henry Popple, *A Map of the British Empire in America,* Harry Margary, 1972; *British Maps of Colonial America,* University of Chicago Press, 1974; (with Hillier, Quinn, and Williams) *Exploration of North America, 1630-1776,* Elek, 1974; (editor with D. Marshall) *North America at the Time of the Revolution: A Collection of Eighteenth-Century Maps,* Harry Margary, 1975; (with H. Rankin) *Fate of a Nation* (Book-of-the-Month Club Bicentennial selection), 1976; *Colonial Charting of the Massachusetts Coast,* Colonial Society of Massachusetts, in press. Contributor of articles to periodicals.

SIDELIGHTS: William Cumming told *CA:* ''If each writer's style and method of writing results from his background and experience, mine developed from extensive memorization of the King James' version including several books and many psalms of the Bible (an unconscious training experience by Ruskin and many other writers); forty years of critical correction of college English themes; and an effort to keep the reader in mind by direct, clear, and interesting phrasing and development of the subject. I try to know what I am writing about before starting.''

*   *   *

CUMMINGS, Jean 1930-

PERSONAL: Born April 19, 1930, in Charles City, Iowa; daughter of William Kinsey (an attorney) and Eathel

(Gibson) Carr; married Dwain W. Cummings (a surgeon), February 2, 1951; children: Bruce, Beth, Brenda. *Education:* Attended Carleton College, 1948-49, and University of Iowa, 1949-51; Drake University, B.A., 1953. *Home:* 4211 South Brooks Rd., Muskegon, Mich. 49444. *Agent:* Curtis Brown, Ltd., 575 Madison Ave., New York, N.Y. 10022.

CAREER: Secretary in Des Moines, Iowa, 1951-54; Des Moines General Hospital, Des Moines, medical secretary, 1954-58. Member of board of directors, Muskegon County Library.

WRITINGS: Why They Call Him the Buffalo Doctor, Prentice-Hall, 1971. Contributor of short stories to newspapers.

WORK IN PROGRESS: Historical novel revolving around the demise of the great buffalo herds; a juvenile historical novel of the Michigan lumbering era; a novel about married medical students; a humorous how-to manual on how to survive country living.

SIDELIGHTS: Since 1964, Jean Cummings and her family have been raising a herd of buffalo, an experience which has led her toward experimental research work on organ transplant serum based on buffalo blood, involvement in life on Indian reservations, assistance to the American Indian in raising buffalo for food and handicrafts, and an interest in conservation, ecology, and historically significant animals.

* * *

CUMMINS, Paul F. 1937-

PERSONAL: Born September 9, 1937, in Chicago, Ill.; son of Paul Stedman (a financier) and Ruth (Wenter) Cummins; married Elizabeth Keyser, June 12, 1965; married second wife, Maryann Huber (a music teacher), February 19, 1972. *Education:* Stanford University, B.A., 1959; Harvard University, M.A.T., 1960; University of Southern California, Ph.D., 1967. *Office:* St. Augustine By-the-Sea School, 1229 Fourth St., Santa Monica, Calif. 90401.

CAREER: English teacher in private schools in North Hollywood, Calif., 1961-70; University of California, Los Angeles, teacher of English, 1968—; St. Augustine By-the-Sea School, Santa Monica, Calif., headmaster, 1970—. Crossroads School, Santa Monica, Calif., founding member of board of trustees, and headmaster, 1973—. *Member:* Modern Language Association of America, National Association of Independent Schools, California Association for Teachers of English.

WRITINGS: Max Rafferty: A Study in Simplicity, Hogarth Press, 1968; *Richard Wilbur,* Eerdmans, 1971.

WORK IN PROGRESS: Several works of children's fiction.

* * *

CUNLIFFE, Elaine

PERSONAL: Born in Burnley, Lancashire, England; daughter of Robert and Mabel (Lupton) Emmott; married James Cunliffe (a dental surgeon; deceased); children: Jennefer (Mrs. Ray Prouse), Jerome, Julienne (Mrs. John Oldfield), Naomi. *Education:* Attended schools in England. *Religion:* Presbyterian. *Home:* Barr Cottage, Orchardton by Castle Douglas, Galloway, Scotland.

CAREER: Writer.

WRITINGS—Published by Dinwiddie & Co. except as indicated; all illustrated with own photographs: *Tomorrow's Country,* 1966; *Unforgettable Journey: 7000 Miles by Greyhound Bus,* 1968; *The Wandering Moon,* 1969; *Elaine's Australian Safari,* 1970; *Hi, Skunks,* Vantage, 1975. Contributor of articles illustrated with her own photographs to periodicals, including *Lancashire Life, The Lady, House Beautiful, Scotland's Magazine, Scottish Field,* and *Homes and Gardens.*

WORK IN PROGRESS: A book on Dr. Livingstone; cookery book; another U.S. travel book.

SIDELIGHTS: Elaine Cunliffe told *CA:* "I had written many novels, mostly historical, without success ... I had always wanted to travel, and writing travel books presents an ideal opportunity. I travel two months, January to March, every year, giving talks and collecting material for my books." Cunliffe has traveled around the world twice, logging three quarters of a million miles in the last ten years.

AVOCATIONAL INTERESTS: Gardening, swimming, knotting, reading, cooking, photography.

BIOGRAPHICAL/CRITICAL SOURCES: Books and Bookmen, November, 1969.

* * *

CURL, Donald Walter 1935-

PERSONAL: Born October 7, 1935, in East Liberty, Ohio; son of Charles N. and Dorothy (Wood) Curl. *Education:* Ohio State University, B.S., 1957, M.A., 1958, Ph.D., 1964. *Politics:* Democrat. *Religion:* Episcopalian. *Home:* 854 Northwest Alamanda, Boca Raton, Fla. 33432. *Office:* Department of History, Florida Atlantic University, Boca Raton, Fla. 33432.

CAREER: Kent State University, Kent, Ohio, instructor in history, 1961-64; Florida Atlantic University, Boca Raton, assistant professor, 1964-67, associate professor, 1967-71, professor of history, 1971—, chairman of department, 1969-75. *Member:* American Historical Society, American Studies Association, Southern Historical Association, Florida Historical Society (member of board of directors). *Awards, honors:* Certificate of commendation from American Association for State and Local History, 1972, for *Pioneer Life in Southeast Florida.*

WRITINGS: (Contributor) Kenneth Wheeler, editor, *For the Union: Ohio Leaders in Civil War,* Ohio State University Press, 1968; (editor) *Pioneer Life in Southeast Florida,* University of Miami, 1970; *The Pioneer Cook in Southeast Florida,* Boca Raton Historical Society, 1975. Contributor to history journals.

WORK IN PROGRESS: A History of Political Parties; A History of the Palm Beaches.

* * *

CURLE, Charles T. W. 1916-
(Adam Curle)

PERSONAL: Born July 4, 1916, in Ile Adam, France; son of Richard (a writer) and Cordelia (Fisher) Curle; married Pamela Hobson, October 13, 1939; married second wife, Anne Edie, May 28, 1958; children: (first marriage) Christina (Mrs. Peter Goldfine), Anna (Mrs. Philip Pollard); (second marriage) Deborah. *Education:* Oxford University, B.A., B.S., M.A., all 1947, D.Phil., 1950. *Religion:* Society of Friends. *Home:* Dear Bought, Townhead Lane, Austwick, Lancaster LA2 8BS, England. *Office:* School of Peace Studies, University of Bradford, Bradford, West Yorkshire BD7 1DP, England.

CAREER: Tavistock Institute, London, England, staff

member, 1947-50; Oxford University, Oxford, England, lecturer in social psychology, 1950-52; University of Exeter, Exeter, England, professor of educational psychology, 1952-56; Government of Pakistan, adviser on social affairs, 1956-59; Ghana University, Legon, professor of education, 1959-61; Harvard University, Cambridge, Mass., professor of education and development, 1961-73; University of Bradford, Bradford, England, professor of peace studies, 1973—. Consultant to World Bank, Ford Foundation, and United Nations special agencies. *Military service:* British Army, 1940-46; became major. *Member:* American Academy of Arts and Science.

WRITINGS—Under name Adam Curle: *Educational Strategies for Developing Societies,* Tavistock, 1963, 2nd edition, 1970; *Planning for Education in Pakistan,* Harvard University Press, 1966; *Problems of Professional Identity* (booklet), Education and World Affairs, 1968 (published as *The Professional Identity of the Educational Planner,* International Institute for Educational Planning, 1969); *Educational Problems of Developing Societies,* Praeger, 1969, expanded and updated edition, 1973; *Making Peace,* Tavistock, 1971; *Mystics and Militants,* Tavistock, 1972; *Education for Liberation,* Wiley, 1973; *Violence, Reconciliation and Anger,* FOR Press, 1975. Also author of papers and lectures on education and peace.

WORK IN PROGRESS: The Children of God, a book on peacemakers.

SIDELIGHTS: Adam Curle's anthropological research has taken him among nomads in the Arctic and the Middle East; he has worked in twenty countries in Africa, Asia, and Latin America. *Avocational interests:* Music.

*   *   *

CURRAN, Charles A(rthur) 1913-

PERSONAL: Born October 9, 1913, in Philadelphia, Pa.; son of Michael and Mary (Daugherty) Curran. *Education:* St. Charles College, Columbus, Ohio, B.A., 1935; studied at St. Mary's Seminary, Cincinnati; Ohio State University, M.A., 1941, Ph.D., 1944. *Office:* Department of Psychology, Loyola University, Lewis Towers, 820 North Michigan Ave., Chicago, Ill. 60611.

CAREER: Roman Catholic priest, ordained in 1939; St. Charles College, Columbus, Ohio, professor of psychology, 1944-53; Loyola University, Graduate School, Chicago, Ill., professor of psychology, 1955—. Visiting professor at University of Louvain, 1953, and Menninger Foundation, 1960. *Peritus,* Vatican Council II. *Member:* Academy of Religion and Health (member of advisory council). *Awards, honors:* Pope Paul VI Medal, 1968, for distinguished contribution to the Catholic priesthood; Pastoral Psychology Prize, 1969, for *Religious Values in Counseling and Psychotherapy.*

WRITINGS: Personality Factors in Counseling, Grune, 1945; *Counseling in Catholic Life and Education,* Macmillan, 1952; *Counseling and Psychotherapy: The Pursuit of Values,* Sheed, 1968, 2nd edition, 1976; *Religious Values in Counseling and Psychotherapy,* Sheed, 1969; *Psychological Dynamics in Religious Living,* Herder & Herder, 1971; *Counseling-Learning: A Whole-Person Model for Education,* Grune, 1972. Also author of *Counseling-Learning in Second Languages,* 1976.

Contributor: R. J. Deferrari, editor, *Guidance in Catholic Colleges and Universities,* Catholic University of America Press, 1949; A. H. Brayfield, editor, *Readings in Modern Methods of Counseling,* Appleton, 1950; Magda Arnold and

John Gasson, editors, *The Human Person,* Ronald, 1954; W. C. Bier, editor, *Perception,* Fordham University Press, 1957; J. E. Haley, editor, *Proceedings of the 1959 Sisters' Institute of Spirituality,* University of Notre Dame Press, 1960; Haley, editor, *Proceedings of the 1960 Sisters' Institute of Spirituality,* University of Notre Dame Press, 1961; *Systems of Human Guidance: Religion and Psychotherapy,* C. C Thomas, 1972. Also editor of "The Word Becomes Flesh: A Psychodynamic Approach to Homiletics, and Catechetics, and Meditation" series, 1973-76. Contributor of about eighty articles to religious and psychology journals. Member of editorial board, *Journal of Pastoral Counseling.*

WORK IN PROGRESS: Community Language Learning; Achieving Understanding.

*   *   *

CURRY, Lerond (Loving) 1938-

PERSONAL: Born September 16, 1938, in Bowling Green, Ky.; son of Bronston Loving (a teacher) and Edith Marie (Owen) Curry; married Rebecca Holbrook, December 28, 1970. *Education:* Western Kentucky State College (now Western Kentucky University), B.A., 1960; Southern Baptist Theological Seminary, B.D., 1963; Florida State University, M.A., 1964, Ph.D., 1967. *Politics:* Liberal Democrat. *Religion:* Ecumenical Christian. *Home:* 157 Jerry Dr., Danville, Va. 24541. *Office:* Department of Religion and Philosophy, Averett College, Danville, Va. 24541.

CAREER: Florida State University, Tallahassee, instructor in humanities, 1964-66; Western Kentucky University, Bowling Green, assistant professor of history and religion, 1967-70; Averett College, Danville, Va., assistant professor of religion, 1970—. *Military service:* U.S. Army Reserve, 1955-63. *Member:* American Academy of Religion, Society for the Arts, Religion, and Contemporary Culture.

WRITINGS: Protestant-Catholic Relations in America: World War I through Vatican II, University Press of Kentucky, 1972.

AVOCATIONAL INTERESTS: International travel.

*   *   *

CURRY, Peggy Simson 1911-

PERSONAL: Born December 30, 1911, in Dunure, Ayrshire, Scotland; daughter of William Andrew (a rancher) and Margaret (Anderson) Simson; married William Seeright Curry (an educator), July 21, 1937; children: Michael Munro. *Education:* University of Wyoming, B.A., 1936. *Politics:* Republican. *Religion:* Presbyterian. *Home and office:* 3125 Garden Creek Rd., Casper, Wyo. 82601. *Agent:* Lenniger Literary Agency, Inc., 437 Fifth Ave., New York, N.Y. 10016.

CAREER: Casper College, Casper, Wyo., instructor in creative writing, 1952—; author. Lecturer at various colleges and writers' conferences, 1952—. Poet-in-residence, State of Wyoming poetry-in-schools program, 1971—. *Member:* Western Writers of America, Kappa Kappa Gamma, P.E.O. Sisterhood. *Awards, honors:* Spur Award, Western Writers of America, 1957, 1970; Kappa Kappa Gamma Distinguished Alumni award, 1964; University of Wyoming Distinguished Alumni award, 1968.

WRITINGS: Fire in the Water (novel), McGraw, 1951; *Red Wind of Wyoming* (poetry), Allan Swallow, 1955; *So Far from Spring* (novel), Viking, 1956; *The Oil Patch* (novel), McGraw, 1959; *Creating Fiction from Experience,* Writer, Inc., 1964, revised edition, 1975; *A Shield of Clover* (juvenile novel), McKay, 1970. Contributor to *New York Times, Saturday Evening Post, Christian Science Monitor, Poet* (India), *Reader's Digest, Audubon, Good Housekeeping, Collier's, Toronto Star,* and *Boys' Life.* Poet's column in *Chicago Sunday Tribune* and in other publications.

WORK IN PROGRESS: Shindig, a novel; a book of poems.

* * *

CUSAC, Marian H(ollingsworth) 1932-

PERSONAL: Surname is pronounced *Kyu*-sic; born February 22, 1932, in Georgetown, Ky.; daughter of A. Hayden (a minister) and Merris (Everett) Hollingsworth; married William L. Cusac (an office manager), May 1, 1965; children: Michael, Sarah. *Education:* Mary Baldwin College, A.B., 1954; University of North Carolina, M.A., 1957, Ph.D., 1964. *Religion:* Protestant. *Home:* 31L Lipscomb St., Marion, S.C. 29571. *Office:* Department of English, Francis Marion College, Florence, S.C. 29501.

CAREER: Wright State University, Dayton, Ohio, assistant professor of English, 1964-65; Erskine College, Due West, S.C., associate professor of English, 1965-67; Francis Marion College, Florence, S.C., lecturer, 1973-77, assistant professor of English, 1977—.

WRITINGS: Narrative Structure in the Novels of Sir Walter Scott, Mouton, 1969. Contributor to *Keats-Shelley Journal* and *Walt Whitman Review.*

* * *

CUTTER, Donald C(olgett) 1922-

PERSONAL: Born January 9, 1922, in Chico, Calif.; son of Alex Ross (a manufacturer and salesman) and Emma (Colgett) Cutter; married Charlotte Leon Lazear, June 22, 1945; children: Diane (Mrs. Robert Haladay), Donald, Jr., Charles, Teresa, Theodore, Andrea, Alex, Douglas, Carmen. *Education:* University of California, Berkeley, A.B., 1943, M.A., 1947, Ph.D., 1950. *Religion:* Presbyterian. *Home:* 2508 Harold Pl. N.E., Albuquerque, N.M. 87106. *Office:* History Department, University of New Mexico, Albuquerque, N.M. 87131.

CAREER: San Diego State College (now University), San Diego, Calif., instructor in history, 1950-51; University of Southern California, Los Angeles, assistant professor, 1951-56, associate professor, 1956-61, professor of history, 1961-62; University of New Mexico, Albuquerque, professor of history, 1962—. Chief of historical research, Council of California Indians, 1953-56; director, American Indian Historical Research Project, University of New Mexico, 1967-70. *Military service:* U.S. Navy, 1943-46. U.S. Naval Reserve, 1946-67; became lieutenant. *Member:* American Historical Association, Latin American Studies Association, Western History Association (vice-president, 1974-75; president, 1975-76), Rocky Mountain Council for Latin American Studies (vice-president, 1966-67; president, 1967-68), Phi Alpha Theta, Sigma Delta Pi. *Awards, honors:* Fulbright research fellow in Spain, 1961-62; Fulbright lecturer in Mexico, 1967, 1969, 1971-72.

WRITINGS: (Translator) R. F. Heizer and J. E. Mills, editors, *The Four Ages of Tsurai,* University of California Press, 1952; *The Diary of Ensign Gabriel Moraga's Expedition of Discovery in the Sacramento Valley, 1808,* Dawson's Book Shop, 1957; *Malaspina in California,* John Howell, 1960; (with Laurio Destefani) *Tadeo Haenke y el final de una vieja polemica,* Departamento de Estudios Historicos

Navales (Argentina), 1966; (editor) *The California Coast,* University of Oklahoma Press, 1969. Contributor to *Revista de Indias, Pacific Northwest Quarterly, Journal of the West, Western Historical Quarterly, American West, Arizona and the West,* and other publications. Editor, *New Mexico Historical Review.*

WORK IN PROGRESS: Spanish naval activity in North America.

* * *

CUTTS, Richard 1923-

PERSONAL: Born November 24, 1923, in Kittery Point, Me.; son of Joseph William (a businessman) and Agnes (Graham) Cutts; married Hazel Starrett (a high school librarian), June 23, 1948; children: Judith Marion, Richard, Sarah, Joseph William. *Education:* University of Maine, B.A., 1948, M.A., 1949; Pennsylvania State University, Ph.D., 1958. *Home:* 7 Shaw Cir., Northfield, Vt. 05663. *Office:* Department of English, Norwich University, Northfield, Vt. 05663.

CAREER: Pennsylvania State University, DuBois Campus, DuBois, instructor, 1952-60, assistant professor of English composition and literature, 1960; Norwich University, Northfield, Vt., assistant professor, 1960-61, associate professor, 1961-70, professor of English, 1970—. *Military service:* U.S. Army, 1943-46. *Member:* Modern Language Association of America, National Council of Teachers of English, American Film Institute, Conference on College Composition and Communication.

WRITINGS: (With Loring E. Hart) *The Norwich Guide to Writing,* Norwich University, 1966; *Index to the Youth's Companion: 1871-1929,* Scarecrow, 1972.

AVOCATIONAL INTERESTS: Music (performs with dance and jazz groups and with a church choir; also plays carillon).

* * *

DAGAN, Avigdor 1912-
(Viktor Fischl)

PERSONAL: Original name, Viktor Fischl; born June 30, 1912, in Hradec Kralove, Czechoslovakia; son of Moritz (a merchant) and Frieda (Ehrenstein) Fischl; married Stella Berger, April 10, 1938; children: Daniel, Gabriel. *Education:* University of Prague, D.rer pol., 1938. *Religion:* Jewish. *Home:* 4 Rabbi Benyamin, Jerusalem, Israel. *Office:* Embassy of Israel, 20 Anton Frankgasse, Wien 18, Austria.

CAREER: Zidovske Zpravy (Zionist weekly), Prague, Czechoslovakia, editor, 1935-39; Czechoslovakian Parliament, Prague, parliamentary secretary of Jewish Party, 1936-39; migrated to Israel, 1949; Israel Ministry of Foreign Affairs, Jerusalem, diplomat, 1950—, serving as counsellor in Tokyo, 1955-59, and Rangoon, 1959-60, director of East European Division, Jerusalem, 1960-61, ambassador to Poland, 1961-64, ambassador to Jugoslavia, 1965-67, ambassador to Norway and Iceland, 1969-72, ambassador to Austria, 1974—. Lecturer on Soviet and eastern European affairs at Columbia University and Harvard University. *Awards, honors:* Melantrich Prize (Czechoslovakia), 1937, for *Hebrejske melodie;* European Literary Club Prize (Prague), 1948, for *Pisen o litosti* (first published as *Shir Harakhamim*).

WRITINGS—Under name Viktor Fischl, except as indicated: *Jaro* (title means "The Spring"; poems), F. J.

Mueller, 1933; *Kniha Noci* (title means "Book of Nights"; poems), Druzstevni Prace, 1936; *Hebrejske melodie* (title means "Hebrew Melodies"; poems), Melantrich, 1936; *Evropske zalmy* (title means "European Psalms"; poems), Vydal Cechoslovak (London), 1941; *Mrtva ves* (war poems), Edice Mladeho Ceskoslovenska (London), 1943, 2nd edition, Pax, 1946, translation by Laurie Lee published as *The Dead Village,* Young Czechoslovakia (London), 1943; *Anglicke sonety* (title means "English Sonnets"; poems), Melantrich, 1946; *Lyricky zapisnik* (title means "Lyrical Notebook"; poems), Vaclav Petr, 1946; *Shir Harakhamim* (novel written in Czech as *Pisen o litosti* [title means "Song of Pity"]), Hebrew translation by Gideon Pollak, Am Oved, 1951; *Hovory s Janem Masarykem* (title means "Conversations with Jan Masaryk"), Izraelske Listy, 1952, Kruh Pratel Ceskoslovenske Knihy (Chicago), 1953; (under name Avigdor Dagan) *Moscow and Jerusalem: Twenty Years of Relations between Israel and the Soviet Union,* foreword by Abba Eban, Abelard, 1970; (under name Avigdor Dagan) *Kuropeni* (title means "The Song of a Rooster"), Konfrontation Verlag, 1975.

Translation of poetry: Antoni Slonimski, *Alarm,* Kruh Pratel Ceskoslovenske Knihy v Anglii (London), 1943; Franz Werfel, *Basne* (title means "Poems"), Vaclav Petr (Prague), 1948.

WORK IN PROGRESS: The Kiosk and the Universe and *Soviet Imperialism.*

SIDELIGHTS: Although *Pisen o litosti* received the European Literary Club Prize in Prague in 1948, the novel was not published until three years later in Israel; publication in Czechoslovakia was forbidden after the Communist coup there. Avigdor Dagan is competent in eight languages—French, German, Polish, Russian, and Serbo-Croatian, in addition to Czech, Hebrew, and English.

AVOCATIONAL INTERESTS: Painting.

BIOGRAPHICAL/CRITICAL SOURCES: Saturday Review, February 6, 1971; *New Leader,* May 3, 1971.

*   *   *

DAIGON, Arthur   1928-

PERSONAL: Surname is pronounced *Day*-gone; born February 8, 1928, in New York, N.Y.; son of Samuel and Nettie (Segal) Daigon; married Ruth Popeski (a poet), April 11, 1952; children: Tom, Glenn. *Education:* New York University, B.A., 1948, M.A., 1949, Ed.D., 1963. *Home:* North Bear Hill Rd., Chaplin, Conn. 06235. *Office:* School of Education, University of Connecticut, Storrs, Conn. 06268.

CAREER: High school English teacher in Valley Stream, N.Y., 1952-63; University of Connecticut, Storrs, assistant professor, 1963-66, associate professor, 1966-70, professor of English education, 1970—. Member of National Commission on the English Curriculum. *Member:* National Council of Teachers of English.

WRITINGS: (With R. T. La Conte) *Challenge and Change in the Teaching of English,* Allyn & Bacon, 1971; (with La Conte) *Dig—U.S.A.: This Generation,* Bantam, 1971; (with La Conte) *Dig—U.S.A.: The Good Life,* Bantam, 1972; *Dig—U.S.A.: Violence,* Bantam, 1972; *Write On!,* Harcourt, 1972; *Nova,* twelve volumes, Prentice-Hall, 1977; *Put It in Writing,* Harcourt, 1977. Contributor to literature journals. Contributing editor, *Media and Methods,* 1969—.

*   *   *

DAILY, Jay E(lwood)   1923-

PERSONAL: Born June 17, 1923, in Pikeview, Colo.; son of Roy R. (a miner) and Anna Olvie (Baker) Daily; married Jennifer Hole, December 17, 1960. *Education:* Attended Southern Colorado State College, 1942-43; New York University, B.A., 1951; Columbia University, M.S., 1952, D.L.S., 1957. *Politics:* Democrat. *Home:* 709 South Negley, Pittsburgh, Pa. 15232. *Office:* Graduate School of Library and Information Science, University of Pittsburgh, 135 Bellefield, Pittsburgh, Pa. 15260.

CAREER: Government of the Union of Burma, Office of the Prime Minister, Rangoon, advisory librarian, 1957-59; University of Mandalay, Mandalay, Burma, consultant librarian, 1959-62; Franklin Book Programs, New York, N.Y., library consultant, 1962-65; University of Pittsburgh, Pittsburgh, Pa., assistant director of libraries, 1965-66, professor of library and information science, 1967—. *Military service:* U.S. Army, 1943-46; became technical sergeant. *Member:* American Library Association (life member; member of cataloging and classification section), Special Libraries Association, American Association of University Professors, American Library Society. *Awards, honors:* Honorary Teacher of Korea, 1948; Paula K. Lazrus Memorial fellowship, 1955-57.

WRITINGS: (With Mildred S. Myers) *Cataloging for Library Technical Assistants,* Gryphon House, 1969, workbook, 1972; (with John Phillip Immroth) *Library Cataloging: A Guide to a Basic Course,* Scarecrow, 1971; (with James Williams and Martha Manheimer) *The Classified List of Library of Congress Subject Headings,* Dekker, 1972; *Organizing Non-Print Materials,* Dekker, 1972; *The Anatomy of Censorship,* Dekker, 1973; *Cataloging Phonorecordings,* Dekker, 1975; *The Looking-Glass Decades, Poems,* Pangloss Press Books, 1977; *Languages for Library and Information Science,* Dekker, 1978. Also editor of *Practical Books in Library and Information Science,* Dekker, and co-editor of *Encyclopedia of Library and Information Science.* Contributor of articles to library journals and of poetry to literary journals, including *Poetry: A Magazine of Verse* and *Voices.* Editor, *Pittsburgh Studies in Library and Information Science.*

WORK IN PROGRESS: Intellectual Freedom Workbook; second edition of *The Anatomy of Censorship.*

SIDELIGHTS: Jay E. Daily told *CA:* "Although I have written poetry from the age of sixteen, I have resisted having it published in book form and I no longer submit verse to periodicals. Poetry should be aged before it becomes truly representative. At the urging of friends, a sequence of short poems [has been] published, but only in a limited, numbered edition. Emily Dickinson had the good fortune of never having to expose her verse in print except for the few that were published in periodicals. The good ones resist decay and the urge to hide them away, possibly forever. My work is writing for the library profession, but my most important book, *The Anatomy of Censorship,* shows my methods. The second edition is in preparation and will represent fifteen years of research and endless rewritings."

AVOCATIONAL INTERESTS: Travel, opera, linguistics, history.

*   *   *

DALCOURT, Gerard J.   1927-

PERSONAL: Born April 30, 1927, in St. Albans, Vt.; son of Albert (a laborer) and Julia (Aubin) Dalcourt; married Catherine Mary McCauley (a physical therapist), June 11, 1960; children: James Socrates, Albert Plato. *Education:* Attended St. Michael's College, 1946-47; University of Montreal, B.A. and M.A., 1950, Ph.D., 1959; University of Southern California, M.S., 1954. *Residence:* Maplewood, N.J. *Office:* Department of Philosophy, Seton Hall University, South Orange, N.J. 07079.

CAREER: University of Kansas, Lawrence, librarian, 1954-56; Villanova University, Villanova, Pa., instructor in philosophy, 1957-62; Seton Hall University, South Orange, N.J., assistant professor, 1962-66, associate professor, 1966-75, professor of philosophy, 1975—. *Military service:* U.S. Army, 1950-52. *Member:* American Philosophical Association, American Catholic Philosophical Association, Metaphysical Society of America, American Association of University Professors (treasurer, N.J. conference, 1968-72), Metropolitan Roundtable of Philosophy (co-chairman, 1967-69).

WRITINGS: The Philosophy of St. Thomas Aquinas, Monarch, 1965; (editor) *The Great Dialogue of Nature and Space,* Magi Books, 1970. Contributor to *New Catholic Encyclopedia,* and to journals, including *International Philosophical Quarterly, America,* and *Catholic Library World.*

WORK IN PROGRESS: Research on the methodology of ethics.

AVOCATIONAL INTERESTS: Playing tennis and the recorder.

* * *

DALE, Richard 1932-

PERSONAL: Born October 22, 1932, in Columbus, Ohio; son of Edgar and Elizabeth (Kirchner) Dale; married Doris Mae Cruger, August 18, 1967. *Education:* Bowdoin College, A.B., 1954; study at Columbia University, 1954-55; Ohio State University, M.A., 1957; Princeton University, M.A., 1961, Ph.D., 1962. *Home:* Union Hill, Route 4, Carbondale, Ill. 62901. *Office:* Department of Political Science, Southern Illinois University, Carbondale, Ill. 62901.

CAREER: University of New Hampshire, Durham, instructor in government, 1962-63; Northern Illinois University, DeKalb, assistant professor of political science, 1963-66; Southern Illinois University at Carbondale, adjunct professor, 1966-67, assistant professor, 1967-71, associate professor of political science, 1971—. Member, Inter-University Seminar on Armed Forces and Society. Has presented papers at conferences of professional organizations. *Military service:* U.S. Army, 1957-59. *Member:* International Studies Association, International African Institute, African Studies Association, American Political Science Association, Political Science Association of South Africa, South African Military History Society, Botswana Society, Royal African Society, South West Africa Scientific Society, Midwest Political Science Association. *Awards, honors:* National Defence foreign language fellow, University of California, Los Angeles, summer, 1964; American Philosophical Society travel grant, summer, 1970.

WRITINGS: Botswana and Its Southern Neighbor: The Patterns of Linkage and the Options in Statecraft (monograph), Ohio University Center for International Studies, 1970; *The Racial Component of Botswana's Foreign Policy* (monograph), Center of International Race Relations, Graduate School of International Studies, University of Denver, 1971; (editor with Christian P. Potholm, and contributor) *Southern Africa in Perspective: Essays in Regional Politics,* Free Press, 1972. Contributor of articles and book reviews to *New Republic, Political Science Quarterly, Africa Report, American Political Science Review, World Affairs,*

Africa Today, Current History, Plural Societies, and other journals.

WORK IN PROGRESS: Botswana and Its Neighbors in Southern Africa, 1945-1976: A Study in Conflict and Cooperation.

* * *

DALESKI, H(illel) M(atthew) 1926-

PERSONAL: Born July 19, 1926, in Johannesburg, South Africa; son of Joseph (a lawyer) and Tilly (Morris) Daleski; married Aviva Prop (a ceramist), June 29, 1950 (divorced); married Shirley Kaufman (a poet), June 20, 1974; children: (first marriage) Deborah, Gil, Arit, Yonat. *Education:* University of the Witwatersrand, B.A., 1947, B.A. (honors), 1949, M.A., 1952; Hebrew University, Ph.D., 1963. *Religion:* Jewish. *Home:* 18 Neve Sha'anan St., Jerusalem, Israel. *Office:* Department of English, Hebrew University, Jerusalem, Israel.

CAREER: Hebrew University, Jerusalem, Israel, assistant, 1954-57, instructor, 1958-63, lecturer, 1963-66, senior lecturer, 1966-70, associate professor, 1970-75, professor of English, 1976—. *Military service:* Sixth South African Armoured Division, 1944-46; Israeli Army, 1948, 1956, 1967.

WRITINGS: The Forked Flame: A Study of D. H. Lawrence, Northwestern University Press, 1965; *Dickens and the Art of Analogy,* Schocken, 1970; *Joseph Conrad: The Way of Dispossession,* Holmes & Meier, 1977. Contributor of articles to academic journals.

WORK IN PROGRESS: A study of the divided self in the English novel of the nineteenth and twentieth centuries.

BIOGRAPHICAL/CRITICAL SOURCES: Contemporary Literature, Volume IX, number 1, winter, 1968.

* * *

DALVEN, Rae 1904-

PERSONAL: Born April 25, 1904, in Prevesa, Greece; daughter of Israel (a merchant) and Esther (Colchamiro) Dalven; married Jack Negrin, August 29, 1928 (divorced, 1938). *Education:* Hunter College (now Hunter College of the City University of New York), B.A., 1925; New York University, M.A., 1928, Ph.D., 1961; Yale University, M.F.A., 1941. *Home:* 11 Fifth Ave., New York, N.Y. 10003. *Agent:* Bertha Klausner International Literary Agency, Inc., 71 Park Ave., New York, N.Y. 10016. *Office:* Department of English, Ladycliff College, Highland Falls, N.Y. 10928.

CAREER: Teacher in the New York City public school system for twenty-two years; member of the faculty of Fairleigh Dickinson University, Rutherford, N.J., for three years; Fisk University, Nashville, Tenn., assistant professor of drama, 1952-53; Pace College (now University), New York, N.Y., adjunct professor of English, 1961-67; Ladycliff College, Highland Falls, N.Y., professor of English and chairman of department, 1962-73, professor emeritus, 1973—. Guest of MacDowell Colony (writers' colony), 1965, 1966, 1977, and of Mishkenot Sha' ananim (writers' colony), Jerusalem, 1977. Translator of military and scientific material from Greek, French, and German for U.S. War Department during World War II. *Member:* Modern Language Association of America, Authors Guild, Modern Greek Studies Association, American Society of Sephardic Studies (president), Janina Sisterhood, Sisterhood of Spanish and Portuguese Synagogue, American Friends of Alliance Israelite Universelle, Ladies Auxiliary of Sephardic Home for the Aged, Hadassah. *Awards, honors:* Grants from Memorial Foundation for Jewish Culture, 1967, 1970, and from National Foundation for Jewish Culture, 1968, to write a history of the Janina Jews of Greece; Jacob Glatstein Memorial Prize, *Poetry* (magazine), 1972, for verse translations from the Greek; elected to Hall of Fame of Hunter College of the City University of New York Alumni Association, 1973; Outstanding Educator of America, 1973; Gold Key Award, Columbia Press Association, 1973; named in National Register of Prominent Americans, 1976-77.

WRITINGS: (Translator from the Greek) Joseph Eliyia, *Poems,* Yanina Brotherhood, 1944; (contributor) *World's Best,* edited by Whit Burnett, Dial, 1950; (translator from the Greek) *Modern Greek Poetry,* Gaer Associates, 1949, new edition, Russell, 1971; (translator from the Greek) *The Complete Poems of Cavafy,* Harcourt, 1961, expanded edition, 1976; (contributor) *European Authors, 1000-1900,* Wilson, 1967; *Anna Comnena,* Twayne, 1972; (translator from the Greek) *Fourth Dimension: Selected Poems of Yannis Ritsos,* David R. Godine, 1977.

Plays: "A Season in Hell" (three-act), produced Off-Broadway at Cherry Lane Theater, 1950; "Hercules," (radio drama), broadcast in Tennessee. Also author of "Judas," translation of drama by Spero Melas. Contributor of articles to *Encyclopedia Judaica, Reader's Encyclopedia of World Drama, Conservative Judaism,* and *Sephardic Scholar;* contributor of short story and verse translations from the Greek to *New Directions, Poetry, Mundus Artium, Odyssey, Epirotiki Estia* (Jannina, Greece), and other publications.

WORK IN PROGRESS: The Jews of Janina Greece; two translations from the Greek, Elly Alexiou, *To Become Great,* a biography of Nikos Kazantzakis, and Anghelo Terzakis' play, "The Ancestor"; an original three-act play, "Esthyr."

*   *   *

D'AMELIO, Dan 1927-

PERSONAL: Born December 5, 1927, in Accadia, Italy; came to United States; son of Frank (an artist) and Nina (Potenza) D'Amelio; married Fanny Di Frenza, November 18, 1956; children: Frank, Dan, Nina, Teresa. *Education:* New York University, B.S., 1953. *Home and office:* Pepper Ridge Rd., Portland, Conn. 06480.

CAREER: Columbia Broadcasting System, Inc. (CBS), New York, N.Y., member of editorial staff, 1956-58; teacher of English in high school in East Islip, N.Y., 1958-59; teacher of retarded children in Brentwood, N.Y., 1959-64; North Shore News Syndicate, Smithtown, N.Y., writer and editor, 1964-68; American Education Publications, Middletown, Conn., staff writer, 1969-74. *Military service:* U.S. Army, 1946-47; served in Italy.

WRITINGS: (With John Mulligan) *Experiences in Journalism,* Lyons & Carnahan, 1966; *Taller Than Bandai Mountain: The Story of Hideyo Noguchi,* Viking, 1968; *Severely Retarded Children: Wider Horizons,* C. E. Merrill, 1971.

WORK IN PROGRESS: Researching and writing a book that focuses on the early life of Saint Francis, from boyhood to his conversion.

SIDELIGHTS: Dan D'Amelio told *CA:* "Writing has been often described as lonely work; I have not found it so. I am apt to feel lonely when I am not writing."

BIOGRAPHICAL/CRITICAL SOURCES: New York

Times Book Review, May 19, 1968; *Book World,* September 22, 1968.

*   *   *

DANA, Robert (Patrick) 1929-

PERSONAL: Born June 2, 1929, in Allston, Mass.; son of Samuel (a milliner) and Margaret (Devine) Dana; married Mary Kowalke, June 2, 1951 (divorced, 1973); married Margaret Sellen, September 14, 1974; children: (first marriage) Lori Ann, Arden Kay, Richard Michael. *Education:* Drake University, A.B., 1951; University of Iowa, M.A., 1954. *Residence:* Solon, Iowa. *Office:* Department of English, Cornell College, Mount Vernon, Iowa 52314.

CAREER: Cornell College, Mount Vernon, Iowa, instructor in English and journalism, 1954-58, assistant professor, 1958-62, associate professor, 1962-68, professor of English, 1968—, chairman of department, 1974-78. Visiting poet and professor of English, University of Florida, 1975-76. Editor, Hillside Press, 1957-67. *Military service:* U.S. Navy, 1946-48; served in South Pacific. *Member:* National Humanities Faculty. *Awards, honors:* Danforth teacher study grant, 1959-60; Mary Roberts Rinehart Foundation poetry fellowship, 1962-63; Ford-Associated Colleges of the Midwest grant, 1966-67.

WRITINGS—Poetry: My Glass Brother and Other Poems, Stonewall Press, 1957; *The Dark Flags of Waking,* Qara Press, 1964; *Journeys from the Skin,* Hundred Pound Press, 1966; *Some Versions of Silence,* Norton, 1967; *The Power of the Visible,* Swallow Press, 1971; *The Watergate Elegy,* Wine Press, 1973; *Tryptych,* Wine Press, 1974; *The Winter and the Snow,* Windhover Press, 1978.

Work represented in anthologies, including: *Poetry for Pleasure,* Doubleday, 1960; *Midland,* Random House, 1961; *On City Streets,* M. Evans, 1968; *The "New Yorker" Book of Poems,* Viking, 1969; *The "New York Times" Book of Verse,* Macmillan, 1970; *Voyages to an Inland Sea III,* University of Wisconsin—LaCrosse, 1973; *Heartland II,* Northern Illinois University, 1975; *Washington and the Poet,* Stinehour, 1977; *I Sing the Song of Myself,* Morrow, 1977. Contributor of poetry to *Poetry, Paris Review, Sewanee Review, New Yorker, Nation, Quarterly Review of Literature, Tri-Quarterly, North American Poetry Review, West Coast Review* (Canada), *Stand* (England), and other periodicals and newspapers. Editor, *North American Review,* 1964-68; contributing editor, *American Poetry Review,* 1973—.

WORK IN PROGRESS: New poems.

BIOGRAPHICAL/CRITICAL SOURCES: Poetry, February, 1968; *New Letters,* summer, 1973.

*   *   *

DANAHER, Kevin 1913-
(Caoimhin O Danachair)

PERSONAL: Born January 30, 1913, in Limerick, Ireland; son of William (a schoolteacher) and Maighread (O'Ryan) Danaher; married Anna Mary Ryan (a high school teacher); children: Donal Maolmhuire, Sean Laoiseach. *Education:* University College, Dublin, B.A., 1936, Diploma in Education (honors), 1937, M.A., 1945, D.Litt., 1974; graduate study at University of Berlin, 1937-38, and University of Leipzig, 1938-39. *Office:* Department of Irish Folklore, University College, National University of Ireland, Dublin, Ireland.

CAREER: National University of Ireland, University College, Dublin, university lecturer in folklore, 1971—. Has lectured in Britain, Germany, Sweden, Denmark, Austria, Hungary, Canada, and the United States, as well as in Ireland. *Military service:* Irish Army, Artillery, 1940-45; became captain.

WRITINGS—Published by Mercier, except as indicated: *In Ireland Long Ago,* 1962; (editor with J. G. Simms) *The Danish Force in Ireland, 1691-1692,* Irish Manuscripts Commission, 1963; *Gentle Places and Simple Things,* 1964; *Irish Country People,* 1966; *Folktales of the Irish Countryside* (Irish full edition), 1967, David White, 1970; *The Pleasant Land of Ireland,* 1970; *The Year in Ireland,* 1972; *Ireland's Vernacular Architecture,* 1975; *A Bibliography of Irish Ethnology and Folk Tradition,* in press. Editor, Irish Government's "Life and Culture" series, 1965—. Contributor of about seventy articles to learned journals. Editor, *Irish Sword,* 1960-71.

SIDELIGHTS: Kevin Danaher speaks German and Swedish fluently, as well as English and Gaelic; he reads French, Norwegian, Danish, Dutch, Spanish, Portuguese, and Italian.

* * *

D'ANGELO, Luciano 1932-
(Lou D'Angelo)

PERSONAL: Surname is pronounced *Dan*-gelo; born April 9, 1932, in New York, N.Y.; son of Giuseppe (a waiter) and Michelina D'Angelo; married Alice B. Grauer (a free-lance copywriter), August 14, 1965. *Education:* City College (now City College of the City University of New York), B.B.A., 1954. *Home:* 345 East 81st St., New York, N.Y. 10028. *Office:* Franklin Spier, Inc., 270 Madison Ave., New York, N.Y. 10016.

CAREER: Diener & Dorskind, Inc. (advertising agency), New York City, layout artist, 1954-65; Franklin Spier, Inc. (advertising agency), New York City, copywriter, 1965—. *Member:* Authors' Guild, Authors League of America. *Awards, honors:* Deutsch, Shea & Evans Award for Product Advertising of Outstanding Social Significance, Rutgers University, 1969.

WRITINGS: How to Be an Italian, Price, Stern, 1968; *What the Ancients Said* (novel), Doubleday, 1971; *A Circle of Friends* (novel), Doubleday, 1977. Work represented in *The Bedside Phoenix Nest,* Washburn, 1965, and *"Saturday Review" Sampler of Wit and Wisdom,* Simon & Schuster, 1966, both edited by Martin Levin.

AVOCATIONAL INTERESTS: Opera and ballet.

* * *

DANIEL, Jerry C(layton) 1937-

PERSONAL: Born June 30, 1937, in Mount Vernon, Mo.; son of Thomas C. (a railroad engineer) and Francis (Smith) Daniel; married Mary G. Columbus, March 15, 1957; children: Stormy Amber, Jerry Clayton II, Dane Thor, Susan Constance. *Education:* University of Denver, B.S.B.A., 1958, J.D., 1960. *Politics:* Republican. *Religion:* Baptist. *Home:* 1925 18th Ave., Greeley, Colo. *Office:* Houthens, Houtchens & Daniel, 1007 9th Ave., Greeley, Colo.

CAREER: Admitted to Bar of Colorado State, 1963; Federal Bureau of Investigation, special agent in Texas and Virginia, 1963-66; Shivers & Banta, Englewood, Colo., attorney, 1967-68; Great Western Sugar Co., Denver, Colo., house counsel, 1968-70, assistant director of legal affairs and assistant secretary, 1970-71; general counsel, Great Western

Producers Cooperative, 1971—; Houthens, Houtchens & Daniel (law firm), Greeley, Colo., partner, 1974—. *Military service:* U.S. Army, Military Police, 1961-63; became lieutenant. *Member:* American Bar Association, Arapahoe County Bar Association, Phi Kappa Sigma.

WRITINGS: The Space Machine, Lenox Hill, 1971. Contributor to magazines.

WORK IN PROGRESS: A detective-mystery novel.

AVOCATIONAL INTERESTS: Fishing, hunting, swimming, bridge, church activities, reading, writing.

* * *

DANIEL, Robert L(eslie) 1923-

PERSONAL: Born May 1, 1923, in Detroit, Mich.; son of Leslie Irvine and Margaret (Sheffler) Daniel; married Barbara Jean Pugh (an instructor), June 12, 1950; children: Robert S., Martha V., Joseph I. *Education:* Attended University of Michigan, 1941-43; Miami University, Oxford, Ohio, B.S., 1948, M.A., 1949; University of Wisconsin, Ph.D., 1953. *Religion:* Episcopalian. *Home:* 7 Arden Pl., Athens, Ohio 45701. *Office:* Department of History, Ohio University, Athens, Ohio 45701.

CAREER: Carnegie Institute of Technology (now Carnegie-Mellon University), Pittsburgh, Pa., instructor in history, 1953-56; Cornell University, Ithaca, N.Y., assistant professor of history, 1956-57; Ohio University, Athens, assistant professor, 1957-61, associate professor, 1961-66, professor of history, 1966—, chairman of department, 1970-75. Fulbright lecturer, University of Utrecht, 1967-68. *Military service:* U.S. Army Air Forces, 1943-46; became first lieutenant. *Member:* American Historical Association, Organization of American Historians, American Studies Association, American Association of University Professors. *Awards, honors:* American Philosophical Society research grants, 1961, 1965.

WRITINGS: (Assistant with others to Merle Curti, senior author) *The Making of an American Community,* Stanford University Press, 1959; *American Philanthropy in the Near East,* Ohio University Press, 1970. Contributor to *Mississippi Valley Historical Review, Mid-America, Middle East Journal,* and other journals, and to *Encyclopedia Americana.*

WORK IN PROGRESS: Women in American History.

* * *

DANIELS, Steven Lloyd 1945-1973

PERSONAL: Born February 11, 1945, in New York, N.Y.; son of Elliott Lawrence and Florence (Stern) Daniels; married Patricia Levinson, 1968. *Education:* Attended secondary schools, 1960-63, in Rome, Italy, Maadi, Egypt, New York, N.Y., Rio de Janeiro, Brazil, and Mexico City, Mexico; attended University of the Americas, 1963-64; University of Michigan, A.B., 1966; Ohio State University, additional study, 1966-67; Temple University, Ed.M., 1971. *Home:* 807 Mount Pleasant, Ann Arbor, Mich. 48103.

CAREER: XEN Radio, Mexico City, Mexico, producer-director of weekly news specials, 1962; junior high school teacher of reading in Philadelphia, Pa., 1967-69; Student-Community Involvement Project (federally funded program), Philadelphia, program director, 1970; public schools of Ann Arbor, Mich., director of curriculum, beginning 1971.

WRITINGS: How 2 Gerbils, 20 Goldfish, 200 Games, 2000

Books and I Taught Them How to Read, Westminster, 1971. Contributor of articles on ghetto education to *Reader's Digest, Philadelphia Sunday Inquirer, Colloquy,* and other publications.

WORK IN PROGRESS: Writing *The Curriculum Office.*†

(Died July 16, 1973)

* * *

DANIELSON, Michael N(ils) 1934-

PERSONAL: Born April 8, 1934, in New York, N.Y.; son of Virgil A. and Dorothy (de Lucas) Danielson; married Ruth P. Shevon (a microbiologist), September 3, 1955; children: Jessica, Jeffrey. *Education:* Rutgers University, B.A., 1955, M.A., 1956; Columbia University, graduate study, 1961-62; Princeton University, Ph.D., 1962. *Home:* 283 Hartley Ave., Princeton, N.J. 08540. *Office:* 231 Woodrow Wilson School, Princeton University, Princeton, N.J. 08540.

CAREER: Omaha University, Omaha, Neb., instructor in political science, 1957-59; Rutgers University, New Brunswick, N.J., instructor in politics, 1961; Institute of Public Administration, New York, N.Y., research associate, 1961-63; Princeton University, Princeton, N.J., visiting lecturer, 1962-63, lecturer, 1963, assistant professor, 1963-67, associate professor, 1967-70, professor of politics and public affairs, 1970—, associate dean and director of graduate program of Woodrow Wilson School of Public and International Affairs, 1971-74. Chairman, Council on Urban Studies, Princeton University, 1969-72. Consultant to Governor Richard J. Hughes, 1966-67, New Jersey Department of Community Affairs, 1966-70, U.S. Department of Housing and Urban Development, 1966-67, Task Force on the Cities, 1967, New Jersey Department of Transportation, 1967-70, New Jersey County and Municipal Government Study Commission, 1968-72, Council for Family Grants, 1968-69, Institute of Public Administration, 1968, Commission on Population Growth and the American Future, 1971, Racine Environment Committee, Ford Foundation, 1971, Kettering Foundation, 1976, and to Governor Brendon Byrne, 1974-76. Former member, Tri-State Regional Planning Commission; member of technical advisory committee, Middlesex-Somerset-Mercer Regional Study Council. Member of board of trustees, Glassboro State College. *Military service:* U.S. Air Force, 1956-59; became first lieutenant. U.S. Air Force Reserve, 1959-64. *Member:* American Political Science Association, American Association of University Professors, National Model Railroad Association, Northeastern Political Science Association.

WRITINGS: Intergovernmental Responsibilities for Water Supply and Sewage Disposal in Metropolitan Areas, Advisory Commission on Intergovernmental Relations, 1962; (contributor) Lyle C. Fitch and others, *Urban Transportation and Public Policy,* Chandler Publishing, 1964; *Federal-Metropolitan Politics and the Commuter Crisis,* Columbia University Press, 1965; (editor) *Metropolitan Politics: A Reader,* Little, Brown, 1966, 2nd edition, 1971; (editor with Walter F. Murphy) *Modern American Democracy,* Holt, 1969; (with Murphy, Marver H. Bernstein, and Robert K. Carr) *American Democracy,* Holt, 1971, 8th edition, 1977; *Differentiation, Segregation, and Political Fragmentation in the American Metropolis,* Commission on Population Growth and the American Future, 1971; *The Politics of Exclusion,* Columbia University Press, 1976; (with Alan M. Hershey and John M. Bayne) *One Nation, So Many Governments,* Lexington Books, 1977. Contributor to *Interna-

tional Journal of Comparative Sociology, National Civic Review, Political Science Quarterly, Public Opinion Quarterly, World Politics,* and other publications.

WORK IN PROGRESS: With J. W. Doig, *The Politics of Development in the New York Region,* for publication by Institute of Governmental Studies, University of California; with Henry Breuen, *The Comparative Politics of Urban Development;* another book.

* * *

D'APRIX, Roger M. 1932-

PERSONAL: Surname is pronounced Da-*pree;* born August 28, 1932, in Utica, N.Y.; son of Charles F. (a photographer) and Mary (Freytag) D'Aprix; married Theresa Collea, December 17, 1955; children: Cynthia, Richard, Laura, Anthony. *Education:* Hamilton College, B.A., 1955; State University of New York at Albany, additional study, 1955-56. *Politics:* Democrat-Liberal. *Religion:* Catholic. *Home:* 103 Gaslight Lane, Rochester, N.Y. 14610. *Office:* Xerox Corp., Xerox Sq. 006, Rochester, N.Y. 14603.

CAREER: Utica Public Schools, Utica, N.Y., English teacher, 1956-59; General Electric Corp., Utica, technical publicist, 1959-65; Consolidated Vacuum Corp., Rochester, N.Y., manager of communications, 1965-68; Xerox Corp., Rochester, manager of employee communication, 1968—. Adjunct associate professor of English, Monroe Community College. Director, Industrial Communication. Trustee, Becket Hall Seminary, St. John Fisher College. *Military service:* U.S. Army Reserve, 1957-63. *Member:* International Association of Business Communicators, Industrial Communications Council, Phi Beta Kappa.

WRITINGS: How's That Again: A Guide to Effective Written and Oral Communication in Business, Dow-Jones-Irwin, 1971; *Struggle for Identity: The Silent Revolution against Corporate Conformity,* Dow-Jones-Irwin, 1972; *In Search of a Corporate Soul,* American Management Association, 1976; *The Believable Corporation,* American Management Association, 1976. Contributor of thirty articles on organizational communication to periodicals.

SIDELIGHTS: Roger M. D'Aprix told *CA:* "My primary motivation is human dignity and freedom and how to preserve it in the face of the power and pressure of large organizations. All of my books address that enormous question in one way or another."

* * *

DARLING, Arthur Burr 1892-1971

December 28, 1892—November 27, 1971; American educator and historian. Obituaries: *New York Times,* November 29, 1971. (See index for *CA* sketch)

* * *

DAS, Gurcharan 1943-

PERSONAL: Born October 3, 1943, in Lyallpur, India; son of Barkat Ram (an engineer) and Vimla (Verma) Das; married Bunu Basnyat, July 24, 1970. *Education:* Harvard University, A.B. (magna cum laude), 1963. *Home:* "Seaglimpse," Gaffar Khan Rd., Tenth Floor, Worli, Bombay, India. *Agent:* Gloria Safier, 667 Madison Ave., New York, N.Y. 10021. *Office:* Richardson-Hindustan, Haines Rd., Bombay-11, India.

AWARDS, HONORS: Sultan Padamsee Prize (India) for best play of 1968, for *Larins Sahib.*

WRITINGS: Larins Sahib: A Play in Three Acts, Oxford University Press, 1970; *Mira* (play), Breakthrough Press, 1971.

WORK IN PROGRESS: A novel about growing up in India.

SIDELIGHTS: Clive Barnes says in his review of "Mira": "It was described as a Krishna rite, and it was remarkable in the way it combined Indian legend with the sophistication of Western total theater.... [The] play has something of the quality of a dream ritual. The language has a plaintive poetry to it, and what the play lacks in immediacy it makes up in pathos. Mira ... is a modern woman being broken on the wheels of convention. The timelessness of the story is emphasized by the very strangeness of the social and dramatic settings surrounding it.... [It] is one of those plays that has the savor of an experience about it. It had all the grace of a lovely alien voice speaking of eternals in a language just delicately opaque. The passion was discreetly in the next room—or the next continent."

AVOCATIONAL INTERESTS: Music, especially Bach.

BIOGRAPHICAL/CRITICAL SOURCES: Show Business, May 30, 1970; *New York Times,* June 3, 1970.†

*   *   *

DASH, Tony 1945-

PERSONAL: Born November 22, 1945, in Liverpool, England; son of Joseph (a painter) and Catherine (Lynn) Dash; married Barbara Kelly; children: Suzanna, Sophie, Barnaby. *Education:* Ethel Wormold College, Teaching Diploma, 1971; Lancashire College of Agriculture, national certificate of horticulture, 1977. *Home:* 478 Stanley Rd., Bootle 20, Lancashire, England.

CAREER: Asylum Publications, Bootle, England, owner and editor of *Asylum Magazine,* 1967.

WRITINGS: (With Brian Wake) *Love Poems for the Insane,* Matrix Publications, 1968; (with Wake) *Old and Pneumatic Poems,* Asylum Press, 1969; (editor) *Anthology of Little Magazine Poets,* Asylum Press, 1969; *Transplants,* Draftwood Publications, 1972. Also author of a television play, "Tea and Friends." Poems and short stories have been published in little literary magazines.

WORK IN PROGRESS: Pages from the Glass Cutter's Window Book.

*   *   *

DAUGHEN, Joseph R(obert) 1935-

PERSONAL: Surname is pronounced Dawn; born June 12, 1935, in Philadelphia, Pa.; son of John J. and Loretta (Sandone) Daughen; married Joan Purdy, December 30, 1961; children: Joan Patrice. *Education:* Temple University, B.S., 1956. *Politics:* Independent. *Office: Philadelphia Bulletin,* 30th and Market Sts., Philadelphia, Pa. 19101.

CAREER: Philadelphia Daily News, Philadelphia, Pa., reporter, 1956-63; *Philadelphia Bulletin,* Philadelphia, Harrisburg correspondent, 1964-65, Washington correspondent, 1965-67, national correspondent, 1969—. *Member:* National Press Club, Philadelphia Press Association, Sigma Delta Chi. *Awards, honors:* National Mass Media Award, National Conference of Christians and Jews, 1966, for study, "The Negro in Philadelphia"; several local press awards.

WRITINGS: (With Peter Binzen) *The Wreck of the Penn Central,* Little, Brown, 1971. Also author of a pamphlet, "The Most Powerful Mayor," and of a special study, "The

Negro in Philadelphia," both published in *Philadelphia Bulletin;* author of a study on the cost of the war in Viet Nam.

WORK IN PROGRESS: A book, with Peter Binzen, on Philadelphia's mayor, Frank Rizzo, to be published by Little, Brown.

SIDELIGHTS: Joseph Daughen has covered the last three presidential elections as a newspaper correspondent. He remarked to *CA:* "National politics is my area of interest and my specific duty and I have traveled the country over in this pursuit. Probably because of my work as a journalist I am concerned mostly about the issues of the day.... I relax with detective stories, spy stories, political novels."

*   *   *

DAVENPORT, Gene L(ooney) 1935-

PERSONAL: Born October 9, 1935, in Sylacauga, Ala.; son of Emmett L. (a cemetery superintendent) and Mildred (Looney) Davenport; married Kay Tibbals, August 23, 1959 (divorced, 1973); children: Pamela, Deborah. *Education:* Birmingham-Southern College, B.A., 1957; Vanderbilt University, B.D., 1960, Ph.D., 1968. *Home:* 1225 North Highland, Jackson, Tenn. 38301. *Office:* Department of Religion and Philosophy, Lambuth College, Jackson, Tenn. 38301.

CAREER: Ordained a minister in the United Methodist Church, 1962; Lambuth College, Jackson, Tenn., assistant professor, 1963-68, associate professor, 1968-71, professor of religion, 1971—, chairman of department of religion and philosophy, 1968—. *Member:* Society of Biblical Literature.

WRITINGS: What's the Church For?, Friendship, 1968; *The Eschatology of the Book of Jubilees,* E. J. Brill, 1971; *King Jesus: Servant, Lord, Soul Brother,* Board of Education, United Methodist Church, 1972. Also author of curriculum materials for the United Methodist Church; contributor of articles and book reviews to *Religion and Life, Christian Advocate,* and *Motive.* Editor and contributor to *Lambuth Review.*

WORK IN PROGRESS: Research on Apocryphal Books of the Old Testament; a collection of theological essays, reflections on Ecclesiastes, and short stories.

*   *   *

DAVENPORT, Guy (Mattison), Jr. 1927-
(Max Montgomery)

PERSONAL: Born November 23, 1927, in Anderson, S.C.; son of Guy Mattison (an express agent) and Marie (Fant) Davenport. *Education:* Duke University, B.A., 1948; Merton College, Oxford, B.Litt., 1950; Harvard University, Ph.D., 1961. *Politics:* "Democrat and Conservative." *Religion:* Baptist. *Home:* 621 Sayre Ave., Lexington, Ky. 40508. *Office:* Department of English, University of Kentucky, Lexington, Ky. 40506.

CAREER: Washington University, St. Louis, Mo., instructor in English, 1952-55; Haverford College, Haverford, Pa., assistant professor of English, 1961-63; University of Kentucky, Lexington, professor of English, 1963—. State secretary, Rhodes Scholarship Selection Committee. *Military service:* U.S. Army, Airborne Corps, 1950-52. *Awards, honors:* Rhodes scholarship, Merton College, Oxford, 1948-50; Anne Flexner Creative Writing award, 1948; Blumenthal-Leviton Prize for Poetry, 1967; Kentucky Research Award, 1976.

WRITINGS: (Editor and author of introduction and notes) *The Intelligence of Louis Agassiz: A Specimen Book of Sci-*

entific Writings, Beacon Press, 1963; (translator) *Carmina Archilochi: The Fragments of Archilochos,* University of California Press, 1964; (translator and author of introduction) *Sappho: Songs and Fragments,* University of Michigan Press, 1965; *Flowers and Leaves: Poema vel sonata, carmina autumni primaeque veris transformationum,* Jargon Society, 1966; *Cydonia Florentia,* Lowell-Adams House Printers, 1966; *Pennant Key-Indexed Guide to Homer's "Iliad,"* Educational Research Associates, 1967; *Pennant Key-Indexed Guide to Homer's "Odyssey,"* Educational Research Associates, 1967; *Do You Have a Poem Book on E. E. Cummings?,* Jargon Society, 1969; (author of introduction) *An Ear in Bartram's Tree: Selected Poems of Jonathan Williams 1957-67,* University of North Carolina Press, 1969; (author of introduction) Ronald Johnson, *Valley of the Many-Colored Grasses,* Norton, 1969; *Jonathan Williams, Poet,* Asphodel Book Shop, 1969.

Illustrator: Hugh Kenner, *The Stoic Comedians,* Beacon Press, 1964; Hugh Kenner, *The Counterfeiters,* Indiana University Press, 1968; Ronald Johnson, *The Spirit Walks, the Rocks Will Talk,* Jargon Society, 1969; Allen Mandelbaum, *The "Aeneid" of Virgil,* University of California Press, 1972.

Contributor: Lewis Leary, editor, *Method and Motive in "The Cantos" of Ezra Pound,* Columbia University Press, 1954; Dominique de Roux, editor, *Les Cahiers de l'Herne: Ezra Pound,* [Paris], 1965; Eva Hesse, editor, *Ezra Pound: 22 Versuche ueber einer Dichter,* Athenaeum Verlag, 1967; *Ezra's "Bowmen of Shu,"* Adams House, 1967; Jonathan Williams, *Sharp Tools for Catullan Gardens,* Indiana University, 1967; Hesse, editor, *New Approaches to Ezra Pound,* Faber, 1969; *Tatlin!,* Scribners, 1975.

Also author of libretti for Lukas Foss's "Carmina Archilochi" and Richard Swift's "Songs of Archilochos." Contributor of short stories to *Hudson Review* and of essays, reviews under pseudonym, Max Montgomery, and articles to *Virginia Quarterly Review, National Review, New York Times Book Review, Life,* and other publications. Contributing editor, *National Review,* 1962—. Illustrator for *Arion,* 1964—, and *Paideuma,* 1972—.

WORK IN PROGRESS: Hellenika, translations of Herakleitos, Sappho, Alkman, and Archilochos, for University of California Press; *Da Vinci's Bicycle; The Daimon of Sokrates,* a novella, for Larkspur.

SIDELIGHTS: Writing about Guy Davenport's *Sappho: Poems and Fragments,* D. S. Carne-Ross comments: "Davenport has justifiably brought into his version the radiance that can surround Sappho's single words. His feeling for what he calls her 'archaic robustness' has helped him to keep the tone bright and clear, instead of going soggy with reverence as so many translators have done."

Davenport told *CA:* "Primarily a teacher, I consider all my writing as extensions of the classroom. The translations (Heraclitus, Alkman, Menander, Sappho, Archilochos) are meant to serve the Greekless, as my stories are lessons in history. My poems are lessons in aesthetics. There is room enough for self-expression in even the most rigorously scholarly writing, and thus I have avoided all temptations to use writing for personal expression. Writing is the one social bond, and should be objective, useful, instructive."

BIOGRAPHICAL/CRITICAL SOURCES: New York Review of Books, March 3, 1966; *Contemporary Literary Criticism,* Volume VI, Gale, 1976; *New Literary History,* autumn, 1977.

DAVID, Stephen M(ark) 1934-

PERSONAL: Born June 18, 1934, in Brooklyn, N.Y.; son of Louis S. (a businessman) and Rose (Pruzan) David; married Janet Cohen (a psychologist), August 23, 1962. *Education:* Columbia University, B.A., 1956, Ph.D., 1967; Harvard University, LL.B., 1959. *Home:* 303 West 66th St., New York, N.Y. 10023. *Office:* Department of Political Science, Fordham University, Bronx, N.Y. 10458.

CAREER: New York State Commission on Government Operations of the City of New York, research assistant, 1959; Institute of Public Administration, New York City, research assistant, 1960-63; Mobilization for Youth, New York City, member of research staff, 1963-64; Fordham University, Bronx, N.Y., 1965—, began as associate professor, currently professor of urban politics, chairman of department of political science. Consultant to WCBS-TV, 1968—, and to Staten Island Community College of the City University of New York, 1970—. *Military service:* U.S. Army, 1959. *Member:* American Political Science Association, American Association of University Professors, New York State Political Science Association, Phi Beta Kappa.

WRITINGS: (Contributor) R. Connery, editor, *Urban Riots: Violence and Social Change,* Doubleday, 1970; (editor with Jewell Bellush, and contributor) *Race and Politics in New York City,* Praeger, 1971; (contributor) William C. Bier, editor, *Alienation: Plight of Modern Man,* Fordham University Press, 1972; *History of the Narcotic Addiction Political Arena in New York City: An Initial Exploration,* National Institute of Mental Health, 1972; (co-editor) *Urban Politics and Policy: The City in Crisis,* Praeger, 1973, 2nd edition, 1976; (contributor) Robert L. Lineberry and Louis H. Masotti, editors, *Urban Problems and Public Policy,* Heath, 1975.

*   *   *

DAVIDSON, E(phraim) E(dward) 1923-

PERSONAL: Born April 11, 1923, in Oxford, Miss.; son of Roy L. and Garna (Ailene) Davidson; married Mary Parks, April 11, 1948; children: Deborah (Mrs. John Myers), Sandra (Mrs. Joe Jameson), Wanda (Mrs. Judd Hurd), Vicki, Brenda. *Education:* University of Mississippi, B.B.A., 1954, M.B.A., 1955; University of Kentucky, additional study, 1957-59; Louisiana State University, Ph.D., 1966. *Politics:* Democrat. *Religion:* Baptist. *Home:* 1101 Graham Dr., Stillwater, Okla. 74074. *Office:* Oklahoma State University, Stillwater, Okla. 74074.

CAREER: University of Mississippi, director of Millsap Center, Jackson, 1955-57, business manager, University, 1957-68; Oklahoma State University, Stillwater, vice-president for business and finance, 1968—. Member of faculty, Business Management Institute, University of Kentucky, 1963-69. Member of board of directors, Stillwater Chamber of Commerce. *Military service:* U.S. Marine Corps, 1943-46; became sergeant.

MEMBER: National Association of College and University Business Officers (member of board of directors, 1964-68), American Council on Education, National Association of State Universities and Land-Grant Colleges, Southern Association of College and University Business Officers (president, 1974), Southern Association of Colleges and Schools, Omicron Delta Kappa, Beta Gamma Sigma, Phi Kappa Phi, Phi Eta Sigma, Pi Kappa Pi, Beta Alpha Psi.

WRITINGS: (With Clarence Scheps) *Accounting for Colleges and Universities,* revised edition, Louisiana State University Press, 1970. Contributor to journals.

AVOCATIONAL INTERESTS: Flying, two-way radio, golf.

*   *   *

DAVIDSON, Marshall B(owman) 1907-

PERSONAL: Born April 26, 1907, in New York, N.Y.; son of Henry Fletcher and Frances A. (Holt) Davidson; married Ruth Bradbury (a former editor), August 20, 1935. *Education:* Princeton University, B.S., 1928. *Home:* 140 East 83rd St., New York, N.Y. 10028. *Office:* American Heritage Publishing Co., 10 Rockefeller Plaza, New York, N.Y. 10020.

CAREER: Metropolitan Museum of Art, New York City, assistant curator, 1935-41, associate curator, American wing, 1941-47, editor of publications, 1947-60; Horizon Books, New York City, editor, 1961-64, editor of *Horizon* (magazine), 1964-66, senior editor, 1966—. *Awards, honors:* Carey-Thomas award for creative publishing, 1951, for *Life in America.*

WRITINGS—Published by American Heritage Publishing, except as indicated: *Life in America,* two volumes, Houghton, 1951; (author of introduction) James J. Audubon, *The Original Water Color Paintings of James J. Audubon,* two volumes, 1966; *American Heritage History of Colonial Antiques,* 1967; *American Heritage History of American Antiques: 1784-1860,* 1968; *American Heritage History of Antiques: 1865-1917,* 1969; *American Heritage History of Notable American Houses,* 1971; *Horizon Concise History of France,* 1972; *The American Heritage History of the Artists' America,* 1973; *The American Heritage History of the Writers' America,* 1973; *Great Historic Places of Europe,* 1974; *The Horizon History of the World in 1776,* 1975; *Architecture in America: A Pictorial Survey,* 1976; *Fifty Early American Tools,* Olivetti Corp., 1976; *New York: A Pictorial History,* Scribners, 1977. Contributor to art, museum, and history journals.

*   *   *

DAVIES, Alan T(rewartha) 1933-

PERSONAL: Born June 24, 1933, in Montreal, Quebec, Canada; son of Albert Victor (a sales manager) and Florence (Clendenning) Davies; married Marilyn Vaughn Kiefer, September 22, 1962; children: Andrew Mark, Alison Anne. *Education:* McGill University, B.A., 1954, B.D., 1957; Union Theological Seminary, New York, N.Y., S.T.M., 1960, Ph.D., 1966; Hebrew Union College—Jewish Institute of Religion, Cincinnati, postdoctoral study, 1967-68. *Home:* 11 Centennial Park Rd., No. 22, Etobicoke, Ontario, Canada M9C 4W8. *Office:* Department of Religious Studies, Victoria College, University of Toronto, Toronto, Ontario, Canada.

CAREER: Clergyman of United Church of Canada; University of Toronto, Victoria College, Toronto, Ontario, assistant professor in department of religious studies, 1969—. *Member:* Canadian Theological Society, American Society of Christian Ethics. *Awards, honors:* McGill Delta Upsilon traveling fellow, 1959-60; J. Clarence and Corale B. Workum fellow at Hebrew Union College—Jewish Institute of Religion, 1967-68; Canada Council leave fellowship, 1975-76.

WRITINGS: Anti-Semitism and the Christian Mind, Herder & Herder, 1969.

BIOGRAPHICAL/CRITICAL SOURCES: Commonweal, February 20, 1970.

DAVIES, R(obert) W(illiam) 1925-

PERSONAL: Born April 23, 1925, in London, England; son of William and Gladys Hilda (Hall) Davies; married Frances Rebecca Moscow (a researcher and teacher), December 29, 1953; children: Maurice William, Catherine Gladys Anne. *Education:* University of London, B.A., 1950; University of Birmingham, Ph.D., 1954. *Office:* Centre for Russian and East European Studies, University of Birmingham, Birmingham B15 2TT, England.

CAREER: University of Glasgow, Glasgow, Scotland, senior research scholar and assistant in department of Soviet institutions, 1954-56; University of Birmingham, Birmingham, England, research fellow, lecturer and senior lecturer in department of economics and institutions of the U.S.S.R., 1956-63, director, Centre for Russian and East European Studies, 1963—, professor of Soviet economic studies, 1965—. *Military service:* Royal Air Force, 1943-46; served as aircraftsman. *Member:* National Association of Soviet and East European Studies (member of National Committee, 1965-76).

WRITINGS: The Development of the Soviet Budgetary System, Cambridge University Press, 1958; (with E. Zaleski and others) *Science Policy in the U.S.S.R.,* Organisation for Economic Cooperation and Development, 1969; (with E. H. Carr) *Foundations of a Planned Economy, 1926-1929,* Volume I, two parts, Macmillan (London), 1969, Macmillan (New York), 1971; (editor with R. Amann and J. Cooper) *The Technological Level of Soviet Industry,* Yale University Press, 1977; (editor) *The Soviet Union,* Allen & Unwin, 1977. Contributor of articles on Soviet science and technology, and history of Soviet economic institutions, to periodicals. Member of editorial board, *Economics of Planning;* member of advisory board, *Soviet Studies.*

WORK IN PROGRESS: Writing on Soviet economic history, 1929-1937, and on economics and organisation of Soviet research and development.

*   *   *

DAVIES, (William) Robertson 1913-

PERSONAL: Born August 28, 1913, in Thamesville, Ontario, Canada; son of William Rupert (a publisher) and Florence (McKay) Davies; married Brenda Matthews, February 2, 1940; children: Miranda, Jennifer (Mrs. C. T. Surridge), Rosamond (Mrs. John Cunnington). *Education:* Attended Upper Canada College, Toronto, Ontario, and Queen's University, Kingston, Ontario; Balliol College, Oxford, B.Litt., 1938. *Home and office:* Massey College, University of Toronto, 4 Devonshire Pl., Toronto, Ontario, Canada M5S 2E1. *Agent:* Curtis Brown Ltd., 575 Madison Ave., New York, N.Y. 10022.

CAREER: Old Vic Company, London, England, teacher and actor, 1938-40; *Saturday Night,* Toronto, Ontario, literary editor, 1940-42; *Examiner,* Peterborough, Ontario, editor and publisher, 1942-62; University of Toronto, Toronto, professor of English, 1960—, master of Massey College, 1962—. Senator, Stratford Shakespearean Festival, Stratford, Ontario. *Member:* Royal Society of Canada (fellow), Authors Guild, Dramatists Guild, Writers' Union (Canada), P.E.N. International. *Awards, honors:* Louis Jouvet Prize for Directing, Dominion Drama Festival, 1949; Stephen Leacock Medal for Humour, 1954, for *Leaven of Malice;* LL.D., University of Alberta, 1957, Queen's University, 1962, University of Manitoba, 1972; D.Litt., McMaster University, 1959, University of Windsor, 1971, York University, 1973, Mount Allison University, 1973, Memorial University of Newfoundland, 1974, University of Western Ontario, 1974, McGill University, 1974, Trent University, 1974; Lorne Pierce Medal, Royal Society of Canada, 1961; D.C.L., Bishop's University, 1967; Companion of the Order of Canada, 1972; Governor-General's Award for fiction, 1973, for *The Manticore;* D.Univ., University of Calgary, 1975.

WRITINGS—Novels: *Tempest-Tost,* Clarke, Irwin, 1951, Rinehart, 1952; *Leaven of Malice,* Clarke, Irwin, 1954, Scribner, 1955; *A Mixture of Frailties,* Scribner, 1958; *Fifth Business,* Viking, 1970; *The Manticore,* Viking, 1972; *World of Wonders,* Macmillan (Canada), 1975, Viking, 1976.

Plays: *Fortune, My Foe* (first produced in Kingston, Ontario by Arthur Sutherland's International Players, 1948), Clarke, Irwin, 1949; *Eros at Breakfast and Other Plays* (contains "Eros at Breakfast" [first produced in Montreal at Montreal Repertory Theatre, 1948], "Overlaid" [first produced in Peterborough, Ontario at Peterborough Little Theatre, 1947], "The Voice of the People" [first produced in Montreal at Montreal Repertory Theatre, 1948], "At the Gates of the Righteous" [first produced in Peterborough at Peterborough Little Theatre, 1948], and "Hope Deferred" [first produced in Montreal at Montreal Repertory Theatre, 1948]), introduction by Tyrone Guthrie, Clarke, Irwin, 1949, published without "Hope Deferred" as *Four Favorite Plays,* 1968; *At My Heart's Core* (first produced in Peterborough at Peterborough Little Theatre, 1950), Clarke, Irwin, 1952; *A Masque of Aesop* (first produced in Toronto at Upper Canada College, May, 1952), Clarke, Irwin, 1952; *A Jig for the Gypsy* (first produced in Toronto at Crest Theatre, 1954), Clarke, Irwin, 1955; *Love and Libel* (dramatization of his novel *Leaven of Malice;* first produced in Toronto at Royal Alexandria Theatre, November, 1960; produced on Broadway at Martin Beck Theatre, December, 1960), Studio Duplicating Service, 1960; *A Masque for Mr. Punch* (first produced in Toronto at Upper Canada College, 1962), Oxford University Press, 1963; *Hunting Stuart and Other Plays* (contains "Hunting Stuart" [first produced in Toronto at Crest Theatre, 1955], "King Phoenix" [first produced in Peterborough, 1950], and "General Confession"), New Press, 1972; "Brothers in the Black Art," produced on CBC-TV, 1974; *Question Time* (first produced in Toronto at St. Lawrence Center, 1975), Macmillan, 1975.

Nonfiction: *Shakespeare's Boy Actors,* Dent, 1939, Russell, 1964; (editor) *Shakespeare for Young Players: A Junior Course,* Clarke, Irwin, 1942; *The Diary of Samuel Marchbanks,* Clarke, Irwin, 1947; *The Table Talk of Samuel Marchbanks,* Clarke, Irwin, 1949; (with Tyrone Guthrie and Grant Macdonald) *Renown at Stratford: A Record of the Shakespearean Festival in Canada,* Clarke, Irwin, 1953; (with Guthrie and Macdonald) *Twice Have the Trumpets Sounded: A Record of the Stratford Shakespearean Festival in Canada,* Clarke, Irwin, 1954; (with Guthrie, Boyd Neal, and Tanya Moiseiwitsch) *Thrice the Brinded Cat Hath Mew'd: A Record of the Stratford Shakespearean Festival in Canada,* Clarke, Irwin, 1955; *A Voice from the Attic,* Knopf, 1960 (published in England as *The Personal Art: Reading to Good Purpose,* Secker & Warburg, 1961); *Le Jeu de centenaire,* Comission du Centenaire, c. 1967; *Samuel Marchbanks' Almanack,* McClelland & Stewart, 1967; *Stephen Leacock,* McClelland & Stewart, 1970; (editor and author of introduction) *Feast of Stephen,* McClelland & Stewart, 1970; (with Michael R. Booth, Richard Southern, Frederick Marker, and Lise-Lone Marker) *The Revels History of Drama in English,* Volume VI: *1750-1880,*

Methuen, 1975; *One Half of Robertson Davies,* Viking, 1978.

WORK IN PROGRESS: A novel and a play.

SIDELIGHTS: Robertson Davies told *CA:* "The theme which lies at the root of all my novels is the isolation of the human spirit. I have not attempted to deal with it in a gloomy fashion but rather to demonstrate that what my characters do that might be called really significant is done on their own volition and usually contrary to what is expected of them. This theme is worked out in terms of characters who are trying to escape from early influences and find their own place in the world but who are reluctant to do so in a way that will bring pain and disappointment to others."

John Skow comments in a *Time* review: "It is a secure kind of pleasure to begin a novel by Canadian writer Robertson Davies. This is not because the reader knows what will happen—Davies does not write formula fiction—but because he is serenely sure of what will not happen. The author will not hunt snarks, nor plant a forest of symbols and then get lost in it. Nor will he fail to have some rather compelling reason to write rather than remain silent." Roger Sale writes in *New York Review of Books:* "Davies is Canadian, old-fashioned, a craftsman, a good storyteller.... Davies is a Jungian Ross Macdonald, a writer who wants to describe contemporary experiences in which people discover the meaning of their lives by discovering the ways those lives conform to ancient patterns."

It was not until the publication of *Fifth Business,* the first of a trilogy of novels that also includes *The Manticore* and *World of Wonders,* that Davies received much critical notice in the United States. L. J. Davis calls *Fifth Business* "a mature, accomplished and altogether remarkable book . . . [which] achieves a richness and depth that are exceptional in a modern novel and rare at any time. On its simplest and most obvious level it is a remarkably colorful tale of ambition, love and weird vengeance. At its deepest, it is a work of theological fiction that approaches Graham Greene at the top of his form." J. D. O'Hara agrees in a review in *Saturday Review,* writing that the novel is "intelligently conceived and intelligently narrated, free from gimmicks and tricks; not at all mod, it makes no appeals to current fashions in style or content, neither pandering to the reader nor taking on the universe, but is full of the art that conceals itself."

William Kennedy writes of *The Manticore:* "The book, being a segment of a kind of saga, is not quite an entity, but refers backward to earlier work and hints broadly at what will probably come next.... Questions about events are raised but left hanging, which is Mr. Davies's way. He is clearly developing a shelf of interlocking books the way Faulkner did . . . and he is telling us: Love me, love my shelf. And we more or less do. He is a highly literate, intelligent man with a mystical and melodramatic imagination, and he conveys a sense of real life lived in a fully imagined if sometimes mythical and magical world. Realists will probably be put off, but then they never even liked Jung."

In a review in *Newsweek,* Peter S. Prescott states that "Davies means to recharge the world with a wonder it has lost, to re-create through the intervention of saints and miracles, psychoanalysts and sleight-of-hand a proper sense of awe at life's mystery and a recognition of the price that must be paid for initiation into that mystery. He is a psychological optimist: the distinctive character of the trilogy that is completed with *World of Wonders* derives from Davies's belief that a man may at some cost gain understanding of his destiny. Not a common idea among novelists nowadays, but then these are uncommon novels; Davies's trilogy is one of the splendid literary enterprises of this decade.''

Claude Bissell writes in *Canadian Forum:* ''I hope that the trilogy will be brought out in a single volume under a single comprehensive title. The three books have been ingeniously constructed so as to have separate existences, and to take advantage of the aura of the murder mystery. But they are essentially parts of a whole: three parallel pilgrimages.... Together these novels comprise the major piece of prose fiction in Canadian literature—in scope, in the constant interplay of wit and intelligence, in the persistent attempt to find a pattern in this 'life of marvels, cruel circumstances, obscenities, and commonplaces.'''

BIOGRAPHICAL/CRITICAL SOURCES: Saturday Night, December 13, 1947; *Canadian Forum,* June, 1950, December, 1975; *MacLean's,* March 15, 1952; *Tamarack Review,* autumn, 1958; *Canadian Literature,* spring, 1960, winter, 1961, spring, 1973, winter, 1974, winter, 1976; *Financial Post,* January 19, 1963; *Library Quarterly,* April, 1969; *Book World,* December 13, 1970; *Saturday Review,* December 26, 1970, April 3, 1976; *Time,* January 11, 1971, May 17, 1976; Elspeth Buitenhuis, *Canadian Writers and Their Works: Robertson Davies,* Forum House Publishing, 1972; *New York Times Book Review,* November 19, 1972, April 25, 1976; *Journal of Canadian Fiction,* winter, 1972; Mavor Moore, *Four Canadian Playwrights,* Holt, 1973; Donald Cameron, *Conversations with Canadian Novelists,* Part 1, Macmillan, 1973; *New York Review of Books,* February 8, 1973; *Contemporary Literary Criticism,* Gale, Volume II, 1974, Volume VII, 1977; *Newsweek,* March 22, 1976; *Canadian Review,* fall, 1976; *Journal of Canadian Studies,* February, 1977.

*   *   *

DAVIS, David C(harles) L.   1928-

PERSONAL: Born February 6, 1928, in Oxnard, Calif.; son of Charles Lester (a physician) and Esther (Reeder) Davis; married Dorothy Ham (a school librarian; co-director of Wayfarer Farm School), March 31, 1958; children: Nils Peter, Erika Ann. *Education:* Santa Barbara College (now University of California, Santa Barbara), A.B., 1950; University of Copenhagen, Diploma, 1955; San Francisco State College (now University), M.A., 1965; U.S. International University, Ph.D., 1969. *Home and office:* Wayfarer Farm School, 33250 King Ridge Rd., Cazadero, Calif. 95421.

CAREER: G. S. Haly Co. (tea importer), San Francisco, Calif., assistant to owner, 1953-54; King Publications, Inc., San Francisco, 1956-57, began as mail clerk, became traffic manager; teacher in Bodega Bay, Calif., 1957; teacher in Cazadero, Calif., 1957-58, teacher-principal, 1958-60; teacher in Work Skills School in Copenhagen, Denmark, 1960-61, and guest lecturer at other Copenhagen schools, 1961; teacher in Cotati, Calif., 1961-62, and Boonville, Calif., 1962-67; Wayfarer Farm School (independent high school), Cazadero, founder and co-director, 1971—. *Military service:* U.S. Navy, 1950-52; served in Korea. *Member:* Association for Supervision and Curriculum Development, California Mathematics Council, California Council for the Social Studies.

WRITINGS: Model for a Humanistic Education: The Danish Folk Highschool, C. E. Merrill, 1971.

*   *   *

DAVIS, John J(ames)   1936-

PERSONAL: Born October 13, 1936, in Philadelphia, Pa.;

son of John James (a salesman) and Cathryn Ann Davis; married Carolyn A. Clark (a bookkeeper), June 26, 1958; children: Debbie Ann. *Education:* Attended Philadelphia Bible Institute, 1955; Trinity College, Fla., B.A., 1959; Grace Theological Seminary, B.D. (cum laude), 1962, Th.M., 1964, Th.D., 1967; Near East School of Archaeology, graduate study, 1963. *Home:* R.R. 8, Warsaw, Ind. 46580. *Office:* Grace Theological Seminary, Winona Lake, Ind. 46590.

CAREER: Clergyman of Grace Brethren Church; pastor in Tampa, Fla., 1953-55, and South Whitely, Ind., 1965-68; Grace College, Winona Lake, Ind., instructor in archaeology, 1963-65; Grace Theological Seminary, Winona Lake, 1965—, currently professor of Old Testament and Hebrew and executive vice-president. Academic dean, Wheaton Summer Institute of Archaeology, Jerusalem, 1968; executive dean, Near East Institute of Archaeology, Jerusalem, 1970, 1971. Member of staff, Tekoa excavations in Israel, 1968, 1970, joint expedition to Ai, 1974, Raddana excavations, 1974, and Heshbon expedition in Jordan, 1976. *Member:* Evangelical Theological Society, Creation Research Society, American Schools of Oriental Research, National Association of Professors of Hebrew, Near East Archaeological Society, Association for Historic Archaeology, Kiwanis Club. *Awards, honors:* D.D., Trinity College, 1968; Book of the Year award, BMH Books, 1975, for *Paradise to Prison.*

WRITINGS—All published by Baker Book: *Biblical Numerology,* 1968; *Conquest and Crisis: Studies in Joshua, Judges, and Ruth,* 1969; *The Birth of a Kingdom: Studies in the Books of Samuel and I Kings,* 1970; *Moses and the Gods of Egypt,* 1971; *Hebrew Language: An Analysis of the Strong Verb,* 1971; *Paradise to Prison: Studies in Genesis,* 1975; *Tombs Tell Tales,* 1978. Also author of *Mummies, Men and Madness,* 1972, and *Pre-Seminary Training and the Bible College Curriculum,* 1975. Contributor to *Wycliffe Bible Encyclopedia, Zondervan Dictionary of Archaeology,* and to religious journals.

SIDELIGHTS: John J. Davis told *CA:* ''Archaeological research in the Near East has produced a staggering amount of material which has direct and indirect relevance for the Biblical scholar. It is my aim to help the student of the Old Testament to confront these discoveries and integrate their results with their various fields of interest. For years pastors and teachers have struggled with commentaries which lacked any visual aids. To fill a critical need in this area, we have included a generous number of maps, charts, photographs and drawings in the various volumes. If a picture is really worth a thousand words, then we have saved both publisher and reader a considerable amount of ink and paper. I have also attempted to carefully document my various subjects at greater depth.

''I must also admit that I detest books that lack some sense of humor. In the light of this, I have attempted to spare the reader the agony of ponderous discussions without some levity and humor. It is my opinion that literary diversification and balance are necessary ingredients to good writing. Merely tacking on humorous and shallow material for the sake of entertainment, however, is about as valuable as painting racing stripes on an arthritic camel. Having one's book serve as a window prop is not my idea of achieving literary goals.''

*   *   *

DAVIS, (John) Michael   1940-

PERSONAL: Born November 29, 1940, in Oklahoma City,

Okla.; son of Clifton Harry (an attorney) and Virginia (Rader) Davis. *Education:* Wabash College, A.B., 1962; Rice University, Ph.D., 1967. *Home:* 7010 Phoenix N.E., No. 509, Albuquerque, N.M. 87110.

CAREER: University of Miami, Coral Gables, Fla., assistant professor of history, 1967-71; U.S. Department of State, Washington, D.C., foreign service officer, 1971—, serving in Paris, Vietnam, and Damascus. *Member:* American Historical Association. *Awards, honors:* National Defense Education Act fellow, 1962, 1965, 1967, 1970; Benjamin Barondess Prize, Civil War Round Table of New York, 1971, for *The Image of Lincoln in the South.*

WRITINGS: The Image of Lincoln in the South, University of Tennessee, 1971. Contributor to *Miami Herald.*

WORK IN PROGRESS: The Idea of Conservatism in American Thought.

* * *

DAVIS, Ralph C(urrier) 1894-

PERSONAL: Born December 24, 1894, in Mohawk, N.Y.; son of Frank Colin (a commission salesman) and Susie Helen (Greene) Davis; married Dorothy Rebecca O'Neil, April 5, 1926; children: Dannette C. Davis Palmer (deceased). *Education:* Cornell University, M.E., 1916; Ohio State University, M.A., 1926. *Home and office:* 1994 Edgemont Rd. N., Columbus, Ohio 43212.

CAREER: Winchester Repeating Arms Co., New Haven, Conn., industrial engineer, 1916-18; Gleason Works, Rochester, N.Y., industrial engineer, 1919; Chamber of Commerce, Cleveland, Ohio, assistant labor commissioner, 1919-23; Ohio State University, Columbus, assistant professor of management, 1923-27; General Motors Institute, Detroit, Mich., head of management department, 1927-30; Ohio State University, associate professor, 1930-36, professor of business organization, 1936-65, professor emeritus, 1965—. Visiting professor at Columbia University, Stanford University, Indiana University, and other universities. *Military service:* U.S. Army, 1918. U.S. Naval Reserve Force, 1918-19; became ensign. U.S. Army Air Forces, Air Materiel Command, 1942-46; became lieutenant colonel.

MEMBER: American Institute of Management (member of board of directors, 1952—), Academy of Management (co-founder, 1936; president, 1948; member of board of directors and dean of fellows, 1966—), International Academy of Management (fellow), Society for Advancement of Management (vice-president, 1942-43, 1946-47, 1953-58), Sons of the American Revolution, Torch Club. *Awards, honors:* Taylor Key, Society for Advancement of Management, 1958; D.Sc., Wayne State University, 1964; Centennial Distinguished Service Award, Ohio State University, 1971.

WRITINGS: The Principles of Factory Organization and Management, Harper, 1928, revised edition published as *Industrial Organization and Management,* 1940, 3rd edition, 1957; *The Principles of Business Organization and Operation,* H. L. Hedrick, 1934, 4th edition, 1937, reprinted, Hive Publishing, 1973; *Purchasing and Storing,* Alexander Hamilton Institute, 1935, 3rd revised edition (with Michael J. Jucius), 1947; *Shop Management for the Shop Supervisor,* Harper, 1941; *The Fundamentals of Top Management,* Harper, 1951; (with Alton W. Baker) *Labor-Management Arbitration,* Bureau of Business Research, Ohio State University, 1951; (with Alan C. Filley) *Principles of Management,* Alexander Hamilton Institute, 1962. Also author of papers and articles on the philosophy of manage-

ment which have been published by Society for Advancement of Management and in journals.

WORK IN PROGRESS: Research in the area of long-range planning for profitable corporate growth; writing a final statement of his philosophy of management.

AVOCATIONAL INTERESTS: Bridge, golf, bowling.

* * *

DAVIS, Richard W. 1935-

PERSONAL: Born December 8, 1935, in Somers, Conn.; son of Fred Cady and Janet (Whitlock) Davis; married Elisabeth Sargent, December 18, 1965; children: Benjamin Whitlock, Matthew Sargent. *Education:* Amherst College, B.A., 1957; Columbia University, M.A., 1958, Ph.D., 1964; Cambridge University, M.Litt., 1962. *Politics:* Democrat. *Religion:* Congregationalist. *Home:* 7106 Waterman Ave., University City, Mo. 63130. *Office:* Department of History, Washington University, St. Louis, Mo. 63130.

CAREER: Cambridge University, Christ's College, Cambridge, England, supervisor in history, 1960-62; University of Rhode Island, Kingston, instructor in history, 1962-64; University of California, Riverside, assistant professor of history, 1964-69; Washington University, St. Louis, Mo., associate professor, 1969-73, professor of history, 1973—, chairman of department, 1974-77. Consultant to National Endowment for the Humanities. *Member:* American Historical Association, Royal Historical Society (fellow), Conference on British Studies, Society of Authors (England), Authors' Club (London). *Awards, honors:* National Endowment for the Humanities, fellowship, 1967-68, research grant, 1973; American Philosophical Society fellowship, summer, 1970; Guggenheim fellowship, 1972-73.

WRITINGS: Dissent in Politics: 1780-1830, Epworth Press, 1971; *Political Change and Continuity: 1760-1885,* David & Charles, 1972; (with F. C. Davis) *Somers: The History of a Connecticut Town,* Somers Historical Society, 1973; *Disraeli,* Little, Brown, 1976. Contributor of articles and reviews to history journals.

WORK IN PROGRESS: Toryism to Tamworth: The Triumph of Reform, 1826-1835; The House of Lords, 1660-1911.

AVOCATIONAL INTERESTS: Swimming, jogging, gardening.

* * *

DAVIS, Robert Murray 1934-

PERSONAL: Born September 4, 1934, in Lyons, Kan.; son of Matthew Cary (a dealer) and Elizabeth (Murray) Davis; married Barbara Hillyer, December 28, 1958; children: Megan, Jennifer, John. *Education:* Rockhurst College, B.S., 1955; University of Kansas, M.A., 1958; University of Wisconsin, Ph.D., 1964. *Religion:* Catholic. *Home:* 736 Nancy Lynn, Norman, Okla. 73069. *Office:* Department of English, University of Oklahoma, 760 Van Vleet, Norman, Okla. 73019.

CAREER: Loyola University, Chicago, Ill., assistant professor of English, 1962-65; University of California, Santa Barbara, assistant professor of English, 1965-67; University of Oklahoma, Norman, 1967—, currently professor of English. *Member:* Modern Language Association of America, South Central Modern Language Association. *Awards, honors:* National Endowment for the Humanities summer stipend, 1969.

WRITINGS: (Editor) *The Novel: Modern Essays in Criticism,* Prentice-Hall, 1969; (editor) *Evelyn Waugh,* B. Herder, 1969; (editor) *Steinbeck,* Prentice-Hall, 1972; (editor) *Modern British Short Novels,* Scott, Foresman, 1972; (with others) *Evelyn Waugh: A Checklist of Primary and Secondary Material,* Whitston Publishing, 1972. Contributor to scholarly journals. Associate editor, *Genre.*

WORK IN PROGRESS: A new edition of *Evelyn Waugh: A Checklist of Primary and Secondary Material;* a catalogue of the Evelyn Waugh collection at University of Texas; with Jerome Klinkowitz and Asa Pieratt, a bibliography of Donald Barthelme, for Shoe String; a study of Waugh; a work on the habits of composition; various articles.

* * *

DAVIS, Wayne H(arry) 1930-

PERSONAL: Born December 31, 1930, in Morgantown, W. Va.; son of Hannibal A. (a professor) and Tyreeca (Stemple) Davis; married Shirley Johnson, June 21, 1958; children: Carolyn, Beverly, Daniel. *Education:* West Virginia University, A.B., 1953; University of Illinois, M.S., 1955, Ph.D., 1957. *Religion:* Unitarian. *Home:* 130 Jesselyn Dr., Lexington, Ky. 40503. *Office:* Department of Biology, University of Kentucky, Lexington, Ky. 40506.

CAREER: University of Minnesota, St. Paul, research fellow in zoology, 1957-59; Middlebury College, Middlebury, Vt., instructor in biology, 1959-61; University of Kentucky, Lexington, assistant professor, 1961-64, associate professor, 1964-70, professor of biology, 1970—. *Member:* American Association for the Advancement of Science (fellow), American Society of Mammalogists, Friends of the Earth, National Audubon Society, Zero Population Growth (member of board of directors, 1971—), Common Cause, Defenders of Wildlife, Sierra Club.

WRITINGS: (With Roger W. Barbour) *Bats of America,* University Press of Kentucky, 1969; (editor) *Readings in Human Population Ecology,* Prentice-Hall, 1971; *Mammals of Kentucky,* University Press of Kentucky, 1974. Environmental columnist for *Louisville Times* and *Courier-Journal* (Louisville); contributor of articles to Metropolitan Sunday Newspapers, Inc., *New Republic,* and other periodicals.

SIDELIGHTS: Wayne Davis told *CA* that "a Sand County Almanac by Aldo Leopold [written in] 1949 (recently reprinted in paperback) has had more influence in developing my philosophy and my writing style in my newspaper and magazine writings than has any other work."

* * *

DAVIS, William H(atcher) 1939-

PERSONAL: Born January 5, 1939, in Frankewing, Tenn.; son of George B. and Lois (Sawyers) Davis. *Education:* Abilene Christian College, B.A., 1960, M.A., 1961; Rice University, Ph.D., 1965. *Politics:* Democrat. *Religion:* Christian. *Office:* Philosophy Department, Auburn University, Auburn, Ala. 36830.

CAREER: University of Houston, Houston, Tex., instructor in philosophy, 1964-66; Auburn University, Auburn, Ala., assistant professor, 1966-71, associate professor of philosophy, 1971—. *Member:* American Philosophical Association, C. S. Peirce Society, Southern Society for Philosophy and Psychology, Southwestern Philosophical Society, Alabama Philosophical Society (secretary-treasurer, 1970-71).

WRITINGS: Science and Christian Faith, Biblical Research Society, 1968; *Philosophy of Religion,* Biblical Research Society, 1969; *The Freewill Question,* Nijhoff, 1971; *Peirce's Epistemology,* Nijhoff, 1972. Contributor to *Southern Journal of Philosophy, Journal of Value Inquiry, Philosophy Today,* and other scholarly journals.

* * *

DAWE, Donald G. 1926-

PERSONAL: Born July 12, 1926, in Detroit, Mich.; son of Gilbert T. and Erma (Vivian) Dawe; married Nancy Jane Simons (an occupational therapist), December 28, 1957; children: Joanna Marie, Stephen Donald. *Education:* Wayne University (now Wayne State University), B.S., 1949; Princeton Theological Seminary, graduate study, 1949-50; Union Theological Seminary, New York, N.Y., B.D., 1952, Th.D., 1960. *Politics:* Democrat. *Home:* 1203 Confederate Ave., Richmond, Va. 23227. *Office:* Department of Theology, Union Theological Seminary, Richmond, Va. 23227.

CAREER: Clergyman of Presbyterian Church; pastor in Sauquoit, N.Y., Lake Forest, Ill., and Chicago, Ill., 1952-57; Union Theological Seminary, New York, N.Y., assistant professor of theology and acting dean of students, 1957-61; Macalester College, St. Paul, Minn., associate professor of religion, 1961-69; Union Theological Seminary, Richmond, Va., professor of theology, 1969—. *Military service:* U.S. Army, 1944-46. *Member:* Society for the Scientific Study of Religion, Council on Religion in Higher Education, American Association of University Professors, American Teilhard Society. *Awards, honors:* Fellowships from Eli Lilly Endowment, 1964-65, and Institute of International Education, 1968-69.

WRITINGS: The Form of a Servant, Westminster, 1964; *No Orthodoxy but the Truth,* Westminster, 1969; *Paul Interpreted for India,* Punjabi University Press, 1974; *Jesus, Lord for All Times,* John Knox, 1975. Contributor to *Christian Century, Scottish Journal of Theology, Interpretation,* and other religious journals in the United States, Europe, and India.

WORK IN PROGRESS: Jesus and the Human Future; Christian Faith in a Religiously Plural World.

BIOGRAPHICAL/CRITICAL SOURCES: Christian Century, August 6, 1969.

* * *

DAWSON, Jerry F. 1933-

PERSONAL: Born December 28, 1933, in Borger, Tex.; son of Frank Alden (a welder) and Nellena (Gibson) Dawson; married Margie Jo Clements (a clerk), June 21, 1952; children: Kim Alden, Carey Austin, Jamie Lynn. *Education:* Attended Wayland Baptist College, 1952-54; Mississippi College, B.A. (with special distinction), 1956; University of Texas, M.A., 1958, Ph.D., 1964. *Home:* 704 Rainey, Marshall, Tex. 75670. *Office:* Office of the President, East Texas Baptist College, Marshall, Tex. 75670.

CAREER: J. M. Huber Corp., Borger, Tex., pipeline worker, 1952-56; pastor of Baptist church in McDade, Tex., 1956-60; Wayland Baptist College, Plainview, Tex., chairman of history department, 1960-68; Texas A & M University, College Station, associate professor of history, 1968-71; Southwest Texas State University, San Marcos, dean of Graduate School, 1971-76; East Texas Baptist College, Marshall, president, 1976—. *Member:* Rocky Mountain Social Science Association.

WRITINGS: Friedrich Schleiermacher: The Evolution of a Nationalist, University of Texas Press, 1966; (with Dennis Dunn) Folktales and Footprints: Stories from the Old World, W. S. Benson, 1973. Assistant editor, Rocky Mountain Social Science Journal and editor, Newsletter of Rocky Mountain Social Science Association, 1967—.

* * *

DAY, James F(rancis) 1917-

PERSONAL: Born April 8, 1917, in Roosevelt, Utah; son of J. Frank (a teacher) and Chloe G. (Huntsman) Day; married Shirley G. Sugerman (a teacher), April 8, 1946; children: Karen F. (Mrs. Stephen Stafford). Education: Utah State University, B.S., 1938, M.S., 1939; Stanford University, Ed.D., 1949. Home: 1308 Mathias Dr., El Paso, Tex. 79903. Office address: Box 91, University of Texas, El Paso, Tex. 79968.

CAREER: Licensed psychologist in Texas. North Sampete High School, Mount Pleasant, Utah, science teacher, 1939-41; State of Utah, Salt Lake City, statistician, 1941-42; Visalia College, Visalia, Calif., director of guidance, 1947-48; Eastern Washington State College (now University), Cheney, director of psychological clinic, 1949-50; Arizona State University, Tempe, assistant professor of psychology, 1950-51; Northwestern University, Evanston, Ill., lecturer in psychology, 1951-52; U.S. Naval Examining Center, Great Lakes, Ill., research psychologist, 1951-52; San Francisco State College (now University), San Francisco, Calif., assistant professor of psychology, 1952-54; U.S. Air Force, Denver, Colo., educational advisor, 1954-55; University of Texas at El Paso, assistant professor, 1955-58, associate professor, 1958-60, professor of educational psychology, 1960—, chairman of department of education and coordinator of teacher education, 1960-66. Member of board of directors, National Conference of Christians and Jews, El Paso, 1967—. Military service: U.S. Navy, 1942-46; became lieutenant. Member: American Psychological Association, American Personnel and Guidance Association, National Society for the Study of Education, Rocky Mountain Psychological Association, Trans Pecos Personnel and Guidance Association (president, 1958-59, 1960-61), Phi Delta Kappa, Kappa Delta Pi. Awards, honors: Certificate of appreciation, El Paso Council for Retarded Children, 1964.

WRITINGS: (Contributor) Stanley Lehrer, editor, Leaders, Teachers, and Learners in Academe, Appleton, 1970; Teacher Retirement in the United States, Christopher, 1971; Migrant Education, Philosophical Library, 1975; (contributor) Christopher J. Lucas, editor, Challenge and Choice in Contemporary Education: Six Major Ideological Perspectives, Macmillan, 1976. Contributor to Educational Yearbook, Macmillan, 1975; also contributor to Eastern Gale, School and Society, Journal of Thought, Guidance Clinic, Journal of Employment Counseling, and Intellect. Member of editorial board, Southwestern Review, 1974—.

* * *

DAY, Richard E. 1929-

PERSONAL: Born November 2, 1929, in St. Joseph, Mo.; son of William E. and Geneva (Miller) Day; married Melissa Blair (a real estate agent), February 2, 1951; children: William E. II, Thomas E. Education: University of Pennsylvania, B.S., 1951; University of Michigan, J.D. (with honors), 1957. Office: School of Law, University of South Carolina, Columbia, S.C. 29208.

CAREER: Kirkland & Ellis, Chicago, Ill., attorney, 1957-58; Howrey & Simon, Washington, D.C., attorney, 1958-61; University of North Carolina at Chapel Hill, assistant professor of law, 1961-64; Ohio State University, Columbus, associate professor, 1964-66, professor of law, 1966-75; University of South Carolina, Columbia, professor of law, 1975—, dean of School of Law, 1977—. National Conference of Commissioners on Uniform State Laws, commissioner from Ohio, 1968-75, commissioner from South Carolina, 1977—; chairman of legislation committee, Governor's Advisory Council on International Trade, 1972-75. Reporter, U.S. Commission on Civil Rights, 1962-64. Military service: U.S. Naval Reserve, 1952-55; became lieutenant. Member: American Bar Association (member of council, antitrust section, 1970-73; secretary, 1973-75).

WRITINGS: The Intensified Course in Antitrust Law, Ohio Legal Center Institute, 1970, 3rd edition, 1974. Antitrust Bulletin, book review editor, 1968-72, member of advisory board, 1972—; member of research staff, Idea, 1971-73; member of advisory board, Antitrust and Trade Regulation Report, 1973-76, and Journal of Reprints for Antitrust Law and Economics, 1974—.

* * *

DAY, Stacey B(iswas) 1927-

PERSONAL: Born December 31, 1927, in London, England; son of Satis Biswas (a barrister) and Emma Lenora (Camp) Day; married Noor Kassim Kanji (a microbiologist), March 17, 1952 (divorced, 1969); married Nasreen Y. Fazalbhoy (a psychologist), June 7, 1970 (divorced, 1973); married Ivana Podvalova (a research pharmacologist), October 18, 1973; children: (first marriage) Kahlil Amyn, Selim Mahommed. Education: Royal College of Surgeons in Ireland, M.D., 1955; McGill University, Ph.D., 1964; University of Cincinnati, D.Sc., 1971. Politics: Democrat. Home: 6 Lomond Ave., Spring Valley, N.Y. 10977. Agent: Robert Feher, c/o Cultural and Educational Productions, 310 Craig St. E., Montreal, Quebec, Canada. Office: Department of Biosciences Communications, Sloan-Kettering Institute, 1275 York Ave., New York, N.Y. 10021.

CAREER: University of Minnesota Hosptials, Minneapolis, surgeon, 1956-60; St. George's Hospital, London, England, honorary clinical assistant in surgery, 1960-61; McGill University, Montreal, Quebec, surgeon in Experimental Division, 1961-65; Hoffman La Roche (pharmaceutical manufacturer), Nutley, N.J., medical director for New England, 1966-68; Shriners Hospital Burns Institute, Cincinnati, Ohio, associate director of basic medical research, 1969-70; University of Minnesota, Minneapolis, conservator, Bell Museum of Pathobiology, associate professor in pathology department, assistant professor of research surgery, Medical School, 1971-73; Cornell University, School of Medical Sciences, New York, N.Y., professor of biology in Sloan-Kettering Division, member and director of biomedical communication and medical education at Sloan-Kettering Institute for Cancer Research, 1974—. Canadian Heart Association, research associate, 1964-66, senior research associate, 1966-67. Arris and Gale Lecturer, Royal College of Surgeons, England, 1971. Visiting professor at Royal College of Surgeons in Ireland, Dublin, 1972, Oncologic Research Institute, 1976, National Academy of Science, 1976; visiting professor and distinguished lecturer, University of Bologna, 1977. Exchange scientist to the Soviet Union for the National Cancer Institute, 1976. Director and vice-president for research and American scientific affairs, Mario Negri Foundation, New York, N.Y., 1974—; director, Cultural and Educational Productions Publishing,

Montreal, Quebec. Former president, India League, Dublin, Ireland; broadcaster and contributor to All India Radio, New Delhi and Calcutta, and Indian statesman. Consulting editor, Van Nostrand, Reinhold Co.; consultant, Charles Scribner's, Sons, Cincinnati Zoological Society, 1969-71, Plenum Publishing Corp., and Pan American Health Organization, 1974. *Military service:* British Army, 1946-49; served in Royal Army Educational Corps.

MEMBER: World Academy of Arts and Sciences (fellow), Society of Pharmacological and Environmental Pathologists, American Association for the Advancement of Science, American Academy of Political and Social Science, American Anthropological Association, International Communication Association, American Cybernetics Society, Zoological Society of London (fellow, 1956—), Royal Microscopical Society (fellow, 1955—), Royal Society of Health (fellow), Harvey Society, American Burns Association, International Society for Burn Injuries (Edinburgh) Candian Authors Association, New York Academy of Sciences, New York Historical Society, Bombay Society of Natural History, Sigma Xi; other medical and non-medical societies and clubs in America and abroad. *Awards, honors:* Royal College of Surgeons in Ireland, first prize and silver medal in biology, 1950, silver medal for best scientific paper of academic year (Biological Society), 1953 and 1954; Triennial Reuben Harvey Memorial Prize and Medal, 1957; second prize in clinical surgery, St. Laurence's Richmond Hospital, Dublin, 1955; Moynihan Prize and Medal, Association of Surgeons of Great Britain and Ireland, 1960; Ciba fellow in Canada, 1963; University of Minnesota, Bell Museum of Pathobiology, Gold Key, 1973. Fellowships from Minnesota Heart Association, 1958-59. American Heart Association, 1959-60, American Cancer Society 1961-62, Canadian Defense Board, 1962-63, Canadian Heart Association, 1964-66, 1966, and other organizations.

WRITINGS—Technical: *The Idle Thoughts of a Surgical Fellow: With an Account of Experimental Surgical Studies, 1956-1966,* Cultural and Educational Productions, 1968; *Gastric Physiologist: Physician and American Statesman,* Cultural and Educational Productions, 1969; *Curling's Ulcer: An Experiment of Nature,* C. C Thomas, 1971; (editor) *Death and Attitudes toward Death,* Bell Museum of Pathobiology Publication, 1972; (editor with Robert A. Good) *Membranes Viruses and Immune Mechanisms in Experimental and Clinical Diseases,* Academic Press, 1972; (editor with Good) *Bulletins of the Bell Museum of Pathobiology,* four volumes, University of Minnesota Medical School, 1972; (author of introduction) Joseph Black, *De Humore Acido a Cibis orto: Et Magnesia Alba,* Bell Museum of Pathobiology Publication, 1973; (editor) *Ethics in Medicine in a Changing Society,* Bell Museum of Pathobiology Publication, 1973; (editor with Good and Ellis S. Benson) *Miscellaneous Papers of the Bell Museum of Pathobiology,* University of Minnesota Medical School, 1973; *Tuluak and Amaulik: Dialogues on Death and Mourning with the Inuit Eskimo of Point Barrow and Wainwright, Alaska,* Bell Museum of Pathobiology Publication, 1974; (editor with Good and J. Yunis) *Molecular Pathology,* C. C Thomas, 1975; (editor) *Trauma: Clinical and Biological Aspects,* Plenum Corp., 1975; (editor) *Communication of Scientific Information,* S. Karger, 1975; (editor with W. P. Myers, W. P. Laird, P. Stansley, S. Garattini, and M. C. Lewis) *Cancer Invasion and Metastasis: Biologic Mechanisms and Therapy,* Raven Press, 1976; (with Good) *Comprehensive Immunology,* Plenum Corp. in press.

Other; all published by Cultural and Educational Produc-

tions, except as indicated: *Collected Lines* (verse), 1966; *By the Waters of Babylon* (four-act play), 1966; *East of West* (three-act play), 1967; *American Lines* (verse), 1967; *The Music Box* (three-act play), 1967; *Poems and Etudes* (verse), 1968; *Rosalita* (novella), 1968; *Three-One Act Plays for Reading: Presenting Portland en Passant, The Cricket Cage, and Little Boy on a Red Horse,* 1968; *Bellechasse* (novella), 1970; *Ten Poems and a Letter from America for Mr. Sinha,* 1971; (author of introduction) George Dahl, *Of Physicians and Fairies,* 1973; (contributor) Louis Safer, editor, *The Broken Glass Factory,* University of Minnesota, 1974. Also author of *East of the Navel and Afterbirth: Reflections and Song Poetry from Rapa Nui.*

WORK IN PROGRESS: Immunologic Words and Phrases, a short dictionary; *Comprehensive Immunology,* for Plenum Corp.; studies in biosciences communications with special emphasis upon interdisciplinary methodologies.

SIDELIGHTS: Stacey Day is a poet-playwright-surgeon-philosopher who "feels that man should not follow a career or profession to the point of boredom," according to a writer for the Montreal *Weekly Post.* Medical writer and journalist Walter C. Alvarez considers him "one of the most remarkable physicians of today . . . [with] a great flair for doing splendid literary research. . . . His *The Idle Thoughts of a Surgical Fellow,* an account of experimental surgical studies carried out from 1956 to 1966, is a remarkable book." Born in England of an English mother and Indian father, Day has traveled widely in Europe, Africa, India, Pakistan, and North America. Calling himself a "perspective humanitarian," Day told *CA* he is especially interested in the region between Europe and Asia, feudal economies coping with advanced technological societies, and the social, moral, and health problems of indigent inhabitants. His medical writings include studies on heart and circulatory disease and on the extinct Irish elk; as poet and philosopher he has studied the American hippie subculture, appeared on radio and television programs, and given poetry readings in Africa, India, England, Canada, and the United States. His novella, *Rosalita,* is described as "a post-Ulysses Joycean psychoanalytic treatment of the generation gap and contemporary hip living." "I'm fascinated by contrasts," Day told a *Los Angeles Times* reporter. "Old, new, East, West. . . . The West is an external society, while the East is internal, more spiritual. . . . We must try to understand each other." Day continues, "I have tried to assimilate things of goodness from many cultures and to bring about synthesis of these expressions to my own life and writings."

BIOGRAPHICAL/CRITICAL SOURCES: Weekly Post (Montreal), September 7, 1967; *Los Angeles Times,* September 19, 1967; *Cincinnati Enquirer,* November 26, 1967; *East African Standard* (Nairobi), February, 1968; *Ananda Bazar Patrika* (Calcutta), March, 1968; *Gastroenterology,* Number 6, 1969.

* * *

DAY LEWIS, C(ecil) 1904-1972
(Nicholas Blake)

April 17, 1904—May 22, 1972; British poet, essayist, novelist, editor, literary critic, and translator. Obituaries: *New York Times,* May 23, 1972; *Washington Post,* May 23, 1972; *L'Express,* May 29-June 4, 1972; *Newsweek,* June 6, 1972; *Time,* June 5, 1972. (See index for *CA* sketch)

* * *

DEAK, Francis 1899-1972

March 5, 1899—January 21, 1972; Hungarian-born American educator, diplomatic advisor, and authority on international law. Obituaries: *New York Times,* January 23, 1972; *Publishers Weekly,* February 28, 1972.

*   *   *

DEAN, Joel 1906-

PERSONAL: Born October 5, 1906, in Vershire, Vt.; son of Benjamin A. (a clergyman) and Eloise (Partridge) Dean; married Phyllis Van Dyk, June 24, 1939 (deceased); children: Joel, Jr., Gretchen, Gillian, Jurrien. *Education:* Pomona College, A.B., 1927; Harvard University, M.B.A., 1929; University of Chicago, Ph.D., 1936. *Home and office:* 14 Hopke Ave., Hastings-on-Hudson, N.Y. 10706.

CAREER: International Business Machines Corp., New York City, salesman, 1930-32; Indiana University, Bloomington, acting assistant professor, 1934, assistant professor of economics, 1934-39; University of Chicago, Chicago, Ill., assistant professor of economics and director of Institute of Statistics, 1939-45; Joel Dean Associates, Inc., Hastings-on-Hudson, N.Y., president, 1940—; Columbia University, New York City, professor of business economics, 1945-70, professor emeritus, 1970—. Visiting fellow, St. Catherine's College, Oxford University, and Oxford Center for Management Studies, 1970. Executive secretary, Conference on Price Research, National Bureau for Economic Research, 1938-39; research associate, Cowles Commission, 1939-45; director of fuel rationing, Office of Price Administration, 1941-44. Director of General Precision Equipment Corp., One William Street Fund, Amerace Corp., and Bureau of University Travel. President, Joel Dean Foundation, beginning 1955.

MEMBER: National Association of Business Economists (fellow), American Economic Association, American Marketing Association, Royal Society of Arts, Century Association. *Awards, honors:* Book of the year award, American Finance Association, 1952, for *Managerial Economics;* honorary doctorates from University of Stockholm, 1959, Pace College (now University), 1964, and University of Torino, 1965; Converse Award, American Marketing Association, 1959; Alpha Kappa Psi award, 1966.

WRITINGS: Statistical Determination of Costs, University of Chicago Press, 1936; *Statistical Cost Functions of a Hosiery Mill,* University of Chicago Press, 1941; (with R. W. James) *Long-Run Behavior of Costs in a Chain of Shoe Stores,* University of Chicago Press, 1942; (with others) *Costs Behavior and Price Policy,* National Bureau of Economic Research, 1943; *Capital Budgeting,* Columbia University Press, 1951; *Managerial Economics,* Prentice-Hall, 1951; *Management of Capital Expenditures* (booklet; J. Anderson Fitzgerald Lectures), College of Business Administration, University of Texas, 1960; *New Methods of Measuring the Productivity of Corporate Capital Investments,* Annual Conference on Financial Administration, Graduate School of Business Administration, New York University, 1962; (with others) *Management Sciences in the Emerging Countries,* Pergamon, 1965; *Evaluation of Industrial Projects,* United Nations, 1968; *Financial Planning of Industrial Projects,* United Nations, 1968; (with others) *Measuring the Investment Performance of Pension Funds,* Bank Administration Institute, 1968; *Conglomerate Mergers,* St. Johns Law Review, 1970; (compiler) *Readings in the Social Control of Industry,* American Economic Association, 1973; *Statistical Cost Estimation,* Indiana University Press, 1977.

Contributor: *Handbook of Wage and Salary Administra-*

tion, American Management Association, 1950; David Solomons, editor, *Studies in Costing,* Sweet & Maxwell, 1952; Wyman P. Fiske and John A. Beckett, editors, *Industrial Accountant's Handbook,* Prentice-Hall, 1954; William Grant Ireson and Eugene L. Grant, editors, *Handbook of Industrial Engineering and Management,* Prentice-Hall, 1955, 2nd edition, 1971; *Federal Tax Policy for Economic Growth and Stability,* Joint Committee on the Economic Report (Washington, D.C.), 1955; Eugene J. Kelley and William Lazare, editors, *Managerial Marketing: Perspectives and Viewpoints,* Irwin, 1958, revised edition published as *Managerial Marketing: Policies, Strategies, and Decisions,* 1973.

Pricing—The Critical Decision, American Management Association, 1961; *Report to Management 5,* Graduate School of Business Administration, University of Southern California, 1962; Thomas L. Whisler and Shirley Harper, editors, *Performance Appraisal: Research and Practice,* Holt, 1962; John O'Donnell and Milton Goldberg, editors, *Elements of Financial Administration,* C. E. Merrill, 1962; W. T. Baxter and S. Davidson, editors, *Studies in Accounting Theory,* Sweet & Maxwell, 1962; Arthur Kroeger, Lawrence C. Lockley, and Charles J. Dirksen, editors, *Readings in Marketing,* Irwin, 1963; Schuyler F. Otteson, William G. Panschar, and James M. Patterson, editors, *Marketing Management: Text and Readings,* Macmillan, 1963; S. H. Britt and H. W. Boyd, editors, *Marketing Management and Administrative Action,* McGraw, 1963; C. T. Devine, editor, *Readings in Accounting Theory,* Universitas Indonesia, 1963; Francis J. Corrigan and Howard A. Ward, editors, *Financial Management: Policies and Practices,* Houghton, 1963; Steven J. Shaw and C. McFerron Gittinger, editors, *Marketing in Business Management,* Macmillan, 1963; Sidney Davidson, David Green, Charles Horngren, and George Sorter, editors, *An Income Approach to Accounting Theory: Readings and Questions,* Prentice-Hall, 1963; R. Cox and W. Alderson, editors, *Theory of Marketing,* Irwin, 1964; J. D. Blazouke, editor, *Readings in Controllership,* General Accounts Association, University of British Columbia, 1964; M. C. Kapoor and H. W. Boyd, editors, *Readings in Marketing Management,* Asia Publishing Co., 1964; V. P. Diatchenko and J. T. Dunlop, editors, *Conference on Labor Productivity,* McGraw, 1964; J. B. Matthews, R. E. Frank, T. Levitt, and R. D. Buzzell, editors, *Marketing: An Introductory Analysis,* McGraw, 1964; Kenneth P. Uhl, editor, *Introduction to Marketing,* State University of Iowa Press, 1964; Edward C. Bursk and John F. Chapman, editors, *Modern Marketing Strategy,* Harvard University Press, 1964; R. S. Hancock and R. J. Halloway, editors, *The Environment of Marketing Behavior,* Wiley, 1964, 2nd edition, 1969.

K. M. Ruppenthal, editor, *Issues in Transportation,* C. E. Merrill, 1965; Perry Bliss, editor, *Readings in the Behavioral Sciences and Marketing,* Allyn & Bacon, 1966; Edwin Mansfield, editor, *Managerial Economics and Operations Research,* Norton, 1966, 3rd edition, 1975; William Alberts and Joel Segall, editors, *The Corporate Merger,* University of Chicago Press, 1966; H. B. Maynard, editor, *Handbook of Business Administration,* McGraw, 1967; Lee Adler, *Plotting Marketing Strategy,* Simon & Schuster, 1967; Stewart H. Rewoldt and others, editors, *Introduction to Marketing Management: Text and Cases,* Irwin, 1969, 3rd edition, 1977; William R. Lamone and Rudolph P. Darden, editors, *Perspectives in Theory, Systems and Operations Research in Marketing,* Irwin, 1969; Victor P. Buell, editor, *Handbook of Modern Marketing,* McGraw, 1970; Edwin

Mansfield, editor, *Elementary Economic and Business Statistics: Readings and Cases,* University of Chicago Press, 1970.

Contributor to numerous periodicals, including *Journal of Industrial Economics, Journal of Marketing, New York University Law Review, Harvard Business Review, Financial Analysis Journal,* and *Journal of Business.*

SIDELIGHTS: Joel Dean's *Managerial Economics* has been published in French, Spanish, and Portuguese.

* * *

DEARDEN, James A(rthur)   1924-1976

PERSONAL: Born April 10, 1924, in Salford, England; son of James Edward and Florrie (Wilson) Dearden; married Audrey Sykes (a private secretary), June 11, 1949; children: Heather Jane. *Education:* Manchester School of Librarianship, A.L.A., 1948, F.L.A., 1956; University College, London, M.A., 1970. *Home:* Bryntyrnol, Machynlleth, Wales. *Office:* Department of Bibliographical Studies, College of Librarianship Wales, Aberystwyth, Wales.

CAREER: John Rylands Library, Manchester, England, assistant librarian, 1940-43; Manchester Public Libraries, Manchester, assistant librarian, 1947-51; Lancashire County Libraries, Lancashire, England, area librarian, 1951-59; College of Technology, Reading, England, librarian, 1959-63; College of Technology, Southampton, England, librarian-tutor, 1963-66; College of Librarianship Wales, Aberystwyth, principal lecturer in department of bibliographical studies, beginning 1966. Assistant examiner, Library Association of Great Britain, 1963-70. *Military service:* British Army, Artillery, 1943-47. *Member:* Library Association, Printing Historical Society.

WRITINGS: Books Are for People: A Librarian's Life, foreword by George Chandler, Educational Explorers, 1969. Contributor to library journals.

WORK IN PROGRESS: History of modern type design.

AVOCATIONAL INTERESTS: Book collecting, photography, gardening, cultivating cacti.†

(Died August, 1976)

* * *

DEARDEN, John   1919-

PERSONAL: Born November 19, 1919, in Lancashire, England; came to United States in 1924; naturalized in 1933; son of Ernest (a machinist) and Florence (Curwen) Dearden; married Helen Marie Borden, June 24, 1945; children: John Curwen, Robert George, Thomas Allen, Rachel Guerin, Ruth Anne. *Education:* American International College, A.B., 1945; University of Pennsylvania, M.B.A., 1946, additional graduate study, 1947-49. *Home:* 33 Summit Rd., Lexington, Mass. 02173. *Office:* Morgan Hall, Soldiers Field, Boston, Mass. 02163.

CAREER: Certified public accountant, 1948—; University of Pennsylvania, Philadelphia, instructor in accounting, 1947-49; Ford Motor Co., Dearborn, Mich., manager of financial systems department, 1949-59; Harvard University, Graduate School of Business Administration, Boston, Mass., faculty member, 1959—, professor of business administration, 1964—. *Military service:* U.S. Naval Reserve, active duty, 1943-46; became petty officer second class. *Member:* Financial Executives Institute, American Accounting Association, American Institute of Certified Public Accountants. *Awards, honors:* M.A., Harvard University,

1964; Fiftieth Anniversary Award, Wharton School of Finance and Commerce, for outstanding contribution to education.

WRITINGS: (With Robert N. Anthony) *Cases and Problems in Management Accounting,* Irwin, 1962; *Cost and Budget Analysis,* Prentice-Hall, 1962; (with Anthony and Richard F. Vancil) *Management Control Systems,* Irwin, 1965, 3rd edition (with Anthony), 1976; (with F. W. McFarlan) *Management Information Systems,* Irwin, 1966; *Computers in Business Management,* Dow Jones-Irwin, 1966; (contributor) Charles A. Myers, editor, *The Impact of Computers on Management,* M.I.T. Press, 1967; *Essentials of Cost Accounting,* Addison-Wesley, 1968; (with McFarlan and W. M. Zani) *Managing Computer-Based Information Systems,* Irwin, 1971; (with Edward C. Bursk, David F. Hawkins, and Victor M. Longstreet) *Financial Control of Multinational Operations,* Financial Executives Institute, 1971; *Cost Accounting and Financial Control Systems,* Addison-Wesley, 1973; (with John Shank) *Financial Accounting and Reporting: A Contemporary Emphasis,* Prentice-Hall, 1975; (with S. K. Bhattacharyya) *Accounting for Management,* Vikas Publishing House (India), 1976. Contributor of about thirty articles and reviews to business journals in the United States, Europe, and Asia.

* * *

DEBRECZENY, Paul   1932-

PERSONAL: Surname is pronounced *Deb*-bret-sen-ee; born February 16, 1932, in Budapest, Hungary; came to United States in 1960, naturalized in 1966; son of Zsigmond (a statistician) and Margit (Csanady) Debreczeny; married Gillian M. Butterworth, October 30, 1959; children: Louise, Martin. *Education:* Eotvos University of Budapest, B.A. in Russian language and literature, 1953, B.A. in Hungarian language and literature, 1955; University of London, Ph.D., 1960. *Politics:* Democrat. *Home:* 304 Hoot Owl Lane, Chapel Hill, N.C. 27514. *Office:* Department of Slavic Languages, University of North Carolina, Chapel Hill, N.C. 27514.

CAREER: Institute of Literature, Hungarian Academy of Sciences, Budapest, Hungary, research fellow, 1955-56; Pergamon Press, Oxford, England, translation editor, 1959-60; Tulane University, New Orleans, La., assistant professor, 1960-66, associate professor of Russian, 1966-67; University of North Carolina at Chapel Hill, associate professor, 1967-74, professor of Russian and chairman of department, 1974—. *Member:* Modern Language Association of America, American Association of Teachers of Slavic and East European Languages, American Association for the Advancement of Slavic Studies. *Awards, honors:* Summer research grants from American Philosophical Society, Tulane University, and University of North Carolina; awarded key to city of New Orleans, 1967; International Research and Exchanges Board research grant, 1973.

WRITINGS: Nikolay Gogol and His Contemporary Critics, American Philosophical Society, 1966; (editor and translator with Jesse Zeldin) *Literature and National Identity: Nineteenth-Century Russian Critical Essays,* University of Nebraska Press, 1970; (editor with Thomas Eekman) *Chekhov's Art of Writing: A Collection of Critical Essays,* Slavica, 1977. Guest editor for two special issues on Pushkin, *Canadian-American Slavic Studies,* summer, 1976, spring, 1977.

WORK IN PROGRESS: A critical study of Alexander Pushkin's prose fiction.

De CASTRO, Josue   1908-1973

PERSONAL: Born September 5, 1908, in Recife, Brazil; son of Manoel Apolonio and Josefa (Barboza) De Castro; married Glauce Pinto, April 11, 1934; children: Fernando, Ana-Maria, Sonia. *Education:* University of Brazil (now Federal University of Rio de Janeiro), Doctor of Medicine, 1929, Doctor in Philosophy, 1930; postgraduate study in the United States. *Home:* Rua Ministro Viveiros de Castra 126, 2000 Rio de Janeiro ZC.07 Brazil. *Agent:* Sanford Jerome Greenburger Associates, 825 Third Ave., New York, N.Y. 10022.

CAREER: Head of Brazilian Students Commission visiting Mexico, 1930; University of Recife, Recife, Brazil, assistant professor of philosophy, College of Medicine, 1932, vice-director, faculty of philosophy, 1933-35; University of Brazil (now Federal University of Rio de Janeiro), Rio de Janeiro, professor of anthropology and director of Institute of Nutrition, 1933-38, professor of human geography, School of Physiology, 1935-38, and School of Sciences and Philosophy, 1939-68; University of Paris, VIII, Paris, France, professor of bio-geography and ecology, 1968-73. Head of National Technical Bureau on Food, department coordinating food problems in Brazil during World War II, 1942-44; member of National Congress of Brazil, 1955-63; president of National Commission for Social Welfare, Brazil, and chairman of council, Food and Agriculture Organization of the United Nations, Rome, Italy, 1952-56; chairman, Governmental Committee of the Freedom from Hunger Campaign, United Nations Organization, 1960; Brazilian ambassador to European office of the United Nations, Geneva, Switzerland, 1962-64; head of Brazilian delegation to the Disarmament Conference, Geneva, 1962-64; chairman, Council of the Intergovernmental Committee for European Migrations, 1963-73. Chairman, International Development Centre, Paris, 1964-73.

MEMBER: World Association of Struggle Against Hunger (president), World Parliament Association (vice-chairman), World Academy of Art and Science, World Constitutional Convention (Denver, Colo.), Academy of Medical Science (U.S.S.R.), International Medical Association for the Study of Life and Health (president). Honorary member of numerous international scientific organizations and academies. *Awards, honors:* American Library Association notable book selection, 1952, and Franklin D. Roosevelt Award, American Academy of Political Science, 1953, for *Geography of Hunger;* International Award of Peace, World Peace Council, 1954; Great Medal of the City of Paris; Officer of the Legion of Honor (France); Grand-Croix du Merite Medical (Brazil); Professor Honoris Causa, University of Santo Domingo, 1945, University of San Marcos, Lima, Peru, 1946, and Universidad Nacional de Ingenierja, Lima, Peru, 1965.

WRITINGS: O Problema da alimentacao no Brasil, Companhia Editora Nacional (Sao Paulo), 1933; *A Questao do salario minimo,* Departamento de Estatistica e Publicidade (Rio de Janeiro), 1935; *Alimentacao e raca,* Civilizacao Brasileira (Rio de Janeiro), 1936; *Documentario do nordeste* (includes "Documentario do nordeste," "Motivos sociais," and "Valores humanos"), J. Olympio (Rio de Janeiro), 1937, 3rd edition, Brasiliense (Sao Paulo), 1965; *A Alimentacao brasileira a luz da geografia humana,* Livraria do Globo (Porto Alegre), 1937; *Science et technique,* Ministerio da Educacao e Saude (Rio de Janeiro), 1937; *Geografia humana: Estudo da paisagem cultural do mundo,* Livraria do Globo, 1939; *Alimentazione e acclimatazione umana nei tropici* (originally written in Portuguese but published in Italian), Edite dall'instituto Biochimico Italiano (Rome), c.1939; *Geografia da fome: A Fome no Brasil* (title means "Geography of Hunger: Hunger in Brazil"; see *Sidelights* below), O Cruzeiro (Rio de Janeiro), 1946, 8th edition (subsequent editions published with varying subtitles), Brasiliense, 1963, translation by George Reed of greatly expanded version published as *Geography of Hunger* (study of world hunger and politics), foreword by Lord John Boyd-Orr, Little, Brown, 1952, Portuguese edition of expanded version published as *Geopolitica da fome: Ensaio sobre os problemas de alimentacao e de populacao do mundo,* Editora Brasiliense, 1957, 6th edition, 1961, translation published as *Geopolitics of Hunger,* Monthly Review Press, 1977; *Fatores de localizacao da cidade do Recife: Um Ensaio de geografia urbana,* Imprensa Nacional (Rio de Janeiro), 1948.

Le Probleme de l'alimentation en Amerique du Sud, published for UNESCO by Dunod (Paris), 1950; *A Cidade do Recife: Ensaio de geografia urbana,* Estudante do Brasil (Rio de Janeiro), 1954; *Ensaios de geografia humana,* Brasiliense, 1954, 5th edtion, 1969; *Ensaios de biologia social,* Brasiliense, 1956, 3rd edition, 1965; *Le Livre noir de la faim* (originally written in Portuguese but published in French), Editions Ouvrieres, Economie et Humanisme, 1958, translation from the Portuguese by Charles Lann Markmann published as *The Black Book of Hunger,* Beacon Press, 1967, Funk, 1968; *Homens e caranguejos* (novel), Brasiliense, 1958, published as *O Ciclo do caranguejo,* Brasilia Editora, 1966, translation by Susan Hertelendy published as *Of Men and Crabs,* Vanguard, 1971; (editor) *Hunger and Food* (published as special issue of *Science and Mankind,* Number 1, 1958), World Federation of Scientific Workers, 1958.

Sete palmos de terra e um caixao: Ensaio sobre o Nordeste, area explosiva, Brasiliense, 1965, 2nd edition, 1967, translation published as *Death in the Northeast,* Random House, 1966; (contributor) *Ou en est revolution en Amerique latine?: Debat public entre Claude Julien, Josue de Castro, Juan Arcocha, Mario Vargas Llosa,* Cahiers du Centre d'Etudes Socialistes (Paris), 1965; *Adonde va la America Latina?: Dinamica del desarrallo, cambios y resistencias sociales,* Editorial Latinoamericana (Lima), 1966; (editor with John Gerassi and Irving Louis Horowitz) *Latin American Radicalism: A Documentary Report on Left and Nationalist Movements,* Random House, 1968; *El Hambre: Problema universal,* Editorial la Pleyade, 1969; *O Drama do terceiro mundo,* Publicacoes Dom Quixote, 1970; (with others) *O Brasil na encruzilhada,* Publicacoes Dom Quixote, 1970; (with others) *A China e o Ocidente,* Cadernos do Seculo, 1971; (with others) *America latina y los problemas del desarrollo,* Monte Avila Editores, 1974. Author of articles for numerous newspapers, journals, and television programs; contributor to *Collier's, Reader's Digest Catholic, Constellation* (France), and other periodicals.

WORK IN PROGRESS: A book, tentatively entitled *Survive or Perish Together.*

SIDELIGHTS: Josue De Castro's books have been translated into 24 languages. He estimated that 400 to 600 articles on him and his work have appeared in journals and periodicals the world over; a large percentage of these focused on *Geography of Hunger,* hailed by many as one of the most significant books on world hunger and poverty ever written. Published in the United States in 1952, it was called by Pearl Buck "the most important book that has been written in these confused, dangerous and ridiculous times of ours. . . . De Castro, the great nutritionist, . . . proves that hunger is a man-made plague."

This famous book began as a study of hunger in Brazil. As De Castro's wife recently told *CA*, ''the author at that time intended to write other volumes applying the same method of analysis to various areas of hunger in the world.'' Instead, he condensed the work on Brazil and added ''a study of the multiple forms of hunger in the world with its political implications and repercussions,'' she explained. In his review of *Geography of Hunger,* Jonathan N. Leonard said: ''The best thing in De Castro's book is this recognition that most of the world's hunger is of social origin and therefore under man's control. The worst thing is his naive and complacent notion that nature, unaided by man and in spite of man, will check automatically the increase of a well-fed population.'' In its obituary, the *New York Times* credited De Castro as ''the first to draw attention to the growing disparity in revenue between the industrialized and the underdeveloped countries.''

His novel, *Homens e caranguejos,* was adapted for the theatre by Gabrile Cousin and published in French as a three-act play entitled *Le Cycle du crabe; ou, Les Aventures de Ze-Luis, Maria et leurs fils Joao,* Gallimard, 1969.

BIOGRAPHICAL/CRITICAL SOURCES: Paris Normandie, February, 1951, October 21, 1966; *Book Find News,* Issue 119; *Yorkshire Observer,* February 7, 1952; *London Times,* February 9, 1952; *Southern Daily Echo,* February 25, 1952; *New York Herald Tribune,* March 2, 1952, May 11, 1952; *New York Times Book Review,* March 9, 1952, October 16, 1966, January 17, 1971, June 6, 1971; *New Republic,* April 7, 1952; *America,* April 12, 1952, December 17, 1966, May 6, 1967; *Defense de l'Homme,* January, 1953; *International Labor Review,* July, 1966; *New Leader,* April 28, 1969; *Nation,* March 3, 1969; *Saturday Review,* June 7, 1969, December 26, 1970; *Atlantic,* October, 1970; *Commonweal,* December 3, 1971; *New York Times,* September 25, 1973.†

(Died September 24, 1973)

* * *

DeCROW, Karen 1937-

PERSONAL: Born December 18, 1937, in Chicago, Ill.; daughter of Samuel Meyer (a businessman) and Juliette (a ballet dancer; maiden name, Abt) Lipschultz; married Alexander Kolben, December 15, 1960 (divorced, 1965); married Roger DeCrow, August 27, 1965 (divorced, 1972). *Education:* Northwestern University, B.S., 1959; Syracuse University, graduate study in journalism, 1967-68, J.D., 1972. *Home:* 116 Benedict Ave., Syracuse, N.Y. 13210. *Agent:* (Literary) Elaine Markson, 44 Greenwich Ave., New York, N.Y. 10011.

CAREER: Golf Digest, Norwalk, Conn., fashion editor, 1959-60; *Zoning Digest* (monthly magazine of American Society of Planning Officials), Chicago, Ill., editor, 1960-61; Center for the Study of Liberal Education of Adults, Chicago, writer and editor, 1961-64; Holt, Rinehart & Winston, Inc., New York City, social studies and adult education editor, 1965; L. W. Singer Co., Inc., New York City, social science editor, 1965-66; Eastern Regional Institute for Education, Syracuse, N.Y., writer, 1967-69; National Organization for Women, Washington, D.C., former Eastern regional director and political chairwoman, national board member, 1968-77, president, 1974-77; admitted to New York State Bar, 1974. Liberal Party candidate for mayor of Syracuse, 1969; speaker at World Congress of Women, Helsinki, 1969, and Moscow, 1975; national coordinator of Women's Strike for Equality, 1970. Consultant on affirmative action, sexism

in the law, and images of women and men in media; lecturer throughout the country; guest on ''Today Show,'' ''Monitor,'' and other network television and radio programs; also has been on radio shows in Europe, Japan, and Canada. *Member:* National Organization for Women, National Women's Political Caucus, Ad Hoc Committee of Women for Human Rights, Working Women United (member of board of advisors), Gay Rights National Lobby (national board member), Onondaga County Bar Association, American Civil Liberties Union, Theta Sigma Phi. *Awards, honors:* Selected by *Time* magazine as one of 200 future leaders of America, 1974, and by Newspaper Enterprise Association as one of fifty most influential women in America, 1975.

WRITINGS: (With Roger DeCrow) *University Adult Education: A Selected Bibliography,* American Council on Education, 1967; (editor) Howard Osofsky, *The Pregnant Teenager,* C. C Thomas, 1968; *The Young Woman's Guide to Liberation,* Bobbs-Merrill, 1971; (editor) Robert Seidenberg, *Corporate Wives, Corporate Casualties,* American Management Association, 1973; *Sexist Justice,* Random House, 1974. Author of columns and editorials, *Do It NOW,* 1974-77. Contributor to *Mademoiselle, Adult Leadership, Judge, Life, Ingenue,* and other periodicals.

WORK IN PROGRESS: A journal on her 1976 visit to The People's Republic of China.

SIDELIGHTS: Karen DeCrow's *Sexist Justice* is an account of discrimination against women in the law. *Atlantic* reviewer Phoebe Adams writes: ''Ms. DeCrow is a lawyer and well equipped to pin down, case by case and statute by statute, the misogyny which permeates both the structure and the application of our laws. She does it clearly, with a minimum of ill temper, and a decent consideration of the historical roots of the situation. This is valuable reading both for feminine activists and for those who still wonder what the girls are complaining about.''

BIOGRAPHICAL/CRITICAL SOURCES: Best Sellers, July 1, 1971; *Atlantic,* March, 1974; *Psychology Today,* June, 1974.

* * *

DEDEK, John F. 1929-

PERSONAL: Born September 20, 1929, in Chicago, Ill.; son of John P. and Anne E. (McDonald) Dedek. *Education:* St. Mary of the Lake Seminary, B.A., 1951, M.A., 1953; Pontifical University of St. Mary of the Lake, S.T.B., 1953, S.T.L., 1955, S.T.D., 1958. *Office:* Pontifical University of St. Mary of the Lake, Mundelein, Ill. 60060.

CAREER: Roman Catholic priest; St. Gilbert Church, Grayslake, Ill., associate pastor, 1958-65; Pontifical University of St. Mary of the Lake, Mundelein, Ill., professor of moral theology, 1966—. *Member:* Catholic Theological Society of America.

WRITINGS: Experimental Knowledge of the Indwelling Trinity, St. Mary of the Lake Seminary, 1958; *Contemporary Sexual Morality,* Sheed, 1971; *Human Life: Some Moral Issues,* Sheed, 1972; *Titius and Bertha Ride Again,* Sheed, 1974; *Contemporary Medical Ethics,* Sheed, 1975. Contributor to *Proceedings* of Catholic Theological Seminary of America and *New Catholic Encyclopedia.* Contributor to *Theological Studies, Chicago Studies, McCormick Quarterly,* and other journals. Associate editor, *Chicago Studies.*

DEDINA, Michel 1933-

PERSONAL: Born April 18, 1933, in Paris, France; son of Daniel and Lotti (Seligman) Dedina; married Josephine Fournier, December 7, 1956; children: Serge, Nicholas. *Education:* Attended University of Southern California, 1969; California State College at Los Angeles (now California State University, Los Angeles), B.A., 1971; San Diego State University, M.A., 1975. *Home:* 1414 Hemlock Ave., Imperial Beach, Calif. 92032.

CAREER: Instructor in television production and film production in San Diego, Calif. Film director and screen writer; involved with film production in Central America. *Member:* National Association of Television Arts and Sciences, Society of Motion Picture and Television Engineers, Society of Authors (London), Alpha Epsilon Rho.

WRITINGS: The Harm in Trying (fiction), Muller, 1964, A. S. Barnes, 1967; *The Mink Steal* (detective fiction), Muller, 1966.

* * *

DEEDY, John 1923-

PERSONAL: Born August 17, 1923, in Worcester, Mass.; son of John G. and Grace (McDonough) Deedy; married Mary M. Noonan, April 22, 1949; children: Joan, John, Justine, Paul. *Education:* College of the Holy Cross, A.B., 1948; Trinity College, Dublin, Ireland, A.B., 1949, M.A., 1957; Institut du Pantheon, Paris, France, Certificate, 1949. *Politics:* Democrat. *Religion:* Roman Catholic. *Home:* 4 Bayard St., Larchmont, N.Y. 10538. *Office:* Commonweal, Commonweal Publishing Co., Inc., 232 Madison Ave., New York, N.Y. 10016.

CAREER: Correspondent or reporter for *Worcester Telegram, Boston Post,* and *Boston Globe,* at intervals, 1940-51; *Catholic Free Press,* Worcester, Mass., editor, 1951-59; *Pittsburgh Catholic,* Pittsburgh, Pa., editor, 1959-67; *Commonweal* (magazine), New York, N.Y., managing editor, 1967—. *Military service:* U.S. Army Air Forces, 1942-44.

WRITINGS: (With Jack Frost) *The Church in Worcester, New England,* Hawthorn, 1956; (with Martin Marty and David Silverman) *The Religious Press in America,* Holt, 1963; (editor) *Eyes on the Modern World,* Kenedy, 1965; *The Vatican* (juvenile), F. Watts, 1970; (with Philip Nobile) *The Complete Ecology Fact Book,* Doubleday, 1972; *What a Modern Catholic Believes about Conscience, Freedom and Authority,* Thomas More Press, 1972; *What a Modern Catholic Believes about the Commandments,* Thomas More Press, 1975; *Literary Places and People: New York, New England,* Sheed Andrews & McMeel, in press.

Contributor: Daniel Callahan, editor, *Federal Aid and Catholic Schools,* Helicon, 1964; Thomas Quigley, editor, *American Catholics and Vietnam,* Eerdmans, 1968; Michael McCauley, editor, *On the Run: Spirituality for the Seventies,* Thomas More Press, 1974; John J. Delaney, editor, *Saints for All Seasons,* Doubleday, in press. U.S. correspondent for *Informations Catholiques Internationales* (Paris). Contributor to *New Republic, Critic, New York Magazine, New York Times,* and other periodicals and newspapers.

WORK IN PROGRESS: A book about seven Catholics who had impact on modern American Catholic history, for Thomas More Press.

* * *

DEFORD, Frank 1938-

PERSONAL: Born December 16, 1938, in Baltimore, Md.; son of Benjamin F., Jr. (a businessman) and Louise (McAdams) Deford; married Carol Penner, August 30, 1965; children: Christian McAdams, Alexandra Miller. *Education:* Princeton University, A.B., 1962. *Politics:* Democrat. *Religion:* Episcopalian. *Address:* Box 98, Westport, Conn. 06436. *Agent:* Sterling Lord Agency, 660 Madison Ave., New York, N.Y. 10021. *Office:* Time, Inc., Time-Life Building, New York, N.Y. 10020.

CAREER: Sports Illustrated (magazine), New York, N.Y., senior writer, 1962—.

WRITINGS: There She Is: The Life and Times of Miss America, Viking, 1971; *Five Strides on the Banked Track,* Little, Brown, 1971; *Cut 'n' Run,* Viking, 1973; *Big Bill Tilder,* Simon & Schuster, 1976; *The Owner,* Viking, 1976.

* * *

de FUNIAK, William Q(uinby) 1901-

PERSONAL: Born November 16, 1901, in Birmingham, Ala.; son of Ernest and Florence (Quinby) de Funiak; married Eleanor Slater, October 30, 1932; children: Olivia, William Slater, Frederick. *Education:* University of Virginia, LL.B., 1924, Jur. D., 1970; University of California, Berkeley, graduate study, 1942; University of San Francisco, LL.M., 1947. *Religion:* Deist.

CAREER: Admitted to state bars of Kentucky, 1923, and California, 1933; legal editor and writer with Edward Thompson Co., 1925-26, Bancroft-Whitney Co., 1926-27, 1930-37, and American Law Book Co., 1928-29; Callaghan & Co., Chicago, Ill., assistant editor-in-chief, 1937-41; University of San Francisco, San Francisco, Calif., professor of law, 1941-66; University of the Pacific, McGeorge School of Law, Sacramento, Calif., professor of law, 1968-71. Visiting professor at Hastings College of Law, 1947, University of Edinburgh, 1963, University of London, 1963, 1965, University of Arizona, 1966-67, and Willamette University, 1967. Senior attorney, War Relocation Authority, 1942. *Military service:* U.S. Coast Guard Reserve, active duty, 1943-45; inactive service, 1946-52. *Member:* California Bar Association, Kentucky Bar Association, Prima County (Ariz.) Bar Association, Marion County (Ore.) Bar Association, Scribes.

WRITINGS: American Notary and Commissioner of Deeds Manual, 5th edition (de Funiak was not associated with earlier editions), Callaghan, 1942; *Principles of Community Property,* two volumes, Callaghan, 1943, revised edition (with M. J. Vaughn), University of Arizona Press, 1971; *Cases and Materials on Community Property,* Bobbs-Merrill, 1947, revised edition, Davis Publishing (Santa Cruz), 1969; *Questions and Answers with Problems and Illustrative Matter on Conflict of Law,* Callaghan, 1949; *Handbook of Modern Equity,* University of San Francisco Press, 1950, 3rd edition, Little, 1961; (editor) *The American-British British-American Dictionary,* privately printed, 1963, 3rd edition printed as *American-British Dictionary and Helpful Hints to Travelers,* 1967, 4th edition, A. S. Barnes, 1977; (with William A. Reppy, Jr.) *Community Property in the United States,* Bobbs-Merrill, 1975. Also author of *Cases on Equitable Relief,* two volumes, 1964-65. Co-author or editor of other legal publications, including *Callaghan's Michigan Digest,* 1941-42, and *Callaghan's Iowa Digest,* 1941. Contributor of articles and book reviews to law journals in a dozen states.

DeGROOD, David H.   1937-

PERSONAL: Born December 25, 1937, in Buffalo, N.Y.; son of Walter F. (a milkman) and Elizabeth (Lilycrop) De-Grood; married Elaine A. Tickner (an organist), 1961. *Education:* University of Buffalo (now State University of New York at Buffalo), B.A., 1960, M.A., 1961; State University of New York at Buffalo, Ph.D., 1966. *Home:* 1329 Main St., Stratford, Conn. 06497. *Office:* Department of Philosophy, University of Bridgeport, Bridgeport, Conn. 06602.

CAREER: Grocery clerk, 1954-64; State University of New York College at Oneonta, instructor in philosophy, 1964-67; University of Bridgeport, Bridgeport, Conn., assistant professor of philosophy, 1967—.

WRITINGS: Haeckel's Theory of the Unity of Nature, Christopher, 1965; *Philosophies of Essence,* Gruener, 1970, 2nd edition, 1976, Humanities, 1977; (editor) *Contemporary East European Philosophy,* six volumes, Spartacus, 1970-71; (with Dale Riepe and John Somerville) *Radical Currents in Contemporary Philosophy,* Warren Green, 1971; (with Riepe and Paul Crosser) *East-West Dialogues,* Gruener, 1973; *Consciousness and Social Life,* Gruener, 1976; *Class Consciousness and Mystification,* Warren Green, 1977; *Dialectics and Revolution,* Volume I, Humanities, 1978. Editor of book series, "Philosophical Currents," for Gruener. Editor, *Revolutionary World.*

WORK IN PROGRESS: Volume II of *Dialectics and Revolution;* research on the development of the United States; study of the origin of Marxism.

*   *   *

DEISS, Joseph Jay   1915-

PERSONAL: Surname is pronounced "dice"; born January 25, 1915, in Twin Falls, Idaho; son of Joseph John (a rancher) and Charlotte (Neilson) Deiss; married Catherine Dohoney, August 3, 1937; children: John Casy (deceased), Susanna (Mrs. Eric Chivian). *Education:* University of Texas, B.A., 1934, M.A., 1935. *Home:* Thoreau House, Wellfleet, Mass. 02667.

CAREER: U.S. Government, Washington, D.C., editor and writer, 1936-44; *Executives' War Digest,* New York City, editor, 1944-46; free-lance writer, 1947-50; Medical & Pharmaceutical Information Bureau (public relations), New York City, partner, 1950-54; free-lance writer, 1954—. Vice-director, American Academy in Rome, 1965-69; writer-in-residence, Currier House, Harvard-Radcliffe, 1975. *Member:* Authors Guild, Thoreau Society, Phi Gamma Delta. *Awards, honors:* Distinguished Alumnus Award, University of Texas, 1970; Cavalier, Order of the Star of Solidarity of Italy, 1971.

WRITINGS: A Washington Story (novel), Duell, Sloan & Pearce, 1950; *The Blue Chips* (novel), Simon & Schuster, 1957; *The Great Infidel; Frederick II of Hohenstaufen* (biographical novel), Random House, 1963; *Captains of Fortune—Profiles of Six Italian Condottieri,* Gollancz, 1966, Crowell, 1967; *Herculaneum: Italy's Buried Treasure,* Crowell, 1966; *The Roman Years of Margaret Fuller,* Crowell, 1969; *The Town of Hercules: A Buried Treasure Trove* (juvenile), Houghton, 1974. Contributor to national magazines, including *Mademoiselle, Cosmopolitan, Town and Country, Harper's, Reader's Digest, American Heritage,* and *Holiday.*

SIDELIGHTS: Deiss' books have been translated into nineteen languages. He has traveled extensively in Latin America and Europe. *Avocational interests:* Swimming, rowing, tennis.

BIOGRAPHICAL/CRITICAL SOURCES: John Bainbridge, *Another Way of Living,* Holt, 1968; *New York Times Book Review,* November 30, 1969; *Book World,* December 7, 1969, January 4, 1970; *New England Quarterly,* March, 1971; *American Literature,* May, 1970; *Virginia Quarterly Review,* summer, 1970; *American Historical Review,* December, 1970; *Psychology Today,* January, 1975; *Social Education,* March, 1975.

*   *   *

de la MARE, Albinia Catherine   1932-

PERSONAL: Born June 2, 1932, in London, England; daughter of Richard Herbert Ingpen (a publisher) and A. Catherine (Donaldson) de la Mare. *Education:* Attended Queen's College, London, 1947-51; Lady Margaret Hall, Oxford, B.A. and M.A.; Warburg Institute, London, Ph.D., 1966. *Religion:* Church of England. *Home:* 24 Kendall Crescent, Oxford OX2 8NG, England. *Office:* Department of Western Manuscripts, Bodleian Library, Oxford University, Oxford OX1 3BG, England.

CAREER: Oxford University, Bodleian Library, Oxford, England, temporary appointment, 1962-64, assistant in department of western manuscripts, 1964—. *Member:* Society for Renaissance Studies, Oxford Bibliographical Society, Society of Scribes and Illuminators (honorary member).

WRITINGS: (With Jonathan James Graham Alexander) *The Italian Manuscripts in the Library of Major J. R. Abbey,* Praeger, 1969; (with R. W. Hunt) *Duke Humfrey and English Humanism in the Fifteenth Century* (exhibition catalogue), Bodleian Library, 1970; (compiler) *Catalogue of the Collection of Medieval Manuscripts Bequeathed to the Bodleian Library by James P. R. Lyell,* Clarendon Press, 1971; *The Handwriting of Italian Humanists,* Association Internationale de Bibliophilie, 1973—. Contributor of articles on Italian humanistic manuscripts to festschrifts and to journals.

WORK IN PROGRESS: Vespasiano and the Badia of Fiesole, for Warburg Institute; collecting material for an Oxford palaeographical handbook on Italian humanistic script.

BIOGRAPHICAL/CRITICAL SOURCES: Times Literary Supplement, May 28, 1970.

*   *   *

DELASANTA, Rodney   1932-

PERSONAL: Born November 6, 1932, in Winchendon, Mass.; son of Fortunato (a weaver) and Adua (Daole) Delasanta; married Frances Thompson, June 6, 1953; children: Deborah, Lisa, Andrea, Peter. *Education:* Providence College, B.A., 1953; Brown University, M.A., 1955, Ph.D., 1962. *Politics:* Democrat. *Religion:* Roman Catholic. *Home:* 346 St. Louis Ave., Woonsocket, R.I. 02895. *Office:* Department of English, Providence College, Providence, R.I. 02918.

CAREER: Brown University, Providence, R.I., instructor in English literature, 1957-61; Providence College, Providence, assistant professor, 1961-64, associate professor, 1964-69, professor of English, 1969—, chairman of department, 1972-74. Lecturer, Catholic Teachers College, 1957-59; visiting professor at University of Fribourg and University of Neuchatel, 1968-70. President, Concordia Music Corp., 1964-70. *Member:* Modern Language Association of America, Mediaeval Academy of America, American Federation of Musicians, Phi Beta Kappa.

WRITINGS: The Epic Voice, Mouton, 1967. Contributor

to *Essays in Criticism, PMLA, Chaucer Review, Modern Language Quarterly, Studies in the Literary Imagination, Neuphilologische Mitteilungen, Neophilologus, Tennessee Studies in Literature, Texas Studies in Literature and Language, Modern Fiction Studies, Explicator, Papers in Language and Literature, Cithara,* and *Annuale Medievale.*

WORK IN PROGRESS: Chaucer's Parodic Imagination, completion expected in 1978.

* * *

DELOUGHERY, Grace L. 1933-

PERSONAL: Surname is pronounced D'Lowry; born January 17, 1933, in Dumont, Iowa; married Henry O. Deloughery (a realtor); children: Paul; (stepchildren) Michael, Kathleen. *Education:* University of Minnesota, B.S., 1955, M.P.H., 1960; Claremont Graduate School, Ph.D., 1966; additional graduate study at University of California, Riverside, 1966-67, and University of North Dakota, 1967-68.

CAREER: Minneapolis (Minn.) Health Department, staff public health nurse, 1955-59; University of Minnesota, School of Public Health, Minneapolis, research fellow in epidemiology, 1960-64; San Jacinto (Calif.) School District, nurse and community coordinator, 1966; University of North Dakota, Grand Forks, associate professor of nursing, 1967-68; University of California, Los Angeles, assistant professor in residence at School of Nursing, 1968-72; Center for Nursing Education, Spokane, Wash., dean, 1972; Winona State University, Winona, Minn., associate professor of nursing and head of department, 1974-77. Summer instructor, Riverside City College, 1966. Consultant, Veterans Administration Out-Patient Clinic, Los Angeles, Calif., 1968. Regional associate, National Commission for the Study of Nursing and Nursing Education, 1970-73.

MEMBER: American Nurses' Association, National League for Nursing, American Association for Social Psychiatry (treasurer, 1974), American Academy of Social and Political Science, American Academy of Political Science, American Public Health Association, Pi Lambda Theta. *Awards, honors:* Certificate of Award, California Educational Research and Guidance Association, 1967; American Public Health Association fellowship, 1970; American Association for Social Psychiatry fellowship, 1973.

WRITINGS: Health Insurance for Braceros under Public Law 78, University of North Dakota Press, 1968; (senior author) *Consultation and Community Organization in Community Mental Health Nursing,* Williams & Wilkins, 1971; *Political Dynamics: Their Impact on Nurses and Nursing,* Mosby, 1975; *History and Trends of Professional Nursing,* Mosby, 1977. Also author of abstracts, monographs and research reports. Contributor of articles to various journals, including about fifteen to nursing journals.

* * *

de MAUNY, Erik 1920-

PERSONAL: Surname is pronounced de Moan-ee; born September 17, 1920, in London, England; son of Lon Jules and Evelyn (Harrison) de Mauny; married Denyse Aghion, January, 1950; married second wife, Elizabeth Bower, May 4, 1970; children: (second marriage) Marc, Alix (daughter). *Education:* Attended Wellington College, Wellington, New Zealand, 1935-38, and Victoria University of Wellington, 1945-46; University of London, B.A. (honors), 1948. *Religion:* Roman Catholic. *Residence:* Yorkshire, England. *Agent:* John Wolfers, 3 Regent Sq., London W.C.1, En-

gland. *Office:* c/o British Broadcasting Corp., Broadcasting House, London W1A 1AA, England.

CAREER: British Broadcasting Corp., London, England, correspondent, 1958—; former correspondent in central and eastern Europe (including five years in Moscow), the Middle East, and United States (based in Washington, D.C.); foreign correspondent in Paris, France, 1966-72, and in Moscow, 1972-74; currently special correspondent for documentary programs based in London. *Military service:* Second New Zealand Expeditionary Force, 1940-45; became sergeant. *Awards, honors:* Denise Clairouin Prize for translation, 1960, for *A Time to Keep.*

WRITINGS: (Editor with John Waller) *Middle East Anthology,* Lindsay Drummond, 1946; (translator) Jean Paul Sartre, *Portrait of the Anti-Semite,* Secker & Warburg, 1948; *The Huntsman in His Career* (novel), Lindsay Drummond, 1949; (translator with Denyse de Mauny) Andre Dupeyrat, *Mitsinari,* Odhams Press (London), 1957; (translator) Andre Chamson, *A Time to Keep (Le Chiffre de nos jours),* Faber, 1957; (translator) Maria Le Hardouin (pseudonym of Sabine Viala), *Colette: A Biographical Study,* Staples Press (London), 1958; *Russian Prospect: Notes of a Moscow Correspondent,* Macmillan (London), 1969, Atheneum, 1970. Contributor to *Penguin New Writing, London Magazine, Encounter, Times Literary Supplement,* and other publications.

WORK IN PROGRESS: A novel, set in the Soviet Union; an autobiography; research into current developments in Soviet literature; genealogical research into Anglo-Norman connections.

AVOCATIONAL INTERESTS: Music, poetry, foreign languages.

BIOGRAPHICAL/CRITICAL SOURCES: National Observer, February 23, 1970; *New Yorker,* February 28, 1970.

* * *

De MORDAUNT, Walter J(ulius) 1925-

PERSONAL: Born August 31, 1925, in Pueblo, Colo.; son of Walter (an architect) and Fredella (Phillips) De Mordaunt; married Virginia Beach, 1954; children: Mary Ann, Jane, Michael. *Education:* University of Colorado, B.A., 1949, M.A., 1950; University of Denver, Ph.D., 1953. *Home:* 888 Glendale, Ashland, Ore. 97520. *Office:* Department of English, Southern Oregon College, Ashland, Ore. 97520.

CAREER: Mesa County Junior College, Grand Junction, Colo., instructor in English, 1953-55; New Mexico State University, Las Cruces, assistant professor of English, 1955-65; California State College at Los Angeles (now California State University, Los Angeles), associate professor of English, 1965-67; Southern Oregon College, Ashland, professor of English, 1967—. *Member:* Alpha Tau Omega.

WRITINGS: Assignments in Rhetoric, Macmillan, 1963; *A Writer's Guide to Literature,* McGraw, 1965. Author of "Accent on Communication," a column in *Library College Journal,* 1969-72. Contributor to professional journals, including *College English.*

WORK IN PROGRESS: Making Your Point and *Thinking and Writing,* both textbooks; *Education as Poetic Drama.*

SIDELIGHTS: Walter De Mordaunt told *CA:* "As a professor of English after more than two decades of teaching, I have found that authorship has offered many advantages.

Not the least of these, of course, is a strong leg up on financial sufficiency, over and above my salary, that has been derived from royalties from my textbooks. These are now both more than ten years old and are still selling to a large market of college students scattered from coast to coast and in Canada and England. Also, through this same period, I have published a long list of non-fiction articles for professional journals. These articles have been almost as satisfying as the textbooks. For one thing, the journals that have published my articles have always reached a large national readership. For another, writing with some regularity for these periodicals has given me a voice in national academic affairs that I would otherwise have had to forgo. I have been able to amplify this voice by way of national and regional conferences and conventions.

"I would certainly agree that the old dictum, 'Publish or Perish,' has been greatly abused both by college teachers and administrators. But with the right attitude on both sides, when it is not a threat to the teacher nor an easy way out for the administrator, publication can yield much fulfillment. At the very least, it can keep the teacher's enemies at bay, and it can help the administrator to validate the wisdom of his procedures of hiring and firing. But there is in publication a solid gratification that can transcend these 'little' matters of keeping body and soul together. It's hard to pin this down, but it has to do with one's mortality and, so far as he can manage it, his immortality. Authorship is parenthood, and one's good progeny, hopefully, will survive him. An author may not believe, today, everything—or even anything—that he wrote and published yesterday. I often think it's even better if he believes almost nothing of his past scribblings.

"Yet there can be a 'tone of voice' in a piece of writing, indelible as a shell-print in onyx, that can survive the printed words themselves. It is this tone, this attitude towards the world that contains implicitly within it the world's attitude towards him, that will forever denote the author himself. I am giving again, here, the old definition that 'Style is the Man Himself.' But I am saying also that if the writing is good enough—no matter where it be published originally or what kind of writing it is—its author can know that he has achieved his best claim to immortality. It is for this, after all, that we all really strive."

*   *   *

DENISOFF, R. Serge   1939-

PERSONAL: Born June 2, 1939, in San Francisco, Calif.; son of Serge A. and I. D. (Golubev) Denisoff; married Ursula Weber, July, 1976; children: Allegra Christine, Racheal. *Education:* San Francisco City College, A.A., 1964; San Francisco State College (now University), B.A., 1965, M.A., 1967; Simon Fraser University, Ph.D., 1969. *Office:* Department of Sociology, Bowling Green State University, Bowling Green, Ohio 43403.

CAREER: California State College (now University), Los Angeles, assistant professor of sociology, 1969-70; Bowling Green State University, Bowling Green, Ohio, associate professor of sociology, 1970—. *Member:* American Sociological Association, American Folklore Society, Popular Culture Association. *Awards, honors:* American Quarterly award, American Studies Association, 1970; Deems Taylor Award, American Society of Composers, Authors, and Publishers, 1974.

WRITINGS: (With Gary B. Rush) *Social and Political Movements,* Appleton, 1971; *Great Day Coming: Folk Music and the American Left,* University of Illinois Press,

1971; (editor with Richard A. Peterson, and contributor) *The Sounds of Social Change: The Uses of Music in Contemporary Society,* Rand McNally, 1972; (co-editor and contributor) *The Sociology of Political Extremism in the United States,* Harcourt, 1972; *Sing a Song of Social Significance: A Sociological View of Protest Songs,* Bowling Green University Press, 1972; (co-editor and contributor) *Sociology: Theories in Conflict,* Wadsworth, 1972; (editor with Charles McCaghy) *Deviance, Criminality and Conflict: Sociology of Criminality and Nonconformity,* Rand McNally, 1973; *Songs of Protest, War and Peace,* American Bibliographic Center-Clio Press, 1973; (editor with O. Callahan and Mark Levine and contributor) *Theories and Paradigms of Contemporary Sociology,* F. T. Peacock, 1974; (editor) *Sociology of Dissent,* Harcourt, 1974; (with Ralph Wahrman) *An Introduction to Sociology,* Macmillan, 1975; *Solid Gold: The Popular Record Industry,* Transaction Books, 1975.

Contributor: Russel B. Nye and others, editors, *Crises on Campus,* Bowling Green University Press, 1969; Michael Prosser, editor, *Intercommunication among Nations and Peoples,* Harper, 1971; Darrell LeRoy Ashby and Bruce M. Stave, editors, *The Discontented Society,* Rand McNally, 1972. Contributor of more than sixty articles, reviews, and record reviews to *Nation, Focus, Western Folklore, Rolling Stone, Phonograph Record, Stereo Review,* and other periodicals. Editor, *Popular Music and Society;* sociology and music editor, *Journal of Popular Culture.*

WORK IN PROGRESS: A revision of *Introduction to Sociology,* for Macmillan; *There's a Meeting Here Tonight: The Folk Music Revival, 1957-1970,* for University of Illinois Press.

*   *   *

DENKER, Henry   1912-

PERSONAL: Born November 25, 1912, in New York, N.Y.; son of Max (a fur manufacturer) and Jennie (Geller) Denker; married Edith Rose Heckman, December 5, 1942. *Education:* New York University, LL.B., 1934. *Politics:* Liberal Democrat. *Religion:* Jewish. *Home:* 241 Central Park W., New York, N.Y. 10024. *Agent:* Owen Laster, William Morris Agency, 1350 Avenue of the Americas, New York, N.Y. 10019.

CAREER: Admitted to the Bar of New York State, 1935; practiced law in New York City, 1935-58; Research Institute of America, New York City, executive, 1938-40; Standard Statistics, New York City, tax consultant, 1940-42; novelist and writer for radio, television, stage, and screen, 1947—. Drama instructor, American Theatre Wing, 1961-63, College of the Desert, 1970. *Member:* Dramatists Guild (member of council, 1967-70), Authors Guild, Authors League of America, Academy of Television Arts and Sciences (member of council, 1967-72), Writers Guild East. *Awards, honors:* Peabody Award, Christopher Award, *Variety* Showmanship award, and Brotherhood award of National Conference of Christians and Jews for radio series "The Greatest Story Ever Told"; Ohio State award.

WRITINGS—Published by Crowell, except as indicated: *I'll Be Right Home, Ma,* 1949; *My Son, the Lawyer,* 1950; *Salome, Princess of Galilee,* 1952; *That First Easter,* 1959; *The Director,* Baron, 1970; *The Kingmaker,* McKay, 1972; *A Place for the Mighty,* McKay, 1973.

All published by Simon & Schuster: *The Physicians,* 1974; *The Experiment,* 1975; *The Starmaker,* 1977; *The Scofield Diagnosis,* 1977.

Plays: (With Ralph Berkey) "Time Limit," first produced on Broadway at Booth Theatre, January 24, 1956; "Olive Ogilvie," first produced on West End at Aldwych Theatre, March 12, 1957; *A Far Country* (three-act; first produced on Broadway at Music Box, April 4, 1961), Random House, 1961; "Venus at Large," first produced on Broadway at Morosco Theatre, April 12, 1962; *A Case of Libel* (three-act; based on *My Life in Court* by Louis Nizer; first produced on Broadway at Longacre Theatre, October 10, 1963), Random House, 1964; "A Sound of Distant Thunder," first produced in Paramus, N.J. at Paramus Playhouse, 1967; "What Did We Do Wrong?" (two-act comedy), first produced on Broadway at Helen Hayes Theatre, October 22, 1967; "The Headhunters," first produced at Bucks County Playhouse, September, 1971; "The Second Time Around," first produced on Broadway at Morosco Theatre, 1976. Also author of "About William" and "The Name of the Game," as yet neither published nor produced.

Television plays: "The Wound Within," networked by CBS for U.S. Steel Hour, February, 1958; "Give Us Barabbas," networked by NBC for "Hallmark Hall of Fame," March, 1961; "A Case of Libel" (based on his play), networked by ABC, February, 1969; "The Choice," networked by NBC for "Prudential On-stage," March, 1969; "The Man Who Wanted to Live Forever," ABC Movie of the Week, December, 1969; "First Easter," networked by NBC for "Hallmark Hall of Fame," February, 1970; "Neither Are We Enemies," networked by NBC for "Hallmark Hall of Fame," March, 1970; "The Heart Farm," ABC Movie of the Week, March, 1971; "The Court Martial of Lieutenant Calley," networked by ABC, 1975.

Screenplays: "Time Limit!" (based on his play), United Artists, 1957; "The Hook" (based on a novel by Vahe Katcha), Metro-Goldwyn-Mayer, 1962; "Twilight of Honor" (based on a novel by Al Dewlen), Metro-Goldwyn-Mayer, 1963.

Radio plays: "Laughter for the Leader," broadcast by CBS for "Columbia Workshop," 1940; "Me? I Drive a Hack," broadcast by CBS for "Columbia Workshop," 1941. Writer for "Radio Reader's Digest," CBS, 1943-46; writer, director, and producer of series "The Greatest Story Ever Told," ABC, 1947-57.

WORK IN PROGRESS: A novel, *Kit.*

SIDELIGHTS: Henry Denker told *CA* that he "found two areas of early education of enormous value in later writing. Early religious education with a view towards becoming a rabbi turned out to be of enormous importance in working on "The Greatest Story Ever Told" and the other religious books and TV specials I have done. Also legal training and experience turned out to be of great help in doing *A Case of Libel,* "Twilight of Honor," and *The Adversaries.* In each instance, the work concerned a trial and much highly technical legal knowledge was required. For the rest, reading of periodicals provides a varied source of ideas. And research on a topic once selected seems to provide information for yet other subjects.

"As for avocations, [I] am devoted to travel and tennis. Though writing is a hobby as well as a profession and one is never at ease when not engaged in writing on some work. As a result the tendency is to work seven days a week when engaged in a long project such as a novel or a play. Days of the week lose their relevance and it is actually a struggle to interrupt the work for any save the gravest of reasons."

DENNING, Basil W. 1928-

PERSONAL: Born August 31, 1928, in Calcutta, India; son of Sir Howard and Margery (Browne) Denning. *Education:* Attended Royal Naval College, Dartmouth, 1942-46, and Royal Naval College, Greenwich, intermittently, 1948-55; Harvard University, M.B.A. (with distinction), 1960. *Religion:* Church of England. *Home:* 37 Kings Rd., Richmond, Surrey, England. *Office:* Harbridge House Europe, 180 Tottenham Court Rd., London W.1, England.

CAREER: Royal Navy, 1945-57; became lieutenant; Excel Continental Ltd., London, England, director of planning and finance, 1963-65; London Business School, London, director of post-experience programmes, 1965-67, senior lecturer in business policy, 1965-70; Harbridge House Europe, London, principal, 1970-72, vice-president and managing partner, 1974—. Director, Pavelle Ltd.; member of management committee, South Bank Housing Society. *Member:* Association of Teachers of Management, Long Range Planning Society (vice-chairman), Institute for International Affairs, Manpower Planning Society.

WRITINGS: Corporate Long Range Planning: Industry's Problems and National Policies, Longmans, Green, 1969; *Corporate Planning: Selected Concepts,* McGraw, 1971. Contributor of about fifteen articles to education and management journals. Chairman of editorial board, *Journal of Long Range Planning,* 1969-74; member of editorial board, *Journal of Business Policy.*

*   *   *

De RUTH, Jan 1922-

PERSONAL: Born July 31, 1922, in Karlsbad, Czechoslovakia; son of Oscar and Olga (Wollner) De Ruth. *Education:* Studied at Rotter Art School, Prague, Czechoslovakia, Ruskin School of Drawing, Oxford, England, two years, Art Students League, New York, N.Y., one year, Taubes-Pierce Art School, two years, and New School for Social Research, one year. *Home:* 1 West 67th St., New York, N.Y. 10023.

CAREER: Artist (painter). Has exhibited paintings in thirty-one national exhibitions, fourteen one-man museum exhibits, and seventy-one one-man gallery exhibits. *Member:* Allied Artists of America (vice-president), American Artists Professional League, Royal Society of Art, Artist Fellowship, Audubon Artists, Knickerbocker Artists, Connecticut Academy of Fine Art. *Awards, honors:* Gold Medal from National Arts Club; Art Achievement Award from Allied Artists of America; purchase awards from Butler Institute of American Art and Audubon Artists.

WRITINGS: Portrait Painting, Pitman, 1965; *Painting the Nude,* Watson-Guptill, 1967.

SIDELIGHTS: "Jan De Ruth is one of the greatest painters of nudes in our time," the *MD* reviewer writes. "*Painting the Nude* is a model of what an advanced treatise on painting should be."

BIOGRAPHICAL/CRITICAL SOURCES: MD Medical Newsmagazine, June, 1967.

*   *   *

DETWEILER, Robert 1932-

PERSONAL: Born August 25, 1932, in Souderton, Pa.; son of Elmer M. (a postal clerk) and Lillian (Clemmer) Detweiler; married Gertrud Frank, September 9, 1955; children: Bettina, Dirk. *Education:* Attended University of Hamburg,

1955-57; Goshen College, B.A. and B.D., 1959; University of Florida, M.A., 1960, Ph.D., 1962. *Office:* Graduate Institute of Liberal Arts, Emory University, Atlanta, Ga. 30322.

CAREER: University of Florida, Gainesville, instructor, 1961-62, assistant professor of English, 1963-65; Hunter College of the City University of New York, New York, N.Y., assistant professor of English, 1965-66; Florida Presbyterian College, St. Petersburg, associate professor of English, 1966-70; Emory University, Atlanta, Ga., associate professor, 1970-74, professor of liberal arts and director of Graduate Institute of Liberal Arts, 1974—. Guest professor of English, University of Salzburg, 1971-72; guest professor of American literature, University of Hamburg, 1976-77. *Member:* American Association of University Professors, South Atlantic Modern Language Association, Southern Humanities Conference (delegate at large, 1970-74). *Awards, honors:* National Endowment for the Humanities fellow, summer, 1967; German Academic Exchange fellow, summer, 1974.

WRITINGS: Four Spiritual Crises in Mid-Century American Fiction (monograph), University of Florida Press, 1964; *Saul Bellow* (monograph), Eerdmans, 1967; *Iris Murdoch's "The Unicorn"* (monograph), Seabury, 1968; *John Updike,* Twayne, 1972; *Story, Sign, and Self,* Fortress, 1977. Contributor to literature and theology journals.

WORK IN PROGRESS: Studies in contemporary fiction.

*   *   *

DETZLER, Jack J.   1922-

PERSONAL: Born July 20, 1922, in South Bend, Ind.; son of John Jacob (an accountant) and Thekla (King) Detzler. *Education:* Indiana University, A.B. (with honors), 1943, Ph.D., 1952; University of Wisconsin, A.M., 1946. *Home:* 50575 Bristol Ave., South Bend, Ind. 46637. *Office:* Department of History, Saint Mary's College, Notre Dame, Ind.

CAREER: South Bend-Mishawaka Center of Indiana University (now Indiana University, South Bend), instructor, 1947-50, assistant professor of history, 1950-67, academic counselor, 1947-50, dean, 1950-64; Saint Mary's College, Notre Dame, Ind., professor of history, 1967—, vice-president, 1967-72. Member of board of directors of Memorial Hospital, 1952-62, and South Bend-Mishawaka Chamber of Commerce, 1971-73; co-chairman of South Bend-Mishawaka Roundtable of National Conference of Christians and Jews, 1968-70. *Member:* American Historical Association, Organization of American Historians, American Association of University Professors, Indiana Historical Society, Northern Indiana Historical Society (president, 1971-77), Indiana Club, Rotary Club, Phi Beta Kappa, Phi Delta Kappa, Phi Alpha Theta.

WRITINGS: History of the Northwest Indiana Conference of the Methodist Church: 1852-1951, Methodist Publishing Co., 1952; *South Bend, 1900-1910: The Awakening of a Small Town,* Northern Indiana Historical Society, 1959; *South Bend, 1910-1920: A Decade Dedicated to Reform,* Northern Indiana Historical Society, 1960; (editor) *Diary of Howard Stillwell Stanfield: 1864-65,* Indiana University Press, 1969. Contributor to *Encyclopaedia Britannica;* contributor of articles to *Ohio History* and *Wisconsin Magazine of History.*

WORK IN PROGRESS: South Bend, 1920-1930: The Emergence of a City; a biography of Paul M. Butler.

DE VAUX, Roland   1903-1971

December 17, 1903—September 10, 1971; French Dominican priest and biblical scholar. Obituaries: *Washington Post,* September 12, 1971; *New York Times,* September 13, 1971; *Time,* September 27, 1971.

*   *   *

de VRIES, Herbert A.   1917-

PERSONAL: Surname is pronounced de Vrees; born October 9, 1917, in New York, N.Y.; son of Hans Gerhard (an accountant) and Antoinette (Hoegen) de Vries; married Mary J. Johnson, 1944; married second wife, Lorane Sherwood, November 24, 1955; children: (first marriage) Herbert E. Johnson. *Education:* Pennsylvania State College (now University), B.S., 1943; University of Texas, M.Ed., 1946; University of Southern California, Ph.D., 1960. *Home:* 32194 Vista de La Luna, South Laguna, Calif. 92677. *Office:* Gerontology Center, University of Southern California, Los Angeles, Calif. 90007.

CAREER: Long Beach State College (now California State University, Long Beach), associate professor of physical education and coordinator of physical education research, 1957-65; University of Southern California, Los Angeles, professor of physical education and physiology, 1965-69, professor of physiology, 1970—, preceptor of Gerontology Center, 1965—. Director of research, Health Enhancement Institute. *Military service:* U.S. Army Air Forces, 1942-45; became lieutenant. *Member:* American College of Sports Medicine (fellow; member of board of trustees, 1966; vice-president, 1967-68), Gerontology Society (fellow), American Heart Association, American Association for Health, Physical Education and Recreation (member of national research council), Orange County Heart Association.

WRITINGS: Physiology of Exercise for Physical Education and Athletics, W. C. Brown, 1966, 2nd edition, 1974; *Laboratory Manual for Physiology of Exercise,* W. C. Brown, 1971; *Vigor Regained,* Prentice-Hall, 1974. Writer of research reports. Contributor to *Encyclopedia of Sports Medicine;* contributor of more than twenty-five articles to professional journals. Associate editor of *Research Quarterly* of American Association for Health, Physical Education and Recreation, 1965—, and of *Science and Medicine in Sports.*

WORK IN PROGRESS: Research on effect of the type of exercise upon the work of the heart in older men, and other topics.

*   *   *

DHAVAMONY, Mariasusai   1925-

PERSONAL: Born November 7, 1925, in Kuthalur, India; son of Marianayagam Pillai and Arulayi Ammal. *Education:* Attended St. Joseph's College, Tiruchirapalli, South India, 1945-47; Sacred Heart College, Shembaganur, India, Licentiate in Philosophy, 1954; St. Mary's College, Kurseong, India, Licentiate in Theology, 1959; Gregorian University, Ph.D., 1962; Oxford University, D.Phil. (oriental studies), 1967. *Home and office:* Gregorian University, Piazza dehla Pilotta 4, Rome 00187, Italy.

CAREER: Roman Catholic priest, member of Society of Jesus (Jesuits), ordained in 1958; Sacred Heart College, Shembaganur, Madras, India, assistant professor of philosophy, 1962-64; Gregorian University, Rome, Italy, 1967—, began as associate professor, currently professor of history of religions and of Indology, dean of faculty of missiology,

1975—. Visiting summer professor at Boston College, 1967, 1968, and University of San Francisco, 1969, 1970, 1971. Consultant, Vatican Secretariate for Non-Christian Religions.

WRITINGS: Subjectivity and Knowledge in the Philosophy of St. Thomas Aquinas, Gregorian University Press, 1965; *Love of God According to Saiva Siddhanta: A Study in the Mysticism and Theology of Saivism,* Clarendon Press, 1971; (with others) *Revelation in Christianity and Other Religions,* Loyola University Press, 1971; (editor) *Evangelization, Dialogue and Development,* Loyola University Press, 1972. Also author of *Phenomology of Religion,* 1973; author of monographs on Indian religion and comparative religion. Editor-in-chief, *Studia Missionalia,* and *Documenta Missionolia.*

SIDELIGHTS: Mariasusai Dhavamony is fluent in English, Italian, Tamil, and Latin, and reads French, Spanish, German, and Sanskrit.

*   *   *

DIAMANT, Lincoln   1923-
(Stan McDougal)

PERSONAL: Born January 25, 1923; son of Rudolph and Rose (Bloom) Diamant; married Joan Champion (an artist); children: three. *Education:* Columbia University, A.B. (cum laude), 1943. *Politics:* "Anti-establishment." *Religion:* "Non-believer." *Agent:* Anita Diamant, 51 East 42nd St., New York, N.Y. 10017.

CAREER: Spots Alive, Inc., New York, N.Y., president, 1958—; founder and proprietor, Pondside Press, Ossining, N.Y. *Member:* Broadcast Pioneers.

WRITINGS: Introduction to Aristotle, Viking, 1952; *The Anatomy of a Television Commercial,* Hastings House, 1970; *Television's Classic Commercials,* Hastings House, 1971; *The Broadcast Communications Dictionary,* Hastings House, 1974.

SIDELIGHTS: Lincoln Diamant writes to *CA,* "Everything I write (and am planning to write) is the issue of a 25-year love affair with the New York Public Library."

*   *   *

DICKIE, George (Thomas)   1926-

PERSONAL: Born August 12, 1926, in Palmetto, Fla.; son of George Harrison (a farmer) and Emily (Brown) Dickie; married Joyce Petty, August 5, 1950 (died April 26, 1975); children: Garrick George, Blake Allen. *Education:* Florida State University, B.A., 1949; University of California, Los Angeles, Ph.D., 1959. *Politics:* Democrat. *Home:* 1506 Wesley, Evanston, Ill. 60201. *Office:* Department of Philosophy, University of Illinois at Chicago Circle, Chicago, Ill. 60680.

CAREER: Washington State University, Pullman, instructor, 1956-59, assistant professor, 1959-63, associate professor of philosophy, 1963-64; University of Houston, Houston, Tex., associate professor, 1964-65; University of Illinois at Chicago Circle, associate professor, 1965-68, professor of philosophy, 1968—. *Military service:* U.S. Marine Corps, 1944-46. *Member:* American Philosophical Association, American Society for Aesthetics (trustee, 1966-69). *Awards, honors:* National Endowment for the Humanities senior fellowship, 1971-72.

WRITINGS: Aesthetics: An Introduction, Pegasus, 1971; *Art and the Aesthetic: An Institutional Analysis,* Cornell

University Press, 1974; (editor with R. J. Sclafani) *Aesthetics: A Critical Anthology,* St. Martin's, 1977. Contributor to philosophy journals.

*   *   *

DICKINSON, H(arry) T(homas)   1939-

PERSONAL: Born March 9, 1939, in Gateshead, England; son of Joseph and Elizabeth (Warriner) Dickinson; married Elizabeth Galtry, August 26, 1961; children: Mark James, Anna Elizabeth. *Education:* Durham University, B.A., 1960, M.A., 1963; Newcastle University, Ph.D., 1968. *Home:* 44 Viewforth Terrace, Edinburgh, Scotland. *Office:* Department of History, University of Edinburgh, Edinburgh, Scotland.

CAREER: Washington Grammar School, Washington, England, history master, 1961-64; University of Newcastle, Newcastle, England, Earl Grey fellow and researcher in history, 1964-66; University of Edinburgh, Edinburgh, Scotland, 1966—, began as lecturer, currently reader in history. *Member:* Historical Association, Royal Historical Society. *Awards, honors:* Fulbright scholar, 1973; visiting fellow, Huntington Library, 1973; visiting senior fellow, Folger Shakespeare Library, 1973.

WRITINGS: (Editor) *The Correspondence of Sir Jame Clavering, 1708-1740,* Surtees Society, 1967; *Bolingbroke,* Constable, 1970; *Walpole and the Whig Supremacy,* English Universities Press, 1973; (editor) *Politics and Literature in the 18th Century,* Dent, 1974; *Liberty and Property: Political Ideology in Eighteenth-Century Britain,* Weidenfeld & Nicholson, in press. Contributor of articles to *English Historical Review, Bulletin of the Institute of Historical Research, Journal of British Studies, Huntington Library Quarterly, History Today,* and other periodicals.

WORK IN PROGRESS: A study of radical ideas and popular politics in the eighteenth century.

BIOGRAPHICAL/CRITICAL SOURCES: Bookseller, January 9, 1971.

*   *   *

DICKSON, Paul   1939-

PERSONAL: Born July 30, 1939, in Yonkers, N.Y.; son of William A. and Isabelle (Cornell) Dickson, Jr.; married Nancy Hartman, April 13, 1968. *Education:* Wesleyan University, B.A., 1961. *Home address:* Box 80, Garrett Park, Md. 20766. *Agent:* Helen Brann Agency, 14 Sutton Place S., New York, N.Y. 10022.

CAREER: McGraw-Hill Book Co., New York, N.Y., regional editor, 1966-69. *Military service:* U.S. Navy, 1962-65. *Awards, honors:* American Political Science Association fellowship for reporters, 1969-70.

WRITINGS: Think Tanks, Atheneum, 1971; *The Great American Ice Cream Book,* Atheneum, 1973; *The Future of the Workplace,* Weybright, 1975; *The Electronic Battlefield,* Indiana University Press, 1976; *The Mature Person's Guide to Kites, Frisbees, Yo-Yos and Other Childlike Diversions,* New American Library, 1977; *Out of This World,* Delacorte, 1977; *Future File: A Handbook for People with One Foot in the 21st Century,* Rawson, 1977. Contributor to national magazines, including *Progressive, Town and Country, American Heritage, Esquire,* and *Washington Monthly.*

WORK IN PROGRESS: Three non-fiction books.

DIERS, Carol Jean 1933-

PERSONAL: Born July 16, 1933, in Bellingham, Wash.; daughter of W. Donald (a skilled laborer) and Alice H. (a teacher; maiden name West) Diers. *Education:* Western Washington State College (now Western Washington University), B.A., 1956; University of British Columbia, M.A., 1958; University of Washington, Seattle, Ph.D., 1961. *Home:* 3004 Cherrywood Ave., Bellingham, Wash. 98225. *Office:* Department of Psychology, Western Washington University, Bellingham, Wash. 98225.

CAREER: Teacher in public schools of Bellevue, Wash., 1956-57, 1958-59; Olympic College, Bremerton, Wash., instructor in psychology, 1961-63; Western Washington University, Bellingham, assistant professor, 1963-65, associate professor, 1965-73, professor of psychology, 1974—, director of honors program, 1970-74. *Member:* American Psychological Association, American Association for the Advancement of Science, Sigma Xi.

WRITINGS: (With H. L. Harris, C. W. Harwood, R. D. Meade, and H. C. Taylor) *An Introduction to the Behavioral Sciences,* W. C. Brown, 1968. Contributor of about a dozen articles to professional journals.

WORK IN PROGRESS: Writing on social behavior in animals and on personal space.

* * *

DIETL, (Kirsten) Ulla 1940-

PERSONAL: Born June 1, 1940, in Copenhagen, Denmark; daughter of Svend Aage (a hotel proprietor) and Ulla (Madsen) Rasmussen; married Ludwig Dietl (an engineer), April 6, 1959 (died November 1, 1963); children: Malene, Christian. *Education:* Tegne- & Kunstindustriskolen (art academy), diploma, 1960. *Religion:* Protestant. *Office:* c/o Fogtdals Bogforlag A/S, Noerre Farimagsgade 49, DK-1364 Copenhagen, Denmark.

CAREER: Film Graphic (posters, etc), Copenhagen, Denmark, designer, 1960-61; *Alt for damerne* (women's magazine), Copenhagen, designer and journalist, 1961-66; *Det Berlingske Hus* (magazine), Copenhagen, designer and sub-editor, 1966-68; Fogtdals Bogforlag, Copenhagen, designer and sub-editor, *Bo Bedre* (architecture and furniture magazine), 1968—. Artist; editor and author of children's books.

WRITINGS: Eva's Dolls and Puppets, Fogtdal, 1969, Crown, 1971; (with Lis Paludan) *Bo Bedre's Boernenes Idebog* (title means "Ideas and Games for Children"), Fogtdal, 1970; *Tee itse neuloen, virkaten ja ommellen nukkeperhe,* Otava (Helsinki), 1970; *Boernenes store legebog* (title means "Games of All Sorts for Children"), Fogtdal, 1971; *Haven paa altanen* (title means "Decorating at the Terrace"), Fogtdal, 1972; *Sommerhusets Have* (title means "The Garden around the Summer Residence"), Fogtdal, 1972.

WORK IN PROGRESS: A long story for children, to be self-illustrated.†

* * *

DIETZ, Peter O(wen) 1935-

PERSONAL: Born April 20, 1935, in Bronx, N.Y.; son of William E. (national treasurer, Young Men's Christian Association) and Elizabeth (Kohl) Dietz; married Elizabeth Candee, June 21, 1958; children: Susan Candee, Karen Elizabeth. *Education:* Dartmouth College, A.B. (cum laude), 1957, M.B.A. (with high distinction), 1958; Columbia University, Ph.D., 1965. *Home:* 1752 Fernside Dr., Tacoma, Wash. *Office:* Frank Russell Co., 1100 Washington Plaza, Tacoma, Wash. 98402.

CAREER: Northwestern University, School of Business, Evanston, Ill., instructor, 1960-64, assistant professor, 1964-67, associate professor of finance, 1967-69; University of Oregon, College of Business Administration, Eugene, associate professor of finance, 1969-76; Frank Russell Co., Inc., Tacoma, Wash., vice-president, 1971—. Researcher for National Bureau of Economic Research, 1958, Financial Executives Research Foundation, 1964-68, and Council of Profit Sharing Industries, 1967-69. *Member:* American Economic Association, American Finance Association, Financial Management Association, Western Finance Association, Portland Financial Analysts Society.

WRITINGS: Pension Funds: Measuring Investment Performance, Free Press and Graduate School of Business, Columbia University, 1966; (contributor) Donald X. Murray, editor, *Successful Profit 'Sharing Plans: Theory and Practice,* Council of Profit Sharing Industries, 1968; (with Bion B. Howard) *A Study of the Financial Significance of Profit Sharing* (monograph), Council of Profit Sharing Industries, 1969; (contributor) Bert L. Metzger, editor, *Investment Practices, Performance, and Management of Profit Sharing Trust Funds,* Profit Sharing Research Foundation, 1969. Co-author of teacher's guide to *Corporate Financial Policy,* 4th edition, Prentice-Hall, 1962; consulting editor of *The Treasurer's Handbook.* Contributor to finance newspapers and journals.

* * *

Di LEO, Joseph H. 1902-

PERSONAL: Born November 16, 1902, in New York, N.Y.; son of Emanuel (a doctor) and Rosa (Cori) Di Leo; married Joan McTague (a social worker), November 10, 1948; children: Judith, Daniel, Paul. *Education:* University of Bologna, M.D., 1927; graduate study at University of Bologna and University of Rome, 1927-32, and Yale University, 1945. *Religion:* Roman Catholic. *Home:* 49 East 86th St., New York, N.Y. 10028. *Office:* Developmental Clinic, New York Foundling Hospital, 1175 Third Ave., New York, N.Y. 10021.

CAREER: New York Foundling Hospital, New York City, director of Developmental Clinic, 1945—; St. Vincent's Hospital, New York City, staff member, 1946—, currently senior assistant pediatrician; New York Hospital, New York City, assistant attending pediatrician, 1954-71; Manhattan Eye, Ear & Throat Hospital, New York City, attending pediatrician at Hearing and Speech Clinic, 1954-74. New York University, instructor, 1947-55, assistant clinical professor of pediatrics, 1955—; instructor in pediatrics, Medical College, Cornell University, 1954—; lecturer in department of special education, Teachers College, Columbia University, 1963—. Member of advisory board, New York City Department of Mental Health and Mental Retardation, 1973-80. Former consultant, St. Joseph's School for the Deaf. Diplomate, American Board of Pediatrics, 1945. *Member:* American Academy of Pediatrics (fellow), Society for Research in Child Development, American Medical Association, New York State Medical Society, New York County Medical Society.

WRITINGS: (Contributor) *The Exceptional Infant,* Volume I, Special Child, 1967; (contributor) *Learning Disabilities,* Developmental Learning Materials (Chicago), 1969; *Young Children and Their Drawings,* Brunner, 1970; *Phys-*

ical Factors in Growth and Development, Teachers College Press, 1970; *Children's Drawings as Diagnostic Aids,* Brunner, 1973; *Child Development: Analysis and Synthesis,* Brunner, 1977. Contributor to professional journals.

WORK IN PROGRESS: Developmental evaluation of children with PKU and other inherited metabolic disorders; research on genetic factor in childhood psychosis; continuing study of children's drawings.

AVOCATIONAL INTERESTS: Art, painting, the ancient world and great writers of classical antiquity, collecting Greek and Roman coins.

*   *   *

DILLE, John M. 1921(?)-1971

1921(?)—July 11, 1971; American editor and author of books on current events. Obituaries: *New York Times,* July 14, 1971; *Publishers Weekly,* August 23, 1971.

*   *   *

DILLON, J(ames) T(homas) 1940-

PERSONAL: Born December 16, 1940, in Chicago, Ill.; son of Thomas James (a bank officer) and Lorraine (Heineman) Dillon. *Education:* St. Mary's College, Winona, Minn., B.A., 1962; University of Chicago, M.A., 1971, Ph.D., 1978. *Home:* 5602 South Drexel, Chicago, Ill. 60637. *Office:* School of Education, Chicago State University, 95th at King, Chicago, Ill. 60628.

CAREER: High school teacher in Chicago, Ill., 1962-65, Lansing, Mich., 1965-67, Lockport, Ill., 1967-69, and Wheaton, Ill., 1969-70; University of Chicago, Chicago, lecturer in education, 1972-74; Northeastern Illinois University, Chicago, instructor in education, 1974-75; University of Illinois at Chicago Circle, instructor in education, 1975-76; Roosevelt University, Chicago, instructor in psychology, 1976-77; Chicago State University, Chicago, assistant dean of education, 1977—.

WRITINGS: (Co-translator) P. Grieger, *Character and Vocation,* University of London Press, 1963; *Catechetics Reconsidered,* Saint Mary's College Press, 1968; *Personal Teaching,* C. E. Merrill, 1971; (contributor with J. W. Getzels) R. M. W. Travers, editor, *Second Handbook of Research on Teaching,* Rand McNally, 1973; (with D. J. Piveteau) *Resurgence of Religious Instruction,* Religious Education Press, 1977. Contributor of articles, book reviews, and translations to education journals. Associate editor, *La Salle Catechist,* 1967-69; member of editorial board, *School Review,* 1971-74.

WORK IN PROGRESS: Psycholinguistic aspects of classroom questioning; pedagogy of Socrates and Jesus.

*   *   *

DIMOND, Stuart J. 1938-

PERSONAL: Born April 30, 1938, in Bristol, England; son of William Henry (a businessman) and Dorothea Madge Dimond; married Bridgit Carolyn Price, March 30, 1968; children: Clare, Rebecca. *Education:* University of Bristol, B.Sc., 1960, Ph.D., 1963. *Politics:* Socialist. *Home:* 16 Highfields, Llandaff, Cardiff, Wales. *Office:* Department of Psychology, University College, University of Wales, Cardiff, Wales.

CAREER: University of Wales, University College, Cardiff, 1966—, began as lecturer, currently reader in psychology. *Member:* European Brain and Behaviour Society,

British Psychological Society, Association for the Study of Animal Behavior, Experimental Psychological Society. *Awards, honors:* M.A., Trinity College, 1966; senior scientist award from North Atlantic Treaty Organization (NATO).

WRITINGS: The Social Behavior of Animals, Harper, 1970; *The Double Brain,* Churchill Livingstone, 1972; (with J. E. Beaumont) *Hemisphere Function of the Human Brain,* Elek, 1974; *Introducitng Neuropsychology,* C. C Thomas, in press.

AVOCATIONAL INTERESTS: Music, travel, reading, walking, gardening.

*   *   *

DIMONDSTEIN, Geraldine 1926-

PERSONAL: Born January 23, 1926, in Detroit, Mich.; daughter of Max (a businessman) and Edythe (Katz) Holtzman; married Morton Dimondstein (an artist-sculptor and instructor), July 26, 1950; children: Carla, Joshua. *Education:* University of California, Berkeley, B.A., 1947; Bank Street College of Education, M.A., 1949; University of California, Los Angeles, M.A., 1959, Ed.D., 1967. *Politics:* "Open-minded." *Religion:* None. *Home:* 749 Longwood Ave., Los Angeles, Calif. 90005. *Office:* Department of Art, California State University, Los Angeles, Calif. 90032.

CAREER: Early childhood and elementary school teacher and music and dance specialist in New York, N.Y., 1947-59; Pacific Oaks College, Pasadena, Calif., instructor, 1959-60; International Overseas School, Rome, Italy, teacher of music and dance, 1960-64; University of California, Los Angeles, extension instructor in elementary education, 1964-67; Central Atlantic Regional Educational Laboratory, Washington, D.C., program coordinator and head of dance, 1968-69; Center for Early Education, Los Angeles, Calif., instructor in teacher education, 1969-72; California State University, Los Angeles, associate professor in department of art, 1972—.

MEMBER: National Art Education Association, Institute for the Study of Art in Education, Los Angeles County Art Education Council. *Awards, honors:* Commendation from White House Conference on Children, 1970, for film "Children Dance"; instructor in Fulbright-Hays teacher exchange program, London, England, 1976-77.

WRITINGS: (Contributor of music arrangements) *Physical Education for Today's Boys and Girls,* Allyn & Bacon, 1960; (with Naima Prevots) *Development of a Dance Curriculum for Young Children,* U.S. Office of Education, 1969; *Children Dance in the Classroom,* Macmillan, 1970; (contributor) Martin Haberman and Toby Meisel, *Dance: An Art in Academe,* Teachers College Press, 1970; *Exploring the Arts with Children,* Macmillan, 1974. Editor, producer, or director of educational films. Contributor to education and art journals.

AVOCATIONAL INTERESTS: Art (history and contemporary performance) in dance and the visual arts, the collection and study of African art.

*   *   *

DIPPLE, Elizabeth 1937-

PERSONAL: Born May 8, 1937, in Perth County, Ontario, Canada. *Education:* University of Western Ontario, B.A., 1959; Johns Hopkins University, M.A., 1961, Ph.D., 1963. *Office:* Department of English, Northwestern University, Evanston, Ill. 60201.

CAREER: University of Washington, Seattle, instructor, 1963-64, assistant professor, 1964-69, associate professor of English, 1969-71; Northwestern University, Evanston, Ill., associate professor of English, 1971—.

WRITINGS: Plot, Barnes & Noble, 1970. Also author of a monograph on Sidney published by University of Wisconsin Press, 1967. Contributor of articles to journals.

WORK IN PROGRESS: Fictions of the 1590's: Studies in Sidney, Spenser and Shakespeare; Studies in George Eliot, Charlotte Bronte, and Iris Murdoch.

* * *

DIVALE, William T(ulio) 1942-

PERSONAL: Born February 18, 1942, in New York, N.Y.; son of Joseph (a chef) and Josephine (Viola) Divale. *Education:* Pasadena City College, A.A., 1966; University of California, Los Angeles, B.A., 1969; California State College (now University), Los Angeles, M.A., 1971; State University of New York at Buffalo, Ph.D. candidate, 1971—. *Politics:* Socialist. *Agent:* Lurton Blassingame, 60 East 42nd St., New York, N.Y. 10017. *Office:* Department of Anthropology, York College of the City University of New York, Jamaica, N.Y. 11432.

CAREER: Trailer Coach Metals, Inc., El Monte, Calif., draftsman, 1963-65; Federal Bureau of Investigation, Washington, D.C., undercover student agent in Los Angeles, Calif., 1965-69; currently staff member in department of anthropology, York College of the City University of New York, Jamaica, N.Y. Research associate, Center for the Study of Armament and Disarmament, California State University, Los Angeles. *Member:* American Anthropological Association, American Ethnological Society, Society for Cross-Cultural Research, Southwestern Anthropological Association.

WRITINGS: (With James Joseph) *I Lived inside the Campus Revolution,* Cowles, 1970; *Warfare in Primitive Societies: A Bibliography,* Center for the Study of Armament and Disarmament, California State College, Los Angeles, 1971, revised edition, American Bibliographic Center-Clio Press, 1973. Contributor to anthropology journals.

WORK IN PROGRESS: A cross-cultural study of population regulation in two hundred primitive societies, hopefully to end up as a book; a book on the FBI and its role on college campuses in the United States; a cross-cultural study of matrilocal post-marital residence and its causes.

BIOGRAPHICAL/CRITICAL SOURCES: Best Sellers, February 1, 1971; *Nation,* February 8, 1971.†

* * *

DIVOKY, Diane 1939-

PERSONAL: Born July 10, 1939, in Cleveland, Ohio; daughter of George J. and Rosemary (Wolf) Divoky; married Peter Schrag (a writer), May 24, 1969; children: David Divoky Schrag, Benaiah Divoky Schrag. *Education:* Trinity College, Washington, D.C., A.B., 1961; Harvard University, M.A.T., 1965. *Home:* 5963 Manchester Dr., Oakland, Calif. 94618. *Office: Learning,* 530 University Ave., Palo Alto, Calif. 94301.

CAREER: New York Civil Liberties Union, New York, N.Y., research director, students rights project, 1970-72; *Learning,* Palo Alto, Calif., senior editor, 1972—. Freelance writer for general and education publications. *Member:* Education Writers Association, American Civil Liberties Union, National Organization for Women (NOW). *Awards, honors:* Carnegie Foundation and Education Writers Association travel grant, 1967; Education Press awards, 1970, 1971; National Council for the Advancement of Education writing award, 1972; Danforth fellow, 1974.

WRITINGS: (Editor) *How Old Will You Be in 1984?: Expressions of Student Outrage from the High School Free Press,* Avon, 1969; (with Alan H. Levine and others) *The Rights of Students,* Avon, 1974; (with husband, Peter Schrag) *The Myth of the Hyperactive Child,* Pantheon, 1975. Contributor to *Saturday Review, Redbook, Nation's Schools, New York Times,* and *Inquiry.* Member of editorial board, *Inquiry,* 1978—.

* * *

DIZNEY, Henry (Franklin) 1926-

PERSONAL: Born April 6, 1926, in Tacoma, Wash.; son of Walter Clark (a salesman) and Mary (Mudge) Dizney; married Nancy Tellis, August 25, 1951; children: Dan, Carroll, Ann, Laurie, Patrick. *Education:* Southeast Missouri State College (now University), B.S., 1954; Wayne State University, M.Ed., 1955; University of Iowa, Ph.D., 1959. *Home:* 2810 Almaden, Eugene, Ore. 97405. *Office:* College of Education, University of Oregon, Eugene, Ore. 97403.

CAREER: Western Reserve University (now Case Western Reserve University), Cleveland, Ohio, assistant professor of statistical measurements, 1959-60; Kent State University, Kent, Ohio, director of university examination service, 1960-67, associate professor of education, 1964-67; University of Oregon, Eugene, associate professor, 1967, professor of educational psychology, 1970—. *Military service:* U.S. Army, 1944-46. *Member:* American Psychological Association, American Educational Research Association, National Council on Measurement in Education, Phi Delta Kappa.

WRITINGS: Classroom Evaluation for Teachers, W. C. Brown, 1971. Contributor of more than thirty articles to education journals.

* * *

DOBSON, (Richard) Barrie 1931-

PERSONAL: Born November 3, 1931, in Stockton on Tees, England; son of R. H. (a railway engineer) and Mary (Kidd) Dobson; married Narda Leon, June 19, 1959; children: Mark, Michelle. *Education:* Oxford University, M.A., 1958, D.Phil., 1962. *Home:* 121 Stockton Lane, York, England. *Office:* Department of History, University of York, York, England.

CAREER: University of York, York, England, senior lecturer, 1968-76, professor of history, 1976—. Founder and chairman, York Film Theatre, 1968-74. *Military service:* British National Service, Royal Education Corps, 1950-51; served in Malaya. *Member:* Royal Historical Society (fellow).

WRITINGS: Selby Abbey and Town, Haynes & Morris (Leeds), 1969; (editor) *The Peasants' Revolt of 1381,* St. Martin's, 1970; (with M. J. Angold) *The World of the Middle Ages,* P. Hamlyn, 1971; *Durham Priory, 1400-1450,* Cambridge University Press, 1974; (with J. Taylor) *Rymes of Robyn Hood: An Introduction to the English Outlaw,* University of Pittsburgh Press, 1975; *The Jews of Medieval York,* Borthwick Institute of Historical Research, 1975. Contributor to British history journals.

WORK IN PROGRESS: A new edition of *Early Chamberlains' Rolls of the City of York;* contributions to forthcoming histories of Oxford University and York Minster.

DODD, Wayne (Donald) 1930-
(Donald Wayne)

PERSONAL: Born September 23, 1930, in Clarita, Okla.; son of Homer D. and Maggie M. (Potts) Dodd; married Betty Coshow, June 7, 1958; children: Elizabeth, Hudson. *Education:* University of Oklahoma, B.A., 1955, M.A., 1957, Ph.D., 1963. *Home:* 46 Grosvenor St., Athens, Ohio 45701. *Office:* Department of English, Ohio University, Athens, Ohio 45701.

CAREER: University of Colorado, Boulder, instructor, 1960-64, assistant professor of English, 1964-68; Ohio University, Athens, associate professor, 1968-73, professor of English, 1973—, director of creative writing program, 1974—. Fellow, Center for Advanced Studies, Wesleyan University, 1964; summer faculty fellow, University of Colorado, 1966. *Military service:* U.S. Navy, 1948-52. *Member:* Phi Beta Kappa. *Awards, honors:* American Council of Learned Societies fellow, 1964-65.

WRITINGS: (Under pseudonym Donald Wayne) *The Adventures of Little White Possum* (juvenile), Putnam, 1970; *We Will Wear White Roses,* Best Cellar Press, 1975; *Made in America,* Croissant, 1976; *A Time of Hunting,* Seabury, 1976. Contributor of poems, reviews, and articles to over forty periodicals and journals, including *American Scholar, Kayak, Discourse, Poetry Northwest, Southern Review,* and *Nation.* Editor, *Ohio Review,* 1971—.

* * *

DODGE, Lowell 1940-

PERSONAL: Born September 11, 1940, in New Haven, Conn.; married Bickley Smith, October 5, 1963; children: Shannon. *Education:* Yale University, B.A. (magna cum laude), 1963; Harvard University, LL.D., 1969.

CAREER: Coro Foundation, Los Angeles, Calif., intern in public affairs, 1963-64; director of tutorial programs with minority groups in South Los Angeles, Calif., and in North Carolina, 1964-66; Community Legal Assistance Office, Cambridge, Mass., staff assistant, 1967-69; Center for Auto Safety (Ralph Nader project), Washington, D.C., director, beginning 1969. Intern in Washington, D.C., with U.S. Bureau of the Budget and Executive Office of the President, summer, 1963, and in Cleveland, Miss., with NAACP Legal Defense Fund, summer, 1967.

WRITINGS: (With Ralph Nader and Ralf Hotchkiss) *What to Do with Your Bad Car,* Grossman, 1971; (project editor with others) *The Volkswagen: An Assessment of Distinctive Hazards,* foreword by Ralph Nader, Center for Auto Safety, 1971, published as *Small—on Safety: The Designed-in Dangers of the Volkswagen,* Grossman, 1972. Contributor to *Moderator.*

SIDELIGHTS: Lowell Dodge spent 1958-59 in England and western Europe as an English-Speaking Union exchange scholar, the summer of 1961 in Yugoslavia under an exchange job program, and participated in Operation Crossroads Africa in Upper Volta the summer of 1962.

BIOGRAPHICAL/CRITICAL SOURCES: Atlantic, June, 1970; *Washington Post,* August 16, 1971.†

* * *

DOLAN, Edward F(rancis), Jr. 1924-

PERSONAL: Born February 10, 1924, in Oakland, Calif.; son of Edward Francis (an engineer) and Zelda (Vieira) Dolan; married Rose Puddefoot (a deputy court recorder),

November 17, 1945; children: Timothy L., Wendy Anne. *Education:* Attended University of Southern California, 1943, San Francisco State College (now University), 1948-50, and University of San Francisco, 1958-59. *Agent:* Barthold Fles Literary Agency, 507 Fifth Ave., New York, N.Y. 10017.

CAREER: Free-lance radio and television writer, 1946-53; free-lance magazine writer, 1946-60; Monticello College, Godfrey, Ill., teacher of radio, television, and drama, 1953-56; *Novato Advance,* Novato, Calif., reporter and feature writer, 1960-68; Novato (Calif.) Unified School District, director of publications, 1968-71. *Military service:* U.S. Army Air Forces, 101st Airborne Division, 1943-46; served in England, France, Germany, Belgium, and Austria.

WRITINGS: Pasteur and the Invisible Giants (juvenile), Dodd, 1958; *Green Universe: The Story of Alexander von Humboldt* (juvenile), Dodd, 1959; *Jenner and the Miracle of Vaccine* (juvenile), Dodd, 1960; *White Battleground: The Conquest of the Arctic,* Dodd, 1961; *Vanquishing Yellow Fever: Dr. Walter Reed* (juvenile), Britannica Press, 1962; *Adventure with a Microscope: A Story of Robert Koch,* Dodd, 1964; *The Camera* (juvenile), Messner, 1965; *Disaster 1906: The San Francisco Earthquake and Fire* (juvenile), Messner, 1967; *Explorers of the Arctic and Antarctic* (juvenile), Crowell Collier, 1968; (with H. T. Silver) *William Crawford Gorgas: Warrior in White* (juvenile), Dodd, 1968.

The Explorers: Adventures in Courage (juvenile), Reilly & Lee, 1970; *Inventors for Medicine* (juvenile), Crown, 1971; *Engines Work Like This* (juvenile), McGraw, 1971; *Legal Action: A Layman's Guide,* Regnery, 1972; (with Frederick J. Hass) *The Foot Book,* Regnery, 1973; (with Hass) *What You Can Do about Your Headache,* Regnery, 1973; *A Lion in the Sun: A Background Book for Young People on the Rise and Fall of the British Empire* (juvenile), Parents' Magazine Press, 1973; *The Complete Beginner's Guide to Bowling* (juvenile), Doubleday, 1974; *The Complete Beginner's Guide to Ice Skating* (juvenile), Doubleday, 1974.

Starting Soccer: A Handbook for Boys and Girls (juvenile), Harper, 1976; *Basic Football Strategy: An Introduction for Young Players* (juvenile), foreword by Duffy Daugherty, Doubleday, 1976; *Amnesty: The American Puzzle* (juvenile), F. Watts, 1976; *The Complete Beginner's Guide to Making and Flying Kites* (juvenile), Doubleday, 1977; *The Complete Beginner's Guide to Magic,* Doubleday, 1977; *How to Leave Home—And Make Everybody Like It* (juvenile), Dodd, 1977; (with Richard B. Lyttle) *Archie Griffin,* Doubleday, 1977; (with Lyttle) *Bobby Clarke* (juvenile), Doubleday, 1977; (with Lyttle) *Martina Navratilova,* Doubleday, 1977; (with Lyttle) *Scott May: Basketball Champion,* Doubleday, 1978; (with Lyttle) *Fred Lynn: The Hero from Boston,* Doubleday, 1978; (with Lyttle) *Janet Guthrie: First Woman Driver at Indianapolis,* Doubleday, 1978.

SIDELIGHTS: Edward F. Dolan, Jr. began writing when he was about twelve and had his first story published at sixteen. He has covered a variety of subjects and found all of them challenging, but prefers to write on medical topics. *Avocational interests:* The theatre, traveling.

BIOGRAPHICAL/CRITICAL SOURCES: Young Readers' Review, November, 1967; *New York Times Book Review,* May 19, 1968; *Best Sellers,* June 1, 1968, December 15, 1971.

DOLBERG, Alexander 1933-
(David Burg)

PERSONAL: Born May 26, 1933, in Moscow, Russia; son of Max Mikhailovich (an economist) and Eugeniya (Berinskaya) Dolberg. *Education:* Moscow State University, diploma (with honors), 1956. *Home:* 63, Drayton Gardens, London S.W.10, England. *Agent:* Deborah Rogers Ltd., 29, Goodge St., London W1P 1FD, England.

CAREER: Cambridge University, King's College, Cambridge, England, researcher and lecturer, 1959-60, 1962-64; Harvard University, Cambridge, Mass., research fellow, Russian Research Center, 1960-62. Writer, journalist, and translator. *Member:* Society of Authors, National Union of Journalists, Institute of Linguists.

WRITINGS: Oppozitsionnye nastroeniia molodezhi v gody posle "ottepeli" (title means "Opposition Trends among Soviet Youth after the Thaw"), Institute for the Study of the USSR, 1960; (contributor) Richard Pipes, editor, *The Russian Intelligentsia,* Columbia University Press, 1961; (with Martin Page) *The Day Khrushchev Fell,* Hawthorn, 1965; (with George Feifer) *Solzhenitsyn: A Biography,* Stein & Day, 1972.

Translator: (With Nicholas Bethell) Alexandr Solzhenitsyn, *Cancer Ward,* Farrar, Straus, 1969; (with Bethell) Solzhenitsyn, *The Love-Girl and the Innocent: A Play,* Bodley Head, 1969, Farrar, Straus, 1970; (with Arthur Boyars) Yuli Daniel, *Prison Poems,* Philip O'Hara, 1972. Contributor to *Statist* (London), *Radio Liberty* (Munich), *Times* (London), *Harper's, Problems of Communism, Der Monat, Osteuropa,* and other magazines and newspapers.

WORK IN PROGRESS: A book on Soviet literature under Khrushchev, *A Revival of Soviet Literature; Fatima: A Totalitarian "Mystery,"* expected completion in 1978.

BIOGRAPHICAL/CRITICAL SOURCES: Saturday Review, February 21, 1970; *Detroit News,* September 10, 1972; *Best Sellers,* November 1, 1972; *Times Literary Supplement,* November 10, 1972; *Listener,* February 8, 1973; *New York Review of Books,* May 17, 1973.

* * *

DOLGOFF, Ralph L. 1932-

PERSONAL: Born November 5, 1932, in Savannah, Ga.; son of Max and Matilda (Yarmovsky) Dolgoff; married Sylvia Miriam Madoff, September 1, 1963; children: Eliana, Shoshana, Aaron, Rachel. *Education:* Columbia University, M.A., 1956, D.S.W., 1974; Adelphi University, M.S.W., 1961. *Religion:* Judaism. *Home:* 25 Farragut Rd., Old Bethpage, N.Y. 11804.

CAREER: Staff member for Jewish Community Centers, 1961-68; Council on Social Work Education, New York, N.Y., 1968—, currently senior program specialist, associate director of division of program services. Visiting professor, Hebrew University, 1975-76; associate professor, School of Social Work, Adelphi University, 1977—. *Military service:* U.S. Army, 1957-59. *Member:* National Association of Social Workers, National Association of Jewish Center Workers, Association of Jewish Communal Service.

WRITINGS: (With Frank Loewenberg) *The Teaching of Practice Skills,* Council on Social Work Education, 1971; (with Loewenberg) *The Practice of Social Intervention: Roles, Goals, and Strategies, A Book of Readings,* F. E. Peacock, 1972. Editor, *Jewish Community Center Program Aids.*

WORK IN PROGRESS: A textbook on social welfare as a social institution.

* * *

DONALDSON, Norman 1922-

PERSONAL: Born December 25, 1922, in Carlisle, England; came to United States in 1957, naturalized in 1963; son of Joseph (an insurance agent) and Rebecca (Irving) Donaldson; married Betty Burgess, March 19, 1947; children: Rosemary, Hilary, Andrew, Heather. *Education:* University of St. Andrews, B.S. (honors in chemistry), 1950. *Politics:* Democrat. *Home:* 1358 Inglis Ave., Columbus, Ohio 43212. *Office:* Chemical Abstracts Service, Ohio State University, Columbus, Ohio 43210.

CAREER: Imperial Chemical Industries, Dyestuffs Division, Manchester, England, technical officer, 1950-57; Chemical Abstracts Service (branch of American Chemical Society), Columbus, Ohio, senior editor, 1957—. *Military service:* British Army, Royal Army Medical Corps, 1942-46.

WRITINGS: Chemistry and Technology of Naphthalene Compounds, Edward Arnold, 1958; *In Search of Dr. Thorndyke* (biography of R. Austin Freeman), Bowling Green University Press, 1971; *Goodbye, Dr. Thorndyke* (pastiche), Luther Norris, 1972. Writer of introductions to Dover paperbacks. Contributor to *Thorndyke File.*

SIDELIGHTS: A *New York Times* critic called *In Search of Dr. Thorndyke* "a brilliant achievement that leaves precious little for future commentators. Mr. Donaldson's style is fresh and lucid, his control of chronology exemplary, his approach affectionate but still objective, his judgments incisive and soundly reasoned, his attention to detail remarkable."

Norman Donaldson writes that "many worthwhile books never get published because publishers' requirements fall, apparently, into a few stereotyped categories. I have tried to interest several of them in the idea of a readable reference book devoted to the deaths of the more interesting personages of history and of recent celebrities. Reference librarians, among others, are convinced the book is needed and would sell, but publishers are so far unenthusiastic."

BIOGRAPHICAL/CRITICAL SOURCES: New York Times, February 28, 1971.

* * *

DONINGTON, Robert 1907-

PERSONAL: Born May 4, 1907, in Leeds, England; son of George Caulton (a teacher) and Ellen (Lowry) Donington; married Gloria Rose (a musicologist; died, 1975); children: Jenny, Laura, Charles, Janie. *Education:* Queen's College, Oxford, B.A., 1930, B.Litt., 1946; studied music privately under Arnold Dolmetsch, H. K. Andrews, R. O. Morris, and Egon Wellesz. *Home:* The Cottage, by 4 Keats Grove, London NW3, England.

CAREER: Played at Haslemere Festivals and was secretary of the Dolmetsch Foundation in the early 1930's; as Leverhulme research fellow, scored and catalogued seventeenth-century English music for viols, 1934-36; member of English Consort of Viols, 1935-39, and London Consort, 1950-60; member of teaching staff of Trinity College of Music, London, England, 1948-60, and Attingham Summer School of Music, 1950-60; founder and director of Donington Consort, 1956-61; University of Pittsburgh, Pittsburgh, Pa., visiting Andrew Mellon Professor of Music, 1961-62; did research, writing, and broadcasting in London, 1962-64; University of

Iowa, Iowa City, visiting professor, 1964-66, professor of music, 1966-73. Visiting professor, Yale University, 1970-71; summer faculty member or visiting professor of music at Stanford University, 1961, 1964, University of Washington, Seattle, 1962, University of Southern California, 1964, Rutgers University, 1968; visiting professor at City University of New York, autumn, 1969, and State University of New York at Buffalo, 1972-74. In addition to his own concerts, performed at Elizabethan Festival in Berlin, 1948, Festival of Britain, 1951, Purcell-Handel celebrations in England, 1959, and Carmel Bach Festival, Carmel, Calif., 1961, 1971; director of recordings of Purcell in Paris and British Council recordings in London; has played in films and on numerous British Broadcasting Corp. and other broadcasts and television shows.

MEMBER: American Musicological Society (member of council, 1967-69, 1970-72), Royal Musical Association, International Musicological Society, Galpin Society (founder-member), Viola da Gamba Society, Stradivarius Association (member of honorary committee), International Bach Society (honorary member), Royal Academy of Music (honorary member), Analytical Psychology Club (vice-chairman, 1960-61). *Awards, honors:* Leverhulme research fellowship, 1935-36; Grand Prix du Disque, 1948; Grand Prix de l'-Academie Charles Cros, 1949; Fellowes Memorial Fund grant, 1958; Composition Prize of Viola da Gamba Society, 1961; guest fellow, Jonathan Edwards College, Yale University, 1970-71.

WRITINGS: The Work and Ideas of Arnold Dolmetsch (booklet), Dolmetsch Foundation, 1932; (with Edgar Hunt) *A Practical Method for the Recorder,* two volumes, Oxford University Press, 1935; (with Barbara Donington) *The Citizen Faces War,* Gollancz, 1936; *The Instruments of Music,* Methuen, 1949, 4th revised edition, 1970; "The Connoisseur Period Guides," Connoisseur, Book I: *Music and Musical Instruments in the Tudor Period, 1500-1603,* 1956, Book II: *Music and Musical Instruments in the Stuart Period, 1603-1714,* 1957, Book III: *Music and Musical Instruments in the Regency Period, 1810-1830,* 1958, Book IV: *Music and Musical Instruments in the Early Victorian Period, 1830-1860,* 1958; *Music for Fun* (quiz book), Hutchinson, 1960; *Tempo and Rhythm in Bach's Organ Music,* Hinrichsen Edition, 1960; (with Margaret Donington) *Scales, Arpeggios and Exercises for the Recorder,* Oxford University Press, 1961; *Wagner's "Ring" and Its Symbols: The Music and the Myth,* St. Martin's, 1963, 3rd edition, 1975; *The Interpretation of Early Music,* St. Martin's, 1963, 3rd edition, 1974; (author of foreword) Francesco Geminiani, *A Treatise of Good Taste in the Art of Musick,* DaCapo Press, 1969; *A Performer's Guide to Baroque Music,* Faber, 1973, Scribner, 1974; *String Playing in Baroque Music,* Scribner, 1977; *The Opera,* Harcourt, 1978.

Contributor: *Unofficial British Peace Aims* (booklet), National Peace Council, 1942; Imogen Holst, editor, *Henry Purcell, 1659-1695,* Oxford University Press, 1959; Ian Kemp, editor, *Michael Tippett: A Symposium on His Sixtieth Birthday,* Faber, 1965; Denis Arnold and Nigel Fortune, editors, *The Monteverdi Companion,* Faber, 1968; H. C. Robbins Landon and Roger E. Chapman, editors, *Studies in Eighteenth-Century Music: A Tribute to Karl Geiringer on His Seventieth Birthday,* Oxford University Press, 1970.

Musical compositions: (Editor) "English Fantasies for Viols," Schott, 1949; (editor with Walter Emery) Henry Purcell, "Two Trio Sonatas," Novello, 1959; "Suite No. I

for Three or More Violins," Elkin, 1960; "Suite No. II for Three or More Violins," Elkin, 1964.

Contributor of about sixty articles to *Grove's Dictionary of Music and Musicians,* 5th edition, Macmillan, 1954, and to *Encyclopaedia Britannica, Pitman's Popular Encyclopaedia, Collier's Encyclopedia, Book of Knowledge, Larousse Dictionnaire de Musique, Die Musik in Geschichte und Gegenwart, Enciclopedia della Musica,* and *Encyclopedia of Music and Musicians.* Contributor of articles and reviews to *Listener, New Statesman, Times Literary Supplement,* and music journals. Editor, *Cherwell,* 1927-29, and *Consort,* 1934-38.

WORK IN PROGRESS: The Rise of Opera, for Faber; a cantata, "Hymn to God the Father," for soloists, chorus, and full orchestra.

SIDELIGHTS: Robert Donington is interested in analytical psychology, "especially as a tool for studying works of art," and in neoplatonic symbolism, "especially for my studies of early opera." *Avocational interests:* Collecting antique clocks, country walks.

*   *   *

DOOB, Anthony N(ewcomb) 1943-

PERSONAL: Born April 28, 1943, in Washington, D.C.; son of Leonard W. and Eveline (Bates) Doob; married Penelope Billings Reed (a professor of English), June 18, 1966 (divorced, 1976). *Education:* Harvard University, A.B., 1964; Stanford University, Ph.D., 1967. *Home:* 22 Langley Ave., Toronto, Ontario, Canada. *Office:* Department of Psychology, University of Toronto, Toronto, Ontario, Canada M5S.

CAREER: Stanford University, Stanford, Calif., instructor in psychology, 1967-68; University of Toronto, Toronto, Ontario, assistant professor, 1968-71, associate professor, 1971-76, professor of psychology, 1976—. *Member:* Canadian Psychological Association, American Psychological Association.

WRITINGS: (With J. L. Freedman) *Deviancy: The Psychology of Being Different,* Academic Press, 1968; (editor with D. T. Regan) *Readings in Experimental Social Psychology,* Appleton, 1971. Contributor to professional journals.

*   *   *

DOROSHKIN, Milton 1914-

PERSONAL: Born August 1, 1914, in New York, N.Y.; son of Jacob I. (a camp director) and Sadie (Weiss) Doroshkin; married Osnas Gelbaum (a librarian), October 23, 1937; children: Tabitha (Mrs. Arthur Gewirtz), Wendy (Mrs. Hartley S. Spatt). *Education:* Jewish Teachers College, Teachers Diploma, 1935; attended New York University, 1936-37, Columbia University, 1942, and City College (now City College of the City University of New York), 1943; New School for Social Research, M.A., 1960, Ph.D., 1968. *Politics:* Liberal independent. *Religion:* "American Jew." *Home:* 22 Farm House Lane, East Hampton, N.Y. 11937. *Office:* Department of Sociology, Bronx Community College of the City University of New York, Bronx, N.Y. 10468.

CAREER: Administrative and executive positions in community relations work and social work, New York, N.Y., 1943-59; New York City Community College of Applied Arts and Sciences of the City University of New York, Brooklyn, N.Y., instructor in sociology, 1959; Bronx Community College of the City University of New York, Bronx, N.Y., 1960—, began as assistant professor, currently professor of sociology. Visiting professor at Yeshiva University, City College of the City University of New York, and Adelphi University. *Member:* American Sociological Association, American Society for Geolinguistics, American Society of Criminology, United Federation of College Teachers. *Awards, honors:* Three research grants from Lucius N. Littauer Foundation; two research grants from Sol and Lillian Ash Foundation.

WRITINGS: Yiddish in America: Social and Cultural Foundations, Fairleigh Dickinson University Press, 1970. Author of articles, book reviews, and scholarly papers. Member of editorial board, *Yiddish* (quarterly journal published by Queens College Press).

WORK IN PROGRESS: Research in sociology of the Jews and in social psychiatry.

AVOCATIONAL INTERESTS: Collecting art, sculpture, music (cello and chamber music), and involvement in community cultural and political activities.

* * *

DOTTS, Maryann J. 1933-

PERSONAL: Born November 11, 1933, in Pittsburgh, Pa.; daughter of Charles A. and Mary J. (Dryer) Dreese; married M. Franklin Dotts (an editor), August 9, 1958; children: Ruthann C. *Education:* National College, Kansas City, Mo., A.B., 1956; Scarritt College for Christian Workers, M.A., 1974; George Peabody College for Teachers, M.L.S., 1975. *Religion:* United Methodist. *Home:* 2514 Blair Blvd., Nashville, Tenn. 37212. *Office:* Belle Meade United Methodist Church, 121 Davidson Rd., Nashville, Tenn. 37205.

CAREER: Director of Christian education at United Methodist churches in Erie, Pa., 1956-58, and Arlington Heights, Ill., 1958-61; Riverside Church, New York, N.Y., teacher and supervisor, 1965-67; Upper Room Library and Museum, Board of Discipleship, Nashville, Tenn., librarian and cataloguer, 1975; Belle Meade United Methodist Church, Nashville, director of Christian education, 1976—. *Member:* Church and Synagogue Library Association (member of board of directors, 1976-77), Christian Educators Fellowship, Tennessee Conference Christian Educators Fellowship.

WRITINGS: I Am Happy, Abingdon, 1971; (with husband, M. Franklin Dotts) *Clues to Creativity: Providing Learning Experiences for Children,* three volumes, Friendship Press, 1974-76; *The Church Resource Library,* Abingdon, 1975. Author of church school curriculum, 1960—.

WORK IN PROGRESS: Librarian's Guide to Displays; a book of chorale readings of the Bible for children; a children's book on the Christmas story; a book on the relationships of colors, sizes, and shapes.

AVOCATIONAL INTERESTS: Camping, Chinese cooking, needlepoint, travel.

* * *

DOUCETTE, Leonard E(ugene) 1936-

PERSONAL: Born February 28, 1936, in Chatham Head, New Brunswick, Canada; son of Frederick J. and Isabelle (Driscoll) Doucette; married Mary Emery, January 19, 1963; children: Julia Glenn, John Frederick. *Education:* St. Thomas University, Chatham, New Brunswick, B.A. (honors), 1955; King's College, London, B.A., 1958; Brown University, Ph.D., 1966. *Home:* 65 Deep Dene Dr., West Hill, Ontario, Canada. *Office:* Department of French, Scarborough College, University of Toronto, Toronto, Ontario, Canada.

CAREER: St. Thomas University, Chatham, New Brunswick, acting professor of modern languages, 1958-61; Brown University, Providence, R.I., assistant in French department, 1961-63; University of Pennsylvania, Philadelphia, instructor, 1965-66, assistant professor of French, 1966-67; University of Toronto, Scarborough College, Toronto, Ontario, assistant professor, 1967-72, associate professor of French, 1972—. Director of English Language School, University of New Brunswick, 1967-70. *Military service:* Royal Canadian Infantry, 1958-61; became captain. *Member:* Modern Language Association of America, Phi Beta Kappa. *Awards, honors:* Humanities Research Council grant, 1970, for *Emery Bigot;* Canada Council grant, 1972-73.

WRITINGS: Emery Bigot: Seventeenth-Century Humanist, University of Toronto Press, 1970.

WORK IN PROGRESS: Research on Pierre-Daniel Huet (1630-1721) and his role in French intellectual history.

* * *

DOUGHERTY, Richard M. 1935-

PERSONAL: Born January 17, 1935, in East Chicago, Ind.; son of Floyd C. and Harriet (Martin) Dougherty; married Carole Mary Low (a secretary), July 8, 1954; children: Jill Ann, Jacquelyn A., Douglas Michael. *Education:* Purdue University, B.S., 1959; Rutgers University, M.L.S., 1961, Ph.D., 1963. *Office:* Library, University of California, Berkeley, Calif. 94720.

CAREER: Inland Steel Corp., East Chicago, Ind., laborer and third helper on open hearth furnaces, 1953-54, 1956-57; Linden Public Library, Linden, N.J., librarian-trainee, 1959-61; Rutgers University, New Brunswick, N.J., research associate, 1961-63; University of North Carolina at Chapel Hill, head of acquisitions department, 1963-66; University of Colorado, Boulder, associate director of libraries, 1966-70; Syracuse University, Syracuse, N.Y., professor of library science, 1970-72; University of California, Berkeley, university librarian, 1972—. Member of biomedical library review committee, National Library of Medicine, 1971-75. President, Mountainside Publishing Co. *Military service:* U.S. Naval Reserve, 1954-56.

MEMBER: American Library Association (member of executive board, 1972-76), American Society for Information Science, New York Library Association, Colorado Library Association, Beta Phi Mu, Xi Sigma Pi, Alpha Zeta. *Awards, honors:* Esther J. Piercy Award, Resources and Technical Services Division, American Library Association, 1969; Council on Library Resources fellowship, 1970.

WRITINGS: (With Fred J. Heinritz) *Scientific Management of Library Operations,* Scarecrow, 1966; (with R. W. Wadsworth and Donald H. Axman) *Politics and Programs Designed to Improve Cooperation and Coordination among Technical Services Operating Units,* Graduate School of Library Service, University of Illinois, 1967; (with James G. Stephens) *Investigation Concerning the Modification of the University of Illinois Computerized Serials Book Catalog to Achieve an Operative System at the University of Colorado Libraries,* Clearinghouse for Federal Scientific and Technical Information, 1968; (with Lawrence E. Leonard and Joan M. Maier) *Centralized Book Processing: A Feasibility*

Study Based on Colorado Academic Libraries, Scarecrow, 1969; (with Leonard and Maier) *Centralized Processing in Academic Libraries,* Scarecrow, 1971; (with Laura Blomquist) *Improving Access to Library Resources,* Scarecrow, 1974.

Contributor to library journals. Assistant editor, *Library Resources and Technical Services,* 1964-69; departmental editor, *Library-College Journal,* 1968-69; member of editorial board, *Journal of Library Automation,* 1968—; editor, *College and Research Libraries* and *ACRL Newsletter,* 1969-74, *Journal of Academic Librarianship,* 1975—.

*   *   *

DOUGLAS-HAMILTON, James   1942-

PERSONAL: Born July 31, 1942, in Lanarkshire, Scotland; son of the Duke and Duchess of Hamilton. *Education:* Balliol College, Oxford, M.A., 1964; University of Edinburgh, LL.B., 1967. *Politics:* Conservative. *Religion:* Church of Scotland. *Home:* 3 Blackie House, Lady Stairs Close, Edinburgh, Scotland. *Agent:* Peter Janson-Smith, 31 Newington Green, London N16 9PU, England.

CAREER: Scots advocate (court attorney) at Parliament House, Edinburgh, Scotland, 1968; House of Commons, London, England, member of Parliament, representing West Edinburgh, 1977—. *Military service:* 6/7 Battalion, Cameronians, Scottish Rifles, 1961-67; Officer, TAVR, Cameronian Company, 2nd Battalion, Lowland Volunteers, 1971-72. *Member:* Oxford Union Society (president, 1964).

WRITINGS: Motive for a Mission: The Story behind Hess's Flight to Britain, Macmillan, 1971.

SIDELIGHTS: James Douglas-Hamilton's book is the result of his investigation into the story behind the mysterious flight to Scotland of Rudolph Hess, Deputy Fuehrer of the Third Reich, on the 10th of May, 1941. The author's father, the Duke of Hamilton, was the man whom Hess asked to see in his quest for a peace settlement between Germany and Great Britain, one month before the Third Reich attacked the Soviet Union.

*   *   *

DOWNER, Alan S(eymour)   1912-1970

July 15, 1912—January 20, 1970; American educator, editor, and author of books on drama. Obituaries: *Variety,* January 18, 1970. (See index for *CA* sketch)

*   *   *

DOWNER, Marion   1892(?)-1971

1892(?)—October 6, 1971; American artist and author of children's books. Obituaries: *Publishers Weekly,* November 8, 1971.

*   *   *

DOWNES, Bryan Trevor   1939-

PERSONAL: Born September 22, 1939, in Vancouver, British Columbia, Canada; came to United States in 1945, naturalized in 1955; married Sharon E. Lenahan, June, 1963; children: Laura Elizabeth, Alexander Bryan. *Education:* University of Oregon, B.S., 1962, Carnegie fellow, 1962-63, M.S., 1963; Washington University, St. Louis, Mo., Ph.D., 1966. *Office:* Division of Public Affairs, School of Community Service and Public Affairs, University of Oregon, Eugene, Ore. 97403.

CAREER: San Francisco State College (now University),

San Francisco, Calif., assistant professor of political science, 1966-67; Michigan State University, East Lansing, assistant professor, 1967-70, associate professor of political science, 1970-71; University of Missouri—St. Louis, associate professor of political science, 1971-76; University of Oregon, School of Community Service and Public Affairs, Eugene, associate professor of public affairs and chairperson of division of public affairs, 1976—. Fellow at Inter-University Consortium for Political Research, University of Michigan, 1964. *Member:* American Political Science Association, Midwest Conference of Political Scientists, Pi Sigma Alpha. *Awards, honors:* National Science Foundation grants, 1965-66 and 1969-70.

WRITINGS: (Editor) *Cities and Suburbs: Selected Readings in Local Politics and Public Policy,* Wadsworth, 1971; *Politics, Change, and the Urban Crisis,* Duxbury, 1976.

Contributor: Terry N. Clark, editor, *Community Structure and Decision-Making: Comparative Analyses,* Chandler Publishing, 1968; Charles M. Bonjean and Norval Glenn, editors, *Blacks in the United States,* Chandler Publishing, 1969; James Riedel, editor, *New Perspectives in State and Local Politics,* Xerox College Publishing, 1971; Harlan Hahn, editor, *Urban Politics and People,* Sage Publications, 1972; Louis H. Masotti and J. K. Hadden, editors, *The Urbanization of the Suburbs,* Sage Publications, 1973. Author or co-author of several papers on political subjects; contributor of articles to *Midwest Journal of Political Science, Urban Affairs Quarterly, Social Science Quarterly, Urban Education, Urban Analysis,* and other journals.

WORK IN PROGRESS: Research on urban migration patterns; compiling research materials on community problem-solving; research on factors affecting public policy decisions, governmental performance, and political change at the local level.

*   *   *

DOWNES, David A(nthony)   1927-

PERSONAL: Born August 17, 1927, in Victor, Colo.; son of David Michael and Julia (Zitnik) Downes; married Audrey Romaine Ernst, September 7, 1949; children: Mary Kathryn, Jane Frances, Daniel Ross, Michelle Marie. *Education:* Regis College, B.A. (cum laude), 1949; Marquette University, M.A., 1950; University of Washington, Ph.D., 1956. *Home:* 1076 San Ramon Dr., Chico, Calif. 95926. *Office:* Educational Development Projects, California State University, Chico, Calif. 95926.

CAREER: Gonzaga University, Spokane, Wash., instructor in English, 1950-53; Seattle University, Seattle, Wash., 1953-68, began as assistant professor, became professor of English and chairman of department; California State University, Chico, professor of English and dean of humanities and fine arts, 1968-72, director of educational development projects, 1972—, director of humanities program, 1972-74. *Awards, honors:* Western Gear Foundation publication grant, 1960; Seattle University research grants, 1961, 1962, 1967, publication grant, 1965; Chico State College (now California State University, Chico) Foundation research grant, 1969.

WRITINGS: Gerard Manley Hopkins: A Study of His Ignatian Spirit, Bookman Associates, 1959; *Victorian Portraits: Hopkins and Pater,* Bookman Associates, 1965; *The Temper of Victorian Belief: Studies in Victorian Religious Fiction; Pater, Kingsley, and Newman,* Twayne, 1972. Contributor to *Thought, Victorian Poetry,* and *Hopkins Quarterly.* Editor, *University Journal,* 1974—.

DOWST, Somerby Rohrer 1926-

PERSONAL: Born January 15, 1926, in Boston, Mass.; son of Robert S. (a writer) and Constance (Rohrer) Dowst; married Aetna Womble, February 24, 1951; children: Aetna, Robert, Talbott. *Education:* Harvard University, A.B., 1948. *Politics:* Democrat. *Religion:* Episcopalian. *Home:* 318 Alpine Dr., Peekskill, N.Y. 10566. *Office:* Purchasing Magazine, 205 East 42nd St., New York, N.Y. 10017.

CAREER: General Aniline & Film Corp., New York City, buyer, 1951-54; Bigelow Sanford Carpet Co., New York City, buyer, 1954; Union Carbide Corp., New York City, purchasing agent, 1954-62; *Purchasing* Magazine, New York City, managing editor, 1962—. *Military service:* U.S. Army Air Forces, 1944-45. *Awards, honors:* Jesse H. Neal Editorial Achievement Award, American Business Press, 1965, for article, "Purchasing at Western Electric."

WRITINGS: Basics for Buyers, Cahners, 1971. Contributor of articles to *Purchasing, Dun's Review, Sales Management, Diners Club, Systems, Health Institution Purchasing,* and *Personal Romances.*

WORK IN PROGRESS: Articles for *Purchasing* (magazine); a book on value analysis.

* * *

DRAKE, Albert (Dee) 1935-

PERSONAL: Born March 26, 1935, in Portland, Ore.; son of Albert Howard and Hildah (Lotten) Drake; married Barbara Robertson (a writer), December 28, 1960; children: Moss Christopher, Monica Durrell, Barbara Ellen. *Education:* Attended Portland State College (now University), 1956-59; University of Oregon, B.A., 1962, M.F.A., 1966. *Politics:* None. *Religion:* None. *Home:* 1790 Grand River Ave., Okemos, Mich. 48864. *Office:* Department of English, Michigan State University, East Lansing, Mich. 48824.

CAREER: Has worked as a laborer, mechanic, gravedigger, and in warehouses; Oregon Research Institute, Eugene, Ore., medical research assistant, 1963-64; Michigan State University, East Lansing, associate professor of English, 1966—. *Military service:* National Guard, 1953-60. *Awards, honors:* National Endowment for the Arts grant, 1975.

WRITINGS: Crap Game (poetry), Stone Press, 1968; (editor and contributor) *Michigan Signatures: An Anthology of Current Michigan Poetry,* Quixote Press, 1969; (with Lawson Inada and Doug Lawder) *Three Northwest Poets,* Quixote Press, 1970; *Pomes,* Stone Press, 1972; *Riding Bike* (poetry), Stone Press, 1973; *By Breathing In and Out* (poetry), Three Rivers Press, 1974; *Cheap Thrills* (poetry), Peaceweed Press, 1975; *Returning to Oregon* (poetry), Cider Press, 1975; *Roadsalt* (poetry), Bieler Press, 1976; *The Post-Card Mysteries and Other Stories* (fiction), Red Cedar Press, 1976; *Tillamook Burn* (fiction and poetry), The Fault Press, 1977. Contributor of fiction to *Best American Short Stories 1971* and to forty-two magazines, including *Redbook, Northwest Review, Fiddlehead,* and *Chicago Review;* contributor of poetry, articles, and reviews to anthologies and more than two hundred magazines, including *Midwest Quarterly, Ann Arbor Review, Wormwood Review, Trace, Western Humanities Review, Descant,* and *West Coast Review.* Editor, *Happiness Holding Tank* (poetry magazine).

WORK IN PROGRESS: A novel, *One Summer;* short and experimental fiction.

SIDELIGHTS: Albert Drake says that he has been influ-enced by experimental poets and fiction writers. He lists his interests as graphics, the visual arts and poetry, and various printing methods. He also enjoys travel.

* * *

DRAKE, Barbara (Ann) 1939-

PERSONAL: Born April 13, 1939, in Abilene, Kan.; daughter of J. Ward and Monica (Lorson) Robertson; married Albert Drake (a writer and teacher at Michigan State University), December 28, 1960; children: Moss Christopher, Monica Durell, Barbara Ellen. *Education:* University of Oregon, B.A., 1961, M.F.A. (with honors), 1966. *Home:* 1790 Grand River Rd., Okemos, Mich. 48864. *Office:* Department of American Thought and Language, Michigan State University, East Lansing, Mich. 48823.

CAREER: Holt, Rinehart & Winston, Inc., New York, N.Y., writer in textbook department, 1966-71; Michigan State University, East Lansing, teacher of women's poetry workshop in Evening School, 1971, instructor in department of American thought and language, 1974—. Work in Michigan Council for the Arts writers-in-the-schools program, 1973—. Gives frequent readings of her own poetry at universities and libraries. *Awards, honors:* National Foundation for the Arts creative writing fellowship, 1966.

WRITINGS: (Contributor) Albert Kitzhaber, editor, *The Oregon Curriculum,* Holt, 1968; (co-author) *The Oregon Curriculum: A Sequential Program in English Literature,* edited by Kitzhaber, Holt, Volume IV, 1969, Volume V, 1970, Volume VI, 1970; *Narcissa Notebook* (chapbook), Stone Press, 1973; *Field Poems,* Stone Press, 1975. Co-author of "Concepts in Literature" series, Holt.

Contributor to anthologies, including *Moving to Antarctic,* Dustbooks, *Echoes from the Moon,* Detroit Women Writers, *The Third Coast,* Wayne State University Press, and *Borestone Mountain Best Poems of 1970.* Contributor of more than fifty poems and of articles, short stories, and reviews to *Epoch, Sumac, Centennial Review, Wisconsin Review, Transpacific, Colorado Quarterly, Wormwood Review, Salt Lick, Northwest Review,* and other publications.

SIDELIGHTS: Barbara Drake tells *CA:* "My husband and I traveled through Europe by foot and motor-scooter for a year (1962-63) including several months on the Greek island of Korfu before returning to graduate school in 1964. It is important to me that since the birth of our first child in 1963 I've consistently been able to combine child-rearing with my graduate school, teaching, and writing career. I support the current women's liberation movement.... I'm an amateur photographer, doing my own darkroom work."

* * *

DRAPER, Alfred 1924-

PERSONAL: Born October 26, 1924, in London, England; son of Richard and Florence (Wills) Draper; married Barbara Pilcher, March 31, 1951; children: Nicholas, Antony. *Education:* Studied at North West Polytechnic, London, four years. *Home:* 31 Oakridge Ave., Radlett, Hertfordshire, England.

CAREER: Journalist in London, England, 1950—, specializing in crime and murder trials at home and reporting from abroad for *Daily Express. Military service:* Royal Navy; served in Atlantic and Pacific theaters; became sub-lieutenant. *Member:* Crime Writers Association. *Awards, honors:* Runner-up in Macmillan/Panther first crime novel competition, 1970, for *Swansong for a Rare Bird.*

WRITINGS: Swansong for a Rare Bird, Coward, 1970; *The Death Penalty,* Macmillan, 1972; *Smoke without Fire,* Arlington Books, 1974; *The Prince of Wales,* New English Library, 1975; *The Story of the Goons,* Everest, 1976. Contributor to British dailies and numerous magazines.

WORK IN PROGRESS: With Leland Stowe, a history of Britain's gold and securities shipped to Canada at the beginning of World War II, for Cassell and Corgi Books.

*   *   *

DRAPKIN, Herbert 1916-

PERSONAL: Born October 26, 1916. *Education:* City College (now City College of the City University of New York), B.S., 1936; Columbia University, M.A., 1938. *Home:* 19812 Burleigh Dr., Yorba Linda, Calif. 92686. *Office:* Department of Biology, Fullerton College, Fullerton, Calif. 92632.

CAREER: Fullerton College, Fullerton, Calif., instructor in biology, 1954—. *Military service:* U.S. Army Air Forces, Aviation Physiology section; became first lieutenant.

WRITINGS: A Manual for Life Sciences, National Press Books, 1959; (with Paul F. Brandwein and others) *Life: Its Forms and Processes,* Harcourt, 1968. Also writer of thirty-five instructional television tapes.

*   *   *

DRAY, William H(erbert) 1921-

PERSONAL: Born June 23, 1921, in Montreal, Quebec, Canada; son of William John and Florence E. (Jones) Dray; married Doris K. Best, September 18, 1943; children: Christopher Reid, Jane Elizabeth. *Education:* University of Toronto, B.A., 1943; Oxford University, M.A., 1955, D.Phil., 1956. *Home:* 166 Rodney Cir., Ottawa, Ontario, Canada. *Office:* Department of Philosophy, University of Ottawa, Ottawa, Ontario, Canada.

CAREER: University of Toronto, Toronto, Ontario, lecturer, 1953-55, assistant professor, 1956-61, professor of philosophy, 1961-68; Trent University, Peterborough, Ontario, professor of philosophy, 1968-76; University of Ottawa, Ottawa, Ontario, professor of philosophy, 1976—. *Military service:* Royal Canadian Air Force, 1941-46. *Member:* Canadian Philosophical Association, American Philosophical Association, Royal Commonwealth Society, Royal Society of Canada (fellow), Aristotelian Society.

WRITINGS: Laws and Explanation in History, Oxford University Press, 1957; *Philosophy of History,* Prentice-Hall, 1964; (editor) *Philosophical Analysis and History,* Harper, 1966.

Contributor: P. Gardiner, editor, *Theories of History,* Free Press, 1959; R. J. Butler, editor, *Analytical Philosophy,* Blackwell, 1962; S. Hook, editor, *Philosophy and History: A Symposium,* New York University Press, 1963; R. S. Peters, editor, *Philosophy and Education,* Ontario Institute for Studies in Education, 1967; L. Gross, editor, *Sociological Theory: Inquiries and Paradigms,* Harper, 1967; P. King and B. C. Parekh, editors, *Politics and Experience,* Cambridge University Press, 1968; H. E. Kiefer and M. K. Munitz, editors, *Science, Mind and History,* State University of New York Press, 1970.

WORK IN PROGRESS: Analysis of the concept of causation in history and of narrative as explanation.

*   *   *

DREIKURS, Rudolph 1897-1972

February 8, 1897—May 25, 1972; Austrian-born American

educator and Adlerian psychiatrist. Obituaries: *New York Times,* May 31, 1972. (See index for *CA* sketch)

*   *   *

DREYFUS, Hubert L(ederer) 1929-

PERSONAL: Born October 15, 1929, in Terre Haute, Ind.; son of Stanley S. (a businessman) and Irene (Lederer) Dreyfus; married Patricia Allen, June 25, 1962 (divorced, 1967); married Genevieve Boissier, December 10, 1974; children: (second marriage) Stephen Daniel. *Education:* Harvard University, B.A. (with highest honors), 1951, M.A., 1952, Ph.D., 1964. *Home:* 1116 Sterling Ave., Berkeley, Calif. 94708. *Office:* Department of Philosophy, University of California, Berkeley, Calif. 94720.

CAREER: Brandeis University, Waltham, Mass., instructor in philosophy, 1957-59; Massachusetts Institute of Technology, Cambridge, instructor, 1960-63, assistant professor, 1963-66, associate professor of philosophy, 1966-68; University of California, Berkeley, associate professor, 1968-72, professor of philosophy, 1972—.

MEMBER: American Philosophical Association, Society for Phenomenology and Existential Philosophy, Phi Beta Kappa. *Awards, honors:* Sheldon traveling fellowship of Harvard University to University of Freiburg, 1953-54; Fulbright fellowship to Husserl Archives, Louvain, Belgium, 1956-57; French Government grants, 1959-60, 1964-65; Baker Award for outstanding teaching, 1966; National Science Foundation grant, 1968; Harbison Prize for outstanding teaching, 1968; American Council of Learned Societies grant, 1968-69; National Endowment for the Humanities fellow, 1976—.

WRITINGS: (With Patricia Allen Dreyfus, translator and author of preface) Maurice Merleau-Ponty, *Sense and Non-Sense,* Northwestern University Press, 1964; *Alchemy and Artificial Intelligence,* RAND Corp., 1965; *What Computers Can't Do: A Critique of Artificial Reason,* Harper, 1972.

Contributor: James Edie, editor, *Phenomenology in America,* Quadrangle, 1967; Lester Embree, editor, *Life-World and Consciousness,* Northwestern University Press, 1970; Marjorie Greene, editor, *Interpretations of Life and Mind,* Routledge & Kegan Paul, 1971; J. T. Fraser and N. Lawrence, editors, *The Study of Time II,* Springer-Verlag, 1975; S. F. Spricker and H. T. Englehardt, editors, *Philosophical Dimensions of the Neuro-Medical Sciences,* Reidel, 1976; M. Ringle, editor, *Philosophical Perspectives in Artificial Intelligence,* Humanities Press, 1978. Contributor to *Akten des XIV Internationalen Kongresses fuer Philosophy,* 1968, *Annals* of American Academy of Political and Social Science, and to journals.

WORK IN PROGRESS: Merleau-Ponty, for Viking; editing *Husserl: Critical Articles,* for University of California Press.

SIDELIGHTS: Hubert Dreyfus told *CA:* "I write because I am a teacher. Teaching helps me clarify and test my ideas, my line of argument, and writing is the natural thing to do afterward. If I write more articles than books, it is because a book, so it seems to me, requires a deeper maturation process.

"At the moment my attention and energy are more than ever focused on the world of Artificial Intelligence. I consider myself to be applying Phenomenology to determine the limits of Computer Science."

Dreyfus lived in Germany for one year and has spent a total

of six years in France. *What Computers Can't Do* has been translated into Russian, Japanese, Portuguese, and Yugoslavian.

* * *

DROESCHER, Vitus B(ernward) 1925-

PERSONAL: Born October 15, 1925, in Leipzig, Germany; son of Gustav (director of the state library) and Frida (Plate) Droescher; married Helga Oppermann (a free-lance science writer), May 28, 1955; children: Lutz, Nicola, Ariane, Till. *Education:* Attended Hannover Institute of Technology, 1948-52. *Religion:* Evangelical Lutheran. *Home:* Koellns Acker 6, Hamburg 54, West Germany. *Agent:* Rosica Colin, 4 Hereford Sq., London SW7 4TU, England.

CAREER: Krupp-Atlas Experimental Laboratories for Submarine Acoustic Research, Bremen, Germany, experimental engineer, 1952-54; free-lance science writer, Hamburg, West Germany, 1954—. *Military service:* German Navy, 1944-45; became ensign. *Member:* Tennis Club (Hamburg; member of executive board). *Awards, honors:* Theodor-Wolff Prize, given by Free University of West Berlin and *Die Welt,* 1965, for the best scientific report in German newspapers; *Die freundliche Bestie* was named the best animal book of the year in the Netherlands, 1970; *Sie lieben und sie toeten sich* was named as the book of the month by the Club Francaise du Livre, 1975.

WRITINGS: Klug wie die Schlangen: Die Erforschung der Tierseele, Stalling, 1962, translation by Eveleen Huggard published as *Mysterious Senses: An Enquiry into Animal Perception,* Hodder & Stoughton, 1964, same translation published as *The Mysterious Senses of Animals,* Dutton, 1965; *Magic der Sinne im Tierreich: Neue Forschungen* (Book of the Month in Germany, October, 1967), Paul List Verlag, 1966, translation by Ursula Lehrburger and Oliver Coburn published as *The Magic of the Senses: New Discoveries in Animal Perception,* Dutton, 1969; *Die freundliche Bestie: Neueste Forschungen,* Stalling, 1968, translation by Richard Winston and Clara Winston published as *The Friendly Beast,* W. H. Allen, 1970, Dutton, 1971; *Die freundliche Bestie im Zoo,* Stalling, 1970; *Sie lieben und sie toeten sich: Naturgeschichte sozialen Verhaltens,* Hoffmann & Campe, 1974, translation by Jan van Heurck published as *They Love and Kill,* Dutton, 1976.

Television documentaries: "African Wildlife," twenty-six programs, 1967-68; "The Last Wild Animals of Europe," twenty-six programs, 1969-71. Contributor of science articles to leading newspapers in Germany.

WORK IN PROGRESS: An encyclopedia on animal behavior (1,200 animals); a thirteen-program television series, "Animal Behavior in the Zoo."

SIDELIGHTS: Vitus Droescher's books have been translated into fifteen languages, with sales of more than 500,000 copies in all editions.

BIOGRAPHICAL/CRITICAL SOURCES: Die Journalisten, Christian Wegner Verlag (Hamburg), 1967.

* * *

DRUMMOND, Harold D. 1916-

PERSONAL: Born June 8, 1916, in Bettsville, Ohio; son of Ray Waldo and Velma (Foor) Drummond; married Catherine Street, August 30, 1939; children: H. Evan. *Education:* Attended Westminster College, Salt Lake City, Utah, 1933-35; Colorado State College (now University of Northern Colorado), A.B., 1937, M.A., 1940; Stanford University,

Ed.D., 1948. *Office:* University of New Mexico, Albuquerque, N.M. 87131.

CAREER: Elementary teacher and principal in Texas, 1938-42; George Peabody College for Teachers, Nashville, Tenn., professor of elementary education, 1947-60; University of New Mexico, Albuquerque, professor of elementary education, 1960—, associate dean for Curriculum and Instruction. Acting professor of education assigned to University of the Philippines, Stanford University, 1954-55. *Military service:* U.S. Naval Reserve, 1942-45; became lieutenant. *Member:* National Education Association, Association for Supervision and Curriculum Development (president, 1965); Professors of Curriculum, American Association of University Professors, National Society for the Study of Education, National Council for the Social Studies, National Council for Geographic Education, Phi Delta Kappa, Phi Kappa Phi.

WRITINGS: (With Charles R. Spain and John I. Goodlad) *Educational Leadership and the Elementary School Principal,* Rinehart, 1956.

Reviser and author of teachers' manuals; texts originally written by De Forest Stull and Roy W. Hatch: *A Journey through Many Lands,* Allyn & Bacon, 1960, 3rd edition, 1969; *Journeys through the Americas,* Allyn & Bacon, 1960, 3rd edition, 1970; *The Western Hemisphere,* Allyn & Bacon, 1961, 4th edition, 1978; *Journeys through the United States and Canada,* Allyn & Bacon, 1966. Contributor to education journals. Member of editorial advisory board, *Childcraft.*

SIDELIGHTS: Drummond has visited sixty countries gathering material for his writings.

AVOCATIONAL INTERESTS: Photography.

* * *

DRURY, John 1898-1972

August 9, 1898—January 11, 1972; American journalist and author of books on local history. Obituaries: *New York Times,* January 13, 1972; *Washington Post,* January 14, 1972. (See index for *CA* sketch)

* * *

DUCKWORTH, George E(ckel) 1903-1972

February 13, 1903—April 5, 1972; American educator and classical scholar. Obituaries: *New York Times,* April 6, 1972; *Washington Post,* April 7, 1972. (See index for *CA* sketch)

* * *

DUFAULT, Peter Kane 1923-

PERSONAL: Born April 22, 1923, in Newark, N.J.; son of Roland Hubert and Christine Joyce (Kane) Dufault; married Joan Pyle; married second wife, Ruth Pauline Tuoti, July, 1963; children: (first marriage) Tadea Christine, Peter Scott, Mark Roland, Ethan Kane. *Education:* Attended Harvard University, 1947. *Home address:* R.D. 2, Hillsdale, N.Y. 12529.

CAREER: Poet; has given readings at Williams College, Amherst College, Bennington College, University of Virginia, Kalamazoo College, Vassar College, and other schools, and at Poetry Center and Lexington Ave. YM-YWHA, New York, N.Y. Narrator of "Forgotten River" and subject of "A Look the Other Way," both produced by CBS-TV. Has worked as a news editor, house painter, tree surgeon, folk singer, actor, fiddler, country dance caller, and as a teacher of writing, U.S. history, soccer, boxing, guitar, and banjo, at Williams College and Berkshire Community College. Peace candidate for Congress, 1968. *Military service:* U.S. Army Air Forces, World War II; served as Liberator bomber co-pilot.

WRITINGS—Poetry: *Angel of Accidence,* Macmillan, 1953; *For Some Stringed Instrument,* Macmillan, 1957; *A Westchester Farewell,* privately printed, 1969. Regular contributor of verse to *New Yorker* and other magazines and anthologies.

WORK IN PROGRESS: A play; a book on U.S. history; a series of "fables"; many poems.

*   *   *

DULANY, Harris 1940-

PERSONAL: Name legally changed, 1945; born January 2, 1940, in McKeesport, Pa.; son of Joseph Hayes Blackburn (a bank clerk) and Anne (a teacher; maiden name, Pollard) Blackburn Dulany; married Barry Leeds (a children's librarian), July 14, 1962; children: Caitlin Barry, Elizabeth Anne. *Education:* Attended Bethany College, Bethany, W. Va., 1957-58; Syracuse University, B.A., 1961; graduate study at Syracuse University and University of Iowa, 1961-63. *Address:* Calle De San Jose 13, Altea (Alicante), Spain.

CAREER: Kennebunk Star, Kennebunk, Me., reporter and editor, 1963-64; Mapes Oil & Gasoline Distributors, Sanford, Me., truck driver, 1964-65; Bowdoin College, Brunswick, Me., assistant director of news services, 1965-67; Three Lions Publishers, Inc., New York City, feature editor, 1967-68; Strand Book Store, New York City, sales clerk, beginning 1968. *Awards, honors:* MacDowell Colony residence fellowship, 1971.

WRITINGS: Falling (novel), McCall Publishing Co., 1971. Contributor to magazines and newspapers.

BIOGRAPHICAL/CRITICAL SOURCES: Publishers Weekly, February 15, 1971; *Washington Star,* May 23, 1971; *Best Sellers,* July 1, 1971; *Saturday Review,* July 3, 1971; *New York Times Book Review,* September 12, 1971; *Rolling Stone,* February 3, 1972.†

*   *   *

DUN, Angus 1892-1971

May 4, 1892—August 12, 1971; American clergyman. Obituaries: *New York Times,* August 13, 1971; *Washington Post,* August 13, 1971; *Newsweek,* August 23, 1971.

*   *   *

DUNBAR, Tony 1949-

PERSONAL: Born June 11, 1949, in Atlanta, Ga.; son of Leslie W. and Peggy (Rawls) Dunbar; married Penny Elizabeth Campbell, 1975. *Education:* Brandeis University, B.A., 1972. *Home:* 809 Cedarcrest Ave., Nashville, Tenn.

CAREER: Worker with civil rights and community development organizations in Georgia, South Carolina, Mississippi, and Kentucky, 1964-70; director of Southern Prison Ministry, 1972-78. *Awards, honors:* Lillian Smith Award, Southern Regional Council, 1971, for *Our Land Too.*

WRITINGS: Our Land Too, Pantheon, 1971; (with Linda Kravitz) *Hard Traveling: Migrant Farm Workers in America,* Ballinger, 1976. Contributor to *New South* and other periodicals.

WORK IN PROGRESS: Research on Christian radicalism and the southern civil rights movement during the depression.

BIOGRAPHICAL/CRITICAL SOURCES: Best Sellers, April 15, 1971.

*   *   *

DUNCAN, A(nthony) D(ouglas) 1930-

PERSONAL: Born July 28, 1930, in Rochester, Kent, England; son of Ronald Leslie (an executive of Shell Mexico BP Ltd.) and Phyllis (Warren) Duncan; married Helga Maria Helene Heinrich, October 13, 1966; children: Iain Michael, Anthony Mark, Fiona Mary. *Education:* Attended grammar schools in Cheshire and Northumberland, England, 1939-47. *Politics:* Scottish National Party. *Home and office:* St. John's Vicarage, 5 Summerhill Grove, Newcastle-upon-Tyre NE4 6EE, England.

CAREER: Articled clerk to chartered accountant in London, England, 1948-52; British Army, regular officer, 1953-60, retired as captain; Church of England, clerk in Holy Orders, 1962—, as assistant curate in Tewkesbury, 1962-65, vicar in Parkend, 1965-69, and rector in Highnam, 1969-73; St. John the Baptist Church, Newcastle-upon-Tyre, England, vicar, 1973—.

WRITINGS: Over the Hill (poems), Mitre Press, 1964; *Pray and Live,* S.P.C.K., 1966; *The Whole Christ,* S.P.C.K., 1968; *The Christ, Psychotherapy and Magic,* Allen & Unwin, 1969; *The Lord of the Dance,* Helios, 1972; *The Priesthood of Man,* S.P.C.K., 1973; *The Fourth Dimension,* Mowbray, 1975.

WORK IN PROGRESS: The Temple of the Spirit; The Sword in the Sun; The Seventh Angel; research projects into Christian spirituality and the perennial philosophy.

SIDELIGHTS: A. D. Duncan's interest in Oriental mysticism evolved from the years he spent in the Far East while a soldier. He is concerned with relating that mysticism and philosophy to orthodox Christian theology. He speaks Malay.

BIOGRAPHICAL/CRITICAL SOURCES: Books and Bookmen, December, 1969, June, 1974.

*   *   *

DUNCAN, Bowie 1941-

PERSONAL: Born February 2, 1941, in Houston, Tex.; son of G. C. (a rancher) and Genevieve (Lykes) Duncan; married Sterett Kelsey (a sculptor), June 30, 1965; children: McKay, Gittings. *Education:* Dartmouth College, B.A., 1964; University of Maryland, M.A., 1970.

CAREER: Wilbraham Academy, Wilbraham, Mass., teacher of English, 1966-68. *Member:* American Studies Association, Phi Kappa Phi.

WRITINGS: The Critical Reception of Howard Nemerov: A Selection of Essays and a Bibliography, introduction by Reed Whitemore, Scarecrow, 1971.

WORK IN PROGRESS: A book, *Stuart Davis: Abstractionist and Activist;* a study of radical pacifism in twentieth-century America.†

*   *   *

DUNHAM, Arthur 1893-

PERSONAL: Born August 3, 1893, in St. Louis, Mo.; son of William A. and Lottie May (Rickart) Dunham; married Esther Frances Schneider, May 31, 1919; children: Ruth

(Mrs. Bruce Hammarstrom), Richard. *Education:* Washington University, St. Louis, Mo., B.A., 1914; University of Illinois, M.A., 1917. *Religion:* Society of Friends. *Home and office:* 1640 Broadway, Ann Arbor, Mich. 48105.

CAREER: Social worker in St. Louis, Mo., 1915-18, Philadelphia, Pa., 1919-23, and Newton, Mass., 1923-25; Public Charities Association of Pennsylvania, Philadelphia, secretary of Child Welfare Division (later Family and Child Welfare Division), 1925-35; University of Michigan, School of Social Work, Ann Arbor, professor of community organization, 1935-63, emeritus professor, 1963—. Fulbright lecturer, University of Manchester, 1967; visiting professor for varying periods since 1962 at University of Hawaii, University of Missouri, University of Alaska, California State University, Fresno, Queen's University of Belfast, and other universities; conducted a seminar at School of Social Welfare, Athens, Greece, 1971. *Member:* National Association of Social Workers, Council on Social Work Education, National Conference on Social Welfare, International Council on Social Welfare, American Association of University Professors.

WRITINGS: Community Welfare Organization: Principles and Practice, Crowell, 1958, revised edition published as *The New Community Organization,* 1970; (editor with Ernest B. Harper) *Community Organization in Action,* Association Press, 1959; (with Monna Heath) *Trends in Community Organization,* School of Social Service Administration, University of Chicago, 1963; (contributor) *Popular Participation in Development: Emerging Trends in Community Development,* United Nations Publications, 1971. Also author of *Ann Arbor Friends Meeting, 1935-1975,* 1976. Contributor to social work and community development journals.

* * *

DUNLEAVY, Gareth W(inthrop) 1923-

PERSONAL: Born February 24, 1923, in Willimantic, Conn.; son of Henry Jay (a high school teacher) and Mabel (Hobbs) Dunleavy; married Elizabeth Lucas, May 31, 1947 (divorced, 1970); married Janet Egleson (a university professor), July 25, 1971; children: (first marriage) Gweneth Anne, Stephen Arthur. *Education:* Clark University, B.A., 1947; Brown University, M.A., 1949; Northwestern University, Ph.D., 1952. *Office:* Department of English, University of Wisconsin, Milwaukee, Wis. 53211.

CAREER: Bradley University, Peoria, Ill., assistant professor of English, 1952-56; University of Wisconsin—Milwaukee, assistant professor, 1956-59, associate professor, 1959-63, professor of English, 1963—, chairman of department, 1964-67, associate dean of Graduate School, 1967-68. *Military service:* U.S. Army, 1942-45; received Purple Heart (wounded in Italy). *Member:* Modern Language Association of America, American Committee for Irish Studies, Mediaeval Academy of America, American Civil Liberties Union, Midwest Modern Language Association, Phi Beta Kappa. *Awards, honors:* American Philosophical Society summer grant, 1971, 1973; American Council of Learned Societies research grant, 1972; American Irish Foundation Research grant, 1973, 1974; Fromkin Research and Lecture award, 1976.

WRITINGS: Colum's Other Island: The Irish at Lindisfarne, University of Wisconsin Press, 1960; (contributor) R. J. McNally, editor, *Old Ireland,* Fordham University Press, 1965; (contributor) John Gardner and N. Joost, editors, *Papers on the Art and Age of Geoffrey Chaucer,*

Southern Illinois University Press, 1967; *Douglas Hyde,* Bucknell University Press, 1974; (with wife, Janet E. Dunleavy) *The O'Conor Papers,* University of Wisconsin Press, 1977.

* * *

DUNMORE, Spencer (Sambrook) 1928-

PERSONAL: Born December 16, 1928, in London, England; son of Sidney Alfred (a civil servant) and Grace Mildred (Sambrook) Dunmore; married Edith Margarete Mueller, November 6, 1953; married second wife, Jean Clare Plant (a secretary), October 23, 1970; children: (first marriage) Janet Lynn. *Education:* Attended Pocklington School, East Yorkshire, England, and Guy's Hospital Medical School, London. *Home:* 830 Danforth Pl., Burlington, Ontario, Canada. *Office:* Steel Company of Canada, Hamilton, Ontario, Canada L8N 3T1.

CAREER: Has worked in advertising and as a copywriter; currently affiliated with Steel Company of Canada, Hamilton, Ontario. *Member:* American Aviation Historical Society.

WRITINGS—Novels; all published by Morrow: *Bomb Run,* 1971; *The Last Hill,* 1973; *Collision,* 1974; *Ashley Landing,* 1976.

WORK IN PROGRESS: Another novel.

SIDELIGHTS: Spencer Dunmore told *CA:* "I think of myself as a classic case of someone who can't write about interesting personal experiences, because I have had none (or none that I'm prepared to admit to). My m.o. has been to badger people who have done interesting things or still do them: e.g. WWII fliers, airline pilots, etc. If, as I've been told, there is an authenticity about my writings, it's because of the patience and excellent memories of my contacts. Without them, I don't know how I could produce."

BIOGRAPHICAL/CRITICAL SOURCES: Bookseller, November 28, 1970; *Bestsellers,* August, 1971, May, 1975, March, 1977.

* * *

DUNN, Donald H(arley) 1929-

PERSONAL: Born November 24, 1929, in Detroit, Mich.; son of Harvey A. (stepfather; an office manager) and Elaine (Hirsh) Vien; married Floracita Weller, January 3, 1953 (separated); children: Christopher, Paul, Elena, Carrie. *Education:* University of Missouri, B.J., 1951. *Politics:* Independent Democrat. *Office: Business Week,* 1221 Avenue of the Americas, New York, N.Y. 10020.

CAREER: Has worked as lyricist, writer of musical comedy books and revues, advertising copywriter, and editor of a television trade magazine, New York City, 1958-66; *Business Week* (magazine), New York City, media and advertising editor, 1967—. *Member:* International Brotherhood of Magicians.

WRITINGS: The Making of "No, No, Nanette" (Book-of-the-Month Club selection), Citadel, 1972; *Ponzi: The Boston Swindler,* McGraw, 1975.

Author of "That's the Spirit," revue produced in St. Louis, Mo., at Artists Guild, 1951, and "It Happened in Hannibal" (musical based on *Tom Sawyer*), produced in St. Louis, Mo., at Maryville College, 1953; wrote lyrics for "This is It," produced in St. Louis at Empress Theater, 1955. Also writer for nightclub reviews and fashion shows. Contributor of articles to *New York Times, Playboy, Show, Electronics Illustrated, Playbill,* and other periodicals.

SIDELIGHTS: Reviewing The Making of "No, No Nanette," Patricia E. Davis writes: "Don Dunn has come up with one of the most enjoyable accounts of the theatrical world in this reader's memory—informative, interesting, colorful and gossipy. It is a chronology of the events that led to the production of a successful Broadway show and the seemingly insurmountable difficulties involved.... The Making of "No, No Nanette"—like the musical it was written about—deserves success."

BIOGRAPHICAL/CRITICAL SOURCES: Variety, March 15, 1972; Detroit News, May 28, 1972; Stage, October 5, 1972.

* * *

DUNN, Katherine (Karen) 1945-

PERSONAL: Born October 24, 1945, in Garden City, Kan.; daughter of Jack (a linotype operator) and Velma (Golly) Dunn; children: Eli Malachy Dunn Dapolonia. Education: Attended Portland State College (now University) and Reed College. Religion: None. Address: 1603 Northwest 23rd, Portland, Ore. 97210.

AWARDS, HONORS: Music Corporation of America writing grant; Rockefeller writing grant.

WRITINGS: Attic (novel), Harper, 1970; Truck (novel), Harper, 1971. Also author of film script of Truck.

WORK IN PROGRESS: A novel entitled Toad, for Harper; a volume of short stories.

SIDELIGHTS: Katherine Dunn told CA: "I have been a believer in the magic of language since, at a very early age, I discovered that some words got me into trouble and others got me out. The revelations since then have been practically continuous.

"There are other inclinations that have shaped the form and direction of my work: rampant curiosity, a cynical inability to accept face-values balanced by lunatic optimism, and the preoccupation with the effervescing qualities of truth that is probably common to those afflicted by absent-mindedness, prevarication, and general unease in the presence of facts. But the miraculous nature of words themselves contains the discipline.

"Writing is, increasingly, a moral issue for me. The evasion of inexpensive facility, the rejection of the flying bridges built so seductively into the language, require a constant effort of will. The determination required for honest exploration and analysis of the human terrain is often greater than I command. But the fruits of that determination seem worthy of all my efforts."

BIOGRAPHICAL/CRITICAL SOURCES: Life, October 24, 1969; New York Times Book Review, June 21, 1970; New York Times, July 1, 1970; Nation, August 3, 1970.

* * *

DUNN, Stephen 1939-

PERSONAL: Born June 24, 1939, in New York, N.Y.; son of Charles F. (a salesman) and Ellen (Fleishman) Dunn; married Lois Kelly (a yoga teacher), September 26, 1965; children: Andrea Ellen, Susanne. Education: Hofstra University, B.A., 1962; New School for Social Research, graduate study, 1964-66; Syracuse University, M.A., 1970. Home: 224 Key Dr., Absecon, N.J. 08201. Agent: Philip G. Spitzer Literary Agency, 111-25 76th Ave., Forest Hills, N.Y. 11375. Office: Stockton State College, Pomona, N.J. 08240.

CAREER: Williamsport Billies, Williamsport, Pa., professional basketball player, 1962-63; National Biscuit Co., New York City, copywriter, 1963-66; Ziff-Davis Publishing Co., New York City, assistant editor, 1967-68; Southwest Minnesota State University, Marshall, assistant professor of creative writing, 1970-73; Stockton State College, Pomona, N.J., poet-in-residence, 1974—. Military service: U.S. Army, 1962. Member: American Association of University Professors. Awards, honors: Academy of American Poets, New York Poetry Center "Discovery '71" Award; National Endowment for the Arts fellowship, 1974.

WRITINGS—Poetry: Five Impersonations, Ox Head Press, 1971; Looking for Holes in the Ceiling, University of Massachusetts Press, 1974; Full of Lust and Good Usage, Carnegie Press, 1976; A Circus of Needs, Carnegie Press, 1978. Contributor of poems to Poetry (Chicago), Atlantic, Poetry Northwest, New York Times, New Republic, and other periodicals.

WORK IN PROGRESS: The Monastery of Work and Love, a book-length poem.

SIDELIGHTS: Dunn lived in Spain for a year and has spent other periods in Europe. He writes: "My poetry must speak for itself; I have no comments about it."

* * *

DUNN, William J. 1906-

PERSONAL: Born July 1, 1906, in Rosedale, Ind.; son of William Nathan (a minister) and Fannie (Miller) Dunn; married Catherine Beltzner, January 10, 1929; children: Patricia Lee (Mrs. G. H. Simmons). Education: Attended Taylor University, two years. Home: 81-11 Pettit Pl., Elmhurst, N.Y. 11373. Agent: Miss Shirley Burke, 370 East 76th St., Suite B-704, New York, N.Y. 10021. Office: British West Indies Airlines International, 610 Fifth Ave., New York, N.Y. 10020.

CAREER: Worked with United Press International and Associated Press in Indianapolis, Ind., Detroit, Mich., New York City, and Washington, D.C., 1926-34; American Airlines, Chicago, Ill., public relations director, 1934-38; Columbia Broadcasting System, editor and correspondent in New York City, and the Far East, 1939-46, war correspondent for Pacific front and chief of Far East Division during World War II; Manila Broadcasting Co., Manila, Philippines, executive vice-president, 1947-53; J. Walter Thompson Co. (advertising agency), Manila, general manager for the Philippines, 1953-59; free-lance writer in Nice, France, and Livorno, Italy, 1959-66; British West Indies Airlines International, New York City, director of public relations for North America, 1969—. Covered Korean War for National Broadcasting Corp. for six months in 1950.

WRITINGS: Enjoy Europe by Car, Nelson, 1962, 3rd edition, Scribner, 1975; Enjoy Europe by Train, Nelson, 1966, revised edition, 1976; Knickerbocker Centennial, Knickerbocker Club (New York, N.Y.), 1971; Out-of-the-Stockpot (cookbook), Scribner, 1971. Contributor to Gourmet, Travel, and other publications.

WORK IN PROGRESS: A third revision of Europe by Train; two specialty cookbooks.

SIDELIGHTS: William Dunn told CA: "Have been a traveler and bon vivant all my life; resided on four continents; circled the globe five times, across North Pole twice; covered the Burma Road on a truck (food was lousy) and have sailed or flown over ... about thirty-five seas, at least. Motivating force is unquenchable curiousity, love of good food, wines, music, and books. Inexcusably lazy but have a knack for meeting deadlines.... Fortunately, my wife is as footloose and hungry as myself.''

* * *

DUTTON, Mary 1922-

PERSONAL: Born November 7, 1922, in El Dorado, Ark.; daughter of Armon Linford (a teacher) and Grace (a teacher; maiden name Harrison) Ball; married Bob Dutton (a refinery worker), June 14, 1946; children: Richard, Bobby, Becky. *Education:* Attended El Dorado Junior College (now Butler County Community Junior College), West Texas State University, and Frank Phillips College. *Agent:* Phoebe Larmore, 44 Greenwich Ave., New York, N.Y. 10011.

CAREER: Teacher in Huttig, Ark., 1941-45; substitute teacher in Borger, Tex., 1951-66. Parks and playgrounds recreation director, Borger, 1960-64. Has also worked as file clerk, cashier, bookkeeper, waitress, typist, shoeclerk, soda jerk, and Avon lady. ''Once during World War II I had a job as a shoe shine girl.''

WRITINGS: Thorpe, World Publishing, 1967. Contributor to Macfadden Bartell publications, *Borger News-Herald,* and *Writer.*

WORK IN PROGRESS: A novel about life in a small town during the last years of World War II, with two sisters as main characters and a working title of *IVA.*

BIOGRAPHICAL/CRITICAL SOURCES: Best Sellers, November 15, 1967.†

* * *

DuVAL, F(rancis) Alan 1916-

PERSONAL: Born December 30, 1916, in Glenwood, Iowa; son of Frank E. and Mary Grace (Cattron) DuVal; married Louise Miller, December 15, 1942; children: Anne Louise. *Education:* Simpson College, B.A., 1939; University of Iowa, M.A., 1941, Ph.D., 1948. *Religion:* Protestant. *Home:* 710 Eighth Ave. N., Mt. Vernon, Iowa 52314. *Office:* Department of Classical and Modern Languages, Cornell College, Mt. Vernon, Iowa 52314.

CAREER: Cornell College, Mt. Vernon, Iowa, instructor, 1941-47, assistant professor, 1947-48, associate professor, 1948-57, professor of German, 1957—, chairman of department, 1960—. Consultant, National Foundation for the Humanities. *Military service:* U.S. Coast Guard, 1942-45; became lieutenant (jg). *Member:* Association of American Teachers of German, Modern Language Association of America, American Council on the Teaching of Foreign Language, Iowa Foreign Language Association, Phi Beta Kappa.

WRITINGS: (With others) *Moderne deutsche Sprachlehre,* Random House, 1967, 2nd edition, 1975; *Arbeitsheft fuer moderne deutsche Sprachlehre,* Random House, 1968, 2nd edition, 1975; (with wife, Louise M. DuVal) *Wiederholung und Fortsetzung,* Harper, 1971. Editor, *Iowa Foreign Language Bulletin,* 1962-64.

AVOCATIONAL INTERESTS: History and operation of American and German railways.

* * *

DWECK, Susan 1943-

PERSONAL: Born July 26, 1943, in Washington, D.C.; daughter of Samuel R. (a real estate financier) and Rena (Cohen) Dweck. *Education:* American University, B.A.,

1965, graduate study, 1966. *Religion:* Jewish. *Home:* 2737 Devonshire Pl. N.W., Washington, D.C. 20008. *Office:* Department of Health, Education and Welfare, 200 Independence Ave. S.W., Washington, D.C. 20201.

CAREER: Gotham Investment Co., Washington, D.C., administrative assistant, 1964-67; teacher in Montgomery County (Md.) Public Schools, 1965-69; University Research Corp., Washington, D.C., administrative and research assistant, Manpower Research Division, 1969-70, research assistant, Research and Education Division, 1970-73; Office of Economic Opportunity, Washington, D.C., research specialist, Office of Evaluation, 1973-74; U.S. Department of Health, Education and Welfare, Washington, D.C., program specialist, Office of Assistant Secretary for Planning and Evaluation, 1974—.

WRITINGS: (With Cheryl Frank) *A Selected Annotated Bibliography on Teacher Effectiveness,* National Computer Systems, 1970; (with Helen S. Astin and Nancy Suniewick) *Women: A Bibliography on Their Education and Careers,* Human Service Press, 1971; (contributor) *Educational Progress of Disadvantaged Students,* Human Service Press, 1971; (contributor) *An Evaluation of Open Admissions at City University of New York,* University Research Corporation, 1972; (contributor) *Higher Education and the Disadvantaged Student,* Human Service Press, 1972. Also author or co-author of various career project directories and reports for U.S. Department of Labor.

AVOCATIONAL INTERESTS: Travel.

* * *

DYCKMAN, Thomas Richard 1932-

PERSONAL: Born February 25, 1932, in Detroit, Mich.; son of Clovis E. and Wildarene (Andrus) Dyckman; married Alice Pletta, November 14, 1955; children: Daniel, James, Linda, David. *Education:* University of Michigan, B.B.A., 1954, M.B.A., 1955, Ph.D., 1962. *Home:* 402 Winthrop Dr., Ithaca, N.Y. 14850. *Office:* 504 Malott Hall, Cornell University, Ithaca, N.Y. 14850.

CAREER: University of California, Berkeley, assistant professor of business administration, 1962-64; Cornell University, Graduate School of Business, Ithaca, N.Y., associate professor, 1964-68, professor of accounting and quantitative analysis, 1968—. *Military service:* U.S. Naval Reserve, 1955-70; became lieutenant. *Member:* American Statistical Association, American Accounting Association, American Institute of Decision Sciences, American Institute of Management Science. *Awards, honors:* Accounting Literature Award from Institute of Certified Public Accountants, 1966.

WRITINGS: Long-Lived Assets, Wadsworth, 1967; (with Seymore Smidt and Alan K. McAdams) *Management Decision Making under Uncertainty,* Macmillan, 1969, 2nd edition, 1976; (with Harold Bierman, Jr.) *Managerial Cost Accounting,* Macmillan, 1971; (with D. Downes and R. Magee) *Efficient Capital Markets and Accounting,* Prentice-Hall, 1975; (with L. J. Thomas) *Fundamental Statistics for Business and Economics,* Prentice-Hall, 1977. Contributor to accounting, management, and statistical journals.

* * *

DYE, Thomas R(oy) 1935-

PERSONAL: Born December 16, 1935, in Pittsburgh, Pa.; son of James C. and Marguerite A. (Dewan) Dye; married Joan G. Wohleber, June, 1957; children: Roy Thomas,

Cheryl Price. *Education:* Pennsylvania State University, B.A., 1957, M.A., 1959; University of Pennsylvania, Ph.D., 1961. *Home:* 2321 Killarney Way, Tallahassee, Fla. 32303. *Office:* Department of Government, Florida State University, Tallahassee, Fla. 32306.

CAREER: University of Wisconsin—Madison, assistant professor of political science, 1962-63; University of Georgia, Athens, assistant professor, 1963-65, associate professor of political science and chairman of department, 1965-68; Florida State University, Tallahassee, professor of government, 1968—, chairman of department, 1969-72. Visiting professor, Bar Ilan University, 1972. *Military service:* U.S. Air Force Reserve, 1957-62; became first lieutenant. *Member:* American Political Science Association (secretary, 1969-72), Southern Political Science Association (member of executive council; president, 1976-77), Phi Beta Kappa, Omicron Delta Kappa. *Awards, honors:* U.S. Office of Education research grants, 1966-67, 1969-70; National Science Foundation grants, 1967, 1970-71; National Institutes of Health research grant, 1973-76.

WRITINGS: (With Oliver P. Williams, S. Charles Liebman, and Harold Herman) *Suburban Differences and Metropolitan Policies,* University of Pennsylvania Press, 1965; *Politics, Economics, and the Public,* Rand McNally, 1966; (editor with Brett W. Hawkins) *Politics in the Metropolis: A Reader in Conflict and Cooperation,* C. E. Merrill, 1967; *Politics in States and Communities,* Prentice-Hall, 1969, 3rd edition, 1977; (with Lee Greene and George S. Parthemos) *American Government: Theory, Structure, and Process,* Wadsworth, 1969; (compiler) *American Public Policy,* C. E. Merrill, 1969; (with Harmon Zeigler) *The Irony of Democracy,* Wadsworth, 1970, 3rd edition, 1975; *The Politics of Equality,* Bobbs-Merrill, 1971; *Understanding Public Policy,* Prentice-Hall, 1972, 2nd edition, 1975; *Who's Running America,* Prentice-Hall, 1976; *Policy Analysis,* University of Alabama Press, 1976.

Contributor: *The Legislative Process in Congress and the States,* Institute of Public Administration, Pennsylvania State University, 1961; Robert E. Crew, editor, *State Politics,* Wadsworth, 1966; Michael N. Danielson, editor, *Metropolitan Politics,* Little, Brown, 1966; Samuel C. Patterson, editor, *American Legislative Process: A Reader,* Van Nostrand, 1967; Peter Woll, editor, *American Government: Readings and Cases,* Little, Brown, 1968; Aaron Wildavsky and Nelson Polsby, editors, *American Governmental Institutions,* Rand McNally, 1968; Donald P. Sprengel, editor, *Comparative State Politics: A Reader,* Wadsworth, 1970; Ira Sharkansky and Richard I. Hofferbert, editors, *Politics and Policies in States and Communities,* Little, Brown, 1970; Walter G. Hack, editor, *Educational Administration: Selected Readings,* Allyn & Bacon, 1970; David A. Morgan and Samuel Kirkpatrick, editors, *Urban Political Analysis: A Systems Approach,* Free Press, 1970; Oliver Walter, editor, *Political Scientists at Work,* Duxbury, 1971; Robert N. Spadaro, editor, *The Policy Vacuum,* Lexington Books, 1975; Frank P. Scioli and Thomas J. Cook, editors, *Methodologies for Analyzing Public Policies,* Lexington Books, 1975; Stuart Nagel, editor, *Policy Studies and the Social Sciences,* Lexington Books, 1975. Editor, "Policy Analysis" series, Bobbs-Merrill. Contributor of about thirty articles and reviews to political science journals.

WORK IN PROGRESS: Writing on urban politics and on inequality, political leadership, and political systems.

DYMENT, Clifford (Henry) 1914-1971

January 20, 1914—1971; English journalist, critic, screenwriter, director, and poet. Obituaries: *Bookseller,* June 19, 1971. (See index for *CA* sketch)

*   *   *

DYRNESS, William A(rthur) 1943-

PERSONAL: Surname is pronounced "*Der*-ness"; born January 23, 1943, in Geneva, Ill.; son of Enock Christen and Grace E. (Williams) Dyrness; married Grace S. Roberts, March 16, 1968; children: Michelle Lynn, Andrea Elizabeth. *Education:* Wheaton College, Wheaton, Ill., B.A., 1965; Columbia Theological Seminary, Decatur, Ga., graduate study, 1965-66; Fuller Theological Seminary, B.D., 1968; University of Strasbourg, D.Theol., 1970; Free University, Amsterdam, Ph.D. candidate. *Address:* P.O. Box 461, Manila, Philippines. *Office:* Department of Theology, Asian Theological Seminary, Manila, Philippines.

CAREER: Hinson Memorial Baptist Church, Portland, Ore., minister to students, 1971-73; Asian Theological Seminary, Manila, Philippines, associate professor of theology, 1974—. Visiting instructor in theology, Regent College, Vancouver, British Columbia, 1971-72.

WRITINGS: Rouault: A Vision of Suffering and Salvation, Eerdmans, 1971.

WORK IN PROGRESS: Christian Art in Asia; Survey of Old Testament Theology; a book on symbolism of the supernatural in early nineteenth-century art.

SIDELIGHTS: William A. Dyrness told *CA:* "I would like to help the Church discover the dimension of art as an expression of faith. For us time is not the moving image of eternity as it was in the Middle Ages, but it has been invaded by God himself at the incarnation as well as marked by his creative hand. Objects of the world can become sacraments; ritual moves toward incarnation. I am especially concerned that Protestants so propositionally oriented develop these other dimensions of their faith."

*   *   *

EADIE, Donald 1919-

PERSONAL: Born January 12, 1919, in Morristown, N.J.; son of Erskine R. (an administrator) and C. Louise (Bell) Eadie; married Ruth J. Hill, February 25, 1944; children: Susan Ruth (Mrs. David L. Willis, Jr.), Carol Ann. *Education:* Lehigh University, B.S.E.E., 1941; University of Florida, M.S.E., 1954. *Politics:* Independent. *Religion:* Presbyterian. *Home:* 2111 Lanai Ave., Belleair Bluffs, Fla. 33540. *Office:* Hillsborough Community College, Tampa, Fla.

CAREER: Armament Laboratory, Wright Field, Dayton, Ohio, radio engineer, 1946-47; Glenn L. Martin Co., Baltimore, Md., electro-mechanical engineer, 1948-49; Ballistics Research Laboratory, Aberdeen Proving Ground, Aberdeen, Md., electronics scientist, 1949-52; University of Florida, Gainesville, assistant professor of electrical engineering, 1952-57; Honeywell, Inc., St. Petersburg, Fla., senior engineer, 1957-75; Hillsborough Community College, Tampa, Fla., associate professor of electronics, 1976—. Teacher of evening classes in electronics, St. Petersburg Junior College, 1957-61. *Military service:* U.S. Army, Ordnance Corps, 1941-42; became first lieutenant. U.S. Army Air Forces, 1942-46; became captain. *Member:* Institute of Electrical and Electronics Engineers, Clearwater Civitan Club (member of board of directors, 1965-68; president, 1968).

WRITINGS: Introduction to the Basic Computer, Prentice-Hall, 1968; *Modern Data Processors and Systems,* Prentice-Hall, 1971. Contributor to technical journals.

WORK IN PROGRESS: Minicomputers: Theory and Operation, for Reston Publishers, completion expected in 1978.

* * *

EALY, Lawrence O(rr) 1915-

PERSONAL: Born September 17, 1915, in Ocean City, N.J.; son of Vance Lawrie (a businessman) and Nellie (Rohm) Ealy; married Margaret Scott, August, 1942 (died, 1943); children: Grant Haertter (adopted). *Education:* University of Pennsylvania, LL.B., 1937, A.M., 1947, Ph.D., 1951. *Politics:* Independent Republican. *Religion:* Episcopalian. *Home:* 2103 Central Ave., Ocean City, N.J. 08226. *Office:* Department of History, Rider College, P.O. Box 6400, Trenton, N.J. 08226.

CAREER: Temple University, Philadelphia, Pa., instructor, 1947-51, assistant professor, 1951-55, associate professor of history, 1955-58; U.S. Naval War College, Newport, R.I., Ernest J. King Professor of History, 1958-59; Hobart and William Smith Colleges, Hobart College, Geneva, N.Y., professor of history, 1959-62, head of department, 1960-62, provost and dean of faculty, 1959-62; Rider College, Trenton, N.J., vice-president and dean, 1962-70, professor of history, 1970—. Visiting lecturer, Rutgers University, 1954-55. President of Trenton branch, International Association of Torch Clubs. *Military service:* U.S. Navy, 1941-46. U.S. Naval Reserve, 1946—; present rank, commander.

MEMBER: American Historical Association, American Bar Association, U.S. Naval Institute, International Platform Association, Pennsylvania Bar Association, Pennsylvania Society of New York, Pi Gamma Mu, Phi Alpha Theta, Pi Delta Epsilon, Delta Sigma Pi, Alpha Chi Rho. *Awards, honors:* Christian and Mary Lindback Award, 1973, for distinguished teaching.

WRITINGS: Under the Puppet's Crown, Meader Press, 1939; *Tacony Farm,* Dorrance, 1942; *The Republic of Panama in World Affairs,* University of Pennsylvania Press, 1951; *Yanqui Politics and the Isthmian Canal,* Pennsylvania State University Press, 1971. Contributor to history and social science journals. Member of editorial board, *American Journal of Legal History.*

WORK IN PROGRESS: Research on American Civil War, with special reference to diplomacy between the United States and Latin America.

AVOCATIONAL INTERESTS: Travel.

* * *

EARNEST, Ernest (Penney) 1901-

PERSONAL: Born September 19, 1901, in Hummelstown, Pa.; son of William H. and Estelle (Penney) Earnest; married Maude Powers, June 25, 1927; children: Barbara Anne Earnest Carrier, Christopher Powers, Ernest Robert. *Education:* Lafayette College, B.S., 1923; Harvard University, additional study, 1923-24; Princeton University, M.A., 1927, Ph.D., 1936. *Politics:* Democrat. *Home:* 428 Righters Mill Rd., Gladwyne, Pa. 19035. *Office:* Department of English, Temple University, Philadelphia, Pa. 19122.

CAREER: Georgia Institute of Technology, Atlanta, instructor in English, 1924-26; Temple University, Philadelphia, Pa., 1927—, began as instructor, professor of English,

1947-69, director of Havertown unit, 1946-51, professor emeritus, 1969—. *Member:* College English Association (member of board of directors, 1953-55), American Association of University Professors, American Civil Liberties Union. *Awards, honors:* Philadelphia Athenaeum Award, 1968, for *Expatriates and Patriots.*

WRITINGS: John and William Bartram, University of Pennsylvania Press, 1940; *A Foreword to Literature,* Appleton, 1944; *S. Weir Mitchell: Novelist and Physician,* University of Pennsylvania Press, 1950; *Academic Procession: An Informal History of the American College, 1636-1953,* Bobbs-Merrill, 1953; *The Uses of Prose,* Harcourt, 1956; *Expatriates and Patriots: American Artists, Scholars, and Writers Abroad, 1789-1930,* Duke University Press, 1968; *The Single Vision: The Alienation of American Intellectuals, 1915-1930,* New York University Press, 1970; *The American Eve in Fact and Fiction, 1775-1914,* University of Illinois Press, 1975. Contributor of essays to *Atlantic, Saturday Review, American Scholar,* and other periodicals.

WORK IN PROGRESS: Always Ready: The American Volunteer Fire Company Past and Present.

AVOCATIONAL INTERESTS: Serving as volunteer fireman (since 1944 has been a volunteer fireman in Gladwyne and Cape May Point, N.J., and has been a director of the Gladwyne Fire Company since 1962).

* * *

EAST, Ben 1898-

PERSONAL: Born July 18, 1898, in Oakland County, Mich.; son of Darwin (a farmer) and Cora (Dorn) East; married Eleanor Lee, July 29, 1919 (deceased); married Helen Gorski, August 16, 1946; children: (first marriage) Barbara (Mrs. Roger Pope), David Carnes. *Education:* Attended high school in Holly, Mich. *Home and office:* 10025 School Lot Lake Dr., Holly, Mich. 48442.

CAREER: Booth Newspapers, Inc. (a chain of eight Michigan daily newspapers), Grand Rapids, Mich., outdoor editor, 1926-46; *Outdoor Life* (magazine), Holly, Mich., Midwest field editor, 1946-66, senior field editor, 1966-70. *Member:* Explorers Club (New York).

WRITINGS: Survival: 23 True Sportsmen's Adventures, Popular Science-Outdoor Life Books, 1968; *Danger: Explosive True Adventures of the Great Outdoors,* Popular Science-Outdoor Life Books, 1970; (with Olive Fredrickson) *The Silence of the North,* Crown, 1972; *The Last Eagle,* Crown, 1974; *The Ben East Hunting Book,* Popular Science-Outdoor Life Books, 1974; (with Anton Money) *This Was the North,* Crown, 1975; *Bears,* Popular Science-Outdoor Life Books, 1977.

* * *

EASTON, David 1917-

PERSONAL: Born June 24, 1917, in Toronto, Ontario, Canada; son of Albert and Mary (Nisker) Easton; married Sylvia Isobel Victoria Johnstone, January 1, 1942; children: Stephen Talbot. *Education:* University of Toronto, B.A., 1939, M.A., 1943; Harvard University, Ph.D., 1947. *Office:* Department of Political Science, University of Chicago, Chicago, Ill. 60637.

CAREER: University of Chicago, Chicago, Ill., assistant professor, 1947-53, associate professor, 1953-55, professor of political science, 1955—, Andrew MacLeish Distinguished Service Professor, 1969—. Member of committee on political and legal philosophy, Social Science Research

Council, 1954-65; member of executive committee, Social Science Education Consortium, 1962-64, and Inter-University Consortium for Political Research, 1962-64; International Committee on Social Science Documentation, member of executive committee, 1965-69, president, 1969-71. Fellow, Center for Advanced Study in the Behavioral Sciences, 1957-58; Ford Professor of Governmental Affairs, 1960-61. Consultant to Brookings Institution, 1953, Mental Health Research Institute, University of Michigan, 1955-56, Royal Commission on Bilingualism and Biculturalism, 1965-67, and Educational Testing Service, 1966-68.

MEMBER: American Political Science Association (president, 1968-69), National Academy of Sciences (chairman of committee on information in the behavioral sciences, 1966-69), Royal Society of Canada. *Awards, honors:* LL.D. from McMaster University, 1971, and Kalamazoo College, 1972.

WRITINGS: The Political System: An Inquiry into the State of Political Science, Knopf, 1953, 2nd edition, 1971; *A Theoretical Approach to Authority,* Department of Economics, Stanford University, 1955; *A Systems Approach to Politics,* Social Science Education Consortium, Purdue University, 1965; *A Framework for Political Analysis,* Prentice-Hall, 1965; *A System Analysis of Political Life,* Wiley, 1965; (editor and contributor) *Varieties of Political Theory,* Prentice-Hall, 1966; (with J. Dennis) *Children in the Political System: Origins of Political Legitimacy,* McGraw, 1969.

Contributor: C. J. Friedrich, editor, *Authority,* Harvard University Press, 1958; S. M. Lipset and L. Lowenthal, editors, *Culture and Social Character,* Free Press, 1961; J. Gould and W. L. Kolb, editors, *A Dictionary of the Social Sciences,* Free Press, 1965; I. Morrissett, editor, *Social Science in the Schools: A Search for Rationale,* Holt, 1971. Contributor to *American Political Science Review, Journal of Politics, International Social Science Journal, Behavioral Science, Antioch Review, World Politics, Administrative Science Quarterly, School Review, Sociological Inquiry,* and other publications. Member of board of editors, *Behavioral Science,* 1956—, *Youth and Society,* 1970—, and *Political Methodology.*

*   *   *

EBLEN, Jack Ericson 1936-

PERSONAL: Born September 20, 1936, in Cincinnati, Ohio; son of Marvin Clinton (a structural design engineer) and Marie (Ericson) Eblen; married Trudi Kramer (a teacher), June 5, 1962; children: Jennifer Anne, Thor Ericson. *Education:* Attended Los Angeles City College, 1955-57; University of Wisconsin, B.S., 1959, M.S., 1961, Ph.D., 1966. *Office:* Population Division, United Nations, New York, N.Y. 10017.

CAREER: Northern Illinois University, DeKalb, instructor in history, 1964-65; Fresno State College (now California State University, Fresno), Fresno, assistant professor of history, 1965-66; University of Connecticut, Storrs, assistant professor of history, 1966-71; University of Oklahoma, Norman, associate professor of history, 1970-73; United Nations, Population Division, New York, N.Y., demographic advisor, 1973; University of Chicago, Chicago, Ill., associate professor of demography and sociology, 1973-74; United Nations, Population Division, population affairs officer, 1976—. Summer instructor, University of Kentucky, 1961; summer lecturer, University of Manitoba, 1962. *Military service:* U.S. Army, Infantry, 1954-55. *Member:* Population Association of America, International Union for the

Scientific Study of Population, and others. *Awards, honors:* Fulbright fellowship to Liberia, 1968-69; National Institutes of Health postdoctoral fellow at University of Pennsylvania Population Studies Center, 1970-71; American Philosophical Society summer grant, 1971; National Institute of Child Health and Human Development special research fellow at Johns Hopkins School of Hygiene and Public Health, Department of Population Dynamics, 1972-73, 1974-76.

WRITINGS: The First and Second United States Empires: Governors and Territorial Government, 1784-1912, University of Pittsburgh Press, 1968; (contributor) *Race and Slavery in the Western Hemisphere: Quantitative Studies,* edited by Stanley Engerman and Eugene D. Genovese, Princeton University Press, 1974. Contributor to *Encyclopedia Americana;* contributor of articles and reviews to journals in demography and history. Editorial consultant to *Reprint Bulletin, Demography,* and other journals.

WORK IN PROGRESS: A global study of recent levels and trends in mortality, analysis of factors related to patterns of morbidity and mortality.

*   *   *

ECKMAN, Frederick (Willis) 1924-

PERSONAL: Born October 27, 1924, in Continental, Ohio; son of Hector Burt (an auto mechanic) and Helen (Osborn) Eckman; married Martha Campbell (a university professor), January 14, 1961. *Education:* Ohio State University, B.A. (cum laude), 1948, M.A., 1949, Ph.D., 1954. *Politics:* "populist (lower case)." *Religion:* Roman Catholic. *Home:* 905 Wallace Ave., Bowling Green, Ohio 43402. *Office:* English Department, Bowling Green State University, Bowling Green, Ohio 43403.

CAREER: Golden Goose Press, Columbus, Ohio, editor and publisher, 1948-54; Glenville State College, Glenville, W. Va., instructor in English, 1949-51; Ohio State University, Columbus, assistant instructor in English, 1952-54; University of Texas, Main University (now University of Texas at Austin), instructor, 1954-57, assistant professor, 1957-59, associate professor of English, 1959-60; Bowling Green State University, Bowling Green, Ohio, assistant professor, 1961-63, associate professor, 1963-67, professor of English, 1967—. *Military service:* U.S. Army, Medical Department, 1943-46; became sergeant. *Member:* Modern Language Association of America, Society for the Study of Midwestern Literature, American Association of University Professors.

WRITINGS: XXV Poems, Golden Goose Press, 1949; *The Exile* (poems), Nordic Press, 1956; *Cobras and Cockle Shells* (criticism), Vagrom, 1958; *The Epistemology of Loss* (poems), Vagrom, 1963; (editor and author of introduction) *Poems from Bowling Green* (anthology), Winesburg Editions, 1966; *The Noon-Day Devil* (poems), Winesburg Editions, 1967; *Sandusky and Back: New and Selected Poems,* Elizabeth Press, 1971; *Nightmare Township* (poems), Newedi Press, 1977. Also editor and author of introduction of *Itinerary 2* (anthology), 1975. Member of editorial staff, *Cronos,* 1947-48, *Texas Studies,* 1956-60, and *Texas Quarterly,* 1958-60.

SIDELIGHTS: Frederick Eckman told *CA:* "I came to writing by a familiar process: the irrepressible need to imitate what I had been reading constantly since early childhood—to poetry from a realization that I was more interested in the infinite metamorphic possibilities of language itself than in words as a vehicle for story-telling, dramatization, explanation, or persuasion." He cites early influences as works of Williams and Pound and the experience of editing and publishing books. His "sustaining force" is "the religious conviction that I am precisely what I was intended to be: a poet who teaches poetry."

* * *

EDDINS, Dwight L. 1939-

PERSONAL: Born July 6, 1939, in Decatur, Ala.; son of Carl Cain and Lorene (Willis) Eddins; married Diane Stevens, December 28, 1963; children: Elizabeth, Miles, Emily. *Education:* University of Alabama, B.A., 1961; Oxford University, B.A. (honors), 1963; Vanderbilt University, Ph.D., 1967. *Home:* 262 Cedar Crest, Tuscaloosa, Ala. 35401. *Office:* Department of English, University of Alabama, University, Ala. 35486.

CAREER: University of Alabama, University, instructor, 1966-67, assistant professor, 1967-70, associate professor of modern British and American literature, 1970—, chairman of department of English, 1972—. *Member:* Modern Language Association of America, Association of American Rhodes Scholars, South Atlantic Modern Language Association, Southern Humanities Association.

WRITINGS: Yeats: The Nineteenth Century Matrix, University of Alabama Press, 1971. Contributor of poems to *Sewanee Review* and *Prairie Schooner* and articles to *Modern Language Quarterly* and *Texas Studies in Language and Literature.*

WORK IN PROGRESS: Research on John Fowles' novels.

* * *

EDELMAN, Murray 1919-

PERSONAL: Born November 5, 1919, in Nanticoke, Pa.; son of Kalman and Sadie (Wiesenberg) Edelman; married Bacia Stepner (a ceramist), June 15, 1952; children: Lauren, Judith, Sarah. *Education:* Bucknell University, A.B., 1941; University of Chicago, M.A., 1942; University of Illinois, Ph.D., 1948. *Home:* 1824 Vilas Ave., Madison, Wis. 53711. *Office:* North Hall, University of Wisconsin, Madison, Wis. 53706.

CAREER: Federal Communications Commission, Washington, D.C., administrative analyst, 1946; University of Illinois, Urbana, instructor, 1948-49, assistant professor, 1949-53, associate professor, 1953-58, professor of political science, 1958-66; University of Wisconsin—Madison, professor of political science, 1966-71, George Herbert Mead Professor of Political Science, 1971—. Visiting professor at Bologna Center, School of Advanced International Studies, Johns Hopkins University, 1956, University of Texas, 1959, and University of Washington, 1971. *Member:* American Political Science Association, Midwest Conference of Political Scientists (vice-president, 1967-68). *Awards, honors:* Fulbright grants to Austria, 1952-53, and Italy, 1956; Guggenheim fellow in Italy, 1962-63; National Endowment for the Humanities senior fellow in England, 1974-75.

WRITINGS: The Licensing of Radio Services in the United States, 1927-1947, University of Illinois Press, 1950; *Channels of Employment: Influences on the Operations of Public Employment Offices and Other Hiring Channels in Local Job Markets,* Institute of Labor and Industrial Relations, University of Illinois, 1952; *National Economic Planning by Collective Bargaining: The Formation of Austrian Wage, Price, and Tax Policy after World War II,* Institute of Labor and Industrial Relations, University of Illinois, 1954; (con-

tributor) Irving Bernstein, Harold Enarson, and R. W. Fleming, editors, *Emergency Disputes and National Policy,* Harper, 1955; (contributor) Milton Derber and Edwin Young, editors, *Labor and the New Deal,* University of Wisconsin Press, 1957; *The Symbolic Uses of Politics,* University of Illinois Press, 1964; (with R. W. Fleming) *The Politics of Wage-Price Decisions,* University of Illinois Press, 1965; (contributor) Gerald Somers, editor, *Essays in Industrial Relations Theory,* Iowa State University Press, 1969; (contributor) Henry Kariel, editor, *Frontiers of Democratic Theory,* Random House, 1970; (with Kenneth Dolbeare) *American Politics: Public Policy, Conflict and Change,* Heath, 1971, 3rd edition, 1977; *Politics as Symbolic Action: Mass Arousal and Quiescence,* Academic Press, 1971; *Political Languages,* Academic Press, 1977. Contributor of about twenty articles to political science journals.

WORK IN PROGRESS: More research on administrative decision-making.

* * *

EDIGER, Peter J. 1926-

PERSONAL: Born August 1, 1926, in Inman, Kan.; son of Jacob H. (a farmer and minister) and Margaret (Wiens) Ediger; married Marjorie Lee Reimer, 1951; children: Irene, Joseph, Janice, Duane. *Education:* Bethel College, North Newton, Kan., B.A., 1951; Mennonite Biblical Seminary, Elkhart, Ind., B.D., 1954. *Home:* 10102 West 64th Pl., Arvada, Colo. 80002. *Office:* Arvada Mennonite Church, 5927 Miller, Arvada, Colo. 80002.

CAREER: Elementary school teacher in public schools in Kansas, 1948-49; pastor of Mennonite church in Fresno, Calif., 1954-61; General Conference of Mennonites, Board of Missions, Newton, Kan., urban church secretary, 1961-64; pastor of Mennonite church in Chicago, Ill., 1964-65; Arvada Mennonite Church, Arvada, Colo., pastor, 1965—. *Wartime service:* Civilian Public Service as conscientious objector to military duty, 1945-46.

WRITINGS: The Prophets' Report on Religion in North America, Faith & Life, 1971. Contributor to *Mennonite.*

* * *

EDMONDS, I(vy) G(ordon) 1917-
(Gary Gordon)

PERSONAL: Born February 15, 1917, in Frost, Tex.; son of Ivy Gordon (an oil field worker) and Delia (Shumate) Edmonds; married Reiko Mimura, July 12, 1956; children: Annette. *Education:* Attended high school in Hillsboro, Tex. *Residence:* Cypress, Calif. *Agent:* Scott Meredith Literary Agency, Inc., 845 Third Ave., New York, N.Y. 10022. *Office:* Northrop Corp., Anaheim, Calif. 92801.

CAREER: U.S. Air Force, aerial photography and public relations assignments, 1940-63, spent half of service in overseas posts and retired as chief master sergeant; Federal Civil Service, public relations work in Los Angeles, Calif., 1963-68; Northrop Corp., Hawthorne, Calif., industrial editor, 1968-72, division public relations in Anaheim, Calif., 1972—. Writer, mainly for young people. *Member:* Writers Guild of America, West. *Awards, honors—*Military: Distinguished Flying Cross, Air Medal, and Bronze Star Medal.

*WRITINGS—*Mainly juvenile: *Solomon in Kimono* (folklore), Pacific Stars and Stripes, 1956; *Ooka: More Tales of Solomon in Komono,* Pacific Stars and Stripes, 1957; *Ooka the Wise* (folklore), Bobbs-Merrill, 1961; *The Bounty's Boy,* Bobbs-Merrill, 1962; *Hollywood RIP,* Regency, 1963; *Iso-*

metric and Isotonic Exercises, Monarch, 1964; *Joel of the Hanging Gardens,* Lippincott, 1966; *Trickster Tales* (folklore), Lippincott, 1966; *Our Heroes' Heroes,* Criterion, 1966; (with John J. Gribbons) *Young Sportsman's Guide to Gymnastics and Tumbling,* Thomas Nelson, 1966, published as *Gymnastics and Tumbling,* Cornerstone Library, 1971; *Lassie and the Wild Mountain Trail,* Whitman Publishing, 1966; *Rat Patrol: Iron Monster Raid,* Whitman Publishing, 1967; *Revolts and Revolutions,* Hawthorn, 1969.

Khmers of Cambodia: The Story of a Mysterious People, Bobbs-Merrill, 1970; *Hot Rodding for Beginners,* Macrae Smith, 1970; *Taiwan: The Other China,* Bobbs-Merrill, 1971; *The Possible Impossibles of Ikkyu the Wise* (folklore), Macrae Smith, 1971; *Motorcycling for Beginners,* Macrae Smith, 1972; *The Magic Man* (biography), Thomas Nelson, 1972; *Thailand, the Golden Land,* Bobbs-Merrill, 1972; *Drag Racing for Beginners,* Bobbs-Merrill, 1972; *Minibikes and Minicycles for Beginners,* Macrae Smith, 1973, published as *Minibikes and Minicycles,* Archway, 1975; *The New Malaysia,* Bobbs-Merrill, 1973; *Rocket and Jet Engines: How They Work,* Putnam, 1973; *Mao's Long March,* Macrae Smith, 1973; *China's Red Rebel: The Story of Mao Tse-tung,* Macrae Smith, 1973; *Micronesia,* Bobbs-Merrill, 1974; *Automotive Tune-ups for Beginners,* Macrae Smith, 1974; *Pakistan,* Holt, 1975; *Ethiopia: Land of the Conquering Lion of Judah,* Holt, 1975; *The Shah of Iran,* Holt, 1976; *The Magic Makers,* Thomas Nelson, 1976; *Allah's Oil: Mideast Petroleum,* Thomas Nelson, 1977; *Second Sight: People Who Saw the Future,* Thomas Nelson, 1977; *Motorcycle Racing for Beginners,* Holt, in press; *The Mysteries of Troy,* Thomas Nelson, in press.

Under pseudonym Gary Gordon: *Rise and Fall of the Japanese Empire,* Monarch, 1962; *Robert F. Kennedy, Assistant President,* Monarch, 1962; *Sex in Business,* Monarch, 1964; *Law and the Marriage Bed,* Monarch, 1965. Has also written over forty additional adult books under five pseudonyms.

WORK IN PROGRESS: Islam: A First Book, for F. Watts; *Buddhism: A First Book,* for F. Watts; *Big U: Universal Pictures in the Silent Days,* for A. S. Barnes; a biography of spiritualist, D. D. Home.

SIDELIGHTS: I. G. Edmonds' interest in folklore began when he was serving in the South Pacific during World War II. Impressed by a native chief's story of how his atoll in the Ellice Islands was created, Edmonds began collecting folk tales in the countries he visited.

*   *   *

EDMONSON, Munro Sterling 1924-

PERSONAL: Born May 18, 1924, in Nogales, Ariz.; son of Everett Sterling and Lillian (Munro) Edmonson; married Barbara Bay Wedemeyer, August 1, 1953; children: Evelyn Mila, Ann Munro, Sallie Ross. *Education:* Harvard University, B.A., 1945, M.A., 1948, Ph.D., 1952. *Home:* 901 Cherokee St., New Orleans, La. 70118. *Office:* Department of Anthropology, Tulane University, New Orleans, La. 70118.

CAREER: Washington University, St. Louis, Mo., instructor in anthropology, 1951; Tulane University, New Orleans, La., assistant professor, 1951-57, associate professor, 1957-60, professor of anthropology, 1960—, chairman of department, 1969-72, research associate, Middle American Research Institute, 1954—. Visiting professor at University of San Carlos, Quezaltenango, Guatemala, 1960-61, Purdue University, 1964, and Harvard University, 1965-66; lecturer at University of Arizona, 1965. Member of research grant

panel, National Endowment for the Humanities, 1976—. Member of fellowship committee, National Science Foundation, 1967-69; member of joint committee on Latin American studies, American Council of Learned Societies-Social Science Research Council, 1968-72. Consultant, Educational Testing Service, 1967-71. *Military service:* U.S. Naval Reserve, 1944-46; became lieutenant junior grade.

MEMBER: American Anthropological Association (fellow; chairman of membership committee, 1968-69), American Association for the Advancement of Science, American Ethnological Society (president, 1966), American Association of University Professors, Southern Anthropological Society, Louisiana Academy of Sciences, New Orleans Academy of Sciences.

WRITINGS: Status Terminology and the Social Structure of North American Indians, University of Washington Press, 1958; (editor with John H. Rohrer) *The Eighth Generation: Cultures and Personalities of New Orleans Negroes,* Harper, 1959, reprinted as *The Eighth Generation Grows Up: Cultures and Personalities of New Orleans Negroes,* Harper, 1964; *Quiche-English Dictionary,* Middle American Research Institute, Tulane University, 1965; *Lore: The Science of Folklore and Literature,* Holt, 1970; *The Book of Counsel,* Middle American Research Institute, 1971. Writer of several Middle American Research Institute studies.

Contributor: Harold I. Lief and others, editors, *The Psychological Basis of Medical Practice,* Harper, 1963; Evon Z. Vogt and Alberto Ruz Lhuiller, editors, *Desarrollo Cultural de los Mayas,* National University of Mexico, 1964; Guy Hunter, editor, *Industrialization and Race Relations,* Oxford University Press, 1965; Vogt and Ethel M. Albert, editors, *People of Rimrock: A Study of Values in Five Cultures,* Harvard University Press, 1966; Robert Wauchope, editor, *Handbook of Middle American Indians,* University of Texas, 1967; John B. Orr and Lydia Pulsipher, editors, *Education and Social Change,* Southwest Educational Development Laboratory, 1967; Vogt and John L. Fischer, editors, *The Anthropology of Clyde Kluckhohn,* University of Southern Illinois Press, 1973. Contributor to *Caribbean Quarterly, Western Folklore,* and other folklore, anthropology, and history journals. Member of editorial board, *Annual Review of Anthropology,* 1971-75.

WORK IN PROGRESS: Antonio: The Life History of a Quiche Indian.

SIDELIGHTS: Munro Edmonson told *CA:* "The common thread in my writing is to recognize the familiarity in what is alien and the alien in what is familiar, and to describe that recognition in a way that is intelligible to other people—whose experience of this polarity is inevitably different from my own. Such an endeavor may be based, as it is in my work, on scientific methods. But it must also transcend them. The challenge of writing lies to me in an awareness that one may know things he cannot communicate and communicate things he doesn't know. The act of writing like that of reading cultivates and develops this awareness. Even when it is only partially successful it is the most important form of creativity; it creates light out of mystery." Edmonson speaks Spanish and French, and has a reading knowledge of Russian, German, Italian, Portuguese, Quiche, and Yucatec Maya.

*   *   *

EDSON, Russell

PERSONAL: Married. *Education:* Completed tenth grade. *Home:* 149 Weed Ave., Stamford, Conn. 06902.

AWARDS, HONORS: Guggenheim fellowship, 1974-75.

WRITINGS: The Very Thing That Happens, New Directions, 1964; *What a Man Can See,* Jargon Society, 1969; *The Childhood of an Equestrian,* Harper, 1973; *The Clam Theater,* Wesleyan University Press, 1973; *The Falling Sickness* (four plays), New Directions, 1975; *The Intuitive Journey and Other Works,* Harper, 1976; *The Reason Why the Closet-Man Is Never Sad,* Wesleyan University Press, 1977. Writer and illustrator of three pamphlets, *Appearances, A Stone Is Nobody's,* and *The Brain Kitchen,* handset and printed at Thing Press, 1961-65. Plays, poetry, and parts of novels have been published in anthologies and in *Nation, Chicago Review, Prairie Schooner, Seventies, Kayak, Dragonfly, Beloit Poetry Journal, Chelsea,* and other periodicals.

SIDELIGHTS: Russell Edson explains the paucity of information about his life: "Take it or leave it, I make it a point not to be a celebrity, most of whom are uncreative scum feeding on the public attention; if I have any public value, it is in my published works, not in my secret dreams. Information as to how I scratched, and where, will make interesting twitterings after I'm dead; not while I still live, and still scratch."

*   *   *

EDWARD VIII   1894-1972
(Duke of Windsor)

June 23, 1894—May 29, 1972; former king of Great Britain and Ireland; after abdication known as Duke of Windsor. Obituaries: *Detroit News,* May 29, 1972; *New York Times,* May 29, 1972; *Washington Post,* May 29, 1972; *Newsweek,* June 5, 1972.

*   *   *

EDWARDS, Allen J(ack)   1926-

PERSONAL: Born June 21, 1926, in Birmingham, Ala.; son of Fletcher F. (a carpenter) and Mamie (Brooks) Edwards; married Geneva Geddie, June 9, 1950; children: Carol Jean, Melanie Sue, Lynn, Joel. *Education:* Birmingham-Southern College, A.B., 1950; University of Alabama, M.A., 1955; University of Iowa, Ph.D., 1958. *Home address:* Route 2, Box 26, Billings, Mo. 65610. *Office:* Department of Psychology, Southwest Missouri State University, Springfield, Mo. 65610.

CAREER: Teacher and principal in public schools of Jefferson County, Ala., 1950-56; University of Kansas, Lawrence, assistant professor, 1958-62, associate professor of education, 1962-63; Southern Illinois University, Carbondale, associate professor of education, 1963-65; University of Missouri—Columbia, professor of education, 1965-73; Southwest Missouri State University, Springfield, professor of psychology and head of department, 1973—. *Military service:* U.S. Army, 1944-46; became staff sergeant. *Member:* American Psychological Association, Gerontological Society, New York Academy of Sciences.

WRITINGS: (With Dale P. Scannelli) *Educational Psychology: The Teaching-Learning Process,* International Textbook Co., 1968; *Individual Mental Testing,* International Textbook Co., Part I: *History and Theories,* 1971, Part II: *Measurements,* 1972, Part III: *Research and Interpretation,* 1975; *Selected Papers of David Wechsler,* Academic Press, 1976. Editor of *Contemporary Educational Psychology.*

EDWARDS, Verne E(rvie), Jr.   1924-

PERSONAL: Born June 23, 1924, in Platteville, Wis.; son of Verne E. (a doctor) and Arlie J. (Stowell) Edwards; married Dolores I. Whitcher (a grade school teacher), June 13, 1947; children: Deborah J., Nancy E. *Education:* Attended Carleton College, 1943-44; Wisconsin State University—Platteville (now University of Wisconsin—Platteville), B.S., 1947; University of Wisconsin, M.S., 1949. *Politics:* Independent. *Religion:* Congregationalist. *Home:* 23 Spencer St., Delaware, Ohio 43015. *Office:* Department of Journalism, Ohio Wesleyan University, Delaware, Ohio 43015.

CAREER: Correspondent for several daily newspapers in Wisconsin and Iowa, 1939-43, 1946-47; Washington State University, Pullman, instructor in journalism, 1949-52; Ohio Wesleyan University, Delaware, assistant professor, 1952-56, associate professor of journalism, 1956-62, acting chairman of department, 1952-53, chairman, 1953-62; *Detroit Free Press,* Detroit, Mich., chief editorial writer, 1962-63; Ohio Wesleyan University, professor of journalism and chairman of department, 1963—. Member, American Council on Education for Journalism (accrediting body), 1963—. *Military service:* U.S. Army Air Forces, 1943-46; became sergeant.

MEMBER: American Society of Journalism School Administrators (president, 1962), Association for Education in Journalism, American Association of University Professors, Sigma Delta Chi. *Awards, honors:* Second prize in Intercollegiate Association Editorial Writing Contest, 1947; first prize in Sigma Delta Chi Foundation Writing Awards, 1965.

WRITINGS: Journalism in a Free Society, W. C. Brown, 1970. Contributor to *Parents' Magazine* and to journalism journals. Associate editor, *Journalism Educator,* 1966-69; member of editorial advisory board, *Journalism Quarterly,* 1972—.

WORK IN PROGRESS: Research on bias inside the staff operations of selected news media.

BIOGRAPHICAL/CRITICAL SOURCES: Journalism Quarterly, summer, 1970.

*   *   *

EGGERS, J(ohn) Philip   1940-

PERSONAL: Born October 1, 1940, in Fort Wayne, Ind.; son of Delmar M. and Margaret (Sprunger) Eggers; married Beth Jennings (a pianist), June 6, 1965; children: David, Michael and Wendy (twins). *Education:* Columbia University, A.B. (magna cum laude), 1962, M.A., 1964, Ph.D., 1968. *Politics:* "Registered in Democratic Party." *Religion:* Protestant. *Home:* 5 Joseph Wallace Dr., Croton, New York, N.Y. 10520. *Office:* Department of English, Manhattan Community College of the City University of New York, 1633 Broadway, New York, N.Y. 10020.

CAREER: Manhattan Community College of the City University of New York, New York, N.Y., 1965—, currently associate professor of English. Part-time lecturer, City College of the City University of New York, 1964, and Pace University, 1973—; adjunct lecturer, Hunter College of the City University of New York, 1970—. *Member:* Modern Language Association of America, Tennyson Society, Phi Beta Kappa. *Awards, honors:* State University of New York summer research fellowship, 1972.

WRITINGS: King Arthur's Laureate: A Study of Tennyson's Idylls of the King, New York University Press, 1971. Contributor to *PMLA, Clio,* and *Victorian Poetry.*

WORK IN PROGRESS: Research on the topic of history in selected English writings of the nineteenth century.

*   *   *

EHRESMANN, Julia M. 1939-

PERSONAL: Born April 12, 1939, in New Orleans, La.; daughter of William Joseph (a demographer) and Mary Ellen (Orebaugh) Moore; married Donald L. Ehresmann (a college teacher and art historian), September 19, 1964; children: Anna Sibylle. *Education:* Pomona College, B.A., 1961; New York University, M.A., 1966; Rutgers University, M.L.S., 1967. *Religion:* Protestant. *Home:* 217 North Third St., Geneva, Ill. 60134. *Office:* William Rainey Harper College, 34 West Palatine Rd., Palatine, Ill. 60067.

CAREER: German National Museum, Nuremburg, apprentice, 1967-68; Bloomfield Public Library, Bloomfield, N.J., assistant librarian, 1968-69; State University of New York College at Brockport, assistant librarian, 1969-71; Geneva Public Library, Geneva, Ill., special services librarian, 1972—; William Rainey Harper College, Palatine, Ill., lecturer, 1972—. *Member:* Beta Phi Mu.

WRITINGS: (Editor) *Pocket Dictionary of Art Terms,* New York Graphic Society, 1971. Contributor to *McGraw-Hill Dictionary of Art,* 1969. Contributor of articles to art publications; regular reviewer for *Choice, RQ,* and *Reference Books Annual.* Editor, *Geneva, Illinois: A History of It's Times and Places,* 1977. Editor of English language entries, *Schrifttum zur deutschen Kunst,* 1967-69.

WORK IN PROGRESS: Revision of *Pocket Dictionary of Art Terms.*

*   *   *

EHRLICH, Arnold 1923-

PERSONAL: Born February 7, 1923, in Philadelphia, Pa.; married Michele Doolan (a fashion editor), June, 1964; children: Christopher, Elizabeth, Michael. *Education:* Johns Hopkins University, A.B., 1947. *Home:* 325 East 57th St., New York, N.Y. 10022. *Office: Publishers' Weekly,* 1180 Avenue of the Americas, New York, N.Y. 10036.

CAREER: United States Information Agency, publications officer in Saigon, Hanoi, and Hongkong, 1951-55; *Holiday,* Philadelphia, Pa., senior editor, 1956-63; *Show,* New York City, senior editor, 1963-64; *Venture,* New York City, senior editor, 1965-68; *Holiday,* Philadelphia, managing editor, 1968-71; *Publishers' Weekly,* New York City, editor-in-chief, 1971—.

WRITINGS: The Beautiful Country: Maine to Hawaii, Viking, 1970. Contributor of articles to *Holiday, Show, Venture, Travel & Leisure,* and *Publishers' Weekly.*

*   *   *

EHRLICH, Jacob Wilburn 1900-1971
(Jake Ehrlich)

October 15, 1900—December 24, 1971; American lawyer. Obituaries: *New York Times,* December 25, 1971; *Washington Post,* December 25, 1971.

*   *   *

EIDT, Robert C. 1923-

PERSONAL: Born January 20, 1923, in Mt. Pleasant, Mich.; son of John C. and Velma (Vance) Eidt; married Marita R. Ritsche (a teacher), July 21, 1956. *Education:* Attended Michigan Technological University, 1940-42;

University of California, Los Angeles, B.A., 1947, M.A., 1951, Ph.D., 1954. *Home:* 1527 West County Line Rd., River Hills, Wis. 53217. *Office:* Department of Geography, University of Wisconsin, Milwaukee, Wis. 53201.

CAREER: University of Wisconsin—Milwaukee, professor of geography, 1967—. Fulbright professor to Peru, 1961. Consultant to U.S. Department of State on Latin America. *Military service:* U.S. Army Air Forces, 1942-46; served in Pacific theater; became first lieutenant. *Member:* Association of American Geographers, American Meteorological Society, Sigma Xi. *Awards, honors:* National Science Foundation senior research grants, 1965, 1970, to Europe and Latin America; Mohan Malaviya Medal, National Geographical Society of India, 1976.

WRITINGS: Pioneer Settlement in Northeast Argentina, University of Wisconsin Press, 1971. Senior editor, *Man, Culture, and Settlement.* Contributing editor, *Handbook of Latin American Studies,* University of Florida Press, 1954—. Contributor to professional journals. Member of board of editors, *Yearbook* of Association of Pacific Coast Geographers; associate editor, *Geoforum.*

WORK IN PROGRESS: A book, *Settlement Geography: Development, Methods, and Research Problems.*

*   *   *

EISENBERG, Larry 1919-

PERSONAL: Born December 21, 1919, in New York, N.Y.; son of Sidney Horace (a furniture salesman) and Yetta (Yellen) Eisenberg; married Frances Brenner (a social worker), October 30, 1950; children: Beth, Michael. *Education:* College of the City of New York (now City College of the City University of New York), B.E.E., 1944; Polytechnic Institute of Brooklyn, M.E.E., 1952, Ph.D., 1966. *Home:* 315 East 88th St., New York, N.Y. 10028. *Office:* Rockefeller University, New York, N.Y. 10021.

CAREER: Rockefeller University, New York, N.Y., assistant professor of electronics, 1958—. *Military service:* U.S. Army Air Forces, 1945-46; became sergeant. *Member:* Writers Guild of America, Science Fiction Writers of America, Sigma Xi, Eta Kappa Nu.

WRITINGS: Limericks for Lantzmen, Citadel, 1965; (with George Gordon) *Games People Shouldn't Play,* Kanrom, 1966; *Best Laid Schemes,* Macmillan, 1971.

WORK IN PROGRESS: A novel and a play.

*   *   *

EISENHOWER, John S(heldon) D(oud) 1922-

PERSONAL: Born August 3, 1922, in Denver, Colo.; son of Dwight David (General of the Army and 34th President of the United States) and Mamie Geneva (Doud) Eisenhower; married Barbara Jean Thomas, June 10, 1947; children: Dwight David II, Barbara Anne (Mrs. Fernando Echavarria-Uribe), Susan Elaine (Mrs. Alexander Hugh Bradshaw), Mary Jean. *Education:* U.S. Military Academy, B.A., 1944; Columbia University, M.A., 1950; U.S. Army Command and General Staff College, graduate, 1955. *Politics:* Republican. *Home:* 1637 Jones Rd., Valley Forge, Pa. 19481.

CAREER: U.S. Army, cadet, 1941-44, regular officer, 1944-63 (resigned commission as lieutenant colonel, 1963), reserve officer, 1963—, with present rank of brigadier general; spent 1965-69 writing his book on World War II; U.S. Ambassador to Belgium, Brussels, 1969-71. Served with Army of Occupation in Europe, 1945-47; instructor in English at U.S. Military Academy, West Point, N.Y., 1948-51; battalion and division officer in Korea, 1952-53; battalion commander at Fort Benning, Ga., 1953-54; instructor in infantry tactics at Fort Belvoir, Va., 1955-57; member of War Plans Division, Army General Staff, Washington, D.C., 1957-58; assistant staff secretary at the White House, Washington, D.C., 1958-61; researched and edited his father's memoirs, *The White House Years,* in Gettysburg, Pa., 1961-64. Chairman, Pennsylvania Citizens for Nixon, 1968 and President's Advisory Committee on Refugees, 1975—. Trustee of Eisenhower College, Seneca Falls, N.Y., and of Eisenhower fellowships.

MEMBER: Army-Navy Country Club (Arlington, Va.). *Awards, honors*—Military: Legion of Merit; Bronze Star; Combat Infantryman's Badge; Belgium Order of the Crown Grand Cross. Academic: L.H.D., Northwood Institute, 1970; Chungmu Distinguished Service medal.

WRITINGS: The Bitter Woods: A Comprehensive Study of the War in Europe (nonfiction), Putnam, 1969; *Strictly Personal* (memoir), Doubleday, 1974.

SIDELIGHTS: Commenting on his famous father, John Eisenhower remarked: "At the age of twenty, when I was a West Point cadet, Dad's name started to get in the papers, and from that time on I was sort of set apart. Friends could finally forget my dad's name, but meeting strangers there was always a little period you had to get over. Of course I felt very partisan in the '52 campaign and watched it like a football game, not realizing what the impact would be on old John if Dad won." Eisenhower went on to say: "Well, it's been a peculiar experience, but it's over now. Most people aren't very familiar with my dad and I'm not active in Washington politics and I try to avoid publicity if I can. I just want to write books. Right now, I'm not much of a curiosity, but 15 years ago, whew! When anonymity finally comes, you're better off."

AVOCATIONAL INTERESTS: Golf.

BIOGRAPHICAL/CRITICAL SOURCES: New York Times, January 23, 1969; *Philadelphia Inquirer,* April 6, 1975.

* * *

EKLUND, Gordon 1945-

PERSONAL: Born July 24, 1945, in Seattle, Wash.; son of Alfred J. (a dental technician) and DeLois (Stewart) Eklund; married Dianna Mylarski, March 12, 1969; children: Jeremy Clark. *Education:* Attended Contra Costa College, San Pablo, Calif. *Address:* Box 641, El Cerrito, Calif. 94530. *Agent:* Kirby McCauley, 220 East 26th St., New York, N.Y. 10010.

CAREER: Worked at numerous odd jobs in the San Francisco area, 1967-71; writer, principally of science fiction, 1968—. *Military service:* U.S. Air Force, 1963-67; became sergeant. *Member:* Science Fiction Writers of America, Lilapa. *Awards, honors:* Nebula Award, 1975, for best science fiction novelette.

WRITINGS: The Eclipse of Dawn, Ace Books, 1971; *A Trace of Dreams,* Ace Books, 1972; *Beyond the Resurrection,* Ace Books, 1973; *All Times Possible,* Daw Books, 1974; (with Poul Anderson) *The Inheritors of Earth,* Chilton, 1974; *Serving in Time,* Laser Books, 1975; *Falling toward Forever,* Laser Books, 1975; *The Grayspace Beast,* Doubleday, 1976; *Dance of the Apocalypse,* Laser Books, 1976; (with Gregory Benford) *If the Stars Are Gods,* Put-

nam, 1977. Contributor to science fiction magazines, including *Galaxy, Fantasy and Science Fiction, Amazing Stories,* and *Fantastic.*

WORK IN PROGRESS: Man with a Million Faces, with Gregory Benford, for Doubleday; "The Lord Tedric" series, with E. E. Smith, ten novels, for Ace Books; *Cosmic Fusion,* for Putnam.

* * *

EKMAN, Rosalind 1933-

PERSONAL: Born October 13, 1933, in Manchester, N.H.; daughter of Nathan and Sonia (Litvin) Ekman; married John Ladd (a professor of philosophy), July, 1963; children: Sarah, Deborah. *Education:* Wheaton College, B.A., 1955; Brown University, M.A., 1956, Ph.D., 1962. *Office:* Department of Philosophy, Wheaton College, Norton, Mass. 02766.

CAREER: Smith College, Northampton, Mass., 1959-67, began as instructor, became assistant professor of philosophy; Wheaton College, Norton, Mass., associate professor, 1967-74, professor of philosophy, 1974—, chairman of department, 1972—. *Member:* American Philosophical Association, Mind Association, Phi Beta Kappa.

WRITINGS: (Editor) *Readings in the Problems of Ethics,* Scribner, 1965.

* * *

ELDER, Michael (Aiken) 1931-

PERSONAL: Born April 30, 1931, in London, England; son of Howard Hugh Aiken (a doctor) and Marjorie Eileen (Adams) Elder; married Sheila Mary Donald (an actress), April 2, 1953; children: Simon Donald Aiken, David John Aiken. *Education:* Royal Academy of Dramatic Art, London, R.A.D.A. diploma, 1951. *Home:* 20 Zetland Pl., Edinburgh 5, Scotland.

CAREER: Actor in films and on stage, television, and radio in Scotland, 1951—; author. Director of Edinburgh Film Festival, 1961-63.

WRITINGS: The Affair at Invergarroch, A. & C. Black, 1950; *Tony behind the Scenes: A Story of the Theatre,* J. Murray, 1955; *The Cabin at Bartonbridge,* J. Murray, 1956; *The Phantom in the Wings,* J. Murray, 1957; *For Those in Peril: The Story of the Life-Boat Service,* J. Murray, 1963; *The Young Martin Luther* (juvenile), Roy, 1966; *The Young James Barrie* (juvenile), Roy, 1968; *Paradise Is Not Enough,* Pinnacle Books, 1971; *The Alien Earth,* Pinnacle Books, 1971; *Nowhere on Earth,* Pinnacle Books, 1973; *Flight to Terror,* Pinnacle Books, 1973; *Down to Earth,* R. Hale, 1973; *A Different World,* R. Hale, 1974; *The Seeds of Frenzy,* R. Hale, 1974; *Centaurian Quest,* R. Hale, 1975; *The Island of Her Dead,* R. Hale, 1975; *Double Time,* R. Hale, 1976; *Mindslip,* R. Hale, 1976; *Gil-Seeker,* R. Hale, 1977. Writer of more than 150 radio dramas for British Broadcasting Corp.

SIDELIGHTS: Michael Elder writes: "I'm not Scottish nationalist though . . . very much concerned with Scotland's 'poor relationship' with England. I am very keen to see the preservation of Scotland's culture—genuine culture rather than the 'tartan and haggis' one."

* * *

ELIAS, Christopher 1925-

PERSONAL: Born May 16, 1925, in New York, N.Y.; son

of Andrew Elias and Mary (Grant) Elias Bastin; married Alyne Elizabeth Franks, September 5, 1953; children: Christopher II, Caroline Mary. *Education:* Hartwick College, B.A., 1952; Columbia University, M.S. (journalism), 1955. *Politics:* Independent. *Religion:* Protestant. *Home and office:* 215 Jacksonville Rd., Lincoln Park, N.J. 07035. *Agent:* Arthur Pine Associates, 1780 Broadway, New York, N.Y. 10019.

CAREER: Reporter and departmental editor for *Oneonta Star,* Oneonta, N.Y., and then *Binghamton Press,* Binghamton, N.Y., 1952-54; *Coal Age,* New York City, news editor, 1955-57; *Business Week,* New York City, member of editorial staff, 1957-63; free-lance writer, principally for business magazines and newspapers, 1963-66; *Magazine of Wall Street,* New York City, editorial director, 1966-67; New York Stock Exchange, New York City, editor of *Exchange* (magazine), 1968-70; free-lance writer, 1970—. *Military service:* U.S. Army, 1945-46.

WRITINGS: Fleecing the Lambs, Regnery, 1971; *The Dollars Barons,* Macmillan, 1973. Contributor to *Economist* (London), *Wall Street Journal, Finance, Signature,* and *Money.*

* * *

ELKINS, William R.   1926-

PERSONAL: Born February 18, 1926, in Birmingham, Ala.; son of James Hill (a civil engineer) and Agnes (Wohler) Elkins; married Eileen Finn, May 26, 1947; children: Stephen James, Susan Gail, William Francis. *Education:* Attended University of Virginia, 1943; Oklahoma City University, B.A., 1949; University of Oklahoma, M.A., 1950, additional study, 1963-65. *Home:* 1610 West St., Emporia, Kan. 66801. *Office:* Department of English, Emporia State University, Emporia, Kan. 66801.

CAREER: Louisville Public Schools, Louisville, Ky., instructor in English and director of University of Louisville cooperative program in English, 1950-63; Central State College (now University), Edmond, Okla., assistant professor of English, 1963-65; Emporia State University, Emporia, Ks., associate professor, 1965-75, professor of English, 1975—. *Military service:* U.S. Army Air Forces, radar instructor and ship's complement navigator, 1943-46. *Member:* American Association of University Professors, National Council of Teachers of English, College English Association, Midwest Modern Language Association, Kansas Association of Teachers of English.

WRITINGS: (With Jack L. Kendall and John R. Willingham) *Literary Reflections,* McGraw, 1967, 3rd edition, 1976; *A New English Primer: An Introduction to Linguistic Concepts and Systems,* St. Martin's, 1974. Editor, *Oklahoma English Bulletin,* 1964-65. Contributor to *English Journal, Kentucky English Bulletin, Kansas University Bulletin of Education, Education Digest, Emporia State Research Studies, Kansas English,* and *Heritage of Kansas.*

WORK IN PROGRESS: A book on linguistic stylistics.

* * *

ELLFELDT, Lois   1910-

PERSONAL: Born August 24, 1910, in Paw Paw, Mich.; daughter of Carl John and Leah (Lowe) Ellfeldt; married Claude Chidamian, October 5, 1954. *Education:* George Washington University, B.S., 1935; Wellesley College, M.S., 1936; University of Southern California, Ph.D., 1946. *Residence:* Laguna Beach, Calif.

CAREER: University of California, Berkeley, instructor in physical education, 1938-40; University of Southern California, Los Angeles, professor of physical education, 1940-71. *Member:* American Academy of Physical Education, American Association for Health, Physical Education and Recreation (chairman of dance section).

WRITINGS: A Primer for Choreographers, National Press Books, 1967; *Folk Dance,* W. C. Brown, 1969; (with Edwin Carnes) *Dance Production Handbook: Or Later Is Too Late,* National Press Books, 1971; (with Charles L. Lowman) *Exercises for the Mature Adult,* C. C Thomas, 1973; (with Virgil L. Morton) *This Is Ballroom Dance,* National Press Books, 1974; *Dance: From Magic to Art,* W. C. Brown, 1976. Contributor to *Anthology of Contemporary Readings,* W. C. Brown, 1970.

WORK IN PROGRESS: Interaction in the Developing of Dance Forms; The Dance Teacher; Great Dancers and Their Times.

* * *

ELLING, Ray H.   1929-

PERSONAL: Born July 23, 1929, in Duluth, Minn.; son of Hadar Eric (an insurance salesman) and Minnie (Lindstam) Elling; married Margit Schreiber, October 14, 1950; children: Ronald Arno, Gerard Bernd, Martin Eric. *Education:* Sorbonne, University of Paris, diploma, 1950; University of Chicago, M.A., 1955; Yale University, Ph.D., 1957. *Office:* Department of Community Medicine, School of Medicine, University of Connecticut Health Center, Farmington, Conn. 06032.

CAREER: Harvard University and Massachusetts General Hospital, Cambridge, research associate, 1958-59; Cornell University, Ithaca, N.Y., assistant professor of hospital administration, 1959-63; University of Pittsburgh, School of Public Health, Pittsburgh, Pa., professor of social sciences and head of social sciences unit, 1963-68; University of Connecticut, Department of Clinical Medicine and Health Care, professor of social sciences and head of Social Science Division, 1968-71; World Health Organization, Geneva, Switzerland, chief of behavioral sciences unit, 1971-73; University of Connecticut Health Center, School of Medicine, Department of Community Medicine, Farmington, professor of sociology, 1973—. Field director, Joint Committee on the Study of Education for Public Health, 1961-65. *Military service:* U.S. Army, Cavalry, 1946-48; became technical sergeant.

MEMBER: International Sociological Association, American Sociological Association, American Public Health Association, Society for the Study of Social Problems, Medical Committee for Human Rights. *Awards, honors:* Commonwealth fellowship, 1955-57; Russell Sage fellowship, 1957-58.

WRITINGS: (With H. G. Fry and W. P. Shepard) *Education and Manpower for Community Health,* University of Pittsburgh Press, 1967; (editor) *National Health Care: Issues and Problems in Socialized Medicine,* Aldine-Atherton, 1971; *Health and Health Care in Hartford's North End,* Connecticut Health Services Research Series, 1972; (editor with Magdalena Sokolowska) *Medical Sociologists at Work,* Transaction Books, 1977; *Cross-National Study of Health Systems* (monograph), Transaction Books, 1978; (editor) *Cross-National Study of Health Systems: An Annotated Bibliography,* Gale, 1978.

Contributor: D. Valdes and D. Dean, editors, *Sociology in*

Use, Macmillan, 1965; W. R. Scott and E. H. Volkart, editors, *Medical Care: Readings in the Sociology of Medical Institutions,* Wiley, 1966; A. Shostak, editor, *Sociology in Action,* Dorsey Press, 1966; R. H. Elling, *National Health Care,* Aldine-Atherton, 1971; E. Friedson, editor, *Medical Men and Their Work,* Aldine-Atherton, 1971; M. Arnold, L. V. Blankenship, and V. Hess, editors, *Administering Health Systems,* Aldine-Atherton, 1971. Contributor to sociology and medical journals, including *Administrative Science Quarterly, Journal of Health and Social Behavior, Milbank Memorial Fund Quarterly,* and *International Journal of Health Services.* Editor of *Comparative Health Systems,* a supplemental issue of *Inquiry,* Volume XII, June, 1975.

SIDELIGHTS: Ray Elling has traveled in Japan, South America, Europe, and Iran. *Avocational interests:* Skiing, tennis.

* * *

ELLIOTT, C(larence) Orville 1913-

PERSONAL: Born December 15, 1913, in El Reno, Okla.; son of C. H. (a doctor) and Elva (Reynolds) Elliott; married Helene Beezley, April 7, 1935; children: Diana J. *Education:* Attended University of Michigan, 1942-43, University of Dayton, 1944-45, and Northern Oklahoma Junior College, 1953-54; Oklahoma State University, B.S., 1955, M.S., 1956; University of Oklahoma, Ph.D., 1958. *Office:* Department of Accountancy and Information Science, Western Illinois University, Macomb, Ill. 61455.

CAREER: Employed as assistant manager and manager for lumber firms in Oilton, Okla., Winfield, Kans., Winston, Mo., and St. Elmo, Ill., 1932-42; Wright-Patterson Air Force Base, Dayton, Ohio, civil service radio engineer, 1942-47; Acme Lumber Co., Hobbs, N.M., manager, 1947; Modern Homes (residential construction firm), Ponca City, Okla., owner and manager, 1947-56; University of Missouri—Columbia, associate professor of accounting, 1958-62; University of Houston, Houston, Tex., professor of accounting, 1964-67; Western Illinois University, Macomb, professor of accountancy and information science, 1967—, chairman of department, 1967-69. Certified public accountant and certified data processor. Visiting professor, University of Colorado, summer, 1964. Member of civic, state, and academic committees. Participant in seminars at universities, and at meetings of professional associations and business institutions. Consultant in accounting and electronic data processing.

MEMBER: American Institute of Certified Public Accountants, American Accounting Association (membership chairman, 1968-70), Data Processing Management Association (member of board of directors, Houston chapter, 1966-67; international director, Gamma chapter, 1967-70), Beta Gamma Sigma, Beta Alpha Psi, Omicron Delta Epsilon. *Awards, honors:* Faculty research grants, North Texas State University, 1959-60, 1960-61, 1961-62; Individual Performance award, Data Processing Management Association, 1970; selected an "Outstanding Educator of America," 1971.

WRITINGS: Card Punching and Verification, Center for Research in Business and Economics, College of Business Administration, University of Houston, 1965; (with Robert S. Wasley) *Business Information Processing Systems,* Irwin, 1965, 4th edition, 1975; *Solution Manual: Business Information Processing Systems,* Irwin, 1965, 3rd edition published as *Solutions Manual and Auxiliary Problems,* 1971,

4th edition, 1975; *Manual of Objective Tests, Business Information Processing Systems,* Irwin, 1965, 3rd edition, 1971; *Introduction to Data Processing,* Learning Systems Co., 1970, 3rd edition, 1975; *Card Punching and Verification: IBM 29 and 59,* Center for Business and Economic Research, School of Business, Western Illinois University, 1972. Contributor to *Accounting Review, Business and Government Review, Journal of Data Management, Texas CPA,* and *Journal of Systems Management.* Contributing editor, *Journal of Data Management* and *Data Processing Management Association Quarterly;* member of editorial advisory board, *Texas CPA,* 1967-70.

* * *

ELLIOTT, Richard V. 1934-

PERSONAL: Born September 27, 1934, in Yonkers, N.Y.; son of George Francis and Eileen Louise (Higgins) Elliott; married Linda Lou Deinhardt, July 14, 1973; children: June Louise. *Education:* U.S. Merchant Marine Academy, B.S., 1958; Georgetown University, graduate study, 1958; New School for Social Research, M.A., 1973. *Home:* 71 Central Ave., Demarest, N.J. 07627. *Office:* Port Authority of New York and New Jersey, One World Trade Center, New York, N.Y. 10048.

CAREER: American Merchant Marine Institute, New York City, assistant to director of information, 1962-63; Marine Index Bureau, New York City, assistant to president, 1963-65; Port Authority of New York and New Jersey, New York City, associate editor of *Via Port of New York,* 1965-67, rail transportation representative, 1967-68, aviation public services representative, 1968-71, supervisor of personnel publications, 1971—. Mayor of Englewood's Citizens' Advisory Committee, 1977-78. *Military service:* U.S. Navy, 1959-61; became lieutenant. *Member:* Steamship Historical Society of America (vice-president of Middle Atlantic States, 1968-70), National Safety Council (vice-president of public relations, Marine Section, 1965), Shipwrites, Historical Society of Delaware, New York Genealogical and Biographical Society. *Awards, honors:* Congressman Wainwright Award for Outstanding Student, American History and Government, 1958.

WRITINGS: Last of the Steamboats: The Saga of the Wilson Line, Tidewater, 1970. High Seas editor, *Steamboat Bill* (journal of Steamship Historical Society of America), 1962-68.

WORK IN PROGRESS: A history of New York Harbor steamboating during the nineteenth and twentieth centuries; research into his family roots since 1770.

SIDELIGHTS: Richard Elliott writes: "I grew up on Yonkers within sight of the Hudson, and like many local people, I really enjoyed the steamboating that was still part of the local summer scene. However, with post-war 'progress' and the elimination of the last steamboat fleets, I became more and more interested in preserving memories of those happy days so that future generations would at least have an idea of what steamboating was like—even if what I had witnessed was the end of an era. Books are a major way of overcoming historic amnesia. I wrote the Wilson Line history first because its staff were among the most generous to youngsters who, like myself, once wrote many a long and detailed letter, requesting photos and seeking answers to specific questions about the boats.... I am more convinced than ever that there is room for special interest books, including steamboat histories."

AVOCATIONAL INTERESTS: History, psychology,

painting maritime and architectural subjects, and promoting civic involvement.

* * *

ELLIOTT, Sheldon D(ouglass) 1906-1972

June 2, 1906—March 7, 1972; American educator and legal scholar. Obituaries: *New York Times,* March 9, 1972.

* * *

ELLIS, Elmo I(srael) 1918-

PERSONAL: Original surname, Israel; name legally changed in 1963; born November 11, 1918, in Birmingham, Ala.; son of Samuel B. and Bertha F. (Seletz) Israel; married Ruth M. Ballinger, December 26, 1944; children: Janet Faye, William Bryan. *Education:* University of Alabama, A.B., 1940; Emory University, M.A., 1948, graduate of advanced management course, 1965. *Religion:* Jewish. *Home:* 6345 Aberdeen Dr. N.E., Atlanta, Ga. 30328. *Office:* WSB Radio, Cox Broadcasting Corp., 1601 West Peachtree N.E., Atlanta, Ga. 30309.

CAREER: Cox Broadcasting Corp., Atlanta, Ga., publicity and production manager of Radio Station WSB, 1940-42; radio writer and producer in New York, N.Y., 1946, working on "We the People," "Great Jury Trials," and other programs; Cox Broadcasting Corp., director of scripts and production for WSB, 1947, production manager of WSB-TV, 1948-52, WSB Radio, manager of programming, 1952-63, vice-president and general manager, 1969—. Commissioner, Governor's Commission on the Georgia White House Conference on Handicapped Individuals; advisory-director, Citizens and Southern Bank, East Point, Ga.; member of advisory board, Consumer Credit Service of Greater Atlanta; member of board of directors, Georgia Safety Council, Governor's Committee on Employment of the Handicapped, Georgia Nutrition Council Advisory Panel, and Georgia State Industry Advisory Committee; member of Georgia Business Task Force, State Chamber of Commerce. Public relations advisor, Georgia Heart Association; member of board of directors, Georgia Arthritis Foundation and Atlanta Mental Health Association; executive board member of Fulton-DeKalb-Clayton Chapter of National Foundation—March of Dimes, chairman of pledge walk, 1975, 1976. Executive committee member of Atlanta chapter, American Jewish Committee; B'nai B'rith, vice-chairman of South East Regional Advisory Board, Anti-Defamation League, and member of executive committee. Member of Atlanta Area Council, Boys Scouts of America; member of advisory committee, Atlanta League of Women Voters; member of board of directors, Junior Achievement of Greater Atlanta. Chairman of Northern Georgia Operational Area Emergency Communications Committee; member of board of directors, International Radio and Television Foundation; member of national board of directors and chairman of executive committee, Radio Advertising Bureau. Member of board of trustees, Atlanta Landmarks, Inc.; member of board of trustees and charter member of president's council, Oglethorpe University. *Military service:* U.S. Army Air Forces, writer and producer of radio programs, 1942-46; became captain.

MEMBER: National Association of FM Broadcasters (former chairman of the board), Georgia Associated Press Broadcasters (president), Sigma Delta Chi; Standard Club and Commerce Club (both Atlanta). *Awards, honors:* More than twenty awards for contributions to his field and for charitable work, including: George Foster Peabody Radio and Television Award, University of Georgia, 1966; Alfred P. Sloan Award, 1966; Freedoms Foundation, Distinguished Service Award, 1970, 1972, George Washington Honor Medal Award, 1972, plus twelve other medals; Southern Baptist Radio and Television Commission Abraham Lincoln Award, 1972, 1977; Distinguished Service Award, Gavin Radio Program Conference, 1973; Atlanta Braves Sportsman Award, 1974; first place for general editorial excellence, United Press International, 1977.

WRITINGS: Sleepy Hollow Poems, Atlanta Journal Co., 1942; (with J. Leonard Reinsch) *Radio Station Management,* Harper, 1948; *Happiness Is Worth the Effort,* Revell, 1970. Contributor of articles and poems to journals and newspapers, including *Quill* and *New York Times.*

WORK IN PROGRESS: How to Live Sanely in an Insane World.

AVOCATIONAL INTERESTS: Painting, golf.†

* * *

ELLIS, Richard N(athaniel) 1939-

PERSONAL: Born June 6, 1939, in Brooklyn, N.Y.; son of Raymond Clark and Gerardine (Slag) Ellis; married Luella Ann Riley (a nurse), August, 1967; children: David D., Sara E. *Education:* Attended Colgate University, 1957-58; University of Colorado, B.A., 1961, M.A., 1963, Ph.D., 1967. *Home:* 1725 Richmond N.E., Albuquerque, N.M. 87106. *Office:* Department of History, University of New Mexico, Albuquerque, N.M. 87131.

CAREER: Murray State University, Murray, Ky., assistant professor of American history, 1967-68; University of New Mexico, Albuquerque, assistant professor, 1968-71, associate professor, 1971-75, professor of history, 1975—, American Indian Historical Research Project, assistant director, 1968-69, director, 1969-71, director of New Mexico Oral History Project, 1976—. *Member:* American Historical Association, Organization of American Historians, American Society for Ethnohistory, American Indian Historical Society, Western History Association (member of council, 1971—), Phi Alpha Theta. *Awards, honors:* Award of Merit, Association for State and Local History, 1974.

WRITINGS: (Author of introduction) Lawire Tatum, *Our Red Brothers and the Peace Policy of Ulysses S. Grant,* University of Nebraska Press, 1970; *General Pope and U.S. Indian Policy,* University of New Mexico Press, 1970; *New Mexico, Past and Present,* University of New Mexico Press, 1971; *The Western American Indian: Case Studies in Tribal History,* University of Nebraska Press, 1972; (contributor) Albert Schroeder, editor, *The Changing Ways of Southwestern Indians,* Rio Grande Press, 1973; *New Mexico Historic Documents,* University of New Mexico Press, 1975; (author of introduction) Luther Standing Bear, *My People the Sioux,* University of Nebraska Press, 1975; (contributor) Robin Higham, *A Guide to the Sources of U.S. Military History,* Archon, 1975. Contributor to *Military Affairs, Southwestern Historical Quarterly, Journal of Arizona History, Colorado Magazine, Montana,* and other publications. Member of editorial board, *American Indian Quarterly, Teaching History, Red River Valley Historical Review; New Mexico Historical Review,* book review editor and member of editorial board.

WORK IN PROGRESS: With Warren Beck, *New Mexico: A History of Four Centuries,* for University of Oklahoma Press; research on U.S. Indian policy.

ELLISON, Virginia H(owell) 1910-
(Virginia Howell, Virginia Howell Mussey, Virginia
T. H. Mussey, V. H. Soskin; pseudonyms: Gor Yun
Leong, Mary A. Mapes)

PERSONAL: Born February 4, 1910, in New York, N.Y.;
daughter of William David (a builder and farmer) and Mary
Augusta (Mapes) Howell; married J. B. Mussey, June 28,
1932 (divorced); married William H. Soskin, April 9, 1941
(deceased); married James W. Ellison (an editor), April 11,
1955 (divorced); children: (second marriage) David Howell,
Nicholas Howell. *Education:* Vassar College, B.A., 1932.
Politics: Independent. *Religion:* Congregationalist. *Home
and office:* Mather Rd., Stamford, Conn. 06903.

CAREER: Howell, Soskin Publishers, Inc., New York
City, editor and part owner, 1940-48; editor with Crown
Publishers, Inc., and Lothrop, Lee & Shephard Co., New
York City, 1948-55; National Council of Churches, New
York City, director of publications and promotion, Wom-
en's Division, 1961-64; Columbia University, New York
City, special writing assignments, 1958-60, 1968-70.

WRITINGS: (Under name Virginia T. H. Mussey) *The
Exploits of George Washington* (postage stamp story and
collectors album), Harper, 1933; (under name Virginia T. H.
Mussey) *The Flying Adventures of Lindberg* (postage stamp
story and collectors album), Harper, 1933; (with Y. K. Chu;
under pseudonym Gor Yun Leong) *Chinatown Inside Out*,
Barrows Mussey, 1936; (under name Virginia Howell
Mussey) *Falla, a President's Dog*, Howell, Soskin, 1941;
(under pseudonym Mary A. Mapes) *Fun with Your Child*,
Howell, Soskin, 1943; (under pseudonym Mary A. Mapes)
Surprise! (juvenile), Howell, Soskin, 1944; (under name Virginia Howell) *Training Pants*, Howell, Soskin, 1946; (under
name Virginia Howell) *Who Likes the Dark?* (juvenile),
Howell, Soskin, 1946; *The Pooh Cook Book* (juvenile) Dut-
ton, 1969; *The Pooh Party Book* (juvenile), Dutton, 1971;
The Pooh Get-Well Book (juvenile), Dutton, 1973. Ghost-
writer of other books.

WORK IN PROGRESS: Research on space, herbs, honey,
and scented geraniums, with books expected to result on all
those subjects; more children's books and fiction.

SIDELIGHTS: Virginia Ellison told *CA:* "I write because I
can't not write. Whatever the distractions, whatever the al-
luring pleasure, I always wind up at the typewriter writing
what I want to write. I would need four or five lives to write
all the books partly written, not to mention my love for
sculpturing and gardening which I'd also like to do full time.
I'd like to stand on street corners with a hat and collect all
the time other people don't know what to do with. I don't
remember when I began or why. I wanted always to write
and always did. I work 5-6 hours daily without interruptions
from telephones or visits. Friends respect my work time as
they do that of office workers."

AVOCATIONAL INTERESTS: Music (especially jazz),
inventing (four inventions in progress), and gardening.

*   *   *

ELSBREE, Langdon 1929-

PERSONAL: Born June 23, 1929, in Trenton, N.J.; son of
Wayland Hoyt (a lawyer and editor) and Miriam (Jenkins)
Elsbree; married Aimee Desiree Wildman (a high school and
college teacher), June 9, 1952; children: Anita. *Education:*
Earlham College, B.A., 1952; Cornell University, M.A.,
1954; Claremont Graduate School, Ph.D., 1963. *Politics:*
Registered Democrat. *Religion:* Quaker. *Home:* 400 Uni-

versity Circle, Claremont, Calif. 91711. *Office:* Department
of English, Bauer Center, Claremont Men's College, Claremont, Calif. 91711.

CAREER: Miami University, Oxford, Ohio, instructor in
English, 1954-57; part-time instructor in English at Harvey
Mudd College and lecturer at Claremont Graduate School,
Claremont, Calif., 1958-59; Scripps College, Claremont, instructor in humanities, 1959-60; Claremont Men's College,
Claremont, instructor, 1960-62, assistant professor, 1963-65,
associate professor, 1966-72, professor of English, 1972—,
chairman of department, 1969-70; Claremont Graduate
School, Claremont, member of English staff, 1965—. Ful-
bright lecturer in American literature, Cairo, Egypt, 1966-
67; lecturer in graduate English, California State College
(now University), Los Angeles, 1968-70. *Member:* Modern
Language Association of America, National Council of
Teachers of English, American Association of University
Professors, Claremont Civic Association. *Awards, honors:*
National Endowment for the Humanities summer stipend,
1975.

WRITINGS—All with Frederick G. Bracher: *Heath's Col-
lege Handbook of Composition* (revised from E. C. Wool-
ley's *College Handbook of Composition*), 7th edition,
Heath, 1967, 9th edition (with Nell Altizer), 1977; *Brief
Handbook of Usage*, Heath, 1968, 9th edition, 1977; *Brief
Guide to Rhetoric*, Heath, 1968, revised edition, 1972. Con-
tributor of articles to *Exercise Exchange*, *Twentieth Century
Literature*, *Claremont Quarterly*, *Nineteenth Century Fic-
tion*, *Philological Quarterly*, *D. H. Lawrence Review*, *South
Atlantic Quarterly*, *Criticism*, and other English journals.

WORK IN PROGRESS: A monograph on archetypal actions in literature, a study of the relationships between ritual
and narrative.

*   *   *

ELSTON, Gene 1922-

PERSONAL: Born March 26, 1922, in Fort Dodge, Iowa;
son of Wesley Herman (a merchant) and Sarah (Mc-
Cormick) Elston; married Anne Crews, August 20, 1944;
children: Robert II, Lynn, Kim. *Education:* Attended Fort
Dodge Junior College and Beloit College. *Residence:* Houston, Tex. *Office:* Houston Sports Association, P.O. Box
288, Houston, Tex. 77001.

CAREER: Sports announcer for stations KVFD, Fort
Dodge, Iowa, 1941, WJW, Cleveland, Ohio, 1945-46,
KXEL, Waterloo, Iowa, 1946-50, KIOA, Des Moines,
Iowa, 1950-53, and WIND, Chicago, Ill., 1954-57; Mutual
Network "Game of the Day," sports announcer, 1957-60;
Houston Sports Association, Houston, Tex., sports an-
nouncer, 1960—. *Military service:* U.S. Navy, aviation ra-
dioman, 1942-44.

WRITINGS: That's the Way the Ball Bounces, C. R. Gibson, 1971.

*   *   *

EMBLEN, D(onald) L(ewis) 1918-
(Bart Reynolds)

PERSONAL: Born October 5, 1918, in Los Angeles, Calif.;
son of Herbert Vern and Edna (Ferner) Emblen; married
Betty Jane Mitchell, 1941 (divorced); children: Cirre, Clovis
(daughters). *Education:* Attended Los Angeles City College
and University of California; San Diego State College (now
University), B.S., 1953; San Francisco State College (now
University), M.A., 1962; University of Lund, language

study, 1971. *Home:* 428 Eighth St., Santa Rosa, Calif. 95401. *Office:* Department of English, Santa Rosa Junior College, Santa Rosa, Calif.

CAREER: Held many jobs, ranging from journeyman laborer to newspaper reporter and editor before entrance into teaching; Santa Rosa Junior College, Santa Rosa, Calif., member of English department, 1959—, chairman of department, 1969—. *Military service:* U.S. Navy, 1941-45; sonar operator on a subchaser. *Member:* American Federation of Teachers, National Council of Teachers of English, American Civil Liberties Union, California Teachers Association.

WRITINGS: There Are Sea Gulls on Our Lawn (poetry), illustrations by wife, Betty Jane Emblen, North Shores Publishing Co., 1947; (with B. J. Emblen) *The Palomino Boy,* illustrations by Lynd Ward, Viking, 1948; *The Crow Tree* (poetry), Grundtvig Press, 1949; (under pseudonym Bart Reynolds) *Paisano,* [Los Angeles], 1957; *Twenty Poems,* Gordon Dixon Press, 1965; *Peter Mark Roget: The Word and the Man,* Crowell, 1970; (with Donald Hall) *A Writer's Reader,* Little, Brown, 1976; (editor) *The Two Hundred Series* (bicentennial papers), Santa Rosa Junior College, 1976. Contributor of poems and articles to periodicals. Co-founder and editor, *Loon: A Journal of Poetry,* 1973—.

WORK IN PROGRESS: Translating modern Swedish poetry.

BIOGRAPHICAL/CRITICAL SOURCES: Show, September 17, 1970.

* * *

ENGLISH, Barbara (Anne) 1933-

PERSONAL: Born September 5, 1933, in Dundee, Scotland; daughter of David Rose (a physician) and Olive (Mackie White) Cameron; married Thomas Anthony English (a surgeon), June 11, 1960; children: Hugh W., Charles E. *Education:* University of St. Andrews, M.A. (honors), 1955, Ph.D., 1977. *Religion:* Anglican. *Home:* Westwood Close, Beverley, Yorkshire, England.

CAREER: National Register of Archives, West Riding, Yorkshire, England, archivist, 1958-62; Thomas Nelson & Sons Ltd. (publishers), Edinburgh, Scotland, assistant editor, 1962-64.

WRITINGS: John Company's Last War, Collins, 1971; *The War for a Persian Lady,* Houghton, 1971.

WORK IN PROGRESS: A book on the Chinese war of 1860.

SIDELIGHTS: Barbara English's chief interest, other than historical research, is the conservation of England's historic towns.

* * *

ENTEMAN, Willard F(inley) 1936-

PERSONAL: Born October 21, 1936, in Glen Ridge, N.J.; son of Verling C. and Elizabeth (Dailey) Enteman; married Kathleen Ffolliott, June 18, 1960; children: Sally Holyoke, David Finley. *Education:* Williams College, B.A., 1959; Harvard University, M.B.A., 1961; Boston University, M.A., 1962, Ph.D., 1965. *Home:* 1333 Lowell Rd., Schenectady, N.Y. 12308. *Office:* Office of the Provost, Union College, Union College and University, Schenectady, N.Y. 12308.

CAREER: Wheaton College, Norton, Mass., instructor, 1963-65, assistant professor of philosophy, 1965-70; Union College and University, Union College, Schenectady,

N.Y., associate professor of philosophy and chairman of department, 1970-72, acting provost, 1972, provost, 1973—. Director, Financial Research, Inc. *Member:* American Philosophical Association, Philosophy of Science Association, American Economic Association.

WRITINGS: (Editor) *The Problem of Free Will,* Scribner, 1967.

WORK IN PROGRESS: Philosophy of economics.

* * *

EPHRON, Phoebe (Wolkind) 1916-1971

January 26, 1916—October 13, 1971; American playwright and screenwriter. Obituaries: *New York Times,* October 14, 1971; *Washington Post,* October 15, 1971.

* * *

EPPINGA, Jacob D. 1917-

PERSONAL: Born June 7, 1917, in Detroit, Mich.; son of Dirk (a contractor) and Sjoerdina (Brolman) Eppinga; married Anne Batts; children: Richard, Jay, Susan, Deanna. *Education:* Calvin College, A.B., 1939; Westminster Theological Seminary, B.D., 1944; graduate study at Calvin Seminary, 1945, Union Theological Seminary, Richmond, Va., 1960, and Cambridge University, 1969. *Home:* 2443 Oakwood S.E., Grand Rapids, Mich. 49506.

CAREER: Minister of Christian Reformed churches in Dearborn, Mich., 1945-53, and Grand Rapids, Mich., 1953-54; LeGrave Christian Reformed Church, Grand Rapids, pastor, 1954—. *Member:* Rotary International.

WRITINGS: Soul of the City, Eerdmans, 1955; *For Sinners Only,* Eerdmans, 1970; *Of Cabbages and Kings,* Zondervan, 1974. Regular contributor to *Banner* (denominational weekly); contributor to other religious periodicals and to "Back to God" radio program.

AVOCATIONAL INTERESTS: Sports, music, travel.

* * *

EPPLE, Anne Orth 1927-

PERSONAL: Born February 9, 1927, in Tuckahoe, N.Y.; daughter of Albert (a fireman) and Anna (Ritter) Orth; married Lewis E. Epple (an electrical engineer), July 17, 1949; children: Lee Scott, Douglas Craig. *Education:* Attended high school in Eastchester, N.Y. *Religion:* Lutheran. *Home:* 14 Lexington Rd., New City, N.Y. 10956. *Agent:* Lenniger Literary Agency, Inc., 437 Fifth Ave., New York, N.Y. 10016.

CAREER: Bronx Zoo, Bronx, N.Y., assistant in education department and school lecturer, 1946-52. *Member:* National Wildlife Federation, National Geographic Society, Clarkstown Garden Club (executive vice-president).

WRITINGS: Nature Quiz Book, Platt, 1955; *Modern Science Quiz Book,* Platt, 1958; *The Beginning Knowledge Book of Ants,* Crowell-Collier, 1969; *The Beginning Knowledge Book of Fossils,* Crowell-Collier, 1969; *The Lookalikes,* St. Martin's, 1971; *Nature Crafts,* Chilton, 1974; *Something from Nothing Crafts,* Chilton, 1976. Also ghost writer of another nature book. Contributor to *Ranger Rick's Nature Magazine,* and to other publications.

WORK IN PROGRESS: Several nature books.

AVOCATIONAL INTERESTS: Hiking, gardening, backpacking, tent-trailering, birding, photography, and all aspects of nature study.

ERHARD, Thomas A.   1923-

PERSONAL: Born June 11, 1923, in West Hoboken, N.J.; son of Herbert Charles and Grace (Agnew) Erhard; married Jean M. Beebe, July 21, 1945 (divorced); married Penelope E. Ryan, July 27, 1972; children: (first marriage) Bruce, Lawrence, Daniel; (second marriage) Kimberly, Corinne. *Education:* Hofstra University, B.A., 1947; University of New Mexico, M.A., 1950, Ph.D., 1960; University of Denver, summer graduate study, 1951. *Home:* 2110 Rosedale Dr., Las Cruces, N.M. 88001. *Office address:* Department of English, Box 3-E, New Mexico State University, Las Cruces, N.M. 88003.

CAREER: Albuquerque (N.M.) public schools, publications sponsor at a high school, 1949-53, public information director for the school system, 1953-57; National Education Association, Washington, D.C., assistant director of Press, Radio, and Television Division, 1957-58; New Mexico State University, Las Cruces, assistant professor, 1960-64, associate professor, 1964-68, professor of English, 1968—. Conducts annual creative writing awards program which reaches into more than five hundred high schools in six southwestern states. *Military service:* U.S. Army, 1943-47; became sergeant. *Member:* National Education Association, National Council of Teachers of English, American Association for Higher Education, American Association of University Professors, Sigma Delta Chi. *Awards, honors:* One first and one third prize in national playwriting contests conducted by community theaters.

WRITINGS: Your Town, on the Map, National Education Association, 1957; *Lynn Riggs: Southwestern Playwright,* Steck, 1970; *Nine Hundred Plays: A Synopsis-History of American Theatre,* Richards Rosen, 1977.

Plays; comedies: *For the Love of Pete* (three-act), Heuer, 1953; *The High White Star* (three-act), Eldridge Publishing, 1957; *Memory, Marlyn, Memory!* (one-act), Ivan Bloom Hardin, 1957; *Tex, Two Knuckles, and a Note* (one-act), National Education Association, 1957; *Command Performance* (one act), National Education Association, 1959; *Standing Room Only* (one act), National Education Association, 1959; *After the Honeymoon* (one-act), National Education Association, 1959; *Rocket in His Pocket* (three-act), Row, Peterson, 1960; *Eleventy Percent* (one act), National Education Association, 1960; *Instant Education* (one-act), National Education Association, 1961; *The Electronovac Gasser* (three-act), Eldridge Publishing, 1962; *Vacation on the Moon* (one-act), National Education Association, 1962; *Reach for the Stars* (one-act), National Education Association, 1963; *The Greatest American* (one-act), National Education Association, 1963; *The Payoff!* (one-act), National Education Association, 1964; *Cathy's Choice* (one-act), National Education Association, 1964; *Two Million Heroes* (one-act), National Education Association, 1964; *A Wild Fight for Spring* (three-act), Baker's Plays, 1966; *The Cataclysmic Loves of Cooper and Looper and Their Friend Who Was Squashed by a Moving Van* (three-act), Eldridge Publishing, 1969; *Francis Asbury: America,* Accent on Youth Magazine, 1974.

Assistant editor, *Current Issues in Higher Education,* Association for Higher Education, 1960, 1964, and associate editor of other A.H.E. yearbooks published under various titles, 1965-71. Contributor of over thirty entries on American and European playwrights to *Worldbook Encyclopedia.* Contributor of short stories and about 130 articles to magazines and about 6,000 articles to newspapers.

WORK IN PROGRESS: Several juvenile suspense novels.

ERICKSON, Erling Arthur   1934-

PERSONAL: Born January 8, 1934, in Portland, N.D.; son of Arthur (a farmer) and Anna (Odegaard) Erickson; married Ruth Hashizume (a teacher), May 25, 1974; children: Robin Elizabeth. *Education:* Luther College, Decorah, Iowa, B.A., 1958; University of North Dakota, M.A., 1959; University of Iowa, Ph.D., 1967. *Politics:* Democrat. *Home:* 8019 Arroyo Way, Stockton, Calif. 95207. *Office:* Department of History, University of the Pacific, Stockton, Calif. 95211.

CAREER: Winnipeg University, Winnipeg, Manitoba, instructor in history, 1959-62; Naval Post-graduate School, Monterey, Calif., assistant professor of history, 1966-68; University of the Pacific, Stockton, Calif., 1969—, began as associate professor, currently professor of history. *Military service:* U.S. Army, 1954-56. *Member:* Organization of American Historians, Newcomen Society in North America. *Awards, honors:* Harvard University Newcomen Society fellowship, 1968-69.

WRITINGS: Banking in Frontier Iowa, Iowa State University Press, 1971; (with Leland Baldwin) *The American Quest,* two volumes, Wadsworth, 1973. Contributor of articles and reviews to *Business History Review, Annals of Iowa, Spiegel Historiael, North Dakota Quarterly, Dictionary of American Biography, Pacific Historian,* and *Journal of American History.*

*   *   *

ESHLEMAN, Clayton   1935-

PERSONAL: Born June 1, 1935, in Indianapolis, Ind.; son of Ira Clayton (an engineer) and Gladys Maine (Spenser) Eshleman; married Barbara Novak, June 17, 1961; married second wife, Caryl Reiter, April 28, 1970; children: (first marriage) Matthew. *Education:* Indiana University, A.B., 1958, M.A.T., 1961. *Home and office:* 852 South Bedford St., Los Angeles, Calif. 90035.

CAREER: Caterpillar (magazine), New York, N.Y. and Sherman Oaks, Calif., publisher and editor, 1967-73; California Institute of the Arts, Valencia, member of faculty of the School of Critical Studies, 1970-73; American College, Paris, France, teacher of American poetry, 1973-74; University of California, Extension Division, Los Angeles, instructor, 1974—. Part-time employee, University of California Press, 1974—. Has given poetry readings of his own works and of translations at more than a hundred schools and universities. Consultant to board of directors, Coordinating Council of Literary Magazines, 1967-70. *Awards, honors:* Coordinating Council of Literary Magazines grants for *Caterpillar,* 1968, 1969, 1970; National Translation Center grants, 1968, 1969; National Translation Center award for translation of *Poemas Humanos,* 1967; *Poetry* magazine award, 1968, for "Five Poems"; Fels nonfiction award, 1975; Carnegie Author's Fund award, 1977; California Arts Council grant, 1977-78.

WRITINGS—Poetry: *Mexico and North,* privately printed (Tokyo), 1961; *The Chavin Illumination,* La Rama Florida (Lima, Peru), 1965; *Lachrymae Mateo: 3 Poems for Christmas, 1966,* Caterpillar, 1966; *Walks,* Caterpillar, 1967; *The Crocus Bud,* Camels Coming Press, 1967; *Brother Stones* (woodcuts by William Paden), Caterpillar, 1968; *T'ai,* Sans Souci Press, 1969; *The House of Ibuki,* Sumac Press, 1969; *The House of Okumura,* Weed/Flower Press, 1969; *The Yellow River Record,* Big Venus Books, 1969; *A Pitchblende,* Maya Quarto, 1969.

The Wand, Capricorn Press, 1971; (editor) *A Caterpillar Anthology,* Doubleday, 1971; *Bearings,* Capricorn Press, 1971; *The Last Judgment: For Caryl Her Thirty-First Birthday, The End of Her Pain,* Plantin Press, 1973; *Realignment,* Treacle Press, 1974; *Portrait of Francis Bacon,* Rivelin Press, 1975; *Cogollo,* Roxbury, 1976; *The Woman Who Saw Through Paradise,* Tansy Press, 1976; *Grotesca,* New London Pride Books, 1977; *The Name Encanyoned River,* Treacle Press, 1977.

All published by Black Sparrow Press: *Cantaloups and Splendour,* 1968; *Indiana,* 1969; *Altars,* 1971; *The Sanjo Bridge,* 1972; *Coils,* 1973; *Human Wedding,* 1973; *Aux Morts,* 1974; *The Gull Wall,* 1975; *Core Meander,* 1977.

Translator: Pablo Neruda, *Residencia en la tierra,* published as *Residence on Earth,* Amber House Press, 1962; (with Denis Kelly) Aime Cesaire, *State of the Union,* Caterpillar, 1966; Cesar Vallejo, *Poemas Humanos,* published as *Human Poems,* Grove, 1968; Antonin Artaud, *Letter to Andre Breton,* Black Sparrow Press, 1974; (with Jose Rubia Barcia) Cesar Vallejo, *Spain, Take This Cup from Me,* Grove, 1974; (with Norman Glass) Antonin Artaud, *To Have Done with the Judgement of God,* Black Sparrow Press, 1975; (with Glass) Artaud, *Artaud the Momo,* Black Sparrow Press, 1976.

SIDELIGHTS: Clayton Eshleman told *CA* that William Blake, Cesar Vallejo, Antonin Artaud, Bud Powell and Chaim Soutine have had a powerful influence on his poetry. He says: "I enjoy giving readings at universities, and since 1966 have read at approximately 100 schools and universities my own poetry and translations. My poetics are the oldest and most engaging human adventure: the emancipation of the self. I should also mention that the writings and therapy of Wilhelm Reich have played an important part in my life and thinking.

"I began to write when I was about 23 years old, at the same time I began to read seriously, so there has always been a constant overlapping between reading and writing, almost as if they are sides of the same coin whose center, or gravity, is experience—my experience which, as all others, in my opinion, is resolutely personal. I write mainly to understand what is happening to me and others, and to express relation or the lack of it. I think that transcendence is a mistake, and that it is much more meaningful to drill through an opaqueness than to try and go over it. I also think that it was a horrendous mistake to say that woman is the muse, and to make woman the source for art done by males. I believe that the earth is my source, and that Caryl, my wife, is my companion. I seek not to be against her, or for her, or at her, or over her, but *with* her.

"As for aspiring writers: believe, I say to you, in apprenticeship. Pick some mature writer or artist and force yourself to know all of his work, from beginning to end, and attempt to assimilate it, and understand why it has the power that it does to move you. Such work takes from between 10 and 20 years, depending on where you are when you make such a move, and who you have picked. The denser the mature artist the more you will get out of such an association, and probably the more difficult your gains will be. University writing workshops and MFA degrees are worthless and in most cases mean that the budding artist is going to be anesthetized in chrysalis."

Hayden Carruth feels that Eshleman's "language has evolved from standard Black Mountainese toward a more personal, driven style, rhythmically intricate, twisted, sometimes obscure and elliptical, experimental, lit by flashes of verbal brilliance; it is always interesting and often moving. Thematically, however, his poetry seems less compelling, since much of it centers on raw neurotic obsessions and Reichian interpretations that give the effect, not of depth, but of shallowness, petulance, and failing concern." In a review of *A Caterpillar Anthology,* Carruth calls the book "the best cross section we have of the Black Mountain movement from 1967 to 1971, or at least of the remains of that movement, which by 1967 had already passed its peak of maturity and begun to split into more strands than one movement can contain. Today the name is at best a historical label. And already we look at *A Caterpillar Anthology* in affection and without regret, as a kind of epitaph."

Diane Wakoski calls *Coils* "a dense rich book about that will to change from an insulated, unthinking, indiscriminately feeling product of the middle class world into a powerful, sensitive real person. It is a book which gives me great faith in the poetic process." However, according to Marjorie G. Perloff, the poems in *Coils* "have an intellectual veneer; they are studded with references to Japanese religion, Reichian psychology, Blakean mythology, and fellow poets.... [This] depressingly trite book ... is, unfortunately, wholly representative of our time and place.... The one redeeming feature of *Coils* may be its unrelenting honesty."

In a review of *The Gull Wall,* Paul Zweig writes: "The impression, finally, is less one of individual poems, than of a pressing flow of images, fragmentary scenes, autobiographical recalls, sprinkled with cultural and historical references which bob through—Lascaux, Japanese movies, medieval gargoyles—like faintly glimpsed road-marks of the space Eshleman's 'creative spirit' gallops through. Often the poems seem to out-run their own words, as if Eshleman believed that grammar were too small and narrow to accommodate the inner lava which he claims as his poetic domain."

BIOGRAPHICAL/CRITICAL SOURCES: Nation, April 24, 1967; *Poetry,* April, 1968, June, 1969; *Hudson Review,* spring, 1970; *New York Times Book Review,* February 13, 1972, February 1, 1976; *American Poetry Review,* July/August, 1973; *Contemporary Literature,* Volume XVI, number 1, winter, 1975; *Contemporary Literary Criticism,* Volume VII, Gale, 1977.

*   *   *

ESKELIN, Neil J(oyner) 1938-

PERSONAL: Born June 7, 1938, in Detroit, Mich.; son of Ernest G. (a minister) and Lurowe (Bullock) Eskelin; married Anne Brewster, January 1, 1966; children: Ian. *Education:* Florida Southern College, B.A., 1959; Ohio State University, M.A., 1961.

CAREER: WYAH-TV, Norfolk, Va., program director, 1961-62; North Dakota State University, Fargo, lecturer, 1963-64; School Assembly Service, Chicago, Ill., conductor of lecture tours, 1965-66; Evangel College, Springfield, Mo., assistant professor of communications, 1967-71; U.S. Office of Education, Training of Teacher Trainers fellow at University of Miami, Miami, Fla., beginning 1971. *Member:* International Platform Association (member of board of governors, 1965-68), Speech Communication Association.

WRITINGS: (Editor with Nonna Dalan) *Speaking to Communicate,* McCutchan, 1969; *How to Make Money Speaking in Public,* Parker Publishing, 1969; *Financing Education,* Mid-America Publishing, 1972; *Comprehensive Medical Care: Six Hundred Pieces of Debate Evidence,* Mid-America Publishing, 1972.

WORK IN PROGRESS: How to Talk Your Way to the Top, for Parker Publishing.

SIDELIGHTS: Neil Eskelin has traveled in forty-five countries. His special interest is personal communication.†

*   *   *

ESPOSITO, John C(abrino) 1940-

PERSONAL: Born June 3, 1940, in New York, N.Y. *Education:* Long Island University, B.A., 1963; Rutgers University, M.A., 1964; Harvard University, J.D., 1967. *Residence:* Washington, D.C.

CAREER: Center for Study of Responsive Law (Ralph Nader Group), Washington, D.C., attorney, 1967-71. Member of board of directors, Project on Corporate Responsibility. *Awards, honors:* Air Conservation Award of National Wildlife Federation, 1970.

WRITINGS: (Contributor) Garrett De Bell, editor, *Environmental Handbook,* Ballantine, 1970; (contributor) Garrett De Bell, editor, *Voter's Guide to Environmental Politics,* Ballantine, 1970; (with Larry J. Silverman) *Task Force Report on Air Pollution,* introduction by Ralph Nader, Center for Study of Responsive Law, 1970, published as *Vanishing Air: The Ralph Nader Study Group Report on Air Pollution,* Grossman, 1970. Also co-director of project report, *Water Wasteland.*

WORK IN PROGRESS: Research on citizens' access to federal regulatory agencies.

BIOGRAPHICAL/CRITICAL SOURCES: New York Times, July 24, 1970, July 23, 1971; *Washington Post,* July 30, 1970; *Show,* September 3, 1970.†

*   *   *

ESSEX, Harry J.

PERSONAL: Born in New York, N.Y.; son of Wolfe Essex; married Lee B. Berman; children: David. *Education:* St. Johns University, New York, N.Y., B.B.A., 1936. *Home:* 9303 Readcrest Dr., Beverly Hills, Calif. 90210.

CAREER: Writer for the stage, television, and motion pictures; worker in New York City Department of Welfare, 1933-35; also painter of boutique items and clerk at various offices. *Military service:* U.S. Army, Signal Corps; served in World War II.

WRITINGS: The Lonely Man, Avon, 1957; *I Put My Right Foot In,* Little, Brown, 1954; *Man and Boy,* Dell, 1971. Also author of *The Amigos,* Dell.

Screenplays: "Man Made Monster," Universal, 1941; (with Hal Smith) "Dangerous Business," Columbia, 1946; "Boston Blackie and the Law," Columbia, 1947; (with Leopold Atlas and Martin Rackin) "Desperate," RKO, 1947; (with Barbara Worth and Maurice H. Conn) "Dragnet," Screen Guild, 1947; "He Walked by Night," Eagle Lion, 1948; (with Fred Niblo, Jr., George W. George, and Robert B. Altman) "Bodyguard," RKO, 1948.

(With Lee Leonard and Robert Hardy Andrews) "Wyoming Mail," Universal, 1950; (with Francis Rosenwald) "Undercover Girl," Universal, 1950; "The Killer That Stalked New York" (based on an article by Milton Lehman), Columbia, 1951; (with Leonard) "The Fat Man," Universal, 1951; (with Earl Felton and Jay Dratler) "Las Vegas Story," RKO, 1952; (with Paul Yawitz and Alyce Canfield) "Models, Inc." Mutual, 1952; (with George Bruce) "Kansas City Confidential," United Artists, 1953; (with Ivan Tors) "The 49th Man," Columbia, 1953; (with Ray

Bradbury) "It Came from Outer Space," Universal, 1953; (and director) "I, the Jury" (from the novel by Mickey Spillane), United Artists, 1953; (adaptor) "Devil's Canyon," RKO, 1953; (with Arthur Ross and Maurice Zimm) "The Creature from the Black Lagoon," Universal, 1954; (with Geoffrey Homes) "Southwest Passage," United Artists, 1954; (and director) "Mad at the World," Film Makers, 1955; (with Ray Buffum) "Teen-Age Crime Wave," Columbia, 1955; (with Buffum) "Jail Bait," Columbia, 1955; (with Robert Hill, William Kozlenko, and James Benson Nablo) "Raw Edge," Universal, 1956; (with Robert Smith) "The Lonely Man," Paramount, 1957.

(With William H. Right, Allan Weiss, and Talbot Jennings) "The Sons of Katie Elder," Paramount, 1965; "Man and Boy" (based on his novel), Jemmin Production Co., 1971; (and director and producer) "The Dune Roller," New World Pictures, 1972; "Fifth Estate" (from the novel by Robin Moore), Paramount, 1976; "The Terrorist," Paramount, 1977.

Plays: "Something for Nothing," produced on Broadway at Windsor Theatre, December 9, 1937; "Stronger Than Brass," produced on Broadway at 48th Street Theatre, November, 1960; "Neighborhood Affair," produced on Broadway at ANTA Theatre, 1960; "One for the Dame," produced in Boston at Colonial Theatre, 1965.

Also author of scripts for "The Untouchables," "Bat Masterson," "77 Sunset Strip," and other television series.

WORK IN PROGRESS: A movie script, entitled "Chrysalis," with Ray Bradbury; a television screenplay, "Martha Was Right," based on the Watergate materials; television adaptation of his novel *Man and Boy,* for Bill Cosby Productions; a novel, *Marina,* for Bantam.

SIDELIGHTS: Harry Essex told *CA:* "My writing (as the listed output might indicate) is almost obsessive. It doesn't embarrass me to admit to a productive 'anxiety,' to a setting down of thoughts and feelings in type. It is precisely this explosive and energized impulse to write that spells (for me, anyway) the difference between mine and a studied or slowly etched writing. That is not to say the man who works slowly and diligently isn't a good writer. Rather the cloth shapes the coat for me, and the surprise is equally entertaining to this writer as to the reader. I write out of a past, out of experience, in strong brush strokes. It comes alive for that reason. Later, I can take my time examining, improving, and finalizing the idea that possessed me and for which I was willing to exchange so many days, weeks, months, *years* for the project.... Writing fiction isn't especially something for the scholar, but rather the 'touched,' the writer with that unique machinery within him that creates a new world to make better, more enjoyable the one in which he lives." He calls his view of the contemporary literary scene "Poor. Suddenly the 'pure' writer finds himself involved in commercial principles established by publishers predicated on profits alone. No longer is the writer with a sense of character and a slight story welcome to the ranks. Today it's like the old Hollywood (and the new, in fact): The measure is Box Office. The poet can sit on the curb and watch the successful boots tapping out a speedy rhythm. The first novel becomes more and more difficult to sell. It usually means loss ... but then ... what does it matter? The true writer goes on with what he must do."

*   *   *

ESTERLY, Glenn 1942-

PERSONAL: Born August 8, 1942, in Luverne, Minn.; son

of Elden R. (a farmer) and Frances (Finke) Esterly. *Education:* South Dakota State University, B.S., 1964; Washington Journalism Center, graduate study, 1968. *Home:* 1964 North Rodney Dr., Los Angeles, Calif. 90027.

CAREER: Sioux City Journal, Sioux City, Iowa, staff writer, 1965; Associated Press, Los Angeles, Calif., staff writer, 1965-69; information and promotion director for television program, "The Advocates", beginning 1970; currently publicity manager, KCET-TV, Los Angeles.

WRITINGS: (With brother, Stanley Esterly) *Freedom from Dependence: Welfare Reform as a Solution to Poverty,* Public Affairs Press, 1971.

* * *

ESTEY, George F. 1924-

PERSONAL: Born January 21, 1924, in Cody, New Brunswick, Canada; son of C. A. (a contractor) and Eileen W. (Fisher) Estey; married Barbara A. Brown, August 25, 1951; children: Roger Scott, Gregory Alan. *Education:* Tufts College (now University), B.A. (magna cum laude), 1952; University of Connecticut, M.A., 1954; University of Illinois, Ph.D., 1960. *Residence:* Lexington, Mass. *Office:* Department of Rhetoric, Boston University, Boston, Mass.

CAREER: University of Connecticut, Storrs, instructor in English, 1953-54; University of Illinois, Urbana, instructor in English, 1954-59; Boston University, Boston, Mass., instructor, 1959-60, assistant professor, 1960-64, associate professor, 1964-67, professor of rhetoric, 1967—. *Military service:* U.S. Army Air Forces, 1942-47, U.S. Air Force, 1947-48; served in the Pacific and in Europe; became sergeant. *Member:* National Council of Teachers of English, College Conference on Composition and Communication, Rhetoric Society, Association for General Liberal Studies, Lexington Historical Society, Phi Beta Kappa.

WRITINGS: (With Harry H. Crosby) *College Writing: The Rhetorical Imperative,* Harper, 1968, 2nd edition, 1975; (editor with Doris Hunter) *Non Violence: A Reader in the Ethics of Action,* Xerox College Publishing, 1971; (editor with Hunter) *Violence: A Reader in the Ethics of Action,* Xerox College Publishing, 1971; (with Crosby) *Just Rhetoric,* Harper, 1972. Also editor, with Hunter, of *Community: A Reader in the Ethics of Action,* Xerox College Publishing. Contributor to literature journals. Editor, *Interdisciplinary Perspectives,* 1976—.

SIDELIGHTS: George F. Estey told *CA:* "As writer, editor, and teacher of writing, I constantly emphasize the importance of the reader to the writer *as he writes.* Without this emphasis, writers miss their mark, and readers go away baffled and confused. On the other hand, writers must avoid underestimating their readers' sense and sensability. In part, the writer-reader relationship accounts for both much of the difficulty in writing, as well as much of the pleasure."

AVOCATIONAL INTERESTS: Camping, still and motion picture photography, travel.

* * *

EVANS, C(harles) Stephen 1948-

PERSONAL: Born May 26, 1948, in Atlanta, Ga.; son of Charles Hinton (a transit operator) and Pearline (a teacher; maiden name, Prewett) Evans; married Jan Walter (a high school teacher), September 6, 1969. *Education:* Wheaton College, Wheaton, Ill., B.A., 1969; Yale University, M.Ph., 1971, Ph.D., 1974. *Politics:* Independent. *Religion:* Protestant. *Home:* 1531 College Ave., Wheaton, Ill. 60187. *Office:*

Department of Philosophy, Wheaton College, 501 East Seminary, Wheaton, Ill. 60187.

CAREER: Trinity College, Deerfield, Ill., assistant professor of philosophy, 1972-74; Wheaton College, Wheaton, Ill., assistant professor of philosophy, 1974—. *Member:* American Philosophical Association, Society for Values in Higher Education (fellow). *Awards, honors:* Marshall fellowship, 1977-78.

WRITINGS: Despair: A Moment or a Way of Life?—An Existential Quest for Hope, Inter-Varsity Press, 1971; *Preserving the Person: A Look at the Human Sciences,* Inter-Varsity Press, 1977; *Subjectivity and Religious Belief,* Eerdmans, 1978.

WORK IN PROGRESS: Research on Soeren Kierkegaard.

* * *

EVANS, David R(ussell) 1937-

PERSONAL: Born October 22, 1937, in Rochester, N.Y.; son of Ralph Merrill (a researcher in color photography and technology) and Pauline (Fowler) Evans; married Judith Ann Lewis, June 12, 1965; children: Daniel. *Education:* Oberlin College, B.A. (cum laude), 1959; University of Illinois, M.Sc., 1961; Makerere University, Kampala, Uganda, Diploma in Education, 1962; Stanford University, Ph.D., 1969. *Address:* c/o Ralph M. Evans, 431 Thomas Ave., Rochester, N.Y. 14617. *Office:* Center for International Education, School of Education, University of Massachusetts, Amherst, Mass. 01002.

CAREER: Makerere Institute of Education, Kampala, Uganda, lecturer in mathematics, 1962-64, research associate, 1967-68; University of Massachusetts—Amherst, assistant professor, 1969-72, associate professor of education, 1973—, director of Center for International Education, 1974—. Consultant to Peace Corps, U.S. Information Agency, U.S. Agency for International Development, Dade County (Fla.) School System, and other institutions. *Member:* African Studies Association, American Educational Research Association, Comparative and International Education Society, Society for International Development, Phi Beta Kappa, Sigma Xi. *Awards, honors:* Ford International Development Study fellowship, 1965-66; Ford Foreign Area fellowship, 1966-68.

WRITINGS: Attitudes and Behavior of Teachers in Uganda: An Aspect of the Process of National Development, International Development Education Center, 1969; (with W. A. Smith and J. Hoteng) *Non-Formal Alternatives to Schooling: A Glossary of Educational Methods,* Center for International Education, University of Massachusetts, 1971; (with Smith and A. Gillette) *Educational Innovations: Issues in Adaptation,* Center for International Education, University of Massachusetts, 1971; *Teachers as Agents of National Development: A Case Study of Uganda,* Praeger, 1971; (with G. L. Schimmel) *The Impact of a Diversified Educational Program on Career Goals: Tororo Girls' School in the Context of Girls' Education in Uganda,* Center for International Education, University of Massachusetts, 1971; (contributor) Harold Lyons, *Learning to Feel—Feeling to Learn,* C. E. Merrill, 1971; (contributor) Kenneth Prewitt, editor, *Education and Political Values,* East African Publishing House, 1971; (with William M. Bass and Richard L. Jantz) *The Leavenworth Site Cemetery: Archaeology and Physical Anthropology,* University of Kansas, 1971; (editor with Frank W. Clark and Leo A. Hamerlynck) *Implementing Behavioral Programs for Schools and Clinics,* Research Press, 1972. Contributor to

Comparative Education Review, Education in Eastern Africa, and other journals.

WORK IN PROGRESS: Doing research and writing on a project to develop non-formal, out-of-school educational materials.

SIDELIGHTS: David R. Evans has lived and worked in Africa for five years. *Avocational interests:* Natural history (particularly study of birds), motorcycles, travel, camping.†

* * *

EVANS, G(ayle) Edward 1937-

PERSONAL: Born January 5, 1937, in Huntingdon, Pa.; son of Thomas R. and LaVonne Evans; married Beverly J. Roe, May 30, 1958 (divorced); married Mary Ann Mills; children: (first marriage) Thomas E. *Education:* University of Minnesota, B.A., 1959, M.A. (anthropology), 1961, M.A. (library science), 1963; University of Illinois, Ph.D., 1968. *Office:* School of Library Service, University of California, Los Angeles, Calif. 90024.

CAREER: Archaeologist at University of Minnesota, St. Paul Science Museum, Illinois State Museum, and New Mexico State Museum, 1957-62; California State College at Hayward (now California State University, Hayward), librarian, 1963-65; Illinois State University, Normal, librarian, 1965-68; University of California, Los Angeles, assistant professor, 1968-72, associate professor of library science, 1972—, library consultant, 1969—. *Member:* American Association of University Professors, American Library Association, American Anthropological Association, California Library Association. *Awards, honors:* National Science Foundation research fellowship, 1960; U.S. Office of Education fellowship, 1966-68; Council on Library Resources fellowship, 1973; Fulbright fellow, 1975.

WRITINGS: (With Marty Bloomberg) *Introduction to Technical Services for Library Technicians,* Libraries Unlimited, 1971, 3rd edition, 1976; *Management Techniques for Librarians,* Academic Press, 1976; *Collection Development* (textbook), Libraries Unlimited, 1977; *Bibliography of Native American Bilingual Materials,* American Indian Studies Center, University of California, Los Angeles, 1977; *Reference Books on American Indians: An Annotated Guide,* Libraries Unlimited, 1978; *Bibliography of Bibliographies on American Indians: An Annotated Union List,* American Bibliographic Center-Clio Press, 1978. Also editor of "Challenge to Change" series, Libraries Unlimited. Book reviewer for *Library Journal* and *Information Storage and Retrieval;* contributor of articles to *Library Journal, Library Quarterly,* and other professional journals.

* * *

EVANS, John W(alker) 1904-

PERSONAL: Born November 16, 1904, in Brooklyn, N.Y.; son of Alfred F. (an architect) and Lucy (Walker) Evans; married Avis Wickins, September 1, 1934. *Education:* Yale University, Ph.B., 1927; New York University, M.A., 1940. *Home:* 3717 Corey Pl. N.W., Washington, D.C. 20016.

CAREER: Henry L. Doherty Co., New York City, assistant sales promotion manager, 1927-30; affiliated with Standard Statistics Co., New York City, 1930-41; U.S. Department of State, Washington, D.C., divisional assistant, 1941-42; U.S. Foreign Economic Administration, Washington, D.C., special assistant to director of Procurement Branch, 1941-45; U.S. Department of Commerce, Washington,

D.C., member of policy staff of Office of International Trade, chairman of Committee for Reciprocity Information, and member of Trade Agreements Committee, 1946-48, director of Commodity Division, 1948-49; U.S. Department of State, Office of International Materials Policy, deputy director, 1949-50, director, 1951-52, director of Office of Economic Defense and Trade Policy, 1952-54, director of commercial policy for General Agreement on Tariffs and Trade, Geneva, Switzerland, 1955-56; U.S. Department of State, Foreign Service, 1956-65, serving as deputy director of Office of Intelligence Research, 1956-57, deputy economic minister in London, England, 1958-60, economic counselor and deputy director of Agency for International Development in Madrid, Spain, 1961, economic minister in Geneva, 1961-65; Harvard University, Center for International Affairs, Cambridge, Mass., research associate, 1965-67; U.S. Executive Office of President, Washington, D.C., assistant special representative for trade negotiations, 1967-70, consultant, 1970-73; consultant, U.S. Department of State, 1973—. Member of U.S. delegation, Preparatory Committee for an International Trade Organization, 1947, 1948; General Agreement on Tariffs and Trade, Geneva, Switzerland, member of U.S. delegation, 1949, 1951, chairman of U.S. delegation, 1948, 1962, U.S. member of Council of Ministers, 1961-65; member of special trade panel, U.S. Chamber of Commerce. Visiting lecturer, Fletcher School of Law and Diplomacy, Tufts University, 1965-66; professorial lecturer, School of Advanced International Studies, Johns Hopkins University, 1967-73. Private consultant in international trade, 1970—. *Member:* Reform Club (London), Cosmos Club (Washington, D.C.).

WRITINGS: U.S. Trade Policy, Harper, 1967; (contributor) *The Global Partnership,* Praeger, 1968; *The Kennedy Round in American Trade Policy: The Twilight of the GATT?,* Harvard University Press, 1971. Contributor to *International Organization, Journal of Common Market Studies,* and other journals.†

* * *

EWY, Donna 1934-

PERSONAL: Born September 1, 1934, in Denver, Colo.; daughter of Lee K. and Irene Lena (Ginsburg) Hohmann; married Rodger Ewy (a photojournalist), March 1, 1958; children: Marguerite, Suzanne, Rodger, Leon. *Education:* University of Colorado, B.A., 1956; University of Northern Colorado, doctoral candidate. *Home:* 1315 Northwood, Boulder, Colo. 80302.

CAREER: Teacher in Denver, Colo., Maryland, San Francisco, Calif., and in France, 1958-61. *Member:* Colorado Association for Prepared Childbirth.

WRITINGS: (With husband, Rodger Ewy) *Preparation for Childbirth,* Pruett, 1970, revised edition, 1976. Contributor to photography journals.

WORK IN PROGRESS: Research on the effects of preparation for childbirth on clinic patients; book for adolescents on childbirth; manual on breastfeeding; film and slides on breastfeeding and childbirth.

* * *

EWY, Rodger 1931-

PERSONAL: Born May 23, 1931, in Denver, Colo.; son of A. W. and M. Jean (Purvis) Ewy; married Donna Hohmann (a photographer), March 1, 1958; children: Marguerite, Suzanne, Rodger, Leon. *Education:* Dartmouth College,

B.F.A. (summa cum laude), 1953. *Home:* 1315 Norwood, Boulder, Colo. 80302.

CAREER: Bechtel Corp., San Francisco, Calif., cost engineer, 1956-57; Ewy Photography, free-lance photojournalist in Europe, 1958-61; National Center for Atmospheric Research, Boulder, Colo., photographer, 1963-68; International Business Machines Corp. (IBM), Boulder, photographer, 1969-74; president, Educational Graphic Aids, Inc.; partner, Ewy Associates (metric consultants). *Member:* Colorado Association for Prepared Childbirth.

WRITINGS: (With wife, Donna Ewy) *Preparation for Childbirth,* Pruett, 1970, revised edition, 1976; *Preparation for Breastfeeding,* Doubleday, 1975. Contributor to photographic journals.

WORK IN PROGRESS: Research on the effects of preparation for childbirth on clinic patients; writing book for teenagers on childbirth; producing film and slides on breastfeeding, childbirth, contraception, and breast examination.

*   *   *

FABRIZIO, Ray 1930-

PERSONAL: Born June 18, 1930, in Cortland, N.Y.; son of Anselmo R. and Mary (Di Donato) Fabrizio; married Allye Hobson (a college teacher), February 10, 1969 (divorced); children: Rita, Carla. *Education:* Los Angeles State College (now California State University, Los Angeles), B.A., 1953; San Francisco State College (now University), M.A., 1957; University of California, Berkeley, additional graduate study, 1957. *Home:* 780 Dry Creek Rd., Monterey, Calif. 93940. *Office:* Department of English, Monterey Peninsula College, Monterey, Calif.

CAREER: Monterey Peninsula College, Monterey, Calif., teacher of English, 1958—; University of California, Santa Cruz, professor of flute, 1969—. Professional flautist; formerly played with San Francisco Symphony Orchestra; currently principal flute with Monterey County Symphony Orchestra. *Military service:* U.S. Army, 1953-55. *Awards, honors:* Borestone Mountain Poetry Award, 1963.

WRITINGS: (With others) *The Inquiring Reader,* Heath, 1967, revised edition, 1974; (compiler) *The Rhetoric of NO,* Holt, 1970; (compiler) *The Rhetoric of YES,* Holt, 1972. Contributor of poems to periodicals published in five countries.

*   *   *

FADER, Daniel 1930-

PERSONAL: Born January 4, 1930, in Baltimore, Md.; son of Maurice A. and Ida (Browne) Fader; married Martha Alice Agnew, October 8, 1955; children: Paul, Lisa. *Education:* Cornell University, B.A., 1952, M.A., 1954; Stanford University, Ph.D., 1963. *Home:* 501 Burson Pl., Ann Arbor, Mich. 48104. *Office:* Department of English, University of Michigan, Ann Arbor, Mich. 48104.

CAREER: University of Michigan, Ann Arbor, instructor, 1961-63, assistant professor, 1963-68, associate professor, 1968-73, professor of English, 1973—, chairman of English composition board, 1976—. Trull Lecturer, Wharton College, University of Pennsylvania, 1960; Forum Lecturer, Brigham Young University; Distinguished Lecturer, Federal City College; Bicentennial Lecturer, University of Nebraska; Herr Memorial Lecturer, College Reading Association; lecturer and keynote speaker at other universities and conferences in United States and Britain. Project director, U.S. Office of Education, at Maxey Boys Training School,

Whitmore Lake, Mich., and Patterson Jr. High School, Washington, D.C.; bibliographer, University Microfilms. Member of educational and policy advisory board, University of California, Los Angeles; consultant to U.S. Office of Education Division of Research in Higher Education, Education Division of Xerox Corp., Kettering Foundation, National Endowment for the Humanities, Children's Department Development Group (Britain), Select Committee on Teacher Preparation (Britain), Corporation for Public Broadcasting, U.S. Senate Committee on Labor and Public Welfare, Carnegie Corp. Conference on the Doctor of Arts Degree, American Bar Association, White House Program on Books for Children, and other government agencies and universities. *Member:* Modern Language Association of America, National Council of Teachers of English, American Association of University Professors. *Awards, honors:* Research scholar, Christ's College, Cambridge University, 1955-57; visiting scholar, Virginia State University; Sigma Chi Scholar, Miami University.

WRITINGS: Hooked on Books, Berkley Publishing, 1966; (with E. B. McNeil) *Hooked on Books: Program and Proof,* Putnam, 1968; *The Periodical Context of English Literature, 1708-1907,* Xerox Corporation, 1970; *The Naked Children,* Macmillan, 1971; (with George Bornstein) *British Periodicals of the Eighteenth and Nineteenth Centuries,* Xerox Corporation, 1972; (with Bornstein) *Two Centuries of British Periodicals,* Xerox Corporation, 1974; *Paul and I Discover America,* Grosset, 1975; (with J. Duggins, T. Finn, and McNeil) *New Hooked on Books,* Berkley Publishing, 1976, hardcover edition, Putnam, 1977. Contributor of articles to *Library Journal, Chicago Tribune, English in Education, Special Libraries, Library Bulletin, Junior College Research Review, Washington Post, Utah Libraries, Source Magazine, Journal of Humanistic Education, Media and Methods,* and other periodicals.

WORK IN PROGRESS: A novel set in America just after World War II.

BIOGRAPHICAL/CRITICAL SOURCES: Life, September 10, 1971; *Detroit News,* November 21, 1971.

*   *   *

FADERMAN, Lillian 1940-

PERSONAL: Born July 18, 1940, in Bronx, N.Y.; daughter of Mary Lifton. *Education:* University of California, Berkeley, A.B., 1962; University of California, Los Angeles, M.A., 1964, Ph.D., 1967. *Office:* Department of English, California State University, Fresno, Calif. 93740.

CAREER: California State University, Fresno, 1967—, associate professor, 1971-72, professor of English, 1973—, chairman of department, 1971-72, dean of School of Humanities, 1972-73, assistant vice-president of academic affairs, 1973-76. *Member:* Modern Language Association of America, American Association of University Women.

WRITINGS: (With Barbara Bradshaw) *Speaking for Ourselves: American Ethnic Writing,* Scott, Foresman, 1969, 2nd edition, 1975; (editor with Luis Omar Salinas) *From the Barrio: A Chicano Anthology,* Canfield Press, 1973.

*   *   *

FADIMAN, James 1939-

PERSONAL: Born May 27, 1939, in New York, N.Y.; son of William James (a story editor for films) and Vera (Racolin) Fadiman; married Dorothy Ostwind (an artist), April 4, 1965; children: Renee, Maria. *Education:* Harvard University, B.A., 1960; Stanford University, M.A., 1962, Ph.D., 1965. *Home:* 1070 Colby Ave., Menlo Park, Calif. 94025. *Office:* 250 Oak Grove Ave., Menlo Park, Calif. 94025.

CAREER: San Francisco State College (now University), San Francisco, Calif., assistant professor of psychology, 1965-66; Brandeis University, Waltham, Mass., assistant professor of psychology, 1967-68; Stanford University, Stanford, Calif., senior counselor, 1969-71; lecturer in design engineering, 1971—, member of faculty, California Institute for Transpersonal Psychology, 1976—; Institute for Executive Research, Menlo Park, Calif., director of education, 1976—. Lecturer and workshop leader, Esalen Institute, 1961—; associate, Patrick Sullivan & Associates (psychological consultants to management), San Francisco, 1965-69; instructor, San Francisco Art Institute, 1969. Lecturer at various universities, colleges, and private institutions. Consultant to International Telephone and Telegraph, University of California, Santa Cruz, Macmillan Co., Wiley, Inc., and Brooks-Cole, Inc., 1968—; consultant, Stanford Research Institute, 1969-71. Director, Institute of Noetic Sciences, and Center for Integral Medicine; vice-president, Transpersonal Institute. *Member:* American Psychological Association, American Association for Humanistic Psychology, Association for Transpersonal Psychology, Sigma Xi.

WRITINGS: (With C. Savage and W. Harman) *Impomea Purpurea: A Naturally Occuring Psychedelic,* International Foundation for Advanced Study, 1963; (with Harman, R. McKin, R. Mogar, and M. Stolaroff) *Use of Psychedelic Agents to Facilitate Creative Problem Solving,* Institute for Psychedelic Research, San Francisco State College, 1965; (contributor) H. Abramson, editor, *Proceedings of the Second International Conference on the Use of LSD in Psychotherapy, 1965,* Bobbs-Merrill, 1967; (contributor) Charles Tart, editor, *Altered States of Consciousness,* Wiley, 1968; *Drugs: The Children Are Choosing,* Bay Area Educational Television Association, 1969.

(Contributor) B. Aaronson and H. Osmond, editors, *The Uses and Implications of Hallucinogenic Drugs,* Doubleday-Anchor, 1970; (editor) *The Proper Study of Man: Perspectives of the Social Sciences,* Macmillan, 1971; (editor with Donald Kewman) *Exploring Madness: Experience, Understanding, and Research,* Brooks-Cole, 1973, 2nd edition, 1978; (editor with G. Hendricks) *Transpersonal Education,* Prentice-Hall, 1976; (editor with J. White) *Relax,* Dell, 1976; (with R. Frager) *Personality and Personal Growth,* Harper, 1976.

Films: "Drugs: The Children Are Choosing," KQED-TV, 1969; "San Francisco Mix: Borning," KQED-TV, 1970; (and co-producer) "San Francisco Mix: Wanting and Needing," KQED-TV, 1971.

Contributor to *Journal of Neuropsychiatry, Psychological Reports, Economic Botany, International Journal of Neuropsychiatry, Journal of Humanistic Psychology, Medical Opinion and Review, Journal of Transpersonal Psychology, Etc., Psychology Today,* and *Whole Earth Catalog. Journal of Humanistic Psychology,* member of editorial staff, 1967-70, member of editorial board, 1970—; associate editor, *Journal of Transpersonal Psychology,* 1969—; member of advisory board, *Humanizing Education.*

WORK IN PROGRESS: Various books and articles on personality theory, weight control, and holistic health; with A. Hastings, an annotated bibliography of holistic health literature.

SIDELIGHTS: James Fadiman told *CA:* "I find that I do so much public speaking as an author that I have little time in which to write. It is clear that we are in the midst of a revolution in our thinking about the body and about medicine. It is also clear that we are overcoming our eagerness to die. I like the alternatives."

* * *

FAGYAS, Maria
(Mary Helen Fay)

PERSONAL: Surname is pronounced *Fudge*-us; born in Budapest, Hungary; daughter of Geza L. (an army officer) and Ilona (Szell) Fagyas; married L. Bush-Fekete (a playwright; deceased). *Education:* Attended Pazmany Peter University, Budapest, two years. *Politics:* Democrat. *Religion:* Protestant. *Address:* P.O. Box 1543, Palm Springs, Calif. 92262. *Agent:* Robert Lantz, 114 East 55th St., New York, N.Y. 10022.

CAREER: Novelist and playwright; screenwriter for Twentieth Century-Fox, Metro-Goldwyn-Mayer, Columbia Pictures, and Warner Brothers, at intervals, 1942-70. *Member:* Writers Guild of America, West. *Awards, honors:* Special award in Edgar Allan Poe Awards, Mystery Writers of America, 1964, for *The Fifth Woman.*

WRITINGS—Novels: *The Fifth Woman,* Doubleday, 1963; *The Widowmaker,* Doubleday, 1966; *The Devil's Lieutenant,* Putnam, 1970; *Dance of the Assassins,* Putnam, 1973.

Plays; under pseudonym Mary Helen Fay, with husband, L. Bush-Fekete: "Embezzled Heaven," produced on Broadway at National Theatre, 1944; "Alice in Arms," produced on Broadway, 1945; "The Big Two," produced on Broadway, 1947; "Faithfully Yours," produced on Broadway at Coronet Theatre, 1951. Under name Maria Fagyas, also author of a play, "The Girl Who Talked to Goldfish."

WORK IN PROGRESS: An untitled novel, for Simon & Schuster.

SIDELIGHTS: Maria Fagyas produced "a fascinating and disturbing book" in *The Devil's Lieutenant,* writes W. G. Rogers. Thomas Lask calls it "a top-drawer psychological thriller that unrolls like a whodunit, so artfully constructed, so smoothly readable that you will find yourself devouring it at a single sitting." Fagyas' novels have been translated into ten foreign languages.

BIOGRAPHICAL/CRITICAL SOURCES: New York Times, May 23, 1970; *New York Times Book Review,* May 24, 1970, January 6, 1974; *Best Sellers,* October 1, 1973; *Book World,* May 11, 1975.

* * *

FAIN, Haskell 1926-

PERSONAL: Born July 1, 1926, in New York, N.Y.; son of Max (a civil engineer) and Ethel (Frankenstein) Fain; married Elaine Folk (a university lecturer), September 14, 1949; children: Jonathan Simon, Madeline Alessandra. *Education:* University of Illinois, B.S., 1948, M.A., 1949; University of California, Berkeley, M.A., 1951, Ph.D., 1956. *Home:* 2306 Van Hise Ave., Madison, Wis. 53705. *Office:* 5185 Helen C. White Hall, University of Wisconsin, Madison, Wis. 53706.

CAREER: University of Wisconsin—Madison, assistant professor, 1956-62, associate professor, 1962-67, professor of philosophy, 1967—, chairman of department, 1968-70.

Fulbright lecturer, University of Bergen, 1961-62; visiting professor at University of British Columbia, 1964-65, Linacre College, Oxford University, 1966-67, and Florida State University, 1970-71. *Military service:* U.S. Army, 1944-46. *Member:* American Philosophical Association, American Civil Liberties Union. *Awards, honors:* Fulbright fellow in Norway, 1954-55; National Endowment for the Humanities fellow, 1974-75.

WRITINGS: Between Philosophy and History: The Resurrection of Speculative Philosophy of History within the Analytic Tradition, Princeton University Press, 1970. Contributor to philosophy journals.

WORK IN PROGRESS: A book about the philosophy of international politics.

* * *

FAINSOD, Merle 1907-1972

May 2, 1907—February 10, 1972; American educator and authority on American and Soviet political affairs. Obituaries: *New York Times,* February 12, 1972; *Washington Post,* February 13, 1972; *Newsweek,* February 21, 1972. (See index for *CA* sketch)

* * *

FAIRBAIRN, Douglas 1926-

PERSONAL: Born December 20, 1926; son of Martin E. and Jean (Fairbairn) Behl; married Gay Vander Woud, December 16, 1966. *Education:* Attended Harvard University, 1946-51. *Politics:* Center. *Religion:* Christian. *Home address:* Box 330552, Coconut Grove Station, Miami, Fla. 33133. *Agent:* Mrs. Roberta Pryor, International Creative Management, 40 West 57th St., New York, N.Y. 10019.

CAREER: Writer. Professional painter working in nonobjective watercolors. *Military service:* Florida National Guard, 1948-51. *Awards, honors:* Seven Emmy nominations, 1962, for television adaptation of novel, *The Voice of Charlie Pont.*

WRITINGS: A Man's World, Simon & Schuster, 1956; *The Joy Train,* Simon & Schuster, 1957; *Money, Marbles & Chalk* (Doubleday Book Club selection, 1959), Simon & Schuster, 1958; *The Voice of Charlie Pont* (play; first produced in Miami at Players Theatre, December 31, 1971), Random House, 1961; *A Gazelle on the Lawn,* Random House, 1964; *A Squirrel of One's Own,* McCall, 1971; *Shoot,* Doubleday, 1973; *A Squirrel Forever,* Simon & Schuster, 1973; *Street 8,* Delacorte, 1977.

Screenplays: "A Man's World" (from his novel of the same title), networked by CBS for "Studio One" in 1956; "The Voice of Charlie Pont" (from his play of the same title), networked by ABC for "Alcoa Premier" in 1962; "Shoot" (from his novel of the same title), produced by Avco Embassy, 1976.

WORK IN PROGRESS: A novel, *Nina and Eric's;* a screenplay based on *Street 8;* an autobiography, *Head above Water.*

* * *

FAIRBROTHER, Nan 1913-1971

December 23, 1913—November 24, 1971; English landscape architect and authority on gardening. Obituaries: *New York Times,* November 26, 1971; *Publishers Weekly,* December 20, 1971. (See index for *CA* sketch)

FAIRFIELD, Roy P(hillip) 1918-

PERSONAL: Born May 17, 1918, in Saco, Me.; son of Wilbur F. and Mary (Smart) Fairfield; married Maryllyn Rumery (a registered nurse), November 30, 1939; children: M. Donna. *Education:* Bates College, A.B., 1943; Harvard University, A.M., 1947, Ph.D., 1953. *Politics:* Democrat. *Religion:* Humanist. *Home:* 1328 Shawnee Dr., Yellow Springs, Ohio 45387. *Office:* Department of Social Science, Union Graduate School, Yellow Springs, Ohio 45387.

CAREER: Bates College, Lewiston, Me., professor of history, 1947-57; Ohio University, Athens, professor of government and social science, 1957-64; Antioch College, Yellow Springs, Ohio, professor of social science and education, 1964-70; Union Graduate School, Yellow Springs, professor of social science, 1970—, director, 1970-75. Adjunct professor of education, Hofstra University, 1956, 1958, 1959. Involved in Peace Corps training, 1962-64. *Member:* American Humanist Association (vice-president and director, 1965-69), York Institute (director), Phi Beta Kappa. *Awards, honors:* Fulbright professorship in Greece, 1953-54; named "Humanist Fellow of the Year," 1973.

WRITINGS: Sands, Spindles and Steeples: A History of Saco, Maine, Falmouth, 1956; (editor) *The Federalist Papers,* Doubleday-Anchor, 1961; (editor) *Humanist Frontiers in American Education,* Prentice-Hall, 1971; (editor) *Humanizing the Workplace,* Prometheus Books, 1974; *Person-Centered Learning,* Prometheus Books, 1977. Poetry included in eight anthologies. Contributor of articles to *Journal of Higher Education, Middle East Journal, School and Society, Phi Delta Kappan, Social Policy,* and other publications. Associate editor, *Humanist,* 1967—.

WORK IN PROGRESS: Dissent in American Society; humanistic studies; haiku and photographic imagery.

SIDELIGHTS: Roy P. Fairfield has traveled in Western Europe, East and West Africa.

* * *

FAIRMAN, Joan A(lexandra) 1935-

PERSONAL: Born April 11, 1935, in Philadelphia, Pa.; daughter of Alexander Daisley and Florence (Wenner) Fairman. *Education:* Peirce Junior College, graduate, 1953. *Politics:* Republican. *Religion:* Episcopalian. *Home:* Salem Harbour, Apt. C-2, 435 Olde Bridge Rd., Andalusia, Pa. 19020.

CAREER: Curtis Publishing Co., Philadelphia, Pa., executive secretary, 1953-70; Towers, Perrin, Forster & Crosby, Inc. (management consultants), Philadelphia, executive secretary, 1970-76, administrative assistant, 1976—.

WRITINGS: (Contributor) Margaret Early, E. K. Cooper, Nancy Santeusanio, and Marian Adell, editors, *Widening Circles,* Harcourt, 1970; *A Penny Saved,* Lantern Press, 1971. Contributor to national children's magazines, including *Jack and Jill* (author of "Baba Yaga" serial) and *Ranger Rick's Nature Magazine.*

* * *

FANTA, J. Julius 1907-

PERSONAL: Born October 1, 1907, in Chicago, Ill.; son of Theodore and Fannie Fanta; married Irene Gross, 1949; children: Steven, Bruce, Ronald, Jayne. *Education:* Attended Marquette University. *Politics:* "Non-partisan." *Home:* 3 Belair Dr., Huntington, N.Y. 11743.

WRITINGS: Sailing with President Kennedy, Sea Lore,

1969; *Winning the America's Cup,* Sea Lore, 1970; *Five Star Finish,* Sea Lore, 1971; *How to Rescue and Cope with Emergencies,* Sea Lore, 1972. Also author of screenplay, "Voyage to Glory."

WORK IN PROGRESS: A novel.

*   *   *

FARBER, Joseph C. 1903-

PERSONAL: Born February 13, 1903, in Cleveland, Ohio; son of Adolph J. and Esther (Selman) Farber; married Caroline Feiss (an artist), May 8, 1930; children: Joan Caroline. *Education:* Attended Columbia University. *Home:* 4 East 88th St., New York, N.Y. 10028. *Agent:* Georges Borchardt, Inc., 136 East 57th St., New York, N.Y. 10022.

CAREER: Photographer and illustrator.

WRITINGS—With photographs by the author: (With Marie Moore) *Portrait of Essex,* Barre, 1969; (with Wendell Garrett) *Thomas Jefferson Redivivus,* Barre, 1971; (with Michael Dorris) *Native Americans: 500 Years After,* Crowell, 1975; (illustrator) Herodotus, *Democracy's First Struggle,* Barre, 1975.

*   *   *

FARLEY, Eugene J. 1916-

PERSONAL: Born September 18, 1916, in Newark, N.J.; son of Matthew E. and Mary (O'Toole) Farley; married Alice Reichl, June 27, 1942; children: David, Dennis. *Education:* Montclair State College, B.A., 1938, M.A., 1946; Rutgers University, Ed.D., 1964. *Home address:* P.O. Box 964, Columbia, Md. 21044.

CAREER: South Orange-Maplewood School District, Maplewood, N.J., teacher, 1947-56, counselor, 1956-76. Director of basic education and high school equivalency in adult school, South Orange, N.J., 1966-69. Consultant, adult education, 1966—, TV High School, 1967, Your Future Is Now, 1972; consultant in pre-retirement counseling, 1977—. *Military service:* U.S. Army, Medical Administration Corps, 1941-45; became captain. *Member:* American Psychological Association, National Association of Public Continuing and Adult Education, National Council of Senior Citizens, Maryland Psychological Association, Maryland Association of Publicly Supported Continuing Education.

WRITINGS—Published by Barron's, except as indicated: (With Clyde Weinhold and Arthur Crabtree) *High School Certification through G.E.D. Tests,* Holt, 1967; *How to Prepare for the High School Equivalency Examination: Reading Interpretation Tests,* 1970; (with wife, Alice R. Farley) *Developing Reading Skills for the High School Equivalency Examinations in Social Studies, Science, and Literature,* 1972; (with A. R. Farley) *Getting Ready for the High School Equivalency Exam: Beginning Preparation in Reading and English,* 1973; *Barron's Preview Examination to Prepare for High School Equivalency Tests,* 1973. Also editor of five books for Barron's.

WORK IN PROGRESS: Revisions of two books and the equivalency exam, for Barron's.

*   *   *

FARNSWORTH, Lee W(infield) 1932-

PERSONAL: Born March 6, 1932, in Salt Lake City, Utah; son of Walter J. (a businessman) and Ethel (Loveridge) Farnsworth; married Zona Gayle Smith, June 16, 1953; children: Carol, David, Kenneth, Ellen, Leonard, Bryan, Steven, Janis, Mary, Paul. *Education:* University of California, Berkeley, A.B. (with highest honors), 1957, M.A., 1960; Stanford University, graduate study, 1960-61, summer, 1963, 1971; Claremont Graduate School, Ph.D., 1963. *Religion:* Church of Jesus Christ of Latter-day Saints. *Home:* 3147 Apache Lane, Provo, Utah 84601. *Office:* Department of Political Science, Brigham Young University, Provo, Utah 84602.

CAREER: Florida State University, Tallahassee, assistant professor of government, 1962-64; Brigham Young University, Provo, Utah, assistant professor, 1964-66, associate professor, 1966-72, professor of political science, 1972—, director of Asian Research Institute, 1965-68. Visiting professor, International Christian University, Tokyo, 1970-71; Fulbright lecturer in the Philippines, summer, 1971. Member of Provo City School Board, 1973-74; elected to Utah House of Representatives, 1973—. *Military service:* U.S. Army, 1953-56. *Member:* American Political Science Association, Association for Asian Studies (chairman of Western Conference, 1967-68), Western Political Science Association (chairman of scholars specializing in the politics of Japan, 1973—). *Awards, honors:* Social Science Foundation fellow, 1968-69; National Science Foundation fellow, summer, 1969; Fulbright research grant to Japan, 1970-71; Japan Foundation fellow, 1975.

WRITINGS: (Editor with R. B. Gray) *Security in a World of Change,* Wadsworth, 1969; *The Story of Japan,* McCormick-Mathers, 1970. Contributor to journals of Asian studies and political science. Editor, *Newsletter of Political Research on Japan,* Brigham Young University, 1970—.

WORK IN PROGRESS: Japan: Government and Politics, a textbook for Harcourt; research on conflict in local and national politics in Japan.

SIDELIGHTS: Lee W. Farnsworth's wife and children traveled with him on his research trips to Japan and Korea in 1970-71, and to Japan in 1975. *Avocational interests:* Handball.

*   *   *

FARR, Roger C.

EDUCATION: State University of New York College at Brockport, B.S., 1961; State University of New York College at Buffalo, M.S., 1965; State University of New York at Buffalo, Ed.D., 1967. *Office:* Reading Clinic, University Schools, Indiana University, Bloomington, Ind. 47405.

CAREER: Junior and senior high school English teacher, Akron, Ohio, 1957-64; State University of New York at Buffalo, instructor in educational psychology, 1966-67; Indiana University at Bloomington, assistant professor, 1967-70, associate professor of education, 1970—, director of Reading Clinic, 1968—. *Member:* International Reading Association (chairman of evaluation of tests committee), National Council on Measurement in Education, American Educational Research Association, National Reading Conference, National Conference on Research in English, Phi Delta Kappa.

WRITINGS: (With Edward G. Summers) *Guide to Tests and Measuring Instruments for Reading,* Indiana University, 1968; (contributor) G. B. Schick and M. M. May, editors, *Multidisciplinary Aspects of College-Adult Reading,* National Reading Conference, 1968; (with James Laffey and Carl Smith) *A Taxonomy of Evaluation Techniques for Reading Programs,* Indiana University for U.S. Office of Education, 1968; (with Nicholas Anastasiow) *Tests of*

Reading Readiness and Achievement: A Review and Evaluation, International Reading Association, 1969; (editor) *Measurement and Evaluation of Reading,* Harcourt, 1970; *Reading: What Can Be Measured?,* International Reading Association, 1970; (contributor) Schick and May, editors, *Reading: Process and Pedagogy,* National Reading Conference, 1970; (with Laffey) *What Research Says to the Teacher of Reading: Reading in the High School,* National Education Association, 1970; *Grade Levels and Test Scores: What Do They Mean?,* National Reading Center, 1971; (compiler) *Measurement of Reading Achievement,* International Reading Association, 1971. Associate editor, *Reading Research Quarterly,* 1968-69; co-editor, *Indiana Reading Quarterly,* 1968-69.

WORK IN PROGRESS: Editing with William Blanton and J. Jaap Tuinman, *Reading Tests for the Secondary Grades: A Review and Evaluation,* for International Reading Association; a section for a book on college-adult reading, for National Reading Conference; a section for a book of readings, for International Reading Association.†

*   *   *

FARRAR, Ronald T(ruman) 1935-

PERSONAL: Born July 3, 1935, in Fordyce, Ark.; son of Truman Langdon and Grace (Johnson) Farrar; married Gayla Hope Dennis, June 3, 1961; children: Janet, Bradley. *Education:* University of Arkansas, B.S., 1957; University of Iowa, M.A., 1962; University of Missouri, Ph.D., 1965. *Religion:* Methodist. *Home:* 3378 Pimlico Pkwy., Lexington, Ky. 40504. *Office:* School of Journalism, University of Kentucky, Lexington, Ky. 40506.

CAREER: Arkansas Democrat, Little Rock, reporter, 1957; *Paragould Daily Press,* Paragould, Ark., news editor, 1958; *Arkansas Gazette,* Little Rock, reporter, 1958-60; *Trumann Democrat,* Trumann, Ark., editor-manager, 1960-61; *Daily Iowan,* Iowa City, Iowa, circulation manager, 1961-62; Indiana University, Bloomington, 1964-70, began as lecturer, became associate professor of journalism; Southern Methodist University, Dallas, Tex., associate professor of journalism and chairman of department, 1970-73; University of Mississippi, University, professor of journalism and chairman of department, 1973-77; University of Kentucky, Lexington, director of School of Journalism, 1977—. *Military service:* U.S. Army, 1957-58; became 2nd lieutenant. U.S. Army Reserve, 1958-65; became captain.

MEMBER: Association for Education in Journalism (chairman-elect of History Division, 1970), Organization of American Historians, American Association of University Professors, Sigma Delta Chi. *Awards, honors:* Distinguished Service Medal of Sigma Delta Chi, 1969, for *Reluctant Servant: The Story of Charles G. Ross.*

WRITINGS: Reluctant Servant: The Story of Charles G. Ross, University of Missouri Press, 1969; (with John Stevens) *Mass Media and the National Experience,* Harper, 1971. Contributor to professional journals.

*   *   *

FARRELL, Kirby 1942-

PERSONAL: Born July 23, 1942, in Boston, Mass. *Education:* Clark University, A.B., 1964; Rutgers University, Ph.D., 1972. *Home:* 59 Revell Ave., Northampton, Mass. 01060. *Office:* Department of English, University of Massachusetts, Amherst, Mass. 01002.

CAREER: Rutgers University, Douglass College, New

Brunswick, N.J., lecturer in English, 1967-70; University of Massachusetts—Amherst, 1970—, began as assistant professor, currently professor of English.

WRITINGS: Cony-Catching (novel), Atheneum, 1971; *Shakespeare's Creation: The Language of Magic and Play* (criticism), University of Massachusetts Press, 1976.

WORK IN PROGRESS: Severance Pay, a novel.

BIOGRAPHICAL/CRITICAL SOURCES: Newsweek, February 15, 1971.

*   *   *

FAULHABER, Martha 1926-

PERSONAL: Born September 6, 1926, in Dayton, Ohio; daughter of Harry Francis (an engineer) and Hildegarde (Elsbernd) Finke; married Robert W. Faulhaber (a professor), June 19, 1950; children: Roberta, Peter, Christina, Elizabeth. *Education:* St. Mary's College, Notre Dame, Ind., B.A., 1948; Chicago Musical College, M.Mus., 1950; Ecole Normale de Musique, Paris, additional study, 1950-52. *Home:* 5653 South Harper, Chicago, Ill. 60637.

CAREER: University of Chicago, Chicago, Ill., teacher in Orthogenic School, 1955-56; currently private teacher of piano. Accompanist for Chicago Children's Choir; pianist with Trio Musicale, 1969-71.

WRITINGS: (With John Hawkinson) *Music and Instruments for Children to Make,* Albert Whitman, 1969; (with Hawkinson) *Rhythms, Music, and Instruments to Make,* Albert Whitman, 1970; (with Janet Underhill) *Music: Invent Your Own,* Albert Whitman, 1974.

*   *   *

FAUST, Irvin 1924-

PERSONAL: Born June 11, 1924, in New York, N.Y.; son of Morris (in insurance business) and Pauline (Henschel) Faust; married Jean Satterthwaite, August 29, 1959. *Education:* City College (now City College of the City University of New York), B.S., 1949; Columbia University, M.A., 1952, Ed.D., 1960. *Residence:* New York, N.Y. *Office:* Garden City High School, Garden City, N.Y.

CAREER: Junior high school teacher, New York, N.Y., 1949-53; high school guidance counselor, Lynbrook, N.Y., 1956-60; Garden City High School, Garden City, N.Y., director of guidance, 1960—. Writer. *Military service:* U.S. Army, 1943-46; served in European theater and in Southwest Pacific. *Member:* New York State Personnel and Guidance Asscoiation, P.E.N. *Awards, honors: New York Times* list of best books of the year included *Roar Lion Roar,* 1965, and *Willy Remembers,* 1971; *Book World* list of best books of 1971 included *Willy Remembers.*

WRITINGS—Fiction, except as indicated: *Entering Angel's World* (nonfiction), Teachers College Press, 1963; *Roar Lion Roar and Other Stories,* Random House, 1965; *The Steagle,* Random House, 1966; *The File on Stanley Patton Buchta,* Random House, 1970; *Willy Remembers,* Arbor House, 1971; *Foreign Devils,* Arbor House, 1973; *A Star in the Family,* Doubleday, 1975. Contributor of short stories to *Esquire, Saturday Evening Post, Paris Review, Carleton Miscellany, New York Magazine, Sewanee Review,* and *Northwest Revue;* contributor of reviews to *Esquire* and *New Republic.*

SIDELIGHTS: " 'Writing a short story,' " Irvin Faust told *New York* magazine, " 'is like living in a one-room apartment: if you furnish it properly, it comes off neatly. Writing a novel is like living in a house. You rummage around in the cellar and the attic, and you can afford to screw up a couple of rooms because there are always others that will be better.'" He has earned praise for both his short stories and his novels. Richard Kostelanetz said of *The Steagle,* in 1967, "Of the many new novels I have read in the past three years, only one struck me as fusing the three virtues of originality, significance and realization at the highest levels of consistency—Irvin Faust's *The Steagle* . . . which may indeed be the most perceptive and sustained portrait of a psychotic breakdown in all novelistic literature." Kostelanetz believes that with this novel "Faust establishes that he is clearly among the most accomplished craftsmen of fiction today." Jerome Charyn wrote that in this book Faust "laid bare the guts, bones, and geography of New York with invention, style and a heartbreaking clarity."

Although *The File on Stanley Patton Buchta* was not as well received as *The Steagle,* it, too, has earned praise. Charyn and others have commented on Faust's ability to evoke the sounds of people and a sense of place peculiar to New York. Faust's use of detail adds to the enjoyment of his stories. George P. Elliott writes of *Roar Lion Roar and Other Stories,* "From the scramble of confrontations and gropings and brief joinings, emerges such a various literary vitality as more than compensates for the stories' shortcomings." The shortcomings being "the great specificity" of locations and references he uses. Elliott concludes, however, that "if you read these stories you may not only enjoy yourself, but also become a little wiser."

Richard R. Lingeman writes: "In *Willy Remembers* Mr. Faust moulds the clay of 90 years of American popular culture into one archetypical hero who is a sort of Vox Pop man of the century. . . . This is a book rich in associations that radiate out from an individual into an era, into America. The quality of Mr. Faust's invention is not strained; he can clot his pages with trivia but not lose the pace of his story."

All of Faust's novels and *Roar Lion Roar* have had paperback editions in this country and some of them have been published in England, France, and Japan. *The Steagle* was made into a motion picture released by Avco Embassy, 1971. Faust's "continuing passion" is history.

BIOGRAPHICAL/CRITICAL SOURCES: Richard Kostelanetz, *The New American Arts,* Avon, 1964; *Harpers,* April, 1965; *Book Week,* July 10, 1966; *New Republic,* July 16, 1966; *Saturday Review,* July 16, 1966; *New York Times Book Review,* July 17, 1966, June 28, 1970; *Newsweek,* July 25, 1966, August 10, 1970; *Christian Science Monitor,* August 18, 1966, October 29, 1970; *Commonweal,* October 28, 1966, December 2, 1966; *Tri-Quarterly,* winter, 1967; *New York,* March 30, 1970; *New York Times,* July 6, 1970, August 30, 1971; *Time,* July 6, 1970, August 30, 1971; *Book World,* August 2, 1970; *New York Review of Books,* August 13, 1970; *Virginia Quarterly Review,* autumn, 1970; *Life,* December 10, 1971; *Contemporary Literary Criticism,* Volume VIII, Gale, 1978.

*　　*　　*

FEATHERSTONE, Joseph (Luke)　1940-

PERSONAL: Born June 13, 1940, in Wilkes-Barre, Pa.; son of Joseph G. (a lawyer) and Rosemary (Trainer) Featherstone; married Helen Jencks (a teacher), 1966; children: Elizabeth, Joseph, Caitlin. *Education:* Harvard University, A.B., 1962; additional study at Harvard University and London School of Economics and Political Science. *Politics:* "Independent liberal-left." *Religion:* Roman Catholic.

Home: 18 Willard St., Newton, Mass. *Office:* Graduate School of Education, Harvard University, Gutman 471, Cambridge, Mass. 02138.

CAREER: Educational Development Center, Newton, Mass., curriculum developer, 1963-65; *New Republic,* Washington, D.C., contributing editor, 1965-67, associate editor, 1967-70; Harvard University, Cambridge, Mass., research fellow, Institute of Politics, 1970-71, currently professor, Graduate School of Education. *Member:* Phi Beta Kappa.

WRITINGS: Schools Where Children Learn, Liveright, 1971; (author of introduction) *Informal Schools in Britain Today,* Citation, 1971; *What Schools Can Do,* Liveright, 1976. Also author of report, *The Primary School Revolution in Great Britain,* 1967. Contributing editor, *New Republic,* 1972—.

WORK IN PROGRESS: A book tentatively entitled *John Dewey: The Mind of an American Progressive;* a study of families and social policy.

*　　*　　*

FEDER, Bernard　1924-

PERSONAL: Surname pronounced Fayder; born October 14, 1924, in New York, N.Y.; son of Joseph George and Clara (Iserovici) Feder; married Elaine Karp (a dance teacher and dance therapist), March 31, 1950; children: Laurie Anne, Karen Lee. *Education:* Attended Ohio University, 1943-44; New York University, B.A., 1948, M.A., 1950, Ph.D., 1957. *Religion:* Jewish. *Home:* 615 Waterside Way, Siesta Key, Sarasota, Fla. 33581.

CAREER: Teacher of social studies, dean, late session coordinator, and administrative assistant in secondary schools of New York, N.Y., 1949-66; Hofstra University, Hempstead, N.Y., assistant professor, 1966-69, associate professor of education, 1969-70; presently engaged in full-time research and writing. Adjunct assistant professor, C. W. Post College, 1959-65; lecturer at Adelphi Suffolk College, 1962-65, and New York University, 1965-66. *Military service:* U.S. Army, 1943-46. *Member:* American Historical Association, National Council for the Social Studies, New York State Conference on Social Education, Florida Council for the Social Studies.

*WRITINGS—*All published by American Book Co., except as indicated: *Viewpoints: USA,* 1967, revised edition, 1972; *Viewpoints in World History,* 1968, revised edition, 1973; *The Process of American Government,* Noble & Noble, 1972; *A Matter of Life and Breath: The Politics of Pollution,* 1973; *Bucking the System: The Politics of Dissent,* 1973; *The Policeman and the Citizen: The Politics of Law and Order,* 1973; *The Price of Maintaining Poverty: The Politics of Welfare,* 1973; *Walking the Straight Line: The Politics of Drug Control,* 1973; *Conscience Versus Law,* Globe Book Co., 1975; *Our Nation of Immigrants,* Globe Book Co., 1976. Contributor to periodicals and journals including *Nation, American West, New York Times, Human Behavior, Psychology Today,* and *Parents' Magazine.*

WORK IN PROGRESS: A book on American history for American Book Co.; a book on testing as the hidden curriculum in schools.

SIDELIGHTS: Bernard Feder told *CA:* "My concern is with the *process* of historical and social science study rather than with the *product.* My writing is based on three major principles: a) to make the study of history and the social sciences more relevant to the casual student than is normally done in traditional books; b) to emphasize the skills of the practitioner rather than memorization; c) to make clear that all conclusions are inferential, not factual, and that there is room for honest differences in interpretation.

"I gave up university teaching, not because I did not enjoy it—I did, very much so—but because I found that administrative and committee assignments kept infringing upon my time. Presently, I feel that my work reaches a wider audience than the few hundred students a year that I taught.... Eventually I should like to return to teaching, along with writing."

*   *   *

FEELEY, Kathleen 1929-

PERSONAL: Born January 7, 1929, in Baltimore, Md.; daughter of Jerome Lawrence (a salesman) and Theresa (Tasker) Feeley. *Education:* College of Notre Dame of Maryland, B.A., 1963; Villanova University, M.A., 1967; Rutgers University, Ph.D., 1970; additional graduate study at Johns Hopkins University and University of Detroit. *Office:* President, College of Notre Dame of Maryland, Baltimore, Md. 21210.

CAREER: Member of religious order, School Sisters of Notre Dame (S.S.N.D.); teacher in elementary schools in Charleston, S.C., Bel Air and Riviera Beach, Md., 1949-59; Notre Dame Preparatory School, Towson, Md., teacher of English, journalism, and creative writing, 1959-65; College of Notre Dame of Maryland, Baltimore, instructor in English, 1965-67; Claremont University Center, Claremont, Calif., fellow in Institute for the Study of Change in the Four-Year College, 1970; College of Notre Dame of Maryland, American Council on Education intern in academic administration, 1970-71, president, 1971—. Appointed to attend general chapter of Congregation of School Sisters of Notre Dame, Rome, Italy, 1968. *Awards, honors:* Rutgers University fellowship, 1969; honorable mention in March-and Literary Contest, 1969, for an article "Thematic Imagery in the Fiction of Flannery O'Connor"; Woman of the Year award from Jewish National Fund Women's Auxiliary, 1975 and from Maryland Colonial Society, 1976; named Goodwill Ambassador to Israel by America-Israel Society, 1976.

WRITINGS: Flannery O'Connor: Voice of the Peacock (literary criticism), Rutgers University Press, 1972. Contributor of articles to *English Journal, Scholastic Teacher, Catholic School Journal, Southern Humanities Review, Liberal Education,* and other periodicals.

*   *   *

FEHL, Philipp P(inhas) 1920-

PERSONAL: Born May 9, 1920, in Vienna, Austria; came to United States in 1940, naturalized in 1943; son of Hugo and Friederike (Beck) Fehl; married Maria R. Schweinburg (a philologist), December 12, 1945; children: Katharine, Caroline. *Education:* Stanford University, B.A., 1947, M.A., 1948; University of Chicago, Ph.D., 1963. *Office:* Department of Art, University of Illinois, Urbana, Ill. 61801.

CAREER: University of Chicago, Chicago, Ill., lecturer in history of art, 1950-52; University of Kansas City, Kansas City, Mo., assistant professor of history of art, 1952-54; University of Nebraska, Lincoln, associate professor of history of art, 1954-63; University of North Carolina at Chapel Hill, professor of history of art, 1963-69; University of Illi-

nois at Urbana-Champaign, professor of history of art, 1969—; artist, with work appearing in numerous journals and in eight one-man exhibitions in the United States and Europe. Research fellow, Warburg Institute, 1957-58; art historian-in-residence, American Academy in Rome, 1967-68; associate, Center for Advanced Study, University of Illinois, 1970-71. *Military service:* U.S. Army, 1942-46. *Member:* International Survey of Jewish Monuments (president, 1977—), College Art Association of America (member of board of directors, 1968-71), Central Illinois Archaeological Society (president, 1973-75), Dunlap Society (member of advisory council). *Awards, honors:* National Endowment for the Humanities fellow, 1977-78.

WRITINGS: The Bird, Finial Press, 1970; *Capricci,* Neue Galerie (Graz, Austria), 1971; *The Classical Monument: Reflections on the Relations of Morality and Art in Greek and Roman Sculpture,* New York University Press, 1972; (editor with wife, M. R. Fehl and Keith Aldrich) *The Literature of Classical Art,* University of California Press, 1978. Contributor to *Art Bulletin, Gazette des Beaux Arts, Burlington,* and other journals. Book review editor, *Art Bulletin,* 1966-69.

WORK IN PROGRESS: The Art of Paolo Veronese, for Phaidon Press.

SIDELIGHTS: Philipp Fehl has traveled and studied in several countries in Europe, including Italy, France, Belgium, and England.

*   *   *

FEIGELSON, Naomi R. 1932-

PERSONAL: Born May 26, 1932, in Pittsburgh, Pa.; daughter of Henry (a judge) and Rachel (Savage) Ellenbogen; divorced; children: Elizabeth, Jonathan. *Education:* Attended Bryn Mawr College, 1950-52; Radcliffe College, B.A. (magna cum laude), 1954; Brandeis University, M.A., 1956. *Politics:* Democrat. *Religion:* Jewish.

CAREER: City of New York, N.Y., director of public information in Department of Consumer Affairs, 1970-71, and in Health Services Administration, beginning 1971.

WRITINGS: The Underground Revolution: Hippies, Yippies and Others, Funk, 1970. Contributor to magazines and newspapers, including *New York Magazine, Village Voice,* and *Dun's Review.*

AVOCATIONAL INTERESTS: Music, literature, the contemporary scene, politics.††

*   *   *

FEIS, Herbert 1893-1972

June 7, 1893—March 2, 1972; American educator, government advisor, economist, and historian. Obituaries: *New York Times,* March 3, 1972; *Washington Post,* March 5, 1972; *Newsweek,* March 13, 1972; *Time,* March 13, 1972; *Publishers Weekly,* March 20, 1972; *Current Biography,* May, 1972. (See index for *CA* sketch)

*   *   *

FELD, Michael 1938-

PERSONAL: Born July 28, 1938, in London, England; son of Benjamin (a tailor) and Ada Rebecca (Brenner) Feld; married Havazelet Drajner, May 11, 1966; children: Guy, Jesse. *Education:* Attended secondary school in London, England, until fifteen. *Politics:* "Sometimes Tory Anarchist—sometimes straight forward Apocalyptic." *Reli-*

gion: Jewish. *Home:* 36A Elm Bank Mansions, The Terrace, London S.W.13, England.

CAREER: English Exporters Ltd., London, England, office boy, 1954-55; Nylon Hosiery Co. Ltd., London, warehouseman, 1955-57; creative director and managing director in advertising agencies, 1958-72; advertising and publicity consultant, 1972—; writer.

WRITINGS: The Sabbatical Year (novel), Alan Ross, 1969; *Super Shelley's Mein Kampf* (novel), Alan Ross, 1969; *Hands of the Philistines* (stories), London Magazine Editions, 1974. Contributor of short stories and reviews to *London Magazine.*

WORK IN PROGRESS: A novel, *The Promotions of Gerald Garfield;* three novellas, *Rituals and Habits of N. 16 Natives, Return of the Tongue,* and *Fender;* a collection of stories.

SIDELIGHTS: Feld wrote in *London Magazine* that when he went to work at fifteen he "hated it in no time." He spent several years trying to get plays produced which he had written in the hopes of acquiring fame and beautiful actresses. When that failed he turned to stories. "Now I hate my writing, because it is so much better than me. It is a penance to make up for the cowardice that affords economic survival." Feld told *CA* he is "keen on association football."

BIOGRAPHICAL/CRITICAL SOURCES: New Statesman, November 22, 1968, October 31, 1969; *Observer Review,* February 9, 1969; *London Magazine,* November, 1969, March, 1970.

* * *

FELD, Ross 1947-

PERSONAL: Born in 1947, in Brooklyn, N.Y.; son of Herman and Lillian (Karmel) Feld; married Ellen Weissman, 1972. *Education:* Attended City College of the City University of New York, 1965-68. *Home:* 570 Westminster Rd., Brooklyn, N.Y. 11230. *Agent:* Mel Berger, William Morris Agency, 1350 Avenue of the Americas, New York, N.Y. 10019.

CAREER: Employed in editorial posts by Time-Life Books and then Grove Press, both New York, N.Y., 1968-70; freelance editor, 1970—. Director of New Novelists Program, City College of the City University of New York, 1975-76; senior contributor, *Kirkus Review,* 1977—. *Awards, honors:* National Endowment for the Arts anthology award, 1970; New York State Council on the Arts grant in fiction, 1976; Pushcart Prize, 1977.

WRITINGS: Winter Poems, Shortstop Press, 1967; *Plum Poems,* Jargon Society, 1971; *Years Out* (novel), Knopf, 1973. Contributor to *Saturday Review, New Republic, Nation, Parnassus,* and other literary magazines.

WORK IN PROGRESS: Prose.

SIDELIGHTS: "Certain ghosts are quite real to me," Ross Feld writes, "and guided and frightened by them, I come to think that writing is given to men who are no more unusual than anyone else, except for the fact that they spend their lives paying court to the world by making it up."

* * *

FELDER, Raoul Lionel 1934-

PERSONAL: Born May 13, 1934, in Brooklyn, N.Y.; son of Morris (an attorney) and Millie (Goldstein) Felder; married Myrna Danenberg (an attorney), May 26, 1963; children:

Rachel Harris, James Harris. *Education:* New York University, B.A., 1955, J.D., 1959; University of Bern, medical studies, 1955-56. *Politics:* Independent. *Religion:* Jewish. *Home:* 985 Fifth Ave., New York, N.Y. 10021. *Office:* 711 Fifth Ave., New York, N.Y. 10022.

CAREER: Private practice of law, New York City, 1959-61; assistant U.S. attorney in New York City, U.S. Department of Justice, 1961-64; private practice of law, New York City, 1964—. Judge, American Bar Association Client Counselling Competition. *Member:* American Bar Association (sustaining member), American Arbitration Association (member of national panel of arbitrators), American Academy of Matrimonial Lawyers (fellow), Society of Medical Jurisprudence, New York State District Attorneys Association, New York State Bar Association, Association of the Bar of the City of New York (member of special committee on matritional law, 1975-77).

WRITINGS: Divorce: The Way Things Are Not—The Way Things Should Be, World Publishing, 1971.

WORK IN PROGRESS: A textbook for the legal profession.

AVOCATIONAL INTERESTS: Collecting cookbooks (has about 1,500 in his collection), skydiving.

* * *

FELDMAN, Burton 1926-

PERSONAL: Born May 3, 1926, in Albany, N.Y.; son of Benjamin and Lena (Tolkin) Feldman; married Margaret Mary Gildea, January, 1953. *Education:* Union College and University, Schenectady, N.Y., B.A., 1949; Columbia University, M.A., 1951; University of Chicago, Ph.D., 1961. *Residence:* Denver, Colo. *Office:* Department of English, University of Denver, Denver, Colo. 80210.

CAREER: University of Chicago, Chicago, Ill., lecturer, 1957-63; University of Denver, Denver, Colo., faculty member in English department, 1965—. *Military service:* U.S. Army, 1944-46.

WRITINGS: (With Robert D. Richardson) *Rise of Modern Mythology 1700-1860,* Indiana University Press, 1971. Editor, *Denver Quarterly,* 1969—.

* * *

FELDMAN, Edmund Burke 1924-

PERSONAL: Born May 6, 1924, in Bayonne, N.J.; married; children: two daughters. *Education:* Syracuse University, B.F.A., 1949; University of California, Los Angeles, M.A., 1951; Columbia University, Ed.D., 1953. *Office:* Department of Art, University of Georgia, Athens, Ga. 30601.

CAREER: Newark Museum, Newark, N.J., curator of painting and sculpture, 1953; Livingston State College (now Livingston University), Livingston, Ala., associate professor of art and head of department, 1953-56; Carnegie Institute of Technology (now Carnegie-Mellon University), Pittsburgh, Pa., associate professor of art, 1956-60; State University of New York College at New Paltz, chairman of art division and director of art education, 1960-66; University of Georgia, Athens, professor of art, 1966—. Consultant to federal, state, and local governmental organizations and to private enterprise. Lecturer on art education at meetings of professional and civic organizations. *Military service:* U.S. Army Air Forces, 1942-46. *Member:* National Art Education Association, College Art Association, Phi Kappa Phi, Tau Sigma Delta, Kappa Delta Pi, Kappa Pi.

WRITINGS: Art as Image and Idea, Prentice-Hall, 1967, 2nd edition published as *Varieties of Visual Experience: Art as Image and Idea,* 1972; *Becoming Human through Art,* Prentice-Hall, 1970; (editor) *Art in American Higher Institutions,* National Art Education Association, 1970.

Contributor: Ralph Smith, editor, *Aesthetics and Criticism in Art,* Rand McNally, 1966; C. D. Gaitskell and Al Hurwitz, editors, *Children and Their Art,* 2nd edition, Harcourt, 1970; Elliott W. Eisner, editor, *Confronting Curriculum Reform,* Little, Brown, 1971. Contributor to *Harvard Educational Review, College Art Journal, Arts in Society, Saturday Review, Art Education Magazine, Arts and Architecture, Studies in Art Education,* and other publications.

WORK IN PROGRESS: History of art.

*   *   *

FELL, H(oward) Barraclough   1917-
(Barry Fell)

PERSONAL: Middle name is pronounced *Bar*-a-cluff; born June 6, 1917, in Lewes, England; came to U.S. in 1964; son of Howard Towne (a mariner) and Elsie (Johnston) Fell; married Irene Clarkson, October 10, 1942; children: Roger Barraclough, Francis Julian, Veronica Irene. *Education:* University of New Zealand, B.Sc., 1938, M.Sc., 1939; University of Edinburgh, Ph.D., 1941, D.Sc., 1955. *Home and office:* Epigraphic Society, 6 Woodland St., Arlington, Mass. 02174.

CAREER: University of Edinburgh, Edinburgh, Scotland, demonstrator in zoology, 1939-41; University of Wellington, Wellington, New Zealand, senior lecturer, 1946-56, associate professor of zoology, 1956-65; Museum of Comparative Zoology, Cambridge, Mass., curator, 1964-77; Harvard University, Cambridge, professor of zoology, 1965-77. Organizer, Sixth Pacific Science Congress, 1947; delgate for New Zealand, Thirteenth International Zoological Congress, 1953. Consultant on epigraphy of ancient inscriptions to U.S. Department of the Interior. Honorary lecturer, University of Maine, 1967—. *Military service:* British Army, Royal E.M. Engineers, 1941-46; became major. *Member:* International Commission for the History of the Sea, New Zealand Association of Science (secretary, 1946; president, 1948), Organization for Tropical Studies, American Academy of Arts and Sciences (fellow), Epigraphic Society (president, 1974—), Royal Society (New Zealand; fellow). *Awards, honors:* Hector Medal and Prize, Royal Society (New Zealand), 1959; Hutton Medal, Royal Society, 1962; A.M., Harvard University, 1965.

WRITINGS: (Compiler with others) *The First Century of New Zealand Zoology, 1769-1868,* Victoria University College, Victoria University of Wellington, 1953; *Tertiary and Recent Echinoidea of New Zealand: Cidaridae,* R. E. Owen, Government Printer (Wellington), 1954; *Deep-sea Echinoderms of New Zealand,* Victoria University of Wellington, 1958.

Synoptic Keys to the Genera of Ophiuroidea, Victoria University of Wellington, 1960; *New Zealand Sea-stars,* A. H. & A. W. Reed (Wellington), 1960; *The Fauna of the Ross Sea,* Part I: *Ophiuroidea,* R. E. Owen, Government Printer, 1961; *Native Sea Stars,* A. H. & A. W. Reed, 1962; *The Phylogeny of Sea-stars,* Royal Society of London, 1963; (with R. Boolootian) *Physiology of Echinoderms,* Wiley, 1966; (with R. C. Moore) *Treatise on Invertebrate Paleontology,* University of Kansas, 1966—; (with J. B. Hersey) *Deep Sea Photography,* Johns Hopkins Press, 1967.

Under name Barry Fell: *Life, Space and Time,* Harper, 1974; *Introduction to Marine Biology,* Harper, 1975; *Dwellers in the Sea,* Reader's Digest Press, 1976; *America B.C.,* Quadrangle, 1976, 4th edition, 1977.

Contributor to *McGraw-Hill Encyclopedia of Science and Technology,* and to *New Zealand Listener, Science, Nature,* and other publications. Editor, *Tuatara* (New Zealand), 1956-64; contributing editor, *Fauna,* 1970—; editor, *Occasional Publications* (journal of the Epigraphic Society), 1974—.

WORK IN PROGRESS: Research on ancient voyages and settlements in the Americas; a book on Egyptian and Iberian colonies in North and Central America; engaged in establishing the first epigraphic museum to house 2000 inscriptions already collected.

SIDELIGHTS: H. B. Fell has traveled in New Britain, various South Pacific countries, Arctic Lapland, and Denmark. *Avocational interests:* Sculpture, archaeology (especially Greco-Roman era), and Mycenaean art.

*   *   *

FELVER, Charles S(tanley)   1916-

PERSONAL: Born October 13, 1916, in Easton, Pa.; son of Jacob Paul (a shop owner) and Caroline (Stanley) Felver; married Marie Alice McRoberts, August 16, 1941; children: Julia Caroline, Madeline Alice, David Stanley. *Education:* Lafayette College, B.A., 1948; Yale University, M.A., 1949; University of Michigan, Ph.D., 1956. *Religion:* Protestant. *Home:* 1069 Woodland Ave., Chico, Calif. 95926. *Office:* Department of English, California State University, Chico, Calif. 95926.

CAREER: Smith, Barney & Co., Easton, Pa., cashier and office manager, 1937-41; Welding Engineers, Inc., Philadelphia, Pa., personnel manager and time study man, 1941-43; University of Kansas, Lawrence, instructor in English, 1949-50; University of Michigan, Ann Arbor, lecturer in English and supervisor of extension program for Saginaw and northeast Michigan, 1952-55; Kent State University, Kent, Ohio, assistant professor, 1955-57, associate professor of English, 1957-61; California State University, Chico, professor of English, 1961—, coordinator of department and chairman of Language Arts Division, 1961-67. Member of Chico City Planning Commission. *Military service:* U.S. Army, Medical Corps, 1943-46; became first sergeant.

MEMBER: National Council of Teachers of English, Phi Beta Kappa, Phi Alpha Theta, Kappa Phi Kappa. *Awards, honors:* Research fellowship at Folger Shakespeare Library, summer, 1961.

WRITINGS: Robert Armin, Shakespeare's Fool: A Biographical Essay (monograph), Kent State University, 1961; (with M. K. Nurmi) *Poetry: An Introduction and Anthology,* C. E. Merrill, 1967; *Joseph Crawhall: The Newcastle Wood Engraver, 1821-1896,* Frank Graham, 1972. Contributor of articles to literature journals. Assistant editor, *Shakespeare Newsletter,* 1957-59.

WORK IN PROGRESS: Research on the pre-Raphaelites and their followers as book and magazine illustrators.

*   *   *

FENNER, Mildred Sandison   1910-

PERSONAL: Born July 9, 1910, in Huntsville, Mo.; daughter of John Forte and Minnielee (Holliday) Sandison; married H. Wolcott Fenner (senior vice-president and director of promotion, Ringling Brothers, Barnum & Bailey Circus), February 1, 1940 (died October 14, 1972). *Education:* Northwest Missouri State College (now University), B.S., 1931; George Washington University, M.A., 1938, Ed.D., 1942. *Politics:* Democratic. *Religion:* Methodist. *Home:* 530 N St., S.W., Washington, D.C. 20024. *Office:* Ringling Brothers, Barnum & Bailey Circus, 1015 18th St. N.W., Washington, D.C. 20036.

CAREER: National Education Association, Washington, D.C., staff member of *NEA Journal*, 1931-43, assistant editor, 1943-49, managing editor, 1949-54, editor of *Today's Education* and *NEA Reporter*, 1954-75; Ringling Brothers, Barnum & Bailey Circus, Washington, D.C., director of educational services, 1975—. Lecturer at summer sessions, Southern Illinois University and American University; conductor of or lecturer at international editors' workshops in Manila, 1956, Amsterdam, 1961, and in Canada and United States. Member of national committee, Educators for Johnson, 1964, and Educators for Humphrey, 1968.

MEMBER: Educational Press Association of America (national secretary-treasurer, 1951-60), National Council of Administrative Women in Education, American Association of University Women, Woman's National Democratic Club, Horace Mann League (national president, 1972-73), Pi Lambda Theta, Sigma Sigma Sigma.

AWARDS, HONORS: Litt.D., Glassboro State College, 1962; several dozen national awards for editorial work with National Education Association, including Gold Medallion Brotherhood Award of National Conference of Christians and Jews, 1969, and Golden Lamp Award of Educational Press Association of America, 1971; Northwest Missouri State College (now University), Distinguished Alumni Award, 1970; named one of the seventy-five most important women in America by *Ladies' Home Journal*, 1971; George Washington University Distinguished Alumni Award, 1972.

WRITINGS: (With Eleanor Fishburn) *Pioneer American Educators*, National Education Association, 1944; *NEA History*, National Education Association, 1945; (editor) *Discipline in the Classroom*, National Education Association, 1969; (editor with husband, H. Wolcott Fenner) *The Circus: Lure and Legend*, Prentice-Hall, 1970; (editor) *Schools Are People*, National Education Association, 1971. Contributor to educational journals.

WORK IN PROGRESS: An anthology of circus fiction; a book to help teacher-authors.

*   *   *

FENTEN, D(onald) X. 1932-

PERSONAL: Born January 3, 1932, in New York, N.Y.; son of Harry J. and Ethel (Scheinwald) Fenten; married Barbara Doris Levy (an elementary school librarian), April 7, 1957; children: Donna Ruth, Jeffrey Allan. *Education:* New York University, B.A., 1953, M.A., 1954; Columbia University, additional graduate study, 1956-57. *Home:* 27 Bowdon Rd., Greenlawn, Long Island, N.Y. 11740.

CAREER: Prior to 1965 held writing and editing positions with Grumman Aircraft Engineering Corp., Perfection on Long Island, Inc., McGraw-Hill Book Co., and other firms; *Progressive Grocer* (magazine), New York, N.Y., associate editor, 1965-70; Syosset High School, Syosset, Long Island, N.Y., teacher of creative writing, journalism, modern communications, and cinematography, 1970—. Regular columnist, *Newsday* (magazine), writing syndicated column "Weekend Gardener," 1974—. *Military service:* U.S.

Army, 1954-56. *Member:* Authors Guild, Authors League of America, Garden Writers Association of America, American Horticultural Society, Indoor Light Gardening Society, Hobby Greenhouse Association, Long Island Horticultural Society.

WRITINGS: Better Photography for Amateurs, Chilton, 1960; *Electric Eye Still Camera Photography*, Chilton, 1961; *Flower and Garden Photography*, Chilton, 1966; *Greenhorn's Guide to Gardening*, Grosset, 1969; *The Clear and Simple Gardening Guide*, Grosset, 1971; *The Organic Grow It, Cook It, Preserve It Guidebook*, Grosset, 1972; *The Concise Guide to Natural Foods*, F. Watts, 1974; *The Weekend Gardener*, New American Library, 1976; *Greenhousing for Purple Thumbs*, 101 Productions, 1976.

Youth books: *Plants for Pots: Projects for Indoor Gardeners*, Lippincott, 1969; *Aviation Careers: Jobs in the Air and on the Ground*, Lippincott, 1969; *Harvesting the Sea*, Lippincott, 1970; *Sea Careers: Jobs on the Waterways of the World*, Lippincott, 1970; *Ins and Outs of Gardening*, Lion Press, 1972; *The Making of a Police Officer*, Westminster, 1972; *Ms.—M.D.*, Westminster, 1973; *Gardening . . . Naturally*, F. Watts, 1973; *Indoor Gardening: A First Book*, F. Watts, 1974; *Ms.—Attorney*, Westminster, 1974; *Strange Differences*, Putnam, 1975; *TV and Radio Careers*, F. Watts, 1976; *Careers in the Sports Industry*, F. Watts, 1977; *The Children's Complete How Does Your Garden Grow Guide to Plants and Planting*, New American Library, 1977; *Ms.—Architect*, Westminster, 1977.

SIDELIGHTS: D. X. Fenten told *CA:* "I have been fortunate that my literary efforts always seem to be the result of 'one thing leading to another'. Because of this I always write in areas of great personal interest and enthusiasm. For example, the arrival of our photogenic daughter sparked my interest in photography. This lead to my first book, and then, two more. The purchase of our suburban home necessitated learning about gardening and after much trial, error, and enjoyment, I wrote *Greenhorn's Guide to Gardening* and *Organic Grow It*.

"Because working in the garden is only feasible during warm months, I became interested in indoor gardening and, with the help of our children wrote my first children's book, *Plants for Pots*. The success of this lead my publisher to request career books, and now the same daughter's interest in medicine resulted in *Ms.—M.D.*, and this in turn was the start of our 'Ms.' series of books for Westminster.

"In 1970, I became tired of hearing people (many near famous, well-educated, well-spoken, etc.), say they 'wished they too could write.' Determined to do something about it, I left my job on the magazine to teach at Syosset High School. I work with students in courses on writing, modern communications, journalism and cinematography—all areas of both proficiency and interest. It is a most marvelous experience for me because the students are honest, willing and interested in working with a 'real' writer—one they know knows, teaches, and cares."

*   *   *

FENTON, Frank 1903-1971

1903—August 23, 1971; American screenwriter and novelist. Obituaries: *Washington Post*, August 27, 1971.

*   *   *

FENTON, Sophia Harvati 1914-

PERSONAL: Born March 23, 1914, in Ambelona, Greece;

daughter of Constantine (a landowner) and Athena (Kondraki) Harvati; married Edward Fenton (a writer), March 23, 1963. *Education:* Athens University, B.A., M.A.; Sorbonne, University of Paris, Ph.D. *Home:* 24 Evrou St., Athens 610, Greece.

CAREER: Moraitis School, Athens, Greece, director and psychologist; University Research Corp., Washington, D.C., former director of therapeutic school. *Awards, honors:* French Government research grant, 1946-54.

WRITINGS: Greece: A Book to Begin On, Holt, 1969; *Ancient Egypt: A Book to Begin On,* Holt, 1971; *Ancient Rome: A Book to Begin On,* Holt, 1971. Contributor of articles on psychology to journals in France and Greece.

*   *   *

FERGUSON, Everett 1933-

PERSONAL: Born February 18, 1933, in Montgomery, Tex.; son of William Everett (a barber) and Edith (Curling) Ferguson; married Nancy Lewis, June 25, 1956; children: Ray, Ann, Patricia. *Education:* Abilene Christian College (now University), B.A., 1953, M.A., 1954; Harvard University, S.T.B., 1956, Ph.D., 1960. *Religion:* Church of Christ. *Home:* 609 East North 16th, Abilene, Tex. 79601. *Office:* Abilene Christian University, Abilene, Tex. 79601.

CAREER: Northeastern Christian Junior College, Villanova, Pa., dean, 1959-62; Abilene Christian University, Abilene, Tex., associate professor, 1962-69, professor, 1969—, director of graduate study in religion, 1970—. *Member:* American Society of Church History, Society of Biblical Literature, Ecclesiastical History Society, Association internationale d'etude patristique. *Awards, honors:* First prize from Christian Research Foundation for his dissertation, "Ordination in the Ancient Church."

WRITINGS: Church History: Early and Medieval, Biblical Research Press, 1966; *Church History: Reformation and Modern,* Biblical Research Press, 1967; *The New Testament Church,* Biblical Research Press, 1968; *Early Christians Speak,* R. B. Sweet, 1971; *A Cappella Music in the Public Worship of the Church,* Biblical Research Press, 1972. Series editor, "Living Word Commentary on the New Testament." Contributor to theological and church history journals.

WORK IN PROGRESS: With A. J. Malherbe, a translation of Gregory of Nyssa's *Life of Moses.*

*   *   *

FERGUSSON, Harvey 1890-1971

1890—August 24, 1971; American novelist. Obituaries: *New York Times,* August 26, 1971; *Washington Post,* August 29, 1971.

*   *   *

FERM, Deane William 1927-

PERSONAL: Born May 22, 1927, in Lebanon, Pa.; son of Vergilius T. A. (a professor) and Nellie A. (Nelson) Ferm; married Paulie E. Swan (a teacher), June 26, 1949 (divorced); married Debra Campbell, December 21, 1976; children: (first marriage) William, Linnea, Robert, Laurie. *Education:* College of Wooster, B.A., 1949; Yale University, B.D., M.Div., 1952, M.A., 1953, Ph.D., 1954. *Religion:* Protestant. *Home:* 79 College St., South Hadley, Mass. 01075. *Office:* Mount Holyoke College, South Hadley, Mass. 01075.

CAREER: Ordained to Presbyterian ministry, 1952; minister on Fisher's Island, N.Y., 1952-54; University of Montana, School of Religion, Missoula, director, 1954-59; Mount Holyoke College, South Hadley, Mass., dean of the college chapel, 1959—. Visiting lecturer, Smith College, 1960-61, 1962-63. *Military service:* U.S. Naval Reserve, 1945-46. *Member:* National Association of College and University Chaplains (member of executive committee). *Awards, honors:* Danforth Foundation campus ministry grant and Poulson fellowship of American Scandinavian Foundation for study and research in Sweden, 1965-66.

WRITINGS: (Contributor) Richard Bender, editor, *On the Work of the Ministry in College and University Communities,* Methodist Church, 1962; *Responsible Sexuality Now,* Seabury, 1971; (contributor) C. K. McFarland, editor, *Intellectual History: The Modern American Tradition,* Holt, 1971. Contributor to *A Dictionary of Pastoral Psychology;* contributor of more than thirty articles to *Christian Century, Redbook, Parents' Magazine,* and professional journals.

WORK IN PROGRESS: Research on the future of American Protestantism and the future of the American family.

AVOCATIONAL INTERESTS: Fishing, hiking, swimming, reading.

BIOGRAPHICAL/CRITICAL SOURCES: Christian Century, March 10, 1971.

*   *   *

FERN, Alan M(axwell) 1930-

PERSONAL: Born October 19, 1930, in Detroit, Mich.; son of Martin (a teacher) and Rose (Coral) Fern; married Lois Ann Karbel (a librarian), March 17, 1957. *Education:* University of Chicago, A.B., 1950, M.A., 1954, Ph.D., 1960. *Home:* 3605 Raymond St., Chevy Chase, Md. 20015. *Office:* Research Department, Library of Congress, Washington, D.C. 20540.

CAREER: University of Chicago, Chicago, Ill., instructor, 1953-60, assistant professor of humanities, 1960-61; Library of Congress, Washington, D.C., Prints and Photographs Division, assistant curator of prints, 1961-62, curator of prints, 1962-64, head of processing and curatorial section, 1964-73, assistant chief of division, 1964-73, chief of division, 1973-76, director of research department, 1976—. Also taught at Art Institute of Chicago, Institute of Design, Pratt Institute, and University of Maryland. *Member:* College Art Association, Special Libraries Association, Print Council of America (former president), American Institute of Graphic Arts (former director), American Antiquarian Society, Cosmos Club, Grolier Club, Baltimore Bibliophiles.

WRITINGS: (Editor) Lucien Pissarro, *Notes on the Eragny Press, and a Letter to J. B. Manson,* privately printed, 1957; (with others) *Art Nouveau,* New York Museum of Modern Art, 1960; *Word and Image: Posters from the Collection of the Museum of Modern Art,* edited by Mildred Constantine, New York Museum of Modern Art, 1968.

Leonard Baskin (catalog of an exhibition), National Collection of Fine Arts, Smithsonian Institution, 1970; (author of introduction) *American Prints in the Library of Congress,* Johns Hopkins Press, 1970; (contributor) J. Sutter, editor, *The Neo-Impressionists,* Ides et Calandes (Neuchatel), 1970, New York Graphic Society, 1971; (co-author) *Revolutionary Soviet Film Posters,* Johns Hopkins Press, 1974; (contributor) *Lasansky: Printmaker,* University of Iowa Press, 1975; (contributor) *Fritz Eichenberg,* C. N. Potter, 1977. Contributor to *Apollo, Architectural Review, Book-*

Collector's Quarterly, Chicago Review, College Art Journal, and other publications. Former book review editor, *Art Journal.*

* * *

FERNANDEZ, Julio A. 1936-

PERSONAL: Born July 27, 1936, in Belize, British Honduras; son of Antonio and Rosalina Fernandez; married Doris Wells, August 26, 1962. *Education:* San Diego State College (now University), B.A., 1963, M.A., 1964; University of California, Santa Barbara, Ph.D., 1967. *Home:* 832 North Lamont Dr., Cortland, N.Y. 13045. *Office:* Department of Political Science, State University of New York College, Cortland, N.Y. 13045.

CAREER: St. John's College, Belize, British Honduras, instructor in Spanish and Latin, 1954-55; University of California, Santa Barbara, lecturer in political science, 1966-67; University of Colorado, Boulder, assistant professor of political science, 1967-71; State University of New York College at Cortland, associate professor of political science, 1971—. *Military service:* U.S. Air Force, 1956-60. *Member:* American Political Science Association, Latin American Studies Association, American Association of University Professors, International Studies Association, Pi Sigma Alpha.

WRITINGS: Political Administration in Mexico, Bureau of Governmental Research, University of California, 1969; *The Challenge of Democracy in Latin America,* Institute for the Comparative Study of Political Systems and Ideologies, University of Colorado, 1969; *The Political Elite in Argentina,* New York University Press, 1970; (contributor) Ben G. Burnett and Kenneth F. Johnson, editors, *Political Forces in Latin America,* Wadsworth, 1970. Contributor to *Journal of Inter-American Studies.*

WORK IN PROGRESS: Research on the problems for an independent Belize in Central America; research on Latin American international relations.

* * *

FERNEA, Robert Alan 1932-

PERSONAL: Surname is pronounced Fur-nee-ah; born January 25, 1932, in Vancouver, Wash.; son of George Jacob and Alta (Carter) Fernea; married Elizabeth Warnock (a writer), June 8, 1956; children: Laura Ann, David Karim, Laila Catherine. *Education:* Reed College, B.A., 1954; University of Chicago, M.A., 1957, Ph.D., 1959. *Home:* 3003 Bowman Rd., Austin, Tex. 78703. *Office:* Center for Middle Eastern Studies, University of Texas, Austin, Tex. 78712.

CAREER: American University, Cairo, Egypt, assistant professor, 1959-63, associate professor of anthropology, 1963-65; Harvard University, Cambridge, Mass., postdoctoral fellow at Center for Middle Eastern Studies, 1965-66; University of Texas at Austin, associate professor, 1966-69, professor of anthropology, 1969—, director of Center for Middle Eastern Studies, 1966-73. Visiting lecturer, University of Alexandria, United Arab Republic, 1963-65; visiting professor at University of California, Los Angeles, 1968, and at University of Washington, 1970. Researcher in Marrakesh, Morocco, 1971-72; director, summer program in Middle East studies, for HEW and University of Texas, 1971; member of board of governors, American Research Center in Egypt. Chairman, Austin Ballet Academy, 1971; member of Austin Committee on Foreign Relations. Consul-

tant to Ford Foundation in the United Arab Republic, 1963-65, to National Endowment for the Humanities, 1977, and to Council for International Education, Department of Health, Education and Welfare, 1977—. *Member:* American Anthropological Association (fellow), Middle East Studies Association (founding fellow), Sigma Xi. *Awards, honors:* Fulbright post-doctoral awards for study in Afghanistan and Morocco; chosen "Texas Writer of the Year," 1970; French government scholar, Paris and Aix-en-Provence, 1976.

WRITINGS: (Editor) *Contemporary Egyptian Nubia,* Volumes I-II, Human Relations Area File Press, 1966; *Shaykh and Effendi: Changing Patterns of Authority among the El Shabana of Southern Iraq,* Harvard University Press, 1970. Also author, with George Gerster, of *The Nubians,* University of Texas Press. Contributor of articles and reviews to academic journals.

WORK IN PROGRESS: Research on Morocco and Afghanistan; problems of developing countries, particularly agrarian reform and land resettlement.

* * *

FERRELL, Mallory Hope 1935-

PERSONAL: Born November 23, 1935, in Portsmouth, Va.; son of Mallory Hope (a contractor) and Laura Evelyn (Bunn) Ferrell; married Gloria Timm, March 8, 1975; children: Susan Constance, Mallory Hope III, Kimberly Lynn, Eric Timm. *Education:* Attended Virginia Polytechnic Institute, 1954-55; University of Miami, Coral Gables, Fla., B.A., 1958, graduate study in architecture, 1958-59; Air University, Command and Staff College, Associate in Military Science, 1963. *Politics:* Independent. *Religion:* Methodist. *Home:* 4759 Dorchester Cir., Boulder, Colo. 80301. *Office:* Chief Pilot's Office, Western Airlines International, Denver, Colo.

CAREER: U.S. Air Force, pilot and instructor pilot, 1960-64, flew more than one hundred jet fighter combat missions and left service as captain; self-employed architectural engineer, Norfolk, Va., 1964-67; Western Airlines International, Denver, Colo., commercial pilot, 1967—. Free-lance photographer. Member of board of directors, Colorado Railroad Museum. *Member:* Air Line Pilots Association, U.S. Junior Chamber of Commerce, Rocky Mountain Railroad Club, New Mexico Railroad Club, Sigma Delta Chi, Kappa Alpha Mu. *Awards, honors—Military:* Air Medal (twelve times). Other: Named photographer of the year by *Life-Encyclopaedia Britannica,* 1959; Golden Spur Award, Western Writers of America, 1975.

WRITINGS: Rails, Sagebrush and Pine, Golden West, 1967; *The Gilpin Gold Tram,* Pruett, 1970; *The 1871 Grant Locomotive,* Pruett, 1971; *Silver San Juan,* Pruett, 1972; *Tweetsie Country,* Pruett, 1976; *West Side,* PFM Books, 1977. Photographic essays have been published in *Photography Annual, Life, Look, This Week, Sports Illustrated, Trains, Fortune, Friends,* and other periodicals.

WORK IN PROGRESS: A two-volume study, *Denver and Rio Grande; Louisiana Plantation Railroads; Slow Train Down South;* preparing his work for a photographic exhibit, "My American West."

SIDELIGHTS: Over the years Mallory Ferrell has gathered together about 80,000 old West railroad scenes, from which he obtains many of the illustrations for his books on narrow gauge and short line railroads. In addition to flying Boeings commercially, he still pilots F-100 fighter aircraft on weekends with the Air Guard and "collects material associated with WWI flying, including an ancient (flyable) Gypsy Moth biwing airplane.'' He also helps rebuild old steam engines and cars at the Colorado Railroad Museum.

BIOGRAPHICAL/CRITICAL SOURCES: Denver Post, August 24, 1969, September 21, 1969, December 19, 1971.

*   *   *

FESS, Philip E.   1931-

PERSONAL: Born November 25, 1931, in Troy, Ohio; son of Charles E. and Lucille (Furlong) Fess; married Suzanne Cuthbert, September 17, 1955; children: Linda, Virginia, Martha. Education: Miami University, Oxford, Ohio, B.S., 1953; University of Illinois, M.S., 1955, Ph.D., 1960. Home: 2408 Melrose Dr., Champaign, Ill. 61820. Office: University of Illinois, 211 Commerce W., Urbana, Ill.

CAREER: Licensed certified public accountant, State of Illinois, 1959; University of Illinois at Urbana-Champaign, instructor in accountancy, 1953-55; University of Alabama, University, instructor in accountancy, 1957-60; University of Illinois at Urbana-Champaign, assistant professor, 1960-63, associate professor, 1963-68, professor of accountancy, 1968—. Arthur Andersen & Co., auditor at various periods, 1953-55, consultant, 1959—; auditor, U.S. Air Force, 1955-57. Member: American Accounting Association, American Institute of Certified Public Accountants, National Association of Accountants, Illinois C.P.A. Society (president of Eastern chapter).

WRITINGS: (With others) Statement of Basic Accounting Postulates and Principles, Center for International Education in Accounting, University of Illinois, 1962; (with C. Rollin Niswonger) Accounting Principles, South-Western Publishing, 9th edition (Fess was not associated with earlier editions), 1965, 12th edition, 1977. Contributor of about forty articles to accounting and management journals.

*   *   *

FICKER, Victor B.   1937-

PERSONAL: Born August 11, 1937, in Brookfield, Ill.; son of Victor A. and Helen Ficker; married, August 3, 1963; wife's name, Merle; children: Ellen, Celene. Education: University of Florida, B.A.E., 1961, M.Ed., 1962, Ed.S., 1966, Ed.D., 1967. Residence: Franklin, Va. Office: Office of the Dean, Paul D. Camp Community College, Franklin, Va. 23851.

CAREER: Polk Community College, Winter Haven, Fla., chairman of Division of Social Science, 1967-71; Paul D. Camp Community College, Franklin, Va., dean of instruction, 1971-73, dean of college, 1973—. Adjunct professor, University of Florida. Military service: U.S. Marine Corps, 1957-59. Member: American Association of University Professors, Phi Beta Kappa, Alpha Kappa Delta, Kappa Delta Pi, Phi Kappa Phi, Lions Club, Ruritan Club.

WRITINGS: (With Herbert S. Graves) Social Science and Urban Crisis, Macmillan, 1971, 2nd edition, 1978; (with Graves) Deprivation in America, Glencoe Press, 1971; (with James Rigterink) Values in Conflict: A Text Reader in Social Problems, with teacher's manual, Heath, 1972; The Revolution in Religion, C. E. Merrill, 1973; Effective Supervision, C. E. Merrill, 1975. Also author, with Carole Wines, of Man's Search for Himself, C. E. Merrill. Contributor to education journals. Member of editorial board, Community College Social Science Quarterly.

FIELD, Arthur J(ordan)   1927-1975

PERSONAL: Born July 1, 1927, in New York, N.Y.; name legally changed; son of Irving J. (a businessman) and Tessie (Gitelson) Feinfeld; married; children: Michael A. Education: University of Pennsylvania, B.S.E., 1947; Columbia University, M.A., 1949; Brown University, Ph.D., 1961. Office: Department of Sociology, College of Staten Island of the City University of New York, 715 Ocean Ter., Staten Island, N.Y. 10301.

CAREER: Settlement house worker in New York City, 1948-51; Group Farming Research Institute, Poughkeepsie, N.Y., researcher, 1950; Office of Social Welfare, Safad, Israel, director, 1951-52; South Shore Temple, Chicago, Ill., executive director, 1952-53; James M. Vicary Co., New York City, senior statistician, 1953-54; University of Massachusetts—Amherst, instructor in sociology, 1954-55; University of Rhode Island, Kingston, instructor in sociology, 1956-57; City Plan Commission, Providence, R.I., research director, 1957-60; University of Saskatchewan, Saskatoon, lecturer in sociology, 1960-61; Flint College of the University of Michigan (now University of Michigan—Flint), assistant professor of sociology, 1961-64; Wayne State University, Detroit, Mich., assistant professor of sociology, 1964-67; Rensselaer Polytechnic Institute, Troy, N.Y., associate professor of sociology, 1967-71; College of Staten Island of the City University of New York, Staten Island, N.Y., professor of sociology, 1971-75. Visiting professor, Hunter College of the City University of New York, 1970-71. Senior research associate, Caribbean Research Institute.

MEMBER: American Sociological Association, Society for the Study of Social Problems, Population Association of America, American Association of University Professors, Regional Science Association, Eastern Sociological Society.

WRITINGS: Communal Life in Palestine, Arts & Science Press, 1948; (editor and contributor) Urbanization and Work in Modernizing Societies, Glengary Press, 1967; (author of introduction) Abraham Epstein, The Negro Migrant in Pittsburgh, Arno, 1969; Urban Power Structures: Problems in Theory and Research, Schenkman, 1970; (editor and contributor) City and Country in the Third World: Issues in the Modernization of Latin America, Schenkman, 1970. Writer of monographs and research reports. Contributor to Caravan, Midwest Folklore, and other journals.

WORK IN PROGRESS: A book on residents of mobile homes in the United States.†

(Died, 1975)

*   *   *

FIELD, John (Leslie)   1910-

PERSONAL: Born September 20, 1910, in Des Moines, Iowa; son of George Albert (a lumberman) and Mary (Ryan) Field; married Marion Leeson, October 2, 1937. Education: University of Iowa, B.S.Ch.E., 1932. Politics: Independent. Religion: Agnostic. Home: 1350 North Portofino Dr., Apt. 401, Sarasota, Fla. 33581.

CAREER: Standard Oil Co. of New Jersey and affiliates, 1934-59, working in technical, administrative, and construction positions in Aruba, Netherlands Antilles, 1934-45, Caracas, Venezuela, 1946-52, Rome, Italy, 1953-55, Siracusa, Sicily, 1956, and New York, N.Y., 1957-59; director and former president of Friends of Arts and Sciences, Sarasota, Fla. Member: Tau Beta Pi.

WRITINGS: Two Seas: Nature and Man around the Mediterranean and Caribbean, Manyland Books, 1970; (translator from the Italian with wife, Marion Field) Pirandello, *Cap and Bells,* Manyland Books, 1974.

WORK IN PROGRESS: Thorn Harvest, a novel on contemporary South America; a play, "A Conrad Cosmorama."

SIDELIGHTS: John Field has traveled from the Arctic to the Antipodes and three times around the world.

BIOGRAPHICAL/CRITICAL SOURCES: Book Exchange (London), September, 1971.

* * *

FINK, Augusta 1916-

PERSONAL: Born December 5, 1916, in New York, N.Y.; daughter of William (an insurance consultant) and Lillian (Graf) Fink. *Education:* University of California, Los Angeles, M.A., 1939. *Address:* P.O. Box 1152, Carmel, Calif. 93921.

CAREER: Los Angeles County Civil Service Department, Los Angeles, Calif., had charge of conducting and developing management and supervisory training programs, 1945-60; Shorebird Bookstore, Palos Verdes Peninsula, Calif., owner and manager, 1960-67. *Member:* California Historical Society, Monterey History and Art Association (chairman of history committee, 1971-73).

WRITINGS: Time and the Terraced Land: A History of the Palos Verdes Peninsula, Howell-North Books, 1966; *To Touch the Sky* (juvenile), Golden Gate, 1971; *Monterey: The Presence of the Past,* Chronicle Publishing, 1972; *Adobes in the Sun,* photographs by Morley Baer, Chronicle Publishing, 1972. Contributor of articles on Western history and travel to *Westways.*

WORK IN PROGRESS: Several works of fiction with historical background in California; a biography of Mary Austin; with Morley Baer, a book illustrating Mary Austin's nature writings.

AVOCATIONAL INTERESTS: Mysticism, music, the outdoors.

* * *

FINKELSTEIN, Marina S. 1921(?)-1972

1921(?)—March 6, 1972; Russian-born editor and authority on international relations. Obituaries: *New York Times,* March 7, 1972; *Washington Post,* March 7, 1972.

* * *

FIORE, Peter Amadeus 1927-

PERSONAL: Born September 8, 1927, in Glens Falls, N.Y.; son of Peter and Virginia Fiore. *Education:* Siena College, A.B., 1949; Catholic University of America, M.A., 1955; University College, London, Ph.D., 1961. *Home and office:* Siena College, Loudonville, N.Y. 12211.

CAREER: Roman Catholic priest of Order of Friars Minor. Siena College, Loudonville, N.Y., instructor, 1956-58, assistant professor, 1961-66, associate professor, 1966-71, professor of English, 1971—, chairman of department, 1962-67, 1975—, dean of Division of Arts, 1966-71. Member of education committee, Saratoga Performing Arts Center; adviser, Lake George Opera Festival Association. *Military service:* U.S. Army, 1946-47. *Member:* Modern Language Association of America, Milton Society of America, National Council of Teachers of English, Association of Departments of English, International Platform Association, Catholic Renascence Society, Delta Epsilon Sigma (president of Beta

Psi chapter). *Awards, honors:* Research grants from Glens Falls Foundation and from a private foundation in London, England.

WRITINGS: (Contributor) A. A. Norton and J. T. Nourse, editors, *A Christian Approach to Western Literature,* Newman, 1961; *Th' Upright Heart and Pure,* Duquesne University Press, 1967; *Just So Much Honor,* Pennsylvania State University Press, 1972. Contributor to *Milton Encyclopedia* and to scholarly journals. Editor, *Greyfriar: Siena Studies in Literature.*

WORK IN PROGRESS: Further studies on Milton.

* * *

FISCH, Max H(arold) 1900-

PERSONAL: Born December 21, 1900, in Elma, Wash.; son of William Frederick (a lumberjack and ship's barber) and Bessie J. (Himes) Fisch; married Ruth A. Bales, June 12, 1927 (died July 9, 1974); children: Emily J. (Mrs. Andrew L. Maverick), Margaret (Mrs. David Kalal), William B. *Education:* Butler University, A.B., 1924; Cornell University, Ph.D., 1930. *Home:* 3211 Nobscot Dr., Apt. A, Indianapolis, Ind. 46222. *Office:* Peirce Education Project, Indiana University-Purdue University at Indianapolis, 420 Blake St., Indianapolis, Ind. 46202.

CAREER: Cornell University, Ithaca, N.Y., instructor in philosophy, 1926-28; Western Reserve University (now Case Western Reserve University), Cleveland, Ohio, assistant professor of philosophy, 1928-43; U.S. Army Medical Library, Cleveland, curator of rare books, 1942-45, chief of history of medicine division, 1946; University of Illinois at Urbana-Champaign, professor of philosophy, 1946-69, professor emeritus, 1969—; associate member, Center for Advanced Study, 1961-63, 1967; Indiana University-Purdue University at Indianapolis, adjunct professor of philosophy, 1975—. Fulbright research professor, University of Naples, 1950-51; visiting professor, University of Chicago, 1955, Keio University, 1958-59, State University of New York at Buffalo, 1969-70, University of Florida, 1970-71, and Texas Tech University, 1973-75; Matchette Lecturer, Purdue University, 1956; Harvard University, George Santayana fellow, 1960, honorary research fellow, 1966-67. Member of administrative board, International Association of Universities, 1950-55; president, C. S. Peirce Bicentennial International Congress, Amsterdam, 1976.

MEMBER: American Philosophical Association (president of Western division, 1955-56; chairman of national board of officers, 1956-58), History of Science Society (council member, 1951-53), Charles S. Peirce Society (president, 1961), Semiotic Society of America, National Society of Sciences, Letters, and Arts (Naples, Italy). *Awards, honors:* Named Knight of the Order of Merit of the Italian Republic, 1976.

WRITINGS: (With Paul R. Anderson) *Philosophy in America from the Puritans to James,* Appleton, 1939; (editor and translator with Thomas G. Bergin) *The Autobiography of Giambattista Vico,* Cornell University Press, 1944; *Nicolaus Pol 1494,* Reichner, 1947; (editor) *Selected Papers of Robert C. Binkley,* Harvard University Press, 1948; (translator and editor with Bergin) *The New Science of Giambattista Vico,* Cornell University Press, 1948, revised and abridged translation with new introduction, Doubleday, 1961, 2nd revised and abridged translation, Cornell University Press, 1970. Member of advisory committee for an edition of the works of William James, American Council of Learned Societies, 1973—.

WORK IN PROGRESS: A two-volume biography of Charles Sanders Peirce; general editor of a new edition of Peirce's works, to be arranged chronologically in fifteen or more volumes.

BIOGRAPHICAL/CRITICAL SOURCES: Richard Tursman, editor, *Studies in Philosophy and in the History of Science: Essays in Honor of Max Fisch,* Coronado Press, 1970; *Books Abroad,* autumn, 1970.

* * *

FISCHER, Wolfgang Georg 1933-

PERSONAL: Born October 24, 1933, in Vienna, Austria; son of R. Heinrich (an art dealer) and Martha Fischer; married April 5, 1961; children: Flora, Bettina, Tobias. *Education:* Attended University of Vienna, 1953-59, and University of Freiburg, 1955; University of Paris, Ph.D., 1960; Harvard University, postdoctoral research fellow, 1961-62. *Home:* 49 Carlton Hill, London N.W.1, England.

CAREER: Smith College, Northampton, Mass., instructor in art history, 1962-63; Marlborough Fine Art Gallery, London, England, director, 1963-71; co-founder and partner, Fischer Fine Art Gallery, 1972—. *Member:* International P.E.N., Reform Club (London). *Awards, honors:* Charles Veillon Literary Prize, 1970.

WRITINGS: Wohnungen (novel), Hanser, 1969, translation with Inge Woodwin published as *Interiors: A Novel Set in Vienna, 1910-1938,* P. Owen, 1971; *Moeblierte Zimmer* (novel), Hanser, 1972, translation with Goodwin published as *Furnished Rooms,* P. Owen, 1971; *Sugarpeople from Sugarland,* Sidgwick & Jackson, 1975.

SIDELIGHTS: Wolfgang Fischer is interested in Jewish and other refugee problems and their history. *Interiors* has been translated into Polish, and *Furnished Rooms* into French and Polish.

BIOGRAPHICAL/CRITICAL SOURCES: Times Literary Supplement, April 16, 1970; *Books Abroad,* autumn, 1970.

* * *

FISHER, Allan G(eorge) B(arnard) 1895-1976

PERSONAL: Born October 26, 1895, in Christchurch, New Zealand; son of Allan Gibson (a Salvation Army officer) and Nellie (Barnard) Fisher; married Eleanor Airini Pope, January 8, 1929; children: Humphrey J., Catherine A. (Mrs. Leonard Lawler). *Education:* Attended Scotch College, Melbourne, 1909-12; University of Melbourne, B.A., 1921; London School of Economics and Political Science, Ph.D., 1925. *Home:* 76 Ormond Ave., Hampton, Middlesex, England.

CAREER: University of Otago, Dunedin, New Zealand, professor of economics, 1925-35; University of Western Australia, Nedlands, professor of economics, 1936-37; Royal Institute of International Affairs, London, England, professor of international economics, 1938-46; International Monetary Fund, Washington, D.C. 1947-60, became chief editor. Economist, Bank of New South Wales, 1934. Counsellor, New Zealand Legation, Washington, D.C., 1944. *Military service:* Australian Imperial Forces, 1916-19. *Member:* Royal Economic Society.

WRITINGS: Some Problems of Wages and Their Regulation, P. S. King & Son, 1926; *The Clash of Progress and Security,* Macmillan, 1935; *Economic Progress and Social Security,* Macmillan, 1945; *International Implications of*

Full Employment, Royal Institute of International Affairs, 1946; (with son, Humphrey J. Fisher) *Slavery and Muslim Society in Africa: The Institution in Saharan and Sudanic Africa and the Trans-Saharan Trade,* C. Hurst, 1970, Doubleday, 1971; (editor and translator with Humphrey J. Fisher) Gustav Nachtigal, *Sahara and Sudan,* Volume IV: *Wadai and Darfur,* University of California Press, 1972, Volume I: *Tripoli and Fezzan, Tibesti or Tu,* Barnes & Noble, 1974. Contributor to *Survey of International Affairs,* 1937, 1938; contributor to *Economic Journal, Economic Record, International Affairs,* and other journals.

WORK IN PROGRESS: Continuation of translation of Gustav Nachtigal's *Sahara and Sudan.*†

(Died January 8, 1976)

* * *

FISHER, Humphrey J(ohn) 1933-

PERSONAL: Born September 20, 1933, in Dunedin, New Zealand; son of Allan G. B. and E. A. (Pope) Fisher; married Helga H. A. Kricke, 1958; children: Clemens, Duncan, Crispin, Thomas. *Education:* Attended Deep Springs Junior College, 1950-52; Harvard University, B.A. (magna cum laude), 1955; Oxford University, D.Phil., 1959. *Religion:* Quaker. *Home:* 66 Ormond Ave., Hampton, Middlesex, England. *Office:* School of Oriental and African Studies, University of London, London W.C.1, England.

CAREER: University of London, School of Oriental and African Studies, London, England, 1952—, began as lecturer, currently reader in African history. *Member:* Association of University Teachers, African Studies Association, Phi Beta Kappa.

WRITINGS: Ahmadiyyah: A Study in Contemporary Islam on the West African Coast, Oxford University Press, 1963; (with father, Allan G. B. Fisher) *Slavery and Muslim Society in Africa: The Institution in Saharan and Sudanic Africa and the Trans-Saharan Trade,* C. Hurst, 1970, Doubleday, 1971; (editor and translator with Allan G. B. Fisher) Gustav Nachtigal, *Sahara and Sudan,* Volume IV: *Wadai and Darfur,* University of California Press, 1972, Volume I: *Tripoli and Fezzan, Tibesti or Tu,* Barnes & Noble, 1974. Contributor to *Journal of African History* and to other journals.

WORK IN PROGRESS: Continuing work on the translation of Nachtigal's *Sahara and Sudan;* a book on the general history and character of Islam in black Africa; work in comparative religious studies; various minor research projects.

SIDELIGHTS: Humphrey Fisher is especially interested in the care and education of children.

* * *

FISHER, J(oseph) Thomas 1936-

PERSONAL: Born November 9, 1936, in Titusville, Pa.; son of Thomas Anthony (an electrician) and Emily (McPherson) Fisher; married Patricia Buchert (an elementary teacher), July 23, 1971; children: Ross Michael, Jill Christina. *Education:* Slippery Rock State College, B.S., 1958; University of Illinois, M.S., 1961; Temple University, doctoral candidate, 1965—. *Religion:* Presbyterian. *Home:* 225 Price St., West Chester, Pa. 19380. *Office:* School of Health and Physical Education, West Chester State College, West Chester, Pa. 19380.

CAREER: University of Illinois, Urbana, instructor in physical education, 1959-61; Springfield Township High

School, Montgomery Co., Pa., teacher of health, coordinator of health and physical education department, and soccer and track coach, 1967-68; West Chester State College, West Chester, Pa., associate professor of health education, and soccer coach, 1968—. Summer instructor in fitness programs at University of Illinois, 1960, 1961, Young Men's Christian Association, Philadelphia, Pa., 1965, 1967, and U.S. Marine Fitness Academy, Quantico, Va., 1970, 1971, 1972. Extension professor at Towson State College, 1971-76. *Military service:* U.S. Marine Corps Reserve, on active duty, 1961-64; served in Far East; on reserve duty, 1964—; current rank, major. *Member:* American Alliance for Health, Physical Education and Recreation, American School Health Association, National Institute on Alcohol Abuse and Alcoholism, Nutrition Today Society, National Soccer Coaches Association of America, Marine Corps Reserve Officers Association, Marine Corps League, Pennsylvania Soccer Coaches Association, Pennsylvania Association for Health, Physical Education and Recreation, Phi Delta Kappa, Phi Epsilon Kappa.

WRITINGS: (Editor with Clint E. Bruess) *Selected Readings in Health,* Macmillan, 1970. Contributor to physical education and education journals.

WORK IN PROGRESS: Research on obesity.

* * *

FISHER, Lee 1908-

PERSONAL: Born August 25, 1908, in Kokomo, Ind.; son of Charles Arthur and Clara Mae (Young) Fisher; married Betty Ruth Ladd (a psychological counselor), April 25, 1920; children: Mary Lee, Carolyn Jean, Larry Ladd. *Education:* Attended University of North Carolina, Winona Lake School of Theology, and American Academy of Art, Chicago, Ill. *Politics:* Republican. *Religion:* Baptist. *Home:* 306 Emerald Pl. E., Indian Harbour Beach, Fla. 32937.

CAREER: Former editor of two evangelical magazines; currently researcher for Evangelist Billy Graham and free-lance writer; has accompanied Billy Graham to more than sixty countries, islands, and provinces. *Member:* American Society of Composers, Authors and Publishers (ASCAP).

WRITINGS: My Treasure Chest, Golden Rule, 1940; *Revelation,* Economy Printing, 1945; (with George Burnham) *Billy Graham and the New York Crusade,* Zondervan, 1957; *Out of This World: The Story of the Greatest Character I Have Ever Known,* Logos International, 1970; *Fire in the Hills,* Abingdon, 1970; *A Funny Thing Happened on the Way to the Crusade,* Creation House, 1974; *So You're Getting Married,* Logos International, 1977. Also author of *A Time to Seek,* Abingdon. Contributor to religious journals.

WORK IN PROGRESS: Let's Face the Music; also writing on satanism and modern occultism.

SIDELIGHTS: Lee Fisher told *CA:* "My regret is that the 'three score and ten' imposed upon us limits our creative productivity. There are so many stories to be told. My particular interest is in writing about unknown people whose story should be known. One can make more money writing about celebrities. But the greatest people, in my estimation, are those who do fascinating things, have great ideals, or a great compassion—and never have the time or desire to publicize it. These never cease to inspire us."

* * *

FISHER, Mary L. 1928-

PERSONAL: Born July 1, 1928, in Fall River, Mass.; married Robert N. Fisher (director of marketing and economic planning, American Optical Corp.); children: Rodney. *Education:* Radcliffe College, A.B., 1949; University of Rhode Island, graduate study, 1960; Simmons College, M.S. in L.S., 1967.

CAREER: Massachusetts Institute of Technology, Cambridge, economics librarian, 1950-51; Warren (R.I.) public schools, librarian, 1958-60; Worcester (Mass.) public schools, assistant to director of school libraries, 1961-63; Lexington (Mass.) public schools, professional curriculum librarian, 1965-66; Harvard University Press, Cambridge, Mass., librarian and bibliographer, beginning 1967. Director, New England Bibliography, Inc. *Member:* American Library Association, Harvard Library Club.

WRITINGS: Cambodia: An Annotated Bibliography of Its History, Geography, Politics, and Economy since 1954, Center for International Studies, Massachusetts Institute of Technology, 1967; (compiler with Elizabeth Williams Miller) *The Negro in America: A Bibliography,* 2nd edition (Fisher was not connected with earlier edition), Harvard University Press, 1970. Contributor of reviews to *New England Quarterly* and other journals.

WORK IN PROGRESS: Revised editions of Cambodia and Negro bibliographies.†

* * *

FISHER, Seymour 1922-

PERSONAL: Born May 13, 1922, in Baltimore, Md.; son of Sam (a cleaning store owner) and Jean (Miller) Fisher; married Rhoda Lee Feinberg (a psychologist), March 22, 1947; children: Jerid Martin, Eve Phyllis. *Education:* University of Chicago, M.A., 1943, Ph.D., 1948. *Home:* 4855 Armstrong Rd., Manlius, N.Y. 13104. *Office:* Department of Psychiatry, Upstate Medical Center, State University of New York, Syracuse, N.Y. 13210.

CAREER: Illinois Neuropsychiatric Institute, Chicago, public health fellow in clinical psychology, 1945-48; Elgin State Hospital, Elgin, Ill., chief psychologist, 1949-51; Veterans Administration Hospital, Houston, Tex., research psychologist, 1952-56; Baylor University, College of Medicine, Houston, U.S. Public Health Service career research investigator and associate professor of psychology, 1957-61; State University of New York Upstate Medical Center, Syracuse, professor of psychology, 1961—. *Member:* American Psychological Association.

WRITINGS: (With Sidney Cleveland) *Body Image and Personality,* Van Nostrand, 1958, revised edition, Dover, 1968; *Body Experience in Fantasy and Behavior,* Appleton, 1970; *The Female Orgasm,* Basic Books, 1973; (with wife, Rhoda Fisher) *What We Really Know about Child Rearing,* Basic Books, 1976; (with Roger Greenberg) *The Scientific Credibility of Freud's Theories and Therapy,* Basic Books, 1977.

* * *

FITE, Gilbert C(ourtland) 1918-

PERSONAL: Born May 14, 1918, in Santa Fe, Ohio; son of Clyde and Mary (McCardle) Fite; married Alberta June Goodwin, July 23, 1941; children: James F., Jack Preston. *Education:* Attended Wessington Springs Junior College, 1935-37, and Seattle Pacific College, 1938; University of South Dakota, B.A. and M.A., 1941; University of Missouri, Ph. D., 1945. *Religion:* Disciples of Christ. *Home:* 150 Horseshoe Cir., Athens, Ga. 30605. *Office:* Department of History, University of Georgia, Athens, Ga. 30602.

CAREER: Wessington Springs Junior College, Wessington Springs, S.D., member of faculty, 1941-42; University of Oklahoma, Norman, assistant professor, 1945-49, associate professor, 1949-54, professor, 1954-58, research professor of history, 1958-68, George Lynn Cross Professor of History, 1968-71; Eastern Illinois University, Charleston, president, 1971-76; University of Georgia, Athens, Richard B. Russell Professor of History, 1976—. Visiting professor at Jadavpur University, 1962-63, and at Vanderbilt University, University of Missouri, University of Illinois, and University of Wisconsin. Director, American Studies Research Center, Hyderabad. Member of board of trustees, Phillips University, 1968-76.

MEMBER: American Historical Association, Organization of American Historians, Agricultural History Society (president, 1960-61), American Association for State and Local History, Economic History Association, Southern Historical Association (president, 1974), Phi Beta Kappa, Phi Alpha Theta. *Awards, honors:* Ford Foundation fellow, 1954-55; Litt.D. from Seattle Pacific College, 1962, and University of South Dakota, 1975; Guggenheim fellow, 1964.

WRITINGS: Peter Norbeck: Prairie Statesman, University of Missouri Studies, 1948; *Mount Rushmore,* University of Oklahoma Press, 1952; (editor with John S. Ezell, R. L. Biesele, and R. C. Cotner) *Readings in American History,* two volumes, Houghton, 1954, 3rd edition, 1964; *George N. Peek and the Fight for Farm Parity,* University of Oklahoma Press, 1954; (with Ladd Haystead) *The Agricultural Regions of the United States,* University of Oklahoma Press, 1955; (with H. C. Peterson) *Opponents of War: 1917-1918,* University of Wisconsin Press, 1957; (with Jim E. Reese) *An Economic History of the United States,* Houghton, 1959, 2nd edition, 1965; (author of introduction) James S. Brisbin, *The Beef Bonanza,* University of Oklahoma Press, 1959.

(Contributor) *Probing the American West,* Museum of New Mexico Press, 1962; *American Agriculture and Farm Policy in the Twentieth Century* (pamphlet), Macmillan, 1964; *Farm to Factory: A History of the Consumers Cooperative Association,* University of Missouri Press, 1965; *The Farmers Frontier: 1865-1900,* Holt, 1966; (contributor) *Great American Co-operators,* American Institute of Cooperation, 1967; (contributor) John Braeman, editor, *Change and Continuity in Twentieth Century America: The 20's,* Ohio State University Press, 1968; (with Norman Graebner and Philip White) *A History of the United States,* two volumes, McGraw, 1970; (with Graebner and White) *A History of the American People,* McGraw, 1970, 2nd edition, 1976; (with J. Carroll Moody) *The Credit Union Movement: Origins and Development,* University of Nebraska Press, 1971; (contributor) *A History of American Presidential Elections,* four volumes, McGraw, 1971; (with Graebner) *The United States since World War I,* Ronald, 1972.

Contributor to *Dictionary of American Biography;* contributor of more than forty articles to history and agriculture journals.

AVOCATIONAL INTERESTS: Travel, photography.

* * *

FitzGERALD, Cathleen 1932-

PERSONAL: Born July 1, 1932, in Dublin, Ireland; daughter of Thomas (a civil servant) and Mona (Hardiman) FitzGerald. *Education:* University College, Dublin, Ireland, B.A., 1953, higher diploma in education, 1954. *Reli-*

gion: Roman Catholic. *Home:* 216 West 89th St., New York, N.Y. 10024.

CAREER: Teacher in Ireland, England, and the United States, 1954-62; Grolier, Inc., New York, N.Y., managing editor of *New Book of Knowledge,* 1964-71, Grolier International, editorial adviser for *Japanese Book of Knowledge,* 1971-72, executive editor, 1973—. *Member:* Association for Supervision and Curriculum Development, Foreign Correspondents Club of Japan. *Awards, honors:* Salzburg Seminar in American Studies fellowship, 1956.

WRITINGS—Juvenile: *Let's Find Out about Words,* F. Watts, 1971; *Let's Find Out about Bees,* F. Watts, 1973. Author of several television and radio scripts for Irish children's programs.

WORK IN PROGRESS: A children's book about the seashore.

* * *

FITZSIMMONS, Thomas 1926-

PERSONAL: Born October 21, 1926, in Lowell, Mass.; son of William and Irene Yvonne (Courtois) Fitzsimmons; married in February, 1952 (divorced, 1977); children: Sean, Ian. *Education:* Attended Fresno State College (now California State University, Fresno), 1947-49, and Sorbonne, University of Paris, and Institut de Science Politique, 1949-50; Stanford University, B.A., 1951; Columbia University, M.A. (with honors), 1952. *Agent:* Anthony Sheil Associates Ltd., 52 Floral St., Covent Garden, London WC2E 9DA, England. *Office:* Department of English, Oakland University, Rochester, Mich. 48063.

CAREER: Office of U.S. Secretary of Defense, Washington, D.C., consultant in historical section, 1952; *New Republic,* Washington, D.C., foreign affairs writer and editor, 1952-55; American University, Washington, D.C., assistant professor of English, 1955-59; Yale University, Human Relations Area File, New Haven, Conn., research chairman, 1955-56, director of research, 1956-58, director and editor, HRAF Press, 1958-59; Oakland University, Rochester, Mich., assistant professor, 1959-60, associate professor, 1961-66, professor of literature, 1966—; chairman of the board of Inscape (growth center). Has given readings of his poetry, lectures, and conducted workshops in eighteen countries, including Japan, Australia, Pakistan, Greece, Italy, France, Netherlands, England, and Mexico. Exhibitor, with artist, Karen Hargreave, of poem/paintings and poem/sculptures in two gallery shows, 1973 and 1974. Visiting professor and poet in residence, Tokyo University of Education, 1973-75; visiting lecturer, Keio University and Japan Women's University, 1973-75. *Military service:* U.S. Merchant Marine, 1942-45. U.S. Army Air Forces, 1945. *Awards, honors:* Fulbright lecturer in Japan, 1962-64, in Pakistan, summer, 1964, in Romania, 1967-68, in Nice, France, summer, 1968; National Endowment for the Arts poetry award, 1967.

WRITINGS: (Principal author) *USSR,* Human Relations Area File Press, 1960; *Downinside* (long poem), Press Zero, 1969; *This Time, This Place* (poems and graphics), Press Zero, 1969; *Morningdew* (long poem), Press Zero, 1970; *Meditation Seeds,* Stone Marrow Press, 1971; *Mooning* (poems), Red Hanrahan Press, 1971; *With the Water,* New Voices Press, 1972; (translator) *Japanese Poetry Now,* Schocken, 1972; (contributor) Chalib, *Ghazals,* Columbia University Press, 1972; *Zenjoints* (poetry-meditation practices), New Voices Press, 1972; *Playseeds* (poem/plays), Pilot Press, 1973; *The Big Huge,* K. T. Did Press, 1975; *The*

House of My Friend (with cassette tape), K. T. Did Press, 1976. Also creator of "Some Other American Poets," a videotape with music accompaniment in which Fitzsimmons reads the works of minority poets, distributed throughout Europe and Asia. Contributor of more than two hundred poems and essays to *Saturday Review, Sewanee Review, New Republic, Commonweal, Road Apple Review, Wormwood,* and numerous other periodicals.

WORK IN PROGRESS: Action poems—continuing experiment.

SIDELIGHTS: Thomas Fitzsimmons has studied meditation/awareness disciplines in the United States and in the Orient. He told *CA* that he feels "the arts have a healing role in 'manipulative' societies such as ours in that they activate the 'other' capacities for harmony and respect and flexibility of response." In order to activate this healing movement, he attempts "to get poetry out of books, onto the breath, onto the walls, and into the life-spaces." He is "interested in ceremony as an interflow that eliminates the distance between maker and taker—so that all both take and make."

BIOGRAPHICAL/CRITICAL SOURCES: Poetry, November, 1967.

* * *

FITZSIMONS, Neal 1928-

PERSONAL: Born September 28, 1928, in Litchfield, Conn.; son of Tom Leffingwell Fitzsimons (an institutional manager) and Alma G. Fitzsimons Thompson; married Mayvis Ellis, January 12, 1952; children: Scott, Gray, Reid. *Education:* Cornell University, B.C.E., 1950. *Home:* 10149 Cedar Lane, Kensington, Md. 20795.

CAREER: Civil engineer in Africa and Asia, designing airfields, highways, and buildings, 1952-55; U.S. Department of Defense, Washington, D.C., civil engineer, 1956-75; WJE Inc., Northbrook, Ill., principal and consulting engineer, 1976—. Has lectured on civil engineering, systems engineering, and engineering history in the United States and Europe. Consultant to National Park Service, National Trust for Historic Preservation, and Smithsonian Institution, on preservation and documentation of engineering historic landmarks, and to television documentary, "It Couldn't Be Done." *Military service:* U.S. Army, Corps of Engineers, 1945-47, 1950-52; served in Europe; became captain; received outstanding achievement award of Seventh Army, 1952.

MEMBER: American Society of Civil Engineers (chairman, national committee on history and heritage; chairman, research council on performance of structures), Engineers Joint Council (chairman, national committee on American Revolution bicentennial), American Concrete Institute, American Geophysical Union, Newcomen Society. *Awards, honors:* Civil Service Commission outstanding performance award, 1959, 1962; Army Commendation Medal, 1967; American Society of Civil Engineers history medal, 1976; Department of the Army Meritorious Service Award, 1976.

WRITINGS: (With Eugene P. Wigner) *Who Speaks for Civil Defense?,* Scribner, 1968; (editor) *The Reminiscences of John B. Jervis: Engineer of the Old Croton,* Syracuse University Press, 1971. Author of "Benchmarks," a monthly column in journal of American Society of Civil Engineers, and of over 100 papers on aspects of engineering.

WORK IN PROGRESS: Pollution Fighters; Benjamin Wright, father of American civil engineering.

FITZSIMONS, Raymund

PERSONAL: Son of James and Elizabeth (Mulvey) Fitzsimons; married Anne O'Brien (a literary researcher), October 5, 1959; children: James, Mary, Lucy, Elizabeth. *Home:* The Retreat, The Green, Wetheral, Carlisle, Cumberland, England. *Agent:* Julian Bach, Jr., 3 East 48th St., New York, N.Y. 10017; and Anthony Sheil Associates Ltd., 52 Floral St., Covent Garden, London WC2E 9DA, England.

WRITINGS: The Baron of Piccadilly: The Travels and Entertainments of Albert Smith, 1816-1860, Bles, 1967; *Barnum in London,* Bles, 1969, St. Martin's, 1970; *Garish Lights: The Public Readings of Charles Dickens,* Lippincott, 1970, published as *The Charles Dickens Show: An Account of His Public Readings, 1858-1870,* Bles, 1970, Fernhill, 1972; *Edmund Kean: Fire from Heaven,* Dial, 1976.

WORK IN PROGRESS: Death and the Magician: A Study of Houdini.

BIOGRAPHICAL/CRITICAL SOURCES: Observer Review, October 8, 1967; *Times Literary Supplement,* October 19, 1967; *Spectator,* December 20, 1969.

* * *

FLAHERTY, Doug(las Ernest) 1939-

PERSONAL: Born April 25, 1939; son of Douglas Ernest (a foreman) and Hazel (Shinkwin) Flaherty; married Anick O'Meara (an Irish poet), June 21, 1973. *Education:* Merrimack College, B.S., 1961; University of Massachusetts, M.A., 1964; University of Iowa, M.F.A., 1966. *Home:* 3263 Shorewood Dr., Oshkosh, Wis. *Office:* Department of English, University of Wisconsin—Oshkosh, Oshkosh, Wis. 54901.

CAREER: University of Wisconsin—Oshkosh, assistant professor of English, 1966—. *Awards, honors:* Kansas City Poetry Award, sponsored by Hallmark, Inc., 1966; National Endowment grant, 1973.

WRITINGS—Poetry: Just a Little Old Wood's Tale, Road Runner Press, 1969; *The Elderly Battlefield Nurse,* Road Runner Press, 1969; *The Tomb of Skulls,* Road Runner Press, 1970; *Their Place in the Heat,* Road Runner Press, 1971; *Digging into Ourselves,* Quixote Press, 1971; *Weaving a Slow Dream of Hands,* Seafront Press, 1972; *Moving All Ways at Once,* Monday Morning Press, 1972; *Fleshed Out,* Prickly Pear Press, 1973; *Near the Bone,* Pentagram Press, 1975; *To Keep the Blood from Drowning,* Second Coming, 1976; *Love: Tangle of Roots,* Ithaca House, 1977. Contributor of poems to more than a hundred literary and popular journals, including *Nation* and *New Yorker.* Founder and editor, *Road Apple Review* (a national poetry quarterly), 1968.

WORK IN PROGRESS: A novel, *The First Cut.*

SIDELIGHTS: Doug Flaherty told *CA* he "write[s] poetry because it's the oldest form of spoken emotional utterance. I like to feel a shared contact with the past. And the poem projects one's feelings into the future, even if we later want to reject what we have said inadequately. Perhaps it is a miracle we can speak at all. In an age of perversity and destruction, the ability to speak a poem is my reason for lugging this body through another day, another century."

* * *

FLANAGAN, Robert (James) 1941-

PERSONAL: Born April 26, 1941, in Toledo, Ohio; son of

Robert John and Minnie Jane (Treloar) Flanagan; married Kathleen Borer (a registered nurse), August 24, 1963; children: Anne, Nora, Joseph. *Education:* University of Toledo, B.A., 1965; University of Chicago, M.A., 1967. *Politics:* Independent. *Religion:* Society of Friends (Quaker). *Home:* 181 North Liberty St., Delaware, Ohio 43015. *Agent:* John Schaffner, 425 East 51st St., New York, N.Y. 10022. *Office:* Department of English, Ohio Wesleyan University, Delaware, Ohio 43015.

CAREER: Central YMCA Community College, Chicago, Ill., instructor in English, 1966-67; Slippery Rock State College, Slippery Rock, Pa., instructor in English, 1967-69; Ohio Wesleyan University, Delaware, associate professor of English, 1969—. *Military service:* U.S. Marine Corps Reserve, 1960-66. *Member:* Ohio Poets' Association. *Awards, honors:* Screen Gems Award for Short Fiction, 1966, for "In His Father's Room."

WRITINGS: Maggot (novel), Paperback Library, 1971; *The Full Round* (poems), Fiddlehead Books, 1973; *Three Times Three* (short fiction), Ithaca House, 1977. Poetry anthologized in *Heartland II: Poets of the Midwest,* edited by Lucien Stryk, Northern Illinois University Press, 1975.

WORK IN PROGRESS: Once You Learn You Never Forget, poems; *So Where Do You Bury Your Dead?,* a novel.

SIDELIGHTS: Robert Flanagan told *CA:* "When I was younger, I used to stay up at night and write. It was very romantic, although in the morning when I read what I'd written I ended up throwing most of it away anyhow. Now, with a family and a job, I try to write regularly a few hours every morning. This demands the ability to bank the fires for the next day. It gives the work continuity, I think.

"I work in both poetry and fiction. I'm a Jekyll and Hyde writer. When I'm working well with poems I am sure I'll never go back to writing fiction; it is so clumsy, fat, such a bucket to hold things. When I'm working well with fiction, particularly with a novel, I know I'll never go back to writing poems; they are so small, so breakable, such teacups for holding things.

"Beneath my poetry and fiction lies the simple story-telling urge. My family always told stories, no matter how uneducated they were. We not only entertained ourselves, but we made our lives more livable by telling stories in which they were changed."

* * *

FLANDERS, Helen Hartness 1890-1972

May 19, 1890—May 24, 1972; American poet, editor, and collector of American folk songs. Obituaries: *New York Times,* May 25, 1972; *Washington Post,* May 25, 1972. (See index for *CA* sketch)

* * *

FLANDERS, Henry Jackson, Jr. 1921-

PERSONAL: Born October 2, 1921, in Malvern, Ark.; son of Henry Jackson and Mae (Hargis) Flanders; married Tommie Lou Pardew (a social worker), 1944; children: Janet (Mrs. A. G. Mitchell), Jack III. *Education:* Baylor University, B.A., 1943; Southern Baptist Theological Seminary, B.D., 1948, Ph.D., 1950. *Home:* 3820 Chateau, Waco, Tex. 74710. *Office:* Department of Religion, Baylor University, Waco, Tex. 76703.

CAREER: Pastor of Baptist Churches in Navasota, Tex., 1940-41, Heltonville, Ind., 1946-49, Indian Fork, Ky., 1949-

50, and Waco, Tex., 1962-69; Furman University, Greenville, S.C., assistant professor, 1950-53, associate professor, 1953-55, professor of religion, chairman of department, and chaplain, 1955-62; Baylor University, Waco, professor of religion, 1969—. President and member of board of directors, Economic Opportunities Advancement Corp.; member of board of directors of Board of Mental Health of Waco, Tex. and Heart of Texas Red Cross; trustee and chairman of board, Golden Gate Baptist Theological Seminary; trustee of Baylor University and Hillcrest Hospital. *Military service:* U.S. Army Air Forces, 1943-45; became first lieutenant; received several medals and multiple clusters. *Member:* American Academy of Religion, Society of Biblical Literature, American Association of University Professors (president, Baylor chapter), Association of Baptist Professors of Religion (president), Baptist General Convention of Texas (member of executive committee), Sigma Tau Delta, Rotary International, Masons.

WRITINGS: (With Robert W. Crapps and David A. Smith) *People of the Covenant: An Introduction to the Old Testament,* Ronald, 1963, 2nd edition, 1973; (with Bruce C. Cresson) *Introduction to the Bible,* Ronald, 1973. Contributor of articles to *Baptist Program, Baptist Courier, Journal of Church and State, Southwestern Journal of Theology,* and other periodicals.

AVOCATIONAL INTERESTS: Flying, skiing, golf, travel.

* * *

FLANIGAN, Lloyd A(llen) 1933-

PERSONAL: Born June 16, 1933, in Parkersburg, W.Va.; son of Paul A. (in steel industry management) and Frances E. (Caldwell) Flanigan; married Betty Clarke Dillon, July 25, 1959; children: Elizabeth Caldwell, Jennifer Holloway. *Education:* Ohio University, B.A. and B.S.Ed., 1957; University of Virginia, M.Ed., 1966; also studied German at University of Munich and Goethe Institute, 1955-56. *Home:* 140 Autumn Dr., Collinsville, Va. 24078.

CAREER: University of Missouri, School of Mines and Metallurgy (now University of Missouri—Rolla), instructor in English, 1958-59; Baker University, Baldwin, Kan., instructor in English and German, 1959-60; Augusta Military Academy, Fort Defiance, Va., chairman, department of English, 1961-66; St. Petersburg Junior College, St. Petersburg and Clearwater, Fla., instructor in English, 1966-74; Maine Maritime Academy, Castiner, Me., associate professor of English and German, 1974-76; Piedmont Virginia Community College, Charlottesville, Va., associate professor of English and German, 1976-77; Nationwide Homes, Martinsville, Va., director of sales, Consumer Division. Consultant-reviewer for several publishers.

WRITINGS: (With Donald J. Tighe) *Source, Idea, Technique,* Holbrook, 1969; (with Sylvia A. Holladay) *Developing Style: An Extension of Personality,* Holbrook, 1972; *Approaches to Exposition: What, How and Why,* Winthrop Publishing, 1974.

WORK IN PROGRESS: A technical writing text.

AVOCATIONAL INTERESTS: Writing, water sports.

* * *

FLEISCHMANN, Glen H(arvey) 1909-

PERSONAL: Born February 23, 1909, in Manley, Neb.; son of Frederick Ferdinand and Sarah Montgomery (Taylor) Fleischmann; married Evelyn Grace Fitzpatrick, February

10, 1931. *Education:* Attended Vogue School of Art, Chicago, Ill., 1929. *Home:* 1160 Midland Ave., Bronxville, N.Y. 10708.

CAREER: Meyer Both Advertising Co., Chicago, Ill., art apprentice, 1932-34, ad creator (layout, copy, and finished art), 1934-37; R. H. Macy & Co., New York, N.Y., executive artist, 1937-39; free-lance illustrator (magazines and advertising), 1939—, with work appearing in *Saturday Evening Post, Good Housekeeping, Collier's, American, Woman's Home Companion, Parents' Magazine, True, Field & Stream, Sports Afield,* and other national magazines, and in ads for General Foods, General Mills, Lever Bros., General Motors, Ford Motor Co., and other firms. *Military service:* U.S. Army, Corps of Engineers, 1943-45. *Member:* Authors Guild, Authors League of America. *Awards, honors:* His ad for Swan soap was voted the most popular in Art Directors Show, 1943.

WRITINGS: While Rivers Flow (novel), Macmillan, 1963; *The Cherokee Removal* (nonfiction; Junior Literary Guild selection), F. Watts, 1971.

WORK IN PROGRESS: Desperate Journey, a novel; *The Artist: His Markets and His World,* nonfiction; *Krug: An Artist in Philistia,* a novel; *The Whitaker Legacy,* a novel.

SIDELIGHTS: Both *While Rivers Flow* and *The Cherokee Removal* had their beginnings in old orderly-room records of the Cherokee Removal of 1838 that Fleischmann saw in the archives of Fort Belvoir when he was stationed there during World War II. After his discharge from the Army he traveled over the route of the story in eight states and made four field trips through the Old Cherokee Nation. Some of his relatives were among the evictors and the evicted in the Cherokee Removal.

BIOGRAPHICAL/CRITICAL SOURCES: Chicago Tribune, June 16, 1963; *New York Times Book Review,* June 23, 1963.

*   *   *

FLEMING, H(orace) K(ingston)   1901-

PERSONAL: Born February 1, 1901, in Birkenhead, England; came to United States, 1924, naturalized citizen, 1937; son of Horace (an educator) and Cecile (Steele) Fleming; married Doris Brown, January 3, 1931; children: Pamela Fleming Johnston, Paula (Mrs. Donald Wharram). *Education:* Attended London School of Economics and Political Science, 1919-21. *Home address:* Apt. M-1, Route 3, Box 194, De Land, Fla. 32720. *Agent:* Laurence Pollinger Ltd., 18 Maddox St., London W1R 0EU, England.

CAREER: Editorial assistant on several newspapers before coming to America; *Baltimore Sun,* Baltimore, Md., member of editorial staff, 1924-41, managing editor, 1941-42; Board of Economic Warfare, Washington, D.C., chief of Blockade Division, 1942-43; U.S. Department of State, Washington, D.C., assistant chief of Eastern Hemisphere Division, 1943-44, assistant chief of International Information Division, 1944-45, assistant to director of Office of American Republics Affairs, 1946-48; Institute for Advanced Study, Princeton, N.J., general manager, 1951-54; U.S. Federal Housing Administration (FHA), Washington, D.C., director of public information, 1955-56; U.S. Housing and Home Finance Agency, Washington, D.C., assistant administrator, 1956-60, special assistant to administrator, 1960-61, area coordinator of urban renewal in regional office, San Francisco, Calif., 1961-66.

WRITINGS: Eden, Eden (novel), Gollancz, 1947; *The Day They Kidnapped Queen Victoria* (novel), Frewin, 1969.

WORK IN PROGRESS: An Edwardian novel and a play.

SIDELIGHTS: A radio adaptation of *The Day They Kidnapped Queen Victoria* has been carried twice in fifteen installments by British Broadcasting Corp. The book has been published in French and a contract has been prepared to make a film of it.

*   *   *

FLEMING, (Robert) Peter   1907-1971

May 31, 1907—August 18, 1971; British novelist. Obituaries: *New York Times,* August 20, 1971; *Washington Post,* August 20, 1971; *Time,* August 30, 1971.

*   *   *

FLETCHER, Ronald   1921-

PERSONAL: Born August 11, 1921, in Hoyland, Yorkshire, England; son of George William (a carpenter) and Winifred M. (Hatswell) Fletcher; married Clarice Roma Phipps, May 27, 1944; children: Paul, Adrian John. *Education:* University of Bristol, B.A. (first class honors), 1951; London School of Economics and Political Science, Ph.D., 1954. *Politics:* ''Puzzled.'' *Religion:* ''Puzzled.'' *Home and office:* Cranmere, Halesworth Rd., Reydon, Southwold IP18 6NH, Suffolk, England. *Agent:* Curtis Brown Ltd., 1 Craven Hill, London W2 3EW, England.

CAREER: University of London, London, England, lecturer in sociology at Bedford College and Birkbeck College, 1953-63; University of York, Heslington, England, professor of sociology and head of department, 1964-68; University of Essex, Colchester, England, visiting professor of sociology, 1968-69; full-time research and writing, 1969-76; University of Reading, Reading, England, visiting lecturer in sociology, 1976-78. Auguste Comte Memorial Trust Lecturer, London School of Economics and Political Science, University of London, 1966; associate lecturer (consultancy), Thames Polytechnic; British Council lecturer in Denmark, Malta, and Rome. Course consultant, Open University. *Member:* British Sociological Association, American Sociological Association, Royal Society of Arts (fellow), Society of Authors, Authors' Club. *Awards, honors:* Rockefeller Foundation fellow, 1962.

WRITINGS: Instinct in Man: In the Light of Recent Work in Comparative Psychology (revised and shortened version of doctoral thesis), International Universities Press, 1957, 2nd edition, Allen & Unwin, 1968; *Issues in Education,* Ethical Union, 1960; *The Family and Marriage: An Analysis and Moral Assessment,* Penguin, 1962, revised edition published as *The Family and Marriage in Britain: An Analysis and Moral Assessment,* 1966; *Human Needs and Social Order,* M. Joseph, 1965, Schocken, 1966; *Auguste Comte and the Making of Sociology* (Auguste Comte Memorial Trust lecture), Athlone Press, 1966; *The Parkers at Saltram: Everyday Life in an 18th Century House,* British Broadcasting Corp., 1970; *The Making of Sociology* (core text), M. Joseph, Volume I: *Beginnings and Foundations,* 1971, Volume II: *Developments,* 1972; (editor and author of introductory essay) *John Stuart Mill: A Logical Critique of Sociology* (complementary volume to core text of *The Making of Sociology),* M. Joseph, 1971; (editor) *The Science of Society and the Unity of Mankind,* Heinemann, 1974; (editor) Auguste Comte, *The Crisis of Industrial Civilization,* Heinemann, 1974; *The Akenham Burial Case,* Wildwood House, 1974; *What's Wrong with Higher Education?,* Metheun, 1975; *The Framework of Society,* Open University Press, 1976; *The Biography of a Victorian Village,* Batsford, 1977;

In a Country Churchyard, Batsford, 1978. Editor-in-chief, "The Making of Sociology" series.

Television scripts include "The Artist in Society," "Human Societies," and "The Parkers at Saltram." Regular reviewer and columnist in *Times Educational Supplement, East Anglian Daily Times.* Contributor to sociology journals.

WORK IN PROGRESS: The Family and Marriage Now, for Penguin; *Creative Humanism,* for Allen & Unwin; *The Promethean Fire* and *The Sovereign Educators,* two volumes on the sociology of education, for Batsford.

SIDELIGHTS: Ronald Fletcher says that he is disillusioned with universities. "Can lead a more satisfying 'academic' life outside rather than inside academic walls. . . ." On television: "Do not believe in the distinction between education and entertainment. The best work is both. Also interested in music (composition) and painting—but, alas, cannot find enough time."

* * *

FLIPPO, Edwin B(ly) 1925-

PERSONAL: Born September 13, 1925, in Fort Worth, Tex.; son of Claude B. (an engineer) and Ada (Watson) Flippo; married Jean Gwin, March 18, 1950; children: Robert D., Susan J., Sallie J. *Education:* University of Missouri, B.S., 1947; Ohio State University, M.B.A., 1948, Ph.D., 1953. *Politics:* Republican. *Religion:* Protestant. *Home:* 1121 Camino de los Padres, Tucson, Ariz. 85718. *Office:* Department of Management, University of Arizona, Tucson, Ariz. 85721.

CAREER: University of Missouri—Columbia, instructor in management, 1948-49; Ohio State University, Research Foundation, Columbus, research associate, 1951-52; Miami University, Oxford, Ohio, assistant professor of industrial management, 1952-57; California State College at Los Angeles (now California State University, Los Angeles), professor of management, 1957-64; University of Arizona, Tucson, professor of management, 1964—. Visiting professor, University of Western Australia, spring, 1971. *Military service:* U.S. Army, 1943-46; became first lieutenant. *Member:* Academy of Management (fellow; chairman of publications committee, 1964-66), Alpha Kappa Psi.

WRITINGS: Profit Sharing in American Business, Bureau of Business Research, Ohio State University, 1954; *Principles of Personnel Management,* McGraw, 1961, 4th edition, 1976; *Management: A Behavioral Approach,* Allyn & Bacon, 1966, 4th edition, 1978.

* * *

FLOETHE, Richard 1901-

PERSONAL: His surname (pronounced "flirta") formerly appeared in umlauted form, but he has used the anglicized form for some years; born September 2, 1901, in Essen, Germany; came to United States in 1928; son of Richard William (in civil service) and Anna Marie (Kerckhoff) Floethe; married Louise Lee (a writer of children's books), June 24, 1937; children: Stephen Lee, Ronald Kerckhoff. *Education:* Studied at art academies in Dortmund, 1920-22, Munich, 1922-23, and at the Bauhaus in Weimar, 1923-24. *Politics:* Republican. *Religion:* Unitarian Universalist. *Home and studio:* 1391 Harbor Dr., Sarasota, Fla. 33579.

CAREER: Painter, print maker, and book illustrator. First major commission as an artist was a mural for the International Exposition in Cologne, Germany, 1928; art director of

Poster Division, Federal Art Project, New York City, 1936-39; instructor in commercial design at Cooper Union, New York City, 1940-41; art director of Poster Division, War Service of City of New York, 1942-43; instructor in illustration at Ringling School of Art, Sarasota, Fla., 1954-67. His water colors and prints are included in the collections of the Library of Congress, Metropolitan Museum of Art, Philadelphia Museum of Art, New York Public Library, and a number of university collections. *Member:* Sarasota Yacht Club, Bath and Racquet Club. *Awards, honors:* Winner of Limited Editions Club international competition for book illustration, 1934, for *Glorious Adventures of Tyl Ulenspiegl,* and 1937, for *The Adventures of Pinocchio.*

WRITINGS—Self-illustrated: Summer Holiday, Brookdale Press (Middletown, N.Y.), 1939.

Illustrator: Allen Chaffee, *Wandy the Wild Pony,* Harrison Smith, 1932; George D. Parrish, *Hung for a Song,* Farrar & Rinehart, 1934; Myron Brinig, *Out of Life,* Farrar & Rinehart, 1934; Charles T. H. Coster, *Glorious Adventures of Tyl Ulenspiegl,* translated by Allan R. Macdougall, Limited Editions Club, 1934; Sterner St. Paul Meek, *The Monkeys Have No Tails in Zambonga,* Morrow, 1935; Marjorie Fischer, *Street Fair,* Random House, 1935; Fischer, *Palaces on Monday,* Random House, 1936; *Cupid's Horn Book,* Peter Pauper, 1936; Daniel Defoe, *Robinson Crusoe,* Peter Pauper, 1937; Nor Burglon, *The Gate Swings In,* Little, Brown, 1937; Noel Streatfeild, *Ballet Shoes,* Random House, 1937; Carlo Lorenzini, *The Adventures of Pinocchio,* translated by Walter S. Cramp. Limited Editions Club, 1937; Helen Follett, *Third Class Ticket to Heaven,* Winston, 1938; Streatfeild, *Tennis Shoes,* Random House, 1938; Giovanni Boccaccio, *Decameron,* Peter Pauper, 1938; Streatfeild, *Circus Shoes,* Random House, 1939; Heluiz C. Washburne, *Friedl, the Mountain Boy,* Winston, 1939; Caroline Cunningham, editor, *The Talking Stone,* Knopf, 1939.

Kathleen Coyle, *Brittany Summer,* Harper, 1940; Elizabeth Goudge, *Smoky House,* Coward, 1940; Streatfeild, *The Secret of the Lodge,* Random House, 1940; William Shakespeare, *All's Well That Ends Well,* Limited Editions Club, 1940; Streatfeild, *The Stranger in Primrose Lane,* Random House, 1941; Mary Treadgold, *Left Till Called For,* Doubleday, 1941; Jack Bechdolt, *Junior Air Raid Wardens,* Lippincott, 1942; Jerome K. Jerome, *Three Men in a Boat,* Scribner, 1942; *The Adventures of Baron Munchausen,* Peter Pauper, 1944; Jerome S. Meyer, *Picture Book of Astronomy,* Lothrop, 1945; Streatfield, *Theater Shoes,* Random House, 1945; Carlo Lorenzini, *Pinocchio,* World Publishing, 1946; Darwin L. O. Teilhet, *The Avion My Uncle Flew,* Appleton, 1946; Meyer, *Picture Book of Molecules and Atoms,* Lothrop, 1947; Charles Lamb, *Dissertation on Roast Pig and Other Essays,* Peter Pauper, 1947; Meyer, *Fun-To-Do,* Dutton, 1948; Streatfeild, *Party Shoes,* Random House, 1948; Hester O'Neill, *Young Patriots,* Thomas Nelson, 1948; Meyer, *Picture Book of the Weather,* Lothrop, 1948; E. M. Orr and others, editors, *Stories Old and New,* Doubleday, 1948; Amy Hogeboom, editor, *Tales from the High Seas,* Lothrop, 1948; Lucy Sprague Mitchell, *A Year on the Farm,* Simon & Schuster, 1948; Walter Havighurst and M. M. Boyd, *Song of the Pines,* Winston, 1949; Meyer, *Picture Book of the Earth,* Lothrop, 1949; Hazel H. Wilson, *Island Summer,* Abingdon-Cokesbury, 1949.

Margaret Wise Brown, *The Dream Book,* Random House, 1950; Edna L. Sterling and others, *English Is Our Language,* Heath, 1950; Meyer, *Picture Book of Chemistry,* Lothrop, 1950; Streatfeild, *Skating Shoes,* Random House, 1951; Elizabeth Goudge, *The Valley of Song,* Coward, 1951;

Meyer, *Picture Book of Radio and Television*, Lothrop, 1951; Paul Witty and others, *Do and Dare* (reader), Heath, 1951; *The World's Best Limericks*, Peter Pauper, 1951; Katherine B. Shippen, *Mr. Bell Invents the Telephone*, Random House, 1952; Meyer, *Picture Book of Electricity*, Lothrop, 1953; Streatfeild, *Family Shoes*, Random House, 1954; Frank R. Stockton, *Ting-A-Ling Tales*, Scribner, 1955; Lee Sutton, *Venus Boy*, Lothrop, 1955; Nancy Nash, *Wumpy's Christmas Gift*, Lothrop, 1956; Meyer, *Picture Book of the Sea*, Lothrop, 1956; Streatfeild, *Dancing Shoes*, Random House, 1957; Charles M. Purin, *Fortunatus*, Heath, 1958; Stella M. Hinz, *Das Geheimisvolle Dorf*, Heath, 1958; Peter Hagboldt, *Das Abenteur der Neujahrsnacht*, Heath, 1958; Arthur Schnitzler, *Der Blinde Geronimo und sein Bruder*, Heath, 1959.

Illustrator of books by wife, Louise Lee Floethe; published by Scribner, except as indicated: *If I Were Captain* (Junior Literary Guild selection), 1956; *The Farmer and His Cows*, 1957; *The Winning Colt*, Sterling, 1957; *Terry Sets Sail*, Harper, 1958; *The Cowboy on the Ranch*, 1959; *The Indian and His Pueblo*, 1960; *Triangle X*, Harper, 1960; *Sara*, Ariel, 1961; *The Fisherman and His Boat*, 1961; *Blueberry Pie*, 1962; *The Story of Lumber*, 1962; *Sea of Grass*, 1963; *The Islands of Hawaii*, 1964; *Bittersweet Summer*, Ariel, 1964; *The New Roof*, 1965; *Fountain of the Friendly Lion*, 1966; *A Thousand and One Buddhas*, Ariel, 1967; *Floating Market*, Ariel, 1969; *Farming around the World*, 1970; *Jungle People*, 1971; *Fishing around the World*, 1972; *Houses around the World*, 1973.

Designer of jackets for *A Year to Remember*, by Louise Lee Floethe, Lothrop, 1957, and many other books. Contributor to *Horn Book*.

AVOCATIONAL INTERESTS: Tennis, sailing.

BIOGRAPHICAL/CRITICAL SOURCES: "Kid Stuff," film produced by Gordon-Kerckhoff Productions, 1970.

*   *   *

FLORENCE, Ronald 1942-

PERSONAL: Born October 14, 1942, in California; son of Harold and Edna Helen (Levy) Florence. *Education:* University of California, Berkeley, A.B., 1964; Harvard University, M.A., 1965, Ph.D., 1969. *Home:* 114 Five Mile River Rd., Darien, Conn. 06820. *Office:* 33 West 42nd St., New York, N.Y. 10036.

CAREER: Sarah Lawrence College, Bronxville, N.Y., member of history faculty, 1968-71; State University of New York College at Purchase, assistant professor, then associate professor of history, 1971-74; research associate, Twentieth Century Fund, 1974; New York Council for the Humanities, New York City, executive director, 1975—. Co-chairman of Conference on the Future of the Intellectual Community, New York, 1976, and International Conference on the Humanities and Social Thought, Italy, 1977. *Awards, honors:* Austrian History Prize (special commendation), Austrian Institute, 1969.

WRITINGS: Fritz: The Story of a Political Assassin, Dial, 1971; *Marx's Daughters*, Dial, 1975.

*   *   *

FLOYD, Barry Neil 1925-

PERSONAL: Born June 29, 1925, in London, England; son of Leslie Gabriel (an engineer) and Ivy (Pearce) Floyd; married Jean Laurie (a teacher and librarian), June 11, 1953; children: James, Laurie, Julia, Valerie, Barrie. *Education:*

Cambridge University, B.A. (honors), 1949; University of Minnesota, M.A., 1951; Syracuse University, Ph.D., 1959. *Politics:* Liberal. *Religion:* Presbyterian. *Home:* 11 Coventry Rd., Newton Hall, Durham DH1 5XD, England. *Office:* Department of Geography, University of Durham, South Rd., Durham DH1 3LE, England.

CAREER: College of Wooster, Wooster, Ohio, instructor in geography and geology, 1951-55; Government of Southern Rhodesia, Department of Native Agriculture, land development officer, 1957-58; assistant professor of geography at Dartmouth College, Hanover, N.H., 1959-61, Michigan State University, East Lansing, 1961, and University of Nigeria, Nsukka, 1962-66; University of the West Indies, Mona, Kingston, Jamaica, head of department of geography, 1966-72; University of Durham, Durham, England, department of geography staff member, 1972—. *Military service:* Royal Air Force, 1943-47; served as flight lieutenant. *Member:* Institute of British Geographers, Geographical Association, Society for Caribbean Studies, Jamaican Geographical Society.

WRITINGS: Eastern Nigeria: A Geographical Review, Macmillan, 1969. Contributor to academic journals.

WORK IN PROGRESS: Spatial aspects of small scale agriculture in the tropics, with particular reference to Africa and West Indies.

*   *   *

FLOYD, W(illiam) E(dward) G(regory) 1939-

PERSONAL: Born November 4, 1939, in New Orleans, La.; son of Jewell Edward and Margaret (Mitchell) Floyd. *Education:* Brown University, B.A., 1961; Oxford University, S.T.L. and B.Litt., 1968. *Home and office:* Portsmouth Abbey, Portsmouth, R.I. 02871.

CAREER: Roman Catholic priest. Portsmouth Abbey School, Portsmouth, R.I., teacher and director of admissions, 1961-73, headmaster, 1973—.

WRITINGS: Clement of Alexandria's Treatment of the Problem of Evil, Oxford University, 1971.

*   *   *

FLUNO, Robert Y(ounger) 1916-

PERSONAL: Born November 27, 1916, in Appleton, Wis.; son of Arthur S. and Elsie M. Fluno; married Ruth Lilja (an artist), January 18, 1944 (deceased). *Education:* Rollins College, B.A., 1938; graduate study at American University, 1938-40, and London School of Economics and Political Science, 1950-51; University of Minnesota, Ph.D., 1952. *Home:* 725 Valencia, Walla Walla, Wash. 99362. *Office:* Department of Political Science, Whitman College, Walla Walla, Wash. 99362.

CAREER: U.S. War Department, Aberdeen, Md., assistant director of civilian personnel, 1940-42; University of Minnesota, Minneapolis, instructor in political science, 1947-48; Mount Union College, Alliance, Ohio, assistant professor of political science, 1948-52; Whitman College, Walla Walla, Wash., associate professor, 1952-56, professor, 1956-60, Miles C. Moore Professor of Political Science, 1960—. Fulbright professor, University of Rajshahi, 1957. *Military service:* U.S. Naval Reserve, 1942-45; became lieutenant.

WRITINGS: (With Chester C. Maxey) *The American Problem of Government*, Appleton, 1957; (contributor) Rocco J. Tresolini and Richard T. Frost, editors, *Case*

Studies in American National Government and Politics, Prentice-Hall, 1966; *The Democratic Community,* Dodd, 1971.

WORK IN PROGRESS: A book on the varieties of American political discourse.

*   *   *

FOLEY, William E. 1938-

PERSONAL: Born September 20, 1938, in Kansas City, Mo.; son of William D. and Lorene (Renner) Foley; married Martha A. Ellenburg, May 30, 1967; children: Laura Ann, David Edward. *Education:* Central Missouri State College (now Central Missouri State University), B.S., 1960, M.A., 1963; University of Missouri—Columbia, Ph.D., 1967. *Religion:* Presbyterian. *Home:* 1418 Grandview Dr., Warrensburg, Mo. 64093. *Office:* Department of History, Central Missouri State University, Warrensburg, Mo. 64093.

CAREER: Central Missouri State University, Warrensburg, assistant professor, 1966-69, associate professor, 1969-73, professor of history, 1973—. *Member:* Organization of American Historians, Western History Association, State Historical Society of Missouri, Missouri Historical Society, Phi Alpha Theta. *Awards, honors:* Award of Merit, American Association for State and Local History, 1974, for *A History of Missouri: 1673-1820.*

WRITINGS: A History of Missouri: 1673-1820, University of Missouri Press, 1971; *Missouri: Then and Now,* Steck, 1976. Contributor to history journals.

WORK IN PROGRESS: A book entitled *Auguste and Pierre Chouteau: River Barons of the Mississippi Valley.*

*   *   *

FORAN, Donald J. 1943-

PERSONAL: Surname is pronounced *For*-un; born February 27, 1943, in Los Angeles, Calif.; son of William Thomas and Eileen (Curran) Foran. *Education:* Gonzaga University, M.A., 1967; University of Southern California, Ph.D., 1973; Jesuit School of Theology, S.T.M., 1975. *Politics:* Progressive democrat. *Office:* Department of English, Seattle University, Seattle, Wash. 98122.

CAREER: Entered Society of Jesus (Jesuits), 1961; Gonzaga Preparatory School, Spokane, Wash., teacher of English and American literature and chairman of English department, 1968-70; Seattle University, Seattle, Wash., assistant professor of English and religious studies, 1975—. *Member:* Modern Language Association of America, National Council of Teachers of English, Wallace Stevens Society, Bread for the World, Kappa Delta Pi.

WRITINGS: Living with Ambiguity: Discerning God in a Complex Society, Alba, 1971. Contributor to literary journals and justice forums.

WORK IN PROGRESS: A book of essays combining literature and contemporary applications, entitled *Life Metaphors;* an article for *Wallace Stevens Journal;* several poems.

*   *   *

FORCIONE, Alban Keith 1938-

PERSONAL: Born November 17, 1938, in Washington, D.C.; son of Eugene (a physician) and Wilda (Ashby) Forcione; married Renate Muehlenstedt, September 5, 1964; children: Michael, Mark. *Education:* Princeton University, B.A., 1960, M.A. and Ph.D., 1968; Harvard University,

M.A., 1961; studied at Goettingen University, 1962-63. *Home:* 14 College Rd., Princeton, N.J. 08540. *Office:* Department of Romance Languages, Princeton University, Princeton, N.J. 08540.

CAREER: Princeton University, Princeton, N.J., assistant professor, 1968-71, associate professor of Romance languages, 1971-75, professor of Romance languages and comparative literature, 1975—. *Member:* Phi Beta Kappa. *Awards, honors:* Woodrow Wilson fellow, 1960-61; Fulbright fellow, 1961-62.

WRITINGS: Cervantes, Aristotle, and the Persiles, Princeton University Press, 1970; *Cervantes' Christian Romance,* Princeton University Press, 1972. Contributor to Romance language journals.

WORK IN PROGRESS: Cervantes and the Humanist Vision.

*   *   *

FORD, Phyllis M(arjorie) 1928-

PERSONAL: Born March 18, 1928, in Ludlow, Mass.; daughter of Wendell Bradford (a management consultant) and Phyllis (Symonds) Ford. *Education:* University of Massachusetts, B.S., 1949; Arizona State University, M.A., 1954; Indiana University, Re.D., 1962. *Office:* Department of Recreation and Park Management, University of Oregon, Eugene, Ore. 97403.

CAREER: University of Massachusetts—Amherst, research technician, 1949-50; Y.W.C.A., Orange, N.J., teenage program director, 1950-51; Florence Union High School, Florence, Ariz., teacher, 1951-54; Technical Vocational High School, Hammond, Ind., teacher, 1954-58; Schools of the City of Hammond, supervisor of girls physical education, 1958-59; University of Oregon, Eugene, associate professor of recreation and park management, 1961-69; University of Iowa, Iowa City, associate professor of recreation and chairman of the department, 1969-71; University of Oregon, associate professor and head of the department, 1971-75, professor of recreation and park management and graduate coordinator, 1975—. Visiting lecturer, Indiana University, 1959-61. Member of board of directors, Western Rivers Girl Scouts. Consultant in outdoor education to various school systems. *Member:* American Camping Association (national secretary, 1969-73), National Park and Recreation Association, American Association for Health, Physical Education, and Recreation, Oregon Parks and Recreation Society (member of board of directors, 1972-73), Pi Lambda Theta.

WRITINGS: GAA Songbook, Indiana League of High School Girls Athletic Associations, 1957; *Leisure and the Senior Citizens,* Department of Recreation, Indiana University, 1962; *Your Camp and the Handicapped Child,* American Camping Association, 1962; (editor) *Professional Preparation Standards in Recreation,* revised edition, Northwest Council on Teacher Education Standards for Health, Physical Education and Recreation, 1965; *The Handicapped Camper and the Regular Camp,* American Camping Association, 1966; *A Guide for Leaders of Informal Recreational Activities,* University of Iowa Press, 1970, published as *Informal Recreation Activities: A Leader's Guide,* American Camping Association, 1977; (editor) Janet Tobitt, *A Counselor's Guide to Camp Singing,* revised edition, American Camping Association, 1971; (with Lynn S. Rodney) *Camp Administration,* Ronald, 1971; (with Effie L. Fairchild) *Kool Summer Fun* (summer playground cards), National Recreation and Parks Association, 1972. Contributor of articles to various periodicals, including *Health Bulletin* (Indiana State Board of Health), *Journal of Health, Physical Education and Recreation, Camping Magazine,* and *Outing Guide.* Author of surveys on recreation for government agencies.

AVOCATIONAL INTERESTS: Natural history, backpacking, and mountaineering.

* * *

FORD, Robert N(icholas) 1909-

PERSONAL: Born February 25, 1909, in North Braddock, Pa.; son of Samuel and Catherine V. (Cox) Ford; married Jane Foust, August 12, 1933; children: Florence Ford Byrne, Raymond F. *Education:* Pennsylvania State University, B.A., 1931; University of Pittsburgh, M.A., 1935, Ph.D., 1940. *Office:* American Telephone and Telegraph Co., 195 Broadway, Room C2270, New York, N.Y. 10007.

CAREER: Teacher in Pennsylvania schools, 1931-40; instructor in sociology at University of Kentucky, Lexington, 1940, and University of Alabama, University, 1940-41; Mississippi State University, State College, associate professor of sociology, 1941-43; Vanderbilt University, Nashville, Tenn., assistant professor of sociology, 1943; U.S. Government, Washington, D.C., Selective Service System, chief of classification system at national headquarters, 1943-44, War Department (now Department of Defense), Office of Chiefs of Staff, statistician in research branch of Information and Education Division, 1944-45, Veterans Administration, Office of Coordination and Planning, assistant chief of Survey Division, 1945-47; American Telephone & Telegraph Co., New York, N.Y., statistician, 1947-49, personnel relations staff, 1949-55, director of communications and social science research, 1955-58, Department of Personnel Relations, supervisor of management training section, 1958-67, director of manpower utilization, 1968-71, director of manpower utilization, development, and research, 1972—.

MEMBER: American Sociological Association, American Statistical Association, American Association for Public Opinion Research (president, 1968-69). *Awards, honors:* Special individual award, American Society for Training and Development, 1970, for his substantial contribution to the profession.

WRITINGS: Motivation through the Work Itself, American Management Association, 1969; (with John R. Maher) *New Horizons in Job Enrichment,* Van Nostrand, 1971. Also author of *The Obstinate Employee.*

* * *

FOREMAN, Harry 1915-

PERSONAL: Born March 5, 1915, in Winnipeg, Manitoba, Canada; naturalized U.S. citizen in 1940; son of Monish and Fannie (Decter) Foreman; married Billie Deane Smith, June 29, 1956; children: Matthew Dean, Pamela Kim. *Education:* Antioch College, B.S., 1938; Ohio State University, M.S. and Ph.D., 1942; University of California, San Francisco, M.D., 1947. *Office:* Center for Population Studies, University of Minnesota, Minneapolis, Minn. 55455.

CAREER: Eldorado Oil Co., Oakland, Calif., research chemist, 1943-44; Mount Zion Hospital, San Francisco, Calif., intern, 1947-48, resident in internal medicine, 1948-49; University of California, Berkeley, National Research Council and Atomic Energy Commission postdoctoral fellow at Crocker Radiation Laboratory, 1949-51; Los Alamos Scientific Laboratory (of University of California), Los Alamos, N.M., staff member of biomedical research

group, 1951-62; University of Minnesota, Minneapolis, associate professor of radiological health at School of Public Health, 1962-69, associate professor in department of obstetrics and gynecology, 1969—, director of Center for Population Studies, 1969—. *Military service:* U.S. Army, 1944-45.

MEMBER: American Association for the Advancement of Science (fellow), Radiation Research Society, Biophysical Society, Society for Experimental Biology and Medicine, American Society for Pharmacology and Experimental Therapeutics, American Public Health Association, Health Physics Society, American Physiological Society, Sigma Xi, Phi Lambda Upsilon.

WRITINGS: (Contributor) Behren, editor, *After the A Bomb,* Thomas Nelson, 1951; (contributor) J. M. Seven and L. A. Johnson, editors, *Metal-Binding in Medicine,* Lippincott, 1960; *Diagnosis and Treatment of Radioactive Poisoning,* International Atomic Energy Agency (Vienna), 1963; (editor) *Nuclear Power and the Public,* University of Minnesota Press, 1970; (contributor) *Handbuch der experimental Pharmakologie,* Springer-Verlag, 1970. Contributor of about forty articles to medical journals.

BIOGRAPHICAL/CRITICAL SOURCES: New York Times Book Review, March 14, 1971.

* * *

FOSTER, Don(ald) 1948-
(Dennis Saint-Eden)

PERSONAL: Born July 17, 1948, in Pilot Point, Tex.; son of Arthur A. and Ina (Fulenwieder) Foster. *Education:* North Texas State University, B.A., 1969. *Address:* Box 8867, NT Station, Denton, Tex. 76203.

*WRITINGS—*Poetry; under pseudonym Dennis Saint-Eden, except as indicated: *Three Poems,* Seven Flowers Press (Cleveland, Ohio), 1967; *Voyage thru Panhandle Street,* Tattoo Press (Glendale, Calif.), 1969; *Jewelry of the Finest Order: For Carol,* Ground Zero Press (Cleveland), 1969; *It's Too Soon to Know if We're Related,* Hors Commerce Press (Torrance, Calif.), 1970; (under name Don Foster) *Laugh,* Shroom Press (Cleveland), 1971; (under name Don Foster) *Southwest Varicose,* Thorp Springs Press (Berkeley, Calif.), 1977.

Poetry represented in *Neo Poetry Anthology 1,* Gato Magazine Press (Los Gatos, Calif.), 1967. Contributor of poetry to magazines, including *Tampa Poetry Review, South Florida Review, Black Sun, Premiere, Outcast, Encore, Descant, Invisible City, West Conscious Review, Wine Rings, Lowlands, Tawte, Forum, Poetry Quarterly,* and *Arx.*

* * *

FOSTER, John (Thomas) 1925-

PERSONAL: Born July 19, 1925, in Chicago, Ill.; son of George Peter (an attorney) and Helen (McLaughlin) Foster; married Elizabeth Rhodes, June 3, 1949; children: Carol W. Faulkner (stepdaughter), Norah S., John, Jr. *Education:* Attended University of Wisconsin, 1943; Florida Southern College, B.A., 1950; University of Florida, further study, 1950-51. *Home:* 4311 Alcove Ave., Studio City, Calif. 91604. *Agent:* Harold Matson Co., Inc., 22 East 40th St., New York, N.Y. 10016.

CAREER: Newspaper reporter in Lakeland, Fla., 1951-53, and Wilmington, N.C., 1953-55; *Dixie Roto,* New Orleans, La., staff writer and assistant editor, 1955-66; *Suffolk Sun,* Deer Park, N.Y., editor of *Dawn* (weekend magazine),

1966-68; Long Island University, Brookville, N.Y., assistant to director of public relations, 1968-70; New York Ocean Science Laboratory, Montauk, technical writer, 1970-75. *Military service:* U.S. Naval Reserve, active duty, 1943-46; served in the Pacific. *Awards, honors:* State (North Carolina) Associated Press award, 1954; Regional Associated Press award, 1965; National Alumni Association award, 1971.

WRITINGS: Rebel Sea Raider, Morrow, 1966; *Marco and the Tiger* (juvenile), Dodd, 1966; *Guadalcanal General,* Morrow, 1967; *Marco and the Sleuth Hound* (juvenile), Dodd, 1967; *Sir Francis Drake,* Garrard, 1967; *Southern Frontiersman: The Story of General Sam Dale,* Morrow, 1968; *Napoleon's Marshall,* Morrow, 1969; *Mississippi Wonderland,* Dodd, 1969; *General John J. Pershing,* Garrard, 1970; *Marco and That Curious Cat* (juvenile), Dodd, 1971; *The Hundred Days,* F. Watts, 1972; *Flight of the Lone Eagle,* F. Watts, 1974; *The Gallant Gray Trotter* (juvenile), Dodd, 1974; *The Sea Miners,* Hastings House, 1977. Contributor to national magazines in Canada, Europe, and the United States.

AVOCATIONAL INTERESTS: Travel, walking, swimming, rowing, reading, watching suspense films.

BIOGRAPHICAL/CRITICAL SOURCES: Christian Science Monitor, October 5, 1967; *New York Times Book Review,* November 5, 1967; *Book World,* November 9, 1969, Part II.

* * *

FOSTER, Lee Edwin   1943-

PERSONAL: Born July 23, 1943, in Omaha, Neb.; son of Russell G. (a manufacturer) and Nellie V. (Lyons) Foster. *Education:* University of Notre Dame, B.A. (summa cum laude), 1965; Stanford University, M.A., 1968. *Agent:* H. N. Swanson, Inc., 8523 Sunset Blvd., West Hollywood, Calif. 90069.

CAREER: Free-lance writer and photographer. *Awards, honors:* Woodrow Wilson fellowship, 1966.

WRITINGS: The Message of April Fools (novel), Pacific Coast Publishers, 1970; *Just Twenty-Five Cents and Three Wheaties Boxtops* (photo essay with text), Pacific Coast Publishers, 1970.

WORK IN PROGRESS: Mexico: The Devil's Pinata, with photographs; *Graeson's House,* a novel; text and photo travel books on China, Japan, and India.††

* * *

FOSTER, Ruel Elton   1916-

PERSONAL: Born November 30, 1916, in Springfield, Ky.; son of Ruel Elton (a banker) and Emily (Russell) Foster; married Margaret O'Connor, August 30, 1947; children: Russell, Alethaire, David, Emily, Robert, Paul. *Education:* University of Kentucky, A.B., 1938, M.A., 1939; Vanderbilt University, Ph.D., 1942. *Religion:* Roman Catholic. *Office:* Department of English, West Virginia University, Morgantown, W.Va. 26505.

CAREER: West Virginia University, Morgantown, instructor, 1941-46, assistant professor, 1946-52, associate professor, 1952-57, professor of English, 1957—, chairman of department, 1967, Benedum Professor of American Literature, 1974—. Associate professor of English, University of Mississippi, summers, 1949, 1951. *Military service:* U.S. Army, Corps of Engineers, 1942-45; became first lieutenant.

Member: International Association of University Professors of English, American Association of University Professors, Modern Language Association of America, Phi Beta Kappa. *Awards, honors:* Ford Foundation fellowship, 1952-53; West Virginia Foundation fellowship, 1960; University of West Virginia writing grant, 1965.

WRITINGS: (With O. J. Anderson) *Work in Progress: Practical Aids to Writing,* Lippincott, 1948; (with Harry M. Campbell) *William Faulkner: A Critical Appraisal,* University of Oklahoma Press, 1951; (with Campbell) *Elizabeth Madox Roberts: American Novelist,* University of Oklahoma Press, 1956; *Jesse Stuart,* Twayne, 1969. Contributor of articles, stories, and poems to literary quarterlies.

WORK IN PROGRESS: The Southern Literary Renaissance; The Keepers; an annotated edition of *The Whaling Logs of Joshua F. Beane; William Faulkner: A Paradigm of Religion in the South.*

* * *

FOULKES, Fred K.   1941-

PERSONAL: Born July 27, 1941; son of Clarence R. and Constance (Klee) Foulkes. *Education:* Princeton University, A.B., 1963; Harvard University, M.B.A., 1965, D.B.A., 1968. *Home:* 50 Follen St., Cambridge, Mass. 02138. *Office:* Graduate School of Business Administration, Harvard University, Boston, Mass. 02163.

CAREER: Chemical Bank New York Trust, New York, N.Y., trainee, 1963; Harvard University, Graduate School of Business Administration, Boston, Mass., research associate in business, 1966; Chrysler Corp., Detroit, Mich., labor relations staff, 1967; Harvard University, Graduate School of Business Administration, currently associate professor of business administration. *Member:* Industrial Relations Research Association, Phi Beta Kappa, Omicron Delta Epsilon.

WRITINGS: Creating More Meaningful Work, American Management Association, 1969; (contributor) Harold L. Sheppard and Neal Q. Herrick, editors, *Where Have All the Robots Gone?: Worker Dissatisfaction in the Seventies,* Free Press, 1972. Contributor to *Compton Yearbook,* 1974. Contributor of articles to *Harvard Business Review* and *Harvard Business School Bulletin.*

WORK IN PROGRESS: Research on job enrichment, personnel's changing role, career planning and development, and personnel practices of large, nonunion employers in the United States.

* * *

FOWLER, Don D.   1936-

PERSONAL: Born April 24, 1936, in Torrey, Utah; son of Eldon C. (a contractor) and Ruby (Noyes) Fowler; married Catherine Sweeney (a professor), June 14, 1964. *Education:* Attended Weber State College, 1954-55; University of Utah, B.A., 1959, graduate study, 1959-62; University of Pittsburgh, Ph.D., 1965. *Home:* 1010 Foothill Rd., Reno, Nev. 89511. *Office:* Desert Research Institute, University of Nevada, Reno, Nev. 89507.

CAREER: University of Pittsburgh, Pittsburgh, Pa., instructor in Evening Division, 1963; University of Nevada, Reno, instructor, 1964-65, assistant professor, 1965-67, associate professor of anthropology and executive director of Human Systems Center of Desert Research Institute, 1968-71, research professor, Desert Research Institute, 1972—, acting chairman of department of anthropology, 1966-67.

Visiting postdoctoral fellow, Smithsonian Institution, 1967-68. Has done field work with Glen Canyon Archaeological Salvage Project, 1957-62, with Shoshoni Indians, 1961, and in areas of Utah, Arizona, and Nevada, 1958-70. Member of advisory board, Regional Studies Center, College of Idaho, 1970—. Research associate, Smithsonian Institution, 1970—.

MEMBER: American Anthropological Association (fellow), Society for American Archaeology, American Society for Ethnohistory (review editor, 1967-71), Society for General Systems Research, Current Anthropology (associate), Southwestern Anthropological Association, Washington Anthropological Society, Sigma Xi. *Awards, honors:* Grants from Fleischmann Foundation, 1966-67, National Endowment for the Humanities, 1967, National Science Foundation, 1969, 1970, Wenner-Gren Foundation, 1970, and Office of Water Resources Research, 1970-71.

WRITINGS: (With Eliot Porter) *Down the Colorado: John Wesley Powell's Diary of the First Trip through the Grand Canyon,* Dutton, 1969; (with C. S. Fowler) *The Anthropology of the Numa: John Wesley Powell's Manuscripts on Great Basin Indians, 1868-1880,* Smithsonian Institution Press, 1971; *"Photographed All the Best Scenery": Jack Hillers' Diary of the Powell Expedition, 1871-1875,* University of Utah Press, 1971; *In a Sacred Manner We Live: Edward S. Curtis' Indian Photographs,* Barre Publishing, 1972. Contributor of about thirty articles to anthropology journals. Associate editor, *Northwestern Anthropological Research Notes,* 1966-71; book review editor, *Ethnohistory,* 1967-71; assistant editor for current research, *American Antiquity,* 1970-75.

WORK IN PROGRESS: John Wesley and the Bureau of American Ethnology; with J. F. Matley and R. H. Royak, *Material Culture of the Numa: The Powell Collection from Western North America,* for Smithsonian Institution; *Great Basin Indians,* for Knopf; *Jack Hillers, Photographer,* for University of Utah Press.

BIOGRAPHICAL/CRITICAL SOURCES: Christian Science Monitor, November 28, 1969.

* * *

FOX, Douglas McMurray 1940-

PERSONAL: Born May 2, 1940, in New London, Conn. *Education:* Yale University, B.A., 1962; Columbia University, Ph.D., 1968. *Home:* 4 Spruce Dr., Sandy Hook, Conn. 06482. *Office:* Department of Political Science, William Paterson College of New Jersey, Wayne, N.J. 07470.

CAREER: Pratt Institute, Brooklyn, N.Y., lecturer in sociology, 1964-66; Bowdoin College, Brunswick, Me., assistant professor of government, 1967-69; University of Connecticut, Storrs, assistant professor of political science, 1970-74; William Paterson College of New Jersey, Wayne, associate professor of political science, 1974—. *Member:* National Center for Public Service Tutorships, American Society for Public Administration. *Awards, honors:* National Center for Education in Politics fellow in urban government, 1965-66; National Water Resources Council grant, 1971.

WRITINGS: The Politics of U.S. Foreign Policy-Making, Goodyear Publishing, 1971; *The New Urban Politics: Cities and the Federal Government,* Goodyear Publishing, 1972; *The Politics of City and State Bureaucracy,* Goodyear Publishing, 1974; *Eighty Thousand Governments,* Allyn & Bacon, 1977. Contributor of about twenty articles to political science and public administration journals.

WORK IN PROGRESS: A book on results-oriented public management.

* * *

FOX, Milton S. 1904-1971

1904—October 25, 1971; American editor, painter, and author of texts for art books. Obituaries: *New York Times,* October 26, 1971; *Washington Post,* October 28, 1971; *Publishers Weekly,* November 1, 1971.

* * *

FRANCE, Beulah Sanford 1891-1971

October 18, 1891—December 29, 1971; American health educator and author of books on child care. Obituaries: *New York Times,* January 1, 1972.

* * *

FRANCK, Thomas M. 1931-

PERSONAL: Born July 14, 1931, in Berlin, Germany; became Canadian citizen. *Education:* University of British Columbia, B.A., 1952, LL.B., 1953; Harvard University, LL.M., 1954, S.J.D., 1959. *Home:* 15 Charlton St., New York, N.Y. 10014. *Office:* Center for International Studies, School of Law, New York University, 40 Washington Sq. S., Room 440, New York, N.Y. 10012.

CAREER: University of Nebraska at Lincoln, assistant professor of law, 1954-56; New York University, New York, N.Y., associate professor, 1960-62, professor of law, 1962—, director of Center for International Studies, 1965—. Visiting professor, Stanford University, 1963; visiting summer lecturer, University of East Africa, 1963-66. Member, Sierra Leone Commission on Legal Education; director, International Law Program. Consultant to U.S. Department of State, 1970—, and to governments of Tanganyika, Zanzibar, Kenya, and Mauritius. Member of advisory committee, Carnegie Endowment for International Peace; member of advisory council, U.S. Institute of Human Rights. *Military service:* Canadian Army, 1950-53; became lieutenant.

MEMBER: American Society of International Law (member of executive committee), International Law Association, American Bar Association, American Foreign Law Association, International Studies Association, International League for the Rights of Man (member of board of directors), African Law Association in America (director, 1970-73).

WRITINGS: Race and Nationalism, Fordham University Press, 1960; (with John Carey) *The Role of the United Nations in the Congo,* Praeger, 1963; *East African Unity through Law,* Yale University Press, 1964; (with others) *African Law,* Praeger, 1964; *Comparative Constitutional Process: Cases and Materials,* Praeger, 1968; *The Structure of Impartiality,* Macmillan, 1968; (editor with Edward Weisband and contributor) *A Free Trade Association,* New York University Press, 1968; (editor and contributor) *Why Federations Fail,* New York University Press, 1968; (with Weisband) *Word Politics: Verbal Strategy among the Superpowers,* Oxford University Press, 1971; (with Weisband) *Resignation in Protest,* Viking, 1975. Also author of *Conflict and Subjectivity.* Contributor to *African Forum, Banker,* and legal periodicals.

* * *

FRANKEL, Sandor 1943-

PERSONAL: Born November 16, 1943, in New York,

N.Y.; son of David and Bessie (Fishman) Frankel. *Education:* New York University, B.A., 1964; Harvard University, LL.B., 1967. *Office:* 225 Broadway, New York, N.Y. 10007.

CAREER: Admitted to the Bar of the State of New York, 1967, and the Bar of the District of Columbia, 1968; assistant United States Attorney for the District of Columbia, 1968-71; attorney in private practice, 1971—. Member, White House Task Force on Crime, 1967; counsel, National Commission on Reform of Federal Criminal Laws, 1968. *Member:* Phi Beta Kappa.

WRITINGS: Beyond a Reasonable Doubt, Stein & Day, 1971.

*   *   *

FRANKLIN, Billy J(oe)   1940-

PERSONAL: Born January 30, 1940, in Honey Grove, Tex.; son of John Asia (a farmer) and Annie Mae (Castle) Franklin; married Sonya Kay Erwin, June 1, 1958; children: Terry Daylon, Shari Dea. *Education:* Attended East Texas State University, 1958-60; University of Texas at Austin, B.A., 1965, M.A., 1967, Ph.D., 1969. *Home:* 1528 Walnut, Nacogdoches, Tex. 75961. *Office:* Office of Academic Affairs, Stephen F. Austin State University, Nacogdoches, Tex. 75961.

CAREER: Baylor University, Waco, Tex., assistant professor of sociology, 1968-69; University of Iowa, Iowa City, assistant professor of sociology, 1969-71; Western Carolina University, Cullowhee, N.C., associate professor of sociology and chairman of department of sociology and anthropology, 1971-73; Wright State University, Dayton, Ohio, professor of sociology and chairman of department of sociology, anthropology, and social work, 1973-75; Southwest Texas State University, San Marcos, professor of sociology and dean of school of liberal arts, 1975-77; Stephen F. Austin State University, Nacogdoches, Tex., vice-president for academic affairs, 1977—. *Member:* American Sociological Association, American Association of Higher Education, Southwest Social Science Association, Southwest Sociological Association, Southern Sociological Society, Texas Academy of Science.

WRITINGS: (With Harold Osborne) *Research Methods: Issues and Insights,* Wadsworth, 1971; (with Frank Kohout) *Social Psychology and Everyday Life,* McKay, 1973. Contributor to *Journal of Health and Social Behavior, Journal of Psychology, Sociometry, Sociological Quarterly, Social Forces, Journal of Social Psychology,* and other journals.

WORK IN PROGRESS: A series of manuscripts concerning interpersonal attraction.

AVOCATIONAL INTERESTS: Reading modern fiction, refinishing old furniture, hiking, fishing, gardening, collecting antique clocks.

*   *   *

FRASE, Robert W(illiam)   1912-

PERSONAL: Born January 1, 1912, in Chicago, Ill.; son of Otto Paul and Lillian (Jones) Frase; married Eleanor Stockwell (an economist), June 10, 1939; children: Mary (Mrs. Raymond S. Williams), Richard Stockwell, Katharine Gordon. *Education:* University of Wisconsin, A.B., 1934; Harvard University, A.M., 1944. *Religion:* Protestant. *Home:* 6718 Montour Dr., Falls Church, Va. 22043. *Office:* National Commission on New Technological Uses of Copyrighted Works, Washington, D.C. 20558.

CAREER: Social Science Research Council, Washington, D.C., staff member, 1934-36; U.S. Government, Washington, D.C., economist in Department of Labor, 1938-40, economist in Department of Agriculture, 1940-42, economist for U.S. War Relocation Authority, 1942-43, special assistant to secretary of commerce, 1945-50; American Book Publishers Council, Washington, D.C., economist and associate managing director, 1950-60; joint office of American Book Publishers Council and American Educational Publishers Institute, Washington, D.C., director and economist, 1960-70; Association of American Publishers, Washington, D.C., vice-president and economist, 1970-72; consulting economist, 1972-75; National Commission on New Technological Uses of Copyrighted Works, Washington, D.C., assistant executive director and economist, 1975—. *Military service:* U.S. Army, Military Intelligence Service, 1943-45; became first lieutenant. *Member:* Phi Beta Kappa, Cosmos Club. *Awards, honors:* Guggenheim fellowship, 1948-49.

WRITINGS: (With H. Guinzburg and T. Waller) *Books and the Mass Market,* University of Illinois Press, 1953; (with Charles McKinley) *Launching Social Security,* University of Wisconsin Press, 1970; (with others) *Book Publishing in the U.S.S.R.,* Harvard University Press, 1971; *Library Funding and Public Support,* American Library Association, 1973. Contributor to professional journals, encyclopedias, and yearbooks.

WORK IN PROGRESS: Economics of publishing.

*   *   *

FRASER, Arvonne S.   1925-

PERSONAL: Born September 1, 1925, in Lamberton, Minn.; daughter of Orland D. (a farmer) and Phyllis (DuFrene) Skelton; married Donald M. Fraser (a U.S. congressman), June 30, 1950; children: Thomas, Mary Mac, John, Lois, Anne (deceased), Jean. *Education:* University of Minnesota, B.A., 1948; George Washington University, graduate study. *Politics:* Democratic-Farmer-Labor Party of Minnesota. *Home:* 1253 Fourth St. S.W., Washington, D.C. 20024. *Office:* Women-in-Development, Agency for International Development, Washington, D.C. 20523.

CAREER: Democratic-Farmer-Labor Party, Minneapolis, Minn., secretary to chairman, 1949-51, state vice-chairman, 1956-62; Minnesota Citizens for Kennedy, assistant manager, 1960; volunteer staff assistant in office of her congressman-husband, Washington, D.C., 1963-76; Agency for International Development, Washington, D.C., coordinator of Women-in-Development, 1977—. Campaign manager, Fraser for Congress Committee, 1972-76; coordinator, Upper Great Lakes Region, Carter/Mondale presidential campaign, 1976. Member of New York advisory board, Alan Guttmacher Institute, 1973-77; member of board, Washington Opportunities for Women. President, Advise and Consult, Inc. *Member:* Women's Equity Action League (vice-president, 1971; national president, 1972-74; treasurer of educational and legal defense fund, 1974-77), Women's Rights Task Force (former chairperson), National Leadership Conference on Civil Rights (member of executive committee, 1977—), National Organization for Women, Nameless Sisterhood of Washington, Democratic Congressional Wives Forum (past secretary).

WRITINGS: Government: Looking Forward to a Career, Dillon, 1970, 2nd edition, 1975; *Secretarial Work: Looking Forward to a Career,* Dillon, 1974. Contributor to *Minnesota Women,* 1977. Contributor to political and other periodicals.

WORK IN PROGRESS: Biographies of La Donna Harris, Indian leader, and Lucy Stone, feminist orator; a juvenile biography of Virginia Woolf.

*   *   *

FRASER, Peter (Shaw) 1932-

PERSONAL: Born March 31, 1932, in Aberdeenshire, Scotland; son of Allan Henry Hector (a writer and agricultural scientist) and Wilhelmine (Shaw) Fraser. *Education:* Glasgow School of Art, Diploma, 1955; St. Andrews School of Occupational Therapy, Diploma, 1960. *Politics:* "Nothing constant, mainly Conservative." *Religion:* Anglican. *Home and office:* 10 Kings Cross Ter., Aberdeen AB2 4BF, Scotland.

CAREER: St. Crispins Hospital, Northampton, England, occupational therapist, 1961-63; St. Andrews Hospital, Northampton, art therapist, 1964-68; Royal Cornhill Hospital, Aberdeen, Scotland, part-time occupational therapist, 1970—; writer and illustrator.

WRITINGS: (Illustrator) W. D. Simpson, *Castles in Britain,* Hastings House, 1966; (self-illustrated) *Introducing Puppetry,* Watson-Guptill, 1968, 2nd edition, 1969; (self-illustrated) *Punch and Judy,* Van Nostrand, 1970; (self-illustrated) *Puppet Circus,* Batsford, 1971. Contributor to art journals.

AVOCATIONAL INTERESTS: Swimming, the outdoors, collecting early English watercolors.

BIOGRAPHICAL/CRITICAL SOURCES: Punch, July 1, 1970.

*   *   *

FRAZIER, Thomas R(ichard) 1931-

PERSONAL: Born May 4, 1931, in Memphis, Tenn.; son of Walter A. (a salesman) and Mildred (Laughter) Frazier; married Marion Goldberg, February 29, 1964; children: Marc, Dawn. *Education:* Baylor University, B.A., 1952; Southern Methodist University, M.A., 1953; Southeastern Baptist Theological Seminary, B.D., 1956; Columbia University, Ph.D., 1967. *Home:* 452 Riverside Dr., Apt. 56, New York, N.Y. 10027. *Office:* Department of History, Bernard M. Baruch College of the City University of New York, 17 Lexington Ave., New York, N.Y. 10010.

CAREER: University of Massachusetts—Amherst, resident theologian, 1963-65; New York Institute of Technology, New York City, assistant professor of history, 1965-67; Queensborough Community College of the City University of New York, Bayside, N.Y., assistant professor of history, 1967-68; Bernard M. Baruch College of the City University of New York, New York City, assistant professor, 1968-72, associate professor, 1972-76, professor of history, 1977—. *Military service:* U.S. Army, 1956-58. *Member:* American Historical Association, American Studies Association, Organization of American Historians, American Academy of Religion.

WRITINGS: (Editor) *Afro-American History: Primary Sources,* Harcourt, 1970; (editor) *The Underside of American History: Other Readings,* two volumes, Harcourt, 1971; (editor) *The Private Side of American History: Readings in Everyday Life,* Volume II: *Since 1865,* Harcourt, 1975.

*   *   *

FREDEMAN, William E(van) 1928-

PERSONAL: Born July 19, 1928, in Pine Bluff, Ark.; be-

came Canadian citizen in 1969; son of Frank Henry (a U.S. Army officer) and Lucille A. (Griffiths) Fredeman; married E. Jane Cowan, April 25, 1964; children: Robert Luke. *Education:* Hendrix College, B.A., 1948; University of Oklahoma, M.A., 1950, Ph.D., 1956. *Home:* 1649 Allison Rd., Vancouver, British Columbia, Canada. *Office:* Department of English, University of British Columbia, Vancouver, British Columbia, Canada.

CAREER: High school teacher in Oklahoma City, Okla., 1948-53; University of British Columbia, Vancouver, instructor, 1956-58, assistant professor, 1958-63, associate professor, 1963-67, professor of English, 1967—. *Military service:* U.S. Naval Reserve, active duty, 1945-46. U.S. Army Reserve, 1949-57; became first lieutenant. *Member:* International Association of University Professors of English, Royal Society of Canada (fellow), Royal Society of Literature (fellow), Modern Language Association of America, Bibliographical Society, Research Society for Victorian Periodicals (vice-president, 1968-70), Canadian Association of University Teachers, Association of Canadian University Teachers of English. *Awards, honors:* Canada Council research fellowships, 1959-60, 1971-72; Guggenheim fellowships, 1965-66, 1972-73; Killam senior research fellowship, 1971-72.

WRITINGS: Pre-Raphaelitism: A Bibliocritical Study, Harvard University Press, 1965; *A Pre-Raphaelite Gazette: The Penkill Letters of Arthur Hughes to William Bell Scott and Alice Boyd,* John Rylands Library, 1967; (contributor) F. E. Faverty, editor, *The Victorian Poets,* 2nd edition, Harvard University Press, 1968; *Prelude to the Last Decade: Dante Gabriel Rossetti in the Summer of 1872,* John Rylands Library, 1971; (editor) W. M. Rossetti, *The PRB Journal: W. M. Rossetti's Diary of the Pre-Raphaelite Brotherhood,* Clarendon Press, 1975; (editor) W. B. Scott, *The Letters of Pictor Ignotus: W. B. Scott's Correspondence with Alice Boyd,* John Rylands Library, 1976. Contributor to *Victorian Studies, Victorian Poetry, University of Toronto Quarterly, Studies in Bibliography, Times Literary Supplement, Bulletin of the John Rylands Library,* and other literary periodicals.

WORK IN PROGRESS: Editing the letters of Dante Gabriel Rossetti, for Clarendon Press.

AVOCATIONAL INTERESTS: Collecting books.

*   *   *

FREDENBURGH, Franz A(lvah) 1906-

PERSONAL: Born November 18, 1906, in Syracuse, N.Y.; son of Alvah C. (a teacher of piano and pipe organ) and Jennie (Blessing) Fredenburgh. *Education:* University of Oklahoma, B.A., 1935; New York University, M.A., 1936, Ph.D., 1939; State University College of Education (now State University of New York at Albany), postdoctoral study, 1959. *Home:* 4115 Poinciana Ave., Miami, Fla. 33133. *Office:* Department of Psychology, Miami-Dade Community College, Miami, Fla. 33156.

CAREER: Director of guidance at public schools in Bellmore, N.Y., 1939-40, and Hudson, N.Y., 1940-42; War Manpower Commission, placement officer and classification analyst in New York City, and Washington, D.C., 1942-43; Gimbel Brothers, Philadelphia, Pa., personnel director, 1943-44; Loft Candy Corp., Long Island City, N.Y., director of industrial relations, 1944-46; Quinnipiac College, Junior College Division, New Haven, Conn., professor of psychology and dean of faculty, 1947-49; Great American Group of Insurance Companies, New York City, personnel director, 1949-57; Duchess County Board of Cooperative Educational Services, Milbrook, N.Y., school psychologist, 1959-60; Duchess Community College, Poughkeepsie, N.Y., lecturer, 1960-61, professor of psychology and coordinator for behavioral sciences, 1961-66; Miami-Dade Community College, South Campus, Miami, Fla., professor of psychology, 1966—, chairman of department of psychology and education, 1966-70. Visiting professor at New York College for Teachers (now State University of New York at Albany), summers, 1940-41, and University of New Hampshire, summer, 1960. Director, Institute for Human Development, Miami, 1973—; president, Scholarships Unlimited, Inc., Miami, 1976—. Certified psychologist, New York State and Florida. *Member:* American Psychological Association, Southeastern Psychological Association, Florida Psychological Association.

WRITINGS: The Psychology of Personality and Adjustment, with teacher's guide and workbook, Cummings, 1971; *Exploring Human Behavior: An Introduction to Psychology,* with teacher's guide and workbook, Wiley, 1973. Also author of other course materials for Duchess Community College and Hudson (N.Y.) schools and a series of career monographs. Contributor to personnel, psychology, and education journals.

SIDELIGHTS: Franz Fredenburgh told *CA:* "Teaching psychology in an 'open-door' community college where students from all sectors of society find their way into college classes made me realize that few textbook writers address themselves to the student whose vocabulary is limited and reading level minimal. I developed my texts with the student's limitations in mind. The workbooks reinforce and synthesize chapter content through programmed instructional materials and self-quizzes. What has been most gratifying has been the highly favorable feedback from students who have found these materials helpful. My advise to aspiring college textbook writers is to write for the student rather than to the teacher who will adopt the book. Adoptions will automatically follow a student-oriented book."

* * *

FREEDMAN, Robert Owen 1941-

PERSONAL: Born April 18, 1941, in Philadelphia, Pa.; son of Clarence (a lawyer) and Anne (Stone) Freedman; married Sharon Center (a teacher), March 12, 1965; children: Debby, David. *Education:* University of Pennsylvania, B.A. (with honors), 1962; Columbia University, M.A., 1965, Certificate of Russian Institute, 1965, Ph.D., 1969. *Home:* 2525 Farringdon Rd., Baltimore, Md. 21209. *Office:* Graduate Department, Baltimore Hebrew College, 5800 Park Heights Ave., Baltimore, Md. 21215.

CAREER: U.S. Army, 1965-70, became captain; U.S. Military Academy, West Point, N.Y., member of faculty, 1967-70; Marquette University, Milwaukee, Wis., assistant professor of political science, beginning 1970; currently professor of political science and dean of Peggy Meyerhoff Pearlstone School of Graduate Studies, Baltimore Hebrew College, Baltimore, Md. *Member:* American Association for the Advancement of Slavic Studies, American Political Science Association, American Association of University Professors, International Studies Association, Middle East Institute, Political Science Honor Society, Social Science Honor Society. *Awards, honors:* National Endowment for the Humanities fellowship, 1971, for research in Zionist Archives, Jerusalem.

WRITINGS: Economic Warfare in the Communist Bloc: A Study of Soviet Economic Pressure against Yugoslavia, Albania, and Communist China, Praeger, 1970; *Soviet Policy toward the Middle East since 1970,* Praeger, 1975.

Contributor: Mark Tessler, editor, *A New Look at the Middle East,* Institute of World Affairs, University of Wisconsin—Milwaukee, 1971; Thomas Hachey, editor, *The Problem of Partition: Peril to World Peace,* Rand McNally, 1972; Norton T. Dodge, editor, *The Soviets in Asia,* Cremona Foundation, 1972; Michael McGwire, editor, *Soviet Naval Policy: Objectives and Constraints,* Praeger, 1975; Roger Kanet and Donna Bahry, editor, *Soviet Economic and Political Relations with the Developing World,* Praeger, 1975; Yonah Alexander, editor, *International Terrorism: National, Regional and Global Perspectives,* Praeger, 1976; Naiem Sherbiny and Tessler, editors, *Arab Oil: Impact on Arab Nations and Global Implications,* Praeger, 1976.

Contributor of articles and book reviews to *Middle East Review, Middle East, Naval War College Review, Soviet Union, Perspective,* and *American Political Science Review.*

WORK IN PROGRESS: Soviet-American Relations in the Nixon Years.

* * *

FREEMAN, Walter (Jackson, Jr.) 1895-1972

November 14, 1895—May 31, 1972; American neurologist. Obituaries: *Washington Post,* June 1, 1972. (See index for *CA* sketch)

* * *

FREY, Henry A. 1923-

PERSONAL: Surname rhymes with "pie"; born June 11, 1923, in Saranac Lake, N.Y.; son of Arthur Jensen (a college business manager) and Margaret (Johnson) Frey; married Iris Frey, November 26, 1959; children: Daniel, Marcus, Michael. *Education:* Harvard University, B.A., 1945, M.A., 1946. *Politics:* Independent. *Religion:* None. *Home:* Goldhaldenstrasse 20a, Zollikon, Zurich, Switzerland 8702.

CAREER: Princeton University, Princeton, N.J., instructor in English, 1947-48; Tufts University, Medford, Mass., instructor in English, 1948-51; University of Lille, Lille, France, lecturer, 1951-52; Hull's School of English, Zurich, Switzerland, teacher of English as a foreign language, 1955—. Translator. *Military service:* U.S. Navy, 1943-44.

WRITINGS—Translator from the German: (With Cedric Wayland) Emil Egli and Emil Schulthess, *The Amazon: A Photographic Survey,* Simon & Schuster, 1962; Thomas Schmid and Carlo Testa, *Systems Building,* Artemis (Zurich), 1969; Willy Boesiger, editor, *Le Corbusier: The Last Works,* Artemis, 1970; Udo Kultermann, editor, *Kenzo Tange 1946-1969,* Artemis, 1970; Karl Fleig, editor, *Alvar Aalto,* Volume II: *1963-1970,* Artemis, 1971.

AVOCATIONAL INTERESTS: Archaeology, history of religion, anthropology.

* * *

FRIED, John J(ames) 1940-

PERSONAL: Surname is pronounced freed; born November 3, 1940, in Quito, Ecuador; came to United States in 1950, naturalized in 1956; son of Philip and Jeanette (Rosenheck) Fried; married Christiane Hommey, September 8, 1968. *Education:* University of Michigan, M.A., 1961; Columbia University, M.S., 1963. *Home:* 1206 Alvira, Los Angeles, Calif. 90035. *Agent:* Julian Bach, 3 East 48th St., New York, N.Y. 10017.

CAREER: Formerly employed as reporter for *Detroit News,* United Press International, and *Life;* now free-lance writer.

WRITINGS: The Mystery of Heredity, John Day, 1971; *Vasectomy: Truth and Consequences,* Saturday Review Press, 1972; *Life along the San Andreas Fault,* Saturday Review Press, 1973; (with E. B. Dietrich) *Code Arrest: A Heart Stops,* Saturday Review Press, 1974; (editor) Howard Wilcox, *Hothouse Earth,* Praeger, 1975; (with Lucas Yanker) *Animal Doctor,* Saturday Review Press, 1976. Contributor to *New Leader, New Republic, Sports Illustrated, Reader's Digest, New York Times Sunday Magazine, Playgirl,* and *Free Enterprise.*

*   *   *

FRIEDMANN, Yohanan 1936-

PERSONAL: Born March 28, 1936, in Zakamenne, Czechoslovakia; son of Moshe (a physician) and Jolana (Klein) Friedmann; married Zafrira Schmidt, October 3, 1968; children: Jasmin, Tamar. *Education:* Hebrew University of Jerusalem, B.A., M.A.; McGill University, Ph.D., 1966. *Religion:* Jewish. *Home:* 115 Uziel, Jerusalem, Israel. *Office:* Hebrew University of Jerusalem, Givat-Ram, Jerusalem, Israel.

CAREER: Hebrew University of Jerusalem, Jerusalem, Israel, presently senior lecturer.

WRITINGS: Shaykh Ahmad Sirhindi, McGill University Press, 1971.

WORK IN PROGRESS: A history of Islam in India and Pakistan.

*   *   *

FRIMMER, Steven 1928-

PERSONAL: Born June 29, 1928, in New York, N.Y.; son of Isidore (a psychiatrist) and Grace (Lipsky) Frimmer; married Barbara Meyers (a speech therapist), June 29, 1952; children: Erica, Andrea, Eliza. *Education:* New York University, B.A., 1950, M.A., 1951. *Home:* 255 Overpeck Ave., Ridgefield Park, N.J. 07660. *Agent:* Joan Korman Raines, 475 Fifth Ave., New York, N.Y. 10017. *Office: Reader's Digest,* 200 Park Ave., New York, N.Y. 10017.

CAREER: Marboro Book Club, New York City, editor, 1959-63; Mid-Century Book Society, New York City, editor, 1963; G. P. Putnam's Sons, New York City, managing editor, 1963-69; McCall Books, New York City, managing editor, 1969-71; Saturday Review Book Club, New York City, editor, 1971-73; Reader's Digest Press, New York City, senior editor, 1973—.

WRITINGS: The Stone That Spoke, Putnam, 1969; *Finding the Forgotten,* Putnam, 1971; *Neverland,* Viking, 1976.

*   *   *

FRISCH, Morton J. 1923-

PERSONAL: Born January 26, 1923, in Chicago, Ill.; son of Harry I. and Gertrude (Glicksman) Frisch; married Joelyn Saltzman, February 20, 1949; children: Hollis, Mark, Seth. *Education:* Roosevelt University, B.A., 1949; University of Chicago, M.A., 1949; Pennsylvania State University, Ph.D., 1953. *Home:* 1626 Schifly Lane, DeKalb, Ill. 60115.

Office: Department of Political Science, Northern Illinois University, DeKalb, Ill. 60115.

CAREER: College of William and Mary, Williamsburg, Va., assistant professor, 1953-61, associate professor of government, 1961-64; Northern Illinois University, DeKalb, associate professor, 1964-66, professor of political science, 1966—. Fulbright professor of political science, University of Stockholm, 1963-64. *Military service:* U.S. Army, 1943-46; received Belgian Croix de Guerre. *Member:* American Political Science Association, Midwest Political Science Association.

WRITINGS: (Editor with Martin Diamond) *The Thirties: A Reconsideration in the Light of the American Political Tradition,* Northern Illinois University Press, 1968; (editor with Richard G. Stevens) *American Political Thought: The Philosophic Dimension of American Statesmanship,* Scribner, 1971; (compiler with Stevens) *The Political Thought of American Statesmen: Selected Writings and Speeches,* F. E. Peacock, 1973; *Franklin D. Roosevelt: The Contribution of the New Deal to American Political Thought and Practice,* Twayne, 1975. Contributor to political science and popular journals, including *Ethics, New Republic, Cambridge Journal, Journal of Politics,* and *Review of Politics.*†

*   *   *

FRITSCHLER, A. Lee 1937-

PERSONAL: Born May 5, 1937, in Schenectady, N.Y.; son of George A. (a civil servant) and Jane (Green) Fritschler; married Aliceann Wohlbruck (a consultant), November 2, 1961; children: Craig A., Eric G. *Education:* Union College, Schenectady, N.Y., B.A., 1959; Syracuse University, M.P.A., 1960, Ph.D., 1965. *Home:* 5534 Nevada Ave. N.W., Washington, D.C. 20015. *Office:* Department of Government, American University, Washington, D.C. 20016.

CAREER: American University, Washington, D.C., assistant professor, 1964-68, associate professor of government and public administration, 1968—, director of public administration programs, 1971—.

WRITINGS: Smoking and Politics: Policymaking in the Federal Bureaucracy, Appleton, 1969, 2nd edition, Prentice-Hall, 1975. Contributor to professional journals.

WORK IN PROGRESS: The Politics of Intergovernmental Relations, with Morley Segal, for Chandler Publishing.

*   *   *

FROST, Peter Kip 1936-

PERSONAL: Born September 26, 1936, in Boston, Mass.; son of Horace Weir (an investment broker) and Mildred (Kip) Frost; married Margaret Parsons, June 16, 1965; children: Jonathan, Michael, Rufus. *Education:* Harvard University, B.A., 1958, M.A., 1962, Ph.D., 1966. *Office:* Department of History, Williams College, Williamstown, Mass. 01267.

CAREER: Williams College, Williamstown, Mass., instructor, 1964-66, assistant professor, 1966-72, associate professor of history, 1972—, associate dean of administration, 1969-72. Director, Williams-in-Hong Kong; trustee, Lingnan College, Hong Kong. *Member:* Signet Society (Harvard University).

WRITINGS: The Bakumatsu Currency Crisis (originally announced as *Coinage Problems of the Late Tokugawa Period*), Harvard University Press, 1970; *Golden Age of China and Japan,* C. E. Merrill, 1971; *China and Japan in the Modern World,* C. E. Merrill, 1972.

WORK IN PROGRESS: A book, *Education in Japan.*†

*   *   *

FROST, Richard 1929-

PERSONAL: Born April 8, 1929, in Palo Alto, Calif.; son of Willis George (a civil engineer) and Ruth (Kettlewell) Frost; married Frances Atkins, September 2, 1951; married second wife, Carol Kydd (a poet and teacher), August 23, 1969; children: (first marriage) Robert Willis, Diana Ruth, Catherine Patricia; (second marriage) Daniel Adam, Joel Richard. *Education:* San Jose State College (now University), A.B., 1951, M.A., 1957. *Religion:* None. *Home address:* R.D. 2, Box 73, Otego, N.Y. 13825. *Office:* Department of English, State University of New York College at Oneonta, Oneonta, N.Y. 13820.

CAREER: Employed as a laborer, chainman on a survey party, jazz drummer, clothing salesman, and opinion poll taker, prior to 1956; San Jose State College (now University), San Jose, Calif., instructor in English, 1956-57; Towson State College, Towson, Md., instructor in English, 1957-59; State University of New York College at Oneonta, assistant professor, 1959-64, associate professor, 1964-71, professor of English, 1971—. *Awards, honors:* Danforth grant, 1961; State University of New York summer writing fellowship, 1966, 1968, 1969, 1972, 1976.

WRITINGS: The Circus Villains (poems), Ohio University Press, 1965; *Getting Drunk with the Birds* (poems), Ohio University Press, 1971. Contributor of poetry to *Harper's, Poetry, Sewanee Review, Carleton Miscellany, Beloit Poetry Journal, New York Times, Prairie Schooner, Paris Review, Massachusetts Review, Poetry Northwest, Esquire, Southern Poetry Review, Southwest Review, Colorado Quarterly, Minnesota Review, Literary Review, Tri-Quarterly,* and other publications. Poetry editor, *Satire Newsletter,* 1964-74.

WORK IN PROGRESS: Another collection of poems.

SIDELIGHTS: Richard Frost told *CA:* "Sometime very early I got the idea that writing poetry was heroic: my brother, Jack, fifteen years older, was a sailor and a poet and of course my standard of manly accomplishment. By the time I learned that poetry was generally ignored and without financial profit, I was too far committed to it to know how to stop. Now I can only wonder why I write. The urge to fill blank pages with lines of my own words is as insistent as sex or eating—I can glorify it with no terms such as 'rage for order.' I often hate and fear it—I find it terribly necessary and satisfying. Occasionally I get the same sort of pleasure, or part of it, building a chair or some shelves; but nothing works as well for me as a new poem. Then I am just right, for a while, until I know it is time to write another." A collection of Frost's papers is in the Boston University Library.

*   *   *

FRUEHLING, Rosemary T(herese) 1933-

PERSONAL: Born January 23, 1933, in Gilbert, Minn.; daughter of John C. (a restaurant owner) and Mary (Scalise) Juiffre; married Donald L. Fruehling (executive vice-president of McGraw-Hill Book Co.), July 23, 1969; children: Shirley. *Education:* Virginia Junior College, A.A., 1952; University of Minnesota, B.S., 1954, M.A., 1968, Ph.D., 1977. *Politics:* Registered Republican. *Religion:* Catholic. *Home:* 6 Raleigh Ct., Morristown, N.J. 07960.

CAREER: Business teacher in high schools in Red Wing, Minneapolis, and Hopkins, Minn., 1954-65; St. Louis Park High School, St. Louis Park, Minn., teacher-coordinator of business, 1965-69; County College of Morris, Dover, N.J., associate professor of secretarial science, 1969-76; currently adjunct professor at University of Minnesota. Author, lecturer, and educational consultant for McGraw-Hill Book Co., Gregg Division, 1967—; educational consultant, Warner-Lambert Pharmaceutical Co., 1971, Jersey Central Power and Light. Member of board of directors, Vocational Youth Camps, State Department of Education, St. Paul, Minn.; member of New Jersey Career Education Advisory Council. *Member:* International Platform Association, National Business Education Association, American Vocation Association, Office Education Association (executive director), New Jersey Office Coordinator's Association, Delta Pi Epsilon. *Awards, honors:* Award for distinguished service to business education in Minnesota, 1967; Distinguished Citation award, National Office Education Association, 1969; Distinguished Service Award, Minnesota Office Education Association, 1977.

WRITINGS: (With S. Bouchard) *Business Correspondence Thirty,* with teacher's manual and key, McGraw, 1971, 2nd edition, 1976; *Tapes for Typing 75,* McGraw, 1971; (with Bouchard) *The Art of Writing Effective Letters,* McGraw, 1972; (with Roy Poe) *Case Study Approach to Letter Writing,* McGraw, 1972; (with Poe) *Business Communication: A Problem-Solving Approach,* McGraw, 1973, revised edition, edited by Joseph Tinervia, 1978; (with W. Porter Swift) *Psychology, Human Relations and Motivation,* 5th edition, McGraw, 1974; (editor with Edwin L. Herr) *Working at Human Relations,* with teacher's manual and key, McGraw, 1977; (with Peres) *Human Relations for the Office Worker,* McGraw, in press. Contributor to *Business Education World, NBEA Forum,* and *Today's Secretary.*

*   *   *

FRYKMAN, John H(arvey) 1932-

PERSONAL: First syllable of surname rhymes with "lick"; born April 19, 1932, in Boston, Mass.; son of Albion Helmer (a carpenter) and Ruth Maria Elizabeth (Kindberg) Frykman; married Nancy Alice Willock (a bookkeeper), June 7, 1957; married second wife, Cheryl Corinne Arnold (a teacher), December 22, 1968; children: (first marriage) Kristin Linnea, Lars Andrew, Erik John. *Education:* Attended University of Massachusetts, 1950-51; Wentworth Institute, Boston, Certificate in Architectural Construction, 1955; Bethany College, Lindsborg, Kan., B.A., 1957; Lutheran Theological Seminary, Philadelphia, M.Div., 1960; further training at University of California Medical Center, San Francisco, 1968-69, and Mental Research Institute, Palo Alto, 1970-71. *Office:* Cypress Institute, 24730 Lower Trail, Carmel, Calif. 93923.

CAREER: Part-time work while student included dairy hand, janitor, singer with jazz combo, and carpenter; ordained to Lutheran ministry, 1960; associate pastor of church in Sacramento, Calif., 1960-62; pastor of church in Oakland, Calif., 1962-68; Haight-Ashbury Medical Clinic, San Francisco, Calif., director of drug treatment program, 1968-70; Carmel Unified School District, Carmel, Calif., community counselor, 1970-72; Cypress Institute, Carmel, president and executive director, 1972—. Instructor in departments of criminology, sociology, and education, University of California Extension, 1970-74; associate staff member of National Drug Abuse Training Center, California State University, Hayward, 1970—. Consultant to Youth Office,

City of Oslo, Norway, 1971. *Military service:* U.S. Army, 1952-54; served in Korea. California Army National Guard, chaplain, 1964-67.

WRITINGS: It's Happening (poems), C/J Press (Oakland, Calif.), 1967; *A New Connection: An Approach to Compulsive Drug Users,* C/J Press, 1970, revised and enlarged edition, Scrimshaw Press (San Francisco), 1971; *Teenage Survival Handbook,* Palo Colorado Press, 1978. Contributor to *A Drug Abuse Anthology,* Holt, 1970, and to symposia on drug treatment programs.

WORK IN PROGRESS: A guide to family counseling, *Making the Impossible Difficult.*

AVOCATIONAL INTERESTS: Music, photography, art, building, crafts, hiking, boating, and a variety of sports.

* * *

FULLMER, Daniel W(arren) 1922-

PERSONAL: Born December 12, 1922, in London Mills, Ill.; son of Daniel Floyd and Sarah Louisa (Essex) Fullmer; married Patricia A. Allen, July 14, 1949; children: Daniel William, Mark Warren. *Education:* Western Illinois University, B.S., 1947, M.S., 1952; University of Denver, Ph.D., 1955. *Office:* Department of Educational Psychology, University of Hawaii, 1776 University Ave., Honolulu, Hawaii 96822.

CAREER: University of Oregon, Portland, assistant professor, 1955-57, associate professor of education, 1957-60; U.S. Office of Education, Portland, specialist in counseling, 1962-63; University of Hawaii, Honolulu, professor of educational psychology, 1966—. Member of State Board for Certification of Psychologists, Hawaii; president, Sussannah Wesley Community Center, Honolulu, 1972. *Military service:* U.S. Navy, Submarine Service, 1944-46. *Member:* American Personnel and Guidance Association, American Psychological Association. *Awards, honors:* Nancy C. Wimmer Award for outstanding contribution to field of counseling and guidance, American Personnel and Guidance Association, 1963; Francis E. Clark Award, Hawaii Personnel and Guidance Association, 1972.

WRITINGS: (With H. W. Bernard) *Counseling: Content and Process,* Science Research Associates, 1964; (editor with Daniel Schreiber and B. A. Kaplan) *Guidance and the School Dropout,* National Education Association and American Personnel and Guidance Association, 1964; (with Bernard) *Family Consultation,* Houghton, 1968; (with Bernard) *Principles of Guidance: A Basic Text,* Harper, 1969, 2nd edition, 1977; (editor with G. M. Gazda) *Theory and Methods of Group Counseling,* C. C Thomas, 1969; *Counseling: Group Theory and System,* Carroll Press, 1971, 2nd edition, 1977; (with Bernard) *The School Counselor-Consultant,* Houghton, 1972; (contributor) Gazda, editor, *Theories and Methods of Group Counseling in the Schools,* C. C Thomas, 1976; (with Carlson) *Focus on Guidance,* Love Publishing, 1977. Contributor to education and guidance journals.

WORK IN PROGRESS: Continuing research on family group consultation and counseling.

* * *

FULTON, Robin 1937-

PERSONAL: Born May 6, 1937, in Isle of Arran, Scotland. *Education:* University of Edinburgh, M.A., 1959, Ph.D., 1972. *Address:* Postboks 467, N 4001 Stavanger, Norway.

CAREER: Poet and translator. Editor of *Lines Review* (Scottish literary quarterly), 1967—. *Awards, honors:* Eric Gregory Award, 1966; University of Edinburgh writer's fellowship, 1969-71; Arts Council bursary, 1972.

WRITINGS—All poetry, except as indicated: *A Manner of Definition, and Other Poems,* Giles Gordon, 1963; *Instances,* M. Macdonald, 1967; *Inventories,* Caithness Books, 1969; *The Spaces between the Stones,* New Rivers Press, 1971; *Quarters,* Castlelaw Press, 1971; *The Man with the Surbahar,* M. Macdonald, 1971; (editor) *Trio: New Poets from Edinburgh* (anthology), New Rivers Press, 1971; *Tree-Lines,* New Rivers Press, 1974; *Contemporary Scottish Poetry: Individuals and Contexts* (criticism), M. Macdonald, 1974.

Translator: *An Italian Quartet: Versions after Saba, Ungaretti, Montale, Quasimodo,* Dufour, 1966; (from the Russian) Aleksandr Aleksandrovich Blok, *Twelve,* Akros Publications, 1968; (from the Swedish) Lars Gustafsson, *Selected Poems,* New Rivers Press, 1972; Gunnar Harding, *They Killed Sitting Bull and Other Poems,* London Magazine Editions, 1973; (from the Swedish) Tomas Transtroemer, *Selected Poems,* Penguin, 1973; (with Anselm Hollo) *Paavo Haavikko and Tomas Transtroemer,* Penguin, 1974; Osten Sjoestrand, *The Hidden Music and Other Poems,* Oleander Press, 1975; Werner Aspenstroem, *Selected Poems,* Oasis Books, 1976. Editor of special Scottish issues of *Spirit,* 1971, and *Literary Review,* 1975.

BIOGRAPHICAL/CRITICAL SOURCES: Saturday Review/World, September 7, 1974; *Choice,* March, 1975.

* * *

FUNK, Robert W(alter) 1926-

PERSONAL: Born July 18, 1926, in Evansville, Ind.; son of Robert Joseph and Ada (Adams) Funk; married Inabelle McKee, 1950; children: Andrea Elizabeth, Stephanie Alyson. *Education:* Attended Johnson Bible College, Evansville; Butler University, A.B., 1947, B.D. (honors), 1950, M.A., 1951; Vanderbilt University, Ph.D., 1953. *Office:* Department of Religious Studies, Univeristy of Montana, Missoula, Mont. 59801.

CAREER: Ordained minister of Disciples of Christ; associate minister of Christian church in Indianapolis, Ind., 1945-49; Butler University, Indianapolis, lecturer in Bible, 1947-49; minister of Christian church in Crawfordsville, Ind., 1949-51; Vanderbilt University, Nashville, Tenn., lecturer in Bible, 1951-53; Texas Christian University, Fort Worth, assistant professor of religion, 1953-56; Harvard University, Divinity School, Cambridge, Mass., instructor, 1956-57; Emory University, Atlanta, Ga., assistant professor of biblical theology, 1958-59; Drew University, Madison, N.J., associate professor of New Testament, 1959-66; Vanderbilt University, Divinity School, professor of New Testament, 1966-69, chairman of graduate department of religion, 1967-69; University of Montana, Missoula, professor of religious studies, 1969—, chairman of department, 1974-76, associate dean, College of Arts and Sciences, 1971-72. Interim pastor at churches in Tennessee, Texas, and Massachusetts, 1951-57; annual professor, American School of Oriental Research, Jerusalem, 1957-58; director of Scholars' Press, 1974—. Member of organizing committee, Drew Consultations, 1962, 1964, and Vanderbilt Consultations, 1968, 1969; Conference on the Coordination of Learned Societies for the Study of Religion, member of committee to form a council for the study of religion, 1968-69, member of task force on scholarly communication and publication,

1970-72; member of various university councils and committees.

MEMBER: American Academy of Religion (member of board of directors, 1968-73), Society of Biblical Literature (executive secretary, 1968-73; president, 1974-75), American Schools of Oriental Research, Studiorum Novi Testamenti Societas, New Testament Colloquium (member of organizing committee and secretary, 1962; member of executive committee, 1965-67; chairman, 1967), Catholic Biblical Association, Association of Disciples for Theological Discussion, Society for the Scientific Study of Religion, Society for Religion in Higher Education (fellow), American Council of Learned Societies (Conference of Secretaries, member of executive committee, 1970-72), American Association of University Professors. *Awards, honors:* Fulbright scholar at University of Tuebingen, 1965-66; Gugenheim fellow, 1965-66; American Council of Learned Societies fellow, 1973-74.

WRITINGS: New Testament Life and Literature: A Syllabus, Texas Christian University Press, 1955; (translator and reviser with Friedrich W. Blass and Albert Debrunner) *A Grammar of the Greek New Testament and Other Early Christian Literature,* University of Chicago Press, 1961; (contributor) James M. Robinson and John B. Cobb, editors, *New Frontiers in Theology,* Volume II: *The New Hermeneutic,* Harper, 1964; *Language, Hermeneutic, and Word of God: The Problem of Language in the New Testament and in Contemporary Theology,* Harper, 1966; (contributor) W. R. Farmer, C.F.D. Moule, and R. R. Niebuhr, editors, *Christian History and Interpretation: Studies Presented to John Knox,* Cambridge University Press, 1967; (contributor) Tony Stoneburner, editor, *Parable, Myth, and Language,* Church Society for College Work, 1968; (editor and author of introduction) Rudolf Bultmann, *Faith and Understanding,* translation by Louise Pettibone Smith, Volume I, Harper, 1969; (contributor) *Jesus and Man's Hope,* Volume II, Pittsburgh Theological Seminary, 1971; *A Beginning-Intermediate Grammar of Hellenistic Greek,* Scholars' Press, 1973; *Jesus as Precursor,* Scholars' Press, 1975.

Contributor to *Interpreter's Dictionary of the Bible,* Abingdon, 1962, and of more than fifty articles and reviews to religion, theology, and archaeology journals. Member of editorial board, "Hermeneia; A Critical Historical Commentary on the New Testament" series, Fortress, 1964—; editor and chairman of editorial board, *Journal for Theology and the Church,* Harper, 1964-74; member of publications committee, Council on the Study of Religion, 1969-73; member of editorial board, *Journal of the American Academy of Religion,* 1970-73; editor, *Semeia* and *Studies in American Biblical Scholarship,* 1974—.

WORK IN PROGRESS: Writing *The Form and Structure of the Pauline Letter,* a book in "Hermeneia: A Critical Historical Commentary on the New Testament" series, for Fortress; articles and pamphlets.

*   *   *

FURER, Howard B(ernard) 1934-

PERSONAL: Born November 28, 1934, in Brooklyn, N.Y.; son of Sidney Lewis and Essie (Glasser) Furer; married Marlene Zimmer, June 28, 1958; children: Cara Beth, Keith. *Education:* New York University, B.A., 1955, M.A., 1956, Ph.D., 1963. *Religion:* Jewish. *Home:* 261 Winthrop Rd., Teaneck, N.J. 07666. *Office:* Department of History, Kean College of New Jersey, Union, N.J. 07083.

CAREER: Teacher in high schools in New York, 1956-60;

Long Island University, Brooklyn, N.Y., instructor in history, 1961-62; Bronx Community College of the City University of New York, Bronx, N.Y., instructor in history, 1962-63; Dutchess Community College, Poughkeepsie, N.Y., assistant professor, 1963; Kean College of New Jersey, Union, assistant professor, 1963-65, associate professor, 1965-68, professor of history, 1968—. *Member:* American Historical Association, Organization of American Historians, American Association of University Professors, American Federation of Teachers.

WRITINGS—All published by Oceana, except as indicated: *William Frederick Havemeyer: A Political Biography,* American Press, 1964; *Harry S. Truman: Documentary History,* 1969; *James A. Garfield and Chester A. Arthur: Documentary History,* 1970; *Lyndon B. Johnson: Documentary History,* 1971; *The British in America, 1578-1970,* 1972; *The Scandinavians in America, 986-1970,* 1972; *The Germans in America, 1607-1970,* 1973; *New York: A Chronological and Documentary History,* 1974; *Washington, D.C.: A Chronological and Documentary History,* 1975. Editor of series "Great American Cities," twenty-one volumes, 1973—, and "Segments of United States History," ten tapes, JAB Press, 1977. Contributor to history journals.

*   *   *

GABEL, Margaret 1938-

PERSONAL: Born October 15, 1938, in Danville, Va.; daughter of John Wesley (a tractor dealer) and Ilah (Tate) Booker; married F. Daniel Gabel, Jr. (an insurance broker), December 30, 1961. *Education:* Duke University, B.A., 1960. *Religion:* Methodist. *Home:* 72 Jane St., New York, N.Y. 10014.

CAREER: Doubleday & Co., New York City, assistant editor, 1960-64; Meredith Press, New York City, associate editor, 1967-70; Thomas Nelson, Inc., New York City, associate editor, 1970-71. Instructor, New School for Social Research, New York City. *Member:* Friends of the Earth. *Awards, honors:* Virginia Press Association award, 1956.

WRITINGS: Sparrows Don't Drop Candy Wrappers (juvenile), Dodd, 1971. Work anthologized in *Intro #1,* edited by R. V. Cassell, Bantam, 1968. Contributor to *Carolina Quarterly.*

WORK IN PROGRESS: Short stories.

SIDELIGHTS: Margaret Gabel told *CA:* "My interest is in fiction—and particularly in characterizations. I find fiction writing a way of recapturing parts of my life and keeping in touch with myself."†

*   *   *

GABLIK, Suzi 1934-

PERSONAL: Born September 26, 1934, in New York, N.Y.; daughter of Anthony J. and Geraldine (Schwarz) Gablik. *Education:* Attended Black Mountain College, summer, 1951; Hunter College (now Hunter College of the City University of New York), B.A., 1955. *Home:* 5 Westmoreland St., London W.1, England. *Agent:* A. D. Peters, 10 Buckingham St., London WC2N 6BU, England.

CAREER: Critic and artist, specializing in collage paintings; since 1966 has had four one-woman shows in New York, the most recent in May, 1972. University lecturer.

WRITINGS: (Compiler with John Russell) *Pop Art Redefined,* Praeger, 1969; *Magritte,* New York Graphic Society, 1970; *Progress in Art,* Rizzoli, 1977.

GAGNON, John H(enry) 1931-

PERSONAL: Born November 22, 1931, in Fall River, Mass.; son of George and Mary (Murphy) Gagnon; married Patricia Orlikoff, 1955 (divorced, 1978); children: Andree, Christopher. *Education:* University of Chicago, B.A., 1955, Ph.D., 1969. *Office:* Department of Sociology, State University of New York, Stony Brook, N.Y. 11790.

CAREER: Northwestern University, Medical School, Evanston, Ill., clinical assistant in psychiatry, 1958-59; Indiana University, Bloomington, lecturer in sociology, 1959-67, senior research sociologist and trustee of Institute for Sex Research, 1959-68; State University of New York at Stony Brook, associate professor, 1968-70, professor of sociology, 1970—, director of Center for Continuing Education, 1970-72. Overseas fellow, Churchill College, Cambridge University, 1972-73; National Institute for Mental Health fellow, 1972-73. Member of board of advisers, National Sex and Drug Forum, 1968-71; member of steering committee, Biological Sciences Curriculum Study, 1968-71.

MEMBER: American Sociological Association, Society for the Study of Social Problems, American Association for the Advancement of Science, National Council on Family Relations, Association for the Study of Abortion, Sex Information and Education Council of the United States (member of board of directors, 1967-70), Illinois Academy of Criminology.

WRITINGS: (With Paul H. Gebhard, Cornelia V. Christenson, and Wardell B. Pomeroy) *Sex Offenders: An Analysis of Types,* Harper, 1965; (editor with William Simon) *Sexual Deviance: A Reader,* Harper, 1967; (with Simon) *The Sexual Scene,* Aldine, 1970, 2nd edition, 1973; (with Simon) *Sexual Conduct: The Social Sources of Human Sexuality,* Aldine, 1973; *Human Sexualities,* Scott, Foresman, 1977; *Human Sexuality in Today's World,* Little, Brown, 1977; (with Cathy S. Greenblat) *Life Designs: Individuals, Marriages and Families,* Scott, Foresman, 1977. Contributor of articles and book reviews to scholarly journals. Associate editor, *Social Problems,* 1970-73; contributing editor, *Change,* 1971—; associate editor, *Teaching Sociology,* 1971-73; former member of editorial boards, *American Journal of Sociology, Social Forces, Demography,* and *American Sociological Review.*

WORK IN PROGRESS: For U.S. Public Health Service, continuing studies in adult socialization; simulation games in health care, sex roles, and travel; research in socio-cultural change and in human sexual conduct.

* * *

GALBRAITH, Clare K(earney) 1919-

PERSONAL: Born July 28, 1919, in Alameda, Calif.; daughter of Raymond Warren (an attorney) and Carrie (Crane) Kearney; married Henry Stephen Galbraith (in lumber business), November 8, 1942 (divorced); children: Henry Thomas, Richard Raymond, Kathleen Kearney (Mrs. Edward Chwekun), Carol Jean. *Education:* Attended Southern Methodist University, 1936-37, and University of Texas, 1937-40; Arizona State University, B.S., 1954, M.A., 1962; Stanford University, graduate study in marine biology, 1964-70. *Politics:* "Have I been radicalized? Probably." *Home:* 4937 Swiss Ave., Dallas, Tex. 75214. *Office:* Dallas Independent School District, Pearl C. Anderson Career Academy, 3400 Garden Lane, Dallas, Tex. 75210.

CAREER: Stenographer for mortgage and loan and for fertilizer companies in Phoenix, Ariz., 1954-55; Scottsdale Public Schools, Scottsdale, Ariz., teacher, 1956-62; teacher in elementary schools in California, 1962-66; Stanford University, Kettering Foundation, Palo Alto, Calif., teacher and art education consultant, 1966-67; Stanford University, Palo Alto, key punch operator, 1968-70; Dallas Independent School District, Dallas, Tex., media specialist, beginning 1970, currently teacher at Pearl C. Anderson Career Academy. Member of advisory board, Dallas Public Library; member of Goals for Dallas. *Member:* National Association for the Advancement of Colored People, Maricopa County Mental Health Association (board member, 1959-62), Women for Change (Dallas), Pi Lambda Theta, Kappa Kappa Gamma.

WRITINGS: *Spanish Speaking Children Communicate,* Association for Childhood Education, 1965; *Victor,* Little, Brown, 1971; (contributor) Murray Cohen, editor, *Cultural Neighbors,* Association for Childhood Education, 1972; (contributor) *Special Happenings,* Holt, 1977. Editor, Alliance for Integrated Education *Newsletter,* 1975-76.

WORK IN PROGRESS: Clean and Dirty: What Do We Really Mean?; What Did the Bear See?; Angelina and the Karate Chop; Sea Lions, Elephant Seals, and Walruses.

SIDELIGHTS: Clare Galbraith writes: "When I am writing fiction, I would like to have children experience beyond their own lives in the thoughts and feelings of those who have been brought up differently, I would hope that those who recognize their own experience in my stories, will think 'someone else understands. I am not alone. It *is* good to be me.'"

* * *

GALE, Vi

PERSONAL: Born in Noret, Dala-Jarna, Sweden; came to United States in 1929, naturalized in 1940; daughter of Erland G. and Mary E. (Petterson) Hokenson; married James C. Gale. *Education:* Attended literature and writing courses at University of Colorado, Portland State University, Lewis and Clark College, and University of Oregon. *Home:* 11519 Northeast Prescott, Portland, Ore. 97220.

CAREER: Free-lance writer. Director of creative writing workshops, Young Women's Christian Association, Portland, Ore., 1962—, and currently conductor of community program; editor and publisher, Prescott Street Press, 1974—. Writer-in-residence, Eastern Oregon College, Le Grande, 1968, and Clatsop Community College, Astoria, Ore., 1969. Lecturer. *Awards, honors:* Oregon Poetry Prize, 1954; Swallow Press New Poetry Series Award, 1958.

WRITINGS: Several Houses, Alan Swallow, 1959; *Love Always,* Alan Swallow, 1965; *Nineteen Ing Poems,* Press-22, 1970; *Clouded Sea,* Press-22, 1971; *Clearwater,* Swallow Press, 1974. Work represented in anthologies, including *Oregon Signatures,* edited by Robert D. Brown and others, Oregon State University Press, 1959, *Golden Year: The Poetry Society of American Anthology (1910-1960),* edited by Melville Cane and others, Fine Editions Press, 1960, and *NW Manuscript Poems,* Reed College Press, 1966. Contributor of poetry, short stories, photography, and articles to *Northwest Review, Poetry Northwest, Poetry* (Chicago), *Pacific Spectator, Colorado Quarterly, December, Kansas Magazine, Midwest Quarterly Review,* and other publications.

* * *

GALINSKY, G(otthard) Karl 1942-

PERSONAL: Born February 7, 1942, in Strassburg, Alsace;

son of Hans Karl (a professor) and Edith (Margenburg) Galinsky; married second wife, Susan Plume, September 17, 1976; children: (first marriage) Robert Charles, John Anthony. *Education:* Bowdoin College, A.B., 1963; Princeton University, M.A., 1965, Ph.D., 1966. *Home:* 2729 Trail of Madrones, Austin, Tex. 78746. *Office:* Department of Classics, University of Texas, Austin, Tex. 78712.

CAREER: Princeton University, Princeton, N.J., instructor in classics, 1965-66; University of Texas at Austin, assistant professor, 1966-68, associate professor, 1968-72, professor of classics, 1972—, chairman of department, 1974. American Academy in Rome, member of classical jury, 1970-72, classicist-in-residence, 1972-73. National Endowment for the Humanities, director of summer and residential seminars, 1975-78, consultant, 1976-78. *Member:* American Philological Association, Archaeological Institute of America, Vergilian Society (trustee, 1972-77; vice-president, 1977-78), Classical Association of the Middle West and South (chairman, Southern section, 1976-78), Texas Classical Association (first vice-president, 1971-72). *Awards, honors:* National Endowment for the Humanities summer grant, 1967; American Council of Learned Societies fellow, 1968-69; Fulbright grant, 1972-73; Guggenheim fellow, 1972-73.

WRITINGS: Aeneas, Sicily, and Rome, Princeton University Press, 1969; (with F. W. Lenz) *Albii Tibulli aliorumque carminum libri tres,* E. J. Brill, 1971; *The Kerakles Theme: The Adaptations of the Hero in Literature from Homer to the Twentieth Century,* Blackwell, 1972; *Perspectives of Roman Poetry: A Classics Symposium,* University of Texas Press, 1974; *Ovid's "Metamorphoses": An Introduction to Its Basic Aspects,* University of California Press, 1975. Contributor to classics journals, including *American Journal of Philology, Classical Philology, Wiener Studien, Latomus, Mnemosyne, Classical Journal, TAPA, Vogt Festschrift.*

WORK IN PROGRESS: A cultural history of the Augustan age.

*　　*　　*

GALLAGHER, Kent G(rey)　1933-

PERSONAL: Born November 9, 1933, in Oak Park, Ill.; son of Charles Joseph (a court reporter) and Lucile (Nussle) Gallagher; married Sonja Ferguson, 1976; children: (previous marriage) Geoffrey Kent, Douglas Grey, Bradford Dean. *Education:* Attended University of Illinois, Chicago, 1951-53; Carleton College, A.B., 1957; Indiana University, M.A., 1960, Ph.D., 1962. *Politics:* Independent. *Religion:* None. *Office:* Department of Theater Arts, Texas Christian University, Ft. Worth, Tex. 76133.

CAREER: Ball State University, Muncie, Ind., director of theater, 1962-64, assistant professor of theater and drama and English, 1964-66; Washington State University, Pullman, 1966-76, began as associate professor, became professor of theater and drama and head of department; Texas Christian University, Ft. Worth, chairman of department of theater arts and drama, 1976—. Member of Pullman advisory council, Washington State Board Against Discrimination and Washington State Human Rights Commission. *Military service:* U.S. Army, 1953-55; became sergeant. *Member:* American Theatre Association, Speech Communication Association, American National Theatre and Academy, American Society for Theatre Research, Washington Association of Theatre Artists (past president), American Civil Liberties Union. *Awards, honors:* Woodrow Wilson travel and study grant, 1967.

WRITINGS: The Foreigner in Early American Drama, Mouton & Co., 1966; (editor) *Curriculum Guidelines in Drama Education,* State of Washington, 1971. Contributor to theater and speech journals.

WORK IN PROGRESS: Graduate Education in Theatre Arts and Drama; a history of the Haymarket Theatre (Boston); research on tragedy in the American theater.

*　　*　　*

GALLUP, Dick　1941-

PERSONAL: Born July 3, 1941, in Mass.; son of Harry Gallup; married Carol Clifford, 1965; children: Christina, Samuel. *Education:* Tulane University of Louisiana, student, 1959-62; Columbia University, B.A., 1968.

WRITINGS: Where I Hang My Hat (poems), Harper, 1970; *Above the Tree Line* (poems), Big Sky Books, 1976.

WORK IN PROGRESS: Poetry.†

*　　*　　*

GAMSON, William A.　1934-

PERSONAL: Born January 27, 1934, in Philadelphia, Pa.; son of Edward (a salesman) and Blanche (Weintraub) Gamson; married Zelda Finkelstein (a sociologist), July 1, 1956; children: Jennifer, Joshua. *Education:* Antioch College, B.A., 1955; University of Michigan, M.A., 1956, Ph.D., 1959. *Home:* 1413 Granger, Ann Arbor, Mich. 48104. *Office:* Department of Sociology, University of Michigan, Ann Arbor, Mich. 48104.

CAREER: Harvard University, Cambridge, Mass., research associate in social psychology, 1959-62; University of Michigan, Ann Arbor, assistant professor, 1962-64, associate professor, 1964-66, professor of sociology, 1966—, chairman of department, 1974—, research sociologist, Center for Research on Conflict Resolution, 1962-71. Visiting fellow, Western Behavioral Sciences Institute, 1964; visiting lecturer, Harvard University, 1968-69; visiting professor, Hebrew University of Jerusalem, 1969, and 1972-73. *Member:* American Sociological Association (chairman of social psychology section, 1971-72), Society for the Psychological Study of Social Issues (member of council, 1968-70). *Awards, honors:* Annual Socio-Psychological Prize, American Association for the Advancement of Science, 1962, for two essays; Sorokin Award, American Sociological Association, 1969, for *Power and Discontent.*

WRITINGS: Power and Discontent, Dorsey, 1968; *SIMSOC: Simulated Society,* with participant's manual and instructor's manual, Free Press, 1969, 3rd edition, 1978; (with Andre Modigliani) *Untangling the Cold War: A Strategy for Testing Rival Theories,* Little, Brown, 1971; (with Modigliani) *Conceptions of Social Life,* Little, Brown, 1974; *Strategy of Social Protest,* Dorsey, 1975.

Contributor: Roger Fisher, editor, *International Conflict and Behavioral Science,* Basic Books, 1964; Leonard Berkowitz, editor, *Advances in Experimental Social Psychology,* Volume I, Academic Press, 1964; Charles Press and Alan Arian, editors, *Empathy and Ideology,* Rand McNally, 1966; Terry N. Clark, editor, *Community Power and Decision-Making: Comparative Analyses,* Chandler Publishing, 1968; Willis D. Hawley and Frederick M. Wirt, editors, *The Search for Power in American Communities,* Prentice-Hall, 1968; John E. Mueller, editor, *Approaches to Measurement in International Relations,* Appleton, 1968; Naomi Rosenbaum, editor, *Readings in International Political Behavior,* Prentice-Hall, 1968; Peter Orleans, editor,

Social Structure and Social Process, Allyn & Bacon, 1969; Tony Tripodi, Phillip Fellin, and Henry J. Meyer, editors, *Exemplars in Social Research,* F. E. Peacock, 1969; Edward F. Borgatta, editor, *Social Psychology: Readings and Perspective,* Rand McNally, 1969.

Michael T. Aiken and Paul E. Mott, editors, *The Structure of Community Power: Readings,* Random House, 1970; Kurt Back, editor, *Social Psychology,* Wiley, 1971; Samuel A. Kirkpatrick, editor, *Quantitative Analysis of Political Data,* C. E. Merrill, 1971; Richard P. Taub, editor, *Tocqueville's America and Today's,* Rand McNally, 1971; Richard Ofshe, editor, *Interpersonal Behavior in Small Groups,* Prentice-Hall, 1971; Robert S. Ross and William C. Mitchell, editors, *Introductory Readings in American Government,* Markham, 1971; James F. Short, Jr. and Marvin E. Wolfgang, editors, *Collective Violence,* Aldine-Atherton, 1971; Michael Inbar and Clarice Stoll, editors, *Simulation and Gaming in Social Science: The Design Process,* Free Press, 1971; Ada Finifter, editor, *Alienation and the Social System,* Wiley, 1972.

Contributor to *International Encyclopedia of the Social Sciences* and to sociology journals. Associate editor, *Sociometry,* 1964-67, and *Simulation and Games,* 1969—; chairman of editorial board, *Journal of Conflict Resolution,* 1969—; member of advisory board, *Politics and Society,* 1970—. Editor with Benjamin D. Paul and S. Stephen Kegeles of special issue of *Journal of Social Issues* on fluoridation, November, 1961.

*　　*　　*

GANDEE, Lee R(auss) 1917-

PERSONAL: Born May 8, 1917, in Kanawha County, W. Va.; son of Jesse Thomas (a postal clerk) and Mary Delcie (Brickey) Gandee; married Aline Phillips (a saleswoman), March 7, 1943 (divorced, 1976; remarried, July 7, 1977); children: Eva Eugenia (Mrs. Juan Suarez Prieto), Sarah Catherine (Mrs. Tom Sawyer), Michael Stephen. *Education:* West Virginia State Normal School (now Marshall University), A.B., 1940; Mexico City College (now University of the Americas), M.A. (cum laude), 1949. *Politics:* Independent. *Religion:* "Syncretist." *Home:* 327 Carpenter St., West Columbia, S.C. 29169.

CAREER: Civilian employee, U.S. Army Air Forces, 1945-47, and South Carolina National Guard, 1950-54; social science teacher in public and private schools, 1954-63; Lenoir Rhyne College, Hickory, N.C., instructor in history, 1964-68; free-lance writer, 1969—; currently a research analyst for the state of South Carolina. *Military service:* U.S. Army Air Forces, 1940-45; became staff sergeant. *Member:* National Trust for Historic Preservation.

WRITINGS: Strange Experience, Prentice-Hall, 1972. Author of "Early County History" column in *Lexington Dispatch News,* 1962-75. Contributor to *Fate* magazine. Contributing editor, *Georgia Genealogical Magazine.*

WORK IN PROGRESS: A book on artifacts, for Prentice-Hall; research on parapsychological phenomena of Hexerei; continuing research on history and genealogy of Lexington County, S.C.; research for a book on Indo-European magic.

*　　*　　*

GANS, Eric L. 1941-

PERSONAL: Born August 21, 1941, in New York, N.Y.; son of Irving and Pearl (Fintell) Gans; children: (second marriage) Gisele, Georges. *Education:* Columbia University, B.A., 1960; Johns Hopkins University, M.A., 1961, Ph.D., 1966. *Office:* Department of French, University of California, Los Angeles, Calif. 90024.

CAREER: State University of New York at Fredonia, instructor in French, 1965-67; Indiana University at Bloomington, assistant professor of French, 1967-69; University of California, Los Angeles, assistant professor, 1969-73, associate professor, 1973-76, professor of French, 1976—, chairman of department, 1974—. *Member:* Modern Language Association of America, American Association of Teachers of French.

WRITINGS: The Discovery of Illusion: Flaubert's Early Works, 1835-1837, University of California Press, 1971; *Un pari contre l'histoire: Les premieres nouvelles de Merimee,* Minard, 1972; *Musset et le "drame tragique,"* Jose Corti, 1974; *Le paradoxe de Phedre,* Nizet, 1975; *Essais d'-esthetique paradoxale,* Gallimard, 1977.

WORK IN PROGRESS: Du langage un discours.

*　　*　　*

GANZGLASS, Martin Richard 1941-

PERSONAL: Born April 1, 1941, in New York, N.Y.; son of Henry S. and Lillian (Ennis) Ganzglass; married Evelyn I. Hirsch (an employment analyst), May 24, 1964. *Education:* City College of the City University of New York, B.A., 1961; Harvard University, LL.B., 1964. *Residence:* Washington, D.C. *Office:* Delson & Gordon, 1900 L St. N.W., Washington, D.C. 20036.

CAREER: National Labor Relations Board, Washington, D.C., attorney, 1964-66; U.S. Peace Corps, Somalia, volunteer, 1966-68; Delson & Gordon, New York, N.Y. and Washington, D.C., attorney, 1968—. *Member:* American Bar Association, Federal Bar Association, New York City Bar Association, Phi Beta Kappa.

WRITINGS: The Penal Code of the Somali Democratic Republic, Rutgers University Press, 1971. Contributor to law journals.

*　　*　　*

GARCIA MARQUEZ, Gabriel 1928-

PERSONAL: Born March 6, 1928, in Aracataca, Colombia; son of Gabriel E. Garcia and Luisa Marquez Iguaran; married Mercedes Barcha; children: Rodrigo, Gonzalo. *Education:* Educated by Jesuits in Colombia; Universidad Nacional de Colombia, studied law and journalism. *Address:* P.O. Box 20736, Mexico City D.F., Mexico. *Agent:* Carmen Balcells, Diagonal 580, Barcelona 11, Spain.

CAREER: Worked as a journalist in Latin America, Europe, and the United States, 1950-65; writer, 1965—. *Awards, honors:* Colombian Association of Writers and Artists award, 1954, for short story, "Un dia despues del sabado"; Premio Literario Esso (Colombia), 1961, for *La mala hora;* Chinchiano Award (Italy), 1969, Prix de Meilleur Livre Etranger (France), 1969, and Romulo Gallegos prize (Venezuela), 1972, all for *One Hundred Years of Solitude;* Books Abroad/Neustadt International Prize for Literature, 1972; honorary doctorate, Columbia University, 1971.

WRITINGS: La hojarasca (novella), Organizacion Continental de los Festivales del Libro (Bogota), 1955, translation published in *Leaf Storm, and Other Stories* (see below); *El coronel no tiene quien lo escriba* (novella), Era (Mexico), 1957, 3rd edition, 1966, published with "La increible y triste historia de la candida Erendira y de su abuela desalmada" (see below), published in *Triple espera: novelas cortas de hispanoamerica* (see below), translation published in *No One Writes to the Colonel, and Other Stories* (see below); *La mala hora* (novel), [Madrid], 1962, Era, 1966; *Los funerales de la Mama Grande* (short stories; contains "La siesta del martes," "Un dia de estos," "En este pueblo no hay ladrones," "La prodigiosa tarde de Baltazar," "La viuda de Montiel," "Un dia despues del sabado," "Rosas artificiales," and "Los funerales de la Mama Grande"), Universidad Veracruzana (Xalapa), 1962, translation published in *No One Writes to the Colonel, and Other Stories* (see below); *Cien anos de soledad* (novel), Sudamericana (Buenos Aires), 1967, translation by Gregory Rabassa published as *One Hundred Years of Solitude,* Harper, 1970; (with Mario Vargas Llosa) *La novela en america latina* (dialogue between Garcia Marquez and Llosa, held at Universidad Nacional de Ingenieria, Lima, Peru, September 4, 1967), C. Milla Batres (Lima), c.1968; *No One Writes to the Colonel, and Other Stories* (contains the novella "No One Writes to the Colonel," and eight stories, "Tuesday Siesta," "One of These Days," "In This Town There Are No Thieves," "Balthazar's Marvelous Afternoon," "Montiel's Widow," "One Day after Saturday," "Artificial Roses," and "Big Mama's Funeral"), translation by J. S. Bernstein, Harper, 1968; *Seis cuentos latinoamericanos,* Sandino, 1969.

Relato de un naufrago, Tusquets Editor (Barcelona), 1970; *Leafstorm, and Other Stories* (contains the novella, "Leafstorm," and six stories, including "The Handsomest Drowned Man in the World," and "Blacaman the Good, Vendor of Miracles"), translation by Gregory Rabassa, Harper, 1972; *La increible y triste historia de la candida Erendira y de su abuela desalmada: siete cuentos* (stories; includes "Un senor muy viejo con unas alas enormes," "El mar del tiempo perdido," "El ahogado mas hermoso del mundo," "Muerte constante mas alla del amor," "El ultimo viaje del buque fantasma," "Blacaman el bueno vendedor de milagros"; "La increible y triste historia de la candida Erendira y de su abuela desalmada" published with "El coronel no tiene quien le escriba" [see below]), Barral Editores (Barcelona), 1972, translation by Gregory Rabassa published as *Innocent Erendira and Other Stories,* Harper, 1978; *El negro qui hizo esperar a los angeles,* Ediciones Alfil (Uruguay), 1972; *Ojos de perro azul: nueve cuentos desconocidos* (stories; includes "La tercera resignacion," "La otra costilla de la muerte," "Eva esta dentro de su gato," "Amargura para tres sonambulos," "Dialogo del espejo," "La mujer que llegaba a las seis," "Nabo, el negro qui hizo esperar a los angeles," "Alguien desordena estas rosas"), Equiseditorial (Argentina), 1972; *Cuando era feliz e indocumentado,* El Ojo del Camello (Caracas), 1973; *El otono del patriarca* (novel), Plaza & Janes (Spain), 1975, translation by Gregory Rabassa published as *The Autumn of the Patriarch,* Harper, 1976; *Todos los cuentos de Gabriel Garcia Marquez (1947-1972),* Plaza & Janes, 1975; *El coronel no tiene quien le escriba* [and] *La increible y triste historia de la candida Erendira y de su abuela desalmada* (novellas), Libreria del Colegio (Buenos Aires), 1975; (contributor) *Triple espera: novelas cortas de hispanoamerica,* edited by Djelal Kadir, Harcourt, 1976. Contributor of short stories to *El Espectador, El Heraldo, Nuevo Mundo, Casa de las Americas,* and other periodicals.

WORK IN PROGRESS: A non-fiction book on the United States' blockade of revolutionary Cuba.

SIDELIGHTS: No One Writes to the Colonel, and Other Stories "introduces the reader to the microcosmic world of Macondo, ostensibly a sleepy, hot, coastal town in which nothing ever happens," writes Robert G. Mead, Jr. "But in truth Macondo exists only in the fantasy of the author, a town which he himself admits is born of his nostalgia for the life he lived as a young boy more than thirty years ago in a vanished Colombia. . . . All the stories communicate incidents in the lives of humble (and a few rich) townspeople, all of whom have been deeply affected by the long and bloody political strife between the liberals and the conservatives in Colombia." Oliver T. Myers calls Gabriel Garcia Marquez a "political novelist . . . because his people, who for the most part are more real than is fashionable today, are operating in a context that could be found only in a place like Colombia, where a type of stability had been achieved through the machinery of a repressive dictatorship." The book is, according to Myers, "the official history of Macondo, [ranging] from detailed realism, through dreamy fragments and images, to political allegory. One story is linked to another by an event, or a person or merely a mood, and no one story can be fully understood without reading them all; it will take *100 Years of Solitude* to understand why Macondo is what it is."

One Hundred Years of Solitude has become an international best seller and prompted comparisons with the work of Cervantes, Faulkner, Joyce, and Guenter Grass. (According to Martha Duffy of *Time,* Garcia Marquez "has acknowledged that reading Faulkner and making a pilgrimage through Yoknapatawpha country helped him to enrich his own private literary property and see its mythic possibilities.") With almost unvarying accord, critics everywhere have termed *One Hundred Years of Solitude* a masterpiece. William McPherson of the *Washington Post* called it a "vast jungle of a novel—at once so rich, so dense and so extravagant as to be overwhelming; a fabulous creation of magic and metaphor and myth. . . . It resists efforts to reduce it in size or to fix it in place. Instead, it lies there in its yeasty mass beating with a life of its own, one that no amount of critical kneading can still." William Kennedy writes for *National Observer:* "*One Hundred Years of Solitude* is the first piece of literature since the Book of Genesis that should be required reading for the entire human race. It takes up not long after Genesis left off and carries through to the air age, reporting on everything that happened in between with more lucidity, wit, wisdom, and poetry than is expected from 100 years of novelists, let alone one man. . . . The book is like *Finnegans Wake* in its ambition to encompass all of man's life on earth, but it is written in simple and beautiful prose, without the incomprehensibility of the Joycean portmanteau puns. It is like Thornton Wilder's *Skin of Our Teeth* and *Our Town* in its reduction of all civilization to the family level, but without Mr. Wilder's sentimentality and with infinitely larger scope and far more toughness. It is like *Pilgrim's Progress* and all the morality plays, fused with a modern tongue and a horizonless surrealism.''

On the surface the novel is the story of the Buendia family and the town of Macondo, but, as John Leonard notes, "it is also a recapitulation of our evolutionary and intellectual experience. Macondo is Latin America in microcosm: local autonomy yielding to state authority; anticlericalism; party politics; the coming of the United Fruit Company; aborted revolutions; the rape of innocence by history. And the Buendias (inventors, artisans, soldiers, lovers, mystics) seem doomed to ride a biological tragi-cycle in circles from solitude to magic to poetry to science to politics to violence back again to solitude. . . . With a single bound, Gabriel Garcia Marquez leaps onto the stage . . . his appetite as enormous as his imagination, his fatalism greater than either. Dazzling.''

Alfred Kazin declares that he read the ''utterly original *One Hundred Years of Solitude* . . . with the same recognition of a New World epic that one feels about *Moby Dick.* . . . [Garcia Marquez] has extraordinary strength and firmness of imagination and writes with the calmness of a man who knows exactly what wonders he can perform. . . . As with Emerson, Poe, Hawthorne, every sentence breaks the silence of a vast emptiness, the famous New World 'solitude' that is the unconscious despair of his characters but the sign of [Garcia] Marquez's genius.''

The Autumn of the Patriarch also won critical acclaim. Dean Flower writes for *Hudson Review:* ''The novel is shaped by a series of bold conceptions: the idea of a centuries-old tyrant so legendary as to be almost immortal; the idea of a non-chronological dream-monologue to unfold this legend, echoing with voices; and the idea of a patriarch given identity *only* by these voices. . . . Garcia Marquez . . . grips us in an authentic nightmare of modern dictatorship.'' The *New York Times Book Review* calls it ''a most complex and terrible vision of Latin America's ubiquitous, unkillable demon . . . mystical and surrealistic in its excesses, its distortions and its exotic language. It is a supreme polemic against any society that encourages or even permits the growth of such a dictator.'' ''Emptiness is the book's great symbol,'' writes Patrick Breslin for *America.* ''Everything is hollow and false. Under a flood of poetic language that sweeps unruffled through everyday occurrences and magical impossibilities, Garcia Marquez depicts the emptiness of a kind of power tragically common in Latin America.'' Though abstract and surrealistic, Flower notes, ''*The Autumn of the Patriarch* . . . is perfectly unified and concentrated, proceeds from particularized places and believable voices, and is resolved by devastating ironies and a myth that transcends history.''

Garcia Marquez's works have been published in more than twenty languages, and in eight Spanish-speaking countries.

BIOGRAPHICAL/CRITICAL SOURCES—Books: Luis Harss and Barbara Dohmann, *Into the Mainstream,* Harper, 1967; Carmen Arnau, *El mundo mitico de Gabriel Garcia Marquez,* Ediciones Peninsula, 1971; Mario Vargas Llosa, *Garcia Marquez: historia de un deicido,* Barral Editores, 1971; Ernesto Gonzalez Barmejo, *Cosas de escritores,* Biblioteca de Marcha, 1971; Helmy F. Giacoman, editor, *Homenaje a G. Garcia Marquez,* Las Americas, 1972; Mario Benedetti, *Nueve asedios a Garcia Marquez,* Editorial Universitaria, 1972; Rita Guibert, *Seven Voices: Seven Latin American Writers Talk to Rita Guibert,* Knopf, 1973; *Contemporary Literary Criticism,* Gale, Volume II, 1974, Volume III, 1975, Volume VIII, 1978.

Periodicals: *New York Times,* September 26, 1968, March 3, 1970, March 17, 1972; *Nation,* December 2, 1968, May 15, 1972, December 25, 1976; *Saturday Review,* December 21, 1968, March 7, 1970, December 11, 1976; *Books Abroad,* winter, 1970, winter, 1971, winter, 1973, summer, 1973; *Commonweal,* March 6, 1970; *New York Times Book Review,* March 8, 1970, February 20, 1972, January 2, 1977; *Washington Post,* March 18, 1970; *New York Review of Books,* March 26, 1970; *National Observer,* April 20, 1970; *New Yorker,* March 11, 1972; *Time,* March 13, 1972, July 10, 1978; *Times Literary Supplement,* September 29, 1972, April 15, 1977; *Books and Bookmen,* March, 1973; *London Magazine,* April/May, 1973; *America,* December 8, 1976; *American Scholar,* spring, 1977; *Virginia Quarterly Review,*

spring, 1977; *Progressive,* April, 1977; *New Republic,* April 9, 1977; *National Review,* May 27, 1977; *Hudson Review,* summer, 1977.

* * *

GARDEN, Nancy 1938-

PERSONAL: Born May 15, 1938, in Boston, Mass. *Education:* Columbia University, B.F.A., 1961, M.A., 1962. *Residence:* Carlisle, Mass. *Agent:* Dorothy Markinko, McIntosh & Otis, Inc., 475 Fifth Ave., New York, N.Y. 10016.

CAREER: ''Knocked around theater a good deal in the past, as an actress, lighting designer, and jack-of-all-trades; have taught, in one way or another, all levels, including adult; have done free-lance editorial work for various publishers''; *Junior Scholastic* magazine, New York City, contributing editor, 1969-70; *American Observer* (magazine), Washington, D.C., contributing editor, 1970-72; Houghton Mifflin Co., New York City, associate editor, 1972, assistant editor, 1973, editor, 1974—.

WRITINGS—For young people: *What Happened in Marston,* Four Winds, 1971; *Berlin: City Split in Two,* Putnam, 1971; *The Loners* (novel), Viking, 1972; *Vampires,* Lippincott, 1973; *Werewolves,* Lippincott, 1973; *Witches,* Lippincott, 1975; *Demons and Devils,* Lippincott, 1976. Contributor of reviews to magazines, including *American Observer.*

WORK IN PROGRESS: A young adult novel, an adult novel, and several shorter books for children.

SIDELIGHTS: Nancy Garden told *CA:* ''I write for young people because I like them, and because I think they are important. . . . Children's books can be mind-stretchers and imagination-ticklers and builders of good taste in a way that adult books cannot, because young people usually come to books with more open minds. It's exciting to be able to contribute to that in a small way.''

Nancy Garden is a refugee from New York City, living ''happily in the country surrounded, after fifteen years of concrete, with dogs and cats and trees and fresh air.''

* * *

GARDNER, R(ufus) H(allette III) 1918-

PERSONAL: Born July 25, 1918, in Mayfield, Ky.; son of Rufus Hallette, Jr. and Kathleen (Moorman) Gardner; divorced. *Education:* Texas Christian University, A.B., 1941. *Politics:* Liberal Democrat. *Residence:* Baltimore, Md. *Agent:* Ann Elmo Agency, Inc., 52 Vanderbilt Ave., New York, N.Y. 10017. *Office:* The Sunpapers, Baltimore, Md. 21203.

CAREER: Glenn L. Martin Co., Middle River, Md., aircraft engineer, 1941-49; *Baltimore Sun,* Baltimore, Md., reporter and feature writer, 1951-54, drama and film critic, 1954—. Visiting lecturer in drama, Goucher College, 1968.

WRITINGS: The Splintered Stage: The Decline of the American Theater, Macmillan, 1965.

Plays: ''I.O.U. Jeremiah,'' first produced in New York, N.Y. at Originals Only Playhouse, 1950; ''Christabel and the Rubicon,'' first produced in Olney, Md. at Olney Theatre, 1969.†

* * *

GARDNER, Richard A. 1931-

PERSONAL: Born April 28, 1931, in New York, N.Y.; son of Irving (an insurance agent) and Amelia (Weingarten) Gardner; married Lee Robbins (a psychiatrist), April 14,

1957; children: Andrew, Nancy, Julie. *Education:* Columbia University, A.B., 1952; State University of New York, M.D., 1956; William A. White Psychoanalytic Institute, Certificate in Psychoanalysis, 1966. *Politics:* Democratic Party. *Religion:* Jewish. *Residence:* Tenafly, N.J. *Office:* 155 County Rd., Cresskill, N.J. 07626.

CAREER: Montefiore Hospital, Bronx, N.Y., intern, 1956-57; New York State Psychiatric Institute-Columbia-Presbyterian Medical Center, New York City, resident in adult psychiatry, 1957-59, in child psychiatry, 1959-60, 1962-63; William A. White Psychoanalytic Institute, New York City, trainee, 1959-60, 1962-66; private practice of adult and child psychiatry and psychoanalysis, Cresskill, N.J., 1966—. Associate attending psychiatrist, Columbia-Presbyterian Medical Center; associate clinical professor of child psychiatry, College of Physicians and Surgeons, Columbia University; associate attending psychiatrist, New York State Psychiatric Institute; member of faculty, William A. White Psychoanalytic Institute. Certified in psychiatry, American Board of Psychiatry and Neurology, 1963, in child psychiatry, 1966. *Military service:* U.S. Army, Medical Corps, 1960-62; served in Germany; became captain.

MEMBER: American Academy of Psychoanalysis (fellow), American Academy of Child Psychiatry (fellow), American Psychiatric Association. *Awards, honors:* Harry Stack Sullivan Award, William A. White Psychoanalytic Institute, 1966, for paper, "The Mutual Storytelling Technique"; Gralnick Foundation Award, 1967, for paper, "The Guilt Reaction of Parents of Children with Severe Physical Disease"; *Psychology and Social Science Review* Book of the Year award, 1971, for *Therapeutic Communication with Children: The Mutual Storytelling Technique.*

WRITINGS: The Child's Book about Brain Injury (juvenile), Association for Brain Injured Children (New York), 1966; (contributor) Jules H. Masserman, editor, *Science and Psychoanalysis,* Volume XIV, Grune, 1969; *The Boys and Girls Book about Divorce* (juvenile), Jason Aronson, 1970; *Therapeutic Communication with Children: The Mutual Storytelling Technique,* Jason Aronson, 1971; (contributor) Robert L. Noland, editor, *Counseling Parents of the Ill and Handicapped,* C. C Thomas, 1971; (author of foreword) Philip Barker, *Basic Child Psychiatry,* Staples, 1971; *Doctor Gardner's Stories about the Real World* (juvenile), Prentice-Hall, 1972; *MBD: The Family Book about Brain Dysfunction,* Jason Aronson, 1973; *On Understanding Children,* Jason Aronson, 1973; *The Talking, Feeling, and Doing Game,* Creative Therapeutics, 1973; *Doctor Gardner's Fairy Tales for Today's Children,* Prentice-Hall, 1974; *Psychotherapeutic Approaches to the Resistant Child,* Jason Aronson, 1975; *Psychotherapy with Children of Divorce,* Jason Aronson, 1976; *Doctor Gardner's Modern Fairy Tales,* George F. Stickley Co., 1977; *The Parents Book about Divorce,* Doubleday, 1977. Contributor to psychiatry yearbooks; contributor of about one hundred articles to psychiatry journals and to popular periodicals, including *Harper's Bazaar* and *Today's Girl.* Editor-in-Chief, *International Journal of Child Psychotherapy,* 1972-73.

WORK IN PROGRESS: The Diagnosis and Treatment of Minimal Brain Dysfunction; books using his knowledge of child psychiatry to help parents deal with various child problems.

SIDELIGHTS: Richard Gardner told *CA:* "Medical school training at the State University of New York's Brooklyn Medical Center was both grueling and immensely rewarding. The dedication to patient care that was instilled in me then

has been central to my professional life. It was there that I had my first experience with psychiatric patients and it was then that I decided that inquiries into the basic mechanisms of psychopathological disorders could be among the most fascinating of intellectual pursuits and the alleviation of such patients' suffering a most noble calling." *The Boys and Girls Book about Divorce* has been published in translation in Argentina, Japan, Holland, and Israel.

BIOGRAPHICAL/CRITICAL SOURCES: Time, October 26, 1970; *New York Times Magazine,* November 22, 1970, November 28, 1971; *New York,* March 1, 1971.

* * *

GARFITT, Roger 1944-

PERSONAL: Born April 12, 1944, in Wiltshire, England; son of Alan (a circuit judge) and Muriel (Jaggers) Garfitt. *Education:* Merton College, Oxford, B.A. (honors), 1968. *Home:* c/o South Weylands Farm, Esher Rd., Walton-on-Thames, Surrey, England.

CAREER: Free-lance writer. *Awards, honors:* Guinness International Poetry Prize, 1973; Gregory Award, 1974; Arts Council Creative Writing fellowship, 1975-77.

WRITINGS: Caught on Blue (poems), Carcanet Press, 1970; *West of Elm* (poems), Carcanet Press, 1975. Work has been anthologized in *British Poetry since 1960,* 1972, and *Two Decades of Irish Writing,* 1975. Contributor of poetry and fiction reviews to *Times Literary Supplement, London Magazine, New Review, Listener,* and *Stand.*

WORK IN PROGRESS: A collection of poems, for Carcanet Press; *Counter Measures,* a critical book on directions in contemporary poetry; a book on the wildlife of a North Devon valley.

* * *

GARNER, (Lafayette) Ross 1914-

PERSONAL: Born March 28, 1914, in Norristown, Pa.; son of Albert Rowland (a doctor) and Margaret (Ross) Garner; married Ann Magaret (a professor of psychology), June 13, 1953; children: David, Margaret. *Education:* Haverford College, A.B., 1936; University of Pennsylvania, LL.B., 1939; University of Hawaii, M.A., 1948; University of Chicago, Ph.D., 1955. *Politics:* Liberal. *Religion:* "Pre-Reformation." *Home:* 2011 Ridgewood Lane, Lake Oswego, Ore. 97034. *Office:* Department of English, Portland State University, P.O. Box 751, Portland, Ore. 97207.

CAREER: University of Nebraska, Lincoln, assistant professor, 1955-59, associate professor, 1959-63, professor of English, 1963-68; Portland State University, Portland, Ore., professor of English, 1968—. *Military service:* U.S. Army, 1941-46; became captain. *Member:* Modern Language Association of America, American Association of University Professors, Renaissance Society of America, Milton Society of America, American Civil Liberties Union, Common Cause, Phi Kappa Phi. *Awards, honors:* Fiske Poetry Award, 1952; Woods research fellowship to England and Wales, 1961-62.

WRITINGS: Henry Vaughan: Experience and the Tradition, University of Chicago Press, 1959; *The Unprofitable Servant in Henry Vaughan,* University of Nebraska Press, 1963. Contributor of articles and reviews to scholarly journals. Editor, "News and Ideas" column in *College English,* 1959-61.

WORK IN PROGRESS: Two monographs, with the tentative titles *Moral Responsibility in Shakespeare* and *Simple Piety and the Death of God;* essays and poems.†

*   *   *

GARNHAM, Nicholas 1937-

PERSONAL: Born June 18, 1937, in London, England; son of Robert (a businessman) and Moira (Sergeant) Garnham; married Barbara Staveley, November 26, 1963; children: Sophie. *Education:* Attended Winchester College, 1950-55; Trinity College, Cambridge, B.A. (second class honors), 1961. *Home:* 4 Park Hill Rd., London N.W.3, England. *Office:* Polytechnic of Central London, 309 Regent St., London W1R 8AL, England.

CAREER: British Broadcasting Corp., London, England, film editor, 1962-65, director, 1965-68; free-lance writer and director, 1968-72; Polytechnic of Central London, London, head of media studies, 1972—. *Military service:* Royal Navy, 1956-58.

WRITINGS: (With Joan Bakewell) *The New Priesthood,* Allen Lane, 1970; *Samuel Fuller,* British Film Institute, 1971; *Structures of Television,* British Film Institute, 1972. Writer of television documentaries, "Has the Past Got a Future?" and "In Search of Paradise." Contributor to *Listener, New Society, New Statesman,* and other periodicals.

WORK IN PROGRESS: Research on the political economy of culture.

*   *   *

GARRETT, James Leo, Jr. 1925-

PERSONAL: Born November 25, 1925, in Waco, Tex.; son of James Leo (an accountant and professor) and Grace (Jenkins) Garrett; married Myrta Ann Latimer, August 31, 1948; children: James Leo III, Robert Thomas, Paul Latimer. *Education:* Baylor University, B.A. (cum laude), 1945; Southwestern Baptist Theological Seminary, B.D., 1948, Th.D., 1954; Princeton Theological Seminary, Th.M., 1949; additional study at Texas Christian University, summers, 1954, 1956, and Catholic University of America, 1963; Harvard University, Ph.D., 1966; postdoctoral study at Oxford University, 1968-69, and St. John's University, summer, 1977. *Home:* 2224 Wooded Acres Dr., Waco, Tex. 76710. *Office address:* Box 380, Baylor University, Waco, Tex. 76703.

CAREER: Pastor of Baptist churches in Texas, 1945-51, visiting pastor, 1951-62; Baylor University, Waco, Tex., interim instructor in Greek, 1948; Southwestern Baptist Theological Seminary, Fort Worth, Tex., instructor, 1949-51, assistant professor, 1951-54, associate professor, 1954-57, professor of theology, 1957-59; Southern Baptist Theological Seminary, Louisville, Ky., professor of Christian theology, 1959-73; Baylor University, professor of religion and director of J. M. Dawson Studies in Church and State, 1973—. Has lectured in Colombia, Brazil, Mexico, Switzerland, and England. Chairman of Study Commission on Cooperative Christianity, Baptist World Alliance, 1968-75. Treasurer, Machaerus Archaeological Excavation, Amman, Jordan, 1968. *Member:* American Society of Church History, American Academy of Religion, Southern Baptist Historical Society. *Awards, honors:* American Association of Theological Schools faculty fellowship at Library of Congress, 1962-63.

WRITINGS: The Nature of the Church according to the Radical Continental Reformation, privately printed, 1957; *Baptist Church Discipline,* Broadman, 1962; *Evangelism for Discipleship,* privately printed, 1964; (editor) *The Teacher's Yoke: Studies in Memory of Henry Trantham,* Baylor University Press, 1964; *Baptists and Roman Catholicism,* Broadman, 1965; (editor) *The Concept of the Believers' Church,* Herald Press, 1970; *Reinhold Niebuhr on Roman Catholicism,* Seminary Baptist Book Store, 1972; (editor) *Baptist Relations with Other Christians,* Judson Press, 1974. Sermons included in *Southwestern Sermons,* Broadman, 1960, and *Christ for the World,* Broadman, 1963. Contributor to encyclopedias, journals, and Baptist periodicals. Managing editor, *Southwestern Journal of Theology,* 1958-59; member of editorial board, *Review and Expositor,* 1963-66; consulting editor, *Mennonite Quarterly Review,* 1969—; editor, *Journal of Church and State,* 1973—.

WORK IN PROGRESS: The Priesthood of All Christians.

SIDELIGHTS: James Garrett has traveled widely in the Near and Middle East, Europe, Japan, and Central and South America. He was a guest at the closing week of the fourth session, Vatican Council II, 1965.

*   *   *

GARRETT, John (Allen) 1920-

PERSONAL: Born July 15, 1920; son of George and Pearl (Dwight) Garrett; married Dorothy Scott-Orr, December 15, 1944 (deceased); married Roberta Riggleman (a journalist), June 14, 1959; children: (first marriage) David, Catherine Garrett Johnson, Peter; (second marriage) Mark, Stephen. *Education:* Attended Scots College, Sydney, Australia; University of Sydney, B.A., 1943, B.D., 1945, M.A., 1948; Camden College, Sydney, further study, 1941-44. *Home and office address:* Private Bag, Suva, Fiji.

CAREER: Ordained Congregational minister, 1946; minister of church in Summer Hill, New South Wales, Australia, 1945-50; Australian Council of Churches, Sydney, New South Wales, general secretary, 1950-54; World Council of Churches, Geneva, Switzerland, director of information, 1954-60; Camden College, Sydney, principal, 1960-66; Pacific Theological College, Suva, Fiji, professor of church history, 1967-74, faculty associate, 1974—. Visiting fellow, Australian National University, 1977—. Freelance journalist. *Member:* Royal Australian Historical Society.

WRITINGS: (With L. W. Farr) *Camden College: A Centenary History,* Camden College, 1964; *Roger Williams: Witness Beyond Christendom, 1603-1683,* Macmillan, 1970. Contributor to religious journals.

WORK IN PROGRESS: Research toward books on the history of Christianity in the Pacific area.

AVOCATIONAL INTERESTS: Music and the arts, sports (especially track and rugby).

*   *   *

GARRISON, Omar V. 1913-

PERSONAL: Born June 2, 1913, in LaJunta, Colo.; son of Jasper and Martha (Anderson) Garrison; married Virginia Leah Herrick, September 11, 1952. *Home:* Edificio Portinyol, 90, 5a, Arenys de Mar, Barcelona, Spain.

CAREER: Reuters (British wire service), London, England, war correspondent, 1942-45; *Fresno Guide,* Fresno, Calif., editor, 1945-48; *Los Angeles Mirror-News,* Los Angeles, Calif., science editor, 1948-59; now free-lance writer. *Awards, honors:* Ogden Reid fellowship, 1954; Freedoms Foundation award, 1957.

WRITINGS: Tantra, Julian Press, 1964; Spy Government, Lyle Stuart, 1967; The Dictocrats, Books for Today, 1970; Howard Hughes in Las Vegas, Lyle Stuart, 1971; Medical Astrology, Lyle Stuart, 1971; Balboa: Conquistador, Lyle Stuart, 1971; Lost Gems of Secret Knowledge, University Books, 1973; Hidden Story of Scientology, Citadel, 1974; The Secret World of Interpol, Ralston-Pilot, 1976; The Encyclopedia of Prophecy, Lyle Stuart, 1977.

BIOGRAPHICAL/CRITICAL SOURCES: Nation, December 11, 1967; Best Sellers, December 1, 1971; Books and Bookmen, December, 1972.

*   *   *

GARSON, Barbara

PERSONAL: Born in Brooklyn, N.Y.; children: Juliet. Education: Attended University of California, Berkeley. Politics: Socialist. Agent: Elaine Markson, 44 Greenwich Ave., New York, N.Y. 10011.

CAREER: Writer. Co-founder of Grassy Knoll Press. Awards, honors: A.B.C. grant to study writing for cameras, administered by Yale University School of Drama, 1967; special commission for the creation of plays for children, New York State Council on the Arts, 1975; Obie (Off-Broadway) Award, Village Voice, 1977, for "The Dinosaur Door"; National Endowment for the Arts creative writing grant, 1977.

WRITINGS: MacBird! (two-act play; first produced Off-Broadway at Village Gate, February 22, 1967), Grassy Knoll Press, 1966, Grove, 1967; (with Fred Gardner) "The Co-op" (two-act play), first produced Off-Broadway at Bartenieff and Fields Theatre for the New City, June, 1972; All the Livelong Day: The Meaning and Demeaning of Routine Work, Doubleday, 1975; "The Dinosaur Door" (children's play), first produced Off-Broadway at Theatre for the New City, June, 1976. Contributor of articles to Harper's, New York Times, Ms., Ramparts, Liberation, Mother Jones, In These Times, Working Papers, and other periodicals.

SIDELIGHTS: One of the most controversial plays produced in the 1960's, Barbara Garson's "MacBird!" has been attacked and defended, dismissed and analyzed by critics in the United States and abroad. Written originally as a street theatre play to be performed for political demonstrations, the play has had advocates and detractors of equal stature. Martin Esslin calls it "a healthy, vigorous and on the whole admirable piece of political cartooning." "The funniest, toughest-minded, and most ingenious political satire I've read in years is Barbara Garson's 'MacBird!' ...," writes Dwight Macdonald in his review. "She has solved, in her own slam-bang way, the problem of satirizing a reality so grotesque that it often seems to defy exaggeration. . . . At last the younger generation has produced a satirist." Robert Brustein praises Garson as "an extraordinarily gifted parodist, for in converting Macbeth to her own uses, she demonstrates an unusual ear for Shakespearean verse and an impressive ability to adapt the rhythms and accents of a past age to a modern idiom. . . . It will very probably go down as one of the [most] brutally provocative works in the American theatre, as well as one of the most grimly amusing."

In one of his highly critical reviews of "MacBird!," Walter Kerr calls the play "a very strange fusion of the more cavalier pronouncements of the extreme left and extreme right both. The upshot is a kind of crackpot consensus, with wan and bewildered smiles doing what they can to keep alive." In another article Kerr suggests that ". . . the jests are random, inconsequential, unmatched—and therein tasteless-

ness lies. . . . Tone is a kind of truth: and that truth, in however bizarre an exercise, must finally be respected. Tone finally goes so far astray in 'MacBird!' that satire is lost sight of altogether."

Many other reviewers have a rather ambivalent attitude towards the play; while they find it ripe with faults, they also see it as an important piece of propaganda reflecting its times. Alan Brien states: "In performance . . . the play succeeds in being both funny and gripping. But it makes no pretence to be more than instant, disposable pop art, concentrate of propaganda—just pour on hot emotion and stir. It is a work of literary collage, junk sculpture of drama, which exists for now and for us not for tomorrow and for posterity. It flashes by like a strip cartoon. Good or bad taste is not applicable—it has the authentic taste of this moment of our age."

"MacBird!" has had more than 300 productions. The play sold over half a million copies and was published in translation in France, Brazil, and Uruguay.

Garson's study of routine work, All the Livelong Day, also received mixed reviews. Garson, a self-styled "socialist agitator and educator," irked several reviewers by her interjection of her political opinions. "Her judgments on the subject will annoy all but the most ardent of socialists," predicts J. D. Moorhead. A Newsweek reviewer notes that "Garson is a playwright; she knows what dialogue is, and how to shape a scene, but she has no sense at all of how to shape an argument that persuades." However, Moorhead characterizes All the Livelong Day as "a loving book. It celebrates man's vitality and ingenuity."

BIOGRAPHICAL/CRITICAL SOURCES: Books, November, 1966; Village Voice, January 12, 1967, March 2, 1967, September 29, 1975; Motive, February, 1967; Times Literary Supplement, February 9, 1967; New York Times Book Review, February 12, 1967, October 5, 1975; New York Times, February 24, 1967, March 12, 1967, March 19, 1967, April 1, 1967, April 16, 1967; Observer, February 26, 1967; National Observer, February 27, 1967; Time, March 3, 1967; Newsweek, March 6, 1967, September 29, 1975; New Republic, March 11, 1967; New Yorker, March 11, 1967; Nation, March 13, 1967, May 22, 1976; Life, March 17, 1967; Listener, March 30, 1967; New Statesman, March 31, 1967; Vogue, April 15, 1967; Ramparts, May, 1967; Christian Century, May 31, 1967; Literary Times, May-June, 1967; London Magazine, June, 1967; Hudson Review, summer, 1967; Cue, June 17, 1972; Christian Science Monitor, October 1, 1975; Ms., November, 1975; Progressive, November, 1975.

*   *   *

GARTNER, Alan 1935-

PERSONAL: Born April 4, 1935, in New York, N.Y.; son of Harold J. (an executive) and Mary (Triner) Gartner; married Audrey Joseph, July 7, 1957; children: Jonathan, Rachel, Daniel. Education: Antioch College, A.B., 1956; Harvard University, M.A., 1961; Union College and University, Ph.D., 1972. Home: 20 Sailfish Pl., Northport, N.Y. 11768. Office: New Human Services Institute, 184 Fifth Ave., New York, N.Y. 10010.

CAREER: Harvard University, Graduate School of Education, Cambridge, Mass., instructor in education, 1962-65; Newton Public Schools, Newton, Mass., teacher, 1962-65; Congress of Racial Equality, New York City, community relations director, 1965-66; Economic Opportunity Council, Patchogue, N.Y., executive director, 1966-67; New Careers

Development Center, New York City, co-director, 1967-72; Queens College of the City University of New York, Flushing, N.Y., professor, 1972-76; Graduate School and University Center of the City University of New York, New York City, member of staff, New Human Services Institute, 1976—. Member, Economic Opportunity Council, Suffolk County, N.Y. *Member:* American Civil Liberties Union (Suffolk County; member of board of directors), Boston Congress of Racial Equality (chairman, 1961-65). *Awards, honors:* Florina Lasker fellow, Brandeis University, 1962; Poynter fellow, Yale University, 1976.

WRITINGS: Paraprofessionals and Their Performance, Praeger, 1971; (with Mary Kohler and Frank Riessman) *Children Teach Children,* Harper, 1971; (with Colin Greer and Riessman) *After Deschooling, What?,* Harper, 1973; (with Russell Nixon and Riessman) *Public Service Employment,* Praeger, 1973; (with Greer and Riessman) *What Nixon Is Doing to Us,* Harper, 1973; (with Greer and Riessman) *The New Assault on Equality,* Harper, 1974; (with Riessman) *The Service Society and the Consumer Vanguard,* Harper, 1974; (with William Lynch and Riessman) *A Full Employment Program for the 1970's,* Praeger, 1976; *The Preparation of Human Service Professionals,* Human Sciences Press, 1976; (with Vivian Jackson and Riessman) *Paraprofessionals Today,* Human Sciences Press, 1977; (with Riessman) *Self-Help,* Jossey-Bass, 1977.

* * *

GARVER, Richard B(ennett) 1934-

PERSONAL: Born November 14, 1934, in Youngstown, Ohio; son of Matthew H. and Mary K. (Clarke) Garver; married Donna Rae Fisher, May 21, 1967; children: Deborah Rae, David Alan. *Education:* Ohio State University, B.Sc., 1956; University of Florida, M.P.H., 1968; University of Northern Colorado, graduate study.

CAREER: U.S. Air Force, career officer, 1956—, present rank, major; U.S. Air Force Academy, Colorado Springs, Colo., 1965-71, began as assistant professor, became associate professor of life and behavioral science, varsity golf coach, 1965-71. *Member:* International Society for Professional Hypnosis, Phi Kappa Phi.

WRITINGS: (With Anthony R. Cillo and Patrick S. Going) *You Can Defend Yourself,* Apollo, 1971. Contributor to *Golf Monthly, Coach and Athlete, Florida JOHPER,* and other periodicals.

WORK IN PROGRESS: Hypnosis in Sport; Hypnosis and Facilitation of Neuro-motor Pathways.

AVOCATIONAL INTERESTS: Judo, karate, and aikido.†

* * *

GATES, Jean Key 1911-

PERSONAL: Born September 23, 1911, in Carthage, Ark.; daughter of William James (a businessman) and Jeannette (Wylie) Key; married Sherwood Gates, July 30, 1949 (deceased). *Education:* Hendrix College, B.A., 1930; Catholic University of America, M.S. in L.S., 1951; summer graduate study at University of Arkansas, 1941-48, and George Washington University, 1956, 1959. *Religion:* Presbyterian. *Home:* 4148 Pine Lake Lane-102, Tampa, Fla. 33624. *Office:* University of South Florida, Tampa, Fla. 33620.

CAREER: Teacher in Briggsville, Ark., 1930-31, Thornton, Ark., 1933-34, and Eudora, Ark., 1934-37; county supervisor of schools, Chicot County, Lake Village, Ark., 1937-49; District of Columbia Teachers College, Washington, li-

brarian, 1951-58, librarian in charge of library instruction, 1958-63; University of Maryland, College Park, lecturer in library education, 1964-66; University of South Florida, Tampa, lecturer, 1966-68, assistant professor, 1968-72, associate professor of library-audiovisual education, 1972—. *Member:* American Library Association, American Association of School Librarians, Association of College and Research Libraries, National Education Association, Southeastern Library Association, Florida Education Association, Florida Library Association, Beta Phi Mu, Delta Kappa Gamma.

WRITINGS: Guide to the Use of Books and Libraries, with instructor's manual, McGraw, 1962, 4th edition, with teacher's manual, 1978; *Introduction to Librarianship,* McGraw, 1968, 2nd edition, 1976. Consulting editor, McGraw's "Series in Library Education"; educational advisor, McGraw's filmstrips "The College Library" series, 1966.

SIDELIGHTS: Jean Gates' *Guide to the Use of Books and Libraries* has been translated into Spanish and Portuguese. *Avocational interests:* Photography, travel.

* * *

GAULDIE, (William) Sinclair 1918-

PERSONAL: Born December 29, 1918, in Dundee, Scotland; son of William (an architect) and Charlotte (Sinclair) Gauldie; married Enid Elizabeth MacNeilage (a historian), May 12, 1949; children: Robin William, Alison Charlotte, Rebecca Ann. *Education:* Attended Dundee College of Art, 1936-39, 1940-43. *Office:* Gauldie Wright & Partners, 2 Osborne Pl., Dundee, Scotland.

CAREER: Architect; Gauldie Wright & Partners (formerly Gauldie, Hardie, Wright & Needham), Dundee, Scotland, senior partner, 1945—; University of Dundee, Dundee, honorary assistant lecturer, 1957—. Former chairman, Scottish Building Contract Committee; member of Broadcasting Council for Scotland, 1965-70, Scottish Housing Advisory Committee, 1966-70, and General Advisory Council of British Broadcasting Corp. (BBC), 1971—. *Military service:* British Army, Royal Corps of Signals, 1939-40. *Member:* Royal Institute of British Architects (fellow), Royal Incorporation of Architects in Scotland (fellow; president, 1963-65), British Society of Aesthetics, Scottish Arts Club, Royal Tay Yacht Club. *Awards, honors:* Created Commander of Order of the British Empire, for services to architecture, 1970.

WRITINGS: (With George Scott-Moncrieff) *Looking at Scottish Buildings,* Serif, 1947; (with Harold Scott) *Fortesquieu,* Dobson, 1953; *Architecture,* Oxford University Press, 1969. Contributor to architecture and aesthetics journals in Great Britain. Member of editorial consultative committee, *British Journal of Aesthetics.*

BIOGRAPHICAL/CRITICAL SOURCES: Time, October 24, 1969; *Christian Century,* October 29, 1969; *Virginia Quarterly Review,* spring, 1970.

* * *

GEERTZ, Clifford 1926-

PERSONAL: Born August 23, 1926, in San Francisco, Calif.; son of Clifford James (an engineer) and Lois (Brigger) Geertz; married Hildred Storey (a professor of anthropology and chairman of department at Princeton University), October 30, 1948; children: Erika, Benjamin. *Education:* Antioch College, A.B., 1950; Harvard University, Ph.D., 1956. *Home:* 5 Newlin Rd., Princeton, N.J. 08540. *Office:*

Department of Social Science, Institute for Advanced Study, Princeton, N.J. 08540.

CAREER: Harvard University, Cambridge, Mass., research associate, Laboratory of Social Relations, and instructor in social relations, 1956-57; Massachusetts Institute of Technology in Indonesia, research associate, Center for International Studies, 1957-58; Center for Advanced Study in the Behavioral Sciences, Stanford, Calif., fellow, 1958-59; University of California, Berkeley, assistant professor of anthropology, 1959-60; University of Chicago, Chicago, Ill., assistant professor, 1960-61, associate professor, 1961-64, professor of anthropology, 1964-70; Institute for Advanced Study, Princeton, N.J., professor of social science, 1970—. Committee for Comparative Study of New Nations, member, 1960-70, chairman, 1968-69. *Military service:* U.S. Navy, 1943-45. *Member:* American Anthropological Association, American Academy of Arts and Sciences, National Academy of Sciences, Association for Asian Studies, Middle East Studies Association. *Awards, honors:* American Sociological Association Sorokin Prize, 1974; American Academy of Arts and Sciences social science prize, 1974.

WRITINGS: The Rotating Credit Association: An Instrument for Development, Center for International Studies, Massachusetts Institute of Technology, 1956; *The Development of the Javanese Economy: A Socio-Cultural Approach,* Center for International Studies, Massachusetts Institute of Technology, 1956; *The Social Context of Economic Change: An Indonesian Case Study,* Center for International Studies, Massachusetts Institute of Technology, 1956; *Modjokuto: Religion in Java,* four volumes, Center for International Studies, Massachusetts Institute of Technology, 1958; *The Religion of Java* (part of material first published in *Modjokuto*), Free Press, 1960; (editor) *Old Societies and New States,* Free Press, 1963; *Agricultural Involution: The Process of Ecological Change in Indonesia,* University of California Press, for Association for Asian Studies, 1963; *Peddlers and Princes: Social Change and Economic Modernization in Two Indonesian Towns,* University of Chicago Press, 1963; *The Social History of an Indonesian Town,* M.I.T. Press, 1965; *Person, Time, and Conduct in Bali: An Essay in Cultural Analysis,* Southeast Asia Studies, Yale University, 1966; *Islam Observed: Religious Development in Morocco and Indonesia,* Yale University Press, 1968; *The Interpretation of Cultures,* Basic Books, 1973; (with wife, Hildred Geertz) *Kinship in Bali,* University of Chicago Press, 1975. Contributor to *New York Review of Books, Daedalus, Encounter,* and other journals.

WORK IN PROGRESS: Further cultural anthropological studies in Indonesia and Morocco.

SIDELIGHTS: Clifford Geertz is competent in Dutch, Indonesian, Javanese, French, and Moroccan Arabic.

* * *

GEHMAN, Richard Boyd 1921-1972
(Frederick Christian, Martin Scott)

May 20, 1921—May 13, 1972; American novelist, magazine writer, and biographer. Obituaries: *New York Times,* May 14, 1972; *Washington Post,* May 14, 1972; *Publishers Weekly,* May 22, 1972. (See index for *CA* sketch)

* * *

GEHRI, Alfred 1896(?)-1972

1896(?)—January 8, 1972; Swiss playwright and translator.

Obituaries: *New York Times,* January 9, 1972; *Washington Post,* January 10, 1972.

* * *

GELLERT, Judith 1925-

PERSONAL: Born July 7, 1925, in New York, N.Y.; daughter of Norbert C. Gellert; children: Jeffrey Tennyson, Noel Tennyson. *Education:* Skidmore College, M.A., 1947. *Politics:* Liberal. *Home:* 5602 Roosevelt St., Bethesda, Md. 20034.

CAREER: Free-lance portrait photographer in Washington, D.C., Baltimore, Md., and New England.

WRITINGS: (Photographic illustrator) Kathleen Costello Beer, *Bumble and Me,* Van Nostrand, 1969; *Wild Jeff* (illustrated with photographs by the author), Pratt & Munk, 1971.

WORK IN PROGRESS: A book of photographs of family life taken during a year on a farm in Vermont.†

* * *

GELPI, Albert 1931-

PERSONAL: Surname is pronounced *Jel*-pi; born July 19, 1931, in New Orleans, La.; son of Albert Joseph (a businessman) and Alice (Delaup) Gelpi; married Barbara Charlesworth (a lecturer in English), June 14, 1965; children: Christopher Francis Cecil, Adrienne Catherine Ardelle. *Education:* Loyola University, New Orleans, A.B., 1951; Tulane University, M.A., 1956; Harvard University, Ph.D., 1962. *Religion:* Roman Catholic. *Home:* 870 Tolman Dr., Stanford, Calif. 94305. *Office:* Department of English, Stanford University, Stanford, Calif. 94305.

CAREER: Harvard University, Cambridge, Mass., assistant professor of English, 1962-67; Stanford University, Stanford, Calif., associate professor, 1967-75, professor of English, 1975—.

WRITINGS: Emily Dickinson: The Mind of the Poet, Harvard University Press, 1965; *The Poet in America: 1650 to the Present,* Heath, 1974; (editor with wife, Barbara Charlesworth Gelpi) *Adrienne Rich's Poetry,* Norton, 1975; *The Tenth Muse: The Psyche of the American Poet,* Harvard University Press, 1975. Contributor of essays, articles, and reviews to periodicals.

WORK IN PROGRESS: The American Poetic Renaissance 1910-1930.

* * *

GEMMETT, Robert J(ames) 1936-

PERSONAL: Born March 11, 1936, in Schenectady, N.Y.; son of A. James and Dorothy (MacFarlane) Gemmett; married Kendra Baxter, January 25, 1964; children: Stephen, Scott, David, Kerry. *Education:* Siena College, B.A., 1959; University of Massachusetts, M.A., 1962; Syracuse University, Ph.D., 1967. *Office:* Department of English, State University of New York College, Brockport, N.Y. 14420.

CAREER: Clarkson College of Technology, Potsdam, N.Y., instructor in English, 1964-65; *English Record,* New York, N.Y., associate editor, 1967-69; State University of New York College at Brockport, associate professor, 1965-70, professor of English, 1970—, chairman of department, 1975—. *Military service:* U.S. Army, 1959; became second lieutenant. *Awards, honors:* Outstanding Educators in America recognition of merit, 1975.

WRITINGS: William Beckford, Twayne, 1977.

Editor: William Beckford, *Biographical Memoirs of Extraordinary Painters*, Fairleigh Dickinson University Press, 1969; Beckford, *Dreams, Waking Thoughts and Incidents*, Fairleigh Dickinson University Press, 1971; (author of introduction) *Men of Letters*, Volume III, Mansell Information Publishing, 1972; (author of introduction) Beckford, *Vathek*, 1786 and 1787 editions, Scholars Facsimiles and Reprints, 1972; Beckford, *Episodes of Vathek*, Fairleigh Dickinson University Press, 1975. Contributor of articles to *English Miscellany, Philological Quarterly, Gazette des Beaux Arts, Papers* of the Bibliographical Society of America, *Library Chronicle, American Book Collector*, and other English journals.

WORK IN PROGRESS: Editing a collection of unpublished letters by William Beckford; a study entitled *Beckford's Fonthill: The Landscape as Art*.

* * *

GENDZIER, Stephen J(ules) 1930-

PERSONAL: Born July 14, 1930, in New York, N.Y.; son of Louis and Sally (Koenig) Gendzier; married; wife's name, Irene (divorced); married Rhea Mendoza Diamond, 1973; children: (first marriage) Alexander A.; stepchildren: Christopher S., Evan A., Josh K. *Education:* Oberlin College, B.A., 1952; Columbia University, M.A., 1953, Ph.D., 1959; University of Paris, Certificats, 1955. *Home:* 36 Hayes Ave., Lexington, Mass. 02173. *Office:* Department of Romance and Comparative Literature, Brandeis University, Waltham, Mass. 02154.

CAREER: Columbia University, Columbia College, New York, N.Y., instructor in French literature, 1956-60; Massachusetts Institute of Technology, Cambridge, Mass., assistant professor of French literature, 1960-62; Brandeis University, Waltham, Mass., assistant professor, 1962-66, associate professor of French literature, 1966—, chairman of department of Romance and Comparative Literature, 1977—. *Member:* American Association of Teachers of French, American Association of University Professors, Modern Language Association of America, Societe Francaise d'Etude du XVIIIe Siecle, American Society for Eighteenth-Century Studies. *Awards, honors:* Fulbright grant, 1954-56.

WRITINGS: (Editor and translator) Denis Diderot, *The Encyclopedia: Selections*, Harper, 1967, 2nd edition, 1969. Contributor of articles, reviews, and translations to *Symposium, Romanic Review, French Review, Studies on Voltaire, Diderot Studies*, and other publications.

* * *

GERARD-LIBOIS, Jules C. 1923-
(G. Heinz)

PERSONAL: Born December 3, 1923, in Liege, Belgium; son of Jules and Christine (Heinz) Gerard; married Andree Libois (an editor); children: Marc, Dominique, Catherine. *Education:* University of Liege, LL.D. *Home:* Avenue du Houx 28, Boitsfort, Belgium B1170. *Office:* Centre de Recherche et d'Information Socio-Politiques, Congres 35, Brussels 1, Belgium 1000.

CAREER: Centre de Recherche et d'Information Socio-Politiques (CRISP), Brussels, Belgium, chairman, 1959—; Centre d'Etudes et le Documentation Africaines (CEDAF), Brussels, chairman, 1970—. Member of board, Institut Belge de Science Politique, Brussels, 1966—; director, Commission of European Communities. *Member:* International Political Science Association. *Awards, honors:* Prix de la libre Academie Picard.

WRITINGS: Secession au Katanga, Centre de Recherche et d'Information Socio-Politiques, 1963, translation by Rebecca Young published as *Katanga Secession*, University of Wisconsin Press, 1966; *Le Role de la Belgique dans l'operation des Nations Unies au Congo, 1960-1964* (title means "The Role of Belgium in the Operations of the United Nations in the Congo, 1960-1964"), Centre de Recherche et d'Information Socio-Politiques, 1965; (with H. Donnay) *Lumumba Patrice: Les cinquante derniers jours de sa vie*, Centre de Recherche et d'Information Socio-Politiques, 1966, translation by J. C. Seitz published as *Lumumba: The Last Fifty Days*, Grove, 1970; (with J. Govitch) *L'An 40* (title means "The Year 40"; on Belgium under German occupation), Centre de Recherche et d'Information Socio-Politiques, 1971. Editor with Benoit Verhaegen and others of *Congo* (yearbook), Centre de Recherche et d'Information Socio-Politiques, 1959—; some of the yearbooks also have been published in America by Princeton University Press. Contributor to *Res Publica, Revue Nouvelle*, and other periodicals.

WORK IN PROGRESS: Studies on the external politics of Belgium, particularly on the relation between size and situation of the country and its international behavior; *Belgique: 1944-45, liberation restauration*.

* * *

GERBER, Dan 1940-

PERSONAL: Born August 12, 1940, in Grand Rapids, Mich.; son of Daniel F. (a businessman) and Dorothy (Scott) Gerber; married Virginia Hartjen, August 12, 1961; children: Wendy, Frank, Tamara. *Education:* Michigan State University, B.A., 1962. *Politics:* Anarchist. *Religion:* Buddhist. *Home:* The Amazing X Ranch, Fremont, Mich. 49412. *Agent:* Robert Dattila, Phoenix Literary Agency, 150 East 74th St., New York, N.Y. 10021.

CAREER: Gerber was a professional racing driver for five years, and a high school teacher of English in Fremont, Mich., for two years; Grand Valley State College, Thomas Jefferson College, Allendale, Mich., poet-in-residence, 1969-70; Michigan State University, East Lansing, writer-in-residence, 1970. *Member:* P.E.N., Authors Guild.

WRITINGS: (With Jim Harrison, Charles Simic, J. D. Reed, and George Quasha) *Five Blind Men* (poems), Sumac Press, 1969; *The Revenant* (poems), Sumac Press, 1971; *Departure* (poems), Sumac Press, 1973; *American Atlas* (novel), Prentice-Hall, 1973; *Out of Control* (novel), Prentice-Hall, 1974; *Indy: The World's Fastest Carnival Ride* (nonfiction), Prentice-Hall, 1977.

Contributor to anthologies: *Heartland*, edited by L. Stryk, Northern Illinois University Press, 1967; *Inside Outer Space*, edited by R. Vas Dias, Anchor Books, 1971; *The Third Coast: Contemporary Michigan Poetry*, edited by C. Hilberry and others, Wayne State University Press, 1976; *The Face of Poetry*, edited by M. L. Macarthur and H. C. Laverne, Gallimaufry Press, 1977. Also contributed poems to *Young American Poets*, published in Japan. Contributor of poetry, essays, and stories to *New York, Playboy, Sports Illustrated, New Yorker, Nation, Partisan Review, Stony Brook, Hearse, Voyages*, and other magazines.

WORK IN PROGRESS: A collection of poems, tentatively entitled *Letters to an Old Friend;* a novel, tentatively entitled *Last Day in the Field;* a book on psyching-up.

SIDELIGHTS: "Randall Jarrel's definition of a good poet, 'a man who, in a lifetime of standing out in thunderstorms, manages to be struck by lightning a half dozen times,' suits me," Dan Gerber told *CA*. "The active business of the poet is to keep his lightning rod polished and his ear tuned to the rumblings of distant thunder.... A man struck by lightning is seldom appeased by house current. In poetry as well as prose, I feel less a creator than an instrument of experience. I write what presents itself to me as necessary. I write about me, in the context of whatever experience, of matter or the imagination, I find myself."

AVOCATIONAL INTERESTS: Calligraphy, farming, tennis, sailing, music, and photography.

* * *

GERGEN, Kenneth J(ay) 1934-

PERSONAL: Born December 9, 1934, in Rochester, N.Y.; son of John Jay (a professor) and Aubeign (Lermond) Gergen; married Eleanor Cowan, June 21, 1957; married second wife, Mary McCanny (a psychologist), October 4, 1969; children: (first marriage) Laura Lynne, John Stanford. *Education:* Yale University, B.A., 1957; Duke University, Ph.D., 1963. *Home:* Rose Valley Rd., Wallingford, Pa., 19086. *Office:* Department of Psychology, Swarthmore College, Swarthmore, Pa. 19081.

CAREER: Harvard University, Cambridge, Mass., instructor, 1963-64, assistant professor of social psychology, 1964-67; Swarthmore College, Swarthmore, Pa., associate professor, 1967-71, professor of psychology, 1971—, chairman of department, 1967—. Visiting summer professor, University of North Carolina, 1963; research fellow in Stockholm, Sweden, 1966; summer lecturer, University of Colorado, 1967. Consultant to National Science Foundation, Eastern Pennsylvania Psychiatric Institute, and Arthur D. Little, Inc. *Military service:* U.S. Naval Reserve, 1957-59; became lieutenant. *Member:* American Psychological Association, American Sociological Association, American Association for Public Opinion Research, American Academy of Political and Social Science. *Awards, honors:* Guggenheim fellow, 1968-69; Fulbright research fellow, 1977-78.

WRITINGS: (Editor with Raymond A. Bauer) *The Study of Policy Formation,* Free Press, 1968; (editor with Chad Gordon) *The Self in Social Interaction,* Volume I, Wiley, 1968; *The Psychology of Behavior Exchange,* Addison-Wesley, 1969; (editor with David Marlowe) *Personality and Social Behavior,* Addison-Wesley, 1970; *The Concept of Self,* Holt, 1971; (editor) *Social Psychology,* CRM Books, 1976; (editor with L. Strickland and F. Aboud) *Social Psychology in Transition,* Plenum, 1977. Writer of fifteen-program television series on the psychology of motivation.

WORK IN PROGRESS: Regenerating Social Knowledge; Social Psychology: Issues and Action.

* * *

GERSHEN, Martin 1924-

PERSONAL: Born August 20, 1924, in Bronx, N.Y.; son of Hyman S. (a tailor) and Jennie (Gerson) Gershen; married Molly Cohen; children: Robert, Susan, Joseph. *Education:* New York University, B.S., 1949; University of Grenoble, Diplome, 1949; University of Paris, additional study, 1949-50; Columbia University, Certificate in Advanced International Reporting (M.A. equivalent), 1966. *Residence:* Israel.

CAREER: Newsman since 1949; former seaman in merchant marine under three flags; *Stars and Stripes* (military newspaper), member of editorial staff of European edition, 1956-62, with assignments as bureau chief in Germany, London, and Washington, D.C., and as roving correspondent in Europe, Middle East, and Africa; *Newark Star-Ledger* and other Newhouse newspapers, member of editorial staff, 1962-70, variously reporter, feature writer, re-write man, photographer, war correspondent, and syndicated columnist, chief of New York Bureau, 1966-70; University of Illinois at Urbana-Champaign, member of journalism faculty, faculty adviser to student chapters of Theta Sigma Phi and Sigma Delta Chi, beginning 1971; currently living in Israel. *Military service:* U.S. Navy, coxswain, 1942-46; received four battle stars for combat in Pacific theater.

MEMBER: Newspaper Reporters Association (chairman, freedom of the press committee), Overseas Press Club, Sigma Delta Chi. *Awards, honors:* Ford Foundation fellow in advanced international reporting, 1965-66; Ernie Pyle Memorial Award for reporting in Vietnam, 1967; Sigma Delta Chi Award for distinguished reporting in Vietnam, 1968; Page One Award for International Reporting from American Newspaper Guild, New York Chapter.

WRITINGS: Destroy or Die: The True Story of Mylai, Arlington House, 1970. Regular contributor to *Time, Life, Parade, Education Age, Columbia Journalism Review,* and United Press International; also has written for *World Digest, New York Herald Tribune, Daily Mail,* and other newspapers.†

* * *

GERSHMAN, Herbert S. 1926-1971

June 3, 1926—March 31, 1971; American educator, editor, and authority on surrealism. Obituaries: *Books Abroad,* summer, 1971. (See index for *CA* sketch)

* * *

GERSON, Wolfgang 1916-

PERSONAL: Born March 18, 1916, in Hamburg, Germany; son of Oskar (an architect) and Marta Sexta (Rosenfeld) Gerson; married Hildegard J. Aronstein, 1944; children: Martin, Ann, Erika, Katherine. *Education:* Studied at Architectural Association, London, England. *Religion:* Unitarian Universalist. *Home:* 1040 Aubeneau Crescent, West Vancouver, British Columbia, Canada. *Office:* School of Architecture, University of British Columbia, Vancouver, British Columbia, Canada.

CAREER: University of Manitoba, Winnipeg, member of faculty of School of Architecture, 1947-56; University of British Columbia, Vancouver, 1956—, professor of architecture and chairman of graduate program in School of Architecture, 1963—.

WRITINGS: Patterns of Urban Living, University of Toronto Press, 1970.

* * *

GHEORGHIU, (Constantin) Virgil 1916-

PERSONAL: Born September 15, 1916, in Razbeoni-Neamtz (a mountain village), Moldavie, Rumania; son of Constantin (a priest of the Rumanian Orthodox Church) and Maria (Scobay) Gheorghiu; married Ecaterina Burbea (a lawyer), July 29, 1939, in Bucharest. *Education:* Attended Royal Military College, Kishiniev, Rumania, and University of Bucharest; took theology courses at University of Heidelberg after his release from wartime internment. *Politics:*

"No party politics." *Home:* 16 Rue de Siam, Paris 16, France.

CAREER: Rumanian novelist, living in exile in France since 1948; priest of the Paris Colony Rumanian Orthodox Church, 1963—. Gheorghiu had published poetry before he was called into the Rumanian Army, and while still in uniform wrote pro-government books when Marshal Ion Antonescu came into power in 1941 (Antonescu was a leader of the militarist movement and a German ally); when Antonescu was overthrown with Soviet help in 1944, Gheorghiu, then a member of the Rumanian diplomatic corps in Yugoslavia, was interned; he was freed from an internment camp in Czechoslovakia by the American advance in 1945, but considered suspect by the new government of Rumania, spent three years as a displaced person before settling in France. *Military service:* Rumanian Army. *Awards, honors:* Royal Poetry Prize (Rumania), 1940, for *Caligrafie pe zapada.*

WRITINGS—In Rumanian: *Viata de toate zilele a poetului* (title means "The Daily Life of a Poet"; poems), Cartea Romanesca, 1938; *Armand Calinescu* (poems), Socec, 1940; *Caligrafie pe zapada* (title means "Calligraphy on the Snow"; poems), Fundatiilor Regale, 1940; *Ard Malurile Nistrului* (title means "The Flaming Banks of the Dniester"; documentary), Nationala, 1941; *Am luptat in Crimeea* (title means "I Fought in the Crimea"; documentary), Nationale, 1942; *Cu submarinul la asediul Sevastopolului* (title means "In Submarine at the Siege of Sebastopol"; documentary), Nationala, 1942; *Ultima ora* (title means "The Last Hour"; novel), Nationala, 1942; *Ceasul de rugaciune* (title means "The Hour of Prayer"; poems), Nationala, 1942.

In French; most books were written in Rumanian and translated by Livia Lamoure for first publication in France; all novels, except as noted: *La Vingt-cinquieme heure* (autobiographical novel; translated from the Rumanian by Monique Saint-Come), Plon, 1949, English translation by Rita Eldon published as *The Twenty-Fifth Hour*, Knopf, 1950, Regnery, 1966.

La Seconde chance (autobiographical novel), Plon, 1952; *L'Homme qui voyagea seul*, Plon, 1954; *Le Peuple des immortels* (stories), Plon, 1955; *Vertu a forte dose*, Plon, c. 1956, retitled *Les Sacrifies du Danube* after first printing; *Saint Jean Bouche d'Or* (fictionalized biography), Plon, 1957; *Les Mendiants de miracles*, Plon, 1958.

La Cravache (postface by the author), Plon, 1960; *Perahim*, Plon, 1961; *La Maison de Petrodava*, Plon, 1961; *La Vie de Mahomet* (biography), Plon, 1962; *Les Immortels d'Agapia*, Plon, 1964, English translation by Milton Stansbury published as *The Immortals of the Mountain*, Regnery, 1969; *De la Vingt-cinquieme heure a l'heure eternelle* (memoir of his father), Plon, 1965; *La Jeunesse du docteur Luther*, Plon, 1965; *Le Meurtre de Kyralessa*, Plon, 1966, English translation by Marika Mihalyi published as *The Death of Kyralessa*, Regnery, 1968; *La Condottiera*, Plon, 1967; *La Tunique de peau*, Plon, 1967; *Pourquoi m'a-t-on appele Virgil?*, Plon, 1968; *La vie du Patriarche Athenagoras* (biography), Plon, 1969.

L'espionne, Plon, 1971; *L'oeil Americain*, Plon, 1972; *Dieu ne recoit que le Dimanche*, Plon, 1975.

In other languages: *Rumaenische Maerchen* (fairy tales), Aehren-Verlag (Heidelberg), 1948; *De Verdenking* (novel), Van Hoeve (The Hague), 1962; *Contrata de Heroes* (novel), Editorial Luis de Caralt (Barcelona), c. 1963. Also author of *Alibi pour Limitroff*, 1962, and *Ambrosius de Milan.*

SIDELIGHTS: Marilyn Gaddis Rose wrote in *Books Abroad:* "In person Father Gheorghiu seems more like a priest than a novelist. He and his gracious wife live comfortably in a pleasantly furnished apartment . . . although as resident aliens without a homeland they could be asked to leave France on very short notice. He is tall, wan, dark-haired, spectacled, somewhat more gaunt than Arthur Miller whom he resembles. A visitor finds it hard to realize that this kind, genial host with a soft Rumanian accent and a whimsical sense of humor has written such violence-filled novels, or could, as he admits in the epilogue of *La Cravache* often have provoked deliberately the controversy that has followed his career as an *emigre* novelist." Gheorghiu's cultural background is both Eastern and Western, his church a blend of Greek Orthodoxy and Roman Catholicism, and his native country has undergone considerable changes in policy in recent years. These forces all contribute to the urgency in his writing, and what Rose called "his search for a spiritual no man's land." She wrote that he was "the oldest child of very young parents. Steadfast piety made existence bearable for these folk who considered oppression normal." Life in the mountain village where his father was the priest was by no means easy.

Both *La Seconde chance* and *The Twenty-Fifth Hour* are autobiographical. In the latter, Rose writes, "Father Gheorghiu says that . . . he himself is Trajan . . . , that the characters are composites of people he knew, and that he himself protested his imprisonment by means of Swiftian petitions." During this time he increased his familiarity with Anglo-American literature. "Walt Whitman, he says, had been a revelation of his adolescence. He gained facility reading the guards' pocketbooks. He went on to T. S. Eliot and W. H. Auden, whom he quotes in *The Twenty-Fifth Hour*, and Ezra Pound."

Relating his childhood and wartime experiences, and his life since that time, Rose comments: "With such conflicting loyalties in his past, Father Gheorghiu is bound to have an apocalyptic, but clouded, world view . . . [his] experiences made his partial, but spiritualizing, perspective necessary. To him death has to be martyrdom; suffering has to be penance. He may suggest unwittingly that oppression requires both a group willing to oppress and a group willing to be oppressed. From his point of view this impasse is never-ending, making necessary a spiritual mid-world. Today, a successful Western novelist for fifteen years, Father Gheorghiu has to keep creating this mid-world, for he says it is clearer than ever that we live in the twenty-fifth hour."

The Twenty-Fifth Hour, begun in one concentration camp and finished in another, is the most widely translated of his books, which in all have been published in thirty-four languages. A film version, released in 1966 featured Anthony Quinn and was directed by Carlo Ponti and Henri Verneuil.

BIOGRAPHICAL/CRITICAL SOURCES: Books Abroad, summer, 1950, spring, 1967, autumn, 1968; *Village Voice*, August 26, 1965; *Le Figaro Litteraire*, June 30, 1966; *Hudson Review*, spring, 1967; *Best Sellers*, May 15, 1968; *Le Monde*, May 9, 1970.†

*   *   *

GIANNETTI, Louis D. 1937-

PERSONAL: Born April 1, 1937, in Natick, Mass.; son of John and Vincenza (Zappitelli) Giannetti; married Justine Gallagher, September 11, 1964; children: Christina. *Education:* Boston University, B.A., 1959; University of Iowa, M.A., 1961, Ph.D., 1967. *Home:* 3374 Ashby Rd., Shaker

Heights, Ohio 44120. *Office:* Department of English, Case Western Reserve University, Cleveland, Ohio 44106.

CAREER: Emory University, Atlanta, Ga., assistant professor of English, 1966-70; Case Western Reserve University, Cleveland, Ohio, 1970—, began as assistant professor of film, currently professor of English and film. Film critic for *Cleveland* magazine. *Member:* American Film Institute.

WRITINGS: Understanding Movies, Prentice-Hall, 1972, 2nd edition, 1976; *Godard and Others: Essays in Film Form,* Fairleigh Dickinson University Press, 1975. Contributor of articles on film, drama, and literature to *Western-Humanities Review, Modern Drama, Literature/Film Quarterly, Comparative Drama, Journal of Aesthetic Education, Film Criticism,* and other journals.

WORK IN PROGRESS: Masters of the American Cinema, for Prentice-Hall; *The Cinema of Fred Zinnemann.*

*   *   *

GIBB, Hamilton (Alexander Rosskeen) 1895-1971

January 2, 1895—October 22, 1971; English educator, translator, and authority on the Middle East. Obituaries: *Washington Post,* October 30, 1971. (See index for *CA* sketch)

*   *   *

GIBBS, A(nthony) M(atthews) 1933-

PERSONAL: Born January 21, 1933, in Ballarat, Victoria, Australia; son of John Frederick Lloyd (a manager) and Stella (Single) Gibbs; married Jillian Irving Holden; children: Samuel Lloyd, James Matthews Irving. *Education:* University of Melbourne, B.A. (honors), 1955; Magdalen College, Oxford, B.A., 1959, M.A., 1970, B.Litt., 1970. *Home:* 32 Middle St., McMahon's Point 2060, New South Wales, Australia. *Office:* School of English and Linguistics, Macquarie University, North Ryde 2113, New South Wales, Australia.

CAREER: University of Adelaide, Adelaide, South Australia, lecturer in English, 1960-66; University of Leeds, Leeds, England, lecturer in English, 1966-69; University of Newcastle, Newcastle, New South Wales, Australia, professor of English and head of department, 1969-75; Macquarie University, North Ryde, New South Wales, professor of English and head of School of English and Linguistics, 1975—. *Member:* International Association for the Study of Anglo-Irish Literature (member of executive committee), Australian Universities Languages and Literature Association, Achilles Club (Oxford). *Awards, honors:* Rhodes scholar, 1956-59.

WRITINGS: Shaw, Oliver & Boyd, 1969; (editor) *Sir William Davenant: The Shorter Poems, and Songs from the Plays and Masques,* Clarendon Press, 1972. Contributor of articles on Shaw, Yeats, and Australian literature to various periodicals. *Southern Review* (Australia), founding co-editor, 1963-64, member of corresponding committee, 1965—.

WORK IN PROGRESS: A further critical study of Shaw; a Shaw volume for Routledge's "Author Guides" series.

SIDELIGHTS: A. M. Gibbs told *CA:* "My interest in Shaw has been a long-standing one. I value him for the breadth and humanity of his comic vision, and for the robust yet subtle engagement of his drama with political and social issues. Davenant interests me as a poet (despite the unevenness of his performance) and as an innovator in matters of literary taste and in theatrical modes."

GIBSON, John 1907-

PERSONAL: Born October 31, 1907, in Wakefield, Yorkshire, England; son of Thomas (a physician) and Evelyn Mary Gibson; married; wife's name, Jennifer Mary. *Education:* University of London, D.P.M., 1939; University of Leeds, M.D., 1961; Royal College of Psychiatrists, F.R.C. Psych., 1971. *Home:* Pineacre, Southfields Rd., Woldingham, Surrey CR3 7BG, England.

CAREER: Consultant psychiatrist. *Member:* British Medical Association, Royal Society of Medicine (London), Society of Authors.

WRITINGS: (With Thomas French) *Mental Deficiency Nursing,* Faber, 1958, 2nd edition published as *Nursing the Mentally Retarded,* 1967, 3rd edition, 1971; *Health, Personal and Communal: A Short Hygiene for Nurses,* Faber, 1959, 4th edition, 1976; *Human Biology: Elementary Anatomy and Physiology for Students and Nurses,* Faber, 1960, 4th edition, 1976; (with Jennifer M. Jarvis) *Psychology for Nurses,* C. C Thomas, 1961, 3rd edition, Blackwell Scientific Publications, 1971; *Psychiatry for Nurses,* F. A. Davis, 1962, 3rd edition, Lippincott, 1971; *A Guide to the Nervous System,* Faber, 1962, 3rd edition, 1975; *A Guide to Psychiatry for Students of Medicine,* F. A. Davis, 1963; *Mental Nursing Examination Questions and Answers,* Faber, 1964, 3rd edition, 1975; *The Nurse's Materia Medica,* Blackwell Scientific Publications, 1965, 3rd edition, Lippincott, 1974; *Great Doctors and Medical Scientists,* St. Martin's, 1967; *The Development of Surgery,* St. Martin's, 1967; *Modern Medicine for Nurses,* F. A. Davis, 1970, 3rd edition, Lippincott, 1975; *John Howard and Elizabeth Fry,* Methuen, 1971; *Modern Physiology and Anatomy for Nurses,* Lippincott, 1976; *Common Symptoms Described for Nurses,* Blackwell Scientific Publications, 1976.

*   *   *

GIBSON, William E(dward) 1944-

PERSONAL: Born April 11, 1944, in Farragut, Idaho; son of William E. and Lucy (Dickehut) Gibson. *Education:* University of Chicago, A.B., 1964, M.A., 1965, Ph.D., 1967. *Home:* 870 United Nations Plaza, New York, N.Y. 10017. *Office:* Smith Barney, Harris Upham & Co., 1345 Avenue of the Americas, New York, N.Y. 10019.

CAREER: Federal Reserve Bank of Chicago, Chicago, Ill., research fellow, 1966-67; University of California, Los Angeles, assistant professor of economics, 1967-70; Brookings Institution, Washington, D.C., economics fellow, 1970-71; U.S. President's Council of Economic Advisers, Washington, D.C., senior staff economist, 1971-73; Brookings Institution, senior fellow, 1973-75; Chase Manhattan Bank, New York City, vice-president and director of monetary affairs, 1975-76; Smith Barney, Harris Upham & Co., New York City, vice-president and manager, Fixed-Income Research Department, 1976—. Director of monetary analysis, G. A. Saxon & Co., 1973-75; supervisory analyst, New York Stock Exchange, 1977—. Consulting editor, Dickenson Publishing Co. Adjunct professor, University of Southern California, 1968. *Member:* American Economic Association, Econometric Society, American Statistical Association, American Finance Association, National Association of Business Economists, International Economists Club, Financial Management Association (director), American Association for the Advancement of Science, Society of Government Economists, American Association of University Professors, University Club (New York), City Tattersalls Club (Sydney, Australia), Cosmos Club (Washington, D.C.).

WRITINGS: (Editor with George G. Kaufman) *Monetary Economics,* McGraw, 1971; (contributor) Alexander Swoboda, editor, *Coping with Uncertainty in Financial Markets,* University of Geneva Press, 1977. Also author of *Effects of Money on Interest Rates,* Board of Governors of the Federal Reserve System, 1970. Writer of research reports; contributor of articles and reviews to journals.

WORK IN PROGRESS: Research in monetary economics, monetary policy, and international finance; *Monetary Theory and Policy,* for Harper.

*   *   *

GIES, Thomas G(eorge) 1921-

PERSONAL: Born January 12, 1921, in Detroit, Mich.; son of Charles George (an advertising man) and Jane Elizabeth (Sturman) Gies; married Thelma Young, September 6, 1941; children: Laura, Thomas, J. Christopher. *Education:* University of Michigan, A.B., 1946, M.A., 1948, Ph.D., 1952. *Politics:* Democrat. *Religion:* Presbyterian. *Home:* 2980 Devonshire, Ann Arbor, Mich. 48104. *Office:* 642 Graduate School of Business, University of Michigan, Ann Arbor, Mich. 48104.

CAREER: University of Michigan, Ann Arbor, lecturer in economics, 1948-51; Federal Reserve Bank, Kansas City, Mo., financial economist, 1951-57; University of Kansas City (now University of Missouri at Kansas City), lecturer in finance, 1956-57; University of Michigan, associate professor, 1957-61, professor of finance, 1961—. Lecturer, Netherlands School of Economics, Rotterdam, 1964-65. Member, Governor of Michigan's Committee for Economic Development, 1959-60, 1961-62; chairman, Governor's Committee for Revision of Michigan's Financial Code, 1964-65; vice-chairman, Governor of Michigan's Council of Financial Advisers, 1965-66. *Military service:* U.S. Army and U.S. Army Air Forces, 1942-46. *Member:* American Economic Association, American Finance Association, American Academy of Arts and Sciences, Midwest Finance Association (president, 1971-72), Alpha Kappa Psi, Phi Kappa Phi.

WRITINGS: (With Martha Seger and Cedric V. Fricke) *Consumer Finance Companies in Michigan,* Bureau of Business Research, University of Michigan, 1961; (with Thomas Mayer and E. C. Ettin) *Portfolio Policies and Regulations of Private Financial Institutions,* Prentice-Hall, 1962; (contributor) James Crutchfield, Charles Henning, and William Pigott, editors, *Money, Financial Institutions and the Economy: A Book of Readings,* Prentice-Hall, 1965; (with W. G. Shepherd) *Utility Regulations: New Directions in Theory and Policy,* Knopf, 1966; (with V. P. Apilado, D. J. Brophy, and S. L. Jones) *Financial Laws and Economic Expansion in Michigan,* Bureau of Business Research, University of Michigan, 1970; (editor with Apilado) *Banking Markets and Financial Institutions,* Irwin, 1971. Contributor to business and economic journals.

*   *   *

GIGLIO, Ernest D(avid) 1931-

PERSONAL: Surname is pronounced *Jail*-yo; born August 16, 1931, in New York, N.Y.; son of Hubert and Mary (Trombetta) Giglio; married Karin Elisabeth Kluge (a German teacher), June 10, 1961; children: Chris, David, Elisabeth. *Education:* Queens College (now Queens College of the City University of New York), B.A., 1953; New York College for Teachers (now State University of New York at Albany), M.A., 1957; Syracuse University, Ph.D., 1964.

Religion: Roman Catholic. *Home:* 709 Lincoln Ave., Williamsport, Pa. 17701. *Office:* Department of Political Science, Lycoming College, Williamsport, Pa. 17701.

CAREER: Dickinson College, Carlisle, Pa., instructor in history and political science, 1963-65; Villanova University, Villanova, Pa., assistant professor of political science, 1965-70; University of Akron, Akron, Ohio, associate professor of political science and director of American Institutions, 1970-72; Lycoming College, Williamsport, Pa., head of department of political science, 1972—. *Military service:* U.S. Army, 1953-55. *Member:* American Political Science Association, American Association of University Professors, American Civil Liberties Union.

WRITINGS: (Contributor) Thomas F. Powell, editor, *The Humanities and the Social Studies,* Council on Social Studies, 1969; (editor) *Contemporary Issues in American Society,* McCutchan, Volume I: *Political,* 1970, Volume II: *Social,* 1971, Volume III: *Economic,* 1971; (editor with John J. Schrems) *Future Politics,* McCutchan, 1971. Contributor of articles and reviews to education and law journals.

*   *   *

GILBERT, Creighton (Eddy) 1924-

PERSONAL: Born June 6, 1924, in Durham, N.C.; son of Allan H. (a professor) and Katharine (a professor; maiden name, Everett) Gilbert. *Education:* Attended Duke University, 1938-40, and Johns Hopkins University, 1940; New York University, B.A., 1942, Ph.D., 1955. *Politics:* Democrat. *Religion:* None. *Office:* Department of History of Art, Cornell University, Ithaca, N.Y. 14850.

CAREER: Emory University, Atlanta, Ga., instructor of fine arts, 1946-47; University of Louisville, Louisville, Ky., instructor, 1947-55, assistant professor of fine arts, 1955-56; Indiana University at Bloomington, assistant professor of fine arts, 1956-58; Ringling Museums, Sarasota, Fla., curator, 1959-61; Brandeis University, Waltham, Mass., associate professor, 1961-65, Sidney and Ellen Wien Professor of History of Art, 1965-69, chairman of department, 1963-66, 1968-69; Queens College of the City University of New York, Flushing, N.Y., professor of art, 1969-77, chairman of department, 1969-72; Cornell University, Ithaca, N.Y., Jacob Gould Schurman Professor of the History of Art, 1977—. Fulbright professor, University of Rome, 1951-52, visiting summer professor at New York University, 1956, University of California, Berkeley, 1959, and Harvard University, 1964; visiting professor, University of Leiden, 1974-75.

MEMBER: College Art Association, Renaissance Society of America (member of council, 1963-65), American Academy of Arts and Sciences (fellow), Ateneo di Brescia (honorary member), Institute of Fine Arts Alumni Association (chairman of board of directors, 1970-74). *Awards, honors:* Mather Award, College Art Association, 1964; Kress fellow, Harvard Center for Italian Renaissance Studies, 1967-68; fellow, Netherlands Institute for Advanced Study, 1972-73.

WRITINGS: (Translator) *Complete Poems and Selected Letters of Michelangelo,* Random House, 1963, revised edition, Modern Library, 1965; *Seventeenth-Century Paintings from the Low Countries,* October House, 1966; *Michelangelo,* McGraw, 1967; *Change in Piero della Francesca,* J. J. Augustin, 1968; (editor) *Renaissance Art,* Harper, 1970; *History of Renaissance Art,* Abrams, 1973. Contributor to *Propyluen Kustgeschichte,* Vol. VIIII, Propyluen Verlag, 1972. Contributor to art history journals in the United States and Europe. Contributing editor, *Arts,* 1961-65.

GILBERT, Glenn Gordon 1936-

PERSONAL: Born September 17, 1936, in Montgomery, Ala.; son of William Harlan (an anthropologist) and Margaret (Christensen) Gilbert; married Erika Wrede, August 7, 1964; children: Alexander, Christa. *Education:* University of Chicago, B.A., 1957; University of Frankfurt, graduate study, 1957-60; University of Paris, Diplome de la Langue Francaise, 1960; Harvard University, Ph.D., 1963. *Politics:* Democrat. *Religion:* Unitarian. *Home:* R.R. 4, Union Hill, Carbondale, Ill. 62901. *Office:* Department of Linguistics, Southern Illinois University, Carbondale, Ill. 62901.

CAREER: University of Texas at Austin, instructor, 1963-65, assistant professor of Germanic languages, 1965-70; Southern Illinois University, Carbondale, associate professor, 1970-75, professor of linguistics, 1975—. Fulbright lecturer in linguistics, University of Marburg, 1966-67, and University of Mainz, 1973-74. *Member:* International Linguistic Association, Linguistic Society of America, American Dialect Society, American Anthropological Association, Midwest American Dialect Society (president, 1970-72).

WRITINGS: (Editor) *Texas Studies in Bilingualism,* Walter de Gruyter, 1970; (editor) *The German Language in America,* University of Texas Press, 1971; *Linguistic Atlas of Texas German,* University of Texas Press, 1972. Contributor to *Language, Orbis, American Speech, Zeitschrift fuer Mundartforschung,* and *La Monda Lingvo-Problemo.* Associate editor, *Journal of Creole Studies.*

WORK IN PROGRESS: Ethnic and creole languages in the U.S. and the Caribbean; a translation and assessment of the work of Hugo Schuchardt in pidgin and creole languages; a history of pidgin and creole studies; pidginization vs. second-language learning.

SIDELIGHTS: Glenn Gilbert speaks and reads German, French, Spanish, and Swedish, and reads Norwegian, Danish, Dutch, Afrikaans, Portuguese, and Italian.

*   *   *

GILBERT, Jarvey 1917-

PERSONAL: Born October 14, 1917, in Minneapolis, Minn.; son of Nathan and Betty (Rosenthal) Gilbert; married Sarah Seligman, September 26, 1948; children: Jean (Mrs. William Seager), Deborah (Mrs. Dennis Ross), Laura. *Education:* University of Minnesota, B.S., 1940, B.M., 1942, M.D., 1943. *Politics:* Democrat. *Religion:* Jewish. *Home:* 828 Grinnell Dr. E., Burbank, Calif. 91501. *Office:* 265 Orange Grove E., Burbank, Calif. 91502.

CAREER: Radio commentator for station KBBQ, Burbank, Calif., 1971-72. City of Burbank, city councilman, 1967—, mayor, 1970-71. President, Southern California Association of Governments, 1974-75; member of hearing board, South Coast Air Quality Management District, 1977—. *Member:* American Medical Association.

WRITINGS: Prescriptions for Living, Price, Stern, 1971.

*   *   *

GILBRETH, Lillian Moller 1878-1972

May 24, 1878—January 2, 1972; American pioneer in time-motion studies. Obituaries: *New York Times,* January 3, 1972; *Washington Post,* January 3, 1972; *Newsweek,* January 17, 1972; *Time,* January 17, 1972.

GILDNER, Gary 1938-

PERSONAL: Born August 22, 1938, in West Branch, Mich.; son of Theodore Edward (a carpenter) and Jean (Szostak) Gildner; married Judith McKibben (editor of *Annals of Iowa*), January 5, 1963; children: Gretchen. *Education:* Michigan State University, B.A., 1960, M.A., 1961. *Home:* 2915 School St., Des Moines, Iowa 50311. *Office:* Department of English, Drake University, Des Moines, Iowa 50311.

CAREER: Wayne State University, Detroit, Mich., writer for department of university relations, 1961-62; Northern Michigan University, Marquette, instructor in English, 1963-66; Drake University, Des Moines, Iowa, associate professor of English, 1966—. *Awards, honors:* Robert Frost fellow at Bread Loaf Writers' Conference, 1970; National Endowment for the Arts fellow, 1971, 1976; Yaddo fellow, 1972, 1973, 1975, 1976; MacDowell Colony fellow, 1974; Theodore Roethke prize, 1976.

WRITINGS—Poetry: *First Practice,* University of Pittsburgh Press, 1969; *Digging for Indians,* University of Pittsburgh Press, 1971; *Nails,* University of Pittsburgh Press, 1975; (editor with wife, Judith Gildner, and contributor) *Out of This World: Poems from the Hawkeye State* (anthology), Iowa State University Press, 1975; *Letters from Vicksburg,* Unicorn Press, 1976; *The Runner and Other Poems,* University of Pittsburgh Press, 1978.

Contributor to anthologies, including: *Best Little Magazine Fiction, 1970,* edited by Curt Johnson, New York University Press, 1970; *I Love You All Day,* edited by Philip Dacey and Gerald Knoll, Abbey Press, 1970; *Poetry Brief,* edited by William Cole, Macmillan, 1971; *An Introduction to Poetry,* edited by X. J. Kennedy, Little Brown, 1971, revised edition, 1976; *Poems One Line and Longer,* edited by Cole, Grossman, 1973; *Poetry: Points of Departure,* Winthrop, 1974; *The American Poetry Anthology,* edited by Daniel Halpern, Avon, 1975; *Heartland II: Poets of the Midwest,* edited by Lucien Stryk, Northern Illinois University Press, 1975; *The Sporting Spirit,* edited by Robert Higgs and Neil Isaacs, Harcourt, 1977.

WORK IN PROGRESS: The Crush and Other Ways of Living and Not Living Together, a book of fiction.

SIDELIGHTS: Gary Gildner writes: "I wrote *Letters from Vicksburg* during a cold, wet week in March of 1975. All winter I hadn't written much that made me happy. *Nails* was finished—had been for a while and was about to come out—and maybe I was pushing too hard to come up with poems that were not like the poems in that book. Or maybe I was doing something else 'wrong,' I don't know. Anyway, I was in a dry spell. And sloppy weather never helps. One day I picked up the civil war letters that Judy had left in my room . . . and right away I was taken with this fellow—this cocky, frightened, proud, lonely, semi-literate young soldier from Iowa who was on his way to Vicksburg and writing home to his wife about it. I began to fool with the idea of using the letters in some kind of exercise that might help open me up. The story was good, that is the bones were there, but his presentation, as the English teacher might say, was ignorant: he spelled mainly by ear, . . . he used no punctuation, and he rambled. I thought, what are these letters *not* like? Well, I decided, they are about as far from the sonnet as Yogi Berra's batting style, so why don't I 'translate' them into that sober shape—just as an exercise, just as a way of getting away from myself, and just to be contrary? I may have been feeling a bit cocky too, at this point, though God knows why. I wrote drafts of the first two or three and liked them; I liked them even better after removing some screws here and there and letting them breathe as fully as they wanted to. Somewhere in the middle of number four, I think, I started to get that feeling which you can't describe but which feels *good,* and the exercise became something else then. ... I departed from the letters, as I say elsewhere, whenever it seemed necessary or fruitful; but I tried to remain faithful to their grammar, their 'stance'. ... I stayed with the sonnet plan throughout, but I felt absolutely no guilt taking out hardware whenever the voice got tight on me.''

* * *

GILIEN, Sasha 1925(?)-1971

1925(?)—November 29, 1971; American satirist and journalist. Obituaries: *Washington Post,* December 4, 1971.

* * *

GILL, Jerry H. 1933-

PERSONAL: Name legally changed, 1965; born February 7, 1933, in Lynden, Wash.; son of Walter and Virginia (McGinnis) Gauthier. *Education:* Westmont College, B.A., 1956; University of Washington, Seattle, M.A., 1957; New York Theological Seminary, B.D., 1960; Duke University, Ph.D., 1966. *Office:* Department of Philosophy, Eastern College, St. Davids, Pa. 19087.

CAREER: Clergyman; ordained, 1956; Seattle Pacific College, Seattle, Wash., assistant professor of philosophy and religion, 1960-64; Southwestern at Memphis, Memphis, Tenn., assistant professor of philosophy, 1966-69; Eckerd College, St. Petersburg, Fla., 1969-77, began as associate professor, became professor of philosphy; Eastern College, St. Davids, Pa., professor of Christianity and culture, 1977—. *Member:* American Philosophical Association.

WRITINGS: Ingmar Bergman and the Search for Meaning, Eerdmans, 1967; (editor) *Philosophy Today,* Macmillan, Number I, 1968, Number II, 1969, Number III, 1970; (editor) *Philosophy and Religion,* Burgess, 1968; (editor) *Essays on Kierkegaard,* Burgess, 1969; *The Possibility of Religious Knowledge,* Eerdmans, 1971; *Ian Ramsey,* Allen & Unwin, 1976. Contributor to theology and philosophy journals.

WORK IN PROGRESS: Books on the thought of Ludwig Wittgenstein and on post-critical philosophy.

* * *

GILLESPIE, Neal C(ephas) 1933-

PERSONAL: Born March 9, 1933, in Canton, N.C.; son of William Dewey (a businessman) and Molley (Shook) Gillespie; married Sarah Calhoun (a librarian), March 27, 1960. *Education:* Emory University, A.B., 1959; Duke University, M.A., 1961, Ph.D., 1964. *Home:* 1049 Clifton Rd. N.E., Atlanta, Ga. 30307. *Office:* Department of History, Georgia State University, University Plaza, Atlanta, Ga. 30303.

CAREER: Georgia State University, Atlanta, assistant professor, 1963-67, associate professor, 1967-72, professor of history, 1972—. *Military service:* U.S. Navy, 1952-56. *Member:* American Historical Association, Organization of American Historians, American Society of Church History, American Association of University Professors, History of Science Society, Southern Historical Association, Phi Beta Kappa. *Awards, honors:* Woodrow Wilson fellow, 1959-60.

WRITINGS: The Collapse of Orthodoxy: The Intellectual Ordeal of George Frederick Holmes, University Press of Virginia, 1972. Contributor of articles to *Journal of Southern History, Journal of the History of Philosophy, South Atlantic Quarterly, Journal of Mississippi History,* and *Isis.*

WORK IN PROGRESS: Research on the place of theological concepts in the development of modern science with emphasis on Darwinism and the rise of positivism.

SIDELIGHTS: Neal Gillespie calls himself "a student of intellectual history especially interested in the response of religious intellectuals to the new scientific world view which emerged in the nineteenth century and the role that they played in transforming both theology and science."

* * *

GILLETT, Charlie 1942-

PERSONAL: Born February 20, 1942, in England; son of Tona Gillett (an engineer) and Diana (a journalist; maiden name, Maltby) Lamb; married Buffy Chessum, December 19, 1964; children: Suzy, Jody, Ivan. *Education:* Peterhouse, Cambridge, B.A., 1964; Redland College, Certificate of Education, 1965; Columbia University, M.A., 1966. *Home:* 11 Liston Rd., London SW4 0DG, England.

CAREER: Kingsway College for Further Education, London, England, lecturer in social studies, film-making, and athletics, 1966-71; British Broadcasting Corp., London, television production assistant, 1971-72, radio disc jockey, host of weekly show, ''Honky Tonk,'' 1972—. Co-founder, co-director, and producer, Oval Records, London, 1974—. *Awards, honors: Sound of the City* was cited as *Rolling Stone* Music Book of the Year and as *New York Times* Popular Music Book of the Year.

WRITINGS: Sound of the City: The Rise of Rock and Roll, Outerbridge & Dienstfrey, 1970; *All in the Game,* Penguin, 1971; (editor) *Rock File,* New English Library, 1972; *Making Tracks: The Story of Atlantic Records,* Dutton, 1974; (editor) *Rock File 2,* Panther, 1974; (editor with Simon Frith) *Rock File 3,* Panther, 1975; (editor with Frith) *Rock File 4,* Panther, 1976; (editor with Stephen Nugent) *Rock Almanac,* Doubleday, 1977. Contributor to *Rolling Stone, Creem, Village Voice, Fusion,* and other periodicals. Contributing editor, *Record Mirror,* 1969-71, *Ink,* 1971, *Cream,* 1971-72, *Let It Rock,* 1973-74, and *New Musical Express,* 1974—.

WORK IN PROGRESS: A complete revision of *Sound of the City,* possibly under a new title and in two volumes.

SIDELIGHTS: Charlie Gillett told *CA:* ''Although I have been making a living from writing since *Sound of the City* came out in 1970, I don't think of myself as *a writer:* I can't type a line without mis-spelling a couple of words, and every time I go back to something I write, it looks clumsy, badly phrased. I'm primarily a music enthusiast, who hopes to make a living as a record producer, and who never tires of discovering yet another previously unknown record that turns out to have a special magic. Once discovered, the secret must be passed on! A weekly radio show, 'Honky Tonk,' is my most efficient means of introducing others to the unearthed treasure, but after a while the itch returns, to try and sort all the mysteries into an order, to find out and tell anyone who cares just who was the astute producer or arranger who enabled each of these records to be made.

''So, I hope readers will forgive my tortured grammar, and follow my leads as they hunt the second hand record shops for used 45's that were forgotten too fast. It is worth all the hard grind of writing to see *Sound of the City* still cited as a useful guide to American popular music, as for instance in . . . *New York Review of Books* where correspondent Carolyn Porter recommends it in a response to a survey of rock books by other writers. However, I am uncomfortably conscious of how many errors and misinterpretations are scattered through the first version—hence my present task, a complete rewrite! Back to the grindstone. . . .''

BIOGRAPHICAL/CRITICAL SOURCES: New York Times, August 21, 1970; *New York Review of Books,* April 14, 1977.

* * *

GILLIN, Donald George 1930-

PERSONAL: Born June 3, 1930, in San Francisco, Calif.; son of George Andrew and Eva Vivian (Ammon) Gillin; married Rose Marie McDowell (a teacher), September 6, 1953; children: Paul D., Lynn J. *Education:* Stanford University, B.A., 1952, M.A., 1953, Ph.D., 1959. *Politics:* Independent. *Religion:* None. *Office:* Department of History, Vassar College, Poughkeepsie, N.Y. 12601.

CAREER: Duke University, Durham, N.C., instructor, 1959-60, assistant professor, 1960-64, associate professor of history, 1964-68; Vassar College, Poughkeepsie, N.Y., professor of history and chairman of East Asian studies, 1968—. Visiting lecturer, University of Michigan, 1959; visiting assistant professor, San Francisco State College (now University), 1963; visiting associate professor, University of North Carolina at Chapel Hill, 1965-66. *Military service:* U.S. Army, 1948-49. *Member:* Association for Asian Studies, Committee of Concerned Asian Scholars. *Awards, honors:* Social Science Research Council, Rockefeller Foundation, and Committee for East Asian Studies fellowship at Stanford University, 1962-63; Social Science Research Council Joint Committee on Contemporary China fellowship in Taiwan, 1966-67.

WRITINGS: Warlord: Yen Hsi-shan in Shansi Province, 1911-1950, Princeton University Press, 1967; *East Asia: A Bibliography for Undergraduate Libraries,* Bro-Dart Foundation, 1970; (contributor) J. A. Harrison, editor, *China: Enduring Scholarship,* University of Arizona Press, 1972. Contributor to Asian studies journals. Editor, China section of *Newsletter* of Association for Asian Studies, 1965-66.

WORK IN PROGRESS: Collapse: The Nationalist Defeat on the Mainland of China, 1945-1950.

BIOGRAPHICAL/CRITICAL SOURCES: New York Times Book Review, March 19, 1967.

* * *

GILLIS, John R. 1939-

PERSONAL: Born January 13, 1939, in Plainfield, N.J.; son of Randall (an engineer) and Ruth (Donaldson) Gillis; married Christina Marsden (a teacher), August 20, 1960; children: Christopher, Benjamin. *Education:* Amherst College, A.B., 1960; Stanford University, Ph.D., 1965. *Politics:* Independent. *Religion:* None. *Home address:* R.D. 2, Whitehouse Station, N.J. 08889. *Office:* Department of History, Livingston College, Rutgers University, New Brunswick, N.J.

CAREER: Stanford University, Stanford, Calif., instructor in history, 1964-65; Princeton University, Princeton, N.J., assistant professor of history, 1965-71; Rutgers University, Livingston College, New Brunswick, N.J., associate professor, 1971-76, professor of history, 1976—. *Member:* American Historical Association.

WRITINGS: The Prussian Bureaucracy in Crisis: 1840-1860, Stanford University Press, 1970; *Youth and History,* Academic Press, 1974; *Development of European Society, 1770-1870,* Houghton, 1977. Contributor to political science and history journals.

WORK IN PROGRESS: A history of male-female relations in nineteenth-century England, based in part on research of the London Foundling Hospital records.

* * *

GILMER, (Frank) Walker 1935-

PERSONAL: Born July 11, 1935, in Chicago, Ill.; son of Frank Bostick (an attorney) and Mary Elizabeth (Swain) Gilmer; married Peggy Platt, August 4, 1962; children: Charles Frederic. *Education:* University of Virginia, B.A., 1957; Harvard University, law student, 1957-58; Northwestern University, M.A., 1959, Ph.D., 1963. *Politics:* Independent. *Religion:* Protestant. *Home:* 108 Taylor Pl., Greencastle, Ind. 46135. *Office:* English Department, DePauw University, Greencastle, Ind. 46135.

CAREER: DePauw University, Greencastle, Ind., assistant professor, 1963-67, associate professor, 1967-75, professor of English, 1975—. *Member:* Modern Language Association of America, Phi Beta Kappa.

WRITINGS: Horace Liveright: Publisher of the Twenties, David Lewis, 1970.

BIOGRAPHICAL/CRITICAL SOURCES: New York Times Book Review, May 31, 1970.

* * *

GILMORE, Charles L(ee)

PERSONAL: Born in Cadiz, Ohio; son of Charles (a United Presbyterian minister) and Elizabeth Josephine (Rippey) Gilmore; married Katherine Warner, August 1, 1941; children: Margaret (Mrs. Chris Rackliff), C. Michael, Charlee (Mrs. Gary Sauls). *Education:* Rensselaer Polytechnic Institute, B.Ch.E., 1942. *Politics:* Independent. *Religion:* Protestant. *Home:* 308 College View, Bryan, Tex. 77801. *Office:* Department of Industrial Engineering, Texas A&M University, College Station, Tex. 77843.

CAREER: Registered professional engineer in Pennsylvania, Texas, and California; engineer with Westinghouse Electric Co., Standard Oil Co., and Hagan Corp. prior to 1951; Monsanto Co., Texas City, Tex., general operating supervisor of vinyl chloride monomer unit, 1951-56, superintendent of loss prevention and safety department, 1956-75; Texas A&M University, College Station, associate professor of industrial engineering, 1975—. Member of general advisory committee, Texas Occupational Safety Board; member emeritus of occupational safety committee, Texas Chemical Council. *Member:* American Society of Safety Engineers (fellow), Sigma Xi, Tau Beta Pi.

WRITINGS: Accident Prevention and Loss Control, American Management Association, 1970. Contributor to engineering and management journals.

* * *

GILMORE, Gene 1920-

PERSONAL: Born February 15, 1920, in Mt. Pleasant, Mich.; son of Selmar F. and Mary (Roethlisberger) Gilmore; married Virginia Smith, March 14, 1948; children: Thomas, Louise, Daniel. *Education:* University of Michigan, A.B., 1942; Syracuse University, M.A., 1961. *Politics:*

Democrat. *Religion:* Quaker. *Home:* 611 Ohio, Urbana, Ill. 61801. *Office:* Department of Journalism, University of Illinois, 119 Gregory Hall, Urbana, Ill. 61801.

CAREER: Times Herald, Port Huron, Mich., reporter-editor, 1947-48; *Gazette & Daily,* York, Pa., reporter-editor, 1949-57; Syracuse University, Syracuse, N.Y., instructor in journalism, 1957-63; University of Illinois, Urbana, assistant professor, 1963-71, associate professor of journalism, 1971—. Copy editor, summers, *Washington Post, Philadelphia Bulletin, Rochester* (N.Y.) *Times Union;* consultant, Newspaper Fund. Urbana City Councilman, 1965-69, 1971—. *Military service:* U.S. Coast Guard, 1942-46; became ensign. *Awards, honors:* McNaught Medal for outstanding journalism student, University of Michigan, 1942.

WRITINGS: (Editor) *High School Journalism Today,* Interstate, 1967, 2nd edition, 1976; (with Robert Root) *Modern Newspaper Editing,* Glendessary, 1971, 2nd edition, 1976. Contributor of articles to *Quill, Nation, Quill & Scroll,* and *Illinois Farmer.*

* * *

GILMORE, J. Herbert, Jr. 1925-

PERSONAL: Born January 7, 1925, in Rutledge, Tenn.; son of Herbert (a builder) and Mabel (Doyal) Gilmore; married Joyce Marie Wade (a teacher), June 17, 1946; children: Victor Alan, Dale Temple, James Winston, Joy Marie. *Education:* Carson-Newman College, A.B., 1945; George Peabody College for Teachers, M.A., 1949; Southern Baptist Theological Seminary, B.D., 1950, Th.M., 1951, Th.D., 1959; additional graduate study at other institutions, including Yale University, 1970. *Politics:* Republican. *Address:* P.O. Box 706, Gatlinburg, Tenn. 37738.

CAREER: Clergyman of the Southern Baptist Church; associate pastor during student days at Baptist churches in Fountain City, Tenn. and Springfield, Tenn.; pastor in Cedar Hill, Tenn., 1947-49, Bloomfield, Ky., 1950-53, Marshall, Mo., 1953-56, Louisville, Ky., 1956-60, and Washington, D.C., 1963-68; professor of applied Christianity, Carver School of Missions and Social Work, 1960-63; First Baptist Church, Birmingham, Ala., pastor, 1968-70; Baptist Church of the Covenant, Birmingham, pastor, 1971-76. Visiting professor at Missouri Valley College, 1954-55, and Southern Baptist Theological Seminary, 1959-60; visiting professor of philosophy, University of Alabama in Birmingham, 1971. Frequent guest lecturer and preacher. Member of board of trustees, Midwestern Baptist Theological Seminary. *Member:* Academy of Parish Clergy, Society of Biblical Literature, National Conference of Christians and Jews, American Society of Christian Ethics, American Academy of Arts and Sciences, Society of Political Science.

WRITINGS: When Love Prevails, Eerdmans, 1971; *Devotions for the Home,* Broadman, 1971; *They Chose to Live,* Eerdmans, 1972. Writer of Sunday school teaching materials; contributor to religious journals.

WORK IN PROGRESS: Two books, *The Crisis in Preaching* and *William Temple: A Man for Our Times;* research on the relationship of religion and culture in the South; a book containing the Bicentennial lectures he delivered for the American Baptist Convention.

SIDELIGHTS: J. Herbert Gilmore told *CA* that he was "instrumental in establishing a church in Birmingham, Alabama that was interracial, intercultural, and international. It was the first church in the city of any denomination to deliberately transcend the racial barrier." *Avocational interests:* Sports.

GILMORE, Jene Carlton 1933-

PERSONAL: Born July 26, 1933, in Stuart, Okla.; son of Charles V. and Pauline (Biggs) Gilmore; married Hella Adamo (a payroll clerk), February 2, 1957; children: Elizabeth Ann, Michael Raymond. *Education:* Attended University of Oklahoma, 1951-52, and Abilene Christian College, 1952-55; Oklahoma State University, B.S., 1958. *Home:* 4653 White Oak Pl., Encino, Calif. 91316.

CAREER: Manager of Crossroads of Sport, Inc., New York, N.Y., 1965-72, Petersen Gallery, 1972-77, and Highland Mall Gallery, 1977—. *Military service:* U.S. Army, 1954-57; became sergeant. *Member:* Ducks Unlimited, Ruffed Grouse Society, Atlantic Brant Association, Anglers Club of New York, Pequest Anglers Club, Indian Head Duck Club.

WRITINGS: Art for Conservation, Barre, 1971.

WORK IN PROGRESS: American Sporting Artist.

AVOCATIONAL INTERESTS: Shooting, fishing, conservation of game.

* * *

GIORNO, John 1936-

PERSONAL: Born December 4, 1936, in New York, N.Y. *Education:* Columbia University, B.A., 1958. *Religion:* Buddhist. *Home:* 222 Bowery, New York, N.Y. 10012.

CAREER: Poet. Associated with Dial-a-Poem record series, 1968-77, Radio Free Poetry, 1970, and Electronic Sensory Poetry Environments (E.S.P.E.). Also involved in project called Consumer Product Poetry, which provides matchbook poems, t-shirt poems, window curtain poems, chocolate bar poems, and silk screen poem prints, and "The Archives," 1972.

WRITINGS—All poetry: Poems by John Giorno, Mother Press, 1967; *C——*(poems translated into German), Marz Verlag, 1969; *Balling Buddha,* Kulchur Press, 1970; *Cum,* Adventures in Poetry, 1971; *Birds,* Angel Hair Books, 1971; *Cancer in My Left Ball,* Something Else Press, 1973. Also author of *The American Book of the Dead,* 1964.

Poetry included in anthologies, including: *Acid,* edited by Rolf O. Brinkman, Marz Verlag, 1969; *The World Anthology,* edited by Anne Waldman, Bobbs-Merrill, 1969; *Silverscreen,* edited by Brinkman, Marz Verlag, 1970; *Possibilities of Poetry,* edited by Richard Kostelanetz, Dell, 1970; *An Anthology of New York Poets,* edited by Ron Padgett and David Shapiro, Random House, 1970; *Another World Anthology,* edited by Waldman, Bobbs-Merrill, 1971. Poetry recorded on "Raspberry and Pornographic Poem," Intravenus Mind, 1967, and on another album with William S. Burroughs, 1976. Also author (with Allen Ginsberg) of film script, "September on Jessore Road," 1972.

SIDELIGHTS: An exponent of "found" poetry, John Giorno creates his work by taking a piece of prose, usually journalistic, and breaking the words into a pattern of lines. "There is no invention in Giorno's poems," Tom Clark writes, "only composition.... They are all concerned with structure." John Perreault describes Giorno's *Poems* as "a literary event, a paradoxical indictment, and a perverse celebration of raw, ad-mass language. Some may say his blank catalogs of brutality and 'pornography' are as dangerous as the 'facts' they point to. But I do not think this point is relevant. And although for those familiar with current art the use of found materials may seem old hat, for poetry at least it is a major innovation, long overdue, particularly since Giorno uses this borrowed technique in a unique way and for his own expressive, or perhaps I should say 'anti-expressive' ends. *Poems by John Giorno* is a disturbing book and an emotional book," Perreault concludes. "Giorno's deadpan shock tactics break down the distance between poetry and the reader, poetry and life."

BIOGRAPHICAL/CRITICAL SOURCES: Village Voice, September 7, 1967, February 27, 1969, May 22, 1969; *National Observer,* October 30, 1967; *New York Times Book Review,* March 31, 1968; *New York Times,* September 30, 1968, January 14, 1969; *Newsweek,* March 3, 1969; *Time,* September 14, 1970.

*   *   *

GIPSON, Lawrence Henry 1880-1971

December 7, 1880—September 26, 1971; American educator and historian. Obituaries: *New York Times,* September 27, 1971; *Washington Post,* September 28, 1971; *Current Biography,* November, 1971. (See index for *CA* sketch)

*   *   *

GLASSBURNER, Bruce 1920-

PERSONAL: Born December 4, 1920, in Beatrice, Neb.; son of Fred Raymond (a teacher) and Edna M. (Morrison) Glassburner; married Eleanor Schlott, September 2, 1942; children: Kay Glassburner Ikranagara, Judith, John, Robert. *Education:* Iowa State College (now Iowa State University of Science and Technology), B.S., 1943, M.S., 1949; University of California, Berkeley, Ph.D., 1953. *Home:* 504 Hermosa Pl., Davis, Calif. 95616. *Office:* Department of Economics, University of California, Davis, Calif. 95616.

CAREER: University of California, Berkeley, lecturer in economics, 1951-53; Federal Reserve Bank of San Francisco, San Francisco, Calif., economist, 1953-55; University of California, Davis, assistant professor, 1955-59, associate professor, 1959-66, professor of economics, 1966—, chairman of department, 1956-63, acting chairman, 1967-69. University of Indonesia, visiting professor, 1957-60, and chairman of field staff, University of California-University of Indonesia economics project, 1958-60; Chinese University of Hong Kong, visiting professor, 1969-71, and associate director of University of California Study Centre, Hong Kong, 1969-70, director, 1970-71. Consultant, Federal Reserve Board of Governors, 1956-57; senior adviser, Pakistan Institute of Development Economics, Karachi, 1964-66; consultant, Agency for International Development, summers, 1966, 1967. *Military service:* U.S. Army, Field Artillery, 1943-46; became captain. *Member:* American Economic Association. *Awards, honors:* Grants from Southeast Asia Development Advisory Group, 1968, 1969-70.

WRITINGS: (Contributor) *Bunga Rampai Ekonomi* (title means "Readings in Economics"), [Djakarta], 1960; (contributor) Frederick Harbison and Charles A. Meyers, editors, *Manpower and Education: Country Studies in Economic Development,* McGraw, 1965; (editor and contributor) *The Economy of Indonesia: Selected Readings,* Cornell University Press, 1971. Contributor of more than twenty articles to economic journals in United States, Indonesia, and Australia. Editor, *Pakistan Development Review,* 1964-66; associate editor, *Ekonomi dan Keuangan Indonesia,* 1969.

WORK IN PROGRESS: Further studies on economic development in Indonesia.

AVOCATIONAL INTERESTS: Tennis, skiing, playing bass viol ("badly, but with enthusiasm").

*   *   *

GLATSTEIN, Jacob 1896-1971

August 20, 1896—November 19, 1971; Polish-born American columnist, editor, and Yiddish poet. Obituaries: *New York Times,* November 20, 1971.

*   *   *

GLAZER-MALBIN, Nona 1932-
(Nona Y. Glazer)

PERSONAL: Born October 27, 1932, in Chicago, Ill. *Education:* University of Oregon, B.A., 1955, M.A., 1957; London School of Economics and Political Science, graduate study, 1959-60; Cornell University, Ph.D., 1965. *Office:* Department of Sociology, 217 Cramer Hall, Portland State University, Portland, Ore. 97207.

CAREER: Western Washington State College (now Western Washington University), Bellingham, instructor in sociology, 1957-59; Portland State University, Portland, Ore., assistant professor, 1964-68, associate professor of sociology, 1968—. *Member:* American Sociological Association, Society for Applied Anthropology.

WRITINGS: (Editor with Carol Greedon; under name Nona Glazer) *Children and Poverty,* Rand McNally, 1968; (with Helen P. Waehrer; under name Nona Glazer-Malbin) *Woman in a Man-made World,* Rand McNally, 1972, 2nd edition, 1977; (under name Nona Glazer-Malbin) *Old Family-New Family,* Van Nostrand, 1975.

WORK IN PROGRESS: Sex-roles; childrearing and housework; women's roles and social policy.

*   *   *

GLUCK, Louise 1943-

PERSONAL: Surname is pronounced *Glick;* born April 22, 1943, in New York, N.Y.; daughter of Daniel (an executive) and Beatrice (Grosby) Gluck; married John Dranow (a professor); children: Noah. *Education:* Attended Sarah Lawrence College and Columbia University. *Home:* 966 Northfield Rd., Woodmere, N.Y. 11598. *Mailing address:* Master of Fine Arts Program, Goddard College, Plainfield, Vt. 05667.

CAREER: Poet. Fine Arts Work Center, Provincetown, Mass., visiting teacher, 1970; Goddard College, Plainfield, Vt., artist-in-residence, 1971-72; visiting lecturer, University of North Carolina, Greensboro, spring, 1973, and University of Virginia, spring, 1975; University of Iowa, Iowa City, affiliated with creative writing program, 1976-77; University of Cincinnati, Cincinnati, Ohio, Elliston Professor of Poetry, spring, 1978. *Awards, honors:* Academy of American Poets Prize, Columbia University, 1967; Rockefeller Foundation grant, 1968; National Endowment for the Arts grant, 1970; Eunice Tietjens Memorial Prize of *Poetry* magazine, 1971; Guggenheim fellowship, 1975-76.

WRITINGS: Firstborn (poems), New American Library, 1968; *The House on Marshland,* Ecco Press, 1975; *The Garden* (chapbook), Antaeus Editions, in press. Work represented in numerous anthologies, including: *The New Yorker Book of Poems,* Viking, 1970; *New Voices in American Poetry,* Winthrop Publishing, 1973; *The American Poetry Anthology,* Avon, 1975.

SIDELIGHTS: Helen Vendler writes that Louise Gluck's

"advance between 1968 (*Firstborn*) and 1975 is phenomenal.... [Her] poems are almost dreamy; they drift in a reflection like the moon in a pool (the moon and the pool recur as powerful counters in her private language).... There is nothing diffident about a poet who dares to call one poem "The Magi," and another "To Autumn," recalling the immortal poems of those titles by Yeats and Keats.... A very peculiar power, and a new style, commanding in its indifference to current modes." Robert Boyers describes Louise Gluck as "a poet of few themes, but these she develops with a ferocity that borders on obsession. She appears to write best when she is least herself, when she writes out of contexts which are relatively unfamiliar to her own experience, and which she need not invest with the accouterments of melodrama or terror in order to make them striking."

BIOGRAPHICAL/CRITICAL SOURCES: Partisan Review, Number 2, 1969; *Poetry,* February, 1971; *New York Times Book Review,* April 6, 1975; *Contemporary Literary Criticism,* Volume VII, Gale, 1977.

*   *   *

GLUECK, William Frank 1934-

PERSONAL: Surname is pronounced Glick; born December 24, 1934, in Cincinnati, Ohio; son of Frank Charles (a businessman) and Alice (Buxsel) Glueck; children: William, Jr., Lisa, David, Melissa. *Education:* Xavier University, B.S. (magna cum laude), 1956, M.B.A., 1963; Michigan State University, Ph. D., 1966. *Home:* 315 Hickory Hill Dr., Watkinsville, Ga. 30677. *Office:* 412 Brooks, College of Business Administration, University of Georgia, Athens, Ga. 30601.

CAREER: Employed in sales, sales management, and management positions in the food industry, 1958-63; Michigan State University, East Lansing, assistant instructor in management, 1963-64, assistant to associate dean for graduate programs in business administration, 1964-66; University of Texas at Austin, assistant professor of management, 1966-68; University of Missouri—Columbia, associate professor of management, faculty research associate, Business and Public Administration Research Center, and faculty research associate, Space Sciences Research Center, 1968-70, professor of management and faculty research professor, 1972-76; University of Georgia, Athens, distinguished professor of management, 1976—. Visiting research fellow, University of Aston, Birmingham, England, 1970-71; Fulbright visiting professor at University of Belgrade, 1971. Consultant to Aluminum Company of America, American Management Association, American College of Hospital Administrators, and Missouri Regional Medical Programs. *Military service:* U.S. Army, 1956-58; became first lieutenant. *Member:* American Association of University Professors, Institute of Management Sciences, Industrial Relations Research Association, Beta Gamma Sigma, Phi Kappa Phi, Alpha Sigma Nu, Tau Kappa Alpha, Sigma Pi. *Awards, honors:* University of Texas excellence fund award, 1968.

WRITINGS: Hemisphere West: El Futuro, Bureau of Business Research, University of Texas, 1968; (with Cary D. Thorp) *Organization Planning and Development,* American Management Association, 1971; *The Management of Scientific Research: An Annotated Bibliography and Synopsis,* Research Center, School of Business and Public Administration, University of Missouri, 1971; *Business Policy: Strategy Formation and Management Action,* McGraw, 1971, 2nd edition, 1976; *The Teaching of Business Policy,* McGraw, 1971, 2nd edition, 1976; *Personnel: A Diagnostic Approach,* Business Publications, 1974, 2nd edition, 1977; *Cases and Exercises in Personnel,* Business Publications, 1974, 2nd edition, 1977; *Management,* Dryden, 1977; *The Managerial Experience,* Dryden, 1977; *Study Guide for Management,* Dryden, 1977; *Readings in Personnel,* Business Publications, 1977; *Readings in Business Policy/Strategic Management from Business Week,* McGraw, 1978.

Contributor: William G. Scott, editor, *Organization Concepts and Analysis,* Dickenson, 1969; Dale S. Beach, editor, *Readings in Personnel,* Macmillan, 1970; Elmer Burack and James Walker, editors, *Manpower Planning,* Allyn & Bacon, 1971; Robert W. Siroka and others, editors, *Sensitivity Training Reader,* Grosset, 1971. Contributor to *Academy of Management Journal, Management Science, Personnel Psychology,* and over thirty other publications.

*   *   *

GLUT, Donald F(rank) 1944-
(Don Grant, Johnny Jason, Victor Morrison, Rod Richmond, Mick Rogers, Dr. Spektor, Dale Steele, Bradley D. Thorne)

PERSONAL: Surname rhymes with "boot"; born February 19, 1944; son of Frank C. (a baker and World War II pilot) and Julia (Blasovits) Glut. *Education:* Attended De Paul University, 1962-64; University of Southern California, B.A., 1967. *Home address:* Box 3143, North Hollywood, Calif. 91609. *Agent:* Forrest J Ackerman, 2495 Glendower Ave., Hollywood, Calif. 90027.

CAREER: Worked as writer, assistant copywriter with advertising agency in Van Nuys, book store clerk in Hollywood, actor, and professional musician and singer, all in Calif., 1965-71; part-time writer, 1966—. *Member:* Writers Guild of America West, International Tom Steele Fan Club (executive president), Academy of Comic Book Artists, American Federation of Musicians, American Federation of Television and Radio Artists, Society of Vertebrate Paleontology, Alpha Chi. *Awards, honors: The Dinosaur Dictionary* was selected as one of the best reference books of 1974 by the American Library Association; Montague Summers Award from Count Dracula Society, 1976, for *The Dracula Book;* Friends of Fandom award from San Diego Comic Convention, 1976.

WRITINGS: (Under pseudonym Mick Rogers) *Freakout on Sunset Strip,* Greenleaf Classics, 1967; *Frankenstein Resucitado* (originally written in English as *Frankenstein Lives Again,* but published in Spanish), Buru Lan (San Sebastian, Spain), 1971; *Frankenstein y el Robot* (originally written in English as *Terror of Frankenstein,* but published in Spanish), Buru Lan, 1971; (with Jim Harmon) *The Great Movie Serials: Their Sound and Fury,* Doubleday, 1971; *True Vampires of History,* H C Publishers, 1972; *The Dinosaur Dictionary,* Citadel, 1972; *The Frankenstein Legend: A Tribute to Mary Shelley and Boris Karloff,* Scarecrow, 1972; *Bugged* (novel), Manor, 1974; *Broeder Bloed* (originally written in English as *Brother Blood,* but published in Dutch), De Schorpioen, 1974; *The Great Television Heroes,* Doubleday, 1975; *The Dracula Book,* Scarecrow, 1975; *Spawn* (novel), Laser Books, 1976; *The Family Funtime Book of Monsters,* Western Publishing, 1977; *Classic Movie Monsters,* Scarecrow, 1977.

Also author of movie script, "Castle of Gore," and scripts for underground films; author of television scripts, "Shazam!," "Land of the Lost," "Dynomutt, Dog Wonder," "The New Superfriends," "The Young Sentinels," and "Tarzan, Lord of the Jungle." Author of record album liner notes for "Frankenstein" and "Dracula" (recordings of old radio broadcasts), produced by Mark 56 Records.

Contributor: Forrest J. Ackerman, editor, *The Frankenscience Monster*, Ace Books, 1970; Dick Lupoff and Don Thompson, editors, *The Comic Book Book*, Arlington House, 1972; *The Rivals of Frankenstein*, Corgi Books, 1977. Contributor of short stories to *Famous Monsters of Filmland #83*, 1971, and to the "Perry Rhodan" series, published by Ace Books. Contributor to numerous comic books, including *Eerie, Vampirella, Tweety and Sylvester, Porky Pig, Tarzan, Ghost Rider, House of Mystery, Grimm's Ghost Stories, Bugs Bunny,* and *Dagar the Invincible* (for which Glut created the character). Contributor of articles and fiction to *Search, Fave, Tiger Beat, Right On, Science Fiction Illustrated, Mystery Comics Digest,* and *Golden Comics Digest.* Editor and publisher, with Richard Anderson, of *Shazam* (fan magazine), 1962-64; editor-author, *Modern Monsters;* contributing editor, *Castle of Frankenstein;* associate editor, *Monsters of the Movies, E-Go Collectors Series, Henry Winkler Magazine, TV's Dynamic Heroes,* and *King of the Monsters.*

WORK IN PROGRESS: Several novels, to be published in England by MEWS Books, *Frankenstein Lives Again, Terror of Frankenstein, Bones of Frankenstein,* and *Frankenstein Meets Dracula.*

SIDELIGHTS: Donald Glut plays the piano, organ, guitar, bass guitar, clarinet, trombone, baritone, and other instruments. He writes songs and is an amateur sleight-of-hand magician, artist, and film-maker, specializing in all areas of horror and science and fantasy fiction. He is also interested in the "nostalgic arts," including old radio shows and comic books, and is a collector in these areas.

Many of Glut's works have been published in Spanish, German, and Dutch, and translations into Swedish are being planned. The University of Southern California produced a "dramatic documentary," entitled "Glut," in 1967.

BIOGRAPHICAL/CRITICAL SOURCES: Dick Lupoff and Don Thompson, editors, *The Comic Book Book,* Arlington House, 1972; Jean-Marie Sabatier, *Les Classiques du Cinema Fantastique,* Ballard (Paris), 1973.

*   *   *

GOETZE, Albrecht E. R. 1897-1971

January 11, 1897—August 15, 1971; German-born scholar and author of books on ancient civilizations. Obituaries: *New York Times,* August 18, 1971; *Time,* August 30, 1971.

*   *   *

GOINS, Ellen H(aynes) 1927-

PERSONAL: Born May 4, 1927, in Amarillo, Tex.; daughter of Eugene B. (a construction engineer) and Bess (Bennett) Haynes; married Otto Goins (a territorial sales manager), August 2, 1946; children: Ellen, Richard Greg, Laura Gail. *Education:* Attended Northeast Louisiana University, 1944-46; American Academy of Art, diploma, 1950. *Residence:* Houston, Tex. *Office address:* Steck-Vaughn Co., P.O. Box 2028, Austin, Tex. 78767.

CAREER: Hoskinson-Rohloff Studios, Chicago, Ill., artist, 1950-55; portrait painter and free-lance artist, 1955—; Steck-Vaughn Co., Austin, Tex., textbook artist, 1968—. *Member:* Houston Writers Workshop, Houston Watercolor Art Society.

WRITINGS—Self-illustrated, except as indicated: *Omar the Undercover Cat,* Steck, 1968; (authored only) *Horror at Hinklemeyer House,* Follett, 1971; *She Was Scared Silly,* Steck, 1971; *David's Pockets,* Steck, 1972; *Big Diamond's Boy* (novel), Thomas Nelson, 1977.

Illustrator: Frances Williams, *Red Mouse,* Steck, 1967; Blanchette, Arnspiger, Brill, Rucker, *Our Values,* Steck, 1969; *The Human Values Series Teaching Pictures,* Steck, 1969; *Myself,* Steck, 1970; *Myself and Others,* Steck, 1970. Contributor of writings and art to periodicals.

WORK IN PROGRESS: Writing and illustrating *The Long Winter Sleep,* for McKay.

*   *   *

GOLANN, Cecil Paige 1921-

PERSONAL: Surname is pronounced Go-*lann;* born January 20, 1921, in New York, N.Y.; daughter of Daniel Leonard (a physician) and Ethel (Block) Golann. *Education:* Barnard College, B.A. (summa cum laude), 1941; Columbia University, M.A., 1942, Ph.D., 1952. *Home:* 425 Riverside Dr., New York, N.Y. 10025. *Agent:* Patricia Lewis, 450 Seventh Ave., Room 602, New York, N.Y. 10001.

CAREER: Hunter College (now Hunter College of the City University of New York), New York City, lecturer in English, 1953-55; Thomas Alva Edison Foundation, New York City, director of mass media awards, 1955-57; National Broadcasting Co. Television, New York City, program researcher, 1958-62; Crowell Collier & Macmillan, Inc., New York City, associate editor, 1962-67, senior editor, 1967-71. *Member:* American Philological Association, New York Classical Club, Metropolitan Opera Guild, Phi Beta Kappa. *Awards, honors:* Fulbright fellowship to Italy, 1952-53; Ford Foundation Fund for the Advancement of Education grant to attend Hunter College, 1954-55.

WRITINGS: Our World: The Taming of Israel's Negev (juvenile) Messner, 1970. Contributor to *New Columbia Encyclopedia,* and more than 100 articles to periodicals.

WORK IN PROGRESS: Impact, a novel about Israel during the Six-Day War, completion expected in 1979; *Bronzebeard,* a novel about Nero and St. Paul, 1980.

*   *   *

GOLDEN, Arthur 1924-

PERSONAL: Born August 22, 1924, in New York, N.Y.; son of Harry and Gussie (Leavitt) Golden; married Bernice P. Landau, June 3, 1956; children: Susan. *Education:* New York University, B.A., 1947, Ph.D., 1962; Columbia University, M.A., 1948. *Home:* 5 Stockbridge Ave., Suffern, N.Y. 10901. *Office:* Department of English, City College of the City University of New York, New York, N.Y. 10031.

CAREER: New York University, New York City, instructor in English, 1959-63; City College of the City University of New York, New York City, instructor, 1963-64, assistant professor, 1965-69, associate professor, 1970-73, professor of English, 1974—. Trustee, Walt Whitman Birthplace Association, Huntington, N.Y. 1967—. *Member:* American Studies Association, Bibliographical Society of America, Modern Language Association of America, Long Island Historical Society, Bibliographical Society of University of Virginia. *Awards, honors:* National Endowment for the Humanities grant, 1970-71; Faculty Research Foundation Award, City University of New York, 1970-71.

WRITINGS: (Editor) *Walt Whitman's Blue Book: The*

1860-61 "Leaves of Grass" Containing His Manuscript Additions and Revisions, two volumes, New York Public Library, Volume I: *Facsimile,* 1968, Volume II: *Textual Analysis,* 1968; (editor) *Walt Whitman: A Collection of Criticism,* McGraw, 1974. Contributor of articles and reviews to PMLA, *Bulletin* of the New York Public Library, *Literature and Psychology, Papers* of the Bibliographical Society of America, *McGraw-Hill Encyclopedia of World Biography,* and to other literary journals. Member of editorial board, *Literature and Psychology.*

WORK IN PROGRESS: Editing manuscript section of Walt Whitman Variorum edition of *Leaves of Grass,* expected completion in 1979; a critical study of nineteenth-century American poetry.

* * *

GOLDEN, Jeffrey S. 1950-

PERSONAL: Born April 24, 1950, in Los Angeles, Calif.; son of Jack (an engineering consultant) and Lane (Kutz) Golden. *Education:* Attended Harvard University, 1968-70. *Politics:* "Wholistic." *Religion:* "Same as politics." *Home:* 2087 Holcomb Springs Rd., Gold Hill, Ore. 97525. *Agent:* Candida Donadio Literary Agency, Inc., 111 West 57th St., New York, N.Y. 10019.

CAREER: Apprentice carpenter in San Rafael, Calif., 1970-71; independent carpenter in Rogue River Valley, Ore., 1972-75; owner of and homebuilder for The Joe Hill Co., 1975—.

WRITINGS: Watermelon Summer, Lippincott, 1970. Contributor of articles on various aspects of establishing rural collectives to periodicals.

WORK IN PROGRESS: Fiction.

BIOGRAPHICAL/CRITICAL SOURCES: San Francisco Chronicle, December 26, 1971.

* * *

GOLDIN, Judah 1914-

PERSONAL: Born September 14, 1914, in New York, N.Y.; son of Gerson David (a merchant) and Rachel (Robkin) Goldin; married Grace Avis Aaronson (a writer), June 21, 1938; children: Robin Elinor (deceased), David Lionel. *Education:* City College of New York (now City College of the City University of New York), B.S., 1934; Jewish Theological Seminary of America, B.H.L., 1934, M.H.L., 1938, D.H.L., 1943; Columbia University, M.A., 1938. *Home:* 405 Thayer Rd., Swarthmore, Pa. 19081. *Office:* Department of Oriental Studies, University of Pennsylvania, Philadelphia, Pa. 19081.

CAREER: University of Iowa, Iowa City, associate professor of religion, 1946-52; Jewish Theological Seminary of America, Seminary College, New York, N.Y., dean and associate professor of Aggadah, 1952-58; Yale University, New Haven, Conn., professor of classical Judaica, 1958-73; University of Pennsylvania, Philadelphia, professor of Oriental studies, 1973—. Visiting associate professor, Duke University, 1943-45. *Member:* American Academy for Jewish Research (fellow), Society of Biblical Literature, American Oriental Society, Middle East Studies Association, Phi Beta Kappa. *Awards, honors:* American Philosophical Society grant, 1957, 1971; Guggenheim fellowship, 1958; Fulbright fellowships, 1958, 1964-65; M.A., Yale University, 1958; H.L.D., Jewish Theological Seminary of America, 1968; D.D., Colgate University, 1973.

WRITINGS: (Translator) *The Fathers According to Rabbi Nathan,* Yale University Press, 1955; (editor and translator) *The Living Talmud: The Wisdom of the Fathers,* New American Library, 1957; (translator and author of introduction) Shalom Spiegel, *The Last Trial,* Pantheon, 1967; (editor and author of introduction) *The Jewish Expression,* Bantam, 1970; *The Song at the Sea,* Yale University Press, 1971. Consultant, *Encyclopaedia Britannica.*

WORK IN PROGRESS: The nature of midrashic literature; *The Nature of Literary Exegesis.*

SIDELIGHTS: Judah Goldin's main interests lie in aspects of Hellenistic civilization and in English literature. He has traveled in Europe, Israel, and South Africa and has competence in Greek, Latin, Hebrew, Aramaic, Syriac, French, and German. *Avocational interests:* Music.

* * *

GOLDMAN, Merle 1931-

PERSONAL: Born March 12, 1931, in New Haven, Conn.; daughter of Jacques A. (a businessman) and Rose (Breslau) Rosenblatt; married Marshall Goldman (an economist), June 14, 1963; children: Ethan, Avra, Karla, Seth. *Education:* Sarah Lawrence College, B.A., 1953; Radcliffe College, M.A., 1957; Harvard University, Ph.D., 1964. *Home:* 17 Midland Rd., Wellesley, Mass. 02181. *Office:* Department of History, Boston University, Boston, Mass. 02215.

CAREER: Wellesley College, Wellesley, Mass., instructor in Far Eastern history, 1963-64; Northeastern University, Boston, Mass., instructor in Chinese history, 1966-68; Harvard University, Cambridge, Mass., research associate at East Asian Research Center, 1967—; Boston University, Boston, associate professor of history, 1971—. Lecturer, Foreign Service Institute, U.S. Department of State, 1968—, Harvard University, 1968—, Radcliffe College, 1968-70. *Member:* Phi Beta Kappa.

WRITINGS: Literary Dissent in Communist China, Harvard University Press, 1967; (editor) *Modern Chinese Literature in the May Fourth Era,* Harvard University Press, 1977.

Contributor: John Lewis, editor, *Party Leadership and Revolutionary Power,* Cambridge University Press, 1970; Benjamin Schwartz, editor, *Reflections on the May Fourth Movement: A Symposium,* Harvard University Press, 1972; Chalmers Johnson, editor, *Ideology and Politics in China,* University of Washington Press, 1972. Contributor to *China Quarterly, Survey, Harvard Papers on China,* and *Current History.*

WORK IN PROGRESS: The role of the intellectual in the Chinese communist movement.

* * *

GOLDSTEIN, Abraham S(amuel) 1925-

PERSONAL: Born July 27, 1925, in New York, N.Y.; son of Isidore and Yetta (Crystal) Goldstein; married Ruth Tessler, August 31, 1947; children: William Ira, Marianne Susan. *Education:* City College (now City College of the City University of New York), B.B.A., 1946; Yale University, LL.B., 1949. *Home:* 545 Ellsworth Ave., New Haven, Conn. 06511. *Office:* Law School, Yale University, 127 Wall St., New Haven, Conn. 06520.

CAREER: Admitted to District of Columbia Bar, 1949; Cook & Berger, Washington, D.C., associate, 1949; law clerk to circuit judge, U.S. Court of Appeals, Washington,

D.C., 1949-51; Donohue & Kaufmann, Washington, D.C., partner specializing in civil and criminal litigation, 1951-56; Yale University, New Haven, Conn., associate professor, 1956-61, professor of law, 1961-67, William Nelson Cromwell Professor of Law, 1967-75, dean of Law School, 1970-75, Sterling Professor of Law, 1975—. Visiting professor, Hebrew University, Jerusalem. Cambridge University, visiting fellow, Institute of Criminology, and fellow of Christ's College, 1964-65; member of faculty, Salzburg Seminar in American Studies, summer, 1969. Vice-president, Connecticut Bar Foundation, 1976—. Consultant, President's Commission on Law Enforcement and Administration of Criminal Justice, 1966-67, Procurador-General of Colombia, 1968; member of Task Force on the Future of Legal Education, Carnegie Commission on Future of Higher Education, 1969. Chairman, Commission on Law, Social Action and Urban Affairs, American Jewish Congress, 1977—. Member of Connecticut Commission to Revise Criminal Statutes, 1966-69, and Governor's Planning Committee on Criminal Administration, 1967-71; member of Connecticut Board of Parole, 1967-69. *Military service:* U.S. Army, 1943-46.

MEMBER: American Academy of Arts and Sciences, American Association of University Professors, Beta Gamma Sigma. *Awards, honors:* M.A., Yale University, 1961; M.A., Cambridge University, 1964; Guggenheim fellow, 1964-65.

WRITINGS: The Insanity Defense, Yale University Press, 1967; (editor with Joseph Goldstein) *Crime, Law and Society* (readings), Free Press, 1971; (with L. Orland) *Criminal Procedure,* Little, Brown, 1974. Contributor of articles and reviews to legal and other journals.

*   *   *

GOLDSTEIN, Alvin H., Sr. 1902-1972

June 19, 1902—May 6, 1972; American journalist. Obituaries: *New York Times,* May 8, 1972; *Washington Post,* May 9, 1972; *Time,* May 22, 1972.

*   *   *

GOLDSTEIN, Kenneth M(ichael) 1940-

PERSONAL: Born October 11, 1940, in New York, N.Y.; son of Abraham and Ethel (Rosenberg) Goldstein; married Elaine Lois Gronner (adjunct lecturer at a college), May 4, 1964; children: Alisha Pam, Stacey Britt, Russell Stewart. *Education:* City College of the City University of New York, B.A., 1961; Princeton University, M.A., 1963, Ph.D., 1964. *Residence:* Staten Island, N.Y. *Office:* Staten Island Children's Community Mental Health Center, 657 Castleton Ave., Staten Island, N.Y. 10301.

CAREER: Wakoff Research Center, Staten Island, N.Y., research psychologist, 1964—, associate director of research; North Richmond Community Mental Health Center, Staten Island, program analyst, 1970-73; Saint Vincent's Medical Center of Richmond, Staten Island, associate director of research, 1970—; Staten Island Children's Community Health Center, Staten Island, director of research and development, 1974—. Clinical instructor in psychology, State University of New York Downstate Medical Center, 1965-67; Richmond College of the City University of New York (now College of Staten Island of the City University of New York), assistant professor, 1967-70, adjunct professor of psychology, 1971-72; adjunct associate professor of psychology, Staten Island Community College of the City University of New York, 1970-76; adjunct professor of psychology, Queens College of the City University of New York,

1977—. Consultant, National Science Foundation, 1971—. *Member:* American Psychological Association, Association for Children with Learning Disabilities, Eastern Psychological Association, Phi Beta Kappa, Sigma Xi, Psi Chi. *Awards, honors:* Woodrow Wilson fellow, 1961-62; National Institute of Mental Health fellow, 1962-64; Gardner Murphy award in psychology, City College of the City University of New York.

WRITINGS: (With Sheldon Blackman) *An Introduction to Data Management in the Behavioral and Social Sciences,* Wiley, 1971; (contributor) P. McReynolds, editor, *Advances in Psychological Assessment,* Volume IV, Jossey-Bass, 1977; *Cognitive Style: Five Approaches and Relevant Research,* Wiley, 1978. Contributor of about two dozen articles to psychology journals.

*   *   *

GOLDSTEIN, Laurence 1937(?)-1972

1937(?)—February 12, 1972; American television journalist and reviewer. Obituaries: *New York Times,* February 14, 1972.

*   *   *

GOLDSTONE, Richard H. 1921-

PERSONAL: Born August 8, 1921, in New York, N.Y.; son of George A. (an educator) and Lena (Dane) Goldstone. *Education:* University of Wisconsin, B.A., 1941; Columbia University, M.A., 1947, Ph.D., 1960. *Home:* 17 Hampton Harbor Rd., Hampton Bays, N.Y. 11946. *Agent:* Rae Pierre Corsini, 12 Beekman Pl., New York, N.Y. *Office:* Department of English, City College of the City University of New York, 138th St. and Convent Ave., New York, N.Y. 10031.

CAREER: Syracuse University, Syracuse, N.Y., instructor in English, 1946-48; University of Kentucky, Lexington, instructor in English, 1948-50, 1952-53; Columbia University, New York City, instructor in English, 1953-61; City College of the City University of New York, New York City, associate professor of English, 1961—, ombudsman, 1972—. Member of executive committee, Legislative Conference of New York. *Military service:* U.S. Army Air Forces, 1941-46, U.S. Air Force, 1947-65; became lieutenant colonel. *Member:* Modern Language Association of America, Andiron Club of New York (business manager).

WRITINGS: (Editor) *Contexts of the Drama,* McGraw, 1968; (editor) *Mentor Masterworks of Modern Drama,* New American Library, 1969; (editor with Abraham Lass) *Mentor Book of Short Plays,* New American Library, 1969; *Thornton Wilder: An Intimate Portrait,* Dutton, 1975. Contributor to *Saturday Review, Paris Review, New York Times Book Review,* and other magazines and newspapers.†

*   *   *

GOLDSWORTHY, David 1938-

PERSONAL: Born September 13, 1938, in Adelaide, Australia; son of John Garfield (a teacher) and Phyllis (Gould) Goldsworthy; married Joanna Wolff (a laboratory technician), April 11, 1964; children: Patrick. *Education:* University of Adelaide, B.A. (honors), 1959; Oxford University, B.Phil., 1962, D.Phil., 1969. *Politics:* Australian Labour Party. *Religion:* Methodist. *Home:* 19 Beaver St., East Malvern, Victoria, Australia 3145. *Office:* Monash University, Wellington Rd., Clayton, Victoria, Australia 3168.

CAREER: Monash University, Clayton, Australia, lecturer, 1965-68, senior lecturer, 1968-76, reader in politics,

1976—. *Member:* Australasian Political Studies Association, Australian Institute of International Affairs (council member, Victoria branch).

WRITINGS: Colonial Issues in British Politics 1945-1961: From Colonial Development to Wind of Change, Oxford University Press, 1971. Editor, *Australian Outlook* (Australian Institute of International Affairs journal).

WORK IN PROGRESS: A book entitled *Tom Mboya's Role in Keyan Politics,* completion expected in 1979.

AVOCATIONAL INTERESTS: Travel, cinema, music (especially jazz).

* * *

GOODALL, John Strickland 1908-

PERSONAL: Born June 7, 1908, in Heacham, Norfolk, England; son of Joseph Strickland (a physician and surgeon) and Amelia (Hunt) Goodall; married Margaret Alison Nicol, March 25, 1933; children: Sarah Strickland (Mrs. H. Stead-Ellis). *Education:* Attended Harrow School, 1922-26; studied art privately under J. Watson Nicol, Sir Arthur Cope, and Harold Speed, and later at Royal Academy School of Art, London. *Politics:* Conservative. *Religion:* Church of England. *Home and studio:* Lawn Cottage, Tisbury, Wiltshire, England.

CAREER: Painter. Illustrator during early part of his career for books, periodicals, and advertising; after the war started landscape painting in water color and gouache and doing "conversation groups," including one of the late Duchess of Kent and her family; has had exhibitions of his Victorian pastiche in London and Canterbury. *Military service:* British Army, Royal Norfolk Regiment, 1939-45; served in India, Burma, and Kashmir. *Member:* Royal Institute of Water Colour Painters, Royal Society of British Artists, National Society of British Artists. *Awards, honors: Boston Globe-Horn Book* Award for excellence in authorship and illustration of a children's book, 1969, for *The Adventures of Paddy Pork.*

WRITINGS—Picture books: *Field Mouse House,* Blackie & Son, 1954; *Dr. Owl's Party,* Blackie & Son, 1954; *The Adventures of Paddy Pork,* Harcourt, 1968; *The Ballooning Adventures of Paddy Pork* (ALA Notable Book, *Horn Book* Honor List), Harcourt, 1969; *Shrewbettina's Birthday,* Harcourt, 1971; *Jacko,* Macmillan, 1971; *Kelly,* Atheneum, 1971; *Dot and Esmerelda,* Atheneum, 1972.

Illustrator: Anthony Robertson, *How to Do and Say in England,* Dickson, 1936; Susan Dorritt, *Jason's Lucky Day,* Abelard, 1958; Edith N. Bland, *Five Children and It,* Looking Glass Library, 1959; Bland, *Story of the Amulet,* Looking Glass Library, 1960; Bland, *Phoenix and the Carpet,* Looking Glass Library, 1960; Barbara Ker Wilson, *Fairy Tales of England,* Dutton, 1960; Lewis Carroll, *Alice in Wonderland* (illustrations after John Tenniel), Blackie & Son, 1965. Also illustrated Read, *All the Village School,* M. Joseph; Nancy Pense Britton, *The Insane Folly,* Basil Blackwood; Simon Dewes, *Suffolk Childhood,* Hutchinson; Dewes, *Essex Schooldays,* Hutchinson; Dewes, *When all the World was Young,* Hutchinson; R. Arkell, *Trumpets over Merriford,* M. Joseph; Arkell, *The Round House,* M. Joseph; Garrick Play Books, Blackie; two books by Chenvix Trench for Blackwood; a number of "Seekers and Finders" books by Amabel Williams-Ellis, for Blackie, and others.

Contributor to *Connoisseur, Radio Times,* and other magazines and newspapers.

WORK IN PROGRESS: An Edwardian Winter; A Village Heritage.

SIDELIGHTS: John Goodall has painted in France, Italy, Yugoslavia, Portugal, Spain, Andorra, Greece, Netherlands, Switzerland, and Sweden. He made a leisurely trip around the world on a cargo ship, 1960-61.

BIOGRAPHICAL/CRITICAL SOURCES: Connoisseur, July, 1968, November, 1971; *Book World,* October 20, 1968; *Times Literary Supplement,* April 16, 1970.

* * *

GOODALL, Marcus C(ampbell) 1914-

PERSONAL: Born March 3, 1914, in London, England; son of Edwin Campbell (a merchant) and Winifrede (Elliott) Goodall; married first wife, Luella Trinterud; married second wife, Helen McKenney, November 28, 1960; children: (second marriage) Stella, Jonathan. *Education:* Attended Oxford University, 1933-36, and Institute for Advanced Study, Princeton, N.J., 1949-50. *Politics:* Radical. *Religion:* None. *Home:* 1724 Saulter Rd., Birmingham, Ala. 35209. *Office:* Department of Biophysics, University of Alabama, Birmingham, Ala. 35233.

CAREER: Luton Aircraft Ltd., Gerrard's Cross, England, draftsman and designer in aerodynamics, 1936-37; Pye Radio Ltd., Cambridge, England, development and vacuum engineer, 1937-42; British Admiralty, Bristol, England, experimental officer in microwave radar, 1942-45; Marconi Wireless Telegraph Co., Chelmsford, England, senior development engineer, 1945-49; Standard Telephones and Cables Ltd., Ilminster, England, research physicist, 1950-51; Institute for Muscle Research, Woods Hole, Mass., research fellow in muscle biophysics, 1951-53; University of Michigan, Ann Arbor, lecturer in zoology, 1953-56; Massachusetts Institute of Technology, Cambridge, research associate in biology, 1956-59; Cornell University, Ithaca, N.Y., research associate at Computation Center, 1959-60; Massachusetts Institute of Technology, staff member, Research Laboratory of Electronics, 1960-65; Boston University, Boston, Mass., research associate in physics, 1965-66; Institute for Biomedical Research, Chicago, Ill., associate member, 1966-70; University of Alabama in Birmingham, associate professor of biophysics, 1970—.

MEMBER: London Mathematical Society, American Mathematical Society, Biophysical Society, General Systems Research Society, Royal Geographical Society, Royal Commonwealth Society. *Awards, honors:* Leverhulme research fellowship in mathematical physics, 1949.

WRITINGS: (Contributor) *Cerebral Systems and Computer Logic,* California Institute of Technology, 1960; *Science and the Politician,* Schenkman, 1965; *Science, Logic and Political Action,* Schenkman, 1970. Contributor of more than thirty articles to scientific journals.

WORK IN PROGRESS: Politics of Survival.

SIDELIGHTS: Marcus Goodall describes himself as a "philosophical activist." His early interest (to age sixteen) was in the literary and classical; at Oxford he concentrated on chemistry; now he is thinking of completing a life-long interest—the foundations of relativistic quantum mechanics. He also is a licensed aircraft pilot.

* * *

GOODHEART, Barbara 1934-

PERSONAL: Born July 13, 1934, in Chicago, Ill.; daughter

of Victor Theodore (a former business executive) and Jean (Smith) Peterson; married Clyde R. Goodheart (a physician and cancer virologist), December 26, 1953; children: Ken, Karen, Diane. *Education:* Northwestern University, B.A., 1955. *Home:* 15 Sheffield Ct., Lincolnshire, Deerfield, Ill. 60015.

CAREER: Free-lance writer. *Member:* American Society of Journalists and Authors (midwest chairperson, 1973-75).

WRITINGS: A Year on the Desert (youth book), Prentice-Hall, 1969; (contributor) G. B. Fulton and W. V. Fasbender, editors, *Health Education in the Elementary School: Guidelines and Program Suggestions,* Goodyear Publishing, 1972; (contributor) L. A. Jacobus, editor, *Issues and Response,* Harcourt, 1972; (contributor) *Health,* Southwestern Co., 1973. Ghost-writer of chapter in *The USA, Customs, and Institutions,* Simon & Schuster, 1970. Writer of features for *Deerfield Review,* 1965-66, studyprint scripts for Society for Visual Education, medical pamphlets, brochures, and press releases. Contributor of chapters to textbooks, and of articles to *Today's Health,* (under her own name and under a pseudonym), *Today's Family, Westways, Lady's Circle, Together, Companion, Direction, Northwestern Report, Better Homes and Gardens, Family Weekly, Discovery,* and other magazines.

WORK IN PROGRESS: Co-authoring a trade book; writing a series of medical "backgrounders," audiotape scripts, workbooks.

*   *   *

GOODIN, Gayle   1938-

PERSONAL: Born March 16, 1938, in Kinston, Ala.; son of Luke Elliott and Neitha (Bedsole) Goodin. *Education:* Troy State University, B.A., 1959; attended Guadalajara Summer School, 1960; University of Mississippi, M.A., 1966, Ph.D., 1978. *Home address:* Route 3, Box 93, Griffin, Ga. 30223.

CAREER: High school teacher of English and Spanish in Decatur, Ga., 1959-61, 1962-65; DeKalb Community College, Clarkston, Ga., instructor, 1966-75. *Military service:* National Guard, 1955. *Member:* Dixie Council of Authors and Journalists, Georgia Writers Association, Atlanta Writers Club, Sigma Tau Delta. *Awards, honors:* Atlanta Prose Writer of the Year, 1971, and Daisy Osborne Gibbs Poetry Award from Atlanta Writers Club.

WRITINGS: Watch for the Morning, privately printed, 1967; *Pre-Writing Encounter,* Holbrook, 1971. Founder, *Between These Lines* (poetry magazine for Georgia high school students). Editor, *DeKalb Literary Arts Journal,* 1968-73.

WORK IN PROGRESS: Editing Neitha Goodin's *Earth-Angel and Moonshine;* co-authoring a freshman composition text; four books, *Behold Our Blood, Sing the Aloneness, The Acid Kingdom, Sahara Storming;* a collection of poems, *The Gene Coleman Trilogy; Deep South Poetry: A Classification of Subjects.*

AVOCATIONAL INTERESTS: Water skiing, wrestling, hiking, weight lifting, tennis.

BIOGRAPHICAL/CRITICAL SOURCES: Decatur-DeKalb News, February 17, 1971, September 29, 1971; *Atlanta Journal,* September 1, 1971.

*   *   *

GOODING, Cynthia   1924-

PERSONAL: Born August 12, 1924, in Rochester, Minn.;

daughter of Arthur Faitoute (a stockbroker) and Frances (Judson) Gooding; married Hasan Ozbekhan (an economist), July, 1948 (divorced, 1957); children: Ayshe, Leyla. *Education:* Graduated from Branksome Hall, Toronto, Canada, 1940.

CAREER: Folksinger; from 1952-62 recorded ten LP albums of folk songs from Mexico, Spain, England, France, and Turkey, most on Elektra label. Writer.

WRITINGS: A Princeton Guide: Walks, Drives and Commentary, photographic illustrations by Mercedes Rogers, foreword by Stringfellow Barr, Middle Atlantic Press, 1971. Also author of a novel, *The Central Place.*

WORK IN PROGRESS: A novel, *Man of Stone.*

BIOGRAPHICAL/CRITICAL SOURCES: Ray McKinley Lawless, *Folk Singers and Folk Songs in America,* Duell, 1960; *Bookman's Yearbook,* 1971.††

*   *   *

GOODMAN, Charles S(chaffner)   1916-

PERSONAL: Born April 5, 1916, in Detroit, Mich.; son of Lawrence M., Sr. (an insurance executive) and Carolyn (Schaffner) Goodman; married Dorothy Irvin, December 4, 1943; children: Carol Suzanne, Charles, Jr. *Education:* University of California, Los Angeles, B.A., 1938, M.A., 1940; University of Michigan, Ph.D., 1948. *Home:* General Washington Rd., Wayne, Pa. 19087. *Office:* Department of Marketing, Wharton School, University of Pennsylvania, Philadelphia, Pa. 19104.

CAREER: University of Pennsylvania, Wharton School, Philadelphia, lecturer, 1946-48, assistant professor, 1948-53, associate professor, 1953-57, professor of marketing, 1957—, chairman of department, 1974—. Director, Silo, Inc. (discount retail appliance chain), 1969—. Consultant to various business, governmental, and trade organizations. *Military service:* U.S. Naval Reserve, active duty, 1942-46; served in Supply Corps, became commander; retired, 1968. *Member:* American Marketing Association (Philadelphia chapter, director, 1961-63, vice-president, 1963-65, president, 1965-66; director, 1966-67), Beta Gamma Sigma. *Awards, honors:* Alpha Kappa Psi award for best article in *Journal of Marketing,* 1968.

WRITINGS: The Control of Customer Returns, Bureau of Business Research, University of Michigan, 1942; *Location of Fashion Industries,* Bureau of Business Research, University of Michigan, 1948; (with Reavis Cox and F. R. Root) *Adaptation to Markets in the Distribution of Building Materials,* Producers' Council, Inc., 1963; (with Cox and T. C. Fichlander) *Distribution in a High-Level Economy,* Prentice-Hall, 1965; *Management of the Personal Selling Function,* Holt, 1971. Contributor to *Journal of Marketing, Journal of Retailing, Industrial Marketing Management* (Amsterdam), and *Personnel Journal.* Managing editor, American Marketing Association *Proceedings,* 1960-68.

*   *   *

GOODMAN, Jonathan   1931-

PERSONAL: Born January 17, 1931, in London, England; son of Jack Arthur (a civil servant) and Margaret-Louise (Hicks) Goodman; married Christine Wylie-Harris (a journalist), October 15, 1959. *Education:* Attended Sir Charles Elliot School, 1941-48. *Home:* 43 Ealing Village, London W5 2LZ, England. *Agent:* Charles Lavell Ltd., 176 Wardour St., London W1V 3AA, England. *Office address:* Anbar Publications, Ltd., P.O. Box 23, Wembley HA9 8DJ, England.

CAREER: Theatrical director and television producer for various companies in England, 1951-64; Anbar Publications Ltd., London, England, director, 1965—. *Military service:* Royal Air Force, 1949-51. *Member:* Royal Society of Arts (fellow), Medico-Legal Society, British Academy of Forensic Sciences, Our Society, Crime Writers Association.

WRITINGS: Matinee Idylls (poetry), Mitre Press, 1954; *Instead of Murder* (novel), Hammond, Hammond, 1961; *Criminal Tendencies* (novel), John Long, 1964; *Hello Cruel World Goodbye* (novel), John Long, 1964; *The Killing of Julia Wallace*, Harrap, 1969, Scribner, 1977; *Bloody Versicles: The Rhymes of Crime*, St. Martin's, 1971; *Posts-Mortem: The Correspondence of Murder*, David & Charles, 1971; (editor) *My Experiences as an Executioner*, David & Charles, 1972; *Trial of Ian Brady and Myia Hindley*, David & Charles, 1974; *The Burning of Evelyn Foster*, Scribner, 1977. Writer of stage plays and television scripts for various organizations. Contributor of articles, short stories, and reviews to several publications. General editor, "Celebrated Trials" series, David & Charles, 1971—.

WORK IN PROGRESS: A Case of Deja Vu, a novel.

BIOGRAPHICAL/CRITICAL SOURCES: Books and Bookmen, May, 1969.

*   *   *

GOODMAN, Philip   1911-

PERSONAL: Born September 6, 1911, in New York, N.Y.; son of Harry D. and Molly (Epstein) Goodman; married Hanna Caspi, August 14, 1932; children: Abraham C., Judith (Mrs. Irving Rubin). *Education:* Attended Yeshiva University and City College (now City College of the City University of New York), 1930; Yeshiva of Rabbi Kook, Rabbi, 1932. *Home:* 63 Shahal St., Jerusalem, Israel.

CAREER: Institutional Synagogue, New York City, rabbi and executive director, 1933-42; National Jewish Welfare Board, New York City, staff member of Committee on Army and Navy Religious Activities (now Commission on Jewish Chaplaincy), 1942-44, director of Jewish education, 1944-68, administrative secretary of World Federation of Young Men's Hebrew Associations and Jewish Community Centers, 1956-68, executive secretary of Jewish Book Council of America, 1944-76, consultant to Services to Small Communities, 1968-76. Former secretary, National Council for Jewish Education; executive secretary, American Jewish Historical Society, 1948-53. *Awards, honors:* Mordecai Ben David Award from Yeshiva University, 1955; first Horeb Award of Teachers Institute Alumni, Yeshiva University, 1960.

WRITINGS: (Compiler) *Purim Anthology,* Jewish Publication Society, 1949; *Hamishah Asar bi-Shevat* (program material for youth and adults), National Jewish Welfare Board, 1950; *Lincoln's Birthday Program Material for Jewish Groups,* National Jewish Welfare Board, 1953; *Rejoice in Thy Festival: A Treasury of Wisdom, Wit, and Humor for the Sabbath and Jewish Holidays,* Bloch Publishing, 1956; (compiler) *The Passover Anthology,* Jewish Publication Society, 1961; (editor) *A Treasury of Jewish Inspiration,* New York Board of Rabbis, 1962; (compiler with wife, Hanna Goodman) *The Jewish Marriage Anthology,* Jewish Publication Society, 1965; (compiler) *The Rosh Hashanah Anthology,* Jewish Publication Society, 1970; *Illustrated Essays on Jewish Bookplates,* Ktav, 1971; (compiler) *The Yom Kippur Anthology,* Jewish Publication Society, 1971; (compiler) *Essays on Jewish Booklore,* Ktav, 1971; *Jewish Bookplate Literature: An Annotated Bibliography,* Ktav, 1971;

(compiler) *The Sukkot and Simhat Torah Anthology,* Jewish Publication Society, 1973; *The Shavuot Anthology,* Jewish Publication Society, 1975; (compiler) *The Hanukkah Anthology,* Jewish Publication Society, 1976.

Booklets include: (Compiler) *American Jewish History* (prose and verse selection), American Jewish Historical Society, 1949; *Jewish History Programs,* American Jewish Historical Society, 1949; *American Jewish History Programs,* American Jewish Historical Society, 1962. Managing editor, *Jewish Book Annual,* 1944-76; associate editor, *In Jewish Bookland,* 1945-76.

*   *   *

GOODRICH, Robert E(dward), Jr.   1909-

PERSONAL: Born June 9, 1909, in Cleburne, Tex.; son of Robert E. and Moye (Wilson) Goodrich; married Thelma Quillian, June 5, 1939; children: Thelma Jean (Mrs. James E. Skinner), Lucy (Mrs. James Caswell), Robert Edward III, Paul Quillian. *Education:* Birmingham-Southern College, B.A., 1931; Southern Methodist University, M.A., 1940. *Home:* 4954 Lindell, 8 E, St. Louis, Mo. 63108. *Office:* 4625 Lindell, Suite 420, St. Louis, Mo. 63108.

CAREER: Prior to entering the ministry was program director of Radio Station KTBS in Shreveport, La.; ordained Methodist minister, 1933; pastor in Port Arthur, Tex., 1935-37, Galena Park, Tex., 1937-39, Houston, Tex., 1939-44, and El Paso, Tex., 1944-46; First Methodist Church, Dallas, Tex., pastor, 1946-72; elected to position of bishop in United Methodist Church and assigned to Missouri area. Producer of first dramatic religious television show in Dallas, 1949, of "A Faith Is Born," for General Conference (Methodist) in San Francisco, 1952, and of "The New Wilderness" for General Conference in Dallas, 1968; preacher on Methodist series of "Protestant Hour" broadcasts. Trustee of Southwestern University and Southern Methodist University. *Awards, honors:* D.D., Centenary College, 1950; Distinguished Alumnus Award, Southern Methodist University, 1967.

WRITINGS: What's It All About?, Revell, 1955; *Reach for the Sky,* Abingdon, 1960; *Lift Up Your Heart,* Tidings, 1961; *On the Other Side of Sorrow,* Abingdon, 1962; *Look at the Burning Bushes,* Spiritual Life, 1963; *Dear God Where Are You?,* Word Books, 1969.

SIDELIGHTS: As a student at Perkins School of Theology, Robert Goodrich directed the Southern Methodist University Rose Bowl Band and the S.M.U. Mustang Band, a popular music group. In his final year as director, the Mustang Band played thirteen weeks in metropolitan theaters under the aegis of the National Broadcasting Co.

*   *   *

GOODSTEIN, Leonard D(avid)   1927-

PERSONAL: Born January 11, 1927, in New York, N.Y.; son of Moses (a salesman) and Stella (Warshar) Goodstein; married Jeanette Treat (a political scientist), August 26, 1972; children: Richard Edward, Steven Michael. *Education:* City College (now City College of the City University of New York), B.S., 1948; Columbia University, M.A., 1948, Ph.D., 1952. *Politics:* Independent. *Religion:* Jewish. *Home:* 9819 North 65 Pl., Scottsdale, Ariz. 85253. *Office:* Department of Psychology, Arizona State University, Tempe, Ariz. 85281.

CAREER: Diplomate in clinical psychology; Hofstra College (now University), Hempstead, N.Y., instructor in psychology, 1948-51; University of Iowa, Iowa City, instructor, 1951-53, assistant professor, 1953-57, associate professor, 1957-61, professor of psychology, 1961-64; University of Cincinnati, Cincinnati, Ohio, professor of psychology, 1964-74; Arizona State University, Tempe, professor of psychology and chairman of department, 1974—. Fulbright senior lecturer, Vrije Universiteit, Amsterdam. Consultant to Veterans Administration, 1953—, and Peace Corps, 1963-70. *Member:* American Psychological Association, Midwestern Psychological Association (member of board of directors, 1970-73).

WRITINGS: (Editor with Richard I. Lanyon) *Readings in Personality Assessment,* Wiley, 1971; (with Lanyon) *Personality Assessment,* Wiley, 1971; *Adjustment, Behavior, and Personality,* Addison-Wesley, 1975; *Consultants with Human Service Systems,* Addison-Wesley, 1978. Contributor of more than a hundred articles to professional journals.

WORK IN PROGRESS: Revisions of *Personality Assessment* and *Adjustment Behavior and Personality.*

BIOGRAPHICAL/CRITICAL SOURCES: Personnel and Guidance Journal, January, 1971.

* * *

GORDON, Alvin J. 1912-

PERSONAL: Born May 5, 1912, in Brookline, Mass.; son of Nathan H. (a motion picture industry businessman) and Sarah (Edinberg) Gordon; married Darley Fuller, January 10, 1938; married second wife, Betty Halstead, May 14, 1966; stepchildren: (second marriage) Lisa Mackenzie, Matt Mackenzie, Peggy Mackenzie, Ann Elkins. *Education:* Wisconsin University, certificate, 1932; Harvard University, A.B., 1938. *Home:* 1975 Sobre Vista Rd., Sonoma, Calif.

CAREER: President, Gateway Productions, Inc. (producers of educational films; distributed by University of Arizona, Tucson), 1946—. President of Nathan H. Gordon Corp. (investment firm), Boston, Mass., 1966, and El Paseo de Sonoma (restaurant and shops), Sonoma, Calif., 1968. *Member:* Press Club, International Platform Association, Explorers Club. *Awards, honors:* Detur Prize, 1938; John Harvard honorary fellowship, 1938; diploma from Mexican Historical Society, 1941.

WRITINGS: (With Darley Gordon) *Our Son Pablo,* Whittlesey House, 1946; *Inherit the Earth,* University of Arizona Press, 1964; *Brooms of Mexico,* University of Arizona Press; 1966; *Journeys with St. Francis,* Best-West, 1968; *Of Vines and Missions,* Northland Press, 1971; *Guaymas,* Vista del Mar (Tucson, Ariz.), 1973. Also author of a motion picture script on Surinam.

WORK IN PROGRESS: Films for the deaf; a book on using one's senses and imagination.

SIDELIGHTS: Alvin Gordon wrote *CA,* "My efforts in writing and film production, as well as architectural building and restoration are constantly influenced by the desire to create beauty as well as to inform."

* * *

GORDON, Ambrose, Jr. 1920-

PERSONAL: Born May 23, 1920, in Savannah, Ga.; son of Ambrose and Lenore (Hunter) Gordon; married Mary Spainhour, September 1, 1960; children: Marion R., Ambrose III. *Education:* Yale University, B.A., 1942, M.A., 1951, Ph.D., 1952. *Home:* 1606 Forest Trail, Austin, Tex.

78703. *Office:* Department of English, University of Texas, Austin, Tex. 78712.

CAREER: University of Texas at Austin, assistant professor, 1958-64, associate professor, 1964-72, professor of English, 1972—. *Military service:* U.S. Navy, 1942-46.

WRITINGS: The Invisible Tent: The War Novels of Ford Madox Ford, University of Texas Press, 1964.

* * *

GORDON, Dane R. 1925-

PERSONAL: Born June 15, 1925, in London, England; son of Leonard (a musician) and Heather (Gibson) Gordon; married Elizabeth May Marshall (a chemist, in personnel work), August 16, 1952. *Education:* Cambridge University, B.A., 1951, M.A., 1958; University of London, B.D., 1956; University of Rochester, M.A., 1960. *Home:* 44 Crestline Rd., Rochester, N.Y. 14618. *Office:* Rochester Institute of Technology, Rochester, N.Y. 14623.

CAREER: Clergyman of Presbyterian Church; Central Presbyterian Church, Rochester, N.Y., minister, 1957-61; Rochester Institute of Technology, Rochester, assistant professor, 1962-65, associate professor, 1965-74, professor, 1974—, chairman of science and humanities department, 1974, assistant dean, 1976, acting dean, 1976—. *Military service:* Royal Navy, 1943-47. *Member:* American Philosophical Association, Society for the Scientific Study of Religion, American Association of University Professors, American Society of Composers, Authors and Publishers, Rochester Poetry Society. *Awards, honors:* Danforth associate, 1966-67.

WRITINGS: Preach Me a Play, Foundation Books (King of Prussia, Pa.), 1965; *Philosophy of Religion,* New York State Department of Education, 1971; (with Milford Fargo) *A Family Christ Mass,* Kendor Music, 1973; (with Fargo) *Away He Run,* Galaxy, 1976. Also author of a three-act play, "Too Little for Milo," published in *Prize Plays,* Abingdon, 1961. Contributor of articles and poetry to *Christian Century, Touchstone, Torch Quarterly,* and other religious and general publications.

WORK IN PROGRESS: A college text, *Introduction to Biblical Studies;* "Pilgrim," a musical adaptation with Milford Fargo.

AVOCATIONAL INTERESTS: Music, playing flute and recorder, wine making, wine drinking, gardening.

* * *

GORDON, George Byron 1911-

PERSONAL: Born July 20, 1911, in New York, N.Y.; son of Milton John (an attorney) and Antoinette (Koscherak) Gordon; married Clara Popper, November 23, 1932; children: William John, Patricia Clare (Mrs. Peter R. Chick), Anthony Charles. *Home and office:* 46 Claremont Dr., Maplewood, N.J. 07040.

CAREER: Private practice as consulting counsel on tax estate matters, 1934-39; Prentice-Hall, Inc., New York, N.Y., executive editor and consulting editor, 1945-48; Mutual Benefit Life Insurance Co., Newark, N.J., 1948-71, held several positions within company including director of advanced underwriting services and second vice-president; currently in private practice as consulting editor. Guest lecturer at University of Connecticut, University of Florida, University of Illinois, and a member of other institutions; lecturer to bar and trust groups. *Military service:* U.S.

Marine Corps, 1942-45; became captain. *Member:* Council of Profit Sharing Industries (member of board of directors of Newark chapter).

WRITINGS: (With James C. Wriggins) *Understanding Federal Income, Estate and Gift Taxes,* Institute for Business Planning, 1952, 2nd edition, 1954; *You, Your Heirs and Your Estate,* Business Reports, Inc., 1952, 2nd edition, Farnsworth Publishing, 1963, 4th edition, 1977; *Repairs vs. Capital Expenditures,* Ronald, 1958; *Profit-Sharing in Business and Estate Planning,* Farnsworth Publishing, 1960, 3rd edition, 1970; *Using Tax Money for the Family,* Prentice-Hall, 1962; (editor and reviser) Robert S. Holzman, *Guide to Pension and Profit-Sharing Plans,* Farnsworth Publishing, 1965; (editor) *The Fifteenth Anniversary Edition of Estate Planners Quarterly* (reader), Farnsworth Publishing, 1969. Contributor to *Estate Tax Techniques,* Matthew Bender, 1955. Also contributor to business journals. Managing editor, *Financial Planning;* member of editorial boards, *Estate Planners Quarterly,* and *Journal of Community Property.*

AVOCATIONAL INTERESTS: Visual, dramatic, and fine arts; collecting rare books, prints, paintings in enamel, paperweights, old Indian baskets, pottery, and sculpture; music.

*   *   *

GORDON, Harold J(ackson), Jr.   1919-

PERSONAL: Born December 30, 1919, in Cleveland, Ohio; son of Harold Jackson and Irene (Mount) Gordon; married Nancy Morehouse (a college instructor), September 10, 1949; children: Elizabeth C., Edward M., Richard M. *Education:* Attended Virginia Polytechnic Institute, 1936-37; University of Richmond, B.A., 1940; Johns Hopkins University, additional study, 1946-47; Yale University, M.A., 1948, Ph.D., 1953. *Politics:* Independent. *Religion:* None. *Home:* 27 Pease Pl., Amherst, Mass. 01002. *Office:* Department of History, University of Massachusetts, Amherst, Mass. 01003.

CAREER: Office of Assistant Chief of Staff, Department of the Army, Washington, D.C., military intelligence research analyst, 1951-55; University of Pittsburgh, Pittsburgh, Pa., instructor, 1955-57, assistant professor of history, 1957-59; University of Massachusetts—Amherst, associate professor, 1959-62, professor of history, 1962—. *Military service:* U.S. Army, 1943-46; received bronze star with cluster; U.S. Army Reserve, 1946-73, served in military intelligence; retired as lieutenant colonel. *Member:* American Historical Association, American Military Institute, Conference Group on Central European History (member of executive board, 1970-73), Conference Group on German Politics, New England Historical Association, Historische Verein von Oberbayern. *Awards, honors:* Grant-in-aid for travel and research in Europe, 1958; Fulbright research grant, 1965-66; German Academic Exchange Service grant, 1969-70.

WRITINGS: The Reichswehr and the German Republic, 1919-1926, Princeton University Press, 1957; *Der Hitlerputsch 1923* (originally written in English; translated by Hans-Juergen Baron von Koskull and published in German), Bernard & Graefe, 1971, published in English as *Hitler and the Beer Hall Putsch,* Princeton University Press, 1972. Contributor to *Military Affairs, Wehrwissenschaftliche Rundschau, Zeitschrift fuer bayerische Landesgeschichte,* and *Politische Studien.*

WORK IN PROGRESS: Four books, *The German Police,*

1919-1933, Freikorps Movement, Reichswehr, 1927-1935, and *Bavarian Politics, 1919-1933.*

SIDELIGHTS: Harold Gordon told *CA:* "My research is aimed at exploring problems which arouse my interest and my writing is intended to show as clearly as possible what I have found and what it means in my estimation. I want both to inform the reader of what I have learned and to stimulate him to examine my ideas critically. The second can be of at least as much value as the first—whether I am wrong or right—since it is often only the clash between discordant viewpoints which leads the reader to formulate his own independent views. Thus the historian should provide the raw material for the reader and initiate a debate with those who wish to go beyond the facts to the meaning, as well as to encourage the reader to apply such lessons as he draws from history and the critical skills he develops by studying it analytically to the problems of his times and his own life."

AVOCATIONAL INTERESTS: Photography, wildlife, firearms and ecology (primarily in the biological aspects), Russian armed forces and military history, travel in Germany.

*   *   *

GORDON, Lois G.   1938-

PERSONAL: Born November 13, 1938, in Englewood, N.J.; daughter of Irving David and Betty (Davis) Goldfein; married Alan Lee Gordon (a psychiatrist), November 13, 1961; children: Robert Michael. *Education:* University of Michigan, B.A. (with honors), 1960; University of Wisconsin, M.A., 1962, Ph.D., 1966. *Religion:* Jewish. *Home:* 300 Central Park W., New York, N.Y. 10024. *Office:* Department of English, Fairleigh Dickinson University, Teaneck, N.J. 07666.

CAREER: City College of the City University of New York, New York, N.Y., lecturer in English, 1964-66; University of Missouri at Kansas City, assistant professor of English, 1966-68; Fairleigh Dickinson University, Teaneck, N.J., assistant professor, 1968-71, associate professor, 1971-75, professor of English, 1975—. *Member:* Modern Language Association of America, National Association for Psychoanalytic Criticism (member of advisory board, 1975—).

WRITINGS: Stratagems to Uncover Nakedness: The Dreams of Harold Pinter, University of Missouri Press, 1969. Writer and narrator of educational tapes on modern drama for Everett Edwards. Contributor to literature journals. Assistant editor, *Literature and Psychology,* 1968-70.

WORK IN PROGRESS: The Terrible Beauty, a study of existential and Freudian thought in modern literature.

AVOCATIONAL INTERESTS: Piano.

*   *   *

GORDON, Sanford D(aniel)   1924-

PERSONAL: Born June 23, 1924, in Newark, N.J.; son of Harry L. (a businessman) and Beatrice S. (Safris) Gordon; married Alice L. Pressman, May 27, 1948; children: Ellen A., Eric A. *Education:* New York University, B.S., (magna cum laude), 1947, M.A., 1948., Ph.D., 1953. *Politics:* Registered Democrat. *Religion:* Jewish. *Home:* 1 Tudor Rd., Albany, N.Y. 12203. *Office:* State University of New York, Central Administration, 99 Washington Ave., Albany, New York 12246.

CAREER: New York University, New York, N.Y., instructor in social studies, 1948-50; State University of New York College at Oneonta, instructor, 1950-52, assistant professor, 1952-54, associate professor, 1954-57, professor of economics, 1957—, chairman of department, 1960—; State University of New York, Central Administration, Albany, director of research and planning, 1972, assistant vice chancellor for policy and planning, 1972-76, provost for policy analysis, 1976—. Visiting summer professor at State University of New York College at Buffalo, 1965, and University of Miami, Coral Gables, 1967; part-time visiting professor, Russell Sage College, 1973—; visiting university fellow, Empire State College of State University of New York at Saratoga Spring, 1971-72. Parks commissioner, City of Oneonta, 1956-60; vice-president, Oneonta Brotherhood Council. Consultant to New York State Bankers Association, 1973—. *Military service:* U.S. Army Air Forces, 1943-45; became sergeant; received Air Medal with three oak-leaf clusters, Purple Heart, and Presidential Citation.

MEMBER: American Economic Association, Association for Evolutionary Economics, Economic History Association, American Association of University Professors, New York State Economics Association, (president, 1967-68). *Awards, honors:* Calvin Kazajian Foundation award, 1967, for innovations in teaching economics at college level.

WRITINGS: (With Jess Witchel) *An Introduction to the American Economy: Analysis and Policy,* Heath, 1967; *A Visual Analysis of the American Economy,* Heath, 1968; (with George Dawson and others) *The American Economy: Analysis and Policy,* Heath, 1969; (with Dawson) *Introductory Economics,* Heath, 1972, 3rd edition, 1976. Editor, Kennikat's reprint series, "Economic Thought, History, and Challenge." Television scripts include twenty-eight program series, "The American Economy," 1968. Contributor to economic and education journals.

*   *   *

GORDON, Walter Kelly 1930-

PERSONAL: Born January 25, 1930, in Brooklyn, N.Y.; son of William Benjamin (a railroad engineer) and Grace Adele (Kelly) Gordon; married Lydia Caroline Fruchtman, August 29, 1959; children: Karyn Gay. *Education:* Clark University, A.B., 1950; University of Pennsylvania, M.A., 1956, Ph.D., 1960. *Home:* 2803 Salem Dr., Cinnaminson, N.J. 08077. *Office:* Office of the Dean, College of Arts and Sciences, Rutgers University, Camden, N.J. 08102.

CAREER: Cedar Crest College, Allentown, Pa., instructor, 1959-60, assistant professor of English, 1960-61; Rutgers University, Camden, N.J., assistant professor, 1961-67, associate professor, 1967-74, professor of English, 1974—, chairman of department, 1971-72, associate dean, 1972-73, dean of College of Arts and Sciences, 1973—. *Military service:* U.S. Navy, 1951-56; became lieutenant; U.S. Naval Reserve. *Member:* Modern Language Association of America, National Council of Teachers of English, American Association of University Professors.

WRITINGS: (Editor with James L. Sanderson) *Exposition and the English Language,* Appleton, 1963, 2nd edition, 1969; (editor) *Literature in Critical Perspectives,* Appleton, 1968. Contributor to literature journals.

WORK IN PROGRESS: A revision of *Literature in Critical Perspectives,* completion expected in 1978.

AVOCATIONAL INTERESTS: Swimming, boating, travel.

GOSE, Elliott B(ickley), Jr. 1926-

PERSONAL: Born May 3, 1926, in Nogales, Ariz.; became a Canadian citizen; son of Elliott and Eleanor (Paulding) Gose; married Kathleen Brittain, 1950; children: Peter C., Sarah E. *Education:* University of Colorado, B.A., 1949, M.A., 1950; Cornell University, Ph.D., 1954. *Office:* Department of English, University of British Columbia, Vancouver, British Columbia, Canada.

CAREER: Louisiana State University, Baton Rouge, instructor in English, 1954-56; University of British Columbia, Vancouver, instructor, 1956-58, assistant professor, 1958-63, associate professor, 1963-67, professor of English, 1967—. *Military service:* U.S. Army, 1946-47. *Member:* Modern Language Association of America, Phi Beta Kappa. *Awards, honors:* Canada Council leave fellowship, 1971-72.

WRITINGS: Imagination Indulged: The Irrational in the Nineteenth-Century Novel, McGill Queens University Press, 1972. Contributor to literary journals.

WORK IN PROGRESS: The Transformation Process in Joyce's Ulysses, a critical, psychoanalytic, aesthetic study.

*   *   *

GOTTESMAN, Ronald 1933-

PERSONAL: Born January 7, 1933, in Boston, Mass.; son of Benjamin (a salesman) and Eva (Glagovsky) Gottesman; married Valerie Anne Kruszyna, June 9, 1956; children: Lann, Grant. *Education:* University of Massachusetts, A.B. (with honors), 1955; Colgate University, M.A., 1957; Indiana University, Ph.D., 1964. *Home:* 10793 Ashton Ave., No. 11, Los Angeles, Calif. 90024. *Agent:* Bertha Klausner International Literary Agency, Inc., 71 Park Ave., New York, N.Y. 10016. *Office:* Center for the Humanities, DML 303, University of Southern California, Los Angeles, Calif. 90007.

CAREER: Northwestern University, Evanston, Ill., instructor in English, 1960-62; Indiana University at Bloomington, lecturer, 1962-64, assistant professor, 1964-68, associate professor of English, 1968, Upton Sinclair Archivist at Lilly Library, 1963-69; Rutgers University, Livingston College, New Brunswick, N.J., associate professor of English, 1969-72; University of Wisconsin—Parkside, professor of English and humanities, 1972-75; University of Southern California, Los Angeles, professor of English and director of Center for the Humanities, 1975—. Visiting professor, University of Zagreb, 1965-66. *Military service:* U.S. Army Reserve, 1955-63. *Member:* Modern Language Association of America, American Studies Association, National Council of Teachers of English, Society for Cinema Studies, American Association of University Professors, University Film Association. *Awards, honors:* International Affairs Center grant, summer, 1966, to work in Central State Archives for Art and Literature, Moscow; Guggenheim fellow, 1970-71.

WRITINGS: A Catalogue of Books, Manuscripts, and Other Materials from the Upton Sinclair Archives, Lilly Library, 1963; (contributor) *Books for Teachers of English: An Annotated Bibliography,* Indiana University Press, 1968; (contributor) *Professional Standards and American Editions,* Modern Language Association of America, 1969; (editor with Scott Bennett) *Art and Error: Modern Textual Editing,* Indiana University Press, 1970; (with Harry M. Geduld) *Sergei Eisenstein and Upton Sinclair: The Making and Unmaking of Que Viva Mexico!,* Indiana University Press, 1970; (editor) *Focus on Citizen Kane,* Prentice-Hall,

1971; (editor) *Studies in Invisible Man*, C. E. Merrill, 1971; (with Geduld) *Guidebook to Film: An Eleven-in-One Reference Work*, Holt, 1972; (with Charles Silet) *Literary Manuscripts of Upton Sinclair*, Ohio State University Press, 1973; *Upton Sinclair: An Annotated Checklist*, Kent State University Press, 1973; *An Illustrated Glossary of Film Terms*, Holt, 1973; (editor) *Focus on Orson Welles*, Prentice-Hall, 1976; (co-editor) *The Girl in the Hairy Paw: King Kong as Movie, Monster and Myth*, Avon, 1976.

Interviewer and editor, "Upton Sinclair: An Oral Memoir," for Oral History Research Office, Columbia University, 1963. Member of executive committee, "A Selected Edition of W. D. Howells," Indiana University Press, 1965—, textual editor, 1965-68, general editor, 1968-69. Co-general editor with Harry M. Geduld of Spectrum "Film Focus" series, Prentice-Hall, 1971—; co-general editor, "Filmguides" series, Indiana University Press, and of reference guides to literature; advisory editor of filmstudies. Field editor, *Reference Guides to Literature: American and English*. Contributor to *Notable American Women;* contributor of more than twenty articles and reviews to academic journals and to newspapers. Editor, *Quarterly Review of Film Studies*.

WORK IN PROGRESS: W. D. Howells: Selected Criticism, Volume III, for Indiana University Press; general editor of Norton's multivolume *Norton Anthology of American Literature*.

* * *

GOTTFRIED, Theodore Mark 1928-
(Leslie Behan, Harry Gregory, Lou Marco, Ted Mark, Katherine Tobias)

PERSONAL: Born October 19, 1928, in Bronx, N.Y.; son of Harry Mark (a toolmaker) and Jennie (Bach) Gottfried; married Leanore Traugot, June 25, 1950 (divorced, 1970); married Harriet Klein, September 25, 1976; children: (first marriage) Julie Ellen, Daniel Mark, Katherine Anne, Toby Jean, Valerie Dawn; stepchildren: Melanie, Lisa. *Education:* Attended University of Miami, Coral Gables, Fla., 1946-47, New York School of Journalism, 1947, and New School for Social Research, 1948-49. *Religion:* Unitarian Universalist. *Home:* 162-30 Powells Cove Blvd., Whitestone, N.Y. 11357. *Agent:* Robert P. Mills Ltd., 156 East 52nd St., New York, N.Y. 10022.

CAREER: Warner Brothers, New York City, publicist, 1947-51; during 1951 was assistant manager of a theater, publicist for Skymaster Airline, and reporter and film reviewer for *Boxoffice* (magazine), all New York City; cab driver for Checker Cab Co., New York City, 1952-55; Premier Peat Moss, New York City, advertising manager, 1955; Penthouse Publications, New York City, editor, 1956-57; Stearn Publications, New York City, successively editor, managing editor, and executive editor, 1957-62; Westpark Publications, New York City, editor of *Dude* and *Gent* (magazines), 1963; free-lance fiction writer, 1963—; editor, *High Society* (magazine), 1976-77; Drake Publications, New York City, publisher, 1977—.

WRITINGS—Under pseudonym Leslie Behan: *The Midway at Midnight*, Domino, 1964; *In Love's Dark Corners*, Domino, 1965; *Circle of Sin*, Lancer Books, 1967, later reprinted under pseudonym Ted Mark.

Under pseudonym Harry Gregory: *The Twisted Sex Trap*, Brandon House, 1969.

Under pseudonym Ted Mark; all published by Lancer Books: *The Man from O.R.G.Y.*, 1965; *The Nine Month

Caper, 1965; *The Girl from Pussycat*, 1965; *The Ted Mark Reader* (short stories), 1966; *The Real Gone Girls*, 1966; also author of screenplay of book produced by Sidney Pink as "The Man from O.R.G.Y.," 1970; *Pussycat, Pussycat*, 1966; *Dr. Nyet*, 1966; *A Hard Day's Knight*, 1966; *My Son the Double Agent*, 1966; *The Unhatched Egghead*, 1966; *The Nude Wore Black*, 1967; *Room at the Topless*, 1967.

Published by Berkley Publishing, except as indicated: *The Square Root of Sex*, 1967; *I Was a Teeny-Bopper for the C.I.A.*, 1967; *Back Home at the O.R.G.Y.*, 1968; *Come Be My O.R.G.Y.*, 1968; *The Pussycat Transplant*, 1968; *This Nude for Hire*, 1969; *Where's Your O.R.G.Y.?*, 1969; *The Nude Who Did*, 1970; *The Man from Charisma*, Dell, 1970; *Right On, Relevant*, Dell, 1970; *Rip Off, Relevant*, Dell, 1971; *Regina Blue*, Dell, 1972; *Beauty and the Bug*, Dell, 1975.

Under pseudonym Katherine Tobias: *The Lady in the Lightning*, Lancer Books, 1966.

Also author of *The Zinger* under pseudonym Lou Marco, 1977. Writer for Playboy Press under various undisclosed pseudonyms.

WORK IN PROGRESS: Dial O for O.R.G.Y.; and an original screenplay about the humorous aspects of the so-called generation gap.

SIDELIGHTS: "My major recreations are personal relationships and chess," Theodore Gottfried writes. "I am concerned about civil rights, have marched in Mississippi, worked to integrate housing in the north, and gone to jail for sitting-in at a landlord's office. I've also been active in the peace movement, was jailed in New York at the 1967 Whitehall Street protest, tear-gassed in Washington, and tear-gassed in Chicago during the 1968 Democratic Convention which I covered for *Status Magazine*, my assignment having been to write a humor piece." Gottfried also told *CA* that he is "concerned with feminism" and supports the Equal Rights Amendment.

All of the Ted Mark books through 1969 have been published in the Scandinavian countries and England. *Pussycat, Pussycat* also has been published in Brazil and Portugal, and *The Lady in the Lightning* in Portugal.

* * *

GOULD, James A(dams) 1922-

PERSONAL: Born July 11, 1922, in Flint, Mich.; son of Edgar Harold (an engineer) and Matilda (Wareham) Gould; married Ruth Goos; children: Leslie, Francesca, Stephanie. *Education:* University of Michigan, B.S., 1947, M.A., 1948, Ph.D., 1953. *Politics:* Democrat. *Religion:* Unitarian-Universalist. *Home:* 4487 Vieux Carre, Lutz, Fla. 33549. *Office:* Department of Philosophy, University of South Florida, Tampa, Fla. 33620.

CAREER: University of Miami, Coral Gables, Fla., instructor in philosophy, 1953-57; Emory University, Atlanta, Ga., assistant professor of philosophy, 1957-62; Florida State University, Tallahassee, associate professor of philosophy, 1962-64; University of South Florida, Tampa, professor of philosophy and chairman of department, 1964—. *Military service:* U.S. Army Air Forces, 1943-46; became first lieutenant. *Member:* American Society for Legal and Political Philosophy, American Civil Liberties Union (chairman of Tampa chapter, 1968-73). *Awards, honors:* Freedom Foundation radio award, 1961; American Philosophical Association lectures awards, 1976.

WRITINGS: (Editor) *Readings on Logic*, Macmillan, 1964,

2nd edition, 1972; (editor) *Readings in Contemporary Logic,* Macmillan, 1965; *Philosophy for a New Generation,* Macmillan, 1970, 3rd edition, 1977; *Freedom: The Philosophical Problems,* Macmillan, 1970; *The Western Humanities,* two volumes, Holt, 1971; *Classical Philosophical Questions,* C. E. Merrill, 1971, 2nd edition, 1975; *Love, Sex, and World Identity,* Boyd & Fraser, 1972; *Violence and Literature in the Twentieth Century,* Boyd & Fraser, 1972; *Religion for a New Generation,* Macmillan, 1972; *Contemporary Political Ideologies,* Macmillan, 1972; *Existentialism,* Dickerson Publishing, 1973; *Person to Person Reader,* Holt, 1973.

*   *   *

GOVE, Samuel K(imball)   1923-

PERSONAL: Born December 27, 1923, in Walpole, Mass.; son of Chester B. (a banker) and Minnie (Allen) Gove. *Education:* University of Massachusetts, B.S., 1947; Syracuse University, M.A., 1949. *Home:* 2006 Bruce Dr., Urbana, Ill. 61801. *Office:* Institute of Government and Public Affairs, University of Illinois, 1201 West Nevada St., Urbana, Ill. 61801.

CAREER: University of Illinois, Urbana, research associate of Institute of Government and Public Affairs, 1951-54, research assistant professor, 1954-57, research associate professor, 1957-60, associate professor, 1960-61, professor in Institute, 1961—, professor of political science in the university, 1966—, acting director of Institute, 1961-62, 1964-65, 1966-67, director, 1967—, advisor, public administration program, 1974—. Staff assistant, National Association of Assessing Officers, 1949; staff fellow, National Municipal League, 1955-56; executive assistant, Illinois auditor of Public Accounts, 1957. Member, Illinois Commission on State Government, 1965-67; secretary, Illinois Local Governments Commission, 1967-69; chairman, Illinois Citizens Task Force on Constitutional Implementation, 1971—. *Military service:* U.S. Naval Reserve, 1943-46; served in Pacific area; became lieutenant junior grade.

MEMBER: American Political Science Association, American Society for Public Administration, National Municipal League, National Association of Schools of Public Affairs and Administration, Governmental Research Association (director, 1969), American Association of Higher Education, American Association of University Professors, Midwest Conference of Political Scientists, Illinois Historical Society.

WRITINGS: (With Thomas Page) *Next Steps in Illinois Personnel Administration,* Institute of Government and Public Affairs, 1955; (with Gilbert Y. Steiner) *Legislative Politics in Illinois,* University of Illinois Press, 1960; (with C. F. Snider) *American State and Local Government,* Appleton-Century-Crofts, 1965; (with Richard J. Carlson) *An Introduction to the Illinois General Assembly,* Institute of Government and Public Affairs, 1968; (editor with Victoria Ranney) *Con Con: Issues for the Illinois Constitutional Convention,* University of Illinois Press, 1970; (editor with Elizabeth Stewart) *The University and the Emerging Federalism: A Conference on Improving University Contributions to State Governments,* Institute of Government and Public Affairs, 1972; (editor with Stephanie Cole) *Home Rule in Illinois,* Institute of Government and Public Affairs, 1973; (with Thomas R. Kitsos) *Revision Success: The Sixth Illinois Constitutional Convention,* National Municipal League, 1974; (editor with Frederick Wirt) *Political Science and School Politics: The Princes and Pundits,* Lexington Books, 1976; (with Richard W. Carlson and Richard J.

Carlson) *The Illinois Legislature: Structure and Process,* University of Illinois Press, 1976. Also author of numerous research and statistical monographs on Illinois government matters. Contributor to many political science books and journals in his field.

WORK IN PROGRESS: Two books, *The Politics of Higher Education* and *State Politics.*

AVOCATIONAL INTERESTS: Tennis.

*   *   *

GOVONI, Laura E.   1914-

PERSONAL: Born September 17, 1914, in Boston, Mass.; daughter of Augustus Govoni. *Education:* Boston City Hospital, nursing diploma, 1936; Boston Lying-In Hospital, diploma in obstetrical nursing; Simmons College, certificate in public health, 1938; Boston University, B.A., 1949, M.A., 1950, Ph.D., 1969. *Office address:* University of Connecticut, Box U59, Storrs, Conn. 06268.

CAREER: Boston Visiting Nurse Association, Boston, Mass., staff nurse, 1938-42; Massachusetts Department of Public Health, Boston, infant welfare field nurse, 1942-46; New England Baptist Hospital, Boston, senior instructor in fundamentals of nursing, 1950-57; Simmons College, Boston, assistant professor of medical-surgical nursing, 1957-63; Boston University, Boston, associate professor of medical-surgical nursing, 1968-70; University of Connecticut, Storrs, associate professor of medical-surgical nursing and behavioral components in health and illness, 1970—. Member of board of advisors, QT Boston, Inc. (self-help organization for ileostomy patients), 1957-63. *Military service:* U.S. Navy, Nurse Corps, 1943-46; became lieutenant senior grade. *Member:* American Anthropological Association, Medical Anthropology Association, American Nurses Association, National League for Nursing, American Association of University Professors, Connecticut Nurses Association, Delta Kappa Gamma, Sigma Theta Tau.

WRITINGS: (With Faye Berzon and Marilyn Fall) *Drugs and Nursing Implications,* Appleton, 1965, 2nd edition (with Janice E. Hayes), 1970.

WORK IN PROGRESS: A third edition of *Drugs and Nursing Implications;* a book on patient care guidelines for nurse practitioners; research on cultural influences on Circadian Rhythm and on ethno-pharmacology.

SIDELIGHTS: Laura Govoni has invented and patented a disposable plastic cover for clinical thermometers which avoids the necessity for chemical sterilization. *Avocational interests:* Astronomy, archaeological digs (especially in American Southwest), rock hounding, nature walks, fishing.

*   *   *

GRABER, Doris A.   1923-

PERSONAL: Born November 11, 1923, in St. Louis, Mo.; daughter of E. and Martha (Insel) Appel; married T. M. Graber (an orthodontist and professor), June 15, 1941; children: Lee W., Thomas W., Jack D., Jim M., Susan D. *Education:* Washington University, St. Louis, Mo., B.A., 1940, M.A., 1941; Columbia University, Ph.D., 1947. *Home:* 2895 Sheridan Pl., Evanston, Ill. 60201. *Office:* Department of Political Science, University of Illinois at Chicago Circle, Chicago, Ill. 60680.

CAREER: Feature writer for newspapers in St. Louis, Mo., 1937-41; U.S. Army Educational Reconditioning Program, Camp Maxey, Tex., civilian director, 1942-43; Commerce

Clearing House, Chicago, Ill., editor of *U.S. Supreme Court Digest* and *Legal Periodicals Digest,* 1945-46; lecturer in political science at Northwestern University, Evanston, Ill., University of Chicago, Chicago, and North Park College, Chicago, 1947-52; University of Chicago, research associate, Center for Study of American Foreign and Military Policy, 1952-71; Harper & Row, Evanston, textbook editor, 1956-63; University of Illinois at Chicago Circle, associate professor, 1963-70, professor of political science, 1970—.

MEMBER: American Political Science Association, American Association for Public Opinion Research, American Society of International Law, Academy of Political Science, American Academy of Political and Social Science, American Society for Education in Journalism, International Communications Association, Midwest Political Science Association (president, 1972-73), Midwest Society for Public Opinion Research, League of Women Voters, Phi Beta Kappa, Pi Sigma Alpha. *Awards, honors:* University of Illinois research professorship, 1971.

WRITINGS: The Development of the Law of Belligerent Occupation, Columbia University Press, 1949; *Crisis Diplomacy: A History of U.S. Intervention Policies and Practices,* Public Affairs Press, 1959; *Public Opinion, the President, and Foreign Policy,* Holt, 1968; *Verbal Behavior and Politics,* University of Illinois Press, 1976. Contributor to political science and world affairs journals.

WORK IN PROGRESS: Learning about Politics from the Mass Media, completion expected in 1979.

* * *

GRAD, Frank P. 1924-

PERSONAL: Born May 2, 1924, in Vienna, Austria; son of Morris (a lawyer) and Clara (Scher) Grad; married Lisa Szilagyi (a pianist and piano teacher), December 6, 1946; children: David A., Catharine A. *Education:* Brooklyn College (now Brooklyn College of the City University of New York), A.B., 1947; Columbia University, LL.B., 1949. *Home:* 315 Central Park W., New York, N.Y. 10025. *Office:* Law School, Columbia University, 435 West 116th St., New York, N.Y. 10027.

CAREER: Admitted to the Bar of New York State, 1949; Columbia University, Law School, New York City, associate in law, 1949-50; House, Grossman, Vorhaus & Hamley, New York City, attorney, 1950-53; Columbia University, Law School, lecturer, 1954-64, adjunct professor, 1964-69, professor of law, 1969—, assistant director of Legislative Drafting Research Fund, 1953-55, associate director, 1955-69, director, 1969—. *Military service:* U.S. Army, 1943-46. *Member:* American Bar Association, American Public Health Association, Association of the Bar of City of New York.

WRITINGS: The Drafting of State Constitutions, National Municipal League, 1963; *Public Health Law Manual,* American Public Health Association, 1965, revised edition, 1970; *Legal Remedies for Housing Code Violations,* National Commission on Urban Problems, 1968; *Alcoholism and the Law,* Oceana, 1971; *Environmental Control: Priorities, Policies and the Law,* Columbia University Press, 1971; *Environmental Law: Sources and Problems,* Matthew Bender, 1971, 2nd edition, 1978; (with Albert J. Rosenthal and others) *The Automobile and the Regulation of Its Impact on the Environment,* Oklahoma University Press, 1975; *Treatise on Environmental Law,* Matthew Bender, Volume I, 1973, Volume II, 1974, Volume III, 1976. Contributor of ar-

ticles on state constitutional law, housing, and public health law to professional journals.

WORK IN PROGRESS: An analysis of the procedures and administration of physician's professional discipline.

* * *

GRAHAM, Clarence H. 1906-1971

January 6, 1906—July 25, 1971; American psychologist and authority on vision. Obituaries: *New York Times,* July 26, 1971; *Washington Post,* July 27, 1971.

* * *

GRAHAM, John 1926-

PERSONAL: Born September 1, 1926, in Washington, D.C.; son of John Thomas and Catherine (O'Neill) Graham; divorced; children: Sarah, John, Christopher, Jane. *Education:* Georgetown University, A.B., 1949; Harvard University, M.A. (English literature), 1954; Johns Hopkins University, M.A. (American literature), 1959, Ph.D., 1960. *Politics:* None. *Religion:* None. *Home:* 701 Bolling Ave., Charlottesville, Va. 22901. *Office:* Department of Speech and Drama, University of Virginia, Charlottesville, Va. 22903.

CAREER: Bullis School, Silver Spring, Md., member of Latin faculty, 1948; Georgetown University, Washington, D.C., instructor in English, 1949-50; English instructor at St. Paul's School, Concord, N.H., 1953, and Marquette University, Milwaukee, Wis., 1953-54; Johns Hopkins University, Baltimore, Md., junior instructor, 1954-57; University of Virginia, Charlottesville, instructor in English, 1958-61, assistant professor in department of speech and drama, 1961-67, associate professor, 1967—, assistant dean of college, 1966-75. *Military service:* U.S. Army Air Forces, 1944-45. *Member:* Modern Language Association of America, Speech Association of America, American Society for Aesthetics, American Forensic Association, The Colonnade Club (past president), Raven Society (University of Virginia), Friday Club (University of Virginia), Farmington Hunt Club. *Awards, honors:* Fulbright fellowship to Germany, 1957-58.

WRITINGS: A Crowd of Cows (juvenile), Harcourt, 1968; (editor) *Great American Speeches, 1898-1963: Texts and Studies,* Appleton, 1970; (editor and contributor), Ernest Hemingway, *Studies in "A Farewell to Arms",* C. E. Merrill, 1971; (editor and contributor) John Hawkes, *Studies in "Second Skin",* C. E. Merrill, 1971; *Craft So Hard to Learn,* Morrow, 1972; *The Writer's Voice,* Morrow, 1973; *I Love You, Mouse* (juvenile), Harcourt, 1976.

Contributor: Carlos Baker, editor, *Hemingway: Critiques of Four Major Novels,* Scribner, 1962; *The Dictionary of the History of Ideas,* Scribner, 1973; Clinton S. Burhans, editor, *A Critical Guide to Ernest Hemingway,* American R.D.M., 1973; Arthur Waldhorn, editor, *Ernest Hemingway: Studies in Contemporary Literature,* McGraw, 1973. Contributor of articles to *Massachusetts Review, Studies in Romanticism, Journal of the History of Ideas, Modern Fiction Studies, Speech Teacher,* and other journals.

Editor, for Caedmon Records, of "Anthologies of Great Speeches" series, including "Great American Speeches," five volumes, 1970, "Great British Speeches," four volumes, 1971, "Great Black Speeches," two volumes, 1972, "The British Parliament Debates and the American Revolution," 1972, and "The Burke-Paine Debate," 1972.

WORK IN PROGRESS: Lavater's "Essays on Physiogno-

my": A Study in the History of Ideas; The Context for Description: Language, Paintings, and Science; Stendhal and the Search for the Truth: A Study in Non-Verbal Communication; ecphrasis; rhetorical portrait.

SIDELIGHTS: John Graham told CA: "I am convinced that the only way to learn anything about language is to write poetry. There is a demand for compression through seeking the exact word or phrase or image that fiction does not seem to insist on. I think I have also learned something about writing through working on very short book reviews where, again, compression is essential." Graham went on to say: "I would like to write a really imaginative book, but I am not at all convinced that I am capable of doing this. Although I write from my own experience I also write from my interest in language. The very words 'once upon a time' seem to me to jar us into dreaming about what could have happened at some time. I think from such dreams one extracts a good story, exciting people, and freedom of language. But at this point I believe I am a 'maker of books,' that my work is essentially analytic rather than genuinely creative."

AVOCATIONAL INTERESTS: Children's literature and illustrators; the relations between poetry and painting.

*   *   *

GRAHAM, John Remington   1940-

PERSONAL: Born November 20, 1940; son of William and Elizabeth (Johnstone) Graham; married Catherine Clark (a musician), October 9, 1971; children: Nathaniel. Education: Attended University of Notre Dame, 1959-60; University of Minnesota, B.A., 1963, LL.B., 1966, graduate study in philosophy, 1967-68. Politics: Independent. Religion: Roman Catholic. Office: School of Law, Hamline University, St. Paul, Minn. 55104.

CAREER: Member of the Bar of the Supreme Court of Minnesota, 1967—, the United States District Court for Minnesota, 1968—, the United States Court of Appeals for the Eighth Circuit, 1968—, and the Supreme Court of the United States, 1971—; attorney at law in Minneapolis, Minn., 1967—; currently associate professor, School of Law, Hamline University, St. Paul, Minn. Candidate for Associate Justice of the Minnesota Supreme Court, 1974. Lecturer at Minnesota Metropolitan State College. Member: Historic Heartland Association (president), Citizens for Governmental Restraint (vice-president), Minnesota Clergy and Laymen Concerned (member of executive committee).

WRITINGS: A Constitutional History of the Military Draft, Ross & Haines, 1971; A Critical View of the Equal Rights Amendment, Women for Responsible Legislation, 1977. Contributor of articles to journals in his field.

WORK IN PROGRESS: A book tentatively entitled Principles of Confederacy; research into the original meaning of the United States Constitution.

SIDELIGHTS: John Graham wrote CA, "My primary interest is restoration of the traditional view of the common law as ideal truth above politics and independent of precedent, and the constitutions of the United States and the several States, as intended by the Framers of these documents." Graham is a co-founder of the School of Law now at Hamline University.

*   *   *

GRAHAM, W(illiam) Fred   1930-

PERSONAL: Born October 31, 1930, in Columbus, Ohio;

son of William Fred and Serena (Clark) Graham; married Marjory Jean Garrett, August 12, 1953; children: Terese, Bonny, Marcy, Geneva. Education: Tarkio College, B.A., 1952; Pittsburgh Theological Seminary, B.D., 1955; Louisville Presbyterian Seminary, Th.M., 1959; University of Iowa, Ph.D., 1965. Home: 332 Chesterfield Parkway, East Lansing, Mich. 48823. Office: Department of Religious Studies, Justin Morrill College, Michigan State University, East Lansing, Mich. 48824.

CAREER: Ordained Presbyterian minister, 1955; Bethel United Presbyterian Church, Waterloo, Iowa, pastor, 1955-61; Michigan State University, East Lansing, instructor, 1963-64, assistant professor in department of religion, 1964-66, Justin Morrill College, assistant professor, 1965-69, associate professor of religious studies, 1969-73, professor in department of religious studies, 1973—. Member: American Society for Church History, American Academy of Religion, Society for Reformation Research, Michigan Academy of Science, Arts and Letters (chairman, Religious Studies Section, 1964-65, 1968-69).

WRITINGS: The Constructive Revolutionary: John Calvin and His Socio-Economic Impact, John Knox, 1971; Picking Up the Pieces, Eerdmans, 1975. Contributor of articles to Ministry, Presbyterian Life, Christian Century, Christianity Today, Reformed Journal, Educational Forum, and other periodicals.

WORK IN PROGRESS: "I am trying to break through some of the problems of secularity and religious belief by writing several 'mystery story/theological novels.'"

SIDELIGHTS: W. Fred Graham told CA he is "most concerned to discover how a Christian can understand society and himself in a world where the transcendent and the 'numinous' are almost deliberately excluded from human experience by the fragmentation of the old sacred universe which the secular world once validated." He is interested in "innovative education at the university level."

A church historian, Graham has done research for his writings in Switzerland and Scotland. Graham also works with Roman Catholic thought in the secular world, teaching a class with a Catholic priest once a year, and working many weeks for the Navy Chaplains Professional Training courses and seminars.

*   *   *

GRAINGER, A(nthony) J(ohn)   1929-

PERSONAL: Born June 19, 1929, in London, England; son of Charles Frederick Henry (a merchant) and Olive Lavell (Kennard) Grainger; divorced; children: Alice Bernadette, James Martin. Education: Cambridge University, B.A. (honors), 1953; Oxford University, Diploma in Education, 1957. Religion: Church of England. Home: 173, Avenue Rd., Leicester, Leicestershire, England.

CAREER: Bushloe High School, Leicestershire, England, head of English department, 1961-66; University of Leicester, Leicester, England, psychological counsellor, 1964-68. Psychotherapist in private practice. Military service: Royal Air Force, 1948-50. Member: British Association of Psychotherapists (London).

WRITINGS: The Bullring: A Classroom Experiment in Moral Education, Pergamon, 1970.

WORK IN PROGRESS: A book, Myths, Dreams and Fairy Tales.

GRAMPP, William D(yer)   1914-

PERSONAL: Born August 22, 1914, in Columbus, Ohio; son of Joseph Frank and Carolyn (Walterscheid) Grampp; children: Wendy Grampp Tockman, Heather M., Christopher W. *Education:* University of Akron, A.B., 1936; Columbia University, additional study, 1941; University of Chicago, A.M., 1942, Ph.D., 1944. *Home:* 5426 Ridgewood Ct., Chicago, Ill. 60615. *Office:* College of Business Administration, University of Illinois at Chicago Circle, Chicago, Ill. 60680.

CAREER: Member of editorial staff of *Akron Times-Press*, Akron, Ohio, 1937-38, Press Wireless, Paris, France, 1938, and London bureau of *Chicago Tribune*, London, England, 1939; Adelphi College (now University), Garden City, N.Y., instructor in economics, 1942; Elmhurst College, Elmhurst, Ill., assistant professor of economics, 1942-44; American Embassy, Rome, Italy, vice-consul in economic section, 1944-45; De Paul University, Chicago, Ill., assistant professor, 1945-47; University of Illinois at Chicago Circle, College of Business Administration, professor of economics, 1947—. Visiting professor at Lake Forest College, University of California, Los Angeles, Indiana University, City College of the City University of New York, and University of Wisconsin.

WRITINGS: (Editor with E. T. Weiler) *Economic Policy*, Irwin, 1953, 3rd edition, 1961; *The Manchester School of Economics*, Stanford University Press, 1960; *Economic Liberalism*, Random House, 1965. Contributor to economic and business journals.

*   *   *

GRANITE, Harvey R.   1927-

PERSONAL: Born November 23, 1927, in Rochester, N.Y.; son of Albert William (a clothing cutter) and Martha (Potter) Granite; married Ursula Blum (a social worker), June 18, 1950; children: Deborah Ruth, Tamara Eve. *Education:* Cornell University, A.B., 1949; University of Rochester, M.A., 1956; Columbia University, graduate study, 1962-63; University of Pittsburgh, Ph.D., 1974. *Politics:* Democrat. *Home:* 108 Colebourne Rd., Rochester, N.Y. 14609.

CAREER: Worker in clothing, auto, and steel plants in Flint, Mich. and Rochester, N.Y., 1949-52; hotel employee and restaurant waiter in Rochester, 1952-56; Rochester Public Schools, teacher of English and head of department, 1956-64, citywide director of English, reading, and libraries, 1964-69, supervising director of instruction, 1969-71, coordinator of urban funded programs, 1971—. Senior lecturer, University of Rochester, 1957-71. Board member, Action for a Better Community; member, Prison Reform Committee. *Member:* United Teachers Federation, National Council of Teachers of English, International Reading Association, John Hay Fellows Alumni, Urban League, Voters for Peace. *Awards, honors:* John Hay fellowships, summer, 1960, 1962-63; Mabel Phelps Dodge fiction award, 1963.

WRITINGS—Contributor: Robert Rosborough Leeper, editor, *Supervision: Emerging Profession*, Association for Supervision and Curriculum Development, 1969; Alvin W. Howard and George C. Stoumbis, editors, *Schools for the Middle Years*, Intext, 1969; Patricia A. Benner and Virginia L. Law, editors, "Troubleshooter: A Program in Basic English Skills" series, Houghton, 1969; Jo M. Stanchfield and others, editors, "Action Series," Houghton, 1970, 1971; George P. Elliott and others, editors, *Themes in World Literature*, Houghton, 1970; Helen M. Nance, editor, *Instruc-*

tional Concerns for Urban Elementary Schools, Illinois State University, 1970; Mary Ellen Chase and Charles Griffiths, editors, *Readings from the Old Testament*, Houghton, 1971; John M. Franco, *American Women Contributors to American Life*, Benefic, 1976. Also author of "A Time to Grow Up," a television documentary about Title I in Rochester schools, 1968. Contributor to *Antioch Review, Epoch, English Record, Jewish Roots*, and other journals.

WORK IN PROGRESS: Vistas, an anthology series for middle and junior high school students; a language text for urban youth; writing on the training of urban secondary school teachers of English; writing and editing fiction.

*   *   *

GRANT, Jane (Cole)   1895-1972

May 29, 1895—March 16, 1972; American journalist and feminist. Obituaries: *New York Times*, March 17, 1972; *Newsweek*, March 27, 1972; *Time*, March 27, 1972. (See index for *CA* sketch)

*   *   *

GRANT, Neil   1938-
(David Mountfield)

PERSONAL: Born June 9, 1938, in the United Kingdom; son of Alastair and Margaret (Sims) Grant. *Education:* St. Johns College, Cambridge, B.A., 1961. *Home:* 2 Avenue Rd., Teddington, Middlesex, England.

CAREER: American Peoples Encyclopedia, New York, N.Y., associate editor, 1962-67.

WRITINGS—For children; published by F. Watts, except as indicated: *Benjamin Disraeli: Prime Minister Extraordinary*, 1969; *Charles V: Holy Roman Emperor*, 1970; *Victoria: Queen and Empress*, 1970; *English Explorers of North America*, Messner, 1970; *The Renaissance: A First Book*, 1971; *Munich, 1938: Appeasement Fails to Bring Peace for Our Time*, 1971; *Cathedrals*, 1972; *Guilds*, 1972; *The Easter Rising: Dublin, 1916*, 1972; *The Industrial Revolution*, 1973; *The Partition of Palestine, 1947: Jewish Triumph, British Failure, Arab Disaster*, 1973; *The New World Held Promise: Why England Colonized North America*, illustrations by Paul Frame, Messner, 1974.

For adults; under pseudonym David Mountfield: *A History of Polar Exploration*, Dial, 1974; *The Coaching Age*, E. M. Hale, 1976.

*   *   *

GRAUMAN, Lawrence, Jr.   1935-

PERSONAL: Born November 8, 1935, in Louisville, Ky.; son of Lawrence S. (an attorney) and Katherine (Heine) Grauman; married Cynthia Whitsell (an actress), August 10, 1962; children: Aimee Elizabeth, Lucia Lawrence. *Education:* Universite de Montpellier, Diploma in French Literature, 1956; University of Chicago, M.A., 1963; New York University, Ph.D., 1966. *Politics:* Independent. *Home:* 254 West Blithedale Ave., Mill Valley, Calif. 94941. *Office:* 22713 Sunset Station, San Francisco, Calif. 94122.

CAREER: Has worked as political reporter and feature writer for newspapers in Chicago, Ill., news director for a New Jersey broadcasting company, correspondent for a national wire service, editor for a Chicago publishing firm, and staff member of *NATO Annual Review*, Paris, France; Wiltwyck School, Esopus, N.Y., teacher of emotionally disturbed children, 1956-57; Illinois Institute of Technology,

Chicago, instructor in English, 1959-62; Antioch College, Yellow Springs, Ohio, assistant professor of literature, 1966-67; Vassar College, Poughkeepsie, N.Y., lecturer in English, 1967-69; Bard College, Annandale, N.Y., acting dean of college, 1968; Antioch College, assistant professor of literature and editor of *Antioch Review*, 1969-75; free-lance writer and editor. *Military service:* U.S. Army, 1955-56. *Member:* American Civil Liberties Union (member of board of directors). *Awards, honors:* Danforth fellow, 1966-67.

WRITINGS: Issues, Little, Brown, 1971; (editor) George Horace Lorimer, *Letters of a Self-Made Merchant to His Son,* Outerbridge & Dientsfrey, 1970. Writer of "Myth in Mississippi," one-hour documentary program for network radio, 1964, and "A World Passed By," documentary for Nassau Broadcasting Co., 1965. Contributor of more than twenty articles to *Nation, Harper's, New Republic, New Leader, New York Times Magazine,* and other periodicals. Member of editorial board, *Civil Liberties Review,* 1975—; contributing editor, *Harper's,* 1976-77.

WORK IN PROGRESS: Directing a study of little magazines for Twentieth Century Fund, and writing a book on the editorial and economic conditions of little magazines and their relationship to contemporary literature.

* * *

GRAVES, Wallace 1922-

PERSONAL: Born September 21, 1922, in Seattle, Wash.; son of Edwin Lyman (a salesman) and Helen (Malson) Graves; married Betty Ross (an educator), July 2, 1944; children: Linda Kristen. *Education:* University of Washington, Seattle, B.A., 1944, M.A., 1952, Ph.D., 1954. *Agent:* Don Congdon, Harold Matson Co., Inc., 22 East 40th St., New York, N.Y. 10016. *Office:* Department of English, California State University, Northridge, Calif. 91324.

CAREER: Lower Columbia College, Longview, Wash., instructor, 1955-57; Venetoklein Gymnasium, Rhodes, Greece, instructor, 1957-59; California State University, Northridge, assistant professor, 1959-62, associate professor, 1963-67, professor of English, 1968—. *Military service:* U.S. Naval Reserve, 1944-46.

WRITINGS: Trixie, Knopf, 1969; (with William G. Leary) *From Word to Story,* Harcourt, 1971. Contributor to *Kenyon Review, Prism International, Western Humanities Review,* and other journals.

BIOGRAPHICAL/CRITICAL SOURCES: Best Sellers, November 15, 1969; *Negro Digest,* February, 1970.

* * *

GRAY, Genevieve S(tuck) 1920-
(Jenny Gray)

PERSONAL: Born August 6, 1920, in Jonesboro, Ark.; daughter of Howard Charles and Bess (Graham) Stuck; married Paul Gray, Jr., October 31, 1941 (divorced, 1946); children: Paul Russell, Howard Axtell. *Education:* University of Arkansas, B.A., 1941; University of Arizona, M.Ed., 1961; University of Southern California, additional study, 1963-64. *Politics:* Democrat. *Religion:* Methodist.

CAREER: Elementary and secondary school teacher in Jonesboro, Ark., 1955-57, and Tucson, Ariz., 1957-63; Litton Industries, Adler-Westrex Division, multi-media education coordinator in anti-poverty program, at Camp Atterbury, Ind., 1964-65; high school teacher in Sacramento, Calif., 1965-67; full-time writer, principally of educational materials, 1967—. *Member:* Authors League of

America. *Awards, honors:* "Our Environment: Sound and Noise" received the Gold Camera Award at U.S. Industrial Film Festival, 1971.

WRITINGS—Under name Jenny Gray: *Two-Too-To* (programmed instruction), Pak Donald, 1962; *The Teacher's Survival Guide,* Fearon, 1967; *Teaching Without Tears: Your First Year in the Elementary School,* Fearon, 1968.

Other writings under name Jenny Gray: "Composition and Language Activities" (series of supplementary booklets to accompany "Elementary School English" textbooks), Addison-Wesley, 1967.

Under name Genevieve S. Gray: (Editor and abridger) Thomas W. Higginson, *Army Life in a Black Regiment,* Grosset, 1970; (editor and abridger) Frederick Douglass, *The Life and Times of Frederick Douglass,* Grosset, 1970; *Jobs in Transportation,* Lothrop, 1973; *Condominiums: How to Buy, Sell, and Live in Them,* Funk, 1975.

All juveniles: *The Yellow Bone Ring,* illustrated by W. T. Mars, Lothrop, 1971; *The Seven Wishes of Joanna Peabody,* illustrated by Elton Fax, Lothrop, 1972; *I Know a Bus Driver,* illustrated by Charles Dougherty, Putnam, 1972; *A Kite for Bennie,* illustrated by Floyd Sowell, McGraw, 1972; *Jam for Angelina,* Scott, Foresman, 1972; *Casey's Camper,* illustrated by Joseph P. Mathieu, McGraw, 1973; *Keep an Eye on Kevin: Safety Begins at Home,* illustrated by Don Madden, Lothrop, 1973; *Send Wendell,* illustrated by Symeon Shimin, McGraw, 1974; *Sore Loser,* illustrated by Beth Krush and Joe Krush, Houghton, 1974.

Ghost Story, illustrated by Greta Matus, Lothrop, 1975; *Varnell Roberts, Super Pigeon,* illustrated by Marvin Friedman, Houghton, 1975; *The Secret of the Mask,* illustrated by Gary Jones, EMC Corp., 1975; *The Spiderweb Stone,* illustrated by Jones, EMC Corp., 1975; *Tall Singer,* illustrated by Jones, EMC Corp., 1975; *The Magic Bears,* illustrated by Jones, EMC Corp., 1975; *How Far Felipe,* Harper, 1978.

"Her Girl Stuff" series; illustrated by Nan Brooks; all published by EMC Corp.: *Break In,* 1973; *Hot Shot,* 1973; *Stand Off,* 1973; *Stray,* 1973.

"Time of Danger, Time for Courage" series; all published by EMC Corp.: *Alaska Woman,* 1977; *The Dark Side of Nowhere,* 1977; *Has Anyone Seen Buddy Bascom?,* 1977; *Two Tickets to Memphis,* 1977.

Other writings under name Genevieve S. Gray: "People Are . . . ," 1968, and "Operation Trek," 1969, both narration scripts for films by Aztec Film Productions. "Love, Rebellion, Conflict and Other Things," tape self-instruction units on literature for high school and junior college students, produced by EMC Corp. and Bantam, 1970. "Our Environment: Sound and Noise," filmstrip, produced by EMC Corp., 1970.

WORK IN PROGRESS: A series of beginning readers, for Benefic.

BIOGRAPHICAL/CRITICAL SOURCES: Sacramento Bee, March 24, 1968; *Arizona Daily Star,* November 5, 1971.†

* * *

GRAY, Gibson 1922-

PERSONAL: Born October 26, 1922, in Lufkin, Tex.; son of Lee Hendrix (an oil refiner and producer) and Jeta (Gibson) Gray; married Mary Anna Wells, November 21, 1973. *Education:* Attended Tyler Junior College, 1939-41; University of Texas, Main University (now University of

Texas at Austin), B.B.A., 1947; Columbia University, M.A., 1950, Ph.D., 1967. *Politics:* Democrat. *Religion:* Protestant. *Home:* 3630 Kale Dr., Lumberton, N.C. 28358. *Office:* Department of Political Science, Pembroke State University, Pembroke, N.C. 28372.

CAREER: State Council for a Pennsylvania Fair Employment Practice Commission, Harrisburg, associate director, 1953-55; Office of the Governor, Harrisburg, assistant to chief clerk, 1961-63; Pennsylvania State Planning Board, Harrisburg, administrative officer, 1963-66; North Texas State University, Denton, assistant professor of government, 1967-69; Central State University, Edmond, Okla., assistant professor of political science, 1969-71; Pembroke State University, Pembroke, N.C., associate professor of political science, 1971—. *Military service:* U.S. Army, 1943-46; served in Sri Lanka. *Member:* American Political Science Association, Southern Political Science Association, Southwestern Political Science Association, Midwest Political Science Association, Oklahoma Academy of Science (chairman of Division of Social Science, 1970), Phi Theta Kappa, Sigma Iota Epsilon.

WRITINGS: (With staff of Pennsylvania State Planning Board) *The Population of Pennsylvania: A Social Profile,* Pennsylvania State Planning Board, 1963; *The Lobbying Game: A Study of the 1963 Campaign of the State Council for a Pennsylvania Fair Employment Practice Commission,* privately printed, 1970. Also author of *Your Local Government at Work: Local Government in the North Carolina Counties of Bladen, Columbus, Cumberland, Hoke, Richmond, Robeson, and Scotland,* privately printed, 1975.

WORK IN PROGRESS: Political Leadership among Mexican-Americans in San Antonio, Texas.

SIDELIGHTS: Gibson Gray wrote *CA* about the motivating factor important to his career: "A reformist element has been an impelling element. Perhaps this element comes partly from the Populist tradition and partly from the Progressive tradition."

BIOGRAPHICAL/CRITICAL SOURCES: Political Science (publication of Victoria University of Wellington, New Zealand), July, 1971.

* * *

GRAY, James R(obert) 1921-

PERSONAL: Born November 10, 1921, in Boise, Idaho; son of John Golden and Elizabeth (Gallimore) Gray; married Bernice Heisner, December 1, 1945; children: James Robert, Jr., Catherine Mary, Elizabeth Anne. *Education:* Boise State College (now University), Diploma, 1941; Utah State University, B.S., 1947, M.S., 1949; Oregon State University, Ph.D., 1957. *Politics:* Independent. *Home:* 2120 Hagerty Rd., Las Cruces, N.M. 88001. *Office:* Department of Agricultural Economics, New Mexico State University, Las Cruces, N.M. 88003.

CAREER: U.S. Department of Agriculture, Bozeman, Mont. and Las Cruces, N.M., agricultural economist, 1949-58; New Mexico State University, Las Cruces, associate professor, 1958-64, professor of agricultural economics, 1964—. *Military service:* U.S. Army Air Forces, 1942-45; became sergeant. *Member:* American Farm Economic Association, American Society of Range Management, Western Farm Economic Association (vice-president, 1967), Sigma Xi, Alpha Zeta, Zi Sigma Pi, Phi Kappa Pi.

WRITINGS: Ranch Economics, Iowa State University Press, 1958. Contributor of over one hundred articles to journals in his field.

WORK IN PROGRESS: Introductory Research Methods in the Social Sciences; research in resource economics, ranch economics, recreation economics, "forestry economics," and feed marketing.

* * *

GRAYBILL, Ron(ald D.) 1944-

PERSONAL: Born March 25, 1944; son of John W. (a carpenter) and Marguerite (Ruckle) Graybill; married Gerte Bacher (a physical therapist), December 21, 1967; children: N. Torsten, Lela J. *Education:* Loma Linda University, B.A., 1966; Andrews University, B.D., 1968. *Home:* 11307 Estonia Dr., Wheaton, Md. 20002.

CAREER: Pastor of Seventh-day Adventist church, 1968-70; Ellen G. White Publications, Inc., Washington, D.C., assistant secretary, 1970—.

WRITINGS: Ellen G. White and Church Race Relations, Review & Herald, 1970; *Mission to Black America,* Pacific Press Publishing Association, 1971. Contributor to *Insight* and *Adventist Heritage.*

WORK IN PROGRESS: Research for a two-volume biography (by another author) of Ellen White, co-founder and leader of the Seventh-day Adventist Church.

SIDELIGHTS: Ron Graybill told *CA,* "Denominational history need be neither parochial nor filiopietistic if the historian can keep his narrative in constant dialogue with the larger culture in which his subject flourished."

* * *

GRAYSON, Robert A. 1927-

PERSONAL: Born October 8, 1927, in New York, N.Y.; son of Jules and Lillian (Davidson) Grayson; married Suzanne Bomse (a marketing consultant), June 18, 1960; children: Peter, Jocelyn, Andrea. *Education:* University of Illinois, B.S., 1948; New York University, M.B.A., 1962, Ph.D., 1968. *Politics:* Independent. *Home:* 269 Fountain Rd., Englewood, N.J. 07631. *Office:* Grayson Associates, Inc., Englewood, N.J.

CAREER: Lever Brothers, New York City, new products manager, 1962-68; Daniels & Charles (advertising agency), New York City, senior vice-president, 1968-71; Grayson Associates, Inc. (marketing and management consultants), Englewood, N.J., chairman, 1971—. *Member:* American Marketing Association (president of New York chapter, 1968-69; member of board of directors, 1966—), Academy of Management, American Association of University Professors.

WRITINGS: Market and the Computer, American Marketing Association, 1968; *Introduction to Marketing,* Appleton, 1971. Editor, *The Grayson Report.*

WORK IN PROGRESS: Market Research; a management textbook, completion expected in 1980.

* * *

GREAVES, Richard L(ee) 1938-

PERSONAL: Born September 11, 1938, in Glendale, Calif.; son of David Moyle (a retail grocer) and Frieda E. (Dietrich) Greaves; married Judith Rae Dieker, September 4, 1959; children: Sherry Elizabeth, Stephany Lynn. *Education:* Bethel College and Seminary, St. Paul, Minn., B.A. (summa cum laude), 1960; Berkeley Baptist Divinity School, M.A. (magna cum laude), 1962; University of London, Ph.D., 1964; University of Missouri, additional study, 1965. *Poli-*

tics: Democrat. *Home:* 910 Shadowlawn Dr., Tallahassee, Fla. 32303. *Office:* Department of History, Florida State University, Tallahassee, Fla. 32306.

CAREER: Florida Memorial College, St. Augustine, associate professor of history, 1964-65; William Woods College, Fulton, Mo., assistant professor of history, 1965-66; Eastern Washington State College (now Eastern Washington University), Cheney, assistant professor of history, 1966-69; Michigan State University, East Lansing, associate professor of humanities, 1969-72; Florida State University, Tallahassee, professor of history, 1972—. *Member:* American Historical Association, American Society of Church History, Historians of Early Modern Europe, Baptist Historical Society, Institute of Historical Research (London). *Awards, honors:* William Andrews Clark Memorial Library, University of California, Los Angeles, research fellow, 1966, Andrew W. Mellon fellow, 1977; National Endowment for the Humanities research fellow, 1967; Walter D. Love Memorial Prize, Conference on British Studies, 1970, for *The Puritan Revolution and Educational Thought;* American Council of Learned Societies fellow, 1977.

WRITINGS: The Puritan Revolution and Educational Thought: Background for Reform, Rutgers University Press, 1969; *John Bunyan,* Sutton Courtenay Press, 1969; (editor with Floyd D. Barrows) *Problems in the History and Thought of Western Man,* Humanities Department, Michigan State University, Volume I: *The Ancient World,* 1971, Volume II: *The Middle Ages, Renaissance, Reformation,* 1972; *An Annotated Bibliography of John Bunyan Studies,* Clifford E. Barbour Library, 1972; (editor) *Elizabeth I: Queen of England,* Heath, 1974; (editor) *The Miscellaneous Works of John Bunyan,* Clarendon Press, Volume II, 1976 (Greaves was not associated with earlier volume), Volume VIII, in press. Contributor of articles and reviews to *Quaker History, Musical Times* (London), *Huntington Library Quarterly, Scottish Journal of Theology, Journal of Modern History, Sixteenth Century Journal, Renaissance and Reformation, Archiv fuer Reformationsgeschichte,* and other journals.

WORK IN PROGRESS: Editing Volume IX of *The Miscellaneous Works of John Bunyan,* for Clarendon Press; co-editing, with Robert Zaller, *A Biographical Dictionary of British Radicals in the Seventeenth Century,* in two volumes for Harvester Press; *Elizabethan Society: Religious Perspectives and Social Practices.*

SIDELIGHTS: Richard Greaves told *CA:* "One of the most difficult hurdles to productive, creative writing faced by scholars in Florida is the prevalent anti-intellectualism in the state and the absence of a spirit of educational responsibility in the state legislature. Aspiring writers working in an academic context would be advised to avoid Florida." *Avocational interests:* Sports, art, music.

*　　　　*　　　　*

GREEN, David E. 1942-

PERSONAL: Born February 9, 1942, in New York, N.Y.; son of Herman J. (a professor) and Selma (a professor; maiden name, Berenson) Green; married Norma J. Stewart, August 6, 1976; children: Shoshana Leslie. *Education:* Cornell University, B.A., 1962, Ph.D., 1967; Stanford University, M.A., 1963. *Politics:* "Anarchist at heart." *Religion:* Jewish. *Office:* Department of History, University of Saskatchewan, Saskatoon, Saskatchewan, Canada.

CAREER: Ohio State University, Columbus, assistant professor of history, 1967-68; University of Saskatchewan, Sas-

katoon, special lecturer, 1969-70, assistant professor, 1970-72, associate professor, 1972-77, professor of history, 1977—. Visiting summer professor, Cornell University, 1969, 1970. *Member:* American Historical Association, Canadian Association of University Teachers, Canadian Association for Latin American Studies. *Awards, honors:* Woodrow Wilson fellow, 1962-63; American Council of Learned Societies postdoctoral fellow, 1971-72.

WRITINGS: (Contributor) Barton J. Bernstein, editor, *Politics and Policies of the Truman Administration,* Quadrangle, 1970; *The Containment of Latin America: A History of the Myths and Realities of the Good Neighbor Policy,* Quadrangle, 1971. Contributor of articles to *Historical Papers* and *Latin American Research Review.*

WORK IN PROGRESS: The Agony of American Conservatism: A Study in Twentieth-Century Thought and Institutions.

AVOCATIONAL INTERESTS: Acting, musical theater, swimming, ping-pong.

*　　　　*　　　　*

GREENAWALT, R(obert) Kent 1936-

PERSONAL: Born June 25, 1936, in New York, N.Y.; son of Kenneth William (a lawyer) and Martha (Sloan) Greenawalt; married Sanja Milic, July 14, 1968; children: Robert Milic, Alexander K. A., Andrei M. K. *Education:* Swarthmore College, A.B. (with honors), 1958; Oxford University, B.Phil., 1960; Columbia University, LL.B., 1963. *Home:* 435 Riverside Dr., New York, N.Y. 10025. *Office:* School of Law, Columbia University, 435 West 116th St., New York, N.Y. 10027.

CAREER: Member of Bar of New York and of U.S. Supreme Court; law clerk to Justice John M. Harlan, U.S. Supreme Court, Washington, D.C., 1963-64; Agency for International Development, Washington, D.C., special assistant to assistant administrator for development finance and private enterprise, 1964-65; Columbia University, School of Law, New York, N.Y., assistant professor, 1965-68, associate professor, 1968-69, professor of law, 1969—. Deputy solicitor general, U.S. Department of Justice, Washington, D.C., 1971-72. Visiting professor of law, Stanford University, summer, 1970. Attorney, Lawyers' Committee for Civil Rights, Jackson, Miss., summer, 1965; member of staff, Mayor John Lindsay's Task Force on Law Enforcement, 1965; associate director, New York Institute for Legal Education, summer, 1969; legal adviser, *Grolier's Encyclopedia,* 1966-71.

MEMBER: American Bar Association, American Civil Liberties Union (member of due process committee, 1969-71), American Society of International Law, American Society for Political and Legal Philosophy, National Association for the Advancement of Colored People, American Association of University Professors, New York Bar Association, New York City Bar Association, Phi Beta Kappa.

WRITINGS: (With Walter Gelhorn) *The Sectarian College and the Public Purse,* Oceana, 1970. Also author of *Legal Protections of Privacy,* 1976. Contributor of articles and reviews to legal journals. Editor-in-chief, *Columbia Law Review,* 1962-63.

*　　　　*　　　　*

GREENBAUM, Sidney 1929-

PERSONAL: Born December 31, 1929, in London, England; son of Lewis and Nellie (Goldfinger) Greenbaum.

Education: University of London, B.A. (Hebrew and Aramaic; honors), 1951, M.A., 1953, Postgraduate Certificate in Education, 1954, B.A. (English; honors), 1957, Ph.D., 1967. *Religion:* Jewish. *Office:* Department of English, University of Wisconsin, Milwaukee, Wis. 53201.

CAREER: Primary school teacher in London, England, 1954-57; head of high school English department in London, 1957-64; University of London, London, tutor in adult evening courses at Goldsmiths College, 1963-66, instructor in English at University College, 1967-68; University of Oregon, Eugene, visiting assistant professor of English, 1968-69; University of Wisconsin—Milwaukee, visiting professor, 1969-70, associate professor, 1970-72, professor of English, 1972—. Visiting professor, Hebrew University of Jerusalem, 1972-73. *Member:* Linguistics Society of America, Modern Language Association of America, International Association of University Professors of English, Linguistic Association of Canada and the United States, Teachers of English to Speakers of Other Languages (member of editorial committee of quarterly publication), American Dialect Society.

WRITINGS: Studies in English Adverbial Usage, Longmans, Green, 1969, University of Miami Linguistics Series, 1970; *Verb-Intensifier Collocations in English: An Experimental Approach,* Mouton, 1970; (with Randolph Quirk) *Elicitation Experiments in English: Linguistic Studies in Use and Attitude,* University of Miami Linguistic Series, 1970; (with Quirk, Geoffrey Leech, and Jan Svartvik) *A Grammar of Contemporary English,* Academic Press, 1972; (with Quirk) *A Concise Grammar of Contemporary English,* Harcourt, 1973 (published in England as *A University Grammar of English,* Longman, 1973); *Acceptability in Language,* Mouton, 1977. Contributor to linguistics journals.

WORK IN PROGRESS: With Leech and Svartvik, *Studies in English Linguistics;* with Morton Bloomfield, *Rhetoric Handbook for Freshman Composition;* revised editions of *A Concise Grammar of Contemporary English* and *A University Grammar of English.*

* * *

GREENBERG, Alvin (David) 1932-

PERSONAL: Born May 10, 1932, in Cincinnati, Ohio; married Marsha Drucker (a teacher), January 30, 1955 (divorced, 1976); children: Matthew, Nicholas, Ann. *Education:* Attended Brown University, 1950-52; University of Cincinnati, B.A., 1954, M.A., 1960; University of Washington, Seattle, Ph.D., 1964. *Home:* 171 Vernon St., St. Paul, Minn. 55105. *Agent:* Theron Raines, 475 Fifth Ave., New York, N.Y. 10017. *Office:* Department of English, Macalester College, St. Paul, Minn. 55105.

CAREER: University of Kentucky, Lexington, instructor in English, 1963-65; Macalester College, St. Paul, Minn., 1965—, began as associate professor, currently professor of English. Fulbright lecturer, University of Kerala, India, 1966-67. *Military service:* U.S. Army, 1954.

WRITINGS: The Small Waves (novel), El Corno Press, 1965; *The Metaphysical Giraffe* (poems), New Rivers Press, 1968; *Going Nowhere* (novel), Simon & Schuster, 1971; *The House of the Would-Be Gardener* (poems), New Rivers Press, 1972; *Dark Lands* (poems), Ithaca House, 1973; *Metaform* (poems), University of Massachusetts Press, 1975; *The Invention of the West* (novel), Avon, 1976. Also author of "A Wall," a play produced by The Theatre Company of the Minneapolis Institute of Arts, 1971, and

"Horspfal," an opera libretto with music by Eric Stokes, produced by Center Opera Company of Milwaukee, 1969. Contributor of short stories and poetry to literary journals, including *New American Review, Antioch Review,* and *New Letters.* Editor, *Minnesota Review,* 1967-71, fiction editor, 1971-73.

WORK IN PROGRESS: A second opera libretto, with Stokes; a novel.

* * *

GREENBERG, Harvey R. 1935-

PERSONAL: Born June 27, 1935, in Philadelphia, Pa.; son of Murry H. (an insurance broker) and Dora (Cohen) Greenberg; married second wife, Rima R. Winchester (a teacher), February 25, 1971; children: (first marriage) Matthew, Paul. *Education:* Columbia University, A.B., 1955; Cornell University, M.D., 1959. *Home and office:* 320 West 86th St., New York, N.Y. 10021.

CAREER: Yeshiva University, Albert Einstein College of Medicine, Bronx, N.Y., assistant clinical professor of child psychology, 1965-76, associate clinical professor of child psychiatry, 1976—. *Military service:* U.S. Army, psychiatrist, 1963-65. *Member:* American Academy of Psychoanalysis, Society of Medical Analysis, New York State Medical Society.

WRITINGS: What You Must Know about Drugs, Scholastic Press, 1971; *Movies on Your Mind,* Saturday Review Press, 1975. Contributor of over thirty articles to psychiatric and psychoanalytic journals.

AVOCATIONAL INTERESTS: Playing organ, piano, harpsichord; writing poetry.

* * *

GREENBERG, Morris S. 1924-
(Morrie Greenberg)

PERSONAL: Born September 26, 1924, in Poland; son of Hyman (a merchant) and Sara (Goldfarb) Greenberg; married Audrey L. Bricker, August 16, 1953; children: Richard, Susan. *Education:* University of California, Los Angeles, B.A., 1949; California State College at Los Angeles (now California State University, Los Angeles), M.A., 1953. *Home:* 9054 Whitaker Ave., Sepulveda, Calif. 91343.

CAREER: Teacher in California schools, 1949-68; Madison Junior High School, Los Angeles, Calif., assistant principal, 1968-76; Los Angeles City Schools, administrative consultant, 1976—.

WRITINGS: (With David Bidna and Gerald Spitz) *We the People: A History of the U.S.A.,* Heath, 1971. Short stories, under name Morrie Greenberg, included in *Happenings, Voices of Youth, Knowing,* and *Now,* all anthologies published by Los Angeles City School District.

WORK IN PROGRESS: A book on how to teach social studies; short stories for juvenile magazines.

* * *

GREENE, Jonathan Edward 1943-

PERSONAL: Born April 19, 1943, in New York, N.Y.; married Alice-Ann Kingston, June 5, 1963 (divorced); married Dobree Adams, May 23, 1974; children: Michal Tara, Kora Radella; stepchildren: Hunter Purdy, John Purdy. *Education:* Bard College, B.A., 1965; additional study at University of California, Wagner College, and University of Kentucky. *Address:* P.O. Box 106, Frankfort, Ky. 40601.

CAREER: Gnomon Press, Frankfort, Ky., publisher, 1965—; University Press of Kentucky, Lexington, production manager and designer, 1967-75.

WRITINGS—Poetry: The Reckoning, Matter Books, 1966; Instance, Buttonwood Press, 1968; The Lapidary, Btack Sparrow Press, 1969; A 17th Century Garner, Buttonwood Press, 1969; An Unspoken Complaint, Unicorn Press, 1970; Glossary of the Everyday, Coach House Press (Toronto), 1974; Scaling the Walls, Gnomon Press, 1974; Once a Kingdom Again, Sand Dollar, 1977; Quiet Goods, Larkspur Press, 1977. Poems included in several anthologies and periodicals.

WORK IN PROGRESS: Two more books of poems, Peripateticks and Anniversaries.

*   *   *

GREENFIELD, Irving A. 1928-

PERSONAL: Born February 22, 1928, in Brooklyn, N.Y.; son of Samuel (a jeweler) and Anna (Berkowitz) Greenfield; married Anita Mittag (a teacher), September 2, 1950; children: Rick, Nat. Education: Brooklyn College (now Brooklyn College of the City University of New York), B.A., 1950. Home and office: 2421 Glenwood Rd., Brooklyn, N.Y. 11210. Agent: Henry Morrison, 58 West Tenth St., New York, N.Y. 10011.

CAREER: Writer. Military service: U.S. Army, 1950-52.

WRITINGS: Waters of Death, Lancer Books, 1967; U.F.O. Report, Lancer Books, 1967; The Others, Lancer Books, 1969; Clorecrest, Belmont Books, 1969.

Succubus, Dell, 1970; The Sexplorer, Dell, 1972; Ichabod Rides Again, Berkley Publishing, 1972; The Carey Blood, Dell, 1972; Carey's Vengeance, Dell, 1972; Making U-Hoo, Dell, 1973; The Ancient of Days: The Chronicles of Ronstrum the Builder, Avon, 1973; The Glow of Morning, Dell, 1973; The Carey Gun, Dell, 1974; The Stars Will Judge, Dell, 1974; The Play of Darkness, Avon, 1974; To Savor the Past, Berkley Publishing, 1975; A Flame on the Wind, Dell, 1975; Alton, Avon, 1975; The Face of Him, Manor, 1976; Who Knows, Manor, 1977; Doesn't Everyone, Manor, 1977. Also author of Adios Oaxaca and Ichabod Encounters.

WORK IN PROGRESS: High Terror; The Hammer of God; Oberfest.

*   *   *

GREENSPAN, Charlotte L. 1921-

PERSONAL: Born August 10, 1921, in Springfield, Mass.; daughter of Hyman and Alta (Yerozolimsky) Litman; married Daniel Greenspan (an executive), November 22, 1947; children: Herbert, Michael, Joel. Education: Smith College, B.A. (with high honors), 1942, M.A., 1944. Politics: Independent. Religion: Jewish. Home: 56 Chesterfield Ave., Springfield, Mass. 01118. Office: Department of English, Western New England College, Springfield, Mass. 01119.

CAREER: Western New England College, Springfield, Mass., lecturer, 1966-67, instructor, 1967-70, assistant professor, 1970-76, professor of English, 1976—. Member: Modern Language Association of America, American Association of University Professors, College English Association, Phi Beta Kappa.

WRITINGS: (Editor with Lester Hirsch) All Those Voices, Macmillan, 1971. Contributor of short stories and poems to newspapers and national periodicals.

WORK IN PROGRESS: Research on science and literature.

GREYSER, Stephen A. 1935-

PERSONAL: Born March 17, 1935, in Boston, Mass.; son of Morris (an artist and teacher) and Gladys (Koven) Greyser; married Linda L. Segel (a teacher), June 30, 1968. Education: Harvard University, A.B. (magna cum laude), 1956, M.B.A., 1958, D.B.A., 1965. Home: 46 Campbell Rd., Wayland, Mass. 01778. Office: School of Business, Harvard University, Boston, Mass. 02163.

CAREER: Radio and television writer and producer of sports and news programs, Boston, Mass., 1952-57; Harvard University, School of Business, Boston, assistant professor, 1966-68, associate professor, 1968-72, professor of business administration, 1972—, Harvard Summer School Institute in Arts Administration, research director, 1969—. Marketing Science Institute, Cambridge, Mass., project director, 1969—, executive director, 1972—; faculty principal, Management Analysis Center, Cambridge. Member of communications committee, U.S. Chamber of Commerce, 1969-70; Federal Trade Commission public witness on social impacts of advertising, 1971; member of board of directors, Advertising Research Foundation, 1977—. Distinguished visiting lecturer, York University, 1972, and University of Western Ontario, 1974. Military service: U.S. Army Reserve, active duty, 1959-65; became sergeant.

MEMBER: American Marketing Association (member of national board of directors, 1967-69; chairman of publications board, 1967-69), American Academy of Advertising (director, 1964-67; vice-president, 1970-72; president, 1972-74; chairman, 1974-76), Association for Consumer Research (member of advisory council, 1974-77), American Association for Public Opinion Research. Awards, honors: Kappa Tau Alpha lecturer, University of Illinois, College of Communications, 1969.

WRITINGS: (Editor) Toward Scientific Marketing, American Marketing Association, 1964; (editor) The Consumer Judgment of Advertising (monograph), American Association of Advertising Agencies, 1965; (with Edward C. Bursk) Advanced Cases in Marketing Management, Prentice-Hall, 1968, 2nd edition published as Cases in Marketing Management, 1975; (with Raymond A. Bauer) Advertising in America: The Consumer View, Division of Research, Harvard Business School, 1968; (with Thomas Raymond and Douglas Schwalbe) Cases in Arts Administration, Institute of Arts Administration, 1971; Cases in Advertising and Communications Management, Prentice-Hall, 1972; (editor) Cultural Policy and Arts Administration, Harvard University Press, 1973. Contributor to marketing, advertising, and communications journals. Harvard Business Review, assistant editor and research director, 1961-66, editorial board secretary, 1966—; member of editorial board, Journal of Marketing, 1967-74, 1976—.

WORK IN PROGRESS: "A book-length report on public attitudes toward consumerism (based on national survey) and also a volume of collected papers on Consumer Affairs and Marketing Management."

*   *   *

GRIBBIN, Lenore S. 1922-
(Petunia Worblefister)

PERSONAL: Born August 31, 1922, in Columbia, Mo.; daughter of John Richard (a bookbinder) and Iva (McMillen) Sipes; married John Hawkins Gribbin (a librarian), March 31, 1951. Education: University of Wisconsin, B.S. and B.L.S., 1944; University of Chicago, M.A., 1954. Home: 511 Westridge Dr., Columbia, Mo. 65201.

CAREER: Cataloger at University of Chicago Library, Chicago, Ill., 1951-53, National Library of Medicine, Washington, D.C., 1954-58, and U.S. Library of Congress, Washington, D.C., 1960-61; University of North Carolina at Chapel Hill, curator of detective story collection, 1964-66.

WRITINGS: The Case of the Missing Detective Stories, University of North Carolina Press, 1966; *Who's Whodunit: A List of 3218 Detective Story Writers and Their 1100 Pseudonyms,* University of North Carolina Press, 1968. Contributor of satire-humor to *Library Journal* and under a pseudonym to *Southeastern Librarian.*

WORK IN PROGRESS: Historical and genealogical articles.

* * *

GRIFFIN, Al 1919-

PERSONAL: Born December 19, 1919, in Chicago, Ill.; son of Albert Fred and Lydia (Pietsch) Gutzmer; married March 17, 1946, wife's name, Catherine; married second wife, Lolita Collyer (a nursery school director), November 1, 1968; children: Margaret. *Education:* Pasadena Junior College (now Pasadena City College), A.A., 1937. *Politics:* Democrat. *Religion:* Unitarian Universalist. *Home and office:* 1212 Maple Ave., Evanston, Ill. 60202.

CAREER: Life, feature writer in Chicago, Ill., and Detroit, Mich., 1959-63; free-lance professional writer, 1963—. *Wartime service:* U.S. Merchant Marine, World War II. *Member:* Authors Guild. *Awards, honors:* Cited as best professional free-lance writer by American Business Press, 1967.

WRITINGS—Published by Regnery, except as indicated: *So You'd Like to Buy an Airplane: A Handbook for Prospective Owners,* Macmillan, 1970; *So You Want to Buy a House,* 1970; *So You Want to Buy a Mobile Home,* 1970; *So You Want to Buy a Motorboat,* 1971; *Credit Jungle,* 1971; *How to Start and Operate a Day Care Home,* 1973; *Recreational Vehicles: A Buyer's and User's Guide,* 1973; *Motorcycles: A Buyer's and Rider's Guide,* 1974; *Step Right Up, Folks,* 1974; *Home and Apartment Security,* 1975. Also author of *The Great American Zoo Explosion.*

Author of a syndicated newspaper column; contributor of more than three hundred articles to magazines.

WORK IN PROGRESS: An expose on psychiatry; a book on organic and macrobiotic foods.†

* * *

GRIFFIN, Jacqueline P. 1927-

PERSONAL: Born December 21, 1927, in Manila, Philippines; daughter of Emil Bates and Amalia (Erbach) Perry; married Charles W. Griffin, Jr. (a free-lance writer), November 26, 1949; children: Janis. *Education:* George Washington University, B.A., 1948; Montclair State College, M.A., 1968. *Politics:* Democrat. *Religion:* Society of Friends. *Home:* 62 Indian Spring Trail, Denville, N.J. 17834. *Office:* Essex County College, 303 University Ave., Newark, N.J. 07102.

CAREER: Essex County College, Newark, N.J., assistant professor of English, 1968—.

WRITINGS: Sentence Strategies: Writing for College, Harcourt, 1971.

* * *

GRIMES, W(illiam) H(enry) 1892-1972

March 7, 1892—January 14, 1972; American journalist and editor. Obituaries: *New York Times,* January 15, 1972; *Washington Post,* January 15, 1972; *Current Biography,* March, 1972.

* * *

GRIMSLEY, Will (Henry) 1914-

PERSONAL: Born January 27, 1914, in Monterey, Tenn.; son of Alvis Chilton (a railroad engineer) and Bertie (Elrod) Grimsley; married Nellie Harris, February 12, 1937; children: Gayle (Mrs. Charles Kennedy), Kelly, Nellie B. *Education:* Educated in Nashville, Tenn. *Religion:* Baptist. *Home:* 2 Prescott St., Garden City, N.Y. 11530. *Office:* 50 Rockefeller Plaza, New York, N.Y. 10022.

CAREER: Evening Tennessean, Nashville, Tenn., sports writer, 1932-35, sports editor and columnist, 1935-43; also sports writer for *Nashville Tennessean;* Associated Press, New York, N.Y., news correspondent and national columnist, 1943—, sports writer, 1947—, special correspondent, 1969—. *Member:* U.S. Lawn Tennis Writers Association (former president), Baseball Writers Association of America, Golf Writers Association of America (president, 1977-78). *Awards, honors:* Finalist in Sports Writer of the Year competition, National Association of Sports Writers, 1959 and 1968; named nation's best sports writer of participant sports by Marlboro and Martini-Rossi, 1965, for articles on tennis.

WRITINGS: Golf: Its History, People and Events, Prentice-Hall, 1966; *Football: The Greatest Moments in the Southwest Conference,* Little, Brown, 1968; *Tennis: Its History, People and Events,* Prentice-Hall, 1971; (editor with Tom Di Lustro) *Century of Sports,* Hammond, Inc., 1971; *Sports Immortals,* Rutledge Books, 1973. Contributor of over 200 articles to magazines, including *Saturday Evening Post, Readers Digest, Golf, Golf World* (Great Britain).

SIDELIGHTS: Member of a special Associated Press (AP) news task force which can be assigned to major news breaks anywhere in the world, Will Grimsley has been called the "most traveled of sports writers." He has logged more than a million miles and written about the entire sports spectrum, covering golf tournaments (the British Open at St. Andrews, the French Open at Paris, the Canada Cup matches around the world), tennis matches (twelve trips to Australia for the Davis Cup), championship fights, Indianapolis "500" races, the Kentucky Derby, the World Series, and other events in mainland China, Japan, Russia, Hungary, Germany, Britain, and France. He has also covered eight Winter and Summer Olympics, including Helsinki in 1952, Melbourne, 1956, Rome, 1960, Tokyo, 1964, Mexico City, 1968, Munich, 1972, Montreal, 1976, and the Winter Olympics at Grenoble, 1968, Sapporo, 1972, and Innsbruck, 1976.

* * *

GROSSBACH, Robert 1941-

PERSONAL: Born December 31, 1941, in Bronx, N.Y.; son of Herman and Mollie Grossbach; married Sylvia Cohen; children: Mitchell, Elliot, Jennifer. *Education:* Cooper Union, B.S.E.E., 1962; Columbia University, M.E.E., 1965. *Home:* 5 Bradford Rd., Plainview, N.Y. 11803. *Agent:* Candida Donadio, 111 West 57th St., New York, N.Y. 10019.

CAREER: Wheeler Laboratories, Long Island, N.Y., engineer, 1962-65; Loral Corp., Bronx, N.Y., senior engineer, 1965-68; Narda Microwaves, Plainview, N.Y., section head, 1970-77; free-lance writer, 1977—. *Member:* Institute of Electrical and Electronics Engineers.

WRITINGS: Someone Great, Harper's Magazine Press, 1971; *Easy and Hard Ways Out,* Harper's Magazine Press, 1974; *The Goodbye Girl* (novelization of screenplay by Neil Simon), Warner Paperback, 1977; *The Cheap Detective* (novelization of screenplay by Simon), Warner Paperback, 1978. Contributor of technical articles to Institute of Electrical and Electronics Engineers *Proceedings,* and to *Microwave Journal.*

WORK IN PROGRESS: Round Trip: An Autonecrographical Novel, for Harper; novelization of screenplay, "California Suite," by Neil Simon.

*   *   *

GROSSMAN, Kurt R. 1897-1972

May 21, 1897—March 2, 1972; German journalist, biographer, and author of books on German-Jewish relations. Obituaries: *New York Times,* March 4, 1972.

*   *   *

GROSSMANN, Reinhardt S. 1931-

PERSONAL: Born January 10, 1931, in Berlin, Germany; son of Willy and Margarete (Neumann) Grossmann; married Anne Marcy, December 27, 1958; children: Marcy, Martin. *Education:* Attended Paedagogische Hochschule, Berlin, Germany, 1949-54; University of Iowa, Ph.D., 1958. *Office:* Department of Philosophy, Indiana University, Bloomington, Ind. 47401.

CAREER: University of Illinois, Urbana, instructor, 1958-61, assistant professor of philosophy, 1961-62; Indiana University at Bloomington, 1962—, began as assistant professor, professor of philosophy, 1969—. *Member:* American Philosophical Association.

WRITINGS: (With Edwin B. Allaire and others) *Essays in Ontology,* Nijhoff, 1963; *The Structure of Mind,* University of Wisconsin Press, 1965; *Reflections on Frege's Philosophy,* Northwestern University Press, 1969; *Ontological Reduction,* Indiana University Press, 1973; *Meinong,* Routledge, Kegan & Paul, 1974.

*   *   *

GROSSWIRTH, Marvin 1931-

PERSONAL: Born August 5, 1931, in Brooklyn, N.Y.; son of Isidore and Ida (Katzoff) Grosswirth; married Marilyn Siegmann (an electronic data processing manager), September 7, 1969. *Education:* Bernard M. Baruch School of Business and Public Administration of the City College (now Bernard M. Baruch College of the City University of New York), B.B.A., 1961. *Home and office:* 151 West 74th St., New York, N.Y. 10023.

CAREER: Has worked as editor and public relations director with various publishing firms, New York, N.Y., 1960-70. Member of board, Workshop in Business Opportunities, Inc. *Member:* American Society of Journalists and Authors (member of executive council), Authors Guild, Mensa (public relations officer; assistant international general secretary; national chairman), National Association to Aid Fat Americans, Inc. (member of board of directors).

WRITINGS: The Art of Growing a Beard, Jarrow Press, 1971; *Fat Pride: A Survival Handbook,* Jarrow Press, 1971; (with Louis J. Rosenfeld) *The Truth about Vasectomy,* Prentice-Hall, 1972; *Beginner's Guide to Home Computers,* Doubleday, 1978. Contributor of articles to *New York Times, Saturday Review, Science Digest, Viva,* and many

other magazines; author of monthly column in *Mensa Bulletin.*

WORK IN PROGRESS: The Impaired Physicians; How to Patent and Market Your Inventions, for McKay.

*   *   *

GRUBAR, Francis S(tanley) 1924-

PERSONAL: Born June 8, 1924, in New Britain, Conn.; son of Frank Stanley (a printer) and Helen (La Gosh) Grubar; married Phyllis Woodlock, September 28, 1962; children: Margot, Patrick. *Education:* University of Maryland, B.A., 1948, M.A., 1949; Johns Hopkins University, M.A., 1952, Ph.D., 1966. *Home:* 5712 27th St. N.W., Washington, D.C. 20015. *Office:* Department of Art, George Washington University, Washington, D.C. 20052.

CAREER: University of Maryland, College Park, instructor, 1948-57, assistant professor of art history, 1957-66; George Washington University, Washington, D.C., associate professor, 1966-74, professor of art history, 1974—, chairman of department, 1972-73. Visiting lecturer in art history, Catholic University of America, summers, 1951-58. *Military service:* U.S. Army, 1943-45; received six battle stars. *Member:* College Art Association, American Association of University Professors, American Studies Association, Connecticut Historical Society, Columbia Historical Society, Phi Delta Kappa, Phi Kappa Phi. *Awards, honors: Evening Star,* Washington, D.C., faculty research grant, 1967-68.

WRITINGS: William Ranney: Painter of the Early West, C. N. Potter, 1962; *Richard Caton Woodville: An Early American Genre Painter* (exhibition catalogue), Corcoran Gallery of Art, 1967; (contributor) Stuart Feld, editor, *The American Vision* (exhibition catalogue), Public Education Association, 1968; (contributor) Ray B. Browne and others, editors, *Challenges in American Culture,* Bowling Green University, 1970; *Minerva J. Chapman* (exhibition catalogue), Adams, Davidson Gallery, 1971. Contributor to *New Catholic Encyclopedia, Notable American Women, 1607-1950,* and art journals.

WORK IN PROGRESS: A book on American genre art; research on Edward Moran, Regis Francois Gignoux, and William Randolph Barbee.

*   *   *

GRUBERG, Martin 1935-

PERSONAL: Born January 28, 1935, in New York, N.Y.; son of Benjamin (a steamfitter) and Mollie (Stolnitz) Gruberg; married Rosaline Kurfirst, March 25, 1967. *Education:* City College (now City College of the City University of New York), B.A. (cum laude), 1955; Columbia University, Ph.D., 1963. *Home:* 2020 Wisconsin St., Oshkosh, Wis. 54901. *Office:* Clow Hall, University of Wisconsin, Oshkosh, Wis. 54901.

CAREER: U.S. Department of State, Passport Agency, New York City, agent-adjudicator, 1960-61; high school teacher of social studies, New York City, 1961-62; Hunter College of the City University of New York, New York City, instructor in political science, 1961-62; high school teacher of social studies, Pelham, N.Y., 1962-63; University of Wisconsin—Oshkosh, assistant professor, 1963-66, associate professor, 1966-69, professor of political science, 1969—, chairman of department, 1969-72. President, Oshkosh Human Rights Council, 1966-68. *Member:* American Political Science Association, American Association of

University Professors (Secretary of Wisconsin conference, 1975-77), Law and Society Association, Midwest Political Science Association, Wisconsin Political Science Association (vice-president, 1973-74; president, 1974-75); Optimist Club, Candlelight Club, Aurelian Society (all Oshkosh).

WRITINGS: Women in American Politics, Academia Press, 1968; (contributor) William C. Spragens and Robert W. Russell, editors, *Conflict and Crisis in American Politics,* Kendall/Hunt, 1970. Contributor to *Encyclopedia Americana* and to political science and history journals. Writer of "Women: Our Largest Minority," a weekly column for *Paper for Central Wisconsin,* 1970-71, and "Spotlight on Women," a weekly column for *Oshkosh Northwestern,* 1971-72.

WORK IN PROGRESS: The Bolters: Some Observations on Party Desertion.

*   *   *

GULICK, Grover C. 1916-
(Bill Gulick)

PERSONAL: Surname is pronounced *Gu*-lick; born February 22, 1916, in Kansas City, Mo.; son of Grover Cleveland (a veterinarian) and Golda Mae (Hall) Gulick; married Marcella Jeanne Abbott (researcher for her husband), June 30, 1946. *Education:* Attended University of Oklahoma, 1935-37, 1939-41. *Home:* Route 3, Walla Walla, Wash. 99362. *Agent:* Carl Brandt, Brandt & Brandt, 101 Park Ave., New York, N.Y. 10017.

CAREER: Professional writer, 1941—. *Member:* Western Writers of America (president, 1955-56). *Awards, honors:* Best Short Story Award, Western Writers of America, 1958, 1960; Western Heritage Award, Cowboy Hall of Fame, 1966, for *They Came to a Valley;* Governors Award, Washington State Arts Commission, 1967, 1972; Pacific Northwest Booksellers Award, 1971, for *Snake River Country.*

WRITINGS—All under name Bill Gulick; novels, except as noted: *Bend of the Snake,* Houghton, 1950; *A Drum Calls West,* Houghton, 1952; *A Thousand for the Cariboo,* Houghton, 1954; *White Men, Red Men and Mountain Men,* Houghton, 1955; *The Land Beyond,* Houghton, 1958; *Showdown in the Sun,* Popular Library, 1958; *The Shaming of Broken Horn,* Doubleday, 1961; *The Moon-Eyed Appaloosa,* Doubleday, 1962; *The Hallelujah Trail,* Doubleday, 1963; *They Came to a Valley,* Doubleday, 1966; *Liveliest Town in the West,* Doubleday, 1969; *Snake River Country* (non-fiction; photographs by Earl Roberge), Caxton, 1971; *The Country Club Caper,* Doubleday, 1971.

Juvenile books with Thomas Rothrock: *Abilene or Bust,* Cupples & Leon, 1946; *Desolation Trail,* Cupples & Leon, 1946.

Screenplays based on novels: "Bend of the River," Universal Pictures, 1951; "The Road to Denver" (based on a *Saturday Evening Post* serial, "The Man from Texas"), Republic Pictures, 1955; "Hallelujah Trail," United Artists, 1965; "Showdown in the Sun," bought by Richmond Productions; "Fandango," bought by Twentieth Century-Fox.

Author of two historical pageants, "The Magic Musket," 1953, and "The First Treaty Council," 1955, both produced regionally; also author of historical outdoor drama, "Trails West," first produced in Walla Walla, Wash., July 1, 1976. About 150 stories have been published in magazines, including *Esquire, Argosy, Collier's, Liberty, Saturday Evening Post,* and *Adventure.*

WORK IN PROGRESS: Treasure in Hell's Canyon, a novel.

SIDELIGHTS: After six-month stays in Greenwich Village, the Berkshires, Mexico, Arizona, southern California, and Oklahoma, Grover Gulick and his wife kept homing to the Pacific Northwest. They finally established a permanent base near Walla Walla, Wash., in an older house with a few acres of land and a view of the Blue Mountains.

AVOCATIONAL INTERESTS: Fishing, golf, photography.

*   *   *

GULLEY, Norman 1920-

PERSONAL: Born August 2, 1920, in Wigan, Lancashire, England; son of William (an engineer) and Miriam (Seddon) Gulley; married Joyce Eastham, September 4, 1945; children: David Michael, Ian Richard, Janet Rachel. *Education:* Attended St. Edmund Hall, Oxford, 1938-41; Oxford University, M.A., 1945. *Politics:* Socialist. *Home:* Delfan, Llanycrwys, Llanwrda, Carmarthenshire, Wales. *Office:* Department of Classics, St. David's University College, Lampeter, Dyfed S A48 7E D, Wales.

CAREER: University of Bristol, Bristol, England, lecturer, 1946-61, senior lecturer, 1961-64, reader in classics and ancient philosophy, 1964-68; St. David's University College, Lampeter, Wales, professor of classics, 1968—. Chief examiner in classics, Southern Universities Joint Board for School Examinations, 1958-63. *Military service:* Royal Air Force, 1941-45; became flight lieutenant. *Member:* Classical Association (president of Bristol branch, 1959-62).

WRITINGS: Plato's Theory of Knowledge, Barnes & Noble, 1962; *The Philosophy of Socrates,* St. Martin's, 1968; *Aristotle on the Purposes of Literature,* University of Wales Press, 1971. Contributor of articles on Greek philosophy and mathematics and reviews to professional journals.

WORK IN PROGRESS: A history of Greek ethics, particularly emphasizing Plato, Aristotle, Epicurus, and the early Stoics; philosophy of literature in Plato and Aristotle.

AVOCATIONAL INTERESTS: Music (especially chamber music), motoring, croquet.

BIOGRAPHICAL/CRITICAL SOURCES: Times Literary Supplement, July 31, 1969.

*   *   *

GUNDERSON, Keith (Robert) 1935-

PERSONAL: Born August 29, 1935, in New Ulm, Minn.; son of Luverne Robert (in sales) and Roslyn (Swark) Gunderson; married Donna Mae Beernink (a speech pathologist), December 29, 1959; children: Christopher Ralph, Jonathan Robert. *Education:* Macalester College, B.A., 1957; Worcester College, Oxford, B.A., 1959; Princeton University, Ph.D., 1963. *Home:* 2401 Sheridan Ave. S., Minneapolis, Minn. 55404. *Office:* Department of Philosophy, University of Minnesota, Minneapolis, Minn. 55455.

CAREER: Princeton University, Princeton, N.J., instructor in philosophy, 1962-64; University of California, Los Angeles, assistant professor of philosophy, 1964-67; University of Minnesota, Minneapolis, professor of philosophy, 1967—, research associate of Minnesota Center for Philosophy of Science, 1967—. Carnegie Visiting Lecturer, University of Redlands, 1973. Active in Minneapolis Poets-in-the-Schools Program, 1967-73. *Member:* American Philosophical Association, Incognoscenti. *Awards, honors:* Fulbright scholar at Oxford University, 1957-59.

WRITINGS: A Continual Interest in the Sun and Sea (poetry), Abelard, 1971; *Mentality and Machines,* Doubleday, 1971; (editor and author of introduction) *Language, Mind, and Knowledge,* University of Minnesota Press, 1975; *To See a Thing* (poetry), Nodin, in press. Contributor of about sixty poems to *Western Humanities Review, Prairie Schooner, Burning Water, South and West, Epoch, Massachusetts Review, Trace,* and other literary journals; contributor of about twenty-five articles and reviews to *Encyclopedia of Philosophy,* and to philosophy and other journals.

WORK IN PROGRESS: Volume II of *A Continual Interest in the Sun and Sea; Prologue to Singing Child-Eye and Mountain Songs,* a long poem; *An Essay on Robots,* a satire in iambic couplets; editing a volume of *Minnesota Studies in the Philosophy of Science.*

SIDELIGHTS: Keith Gunderson's "main philosophical interests have to do with philosophy of mind," but he also teaches courses in aesthetics and on John Locke, "especially his views on language and mind"; he hopes eventually to integrate all these interests in a large book on *Mind, Language, and Art.* Gunderson told *CA:* "Unlike many, I see no conflict between doing philosophy on the one hand and writing poetry on the other. Differences in the type of activity involved as well as the (alleged) difference between constructing a scientific theory and producing art seem to me highly exaggerated. All strike me as being highly complicated kinds of problem-solving activity specific to a given medium (words, concepts, paint, etc.)."†

*   *   *

GUNTER, P(ete) A(ddison) Y(ancey) 1936-

PERSONAL: Born October 20, 1936, in Hammond, Ind.; son of Addison Yancey (an engineer) and Anna Ruth (Morris) Gunter; married Barrye Ingram (an English teacher), 1965 (divorced); married Elizabeth Ellington (an environmental consultant), April 12, 1969; children: Sheila Dewing. *Education:* University of Texas, Main University (now University of Texas at Austin), B.A., 1958; Cambridge University, B.A., 1960; Yale University, Ph.D., 1963. *Politics:* Liberal democrat. *Home:* 225 Jagoe St., Denton, Tex. 76201. *Office:* Department of Philosophy, North Texas State University, Denton, Tex. 76203.

CAREER: Auburn University, Auburn, Ala., assistant professor of philosophy, 1962-65; University of Tennessee, Knoxville, associate professor of philosophy, 1965-69; North Texas State University, Denton, professor of philosophy, 1969—, chairman of department, 1969-76. Consultant to Society for Philosophy of Creativity. *Member:* American Philosophical Association, American Association of University Professors, American Civil Liberties Union (member of local executive committee), Southern Society for Philosophy and Psychology, Southwestern Philosophical Association, Texas Institute of Letters, Big Thicket Association (president, 1971-73; chairman of coordinating committee). *Awards, honors:* National Endowment for the Humanities young scholar grant, 1968.

WRITINGS: (Editor) *Bergson and the Evolution of Physics,* University of Tennessee Press, 1969; *The Big Thicket: A Challenge for Conservation,* Jenkins Publishing, 1972; *Henri Bergson: A Bibliography,* Philosophy Documentation Center, 1974. Contributor to philosophy journals and conservationist magazines. Member of editorial board, *Southern Humanities Review;* co-editor, *Liberal Voice* (published in Denton), 1969-71.

WORK IN PROGRESS: Readings in Process Philosophy; Bergson's Philosophy of Science; Theory of Personality; The Nameless War, a novel concerning the Civil War.

SIDELIGHTS: P.A.Y. Gunter told *CA:* "It would be very difficult for me to explain what sort of writer I am or where my writing is tending. A philosopher of science and historian of modern philosophy by profession, I am drawn to write on environmental problems. But at the same time, a contrary impulse to write poetry, music, and fiction continues to make the process of nature and science writing extremely frustrating. It would be nice if one had more than one lifetime—at the same time."

*   *   *

GUNTHER, Gerald 1927-

PERSONAL: Name legally changed; born May 26, 1927, in Usingen, Germany; naturalized U.S. citizen; son of Otto (a butcher) and Minna (Floersheim) Gutenstein; married Barbara Kelsky, June 22, 1949; children: Daniel Jay, Andrew James. *Education:* Brooklyn College (now Brooklyn College of the City University of New York), A.B., 1949; Columbia University, M.A., 1950; Harvard University, LL.B., 1953. *Religion:* Jewish. *Home:* 858 Lathrop Dr., Stanford, Calif. 94305. *Office:* School of Law, Stanford University, Stanford, Calif. 94305.

CAREER: Law clerk to Judge Learned Hand, New York City, 1953-54, and to U.S. Chief Justice Earl Warren, Washington, D.C., 1954-55; Cleary, Gottlieb, Friendly & Hamilton (law firm), New York City, associate, 1953, 1954, 1955-56; Columbia University, School of Law, New York City, associate professor, 1956-60, professor of law, 1960-62; Stanford University, Stanford, Calif., professor in School of Law, 1962—, William Nelson Cromwell Professor of Law, 1972—. Fellow, Center for Advanced Study in the Behavioral Sciences, 1970-71. Visiting professor, Harvard University, 1972-73; Fulbright lecturer in Ghana, 1970. Member of faculty, Salzburg Seminar in American Studies, 1976. *Military service:* U.S. Naval Reserve, 1945-46. *Member:* American Law Institute, Organization of American Historians, American Historical Association, American Academy of Arts and Sciences (fellow). *Awards, honors:* Distinguished Alumnus Award, Brooklyn College of the City University of New York, 1961; Guggenheim fellow, 1962-63.

WRITINGS: (Editor) *Cases and Materials on Constitutional Law,* 7th edition (Gunther was not associated with earlier editions), Foundation Press, 1965, 9th edition, 1975, and annual supplements, 1966—; (editor) *John Marshall's Defense of McCulloch v. Maryland,* Stanford University Press, 1969; (editor) *Cases and Materials on Individual Rights in Constitutional Law,* Foundation Press, 1970, 2nd edition, 1975, annual supplements, 1971; (contributor) *Aspects of American Liberty: Philosophical, Historical, and Political,* American Philosophical Society, 1977. Contributor to legal and other journals.

WORK IN PROGRESS: Several volumes on the Marshall Court for the multi-volume *History of the United States Supreme Court,* for Macmillan; designated biographer of Judge Learned Hand, with a book in process.

*   *   *

GURR, Andrew (John) 1936-

PERSONAL: Surname rhymes with "fur"; born December 23, 1936, in Leicester, England; son of John V. and Elsie R. (Dow) Gurr; married Elizabeth Ann Gordon (a teacher), July 1, 1961; children: Robin, Douglas, Corin. *Education:* University of Auckland, B.A., 1957, M.A., 1958; Cambridge University, Ph.D., 1963. *Office:* Department of English, University of Reading, Whiteknights Park, Reading, England.

CAREER: Victoria University of Wellington, Wellington, New Zealand, lecturer in English, 1959; University of Leeus, Leeds, England, lecturer in English, 1962-69; University of Nairobi, Nairobi, Kenya, lecturer in English and head of department, 1969-73; University of Reading, Reading, England, professor of English, 1976—. *Member:* Association of Commonwealth Literature and Language Studies.

WRITINGS: (Editor) Francis Beaumont, *The Knight of the Burning Pestle,* University of California Press, 1968; (editor) Beaumont and John Fletcher, *The Maid's Tragedy,* University of California Press, 1969; (editor) Beaumont and Fletcher, *Philaster,* Methuen, 1969; *The Shakespearean Stage, 1574-1642,* Cambridge University Press, 1970. Director. ''Northern House Pamphlet Poets.''

WORK IN PROGRESS: African literature.

* * *

GUTHMAN, Edwin 1919-

PERSONAL: Born August 11, 1919, in Seattle, Wash.; son of Otto and Hilda (Leiser) Guthman; married Jo Ann Cheim, July 6, 1947; children: Lester, Edwin, Gary, Diane. *Education:* University of Washington, B.A., 1941; Harvard University, additional study, 1950-51. *Home:* 283 Locust St., Philadelphia, Pa. 19106. *Agent:* Theodore Sorensen, 345 Park Ave., New York, N.Y. 10022. *Office: Philadelphia Inquirer,* 400 North Broad St., Philadelphia, Pa. 19101.

CAREER: Seattle Star, Seattle, Wash., reporter, 1941, 1946-47; *Seattle Times,* Seattle, reporter, 1947-60; U.S. Department of Justice, Washington, D.C., special assistant for public information, 1961-64; press secretary for Senator Robert Kennedy, Washington, D.C., 1965; *Los Angeles Times,* Los Angeles, Calif., national editor, 1965-77; *Philadelphia Inquirer,* Philadelphia, Pa., editor, 1977—. Member of board of directors, Ryther Child Center, 1953-60. *Military service:* U.S. Army, 1941-45; became captain; received Silver Star and Purple Heart. *Member:* Sigma Delta Chi, Society of Nieman Fellows. *Awards, honors:* Pulitzer Prize for national news reporting, 1950; University of Washington Distinguished Alumnus award, 1975.

WRITINGS: (Editor with Pierre Salinger, Frank Mankiewicz, and John Seigenthaler) *An Honorable Profession,* Doubleday, 1968; *We Band of Brothers,* Harper, 1971.

BIOGRAPHICAL/CRITICAL SOURCES: Washington Post, May 27, 1971.

* * *

GUTHRIE, James Shields 1931-
(David Creed)

PERSONAL: Born December 14, 1931, in Kandy, Ceylon; son of William Alexander (a civil engineer) and Eleanor (Crowden) Guthrie; married Raye Pelling (a novelist), July 20, 1958. *Education:* Attended Eton College, 1945-50; Cambridge University, B.A. (honors), 1953, M.A. 1966; University of London, further graduate study, 1965-55. *Residence:* Powys, Bahrain. *Agent:* RSS Ltd., 32 College Cross, London N1, England.

CAREER: Has held various positions including administrative officer in Tanzania, H.M. Overseas Civil Service, 1954-56; welfare officer in New Guinea, Department of Native Affairs, Government of Australia, 1961-63; teacher, Ministry of Education, Kuwait, 1965-66; teacher Markham College, Lima, Peru, 1968-69; currently inspector of schools, Government of Bahrain.

WRITINGS: (Under pseudonym David Creed) *The Noncombatants* (novel), Collins, 1969; *The Trial of Lobo Icheka* (novel), Macmillan, 1971. Contributor to newspapers and journals in India, 1959-60.

WORK IN PROGRESS: A novel, *The Wather of Chimor.*

SIDELIGHTS: Guthrie also has lived and worked in Pakistan, Hong Kong, Australia, Netherlands, and Spain. He speaks Swahili, neo-Melanesian, Dutch, Spanish, French, and some Hindi and Arabic.

BIOGRAPHICAL/CRITICAL SOURCES: Times Literary Supplement, June 12, 1969.

* * *

GWALTNEY, John L(angston) 1928-

PERSONAL: Born September 25, 1928, in Orange, N.J.; son of Stanley and Mabel (Harper) Gwaltney; married; wife's name, Judith; children: Karen, Peter. *Education:* Upsala College, B.A., 1952; New School for Social Research, M.A., 1957; Columbia University, Ph.D., 1967. *Politics:* ''Reason.'' *Religion:* ''Reason.'' *Home:* 153 Strong Ave., Syracuse, N.Y. 13210. *Office:* Department of Anthropology, Syracuse University, 500 University Pl., Syracuse, N.Y. 13210.

CAREER: State University of New York, assistant professor, 1967-69, associate professor, 1969-71; Syracuse University, Syracuse, N.Y., associate professor of anthropology, 1971—. Senior fellow, National Endowment for the Humanities, 1973-74; fellow, American Council of Learned Societies, 1976-77. *Member:* American Anthropological Association (fellow), American Ethnological Society, American Association for the Advancement of Science, Society for Applied Anthropology.

WRITINGS: The Thrice Shy: Cultural Accomodation to Blindness and Other Disasters in a Mexican Community, Columbia University Press, 1970. Contributor to journals.

WORK IN PROGRESS: Research on native anthropology, myth charter, and black studies.

SIDELIGHTS: John Gwaltney, blind since birth, did his research for *The Thrice Shy* in a community where marginal living made blindness a constant threat to the entire community. His anthropological field work has been among Mexican Indians, American Indians, Jamaican Maroons, and northeastern United States urban Afro-Americans.

* * *

HAABY, Lawrence O. 1915-

PERSONAL: Born August 9, 1915, in Roseau, Minn.; married Delores K. Syverud, 1940; children: Kaydell, Gary, DeAnn. *Education:* Moorhead State College, B.A., 1939; Columbia University, M.A., 1940, Ed.D., 1950; graduate study at University of Michigan and University of Southern California, 1946-48. *Office:* College of Education, University of Tennessee, Knoxville, Tenn. 37916.

CAREER: Teacher in Riverdale, N.Y., 1939, Fergus Falls, Minn., 1940-42, and Minneapolis, Minn., 1942-43; Western Michigan University, Kalamazoo, resident teacher in Laboratory School and associate professor of education, 1945-48; Columbia University, Teachers College, New York, N.Y., instructor in education, 1949-50; University of Tennessee, Knoxville, associate professor, 1950-53, professor of education, 1953—. Visiting summer professor at University of Florida, 1950, and Boston University, 1956; UNESCO education expert at Seminar on Teacher Education for Latin

America, University of Chile, 1961-62. Executive director, Tennessee Council on Economic Education, 1955-61. *Military service:* U.S. Army, 1943-45.

MEMBER: National Education Association, National Council for the Social Studies, American Association of University Professors, Tennesee Education Association, Phi Delta Kappa, Gamma Theta Upsilon, Kappa Delta Pi.

WRITINGS: (With John V. D. Southworth and Ernest L. Thurston) *Our Homeland and the World,* 2nd edition (Haaby was not associated with earlier edition), Iroquois Publishing, 1960, revised edition, C. E. Merrill, 1964; (with Hankins and Thurston) *Homelands of the World,* 2nd edition (Haaby was not associated with earlier edition), Iroquois Publishing, 1960; (with Hankins and Thurston) *Homelands Beyond the Seas,* revised edition (Haaby was not associated with earlier edition), C. E. Merrill, 1964; (editor) *Our American Democratic Republic and Contrasting Totalitarian Systems Including Communism and Fascism,* revised edition (Haaby was not associated with earlier editions), Tennessee State Department of Education, 1965. Contributor to *Britannica Junior Encyclopedia* and to education journals.

*   *   *

HAAC, Oscar A(lfred) 1918-

PERSONAL: Born January 28, 1918, in Frankfurt, Germany; son of Oscar Eugen (a merchant and judge) and Charlotte L. (Sternberg) Haac; married Clare E. Lytle (a college teacher), December 6, 1942 (died May, 1970); married Gunilla Nohrlander (an attorney), June 22, 1972; children: (first marriage) Alice Winfield (Mrs. Hermond Vessell), Oscar Clifford. *Education:* Attended College Francais in Berlin; Yale University, B.A., 1939, M.A., 1942, Ph.D., 1948; University of Paris, Doctorat, 1948; summer study at Middlebury College, 1940, 1941, National University of Mexico, 1950, 1951, and Yale University, 1952. *Religion:* Unitarian Universalist. *Home:* 157 Quaker Path, Setauket, N.Y. 11733. *Office:* Department of French, State University of New York, Stony Brook, N.Y. 11794.

CAREER: Teacher at private secondary school, 1939-40; Pennsylvania State University, University Park, assistant professor of Romance languages, 1948-54; Emory University, Atlanta, Ga., associate professor, 1954-62, professor of French, 1962-65; State University of New York at Stony Brook, professor of French, 1965—. Visiting professor, University of Wyoming, summer, 1959, Georgia College, Milledgeville, summer, 1964. Interpreter at World Assembly of World Council of Churches, 1954. Director of National Defense Education Act French institutes in Atlanta and Besancon, France, 1960-63. *Military service:* U.S. Army, 1941-45; intelligence officer in Normandy landing and French and German campaigns; received Bronze Star Medal.

MEMBER: Modern Language Association of America, American Association of Teachers of French, American Society for Eighteenth-Century Studies, American Association of University Professors, Societe des Professeurs Francais, Societe des Textes Francais Modernes, New York State Association of Foreign Language Teachers, Phi Sigma Iota (national president, 1964-67; national treasurer, 1974—). *Awards, honors:* Guggenheim fellowship, 1957-58; Palmes Academiques (France), 1963; research grants from American Philosophical Society, French Government, Modern Language Association of America, and various universities.

WRITINGS: Les Principes inspirateurs de Michelet: Sensibilite et philosophie de l'histoire, Yale University Press, 1951; (editor and contributor) Jules Michelet, *Cours professe au College de France en 1839* (critical edition; special supplement to *Revue d'Histoire Litteraire*), A. Colin, 1954; (contributor of translation) *To Dr. Albert Schweitzer: A Festschrift,* Friends of Albert Schweitzer, 1955; (translator) Max Scheler, *Philosophical Perspectives,* Beacon Press, 1958; (editor with William A. Strozier and William S. Willis) *Points de vue,* Appleton, 1959; (editor and contributor) Pierre Simon Ballanche, *La Theodicee et la Virginie romaine* (critical edition), Droz, 1959; (contributor) *The Persistent Voice: Festschrift to Henri Peyre,* New York University Press, 1971; (with Arthur Bieler, Pierre Leon, and Monique Leon) *Perspectives de France,* with teacher's manual, workbook, and tapes, Prentice-Hall, 1968, revised edition, 1972; *Marivaux,* Twayne, 1973; (with Bieler) *Actualite et Avenir* (interviews with prominent Frenchmen and authors), Prentice-Hall, 1975. Contributor of bibliographies, articles, and reviews to professional journals.

WORK IN PROGRESS: A study of Jules Michelet, the French historian; an edition in English translation of the correspondence between J. S. Mill and Auguste Comte, in collaboration with B. Semmell.

SIDELIGHTS: Oscar A. Haac told *CA,* "I try to convey the fundamental literary and ideological objectives of the author discussed, the world he tries to communicate; also the civilization and intellectual world of France, presented in new and diverse ways; as in teaching, I try to share my enthusiasm."

*   *   *

HAAR, Charles M(onroe) 1920-

PERSONAL: Born December 3, 1920, in Antwerp, Belgium; brought to United States in 1921, naturalized citizen in 1926; son of Benjamin (a businessman) and Dora (Eisner) Haar; married Natalie Zinn (a psychologist), 1946; children: Jeremy, Susan, John. *Education:* New York University, A.B., 1940; University of Wisconsin, M.A., 1941; Harvard University, LL.B., 1948. *Home:* 1 Kennedy Rd., Cambridge, Mass. 02138. *Office:* Law School, Harvard University, Cambridge, Mass. 02138.

CAREER: Admitted to Bar of the State of New York, 1949; private practice of law, New York, N.Y., 1949-52; Harvard University, Cambridge, Mass., assistant professor, 1952-54, professor of law, 1954-66; U.S. Department of Housing and Urban Development, assistant secretary and undersecretary for metropolitan development, 1966-69; Harvard University, professor of law, 1969-72, Louis D. Brandeis Professor, 1972—. Chairman of President's Task Force on Preservation of Natural Beauty, Task Force on Model Cities, and of Task Force on Suburban Problems. Chief reporter, American Land Institute project on model code for land development, 1964-66; vice-president, Doxiadis Associates; president, Regional and Urban Dynamics, Inc. Director of Charles River Associates and Zelda Zinn Foundation. *Military service:* U.S. Navy, 1942-46; became lieutenant junior grade. *Member:* American Academy of Arts and Sciences, American Bar Association (fellow), American Law Institute, British Town Planning Institute, Phi Beta Kappa. *Awards, honors:* LL.D., Lake Erie University, 1968; Rockefeller Foundation fellow.

WRITINGS: Land Planning Law in a Free Society, Harvard University Press, 1951; *Land-Use Planning: A Casebook in Use, Misuse, and Reuse of Urban Land,* Little,

Brown, 1959, 3rd edition, 1976, supplement, 1966; *Report on Possible Work by the American Law Institute on Land-Use Planning and Controls,* American Law Institute, 1960; *Federal Credit and Private Housing: The Mass Financing Dilemma,* McGraw, 1960; (editor) *Law and Land: Anglo-American Planning Practice,* Harvard University Press, 1964; (editor and author of introduction and notes) *The Golden Age of the American Law,* Braziller, 1965; *The End of Innocence: A Suburban Reader,* Scott, Foresman, 1972; (with Demetrius S. Iatridis) *Housing the Poor in Suburbia: Public Policy at the Grass Roots,* Ballinger, 1974; (editor) *The President's Task Force on Suburban Problems: Final Report,* Ballinger, 1974; *Between the Idea and the Reality: A Study in the Origin, Fate, and Legacy of the Model Cities Program,* Little, Brown, 1975. Contributor to legal and land use journals.

WORK IN PROGRESS: The Idea of Equality.

* * *

HAASE, Ann Marie Bernazza   1942-
(Ann Marie Bernazza)

PERSONAL: Born January 3, 1942, in Poughkeepsie, N.Y.; daughter of Leonard David and Ann (Peluse) Bernazza; married Richard Frank Haase (a psychologist), March 27, 1971. *Education:* State University of New York College at New Paltz, B.S., 1963; Syracuse University, graduate study, 1963; University of Connecticut, M.A., 1967, Ph.D., 1969. *Home:* 4500 East Sunrise, No. E-8, Tucson, Ariz. 85718. *Office:* College of Education, University of Arizona, Tucson, Ariz. 85721.

CAREER: Junior high school teacher of English and social studies in Liverpool, N.Y., 1955-57; coordinator and instructor in projects and institutes, Connecticut State Department of Education, 1968-69; University of Hartford, West Hartford, Conn., associate professor of education, 1968-72; University of Massachusetts—Amherst, consultant to graduate psychiatric nursing program, 1971-72, associate professor of nursing research, 1972-76; University of Arizona, Tucson, associate professor of educational psychology, 1976—, assistant dean of research, 1977—. Visiting scholar, Center for Educational Management Studies, University of Massachusetts, 1975-76. Licensed psychologist in Massachusetts and Arizona. Has presented papers at numerous professional conferences. *Member:* American Educational Research Association, American Psychological Association, National Reading Conference, International Reading Association, New England Educational Research Organization (vice-president, 1970-71; program chairwoman, 1971-72; president, 1972-73), Rocky Mountain Education Research Association, Gerontological Society, Phi Kappa Phi, Phi Delta Kappa.

WRITINGS—Under name Ann Marie Bernazza: (With R. H. Bloomer) *Reading and Typing: A Linguistic Phonetic Approach* (for primer, grade one, and grade two, with workbooks and teacher's manuals), Olivetti-Underwood Corp., 1967-68; (with Bloomer) *Reading and Typing: A Linguistic Approach,* Leonard Hutcheson Publishing, 1970. Writer of research reports; contributor to education journals.

* * *

HABER, Audrey   1940-

PERSONAL: Born February 4, 1940, in New York, N.Y.; daughter of Louis Larry and Sally (Reit) Bloom; married Jerome Jassenoff (a manufacturer's representative), December 19, 1969; children: Laurie Beth, David Scott. *Edu-*

cation: Adelphi University, B.A., 1960, Ph.D., 1963; New York University, postdoctoral study, 1965-68. *Religion:* Jewish. *Home:* 1315 Carmelina Ave., Los Angeles, Calif. 90025. *Office:* Department of Pediatrics, University of California, Los Angeles, Calif. 90024.

CAREER: Adelphi University, Garden City, N.Y., member of faculty of psychology, 1961-65; Long Island University, C. W. Post Center, Greenvale, N.Y., assistant professor, 1964-67, associate professor of psychology, 1967-70; University of California, Los Angeles, research psychologist, 1970—. Instructor and senior research associate in psychiatry, New York Medical College, 1963-64; research psychologist, Long Island Jewish Hospital, 1964-66. *Member:* American Psychological Association, Western Psychological Association, Psi Chi.

WRITINGS: (With Richard P. Runyon) *Fundamentals of Behavioral Statistics,* Addison-Wesley, 1967, 3rd edition, 1976; (with Runyon) *General Statistics,* published with *Workbook,* Addison-Wesley, 1969, 3rd edition, 1977; (with Pietro Badia and Runyon) *Readings in Statistics,* Addison-Wesley, 1970; (with Runyon and Badia) *Problems in Psychological Research,* Addison-Wesley, 1970; (with Runyon) *Fundamentals of Psychology,* Addison-Wesley, 1974, 2nd edition, 1978. Contributor to psychology journals.

* * *

HABER, Ralph Norman   1932-

PERSONAL: Born May 15, 1932, in Lansing, Mich.; son of William (a professor and dean) and Fannie (Gallas) Haber; married Ruth Boss, 1961 (divorced); married Lyn Roland, 1974; children: (first marriage) Sabrina, Rebecca. *Education:* University of Michigan, B.A. (with honors), 1953; Wesleyan University, Middletown, Conn., M.A., 1954; Stanford University, Ph.D., 1957. *Politics:* Democrat. *Religion:* Jewish. *Home:* 1209 Clover St., Rochester, N.Y. 14610. *Office:* Department of Psychology, University of Rochester, Rochester, N.Y. 14627.

CAREER: Stanford University, Stanford, Calif., research associate, Institute for Communications Research, 1957-58; San Francisco State College (now University), San Francisco, Calif., instructor in psychology, 1957-58; Yale University, New Haven, Conn., assistant professor of psychology, 1958-64; University of Rochester, Rochester, N.Y., associate professor, 1964-67, professor of psychology, 1967—, professor of visual science, 1970—, chairman of department of psychology, 1967-70. Visiting scientist, Medical Research Council, Cambridge, England, 1970-71; visiting professor, Hebrew University, Jerusalem, Israel, 1976. Advisory editor, Holt, Rinehart & Winston, Inc., 1969—. *Member:* American Psychological Association (fellow), American Association for the Advancement of Science (fellow), Psychonomics Society, Linguistics Society of America, Optical Society of America.

WRITINGS—Published by Holt, except as indicated: (Editor) *Current Research in Motivation,* 1966; (editor) *Contemporary Theory and Research in Visual Perception,* 1968; (editor) *Information Processing Approaches to Visual Perception,* 1969; (with Maurice Hershenson) *The Psychology of Visual Perception,* 1973; (with Ahran Fried) *Introduction to Psychology,* 1975; (with Bernard Weiner and others) *Discovering Psychology,* Science Research Associates, 1978. Contributor of more than seventy articles and monographs to psychology journals.

WORK IN PROGRESS: With Maurice Hershenson, a revision of *The Psychology of Visual Percepion;* further research on visual perception, especially on the perceptual components of reading.

*   *   *

HACIKYAN, A(gop) J. 1931-

PERSONAL: Born November 25, 1931, in Istanbul, Turkey; son of Stephan (a businessman) and Pergruhi Hacikyan; married Mimi Cerkezyan, September 30, 1956; married second wife, Brigitte Chabert, February 20, 1971; children: (first marriage) Talleen (daughter); (second marriage) Stephen. *Education:* American College of Istanbul, B.A.; University of Montreal, M.A., Ph.D. *Home and office:* College Militaire Royal, Saint-Jean, Quebec, Canada.

CAREER: University of Sherbrooke, Sherbrooke, Quebec, 1962-65, began as instructor, became associate professor; College Militaire Royal, Saint-Jean, Quebec, professor of English and chairman of department, 1965—. Administrative officer in charge of examinations and language programs, United Nations, Geneva, Switzerland, 1974-76. Canadian exchange scholar in France and Canada. *Military service:* Turkish Army Reserve, 1954-56; became lieutenant. *Member:* Modern Language Association of America, Modern Humanities Research Association, Canadian Association of University Teachers. *Awards, honors:* Canada Council awards; Atherton Literary Prize; Department of National Defense grants.

WRITINGS: A Linguistic and Literary Analysis of Old English Riddles, Casalini (Florence), 1966; *Handbook of Methodology of Teaching English as a Second Language*, Librairie Beauchemin (Montreal), 1967; *English Pronunciation*, Librairie Beauchemin, 1969; *The Gigo Cycle* (novel), Giligia Press, 1969; *Tomas* (novel), Giligia Press, 1970; *Runes of Old English Poetry* (monograph), University of Ottawa Press, 1972; *The Problems of the French-Speakers*, Librairie Beauchemin, 1975. Contributor of articles to literary journals. Editor, *Sun Literary Review*.

WORK IN PROGRESS: Two novels, *The Accident Makers* and *The Battle of the Prophets; Dialogues and Exercises in Business English*.

SIDELIGHTS: A. J. Hacikyan told *CA* he used the Middle East, especially Turkey, his native country, as the background for his novels. He has traveled widely in the Middle East, Europe, Canada, and the United States, speaks French in addition to Turkish and Armenian, and considers "teaching and travels vital for my writing career."

*   *   *

HAENICKE, Diether H. 1935-

PERSONAL: Born May 19, 1935, in Hagen, Germany; naturalized U.S. citizen in 1972; son of Erwin O. (an official of state of Northrhine-Westphalia) and Helene (Wildfang) Haenicke; married Carol Ann Colditz, September 29, 1962; children: Jennifer Ruth, Kurt Robert. *Education:* Studied at University of Goettingen, 1955-56, and University of Marburg, 1957-59; University of Munich, Ph.D. (magna cum laude), 1962. *Home:* 215 Mount Vernon Blvd., Royal Oak, Mich. 48073. *Office:* Office of Vice-President and Provost, Wayne State University, Detroit, Mich. 48202.

CAREER: Junior Year Abroad programs in Munich and Freiburg, Germany, instructor in German, 1959-63; Wayne State University, Detroit, Mich., assistant professor, 1963-68, associate professor, 1968-72, professor of German, 1972—, chairman of department of Romance and Germanic languages and literatures, 1971-72, resident director of

Junior Year in Freiburg, 1965-66, 1969-70, director of Junior Year Abroad programs, 1970-75, associate dean of College of Liberal Arts, 1972-75, provost, 1975-77, vice-president and provost, 1977—. *Member:* American Association of Teachers of German, Modern Language Association of America, American Council on the Teaching of Foreign Languages, Deutscher Wissenschafter Verband, Hoelderlin Gesellschaft, American Association of University Professors, Michigan Academy of Arts and Sciences. *Awards, honors:* Fulbright scholar, 1963-65.

WRITINGS: Untersuchungen zum Versepos des 20. Jahrhunderts, University of Munich, 1962; (editor) L. Tieck, *Liebesgeschichte der schoenen Magelone*, Goldmann, 1969; (editor) Tieck, *Der blonde Eckbert u.a. Novellen*, Goldmann, 1969; (editor) Tieck, *Franz Sternbalds Wanderungen*, Goldmann, 1970; (editor and author with Horst S. Daemmrich) *The Challenge of German Literature*, Wayne State University Press, 1971. Contributor of articles and reviews to academic and literary journals.

WORK IN PROGRESS: Research in early nineteenth-century German Romanticism and in twentieth-century German literature.

AVOCATIONAL INTERESTS: Music, fine arts.

*   *   *

HAGERTY, Nancy K. 1935-

PERSONAL: Born September 25, 1935, in Murray, Utah; daughter of Leland Albert (a sheet metal worker and inventor) and Bernice (a poet; maiden name Burbidge) Daines; married Everett L. Hagerty (an assistant professor), July 18, 1958; children: Lonn James, Colleen K., Shawn Marie. *Education:* Brigham Young University, B.S., 1961; Columbia University, M.A., 1964; Florida State University, Ph.D., 1970. *Religion:* Church of Jesus Christ of Latter-day Saints.

CAREER: Worked in banks, operating IBM proof machines while taking college courses, and also as a welfare worker, 1953-61; teacher of four grades in the mountain mining community of Scofield, Utah, 1960-61; teacher of sixth grade in a residence school for the disadvantaged, Hope Farm, N.Y., 1966-67; Florida State University, Tallahassee, instructor and fellow in computer-assisted instruction, 1967-70; University of British Columbia, Vancouver, lecturer in educational psychology, beginning 1970. *Member:* American Psychological Association, American Educational Research Association.

WRITINGS: (With Walter Dick) *Topics in Measurement: Reliability and Validity*, McGraw, 1971; *A General Systems Approach Model for Developing Instructional Materials: A Manual of Instructions*, Western Washington State College, 1971; (editor with Raymond F. Latta) *Computer-Assisted Instruction: Implications for the Northwest*, Western Washington State College, 1971; (contributor with husband, Everett Hagerty) Michael Jackson, *Cases and Materials on Family Law*, Village Printwrights (Vancouver, B.C.), 1971. Also author of *Individualized Instruction: Techniques for Implementation and Management*, Center for Continuing Education, University of British Columbia. Poems included in *Encounter: An Anthology of Modern Poetry*, Idlewild, 1968, and *Generation*.

WORK IN PROGRESS: Developing Instructional Materials: A Systems Approach, with Stanley S. Blank; editing *Readings in Programmed Instruction Research*, with Stanley S. Blank; *Communal Living: A Search for Meaning*, with husband, Everett L. Hagerty.

AVOCATIONAL INTERESTS: Weaving, pottery, painting, house-building.††

* * *

HAHN, Harlan 1939-

PERSONAL: Born July 9, 1939, in Osage, Iowa; son of Harold E. (a teacher) and Ada (Tollefson) Hahn. *Education:* Attended University of Minnesota, 1957-58, 1965-66, American University, 1959; St. Olaf College, B.A. (magna cum laude), 1960; attended Drake University, 1961; Harvard University, M.A., 1963, Ph.D., 1964. *Home:* 717 11th St., Santa Monica, Calif. 90402. *Office:* Department of Political Science, University of Southern California, Los Angeles, Calif. 90007.

CAREER: Newspaper reporter, 1955-57; radio announcer, 1959-60; U.S. Bureau of the Budget, Washington, D.C., budget examiner, 1962; University of Michigan, Ann Arbor, assistant professor of political science, 1964-67; University of California, Riverside, visiting assistant professor, 1967-68, associate professor, 1968-71, professor of political science, 1971-72; University of Southern California, Los Angeles, professor of political science, 1972—. Clerk for Senator Eugene J. McCarthy, 1959; program analyst, U.S. Office of Education, 1964. Participant, Symposium on Political Science and Public Health, Harvard School of Public Health, 1969; lecturer, Executive Development Seminar for Police Officials, 1970-71. *Member:* American Political Science Association, Phi Beta Kappa, Pi Gamma Mu, Pi Kappa Delta. *Awards, honors:* Grants from Michigan State Department of Health, 1965, Horace H. Rackham Foundation, 1966-67, University of Michigan, 1967, and University of California, 1967-72.

WRITINGS: Urban-Rural Conflict: The Politics of Change, Sage Publications, 1971; (editor and contributor) *Police in Urban Society,* Sage Publications, 1971; (editor) *People and Politics in Urban Society,* Sage Publications, 1972; (with Joe R. Feagin) *Ghetto Revolts,* Macmillan, 1973; (with R. William Holland) *American Government: Minority Rights Versus Majority Rule,* Wiley, 1976; (with Larry L. Berg and John R. Schmidhauser) *Corruption in the American Political System,* General Learning Press, 1976.

Contributor: *Winning Orations,* Interstate Oratorical Society (East Lansing, Mich), 1958; Lionel D. Feldman and Michael D. Goldrick, editors, *Politics and Government of Urban Canada,* Methuen, 1969; Robert P. Swierenga, editor, *Quantification in American History: Theory and Research,* Atheneum, 1970; Bryan T. Downes, editor, *Cities and Suburbs: Selected Readings in Local Politics and Public Policy,* Wadsworth, 1971; Peter Orleans and Russell Ellis, editors, *Race and Change in Urban Society,* Sage Publications, 1971; Daniel N. Gordon, editor, *Social Change and Urban Politics,* Prentice-Hall, 1973.

Contributor to *Journal of Politics, Polity, Public Opinion Quarterly, Dissent, Social Science Quarterly, Phylon, American Behavioral Scientist, Journal of Black Studies, American Political Science Review, Soundings, Science and Society, Journal of Political Studies, Mental Hygiene,* and other journals. Editor, *American Behavioral Scientist,* 1970, *American Politics Quarterly,* 1971-77; member of advisory board, *Journal of Political Studies,* 1968—; advisory editor, *Social Science Quarterly,* 1970-72; member of board of editors, *Politics and Society,* 1970-71; member of editorial board, *American Journal of Community Psychology,* 1975—.

HAHN, Roger 1932-

PERSONAL: Born January 5, 1932, in Paris, France; son of Jean (now John) Pierre (a businessman) and Therese (Levy) Hahn; married Ellen Isabel Leibovici (a musician), September 11, 1955; children: Elisabeth Louise, Sophie Anne. *Education:* Harvard University, B.A. (magna cum laude), 1953, M.A.T., 1954; Ecole Pratique des Hautes Etudes, Paris, Diploma, 1955; Cornell University, Ph.D., 1962. *Politics:* None. *Religion:* Jewish. *Home:* 686 Santa Barbara Rd., Berkeley, Calif. 94707. *Office:* Department of History, University of California, Berkeley, Calif. 94720.

CAREER: University of Delaware, Newark, instructor in history, 1960-61; University of California, Berkeley, instructor, 1961-62, assistant professor, 1962-68, associate professor of history, 1968—. Special assistant to director of Bancroft Library, Berkeley. *Military service:* U.S. Army, 1955-57. *Member:* American Historical Association, History of Science Society (member of council), American Association for the Advancement of Science (fellow; member of council), Society for French Historical Studies, American Society for Eighteenth-Century Studies, Academie Internationale d'Histoire des Sciences (corresponding member). *Awards, honors:* Fulbright scholar in Paris, 1954-55; National Science Foundation fellow, 1964-65; Book Prize award, American Historical Association, Pacific Coast branch, 1972; American Council of Learned Societies fellow, 1973-74.

WRITINGS: L'Hydrodynamique au XVIIIe siecle, Palais de la Decouverte (Paris), 1965; *Laplace as a Newtonian Scientist,* William A. Clark Library (Los Angeles), 1967; *The Anatomy of a Scientific Institution: The Paris Academy of Sciences (1666-1803),* University of California Press, 1971. Advisory editor, *Isis, History of Science, Social Studies of Science,* and *Eighteenth-Century Studies.*

WORK IN PROGRESS: A biography of Pierre Simon Laplace, 1749-1827; editing the correspondence of Rudjer Boskovic, 1711-1787.

* * *

HAIG, (Irvine Reid) Stirling 1936-

PERSONAL: Born May 20, 1936, in Washington, D.C.; son of I. T. and Helen (Rothwell) Haig; married Sara Lochridge, June 25, 1960; children: Christopher L., Alan T. *Education:* University of North Carolina at Chapel Hill, B.A., 1958; University of Lyon, graduate study, 1958-59; Yale University, Ph.D., 1964. *Office:* Department of Romance Languages, University of North Carolina, Chapel Hill, N.C. 27514.

CAREER: Yale University, New Haven, Conn., instructor in French, 1962-64; Princeton University, Princeton, N.J., instructor, 1964-65, assistant professor of French, 1965-67; University of North Carolina at Chapel Hill, assistant professor, 1967-68, associate professor, 1968-73, professor of French, 1973—. Chairman of graduate school foreign language test in French, Educational Testing Service. *Member:* American Association of Teachers of French, Modern Language Association of America, Association Internationale des Etudes Francaises. *Awards, honors:* French Government award, 1958; Fulbright scholar in France, 1958-59; Princeton Committee for Research in the Humanities grant, 1966.

WRITINGS: (Co-editor) *Contes et Nouvelles d'aujourd'hui,* Harper, 1966; *Madame de Lafayette,* Twayne, 1970. Contributor of articles to French, English, Italian, and

American journals. *French Review,* assistant editor, 1968-72, managing editor, 1971-74, editor-in-chief, 1974—.

WORK IN PROGRESS: Research on Stendhal.

SIDELIGHTS: Stirling Haig lived in Rome, 1951-54, in Lyon, 1958-59, 1969-70, and in Paris, 1966. *Avocational interests:* Trout fishing, tennis.

* * *

HAINES, George H(enry), Jr. 1937-

PERSONAL: Born September 17, 1937, in Syracuse, N.Y.; son of George Henry (an educator) and Mary (Garber) Haines; married Judith Phillips, June 10, 1961; children: George Emory, John Howard, David Jeremy. *Education:* Massachusetts Institute of Technology, S.B., 1958; Carnegie Institute of Technology (now Carnegie-Mellon University), M.S., 1960, Ph.D., 1964. *Office:* Faculty of Management Studies, University of Toronto, Toronto, Ontario, Canada M55 1U4.

CAREER: U.S. Army, Natick Laboratories, Natick, Mass., statistician, 1962-64; University of California, Los Angeles, assistant professor of business administration, 1964-66; University of Rochester, Rochester, N.Y., assistant professor, 1966-68, associate professor of business administration, 1969-73; University of Toronto, Toronto, Ontario, professor of business administration, 1973—. Director, Consumer Council of Monroe County, 1970-71. *Military service:* U.S. Army Reserve, 1958-68; became captain. *Member:* Association for Consumer Research (treasurer), Institute of Management Science, American Economic Association, Econometric Society, American Marketing Association, Society for Management Information Systems.

WRITINGS: Consumer Behavior: Learning Models of Purchasing, Free Press, 1969; *Problems in Consumer Affairs,* University of Toledo, 1977. Contributor to economics and management journals.

WORK IN PROGRESS: With Marcus Alexis and Leonard S. Simon, *Operation of the Inner City Marketplace.*

* * *

HAISLIP, John 1925-

PERSONAL: Born August 25, 1925, in Lancaster, Pa.; son of Thomas H. (a laborer) and Dorothy (Eaton) Haislip; married Arlene Shaneyfelt Downs, September 14, 1962; children: Linda Downs, Susan Downs, John Downs; stepchildren: Jeanne Elizabeth. *Education:* University of Washington, B.A., 1950, Ph.D., 1965. *Office:* Department of English, University of Oregon, Eugene, Ore. 97403.

CAREER: Oregon State University, Corvallis, instructor, 1958-62, assistant professor, 1962-66, associate professor of English, 1966-67; University of Oregon, Eugene, associate professor, 1967-76, professor of English, 1976—, former director of Creative Writing Program.

WRITINGS: Not Every Year (poems), University of Washington Press, 1971. Contributor of poetry to literary magazines. Former editor, *Northwest Review.*

WORK IN PROGRESS: A second book of poetry.

* * *

HALE, Allean Lemmon 1914-

PERSONAL: Given name is pronounced Al-lean; born July 13, 1914, in Bethany, Neb.; daughter of Clarence Eugene (a clergyman and writer) and Constance (Harlan) Lemmon;

married Mark Pendleton Hale (former director of Jane Addams School of Social Work, University of Illinois), December 31, 1936; children: Susanna (Mrs. James Wolf), Mark Pendleton, Jr. *Education:* Christian College (now Columbia College), Columbia, Mo., A.A., 1933; University of Missouri, B.A., 1935; University of Iowa, M.A., 1963. *Politics:* Democrat. *Religion:* Disciples of Christ. *Home:* 22 G. H. Baker Dr., Urbana, Ill. 61801.

CAREER: Chicago Theological Seminary, Chicago, Ill., production assistant in drama, 1941; Christian College (now Columbia College), Columbia, Mo., alumnae director and editor of college magazine, 1951-56; University of Iowa, Iowa City, instructor in communication skills, 1960-62; instructor in fiction writing in adult education program, Urbana, Ill., 1965; editorial assistant to Oscar Lewis, writer-anthropologist, Urbana, 1966-69; free-lance writer. Member of board of directors, Lenoir Memorial Home, Columbia, 1972-77. *Member:* Phi Beta Kappa, University of Illinois Women's Club, Champaign-Urbana Social Science Club, Columbia College Alumni Association (member of board of directors, 1968-75). *Awards, honors:* First prize in Zeta Phi Eta National Playwriting Contest for "The Hero," 1933, and "Last Flight Over," 1935; first prize in Midwestern Intercollegiate Folk Playwriting Contest for "Last Flight Over," 1935; four awards from National Federation of Press Women, 1953; Distinguished Alumna Award, Christian College, 1964.

WRITINGS: Petticoat Pioneer (history of Christian College), Christian College, 1957, revised edition, 1968; (contributor) *Witness against Odds,* Friendship, 1975.

Plays: *Last Flight Over,* Row, Peterson, 1935; *Remind Me to Live,* Friendship, 1960; *Two in a Trap,* Friendship, 1966; *A Whole New Life,* Friendship, 1969; *The Second Coming of Mrs. C.,* Friendship, 1971. Also author of play, "The Hero" published in *Christian College Prize Plays,* 1934.

Poems have been published in *Saturday Evening Post* and *Parents' Magazine.*

WORK IN PROGRESS: An analytical book on Tennessee Williams' later work.

AVOCATIONAL INTERESTS: Languages, art history.

BIOGRAPHICAL/CRITICAL SOURCES: Champaign News Gazette, January 4, 1969; *Christian College Magazine,* February, 1969.

* * *

HALL, Donald Ray 1933-

PERSONAL: Born October 2, 1933, in Cherokee County, Kan.; son of Arthur Logan and Virginia B. (Hollowell) Hall. *Education:* Columbia University, B.A., 1955; attended University of Bordeaux, 1955-56, and University of Strasbourg, 1956-57; Yale University, Ph.D., 1966. *Home:* 280 Riverside Dr., New York, N.Y. 10025.

CAREER: Yale University, New Haven, Conn., instructor in French, 1962-66; Columbia University, New York, N.Y., assistant professor of French language and literature and Romance philology, 1966-72; Brooklyn College of the City University of New York, Brooklyn, assistant professor of French, 1972-77; free-lance author and library researcher in French literature and in music, 1977—. Vocal coach and accompanist; translator from the French. *Military service:* U.S. Army, 1958-60. *Member:* Modern Language Association of America, American Translators' Association, Phi Beta Kappa. *Awards, honors:* Woodrow Wilson fellowship, 1958; Council for Research in the Humanities award, 1971.

WRITINGS: (Editor with Eve G. Katz) Georges Simenon, *Le Chien jaune,* Harper, 1967; (with Katz) *Explicating French Texts* (textbook), Harper, 1970.

WORK IN PROGRESS: A critical biography of Jules Valles, the nineteenth-century French novelist and journalist.

SIDELIGHTS: Citing French literature as his chief professional activity, Donald Hall told *CA* that "music is a secondary field of great importance to me, as teacher of vocal repertoire, and scholar interested in music's place in intellectual history and its relationships with literature. . . . Fascination with languages has led me to study (apart from French) Spanish, Italian, Portuguese, Latin, Greek, German, Russian, Modern Greek and Japanese."

* * *

HALL, Douglas Kent 1938-

PERSONAL: Born December 12, 1938, in Vernal, Utah; son of C. W. (a carpenter) Hall and Phyllis (Hiatt) Hall Gatzemeyer; married Claire Nicholson (a fashion buyer), June 26, 1960 (divorced, 1972). *Education:* Brigham Young University, B.A., 1960; University of Iowa, M.F.A., 1964.

CAREER: University of Portland, Portland, Ore., instructor in creative writing and literature, 1965-68; free-lance photographer, 1968—.

WRITINGS: (With Sue C. Clark) *Rock: A World Bold as Love,* Cowles, 1970; *On the Way to the Sky,* Saturday Review Press, 1972; *The Superstars in Their Own Words,* Music Sales, 1972; *Let 'er Buck,* Dutton, 1973; *Rock & Roll Retreat Blues,* Avon, 1974; *The Master of Oakwindsor,* Crowell, 1976; *Rodeo,* Ballantine, 1976; *Van People: The Great American Rainbow Boogie,* Crowell, 1977; (with Arnold Schwarzenegger) *Arnold: The Education of a Body Builder,* Simon & Schuster, 1977.

WORK IN PROGRESS: A novel entitled *Inbetween;* a film script; a photographic work on American Indians.†

* * *

HALL, Geraldine M(arion) 1935-

PERSONAL: Born March 24, 1935, in Chicago, Ill.; daughter of Joseph A. (a farmer) and Alice (Geeraerts) Van Mullem; married Bradley J. Hall (a teacher), November 25, 1954; children: James, Philip, Susan, Theresa, Timothy, Jonathan. *Education:* Mount Senario College, B.S., 1967; Northern Arizona University, M.A., 1972. *Religion:* Catholic. *Home:* 613 Camino del Bosque N.W., Albuquerque, N.M. 87114.

CAREER: Taught elementary grades in one-room rural schools in Wisconsin and operated dairy farm with husband, 1956-67; Many Farms School, Chinle, Ariz. (Navajo Indian reservation), music teacher, librarian, and teacher in Title I Reading Clininc, 1967-72; New Mexico State University, Grants Branch, Grants, instructor, 1973-76; Albuquerque Indian School, Albuquerque, N.M., teacher, 1976; Isleta Pueblo Elementary School, Albuquerque, reading specialist and Title I Project director, 1976—. *Awards, honors:* Southern Books Competition award, 1973, for *Kee's Home.*

WRITINGS: Kee's Home (Navajo-English elementary reader), Northland Press, 1971.

WORK IN PROGRESS: Continuing work on series of Navajo-English readers, including *The Trading Post, The Rodeo.*

SIDELIGHTS: Geraldine Hall explains the motivation behind her series of readers: "As a teacher working with Navajo-speaking primary children, I found them much more eager to learn to read when words from their own language were placed before them. They could not relate to ordinary textbooks. As suitable and easy materials were not available, I decided to make some. Many more such books are needed."

* * *

HALL, Mark W. 1943-

PERSONAL: Name legally changed at birth; born June 3, 1943, in Columbia, S.C.; son of George (a professor) and Hannah (Leibner) Hallowitz; married Merryl Martin (a horse breeder), August 27, 1965; children: Tabatha, Woodlad, Pootan. *Education:* College of Marin, A.A., 1963; San Jose State College (now University), B.A., 1965, B.A., 1966; University of Missouri, M.A., 1967. *Politics:* "Independent radical socialist." *Religion:* "Humanist." *Home:* 1296 Howard Dr., Chico, Calif. 95926. *Office:* Department of Mass Communication, Butte College, Box 556, Durham, Calif. 95938.

CAREER: KOMU-TV, Columbia, Mo., reporter, 1967-69; Chico State College (now California State University, Chico), assistant professor of mass communications, 1969-71; Butte College, Durham, Calif., instructor in mass communications, 1971—. Program consultant, Western Telecommunications, Inc.; director, People's Radio Foundation. *Member:* Sigma Delta Chi, Kappa Alpha Mu. *Awards, honors:* National Documentary Writing Award from Sigma Delta Chi, 1969.

WRITINGS: An Introduction to Broadcast Journalism, Hastings House, 1971, 2nd edition published as *Broadcast Journalism: An Introduction to News Writing,* 1977. Contributor of articles to communications journals and to newspapers.

WORK IN PROGRESS: Mass Media in America; research on nuclear fear in cinema, for a chapter in a film textbook.†

* * *

HALL, Martin Hardwick 1925-

PERSONAL: Born August 30, 1925, in Calexico, Calif.; son of Martin Van Buren (a rancher) and Lillian Marie (Hardwick) Hall. *Education:* Attended San Diego State College (now University), 1946; University of New Mexico, B.A., 1950; University of Alabama, M.A., 1951; Louisiana State University, Ph.D., 1957. *Politics:* American Party. *Religion:* Agnostic. *Home:* 1620 Dale Dr., Arlington, Tex. 76010. *Office:* Department of History, University of Texas, Arlington, Tex. 76010.

CAREER: Arkansas Agricultural and Mechanical College (now University of Arkansas at Monticello), Monticello, assistant professor of social science, 1956-57; Arkansas State University, Jonesboro, assistant professor of social science, 1957-58; Louisiana State University in New Orleans, assistant professor of history, 1958-60; McNeese State University, Lake Charles, La., associate professor of history, 1960-64; University of Texas at Arlington, associate professor, 1964-71, professor of history, 1971—. Member of board of directors, Southwestern Historical Wax Museum, Grand Prairie, Tex. *Military service:* U.S. Army, 1943-46; served in Asiatic-Pacific theater.

MEMBER: Organization of American Historians, Southern Historical Association, Western History Association, Texas State Historical Association, Louisiana Historical Association, Arizona Historical Society, El Paso Historical Society, Phi Kappa Phi, Phi Alpha Theta, Alpha Kappa Delta, Pi Gamma Mu, Sons of the Republic of Texas (honorary member).

WRITINGS: Sibley's New Mexico Campaign, University of Texas Press, 1960; (editor with Edwin A. Davis) *Theophilous Noel, A Campaign from Santa Fe to the Mississippi,* Stagecoach Press, 1961; (with Frank E. Vandiver and Homer L. Kerr) *Essays on the American Civil War,* University of Texas Press, 1968; (contributor) Richard N. Ellis, editor, *New Mexico Past and Present: A Historical Reader,* University of New Mexico Press, 1971. Contributor to *Handbook of Texas;* contributor of more than thirty articles and reviews to historical journals. Associate editor, *Journal of Arizona History.*

WORK IN PROGRESS: The Army of New Mexico: Annotated Muster Rolls with Biographical Sketches of Company and Regimental Commanders.

* * *

HALLIBURTON, Warren J.   1924-

PERSONAL: Born August 2, 1924, in New York, N.Y.; son of Richard H. (a book shipping manager) and Blanche (Watson) Halliburton; married Marion Jones, December 20, 1947; married second wife, Frances Fletcher (a teacher), February 11, 1971; children: (first marriage) Cheryl, Stephanie, Warren, Jr., Jena. *Education:* New York University, B.S., 1949; Columbia University, M.Ed., 1975, D.Ed., 1977. *Address:* 90 La Salle St., New York, N.Y. 10027.

CAREER: Prairie View Agricultural and Mechanical College, Prairie View, Tex., instructor in English, 1949; Bishop College, Dallas, Tex., instructor in English, 1951; associate, Institute of International Education, 1952; *Recorder* (newspaper), New York City, reporter and columnist, 1953; teacher and dean in Brooklyn, N.Y. high school, 1958-60; coordinator for New York City Board of Education, and associate of New York State Department of Education, 1960-65; McGraw Hill, Inc., New York City, editor, 1967; Hamilton-Kirkland Colleges, Clinton, N.Y., visiting professor of English, 1971-72; currently editor, research associate, and director of scholarly journal, government program, and Ethnic Studies Center, Teachers College, Columbia University. Free-lance editor and writer. *Military service:* U.S. Army Air Forces, 1943-46.

WRITINGS: (Editor with Mauri E. Pelkonen) *New Worlds of Literature,* Harcourt, 1966; *The Heist* (novel), McGraw, 1969; *Cry, Baby!* (novel), McGraw, 1969; *Some Things that Glitter* (novel), McGraw, 1969; (with William L. Katz) *American Majorities and Minorities: A Syllabus of United States History for Secondary Schools,* Arno, 1970; (with Laurence Swinburne and Steve Broudy) *They Had a Dream,* Pyramid Publications, 1970; (editor and contributor) *America's Color Caravan,* four volumes, Singer Graflex, 1971. Editor of text editions of Jack London's *Call of the Wild,* Douglas Wallop's *The Year the Yankees Lost the Pennant,* and Paddy Chayefsky's *Marty* and *Printer's Measure,* all McGraw, 1968. Contributor of about one hundred short stories, adaptations, and articles to periodicals; writer of fifteen filmstrips and a motion picture, "Dig!"

WORK IN PROGRESS: A biography of Jesse Jackson, for F. Watts; *The History of Black Americans,* for Harcourt; *Harlem: A History of Broken Dreams,* for Doubleday; *Pathways to the World of English,* for Globe; and other writings.

SIDELIGHTS: Warren Halliburton told *CA:* "Writing is a

sanctuary of self-realization, affording me the opportunity for adventure and discovery of my relation with the world. This is a rare if not unique privilege in today's pigeon-holing society." *Avocational interests:* Jogging, a follow-through of his days in track and field competition.

* * *

HALPERN, Daniel   1945-

PERSONAL: Born September 11, 1945, in Syracuse, N.Y.; son of Irving (a scrap dealer) and Rosemary (Glueck) Halpern. *Education:* Columbia University, M.F.A., 1972. *Office:* Ecco Press, 1 West 30th St., New York, N.Y. 10001.

CAREER: Ecco Press, New York City, editor-in-chief, 1969—; New School of Social Research, New York City, instructor in poetry and fiction workshops, 1971-76; Princeton University, Princeton, N.J., instructor in poetry workshops, 1975-76; Columbia University, Graduate School, New York City, instructor in poetry workshops, 1976—. Free-lance editor, Bobbs-Merrill Co. *Awards, honors:* Jessie Rehder Poetry Award, 1971; YMHA Discovery Award; National Endowment for the Arts fellowships; Robert Frost fellowship; Great Lakes Colleges National Book Award.

WRITINGS: Traveling on Credit, Viking, 1972; (co-editor) *Borges on Writing,* Dutton, 1973; (translator with Paula Paley) *Songs of Mririda,* Unicorn Press, 1974; *Street Fire,* Viking, 1975; (editor) *The American Poetry Anthology,* Avon, 1975; *Life Among Others,* Penguin, 1978. Editor, *Antaeus,* 1969—.

* * *

HALS, Ronald M.   1926-

PERSONAL: Born September 4, 1926, in Minneapolis, Minn.; son of Rolf M. (a clerk) and Doris (Nelson) Hals; married Laura Fahrenholz, June 14, 1947; children: Eric, Gary. *Education:* Attended University of California, Berkeley, 1943-44; Capital University, A.B., 1946; Evangelical Lutheran Theological Seminary, B.D., 1950; Hebrew Union College, Ph.D., 1953. *Politics:* Independent. *Home:* 1340 Coburg Rd., Columbus, Ohio 43227. *Office:* Evangelical Lutheran Theological Seminary, 2199 East Main St., Columbus, Ohio 43209.

CAREER: Clergyman of Lutheran Church; St. Luke's Lutheran Church, Toledo, Ohio, pastor, 1954-57; Evangelical Lutheran Theological Seminary, Columbus, Ohio, professor of Biblical theology, 1957—. *Member:* Society of Biblical Literature. *Awards, honors:* Fulbright scholar in Germany, 1953-54; American Association of Theological Schools fellowship, 1962-63; Fredrik A. Schiotz Award, Aid Association for Lutherans, 1970-71.

WRITINGS: The Theology of the Book of Ruth, Fortress, 1969. Contributor to theology journals.

* * *

HALSALL, Elizabeth   1916-

PERSONAL: Surname is pronounced Hol-sel; born December 29, 1916, in Dalton-in-Furness, Lancashire, England; daughter of Thomas (an engineer) and Anne Halsall. *Education:* Oxford University, B.A. (second class honors), 1938, Diploma in Education, 1939; University of London, Ph.D., 1963. *Religion:* Roman Catholic. *Home:* Cottage, Ferry Rd., Wawne, Hull, England. *Office:* Institute of Education, University of Hull, Hull, England.

CAREER: Teacher in various schools in England as assistant and as head of department, 1939-55; St. Gregory's Comprehensive School, Kirkby, England, deputy head, 1959-64; University of Hull, Hull, England, lecturer in comparative education, 1964—. *Member:* Comparative Education Society of Europe, Comparative Education Society of Great Britain (member of executive committee, 1964-66), Modern Language Association (member of national council, 1951-55).

WRITINGS: French as a Second Language: Levels of Attainment in Three Countries, Institute of Education, University of Hull, 1968; (contributor) H. J. Noah and Max A. Eckstein, editors, *Scientific Studies in Comparative Education,* Macmillan, 1969; (editor) *Becoming Comprehensive: Case Histories,* Pergamon, 1970; *The Comprehensive School: Guidelines for the Reorganization of Secondary Education,* Pergamon, 1973. Contributor to language and education journals.

WORK IN PROGRESS: A bibliography of modern language teaching textbooks published in selected countries of western Europe up to 1800; a study of modern language teaching methods in Netherlands, Belgium, and Denmark.

* * *

HAMILTON, Dorothy 1906-

PERSONAL: Born September 25, 1906, in Selma, Ind.; daughter of Garry C. (a farmer) and Mary (Bartle) Drumm; married Harry D. Hamilton (a farmer), September 29, 1927; children: Dale, Kathryn (Mrs. Malcolm Julian), Carolyn (Mrs. Bill Necessary), Lois (Mrs. Leonard Benson), Stephen, Frances (Mrs. John Parkison), David. *Education:* Attended Ball State University, 1925-27, and correspondence courses at Indiana University, 1961, 1965, writing courses at Writer's Digest Schools. *Home address:* R.R. 1, Box 351, Selma, Ind. 47383.

CAREER: Liberty-Perry School Corp., Selma, Ind., private tutor, 1964—. Teacher of writing classes for Young Women's Christian Association in Muncie, Ind. and community education programs of Muncie Community Schools; member of executive committee, teacher, and co-director of Midwest Writers' Workshop, Ball State University. *Member:* Women in Communications, Delta Kappa Gamma.

WRITINGS—Young people's books; published by Herald Press: *Anita's Choice,* 1971; *Charco,* 1971; *Christmas for Holly,* 1971; *Tony Savala,* 1972; *Jim Musco, Delaware Indian,* 1972; *The Blue Caboose,* 1972; *Kerry,* 1973; *Mindy,* 1973; *Jason,* 1974; *Gift of a Home,* 1974; *Busboys at Big Bend,* 1974; *Cricket,* 1975; *Neva's Patchwork Pillow,* 1975; *The Castle,* 1975; *Linda's Raintree,* 1975; *Winter Girl,* 1976; *Straight Mark,* 1976; *Rosalie,* 1977.

Other; published by Herald Press: *The Killdeer,* 1972; *Settled Furrows,* 1972; *The Quail,* 1973; *The Eagle,* 1974.

WORK IN PROGRESS: Mary Jane: A Bound Girl; Daniel Forbes: Frontier Boy; Maris Mountain; Rosalie at Eleven; Bittersweet Days.

SIDELIGHTS: Dorothy Hamilton published her first book at the age of 65. She told *CA:* "In a TV interview I was asked, 'How do you account for the late blooming of your writing career?' My answer was 'Prayer, persistence and the resolve to work to attain a professional attitude.' My urge to write was inborn. My material is people and a kind of total immersion in my setting. My goal is to make each book better than the one before."

HAMILTON, Franklin Willard 1923-

PERSONAL: Born November 22, 1923, in Benton, Ill.; son of James A. (a mail carrier) and Georgia B. (Dowell) Hamilton; married Betty Jean Spellmeyer (a registered nurse), September 29, 1956; children: Douglas James, Karen Joyce. *Education:* Southern Illinois University, B.A., 1949, M.A., 1949; Kansas State Teachers College, M.S., 1955; University of Kansas, Ed.D., 1961; also studied at Washington University, St. Louis, University of Illinois, Western Kentucky University, State University of Iowa, and St. Louis University. *Religion:* Methodist. *Residence:* Flint, Mich. *Office:* Walden Press, 423 South Franklin Ave., Flint, Mich. 48503.

CAREER: English instructor at Hiwassee College, Madisonville, Tenn., 1951-52, College of Emporia, Emporia, Kan., 1953-55, Illinois State University, Normal, 1955, and University of Kansas, Lawrence, 1960-61; Genesee Community College, Flint, Mich., instructor in English, 1956—. Editor, Walden Press, Flint. Journalist. *Member:* National Council of Teachers of English.

WRITINGS: Leaf Scar (poetry), Brookside Press, 1965; *Thoreau on the Art of Writing* (literary criticism), Walden Press, 1967; *Love Cry* (poetry), Brookside Press, 1970. Contributor of poetry to numerous periodicals, including *American Bard, Poetry and Drama Magazine, Odyssey, Saturday Review, Pegasus, Artesian, New Athenaeum, Trace, College English, Cardinal Poetry Quarterly, Bitterroot,* and *Manhattan Review.*

AVOCATIONAL INTERESTS: Youth hockey, Boy and Girl Scouting, camping, fishing, stamp and coin collecting, and collecting little magazines.

* * *

HAMILTON, Henry W. 1898-

PERSONAL: Born June 11, 1898, in Fulton, Mo.; son of George Wilson (a farmer) and Anna (Heuermann) Hamilton; married Jean Tyree, February 24, 1940; children: James Tyree, Anne. *Education:* Attended Westminster College, Fulton, Mo., 1917-18; University of Missouri, B.S., 1922. *Politics:* Democrat. *Home:* 537 East Eastwood, Marshall, Mo. 65340.

CAREER: American Friends Service Committee, rehabilitation worker in Russia, Poland, and Germany, 1923-24; University of Missouri, Columbia, agricultural extension agent, 1927-42; Wood & Huston Bank, Marshall, Mo., agricultural representative, 1942-58, vice-president, 1946-58; grain farmer in Marshall, 1958—. Past president, Vanmeter District Levee; secretary of committee for recovery of archaeological remains, National Park Service, 1958—; chairman of advisory council, Missouri State Park Board, 1966—.

MEMBER: Society for American Archaeology, Missouri Archaeological Society (president, 1958—), Iowa Archaeological Society, Arkansas Archaeological Society, Oklahoma Anthropological Society, Manitoba Archaeological Society, State Historical Society of Missouri, Montana Historical Society, Nebraska Historical Society, South Dakota Historical Society, Alpha Gamma Rho, Gamma Sigma Delta, Epsilon Sigma Rho. *Awards, honors:* Distinguished service award, Missouri Archaeological Society, 1952; distinguished service award in agriculture, Gamma Sigma Delta, 1961; University of Missouri's Hamilton Field School of Archaeology was named in honor of Hamilton and his brother in 1965.

WRITINGS: The Spiro Mound, Missouri Archaeological Society, 1952; Tobacco Pines of the Missouri Indians, Missouri Archaeological Society, 1967; (with wife, Jean Tyree Hamilton) Remington Schuyler: Artist and Writer, Missouri Historical Society, 1969; (with J. T. Hamilton) The Sioux of the Rosebud, University of Oklahoma Press, 1971; (with J. T. Hamilton) Clay Pipes from Pamplin, Missouri Archaeological Society, 1972; (with J. T. Hamilton and Eleanor F. Chapman) Spiro Mound Copper, Missouri Archaeological Society, 1974. Contributor of articles to history, anthropology, and archaeology journals.

WORK IN PROGRESS: Remington Schuyler: His Life and His Work; with J. T. Hamilton, Alfred Montgomery: Itinerant Artist, 1857-1922, and Fruit Drying: A Forgotten Facet of Missouri History; a book based on Hamilton's own experiences, Housing and Agricultural Reconstruction in White Russia after World War I.

SIDELIGHTS: Henry Hamilton told CA: "Writing is work, but it is also a lot of fun. Both my wife, Jean Tyree Hamilton, and I never look for things to write about, they simply present themselves. We do not write for a financial return. We write because we feel that certain things should be down in the written record, before the information is lost."

*   *   *

HAMILTON, Jean Tyree 1909-

PERSONAL: Born June 6, 1909, in Lexington, Mo.; daughter of Clement (a farmer) and Maude (Duncan) Tyree; married Henry W. Hamilton (a farmer), February 24, 1940; children: James Tyree, Anne. Education: Christian College (now Columbia College), Columbia, Mo., A.A., 1929; University of Missouri, B.S., 1932. Politics: Democrat. Religion: Christian. Home: 537 East Eastwood, Marshall, Mo. 65340.

CAREER: Former secretary. Lafayette County, Mo., deputy assessor, 1932-36, treasurer, 1936-40; Saline County American Red Cross, chairman of Women's Division, 1954; Saline County Lewis & Clark Commission, chairman, 1967—. Member of Governor's Council on Natural Beauty; chairman, Sites House Restoration Committee. Member: Daughters of the American Revolution (past regent of Marshall chapter), Colonial Dames of America, National Trust for Historic Preservation, Missouri Museums Association, Friends of Arrow Rock, Inc. (vice-president).

WRITINGS: Arrow Rock, Where Wheels Started West, American Press (Columbia, Mo.), 1963; (with husband, Henry W. Hamilton) Remington Schuyler: Artist and Writer, Missouri Historical Society, 1969; (with H. W. Hamilton) The Sioux of the Rosebud, University of Oklahoma Press, 1971; Abel Vanmeter: His Park and His Diary, Missouri Historical Society, 1971; (with H. W. Hamilton) Clay Pipes from Pamplin, Missouri Archaeological Society, 1972; (with H. W. Hamilton and Eleanor F. Chapman) Spiro Mound Copper, Missouri Archaeological Society, 1974. Contributor to Missouri history journals. Also author of radio scripts for "Museum Hour," a program presented by KXTR-FM Radio, Independence, Mo.

WORK IN PROGRESS: L. M. Hardin: Physician to the Sioux; Col. Charles P. Jordan: Showman Extraordinary; Mr. Bingham's Tombstone; editing Early Days in Cherry County, by Alma Carlson Roosa; with H. W. Hamilton, Alfred Montgomery: Itinerant Artist, 1857-1922, and Fruit Drying: A Forgotten Facet of Missouri History.

BIOGRAPHICAL/CRITICAL SOURCES: Jack D. Rittenhouse, The Santa Fe Trail: A Historical Bibliography, University of New Mexico Press, 1971.

*   *   *

HAMMERMAN, Gay M(orenus) 1926-

PERSONAL: Born May 14, 1926, in Richmond, Va.; daughter of Richard Thomas (an architect) and Constance (Gay) Morenus; married Herbert Hammerman (an economist), September 3, 1955; children: Joseph Richard, Daniel Aaron. Education: Attended Women's College of the University of North Carolina (now University of North Carolina at Greensboro), 1943-45; University of North Carolina at Chapel Hill, A.B., 1947; Radcliffe College, M.A., 1949. Politics: Democrat. Residence: Arlington, Va. Office address: Historical Evaluation & Research Organization, P.O. Box 157, Dunn Loring, Va. 22027.

CAREER: Mount Vernon Seminary and Junior College, Washington, D.C., teacher of history and government, 1949-51; U.S. Department of Defense, Department of the Army, Office of the Chief of Military History, Washington, D.C., 1951-55, began as copy editor, became editor and indexer; U.S. Department of State, Washington, D.C., editor, 1955-57; Historical Evaluation & Research Organization (HERO), Dunn Loring, Va., writer and editor, 1963—. Member: Phi Beta Kappa.

WRITINGS: (Contributor) Trevor Nevitt Dupuy, editor, Holidays: Days of Significance for All Americans, F. Watts, 1965; (with Dupuy) The Military History of World War I, Volume III: Stalemate in the Trenches: November 1914-March 1918, F. Watts, 1967; (contributor) Dupuy, editor, The Almanac of World Military Power, T. N. Dupuy Associates, in association with Stackpole, 1970; (with Dupuy) The Military History of Revolutionary War Land Battles (juvenile), F. Watts, 1970; (editor with Dupuy) A Documentary History of Arms Control and Disarmament, Bowker, 1973; (with Dupuy) People and Events of the American Revolution, Bowker, 1974; (with R. Ernest Dupuy and Grace P. Hayes) The American Revolution: A Global War, McKay, 1977. Editor, History, Numbers, and War.

WORK IN PROGRESS: A personal journal.

SIDELIGHTS: Leo Schwarzkopf describes A Documentary History of Arms Control and Disarmament as "a useful, compact reference book that provides in one volume the text and historical background of the most significant documents on arms control and disarmament throughout world history. The excellent commentary and analysis enhance the value of this work, but the lack of a subject index somewhat limits its usefulness."

Gay Hammerman writes: "Somehow I became a military historian, something I never would have chosen. War is a central human experience, however, and writing about it is sometimes very moving. . . . In the past three years, I have gone back to dance very seriously. It is something that has been important to me since childhood. Because I didn't excel at it, I was never willing to risk giving it a high priority in my life, but for the past twenty years, off and on, it has been my chief creative recreation. I have studied with Erika Thimey and other Washington dancers, and have studied dance therapy at George Washington University and the Effort/Shape system of body movement analysis at American University."

AVOCATIONAL INTERESTS: Modern dance, improvisational theater.

BIOGRAPHICAL/CRITICAL SOURCES: American Reference Books Annual, sixth edition, 1975; *Saturday Review,* May 17, 1975.

* * *

HAMMOND, Ross W(illiam) 1918-

PERSONAL: Born March 20, 1918, in New York, N.Y.; son of Elsie (Richards) Hammond; married Faye Keith, May 5, 1946. *Education:* University of Texas, B.S., 1951, M.S., 1952. *Politics:* Republican. *Religion:* Presbyterian. *Home:* 1571 Rochelle Ct., Atlanta, Ga. 30341. *Office:* Office of International Programs, Georgia Institute of Technology, Atlanta, Ga. 30332.

CAREER: Texas Electric Service Co., Fort Worth, area development engineer, 1952-60; Lubbock Chamber of Commerce, Lubbock, Tex., industrial manager, 1960-61; Georgia Institute of Technology, Atlanta, chief of industrial development division, 1961-62; American Institute of Industrial Engineers, New York, N.Y., executive director, 1962-63; Georgia Institute of Technology, chief of industrial development division, 1965-77, director, Office of International Programs, 1977—. Partner, Development Research Services (consultants). Chairman, Governor's Committee on Housing in Georgia, 1970. *Military service:* U.S. Army Air Forces, 1943-46; became lieutenant. *Member:* American Institute of Industrial Engineers (president, 1966-67), Southern Industrial Development Council, Georgia Industrial Developers Association (president, 1967), Tau Beta Pi, Eta Kappa Nu.

WRITINGS: Your Career in Industrial Engineering, Rosen Press, 1964; (contributor) H. B. Maynard, editor, *Handbook of Modern Manufacturing Management,* McGraw, 1970; (contributor) W. H. Shabacker, R. S. Clark, and H. C. Cooper, editors, *Focus on the Future of Georgia,* Georgia Department of Education, 1970; (contributor) Maynard, editor, *Handbook of Industrial Engineering,* McGraw, 1971; *Economic Development Trends in the Sixteen-State South,* Georgia Institute of Technology, 1972.

AVOCATIONAL INTERESTS: Model railroads, photography.

* * *

HAMPDEN-TURNER, Charles M. 1934-

PERSONAL: Born September 29, 1934, in London, England; son of Charles (a soldier) and Eleanor (Clark) Hampden-Turner; married Marion Shelley (an architect), May 6, 1966; children: Charles Michael. *Education:* Trinity College, Cambridge, B.A., 1957, M.B.A., 1963; Harvard University, D.B.A., 1967. *Politics:* Radical. *Religion:* Agnostic. *Home:* 1435 Arch St., Berkeley, Calif. 94708. *Agent:* Sterling Lord Agency, 660 Madison Ave., New York, N.Y. 10021. *Office:* Wright Institute, 2728 Durant Ave., Berkeley, Calif. 94704.

CAREER: Visiting lecturer at Laboratory for Community Psychiatry, Harvard Medical School, Boston, Mass., and at Kennedy Institute of Politics, Harvard Universy, Cambridge, Mass., 1967-69 Cambridge, fellow, 1969-75; Wright Institute, Berkeley Calif., director, 1975—. *Member:* Association of Humanistic Psychology (president, 1977). *Awards, honors:* Douglas McGregor Award, National Training Laboratories, 1966, for article, "Existential Learning Theory," in *Journal of Applied Behavioral Science;* Guggenheim fellowship, 1972.

WRITINGS: (Contributor) Richard S. Rosenbloom and Robin Maris, editors, *Social Innovation in the City,* Harvard University Press, 1969; (contributor) Paul R. Lawrence and J. W. Lorsch, editors, *Studies in Organizational Design,* Irwin, 1970; *Radical Man: The Process of Psycho-Social Development,* Schenkman, 1970; *A Strategy for Poor Americans,* Doubleday, 1973; *Sane Asylum: Inside the Delancey Street Foundation,* Morrow, 1977.

WORK IN PROGRESS: Gentlemen and Tradesmen, for Routledge & Kegan Paul.

* * *

HAMPTON, H(arold) Duane 1932-

PERSONAL: Born June 21, 1932, in Walden, Colo.; married Suzanne Galloway, June 11, 1961; children: Andrew, Wade, Mathew. *Education:* University of Colorado, B.A., 1959, M.A., 1961, Ph.D., 1965. *Office:* Department of History, University of Montana, Missoula, Mont. 59801.

CAREER: Ohio State University, Columbus, instructor in history, 1964-65; University of Montana, Missoula, associate professor of history, 1965—. Consultant, VISTA. *Military service:* U.S. Army, 1954-56. *Member:* American Historical Association, Organization of American Historians, Western History Association. *Awards, honors:* National Endowment for the Humanities grant, 1970.

WRITINGS: How the U.S. Army Saved the National Parks, Indiana University Press, 1971. Contributor of articles to *Montana Western History, Colorado, Forest History,* and of articles and reviews to *New Mexico Historical Review* and *Arizona Historical Review.*

WORK IN PROGRESS: A biography of George Bird Grinnell.

* * *

HAMPTON, Robert E. 1924-

PERSONAL: Born July 26, 1924, in Oakland, Calif.; son of Edwin Muir (an engineer) and Edith (Diehl) Hampton; married Claire L. Oliveira, September 3, 1948. *Education:* Golden Gate College (now University), B.B.A., 1949; Chico State College (now California State University, Chico), M.A., 1951; Stanford University, Ed.D., 1961. *Politics:* Republican. *Religion:* Methodist. *Home:* 2526 West Scott, Fresno, Calif. 93705. *Office:* Business School, California State University, Fresno, Calif. 93726.

CAREER: Santa Rosa Junior College, Santa Rosa, Calif., head of Business Division, 1953-56; California State University, Fresno, assistant professor, 1956-60, associate professor, 1961-66, professor of marketing and assistant dean of Business School, 1967—. *Military service:* U.S. Army, 1943-46. *Member:* American Academy of Advertising, Sales and Marketing Executives, California Teachers Association, Beta Gamma Sigma (national secretary), Delta Pi Epsilon. *Awards, honors:* Named top faculty adviser (nationally) by Pi Sigma Epsilon, 1969; Direct Mail Advertising Association fellowships, 1967, 1969.

WRITINGS: (Contributor) *Principles of Retailing,* Pitman, 1955; (with J. B. Zabin) *College Salesmanship,* McGraw, 1970. Contributor to National Business Education Association *Yearbook,* 1966.

* * *

HAMPTON, William (Albert) 1929-

PERSONAL: Born July 26, 1929, in London, England; son of William John (a printer) and Sarah (Edwards) Hampton;

married Hazel Starling (a teacher), December 29, 1951; children: Joseph, Sarah. *Education:* London School of Economics and Political Science, B.Sc. (first class honors), 1963; University of Sheffield, Ph.D., 1970. *Politics:* Labour Party. *Religion:* None. *Home:* 26 Meadow Bank Ave., Sheffield S71PB, England. *Office:* Department of Extramural Studies, University of Sheffield, Sheffield S10 29S, England.

CAREER: Compositor in printing industry in Colchester, England, 1944-60; University of Sheffield, Department of Extramural Studies, Sheffield, England, assistant lecturer, 1963-64, lecturer, 1964-70, senior lecturer in politics, 1970—, research coordinator in department of environment, 1973-77. *Military service:* British Army, 1947-49. *Member:* Political Studies Association, Society for the Study of Labour History, Society of Industrial Tutors, Association of University Teachers. *Awards, honors:* Imperial Relations Trust grant to study social work teaching in Australia and New Zealand, 1972.

WRITINGS: Democracy and Community: A Study of Politics in Sheffield, Oxford University Press, 1970; (contributor) J. T. Coppock and W. R. D. Sewell, editors, *Public Participation in Planning,* Wiley, 1977; (contributor) George Jones and Alan Norton, editors, *Leadership in Local Government,* Knight, 1978. Contributor to political science and social policy journals. Member of editorial advisory committee, *Politics and Policy.*

WORK IN PROGRESS: Planning and Participation in Practice, with Noel Boaden, Michael Goldsmith, and Peter Stringer.

*   *   *

HANCHETT, William 1922-

PERSONAL: Born May 25, 1922, in Evanston, Ill.; son of William F. (a businessman) and Alice (Trowbridge) Hanchett; married Jean Forster, September 30, 1945 (divorced 1970); married Elizabeth Riddle (a French professor), September 5, 1970 (divorced 1975); children: (first marriage) Thomas, Emily. *Education:* Attended Black Mountain College, 1941-42, and Roosevelt University, 1946-47; Southern Methodist University, B.A., 1948; University of California, Berkeley, M.A., 1949, Ph.D., 1952. *Home:* 3515 State St., San Diego, Calif. 92103. *Office:* Department of History, San Diego State University, San Diego, Calif. 92115.

CAREER: Historian with United States Air Force, 1952-54; University of Colorado, Boulder, acting assistant professor of U.S. history, 1954-55; Colorado State University, Fort Collins, assistant professor of history, 1955-56; San Diego State University, San Diego, Calif., associate professor, 1956-65, professor of history, 1965—. *Military service:* U.S. Army Air Forces, 1942-45; became lieutenant. *Member:* American Historical Association, Organization of American Historians.

WRITINGS: (Editor with Richard T. Ruetten) *Transformation of America,* W. C. Brown, 1963; *Irish: Charles G. Halpine in Civil War America,* Syracuse University Press, 1970.

WORK IN PROGRESS: Research on Abraham Lindoln; a book, *The Literature of Lincoln's Assassination.*

*   *   *

HANCOCK, M. Donald 1939-

PERSONAL: Born August 20, 1939, in McAllen, Tex.; son of Robert Nicklas and Florence (Nordquest) Hancock; mar-

ried Kay Lorans (an editor), May 29, 1965; children: Erik, Kendra. *Education:* Attended University of Bonn, 1959-60; University of Texas, B.A., 1961; Columbia University, M.A., 1962, Ph.D., 1966; University of Stockholm, graduate study, 1963-64. *Office:* Department of Government, University of Texas, Austin, Tex. 78712.

CAREER: Columbia University, New York, N.Y., instructor in government, spring, 1965; University of Texas at Austin, assistant professor, 1965-69, associate professor, 1969-75, professor of government, 1975—, associate dean of college of social and behavioral sciences, 1976—. *Member:* American Political Science Association, Society for the Advancement of Scandinavian Studies, Southwest Social Science Association, Phi Beta Kappa. *Awards, honors:* Council on Foreign Relations international fellow, 1972.

WRITINGS: (Editor with Dankwart A. Rostow) *American Foreign Policy in International Perspective,* Prentice-Hall, 1971; (editor with Herbert Hirsch) *Comparative Legislative Systems,* Free Press, 1971; (editor with Gideon Sjoberg, and contributor) *Politics in the Post-Welfare State: Responses to the New Individualism,* Columbia University Press, 1972; *Sweden: The Politics of Postindustrial Change,* Holt, 1972. Contributor of articles on Sweden and Germany to periodicals.

WORK IN PROGRESS: A book on West German politics; a comparative study on the public sector in Sweden and West Germany.

*   *   *

HANDLER, Philip 1917-

PERSONAL: Born August 13, 1917, in New York, N.Y.; son of Jacob and Lena (Heisen) Handler; married Lucille Marcus, 1939; children: Mark, Eric Paul. *Education:* City College (now City College of the City University of New York), B.S., 1936; University of Illinois, Ph.D., 1939. *Office:* National Academy of Sciences, 2101 Constitution Ave. N.W., Washington, D.C. 20418.

CAREER: U.S. Department of Agriculture, junior chemist at Regional Soybean By-products Laboratory, 1937-39; Duke University, School of Medicine, Durham, N.C., instructor, 1939-42, assistant professor of physiology and nutrition, 1942-45, associate professor, 1945-50, professor of biochemistry, 1950-61, James B. Duke Professor of Biochemistry, 1961—, chairman of department of biochemistry, 1950-69, on extended leave, 1969—; National Academy of Sciences, Washington, D.C., president, 1969—. National Institutes of Health, member of biochemistry study section, 1953-58, chairman, 1956-58, chairman of advisory committee on radiation and aging, 1957-61, member of national advisory council on research resources and facilities, 1963-67; National Science Foundation, member of national science board, 1962-72, chairman, 1966-70; member, President Nixon's Task Force on Science Policy, 1969-70; member of council, Smithsonian Institution, 1969-74; member of corporation, Woods Hole Oceanographic Institution, 1970—. Member of visiting committees for universities, including Johns Hopkins University, 1964-69, University of Notre Dame, 1964, and Yale University, 1968; member of board of governors, Hebrew University of Jerusalem, 1969—; member of board of trustees, Rockefeller Foundation, 1971. Aharon Katzir Memorial Lecturer, Jerusalem, 1973.

MEMBER: American Academy of Arts and Sciences (fellow), American Association for the Advancement of Science (fellow), American Chemical Society, American Institute of Biological Sciences, American Institute of Nutrition,

American Philosophical Society, American Society of Biological Chemists (president, 1962-63), Biochemical Society (Great Britain), Federation of American Societies for Experimental Biology (member of board, 1953-66; chairman, 1959-65), Foundation for Advancement of the Sciences, German Academy of Natural Sciences, Japanese Biochemical Society, National Academy of Medicine of Mexico, Swiss Academy of Natural Sciences, Royal Society for the Encouragement of Arts, Manufacture and Commerce, International Union of Biochemistry, Society of Experimental Biology and Medicine, Society of Naval Architects and Marine Engineers, New York Academy of Sciences (honorary life member).

AWARDS, HONORS: C. B. Mayer Award of New York Academy of Medicine, 1943; Townsend Harris Medal of City College, New York, N.Y., 1964; American Medical Association Annual Award for distinguished contributions to medical science, 1969; North Carolina Award for Science, 1970; Alumni Association Achievement Award from University of Illinois, 1972. D.Sc. from Case Western Reserve University, 1968, Colorado State University and Carnegie-Mellon University, 1970, University of North Carolina, Yeshiva University, and New York Medical College, 1971, Temple University and Medical College of Wisconsin, 1972, George Washington University and Hahnemann Medical College, 1973, Michigan State University, 1975, Polytechnic Institute of New York, 1976, University of Alaska, Butler University, and Southwestern at Memphis, 1977; LL.D., Emory University, 1969, City College of the City University of New York, 1972; Ph.D., Hebrew University of Jerusalem, 1971; Litt.D., Nova University, 1972; L.H.D., Florida State University, 1975.

WRITINGS: (With Abraham White and Emil L. Smith) *Principles of Biochemistry*, McGraw, 1954, 5th edition, 1973; (editor) *Biology and the Future of Man*, Oxford University Press, 1970. Contributor of about two hundred articles to professional journals.

WORK IN PROGRESS: With Abraham White, Robert Lehman, and Emil L. Smith, 6th edition of *Principles of Biochemistry*, for McGraw.

* * *

HANSEN, Donald Charles 1935-

PERSONAL: Born July 14, 1935, in Presque Isle, Me.; son of Daniel Emil (a clerk) and Blanche (Stevenson) Hansen; married Jill McAnney, May 2, 1959; children: Burnett, Wells. *Education:* Boston University, B.S., 1957; Syracuse University, additional study, 1967-69. *Politics:* Independent. *Religion:* Episcopalian. *Home:* Prince's Point, Yarmouth, Me. 04096. *Agent:* Harold Ober Associates, Inc., 40 East 49th St., New York, N.Y. 10017. *Office:* Guy Gannett Publishing Co., Congress St., Portland, Me. 04111.

CAREER: Guy Gannett Publishing Co., Portland, Me., political writer, 1961-73, editorial pages director, 1974—. *Member:* Sigma Delta Chi. *Awards, honors:* American Political Science Association fellowship, 1967.

WRITINGS: (With Theo Lippman, Jr.) *Muskie*, Norton, 1971.

* * *

HANSON, Joan 1938-

PERSONAL: Born June 25, 1938, in Appleton, Wis.; daughter of Jack Ray (a dentist) and Jeanne (Glennon) Benton; married Dale Hanson (a banker), July 15, 1961; chil-

dren: Tucker, Timmy. *Education:* Carleton College, B.A., 1960. *Home:* 15707 Afton Hills, Afton, Minn. 55043.

CAREER: New England Deaconess Hospital, Boston, Mass., laboratory technician, 1960-62; University of Minnesota, Medical School, Minneapolis, cancer research laboratory technician, 1963-66; writer and illustrator of children's books.

WRITINGS—Self-illustrated: *The Monster's Nose Was Cold*, Carolrhoda, 1970; *I Don't Like Timmy*, Carolrhoda, 1971; *Alfred Snood*, Putnam, 1972; *I Won't Be Afraid*, Lerner, 1974; *I'm Going to Run Away*, Platt, 1976.

"Joan Hanson Word Books" series; published by Lerner: *Homonyms*, 1972; *Homographs*, 1972; *Antonyms*, 1972; *Synonyms*, 1972; *British-American Synonyms*, 1972; *More Synonyms*, 1973; *More Antonyms*, 1973; *Homographic Homophones*, 1973; *More Homonyms*, 1973; *Similes*, 1976; *Sound Words*, 1976; *Still More Antonyms*, 1976; *Still More Homonyms*, in press.

Illustrator: Gloria Patrick, *This Is . . .*, Carolrhoda, 1969; Eve Holmquist, *The Giant Giraffe*, Carolrhoda, 1973.

WORK IN PROGRESS: Still More Synonyms, for Lerner.

* * *

HANSTEN, Philip D. 1943-

PERSONAL: Born August 21, 1943, in Chicago, Ill.; son of Herman W. (a teacher) and Cecile (Dusenbury) Hansten; married Martha Kay Dow, September 12, 1964; children: Michelle, Christopher, Martin. *Education:* Attended Modesto Junior College, 1961-63; University of California, Pharm.D., 1968. *Politics:* Independent. *Religion:* Episcopalian. *Home:* 790 Meadow Vale, Pullman, Wash. 99163. *Office:* College of Pharmacy, Washington State University, Pullman, Wash. 99163.

CAREER: University of California, San Francisco, assistant professor of clinical pharmacy, 1968-70; Washington State University, Pullman, assistant professor, 1970-76, associate professor of clinical pharmacy, 1976—. Director of drug information center, Alta Bates Hospital, 1968-70. *Member:* American College of Clinical Pharmacology, American Society of Hospital Pharmacists, American Association of Colleges of Pharmacy, Washington State Pharmaceutical Association.

WRITINGS: Drug Interactions, Lea & Febiger, 1971.

SIDELIGHTS: Drug Interactions has been translated into Japanese, German, and Spanish.

* * *

HARBERT, Earl N(orman) 1934-

PERSONAL: Born April 1, 1934, in Cleveland, Ohio; son of Elmer William and Elsie (Francis) Harbert; married Ellen Mayo, May 24, 1971. *Education:* Hamilton College, A.B., 1956; Johns Hopkins University, M.A., 1961; University of Wisconsin, Ph.D., 1966. *Home:* 67 Glenwood Ave., Harahan, La. 70123. *Office:* Department of English, Tulane University, New Orleans, La. 70118.

CAREER: George Washington University, Washington, D.C., instructor in English, 1961-62; Tulane University, New Orleans, La., 1966—, began as associate professor, currently professor of English. Fulbright-Hays lecturer, 1967-68. *Military service:* U.S. Navy, 1957-60; became lieutenant. *Member:* Modern Language Association of America. *Awards, honors:* American Philosophical Society research grant, 1972; Kellogg Essay Prize from Hamilton College.

WRITINGS: (Editor with Robert A. Rees) *Fifteen American Authors before 1900,* University of Wisconsin Press, 1971; *The Force So Much Closer Home: Henry Adams and the Adams Family,* New York University Press, 1977; *Henry Adams: A Reference Guide,* G. K. Hall, 1977. Also author of *John T. Hayward: Creative Engineer.* Contributor to *American Literature, Journal of American Studies, Tulane Studies in English,* and other publications.

* * *

HARDIE, Frank 1911-

PERSONAL: Born June 14, 1911, in London, England; son of Martin and Madeline (Pattisson) Hardie; married Gertrude Alman, March 6, 1957. *Education:* Attended Westminster School, London, England, 1925-29; Christ Church, Oxford, M.A., 1933; Merton College, Oxford, D.Phil., 1937. *Politics:* Social Democrat. *Religion:* "Of all men of sense." *Home and office:* 18 Kensington Gate, London W.8, England.

CAREER: Hardie taught briefly before World War II, then worked in industry, mainly steel; he retired in 1964 to resume historical writing.

WRITINGS: *The Political Influence of Queen Victoria, 1861-1901,* Oxford University Press, 1935, 2nd edition, 1938, reprinted, Cass & Co., 1963; *The Political Influence of the British Monarchy, 1868-1952,* Harper, 1970; *The Aryssinian Crisis,* Archon Books, 1974; (editor) *The Prints of Martin Hardie,* Ashmolean Museum, 1975. Contributor to *Dictionary of National Biography;* contributor of articles and reviews to periodicals.

WORK IN PROGRESS: *Britain and Zion: The Fateful Entanglement,* with Irwin Herrman.

SIDELIGHTS: Frank Hardie told *CA:* "A writer sentences himself to long terms of solitary confinement and exceptionally hard labour. Why? I can think of only two reasons: to make money, or because he feels that there is something he *must* say, some aspect of truth he must put on the record before he passes away. Good luck to the money-makers, and Valiant-for-Truth is by no means above making money, but that is the least part of his reward. Both types of writer no doubt share one satisfaction, doing the job, whatever it is, well, but the only real reward of the writer whose arduous efforts are aimed at giving others a piece of his mind is to be made aware of readers who appreciate the proferred gift at its full value—which does not necessarily mean accepting every bit of it!"

* * *

HARDIMAN, James W. 1919-

PERSONAL: Born July 10, 1919, in Brighton, England; son of James Michael (a showman) and Emily (Rolfe) Hardiman; married Anneliese Huttig, February 11, 1956; children: Joan, Donna, Donald, Roy, Scott, James W., Jr. *Education:* Attended University of Toronto. *Religion:* Nichiren (Japan Buddhist).

CAREER: J. Arthur Rank Organisation of Canada, Toronto, Ontario, director of advertising and publicity, 1947-56; National Theatres, Inc., Los Angeles, Calif., assistant director of advertising and publicity, 1956-58; Columbia Broadcasting System Television Network, Los Angeles, manager of special promotions, 1958-59, Hollywood, Calif., director of press information, 1964-67; Walt Disney Productions, Burbank, Calif., director of radio and television, 1959-60; Screen Gems, Inc., Hollywood, director of publicity,

1960-64, studio director of publicity and promotions, 1967-70; Sijojano Enterprises, Inc., Tokyo, Japan, vice-president and director, 1970-71; UNI Public Relations Corp., Tokyo, Japan, managing director of international department, beginning 1972. Member, Los Angeles Chamber of Commerce. *Military service:* Canadian Army, 1939-45; became major. U.S. Marine Corps Reserve; became major.

MEMBER: Screen Publicists Guild, Los Angeles Press Club, Hollywood Press Club. *Awards, honors:* Three Quigley Awards and four box office blue ribbons from Quigley Publications, 1948-51; named Champion Showman of Odeon Theatres of Canada by *Box Office Magazine,* 1950; named Hollywood Showman of the Year by Screen Publicists Guild, 1968.

WRITINGS—Published by Hammond, Inc., except as indicated: *Windjammer,* Random House, 1958; *The Big Fisherman,* Random House, 1960; *The Crowning Experience,* Random House, 1962; (with Charles E. Cochard) *Japan,* 1971; (with Cochard) *South East Asia,* 1971; (with Cochard) *Mexico,* 1971; (with Cochard) *Tahiti,* 1972; (with Cochard) *The Orient,* 1972; (with Cochard) *Hawaii,* 1972.

Also author of screenplays "Crashout," and "OZ."

Contributor to numerous magazines and newspapers. Editor, *Aldershot News, Odeonews.* CBS war correspondent in South Viet Nam, 1965; war correspondent, *Los Angeles Herald-Examiner* and *Denver Post,* South Viet Nam, 1966.††

* * *

HARDING, James 1929-

PERSONAL: Born May 30, 1929, in Bath, Somerset, England; married Gillian Russell, January 28, 1956; children: Rupert, Lucy. *Education:* Sorbonne, University of Paris, Diplome de la civilisation francaise, 1948; University of Bristol, B.A. (with honors), 1950; University of London, Ph.D., 1973. *Home:* 3 Montagu Square, London W.1, England. *Agent:* H. van Thal, London Management, 235-241 Regent St., London W1A 2JT, England; and Kurt Hellmer, 52 Vanderbilt Ave., New York, N.Y. 10017.

CAREER: Copywriter and advertising executive in advertising agencies and mass-magazine publishing houses, London, England, 1952-64; lecturer, broadcaster, and author in French and English, 1965—. *Military service:* Royal Air Force, 1950-52; served as flying officer. *Member:* Classical Association.

WRITINGS: *Saint-Saens and His Circle,* Fernhill, 1965; *Sacha Guitry: The Last Boulevardier,* Scribner, 1968; *The Duke of Wellington,* Morgan Grampian, 1968, published as *Wellington,* A. S. Barnes, 1969; (author of introduction) Richard Doddridge Blackmore, *The Maid of Sker,* Anthony Blond, 1968; *Massenet,* Dent, 1970, St. Martin's, 1971; *Boulanger,* Scribner, 1971 (published in England as *General Boulanger,* W. H. Allen, 1971); *Rossini,* Crowell, 1971; *The Ox on the Roof,* St. Martin's, 1972; (editor and author of preface) *Lord Chesterfield's Letters to His Son,* Folio Society, 1973; *Gounod,* Stein & Day, 1973; *Lost Illusions: Paul Leautaud and His World,* Allen & Unwin, 1974, Fairleigh Dickinson University Press, 1975; *Eric Satie,* Praeger, 1975. Contributor to numerous journals, periodicals, reference works, and dictionaries.

WORK IN PROGRESS: *French Operetta,* for Chappell; a biography of Andre Gide.

AVOCATIONAL INTERESTS: French music, literature, and theatre, and English literature of the 18th, 19th, and 20th centuries; collecting manuscripts of French authors, musicians, and composers.

* * *

HARDOY, Jorge Enrique 1926-

PERSONAL: Born September 15, 1926, in Buenos Aires, Argentina; son of Jorge B. (an architect) and Magdalena (Noetinger) Hardoy; married Ana Maria Noguerol (an architect), December 21, 1956; children: Maria, Ines, Isabel, Agustina, Jorgelina. *Education:* University of Buenos Aires, Architect, 1950; Harvard University, Master in City Planning, 1955, Ph.D., 1965.

CAREER: Universidad de Litoral, Rosario, Argentina, professor of planning, 1956-65, director, Institute of Urban and Regional Planning, 1962-65; Instituto ki Tella, Buenos Aires, Argentina, director, Center of Urban and Regional Studies, 1966-69, head researcher, 1971—. Visiting professor in Department of City Planning, Yale University, 1970. Advisor, United Nations and World Council of Churches. *Member:* Interamerican Planning Society (director, 1962-66, president, 1966-70). *Awards, honors:* Guggenheim fellow, 1961, 1968.

WRITINGS: Bibliography on the Evolution of Cities in Latin America: The Cities of Pre-Columbian America, the Colonial Cities, the Period following Independence, Council of Planning Librarians (Oakland), 1962; *Ciudades Precolombianas,* Ediciones Infinito (Buenos Aires), 1964, revised translation by Judith Stranton published as *Pre-Columbian Cities,* Walker & Co., 1972; (with others) *Plan fisico para S. C. de Bariloche,* Fundacion Bariloche, 1965; *Bases de un programa de asistencia tecnica y financiera para el desarrollo urbano en la America Latina,* Sociedad Interamericana de Planificacion (San Juan), 1965; (with Raul O. Basaldua and Oscar A. Moreno) *Politica de la tierra urbana y mecanismos para su regulacion en America del Sur,* Editorial del Instituto di Tella, 1968; *Urban Planning in Pre-Columbian America,* Braziller, 1968; (editor with Carlos Tabar) *La Urbanizacion en America Latina,* Editorial del Instituto di Tella, 1969, translation published as *Urbanization in Latin America: Approaches and Issues,* Doubleday, 1975; (editor with R. P. Schaedel) *El Proceso de urbanizacion en America Latina,* Editorial del Instituto di Tella, 1969.

(With Maruja Acosta) *Reforma urbana en Cuba revolucionaria,* Sintesis Dos Mil (Caracas), 1971, translation published as *Urban Reform in Revolutionary Cuba,* Yale University Press, 1973; (with Moreno) *Aspectos politicos de la reforma urbana,* Editorial del Instituto di Tella, 1971; (with Moreno) *Teoria y practica de la reforma urbana en America Latina,* Editorial del Instituto di Tella, 1971; *Las Ciudades de America Latina,* Editorial Paidos (Buenos Aires), 1972; (editor with Guillermo Geisse) *Urban and Regional Development Policies in Latin America,* Sage Publications, 1972; (editor with others) *Urbanizacion en America Latina: una bibliografia sobre su historia,* Editorial del Instituto di Tella, 1975. Contributor of articles on urban planning to journals.†

* * *

HARE, Peter H. 1935-

PERSONAL: Born March 12, 1935, in New York, N.Y.; son of Michael M. (an architect and author) and Jane (Jopling) Hare; married Daphne Kean (a professor of medicine and biophysics), May 30, 1959; children: Clare Kean (son), Gwendolyn Meigs. *Education:* Yale University, B.A., 1957; Columbia University, M.A., 1962, Ph.D., 1965. *Politics:* Republican (registered). *Religion:* None. *Home:* 219 Depew

Ave., Buffalo, N.Y. 14214. *Office:* Department of Philosophy, State University of New York, 664 Baldy Hall, Buffalo, N.Y. 14260.

CAREER: State University of New York at Buffalo, lecturer, 1962-65, assistant professor, 1965-67, associate professor, 1967-71, professor of philosophy, 1971—, director of graduate studies in philosophy, 1966-68, chairman of department, 1971-76. *Member:* American Philosophical Association, New York State Philosophical Association (secretary-treasurer, 1971-73; vice-president, 1973-75; president, 1975—), Charles S. Peirce Society (president, 1976). *Awards, honors:* National Endowment for the Humanities fellowship, 1968-69.

WRITINGS: (With E. H. Madden) *Evil and the Concept of God,* C. C Thomas, 1968; (with Madden) *Causing, Perceiving, and Believing: An Examination of the Philosophy of C.J. Ducasse,* D. Reidel, 1975. Contributor of more than thirty articles to philosophy journals. Assistant director of U.S. Office of *Bibliography of Philosophy,* 1965-68; *Transactions of the Charles S. Peirce Society,* consulting editor, 1971-74, editor, 1974—.

WORK IN PROGRESS: Major Themes in Recent American Metaphysics and Epistemology.

* * *

HARGRAVE, O. T. 1936-

PERSONAL: Born December 28, 1936, in Mt. Vernon, Tex.; son of Vessie Dee (a minister) and Bessie Mae (Davis) Hargrave; married Patsy Ann Newman, August 24, 1957; children: Lisa Ann, Charles Mark, Karin Lee. *Education:* Trinity University, San Antonio, Tex., B.A., 1957, M.A., 1958; Vanderbilt University, B.D., 1961, Ph.D., 1966; also attended Cambridge University, 1963-64. *Politics:* Independent. *Home:* 9450 Dartcrest Dr., Dallas, Tex. 75238. *Office:* Department of History, Southern Methodist University, Dallas, Tex. 75222.

CAREER: Florida Southern College, Lakeland, assistant professor of history, 1964-66, chairman of department, 1966-67; Southern Methodist University, Dallas, Tex., assistant professor, 1967-70, associate professor of history, 1970—. *Member:* American Historical Association, American Society of Church History, American Association of University Professors.

WRITINGS: (Editor with Charles R. Ritcheson) *Current Research in British Studies,* Southern Methodist University Press, 1969. Contributor of articles and reviews to church history journals.

WORK IN PROGRESS: Research on the iconography of John Foxe's *Book of Martyrs.*

* * *

HARGRAVE, Rowena 1906-

PERSONAL: Born December 12, 1906, in Boonville, Ind.; daughter of Berry Little (a trucker) and Anna (Stephens) Hullett; married Harold Hargrave (superintendent of La Porte Community Schools), June 4, 1935; children: Ruth (Mrs. Richard Bersin). *Education:* Attended Oakland City College, 1924-25; Indiana State University, B.S., 1949; University of Chicago, M.A., 1962. *Religion:* Baptist. *Home:* 1808 Monroe St., La Porte, Ind. 46350.

CAREER: Elementary teacher in Boonville, Ind., 1925-29, and La Porte, Ind., 1929-39, 1942-71. Summer teacher in reading clinic, University of Chicago, 1963, 1965. *Member:*

National Retired Teachers Association, International Reading Association, American Association of University Women, Indiana State Retired Teacher's Association, Pi Lambda Theta, Delta Kappa Gamma, Civic Music Association, Woman's Literary Club, La Porte Community Hospital Auxiliary, Little Theatre Club.

WRITINGS: "Building Reading Skills" series, six books, McCormick-Mathers, 1951, 5th revised edition, 1971; "Extending Reading Skills" series, McCormick-Mathers, 1976. Contributor to education journals.

SIDELIGHTS: Rowena Hargrave writes, "Children and their love of reading have been my inspiration for writing."

* * *

HARGROVE, Barbara Watts 1924-

PERSONAL: Born April 10, 1924, in Fort Collins, Colo.; daughter of Robert H. (a dairy farmer) and Vera (Sherred) Watts; married Howard C. Hargrove, December 27, 1942 (deceased); children: Stanley H., Kathleen J., Kenneth L., Dorothy E. *Education:* Colorado State University, B.S., 1962, M.S., 1963, Ph.D., 1968. *Religion:* Presbyterian. *Home:* 350 Conner St., Apt. 400, New Haven, Conn. 06511. *Office:* Divinity School, Yale University, 409 Prospect, New Haven, Conn. 06510.

CAREER: Colorado State University, Fort Collins, instructor in sociology, 1964-67; Hollins College, Hollins College, Va., assistant professor of sociology, 1967-72, chairman of department, 1971-72; University of California, Berkeley, research associate, 1972-73; University of North Florida, Department of Sociology and Social Welfare, Jacksonville, associate professor and chairman of department, 1973-75; Yale University, Divinity School, New Haven, Conn., associate professor of religion, 1975—, member of advisory board, Program for the Study of New Religious Movements, Graduate Theological Union. Secretary, Citizens' Committee for Public Schools, Fort Collins, Colo., 1963-65; president, Roanoke Valley Council on Human Relations, 1971-72; member of organizing board, Citizens Association for Justice in Virginia, 1972; member of board, Christian Community Action, New Haven. *Member:* American Sociological Association, Society for the Scientific Study of Religion, Religious Research Association (vice-president, 1976—), Phi Kappa Phi, Pi Gamma Mu. *Awards, honors:* National Endowment for the Humanities Younger Humanist Award, 1972-73.

WRITINGS: Reformation of the Holy: A Sociology of Religion, F. A. Davis, 1971; (contributor) Charles Y. Glock and Robert Bellah, editors, *The New Religious Consciousness,* University of California Press, 1976. Contributor to journals in her field.

WORK IN PROGRESS: A book on church youth and campus ministry and response to new religious movements.

* * *

HARGROVE, Katharine T.

PERSONAL: Born in New York, N.Y. *Education:* Manhattanville College, B.A., 1931; Catholic University of America, M.A. (philosophy), 1945; Providence College, M.A. (religious education), 1956; film studies at New York University, British Film Institute, and New School for Social Research. *Home and office:* Manhattanville College, Purchase, N.Y. 10577.

CAREER: Roman Catholic nun, member of Religious of the Sacred Heart (R.S.C.J.); Manhattanville College, Purchase,

N.Y., associate professor of religion, 1951—. Member of board of directors, National Conference of Christians and Jews; U.S. representative, International Conference of Christians and Jews; member of Christopher's Film Award Board. Member of religious advisory board, New York State Division of Human Rights; chaplain of Westchester Cerebral Palsy, Inc. Conductor of film seminars, mostly on Fellini and Bergmann, in Canada and the United States; also conductor of film study tours in England and Europe. Speaker on radio and television in Berlin, Germany, London, England, Dublin, Ireland, and the United States.

MEMBER: American Academy of Religion, Society for the Scientific Study of Religion, Religious Education Association (member of board of directors; member of executive board; member of editorial board), College Theology Society (former vice-president), American Schools of Oriental Research, University Film Association, American Catholic Philosophical Association, American Association of University Professors. *Awards, honors:* Three grants from David G. Osterer Foundation; Torch of Liberty Award from Westchester Anti-Defamation League; Brotherhood Award from Westchester Cerebral Palsy, Inc.; Edith Stein Award for Judaeo-Christian Work, 1966.

WRITINGS: (Editor) *The Star and the Cross,* Bruce, 1966; *On the Other Side,* Prentice-Hall, 1967; *The Paradox of Religious Secularity,* Prentice-Hall, 1968. Contributor to *New Catholic Encyclopedia* and *Catholic Youth Encyclopedia;* also contributor of articles and reviews to publications in France, Italy, and the United States.

WORK IN PROGRESS: A reader on Jewish-Christian dialogue for adult students.

* * *

HARING, Joseph E(merick) 1931-

PERSONAL: Born July 19, 1931, in Mansfield, Ohio; son of Joseph (a businessman) and Kathryn (Woerner) Haring; married Loreen Carolyn Stuber (a designer), June 2, 1956; children: Crystal, Arianne, Elisa, Peter. *Education:* Ohio State University, B.S., 1952; Columbia University, Ph.D., 1959. *Office:* Department of Economics, Occidental College, 1600 Campus Rd., Los Angeles, Calif. 90041.

CAREER: City College (now City College of the City University of New York), New York City, lecturer in economics, 1957; Columbia University, New York City, lecturer, 1957-58, instructor in economics at Barnard College, 1958-59; Occidental College, Los Angeles, Calif., assistant professor, 1959-63, associate professor, 1963-65, Richard W. Millar Associate Professor, 1965-76, Richard W. Millar Professor of Economics and Finance, 1976—, chairman of department of economics, 1962-73. Brookings National Research Professor in Economics, 1961-62; National Science Foundation visiting research professor, University of Vienna, 1974; Fulbright visiting professor, University of Munich, 1974-75. President, Pasadena Research Institute; research coordinator, Southern California Research Council. Member, State Mining and Geology Board. *Military service:* U.S. Army, 1953-55. *Member:* American Economic Association, Royal Economic Society, Econometric Society, Western Economic Association, Western Finance Association, Western Regional Science Association, Southern California Economic Association (president, 1965).

WRITINGS: (Editor) *Migration and the Southern California Economy,* Southern California Research Council, 1964; (editor) *New Economics of Regulated Industries,* Occidental College, 1968; *Arresting Slums,* Southern California

Research Council, 1968; (editor with Joseph F. Humphrey) *Utility Regulation during Inflation*, Occidental College, 1971; (editor) *Urban and Regional Economics*, Houghton, 1972. Contributor to *American Economic Review, Western Economic Journal, Asian Survey, Kyklos, Metroeconomica, Journal of Urban Economics, Review of Economics and Statistics*, and other publications. Associate editor, *Journal of Financial and Quantitative Analysis*, 1964-68; member of editorial board, Southern California Academy of Science.

WORK IN PROGRESS: Pricing of Public Services: Electricity, Telephone Service, Medical Care.

SIDELIGHTS: Joseph Haring told *CA:* "My writings are motivated by needs I see in two areas: (1) public policy issues on which economics and related subjects can shed light; (2) student interest and motivation, in the relationships between economics and related fields. Some of my books on population have resulted in testimony before Senate and Congressional Committees, and a number of books are expressly designed for student use as textual materials."

* * *

HARKINS, William E(dward) 1921-

PERSONAL: Born November 10, 1921, in State College, Pa.; son of John Franklin and Mary K. (Wagner) Harkins. *Education:* Pennsylvania State University, B.A., 1942; Columbia University, M.A., 1946, Ph.D., 1950; additional study at Charles University, Prague, Czechoslovakia, 1947-48. *Home:* 100 La Salle St., New York, N.Y. 10027. *Office:* Department of Slavic Languages, Columbia University, New York, N.Y. 10027.

CAREER: University of Pennsylvania, Philadelphia, instructor in Slavic languages, 1948-49; Columbia University, New York, N.Y., instructor, 1949-52, assistant professor, 1952-57, associate professor, 1957-64, professor of Slavic languages, 1964—, chairman of department, 1965-71. President, Masaryk Institute, 1968-74. *Military service:* U.S. Naval Reserve, 1942-45; became lieutenant junior grade. *Member:* Modern Language Association of America, American Association for the Advancement of Slavic Studies (treasurer, 1967—), American Association of Teachers of Slavic and East European Languages (president, 1974-76). *Awards, honors:* Guggenheim fellow, 1958-59.

WRITINGS: The Russian Folk Epos in Czech Literature, Kings Crown Press, 1951; *A Modern Czech Grammar*, Kings Crown Press, 1953; (compiler) *Anthology of Czech Literature*, Kings Crown Press, 1953; *A Dictionary of Russian Literature*, Philosophical Library, 1956; *Karel Capek*, Columbia University Press, 1962; (with Galina Stilman and Leon Stilman) *Introductory Russian Grammar*, Blaisdell, 1964, revised edition, Xerox College Publishing, 1971.

WORK IN PROGRESS: A book on Czech literature, 1956-1970.

SIDELIGHTS: William Harkins has made four trips to the Soviet Union and seven to Czechoslovakia.

* * *

HARLAN, John Marshall 1899-1971

May 20, 1899—December 29, 1971; American jurist. Obituaries: *New York Times*, December 30, 1971; *Washington Post*, December 30, 1971; *Newsweek*, January 10, 1972; *Time*, January 10, 1972.

HARMON, William (Ruth) 1938-

PERSONAL: Born June 10, 1938, in Concord, N.C.; son of William Richard (a textile executive) and Virginia (Pickerel) Harmon; married Lynn Chadwell, December 20, 1965; children: Sally Frances, William Richard Harmon II. *Education:* University of Chicago, A.B., 1958, A.M., 1968; University of North Carolina at Chapel Hill, M.A., 1968; University of Cincinnati, Ph.D., 1970. *Politics:* Democrat. *Religion:* None. *Home:* 350 Wesley Dr., Chapel Hill, N.C. 27514. *Office:* Department of English, University of North Carolina, Chapel Hill, N.C. 27514.

CAREER: U.S. Navy, active duty as officer, 1960-67, reserve service, 1967—, with current rank of lieutenant commander; University of North Carolina at Chapel Hill, instructor, 1970-71, assistant professor, 1971-72, associate professor, 1973-77, professor of English, 1977—, department chairman, 1972-77. *Member:* Modern Language Association of America, Academy of American Poets, American Anthropological Association, South Atlantic Modern Language Association. *Awards, honors*—Military: Navy Commendation Medal with V; Vietnamese Staff Service Honor Medal, first class. Civilian: Fellowships include Rockefeller Foundation Humanities fellowship, Ford Foundation fellowship, and Elliston Poetry Fund scholarship; research grants from Kenan Fund.

WRITINGS—All poetry, except as indicated: *Treasury Holiday*, Wesleyan University Press, 1970; *Legion: Civic Choruses*, Wesleyan University Press, 1973; *The Intussuception of Miss Mary America*, Kayak Books, 1976; *Time in Ezra Pound's Work* (criticism), University of North Carolina Press, 1977. Anthologized in *Quickly Aging Here: Some Poets of the 1970's*, edited by Geof Hewitt, Doubleday, 1969. Contributor to journals, including *Antioch Review, Kayak, Beloit Poetry Journal, Carolina Quarterly,* and *San Francisco Review.*

WORK IN PROGRESS: The Oxford Book of American Light Verse; critical studies of T. S. Eliot and A. R. Ammons; a volume of poems.

SIDELIGHTS: William Harmon writes: "I try to avoid subjecting what I do to any very agonizing scrutiny. Poetry is so demanding that, certainly, I would not write it if I did not absolutely as a matter of necessity have to. Teaching, criticism, editing, and other such academic or belletristic pastimes make up a much less ulcerating regimen."

BIOGRAPHICAL/CRITICAL SOURCES: Antioch Review, fall/winter, 1970-71.

* * *

HARO, Robert P(eter) 1936-

PERSONAL: Born September 9, 1936, in Sacramento, Calif.; son of Tereso Nunez (a farmer) and Catalina (Herreros) Haro; married Pauline Kessemeier (a high school teacher), June 10, 1961; children: Richard T., Robert P. *Education:* University of California, Berkeley, B.A., 1958, M.A., 1959, M.L.S., 1962. *Religion:* Roman Catholic. *Home:* 1007 Alice St., Davis, Calif. 95616.

CAREER: California State College (now California State University, Hayward), Hayward, librarian, 1962-63; State University of New York at Buffalo, librarian, 1963-65; University of California Library, Davis, social science bibliographer, 1965-67, librarian in Institute of Government Affairs, 1967-69; University of Maryland, School of Librarianship, College Park, librarian and lecturer, 1969-71; University of Southern California Library, Los Angeles, librarian, beginning 1971. *Military service:* U.S. Army, 1959-61; became staff sergeant. *Member:* American Library Association, Special Libraries Association, American Association of University Professors, California Library Association.

WRITINGS: Directory of Government, Public, and Urban Affairs Research Centers, Institute of Governmental Affairs, University of California, 1969; *Latin Americana Research in the United States and Canada: A Guide and Directory,* American Library Association, 1971. Contributor to *Parent's Encyclopedia;* contributor of over twenty articles to library journals.

WORK IN PROGRESS: Library and Information Services to Spanish Origin Americans.

AVOCATIONAL INTERESTS: Hiking, camping, photography, touch football, surfing, skindiving, sports cars and rallying.†

*   *   *

HARPER, J(ohn) Russell 1914-

PERSONAL: Born April 15, 1914, in Caledonia, Ontario, Canada; son of Alexander Turnbull (a farmer) and J. Evelyn (Taylor) Harper; married Elizabeth M. Goodchild, May 10, 1945; children: Jennifer Elizabeth. *Education:* Attended Hamilton Teachers College, Ontario, 1932, McMaster University, 1934, and Ontario College of Art, 1938-42; University of Toronto, B.A., 1947, M.A., 1949. *Home:* R.R. 3, Alexandria, Ontario, Canada. *Office:* Department of Fine Arts, Sir George Williams University, Montreal, Quebec, Canada.

CAREER: University of Toronto, Toronto, Ontario, curator of Lee College, 1947-50; Royal Ontario Museum, Toronto, chief cataloguer, 1948-52; New Brunswick Museum, Saint John, archivist, 1952-56; Lord Beaverbrook Art College, New Brunswick, curator, 1957-59; National Gallery of Canada, Ottawa, Ontario, curator of Canadian art, 1960-64; McGill University, Montreal, Quebec, chief curator of McCord Museum, 1964-67; Sir George Williams University, Montreal, professor of fine arts, 1967—. *Military service:* Royal Canadian Air Force, 1942-46. *Member:* Royal Society of Canada (fellow). *Awards, honors:* Royal Canadian fellowship for research in Paris, 1956; Doctor of Letters, University of Guelph, 1972; Officer, Order of Canada, 1975.

WRITINGS: Portland Point, Crossroads of New Brunswick History, New Brunswick Museum, 1956; *Historical Directory of New Brunswick Newspapers and Periodicals,* University of New Brunswick Press, 1961; *Painting in Canada: A History,* University of Toronto Press, 1966; (editor with Stanley Triggs) *Portrait of a Period,* McGill University Press, 1967; *Early Painters and Engravers in Canada,* University of Toronto Press, 1970; *Dictionary of Canadian Artists,* University of Toronto Press, 1970; *Paul Kane's Frontier,* University of Texas Press, 1971; *A People's Art,* University of Toronto Press, 1974; *William G. R. Hind,* National Gallery of Canada (Ottawa), 1976. Contributor to professional journals.

WORK IN PROGRESS: Cornelius Krieghoff and His Associates; Painters in the Arctic, 1820-1880.

*   *   *

HARPER, Michael S. 1938-

PERSONAL: Born March 18, 1938, in Brooklyn, N.Y.; son of Walter Warren and Katherine (Johnson) Harper; married Shirley Ann Buffington, December 24, 1965; children: Ro-

land Warren, Patrice Cuchulain, Rachel Maria. *Education:* Los Angeles City College, A.A., 1959; Los Angeles State College of Applied Arts and Sciences (now California State University, Los Angeles), B.A., 1961, M.A., 1963; University of Iowa, M.A., 1963; additional study, University of Illinois, 1970-71. *Home:* 397 Tremont St., Taunton, Mass. 02780. *Office:* Department of English, Brown University, Providence, R.I. 02912.

CAREER: Contra Costa College, San Pablo, Calif., instructor in English, 1964-68; Lewis and Clark College, Portland, Ore., poet-in-residence, 1968-69; Reed College, Portland, visiting professor, 1968-69; California State College (now University), Hayward, associate professor of English, 1970; Brown University, Providence, R.I., associate professor, 1971-73, professor of English, 1973—, director of writing program. Visiting professor at Harvard University, 1974, and Yale University, 1977. Travelled to England on bicentenary tour, 1976. Original founding member, African Continuum, St. Louis, Mo.

MEMBER: American Academy of Arts and Letters. *Awards, honors:* Center for Advanced Study, University of Illinois fellow, 1970-71; Black Academy of Arts and Letters award, 1972, for *History Is Your Own Heartbeat;* National Institute of Arts and Letters award, 1972; Guggenheim fellowship, 1976; National Endowment for the Arts grant, 1977; American Specialist grant to Africa, 1977; National Book Award for poetry nomination, Association of American Publishers, 1978, for *Images of Kin.*

WRITINGS: Dear John, Dear Coltrane (poems), University of Pittsburgh Press, 1970; *History Is Your Own Heartbeat,* University of Illinois Press, 1971; *Photographs: Negatives: History as Apple Tree,* Scarab Press, 1972; *Song: I Want a Witness,* University of Pittsburgh Press, 1972; *Debridement,* Doubleday, 1973; (editor) *Heartblow: Black Veils* (antology), University of Illinois Press, 1974; *Nightmare Begins Responsibility,* University of Illinois Press, 1975; *Images of Kin,* University of Illinois Press, 1977; (editor) *Chant of Saints,* University of Illinois Press, 1978; (editor) *Heartblow: Black Veils,* University of Illinois Press, 1978. Poetry has appeared in several anthologies, including *The Poetry of Black America, To Gwen with Love, Starting with Poetry, Understanding the New Black Poetry, The Black Poets, Natural Process,* and others. Contributor to periodicals, including *Black Scholar, Black World, Chicago Review, Negro American Literature Forum, Negro Digest, Poetry,* and many others. Guest editor, *Iowa Review, Massachusetts Review,* and *American Poetry Review.*

SIDELIGHTS: Michael Harper told *CA:* "In the late sixties [I] traveled to Mexico and Europe where those landscapes broadened my scope and interest in poetry and culture of other countries while I searched my own family and racial history for folklore, history and myth for themes that would give my writing the tradition and context where I could find my own voice. My travels made me look closely at the wealth of human materials in my own life, its ethnic richness, complexity of language and stylization, the tension between stated moral idealism and brutal historical realities, and I investigated the inner reality of those struggles to find the lyrical expression of their secrets in my own voice."

A reviewer for the *Virginia Quarterly Review* writes: "Mr. Harper claims that his prosody grows rather out of jazz than out of traditional Western poetics, and . . . much of his work is given to what we are learning to call 'the black theme'. . . . Whatever his ideological loyalties, however, Mr. Harper's is a poetry of classically unadorned statement, a direct, unflinching record of a man alive in his time. When he is at his best, in both his public and private voice, he creates a language humming with emotion and ennobled by a deeply felt human dignity.''

In reviewing *Debridement,* Laurence Lieberman remarks that ''Harper's deadpan style is deceptive; when it most wears the guise of expressionless immobility, just under the chilled surface a cunning of insurgency lurks to spring.... The author's passions, like [John Brown's] his protagonist's, are ordered, shaped, controlled by intelligence, rage, or pain, transfigured by vision.... A hasty reader may miss the abiding qualities of the art which selects and rescues the salient moments ... of history ... as the facts are salvaged by the careful eye and ear informed by a remarkable imagination which balances the American present and past.''

BIOGRAPHICAL/CRITICAL SOURCES: Saturday Review, August 8, 1970; *Virginia Quarterly Review,* autumn, 1970; *Yale Review,* October, 1973; *Poetry,* December, 1973; John O'Brian, editor, *Interviews with Black Writers,* Liveright, 1973; *Parnassus: Poetry in Review,* fall/winter, 1975; *Contemporary Literary Criticism,* Volume VII, Gale, 1977.

* * *

HARRIMAN, Richard L(evet) 1944-

PERSONAL: Born October 7, 1944, in Buffalo, N.Y.; son of Thomas Jarvis (a corporation executive) and Eleanor (Levet) Harriman. *Education:* Stanford University, A.B. (English), 1967, A.B. (political science), 1971; University of California, Davis, J.D., 1975. *Home:* 2406 Katherine Ave., Modesto, Calif. 95350. *Office:* Haight & Harriman, 719 14th St., P.O. Box 3386, Modesto, Calif. 95353.

CAREER: Stanford Research Institute, Stanford, Calif., editor, administrative assistant, and project administrator in Menlo Park, Calif. and Bangkok, Thailand, 1967-68. Assistant campaign manager for mayoral and city council campaigns in Buffalo, N.Y., 1969; volunteer at California State Democratic Headquarters, San Francisco, 1969; private practice of law in Modesto, Calif. Co-founder and vice-president, Consumer Alliance, Palo Alto; former committee member, Palo Alto Land Use Coalition. *Member:* Zero Population Growth (founder of Stanford chapter).

WRITINGS: (With Paul R. Ehrlich) *How to Be a Survivor: A Plan to Save Spaceship Earth,* Ballantine, 1971. Contributor to journals.

WORK IN PROGRESS: Articles on the environment of the Central Valley in California.

* * *

HARRIS, Ernest E(dward) 1914-

PERSONAL: Born August 26, 1914, in Gadsden, Ala.; son of Walker F. and Viola (Gilmore) Harris; married Evelyn Arthurs (a teacher), June 22, 1939; children: Rose Marie (Mrs. Norman Luetters), Ernest Edward, Jr. *Education:* Attended Cincinnati Conservatory of Music, 1932-33; Catawba College, B.A., 1936; Columbia University, M.A., 1940, Ed. D., 1944; attended Juilliard School of Music, 1941. *Home:* 21 Chestnut Dr., Hastings-on-Hudson, N.Y. 10706. *Office address:* Teachers College, Columbia University, 525 West 120th St., Box 87, New York, N.Y. 10027.

CAREER: Catawba College, Salisbury, N.C., conductor of band, 1935-36; Junior Order United American Mechanics Orphanage, Lexington, N.C., conductor of orchestra, 1935-38; Yadkin County School System, N.C., director of instrumental music, 1936-38; Georgia Teachers College (now

Georgia Southern College), Statesboro, instructor in music, 1938-41; Columbia University, Teachers College, New York, N.Y., instructor, 1941-44, associate, 1945-46, assistant professor, 1946-50, associate professor, 1950-55, professor of music education, 1955—, director of Instructional Support Services, 1969—. Clinician and director of workshops for music educators, conductor of state music festivals, and consultant to public school systems.

MEMBER: National Music Council (member of executive board, 1946-62), Acoustical Society of America, National Association of American Composers and Conductors, Music Educators National Conference (national chairman, 1951-54), Music Teachers National Association, American String Teachers Association (national president, 1952-54), National School Orchestra Association, College Band Directors Association, Association for Educational Communications and Technology, New York State Educational Communications Association, New York String Teachers Guild (member of advisory board), Phi Mu Alpha (Eastern Province Governor, 1948-52), Phi Delta Kappa. *Awards, honors:* House Resolution, 3rd Legislature of Hawaii, 1965, for major contribution to artistic and aesthetic development of youth; LL. D. from Catawba College, 1971.

WRITINGS: The Solo Drummer (method book), G. Ricordi, 1949; (with Raymond Burrows and Ella M. Ahearn) *Young America at the Violin,* C. C. Birchard, 1955; (with Robert H. Klotman) *Learning to Teach through Playing,* Addison-Wesley, 1971; (editor) *Music Education: A Guide to Information Sources,* Gale, 1977. Also author of three music education manuals for the U.S. Department of Defense.

Arranger of compositions for school orchestra, all published by Bourne: *Larghetto from ''Concerto Grosso''—Opus 6, No. 12—Handel,* 1949; *''Promenade'' from Opus 100—Schubert,* 1950; *Folk Fantasy* (based on American folk tunes), 1951; *The ''Famous Largo'' from Opus 76, No. 5—Haydn,* 1952; (with Harry R. Wilson) *Festival Song of Praise, from ''Oedipus in Colonos,'' Opus 93—Mendelssohn,* for Chorus and Orchestra, 1953; *Death and the Maiden—Schubert,* 1956; *Gay Parade—Schubert,* 1956.

Arranger of compositions for school bands, all published by Bourne: *Larghetto from ''Concerto Grosso''—Opus 6, No. 12—Handel,* 1952; *Death and the Maiden—Schubert,* 1955; (and contributor) *Classics for Band: An Album,* 1961.

Contributor: Richard Harry Werder, editor, *Specialized Activities in Music Education,* Catholic University of America Press, 1956; *Music Activities in the Elementary School,* Catholic University of America Press, 1957; *Developing Teaching Skills in Music,* Catholic University of America Press, 1959; *Music Teaching Methods and Techniques,* Catholic University of America Press, 1960; Archie Neff Jones, editor, *Music Education in Action: Basic Principles and Practical Methods,* Allyn & Bacon, 1960; *Procedures and Techniques of Music Teaching,* Catholic University of America Press, 1961; *Music Pedagogy,* Catholic University of America Press, 1963. Contributor of articles on music education to *Teachers College Record, Research Council Bulletin* (Music Educators National Conference), *Music Educators Journal, Orchestra News,* and other professional journals.

* * *

HARRIS, Janet 1932-

PERSONAL: Born April 17, 1932, in Newark, N.J.;

daughter of Nathan (an attorney) and Ida (Lachow) Urovsky; formerly married to Martin Harris; children: Michael, Clint. *Education:* Ohio University, Athens, B.S.Ed., 1951. *Home:* 120 West Lena Ave., Freeport, N.Y. 11520. *Agent:* Dorothy Markinko, McIntosh & Otis, Inc., 475 Fifth Ave., New York, N.Y. 10017.

CAREER: Worked as a fund raiser and in public relations and wrote for radio, 1952-60; full-time writer, 1960—. Lecturer in English department, C. W. Post College, Long Island University, 1969, and Glen Cove Community College, State University of New York, 1970. Chairman for South Nassau, Women's Strike for Peace, 1964-65. *Member:* Authors League, Congress of Racial Equality (secretary of Long Island chapter, 1966-69). *Awards, honors:* Women's Press Club of New York City Award for "contribution to the literature of social protest," 1969.

WRITINGS: The Long Freedom Road: The Civil Rights Story, foreword by Whitney Young, McGraw, 1967; (with Julius Hobson) *Black Pride: A People's Struggle* (juvenile), McGraw, 1969; *Students in Revolt,* McGraw, 1970; *A Single Standard,* McGraw, 1971; *Crisis in Corrections,* McGraw, 1973; *The Prime of Ms. America,* Putnam, 1975; *Thursday's Children,* Harper, 1977. Reviewer, *New York Times Book Review,* 1970-71.

WORK IN PROGRESS: One juvenile book; a magazine series.

SIDELIGHTS: Janet Harris writes: "The theme of all my writing centers around my belief in the rights of the individual for freedom and self-expression, at the cost of non-violent revolution against authority. I am opposed to racism, sexism, to war, to the placing of property rights above human rights. I believe we are in the midst of a social revolution in which authoritarian values are being replaced with humane concepts and my work and my life are dedicated to this change in consciousness."

BIOGRAPHICAL/CRITICAL SOURCES: Listener, May 16, 1968; *New York Times Book Review,* May 4, 1969, November 9, 1969; *Commonweal,* May 23, 1969; *Young Reader Readers Review,* October, 1969.

*   *   *

HARRIS, Jessica L(ee) 1939-

PERSONAL: Born June 4, 1939, in Bryans Road, Md.; daughter of Jesse Woodrow and Margret (Downs) Milstead; married Robert Harris (a plastics engineer), June 4, 1960. *Education:* Eastern Nazarene College, A.B., 1960; Columbia University, M.S., 1965, D.L.S., 1969. *Home:* 43 Wilson Pl., Freeport, N.Y. 11520. *Office:* Division of Library and Information Science, St. John's University, Jamaica, N.Y. 11439.

CAREER: High school library assistant in Shorewood, Wis., 1960-61; Midwest Translation Bureau, Milwaukee, Wis., editor and translator, 1961-62; Bethel (Conn.) Public Library, library assistant, 1963-64; Rothines Associates, New York City, research associate, 1965-69; Columbia University, New York City, assistant professor of library service, 1969-72; Queens College of the City University of New York, Flushing, N.Y., assistant professor of library science, 1972-74; St. John's University, Jamaica, N.Y., associate professor of library and information science, 1974—. *Member:* American Library Association, American Society of Indexers (secretary, 1968-69), Society of Indexers (London), Association for Computing Machinery, American Society for Information Science, Special Libraries Associa-

tion, New York Technical Services Librarians, New York Library Club, Beta Phi Mu, Phi Delta Lambda.

WRITINGS: (With Theodore C. Hines) *Computer Filing of Index, Bibliographic, and Catalog Entries,* Bro-Dart Foundation, 1966; *Subject Analysis: Computer Implications of Rigorous Definition,* Scarecrow, 1970. Contributor of articles and reviews to professional journals. *Annual Review of Information Science and Technology,* index and bibliographic editor, 1974-75, compiler of cumulative index for volumes 1-10, 1976.

WORK IN PROGRESS: Studies of indexing language development.

*   *   *

HARRIS, Rosemary (Jeanne)

PERSONAL: Born in London, England; daughter of Arthur Travers (in Royal Air Force) and Barbara D. K. (Money) Harris. *Education:* Studied at Chelsea School of Art, London, and Courtauld Institute, London. *Politics:* Liberal. *Religion:* Christian. *Home:* 33 Cheyne Court, Flood St., London SW3 5TR, England. *Agent:* Michael Horniman, A. P. Watt & Son, 26/28 Bedford Row, London WC1R 4HL, England.

CAREER: Writer; picture restorer; reader for Metro-Goldwyn-Mayer. *Member:* Society of Authors. *Awards, honors:* Carnegie Medal of Library Association (England) for outstanding children's book of 1968, *The Moon in the Cloud;* Arts Council grant for research, 1971.

WRITINGS: The Summer House, Hamish Hamilton, 1956; *Voyage to Cythera,* Bodley Head, 1958; *Venus with Sparrows,* Faber, 1961; *All My Enemies,* Faber, 1967, Simon & Schuster, 1972; *The Nice Girl's Story,* Faber, 1968, published as *Nor Evil Dreams,* Simon & Schuster, 1973; *A Wicked Pack of Cards,* Faber, 1969, Walker & Co., 1970; *Sea Magic and Other Stories of Enchantment,* Macmillan (New York), 1974 (expanded version published in England as *The Lotus and the Grail: Legends from East and West,* Faber, 1974); *The Double Snare,* Faber, 1974, Simon & Schuster, 1975; *Three Candles for the Dark,* Faber, 1976.

Juveniles: *The Moon in the Cloud,* Faber, 1968, Macmillan (New York), 1970; *The Shadow on the Sun,* Macmillan (New York), 1970; *The Seal-Singing,* Macmillan (New York), 1971; *The Child in the Bamboo Grove,* illustrations by Errol le Cain, Faber, 1971; *The Bright and Morning Star,* Macmillan (New York), 1972; *The King's White Elephant,* Faber, 1973; *The Flying Ship,* Faber, 1975; *The Little Dog of Fo,* Faber, 1976; *I Want to Be a Fish,* Kestrel Books, 1977. Also author of television play for children, "Peronik," 1976.

WORK IN PROGRESS: A book for children, *A Quest for Orion,* and its sequel.

SIDELIGHTS: Rosemary Harris writes: "There are many, many different things which turn someone into a writer by profession, rather than someone who writes a book or two on the side as a relief from other activities. I always wrote—but equally I always painted, and was interested in music. Writing as a way of life is perhaps something that tends to happen, instead of being deliberately chosen—unless one starts off with serious intentions as a journalist, and then gravitates to books.

"The turning point in my work was definitely my first book for children, *The Moon in the Cloud,* which got the Carnegie Medal. It was a book that almost seemed to write itself, everything fell into place with such ease; but, looking back, I see that it owed a great deal to my years of training as a painter in Chelsea. It was certainly there that I got a lot of my visual training which was a very strong element in that book, and one which the critics over here particularly noticed. And it was in the sculpture class with F. E. McWilliam and Henry Moore that I learned to love the Egyptians—particularly the sculpture of the Old Kingdom. Curiously enough, several people have asked me if I was influenced by Thomas Mann's *Joseph and His Brethren,* and the answer is 'Yes, I was,' but only *after* I'd written *The Moon in the Cloud.* I didn't read Mann's great work until later on; then I think it was a strong influence on my writing two other books to complete the trilogy—*The Shadow on the Sun* and *The Bright and Morning Star.*"

AVOCATIONAL INTERESTS: Theater, music, photography.

BIOGRAPHICAL/CRITICAL SOURCES: Books and Bookmen, March, 1968, December, 1971; *New York Times Book Review,* April 12, 1970; *Times Literary Supplement,* July 20, 1970.

* * *

HART, John E(dward) 1917-

PERSONAL: Born February 16, 1917, in Barnard, Kan.; son of Harriss L. (in real estate) and Anna (Hunter) Hart; married Mary Helen Negus (an art consultant), December 29, 1942. *Education:* Kansas Wesleyan University, B.A., 1938; Northwestern University, graduate study, 1938; Syracuse University, M.A., 1940, Ph.D., 1954; Cambridge University, graduate study, 1951. *Politics:* Democrat. *Religion:* Methodist. *Home:* 412 Fitch St., Albion, Mich. 49224. *Office:* Department of English, Albion College, Albion, Mich. 49224.

CAREER: Syracuse University, Syracuse, N.Y., instructor in English literature, 1940-42, 1953-54; Cincinnati University, Cincinnati, Ohio, instructor in English literature, 1946-49; Albion College, Albion, Mich., assistant professor, 1954-60, associate professor, 1960-65, professor of English and American literature, 1965—. Lecturer, Odenwaldschule, Heppenheim, Germany, 1950-51; lecturer for community education classes, 1962-63. *Military service:* U.S. Army, 1942-45; became sergeant; received three battle stars. *Member:* Modern Language Association of America, American Association of University Professors, Omicron Delta Kappa, Pi Gamma Mu.

WRITINGS: History of 334th Field Artillery Battalion, U.S. Department of the Army, 1946; *Floyd Dell,* Twayne, 1971; *Albert Halper,* Twayne, 1978.

Contributor: Richard Lettis and others, editors, *The Red Badge of Courage: Text and Criticism,* Harcourt, 1960, 2nd edition, 1976; Sculley Bradley and others, editors, *The Red Badge of Courage: An Annotated Text, Background and Sources,* Norton, 1962; John Vickery, editor, *Myth and Literature,* University of Nebraska Press, 1966; *The Red Badge of Courage: Analytic Notes and Review,* American R.D.M., 1966; Arlin Turner, editor, *Merrill Studies in "The Scarlet Letter,"* C. E. Merrill, 1970. Member of *Experiment* Poetry Group, 1948-59. Poetry anthologized in *New Directions Anthology,* edited by James Laughlin, New Directions, 1942. Contributor to *New Mexico Quarterly Review, Experiment, New England Quarterly, Modern Fiction Studies,* and other publications.

WORK IN PROGRESS: A critical essay on *The Picture of Dorian Gray;* study in American self-achievement, *Heroes and Progresses;* essays on American novelists.

HART, Larry 1920-

PERSONAL: Born March 17, 1920, in Schenectady, N.Y.; son of Harry H. and Everil (Reed) Hart; married Ruth Brooks (a school teacher), April, 1943; children: Bonnilyn, Alan. *Education:* Attended Union College, Schenectady, N.Y. *Religion:* Protestant. *Home:* 195 Droms Rd., Scotia, N.Y. 12302. *Office: Schenectady Gazette,* 332 State St., Schenectady, N.Y. 12301.

CAREER: News photographer in Schenectady, N.Y., 1945-61; *Schenectady Gazette,* Schenectady, political writer, 1961-70, editorial writer, 1970-76, editor of editorial page, 1977—. Frequent speaker throughout northeastern New York on history of Mohawk Valley; Schenectady city and county historian. *Military service:* U.S. Army Air Forces, 1942-45; became staff sergeant. *Member:* Schenectady County Historical Society (president, 1965-68), Ballston Spa Historical Society, Lake George Historical Association.

WRITINGS: The Sacandaga Story, Riedinger, 1967; *Did I Wake You Up?,* Riedinger, 1970; *Schenectady's Golden Era,* Old Dorp Books, 1974, revised edition, 1976; *Tales of Old Schenectady,* Volume I, Old Dorp Books, 1975.

WORK IN PROGRESS: Research on history of Schenectady County.

SIDELIGHTS: Larry Hart told *CA:* "As long as I can remember, I have always been fascinated with the history and folklore of the community where I was born—and Schenectady happens to be replete with Americana dating back to the mid-17th century. In more recent years, I became painfully aware of the fact that not enough had been written of long-forgotten events, especially of the so-called common people who helped develop Schenectady in so many ways—they were very much a part of its industrial, economic and social growth. So I have dedicated my spare time to writing this history as well as talking about it."

* * *

HARTH, Robert 1940-

PERSONAL: Born June 14, 1940, in New York, N.Y.; son of Isidore and Eva (Gelman) Harth; married Linda Gruenberg, November 23, 1963; children: Rona, Ira, Benjamin. *Education:* San Fernando Valley State College (now California State University, Northridge), B.A., 1964; George Peabody College for Teachers, M.A., 1965, Ed.D., 1969. *Home:* 505 Laurel Dr., Columbia, Mo. 65201. *Office:* Department of Special Education, University of Missouri, 515 South Sixth St., Columbia, Mo. 65201.

CAREER: Laurence School, Van Nuys, Calif., physical education teacher for emotionally disturbed children, 1962-63; Burbank Retarded Children's Center, Burbank, Calif., teacher, 1963-64; Monroe Harding Children's Home, Nashville, Tenn., teacher, 1964; Wright School, Durham, N.C., liaison teacher-counselor, 1965-66; California State College at Fullerton (now California State University, Fullerton), assistant professor of special education, 1967; Cumberland House Elementary School, Nashville, Tenn., liaison teacher-counselor, 1968; Cloverbottom Hospital and School, Donelson, Tenn., coordinator of in-service education, 1969; University of Missouri—Columbia, assistant professor of special education, 1969—. Director, Young Adult Summer Day Camp for the Physically Handicapped, 1963. *Member:* Council for Exceptional Children, Phi Delta Kappa.

WRITINGS: (Editor) *Issues in Behavior Disorders: A Book of Readings,* C. C Thomas, 1971. Contributor to *Interna-*

tional Journal for the Education of the Blind, Exceptional Children, and *Education and Training of the Mentally Retarded.*

WORK IN PROGRESS: Research on the assessment of attitudes towards mental retardation.†

* * *

HARTMAN, Rachel (Frieda) 1920-1972

August 16, 1920—May 26, 1972; American editor and poet. Obituaries: *New York Times,* May 27, 1972. (See index for *CA* sketch)

* * *

HARVEY, Van A(ustin) 1926-

PERSONAL: Born April 23, 1926, in Hankow, China; son of Earle R. (a minister) and Mary (Mullis) Harvey; married Margaret Lynn, August 31, 1950; children: Jonathan Lynn, Christopher Earle. *Education:* Occidental College, B.A., 1948; Yale University, B.D., 1951, Ph.D., 1957. *Politics:* Democrat. *Office:* Department of Religious Studies, Stanford University, Stanford, Calif. 94305.

CAREER: Princeton University, Princeton, N.J., instructor, 1954-55, lecturer, 1955-56, assistant professor of religion, 1956-58; Southern Methodist University, Perkins School of Theology, Dallas, Tex., assistant professor, 1958-62, associate professor, 1962-65, professor of theology, 1965-68; University of Pennsylvania, Philadelphia, professor of religious thought, 1968-77, chairman of department, 1971-76; Stanford University, Stanford, Calif., professor of religious studies, 1977—. *Military service:* U.S. Naval Reserve, 1944-46; became ensign. *Member:* American Academy of Religion, Society on Religion in Higher Education, American Theological Society. *Awards, honors:* Bollingen fellow at University of Marburg, 1960-61; D.Hum., Occidental College, 1963; Guggenheim fellow, 1966 (at Oxford University), and 1972.

WRITINGS: Handbook of Theological Terms, Macmillan, 1964; *The Historian and the Believer,* Macmillan, 1966. Contributor to theology journals.

WORK IN PROGRESS: Secularization and Unbelief: A Study of Unbelief in Theologians.

* * *

HASKINS, James 1941-
(Jim Haskins)

PERSONAL: Born September 19, 1941, in Montgomery, Ala.; son of Henry and Julia (Brown) Haskins. *Education:* Georgetown University, B.A., 1960; Alabama State University, B.S., 1962; University of New Mexico, M.A., 1963; graduate study at New School for Social Research, 1965-67, and Queens College of the City University of New York, 1967-68. *Home:* 325 West End Ave., New York, N.Y. 10023.

CAREER: Smith Barney & Co., New York City, stock trader, 1963-65; New York (N.Y.) Board of Education, teacher, 1966-68; New School for Social Research, New York City, visiting lecturer, 1970-72; Staten Island Community College of the City University of New York, Staten Island, N.Y., associate professor, 1970-77. Visiting professor, Indiana University—Purdue University at Indianapolis, 1973—. Consultant, Education Development Center, Newton, Mass., 1975—. *Awards, honors: The Creoles of Color of New Orleans* was selected as a finalist for Spur Award of

Western Writers of America, 1975; *The Story of Stevie Wonder* was awarded the eighth annual Coretta Scott King Award.

WRITINGS: Pinckney Benton Stewart Pitchback: A Biography, Macmillan, 1973; *Street Gangs: Yesterday and Today,* Hastings House, 1974; *Witchcraft, Mysticism and Magic in the Black World,* Doubleday, 1974; *Snow Sculpture and Ice Carving,* Macmillan, 1974; *A New Kind of Joy: The Story of the Special Olympics,* Doubleday, 1976; *Scott Joplin: The Search for the Man,* Doubleday, in press; *The Cotton Club Papers,* Random House, in press.

Juvenile books: *Resistance: Profiles in Nonviolence,* Doubleday, 1970; *The War and the Protest: Viet Nam,* Doubleday, 1971; *Revolutionaries: Agents of Change,* Lippincott, 1971; *From Lew Alcindor to Kareem Abdul Jabbar,* Lothrop, 1972; *A Piece of the Power: Four Black Mayors,* Dial, 1972; *Profiles in Black Power,* Doubleday, 1972; *Religions,* Lippincott, 1973; *Adam Clayton Powell: Portrait of a Marching Black,* Dial, 1974; *Babe Ruth and Hank Aaron: The Home Run Kings,* Lothrop, 1974; *Jobs in Business and Office,* Lothrop, 1974; *The Creoles of Color of New Orleans,* Crowell, 1975; *Fighting Shirley Chisholm,* Dial, 1975; *The Consumer Movement,* F. Watts, 1975; *The Picture Life of Malcolm X,* F. Watts, 1975; *Dr. J.: A Biography of Julius Erving,* Doubleday, 1975; *Pele: A Biography,* Doubleday, 1976; *The Story of Stevie Wonder,* Lothrop, 1976; *Always Movin' On: The Life of Langston Hughes,* F. Watts, 1976; *The Story of Barbara Jordan,* Dial, 1977; *Who Are the Handicapped?,* Doubleday, in press.

Under name Jim Haskins: *Diary of a Harlem Schoolteacher,* Grove, 1970; (editor) *Black Manifesto for Education,* Morrow, 1973; (with Hugh Butts) *The Psychology of Black Language,* Barnes & Noble, 1973; *Jokes from Black Folks,* Doubleday, 1973; *Ralphe Bunche: A Most Reluctant Hero* (juvenile), Hawthorn, 1974; *Your Rights: Past and Present* (juvenile), Hawthorn, 1975; *Teenage Alcoholism* (juvenile), Hawthorn, 1976; *The Long Struggle: The Story of American Labor* (juvenile), Westminster, 1976.

WORK IN PROGRESS: James Van Dertee: A Biography, for Dodd; *The Quiet Revolution: The Struggle for the Rights of Disabled Americans,* for Crowell; *Aging: The Great Exclusion,* for Hastings House; *The Stevie Wonder Scrapbook,* for Grosset.

BIOGRAPHICAL/CRITICAL SOURCES: New York Post, February 7, 1970; *Manhattan Tribune,* March 7, 1970; *Christian Science Monitor,* March 12, 1970; *New Leader,* April 16, 1970; *Washington Post,* November 15, 1973; *Children's Literature Review,* Volume III, Gale, 1978.

* * *

HASLING, John 1928-

PERSONAL: Born March 2, 1928, in San Mateo, Calif.; son of John and Nora (Beyer) Hasling; married Patricia Dawn O'Day, August 9, 1953 (divorced); married Elsie Ruth Wale, September 10, 1977; children: (first marriage) William Michael, James Patrick, Paige Kimberly. *Education:* Attended University of California, Berkeley, 1949-51; Sacramento State College (now California State University, Sacramento), B.A., 1962, M.A., 1963. *Politics:* Democrat. *Religion:* Agnostic. *Home:* 1137 Reed Ave., Sunnyvale, Calif. 94086. *Office:* Department of Broadcasting and Speech, Foothill College, Los Altos Hills, Calif. 94022.

CAREER: Sacramento State College (now California State University, Sacramento), Sacramento, Calif., instructor in speech and debate, 1965-66; Foothill College, Los Altos Hills, Calif., associate professor of broadcasting and speech, 1966—. *Military service:* U.S. Army, paratrooper, 1946-48.

WRITINGS: The Message, the Speaker, the Audience, McGraw, 1971, 2nd edition published as *The Audience, the Message, the Speaker,* 1976; *Group Discussion and Decision Making,* Crowell, 1975.

WORK IN PROGRESS: The Professional Radio Broadcaster, for McGraw.

* * *

HASSAN, William Ephraim, Jr. 1923-

PERSONAL: Born October 13, 1923, in Brockton, Mass.; son of William E. and Matilda (Salamy) Hassan; married Rosetta T. Amodeo; children: William A., Thomas E. *Education:* Massachusetts College of Pharmacy, B.S., 1945, M.S., 1947, Ph.D., 1951; Boston University, additional study, 1947-48; Suffolk University, LL.B., 1965. *Home:* 18 Joseph Rd., Newton, Mass. 02160. *Office:* Peter Bent Brigham Hospital, 721 Huntington Ave., Brockton, Mass. 02115.

CAREER: Registered pharmacist; notary public; admitted to Bar of Massachusetts State, 1966; Massachusetts College of Pharmacy, Boston, instructor in pharmacology and biology, 1949-53, adjunct professor of hospital pharmacy, 1967-69, adjunct professor of jurisprudence and hospital pharmacy, 1969-71, trustee, 1971, 1973, vice-chairman, 1975; Peter Bent Brigham Hospital, Brockton, Mass., pharmacist-in-chief, 1951-56, assistant director, 1956-57, 1958-59, acting associate director, 1957-58, associate director, 1959-67, director, 1967—. Vice-president of operations and associate general counsel, National Medical Care, Inc., 1968-71; vice-president for administration, Affiliated Hospitals Center, Inc., 1976—. Harvard University, visiting lecturer, School of Public Health, 1969—, faculty member, Medical School, 1969—; preceptor, graduate programs in health care administration, George Washington University, 1967-68. Participant in various programs and conferences on medical and legal topics. Member of state and local health and civic committees. *Military service:* U.S. Public Health Service Reserves, 1960—; present rank, lieutenant commander.

MEMBER: International Academy of Law and Science (fellow), American Pharmaceutical Association, American Society of Hospital Pharmacists, American College of Apothecaries (hospital fellow), American Hospital Association, American College of Hospital Administrators (fellow), National League for Nursing, Society of Hospital Attorneys, Hospital Laundry Association (trustee, 1970—), New England Hospital Assembly, Massachusetts Hospital Association (member of board of trustees, 1968-71), Massachusetts Society of Hospital Pharmacists (vice-president, 1953-54; president, 1954-55), Massachusetts Public Health Association, Massachusetts Medical Society, Alumni Association of Massachusetts College of Pharmacy (second vice-president, 1965-66; president, 1967-68), Alumni Association of Suffolk University Law School, Boston Druggists' Association (president, 1961-63), Boston Bar Association, Greater Boston Hospital Association (director, 1968—; member of executive committee, 1968-71; vice-president, 1969-70; president, 1970-71), Wig and Robe Society, Century Club (president, 1969-70).

WRITINGS: Textbook of Hospital Pharmacy, Lea & Febiger, 1965, 3rd edition, 1973; (editor) *Techniques of Medication,* Lippincott, 1969; (editor) *Hazards of Medication,* Lippincott, 1971; *Law for the Pharmacy Student,* Lea &

Febiger, 1971. Contributor to *Journal of the American Pharmaceutical Association, Modern Hospital, Drug Topics, Hospitals,* and other publications. Hospital pharmacy editor, *Drug Topics,* 1966-72.

* * *

HATCH, (Alden) Denison 1935-

PERSONAL: Born August 15, 1935, in New York, N.Y.; son of Alden (an author) and Ruth (Brown) Hatch; married Margaret Cook, July 12, 1970. *Education:* Columbia University, B.A., 1958. *Politics:* Independent. *Religion:* Episcopalian. *Home:* 65 Riverside Ave., Stamford, Conn. 06905. *Agent:* Marvin Moss, 9200 Sunset Blvd., Los Angeles, Calif. 90069.

CAREER: Franklin Watts, Inc. (publisher), New York City, sales manager, 1961-64; *Library Journal,* New York City, advertising representative, 1964; Grolier Enterprises, New York City, product manager, 1965-67; Crowell Collier Macmillan, New York City, book club manager, 1968-69; Meredith Corp., Manhasset, N.Y., director of book clubs, 1969-71; Walter Weintz & Co., Stamford, Conn., vice-president and copywriter, 1972-75; free-lance direct response copywriter, 1976—. *Military service:* U.S. Army, 1957-59. *Member:* Authors Guild, Players Club (New York), Nutmeg Curling (Darien, Conn.).

WRITINGS: Statuary Rape, Coward, 1959; *Statues of Limitations,* Coward, 1961; *The Fingered City,* Eriksson, 1969; *Cedarhurst Alley,* Eriksson, 1970; *The Stork,* Morrow, 1977.

WORK IN PROGRESS: A novel, tentatively entitled *Ribbons of Steel.*

SIDELIGHTS: Film rights to *The Stork* have been sold to Universal Pictures. *Avocational interests:* Horse racing.

* * *

HATCHER, John 1942-

PERSONAL: Born January 7, 1942, in London, England; son of John Edward (a janitor) and Lilian (Lepper) Hatcher; married Janice Ranson (a physiotherapist). *Education:* London School of Economics and Political Science, B.Sc. (first class honors), 1964, Ph.D., 1967. *Home and office:* Corpus Christi College, Cambridge University, Cambridge, England.

CAREER: University of Kent, Canterbury, England, lecturer, 1967-73, senior lecturer in history, 1973-75; University of Colorado, Boulder, visiting professor of history, 1975-76; Cambridge University, Cambridge, England, lecturer in history and fellow of Corpus Christi College, 1976—. *Member:* Royal Historical Society (fellow).

WRITINGS: Rural Economy and Society in the Duchy of Cornwall, 1300-1500, Cambridge University Press, 1970; *English Tin Trade to 1550,* Oxford University Press, 1973; (with Theodore C. Barker) *History of British Pewter,* Longman, 1974. Also author of *Plague, Population and the English Economy, 1348-1530,* 1977, and *Enterprise and Poverty: Rural Society and Economic Change,* with E. Miller, in press. Contributor to history journals.

* * *

HAVEMEYER, Loomis 1886-1971

June 7, 1886—August 14, 1971; American educator and anthropologist. Obituaries: *New York Times,* August 16, 1971.

HAVIGHURST, Alfred F(reeman) 1904-

PERSONAL: Born September 30, 1904, in Mount Pleasant, Iowa; son of Freeman Alfred and Winifred (Weter) Havighurst; married Mildred Linscott, November 23, 1966. Education: Ohio Wesleyan University, B.A., 1925; University of Chicago, M.A., 1928; Harvard University, M.A., 1930, Ph.D., 1936. Religion: Methodist. Home: 11 Blake Field, Amherst, Mass. 01002. Office: Department of History, Amherst College, Amherst, Mass. 01002.

CAREER: High school history teacher in Covington, Ky., 1925-27; Pacific University, Forest Grove, Ore., professor of history and political science, 1928-29; Amherst College, Amherst, Mass., instructor, 1931-38, assistant professor, 1938-42, associate professor, 1942-54, professor of history, 1954-70, professor emeritus, 1970—. Visiting assistant professor, Mount Holyoke College, 1942. Military service: U.S. Army, 1942-46; served in Europe; became second lieutenant. Member: American Historical Association, Conference on British Studies, Historical Association (England), American Association of University Professors, Anglo-American Associates, Royal Historical Society (fellow), Phi Delta Theta. Awards, honors: A.M., Amherst College, 1954.

WRITINGS: (Editor) The Pirenne Thesis, Heath, 1958, 3rd edition, 1976; Twentieth-Century Britain, Harper, 1962, 2nd edition, 1966; Radical Journalist: H. W. Massingham, 1860-1874, Cambridge University Press, 1974; (editor) Modern England, 1901-1970, Cambridge University Press, 1976. Contributor to World Book Encyclopedia, Encyclopedia of World Biography, Encyclopaedia Britannica, and to historical journals.

WORK IN PROGRESS: Third edition of Twentieth-Century Britain, for University of Chicago Press.

*   *   *

HAWES, Judy 1913-

PERSONAL: Born October 16, 1913, in New York, N.Y.; daughter of Edward Harris (a manufacturers' agent) and Lester (Baker) Mays; married John Hawes (a banker), June 6, 1936; children: John, Amanda (Mrs. Theodore Smith), Jane, Lester Ann. Education: Vassar College, A.B., 1934; Paterson State College (now William Paterson College of New Jersey), Teacher's Certificate, 1962. Politics: Democrat ("McCarthy delegate to Chicago"). Religion: Protestant. Home: 79 Abbington Ter., Glen Rock, N.J. 07452.

CAREER: Teacher of the handicapped, 1958-76, most recently at Coleman School, Glen Rock, N.J. Member: Council for Exceptional Children (chapter president, 1968-69). Awards, honors: New Jersey Association of English Teachers Book Award for each publication; Spring Peepers won awards from New York Academy of Sciences, National Association of Science Teachers, and Childrens Book Council.

WRITINGS—"Let's-Read-and-Find-Out Science" series, published by Crowell: Fireflies in the Night, 1963; Bees and Beelines, 1964; Watch Honeybees with Me, 1964; Shrimps, 1967; Ladybug, Ladybug, Fly Away Home, 1967; Why Frogs Are Wet, 1968; What I Like about Toads, 1968; The Goats Who Killed the Leopard, 1970; Daddy Longlegs, 1972; Spring Peepers, 1975.

*   *   *

HAYDEN, Albert A(rthur) 1923-

PERSONAL: Born September 18, 1923, in Cape Girardeau

County, Mo.; son of Howard E. and Clara A. (Rust) Hayden; married Priscilla Anne Redin, September 11, 1954; children: Keith Alan, Anne Marie. Education: Attended Chicago City Junior College, 1946-48; University of Illinois, B.A., 1950; University of Chicago, graduate study, 1950; Bucknell University, M.A., 1952; University of Wisconsin, Ph.D., 1959. Home: 1329 Eastgate Rd., Springfield, Ohio 45503. Office: Department of History, Wittenberg University, Springfield, Ohio 45501.

CAREER: Wittenberg University, Springfield, Ohio, instructor, 1959-61, assistant professor, 1961-63, associate professor, 1963-70, professor of history, 1970—. Visiting associate professor of history, Kent State University, 1964. Military service: U.S. Army Air Forces, 1943-46; became technical sergeant. Member: American Historical Association, American Association of University Professors, Conference on British Studies, Ohio Academy of History. Awards, honors: Fulbright grant to Australia, 1954-55.

WRITINGS: New South Wales Immigration Policy, 1856-1900, American Philosophical Society, 1971. Contributor to Dictionary of Australian Biography and Journal of Royal Australian Historical Society.

WORK IN PROGRESS: A study of the Reform Bill of 1832.

*   *   *

HAYDEN, Carl T(rumbull) 1877-1972

October 2, 1877—January 25, 1972; American congressional leader. Obituaries: New York Times, January 26, 1972; Washington Post, January 27, 1972; Newsweek, February 7, 1972; Time, February 7, 1972.

*   *   *

HAYES, Grace Person 1919-

PERSONAL: Born February 11, 1919, in Ware, Mass.; daughter of Flynn Russell and Effie (Spencer) Person; married Robert Cary Hayes (a labor economist), October 21, 1950; children: Martha Anne, Benjamin Russell. Education: Wellesley College, B.A., 1940; Columbia University, M.A., 1941. Home: 5425 Harwood Rd., Bethesda, Md. 20014. Office: T. N. Dupuy Associates, P.O. Box 157, Dunn Loring, Va. 22027.

CAREER: U.S. Navy, officer, 1943-53, assigned as historian to Historical Section, Joint Chiefs of Staff, to write a history of the war against Japan, 1946-53; retired as lieutenant; Historical Evaluation and Research Organization and T. N. Dupuy Associates, Dunn Loring, Va., staff associate and director of research, 1963—.

WRITINGS: (With Trevor Nevitt Dupuy) The Military History of World War I, F. Watts, Volume V: The Campaigns on the Turkish Fronts, 1967, Volume X: Naval and Overseas War, 1916-1918, 1967; (with Dupuy) The Military History of Revolutionary War Battles, F. Watts, 1970; The Compact History of World War I, Hawthorn, 1972; (with Dupuy and J. A. C. Andrews) The Almanac of World Military Power, Bowker, 1974; (with Paul Martell) World Military Leaders, Bowker, 1974; (with Dupuy and Gay M. Hammerman) The American Revolution: A Global War, McKay, 1977.

*   *   *

HAYES, Nelson (Taylor) 1903-1971

October 9, 1903—August 28, 1971; American businessman

and novelist. Obituaries: *New York Times,* September 2, 1971. (See index for *CA* sketch)

*   *   *

HAYMES, Robert C.   1931-

PERSONAL: Born July 3, 1931, in New York, N.Y.; son of Michael and Winifred (Koenig) Haymes; married Jamie Buswell, January 22, 1965; children: Douglas Fletcher, Lisa Melanie, Nancy Shannon. *Education:* New York University, B.A., 1952, M.S., 1953, Ph.D., 1959. *Home:* 10611 Candlewood, Houston, Tex. 77042. *Office:* Department of Space Physics and Astronomy, Rice University, Houston, Tex. 77001.

CAREER: New York University, New York, N.Y., assistant professor of physics, 1959-62; Jet Propulsion Laboratory, Pasadena, Calif., research appointee, 1962-64; Rice University, Houston, Tex., assistant professor, 1964-66, associate professor of space science, 1966-72, professor of space physics and astronomy, 1972—. *Member:* American Astronomical Society, American Geophysical Union, American Association for the Advancement of Science, American Association of University Professors, Sigma Xi.

WRITINGS: Introduction to Space Science, Wiley, 1971. Contributor of about thirty articles to science journals.

WORK IN PROGRESS: Research in gamma ray astronomy.

*   *   *

HAYS, Peter L.   1938-

PERSONAL: Born April 18, 1938, in Bremerhaven, Germany; son of Eric (a grocer) and Elsa (Nussbaum) Hays; married Myrna Mantel (a teacher), September 14, 1963; children: Melissa Anne, Eric Lee, Jeffrey Michael. *Education:* University of Rochester, A.B., 1959; New York University, M.A., 1961; Ohio State University, Ph.D., 1965. *Residence:* Davis, Calif. *Office:* Department of English, University of California, Davis, Calif. 95616.

CAREER: Ohio State University, Columbus, instructor in English, 1965-66; University of California, Davis, assistant professor, 1966-72, associate professor, 1972-77, professor of English and comparative literature, 1977—, chairman of English department, 1974-77. Fulbright lecturer in Mainz, Germany, 1977-78. Instructor in department of independent instruction, University of California, Berkeley. *Military service:* U.S. Army, 1959-60. U.S. Army Reserve, 1960-66. *Member:* Modern Language Association of America, Philological Association of the Pacific Coast, Society for the Study of Southern Literature.

WRITINGS: The Limping Hero, New York University Press, 1971. Contributor of numerous articles to literature journals.

WORK IN PROGRESS: Research on folklore and literature.

SIDELIGHTS: Peter Hays told *CA,* ''Although faculty may be paid only for their teaching and promoted . . . largely for their publications, publication, for me, is not separate from teaching, but rather, extends the podium offered in the classroom and allows professors further scope 'to profess' their views, to educate more widely.''

*   *   *

HAZELRIGG, Meredith K(ent)   1942-

PERSONAL: Born March 28, 1942, in Allegan, Mich.; son

of Burke Browning (a bookkeeper) and Genevieve (Sakal) Hazelrigg; married Gail Marie Stillman (deceased); married Noel Fields (an artist). *Education:* Michigan State University, B.A., 1965, M.A., 1967. *Address:* P.O. Box 18202, Lansing, Mich. 48901.

CAREER: Michigan Department of Social Services, Boys Training School, Lansing, Mich., member of staff, 1964-68; teacher of adult education in public schools in Lansing, 1965-67; Lansing Community College, Lansing, instructor in English, 1966-69; Malcolm X Communications Skills Academy, Lansing, instructor in language skills and administrative assistant, 1970-71; *Westside News,* Lansing, staff writer and advertising director, 1970-71; commissioner, Allegan City Planning Commission, 1971—. Member of board of directors, Allegan Community Development Corp., 1971-74. Volunteer consultant to community groups throughout state of Michigan.

WRITINGS: (With John Antico) *Insight through Fiction: Dealing Effectively with the Short Story,* Cummings, 1970. Author of newspaper columns, ''Views from Other Perspectives,'' ''The Armchair Gardener,'' and ''Bookmark,'' appearing in *Allegan County Photo Journal, Allegan News Gazette,* and other local weeklies. Contributor of various articles ranging in subjects from credit to ceramics to periodicals.

WORK IN PROGRESS: Story of Frederick Douglas and *Story of Marcus Garvey,* books for children, with wife, Noel Fields; *Hegel's Dialectical Method: An Introduction to Its Practical Use; Third World Reader,* a historical anthology, with Kimathi Mohammed; a ceramic text for studio and classroom; an introduction to conversational Chinese.

SIDELIGHTS: Meredith Hazelrigg told *CA:* ''[I] do not like to see academic knowledge or awareness . . . exist without practical application. I have . . . 'retired' through the benefit of playing the stock market and accepting a lower standard of living, thus freeing myself to undertake social experiments and apply myself in volunteer activities where funds are not available to sustain an effort.'' Hazelrigg is presently building low fire pottery works with his wife while he is ''biding time until publishers are less afraid of political implications widely accepted outside of print.''

*   *   *

HEATH, Edward Richard George   1916-

PERSONAL: Born July 9, 1916, in Broadstairs, Kent, England; son of William George (a builder and carpenter) and Edith Anne (Pantony) Heath. *Education:* Balliol College, Oxford, M.A., 1939. *Office:* House of Commons, Westminster, London SW1, England.

CAREER: Served with British Civil Service, 1946-47, resigned to become prospective Conservative candidate for Bexley; House of Commons, London, England, member of Parliament from Bexley, 1950-74, from Bexley, Sidcup, 1974—, with successive posts as assistant Conservative whip and Lord Commissioner of the Treasury, 1951, joint deputy government chief whip, 1952, deputy government chief whip, 1953-55, Parliamentary Secretary to the Treasury and government chief whip, 1955-59, Minister of Labour, 1959-60, Lord Privy Seal with Foreign Office responsibilities, 1960-63, Secretary of State for Industry, Trade, and Regional Development and president of the Board of Trade, 1963-64, Conservative leader of opposition, 1965-70, Prime Minister and first Lord of the Treasury, 1970-74, Conservative leader of opposition, 1974-75, president of Conservative Commonwealth and Overseas Council, 1975—. Visiting fellow, Nuffield College, Oxford University, 1962-69; Cyril Foster Memorial Lecturer, Oxford University, 1965; Godkin Lecturer, Harvard University, 1966; visiting Chubb Fellow, Yale University, 1975. President, Federation of University Conservative and Unionist Associations, 1959—. Member of council, Royal College of Music, 1961-70; chairman, London Symphony Orchestra Trust, 1963-70. *Military service:* British Army, 1940-46; served in France, Belgium, Netherlands, and Germany; became lieutenant colonel; mentioned in dispatches. Territorial Army, regimental commander, 1947-51, master gunner within the Tower of London, 1951-54.

MEMBER: Bucks Club, Carlton Club, Royal Yacht Squadron, New York Yacht Club (honorary member). *Awards, honors:* Member of the Order of the British Empire, 1946; Smith-Mundt fellowship in the United States, 1953; Charlemagne Prize from Aachen, West Germany, 1963; honorary fellow, Baliol College, Oxford University, 1970; Estes J. Kefauver Union of the Free Award, Edward J. Meeman Foundation, 1971; Freiherr von Stein Foundation prize, 1971; Stresseman Gold Medal, 1971; D.C.L., Oxford University, 1971; D.Tech., Bradford University, 1972; LL.D., Westminster College, Salt Lake City, Utah, 1976; Dr.h.c., Sorbonne, University of Paris, 1976.

WRITINGS: (With others) *One Nation—A Tory Approach to Social Problems,* Conservative Political Centre, 1950; *Parliament and People* (booklet), Conservative Political Centre, 1960; *The Conservative Goal: A Call to Action* (booklet), Conservative Political Centre, 1966; *Keeping the Peace: A New Look at the Role of the United Nations,* United Nations Association, 1968; *Old World, New Horizons: Britain, Europe, and the Atlantic Alliance* (Godkin lectures, 1967), Harvard University Press, 1970; *My Style of Government,* Evening Standard, 1972; *Sailing: A Course of My Life,* Sidgewick & Jackson, 1975; *Music: A Joy for Life,* Sidgewick & Jackson, 1976.

SIDELIGHTS: Edward Heath brought an unlikely background to the leadership of the Conservative Party of Great Britain. Lacking the aristocratic or political connections often found in that office, Heath originally had planned for a career in music. As a child, he sang in a church choir and played the organ. Although he went to Balliol College on an organ scholarship, he developed an interest in politics and economics while there. His student political affiliations included the presidencies of the Oxford University Conservative Association and the Oxford Union.

During the summer of 1939, Heath hitchhiked across northern Europe visiting the politically troubled Poland and Danzig. Although philosophically a Conservative, Heath opposed the Conservative appeasement of Germany in the 1930's and volunteered for the British Army in 1940. After the war he rejected music as a career, although it remained a favorite pastime—demonstrated not only by his book on the subject but also by his vice-presidency of the Bach Choir since 1970 and by the fact that he has been an honorary member of the London Symphony Orchestra since 1974.

After being elected to Parliament from a former Labour district, Heath rose through the Conservative Party ranks to become the party's leader. Throughout his political career, he has especially espoused unity for Western Europe and was instrumental in bringing Britain into the European Economic Community (EEC) and into the Common Market. In 1970 he led the Conservative Party to a narrow victory which established Heath as Prime Minister until his party was defeated in 1974.

Heath took up sailing after he was well-established in his political career. He was the winner of the Sydney to Hobart Ocean Race in 1969 and captained Britain's winning Admiral's Cup team in 1971. Reviewing *Sailing: A Course of My Life,* John Prentice writes: "It is so difficult to write about a complex technical art in a manner which will interest the general public—which is what one guesses Mr. Heath is aiming at—and at the same time not appear mundane to practicioners of the art. . . . It will be obvious to the reader of *Sailing,* as it always has been to those who race against him, that Mr. Heath enjoys winning. . . . He describes the reasons for which after he had become Leader of the Opposition in 1965, he decided to take up sailing and the manner in which he did it." Prentice adds that Heath "is careful to avoid analogues between his recreation and politics: but it remains a fact that great physical strength and endurance are required even for short races in the modern large ocean-racing yacht." J. A. Phillips finds Heath in this book "disarmingly charming" and relates Heath's report that "he gave up golf because the players talked politics." Calling the book "a British best-seller" David Anable finds Heath taking a philosophical stance: "He is trying to get across to his compatriots an attitude of mind. He calls it at one point 'a more effective effort to attain the highest standards to which we can aspire.'" Anable adds that as Prime Minister, Heath "could not persuade his countrymen to back him up against the striking coal miners in 1974; the people threw him out of office. But as author and sailor he bridges the gap."

BIOGRAPHICAL/CRITICAL SOURCES: George Hutchinson, *Edward Heath: A Personal and Political Biography,* Longmans, Green, 1970; Marian Evans, *Ted Heath: A Family Portrait,* Kimber & Co., 1970; *Reader's Digest,* April, 1972; *Newsweek,* May 28, 1972, October 1, 1973; Margaret Laing, *Edward Heath: Prime Minister,* Third Press, 1973; *New Statesman,* November 28, 1975; *Christian Science Monitor,* June 3, 1976; *Best Sellers,* July, 1976; *Yachting,* July, 1976.

*   *   *

HECHT, James L(ee) 1926-

PERSONAL: Born December 21, 1926, in New York, N.Y.; son of Leo (a businessman) and Edith (Hoffheimer) Hecht; married Amy Blatchford (a university professor), October 10, 1953; children: Charles Blatchford, Margaret Williams, Andrew Clark (deceased). *Education:* Cornell University, B.Ch.E., 1949; Georgia Institute of Technology, M.S., 1951; Yale University, Ph.D., 1955. *Home:* 111 South Spring Valley Rd., Wilmington, Del. 19807.

CAREER: E. I. du Pont de Nemours & Co., research engineer, 1953-59, staff engineer, 1959-60, research supervisor, 1960-68, research associate, 1968-70, all in Buffalo, N.Y., research associate in Richmond, Va., 1970-76, research associate in Wilmington, Del., 1976—. Housing Opportunities Made Equal, president and chairman of board, Buffalo chapter, 1965-70, president, Richmond chapter, 1973-77; vice-president, Niagara Frontier Housing Development Co., 1968-70. *Military service:* U.S. Army, 1945-47. *Member:* American Chemical Society (chairman of western New York section, 1966-67).

WRITINGS: Because It Is Right: Integration in Housing, Little, Brown, 1970.

*   *   *

HEDLUND, Ronald D(avid) 1941-

PERSONAL: Born June 16, 1941, in Joliet, Ill.; son of

Henry G. (a minister) and Betty (Nelson) Hedlund; married Ellen Parrish (a guidance counselor), August 22, 1964; children: Karen M., David P. *Education:* Augustana College, Rock Island, Ill., B.A., 1963; University of Iowa, M.A., 1964, Ph.D., 1967. *Politics:* Independent. *Religion:* Lutheran. *Home:* 2114 East Wood Pl., Shorewood, Wis. 53211. *Office:* Department of Political Science, University of Wisconsin, Milwaukee, Wis. 53201.

CAREER: University of Wisconsin—Milwaukee, assistant professor, 1967-73, associate professor of political science, 1973—, director of political research laboratory, 1968-70, director of social science research facility, 1970—, scientist, Urban Research Center, 1976—. Managing partner and consultant, Wisconsin Public Opinion and Marketing Research. Wisconsin legislative service fellow, American Political Science Association, 1967—. *Member:* International Political Science Association, American Political Science Association, American Association for Public Opinion Research, Midwest Political Science Association, Southern Political Science Association. *Awards, honors:* Social Science Research Council faculty research grant, 1967-68; American Political Science Association grant, 1970; University of Wisconsin—Milwaukee research grants, 1974-75, 1976-77.

WRITINGS: (With Robert Paul Boynton and Garrison Nelson) *Political Analysis: Theory and Research in American Politics,* Sernoll, 1965; (contributor) Samuel C. Patterson, editor, *Midwest Legislative Politics,* Institute of Public Affairs, University of Iowa, 1967; (with Wilder W. Crane) *The Job of the Legislator: Wisconsin,* American Political Science Association, 1969; (editor with Louis D. Hayes, and contributor) *The Conduct of Political Inquiry: Behavioral Political Inquiry,* Prentice-Hall, 1970; (with Crane) *The Job of the Wisconsin Legislator,* American Political Science Association, 1971; (with Patterson and G. Robert Boynton) *Representatives and Represented,* Wiley, 1975. Contributor to *New Republic, Milwaukee Journal, American Journal of Sociology, Experimental Study of Politics,* and other journals in his field. Member of editorial board, *Legislative Studies Quarterly.*

WORK IN PROGRESS: Research on measuring performance levels in legislative bodies and on factors affecting performance.

*   *   *

HEDRICK, Basil C(alvin) 1932-

PERSONAL: Born March 17, 1932, in Lewistown, Mo.; son of Truman B. (a merchant marine captain) and M. LaVeta (Stice) Hedrick; married Anne Lanier Kehoe (co-owner of a travel agency), January 19, 1957; children: Anne Lanier. *Education:* Universidad Nacional Autonoma de Mexico, student, 1952, 1953; Augustana College, Rock Island, Ill., A.B., 1956; University of Florida, M.A., 1957, doctoral study, 1958-59; Southern Illinois University, doctoral work, 1962-63; Inter-American University, Ph.D., 1966; summer graduate study at University of Vienna, 1956, and University of the Americas, 1962. *Politics:* Independent. *Home:* 805 Twisdale, Carbondale, Ill. 62901. *Office:* University Museum and Art Galleries, Southern Illinois University, Carbondale, Ill. 62901.

CAREER: Intermittently self employed as translator and interpreter, 1951—; Rock Island County (Ill.) Public School System, elementary teacher, 1954-55; head of elementary language problems and remedial reading programs in public schools and teacher of adult education courses, Alamogordo, N.M., 1957-58; University of Florida, Gainesville,

assistant director of School of Inter-American Studies, 1958-59; Southern Illinois University, Carbondale, lecturer in Spanish, 1959-63, Latin American Institute, acting director, 1959-60, assistant director, 1960-63, University Museum, curator of exhibits, 1963, coordinator and leader of Summer Study Abroad Program and Summer Study Tour, 1963; Fullerton Junior College, Fullerton, Calif., faculty member in foreign language and social science division and assistant to the president, 1963-67; Southern Illinois University, assistant professor of anthropology, 1967-69, associate professor of conservation and outdoor education, 1969-72, professor of conservation and outdoor education, 1972—, University Museum, assistant director, 1967-69, acting director, 1969-70, director, 1970-72, curator of anthropology section, 1972-74, director, and curator of anthropology section, 1974, University Museum and Art Galleries, director, and curator of anthropology section, 1974—, Division of International Education, dean, 1972-74, director, 1974. Senior Fulbright-Hays lecturer, Brazil, 1972. Project director for Fort Massac Restoration Project, Illinois Department of Conservation. Member of zoning board of appeals, City of Carbondale, 1976-80; chairman of steering committee, Goals for Carbondale.

MEMBER: Association for Latin American Studies, American Association of Museums, Association of Science Museum Directors, National Association for Nepalese Studies, National Association for Afghan Studies, Mid-West Conference of Museums, Illinois Archaeological Survey, Jackson County Historical Society, Frankfort Area Historical Society, Sigma Delta Pi, Phi Alpha Theta, Phi Kappa Pi. *Awards, honors:* Cross of Eloy Alfaro; Best Teacher of the Year award, Fullerton Junior College, 1966; U.S. Department of State grant to Bangladesh, 1973.

WRITINGS: Fray Bernardino de Sahagun, School of Inter-American Studies, University of Florida, 1959; (editor) *Investigations in Progress in the Field of Latin American Studies,* Pan American Union, 1959; *Seis Cosas de Papel: Poesias,* Instituto Norteno de Cultura, 1964; (with wife, Anne K. Hedrick) *Historical Dictionary of Panama,* Scarecrow, 1970; (contributor) *Man across the Sea,* University of Texas Press, 1971; (editor with J. Charles Kelley and Carroll L. Riley) *The North Mexican Frontier: Readings in Archaeology, Ethnohistory, and Ethnography,* Southern Illinois University Press, 1971; (with A. K. Hedrick) *Historical and Cultural Dictionaries of Asia: Nepal,* Scarecrow, 1972; (editor with Kelley and Riley) *The Classic Southwest: Readings in Archaeology, Ethnohistory, and Ethnology,* Southern Illinois University Press, 1973; (editor with Kelley and Riley) *The Mesoamerican Southwest: Readings in Archaeology, Ethnohistory, and Ethnology,* Southern Illinois University Press, 1974; (with Riley) *Across the Chichimec Sea,* Southern Illinois University Press, in press. General editor of Scarecrow's "Historical and Cultural Dictionaries of Asia" series, 1972-76; co-editor of Southern Illinois University "Centennial Publications" series, 1971-74; chief editor of "Mesoamerican Studies," "Southern Illinois Studies," and "Museum Studies" series, all published by Southern Illinois University. Contributor to *Encyclopedia Americana, Worldmark Encyclopedia,* and *American Oxford Encyclopedia;* contributor of articles and reviews to magazines and journals.

*   *   *

HEDRICK, Floyd D(udley) 1927-

PERSONAL: Born January 19, 1927, in Lynchburg, Va.; son of Silas Dudley and Alice Maude (Stowe) Hedrick; married Rachel Childress, May 27, 1950; children: Susan, Alice. *Education:* Virginia Commercial College, B.S., 1948; attended Lynchburg College, 1954-55, and American University, 1963-65; additional study at George Washington University and Harvard University. *Politics:* Independent. *Religion:* Protestant. *Home:* 3824 King Arthur Rd., Annandale, Va. 22003. *Office:* Department of Procurement and Contracting, Library of Congress, Washington, D.C. 20540.

CAREER: Trailways, Inc., Lynchburg, Va. and Washington, D.C., purchasing manager and superintendent of stores, 1948-66; Macke Co. (food service), Cheverly, Md., corporate vice-president of purchasing, 1966-72; Atlantic Supply Co. (wholly-owned subsidiary of Macke Co.), Hyattsville, Md., vice-president, 1967-71, president, 1971-72; Library of Congress, Washington, D.C., chief of procurement and contracting department, 1973—. Member of Interagency Procurement Policy Committee, 1973—, and Interagency Metrication Policy Committee, 1976—. Consultant to Interracial Council of Business Opportunity of Greater Washington Area, 1966-72. *Military service:* U.S. Naval Reserve, 1944-46, 1950-52; became commander. *Member:* National Association of Purchasing Management (member of board of directors, 1972-73), American Management Association, Purchasing Management Association of Washington, D.C. (president, 1969-70), 32nd Degree Mason.

WRITINGS: Purchasing Management in the Smaller Company, American Management Association, 1971; (contributor) George Alijian, editor, *Purchasing Handbook,* 3rd edition, McGraw, 1973; *Purchasing for Owners of Small Plants,* Small Business Administration, 1976. Contributor to business and purchasing journals.

AVOCATIONAL INTERESTS: Motorboating.

*   *   *

HEER, Nancy Whittier

PERSONAL: Surname is pronounced Hare; born in Swampscott, Mass.; daughter of Philip Page and Gladys (Reid) Whittier; married David M. Heer (a professor), June 29, 1957; children: Laura Page, Catherine Reid. *Education:* Syracuse University, A.B., 1954; Radcliffe College, A.M., 1956; Harvard University, Ph.D., 1968. *Home:* 2120 East Live Oak Dr., Los Angeles, Calif. 90068. *Office:* Office of the President, Immaculate Heart College, 2021 Western Ave., Los Angeles, Calif. 90027.

CAREER: Wheaton College, Norton, Mass., associate professor of government, 1968-72, provost, 1974-76; Harvard University, Russian Research Center, Cambridge, Mass., research associate, 1968-76; Immaculate Heart College, Los Angeles, Calif., president, 1977—. *Member:* American Political Science Association, American Association for the Advancement of Slavic Studies.

WRITINGS: Politics and History in the Soviet Union, M.I.T. Press, 1971; (editor and contributor) *The Dynamics of Soviet Politics,* Harvard University Press, 1976; (editor and contributor) *Windows on the Russian Past,* American Association for the Advancement of Slavic Studies, 1977.

*   *   *

HEGER, Theodore Ernest 1907-

PERSONAL: Born February 27, 1907, in St. Paul, Minn.; son of Hermann Henry (a manufacturer) and Mathile (Taufmann) Heger; married Dorothy Johnson (a church organist), March 1, 1930; children: Theodore Charles, Diane Virginia

Heger Kvamme. *Education:* University of Minnesota, B.A., 1929; University of Michigan, M.Mus., 1939. *Home:* 1502 Golden Ave., Ann Arbor, Mich. 48104. *Office:* School of Music, University of Michigan, Ann Arbor, Mich. 48105.

CAREER: Virginia State Junior College (now Mesabi State Junior College), Virginia, Minn., chairman of department of music, 1929-45; University of Michigan, Ann Arbor, assistant professor, 1945-54, associate professor, 1954-62, professor of music history and musicology, 1962—. *Member:* American Musicological Society, American Association of University Professors, Pi Kappa Lambda.

WRITINGS: (With Earl V. Moore) *The Symphony and the Symphonic Poem: Analytical and Descriptive Charts of the Standard Symphonic Repertory,* Educational Music Service, 1949, 6th edition, Ulrich's Books, 1974; *Music of the Classic Period,* W. C. Brown, 1969.

SIDELIGHTS: Theodore Heger traveled in Europe, the Near East, and Africa in 1960 and 1967.

*   *   *

HEIM, Alice (Winifred) 1913-

PERSONAL: Born April 19, 1913, in London, England; daughter of Felix (a company director) and Lucie (Steinhard) Heim; children: (adopted) Jessica Lucie, Quentin Felix. *Education:* Newnham College, Cambridge, M.A., 1935, Ph.D., 1939. *Home:* 8 Bateman St., Cambridge CB2 1NB, England. *Office:* Psychological Laboratory, Cambridge University, Downing St., Cambridge, England.

CAREER: Cambridge University, Cambridge, England, instructor and researcher in educational, clinical, and psychometric psychology, 1939—. Has given talks on BBC radio. *Member:* British Psychological Society (fellow), British Association for the Advancement of Science, Experimental Psychology Society, Cambridge Womens Research Club, Clare Hall (Cambridge; fellow), Cambridge Scientists Lunch Club (president, 1970-72).

WRITINGS: The Appraisal of Intelligence, Methuen, 1954, N.F.E.R. Publishing Co., 1970; *Intelligence and Personality,* Penguin, 1970; *Psychological Testing,* Oxford University Press, 1974; *Teaching and Learning in Higher Education,* N.F.E.R. Publishing Co., 1976. Deviser of various tests of intelligence, interests, and personality. Contributor of papers to British, American, and French psychological journals. Member of editorial board, *Occupational Psychology,* 1970-73.

WORK IN PROGRESS: Currently developing a test of perceptual reasoning for five- to ten-year olds, a vocabulary scale, and a test of verbal reasoning; researching on French and English versions of the Brook Reaction Test of interests and personality.

SIDELIGHTS: Alice Heim has traveled in Corsica, Turkey, Israel, France, Austria, Yugoslavia, Germany, and the United States. She told *CA,* "Unlike most experimental psychologists, I consider that experience is as important as behavior, that human beings are more interesting than rats—but that the latter deserve humane treatment."

*   *   *

HEIMANN, Susan 1940-

PERSONAL: Born March 12, 1940, in New York, N.Y.; daughter of Heinrich (a patent attorney and engineer) and Netta (Oppler) Heimann; married Richard Llewellyn, 1974. *Education:* Barnard College, B.A., 1961; New York University, M.A., 1963. *Home:* 41 Terenuse Rd. W., Dublin 6, Ireland.

CAREER: Grolier, Inc., New York, N.Y., associate editor, *New Book of Knowledge* and *Lands and People,* 1964-72; currently free-lance editor.

WRITINGS: (With Michael Edison) *Public Opinion Polls,* F. Watts, 1972; *Christopher Columbus,* F. Watts, 1973.

WORK IN PROGRESS: Research on Field Marshal Mannerheim and Leigh Hunt.

AVOCATIONAL INTERESTS: People, art, films, travel, music, wine, photography.

* * *

HEISER, Victor George 1873-1972

February 5, 1873—February 27, 1972; American physician and public health authority. Obituaries: *New York Times,* February 28, 1972; *Washington Post,* March 1, 1972; *Time,* March 13, 1972; *Current Biography,* May, 1972.

* * *

HELD, Jack Preston 1926-

PERSONAL: Born May 3, 1926; son of Preston Clare and Mary Agnes (Cunningham) Held. *Education:* Western Reserve University (now Case Western Reserve University), B.A., 1951; University of California, Los Angeles, M.A., 1954. *Home:* 3954 Pepper Tree Lane, San Jose, Calif. 95127.

CAREER: Lyric Theatre, Cleveland, Ohio, professional actor, 1947-50; English and speech teacher in high school in Lancaster, Calif., 1957-60; Antelope Valley College, Lancaster, instructor in speech and theater, beginning 1960. Community theater director and adviser in Lancaster, Calif.; member and adviser, English-American Reading Room, Krems, Austria. *Military service:* U.S. Army, Infantry, 1944-46. *Member:* American Educational Theatre Association, National Education Association, Speech Communication Association, American Association of University Professors, California Teachers Association.

WRITINGS: Improvisational Acting: A Handbook of Exercises for the Student Actor, Wadsworth, 1971. Also adapter for theater, Anton Koolhaas, *Don't Do It, Snow White,* translated from the Dutch by Wim Gietema and Guus Pieter Vis, Netherlands Centre of International Theatre Institute. Contributor to *Speech Teacher.*

WORK IN PROGRESS: Editing a collection of plays, a novella, and short stories by Anton Koolhaas, translated by Guus Pieter Vis.†

* * *

HELD, R(oyer) Burnell 1921-

PERSONAL: Born October 30, 1921, in Hinton, Iowa; son of Albert Herbert (a farmer) and Neva Lucille (Royer) Held; married Edith M. Ladue (an office manager), April 9, 1949; children: Royer L., Marcia L., Eunice L., Karl E., Karen A. *Education:* Iowa State College (now University), B.S., 1947, M.S., 1949, Ph.D., 1953. *Politics:* Democrat. *Religion:* Unitarian Universalist. *Home:* 4760 Venturi Lane, Fort Collins, Colo. 80521. *Office:* Department of Economics, Colorado State University, Fort Collins, Colo. 80521.

CAREER: U.S. Bureau of the Budget, Washington, D.C., junior budget examiner, 1948-49; Iowa Agricultural Experiment Station, Ames, agricultural economist, 1950-53; Michigan State University, East Lansing, assistant professor of agricultural economics, 1953-54; Pennsylvania State Univer-

sity, State College, associate professor of agricultural economics, 1954-55; Resources for the Future, Inc., Washington, D.C., research associate, 1955-64; U.S. Department of Commerce, Washington, D.C., study director, 1964-65; U.S. Department of Interior, Bureau of Outdoor Recreation, Washington, D.C., chief of Division of Research and Education, 1965-67; Colorado State University, Fort Collins, professor of economics and professor of outdoor recreation, 1967—. Visiting summer lecturer, University of Colorado, 1961. President, Poudre Valley Greenbelt Association, 1970. *Military service:* U.S. Army, 1943-46; became first lieutenant; received Bronze Star with cluster and Purple Heart.

MEMBER: American Economic Association, American Agricultural Economics Association, American Association for the Advancement of Science, Society of Park and Recreation Educators, Western Regional Science Association, Alpha Zeta, Sigma Xi, Phi Kappa Phi, Gamma Sigma Delta.

WRITINGS: (With Marion Clawson) *The Federal Lands,* Johns Hopkins Press, 1957; (with Clawson) *Land for the Future,* Johns Hopkins Press, 1960; (with Clawson) *Soil Conservation in Perspective,* Johns Hopkins Press, 1965; (contributor) *A Proposed Program for Scenic Roads and Parkways,* U.S. Department of Commerce, 1966; (contributor) *Fish and Wildlife Resources on Public Lands,* Public Land Law Review Commission Report, 1969. Contributor to land use journals.

WORK IN PROGRESS: Studies on the value of nonpriced, nonmarket goods such as water, natural areas, and the value of a pollution-free environment.

* * *

HELLIE, Richard 1937-

PERSONAL: Born May 8, 1937, in Waterloo, Iowa; son of Ole I. (a journalist) and Elizabeth (a teacher; maiden name, Larsen) Hellie; married Jean Laves (an instructor in Russian literature), December 23, 1961; children: Benjamin. *Education:* University of Chicago, A.B., 1958, A.M., 1960, Ph.D., 1965; graduate study at Russian Research Center, Harvard University, 1962-63, and University of Moscow, 1963-64. *Religion:* Atheist. *Home:* 4917 South Greenwood Ave., Chicago, Ill. 60615. *Office address:* Department of History, University of Chicago, 1126 East 59th St., Box 78, Chicago, Ill. 60637.

CAREER: Rutgers University, New Brunswick, N.J., assistant professor of Russian history, 1965-66; University of Chicago, Chicago, Ill., assistant professor, 1966-71, associate professor of Russian history, 1971—. *Member:* American Historical Association, American Association for the Advancement of Slavic Studies, American Society for Legal History, Labor History Society, Peasant History Society. *Awards, honors:* Herbert Baxter Adams Prize in European history, American Historical Association, 1972, for *Enserfment and Military Change in Muscovy;* Guggenheim fellowship, 1973-74.

WRITINGS: (Compiler, editor, and translator) *Muscovite Society: Readings for Introduction to Russian Civilization,* Syllabus Division, University of Chicago, 1967; *Enserfment and Military Change in Muscovy,* University of Chicago Press, 1971.

WORK IN PROGRESS: Slavery in Muscovy.

* * *

HELLMANN, Anna 1902(?)-1972

1902(?)—January 15, 1972; American poet and lecturer.

Obituaries: *New York Times,* January 17, 1972.

* * *

HELLSTROM, Ward   1930-

PERSONAL: Born February 2, 1930, in Evanston, Ill.; son of Klaus Edward and Bernice Lois (Tompkins) Hellstrom; married Phyllis Joan Wyman, December 19, 1953; children: Lory, Joshua Klaus, Nathaniel, Zachary. *Education:* Northwestern University, B.S., 1952; University of Illinois, M.A., 1956, Ph.D., 1961. *Politics:* Democrat. *Home:* 1000 Southwest 25th Pl., Gainesville, Fla. 32601. *Office:* Department of English, University of Florida, Gainesville, Fla. 32601.

CAREER: University of Florida, Gainesville, assistant professor, 1961-67, associate professor, 1967-71, professor of English, 1971—. *Member:* Modern Language Association of America, National Council of Teachers of English, College Conference on Composition and Communication, Southeastern Conference on English in the Two-Year College, South Atlantic Modern Language Association, Florida College English Association (president, 1971-72).

WRITINGS: On the Poems of Tennyson, University of Florida Press, 1972. Contributor to *Studies in English Literature, New Orleans Review* and other journals.

WORK IN PROGRESS: A handbook of English usage.

* * *

HELMER, William F.   1926-

PERSONAL: Born November 12, 1926, in Oneida, N.Y.; married Joan Smith, August 27, 1955; children: William S., Stephen, Mary, Michael. *Education:* New York College for Teachers (now State University of New York at Albany), B.A., 1953; University of Pennsylvania, M.A., 1955, Ph.D., 1963. *Address:* P.O. Box 157, Morrisville, N.Y. 13408. *Office:* Division of Liberal Arts, State University of New York Agricultural and Technical College, Morrisville, N.Y. 13408.

CAREER: Has worked as a machinist, a postal clerk, a technical writer, a race track pari-mutuel clerk, and an amateur printer; State University of New York Agricultural and Technical College at Morrisville, instructor, 1956-57, assistant professor, 1957-62, associate professor, 1962-64, professor of English, 1964—, chairman of Liberal Arts Division, 1971—. *Military service:* U.S. Army, Corps of Engineers, 1945-46, 1950-51. *Member:* Modern Language Association of America, American Association of University Professors, Railway and Locomotive Historical Society, Society for Industrial Archeology.

WRITINGS: O. & W.: The Long Life and Slow Death of the New York, Ontario & Western Railway, Howell-North Books, 1959; *Rip Van Winkle Railroads,* Howell-North Books, 1970.

WORK IN PROGRESS: A book, tentatively entitled *A History of New York State Railroads.*

* * *

HELMKER, Judith Anne   1940-

PERSONAL: Born January 22, 1940, in Highland Park, Mich.; daughter of Theodore Carl (a banker) and Dorothea (Blitz) Huebner; married Lewis J. Helmker (an accountant), August 20, 1960; children: Jon Lewis, Hollie Anne, Shellie Dee. *Education:* Central Michigan University, B.S., 1961; Michigan State University, M.S., 1968, Ed.S., 1972. *Poli-*

tics: Republican. *Religion:* Methodist. *Home:* 2300 Wellington Dr., Owosso, Mich. 48867.

CAREER: Owosso (Mich.) public schools, teacher of physical education, 1961—. Chairperson of Owosso Health and Science Committee; member of Owosso Elementary Curriculum Council; Owosso Memorial Hospital Auxiliary, director of volunteers, member of board of directors. First United Methodist Church, member of administrative board, council on missions, and education committee, children's coordinator. *Member:* American Association for Health, Physical Education and Recreation, American Association of Tension Control, International Biographical Association, International Platform Association, Michigan Education Association, Michigan Association for Health, Physical Education and Recreation, Delta Psi Kappa. *Awards, honors:* American Red Cross service award; named outstanding elementary teacher of America, 1974.

WRITINGS: High School Girls' Athletic Associations: Their Organization and Administration, A. S. Barnes, 1961; *A Manual of Snowmobiling,* A. S. Barnes, 1971, 2nd edition, 1976; *The Autobiography of Pain,* New Voices Publishing, 1976. Contributor to journals.

WORK IN PROGRESS: Fitness Is Forever, a book stressing the importance of physical fitness for senior citizens.

AVOCATIONAL INTERESTS: Sewing, knitting, bridge, interior decorating, gardening, sports.

* * *

HELWIG, David (Gordon)   1938-

PERSONAL: Born April 5, 1938, in Toronto, Ontario, Canada; son of William Gordon (a cabinetmaker) and Ivy (Abbott) Helwig; married Nancy Keeling, September 19, 1959; children: Sarah Magdalen, Kathleen Rebecca. *Education:* University of Toronto, B.A., 1960; University of Liverpool, M.A., 1962. *Address:* c/o Oberon Press, 555 Maple Lane, Ottawa, Ontario, Canada K1M 0N7.

CAREER: Queen's University, Kingston, Ontario, assistant professor of English, 1962-74; literary manager, Canadian Broadcasting Corp. Television Drama, 1974-76. Editor-at-large, Oberon Press, 1973-74. *Awards, honors:* Centennial Award for play, "A Time of Winter."

WRITINGS—All published by Oberon Press: *Figures in a Landscape* (poems and three plays, "A Time of Winter," "The Dreambook," and "The Dancers of Colbek"; "A Time of Winter" produced in Kingston, Ontario, by Domino Theatre, 1967), 1968; *The Streets of Summer* (poems), 1969; *The Sign of the Gunman* (poems), 1969; *The Day before Tomorrow* (novel), 1971; (editor) *Fourteen Stories High* (short story anthology), 1971; *A Book about Billie* (documentary), 1972; *The Best Name of Silence* (poems), 1972; *Atlantic Crossings* (poems), 1974; *The Glass Knight* (novel), 1976. Also editor of *New Canadian Stories,* short story anthology series, 1972-75. Work represented in numerous anthologies, including *Canadian Short Stories,* edited by Robert Weaver, Oxford University Press, 1968, and *Canadian Poetry: The Modern Era,* edited by Newlove, McClelland & Stewart, 1977.

BIOGRAPHICAL/CRITICAL SOURCES: Canadian Forum, January, 1969, March, 1970; *Fiddlehead,* January-February, 1969.

* * *

HEMBREE, Charles R.   1938-

PERSONAL: Born April 23, 1938, in Zincville, Okla.; son

of Charles Fred (a minister) and Lucy (King) Hembree; married Shirley Ann Thompson, September 28, 1957; children: Robin Denise, Charles Rodney. *Education:* Attended Central Bible College, Southwestern Assemblies of God College at Waxahachie, Tex., Southwest Missouri State College, and Evangel College. *Home:* 18451 Clifton Way, Castro Valley, Calif. 94546. *Office:* Bethel Temple, 354 Hayward Blvd., Hayward, Calif. 94542.

CAREER: Former colonel in Salvation Army, working on *War Cry* in Chicago, Ill.; State of Arkansas, Little Rock, assistant commissioner of prisons, 1967-70; Bethel Temple (Assemblies of God church), Hayward, Calif., pastor, 1970—. Member of California State Advisory Board of Religion for Institutional Religion.

WRITINGS—Published by Baker Book, except as indicated: *Pocket of Pebbles,* 1969; *Voice of the Turtle Dove,* 1970; *Songs in a Strange Land,* Gospel Publishing, 1971; *Fruits of the Spirit,* 1971; *Spiritual Stirrings,* 1973; *Know and Grow: Devotions through the Bible,* 1975; *The Shepherd's Psalm,* 1975.

"Good Morning Lord" series: *Devotions for Everyday Living,* 1971; *Five Minute Devotions,* 1973; *Devotions on Bible Prayers,* 1976; *Sixty Seconds with God,* in press.

Also author of weekly column, "Life Lines," in *War Cry,* a Salvation Army publication. Contributor of more than 450 articles to various magazines.†

*   *   *

HEMENWAY, Robert 1921-

PERSONAL: Born July 15, 1921, in South Haven, Mich.; son of Earl Lee (a statistician) and Freda (Penoyar) Hemenway. *Education:* University of Chicago, A.B., 1946, A.M., 1951. *Home:* 88 Michigan Ave., South Haven, Mich. 49090.

CAREER: Juilliard School of Music, New York City, teacher of English, 1948-50; Great Books Foundation, Chicago, Ill., academic director, 1951-55; World Affairs Center, New York City, associate director, 1956-58; *New Yorker* (magazine), New York City, fiction editor, 1959-71. *Military service:* U.S. Army, Signal Corps Intelligence Service, 1942-45. *Member:* Phi Beta Kappa. *Awards, honors:* O. Henry Prize Story Award, 1970.

WRITINGS: The Girl Who Sang with the Beatles and Other Stories, Knopf, 1970.

WORK IN PROGRESS: A novel.

BIOGRAPHICAL/CRITICAL SOURCES: New York Times, April 14, 1970; *Best Sellers,* April 15, 1970; *Nation,* April 27, 1970; *New York Times Book Review,* July 26, 1970; *Observer Review,* December 20, 1970.

*   *   *

HENAULT, Marie (Josephine) 1921-

PERSONAL: Born July 16, 1921, in Oakville, Wash.; daughter of Ernst Carl (a contractor) and Amanda Sophia (Anderson) Philipsen; married Robert J. Henault (a professor), August 16, 1952; children: Martial Ernst. *Education:* University of Washington, Seattle, B.A., 1945, M.A., 1946; University of Maryland, Ph.D., 1952. *Religion:* Roman Catholic. *Home:* 61 Jericho Rd., Essex Junction, Vt. 05452. *Office:* Department of English, St. Michael's College, Winooski, Vt. 05404.

CAREER: University of Utah, Salt Lake City, instructor in English, 1946-49; University of Maryland, College Park, instructor in English, 1954-55; St. Joseph's College, Emmitsburg, Md., instructor in English, 1960-61; St. Michael's College, Winooski, Vt., lecturer, 1962-65, assistant professor, 1965-70, associate professor, 1970-73, professor of English, 1973—, chairman of department, 1969-72.

WRITINGS: Peter Viereck, Twayne, 1969; *Checklist of Ezra Pound,* C. E. Merrill, 1970; *Guide to Ezra Pound,* C. E. Merrill, 1970; (editor) *Studies in the "Cantos",* C. E. Merrill, 1971; *Stanley Kunitz,* Twayne, 1978. Contributor to literature journals.

*   *   *

HENDERSON, Bill 1941-
(Luke Walton)

PERSONAL: Born April 5, 1941, Philadelphia, Pa.; son of Francis L. and Dorothy (Galloway) Henderson. *Education:* Hamilton College, B.A., 1963; University of Pennsylvania, graduate study, 1965-66. *Politics:* Independent. *Religion:* Independent. *Residence:* New York, N.Y. *Office address:* Pushcart Press, P.O. Box 845, Yonkers, N.Y. 10701.

CAREER: Pushcart Press, Yonkers, N.Y., publisher, 1972—; Doubleday & Co., New York City, editor, 1972-73; Coward, McCann & Geoghegan, New York City, senior editor, 1973-75; Harper & Row, New York City, consulting editor, 1975—. *Awards, honors:* Citation, New Jersey Association of Teachers of English, 1972, for *The Galapagos Kid.*

WRITINGS: (Under pseudonym Luke Walton) *The Galapagos Kid* (novel), Nautilus Books, 1971; (editor) *The Publish-It-Yourself Handbook,* Pushcart Press, 1973; (editor) *The Pushcart Prize: Best of the Small Presses* (annual anthology), Pushcart Press, 1976—. Contributor of short stories and essays to *Carolina Quarterly, Chicago Review, Ontario Review,* and *New York Times Book Review.*

WORK IN PROGRESS: Several books.

SIDELIGHTS: In a *Publishers Weekly* interview with Robert Dahlin, Bill Henderson discusses the functions of small presses, including his own Pushcart Press: "Most small presses, even if they are good, never make it out of the garage. But they provide a great chance for the writer to write freely, without commercial restraint. They are just about the only place a new writer can get a hearing, the only place a writer can learn."

BIOGRAPHICAL/CRITICAL SOURCES: Publishers Weekly, June 5, 1978.

*   *   *

HENDERSON, James 1934-

PERSONAL: Born November 13, 1934, in Abadan, Iran; married Carole Judith Proulx, 1969. *Education:* University of Wales, B.A. (honors), 1957, Dip.Ed., 1956, M.A., 1959. *Home:* R.R. 4, Acton, Ontario, Canada. *Agent:* William Morris Agency, 1350 Avenue of the Americas, New York, N.Y. 19000.

CAREER: High school teacher of English in British Columbia, 1959-60, and Ontario, 1962-67; Canadian Broadcasting Corp., Vancouver, British Columbia, radio producer, 1960-62; Ontario Department of Education, Toronto, television consultant, 1967-68; Halton County Board of Education, Burlington, Ontario, coordinator of language arts, 1968-73; currently co-ordinator of Language Study Centre, Toronto Board of Education. Teaching associate in College of Education, Western University, London, Ontario, 1967-68.

WRITINGS: (Editor) Robert Louis Stevenson, *The Black Arrow,* Macmillan, 1965, St. Martin's, 1967; (editor) J. Meade Falkner, *Moonfleet,* Macmillan, 1967; (editor) Dylan Thomas, *Under Milk Wood,* Dent, 1967; (editor) *The Time of Your Life* (short story anthology), Macmillan, 1967; *Discussion and Debate,* Dent, 1970; (editor) *Writers in Conflict* (prose anthology), Macmillan, 1971; *Copperhead* (novel), Knopf, 1971; (with Ronald T. Shephard) *Language Moves* (textbook), Thomas Nelson, 1973; *Language Matters* (textbook), Thomas Nelson, 1975; *Mediascan,* Thomas Nelson, 1976; *Electric English* (grammar textbook), Thomas Nelson, 1976.

WORK IN PROGRESS: A novel.

AVOCATIONAL INTERESTS: Travel, particularly in the Caribbean, and Europe.

* * *

HENDERSON, Robert M. 1926-

PERSONAL: Born January 14, 1926, in Muskegon, Mich.; son of James Fournier and Marion (Rann) Henderson; married Mary Carmen Malanga (a museum curator), February 14, 1953; children: James M., Douglas A., Stuart A. *Education:* Michigan State University, B.A., 1950; Carnegie Institute of Technology (now Carnegie-Mellon University), M.F.A., 1953; New York University, Ph.D., 1965. *Home:* 859 Meadow Lane, Franklin Lakes, N.J. 07471. *Office:* Library and Museum of the Performing Arts, 111 Amsterdam Ave., New York, N.Y. 10023.

CAREER: Adelphi University, Garden City, N.Y., assistant professor of drama, 1955-60; American University, Washington, D.C., associate professor of drama and film and director of theatre, 1960-64; New York Public Library, Library and Museum of the Performing Arts, New York, N.Y., chief of general library and museum, 1965—. Consultant to Long Island Community Theatre Association, 1956-59, and film consultant for SDC., Inc., 1963. *Military service:* U.S. Navy, 1943-46. *Member:* Theatre Library Association (vice-president, 1970-72; president, 1972-76), Council of National Library Associations (chairman, 1977).

WRITINGS: (Editor with Jack Yocum) *Baroque Architectural Drawings,* Speech Arts Press, 1962; *D. W. Griffith: The Years at Biograph,* Farrar, Straus, 1970; *D. W. Griffith: His Life and Work,* Oxford University Press, 1972. Contributor of articles to *Encyclopaedia Britannica.*

SIDELIGHTS: John McCabe describes *D. W. Griffith: His Life and Work* as a "definitive biography, an unsentimental yet affecting portrait of a complex and contradictory personality who, more than any other single individual, can be called the man who invented Hollywood."

Reviewing *D. W. Griffith: The Years at Biograph,* Robert Sklar writes: "Robert M. Henderson's study of the director's early career provides an essential start to a full understanding of Griffith's place in film history.... Henderson's valuable book is as much a source work as a critical study of Griffith's early films.... The chief failing of the book is its slighting of the four-reel feature Griffith made in 1913 before leaving Biograph, *Judith of Bethulia. Judith* marks a great turning point in Griffith's career, focusing for the first time all his developing ability to make the motion picture a work of psychological and emotional force, and in a *concise* epic form."

BIOGRAPHICAL/CRITICAL SOURCES: *Best Sellers,* September 15, 1970; *Nation,* September 21, 1970; *Cue,* October 31, 1970; *Washington Post,* April 3, 1972; *Detroit News,* June 14, 1972.

HENDERSON, William L(eroy) 1927-

PERSONAL: Born August 23, 1927, in St. Clairsville, Ohio; son of Leroy Twinem (a draftsman) and Gladys (Whittock) Henderson; married Irma Pogany, March 19, 1960; children: Carol A. *Education:* Ohio State University, B.S., 1951, M.A., 1954, Ph.D., 1962; postdoctoral study at Indiana University, 1962, and University of Virginia, 1966. *Home:* 44 Whipkey Dr. S.W., Granville, Ohio 43023. *Office:* Department of Economics, Denison University, Granville, Ohio 43023.

CAREER: Ohio State University, Columbus, instructor in public finance and statistics, 1957-60; Denison University, Granville, Ohio, assistant professor of public finance, 1960-63; University of Arizona, Tucson, associate professor of economics and assistant director of Bureau of Business Research, 1963-65; Denison University, associate professor, 1965-68, John G. Harris Professor of Economics, 1968—, chairman of department, 1965-70, assistant to president, 1970-73. Summer lecturer, University of Ljubljana, 1967; director of planning and development, Wabash College, 1973-75. *Military service:* U.S. Army Air Forces, 1945-46. *Member:* American Economic Association, National Tax Association, Association for Evolutionary Economics, Omicron Delta Epsilon, Omicron Delta Kappa. *Awards, honors:* Ford Foundation postdoctoral fellow at Indiana University, 1962.

WRITINGS: (Editor with Helen Cameron) *Public Finance: Selected Readings,* Random House, 1966; (with Cameron) *The Public Economy: An Introduction to Government Finance,* Random House, 1969; *Economic Disparity: Problems and Strategy for Black America,* Free Press, 1970. Also author of *Urban Economics: Processes and Problems,* Wiley. Contributor of about twenty-five articles to economics journals.

WORK IN PROGRESS: *Introduction to Economics,* for Holden-Day.

* * *

HENDRICK, Ives 1898-1972

May 10, 1898—May 28, 1972; American psychiatrist and educator. Obituaries: *New York Times,* May 31, 1972. (See index for *CA* sketch)

* * *

HENKES, Robert 1922-

PERSONAL: Born October 28, 1922, in Kalamazoo, Mich.; son of Peter John (a policeman) and Veronica (Itsenhuiser) Henkes; married Frances Malerney, April 21, 1956; children: Catherine, Anne, Susan, Jane. *Education:* Drake University, B.F.A., 1948; University of Wisconsin, M.A., 1950; attended summer painting workshops at University of Michigan, 1955, and Michigan State University, 1956. *Religion:* Roman Catholic. *Home:* 1124 Bretton Dr., Kalamazoo, Mich. 49007. *Office:* Department of Art, Kalamazoo Institute of Arts, Kalamazoo, Mich. 49001.

CAREER: Kalamazoo Institute of Arts, Kalamazoo, Mich., instructor in painting, 1954—; Nazareth College, Kalamazoo, professor of art, 1966-72. Instructor in art, Barbour Hall Boys School, Kalamazoo, 1968—; director of community art education workshops for children and painting instructor at Adult Community Center, Kalamazoo. Has had one-man shows in Des Moines, Milwaukee, Racine, and at Nazareth College, Kalamazoo College, Western Michigan University, and Luther College. *Member:* National Art

Education Association, Western Arts Association, Michigan Art Education Association, Kalamazoo Council of the Arts, Delta Phi Delta. *Awards, honors:* Painting awards from South Bend Art Association, Grand Rapids Art Association, Detroit Artists, and Kalamazoo Institute of Arts.

WRITINGS: Orientation to Drawing and Painting, International Textbook, 1965; *Notes on Art and Art Education,* MSS Educational Publishing, 1969; *Eight American Women Painters,* Gordon Press, 1977; (contributor) *Great Men,* Dial, 1978; *The Crucifixion in American Painting,* Gordon Press, 1979; *Insights in Art and Education,* Gordon Press, 1979. Contributor of more than 115 articles to art and education journals.

WORK IN PROGRESS: New Vision in Painting; Artistic Expression of the Child; Ten American Humanist Painters; Painting Styles; Drawing in the Junior High School; Ten American Religious Painters; The Life and Works of Umberto Romano.

SIDELIGHTS: Robert Henkes told *CA:* "Writing is essential to teaching and painting as the latter are essential to my writing. Successful teaching only reaches a small segment of society while the printed word reaches thousands in a single moment. Aside from contribution, word manipulation arouses the aesthetic experience. It is quite similar to composing a painting. Words can change man's spiritual condition as much as the color images of a canvas."

AVOCATIONAL INTERESTS: Track (member of national collegiate cross-country championship team, 1944-45), collecting antique glass.

* * *

HENKIN, Louis 1917-

PERSONAL: Born November 11, 1917, in Russia; brought to United States in 1923, naturalized citizen, 1930; son of Yoseph Elia (a rabbi) and Frieda Rebecca (Kreindel) Henkin; married Alice Barbara Hartman (an attorney), June 19, 1960; children: Joshua Herbert, David Michel, Daniel Joseph. *Education:* Yeshiva University, A.B., 1937; Harvard University, LL.B., 1940. *Religion:* Jewish. *Home:* 460 Riverside Dr., New York, N.Y. 10027. *Office:* School of Law, Columbia University, New York, N.Y. 10027.

CAREER: Law clerk to Judge Learned Hand of U.S. Court of Appeals, 1940-41, and to Justice Felix Frankfurter of U.S. Supreme Court, 1946-47; U.S. Department of State, Washington, D.C., officer, 1945-46; United Nations, New York City, consultant to legal department, 1947-48; U.S. Department of State, Washington, D.C., officer, 1948-57, and U.S. representative to United Nations Committee on Refugees and Stateless Persons, 1950, adviser to U.S. delegation to United Nations Economic and Social Council, 1950, and to U.N. General Assembly, 1950-53; Columbia University, School of Law, New York City, lecturer in law and associate director of Legislative Drafting Research Fund, 1956-57; University of Pennsylvania, School of Law, Philadelphia, visiting professor, 1957-58, professor of law, 1958-62; Columbia University, School of Law, professor of international law and diplomacy, 1962-63, Hamilton Fish Professor of International Law and Diplomacy, 1963—, member of Institute of War and Peace Studies, 1962—. Member of Bar of New York State and Bar of U.S. Supreme Court. U.S. member, Permanent Court of Arbitration, 1963-69; president, U.S. Institute of Human Rights, 1969—; Carnegie Lecturer, Hague Academy of International Law, 1965. *Military service:* U.S. Army, 1941-45; became staff sergeant; received Silver Star.

MEMBER: American Society of International Law, International Law Association (American branch), American Society for Political and Legal Philosophy, American Political Science Association, Council on Foreign Relations. *Awards, honors:* D.H.L., Yeshiva University, 1963.

WRITINGS: Arms Control and Inspection in American Law, Columbia University Press, 1958; *The Berlin Crisis and the United States,* Carnegie Endowment for International Peace, 1959; (editor) *Arms Control: Issues for the Public,* Prentice-Hall, 1961; *Law for the Sea's Mineral Resources,* Columbia University Press, 1968; *How Nations Behave: Law and Foreign Policy,* Praeger, 1968; *Foreign Affairs and the Constitution,* Foundation Press, 1972; (editor) *World Politics and Jewish Concerns,* Quadrangle, 1972; (editor with Wolfgang G. Friedmann and others) *Transnational Law in a Changing Society,* Columbia University Press, 1972. Also author of *The Rights of Man Today.* Contributor to legal and political journals. Member of board of editors, *American Journal of International Law,* 1967—.

WORK IN PROGRESS: Research on international law and politics, including the law of the sea and of human rights, and on American constitutional law and government.

* * *

HENLE, Mary 1913-

PERSONAL: Born July 14, 1913, in Cleveland, Ohio; daughter of Leo (a businessman) and Pearl (Hahn) Henle. *Education:* Smith College, A.B., 1934, A.M., 1935; Bryn Mawr College, Ph.D., 1939. *Home address:* Box 404, Ridgefield, Conn. 06877. *Office:* Department of Psychology, New School for Social Research, 66 West 12th, New York, N.Y. 10011.

CAREER: Swarthmore College, Swarthmore, Pa., research associate, 1939-41; University of Delaware, Newark, instructor in psychology, 1941-42; Bryn Mawr College, Bryn Mawr, Pa., instructor in psychology, 1942-44; Sarah Lawrence College, Bronxville, N.Y., teacher of psychology, 1944-46; New School for Social Research, Graduate Faculty, New York, N.Y., assistant professor, 1946-48, associate professor, 1948-54, professor of psychology, 1954—. Research fellow and lecturer on social relations, Harvard University, 1963-64; Educational Services, Inc., senior scholar, 1964-65, consultant, 1965-67. *Member:* American Psychological Association, American Association for the Advancement of Science (fellow), American Association of University Professors, Eastern Psychological Association, Sigma Xi, Cheiron Society. *Awards, honors:* Guggenheim fellowships, 1951-52, 1960-61.

WRITINGS: (Editor) *Documents of Gestalt Psychology,* University of California Press, 1961; (editor) *Selected Papers of Wolfgang Koehler,* Liveright, 1971; (editor with John Sullivan) *Historical Conceptions of Psychology,* Springer Publishing, 1973; (editor) *Vision and Artifact,* Springer Publishing, 1976. Contributor to scholarly journals.

WORK IN PROGRESS: Studies on human reasoning and on systematic psychology and history of psychology.

* * *

HENLE, Theda O. 1918-

PERSONAL: Born March 21, 1918, in San Diego, Calif.; daughter of Frank S. (a reporter) and Katherine (Burnham) Ostrander; married Peter Henle (an economist), August 25, 1941; children: Michael, James, Paul. *Education:* Swarthmore College, B.A. (with honors). *Politics:* Democrat.

MEMBER: League of Women Voters, Arlington League (president, 1956-58).

WRITINGS: Death Files for Congress, Vanguard, 1971.

WORK IN PROGRESS: Death Tips the Scales, a second novel of suspense.

SIDELIGHTS: Theda Henle wrote to *CA:* "Children grown—tired of hours of unpaid work (my book jacket says I am a 'retired volunteer'!) Decided to try who-dun-its because it is still respectable to write one without the inevitable sex chapter."††

*   *   *

HENNESEY, James J. 1926-

PERSONAL: Born October 6, 1926, in Jersey City, N.J.; son of Charles Gregory and Loretta (Beggans) Hennesey. *Education:* Attended Fordham University, 1945-47; Loyola University, Chicago, B.A., 1948; Woodstock College, Ph.L., 1951, S.T.B., 1956, S.T.L., 1958; Catholic University of America, M.A., 1960, Ph.D., 1963. *Home and office:* 140 Commonwealth Ave., Chestnut Hill, Mass. 02167.

CAREER: Roman Catholic priest of Society of Jesus (Jesuits); high school teacher in Buffalo, N.Y., 1951-54; Fordham University, Bronx, N.Y., instructor, 1962-64, assistant professor, 1964-68, associate professor of church history, 1968-71; Graduate Theological Union, Berkeley, Calif., professor of history, 1971-73; Jesuit School of Theology, Chicago, Ill., professor of church history and president, 1973-76; Boston College, Chestnut Hill, Mass., professor of church history, 1977—. Visiting lecturer at Gregorian University, Rome, 1963-64, 1972, Union Theological Seminary, New York, 1964-65, 1967-68, Regis College, Toronto, 1966-67, Stanford University, 1973, and University of Chicago, 1974-75. Assistant regional superior, Jesuit Order in New York, 1965-67; rector, Fordham Jesuit Community, 1968-70.

MEMBER: American Society of Church History (member of council, 1970-72), American Catholic Historical Association (member of council, 1966-68), American Jesuit Historical Conference (national chairman, 1965-66). *Awards, honors:* Peter Guilday History Prize, 1960; Jesuit grant to study in Europe, 1961-62.

WRITINGS: The First Council of the Vatican: The American Experience, Herder & Herder, 1963; (contributor) Eugene Culhane, editor, *American Catholic Horizons,* Doubleday, 1966; (contributor) Phillip Gleason, editor, *Catholicism in America,* Harper, 1970; (contributor) J. A. Coriden, editor, *The Once and Future Church,* Alba, 1971; (contributor) T. M. McFadden, editor, *America in Theological Perspective,* Seabury, 1976; (contributor) R. Triscoe, editor, *Catholics in America, 1776-1976,* United States Catholic Conference, 1976. Contributor to *Encyclopedia Americana, New Catholic Encyclopedia,* and other encyclopedias; also contributor to historical and theological journals in United States, Italy, Germany, and the Netherlands, and to Catholic magazines.

WORK IN PROGRESS: Research on English origins of the American Roman Catholic community.

SIDELIGHTS: James J. Hennesey is interested in history "as a liberating force in men's life, to avoid the immobility of conservatism, and at the same time realize that, if patterns be not cyclic, men in succeeding eras do indeed resemble one another."

HENRY, Shirley 1925(?)-1972

1925(?)—February 15, 1972; American songwriter and television writer. Obituaries: *Variety,* February 23, 1972.

*   *   *

HENSLEY, Joe L. 1926-

PERSONAL: Born March 19, 1926, in Bloomington, Ind.; son of Ralph Ramon and Frances Mae (Wilson) Hensley; married Charlotte R. Bettinger, June 18, 1950; children: Michael Joseph. *Education:* Indiana University, A.B., 1950, LL.B., 1955. *Politics:* Democrat. *Religion:* Presbyterian. *Home:* 2315 Blackmore, Madison, Ind. 47250. *Office:* Fifth Judicial Circuit Courthouse, Madison, Ind. 47250.

CAREER: Admitted to State Bar of Indiana, 1955; Metford & Hensley, Attorneys at Law, Madison, Ind., associate, 1955-71; Ford, Hensley & Todd, Attorneys at Law, Madison, partner, 1971-73; Hensley, Todd, & Castor, Madison, partner, 1973-75; Eightieth Judicial Circuit, Indiana, judge pro-tempore, 1975-76; Fifth Judicial Circuit, Indiana, judge, 1977—. Indiana General Assembly, member of Assembly, 1961-62, prosecuting attorney of Fifth Judicial Indiana Circuit, 1963-66. *Military service:* U.S. Navy, hospital corpsman, 1944-46, journalist in Korea, 1951-52. *Member:* Indiana State Bar Association, Jefferson County Bar Association, Mystery Writers of America, Science Fiction Writers of America (chairman of legal committee).

WRITINGS—All published by Doubleday, except as indicated: *The Color of Hate,* Ace, 1961; *Deliver Us to Evil,* 1971; *Legislative Body,* 1972; *The Poison Summer,* 1974; *Song of Corpus Juris,* 1974; *Rivertown Risk,* 1977; *A Killing in Gold,* 1978. Contributor of more than fifty science fiction and suspense stories to magazines.

SIDELIGHTS: Joe Hensley told *CA:* "Time is a very difficult thing. I must find mine in odd places. I have no intention, at least now, of stopping being a judge. My stories are at least partially the result of that life. Although they usually take the suspense form, my books are about people who must live in this complicated and devious world all of us try our best to exist within. I find that I can't easily stop writing. So I get up earlier, work harder, and hope to get more done. It isn't fun anymore, but it's something I do. I'm glad I do it and I doubt that anything could make me stop."

*   *   *

HERBERS, John N. 1923-

PERSONAL: Born November 4, 1923, in Memphis, Tenn.; son of John N. and Mable (Foster) Herbers; married Mary E. Wood, September 17, 1952; children: Claudia (Mrs. Paul Stein), Mary, Anne, Jill. *Education:* Emory University, B.A., 1949; Harvard University, additional study, 1961. *Religion:* Presbyterian. *Home:* 7514 Glenbrook Rd., Bethesda, Md. 20014. *Office: New York Times,* 1920 L St. N.W., Washington, D.C.

CAREER: Correspondent and manager, United Press International (UPI), 1953-63; *New York Times,* New York City, correspondent in Washington, D.C., 1963-75, assistant national editor in New York City, 1975-76, deputy bureau chief in Washington, D.C., 1976—.

WRITINGS: The Lost Priority, Funk, 1970; *The Black Dilemma,* John Day, 1973; *No Thank You, Mr. President,* Norton, 1976.

HERBERT, A(lan) P(atrick) 1890-1971

September 24, 1890—November 11, 1971; English social reformer, humorist, poet, lyricist, playwright, and novelist. Obituaries: *New York Times,* November 12, 1971; *Washington Post,* November 12, 1971; *Newsweek,* November 22, 1971; *Time,* November 22, 1971; *Publishers Weekly,* December 6, 1971.

* * *

HERNDL, George C. 1927-

PERSONAL: Born September 20, 1927, in Atlanta, Ga.; son of George P. (a businessman) and Margaret (Keane) Herndl; married Adeline Vogel (a businesswoman), September 1, 1951; children: Christopher, Carl. *Education:* Catholic University of America, A.B., 1950; University of North Carolina at Chapel Hill, M.A., 1957, Ph.D., 1965. *Home:* 132 Oak Trail, Belmont, N.C. 28012. *Office:* Humanities Division, Belmont Abbey College, Belmont, N.C. 28012.

CAREER: Has worked as a seaman, salesman, carpenter, insurance agent, cab driver, civil servant, factory foreman, and stevedore; Belmont Abbey College, Belmont, N.C., instructor, 1958-60, assistant professor, 1960-62, associate professor, 1962-64, professor of English, 1964—, chairman of department, 1958—, chairman of Humanities Division, 1969—. *Military service:* U.S. Marine Corps, 1944-46. *Member:* Modern Language Association of America, American Association of University Professors, Southern Atlantic Modern Language Association. *Awards, honors:* Danforth associate, 1965—; Southeastern Medieval and Renaissance Institute, fellow, 1965; Cooperative Program in the Humanities, humanities fellow, 1966-67; South Atlantic Modern Language Association SAMLA Studies award for *The High Design,* 1969; National Endowment for the Humanities fellowships, 1973, 1975; Lily Foundation fellowship, 1976-77.

WRITINGS: The Liberal Arts (pamphlet), Belmont Abbey College Press, 1962; (editor) *Report on Organized Crime,* Pennsylvania State Crime Commission, 1970; *The High Design: English Renaissance Tragedy and the Natural Law,* University Press of Kentucky, 1970. Contributor of articles to education journals and literary magazines.

WORK IN PROGRESS: A survey of contemporary schools of literary criticism.

* * *

HEROLD, Brenda 1948-

PERSONAL: Born December 27, 1948, in Shreveport, La.; daughter of Arthur Anselm (a physician) and Lucille (Tremblay) Herold. *Home:* 1267 Jilla St., Mountainview, Calif. 94040. *Agent:* Ted Wilentz, 29 Perry St., New York, N.Y. 10014.

CAREER: Street singer in New Orleans, La. and New York, N.Y., 1968-70; affiliated with Austin MacCormick Center (a halfway house), San Francisco, Calif., 1970; Pedregal House (a residential treatment center and halfway house), San Mateo, Calif., house manager, beginning 1970; currently teaching in community bilingual education program and finishing third year of night law school. *Awards, honors:* First prize in Sigma Tau Delta Literary Contest, 1967, for "Tin Stars"; Southern Literary Festival first prize in poetry, for "Beneath a Reign of Uncouth Stars."

WRITINGS: The St. Charles Gig (poems), Corinth Books, 1971.

WORK IN PROGRESS: A second book of poems, *Waking Up.*

* * *

HERRNSTADT, Richard L. 1926-

PERSONAL: Born November 4, 1926, in New York, N.Y.; son of Oscar Edward (a businessman) and Helen (Lidz) Herrnstadt; married Helen Appel (an academic adviser), June 18, 1950; children: Steven, Ellen, Owen. *Education:* University of Wisconsin, B.S., 1948, M.S., 1950; University of Maryland, Ph.D., 1960. *Politics:* Democrat. *Religion:* Jewish. *Home:* 2121 Hughes, Ames, Iowa 50010. *Office:* Department of English, Iowa State University, Ames, Iowa 50011.

CAREER: Iowa State University, Ames, instructor, 1954-58, assistant professor, 1958-61, associate professor, 1961-65, professor of English, 1965—. Member of boards of directors, Ames Community School District, 1967-74, and Iowa Public Programs in the Humanities, 1973-79. *Military service:* U.S. Navy, 1945-46. *Member:* American Studies Association (member of executive council, 1969-76), American Association of University Professors (president of Iowa State University chapter, 1965-66), Modern Language Association of America, Midcontinent American Studies Association (president, 1962-63), Phi Delta Kappa.

WRITINGS: (Editor) *The Letters of A. Bronson Alcott,* Iowa State University Press, 1969. Contributor to journals in his field.

WORK IN PROGRESS: The Poetry of A. Bronson Alcott; research on nineteenth-century American literature.

* * *

HERSCHBERGER, Ruth (Margaret) 1917-
(Josephine Langstaff)

PERSONAL: Born January 30, 1917, in Philipse Manor, N.Y.; daughter of Clarence Bertram (a former All-American fullback, now a realtor) and Grace Josephine (executive secretary of Renaissance Society, University of Chicago, 1942-56; maiden name, Eberhart) Herschberger. *Education:* Attended University of Chicago, 1935-38, and Black Mountain College, Black Mountain, N.C., 1938-39; further courses in theater and poetry at University of Michigan, New School for Social Research, and Union Theological Seminary, New York. *Home:* D-717 Westbeth, 463 West St., New York, N.Y. 10014.

CAREER: Poet, playwright, writer. Producer of verse plays and staged readings of plays and poems at Poetry Library, University of Chicago, and elsewhere in Chicago and New York City during the 1950's. Playwright-in-residence, Wisconsin Idea Theatre, 1951-53. Former sponsor and advisor, Women's Interart Center. *Awards, honors:* Avery and Jule Hopwood Award in poetry, University of Michigan, 1941; Harriet Monroe Memorial Prize of *Poetry Magazine,* 1953; Grace Thayer Bradley Award for Poetry of Friends of Literature, 1957; Bollingen Foundation grant, 1963; Society of Midland Authors Poetry Award, 1969.

WRITINGS: Adam's Rib (nonfiction), Pellegrini & Cudahy, 1948, reprinted, Harper, 1970; *A Way of Happening* (poems), Pellegrini & Cudahy, 1948; (contributor) R. A. Baker, editor, *Psychology in the Wry,* Van Nostrand, 1963; *Nature and Love Poems* (includes six poems from *A Way of Happening*), Eakins, 1969; (contributor) Betty Roszak and Theodore Roszak, editors, *Masculine and Feminine,* Harper, 1970. Chapters of *Adam's Rib* included in several textbooks.

Plays: "Edgar Allan Poe," produced in New York on radio, 1943; "A Ferocious Incident" and "Andrew Jackson," jointly produced in Chicago at Playwrights Theatre Club for the Poets Company, 1953; "Luther," read on radio in Chicago, 1955, with subsequent staged readings at little theaters in Chicago; "A Dream Play," published in *Botteghe Oscure*, spring, 1957, first produced in Chicago at Reynolds Club Theatre, 1957, produced Off-Off Broadway at Off Center Theatre, 1966; "Delphine" (three-act in couplets, based on the Balzac novel *Pere Goriot*), given staged reading by poets and actors in New York at Guggenheim Museum under sponsorship of Academy of American Poets, 1968; "The Decision" (feminist skit on abortion), produced Off-Off Broadway at The Assembly, 1971.

Poems have been included in many collections, among them *The Golden Treasury*, revised edition, New American Library, *A Little Treasury of American Poetry*, Scribner, *A New Anthology of Modern Poetry*, revised edition, Random House, *The Pocket Book of Modern Verse*, and *Illustrated Treasury of Children's Poetry*, Grosset, 1969, *Fine Frenzy*, McGraw, 1972, *The Women Poets in English*, McGraw, 1972, *We Become New*, Bantam, 1975, and *Celebration*, Winthrop Publishing, 1977. Poems have been recorded in "Library Album of Modern Poetry," Gryphon Records, for Library of Congress, 1960, edited and published version, Collectors Guild, 1963, and in "Patterns in God's World," Lutheran Church Press, 1971. Poems have also appeared in more than thirty national and literary magazines. Translations of poems by Mayakovsky included in *Translations by American Poets*, Ohio University Press, 1970.

Contributed a literary essay to *Accent Anthology*, Harcourt, 1946, and a story to *Best American Short Stories*, 1949. Editor (and publisher) of *Broadsides from Buckfastleigh* and *Broadsides from America*. Reviewer of verse plays for *Village Voice*, 1961-62.

SIDELIGHTS: Ruth Herschberger is classed among five "outstanding woman-poets alive today" by Selden Rodman, who adds, "She defers to none of them in expressing the sheer joy and pain of being a woman." While she is identified with poetry, the most successful of Ruth Herschberger's work is the nonfiction *Adam's Rib* (now out of print), originally published under the pseudonym Josephine Langstaff in England, 1954, and under the same pseudonym in Finnish, Norwegian, and Swedish editions.

Herschberger told *CA:* "I am interested in combining verse and film/video. . . . To finance the experiments of poetry and film I think we need two species of judges: the literary and the visual art type. So far, the antiverbalists are subsidizing film." She has lived at Yaddo, Taos, and Ossabaw writers' colonies.

BIOGRAPHICAL/CRITICAL SOURCES: New York Times, November 30, 1969.

* * *

HERSHAN, Stella K.   1915-

PERSONAL: Born February 7, 1915, in Vienna, Austria; came to United States as a refugee in 1939; daughter of Felix (a businessman) and Lucy (Pick) Kreidl; married Rudolf Hershan (an engineer), November 19, 1933 (deceased); children: Lisa (Mrs. Allan Grabell). *Education:* New York University, Certificate in General Education, 1962; New School for Social Research, Certificate in Human Relations, 1968. *Politics:* Democrat. *Religion:* Jewish. *Home:* 2 Fifth Ave., New York, N.Y. 10011. *Agent:* Roslyn Targ Literary Agency, 250 West 57th St., New York, N.Y. 10019.

WRITINGS: A Woman of Quality, Crown, 1970; *The Naked Angel* (novel), R. Hale, 1973, Pinnacle Books, 1977. Contributor to journals in the United States and Austria.

WORK IN PROGRESS: The Corset, a novel about a woman trying to liberate herself in Vienna in 1900.

SIDELIGHTS: Stella Hershan lives in Greenwich Village with her cat, Catherine the Great. *The Naked Angel* has been published in Austria, Germany, Italy, Netherlands, and Scandinavia.

* * *

HERSHEY, Burnet   1896-1971

December 13, 1896—December 13, 1971; Romanian-born American journalist, dramatist, screenwriter, biographer, editor, and author of books on modern history. Obituaries: *Detroit News*, December 14, 1971; *New York Times*, December 14, 1971; *Washington Post*, December 16, 1971. (See index for *CA* sketch)

* * *

HERSHON, Robert   1936-

PERSONAL: Born May 28, 1936, in Brooklyn, N.Y.; son of Mark and Barbara (Pernick) Hershon; married Michaeleen Waldron (an artist), February, 1962; children: Elizabeth, Jedediah. *Education:* New York University, B.S., 1957. *Home:* 231 Wyckoff St., Brooklyn, N.Y. 11217.

CAREER: Hanging Loose (magazine), Brooklyn, N.Y., co-editor, 1966—.

WRITINGS—All poems: *Swans Loving Bears Burning the Melting Deer*, New-Books, 1967; *Atlantic Avenue*, Unicorn Press, 1970; (with Dick Lourie, Emmett Jarrett, and Marge Piercy) *4-Telling*, New-Books, 1971; *Grocery Lists*, New-Books/Crossing Press, 1972; *Little Red Wagon Painted Blue*, Unicorn Press, 1972; *Rocks and Chairs*, Some of Us Press, 1975.

* * *

HERSKOVITS, Frances Shapiro   1897-1972

1897—May 4, 1972; American anthropologist. Obituaries: *New York Times*, May 8, 1972.

* * *

HERZOG, Stephen J(oel)   1938-

PERSONAL: Born September 17, 1938, in Chicago, Ill.; son of Paul (a physician) and Florence (Glickman) Herzog; married Elane Schwartz (a musician), August 20, 1961; children: Cheryl, Paul. *Education:* University of California, Los Angeles, B.A., 1960, M.A., 1963, Ph.D., 1967. *Politics:* Democrat. *Religion:* Jewish. *Home:* 1477 Fordham, Thousand Oaks, Calif. 91360. *Office:* Urban Studies Institute, Moorpark College, Moorpark, Calif. 93021.

CAREER: Instructor in history and political science, Los Angeles City College and Santa Monica City College, 1963-64; Ventura College, Ventura, Calif., instructor in political science, 1964-67; Moorpark College, Moorpark, Calif., instructor in political science, 1967—. *Member:* American Federation of Teachers (president, Ventura County), Conejo Environmental League (member of council), Conejo Valley Human Relations Club.

WRITINGS: (Editor) *Minority Group Politics: A Reader*, Holt, 1971; *The Survival Kit*, Wadsworth, 1971.

WORK IN PROGRESS: Contemporary Urban Issues.†

HESLA, David H(eimarck) 1929-

PERSONAL: Born October 14, 1929, in Stevens Point, Wis.; son of O. E. and Alma (Heimarck) Hesla; married Mary Stegner (a musician), June 16, 1956; children: Maren, Thor David. *Education:* St. Olaf College, B.A., 1951; University of Chicago, A.M., 1956, Ph.D., 1964. *Residence:* Decatur, Ga. *Office:* Graduate Institute of the Liberal Arts, Emory University, Atlanta, Ga. 30322.

CAREER: St. Olaf College, Northfield, Minn., instructor in English, 1955-56; Cornell College, Mt. Vernon, Iowa, assistant professor of English, 1961-65; Emory University, Atlanta, Ga., assistant professor, 1965-69, associate professor of humanities and of literature and theology, 1969—. Fulbright professor, University of Oulu, Finland, 1972-73. *Military service:* U.S. Marine Corps, 1952-54. *Member:* Modern Language Association of America, American Academy of Religion, American Association of University Professors. *Awards, honors:* Emory University Research Committee summer grants, 1965, 1970; National Endowment for the Humanities grant, 1968; McKnight Award, 1973, for *The Shape of Chaos.*

WRITINGS: (Contributor) Robert O. Evans, editor, *Graham Greene: Some Critical Considerations,* University of Kentucky Press, 1963; (contributor) Nathan A. Scott, editor, *Adversity and Grace: Studies in Recent American Literature,* University of Chicago Press, 1968; *The Shape of Chaos: An Interpretation of the Art of Samuel Beckett,* University of Minnesota Press, 1971. Contributor to *Critique, Emory College Today, Choice, Christian Scholar, North American Review,* and *Christian Advocate.*

WORK IN PROGRESS: Inter-relations of literature, theology, and philosophy; literary criticism; religious dimensions of American literature.

*　　*　　*

HESS, Lilo 1916-

PERSONAL: Born in 1916 in Erfurt, Germany. *Education:* Educated in European schools. *Home:* R.D. 1, Stroudsburg, Pa. 18360.

CAREER: Animal photographer for magazines; writer and illustrator of children's books. *Awards, honors: Animals That Hide, Imitate and Bluff* was selected one of the Child Study Association's Books of the Year.

WRITINGS—Author and photographic illustrator; published by Crowell, except as indicated: *Christine, the Baby Chimp,* G. Bell, 1954; *Rabbits in the Meadow,* 1963; *Easter in November,* 1964; *Shetland Ponies,* 1964; *The Timid Sheep,* 1965.

All published by Scribner: *Sea Horses,* 1966; *Foxes in the Woodshed,* 1966; *Pigeons Everywhere,* 1967; *The Curious Raccoons,* 1968; *The Remarkable Chameleon,* 1968; *The Misunderstood Skunk,* 1969; *Animals That Hide, Imitate and Bluff,* 1970; *The Praying Mantis, Insect Cannibal,* 1971; *Mouse and Company,* 1972; *Problem Pets,* 1972; *Monkeys and Apes without Trees,* 1973; *A Snail's Pace,* 1974; *A Pony to Love,* 1975; *Small Habitats,* 1976; *A Puppy for You,* 1976; *A Dog by Your Side,* 1977; *Life Begins for Puppies,* 1978.

Illustrator: Dorothy C. Hogner, *Odd Pets,* Crowell, 1951; Irmengarde Eberle, *Fawn in the Woods,* Crowell, 1962. Photographs published in *Natural History Magazine, Life, Look, Parents' Magazine, New York Times Magazine, This Week,* and in European periodicals.

WORK IN PROGRESS: The Busy Earthworm, for Scribner.

HESSERT, Paul 1925-

PERSONAL: Born September 17, 1925, in Fort Wayne, Ind.; son of Christian G. (an accountant) and Edith F. (Ulenhake) Hessert; married Alta Mae Adams, February 11, 1953; children: Lynne, Judith, Christian. *Education:* Purdue University, B.S., 1945; Garrett Theological Seminary, B.D., 1949; Northwestern University, M.A., 1949; University of St. Andrews, Scotland, graduate study, 1950; Edinburgh University, Ph.D., 1951. *Religion:* Methodist. *Home:* 324 Hamilton St., Evanston, Ill. 60202. *Office:* Department of Systematic Theology, Garrett Theological Seminary, Evanston, Ill. 60201.

CAREER: Garrett Theological Seminary, Evanston, Ill., associate professor, 1963-66, professor of systematic theology, 1967—. *Member:* American Theological Society, Society of Biblical Literature, American Academy of Religion, American Association of University Professors.

WRITINGS: Introduction to Christianity, Prentice-Hall, 1958; *New Directions in Theology Today,* Westminster, 1967; (contributor) *Theologie: Zwischen Gestern and Morgen,* Kaiser Verlag, 1968; (contributor) Dow Kirkpatrick, editor, *The Living God,* Abingdon, 1970.

WORK IN PROGRESS: Writing on theology of the photographic medium; a study of the relation of theological structures to those of the cultures from which they come; a study of the relation of word to image.

SIDELIGHTS: Paul Hessert told *CA:* "I have been impressed with the inextricability of religious concerns from the culture at large and the way dominant cultural forms shape theological expression. These forms derive from the basic assumptions and categories a culture uses to work and think and understand itself. The cultural transition in which we are currently involved offers a unique opportunity to come to terms with cultural formations throughout history. Particularly we are called back today to the natural structures which make life possible and viable."

*　　*　　*

HESSION, Charles H(enry) 1911-

PERSONAL: Born May 1, 1911, in Brooklyn, N.Y.; son of Charles H. and Lillian (Carroll) Hession; married Marie N. Struever, 1946; children: William J., John C., Edwin A., Ann Marie. *Education:* College of the City of New York (now City College of the City University of New York), B.A., 1932; Columbia University, M.A., 1933, Ph.D., 1948. *Politics:* Democrat. *Religion:* Unitarian Universalist. *Home:* 6 Bayberry Rd., Bellport, N.Y. 11713. *Office:* Department of Economics, Brooklyn College of the City University of New York, Brooklyn, N.Y. 11210.

CAREER: Brooklyn College of the City University of New York, Brooklyn, N.Y., instructor, 1934-42, assistant professor, 1946-53, associate professor, 1953-64, professor of economics, 1965-73, professor emeritus, 1973—, chairman of social science program, 1967-73. Senior economist, Economics Institute, University of Colorado, summer, 1960; Fulbright professor, University College Galway, 1976-77. Member of board of directors, New York Metropolitan District, Unitarian Universalist Association, 1968-69. Consultant to U.S. Department of Justice, 1960-63, and to private firms on trade regulation matters. *Military service:* U.S. Army, Corps of Engineers, 1942-46; became second lieutenant; received Bronze Star Medal and Purple Heart. *Member:* American Economic Association, Economic History Association, Association for Evolutionary Economics,

Metropolitan Economics Association (co-founder and president, 1951-52), Vandeveer Park Civic Association (president, 1955-57; member of board of directors, 1959-61). *Awards, honors:* National research professor at Brookings Institution, 1957-58.

WRITINGS: (With W. H. Steiner and Ezra Bowen) *Problems in Economics,* Holt, 1934; (editor with Curwen Stoddart and others) *Readings in Economic Institutions,* two volumes, Brooklyn College Press, 1941; (with S. M. Miller and Stoddart) *The Dynamics of the American Economy,* Knopf, 1956; (with Hyman Sardy) *Ascent to Affluence: A History of American Economic Development,* Allyn & Bacon, 1970; (contributor) Walter Adams, editor, *The Structure of American Industry,* Macmillan, 1950, 4th edition, 1970; *John Kenneth Galbraith and His Critics,* Norton, 1972.

WORK IN PROGRESS: A psycho-biography tentatively entitled *The Creative Genius of John Maynard Keynes.*

*   *   *

HESTER, Marcus B.   1937-

PERSONAL: Born June 20, 1937, in Raleigh, N.C.; son of John Lee (a game warden) and Beatrice (Baker) Hester; married Joan Hill (a high school teacher), June 14, 1960. *Education:* Wake Forest University, B.A., 1960; Vanderbilt University, Ph.D., 1964. *Politics:* Democrat. *Religion:* Baptist. *Home:* 2061 Royall Dr., Winston-Salem, N.C. 27106. *Office:* Department of Philosophy, Wake Forest University, Winston-Salem, N.C. 27109.

CAREER: Wake Forest University, Winston-Salem, N.C., associate professor, 1963-76, professor of philosophy, 1976—. Fellow of Cooperative Program in the Humanities, University of North Carolina, 1966-67. *Member:* American Society for Aesthetics, American Association of University Professors, Southern Society for Philosophy, Phi Beta Kappa.

WRITINGS: The Meaning of Poetic Metaphor, Mouton, 1967. Contributor to professional journals.

WORK IN PROGRESS: A book on the nature of criticism of painting; writing on aesthetics and philosophy of mind.

AVOCATIONAL INTERESTS: Music, painting, astronomy.

*   *   *

HETZRON, Robert   1937-

PERSONAL: Name legally changed, 1961; born December 31, 1937, in Budapest, Hungary; son of Vilmos J. (a wholesaler) and Olga (Mandel) Herzog; married Gabriella Paloczi, May 15, 1966; children: Gabriel Fenteany, Rita Ennemore, George Tardenat. *Education:* School of Oriental Languages, Paris, France, diploma in Hebrew, 1959, diploma in Amharic, 1960; Hebrew University, M.A., 1964; University of California, Los Angeles, Ph.D., 1966. *Politics:* None. *Religion:* Jewish. *Home:* 1346 San Rafael Ave., Santa Barbara, Calif. 93109. *Office:* Department of Eastern Languages, University of California, Santa Barbara, Calif. 93106.

CAREER: University of California, Santa Barbara, assistant professor, 1966-69, associate professor of Hebrew, 1969—. *Military service:* Israeli Army, 1962-64. *Member:* American Oriental Society, Linguistic Society of America, International Linguistic Association, Linguistic Society (Paris). *Awards, honors:* Guggenheim fellowship, 1976-77.

WRITINGS: The Verbal System of Southern Agaw, University of California Press, 1969; *Ethiopian Semitic: Studies in Classification,* Manchester University Press, 1972; *Surfacing,* Liviana, 1975; *The Gunnan-Gurage Languages,* Instituto Orientale di Napoli, 1977. Contributor of articles on linguistics to professional journals.

WORK IN PROGRESS: Semito-Cushitica.

*   *   *

HEWITT, Geof (George F.)   1943-

PERSONAL: Born September 1, 1943, in Glen Ridge, N.J.; son of George F. (an engineer) and Nadine (Easter) Hewitt; married Janet Lind, April 18, 1971; children: Benjamin Starr. *Education:* Cornell University, B.A., 1966; Johns Hopkins University, M.A., 1967; University of Iowa, M.F.A., 1969. *Politics:* "People's Poetry Party." *Home and office address:* R. D. 4, Enosburg, Vt. 05450.

CAREER: Johns Hopkins University, Baltimore, Md., instructor in English, 1966-67; University of Iowa, Iowa City, instructor in English, 1967-69; University of Hawaii, Honolulu, instructor in English, 1969-70; *Cornell Alumni News,* Ithaca, N.Y., contributing editor, 1970—. Founder and editor, Kumquat Press, 1966—; participant in "Poetry in the Schools" program in New York and Vermont. *Awards, honors:* Academy of American Poets Prize, 1966; Coordinating Council of Literary Magazines grants, 1968, 1970.

WRITINGS—Poems, except as indicated: *Poem and Other Poems,* Kumquat, 1966; *Waking Up Still Pickled,* Lillabulero, 1967; (editor) *Quickly Aging Here,* Doubleday, 1969; (editor) *Selected Poems of Alfred Starr Hamilton,* Jargon Society, 1970; (editor) *Living in Whales,* Vermont Council on Arts, 1972; *Stone Soup,* Ithaca House, 1974; *The Corn,* Blue Moon Press, 1975; *I Think They'll Lay My Egg Tomorrow,* Stinehour Press, 1976; *Working for Yourself* (nonfiction), Rodale Press, 1977.

Contributor of critical essays to *Contemporary Poets of the English Language,* St. James Press, 1970, and *New American and Canadian Poetry,* Beacon Press, 1971. Contributor of poetry to *Carolina Quarterly, Paris Review, Poetry Now, New Letters, Harper's, Chicago Review, Foxfire, Greenfield Review, Shenandoah,* and other periodicals. Contributing editor, *New Letters* (University of Missouri review).

SIDELIGHTS: Geof Hewitt told *CA:* "I worked in Honduras. I sang in Europe. I taught in Hawaii. I would be a musician if I could, or a full-time poet, if that were possible."

BIOGRAPHICAL/CRITICAL SOURCES: Poetry, December, 1968; *New York Times,* February 20, 1970.

*   *   *

HEY, Nigel S(tewart)   1936-

PERSONAL: Born June 23, 1936, in Morecambe, Lancashire, England; son of Aaron and Margery (Kershaw) Hey; married Miriam Lamb, October 13, 1960 (divorced, 1977); children: Brian, Jocelyn. *Education:* University of Utah, B.A., 1958. *Home:* 12 Briston Grove, London N8 9EX, England. *Office:* IMS World Publications, York House, 37 Queen Sq., London WCIN 3BH, England.

CAREER: United Press International, newsman in Salt Lake City, Utah, 1958; *Kentish Express* (weekly newspaper), Ashford, Kent, England, copy editor, 1959-60; *Bermuda Mid-Ocean News* (daily newspaper), Hamilton, Bermuda, associate editor, 1958-59, 1960-61; Weltech College,

Salt Lake City, director, 1962-64; Newspaper Printing Corp., Albuquerque, N.M., editor, 1964-66; Sandia Laboratories (research and development firm), Albuquerque, science writer, 1966-72; IMS World Publications, London, England, editorial director, 1972—. Member of board of directors, New Mexico Conference on Social Welfare, 1966-70. *Member:* American Institute of Aeronautics and Astronautics, National Association of Science Writers, International Association of Science Writers, Association of British Science Writers. *Awards, honors:* New Mexico State Press Association awards for editorial and feature writing in weekly newspapers.

WRITINGS—Youth books: *The Mysterious Sun,* Putnam, 1971; (with Science Book Associates editors) *How Will We Feed the Hungry Billions?,* Messner, 1971; *How We Will Explore the Outer Planets,* Putnam, 1973. Writer of film, "The Space Age and You," and short television film clips on science; co-writer of other full-length science films.

WORK IN PROGRESS: Juvenile books on wildlife, space, electron microscopy, and astronomical instrumentation.

SIDELIGHTS: Nigel Hey, who has speared barracuda off Bermuda and driven a tunnel into a Greek mountain, looks on research for books as another, semi-vicarious, type of adventure. He writes: "We must . . . learn to think of technology as the farmer thinks of his plow—as a means of husbanding the finite fields of earth. Most vital subject? Easy—it's the race between population, the restoration of natural ecological balances, and the management of world food, water and energy resources."

* * *

HEYEN, William 1940-

PERSONAL: Born November 1, 1940; son of Henry Jurgen (a cabinet maker) and Wilhelmina (Woermke) Heyen; married Hannelore Greiner, July 7, 1962; children: William, Kristen. *Education:* State University of New York College at Brockport, B.S.Ed., 1961; Ohio University, M.A., 1963, Ph.D., 1967. *Home:* 142 Frazier St., Brockport, N.Y. 14420. *Office:* Department of English, State University of New York College, Brockport, N.Y. 14420.

CAREER: State University of New York College at Cortland, instructor in English, 1963-65; State University of New York College at Brockport, assistant professor, 1967-70, associate professor of English, 1970—. Fulbright lecturer to Germany, 1971-72.

WRITINGS: Depth of Field: Poems, Louisiana State University Press, 1970; (editor) *A Profile of Theodore Roethke,* C. E. Merrill, 1971; *Noise in the Trees: Poems and a Memoir,* Vanguard Press, 1974; *Of Palestine: A Meditation,* Abattoir Editions, 1976; (editor) *American Poets in 1976,* Bobbs-Merrill, 1976; *XVII Machines,* Rook Press, 1976; *The Swastika Poems,* Vanguard Press, 1977. Contributor of poems, articles, and essays to periodicals, literary magazines, and newspapers, including *Poetry, New Yorker, American Scholar, Prose, Southern Review, Nation, Texas Studies in Literature and Language, Prairie Schooner, New York Times, Quarterly Review of Literature,* and *Saturday Review.*

WORK IN PROGRESS: A volume of poems; a collection of essays on modern American poets.

SIDELIGHTS: Reviewing *Noise in the Trees: Poems and a Memoir,* a *Poetry* critic writes: "Just as the Memoir needs restraint . . . the poems want spirit. . . . In the first section, Heyen begins well enough, with several tight narratives

drawn from American history: Indian dog-sacrifice, a bareback bull-ride which established Smithtown's boundaries. . . . However, in some of the historical and natural accounts, the advantage of setting the facts in verse isn't always apparent. . . .''

A *Choice* reviewer states that *The Swastika Poems* "crudely and concretely convey the 1935-45 experiences and the present-day memorials to genocide. More memorable is the tone: urgent, keenly lyrical, poignant, disciplined by the forms despite subject matter that screams for titanic hyperbole. Highly recommended."

BIOGRAPHICAL/CRITICAL SOURCES: Western Humanities Review, summer, 1969; *Prose,* spring, 1972; *Poetry,* July, 1975; *Virginia Quarterly Review,* summer, 1977; *New York Times Book Review,* October 2, 1977; *Choice,* October, 1977.

* * *

HICKS, Warren B(raukman) 1921-

PERSONAL: Born July 25, 1921, in Denver, Colo.; son of Earl Gregory (an actor and executive) and Catherine (Howard) Hicks; married Wilhelmina R. Kuster, April 17, 1944; children: Joel, Darren. *Education:* University of Denver, B.B.A., 1948, M.B.A., 1950; also attended Western State College of Colorado, 1950-53, University of the Pacific, 1954-60, and University of San Francisco, 1961-63. *Religion:* Methodist. *Home:* 1672 Orchard Way, Pleasanton, Calif. 94566. *Office:* Chabot College, 25555 Hesperian Blvd., Hayward, Calif. 94545; and Department of Librarianship, San Jose State University, 125 South Seventh, San Jose, Calif. 95114.

CAREER: Western State College of Colorado, Gunnison, head librarian, 1949-53; Lodi Union High School District, Lodi, Calif., head librarian, 1953-61; University of San Francisco, San Francisco, Calif., lecturer in library science, 1958-68; Chabot College, Hayward, Calif., 1963—, began as director of library services, currently associate dean of instruction-learning resources; San Jose State University, San Jose, Calif., assistant professor of librarianship, 1968—. Supervisor of school libraries, Berkeley Unified School District, Berkeley, Calif., 1961-63. Library consultant to various schools and colleges in United States, and to federal government of Australia, 1967, state governments of New South Wales, Victoria, and Tasmania, Australia, 1967.

MEMBER: American Library Association, California Association of School Librarians (treasurer, 1957; president of Northern section, 1961-62; vice-president and president elect, 1968; president, 1969-70), Audio-Visual Educational Association of California, California Teachers Association, California Library Association (coordinator of Northern region, California Community Colleges Library Cooperative). *Awards, honors:* Kirkbride Award for most original research in California history, California Historical Society, 1954, for *The History of Lodi, California, from Early Times to 1906.*

WRITINGS: The History of Lodi, California, from Early Times to 1906, Lodi Public Library, 1954; *The Organization of Non-Book Materials in School Libraries,* California State Department of Education, 1967; *Developing Multi-Media Libraries,* Bowker, 1970; *Managing Multi-Media Libraries,* Bowker, 1976. Also author of a pamphlet, *Preparation and Cataloging Time for School Libraries,* Northern Section, School Library Association of California, 1959. Contributor of articles on school libraries to *College and Research Libraries, California Education, California Librarian, Junior College Journal,* and *Library Journal.*

WORK IN PROGRESS: A revision of *Developing Multi-Media Libraries.*

*   *   *

HIGGINS, Colin 1941-

PERSONAL: Born July 28, 1941, in Noumea, New Caledonia; now a U.S. citizen; son of John Edward (a chief purser) and Joy (Kelly) Higgins. *Education:* Stanford University, B.A., 1967; Sorbonne, University of Paris, graduate study, 1965; University of California, Los Angeles, M.F.A., 1970. *Home:* 2844 Hutton Dr., Beverly Hills, Calif. 90210. *Agent:* Steve Roth, Ziegler, Diskant & Roth, Inc., 9255 Sunset Blvd., Los Angeles, Calif. 90069.

CAREER: Professional actor in California, 1960-70; merchant seaman in California, 1967. Writer, director. *Military service:* U.S. Army, 1962-65. *Awards, honors:* "Silver Streak" was nominated for the Writers Guild Award for best comedy of 1976.

WRITINGS: Harold and Maude (novel; based on his screenplay of same title), Lippincott, 1971; (with Dennis Cannon) "The Ik" (play; based on *The Mountain People* by Colin Turnbull), French translation by Jean-Claude Carrier first produced as "Les Iks" in Paris at Theatre des Bouffes du Nord, January, 1975, first produced in English at Round House, London, January 15, 1976, produced at George Washington University, Washington, D.C., October 20, 1976.

Screenplays: "Harold and Maude," Paramount, 1971; "The Devil's Daughter," ABC-TV, 1972; "Silver Streak," Twentieth Century-Fox, 1976; "Foul Play," Paramount, 1978.

SIDELIGHTS: Although Colin Higgins' "Silver Streak" was nominated for the Writers Guild's best comedy of 1976, critics were not enthusiastic in their response to the film. Judith Crist writes: "Higgins, author of the delightful 'Harold and Maude,' has come up with a 1940s comedy-chase version of 'The Lady Vanishes'.... There is a nagging consciousness that things should be funnier than they are."

Higgins' "The Ik" was presented as a bicentennial gift from the French government to the American people. The play toured U.S. college campuses in the summer of 1976. Both "The Ik" and a stage-play version of "Harold and Maude" have been translated into French.

BIOGRAPHICAL/CRITICAL SOURCES: New York Times Book Review, September 26, 1971; *Best Sellers,* October 1, 1971; *Film Quarterly,* fall, 1972; *Newsweek,* December 13, 1976; *Time,* December 13, 1976; *New Yorker,* January 17, 1977; *Saturday Review,* January 22, 1977.

*   *   *

HIGHAM, Charles 1931-

PERSONAL: Born February 18, 1931, in London, England; emigrated to Australia in 1954; came to United States in 1969; son of Sir Charles Frederick (a publicist and author) and Josephine (Webb) Higham. *Education:* Studied privately. *Residence:* Hollywood, Calif. *Agent:* John Cushman Associates, Inc., 25 West 43rd St., New York, N.Y. 10036.

CAREER: Literary and film critic in London, England and then in Sidney, Australia, 1954-63; *Bulletin* (weekly), Sidney, literary editor, 1963-68; University of California, Santa Cruz, Regents Professor, 1969; KPFK Radio, Los Angeles, Calif., film critic, 1969-71; Hollywood correspondent for

New York Times, 1970—, and *Us* (magazine), 1977—. Official historian for audio history of the movies presented to the American Film Institute in 1973, Time-Life Books. *Awards, honors:* Poetry prizes from Poetry Society of London, 1949, and *Sidney Morning Herald,* 1956.

WRITINGS: A Distant Star (poems), Hand & Flower Press, 1951; *Spring and Death* (poems), Hand & Flower Press, 1953; (translator of poems of Marc Chagall) H. F. S. Bauman, editor, *Eight European Artists,* Heinemann, 1954.

The Earthbound and Other Poems, Angus & Robertson, 1960; (editor with Alan Brissenden) *They Came to Australia: An Anthology,* F. W. Cheshire, 1961; *Noonday Country: Poems, 1954-1965,* Angus & Robertson, 1966; (editor with Michael Wilding) *Australians Abroad: An Anthology,* F. W. Cheshire, 1967; (editor) *Australian Writing Today,* Penguin, 1968; (with Joel Greenberg) *Hollywood in the Forties,* A. S. Barnes, 1968; (with Greenberg) *The Celluloid Muse: Hollywood Directors Speak,* Angus & Robertson, 1969, Regnery, 1971.

The Films of Orson Welles, University of California Press, 1970; *Hollywood Cameramen: Sources of Light,* Indiana University Press, 1970; *The Voyage to Brindisi and Other Poems, 1966-1969,* Angus & Robertson, 1970; *Hollywood at Sunset,* Saturday Review Press, 1972; *Ziegfield,* Regnery, 1972; *The Art of the American Film,* Doubleday, 1973; *Cecil B. De Mille: A Biography,* Scribner, 1973; *Ava: A Life Story,* Delacorte, 1974; *Kate: The Life of Katharine Hepburn,* Norton, 1975; *Charles Laughton: An Intimate Biography,* Doubleday, 1975; *The Adventures of Conan Doyle,* Norton, 1976; *Marlene: The Life of Marlene Dietrich,* Norton, 1977; *The Changeling: A Fairy Tale of Terror* (novel), Simon & Schuster, 1978.

Poetry represented in numerous anthologies, including: *New Poems, 1954: A P.E.N. Anthology,* edited by Rex Warner and others, M. Joseph, 1954; *Australian Poetry, 1954,* edited by Ronald McCuaig, Angus & Robertson, 1955; *Australian Poetry, 1956,* edited by A. A. Phillips, Angus & Robertson, 1956; *Australian Poetry, 1963,* edited by G. A. Wilkes, Angus & Robertson, 1963; *Best Poems of 1962: Borestone Mountain Poetry Awards,* edited by Lionel Stevenson and others, Pacific Books, 1963; *Poetry in Australia II,* edited by D. Stewart, Angus & Robertson, 1964, University of California Press, 1965; *New Poems, 1965: A P.E.N. Anthology of Contemporary Poetry,* edited by C. V. Wedgwood, Hutchinson, 1966; *Australian Poetry, 1966,* edited by David Campbell, Tri-Ocean, 1967; *Best Poems of 1967: Borestone Mountain Poetry Awards,* edited by Stevenson and others, Pacific Books, 1967.

Contributor of poems, articles, reviews, and interviews to magazines and newspapers, including *London Magazine, Sight and Sound, Hudson Review, Yale Review,* and *New York Times.*

WORK IN PROGRESS: Tango, a novel of the 1920's; *Blessed Are the Rich,* a novel set in nineteenth-century California; a screenplay based on *The Changeling; The Adventures of Errol Flynn.*

SIDELIGHTS: Charles Higham told *CA:* "Fundamentally, I am a poet, of the Romantic school, out of sympathy with most American and British verse of my period, but very much in sympathy with the poetry of Australia, where I lived for fifteen years. I deeply admire Patrick White (a poet-novelist), A. D. Hope, W. Hart-Smith, James McAuley, and other Australian poets; American poets I do warm to are Elizabeth Bishop, Howard Moss, James Dickey, and W. S. Merwin. I write biographies for a professional occupation, much as some poets might teach or practise law or medicine, but recently my biography of Conan Doyle provided a rare opportunity to provide a book of literary content and (I hope) quality. I love writing, and am restless and unhappy only when not busy on a new project. I have never had writer's block; writing *is* my holiday. Now I have found a way to blend my poetic and more commercial talents; I have discovered, rather in the middle of life, a gift for fiction. This has been the greatest joy of my life. Since the masses do not read poetry, I can bring a poetic sensibility to bear on writing for a mass market. I am overjoyed.

"I have found most writers, if not all I have met, unhappy, tormented creatures. I am not unhappy and not tormented; I enjoy my work (especially verse). My view of literary criticism is that like so much cultural activity today it is fighting a rearguard action against the force of mass culture.... The result is that literary critics are increasingly nervous, tense and mistrustful; they tend to prefer fragmented, collapsed narrative structures and books which deal in mental breakdown and disorder because, in American culture, they can identify with plights rather than triumphs, with disease rather than health. I have preferred the Victorian solution: prose is made to earn the right to the luxury of verse; all work is valuable, if seriously and sincerely intended; life and humanity are to be encouraged and nurtured; progress is a reality, though man has preferred that progress to be toward his general medical and social welfare rather than that of an intellectual elite; humankind is fundamentally a species to be optimistic about; let us write solid, worthwhile, straight-forward stories about people; let us not be cynical, disruptive, destructive, elliptical, abstruse, obscure, or inverted, when we embark on the voyage of literature. I admire the novelists of security and substance: the Bronte sisters, Dickens, Balzac, Flaubert, Svevo, rather than those of breakdown and despair, Kafka, Joyce, Virginia Woolf, Celine, Sartre. I believe in joy and aspiration; I am not, therefore, too happy with much of the literature of the century, but prefer earlier inspirations and models."

AVOCATIONAL INTERESTS: Rare old movies, health foods, physical fitness.

BIOGRAPHICAL/CRITICAL SOURCES: London Magazine, April, 1967; *New Statesman,* November 29, 1968, February 6, 1970, January 1, 1971, November 26, 1976; *Christian Science Monitor,* May 14, 1971, June 26, 1975; *New York Times Book Review,* December 2, 1973, June 20, 1976, November 7, 1976; *Times Literary Supplement,* August 30, 1974, September 10, 1976.

* * *

HIGHAM, Roger 1935-

PERSONAL: Born June 23, 1935, in Dartford, Kent, England; son of H. G. and Winifred (Loveland) Higham; married Isobel Gemmill, July 29, 1967. *Education:* University of Kent at Canterbury, B.A. (with honors), 1973. *Religion:* Church of England. *Home:* 39 High St., Sturry, Canterbury, Kent, England. *Agent:* David Higham Associates Ltd., 5/8 Lower John St., London WIR 4HA, England.

CAREER: Farmed in Kent and Sussex, England, 1952-58; Barclays Bank Ltd., London, England, cashier and other work, 1958-62; *Church of England Newspaper,* London, circulation manager, 1962-64; writer, beginning 1964; Junior King's School, Canterbury, England, schoolmaster, 1973—. *Military service:* National Service in Royal West Kent Regiment, 1954-56.

WRITINGS: (Self-illustrated) *Island Road to Africa,* Dent,

1968; (self-illustrated) *Provencal Sunshine,* Dent, 1969; (self-illustrated) *Road to the Pyrenees,* Dent, 1971; (self-illustrated) *The South Country,* Dent, 1972; *Kent,* Batsford, 1974; *Berkshire,* Batsford, 1977. Contributor to local histories; also contributor to *Blackwood's* and other magazines.

* * *

HILBERG, Raul 1926-

PERSONAL: Born June 2, 1926, in Vienna, Austria; son of Michael and Gisela (Schachter) Hilberg; married Christine Hemenway (an instructor), March 14, 1964 (divorced); children: David, Deborah. *Education:* Brooklyn College (now Brooklyn College of the City University of New York), B.A., 1948; Columbia University, M.A., 1950, Ph.D., 1955. *Politics:* Independent. *Home:* 236 Prospect Parkway, Burlington, Vt. 05401. *Agent;* Theron Raines, 475 Fifth Ave., New York, N.Y. 10017. *Office:* Department of Political Science, University of Vermont, Burlington, Vt. 05401.

CAREER: VIVO Institute, Alexandria, Va., member of research mission, 1955; University of Vermont, Burlington, assistant professor, 1956-61, associate professor, 1961-67, professor of political science, 1967—. *Military service:* U.S. Army, 1944-46. *Member:* American Political Science Association, American Society of International Law, Jewish Studies Association, Phi Beta Kappa. *Awards, honors:* Jewish Cultural Reconstruction fellowship, 1956; University of Vermont faculty summer research fellowships, 1958, 1966; *Saturday Review* Anisfield-Wolf Award, 1968.

WRITINGS: The Destruction of the European Jews, Quadrangle, 1961; (editor) *Documents of Destruction,* Quadrangle, 1971; (editor with Stanislaw Staron and Josef Kermisz) Adam Czerniakow, *The Diary of the Warsaw Ghetto,* Stein & Day, 1978. Contributor to *Midstream* and *Societas.* Editor, *Jewish Encyclopedia Handbooks,* 1962-63.

* * *

HILDEBRAND, Verna 1924-

PERSONAL: Born August 17, 1924, in Dodge City, Kan.; daughter of Carrell E. (a farmer) and Florence Butcher; married John R. Hildebrand (an economist), June 24, 1946; children: Carol, Steve. *Education:* Kansas State University, B.S., 1945, M.S., 1957; University of California, Berkeley, graduate study, 1946-48; Texas Woman's University, Ph.D., 1970. *Home:* 724 Albert St., East Lansing, Mich. 48823. *Office:* College of Human Ecology, Michigan State University, East Lansing, Mich. 48823.

CAREER: Kansas State University, Manhattan, instructor in family relations, 1953-54, instructor in student counseling center, 1958; Oklahoma State University, Stillwater, instructor in family relations and child development, 1955-56; Texas Technological College (now Texas Tech University), Lubbock, assistant professor of home and family life, 1962-67; Michigan State University, East Lansing, 1967—, currently professor of family and child science and of family ecology. *Member:* National Association for the Education of Young Children, American Home Economics Association (chairman of family relations and child development station, 1975-77), Association for Childhood Education International.

WRITINGS: Introduction to Early Childhood Education, with *Laboratory Workbook,* Macmillan, 1971, 2nd edition, 1976; *Guiding Young Children,* Macmillan, 1975. Contributor of articles to journals.

WORK IN PROGRESS: Parenting and Teaching Young

Children, for McGraw; *Administration of Child Development Centers,* for Macmillan.

SIDELIGHTS: Verna Hildebrand writes: "I am strongly committed to improving the quality of early childhood nursery schools, child care centers, and kindergartens. Quality care and education for young children is an investment in our future."

* * *

HILL, Earle 1941-

PERSONAL: Born January 9, 1941, in Newnan, Ga.; son of Robert Earl (a newspaper man) and Ozella (Yeatman) Jones; married; wife's name, Joanne; children: Cynthia, Lisa, Kimberly, David. *Education:* Jacksonville State University, B.S. *Politics:* None. *Religion:* None. *Residence:* Macon, Ga.

CAREER: Optician in Orlando, Fla., and Chicago, Ill., 1962-65; now free-lance writer.

WRITINGS: Quietly Crush the Lizard (novel), Vanguard, 1972.

WORK IN PROGRESS: A novel, *The Covenant.*

* * *

HILL, James N(ewlin) 1934-

PERSONAL: Born November 30, 1934, in Pomona, Calif.; son of Mason Lowell (a geologist) and Katherine (Maple) Hill; married Mary Ann Hepp, August 28, 1958; children: Kraig Mason, Laura Katherine, Karlyn McCleod. *Education:* Pomona College, B.A., 1957; University of Chicago, M.A., 1963, Ph.D., 1965. *Home:* 20544 Seaboard Rd., Malibu, Calif. 90265. *Office:* Department of Anthropology, University of California, 405 Hilgard, Los Angeles, Calif. 90024.

CAREER: University of California, Los Angeles, assistant professor, 1965-70, associate professor of anthropology, 1970—, acting director of archaeological survey, 1966-70. *Military service:* U.S. Navy, 1957-60; became lieutenant. *Member:* American Anthropological Association (fellow), Society for American Archaeology, Society for California Archaeology. *Awards, honors:* National Science Foundation grant for archaeological research in Central America.

WRITINGS: Broken Pueblo: Prehistoric Social Organization in the American Southwest, University of Arizona Press, 1970. Contributor to anthropology and archaeology journals.

WORK IN PROGRESS: Research on the evolution of aspects of prehistoric social organization in central Arizona; research on identification of individual potters from motor-habit characteristics of potsherds.

SIDELIGHTS: James Hill writes: "I became interested in archaeology from childhood reading and from a slide course on Mesoamerican archaeology as an undergraduate. I had originally intended to specialize in Mesoamerican archaeology, but my first field work was in the American Southwest, and I changed interest to that area. However, I am primarily interested in theory and methods, and in the question of how to explain prehistoric organizational change. . . . I have traveled extensively throughout the American Southwest and Mexico. While in the U.S. Navy, I visited Hawaii, Japan, Panama, and several Pacific islands." *Avocational interests:* Tennis, basketball, football.

BIOGRAPHICAL/CRITICAL SOURCES: American Anthropologist, Volume LXXII, number 3, 1970.

HILL, Peter Proal 1926-

PERSONAL: Born October 4, 1926, in Concord, Mass.; son of George Alfred (a shoe manufacturer) and Ruth (Proal) Hill; married Barbara Rykken, November 28, 1953; children: George Alfred II. *Education:* Tufts University, A.B., 1948; Boston University, A.M., 1953; George Washington University, Ph.D., 1966. *Politics:* Democrat. *Religion:* Unitarian-Universalist. *Home:* 6636 31st Pl. N.W., Washington, D.C. 20015. *Office:* Department of History, George Washington University, Washington, D.C. 20052.

CAREER: George Washington University, Washington, D.C., assistant professor, 1960-66, associate professor, 1966-74, professor of history, 1974—. Part-time lecturer in U.S. diplomatic history, National War College. *Member:* American Historical Association, Organization of American Historians, Society for French Historical Studies.

WRITINGS: William Vans Murray, Federalist Diplomat: The Shaping of Peace with France, 1797-1801, Syracuse University Press, 1971.

WORK IN PROGRESS: Research on the early national period of American history, and on sources of French revolutionary policy toward the United States.

* * *

HILL, Philip G(eorge) 1934-

PERSONAL: Born September 19, 1934, in Christiansburg, Va.; son of Clifton Carr (a teacher) and Thelma (Huntoon) Hill; married Marjorie Ellen Fyfe (a homemaker), January 19, 1957; children: Robert Clifton, Judith Lynne, Thomas Alan. *Education:* University of Florida, B.A., 1956; University of North Carolina at Chapel Hill, M.A., 1960; Tulane University, Ph.D., 1964. *Religion:* Presbyterian. *Home:* 16 North Warwick Rd., Greenville, S.C. 29609. *Office:* Department of Drama and Speech, Furman University, Greenville, S.C. 29613.

CAREER: Allegheny College, Meadville, Pa., instructor in theater, and technical director, 1960-62; Furman University, Greenville, S.C., chairman of department of drama and speech, 1964—. *Military service:* U.S. Air Force, 1956-59; became first lieutenant. *Member:* American Theatre Association, U.S. Institute for Theatre Technology, Southeastern Theatre Conference (executive secretary-treasurer, 1968-72; vice-president, 1973-74; president, 1974-75), South Carolina Theatre Association (president, 1969-70), South Carolina Speech Association (president, 1971-72), Phi Beta Kappa, Phi Kappa Phi. *Awards, honors:* Woodrow Wilson fellow, 1959-60; Suzanne M. Davis Award, 1976, for distinguished service to Southern theatre, 1976.

WRITINGS: The Living Art, Holt, 1971. Contributor to speech and theater journals.

* * *

HILL, Richard (Fontaine) 1941-

PERSONAL: Born October 15, 1941; son of Robert Richards (a salesman) and Bertha (Fontaine) Hill; married Karen Anderson, February 16, 1962 (divorced, 1971); children: Miles Anthony, Patrick Fontaine. *Education:* St. Petersburg Junior College, A.A., 1961; attended Florida State University, 1961-62; University of South Florida, B.A., 1965, M.A., 1967. *Home:* 4026 Fourth Ave. S., St. Petersburg, Fla. 33711. *Agent:* Elaine Markson, 44 Greenwich Ave., New York, N.Y. 10011.

CAREER: Northeast High School, St. Petersburg, Fla.,

English teacher, 1965-67; University of South Florida, Tampa, instructor in English, 1968; St. Petersburg Junior College, St. Petersburg, humanities teacher, 1969; free-lance writer, 1969—. *Military service:* U.S. Navy, 1962-64, served as journalist 2nd class; U.S. Coast Guard Reserve, 1967, served as ensign. *Member:* Science Fiction Writers of America. *Awards, honors:* O. Henry Award, Doubleday & Co., 1974; creative writing grant, National Endowment for the Arts, 1976.

WRITINGS: Ghost Story (novel), Liveright, 1971. Also author of a novel, *Brave Salt.* Contributor of articles to *Los Angeles Free Press, Rolling Stone, Esquire,* and *Playboy;* contributor of thirty short stories and over fifty articles to magazines and anthologies, including *New American Review.*

WORK IN PROGRESS: A novel and screenplay about working construction in Atlanta, *Fox Chase Punchout; Self Help Book for People Who Have Trouble Helping Themselves without Taking Too Much;* an autobiographical novel, tentatively entitled *Flight of the Bolo Bat.*

SIDELIGHTS: A free-lance writer, Richard Hill told *CA* he's "tired of hustling.... I'm interested in slowing down, finding a peaceful situation in which I can work on projects of real interest to me.... My friend, Jack Kerouac [who died in 1969], drank himself to death at 47. I don't owe anybody that. My most vital concern is my own health and happiness."

Hill added, "I'm presently writing, teaching Zen karate, living with my sons, and thinking about writing a book on survival."

*   *   *

HILL, Richard E.   1920-

PERSONAL: Born October 28, 1920, in Snoqualmie Falls, Wash.; son of Eugene Shoudy (a merchant) and Adalaide (Snyder) Hill; married Jeanne Cazenave (a French teacher), July 6, 1946; children: David Richard, Nicole Ann. *Education:* Attended State College of Washington (now Washington State University), 1938-40; University of Chicago, A.B., 1942; Harvard University, M.B.A., 1947; University of Washington, D.B.A., 1969. *Politics:* Republican. *Religion:* "No preference." *Home:* 840 Piccadilly Circle, Sacramento, Calif. 95825. *Office:* Department of Business Administration, California State University, 6000 J St., Sacramento, Calif. 95819.

CAREER: Carnation Co., Los Angeles, Calif., assistant purchasing agent, 1948-51, assistant to vice-president in charge of production, 1951-52, assistant plant manager, 1952-53, Oakland, Calif., assistant plant manager, 1953-57; Basic Vegetable Products, Inc., Vacaville, Calif., plant manager, 1957-63; California State University, Sacramento, lecturer, 1963-69, professor of production and management, 1969—. Trustee, Vaca Valley Unified School District, 1955-57. *Military service:* U.S. Army, 1943-46; became lieutenant.

MEMBER: American Production and Inventory Control Society (president of Sacramento chapter, 1971-72), National Association of Purchasing Managers (Capitol City group), Academy of Management, Association of Operative Millers (regional president, 1957).

WRITINGS: A Comprehensive Model of Aggregate Inventory Management, University Microfilms, 1969; (with John P. Van Gigch) *Using Systems Analysis to Implement Cost Effectiveness and Program Budgeting in Education,* Educa-

tional Technology, 1971. Contributor to management journals. Member of editorial board, *Journal of American Production and Inventory Control Society.*

WORK IN PROGRESS: Studying aggregate inventory management.

AVOCATIONAL INTERESTS: Skiing, tennis, gardening, reading, travel, dancing, dinner parties.†

*   *   *

HILL, Susan   1942-

PERSONAL: Born February 5, 1942; daughter of R. H. and Doris Hill. *Education:* King's College, London, B.A. (honors), 1963. *Religion:* Anglican. *Home:* 3 Jephson Pl., Royal Leamington Spa, Warwickshire, England. *Agent:* Curtis Brown, Ltd., 1 Craven Hill, London W2 3EW, England; and John Cushman Associates, Inc., 25 West 43rd St., New York, N.Y. 10036.

CAREER: Novelist and playwright, 1960—.

WRITINGS: The Enclosure (novel), Hutchinson, 1961; *Do Me a Favour* (novel), Hutchinson, 1963; *Gentlemen and Ladies* (novel), Walker & Co., 1969; *A Change for the Better* (novel), Hamish Hamilton, 1969; *I'm the King of the Castle* (novel), Viking, 1970; *The Albatross and Other Stories,* Hamish Hamilton, 1971, Saturday Review Press, 1975; *Strange Meetings* (novel), Saturday Review Press, 1972; *The Bird of the Night* (novel), Saturday Review Press, 1972; *The Custodian* (stories), Covent Garden Press, 1972; *A Bit of Singing and Dancing* (stories), Hamish Hamilton, 1973; *In the Springtime of the Year* (novel), Saturday Review Press, 1974; *"The Cold Country" and Other Plays for Radio,* British Broadcasting Corp., 1975; *The Elephant Man,* Cambridge University Press, 1975. Two stories included in *Penguin New Short Stories,* Penguin.

Also author of radio plays, "Miss Lavender Is Dead," 1970, "Taking Leave," 1971, "White Elegy," 1973, and "A Window on the World," 1974.

SIDELIGHTS: Susan Hill's novels tend to deal with small people, small in the sense that they are out of what is considered as the mainstream of life. In *Gentleman and Ladies,* Vernon Scannell writes, she "takes a brave and honest look at the business of ageing and dying, the unconsoling irony of existence. All of her characters are middle-aged, elderly or ancient," and Scannell says that she uses the "dialogue of stately, formal speech." A. C. Ringer states that "the book's considerable charm lies in Miss Hill's insight into and sympathetic understanding of her eccentric characters ... and it is written with a light touch that still manages to encompass the inherent tragedy of the declining years and the coming of old age." Martin Levin writes that "Miss Hill's style, briskly impressionistic, is better than its substance."

A Change for the Better is in the tradition of British comic novels. Jonathan Raban writes that the book "is artfully composed of the dead and rotting language of Westbourne itself; a destitute society finds its linguistic correlative in a dialect of sad cliches.... The language of the narrative strictly follows the airless corridors of the characters' own thoughts, reproduced in every colourless detail—mean, complaining, platitudinous.... But the tone of *A Change for the Better* is rooted in its dialogue: Miss Hill has created a stylized, yet brilliantly accurate grammar and vocabulary for her distressed gentlefolk—an entirely authentic idiom to be spoken by the living dead as they inhabit their shabby-genteel wasteland. Their language is rigid, archaic, and metrical, a mixture of drab proverbs, oratorical flourishes borrowed from popular romance, and catch phrases from the more sober varieties of adman's English.'' Raban finds that Miss Hill has ''a fine sense of pace and timing and a delicious eye for incongruous detail.''

The title story of *The Albatross and Other Stories* is ''about fear, anxiety and inadequacy in which the atmosphere and environment are evoked with great skill and feeling and the characters are presented and developed with a kind of austere compassion,'' J. A. Cuddon writes. ''The language is spare, the dialogue terse and the tone beautifully adjusted to the severe vision.... The narrative, the events, are simple enough, but long after one has read these stories one is left with a curious, hard-edged almost physical sensation; a feeling of chill and desolation. But not depression. Miss Hill's art brings an elation of its own.''

In a review of *Strange Meetings*, Diane Leclercq writes: ''Coming hard on the heels of Susan Hill's very considerable achievements in her most recent work, one expects great things from [this book]. In many respects one gets them: the hard-edged prose, the painstaking detail, some aspects of the portrayal of Hilliard, and many of the minor characters. But the book has inbuilt defects that make it, in the final analysis, a failure.... The radical weakness is, perhaps, a failure to realize any of the attitudes that people must have had in the situation at the Western Front.''

Michele Murray believes that ''*The Bird of Night* lacks all those elements that automatically stamp a new novel as 'profound' or 'important,' and worth noticing. What it has instead are qualities rarely found in contemporary fiction and apparently not much valued, which is a pity. It is a thoroughly *created* piece of work, a novel wrought of language carefully designed to tell a story drawn, not from the surface of the author's life or fragments of her autobiography, but from the heart of the imagaination.... The careful shaping of material to make its effect with the utmost economy, adhered to and practiced by such modern masters as Gide, Woolf, Colette, and Pavese, seems to have fallen into abeyance, and it is good to see it once again employed with such great skill.''

Murray calls *In the Springtime of the Year* ''another triumph by an artist who, in her quiet, steady way, is fast becoming one of the outstanding novelists of our time.'' She goes on to say that Susan Hill ''has already demonstrated her mastery of character-drawing and fictional technique in her earlier novels, but *In the Springtime of the Year*, with its deliberate stripping away of almost all the elements of conventional fiction, represents a remarkable advance in what is turning out to be a considerable *oeuvre* for such a young writer....'' Margaret Atwood feels that despite ''lapses into simplemindedness, *In the Springtime of the Year* justifies itself by the intensity of those things it does well: moments of genuine feeling, moments of vision. It is less a novel than the portrait of an emotion, and as this it is poignant and convincing.''

BIOGRAPHICAL/CRITICAL SOURCES: New Statesman, January 31, 1969, January 25, 1974; *New York Times Book Review*, March 30, 1969, May 27, 1973, May 18, 1974; *London Magazine*, November, 1969; *Best Sellers*, October 1, 1970; *Listener*, October 8, 1970; *Books & Bookmen*, April, 1971, January, 1972, June, 1974; *Bookseller*, October 23, 1971; *New Republic*, February 16, 1974, May 18, 1974; *Washington Post*, May 19, 1974.†

*   *   *

HILLEGAS, Mark R(obert)   1926-

PERSONAL: Born December 26, 1926, in Glendale, Calif.;
son of Elwyn Guy (a teacher) and Louise (Westervelt) Hillegas; married Elizabeth Connolly (an academic adviser), August 12, 1951; children: Jane Carr, Richard Newton. *Education:* Columbia University, A.B., 1949, M.A., 1950, Ph.D., 1957. *Home:* 1218 Carter St., Carbondale, Ill. 62901. *Office:* Department of English, Southern Illinois University, Carbondale, Ill. 62901.

CAREER: Columbia University, New York, N.Y., lecturer, 1952-57, instructor in English, 1957-58; University of Michigan, Ann Arbor, instructor in English, 1958-61; Colgate University, Hamilton, N.Y., assistant professor of English, 1961-65; Southern Illinois University, Carbondale, associate professor, 1965-70, professor of English, 1970—. *Member:* Modern Language Association of America. *Awards, honors:* Lucius N. Littauer Foundation, Alfred P. Sloan Foundation, and Research Corp. fellowship, 1963.

WRITINGS: (Editor) H. G. Wells, *A Modern Utopia*, University of Nebraska Press, 1967; *The Future as Nightmare: H. G. Wells and the Anti-Utopians*, Oxford University Press, 1967; (editor) *Shadows of Imagination: The Fantasies of C. S. Lewis, J. R. R. Tolkien, and Charles Williams*, Southern Illinois University Press, 1969; (contributor) Jerome H. Buckley, editor, *The Worlds of Victorian Fiction*, Harvard University Press, 1975. Contributor to *Saturday Review, Nation,* and scholarly journals.

WORK IN PROGRESS: A Utopian Speculation.

SIDELIGHTS: Mark Hillegas writes: ''Increasingly my interest shifts from literary analysis to the complex issues of social organization and the relationship of scientific and technological advance to human life. I feel that lucid prose exposition is a more useful instrument for discussing such issues than poetry, fiction, or drama.''

BIOGRAPHICAL/CRITICAL SOURCES: New York Times Book Review, October 22, 1967; *Book World*, December 31, 1967; *Virginia Quarterly Review*, spring, 1968; *New York Review*, March 14, 1968; *Carleton Miscellany*, winter, 1968.

*   *   *

HILLIKER, Grant   1921-

PERSONAL: Born June 26, 1921, in Tomah, Wash.; son of Vernon Gilbert (a forest ranger) and Celeste (Reich) Hilliker; married Miriam L. Chrisler, April 3, 1943; children: Janet Lee, Laurie Ann. *Education:* University of Wisconsin—Madison, B.A. (with high honors), 1942; further study at Northwestern University Technological Institute, 1943, and George Washington University, 1950-55. *Residence:* Columbus, Ohio. *Office address:* Urban Alternatives Group, Inc., Box 303, Worthington, Ohio 43085.

CAREER: U.S. Department of State, Washington, D.C., foreign service officer, 1947-50, 1955-71, civil service officer, 1950-55; Ohio State University, Columbus, adjunct professor of political science and public policy, 1971-75; Urban Alternatives Group, Inc., Worthington, Ohio, program development director, 1976—. Member of city council, Falls Church, Va., 1953-55; president, Citizens for a Better City, Falls Church, 1961-63; co-chairman, Operation Breakthrough, Inc., Falls Church, 1970-71. *Military service:* U.S. Army Air Forces, 1943-45. U.S. Army, Signal Corps, 1945-46; became first lieutenant. *Member:* International Studies Association, Phi Beta Kappa.

WRITINGS: The Politics of Reform in Peru, Johns Hopkins Press, 1971.

WORK IN PROGRESS: Research on citizen influence on urban policymaking.

HILLS, Stuart Lee 1932-

PERSONAL: Born August 18, 1932, in Orange, N.J.; son of Frederic Wheeler and Mildred (Chambers) Hills; married Wilma Smith, September 8, 1956; children: Darrick, Marc, Michael. *Education:* College of Wooster, B.A., 1955; Indiana University, M.A., 1958, Ph.D., 1964. *Home:* 40 State St., Canton, N.Y. 13617. *Office:* Department of Sociology, St. Lawrence University, Canton, N.Y. 13617.

CAREER: Central Michigan University, Mt. Pleasant, assistant professor of sociology, 1961-62; Muskingum College, New Concord, Ohio, chairman of department of sociology, 1962-71; St. Lawrence University, Canton, N.Y., associate professor of sociology, 1971—. Summer instructor, American College of Switzerland. *Member:* American Sociological Association, Society for the Study of Social Problems, American Association of University Professors. *Awards, honors:* Distinguished Teacher award, Muskingum College, 1968.

WRITINGS: Crime, Power, and Morality: The Criminal-Law Process in America, Chandler Publishing, 1971. Contributor to *Sociological Focus, Crime and Delinquency, Federal Probation, Land Economics, Sociological Quarterly,* and other publications.

SIDELIGHTS: Stuart Hills has led students on research projects to Israel and Jamaica.

* * *

HIMELICK, (James) Raymond 1910-

PERSONAL: Born October 7, 1910, in Jonesboro, Ind.; son of Earl Leroy (a mould cutter in a glass factory) and Dora Lydia (Nelson) Himelick; married Mary Kathryn Thomas, 1940; children: Thomas Earl. *Education:* Ball State Teachers College (now Ball State University), B.A., 1932; University of Michigan, M.A., 1943; Indiana University, Ph.D., 1950. *Politics:* Democrat. *Religion:* Methodist. *Home:* 708 Avondale Dr. W., Lafayette, Ind. 47906.

CAREER: English teacher in public schools in Indiana, 1932-45; Indiana University at Bloomington, member of English faculty, 1948-50; Purdue University, Lafayette, Ind., instructor, 1950-52, assistant professor, 1952-59, associate professor, 1959-64, professor of English, 1964-76, professor emeritus, 1976—. *Member:* Modern Language Association of America, Midwest Modern Language Association, American Association of University Professors, Renaissance Society of America.

WRITINGS: (Translator and author of introduction and notes) *The Enchiridion of Erasmus,* Indiana University Press, 1963; (editor and author of introduction and notes) Samuel Daniel, *Musophilus,* Purdue University, 1965; (translator and author of introduction and notes) *Erasmus and the Seamless Coat of Jesus,* Purdue University, 1971. Contributor of articles to *Modern Fiction Studies, South Atlantic Quarterly, American Literature, Modern Language Notes, Philological Quarterly,* and other literary journals.

WORK IN PROGRESS: Contrasting Renaissance and modern views of death.

AVOCATIONAL INTERESTS: Music.

* * *

HINTON, Bernard L. 1937-

PERSONAL: Born March 26, 1937, in Detroit, Mich.; married Linda Kay Rich (an instructor), September 25, 1971; children: Linda Sue, Sandra Lee. *Education:* Wayne State University, B.S., 1960, M.B.A., 1962; Stanford University, Ph.D., 1966. *Home:* 2751 Spicewood Lane, Bloomington, Ind. 47401. *Office:* Graduate School of Business, Indiana University, Bloomington, Ind. 47401.

CAREER: Steelcote Distributing Co., Mt. Clemens, Mich., manager of wholesale and retail sales, 1955-58; Paint Can, Inc., Mt. Clemens, manager of retail sales and inventory control, 1958-60; Wayne State University, Detroit, Mich., instructor in business, 1960-62; Indiana University at Bloomington, assistant professor, 1966-69, associate professor, 1969-74, professor of organizational behavior, 1974—, chairman of administrative and behavioral studies department, 1971—. *Member:* American Institute for Decision Sciences, American Psychological Association, Creative Education Foundation, Beta Gamma Sigma, Sigma Iota Epsilon.

WRITINGS: (With H. Joseph Reitz) *Groups and Organizations: Integrated Readings in the Analysis of Social Behavior,* Wadsworth, 1971. Contributor of over twenty articles to psychology journals.

WORK IN PROGRESS: Writing on organizational behavior, motivation, and organizational structure.

* * *

HIRSCH, Seev 1931-

PERSONAL: Born July 1, 1931, in Duisburg, Germany; son of Benjamin Berchard (a hotel manager) and Ettel (Siegelwachs) Hirsch; married Shirley Schalit (an artist), July 22, 1956; children: Yael, Raphael. *Education:* Hebrew University, B.A., 1960; Harvard University, M.B.A., 1962, D.B.A., 1965. *Religion:* Jewish. *Home:* Shlomo Hamelech, 26 Herzliya B, Israel. *Office:* Leon Recarati Graduate School of Business Administration, Tel Aviv University, Tel Aviv, Israel.

CAREER: Member of kibbutz, 1951-59; Tel Aviv University, Leon Recarati Graduate School of Business Administration, Tel Aviv, Israel, senior lecturer, 1965-71, associate professor of international economics and international business, 1971—, dean, 1971-73. Visiting fellow, Economic Development Institute, World Bank, 1976. *Military service:* Israeli Army, 1948-50. *Awards, honors:* Rockefeller Brothers fellowship, 1974.

WRITINGS: Location of Industry and International Competitiveness, Oxford University Press, 1967; *The Export Performance of Six Manufacturing Industries: A Comparative Study of Denmark, Holland, and Israel,* Praeger, 1971; (with others) *Profiles of Six Export-Oriented Industries,* United Nations Industrial Development Organization, 1974; *Rich Man, Poor Man and Every Man's Goods: Aspects of Industrialization and Trade,* Mohr, 1977.

* * *

HISS, Alger 1904-

PERSONAL: Born November 11, 1904, in Baltimore, Md.; son of Charles Alger (a businessman) and Mary Lavinia (Hughes) Hiss; married Priscilla Fansler Hobson, December 15, 1929 (separated, 1959); children: Timothy Hobson (stepson), Anthony. *Education:* Attended Maryland Institute of Art, 1921-22; Johns Hopkins University, A.B., 1926; Harvard University, LL.B., 1929. *Politics:* Democrat. *Religion:* Episcopalian. *Agent:* Marie Rodell, 141 East 55th St., New York, N.Y. 10022. *Office:* Davison-Bluth, 295 Lafayette St., New York, N.Y. 10012.

CAREER: Law clerk for Justice Oliver Wendell Holmes,

Washington, D.C., 1929; Choate, Hall, & Stewart (law firm), Boston, Mass., staff lawyer, 1930-32; Cotton, Franklin, Wright, & Gordon (law firm), New York City, staff lawyer, 1932-33; U.S. Government, Washington, D.C., assistant general counsel in Agricultural Adjustment Administration, 1933-35, legal assistant to Nye Committee, 1935, assistant in Solicitor General's Office, 1935-36, staff member to assistant secretary of state, 1936-39, assistant to the adviser on political relations, 1939-44, deputy director of Office of Special Political Affairs, 1944-45, director of Office of Special Political Affairs, 1945-47; Carnegie Endowment for International Peace, New York City, president, 1947-48; indicted for perjury by New York Grand Jury, 1948, found guilty after second trial, 1950, served prison term, 1951-54; Feathercombs, Inc. (manufacturing firm), New York City, general manager, 1956-59; Davison-Bluth (printing and office supplies firm), New York City, salesman, 1960—. Lecturer and conductor of seminars on the United Nations, U.S. Foreign Policy, the New Deal, and the McCarthy era. *Member:* Phi Beta Kappa. *Awards, honors:* LL.D., Johns Hopkins University, 1947.

WRITINGS: In the Court of Public Opinion, Knopf, 1957; (editor) *The Holmes-Laski Letters,* Atheneum, 1963. Contributor of articles on the United Nations to various journals.

WORK IN PROGRESS: A book on the New Deal.

SIDELIGHTS: The Alger Hiss-Whittaker Chambers case has been a subject of controversy for the past thirty years. In 1948, Chambers, then a senior editor of *Time,* accused Hiss of passing him secret State Department documents in the late 1930's, when Chambers was said to have been a Communist. Hiss denied it. He could not be tried for espionage because of the statute of limitations, but *was* indicted and found guilty of lying to a federal grand jury for claiming he never gave Chambers secret documents nor met with him in February or March of 1938.

Evidence produced by Chambers included four memos said to be in Hiss's handwriting and sixty-five pages of retyped State Department documents, sixty-four of which were allegedly typed on the now-famous Woodstock typewriter once owned by Hiss. Chambers showed House Un-American Activities Committee (HUAC) agents the hollowed-out pumpkin in which he had hidden five rolls of film, now referred to as the "pumpkin papers." Two of these rolls contained secret government information.

A reviewer in *Time* asks: "Who was telling the truth? Was it the serene and unfailingly courteous Hiss, who went to Lewisburg prison for 44 months and today, at age 73, still professes innocence? Or was it the brooding, tormented accuser, Whittaker Chambers, who died on his Maryland farm in 1961? Despite a dozen books and articles about the case, many of them little more than briefs for one side or the other, the question has not been answered conclusively."

Recently, Allen Weinstein has written *Perjury: The Hiss-Chambers Case,* the latest book on the subject to date. A *Time* reviewer writes that Weinstein, ". . . has turned up previously undisclosed evidence that inexorably led him to this unqualified verdict: 'The jurors made no mistake in finding Alger Hiss guilty as charged. . . .' [Weinstein] set out convinced that Hiss was innocent. He changed his mind during five years of research into a mass of records that had never been studied. Among them were more than 40,000 pages of FBI files, which Weinstein obtained by suing under the Freedom of Information Act. The files of Hiss's own attorneys, which Hiss opened to Weinstein, yielded other

revealing facts that were kept hidden during the trial. The author also questioned more than 80 people who were connected with the Hiss-Chambers drama, including five former Soviet agents, and talked with Hiss on six occasions."

Already, articles attacking *Perjury: The Hiss-Chambers Case* are appearing. In *Nation,* Victor Navasky states that "*Perjury* settles nothing about the Hiss case. It sets forth some new riddles, fails to solve them and ignores some old ones. The target of *Perjury* is Alger Hiss and his claim of innocence, but its temporary victim is historical truth." Navasky disputes Weinstein's claim to an earlier "commitment to the innocence of Alger Hiss," and says a "review of [Weinstein's] previous writings" shows he had never said so in print before.

John Chabot Smith, author of *Alger Hiss: The True Story,* covered the Hiss trials as a correspondent for the *New York Herald Tribune.* He and Allen Weinstein appeared in a debate over the controversy at Princeton University on April 13, 1976. In *Harper's,* Smith analyses some of the newly released government documents not mentioned by Weinstein, and finds new evidence of Hiss's innocence. He writes: "Weinstein's judgments . . . can be faulted on every page of *Perjury.* The case has defied explanation so far because nobody could believe Chambers had made up such an elaborate story, . . . nor was it credible that Alger Hiss could have been as innocent as he claimed. . . . The easy answer in those days was that Hiss *must* be lying because the government and leading politicians of the day said he was. . . . But by itself it didn't answer the big question: If Chambers lied about Hiss, why couldn't Hiss prove it? . . . He could not disprove the lies because he didn't know what they were. By the time he heard them, they were already accepted by most people as truth, on the authority of a Congressional committee (HUAC) better known to the public than he." Smith told *CA* that "groundwork for the committee's attack had been laid for them by the FBI and then Secretary of State James F. Byrnes, who condemned Hiss unheard, without revealing his accuser or the charges against him. Thus, . . . they sealed his fate before he or the public knew anything about it.'"

The Hiss-Chambers trial represented far more than one man versus another. According to a *Time* reviewer, it was a struggle between the leftist backers of the New Deal and the conservative anti-Communists. The case acted as a catalyst for McCarthyism and its search for Communists. Victor Navasky writes that if Hiss were guilty, then, for many people, it would mean ". . . the New Deal was corrupt, the State Department had been subverted, Yalta was a sellout, the U.N. was a Communist plot, the possibilities of peaceful coexistence with the Soviet Union were shattered, and incipient cold-war repression became defensible."

Alger Hiss has not given up. He has been suing the government for all material pertaining to him under the Freedom of Information Act. As a result of information found in documents obtained thus far, Hiss plans on filing a petition of *coram nobis* (used by defendants who feel misrepresentations of fact led to their conviction), announced Victor Rabinowitz of the law firm representing him. After thirty years, the controversy continues.

BIOGRAPHICAL/CRITICAL SOURCES: Earl Jowitt, *The Strange Case of Alger Hiss,* Doubleday, 1953; Fred J. Cook, *The Unfinished Story of Alger Hiss,* Morrow, 1957; Richard M. Nixon, *Six Crises,* Doubleday, 1962; Meyer A. Zeligs, *Friendship and Fratricide: An Analysis of Whittaker Chambers and Alger Hiss,* Viking, 1967; *New York Times,*

September 16, 1967; *Newsweek*, October 21, 1974, August 11, 1976; *Time*, August 11, 1975, March 29, 1976, February 13, 1978; John Chabot Smith, *Alger Hiss, The True Story*, Holt, 1976, updated edition, Penguin, 1977; *New York Review*, November 25, 1976; Anthony Hiss, *Laughing Last: Alger Hiss*, Houghton, 1977; Allen Weinstein, *Perjury: The Hiss-Chambers Case*, Knopf, 1978; *New York Times Book Review*, April 9, 1978; *Harper's*, June, 1978.

*   *   *

HITCHCOCK, George 1914-

PERSONAL: Born June 2, 1914, in Hood River, Ore. *Education:* University of Oregon, B.A., 1935. *Politics:* Communist. *Religion:* None. *Home:* 325 Ocean View Ave., Santa Cruz, Calif. 95062.

CAREER: Kayak, San Francisco, Calif., editor and publisher of books and magazine, 1964—. *Awards, honors:* "The Busy Martyr" was chosen Play of the Year by Southeast Theatre Conference.

WRITINGS—Poetry; published by Kayak, except as indicated: (With Mel Fowler) *Poems & Prints*, San Francisco Review, 1962; *Tactics of Survival, and Other Poems*, Bindweed Press, 1964; (editor with R. L. Peters) *Pioneers of Modern Poetry* (see *Sidelights* below), 1966, 4th edition, 1969; *The Dolphin with the Revolver in Its Teeth*, Unicorn Press, 1967; *Two Poems*, Unicorn Press, 1967; *Poetry Card* (consists of poem "The One Whose Reproach I Cannot Evade"), Unicorn Press, c. 1967; (compiler and translator with Heiner Bastian) *Eight Poets of Germany and America*, German and English edition, 1967; *A Ship of Bells*, contains prints by Mel Fowler, 1968; (illustrator) Lennart Bruce, *Observations: An Agenda* (poem by Bruce, prints by Hitchcock), 1968; (editor) *Losers Weepers: Poems Found Practically Everywhere*, 1969; *Twelve Stanzas in Praise of the Holy Chariot*, 1969; *The Rococo Eye*, Juniper Books, 1971; *Another Shore*, 1971; *Notes of the Siege Year*, 1974; (translator with A. Fernando) Ludwig Zeller, *Dream Woman*, 1975; *Lessons in Alchemy*, West Coast Poetry Review, 1977; *The Piano beneath the Skin*, Copper Canyon Press, 1978.

Plays: "The Discovery and Perilous Ascent of Kan-Chen-Chomo" (first produced in San Francisco by The Interplayers, 1955), published in *First Stage*, Volume III, number 3, 1964; "Prometheus Found" (first produced in San Francisco at Actors Workshop, 1958), published in *San Francisco Review*, Volume I, number 1, 1958; "The Housewarming" (first produced in San Francisco at Actors Workshop, 1958), published in *Masses & Mainstream*, 1957; "The Busy Martyr" (first produced in San Francisco at Actors Workshop, 1959), published in *First Stage*, Volume II, number 1, 1962; "The Magical History of Doctor Faustus," first produced in San Francisco by The Interplayers, 1966; "The Ticket" (first produced in San Francisco, 1967), published in *Chelsea*, number 14; *The Counterfeit Rose: A Baroque Comedy* (first produced in Memphis, Tenn., at Circuit Theater, March, 1978), Kayak, 1967.

Contributor to anthologies, including: *The Modern Short Story in the Making*, edited by W. Burnett and H. Burnett, Hawthorn, 1964; *Poets of Today*, edited by Walter Lowenfels, International Publishers, 1964; *Of Poetry and Power: Poems on the Presidency of J. F. Kennedy*, edited by Glikes and Schwaber, Basic Books, 1964; *A Poetry Reading against the Vietnam War*, Sixties Press, 1966; *Where Is Vietnam? American Poets Respond*, edited by Lowenfels, Anchor, 1967; *The Voice That Is Great within Us*, edited by

Hayden Carruth, Bantam, 1972; *A Geography of Poets*, edited by Edward Field, Bantam, 1978; *The Oxford Book of American Popular Verse*, edited by William Harmon, Oxford University Press, 1978; *Surrealism in English*, edited by Edward Germain, Penguin, 1978. Editor, *San Francisco Review*.

SIDELIGHTS: George Hitchcock's *Pioneers of Modern Poetry* was described by Edgar Robinson as "a compilation of bits of Victorian (and a trifle later) prose arranged as verse with mock-erudite footnotes attached.... For all I know, the Editors may be putting me on.... Anyway, this variety of humor leaves me cold." Hitchcock told *CA* that the book is "a form of satire."

BIOGRAPHICAL/CRITICAL SOURCES: Carleton Miscellany, fall, 1967; *Chicago Review*, Volume XX, number 1, 1968, January-February, 1971; *Virginia Quarterly Review*, summer, 1969.

*   *   *

HITCHCOCK, James 1938-

PERSONAL: Born February 13, 1938, in St. Louis, Mo.; son of George F. (an auto worker) and Stella (Martin) Hitchcock; married Helen L. Hull, November 25, 1966; children: Alexandra Katherine, Consuelo Justine, Hilary Caroline. *Education:* St. Louis University, A.B., 1960; Princeton University, M.A., 1962, Ph.D., 1965. *Politics:* Independent. *Religion:* Roman Catholic. *Home:* 6158 Kingsbury Ave., St. Louis, Mo. 63112. *Office:* Department of History, St. Louis University, St. Louis, Mo. 63103.

CAREER: St. John's University, Jamaica, N.Y., assistant professor of history, 1964-66; St. Louis University, St. Louis, Mo., assistant professor, 1966-68, associate professor, 1968-71, professor of history, 1971—. *Member:* American Historical Association, American Society for Reformation Research, Sixteenth Century Studies Conference, Renaissance Society of America, Phi Beta Kappa. *Awards, honors:* National Endowment for the Humanities grant, 1968; D.H.L., Benedictine College, 1972.

WRITINGS: The Decline and Fall of Radical Catholicism, Herder & Herder, 1971; *The Recovery of the Sacred*, Seabury, 1974.

WORK IN PROGRESS: Elizabethan Folk Religion; The Mind of Thomas More; A Social History of Western Europe.

*   *   *

HJORTSBERG, William (Reinhold) 1941-

PERSONAL: Surname is pronounced Yorts-berg; born February 23, 1941, in New York, N.Y.; son of Helge (a restaurateur) and Ida (Welti) Hjortsberg; married Marian Renken, June 2, 1962; children: Lorca Isabel, Max William. *Education:* Dartmouth College, B.A., 1962; graduate study at Yale University, 1962-63, and Stanford University, 1967-68. *Home:* Pine Creek, Mont. 59047. *Agent:* Robert Dattila, Phoenix Literary Agency, 150 East 74th St., New York, N.Y. 10021.

CAREER: Has always considered himself a full-time writer, "although in the past necessity often required me to seek employment"; worked while in college as dishwasher, pizza cook, and graphic design assistant; since then has been a teacher in St. Croix, Virgin Islands, 1963-64, 1966-67, draughtsman in New Haven, Conn., 1965, and stock boy in a grocery in Bolinas, Calif., for three months of 1968. *Awards, honors:* Wallace Stegner creative writing fellowship, 1967; *Playboy* Editorial Award for best new fiction contributor, 1971, for short version of *Gray Matters;* National Endowment for the Arts creative writing fellowship grant, 1976.

WRITINGS: (Contributor) *Prize College Stories,* Random House, 1963; *Alp,* Simon & Schuster, 1969; *Gray Matters,* Simon & Schuster, 1971; *Symbiography,* Sumac Press, 1973; *Toro! Toro! Toro!,* Simon & Schuster, 1974. Also author of filmscript, "Thunder and Lightening," for Twentieth-Century Fox. Contributor to *Look, Sports Illustrated, Playboy, Last Supplement of the Whole Earth Catalog, New York Times Book Review, Catholic World,* and other periodicals.

WORK IN PROGRESS: Fallen Angel, a novel; an adaption of *A River Runs through It* for Paramount Pictures Corp., and a comedy for New World Pictures, Inc.

SIDELIGHTS: Before settling in Montana in 1971, Hjortsberg spent almost nine years abroad—mainly in Mexico, St. Croix, on the island of Formentera in Spain, and in Puerto Limon, Costa Rica. He writes: "I enjoy fly fishing, both for trout and in salt water; upland game shooting, skiing, riding horses, body surfing, sketching, exploring unfamiliar places, and conversation. Although born in New York, I tend now to avoid cities. As a boy, I wanted to be a painter. I believe that the land and sky and water belong to the people and are not the exclusive property of industry and commerce ... I don't believe in nationalism, flags, boundary lines, systems, or nineteenth-century technology. I like the Apollo Project photos of earth; one world, alive and green."

Gray Matters has been translated into several European languages and will soon appear in Japanese.

BIOGRAPHICAL/CRITICAL SOURCES: Life, October 24, 1969; *New York Times,* December 16, 1969; *Los Angeles Times Calendar,* October 17, 1971; *New York Times Book Review,* October 31, 1971, August 25, 1974; *New Republic,* September 13, 1974.

*   *   *

HOAGLAND, Everett (III) 1942-

PERSONAL: Born December 18, 1942, in Philadelphia, Pa.; son of Everett, Jr. and Estelle (Johnson) Hoagland; married Alice Trimiew; children: Kamal (son). *Education:* Lincoln University, Lincoln University, Pa., A.B., 1964; Brown University, M.A., 1973. *Office:* Department of English, Southeastern Massachusetts University, North Dartmouth, Mass. 02747.

CAREER: Teacher of English in public schools of Philadelphia, Pa., 1964-67; Lincoln University, Lincoln University, Pa., assistant director of admissions, 1967-69; Claremont College, Claremont, Calif., administrative assistant and teacher of Black poetry at Black Studies Center, 1969-70, poet in residence, 1970-71; Southeastern Massachusetts University, North Dartmouth, staff position in department of English, 1973-76, associate professor of English, 1976—. *Awards, honors:* Fellowship in creative writing, Brown University, 1971-73; Gwendolyn Brooks Award for Fiction, *Black World* (magazine), 1974; Massachusetts Arts & Humanities Foundation award for poetry, 1975.

WRITINGS: Black Velvet, Broadside Press, 1970; *Scrimshaw* (poetry) Patmos Press, 1976. Contributor of poems to anthologies, including *The New Black Poetry, The Black Poets, Giant Talk,* and *Significance: The Struggle We Share.* Contributor of poetry and fiction to *American Poetry Review, Black World, Essence, Nimrod,* and other periodicals.

WORK IN PROGRESS: Two novels, *King Dust* and *Bedrock Mass.*

BIOGRAPHICAL/CRITICAL SOURCES: Don Lee, *Dynamite Voices,* Broadside Press, 1971.

*   *   *

HOBSON, Anthony (Robert Alwyn) 1921-

PERSONAL: Born September 5, 1921, in North Wales; son of Geoffrey Dudley and Gertrude Adelaide Hobson; married Tanya Vinogradoff, 1959; children: one son, two daughters. *Education:* New College, Oxford, M.A. *Home:* The Glebe House, Whitsbury, Fordingbridge, Hampshire, England. *Office:* Sotheby & Co., 34 New Bond St., London W1A 2AA, England.

CAREER: Sotheby & Co., London, England, director, 1949-70, associate, 1970—. *Military service:* British Army, Scots Guards, 1941-46; became captain; mentioned in dispatches.

WRITINGS: French and Italian Collectors and Their Bindings, Illustrated from Examples in the Library of J. R. Abbey, Oxford University Press, 1953; *Great Libraries,* Putnam, 1970; *Apollo and Pegasus: An Enquiry into the Formation and Dispersal of a Renaissance Library,* Gerard Th. Van Heusden (Amsterdam), 1975.

WORK IN PROGRESS: The Library of Diego Hurtado de Mendoza.

*   *   *

HODES, Aubrey 1927-

PERSONAL: Born December 1, 1927, in Cape Town, South Africa; son of Leon (a farmer) and Rachel (Rabinowitz) Hodes; married Rhoda Kroll (a painter), October 6, 1953 (separated, 1975); children: Gabriel, Tamar. *Education:* University of Cape Town, B.S., 1947; Oxford University, graduate study, 1955. *Politics:* "Liberal and committed to compassion." *Religion:* "Jewish Humanist." *Home:* 35 Belsize Park Gardens, London NW3, England. *Agent:* Lucy Kroll, 390 West End Ave., New York, N.Y. 10024.

CAREER: Writer, 1949—; shepherd on kibbutz near Nazareth, Israel, 1949-54; W. Turnowsky & Son (publishing house), Tel Aviv, Israel, senior editor, 1954-59; U.S. Embassy, Tel Aviv, senior translator and press analyst, 1959-65; Institute of World Affairs, New York, N.Y., fellow, 1965-67; U.S. Embassy, London, England, employee in international press section, 1967-69; Holloway School, London, teacher of English, 1973—. *Military service:* Israeli Army, 1956-57. *Awards, honors:* Second prize, *New York Herald Tribune* World Short Story Contest, 1955.

WRITINGS: (Translator from the Hebrew) Moses Shamir, *The Fifth Wheel,* Bodley Head, 1961; (translator from the Hebrew) Aharon Megged, *Fortunes of a Fool,* Random House, 1962; *Dialogue with Ishmael: Israel's Future in the Middle East,* Funk, 1969; *Martin Buber: An Intimate Portrait,* Viking, 1971 (published in England as *Encounter with Martin Buber,* Allen Lane, 1972); (translator from the Hebrew) David Ben-Gurion, *Letters to Paula,* Vallentine, Mitchell, 1971, University of Pittsburgh Press, 1972; *Journey from Ice,* Viking, 1978; *Ben-Gurion,* Penguin, 1979. Also translator of *Dianes,* by Moshe Sharett. Contributor of articles, stories, and poems to *Commentary, Encounter,* and other periodicals. Editor, *New Outlook* (Israel), 1957-65.

WORK IN PROGRESS: The Gardenia Dwarf, a novel about an artists' colony in Greece.

SIDELIGHTS: Thomas Lask describes Aubrey Hodes as "an Israeli journalist who desires a genuine accommodation with the Arabs and . . . [who] wants Israel to be motivated as much by moral principles as by military and chauvinistic ones." Lask believes that Hodes' book on Buber "breathes such a largeness of spirit, such a concern for one's fellow man, such a striving for international understanding that reading it is like entering on a personal retreat." His papers are now in the twentieth-century archives of Boston University Library.

Hodes lived on the Greek island of Hydra from 1965 to 1966.

AVOCATIONAL INTERESTS: Archaeology; collecting rocks and fossils, and autographed letters of modern writers, classical music (especially Mozart), good jazz, theatre, conversation, walking on Hampstead Heath, and "anyone who is their own man or woman and goes at their own pace."

BIOGRAPHICAL/CRITICAL SOURCES: New York Times, January 29, 1969, August 18, 1971; *Carleton Miscellany,* summer, 1969; *National Review,* July 1, 1969; *Saturday Review,* July 31, 1971; *New Yorker,* August 28, 1971; *New York Times Book Review,* August 29, 1971.

* * *

HODGE, Francis (Richard) 1915-

PERSONAL: Born December 17, 1915, in Geneva, N.Y.; son of Richard Duane (a barber) and Mabel Ella (Clark) Hodge; married Beulah Bernice Wiley (a television producer), June 1, 1942; children: Elizabeth Jean (Mrs. James Flack II). *Education:* Hobart College, B.A., 1939; Cornell University, M.A., 1940, Ph.D., 1948. *Home:* 1109 Bluebonnet Lane, Austin, Tex. 78704. *Office:* Department of Drama, University of Texas, Austin, Tex. 78712.

CAREER: Carroll College, Waukesha, Wis., instructor in drama, 1940-42; Cornell University, Ithaca, N.Y., instructor in drama, 1948; University of Texas at Austin, assistant professor, 1949-55, associate professor, 1955-62, professor of drama, 1962—. Director of plays in U.S. and Canada. Visiting assistant professor, University of Iowa, 1948-49; professor of drama, summers, University of Colorado, 1960, Banff School of Fine Arts, 1961-68, and University of British Columbia, 1962. *Military service:* U.S. Army Air Forces, 1942-45; became staff sergeant. *Member:* International Society for Theatre Research, American Theatre Association (fellow), Speech Communication Association, American Society for Theatre Research, Theatre Library Association, Phi Kappa Phi. *Awards, honors:* Golden Anniversary award, Speech Association of America, 1965, for *Yankee Theatre.*

WRITINGS: (Contributor) Leroy Robert Shaw, editor, *German Theatre Today,* University of Texas Press, 1964; *Yankee Theatre: The Image of America on the Stage, 1825-1850,* University of Texas Press, 1964; (author of introduction) Noah Ludlow, *Dramatic Life As I Found It,* Benjamin Blom, 1966; *Play Directing: Analysis, Communication, and Style,* Prentice-Hall, 1971; (editor) *Innovations in Stage and Theatre Design* (essays), American Society for Theatre Research and Theatre Library Association, 1972. Articles appear in several anthologies. Contributor to *Theatre Annual, Quarterly Journal of Speech, Educational Theatre Journal, Western Speech, Texas Quarterly, Southern Speech,* and *Theatre Survey.* Editor, *Educational Theatre Journal,* 1966-68.

WORK IN PROGRESS: New Directions in the Theatre in the Light of Theatre History; nonverbal theatricals; the director-interpreter versus the artist-leader; audiences in America.

SIDELIGHTS: Francis Hodge has traveled extensively in Europe studying folk festivals, antique theatres, and contemporary stagings.

BIOGRAPHICAL/CRITICAL SOURCES: Writer, November, 1971; *Quarterly Journal of Speech,* April, 1972.

* * *

HODGE, P(aul) W(illiam) 1934-

PERSONAL: Born November 8, 1934, in Seattle, Wash.; son of Paul H. and Frances (Bakeman) Hodge; married Ann Uran, June 14, 1961; children: Gordon, Erik, Sandra. *Education:* Yale University, B.S., 1956; Harvard University, Ph.D., 1960. *Residence:* Seattle, Wash. *Office:* Department of Astronomy, University of Washington, Seattle, Wash. 98195.

CAREER: Harvard University, Cambridge, Mass., lecturer in astronomy, 1960; University of California, Berkeley, assistant professor of astronomy, 1961-65; University of Washington, Seattle, associate professor, 1965-69, professor of astronomy, 1969—. Physicist at Smithsonian Astrophysical Observatory, 1956-75. *Member:* American Astronomical Society, American Geophysical Union, International Astronomical Union, Committee on Space Research of International Council of Scientific Unions. *Awards, honors:* National Science Foundation fellow, 1960-61.

WRITINGS: (With J. C. Brandt) *Solar System Astrophysics,* McGraw, 1963; *Galaxies and Cosmology,* McGraw, 1965; *The Large Magellanic Cloud,* Smithsonian Press, 1967; *Concepts of the Universe,* McGraw, 1969; *The Revolution in Astronomy,* Holiday House, 1970; (reviser) Harlow Shapley, *Galaxies,* Harvard University Press, 1972; *Astronomy Study Guide,* McGraw, 1973; *Concepts of Contemporary Astronomy,* McGraw, 1974; (with F. Wright) *The Small Magellanic Cloud,* University of Washington Press, 1977. Contributor of about two hundred papers to astronomy journals.

WORK IN PROGRESS: Second edition of *Concepts of Contemporary Astronomy.*

* * *

HOFFMANN, Erik P(eter) 1939-

PERSONAL: Born August 7, 1939, in New York, N.Y.; son of William H. (a management consultant) and Helene (Grasshoff) Hoffmann; married Jenet Fogman (an artist), July 14, 1969. *Education:* Haverford College, B.A., 1961; Indiana University, M.A., 1965, Ph.D., 1967. *Home:* 1175 Stratford Rd., Schenectady, N.Y. 12308. *Office:* Department of Political Science, Graduate School of Public Affairs, State University of New York, Albany, N.Y. 12222.

CAREER: Temple University, Philadelphia, Pa., instructor, 1965-67, assistant professor of political science, 1967-69; State University of New York at Albany, assistant professor, 1969-72, associate professor of political science, 1972—. Columbia University, seminar associate, 1972—, senior research fellow, 1975-76. Member of board of trustees, Citizen Exchange Corps. *Member:* American Political Science Association, American Association for the Advancement of Slavic Studies. *Awards, honors:* American Council of Learned Societies and Social Science Research Council grant for Soviet studies, 1975-76.

WRITINGS: (Editor with Frederic J. Fleron, Jr.) *The Con-*

duct of Soviet Foreign Policy, Aldine-Atherton, 1971. Contributor of chapters to numerous scholarly books. Contributor to World Politics, Problems of Communism, Soviet Union, Canadian-American Slavic Studies, and other journals. Coordinating editor, Soviet Union.

WORK IN PROGRESS: Research on Soviet domestic politics and foreign policy.

* * *

HOFSTADTER, Albert 1910-

PERSONAL: Born March 28, 1910, in New York, N.Y.; son of Louis and Henrietta (Koenigsberg) Hofstadter; married Manya Huber, February 12, 1936; children: Marc Elihu. Education: City College (now City College of the City University of New York), B.S., 1929; Columbia University, M.A., 1934, Ph.D., 1935. Office: Department of Philosophy, Graduate Faculty, New School for Social Research, New York, N.Y. 10011.

CAREER: New York University, New York City, began as instructor, became associate professor; Columbia University, New York City, associate professor, 1950-52, professor of philosophy, 1952-67, chairman, department of fine arts and archaeology, 1955-57; University of California, Santa Cruz, professor of philosophy, 1967-76; New School for Social Research, Graduate Faculty, New York City, professor of philosophy and chairman of department, 1976—. Member: American Philosophical Association (vice-president, Eastern division, 1970-71), American Metaphysical Society, American Society for Aesthetics (trustee, 1963-66), American Society for Phenomenology and Existential Philosophy, Conference on Science, Philosophy, and Religion in Relation to the Democratic Way of Life (fellow), New York Philosophy Club (secretary, 1950-64). Awards, honors: Guggenheim fellow, 1943; Center for Advanced Study in the Behavioral Sciences fellow, 1966-67; Nicholas Murray Butler Silver Medal, Columbia University, 1971.

WRITINGS: Locke and Scepticism, Albee Press, 1936; (editor with Richard F. Kuhns) Philosophies of Art and Beauty: Selected Readings in Aesthetics from Plato to Heidegger, Modern Library, 1964; Truth and Art, Columbia University Press, 1965; Agony and Epitaph: Man, His Art, and His Poetry, Braziller, 1970; (translator from the German and author of introduction) Martin Heidegger, Poetry, Language, Thought, Harper, 1971.

WORK IN PROGRESS: Projected volumes on aesthetics, Hegel's philosophy, the philosophy of Martin Heidegger, and philosophy of the human spirit.

SIDELIGHTS: Albert Hofstadter told CA: "My main effort is to keep alive the true philosophical spirit, which seeks to comprehend reality by fundamental thinking, and which has been largely abandoned in academic circles in American and British universities, which have been dominated by positive science and the analytic-logical intellect. I am interested, philosophically, in everything pertaining to the adventure of the human spirit in the world of reality. It is, obviously, a heart-breaking task to try to keep in touch!"

AVOCATIONAL INTERESTS: Poetry and the other arts; anthropological and similar subject matters.

* * *

HOGNER, Dorothy Childs

PERSONAL: Born in New York, N.Y.; daughter of Albert Ewing (a physician) and Amelia (McGraw) Childs; married Nils Hogner (an artist, illustrator, and mural painter), July

23, 1932 (died July 30, 1970). Education: Attended Wellesley College, 1923-24; University of New Mexico, B.A., 1936. Politics: Republican. Home: Hemlock Hill Herb Farm, Litchfield, Conn. 06759.

CAREER: Writer, principally of juvenile books illustrated by her husband. Runs Hemlock Hill Herb Farm in the Berkshires and sells herb plants. Member: Authors League of America, Garden Club of America, Herb Society of America.

WRITINGS—Adult: South to Padre (travel), Lothrop, 1936; Westward: High, Low and Dry (travel), Dutton, 1938; Summer Roads to Gaspe (travel), Dutton, 1939; Herbs from the Garden to the Table, Oxford University Press, 1953; A Fresh Herb Platter, Doubleday, 1961; Gardening and Cooking on Terrace and Patio, Doubleday, 1964.

Juvenile; all illustrated by husband, Nils Hogner, except as indicated: Navajo Winter Nights, Thomas Nelson, 1935; Education of a Burro, Thomas Nelson, 1936; Santa Fe Caravans, Thomas Nelson, 1937; Little Esther, Thomas Nelson, 1937; Lady Bird, Oxford University Press, 1938; Old Hank Weatherbee, Oxford University Press, 1939; Pancho, Thomas Nelson, 1939.

Don't Blame the Puffins, Oxford University Press, 1940; Stormy, the First Mustang, Oxford University Press, 1941 (published in England as Stormy, the First American Mustang, Hutchinson, 1944); Children of Mexico, Heath, 1942; The Animal Book: American Mammals North of Mexico, Oxford University Press, 1942; The Bible Story, Oxford University Press, 1943; Our American Horse, Thomas Nelson, 1944; Reward for Brownie, Oxford University Press, 1944; Farm Animals, and Working and Sporting Breeds of the United States and Canada, Oxford University Press, 1945; Unexpected Journey: The Story of a Dog, Creative Age Press, 1945; Winky, King of the Garden, Oxford University Press, 1946; Blue Swamp, Oxford University Press, 1947; Barnyard Family, Oxford University Press, 1948; Daisy: A Farm Fable, Oxford University Press, 1949.

Dusty's Return, Oxford University Press, 1950; Odd Pets, illustrated with photographs by Lilo Hess, Crowell, 1951; Wild Little Honker, Oxford University Press, 1951; Snowflake, Oxford University Press, 1952; Earthworms, Crowell, 1953; The Horse Family, Oxford University Press, 1953; The Dog Family, Oxford University Press, 1954; Wide River, Lippincott, 1954; Spiders, Crowell, 1955; Rufus, Lippincott, 1955; Frogs and Polliwogs, Crowell, 1956; The Cat Family, Oxford University Press, 1956; Conservation in America, Lippincott, 1958; Snails, Crowell, 1958.

Grasshoppers and Crickets, Crowell, 1960; Water Over the Dam, Lippincott, 1960; Butterflies, Crowell, 1962; Water Beetles, Crowell, 1963; Moths, Crowell, 1964; A Book of Snakes, Crowell, 1966; Weeds, Crowell, 1968; Birds of Prey, Crowell, 1969; Good Bugs and Bad Bugs in Your Garden: Backyard Ecology, illustrations by Grambs Miller, Crowell, 1974; Water Plants, illustrated with photographs from various sources, Holiday House, 1977; Endangered Plants, illustrations by Arabelle Wheatley, Crowell, 1977.

WORK IN PROGRESS: Sea Mammals, for Crowell.

SIDELIGHTS: Dorothy Hogner wrote CA that sea mammals, the subject of her new book, are "a fascinating subject and . . . much in the news today, with headlines on the tuna fish-porpoise battle, the Eskimos and the bowhead whales, the Florida manatee in danger of extinction, [and] the stranded whales."

HOLDREN, John P(aul) 1944-

PERSONAL: Born March 1, 1944, in Sewickley, Pa.; son of Raymond Andrew (a realtor) and Virginia June (Fuqua) Holdren; married Cheryl Lea Edgar (a poet); February 5, 1966; children: John Craig, Jill Virginia. *Education:* Massachusetts Institute of Technology, S.B., 1965, S.M., 1966; Stanford University, Ph.D., 1970. *Home:* 6668 Colton Blvd., Oakland, Calif. 94611. *Office:* 100 T-4, University of California, Berkeley, Calif. 94720.

CAREER: University of California, Lawrence Livermore Laboratory, Livermore, physicist in controlled thermonuclear research, 1970-71; University of California, Berkeley, lecturer in electrical engineering, 1971; California Institute of Technology, Pasadena, senior research fellow in environmental quality laboratory and in population program, 1972-73; University of California, Berkeley, assistant professor, 1973-75, associate professor of energy and resources, 1975—. National Academy of Sciences, member of international environmental programs committee, 1970-75, steering committee for study of nuclear and alternative energy systems, 1975-77, and committee to review the literature of nuclear risks, 1975-77. *Member:* American Physical Society, American Association for the Advancement of Science, Federation of American Scientists, American Nuclear Society, Sigma Xi, Tau Beta Pi.

WRITINGS: (Editor with Paul R. Ehrlich) *Global Ecology,* Harcourt, 1971; (editor with P. Ehrlich and Richard W. Holm) *Man and the Ecosphere,* W. H. Freeman, 1971; (with Phillip Herrera) *Energy,* Sierra Club, 1971; (with P. Ehrlich and Anne Ehrlich) *Human Ecology,* W. H. Freeman, 1973; (editor with Harrison Brown, Alan Sweezy, and Barbara West) *Population: Perspective 1973,* Freeman, Cooper, 1974; (with P. Ehrlich and A. Ehrlich) *Ecoscience,* W. H. Freeman, 1977. Contributor, with P. Ehrlich, of regular monthly science articles to *Saturday Review,* 1970-72; contributor to *Science, Bioscience, Physics of Fluids, Nuclear Fusion, Plasma Physics, Daedalus, Energy Systems and Policy, American Scientist, New York Times, London Times,* and *Bulletin of the Atomic Scientists.*

* * *

HOLLAND, Francis Ross, Jr. 1927-

PERSONAL: Born August 24, 1927, in Savannah, Ga.; son of Francis Ross (a credit manager) and Eleanor (Struck) Holland; married June Agee (a high school teacher), July 24, 1948; children: Henry Ross. *Education:* University of Georgia, Atlanta Division, B.C.S., 1950; University of Texas (now University of Texas at Austin), M.A., 1958. *Politics:* Democrat. *Home:* 2117 E. St. N.W., Washington, D.C. 20037. *Office:* Division of Cultural Resources Management, National Park Service, Department of the Interior, Washington, D.C. 20242.

CAREER: National Park Service, Washington, D.C., historian, 1958—; has worked for National Park Service at Shiloh National Military Park, Morristown National Historical Park, Cabrillo and Channel Islands National Monuments, Chesapeake and Ohio Canal National Monument, Eastern, Western, and Denver Service Centers, North Atlantic Regional Office, and at the Washington office. *Military service:* U.S. Navy, 1945-46, 1953-55; became lieutenant junior grade. *Member:* North American Society for Oceanic History, Society for the History of Discoveries, Southern History Association, Western Historical Association, California Historical Society, Alaska Historical Society.

WRITINGS: America's Lighthouses: Their Illustrated His-

tory *Since 1716,* Greene, 1972. Also author of *The Aransas Pass Light Station: A History,* 1976. Contributor to history journals. Editor, *Western Explorer,* 1961-64.

WORK IN PROGRESS: History of early West Coast lighthouses.

* * *

HOLLAND, Kenneth J(ohn) 1918-

PERSONAL: Born July 19, 1918, in Minneapolis, Minn.; son of John Olaf (a miller) and Olga (Dahlberg) Holland; married Maurine Strom (an accountant), August 15, 1948; children: Laurence, Wesley. *Education:* Union College, Lincoln, Neb., B.A., 1949; attended Vanderbilt University, 1969-71. *Religion:* Seventh-day Adventist. *Home:* 5956 Port Yakima Ct., Hermitage, Tenn. 37076. *Office address:* Southern Publishing Association, P.O. Box 59, Nashville, Tenn. 37202.

CAREER: Southern Publishing Association, Nashville, Tenn., copy editor, 1949-51, assistant editor, 1951-58, editor, *These Times,* 1958—. Has conducted editorial councils and writers' conferences in the United States and overseas. Member of advisory committee, publishing department of Seventh-Day Adventists. *Military service:* U.S. Army, 1941-43; U.S. Army Air Forces, 1943-45. *Member:* International Platform Association, Associated Church Press (board member). *Awards, honors:* Associated Church Press Award of Merit, 1969, 1976; graphic arts awards from Printing Industry of America and Society of Publication Designers, 1977.

WRITINGS: Great Churches of America, Southern Publishing, 1957; (compiler) *Those Sabbath Hours,* Southern Publishing, 1966; *This Day Is Yours,* Southern Publishing, 1969; *The Magnificent Seventh,* Pacific Press, 1970; *A New Kind of Life,* Pacific Press, 1973; *The Choice,* Southern Publishing, 1977. Also author of *Southern Publishing Association Stylebook,* 1952. Contributor to *Liberty, Review & Herald,* and *Message.*

SIDELIGHTS: Kenneth J. Holland told *CA* he is "fascinated" by the seventh-day Sabbath and Bible prophecy. He would like "to show that the God of the Bible is trustworthy—because of His character, creative works, and activities in behalf of ancient Israel." Holland has traveled around the world, twice to the Holy Land.

* * *

HOLLAND, Robert 1940-

PERSONAL: Born February 27, 1940; son of Roy Theurer and Alice (Landeen) Holland; married Leslie Roberts (a photographer), August 28, 1971. *Education:* Attended Colby College, Waterville, Me., 1957-58, and Southern Connecticut State College, 1958-60; University of Connecticut, B.A., 1962, graduate study, 1963-64; Trinity College, Hartford, Conn., graduate study, 1977-78. *Religion:* Congregationalist. *Home and office:* Pea Hill Rd., Killingworth, Conn. 06417. *Agent:* James Brown Associates, Inc., 25 West 43rd St., New York, N.Y. 10036.

CAREER: Grove School, Madison, Conn., teacher, 1962-63; *New Haven Register,* New Haven, Conn., reporter, writer, editor, 1966-67, 1968-71; Gannett Newspapers, Rochester, N.Y., reporter and columnist, 1967-68; full-time writer, 1971—. *Military service:* U.S. Naval Reserve, 1965-71; became lieutenant junior grade. *Member:* Authors Guild.

WRITINGS: The Hunter, Stein & Day, 1971. Contributor

of articles, stories, and photographs to magazines, including *Connecticut Magazine.*

WORK IN PROGRESS: Four novels and a play, completed and awaiting publication; two other novels.

SIDELIGHTS: Robert Holland told *CA* he believes that "today a writer must compete with the most pernicious of forces: television. To do so I write short books which may be read in a single sitting. The story, therefore, has to come first. Theme and ideas which I try to get across are subtle and operate at another level from the story. A writer is an entertainer. . . . Success depends on whether you are able to create the kinds of images and characters which stay with your reader beyond his reading."

Holland feels that "books about New Englanders" seem to be ". . . last on the selection lists of most publishers." He went on to say: ". . . if you look at current fiction, it is clear that the only acceptable rural novel is from the South. Even then, nearly all rural novels have a decidedly urban cast. It is as if those who live in the cities, those who control the publishing business, no longer find any virtue in country ways. They tell me such books won't sell, and though I suspect they may be right, it seems odd that so noble an art as fiction should finally be determined on a balance sheet."

*   *   *

HOLLEY, Bobbie Lee 1927-

PERSONAL: Born June 9, 1927, in Chattanooga, Tenn.; daughter of Clifford Lee and Ella (Boyd) Gault; married Edward G. Holley (dean of School of Library Science, University of North Carolina), June 19, 1954; children: Gailon Boyd, Edward Jens, Amy Lin, Beth Alison. *Education:* Attended Freed-Hardeman College, 1945-46; David Lipscomb College, B.A. (magna cum laude), 1950; Northwestern University, M.A., 1951. *Religion:* Church of Christ. *Home:* 1508 Ephesus Church Rd., Chapel Hill, N.C. 27514.

CAREER: High school English teacher in Nashville, Tenn., 1951-54, and Arlington, Va., 1954-56. Lecturer to women's church groups and conductor of workshops. *Awards, honors:* Twentieth-century Christian Journalism Award, 1970.

WRITINGS: Person to Person, R. B. Sweet, 1969; *To Persons with Love,* Sweet Publishing, 1974; *Jesus Calls Me,* Sweet Publishing, 1975. Writer of "God's Design: Woman's Dignity," an address for a seminar on Christian womanhood, later published in *Mission Journal.* Regular contributor to *Christian Woman;* contributor to other religion journals.

*   *   *

HOLM, Don(ald Raymond) 1918-
(Peter Denali)

PERSONAL: Born January 3, 1918, in Velva, N.D.; son of Ralph Edward (a blacksmith) and Minnie V. (Luke) Holm; married Mary Beazley, July 17, 1941; married Myrtle Tate (a newspaper advertising employee), May 31, 1963; children: (first marriage) Rebecca Lee (Mrs. Gene Hilby), Douglas Kimball. *Education:* Attended Portland State University, 1946-48, and Multnomah College (now Multnomah School of Engineering, University of Portland), 1948; Lewis and Clark College, B.A., 1950. *Home:* 9995 Southwest Maplecrest Ct., Beaverton, Ore. 97005. *Agent:* August Lenniger, Lenniger Literary Agency, Inc., 437 Fifth Ave., New York, N.Y. 10016. *Office: The Oregonian,* 1320 Southwest Broadway, Portland, Ore. 97201.

CAREER: After graduation from high school in 1936, worked as dish washer, logger, miner, commercial fisherman, carpenter, construction worker, and steelworker; mining and sawmill worker, Howe Sound Mining Co., Chelan, Wash., 1938-39, and Alaska-Juneau Mining Co., 1939-40; construction worker in Fairbanks, Alaska, 1940-41; Kaiser Co. (construction), Oakland, Calif., construction foreman, 1941-44; KPOJ Radio Station, Portland, Ore., script writer, 1948-49; Hyster Co. (manufacturer of heavy machinery), Portland, publicity-promotion worker, 1950-54; Mobil Oil Co., Portland, northwest public relations representative, 1954-60; *The Oregonian* (daily newspaper), Portland, political and feature writer, 1960—, outdoor-wildlife columnist and editor, 1968—. Free-lance writer on outdoors and related fields. *Military service:* U.S. Navy, 1945-46.

MEMBER: Authors Guild, Authors League of America, Western Writers of America, Outdoor Writers Association of America, National Rifle Association, Oregon Historical Society, Montana Historical Society, Oregon Freelance Club (former president), Willamette Writers Club, Lewis & Clark Heritage Foundation (member of Governor's Committee), Explorers Club of New York, Port Ludlow Yacht Club, Masons, Scottish Rites, Slocum Society. *Awards, honors:* James C. Henshall awards, American Fishing Tackle Manufacturers Association, 1st place in 1968, 2nd place in 1969, for best sport fishing column in nation.

WRITINGS: Reunion Summer, Buffalo Books, 1963; *Old Fashioned Dutch Oven Cookbook,* Caxton, 1969; *Pacific North!,* Caxton, 1969; *101 Best Fishing Trips in Oregon,* Caxton, 1970; *Anglers Guide to Pacific Game Fish,* Winchester Western Press, 1971; *The Complete Sourdough Cookbook,* Caxton, 1972; *The Circumnavigators,* Prentice-Hall, 1975; *Cruising the Northwest,* Prentice-Hall, 1977; *Drying, Pickling, and Smoke Cooking,* Caxton, 1977.

Also author of several corporation histories; contributor of 2000 feature articles, some under pseudonym Peter Denali, to newspapers and magazines, and 150 fiction short stories to periodicals. Work anthologized in several collections, including *The Ten Best Outdoor Adventures,* Dutton, 1963, *Depth Reporting: An Approach to Journalism,* by Neale Copple, Prentice-Hall, 1964, *This Land Around Us: A Treasury of Pacific Northwest Writing,* edited by Ellis Lucia, Doubleday, 1969, and *The Best Outdoor Adventure Stories of Outdoor Life,* Harper, 1976.

WORK IN PROGRESS: A biographical narrative of America's first "mountain man," John Colter, member of Lewis and Clark expedition and discoverer of the area now encompassed by Yellowstone Park; *The Islands of the Four Mountains,* a novel of a commercial fishing fleet in Alaska; a nonfiction book, *The Return of the Sea Otter;* three other books, *The Globe Mutiny, Winter of '38,* and *City Hall Beat.*

AVOCATIONAL INTERESTS: Ecology and the environment, oceanography, geology, marine and freshwater fisheries, sport fishing and hunting, outdoor recreation, history, Western Americana, contemporary world affairs, travel and exploration, boating, flying, politics, cooking of specialties, photography, home workshop and craftsmanship, books and reading.

*   *   *

HOLMES, Arthur F. 1924-

PERSONAL: Born March 15, 1924, in Dover, England; son of Frank A. (a schoolteacher) and Annie (Fairs) Holmes; married Alice Henderson, June 25, 1949; children: Paul,

Mark. *Education:* Wheaton College, Wheaton, Ill., A.B., 1950, M.A., 1952; Northwestern University, Ph.D., 1957. *Home:* 911 North Washington St., Wheaton, Ill. 60187. *Office:* Department of Philosophy, Wheaton College, Wheaton, Ill. 60187.

CAREER: Wheaton College, Wheaton, Ill., assistant professor, 1953-57, associate professor, 1957-66, professor of philosophy, 1966—. Summer visiting professor, University of the Pacific and Garrett Theological Seminary. *Military service:* Royal Air Force, 1942-47. *Member:* American Philosophical Association, Metaphysical Society of America, Illinois Philosophy Conference. *Awards, honors:* Danforth Foundation teacher study grant, 1955-56.

WRITINGS: Christianity and Philosophy, Inter-Varsity Press, 1960, revised edition published as *Philosophy: A Christian Perspective,* 1975; *Christian Philosophy in the Twentieth Century,* Craig Press, 1969; *Faith Seeks Understanding,* Eerdmans, 1971; *The Idea of a Christian College,* Eerdmans, 1975; (editor) *War and Christian Ethics,* Baker Book, 1976; *All Truth Is God's Truth,* Eerdmans, 1977. Contributor to *Encyclopaedia Britannica* and to religion and philosophy journals. Contributing editor, *Reformed Journal.*

* * *

HOLMES, David M(orton) 1929-

PERSONAL: Born June 4, 1929, in Walkerville, Ontario, Canada; son of William Morton and Alice E. (Bennett) Holmes; married Marian Isabelle Brough, September 22, 1950; children: Leslie Constance, Ruth Emily, Alison Stephanie. *Education:* University of Western Ontario, B.A., 1959; University of Windsor, M.A., 1964; Merton College, Oxford, D.Phil., 1968. *Home:* 27 Oxford Rd., Old Marston, Oxford, England. *Agent:* David Higham Associates Ltd., 5-8 Lower John St., London W1R 4HA, England. *Office:* Department of English, University of Dakar, Dakar-Fann, Senegal.

CAREER: University of Windsor, Windsor, Ontario, associate professor of English, 1964-73; University of Dakar, Dakar-Fann, Senegal, professor of English, 1975—. *Military service:* Royal Canadian Air Force, Flying Officer, 1951-57. *Member:* Commonwealth Society, Merton Society.

WRITINGS: The Art of Thomas Middleton, Clarendon Press, 1970; (with H. D. Janzen) *A Note on the Editing of Jacobean Drama,* University of Toronto Press, 1972. Contributor to *Baker Street Journal, Holmesian Quarterly, Modern Language Review,* and other journals.

WORK IN PROGRESS: Writing fiction; research on English renaissance literature.

SIDELIGHTS: David M. Holmes has traveled in South and Central America, the Arctic, Greenland, Iceland, Europe, the British West Indies, and Africa.

BIOGRAPHICAL/CRITICAL SOURCES: Books & Bookmen, February, 1971.

* * *

HOLMES, Lowell D(on) 1925-

PERSONAL: Born June 15, 1925, in Sioux City, Iowa; son of Emmit L. (in railroad passenger traffic department) and Marie P. (Tall) Holmes; married Jeanette R. Timmcke, November 17, 1951 (divorced, 1975); children: Loreen, Jonathan, Jill. *Education:* Northwestern University, B.S., 1950, Ph.D., 1957; University of Wisconsin, graduate study, 1950-51. *Politics:* Democrat. *Religion:* Protestant. *Home:* 2950

North Terrace Dr., Wichita, Kan. 67208. *Office:* Department of Anthropology, Wichita State University, Wichita, Kan. 67208.

CAREER: Missouri Valley College, Marshall, assistant professor of anthropology and chairman of department of sociology and anthropology, 1956-59; Wichita State University, Wichita, Kan., assistant professor, 1959-62, associate professor, 1962-66, professor of anthropology, 1966—, chairman of department, 1966-69. National Science Foundation lecturer, 1965—. Anthropological research in American Samoa, 1953-54, 1962-63. *Military service:* U.S. Coast Guard, 1943-45. *Member:* American Anthropological Association (fellow), American Ethnological Society, Central States Anthropological Society (first vice-president, 1971-72), Sigma Xi, Alpha Kappa Delta, Lambda Alpha (founder).

WRITINGS: Ta'u Stability and Change in a Samoan Village, Polynesian Society (Wellington, New Zealand), 1958; *Anthropology: An Introduction,* Ronald, 1965, 2nd edition, 1971; (contributor) D. H. Efron, editor, *Ethnopharmacologic Search for Psychoactive Drugs,* U.S. Department of Health, Education, and Welfare, 1967; *The Story of Samoa,* McCormick-Mathers, 1967; (editor) *Readings in General Anthropology,* Ronald, 1971; (contributor) Ron Crocombe, editor, *Land Tenure in the Pacific,* Oxford University Press (Melbourne), 1971; (editor with Donald Cowgill) *Aging and Modernization: A Cross-Cultural Analysis,* Appleton, 1972; *Samoan Village,* Holt, 1974. Contributor of more than thirty articles and reviews to journals, including *Pacific Islands Monthly, Journal of American Folklore,* and *Science of Man.* Editor, *Lambda Alpha Journal of Man,* 1968—.

WORK IN PROGRESS: A Samoan Islands bibliography, for Australian National University Press; cross-cultural studies of aging and of education; research on the distribution, function, and effects of the drug kava *(Piper methysticum).*

* * *

HOLMSTROM, Lynda Lytle 1939-

PERSONAL: Born April 23, 1939, in Seattle, Wash. *Education:* Stanford University, B.A., 1961; Boston University, M.A., 1965; Brandeis University, Ph.D., 1970. *Office:* Department of Sociology, Boston College, Chestnut Hill, Mass. 02167.

CAREER: Stanford University, Stanford, Calif., research assistant, 1961-63; Human Sciences Research, McLean, Va., research assistant, 1964; Boston College, Chestnut Hill, Mass., instructor, 1969-70, assistant professor, 1970-74, associate professor of sociology, 1974—, chairperson of department, 1974-75, 1977—. *Member:* International Sociological Association, American Sociological Association, American Civil Liberties Union.

WRITINGS: (Assistant editor with senior editors W. Richard Scott and Edmund H. Volkart) *Medical Care,* Wiley, 1966; *The Two-Career Family,* Schenkman, 1972; (with Ann Wolbert Burgess) *Rape: Victims of Crisis,* Robert J. Brady, 1974; *The Victim of Rape: Institutional Response,* Wiley, 1978.

WORK IN PROGRESS: Research on rape victims.

AVOCATIONAL INTERESTS: Skiing, travel.

* * *

HOLTAN, Orley I. 1933-

PERSONAL: Born April 19, 1933, in Duluth, Minn.; son of

Sigurd and Edna (Bjerkan) Holtan; married Judith Hirsch, September 8, 1963. *Education:* Attended Eastern Montana College, 1950-52; St. Olaf College, B.A., 1954; University of North Dakota, M.A., 1960; University of Minnesota, Ph.D., 1966. *Home:* 438 North Main St., Slippery Rock, Pa. 16057. *Office:* Department of Communication, Slippery Rock State College, Slippery Rock, Pa. 16057.

CAREER: High school teacher of English and speech in Broadview, Mont., 1957-58; Morehead State College, Morehead, Ky., instructor in speech and theater, 1960-61; University of Minnesota, Minneapolis, instructor in speech and communication, 1962-67; Slippery Rock State College, Slippery Rock, Pa., associate professor of speech and theater and play director, 1967—. *Military service:* U.S. Army, 1954-57. *Member:* American Educational Theatre Association, Speech Communication Association, Theatre Association of Pennsylvania (president, 1976-77), Pennsylvania Speech Association, Rotary Club (Slippery Rock).

WRITINGS: Mythic Patterns in Ibsen's Last Plays, University of Minnesota Press, 1970; *Introduction to Theatre: Mirror to Nature,* Prentice-Hall, 1976. Contributor of about a dozen articles and reviews to literature journals. Associate editor, *Quarterly Journal of Speech,* 1972-74.

WORK IN PROGRESS: Research on Scandinavian theater and drama and on theater in the frontier West.

SIDELIGHTS: Orley Holtan speaks Norwegian, reads Swedish, Danish, German, and some Spanish and French.

*   *   *

HOLTZMAN, Paul D(ouglas) 1918-

PERSONAL: Born April 4, 1918, in Los Angeles, Calif.; son of Albert and Esther (Goldberg) Holtzman; married Ingrid Pearson, September 5, 1951; children: Douglas. *Education:* Louisiana State University, B.A., 1941; University of Southern California, M.A., 1948, Ph.D., 1950. *Home:* 459 Martin Ter., State College, Pa. 16801. *Office:* 317 Sparks Building, Pennsylvania State University, University Park, Pa. 16802.

CAREER: San Francisco State College (now University), San Francisco, Calif., instructor in speech and director of speech laboratory, 1948-51; Queens College (now Queens College of the City University of New York), Flushing, N.Y., instructor in speech, 1951-57; Pennsylvania State University, University Park, associate professor, 1957-65, professor of speech communication, 1965—. Visiting professor at State University of New York College at Albany, 1956, and University of Hawaii, 1968. *Military service:* U.S. Army Air Forces, 1943-46; became sergeant. *Member:* International Communication Association, Speech Communication Association, American Association for the Advancement of Science, Teachers of English to Speakers of Other Languages, National Association for Foreign Student Affairs, American Psychological Association.

WRITINGS: (With Robert T. Oliver and Harold P. Zelko) *Communicative Speech,* 3rd edition (Holtzman was not associated with earlier editions), Holt, 1962; (with Oliver and Zelko) *Communicative Speaking and Listening,* 4th edition (originally published as *Essentials of Communicative Speech,* Dryden, 1949; Holtzman was not associated with earlier editions), Holt, 1968; *The Psychology of Speakers' Audiences,* Scott, Foresman, 1970; (with Donald H. Eckroyd) *Communication Concepts and Models,* National Textbook Co., 1976. Contributor to speech journals. Editor, *Journal of Communication,* 1971-76.

WORK IN PROGRESS: With Kenneth Frandsen, 5th edition of *Communicative Speaking and Listening;* research on second language proficiency testing, in persuasion, and in second language learning.

*   *   *

HOMZE, Edward L. 1930-

PERSONAL: Born October 13, 1930, in Canton, Ohio; son of John Frank (a welder) and Mary Ann (Granchi) Homze; married Alma Betty Cross (a university professor), March 21, 1959; children: Eric John, Heidi Ann. *Education:* Bowling Green State University, B.A., 1952, M.A., 1953; Pennsylvania State University, graduate study, 1956-57, 1959-61, Ph.D., 1963; Free University of Berlin, graduate study, 1957-59. *Politics:* Democratic. *Religion:* Roman Catholic. *Home:* 3450 Woodshire Pkwy., Lincoln, Neb. 68502. *Office:* Department of History, University of Nebraska, Lincoln, Neb. 68504.

CAREER: Kansas State Teachers College (now Emporia Kansas State College), Emporia, assistant professor of history, 1961-65; University of Nebraska, Lincoln, 1965—, began as associate professor, currently professor of history. Visiting professor, U.S. Naval War College, Newport, R.I., 1975-76. *Military service:* U.S. Air Force, 1954-56; became first lieutenant. *Member:* American Historical Association, American Association for the Advancement of Slavic Studies, American Association of University Professors, Conference Group for Central European History. *Awards, honors:* National Foundation for the Arts and Humanities fellow, 1968; Danforth associate, 1972.

WRITINGS: Foreign Labor in Nazi Germany, Princeton University Press, 1967; (with wife, Alma Homze) *Germany: Divided Nation,* Thomas Nelson, 1970; (with A. Homze) *Willy Brandt,* Thomas Nelson, 1974; *Arming the Luftwaffe,* University of Nebraska Press, 1976. Contributor of reviews to history journals.

WORK IN PROGRESS: Research on the German air industry during World War II.

SIDELIGHTS: Edward Homze told *CA* that his writing "deals with my teaching area of modern German history. I have lived in Germany a number of years since my student days at the University of West Berlin. I have traveled widely in Europe...." *Avocational interests:* Travel, camping, photography, tennis, skiing, sailing.

*   *   *

HONDERICH, Ted 1933-

PERSONAL: Born January 30, 1933, in Baden, Ontario, Canada; son of John William (a pamphleteer and printer) and Rae Laura (a teacher; maiden name Armstrong) Honderich; married Margaret Penman, 1957; married second wife, Pauline Goodwin, 1964; children: Kiaran, John Ruan. *Education:* University of Toronto, B.A., 1959; University of London, Ph.D., 1969. *Politics:* Socialist. *Religion:* None. *Home:* 4 Keats Grove, Hampstead, London N.W.3, England. *Office:* Department of Philosophy, University College, University of London, Gower St., London W.C.1, England.

CAREER: Previously taught at University of Sussex, Sussex, England; University of London, University College, London, England, member of department of philosophy, 1964—. Visiting professor at Yale University and City University of New York, 1970-71.

WRITINGS: Punishment. The Supposed Justifications,

Harcourt, 1969, revised edition, Penguin, 1971; (editor) *Essays on Freedom of Action*, Routledge & Kegan Paul, 1973; (editor) *Social Ends and Political Means*, Routledge & Kegan Paul, 1976; *Three Essays on Political Violence*, Basil Blackwell, 1977. Contributor of articles to books and periodicals. Editor, "International Library of Philosophy and Scientific Method."

WORK IN PROGRESS: A book on determinism, for Penguin.

* * *

HONEY, William (Houghton) 1910-

PERSONAL: Born April 23, 1910, in Sydney, Australia; son of William Henry (a journalist) and Florence Eva (Houghton) Honey. *Education:* Studied grand opera and Russian ballet in Rome, Italy and London, England, 1935-39; attended University of Sydney, 1934, and Sorbonne, University of Paris, 1948. *Politics:* "Non-political." *Religion:* Agnostic. *Address:* c/o Mitre Press, Sardinia House, Kingsway, London, W.C.2, England.

CAREER: Worked in tourist industry, 1947-61, in western Europe, the Middle East, Morocco, and Tunisia; free-lance author and journalist, 1962—. One of four members of Shakespeare Action Committee, which is dedicated to the opening of the Shakespeare tomb in Stratford-upon-Avon and the establishment of the true identity of Shakespeare. *Military service:* Royal Navy, Fleet Air Arm, 1941-45; became lieutenant; served in South Africa, India, and Ceylon; received wound certificate.

WRITINGS: Trials of a Travel-Courier, R. Hale, 1959; *Travel-Courier in Spain*, R. Hale, 1960; *The Somnambulist* (novel), R. Hale, 1961; *The Shakespeare Epitaph Deciphered*, Mitre Press, 1969. Contributor to newspapers and magazines. Travel correspondent, *Sunday Times*, 1954-55.

WORK IN PROGRESS: The Life and Achievements of Christopher Marlowe Alias Shakespeare, a book to prove that the true author of Shakespeare's plays was Christopher Marlowe; a full-scale life of Marlowe-"Shakespeare" in fictional form, as yet untitled.

* * *

HOOD, Joseph F. 1925-

PERSONAL: Born August 12, 1925, in Philadelphia, Pa.; son of Joseph A. (an insurance broker) and Mary F. (McNally) Hood; married Helen Chopko (a department store executive), 1947. *Education:* "Preferred to continue flying career rather than college. But I can't remember a time when I wasn't an omnivorous and almost compulsive reader...." *Politics:* Independent. *Home:* 704 Prospect Row, San Mateo, Calif. 94401. *Agent:* Curtis Brown Ltd., 575 Madison Ave., New York, N.Y. 10022.

CAREER: Commercial pilot and instrument flight instructor, 1947-56; Pan-American World Airways, pilot, 1956-64 (medical retirement). Free-lance writer and editor. *Military service:* U.S. Army Air Forces, 1943-46. *Member:* American Aviation Historical Society, Wingfoot Light-Than-Air Society, California Writers' Club.

WRITINGS—For teen-agers, except as indicated: *When Monsters Roamed the Skies: The Saga of the Dirigible Airship* (juvenile), Grosset, 1968 (published in England as *The Story of Airships: When Monsters Roamed the Skies*, Arthur Barker, 1968); *Skyway Round the World: The Story of the First Global Airway*, Scribner, 1968; *The Sky Racers: Speed Kings of Aviation's Golden Age*, Grosset, 1969; (with

Ralph A. O'Neill) *A Dream of Eagles* (adult), Houghton, 1973. Contributor of adult articles on aviation and American history to magazines, including *American West*. Consulting editor, Sunset Books.

AVOCATIONAL INTERESTS: Photography, music, theatre pipe organ.

* * *

HOOPES, Donelson F(arquhar) 1932-

PERSONAL: Born December 3, 1932, in Philadelphia, Pa.; son of Donelson W. and Esther T. (Dechert) Hoopes. *Education:* Attended Pennsylvania Academy of the Fine Arts, 1950-53, and University of Florence, 1958-59; University of Pennsylvania, A.B., 1960. *Home:* 8262 West Norton Ave., Los Angeles, Calif. 90046. *Agent:* Toni Mendez, 140 East 56th St., New York, N.Y. 10022.

CAREER: Portland Museum of Art, Portland, Me., director, 1960-62; Corcoran Gallery of Art, Washington, D.C., curator, 1962-64; Brooklyn Museum, Brooklyn, N.Y., curator of painting and sculpture, 1965-69; Los Angeles County (Calif.) Museum of Art, curator of American art, 1972-75. State advisor for Maine, American Federation of Art, 1960-62; consultant to New York State Council for the Arts, 1965-69, High Museum of Art, Atlanta, Ga., 1971-72, Archives of American Art, 1974—, and Committee for the Preservation of the White House, 1977—; visiting curator-in-charge of American galleries, M. H. de Young Memorial Museum, San Francisco, Calif., 1976-77. *Military service:* U.S. Army, 1953-55; received Commendation Medal. *Member:* American Association of Museums, Victorian Society in America, National Trust for Historic Preservation, College Art Association of America, Association of Ex-Members of Squadron A (New York). *Awards, honors:* *Winslow Homer Watercolors* was included on American Library Association list of notable books of 1969.

WRITINGS: (Contributor) E. F. Wilder and G. A. Mellon, editors, *Maine and Its Role in American Art*, Studio Viking, 1963; *Winslow Homer Watercolors*, Watson-Guptill, 1969; *Sargent Watercolors*, Watson-Guptill, 1970; *Eakins Watercolors*, Watson-Guptill, 1971; *The American Impressionists*, Watson-Guptill, 1972; *American Watercolor Painting*, Watson-Guptill, 1977. Contributor to *Encyclopaedia of World Art, Notable American Women*, and to art and antiques journals. Contributing editor, *American Art & Antiques*, 1978—.

BIOGRAPHICAL/CRITICAL SOURCES: Apollo, May, 1972; *Time*, December 4, 1972; *Book World*, December 19, 1972; *American Artist*, June, 1973.

* * *

HOOVER, Dwight W(esley) 1926-

PERSONAL: Born September 15, 1926, in Oskaloosa, Iowa; son of Homer S. (a farmer) and Ruth (Hull) Hoover; married Nannie Crosley (a social worker), August 14, 1954; children: Polly, Sara, Elizabeth. *Education:* William Penn College, B.A., 1948; Haverford College, M.A., 1949; University of Iowa, Ph.D., 1953. *Politics:* Republican. *Religion:* Society of Friends. *Home:* 301 Wheeling Ave., Muncie, Ind. 47303. *Office:* Department of History, Ball State University, Muncie, Ind. 47306.

CAREER: Bethune-Cookman College, Daytona Beach, Fla., professor of history, chairman of department, and head of Division of Social Science, 1953-55, 1958; Kansas State University, Manhattan, assistant professor of general studies, 1958-59; Ball State University, Muncie, Ind., assistant professor, 1959-63, associate professor, 1963-67, professor of history, 1967—. Professor of historical sociology, University of Virginia, 1977. Consultant on urban history and on a national organization of state-based committees, National Endowment for the Humanities. Member of advisory board, Indiana Civil Rights Commission, 1961; member, Muncie Human Rights Commission, 1966. *Military service:* U.S. Navy, 1955-58; stationed in Japan two years. U.S. Naval Reserve, 1958-69; became lieutenant commander. *Member:* American Historical Association, Organization of American Historians, American Association of University Professors, American Studies Association, Indiana Academy of Social Science, Christian Rural Overseas Program (CROP).

WRITINGS: (Editor) *Understanding Negro History,* Quadrangle, 1968; *Henry James Senior and the Religion of Community,* Eerdmans, 1969; (contributor) Martin Ballard, editor, *New Movements in the Study and Teaching of History,* Indiana University Press, 1970; *A Teacher's Guide to American Urban History,* Quadrangle, 1971; (editor with C. Warren Vander Hill) *Readings in Twentieth Century American Social History,* Wiley, 1972; (editor with John T. A. Koumoulides) *Conspectus of History: Focus on Biography,* Cambridge University Press, 1975; (editor with Koumoulides) *Conspectus of History: Focus on Issues in World Diplomacy,* Cambridge University Press, 1976; *The Red and the Black,* Rand McNally, 1976; *Cities,* Bowker, 1976. Contributor to history journals.

WORK IN PROGRESS: A history of Muncie, Indiana; a psychobiography of Franklin D. Roosevelt.

SIDELIGHTS: Dwight Hoover told *CA:* "I write in order to educate myself; my prospective audience is less important to me than is my own personal understanding. I find that writing, like many other things in life, is a matter of discipline. I try to write every day; I do not wait for inspiration because I might not have it. I do have barren days but find I need to ignore these and continue on. . . . I began my career with an article which led to a book, although not the one I intended to write. This book led to another and so on."

Hoover spent three months in Mexico and eight months in London on sabbaticals. He also lived in Japan for two years.

AVOCATIONAL INTERESTS: Travel, fishing, reading, gardening, and antique collecting.

* * *

HOOVER, J(ohn) Edgar 1895-1972

January 1, 1895—May 3, 1972; American director of the Federal Bureau of Investigation. Obituaries: *New York Times,* May 3, 1972; *Washington Post,* May 3, 1972; *Time,* May 15, 1972. (See index for *CA* sketch)

* * *

HOPKINS, George E(mil) 1937-

PERSONAL: Born March 6, 1937, in Shawnee, Okla.; son of Homer N. and Lillian (Hunt) Hopkins; married Elaine Bridges (a newspaper reporter), December 30, 1959; children: Jennifer Ellen, Paul Wilson. *Education:* Southern Methodist University, B.A., 1959; University of Texas at Austin, M.A., 1967, Ph.D., 1969. *Religion:* Methodist. *Home address:* R.F.D.1, Colchester, Ill. 62326. *Office:* Department of History, Western Illinois University, Macomb, Ill. 61455.

CAREER: Western Illinois University, Macomb, assistant professor, 1968-74, associate professor of history, 1974—.

Military service: U.S. Navy, Naval Aviator, 1959-64; became lieutenant junior grade. *Member:* American Historical Association, Organization of American Historians, Southern Historical Association, Phi Alpha Theta. *Awards, honors:* Phi Alpha Theta national prize paper award, 1965.

WRITINGS: The Airline Pilots: A Study in Elite Unionization, Harvard University Press, 1971. Contributor to *Historian, American Heritage, Washington Monthly, New Republic,* and *Air Line Pilot.*

WORK IN PROGRESS: Research on aviation history, labor history, and economic history.

AVOCATIONAL INTERESTS: Far eastern travel and history, flying.

* * *

HOPPER, Columbus B(urwell) 1931-

PERSONAL: Born December 22, 1931, in Forest City, N.C.; son of Walter M. and Ellen (Bland) Hopper; married Patricia Benoy, November 6, 1954; children: Christopher Brian, Arthur Walter. *Education:* Gardner-Webb Junior College (now Gardner-Webb College), A.A., 1952; Furman University, B.A., 1954; University of North Carolina at Chapel Hill, M.A., 1957; Florida State University, Ph.D., 1964. *Politics:* Democrat. *Religion:* Baptist. *Home:* 1303 South 11th St., Oxford, Miss. 38655. *Office:* Department of Sociology, University of Mississippi, University, Miss. 38677.

CAREER: University of Mississippi, University, assistant professor of sociology, 1957-64; Southeast Missouri State College (now University), Cape Girardeau, associate professor of sociology, 1964-65; University of Mississippi, associate professor, 1965-68, professor of sociology, 1968—. *Military service:* U.S. Army, 1954-56. *Member:* American Sociological Association, American Correction Association, Southern Sociological Association, Southern Correctional Association, Alpha Kappa Delta. *Awards, honors:* Research grant from U.S. Department of Health, Education, and Welfare, 1967-68.

WRITINGS: Sex in Prison, Louisiana State University Press, 1969. Contributor to law and sociology journals.

WORK IN PROGRESS: Continuing research on conjugal visitation in prisons, medical sociology, criminology, and penology.

* * *

HOROVITZ, Israel 1939-

PERSONAL: Born March 31, 1939, in Wakefield, Mass.; son of Julius Charles (a lawyer) and Hazel (Solberg) Horovitz; married second wife, Doris Keefe (an artist), December 25, 1959 (divorced December, 1972); children: (second marriage) Rachael Keefe, Matthew Keefe, Adam Keefe. *Education:* Royal Academy of Dramatic Art, London, M.A., 1963; New School for Social Research, student, 1963-66; City University of New York, M.A., 1977, Ph.D., candidate. *Religion:* Jewish. *Agent:* Gloria Safier, 667 Madison Ave., New York, N.Y. 10021; Margaret Ramsay Ltd., 14a Goodwin's Ct., London WC2N 4LL, England; and Les Editions de Minuit, 9 rue Bernard-Palissy, Paris, France. *Office:* The Actors Studio, 432 West 44th St., New York, N.Y. 10036.

CAREER: Playwright and director. Stagehand, Paper Mill Playhouse, Millburn, N.J., 1963-65; playwright-in-residence, Royal Shakespeare Co., London, England, 1965; instructor in playwriting, Circle in the Square Theatre School, New York City, 1968-70; playwright-in-residence, City College of the City University of New York, New York City, 1969-74; part-time professor of playwriting, New York University, New York City, 1970-76; director of the playwrights unit of The Actors Studio, 1977—. Fannie Hurst Visiting Professor of Theatre Arts, Brandeis University, Waltham, Mass., 1974-75. Founding member, Eugene O'Neill Memorial Theatre Foundation.

MEMBER: International P.E.N., Authors League of America, Societe de Compositeurs Dramatique (Paris), Dramatists Guild, New Dramatists, Inc., Actors Studio (member of playwrights unit), Players. *Awards, honors:* Rockefeller fellowships in playwriting, 1968, 1969; Vernon Rice Award, 1968, for *The Indian Wants the Bronx;* Drama Desk Best Play award, 1968, for *The Indian Wants the Bronx* and *It's Called the Sugar Plum;* Obie awards for Best American play, for *The Indian Wants the Bronx,* 1968, and *The Honest-to-God Schnozzola,* 1969; *Jersey Journal* Best Play award, 1968, for *The Indian Wants the Bronx; Plays and Players* Best Foreign Play award, 1969, for *It's Called the Sugar Plum; Show Business* award for best Off-Broadway play, 1969, for *Line* and *Rats; Village Voice* Off-Broadway award, 1969, for *The Honest-to-God Schnozzola;* Cannes Film Festival Prix de Jury, 1971, for "The Strawberry Statement"; American Academy of Arts and Letters Award in Literature, 1972; New York State Council on the Arts grant, 1972, 1974; co-recipient of Academy of Television Arts and Sciences (Emmy) award, for *VD-Blues;* Christopher Award, for *VD-Blues;* French Critics Prize, 1973, for *Line;* National Endowment of the Arts Award, 1974-75; Fulbright Foundation grant, 1975; Guggenheim fellowship, 1977-78, and other awards.

WRITINGS: Cappella (novel), Harper, 1973; *Spider Poems and Other Writings* (verse), Harper, 1973.

Published plays: *It's Called the Sugar Plum* (one-act; first produced with "The Indian Wants the Bronx," Off-Broadway at Astor Place Theatre, January 17, 1968), Dramatists Play Service, 1968; *The Indian Wants the Bronx* (one-act; first produced with "It's Called the Sugar Plum," Off-Broadway at Astor Place Theatre, January 17, 1968; produced with "Rats" in London at Open Space Theatre, August 26, 1969), Dramatists Play Service, 1968; *Line* (first produced as one-act Off-Off-Broadway at Cafe LaMama, November, 1967; produced as two-act in Los Angeles at Mark Taper Forum, October, 1969; produced as one-act with "Acrobats" Off-Broadway at Theatre De Lys, February 15, 1971), Dramatists Play Service, 1968; *Rats* (one-act; first produced with ten other one-acts Off-Broadway at Cafe Au Go Go, May 8, 1968; produced with "The Indian Wants the Bronx" in London at Open Space Theatre, August 26, 1969), Dramatists Play Service, 1968; *Morning* (one-act; first produced in Spoleto, Italy at Festival of Two Worlds, directed by Horovitz as "Chiaroscuro," July, 1968; produced with "Noon" by Terrence McNally and "Night" by Leonard Melfi on Broadway at Henry Miller's Theatre, November 29, 1968), Random House, 1968.

The Honest-to-God Schnozzola (one-act; first produced in Provincetown, Mass. at Act IV Theatre, August 8, 1968; produced with "Leader," Off-Broadway at Gramercy Arts Theatre, April 21, 1969), Breakthrough Press, 1971; *Acrobats* (one-act; first produced in Amsterdam at Mickery Theatre, May 20, 1968; produced with "Line" Off-Broadway at Theatre De Lys, February 15, 1971), Dramatists Play Service, 1971; *Clair-Obscur* (first produced in Paris at Theatre Lucernaire, April 10, 1970), Gallimard,

1972; *Dr. Hero* (originally titled "The World's Greatest Play"; first produced, under title "Hero," in New York, 1971; produced under title "Dr. Hero," Off-Broadway at New York Public Theatre, May 25, 1971), Dramatists Play Service, 1973; *Play for Trees* (television play; networked by NET, November, 1969) [and] *Leader* (one-act, first produced with "The Honest-to-God Schnozzola," Off-Broadway at Gramercy Arts Theatre, April 21, 1969), Dramatists Play Service, 1973; *Shooting Gallery* (produced at the WPA New Plays Festival) [and] *Play for Germs* (based on television play, "VD-Blues"; see below), Dramatists Play Service, 1973; *The Primary English Class* (first produced Off-Off Broadway at The Cubicula, 1975; produced Off-Broadway at the Circle-in-the-Square Theatre, 1975), Dramatists Play Service, 1976.

Unpublished plays: "The Comeback," first produced in Boston at Emerson College, November 1, 1960; "The Hanging of Emanuel," first produced in South Orange, N.J. at Il Cafe Cabaret Theatre, December 20, 1962; "This Play Is about Me," first produced in South Orange, N.J. at Il Cafe Cabaret Theatre, January 15, 1963; "The Killer Dove" (two-act), first produced in West Orange, N.J. at Theatre-on-the-Green, May 10, 1966; "Le Premiere," first produced in Paris, directed by Horovitz, at Theatre de Poche, September, 1972; "The Reason We Eat," first produced in Stamford, Conn., at Hartman Theatre, November, 1976, produced in Boston, Mass. at Boston Repertory Co., November, 1977; "The Former One-on-One Basketball Champion," first produced in New York at the Actors Studio, December, 1977; "Man with Bags" (an adaptation of Ionesco's *l'Homme Aux Valises*), first produced in Towson, Md. at Towson State University Theatre, 1977; "Cappella" (an adaptation of Horovitz's novel of the same title; see above), first produced Off-Broadway at the Off-Center Theatre, January, 1978. Also author of "The Death of Bernard the Believer," "The Simon Street Harvest," "Mackerel," and "The Lounge Player," as yet unproduced.

"Wakefield Series" (seven plays): *Alfred the Great* (three-act; first produced in Paris at American Center Theatre, directed by Horovitz, January 28, 1972; produced in Great Neck, N.Y., 1972; produced with "Our Father's Failing" and "Alfred Dies," under program title "The Wakefield Plays," in New York at Actor's Studio, January, 1978), Harper, 1974; *Stage Directions* [and] *Spared* ("Stage Directions" first produced in New York at Actors Studio, produced with "Spared," "Hopscotch," and "The 75th," under program title "The Quannapowitt Quartet," at New York Shakespeare Festival, February, 1978; "Spared" first produced with "Hopscotch" in Paris at Theatre du Centre Cultural Americain, directed by Horovitz, 1974, produced in New York at Actors Studio, produced with "Stage Directions," "Hopscotch," and "The 75th," under program title "The Quannapowitt Quartet," at New York Shakespeare Festival, February, 1978), Dramatists Play Service, 1976; "Hopscotch," first produced with "Spared" in Paris at Theatre du Centre Cultural Americain, 1974, produced with "The 75th," "Stage Directions," and "Spared," under program title "The Quannapowitt Quartet," February, 1978; *The 75th* (first produced with "Hopscotch," "Stage Directions," and "Spared," under program title "The Quannapowitt Quartet," February, 1978), Dramatist Play Service, 1976; "Our Father's Failing," first produced with "Alfred the Great," and "Alfred Dies," under program title "The Wakefield Plays," January, 1978; "Alfred Dies," first produced with "Alfred the Great," and "Our Father's Failing," under program title "The Wakefield Plays," January, 1978.

Screenplays: "The Strawberry Statement" (based on the book by James Simon Kunen), Metro-Goldwyn-Mayer, 1970; "Line" (adapted from his play of same title; see above), Kaleidoscope Films, 1970 (film as yet not released); "Believe in Me" (originally titled "Speed Is of the Essence"), Metro-Goldwyn-Mayer, 1971; "Acrobats" (adapted from his play of same title; see above), Walker Stuart Productions, 1972.

Television plays: (With Jules Feiffer) *VD-Blues* (networked by NET, 1972, directed and produced by Horovitz), Avon, 1974; "Start To Finish," produced by Columbia Broadcasting Corp., 1977-78; "The Making and Breaking of Splinters Braun," produced by CBS-TV, 1977-78; "The Primary English Class" (based on Horovitz's play of same title; see above), produced in 1976; "Bartleby, the Scrivener" (adapted from the Melville novel of same title), produced for Public Television, Baltimore, Md., January 1978. Author of several television plays for British Broadcasting Corp. Also author of television plays, "Funny Books," "D.C.A.C.," and "The Indian Wants the Bronx" (based on his play of the same title; see above), as yet unproduced.

Collections: *First Season* (contains "The Indian Wants the Bronx," "Line," "It's Called the Sugar Plum," and "Rats"), Random House, 1968; (with Terrence McNally and Leonard Melfi) *Morning, Noon,* [and] *Night* (the first by Horovitz, the second by McNally, the third by Melfi; see above), Random House, 1969.

Plays anthologized in *Collision Course,* edited by Edward Parone, Random House, 1968, *The Waterford Plays,* edited by John Lahr, Grove, 1968, *The Best Short Plays,* edited by Stanley Richards, Chilton, 1968, 1969, 1975, 1977, and 1978, *The Best Short Plays of 1970,* edited by Richards, Chilton, 1970, and *Famous American Plays of the 1960's,* edited by Harold Clurman, Dell, 1972. Contributor of poetry to various publications including *Village Voice, Poetry, Painted Bride Quarterly, Paris Review,* and others. Also contributor to Dramatist Guild *Quarterly,* 1976.

WORK IN PROGRESS: A filmscript, "Town and Country."

SIDELIGHTS: Despite his experimental approach to theatre, Israel Horovitz has received praise from various critics who describe him as one of the playwrights who may yet infuse new life into American theatre. Clive Barnes characterizes him as "a superb comic writer" who "has fantasies where other people keep their thoughts and translates those fantasies into a mockingly careful realism that is ironically thought-provoking." Edith Oliver believes that Horovitz "can delineate a character with a flick of a line or a piece of business, he can write dialogue that is dramatic and rings true, and he can explore an atmosphere or state of mind."

Horovitz sees his work as an expression of his own personal being. "Writers must never discuss the process of writing," he told *CA.* "It is precisely as ridiculous as a snail discussing his shell." Most of Horovitz's plays have been translated in over twenty languages and performed worldwide.

BIOGRAPHICAL/CRITICAL SOURCES: Nation, February 12, 1968; *New Statesman,* September 6, 1968; *New York Times,* November 29, 1968, January 28, 1972; *Village Voice,* December 5, 1968, April 24, 1969, October 28, 1971; *Show Business,* December 14, 1968; *New Yorker,* May 3, 1969; Stuart Little and Arthur Cantor, *The Playmakers,* Norton, 1970; Martin Gottfried, *Opening Nights,* Putnam,

1970; Walter Kerr, *Thirty Days Hath November: Pain and Pleasure in the Contemporary Theatre,* Simon & Schuster, 1970; *Christian Science Monitor,* July 22, 1970; *Variety,* August 5, 1970.

*   *   *

HOROWITZ, Mardi J(on)   1934-

PERSONAL: Born May 16, 1934, in Los Angeles, Calif.; married Nancy Florence Holzworth, 1959; children: Ariana, Jordan, Joshua. *Education:* University of California, B.A., 1955, M.D., 1958. *Office:* Medical School, University of California, San Francisco, Calif. 94143.

CAREER: Resident in psychiatry at University of California School of Medicine and Langley Porter Neuropsychiatric Institute, 1959-62; University of California, San Francisco, Medical School, clinical instructor, 1962-65, assistant clinical professor, 1965-71, associate clinical professor, 1971-72, associate professor, 1972-74, professor of psychiatry, 1974—; Mount Zion Hospital and Medical Center, San Francisco, Calif., research scientist, 1964-72. *Military service:* U.S. Naval Reserve, 1962-64; became lieutenant commander. *Member:* American Psychiatric Association (fellow), American Medical Association.

WRITINGS: (With Thomas Lowry and others) *Hyperventilation and Hysteria,* C. C Thomas, 1968; (with others) *Psychosocial Function in Epilepsy,* C. C Thomas, 1970; *Image Formation and Cognition,* Appleton, 1970; *Stress Response Syndromes,* Aronson, Jason, 1976; *Hysterical Personality,* Aronson, Jason, 1977.

*   *   *

HOTCHKISS, Ralf D.   1947-

PERSONAL: Born December 6, 1947, in Rockford, Ill.; son of Hilton Delos (in fruit processing) and Katherine Ruth (a musician; maiden name Huffer) Hotchkiss. *Education:* Oberlin College, B.A., 1970. *Religion:* Unitarian Universalist. *Home:* (Permanent) 4209 Cushman Rd., Rockford, Ill. 61111.

CAREER: Woodward Governor Co., Rockford, Ill., 1962-71, began as summer lawn boy, later carpenter's assistant, machinist, and laboratory technician, electronic engineer and worker on fluidics and medical safety devices, 1967-71; Center for Concerned Engineering (nonprofit group working with Ralph Nader), Washington, D.C., director, beginning 1971. Independent researcher in design of electronic guidance and obstacle detection systems for the blind; professional drummer with rock bands, 1964—. Member of planning committee for design of new Rehabilitation Institute of Chicago, 1969. *Awards, honors:* American Society of Metals Science Award, 1964; winner of science talent search of Illinois State Academy of Science, and the Honeywell selection of science projects for national broadcast, 1965; included in honors group of Westinghouse science talent search.

WRITINGS: (With Ralph Nader and Lowell Dodge) *What to Do with Your Bad Car: An Action Manual for Lemon Owners,* Grossman, 1971; (editor with Dodge, Steven Oesch, Carl Nash, and Bernard O'Meara) *Small on Safety: The Designed-In Dangers of the Volkswagen,* Center for Auto Safety, 1971.

SIDELIGHTS: As a hobby Ralf Hotchkiss has designed and built gadgets ranging from a four-seat bicycle to resonant column bass bongoes to a wheelchair (the "Tank") which climbs stairs and mountains.

BIOGRAPHICAL/CRITICAL SOURCES: Medical World News, April 2, 1965; *Atlantic,* June, 1970.†

HOUGH, John T., Jr. 1946-

PERSONAL: Surname rhymes with "puff"; born January 31, 1946, in York, Pa.; son of John T. and Mary (Kurtz) Hough. *Education:* Haverford College, B.A., 1968. *Politics:* "Farthest left edge of the Democratic Party." *Religion:* Episcopalian. *Home:* 15 Inman St., Apt. 1, West Tisbury, Mass. 02139.

CAREER: Falmouth Enterprise, Falmouth, Mass., reporter, summers, 1966, 1967; Volunteers in Service to America (VISTA), tutor and counselor in ghetto junior high school in Detroit, Mich., 1968-69; member of staff of Senator Charles McC. Mathias, Jr. of Maryland, 1969-70; Massachusetts Correctional Association, Boston, writer and social worker (as conscientious objector, in lieu of military service), 1970-72; speech writer for Senator Charles McC. Mathias, Jr., 1976-77; *New York Times,* New York, N.Y., assistant to James Reston, Washington Bureau, 1977—.

WRITINGS: A Peck of Salt: A Year in the Ghetto, Atlantic, 1970; *A Two Car Funeral* (novel), Little, Brown, 1973; *The Guardian* (novel), Little, Brown, 1975.

BIOGRAPHICAL/CRITICAL SOURCES: Best Sellers, October 15, 1970.

* * *

HOUSEPIAN, Marjorie 1923-

PERSONAL: Born November 21, 1923, in New York, N.Y.; daughter of Moses M. (a physician) and Makrouhie (Ashjian) Housepian; married Donald S. Johnson, 1943 (divorced, 1956); married Machbi Dobkin, March 23, 1957; children: (first marriage) Stephen Andrew; (second marriage) Daniel, Jonathan. *Education:* Attended Smith College, 1940-42; Barnard College, A.B., 1944; Columbia University, M.A., 1971. *Office:* Department of English, Barnard College, 606 West 120th St., New York, N.Y. 10027.

CAREER: Dun & Bradstreet, New York City, market researcher, 1945-46; Barnard College, New York City, secretary to president, 1954-57, lecturer, 1957-67, associate in English, 1967—, associate dean of studies, 1971—. *Member:* International P.E.N., Authors League of America, American Association of University Professors.

WRITINGS: A Houseful of Love, Random House, 1957; *The Smyrna Affair,* Harcourt, 1971. Contributor to *Collier Encyclopedia;* contributor to literary and popular journals, including *Atlantic, Paris Review, Commentary, Saturday Review, Vogue,* and *Ararat Quarterly.*

WORK IN PROGRESS: Editing the personal letters of M. Carey Thomas of Bryn Mawr.

SIDELIGHTS: Marjorie Housepian told *CA:* "I write when I have something to say that no one else is saying better (as far as I can tell). Judging by the contemporary literary scene, this is not a widely held practice. More dismaying is the evidence that publishers are increasingly 'merchandising' books, as though they were processing cheese, and the fact that young people who aspire to be writers—and I see this in my writing courses at Barnard—are all too seldom readers." Housepian has traveled to Turkey, Yugoslavia, and Greece, and twice to Soviet Armenia. *A Houseful of Love* has been published in Japan, Norway, Germany, and Italy.

* * *

HOWARD, Alvin Wendell 1922-1975

PERSONAL: Born April 12, 1922, in Everett, Wash.; son of

Arthur Henry and Ruth V. (Beckman) Howard; married Ruth A. Ritchie (a high school teacher of French), September 9, 1944; children: Arthur R., Arley Anne, John Robert, Alix Susanne. *Education:* University of Washington, Seattle, B.A., 1943; Western Washington State College (now Western Washington University), B.Ed., 1949, M.Ed., 1953; University of Oregon, Ed.D., 1966. *Politics:* Republican. *Religion:* Presbyterian. *Office:* College of Education, University of New Mexico, Albuquerque, N.M. 87106.

CAREER: Elementary teacher in Cashmere, Wash., 1949-50; junior high school teacher, counselor, and then principal in Bellingham, Wash., 1950-64; University of Oregon, Eugene, instructor and supervisor of intern teachers, 1965-66; University of New Mexico, Albuquerque, assistant professor, 1966-69, associate professor of secondary education, 1969-75, assistant to dean of College of Education, 1968-70. Visiting summer professor, Eastern Oregon College, 1966. *Member:* National Association of Secondary School Principals, Association for Supervision and Curriculum Development, National Education Association (life member), New Mexico Education Association, New Mexico Association of Secondary School Principals (member of executive committee, 1969-70), Phi Delta Kappa, Alpha Kappa Psi, North Central Association (assistant state director, beginning 1969).

WRITINGS: Teaching in Middle Schools, International Textbook, 1968; (editor with G. C. Stoumbis, and contributor) *Schools for the Middle Years: A Book of Readings,* International Textbook, 1969; (with Stoumbis) *Junior High and Middle Schools: Issues and Practices,* International Textbook, 1970; (contributor) Jean S. Kujoth, editor, *The Teacher and School Discipline,* Scarecrow, 1970; (contributor) Charles Bucher, editor, *A Book of Readings in Physical Education,* Mosby, 1971; (contributor) John H. Hansen and A. C. Hearn, editors, *The Middle School Program,* Rand McNally, 1971. Contributor of about forty articles to education journals.

WORK IN PROGRESS: A book on teacher preparation.†

(Died January, 1975)

* * *

HOWARD, J. Woodford, Jr. 1931-

PERSONAL: Born July 5, 1931, in Ashland, Ky.; son of J. Woodford (a lawyer) and Florence (Stephens) Howard; married Valerie Hope Barclay, April 10, 1960; children: Elaine Hope. *Education:* Duke University, A.B. (summa cum laude), 1952; Princeton University, M.P.A., 1954, M.A., 1955, Ph.D., 1959. *Office:* Department of Political Science, Johns Hopkins University, Baltimore, Md. 21218.

CAREER: Lafayette College, Easton, Pa., instructor, 1958-59, assistant professor of government and law, 1959-61; Harvard University, Cambridge, Mass., fellow in law and political science, 1961-62; Duke University, Durham, N.C., assistant professor, 1962-66, associate professor of political science, 1966-67; Johns Hopkins University, Baltimore, Md., associate professor, 1967-69, professor of political science, 1969-75, Thomas P. Stran Professor, 1975—, chairman of department, 1973-75. *Military service:* U.S. Air Force, 1955-57; became first lieutenant. *Member:* American Political Science Association, Law and Society Association (trustee), American Judicature Society, Southern Political Science Association, Omicron Delta Kappa, Phi Beta Kappa.

WRITINGS: (Contributor) Gottfried Dietze, editor, *Es-*

says on the American Constitution, Prentice-Hall, 1964; *Mr. Justice Murphy: A Political Biography,* Princeton University Press, 1968; (contributor) Howard Ball and Thomas P. Lauth, Jr., editors, *Changing Perspectives in Contemporary Political Analysis,* Prentice-Hall, 1971; (contributor) Joel B. Grossman and Richard S. Wells, editors, *Constitutional Law and Judicial Policymaking,* Wiley, 1972; (contributor) F. Murphy and C. Herman Pritchett, editors, *Courts, Judges, and Politics,* 2nd edition (Howard was not associated with earlier edition), Random House, 1974. Contributor of articles and reviews to political science, history, and law journals. Member of editorial board, *American Political Science Review* and *Law and Society Review.*

WORK IN PROGRESS: A monograph on the U.S. Courts of Appeals for the District of Columbia and the second and fifth circuits.

BIOGRAPHICAL/CRITICAL SOURCES: Virginia Quarterly Review, spring, 1969.

* * *

HOWE, Nelson 1935-

PERSONAL: Born November 5, 1935, in Lansing, Mich.; son of Nelson Scott, Jr. (a veterinarian) and Margaret (Moon) Howe; married Linda Lutes (an artist), November 13, 1961. *Education:* University of Michigan, B.A., 1957, M.A., 1961. *Home:* 307 West Broadway, New York, N.Y. 10013.

CAREER: Self-employed artist, 1961-68; New Jersey Institute of Technology, Newark, N.J., instructor in art, 1968-77. Part-time instructor, Parsons School of Design, New York, N.Y., 1968. Co-founder and vice-president, Jacob Cram Cooperative, Inc. *Member:* John Barton Walgomot Society. *Awards, honors:* American Institute of Graphic Arts listed *To the Sincere Reader* as one of the fifty best designed books of the year, 1969.

WRITINGS: (With Steve Hesterman, programmer) *Job Art* (computer generated book), Wittenborn, 1971; (author and designer) *Daily Translating System,* Circle Press Publications, 1971. Contributor to education journals and other periodicals.

Designer: Keith Waldrop, *To the Sincere Reader* (poetry), Wittenborn, 1969, 2nd edition, 1971; (and writer of instructions) Rosmarie Waldrop, *Body Image* (poetry), Wittenborn, 1970; *No Surprises,* Wittenborn, 1971.

WORK IN PROGRESS: Further work on notation systems and scores (which use both visual design and writing) as an art form.

BIOGRAPHICAL/CRITICAL SOURCES: Print Magazine, January/February, 1971.

* * *

HOWELL, John M(ichael) 1933-

PERSONAL: Born March 2, 1933, in Oshawa, Ontario, Canada; came to United States in 1950, naturalized in 1957; son of Percy Thomas (a physician) and Madge (Reekie) Howell; married Suzanne Firmin (a teacher), August 10, 1963; children: Evan Thomas. *Education:* Millsaps College, B.A., 1954; University of Southern California, M.A., 1960; Tulane University, Ph.D., 1963. *Office:* Department of English, Southern Illinois University, Carbondale, Ill. 62901.

CAREER: Southern Illinois University at Carbondale, assistant professor, 1963-68, associate professor of American literature, 1968—. *Member:* American Association of Uni-

versity Professors, National Council of Teachers of English, Modern Language Association of America.

WRITINGS: Hemingway's African Stories: The Stories, Their Sources, Their Critics, Scribner, 1969. Contributor of numerous articles on modern American authors to periodicals.

WORK IN PROGRESS: A study of John Gardner.

* * *

HOWELL, Wilbur Samuel 1904-

PERSONAL: Born April 22, 1904, in Wayne, N.Y.; son of Wood Augustus (a high school teacher) and Edna (Hanmer) Howell; married Charlotte Coombe, June 26, 1928 (died April 5, 1956); married Cecilia Jonkman Van Eerden, June 27, 1962; children: (first marriage) Samuel Coombe. *Education:* Cornell University, A.B., 1924, A.M., 1928, Ph.D., 1931; also studied at Sorbonne, University of Paris, 1928-29. *Politics:* Democrat. *Religion:* Episcopalian. *Home:* 20 Armour Rd., Princeton, N.J. 08540. *Office:* Department of English, Princeton University, Princeton, N.J. 08540.

CAREER: Iowa State College of Agriculture and Mechanic Arts (now Iowa State University of Science and Technology), Ames, instructor in public speaking, 1924-25; Washington University, St. Louis, Mo., instructor in public speaking, 1925-27; Cornell University, Ithaca, N.Y., instructor in public speaking, 1927-28, 1929-30; Harvard University, Cambridge, Mass., instructor in public speaking, 1930-33; Dartmouth College, Hanover, N.H., assistant professor of public speaking, 1933-34; Princeton University, Princeton, N.J., assistant professor, 1934-40, associate professor, 1940-55, professor of rhetoric and oratory, 1955-72, professor emeritus, 1972—. *Member:* Modern Language Association of America, Renaissance Society of America, Speech Communication Association, American Association of University Professors, Phi Beta Kappa. *Awards, honors:* Guggenheim fellowships, 1948-49, 1957-58; Huntington Library fellowships, 1951-52, 1962-63; Council of Humanities, Princeton, senior fellow, 1966; Golden Anniversary Book Fund Prize from Speech Communication Association, 1972, and 1976.

*WRITINGS—*Published by Princeton University Press, except as indicated: *The Rhetoric of Alcuin and Charlemagne,* 1941; *Problems and Styles of Communication,* F. S. Crofts & Co., 1945; *Fenelon's Dialogues on Eloquence,* 1951; *Logic and Rhetoric in England: 1500-1700,* 1956; *Eighteenth-Century British Logic and Rhetoric,* 1971; *Poetics, Rhetoric, and Logic: Studies in the Basic Disciplines of Criticism,* Cornell University Press, 1975. Contributor of articles to professional journals; contributor to *Encyclopaedia Britannica.* Editor-in-chief, *Quarterly Journal of Speech,* 1954-56.

WORK IN PROGRESS: Preparing critical editions of Thomas Jefferson's "Parliamentary Manual" and "Parliamentary Pocket-Book," for inclusion in *The Papers of Thomas Jefferson,* edited by Julian P. Boyd.

* * *

HOWICK, William Henry 1924-

PERSONAL: Born October 6, 1924, in Paris, Ontario, Canada; son of Harry A. (a clergyman) and Eva (Plumley) Howick; married Nettie Frances Tucker (a teacher), September 1, 1954. *Education:* Canadian College, Th.B., 1949; Trevecca Nazarene College, A.B., 1950; George Peabody College for Teachers, M.A., 1952, M.Ed., 1953, Ph.D.,

1963; also studied at University of Tennessee, 1956-65. *Religion:* Methodist. *Address:* P.O. Box 11003, Memphis, Tenn. 38111. *Office:* Department of Education, Memphis State University, Memphis, Tenn. 38111.

CAREER: Edmonton Journal, Edmonton, Alberta, newspaper distributor and reporter, 1947-49; high school teacher and band director in Red Deer, Alberta, 1947-49; Trevecca Nazarene College, Nashville, Tenn., teacher in Demonstration School, 1949-54, associate professor of education and philosophy and supervisor of student teachers, 1954-57; teacher in public schools in Los Angeles, Calif., 1957-58; Trevecca Nazarene College, associate professor of education and philosophy and head of department, 1958-63; George Peabody College for Teachers, Nashville, supervisory teacher in Demonstration School, 1963-65; Southeast Missouri State College (now University), Cape Girardeau, associate professor of education, 1965-67; Memphis State University, Memphis, Tenn., associate professor, 1967-72, professor of education and educational foundations, 1972—. *Member:* American Educational Studies Association (charter member and historian; member of national council, 1969—), Philosophy of Education Society, Phi Delta Kappa.

WRITINGS: Philosophies of Western Education, Interstate, 1971. Contributor to education journals.

WORK IN PROGRESS: A history of Western education.

AVOCATIONAL INTERESTS: Travel, fishing, outdoor sports.

*   *   *

HOYER, H(arvey) Conrad   1907-

PERSONAL: Born July 21, 1907, in Clay County, S.D.; son of Gust (a farmer) and Johanna (Norder) Hoyer; married E. Margaret Larson (an assistant librarian), September 3, 1930; children: Gustav Adolph, Helen JoAnn (Mrs. William Kahl), Marcus Conrad, Ruth, Bernard Eric. *Education:* Attended University of South Dakota, 1925-27; Augustana College, Sioux Falls, S.D., A.B., 1931; Augustana Seminary, Rock Island, Ill., B.D., 1936. *Politics:* Independent. *Address:* Box 180, Phillips, Wis. 54555.

CAREER: Grade school teacher in South Dakota, 1926-29, and principal, 1931-32; ordained Lutheran minister, 1936; pastor of Lutheran churches in Madison, Wis., 1936-40, and Chicago, Ill., 1940-43; National Lutheran Council, Chicago, director of American missions, 1943-60; National Council of Churches of Christ in the U.S.A., New York, N.Y., associate executive secretary, Division of Home Missions, 1960-64, associate executive secretary, department for councils of churches, 1965-70; associate executive director, Commission for Regional and Local Ecumenicism, 1970-72; Luther College, Teaneck, N.J., president, 1974-75. President, Illinois Conference Luther League, 1938-42; vice-president, Augustana Synod Luther League, 1947-49. *Member:* Association of Council Secretaries (vice-president, 1964-65), National Association of Ecumenical Staff. *Awards, honors:* D.D., Augustana College, Sioux Falls, 1950.

WRITINGS: (Editor) *Christ for the Moving Millions,* National Lutheran Council, 1950; *Ecumenopolis U.S.A.: The Church Mission in Community,* Augsburg, 1971. Also author, co-author, and editor of religious pamphlets. Editor, *American Missions Together,* 1947-60, and *ACS Journal* (quarterly publication of Association of Council Secretaries), 1965-72.

WORK IN PROGRESS: Church and Community in the Late 20th Century.

AVOCATIONAL INTERESTS: Fishing, music.

HOYT, Charles Alva   1931-

PERSONAL: Born September 26, 1931, in Middletown, Conn.; son of Carlyle Goodrich (a teacher and administrator) and Agnes (Paige) Hoyt; married Anna McLellan, June 17, 1960 (divorced); married Mariana Schackne, August 17, 1974; children: (first marriage) Carlyle Goodrich, Thomas Hale, George Paige; (second marriage) Samuel Webster. *Education:* Wesleyan University, Middletown, Conn., A.B. (with distinction), 1953, M.A.T., 1955; Columbia University, M.A. (with high honors), 1956, Ph.D., 1961. *Politics:* Independent. *Religion:* Radical Protestant. *Home:* Ramble Hill, Millbrook, N.Y. 12545. *Agent:* Gunther Stuhlmann, 65 Irving Pl., New York, N.Y. 10003. *Office:* Department of English, Marist College, Poughkeepsie, N.Y. 12601.

CAREER: Wayne State University, Detroit, Mich., instructor in English, 1957-60; Bennett College, Millbrook, N.Y., assistant professor, 1960-64, associate professor, 1964-68, professor of English and chairman of department, 1968-77; Marist College, Poughkeepsie, N.Y., associate professor of English, 1977—. Has played piano professionally, mainly with jazz groups. Consultant, National Endowment for the Humanities. *Member:* American Federation of Musicians.

WRITINGS: (Editor) *Minor British Novelists,* Southern Illinois University Press, 1967; (editor) *Minor American Novelists,* Southern Illinois University Press, 1971. Contributor to *Encyclopedia Americana, Saturday Review, Gourmet, New York Times, Louisville Courier-Journal, Cavalier, Commonweal,* and other publications.

WORK IN PROGRESS: A book on witchcraft; fiction and poetry.

SIDELIGHTS: Charles Hoyt released an album, "Last Chance Jazz Band," in 1977. *Avocational interests:* Witchcraft (Hoyt is a specialist in that field).

*   *   *

HSIA, David Yi-Yung   1925-1972

August 22, 1925—January 27, 1972; Chinese-born American educator, pediatrician, and author of books on genetics. Obituaries: *New York Times,* January 28, 1972.

*   *   *

HUBBARD, David Allan   1928-

PERSONAL: Born April 8, 1928, in Stockton, Calif.; son of John King (a minister) and Helena (White) Hubbard; married Ruth Doyal, August 12, 1949; children: Mary Ruth. *Education:* Westmont College, B.A., 1949; Fuller Theological Seminary, B.D., 1952, Th.M., 1954; University of St. Andrews, Ph.D., 1957. *Home:* 330 West California Blvd., Pasadena, Calif. 91105. *Office:* Fuller Theological Seminary, 135 North Oakland Ave., Pasadena, Calif. 91101.

CAREER: Clergyman of Conservative Baptist Association, ordained in 1952; Westmont College, Santa Barbara, Calif., assistant professor of Bible and Greek, 1957, chairman of department of Biblical studies, 1958-63; Fuller Theological Seminary, Pasadena, Calif., president, and professor of Old Testament, 1963—. Interim pastor in Montecito, Calif., 1960-62; Fuller Evangelistic Association, Pasadena, executive vice-president and speaker on "The Joyful Sound" (international radio broadcast), 1969—. Chairman, Pasadena Urban Coalition, 1967-71. Member, California State Board of Education, 1972-75; member of board of directors, National Institute of Campus Ministries, 1974—. *Member:*

American Academy of Religion, Association of Theological Schools (member of executive committee, 1972-76; president, 1976—), Society of Biblical Literature, Rotary Club.

WRITINGS: With Bands of Love, Eerdmans, 1968; Is Life Really Worth Living?, Regal Books, 1969; What's God Been Doing All This Time?, Regal Books, 1970; What's New?, Word, Inc., 1970; Does the Bible Really Work?, Word, Inc., 1971; Psalms for All Seasons, Eerdmans, 1971; Is the Family Here to Stay?, Word, Inc., 1971; The Problem with Prayer Is . . ., Tyndale, 1972; How to Face Your Fears, A. J. Holman, 1972; The Holy Spirit in Today's World, Word, Inc., 1973; Church: Who Needs It?, Regal Books, 1974; They Met Jesus, A. J. Holman, 1974; An Honest Search for a Righteous Life, Tyndale, 1975; More Psalms for All Seasons, Eerdmans, 1975; Beyond Futility, Eerdmans, 1976; Colossians Speaks to the Sickness of Our Times, Word, Inc., 1976; Happiness: You Can Find the Secret, Tyndale, 1976; Will We Ever Catch Up with the Bible?, Regal Books, 1977; Galatians: Gospel of Freedom, Word, Inc., 1977; Strange Heroes, A. J. Holman, 1977. Contributor to theological dictionaries, KJV Holman Family Bible, and to religious journals.

*   *   *

HUBBARD, David G(raham) 1920-

PERSONAL: Born October 5, 1920, in Dexter, N.M.; son of Ethelbert Jackson (a physician) and Rose (Graham) Hubbard; married Bettie Daniel Broach, December 23, 1966; children: Sharon O'Bryant, Joseph David, Patrick Graham, Marianna Magee. Education: University of Texas, M.D., 1944; Chicago Institute for Psychoanalysis, additional study, 1948-51. Politics: "Middle of the road." Religion: Episcopalian. Home: 5122 Deloach Ave., Dallas, Tex. 75220. Office: 8333 Douglas, Suite 1238, Dallas, Tex. 75225.

CAREER: University of Chicago Hospital, Chicago, Ill., resident, 1947-49; Veteran's Administration Hospital, Chicago, resident, 1949-50; Aberrant Behavior Center, Dallas, Tex., director, 1969—. Private practice of psychiatry, Dallas, 1952—. Teaching consultant, U.S. Public Health Service Research Center, Fort Worth, 1953-71; psychiatric consultant to Family Guidance Center, Dallas, 1953-70, Texas State Department of Child Welfare, 1955-60, Texas Presbyterian Child Placement Agency, 1955-60, U.S. Medical Center for Federal Prisoners, Springfield, Mo., 1968-70, and to Federal Aviation Administration, 1971. Military service: U.S. Navy, intern, 1944-45. U.S. Naval Reserve, 1944-46, 1951-52; became lieutenant.

MEMBER: American Medical Association, American Psychiatric Association, American Academy of Air Traffic Control Medicine, Texas Medical Association, Texas Psychiatric Association, United Association of Texas Law Enforcement Officials, Dallas County Medical Association, Dallas County Psychiatric Association.

WRITINGS: The Skyjacker: His Flights of Fancy, Macmillan, 1971. Also author of Some Skunks and Other Cases, Genesis. Contributor to journals.

WORK IN PROGRESS: A book on the inner ear.

*   *   *

HUBBARD, Lucien 1889(?)-1971

1889(?)—December 31, 1971; American film director and producer, screenwriter, correspondent, and novelist. Obituaries: New York Times, January 1, 1972.

HUBER, Richard M(iller) 1922-

PERSONAL: Born July 27, 1922, in Ardmore, Pa.; son of John Y., Jr. and Caroline (Miller) Huber; married Cintra Carter, June, 1950; married second wife, Suzanne Keller (a professor of sociology at Princeton University), December 21, 1968; children: (first marriage) Cintra, Richard M., Jr., Casilda. Education: Princeton University, B.A., 1945; Yale University, Ph. D., 1953. Religion: Episcopalian. Home: 444 East 86th St., New York, N.Y. 10028. Office: Division of Continuing Education, Hunter College of the City University of New York, 695 Park Ave., New York, N.Y. 10021.

CAREER: Hunter College of the City University of New York, New York, N.Y., dean of School of General Studies, 1971-77, executive director of Division of Continuing Education, 1977—. Member of literature committee, Governor's Commission on the Arts in New Jersey, 1966-67; director, Oral History Project, Princeton, N.J., 1969—; member, New Jersey Bicentennial Consultant Team for Television, 1972—. Former moderator of radio and television programs. Military service: U.S. Army Air Forces, World War II; became lieutenant.

MEMBER: American Historical Association, American Studies Association, Society of American Historians, American Association of University Administrators, Association for Continuing Higher Education, New Jersey Historical Society, Historical Society of Princeton, Nassau Club, Pretty Brook Club. Awards, honors: Danforth teaching fellowship, 1953-54; award of merit, American Association of State and Local History, 1965, for outstanding work in history; New Jersey Historical Society award, 1965, for distinguished work in the history of New Jersey.

WRITINGS: Big All the Way Through: The Life of Van Santvoord Merle-Smith, Princeton University Press, 1952; The American Idea of Success, McGraw, 1971. Editor, with Wheaton J. Lane of "The New Jersey Historical Series," thirty-one volumes, Van Nostrand, 1964-65.

WORK IN PROGRESS: Various essays on education and television; The American Idea of Happiness.

BIOGRAPHICAL/CRITICAL SOURCES: Washington Post, March 23, 1972.

*   *   *

HUBIN, Allen J. 1936-

PERSONAL: Born March 5, 1936, in Crosby, Minn.; son of Edwin Gustav (a physician) and Elizabeth (Wall) Hubin; married Marilyn Hagstrom, May 3, 1958; children: Loren, Jennifer, Wendy, Daniel, Joy. Education: Attended Bethel College, St. Paul, Minn., 1953-56; Wheaton College, Wheaton, Ill., B.S., 1958; University of Minnesota, M.S., 1961. Religion: Presbyterian. Home: 3656 Midland, White Bear Lake, Minn. 55110.

CAREER: Minnesota Mining & Manufacturing Co., St. Paul, Minn., 1961—, began as technical patent specialist, currently manager of Technical Education and Training. Member: American Society for Engineering Education, Mystery Writers of America.

WRITINGS: (Editor) Best Detective Stories of the Year, Dutton, 24th edition (Hubin was not associated with earlier editions), 1970, 29th edition, 1975; (editor) Best of the Best Detective Stories, Dutton, 1971; (contributor) John Ball, editor, The Mystery Story, University of California, San Diego, 1976. Editor and publisher, Armchair Detective, 1967—; author of weekly crime fiction review, New York

Times Book Review, 1968-71. Contributor to *Encyclopaedia Britannica* and *Encyclopedia Americana.* Contributing editor, *Encyclopedia of Mystery and Detection,* McGraw, 1976.

WORK IN PROGRESS: Editing, *The Best of the Armchair Detective,* for University of California, San Diego; *Bibliography of Crime Fiction,* also for University of California, San Diego.

AVOCATIONAL INTERESTS: Reading and collecting mystery and detective fiction (collection includes about fourteen thousand titles).

* * *

HUCKABY, Gerald 1933-

PERSONAL: Born May 3, 1933, in Santa Barbara, Calif.; son of William Aubrey (a clothing salesman) and Regina (Delaney) Huckaby; married Mary Pjerrou (a teacher and poet), May 31, 1969. *Education:* Loyola University of Los Angeles, B.A., 1955, M.A., 1961; University of California, Los Angeles, graduate study, 1961-66. *Politics:* ''Dirigiblist.'' *Religion:* ''Dirigiblest.'' *Residence:* Los Angeles, Calif. *Agent:* Audrey Soracco, 145 East 27th St., New York, N.Y. 10016. *Office:* Department of English, Immaculate Heart College, 2021 North Western Ave., Los Angeles, Calif. 90027.

CAREER: Immaculate Heart College, Los Angeles, Calif., assistant professor of English, 1961—. *Military service:* U.S. Air Force, 1955-58; became captain.

WRITINGS: City, Uncity (poems), illustrated by Corita Kent, Doubleday, 1969.

WORK IN PROGRESS: Koberly's Easy Lay, a book of poems; *Phoebus Koberly's Moon-Shot,* an epic poem.†

* * *

HUDDLESTON, Rodney D(esmond) 1937-

PERSONAL: Born April 4, 1937, in Bowdon, Cheshire, England; son of Denis Wilson and Dorothy (Marsland) Huddleston; married Joan Mulholland (a university tutor), December 18, 1965. *Education:* Corpus Christi College, Cambridge, B.A. (honours), 1960; University of Edinburgh, Ph.D., 1963. *Home:* 5 Holdway St., Kenmore, Queensland, Australia 4069. *Office:* Department of English, Queensland University, St. Lucia, Queensland, Australia 4067.

CAREER: University of Edinburgh, Edinburgh, Scotland, lecturer in linguistics, 1963-64; University of London, London, England, research assistant in linguistics, 1964-67; University of Reading, Reading, Berkshire, England, lecturer in linguistics, 1967-68; University of London, lecturer in linguistics, 1968-69; Queensland University, Brisbane, Queensland, Australia, 1969—, began as lecturer, currently reader in linguistics. *Member:* Linguistic Society of America, Linguistics Association of Great Britain, Linguistic Society of Australia.

WRITINGS: The Sentence in Written English: A Syntactic Study Based on an Analysis of Scientific Texts, Cambridge University Press, 1971; *An Introduction to English Transformational Syntax,* Longman, 1976. Contributor to linguistics journals.

WORK IN PROGRESS: Research in general linguistics and English syntax.

* * *

HUDGINS, H(erbert) C(ornelius), Jr. 1932-

PERSONAL: Born October 9, 1932, in Trotville, N.C.; son of Herbert Cornelius and Lucille (Simpson) Hudgins. *Education:* High Point College, A.B., 1954; University of North Carolina, M.Ed., 1959; Duke University, Ed.D., 1966. *Religion:* Methodist. *Home:* 119 Debaran Lane, Rosemont, Pa. 19010. *Office:* Department of Educational Administration, Temple University, Broad and Montgomery, Philadelphia, Pa. 19122.

CAREER: Teacher of social studies in Thomasville, N.C., 1954-59, and principal of high school, 1959-64; University of North Carolina at Greensboro, assistant professor of education, 1966-69; Temple University, Philadelphia, Pa., associate professor, 1969-73, professor of educational administration, 1973—. *Member:* National Organization on Legal Problems of Education, American Association of School Administrators, National Association of Secondary-School Principals, Pennsylvania Association of Secondary-School Principals, Pennsylvania Professors of Educational Administration, Horace Mann League, Kappa Delta Pi, Phi Delta Kappa.

WRITINGS: The Warren Court and the Public Schools, Interstate, 1970. Also author of a monograph *Public School Desegregation: Legal Issues and Judicial Decisions,* Educational Resources Information Center, and *School Administrators and the Courts,* Educational Service. Contributor to *Yearbook of School Law,* National Organization on Legal Problems of Education, 1974, 1975, 1976, and to *1977 Yearbook,* National Society for the Study of Education. Contributor to legal and education journals.

* * *

HUDSON, Charles M(elvin, Jr.) 1932-

PERSONAL: Born December 24, 1932, in Monterey, Ky.; son of Charles Melvin (a farmer) and Sarah (Long) Hudson; married Jo Ann Rodgers, 1954; married second wife, Joyce Rockwood (a writer and anthropologist), May 28, 1968; children: (first marriage) Charles Melvin III, Ann Rebecca. *Education:* University of Kentucky, A.B., 1959; University of North Carolina, Ph.D., 1965. *Office:* Department of Anthropology, University of Georgia, Athens, Ga. 30602.

CAREER: University of Georgia, Athens, assistant professor, 1964-68, associate professor, 1968-77, professor of anthropology, 1977—. Senior fellow, Center for the History of the American Indian, Newberry Library, Chicago, Ill., 1977-78. *Member:* American Anthropological Association (fellow), American Ethnological Society, American Society for Ethnohistory, Royal Anthropological Institute of Great Britain and Ireland (fellow). *Awards, honors:* Woodrow Wilson scholar, 1959-60.

WRITINGS: The Catawba Nation, University of Georgia Press, 1970; (editor) *Red, White and Black: Symposium on Indians in the Old South,* University of Georgia Press, 1971; (editor) *Four Centuries of Southern Indians,* University of Georgia Press, 1975; *The Southeastern Indians,* University of Tennessee Press, 1976. Editor, *Proceedings* of Southern Anthropological Society, 1967-71.

WORK IN PROGRESS: The southeastern Indians in the mid-eighteenth century; the world view of the southeastern Indians.

* * *

HUDSON, Gladys W(atts) 1926-

PERSONAL: Born July 23, 1926, in McKinney, Tex.; daughter of Robert A. (a baker) and Gertrude (Rickerson) Watts; married Thomas Earl Waden (a minister), December

22, 1945 (deceased); married Jack W. Hudson (a systems analyst), November 25, 1964; children: (first marriage) Thomas Earl Waden, Jr., Andrew Franklin Waden. *Education:* East Texas Baptist College, B.A., 1947; Southwestern Baptist Theological Seminary, further study, 1947-49; Baylor University, M.A., 1964. *Religion:* Baptist. *Home:* 3030 Lasker, Waco, Tex. 76707.

CAREER: Teacher of English in public schools in Walterboro, S.C., 1958-61; East Texas Baptist College, Marshall, instructor in English, 1964-65; Baylor University, Waco, Tex., instructor in English, 1965-74; Success Motivation Institute, Inc., Waco, director of product development, 1974—. *Member:* International Transactional Analysis Association.

WRITINGS: Paradise Lost: A Concordance, Gale, 1970. Contributor to Baptist publications.

*   *   *

HUDSON, James A(lbert)   1924-

PERSONAL: Born May 28, 1924, in Brownsville, Tenn.; son of James Albert (a postmaster) and Gladys (Bruce) Hudson; divorced. *Education:* Attended Vanderbilt University, 1942-43, 1947, Emory University, 1943-44, and Columbia University, 1944. *Politics:* Independent. *Religion:* Methodist. *Address:* P.O. Box 555, Brownsville, Tenn. 38012. *Agent:* William Morris, 1350 Avenue of the Americas, New York, N.Y. 10019.

CAREER: United Press International, New York, N.Y., rewriteman and feature writer, 1948-65, news editor, 1965-67; full-time free-lance writer, 1967—. *Military service:* U.S. Navy, World War II, served in Pacific; became lieutenant junior grade. *Awards, honors:* Scripps-Howard Award, 1947, for feature writing.

WRITINGS: Stalin's Daughter: Flight to Freedom, Tower, 1967; *The Blunderers: A Medical Expose,* Tower, 1968; *The Mysterious Death of Marilyn Monroe,* Volitant, 1968; *RFK, 1925-1968,* Scholastic Book Services, 1969; *Flip Wilson Close-Up,* Avon, 1971; *Latin America,* Scholastic Book Services, 1972; *The Osmonds,* Scholastic Book Services, 1972; *Young Mr. Cassidy,* Scholastic Book Services, 1973; *Nashville: City of Sound,* Scholastic Book Services, 1976. Contributor of more than 100 articles and short stories to periodicals.

WORK IN PROGRESS: The Last Blackout, a novel.

SIDELIGHTS: James Hudson writes: "Free advice to any discouraged young freelancer: Don't forget, writing sure beats working for a living! But after ten years of having fun at it, I've run out of excuses and have settled down to finish that first novel."

*   *   *

HUDSON, Michael Huckleberry   1939-

PERSONAL: Born March 14, 1939; son of Nathanial Carlos (an editor) and Madeline (Burke) Hudson; children: Peter, Gabriella. *Education:* University of Chicago, B.A., 1959; New York University, M.A., 1965, Ph.D., 1968. *Politics:* "Anti-nationalist." *Home:* 191 East Second St., New York, N.Y. 10009.

CAREER: Chase Manhattan Bank, New York City, balance-of-payments economist, 1964-67; Arthur Andersen, New York City, balance-of-payments economist, 1968-69; New School for Social Research, New York City, assistant professor of economics, 1969-72; senior economist, Hudson

Institute, 1972-76; Institute for Development Strategies, New York City, president, 1977—. Senior economist, Continental Oil Co., 1970-71.

WRITINGS: A Payments-Flow Analysis of U.S. International Transactions 1960-1968, Graduate School of Business Administration, New York University, 1970; (with Denis Goulet) *The Myth of Aid,* IDOC International, 1970; *Super Imperialism: The Economic Strategy of American Empire,* Holt, 1972; *Economics and Technology in Nineteenth Century American Thought: The Neglected American Economists,* Garland Publishing, 1974; *Global Fracture: The New International Economic Order,* Harper, 1977. Contributor to economics journals.

WORK IN PROGRESS: The New American Depression: America's Confusion between Wealth and Overhead; Theories of Trade and Development: A Reexamination of International Economic Thought; The Inversion of American Civilization; Theories of Technology and Society; "Mesmer," a play.

SIDELIGHTS: Michael Hudson told *CA* he "prefers to write for intelligent people rather than for other economists. All of [my] books describe the changing structure of the world's economic and political organization, and the transformation of productive powers and financial relationships in response to changed perceptions of the world and the past."

*   *   *

HUDSON, Wilma J(ones)   1916-

PERSONAL: Born January 29, 1916, in Walnut Grove, Mo.; daughter of William Henry (a merchant) and Myrtle (McLemore) Jones; married Marion B. Hudson (an electrical engineer), December 25, 1941 (died February 27, 1975); children: Jack Alan, Tom Scott, Janet Sue. *Education:* Drury College, A.B., 1936; Washington University, St. Louis, Mo., M.A., 1937; summer graduate study at Southwest Missouri State Teachers College (now Southwest Missouri State University), 1937, University of Illinois, 1941, and Butler University, 1966-67. *Home:* 10550 Zionsville Rd., Zionsville, Ind. 46077.

CAREER: High school teacher of English in Edwardsville, Ill., 1937-42, in Indianapolis, Ind., 1943-47, and 1963-66; librarian and audiovisual specialist at schools in Zionsville, Ind., 1966—. *Member:* National Council of Teachers of English, Indiana School Librarian Association, Indiana State Teachers Association, Delta Delta Delta, Psi Iota Xi, Mortar Board.

WRITINGS—Juveniles; all published by Bobbs-Merrill: *Dwight D. Eisenhower: Young Military Leader,* 1970; *J. C. Penney: Golden Rule Boy,* 1972; *Harry S Truman: Missouri Farm Boy,* 1973.

SIDELIGHTS: Wilma J. Hudson told *CA:* "Writing is my avocation. The three books which have been published were written while working full-time as a school librarian and keeping a home for a cooperative husband and children. Summer vacation time was devoted to travel for research by the entire family. With much patience we hunted for specific details of how something was made or how it worked from some decade in the past. The demanding part of research for children's books is to present not only accurate biographical material but also to provide correct, geographical, historical, and socio-economic details. Reading teachers generally stress that young children find satisfaction in reading about children their own age. Psychologists generally stress that young people must have goals that appear to be attainable.

When a biography can emphasize the experiences and the problems encountered during the childhood years and then present the outstanding achievements of men and women who have contributed to our society, the book becomes both readable, relevant, and worthwhile. Idealistic as it may seem, to write such books is my purpose in the biographies which I have written.''

BIOGRAPHICAL/CRITICAL SOURCES: Indianapolis News, January 7, 1970.

* * *

HUGHES, Daniel 1929-

PERSONAL: Born June 14, 1929, in Dover, N.H.; son of Daniel John and Beatrice (Ashby) Hughes; married Mary Yewell Small, August 7, 1954. *Education:* University of New Hampshire, B.A., 1950; Brown University, M.A., 1953, Ph.D., 1958. *Religion:* Manichean. *Home:* 17524 Third Ave., Detroit, Mich. 48203. *Office:* Department of English, Wayne State University, Detroit, Mich. 48202.

CAREER: Brown University, Providence, R.I., assistant professor of English, 1959-64; Wayne State University, Detroit, Mich., associate professor, 1964-69, professor of English, 1969—. *Military service:* U.S. Army, 1951-53; became lieutenant. *Member:* Modern Language Association of America, Phi Beta Kappa. *Awards, honors:* Borestone Mountain awards, 1959, 1962.

WRITINGS: Waking in a Tree (poetry), October House, 1964; *Lost Title,* Copper Beech Press, 1975. Contributor to *Massachusetts Review, Poetry, Criticism, Nation, Southern Review, Quarterly Review,* and other publications.

WORK IN PROGRESS: A third book of poems.

SIDELIGHTS: X. J. Kennedy describes Daniel Hughes' poetry as ''hard, subtle, and controlled...,'' adding: ''In an excellent book that seems the finely chiseled product of years, he wins victories over much recalcitrant matter.... There is nothing tentative about his handling of his language, his merciless intelligence.''

Hughes is interested in Italian Renaissance art and history, poetic theory (especially Paul Valery and French symbolism), modern fiction (especially Nabokov and Bellow), modern poetry from Eliot to the present, and ancient historians and fathers of the church. He told *CA,* ''My poetry seeks a cracked, if elegant, surface and a steady, mysterious depth.''

BIOGRAPHICAL/CRITICAL SOURCES: New York Times Book Review, December 22, 1963.

* * *

HUGHES, Felicity 1938-

PERSONAL: Born June 15, 1938, in Lancashire, England; daughter of Patrick Edward (a clergyman) and Estelle (Connor) Craig; married Glyn Hughes, August 18, 1962; children: Helen Elizabeth, Gwynneth Patricia. *Education:* Attended Knox College, Jamaica, 1951-57; Salem College, Salem, N.C., B.A. (cum laude), 1961. *Politics:* Socialist. *Religion:* Moravian. *Home:* Yacht Moon Deep, c/o G.P.O. Dartmouth, Devonshire, England.

CAREER: Teacher.

WRITINGS: Reading and Writing Before School, J. Cape, 1971, St. Martin's, 1972.

WORK IN PROGRESS: The Ways We Read, a comprehensive theory of reading for teachers and mothers; exploring ways of helping deaf babies to read, using film.

SIDELIGHTS: Felicity Hughes, who describes herself as ''boatwife,'' told *CA:* ''I am primarily interested in the idea that learning to read is exactly like learning to hear, and is therefore a non-academic, natural process. It is this idea which I am exploring in all my projects. Teaching methods follow from this idea. As far as I know, my work is the first to show that written language really does operate like spoken language all along the line, phonetics and all.''††

* * *

HUGHES, Glyn 1935-

PERSONAL: Born May 25, 1935, in Middlewich, Cheshire, England; son of Percival (a bus conductor) and Evelyn (Green) Hughes; married Elizabeth Slater, August 18, 1958 (divorced); married Roya Liakopoulos, 1974; children: (first marriage) Gwilym. *Education:* Regional College of Art, Manchester, England, N.D.D., 1957, A.T.D., 1958. *Agent:* David Higham Associates, 5-8 Lower John St., London W1R 4HA, England.

CAREER: Art teacher in secondary schools in Lancashire and Yorkshire, England, 1958-65; author. Part-time lecturer in literature, University of Manchester, 1970-73; has also taught part time in colleges and centers for further education and at H. M. Prison, Manchester. Has given poetry readings on Arts Council writers tours and at Royal College of Art, University of London, University of Oxford, and at various other universities in England; also read poetry at Kenyon College, Ohio State University, and other Ohio colleges, 1970. Member of committee, Manchester Institute of Contemporary Arts, 1966-69. *Awards, honors:* Welsh Arts Council Young Poet's Prize, 1969, for *Neighbours;* Arts Council bursaries, 1970 and 1974.

WRITINGS—Poetry: Love on the Moor, Phoenix Poets Press, 1968; *Neighbours* (Poetry Book Society recommendation in England), Dufour, 1970; *Towards the Sun,* Phoenix Poets Press, 1971; *Rest the Poor Struggler,* Dufour, 1972; *Prose Millstone Grit,* Gollancz, 1975; *Fair Prospects,* Gollancz, 1976. Also author of *Alibis and Convictions,* 1977. Author of plays, ''Alone On the Moon,'' and ''One Man Alone,'' both produced for British Broadcasting Corp., 1975. Contributor of poetry to magazines.

WORK IN PROGRESS: A novel; a book on the eighteenth-century Yorkshire Methodist Parson, William Grimshaw.

BIOGRAPHICAL/CRITICAL SOURCES: Irish Times, June 13, 1970; *Guardian,* June 20, 1970; *Times Literary Supplement,* July 2, 1970, September 24, 1976; *Observer,* July 19, 1970; *Review,* September, 1970; *Listener,* October 8, 1970, October 28, 1971, March 20, 1975; *Guardian,* April 10, 1975, August 5, 1976.

* * *

HUGHES, Judith M(arkham) 1941-

PERSONAL: Born February 20, 1941; daughter of Sanford H. (a lawyer) and Sylvia (Kovner) Markham; married H. Stuart Hughes (a professor), March 26, 1964; children: David Markham. *Education:* Swarthmore College, B.A., 1962; Harvard University, M.A., 1963, Ph.D., 1970. *Home:* 8531 Avenida de las Andas, La Jolla, Calif. 92037. *Office:* Department of History, University of California, San Diego, La Jolla, Calif. 92093.

CAREER: Harvard University, Cambridge, Mass., assistant professor of social studies, 1970-75; University of California, San Diego, La Jolla, associate professor of history,

1975—. *Member:* American Historical Association, Society for French Historical Studies, Conference on British Studies, Phi Beta Kappa. *Awards, honors:* Woodrow Wilson fellowship, 1962-63; National Endowment for the Humanities fellowship, 1974.

WRITINGS: To the Maginot Line: The Politics of French Military Preparations in the 1920's, Harvard University Press, 1971.

*   *   *

HULSE, Stewart H(arding), Jr. 1931-

PERSONAL: Surname rhymes with "pulse"; born August 25, 1931, in Elizabeth, N.J.; son of Stewart Harding and Katharine (Jones) Hulse; married Nancy Huppertz, August 14, 1954; children: Stephen, Jennifer, Melissa. *Education:* Williams College, A.B., 1953; Brown University, Sc.M., 1955, Ph.D., 1957. *Home:* Chapel Ridge Rd., Lutherville, Md. 21093. *Office:* Department of Psychology, Johns Hopkins University, Baltimore, Md. 21218.

CAREER: Johns Hopkins University, Baltimore, Md., instructor, 1957-58, assistant professor, 1958-63, associate professor, 1963-69, professor of psychology, 1969—. *Member:* American Psychological Association (fellow), American Association for the Advancement of Science (fellow), Psychonomic Society, Eastern Psychological Association, Sigma Xi.

WRITINGS: (With James Deese) *The Psychology of Learning,* 3rd edition (Hulse was not associated with earlier editions), McGraw, 1967, 4th edition, 1976; (contributor) G. H. Brown, editor, *The Psychology of Learning and Motivation,* Volume VII, Academic Press, 1973; (with H. Fowler and W. K. Honig) *Cognitive Processes in Animal Behavior,* Erlbaum, in press. Contributor to psychology journals. Associate editor, *Animal Learning and Behavior.* Consulting editor, *Journal of Experimental Psychology.*

*   *   *

HULTENG, John L. 1921-

PERSONAL: Born April 1, 1921, in Grand Forks, N.D.; son of John L. and Ragnhild (Anderson) Hulteng; married Elizabeth Jean Rucker, June 18, 1947; children: Robert G., Karen E., Richard J. *Education:* University of North Dakota, Ph.B., 1943; Columbia University, M.S., 1947; Harvard University, additional study, 1949-50. *Home address:* Box 423, Hayden Lake, Idaho 83835. *Office:* Department of Communication, Stanford University, Stanford, Calif. 94305.

CAREER: Editorial writer, foreign correspondent, and editorial page editor for *Providence Journal* and *Evening Bulletin,* Providence, R.I., 1947-55; University of Oregon, Eugene, associate professor, 1955-61, professor of journalism, 1961-77, dean of School of Journalism, 1962-68, 1975-76; East-West Communication Institute, Honolulu, Hawaii, assistant director, 1974-75; Stanford University, Stanford, Calif., professor of journalism, 1977—. Visiting professor, Stanford University, 1970-71. *Military service:* U.S. Army Air Forces, 1943-46; became first lieutenant. *Member:* Association for Education in Journalism, American Association of Schools and Departments of Journalism (president, 1966-67), American Association of University Professors, Phi Beta Kappa, Kappa Tau Alpha, Sigma Delta Chi, Alpha Delta Sigma. *Awards, honors:* Pulitzer scholar, 1947; Nieman fellow, 1949-50; University of Oregon Ersted Award for distinguished teaching, 1961; National Sigma Delta Chi award for distinguished teaching, 1970.

WRITINGS: The Fourth Estate, Harper, 1971; *The Opinion Function,* Harper, 1973; *The Messenger's Motives,* Prentice-Hall, 1976. Contributor of many chapters to books; also contributor to *Journalism Quarterly, Columbia Journalism Review, Nieman Reports, Bulletin of American Society of Newspaper Editors,* and other periodicals.

WORK IN PROGRESS: An introductory textbook series.

*   *   *

HUMMEL, Ray O(rvin), Jr. 1909-

PERSONAL: Born October 2, 1909, Lincoln, Neb.; son of Ray O. (a physician) and Charlotte (Hullhorst) Hummel; married former wife, Roberta Harrison (a school librarian), August 15, 1939; children: Ray O. III, Charlotte H. *Education:* University of Nebraska, A.B., 1930, A.M., 1931, Ph.D., 1934; attended University of Iowa, 1932-33; University of Michigan, A.B.L.S., 1936. *Religion:* Methodist. *Home:* 5107 Sylvan Rd., Richmond, Va. 23225. *Office:* Cabell Library, Virginia Commonwealth University, Richmond, Va. 23220.

CAREER: Folger Shakespeare Library, Washington, D.C., cataloger, 1936-46; University of Minnesota Library, Minneapolis, professor and head of cataloging division, 1946-48; Virginia State Library, Richmond, assistant state librarian, 1948-75, consultant, 1975—; Virginia Commonwealth University, Cabell Library, Richmond, scholar-in-residence, 1975—. Part-time instructor, Catholic University, 1938-42. *Military service:* U.S. Navy, 1942-45; became lieutenant commander. *Member:* American Library Association (member of council, 1950-59), Bibliographical Society, Virginia Library Association (president, 1957-58).

WRITINGS: A List of Places Included in Nineteenth Century Virginia Directories, Virginia State Library, 1960; *Virginia Local History: A Bibliography,* Virginia State Library, 1971, revised edition, 1976; *Southeastern Broadsides before 1877: A Bibliography,* University Press of Virginia, 1971; *More Virginia Broadsides,* Virginia State Library, 1975; *Portraits and Statuary of Virginians,* Virginia State Library, 1977. Managing editor, *Library Resources and Technical Services,* 1960-65.

*   *   *

HUMPHREYS, Alexander J(eremiah) 1913-

PERSONAL: Born July 15, 1913, in San Francisco, Calif.; son of Milton Alexander and Hannah Mary (Riordan) Humphreys. *Education:* Attended University of Santa Clara, 1933-35; Gonzaga University, A.B., 1937, M.A. (philosophy), 1938; Fordham University, M.A. (sociology), 1942; Alma College (now The Jesuit School of Theology at Berkeley), S.T.L., 1946; Harvard University, Ph.D., 1953. *Politics:* "Democrat—open-ended." *Home and office:* Loyola Marymount University, 7101 West 80th St., Los Angeles, Calif. 90045.

CAREER: Roman Catholic priest of Society of Jesus (Jesuits); University of Santa Clara, Santa Clara, Calif., instructor in philosophy, 1938-40; Loyola Marymount University, Los Angeles, Calif., assistant professor, 1953-61, associate professor, 1961—, chairman of department of sociology, 1960-69, coordinator of accreditation report, 1962. Member of Western College Association accrediting committees for Fresno State College (now California State University, Fresno), 1956, College of the Pacific, 1957, University of California, San Diego, 1965, and Claremont Men's College, 1969. Instructor in philosophy, University of San Francisco, summer, 1969.

MEMBER: American Sociological Association, American Association of University Professors, American Catholic Sociological Society (now Association for the Sociology of Religion), American Committee for Irish Studies, Pacific Sociological Society.

WRITINGS: New Dubliners, Fordham University Press, 1965; (contributor) Meyer Nimkoff, editor, *Comparative Family Systems,* Houghton, 1965. Contributor of articles and reviews to professional journals.

WORK IN PROGRESS: Research on the family in a federal housing authority project in the wider Los Angeles community.

SIDELIGHTS: Alexander Humphreys told *CA:* "I am interested in the whole process of modern urbanization and its effect upon the major institutions of human societies. I have focused on the family because it not only is valuable in its own right but because every other institution in society impinges on the family. Consequently the study of the family forces one to understand the structure, the function, the de facto influence of all other institutions on the family. I am also—indeed, primarily—interested in teaching and in training young men and women to have a deep and imbibing interest in as well as the abilities and skills to cope with our human society and culture, and a real knowledge and love of truly human life in a truly human society—which I don't believe can be realized without a touch of the divine."

* * *

HUNGERFORD, Harold R(alph)   1928-

PERSONAL: Born January 21, 1928, in Kankakee, Ill.; son of Harold Norton (a teacher) and Alice (Hardy) Hungerford; married Patricia Clapper, June 17, 1951; children: Linda Elise, Suzanne Mary. *Education:* Blackburn College, A.A., 1947; Illinois State Normal University (now Illinois State University), B.S.Ed., 1949, M.S.Ed., 1953; University of Oklahoma, graduate study, 1953; University of Illinois, Advanced Certificate in Education, 1963; Southern Illinois University at Carbondale, Ph.D., 1970. *Religion:* Protestant. *Home:* RFD 4, Carbondale, Ill. 62901. *Office:* Department of C.I.M., College of Education, Southern Illinois University, Carbondale, Ill. 62901.

CAREER: Public schools of Kankakee, Ill., high school science teacher, 1949-51, 1956-57, elementary teacher, 1954-56, elementary school principal, 1957-58, junior high principal, 1958-65; Southern Illinois University at Cardondale, science methods instructor in elementary education, 1969—. Resource consultant, North American Regional Conference on Environmental Education (sponsored by UNESCO), 1976. *Military service:* U.S. Air Force, 1951-54. *Member:* National Science Teachers Association, National Association for Research in Science Teaching, Photographic Society of America, National Wildlife Federation, National Audubon Society, Nature Conservancy, Central Association of School Science and Mathematics Teachers, Illinois Science Teachers Association. *Awards, honors:* Ranking of five-star nature photographer from Photographic Society of America; awards for photographs in international competition, including Authentic Wildlife Medal from Chicago Nature Exhibit, 1970.

WRITINGS—All published by J. Weston Walch, except as indicated: (With R. E. Drew) *Teaching Elementary School Science,* 1959; *Adventures in Science,* 1962; *Science and the Science Student,* 1964; (editor with Nancy Shephard) *The Natural Resources of Kankakee County,* Kankakee County Conservation Committee, 1964; (with A. N. Tomera) *Re-*

production: An Important Life Function, 1966; (with Donald G. Hertz) *Cells: Diversity of Structure and Function,* 1967; (contributor) Laurence P. Pringle, editor, *Discovering the Outdoors,* Natural History Press, 1969; (with Tomera) *Understanding Science and the Scientist,* Benefic, 1969; *Science and Conservation in the Field,* 1969; *Ecology: The Circle of Life,* Childrens Press, 1971; (with Tomera) *Ecological Factors,* 1971; (with Tomera) *Communities and Ecosystems,* 1971; (with Tomera) *Communities in Nature* (eight sound filmstrips), Society for Visual Education, 1976; (with Peyton) *Teaching Environmental Education,* 1976; (with Tomera) *Science in the Elementary School: A Worktext,* Stipes, 1977. Writer of filmstrips and other curriculum materials. Contributor of about a dozen articles to education journals.

WORK IN PROGRESS: A teaching module in ecology, for Society for Visual Education.

SIDELIGHTS: "For me, the ultimate responsibility of a professional educator must be to improve general education instruction at all grade levels," Harold Hungerford wrote *CA.* He continued: "In particular, the science/environmental educator must bear the tremendous burden of helping human beings in all walks of life perceive their own cultural and natural relationships to science, technology, and the biosphere in which they live. To do less is an abdication of responsibility even though the victories are sometimes few and the margins of success frustratingly small."

* * *

HUNSAKER, David M(alcolm)   1944-

PERSONAL: Born July 30, 1944, in Riverside, Calif.; son of Perry L. (a business executive) and Lois B. (Coogan) Hunsaker; married Karen A. Metz (a career consultant), June 25, 1966; children: Justin Scott. *Education:* University of California, Santa Barbara, B.A., 1966; Columbia University, J.D., 1969; Bradley University, M.A., 1972; University of Virginia, LL.M., 1977. *Office address:* Putbrese & Kennedy, Attorneys, P.O. Box 539, McLean, Va. 22101.

CAREER: Clark Carr & Ellis, Attorneys, New York City, junior associate, 1968; Queens College of the City University of New York, New York City, lecturer, 1968-69; Bradley University, Peoria, Ill., instructor, 1969-71; San Diego State University, San Diego, Calif., assistant professor of speech, 1971-74; University of San Diego, School of Law, San Diego, Calif., adjunct professor of law, 1972-74; University of Virginia, Charlottesville, associate professor of speech communication, 1974-77; Putbrese & Kennedy, Attorneys, McLean, Va., associate, 1977—. Consultant, United States Army, 1975-77, and South Eastern Theatre Conference, 1977. *Member:* California Bar Association, District of Columbia Bar Association, Federal Communications Bar Association.

WRITINGS: Cases and Materials on Freedom of Speech, Simon & Schuster, 1970; (with Craig R. Smith) *The Bases of Argument: Ideas in Conflict,* Bobbs-Merrill, 1972. Contributor to *1970 Yearbook of Freedom of Speech.* Contributor to *Columbia Journal of Transnational Law, Western Speech Communication Journal, San Diego Law Review, Rendezvous, Psychological Reports, Freedom of Information Center Reports, Southern Speech Communication Journal, Duquesne Law Review,* and *Journal of Legal Education.*

WORK IN PROGRESS: Articles on the oral argument before the Supreme Court on the Watergate tapes, adverse publicity by administrative agencies, and legal and medical definitions of death.

HUNSINGER, Paul 1919-

PERSONAL: Born March 23, 1919, in Findlay, Ohio; son of C. S. and Gertrude Hunsinger; married Pat Wedell; children: Kay Bergstrom, Marya McConnell, Steve. Education: North Central College, B.A., 1941; Evangelical Theological Seminary, B.D., 1944; Northwestern University, M.A., 1946, Ph.D., 1951. Politics: Democrat. Religion: Methodist. Home: 1157 South Vine, Denver, Colo. 80209. Office: Department of Speech Communication, University of Denver, Denver, Colo. 80210.

CAREER: Ordained minister of Evangelical United Brethren Church (now United Methodist), 1945; minister in Chicago, Ill. at Salem Evangelical Church, 1944-46, and Diversey Parkway Church, 1946-48; North Central College, Naperville, Ill., instructor in speech, 1941-44; Northwestern University, Evanston, Ill., lecturer in oral interpretation, 1946-48; Morningside College, Sioux City, Iowa, assistant professor of public speaking and debate, 1948-49; Southern Illinois University at Carbondale, associate professor of oral interpretation and associate dean of College of Vocation and Professions, 1949-58; Occidental College, Los Angeles, Calif., associate professor of speech, 1958-62; University of Denver, Denver, Colo., professor of speech communication, 1962—, chairman of department, 1962-69. Guest professor, University of Hawaii, Honolulu, 1972 and 1976. Consultant to Department of Health, Education and Welfare, Peace Corps, Mountain States Telephone Co., Colorado Public Service, and Department of Personnel Services (Hawaii).

MEMBER: International Society for General Semantics (president, 1967-71), International Communication Association, American Association of University Professors, Speech Communications Association (member of executive council), Institute of General Semantics (trustee), Pacific Communication Association (president). Awards, honors: Southern Illinois University and University of Denver Outstanding Teacher awards; North Central College Outstanding Alumnus award.

WRITINGS: (With William Buys and others) Creative Speaking, National Textbook Co., 1964; Communicative Interpretation, W. C. Brown, 1967; (with Roy Wood) Managing Forensic Tournaments, National Textbook Co., 1970. Also author of Using Words Effectively, National Textbook Co.

WORK IN PROGRESS: Interpretive Communication, for Houghton.

*   *   *

HUNT, David 1942-

PERSONAL: Born March 1, 1942, in Buffalo, N.Y.; son of James J. (a social worker) and Freda (Greenberg) Hunt; married Persis Charles, August 26, 1967. Education: Haverford College, B.A., 1963; Harvard University, Ph.D., 1969. Home: 20 Dudley St., Cambridge, Mass. 02140. Office: Department of History, University of Massachusetts, Boston, Mass. 02116.

CAREER: University of Massachusetts—Boston, 1969—, began as assistant professor, currently associate professor of history.

WRITINGS: Parents and Children in History: The Psychology of Family Life in Early Modern France, Basic Books, 1970. Contributor to Radical America.

HUNT, John J. 1929-

PERSONAL: Born June 29, 1929, in Kansas City, Mo.; son of Charles E. (a florist) and Norah (Mullins) Hunt; married Madgie Leeper, March 9, 1951; children: J. Kevin. Education: Missouri Valley College (now University), B.S., 1950; Central Missouri State College (now University), M.S., 1955; Colorado State College (now University of Northern Colorado), Ed.D., 1959, post-doctoral study, 1963; University of Colorado, post-doctoral study, 1965. Home: 308 Parkside Lane, Missoula, Mont. 59801. Office: School of Education, University of Montana, Missoula, Mont. 59801.

CAREER: Teacher of the orthopedically handicapped in Marshall, Mo., 1950; high school teacher and coach in Kansas City, Mo., 1950-55; Missouri Valley College (now University), Marshall, assistant professor and coach, 1955-56; junior high school teacher in Kansas City, 1956-57; public schools of Boulder Valley, Colo., director of educational services, 1959-66; University of Montana, Missoula, associate professor, 1966-72, professor of education, 1972—, staff associate of Division of Educational Research and Services, 1966—, director of Project Upward Bound, 1966-68, coordinator of Division of Educational Administration, Curriculum, and Supervision, 1970—. Associate director of project for National Right to Read Program, Institute for Educational Management, 1972. Visiting lecturer at Adams State College, University of Lethbridge, University of Calgary, and other institutions. Military service: U.S. Army, 1951-53.

MEMBER: Association for Supervision and Curriculum Development, National Education Association, National Association of Secondary School Principals, National Community School Education Association, International Platform Association, Montana Education Association, Tau Kappa Epsilon, Delta Tau Kappa, Phi Delta Kappa, Lions Club.

WRITINGS: (With Robert H. Johnson, Jr.) Rx for Team-Teaching, Burgess, 1968. Writer or contributor to more than fifty educational studies; contributor of over thirty articles to education journals. Editor, Recreation at the Top of the Nation, 1957-58.

WORK IN PROGRESS: Writing on individualized instruction.

*   *   *

HUNT, John P. 1915-

PERSONAL: Born July 1, 1915, in Kalona, Iowa; son of William Anderson (a judge) and Grace (Toulouse) Hunt; married Pauline Strong, August 23, 1943; children: Regan G. (daughter), John P., Jr. Education: University of Missouri, B.J., 1937, graduate study, 1938. Home: 11152 White Oak Ave., Granada Hills, Calif. 91344. Office: City Hall, Room 278, Los Angeles, Calif. 91344.

CAREER: Worked for newspapers in Iowa, prior to World War II, and for Hollywood Citizen News, Hollywood, Calif., 1947-48; Los Angeles Mirror-News, Los Angeles, Calif., reporter, 1948-60; Los Angeles County District Attorney's Office, Los Angeles, press secretary, 1960-61; Office of the Mayor, Los Angeles, press secretary, 1961-63; Los Angeles Zoo, Los Angeles, community relations director, 1963-65; City Economic Development Board Community, Los Angeles, area economic coordinator, 1965—. Military service: U.S. Army Air Forces, 1941-46. U.S. Air Force, 1951-53. U.S. Air Force Retired Reserve; now lieutenant colonel.

WRITINGS: A World Full of Animals, McKay, 1969. Contributor to popular periodicals, including *McCall's, True,* and *Gentlemen's Quarterly.* Supervising editor, *Scope* (publication of the city of Los Angeles).

WORK IN PROGRESS: Further writing on the Los Angeles Zoo and its role in saving endangered species from extinction; research on the march of the Mormon Battalion from Iowa to California, 1846-47.

SIDELIGHTS: John P. Hunt writes: "I support a new ethic that wild animals are a vastly depleted resource now to be absolutely protected with no open seasons, a heritage to protect rather than a game crop to be harvested. Hunting is not a sport and hasn't been since the mid-1850's when the rifle became generally available at a reasonable price. No animal, including an elephant, is equipped to cope on a 'sporting' basis with a high-powered rifle and expensive scope. . . ."

BIOGRAPHICAL/CRITICAL SOURCES: Best Sellers, April 1, 1969.

* * *

HUNT, William Dudley, Jr. 1922-

PERSONAL: Born March 23, 1922, in New Orleans, La.; son of William Dudley (a civil engineer) and Ruth (Lee) Hunt; married Julia Wellborn, June 9, 1942 (divorced, 1953); married Gwendolyn Munson, June 19, 1954; children: (first marriage) William Dudley III, Walter W.; (second marriage) Ruth Lee II, Stephen C. M., Gwendolyn M. II, John M. *Education:* Jacksonville State University, B.A., 1949; Tulane University, B.Arch., 1957. *Religion:* Episcopal. *Home address:* Box 228A, Route 3, Gloucester, Va. 23061. *Office address:* Box 670, Gloucester, Va. 23061; and John Wiley & Sons, Inc., 605 Third Ave., New York, N.Y. 10016.

CAREER: Private practice of architecture, 1951-64; *Architectural Record,* New York City, senior editor, 1958-63; American Institute of Architects, Washington, D.C., publisher of *American Institute of Architects Journal,* 1964-72, publishing director, 1970-72; John Wiley & Sons, Inc., New York City, architecture editor, 1972—. Director, Product Systems for Architects and Engineers, 1970-71. Consultant to Alcoa and U.S. Steel Co., 1963-68; consulting editor, Dodge Books, 1958-65, McGraw-Hill Book Co., 1965—. Member of architectural review board, Town of Rye, N.Y., 1963. *Military service:* U.S. Army Air Forces, pilot and engineering officer, 1942-45; became first lieutenant. U.S. Air Force Reserve, 1945—; present rank, lieutenant colonel. *Member:* American Institute of Architects (fellow), Authors Guild, Authors League of America, Tau Sigma Delta. *Awards, honors:* Design award, Dallas Museum of Fine Arts, 1958.

WRITINGS: Contemporary Curtain Wall, Dodge Books, 1958; (editor and contributor) *Hotels, Motels, Restaurants, and Bars,* Dodge Books, 1960; (editor and contributor) *Hospitals, Health Centers and Clinics,* Dodge Books, 1961; (editor and contributor) *Office Buildings,* Dodge Books, 1961; (editor and contributor) *Organizing for Successful Practice,* Dodge Books, 1962; *Comprehensive Architectural Services,* McGraw, 1965; *Creative Cost Control,* McGraw, 1967; *Total Design,* McGraw, 1972. Contributor of many articles to *American Institute of Architects Journal, Architectural Record,* and other professional architectural magazines.

WORK IN PROGRESS: Encyclopedia of American Architecture, for McGraw.

HUNTER, Frederick J(ames) 1916-

PERSONAL: Born May 31, 1916, in Denver, Colo.; son of John Lauren (an advertising manager) and Mary (Affolter) Hunter; married Elberta Casey (an artist), August 15, 1945; children: James L., Casey S., Kirk L. *Education:* Attended Los Angeles City College, 1935-38; University of California, Berkeley, B.A., 1940; University of North Carolina, M.A., 1942; Stanford University, Ph.D., 1954. *Politics:* Independent. *Religion:* Protestant. *Home:* 4803 Timberline Dr., Austin, Tex. 78746. *Office:* Department of Drama, University of Texas, Austin, Tex. 78712.

CAREER: Iowa State College (now University), Ames, instructor in English and drama, 1946; Whitman College, Walla Walla, Wash., assistant professor of English, 1946-48; Santa Barbara College (now University of California, Santa Barbara), lecturer in drama, 1950; University of Oregon, Eugene, assistant professor of theater, 1950-57; University of Texas at Austin, assistant professor, 1957-62, associate professor, 1962-68, professor of drama, 1969—, acting chairman of department, 1976—. Has appeared in plays in Los Angeles, Calif., and in North Carolina. Curator, Hoblitzelle Theatre Arts Library, 1960-71. *Military service:* U.S. Army Air Forces, 1942-46; became captain. *Member:* American Theater Association, American Society for Theatre Research, American Society for Aesthetics, American Library Association, Tau Sigma Delta.

WRITINGS: A Guide to Theatre and Drama Collections at the University of Texas, Humanities Research Center, University of Texas, 1967; *Drama Bibliography: A Guide to Extended Reading in Dramatic Art,* G. K. Hall, 1971; *A Catalog of the Norman Bel Geddes Theatre Collection,* G. K. Hall, 1973; *The Power of Dramatic Form,* Exposition Press, 1974. Contributor to theater and aesthetics journals.

SIDELIGHTS: Frederick Hunter told *CA:* "Analyses and compilations are not artistic writings, but they are clues to the availability of art and to its meaning and value. As the products of art, including theatre art become more pervasive in our culture, the more need there will be for catalogs, bibliographies, and analyses. If there is any good art, where is it?"

* * *

HUNTER, Geoffrey (Basil Bailey) 1925-

PERSONAL: Born December 14, 1925, in Leeds, England; son of Joseph Walter (a clergyman, missionary, and university teacher, who spent twenty-seven years in China) and Margaret Christina (a teacher before her marriage; maiden name, Brownlee) Hunter; married Patience Margaret Tate (partner in a second-hand book shop), June 12, 1951; children: Katy, Elizabeth, Lucy. *Education:* Had his first schooling in Shantung Province, China; later attended schools in Sussex, England, and then Eton College; New College, Oxford, B.A., 1950, M.A., 1953. *Politics:* Labour. *Religion:* None. *Home:* Priormuir, by St. Andrews, Fife, Scotland. *Office:* Department of Logic and Metaphysics, University of St. Andrews, St. Andrews, Fife, Scotland.

CAREER: Queen's University at Kingston, Kingston, Ontario, lecturer in philosophy, 1950-52; University of Leeds, Leeds, England, lecturer in philosophy, 1952-65; University of St. Andrews, St. Andrews, Scotland, lecturer, 1965-66, senior lecturer, 1966-72, reader in logic and metaphysics, 1972—. Visiting associate professor, University of North Carolina at Chapel Hill, spring, 1964. *Military service:* Royal Navy, 1944-46; became sub-lieutenant. *Member:* Aristotelian Society, Mind Association, Association for Symbolic Logic, Association of University Teachers, Society of Authors.

WRITINGS: Metalogic: An Introduction to the Metatheory of Standard First Order Logic, University of California Press, 1971, revised edition, 1973.

Contributor: V. C. Chappell, editor, Hume, Doubleday, 1966; W. D. Hudson, editor, The Is-Ought Question, Macmillan, 1969; W. B. Todd, editor, Hume and the Enlightenment, Humanities Research Center, University of Texas, 1974. Contributor to philosophy journals, to Queen's Quarterly, Texas Studies in Literature and Language, and Scope (film periodical).

WORK IN PROGRESS: On the logic of "if."

* * *

HUNTLEY, Frank Livingstone 1902-

PERSONAL: Born October 10, 1902, in Hanyang, Hupeh, China; son of George Arthur (a medical missionary) and Eliza (Reid) Huntley; married Katharine Burgner, June 16, 1926; children: John, Janet (Mrs. Richard Linde), Sylvia (Mrs. Michael Horowitz), Christopher, James. Education: Oberlin College, A.B., 1924; University of Chicago, M.A., 1926, Ph.D., 1938; attended Japanese Language School, Tokyo, Japan, 1929. Politics: Democrat. Religion: Episcopalian. Home: 1048 Martin Pl., Ann Arbor, Mich. 48104. Office: Department of English, University of Michigan, Ann Arbor, Mich. 48104.

CAREER: Washington University, St. Louis, Mo., instructor in English, 1925-27; Oberlin College, Oberlin, Ohio, instructor in English, 1927-29; Doshisha University and Kyoto University, Kyoto, Japan, professor of English, 1929-35; Stout Institute (now University of Wisconsin—Stout), Menominee, Wis., chairman of English department, 1938-43; Carleton College, Northfield, Minn., associate professor of English, 1943-44; University of Michigan, Ann Arbor, associate professor, 1944-55, professor of English, 1955-72, professor emeritus, 1972—, secretary of Barbour Scholarships for Oriental Women, 1946-72. Civilian adviser on Japanese language and area, U.S. Army, 1942-45. Member: Renaissance Society of America, Modern Language Association of America. Awards, honors: Fulbright fellow in Japan, 1958; fellowship to Folger Shakespeare Library, 1970; fellowship to William Andrews Clark Memorial Library, University of California, Los Angeles, 1972.

WRITINGS: On Dryden's Essay of Dramatic Poesy, University of Michigan Press, 1951; (editor) Two Funeral Sermons, William Andrews Clark Memorial Library, University of California, 1956; Sir Thomas Browne: A Biographical and Critical Study, University of Michigan Press, 1962; (editor) Sir Thomas Browne, Hydriotaphia [and] The Garden of Cyprus, Appleton, 1966; (editor) Sir Thomas Browne, Religio Medici, Appleton, 1966; Jeremy Taylor and the Great Rebellion: A Study of His Mind and Temper in Controversy, University of Michigan Press, 1970; Bishop Joseph Hall, 1574-1656: A Biographical and Critical Study, [Cambridge, England], 1977. Contributor of about seventy-five articles on seventeenth-century literature to journals.

AVOCATIONAL INTERESTS: House renovation, sailing.

* * *

HURLEY, John 1928-

PERSONAL: Born March 10, 1928, in Medford, Mass.; son of James and Bess (Cullen) Cotter; children: Stephen,

Sheila. Education: Attended Saint Bonaventure University, 1949-52; Saint Mary College, Xavier, Kan., B.S., 1956; University of Connecticut, M.A., 1958. Residence: Anaheim, Calif. Office: Department of English, Santa Ana College, Santa Ana, Calif. 92706.

CAREER: Santa Ana College, Santa Ana, Calif., instructor in English, 1964—. Accountant and auditor in private industry. Military service: U.S. Army, 1952-54.

WRITINGS: A Practical Rhetoric, W. C. Brown, 1971. Also author of "Twice in Eden," a musical drama. Contributor to English Journal, Grit, Media and Methods, Creative Moment, Today's Writer, and other journals and newspapers.

WORK IN PROGRESS: A musical drama; a novel; a textbook; a biography.

AVOCATIONAL INTERESTS: Skiing, ice skating, tennis, hiking, swimming, traveling in the United States, reading, music, playing piano, plays.

* * *

HURWITZ, Ken 1948-

PERSONAL: Born April 21, 1948, in Milwaukee, Wis.; son of Herman (a lawyer) and Thelma (Wein) Hurwitz. Education: Harvard University, A.B. (cum laude), 1970. Religion: Jewish. Home: 10847½ Wilshire, Los Angeles, Calif. 90024. Agent: Carl Brandt, Brandt & Brandt, 101 Park Ave., New York, N.Y. 10017; and Ben Benjamin, International Creative Management, 8899 Beverly Blvd., Los Angeles, Calif. 90048.

CAREER: Writer.

WRITINGS: Marching Nowhere, Norton, 1971; The Line of David, Norton, 1973; (with Vincent Bugliosi) Till Death Do Us Part: A True Murder Mystery, Norton, 1978.

* * *

HUTCHINGS, Raymond 1924-

PERSONAL: Born November 18, 1924, in Westcliff-on-Sea, England; son of Dudley Albert and Winifred Alice (Bennett) Hutchings; married Karen Langemark, April 2, 1949; children: Stella, Theresa (Mrs. Nigel Philip Repper), Julian, Nicholas. Education: St. John's College, Cambridge, B.A., 1947, M.A., 1953; University of London, Ph.D., 1958. Home and office: 168 Turnpike Link, Croydon CRO 5NZ, England.

CAREER: Member of British Foreign Office and Foreign Service, 1952-68, 1973-75; British Embassy, Moscow, Soviet Union, junior attache, 1954, second secretary, 1957-59; Royal Institute of International Affairs, London, England, research specialist in Soviet studies, 1968-72; Harvard University, Russian Research Center, Cambridge, Mass., research fellow, 1972-73. University of Maryland, lecturer, 1962, visiting professor, 1972; lecturer, University of Southern California, 1962; senior research fellow in economic history, Australian National University, 1964-68; visiting professor, Pennsylvania State University, 1973, University of Texas, 1976. Has given annual lecture tours in North America, 1973—. Military service: British Army, 1943-46; became sergeant. Member: National Association for Soviet and East European Studies (treasurer, 1968-72), American Association for the Advancement of Slavic Studies, Royal United Services Institute for Defence Studies.

WRITINGS: Soviet Economic Development, Basil Blackwell, 1971; Seasonal Influences in Soviet Industry, Oxford

University Press, for Royal Institute of International Affairs, 1971; *Soviet Science Technology Design: Interaction and Convergence,* Oxford University Press, for Royal Institute of International Affairs, 1976.

Contributor: G. Schoeplin, editor, *The Soviet Union and Eastern Europe,* Anthony Blond, 1970; W. Gumpel and Dietmar Keese, editors, *Probleme des Industrialismus im Ost und West,* Gunter Olzog, 1973; M. McGuire, editor, *Soviet Naval Developments,* Praeger, 1973; J. Hardt, editor, *Soviet Economic Prospects for the Seventies,* Joint Economic Committee, 1973. Contributor of over forty articles and reviews to journals of Soviet and international affairs.

WORK IN PROGRESS: Research on Soviet design practices and their influence on Soviet naval design and on patterns and trends in the provision of Soviet economic statistics.

SIDELIGHTS: Raymond Hutchings told *CA:* "I began to read about Russia in 1942 and have been reading, writing, or reflecting about Russia, or looking at Russia, ever since. . . . I worked for a long time as an economist which is still my chief specialization, but have now broadened out, I hope, to a point where I am not quite sure how to describe myself. . . . I have traveled much, lived in four continents, . . . and would like to travel much more, especially in hot, dry, and lonely places. . . . I got into the academic world rather late, but with a big reserve of material and an urge to communicate, and am trying now to make up for lost time. I hope to go on doing research forever."

* * *

HYDER, Clyde Kenneth 1902-

PERSONAL: Born January 4, 1902, in West Plains, Mo.; son of Lewis Marvin and Mae Lou (Turner) Hyder; married Allena Hicks, October 14, 1941 (died, 1968); children: Catherine Alison (Mrs. Ross H. Ogden). *Education:* Drury College, A.B., 1924; Harvard University, A.M., 1926, Ph.D., 1933. *Politics:* Independent. *Home and office:* 233 Dakota St., Lawrence, Kan. 66044.

CAREER: University of Texas, Main University (now University of Texas at Austin), instructor in English, 1926-27; University of Kansas, Lawrence, assistant professor, 1930-37, associate professor, 1937-47, professor of English, 1947-68, professor emeritus, 1968—. University of Kansas Press, editor, 1946, editor and director, 1953-68. *Military service:* U.S. Army Air Forces, 1942-44; became staff sergeant. *Member:* American Association of University Professors, Modern Language Association of America, Theta Kappa Nu, Sigma Tau Delta.

WRITINGS: Swinburne's Literary Career and Fame, Duke University Press, 1933; (editor with Lewis Chase) *The Best of Swinburne,* Thomas Nelson, 1937; (editor with J. E. Hankins) *Selected Nineteenth Century Essays,* F. S. Crofts, 1938; (compiler) *A Concordance to the Poems o9 A. E. Housman,* privately printed, 1940, reprinted, Peter Smith, 1966; (compiler with W. D. Paden) *A Concordance to the Poems of Oliver Goldsmith,* privately printed, 1940, reprinted, Peter Smith, 1966; *Snow of Kansas: The Life of Francis Huntington Snow,* University of Kansas Press, 1953; *George Lyman Kittredge: Teacher and Scholar,* University of Kansas Press, 1962; (editor) *Swinburne Replies,* Syracuse University Press, 1966; (editor) *Swinburne: The Critical Heritage,* Routledge & Kegan Paul, 1970; *Swinburne as Critic,* Routledge & Kegan Paul, 1972. Contributor to *Collier's Encyclopedia* and to various periodicals.

SIDELIGHTS: Clyde Hyder has traveled in England, France, Italy, Switzerland, Australia, Canada, Mexico, and most states of the United States. His special interests include English and American history and folklore.

* * *

HYERS, M. Conrad 1933-

PERSONAL: Born July 31, 1933, in Philadelphia, Pa.; son of A. Melvin (a minister) and Miriam (Soper) Hyers; married Gerry Ort (a teacher), September 6, 1955; children: Jon, Dean, Lauri. *Education:* Carson-Newman College, B.A., 1954; Eastern Baptist Theological Seminary, B.D., 1958; Princeton Theological Seminary, Th.M., 1959, Ph.D., 1965; University of Hawaii, postdoctoral study, 1970. *Home:* Scandia Heights, R.R. 1, St. Peter, Minn. 56082. *Office:* Department of Religion, Gustavus Adolphus College, St. Peter, Minn. 56082.

CAREER: Ordained American Baptist minister, 1960; Beloit College, Beloit, Wis., instructor, 1965-67, assistant professor, 1967-69, associate professor of comparative mythology and history of religions, 1969-77; Gustavus Adolphus College, St. Peter, Minn., associate professor, 1977—. *Member:* American Academy of Religion, Society for the Scientific Study of Religion. *Awards, honors:* Younger humanist fellow, National Endowment for the Humanities, 1970-71.

WRITINGS: (Editor) *Holy Laughter: Essays on Religion in the Comic Perspective,* Seabury, 1969; *Zen and the Comic Spirit,* Westminster, 1974; *The Chickadees: A Contemporary Fable,* Westminster, 1974. Contributor to theology and philosophy journals.

WORK IN PROGRESS: Prophet and Mystic: The Perennial Dialectic; The Mythology of Comedy.

* * *

IDUARTE (Foucher), Andres 1907-

PERSONAL: Born May 1, 1907, in Villahermosa, Tabasco, Mexico; son of Andres (a professor and chief justice) and Adela Foucher Iduarte; married Graciela Frias-Amescua, May 21, 1932. *Education:* National University of Mexico, B.S. & L., 1925, Licenciado en Derecho, 1933; attended University of Paris and studied at Musee de Louvre, 1928-30; Central University of Madrid, LL.D., 1935; Columbia University, D.Phil., 1944.

CAREER: National University of Mexico, Mexico City, professor of history, member of University Council, 1930-32; Ateneo Cientifico y Literario, Ibero-American Section, Madrid, first secretary, 1933-36; Columbia University, New York City, instructor in Spanish, 1939-45, assistant professor, 1945-50, associate professor, 1950-60, professor of Spanish-American literature, 1960-72, acting director, Hispanic Institute, 1949-50. Director-general, National Institute of Fine Arts, Mexico City, Mexico, 1952-54; cultural advisor for Government of Mexico, New York City, 1947-70. Visiting professor at American and Latin American universities, 1946-72. Member, Committee for Romulo Gallegos International Novel Contest, 1967.

MEMBER: Instituto International de Literatura Iberoamericana (president, 1957-59), Cuban Academy of History (elected, 1946—), Mexican Academy of International Law, Academy of the Spanish Language (Mexican branch), Societe Europeene de Culture (Venice), Hispanic Institute (Columbia University). *Awards, honors:* First prize in *Revista de Revistas* short novel contest, 1928, for *El Himno a la sangre;* first prize in Universidad Nacional Autonoma de Mexico contest, 1931, for essay "El Liberatador Simon Bolivar"; *Letras de Mexico* award for best book of 1945, Order of Cespedes (Cuba), 1946, and Cuban Government award for best essay on Marti, 1955, all for *Marti, escritor;* Doctor Honoris Causa, University of San Nicolas de Hidalgo, Mexico, 1953; Commander Order of the British Empire, 1954.

WRITINGS: (Contributor) *Homenaje a Bolivar en el Primer centenario,* Senoria de Relaciones Exteriores (Mexico), 1931; *El Caballero Maton* (novel), Imprenta Mundial (Mexico), 1932; *El Problema moral de la juventud mexicana,* Grupo Unificacion (Mexico), 1932; *Marti, escritor* (essay), Cuadernos Americanos (Mexico), 1945, 2nd edition, Ministerio de Educacion (Havana), 1951; *En torno a Gabriela Mistral,* Cuadernos Americanos, 1946; (editor with James F. Shearer) *Sarmiento! a traves de sus mejores paginas,* Dryden, 1949.

(Compiler and author of prologue and notes) Jose Marti, *Prosas,* Union Panamericana (Washington D.C.), 1950; *Platicas hispanoamericanas,* Fondo de Cultura Economica (Mexico), 1951; *Un Nino en la Revolucion Mexicana* (novel; originally announced as "Tabasco: Un Nino en la Revolucion Mexicana"; one chapter, "El Mundo primero," first published in *Hora de Espana,* December, 1937), Ruta (Mexico), 1951, 2nd edition, Obregon (Mexico), 1954, translation and adaptation by James F. Shearer published as *Nino: Child of the Mexican Revolution,* Praeger, 1971; *Veinte anos con Romulo Gallegos,* Ediciones Humanismo (Mexico), 1954, 2nd edition published as *Con Romulo Gallegos,* Avila (Caracas), 1969; *La Isla sin veneno,* Universidad de Oriente (Santiago de Cuba), 1954; *Sarmiento, Marti y Rodo,* Academia de la Historia de Cuba (Havana), 1955; *Elogio de Mexico,* [New York], 1956; *Alfonso Reyes: El Hombre y su mundo* (originally published in *Revista Hispanica Moderna,* July-October, 1956), Hispanic Institute, Columbia University, 1956; (author of prologue) Eugenio Florit, *Antologia poetica,* Ediciones de Andrea (Mexico), 1956; *Gabriela Mistral, santa a la jineta,* Cuadernos Americanos, 1958.

Martin Luis Guzman en sus libros (essay; published in *Obras Completas de Martin Luis Guzman*), Compania General de Ediciones (Mexico), 1961; *Don Pedro de Alba y su tiempo,* Editorial Cultura (Mexico), 1962; *Homenaje a Cuauhtemoc,* [Mexico], 1963; *Mexico en la nostalgia,* Editorial Cultura, 1965; *Tres escritores mexicanos,* Editorial Cultura, 1967; *Juarez: Maximo simbolo,* Secretaria de Hacienda (Mexico), 1967; *El Mundo sonriente* (novel; sequel to *Un Nino en la Revolucion Mexicana*), Fondo de Cultura Economica, 1968; *Diez estampas mexicanas,* Secretaria de Hacienda y Credito Publico, 1971; *Lunes de El National,* foreword by Andres Henestrosa, Secretary of Public Education (Mexico), 1975. Also author of a short novel, *El Himno a la sangre,* first published in *Revista de Revistas,* March, 1928. Contributor of essays and articles to Mexican, Spanish, and American periodicals. Editor, *Universidad de Mexico,* 1930-32.

WORK IN PROGRESS: Several books: *Otra vez Paris* and *Bajo el sol del diablo* (sequels to *El Mundo sonriente*), *En el fuego de Espana, Preparatoria,* 3rd edition of *Marti, escritor,* and a collection of articles which appeared in the press, entitled *Familia y patria;* writing on the Latin American essay, the political Mexican essay; research on Louisiana and the Yucatan.

SIDELIGHTS: Andres Iduarte has traveled extensively throughout Europe, Latin America, and the United States. He is fluent in French, Italian, and Portuguese, as well as Spanish and English. Iduarte is currently living in Mexico. *Avocational Interests:* Horseback riding, swimming, and rowing.

BIOGRAPHICAL/CRITICAL SOURCES: El Universal, June 23, 1945, May 20, 1968; *Letras de Mexico,* September 15, 1946; *El Nacional* (Mexico), December 9, 1951; *Revista Hispanica Moderna* (New York), Numbers 1-2, 1954; *Books Abroad,* November, 1955; Enrique Anderson Imbert and Eugenio Florit, *Literatura hispanoamericana,* Holt, 1960; Carlos J. Sierra, *Hemerografia de Andres Iduarte Foucher,* Boletin Bibliografico de la Secretaria de Hacienda (Mexico), 1965; *Excelsior: Diorama de la Cultura,* October 17, 1967, May 3, 1968, August 11, 1968, September 22, 1968; *El Dia: El Gallo Ilustrado,* May 19, 1968; *La Gaceta* (Fondo de Cultura), June, 1968; *New Yorker,* July 17, 1971.†

* * *

IHDE, Don 1934-

PERSONAL: Born January 14, 1934. *Education:* University of Kansas, B.A., 1956; Andover Newton Theological School, M.Div., 1959; Boston University, Ph.D., 1964. *Office:* Department of Philosophy, State University of New York, Stony Brook, N.Y. 11790.

CAREER: Southern Illinois University at Carbondale, assistant professor, 1964-67, associate professor of philosophy, 1968-69; State University of New York at Stony Brook, associate professor, 1969-71, professor of philosophy, 1971—.

WRITINGS: Hermeneutic Phenomenology, Northwestern University Press, 1971; *Listening and Voice,* Ohio University Press, 1976.

WORK IN PROGRESS: A philosophy of technology.

BIOGRAPHICAL/CRITICAL SOURCES: Philosophy Today, winter, 1971-72.

* * *

IHNAT, Steve 1935(?)-1972

1935(?)—May 12, 1972; Canadian film actor, director, and screenwriter. Obituaries: *New York Times,* May 20, 1972; *Washington Post,* May 20, 1972.

* * *

INADA, Lawson Fusao 1938-

PERSONAL: Born May 26, 1938, in Fresno, Calif.; son of Fusaji and Masako (Saito) Inada; married Janet Francis, February 19, 1962; children: Miles Fusao, Lowell Masao. *Education:* Attended University of California, Berkeley, 1956-57; Fresno State College (now California State University, Fresno), B.A., 1959; University of Iowa, graduate study, 1960-62; University of Oregon, M.F.A., 1966. *Home:* 2320 Morada Lane, Ashland, Ore. 97520. *Office:* Department of English, Southern Oregon State College, Ashland, Ore. 97520.

CAREER: University of New Hampshire, Durham, instructor in English, 1962-65; Southern Oregon State College, Ashland, associate professor, 1966-77, professor of English, 1977—. Director of Students of Other Cultures project, 1970-72, and Combined Asian-American Resources project, 1971—. Visiting lecturer at Lewis and Clark College, 1969, and University of Hawaii, 1978. Host of radio program, "Talk Story: The Written Word," on KSOR-FM, Ashland, Ore. Seminar leader at various poetry and creative writing workshops, including Asian-Americans for a Fair Media Conference, 1975, Siskiyou Writers Conference, 1977, and Iowa State Department of Education Conference, 1978. Judge, Coordinating Council of Literary Magazines College Contest, 1976. Has given readings of his poetry at numerous universities and seminars, including University of California, Berkeley, University of California, Los Angeles, University of Michigan, University of Oregon, San Francisco State University, University of Washington, Oregon Poetry-in-the-Schools, Minnesota Poetry-in-the-Schools, Seattle Arts Commission Festival, and National Poetry Festival. Lecturer on Asian-American literature to community groups and scholarly conferences. Consultant to many literary organizations, including Third World Writers Festival, Central Washington State College, 1974, Society for the Study of Multi-Ethnic Literature of the United States, 1977, and Asian-American Writers Conference, 1978.

MEMBER: Japanese American Citizens League. *Awards, honors:* University of Iowa Writers Workshop fellowship, 1960-62; National Endowment for the Arts Creative Writing fellowship, 1972; Pioneer Writers Award from Asian-American Writers Conference, 1975.

WRITINGS: Three Northwest Poets: Drake, Inada, Lawder, Quixote Press, 1970; *Before the War: Poems As They Happen,* Morrow, 1971; (editor) *Aiiieeeee!: An Anthology of Asian-American Writers,* Howard University Press, 1974.

Poetry represented in numerous anthologies, including *Down At the Santa Fe Depot: Twenty Fresno Poets,* David Kherdian, editor, Giligia Press, 1970, *The Modern Idiom,* Lio Hamalian, editor, Crowell, 1972, *Settling America,* David Kherdian, editor, Macmillan, 1974, *Modern Poetry of Western America,* William Stafford, editor, Brigham Young University Press, 1975, and *Focus on Forms,* Philip J. McFarland, editor, Houghton, 1977.

Contributor of poetry to many periodicals, including *Amerasia Journal, Bridge, Carleton Miscellany, Chicago Review, Evergreen Review, Kayak, Massachusetts Review, Mother Jones, Northwest Review, San Francisco Review,* and *Southwest Review.* Member of editorial boards, *Directory of American Poets* and *Directory of American Fiction Writers,* 1976—; member of editorial board, Associated Writing Programs, *Contemporary Poetry,* 1977—. Assistant editor, *Northwest Review,* 1965-66; editor, *Rogue River Gorge,* 1970—; contributing editor, *Dues: Third World Writing,* 1972-74; guest editor, *Hawaii Review,* summer, 1978.

WORK IN PROGRESS: The Buddha Bandits on the Tokaido 99: Hongo, Inada, Lau, a book of poetry.

SIDELIGHTS: Lawson Inada told *CA:* "There are a lot of foolish categories, a lot of important terms; somehow, we've got to see our way through, respecting differences and recognizing similarities. Put it this way: I am a man trying to do right by my word."

*   *   *

INDIK, Bernard P(aul) 1932-

PERSONAL: Born April 30, 1932, in Philadelphia, Pa.; son of J. Joseph (a sales agent) and Ida (Kaplan) Indik; married Harriet S. Simberloff (a teacher), June 26, 1955; children: Joyce Janet, Martin Karl, Jay Joseph, Debra Ruth, William Aaron. *Education:* University of Pennsylvania, B.S., 1954, M.B.A., 1955; University of Michigan, A.M., 1959, Ph.D., 1961. *Home:* 32 Kendall Rd., Kendall Park, N.J. 08824. *Office:* Graduate School of Social Work, Rutgers University, New Brunswick, N.J. 08903.

CAREER: Textured Yarn Co., Philadelphia, Pa., assistant plant manager, 1955; University of Michigan, Ann Arbor, assistant study director and study director in Survey Research Center, 1957-61; Rutgers University, New Brunswick, N.J., assistant research specialist, 1961-65, associate research specialist, 1965-68, associate professor, 1968-69, professor of social work, 1969—. Trustee, South Brunswick Township Library Board, 1967-70; member, South Brunswick Planning Board, 1976—. Consultant, New Jersey Department of Labor and Industry, 1963-65, 1975-76. *Military service:* U.S. Army, Medical Corps, 1955-57. *Member:* American Psychological Association (fellow), American Academy of Political and Social Science, Council on Social Work Education, Society for General Systems Research, Society for the Psychological Study of Social Issues (fellow), Eastern Psychological Association.

WRITINGS: (Editor with F. K. Berrien) *People, Groups, and Organizations,* Teachers College Press, 1968; (with George Sternlieb) *Ecology of Welfare,* Transaction Press, 1973.

Monographs include: (With Basil S. Georgopoulos and Stanley E. Seashire) *Some Models of Organizational Effectiveness,* Institute for Social Research, University of Michigan, 1960; (with B. G. Becker and A. M. Beeuwkes) *Dietary Intake Methodologies: A Review,* Institute for Social Research, University of Michigan, 1960; *Three Studies on Organizational and Individual Dimensions of Organizations,* Rutgers University, 1965; (with others) *The Mediator: Background, Self Image and Attitudes,* Institute of Management and Labor Relations, Rutgers University, 1966; *The Motivation to Work,* Institute of Management and Labor Relations, Rutgers University, 1966; (with Jack Chernick and Roger Craig) *The Selection of Trainees under M.D.T.A.,* Institute of Management and Labor Relations, Rutgers University, 1966; (with R. Beauregard) *Labor Market Planning to Serve the Developmentally Disabled,* Rutgers University, 1976. Contributor of chapters to seven books. Contributor of about thirty articles and reviews to journals.

WORK IN PROGRESS: Making Social Welfare Organizations Work Effectively: A Text.

SIDELIGHTS: Bernard P. Indik told *CA:* "What a teacher and researcher should do is find out what it is useful to know and present it in a manner that can be understood and used. Writing in technical jargon is useless unless the writer clearly presents and uses definitions and has something worth saying."

*   *   *

INGARD, K(arl) Uno 1921-

PERSONAL: Born February 24, 1921, in Gothenburg, Sweden; naturalized U.S. citizen; son of Carl and Anna (Nilsson) Ingard; married Doris Karlsson, 1948; children: John, Sven, Marianne, Karl. *Education:* Chalmers Institute of Technology (now Chalmers University of Technology), Gothenburg, E.E., 1944, Technical Licentiate, 1948; Massachusetts Institute of Technology, Ph.D., 1950. *Home:* Kittery Point, Me. 03905. *Office:* Gas Turbine Lab 31-264, Massachusetts Institute of Technology, Cambridge, Mass. 02139.

CAREER: Technical Gymnasium, Sweden, lecturer in electrical engineering, 1943-45; Technical Institute, Sweden, lecturer in mathematics, 1945-46; Chalmers Institute of Technology (now Chalmers University of Technology), Gothenburg, Sweden, lecturer in acoustics and director of acoustics laboratory, 1946-48; Massachusetts Institute of Technology, Cambridge, assistant professor, 1952-56, associate professor, 1956-66, professor of physics, 1966—, professor of aeronautics and astronautics, 1971—. Research engineer, National Laboratory for Defense, Stockholm, 1945-46.

MEMBER: Acoustical Society of America (fellow; member of executive council, 1970—), American Physical Society (fellow), American Association of Physics Teachers, Sigma Xi. *Awards, honors:* Biennial Award of Acoustical Society of America, 1954; Guggenheim fellowship, 1960; Gustaf Dalen Medal for contribution to physical acoustics, 1970.

WRITINGS: (With William L. Kraushaar) *Introduction to Mechanics, Matter and Waves,* Addison-Wesley, 1960; (with Philip M. Morse) *Theoretical Acoustics,* McGraw, 1968; (editor with Herman Feshbach) *In Honor of Philip M. Morse,* M.I.T. Press, 1969.

Contributor: Cyril M. Harris, editor, *Handbook of Noise Control,* McGraw, 1957; E. U. Condon and Hugh Odishaw, editors, *Handbook of Physics,* McGraw, 1958, 2nd edition, 1967; Siegfried Flugge, editor, *Handbuch der Physik,* Springer-Verlag, 1961. Contributor of more than thirty articles to physics and acoustical journals and to *Nature.*

*   *   *

INGRAHAM, Vernon L. 1924-

PERSONAL: Born October 1, 1924, in Milford, N.H.; son of Clayton Russell (a machinist) and Eva (Mason) Ingraham; married Marcia Burd (an artist), June 16, 1960 (divorced, 1975); children: Christopher, David, Jason. *Education:* University of New Hampshire, B.A., 1949; Amherst College, M.A., 1951; University of Pennsylvania, Ph.D., 1965. *Home:* 78 Pleasant St., Marion, Mass. 02738. *Office:* Department of English, Southeastern Massachusetts University, North Dartmouth, Mass. 02747.

CAREER: Dean Junior College, Franklin, Mass., instructor in English, 1953-58; University of Delaware, Newark, instructor in English, 1960-62; Haverford College, Haverford, Pa., instructor in English, 1962-63; Gettysburg College, Gettysburg, Pa., instructor in English, 1963-65; Southeastern Massachusetts University, North Dartmouth, assistant professor, 1965-67, associate professor, 1967-71, professor of English, 1971—, chairman of department, 1968-72. *Military service:* U.S. Army, 1943-46; became sergeant; received Bronze Star Medal, Purple Heart, and Combat Infantry Badge. *Member:* Modern Language Association of America, American Association of University Professors.

WRITINGS: (Editor) *Survival: Readings on Environment,* Holbrook, 1971. Literary editor, G. & C. Merriam Co., 1951-53.

WORK IN PROGRESS: Death and Dying in Literature.

*   *   *

INGRAMS, Doreen 1906-

PERSONAL: Born January 24, 1906, in London, England; daughter of Edward (a member of Parliament and privy councillor) and Isabella (Scott) Shortt; married Harold Ingrams (a political officer with service in Arabia), June 3, 1930; children: two daughters. *Education:* Privately educated in London, England, and in Switzerland. *Home:* 3 Westfield House, Tenterden, Kent, England.

CAREER: British Broadcasting Corp., London, England, senior assistant in Arabic Service, 1956-68. Lecturer for Central Office of Information. Member of executive committee, Council for the Advancement of Arab-British Understanding. *Member:* United Nations Association (vice-chairman of Tenterden branch). *Awards, honors:* Co-winner with her husband of Founders Medal of Royal Geographical Society and of Lawrence of Arabia Medal of Royal Central Asian Society.

WRITINGS: A Survey of Social and Economic Conditions in the Aden Protectorate, H.M.S.O., 1949; *A Time in Arabia,* J. Murray, 1970; *Palestine Papers 1917-1922: Seeds of Conflict,* J. Murray, 1972; *The Arab World* (booklets and film strip), EMC Corp., 1974. Contributor to *Middle East Handbook,* 1971, and to *Gulf Handbook,* 1976-77.

BIOGRAPHICAL/CRITICAL SOURCES: Listener, December 31, 1970.

*   *   *

IPSEN, D(avid) C(arl) 1921-

PERSONAL: Born February 15, 1921, in Schenectady, N.Y.; son of Carl L. (an engineer) and Miriam (Grover) Ipsen; married Heather Zoccola (an elementary teacher), August 28, 1949; children: Carl David, Eric Mark. *Education:* University of Michigan, B.S.E., 1942; University of California, Ph.D., 1953. *Home:* 655 Vistamont Ave., Berkeley, Calif. 94708.

CAREER: General Electric Co., engineer at plants in Schenectady, N.Y., and Lynn, Mass., 1942-49; University of California, Berkeley, lecturer, 1950-53, assistant professor of mechanical engineering, 1953-57, assistant director of elementary school science project, 1959-66, consultant to biomedical curriculum project, 1970-75.

WRITINGS: Units, Dimensions, and Dimensionless Numbers, McGraw, 1960.

Juvenile books; all published by Addison-Wesley: *The Riddle of the Stegosaurus,* 1969; *Rattlesnakes and Scientists,* 1970; *What Does a Bee See?,* 1971; *The Elusive Zebra,* 1971; *Eye of the Whirlwind: The Story of John Scopes,* 1973.

*   *   *

IRVINE, Demar (Buel) 1908-

PERSONAL: Born May 25, 1908, in Modesto, Calif.; married Greta Eickenscheidt, June 12, 1934. *Education:* Attended University of California, Los Angeles, 1925-27; University of California, Berkeley, B.A., 1929, M.A., 1931; private study of music in Paris, Berlin, and Vienna, 1931-34; Harvard University, Ph.D., 1937. *Home:* 4904 Northeast 60th St., Seattle, Wash. 98115. *Office:* School of Music, University of Washington, Seattle, Wash. 98195.

CAREER: Substitute teacher of music in Potsdam, N.Y., 1935-36; American International College, Springfield, Mass., music director, 1936-37; University of Washington, Seattle, instructor, 1937-38, assistant professor, 1938-47, associate professor, 1947-60, professor of musicology, 1960—, acting director of School of Music, 1959, 1962-63. *Member:* American Musicological Society. *Awards, honors:* George Ladd Prix de Paris, 1931.

WRITINGS: Writing about Music: A Style Book for Reports and Theses, University of Washington Press, 1956, 2nd edition, revised and enlarged, 1969; (editor) Hans Moldenhauer, *Anton von Webern: Perspectives,* University of Washington Press, 1966. Also author of *Jules Massenet: A Chronicle of His Life and Times,* 1974.

IRWIN, Vera Rushforth 1913-

PERSONAL: Born November 4, 1913, in Yonkers, N.Y.; daughter of Robert Roy (a teacher) and Elizabeth K. (Streb) Rushforth; married William M. Irwin (an electrician), August 11, 1951. *Education:* Attended State Normal School (now State University of New York College at New Paltz), 1930-33; New York University, B.A., 1937, M.A., 1947; graduate study at University of Colorado, 1940, Columbia University, 1942, Institute of Advanced Studies in Theatre Arts, 1955-65. *Home:* 51 Elting Ave., New Paltz, N.Y. 12561. *Office:* Department of Theater Arts, State University of New York College, New Paltz, N.Y. 12561.

CAREER: Carmel High School, Carmel, N.Y., teacher, 1933-37; Croton-Harmon High School, Croton-on-Hudson, N.Y., director and English teacher, 1937-47; State University of New York College at New Paltz, assistant professor, 1947-49, associate professor and director of drama, 1949-69, professor of theatre arts and dramatic literature and chairman of department of theatre arts, 1969—. *Member:* American Association of University Professors, American Society for Theatre Research, American Theatre Association. *Awards, honors:* Ford fellowship, 1955-56; Institute for Advanced Study in Theatre Arts scholarship, 1962; Outstanding Alumni award, State University of New York College at New Paltz, 1969.

WRITINGS: (Editor) *Four Classical Asian Plays,* Penguin, 1972.

WORK IN PROGRESS: Outstanding Women in Today's American Theatre.

SIDELIGHTS: Vera Irwin has traveled in U.S., Canada, Mexico, England, Scotland, Wales, France, Italy, Germany, and Switzerland.

*   *   *

ISAAC, Stephen 1925-

PERSONAL: Born January 11, 1925, in Medford, Ore.; son of Clayton Harrison and Alice (Palmer) Isaac; married Phyllis Jean Day, June 20, 1953; children: Kent, Merrily, Felice, Blake. *Education:* University of California, Berkeley, B.A., 1951; Claremont Graduate School, M.A., 1953, Ph.D., 1963. *Religion:* Protestant. *Home address:* Route 5, Box 206, Escondido, Calif. 92025. *Office:* San Diego City Schools, 4100 Normal St., San Diego, Calif. 92103.

CAREER: Teacher of special education in Ontario, Calif., 1953-55; Orange Coast College District, Costa Mesa, Calif., instructor, testing coordinator, and counselor, 1955-59; System Development Corp., Santa Monica, Calif., training consultant in computer systems, operations analyst, research specialist, human factors scientist, 1959-65; Department of Education, San Diego County, San Diego, Calif., guidance coordinator, 1965-73; San Diego City Schools, San Diego, director of evaluation services, 1973—. Evening instructor in adult education, San Bernardino Valley College, 1961-63; lecturer in group dynamics and counseling, Extension Division, University of California, Los Angeles, 1963-64; assistant professor of quantitative methods, San Fernando Valley State College, 1964-65; lecturer in educational psychology and research methods, University of San Diego, 1965-68. Questhaven Retreat, Escondido, Calif., minister, 1953—, vice-president of board of directors, 1959—. Consulting psychologist, Children's Medical Group, Escondido, Calif., 1966—. *Military service:* U.S. Army, 1943-46; served in European and Pacific theaters. *Member:* American Psychological Association, Western Psychological Association, California Educational Research Association.

WRITINGS: (With William B. Michael) *Handbook in Research and Evaluation,* Robert R. Knapp, 1971; *Songs from the House of Pilgrimage,* Branden Press, 1971; *The Way of Discipleship to Christ,* Christward Ministry Press, 1976.

WORK IN PROGRESS: Research on the usefulness and validity of the Jungian Type theory to illuminate the problem of individual differences as they interact with educational programs and teacher approaches, with a book expected to result; studying higher states of consciousness and personal growth, with a series of books anticipated.

AVOCATIONAL INTERESTS: Christian mysticism and the experience of higher states of consciousness; New World archaeology, writing, travel, wilderness preservation.

*   *   *

ISENBERG, Seymour 1930-

PERSONAL: Born September 10, 1930; son of Harry (a dentist) and Mildred (Shield) Isenberg; married Anita De Moncada (a stained glass artist), December 20, 1958; children: Arthur. *Education:* Syracuse University, A.B., 1951; Columbia University, graduate student, 1951-53; Kansas City College of Osteopathy, D.O., 1957. *Religion:* Jewish. *Home:* 8 Frasco Lane, Norwood, N.J. 07648.

CAREER: Has worked as a printer, photographer, musician, surgeon, and stained glass artist; private practice of osteopathy in Northvale, N.J., and obesity control in Teaneck, N.J., 1959—.

WRITINGS: (Ghostwriter) Eugene F. DiPaola, *How to Multiply Your Real Estate Sales,* Prentice-Hall, 1963.

With wife, Anita Isenberg; all published by Chilton: *Start Off in Stained Glass,* 1972; *How to Work in Stained Glass,* 1972; *Stained Glass Lamps,* 1973; *Stained Glass: Advanced Projects and Techniques,* 1974.

With L. M. Elting; all published by St. Martin's: *You Can Be Fat-Free Forever,* 1973; *The Consumer's Guide to Successful Surgery,* 1976; *The Nine-Day Super Diet,* 1978. Contributor of articles to *Creative Crafts, Defenders of Wildlife, Medical Times, Medical Economics, Medical Opinion and Review, Osteopathic Physician, Leonardo,* and of fiction to *Diagnostica.* Editor, *Glass Workshop Magazine.*

WORK IN PROGRESS: Painting On Glass and *Beginner's Guide to Stained Glass,* with A. Isenberg; *Emergency Exit,* a hospital mystery novel.

SIDELIGHTS: Seymour Isenberg told *CA* that he has been writing since the age of eleven and has "enough unpublished ephemera to stuff the corners of the draftiest house; mostly fiction. I prefer to write fiction but it is my nonfiction that mostly gets published, probably because it is tailored to specific markets and my fiction is tailored only to myself. But then, I don't buy it either. I started to write because I was reading so many things I felt needed improving; once I had it down on paper I found it was my own stuff that *really* needed improving. That's never changed. I suppose each new book is an attempt to improve upon the last, whatever the subject matter. It's an attempt that, for me, is inevitably self-defeating. Long ago I gave up reading anything of my own once it was in print; it's an experience similar to skating on thin ice. You keep going through the holes.

"When my first book came out, I wanted to buy up all the copies and re-write the whole thing; the same with my first book on stained glass—which is now somewhere in the neighborhood of 70,000 copies, a number too awesome for mere caprice to mess with. Perhaps the answer is to write fast and write a lot, which I do, and hope someday you'll even write well. I have a feeling I could do this if I learned to type properly. Perhaps this is the reason I never learned to type properly. I'd hate to challenge the assumption on which my ego seems to rest."

AVOCATIONAL INTERESTS: Travel, especially the South Seas and the Mediterranean where he has taught stained glass work.

*   *   *

ITZKOFF, Seymour W(illiam) 1928-

PERSONAL: Born July 22, 1928, in Brooklyn, N.Y.; son of Jacob J. (operator of a small business) and Rose (Pekar) Itzkoff; married Patricia Stroman (a violinist and teacher of violin), September 7, 1954; children: Julia Louise, Gerald Hill. *Education:* University of Hartford, B.A., 1950; Columbia University, M.A., 1956, Ed.D., 1965. *Religion:* Jewish. *Home:* 57 Dryads Green, Northampton, Mass. 01060. *Office:* Department of Education, Smith College, Northampton, Mass. 01060.

CAREER: Hartford Symphony Orchestra, Hartford, Conn., cellist, 1948-50; elementary and secondary teacher in schools of Suffolk County, N.Y., 1955-60; Hunter College of the City University of New York, New York, N.Y., lecturer in education, 1960-65; Smith College, Northampton, Mass., assistant professor, 1965-70, associate professor, 1970-75, professor of education, 1975—. Cellist in string quartet. *Military service:* U.S. Army Symphony Orchestra, cellist, 1950-53; became staff sergeant.

WRITINGS: Cultural Pluralism and American Education, Crowell, 1969; *Ernst Cassirer: Scientific Knowledge and the Concept of Man,* University of Notre Dame Press, 1971; *New Public Education,* McKay, 1976; *Ernst Cassirer: Philosopher of Culture,* G. K. Hall, 1977. Also author of scripts for radio. Contributor of articles to professional journals.

*   *   *

JACKSON, Mahalia 1901-1972

October 26, 1901—January 27, 1972; American gospel singer. Obituaries: *New York Times,* January 28, 1972; *Washington Post,* January 28, 1972; *L'Express,* January 31-February 6, 1972; *Time,* February 7, 1972; *Current Biography,* March, 1972.

*   *   *

JACKSON, S. Wesley 1936-

PERSONAL: Born June 15, 1936, in Topeka, Kan.; son of Howard Taylor and Nettie (Stover) Jackson; married Dana Lee Percival, December 22, 1957; children: Laura, Scott, Sara. *Education:* Kansas Wesleyan University, B.A., 1958; University of Kansas, M.A., 1960; North Carolina State University, Ph.D., 1967. *Home and office:* R.R. 3, Salina, Kan.

CAREER: Kansas Wesleyan University, Salina, instructor, then assistant professor, 1962-67, associate professor of biology, 1967-71; California State University, Sacramento, associate professor and chairman of environmental studies, 1971-76; The Land Institute, Salina, Kan., director, 1976—. *Member:* Botanical Society of America, Genetics Society of America, American Institute of Biological Sciences, American Association for the Advancement of Science, International Association of Plant Taxonomy, Wilderness Society, Kansas Academy of Science (chairman of conservation committee).

WRITINGS: Man and the Environment, W. C. Brown, 1971. Contributor to journals.

WORK IN PROGRESS: A book, *Planning for Survival;* revised edition of *Man and the Environment.*

AVOCATIONAL INTERESTS: Travel, carpentry, welding, gardening.

*   *   *

JACOBSEN, Josephine 1908-

PERSONAL: Born August 19, 1908, in Cobourg, Ontario, Canada; daughter of Joseph Edward (a doctor) and Octavia (Winder) Boylan; married Eric Jacobsen, March 17, 1932; children: Erlend Ericsen. *Education:* Educated by private tutors and at Roland Park Country School, 1915-18. *Politics:* Democrat. *Religion:* Roman Catholic. *Home:* 220 Stony Ford Rd., Baltimore, Md. 21210. *Agent:* McIntosh & Otis, 475 Fifth Ave., New York, N.Y. 10017. *Office:* Poetry Office, Library of Congress, Washington, D.C. 20540.

CAREER: Library of Congress, Washington, D.C., poetry consultant, 1971-73, honorary consultant in American letters, 1973—. *Member:* Baltimore Citizens' Planning and Housing Association, Baltimore Center Stage Association, Baltimore Museum of Art, Walters Art Gallery, Hamilton Street Club. *Awards, honors: The Shade-Seller* was nominated for a National Book Award.

WRITINGS—Poetry, except as indicated: *For the Unlost,* Contemporary Poetry, 1946; *The Human Climate,* Contemporary Poetry, 1953; (with William R. Mueller) *The Testament of Samuel Beckett* (dramatic criticism), Hill & Wang, 1964; *The Animal Inside,* Ohio University Press, 1966; (with Mueller) *Ionesco and Genet, Playwrights of Silence* (dramatic criticism), Hill & Wang, 1968; *The Instant of Knowing,* Library of Congress, 1974; *The Shade-Seller: New and Selected Poems,* Doubleday, 1974; *One Poet's Poetry,* Agnes Scott College, 1975. Work represented in anthologies, including *Best American Short Stories,* 1966, *O. Henry Prize Stories,* 1967, 1971, 1973, and 1976, and *Fifty Years of the American Short Story,* 1970, as well as in poetry collections.

WORK IN PROGRESS: A new collection of poems; *A Walk with Raschid,* a collection of short stories.

SIDELIGHTS: Josephine Jacobsen is "extremely interested" in the theatre, and has acted with the Vagabond Players in Baltimore. Equally interested in travel, she has visited Mexico, Guatemala, Venezuela, the Caribbean Islands, France, Italy, Greece, Morocco, Kenya, Tanzania, Portugal, Madeira, Spain, and Canada.

*   *   *

JACOBUS, Elaine Wegener 1908-

PERSONAL: Surname is pronounced Ja-*co*-bus; born September 2, 1908, in St. Louis, Mo.; daughter of Albert Benjamin (a professor of physical education) and Helen (DuBois) Wegener; married Everett Franklin Jacobus (an office manager), November 16, 1935; children: Everett Franklin, Jr., Jay Albert. *Education:* Attended Elmira College, 1926-27; Beaver College, A.B., 1929. *Politics:* Republican. *Religion:* United Methodist. *Home:* 427 Circlewood Dr., Venice, Fla. 33595.

CAREER: Kindergarten teacher in public schools in Caldwell, N.J., 1929-32, Cheltenham Township, Pa., 1932-41, and Florham Park, N.J., beginning 1952. *Member:* National Education Association, Association of Kindergarten Educators, American Association of University Women (membership chairman, 1962-64), New Jersey Education Association, Morris County (N.J.) Association of Kindergarten Educators (treasurer, 1967-72), Morris County Educators, Audio-Visual Association.

WRITINGS: (Contributor) Jerome Edward Leavitt, editor, *Readings in Elementary Education,* W. C. Brown, 1961; *The World of Kindergarten: A Way to Reading,* Macmillan, 1971. Contributor to *Grade Teacher, Instructor,* and other professional journals.

WORK IN PROGRESS: Barney's Gull, Sherm Does His Share, and *Too Many Teeth,* all juvenile books.

SIDELIGHTS: Elaine Wegener Jacobus told *CA* that she was "fortunate enough to come from a read-aloud family with a father who wrote and illustrated three books on athletics. I was urged to 'write it down; send it in.' Our table conversation was never personalities, but rather ideas, thoughts, and reports of what we had read. I write when an idea strikes me, and have no admirable writing habits.

"The purpose of writing my kindergarten text was to help and encourage young teachers with suggestions gleaned from 32 years of teaching the delightful five-year-old child. Many of the chapters were published in educational periodicals, but were cut and changed to fit the compact space allotted in this paperback.... The stories I am writing now are perhaps too long for the 1,000 word tops in children's periodicals, but I keep trying."

AVOCATIONAL INTERESTS: Travel, sewing, knitting and tatting, painting, social dancing, shell crafts, stamps.

*   *   *

JACOBUS, Lee A.   1935-

PERSONAL: Born August 20, 1935, in Orange, N.J.; son of Ernest W. and Julia R. (Byrne) Jacobus; married Joanna J. Miller (a teacher of modern dance), April 5, 1958; children: Sharon Grania, James Diarmuid. *Education:* Brown University, A.B., 1957, A.M., 1959; Claremont University Center (now Claremont Graduate School), Ph.D., 1968. *Home:* 111 River Rd., Mansfield Center, Conn. 06250. *Office:* Department of English, University of Connecticut, U-25, Storrs, Conn. 06268.

CAREER: Mary C. Wheeler School, Providence, R.I., teacher of English, 1959-60; Western Connecticut State College, Danbury, instructor in English, 1960-66; University of Connecticut, Storrs, assistant professor, 1968-71, associate professor, 1971-77, professor of English, 1977—. Summer instructor at Phillips Exeter Academy, 1962, and Columbia University, 1967. Advisory editor, Longman, Inc., 1976—. *Member:* Modern Language Association of America, American Society for Aesthetics, Milton Society of America, Soho Photographic Foundation. *Awards, honors:* Fellow of William Andrews Clark Memorial Library, University of California, Los Angeles, 1968; University of Connecticut Research Foundation grants, 1968, 1971, 1972; Connecticut Commission on the Arts grant, 1975-76.

WRITINGS: Improving College Reading, Harcourt, 1967, 3rd edition, 1978; (editor) *Issues and Response,* Harcourt, 1968, revised edition, 1972; (editor) *Aesthetics and the Arts,* McGraw, 1968; *Developing College Reading,* Harcourt, 1970; (editor) *17 from Everywhere: Short Stories of the World,* Bantam, 1971; (with F. David Martin) *Humanities through the Arts,* McGraw, 1975; *John Cleveland,* Twayne, 1975; *Sudden Apprehension: Aspects of Knowledge in "Paradise Lost,"* Mouton, 1975; (contributor) Donald B. Gib-

son, editor, *Black American Poets,* Prentice-Hall, 1975; *The Sentence Book,* Harcourt, 1976; *The Paragraph and Essay Book,* Harcourt, 1977. Contributor of articles to scholarly journals; contributor of poems and short stories to literary magazines, 1960—.

WORK IN PROGRESS: Shakespeare and the Quest for Certainty; Anthology of Modern Irish Literature, for Longman; a book of photographs of northeast Connecticut; a collection of American plays; a novel, *Coming to Terms;* second edition of *Humanities through the Arts.*

AVOCATIONAL INTERESTS: Music (plays drums with an academic jazz group), art, woodworking and furniture building, tree work and landscaping, photography.

*   *   *

JADOS, Stanley S.   1912-1977

PERSONAL: Born February 16, 1912, in Gorlice, Poland; naturalized U.S. citizen; son of Albert J. and Catherine (Plonka) Jados; married Florence Lubash, May 30, 1942; children: Catherine (Mrs. James Truschke), Mary Ann (Mrs. Dave Steiner), Paulette, Paul. *Education:* DePaul University, Ph.B., 1940, A.M., 1941; Northwestern University, additional graduate study, 1941-42, 1945-47; University of Ottawa, Ph.D., 1952. *Religion:* Roman Catholic. *Home:* 1945 Kennicott Ct., Des Plaines, Ill. 60018. *Office:* Department of Political Science, DePaul University, 2323 North Seminary Ave., Chicago, Ill. 60614.

CAREER: DePaul University, Chicago, Ill., assistant professor, 1945-52, associate professor, 1953-62, professor of political science, 1963-77. Part-time translator and interpreter of Slavic languages, U.S. Department of Justice, 1961-65. *Military service:* U.S. Army, 1942-44; served in Africa and Italy; became captain; received Purple Heart. *Member:* American Political Science Association, American Academy of Political and Social Science, American Association of University Professors, Midwest Political Science Association. *Awards, honors:* Fellow at Oak Ridge Research Center for Use of Computers in Social Sciences, 1967.

WRITINGS: Russian-American Relations: Washington to Eisenhower, Catholic University of America Press, 1965; *The Consulate of the Sea: International Law,* University of Alabama Press, 1973. Contributor to political science journals and *Chicago Sun-Times.*

WORK IN PROGRESS: A book, *American Contribution to the Evolution of International Law.*†

(Died March 3, 1977)

*   *   *

JAFFA, Harry V(ictor)   1918-

PERSONAL: Born October 7, 1918, in New York, N.Y.; son of Arthur S. and Frances (Landau) Jaffa; married Marjorie E. Butler (a research secretary), April 25, 1942; children: Donald Allen, Philip B., Karen Louise. *Education:* Yale University, B.A., 1939; New School for Social Research, Ph.D., 1951. *Politics:* Republican. *Home:* 549 Baughman, Claremont, Calif. 91711. *Office:* Claremont Men's College, Claremont, Calif. 91711.

CAREER: Queens College (now Queens College of the City University of New York), Flushing, N.Y., member of faculty, 1945-48; member of faculty, College of the City of New York (now City College of the City University of New York), New York, N.Y., 1948-49; member of faculty, University of Chicago, Chicago, Ill., 1949-51; Ohio State University, Columbus, assistant professor, 1951-57, associate professor, 1957-59, professor of political science, 1959-64; Claremont Men's College and Claremont Graduate School, Claremont, Calif., professor of political philosophy, 1964-71, Henry Salvatori Research Professor, 1971—. *Member:* Winston S. Churchill Association (founding president). *Awards, honors:* Guggenheim fellow; Relm Foundation fellow; Mershon fellow; Salvatori fellow; Ohioana Book Award in nonfiction, 1960, for *Crisis of the House Divided.*

WRITINGS: Thomism and Aristotelianism: A Study of the Commentary by Thomas Aquinas on the Nichomachean Ethics, University of Chicago Press, 1952; (editor with Robert W. Johannsen) *In the Name of the People: Speeches and Writings of Lincoln and Douglas in the Ohio Campaign of 1858,* Ohio State University Press, 1959; *Crisis of the House Divided: An Interpretation of the Issue in the Lincoln-Douglas Debates,* Doubleday, 1959; (with Allan Bloom) *Shakespeare's Politics,* Basic Books, 1965; *Equality and Liberty: Theory and Practice in American Politics,* Oxford University Press, 1965; *The Conditions of Freedom: Essays in Political Philosophy,* Johns Hopkins Press, 1975. Also author of *How to Think about the American Revolution: A Bicentennial Celebration.*

Contributor: *Goals and Values in Agricultural Policy,* Iowa State University Press, 1961; *Political Parties, U.S.A.,* Rand McNally, 1961; Leo Strauss and Joseph Cropsey, editors, *A History of Political Philosophy,* Rand McNally, 1962; Melvin A. Laird, editor, *The Conservative Papers,* Doubleday-Anchor, 1964; Robert A. Goldwin, editor, *100 Years of Emancipation,* Rand McNally, 1964; Goldwin, editor, *A Nation of Cities,* Rand McNally, 1966; Goldwin, editor, *Reflections on Thoreau and Lincoln,* Rand McNally, 1969; Don E. Fehrenbacher, editor, *The Leadership of Abraham Lincoln,* Wiley, 1970; Morton Frisch and Richard Stevens, editors, *American Political Thought,* Scribner, 1971. Contributor of about twenty articles and reviews to periodicals, including *National Review* and *Chicago Review;* contributor to *International Encyclopedia of the Social Sciences.*

*   *   *

JAMES, Edward T(opping) 1917-

PERSONAL: Born July 26, 1917, in Chicago, Ill.; son of Sydney Vincent (a mechanical engineer) and Beatrice (Topping) James; married Janet Wilson (a college history teacher), May 12, 1945; children: Edward Topping, Lucy Wilson. *Education:* Harvard University, A.B., 1938, A.M., 1941, Ph.D., 1954. *Politics:* Democrat. *Home:* 62 Gorham St., Cambridge, Mass. 02138. *Office:* Schlesinger Library, Radcliffe College, 3 James St., Cambridge, Mass. 02138.

CAREER: Mills College, Oakland, Calif., assistant professor of history and government, 1950-53; *Dictionary of American Biography,* New York, N.Y., associate editor, 1954-58; Radcliffe College, Cambridge, Mass., editor, *Notable American Women,* 1958-69; *Dictionary of American Biography,* Cambridge, editor, 1960-73; Radcliffe College, Schlesinger Library, Cambridge, editor, Women's Trade Union League Microfilm Project, 1975—. *Military service:* U.S. Naval Reserve, 1942-46; became lieutenant commander. *Member:* American Historical Association, Organization of American Historians, Colonial Society of Massachusetts.

WRITINGS: (Associate editor) *Dictionary of American Biography,* Supplement Two (James was not associated with

earlier edition), Scribner, 1958; (editor) *The American Plutarch,* Scribner, 1964; (editor) *Notable American Women: 1607-1950,* Belknap-Harvard, 1971; (editor) *Dictionary of American Biography,* Supplement Three, Scribner, 1973; (co-editor) *Dictionary of American Biography,* Supplement Four, Scribner, 1975.

AVOCATIONAL INTERESTS: Films, American architectural history.

*   *   *

JAMES, Theodore, Jr. 1934-

PERSONAL: Born August 10, 1934, in Irvington, N.J.; son of Theodore and Marian (Ziebko) James. *Education:* Princeton University, A.B., 1957. *Politics:* Liberal. *Religion:* Episcopalian. *Home address:* Box 204, Peconic, N.J. 11958.

CAREER: McCann, Erickson, New York City, television copywriter, 1959-60; Cunningham & Walsh, New York City, television copywriter, 1960-62; *Women's Wear Daily,* New York City, columnist and feature writer (corresponded from Paris, Poland, Hungary, and Czechoslovakia), 1963-66; General Learning Corp., New York City, writer of educational audio-visual and book material, 1971-73; writer and music consultant, Time Films Inc., 1975—. *Military service:* U.S. Army, 1957-58.

WRITINGS: (With Alexis Obolensky) *Backgammon: The Action Game,* Macmillan, 1969; (with Rosalind Cole) *Waldorf-Astoria Cookbook,* Bobbs-Merrill, 1969; *Fifth Avenue,* Walker & Co., 1971; (with Cole) *Europe: Second Time Around,* Funk, 1971; (with Gene Cavallero, Jr.) *Colony Cookbook,* Bobbs-Merrill, 1972; *The Empire State Building,* Harper, 1975. Contributor to *New York, Town and Country,* and *Smithsonian.*

WORK IN PROGRESS: Research on social history, history of architecture; comedy material; a novel.

*   *   *

JANSEN, Clifford J. 1935-

PERSONAL: Born February 11, 1935, in Cape Town, South Africa; son of Alfred P. (a platen pressman) and Fanny (Meugens) Jansen. *Education:* Catholic University of Louvain, License in Economics, 1963, License in Sociology and Political Science, 1964; Bath University of Technology, Ph.D., 1968. *Home:* 549 Steeles Ave. W., Apt. 46, Toronto, Ontario, Canada M2M 3Y1. *Office:* Department of Sociology, York University, Toronto, Ontario, Canada M3J 1P3.

CAREER: Gregorian University, Rome, Italy, research assistant, 1964; York University, Toronto, Ontario, assistant professor, 1968-73, associate professor of sociology, 1973—. *Member:* American Sociological Association, Canadian Society of Sociology and Anthropology.

WRITINGS: (Editor) *Readings in the Sociology of Migration,* Pergamon, 1970.

WORK IN PROGRESS: Research on ethnic groups in Canada and on students during and after university education.

*   *   *

JARES, Joe 1937-

PERSONAL: Surname is pronounced Jars; born September 2, 1937, in Huntington Park, Calif.; son of Frank August (a wrestler) and Dorothy (Pepper) Jares; married Sue Ellen Wolins (a photo editor, writer, and researcher), May 14,

1967; children: Hayley Joanne, Julie Michelle. *Education:* University of Southern California, B.A., 1959. *Religion:* Agnostic. *Home:* 9701 Cresta Dr., Los Angeles, Calif. 90035. *Agent:* Julian Bach, Jr., 3 East 48th St., New York, N.Y. 10017. *Office: Sports Illustrated,* Suite 400, 450 North Roxbury Dr., Beverly Hills, Calif. 90210.

CAREER: United Press International (UPI), Los Angeles, Calif., staff writer, 1959; *Los Angeles Herald-Express,* Los Angeles, sports writer, 1959-60; United Press International, staff writer, 1960-61; *Los Angeles Times,* Los Angeles, staff writer, 1961-65; *Sports Illustrated* (magazine), associate editor in New York, N.Y., then Beverly Hills, Calif., 1965—. *Military service:* Air National Guard, 1959-62; Air Reserve, 1962-65. *Member:* U.S. Basketball Writers Association, Phi Beta Kappa, Sigma Delta Chi, Phi Kappa Phi. *Awards, honors:* Award for best sports story of the year from California Associated Press, 1964; award for best sports story of the year from Los Angeles Press Club, 1964.

WRITINGS: (With Ed Lindop) *White House Sportsmen,* Houghton, 1964; (with Walt Frazier) *Clyde,* Holt, 1970; *Basketball: The American Game,* Follett, 1971; *Whatever Happened to Gorgeous George?,* Prentice-Hall, 1974.

WORK IN PROGRESS: A mystery novel.

*   *   *

JARVIS, Fred(erick) G(ordon, Jr.)   1930-
(Fritz Gordon)

PERSONAL: Born July 25, 1930; son of Frederick Gordon (an insurance consultant) and Ruth (Bisbee) Jarvis; married Helen Norris Smith, September 2, 1967; children: Emily Ruth. *Education:* Yale University, B.A., 1952; Manhattan School of Music, additional study, 1953. *Politics:* Republican. *Religion:* Episcopalian. *Home:* 190 Riverside Dr., New York, N.Y. 10024.

CAREER: Metropolitan Host (magazine), New York City, restaurant reviewer, 1956-61; New York Athletic Club, New York City, editor of *Winged Foot* (magazine), 1961-70; F. J. Corp. (magazine publishing), New York City, president, 1970—. *Military service:* U.S. Army, 1953-56.

WRITINGS: (Under pseudonym Fritz Gordon) *The Flight of the Bamboo Saucer,* Award Books, 1967; (under pseudonym Fritz Gordon) *Tonight They Die to Mendelssohn,* Award Books, 1968; (with Bob Considine) *The First Hundred Years,* Macmillan, 1969; *Murder at the Met,* Coward, 1971. Contributor of articles and music reviews to magazines.

WORK IN PROGRESS: Deliver Us from Evil, a mystery novel.

AVOCATIONAL INTERESTS: Cooking, badminton, playing bridge, travel in Europe.

*   *   *

JEFFERSON, Alan   1921-

PERSONAL: Born March 20, 1921, in Surrey, England; son of H. E. and Dorothy (Clark) Jefferson; married Elisabeth Ann Grogan (a dancer), 1944 (divorced, 1949); married Joan Pamela Bailey (a singer), July 22, 1955 (divorced, 1976); married Antonia Raeburn (an author), 1976; children: (first marriage) one son; (second marriage) two sons, one daughter; (third marriage) two sons. *Education:* Attended Rydal School, 1935-37, and Old Vic Theatre School, 1947-48. *Home:* Higher Clicker Farm, Horningtops, Liskeard, Cornwall PL14 3QA, England. *Agent:* David Higham Asso-

ciates Ltd., 5-8 Lower John St., London WIR 4HA, England.

CAREER: Stage manager and producer in theaters in London and Stratford-on-Avon, England, 1948-54; worked for various advertising agencies in London, England, 1954-62, and for Shell-Mex and B. P. Ltd., London, 1962-66; London Symphony Orchestra, London, administrator, 1967-68; British Broadcasting Corp. (BBC), London, orchestral and concerts manager, 1968-73. Professor of vocal interpretation, Guildhall School of Music and Drama, 1967-74. *Military service:* British Army, Duke of Cornwall's Light Infantry, Reconnaissance Corps, Parachute Regiment, 1939-46; became captain.

WRITINGS: The Operas of Richard Strauss in Great Britain: 1910-1963, Putnam, 1964; *The Lieder of Richard Strauss,* Praeger, 1971; *Delius,* Octagon, 1972; *The Life of Richard Strauss,* David & Charles, 1973; *Inside the Orchestra,* Reid, 1974; *Richard Strauss* (biography), David & Charles, 1975; *The Glory of Opera,* Putnam, 1976.

WORK IN PROGRESS: Sir Thomas Beecham: A Centenary Tribute, for Macdonald & Jane's; *Encyclopedia of Recorded Opera,* for Salamander Books.

*   *   *

JENNINGS, Jesse David   1909-

PERSONAL: Born July 7, 1909, in Oklahoma City, Okla.; son of Daniel Wellman and Grace B. (Cruce) Jennings; married Jane Noyes Chase (a weaver), September 7, 1935; children: Jesse David, Jr., Herbert Lee. *Education:* Montezuma College, B.A., 1929; University of Chicago, Ph.D., 1943. *Office:* Department of Anthropology, University of Utah, Salt Lake City, Utah 84112.

CAREER: Did archaeological work in Illinois, Tennessee, North Carolina, Florida, New Mexico, and Guatemala, 1930-36; U.S. National Park Service, 1937-48, ranger in Camp Verde, Ariz., 1937-38, acting superintendent of Ocmulgee National Monument, Macon, Ga., 1938-39, archaeologist for Natchez Trace Parkway, 1938-39, 1945-46, regional archaeologist in Omaha, Neb., 1947-48; University of Utah, Salt Lake City, professor of anthropology, 1948—, head of department, 1952-60, distinguished research professor, 1970-71. Visiting professor at Northwestern University, 1960, University of Minnesota, 1961, and University of Hawaii, 1965, 1967; summer lecturer at University of Colorado, 1961, and Fairmont College and Rice University, 1962; director, Glen Canyon Archaeological Salvage Project, 1957-65; director, Utah Museum of Natural History, 1965—; consultant, National Science Foundation, 1964-66. *Military service:* U.S. Naval Reserve, 1942-45; became lieutenant.

MEMBER: American Anthropological Association (member of executive board, 1953-56), Society for American Archaeology (president, 1959-60), American Association for the Advancement of Science (section vice-president, 1961), Sigma Xi, Phi Kappa Phi. *Awards, honors:* Viking medalist in archaeology, 1958.

WRITINGS: (With A. V. Kidder and E. M. Shook) *Excavations at Kaminal Juyu, Guatemala,* Carnegie Institution, 1946; (contributor) J. B. Griffin, editor, *Archeology of the Eastern United States,* University of Chicago Press, 1952; (with E. A. Hoebel and E. R. Smith) *Readings in Anthropology,* McGraw, 1955; *Danger Cave,* University of Utah Anthropological Papers, 1957; (editor with Edward Norbeck and contributor) *Prehistoric Man in the New World,* University of Chicago Press, 1964; (editor with Robert F. Spencer and contributor) *Native Americans,* Harper, 1965; *Prehistory of North America,* McGraw, 1968; (editor and contributor) *Ancient Native Americans,* Addison-Wesley, 1977; *Prehistory of the Eastern Great Basin,* University of Utah Press, 1977. Also author of research monographs; contributor to *Encyclopaedia Britannica;* contributor of about fifty articles and reviews to archaeological and anthropological journals. Editor of *American Antiquity,* 1950-54, and *University of Utah Anthropological Papers,* 1950-53, 1963—.

*   *   *

JENSEN, Richard J.   1941-

PERSONAL: Born October 24, 1941, in South Bend, Ind.; son of Jens E. (a salesman) and Josephine (Dominick) Jensen; married D'Ann Campbell, July 16, 1976. *Education:* University of Notre Dame, B.A., 1962; Yale University, M.A., 1965, Ph.D., 1966. *Politics:* Republican. *Home:* 400 East Randolph, Chicago, Ill. 60601. *Office:* Department of History, University of Illinois at Chicago Circle, Chicago, Ill. 60680.

CAREER: Washington University, St. Louis, Mo., assistant professor of history, 1966-70; University of Illinois at Chicago Circle, associate professor, 1970-73, professor of history, 1973—. Visiting professor, University of Michigan, 1968, and Harvard University, 1973. Senior staff associate, President's Commission on Campus Unrest (Scranton Commission), 1970. Director of Family and Community History Center, Newberry Library, 1971—. *Member:* American Historical Association, Organization of American Historians. *Awards, honors:* Grants from Rockefeller Foundation, Spencer Foundation, National Endowment for the Humanities, National Institute of Mental Health, National Institute on Aging, and National Institute of Education.

WRITINGS: The Winning of the Midwest: Social and Political Conflict, 1888-1896, University of Chicago Press, 1971; (with Charles Dollar) *Historian's Guide to Statistics: Quantitative Analysis and Historical Research,* Holt, 1971; *Illinois: The Bicentennial History,* Norton, 1977; *Education and the Modernization of the Midwest,* Harvard University Press, 1978.

Contributor: S. M. Lipset, editor, *Politics and the Social Sciences,* Oxford University Press, 1969; Robert Swierenga, editor, *Quantification in American History,* Atheneum, 1970; Joel Silbey and Samuel McSeveney, editors, *Voters, Parties, and Elections,* Xerox College Publishing, 1972; Michael Gordon, editor, *The Family in Historical Perspective,* St. Martin's, 1972; Frederick Jaher, editor, *The Rich, the Well-Born, and the Powerful,* University of Illinois Press, 1974. Also contributor to *Coalition Politics,* edited by S. M. Lipset. Contributor to historical and political science journals and newspapers.

WORK IN PROGRESS: Development of American parties, voting behavior, and campaign techniques; quantitative studies in demographic and social history; *Theory of Modernization;* secondary analysis of public opinion polls.

*   *   *

JEWELL, Derek   1927-

PERSONAL: Born June 6, 1927, in London, England; son of John George and Maud (Green) Jewell; married Elizabeth Margaret Benson (a free-lance writer and crossword compiler), September 15, 1953; children: Nicholas, Sarah. *Education:* Wadham College, Oxford, B.A., 1948, M.A., 1950.

Religion: Church of England. *Home:* 25 Spencer Rd., East Molesey, Hampton Court, Surrey, England. *Agent:* George Greenfield, John Farquharson Ltd., 15 Red Lion Square, London WCIR 4QW, England. *Office:* Times Newspapers Ltd., New Printing House Square, Gray's Inn Rd., London WC1X 8EZ, England.

CAREER: Oxford University, Oxford, England, instructor, 1950; *Liverpool Daily Post,* Liverpool, England, reporter and news writer, 1951-62, deputy editor, 1960-62; *St. Louis Post Dispatch,* St. Louis, Mo., reporter, 1956; *Sunday Times,* London, England, personal assistant to editor, 1962-63, deputy editor of color magazine, 1963-68; Times Newspapers Ltd., London, publishing director, 1968—. Director, Sphere Books Ltd.; chairman, Newspaper Archives Development Ltd. *Military service:* Royal Air Force, flying officer, 1948-50. *Member:* National Union of Journalists. *Awards, honors:* Design and Art Directors Association award as best U.K. editorial feature of 1968, for editing of seven-week series, ''America Hurrah!,'' published in *Sunday Times Magazine.*

WRITINGS: (Editor) *Man and Motor: The 20th Century Love Affair,* Hodder & Stoughton, 1966, Walker & Co., 1967; (editor) *Alamein and the Desert War,* Sphere, 1967, Ballantine, 1968; *Come in Number One, Your Time Is Up* (novel), Doubleday, 1971; *Sellout,* Ballantine, 1974; *Duke: A Portrait of Duke Ellington* (biography), Norton, 1977; (with wife, Elizabeth Jewell) *The Sunday Times Book of Crosswords,* Numbers 1 and 2, Penguin, 1976. Contributor of articles to newspapers and magazines; jazz and popular music critic, *Sunday Times.*

WORK IN PROGRESS: A second musical biography; more crossword books with E. Jewell.

*   *   *

JOHANNIS, Theodore B(enjamin), Jr.   1914-

PERSONAL: Born December 29, 1914, in Claremont, N.H.; son of Theodore B. (a mechanical engineer) and Jeannetta (Browning) Johannis; married Mary Deming (a curriculum associate), May 16, 1942; children: Rhonda (Mrs. John Refsnider), Reeve. *Education:* Washington State University, B.A., 1948, M.A., 1948; Florida State University, Ph.D., 1955. *Home:* 3524 High St., Eugene, Ore. 97405. *Office:* Department of Sociology, University of Oregon, Eugene, Ore. 97403.

CAREER: Johannis Studio, Claremont, N.H., owner, 1939-41; Linfield College, McMinnville, Ore., assistant professor of sociology, 1948-50; University of Oregon, Eugene, assistant professor, 1953-61, associate professor, 1961-67, professor of sociology, 1968—. Business manager, *Pacific Sociological Review,* 1958-70; director, E. C. Brown Foundation, Portland, Ore., 1971-75. *Military service:* U.S. Navy, 1942-45. *Member:* National Council on Family Relations (former member of board of directors), American Sociological Association, American Home Economics Association, National Recreation and Parks Association, Pacific Sociological Association (past vice-president, Northern Division).

WRITINGS: (With Curtis E. Avery) *Love and Marriage: A Guide for Teenagers,* Harcourt, 1971; (editor with C. Neil Bull) *Sociology of Leisure,* Sage Publications, 1971. Co-editor, *Family Life Coordinator,* 1958-68.

WORK IN PROGRESS: Research on leisure and the family, and division of labor in the family.

BIOGRAPHICAL/CRITICAL SOURCES: Best Sellers, August 15, 1971.

JOHNSON, Barry L(ynn) 1934-

PERSONAL: Born August 11, 1934, in De Kalb, Tex.; son of George S. (a salesman) and Pauline (Hibbs) Johnson; married Marie Desadier, September 7, 1956; children: Marissa Lyn, Michelle R., Eric Lynn. *Education:* Northwestern State College of Louisiana, B.S., 1957; Baylor University, M.S., 1959; Louisiana State University in New Orleans, Ed.D., 1965. *Religion:* Baptist. *Office:* Department of Physical Education, Northeast Louisiana State College, Monroe, La. 71201.

CAREER: Physical education instructor at Northwestern College of Louisiana, Natchitoches, 1958-59, and Centenary College of Louisiana, Shreveport, 1959-60; Northeast Louisiana State College, Monroe, instructor, 1960-64, assistant professor of physical education, 1966-67; East Texas State University, Commerce, associate professor of physical education, 1967-68; Northeast Louisiana State College, associate professor of physical education and head of department, 1968—. President, Barry Johnson Creations (physical education equipment), 1972—. *Military service:* U.S. Army Reserve, 1957-65; became captain. *Member:* American Association of Health, Physical Education and Recreation, Southern Association of Health, Physical Education and Recreation (delegate, 1969-70), Louisiana Association of Health, Physical Education and Recreation (president, 1971-72), Monroe Jaycees (president, 1970-71).

WRITINGS: A Beginner's Book of Gymnastics, Appleton, 1965; (with Jack K. Nelson) *Practical Measurements for Evaluation in Physical Education,* Burgess, 1969, 2nd edition, 1974; (with Patricia D. Boudreaux) *Basic Gymnastics for Girls and Women,* Appleton, 1971; (with Mary Jane Garcia) *Gymnastics for the Beginner: A Coeducational Approach,* Swift, 1976; (with Garcia) *Fitness and Conditioning for Everyone,* Swift, 1978. Contributor of articles to *Journal of American Association of Health, Physical Education and Recreation* and *Research Quarterly.*

SIDELIGHTS: Barry Johnson's company, Barry Johnson Creations, is concerned with the development of physical education equipment, such as the tennis and badminton set-up machine.†

*   *   *

JOHNSON, Bernard 1933-

PERSONAL: Born November 5, 1933, in Lutterworth, Leicestershire, England; son of H. R. and M. E. (Grant) Johnson; married Annie Pourcel, June, 1959; children: Nicholas, Isabel. *Education:* University of Nottingham, B.A., 1957, Ph.D., 1960; also studied at Cambridge University and University of Belgrade. *Home:* 25 Eton Ave., Sudbury Town, Wembley, England. *Office:* London School of Economics and Political Science, University of London, London WC2A 2AE, England.

CAREER: University of Nottingham, Nottingham, England, lecturer in Slavonic languages and literature, 1960-65; University of London, London School of Economics and Political Science, London, England, lecturer in Slavonic languages and literature, 1965—. *Military service:* Royal Air Force, 1952-54.

WRITINGS: New Writing in Yugoslavia, Penguin, 1970.

WORK IN PROGRESS: Research on Serbian, Croatian, and Russian languages and literature.

*   *   *

JOHNSON, Bruce 1933-

PERSONAL: Born April 29, 1933, in Chicago, Ill.; son of George A. (a railroad clerk) and Elsie (Clausing) Johnson; married Jean C. Kruger (a commercial artist), June 29, 1957; children: Abram. *Education:* University of Chicago, A.B., 1952; Northwestern University, B.A., 1954, M.A., 1955, Ph.D., 1959. *Politics:* Democrat. *Religion:* None. *Home:* 16 Kirklees Rd., Pittsford, N.Y. 14534. *Office:* Department of English, University of Rochester, Rochester, N.Y. 14627.

CAREER: University of Michigan, Ann Arbor, instructor in English, 1958-62; University of Rochester, Rochester, N.Y., 1962—, currently professor of English, director of undergraduate English studies, 1963-68, chairman of interdepartmental studies, 1970-71. *Member:* Modern Language Association of America. *Awards, honors:* National Endowment for the Humanities senior fellow, 1974-75; Guggenheim fellow, 1977-78.

WRITINGS: Conrad's Models of Mind, University of Minnesota Press, 1971. Also author of a book on Thomas Hardy's novels, and of essays on Conrad and Hardy.

WORK IN PROGRESS: A study of the relations between American literature and painting.

*   *   *

JOHNSON, Cecil Edward 1927-

PERSONAL: Born January 23, 1927, in Iola, Kan.; son of Louis E. and June (Cameron) Johnson; married Edith J. Dunn, September 3, 1947; children: Edward and Eric (twin sons), Elizabeth A. (Mrs. Stephen Pope), Ernest R. *Education:* University of Southern California, B.S., 1950; Los Angeles State College of Applied Arts and Sciences (now California State University, Los Angeles), M.A., 1954; University of Buenos Aires, D.Litt., 1976. *Home:* 3958 Chapman Pl., Riverside, Calif. 92506. *Office:* Department of Biology, Riverside City College, Riverside, Calif. 92506.

CAREER: Riverside City College, Riverside, Calif., instructor, 1952-58, associate professor of biology, 1958—. *Military service:* U.S. Navy, 1944-46; U.S. Army Reserve, 1959. *Member:* World Population Society, Environmental Fund, Citizens Rights Organization, Cooper Ornithological Society, Phi Beta Kappa.

WRITINGS: The Subtle Menace of Illegal Aliens in Times of Economic Recession, World Population Society, 1976; *The Takeover of America,* Town Hall of California, 1977.

Editor: *Social and Natural Biology: Selections from Contemporary Classics,* Van Nostrand, 1968; *Sex and Human Relationships,* C. E. Merrill, 1970; *Human Biology: Contemporary Readings,* Van Nostrand, 1970; *Contemporary Readings in Behavior,* McGraw, 1970; *Eco-Crisis,* Wiley, 1970; (with Malcolm M. MacDonald) *Society and the Environment: Contemporary Readings,* Van Nostrand, 1971; *The Natural World,* McGraw, 1972. Contributor to *Mark Twain Journal, National Geographic,* and *International Journal of Neuropsychiatry.*

WORK IN PROGRESS: A novel, *The Professors.*

SIDELIGHTS: Cecil Edward Johnson told *CA:* "Since 1967, I have appeared on the national media in regard to the illegal alien cancer as it effects jobs for out-of-work Americans.... I debated Lionel J. Castillo, Carter's new appointee as commissioner of the Immigration and Naturalization Service." He will appear before the Senate Hearing on Illegal Aliens as an expert in this field.

JOHNSON, Curt(is Lee) 1928-
(Lee Wallek, Walter Whiz)

PERSONAL: Born May 26, 1928, in Minneapolis, Minn.; son of Hjalmar Nathaniel (a traffic manager) and Gladys (Goring) Johnson; married Jo Ann Lekwa, June 30, 1950 (divorced, 1974); married Rochelle Hickey, January 11, 1975; children: (first marriage) Mark Alan, Paula Catherine; stepchildren: Harry, Eugene. *Education:* University of Iowa, B.A., 1951, M.A., 1952. *Home:* 4343 North Clarendon, Chicago, Ill. 60613. *Office:* 4 East Huron, Chicago, Ill. 60611.

CAREER: Popular Mechanics Press and Windsor Press, New York, N.Y., assistant editor, 1953-54; *American Peoples Encyclopedia,* Chicago, Ill., department editor, 1954-56; Davis Publications, Chicago, handbook editor and promotion director, 1956-60; Scott, Foresman & Co., Glenview, Ill., head of production unit in College Division, 1960-61; Britannica Schools, Inc. and Britannica Press, Chicago, editor of educational and programmed study materials, 1961-63; Scott, Foresman & Co., program director for college texts in English, speech, and children's literature, 1963-66; free-lance writer, editor, and indexer for publishers and industries, 1966-72; Aldine Publishing Co., Chicago, managing editor, 1972-73; St. Clair Press, Chicago, vice-president, 1973—. *Military service:* U.S. Navy, 1946-48. *Member:* Phi Beta Kappa. *Awards, honors:* National Endowment for the Arts Creative Writing fellowship, 1973.

WRITINGS: (Editor with George Uskali) *How to Restore Antique and Classic Cars,* Popular Mechanics Press, 1954; *Hobbledehoy's Hero,* Pennington Press, 1959; (editor with Jarvis Thurston) *Short Stories from the Literary Magazines,* Scott, Foresman, 1970; (editor) *Best Little Magazine Fiction: 1970,* New York University Press, 1970; (editor with Alvin Greenberg) *Best Little Magazine Fiction: 1971,* New York University Press, 1971; (editor with Jack Conroy) *Writers in Revolt,* Lawrence Hill, 1973; *Nobody's Perfect,* Carpenter Press, 1974; *Lace and a Bobbitt,* Vagabond, 1976; *The Morning Light,* Carpenter Press, 1977; *The Forbidden Writings of Lee Wallek* (essays), December Press, 1978. Contributor of about two hundred articles, columns, and reviews and fifty short stories to periodicals, some under pseudonyms Lee Wallek and Walter Whiz. Editor and publisher, *December,* 1962—; consulting editor, *Panache,* 1967-74.

WORK IN PROGRESS: A novel and a collection of short stories.

* * *

JOHNSON, D(onald) Barton 1933-

PERSONAL: Born June 15, 1933, in Indianapolis, Ind.; son of Waylan Eugene (a professor) and Mary Helen (Barton) Johnson; married Sheila Moody, January 23, 1976. *Education:* Indiana University, B.A., 1954; University of California, Berkeley, M.A., 1959; University of California, Los Angeles, Ph.D., 1966. *Home:* 1498 Tunnel Rd., Santa Barbara, Calif. 93105. *Office:* Department of Russian, University of California, Santa Barbara, Calif. 93106.

CAREER: U.S. Department of Defense, Washington, D.C., intelligence research analyst, 1954-59; Ohio State University, Columbus, assistant professor of Russian, 1965-66; University of California, Santa Barbara, associate professor of Russian, 1966—, chairman of Russian area studies program, 1970-75. Visiting professor of Russian and chairman of department, Monash University, Melbourne, Australia, 1975-76. Consultant, Rand Corp., 1966-68. *Member:* American Association of Teachers of Slavic and East European Languages, Philological Association of the Pacific Coast. *Awards, honors:* Grant for research in Eastern Europe, 1968-69.

WRITINGS: Transformations and Their Use in the Resolution of Syntactic Homomorphy, Mouton, 1970; (with D.S. Worth and A.S. Kozak) *Russian Derivational Dictionary,* Elsevier, 1970; (editor with Albert Kaspin and M.W. Kostruba) *Eyewitness: Selections from Russian Memoirs,* Harcourt, 1971; (translator and editor) Yury Lotman, *Analysis of the Poetic Text,* Ardis, 1976. Contributor of articles and reviews to professional journals.

WORK IN PROGRESS: A collection of articles about Vladimir Nabokov.

* * *

JOHNSON, E(arly) Ashby 1917-

PERSONAL: Born December 3, 1917, in Columbus, Ga.; son of Clifford Ross (a cotton broker) and Janie (Bishop) Johnson; married Anne Martin, August 24, 1940 (divorced, 1963); married Janice M. Platt (an advertising consultant), July 28, 1964; children: (first marriage) David Ashby, Paul Martin. *Education:* Presbyterian College, Clinton, S.C., A.B., 1938; University of Richmond, graduate study, 1940-42; Union Theological Seminary, Richmond, Va., B.D., 1941, Th.M., 1942, Th.D., 1948; Yale University, postdoctoral study, 1955-56. *Politics:* Democrat. *Home:* 134 23rd Ave. S., St. Petersburg, Fla. 33705. *Office:* Eckerd College, 5401 34th St. S., St. Petersburg, Fla. 33733.

CAREER: Clergyman of Presbyterian Church; pastor in Brevard, N.C., 1942-47, and Louisville, Ky., 1947-51; King College, Bristol, Tenn., professor of philosophy, 1951-55; Austin College, Sherman, Tex., professor of philosophy and religion, 1956-60; Eckerd College, St. Petersburg, Fla., professor of philosophy and religion, 1960—. *Member:* American Philosophical Association, American Academy of Religion, American Association of University Professors, Presbyterian Education Association of the South.

WRITINGS: The Crucial Task of Theology, John Knox, 1958; *Communion with Young Saints,* John Knox, 1959; *Saved from What?,* John Knox, 1966. Author of youth study materials for Presbyterian Board of Christian Education.

WORK IN PROGRESS: Three novels, *Adieu Odysseus, The Damnation of Lucky John,* and *The Young Pretender.*

AVOCATIONAL INTERESTS: Mythic themes in literature and theology; travel, sailing in American and Mediterranean waters.

* * *

JOHNSON, Halvard 1936-

PERSONAL: Born September 10, 1936, in Newburgh, N.Y.; son of Merrill Carl (a clergyman) and Margaret (Hornwall) Johnson; married Dorothy Anne Trimble, September 12, 1959 (divorced, 1966); married Barbara Jean Toone (a teacher), February 7, 1967. *Education:* Ohio Wesleyan University, B.A., 1958; University of Chicago, M.A., 1960. *Address:* c/o University of Maryland, European Division, APO New York, N.Y. 09403.

CAREER: Chicago City Junior College, Wright Branch, Chicago, Ill., English teacher, 1961-63; Chicago Teachers College North, Chicago, Ill., instructor in English, 1963-64; University of Texas at El Paso, instructor in English, 1964-

68; University of Puerto Rico, Cayey, Puerto Rico, assistant professor of English, 1968-72; lecturer, European Division, University of Maryland, 1973—. *Member:* American Association of University Professors, Associacion de Maestros de Puerto Rico. *Awards, honors:* Woodrow Wilson special fellowship, University of Chicago, 1960.

WRITINGS—Poetry: *Transparencies and Projections,* New Rivers Press, 1969; *The Dance of the Red Swan,* New Rivers Press, 1971; *Eclipse,* illustrated with photographs by Melissa Shook, New Rivers Press, 1974. Contributor of poems to *Minnesota Review, Stony Brook, Sumac, Cafe Solo, Hanging Loose,* and other periodicals. Guest editor, *Fragments* (poetry magazine).

WORK IN PROGRESS: Poetry.

SIDELIGHTS: Halvard Johnson and his wife left their teaching positions in Puerto Rico at the end of the 1971-72 school year to live and travel in Europe, North Africa, and Asia. He told *CA:* "I hope one day to do a one-man poetry magazine; that is, a mimeo magazine that would be given away on a small scale. No production or distribution hassles. . . . I really have no set theory or dogma about poetry, but I am interested in expanding the impact and possibilities of poetry in an age of mass communications. For me, immediately, this seems to mean travel and language learning. Ultimately, it means prophecy—assessing the needs of the future."†

* * *

JOHNSON, James J(ay) 1939-

PERSONAL: Born December 25, 1939, in Emporia, Kan.; son of Donald Warren and Dixie O. (Oppliger) Johnson; married Patricia Ann Roth, August 26, 1962; children: Amy Lynne, Erik James. *Education:* Washington University, A.B., 1961; Illinois State University, M.A., 1964; Northwestern University, Ph.D., 1966. *Religion:* Protestant. *Home:* 813 Cottage Ave., Normal, Ill. 61761. *Office:* Department of Psychology, Illinois State University, Normal, Ill. 61761.

CAREER: Northwestern University, Evanston, Ill., assistant director of guidance laboratory, 1964-66; Illinois State University, Normal, assistant professor, 1966-70, associate professor, 1970-74, professor of psychology, 1975—. *Military service:* U.S. Army Reserve, 1961-68. *Member:* American Personnel and Guidance Association, American Educational Research Association, Midwest Psychological Association, Illinois Psychological Association (secretary-treasurer of academic section, 1971-73), Illinois Guidance and Personnel Association.

WRITINGS: (With William J. Gnagey and Patricia Chesebro) *Student Guide for the Psychology of Classroom Learning,* Holt, 1968; (editor with Gnagey and Chesebro) *Learning Environments: Readings in Educational Psychology,* Holt, 1972. Contributor to *Illinois School Research, Journal of College Student Personnel, I.G.P.A. Newsletter, Adolescence,* and other publications. *Illinois Psychologist,* co-editor, 1972-74, editor, 1974—.

WORK IN PROGRESS: Research on personality dimensions and preference for counseling approach.

* * *

JOHNSON, Kathryn 1929-

PERSONAL: Born May 18, 1929, in Columbus, Ga.; daughter of John Lewis and Lula (Boondry) Johnson. *Education:* Agnes Scott College, B.A. *Office:* Associated Press, Title Bldg., 10th floor, 30 Pryor St., Atlanta, Ga.

CAREER: Associated Press, Atlanta, Ga., news reporter, 1959—. *Member:* Sigma Delta Chi (vice-president of Atlanta chapter, 1971-72). *Awards, honors:* Nieman fellow at Harvard University, 1976-77.

WRITINGS: (With Arthur Everett and Harry F. Rosenthal) *Calley,* Dell, 1971.

* * *

JOHNSON, L.D. 1916-

PERSONAL: Born February 18, 1916, in Walters, Okla.; son of Ray (a farmer) and Maude (Goodman) Johnson; married Marion Ervin (a librarian), September 2, 1937; children: Elaine (Mrs. Archer L. Yeatts III), Roland. *Education:* George Washington University, A.B., 1937; Southern Baptist Theological Seminary, Th.M., 1940, Th.D., 1942. *Home:* 306 Chantilly Dr., Greenville, S.C. 29613. *Office:* Department of Religion, Furman University, Greenville, S.C. 29613.

CAREER: Pastor of Baptist church in Danville, Va., 1943-59; University of Richmond, Richmond, Va., professor of religion, 1959-62; pastor of Baptist church in Greenville, S.C., 1962-67; Furman University, Greenville, professor of religion and chaplain, 1967—. *Member:* Association of Baptist Professors of Religion. *Awards, honors:* George Washington Honor Medal of Freedoms Foundation 1964, for newspaper column.

WRITINGS: An Introduction to the Bible, Convention Press, 1969; *Out of the Whirlwind: The Major Message of Job,* Broadman, 1971; *Israel's Wisdom: Learn and Live,* Broadman, 1975; *The Morning after Death,* in press. Author of weekly column appearing in Sunday newspapers in Virginia, 1955—, and in South Carolina and North Carolina, 1962—.

* * *

JOHNSON, Marshall D. 1935-

PERSONAL: Born November 15, 1935, in Middle River, Minn.; son of Ingvald (a farmer) and Bertha (Maijala) Johnson; married Alice Joy Peterson, May 31, 1959; children: Nathan Erick, Catherine Florence, Jennifer Beth. *Education:* Augsburg College, B.A., 1957; University of Minnesota, graduate study, 1959-60; Augsburg Theological Seminary, B.Th., 1961; Union Theological Seminary, New York, N.Y., Th.D., 1966. *Home:* 608 Tenth Ave. N.W., Waverly, Iowa 50677. *Office:* Department of Religion, Wartburg College, Waverly, Iowa 50677.

CAREER: Clergyman of American Lutheran Church; pastor in Bronx, N.Y., 1961-63; Lutheran Theological Seminary, Philadelphia, Pa., visiting instructor, 1965-66; Wartburg College, Waverly, Iowa, assistant professor, 1966-71, associate professor, 1971-77, professor of religion, 1977—. Fulbright lecturer, University of Bergen, Norway, 1976. *Member:* Society of Biblical Literature. *Awards, honors:* Rockefeller fellow, 1963-65.

WRITINGS: The Purpose of the Biblical Genealogies, Cambridge University Press, 1969; (contributor) James Charlesworth, editor, *Apocrypha and Pseudepigrapha of the Old Testament,* Doubleday, in press. Contributor to *Catholic Biblical Quarterly.*

WORK IN PROGRESS: The relation of New Testament theology to first-century Judaism.

SIDELIGHTS: Marshall Johnson reads Norwegian, German, French, Koine Greek, and Biblical Hebrew. *Avocational interests:* Music, playing piano.

JOHNSON, Maryanna   1925-

PERSONAL: Born December 5, 1925, in Brussels, Belgium; daughter of Jonathan Guest (a missionary and professor) and Margaret (Kimber) Williams; married Deryl F. Johnson (a professor of philosophy), September 3, 1949 (separated); children: Glenn, George, Tom. *Education:* Wheaton College, Wheaton, Ill., B.A., 1949; Asbury Theological Seminary, M.R.E., 1952. *Religion:* Presbyterian. *Home:* 9712 Summit Ave., Kensington Park, Md. 20795.

CAREER: Central College, McPherson, Kan., teacher of Christian education of children, 1957; London College, London, Ontario, teacher of Christian education, 1966; First Presbyterian Church, Fayetteville, N.C., director of Christian education, 1969-70; Cumberland County Department of Social Services, Fayetteville, volunteer coordinator, 1972-73; Cumberland County Mental Health Center, Fayetteville, research assistant, 1974-77.

WRITINGS: (With Patti Bard) *At the Risk of Being a Wife,* Zondervan, 1971. Contributor to *Eternity.*

SIDELIGHTS: The Johnson-Bard collaboration began with casual correspondence and resulted in a book consisting of a series of letters. Patti Bard lives in New York and the two collaborators have never met.

*   *   *

JOHNSON, Richard C.   1919-

PERSONAL: Born January 17, 1919, in Eau Claire, Wis.; son of Carl Adolph (a foundry foreman) and Julia (Matson) Johnson; married Gladys Ditter (a teacher), December 25, 1942; children: Richard William. *Education:* Northern Illinois University, B.E., 1941, M.S., 1952; Northwestern University, graduate study, summers, 1953-59. *Home:* 302 East Hillside Ave., Barrington, Ill. 60010. *Office:* Barrington High School, Barrington, Ill. 60010.

CAREER: Barrington High School, Barrington, Ill., chairman of performing arts department, 1946—. Chairman of drama department, Georgia Governor's Honors Program. *Military service:* U.S. Army Air Forces, 1942-46; became staff sergeant. *Member:* Children's Theater Association (program chairman, 1959), Secondary School Theatre Association (president), Council of National Organizations for Children and Youth (member of executive committee), National Education Association, Illinois Education Association, Barrington High School Education Association (president).

WRITINGS: (With Robert C. Seaver) *A Guide to Makeup for the Stage,* Paramount Press, 1955; *Theatre for Children* (series of articles originally appearing in *Dramatics),* International Thespian Society, 1966; *Producing Plays for Children,* Rosen Press, 1971. Also author of script for filmstrip, "Makeup for the Stage."

*   *   *

JOHNSON, Robert L.   1919-

PERSONAL: Born June 21, 1919, in Detroit, Mich.; son of Delbert and Loretta Johnson; married Mary E. Sowell, March 17, 1942; children: Thomas A., Mary E. *Education:* Abilene Christian College (now University), B.A., 1948; Butler University, M.A., 1949; New York University, Ph.D., 1957. *Office:* John Brown University, Siloam Springs, Ark. 72761.

CAREER: Abilene Christian College (now University), Abilene, Tex., associate professor of religion, 1953-68;

Friends University, Wichita, Kan., professor of religion, 1968-71; Malone College, Canton, Ohio, professor of religion and philosophy, 1972-75; currently affiliated with John Brown University, Siloam Springs, Ark. Lecturer at Oklahoma Christian College, 1959, Oklahoma State University, 1960, and Pepperdine College (now University), 1963. *Military service:* U.S. Army Air Forces, 1940-45; served in Europe; became captain. U.S. Air Force Reserve, 1945-71; became lieutenant colonel. *Member:* American Academy of Religion, Southwestern Philosophical Society.

WRITINGS: The Letter of Paul to the Galatians, R. B. Sweet, 1969; *Humanism and Beyond,* Pilgrim Press, 1973. Contributor to *Wycliffe Bible Encyclopedia.*

*   *   *

JOHNSON, Robert L(eon, Jr.)   1930-

PERSONAL: Born November 6, 1930; son of Robert Leon, Sr. (a citrus grower) and Loralee (Watkins) Johnson; married Barbara J. Park, September 9, 1955; children: Robert Paul, Christopher Andrew. *Education:* University of North Carolina at Chapel Hill, B.A., 1952; Union Theological Seminary, New York, N.Y., B.D., 1955; Harvard University, Th.M., 1968. *Politics:* Democrat. *Home:* 413 Smith Ave., Chapel Hill, N.C. 27514. *Office address:* Box 4694, Duke Station, Durham, N.C. 27706.

CAREER: Methodist minister; associate pastor of Methodist church in Miami, Fla., 1955-57; Wesley Foundation, Chapel Hill, N.C., director, beginning 1957; currently Southern director of National Institute for Campus Ministries. *Member:* American Association for Higher Education, Association of Wesley Foundations (president), National Campus Ministry Association (president, 1972-73), Common Cause. *Awards, honors:* Danforth Foundation study grant, 1967-68.

WRITINGS: Counter Culture and the Vision of God, Augsburg, 1971. Contributor to religious periodicals.

WORK IN PROGRESS: A commentary on the theological significance of William Faulkner; a novel about the South.

AVOCATIONAL INTERESTS: Gardening, sailing.

*   *   *

JOHNSON, Robert Owen   1926-

PERSONAL: Born July 16, 1926, in Englewood, N.J.; son of Walter Knute (a salesman) and Adele (de Castro) Johnson; married Barbara Anderson (an instructor in Spanish, and language laboratory coordinator), August 16, 1952; children: Susan Lee, David Paul. *Education:* U.S. Merchant Marine Academy, B.S., 1947; Yale University, A.B., 1950; University of Washington, Seattle, M.A., 1955, Ph.D., 1964. *Politics:* Republican. *Religion:* Congregational. *Home:* 1305 Clifford St. N.W., Pullman, Wash. 99163. *Office:* Department of English, Washington State University, Pullman, Wash. 99163.

CAREER: Washington State University, Pullman, instructor, 1957-65, assistant professor, 1965-71, associate professor of English, 1971—, member of Council of Faculty Representatives, 1975—, director of American studies program, 1976—. *Military service:* U.S. Naval Reserve, 1947-69; active duty, 1950-53; became lieutenant commander. *Member:* Philological Association of the Pacific Coast, Rocky Mountain Modern Language Association, Kiwanis Club.

WRITINGS: An Index to Literature in "The New Yorker,"

Scarecrow, Volume I, 1969, Volume II, 1970, Volume III, 1971, Volume IV, 1976; *An Index to Profiles in "The New Yorker,"* Scarecrow, 1972.

WORK IN PROGRESS: Supplemental volumes to *An Index to Literature in "The New Yorker."*

* * *

JOHNSON, Ruby Kelley 1928-
(Ruby M. Kelley)

PERSONAL: Born September 7, 1928, in Houston, Tex.; daughter of Timothy Ernest (a cleaner and dyer) and Ruby (Bruce) Kelley; married Kenneth H. Johnson (a teacher), July 9, 1966; children: Kelley Tina, Joan Doris. *Education:* Texas Woman's University, B.A., 1949; University of Bridgeport, M.A., 1956; New York University, Ph.D., 1965. *Home:* R.F.D.1, Chestnut Hill Rd., Sandy Hook, Conn. 06482.

CAREER: University of Bridgeport, Bridgeport, Conn., reading specialist, 1954-56; English teacher in public school in Westport, Conn., 1956-66. *Member:* National Council of Teachers of English, Linguistic Society of America.

WRITINGS: (Under name Ruby M. Kelley) *A Study to Identify the Contents of a Linguistically Based Grammar Program in the Junior High,* Connecticut State Department of Education, 1963; *Contemporary English I and II,* Hayden, 1971.

WORK IN PROGRESS: A sequel to *Contemporary English I and II.*

* * *

JOHNSON, Warren Arthur 1937-

PERSONAL: Born June 12, 1937, in Oakland, Calif.; son of Arthur Alexander (a real estate salesman) and Linnea M. (Anderson) Johnson; married Martha Ann Davidson, December 20, 1958; children: Aaron David, Blake Eliot. *Education:* University of California, Berkeley, B.S., 1959; University of Michigan, M.S., 1966, Ph.D., 1969. *Politics:* Independent. *Home:* 5359 East Falls View Dr., San Diego, Calif. 92115. *Office:* Department of Geography, San Diego State University, San Diego, Calif. 92182.

CAREER: National Park Service, civil engineer, 1960-65, 1966-67; San Diego State University, San Diego, Calif., assistant professor, 1969-71, associate professor, 1971-75, professor of geography, 1975—, chairman of department, 1976—. Fulbright lecturer, University of Leicester, 1974-75. *Member:* Association of American Geographers, Sierra Club. *Awards, honors:* National Park Service grant, 1966; San Diego State University faculty fellowship, 1976.

WRITINGS: Public Parks on Private Land in England and Wales, Johns Hopkins Press, 1971; (editor with John Hardesty and contributor) *Economic Growth vs. the Environment,* Wadsworth, 1971; (contributor) Herman Daly, editor, *Toward a Steady State Economy,* Freeman, 1972. Contributor to *Sierra Club Bulletin.*

WORK IN PROGRESS: A book, tentatively entitled *Out of the Corner: Muddling towards Frugality.*

BIOGRAPHICAL/CRITICAL SOURCES: Bulletin of the International Union for the Conservation of Nature, October-December, 1971; *Growth and Change,* April, 1972.

* * *

JOHNSTON, William 1925-

PERSONAL: Born July 30, 1925, in Belfast, Northern Ireland; son of William and Winifred (Clearkin) Johnston. *Education:* National University of Ireland, B.A. (first class honors), 1948; St. Stanislaus College, Tullamore, Ireland, Lic.Phil., 1951; studied Japanese language and culture at Eiko Gakuen, Yokosuka, Japan, 1951-53; Sophia University, Tokyo, Japan, Lic.Theol., 1958, S.T.D., 1968; Queen's University, Ireland, M.A., 1959. *Office:* Sophia University, Chiyoda-ku, Kioicho 7, Tokyo, Japan.

CAREER: Roman Catholic priest of the Society of Jesus (Jesuits); Sophia University, Tokyo, Japan, lecturer, 1960, associate professor, 1962-68, professor, 1968-74, professor of religious studies, 1974—. Lecturer at Tokyo University, 1964-68; visiting lecturer, Seton Hall University, 1965, and University of San Francisco, 1970.

WRITINGS: (Contributor) E.W.F. Tomlin, editor, *T.S. Eliot: A Tribute from Japan,* Kenkyusha (Japan), 1966; *The Mysticism of "The Cloud of Unknowing,"* Desclee, 1967; (translator) Shusaku Endo, *Silence,* Tuttle, 1969; *The Still Point: Reflections on Zen and Christian Mysticism,* Fordham University Press, 1970; *Christian Zen,* Harper, 1971; (translator) *"The Cloud of Unknowing" and the Book of Privy Counselling,* Doubleday, 1973; *Silent Music: The Science of Meditation,* Harper, 1974. Contributor of articles to *Thought, International Philosophical Quarterly, Theological Studies, Cosmos, Japan Missionary Bulletin, Monumenta Nipponica, Concilium, Eastern Buddhist, Cistercian Studies,* and other journals.

WORK IN PROGRESS: A book on East-West mysticism, *The Eye of Love.*

SIDELIGHTS: William Johnston told *CA:* "My work has been greatly influenced by the twenty years I have spent in Japan and by my experience as a Christian meeting Buddhists in friendly dialogue. *Christian Zen* is somewhat autobiographical. I believe that friendly dialogue between Christianity and Buddhism is of great importance in our day."

* * *

JONAS, Ilsedore B. 1920-

PERSONAL: Born August 31, 1920, in Stettin, Germany; daughter of Theodore Barkow; married Klaus W. Jonas (a professor). *Education:* University of Heidelberg, Certificate; graduate study at University of Muenchen, 1942-44, and University of Wuerzburg, 1944-45; Rutgers University, M.A., 1955; University of Pittsburgh, Ph.D., 1967. *Home:* 5349 Beeler St., Pittsburgh, Pa. 15217. *Office:* Department of Modern Languages, Carnegie-Mellon University, Pittsburgh, Pa. 15213.

CAREER: Rutgers University, New Brunswick, N.J., instructor in German, 1955-56; Yale University Library, New Haven, Conn., assistant in historical manuscripts, 1956-57; University of Pittsburgh, Pittsburgh, Pa., instructor in modern languages, 1958; Carnegie-Mellon University, Pittsburgh, instructor, 1958-64, assistant professor, 1964-69, associate professor, 1969-72, professor of modern languages, 1972—. *Member:* Modern Language Association of America, American Association of Teachers of German.

WRITINGS: (Editor) Erich Kaestner, *Als ich ein kleiner Junge War,* Holt, 1960; (with husband, Klaus W. Jonas) *Thomas Mann Studies,* Volume II (bibliography of criticism), University of Pennsylvania Press, 1967; *Thomas Mann und Italien,* Carl Winter Universitaetsverlag, 1969, revised translation published as *Thomas Mann and Italy,* University of Alabama Press, 1978; (contributor) Hermann Kunisch, editor, *Handbuch der Deutschen Gegenwarts Lit-*

eratur, Volume II, Nymphenburger Verlagshandlung, 1970. Contributor of articles and reviews to literary and scholarly journals, including *Books Abroad, Deutsche Literaturzeitung, German Quarterly, Modern Language Notes,* and *Etudes Germaniques.* Former associate editor, *Journal of Modern Austrian Literature.*

*   *   *

JONES, Adrienne 1915-

PERSONAL: Born July 28, 1915, in Atlanta, Ga.; daughter of Arthur Washington and Orianna (Mason) Applewhite; married Richard Morris Jones, 1939; children: Gregory, Gwen. *Education:* Educated at Theosophical School of the Open Gate and in Beverly Hills (Calif.) public schools; attended University of California, Los Angeles, 1958-59, and University of California, Irvine, 1972. *Politics:* Liberal Democrat. *Religion:* Grew up a Theosophist; later Episcopalian; more recently Unitarian-Universalist. *Home:* 24491 Los Serranos Dr., Laguna Niguel, Calif. 92677.

CAREER: Professional free-lance writer and novelist; has also worked as an office and managerial worker, cattle rancher, and with youth groups. Speaker at conferences, schools, libraries, and writers' groups. *Member:* Authors Guild, Society of Children's Book Writers, P.E.N., American Civil Liberties Union, National Association for the Advancement of Colored People, Southern California Council on Literature for Children and Young People, California Writers Guild, Southern Christian Leadership Conference. *Awards, honors:* Southern California Council on Children and Young People award for best book by a Southern California author, 1972, for *Another Place, Another Spring.*

WRITINGS: Thunderbird Pass, Lippincott, 1952; *Where Eagles Fly,* Putnam, 1957; *Ride the Far Wind* (juvenile), Little, Brown, 1964; *Wild Voyageur: Story of a Canada Goose* (juvenile), Little, Brown, 1966; *Sail, Calypso!* (juvenile), Little Brown, 1968; *Another Place, Another Spring,* Houghton, 1971; *Hawk* (short story), Bank Street College of Education, 1972; *My Name Is Gnorr with an Unsilent G* (short story), Bank Street College of Education, 1972; *Old Witch Hannifin and Her Shoonaget* (short story), Bank Street College of Education, 1972; *Niki and Albert and the Seventh Street Raiders,* Bank Street College of Education, 1972; *Who Needs a Hand to Hold?,* Bank Street College of Education, 1973; *The Mural Master,* Houghton, 1974; *So, Nothing Is Forever,* Houghton, 1974; *The Hawks of Chelney,* Harper, 1977. Excerpts from books represented in anthologies, including: *Bright Horizons: A Collection,* Scott, Foresman, 1969; *On the Edge,* Ginn, 1970; *Measure Me, Sky,* Ginn, 1976; *Young Life,* Orthodox Christian Education Commission, 1976; *Phantoms and Fantasies,* Harper, 1977.

WORK IN PROGRESS: Two novels.

SIDELIGHTS: Adrienne Jones told *CA:* "My endeavor is to learn and understand the feelings and reasons behind the human act, the human mind and heart. In my writing the effort is to portray the brotherhood and friendship that is found in its most vital and active form in the world of the young, yet to understand and reveal the personal tragedies and failures which are so much a part of life. I have chosen to write mainly for young people, as this is the nearest one can come to touching the future. To me it is the most exciting field of writing." Mrs. Jones' books have been published in Germany, Austria, Denmark, Italy, Great Britain, Netherlands, and Japan.

AVOCATIONAL INTERESTS: Travel, books, music, beach-rambling, mountaineering, conservation activities, conversation.

*   *   *

JONES, E(ndsley) Terrence 1941-

PERSONAL: Born August 25, 1941, in Kansas City, Mo.; son of Endsley (a businessman) and Mary (Donovan) Jones; married Ruth Schuessler (a college professor), February 12, 1966; children: Mark. *Education:* St. Louis University, B.S., 1963; Georgetown University, Ph.D., 1967. *Home:* 514 Midvale, University City, Mo. 63130. *Office:* University of Missouri, 8001 Natural Bridge, St. Louis, Mo. 63121.

CAREER: Kansas State University, Manhattan, assistant professor of political science, 1966-69; University of Missouri—St. Louis, associate professor of political science, 1969—. *Military service:* U.S. Army Reserve, 1966-72; became staff sergeant. *Member:* American Political Science Association.

WRITINGS: Conducting Political Research, Harper, 1971.

Contributor: Lee R. McPheters, editor, *The Economics of Crime and Law Enforcement,* C. C Thomas, 1975; Thomas Cook and Frank Scioli, editors, *Methodologies for Analyzing Public Policies,* Heath, 1975; Robert Lineberry and Louis Masotti, editors, *Urban Problems and Public Policy,* Heath, 1976; Lineberry and Masotti, editors, *The New Urban Politics,* Ballinger, 1976. Contributor to history, business, and political science journals.

WORK IN PROGRESS: Research on public policy analysis.

*   *   *

JONES, George Hilton 1924-

PERSONAL: Born January 11, 1924, in Baton Rouge, La.; son of William Carruth (a lawyer and judge) and Elizabeth (Kirkpatrick) Jones. *Education:* Louisiana State University, B.A., 1947; Oxford University, D.Phil., 1950. *Politics:* Democrat. *Home:* 1536 Third St., Apt. 3, Charleston, Ill. 61920. *Office:* Department of History, Eastern Illinois University, Charleston, Ill. 61920.

CAREER: Hofstra College (now Hofstra University), Hempstead, N.Y., instructor in history, 1950-51; Indiana University at Bloomington, visiting assistant professor, 1951-52; Washington College, Chestertown, Md., assistant professor of history, 1954-56; Southern Regional Education Board, research associate, 1957-58; Texas Technological College (now Texas Tech University), Lubbock, assistant professor of history, 1958-60; Kansas State University, Manhattan, assistant professor, 1961-62, associate professor of history, 1962-64; Olivet College, Olivet, Mich., associate professor of history, 1964-66; Eastern Illinois University, Charleston, associate professor, 1966-72, professor of history, 1972—. Editor and commissioned writer, 1953-54, 1956-58. *Military service:* U.S. Army, 1943-45.

MEMBER: American Historical Association, Royal Historical Society (fellow), Conference on British Studies, Society for Italian Historical Studies, American Association of University Professors, American Society for Eighteenth-Century Studies. *Awards, honors:* Rhodes scholarship, 1947-50; Newberry Library fellowship, 1959; Guggenheim fellowship, 1960-61.

WRITINGS: The Main Stream of Jacobitism, Harvard University Press, 1954; (with Redding Sugg) *The Southern Regional Education Board,* Louisiana State University

Press, 1960; *Charles Middleton: The Life and Times of a Restoration Politician,* University of Chicago Press, 1967. Contributor to literature and history journals.

WORK IN PROGRESS: Research for a book on the English revolution of 1688.

SIDELIGHTS: George Jones writes: "I began writing as a requirement for the doctorate. My first subject was rejected as 'already done', and the one which was accepted, Jacobitism, I chose without much premeditation. It has been published. When that was done, I had found writing much too much fun to stop. As a research writer, I have done almost as much for institutional purposes or other uses as I have had published. In all cases, my aim has always been to extend or deepen available knowledge. I do not think highly of most reviews or reviewers of books."

* * *

JONES, Gwendolyn

PERSONAL: Born in Washington, D.C.; daughter of David Breese (in protein and nutrition research) and Clara (Chase) Jones. *Education:* Cornell University, A.B., 1938; Columbia University, M.L.S., 1951. *Politics:* Republican. *Religion:* Unitarian Universalist. *Home:* 132 East 36th St., New York, N.Y. 10016. *Office:* St. Regis Paper Co., 150 East 42nd St., New York, N.Y. 10017.

CAREER: New York Academy of Medicine Library, New York City, reference assistant, 1949-51; Bankers Trust Co., New York City, library cataloger, 1951-52; Consumers Union, New York City, reference assistant, 1952-56; St. Regis Paper Co., New York City, librarian, 1956—. *Member:* Special Libraries Association, Appalachian Mountain Club, Adirondack Mountain Club.

WRITINGS: Packaging Information Sources, Gale, 1967.

AVOCATIONAL INTERESTS: Painting, hiking, travel.

* * *

JONES, H(ouston) G(wynne) 1924-

PERSONAL: Born January 7, 1924, near Yanceyville, N.C.; son of Paul Hosier (a farmer) and Lemma (Fowlkes) Jones. *Education:* Appalachian State Teachers College (now Appalachian State University), B.S. (magna cum laude), 1949; George Peabody College for Teachers, M.A., 1950; Duke University, Ph.D., 1965. *Home:* 302 Country Club Rd., Chapel Hill, N.C. 27514. *Office:* North Carolina Collection, University of North Carolina, Chapel Hill, N.C. 27514.

CAREER: Editor of weekly newspaper in Blowing Rock, N.C., 1949; Oak Ridge Military Institute, Oak Ridge, N.C., professor of history and political science, 1950-53; West Georgia College, Carrollton, professor of history and chairman of division of Social Sciences, 1955-56; North Carolina Department of Archives and History, Raleigh, state archivist, 1956-68, director, 1968-74; University of North Carolina Library, North Carolina Collection, Chapel Hill, curator, 1974—. Visiting instructor in history, Western Carolina College (now University), summer, 1955; visiting instructor in history and archives management, Radcliffe College, summer, 1960; adjunct professor of history, North Carolina State University, 1966-71. Weekly columnist, writing "In the Light of History" for Associated Press, 1969—. Archival consultant to several states. *Military service:* U.S. Naval Reserve, active duty, 1942-46.

MEMBER: American Historical Association, American Association for State and Local History (member of council, 1972-76), Society of American Archivists (fellow; treasurer, 1961-67; vice-president, 1967; president, 1968), Institute of Early American History and Culture (member of council, 1970-73), Joint Committee on the Status of the National Archives (secretary, 1967-69), Southern Historical Association, North Carolina Literary and Historical Association (secretary-treasurer, 1969-75; president, 1976), North Carolina Society (secretary-treasurer, 1975—). *Awards, honors:* R.D.W. Connor Award, 1965, for best article in *North Carolina Historical Review;* Waldo G. Leland Prize of Society of American Archivists, 1967, and Award of Merit of American Association for State and Local History, 1968, for *For History's Sake;* Cannon Cup, North Carolina Society for the Preservation of Antiquities, 1971; recipient of first Distinguished Alumni Award, Appalachian State University, 1971; Halifax Resolves Award for historic preservation, 1974.

WRITINGS: Bedford Brown: State Rights Unionist, privately printed, 1956; *Guide to State and Provincial Archival Agencies: 1961,* Society of American Archivists, 1961; (editor with Julius H. Avant) *Union List of North Carolina Newspapers: 1751-1900,* North Carolina Department of Archives and History, 1963; *For History's Sake,* University of North Carolina Press, 1965; *The Records of a Nation,* Atheneum, 1969. Contributor to professional journals. Editor-in-chief, *North Carolina Historical Review,* 1968-74; member of editorial board, *William and Mary Quarterly,* 1970-73; member of advisory board, *Appalachian Journal,* 1972—; editor, *North Carolina Society Imprints,* 1977—.

WORK IN PROGRESS: North Carolina: A Guide to Information and Reference Sources, for Research and Reference Publications; an illustrated history of North Carolina.

* * *

JONES, Jo

PERSONAL: Born in Sussex, England. *Education:* Studied art in London and Paris, and in Italy. *Home:* 53 Whitelands House, Cheltenham Ter., London S.W.3, England. *Agent:* Wildenstein & Co. Ltd., Picture DLRs, 147 New Bond St., London W.1, England.

CAREER: Artist, painting mainly in oils. Her work has been exhibited frequently in Europe, starting in 1938; has had one-woman exhibitions in London, England, Paris, France, and Zurich, Switzerland; during the years 1952-60, she lived "mainly among the gypsies of Granada, Spain"; since 1965, she has painted mainly in Morocco, where she held an exhibit in Rabat. Her paintings are included in the French State Collection, the Gypsy Museum at University of Leeds, and many private collections in America and Europe.

WRITINGS: Paintings and Drawings of the Gypsies of Granada, text by Augustus John and others, Folklore Associates, 1969. Contributor of drawings to *Journal of the Gypsy Lore Society.*

WORK IN PROGRESS: Preparing for exhibitions in London and Zurich.

SIDELIGHTS: Sacheverell Sitwell wrote in the catalog of Jo Jones' 1971 exhibit in London: "... It is somewhat of a relief to come into a gallery full of paintings and be able to name the places depicted, even point to them on the map. Their happy impression is heightened when the paintings in question, far from being behind the times, have made full use of the most up-to-date techniques. I believe these remarks are of particular application to this present exhibition of paintings by Jo Jones who, having worked for long in Spain, now tackles the wonders of Morocco . . . Her talents seem to have fulfilled themselves especially at Tafraout, and I think that her paintings of this fantastic valley with its rocks of blazing colours are her best works so far. . . . I cannot see them without thinking how much Augustus John . . . would have admired this fruition of her talents.''

*   *   *

JONES, John Bush 1940-

PERSONAL: Born August 3, 1940, in Chicago, Ill.; son of Aaron J., Jr. (a theater owner) and Dorothy (Bush) Jones; married Sandra Carson (a law student), May 18, 1968; children: Aaron Carson. *Education:* Attended Harvard University, 1958-59; Northwestern University, B.S. (with distinction), 1962, M.A., 1963, Ph.D., 1970. *Residence:* Lawrence, Kan. *Office:* Department of English, University of Kansas, Lawrence, Kan. 66045.

CAREER: Happy Medium Theatre, Chicago, Ill., assistant stage manager, 1960-61; Wagon Wheel Playhouse, Warsaw, Ind., lighting designer and stage manager, 1962; Northwestern University, Evanston, Ill., instructor in English, 1965-68; University of Kansas, Lawrence, assistant professor, 1968-72, associate professor, 1972-77, professor of English, 1977—. Founder and stage director, Northwestern University Gilbert and Sullivan Guild and, with wife, of University of Kansas Mount Oread Gilbert and Sullivan Company; chairman, International Conference on Gilbert and Sullivan held at Lawrence, Kan., 1970. *Member:* Modern Language Association of America, American Educational Theatre Association, Savage Club (London). *Awards, honors:* Newberry Library grant, 1971; American Philosophical Society grant, 1972.

WRITINGS: W. S. Gilbert: A Century of Scholarship and Commentary, New York University Press, 1970; (editor) *Readings in Descriptive Bibliography,* Kent State University Press, 1974. Contributor to *Encyclopedia Americana* and to literary and library journals. Special drama correspondent, *Kansas City Star.*

WORK IN PROGRESS: Research on printing and publishing of Victorian periodicals and drama.

*   *   *

JONES, Major J. 1919-

PERSONAL: Born 1919, in Rome, Ga.; son of Pleas and Bertha (Freeman) Jones; married Mattie Parker; children: Chandra. *Education:* Clark College, A.B., 1941; Gammon Theological Seminary, B.D., 1944; Oberlin College, S.T.M., 1950; Boston University, Th.D., 1957. *Office:* Office of the President, Gammon Theological Seminary, 653 Beckwith St. S.W., Atlanta, Ga. 30314.

CAREER: Ordained Methodist minister; pastor in Georgia, East Tennessee, and Gennessee, Ky. Conference, of United Methodist Church, 1952-53; Wiley College, Marshall, Tex., college minister and professor of religion; Fisk University, Nashville, Tenn., dean of chapel, 1956—; Tennessee-Kentucky Conference, Nashville, Tenn., district superintendent; Gammon Theological Seminary, Atlanta, Ga., president and director, 1968—; Interdenominational Theological Center, Atlanta, member of faculty, 1968—. Fellow, Yale University Center for Continuing Education, 1967-68. Lecturer, Berkeley Theological Union, Center for Urban-Black Studies, 1969, Emory University, 1971. Participant in

professional workshops and conferences. Member of board of directors, Southern Christian Leadership Conference, Black Methodists for Church Renewal. Member of board of trustees, Clark College; member of board of visitors, Duke University Divinity School. Member of board of managers, Butler Street YMCA.

MEMBER: American Society of Christian Ethics, United Methodist Association of Deans and Presidents, Committee of Southern Churchmen (member of board of directors), Theta Phi. *Awards, honors:* Alpha Achievement award, Psi Lambda chapter, 1967; declaration from President William Tubman in Liberia, 1971; Distinguished Alumni award, Boston University, School of Theology, 1971; Doctor of Ministry, Vanderbilt University.

WRITINGS: (Contributor) Wilson O. Weldon, editor, *When Fires Burn,* Upper Room, 1969; *Black Awareness: A Theology of Hope,* Abingdon, 1971. Contributor to *Risk and Reality,* Women's Division Study Book, Board of Missions, United Methodist Church. Contributor to *Church School, Adult Student, Advocate,* and *Christian Century.* Booknote editor, *Central Christian Advocate.*

*   *   *

JONES, Marc Edmund 1888-

PERSONAL: Born October 1, 1888, in St. Louis, Mo.; son of Edmund Henry (a sales manager) and Lulu (Holmes) Jones; married Lela Liebrand, 1918 (divorced); married Priscilla Kennedy, June 11, 1926. *Education:* Occidental College, B.A., 1932; San Francisco Theological Seminary, B.D., 1935; Columbia University, Ph.D., 1948. *Politics:* Independent (registered Republican). *Home:* 2324 Norman Rd., Stanwood, Wash. 98292.

CAREER: Employed by Pullman Co., a machine shop and foundry in Calif., and Western Electric Co. until age 24; free-lance writer and editor, 1913—. Ordained minister of United Presbyterian Church; served brief pastorate with Presbyterian church in Esparto, Calif., 1933-38; occasional professional psychological, lay psychoanalytical, and astrological counselling, 1914—. *Military service:* U.S. Army, 1918; edited *Barbed Wire* in Sackett's Harbor, N.Y. *Member:* Authors League of America, American Guild of Authors and Composers, American Society of Church History, American Federation of Astrologers, Advertising Club of New York, Phi Beta Kappa, Phi Delta Kappa, Sigma Alpha Epsilon, three astrological associations, in New York, N.Y., Tempe, Ariz., and Seattle, Wash.

WRITINGS: The New Genesis, privately printed, 1915; *Key Truths of Occult Philosophy: An Introduction to the Codex Occultus,* J. F. Rowny, 1925, reprinted as *Occult Philosophy: An Introduction, the Major Concepts and a Glossary,* McKay, 1948; *The Ritual of Living: An Occult Manual,* J. F. Rowny, 1930, revised and expanded edition published as *The Sabian Manual: A Ritual for Living,* Sabian Publishing Society, 1957; *How to Learn Astrology,* McKay, 1941, revised edition, Sabian Publishing Society, 1969; *The Guide to Horoscope Interpretation,* McKay, 1941; *Problem Solving by Horary Astrology* ("a complete analysis and demonstration comprising a clarification and modernization of an interestingly effective seventeenth-century psychology"), McKay, 1943, revised edition, Sabian Publishing Society, 1971; *Astrology: How and Why It Works,* McKay, 1945, revised edition published as *Astrology; How and Why It Works: An Introduction to Basic Horoscopy,* Sabian Publishing Society, 1969; *Gandhi Lives,* illustrations and afterword by Paramhansa Yogananda,

McKay, 1948 (withdrawn for revision after first printing); *George Sylvester Morris: His Philosophical Career and Theistic Idealism*, McKay, 1948.

The Sabian Symbols in Astrology, Illustrated by One Thousand Horoscopes of Well-Known People, Sabian Publishing Society, 1953, 4th edition, 1972; *The Essentials of Astrological Analysis, Illustrated in the Horoscopes of One Hundred and Seventy-Four Well-Known People*, Sabian Publishing Society, 1960; *The Scope of Astrological Prediction: An Introduction to the Dynamic Horoscopy*, Sabian Publishing Society, 1969; *Mundane Perspectives in Astrology: The Expanded Dynamic Horoscopy*, Shabhala Publications, 1975; *How to Live with the Stars: Simplified Personal Astrology*, Theosophical Publishing, 1976. Screen writer, 1912—; contributor of pulp fiction to magazines, 1918-46; author of approximately 3,000 mimeographed lessons in philosophy and occultism for Sabian Assembly, 1924-45. Ghost writer and author of miscellaneous publications.

WORK IN PROGRESS: Fundamentals of Number Significance; A Handbook of Fantasy; The Magical Squares of Solomon Ben Judah ibn Gabirol.

SIDELIGHTS: Marc E. Jones calls himself "a pioneer scenario writer," and was founder in 1912-13 of what has become the Screen Writers' Guild. He told *CA:* "Because my course has been consistently offbeat with first prominence in movies (my mother wouldn't go to see my first release in a top Chicago theater in 1912) and present major prominence in astrology (still very carnival in its public manifestation), I have avoided all possible publicity except in narrow technical areas. Thus I am seldom written up and have kept no special record of instances. This has spared me interruption. Fundamentally I am insatiably curious about everything that lives or moves or exhibits anything by way of special character, and I find circumstances provide me with more than enough to fill my hours."

Jones has varying degrees of competence in French, Greek, Hebrew, German, Spanish, Latin, Sanskrit, Egyptian, and Assyrian. His 1930 publication, *The Ritual of Living: An Occult Manual*, is now considered a collector's item.

* * *

JONES, William M(cKendrey) 1927-

PERSONAL: Born September 19, 1927, in Dothan, Ala.; son of William M. (a salesman) and Margaret (Farmer) Jones; married Ruth Ann Roberts, August 14, 1952; children: Margaret, Elizabeth, Bronwen. *Education:* University of Alabama, B.A., 1949, M.A., 1950; Northwestern University, Ph.D., 1953. *Home:* 209 Russell Blvd., Columbia, Mo. 65201. *Office:* Department of English, University of Missouri, Columbia, Mo. 65201.

CAREER: Wisconsin State College—Eau Claire (now University of Wisconsin—Eau Claire), associate professor of English, 1953-55; University of Michigan, Ann Arbor, assistant professor of English, 1955-59; University of Missouri—Columbia, assistant professor, 1959-60, associate professor, 1960-65, professor of English, 1965—, associate dean of Graduate School, 1966-68. Communications consultant; lecturer on communications and on Shakespeare. *Military service:* U.S. Army, 1946-47. U.S. Naval Reserve, 1949-56; became lieutenant junior grade. *Member:* Modern Language Association of America, Renaissance Society of America, Shakespeare Society of America. *Awards, honors:* Folger Shakespeare Library research fellow, 1955.

WRITINGS: Stages of Composition, Heath, 1964; *Fiction:*

Form and Experience, Heath, 1969; *Guide to Living Power*, John Knox, 1975; (with wife, Ruth Ann Jones) *Living in Love*, John Knox, 1976; *Speaking Up in Church*, Broadman, 1977. Contributor to *Camera 35, Historian*, and other journals.

WORK IN PROGRESS: Shakespeare's Comic Resurrections.

* * *

JORDAN, Alma Theodora 1929-

PERSONAL: Born December 29, 1929, in Tunapuna, Trinidad, West Indies; daughter of Aaron T. (an agriculturist) and Lucy (Gibbs) Warner; married Lennox Jordan (a medical practitioner), October 20, 1962. *Education:* University of London, B.A. (honors), 1951; Eastern Caribbean Regional Library School, A.L.A., 1955; Royal College of Music, London, A.R.C.M., 1957; Columbia University, M.S., 1958, D.L.S., 1966. *Religion:* Roman Catholic. *Home:* 28 Gilweil Rd., Valsayn Park, Curepe, Trinidad, West Indies. *Office:* Library, University of the West Indies, St. Augustine, Trinidad, West Indies.

CAREER: Carnegie Free Library, San Fernando, Trinidad, librarian, 1955-56; Industrial Development Corp., Port of Spain, Trinidad, librarian, 1959-60; University of the West Indies, St. Augustine, Trinidad, librarian-in-charge, 1960—. Member of executive board, Seminar on the Acquisition of Latin American Library Materials, 1969-72. *Member:* American Library Association, Library Association (United Kingdom), Association of Caribbean Universities and Research Libraries (president, 1969-70; member of executive board, 1969-71), Library Association of Trinidad and Tobago (chairman, 1961-63). *Awards, honors:* Grolier Society fellowship at Columbia University School of Library Science, 1957-59.

WRITINGS: The Development of Library Service in the West Indies through Inter-Library Co-operation, Scarecrow, 1970; (editor) *Research Library Cooperation in the Caribbean*, American Library Association, 1973; (contributor) K. E. Ingram and A. Jefferson, editors, *Libraries and the Challenge of Change*, Mansell, 1975. Contributor to library journals.

WORK IN PROGRESS: A bibliography of West Indian bibliographies.

AVOCATIONAL INTERESTS: Music.

* * *

JORDAN, Amos A(zariah) 1922-

PERSONAL: Born February 11, 1922, in Twin Falls, Idaho; son of Amos Azariah and Olive (Fisher) Jordan; married Mardeane Carver, June 5, 1946; children: Peggy, Diana (Mrs. Dan Paxton), Keith, David, Linda (Mrs. Dan Mobey), Kent. *Education:* Idaho State College (now University), student, 1942; U.S. Military Academy, B.S., 1946; Oxford University, B.A., 1950, M.A., 1955; Columbia University, Ph.D., 1961. *Religion:* Church of Jesus Christ of Latter-day Saints (Mormon). *Home:* 4000 Oak Hill Dr., Annandale, Va. 22003. *Office:* Center for Strategic and International Studies, Georgetown University, 1800 K St. N.W., Washington, D.C. 20006.

CAREER: U.S. Army, cadet, 1943-46, officer, 1946-72, became brigadier general. U.S. Military Academy, West Point, N.Y., instructor in political science and economics, 1950-53, professor of social science, 1955-72, head of department, 1969-72; director, Aspen Institute for Humanistic

Studies, 1972-74; U.S. Department of Defense, Washington, D.C., principal deputy assistant secretary of defense for international security affairs, 1974-76; U.S. Department of State, Washington, D.C., deputy under secretary of state and acting under secretary for security assistance, 1976-77; Georgetown University, Washington, D.C., executive director, Center for Strategic and International Studies, 1977—. Has lectured at Harvard University, Princeton University, University of Pennsylvania, Columbia University, and numerous other colleges, universities, and various war colleges and service academies. Advisor, U.S. Economic Aid Mission to Korea, 1955; staff member, President's Committee to Study the Military Assistance Program, 1959; staff director, Advisory Committee to Secretary of Defense on Non-Military Instruction, 1962; special political adviser to U.S. Ambassador to India, New Delhi, 1963-64; director of Near East and Southern Asia Region, Office of Secretary of Defense, 1966-67.

MEMBER: Institute for Strategic Studies (London), Council on Foreign Relations, Association of American Rhodes Scholars. *Awards, honors*—Military: Distinguished Service Medal; Legion of Merit with oak-leaf cluster; Army Commendation Medal with oak leaf-cluster. Other: Rhodes scholar at Oxford University, 1947; Einstein Prize, Columbia University, 1961.

WRITINGS: (Contributor) G. A. Lincoln, and others, *Economics of National Security,* Prentice-Hall, 1950; (contributor) U.S. Military Academy, Department of Social Sciences, *Contemporary Foreign Governments,* Rinehart, 1953; *Foreign Aid and the Defense of Southeast Asia,* Praeger, 1962; (contributor) *Southeast Asia: Problems of United States Policy,* Massachusetts Institute of Technology, 1963; (editor and contributor) *Issues of National Security in the 1970's,* Praeger, 1967; (contributor) *Handbook of Military Institutions,* Sage Publications, 1971. Contributor to *Encyclopedia Americana, Annals of the American Academy of Political and Social Sciences, Journal of International Affairs, Orbis,* and to other journals and periodicals.

WORK IN PROGRESS: American Defense Policy.

*   *   *

JORDAN, David M(alcolm)   1935-

PERSONAL: Born January 5, 1935, in Philadelphia, Pa.; son of Robert N. (a realtor) and Mary (McCulken) Jordan; married Barbara James, February 6, 1960; children: Diana, Laura, Sarah. *Education:* Princeton University, A.B., 1956; University of Pennsylvania, J.D., 1959. *Politics:* Democrat. *Religion:* Presbyterian. *Home:* 410 Rodman Ave., Jenkintown, Pa. 19046. *Office:* 515 Swede St., Norristown, Pa. 19401.

CAREER: Attorney in Philadelphia, Pa., 1960-65, and Norristown, Pa., 1965—. Jenkintown (Pa.) Borough Council, councilman, 1966-76, president, 1976—. Member of Pennsylvania Democratic State Committee, 1968-70; chairman of Montgomery County Democratic Committee, 1972-75. *Military service:* U.S. Army, 1960. *Member:* Abington Library Society (president, 1970-71).

WRITINGS: Roscoe Conkling of New York, Cornell University Press, 1971.

WORK IN PROGRESS: Democratic General: The Postwar Career of Winfield Scott Hancock.

JORDAN, June   1936-
(June Meyer)

PERSONAL: Born July 9, 1936, in Harlem, New York, N.Y.; daughter of Granville Ivanhoe (a postal clerk) and Mildred Maude (Fisher) Jordan; married Michael Meyer, 1955 (divorced, 1965); children: Christopher David. *Education:* Attended Barnard College, 1953-57, and University of Chicago, 1955-65. *Politics:* ''Politics of survival and change.'' *Religion:* ''Humanitarian.'' *Residence:* New York, N.Y. *Agent:* Joan Daves, 515 Madison Ave., New York, N.Y. 10022. *Office:* Department of English, City College of the City University of New York, New York, N.Y. 10033.

CAREER: Assistant to producer for motion picture ''The Cool World,'' New York City, 1963-64; Mobilization for Youth, Inc., New York City, associate research writer in technical housing department, 1965-66; City College of the City University of New York, New York City, instructor in English and literature, 1966-68; teacher of English and director of Search for Education, Elevation and Knowledge (SEEK Program), Connecticut College, New London, 1967-69; Sarah Lawrence College, Bronxville, N.Y., instructor in literature, 1969-74; City College of the City University of New York, assistant professor of English, 1975—. Visiting poet at State University of New York at Stoney Brook and writer-in-residence, City College of the City University of New York. Visiting lecturer in English and Afro-American Studies, Yale University, 1974-75. Has given poetry readings in schools and colleges around the country and at the Guggenheim Museum. Founder and co-director, Voice of the Children, Inc.; co-founder, Afro-Americans against the Famine, 1973—. Member of board of directors, Teachers and Writers Collaborative, Inc.

AWARDS, HONORS: Rockefeller grant for creative writing, 1969-70; Prize of Rome in Environmental Design, 1970-71; Nancy Bloch Award, 1971, for *The Voice of the Children; New York Times* selection as one of the year's outstanding young adult novels, 1971, and nominee for National Book Award, 1971, for *His Own Where;* New York Council of the Humanities award, 1977.

WRITINGS: Who Look at Me, Crowell, 1969; (editor) *Soulscript,* Doubleday, 1970; (editor with Terri Bush) *The Voice of the Children* (a reader), Holt, 1970; *Some Changes* (poems), Dutton, 1971; *His Own Where* (young adult), Crowell, 1971; *Dry Victories* (juvenile and young adult), Holt, 1972; *Biography of Fannie Lou Hamer,* Crowell, 1972; *New Days: Poems of Exile and Return,* Emerson Hall, 1973; *New Room: New Life,* Crowell, 1975; *Selected Poems of June Jordan: Things That I Do in the Dark,* Random House, 1977; *Okay Now,* Simon & Schuster, 1977. Contributor of stories and poems, prior to 1969 under name June Meyer, to national periodicals, including *Esquire, Nation, Evergreen, Partisan Review, Black World, Black Creation, Essence,* and to newspapers including *Village Voice, New York Times,* and *New York Times Magazine.*

SIDELIGHTS: June Jordan expressed her views on poetry in this way, ''A great variety of black people are writing poetry today—it is not any elitist preoccupation but an activity involving everybody.'' Jordan continues: ''Black youths are finding they don't have to worry about putting together someone else's idea. Frequently, in their own poetic way, they express themselves in classrooms and a teacher will ask, 'What are you trying to say?' Actually, he has already said it—communicated it very well and poetically—but the teacher, who is not tuned in, did not understand it.''

In her book, *Fannie Lou Hamer,* June Jordan describes the life of a woman who was born in Mississippi in 1917, the youngest child in a family of twenty. After years of working a twelve to fourteen hour day, Fannie Hamer became involved in black voter registration in Mississippi in 1962. As a result of this involvement Fannie Hamer was beaten, jailed, and left homeless until Martin Luther King came to her aid and brought her plight to public attention. Her hard work led eventually to the formation of a six-hundred-forty acre Mississippi farm named, The Freedom Farm Cooperative.

The Academy of American Poets sponsored June Jordan's poetry readings in the New York City public schools.

BIOGRAPHICAL/CRITICAL SOURCES: New York Times, April 25, 1969; *Negro Digest,* February, 1970; *Saturday Review,* April 17, 1971; *New York Times Book Review,* November 7, 1971; *Christian Science Monitor,* November 11, 1971; *Redbook,* August, 1972; *Contemporary Literary Criticism,* Volume V, Gale, 1976; *Washington Post,* October 13, 1977; *San Francisco Examiner,* December 7, 1977.

*   *   *

JORDAN, Norman   1938-

PERSONAL: Born July 30, 1938, in Ansted, W.Va.; son of Harold and Rose (Rogers) Jordan; married Brucella Wiggins (a student), July 24, 1965; children: Shirie, Eric. *Education:* Dropped out of junior high school. *Politics:* "Life." *Religion:* None. *Office:* Department of English, Case Western Reserve University, Cleveland, Ohio 44106.

CAREER: Worked as a laborer, 1960-63, state highway inspector, 1963-65, and youth worker at a neighborhood center, 1966-77; Hough Youth Center, Cleveland, Ohio, technical writer, 1967-69; Karamu House (center for the arts and multiracial communication), Cleveland, writer-in-residence, 1970-71; Case Western Reserve University, Cleveland, assistant professor of English, 1971-72. Artistic director, One World Theatre (summer theater at Cuyahoga Community College), 1971-72; member of executive committee, Hough Development Corp. *Military service:* U.S. Navy, 1955-59. *Awards, honors:* Recipient of first Harriett Eells Performing Arts fellowship at Karamu House.

WRITINGS: Destination: Ashes (poems), Third World Press, 1971; *Above Maya* (poems), RA Press, 1971. Poetry represented in numerous anthologies, including *Black Fire* and *The New Black Poetry;* contributor of poetry to little magazines.

Plays produced: "Cadillac Dreams," Bed-Study Theatre, Brooklyn, N.Y., March, 1970; "In the Last Days," Karamu House, Cleveland, Ohio, May, 1971.

WORK IN PROGRESS: "Norman Jordan," a documentary film.†

*   *   *

JORDAN, Pat(rick M.)   1941-

PERSONAL: Born April 22, 1941, in Bridgeport, Conn.; son of Pat M. (a salesman) and Florence (Diamond) Jordan; married Carol Pruzinsky, February 11, 1961; children: Lisa, Jacqueline, Christopher, Stephanie, Robert. *Education:* Fairfield University, A.B., 1965. *Religion:* Roman Catholic. *Home:* 1134 Valley Rd., Bridgeport, Conn. 06604. *Agent:* Sterling Lord Agency, 660 Madison Ave., New York, N.Y. 10021.

CAREER: Professional baseball player, 1959-62; construc-

tion worker, 1962; newspaper reporter, 1962-65; auto racer, 1964-67; high school English teacher, 1965-70.

WRITINGS—All published by Dodd: *Black Coach,* 1971; *Suitors of Spring,* 1973; *A False Spring,* 1975; *Broken Patterns,* 1977. Contributor to *Sports Illustrated.*

WORK IN PROGRESS: A collection of previously published articles; a novel; biographies of three ghetto basketball players.

*   *   *

JORDAN, William A.   1928-

PERSONAL: Born September 10, 1928, in Chicago, Ill.; son of Marion (an educator) and Katie (Allison) Jordan; married Gretchen Bickell (a school principal), June 13, 1964. *Education:* Antioch College, B.S., 1950; Columbia University, M.S., 1955; University of California, Los Angeles, Ph.D., 1968. *Residence:* Nobleton, Ontario, Canada. *Office:* York University, 4700 Keele St., Toronto, Ontario, Canada M3J 2R6.

CAREER: James C. Buckley, Inc. (consultants), New York, N.Y., air route analyst, 1955-57; Northwestern University, Evanston, Ill., assistant to research director, 1958-60; Western Air Lines, Los Angeles, Calif., economist, 1960-64; Stanford University, Stanford, Calif., assistant professor of business economics, 1965-67; York University, Toronto, Ontario, associate professor, 1967-74, professor of business economics, 1974—. Adviser to United States Senate and to Civil Aeronautics Board. Economic consultant to airlines and U.S. Department of Justice. *Military service:* U.S. Marine Corps, 1951-53; became staff sergeant. U.S. Air Force Reserve, 1955—; present rank, colonel. *Member:* American Economic Association, Canadian Economic Association, Transportation Research Forum, Western Economic Association, Beta Gamma Sigma.

WRITINGS: Airline Regulation in America: Effects and Imperfections, Johns Hopkins Press, 1970.

WORK IN PROGRESS: Evaluation of Civil Aeronautics Board activities; airline regulation in Canada.

*   *   *

JUDELLE, Beatrice   1908-

PERSONAL: Born April 18, 1908, in New York, N.Y.; daughter of Samuel and Lena (Sperber) Judelle; married Alexander J. Mittelman, March 29, 1938; children: Richard (stepson). *Education:* Hunter College (now Hunter College of the City University of New York), A.B., 1929. *Residence:* Yountville, Calif.

CAREER: National Retail Merchants Association, New York City, researcher, 1933-41; Haire Publications (publishers of trade magazines), New York City, research director, 1943-50; *Stores* (magazine), New York City, research editor, 1950-55; research consultant in New York City, San Rafael, and Yountville, Calif., 1955—.

WRITINGS: (With Jeannette Jarnow) *Inside the Fashion Business,* Wiley, 1965, 2nd edition, 1974; (with Charles Binder) *Branch Manager's Manual,* National Retail Merchants Association, 1968; *Management Manual for Independent Stores,* National Retail Merchants Association, 1969; (with Mary Troxell) *Fashion Merchandising,* McGraw, 1970; *The Fashion Buyer's Job,* National Retail Merchants Association, 1971. Contributor of research articles and statistical studies to trade publications.

WORK IN PROGRESS: Third edition of *Inside the Fashion Business.*

JUDY, Marvin T(hornton) 1911-

PERSONAL: Born July 10, 1911, in Thayer, Mo.; son of William Edwin (a clergyman) and Alice (Sheible) Judy; married Murlene Oleta Garrett (a bibliographical researcher), June 3, 1934; children: Marvin Garrett, Dwight Henry. *Education:* Central Methodist College, A.B., 1933; Eden Theological Seminary, B.D., 1945; Iowa State College of Agriculture and Mechanical Arts (now Iowa State University of Science and Technology), M.S., 1952. *Home:* 5734 Vanderbilt, Dallas, Tex. 75206. *Office:* Perkins School of Theology, Southern Methodist University, Dallas, Tex. 75275.

CAREER: Clergyman of United Methodist Church; pastor in Birch Tree, Mo., 1933-41, and St. Louis, Mo., 1941-44; Harrison County Larger Parish, Cainsville, Mo., director, 1944-51; Methodist Church in Iowa, Des Moines, director of town and country work, 1951-52; Southern Methodist University, Perkins School of Theology, Dallas, Tex., professor of sociology of religion, 1952—, director of Center for Research in Parish Leadership and Community Development, 1967—. *Member:* American Sociological Association, Rural Sociological Association, Religious Research Association, Association for the Scientific Study of Religion, United Methodist Rural Fellowship (president, 1968-72). *Awards, honors:* D.D., Central Methodist College, Fayette, Mo., 1964; Lilly Endowment research grant, 1964-68.

WRITINGS—All published by Abingdon: *The Larger Parish and Group Ministry,* 1959; *Parish Development Aids,* 1964; *The Cooperative Parish in Nonmetropolitan Areas,* 1967; (with wife, Murlene O. Judy) *The Multiple Staff Ministry,* 1969; *The Parish Development Process,* 1973. Also author of about twenty-two research reports on religious topics.

*   *   *

JUNKINS, Donald 1931-

PERSONAL: Born December 19, 1931, in Saugus, Mass.; son of Ralph Chester (a businessman) and Evelyn (Keyes) Junkins; married Martha Luppold (an artist), June 28, 1958; children: Karn, Daniel, Theodore. *Education:* University of Massachusetts, B.A., 1953; Boston University, S.T.B., 1956, S.T.M., 1957, A.M., 1959, Ph.D., 1963. *Politics:* Democrat. *Religion:* Christian. *Home:* Hawks Rd., Deerfield, Mass. 01342. *Office:* Department of English, University of Massachusetts, Amherst, Mass. 01003.

CAREER: Emerson College, Boston, Mass., instructor, 1961-62, assistant professor of English, 1962-63; Chico State College (now California State University), Chico, assistant professor of English, 1963-66; University of Massachusetts—Amherst, 1966—, began as assistant professor, currently professor of English, director of M.F.A. program in English, 1970—. *Awards, honors:* Bread Loaf Writers' Conference poetry scholarship, summer, 1959; Jennie Tane Award for Poetry, 1968; National Endowment for the Arts Reprint Award, 1969; John Masefield Memorial Award, 1973; National Endowment for the Arts Creative Writing Fellowship grant, 1974.

WRITINGS: The Sunfish and the Partridge (poems), Pym-Randall, 1965; *The Graves of Scotland Parish* (poems), Heron House, 1969; *Walden, One Hundred Years after Thoreau* (poem), Yorick, 1969; *And Sandpipers She Said* (poems), University of Massachusetts Press, 1970; (editor) *The Contemporary World Poets,* Harcourt, 1976; *The Uncle Harry Poems and Other Maine Reminiscences,* Out-

land Press, 1977; *Crossing by Ferry: Poems New and Selected,* University of Massachusetts Press, 1978.

Poetry included in anthologies, including *Classic Short Fiction,* edited by James K. Bowen, Bobbs-Merrill, 1972, *Themes in American Literature,* edited by Charles Genthe and George Keithley, Heath, 1972, and *The "New Yorker" Book of Poems,* edited by staff of *New Yorker,* Viking, 1974. Contributor of poetry to *New Yorker, Atlantic, Sewanee Review, Sumac, Poetry, Northwest Review, Antioch Review,* and other periodicals, and of articles to *Atlantic, Harpers, American Literature, Early American Literature, Studies in Short Fiction, Critique,* and others. Poetry editor, *Massachusetts Review,* 1970-74.

WORK IN PROGRESS: A translation of Euripedes' *Andromache,* for Oxford University Press.

SIDELIGHTS: Donald Junkins summers with his family on Swan's Island, Maine, where they own a twenty-two foot Muscongus Bay sloop, and where he built his own house with the help of Gleason Scott.

Junkins told *CA:* "Most of my poems start out as reminders, and end up as explorations of moments of deep feeling. I write to get in touch with parts of myself I can't contact in any other way. Writing a poem is not like anything else; it takes almost infinite patience and you've got to be willing to explore a lot of branches of feeling that lead you to a possible beginning. Revisions extend the phases of the poem as you listen to the overtones of your voice and get glimpses of the changeling states of a moment revealing itself to you.

"In my own career, knowing other writers who were good human beings helped me. One of my teachers, Amiya Chakravarty, brought me to visit Robert Frost several times. Gerald Warner Brace and Robert Lowell were writing teachers who befriended me, and their approval helped. So did publishing my own poems. There's a terrific satisfaction in finishing and publishing a piece of writing that pleases you and those you respect. Contrary to what others say about the process being its own reward, the reward for me has been the pleasure after. The writing itself is painful, as all writers know.

"I began to write seriously when I reached a dead-end in a Protestant seminary. The start of my way out was two graduate courses at Boston University with Brace and Lowell. Now that I look back twenty years, I can say that the only thing that I hoped to achieve through my books of poems is whatever it is that published books do for those who write them—give one a sense of achievement and some part of oneself that only writing can get you in touch with.

"Ultimately, there's no distinction between a good prose style and a good poetic style, and the quality of much contemporary American poetry would improve if more of our poets practiced the art of the basic American sentence. It's all a matter of concentration and strategy, the music of times effects. Contemporary American poetry needs fewer indulgent (and fragmented) rhapsodies, and more good American sentences."

*   *   *

KAHAN, Gerald 1923-

PERSONAL: Born November 28, 1923, in New York, N.Y.; son of Jacob and Annetta (Zeiken) Kahan; married Rae Ellen Moore, June, 1954; married second wife, Sara Nelle Maloney, June, 1967; children: (first marriage) Deirdre Ellen, Megan Martha. *Education:* University of Wisconsin, B.A., 1947, M.A., 1948, Ph.D., 1954. *Home:*

165 Chinquapin Way, Athens, Ga. 30605. *Office:* Department of Drama and Theatre, University of Georgia, Athens, Ga. 30602.

CAREER: Community Players of Sheboygan, Sheboygan, Wis., director, 1948-52; Western Washington College of Education (now Western Washington University), Bellingham, assistant professor of speech, 1954-56; Reed College, Portland, Ore., assistant professor of theatre, 1956-59; University of Georgia, Athens, associate professor, 1959-67, professor of theatre, 1967—. Guest professor, University of Colorado, 1958, 1960. *Military service:* U.S. Army Air Forces, 1944-45; became first lieutenant. *Member:* American Theatre Association, Southeastern Theatre Conference (president, 1968). *Awards, honors:* George Freedley Memorial Book Award, Theatre Library Association, 1976, for *Jacques Callot: Artist of the Theatre.*

WRITINGS: (Contributor) T. J. Shank, editor, *A Digest of 500 Plays* (summaries of classics), Crowell-Collier, 1963; (author of critical introduction and notes) William B. Maxwell, *The Mysterious Father,* University of Georgia Press, 1965; *Jacques Callot: Artist of the Theatre,* University of Georgia Press, 1976. Contributor to *Educational Theatre Journal, Players, Southern Theatre, Wisconsin Idea Theatre Quarterly,* and other publications. Editor of *Southern Theatre,* 1976—, *Curtain Call,* 1977—, and *Wisconsin Idea Theatre Quarterly.*

AVOCATIONAL INTERESTS: Gardening, bird watching, photography, and stamp collecting.

* * *

KAHLE, Roger (Raymond) 1943-

PERSONAL: Surname is pronounced *Call-ee;* born May 1, 1943, in Everett, Wash.; son of Walter Raymond (a horticulturist) and Dorothy (Schaus) Kahle; married Susan Jane Findling (a teacher), March 26, 1967; children: Michael Alan, Sara Anne. *Education:* Concordia Senior College, Fort Wayne, Ind., B.A., 1965; Concordia Seminary, St. Louis, Mo., M.Div., 1969; Columbia University, M.S., 1970; University of Missouri—Columbia, Ph.D., 1974. *Religion:* Lutheran. *Home:* 11 Charlesbank Ter., Newton, Mass. 02158. *Office:* School of Public Communication, Boston University, Boston, Mass. 02215.

CAREER: KFUO-AM/FM, St. Louis, Mo., announcer and producer, 1966-69; Humboldt State Teacher's College (now Humboldt State University), Arcata, Calif., lecturer in journalism, 1970-71; KBIA-FM, Columbia, Mo., newscaster, producer, and film critic, 1972; Neds-Wardlow Advertising Agency, Columbia, copywriter, 1972; University of Missouri—Columbia, instructor and research associate, 1972-74; Boston University, School of Public Communication, Boston, Mass., assistant professor of communications and associate dean, 1974—. *Member:* Association for Education in Journalism, Society of Professional Journalists, National Academy of Television Arts and Sciences, Kappa Tau Alpha.

WRITINGS: (With Robert E. A. Lee) *Popcorn and Parable: A New Look at the Movies,* Augsburg, 1971; *Implications for Using Mass Media in Dissemination of Water Research Results,* National Technical Information Service, U.S. Department of Commerce, 1974; *Mass Media Handbook for Water Resources Research Directors,* University of Missouri and U.S. Department of the Interior, 1975; (contributor) Bernard Rubin, editor, *Big Business and the Mass Media,* Lexington Books, 1977. Also co-author of a multimedia eighth-grade Lutheran catechism in "Mission: Life" series, Concordia Publishing House, 1973.

KAHN, Frank J(ules) 1938-

PERSONAL: Born April 3, 1938, in New York, N.Y.; son of Ernest L. (in finance) and Martha (Kwal) Kahn; married Abby Pearlman (a social worker), April 28, 1968; children: Julie, Leora. *Education:* Queens College (now Queens College of the City University of New York), B.A., 1958; Syracuse University, M.S., 1961; New York University, Ph.D., 1967. *Office:* Herbert H. Lehman College of the City University of New York, Bronx, N.Y. 10468.

CAREER: Queens College of the City University of New York, Flushing, N.Y., lecturer in mass communication, 1963-67; Herbert H. Lehman College of the City University of New York, Bronx, N.Y., assistant professor, 1967-70, associate professor of mass communication, 1971—. *Military service:* U.S. Army Reserve, 1962-68. *Member:* International Communication Association, Broadcasting Education Association. *Awards, honors:* Broadcast Preceptor award, San Francisco State College (now University), 1968, for *Documents of American Broadcasting;* H.A. Wichelns Award, Speech Communication Association, 1974, for article in *Free Speech Yearbook.*

WRITINGS: (Editor) *Documents of American Broadcasting,* Appleton, 1968, 2nd edition, Prentice-Hall, 1973. Contributor to *Free Speech Yearbook, Catholic University Law Review, Journal of Broadcasting, Federal Communications Bar Journal, Today's Speech,* and other publications.

WORK IN PROGRESS: A third edition of *Documents of American Broadcasting.*

* * *

KAHN, Si(mon) 1944-

PERSONAL: Born April 23, 1944, in Sussex County, Mass.; married Charlotte Brody (an organizer and registered nurse), June 6, 1974; children: (previous marriage) Simon, Jesse. *Education:* Harvard University, A.B., 1965. *Politics:* "Believe in right of folks to control their destinies." *Home:* 817 Carolina St., Roanoke Rapids, N.C. 27870.

CAREER: Organizer and consultant on organizing; worked on the Brookside strike in Harlan County, Kentucky; currently working on the J. P. Stevens campaign in the South. *Military service:* U.S. Army Reserve, 1965-1971.

WRITINGS: How People Get Power: Organizing Oppressed Communities for Action, McGraw, 1970; *The National Forests and Appalachia,* John Hay Whitney Foundation, 1972. Also writer of songs recorded on album, "New Wood," 1974, and of an historical musical, "200 RPM." Contributor to journals, including *New South, Mountain Life and Work, Sing Out, Youth,* and *Southern Exposure.*

WORK IN PROGRESS: Power Strategy, a sequel to *How People Get Power,* dealing with organizing techniques in conflict situations; collections of songs and poetry; a book of Southern textile songs; oral histories of mill workers.

AVOCATIONAL INTERESTS: Mountain and country music, songwriting, singing, playing the fiddle, auto mechanics, carpentry, fishing, "and especially my family."

* * *

KAHN, Theodore C(harles) 1912-

PERSONAL: Born October 13, 1912, in Germany; came to United States in 1922, naturalized in 1927; son of Samuel (a librarian) and Julia (Mayer) Kahn; married Shirley Rich, June 7, 1948; children: Donald Alan, Susan, Steven James. *Education:* Yale University, B.A., 1935; Columbia University, M.A. (counseling and guidance), 1940; University of Southern California, Ph.D., 1950; Mills College, M.A. (clinical psychology), 1952; University of Mainz, Dr. Rer. Nat. (anthropology), 1960. *Home:* 2103 Comanche Rd., Pueblo, Colo. 81001. *Office:* School of Social and Behavioral Science, University of Southern Colorado, Pueblo, Colo. 81001.

CAREER: U.S. Army, 1940-46, became major; University of California, Los Angeles, senior vocational counselor, 1946-48; Los Angeles City College System, Los Angeles, Calif., instructor in psychology, 1948-50; U.S. Air Force, Medical Science Corps, 1950-65, serving in Germany as chief clinical psychologist, retired as colonel; University of Southern Colorado, School of Social and Behavioral Science, Pueblo, professor, 1965—. Diplomate in clinical psychology, American Board of Professional Psychology. Lecturer at Wittenburg College, 1955-56. Consultant to National Association for Brain-Damaged Children, Montgomery County Mental Health Clinic, and other groups.

MEMBER: American Psychological Association (fellow), American Anthropological Association (past liaison fellow), American Association for the Advancement of Science (fellow), International Association for the Study of Symbols (founder and past president), Japanese Society for the Study of the Kahn Test of Symbol Arrangement (honorary president). *Awards, honors*—Military: Purple Heart. Civilian: Outstanding Educator of America award.

WRITINGS: The Kahn Test of Symbol Arrangement, Psychological Test Specialists, 1953; *The Kahn Intelligence Test (Culture Free),* Psychological Test Specialists, 1957; *Psychological Techniques in Diagnosis and Evaluation,* Pergamon, 1960; *An Introduction to Hominology: The Study of the Whole Man,* C. C Thomas, 1969, revised edition, 1972, third edition published as *An Introduction to Hominology: An Integrated View of Mankind and Self,* Nationwide Press, 1976; *Methods and Evaluation in Clinical and Counseling Psychology,* Pergamon, 1975; *Workbook on Moral Values,* Nationwide Press, 1977. Contributor to psychology journals.

WORK IN PROGRESS: Writing on the eight ages of man, a philosophical-evolutionary theory for explaining contemporary events, and on exploring the self-image by means of hominolograms; experiments in audiovisual-tactile rhythm induction therapy; a book, *Hominological Therapy.*

BIOGRAPHICAL/CRITICAL SOURCES: Mayo Clinical Proceedings, August, 1972.

*   *   *

KAKAR, Sudhir 1938-

PERSONAL: Born September 25, 1938, in Nainital, India; son of Sardarilal and Bimla (Kapoor) Kakar; married Apeksha Kilachand, December 22, 1969. *Education:* Gujarat University, B.E., 1958; University of Mannheim, D.K.M., 1964; University of Vienna, Dr. Rer. Comm., 1968; training candidate in psychoanalysis, Sigmund Freud Institute, Frankfurt, 1972—. *Home:* 1 Tilak Marg, Jaipur, India.

CAREER: Harvard University, Cambridge, Mass., lecturer in general education, 1966-67, research fellow, 1967-68; Indian Institute of Management, Ahmedabad, India, professor of organizational behavior, beginning 1969; Indian Institute of Technology, New Delhi, India, head of department of humanities and social sciences, 1976-77. Visiting professor in Vienna, 1974-75, and at McGill University, 1977—.

Member: Indian Psychological Association. *Awards, honors:* Karolyi Foundation Award for young writers, 1962.

WRITINGS: Frederick Taylor: A Study in Personality and Innovation, M.I.T. Press, 1970; (with Kamla Chowdhry) *Conflict and Choice: Indian Youth in a Changing Society,* Somaiya Publications (Bombay), 1970; (editor with Chowdhry) *Understanding Organizational Behavior,* Tata-McGraw-Hill (Delhi), 1971; *Personality and Authority in Work,* Somaiya Publications, 1976; *The Inner World,* Oxford University Press, 1977.

WORK IN PROGRESS: Traditional Indian Approaches to Mental Health and Healing.

AVOCATIONAL INTERESTS: Literature, music.

*   *   *

KALB, S(am) William 1897-

PERSONAL: Born November 12, 1897, in Newark, N.J.; son of Morris (in real estate) and Bertha (Roth) Kalb; married Amelia Segal, May 2, 1926; children: Patricia Irene (Mrs. Harvey Einhorn), Barbara Rose (Mrs. Edward Rachlin). *Education:* Valparaiso University, B.Sc., 1920, Ph.G., 1921; Cincinnati Medical School, M.D., 1925. *Religion:* Hebrew. *Home:* 377 South Harrison St., East Orange, N.J. 07018.

CAREER: Licensed to practice medicine in Ohio, 1925, and New Jersey, 1930; Newark City Hospital, Newark, N.J., intern, 1925; Washington Park Hospital, Chicago, Ill., intern, 1926; Berwind Clinics, New York, N.Y., intern 1927; Rotunda Hospital, Dublin, Ireland, resident, 1927; Allgemeines Krankenheim, Vienna, Austria, resident, 1928; Frauenklinik, Berlin, Germany, resident, 1928; physician in private practice, 1925-67. Adjunct attending physician, Beth Israel Hospital, Newark, 1932-45; lecturer and clinician, New York Post-Graduate Medical School, Columbia University, 1938-48; consultant in nutrition to U.S. Food and Drug Administration, U.S. Post Office Department, and Federal Trade Commission, 1953-63; chief of nutrition service, Clara Maas Memorial Hospital, Belleville, N.J., 1967-68; president, Essex County Blood Bank, 1966-70. *Military service:* U.S. Marine Corps, 1918-19.

MEMBER: American College of Gastroenterology, American College of Nutrition (president, 1961-65), American Medical Association, American Diabetes Association, Endocrine Society, American Jewish Congress (president of New Jersey division, 1935-36), Non-Sectarian Anti-Nazi League (president, 1937-41), Pan-American Medical Association, Future Physicians Club (founder), New Jersey Gastroenterological Society (president, 1959), Medical Society of New Jersey, Academy of Medicine of New Jersey, New Jersey Nutrition Council (president, 1956-58), Essex County Medical Society (president, 1960). *Awards, honors:* American Medical Association, Award in Health Education, 1949, Humanitarian Award for Service in Vietnam, 1966; Humanitarian Award, Independent Order of Odd Fellows, 1966; New Jersey Dietetic Association Award, 1967; City of Newark Humanitarian Award, 1967; Humanitarian Award, North Jersey Blood Bank, 1967; Future Physicians and Health Career Citation, 1968; New Jersey Health Careers Award, 1970.

WRITINGS: Counting Calories for the Patient, Rubin Press, 1959; *Calories to Burn,* Hammond, Inc., 1962; (with Christian A. Hovde) *Your Body: Its Anatomy and Nutrition,* Hammond, Inc., 1962, 2nd edition, 1964; *Your Future as a Physician,* Rosen Press, 1963, 3rd edition, 1972; *Wrap-*

ping Yourself in a Blanket of Fat, Minturn Press, 1973; *Nutrition: Its Past, Present and Future*, Minturn Press, 1973. Contributor to *Nutrition in Every Day Practice* and *Journal of the Medical Society of New Jersey*.

SIDELIGHTS: S. William Kalb has traveled in 152 countries studying conditions relating to nutritional problems.

* * *

KALLAUS, Norman F. 1924-

PERSONAL: Born March 30, 1924, in Richmond, Iowa; son of Roy J. and Maude E. Kallaus; married Alberta Sinn, 1953; children: Anne Marie, Margaret Mary, Clare Ellen. *Education:* University of Iowa, B.S.C., 1949, M.A., 1951, Ph.D., 1956. *Religion:* Roman Catholic. *Home:* R.R. 1, North Liberty, Iowa 52317. *Office:* Department of Business Education, University of Iowa, Iowa City, Iowa 52240.

CAREER: Teacher of business education in Iowa high schools, 1951-53; Arizona State University, Tempe, associate professor of business, 1961-62; senior editor, McGraw-Hill Book Co., 1962-63; University of Iowa, Iowa City, associate professor of business, 1963-67, professor of business education, 1967—, chairman of department of business education, 1965-71, 1973—. Visiting professor, Catholic University of America, 1961, Portland State University, summer, 1972. *Military service:* U.S. Army, 1943-46. *Member:* Administrative Management Society, American Administrative Management Society, American Business Communication Association, National Business Education Association, Iowa Business Education Association.

WRITINGS: Data Communications in Business, American Telephone & Telegraph Corp., 1966; (with Mina Johnson) *Records Management*, South-Western Publishing, 1967, 2nd edition, 1974; (with James Clark) *College Business Machines*, McGraw, 1970; (editor) *Iowa Business Education Handbook*, Iowa State Department of Public Instruction, 1972; (with John W. Neuner and B. Lewis Keeling) *Administrative Office Management*, South-Western Publishing, 6th edition (Kallaus was not associated with earlier editions), 1972, 7th edition, 1978; *An Office Employment Profile*, Iowa Business Education Association, 1973. Contributor to business journals.

* * *

KALLET, Arthur 1902-1972

December 15, 1902—February 24, 1972; American consumer advocate. Obituaries: *New York Times*, February 26, 1972; *Washington Post*, February 27, 1972.

* * *

KALT, Bryson R. 1934-

PERSONAL: Born August 7, 1934, in New York, N.Y.; son of Bryson Francis (a lumber executive) and Eleanor (VanBuskirk) Kalt; married Rhoda Knight Steel, April 6, 1957; children: Melissa Knight. *Education:* Columbia University, A.B., 1958, M.S., 1959. *Religion:* Dutch Reformed. *Residence:* New York, N.Y.

CAREER: Ted Bates & Co. (advertising agency), New York, N.Y., vice-president and account supervisor, 1960-70. *Military service:* U.S. Army, Infantry, 1959-64; became staff sergeant. *Member:* Baker Street Irregulars, Veterans of the 7th Regiment.

WRITINGS: The Mothers Guide to Child Safety, Grosset, 1971.

WORK IN PROGRESS: Two books on safety.

SIDELIGHTS: Bryson Kalt told *CA:* "Shortly after the birth of our little girl in 1966, I became aware of the amazing statistic that 'accidents kill and cripple more children than disease.' First for her protection and later because of a conviction that someone should be sounding the trumpet about Child Safety, I left a successful advertising career to tackle this topic on a number of fronts."

AVOCATIONAL INTERESTS: Travel, photography, book collecting.††

* * *

KAMINSKY, Alice R.

PERSONAL: Born in New York, N.Y.; daughter of Morris and Ida (Spivack) Richkin; married Jack Kaminsky (a professor of philosophy); children: Eric. *Education:* New York University, B.A., 1946, M.A., 1947, Ph.D., 1952. *Office:* Department of English, State University of New York College, Cortland, N.Y. 13045.

CAREER: Hunter College (now Hunter College of the City University of New York), New York, N.Y., instructor in English, 1952-53; Cornell University, Ithaca, N.Y., instructor in English, 1953-62; State University of New York College at Cortland, assistant professor, 1962-65, associate professor, 1965-68, professor of English, 1968—. *Member:* Modern Language Association of America.

WRITINGS: (Editor) *The Literary Criticism of George Henry Lewes*, University of Nebraska Press, 1964; *George Henry Lewes as Literary Critic*, Syracuse University Press, 1968; (contributor) J. Halperin, editor, *The Theory of the Novel: New Essays*, Oxford University Press, 1974; (with husband, Jack Kaminsky) *Logic: A Philosophical Introduction*, Addison-Wesley, 1974. Contributor to *PMLA*, *Midwest Quarterly*, *Bibliography of Philosophy*, and *Nineteenth Century French Studies*.

WORK IN PROGRESS: "Troilus and Criseyde" and the *Critics;* with Jack Kaminsky, *Romance of Reason*.

SIDELIGHTS: A reviewer for *Nineteenth Century Fiction* calls Alice Kaminsky's study of George Lewes "a balanced, original, and long overdue study; one could only wish that Lewes had been as important a critic as Mrs. Kaminsky would have us believe." The reviewer calls Lewes, who was novelist George Eliot's common-law husband, "a rather fusty and occasionally perverse critic, lacking the broadness of vision and concept that would place him, or any of the early Victorians, in the same class with Coleridge or Arnold. It is enough to say that Lewes was a responsible, mildly influential, and at times sensitive reviewer, whose comments are of sufficient interest and importance to justify the present survey of his work."

Timothy Gross writes of *Logic: A Philosophical Introduction:* "The clear style in which this text is written should enhance both the student's understanding of and interest in contemporary logic. Pragmatically, it contains extensive discussions of various forms of fallacious argumentation."

BIOGRAPHICAL/CRITICAL SOURCES: Nineteenth Century Fiction, September, 1969; *Dialogue*, April, 1976.

* * *

KAMINSKY, Peretz 1916-

PERSONAL: Born March 9, 1916, in New York, N.Y.; son of Joshua (a writer) and Bluma (Lieberman) Kaminsky; married Mintzie Schwartzman (an occupational counselor), 1939; children: Marc, Akiva, Riva Kaminsky Danzig. *Home:* 120 Gale Pl., Bronx, N.Y. 10463.

CAREER: Has worked in the publishing field, 1938—; currently a free-lance book designer.

WRITINGS—Poetry: *Reflection in the Eye of God,* Benjamin Blom, 1969; *Adam, Cain, and Other Prayers,* Benjamin Blom, 1970; *The Book of Rituals,* Horizon Press, 1971; *The Book of Questions,* Horizon Press, 1972; *Something Long Ago Paid For,* privately printed, 1977.

WORK IN PROGRESS: Two books of poetry, *A Matter of Time,* about old age, and *In the Absence of God,* about the orphaning of man.

* * *

KAMPF, Louis 1929-

PERSONAL: Born May 12, 1929, in Vienna, Austria; naturalized U.S. citizen; son of Oscar (a diamond-polisher) and Helen (Kuhl) Kampf; married Ellen Cantarow (a professor), 1969. *Education:* Long Island University, B.A., 1951; graduate study at University of Iowa, 1954-58, and Harvard University, 1958-61. *Office:* Department of Humanities, 14N418, Massachusetts Institute of Technology, Cambridge, Mass. 02139.

CAREER: Massachusetts Institute of Technology, Cambridge, assistant professor, 1961-66, associate professor, 1966-70, professor of literature, 1970—, head of department of humanities, 1967—. *Military service:* U.S. Army, 1951-53. *Member:* Modern Language Association of America (president, 1971), New University Conference. *Awards, honors:* Old Dominion fellowship, 1964.

WRITINGS: On Modernism, M.I.T. Press, 1967; *The Dissenting Academy,* Pantheon, 1968; *The Politics of Literature,* Pantheon, 1972. Contributor to *Harper's, Nation, Change,* and to scholarly journals.

BIOGRAPHICAL/CRITICAL SOURCES: New York Review of Books, October 26, 1967; *Criticism,* fall, 1968.

* * *

KANDAOUROFF, Berice 1912-

PERSONAL: Surname is accented on third syllable; born May 24, 1912, in London, England; daughter of Lewis (an industrialist) and Beatrice (Tannenbaum) Lindon; married Dmitry Kandaouroff, January 12, 1935; children: Maria Elisabeth Victoria. *Education:* Attended Benenden School, Cranbrook, Kent, England. *Home:* 27 Rue des Martyrs, Paris, France.

CAREER: Painter and writer; employed in television work; Paris correspondent for *Tableau;* free-lance writer for other newspapers. *Awards, honors:* Effemina prize, for *Adam sans Eve.*

WRITINGS: The Art of Living, Citadel, 1972; *Adam sans Eve,* Jean Dullis, 1973. Also co-author of filmscript, "The Permissive Lady."

WORK IN PROGRESS: Sex at Sixty; another book.

SIDELIGHTS: Berice Kandaouroff writes: "I wrote my first book, *The Art of Living,* when feeling depressed having lost all I possessed in a financial crack. I thought I should tell people what precautions to take so as not to do what foolishness I had done."

* * *

KANDELL, Alice S. 1938-

PERSONAL: Born November 6, 1938, in New York, N.Y.; daughter of Leonard S. (a realtor) and Florence (Levine) Kandell; married William H. Joseph (a lawyer), September 9, 1971; children: Andrew, Benjamin. *Education:* Sarah Lawrence College, B.A., 1960; Harvard University, Ph.D., 1967. *Home:* 11 East 68th St., New York, N.Y. 10021.

CAREER: Jewish Board of Guardians, New York City, research psychologist, 1963-66; Mt. Sinai Hospital, New York City, clinical psychologist, 1967-70; Mt. Sinai School of Medicine, New York City, instructor in clinical psychology, 1968-70; writer and photographer, 1968—. Has had photographs exhibited in one-woman show in New York City and in several group shows. *Member:* American Psychological Association, Asia Society (New York), Sikkim Committee of Himalayas Council (chairman). *Awards, honors: Sikkim: The Hidden Kingdom* was selected by Children's Book Council as a noted book in social studies.

WRITINGS: (Illustrated with own photographs) *Sikkim: The Hidden Kingdom* (juvenile), Doubleday, 1971; (photographic illustrator) Charlotte Salisbury, *Mountaintop Kingdom: Sikkim,* Norton, 1971. Contributor to psychology textbooks; contributor of articles to *Redbook, M.D. Publications,* and *Scholastic Magazine.*

WORK IN PROGRESS: Preparing photographs and story, "Kingdom in the Sky," for book to be published by Bank Street College of Education; a second book of photographs.

SIDELIGHTS: Alice Kandell told *CA* she has traveled to the Himalayan regions many times, and is especially interested in the arts and crafts of Sikkim and the life of the people. A child psychologist by profession, she has spent "considerable time in a high mountain northern village in Sikkim studying child-rearing" and photographing the people.

BIOGRAPHICAL/CRITICAL SOURCES: Women's Wear Daily, November 9, 1967; *New York Post,* November 14, 1967; *Newsday,* November 20, 1967; *McCall's,* November, 1968.

* * *

KANET, Roger E(dward) 1936-

PERSONAL: Born September 1, 1936, in Cincinnati, Ohio; son of Robert George (a skilled worker) and Edith Mary (Weaver) Kanet; married Joan Alice Edwards (a registered nurse), February 16, 1963; children: Suzanne Elise, Laurie Alice. *Education:* Xavier University, Cincinnati, Ohio, student, 1954-58, 1961, A.B., 1961; Berchmanskolleg, Pullach/Munich, Germany, student, Ph.B., 1960; Lehigh University, M.A., 1963; Princeton University, M.A., 1965, Ph.D., 1966. *Religion:* Roman Catholic. *Home:* 1007 South Victor St., Champaign, Ill. 61820. *Office:* Department of Political Science, University of Illinois at Urbana-Champaign, Urbana, Ill. 61801.

CAREER: University of Kansas, Lawrence, assistant professor, 1966-69, associate professor of political science, 1969-74; University of Illinois at Urbana-Champaign, visiting associate professor, 1973-74, associate professor of political science, 1974—, director of graduate studies, 1975—. Program chairman, First International Slavic Conference, 1974. Kansas State Parents' Association for Hearing-Handicapped Children, co-founder, vice-president, 1969-70, president, 1970-71. *Member:* American Political Science Association, American Association for the Advancement of Slavic Studies (chairman of bibliography and documentation committee, 1971-74), International Studies Association, Midwest Political Science Association, Midwest Slavic Conference, Central Slavic Conference (president, 1966-67), Kansas Political Science Association (program chairman, 1970).

WRITINGS: (Editor) *The Behavioral Revolution and Communist Studies: Applications of Behaviorally Oriented Political Research on the Soviet Union and Eastern Europe,* Free Press, 1971; (with others) *The Political and Legal Implications of the Development and Implementation of Remote Sensing Devices,* Center for Research, University of Kansas, 1971; (editor with Ivan Volgyes) *On the Road to Communism: Essays on Soviet Domestic and Foreign Politics,* University Press of Kansas, 1972; (editor) *The Soviet Union and the Developing Nations,* Johns Hopkins Press, 1974; (compiler) *Soviet and East European Foreign Policies: A Bibliography of English and Russian Language Publications, 1967-71,* Clio Press, 1974; (editor with Donna Bahry) *Soviet Economic and Political Relations with the Developing World,* Praeger, 1975.

Contributor: Harry G. Shaffer and Jan S. Prybyla, editors, *From Underdevelopment to Affluence: Western, Soviet, and Chinese Views,* Appleton, 1968; Prybyla, editor, *Communism and Nationalism,* Pennsylvania State University, 1969; Erik Hoffman and Frederic Fleron, Jr., editors, *The Soviet Foreign Policy Process,* Aldine, 1971; Edward J. Czerwinski and Jaroslaw Piekalkiewicz, editors, *The Soviet Invasion of Czechoslovakia: Its Effects on Eastern Europe,* Praeger, 1972; Charles Gati, editor, *The Politics of Modernization in Eastern Europe: Testing the Soviet Model,* 1974; Bernard Eissenstat, editor, *The Soviet Union: The Seventies and Beyond,* Lexington Books, 1975; Gati, editor, *The International Politics of Eastern Europe,* Praeger, 1976; Francis Heller, editor, *The Korean War: A Twenty-five year Perspective,* Regents Press of Kansas, 1977. Compiler of bibliography of Soviet writings on international politics for *Canadian Slavic Studies* for each issue, 1967—; also contributor of more than thirty articles and seventy reviews to professional journals.

WORK IN PROGRESS: Policy Change in People's Poland; a book on integration in Eastern Europe and on East-West relations.

*   *   *

KANG, Shin T.   1935-

PERSONAL: Born December 20, 1935, in Kyong-Kee, Korea; son of Young Hee (a farmer) and Keum (Soon) Kang; married Tae Su Chong, June 8, 1964; children: Mee Na, Mee A, Ishak Lugal. *Education:* Hankook Theological Seminary, B.D., 1960, M.Th., 1962; Hebrew Union College, Cincinnati, Ohio, Ph.D., 1968; Yale University, postdoctoral study, 1968-69. *Home:* 1105 Foothill Dr., Champaign, Ill. 61820. *Office:* World Heritage Museum, University of Illinois at Urbana-Champaign, L.H. 484, Urbana, Ill. 61801.

CAREER: Hankook Theological Seminary, Seoul, Korea, lecturer in English, 1960-61; Korea Christian College, Seoul, lecturer in Greek, Hebrew, and Old Testament, 1960-63; Christian minister in Florence, Ky., 1966-68; Yale University, New Haven, Conn., lecturer in Sumerian, 1968-69; University of Illinois at Urbana-Champaign, research associate in World Heritage Museum, 1969—, curator of Ancient Near Eastern Collection, 1972. *Military service:* Korean Army, 1958-59. *Member:* American Oriental Society.

WRITINGS: (With C. E. Keiser) *Neo-Sumerian Accounts: Texts from Drehem (BIN III),* Yale University Press, 1971; *Sumerian Economic Texts from the Drehem Archive,* University of Illinois Press, 1972; *Sumerian Economic Texts from the Umma Archive,* University of Illinois Press, Volume I, 1973, Volume II, 1978; *Sumerian, Akkadian,*

English Dictionary, University of Illinois Press, 1978. Contributor to newspapers.

SIDELIGHTS: The languages in which Shin Kang is competent include Sumerian, Akkadian, Hebrew, Aramaic, Biblical Greek, French, German, and Syriac.

*   *   *

KANOVSKY, Eliyahu   1922-

PERSONAL: Born March 25, 1922, in Winnipeg, Manitoba, Canada; son of Manuel and Anne (Lifshitz) Kanovsky; married Tamar Parnes (a teacher), October 16, 1945; children: Nachman, Yaakov, Gilah, Mecheal, Chana Rina. *Education:* Yeshiva College (now University), B.A., 1942; Columbia University, Ph.D., 1961. *Religion:* Jewish. *Home:* 7 Meltzer St., Rehovot, Israel. *Office:* Shiloah Center for Middle-Eastern Studies, Tel-Aviv University, Ramat-Aviv, Israel.

CAREER: State University of New York at Stony Brook, assistant professor, 1962-66, associate professor of economics, beginning 1966; Tel-Aviv University, Tel-Aviv, Israel, research fellow, Horowitz Institute, 1972-76, and Shiloah Institute, 1976-77, currently research associate, Shiloah Center for Middle-Eastern Studies. *Awards, honors:* Center for Middle Eastern Studies grants, 1963, 1968-69; Social Science Research Council grant, 1965; Ford Foundation faculty fellowship at Columbia University, 1965-66; Littauer Foundation supplementary fellowship, 1968-69, 1974-75.

WRITINGS: The Economy of the Israeli Kibbutz, Center for Middle Eastern Studies, Harvard University, 1966; (contributor) J. S. Nye, editor, *International Regionalism,* Center for International Affairs, Harvard University, 1968; *The Economic Impact of the Six Day War: Israel, the Occupied Territories, Egypt, and Jordan,* Praeger, 1970; (contributor) Michael Curtis, editor, *People and Politics in the Middle East,* Transaction Books, 1971; (contributor) Abid A. al-Marayati, editor, *The Middle East: Its Governments and Politics,* Duxbury, 1972; *The Economic Development of Jordan,* University Publishing Projects, Tel-Aviv University, 1976; (contributor) A. Hareven, editor, *Between War and Arrangements: The Arab-Israeli Dispute after 1973,* Shiloah Institute, Tel-Aviv University, 1977; *The Economic Development of Syria,* University Publishing Projects, Tel-Aviv University, 1977. Contributor to *Proceedings* of the Shiloah Institute conference, Tel-Aviv University. Contributor to *Middle East Journal, Jerusalem Quarterly, New Middle East,* and *American Journal of Economics and Sociology.*

WORK IN PROGRESS: The Economic Development and Problems of Egypt, and *The Economic Development and Problems of Iraq.*

*   *   *

KANTONEN, T(aito) A(lmar)   1900-

PERSONAL: Surname is accented on first syllable; born April 24, 1900, in Karstula, Finland; naturalized U.S. citizen; son of David (a laborer) and Elina (Paajanen) Kantonen; married Frances Sainio, June 1, 1932; children: Mary Frances (Mrs. John E. Berger), William Almar, Nancy Elaine (Mrs. Victor E. Duane), Martha Sue (Mrs. Thomas W. Lentz). *Education:* Attended Suomi Theological Seminary, 1917-20; University of Minnesota, A.B., 1924; Harvard University, A.M., 1926; Boston University, S.T.B., 1928, Ph.D., 1931. *Politics:* Republican. *Religion:* Lutheran. *Home:* 816 Snowhill Blvd., Springfield, Ohio 45504.

CAREER: Suomi College, Hancock, Mich., instructor in philosophy, 1928; Wittenberg University, Springfield, Ohio, acting professor, 1932-33, professor of systematic theology at Hamma School of Theology, 1933-68, emeritus professor, 1968—. Guest professor, University of Helsinki, 1949. Member of Faith and Order Commission, World Council of Churches; member of Commission on Theology, Lutheran World Federation. *Member:* American Philosophical Association, American Society for Reformation Research. *Awards, honors:* D.D., Augustana College, 1943; Knight of the Order of the White Rose bestowed by president of Finland, 1953; Th.D., University of Helsinki, 1955; L.H.D., Ohio Wesleyan University, 1958.

WRITINGS: *The Message of the Church,* Augsburg, 1941; *Resurgence of the Gospel,* Muhlenberg, 1948; *Risti ja Tahtilippu* (title means "The Cross and the Stars and Stripes"), Soederstroem, 1950; *The Theology of Evangelism,* Muhlenberg, 1954; *The Christian Hope,* Muhlenberg, 1954; *A Theology for Christian Stewardship,* Muhlenberg, 1956; *Life after Death,* Fortress, 1962; *Man in the Eyes of God,* CSS Publishing, 1972; *Christian Faith Today,* CSS Publishing, 1974; *Good News for All Seasons,* CSS Publishing, 1975.

Contributor: E. C. Fendt, editor, *What Lutherans Are Thinking,* Wartburg Press, 1947; Vilmos Vajta, editor, *The Unity of the Church,* Augustana Book, 1957; Harold C. Letts, editor, *Christian Social Responsibility,* Muhlenberg, 1957; T. K. Thompson, editor, *Stewardship in Contemporary Theology,* Association Press, 1960; Lennart Pinomaa, editor, *Teologia Etsii Suuntaa* (title means "Theology Seeks Direction: A Symposium on Contemporary Theologians"), Soederstroem, 1965; Ralph J. Jalkanen, editor, *The Finns in North America,* Michigan State University Press, 1969. Contributor to *Encyclopedia of Religion, Encyclopedia of the Lutheran Church,* and to philosophy and religion journals.

SIDELIGHTS: *The Theology of Evangelism* has been published in German, Spanish, and Japanese; *A Theology for Christian Stewardship* has been published in German, Spanish, Portuguese, and Japanese. There is a Japanese edition of *Life after Death.*

AVOCATIONAL INTERESTS: Golf—has played famous courses from Pebble Beach to St. Andrews.

*   *   *

KAPFER, Miriam B(ierbaum) 1935-

PERSONAL: Born May 8, 1935, in Atlantic, Iowa; daughter of Roy Christopher and Alma (Bees) Bierbaum; married Philip Gordon Kapfer (an education researcher), August 21, 1960; children: Paul Christopher, Stephanie Anne. *Education:* Drake University, B.M.E., 1956; University of Kansas, M.M.E., 1958; graduate study at University of Aberdeen, 1958-59, and University of Kansas, 1960; Ohio State University, Ph.D., 1964; postdoctoral study at Pepperdine College (now University), 1968. *Religion:* Lutheran. *Home:* 4344 Pin Oak St., Salt Lake City, Utah 84117. *Office:* Bureau of Educational Research, 308W Milton Bennion Hall, University of Utah, Salt Lake City, Utah 84112.

CAREER: Concordia Teachers College, Seward, Neb., music teacher, 1958; St. John's College and Academy, Winfield, Kan., teacher, 1959-61; Hamilton Local Elementary Schools, Columbus, Ohio, teacher, 1962-64; Clark County School District, Las Vegas, Nev., teacher, 1964-66, Education Center, professional librarian, 1966-67, and research consultant, 1967-70; University of Utah, Salt Lake City, Center to Improve Learning and Instruction, curriculum and

publications specialist, 1970-73, Bureau of Educational Research, co-director of Life-Involvement Model project, 1973—, research professor of special education, 1975—. State certification board member, Nevada Music Teachers Association, and music advisory board member, Las Vegas Chapter of Young Audiences, Inc., 1967-70; secretary, Allied Arts Council, Las Vegas, 1968.

MEMBER: American Educational Research Association, Music Educators National Conference (life member), National Society for the Study of Education, National Association for Music Therapy, Phi Delta Kappa, Mu Phi Epsilon.

WRITINGS: (Contributor) Samuel G. Fletcher and Frederick S. Berg, editors, *The Hard of Hearing Child: Clinical and Educational Management,* Grune, 1970; (with husband, Philip G. Kapfer, Asahel D. Woodruff, and Rowan C. Stutz) *Toward the Life-Internship Curriculum,* Nevada State Department of Education, 1970; (editor) *Behavioral Objectives in Curriculum Development: Selected Readings and Bibliography,* Educational Technology Publications, 1971; (editor with P. G. Kapfer) *Learning Packages in American Education,* Educational Technology Publications, 1972; (with P. G. Kapfer) *Inquiry ILPs: Individualized Learning Plans for Life-Based Inquiry,* Educational Technology Publications, 1977; (with P. G. Kapfer) *Project ILPs: Individualized Learning Plans for Life-Based Projects,* Educational Technology Publications, 1977.

Author or co-author of numerous published and unpublished reports, papers, and theses on music education, curriculum development, and instructional technology. Reviewer, *Winfield (Kan.) Courier,* 1959-61. Contributor of more than twenty articles to *Nebraska Music Teacher, Journal of Research in Music Education, Educational Technology, Music Educators Journal,* and other educational publications. *Nevada Notes* (Nevada Music Educators Association publication), co-editor, 1965-66, 1968-70, editor, 1966-68; editor, *Educational Progress Reports,* Center to Improve Learning and Instruction, University of Utah, 1970-72; guest editor, *Educational Technology,* 1972 and 1977.

WORK IN PROGRESS: Projects on life-based curricular and instructional designs, and career education.

*   *   *

KAPFER, Philip G(ordon) 1936-

PERSONAL: Born July 4, 1936, in Detroit, Mich.; son of Joseph A. and Viola (Martens) Kapfer; married Miriam Bierbaum (an educational researcher and editor), August 21, 1960; children: Paul Christopher, Stephanie Anne. *Education:* University of Northern Iowa, B.A., 1958, M.A., 1959; Ohio State University, Ph.D., 1964; postgraduate study at Southwestern College, Winfield, Kan., 1960-61, and University of Nevada, 1968-70. *Religion:* Lutheran. *Home:* 4344 Pin Oak St., Salt Lake City, Utah 84117. *Office:* Bureau of Educational Research, 308 Milton Bennion Hall, University of Utah, Salt Lake City, Utah 84112.

CAREER: St. John's College and Academy, Winfield, Kan., chemistry teacher, 1959-61; Clark County School District, Las Vegas, Nev., teacher, 1964-65, curriculum and research consultant, 1965-67, research and dissemination specialist, 1967-70; University of Utah, Salt Lake City, 1970—, began as visiting associate professor of education, currently research professor in department of education and Eccles Medical Library. *Member:* National Science Teachers Association (life member), American Educational Research Association, Association for Supervision and Curriculum Development, National Education Association (life member), National Society for the Study of Education, Phi Delta Kappa. *Awards, honors:* Fellow of Kettering Foundation's Institute for Development of Educational Activities, 1967, 1977.

WRITINGS: (With wife, Miriam Bierbaum Kapfer, Asahel D. Woodruff, and Rowan C. Stutz) *Toward the Life-Internship Curriculum,* Nevada State Department of Education, 1970; (with Glen F. Ovard) *Preparing and Using Individualized Learning Packages for Ungraded, Continuous Progress Education,* Educational Technology Publications, 1971; (editor with M. B. Kapfer) *Learning Packages in American Education,* Educational Technology Publications, 1972; (with M. B. Kapfer) *Inquiry ILPs: Individualized Learning Plans for Life-Based Inquiry,* Educational Technology Publications, 1977; (with M. B. Kapfer) *Project ILPs: Individualized Learning Plans for Life-Based Projects,* Educational Technology Publications, 1977. Contributor to more than seventeen books of readings. Author or co-author of various research reports, symposia, and papers on education. Contributor of articles to *Science Teacher, Phi Delta Kappan, Educational Screen and Audiovisual Guide, Clearing House, Educational Technology,* and other educational journals. Guest editor, *Educational Technology,* 1972.

WORK IN PROGRESS: Research on "life-based curricular and instructional design, administration, and teacher education."

* * *

KAPLAN, Allan 1932-

PERSONAL: Born February 19, 1932, in New York, N.Y. *Education:* University of Miami, B.A., 1956; New York University, M.A., 1960. *Office:* Department of English, Hofstra University, Hempstead, N.Y. 11553.

CAREER: Hofstra University, Hempstead, N.Y., instructor in English, 1968—. *Military service:* U.S. Army, 1957-59. *Awards, honors:* Poets Foundation grant, 1968; Cultural Council Foundation grant, 1972.

WRITINGS: Paper Airplane (poems), Harper, 1971.

* * *

KAPLAN, Lawrence S(amuel) 1924-

PERSONAL: Born October 28, 1924, in Cambridge, Mass.; son of Jacob C. (a physician) and Julia (Starnfield) Kaplan; married Janice Eyges (a psychologist), September 5, 1948; children: Deborah J., Joshua C. *Education:* Colby College, B.A., 1947; Yale University, M.A., 1948, Ph.D., 1951. *Religion:* Jewish. *Home:* 308 Wilson Ave., Kent, Ohio 44240. *Office:* Department of History, Kent State University, Kent, Ohio 44242.

CAREER: University of Bridgeport, Bridgeport, Conn., lecturer in history, 1950; U.S. Department of Defense, Washington, D.C., historian, 1951-54; Kent State University, Kent, Ohio, instructor, 1954-56, assistant professor, 1956-60, associate professor, 1960-65, professor of history, 1965—. Fulbright lecturer at University of Bonn, 1959-60, University of Louvain, 1964-65, and University of Nice, summer, 1965; visiting associate professor, Michigan State University, summer, 1962; visiting research scholar, University of London, 1969-70. Consultant to Pennsylvania Distinguished Faculty Awards Program, 1974-76, and to Historian's Office, U.S. Department of Defense, 1975-77. *Military service:* U.S. Army, Signal Corps, 1943-46.

MEMBER: American Historical Association, Organization of American Historians, Society of Historians of American

Foreign Relations, American Association of University Professors, Ohio Academy of History, Phi Beta Kappa, Pi Gamma Mu, Omicron Delta Kappa. *Awards, honors:* Clements Library-Lilly Endowment fellowship at University of Michigan, summer, 1961; American Philosophical Association grants, 1967, 1969.

WRITINGS: Jefferson and France: An Essay on Politics and Political Ideas, Yale University Press, 1967; (editor) *NATO and the Politics of Containment,* Heath, 1968; (editor) *Recent American Foreign Policy: Conflicting Interpretations,* Dorsey, 1968; *Colonies into Nations: American Diplomacy, 1763-1801,* Macmillan, 1972; *Culture and Diplomacy: The American Experience,* Greenwood Press, in press. Contributor to history, political, and literary journals.

WORK IN PROGRESS: A study of the U.S. military assistance program to NATO, 1948-52, for Historian's Office, U.S. Department of Defense.

* * *

KARANIKAS, Alexander 1916-

PERSONAL: Surname is pronounced Ka-ra-*ni*-kas; born September 23, 1916, in Manchester, N.H.; son of Stephen and Vaia (Olgas) Karanikas; married Helen J. Karagianes, January 2, 1949; children: Marianthe Vaia, Diana Christine, Cynthia Maria. *Education:* Attended University of New Hampshire, 1934-36; Harvard University, A.B. (cum laude), 1939; Northwestern University, M.A., 1950, Ph.D., 1953. *Politics:* Independent Democrat. *Religion:* Greek Orthodox Church. *Home:* 618 North Harvey Ave., Oak Park, Ill. 60302. *Office:* Department of English, University of Illinois at Chicago Circle, Chicago, Ill. 60680.

CAREER: Kendall College, Evanston, Ill., instructor in English, 1952-53; Northwestern University, Evanston, instructor in English, 1953-54; University of Illinois at Chicago Circle, assistant professor, 1954-61, associate professor, 1961-68, professor of English, 1968—. Instructor, Evening Division, Northwestern University, Chicago Campus, 1957-59. Publicity director, Independent Voters of New Hampshire, 1946; candidate for U.S. Congress from 1st District of New Hampshire, 1948. Executive secretary, American Council for a Democratic Greece, 1947; co-chairman, National Bicentennial Symposium on the Greek Experience in America, Modern Greek Studies Association, 1976. Consultant to Peter D. Gianukos Scholarship Fund, 1967—, and to "Greeks in America" film project, National Endowment for the Humanities, 1976—. *Military service:* U.S. Army Air Forces, 1942-46; served in Alaska; became sergeant.

MEMBER: Modern Language Association of America, Modern Greek Studies Association, American Association of University Professors, Society for the Study of Southern Literature, Hellenic Professional Society of Illinois, Friends of Literature (Chicago), Phi Eta Sigma. *Awards, honors:* First prize in New England universities annual poetry contest, 1936; Friends of Literature Award in nonfiction, 1967, for *Tillers of a Myth.*

WRITINGS: When a Youth Gets Poetic, privately printed, 1934; *In Praise of Heroes* (war poems), privately printed, 1945; *Tillers of a Myth: Southern Agrarians as Social and Literary Critics,* University of Wisconsin Press, 1966; (with wife, Helen Karanikas) *Elias Venezis,* Twayne, 1969. Poetry represented in anthologies, including *An Anthology of New Hampshire Poetry,* 1938, *Port Chicago Poets,* 1966, and *Hold Fast to Dreams,* edited by Arna Bontemps, 1969. Contributor of stories, poems, articles, and reviews to *New Hampshire Profiles, World Youth, Yankee, Texas Quar-*

terly, Army Times, Ladd Field Midnight Sun, Athene, Chicago Tribune Sunday Magazine, and other publications. Editor, Allegheny-Kiski Valley edition of *CIO News,* 1941-42; Alaska correspondent, *Yank* (military magazine), 1944-45.

WORK IN PROGRESS: Peter Saw the Wind, a novel; *Tales of Joppa,* short stories; *Fatty,* stories for children; *The Poison Jar,* a collection of poems; *Hellenes and Hellions: A Survey of Greek Characters in American Literature, 1825-1975;* revising two other novels, *Skull* and *The Rogues of Cling Alley.*

SIDELIGHTS: The first big reward that Alexander Karanikas received for his writing was a trip to the 1933 Century of Progress in Chicago as regional winner in a national essay contest. He was aiming for the second prize, a new typewriter, but "overshot my mark." The fiction writing he has underway now is largely based in a small New Hampshire town where Karanikas grew up and where he and his family spend summers. They have nine acres of young apple trees and about eighty acres of unspoiled forest at their Deerhaven Farm in Goffstown.

* * *

KARSH, Yousuf 1908-

PERSONAL: Given name is pronounced *Yoo*-suf; born December 23, 1908, in Mardin, Armenia-in-Turkey; emigrated to Canada in 1924, naturalized Canadian citizen in 1946; son of Amsih (an import-export agent) and Bahia (Nakash) Karsh; married Solange Gauthier, April 27, 1939 (died, 1960); married Estrellita Nachbar, August 28, 1962. *Education:* Attended public school in Sherbrooke, Quebec, Canada, 1925; studied photography under John H. Garo, Boston, Mass., 1929-31. *Home:* "Little Wings," Prescott Hwy., Ottawa, Ontario, Canada. *Office:* Chateau Laurier, Suite 660, Ottawa, Ontario, Canada K1N 8S7.

CAREER: Photographer; has maintained photographic studio in Ottawa, Ontario since 1932; sent to England by Canadian Government during World War II to make portraits of many dignitaries, including King George VI and Princess Elizabeth; has photographed numerous celebrities, including the British Royal Family, King Haakon of Norway, King Constantine and Queen Anne Marie of Greece, General Eisenhower, John L. Lewis, Eleanor Roosevelt, Sir Winston Churchill, Albert Einstein, George Bernard Shaw, Bertrand Russell, H. G. Wells, Malraux, Maugham, Hemingway, Steinbeck, Thomas Mann, Tennessee Williams, Albert Schweitzer, Picasso, Casals, and Sibelius; industrial photographer for Atlas Steel Ltd., Wellington, Ontario, 1950-51, and Ford of Canada Ltd., 1951; first photographer to have one-man exhibition at National Gallery of Canada, 1959, and only one-man exhibitor at Expo '67, Montreal, Quebec; has had numerous other one-man exhibitions; photographic adviser for Expo '70, Osaka, Japan. Represented in permanent collections of Museum of Modern Art (New York City), Metropolitan Museum of Art (New York City), George Eastman House (Rochester, N.Y.), Art Institute of Chicago, St. Louis Art Museum, Philadelphia Art Museum, Huntington Library (San Marino, Calif.), National Portrait Gallery (London), and National Gallery of Canada. Lecturer on photography at Boston Museum of Fine Arts, St. Louis Art Museum, and at world photographic and art congresses in Europe and the United States; visiting professor of photography, Ohio University, Athens, 1968-70; visiting professor of fine arts, Emerson College, 1972. Chairman, subcommittee on immigrant problems, Canadian Citizenship Council; trustee, Photographic Arts and Sciences Foundation, 1965-78.

MEMBER: Royal Photographic Society (England; honorary fellow), Royal Canadian Academy of Arts, Photographic Society of America, Canadian Photographic Society (honorary life member), Canadian-Armenian Congress (honorary president), Muscular Dystrophy Associations of America (corporate member). *Awards, honors:* Canada Council Medal, 1965; Medal of Service of the Order of Canada, and Centennial Medal (Canada), both 1968; Master of Photographic Arts, Professional Photographers Association of Canada, 1970; U.S. Presidential Citation for meritorious service on behalf of the handicapped, 1971; Rochester Science Museum fellow, 1972. LL.D. from Queen's University, Kingston, Ontario, and Carleton University, both 1960; D.H.L. from Dartmouth College, 1961, Ohio University, Athens, 1965, Mount Allison University, 1969, and Emerson College, 1969; D.C.L. from Bishop's University, Lennoxville, Quebec, 1969.

WRITINGS: Faces of Destiny, Prentice-Hall, 1946; (with Bishop Fulton J. Sheen and Henri Daniel-Rops) *This Is the Mass,* translation from the French by Alastair Guinan, Hawthorn, 1958, 3rd edition, 1965; *Portraits of Greatness,* Thomas Nelson, 1959; (with John Fisher) *Canada as Seen by the Camera of Yousuf Karsh and Described in Words by John Fisher,* Thomas Allen, 1960; (with Sheen and H. V. Morton) *This Is Rome: A Pilgrimage in Words and Pictures,* Hawthorn, 1960; (with Sheen and Morton) *This Is the Holy Land: A Pilgrimage in Words and Pictures,* Hawthorn, 1961; (with Sheen) *These Are the Sacraments,* Hawthorn, 1962; *In Search of Greatness: Reflections* (autobiography), Knopf, 1962 (published in Canada as *In Search of Greatness: Reflections of Yousuf Karsh,* University of Toronto Press, 1962); (illustrator) John P. Frank, *The Warren Court,* Macmillan, 1965; *Karsh Portfolio,* Thomas Nelson, 1967; *Faces of Our Time,* University of Toronto Press, 1971; *Karsh Portraits,* New York Graphic Society, 1976.

SIDELIGHTS: Yousuf Karsh grew up in Turkey during the Armenian massacres, and at the age of fifteen was sent to live with an uncle who ran a photographic studio in Sherbrooke, Quebec. His uncle, A. G. Nakash, sent him to Boston in 1929 to study with photographer John Garo, also of Armenian descent. In a *Saturday Review* interview, Karsh said he spent three years of apprenticeship study at Garo's Boylston Street studio: "John Garo was a Mark Twain character, with a flowing mustache. He stopped working every day at four o'clock—when the lights stopped. Then he would hold court. My job was not only mixing the chemicals for the photography but also for the drinks. . . . Garo was a great photographer. But he did not enjoy the kind of wide, geographical dissemination of reputation that is possible today. If you cannot learn by observing, you cannot be a photographer. . . . 'No two people ever see the same [Garo told Karsh]. If you saw what I see, you would only copy me and and you would be nothing.'" Karsh first attracted public attention with a portrait of Sir Winston Churchill, taken after Churchill had addressed the Canadian Parliament on December 30, 1941. As the story goes, Karsh snapped the picture after removing the omnipresent cigar from the lips of a reluctant Churchill, and the ensuing portrait, now internationally famous, reflected the "indomitable spirit of the British nation." *Lens Magazine* calls it "the most reproduced photograph in the history of photography." This portrait was later used as the basis of Churchill commemorative stamps in seven countries, and launched Karsh on his career as portrait photographer of artists, actors, musicians, statesmen, millionaires, popes, presidents, and kings. He has traveled throughout North America, Europe, Asia, and the Arctic to photograph his subjects in their own environments, and is generally considered to be among the world's ten most talented portrait photographers. He is most famous for his ability to capture the characteristic pose or gesture of his subject; according to J. L. McConaughy of *Reader's Digest,* British statesman and publisher Lord Beaverbrook, photographed by Karsh in 1943, on seeing his proofs said, "Karsh, you have immortalized me."

His "unmannered but masterly portraits...confirm a view that Armenian-born Karsh is among the greatest since photography began," writes a *Times Literary Supplement* reviewer. He continues, "Not only does the composing and the portrayal of inner character impress but also the perfect technique of chiaroscuro." But Roy Strong, in a *Books and Bookmen* review of *Karsh Portraits,* calls the photographs "the epitome of the safe. . . . Every mask is composed to fulfill his and their wish to be thought of as intellectual, benign, inspired, humane or whatever quality a particular great person is renowned for. Karsh supplies the halo. . . . In this way, the myths of the great are maintained and propagated." In his review of the same book, the *Best Sellers* critic warns: "To appreciate Karsh's talent one must not quibble with his tendency to idealize his subjects. . . . [His photographs] are masterful exploitations of light and shade. . . . Between the covers of this handsome book [the great] live, breathe, and put their best face forward." Karsh "is the consummate classical portraitist with all the positive qualities which that distinction implies" writes a *Lens Magazine* reviewer, adding, "Karsh's secret is his humanity and his appreciation of humanity."

Karsh keeps photographic equipment in Ottawa, London, Paris, and New York, and often travels with two to three hundred pounds of cameras and lighting equipment. Of all the portraits he has taken (more than 15,000), his favorite is always "the one I will take tomorrow." He told the editors of *Saturday Review:* "When I opened my own studio I was concerned with pleasing the people I photographed. Now I am only concerned with pleasing myself. And there is another thing. Now I am known for pictures of men—but up to my Churchill portrait, I was doing ninety per cent women." Karsh, who has been married twice and has no children, concluded, "If I keep making good photographs, they will be my children." (The only children Karsh photographs are the national poster children of the Muscular Dystrophy Associations of America, as his contribution. He is vitally interested in the education of young people.) He has said, "To make enduring photographs, one must learn to see with one's mind's eye, for the heart and the mind are the true lens of the camera."

Among Karsh portraits which have been used for postage stamps are those of Dag Hammarskjold, Chief Justice Harlan Stone, Canadian Prime Minister William Lyon Mackenzie King, Queen Elizabeth and Prince Philip, Prince Rainier and Princess Grace of Monaco, Pope Pius XII, General George C. Marshall, Jawaharlal Nehru, and Konrad Adenauer. Over 100 portraits of world personalities were included in his exhibit "Men Who Make Our World," first shown at the Art Gallery of the Canadian Pavilion at Expo '67 in Montreal, and subsequently exhibited at galleries and museums in numerous countries. It is now part of the permanent collections of the Museum of Modern Art in Tokyo, Japan, the National Gallery of Australia and the province of Alberta, Canada.

Portraits of Karsh himself have appeared in publications throughout the world. Known for his wit and narrative skill, Karsh has appeared on television shows in the United States and Canada. In 1967 the Canadian Broadcasting Corp. produced a color television special on Karsh, entitled "Diary of a Portraitist," and in 1970 the CBC offered an hour-long "Profile of Karsh." Columbia Broadcasting System's "Sixty Minutes" profiled him in 1977.

BIOGRAPHICAL/CRITICAL SOURCES: Maclean's Magazine, September 1, 1942, February 1, 1944, November 15, 1949; *New York Post Magazine,* March 18, 1947; *Popular Photography,* May, 1947, May 1958; *Reader's Digest,* November, 1947, March, 1976, February, 1977; *Life,* November 30, 1959; *Time,* October 10, 1960; *Saturday Review,* December 9, 1961, April 29, 1967, May 9, 1970, October 16, 1971, November 27, 1976; Yousuf Karsh, *In Search of Greatness: Reflections* (autobiography), Knopf, 1962; *U.S. Camera,* July, 1967; *Times Literary Supplement,* December 14, 1967; Aylesa Forsee, *Famous Photographers,* Macrae, 1968; *Canadian Book Review Annual,* 1976; *American Medical News,* February 16, 1976; *Lens Magazine,* July/August, 1976, March/April, 1977; *Christian Science Monitor,* November 24, 1976; *New York Times Book Review,* December 5, 1976; J. Danziger and B. Conrad, *Interviews with Master Photographers,* Paddington, 1977; *Best Sellers,* March, 1977; *Books and Bookmen,* April, 1977.

* * *

KARSHNER, Roger 1928-

PERSONAL: Born November 10, 1928, in Columbus, Ohio; son of Noble and Edith (Maag) Karshner; married Mary Rockfield, August 5, 1948; children: Juliann, David, Sally, Molly. *Education:* Attended schools in Springfield, Ill. *Home:* 3650 Barham Blvd., T-323, Los Angeles, Calif. 90068.

CAREER: Capitol Records, Hollywood, Calif., worked in sales, 1953-62, marketing, and promotion, 1962-70, vice-president of promotion, 1970-71. *Member:* American Federation of Musicians, Dramatists Guild of America, Broadcast Music, Inc. (songwriter lister). *Awards, honors:* National winner, Gene Krupa drum contest, 1947; president's award, Capitol Records, 1954; Burns Mantle Award, 1975, for "The Dream Crust."

WRITINGS: The Music Machine, Nash Publishing, 1971.

Plays: *Hot Turkey at Midnight,* Samuel French, 1975; *Monkey's Uncle,* Samuel French, 1975. Also author of "The Dream Crust," "Cheeseburg, A La Carte," "Doors," "Lester," "Rodney," "Love on the Cusp," "The Ring," "40-Love," "To Live at the Pitch," and "Blue Tuesday." Author of screenplays, "Willy Kaplow Is a Cue Ball" and "The Way of Eagles."

WORK IN PROGRESS: A play, "Concerto for a Faded Lady."

SIDELIGHTS: Roger Karshner told *CA* he has "no formal literary background. Failed English, rotten speller, poor student. Have always enjoyed words. Their look their sound. Since I can remember I've always been busy writing bits of stuff—stories, poems, articles. I love working with words. *The Music Machine* is my first published work and it deals with the dirty, rotten side of todays record business. I wrote it in longhand and wrote it fast following no particular format. My feelings while writing dictate style, form and all that.

"I'm either writing or thinking about writing most of the time. A fact that is a mixture of great pleasure and great pain—especially pain for those around me, I'm sure. I'm attempting to do something solid, I'm reaching out, exploring right now. Haven't the slightest idea of where I'm heading but I'm on the road walking. I'm most comfortable with the play form. Too bad because it's a rough way to make a living. But—what the hell? I'm thinking about a novel and maybe some screen stuff, although screen people are a pain in the participle.''

*   *   *

KATZ, Michael B(arry) 1939-

PERSONAL: Born April 13, 1939, in Wilmington, Del.; son of George J. (a chemical engineer) and Beatrice (Goldstein) Katz; married Edda Gering (a teacher), August 27, 1970; children: Paul, Rebecca, Sarah. *Education:* Harvard University, B.A., 1961, M.A..T., 1962, Ed.D., 1966. *Office:* Department of History, York University, Toronto, Ontario, Canada.

CAREER: Ontario Institute for Studies in Education, Toronto, associate professor of educational theory, 1966-74; University of Toronto, Toronto, Ontario, associate professor of history, 1966-74; currently professor of history, York University, Toronto. Speaker, Institute Assembly, Ontario Institute for Studies in Education, 1971-72; fellow, Institute for Advanced Studies, Princeton University, 1973-74. *Member:* History of Education Society (director; president, 1975-76), Social Science History Association, Canadian Historical Association, Organization of American Historians.

WRITINGS: *The Irony of Early School Reform: Educational Innovation in Mid-Nineteenth Century Massachusetts,* Harvard University Press, 1968; *School Reform: Past and Present,* Little, Brown, 1971; *Class, Bureaucracy and Schools: The Illusion of Educational Change in America,* Praeger, 1971, revised edition, 1973; (editor) *Education and American History,* Praeger, 1973; (with Paul Mattingly) *Education and Social Change: Themes from Ontario's Past,* New York University Press, 1975; *The People of Hamilton, Canada West: Family and Class in a Mid-Nineteenth-Century City,* Harvard University Press, 1976.

WORK IN PROGRESS: *The Social Organization of Early Industrial Capitalism.*

*   *   *

KATZ, Sanford N. 1933-

PERSONAL: Born December 23, 1933, in Holyoke, Mass.; son of Jacob and Rebecca (Ricklas) Katz; married Joan Raphael (a social worker), June 15, 1958; children: Daniel R., Andrew D. *Education:* Boston University, A.B., 1955; University of Chicago, J.D., 1958; Yale University, visiting scholar at Law School, 1963-64. *Office:* School of Law, Boston College, Brighton, Mass. 02135.

CAREER: Catholic University of America, Washington, D.C., instructor, 1959-60, assistant professor, 1960-62, associate professor of law, 1963-64; University of Florida, Gainesville, professor of law, 1964-68; Boston College, School of Law, Brighton, Mass., professor of law, 1968—. Member of Massachusetts Governor's Committee on Adoption and Foster Care. *Member:* American Bar Association (chairman, Adoption Committee), Massachusetts Bar Association, Order of the Coif (honorary member), Sheldon Society.

WRITINGS: *When Parents Fail,* Beacon Press, 1971; *The Youngest Minority: Lawyers in Defense of Children,* Amer-

ican Bar Association Press, 1974; *Creativity in Social Work: Selected Writings of Lydia Rapoport,* Temple University Press, 1975. Editor-in-chief, *Family Law Quarterly.*

*   *   *

KAUFMAN, Burton I. 1940-

PERSONAL: Born November 26, 1940, in Boston, Mass.; son of Samuel (an upholsterer) and Ruth (Slavinsky) Kaufman; married Diane Kallison (a teacher), January 29, 1966; children: Victor Scott, Heather Dawn. *Education:* Brandeis University, B.A., 1962; Rice University, M.A., 1964, Ph.D., 1966. *Home:* 2909 Nevada, Manhattan, Kan. 66502. *Office:* Department of History, Kansas State University, Manhattan, Kan. 66502.

CAREER: Louisiana State University in New Orleans, assistant professor, 1966-69, associate professor of history, 1969-73; Kansas State University, Manhattan, associate professor, 1973-77, professor of history, 1977—. *Member:* Organization of American Historians. *Awards, honors:* American Philosophical Society Research grant, 1969—; Newcomen Prize, 1972.

WRITINGS: (Editor) *Washington's Farewell Address: The View from the Twentieth Century,* Quadrangle, 1969; *Efficiency and Expansion: Foreign Trade Organization in the Wilson Administration, 1913-1921,* Greenwood Press, 1972, new edition, 1974; *The Oil Cartell Case: A Documentary History of the Antitrust Question in the Cold War Era,* Greenwood Press, 1978.

WORK IN PROGRESS: *U.S. Foreign Economic Policy in the Eisenhower Administration.*

*   *   *

KAWABATA, Yasunari 1899-1972

June 11, 1899—April 16, 1972; Japanese novelist, playwright, short story writer, and film actor. Obituaries: *New York Times,* April 17, 1972; *Washington Post,* April 17, 1972; *L'Express,* April 24-30, 1972; *Newsweek,* May 1, 1972; *Time,* May 1, 1972.

*   *   *

KAWAKAMI, Toyo S(uyemoto) 1916-

PERSONAL: Born January 14, 1916, in Oroville, Calif.; daughter of Tsutomu Howard and Mitsu (Hyakusoku) Suyemoto; divorced; children: Kay (son). *Education:* Sacramento Junior College (now Sacramento City College), A.A., 1935; University of California, Berkeley, B.A., 1937; studied at University of Cincinnati in poetry workshops conducted by Randall Jarrell, 1958, and Karl Shapiro, 1959; University of Michigan, M.L.S., 1964. *Religion:* Protestant. *Home:* 30 Orchard Lane, Columbus, Ohio 43214. *Office:* Education Library, Ohio State University, Columbus, Ohio 43210.

CAREER: Librarian in public library in Topaz, Utah, 1943-45; University of Cincinnati, Cincinnati, Ohio, librarian in College of Nursing and Health, 1946-57, librarian in periodical room in university library, 1957-59; Cincinnati Art Museum, Cincinnati, assistant librarian, 1959-63; Ohio State University, Columbus, assistant head librarian of Education Library, 1964—, head librarian of Social Work Library, 1975—. *Member:* American Library Association, American Society for Information Science, Ohio Library Association, Ohio State University Faculty Women's Club, Ohio State University Library Staff Association, University of Michigan Library Science Alumni Association. *Awards, honors:*

Ohio Poetry Day haiku prize, 1961; Best Article of the Year award, Ohio Library Association, 1974; Asian American Writers Award, Asian American Writers Conference, 1975.

WRITINGS: (Contributor) Isshin H. Yamasaki, editor, *American Bungaku,* Keigan Sha (Tokyo), 1938; *Acronyms in Education and the Behavioral Sciences,* American Library Association, 1971; (contributor) E. J. Josey and Kenneth Peeples, Jr., editors, *Opportunities for Minorities in Librarianship,* Scarecrow, 1977. Also contributor to *Ohioana Library Yearbook,* 1977.

Poetry represented in anthologies, including *Japan: Theme and Variations,* Tuttle, 1951 and *Speaking for Ourselves: American Ethnic Writing,* edited by Lillian Faderman and Barbara Bradshaw, Scott, Foresman, 1969. Contributor to Japanese and other small West Coast and Hawaiian magazines and newspapers, and to national literary journals. Formerly author of "Potpourri," a column appearing in *Hokubei Asahi* and of "Medley," a column appearing in *Seattle Courier.*

WORK IN PROGRESS: How Small a Whisper, poems, for Swallow Press; a narrative of her family's evacuation from the West Coast and internment during World War II because of their ethnic origin; several poems, to be published in *Japanese American Anthology.*

SIDELIGHTS: Toyo Kawakami told *CA:* "Although I write prose, poetry has been the primary interest since I was in grade school. The writing of poetry, in conventional or the brief Japanese forms, was encouraged by my mother, who could quote and explicate so many of the Japanese poets, and who wrote herself. My father, who painted in oils, taught me to perceive beauty in nature. And the fact that I am American-born has endowed me with a bicultural appreciation.

"Poetry is my observation of the world around me, and through it, I record my impressions. I read, and admire, many of the English and American poets, but it is Emily Dickinson who has had the greatest influence on me. David Daiches, the British critic, wrote to me in 1960: 'I am sure you are right to employ a certain regularity of stanza, it clearly suits your talent with its quiet precision and obvious gift for verbal and rhythmic discipline . . . a talent both so controlled and so genuine, a use of language at once delicate and firm.'

"The late quiet hours of the night are, for me, the most conducive for reflective thinking and the writing of poetry. Although the poems are quickly written, they have actually gone through a long period of gestation, from the first impact of thought to the finished lines. The words shape themselves according to the image retained within the mind. In writing the *haiku* and the *tanka* in English, I find the forms demand a discipline at once acerbic and refreshing.

"For the past number of years I have been writing a prose narrative of my experiences of three and a half years in internment camps. Currently I am revising the chapters to include the poems I set down during those years. The manuscript is an attempt to portray how the West Coast Japanese, suddenly deprived of homes and possessions and isolated in desolate places during World War II, adjusted and lived in internment camps. I learned so much from them of patience and endurance."

AVOCATIONAL INTERESTS: Reading, needlework, collecting poetry books.

KAYSING, William C. 1922-
(Bill Kaysing)

PERSONAL: Born July 31, 1922, in Chicago, Ill.; son of Charles and Eleanor (Sturm) Kaysing; married Carol de Ridder, January, 1947 (divorced, 1969); married Ruth Cole Kay, September, 1971; children: (first marriage) Wendy, Jill. *Education:* University of Southern California, B.A., 1949. *Politics:* Libertarian. *Religion:* "My own."

CAREER: Has worked as a fisherman and technical writer; Rocketdyne, Canoga Park, Calif., publications engineer, 1956-63; free-lance writer, 1963—. *Military service:* U.S. Naval Reserve, engineer on destroyer, 1942-46.

WRITINGS—Under name Bill Kaysing: (With wife, Ruth Kaysing) *The Exurbanites Compleat and Illustrated Easy Does It First Time Farmers Guide,* Straight Arrow, 1971; *How to Live in the New America,* Prentice-Hall, 1972; *The Robin Hood Handbook,* Links Books, 1974; *Great Hot Springs of the West,* foreword by Leon Elder, Capra, 1974; (with R. Kaysing) *Eat Well on a Dollar a Day: Live a Healthier Life at a Fraction of the Cost,* Chronicle Books, 1975; *Fell's Beginner's Guide to Motorcycling,* Fell, 1976; (with R. Kaysing) *Dollar a Day Cookbook,* Chronicle Books, 1977. Also author, under name William Kaysing, of *Twenty-five Ways to Advertise a Small Business without Spending More than Ten Dollars,* 1970, *Twenty-five Ways Young People Can Make a Living in the Country,* 1970, and *Land and How to Buy it for a Few Dollars an Acre,* 1970. Contributor to national magazines.†

* * *

KEANE, Bil 1922-

PERSONAL: Born October 5, 1922, in Philadelphia, Pa.; son of Aloysius William and Florence R. (Bunn) Keane; married Thelma Carne, October 23, 1948; children: Gayle, Neal, Glen, Chris, Jeff. *Education:* Attended parochial schools in Philadelphia. *Religion:* Roman Catholic. *Home:* 5815 East Joshua Tree Lane, Paradise Valley, Ariz. 85253.

CAREER: Philadelphia Bulletin, Philadelphia, Pa., staff artist, 1945-59; free-lance artist doing cartoons for major magazines, 1952-60; creator of syndicated newspaper cartoons, "Channel Chuckles," 1954—, and "The Family Circus," 1960—, both cartoons syndicated by Register & Tribune Syndicate to more than five hundred newspapers. *Military service:* U.S. Army, 1942-45; while in service drew cartoons for *Yank* and *Pacific Stars and Stripes;* became staff sergeant. *Member:* National Cartoonists Society, Newspaper Comics Council, Magazine Cartoonists Guild. *Awards, honors:* Named best syndicated panel cartoonist by National Cartoonists Society, 1967, 1971, and 1974; Ohioana Book Award, 1972, for *Just Wait Till You Have Children of Your Own.*

WRITINGS: Channel Chuckles, Scholastic Book Services, 1964; *The Family Circus,* Register & Tribune Syndicate, Volume I, 1965, Volume II, 1966; *Sunday with the Family Circus,* Judson, 1966; *Jest in Pun,* Scholastic Book Services, 1966; *Pun-Abridged Dictionary,* Scholastic Books Services, 1968; *Through the Year with the Family Circus,* Judson, 1969; (with Erma Bombeck) *Just Wait Till You Have Children of Your Own,* Doubleday, 1971; *It's Apparent You're a Parent,* Doubleday, 1971; *More Channel Chuckles,* Scholastic Book Services, 1972; *Deuce and Don'ts of Tennis,* O'Sullivan, Woodside, 1975.

All published by Fawcett: *The Family Circus,* 1967; *I Need a Hug,* 1968; *Peace, Mommy, Peace!,* 1969; *Wanna Be*

Smiled At?, 1970; *Peekaboo! I Love You!*, 1971; *Look Who's Here*, 1972; *Hello, Grandma*, 1973; *When's Later, Daddy?*, 1974; *Mine*, 1975; *I Can't Untie My Shoes*, 1975; *Smile*, 1976; *Jeffy's Lookin' at Me*, 1976; *For This I Went to College*, 1977.

SIDELIGHTS: Bil Keane told *CA:* "I have never taken a formal art course, but taught myself to draw by imitating my favorite cartoonists in the newspapers and magazines while in my teens. I was art editor of the monthly magazine in high school and after three years in the army, I joined the news art staff of the *Philadelphia Bulletin.* My cartoons went unnoticed by 'nearly everybody.' When television was coming into its own in 1954, I started a feature lampooning the boob-tube and called it 'Channel Chuckles.' I still draw it daily for the *Register* and *Tribune* Syndicate. 'The Family Circus' first came to town on February 29th, 1960. Taking advantage of the leap year date, I have determined that the characters in 'The Family Circus' are growing older at the rate of one year in every four. Now if I could only make that work for myself! The feature has grown in popularity and scores at the top of most readership surveys, for which I am thankful. It takes one day a week just to answer the fan mail. I am happy to get writer's cramp that way. American newspaper readers are the sincerest and most appreciative audience in the world and 'Family Circus' now appears in more than five hundred newspapers throughout the U.S. and Canada.

"I am now residing in Arizona where I am studying to be a cactus. . . . My wife Thel, whom I met while hiding in a kangaroo's pouch during World War II in Australia, is my technical adviser, model for the 'Family Circus' mommy, and my editor. She is the most kissable editor I have ever met." Asked by an interviewer if his cartoons are based on his own family life, Keane replied: "On the contrary, my real life is based on the cartoons. If something gets a laugh in the cartoon, I try to work it in around the house." In reality, however, "the cartoons and characters are the Keanes."

Bil and Thel Keane are both avid tennis players. They prefer Arizona living where Keane claims "the desert air makes drawing ink dry faster allowing more time on the tennis court." One of their sons, Glen, is now an animator at Disney Productions.

*   *   *

KEATING, Charlotte Matthews 1927-

PERSONAL: Born September 9, 1927, in Peking, China; daughter of Harold S. (a missionary) and Grace (Waters) Matthews; married Kenneth Lee Keating (a professor and industrial consultant), June 15, 1947; children: Roger Lee, Kevin Jackson. *Education:* Attended Kalamazoo College, 1945-46, Simmons College, 1946-47, and University of Missouri School of Mines and Metallurgy (now University of Missouri—Rolla), 1949-50; Stanford University, B.A., 1954; University of Arizona, further study, 1965-68. *Politics:* Democrat. *Religion:* Unitarian. *Home:* 7054 North Magic Lane, Tucson, Ariz. 85704.

CAREER: University of Missouri School of Mines and Metallurgy (now University of Missouri—Rolla), secretary to librarian, 1950-51; Stanford University Libraries, Stanford, Calif., library assistant, Serials Division, 1951-53; volunteer, Lehigh County Community Council, 1954-55; member of steering committee to organize Lehigh County League of Women Voters, 1954-55; Holy Cross House, Inc., adult literacy volunteer and secretary to board of directors, 1966-69, deputy registrar of voters (volunteer); currently sales associate with Rowena Sinclair Realty; member,

Tucson Board of Realtors. *Member:* League of Women Voters (member of board of directors of Phoenix branch, 1956-57; presently member of Tucson branch), National Federation of Democratic Women, U.S.-China Peoples Friendship Association (Tucson chapter), United Nations Association (Tucson chapter), Common Cause, Unitarian-Universalist Fellowship for Social Justice (president, 1964-65), National Association for the Advancement of Colored People (Tucson chapter), Arizona Federation of Democratic Women's Clubs, Tucson Territorial Democratic Women's Clubs (charter member), Friends of the Tucson Library (member of board of directors).

WRITINGS: Building Bridges of Understanding, Palo Verde Press, 1967; *Building Bridges of Understanding between Cultures*, Palo Verde Press, 1971.

SIDELIGHTS: Charlotte Keating told *CA:* "My enjoyment of reading and my desire to work toward developing intercultural understanding were the primary motivating factors toward the writing of my books. I was determined to combine my roles as parent, volunteer tutor, and student as effectively as possible. My first book began as a term paper and grew as I discovered the need for such a book and the enjoyment I gained from sharing research materials with others. It was fun, it was a challenge, and I'm still amazed that my dream of publishing my annotations came true."

AVOCATIONAL INTERESTS: Traveling in camper trailer, making home improvements.

*   *   *

KEATING, H(enry) R(eymond) F(itzwalter) 1926-

PERSONAL: Born October 31, 1926, in St. Leonards-on-Sea, Sussex, England; son of John Hervey (a schoolmaster) and Muriel Marguerita (Clews) Keating; married Sheila Mary Mitchell (an actress), October 3, 1953; children: Simon, Bryony (daughter), Piers, Hugo. *Education:* Trinity College, Dublin, B.A., 1952. *Home:* 35 Northumberland Pl., London W2 5AS, England. *Agent:* A. D. Peters and Co., 10 Buckingham St., London WC2N 6BU, England.

CAREER: Sub-editor for *Evening Advertiser*, Swindon, Wiltshire, England, 1952-55, *Daily Telegraph*, London, England, 1955-57, and London *Times*, London, 1957-60; mystery writer and novelist, 1959—. *Military service:* British Army, 1945-48; became acting lance-corporal. *Member:* Crime Writers Association (chairman, 1970-71), Society of Authors, Detection Club. *Awards, honors:* Golden Dagger, Crime Writers Association, 1964, for *The Perfect Murder*; Edgar Allan Poe special award, Mystery Writers of America, 1965, for *The Perfect Murder*.

WRITINGS: Death and the Visiting Firemen, Gollancz, 1959; *Zen There Was Murder*, Gollancz, 1960, Penguin, 1963; *A Rush on the Ultimate*, Gollancz, 1961; *The Dog It Was That Died*, Gollancz, 1962, Penguin, 1968; *Death of a Fat God*, Collins, 1963, Dutton, 1966; *The Perfect Murder*, Collins, 1964, Dutton, 1965; *Is Skin-Deep, Is Fatal*, Dutton, 1965; *Inspector Ghote's Good Crusade*, Dutton, 1966; *Inspector Ghote Caught in Meshes*, Collins, 1967, Dutton, 1968; *Inspector Ghote Hunts the Peacock*, Dutton, 1968; *Inspector Ghote Plays a Joker*, Dutton, 1969.

Inspector Ghote Breaks an Egg, Collins, 1970, Doubleday, 1971; *Inspector Ghote Goes by Train*, Collins, 1971, Doubleday, 1972; *The Strong Man*, Heinemann, 1971; *Inspector Ghote Trusts the Heart*, Collins, 1972, Doubleday, 1973; *Bats Fly Up for Inspector Ghote*, Collins, 1974, Doubleday, 1975; *The Underside*, Macmillan, 1974; *A Remarkable Case of Burglary,* Collins, 1975, Doubleday, 1976; *Murder Must Appetize,* Lemon Tree Press, 1975; *Filmi, Filmi, Inspector Ghote,* Collins, 1976, Doubleday, 1977; (editor) *Agatha Christie, First Lady of Crime,* Holt, 1977; *A Long Walk to Wimbledon,* Macmillan, 1978. Contributor to *Ellery Queen's Mystery Magazine;* crime book reviewer, *Times* (London), 1967—.

WORK IN PROGRESS: Research on modern India for future "Inspector Ghote" novels.

SIDELIGHTS: H.R.F. Keating told *CA* he "became a writer because my father, a schoolmaster, had always wanted to be one and had given me the forename REYMOND 'To look good on the spine of his books.' But on leaving college, I decided I had nothing to write about and became a journalist. Met my wife after reviewing her (favourably) at the repertory theatre in Swindon, Wiltshire. She encouraged me to try a detective story. After two unsuccessful attempts the rest followed." Keating started writing crime novels about India because his agent had been unable to sell his previous books in America where "they were said to be 'too English.'" He then wrote a book "in which there were no English characters at all, but one Swede. This, though not intended to be the start of a series, was so much liked that its hero, Inspector Ghote of the Bombay CID, has featured in almost all subsequent books."

BIOGRAPHICAL/CRITICAL SOURCES: Times (London), January 7, 1971; Julian Symons, *Bloody Murder,* Harper, 1972.

*   *   *

KEAY, Frederick 1915-

PERSONAL: Surname rhymes with "ray"; born February 12, 1915, in Madras, India; son of Lyle (a foreign exchange broker) and Jane Helen (Hendry) Keay; married Betty Margaret Bunting, June 26, 1943; children: Peter Lyle, Kathleen Mary (Mrs. John Murray Parkinson). *Education:* University of Edinburgh, M.A. (honors), 1937. *Politics:* Conservative. *Religion:* Presbyterian. *Home and office:* 23 Royston Park Rd., Hatch End HA5 4AA, Middlesex, England. *Agent:* A. D. Peters & Co. Ltd., 10 Buckingham St., Adelphi, London WC2N 6BU, England.

CAREER: Ashridge Management College, near Berkhamstead, Hertfordshire, England, head of faculty of management sciences, 1964—; Apta Teaching and Training Aids Ltd., Glasgow, Scotland, chairman, 1965—. *Military service:* Royal Air Force, 1943-46; became flight lieutenant; mentioned in dispatches. *Member:* Chartered Institute of Secretaries, Business Equipment Trade Association (member of council, 1963), Royal Overseas League, Caledonian Club. *Awards, honors:* Garton Memorial Award, National Institute of Social and Economic Research, for research paper, "Factors affecting Productivity in the Canning Industry."

WRITINGS: The Numerate Manager, Allen & Unwin, 1969; (with G. F. Wensley) *Marketing through Management,* Pergamon, 1970; *Marketing and Sale Forecasting,* Pergamon, 1971. Contributor to *Times, Scotsman, Illustrated London News, A.D. 1977,* and *Colour Review.*

SIDELIGHTS: Frederick Keay has an interest in nineteenth-century American history which stems from an interval that his forefathers spent in the United States and possession of a collection of letters written from America in the period 1830-1870, including two from Jefferson Davis. His great-grandfather emigrated to America in 1820 and his grandfather was born in New Orleans. With the exception of two members, the family returned from New Orleans to Scotland in 1860.

*   *   *

KEEN, (John) Ernest 1937-

PERSONAL: Born February 15, 1937, in Indianapolis, Ind.; son of Isaac William (a painter) and Magdalene (Eberhardt) Keen; married Dorris Jean Prugh (a teacher), 1958; children: Andrew Warren, Christa Melanie, Whitney Ryan. *Education:* Heidelberg College, A.B. (cum laude), 1959; Harvard University, Ph.D., 1963. *Home:* R.D. 1, Verna Rd., Lewisburg, Pa. 17837. *Office:* Department of Psychology, Bucknell University, Lewisburg, Pa. 17837.

CAREER: Veterans Administration Hospital, Boston, Mass., postdoctoral trainee, 1963-64; Bucknell University, Lewisburg, Pa., assistant professor, 1964-69, associate professor, 1969-74, professor of psychology, 1974—. Clinical psychologist, Capital District Psychiatric Center, Albany, N.Y., 1971-72. Psychological consultant to Pennsylvania Bureau of Vocational Rehabilitation, 1964-74, and to Federal Penitentiary, Lewisburg, Pa., 1965-68; fellow, National Humanities Institute, Yale University, 1976-77. *Awards, honors:* Limbach Award for distinguished teaching, Bucknell University, 1970.

WRITINGS: Three Faces of Being: Toward an Existential Clinical Psychology, Appleton, 1970; *Psychology and the New Consciousness,* Brooks/Cole, 1972; *Primer in Phenomenological Psychology,* Holt, 1975; (with Douglas K. Candland and others) *Emotion,* Brooks/Cole, 1977; (contributor) D. Rimm and R. Sommerville, editors, *Abnormal Psychology,* Academic Press, 1977; (contributor) M. King and R. Valle, editors, *Psychopathology,* Williams & Wilkins, 1978. Contributor to psychology and psychiatry journals.

WORK IN PROGRESS: Research on the shift in professional identity within the treatment professions toward community and political involvement, on the history of psychology, and on the history of the social sciences.

SIDELIGHTS: His work in the history of the social sciences has led Ernest Keen to a greater awareness of the quality of writing in his field. He told *CA:* "Engaging a reader in your own thoughts is a moral and aesthetic act, as well as an intellectual one. . . . I wish more social scientists, past and present, understood this layered integrity of writing, but, alas, the social science tradition does not see itself as a tradition of writing at all. I believe this hurts us intellectually more than we know."

BIOGRAPHICAL/CRITICAL SOURCES: Contemporary Psychology, January, 1977.

*   *   *

KEEN, Martin L. 1913-

PERSONAL: Born February 14, 1913, in Atlantic City, N.J.; married Laurel Hochstein Veith, October 18, 1964; children: (wife's prior marriage) Rena Veith Shenk, Linda Veith Goukler. *Education:* Columbia University, B.S., 1953. *Politics:* Democrat. *Home and office:* 11 Tanglewood W., Piscataway, N.J. 08854. *Agent:* Curtis Brown Ltd., 575 Madison Ave., New York, N.Y. 10022.

CAREER: At varying times worked as industrial chemist, biochemist, bacteriologist, staff editor and writer for *Home Illustrated Encyclopedia,* free-lance editor and writer for National Lexicographic Board, Dell Publishing Co., Grolier, Inc., McGraw-Hill Book Co., New American Library,

Doubleday & Co., and others; *Collier's Encyclopedia,* New York City, senior science editor, 1961-64; *Funk & Wagnalls Encyclopedia,* New York City, senior editor and contributor, 1967-68. *Military service:* U.S. Army, 1942-46. *Member:* Authors Guild, American Veterans Committee.

WRITINGS—"How and Why Wonder Book" series; published by Grosset: *How and Why Wonder Book of the Human Body,* 1961; . . . *of the Microscope,* 1961; . . . *of Chemistry,* 1961; . . . *of Wild Animals,* 1962; . . . *of Science Experiments,* 1962; . . . *of Sound,* 1962; . . . *of Prehistoric Animals,* 1962; . . . *of Magnets and Magnetism,* 1963; . . . *of Electronics,* 1969; (with C. C. Cunniff) . . . *of Air and Water,* 1969.

Other juvenile books: *The Wonders of the Human Body,* Grosset, 1966; *The Wonders of Space: Rockets, Missiles and Spacecraft,* Grosset, 1967; *Let's Experiment,* Grosset, 1968; *Lightning and Thunder,* Messner, 1969; *Hunting Fossils,* Messner, 1970; *How It Works,* Grosset, Volume I, 1972, Volume II, 1974; *The World beneath Our Feet: The Story of Soil,* Messner, 1974; *Be a Rockhound,* Messner, 1977.

Ghost-writer of about a dozen elementary science textbooks and teachers' manuals for several publishers; major contributor to *New York Times Encyclopedia Almanac,* 1970.

SIDELIGHTS: "Undoubtedly I have written—as a signed or unsigned contributor, as a rewriter, and as a ghost-writer—more encyclopedia articles than anyone else in the world," Martin Keen says. "They number in the thousands. This is my claim to fame."

BIOGRAPHICAL/CRITICAL SOURCES: Times Literary Supplement, June 26, 1969; *New York Times Book Review,* February 16, 1975; *Appraisal: Children's Science Books,* winter, 1975; *Social Education,* March, 1975; *Science Books,* May, 1975.

*   *   *

KEESECKER, William Francis   1918-

PERSONAL: Born August 28, 1918, in Washington, Kan.; son of Glen Fisler (a farmer) and Maude (King) Keesecker; married Mary Jane Murray, June 10, 1942; children: Mary Elizabeth, Rebecca Ann, Sharon Rachel. *Education:* College of Emporia, A.B., 1940; McCormick Theological Seminary, B.D., 1943; Union Theological Seminary, New York, N.Y., graduate, 1949. *Home:* 114 North Ridgewood, Wichita, Kan. 67208. *Office:* Grace Presbyterian Church, 5002 East Douglas, Wichita, Kan. 67208.

CAREER: Ordained Presbyterian minister, 1943; pastor of Presbyterian churches, 1943—; Grace Presbytrian Church, Wichita, Kan., pastor, 1958—. *Military service:* U.S. Navy, 1945-46. *Member:* Masonic Fraternity.

WRITINGS: A Calvin Treasury, Harper, 1961; *The Wisdom of the Psalms,* World Publishing, 1970; *A Layperson's Guide to the Theology of the Book of Confessions,* United Presbyterian Church in U.S.A., 1976. Contributor of articles on the writings of John Calvin to religious magazines.

*   *   *

KEGAN, Adrienne Koch   1912-1971

September 10, 1912—August 21, 1971; American historian and educator. Obituaries: *Washington Post,* August 23, 1971.

KEHL, D(elmar) G(eorge)   1936-

PERSONAL: Surname is pronounced Kale; born September 12, 1936, in Mount Carroll, Ill.; son of Harry (a farmer) and Anna (Albrecht) Kehl; married Wanda Sue Thomas (a teacher), August 10, 1963; children: Kevin Lane, Kenyon Lee. *Education:* Bob Jones University, B.A., 1957; University of Wisconsin, M.S., 1958; University of Southern California, Ph.D., 1967; also studied at University of Pennsylvania, Fordham University, and Occidental College. *Religion:* Christian. *Home:* 8725 East Citrus Way, Scottsdale, Ariz. 85253. *Office:* Department of English, Arizona State University, Tempe, Ariz. 85281.

CAREER: Teacher in Stamford, Conn., 1959-60; University of Southern California, Los Angeles, lecturer in English, 1963-64; Arizona State University, Tempe, assistant professor, 1965-70, associate professor, 1970-75, professor of English, 1975—. *Member:* National Council of Teachers of English, Rocky Mountain Modern Language Association.

WRITINGS: The Literary Style of the Old Bible and the New, Bobbs-Merrill, 1970; *Poetry and the Visual Arts,* Wadsworth, 1975. Contributor to language and literature journals.

WORK IN PROGRESS: The Rhetoric of Advertisement, for Harcourt; *Rhetoric and Writing: Essay, Story, Poem,* for Prentice-Hall; *Dialectics of Reality in the Fiction of Robert Penn Warren; Diaries of a Novel: "The Grapes of Wrath"; The Handwriting on the Wall: A Study of Graffiti; "An American Tragedy" and Dreiser's Cousin, Mr. Poe.*

*   *   *

KEIM, Charles J.   1921-

PERSONAL: Surname is pronounced Kime; born November 2, 1921, in Judith Gap, Mont.; son of Francis F. (a druggist and chemist) and May T. Keim; married Betty Boyd, April 16, 1944; children: Janet (Mrs. Warren L. Griese), Ann Theresa, Bruce Charles. *Education:* University of Washington, Seattle, B.A., 1948, M.A., 1950. *Religion:* Roman Catholic. *Home address:* P.O. Box 80-242, College, Alaska 99701. *Office:* Department of English and Journalism, University of Alaska, College, Alaska 99701.

CAREER: United Press (now United Press International), correspondent, 1940; *Port Angeles Evening News,* Port Angeles, Wash., news editor, 1950-54; University of Alaska, College, instructor, 1954-55, assistant professor, 1955-57, associate professor, 1957-61, professor of English and journalism, 1961—, dean of College of Arts and Letters, 1963-70. Member, National Commission on Arts and Sciences, 1966-68. Registered big game guide for all Alaska, except the Panhandle and Aleutians. *Military service:* U.S. Army, 1940-45; became first sergeant; received Bronze Star, Combat Infantryman's Badge, and Presidential Unit Citation.

MEMBER: Modern Language Association of America, Rocky Mountain Modern Languages Association, Philological Association of the Pacific Coast, Council of Colleges of Arts and Sciences (member of board, 1968-70), Pacific Northwest Conference on Higher Education (member of board, 1968-70), Alaska Press Club, Explorers Club of New York (fellow), Sigma Delta Chi. *Awards, honors:* Washington State Press award, 1954; Alaska Press Club awards, 1955, 1957, 1964, 1969, 1970; American College Public Relations Association award, jointly with Lowell Thomas, Jr., and University of Alaska, 1963; named Alaska 49'er for cultural contributions to the state, by Alaska Press Club, 1963; two Alaska Centennial literary awards, 1967.

WRITINGS: Aghvook: White Eskimo, University of Washington-University of Alaska Press, 1969; *The Gallant Try,* Alatna Press, 1971; (with Hal Waugh) *Fair Chase with Alaskan Guides,* Alaska Northwest Publishing, 1972; *Change and Other Short Stories about Contemporary Alaska,* AMV Press, 1976. Contributor of articles, short fiction, and photographs to American and foreign publications.

WORK IN PROGRESS: Speak to the Earth, a novel; *The Mystery of the Arctic Ghost,* a juvenile novel; working on a non-fiction book, *Bear Tales from Alaska,* as a co-author.

BIOGRAPHICAL/CRITICAL SOURCES: Alaska Call, March, 1960; *Alaska Review,* fall, 1964; Ingeborg Wilson, *Alaskans I Have Met,* Wilson Publishers, 1968; *Saturday Review,* July 5, 1969.

*   *   *

KEITH, K. Wymand 1924-

PERSONAL: Original name, Leonard Claude Bowen; name legally changed in 1961; born November 16, 1924, in Henryetta, Okla.; son of Claude Monroe (a farmer) and Nellie Ann (Brown) Bowen; married Evelyne Eunice Finley (a dietician), 1944; married second wife, Joyce Cook (a bookkeeper, February 21, 1961; children: (first marriage) Patricia Carole; (second marriage) Jason Christopher; stepchildren: Bruce, Liane, William. *Education:* Self-educated in prison; studied creative writing via correspondence courses, University of Oregon, 1961-65. *Politics:* ''The man and not the party.'' *Religion:* ''Some of each, but all of none.''

CAREER: Spent fifteen years of sentences totaling twenty-five years in penitentiaries on bad check charges, serving approximately three years each in prisons at Leavenworth, Kan., Gould, Ark., McAlester, Okla., Lincoln, Neb., and Salem, Ore.; adjudged criminally insane in Woodland, Calif., 1953; now has been pardoned on most convictions and has been free since 1965; works independently for prison reform, speaking to various groups and on radio and television. *Military service:* U.S. Army, Parachute Infantry, seven months in 1943 (''first Army dropout; honorably discharged'').

WRITINGS: Long Line Rider: The Story of Cummins Prison Farm, McGraw, 1971. Associate editor, *Eyeopener* (prison newspaper), 1957-58; editor, *Shadows* (prison magazine), 1963-64.

WORK IN PROGRESS: Secret of Mendocino, nonfiction in novel form about an ex-convict's adjustment after his release; *Portrait of a Criminal Mind.*

SIDELIGHTS: K. Wymand Keith thought up his adopted name during his check-passing heyday when he was riding through Colorado with a warning, ''Keep Wide of Kansas'' flashing through his mind. The warning about a state where he had done time evolved into K. Wymand Keith. He believes that we must eventually consider men who break laws ill men, not criminals, but in the meantime advocates humanitarianism and sweeping change in prisons, mental hospitals, and other institutions. ''Love to fish, do woodwork, play scrabble, play guitar and write songs (both lyrics and melodies),'' he writes. ''My one great ambition: To become sheriff of Yavapai County, Arizona some day, for one term only.'' He has appeared with John Bartholomew Tucker on the ''A.M. New York Show,'' and on the Garry Moore television show, ''To Tell the Truth.''††

*   *   *

KEMENY, John G(eorge) 1926-

PERSONAL: Born May 31, 1926, in Budapest, Hungary; came to United States in 1940, naturalized citizen in 1945; son of Tibor (an exporter-importer) and Lucy (Fried) Kemeny; married Jean Alexander, November 5, 1950; children: Jennifer M. (Mrs. Charles Carner), Robert A. *Education:* Princeton University, A.B. (summa cum laude), 1947, Ph.D., 1949. *Home:* 1 Tuck Dr., Hanover, N.H. 03755. *Office:* Office of the President, 207 Parkhurst Hall, Dartmouth College, Hanover, N.H. 03755.

CAREER: Assistant to Albert Einstein at Institute for Advanced Study, Princeton, N.J., 1948-49; Princeton University, Princeton, Fine Instructor and Office of Naval Research fellow in mathematics, 1949-51, assistant professor of philosophy, 1951-53; Dartmouth College, Hanover, N.H., professor of mathematics, 1953-70, Albert Bradley Third Century Professor, 1969-72, chairman of department of mathematics, 1955-67, president of the college, 1970—. Visiting professor, New York University, 1952-53; lecturer in Austria, India, and Japan, 1964-65; Sigma Xi national lecturer, 1967. Consultant, RAND Corp., 1953-69; chairman, U.S. Commission on Mathematics Instruction, 1958-60; member of National Research Council, 1963-66, National Commission on Libraries and Information Science, 1971-73, and U.S. Department of Health, Education and Welfare Regional Director's Advisory Committee, 1971-73; vice-chairman, National Science Foundation Committee on Computing, 1968-69; director, Council for Financial Aid to Education, 1976—. Trustee of Foundation Center, 1970-76, and Carnegie Foundation for Advancement of Teaching, 1970—. Member, Hanover School Board, 1961-64; New Hampshire state chairman, United Negro College Fund, 1972—. Co-inventor of computer language BASIC. *Military service:* U.S. Army, assistant in Theoretical Division, Manhattan Project, 1945-46; became sergeant.

MEMBER: Association for Symbolic Logic, Mathematical Association of America (chairman of New England section, 1959-60; member of board of governors, 1960-63; chairman of panel on biological and social sciences, 1963-64), American Academy of Arts and Sciences (fellow), American Mathematical Society, American Philosophical Association, Phi Beta Kappa, Sigma Xi. *Awards, honors:* D.Sc., Middlebury College, 1965, Boston College, 1973, University of Pennsylvania, 1975; LL.D., Columbia University, and Princeton University, both 1971, University of New Hampshire, 1972, Colby College, 1976; Joseph Priestly Award, Dickinson College, 1976.

WRITINGS: (With J. L. Snell and G. L. Thompson) *Introduction to Finite Mathematics,* Prentice-Hall, 1957, 3rd edition, 1974; (with Snell, Thompson, and Hazleton Mirkil) *Finite Mathematical Structures,* Prentice-Hall, 1959; *A Philosopher Looks at Science,* Van Nostrand, 1959; (with Snell) *Finite Markov Chains,* Van Nostrand, 1960, 2nd edition, Springer-Verlag, 1976; (contributor) Daniel Lerner, editor, *Quantity and Quality,* Free Press, 1961; (with Snell) *Mathematical Models in the Social Sciences,* Ginn, 1962; (with Snell, Thompson, and Arthur Schleifer) *Finite Mathematics with Business Applications,* Prentice-Hall, 1962, 2nd edition, 1972; (with Robin Robinson) *New Directions in Mathematics,* Prentice-Hall, 1963; *Random Essays on Mathematics, Education and Computers,* Prentice-Hall, 1964; (with Snell and A. W. Knapp) *Denumberable Markov Chains,* Van Nostrand, 1966; (contributor) Francis Sweeney, *The Knowledge Explosion,* Farrar, Straus, 1966; (with T. E. Kurtz) *Basic Programming,* Wiley, 1967, 2nd edition, 1971; *Man and the Computer,* Scribner, 1972.

Collaborator on the following experimental texts as member of Mathematical Association of America committee on the undergraduate program: *Universal Mathematics*, Part II, Tulane University, 1955; *Modern Mathematical Methods and Models*, Volumes I-II, Mathematical Association of America, 1958-59. Contributor to *Encyclopaedia Britannica*. Consulting editor, *Journal of Symbolic Logic*, 1950-59; associate editor, *Journal of Mathematical Analysis and Applications*, 1959-70.

SIDELIGHTS: John G. Kemeny revolutionized the mathematics program at Dartmouth through a series of innovations which were widely imitated in other colleges. In addition, his invention of the simplified computer code BASIC made possible the use of computers in many areas of education. Kemeny's *Introduction to Finite Mathematics* has been translated into French, Spanish, Russian, and German.

BIOGRAPHICAL/CRITICAL SOURCES: New York Times, January 24, 1970; *Newsweek*, February 2, 1970; *Time*, February 9, 1970; *Dartmouth Alumni*, June, 1970.

*   *   *

KEMPTON, James Murray, Jr.   1945(?)-1971

1945(?)—November 26, 1971; American journalist. Obituaries: *New York Times*, November 28, 1971.

*   *   *

KEMPTON, Jean Goldschmidt   1946(?)-1971

1946(?)—November 26, 1971; American poet and short story writer. Obituaries: *New York Times*, November 28, 1971.

*   *   *

KENNEDY, Gail   1900-1972

September 17, 1900—April 18, 1972; American educator and author of books on philosophy. Obituaries: *New York Times*, April 20, 1972.

*   *   *

KENNERLY, Karen   1940-

PERSONAL: Born July 17, 1940, in New York, N.Y.; daughter of Albert (an architect) and Helen (Wolff) Kennerly. *Education:* Pembroke College, B.A. (with distinction), 1962. *Politics:* Liberal. *Religion:* None. *Office:* Dial Press, 1 Dag Hammarskjold Plaza, 245 East 47th St., New York, N.Y. 10017.

CAREER: Dial Press, New York, N.Y., editor, 1969—.

WRITINGS: The Slave Who Bought His Freedom, Dutton, 1971; (editor and author of introduction) *Hesitant Wolf and Scrupulous Fox: Fables Selected from World Literature*, Random House, 1973.†

*   *   *

KERN, Alfred   1924-

PERSONAL: Original surname Cohen; name legally changed in 1946 ("at the request of an older brother who had already done so"); born August 8, 1924, in Alliance, Ohio; son of Harry (a merchant) and Mollie (Eisenstadt) Cohen; married Carole Franklin (an elementary teacher), August 7, 1947; children: Sheridan (daughter), Pamela, Stephen. *Education:* Allegheny College, A.B., 1948; New York University, M.A., 1954. *Politics:* Democrat. *Residence:* Meadville, Pa. *Agent:* Russell & Volkening, Inc., 551 Fifth Ave., New York, N.Y. 10017. *Office:* Department of English, Allegheny College, Meadville, Pa. 16335.

CAREER: Allegheny College, Meadville, Pa., instructor,

1949-53, assistant professor, 1953-60, associate professor, 1960-67, Frederick F. Seely Professor of English, 1968—, chairman of department, 1968-71. *Military service:* U.S. Army Air Forces, 1942-46; became sergeant. *Member:* Authors Guild.

WRITINGS—Novels: *The Width of Waters*, Houghton, 1959; *Made in U.S.A.*, Houghton, 1966; *The Trial of Martin Ross*, Norton, 1971.

WORK IN PROGRESS: A new novel, *Vows and Infidelities*.

SIDELIGHTS: Alfred Kern's concern with the total nationalization of American life is reflected in the small town settings of his books. All of them, he says, "deal with major characters who work within and serve important American institutions and professions. All the characters seek to improve the quality of the American social order but finally each is personally frustrated by the very institution that he serves. *Made in U.S.A.* . . . came after my 20 year involvement with unions—a number of those years as a consultant to the United Steelworkers of America."

Granville Hicks commented on *Made in U.S.A.*, "The style is lively, tough, and not always for the genteel." In an essay for *Kenyon Review* (later anthologized in *Proletarian Writers of the Thirties*), Gerald Green says *Made in U.S.A.* "is a splendid book. Sharply written, original in plot and characterization, full of the nuances and specifics and argot of the union world, thoroughly entertaining, it is a realistic novel—a social novel, if you will—in the honored tradition."

BIOGRAPHICAL/CRITICAL SOURCES: Saturday Review, February 26, 1966; *Sunday Herald Tribune*, February 27, 1966; *Book Week*, February 27, 1966; *Best Sellers*, March 1, 1966; *New York Times Book Review*, March 13, 1966; David Madden, editor, *Proletarian Writers of the Thirties*, Southern Illinois University Press, 1968.

*   *   *

KETCHUM, William C(larence), Jr.   1931-

PERSONAL: Born March 29, 1931, in Columbia, Mo.; son of William Clarence and Mildred Ann (Roberts) Ketchum; married Patricia McGuigan Forbes, July 8, 1963; children: Rachael Forbes, Aaron Roberts. *Education:* Union College and University, Schenectady, N.Y., B.A., 1953; Columbia University, J.D., 1956. *Home:* 312 West 20th St., New York, N.Y. 10011. *Office:* New School for Social Research, New York, N.Y. 10011.

CAREER: Member of Bar of State in New York; attorney with law firms in New York City, prior to 1969; Civil Court, New York City, attorney, 1969-76; New School for Social Research, New York City, instructor in fine arts, 1971—. *Military service:* U.S. Naval Reserve, active duty, 1956-60; became lieutenant. *Member:* New York Historical Society, New York State Bar Association, Association of the Bar (New York City).

WRITINGS: Early Potters and Potteries of New York State, Funk, 1970; *The Pottery and Porcelain Collector's Handbook*, Funk, 1971; *American Basketry and Woodenware*, Macmillan, 1974; *A Treasury of American Bottles*, Bobbs-Merrill, 1975; *Hooked Rugs*, Harcourt, 1976; *The Catalog of American Antiques*, Rutledge Books, 1977. Contributor to *Western Collector* Magazine, *Pontil* (newsletter), *Spinning Wheel*, *Antiques Journal*, *Early American Life*, *Americana*, and *Pottery Collectors Newsletter*.

WORK IN PROGRESS: A book on Victorian crafts; a book on international furniture styles.

SIDELIGHTS: William Ketchum has had "extensive foreign travel and residence abroad," including Spain, France, British Isles, Portugal, Italy, Morocco, Switzerland, Canada, Mexico, Chile, Japan, Taiwan, Philippines, Korea, and Hong Kong. *Avocational interests:* Antique collecting and dealing, fishing, historical research.

* * *

KIDDLE, Lawrence B(ayard) 1907-

PERSONAL: Born August 20, 1907, in Cleveland, Ohio; son of Bayard Taylor (a businessman) and Emma (Volmar) Kiddle; married Allene Houglan, June 29, 1932; children: Sue Carolyn (Mrs. Edward F. Meyer), Mary Ellen. *Education:* Oberlin College, A.B. (magna cum laude), 1929; University of Wisconsin, A.M., 1930, Ph.D., 1935. *Home:* 2654 Englave Dr., Ann Arbor, Mich. 48103. *Office:* Department of Spanish, University of Michigan, 4144 MLB, Ann Arbor, Mich. 48109.

CAREER: University of New Mexico, Albuquerque, instructor, 1935-37, assistant professor of Romance languages, 1937-38; Princeton University, Princeton, N.J., instructor in Spanish, 1938-40; Tulane University, New Orleans, La., assistant professor, 1940-41, associate professor of Romance languages, 1941-43; University of Michigan, Ann Arbor, assistant professor, 1947-48, associate professor, 1948-54, professor of Spanish, 1954—. Fulbright professor of linguistics, Institute Caro y Cuervo, Bogota, Colombia, 1963-64. *Military service:* U.S. Naval Reserve, active duty, 1943-47; became lieutenant commander. *Member:* Modern Language Association of America, Linguistic Society of America, American Association of Teachers of Spanish and Portuguese, Hispanic Society of America (corresponding member). *Awards, honors:* Military Order of Ayacucho, Peru, 1947.

WRITINGS: (Editor with John E. Englekirk) Mariano Azuela, *Los de abajo,* Appleton, 1939, revised edition, 1971; (editor with Enrique Anderson-Imbert) *Veinte cuentos hispano-americanos del siglo veinte,* Appleton, 1956; (editor) Vicente Blasco Ibanez, *La Barraca,* Holt, 1960; (editor) *Veinte cuentos Espanoles del siglo veinte,* Appleton, 1961; (editor with Lloyd A. Kasten) Alfonso X, *El Libro de las cruces,* Consejo Superior de Investigaciones Cientificas (Madrid), 1961; (editor) *Cuentos americanos y algunas poesias,* Norton, 1970. Contributor to language journals.

AVOCATIONAL INTERESTS: Travel.

* * *

KILGORE, James C(olumbus) 1928-

PERSONAL: Born May 2, 1928, in Ansley, La.; son of James Wilson and Ruth (Bell) Kilgore; married Alberta Gunnels (a teacher), June, 1960; children: Kenneth, Steven, Sheila. *Education:* Wiley College, B.A., 1952; attended Texas Southern University, 1955, and University of Arkansas, summers, 1956-57; University of Missouri, M.A., 1963; graduate study at San Diego State College (now University), 1969, and Kent State University. *Politics:* Independent. *Religion:* Protestant. *Home:* 16604 Talford Ave., Cleveland, Ohio 44128. *Office:* Department of English, Cuyahoga Community College, 25444 Harvard Ave., Warrensville Township, Ohio 44122.

CAREER: English teacher in high schools of Hot Springs, Ark., 1954-58, Fair Lawn, N.J., 1959-60, Hayti, Mo., 1960-61, and Kansas City, Mo., 1963-66. Agricultural, Mechanical and Normal College (now University of Arkansas at

Pine Bluff), instructor in English, 1958-59; Cuyahoga Community College, Cleveland, Ohio, assistant professor, 1966-68, associate professor, 1968-70, professor of English, 1970—. Adjunct professor of Afro-American literature, University of Akron, 1972; participant in Bread Loaf Writers' Conference, annual Asland College Poetry Festival, and International Black Writer's Conference, all 1971. *Military service:* U.S. Army, telegrapher, 1952-54. *Member:* Modern Language Association of America, Renaissance Society of America, National Council of Teachers of English, Ohio Poets Association, Ohioana. *Awards, honors:* Fellowships from Case Western Reserve University, 1964, University of Nebraska, 1966, and University of California, Santa Barbara, 1968.

WRITINGS: The Big Buffalo and Other Poems: A Sampler of the Poetry of James C. Kilgore, Cuyahoga Community College Press, 1970; *Midnight Blast and Other Poems,* King Publishing, 1971; *A Time of Black Devotion,* Ashland Poetry Press, 1971; *Let It Pass* (poems), Sharagun, 1976. Also author of *A Black Bicentennial* (poem), Black River Writers. Represented in several anthologies, including *Sixty on the Sixties: A Decade's History in Verse,* edited by Robert McGovern and Richard Snyder, Ashland Poetry Press, 1970, and *The World of Informative-Persuasive Prose,* edited by K. F. McKean and C. Wheeler, Holt, 1971. Contributor to *Essence, Haiku Highlights, Phylon, Prairie Schooner, Green Apple, Negro Digest, Black World, Crisis,* and other publications.

BIOGRAPHICAL/CRITICAL SOURCES: Negro Digest, July, 1969; *Black World,* June, 1970.

* * *

KILLE, Mary F. 1948-

PERSONAL: Surname rhymes with "chilly"; born January 9, 1948, in Wilmington, Del.; daughter of Walter Bertram and Mary (Stewart) Kille; married David L. Norton (a professor at University of Delaware), August 22, 1970; children: Timothy Tucker, Cory Dana. *Education:* University of Delaware, B.A. (with high honors), 1970, M.A., 1975. *Home:* 6 Windflower Dr., Meadowood, Newark, Del. 19711. *Office:* Department of Philosophy, University of Delaware, Newark, Del. 19711.

CAREER: Received a teaching assistantship while an undergraduate at the University of Delaware, Newark, to help design and assist her (now) husband in presenting a course there on the philosophy of love; since then they have collaborated on a course in the philosophy of death. *Member:* Phi Kappa Phi, Mortar Board.

WRITINGS: (Editor with husband, David L. Norton) *Philosophies of Love,* Chandler Publishing, 1971. Contributor to *Journal of Value Inquiry.*

WORK IN PROGRESS: Research in the aesthetics of Samuel Taylor Coleridge.

* * *

KIM, Yoon Hough 1934-1976

PERSONAL: Born May 10, 1934, in Hamhung, Korea; son of Chul Soo (an educator) and Hih Sook (Huh) Kim; married Jeng Ja Chang, January 16, 1958; children: Nam Ji (daughter), Hih Song (daughter), Won (son). *Education:* Dong Ah University, LL.B., 1958; University of Minnesota, M.A., 1964, Ph.D., 1967. *Office:* Department of Sociology, East Carolina University, Greenville, N.C. 27835.

CAREER: Foster Parents' Plan, Pusan, Korea, caseworker, 1958-60, office manager, 1960-62; East Carolina University, Greenville, N.C., 1967-76, assistant professor, 1967-71, became professor of sociology. *Member:* American Sociological Association, National Conference on Family Relations, Southern Sociological Society.

WRITINGS: (Contributor) Gerhard Neubeck, editor, *Extramarital Relations,* Prentice-Hall, 1969; *The Community of the Blind: Applying the Theory of Community Formation,* American Foundation for the Blind, 1971. Contributor to sociology journals.

WORK IN PROGRESS: Research involving cross-racial acceptance in desegregated schools in the South.†

(Died, 1976)

* * *

KIMBRELL, Grady 1933-

PERSONAL: Born April 6, 1933, in Tallant, Okla.; son of Virgil LeRoy (a welder) and LaVera (Underwood) Kimbrell; married Marilyn King, May 30, 1953 (divorced); married Mary Ellen Harris, April 11, 1973; children: (first marriage) Mark LeRoy, Joni Lynne; (second marriage) Lisa Christine. *Education:* Southwestern College, Winfield, Kan., B.A., 1956; Colorado State College, Greeley, M.A., 1968. *Home:* 4379 Via Esperanza, Santa Barbara, Calif. 93110. *Office:* 720 Santa Barbara St., Santa Barbara, Calif. 93101.

CAREER: High school teacher of business education in Peabody, Kan., 1956-58; Santa Barbara High School, Santa Barbara, Calif., teacher of business education, 1958-60, work-experience counselor, 1960-67, work-experience coordinator, 1967-71; San Marcos High School, Santa Barbara, career development adviser, 1971-75; Santa Barbara High School District, Santa Barbara, research analyst, 1975—. *Military service:* U.S. Army, 1953-55. *Member:* California Association of Work-Experience Education (vice-president), Santa Barbara County Association of Work-Experience Educators (president), Kiwanis Club (secretary).

WRITINGS—All published by McKnight: (With Ben Vineyard) *Succeeding in the World of Work,* 1970, revised edition, 1975; *Strategies for Implementing Work Experience Programs,* 1973; *Individualized Related Instruction,* 1973; *Introduction to Business and Office Careers,* 1974; *Student Activities for Succeeding in the World of Work,* 1975. Contributor to education journals.

AVOCATIONAL INTERESTS: Breeding, training, and racing thoroughbreds and quarterhorses.

* * *

KING, Alvy L(eon) 1932-

PERSONAL: Born August 11, 1932, in Portales, N.M.; son of Raymond Leon (a service station manager) and Anna (Robinson) King; children: Twyla Ann, Lowell Leon, Nancy Joy, Lori D'Ann. *Education:* West Texas State University, B.S., 1959, M.A., 1960; University of Texas, Main University (now University of Texas at Austin), graduate study, 1960-61; Texas Technological College (now Texas Tech University), Ph.D., 1967; Howard University, postdoctoral study, 1970-71. *Home:* 203 Adams Blvd., Terre Haute, Ind. 47803. *Office:* Department of Education, Indiana State University, Terre Haute, Ind. 47809.

CAREER: Oklahoma Christian College, Oklahoma City, chairman of Social Science Division, 1961-62; University of Southwestern Louisiana, Lafayette, instructor in history,

1965-67; Texas Christian University, Fort Worth, assistant professor of history, 1967-71; Indiana State University, Terre Haute, associate professor of Afro-American studies and assistant director of Afro-American Studies Program, 1971-73, associate professor of education and education coordinator of Midwest Center for Equal Education Opportunity, 1973—. *Military service:* U.S. Army, 1954-55; became sergeant. *Member:* Organization of American Historians, Association for the Study of Negro Life and History, American Civil Liberties Union, Southern Historical Association, Western Association for Africanists, Indiana Association for Afro-American Studies, Phi Alpha Theta.

WRITINGS: Louis T. Wigfall: Southern Fire-Eater, Louisiana State University Press, 1970; (co-author) *Pluralism and the American Teacher,* American Association of Colleges for Teacher Education, 1977. Contributor to *Louisiana Studies,* and to *Encyclopedia for Southern History.*

WORK IN PROGRESS: Researching and writing *A History of Ethnic Minorities in the United States;* research projects on desegregation and resegregation, and on the status of black teachers.

* * *

KING, Annette 1941-

PERSONAL: Born November 14, 1941. *Education:* Attended Boston University and Smith College. *Politics:* Radical. *Religion:* None. *Agent:* Toni Strassman, 130 East 18th St., Apt. 7-D, New York, N.Y. 10003.

CAREER: Clinical and staff psychologist in Chattanooga, Tenn., 1971—. *Member:* American Psychological Association, Phi Beta Kappa.

WRITINGS: The Magic Tortoise Ranch (novel), Crown, 1972.

WORK IN PROGRESS: A novel entitled *Last Man Alive.*

BIOGRAPHICAL/CRITICAL SOURCES: San Bernardino Sun-Globe, January 23, 1972; *New York Times Book Review,* February 6, 1972.††

* * *

KING, Edith W(eiss) 1930-

PERSONAL: Born July 16, 1930, in Detroit, Mich.; daughter of Otto A. and Fay (Eskay) Weiss; married Marvin M. King (chief product engineer and manager, Products Division of Samsonite Corp.), December 22, 1951; children: Melissa, Matthew. *Education:* University of Michigan, B.A., 1951; Wayne State University, M.A., 1961, Ed.D., 1966. *Politics:* Democrat. *Religion:* Jewish. *Home:* 3734 South Niagara Way, Denver, Colo. 80237. *Office:* School of Education, University of Denver, Denver, Colo. 80210.

CAREER: Teacher at elementary schools in Michigan, 1951-64; director of cooperative nursery school in Oak Park, Mich., 1959-60; University of Denver, School of Education, Denver, Colo., 1966—, began as associate professor, currently professor of education. Reader and consultant for Allyn & Bacon, Coronet Films and Filmstrips, American Book Co., University of Illinois Press, and other publishers; consultant to Denver Head-Start Child Development Centers. *Member:* American Sociological Association, National Council for the Social Studies, National Council for Social Studies, American Association of University Professors, Sociologists for Women in Society, Western Social Science Association, Phi Beta Kappa, Phi Delta Kappa.

WRITINGS: (With August Kerber) *The Sociology of Early*

Childhood Education, American Book Co., 1968; *The World: Context for Teaching in the Elementary School*, W. C. Brown, 1971; *Educating Young Children: Sociological Interpretations*, W. C. Brown, 1973; (with Joseph Stevens, Jr.) *Administering Early Childhood Education Programs*, Little, Brown, 1976; (with R. P. Cuzzort) *Humanity and Modern Social Thought*, 2nd edition (King was not associated with earlier edition), Dryden, 1976. Also author of "Discovering the World!," filmstrip, records, and teacher's guide on world awareness for young children, Spoken Arts, 1971. Contributor to education journals.

* * *

KING, Edmund L(udwig) 1914-

PERSONAL: Born January 10, 1914, in St. Louis, Mo.; son of William F. B. Seifert and Lydia (Ludwig) Seifert King; stepson of Henry Grady King (a lumberman); married Willard Fahrenkamp (a professor), January 29, 1951. *Education:* University of Texas, Main University (now University of Texas at Austin), A.B., 1933, M.A., 1934, Ph.D., 1949. *Politics:* Democrat. *Religion:* Episcopalian. *Home:* 171 Western Way, Princeton, N.J. 08540. *Office:* Department of Romance Languages, Princeton University, Princeton, N.J. 08540.

CAREER: Mississippi State College (now University), State College, assistant professor of Spanish, 1936-41; University of Texas, Main University (now University of Texas at Austin), instructor in English, 1946; Princeton University, Princeton, N.J., instructor, 1946-50, assistant professor, 1950-55, associate professor, 1955-66, professor of Spanish, 1966—, Walter S. Carpenter, Jr. Professor of the Language, Literature, and Civilization of Spain, 1975—, chairman of department of Romance languages, 1966-72. President of board of directors, International Institute in Spain, Madrid. *Military service:* U.S. Army, 1941-45; became major; received Bronze Star Medal and Golden Cross of Merit (Poland). *Member:* Modern Language Association of America, Hispanic Society of America (corresponding member).

WRITINGS: Becquer: From Painter to Poet, Editorial Porrua S.A., 1953; (translator) Americo Castro, *The Structure of Spanish History*, Princeton University Press, 1954; (editor) Gabriel Miro, *El Humo Dormido*, Dell, 1967; (editor and translator with S. Gilman) *An Idea of History: Selected Essays of Americo Castro*, Ohio State University Press, 1977. Contributor to Romance language journals.

WORK IN PROGRESS: Research on the life and work of Gabriel Miro (1879-1930).

* * *

KING, Helen H(ayes) 1937-

PERSONAL: Born October 15, 1937, in Clarksdale, Miss.; daughter of Emmit (a postal worker) and Mary (Gage) Hayes; married James D. King, Jr. (a sculptor), December 26, 1962 (divorced); children: Chad, Fenote (daughter). *Education:* Attended De Paul University, 1955; Wilson Junior College, Chicago, A.A., 1958; University of Michigan, B.A., 1960. *Religion:* Protestant. *Home:* 2001 South Michigan, Chicago, Ill. 60616.

CAREER: Teacher in public schools in Pontiac, Mich., 1955-59, and Chicago, Ill., 1959, 1963-64; Johnson Publishing Co., Chicago, member of editorial staff of *Ebony* and *Jet* (magazines), 1960-61, 1969-71; associate editor and freelance writer, *Chicago Courier*, Chicago.

WRITINGS: Willy (juvenile), Doubleday, 1971; (contrib-utor) *To Gwen with Love: A Tribute to Gwendolyn Brooks* (poetry anthology), edited by Patricia L. Brown and others, Johnson Publishing Co., Chicago, Ill., 1971; *The Soul of Christmas* (juvenile), Johnson Publishing Co., Chicago, Ill., 1972. Contributor to *Ebony, Jet,* and *Chicago Courier.*

WORK IN PROGRESS: A novel, *A Place for Hating;* a children's book, *Uncle Oscar,* completed and awaiting publication.†

* * *

KING, Lester S(now) 1908-

PERSONAL: Born April 18, 1908, in Cambridge, Mass.; son of Myron L. (a physician) and Sophie (Snow) King; married Marjorie C. Meehan (a physician), December 23, 1931; children: Alfred, Frances (Mrs. Donald E. Widmann). *Education:* Harvard University, A.B. (magna cum laude), 1927, M.D., 1932. *Politics:* Independent. *Religion:* Unitarian Univeralist. *Home:* 360 Wellington Ave., Chicago, Ill. 60657. *Office:* American Medical Association, 535 North Dearborn Ave., Chicago, Ill. 60610.

CAREER: Harvard University, Cambridge, Mass., teaching fellow, 1933-35, Moseley Traveling Fellow in Madrid and London, 1935-36; Rockefeller Institute for Medical Research, Princeton, N.J., assistant, 1937-40; assistant in pathology at Yale University, New Haven, Conn., and pathologist at Fairfield State Hospital, Fairfield, Conn., 1940-42; Illinois Masonic Hospital, Chicago, Ill., pathologist, 1946-63; University of Illinois at the Medical Center, Chicago, clinical assistant professor, 1946-49, clinical associate professor, 1949-56, clinical professor of pathology, 1956-64; *Journal* of the American Medical Association, Chicago, senior editor, 1963-73, contributing editor, 1973—. Professorial lecturer in history of medicine, University of Chicago, 1965—; Garrison Lecturer, American Association for the History of Medicine, 1975. *Military service:* U.S. Army, Medical Corps, 1942-46; became lieutenant colonel.

MEMBER: American Medical Association, American Association for the History of Medicine (president, 1974-76), International Academy of the History of Medicine, Chicago Literary Club, Phi Beta Kappa. *Awards, honors:* National Cancer Institute research grant, 1947-49; Boerhaave Medal, University of Leiden, 1964; Welch Medal, American Association for the History of Medicine, 1977.

WRITINGS: The Medical World of the Eighteenth Century, University of Chicago Press, 1958; *The Growth of Medical Thought*, University of Chicago Press, 1963; (contributor) *Medical Investigations in Seventeenth Century England*, William Andrews Clark Memorial Library, University of California, 1968; (with Charles G. Roland) *Scientific Writing*, American Medical Association, 1968; *The Road to Medical Enlightenment, 1650-1695*, American Elsevier, 1970; (translator) Friedrich Hoffmann, *Fundamenta Medicinae*, American Elsevier, 1971; (editor) *Mainstreams of Medicine: Essays on the Social and Intellectual Context of Medical Practice*, University of Texas Press, 1971; (editor) *A History of Medicine*, Penguin, 1971; *The Philosophy of Medicine: The Early Eighteenth Century*, Harvard University Press, 1978. Contributor of research papers on medical topics and articles on the history of medicine to journals. Editor, *Clio Medica*, 1973-76.

* * *

KING, Marjorie Cameron 1909-
(Peggy Cameron King)

PERSONAL: Born September 3, 1909, in Midland, Ontario,

Canada; daughter of Angus (a salesman) and Ada (Millar) Cameron; married Harry Molyneux King, Jr. (an engineer), July 4, 1935; children: Patricia (Mrs. Clare Mullett), Garrison, Susan (Mrs. George Rabick). *Education:* University of Toronto, B.A., 1932; Ontario College of Education, Specialist in Art, 1933. *Home address:* Route 2, Box S-76, Stephens City, Va. 22655.

CAREER: High school teacher of English and art in Stevensville, Ontario, 1933-35; substitute teacher in Dearborn, Mich., 1952-56, and teacher of magazine writing in adult education classes, 1959-63; teacher of magazine writing in adult education classes in Birmingham, Mich., 1964; writer for magazines. Professional lecturer, speaking before Town Hall and Celebrity Series audiences, for clubs, and at writers conferences. *Member:* Women's National Book Association, National League of American Pen Women, Detroit Women Writers (honorary member), Women in Communications. *Awards, honors:* Headliner Award of Detroit chapter of Women in Communications, 1971; National League of American Pen Women award, 1976.

WRITINGS—All under name Peggy Cameron King: *Ladies, Please Come to Order,* Grosset, 1968; *Ladies, Let's Travel,* Grosset, 1970. Work included in *The Writer's Handbook* and *Guideposts Treasury of Faith.* More than three hundred articles published in fifty magazines and newspaper supplements, including *House Beautiful, Chatelaine, Modern Bride, American Girl, Ingenue, Family Circle, Toronto Star Weekly,* and *Christian Science Monitor.*

WORK IN PROGRESS: A book, *My Cottage Career.*

AVOCATIONAL INTERESTS: Art, interior decoration, summering on a remote island in Algonquin Park in Ontario ("without plumbing or electricity, and thus no television, praise be!").

*   *   *

KINGDON, Frank 1894-1972

February 27, 1894—February 24, 1972; English-born American educator, columnist, political commentator, historian, and author of books on contemporary America. Obituaries: *New York Times,* February 25, 1972; *Washington Post,* February 26, 1972; *Current Biography,* April, 1972.

*   *   *

KINGSTON, (Frederick) Temple 1925-

PERSONAL: Born December 30, 1925, in Toronto, Ontario, Canada; son of George Frederick (an Anglican primate) and Florence B. (Brown) Kingston; married Pauline Boyd Smith, June 15, 1951; children: Frederick, Elizabeth, Paul, Rebecca. *Education:* University of Toronto, B.A., 1947, M.A., 1950, L.Th., 1950, B.D., 1952; Oxford University, D.Phil., 1954; University of Basel, postdoctoral study, 1957. *Home:* 833 Kildare Rd., Windsor, Ontario, Canada. *Office:* Canterbury College, University of Windsor, 172 Patricia Rd., Windsor, Ontario, Canada.

CAREER: Anglican clergyman; Anglican College of British Columbia, Vancouver, professor of theology, 1953-59; University of Windsor, Canterbury College, Windsor, Ontario, professor of philosophy, 1959—, principal, 1965—. *Military service:* Royal Canadian Naval Reserve, chaplain, 1945—. *Member:* Canadian Philosophical Association, Aristotelian Society, Mind Association, Royal Institute of Philosophy. *Awards, honors:* Canada Council fellowship to Oxford University, 1968-69; Cultural Exchange scholarship to France, 1974; Canada Council research grant, France, 1975.

WRITINGS: French Existentialism: A Christian Critique, University of Toronto Press, 1961; (editor) *Anglicanism and Principles of Christian Unity,* Canterbury College, University of Windsor, 1972; (contributor) Gilbert Ryle, editor, *Contemporary Aspects of Philosophy,* Ariel Press, 1976. Also editor of *Anglicanism and Contemporary Social Issues,* 1973, *The Church and Industry,* 1974, and *The Church and Ethics in Public Life,* 1975; author of *On the Importance of Residence Life to Higher Education.*

WORK IN PROGRESS: George Berkeley: Doctrine of Spirit; research on contemporary moral issues; *Contemporary French Philosophy.*

*   *   *

KINSTLER, Everett Raymond 1926-

PERSONAL: Born August 5, 1926; son of Joseph Eugene (a businessman) and Essie (Hazel) Kinstler; married Lea Cummings Nation, June 23, 1958; children: Kate Galloway, Dana Cummings. *Education:* Studied art at National Academy of Design, 1943-45, and Art Students' League, New York, N.Y. *Politics:* Republican. *Religion:* Quaker. *Home:* 15 Gramercy Park, New York, N.Y. 10003. *Office:* 119 East 19th St., New York, N.Y. 10003.

CAREER: Started career as illustrator, New York City, 1943—, specializing in portraiture, 1955—; instructor in painting and drawing, Art Students' League, New York City, 1970—. Portraits include Mrs. Irene Dupont, Jr., astronaut A. B. Shepard, Jr., General Mark W. Clark, Admiral David McDonald, Ambassador David Kennedy, Governor John B. Connally, Elliot Richardson, Roy Rogers and Dale Evans, and numerous others; has exhibited works in one-man shows at Grand Central Art Galleries, New York City, 1960—; represented in permanent collections of New York Stock Exchange, Metropolitan Museum of Art, Brooklyn Museum, Mystic Seaport Museum, U.S. Military Academy, Smithsonian Institution, and numerous colleges, universities, and business firms. *Military service:* U.S. Army, 1945-46; became staff sergeant; received World War II Victory Medal.

MEMBER: National Arts Club (vice-president), Artists Fellowships, Inc. (president, 1967-70), National Academy of Design (academician), American Watercolor Society, Audubon Artists, Players Club, Century Association (trustee), Lotos Club (life member), Dutch Treat. *Awards, honors:* Gold Medal, National Arts Club, 1956-64; U.S. Navy Combat Art Medal, 1965; Salmagundi Medal, 1969; Lotos Club Gold Medal, 1972.

WRITINGS: Painting Portraits, edited by Susan E. Meyer, Watson-Guptill, 1971.

Contributor; all published by Watson-Guptill: Helen Rosenbaum, *Don't Swallow the Avocado Pit,* 1972; Lee R. Bobker, *Making Movies,* 1974; Brendan Gill, *Up Here at the "New Yorker",* 1975; Meyer, *Watercolorists at Work,* 1975; Meyer, *James Montgomery Flagg,* 1975; Joe Singer, *Painting Women's Portraits,* 1976; Singer, *Painting Men's Portraits,* 1977; John Kobler, *Damned in Paradise,* 1978.

Illustrator: Patricia Acheson, *Our Federal Government,* Dodd, 1960; George Martin, *The Opera Companion,* Dodd, 1961; George Martin, *Verdi,* Dodd, 1963. Contributor of articles to *American Artist* magazine.

*   *   *

KIRKPATRICK, Lyman B(ickford), Jr. 1916-

PERSONAL: Born July 15, 1916, in Rochester, N.Y.; son

of Lyman B. (a businessman) and Lyde (Paull) Kirkpatrick; married Jeanne Courtney, February 21, 1939; married second wife, Rita Meade, September 3, 1965; children: (first marriage) Lyman Bickford III, Jeanne Barclay, Paull Timothy, Helen Paull. *Education:* Princeton University, A.B., 1938. *Politics:* Independent. *Religion:* Episcopal. *Home:* Anawan Cliffs, Narragansett, R.I. 02882. *Agent:* Brandt & Brandt, 101 Park Ave., New York, N.Y. 10017. *Office:* Department of Political Science, Brown University, Providence, R.I. 02912.

CAREER: United States News Publishing Corp., Washington, D.C., member of editorial staff of *U.S. News,* 1938-42, of *World Report,* 1946-47; Central Intelligence Agency, Washington, D.C., staff officer, 1947-48, division chief, 1948-50, executive assistant to director, 1950-51, assistant director, 1951-53, inspector general, 1953-62, executive director, 1962-65; Brown University, Providence, R.I., professor of political science, 1965—. U.S. Naval War College, guest lecturer, 1966—, Chester A. Nimitz professor of Political and Social Philosphy, 1971-72. *Military service:* U.S. Army, 1943-46; became major; received Legion of Merit, Croix de Guerre (France and Belgium), Bronze Star, and five battle stars. *Member:* National Press Club, Princeton Club of Washington. *Awards, honors:* National Civil Service League award, 1960, as one of ten outstanding career officers; President's award for distinguished federal civilian service, 1964; Distinguised Intelligence Medal, 1965.

WRITINGS: The Real CIA, Macmillan, 1967; *American Security Policy,* U.S. Department of Navy, 1968; *Captains without Eyes: Major Intelligence Failures in World War II,* Macmillan, 1969; *The U.S. Intelligence Community,* Hill & Wang, 1973. Contributor to *Britannica Year Book,* 1948-60, and to political science and military journals.

BIOGRAPHICAL/CRITICAL SOURCES: Best Sellers, January 15, 1968; *New Yorker,* April 13, 1968.

* * *

KIRSCH, Robert R. 1922-
(Robert Bancroft, Robert Dundee)

PERSONAL: Born October 18, 1922, in Brooklyn, N.Y.; son of Abraham (a salesman) and Pauline (Alterwein) Kirsch; married Nancy Harris (a counselor), June 15, 1951; children: Paul, Eric, Jonathan, Marya. *Education:* University of California, Los Angeles, B.A., 1949, M.A., 1951, C.Phil., 1970. *Agent:* Robert Lescher, 155 East 71st St., New York, N.Y. 10021. *Office: Los Angeles Times,* Los Angeles, Calif. 90053.

CAREER: Hitchhiked to California after graduating from high school, and worked as a library page and in a bakery in Los Angeles, sold shoes in Merced, and later became a reporter for the *Merced Sun-Star,* remaining there until 1941; worked for City News Service and later the United Press in Los Angeles, Calif., 1946-51; *Los Angeles Times,* Los Angeles, staff member, 1951—, first on copy desk, then daily columnist, literary editor, 1957—. Lecturer in journalism, University of California, Los Angeles, 1951-71; dean of college, International Community College, Los Angeles, 1971—. Executive story consultant, Universal Studios, 1965-67. *Military service:* U.S. Navy, 1941-45. *Awards, honors:* Litt.D., University of Redlands.

WRITINGS—Novels, except as indicated: *In the Wrong Rain,* Little, Brown, 1958; *Madeleine Austrian,* Simon & Schuster, 1960; *The Wars of Pardon,* Simon & Schuster, 1965; (with William S. Murphy) *West of the West: Witnesses to the California Experience, 1542-1906* (anthology), Dut-

ton, 1968. Also author, under pseudonym Robert Dundee, of *The Restless Lovers, Pandora's Box,* and *Inferno,* and, under pseudonym Robert Bancroft, of *Knight of the Scimitar,* and *The Castilian Rose.* Author of short stories and novellas; contributor of articles and reviews to *New York, Times, Saturday Review,* and other publications.

SIDELIGHTS: "As a writer, I write the kind of books I would like to read," Kirsch wrote in *Conversations.* "When I have written a book I think the critics would like to read, I have been dissatisfied with myself. As a critic I find that I want first to enjoy the reading experience." He gives the following advice to young writers: "Write for the reader, not for the critic. Write a damned good story and pray that it means something more than a good story. Trust yourself . . . accept the influence of people who really have something to say to you. Live, grow, be a *mensch.* That's all I can say."

Frederick Schroyer wrote of *In the Wrong Rain* in *Saturday Review:* "Kirsch handles . . . [his story] with a deft hand and a warm heart. The result is a remarkable first novel that carries an impact of authenticity, derived from acute observation and transmitted with great sensitivity."

AVOCATIONAL INTERESTS: Walking on the beach, surfing; watching baseball, football, and basketball.

BIOGRAPHICAL/CRITICAL SOURCES: Saturday Review, July 11, 1959; Roy Newquist, *Conversations,* Rand McNally, 1967; *New York Times Book Review,* February 25, 1968; *Show,* June 25, 1970; *Publishers Weekly,* December 12, 1977.

* * *

KIRSCHENBAUM, Aaron 1926-

PERSONAL: Born March 11, 1926, in Brooklyn, N.Y.; son of Philip (a basket weaver) and Tillie (Brill) Kirschenbaum; married Judith Pollak, June 14, 1948; children: Beruriah S. (Mrs. N. Samuel Adler), Elisheva (Mrs. C. H. Sompolinsky), Avigail H., Avraham M., Nehamah L. *Education:* Brooklyn College (now Brooklyn College of the City University of New York), B.A. 1946; Jewish Theological Seminary of America, rabbinical degree and M.H.L., 1950, D.H.L., 1967; Columbia University, Ph.D., 1969. *Home:* 23 Rehob Hagilgal, Ramat Gan, Israel. *Office:* Tel Aviv University Law School, Tel Aviv, Israel.

CAREER: Rabbi; Herzliah Hebrew Teachers Institute, New York City, instructor in Bible and Talmud, 1946-57; City College of New York (now City College of the City University of New York), New York City, lecturer in Hebrew, 1952-57; Fund for the Republic (Ford Foundation), New York City, research fellow in rabbinic literature, 1957-58; Jewish Theological Seminary of America, New York City, associate professor of rabbinic law, 1959-70; Tel Aviv University Law School, Tel Aviv, Israel, associate professor of Jewish law, 1970—. *Member:* Eta Sigma Phi, Propylaea.

WRITINGS: The Talmud and You, Hadassah Education Department, 1967; *Self-Incrimination in Jewish Law,* Burning Bush Press, 1970. Also author of *Non-Contractual Agency in Roman Law,* 1977, and *Jewish Law,* 1978. Editor, *Dine Israel,* 1971-77.

* * *

KIRSCHNER, Linda Rae 1939-

PERSONAL: Born April 25, 1939, in Charleston, Ill.; daughter of Crayton McGee and Irma (Dennis) Heinlein; married Allen Kirschner (a teacher and writer), December

20, 1968; children: Scott Smith, Kenneth, Edward. *Education:* Attended College of Wooster, 1957-58; Hamline University, B.A. (magna cum laude), 1961. *Home:* 32 Randall Rd., Princeton, N.J. 08540.

CAREER: Princeton High School, Princeton, N.J., teacher and director of dramatics, 1961-65; College Entrance Examination Board, New York City, editor, 1965-65; Rhodes School, New York City, dean of girls, 1966-68; St. Hilda's and St. Hugh's School, New York City, chairman of English department, 1968. Edward Ford Foundation visiting scholar in women's literature, Hun School, Princeton University, 1975-76.

WRITINGS—With husband, Allen Kirschner, except as indicated: *Blessed Are the Peacemakers,* Popular Library, 1971; (editors) *Film: Readings in the Mass Media,* Bobbs-Merrill, 1971; (editors) *Journalism: Readings in the Mass Media,* Bobbs-Merrill, 1971; (editors) *Radio and Television: Readings in the Mass Media,* Bobbs-Merrill, 1971; (sole editor) *By Women: An Anthology of Literature,* Houghton, 1976; (sole author) *Regional American Literature,* Visual Education Corp., 1976.

* * *

KISMARIC, Carole 1942-

PERSONAL: Born April 28, 1942, in Orange, N.J.; daughter of John Joseph and Alice (Gruskos) Kismaric; married Charles Mikolaycak (a book illustrator and designer), October 1, 1970. *Education:* Pennsylvania State University, B.F.A., 1964. *Home:* 64 East 91st St., New York, N.Y. 10028. *Office:* Aperture, 226 East 51st St., New York, N.Y. 10022.

CAREER: Time-Life, Inc., New York City, picture editor, 1969-73, assistant editor, 1973-75; Photo-200 (photo project to document United States bicentennial), assistant director, 1975-76; *Aperture,* New York City, managing editor, 1976—.

WRITINGS—For children: *Duel of the Ironclads,* Time-Life, 1968; (with husband, Charles Mikolaycak) *The Boy Who Tried to Cheat Death,* Doubleday, 1971; (editor with Norman Snyder) *The Photography Catalogue,* Harper, 1976; (author of introduction) *Exposure: Ten Photographers' Work* (Creative Artists Public Service Exposure Project), Creative Artists Public Service, 1976; (author of introduction) George Krause, *Saints and Martyrs,* Photopia Gallery, 1976; (author of introduction) Andre Kertesz, *Andre Kertesz,* Aperture, 1977. Contributor to *Camera.* Picture editor, Time-Life photography series and Old West series.

WORK IN PROGRESS: A biography of Andre Kertesz.

AVOCATIONAL INTERESTS: Travel.

* * *

KLAPPERT, Peter 1942-

PERSONAL: Born November 14, 1942, in Rockville Center, N.Y.; son of Herman Emil (a film producer) and Barbara (Rupp) Klappert. *Education:* Cornell University, B.A., 1964; University of Iowa, M.A., 1967, M.F.A., 1968. *Politics:* "All political associations corrupt." *Religion:* None. *Office:* Department of English, George Mason University, 4400 University Dr., Fairfax, Va. 22030.

CAREER: Rollins College, Winter Park, Fla., instructor in English, 1968-71; Harvard University, Briggs-Copeland Lecturer in English and General Education, 1971-74; College of William and Mary, Williamsburg, Va., writer-in-residence, 1976-77, assistant professor, 1977-78; George Mason University, Fairfax, Va., assistant professor of English, 1978—. Visiting lecturer, New College, Sarasota, Fla., 1972. *Member:* Modern Language Association of America, College English Association, Associated Writing Programs, Poetry Society of America. *Awards, honors:* Yale Series of Younger Poets award, 1970, for *Lugging Vegetables to Nantucket;* resident fellowships at Yaddo, 1972, 1973, 1975, at MacDowell Colony, 1973, 1975, at Virginia Center for the Creative Arts, 1978, and at Millay Colony for the Arts, 1978; National Endowment for the Arts fellowship in creative writing, 1973; Lucille Medick Award, Poetry Society of America, 1977.

WRITINGS: *Lugging Vegetables to Nantucket* (collection of poems), Yale University Press, 1971; *After the Rhymer's Guild* (essay, chapbook), New College Press, 1971; (contributor) Hugh Rank, *Language and Public Policy,* National Council of Teachers of English, 1973; *Circular Stairs, Distress in the Mirrors* (poems), Griffin Press, 1975; *Non Sequitur O'Connor* (poems), Bits Press; (contributor) Albert Turner, editor, *Fifty Contemporary Poets: The Creative Process,* McKay, 1977. Poetry anthologized in *The Young American Poets,* edited by Paul Carroll, Follett, 1972; *Best Poems of 1971,* Borestone Mountain, 1972; *Our Only Hope Is Humor,* Ashland Poetry Press, 1972; *The Ardis Anthology of Contemporary American Poetry,* edited by David Rigsbee and Elleanda Proffer, Ardis, 1976; *The American Poetry Anthology,* edited by Daniel Halpern, Avon, 1976. Contributor of poems to numerous magazines, including *Atlantic Monthly, Epoc, Massachusetts Review, Nation, New American Review, New Yorker, American Poetry Review, Agni Review, Falcon, Antaeus, Saturday Review, Parnassus,* and *CEA Forum.*

WORK IN PROGRESS: *The Idiot Princess of the Last Dynasty,* a book of poems.

SIDELIGHTS: Peter Klappert told *CA:* "I did the important part of my growing up in Rowayton, Connecticut. Between Cornell and Iowa I spent 6 months travelling in Europe, the Mid East & Central Asia, and while at Iowa I worked as an attendant in a hospital for alcoholics and as a disc jockey. Teaching is an important part of my life—I would teach even if I were financially independent (though perhaps not so much!)—but *poems* are events, not lessons. I am drawn to the amoral quality of art, the way it stands outside moral codes or, more accurately, creates its own moralities. In any case, that's why I write; to locate myself in time and space, to discover what I truly believe and feel.

"For the past six years I have been working on a long series of dramatic monologues, all set in Paris on the eve of the Nazi Occupation and all spoken by 'Doctor Matthew Mighty-grain-o-salt Dante O'Connor,' the character in Djuna Barnes's novel *Nightwood,* 1936. An important concern of these poems is certainly 'morality,' and they are (I hope) at odds with many elements of conventional morality: in that sense, I hope they 'create their own moralities'. . . . I suppose I would like to be considered a careful and caring poet—one careful enough to try to disguise the care with which the poems are made—and a 'moralist' in an old-fashioned sense of that word, i.e. someone looking for reasons to stay alive."

In a statement for *The Young American Poets,* Klappert said about poetics: "Five years ago I was quite deliberately a disciple of Wallace Stevens, but I find, now, that I am much more interested in poems than in the theory of poetry.

Let's leave that to the politicians. Fascism is as obnoxious in the arts as anywhere else, and there are simply too many poetry gangs running around (each with its own tattoo, swinging chains and marking turf). When a poem gets hold of me I try to do the best job I can with whatever resources I have. In a way I do envy those poets who work from a specific conscious aesthetic, but in poetry, as in metaphysics, it seems to me we have gotten past the point where one can commit himself to a particular faith. Except perhaps arbitrarily.... Poetry has gotten softheaded again, and while in the short term this may be good for our society as a whole (given our national inability to feel), I do not think it is good for our poetry."

BIOGRAPHICAL/CRITICAL SOURCES: Paul Carroll, editor, *The Young American Poets,* Follett, 1972; *Falcon,* 1977; *Agni Review,* 1978.

* * *

KLEIN, Maury 1939-

PERSONAL: Born March 14, 1939, in Memphis, Tenn.; son of Harry (a manager of a clothing store) and Alice Lena (Nickell) Klein; married Joan Kupskey, July 2, 1960 (divorced, 1964); married Sara Julia Hawkins, November 27, 1964 (divorced, 1968); children: (first marriage) Stephanie Lee. *Education:* Knox College, B.A., 1960; Emory University, M.A., 1961, Ph.D., 1965. *Politics:* Independent. *Religion:* None. *Home:* 65 Stonehenge Rd., Kingston, R.I. 02881. *Office:* Department of History, University of Rhode Island, Kingston, R.I. 02881.

CAREER: University of Rhode Island, Kingston, assistant professor, 1965-68, associate professor, 1968-73, professor of history, 1973—. *Member:* Organization of American Historians, Southern Historical Association.

WRITINGS: The Great Richmond Terminal, University Press of Virginia, 1970; *Edward Porter Alexander,* University of Georgia Press, 1971; *A History of the Louisville & Nashville Railroad,* Macmillan, 1972; (with H. A. Kantor) *Prisoners of Progress: American Industrial Cities 1850-1920,* Macmillan, 1976. Contributor to *American Historical Review, Georgia Review, Business History Review, American History Illustrated, Sports Illustrated,* and other periodicals.

WORK IN PROGRESS: A biography of Jay Gould; a historical novel on the Andree expedition of 1897.

* * *

KLEINMUNTZ, Benjamin 1930-

PERSONAL: Born January 15, 1930, in Cologne, Germany; son of Nathan Lewis and Anna (Kuflik) Kleinmuntz; married Dalia Segal (an artist and potter), June 24, 1955; children: Don N., Ira M., Oren J. *Education:* Brooklyn College (now Brooklyn College of the City University of New York), B.A., 1952; University of Minnesota, Ph.D., 1958. *Religion:* Jewish. *Home:* 819 La Crosse Ct., Wilmette, Ill. 60091. *Office:* Department of Psychology, University of Illinois at Chicago Circle, Chicago, Ill. 60680.

CAREER: University of Nebraska, Student Health Center, Lincoln, clinical psychologist, 1958-59; Carnegie-Mellon University, Pittsburgh, Pa., assistant professor, 1959-63, associate professor, 1936-67, professor of psychology, 1967-73; University of Illinois at Chicago Circle, professor of psychology and director of graduate training in clinical psychology, 1973—. Clinical psychologist, Craig-House for Children, 1959-72, and Eye and Ear Hospital, 1964-67; Na-

tional Institute of Mental Health, member of Personality and Cognition Review committee, and grant proposal reviewer, 1967-71. Member of educational board and board of directors, Hebrew Institute of Pittsburgh, beginning 1968. *Military service:* U.S. Army, Military Intelligence, 1952-54. *Member:* American Psychological Association (fellow).

WRITINGS: (Editor) *Problem Solving: Research, Method and Theory,* Wiley, 1966; (editor) *Concepts and the Structure of Memory,* Wiley, 1967; *Personality Measurement,* Dorsey, 1967; (editor) *Formal Representation of Human Judgment,* Wiley, 1968; *Clinical Information Processing by Computer,* Holt, 1969.

(With K. H. Craik, R. L. Rosnow, Robert Rosenthal, J. A. Cheyne, and R. H. Walters) *New Directions in Psychology,* Volume IV, Holt, 1970; (contributor) J. A. Jacquez, editor, *Diagnostic Process,* C. C Thomas, 1972; *Computers in Personality Assessment* (booklet), General Learning Press, 1972; *Essentials of Abnormal Psychology,* Harper, 1974; *Readings in the Essentials of Abnormal Psychology,* Harper, 1974; (with B. Weiner and others) *Discovering Psychology,* Science Research Associates, 1977. Contributor of over thirty-five articles to professional journals.

* * *

KLINE, Lloyd W. 1931-

PERSONAL: Born September 26, 1931. *Education:* Franklin and Marshall College, A.B., 1953; Middlebury College, M.A., 1962; University of Massachusetts, Ed.D., 1970; also attended Temple University and University of Pennsylvania. *Office:* International Reading Association, 6 Tyre Ave., Newark, Del. 19711.

CAREER: International Reading Association, Newark, Del., director of publications. Millersville State College, adjunct professor. *Member:* Phi Delta Kappa.

WRITINGS: Education and the Personal Quest, C. E. Merrill, 1971. Author of weekly newspaper column, "Your Child in School." Contributor of many articles to various publications.

* * *

KLINGER, Eric 1933-

PERSONAL: Born May 23, 1933, in Vienna, Austria; came to United States in 1943, naturalized in 1946; son of Alfred (a lawyer and wholesaler) and Auguste (Stiasny) Klinger; married Karla A. Michelke, April 11, 1960; children: Heather Jill, Roderick Michael, Benjamin Karl. *Education:* Harvard University, A.B., 1954; University of Chicago, Ph.D., 1960. *Home:* 307 East Fifth St., Morris, Minn. 56267. *Office:* Division of Social Sciences, University of Minnesota, Morris Campus, Morris, Minn. 56267.

CAREER: Association of American Medical Colleges, Evanston, Ill., research assistant, 1954-57, research associate, 1957-60; Veterans Administration Hospitals at Hines and Chicago, Ill., clinical psychology trainee, 1957-60; University of Wisconsin—Madison, instructor in psychology, 1960-62; University of Minnesota, Morris, assistant professor, 1962-63, associate professor, 1963-69, professor of psychology, 1969—, vice-chairman of Division of Social Sciences, 1969-73. *Member:* American Psychological Association, American Association for the Advancement of Science, Society for the Psychophysiological Study of Sleep, American Association of University Professors, Sigma Xi.

WRITINGS: Structure and Functions of Fantasy, Wiley,

1971; *Meaning and Void: Inner Experience and the Incentives in People's Lives,* University of Minnesota Press, 1977. Contributor of articles to psychology journals.

WORK IN PROGRESS: Research on fantasy processes, incentive motivation and personality, and personality theory and measurement.

*   *   *

KNECHT, Robert Jean 1926-

PERSONAL: Initial "K" of surname is pronounced; born September 20, 1926, in London, England; son of Jean Joseph Camille (a hospital secretary) and Odette (Mioux) Knecht; married Sonia Mary Fitzpatrick Hodge, August 8, 1956. *Education:* University of London, B.A. (honors), 1948, M.A., 1953. *Home:* 22 Warwick New Rd., Leamington Spa, England. *Office:* Department of History, University of Birmingham, Birmingham, England.

CAREER: History of Parliament Trust and Victoria County History, London, England, research assistant, 1954; Richard Lonsdale-Hands Associates, London, research assistant, 1954-56; University of Birmingham, Birmingham, England, lecturer, 1956-69, senior lecturer in modern history, 1969—. *Member:* Royal Historical Society (fellow), Societe de l'Histoire de France.

WRITINGS: (Editor) *The Voyage of Sir Nicholas Carewe to the Emperor Charles V in the Year 1529,* Cambridge University Press, 1959; *Francis I and Absolute Monarchy,* Historical Association, 1969; *Renaissance and Reformation,* P. Hamlyn, 1969; (contributor) Douglas Johnson, editor, *The Making of the Modern World,* Benn, 1971; *The Fronde,* Historical Association, 1975; (contributor) A. G. Dickens, editor, *The Courts of Europe,* Thames & Hudson, 1977. Contributor to *Encyclopaedia Britannica;* contributor of articles and reviews to historical journals and to newspapers.

WORK IN PROGRESS: Francis I of France, for Allen & Unwin.

AVOCATIONAL INTERESTS: Travel, music, art, photography.

*   *   *

KNIGHT, Everett 1919-

PERSONAL: Born December 15, 1919, in Providence, R.I.; son of Everett and Elizabeth (Holdsworth) Knight; married Myrtle Christine Morris (a teacher), November 22, 1951; children: Paul, Peter, Julian. *Education:* Brown University, A.B., 1947; Sorbonne, University of Paris, Doctorat de l,universite, 1950. *Home:* 53 Whitton Rd., Hamilton, Ontario, Canada. *Office:* Department of Romance Languages, McMaster University, Hamilton, Ontario, Canada.

CAREER: McMaster University, Hamilton, Ontario, professor of French. *Military service:* U.S. Army, 1942-45; became sergeant.

WRITINGS: Literature Considered as Philosophy: The French Example, Routledge & Kegan Paul, 1957, Macmillan (New York), 1958; *The Objective Society,* Routledge & Kegan Paul, 1959, Braziller, 1960; *A Theory of the Classical Novel,* Routledge & Kegan Paul, 1969, Barnes & Noble, 1970. Also author of *The Novel as Structure and Praxis.*

*   *   *

KNIGHT, Frank H(yneman) 1885-1972

November 7, 1885—April 15, 1972; American educator and economist. Obituaries: *New York Times,* April 21, 1972.

KNOBLER, Nathan 1926-

PERSONAL: Born March 13, 1926, in Brooklyn, N.Y.; son of Solomon H. (a cleaning contractor) and Edna (Rothenberg) Knobler; married Lois Jean Mandell (a painter), September 3, 1950; children: Adam. *Education:* Syracuse University, B.F.A., 1950; Florida State University, M.A., 1951. *Home:* 564 Storrs Rd., Mansfield Center, Conn. 06250. *Office:* School of Fine Arts, University of Connecticut, Storrs, Conn. 06268.

CAREER: Professional sculptor; University of Connecticut, Storrs, assistant professor, 1959-62, associate professor, 1962-67, professor of art, 1967—, head of department, 1962-68. Has exhibited work in more than forty shows and institutions, and work is displayed at Florida State University, Munson-Williams-Proctor Institute, Smith College, and U.S. Information Center. *Member:* College Art Association, American Society for Aesthetics.

WRITINGS: The Visual Dialogue, Holt, 1967, revised edition, 1970.

WORK IN PROGRESS: A book on figure drawing.

BIOGRAPHICAL/CRITICAL SOURCES: National Observer, December 18, 1967.

*   *   *

KNUDSON, Rozanne 1932-
(R. R. Knudson)

PERSONAL: "K" in surname is silent; born June 1, 1932, in Washington, D.C., daughter of James K. (a lawyer and statesman) and Ruth (Ellsworth) Knudson. *Education:* Brigham Young University, B.A., 1954; University of Georgia, M.A., 1958; Stanford University, Ph.D., 1967. *Religion:* Mormon. *Home:* 73 The Boulevard, Sea Cliff, N.Y. 11579. *Agent:* McIntosh & Otis, 475 Fifth Ave., New York, N.Y. 10017.

CAREER: English teacher in various public high schools in Florida, 1957-60; Purdue University, Lafayette, Ind., assistant professor of English, 1965-67; Hicksville Schools, Long Island, N.Y., supervisor of English, 1967-70; York College of the City University of New York, Jamaica, N.Y., assistant professor, 1970-71; full-time writer, 1972—. Instructor in English, University of Lethbridge, Lethbridge, Alberta, summer, 1969. *Member:* National Council of Teachers of English, Modern Language Association of American, Authors League of America, American Civil Liberties Union, various ecology clubs.

WRITINGS—Under name R. R. Knudson, except as indicated: (Under name Rozanne Knudson; with Arnold Leslie Lazarus) *Selected Objectives for the English Language Arts* (grades 7-12), Houghton, 1967; (with P. K. Ebert) *Sports Poetry,* Dell, 1971; (with J. A. Wilson and others) *Books for You* (youth book), Washington Square Press, 1971; *Zanballer* (teen novel), Delacorte, 1972; *Jesus Song* (teen novel), Delacorte, 1973; *You Are the Rain* (teen novel), Delacorte, 1974; *Fox Running* (teen novel), Harper, 1975; (contributor) *The Scribner's Anthology for Young People,* Scribner, 1976; *Zanbanger* (teen novel), Harper, 1977. Contributor of articles and reviews to *School Library Journal, American Libraries, Scholastic Scope, English Journal,* and many others. Co-editor, *Quartet* magazine, 1966-68.

WORK IN PROGRESS: Rinehart's Story and Other Stories.

SIDELIGHTS: Rozanne Knudson told *CA:* "I have never wanted to be a writer. I would much rather read and do, at the rate of usually two books a day, mostly fiction and poetry. I consider myself a friend of writers, buy tons of books, hound librarians and English teachers to supply me. I live with May Swenson so have even met lots of writers, all of whom I lionize. I started writing to survive in the publish-or-perish business of professoring: articles for professional journals, reviews, ghost writing for full professors who helped pay my way through graduate schools.'' On the advice of an editor at Delacorte, Miss Knudson wrote her football novel, *Zanballer,* and completed it in 38 days. ''It's an autobiography and led to my downfall as a professor ('fiction doesn't count' I was told by a dean). I'm now a full-time writer. All but one of my novels have been about sports. I suppose I'm sort of a reputation as a sports writer for girls and women.''

* * *

KOENIGSBERGER, H(elmut) G(eorg) 1918-

PERSONAL: Born October 24, 1918, in Berlin, Germany; son of Georg Felix (an architect) and Kaethe (Born) Koenigsberger; married Dorothy Romano (a historian), August 10, 1938; children: K. Francesca, Laura H. *Education:* Cambridge University, B.A., 1940, M.A., 1944, Ph.D., 1948. *Home:* 7B, Hollycroft Ave., London NW3 7QA, England. *Office:* Department of History, King's College, University of London, Strand, London WC2R 2LS, England.

CAREER: University of Belfast, Belfast, Northern Ireland, lecturer in history, 1948-51; University of Manchester, Manchester, England, senior lecturer in history, 1951-60; University of Nottingham, University Park, Nottingham, England, professor of history, 1960-66; Cornell University, Ithaca, N.Y., professor of history, 1966-73; University of London, King's College, London, England, professor of history, 1973—. *Military service:* Royal Navy, 1944-45. *Member:* International Commission for the History of Representative and Parliamentary Institutions, Royal Historical Society, Real Academia de la Historia de Madrid, Historisch Genootschap te Utrecht.

WRITINGS: The Government of Sicily under Philip II of Spain: A Study in the Practice of Empire, Staples Press, 1951, revised edition published as *The Practice of Empire,* Cornell University Press, 1969; (with George L. Mosse) *Europe in the Sixteenth Century,* Holt, 1968; (editor with J. H. Elliott) *The Diversity of History,* Cornell University Press, 1970; *Estates and Revolutions: Essays in Modern European History,* Cornell University Press, 1971; *The Habsburgs and Europe, 1516-1660,* Cornell University Press, 1971; (editor) *Luther: A Profile,* Hill & Wang, 1972. Contributor to *Transactions* of Royal Historical Society and to *Encyclopaedia Britannica.*

WORK IN PROGRESS: The History of European Parliaments, 15th-17th Centuries.

* * *

KOGIKU, K(iichiro) C(hris) 1927-

PERSONAL: Born July 30, 1927, in Okayama, Japan; came to United States in 1952, naturalized in 1967; son of Sotojiro and Tamayoshi (Hamauzu) Kogiku; married Yoshiko Kato, 1969; children: John, Ann. *Education:* University of Denver, B.S., 1954; University of Wisconsin, M.A., 1957, Ph.D., 1959. *Home:* 2846 Sandberg St., Riverside, Calif. 92506. *Office:* Department of Economics, University of California, Riverside, Calif. 92502.

CAREER: University of Wisconsin—Madison, assistant

economist and statistician, 1957-59; Western Michigan University, Kalamazoo, assistant professor of economics, 1959-62; University of California, Riverside, assistant professor, 1962-66, associate professor, 1966-71, professor of economics, 1971—. *Member:* American Economic Association, Econometric Society. *Awards, honors:* Brookings Foundation research professorship, 1965-66.

WRITINGS: An Introduction to Macroeconomic Models, McGraw, 1968; *Microeconomic Models,* Harper, 1971. Contributor to tax and economics journals.

* * *

KOLLER, John M. 1938-

PERSONAL: Born March 23, 1938, in Glen Ullin, N.D. *Education:* College of St. Thomas, B.A., 1960; University of Chicago, M.A., 1961; University of Hawaii, Ph.D., 1966. *Office:* Department of Philosophy, Rensselaer Polytechnic Institute, Troy, N.Y. 12181.

CAREER: Rensselaer Polytechnic Institute, Troy, N.Y., associate professor, 1967-77, professor of philosophy, 1977—. *Member:* American Philosophical Association, American Association for the Advancement of Science, Association for Asian Studies, Society for Asian and Comparative Philosophy, American Association of University Professors. *Awards, honors:* Award from National Humanities Foundation, 1967.

WRITINGS: Oriental Philosophies, Scribner, 1970.

WORK IN PROGRESS: Quest for Self.

* * *

KOLLOCK, Will(iam Raymond) 1940-

PERSONAL: Born March 1, 1940, in Lewes, Del.; son of Joseph Addison (a farmer) and Kathleen (Chandler) Kollock; married Zola Shaulis (a concert pianist), June 8, 1963; children: Milangela Stella. *Education:* University of Delaware, A.B. (with highest honors and distinction), 1962; attended Georgetown University Law School, 1962-63; Stanford University, M.A., 1966. *Home:* 95 Cedar Rd., Ringwood, N.J. 07456. *Office address:* P.O. Box 542, Mahwah, N.J. 07430.

CAREER: Surveying and drafting assistant, Aspen, Colo., summer, 1962; Valley Forge Military Junior College, Wayne, Pa., instructor in creative writing, composition, and corrective reading, 1963-64; Gallup & Robinson, Princeton, N.J., assistant to vice-president of advertising research, 1964-65; University of the Pacific, Stockton, Calif., assistant professor of English, 1967-71, also founder and director of Pacific Writers' Workshop, creator of Poetry Theater, and director of journalism; free-lance writer, Almunecar, Spain, 1971-73; Ramapo College, Mahwah, N.J., associate professor, 1973—. Conductor of classes in poetry therapy, Stockton Day Care Center, 1970-71; director, Ramapo College Poetry Award; director, New Audiences, Inc. *Member:* Phi Beta Kappa, Phi Kappa Phi. *Awards, honors:* President's Fellowship for Public Affairs Communication from Stanford University, 1967-68; recipient of several grants to develop a new art form, Poetry Theatre.

WRITINGS: Are You a Mother (poems), Willow House, 1970. Originator and editor, *Concept* (a philosophy journal), 1962, and *Calliope* (a literary journal), 1969.

WORK IN PROGRESS: Editing *Tales,* a collection of American Indian stories, for Willow House; *I Wish I Were a Rabbit,* a collection of poems; a text on poetry as oral and dramatic literature; editing *The Delaware Dream,* a historical anthology, for Cornell Maritime Press; revised edition of *Are You a Mother.*

SIDELIGHTS: Will Kollock told *CA:* "My love of poetry has increasingly led me to bring poetry to people. While Poetry Theatre is an on-going experiment and while each show has been quite different from every other, the underlying hope has been that audiences will turn on to poetry. I really believe that poetry is humanizing. It follows that I believe it is important for people to have a gut-level response to poetry. Poetry Theatre shows what a poem *is,* from the inside out. The response so far has been encouraging, not just grants or publicity but letters, poems, and drawings inspired by Poetry Theatre and sent to me."

* * *

KOMISAR, Lucy 1942-

PERSONAL: Born April 8, 1942, in New York, N.Y.; daughter of David (a salesman) and Frances (a school secretary; maiden name, Munshin) Komisar. *Education:* Queens College of the City University of New York, B.A., 1964. *Home:* 100 West 12th St., New York, N.Y. 10011. *Agent:* Rhoda Weyr, William Morris Agency, 1350 Avenue of the Americas, New York, N.Y. 10019.

CAREER: Campaign manager for City Council candidate James McNamara, New York City, 1965; Human Resources Administration, New York City, special assistant to deputy administrator, 1967-1968; press secretary, Congressional primary campaign of Allard Lowenstein, 5th District, Long Island, N.Y., 1968; WBAI Radio, New York City, writer, reporter, and producer of six one-hour documentaries on hospitals and health care in New York, 1968; Public Broadcast Laboratory, New York City, researcher reporter, 1968; National Educational Television, New York City, and associate producer, 1968-69; press secretary, City Council President campaign of Elinor Guggenheimer, 1969; commentator for syndicated radio show "In the Public Interest," 1971 and 1974; WBAI, New York City, producer, writer, and host, 1973; free-lance writer. *Member:* P.E.N., National Organization for Women (national vice-president for public relations, 1970-71), National Women's Political Caucus, American Civil Liberties Union. *Awards, honors:* Center for Education in Politics grant to study political activity of International Ladies Garment Workers Union, 1963.

WRITINGS: The New Feminism (youth book), F. Watts, 1971; *Down and Out in the U.S.A.: A History of Public Welfare,* F. Watts, 1973, revised edition, 1977; *The Machismo Factor,* Macmillan, 1976. Contributor of articles on feminism and other social issues to periodicals, including *Washington Monthly, Saturday Review, New York Magazine, Newsweek, New York Times, Washington Post,* and *Village Voice.* Editor, *Mississippi Free Press* (weekly civil rights newspaper), 1962-63; assistant editor and contributor, *Hat Worker* (house organ of United Hatters, Cap and Millinery International), 1966-67.

SIDELIGHTS: Lucy Komisar told *CA:* "The theme of my writing and perhaps the overriding problem of twentieth-century society is the need for people to take personal and political responsibility for the social good. Discrimination against women and the poor, described in my first books, are related to the militarism and authoritarianism analyzed in *The Machismo Factor* in that they all are based on desires for power, dominance and superiority rather than the sensitivity, the empathy and the compassion that would serve the world and all of us better."

KONRAD, Evelyn 1930-

PERSONAL: Born December 28, 1930, in Vienna, Austria; came to United States in 1940, naturalized in 1949; daughter of Eugene and Margarethe Dukler-Breitner Konrad; married Bernard Jereski (a corporation executive), March 10, 1960; children: Laura Diane, Elisabeth Merrilee, Richard Perry and Robert William (twins). *Education:* Stanford University, B.A., 1948, M.A., 1949; New York School of Interior Design, graduate, 1965; New York University, Ph.D., 1973. *Home:* 955 Park Ave., New York, N.Y. 10028. *Office:* Evelyn Konrad Associates, 750 Park Ave., New York, N.Y. 10021.

CAREER: UN World (magazine), New York City, columnist, 1950-51; *Everybody's Digest and World Digest,* New York City, associate editor, 1950-51; *Today's Woman* (magazine), New York City, assistant to fiction editor, 1951-52; *Sponsor* (magazine), New York City, senior editor, 1952-58; Evelyn Konrad Associates (marketing consultants), New York City, owner, 1958—. Free-lance translator of German, French, Italian, Spanish, and Portuguese books and articles, 1950-57. President, The Computer in Marketing, Inc. Member of board of directors and vice-president, Parents League of New York, 1968-71; member of board of directors, Yorkville Youth Council, 1970-74. Economic affairs correspondent, "Nightly News" and "Today Show," NBC-TV, 1976-77. *Member:* International Radio and Television Society, Public Relations Society of America, Stanford Club of New York, Connecticut, and New Jersey.

WRITINGS: (Editor with Rod Erickson) *Marketing Research: A Management Overview,* American Management Association, 1965; (with others) *Computer Innovations in Marketing,* American Management Association, 1970. Author of television scripts for "The Hunter" and "Man against Crime" series. Contributor of articles to national magazines, including *Pageant* and *Seventeen.* Editor, Parents League of New York *Review,* 1970-71, and *Parents League Bulletin,* 1971.

WORK IN PROGRESS: A book on marketing, for American Management Association; four hour-long specials on economics for national television.

* * *

KOOSER, Theodore 1939-
(Ted Kooser)

PERSONAL: Born in April, 1939, in Ames, Iowa; son of Ted, Sr. (a merchant) and Vera (Moser) Kooser; married Diana Tressler (a teacher), November 17, 1962 (divorced); children: Jeffrey Charles. *Education:* Iowa State University, B.S., 1962; University of Nebraska, M.A., 1968. *Home:* 1447 Washington, Lincoln, Neb. 68502.

CAREER: Bankers Life Nebraska (insurance firm), Lincoln, underwriter, 1964—. Part-time instructor in creative writing, University of Nebraska, 1968—. *Awards, honors:* John H. Vreeland Award for Creative Writing, 1964; National Endowment for the Arts fellowship, 1976.

WRITINGS—All poems: Official Entry Blank, University of Nebraska Press, 1969; *Grass County,* Windflower, 1971; *Twenty Poems,* Best Cellar Press, 1973; *A Local Habitation and a Name,* Solo Press, 1974; *Not Coming to Be Barked At,* Pentagram Press, 1976.

SIDELIGHTS: Theodore Kooser told *CA:* "I work with all subject matter and in all forms. I am primarily interested in presenting a regional picture of the midwest, and most of my work reflects my interest in my surroundings here on the Great Plains."

KOPLIN, H(arry) T(homas) 1923-

PERSONAL: Born May 2, 1923, in Elyria, Ohio; son of Perry Orin (a druggist) and Jennette (Thomas) Koplin; married Roberta E. McKown, June 13, 1943 (divorced, 1964); children: Bruce Nicholas, Kathleen Mara (Mrs. David Everett), Therese Elizabeth. *Education:* Oberlin College, B.A., 1947; Cornell University, Ph.D., 1952; Oxford University, postdoctoral study, 1954-55, 1962-63. *Home:* 2531 Chula Vista, Eugene, Ore. 97403. *Office:* Department of Economics, University of Oregon, Eugene, Ore. 97403.

CAREER: University of Oregon, Eugene, instructor, 1950-53, assistant professor, 1953-59, associate professor, 1959-65, professor of economics, 1965—, director of Honors College and assistant dean of College of Liberal Arts, 1959-61. *Military service:* U.S. Army, 1943-46. *Member:* American Economic Association, American Civil Liberties Union, Western Economic Association.

WRITINGS: Microeconomic Analysis, Harper, 1971. Contributor to law and economics journals.

WORK IN PROGRESS: Research on a theory of public goods and externalities.

*   *   *

KOPP, O(swald) W. 1918-

PERSONAL: Born December 16, 1918, in Dolgeville, N.Y.; son of Robert and Olga (Bajor) Kopp; married Marie Hildenbrand, June 28, 1941; children: Janice M. (Mrs. Lawrence E. Rogers). *Education:* New York State College for Teachers (now state University of New York at Albany), B.S., 1944; St. Lawrence University, M.A., 1948; Columbia University, Ed.D., 1952. *Home:* 3316 South 29th St., Lincoln, Neb. 68502. *Office:* Teachers College, University of Nebraska, Lincoln, Neb. 68508.

CAREER: National Education Association, Washington, D.C., assistant executive secretary, department of elementary school principals, 1957-58; University of Nebraska, Teachers College, Lincoln, chairman of department of elementary education, 1962—. Director of project for writing aerospace resource publications for children and teachers, National Aeronautics and Space Administration, 1971—. Adviser, Nebraska Association for Elementary School Principals.

WRITINGS: The Elementary School Transfer: Problems, Principles, and Recommended Procedures, Teachers College Press, 1953; (contributor) *Research in Oral Language,* National Council on Research in English, 1967; *Personalized Curriculum: Method and Design,* C. E. Merrill, 1971; *Personalized Curriculum through Excellence in Leadership,* Interstate, 1974; *Environmental Education: Guidelines and Activities for Teachers,* C. E. Merrill, 1976. Contributor to education yearbooks and journals.

*   *   *

KOPP, Richard L. 1934-

PERSONAL: Born June 23, 1934, in New York, N.Y. *Education:* Queens College of the City of New York (now Queens College of the City University of New York), B.A., 1955; State University of Iowa, M.A., 1957; New York University, Ph.D., 1967. *Office:* Department of Modern Languages, Fairleigh Dickinson University, 285 Madison Ave., Madison, N.J. 07940.

CAREER: New York University, New York, N.Y., instructor in French, 1967; College of the Holy Cross, Worcester, Mass., assistant professor of French, 1959-69; Fairleigh Dickinson University, Madison, N.J., assistant professor of French, 1969-73, associate professor of languages, 1973—, chairman of department of modern languages, 1973-76. *Member:* Modern Language Association of America, American Comparative Literature Association, Societe des Amis de Marcel Proust, Societe des Amis d'Andre Gide. *Awards, honors:* New York University Founder's Day Award, 1968.

WRITINGS: Marcel Proust as a Social Critic, Fairleigh Dickinson University Press, 1971. Contributor to professional journals.

WORK IN PROGRESS: A book on Jean Santeuil.

*   *   *

KOPYCINSKI, Joseph V(alentine) 1923-

PERSONAL: Born February 14, 1923, in Lowell, Mass.; son of Joseph and Anna (Cizius) Kopycinski. *Education:* Attended Virginia Polytechnic Institute, 1943-44; Lowell Technological Institute (now University of Lowell), B.S., 1948, M.S., 1950; Simmons College, M.S.L.S., 1960. *Religion:* Roman Catholic. *Residence:* North Chelmsford, Mass. 01863. *Office:* Alumni/Lyden Library, University of Lowell, Lowell, Mass. 01854.

CAREER: University of Lowell, Lowell, Mass., librarian, 1950-75, director of Alumni/Lyden Library, 1975—, bowling coach, 1965—. Chairman, Lowell Historic District Study Committee, 1971; chief adviser, WLTI-FM (education radio station). *Military service:* U.S. Army, 1943-46; received Combat Infantry Badge. *Member:* American Society for Engineering Education (chairman of Engineering Libraries Division, 1968-69), Massachusetts Conference of Chief Librarians of Public Higher Educational Institutions (president, 1971-72), Lowell Historical Society (member of board of directors, 1970), Middlesex Canal Association.

WRITINGS: Textile Industry Information Sources, Gale, 1964.

AVOCATIONAL INTERESTS: Sports, travel, photography, marshals and outlaws of the old west, local history.

*   *   *

KORMONDY, Edward J(ohn) 1926-

PERSONAL: Surname rhymes with "Normandy"; born June 10, 1926, in Beacon, N.Y.; son of Anthony (a salesman) and Frances (Glover) Kormondy; married Peggy V. Hedrick, June 5, 1950; children: Lynn Ellen, Eric Paul, Mark Hedrick. *Education:* Tusculum College, B.S., 1950; University of Michigan, M.S., 1951, Ph.D., 1955. *Home:* 2505 43rd Ave. N.W., Olympia, Wash. 98502. *Office:* Evergreen State College, Olympia, Wash. 98505.

CAREER: University of Michigan, Ann Arbor, instructor in zoology, 1955-57, curator of insects in Museum of Zoology, 1956-57; Oberlin College, Oberlin, Ohio, assistant professor, 1957-63, associate professor, 1963-67, professor of biology, 1967-69, acting associate dean of College of Arts and Sciences, 1966-67; American Institute of Biological Sciences, Washington, D.C., director of Commission on Undergraduate Education in the Biological Sciences and director of Office of Biological Education, 1968-71; Evergreen State College, Olympia, Wash., member of faculty, 1971—, academic dean, 1972-73, vice-president and provost, 1973—. Visiting summer professor, University of Pittsburgh, 1960-62. Trustee of Tusculum College and National Foundation for Environmental Education, 1971-73. Curriculum consultant to numerous colleges and universities, including Universidad Simon Bolivar, Venezuela. *Member:* American Association for the Advancement of Science, Ecological Society of America, American Society of Limnology and Oceanography, Sigma Xi. *Awards, honors:* Grants from Sigma Xi and from National Academy of Sciences, summer, 1960, and from American Philosophical Society and National Science Foundation, 1961-62; U.S. Public Health Service, post-doctoral fellowship, 1963-64; grant from Atomic Energy Commission, 1964-67.

WRITINGS: Introduction to Genetics: A Program for Self-Instruction, McGraw, 1964; *Readings in Ecology,* Prentice-Hall, 1965; *Readings in General Biology,* Volume I: *Molecules and Cells,* Volume II: *Organisms, Populations, and Ecosystems,* W. C. Brown, 1966; *Concepts of Ecology,* Prentice-Hall, 1969, 2nd edition, 1976; *Environmental Education: The Adult Public,* American Institute of Biological Sciences, 1970; (editor with R. S. Leisner) *Pollution,* W. C. Brown, 1971; (editor with Leisner) *Ecology,* W. C. Brown, 1971; (editor with Leisner) *Population and Food,* W. C. Brown, 1971; (with James Aldrich) *Environmental Education: Academia's Response,* Commission on Undergraduate Education in the Biological Sciences, 1972; (contributor) W. H. Johnson and W. H. Steere, editors, *Challenge to Survival,* Holt, 1974; (contributor) F. Sargent, editor, *Human Ecology,* American Elsevier, 1974; (contributor) *Biology Today,* Random House, 1975; (with T. Sherman and others) *General Biology: The Integrity and Natural History of Organisms,* Wadsworth, 1977.

Contributor of about seventy-five articles and reviews to journals. Editor of Biological Sciences Curriculum Study's "Science and Society" series, 1969-73, and of "Films in Social Biology," 1971-73; member of editorial board, *Journal of Biological Education,* 1968-71, *International Journal of Environmental Studies,* 1971-73.

WORK IN PROGRESS: Editing, with Frank McCormick, *Contemporary Developments in World Ecology,* for Greenwood Press; editing, with B. Essenfeld and P. Richards, *Biology,* a secondary school text, for Addison-Wesley.

AVOCATIONAL INTERESTS: Music, sailing, reading.

*   *   *

KORNEICHUK, Aleksandr Y. 1905-1972

May 25, 1905—May 14, 1972; Soviet playwright and party official. Obituaries: *New York Times,* May 16, 1972; *Washington Post,* May 16, 1972; *L'Express,* May 22-28, 1972; *Time,* May 29, 1972.

*   *   *

KORTNER, Peter 1924-

PERSONAL; Born December 4, 1924, in Berlin, Germany; son of Fritz (a director and actor) and Johanna (Hofer) Kortner. *Education:* University of California, Los Angeles, B.A., 1948. *Politics:* Socialist. *Religion:* "Treat all religions with contempt." *Home and office:* 1441 South Beverly Glen Blvd., Los Angeles, Calif. 90024. *Agent:* Claire Smith, Harold Ober Associates, Inc., 40 East 49th St., New York, N.Y. 10017.

CAREER: Former television writer and producer in Hollywood, Calif.; producer for "Playhouse 90," 1957-60, for "General Electric Theater," 1960, for "The Dupont Show with June Allyson," 1961-62, and for "The Farmer's Daughter," 1964-65; left Hollywood for London in 1966 because of "the drift towards extremism in politics and to-

wards mediocrity in television"; full-time novelist and screenwriter in London, 1966-75, and in Los Angeles, 1975—. *Military service:* U.S. Army, 1943-44 ("Reluctantly!"). *Member:* Writers Guild of America West. *Awards, honors:* Emmy Award of National Academy of Television Arts and Sciences (twice), and Sylvania Award, for "Playhouse 90" programs; Golden Globe Award for "The Farmer's Daughter."

WRITINGS—Novels: Jim for Sale, W. H. Allen, 1970, McKay, 1971; *The Final Twist,* Dell, 1971; *A Slightly Used Woman,* W. H. Allen, 1972, Pinnacle Books, 1974; *Breakfast with a Stranger,* W. H. Allen, 1975, St. Martin's, 1977.

WORK IN PROGRESS: The Severed Threads, a novel; *The Return,* a semi-autobiographical work on Kortner's return to the United States.

SIDELIGHTS: Peter Kortner told *CA:* "As television writers and producers are messenger boys who must conform to the strict specifications laid down by the networks, I started to write novels in the hope of finding greater freedom to express myself about topics which concern me strongly. When I am actually caught up in the process of writing a book, I thoroughly enjoy the long hours and the hard work this entails, and never for a moment regret leaving television and the gold that pours into the coffers of those who labor for it. But when I have finished a book, and turn it over to my publisher, then doubts and strong anxieties begin to take hold of me. The relationship, particularly in America, between publisher and author is unsatisfactory—to understate matters considerably. American publishing seems to me in a deplorable state of decay. Books which were once beautifully produced and carefully proofread are now shockingly cheaply produced, outrageously priced, and full of the most crass kind of errors. The consequences of this are tragic: if publishers no longer take pride in the books they produce, the author is the one who suffers most deeply. Thus it is not surprising that authors are treated shabbily, paid appallingly, and worst of all (unless they are bestsellers), no real effort is made to place their books in bookstores. This is a situation that cannot be allowed to continue. A militant author's guild must be formed which will stand up to publishers and fight for the fundamental rights of authors. This is happening in Germany, and must now happen here. And soon! Otherwise the once-proud American author will wind up as sadly subservient to his publisher as his pathetic Russian counterpart."

BIOGRAPHICAL/CRITICAL SOURCES: Saturday Review, April 30, 1960; *International Herald Tribune,* May 26, 1970; *Der Spiegel,* August 30, 1970; *The Jewish Chronicle,* May, 1973; *Times Literary Supplement,* September 3, 1975; *Publishers Weekly,* January 24, 1977; *Hollywood Reporter,* May 13, 1977; *West Coast Review of Books,* June, 1977.

*   *   *

KOSHLAND, Ellen 1947-

PERSONAL: Born January 1, 1947, in Chicago, Ill.; daughter of Daniel Edward (a professor) and Marian (a professor; maiden name, Elliott) Koshland; married James McCoughey. *Education:* Pomona College, B.A., 1968; University of Michigan, M.A., 1971; Princeton University, visiting student, 1971-72. *Address:* c/o Ormond College, Parkville, Victoria, Australia 3052.

WRITINGS: The Magic Lollipop, Knopf, 1971.

WORK IN PROGRESS: A poetry anthology for people who don't like poetry; poems.

KOTHARI, Rajni 1928-

PERSONAL: Born August 13, 1928, in Palanpur, India; son of Fojalal Jivraj (a merchant) and Parvati (Sanghvi) Kothari; married Hansa Mehta, April 23, 1947; children: Smitu, Miloon, Ashish. *Education:* London School of Economics and Political Science, B.Sc., 1957. *Religion:* Jain. *Home:* 1 Court Rd., Delhi, India. *Office:* Centre for the Study of Developing Societies, 29 Rajpur Rd., Delhi, India.

CAREER: M.S. University of Baroda, Baroda, India, lecturer in economics, 1958-60, reader in political science, 1960-62; National Institute of Community Development (research and training institute), Mussoorie, India, deputy director of research, 1962-63; Centre for the Study of Developing Societies, Delhi, India, director, 1963—. Chairman of panel of sociologists, Indian Agriculture Commission; director of Indian Section, World Order Models Project; member, Indian Council of Social Science Research; trustee, Indian School of Political Economy, Poona. *Member:* Indian Political Science Association, Academy for Political and Social Research (secretary, 1967—), Indian Council of World Affairs (member of executive committee, 1971-74), International Social Science Council (member of board, 1970-73). *Awards, honors:* Center for Advanced Study in Behavioral Sciences fellow, Stanford, 1968-69.

WRITINGS: (Editor with Myron Weiner) *Voting Behaviour in India,* Firma K. L. Mukhopadyay, 1965; (editor) *Party System and Election Studies,* Allied Publishers, 1967; (editor) *Context of Electoral Change in India,* Academic Books, 1969; *Politics in India,* Little, Brown, 1970; (editor) *Caste in Indian Politics,* Humanities, 1970; *Footsteps into the Future: Diagnosis of the Present World and a Design for an Alternative,* Orient Longman, 1974, Free Press, 1975; *State and Nation Building: A Third World Perspective,* South Asia Books, 1976; *Democratic Party and Social Change in India: Crisis and Opportunities,* South Asia Books, 1976. Regular contributor to *Times of India* and *Economic and Political Weekly.*

WORK IN PROGRESS: Survey of Political Science in India, editing five volumes, for Indian Council of Social Science Research; with Rushikesh Maru, editing *India and China: Contrasts in Development; Oppositions in India,* cross-cultural collaborative research on political development with Japanese, Nigerian, American, Polish, and Yugoslav scholars; research on urban violence in India.†

* * *

KOTLER, Philip 1931-

PERSONAL: Born May 27, 1931, in Chicago, Ill.; son of Maurice and Betty (Bubar) Kotler; married Nancy Ruth Kellum, January 31, 1955; children: Amy, Melissa, Jessica. *Education:* Attended DePaul University, 1948-50; University of Chicago, M.A., 1953, postdoctoral study, 1957; Massachusetts Institute of Technology, Ph.D., 1956; Harvard University, postdoctoral study, 1960. *Politics:* Independent. *Religion:* Jewish. *Home:* 624 Central St., Evanston, Ill. 60201. *Office:* Department of Marketing, Northwestern University, Evanston, Ill. 60201.

CAREER: Westinghouse Corp., Pittsburgh, Pa., management trainee, 1953; Roosevelt University, Chicago, Ill., assistant professor, 1957-58, associate professor of economics, 1959-60; Northwestern University, Evanston, Ill., assistant professor, 1962-64, associate professor, 1965-66, professor of marketing, 1967—. *Member:* American Economic Association, American Marketing Association (member of board

of directors), Marketing Science Institute (member of board), Institute of Management Sciences.

WRITINGS: Marketing Management: Analysis, Planning and Control, Prentice-Hall, 1967, 3rd edition, 1976; *Marketing Decision Making: A Model Building Approach,* Holt, 1971; (with Harold Guetzkow and Randall Schultz) *Simulation in Social and Administrative Science,* Prentice-Hall, 1972; (with Gerald Zaltman and Ira Kaufman) *Creating Social Change,* Holt, 1972; (editor with Keith Cox) *Readings in Marketing Management,* Prentice-Hall, 1972; *Marketing for Non-profit Organizations,* Prentice-Hall, 1975. Contributor to journals in management, marketing, and the behavioral sciences.

WORK IN PROGRESS: Books on social change and social marketing.

AVOCATIONAL INTERESTS: Tennis, bridge, reading, travel (has been to Europe and India).

* * *

KOTLOWITZ, Robert 1924-

PERSONAL: Born November 21, 1924, in New York, N.Y.; son of Max and Debra (Kaplan) Kotlowitz; married Carol Naomi Leibowitz, October 15, 1950; children: Alexander William, Daniel Justin. *Education:* Johns Hopkins University, B.A., 1948. *Home:* 54 Riverside Dr., New York, N.Y. 10024. *Agent:* Harold Ober Associates, 40 East 49th St., New York, N.Y. 10017. *Office:* WNET/Channel 13, 304 West 58th St., New York, N.Y. 10019.

CAREER: Discovery Magazine, New York City, associate editor, 1952-55; RCA Victor Records, New York City, manager of press and information, 1955-60; *Show,* New York City, senior editor, 1960-64; *Harper's,* New York City, senior editor, 1965-67, managing editor, 1967-71; WNET/Channel 13, New York City, vice-president of programming, 1971—. Guest lecturer, Queens College (now Queens College of the City University of New York), 1954-55. Member of advisory board, University of Minnesota Drama Publications. *Military service:* U.S. Army, infantry, 1943-46. *Member:* National Association for the Advancement of Colored People (life member), Century Association, Coffee house.

WRITINGS: Somewhere Else (novel), Charterhouse Books, 1972; *The Boardwalk* (novel), Knopf, 1977. Contributor to *New York Times Magazine, Harper's, Esquire, Holiday,* and *Show.* Contributing editor, *Atlantic,* 1971-76.

BIOGRAPHICAL/CRITICAL SOURCES: New York Times, November 18, 1972, March 9, 1977; *Contemporary Literary Criticism,* Volume IV, Gale, 1975.

* * *

KOWITZ, Gerald T(homas) 1928-

PERSONAL: Surname is pronounced *Co*-its; born March 30, 1928, in Port Huron, Mich.; son of William and Martha (Hochleitner) Kowitz; married Norma Giess, November 25, 1952; children: Kristine, Louise, Marlane. *Education:* Michigan State University, B.A., 1948, M.A., 1950, Ph.D., 1954. *Office:* College of Education, University of Oklahoma, Norman, Okla. 73069.

CAREER: Teacher in Lansing, Mich., 1953-54; Greenfield Village Schools, Dearborn, Mich., school psychologist and coordinator of research, 1954-55; University of Arkansas, Graduate Center, Little Rock, associate professor of education, 1955-57; New York State Education Department, Albany, associate in educational research, 1957-60, coordinator of experimental programs, 1960-63; University of Houston, Houston, Tex., associate professor of education, 1963-66, director of Bureau of Educational Research and Services, 1964-66; University of Oklahoma, Norman, professor of education, 1966—, chairman of department of guidance and counseling, 1967, assistant dean, College of Education, 1970—. Licensed psychologist, State of Oklahoma, 1968—. Visiting professor, University of California, Santa Barbara, summer, 1959. Consultant to Battelle Memorial Laboratories, 1969, Tulsa Model Cities, 1969-70, El Reno Federal Reformatory, 1971, and other groups and institutions. *Military service:* U.S. Navy, 1945-47. U.S. Army, 1950-53.

MEMBER: American Educational Research Association, American Personnel and Guidance Association, American Psychological Association, Association for Educational Data Systems, National Education Association (life member), Phi Delta Kappa, Psi Chi.

WRITINGS: (With wife, Norma Kowitz) *Guidance in the Elementary Classroom,* McGraw, 1959; (with N. Kowitz) *Operating Guidance Services in the Modern School,* Holt, 1968; (with N. Kowitz) *An Introduction to Modern Guidance,* Holt, 1971.

Contributor: Jerome M. Seidman, editor, *Education for Mental Health,* Crowell, 1963; Joseph L. French, editor, *Educating the Gifted,* revised edition, Holt, 1964; Richard E. Ripple, editor, *Readings in Learning and Human Abilities,* Harper, 1964; Milton Kornrich, editor, *The Underachieving Student,* C. C Thomas, 1965; F. R. Smith and R. B. McQuigg, editors, *Secondary Schools Today: Readings for Educators,* Houghton, 1965, 2nd edition, 1969; E. W. Courtney, editor, *Applied Research in Education,* Littlefield, 1965; R. G. Dixon, editor, *Concepts in Teacher Education,* Ontario Teachers Federation, 1971; and other symposia.

Author or co-author of a dozen monographs. Contributor of more than forty articles to education and psychology journals. Associate editor, *ARGR Journal* (publication of Association for Research in Growth Relationships), 1960-62; reviewer for Curriculum Advisory Service, 1963—, *Educational and Psychological Measurements,* 1965—, *Phi Delta Kappan,* 1966, and *Contemporary Psychology,* 1967—.

WORK IN PROGRESS: Partial-knowledge testing; evaluating adult education programs.

*   *   *

KRAFT, William F.   1938-

PERSONAL: Born July 8, 1938, in Pittsburgh, Pa.; son of William Frederick and Margaret (Sem_n) Kraft; married Patricia Anne O'Brien, June 17, 1967. *Education:* Duquesne University, B.A., 1960, M.A., 1962, Ph.D., 1965. *Politics:* Independent. *Religion:* Roman Catholic. *Home:* 106 North Harleston Dr., Pittsburgh, Pa. 15237. *Office:* Department of Psychology, Carlow College, 3333 Fifth Ave., Pittsburgh, Pa. 15213.

CAREER: Atascadero State Hospital, Atascadero, Calif., psychology intern, 1964-65; Somerset State Mental Hospital, Somerset, Pa., director of psychology, 1965-67; Dixmont State Mental Hospital, Pittsburgh, Pa., director of psychology, 1967-69; Carlow College, Pittsburgh, 1969—, began as associate professor, currently professor of psychology. In private practice in psychological services. *Member:* American Psychological Association, Psycholo-

gists Interested in Religious Issues, Pennsylvania Psychological Association.

WRITINGS: The Search for the Holy, Westminster, 1971; *A Psychology of Nothingness,* Westminster, 1974. Also author of *Celibate Sexuality,* and *Coming of Age.* Contributor of articles and reviews to professional journals.

WORK IN PROGRESS: Psychospiritual Growth throughout the Life-Cycle.

AVOCATIONAL INTERESTS: Sports, gardening, the performing arts.

*   *   *

KRAMER, Edith   1916-

PERSONAL: Born August 29, 1916, in Vienna, Austria; came to United States in 1938, naturalized in 1944; daughter of Richard (a businessman) and Josephine (Neumann) Kramer. *Education:* Attended Realgymnasium, Vienna. *Politics:* Liberal. *Home:* 80 Delancey St., New York, N.Y. 10002.

CAREER: Representational artist, painter, sculptor, and graphic artist; New School for Social Research, New York, N.Y., instructor, 1957-74; George Washington University, Washington, D.C., instructor, 1972—. Adjunct professor, New York University, 1973—. Art therapist, Wiltwyck School for Boys, 1950-57, Albert Einstein Medical College, 1963—, and Jewish Guild for the Blind School, 1965-74. Has had one-woman shows in New York, Washington, and Munich. *Member:* National Association of Women Artists, American Art Therapy Association (honorary life).

WRITINGS: Art Therapy in a Children's Community, C. C Thomas, 1958; (contributor) Gerd Biermann, editor, *Handbuch der Kinderpsychotherapy,* Ernst Reinhardt Verlag (Munich), 1969; *Art as Therapy with Children,* Schocken, 1971; (contributor) Elinor Ulman and Penny Dachinger, editors, *Art Therapy in Theory and Practice,* Schocken, 1975. Contributor to *Bulletin of Art Therapy* and *American Journal of Art Therapy.*

WORK IN PROGRESS: Writing on the practice of art as therapy with children.

*   *   *

KRANZ, E(dwin) Kirker   1949-

PERSONAL: Born January 12, 1949, in Flint, Mich.; son of Edwin Earl (a factory worker) and Mary (Kirker) Kranz. *Education:* Delta College, A.A.S., 1969; attended Saginaw Valley College. *Politics:* "Has yet to snare my active participation." *Religion:* "Has not either."

CAREER: Employed as library clerk, salesman, stockman, and audio-visual operator while attending college.

WRITINGS: The Clouded Mirror, Lenox Hill Press, 1971.

WORK IN PROGRESS: Child Earth's Children, a story of a non-technological race and their conquest of the spatial void; exploring the medium of videotapes.

AVOCATIONAL INTERESTS: Music, outdoors.††

*   *   *

KRASNER, Leonard   1924-

PERSONAL: Born December 17, 1924, in Brooklyn, N.Y.; son of Samuel (a chemist) and Helen (Randell) Krasner; married Miriam Shostak (a school teacher), August 10, 1947; children: Wendy, David, Charles, Stefanie. *Education:* City College (now City College of the City University of New

York), B.S., 1946; Columbia University, M.A., 1947, Ph.D., 1950. *Home:* 33 Intervale Rd., Setauket, N.Y. 11733. *Office:* Department of Psychology, State University of New York, Stony Brook, N.Y. 11790.

CAREER: University of Massachusetts, Amherst, instructor in psychology, 1950-51; Veterans Administration Regional Office, Brooklyn, N.Y., clinical psychologist in mental hygiene clinic, 1951-53; University of Colorado, Boulder, assistant professor of psychology, 1953-54; Veterans Administration Hospital, Lexington, Ky., assistant chief of clinical psychological service, 1954-56; Veterans Administration Hospital, Palo Alto, Calif., chief of psychological training unit, 1956-64; Educational Testing Service, Princeton, N.J., visiting scholar, 1964-65; State University of New York at Stony Brook, professor of psychology and director of clinical training, 1966—. Diplomate of American Board of Examiners in Professional Psychology, 1955. Associate consultant professor, Stanford University, 1956-64. *Military service:* U.S. Army, 1943-46. *Member:* American Psychological Association (fellow; chairman of board of professional affairs, 1970-71), American Association for the Advancement of Science (fellow), Phi Beta Kappa.

WRITINGS: (Editor with Leonard P. Ullmann) *Research in Behavior Modification,* Holt, 1965; (editor with Ullmann) *Case Studies in Behavior Modification,* Holt, 1965; (with Ullmann) *A Psychological Approach to Abnormal Behavior,* Prentice-Hall, 1969, 2nd edition, 1975; (with Ullmann) *Behavior Influence and Personality,* Holt, 1973; *Environmental Design: Theory and Application,* Pergamon Press, 1977. Contributor to psychology journals. Psychology co-editor for Pergamon Press.

WORK IN PROGRESS: A book on the history of behavior modification as a scientific paradigm and as a social movement from 1946 through 1976.

*   *   *

KRAUS, Robert 1925-

PERSONAL: Born June 21, 1925, in Milwaukee, Wis.; son of Jack and Esther (Rosen) Kraus; married Pamela Wong, December 11, 1946; children: Bruce, William. *Education:* Studied at Layton Art School, Milwaukee, 1942, and at Art Students' League of New York, 1945. *Residence:* Ridgefield, Conn. *Office:* Windmill Books, Inc., 201 Park Ave. S., New York, N.Y. 10003.

CAREER: Cartoonist for national magazines, and author and illustrator of children's books; president of Windmill Books, Inc., New York, N.Y., 1966—; president of Springfellow Books, Inc., 1972—. Had a cartoon published in the *Milwaukee Journal* when he was eleven; drew cartoons and covers for magazines, chiefly the *New Yorker. Awards, honors: Whose Mouse Are You?,* illustrated by Jose Aruego, appeared on the American Library Association list of the most notable books of 1970.

WRITINGS—Author and illustrator; published by Harper, except as indicated: *Junior the Spoiled Cat,* Oxford University Press, 1955; *All the Mice Came,* 1955; *Ladybug, Ladybug,* 1956; *The Littlest Rabbit,* 1957; *I, Mouse,* 1958; *The Trouble with Spider,* 1962; *Miranda's Beautiful Dream,* 1964; *Penguin's Pal,* 1964; *Mouse at Sea,* 1964; *Amanda Remembers,* 1965; *My Son, the Mouse,* 1967; *Little Giant,* 1967; *Hello Hippopotamus,* Windmill Books, 1969; *Daddy Long Ears,* Windmill Books, 1970; *How Spider Saved Christmas,* Windmill Books, 1970; *Vip's Mistake Book,* Windmill Books, 1970; *The Tale Who Wagged the Dog,* Windmill Books, 1971.

Author; all published by Windmill Books, except as indicated: *Harriet and the Promised Land,* 1968; *Unidentified Flying Elephant,* 1968; *The Children Who Got Married,* 1969; *Animal Etiquette,* 1969; *Don't Talk to Strange Bears,* 1969; *Rumple-Nose Dimple and the Three Horrible Snaps,* 1969; *The Christmas Cookie Sprinkle Snitcher,* 1969; *I'm Glad I'm a Boy, I'm Glad I'm a Girl,* 1970; *Whose Mouse Are You?,* Macmillan, 1970; *Bunya the Witch,* 1971; *Shaggy Fur Face,* 1971; *Ludwig, the Dog Who Snored Symphonies,* 1971; *Pipsqueak, Mouse in Shining Armor,* 1971; *Lillian Morgan and Teddy Morgan,* 1971; *The Tree That Stayed Up Until Next Christmas,* 1971; *Leo the Late Bloomer,* 1971; *Milton the Early Riser* (Junior Literary Guild selection), 1972; *Boris Bad Enough,* 1976; *Dinosaur Do's and Don'ts,* 1976; *The Good Housekeeper,* 1977.

''The Bunny's Nutshell Library''; all published by Harper: *The Silver Dandelion,* 1965; *Juniper,* 1965; *The First Robin,* 1965; *Springfellow's Parade,* 1965.

''The Night Light Library''; all published by Springfellow Books: *Good Night Little One,* 1972; *Good Night Little ABC,* 1972; *Good Night Little Richard Rabbit,* 1972.

Illustrator: Paul Anderson, *Red Fox and the Hungry Tiger,* Addison-Wesley, 1962; Carla Stevens, *Rabbit and Skunk and the Spooks,* Scholastic Book Services, 1968; Stevens, *Rabbit and Skunk and the Scary Rock,* Scholastic Book Services, 1970; Cleveland Amory, *Cleveland Amory's Animal,* Dutton, 1976; Stevens, *Rabbit and Skunk and the Big Fight,* Scholastic Book Services, 1976.

*   *   *

KRAUSE, Harry D(ieter) 1932-

PERSONAL: Born April 23, 1932, in Germany; came to United States in 1951, naturalized in 1954; son of Renatus (an industrialist) and Ellen (Abel-Musgrave) Krause; married Eva Disselnkoetter, 1957; children: Philip R., Thomas W., Peter H. *Education:* Attended Free University of Berlin, 1950-51; University of Michigan, B.A., 1954, J.D., 1958. *Home:* 903 Silver St., Urbana, Ill. 61801. *Office:* College of Law, University of Illinois, Urbana, Ill. 61801.

CAREER: Member of Bars of Illinois, Michigan, District of Columbia, and U.S. Supreme Court; Covington & Burling, Washington, D.C., associate attorney, 1958-60; Ford Motor Co., Dearborn, Mich., staff attorney (international), 1960-63; University of Illinois at Urbana-Champaign, College of Law, professor of law, 1963—, associate, Center for Advanced Study, 1970. Illinois State Bar Association, member of Council, Section on Family Law, 1967-70, member of Study Committee on a Code of Marriage and Divorce, 1968-70. Visiting associate, Centre for Socio-Legal Studies, Oxford University, 1977. Co-chairman, American Bar Association/American Medical Association Joint Committee on Judicial Application of Blood Typing Tests to Determine Paternity. Special consultant, Family Study Commission, State of Illinois, 1968-69. *Military service:* U.S. Army, 1954-56.

MEMBER: American Bar Association (chairman of family law committees and council), Law Association for Asia and the Western Pacific (LAWASIA), Deutsche Gesellschaft fuer Rechtsvergleichung. *Awards, honors:* Guggenheim fellow, 1969-70; Fulbright scholar, University of Bonn, 1976-77; German Marshall Fund of the United States fellow, 1977-78; Order of the Coif.

WRITINGS: Illegitimacy: Law and Social Policy, Bobbs-Merrill, 1971; *Family Law: Cases and Materials,* West Publishing, 1976; *Family Law in a Nutshell,* West Publishing, 1977.

Contributor: Wayne R. LaFave and Peter Hay, editors, *International Trade, Investment and Organization,* University of Illinois Press, 1967; J. S. Bradway, editor, *Progress in Family Law,* American Academy of Political and Social Science, 1969; A. Wilkerson, editor, *The Rights of Children,* Temple University Press, 1973; *International Encyclopedia of Comparative Law,* Mouton, 1976. Also contributor to *The Youngest Minority,* edited by S. Katz, 1974. Contributor of articles to *Business Lawyer, Personal Injury Commentator, Duke University Law Journal, University of Michigan Law Review, University of Chicago Law Review, University of Texas Law Review, New York Law Journal, American Journal of Comparative Law, Family Law Quarterly,* and other law journals. Member of board of editors, *Family Law Quarterly,* 1971—; member of advisory board, *American Bar Association Journal,* 1973—.

WORK IN PROGRESS: Child Support: Paternity, Medicine, and Law, for University of Illinois Press.

SIDELIGHTS: Harry Krause has worked on comparative legal research projects in Germany, Scandinavia, Spain, Italy, Mexico, India, Philippines, and Japan.

*   *   *

KREFETZ, Gerald 1932-

PERSONAL: Born July 26, 1932, in New York, N.Y.; son of Samuel F. (a businessman) and Dorothy (Karlikow) Krefetz; married Ruth Marossi (a writer), July 19, 1959 (died, 1972); children: Nadine, Adriene. *Education:* Brooklyn College (now Brooklyn College of the City University of New York), B.A., 1954; Columbia University, M.A., 1957. *Office:* Page Proofs Literary Agency, 55 Bethune St., New York, N.Y. 10014.

CAREER: Page Proofs Literary Agency, New York, N.Y., partner, 1962—. *Military service:* U.S. Army, 1954-56.

WRITINGS: (With wife, Ruth Marossi) *Investing Abroad: A Guide to Financial Europe,* Harper, 1965; (with R. Marossi) *Money Makes Money and the Money Money Makes Makes More Money: The Men Who Are Wall Street,* World Publishing, 1970; *The Dying Dollar,* Playboy Press, 1972, revised edition, 1975.

WORK IN PROGRESS: Where the Jewish Money Is: The Economic Role of Jews in America.

*   *   *

KREMPEL, Daniel S(partakus) 1926-

PERSONAL: Surname is pronounced Krem-*pell;* born July 26, 1926, in Brooklyn, N.Y.; son of Benjamin (a plumber) and Eva (Lieder) Krempel; married Joyce Fisher (an actress), June 18, 1948; children: Jenna Gail, Henry B. James. *Education:* Brooklyn College (now Brooklyn College of the City University of New York), B.A., 1947; Ohio State University, M.A., 1948; University of Illinois, Ph.D., 1953. *Politics:* Independent. *Home:* 1016 Meadowbrook Dr., Syracuse, N.Y. 13224. *Office:* Department of Drama, Syracuse University, 820 East Genesee, Syracuse, N.Y. 13210.

CAREER: University of Oregon, Eugene, instructor, 1954-57, assistant professor of speech and drama, 1957-58; Elmira College, Elmira, N.Y., assistant professor of speech and theater, 1958-62; Franklin College, Franklin, Ind., assistant professor of speech and theater, 1962-63; Skidmore College, Saratoga Springs, N.Y., assistant professor of speech and

drama, 1963-66; Syracuse University, Syracuse, N.Y., associate professor, 1966-73, professor of drama, 1973—. Artistic director, Comedy Arts Theatre, Saratoga Springs, 1965, 1966. *Member:* American Theatre Association, University and College Theatre Association, Speech Communication Association, American Association of University Professors.

WRITINGS: (With James H. Clay) *The Theatrical Image,* McGraw, 1967. Has translated plays from the French, for production. Contributor to speech and theater journals. Associate editor, *Quarterly Journal of Speech,* 1968-71.

SIDELIGHTS: Daniel Krempel told *CA:* "I consider myself a theatre artist and critic-historian; I have a very substantial interest in cinema as well, and look at both theatre and cinema in terms of their role within the total context of our civilization. This is the central thrust of my teaching and any writing I do. My main motivation is to train *aware* artists for tomorrow's entertainment arts."

*   *   *

KRIEGEL, Leonard 1933-

PERSONAL: Born May 25, 1933, in Bronx, N.Y.; son of Fred and Sylvia (Breittholz) Kriegel; married Harriet May Bernzweig, August 24, 1957; children: Mark Benjamin, Eric Bruce. *Education:* Hunter College (now Hunter College of the City University of New York), B.A., 1955; Columbia University, M.A., 1956; New York University, Ph.D., 1960. *Politics:* Socialist. *Religion:* Jewish. *Residence:* New York, N.Y. *Agent:* Owen Laster, William Morris Agency, 1350 Avenue of the Americas, New York, N.Y. 10019. *Office:* Department of English, City College of the City University of New York, New York, N.Y. 10033.

CAREER: Long Island University, Brooklyn, N.Y., assistant professor of English, 1960-61; City College of the City University of New York, New York, N.Y. 1961—, began as assistant professor, currently professor of English. Fulbright lecturer, University of Leiden, 1964-65, University of Groningen, 1968-69. *Awards, honors:* Guggenheim fellow, 1971-72; Rockefeller fellow, 1976.

WRITINGS: (Editor) *The Essential Works of the Founding Fathers,* Bantam, 1964; *The Long Walk Home,* Appleton, 1964; *Edmund Wilson,* Southern Illinois University Press, 1971; *Working Through: An Autobiographical Journey in the Urban University,* Saturday Review Press, 1973; (with Abraham Lass) *Stories of the American Experience,* New American Library, 1973; *Notes for the Two Dollar Window,* Dutton, 1976.

WORK IN PROGRESS: American Manhood.

*   *   *

KROEGER, Frederick P(aul) 1921-

PERSONAL: Surname is pronounced Kraig-er; born April 25, 1921, in Minneapolis, Minn.; son of Paul Mateson and Ruth (Hunkins) Kroeger; married Carolyn C., May 10, 1946 (divorced June 1, 1967); children: Frederick C., Deborah Sue. *Education:* Grinnell College, B.A., 1942; University of Minnesota, M.A., 1949; Oxford University, additional study, 1953-54; University of Michigan, Ph.D., 1967. *Politics:* None. *Religion:* None. *Home:* 3202 Nassau, Corpus Christi, Tex. 78418. *Office:* Department of English, Corpus Christi State University, Corpus Christi, Tex. 78411.

CAREER: Northern Montana College, Havre, instructor in English, 1949-52; University of North Dakota, Grand Forks, instructor in English, 1954-56; Flint Community

Junior College, Flint, Mich., member of faculty, 1956-68; Illinois State University, Normal, 1968-73, began as associate professor, became professor of English; Corpus Christi State University, Corpus Christi, Tex., professor of English, 1973—. *Military service:* U.S. Naval Reserve, 1943-46; became lieutenant. *Member:* Modern Language Association of America, National Council of Teachers of English, Conference on College Composition and Communication, American Educational Research Association, American Association of University Professors, Southwest Modern Language Association, Texas Association of College Teachers, Texas College English Association.

WRITINGS: (With Samuel Weingarten) *English in the Two Year College,* National Council of Teachers of English, 1964. Also author of *A National Study of Humanities Offered in the Occupational Curricula of the Two-year College.*

* * *

KRUEGER, Christoph 1937-

PERSONAL: Born February 20, 1937, in Allenstein, Germany (area now belongs to Poland); son of Heinrich (a librarian) and Marie-Louise (Albert) Krueger; married Eva Bulan, January 18, 1964. *Education:* Attended elementary and high schools in Austria. *Religion:* Evangelical. *Home and office:* Untere Augartenstrasse 7/1/12, Vienna 1020, Austria.

CAREER: Teacher in Vienna, Austria. *Member:* Museum fuer Voelkerkunde (Museum of Ethnology; Vienna). *Awards, honors:* Winner of gold, silver, and bronze medals in Oesterreichiste Staatsmeisterschaft fuer Fotographie (Austrian national photography competition).

WRITINGS: (Editor with Alfons Gabriel) *Sahara,* Schroll, 1967, translation published under same title, Putnam, 1969; *Vulkane* (title means "Volcanoes"), Schroll, 1970.

WORK IN PROGRESS: Persia, a book on the country and its religions; *Islam;* also writing on his experiences and adventures in the Sahara.

AVOCATIONAL INTERESTS: Photography.

* * *

KRUSE, Alexander Z. 1888(?)-1972

1888(?)—March 31, 1972; American art critic, painter, and educator. Obituaries: *New York Times,* April 1, 1972.

* * *

KRUSKAL, William H(enry) 1919-

PERSONAL: Born October 10, 1919, in New York, N.Y.; married Norma Jane Evans, 1942; children: Vincent Joseph, Thomas Evans, Jonas David. *Education:* Harvard University, S.B. (summa cum laude), 1940, M.S., 1941; Columbia University, Ph.D., 1955. *Office:* Department of Statistics, University of Chicago, Chicago, Ill. 60637.

CAREER: U.S. Naval Proving Ground, Dahlgren, Va., mathematician as civilian, 1941-44, as lieutenant junior grade, U.S. Naval Reserve, 1944-46; Kruskal & Kruskal, New York City, vice-president, 1946-48; Columbia University, New York City, lecturer in mathematics, 1949-50; University of Chicago, Chicago, Ill., instructor, 1950-51, assistant professor, 1951-57, associate professor, 1957-62, professor of statistics, 1962—, Ernest DeWitt Burton Distinguished Service Professor, 1973—, chairman of department, 1966-73, dean of Division of the Social Sciences, 1974—.

Visiting assistant professor, University of California, Berkeley, 1955-56; visiting associate professor, Harvard University, summer, 1959. Trustee, National Opinion Research Center, 1970—. Member, President's Commission on Federal Statistics, 1970-71; chairman, Committee on National Statistics, 1971—. Director, Social Science Research Council, 1975—.

MEMBER: Institute of Mathematical Statistics (fellow; president, 1970-71), American Statistical Association (fellow; vice-president, 1972-74), International Statistical Institute, American Association for the Advancement of Science (fellow), American Academy of Arts and Sciences, American Mathematical Society, Mathematical Association of America, Biometric Society, International Association for Statistics in the Physical Sciences, Royal Statistical Society, Phi Beta Kappa, Sigma Xi. *Awards, honors:* Center for Advanced Study in the Behavioral Sciences fellow, 1970-71; National Science Foundation senior postdoctoral fellow, 1970-71.

WRITINGS: (Contributor) Arnold Zellner, editor, *Readings in Economic Statistics and Econometrics,* Little, Brown, 1968; (editor and contributor) *Mathematical Sciences and Social Sciences,* Prentice-Hall, 1970; (contributor) Lennart Raade, editor, *The Teaching of Probability and Statistics,* Wiley, 1970; (contributor) Yehuda Elkana and others, editors, *Toward a Metric of Science: Essays Occasioned by the Advent of Science Indicators,* Wiley, 1977. Contributor of about forty articles to professional journals. Chairman of editorial board, *Statistical Research Monographs,* 1953-58. *Annals of Mathematical Statistics,* editor, 1958-61, associate editor, 1962-65; associate editor, *International Encyclopedia of the Social Sciences,* 1962-67; member of advisory committee, *Encyclopaedia Britannica,* 1966-76.

* * *

KUBIAK, William J. 1929-

PERSONAL: Born May 29, 1929, in Grand Rapids, Mich.; son of Joseph Thomas and Gertrude (Zelenski) Kubiak; married Barbara Fortner (a registered nurse), January 27, 1951; children: Heidi, Robin, Joseph, Anthony. *Education:* Attended Davenport College. *Religion:* Roman Catholic. *Home:* 539 Michigan St. N.E., Grand Rapids, Mich. 49503.

CAREER: Grand Rapids Press, Grand Rapids, Mich., staff artist, 1954—. President, Grand Valley Artists, Inc., 1956-57. *Military service:* U.S. Army, 1951-52.

WRITINGS—Self-illustrated: *Great Lakes Indians,* Baker Book, 1970.

WORK IN PROGRESS: Further research on American Indians.

SIDELIGHTS: William Kubiak told *CA:* "My first serious interest in Indians came when I met Harold Yeiter, an old friend and art associate of fifteen years. He was and still is a wonderful painter of Western Indians. Our conversations about Indians and art stimulated me enough to light the spark and ever since I have been completely fascinated by the subject. I have noticed that the more one reads and learns about the Indians, the less one feels he knows about them. It is difficult to find source material, because there just isn't that much to be found. The popular history of the Western Indians took place mainly in the nineteenth century, whereas that of the Indians in the Great Lakes area was just coming to a close at that time. The facts on Western Indians are still fairly fresh—even photographs are obtainable—but this is not true of Indians of the Great Lakes area in earlier times. . . .

"History books in our schools today seldom, if ever, devote more than one short chapter to the subject, and this usually is poorly written and illustrated. The popular opinion of the Indian has been based upon prejudice and ignorance, for students too often receive just enough information to let them know there were some red savages who inhabited North America at one time. It is to be regretted that we don't have the Indians' side of the story to compare with that of his white counterpart.''

AVOCATIONAL INTERESTS: History, book collecting, painting, sculpture.

*   *   *

KUGELMASS, J. Alvin 1910-1972

September 25, 1910—March 11, 1972; American biographer, magazine writer, and newspaper editor. Obituaries: *Washington Post,* March 13, 1972. (See index for *CA* sketch)

*   *   *

KUJAWA, Duane 1938-

PERSONAL: Born October 16, 1938, in Detroit, Mich.; son of Peter Paul (an engineer) and Lucille (Zinger) Kujawa; married Sharon Lee McAleer, June 11, 1966; children: David Anthony, Laura Marie, Matthew Deschene. *Education:* University of Detroit, B.S. in E.E., 1962; University of Santa Clara, M.B.A., 1965; University of Michigan, fellow of Institute of International Commerce, 1966-69, Ph.D., 1970. *Home:* 15000 Southwest 80th Ave., Miami, Fla. 33158. *Office:* Florida International University, Miami, Fla. 33199.

CAREER: Lockheed Missiles & Space Co., Sunnyvale, Calif., manufacturing engineer, 1962-65; Georgia State University, Atlanta, associate professor of economics in Institute of International Business, 1970-76; Florida International University, Miami, professor of international business, 1976—. *Member:* Industrial Relations Research Association, Academy of International Business (executive secretary, 1976—), Academy of Management.

WRITINGS: International Labor Relations Management in the Automotive Industry: A Comparative Study of Chrysler, Ford and General Motors, Praeger, 1971; (editor) *American Labor and the Multinational Corporation,* Praeger, 1973; (editor) *International Labor and the Multinational Enterprise,* Praeger, 1975; (contributor) *Foreign Direct Investment in the United States,* U.S. Department of Commerce, 1976; (contributor) Robert Hawkins, editor, *The Economic Effects of Multinational Corporations,* Jai Press, 1977. Member of editorial board, *Journal of International Business Studies,* 1971-74.

WORK IN PROGRESS: A book, *Foreign Multinationals in the United States: Management Patterns and Practices,* for Lexington Books; a research project on employment regularization in multi-national enterprise.

*   *   *

KUMMEL, Bernhard 1919-

PERSONAL: Born August 13, 1919, in Racine, Wis.; son of Bernhard and Meta (Storgyard) Kummel; married Gilda Devescovi, December 20, 1946; children: Alex. *Education:* University of Wisconsin, B.A., 1940, M.A., 1941; Columbia University, Ph.D., 1946. *Home:* 228 Common St., Belmont,

Mass. 02178. *Office:* Museum of Comparative Zoology, Harvard University, Cambridge, Mass. 02138.

CAREER: Geologist for the Peruvian government, 1943-46, and for the Bureau of Economic Geology in Texas, 1947-48; University of Illinois at Urbana-Champaign, assistant professor, 1948-49, associate professor of geology, 1949-52; Harvard University, Cambridge, Mass., associate professor, 1952-62, professor of geology, 1962—.

MEMBER: Paleontological Society (president, 1970), Geological Society of America, American Association of Petroleum Geologists, Palaeontological Association, American Academy of Arts and Sciences, Society for Evolution.

WRITINGS: History of the Earth: An Introduction to Historical Geology, W. H. Freeman, 1961, 2nd edition, 1970; (editor with David Raup) *Handbook of Paleontological Techniques,* W. H. Freeman, 1965; (editor with Curt Teichert) *Stratigraphic Boundary Problems: The Permian and Triassic of West Pakistan,* University of Kansas Press, 1970. Contributor to bulletins of the Harvard University Museum of Comparative Zoology, and other paleontological musuem publications.

WORK IN PROGRESS: Permian Triassic History of the World.

*   *   *

KUNNES, Richard 1941-

PERSONAL: Surname is pronounced *Cue*-ness; born August 2, 1941, in Reading, Pa.; son of Albert (an optometrist) and Maryan (Deutsch) Kunnes; married Judith Roehrs (a psychiatric occupational therapist), August 9, 1969. *Education:* Johns Hopkins University, B.A., 1962; Temple University, M.D., 1966. *Politics:* Socialist. *Religion:* None. *Home:* 19920 Lichfield, Detroit, Mich. 48221. *Office:* Department of Psychiatry, University of Michigan, Ann Arbor, Mich. 48104.

CAREER: Columbia University, New York, N.Y., resident in psychiatry, 1969-71; Yeshiva University, Albert Einstein College of Medicine, Bronx, N.Y., research fellow in social and community psychiatry, 1969-71; University of Michigan, Ann Arbor, assistant professor of psychiatry, 1971—. Director of pre- and after-care services, University of Michigan-Washtenaw County Community Mental Health Center. Chairperson, Health Commission of the New American Movement. *Member:* Medical Committee for Human Rights, Physicians Forum, Scientists and Engineers for Political and Social Action.

WRITINGS: Your Money or Your Life: The Medical Market Place, Dodd, 1972; *The American Heroin Empire: Power, Politics, and Profits,* Dodd, 1973; *Therapy and Revolution,* Harper, 1973. Contributor to professional journals. Contributing editor, *McGill Medical Journal, Interface,* and *Radical Therapist.*

BIOGRAPHICAL/CRITICAL SOURCES: Avant-Garde, January, 1970.

*   *   *

KUPPERMAN, Joel J. 1936-

PERSONAL: Born May 18, 1936, in Chicago, Ill.; son of Solomon J. (an engineer) and Sara (Fisher) Kupperman; married Karen Ordahl (a teacher), June 20, 1964; children: Michael, Charles. *Education:* University of Chicago, A.B., 1954, S.B., 1955, A.M., 1956; Harvard University, additional study, 1959-60; Cambridge University, Ph.D., 1963.

Home: R.R. 2, Mansfield Center, Conn. 06250. *Office:* Department of Philosophy, University of Connecticut, Storrs, Conn. 06268.

CAREER: University of Connecticut, Storrs, instructor, 1960-63, assistant professor, 1963-67, associate professor, 1967-72, professor of philosophy, 1972—. Visiting lecturer, Trinity College, Oxford University, 1970.

WRITINGS: (With A. S. McGrode) *Fundamentals of Logic,* Doubleday, 1966; *Ethical Knowledge,* Humanities, 1971; *Philosophy: The Fundamental Problems,* St. Martin's, 1978.

*   *   *

KURIEN, C(hristopher) T(homas)   1931-

PERSONAL: Born July 2, 1931, in Vadasserikara, Kerala, India; son of Thomas Vadakumkara (a professor) and Annamma (Thomas) Kurien; married Susy Oommen, April 24, 1958; children: Prema Ann, Priya Elizabeth. *Education:* University of Madras, B.A. (honors), 1953, M.A., 1955; Stanford University, Ph.D., 1962; Yale University, post-doctoral study, 1968-69. *Religion:* Christian. *Office:* Madras Institute of Development Studies, 74 Second Main Rd., Gandhinagar, Adyar, Madras 20, India.

CAREER: Madras Christian College, Tambaram, Madras, India, tutor, 1953-54, lecturer, 1954-62, professor of economics and head of department, 1962-78; Madras Institute of Development Studies, Gandhinagar, Adyar, Madras, director, 1978—. Director, First South India Workshop on Research Methodology in Economics, 1971. Member, Madras Institute of Development Studies; member of governing body, Centre for Development Studies, Trivandrum, Kerala. Member of advisory council for technical services, World Council of Churches, Geneva. Consultant to State Planning Commission, Tamil Nadu.

MEMBER: Indian Economic Association (life member), Royal Economic Society (London). *Awards, honors:* Fulbright travel grants, 1958, 1962; Woodrow Wilson fellowship, 1960-62; national award for research, University Grants Commission, 1964-65; Hazen-Danforth postdoctoral fellowship, 1968-69; University Grants Commission national fellow in economics, 1975-77.

WRITINGS: Our Five Year Plans, Christian Institute for the Study of Religion and Society (Bangalore), 1966; (editor with S. V. Ananthakrishnan, C. T. Krishnamachari, and Stanley Ragiva) *India Today,* Christian Literature Society (Madras), 1967; *Indian Economic Crisis,* Asia Publishing House, 1969; *A Theoretical Approach to the Indian Economy,* Asia Publishing House, 1970; *A Guide to Research in Economics,* Madras Institute of Development Studies, 1973; *Poetry and Development,* Christian Literature Society (Madras), 1974; *Economic Change in Tamil Nadu,* Allied Publishers (New Delhi), 1977; *Planning and Social Transformation,* Indian Council of Social Science Research, 1977.

WORK IN PROGRESS: Dynamics of Rural Transformation.

AVOCATIONAL INTERESTS: Photography, tennis.

*   *   *

KURTZ, Kenneth H(assett)   1928-

PERSONAL: Born November 7, 1928, in Buffalo, N.Y.; son of Kenneth Hassett (an insurance agent) and Elsie (Trask) Kurtz; married Joan C. Goldstein, August 5, 1956; children: Robert David, Stuart Alan. *Education:* University

of Buffalo (now State University of New York at Buffalo), B.A., 1949; Yale University, M.S., 1951, Ph.D., 1953. *Residence:* Buffalo, N.Y. *Office:* Department of Psychology, State University of New York at Buffalo, Buffalo, N.Y. 14214.

CAREER: Research psychologist in industry, 1953-55; State University of New York at Buffalo, assistant professor, 1957-60, associate professor, 1960-66, professor of psychology, 1966—. *Military service:* U.S. Army, 1955-57. *Member:* American Psychological Association, Psychonomic Society, Eastern Psychological Association.

WRITINGS: Foundations of Psychological Research: Statistics, Methodology, and Measurement, Allyn & Bacon, 1965. Contributor to psychology journals.

*   *   *

KURZMAN, Paul A(lfred)   1938-

PERSONAL: Born November 25, 1938, in New York, N.Y.; son of Harold P. and Eleanor (Hess) Kurzman; married Margaret Frelinghuysen (a potter), January 9, 1965; children: Katherine, David. *Education:* Princeton University, B.A. (magna cum laude), 1960; Columbia University, M.S., 1964; New York University, Ph.D., 1970. *Home:* 75 Montgomery St., New York, N.Y. 10002. *Office:* School of Social Work, Hunter College of the City University of New York, 695 Park Ave., New York, N.Y. 10021.

CAREER: Lower Eastside Neighborhoods Association, New York City, acting executive director, 1964-67; City of New York, assistant commissioner, Youth Services Agency, 1970-72; Columbia University, Industrial Social Welfare Center, New York City, program director, 1972-74; Hunter College of the City University of New York, School of Social Work, New York City, associate professor and chairman of Community Organization and Planning Program, 1974—. Member of board of directors, United Neighborhood Houses, Hamilton-Madison House, Michael Schwerner Memorial Fund, and National Register of Clinical Social Workers. Member of State Licensing Board for Certified Social Work, 1977-82. Consultant and lecturer to numerous organizations and institutions. *Military service:* U.S. Army, 1960-62; became first lieutenant. *Member:* National Association of Social Workers (vice-president, New York City chapter); various professional organizations. *Awards, honors:* Association of the U.S. Army award, 1961; Martin E. Dworkis Award, New York University, 1970, for original contributions to research in public administration; Founders Day Award, New York University, 1971.

WRITINGS: (Contributor) *Social Work Practice* (National Conference on Social Welfare, 1970), Columbia University Press, 1970; (contributor) *Mississippi Casebook,* Michael Schwerner Memorial Fund, 1970; (editor) *The Mississippi Experience: Strategies for Welfare Rights Action,* Association Press, 1971; (contributor) James Goodman, editor, *Dynamics of Racism in Social Work Practice,* National Association of Social Workers, 1973; *Harry Hopkins and the New Deal,* Burdick, 1974; (contributor) B. J. Piccard, editor, *An Introduction to Social Work,* Dorsey, 1975; (contributor) John Turner, editor, *Encyclopedia of Social Work,* 17th edition (Kurzman was not associated with earlier editions), National Association of Social Workers, 1977.

Also author of papers presented to various social work conferences and institutes. Contributor to professional journals, including *Social Work, Journal of Administrative Studies, Social Casework, Child Welfare, Social Welfare in Appalachia, Training and Development Journal,* and *Social Service Quarterly.*

WORK IN PROGRESS: The Organization and Delivery of Social Services to Workers and Their Families through Union and Industrial Settings.

* * *

KUSIN, Vladimir V(ictor) 1929-

PERSONAL: Born December 2, 1929, in Czechoslovakia; married Daniela Cihackova, 1953; children: Victor J., Daniella M. *Education:* Prague School of Economics and Political Science, Prom. Hist., 1953; Charles University, Prague, Ph.D., 1968. *Residence:* Glasgow, Scotland. *Office:* University of Glasgow, 15 Bute Gardens, Glasgow G12 8QQ, Scotland.

CAREER: University teacher, professional abstractor, translator, and journalist in Czechoslovakia, 1953-68; University of Lancaster, Lancaster, England, research fellow, 1968-69; University of Glasgow, Glasgow, Scotland, senior editor, ABSEES (Soviet and East European abstracts series), 1970-76, director, International Information Centre for Soviet and East European Studies, 1976—. Lecturer at universities in England, Germany, France, Sweden, Canada, and the United States. *Member:* National Association for Soviet and East European Studies of Great Britain, International Committee for Soviet and East European Studies (member of executive committee).

WRITINGS: The Intellectual Origins of the Prague Spring: The Development of Reformist Ideas in Czechoslovakia, 1958-1967, Cambridge University Press, 1971; *Political Grouping in the Czechoslovak Reform Movement,* Macmillan, 1972; (editor) *The Czechoslovak Reform Movement,* American Bibliographical Center-Clio Press, 1973; (with Z. Hejzlar) *Czechoslovakia, 1968-1969: Chronology, Bibliography, Annotation,* Garland Publishing, 1975.

Translator into Czech: G. Bocca, *The Life and Death of Harry Oakes,* [Prague], 1965; Bocca, *Bikini Beach,* [Prague], 1967; T. Stoppard, *Rosencrantz and Guildenstern Are Dead,* [Prague], 1968. Contributor of articles and reviews to *Soviet Studies, Times Literary Supplement,* and other publications.

WORK IN PROGRESS: Normalization in Czechoslovakia, 1968-1976: Reinstitution of Political Control.

* * *

KUZMA, Greg 1944-

PERSONAL: Surname is pronounced Koozma; born July 14, 1944, in Rome, N.Y. *Education:* Syracuse University, B.A., 1966, M.A., 1967, *Office:* Department of English, University of Nebraska, Lincoln, Neb. 68508.

CAREER: University of Nebraska, Lincoln, assistant professor of English, 1969—; conducts poetry writing workshops.

WRITINGS—Poetry: Something at Last Visible, Zeitgeist, 1969; *Sitting Around,* Lillabulero, 1969; *Eleven Poems,* Portfolio, 1971; *The Bosporus,* Hellric, 1971; *Harry's Things,* Apple Magazine, 1971; *Song for Someone Going Away,* Ithaca House, 1971; *Good News: Poems,* Viking, 1973; *A Problem of High Water,* West Coast Poetry Review, 1973; *The Buffalo Shoot: Poems,* Basilisk, 1974; *The Obedience School,* Three Rivers Press, 1974; *A Day in the World,* Abattoir, 1976. Contributor of poems to *New Yorker, Nation, Poetry, Shenandoah, North American Review, Carleton Miscellany, Commonweal, Antioch Review, New York Quarterly,* and other magazines. Poetry-book review editor, *Prairie Schooner;* editor of *Pebble* and of Best Cellar Press pamphlet series.

BIOGRAPHICAL/CRITICAL SOURCES: Poetry, March, 1971, December, 1974; *Shenandoah,* winter, 1976; *Contemporary Literary Criticism,* Volume VII, Gale, 1977.†

* * *

LACEY, Robert 1944-

PERSONAL: Born January 3, 1944, in Guildford, Surrey, England; son of Leonard John (a banker) and Vida (Winch) Lacey; married Alexandra Jane Avrach (a graphic designer), April 3, 1971; children: Sasha (son), Scarlett. *Education:* Selwyn College, Cambridge, B.A., 1966, Diploma of Education, 1967, M.A., 1970. *Home:* 38 Kingsmead Rd., London S.W.2, England. *Agent:* John Cushman Associates, 25 West 43rd St., New York, N.Y. 10036.

CAREER: Illustrated London News, London, England, writer, 1968; *Sunday Times,* London, assistant editor of *Sunday Times Magazine,* 1969-73, "Look!" page editor, 1973-74.

WRITINGS: The French Revolution I: The Fall of the Bastille, Grossman, 1968; *The French Revolution II: The Terror,* Grossman, 1968; *The Rise of Napoleon,* Grossman, 1971; *The Peninsular War,* Grossman, 1971; *1812: The Retreat from Moscow,* Grossman, 1971; *Robert, Earl of Essex,* Atheneum, 1971; *Henry VIII,* Doubleday, 1972; *Sir Walter Raleigh,* Atheneum, 1974; *Sir Frances Drake,* Grossman, 1975; *Majesty: Elizabeth II and the House of Windsor,* Harcourt, 1977.

BIOGRAPHICAL/CRITICAL SOURCES: New York Times, June 9, 1971, and February 23, 1977; *Books & Bookmen,* June, 1971; *Book World,* March 17, 1974.

* * *

LaCROSSE, E. Robert 1937-

PERSONAL: Born May 27, 1937, in Bridgeport, Conn.; son of Edwin Robert and Caroline Bassett LaCrosse Hill; married Jean Eder, August 26, 1962; children: Benjamin Tudor and Thomas Harner (twin sons). *Education:* Harvard University, A.B. (cum laude), 1959; University of North Carolina, M.A., 1964, Ph.D., 1966. *Home:* 6191 Highway 73, Evergreen, Colo. 80439.

CAREER: University of North Carolina at Chapel Hill, instructor in psychology, Memorial Hospital, 1965-66; Harvard University, Cambridge, Mass., research associate on pre-school project and assistant professor of psychology, Graduate School of Education, 1966-69; Pacific Oaks College, Pasadena, Calif., president, 1969-76; consultant in private practice, 1977—. Adjunct professor of psychology, Claremont Graduate School, 1969-76. Visiting lecturer, Brandeis University, 1969. Director, Early Childhood Project Education Commission of the States, Denver, Colo., 1977—. *Member:* American Psychological Association, Society for Research in Child Development, Day Care and Child Development Council of America, Inc. (vice-president, board of directors), Association of Upper Level Colleges and Universities (first vice-chairman), National Association for the Education of Young Children (member of editorial advisory board).

WRITINGS: (Contributor) Dwight Allen and Eli Seifman, editors, *The Teacher's Handbook,* Scott, Foresman, 1971; *Day Care for America's Children* (pamphlet), Public Affairs Committee and Child Development Council of America, 1971; (editor) *The Early Childhood Education Directory,* Bowker, 1971. Contributor to several reports and studies on education and contributor to *Genetic Psychology Monographs, Young Children,* and *Claremont Reading Conference Yearbook* (1971).

WORK IN PROGRESS: The Politics of Children.

SIDELIGHTS: E. Robert LaCrosse told *CA:* "Children are on the bottom of the political pecking order. What happens to them now, shapes our future later. Politically, children are where women were fifty years ago—they are still very much a piece of property. In my writing I am trying to help child advocates move from wishing to doing. The doing is hard because the rewards are a long time in coming, but our future hinges on our children and their children. There is some comfort from that as we flail away at the system! . . . I write, I suppose, because words can help or actually make people go and do things. They may know the reality (grim), but words can give them perspective and energy. Mine don't always, but I try to use them to create a positive reality."

*   *   *

LACY, Leslie Alexander   1937-

PERSONAL: Born in 1937, in Franklin, La.; son of Nathaniel Lenard (a physician) and Lillie Lacy. *Education:* Attended private schools in the South before going to New England to college; University of Southern California, M.A.; also attended University of California, Berkeley, and University of Ghana.

CAREER: Active with political groups embracing "explicit socialist alternatives to capitalism" while a law student in California, where he eventually joined the Afro-American Association; went to Africa in 1963 and spent four years studying and teaching at University of Ghana, Legon; returned to United States after Ghana's President Kwame Nkrumah was deposed in 1967; lecturer at New York University, New York City, 1968-70, Howard University, Washington, D.C., 1968-70, and New School of Social Research, New York City, 1969-70.

WRITINGS: (Contributor) Gwendolyn Carter, editor, *Politics in Africa,* Harcourt, 1966; (contributor) LeRoi Jones and Larry Neal, editors, *Black Fire,* Morrow, 1968; *Black Africa on the Move* (juvenile), F. Watts, 1969; (contributor) John Henrik Clark, editor, *Malcolm X,* Macmillan, 1969; *Cheer the Lonesome Traveler: The Life of W.E.B. DuBois* (young adult book), Dial, 1970; *The Rise and Fall of a Proper Negro* (autobiography), Macmillan, 1970; (author of introduction) Wole Soyinka, *The Interpreter,* Macmillan, 1970; *The Soil Soldiers: The Civilian Conservation Corps in the Great Depression,* Chilton, 1970; *Native Daughter,* Macmillan, 1974. Contributor to magazines and journals.

SIDELIGHTS: Hollie I. West wrote that "Leslie Alexander Lacy's self-imposed four-year exile to Africa ended in 1967. As a black American who had gone to the mother country in search of identity, he found, as do many Americans who expatriate themselves, that he was rootless in another country and assimilation was uncertain." In his autobiography, *The Rise and Fall of a Proper Negro,* Lacy writes: "I discovered that trying to belong, to be saved, was at best ritualistic and misleading, covering over my disintegration rather than bringing to myself some reasonable kind of order. . . . Some of us, as I did, soon discovered that our Africa was an illusion, and tried to relate to and love what they saw. The psychologically weak could not make this adjustment."

BIOGRAPHICAL/CRITICAL SOURCES: Washington Post, August 31, 1970.†

LaFAUCI, Horatio M(ichael)   1917-

PERSONAL: Born August 12, 1917, in Providence, R.I.; son of Horatio Domenico (a barber) and Virginia (Camardo) LaFauci; married Bertha Beatrice Lukas, June 29, 1946; children: Roger John, David Michael. *Education:* Brown University, B.A., 1938, M.A., 1949; Harvard University, Ed.D., 1957. *Home:* 238 Park Ave., Arlington, Mass. 02174. *Office:* College of Basic Studies, Boston University, 781 Commonwealth Ave., Boston, Mass. 02215.

CAREER: High school teacher of Latin in Providence, R.I., 1939-40; East Greenwich Academy, East Greenwich, R.I., head of history department and athletic director, 1940-41; Becker Junior College, Worcester, Mass., teacher of economics and accounting and head of department of accounting, 1946-50; Boston University, Boston, Mass., registrar of College of General Education, 1951-53, registrar of Junior College, 1952-56, assistant dean of Junior College, 1953-58, associate professor of psychology and guidance, 1957-58, assistant to dean of the university, 1958, director of university budget, 1958-61, executive assistant to president of the university, 1959-62, dean of College of Basic Studies, 1961-74, professor of education, 1961—. *Military service:* U.S. Army, Medical Administrative Corps, 1941-45; became first lieutenant. *Member:* Association for Higher Education, National Society for the Study of Education, Association for General and Liberal Studies (president, 1970).

WRITINGS: (With Peyton E. Richter) *Team Teaching at the College Level,* Pergamon, 1970. Contributor to education journals.

*   *   *

LaGRAND, Louis E.   1935-

PERSONAL: Born September 18, 1935, in Utica, N.Y.; son of Louis Willard and Doris (VerSchneider) LaGrand; married Barbara Schwab (a teacher), July 6, 1963; children: Christopher, Gregory, Scott. *Education:* Cortland State Teachers College (now State University of New York College at Cortland), B.S., 1957; University of Notre Dame, M.A. (guidance), 1958; Columbia University, M.A. (physical education), 1962; New York University, graduate study, 1964; Florida State University, Ph.D., 1970. *Religion:* Roman Catholic. *Home:* Route 2, Potsdam, N.Y. 13676. *Office:* Department of Health and Physical Education, State University of New York College, Potsdam, N.Y. 13676.

CAREER: Columbia University, New York, N.Y., instructor in physical education, 1958-62; State University of New York College at Potsdam, assistant professor, 1962-65, associate professor of health and physical education, 1965—, head basketball coach, 1962—, varsity tennis coach, 1970—, director of health and physical education, 1970—. Director, Institute of Alcohol Problems, 1976. *Member:* College Physical Education Association, National Association of Basketball Coaches, American Association for Health, Physical Education and Recreation, New York State Association for Health, Physical Education and Recreation, Phi Delta Kappa, Pi Epsilon Kappa.

WRITINGS: (Contributor) *The Best of Basketball from the Coaching Clinic,* Parker Publishing, 1966; *Coach's Complete Guide to Winning Basketball,* Parker Publishing, 1967; *Discipline in the Secondary School,* Parker Publishing, 1969; (contributor) *The Best in Basketball from Scholastic Coach,* Scholastic Coach Book Services, 1970; *Hatha Yoga in Health and Physical Education,* State University of New York Press (Potsdam), 1974; (contributor) *Encyclopedia of*

Physical Education, Addison-Wesley, 1977. Contributor of about twenty-five articles to physical education journals.

WORK IN PROGRESS: Establishing student-teacher relationships; *A Semantic Differential Analysis of Yoga.*

AVOCATIONAL INTERESTS: Travel; stamp and coin collecting.

*   *   *

LAIRD, Betty A(nn) 1925-

PERSONAL: Born December 19, 1925, in Grand Island, Neb.; daughter of Myron E. (a railroad engineer and businessman) and Anna L. (Youtsey) Olson; married Roy D. Laird (a professor of political science at University of Kansas), September 3, 1946; children: Claude Myron, David Alan, Heather Lea. *Education:* Hastings College, B.A. (cum laude), 1948; graduate study at University of Nebraska, 1947-48, University of Washington, Seattle, 1955-56, and University of Kansas, 1960, 1967-68. *Politics:* Democrat. *Religion:* Unitarian Universalist. *Home:* 1641 Mississippi, Lawrence, Kan. 66044.

CAREER: Teacher of English in junior high school, Grand Island, Neb., 1949-50; University of Washington, School of Business, Seattle, curriculum adviser, 1955-56; University of Kansas, Lawrence, assistant instructor in English, 1958-62, research assistant in political science, 1969-70, Slavic and Soviet Area Studies, Polish program administrator, 1972-73. Independent research analyst, 1970—. Centron Corp. (film producers), Lawrence, actress in educational and commercial films since 1958. *Member:* Western Social Science Association, American Association for the Advancement of Slavic Studies.

WRITINGS: (With husband, Roy D. Laird) *Soviet Communism and Agrarian Revolution,* Penguin, 1970; (with R. D. Laird), *To Live Long Enough: The Memoirs of Naum Jasny, Scientific Analyst,* University Press of Kansas, 1976; (with Martha Parker) *Soil of Our Souls,* Coronado Press, 1976; (editor with R. D. Laird and Joseph Hajda) *The Future of Agriculture in the Soviet Union and Eastern Europe,* Westview Press, 1977. Contributor to newspapers and academic journals.

WORK IN PROGRESS: Continuing research in Kansas local history and in collectivized agriculture.

SIDELIGHTS: The Lairds have done research on collective farming in Mexico, the Soviet Union, Yugoslavia, and Poland.

*   *   *

LAIRD, Roy D(ean) 1925-

PERSONAL: Born July 15, 1925, in Blue Hill, Neb.; son of Claud Ross (a psychiatrist) and Amelia Frances (Krula) Laird; married Betty Ann Olson (a writer and editor), September 3, 1946; children: Claude Myson, David Alan, Heather Lea. *Education:* Hastings College, B.A., 1947; University of Nebraska, M.A., 1952; University of Glasgow, graduate study, 1952-53; University of Washington, Seattle, Ph.D., 1956. *Religion:* Unitarian Universalist. *Home:* 1641 Mississippi, Lawrence, Kan. 66044. *Office:* Department of Political Science, University of Kansas, Lawrence, Kan. 66045.

CAREER: U.S. Government, Washington, D.C., research analyst, 1956-57; University of Kansas, Lawrence, assistant professor, 1957-62, associate professor, 1962-66, professor of political science, 1968—, graduate director of department,

1975—, acting chairman of Slavic and Soviet Area Center, 1967-68, 1969. Visiting lecturer at London School of Economics and Political Science, University of London, Oxford University, Warsaw University, University of Glasgow, University of Marburg, University of Munich, Pittsburg State University, Pennsylvania State University, Arizona State University, Yale University, and numerous other colleges and universities.

MEMBER: International Association of Agricultural Economists, International Geographical Union, American Agricultural Economics Association, American Association for the Advancement of Slavic Studies, American Political Science Association, American Academy of Political and Social Sciences, Conference on Soviet Agricultural and Peasant Affairs (founder; member of executive board, 1962—), International Symposium on Soviet Agriculture (founder), American Association of University Professors, Midwest Association for the Advancement of Slavic Studies (member of executive board, 1968-69), Central Slavic Association, Midwest Conference of Slavic Studies, Midwest Political Science Association, Western Social Science Association, Western Slavic Studies Association, Kansas Political Science Association, Pi Sigma Alpha. *Awards, honors:* Elizabeth Watkins Faculty Research fellowship, 1960; Rockefeller Foundation grant to do research in Europe, 1963-64; National Science Foundation grants to do research in Mexico, 1966, 1967-68; Fulbright grant to do research in Eastern Europe, 1967; Hesston Foundation grant, 1976-79.

WRITINGS: Collective Farming in Russia, University of Kansas Press, 1958; *The Rise and Fall of the M.T.S. as an Instrument of Soviet Rule,* University of Kansas Press, 1960; (editor) *Soviet Agricultural and Peasant Affairs,* University of Kansas Press, 1963; (editor with Edward L. Crowley) *Soviet Agriculture: The Permanent Crisis,* Praeger, 1965; *Government of the U.S.S.R.,* Extramural Independent Study Center, University of Kansas, 1970; (with wife, Betty A. Laird) *Soviet Communism and Agrarian Revolution,* Pelican, 1970; *The Soviet Paradigm: An Experiment in Creating a Monohierarchical Polity,* Free Press, 1970; (with Betty A. Laird) *To Live Long Enough: The Memoirs of Naum Jasny, Scientific Analyst,* University of Kansas Press, 1976; (author of introduction) Martha Parker and Betty A. Laird, *Soil of Our Souls,* House of Usher, 1976; (editor with Betty A. Laird and Joseph Hajda) *The Future of Agriculture in the Soviet Union and Eastern Europe,* Westview Press, 1977.

Contributor: Franklyn D. Holzman, editor, *Readings on the Soviet Economy,* Rand McNally, 1962; Harry G. Shaffer, editor, *The Soviet Economy,* Appleton, 1963; Calude E. Hawley and Ruth G. Wentraub, editors, *Administrative Questions and Political Answers,* Van Nostrand, 1966; Jan S. Prybyla, editor, *The Triangle of Power, Conflict, and Accommodation: The United States, the Soviet Union, Communist China,* Pennsylvania State University Press, 1966; Vladimir G. Treml and Robert Farrell, editors, *The Development of the Soviet Economy: Plan and Performance,* Praeger, 1968; Shaffer and Prybyla, editors, *From Underdevelopment to Affluence: Western, Soviet, and Chinese Views,* Appleton, 1968; Shaffer, editor, *The Soviet Economy: A Collection of Western and Soviet Views,* 2nd edition, Appleton, 1969; Richard Cornell, editor, *The Soviet Political System: A Book of Readings,* Prentice-Hall, 1970; Bernard W. Eissenstat, editor, *Lenin and Leninism,* Lexington Books, 1971; Joseph L. Nagie, editor, *Man, State and Society in the Soviet Union,* Praeger, 1972; Ellen Mickiewicz, editor, *Handbook of Soviet Social Science Data,*

Free Press, 1973; Eissenstat, editor, *The Soviet Union in the Seventies and Beyond,* Lexington Books, 1975; Zbigniew M. Fallenbuchl, editor, *Economic Development in the Soviet Union and Eastern Europe,* Volume II, Praeger, 1976.

Editor of "Slavic Series," University of Kansas, 1970. Contributor of about sixty articles and reviews to *New Republic, Kansas City Times, Christian Science Monitor,* and social science journals in the United States and elsewhere.

WORK IN PROGRESS: Writing on trends in Soviet agriculture, on political trends in the Soviet system, and on world food problems.

* * *

La LONDE, Bernard J. 1933-

PERSONAL: Born June 3, 1933, in Detroit, Mich.; son of John B. and Fannie (Napier) La Londe; married Barbara Elaine Eggenberger, September 8, 1958; children: Lisa, Michelle, Christopher. *Education:* University of Notre Dame, B.A., 1955; University of Detroit, M.B.A., 1957; Michigan State University, Ph.D., 1961. *Home:* 2355 Onandaga Dr., Columbus, Ohio 43221. *Office:* Ohio State University, 1775 South College, Columbus, Ohio 43210.

CAREER: Ford Motor Co., Detroit, Mich., member of staff of vice-president for sales, 1955-57; University of Colorado, Boulder, assistant professor, 1961-64, associate professor of marketing, 1964-65; Michigan State University, East Lansing, associate professor, 1965-66, professor of marketing and coordinator of food marketing, 1966-69; Ohio State University, Columbus, J. R. Riley Professor of Marketing and Logistics, 1969—. Speaker at executive development programs in United States and abroad, including England, Switzerland, Canada, Japan; consultant on marketing and logistics problems to more than fifty companies and to several trade associations, 1961—.

MEMBER: National Council of Physical Distribution Management (chairman of education committee, 1965-68), American Marketing Association, Transportation Research Foundation (president, 1971), Regional Science Association, Society of Logistics Engineers.

WRITINGS: (Contributor) Stephen A. Greyser, editor, *Toward Scientific Marketing,* American Marketing Assn., 1964; (with Edward W. Smykay) *Physical Distribution: The New and Profitable Science of Business Logistics,* Darnell, 1967; (contributor) David McConaughy and C. Joseph Clawson, editors, *Business Logistics: Policies and Decisions,* Research Institute for Business and Economics, University of Southern California, 1968; (with Smykay and Donald Bowersox) *Physical Distribution Management,* Macmillan, 1968; (editor with Smykay and Bowersox) *Readings in Physical Distribution Management,* Macmillan, 1969; (with P. Zinszer) *Customer Service: Meaning and Measurement,* National Council of Physical Distribution Management, 1976.

Monographs: *Differentials in Super Market Drawing Power,* Bureau of Business and Economic Research, Michigan State University, 1962; (with F. C. Hammerness and Hugh A. Cotton) *Cost of Possession Study,* National Wholesale Druggist's Association, 1965; *Bibliography on Physical Distribution Management,* Marketing Publications Inc., 1967, annual supplements, 1968—; (with Paul Smith) *Shopping Center Management: A Selected and Annotated Bibliography,* Bureau of Business and Economic Research, Michigan State University, 1968.

Contributor of over fifty articles to distribution and management journals. North American editor, *International Journal of Physical Distribution;* books and monographs editor, American Marketing Association; member of editorial advisory board, *Distribution World Wide.*

WORK IN PROGRESS: Research on design of logistics systems, on simulation applications to distribution problems, and on functional organization of the logistics or physical distribution function.

* * *

LAMB, Elizabeth Searle 1917-
(K. L. Mitchell)

PERSONAL: Born January 22, 1917, in Topeka, Kan.; daughter of Howard Sanford (in insurance) and Helen (a musician; maiden name, Shaver) Searle; married F. Bruce Lamb (a forester and writer), December 11, 1941; children: Carolyn (Mrs. Michael Kaye). *Education:* University of Kansas, B.A., 1939, B.M., 1940. *Religion:* Protestant. *Home:* 970 Acequia Madre, Santa Fe, N.M. 87501. *Agent:* Bertha Klausner International Literary Agency, Inc., 71 Park Ave., New York, N.Y. 10016.

CAREER: Professional harpist and composer in earlier years; Canon City correspondent for *Pueblo Chieftain,* Pueblo, Colo., 1957-59. Has given poetry readings and led poetry and haiku workshops; also judge for various haiku contests. *Member:* National League of American Pen Women, American Harp Society, Haiku Society of America (charter member; president, 1971), Women Poets of New York, Society of Children's Book Writers, Phi Beta Kappa, Pi Kappa Lambda, Mu Phi Epsilon. *Awards, honors:* Awards from National League of American Pen Women for writings, annually, 1965-69, 1971-72, 1974-76; second prize in Ruben Darin International Memorial Poetry Contest sponsored by Organization of American States, 1967; other awards for poetry, including haiku and concrete poetry.

WRITINGS: (With Jean Bailey and Patricia Maloney Markun) *The Pelican Tree and Other Panama Adventures* (juvenile), North River Press, 1953; *Today and Every Day,* Unity Books, 1970; *Inside Me, Outside Me* (juvenile), Unity Books, 1974; *In This Blaze of Sun* (haiku), From Here Press, 1975; (with husband, F. Bruce Lamb) *Picasso's "Bust of Sylvette"* (haiku), Garlinghouse Printers, 1977. Writer of inspirational material under pseudonym, K. L. Mitchell. Contributor of articles to music magazines, of poetry and prose to religious magazines, of music and dance entries to *Young Students Encyclopedia,* 1973, and *My Weekly Reader,* 1974, and of juvenile material to *Children's Activities, Jack and Jill, Highlights for Children,* and *Wee Wisdom;* contributor of poetry to anthologies and to *New York Herald Tribune, Christian Science Monitor, Poetry Digest, Lyric, Haiku* (Toronto), *American Haiku, Haiku Highlights, Tweed, Bonsai, Cicada,* and other publications. Wrote lyrics for six songs in "New Dimensions in Music" series, American Book Co., 1970.

WORK IN PROGRESS: With husband, F. Bruce Lamb, *Tales of the Caxinauas,* adaptation of Amazon Indian stories; three books of poetry, *Readings from a Double Compass, Let All the Banners Fly,* and *39 Blossoms* (haiku).

SIDELIGHTS: During the years 1941-61, Elizabeth Lamb lived mostly in Trinidad, Brazil, Colombia, Panama, and Puerto Rico. *Avocational interests:* Music, including amateur chamber music.

BIOGRAPHICAL/CRITICAL SOURCES: Haiku Highlights, July-August, 1971.

LAMB, F(rank) Bruce 1913-

PERSONAL: Born July 27, 1913, in Cotopaxi, Colo.; son of Frank Richard (an agricultural technician) and Maude (a teacher and school administrator; maiden name, Conover) Lamb; married Elizabeth Searle (a writer), December 11, 1941; children: Carolyn (Mrs. Michael Kaye). *Education:* University of Michigan, B.S., 1940, M.F., 1941, Ph.D., 1954. *Home:* 970 Acequia Madre, Santa Fe, N.M. 87501. *Agent:* Bertha Klausner International Literary Agency, 71 Park Ave., New York, N.Y. 10016.

CAREER: U.S. Department of Engineers, British West Indies, engineer, 1941-42; Rubber Development Corp., Brazil, field technician (mapped unknown tributary of Tapajos River, now known as Rio Novo, in Amazon Valley), 1943-45; international forestry consultant in Latin America, 1945-58; U.S. Forest Service, Rio Pedras, P.R., training officer and research forester in tropical forest research center, 1958-60; U.S. Plywood-Champion Papers, Inc., New York, N.Y., forester in new materials procurement, 1960-65; technical director of forest resources, Champion International Corps., 1966-75; consulting forester, 1975—. *Wartime service:* U.S. Corps of Engineers, civilian employee, 1941-42. *Member:* Society of American Foresters, New York Academy of Sciences, Explorers Club of New York, International Society of Tropical Foresters. *Awards, honors:* Diploma of Honor of Government of Guatemala, 1956.

WRITINGS: (With L. R. Holdridge and Bertel Mason) *Bosques de Guatemala* (title means "Forests of Guatemala"), Instituto de Fomento de Produccion (Guatemala), 1952; *Mahogany of Tropical America,* University of Michigan Press, 1966; (with Manuel Cordova) *Wizard of the Upper Amazon,* Atheneum, 1971, 2nd edition, Houghton, 1975; (with wife, Elizabeth S. Lamb) *Picasso's "Bust of Sylvette"* (haiku), Garlinghouse Printers, 1977. Contributor to natural history and botany journals, and to *American Speech.* Editor, *Caribbean Forester,* 1958-60.

WORK IN PROGRESS: Another sequel to *Wizard; Rio Tigre and Beyond; Kid Curry; Life with the Wild Bunch;* with wife, Elizabeth Lamb, *Tales of the Caxinauas,* adaptation of Amazon Indian stories.

* * *

LAMB, Sydney M(acDonald) 1929-

PERSONAL: Born May 4, 1929, in Denver, Colo.; son of Sydney Bishop (an engineer) and Jean (MacDonald) Lamb; married Sharon Rowell, June 17, 1956 (divorced, 1971); married Susan Tulkington, May 15, 1977; children: (first marriage) Christina, Sarah, Nancy. *Education:* Yale University, B.A., 1951; University of California, Berkeley, Ph.D., 1958. *Religion:* Christian. *Home:* 2905 Garber St., Berkeley, Calif. 94705. *Office:* Semionics Associates, 41 Tunnel Rd., Berkeley, Calif. 94705.

CAREER: University of California, Berkeley, instructor, 1956-58, assistant research linguist, 1958-61, associate professor of linguistics, 1961-64; Yale University, New Haven, Conn., associate professor, 1964-68, professor of linguistics, 1968-77; Semionics Associates, Berkeley, Calif., general partner, 1977—. *Member:* Linguistic Society of America (member of executive committee, 1966-68). *Awards, honors:* National Science Foundation research grants, 1958, 1959, 1961, 1963, 1966, 1968.

WRITINGS: (With S. E. Martin and C. Y. Dougherty) *Chinese Character Indexes,* University of California Press, 1963; *Outline of Stratificational Grammar,* Georgetown

University Press, 1966. Contributor to anthologies and linguistics journals.

WORK IN PROGRESS: Research on structure of language and on conceptual structure.

* * *

LAMONT, Rosette C(lementine)
(R. L. Farmer)

PERSONAL: Born in Paris, France; came to United States in 1941, naturalized in 1944; daughter of Alexandre and Loudmilla Lamont; married Frederick Hyde Farmer (a lawyer and urbanist), August 9, 1969. *Education:* Attended Lycee Moliere and Lycee La Fontaine, Paris, France; Hunter College (now Hunter College of the City University of New York), B.A., 1947; Yale University, M.A., 1948, Ph.D., 1954. *Home:* 260 West 72nd St., New York, N.Y. 10023. *Office:* Graduate Center, City University of New York, 33 West 42nd St., New York, N.Y. 10036.

CAREER: Queens College of the City University of New York, Flushing, N.Y., instructor, 1950-61, assistant professor, 1961-64, associate professor, 1964-67, professor of French, 1967-69; City University of New York, Graduate Center, New York, N.Y., professor of French and comparative literature, 1968—. U.S. State Department envoy in the scholar exchange program with the Soviet Union, 1974. *Member:* P.E.N., Modern Language Association of America, American Comparative Literature Association, American Association of Teachers of French, Phi Beta Kappa, Sigma Tau Delta, Pi Delta Phi. *Awards, honors:* Hunter College Outstanding Achievement Award, 1957; Yaddo Foundation writing fellowships, 1962, 1963, 1965; Chevalier des Palmes Academiques, 1972; Guggenheim fellowship, 1973-74; U.S. State Department fellowship research leave, 1976.

WRITINGS: La Vie et l'oeuvre de Boris Pasternak, Les Presses Du Compagnonnage, 1965; (editor with Kenneth Douglas) *De vive voix: Lectures dramatiques,* Harcourt, 1971; *Ionesco,* Prentice-Hall, 1973; (with Melvin J. Friedman) *The Two Faces of Ionesco,* Whitston Publishing, 1977. Contributor of essays to *Publication of the Modern Language Association, Yale French Studies, French Review, First Stage, Horizon, Massachusetts Review, Town and Country, Harper's Bazaar, Theatre Arts, La Revue des Lettres Modernes, L'Esprit Createur, The Review of National Literature, Studies in the Literary Imagination, Mosaic, Performing Arts Journal, Modern Drama,* and *Modern Occasions.* Member of editorial board and contributor to *Performing Arts Journal.*

WORK IN PROGRESS: The Anti-Hero.

SIDELIGHTS: Rosette Lamont told *CA:* "I have always wanted to be a writer, and since my childhood have lived in books. I feel that literature is a kind of greater life, and that by reading I fill myself with life. When I write I enter into communication with life forces, and with other human beings. In a sense all writing is an act against our inevitable death. Having lived through the Occupation of France I came to realize that we must affirm our existence."

* * *

LANA, Robert E(dward) 1932-

PERSONAL: Born August 9, 1932, in Hoboken, N.J.; son of Edward Vincent (a draftsman) and Daisy (Taborelli) Lana; married Mary Jean Harris, June 16, 1965; children: Renata. *Education:* Rutgers University, B.A., 1954; University of Iowa, graduate study, 1954-55; University of Maryland, M.A., 1956, Ph.D., 1958. *Home:* 233 Righters Mill Rd., Narberth, Pa. 19072. *Office:* Department of Psychology, Temple University, Philadelphia, Pa. 19122.

CAREER: American University, Washington, D.C., associate professor of psychology, 1958-62; Alfred University, Alfred, N.Y., associate professor of psychology and chairman of department, 1962-66; Temple University, Philadelphia, Pa., associate professor, 1966-69, professor of psychology and chairman of department, 1969—. *Member:* American Psychological Association (fellow), Eastern Psychological Association. *Awards, honors:* Fulbright fellow at University of Rome, 1965-66.

WRITINGS: Assumptions of Social Psychology, Appleton, 1969; (with R. L. Rosnow) *Introduction to Contemporary Psychology,* Holt, 1972; (editor with Rosnow) *Readings in Contemporary Psychology,* Holt, 1972; *The Foundations of Psychological Theory,* Halsted, 1976. Member of board of editors of *Educational and Psychological Measurement* and *Journal of Educational Psychology.*

*   *   *

LANCASTER, Kelvin (John) 1924-

PERSONAL: Born December 10, 1924, in Sydney, Australia; son of Jack K. and Margaret (Gray) Lancaster; married Lorraine Cross; married second wife, Deborah Grunfeld (an attorney), June 10, 1963; children: Clifton John, Gilead Saul. *Education:* University of Sydney, B.Sc., 1948, B.A., 1949, M.A., 1953; University of London, B.Sc., 1953, Ph.D., 1958. *Home:* 35 Claremont Ave., New York, N.Y. 10027. *Office:* Department of Economics, Columbia University, New York, N.Y. 10027.

CAREER: University of London, London School of Economics and Political Science, London, England, 1955-61, began as lecturer, became reader in economics; Johns Hopkins University, Baltimore, Md., professor of political economy, 1961-66; Columbia University, New York, N.Y., professor of economics, 1966—. *Military service:* Royal Australian Air Force, 1943-45; became lieutenant. *Member:* American Economic Association, Econometric Society.

WRITINGS: Mathematical Economics, Macmillan, 1968; *Introduction to Modern Microeconomics,* Rand McNally, 1969; *Consumer Demand: A New Approach,* Columbia University Press, 1971; *Modern Economics: Principles and Policies,* Rand McNally, 1973.

*   *   *

LANDAR, Herbert (Jay) 1927-

PERSONAL: Born December 7, 1927, in New York, N.Y.; son of Leo and Mildred (Mann) Landar. *Education:* Queens College (now Queens College of the City University of New York), B.A., 1949; Yale University, M.A., 1955, Ph.D., 1960. *Home:* 1312 South Fremont Ave., Alhambra, Calif. 91803. *Office:* Department of English, California State University, Los Angeles, Calif. 90032.

CAREER: C. L. Barnhart, Inc., Bronxville, N.Y., associate editor, 1949-50; Reed College, Portland, Ore., instructor in humanities and linguistics, 1957-59; California State University, Los Angeles, 1960—, began as assistant professor, currently professor of English. Visiting professor of anthropology, Indiana University, 1976. *Military service:* U.S. Army, 1950-52. *Member:* Linguistic Society of America, American Anthropological Association (fellow), Societe des Americanistes de Paris, New York Historical Society,

New York Academy of Sciences. *Awards, honors:* Guggenheim fellow, 1967-68.

WRITINGS: Navaho Syntax, Linguistic Society of America, 1963; *Language and Culture,* Oxford University Press, 1966. Contributor to linguistics and anthropology journals, including *Language, Ethnology, International Journal of American Linguistics,* and *American Anthropologist.*

WORK IN PROGRESS: Bibliography of American Indian Language Families.

*   *   *

LANDER, Jeannette 1931-

PERSONAL: Born September 8, 1931, in New York, N.Y.; daughter of Harry (a businessman) and Anna (Silverzweig) Lander; married Joachim Seyppel (a writer), August 13, 1950 (separated); children: Marcel, Tove. *Education:* Attended Brandeis University and Bryn Mawr College; Southeastern Louisiana University, B.A., 1957; Free University of Berlin, Ph.D., 1966. *Home:* Rheinstrasse 17, West Berlin 41, Germany.

MEMBER: International P.E.N. Club. *Awards, honors:* While student received prizes from Southeastern Literary Association for essay, 1954, for short story, 1955, and for one-act play, 1956; Villa Massimo Prize, 1976.

WRITINGS—All published by Insel Verlag, except as indicated: *William Butler Yeats: Die Bildersprache seiner Lyrik,* Kohlhammer, 1967; *Ezra Pound,* Colloquim Verlag, 1968, translation published under the same title, Ungar, 1971; *Ein Sommer in der Woche der Itke K.* (novel), 1971; *Auf dem Boden der Frende* (novel), 1972; *Ein Spatz in der Hand . . .* (short stories), 1973; *Die Toechter* (novel), 1976.

*   *   *

LANDIS, Jessie Royce 1904-1972

November 25, 1904—February 3, 1972; American actress. Obituaries: *New York Times,* February 3, 1972; *Washington Post,* February 4, 1972; *Newsweek,* February 14, 1972; *Time,* February 14, 1972.

*   *   *

LANDIS, Judson R(ichard) 1935-

PERSONAL: Born February 21, 1935, in Fremont, Ohio; son of Judson Taylor (a professor and author) and Mary (Green) Landis; married Sheron Chavoor, October 21, 1965; children: Jeffrey Michael, Brian Judson, Kevin Phillip. *Education:* University of California, Berkeley, B.A., 1957; Ohio State University, M.A., 1959, Ph.D., 1962. *Politics:* Democrat. *Religion:* Protestant. *Home:* 3701 Winding Creek Rd., Sacramento, Calif. 95825. *Office:* Department of Sociology, California State University, 6000 J. St., Sacramento, Calif. 95819.

CAREER: California State University, Sacramento, assistant professor, 1963-67, associate professor, 1967-71, professor of sociology, 1971—. *Military service:* U.S. Marine Corps Reserve, 1958-63. *Member:* American Sociological Association, American Association of University Professors, American Criminology Society, Pacific Sociological Association.

WRITINGS: (Editor) *Current Perspectives on Social Problems,* Wadsworth, 1966, 3rd edition, 1973; *Sociology: Concepts and Characteristics,* Wadsworth, 1971, 3rd edition, 1977.

LANDSBERGIS, Algirdas J. 1924-

PERSONAL: Surname is accented on first syllable; born June 23, 1924, in Kybartai, Lithuania; son of Jeronimas and Emilija (Meilunaite) Landsbergis; married Joan Jacobi (a college instructor in philosophy), June 23, 1951; children: Paul, Jon. *Education:* Attended University of Kaunas, 1941-43, and University of Mainz, 1946-49; Brooklyn College (now Brooklyn College of the City University of New York), A.B., 1951; Columbia University, A.M., 1960. *Home:* 87-20 125th St., Richmond Hill, N.Y. 11418. *Agent:* Bertha Klausner, International Literary Agency, Inc., 71 Park Ave., New York, N.Y. 10016. *Office:* Department of History, Fairleigh Dickinson University, Rutherford, N.J. 09090.

CAREER: After Lithuania (annexed by the Soviet Union, 1940) was overrun by the German Army in 1941, Landsbergis did a stint at forced labor in a German factory alongside French war prisoners and Dutch deportees; spent 1945-49 in displaced persons camps in Wiesbaden and Kassel, Germany, and was a high school teacher in Wiesbaden; emigrated to United States with his parents and brother and sister, 1949, working first as a dishwasher in New York City; Brooklyn Public Library, Brooklyn, N.Y., library assistant, 1949-53; Assembly of Captive European Nations, New York City, writer and researcher, 1956-66; Fairleigh Dickinson University, Rutherford, N.J., instructor in history, 1965-66, assistant professor of history, 1966—. Writer; lecturer on East European history and literature. *Member:* P.E.N. International (vice-chairman, U.S. branch, P.E.N.-in-Exile), American Historical Association, American Association for the Advancement of Slavic Studies, Association for the Advancement of Baltic Studies, Dramatists Guild, Authors League of America, Delta Tau Kappa. *Awards, honors: Daily Draugas,* Chicago, 1953, for *Kelione;* Ohio Lithuanian Cultural Association, 1957, for *Penki stulpai turgaus aiksteje;* Los Angeles Drama Association, 1970, for "Paskutinis piknikas."

WRITINGS: Kelione (novel; title means "The Journey"), Draugas (Chicago), 1955; *Ilgoji Naktis* (short stories; title means "The Long Night"), Nida (London), 1956; (editor with Clark Mills) *The Green Oak: Selected Lithuanian Poetry in English Translation,* Voyages Press, 1961; (editor with Mills) *The Green Linden: Selected Lithuanian Folksongs,* Voyages Press, 1964; *Penki stulpai turgaus aiksteje* (play; title means "Five Posts in a Market Place"), Santara-Sviesa, 1965, translation by the author published as *Five Posts in the Market Place* (first produced Off-Broadway, 1961), Manyland Books, 1969; *Meiles Mokykla* (play; title means "The School for Love"), Santara-Sviesa (Chicago), 1966; *Vejas Gluosniuose* (play; title means "Wind in the Willows"), Santara-Sviesa, 1971; *Gluosniai Vejuje* (play; title means "Willows in the Wind"), Santara-Sviesa, 1971; *The Last Picnic* (play; produced in Lithuanian as "Paskutinis piknikas" by The Los Angeles Drama Group Chicago, November 28, 1971), Manyland Books, 1977.

Unpublished plays: "Barzda" (title means "The Beard"), produced by The Toronto Lithuanian Theatre, 1965; "Sudiev, mano karaliau" (title means "Farewell, My King"), produced at Chicago Lithuanian Theatre, January 15, 1967; "Sventasis narvas" (title means "The Holy Cage"), produced at Cleveland Lithuanian Theatre, September 3, 1977. Writer of television scripts. Contributor to *Encyclopedia of World Drama, Encyclopedia Lituanica,* and *Midcentury Authors.* Editor of American-English literature section, *Lietuviu Enciklopedija.* Associate editor of *Arena,* 1962-66, and

Cinema-TV-Digest, 1964—; special issue editor, *Literary Review,* spring, 1965; reviewer for *Books Abroad.* Contributor to *Lituanus Quarterly.*

WORK IN PROGRESS: Two plays, "The Chinese Passion," and "Mary of the Camps."

SIDELIGHTS: Algirdas Landsbergis is competent in German, French, Russian, and Latin, as well as in English and his native Lithuanian.

BIOGRAPHICAL/CRITICAL SOURCES: Frank R. Silbajoris, *Perfection of Exile: Fourteen Contemporary Lithuanian Writers,* University of Oklahoma Press, 1970; Aleksis Rubulis, *Baltic Literature,* University of Notre Dame Press, 1970.

*   *   *

LANG, Kurt 1924-

PERSONAL: Born January 25, 1924, in Berlin, Germany; son of Ernst (a physician) and Ilse (Kass) Lang; married Gladys Engel (a sociologist), June 9, 1950; children: Glenna, Kevin. *Education:* University of Chicago, B.A., 1949, M.A., 1952, Ph.D., 1953. *Religion:* None. *Home:* Christian Ave., Box 63, Stony Brook, N.Y. 11790. *Office:* Department of Sociology, State University of New York, Stony Brook, N.Y. 11790.

CAREER: U.S. Office of Military Government, Germany, research assistant, 1946-47; University of Chicago, Chicago, Ill., research associate in psychological warfare, 1949-51; University of Miami, Coral Gables, Fla., assistant professor of sociology, 1953-54; Canadian Broadcasting Corp. (CBC), Ottawa, Ontario, research sociologist, 1954-56; Queens College of the City University of New York, New York, N.Y., instructor, 1956-59, assistant professor, 1959-62, associate professor of sociology and chairman of department, 1962-64; State University of New York at Stony Brook, professor of sociology, 1964—, chairman of department, 1965-67. Member of faculty, American Studies Seminar, Salzburg, 1961; visiting associate professor, University of California, Berkeley, 1962-63; senior research associate, Center for Policy Research, 1970—. *Military service:* U.S. Army, 1943-46; became sergeant. *Member:* Phi Beta Kappa. *Awards, honors:* Edward L. Bernays Award from American Sociological Society for research on effects of radio and television on American life, 1952; National Endowment for the Humanities grant, 1971-72.

WRITINGS: (With wife, Gladys Engel Lang) *Collective Dynamics,* Crowell, 1961; (with G. E. Lang) *Politics and Television,* Quadrangle, 1968; (with G. E. Lang) *Voting and Non-voting,* Blaisdell, 1968; *Military Institutions and Sociology of War,* Sage Publications, 1972. Contributor to *American Sociological Review.*

SIDELIGHTS: While the Langs' observations on how television is changing American politics are termed "not startlingly new" by Elliott Fremont-Smith, a *Virginia Quarterly Review* critic says of *Politics and Television:* "This book is a welcome first approach to the problem. Its authors are objective; their objectivity and refusal to give in to sensationalism gives their warning its real force. It is a warning we cannot ignore."

BIOGRAPHICAL/CRITICAL SOURCES: Virginia Quarterly Review, autumn, 1968; *New York Times,* October 7, 1968; *New Leader,* November 18, 1968.

*   *   *

LANGENDOEN, D(onald) Terence 1939-

PERSONAL: Surname is pronounced Lan-gan-dan; born

June 7, 1939, in Paterson, N.J.; son of Gerrit (a house-painter) and Wilhelmina (Van Dyk) Langendoen; married Sally Wicklund (a childbirth educator and cabinet maker), 1964; children: David Terence. *Education:* Massachusetts Institute of Technology, S.B., 1961, Ph.D., 1964. *Home:* 219 Kane St., Brooklyn, N.Y. 11231. *Office:* Graduate School and University Center of the City University of New York, 33 West 42nd St., New York, N.Y. 10036.

CAREER: Ohio State University, Columbus, assistant professor, 1964-68, associate professor of linguistics, 1968-69; City University of New York, Brooklyn College, Brooklyn, N.Y., professor of English, 1969—, Graduate School and University Center, New York, N.Y., professor of English and linguistics, 1969—. Visiting lecturer, University of Pennsylvania, fall, 1967; visiting associate professor, Rockefeller University, 1968-69; adjunct professor, State University of New York at Buffalo, 1970, 1971. *Member:* Linguistic Society of America (member of executive committee, 1972-74). *Awards, honors:* National Science Foundation grant, 1967-68; City University of New York faculty research grants, 1971-76; senior Fulbright lectureship to the Netherlands, 1977.

WRITINGS: The London School of Linguistics, M.I.T. Press, 1968; *The Study of Syntax,* Holt, 1969; *Essentials of English Grammar,* Holt, 1970; (editor with Charles J. Fillmore) *Studies in Linguistic Semantics,* Holt, 1971; (editor with T. G. Bever and J. J. Katz) *An Integrated Theory of Linguistic Ability,* Crowell, 1976. Contributor to language journals. Associate editor, *Linguistic Inquiry,* 1969-72; member of associate editorial board, *Language,* 1977—.

WORK IN PROGRESS: General studies on English syntax and linguistic theory.

*   *   *

LANGER, Jonas 1936-

PERSONAL: Born May 2, 1936, in Antwerp, Belgium; son of Samuel (a diamond merchant) and Rachel (Gartner) Langer; married Marilyn May, August 2, 1964; children: Samantha Alexandra. *Education:* College of the City of New York (now City College of the City University of New York), B.A., 1957; Clark University, Worcester, Mass., Ph.D., 1962. *Home:* 2780 Buena Vista Way, Berkeley, Calif. 94720. *Office:* Department of Psychology, University of California, Berkeley, Calif. 94720.

CAREER: University of California, Berkeley, member of psychology department faculty, 1962—. *Member:* Society for Research in Child Development. *Awards, honors:* United States Public Health Service special fellow, 1965-66; James McKeen Cattel fellow, 1976-77.

WRITINGS: Theories of Development, Holt, 1969; (editor with P. H. Mussen and M. Covington) *Trends and Issues in Developmental Psychology,* Holt, 1969. Member of board of editors, *Youth and Adolescence.*

WORK IN PROGRESS: Research on cognitive development; a book entitled *Origins of Logic in Babies.*

*   *   *

LANGFORD, Walter McCarty 1908-

PERSONAL: Born June 27, 1908; son of George Earl (a banker) and Ethel (McCarty) Langford; married Alice Joubert, December 29, 1931 (deceased); children: Lois (Mrs. William B. Berry), Walter McCarty, Jr., James R., Elizabeth (Mrs. Robert P. Jones). *Education:* University of Notre Dame, B.A., 1930; Universidad Nacional Autonoma de Mexico, M.A., 1937. *Politics:* Democrat. *Religion:* Catholic. *Home:* 245 Rue Bossuet, Apt. 1830, South Bend, Ind. 46615. *Office:* University of Notre Dame, Notre Dame, Ind. 46556.

CAREER: First National Bank, Pharr, Tex., assistant cashier, 1930-31; University of Notre Dame, Notre Dame, Ind., instructor, 1931-34, assistant professor, 1934-37, associate professor, 1937-43, professor of modern languages, 1943-73, professor emeritus, 1973—, chairman of department, 1946-59, tennis coach, 1940-53, fencing coach, 1940-43, 1951-61. Director of Chile I Project, Peace Corps in Santiago, Chile, 1961-63; president, C.H.I.L.E., Inc. (non-profit organization which raises funds for Chilean youth), 1966-74. Executive director, Fundacion Gulf & Western Dominicana in Dominican Republic, 1973-76. Consultant to Gulf & Western Corp. on educational projects in Dominican Republic. *Member:* Modern Language Association of America, American Association of Teachers of Spanish and Portuguese (president, Indiana chapter, 1946-47), Latin American Studies Association, American Association of University Professors, National Fencing Coaches Association of America, Catholic Association of Foreign Language Teachers (president, 1955), Midwest Modern Language Association, Notre Dame Club of St. Joseph Valley (president, 1943).

WRITINGS: (With Gordon J. Hempel) *The Use of the Foreign Feature-Length Film in a College Community,* University Services (Notre Dame), 1950; (with Charles E. Parnell and M. Raymond) *Elementary Spanish Series,* Allyn & Bacon, Volume I: *Buenos dias,* Volume II: *Venga a ver,* Volume III: *Yo se leer,* Volume IV: *Me gusta leer,* 1961; *The Mexican Novel Comes of Age,* University of Notre Dame Press, 1971; *La novela mexicana: Realidad y valores,* Editorial Diana, 1975. Contributor of articles, on modern languages and literature and Latin American history, and reviews to popular periodicals and scholarly journals.

WORK IN PROGRESS: Research on the Latin American novel, especially Mexican.

*   *   *

LARKIN, Rochelle 1935-
(R. T. Larkin)

PERSONAL: Born May 6, 1935, in Brooklyn, N.Y.; daughter of Moses and Sarah Dorothy (Kramer) Richter; married Tippy Larkin (a musician), November 24, 1965 (divorced, 1977); children: Julie, Kim, Theodore. *Politics:* Democrat. *Religion:* Jewish. *Home:* 351 East 84th St., New York, N.Y. 10028.

CAREER: Countrywide Publications (magazine publisher), New York City, editor, 1963; Kanrom, Inc. (publisher), New York City, editor, 1964-70; Pinnacle Books, New York City, editor, 1970; Lancer Books, New York City, editor-in-chief, 1973.

WRITINGS: Soul Music, Lancer Books, 1970; (with Milburn Smith) *Teen Scene,* Pyramid Publications, 1970; *Supermarket Superman,* Lancer Books, 1971; *The Godmother,* Lancer Books, 1971; *The Beatles,* Scholastic Book Services, 1974; *Hail Columbia,* Arlington House, 1975; (with Robin Moore) *Valency Girl,* Ballantine, 1976; *Harvest of Desire,* New American Library, 1977; (with Moore) *Mafia Wife,* Macmillan, 1977; *Kitty,* Playboy Press, 1977; *Instant Beauty,* Simon & Schuster, 1978; *Mistress of Desire,* New American Library, 1978.

Under name R. T. Larkin: *For Godmother and Country,*

Lancer Books, 1972; *Cherry Delight,* six volumes, Leisure Books, 1974; *Black Magic,* Dell, 1974; *The Raging Flood,* Belmont-Tower, 1975; *Call Me Anytime,* Zebra Publications, 1975; *The Greek Goddess,* Zebra Publications, 1975; *The International Joke Book,* Nordon Publications, 1975; *Pusher: The Dirty World of a Dope Peddler,* Leisure Books, 1975; *The First One,* Belmont-Tower, 1976; *The Sexual Superstars,* Nordon Publications, 1976; *Living Together,* Belmont-Tower, 1976.

WORK IN PROGRESS: Children of Desire, for New American Library.

AVOCATIONAL INTERESTS: Travel, jewelry.

* * *

LARSEN, Charles E(dward) 1923-

PERSONAL: Born January 9, 1923, in San Francisco, Calif.; son of Charles James and Elizabeth (Scully) Larsen; married Grace Hutchison (an academic dean), November 27, 1943; children: Charles Eric, Douglas Edward. *Education:* University of California, Berkeley, A.B. and M.A., 1945; Columbia University, Ph.D., 1952. *Politics:* Democrat. *Home:* 4649 Meldon Ave., Oakland, Calif. 94619. *Office:* Department of History, Mills College, Oakland, Calif. 94613.

CAREER: Rutgers University, Newark, N.J., lecturer, 1947-48, instructor, 1948-52, assistant professor of government, 1952-55; Mills College, Oakland, Calif., assistant professor, 1957-61, associate professor, 1961-67, professor of history and government, 1967-75, May Treat Morrison Professor of American History, 1975—, chairman of social science division, 1960-63. Reader, Educational Testing Service, Princeton, N.J., 1952-54, 1972—. *Member:* Organization of American Historians, American Studies Association, Phi Beta Kappa, Alpha Mu Gamma. *Awards, honors:* Fulbright scholar in Taiwan, 1962.

WRITINGS: (Editor with Harold M. Hyman) *Freedom and Reform: Essays in Honor of Henry Steele Commager,* Harper, 1967; (author of introduction) Ben B. Lindsey and Harvey O'Higgins, *The Beast,* University of Washington Press, 1970; (author of introduction) Lindsey and Wainwright Evans, *The Companionate Marriage,* Arno, 1972; *The Good Fight: The Life and Times of Ben B. Lindsey,* Quadrangle, 1972. Contributor to *Encyclopedia Americana* and *Dictionary of American Biography.* Contributor of articles to *American Journal of Legal History, Pacific Historical Review, Pacific Northwest Quarterly, Journal of American History,* and *American West.*

WORK IN PROGRESS: Westbrook Pegler and American Journalism in the McCarthy Era.

AVOCATIONAL INTERESTS: Travel, conversation, and old movies.

* * *

LARSON, T(aft) A(lfred) 1910-

PERSONAL: Born January 18, 1910, in Wakefield, Neb.; son of Fred and Jennie (Larson) Larson; married Aylein Eckles Hunt, June 11, 1941 (divorced November 11, 1947); married Mary A. Hawkins (a librarian), August 20, 1949; children: (first marriage) Nancy Jo Larson Gennuso; (second marriage) Mary Lou. *Education:* University of Colorado, A.B., 1932, M.A., 1933; University of Chicago, additional study, 1934-35; University of Illinois, Ph.D., 1937; University of London, postdoctoral study, 1937-38. *Home:* 810 Clark St., Laramie, Wyo. 82070. *Office:* Department of

History, University of Wyoming, University Station, Box 3334, Laramie, Wyo. 82070.

CAREER: University of Wyoming, Laramie, 1936—, began as instructor, professor of history, 1948-69, William Robertson Coe Professor of American Studies, 1969-75, professor emeritus, 1975—, head of department, 1948-68, director of School of American Studies, 1959-69. Visiting professor, Columbia University, 1950-51. Elected member, Wyoming State House of Representatives, 1976—. Member U.S. National Commission for UNESCO, 1963-66. *Military service:* U.S. Naval Reserve, 1943-46; became lieutenant. *Member:* American Historical Association, Organization of American Historians, Western History Association (president, 1970-71), Phi Beta Kappa, Phi Kappa Phi, Delta Sigma Phi, Rotary International.

WRITINGS: Wyoming's War Years: 1941-45, University of Wyoming, 1954; *History of Wyoming,* University of Nebraska Press, 1965; (editor) *Bill Nye's Western Humor,* University of Nebraska Press, 1968; *Wyoming: A Bicentennial History,* Norton, 1977.

WORK IN PROGRESS: A revised edition of the *History of Wyoming,* to be published by University of Nebraska Press; a book on the woman's rights movement in western America, completion expected in 1980.

* * *

LARTIGUE, Jacques-Henri 1894-

PERSONAL: Born June 13, 1894, in Courbevoie, France; son of Henry (a financier) and Marie (Haguet) Lartigue; married Madeleine Messager, December 17, 1919; married second wife, Marcelle Paolucci; married third wife, Florette Ormea, August 28, 1945; children: (first marriage) Dany. *Education:* Academic studies at the Sorbonne, University of Paris, and art studies at Atelier Jullian. *Religion:* Roman Catholic. *Home:* 102 rue de Longchamp, Paris 16, France. *Agent:* Candida Donadio & Associates, Inc., 111 West 57th St., New York, N.Y. 10019.

CAREER: Painter, 1916—, with one-man shows in Paris, 1924-39, in France and New York, 1952-65. Collections of his photographs were exhibited at Museum of Modern Art in New York, summer, 1963, in Germany, 1966, London, 1970, and Paris, 1975. *Awards, honors:* Silver Medal of the City of Paris; Chevalier de la legion d'honneur.

WRITINGS: Photographs, Museum of Modern Art, 1963; *Boyhood Photos of J.-H. Lartigue: The Family Album of a Gilded Age,* A. Guichard, 1966, translation by Carla van Splunteren, edited by Richard Avedon, published as *Diary of a Century,* Viking, 1970; *Memoires sans Memoire,* Laffont, 1975; *Jacques-Henri Lartigue et les Femmes,* Dutton, 1975; *J.-H. Lartigue et les Autos,* Chene, 1976.

WORK IN PROGRESS: Journal illustre, with his own photographs, on the years 1902 to 1971.

SIDELIGHTS: In France, Jacques-Henri Lartigue is known primarily as a painter, although he has been a photographer since the age of seven. Reviewing *Diary of a Century,* Cecil Beaton writes, ''It will astonish a great number of people to discover that some of the most far influencing and beautiful photographs of this century were taken by a mere boy.'' He continues: ''Jacques was fascinated by the attempt to catch the feeling of movement. . . . [He] was influenced by nobody. He contrived nothing. . . . His aim was that the picture should come out clearly: it is this utter straight forwardness that gives his work an abiding quality, a quality that by its total reality often becomes mysterious and weird. . . . Altogether this is the most exciting book of photographs that has appeared for many years.''

Lartigue photographed the official portrait of French president Valery Giscard d'Estaing in 1974.

AVOCATIONAL INTERESTS: Tennis, skiing.

BIOGRAPHICAL/CRITICAL SOURCES: Atlantic, June, 1970; *Time,* December 14, 1970; *Books and Bookmen,* June, 1971.

* * *

LaRUSSO, Dominic A(nthony)   1924-
(Jon Domini)

PERSONAL: Born December 29, 1924, in New Rochelle, N.Y.; son of Frank (an engineer) and Anna Marie (Manfredi) LaRusso; married Carol Bruner, June 24, 1945; children: Kim, Mark Anthony. *Education:* University of Washington, Seattle, B.A., 1950, M.A., 1951; Northwestern University, Ph.D., 1956. *Politics:* Independent. *Home:* 244 West 37th Ave., Eugene, Ore. 97405. *Office:* Department of Speech, University of Oregon, Eugene, Ore. 97403.

CAREER: University of Washington, Seattle, assistant professor, 1956-60, associate professor of speech, 1960-68, director, Evening Division, 1963-68; University of Oregon, Eugene, professor of speech, 1968—. Chairman, Oregon State Board of Health. *Military service:* U.S. Cavalry, 1942-44. *Member:* International Communication Association, Renaissance Society, American Association of Teachers of Italian, Speech Communication Association, Phi Beta Kappa. *Awards, honors:* Fulbright award, 1958-59; Sons of Italy research award, 1964; named Oregon State Speaker of the Year, 1975.

WRITINGS: (With John M. Palmer) *Anatomy for Speech and Hearing,* Harper, 1965; (contributor) Horace G. Rahskopf, editor, *Basic Speech Improvement,* Harper, 1965; *Conferences: Models of Muddles,* U.S. Army, 1966; *Basic Skills of Oral Communication,* W. C. Brown, 1967; *Oral Communication in Secondary School Classrooms,* Prentice-Hall, 1970; *Mind the Shadows,* W. C. Brown, 1971; *Parliamentary Procedure Ring,* Academy of Executive Arts, 1973; (contributor) *The Shadows of Communication,* Kendall/Hunt, 1977. Author of poems under the name Jon Domini. Contributor of articles to *Western Speech* and *Speech Monographs,* of poems to *Argus* and *Christianity Today,* and of reviews to *Rhetoric* and *Philosophy.*

WORK IN PROGRESS: A novel, *Signor Leone;* a book of poems, *Presents of Mind;* a book, *Renaissance Rhetoric: Nonverbal Communication for Parents.*

SIDELIGHTS: Dominic LaRusso is an artist, with one-man shows of his work in wood and leather sculpting, and oil and water-color. *Avocational interests:* Piloting, sky-diving, horseback riding, canoeing in the rapids.

* * *

LASSITER, Isaac Steele   1941-

PERSONAL: Born July 4, 1941, in Johnson County, N.C.; son of David Bruce (a farmer) and Mabel (Byrd) Lassiter; married Elsie Bugg (a teacher), June 13, 1970. *Education:* Campbell College, B.S., 1970; further study at East Carolina University, North Carolina State University, and University of North Carolina. *Politics:* Democrat. *Religion:* Missionary Baptist. *Home address:* Route 1, Box 46-C, Boydton, Va. 22917. *Office:* Norfolk Southern Railway Co., Gold St., Chesapeake, Va. 23324.

CAREER: Worked on bridge construction crews in North Carolina and Virginia, 1962-63; Permaline Atlantic Corp., Alexandria, Va., worked in traffic markings and traffic engineering, 1963-65; Victory Van Co., Alexandria, supervisor of mail handling, 1965-66; teacher of language arts in public schools in Johnson County, N.C., 1966-71; Norfolk Southern Railway Co., Norfolk, Va., maintenance of way workman, 1971-74, track foreman, 1974—. *Member:* International Poetry Society, World Poetry Society, North Carolina Poetry Society, Florida State Poetry Society.

WRITINGS: The Owl's Nest Betrayal (poems), Editions, 1971. Contributor to anthologies and to small literary journals.

WORK IN PROGRESS: Short stories, poems, and a collection of poems.

SIDELIGHTS: Isaac Lassiter told *CA:* "The organization of words used to communicate has appealed to me ever since I can recall. Early in my life I learned I could be more effective and convincing by writing my thoughts and emotions than in oral articulation. Gradually I learned to be more disciplined and subjective in ordering experiences and thoughts on paper. My creative writings reflect my growth as a writer, and in time I believe they will be more successful and artistically mature." Lassiter comments further, "My view of the contemporary literary scene is there are times and places for all aspiring efforts and contributions, both traditional and experimental. Knowledge of the traditional is helpful for understanding the experimental because a writer needs to know from what he is deviating. Perhaps simplifying the traditional, even if disjointedly, reflects growth and change, and therefore enhances the cultural aspects of our current era. Changing a foundation is not worthwhile if the result fails to accommodate and gratify."

AVOCATIONAL INTERESTS: Listening to American folk music, hiking in wooded areas, visiting historical places and museums, and studying the customs and language patterns used in various levels of society.

* * *

LASSON, Kenneth (Lee)   1943-

PERSONAL: Surname is pronounced *Las*-son; born March 24, 1943, in Baltimore, Md.; son of Nelson Bernard (an attorney and professor) and Nanette (Macht) Lasson. *Education:* Johns Hopkins University, A.B., 1963, M.A., 1967; University of Maryland, J.D., 1966. *Home:* 3808 Menlo Dr., Baltimore, Md. 21215. *Office:* School of Law, University of Baltimore, Baltimore, Md. 21201.

CAREER: Constitutional Convention Commission of Maryland, Baltimore, research assistant, 1966; Johns Hopkins University, Baltimore, teaching fellow and lecturer, 1966-68; University of Maryland, Baltimore, assistant to Dean of School of Law, 1967-69; Ralph Nader's Center for the Study of Responsive Law, Washington, D.C., editorial and administrative consultant, 1969—; Goucher College, Towson, Md., lecturer in English, 1970-72, assistant to president, 1970-71; University of Baltimore, School of Law, Baltimore, assistant professor of law, 1977—. Assistant professor of political science and communication arts, and affirmative action officer, Loyola College, Baltimore. Member of board of directors, Center for Science in the Public Interest. *Member:* Maryland Bar, American Civil Liberties Union (member of legal panel, Maryland chapter).

WRITINGS: The Workers: Portraits of Nine American Jobholders (afterword by Ralph Nader), Viking, 1971;

Proudly We Hail: Profiles of Public Citizens in Action, Viking, 1975; _Private Lives of Public Servants,_ Indiana University Press, 1978. Contributor of articles to _Atlantic Monthly,_ to law journals, research documents, and poetry magazines. Contributing editor to _Washingtonian_ magazine.

WORK IN PROGRESS: Muriel the Oriole, a children's book on environmental problems; _Bo Williams' Diary,_ a book about prison life; various articles and anthologies.

AVOCATIONAL INTERESTS: Tennis, softball, pencil sketching, metal sculpture, travel.

* * *

LATHAM, Aaron 1943-

PERSONAL: Born October 3, 1943, in Spur, Tex.; son of Clyde C. and Launa (Cozby) Latham. _Education:_ Amherst College, B.A., 1966; Princeton University, Ph.D., 1970. _Home:_ 2801 New Mexico Ave. N.W., Washington, D.C. 20007. _Agent:_ Sterling Lord Agency, 660 Madison Ave., New York, N.Y. 10022.

CAREER: Washington Post, Washington, D.C., reporter, 1969-71; _Esquire,_ New York, N.Y., associate editor, 1971-74. _Member:_ Phi Beta Kappa.

WRITINGS: Crazy Sundays: F. Scott Fitzgerald in Hollywood, Viking, 1971; _Orchids for Mother,_ Little, Brown, 1977. Contributor to _Harper's_ and _New York Times Magazine._

WORK IN PROGRESS: A biography of Jack Kerouac.

SIDELIGHTS: Aaron Latham spent 1961 in Germany as an exchange student with the American Field Service, and did further traveling through Europe while studying at the University of Montpelier in 1963-64. He says that he "has done a lot of marching: the 1967 March on the Pentagon, the 1969 People's Park March in Berkeley, the Moratorium marches in Washington in the fall of 1969."

BIOGRAPHICAL/CRITICAL SOURCES: New York Review of Books, January 27, 1972.†

* * *

LATTIN, Harriet Pratt 1898-

PERSONAL: Born November 29, 1898, in Corning, N.Y.; daughter of Harry Hayt (a newspaper editor and congressman) and Clarissa C. (Spencer) Pratt; married Norman D. Lattin (a professor of law), June 18, 1918; children: Philip Norman. _Education:_ Smith College, A.B., 1920; further study at University of Michigan, 1923-24; Ohio State University, M.A., 1926, Ph.D., 1928. _Politics:_ Republican. _Religion:_ Congregationalist. _Home:_ 16017 110th Ave., Sun City, Ariz. 85351.

CAREER: Teacher of mathematics, English, and biology in Corning, N.Y., 1920-22; teacher of history, chemistry, and Latin in high school in Chelsea, Mich., 1922-24; Denison University, Granville, Ohio, assistant professor of English and European history, 1929; U.S. Army, Chemical Warfare Services, Columbus, Ohio, inspector, 1943. _Member:_ American Historical Association, Mediaeval Academy of America, History of Science Society, International Society of Planetarium Educators, Phi Beta Kappa, Sigma Alpha Iota.

WRITINGS: The Peasant Boy Who Became Pope: Story of Gerbert, Henry Schuman, 1951; _The Letters of Gerbert with His Papal Privileges as Sylvester II,_ Columbia University Press, 1961; _Star Performance,_ Whitmore, 1969; _Brick and the Abacus,_ Vantage, 1977. Contributor to scholarly journals in the United States and abroad and to _Encyclopaedia Britannica._

WORK IN PROGRESS: Studying history of astronomy and of mediaeval Spanish libraries; research on biographies of Gerbert and Emperor Otto III.

AVOCATIONAL INTERESTS: Playing chamber music on the viola.

* * *

LAUMANN, Edward O. 1938-

PERSONAL: Born August 31, 1938, in Youngstown, Ohio; son of Otto (an investment counselor) and Emalyn (Bauch) Laumann; married Susan Gene Kroto, August 8, 1964; children: Eric Kroto, Lisa Anne. _Education:_ Oberlin College, A.B. (summa cum laude), 1960; Harvard University, A.M., 1962, Ph.D., 1964. _Home:_ 6754 South Euclid, Chicago, Ill. 60649. _Office:_ Department of Sociology, University of Chicago, 1126 East 59th St., Chicago, Ill. 60637.

CAREER: U.S. Bureau of the Census, Washington, D.C., analytical statistician, summers, 1960-62; University of Michigan, Ann Arbor, assistant professor, 1964-69, associate professor of sociology, 1969-73, acting associate chairman of department, 1968-69, director of Center for Research on Social Organization, 1971-73; University of Chicago, Chicago, Ill., professor of sociology and director of Center for Social Organization Studies, 1973—. Faculty research fellow, University of Cologne, 1970-71; visiting professor, University of Kent, 1971. Member of sociology panel, National Science Foundation. _Member:_ International Sociological Association, American Association for the Advancement of Science, American Sociological Association (fellow), Sociological Research Association, Phi Beta Kappa. _Awards, honors:_ Woodrow Wilson fellowship, 1960; Horace H. Rackham faculty research grant, 1965-67, travel and research grant, 1970-71; National Institute of Mental Health grant, 1967-68; National Science Foundation grants, 1968-70, 1972-77; Ford Foundation research grant to work in Germany and England, 1970-71.

WRITINGS: Prestige and Association in an Urban Community, Bobbs-Merrill, 1966; (with Paul Siegel and Robert W. Hodge) _The Logic of Social Hierarchies,_ Markham, 1970; _Stratification Theory and Research,_ Bobbs-Merrill, 1970; _Bonds of Pluralism: The Form and Substance of Urban Social Networks,_ Wiley Interscience, 1973; (with Franz U. Poppi) _Networks of Collective Action: A Perspective on Community Influence Systems,_ Academic Press, 1976. Contributor of over twenty-five articles and reviews to social science journals. Associate editor, _Sociological Inquiry,_ 1967—, _American Sociological Review,_ 1970-72, and _American Journal of Sociology,_ 1974-76.

WORK IN PROGRESS: With John P. Heinz, an intensive study of the sociology of the legal profession in Chicago and the politics of the organized bar; in collaboration with Peter Marsden and Joseph Galaskiewicz, a comparative study of elite decision-making in two Illinois communities.

* * *

LAURENCE, Michael M(arshall) 1940-

PERSONAL: Born May 22, 1940, in New York, N.Y.; son of Frank M., Jr. (a minor capitalist) and Edna (Roeder) Laurence; married Patricia McDonald, March 1, 1969; children: Elizabeth Sarah, John Marshall. _Education:_ Harvard University, B.A., 1963. _Residence:_ Chicago, Ill.

CAREER: Memphis Press-Scimitar, Memphis, Tenn., reporter, 1959-62; _Advance_ magazine, Washington, D.C., managing editor, 1960-63; _Playboy_ magazine, Chicago, Ill., assistant editor, 1963-64, associate editor, 1964-66, senior editor, 1966-72; *OUI* magazine, managing editor, 1972-75. *Member:* Harvard Club, Playboy Club, Collectors Club of Chicago. *Awards, honors:* G. M. Loeb Magazine Award, University of Connecticut, for best magazine article of a business or financial subject, 1969, for article "Playboy Plays the Commodities Market"; Elliott Perry Cup, 1975, for distinguished postal history research.

WRITINGS: Playboy's Investment Guide, Playboy Press, 1971. Also editor, *U.S. Mail and Post Office Assistant,* 1975. Contributor to *Playboy* and *New York Times Magazine.*

WORK IN PROGRESS: Researching a book about the U.S. ten cent postage stamp of 1869.

* * *

LAUX, James M(ichael)   1927-

PERSONAL: Born November 4, 1927, in La Crosse, Wis.; son of William M. and Clara (Smelser) Laux; married Barbara Robertson, 1952; children: Robert, Stephen, Frederick. *Education:* Attended State Teachers College (now University of Wisconsin—La Crosse), 1946-48; University of Wisconsin—Madison, B.S., 1950; University of Connecticut, M.A., 1952; Northwestern University, Ph.D., 1957. *Residence:* Cincinnati, Ohio. *Office:* History Department, University of Cincinnati, Cincinnati, Ohio 45221.

CAREER: Wisconsin State College—La Crosse (now University of Wisconsin—La Crosse), instructor in history, 1955-57; University of Cincinnati, Cincinnati, Ohio, assistant professor, 1957-64, associate professor, 1964-69, professor of history, 1969—. *Military service:* U.S. Naval Reserve, 1945-46. *Member:* American Historical Association, Society for French Historical Studies, Association des Amis du Musee de l'Air, Society of Automotive Historians, Woodside Philosophical Society.

WRITINGS: Wars, Crises and Transformation, privately printed, 1961; (translator) R. Remond, *The Right Wing in France,* University of Pennsylvania Press, 1966, 2nd edition, 1969; (editor with F. Kafker) *The French Revolution: Conflicting Interpretations,* Random House, 1968, 2nd edition, 1976; *In First Gear: The French Automobile Industry to 1914,* McGill-Queens University Press, 1976. Contributor of articles to *French Historical Studies, The French Review, Business History,* and *Le Mouvement Social.*

WORK IN PROGRESS: A translation of Albin Michel's *La Revolution Automobile,* with P. Fridenson and others.

* * *

LaVALLE, Irving H(oward)   1939-

PERSONAL: Surname is accented on second syllable; born April 24, 1939, in Hancock, N.Y.; son of Irving Howard (a physician) and Louise (Wood) LaValle; married Julia Baltazzi, August 21, 1965 (separated). *Education:* Trinity College, Hartford, Conn., B.A., 1960; Harvard University, M.B.A., 1965, D.B.A., 1966. *Politics:* Republican. *Religion:* Episcopalian. *Home:* 726 Foucher St., New Orleans, La. 70115. *Office:* Department of Management Science, Tulane University, New Orleans, La. 70118.

CAREER: Abbott, Proctor & Paine, New York, N.Y., security analyst, 1960-61; Tulane University, New Orleans, La., assistant professor, 1965-68, associate professor, 1968-71, professor of management science, 1971—, secretary of university senate, 1975-78. Former director, Management Optimization Systems, Inc. Consultant on analysis of complex decision problems under uncertainty. *Member:* American Mathematical Society, American Statistical Association, American Economic Association, Institute of Management Science, Institute of Mathematical Statistics, Operations Research Society of America, Royal Statistical Society, Econometric Society, Phi Beta Kappa, Pi Gamma Mu, Beta Gamma Sigma, Audubon Golf Club.

WRITINGS: An Introduction to Probability, Decision, and Inference, Holt, 1970; *Fundamentals of Decision Analysis,* Holt, 1977. Contributor to operations research and statistical journals.

* * *

LAVIN, J(oseph) A(nthony)   1932-

PERSONAL: Born January 20, 1932, in Wigan, England; son of Joseph P. (a teacher) and Mary (Sharkey) Lavin. *Education:* University of Birmingham, B.A., 1954, Ph.D., 1963. *Office:* Department of English, University of British Columbia, Vancouver 8, British Columbia, Canada.

CAREER: University of Iowa, Iowa City, instructor in English, 1956-60; University of British Columbia, Vancouver, professor of English, 1962—. Executive secretary, World Shakespeare Congress of 1971. *Member:* Modern Language Association of America, Bibliographical Society, Renaissance English Text Society, Association of Canadian University Teachers of English, Canadian Association of University Teachers, Philological Association of the Pacific Coast, Bibliographical Society of University of Virginia. *Awards, honors:* Canada Council leave fellowship.

WRITINGS: (Editor) Robert Greene, *The Scottish History of James IV,* Benn, 1967; (editor) William Shakespeare, *Twelfth Night,* Macmillan, 1968; (editor) Greene, *Friar Bacon and Friar Bungay,* Benn, 1969, Norton, 1976. Contributor to academic journals.

WORK IN PROGRESS: English Printers' Ornaments, Volume I, 1475-1557.†

* * *

LAWFORD, J(ames) P(hilip)   1915-

PERSONAL: Born December 29, 1915, in Peking, China; son of Lancelot Henry (an officer in the Chinese Maritime Customs) and Laura Hamilla (Taylor) Lawford; married Joan Mary Spencer, December 16, 1944; children: Nigel Philip Charles, Diana Mary, Sylvia Hamilla. *Education:* Cambridge University, M.A., 1937. *Religion:* Church of England. *Home:* Shapley Heath, Winchfield, Basingstoke, Hampshire, England. *Agent:* Herbert van Thal, London Management, 235-241 Regent St., London W1A 2JT, England. *Office:* Officers' Mess, Royal Military Academy, Sandhurst, Camberley, Surrey, England.

CAREER: Indian Army, infantry officer, 1937-47, serving in India and Far East; British Army officer, 1947-61, serving in North Africa and Middle East and retiring as lieutenant colonel, 1961; Royal Military Academy, Sandhurst, Camberley, England, 1967—, began as senior lecturer in international affairs, currently senior lecturer in communication. *Member:* Royal Commonwealth Society, Officers' Club (Aldershot). *Awards, honors:* Military Cross.

WRITINGS: (Editor with W. E. Catto) *Solah Punjab: The History of the 16th Punjab Regiment,* Gale & Polden, 1967; (with Peter Young) *Charge: Or How to Play War Games,* A. S. Barnes, 1969; (editor with Young) *History of the British Army,* Putnam, 1970; *History of the 30th Punjabis,* Osprey, 1972; *History of the Battle of Salamanca,* Allen &

Unwin, 1973; *Wellington's Peninsula Army,* Osprey, 1973; *The Battle of Vitoria 1813,* Knight & Co., 1973; *Clive: Proconsul of India,* Allen & Unwin, 1976; (editor and contributor) *The Cavalry,* Bobbs-Merrill, 1976.

WORK IN PROGRESS: A book on Napoleon's last three campaigns; a book on Britain's army in India from its origins to the Battle of Buxar, 1764.

*   *   *

LAWRENCE, Margaret Morgan   1914-

PERSONAL: Born August 19, 1914, in New York, N.Y.; daughter of Sandy Alonzo (a clergyman) and Mary (a teacher; maiden name, Smith) Morgan; married Charles R. Lawrence II (a college professor), June 5, 1938; children: Charles R. III, Sara Lawrence Lightfoot, Paula Lawrence Wehmiller. *Education:* Cornell University, A.B., 1936; Columbia University, M.D., 1940, M.S., 1943, Certificate in Psychoanalysis, 1951. *Home:* 34 Dogwood Lane, North Pomona, N.Y. 10970. *Office:* College of Physicians and Surgeons, Columbia University, New York, N.Y. 10027.

CAREER: Licentiate, American Board of Pediatrics, 1948; Meharry Medical College, Nashville, Tenn., instructor, 1943-44, assistant professor, 1944-45, associate professor of pediatrics, 1945-47; New York State Psychiatric Institute and Hospital, New York City, resident in psychiatry, 1948-51; Council Child Development Center, New York City, fellow in child psychiatry and staff pediatrician, 1949-51; Northside Child Development Center, New York City, staff therapist, 1951-54; Columbia University, College of Physicians and Surgeons, New York City, assistant in psychiatry, 1951-56; Rockland County (N.Y.) Center for Mental Health, associate director in charge of children's therapy, 1954-57; Rockland County Community Mental Health Board, director of School Mental Health Unit, 1957-63; medical director, Day Treatment Center, Rockland County Organization for Mentally Ill Children, 1962-68; director, Child Development Center, Pomona, N.Y., 1968—; practicing child psychiatrist and psychoanalyst in Pomona, 1951—; Columbia University, College of Physicians and Surgeons, associate clinical professor of psychiatry, 1975—. Supervising child psychiatrist, Developmental Clinic, Division of Child Psychiatry, Harlem Hospital Center, 1963—. Psychiatric consultant to various schools, colleges, and hospitals, 1952—.

MEMBER: American Psychoanalytic Association, American Psychiatric Association (fellow), American Academy of Psychoanalysis (fellow), American Orthopsychiatric Association (fellow and member of board of directors), New York State Committee for Children, Standing Committee, Diocese of New York, Episcopal Church. *Awards, honors:* Rosenwald fellow, 1942-43; National Research Council fellow, 1947-48; Mental Health Act fellow, U.S. Public Health Service, 1948-50.

WRITINGS: (Contributor) *Current Psychiatric Therapies,* Grune, 1968; *Mental Health Team in the Schools,* Behavioral Publications, 1971; *Young Inner City Families: The Development of Ego Strength under Stress,* Human Sciences Press, 1971. Contributor of articles to *Comprehensive Psychiatry, American Journal of Orthopsychiatry,* and other professional journals.

WORK IN PROGRESS: Infant Caretaker Interaction in an Inner City Community.

LAWRENCE, William Howard   1916-1972

January 29, 1916—March 2, 1972; American journalist and political commentator. Obituaries: *New York Times,* March 3, 1972; *Washington Post,* March 4, 1972; *Newsweek,* March 13, 1972; *Time,* March 13, 1972.

*   *   *   .

LAWTON, Harry Wilson   1927-

PERSONAL: Born December 3, 1927, in Long Beach, Calif.; son of Harry Wilson (a salesman) and Ruhamah (Hedges) Lawton; married Georgeann Leona Honegger, August 7, 1952; children: Deborah, George, Daniel, Jonathan, Richard. *Education:* Riverside City College, A.A., 1948; attended University of California, Berkeley, 1948-50; University of California, Riverside, B.A., 1969. *Politics:* Democrat. *Home:* 795 Spruce St., Riverside, Calif. 92507. *Agent:* Gordon Molson, 9418 Wilshire Blvd., Beverly Hills, Calif. 90212. *Office:* Dean's Office, College of Natural and Agricultural Sciences, University of California, Riverside, Calif. 92502.

CAREER: San Clemente Sun (weekly newspaper), San Clemente, Calif., editor, 1953-54; Press-Enterprise Co., Riverside, Calif., bureau chief in Banning, Calif., 1954-56, chief special feature writer and general assignment reporter, *Daily Enterprise,* 1956-60; Lockheed Propulsion Co., Redlands, Calif., technical editor, 1960-62, supervisor of editing, 1962-64; free-lance writer, 1964-65; University of California, Riverside, principal editor, Department of Horticulture, 1965-70, administrative analyst, Dean's Office, College of Natural and Agricultural Sciences, 1970—. Lecturer in creative writing, University of California. Owner and operator, with F. W. Howton, of The Haunted Bookshop, Berkeley, Calif., 1951-53. Part-time public relations representative, Riverside City Schools, 1956-60; member of board of directors, Malki Museum Inc., Morongo Indian Reservation, Banning, Calif., 1965—. Chairman of editorial board, Malki Museum Press, 1965—.

AWARDS, HONORS: Winner of journalism awards from California Newspaper Publisher's Association, 1953, Twin Counties Press Club, Riverside, Calif., 1958, and Twin Counties Press Club and San Bernardino Counties, 1959; Editorial Citation first prize, California Newspaper Publisher's Association, 1954, for six-part series on life and times of Sadakichi Hartmann, 1957, for series on Mexican-American and Negro housing problems, and 1959, for series (with Al Perrin) on vice in Tijuana, Mexico; California State Fair Gold Medal, 1959, for series on vice in Tijuana; James D. Phelan Award in Literature, and Southwest Literature Award, both 1960, for *Willie Boy: A Desert Manhunt.*

WRITINGS: Willie Boy: A Desert Manhunt, Paisano, 1960, reissued as *Tell Them Willie Boy Is Here,* Award Books, 1969; (editor and author of introduction and bibliography) *Wallace W. Elliott's History of San Bernardino and San Diego Counties, 1882,* Riverside Museum Press, 1965; (author of introduction with Lowell John Bean and William Bright) David Prescott Barrows, *The Ethnobotany of the Coahuilla Indians of California,* Malki Museum Press, 1967; (contributor) Walter Reuther, editor, *The Citrus Industry,* Volume I, Division of Agricultural Sciences, University of California, Berkeley, 1967; (editor with George Knox) Sadakichi Hartmann, *White Chrysanthemums: Literary Fragments and Pronouncements,* forword by Kenneth Rexroth, Herder & Herder, 1971; (editor with Knox) Hartmann, *Confucius, Buddha, and Christ: Three Prophetic Plays,* Herder & Herder, 1971; (editor with Philip Wilke)

The Expedition of Captain J. W. Davidson from Fort Tejon to the Owens Valley in 1859, Ballena, 1976; (editor with Knox) Hartmann, *The Valiant Knights of Daguerre: Selected Critical Essays on Photography and Profiles of Photographic Pioneers,* University of California Press, 1977.

Booklets: (With Lowell John Bean) *The Cahuilla Indians of Southern California,* Malki Museum Press, 1965; *A Bibliography of the Cahuilla Indians of California,* Malki Museum Press, 1967; (editor with Esther Klotz and Joan Hall) *A History of Citrus in the Riverside Area,* Riverside Museum Press, 1968. Contributor of articles to *Indian Historian, Proceedings* of the Southwestern Anthropological Association, and other journals; contributor of short stories to *Mosaic, Chicago, Magazine of Fantasy and Science Fiction,* and *Occident.* Editor and contributor, with Knox, *Sadakichi Hartmann Newsletter,* 1969-1975; managing editor and contributor, *Journal of California Anthropology,* 1974—.

WORK IN PROGRESS: A biography of Sadakichi Hartmann.

SIDELIGHTS: A collector of Western Americana and student of anthropology and history for many years, Harry Lawton first heard legendary accounts of the 1909 Willie Boy manhunt from Cahuilla Indian friends on the Morongo Reservation in Banning, Calif. during the late 1950's. He was "fascinated by the power of the legend and its survival as an affair of historical significance in the minds of the participants. The story had a certain archetypal quality and to the Indians the death of Willie Boy by his own hand represented a last victory over the white man's world." For three years Lawton researched "California's last western manhunt; the result was publication of his first book in 1960, and the Universal release in 1970 of the film version, "Tell Them Willie Boy Is Here." Lawton is presently engaged in writing a biography of Sadakichi Hartmann, working closely with Mrs. Wistaria Linton, Hartmann's daughter, in assembling the letters, manuscripts, and papers of her father.

* * *

LAY, S(amuel) Houston 1912-

PERSONAL: Born January 31, 1912, in Virden, Ill.; son of S. H. and Pearl (Jones) Lay; married Eleanore Erikson, September 9, 1939; children: Samuel Houston III. *Education:* Blackburn College, A.A., 1932; University of Illinois, B.A., 1935, J.D., 1937; Columbia University, LL.M., 1938; U.S. Foreign Service Institute, Certificate, 1939. *Politics:* Republican. *Religion:* Protestant. *Home:* 3882 Liggett Dr., San Diego, Calif. 92106. *Office:* School of Law, California Western University, San Diego, Calif. 92106.

CAREER: Admitted to the Bar of the State of Illinois, 1937; also admitted to Court of Claims Bar, District of Columbia, Court of Military Appeals, and U.S. Supreme Court Bar; U.S. Government attorney, 1938-42; U.S. Department of State, Washington, D.C., international lawyer with office of U.S. High Commissioner for Germany, 1946-54, deputy director, Office of Special Consular Services, 1954-55, Foreign Service inspector, 1955-58, principal officer in Hong Kong, 1959-62; American Bar Foundation, Chicago, Ill., director of international law program, 1962-67; California Western University, School of Law, San Diego, professor of international law, 1967—. *Military service:* U.S. Naval Reserve, active duty, 1942-46; became commander.

MEMBER: American Society of International Law, American Foreign Service Association, Inter-American Bar Association, International Bar Association, Illinois Bar Association, San Diego County Bar Association, Phi Alpha Delta, Phi Rho Pi.

WRITINGS: (With Howard Taubenfeld) *Law of Man's Activities in Space,* University of Chicago Press, 1970; *New Directions in Law of the Sea,* six volumes, Oceana, 1972-77. Contributor of articles on international law to legal publications.

WORK IN PROGRESS: A multivolume work, *New Directions in International Air Law.*

* * *

LAZAREFF, Pierre 1907-1972

April 16, 1907—April 21, 1972; French publisher and editor. Obituaries: *New York Times,* April 21, 1972; *Washington Post,* April 22, 1972; *Newsweek,* May 1, 1972; *Time,* May 1, 1972.

* * *

LEBRA, William P(hilip) 1922-

PERSONAL: Born September 2, 1922, in St. Paul, Minn.; son of William Charles (a lawyer) and Stella (Welker) Lebra; married Takie Sugiyama (an associate professor of anthropology), April 25, 1963. *Education:* University of Minnesota, B.A., 1948, M.A., 1949; Harvard University, Ph.D., 1958. *Home:* 3625 Woodlawn Terrace Pl., Honolulu, Hawaii 96822. *Office:* University of Hawaii, 2424 Maile Way, N. 704, Honolulu, Hawaii 96822.

CAREER: University of Pittsburgh, Pittsburgh, Pa., instructor, 1957-58, assistant professor of anthropology, 1958-61; University of Hawaii, Honolulu, visiting scholar at East West Center, 1961-62, associate professor, 1962-64, professor of anthropology, 1964—, director of Social Science Research Institute, 1962-70. Did ethnographic field research on Okinawa, 1953-54, 1956-57, 1960, 1961, 1974. *Military service:* U.S. Army, 1943-46. *Member:* American Anthropological Association (fellow), Royal Anthropological Institute of Great Britain and Ireland (fellow), American Association for the Advancement of Science, American Ethnological Society, Association for Asian Studies, Society for Applied Anthropology, Asiatic Society of Japan, Japanese Society for Ethnology. *Awards, honors:* National Institute of Mental Health research grants, 1959-62, 1967-77.

WRITINGS: (With F. R. Pitts and W. P. Suttles) *Post-war Okinawa,* National Research Council, 1955; *Okinawan Religion,* University Press of Hawaii, 1966; (contributor) William Caudill and Tsung-yi Lin, editors, *Mental Health Research in Asia and the Pacific,* East-West Center, 1969; (contributor) Edward Norbeck and Susan Parman, editors, *The Study of Japan in the Behavioral Sciences,* Rice University Studies, 1970; (editor) *Transcultural Research in Mental Health,* University Press of Hawaii, 1972; *Okinawa no Shukyo to Shakai Kozo,* Kobundo (Tokyo), 1974; (editor with T. S. Lebra) *Japanese Culture and Behavior,* University Press of Hawaii, 1974; (editor) *Youth, Socialization, and Mental Health,* University Press of Hawaii, 1974; (editor) *Culture–Bound Syndromes, Ethnopsychiatry, and Alternate Therapies,* University Press of Hawaii, 1976. Contributor to professional journals.

* * *

Le CAIN, Errol John 1941-

PERSONAL: Surname is pronounced Lee Cane; born March 5, 1941, in Singapore; son of John and Muriel (Kronenburgh) Le Cain; married Dean Alison Thomson, December, 1976. *Education:* Attended St. Joseph's Institution, Singapore. *Religion:* Buddhist. *Home and office:* 14 Douglas Rd., Herne Bay, Kent, England.

CAREER: Richard Williams Studios, London, England, designer and animator, 1965-69; free-lance designer, 1969—, producing animation sequences for television commercials and motion pictures, including "The Apple Trees," "The Spy with a Cold Nose," "Gawain and the Green Knights," "Casino Royale," "Prudence and the Pill," "The Charge of the Light Brigade," and "The Last Valley." Designed sets for the British Broadcasting Corp. television production, "The Snow Queen," 1976. Writer and illustrator of children's books. *Awards, honors:* Top Ten Best Award from *Amateur Cine World,* 1963, for cartoon, "Victoria's Rocking Horse."

WRITINGS—Self-illustrated juveniles: *King Arthur's Sword,* Faber, 1968; *The Cabbage Princess,* Faber, 1969; *The White Cat* (retold), Faber, 1973.

Illustrator: Anthea Davies, *Sir Orfeo,* Faber, 1970; *Rhymes and Verses of Walter de la Mare,* Faber, 1970; *The Faber Book of Songs for Children,* Faber, 1970; Rosemary Harris, *The Child in the Bamboo Grove,* Faber, 1971; *Cinderella,* Faber, 1971; *The Rhyme of the Ancient Mariner,* Arcadia Press, 1971; Daphne Du Maurier, *My Cousin Rachel,* Heron Books, 1971; De Maurier, *The House on the Strand,* Heron Books, 1971; *Let's Find Out about Halloween,* F. Watts, 1971; Helen Cresswell, *The Beachcombers,* Faber, 1971; *Early Britain,* F. Watts, 1972; Herman Wouk, *The Caine Mutiny,* Heron Books, 1972; Kathleen Abell, *King Orville and the Bullfrogs,* Little, Brown, 1972; Anthony Lewis, *The Dragon Kite,* Holt, 1972; Harris, *The King's White Elephant,* Faber, 1973; Harris, *The Lotus and the Grail,* Faber, 1974; John Keats, *The Eve of St. Agnes,* Arcadia Press, 1974; Elaine Andrews, *Judge Poo and the Mystery of the Dream,* Macmillan, 1974; Harris, *The Flying Ship,* Faber, 1975; Brothers Grimm, *Thorn Rose,* Faber, 1975; Dorothy Van Woerkom, *The Rat, the Ox, and the Zodiac,* Crown, 1976; Walter Pater, *Cupid and Psyche,* Faber, 1977; Brian Patten, *The Sly Cormorant,* Kestrel, 1977.

WORK IN PROGRESS: Designs for a BBC-TV Christmas production of "The Light Princess" (a combination of drawings, cartoons, and acting); illustrations for "The Beauty and the Beast," retold by Rosemary Harris, for Faber; illustrations for Hans Christian Anderson's "The Snow Queen," for Kestrel.

SIDELIGHTS: Errol Le Cain was born in Singapore, and spent his childhood in the Far East. He lived in India for five years, and has traveled extensively through Japan, Hong Kong, and Saigon.

BIOGRAPHICAL/CRITICAL SOURCES: Times Literary Supplement, April 16, 1970; *Graphis,* 1971/72; *She,* October, 1972.

* * *

LECHNER, Robert F(irman) 1918-

PERSONAL: Born February 11, 1918, in Nebraska City, Neb.; son of John George (a railroad employee) and Mary (Tongish) Lechner. *Education:* St. Joseph's College, Rensselaer, Ind., A.B., 1942; University of Fribourg, Ph.D., 1950. *Home:* Carthagena Station, Celina, Ohio 45822. *Office:* Department of Philosophy, DePaul University, Chicago, Ill. 60614.

CAREER: Roman Catholic priest, ordained, 1946; St. Jo-

seph's College, Rensselaer, Ind., 1950-59, became professor of philosophy and head of department; St. Charles Seminary, Celina, Ohio, professor of philosophy, 1959-67; DePaul University, Chicago, Ill., professor of philosophy, 1967—. *Member:* American Philosophical Association, American Catholic Philosophical Association (president, 1960).

WRITINGS: The Aesthetic Experience, Regnery, 1953. Also author of *Doors to the Sacred,* Pio Decimo. Founder and editor, *Philosophy Today,* 1957—.

WORK IN PROGRESS: A critical anthology of writings of contemporary French philosophers.

* * *

LECLERC, Ivor 1915-

PERSONAL: Born February 9, 1915, in South Africa; now a British citizen; married Joan Pirie, September 6, 1975. *Education:* University of South Africa, B.A., 1941; University of Cape Town, M.A., 1946; King's College, London, Ph.D., 1949. *Office:* Department of Philosophy, Emory University, Atlanta, Ga. 30322.

CAREER: University of London, London, England, extension lecturer, 1949-50; University of Glasgow, Glasgow, Scotland, lecturer in aesthetics, 1950-55, lecturer in logic and metaphysics, 1956-61, senior lecturer, 1962-64; Emory University, Atlanta, Ga., visiting professor, 1963-64, professor of philosophy, 1964—. Assistant secretary for London Services Education Committee, and lecturer at London County Council Evening Institute, 1949-50. Visiting professor of philosophy, Bonn University, 1961 and 1973. *Military service:* South African Armed Forces, 1941-45; became captain. *Member:* American Philosophical Association, Metaphysical Society of America, Royal Institute of Philosophy, Kant-Gesellschaft, Cottfried-Wilhelm-Liebniz-Gesellschaft, International Society for Metaphysics, American Association of University Professors, Southern Society for Philosophy and Psychology, Georgia Philosophical Society (president, 1965-66), University Center for Rational Alternatives (president, Emory chapter, 1970-72). *Awards, honors:* Leverhulme research award; Carnegie Trust for Universities of Scotland award and Yale University research award, 1957-58.

WRITINGS: Whitehead's Metaphysics: An Introductory Exposition, Humanities, 1958; (editor and contributor) *The Relevance of Whitehead* (philosophical essays), Humanities, 1961; (translator with Eva Schaper) Gottfried Martin, *An Introduction to General Metaphysics,* Humanities, 1961; (contributor) G. L. Kline, editor, *Alfred North Whitehead: Essays in His Philosophy,* Prentice-Hall, 1963; (contributor) William L. Reese and Eugene Freeman, editors, *Process and Divinity: The Hartshorne Festschrift,* Open Court, 1964; *The Nature of Physical Existence,* Humanities, 1972; *The Philosophy of Leibniz and the Modern World,* Vanderbilt University Press, 1973.

Contributor of articles and essays to numerous philosophical journals, including *Review of Metaphysics, International Philosophical Quarterly, Philosophy, Kant-Studien, Studi Internazionale di Filosofia, Journal of Philosophy,* and to the *Proceedings* of various international philosophy congresses.

WORK IN PROGRESS: A book on metaphysics.

* * *

LECOIN, Louis 1888(?)-1971

1888(?)—June 23, 1971; French editor and pacifist. Obituaries: *New York Times,* June 24, 1971.

* * *

LEDUC, Violette   1907-1972

April 8, 1907—May 28, 1972; French novelist. Obituaries: *New York Times,* May 30, 1972; *Washington Post,* May 30, 1972; *Newsweek,* June 12, 1972; *Time,* June 12, 1972. (See index for *CA* sketch)

* * *

LEE, Alvin A.   1930-

PERSONAL: Born September 30, 1930, in Woodville, Ontario, Canada; son of Norman Osborne and Susanna Elizabeth (Found) Lee; married A. Hope Arnott (an author), December 21, 1958; children: Joanna, Monika, Fiona, Alison, Margaret. *Education:* University of Toronto, B.A., 1953, M.A., 1958, Ph.D., 1961; Emmanuel College, Victoria University, B.D., 1957. *Religion:* Protestant. *Home:* Stormont, West Flamborough, Ontario, Canada L0R 2K0. *Office:* Department of English, McMaster University, Hamilton, Ontario, Canada.

CAREER: McMaster University, Hamilton, Ontario, assistant professor, 1960-66, associate professor, 1966-70, professor of English, 1970—, dean of graduate studies, 1971—, academic vice-president, 1974—. *Member:* Association of Canadian University Teachers of English, Modern Language Association of America, Mediaeval Academy of America, Royal Commonwealth Society (London).

WRITINGS: James Reaney, Twayne, 1968; *The Guest-Hall of Eden: Four Essays on the Design of Old English Poetry,* Yale University Press, 1972; (with wife, Hope Arnott Lee) *Wish and Nightmare,* Harcourt, 1972; (with H. A. Lee) *Circle of Stories,* two volumes, Harcourt, 1972. Also author of *The Garden and the Wilderness,* 1973, *The Temple and the Ruin,* 1973, and *The Peaceable Kingdom,* 1974.

WORK IN PROGRESS: Chief advisory editor for *McMaster Old English Studies and Texts,* for University of Toronto Press.

* * *

LEE, Calvin B. T.   1934-

PERSONAL: Born February 18, 1934, in New York, N.Y.; son of George G. (a restaurateur) and Lin (Hong) Lee; married Audrey Evans; children: Christopher, Craig. *Education:* Columbia University, B.A., 1955, LL.B., 1958; New York University, LL.M., 1965, J.S.D., 1968. *Office:* Prudential Insurance Company of America, Prudential Plaza, Newark, N.J. 07101.

CAREER: Admitted to New York State Bar, 1959; admitted to practice before U.S. Supreme Court, 1966; Columbia University, New York, N.Y., assistant dean of Columbia College, 1961-68; Boston University, Boston, Mass., dean of College of Liberal Arts, 1968-70, executive vice-president, 1970-71; University of Maryland Baltimore County, Baltimore, chancellor, 1971-76; Prudential Insurance Company of America, Newark, N.J., vice-president, 1976—. Staff associate, American Council on Education, 1965-67; assistant director, U.S. Office of Education, Division of College Support, 1967-68.

WRITINGS: Chinese Cooking for American Kitchens, Putnam, 1958; *Chinatown: U.S.A.,* Doubleday, 1965; *One Man, One Vote,* Scribner, 1967; (editor) *Improving College*

Teaching, American Council on Education, 1967; (editor with Charles Dobbins) *Whose Goals for American Higher Education,* American Council on Higher Education, 1968; *The Campus Scene: 1900-1970,* McKay, 1970; (with Alexander Astin) *The Invisible Colleges,* McGraw, 1972; (with Audrey Lee) *The Gourmet Chinese Regional Cookbook,* Putnam, 1976.

SIDELIGHTS: Louis Kronenberger writes in an *Atlantic* review, "The product of considerable research, *The Campus Scene* mixes the essential in themes and movements with the anecdotal and Memory Lane."

BIOGRAPHICAL/CRITICAL SOURCES: Atlantic, October, 1970.

* * *

LEE, Charles   1913-

PERSONAL: Name legally changed in 1938; born January 2, 1913, in Philadelphia, Pa.; son of Benjamin (an accountant) and Lillian (Potash) Levy; divorced; children: Myles Edwin, Gail Margery (Mrs. Richard Snyder). *Education:* University of Pennsylvania, B.A., 1933, M.A., 1936, Ph.D., 1955. *Home:* Presidential Apartments, D., Philadelphia, Pa. 19131. *Office:* Department of English, University of Pennsylvania, Philadelphia, Pa. 19104.

CAREER: Boston Herald–Traveler, Boston, Mass., editor, 1936-40; *Philadelphia Record,* Philadelphia, Pa., editor, 1940-47; *Philadelphia Evening Bulletin,* Philadelphia, contributing editor, 1947-49; University of Pennsylvania, Philadelphia, assistant instructor, 1933-36, lecturer, 1942-55, associate professor, 1955-58, professor of English, 1958—, Annenberg School of Communications, professor of communications and vice dean, 1958-65. Roving critic, WCAU-TV, Philadelphia, 1966-73; entertainment editor, WCAU-Radio, Philadelphia, 1974—. Creative consultant to Four-Star International, Hollywood, Calif. Held one-man art exhibition at the Janet Fleisher Gallery, Philadelphia, 1972. *Member:* American Association of University Professors, Phi Beta Kappa.

WRITINGS: (Self-illustrated) *How to Enjoy Reading,* Waverly House, 1939; *An Almanac of Reading,* Coward, 1940; (editor with others) *North, East, South, West: A Regional Anthology of American Writing,* Howell, Soskin, 1945; *Weekend at the Waldorf* (novelization of the screenplay by Sam and Bella Spewak), Grosset, 1945; (editor) *The Twin Bedside Anthology,* two volumes, Howell, Soskin, 1946; (editor) *Snow Ice, and Penguins: A Cavalcade of Antarctic Adventures,* Dodd, 1950; *The Hidden Public: The Story of the Book-of-the-Month Club,* Doubleday, 1958; (editor) Karl R. Bopp, *The State of the Nation: Retrospect and Prospect,* University of Pennsylvania Press, 1963; *Sevens Come Eleven,* Livingston Press, 1972. Also author of *Exile: A Book of Verse,* 1936, and *I'll Be Waiting,* 1958.

WORK IN PROGRESS: A novel.

* * *

LEE, Janice (Jeanne)   1944-

PERSONAL: Born October 15, 1944, in Hastings, Mich.; daughter of Roger Kenneth (a farmer) and Elsie (Conklin) Davis; married Phillip Lynn Lee (a mobile home salesman), June 17, 1967. *Education:* Western Michigan University, B.A. (magna cum laude), 1966, M.A., 1967. *Politics:* Independent. *Religion:* Protestant. *Home:* 474 Pershing Dr., Mattawan, Mich. 49071.

CAREER: Portage Central High School, Portage, Mich.,

teacher of English and journalism, 1967—. *Member:* National Council of Teachers of English, United Teaching Association, Michigan Council of Teachers of English (member of language and linguistics study committee, 1967-71).

WRITINGS: (With Jean Malmstrom) *Teaching English Linguistically: Principles and Practices for High School,* Appleton, 1971. Contributor to education journals.

*   *   *

LEE, John Eric   1919-

PERSONAL: Born December 12, 1919, in London, England; son of Joseph (a photographer) and Yetta (Kirsch) Lee; divorced. *Education:* University of London, B.A., 1940; Psychology Foundation, Durban, South Africa, Diploma, 1950. *Religion:* Jewish.

CAREER: General manager and chairman, Messrs. Hillman, Millman, Lee & Co. Ltd. (discount stores); self-employed specialist consultant, primarily for retail trade. Organizer of charity theatrical and musical shows. *Member:* British Institute of Management, British Institute of Marketing, Institute of Personnel Management.

WRITINGS: Five Basic Steps in Planned Retail Selling, Pergamon, 1969. Writer of radio scripts; contributor of humorous stories to magazines.

WORK IN PROGRESS: A book on advanced and bolder selling techniques for the retail salesman and the commercial representative.

AVOCATIONAL INTERESTS: Music.††

*   *   *

LEE, Jung Young   1935-

PERSONAL: Born August 20, 1935, in Sunchun, Korea; son of Dong Hi and Induck (Cho) Lee; married Gy Whang, June 6, 1965; children: Sue, Jong. *Education:* Findlay College, B.S., 1957; Garrett Theological Seminary, B.D., 1961; Case Western Reserve University, M.S.L.S., 1962; Boston University, Th.D., 1968. *Home:* 13 Forrest Ct., East Grand Forks, Minn. 56721. *Office:* Department of Religious Studies, University of North Dakota, Grand Forks, N.D. 58202.

CAREER: Ordained Methodist minister, 1961, served churches in Toledo, Cleveland, and Dayton, Ohio; Howard University, Washington, D.C., acting librarian, School of Religion, 1963-64; Otterbein College, Westerville, Ohio, assistant professor of religion and philosophy, 1968-72; University of North Dakota, Grand Forks, 1972—, began as assistant professor, currently associate professor of religious studies. Visiting lecturer in Chinese and Japanese religions, Capital University, 1970. Founder, Foundation for the Continuing Education of Christian Ministers, Inc. Director, Korean Studies Institute in America and Far Eastern Cultural Institute. *Member:* American Academy of Religion, Association for Asian Studies, American Theological Library Association, American Philosophical Association, American Association of University Professors, North American Academy of Ecumenists, Korean Society for Religious Studies in North America (president), Center for the Study of Democratic Institutions, International Platform Association, Ohio West Conference of the United Methodist Church, Martha Kinney Cooper Ohioana Library Association. *Awards, honors:* Senior Fulbright-Hays scholar, 1977.

WRITINGS: The Principle of Changes: Understanding the

"*I Ching,*" University Books, 1971; *The I: A Christian Concept of Man,* Philosophical Library, 1971; *Cosmic Religion,* Philosophical Library, 1973; *God Suffers for Us: A Systematic Inquiry into the Concept of Divine Possibility,* Nijhoff, 1974; *Death and Beyond in the Eastern Perspective: A Study Based on the Bardo Thoedol and the I Ching,* Gordon & Breach, 1974; *The I Ching and Modern Man: Essays on Metaphysical Implications of Change,* University Books, 1975; *Patterns of Inner Process: The Rediscovery of Jesus' Teachings in the I Ching and Preston Herald,* Citadel, 1976; *Sokdam: Capsules of Eastern Wisdom,* Korean Studies Institute in America, 1977; *Korean Shamanistic Rituals,* Mouton, 1977; *The Theology of Change: A Christian Concept of God in Eastern Perspective,* Orbis, 1978.

Contributor to theology and religion journals, including *The Scottish Journal of Theology, The Journal of Religious Thought, Novum Testamentum, Numen: International Review for the History of Religions, International Review of Mission, Current Topics on Contemporary Thought, Systematics, Encounter, Journal of Asian and African Studies, Chinese Culture,* and *Korean Journal.*

WORK IN PROGRESS: Korean Shamanism; "Death Control," to be included in a volume for "Current Topics on Contemporary Thought," a series published by Gordon & Breach; further research on the *I Ching,* "Process of Enlightenment," and myths.

*   *   *

LEE, M(ark) Owen   1930-

PERSONAL: Born May 28, 1930, in Detroit, Mich.; son of Robert L. and Helen (Miller) Lee. *Education:* University of Toronto, B.A., 1953, M.A., 1957; University of St. Michael's College, S.T.B., 1957; University of British Columbia, Ph.D., 1960. *Home and office:* St. Michael's College, University of Toronto, 81 St. Mary St., Toronto, Ontario, Canada M5S 1J4.

CAREER: Roman Catholic priest of Congregation of St. Basil; University of Toronto, St. Michael's College, Toronto, Ontario, lecturer, 1960-63, assistant professor of classics, 1963-68; University of St. Thomas, Houston, Tex., associate professor, 1968-70, professor of classics, 1970-72; Loyola University, Chicago, Ill., associate professor of classics, 1972-75; currently affiliated with St. Michael's College, University of Toronto. *Member:* American Philological Association, American Association of University Professors, American Classical League, Houston Area Teachers of Foreign Languages. *Awards, honors:* Summer session scholarship at American School of Classical studies, Athens, Greece, 1963; Canada Council research grant, 1966.

WRITINGS: Word, Sound, and Image in the Odes of Horace, University of Michigan Press, 1969; *Top Ten: A Personal Approach to the Movies,* Vantage, 1973. Contributor of articles on classical literature and on music to journals in United States, Canada, England, Italy, Denmark, and Germany.

WORK IN PROGRESS: Research on opera and on the Roman poets Horace, Virgil, and Catullus.

SIDELIGHTS: M. Owen Lee is fluent in German, Italian, French, Spanish, modern and classical Greek, and Latin.

BIOGRAPHICAL/CRITICAL SOURCES: Houston Chronicle, September 28, 1969.

LEECING, Walden A. 1932-

PERSONAL: Born September 6, 1932, in Glendale, Calif.; son of Horace W. (a physician and surgeon) and Leona (Dudek) Leecing; married Elizabeth Joan Miller (a teacher), August 16, 1958; children: Jeffrey Scott, Brian Walden. *Education:* University of Redlands, B.A., 1954; Stanford University, M.A., 1956, Ph.D. candidate. *Politics:* Republican. *Religion:* Congregationalist. *Home:* 7540 Northland Ave., San Ramon, Calif. 94583. *Office:* Chabot College, Hayward, Calif. 94545.

CAREER: Santa Ana Senior High School, Santa Ana, Calif., head of drama department, 1959-66; Chabot College, Hayward, Calif., assistant professor, 1970-72, associate professor of language arts, 1972—. Vice-president, Santa Ana Community Players, 1964-66. *Member:* National Council of Teachers of English, American Association of University Professors, Northern California Forensics Association. *Awards, honors:* John Hay-Ford Foundation fellowship, 1963-64; Chabot College faculty research grant to study and analyze students with learning difficulties, 1972; Ernest Crozier Phillips Trophy for outstanding director, 1963; Helena Modjeska Memorial Award, for best actor, 1966; Santa Ana Community Players Award, for actor of the year, 1966.

WRITINGS: (With James Armstrong) *The Curious Eye,* McGraw, 1970. Manuscript reviewer, Cummings Publishing Co., Inc. and Dickenson Publishing Co., Inc.

WORK IN PROGRESS: An anthology of contemporary issues, for Prentice-Hall.

* * *

LEES, Dan 1927-

PERSONAL: Born March 31, 1927, in Manchester, England; son of Edwin Pearson (a rail executive) and Norah (Wilson-Williams) Lees; married Molly Ashworth, October 15, 1955; children: Venetia Elizabeth. *Education:* Attended University of Sheffield, 1948-51. *Politics:* Conservative. *Religion:* Church of England. *Home:* 107 Coronation Rd., Bristol, England. *Office:* British Broadcasting Corp., White Ladies Rd., Bristol, England.

CAREER: Reporter for *Newcastle Chronicle,* Newcastle upon Tyne, England, 1951-55, and *Daily Express,* Manchester, England, 1956-65; free-lance feature writer in southern France, 1965-69; British Broadcasting Corp., Overseas Service, Bristol, England, broadcaster in English, French, and German, 1970—. Has done public relations work in England and France. *Military service:* British Army, Intelligence Corps, 1944-48; became sergeant. *Member:* Crime Writers' Association, National Book League, Western Bookmen, B.B.C. Club, Bristol Literary Society. *Awards, honors:* Lord Kemsley Prize of Kemsley newspapers, for article on Lees' defeat in bout with British middleweight boxing champion.

WRITINGS: The Rainbow Conspiracy, Constable, 1971, Walker & Co., 1972; *Zodiac,* Constable, 1972, Walker & Co., 1973; *Rape of a Quiet Town,* Walker & Co., 1973; *Elizabeth R.I.P.,* Constable, 1974, St. Martin's, 1975.

WORK IN PROGRESS: Our Man in Morton Episcopi; "The Reluctant Jester," a play in three acts for children.

SIDELIGHTS: Dan Lees told *CA:* "I've been writing—for newspapers—since I was at school, but it was Harold Robbins who persuaded me to write books, Irving Wallace who found me an agent and Thornton Wilder who warned me not to tell stories but to write them down. Wilder, who was a marvellous raconteur, explained that all any writer really wants is applause and that once an author has told his story he is reluctant to undertake the chore of putting it on paper. Ever since then I have been getting some of my yarns written down, but, as a story teller and applause seeker, my aim is still to entertain, and although my books contain subliminal warnings and comment these are never allowed to get in the way of the action. My books have been translated into most European languages, which I hope means that more people are being entertained. Meanwhile, I'm still telling more stories than I write—but then, so did Wilder.''

* * *

LE FORT, Gertrud (Petrea) von 1876-1971

October 11, 1876—November 1, 1971; German-Swiss novelist and short story writer. Obituaries: *New York Times,* November 5, 1971. (See index for *CA* sketch)

* * *

LEGTERS, Lyman H(oward) 1928-

PERSONAL: Born February 15, 1928, in Jamestown, N.Y.; son of Lyman H. and Nettie (Saunders) Legters; married Barbara Schoenrock; married second wife, Phyllis Stoneback (a teacher of modern dance), August 4, 1956; children: (second marriage) Lyman Howard, Walter Matthew, Nettie Elisabeth, Douglas Roland. *Education:* University of Michigan, A.B., 1949; Boston University, M.A., 1956; Free University of Berlin, Ph.D., 1958. *Home:* 147 Madrona Pl. E., Seattle, Washington 98112. *Office:* 501 Thomson, University of Washington, Seattle, Wash. 98195.

CAREER: Army Education Center, Berlin, Germany, instructor in American history and English at various periods, 1952-57; University of Pittsburgh, Pittsburgh, Pa., assistant director, Office of Cultural and Educational Exchange, 1958-59; American University, Washington, D.C., associate professor in research and senior research associate, Foreign Areas Studies Division, 1959-62, professorial lecturer, 1962-64; U.S. Office of Education, Washington, D.C., specialist in language and area studies, 1962-64, chief of Language and Area Centers, 1964-65; George Washington University, Washington, D.C., visiting professor, Institute for Sino-Soviet Studies, 1965-66; University of Washington, Seattle, professor of Russian and East European studies, 1966—, associate director of Far Eastern and Russian Institute, and director of Far Eastern and Russian Language and Area Center, 1966-69, chairman of program in social theory, 1974—. Adjunct professor, George Washington University, summer, 1961; professorial lecturer, University of Maryland, 1964-65; visiting professor of history and senior fellow, Russian Institute, Columbia University, 1973. *Military service:* U.S. Army, 1950-53; became sergeant. *Member:* International Society for Comparative Study of Civilization, World Union of Jewish Studies, Institute for the Study of Contemporary Social Problems (fellow), Northwest Dance Foundation (president).

WRITINGS: (Contributor) *Forschungen zur osteuropaeischen Geschichte,* Volume VII, [Berlin] 1959; (with D. N. Bigelow) *NDEA Language and Area Centers,* U.S. Office of Education, 1964; (with Sherman D. Spector) *Checklist of Paperbound Books on Russia and Eastern Europe,* State University of New York, 1966; *Research in the Social Sciences and Humanities,* American Bibliographical Center-Clio Press, 1967; (contributor) Charles Jelavich, editor, *Language and Area Studies: East Central and Southeastern Europe,* University of Chicago Press, 1969; (contributor) Paul Horecky, editor, *East Central Europe: A*

Guide to Basic Publications, University of Chicago Press, 1969; (author of introduction) Peter Sugar, editor, *Native Fascism in the Successor States*, American Bibliographical Center-Clio Press, 1971; (editor) *Essays in Russian History and Literature*, E. J. Brill, 1972. Also editor of *The German Democratic Republic*, 1977.

Co-author of handbooks on Germany, Nigeria, and Brazil, co-editor of handbooks on Columbia and Bolivia, and editor of handbook on Panama published by Foreign Areas Studies Division, American University, 1959-62; editor, "20th Century" series, American Bibliographical Center-Clio Press, 1966—. Contributor to *Sowjetsystem and demokratische Gesellschaft* and to professional journals. Co-editor of special issue of *Annals of the American Academy*, "The Non-Western World in Higher Education," November, 1964; member of advisory board, *Historical Abstracts*.

WORK IN PROGRESS: Writing *East German Higher Education*, a monograph for U.S. Office of Education; *Berlin under the Last Hohenzollerns*, a volume for "Centers of Civilization" series, University of Oklahoma Press; *The Educational Process in Marxist-Leninist Theory; The Global Dimension of Marxism*.

*   *   *

LEHMANN, Winfred P(hilipp) 1916-

PERSONAL: Born June 23, 1916, in Surprise, Neb.; son of Philipp Ludwig and Elenore Friederike (Grosnick) Lehmann; married Ruth Preston Miller, October 12, 1940; children: Terry Jon, Sandra Jean. *Education:* Northwestern College, Watertown, Wis., B.A., 1936; University of Wisconsin, M.A., 1938, Ph.D., 1941. *Home address:* Route 7, Box 524, Austin, Tex. 78703. *Office:* Department of Germanic Languages, University of Texas, Austin, Tex. 78712.

CAREER: Washington University, St. Louis, Mo., instructor, 1946, assistant professor of German, 1946-49; University of Texas at Austin, associate professor, 1949-51, professor of Germanic languages, 1951—, Ashbel Smith Professor, 1963—, chairman of department, 1953-64, director, Linguistics Research Center, 1961—, chairman of department of linguistics, 1964-72. Professor at Linguistic Institute, University of Chicago, 1954; director, Georgetown English Language Program, Ankara, Turkey, and visiting professor of linguistics, Ankara University, 1955-56; visiting professor, Phillipps University, Marburg, Germany, 1964; Collitz Professor, Linguistic Institute, University of Illinois, 1968; associate director, Linguistic Institute, State University of New York, summer, 1976. Member of the linguistic delegation to the People's Republic of China, 1974. *Military service:* U.S. Army, 1942-46; served in Signal Corps.

MEMBER: Linguistic Society of America (vice-president, 1972; president, 1973), Modern Language Association of America (member of executive committee, 1977—), American Council of Learned Societies (member of board of directors), Society for the Advancement of Scandinavian Studies, American Oriental Society, Association for Computational Linguistics (president, 1964), Center for Applied Linguistics (chairman of board of trustees, 1974—), Societe de Linguistique de Paris, Indogermanische Gesellschaft, Linguistic Society of India, Societas Linguisticae Europeae, Early English Text Society, Institut fuer Deutsche Sprache (corresponding fellow), Royal Danish Academy of Sciences (fellow). *Awards, honors:* Fulbright research fellow in Norway, 1950-51; Guggenheim fellow, 1972-73; Brueder-Grimm Prize, University of Marburg, 1974.

WRITINGS: (With Alfred Senn) *A Word Index to Wol-*

fram's "Parzival," University of Wisconsin—Madison, 1938; (with Roe-Merrill S. Heffner) *A Word-Index to the Poems of Walther von der Vogelweide*, University of Wisconsin—Madison, 1940; (with Lloyd Faust) *A Grammar of Formal Written Japanese*, Harvard University Press, 1951; *Proto-Indo-European Phonology*, University of Texas Press and Linguistic Society of America, 1952; *The Alliteration of Old Saxon Poetry* (supplementary volume III to *Norsk Tidsskrift for Sprogvidenskap*), Aschehoug (Oslo), 1953; (with J. L. Dillard) *The Alliterations of the Edda*, Department of Germanic Languages, University of Texas, 1954; *The Development of Germanic Verse Form*, University of Texas Press and Linguistic Society of America, 1956; (with Helmut Rheder and George Schulz-Behrend) *Active German* (elementary reader; includes *Laboratory Handbook* by Gerhard Schmidt and others), Dryden, 1958, 2nd edition, including revised *Handbook*, records, and tapes, published as *Active German Revised*, Holt, 1962; (with Takemitsu Tabusa) *The Alliterations of the Beowulf*, Department of Germanic Languages, University of Texas, 1958; (with Helmut Rehder, L. Shaw, and S. N. Werbow) *Review and Progress in German*, Holt, 1959.

(With Virginia F. Dailey) *The Alliterations of the Christ, Guthlac, Elene, Juliana, Fates of the Apostles, and Dream of the Road*, Department of Germanic Languages, University of Texas, 1960; *Historical Linguistics: An Introduction*, Holt, 1962; *Exercises to Accompany Historical Linguistics: An Introduction*, Holt, 1962, 2nd edition, 1973; (with Helmut Rehder and Hans Beyer) *Spectrum: Modern German Thought in Science, Literature, Philosophy and Art*, Holt, 1964; (with H-J. Hewitt) *Selected Vowel Measurements of American English Speech*, University of Texas, 1965; *Computational Linguistics: Procedures and Problems*, Linguistics Research Center, University of Texas, 1965; (editor and translator) *A Reader in Nineteenth Century Historical Indo-European Linguistics*, Indiana University Press, 1967; (editor and contributor with Yakov Malkiel) *Directions for Historical Linguistics: A Symposium*, University of Texas Press, 1968; *Descriptive Linguistics: An Introduction* (includes *Instructor's Manual*), Random House, 1972, 2nd edition, 1976; (with T. J. O'Hare and Christoph Cobet) *German: Language and Culture* (includes student workbook and teacher's manual), Holt, 1972; *Proto-Indo-European Syntax*, University of Texas Press, 1974; (editor) *Language and Linguistics in the People's Republic of China*, University of Texas Press, 1975; (with wife, R. P. M. Lehmann) *An Introduction to Old Irish*, Modern Language Association of America, 1975.

Contributor: Roe-Merrill S. Heffner, editor, *Collected Indexes to the Works of Wolfram von Eschenbach*, University of Wisconsin Press, 1961; Paul E. Howerton, editor, *Vistas in Information Handling*, Spartan, 1963; Helmut Rehder, editor, *Literary Symbolism*, University of Texas Press, 1965; Henrik Burnbaum and Jaan Puhvel, editors, *Ancient Indo-European Dialects*, University of California Press, 1966; Walter Werner Arndt and others, editors, *Studies in Historical Linguistics in Honor of George Sherman Lane*, University of North Carolina Press, 1967; Allan H. Orrick, editor, *Studies in Honor of Stefan Einarsson*, Mouton, 1968; Charles T. Scott and J. L. Erickson, editors, *Readings for the History of the English Language*, Allyn & Bacon, 1968; Edgar G. C. Polome, editor, *Old Norse Literature and Mythology*, University of Texas Press, 1969; E. B. Atwood and Archibald Anderson Hill, editors, *Studies in Language, Literature and Culture of the Middle Ages, and Later*, University of Texas Press, 1969; Archibald Anderson Hill, editor, *Linguistics Today*, Basic Books, 1969.

Ruke Dravina, editor, *Donum Balticum*, Almquist & Wiksell, 1970; Hreinn Benediktsson, editor, *The Nordic Languages and Modern Linguistics*, Visindafelag Islendinga (Reykjavik), 1970; George Cardona, H. M. Hoenigswald, and Alfred Senn, editors, *Indo-European and Indo-Europeans*, University of Pennsylvania Press, 1970; Maria Tsiapera, editor, *Generative Studies in Historical Linguistics*, Linguistic Research, Inc., 1971; V. Lang and Hans-Gert Roloff, editors, *Dichtung Sprache Gesellschaft*, Athenaeum (Frankfurt), 1971; K. G. Schweisthal, editor, *Grammatik Kybernetik Kommunikation*, Dummler, 1971; W. K. Wimsatt, editor, *Versification: Major Language Types*, New York University Press, 1972; E. S. Firchow and others, editors, *Studies for Einar Haugen*, Mouton, 1972; Frans van Coetsem and Herbert L. Kufner, editors, *Toward a Grammar of Proto-Germanic*, Niemeyer, 1972; John M. Weinstock, editor, *Saga og sprak: Studies in Language and Literature*, Pemberton Press, 1972; *Sprachsystem und Sprachgebrauch*, Schwann, 1974; Charles N. Li, editor, *Word Order Change*, University of Texas Press, 1975; R. Austerlitz, *The Scope of American Linguistics*, Peter de Ridder Press, 1975; C. N. Li, editor, *Subject and Topic*, Academic Press, 1976.

Contributor to *Georgetown Monograph Series on Languages and Linguistics*, published by Institute of Languages and Linguistics, Georgetown University, to *Proceedings* of various international linguistic congresses and institutes, and to *Encyclopedia Americana*. Contributor of essays to numerous scholarly journals, including *American Speech, Language, Modern Language Notes, Germanic Review, Studies in English* (University of Texas), *Studies in Literature and Language, Voprosy Jazykoznanija* (U.S.S.R.), *Zeitschrift fuer Mundartforschung*, and *Publication of the Modern Language Association*; contributor of reviews to *Language, Journal of the American Oriental Society, Romance Philology, Computers and the Humanities*, and other professional journals.

WORK IN PROGRESS: Proto-Indo-European Culture; Types of Language.

* * *

LEHRMANN, Charles C(uno) 1905-1977
(Chanan Lehrmann, Cuno Chanan Lehrmann)

PERSONAL: Born June 15, 1905, in Stryzow, Austria; son of Chaim and Blima (Kranzler) Lehrmann-Frieder; married Graziella Marc Gandolfi (a writer and chief of the European division, Parliament of Luxembourg), April 29, 1937; children: Myriam Mali (Mrs. Uri Be'er). *Education:* Attended Teachers Seminary, Wuerzburg and Rabbinical Seminary, Berlin; University of Wuerzburg, Ph. D., 1932; University of Lausanne, Licence es lettres, 1934; attended Dropsie College for Hebrew and Cognate Learning (now Dropsie University), 1948-49. *Home:* 139 Avenue Fayencerie, Luxembourg.

CAREER: Rabbi in Fribourg, Switzerland, 1936-48; University of Lausanne, Lausanne, Switzerland, lecturer in Jewish and French literature, 1938-48; rabbi in Bristol, Conn., 1948-49; grand rabbi of Luxembourg, 1949-58; Bar-Ilan University, Ramat-Gan, Israel, guest lecturer, 1958-60; senior rabbi of Berlin, Germany, 1960-71, and of Hanover and Lower Saxony, 1971-77; professor of Roman philology, University of Wuerzburg, Wuerzburg, Germany, 1967-77. Secretary, Leo Baeck Federation of Rabbis, 1953-55;

member of board, Conference of German Rabbis, 1967-70. *Awards, honors:* National Award of Grand Duchy of Luxembourg, 1959, for published works and public lectures on Luxembourg history.

WRITINGS—Under name Chanan Lehrmann: *Bergsonisme et Judaisme*, [Geneva], 1937; *L'Element juif dans la litterature francaise*, Editions Die Gestaltung (Zurich and New York), 1941, new edition, Albin Michel (Paris), 1969, translation by George Klin published as *The Jewish Element in French Literature*, Fairleigh Dickinson University Press, 1971; *Das goldene Zeitalter der juedischen Dichtung*, Editions Migdal, 1944; *Stacheldraht um Jacobs Zelte*, Editions Migdal, 1946; *L'Element juif dans le pensee europeene*, Editions du Chant Nouveau, 1947, translation by Klin and Victor Carpenter published as *Jewish Influences on European Thought*, Fairleigh Dickinson University Press, 1976; (with wife, Graziella Lehrmann) *La Communaute juive de Luxembourg dans le passe et dans le present* (title means "The Jewish Community of Luxembourg in the Past and in the Present"), Imprimerie Cooperative Luxembourgeoise, 1953; *Heinrich Heine, Kaempfer und Dichter* (title means "Heinrich Heine, Fighter and Writer"), Francke (Bern), 1957; *L'Ame Luxembourgeoise* (title means "The Luxembourger Soul"), Librairie du Centre (Luxembourg), 1963. Also editor of *Reise in die Vergangenheit*, 1976. Contributor of articles on Jewish literature and other topics to periodicals in Switzerland, France, Germany, United States, and Israel. Editor, *Revue mensuelle pour les communautes Israelites*, 1950-53; co-editor, *Udim* (magazine), 1970-77.

WORK IN PROGRESS: Mirror of a Jewish Family in Our Time; contributions to *The Book of the Jews of Stuttgart, The Book of the Jews of Stryzow,* and *The Book of the Jews of Tuebingen.*

SIDELIGHTS: Charles Lehrmann's literary research was focused on Jewish contributions to Western civilization. He was competent in German, French, Hebrew, Yiddish, Italian, and English. A complete bibliography of his work is being compiled by Lili Zapf of Tuebingen.

(Died September 6, 1977)

* * *

LEIBEL, Charlotte P(ollack) 1899-

PERSONAL: Born July 26, 1899, in Boston, Mass.; daughter of Jacob and Fannie (Fisher) Pollack; married Charles Leibel, December 30, 1931. *Education:* New England School of Law, L.L.B., 1922; also studied psychology at Harvard University, 1930-31, family casework at Simmons College, Boston, Mass., 1928-33, and clinical psychiatry at Boston Psychopathic Hospital, 1929-31. *Home:* 1210 Lenox Ave., Miami Beach, Fla. 33139. *Agent:* Jay Garon-Brooke Associates, Inc., 415 Central Park W., 17 D, New York, N.Y. 10025.

CAREER: Lawyer in Boston, Mass., 1922-28; Associated Jewish Philanthropies, Boston, legal and psychiatric caseworker, 1928-33; graphologist and handwriting expert, 1947—.

WRITINGS: Change Your Handwriting—Change Your Life, Stein & Day, 1972.

WORK IN PROGRESS: Research in graphology, concerning emotional and mental disturbance.

SIDELIGHTS: More than thirty years ago, Charlotte Leibel, then a psychiatric case worker, read a book on graphology which aroused her interest in handwriting as related to personality. She studied the subject with European teachers and became a professional graphologist. As she told *CA*, she "experimented with handwriting therapy, which is used extensively at The Sorbonne in France, and found it very effective in helping people by teaching them how to change their handwritings and thereby change their personalities, i.e., from a negative to a positive approach. I did considerable research on graphotherapy and wrote *Change Your Handwriting—Change Your Life . . .* with a view of helping people to learn this method and thus enable them to realize their potentialities."

* * *

LEIBSON, Jacob J. 1883(?)-1971

1883(?)—October 8, 1971; American educator, poet, short story writer, and playwright. Obituaries: *New York Times*, October 10, 1971.

* * *

LEIBY, James 1924-

PERSONAL: Born June 5, 1924, in Allentown, Pa.; son of James T. H. (a newspaperman) and Pearl (Wetmore) Leiby; married Jean Griest (a librarian), November 26, 1948; children: Ellen, Adlai. *Education:* Attended Pennsylvania State University, 1942-43; Muhlenberg College, A.B., 1948; Harvard University, Ph.D., 1954. *Home:* 2425 Woolsey St., Berkeley, Calif. 94705. *Office:* Department of Social Welfare, University of California, Berkeley, Calif. 94720.

CAREER: Rutgers University, New Brunswick, N.J., assistant professor of history, 1955-61; University of California, Berkeley, 1961—, began as associate professor, currently professor of social welfare. *Military service:* U.S. Army, 1943-46. *Member:* American Historical Association, Organization of American Historians, American Studies Association, Council on Social Work Education.

WRITINGS: Carroll Wright and Labor Reform, Harvard University Press, 1960; *Charity and Correction in New Jersey*, Rutgers University Press, 1967.

WORK IN PROGRESS: Research on the history of social welfare; research on American social and intellectual history.

* * *

LEININGER, Madeleine M. 1925-

PERSONAL: Born July 13, 1925, in Sutton, Neb.; daughter of George W. and Irene (Sheedy) Leininger. *Education:* Mount St. Scholastica College, B.S., 1950; Catholic University of America, M.S.N., 1954; University of Washington, Seattle, Ph.D., 1965. *Office:* College of Nursing, University of Utah, Salt Lake City, Utah 84112.

CAREER: University of Cincinnati, Cincinnati, Ohio, director of graduate program in psychiatric nursing, 1954-60; University of Colorado, Boulder, professor and director of nurse-scientist program, 1966-69; University of Washington, School of Nursing, Seattle, professor of nursing, lecturer in anthropology, and dean, 1969-74; University of Utah, College of Nursing, Salt Lake City, professor of nursing, adjunct professor of anthropology, and dean, 1974—. Green Chair Professor, Harris College of Nursing, Texas Christian University, 1977. Did anthropological field study with Gadsup people in eastern highlands of New Guinea, 1963-65. *Member:* International World Health Organization, American Anthropological Association, American Nurses' Association, National League for Nursing, American Association of Colleges of Nursing, Western Council for Higher

Education in Nursing, Western Interstate Commission on Higher Education, Sigma Theta Tau. *Awards, honors:* National Institutes of Health award, 1953; National League for Nursing fellowship, 1959; Outstanding Alumni Award, Catholic University, 1969; American Academy of Nursing fellowship, 1974; Lh. D., Benedictine College, 1975; Book of the Year Award from *American Journal of Nursing*, 1976, for *Transcultural Health Care Issues and Conditions*.

WRITINGS: (With Charles Hofling and Elizabeth Bregg) *Basic Psychiatric Concepts in Nursing*, Lippincott, 1960, revised edition, 1967; *Nursing and Anthropology: Two Worlds to Blend*, Wiley, 1970; *Contemporary Issues in Mental Health Nursing*, Little, Brown, 1973; (editor) *Health Care Issues*, F. A. Davis, 1974; (editor) *Barriers and Facilitators to Quality Health Care*, F. A. Davis, 1975; (editor) *Transcultural Health Care Issues and Conditions*, F. A. Davis, 1976; (editor) *Transcultural Nursing Care of Infants and Children*, College of Nursing, University of Utah, 1977; *Transcultural Nursing Concepts, Theories and Practices*, Wiley, 1978.

WORK IN PROGRESS: A book on the ethnography of the Gadsup people of New Guinea; research on cross-cultural caring constructs, and on cross-cultural child rearing practices.

* * *

LEKAI, J(ulius) Louis 1916-

PERSONAL: Born February 4, 1916, in Budapest, Hungary; came to United States in 1947, naturalized in 1953. *Education:* Attended Cistercian School of Theology, Budapest, Hungary, 1934-41; University of Budapest, Ph.D., 1942. *Home address:* Route 2, Box 1, Irving, Tex. 75062. *Office:* Department of History, University of Dallas, Irving, Tex. 75061.

CAREER: Roman Catholic priest of the Cistercian Order, ordained 1941; Canisius College, Buffalo, N.Y., assistant professor of history, 1952-56; University of Dallas, Irving, Tex., associate professor, 1956-58, professor of history, 1958—. *Member:* American Historical Association, American Catholic Historical Association, Mediaeval Academy of America, Renaissance Society of America, Archaeological Institute of America. *Awards, honors:* American Philosophical Society grants, 1956, 1958, 1969.

WRITINGS: A Magyar tortenetiras, 1790-1830 (title means "The Hungarian Historiography, 1790-1830"), University of Budapest Press, 1942; *The White Monks: A History of the Cistercian Order*, Cistercian Fathers, 1953; *The Rise of the Cistercian Strict Observance*, Catholic University of America Press, 1968; *The Cistercians: Ideals and Reality*, Kent State University Press, 1977. Contributor of numerous articles to *New Catholic Encyclopedia, Catholic Encyclopedia for School and Home*, and *Dizionario Enciclopedico dei Religiosi;* contributor of more than forty articles to religion and history journals.

WORK IN PROGRESS: The history of the Cistercian College of Saint Bernard in Paris; an edition of Dom Nicolas Cotheret's history of Citeaux.

SIDELIGHTS: The Cistercians: Ideals and Reality, which J. Louis Lekai describes as "a completely updated and comprehensive history of the Cistercian Order, covering both the Common and Strict Observances from their beginnings to the present" has been translated into Spanish. *The White Monks* has been translated into French and German.

LELAND, Jeremy (Francis David) 1932-

PERSONAL: Born October 18, 1932, in Aldershot, Hampshire, England; son of Francis John (an Army officer) and Violet (Butler) Leland; married Joanna Hall (an instructor in horseback riding), October 16, 1957 (divorced, 1976); children: Jonathan, Susanna. *Education:* Slade School of Fine Arts, London, Diploma, 1955. *Politics:* None. *Religion:* None. *Home:* Crossingford Farm, Pulham St. Mary, Norfolk, England. *Agent:* John Johnson, 51-54 Goschen Buildings, 12-13 Henrietta St., London WC2E 8LF, England.

CAREER: Farmed family estate in Ireland until 1962; painter and exhibitor in Ireland, 1962-67; novelist, 1967—. Presently free-lance designer of towels and renovator of a fifteenth-century geriatric dwelling.

WRITINGS—Novels; all published by Gollancz: *A River Decrees*, 1969; *The Jonah*, 1970; *The Tower*, 1972; *Lirri*, 1973. Contributor of short stories to *Argosy, Transatlantic Review*, and *Mademoiselle*.

WORK IN PROGRESS: Novels and short stories.

SIDELIGHTS: Jeremy Leland lived as a child in Egypt; he spent many years in Ireland where the family settled after fleeing as Huguenots from sixteenth-century France. He told *CA* that, although trained as a painter, he finds visual expression too uninvolving, and prefers the personal intimacy of novels.

* * *

LeMASTER, J(immie) R(ay) 1934-

PERSONAL: Born March 29, 1934, in Pike County, Ohio; son of Dennis (a truck driver) and Helen (Smith) LeMaster; married Donna Thompson, May 31, 1952; married second wife, Wanda May Ohnesorge, May 21, 1966; children: (first marriage) Lisa, Lynne, Lon Keith. *Education:* Defiance College, B.S., 1959; Bowling Green State University, M.A., 1962, Ph.D., 1970. *Politics:* "Largely Republican." *Religion:* Lutheran. *Home:* R.R. 8, Defiance, Ohio 43512. *Office:* Department of English, Defiance College, North Clinton St., Defiance, Ohio 43512.

CAREER: High school English teacher in Stryker, Ohio, 1959-61, and Bryan, Ohio, 1961-62; Defiance College, Defiance, Ohio, instructor, 1962-65, assistant professor, 1965-69, associate professor of English, 1969—. Indiana University at Fort Wayne, part-time instructor, 1965-66. *Military service:* U.S. Navy, 1951-55. *Member:* Modern Language Association of America, Midwest Modern Language Association, American Association of University Professors, Ohio Language Association.

WRITINGS: (Editor) *Poets of the Midwest*, Young Publications, 1966; *The Heart Is a Gypsy* (poems), South & West, 1967; (editor) *Morning in the Sun*, Defiance College Publications, 1968; (editor with Sanford Sternlicht) *Symposia Poets*, South & West, 1969; *Children of Adam*, South & West, 1971; (editor with William Chaney) *There Comes a Time*, Defiance College Publications, 1971; *Weeds and Wildflowers* (poems), Defiance College Poetry Center, 1975; *The World of Jesse Stuart: Selected Poems*, McGraw, 1975; *Jesse Stuart: Selected Criticism*, Valkyrie Press, in press; (translator from the French, with Kenneth Lawrence Beaudoin), Claude Vigee, *Indian Summer* (poems), Olivant, in press. Contributor to literary journals.

WORK IN PROGRESS: Jesse Stuart: Kentucky's Chronicler-Poet, for Memphis State University Press; editing and writing introduction to John Clark Jordan's *Understanding Grammar*.

LENARDON, Robert J(oseph) 1928-

PERSONAL: Born September 8, 1928, in Fort William (now Thunder Bay), Ontario, Canada; son of Louis (a businessman) and Nina (Boffa) Lenardon. *Education:* University of British Columbia, B.A. (first class honors), 1949; University of Cincinnati, M.A., 1950, Ph.D., 1954. *Home:* 47 West Third Ave., Columbus, Ohio 43201. *Office:* Department of Classics, Ohio State University, University Hall, North Oval Mall, Columbus, Ohio 43210.

CAREER: Columbia University, New York, N.Y., instructor in Greek and Latin, 1954-57; University of Washington, Seattle, assistant professor of classics, 1957-59; Ohio State University, Columbus, assistant professor, 1959-63, associate professor, 1963-69, professor of classics and director of graduate studies, 1969—. *Member:* American Philological Association, Archaeological Institute of America, American Association of University Professors, Classical Association of the Middle West and South, Ohio Classical Association.

WRITINGS: (With Mark P. O. Morford) *Classical Mythology*, McKay, 1971, revised edition, 1977; *The Saga of Themistocles*, Thames & Hudson, 1977. Contributor to professional journals. Book review editor, *Classical Journal*, 1961-68.

WORK IN PROGRESS: Hellanikos, Thucydides and the Development of Greek Historiography; Greek and Roman Themes in Music.

AVOCATIONAL INTERESTS: Classical music (especially opera), collecting books, records, and tapes.

* * *

LENNON, Joseph Luke 1919-

PERSONAL: Born September 21, 1919, in Providence, R.I.; son of John Joseph and Marjorie (McCabe) Lennon. *Education:* Providence College, A.B., 1940; Immaculate Conception College, S.T.B., 1947; University of Notre Dame, M.A., 1950, Ph.D., 1953. *Politics:* Democrat. *Home and office:* Providence College, River and Eaton Sts., Providence, R.I. 02918.

CAREER: Roman Catholic priest of Dominican Order (O.P.), ordained 1947; University of Notre Dame, South Bend, Ind., instructor, 1948-50; Providence College, Providence, R.I., instructor in education department, 1950-51, assistant dean of men, 1953-54, dean of men, 1955-57, dean of college, 1957-68, vice president for community affairs, 1968—. Director, Teachers Guild of Thomistic Institute, 1953-56. Arbitrator, Rhode Island State Board of Labor; member of board of directors of Blue Shield, Rhode Island Legal Services, Inc., Federal Hill House, Rhode Island Heart Association, Big Sisters, and other civic and charitable groups; member of board of governors, Irish Scholarship Foundation; member of board of trustees, Rhode Island chapter, Leukemia Society of America; member of advisory board, Parents without Partners; member of Governor's Advisory Council on Mental Retardation, Rhode Island Advisory Committee for Vocational Education, and other civic and educational organizations; consultant, Rhode Island State Board of Nursing.

MEMBER: National Society for the Study of Education, National Committee for Civic Responsibility (member of ethics committee), National Association for Retarded Children (member of committee on religious nurture), National Catholic Education Association, American Catholic Sociological Society, American Philosophers of Education Association, American Conference of Academic Deans, Eastern Association of College Deans, New England Educational Association, New England Guidance and Personnel Association, New England Philosophy of Education Society, Alpha Epsilon Delta, Delta Epsilon Sigma (past president; member of executive committee). *Awards, honors:* LL.D., Bradford Durfee College of Technology, 1963.

WRITINGS: College Is for Knowledge, 1959, revised edition published as *Thirty Ways to Get Ahead at College,* Alba, 1964. Contributor to *New Catholic Encyclopedia, Harvard Educational Review, Thomist, New Scholasticism, Modern Schoolman, Catholic Educational Review, Rhode Island Medical Journal, Catholic Educator, Columbia,* and other journals.

WORK IN PROGRESS: Growing toward Maturity; Your Emotions Are Your Allies, a revision of a series of television lectures; *Thomistic Philosophy of Education.*

*   *   *

LEONARD, Charlene M(arie) 1928-

PERSONAL: Born May 16, 1928, in San Diego, Calif.; daughter of Charles Berdan (a professor) and Cecyl Marie (Claydon) Leonard. *Education:* Smith College, A.B., 1949; University of California, Berkeley, M.A., 1951, Ph.D., 1958. *Residence:* San Jose, Calif. *Office:* Department of History, San Jose State University, San Jose, Calif. 95114.

CAREER: Teacher in public schools in San Francisco, Calif., 1951-58; San Jose State University, San Jose, Calif., assistant professor, 1958-63, associate professor, 1963-69, professor of history, 1969—. *Member:* American Historical Association, Society for French Historical Studies. *Awards, honors:* Fulbright scholarship, 1953; American Philosophical Society grant, 1965-66.

WRITINGS: Lyon Transformed: Public Works of the Second Empire, 1853-1863, University of California Press, 1961. Editor, "Great Concepts of the Modern World," a series of books published by Schenkman.

WORK IN PROGRESS: A volume in the "Great Concepts" series, *To Build a City,* a history of European urban planning in the nineteenth and twentieth centuries, for Schenkman; a book on public works in Bordeaux under the Second Empire.

AVOCATIONAL INTERESTS: Lapidary.

*   *   *

LERRO, Anthony Joseph 1932-

PERSONAL: Born February 2, 1932, in Pittsburgh, Pa.; son of Joseph P. and Ann (Volpe) Lerro; married Frances M. Brewer, June, 1957; children: Scott Christian. *Education:* University of Alabama, B.S., 1962, M.Sc., 1964, Ph.D., 1964. *Home:* 1252 Wendy Rd., Rock Hill, S.C. 29730. *Office:* School of Business, Winthrop College, Rock Hill, S.C. 29733.

CAREER: Virginia Polytechnic Institute and State University, Blacksburg, assistant professor, 1966-70, associate professor of finance, 1970-75; Winthrop College, School of Business, Rock Hill, S.C., Springs Professor of Finance, 1975—. *Military service:* U.S. Navy, 1953-57. *Member:* American Finance Association, Financial Management Association, Southern Economic Association, Eastern Finance Association.

WRITINGS: (With C. B. Swayne, Jr.) *Selection of Securities,* D. M. Mark, 1970, 2nd edition, Scott, Foresman, 1973. Contributor to professional journals.

LESLIE, Robert C(ampbell) 1917-

PERSONAL: Born October 20, 1917, in Concord, Mass.; son of Elmer A. (a professor) and Helen (Noon) Leslie; married Paula Eddy, June 14, 1941; children: William, Heather (Mrs. Dana W. Smith). *Education:* DePauw University, A.B., 1939; Boston University, S.T.B., 1942, Ph.D., 1948; University of Vienna, postdoctoral study, 1960-61; Marriage Council of Philadelphia, postdoctoral study, 1967-68. *Politics:* Independent. *Home:* 646 Santa Rosa Ave., Berkeley, Calif. 94707. *Office:* Pacific School of Religion, 1798 Scenic Ave., Berkeley, Calif. 94709.

CAREER: Minister of Methodist church in Peabody, Mass., 1941-43; ordained in Methodist ministry, 1943; Boston University, Boston, Mass., instructor in psychology of religion, 1948-54; Boston State Hospital, Boston, chaplain, 1948-54; Pacific School of Religion, Berkeley, Calif., associate professor, 1954-59, professor of pastoral psychology and counseling, 1959—, director of pastoral counseling service, 1959-67; Graduate Theological Union, Berkeley, professor of theology and personality sciences, 1964—. Chairman of regional personnel committee, United Methodist Church, Board of Missions; president, Fred Finch Youth Center, 1975—. *Military service:* U.S. Army, chaplain, 1943-46; became major. *Member:* American Psychological Association, American Association of Pastoral Counselors, Phi Beta Kappa. *Awards, honors:* American Association of Theological Schools fellow, 1960; National Institute of Mental Health fellow, 1968.

WRITINGS: Jesus and Logotherapy, Abingdon, 1965; *Man's Search for a Meaningful Faith,* Graded Press, 1967; (editor with Emily H. Mudd and contributor) *Professional Growth for Clergymen,* Abingdon, 1970; *Sharing Groups in the Church,* Abingdon, 1971; *Health, Healing, and Holiness,* Graded Press, 1971. Contributor to pastoral psychology journals.

WORK IN PROGRESS: Research on marriage counseling and group therapy.

SIDELIGHTS: Robert Leslie's book, *Man's Search for a Meaningful Faith,* has been translated into Spanish. *Avocational interests:* Sailing a twenty-five foot sloop.

BIOGRAPHICAL/CRITICAL SOURCES: Pastoral Psychology, April, 1955.

*   *   *

LESLIE, (John Randolph) Shane 1885-1971
(Sir Shane Leslie)

1885—August 13, 1971; British author. Obituaries: *New York Times,* August 14, 1971; *Washington Post,* August 15, 1971.

*   *   *

L'ESPERANCE, Wilford L(ouis) III 1930-

PERSONAL: Born December 9, 1930, in New York, N.Y.; son of Wilford L., Jr. (a clerk) and Marguerite (Destephen) L'Esperance; married Barbara Manochio, May 4, 1957; children: Annette, Suzanne, Claire, Wilford IV. *Education:* Columbia University, A.B., 1951, M.S., 1952; University of Michigan, Ph.D., 1963. *Office:* Department of Economics, Ohio State University, Columbus, Ohio 43214.

CAREER: General Electric Co., New York, N.Y. and Fort Wayne, Ind., marketing research assistant, 1952-60; Ohio State University, Columbus, assistant professor, 1963-66, associate professor, 1966-70, professor of economics,

1970—. President, Midwest Econometrics, 1974—. *Member:* American Economic Association, American Statistical Association, Econometric Society.

WRITINGS: Modern Statistics for Business and Economics, Macmillan, 1971. Contributor to journals.

WORK IN PROGRESS: The Structure and Control of a State Economy.

* * *

LESTER, David 1942-

PERSONAL: Born June 1, 1942, in London, England; U.S. citizen; son of Harry and Kathleen (Moore) Lester; married Gene Mercer (a psychologist), April 15, 1967 (divorced, 1977); children: Simon. *Education:* Cambridge University, B.A., 1964, M.A., 1968; Brandeis University, M.A., 1966, Ph.D., 1968. *Politics:* None. *Religion:* None. *Address:* R. D. 1, Box 45G, Berlin, N.J. 08009. *Office:* Psychology Program, Richard Stockton State College, Pomona, N.J. 08240.

CAREER: Wellesley College, Wellesley, Mass., instructor, 1967-68, assistant professor of psychology, 1968-69; Suicide Prevention and Crisis Service, Buffalo, N.Y., research director, 1969-71; Richard Stockton State College, Pomona, N.J., associate professor, 1971-74, professor of psychology, 1975—, chairman of the department, 1971—. Instructor and clinical associate, State University of New York at Buffalo, 1969-71; research associate, Philadelphia General Hospital, 1971—. *Awards, honors:* National Institute of Mental Health research grant, 1967-68.

WRITINGS: (Editor) *Explorations in Exploration,* Van Nostrand, 1969; (contributor) A. Godin, editor, *Mort et presence,* Lumen Vitae, 1971; (with Gene Lester) *Suidice: The Gamble with Death,* Prentice-Hall, 1971; *Why Men Kill Themselves,* C. C Thomas, 1972; (editor with G. Brockopp) *Crisis Intervention and Counseling by Telephone,* C. C Thomas, 1973; *Comparative Psychology: Phyletic Differences in Behavior,* Alfred Publishing, 1973; *A Physiological Basis for Personality Traits,* C. C Thomas, 1974; (with G. Lester) *Crime of Passion: Murder and the Murderer,* Nelson-Hall, 1975; *Unusual Sexual Behavior: The Standard Deviations,* C. C Thomas, 1975; *The Use of Alternative Modes for Communication in Psychotherapy: The Computer, the Book, the Telephone, the Television, the Tape Recorder,* C. C Thomas, 1977. Contributor of over one hundred articles to *Journal of Clinical Psychology, American Anthropologist, Journal of General Psychology, Nature, Clinical Psychologist, Omega,* and other professional journals. Founder and co-editor, *Crisis Intervention,* 1969-71; member of editorial advisory board, Institute for Scientific Information, 1969-70, and *Current Contents (Social and Behavioral Sciences);* member of editorial board, *Omega,* 1971—.

WORK IN PROGRESS: Books on criminal justice and juvenile delinquency; *Suicide: A Guide to Information Sources.*

* * *

LESTER, Gene 1941-
(Jean Mercer)

PERSONAL: Born October 16, 1941, in San Antonio, Tex.; daughter of Harry Eugene (an Air Force officer) and Laura (Leudecke) Mercer; married David Lester (a college professor), April 15, 1967 (divorced, 1977); children: Simon Nicholas. *Education:* Attended Mt. Holyoke College, 1959-61;

Occidental College, A.B., 1963; Brandeis University, Ph.D., 1968. *Politics:* Democrat. *Religion:* None. *Home address:* Box 238, R. D. 1, Hammonton, N.J. 08037. *Office:* Department of Psychology, Richard Stockton State College, Pomona, N.J. 08240.

CAREER: Wheaton College, Norton, Mass., assistant professor of psychology, 1967-69; State University of New York College at Buffalo, assistant professor of psychology, 1969-71; Richard Stockton State College, Pomona, N.J., assistant professor of psychology, 1974—.

WRITINGS: (With David Lester) *Suicide: The Gamble with Death,* Prentice-Hall, 1971; (with D. Lester) *Crime of Passion: Murder and the Murderer,* Nelson-Hall, 1975; (under name Jean Mercer) *Small People: How Children Develop,* Nelson-Hall, in press.

* * *

LEVIN, Gerald H. 1929-

PERSONAL: Born May 18, 1929, in Chicago, Ill.; son of Harry and Eve (Cohen) Levin; married Lillian Cicurel, June 24, 1956; children: Sylvia, Elizabeth. *Education:* Attended Vanderbilt University, 1947-49; University of Chicago, M.A., 1952; University of Michigan, Ph.D., 1956. *Religion:* Jewish. *Residence:* Akron, Ohio. *Office:* Department of English, University of Akron, Akron, Ohio 44325.

CAREER: University of Michigan, Ann Arbor, instructor in English, 1955-56; University of Colorado, Boulder, instructor in English, 1956-57; Eastern Illinois University, Charleston, assistant professor of English, 1957-60; University of Akron, Akron, Ohio, assistant professor, 1960-65, associate professor, 1965-68, professor of English, 1969—, director of English composition, 1967-69. Consultant on rhetoric and literature, Conference on College Communication and Composition, 1964, 1965; regional judge, National Council of Teachers of English National Achievement awards; reader at Advanced Placement examinations for Educational Testing Service, 1966. *Member:* Modern Language Association of America.

WRITINGS—All published by Harcourt, except as indicated: *Prose Models,* 1964, 3rd edition, 1975; *A Brief Handbook of Rhetoric,* 1966; (editor) *The Short Story,* 1967; (editor) Francis Connolly, *The Art of Rhetoric,* 1968; (with Francis Connolly), *A Rhetoric Case Book,* 3rd edition (Levin was not associated with earlier editions), 1969; *Styles for Writing,* 1972; *Sigmund Freud,* Twayne, 1975; *Short Essays: Models for Composition,* 1977. Also author of teaching manuals for *Prose and Criticism,* 1966, and *The Cosmos Reader,* 1971. Contributor to literature journals.

* * *

LEVINSON, Boris M(ayer) 1907-

PERSONAL: Born July 1, 1907, in Kalvarijah, Lithuania; came to United States in 1923, naturalized in 1930; son of Moses (a merchant) and Rose (Lev) Levinson; married Ruth M. Berkowitz, June 16, 1934 (divorced); married Aida Penaranda, October 30, 1974; children: (first marriage) Martin R., David J. *Education:* City College (now City College of the City University of New York), B.S. (cum laude), 1937, M.S., 1938; New York University, Ph.D., 1947. *Religion:* Hebrew. *Home and office:* 86-35 Queens Blvd., Suite 7K, Elmhurst, N.Y. 11373.

CAREER: Board of Education, Adult Guidance Service, New York City, psychologist and later chief psychologist, 1938-40; Jewish Hospital, Brooklyn, N.Y., clinical psychologist in Veterans Rehabilitation and Mental Hygiene Clinics, 1944-48; Yeshiva University, Ferkauf Graduate School of Humanities and Social Sciences, New York City, with Psychological Center as supervising clinical psychologist, 1951-54, chief psychologist, 1954-56, director, 1956-63, on teaching faculty as assistant professor, 1951-53, associate professor, 1953-56, professor of psychology, 1956-73, professor emeritus, 1973—. Lecturer at City College (now City College of the City University of New York), 1947-52, and Hunter College (now Hunter College of the City University of New York), 1949-58; adjunct professor of psychology, John Jay College of Criminal Justice of the City University of New York, 1973-74; professor of psychology, Touro College, 1973-75. Part-time private practice as consulting psychologist, 1938—; chief psychologist at Jewish Memorial Hospital, New York, 1957-59. Diplomate in clinical psychology, American Board of Examiners in Professional Psychology, 1954; certified psychologist, State of New York, 1958.

MEMBER: American Psychological Association (fellow), Society for Personality Assessment (fellow), Inter-American Society of Psychology, Eastern Psychological Association, New York, Society of Clinical Psychologists, Phi Delta Kappa, Psi Chi. *Awards, honors:* Humane Service Award, Bide-A-Wee Home Association, 1970; Scroll of Honor, Yeshiva University, 1973.

WRITINGS: Pet-Oriented Child Psychotherapy, C. C Thomas, 1969; *Pets and Human Development,* C. C Thomas, 1972.

Contributor: A. A. Schneider and P. T. Centi, editors, *Selected Papers from the AGPA Meetings,* American Catholic Association, 1962; N. Kiell, editor, *The Psychodynamics of Jewish Religious Life,* Twayne, 1967; M. W. Fox, editor, *Abnormal Behavior in Animals,* Saunders, 1968; Austin H. Kutscher, editor, *Death and Bereavement,* C. C Thomas, 1969; Tina Levitan, editor, *The Scientist and Religion,* Jewish Agency Publications, 1970; A. H. Kutscher and L. G. Kutscher, editors, *For the Bereaved,* Fell, 1971; J. K. Whittaker and A. E. Fleischman, editors, *Children Away from Home,* Aldine-Atherton, 1972; *Proceedings of the National Conference on the Ecology of the Surplus Dog and Cat Problem,* American Humane Association, 1974; Charles E. Schaefer, editor, *Therapeutic Use of Play,* Aronson, 1975; R. S. Anderson, editor, *Pet Animals and Society,* Bailliere Tindall, 1975; Levitan, editor, *Viewpoints on Science and Judaism,* Board of Jewish Education, 1977.

Contributor to *Encyclopaedica Judaica;* contributor of more than one hundred articles and reviews to psychology journals in the United States and abroad. Contributing editor, *Pet News,* 1976—.

SIDELIGHTS: In a review of *Pets and Human Development,* Carl J. Tuss writes: "A fundamental theme of Dr. Levinson's work recognizes that pets can serve as a palliative for modern urban man's symptoms of alienation from himself and the natural world. A companion theme developed throughout the majority of the book focuses on the role of pets in the individual's quest for mastery of various developmental tasks in the areas of emotional differentiation, relationship formation, and cognition. . . . Finally, the reader is sobered by a wise, pithy epilogue: 'animals are a symbol of the rehumanization of society to the extent that they are allowed to function as members of the animal world, rather than as four-footed humans whose very nature is denied, and are permitted to bring their owners into that world of life, impulse and love.' "

AVOCATIONAL INTERESTS: Poetry, astronomy, microbiology.

BIOGRAPHICAL/CRITICAL SOURCES: Star Weekly (Toronto), June 25, 1966; *Newsday,* February 10, 1971; *Journal of Personality Assessment,* Volume XXXVIII, number 2, 1974.

*   *   *

LEVY, Harry L(ouis) 1906-

PERSONAL: Born December 5, 1906, in New York, N.Y.; son of William W. (a salesman) and Bertha (Haber) Levy; married Muriel Erdreich, April 28, 1928 (deceased); married Ernestine Friedl (a university professor), September 27, 1942; children: (first marriage) Charles S., Ann (Mrs. Arthur L. Lathrop). *Education:* City College (now City College of the City University of New York), B.A., 1925; Columbia University, M.A., 1926, Ph.D., 1936. *Politics:* Democrat. *Religion:* Jewish. *Home and office:* 3080 Colony Rd., Durham, N.C. 27705.

CAREER: Hunter College of the City University of New York, New York City, instructor, 1928-39, assistant professor, 1939-48, associate professor, 1948-53, professor of classics, 1953-63, assistant dean, 1948-49, associate dean, 1951-52, dean of men, 1952-53, 1959-63; City University of New York, New York City, dean of studies, 1963-66, vice-chancellor, 1966-68, emeritus vice-chancellor, 1968—. Professor of humanities, Fordham University, 1967-71; visiting professor, Duke University, 1973—. U.S. Army Reserve Office, member of advisory council for junior science and humanities symposium, 1960-74, acting chairman, 1962; American School of Classical Studies, Athens, member of managing committee, 1962—, research fellow, 1971-72, visiting professor, 1976. *Military service:* U.S. Army, 1943-45; served in China-Burma-India theater. U.S. Army Reserve, 1949-64; became lieutenant colonel.

MEMBER: American Philological Association (secretary-treasurer, 1959-62; member of board of directors, 1967—; second vice-president, 1971-72; first vice-president, 1972-73; president, 1973-74), American Council of Learned Societies (delegate, 1967-71), Phi Beta Kappa. *Awards, honors:* Chancellor's Medal, City University of New York, 1967; President's Medal, Brooklyn College of the City University of New York, 1967, and Hunter College of the City University of New York, 1970; Annual Award, Northeast Conference on the Teaching of Foreign Languages, 1970; American Council of Learned Societies grant, 1971, for work on Claudian in Rome, Paris, and London, and 1976, for work on Ovid in Paris and London; American Philosophical Society grant, 1977, for work on Ovid.

WRITINGS: (Editor) *Language Teacher,* Modern Language Association of America, 1958; *A Latin Reader for Colleges,* University of Chicago Press, 1962; (contributor) Julian A. Pitt-Rivers, editor, *Mediterranean Countrymen: Essays in the Social Anthropology of the Mediterranean,* Mouton (Paris), 1963; *Claudian's "In Rufinum": An Exegetical Commentary,* Press of Case Western Reserve University, 1971; (editor) *Lucian: Seventy Dialogues,* Oklahoma University Press, 1976. Contributor, with Amy K. Clarke, to *Catalogus Translationum et Commentariorum,* Volume III, 1976. Contributor of articles to classical journals. Editor, *Classical Weekly* of Classical Association of Atlantic States, 1949-52; editor, reports of the working committees, Northeast Conference on the Teaching of Foreign Languages, 1958.

WORK IN PROGRESS: Writing on Ovid's *Metamorphoses,* for *Catalogus Translationum et Commentariorum.*

SIDELIGHTS: Harry L. Levy told *CA:* "My writing has been an outgrowth of my more than half-century of college and university teaching and research; except for the articles and books which sprang from my doctoral work on Claudian's *In Rufinum,* most of my articles arose out of observations made on classical texts which I was reading with a class, and my two college text-books were written with the needs of my students in mind. My work in Greece with my anthropologist wife Ernestine Friedl has been the source of another large group of articles devoted to parallel culture traits in Ancient and Modern Greece. Finally, bibliographical studies for the *Catalogus Translationum et Commentariorum,* a reference work dealing with the classical literatures as read and understood by men of the Middle Ages and the Renaissance in Western Europe, have given me a steady scholarly occupation for the last several years, as I have worked on Claudian and Ovid."

* * *

LEWIS, Beth Irwin 1934-

PERSONAL: Born February 28, 1934; daughter of John Mark and Ruth (Hoffman) Irwin; married Dudley Arnold Lewis (a professor of art history), June 24, 1958; children: Martha, David, Paul. *Education:* College of Wooster, B.A., 1956; University of Wisconsin, M.A., 1958; Ph.D., 1969. *Politics:* Democratic. *Religion:* Presbyterian. *Home:* 614 Kieffer St., Wooster, Ohio 44691.

CAREER: Wells College, Aurora, N.Y., part-time instructor in history, 1963-64; College of Wooster, Wooster, Ohio, part-time instructor in history, 1965, 1969, 1972-73, 1974-75. *Member:* American Historical Association, Coordinating Committee on Women in the Historical Profession, Ohio Academy of History, Phi Beta Kappa.

WRITINGS: George Grosz: Art and Politics in the Weimar Republic, University of Wisconsin Press, 1971.

WORK IN PROGRESS: Writing on the interrelationship of history and art, patronage in Weimar Germany, symbols, language about God, and women.

* * *

LICHTENSTADTER, Ilse 1907-

PERSONAL: Born September 10, 1907, in Hamburg, Germany; came to United States in 1938, naturalized in 1944; daughter of Jacob (an educator) and Flora (Levi) Lichtenstadter. *Education:* University of Frankfurt am Main, Ph.D., 1931; Oxford University, D.Phil., 1937. *Politics:* Independent. *Religion:* Jewish. *Home:* 14 Concord Ave., Cambridge, Mass. 02138. *Office:* Center for Middle Eastern Studies, Harvard University, 1737 Cambridge St., Cambridge, Mass. 02138.

CAREER: Cambridge University, Queen's College Library, Cambridge, England, librarian, 1933-35; Oxford University Press, Oxford, England, specialist in Semitic languages, 1935-38; Jewish Theological Seminary, New York City, library cataloguer, 1938-45; Asia Institute, New York City, assistant professor, 1942-44, associate professor, 1944-45, professor of Arabic language and literature and contemporary Islam, 1945-52; New York University, New York City, lecturer in contemporary Islam, 1952-60; Rutgers University, New Brunswick, N.J., lecturer in history of Islam, 1959-60; Harvard University, Cambridge, Mass., lecturer on Arabic, 1960-74, emeritus lecturer, 1974—. *Member:* American Oriental Society, Middle East Studies Association, New York Oriental Club (president, 1945). *Awards,*

honors: Notgemeinschaft der Deutschen Wissenschaft fellow, 1932-33; Social Science Research Council fellow, 1950, 1955; Fulbright travel fellow in Middle East, 1963.

WRITINGS: Women in the Aiyam al-'Arab: A Study of Female Life During Warfare in Preislamic Arabia, Royal Asiatic Society, 1935; (editor) Muhammad ibn Habib, *The Kitab al-Muhabbar,* Da'irat al-Ma'arif (Hyderabad, India), 1942; (translator) Gustave Edmund Von Grunebaum, *Studies in Islamic Cultural History,* American Anthropological Association, 1954; *Islam and the Modern Age: An Analysis and Appraisal,* Twayne, 1959; (editor) Ibn Tufayl, *Hayy ibn Yaqzan: A Philosophical Tale,* translated from classical Arabic with an introduction by Lenn Evan Goodman, Twayne, 1972; *Introduction to Classical Arabic Literature,* Twayne, 1974. Also author of interpretative articles on the Koran. Contributor of articles on classical Arabic poetry, the problems of minorities in Islamic society, and women to encyclopedias and periodicals.

WORK IN PROGRESS: General editor of series, "Library of Classical Arabic Literature"; continued research on Arabic and Islamic literature, especially on the origins of Islam and on the Koran.

SIDELIGHTS: Ilse Lichtenstadter has traveled extensively in the Arabic and Middle Eastern countries. Her main interest is "to study the impact of 'modernization' and 'Westernization' on contemporary Islam and Muslims."

* * *

LICKLIDER, Roy E(ilers) 1941-

PERSONAL: Born January 27, 1941, in Seattle, Wash.; son of Woodburn Jennings (an auto dealer) and Agnes (a certified public accountant; maiden name, Eilers) Licklider; married Patricia Minichino (an assistant professor at City University of New York), July 10, 1971; children: Virginia Anne. *Education:* Boston University, B.A., 1963; Yale University, M.A., 1964, Ph.D., 1968. *Home:* 39 South Adelaide Ave., Highland Park, N.J. 08904. *Office:* Political Science Department, Douglass College, Rutgers University, New Brunswick, N.J. 08903.

CAREER: Tougaloo College, Tougaloo, Miss., assistant professor of political science, 1967-68; Rutgers University, Douglass College, New Brunswick, N.J., assistant professor, 1968-72, associate professor of political science, 1972—, chairman of department, 1974-77; program officer, Exxon Education Foundation, 1977-78 (on leave from Rutgers University). *Member:* International Studies Association, American Political Science Association, American Association of University Professors, Inter-University Seminar on Armed Forces and Society.

WRITINGS: The Private Nuclear Strategists, Ohio State University Press, 1971; (contributor) Irving L. Horowitz, editor, *The Use and Abuse of Social Science,* Dutton, 1971. Contributor to *Political Science Quarterly* and *Simulation and Games.*

WORK IN PROGRESS: A reader in comparative foreign policy; research on the morality of nuclear weapons research and on the utility of instruments of foreign policy.

* * *

LIEBERT, Burt 1925-

PERSONAL: Surname is pronounced Lee-burt; born September 17, 1925, in New York, N.Y.; son of Abraham (a businessman) and Paula (Gilberg) Liebert; married Marjorie Nack (a teacher), September 10, 1950; children: Mark,

Nina, Scott, Judy. *Education:* University of Arizona, B.A., 1948; Art Institute of Chicago, M.F.A., 1950. *Home:* 120 Wisteria Way, Davis, Calif. 95616. *Office:* Department of Education, University of California, Davis, Calif. 95616.

CAREER: High school teacher in Pueblo, Colo., 1951-53; high school teacher of English and drama in Pomona, Calif., 1953-55; American River College, Sacramento, Calif., part-time instructor in English, 1958-63; high school teacher of English, speech, and drama in Sacramento, Calif., 1955-65; University of California, Davis, lecturer and supervisor in teacher education, 1965—. *Member:* National Council of Teachers of English, American Federation of Teachers, California Council of Teachers of English, California Teachers Association.

WRITINGS: Linguistics and the New English Teacher, Macmillan, 1971.

WORK IN PROGRESS: Editing Henrietta Baron's *Everybody Can Cook;* a course of study in home economics for orthopedically-handicapped children, for Special Child Publications.

*   *   *

LIETAER, Bernard A(rthur) 1942-

PERSONAL: Born February 7, 1942, in Lauwe, Belgium; son of Gerard and Agnes (Catry) Lietaer. *Education:* Attended College of St. Paul, Godinne, Belgium, 1955-61, and College of St. Michel, Brussels, 1961-62; University of Louvain, B.S., 1964, M.S., 1967; Massachusetts Institute of Technology, M.S., 1969. *Residence:* Belgium.

CAREER: Cresap, McCormick & Paget, Inc. (management consultants), New York, N.Y., senior associate, 1969-73.

WRITINGS: Financial Management of Foreign Exchange: An Operational Technique to Reduce Risk, M.I.T. Press, 1971. Contributor of articles to *Harvard Business Review.*

WORK IN PROGRESS: Books on planning models in diversified companies, international cash flow management, and financial implications of European integration.

AVOCATIONAL INTERESTS: 17th-century Dutch painting, photography, sailing, classical music.†

*   *   *

LIFSHIN, Lyn

PERSONAL: Born in Burlington, Vt.; daughter of Ben and Frieda (Lazarus) Lipman. *Education:* Syracuse University, B.A., 1960; University of Vermont, M.A., 1963. *Home:* 2142 Appletree Lane, Niskayuna, N.Y. 12309.

CAREER: State University of New York at Albany, teaching fellow, 1964-66; educational television writer, Schenectady, N.Y., 1966; writing consultant, Mental Health Department, Albany, N.Y., 1969, and Empire State College of the State University of New York, 1973; poet-in-residence, Mansfield State College, Mansfield, Pa., beginning 1974; poet. *Awards, honors:* Hart Crane award; Bread Loaf scholarship; Harcourt Brace poetry fellowship; Boulder poetry award; Yaddo fellowship; Millay fellowship; Mac Dowell fellowship; New York Creative Artists Public Service grant; San Jose Poetry award.

WRITINGS—Poetry: Why Is the House Dissolving, Open Skull Press, 1968; *Femina 2,* Abraxas, 1970; *Black Apples,* New Books, 1971; *Leaves and Night Things,* Baby John Press, 1971; *Lady Lyn,* Morgan & Morgan, 1972; *Museum,* November Press, 1972; *I'd Be Jeanne Moreau,* Morgan & Morgan, 1972; *Mercurochrome Sun Poems,* Charis Press,

1972; *Tentacles, Leaves,* Helleric Press, 1972; *Undressed,* Cotyledon Press, 1972; *Moving by Touch,* Cotyledon Press, 1972; *Love Poems,* Zahir Press, 1972; *Forty Days, Apple Nights,* Morgan & Morgan, 1973; *Audley End Poems,* Mag Press, 1973; *The First Week Poems,* Zahir Press, 1973; *All the Women Poets I Ever Liked Didn't Hate Their Fathers,* Konglomerat, 1973; *The Old House on the Croton,* Shameless Hussy Press, 1973.

Poems, Konglomerat, 1974; *Selected Poems,* Crossing Press, 1974; *The Old House,* Capra, 1974; *Shaker Poems,* Omphalos Press, 1974; *Blue Fingers,* Shelter Press, 1974; *Mountain Moving Day,* Crossing Press, 1974; *Green Bandager,* Hidden Springs, 1975; *Paper Apples,* Wormwood Press, 1975; *North,* Morgan & Morgan, 1976; *Shaker House Poems,* Sagariw Press, 1976; *Naked Charm,* Firewood, 1977; *Some Madonnas,* Buffalo Press, 1977; *Leaving South,* Red Dust Press, 1977; *Pantagonia,* Wormwood Press, 1977; *Some January Poems,* Waters Press, 1977; *Plymouth Women,* Morgan & Morgan, 1977; *Mad Girl Poems,* Out of Sight Press, 1977; *Crazy Arms,* Mati Press, 1977; *Twisted Vines,* Beacon Press, 1978; *Thru Blue Dust,* Basilisk, 1978; *Glass,* Morgan & Morgan, 1978.

Contributor of poetry to anthologies, including: *New American and Canadian Poetry,* edited by John Gill, Beacon Press, 1971; *Writing While Young and Seeing Thru Shucks,* Ballantine, 1972; *Rising Tides,* Simon & Schuster, 1973; *Psyche,* Dell, 1974; *In Youth,* Ballantine, 1974; *Pictures That Storm Inside My Head,* Avon, 1975; *I Hear My Sisters Saying,* Crowell, 1976. A recording of Lifshin reading her poetry, "Lyn Lifshin Reads Her Poems," was produced by Women's Audio Exchange, 1977.

WORK IN PROGRESS: A journal; short stories; a novel.

SIDELIGHTS: Lyn Lifshin's papers are being collected by the University of Texas at Austin.

*   *   *

LIFSON, David S. 1908-

PERSONAL: Born December 29, 1908, in New York, N.Y.; son of Louis (a merchant) and Sarah (Saffro) Lifson; married Dorothy Marburger (a librarian), November 27, 1932; children: Hugh A. *Education:* New York University, B.S., 1931, M.A., 1957, Ph.D., 1962. *Home:* 40 East Tenth St., New York, N.Y. 10003. *Agent:* Bertha Klausner, 71 Park Ave., New York, N.Y. 10016. *Office:* Department of English, Monmouth College, West Long Branch, N.J. 07764.

CAREER: Playwright and director; 20th Century Paint and Varnish Manufacturing Corp., New York, N.Y., founder and president, 1937-57; Maryland State College (now University of Maryland Eastern Shore), Princess Anne, Md., professor and director of drama, 1957-58; Pratt Institute, Brooklyn, N.Y., assistant professor and director of drama, 1957-63; Jersey City State College, Jersey City, N.J., assistant professor, 1963-64; Monmouth College, West Long Branch, N.J., associate professor, 1964-65, professor of English, 1965—. Member of board of directors, Brooklyn Heights Youth Center. *Member:* P.E.N., Drama Desk, Actors Equity Association, Outer Critics Circle, Players Club. *Awards, honors:* Otto Kahn Award, Metropolitan Opera, 1930; Founders Day Award, New York University, 1963; Fulbright-Hays scholar, 1970-71.

WRITINGS: The Yiddish Theatre in America, Yoseloff, 1965; (contributor) George Freedley and J. A. Reeves, editors, *A History of the Theatre,* 3rd edition (Lifson was not associated with earlier editions), Crown, 1968; *Epic and Folk Plays of the Yiddish Theatre,* Associated University Presses, 1975; *Headless Victory* (novel), A. S. Barnes, 1978.

Plays: "Familiar Pattern," first produced Off-Broadway at Provincetown Playhouse, 1943; "Mummers and Men," first produced Off-Broadway at Provincetown Playhouse, 1962; "Le Poseur," first produced in New York at Italian Drama Festival, 1974; "How to Rob a Bank," first produced in New York at PAF Playhouse, 1976. Also author of plays, "Greet Tomorrow," "Buffoons," "New Item," "At the Gate," "The Troubador," "Gift of the Magi," "Children," "Gimpy," "Recruits," "Hurrah for Us," "Ivory Tower," "Eye of the Storm," and "Masquerade."

Contributor to *Encyclopaedia Britannica, Encyclopaedia Judaica, Jewish Quarterly,* and *Jewish Currents.* Drama critic, *Gramercy Herald.*

WORK IN PROGRESS: The Closing Door, a novel; two plays, "Banco" and "Oh! Careless Love!."

* * *

LIFTON, Walter M. 1918-

PERSONAL: Born November 2, 1918, in Brooklyn, N.Y.; son of Samuel S. (a salesman) and Sarah (Berman) Lifton; married Ruth Knoppow (a consultant in early childhood education), October 1, 1940; children: Hazel Miriam Lifton Kroesser, Robert William. *Education:* Brooklyn College (now Brooklyn College of the City University of New York), B.A., 1942; New York University, M.A., 1947, Ph.D., 1950. *Home:* 106 Greenleaf Dr., Newtonville, N.Y. 12128. *Office:* Department of Counseling, School of Education, State University of New York at Albany, 1400 Washington Ave., Albany, N.Y. 12203.

CAREER: Worked as cashier, bookkeeper, drug salesman, pharmaceutical detail man, and apprentice machinist while attending evening college; Hunter College (now Hunter College of the City University of New York), New York City, 1946-48, began as interviewer in Veterans Guidance Center, became senior vocational appraiser; New York University, New York City, research psychologist, 1948-50; University of Illinois, Urbana, associate professor of education, 1950-59; Science Research Associates, Inc., Chicago, Ill., director of guidance publications and services, 1959-64; Rochester City School District, Rochester, N.Y., coordinator of pupil personnel services, 1964-70; State University of New York at Albany, professor of education and director of counseling program, 1970—. Visiting summer professor at Boston University, 1953, and University of Southern California, 1957; guest lecturer at other colleges and universities, including Utah State University, University of Toronto, and University of Chicago. *Military service:* U.S. Army, 1942-46.

MEMBER: American Personnel and Guidance Association (chairman of committee on ethical practices, 1965), American Psychological Association, American School Counselors Association, National Association of Pupil Personnel Administrators (president, 1970), National Vocational Guidance Association, Association for Specialists in Group Work (secretary).

WRITINGS: Working with Groups: Group Process and Individual Growth, Wiley, 1960, 2nd edition, 1966; (editor) *Keys to Vocational Decisions,* Science Research Associates, 1964; (contributor) Don C. Dinkmeyer, editor, *Guidance and Counseling in the Elementary School,* Holt, 1968; (contributor) George M. Gazda, editor, *Basic Approaches*

to *Group Psychotherapy and Group Counseling,* C. C Thomas, 1968; (editor and contributor) *Educating for Tomorrow: The Role of Media, Career Development, and Society,* Wiley, 1970; *Groups: Facilitating Individual Group and Societal Change,* Wiley, 1972; (contributor) Gazda, editor, *Theories and Methods of Group Counseling in the Schools,* C. C Thomas, 1976.

Monographs and booklets: (With others) *Counselor Training Methods and Procedures,* University of Missouri Press, 1952; *A Pilot Study to Investigate the Effects of Supervision on the Empathic Ability of Counseling Trainees,* Bureau of Educational Research, University of Illinois, 1952; *A Pilot Study of the Relationship of Empathy to Aesthetic Sensitivity,* Bureau of Educational Research, University of Illinois, 1956; *Introducing the World of Work to Children,* Science Research Associates, 1960; *What Could I Be?,* Science Research Associates, 1960.

Contributor to encyclopedias, including *World Book Encyclopedia, Britannica Junior Encyclopaedia,* and *Encyclopedia of Education;* contributor of about thirty articles to *Saturday Evening Post, Reader's Digest,* and education journals.

* * *

LIGHTWOOD, Martha B. 1923-

PERSONAL: Born January 24, 1923, in Natrona Heights, Pa.; daughter of Andrew J. and Edith (Dunn) Bolar; married M. H. Lightwood, May 18, 1946; children: Andrew B. *Education:* University of Pittsburgh, A.B. (summa cum laude), 1943; Drexel University, M.L.S., 1963; University of Pennsylvania, M.A., 1967, Ph.D., 1978. *Religion:* Quaker. *Home:* 121 Upper Gulph Rd., Strafford, Pa. 19087. *Office:* Lippincott Library, Wharton School, University of Pennsylvania, Philadelphia, Pa. 19104.

CAREER: University of Pennsylvania, Wharton School, Lippincott Library, Philadelphia, head of public services, 1963-72, assistant librarian, 1972—. *Member:* American Political Science Association, Special Libraries Association, League of Women Voters (Philadelphia; member of board of directors).

WRITINGS: Public and Business Planning in the United States: An Annotated Bibliography, Gale, 1972. Contributor to *Special Libraries.*

* * *

LIMBURG, Peter R(ichard) 1929-

PERSONAL: Born November 4, 1929, in New York, N.Y.; son of Richard P. and Edith (Reckford) Limburg; married Margareta Fischerstroem, May 26, 1952; children: Richard, Karin, David, Ellen. *Education:* Yale University, B.A., 1950; Georgetown University, B.S.F.S., 1951; Columbia University, M.A., 1957. *Religion:* Jewish. *Address:* R.R. 2, Box 291, Bedford, N.Y. 10506. *Agent:* Patricia Lewis, Room 602, 450 Seventh Ave., New York, N.Y. 10001.

CAREER: Collier's Encyclopedia, New York City, editorial assistant, 1957-59; Artists & Writers Press, New York City, editor, 1959-61; Grolier, Inc., New York City, head of products and industries department, *The New Book of Knowledge,* 1961-66; Harcourt, Brace & World, Inc., New York City, editor, 1966-69; Crowell-Collier Macmillan, New York City, coordinating editor, 1969-70. *Military service:* U.S. Army Reserve, 1951-53. U.S. Army, 1953-55; became sergeant. *Awards, honors: Termites* was selected one of the outstanding science books for children in 1974 by the National Science Teachers Association and the Childrens Book Council.

WRITINGS—All juveniles: *The First Book of Engines,* F. Watts, 1969; *The Story of Corn,* Messner, 1971; *Watch Out, It's Poison Ivy!,* Messner, 1973; (with James B. Sweeney) *Vessels for Underwater Exploration: A Pictorial History,* Crown, 1973; *Termites,* Hawthorn, 1974; (with Sweeney) *102 Questions and Answers about the Sea,* Messner, 1975; *Chickens, Chickens, Chickens,* Thomas Nelson, 1975; *Poisonous Plants,* illustrations by Marjorie Zaum, Messner, 1976; *Oceanographic Institutions,* Thomas Nelson, 1977; *The Story of Your Heart,* Coward, 1978; *Life on a Sunflower,* Lippincott, 1978.

"What's behind the Word" series; all published by Coward: *What's in the Names of Fruit,* 1972; *What's in the Names of Antique Weapons,* 1973; *What's in the Names of Flowers,* 1974; *What's in the Names of Birds,* 1975; *What's in the Names of Stars and Constellations,* 1976; *What's in the Names of Wild Animals,* 1977.

Contributor to *Encyclopedia Science Supplement,* Grolier, 1972-74; contributor to "Reader's Digest General Books" series on natural sciences and U.S. history, 1972—. Contributing editor, *Science World,* 1974-75.

SIDELIGHTS: Peter Limburg told *CA:* "I cannot say that I always wanted to be a writer. Actually, I wanted to become a chemist, but I flunked freshman math in college too disastrously for any sort of a career in science. My writing career began in a roundabout way, through having been an editor on a variety of reference works. This position called for me to spend a great deal of time rewriting the material our contributors sent in so that ordinary people like our readers could understand it. Since I had to understand what the contributors were talking about myself in order to translate it into plain, straightforward English, I picked up a good deal of knowledge about science, technology, history, geography, foreign languages, and other things. After years of rewriting other people's stuff, I began to think that perhaps I could do as well as they. Encouraged by a former boss, I began my first book during a period between jobs. Eventually I went into writing full-time.

"I write for readers from third grade through high school. My favorite level is junior high on up. On this level one can give a great deal more information than one can for younger kids, and one doesn't have to spend so much time worrying over whether the readers will understand it. Still, writing for younger readers is very good training. At all levels, I think that clarity, accuracy, and honesty are vital to good writing. I have no patience with obscurity or sloppiness. The writer must get his message across as clearly and simply as he can—otherwise he's not doing his job. I think this holds as true of writing for adults as it does of writing for third-graders.

"In my own writing, I try to explain the *how* and *why* of things as well as the *what.* I try to write simply and directly enough for children to understand, but with enough respect for my readers' intelligence so that adults can read my books without embarrassment. And I try to keep my writing interesting—I go on the possibly egocentric theory that what interests me will interest my readers too."

Peter Limburg is fluent in Swedish and Spanish, and has a working knowledge of French and German.

AVOCATIONAL INTERESTS: Gardening, fruit growing, hiking, fishing, history, do-it-yourself projects.

LINDBERG, Leon N. 1932-

PERSONAL: Born June 18, 1932, in Chicago, Ill.; son of Edvin and Thyra (Nord) Lindberg; married Beatrice Ransom, February 5, 1955; children: Andrea Marie, Kaia Nicole. *Education:* University of California, Berkeley, B.A., 1955, M.A., 1957, Ph.D., 1962. *Home:* 109 Chestnut St., Madison, Wis. 53705. *Office:* Department of Political Science, University of Wisconsin, 413 North Hall, Madison, Wis. 53706.

CAREER: University of Wisconsin—Madison, assistant professor, 1961-65, associate professor, 1965-69, professor of political science, 1969—. Research fellow, Center for International Affairs, Harvard University, 1964-65, 1967; visiting research scholar, Carnegie Endowment for International Peace, Geneva, 1972-73; visiting scholar, Brookings Institution, 1976-77. Chairman, Council for European Studies, 1971-72.

WRITINGS: The Political Dynamics of European Economic Integration, Stanford University Press, 1963; *Europe's Would Be Polity,* Prentice-Hall, 1970; (with Stuart A. Scheingold) *Regional Integration,* Harvard University Press, 1971; (editor and contributor) *Stress and Contradiction in Modern Capitalism,* Lexington Books, 1975; *Politics and the Future of Industrial Society,* McKay, 1976; (co-editor) *The Political Economy of Energy Policy,* Institute for Environmental Studies, University of Wisconsin, 1976; *The Energy Syndrome: Comparing National Responses to the Energy Crisis,* Lexington Books, 1977.

WORK IN PROGRESS: The Politics of Economic Instability: Inflation and Energy Policies in Capitalist Nations; director, with Charles S. Maier, of a research project on the politics and sociology of global inflation and recession for the Brookings Institution; research on political and organizational obstacles to energy conservation.

*   *   *

LINDENFELD, Frank 1934-

PERSONAL: Born March 4, 1934, in Vienna, Austria; son of Rudolph and Marianne (Berditchevsky) Lindenfeld; married Bernardine Priven, 1954 (divorced, 1959); married Jacqueline Systermans, 1960 (divorced, 1969); married Josephine M. Ward (an artist), June 15, 1970; children: (first marriage) David; (second marriage) Annette. *Education:* Cornell University, B.A., 1955; Columbia University, M.A., 1958, Ph.D., 1961. *Office:* Department of Sociology-Anthropology, Cheyney State College, Cheyney, Pa. 19319.

CAREER: U.S. Department of Health, Education and Welfare, Office of Education, Washington, D.C., research associate, 1959-61; University of Maryland, College Park, lecturer, 1961-62, assistant professor of sociology, 1962-63; California State College (now University), Los Angeles, assistant professor of sociology, 1964-70; Los Angeles Summerhill Society, Los Angeles, Calif., president, 1967-70; Summerhill West, Los Angeles, and Pegasus, Hayward, Calif., director, 1967-70; California Polytechnic State University, San Luis Obispo, lecturer in sociology, 1973-74; Cheyney State College, Cheyney, Pa., professor and chairman of department of sociology-anthropology, 1974—. Public affairs director, KPFK-FM, 1966.

WRITINGS: (Editor) *Reader in Political Sociology,* Funk, 1968; (editor) *Radical Perspectives on Social Problems: Readings in Critical Sociology,* Macmillan, 1968, 2nd edition, 1973; (editor with Joyce Rothschild-Whitt) *Economic Democracy and Social Change,* Sargent, 1978.

LINDERMAN, Earl W. 1931-

PERSONAL: Born January 1, 1931, in Endicott, N.Y.; son of Earl Williams and Vera (Hickox) Linderman; married Marlene Melamed, February 7, 1953; children: Bill, Mark, Heather, Gwen, Cheryl. *Education:* State University of New York College of Education at Buffalo (now State University of New York College at Buffalo), B.S., 1953; Pennsylvania State University, M.Ed., 1956, Ed.D., 1960. *Home:* 6702 East McDonald Dr., Scottsdale, Ariz. 85252. *Office:* Department of Art, Arizona State University, Tempe, Ariz. 85281.

CAREER: Art teacher in public schools of Schenectady, N.Y., 1956-58; Sacramento State College (now California State University, Sacramento), Sacramento, Calif., assistant professor of art, 1960-65; Oregon State University, Corvallis, associate professor of art, 1965-66; Arizona State University, Tempe, member of art department faculty, 1966—, chairman of department, 1966-74. Art exhibited at Arizona State University, 1976, and Scottsdale Center for the Arts, 1977. *Military service:* U.S. Army, 1953-55. *Member:* National Art Education Association, College Art Association.

WRITINGS: (With Donald W. Herberholz) *Developing Artistic and Perceptual Awareness,* W. C. Brown, 1964, 4th edition, 1978; *Invitation to Vision,* W. C. Brown, 1967; *Teaching Secondary School Art,* W. C. Brown, 1971; (with wife, Marlene M. Linderman) *Crafts for the Classroom,* Macmillan, 1977. Also author of *Artistic Appreciation Today.* Editor of W. C. Brown's "Trends in Art Education" series.

*   *   *

LINTON, Barbara Leslie 1945-
(Barbara Leslie Austin)

PERSONAL: Born September 2, 1945, in Los Angeles, Calif.; daughter of William E. (a physician) and C. Maxine (Potts) Linton. *Education:* Marymount College, Palos Verdes, Calif., B.A., 1968; additional study at University of Arizona, 1970, and San Francisco State University, 1971—. *Politics:* Independent.

CAREER: As a nun, taught grammar school at Marymount, Palos Verdes, Calif., 1967-69, taught children of adults living at Synanon (drug rehabilitation center), Santa Monica, Calif., 1968; left convent in 1969, taught journalism at Summerhill, North Hollywood, Calif.; Gould & Associates, Inc. (industrial designers), Westwood, Calif., director of public relations, 1969-70; University of Arizona, Tucson, instructor in English, 1970-71. *Member:* International Catholic Society for Outstanding Academic Achievement. *Awards, honors:* Gold medals in history and English, Marymount College.

WRITINGS: (Under pseudonym Barbara Leslie Austin) *Sad Nun at Synanon,* Holt, 1970.

WORK IN PROGRESS: A novel, to be published by Holt, *Refugee from a Dying Butterfly;* a long short story, *Kill a Leprechaun for the Lord;* a nonfiction book, *Father, Son, and Holy Dog.*

SIDELIGHTS: Barbara Linton told *CA:* "I am the adopted child of WASP conservative-Republican parents in a lovely suburb of L.A. I was sent away to Marymount at 15; there I became a Catholic and a nun." A "serious" writer since she was a novice in her order (at the age of 19), her experiences with drug addicts and their children and the "attack technique" associated with Synanon led to intense self-examina-

tion and, eventually, to leaving the convent for secular life. Since then she has worked in the business world, lived on a dude ranch, studied creative writing at the University of Arizona ("a colossal bore") and San Francisco State College, and, for four months, joined a "contemplative co-ed commune," MacDowell Colony, in Sedona, Ariz., to work on her second novel, *Refugee from a Dying Butterfly.* She says: "I want to be an excellent writer, someone who makes you laugh and cry, who supports and even sometimes threatens you, like a good friend (c.f. Holden Caulfield in *Catcher in the Rye*)."

BIOGRAPHICAL/CRITICAL SOURCES: New York *Times,* June 1, 1970; *Christian Century,* July 8, 1970.††

*   *   *

LINTON, Ron(ald) M. 1929-

PERSONAL: Born May 7, 1929, in Detroit, Mich.; son of Louis D. and Lillian (Gordon) Linton; married Nancy Gault, November 5, 1955; children: Cynthia, Victoria. *Education:* Michigan State University, B.A., 1951. *Politics:* Democrat. *Religion:* Unitarian Universalist. *Home:* 4830 Broad Branch Rd. N.W., Washington, D.C. 20008. *Office:* Ron M. Linton Consultant, 1015 18th St. N.W., Washington, D.C. 20006.

CAREER: Entered newspaper field in 1951, working for United Press in Michigan and Iowa, with papers in Texas, and as labor editor of *Courier-Journal,* Louisville, Ky.; Michigan State Department of Economic Development, Lansing, staff member, 1954-55; Michigan Department of Workmen's Compensation, Lansing, secretary of department, 1955-56; joined the campaign staff of Senator John F. Kennedy in 1960; U.S. Department of Defense, Washington, D.C., director of economic utilization policy, 1961-63; U.S. Senate, Washington, D.C., chief clerk and staff director of Committee on Public Works, 1963-67; U.S. Department of Health, Education and Welfare, Washington, D.C., chairman of Secretary's Task Force on Environmental Health and Related Problems, 1966-67; Urban American, Inc., Washington, D.C., director of special projects, 1966-67; National Urban Coalition, Washington, D.C., national coordinator, 1967-68; Linton & Co., Inc., Washington, D.C., chairman, 1968—; Ron M. Linton Consultant, Washington, D.C., managing associate, 1968—; K&L Enterprises, Washington, D.C., partner, 1968—. Visiting professor, Rensselaer Polytechnic Institute, 1960-70.

MEMBER: American Public Health Association, National Urban Coalition (co-founder). *Awards, honors:* American Political Science Association fellow in Washington, 1959-60.

WRITINGS: Terracide: America's Destruction of Her Living Environment, Little, Brown, 1970. Writer of government research reports.

*   *   *

LIPETZ, Ben-Ami 1927-

PERSONAL: Born March 14, 1927, in Fargo, N.D.; son of Elijah Yekusiel (a manufacturer) and Ruth (Leavitt) Lipetz; married Carolyn Aikin, March 11, 1950. *Education:* Cornell University, B.M.E., 1948, Ph.D., 1959. *Home:* 20 Acorn Hill Rd., Woodbridge, Conn. 06525. *Office:* Computer Science Department, Yale University, New Haven, Conn. 06520.

CAREER: Brookhaven National Laboratory, Upton, N.Y., editor, 1948-50; Battelle Memorial Institute, Columbus, Ohio, Information Center management, in research and development, 1953-57, assistant department head, 1957-59; Itek Corp., Lexington, Mass., section head, Document Operations information management, 1959-62; consultant on research and management in Carlisle, Mass., 1962-66; Yale University, New Haven, Conn., head of research department in university library, 1966-74, senior research associate in computer science department, 1974—. Constable and chairman of Long-Range Plan Committee, Carlisle, Mass., 1963-65; president of Intermedia, Inc. (publishing company); consultant to various government agencies and nonprofit organizations. *Military service:* U.S. Navy, 1945-46. *Member:* American Society for Information Science (national councilor, 1970-73; chairman, Boston chapter, 1964-66; chairman, standards committee, 1976—), American Library Association (council member, Library Research Round Table, 1967-68; chairman, research committee, 1976—), Special Libraries Association, American Society of Indexers (council member, 1968-70), American Society for Public Administration, Society for Social Studies of Science.

WRITINGS: (Compiler) *Volume 17: Index to Geneva Conference on Peaceful Uses of Atomic Energy,* United Nations, 1958; *The Measurement of Efficiency of Scientific Research,* Intermedia, 1965; (with C. P. McLaughlin) *A Guide to Case Studies of Scientific Activity,* Intermedia, 1965; *User Requirements in Identifying Desired Works in a Large Library,* Yale University Library, 1970. Contributor of numerous papers on information science and librarianship to professional journals. Editor, *Cornell Engineer,* 1946-48, *Information Science Abstracts,* 1966—.

WORK IN PROGRESS: Research on the fundamentals of information storage and retrieval.

SIDELIGHTS: Ben-Ami Lipetz told *CA:* "I do not aspire to be a creative writer or stylist. My objective is to be a creative research planner and a good analyst of important problems. In writing, I try only to achieve spare clarity."

* * *

LIPMAN, Matthew 1923-

PERSONAL: Born August 24, 1923, in Vineland, N.J.; son of William Leo (a manufacturer) and Sophie (Kenin) Lipman; children: Karen, Will. *Education:* Attended Stanford University, 1943-44; Columbia University, B.S., 1948, Ph.D., 1953. *Home:* 40 Park St., Montclair, N.J. 07042. *Office:* Department of Philosophy and Religion, Montclair State College, Upper Montclair, N.J. 07043.

CAREER: Columbia University, New York, N.Y., instructor in philosophy, social science, and fine arts, 1954-57, assistant professor, 1957-61, associate professor, 1961-66, professor of philosophy, 1966-72, research associate in department of philosophy, 1971-72, chairman of department of general education, College of Pharmacy, 1962-72, instructor in contemporary civilization, Columbia College, 1954-63; Montclair State College, Upper Montclair, N.J., professor of philosophy, 1972—. Adjunct associate professor of philosophy, City College of the City University of New York, 1953-75; visiting professor, Sarah Lawrence College, 1963-64. Director, Institute for the Advancement of Philosophy for Children, 1974—. *Military service:* U.S. Army, Infantry, 1943-46; received two Bronze Star Medals. *Member:* American Philosophical Association, American Society for Aesthetics. *Awards, honors:* Fulbright scholar at Sorbonne, University of Paris, 1950-51; Matchette Prize for Aesthetics, 1956; American Council of Learned Societies grant, 1967; National Endowment for the Humanities grant, 1970—.

WRITINGS—Published by Institute for the Advancement of Philosophy for Children, except as indicated: *What Happens in Art,* Appleton, 1967; *Discovering Philosophy,* Appleton, 1969, 2nd edition, Prentice-Hall, 1977; *Contemporary Aesthetics,* Allyn & Bacon, 1973; *Harry Stottlemeier's Discovery,* 1974; (with Ann M. Sharp) *Instructional Manual for Harry,* 1975; *Lisa,* 1976; (with Sharp and Frederick S. Oscangan) *Instructional Manual for Lisa,* 1977; *Suki,* 1977. Contributor to philosophy, psychiatry, and aesthetics journals.

WORK IN PROGRESS: With Ann M. Sharp, *Growing Up with Philosophy,* for Temple University Press.

* * *

LIPPMAN, Theo, Jr. 1929-

PERSONAL: Born September 7, 1929, in Brunswick, Ga.; son of Theo and Louise (Deaver) Lippman; married Madeline Mabry (a librarian), July 16, 1955; children: Susan, Laura. *Education:* Emory University, B.A., 1952. *Office:* *Baltimore Sun,* Baltimore, Md. 21207.

CAREER: *Atlanta Constitution,* Atlanta, Ga., reporter and editor, 1955-65; *Baltimore Sun,* Baltimore, Md., editorial writer, 1965—. *Military service:* U.S. Naval Reserve, 1948-54. *Member:* National Press Club, 14 West Hamilton Street Club (Baltimore).

WRITINGS: (With Donald C. Hansen) *Muskie,* Norton, 1971; *Spiro Agnew's America,* Norton, 1972; (editor) H. L. Mencken, *A Gang of Pecksniffs,* Arlington House, 1975; *Senator Ted Kennedy,* Norton, 1976; *The Squire of Warm Springs,* Playboy Press, 1977.

SIDELIGHTS: Reviewing *Senator Ted Kennedy* for *Harper's,* Richard Condon says, "Mr. Lippman preserves the political record with grace, skill, and attention to historical form."

BIOGRAPHICAL/CRITICAL SOURCES: Life, April 7, 1972; *Best Sellers,* November, 1975, March, 1976; *Commonweal,* November 7, 1975; *Nation,* November 29, 1975; *New York Times Book Review,* January 11, 1976; *Critic,* spring, 1976; *New York Review of Books,* April 29, 1976; *Harper's,* May, 1976; *National Review,* May 14, 1976; *National Observer,* May 22, 1976; *New Republic,* July 24, 1976.

* * *

LIPSON, Goldie 1905-

PERSONAL: Born November 18, 1905, in New York, N.Y.; daughter of Herman and Tillie (Schroff) Goldman; married Morris J. Lipson (a furrier), July 13, 1924 (died July 22, 1975); children: Adylin (Mrs. Murray Rosenblatt), Stanley Z. *Education:* Studied at Columbia University and in Works Progress Administration (WPA) art classes. *Religion:* "All religions as a yoga teacher." *Home and office:* R.R. 6, Box 360, Lake of the Hills, Lake Wales, Fla. 33853.

CAREER: Artist, writer, and teacher of art and yoga; founder of Mount Vernon School of Fine Arts (later the Goldie Lipson Studio Workshop), Mount Vernon, N.Y., 1943 and director there and at its subsequent location in New Rochelle, N.Y., 1945-61; instructor in yoga and the arts at International Center for Self Analysis, Orchid Springs, Fla., 1968—; created sculpture in Orchid Springs permanent collection, 1968—; also conducted classes in yoga and the arts at Florida Central College, Lakeland, 1971, and Lake Wales, 1970, 1971, 1972. Work as an artist has been shown in more than thirty one-woman shows, and exhibited at Metropolitan Museum of Art, Museum of Modern Art, and other galleries. *Member:* Artist Equity Association, National Association of Women Artists, Florida Federation of Art (publicity chairman, 1971-73), Ridge Art Association (Winter Haven, Fla., member of board, 1970-71), Florida Artists Group.

WRITINGS—Self-illustrated: (Compiler) *Rejuvenation: A Handbook of Hatha Yoga-Water Hatha Yoga,* edited by Hilda F. Berkowitz, Lipson Studios, 1963, reprinted as *Rejuvenation through Yoga,* Pyramid Publications, 1965, revised edition, 1977; *We,* Lipson Studios, 1965; *Beyond Yoga,* Pyramid Publications, 1970, revised edition, 1977.

Illustrator: Jess Stearn, *Yoga, Youth, and Reincarnation,* Doubleday, 1965. Writer and illustrator of weekly Sunday feature, "My Guru Says," in *Daily Hylander,* Lake Wales, Fla., 1971-73.

WORK IN PROGRESS: Art through Yoga, for Pyramid Publications.

BIOGRAPHICAL/CRITICAL SOURCES: Tampa Tribune (Tampa, Fla.), September 16, 1968; *The Ledger* (Lakeland, Fla.), February 17, 1971.

* * *

LITZ, A(rthur) Walton (Jr.)   1929-

PERSONAL: Born October 31, 1929, in Nashville, Tenn.; son of A. Walton (an executive) and Lucille (Courtney) Litz; married Marian Ann Weller, February 2, 1958; children: Katharine, Andrew, Victoria, Emily. *Education:* Princeton University, B.A., 1951; Oxford University, D.Phil., 1954. *Home:* 187 Prospect St., Princeton, N.J. 08540. *Office:* Department of English, Princeton University, Princeton, N.J. 08540.

CAREER: Princeton University, Princeton, N.J., instructor, 1956-58, assistant professor, 1958-63, associate professor, 1963-68, professor of English, 1968—, chairman of department, 1975—. *Military service:* U.S. Army, 1954-56. *Awards, honors:* Rhodes scholar, 1951-54; American Council of Learned Societies fellow, 1960-61; National Endowment for the Humanities fellow, 1974-75.

WRITINGS: The Art of James Joyce, Oxford University Press, 1961; *Modern American Fiction,* Oxford University Press, 1963; *Jane Austen,* Oxford University Press, 1965; *James Joyce,* Twayne, 1966; (editor) Thomas Hardy, *Return of the Native,* Houghton, 1967; (editor) James Joyce, *Dubliners,* Viking, 1969; *Modern Literary Criticism, 1900-1970,* Atheneum, 1972; *The Poetic Development of Wallace Stevens,* Oxford University Press, 1972; *Eliot in His Time,* Princeton University Press, 1973; *Major American Short Stories,* Oxford University Press, 1975. Member of editorial board, Princeton University Press, 1967-71.

WORK IN PROGRESS: A study of modern British and American literature.

BIOGRAPHICAL/CRITICAL SOURCES: Books Abroad, winter, 1967; *Modern Language Journal,* December, 1967; *New York Times Book Review,* October 7, 1973; *Nation,* February 23, 1974; *Times Literary Supplement,* May 3, 1974; *New York Review of Books,* September 19, 1974; *Sewanee Review,* October, 1974; *Modern Language Review,* October, 1974; *Virginia Quarterly Review,* winter, 1974; *Review of English Studies,* May, 1975.

* * *

LIVINGSTONE, Harrison Edward   1937-
(John Fairfield)

PERSONAL: Born May 23, 1937. *Education:* Eastern College (now merged with University of Baltimore), LL.B., 1965; Harvard University, B.A., 1970. *Politics:* "Neutral." *Religion:* "Episcopal—not a formal member." *Home:* 312 South Eden St., Baltimore, Md. 21231.

CAREER: Writer. Teacher at seminars in creative writing at Harvard University, 1969-70. *Military service:* U.S. Air Force.

WRITINGS: Poems, privately printed, 1967; (under pseudonym John Fairfield) *David Johnson Passed through Here,* Little, Brown, 1971. Also author of an unpublished novel, "The Wild Rose."

WORK IN PROGRESS: A novel about Baltimore; a novel about Harvard during the campus troubles.

AVOCATIONAL INTERESTS: Back-packing, sailing.

BIOGRAPHICAL/CRITICAL SOURCES: Baltimore Sun, November 28, 1971.

* * *

LIVINGSTONE, Leon   1912-

PERSONAL: Born August 23, 1912, in Boston, Mass.; son of Alexander (an investment broker) and Annie (Sive) Livingstone; married Alicia Arce, February 4, 1948; children: Andrea D., Marco E., Alexa P. *Education:* University of Toronto, B.A. (with honors), 1934; attended University of Paris, 1934-35; Brown University, A.M., 1938, Ph.D., 1947. *Residence:* London, England. *Office:* Department of Languages and Literature, State University of New York at Buffalo, Buffalo, N.Y. 14260.

CAREER: Brown University, Providence, R.I., instructor, 1941-42, assistant professor of Spanish, 1947-50; Wayne State University, Detroit, Mich., assistant professor, 1950-57, associate professor of Spanish, 1957-61; State University of New York at Buffalo, professor of Spanish, 1961—, acting chairman, department of modern languages, 1963-64, director, Programa de Estudios Hispanicos in Barcelona, Spain, 1967-70, chairman, department of Spanish, Italian, and Portuguese, and chairman, Council of Modern Languages, 1967-69. Visiting professor of Spanish, University of California, Los Angeles, 1964-65. *Military service:* U.S. Army, 1942-46; special agent in Counterintelligence Corps. *Member:* American Association of University Professors, American Association of Teachers of Spanish and Portuguese, Modern Language Association (program chairman, Spanish group, 1970; member of executive committee, Spanish group V, 1967-70). *Awards, honors:* French Government Bourse d'Etudes, 1934; faculty fellowship, Fund for the Advancement of Education, 1954-55; Guggenheim fellowship, 1974-75.

WRITINGS: (Contributor) *Homenaje a Rodriguez Monino,* Castalia (Madrid), 1966; (contributor) Jose Rubia Barcia and Marion A. Zeitlin, editors, *Unamuno: Creator and Creation,* University of California Press, 1967; (editor) Azorin, *Dona Ines,* Appleton, 1969; *Tema y forma en las novelas de Azorin,* Gredos (Madrid), 1970; (contributor) *Homenaje al professor Fichter,* Castalia, 1971; (contributor) *Galdos II,* Tamesis, 1974. Contributor of articles and reviews to *Publications of the Modern Language Association of America, Hispanic Review, Symposium, Hispania, Romanic Review, Anales Galdosianos,* and other journals.

WORK IN PROGRESS: A book, *The Elusive I: Identity and Form, Self and Society in the Twentieth-Century Spanish Novel.*

LOCKE, Louis G(lenn) 1912-

PERSONAL: Born May 3, 1912, in Woodstock, Va.; son of Thomas Glenn and Turah (Funk) Locke; married Jeanette Wolfe, September 3, 1940; children: Sarah Anne (Mrs. Walter D. Clark, Jr.), Elizabeth Louise. Education: Bridgewater College, A.B., 1933; George Washington University, A.M., 1934; Harvard University, A.M., 1937, Ph.D., 1938. Home: 474 Ott St., Harrisonburg, Va. 22801. Office: Madison College, South Main St., Harrisonburg, Va. 22801.

CAREER: University of New Brunswick, Fredericton, acting professor of English, 1938-39; University of Virginia, Mary Washington College, Fredericksburg, assistant professor of English, 1939-43; U.S. Army Air Forces, 20th College Training Detachment, Centre College, Danville, Ky., head of English department, 1943-45; Southwestern University, Memphis, Tenn., associate professor of English, 1945-47; Mary Baldwin College, Staunton, Va., professor of English, 1947-56; Madison College, Harrisonburg, Va., chairman of department of English, 1956-67, director of Division of Humanities, 1956-69, dean of School of Humanities, 1969-72, James Madison Distinguished Professor, 1972—. Visiting summer professor at Pennsylvania State University, 1948, and at University of New Mexico, 1950. Director and secretary, Explicator Literary Foundation. Member: Modern Language Association of America, National Council of Teachers of English, College English Association, English Institute, Omicron Delta Kappa. Awards, honors: Dexter travelling fellow of Harvard University, 1937; Ford Foundation fellow, 1953-54.

WRITINGS: (With William Gibson and George Arms) Toward Liberal Education, Rinehart, 1948, 5th edition, Holt, 1967; (with Gibson and Arms) Readings for Liberal Education, Rinehart, 1948, 5th edition, Holt, 1967; (with Gibson and Arms) Introduction to Literature, Rinehart, 1948, 5th edition, Holt, 1967; (with J. P. Kirby and M. E. Porter) Literature of Western Civilization, two volumes, Ronald, 1952; (with Arms) Symposium, Rinehart, 1954; Tillotson: A Study in Seventeenth-Century Literature, Rosenkilde & Bagger (Copenhagen), 1954; (with Harris Wilson) University Readings, Holt, 1961; (with Wilson) The University Handbook, Holt, 1961, 2nd edition, 1966; (with Arms, Gibson, and George Petty, Jr.) TLE6: Options for the '70s, Holt, 1972; (with Gibson and Arms) The College Reader, St. Martin's, 1978. Explicator, co-founder and co-editor, 1942-76, co-executive editor, 1976—.

*   *   *

LOCKE, Wende 1945-

PERSONAL: Born June 6, 1945, in New York, N.Y.; daughter of Milton (an executive) and Gladyce (Sherr) Gluckman. Education: New York University, B.A., 1967, M.A., 1970. Agent: Curtis Brown Ltd., 575 Madison Ave., New York, N.Y. 10022.

CAREER: Has held various jobs in the publishing field.

WRITINGS: Split Hairs (poems), New York University Press, 1970.

WORK IN PROGRESS: Birthmarks (tentative title), a book of poems.

AVOCATIONAL INTERESTS: Sculpturing.†

*   *   *

LOEWENBERG, J(orn) Joseph 1933-

PERSONAL: Born November 22, 1933, in Hamburg, Germany; son of Ernst Lutwin (a teacher) and Margarete (Oettinger) Loewenberg; married Betty Binder, June 26, 1968; children: David, Benjamin. Education: Harvard University, A.B. (cum laude), 1955, M.B.A. (with distinction), 1959, D.B.A., 1962. Home: 1364 Indian Creek Dr., Wynnewood, Pa. 19151. Office: School of Business Administration, Temple University, Philadelphia, Pa. 19122.

CAREER: U.S. Department of Labor, Washington, D.C., labor economist, 1962-66; Temple University, Philadelphia, Pa., assistant professor, 1966-69, associate professor, 1969-74, professor of business administration, 1974—. Part-time instructor, George Washington University and Georgetown University, 1962-66; visiting senior lecturer, Tel Aviv University, 1970-71. Member of national labor panels, American Arbitration Association and Federal Mediation and Conciliation Service. Military service: U.S. Army, 1955-57. Member: Industrial Relations Research Association, American Arbitration Association.

WRITINGS: (Contributor) Martin S. Estey and others, editors, Regulating Union Government, Harper, 1964; The Operation of Severance Pay Plans and Their Implications for Labor Mobility, U.S. Government Printing Office, 1966; (contributor) Seymour Wolfbein, editor, Emerging Sectors of Collective Bargaining, D. H. Mark, 1970; (editor with Michael H. Moskow and Edward C. Koziara) Collective Bargaining in Public Employment, Random House, 1970; Compulsory Binding Arbitration in the Public Sector, International Symposium on Public Employment Labor Relations, 1971; (editor with Moskow) Collective Bargaining in Government: Readings and Cases, Prentice-Hall, 1972; (with James L. Stern and others) Final-Offer Arbitration: The Effects on Public Safety Employee Bargaining, Lexington Books, 1975; (editor with others) Compulsory Arbitration: An International Comparison, Lexington Books, 1976; (editor with Walter J. Gershenfeld) Scope of Public Sector Bargaining, Lexington Books, 1977. Contributor to Monthly Labor Review, Economic and Business Bulletin, Labor Law Journal, Industrial and Labor Relations Review, and Arbitration Journal.

*   *   *

LOFLAND, John (Franklin) 1936-

PERSONAL: Born March 4, 1936, in Milford, Del.; married Lyn Hebert (a university professor), January 2, 1965. Education: Swarthmore College, B.A., 1958; Columbia University, M.A., 1960; University of California, Berkeley, Ph.D., 1964. Home: 523 E St., Davis, Calif. 95616. Office: Department of Sociology, University of California, Davis, Calif. 95616.

CAREER: University of Michigan, Ann Arbor, assistant professor of sociology, 1964-68; Sonoma State College (now California State College, Sonoma), Rohnert Park, Calif., associate professor of sociology, 1968-70; University of California, Davis, associate professor, 1970-74, professor of sociology, 1974—.

WRITINGS: Doomsday Cult: A Study of Conversion, Proselytization and Maintenance of Faith, Prentice-Hall, 1966, enlarged revised edition, Irvington Books, 1977; (with wife, Lyn H. Lofland) Deviance and Identity, Prentice-Hall, 1969; Analyzing Social Settings: A Guide to Qualitative Observation and Analysis, Wadsworth, 1971; Doing Social Life, Wiley, 1976; (with H. Bleackley) State Executions, Patterson Smith, 1977; (editor) Social Strategies, Sage Publications, 1977. Editor, Urban Life: A Journal of Ethnographic Research, 1972-75.

WORK IN PROGRESS: Public Place Politics: Demonstrations at a State Capitol; Sociological Analysis: Qualitative Forms; Social Movements.

* * *

LOH, Jules 1931-

PERSONAL: Born May 29, 1931, in Macon, Ga.; son of Julius E. and Mary (Cassidy) Loh; married Jean Brown, October 25, 1952; children: Stephen, Catherine, Christine, Dennis, Maureen, Carolyn, Michael, Eileen. *Education:* Attended Georgetown University, 1948-51, and Baylor University, 1952-53. *Home:* 111 Willow Dr., Old Tappan, N.J. 07675. *Office:* Associated Press, 50 Rockefeller Plaza, New York, N.Y. 10020.

CAREER: Washington Post, Washington, D.C., reporter, 1948-50; *Waco Tribune-Herald,* Waco, Tex., reporter, 1953-55, regional editor, 1955-58; Associated Press, reporter in Louisville, Ky., 1958-60, feature writer in New York, N.Y., 1960-77, special correspondent, 1977—. *Military service:* U.S. Air Force, 1950-53. *Awards, honors:* Western Writers Association "Spur" award for non-fiction, 1972, for *Lords of the Earth: A History of the Navajo Indians.*

WRITINGS: Lords of the Earth: A History of the Navajo Indians, Macmillan, 1971. Contributor to national periodicals, including *Esquire, Saturday Review,* and *Reader's Digest.*

* * *

LONDON, Herbert I(ra) 1939-

PERSONAL: Born March 6, 1939, in New York, N.Y.; son of Jack (a salesman) and Esta (Epstein) London; married Vicki London, November 27, 1977; children: Stacy, Nancy. *Education:* Columbia University, B.A., 1960, M.A., 1961; New York University, Ph.D., 1966. *Religion:* Jewish. *Home:* 2 Washington Sq. Village, New York, N.Y. 10012. *Office:* Department of Social Studies, New York University, 25 Waverly Pl., New York, N.Y. 10003.

CAREER: New School for Social Research, New York City, instructor in American studies, 1966; Australian National University, Canberra, Australia, research associate, 1966-67; New York University, New York City, assistant professor, 1967-69, associate professor of social studies, 1969—, director of "University Without Walls," 1971-76, director of Gallatin Division, 1976-77. Consultant, Hudson Institute, Institute for Advancement of Urban Education. *Member:* American Association of University Professors, American Historical Association, American Political Science Association, Pop Culture Association. *Awards, honors:* Anderson fellowship; Fulbright award.

WRITINGS: (Editor with Arnold Spinner) *Education in the 21st Century* (papers from symposium sponsored by Center for Field Research and School Services, New York University), Interstate, 1969; *Non-White Immigration and the White Australian Policy,* New York University Press, 1970; *Fitting In,* Grosset, 1974; *Social Science Theory, Structure and Application,* New York University Press, 1975; *The Overheated Decade,* New York University Press, 1976. Contributor of articles to *Orbis, Dissent, University of Colorado Quarterly, New School Bulletin, New York University Quarterly, American Scholar, Arts and Sciences, Dublin Review, Australian Outlook,* and other periodicals.

WORK IN PROGRESS: Left Meets Right, a book describing political convergence in the sixties.

SIDELIGHTS: Herbert London was the director of New York University's "University Without Walls," a program established by nineteen American colleges and universities in 1971 to make college-level education more flexible and available to persons of all ages. Funded by grants from the U.S. Office of Education and the Ford Foundation, and administered by the Union for Experimenting Colleges and Universities at Antioch College, "University Without Walls" offers degree credit for such off-campus activities as government and business internships, service in VISTA and the Peace Corps, travel abroad, and independent study.

London told *CA* that "playing college and professional basketball as well as making rock records in the late '50's" account for his current interest in pop culture.

* * *

LONEY, Glenn (Meredith) 1928-
(Jeff Meredith)

PERSONAL: Born December 24, 1928, in Sacramento, Calif.; son of David Merton (a farmer) and Marion (Busher) Loney. *Education:* University of California, Berkeley, A.B., 1950; University of Wisconsin—Madison, M.A., 1951; Stanford University, Ph.D., 1954. *Home:* 3 East 71st St., New York, N.Y. 10021. *Office:* Department of Theatre, Brooklyn College of the City University of New York, Bedford Ave. & Ave. H., Brooklyn, N.Y. 11210.

CAREER: San Francisco State College (now University), San Francisco, Calif., instructor in language arts, 1955-56; Nevada Southern University (now University of Nevada, Las Vegas), instructor in English and theatre, 1955-56; University of Maryland Overseas, professor of English and speech, 1956-59; Hofstra University, Hempstead, N.Y., instructor in theatre, 1959-61; Adelphi University, Garden City, N.Y., instructor in theatre, 1959-61; Brooklyn College of the City University of New York, Brooklyn, N.Y., assistant professor, 1961-67, associate professor, 1967-70, professor of theatre, 1970—; Graduate School and University Center of the City University of New York, New York, N.Y., professor of theatre, 1970—. Member of ad hoc committees, Save the Forum and Save the Library of Performing Arts. *Military service:* U.S. Army, 1953-55. *Member:* International Theatre Institute, American Society for Theatre Research, American Theatre Association, Speech Communication Association, Children's Theatre Conference, International Federation of Theatre Research, United States Institute for Theatre Technology, American-Scandinavian Foundation (fellow), Drama Desk, Outer Circle of Drama Critics, Phi Beta Kappa, Alpha Mu Gamma.

WRITINGS: Briefing and Conference Techniques, McGraw, 1959; (editor) John Gassner, *Dramatic Soundings,* Crown, 1968; (with Robert Corrigan) *Tragedy,* Houghton, 1971; (with Corrigan) *Comedy,* Houghton, 1971; (with Corrigan) *The Forms of Drama,* Houghton, 1972. Theatre critic for *Educational Theatre Journal,* 1965-71, *New York Daily Column,* and *After Dark.* Contributor to *Christian Science Monitor, New York Herald Tribune, New York Times, Life, Reporter, Saturday Evening Post,* and other publications. Contributing editor to *Cue, After Dark, Dance, Players, Theatre Today, Theatre Crafts,* and other publications.

WORK IN PROGRESS: A chapter on U.S. government and the arts in a book on U.S. and Canadian governments; a study on theatre history, for Scott, Foresman; *Opera as Theatre,* for Summit Books; *Musical Comedy at Home and Abroad,* for Summit Books; *Cue Lines,* a book of interviews; *Who Needs Theatre?*.

LONG, A(nthony) A(rthur) 1937-

PERSONAL: Born August 17, 1937, in Manchester, England; son of Tom Arthur (a teacher) and Joan (LeGrice) Long; married Janice Calloway (a teacher), 1960; married second wife, Kay Flavell (a university lecturer), 1970; children: Stephen Arthur, Rebecca Jane. *Education:* University College, London, B.A., 1960, Ph.D., 1964. *Office:* School of Classics, University of Liverpool, Liverpool L69 3BX, England.

CAREER: University of Otago, Dunedin, New Zealand, lecturer in classics, 1961-64; University of Nottingham, Nottingham, England, lecturer in classics, 1964-66; University of London, University College, London, England, lecturer, 1966-71, reader in Greek and Latin, 1971-73; University of Liverpool, Liverpool, England, Gladstone Professor of Greek, 1973—. Visiting professor of classical philology, University of Munich, 1973. Member, Institute for Advanced Study, Princeton, N.J., 1969-70. Treasurer, Council of University Classical Departments, 1970-75. *Military service:* British Army, 1955-57; became lieutenant. *Member:* Aristotelian Society, Classical Association (member of council, 1974-77), Society for Promotion of Hellenic Studies (member of council, 1972-75), Institute of Classical Studies (member of board of management, 1970-73). *Awards, honors:* Cromer Greek Prize, British Academy, 1968, for *Language and Thought in Sophocles: A Study of Abstract Nouns and Poetic Technique.*

WRITINGS: Language and Thought in Sophocles: A Study of Abstract Nouns and Poetic Technique, Oxford University Press, 1968; (editor) *Problems in Stoicism,* Oxford University Press, 1971; *Hellenistic Philosophy,* Scribner, 1974. Contributor to books on Greek philosophy, Greek literature and ancient philosophy, and to *Dictionary of the History of Ideas.* Contributor to *Classical Review, Classical Quarterly, Journal of Hellenic Studies, Philosophical Quarterly, Phronesis,* and other scholarly journals. Editor, *Bulletin* of University College, London, 1971-73, *Classical Quarterly,* 1975—.

WORK IN PROGRESS: The Hellenistic Philosophers, with T. G. Kidd, for Cambridge University Press; *Studies in Greek Tragedy,* for Duckworth.

AVOCATIONAL INTERESTS: Music, talking, travel, cricket.

BIOGRAPHICAL/CRITICAL SOURCES: New York Times, May 28, 1971.

*   *   *

LONSDALE, Kathleen (Yardley) 1903-1971

January 28, 1903—April 1, 1971; British crystallographer and educator. Obituaries: *New York Times,* April 2, 1971. (See index for *CA* sketch)

*   *   *

LOOMIS, Chauncey C(hester), Jr. 1930-

PERSONAL: Born June 1, 1930, in New York, N.Y.; son of Chauncey C., Sr. (a business executive) and Elizabeth (McClannahan) Loomis. *Education:* Princeton University, A.B., 1952, Ph.D., 1962; Columbia University, A.M., 1956. *Home address:* Box 924, Hanover, N.H. 03755. *Office:* Department of English, Dartmouth College, Hanover, N.H. 03755.

CAREER: University of Vermont, Burlington, instructor in English, 1956-59; Dartmouth College, Hanover, N.H., in-

structor, 1961-62, assistant professor, 1962-66, associate professor, 1967-71, professor of English, 1972—. Professional still and motion picture photographer. *Military service:* U.S. Army, 1952-54. *Member:* Explorers Club. *Awards, honors:* Smithsonian postdoctoral fellow, 1966.

WRITINGS: Weird and Tragic Shores, Knopf, 1971.

WORK IN PROGRESS: A book, *The Settlers of Kenya.*

SIDELIGHTS: Chauncey Loomis has made three expeditions to the Peruvian Andes and five to the Canadian and Alaskan Arctic. He was consultant for the Canadian Broadcasting Corp. television documentary based on his book, entitled "Two Arctic Tales" produced by CBC and NET in 1972, and also shot the film used on the television special, "Wild River, Wild Beasts," produced in 1970 by CBS.

*   *   *

LOPREATO, Joseph 1928-

PERSONAL: Surname is pronounced Lopre-*ah*-toh; born July 13, 1928, in Stefanaconi, Italy; came to United States in 1947; son of Francesco (a farmer) and Marianna (Pavone) Lopreiato; married Carolyn H., 1954 (divorced); children: Gregory F., Marisa S. *Education:* University of Connecticut, B.A., 1956; Yale University, M.A., 1957, Ph.D., 1960. *Office:* Department of Sociology, University of Texas, Austin, Tex. 78712.

CAREER: University of Massachusetts—Amherst, assistant professor of sociology, 1960-62; University of Rome, Rome, Italy, visiting lecturer, 1962-64; University of Connecticut, Storrs, associate professor of sociology, 1964-66; University of Texas at Austin, professor of sociology, 1966—, chairman of department, 1969-72. *Military service:* U.S. Army, 1952-54. *Member:* American Sociological Association, American Italian Historical Association, Southwestern Sociological Association, Southern Sociological Association. *Awards, honors:* Fulbright scholar in Italy, 1962-64; Social Science Research Council fellow, 1963-64; National Science Foundation grant, 1965-68.

WRITINGS: Vilfredo Pareto, Crowell, 1965; *Peasants No More,* Chandler Publishing, 1967; *Italian Americans,* Random House, 1970; *Class, Conflict, and Mobility,* Chandler Publishing, 1972. Contributor to sociology journals. Associate editor, *American Sociological Review,* 1970-72.

WORK IN PROGRESS: Several research projects on the political behavior of the social-class mobile.

*   *   *

LORD, Beman 1924-

PERSONAL: Born November 22, 1924, in Delaware County, N.Y.; son of Harold Beman (a printer) and Eloisae (Judd) Lord; married Patricia Cummings (an editor), September 26, 1959; children: Edwin, Patricia Duffy. *Religion:* Presbyterian. *Home:* 106 East 85th St., New York, N.Y. 10028. *Office:* Charles Scribner's Sons, 597 Fifth Ave., New York, N.Y. 10017.

CAREER: Employed with Library Services Associates, Lord Associates, Lord Book Representatives, Inc.; currently with Charles Scribner's Sons, New York, N.Y. Writer for young people. Head of *New York Times* and Children's Book Council Reading Is Fun Exhibit, 1949-54. *Member:* Library Public Relations Council (president, 1968), American Library Association.

WRITINGS—All published by Walck: The Trouble with Francis, 1958; *Quaterback's Aim,* 1960; *Guards for Matt,*

1961; *Look at Cars*, 1962, revised edition, 1970; *Bats and Balls*, 1962; *Look at Guns*, 1963; *Rough Ice*, 1963; *Mystery Guest at Left End*, 1964; *Our New Baby's ABC*, 1964; *The Perfect Pitch*, 1965; *Look at the Army*, 1965; *A Monster's Visit*, 1967; *The Day the Spaceship Landed*, 1967; *Days of the Week*, 1968; *Shot-Put Challenge*, 1969; *Shrimp's Soccer Goal*, 1970; *The Spaceship Returns*, 1970; *On the Banks of the Delaware*, 1971; *On the Banks of the Hudson*, 1971.

BIOGRAPHICAL/CRITICAL SOURCES: New York Times Book Review, May 2, 1971.

* * *

LORENZEN, David N(eal) 1940-

PERSONAL: Born June 7, 1940, in New Haven, Conn.; son of Stanley H. (a school administrator) and Elena (Sbrega) Lorenzen; married Sheila Breen, October 26, 1961; children: Jesse, Sarah. *Education:* Wesleyan University, Middletown, Conn., B.A., 1962; attended University of London, 1962-65; Australian National University, Ph.D., 1968. *Religion:* None. *Home:* 8 Guyer Rd., Westport, Conn. 06880. *Office:* El Colegio de Mexico, Guanajuato 125, Mexico 11 D.F., Mexico.

CAREER: Wisconsin State University, Whitewater (now University of Wisconsin—Whitewater), assistant professor of history, 1968-70; El Colegio de Mexico, Mexico City, visiting professor of oriental studies, 1970—.

WRITINGS: The Kapalikas and Kalamukhas, University of California, 1972. Contributor of articles to *Estudios Orientales* and of reviews to *Journal of Asian Studies* and other journals.

WORK IN PROGRESS: Translating Madhava's *Sankaradigvigaya;* a project on social dissent in bhakti religion.

* * *

LOURIE, Dick 1937-
(H. Loose, Alvin Wonder)

PERSONAL: Surname rhymes with "jury"; born December 31, 1937, in Hackensack, N.J.; son of Norman Victor Lourie (a social worker) and Doris (a social worker; maiden name, Kaplan) Rosenberg. *Education:* Princeton University, A.B., 1959; Columbia University, M.A., 1960. *Residence:* Ithaca, N.Y.

CAREER: Poet; professional singer and jazz and folk music performer; Ithaca College, Ithaca, N.Y., instructor in English, 1961-63; New York City Department of Welfare, New York City, caseworker, 1965-69; Forest House Headstart, Bronx, N.Y., music teacher, 1968-70; Teachers and Writers Collaborative, New York City, poetry teacher, 1970-71; junior high school teacher of English in Fishkill, N.Y., 1971-72; Moon Associates, Peekskill, N.Y., creations analyst, 1972-73; member of musical group, New York Central, 1977—. Performer in multi-media show touring under the auspices of New York State Council on the Arts, 1970-71; affiliated with New York State Poets in the Schools program, 1972—; has given poetry readings at Cornell University, Brown University, Vassar College, Guggenheim Museum, and at numerous schools, cafes, and coffeehouses. Music consultant, Volt Technical Services, 1968-70. *Military service:* U.S. Army, 1961-62. U.S. Army Reserve. *Member:* Jewish Association for Blacks (northeast regional co-chairman, 1968—), Lower Hudson Valley Verse Club, Northern Westchester Sonneteers, Peekskill Poets Committee (co-chairman, 1972).

WRITINGS—Poetry: The Dream Telephone, The Cross-

ing, 1968; (with Marge Piercy, Emmett Jarrett, and Robert Hershon) *4-Telling*, The Crossing, 1971; *Lies*, Radical America, 1971; *Stumbling*, The Crossing, 1972; *Letter for You to Answer*, Unicorn Press, 1972; *Anima*, Hanging Loose Press, 1977.

Poetry represented in anthologies, including *New Poetry Anthology I*, edited by M. Anania, Swallow Press, 1968, *31 New American Poets*, edited by Ron Schreiber, Hill & Wang, 1968, *American Literary Anthology 3*, edited by George Plimpton and Peter Ardery, Penguin, 1970, and *New American and Canadian Poetry*, edited by John Gill, Beacon Press, 1971. Co-editor, *Hanging Loose.*

BIOGRAPHICAL/CRITICAL SOURCES: Poetry, April, 1970.

* * *

LOVELL, Michael Christopher 1930-

PERSONAL: Born April 11, 1930, in Cambridge, Mass.; son of R. Ivan (an historian) and Rose Mary (Chittenden) Lovell; married Adrienne Ann Goolkasian, June 21, 1959; children: Leslie, Stacie, George, Martin. *Education:* Reed College, B.A., 1952; Stanford University, M.A., 1954, summer graduate study, 1957; University of Michigan, summer graduate study, 1955; Harvard University, Ph.D., 1959. *Home:* Carriage Dr., Durham, Conn. 06422. *Office:* Department of Economics, Wesleyan University, Middletown, Conn. 06457.

CAREER: Yale University, New Haven, Conn., instructor, 1958-59, assistant professor of economics, 1959-63; Carnegie-Mellon University, Pittsburgh, Pa., associate professor, 1963-66, professor of economics, 1966-69; Wesleyan University, Middletown, Conn., professor of economics, 1969—. Visiting lecturer, Wesleyan University, 1960-62; staff member, Cowles Foundation, 1958-63; member of executive committee, Universities-National Bureau Committee for Economic Research, 1966-67; member of board of directors, NEED, 1968-69, Dwelling House Building and Loan Association, 1969-70; member of steering committee, National Bureau of Economic Research-Census Bureau Conference on Seasonal Analysis of Economic Time Series, 1975-76. Consultant, Council of Economic Advisers, 1964, 1967; adviser, Subcommittee on Controlling the New Inflation, Committee for Economic Development, 1974-76; senior adviser, Brookings Panel on Economic Activity, 1974—. *Military service:* U.S. Army, 1953-55. *Member:* American Economics Association (chairman of publications committee, 1976-77), Econometric Society. *Awards, honors:* National Science Foundation grants, 1962-64, 1966-68, 1970-72; Ford Foundation faculty research fellowship, 1964-65; first prize of Kazanjian Foundation Awards Program for the Teaching of Economics, 1973-74.

WRITINGS: (With Albert Hirsch) *Sales Anticipations and Inventory Behavior*, Wiley, 1969; *Macroeconomics: Measurement, Theory, and Policy*, Wiley, 1975.

Contributor: *Inventory Fluctuations and Economic Stabilization*, Part II, U.S. Government Printing Office, 1961; Arnold Zellner, editor, *Readings in Economic Statistics and Econometrics*, Little, Brown, 1963; James Duesenberry, Gary Fromm, Lawrence Klein, and Edwin Kuh, editors, *The Brookings-SSRC Quarterly Econometric Model of the U.S. Economy*, Rand McNally, 1965; Robert Ferber, editor, *Determinants of Investment Behavior*, National Bureau of Economic Research, 1967; Duesenberry, Fromm, Klein, and Kuh, editors, *The Brookings Model: Some Further Results*, North-Holland Publishing, 1969; *The Economic*

Outlook for 1969, University of Michigan Press, 1969; D. N. Thompson, editor, *Contractual Marketing Systems*, Heath, 1971. Contributor of more than thirty articles and reviews to economics journals. Associate editor, *Econometrica*, 1965-68; foreign editor, *Review of Economic Studies*, 1968-70; associate editor, *Journal of the American Statistical Association*, 1975-77.

WORK IN PROGRESS: Writing on the financing of education.

*   *   *

LOVERIDGE, Ronald O. 1938-

PERSONAL: Born August 20, 1938, in Antioch, Calif.; son of Oliver Fay (a civil engineer) and Doris (Lundquist) Loveridge; married Marsha White, June 17, 1961; children: Joan Gay, Kelly Noel. *Education:* University of the Pacific, B.A., 1960; Stanford University, M.A., 1961, Ph.D., 1965. *Politics:* Registered Democrat. *Religion:* Methodist. *Home:* Muirfield Rd., Riverside, Calif. 92506. *Office:* Department of Political Science, University of California, Riverside, Calif. 92507.

CAREER: University of California, Riverside, assistant professor, 1965-71, associate professor of political science, 1971—, chairman of department, 1974-78, associate dean of College of Social and Behavioral Sciences, 1970-74. Chairman of City of Riverside Environmental Protection Commission; chairman of California Assembly fellow selection committee. *Member:* American Political Science Association, Sierra Club.

WRITINGS: (Contributor) Arthur Atkisson and Richard Gaines, editors, *Development of Air Quality Standards*, C. E. Merrill, 1970; *City Managers in Legislative Politics*, Bobbs-Merrill, 1971; (contributor) Paul Downing, editor, *The Contribution of the Social Sciences to the Solution of the Air Pollution Problem: Task Force Assessment*, Praeger, 1972; (contributor) Harlan Hahn, editor, *Urban Affairs Annual Review*, Sage Publications, 1972.

WORK IN PROGRESS: Environmental politics, especially air pollution.

*   *   *

LOVETT, Robert W. 1913-

PERSONAL: Born September 18, 1913, in Beverly, Mass.; son of Merton R. (a leather salesman) and Margaret (Woodberry) Lovett; married Dorothy T. Merrow (librarian), September 7, 1946. *Education:* Harvard University, B.A., 1935, M.A., 1936; Columbia University, B.S., 1947. *Religion:* Congregationalist. *Home:* 27 Conant St., Beverly, Mass. 01915. *Office:* 124 Baker Library, Business School, Harvard University, Boston, Mass. 02163.

CAREER: Harvard University, assistant in archives, Widener Library, Cambridge, Mass., 1937-42, 1945-48, curator of manuscripts, Baker Library, Business School, Boston, Mass., 1948—. Member of board of directors, Essex Institute; chairman of board of directors, Salem Library Committee. *Military service:* U.S. Army, Second Corps, Medical Battalion, 1942-45; served in Sicily and Italy. *Member:* Society of American Archivists (fellow), Business Archives Committee, Massachusetts Historical Society, Colonial Society of Massachusetts, Appalachian Mountain Club (corresponding member), Beverly Historical Society (president, 1970—), Phi Beta Kappa.

WRITINGS—Compiler: (With Eleanor C. Bishop) *List of Business Manuscripts in Baker Library*, Baker Library,

Harvard Business School, 1969; *American Economic and Business History: A Guide to Information Sources*, Gale, 1971; *Documents from the Harvard University Archives, 1638-1750*, Colonial Society of Massachusetts, 1975. Contributor to library and history journals.

AVOCATIONAL INTERESTS: Local history, library history.

*   *   *

LOW, Alfred D(avid) 1913-

PERSONAL: Born February 28, 1913, in Vienna, Austria; came to United States in 1939, naturalized in 1945; son of Samuel and Klara (Warenreich) Low; married Rose Seelenfreund (a college professor), June 30, 1938; children: Suzanne, Ruth. *Education:* University of Vienna, Ph.D., 1936; attended Haverford College, 1940-41, and Harvard University, 1941; Columbia University, A.M., 1956, Certificate of Russian Institute, 1957. *Home:* 9131 West Chambers St., Milwaukee, Wis. 53222. *Office:* Department of History, Marquette University, 1309 West Wisconsin, Milwaukee, Wis. 53233.

CAREER: Waynflete School, Waynflete, Me., instructor, 1942-43; Syracuse University, Syracuse, N.Y., instructor in geography and German, 1943-44; Wells College, Aurora, N.Y., assistant professor of history and political science, 1944-46; Marietta College, Marietta, Ohio, assistant professor, 1946-47, associate professor of history and political science, 1947-57; Youngstown University, Youngstown, Ohio, associate professor, 1957-60, professor of history and political science, 1960-63; Iowa Wesleyan College, Mount Pleasant, professor of history and political science and chairman of the departments, 1964-65; Marquette University, Milwaukee, Wis., professor of history, 1965—, director of German Institute, 1966-69, director of European Colloquium, 1969—. Visiting professor at Brooklyn College (now Brooklyn College of the City University of New York), 1945, New York College for Teachers (now State University of New York at Albany), 1953, State University Teachers College (now State University of New York at Oneonta), summer, 1957, Washington University, summers, 1959, 1962, University of Nebraska, 1963-64, University of Wisconsin—Milwaukee, spring, 1968, Carroll College, spring, 1970, University of Michigan, summer, 1973, and University of Wisconsin—Madison, summer, 1976. Consultant to university presses. Member of Fulbright-Hays Selection Committee. Member of board of directors, Goethe House.

MEMBER: American Historical Association, American Political Science Association, American Association of University Professors, Association of Central European Historians, American Association for the Advancement of Slavic Studies. *Awards, honors:* American Philosophical Society awards, 1958, 1966, 1972; awards from Council of Wisconsin Writers, 1976, for *The Anschluss Movement*, and 1977, for *The Sino-Soviet Dispute;* numerous grants from Marquette University.

WRITINGS: Lenin on the Question of Nationality, Bookman Associates, 1958; *The Anschluss Movement in Austria and Germany, 1918-1919, and the Paris Peace Conference*, American Philosophical Society, 1974; *The Sino-Soviet Dispute*, Fairleigh Dickinson University Press, 1976; *Jews and Judaism in the Eyes of the Germans: From the Enlightenment to Imperial Germany*, Fairleigh Dickinson University Press, in press. Contributor to professional journals, including *Social Studies, American Historical Review, Russian Review, Austrian History Yearbook, Journal of*

Central European Affairs, and *Transactions* of American Philosophical Society.

WORK IN PROGRESS: A political biography of Ulrich von Brockdorff-Rantzau; *The Anschluss Movement, 1919-1938.*

SIDELIGHTS: Alfred Low has a working knowledge of ten languages. He has traveled and done research in Europe every summer since 1966.

* * *

LOWE, Jeanne R. 1924(?)-1972

1924(?)—April 28, 1972; American editor, consultant, and lecturer on urban affairs. Obituaries: *New York Times,* April 29, 1972; *Washington Post,* May 1, 1972.

* * *

LOWE, Richard Barrett 1902-1972

July 8, 1902—April 16, 1972; American educator and government official. Obituaries: *Washington Post,* April 20, 1972.

* * *

LOYE, David (Elliot) 1925-

PERSONAL: Born April 25, 1925, in Palo Alto, Calif.; son of Percival Elliot (an engineer) and Winifred (Sanders) Loye; married Billy Henslee, May 15, 1949 (divorced September 19, 1977); children: Jenella, Kathryn, David Christopher, Jonathan. *Education:* Attended Tulane University, 1945-46; Dartmouth College, B.A., 1948; New School for Social Research, M.A., 1967, Ph.D., 1974. *Politics:* Democrat. *Home:* 1028 Selby Ave., Los Angeles, Calif. 90024. *Office:* School of Medicine, University of California, Los Angeles, Calif. 90024.

CAREER: Worked during his early years as farmhand, factory hand, waiter, and newspaper correspondent; WKY-TV, Oklahoma City, Okla., newsman, 1953-57; *Oklahoma Today* (magazine), Oklahoma City, editor, 1957-60; Carl Byoir & Associates (advertising agency), New York City, writer, 1960-61; Cunningham & Walsh, Inc. (public relations agency), New York City, account executive, 1961-66; Educational Testing Service, Princeton, N.J., senior writer, 1965-70, professional associate, 1970-74; University of California, School of Medicine, Los Angeles, associate research psychologist and research director of Program on Psychosocial Adaptation and the Future, 1974—. Visiting lecturer, Princeton University, 1973-74. *Military service:* U.S. Navy, 1943-46. *Awards, honors:* Anisfield-Wolf Award in Race Relations, 1971, for *The Healing of a Nation.*

WRITINGS: (Editor) *The Future by Design,* New York City Planning Commission, 1964; (editor) *The Troubled Environment,* Urban America, 1965; (editor) *On Evaluating Title I Programs,* Educational Testing Service, 1966; (editor with Richard Peterson) *Conversations toward a Definition of Institutional Vitality,* Educational Testing Service, 1967; (editor) *Strategies for Vocational Research,* Educational Testing Service, 1968; (editor with Harry Harman and Carl Helm) *Computer Assisted Testing,* Educational Testing Service, 1968.

(Editor) *Research at ETS,* Educational Testing Service, 1970; *The Healing of a Nation,* Norton, 1971; *The Leadership Passion,* Jossey-Bass, 1977; *The Knowable Future: A Psychology of Forecasting and Prophesy,* Wiley, 1978. Contributor to journals.

WORK IN PROGRESS: The Psychology of the Middle; The Castle and the Quest; 100 Days of Love, with Riane Tennenhaus; *Adventures of a Sunday Psychic; Journey into a Pocket Utopia; The Case of the Sultry Seeress.*

SIDELIGHTS: David Loye told *CA:* "Having now completed almost half my intended quota of serious, highly theoretical non-fiction works in social science, I hope to succeed with some more enjoyable works of fiction and autobiography. My models in this, I suppose, are A. Conan Doyle and Aldous Huxley."

* * *

LUCKEY, Eleanore Braun 1915-

PERSONAL: Born February 27, 1915, in La Junta, Colo.; daughter of Clarence Eugene (an engineer) and Atha (Brown) Braun; married Robert E. Luckey, 1937 (died, 1953); children: David (deceased), Michael, Robert Allen. *Education:* Colorado State College of Education (now University of Northern Colorado), A.B., 1937, M.A., 1942; University of Minnesota, Ph.D., 1959. *Home:* 1747 Oak Springs Dr., Salt Lake City, Utah 84108. *Office:* Department of Family and Consumer Studies, University of Utah, Salt Lake City, Utah 84112.

CAREER: Secondary school teacher in Portales, N.M., 1937-40, Palo Alto, Calif., 1941-44, Albuquerque, N.M., 1944-46, and Minneapolis, Minn., 1948-50; U.S. Department of State, Porto Alegre, Brazil, assistant executive secretary of Institute Brasiliero-Norteamericano, 1946-48; *Minnesota Journal of Education,* St. Paul, editorial assistant, 1950-53; University of Minnesota, Minneapolis, instructor in marriage and family, 1953-58; University of Iowa, Iowa City, assistant professor of family life, 1958-61; University of Connecticut, Storrs, professor of child development and family relations and head of department, 1961-74; University of Utah, Salt Lake City, professor and chairman of department of family and consumer studies, 1974—. Visiting professor, Ohio University, summers, 1962-64; director, Family Life Institute, University of Connecticut, summers, 1967-68, 1970; instructor, State Department of Education, Virgin Islands, summers, 1968-70. Member, White House Conference on Children and Youth, 1960, 1970, Governor's Commission on Day Care, 1972. Consultant to Children's Bureau, U.S. Department of Health, Education and Welfare, 1966-68.

MEMBER: National Council on Family Relations (president; vice-chairman of affiliated councils and state chapters committee), American Association of Marriage and Family Counselors (member of executive board), American Personnel and Guidance Association, American Psychological Association, American Association of University Professors, Pi Kappa Delta, Psi Chi, Pi Lambda Theta, Phi Kappa Phi. *Awards, honors:* Postdoctoral fellowship, Bowman Gray School of Medicine, 1968; Outstanding Educational Book of the Year award, Pi Lambda Theta, 1970, for *Guidance for Children in Elementary Schools.*

WRITINGS: (With George E. Hill) *Guidance for Children in Elementary Schools,* Appleton, 1969; (with George W. Wise) *Human Growth and the Family,* Graded Press, 1970. Contributor to *Counseling Psychology, Sociometry, Social Forces, Personnel and Guidance, Journal of Marriage and the Family, Family Coordinator, Journal of Consulting Psychology,* and *Medical Aspects of Sexuality.*

WORK IN PROGRESS: Research in correlates of marital satisfaction; articles on parent education, adolescent sexuality, relationship of family to vocational choice, adolescent counseling, and medical training in human sexuality.

SIDELIGHTS: Eleanore Luckey told *CA:* "Children are the world's tools with which to work. They are our charges—ours, the family's and the school's. Children are tomorrow—tomorrow's mind, tomorrow's hands, tomorrow's heart. Today this child is mine—and yours. What will we do with our tomorrow?"

*   *   *

LUDLUM, Robert 1927-
(Jonathan Ryder)

PERSONAL: Born May 25, 1927, in New York, N.Y.; son of George Hartford (a businessman) and Margaret (Wadsworth) Ludlum; married Mary Ryducha (an actress), March 31, 1951; children: Michael, Jonathan, Glynis. *Education:* Wesleyan University, B.A., 1951. *Politics:* Independent. *Home:* 125 Crescent Ave., Leonia, N.J. 07605. *Agent:* Henry Morrison, 58 West 10 St., New York, N.Y. 10011.

CAREER: Actor on Broadway and in television, 1952-60; Playhouse-on-the-Mall, Paramus, N.J., producer, 1960-69; producer in New York, N.Y., 1960-69; writer, 1969—. *Military service:* U.S. Marine Corps, 1944-46. *Member:* Authors League, American Federation of Television and Radio Artists, Screen Actors Guild. *Awards, honors:* New England Professor of Drama award, 1951; awards and grants from American National Theatre and Academy, 1959, and from Actors' Equity Association and William C. Whitney Foundation, 1960; Scroll of Achievement, American National Theatre and Academy, 1960.

WRITINGS: The Scarlatti Inheritance (novel), World Publishing, 1971; *The Osterman Weekend* (novel), World Publishing, 1972; *The Chancellor Manuscript,* Dial, 1972; *The Matlock Paper,* Dial, 1973; (under name Jonathan Ryder) *Trevayne,* Delacorte, 1973; (under name Jonathan Ryder) *The Cry of the Halidon,* Delacorte, 1974; *The Rhinemann Exchange,* Dial, 1974; *The Gemini Contenders,* Dial, 1976.

WORK IN PROGRESS: Cable Tortugas, a novel, for World Publishing.

SIDELIGHTS: Having worked in the theatre both as an actor and writer, Robert Ludlum feels there will be a significant change in American theater as we know it today. He believes: "Within 15 years there will be no New York theater. You can't take a piece of real estate and confine an explosive art form to it. We'll have to go back to the subway circuit—the way it used to be—neighborhood playhouses in the Bronx and Brooklyn and the same thing all over the country. And there will also have to be subsidy. It's the only answer."

The Scarlatti Inheritance was filmed by Universal; *The Osterman Weekend* was filmed by Warner Brothers.

BIOGRAPHICAL/CRITICAL SOURCES: Time, March 8, 1971; *Book World,* March 21, 1971; *New York Times Book Review,* April 4, 1971; *Best Sellers,* June 1, 1971; *Publishers Weekly,* February 2, 1972.†

*   *   *

LUEBKE, Frederick Carl 1927-

PERSONAL: Born January 26, 1927, in Reedsburg, Wis.; son of Frederick J. (a teacher) and Martha (Kretzmann) Luebke; married Norma Wukasch (an editor), August 12, 1951; children: Christina, John, David, Thomas. *Education:* Concordia Teachers College, River Forest, Ill., B.S., 1950; Clarement College (now Claremont Graduate School), M.A., 1958; University of Nebraska, Ph.D., 1966. *Home:* 3117 Woodsdale Blvd., Lincoln, Neb. 68502. *Office:* De-

partment of History, University of Nebraska, Lincoln, Neb. 68508.

CAREER: Teacher in elementary and secondary schools in Los Angeles, Calif., 1951-61; Concordia Teachers College, Seward, Neb., 1961-68, began as assistant professor, became associate professor of history; University of Nebraska, Lincoln, associate professor, 1968-72, professor of history, 1972—. *Member:* Organization of American Historians, Immigration History Society, Social Science History Association. *Awards, honors:* Danforth Foundation teacher grants, 1964, 1965; National Endowment for the Humanities fellowship, 1967; senior Fulbright research fellowship, University of Stuttgart, 1974-75; Newberry Library fellowship, 1977.

WRITINGS: Immigrants and Politics: The Germans of Nebraska, 1880-1900, University of Nebraska Press, 1969; (editor and contributor) *Ethnic Voters and the Election of Lincoln,* University of Nebraska Press, 1971; *Bonds of Loyalty: German-Americans and World War I,* Northern Illinois University Press, 1974. Contributor of articles to scholarly journals.

WORK IN PROGRESS: A study of the ethnic groups on the Great Plains.

*   *   *

LUKAS, Richard C. 1937-

PERSONAL: Born August 29, 1937, in Lynn, Mass.; son of Frank J. and Elizabeth (Kapuscinska) Lukas; married Marita Rokicki, August 7, 1966; children: Jennifer, Renee. *Education:* Florida State University, B.A., 1957, M.A., 1960, Ph.D., 1963. *Politics:* Democrat. *Religion:* Roman Catholic. *Home address:* Route 6, Box 141, Cookeville, Tenn. 38501. *Office:* Department of History, Tennessee Technological University, Cookeville, Tenn. 38501.

CAREER: Tennessee Technological University, Cookeville, assistant professor, 1963-66, associate professor, 1966-69, professor of history, 1969—. Research consultant to U.S. Air Force, 1957-58. *Military service:* U.S. Army Reserve, 1960-66. *Member:* American Historical Association, Society of Historians of American Foreign Relations, American Committee on History of the Second World War, American Association of University Professors, Polish American Historical Association, Polish Institute of Arts and Sciences, Phi Kappa Phi, Phi Alpha Theta. *Awards, honors:* National Endowment for the Humanities grant, 1968; history book award from American Institute of Aeronautics and Astronautics, 1971, for *Eagles East: The Army Air Forces and the Soviet Union, 1941-1945;* American Philosophical Society grant, 1972.

WRITINGS: (Contributor) *Air Force Combat Units of World War II,* U.S. Government Printing Office, 1961; *Eagles East: The Army Air Forces and the Soviet Union, 1941-1945,* Florida State University Press, 1970; (editor) *From Metternich to the Beatles,* New American Library, 1973; *The Strange Allies: The United States and Poland, 1941-1945,* University of Tennessee Press, 1978. Contributor to historical and military affairs journals.

AVOCATIONAL INTERESTS: Motor travel, walking in forests, tennis, paddle ball.

*   *   *

LUKASHEVICH, Stephen 1931-

PERSONAL: Born June 22, 1931, in Nice, France; son of George Lukashevich; married Olga K. Koostov, June 16,

1957. *Education:* University of California, Berkeley, B.A., 1957, M.A., 1958, Ph.D., 1961. *Office:* Department of History, University of Delaware, Newark, Del. 19711.

CAREER: University of Delaware, Newark, 1961—, currently professor of history. *Military service:* U.S. Army, 1953-56. *Member:* American Association for the Advancement of Slavic Studies. *Awards, honors:* Ford Foundation fellow, 1960-61.

WRITINGS: Ivan Aksakov, 1823-1886: A Study in Russian Thought and Politics, Harvard University Press, 1965; *Konstantin Leontev, 1831-1891: A Study in Russian "Heroic Vitalism,"* Pageant, 1967; *N. F. Fedorov, 1828-1903: A Study in Russian Eupsychian and Utopian Thought,* University of Delaware Press, 1977.

WORK IN PROGRESS: Books on Otto Rank, 1884-1939, and Chuang Tzu.

* * *

LUND, Gerald N. 1939-

PERSONAL: Born September 12, 1939, in Fountain Green, Utah; son of Jewell Grover (a pipefitter) and Mary Evelyn (Mortensen) Lund; married Lynn Stanard, June 5, 1963; children: Cynthia, Julie, Gerald Scott, Steven, Lori, Rebecca. *Education:* Brigham Young University, B.A. (cum laude), 1965, M.S., 1969; Pepperdine University, additional study. *Politics:* Independent. *Religion:* Church of Jesus Christ of Latter-day Saints. *Home:* 2351 South 150 East, Bountiful, Utah 84010. *Office:* 50 East North Temple St., Salt Lake City, Utah 84150.

CAREER: Teacher in Mormon schools in Salt Lake City, Utah, 1965-67, Provo, Utah, 1967-69, and California, 1969-74; Walnut Institute of Religion, Walnut, Calif., director, 1971-74; Mormon Church, Salt Lake City, director of college curriculum, 1974—. *Military service:* U.S. Army Reserve, 1958-64.

WRITINGS: The Coming of the Lord, Bookcraft (Salt Lake City), 1971; *This Is Your World,* Bookcraft, 1973.

WORK IN PROGRESS: A book on scriptural symbolism.

* * *

LUND, Thomas A. 1922-

PERSONAL: Born March 16, 1922, in Eau Claire, Wis.; son of Otto E. (a newspaper editor) and Blanche (Patrie) Lund; married Jo Cerney, August 7, 1952; children: Bobbi Jo, Judy, Tim, Kristin, Bill. *Education:* Wisconsin State College (now University of Wisconsin—Stevens Point), B.S., 1953; University of Wisconsin—Milwaukee, M.S., 1970. *Politics:* "... of compromise." *Home:* 542 North 91st St., Milwaukee, Wis. 53226. *Office:* Longfellow Junior High School, 7600 West North St., Wauwatosa, Wis. 53213.

CAREER: U.S. Rubber Co., Eau Claire, Wis., mail clerk, form control manager, and timekeeper, 1939-42, 1945-49; bartender in Stevens Point, Wis., 1949-51; WSPT-Radio, Stevens Point, radio announcer and program director, 1951-56; Longfellow Junior High School, Wauwatosa, Wis., English teacher, 1956—. *Military service:* U.S. Army Air Forces, 1943-45; became staff sergeant; received Distinguished Flying Cross and Air Medal with cluster. *Member:* National Education Association, Wisconsin Education Association, Wauwatosa Education Association.

WRITINGS: The Modern Practical Approach to Teaching English, Parker Publishing, 1971. Also author of a novel. Contributor to English and education journals.

WORK IN PROGRESS: A novel for young adults, *Laurie and Me.*

* * *

LUNDBERG, Donald E(mil) 1916-

PERSONAL: Born June 10, 1916, in Waterloo, Iowa; son of Emil T. (a moulder) and Jennie (Hampton) Lundberg; married Carolyn Brown, 1942; children: Alan, Derek, Lance. *Education:* Iowa State Teachers College (now University of Northern Iowa), B.A., 1941; Duke University, M.A., 1942; Cornell University, Ph.D., 1946. *Religion:* Protestant. *Office:* Department of Hotel and Restaurant Management, California State Polytechnic University, Pomona, Calif. 91768.

CAREER: Cornell University, Ithaca, N.Y., assistant professor of hotel administration, 1946-49; Idaho State College (now University), Pocatello, professor of psychology and dean of students, 1949-50; Florida State University, Tallahassee, professor of hotel and restaurant management and head of department, 1950-59; University of New Hampshire, Durham, chairman of department of hotel administration, 1959-62; University of Massachusetts—Amherst, head of department of hotel, restaurant, and travel administration, 1963-73; California State Polytechnic University, Pomona, chairman of department of hotel and restaurant management, 1973—. Visiting lecturer, Ithaca College, 1946-50; lecturer, Ealing Technical College and University of Surrey, 1968, and University of Kentucky, 1968-70. Research associate, University of Hawaii, 1970. Lecturer for Club Managers Association of America, and to personnel management workshops in United States and Canada. Manager of resorts. Consultant, U.S. Department of Commerce, Catering Education Research Institute, Industrial Training Board for Hotel and Catering Industry, and to universities and businesses. *Military service:* U.S. Navy, 1942-45; became lieutenant. U.S. Naval Reserve, 1945-68; became commander. *Member:* International Society of Food Service Consultants (former president), International Epicurean Circle, Sigma Xi.

WRITINGS: Personnel Practices in Hotels, Cornell University, 1947; *Personnel Management in Hotels and Restaurants,* Burgess, 1949.

(With Vernon C. Kane) *Business Management: Hotels, Motels, and Restaurants,* Peninsular Press, 1952; (editor) *Motel Management Correspondence Course,* American Motels, Inc., 1953; *Operating Manual for Navy Messes and Clubs Ashore,* Bureau of Naval Personnel and U.S. Air Force, 1954; (editor) *Readings in Club Management,* privately printed, 1956; *Inside Innkeeping,* W. C. Brown, 1956.

Adventure in Costa Rica, Dixie Publishers, 1960, revised edition published as *Costa Rica,* 1968; (with Peter Dukas) *How to Operate a Restaurant,* Ahrens, 1960; (with James A. Armatas) *The Management of People in Hotels, Restaurants and Clubs,* W. C. Brown, 1964; *The Logic of Cookery,* privately printed, 1964, revised edition published as *The Logic of Cooking,* 1977; (with Lendal H. Kotschevar) *Understanding Cooking,* University of Massachusetts, 1965, revised edition, 1976.

The Hotel and Restaurant Business, Cahners, 1970, revised edition, 1976; (with Joseph Amendola) *Understanding Baking,* Cahners, 1971; *The Tourist Business,* Cahners, 1971, revised edition, 1976. Contributor to *American Motel Magazine, Club Management, Hotel Management, Institutions,* and other publications. Consulting editor, *Drive-In Management.* Editorial director, Ahrens Publishing Co.; book editor, "Hotel and Restaurant Book" series, W. C. Brown, 1956-70.

*   *   *

LUNN, Janet 1928-

PERSONAL: Born December 28, 1928, in Dallas, Tex.; naturalized Canadian citizen in 1963; daughter of Herman Alfred (a mechanical engineer) and Margaret (Alexander) Swoboda; married Richard Lunn (a teacher); children: Eric, Jeffrey, Alexander, Katherine, John. *Education:* Attended Queen's University at Kingston, 1947-50. *Politics:* New Democratic Party. *Home address:* R.R. 2, Hillier, Ontario, Canada.

CAREER: Clarke Irwin & Co., Toronto, Ontario, children's editor, 1972-75; currently free-lance editor and writer, editorial consultant, and lecturer. *Member:* Writers Union of Canada. *Awards, honors:* Canada Council grant, 1967.

WRITINGS: (With husband, Richard Lunn) *The County* (history of Prince Edward County, Ontario), County of Prince Edward, 1967; *Twin Spell* (juvenile), Harper, 1969; *The Twelve Dancing Princesses* (juvenile), illustrations by Laszlo Gla, Methuen, in press; *Larger than Life* (juvenile), Press Porcepic, in press. Has written scripts for Canadian Broadcasting Co. Contributor of articles and short stories to Canadian periodicals, including *Starting Points in Language Arts.*

WORK IN PROGRESS: A children's novel tentatively entitled *Mrs. Morrissay.*

SIDELIGHTS: Janet Lunn told *CA:* "I work in the children's field because I'm most at home in it. I write articles and lectures for adult audiences but, when it comes to fiction, my greatest love, although I often mean to write for adults, the excitement of pure magic gets to me every time. I have the feeling that only in children's writing and in poetry (which I sometimes write—badly) can I get to the roots of an idea. As well, under my middle-aged skin, I am really ten years old."

AVOCATIONAL INTERESTS: Art, archeology, history, sketching, gardening, and compulsive reading.

*   *   *

LUNT, Elizabeth Graves 1922-

PERSONAL: Born August 7, 1922, in Kansas City, Mo.; daughter of Ludwick (an attorney) and Ozelle (Miller) Graves; married William Charles Lunt (a sales manager), June 19, 1948; children: Lucy Elizabeth, Lindsay Alice. *Education:* Attended Kansas City Art Institute. *Politics:* Democrat. *Religion:* None. *Home and office:* 921 Valentine Rd., Kansas City, Mo. 64111. *Agent:* Evelyn Singer Agency, Inc., Box 163, Braircliff Manor, N.Y. 10510.

CAREER: Kansas City Star, Kansas City, Mo., member of staff and editor of society, women's news, and features sections, 1963-66; Meredith Publishing Co., Des Moines, Iowa, editorial scout and supervisor of photography and writing, 1966-78; free-lance writer. Member of board of directors, Kansas City Planned Parenthood Association, 1968—; chairman of public relations, Kansas City Mayor's Commission for the Sister Cities, 1972—. Member of Jackson County Grand Jury, 1970.

WRITINGS: Stormy, the Squirrel (juvenile; illustrated with own photographs), Harvey House, 1972. Author of weekly column for *Independent Magazine,* 1966-71. Contributor to *Midwest Motorist* (Automobile Club of Missouri magazine).

WORK IN PROGRESS: The Pet Sitter (sequel to *Stormy, the Squirrel*).

*   *   *

LUSKIN, Bernard J(ay) 1937-

PERSONAL: Born June 3, 1937, in Pittsburgh, Pa.; son of Morris Luskin. *Education:* Long Beach City College, A.A., 1959; California State College (now University), Los Angeles, B.A., 1961; California State College (now University), Long Beach, M.A., 1963; University of California, Los Angeles, Ed.D., 1970. *Office:* Coastline Community College, 10231 Slater Ave., Fountain Valley, Calif. 92708.

CAREER: Orange Coast College, Costa Mesa, Calif., associate professor of business and data processing, 1962-65, associate dean of admissions and records, 1965-67; Coast Community College District, Costa Mesa, associate dean of federal projects, 1967-69, vice-chancellor, 1969-76; Coastline Community College, Fountain Valley, Calif., president, 1976—. American Association of Junior Colleges, president of National Council for Resource Development, member of Commission on Governmental Affairs; member of Advisory Committee for Science Education, National Science Foundation. Consultant, American Association of Junior Colleges and U.S. Office of Education. *Military service:* U.S. Navy, 1956-58. *Member:* California State Marriage, Family, Child Counselors Association. *Awards, honors:* Kellogg fellow, 1967-70; National and United Business Education Association award, for outstanding achievement in business education.

WRITINGS: Data Processing: A Practice Set, McBee Systems, 1966; (with Richard L. Howe) *Problems in Data Processing,* Macmillan, 1968, revised edition, 1971; (with Richard Brightman and Theodore Tilton) *Data Processing for Decision Making: An Introduction to Third Generation Information Systems,* Macmillan, 1968, revised edition, 1971; *Everything You Always Wanted to Know about CAI but Were Afraid to Ask,* C.V.E. Publications, 1972; (editor with others) *Contemporary California Issues,* [Boston], 1975. Also editor of *Outreach,* 1974. Contributor to *Computerworld, Junior College Journal,* and *AEDS Monitor.*

*   *   *

LUTZ, Frank W. 1928-

PERSONAL: Born September 24, 1928, in St. Louis, Mo.; son of Vincent J. (a businessman) and Helen (Scrivens) Fritsch; married Susan Bleikamp, July 14, 1958; children: Paul, Andrew, Lynn. *Education:* Attended Harris Teachers College, 1946-48; Washington University, St. Louis, Mo., B.S., 1950, M.S., 1954, Ed.D., 1962; additional graduate study at University of Hawaii, summer, 1951. *Home:* 1315 Trout Rd., State College, Pa. 16801. *Office:* Division of Education Policy Studies, Pennsylvania State University, 303A Rackley Building, University Park, Pa. 16802.

CAREER: New Mexico State Department of Education, Santa Fe, state director of research project, 1963-64; New York University, New York, N.Y., assistant professor, 1964-65, associate professor of educational administration, 1965-68; Pennsylvania State University, University Park, professor of educational administration and director of Division of Education Policy Studies, 1968-73, professor of education and senior member of Graduate School, 1973—. Visiting summer professor, University of New Mexico, 1963. *Member:* American Educational Research Association, American Association of School Administrators, National Conference of Professors of Educational Administration,

American Anthropological Association, Phi Delta Kappa, Kappa Delta Pi.

WRITINGS: (Editor with Joseph Azzarelli) *The Struggle for Power in Education,* Center for Applied Research, 1966; (with Lou Kleinman and Seymour Evans) *Grievances and Their Resolution,* Interstate, 1967; (with Laurence Iannaccone) *Understanding Educational Organizations,* C. E. Merrill, 1969; (with Iannaccone) *Politics, Power, and Policy: The Governance of Local School Districts,* C. E. Merrill, 1970; (editor) *Toward Improved Urban Education,* Charles A. Jones Publishing, 1970; (with Iannaccone) *Public Participation in School Politics: The Dissatisfaction Theory of Democracy,* Lexington Books, in press. Contributor of about forty articles to education journals.

WORK IN PROGRESS: Anthropologized Methods in Educational Organizations, with Iannaccone and Ramsey; writing on anthropology of education, local school boards, governance and organization in higher education.

SIDELIGHTS: Frank Lutz told *CA:* "Writing is not 'easy' for anyone. It may be 'fun' but *not* 'easy.' Why then does a professor do it? There may be many reasons but, in my view, the *proper* reason is to communicate with one's colleagues, stimulate discussion and criticism, and contribute to one's field or discipline. The area of politics and anthropology of education is young and growing rapidly. It is essential that it grow well. This can only occur in the open market of discussion and criticism provided through publication. Publication is the keystone of new knowledge production-dissemination. New knowledge production-dissemination is the essence of the professorship."

*   *   *

LUTZ, Gertrude May   1899-

PERSONAL: Born December 30, 1899, in Oakland, Calif.; daughter of Hugo Albert (a building contractor) and Gertrude (Scrivener) Stenbiht; married Leslie Herman Lutz (an automobile dealer), July 20, 1922; children: Richard Duane. *Education:* Attended Heald's Business College, Reno, Nev., 1918; studied poetry, literature, and public speaking in University of California extension courses. *Politics:* Republican. *Religion:* Presbyterian. *Home:* 1850 Willow Rd., Apt. 27, Palo Alto, Calif. 94304.

CAREER: Poet. Volunteer teacher of poetry and appreciation to handicapped children at Stanford Children's Hospital, Palo Alto, Calif., and Loma Vista Orthopedic Unit of Palo Unified School System. Reader and lecturer on poetry and appreciation to elementary, secondary, and college students and to clubs.

MEMBER: Poetry Society of America, National League of American Pen Women (former president of Palo Alto branch; director of Poetry Workshop), California Writers' Club (former member of board of directors), California Federation of Chaparral Poets, Poetry Society of Virginia, California Olympiad of the Arts, Ina Coolbrith Circle, San Francisco Browning Society (artist), Women's Club of Palo Alto (former music and drama chairman; vice president, 1952). *Awards, honors:* Numerous state and national poetry prizes, including John Barton Seymour Memorial Prize, Norfolk Sonnet Sequence Prize, Aleda Hall Portrait Award, California Federation of Women's Clubs State Poetry Award, Dr. Henry Meade Bland Award, Leitch Memorial Prize, Florence Dickinson Stearns Award, Leonora Speyer Prize, San Francisco Browning Society dramatic monologue award, National League of American Pen Women award for work in imagery poetry, and Karma Dean Ogden Memorial Prize of Poetry Society of Virginia.

WRITINGS—All poetry; published by Golden Quill: *Point the Sun Tomorrow,* 1956; *More Than Image,* 1966; *Song for a New Generation,* 1971; *Leis of Remembrance,* 1975; *Time Is the Traveler,* 1977.

Poems anthologized in several collections, including *Contemporary Poetry,* 1944, *This Is My America,* edited by Kenton Kilmer, 1946, *Poetry and Prizes,* edited by M. S. Sloss, 1950, *Sophisti-Cats,* edited by Lynn Hamilton, 1952, *Varied Verses,* Dierkes Press, 1959, and in three Poetry Society of America collections, *Diamond Anthology,* 1971, four Golden Quill collections, and six Ina Coolbrith anthologies. Contributor of poems to *Accent, American Poet, American Mercury, Arizona Highways, Caraval, Christian Science Monitor, Educational Forum, Household, Literary Review, Oregonian, Lyric, Poet Lore, Recurrence, Sunset, Variegation, Washington Post,* and other literary quarterlies and periodicals; contributor of poetry reviews to *Peninsula Living.*

WORK IN PROGRESS: A book on teaching poetry to blind children, to include poems written by a 10-year-old blind, paralyzed boy.

AVOCATIONAL INTERESTS: Theatre, bird watching, choral group.

*   *   *

LUTZ, William D.   1940-

PERSONAL: Born December 12, 1940, in Racine, Wis. *Education:* Dominican College, Racine, Wis., B.A., 1962; Marquette University, M.A., 1963; University of Nevada, Reno, Ph.D., 1971. *Politics:* "Nebulous." *Religion:* "Same as politics." *Residence:* Moorestown, N.J. *Office:* Department of English, Rutgers University, Camden, N.J. 08102.

CAREER: Rutgers University, Camden, N.J., 1971—, began as assistant professor, currently associate professor of English. *Member:* Modern Language Association of America, National Council of Teachers of English, Conference on College Composition and Communication, Rhetoric Society of America.

WRITINGS: Underground Press Directory, privately printed, 1968; (editor with Harry Brent) *On Revolution,* Winthrop, 1971; (compiler with Brent) *Rhetorical Considerations: Essays for Analysis,* Winthrop, 1974; *The Age of Communication,* Goodyear Publishing, 1974; (editor with Charleton Laird, Robert Gorrell, and Ronald Freeman) *Modern English Reader,* Prentice-Hall, 1977. Contributor to *College Composition and Communication, College English, Notes and Queries,* and *Freshman English News.*

WORK IN PROGRESS: Cambridge College Rhetoric, for Winthrop.

*   *   *

LUZBETAK, Louis J(oseph)   1918-

PERSONAL: Surname is pronounced *Luzz*-buh-tack; born September 19, 1918, in Joliet, Ill.; son of Thomas J. (a mechanic) and Theresa (Tomcik) Luzbetak. *Education:* Divine Word Seminary, Techny, Ill., B.A., 1942; Gregorian University, Rome, Italy, S.T.L., 1946, J.C.B., 1947; University of Fribourg, Switzerland, Ph.D., 1951; also attended University of Vienna, 1950, and University of Oklahoma, 1956. *Home:* Anthropos-Institut, D-5202, St. Augustin, West Germany.

CAREER: Ordained a Roman Catholic priest, 1945; anthropological field worker in New Guinea, 1952-56; professor of cultural anthropology and linguistics at various schools, including Divine Word Seminary, Techny, Ill., Divine Word College, Washington, D.C., Catholic University of America, Washington, D.C., and Georgetown University, Washington, D.C., 1956-65; Divine World College, Washington, D.C., rector and director of Post-Ordination "Pastoral Year," 1958-63; Center for Applied Research in the Apostolate, Washington, D.C., executive director, 1965-73, vice-president, 1973—; Divine Word College, Epworth, Iowa, president, 1973-79 (on leave, 1978-79); Anthropos-Institut, St. Augustin, West Germany, editor of *Anthropos International Review of Ethnology and Linguistics,* 1979—. Lecturer, Center for Intercultural Communication, Catholic University of Puerto Rico, Center for Intercultural Formation, Cuernavaca, Mexico, and other schools. Member of research committee, National Council of Churches, New York, N.Y., 1967-69.

MEMBER: International Association of Mission Studies, American Anthropological Association (fellow), Linguistic Society of America, Society for Applied Anthropology, Catholic Anthropological Association (member of board, 1960; vice-president, 1961-62; president, 1962-69), American Society of Missiology (vice-president, 1974-75; president, 1975-76), Catholic Theological Union (member of board of trustees, 1974—), Association of Professors of Missions, Society for the Scientific Study of Religion, Academy for Studies in Church-Related Education, Religious Research Association, Anthropos Institute (Germany), Institute for Religion and Culture (Japan; member of advisory council). *Awards, honors:* Ford Foundation overseas fellow, 1952-54; Pierre Charles Award, Fordham University, 1963.

WRITINGS: Marriage and the Family in Caucasia: A Contribution to the Study of North Caucasian Ethnology and Customary Law, Anthropos Institute, 1951; *Middle Wahgi Dialects: Grammar,* Catholic Mission (Banz, New Guinea), 1954; (with Paul McVinney) *Tabare Dialect: Grammar,* Catholic Mission (Alexishafen, New Guinea), 1954; *Middle Wahgi Phonology: A Standardisation of Orthographies in the New Guinea Highlands,* University of Sydney, 1956.

The Church and Cultures: An Applied Anthropology for the Religious Worker, Divine Word Publications, 1963, 4th edition, William Carey Library, 1977; (editor) *The Church in the Changing City,* Divine Word Publications, 1966; *Clergy Distribution U.S.A.: A Preliminary Survey of Priest Utilization, Availability, and Demand,* Center for Applied Research in the Apostolate, 1967; (contributor) *Men and Nations,* Catholic Action Federation, 1968; (contributor) *The Church Is Mission,* Geoffrey Chapman, 1969.

(Contributor) *Diocesan Pastoral Council,* National Council of Catholic Men, 1970. Contributor to *Encyclopedic Dictionary of Religion.* Contributor of articles on cultural anthropology, linguistics, missiology, and church-related topics to various periodicals, including *Anthropos* (Siegburg, Germany), *Anthropological Quarterly, Missionsstudien, Living Light,* and *Missiology.* Associate editor, *Anthropological Quarterly,* 1962-67; member of editorial board, American Society of Missiology, 1973-76.

WORK IN PROGRESS: Various studies in anthropology and missiology.

* * *

LYDAY, Leon F(aidherbee) III 1939-

PERSONAL: Born September 24, 1939, in Danville, Va.; son of Leon F., Jr. (a soil conservationist) and Dorothy (White) Lyday; married Bettie Smith, September 1, 1962; children: Andrew, Rachel, John. *Education:* University of North Carolina at Chapel Hill, A.B., 1961, M.A., 1964, Ph.D., 1966. *Home:* 317 Hartswick Ave., State College, Pa. 16801. *Office:* Department of Spanish, Pennsylvania State University, University Park, Pa. 16802.

CAREER: University of North Carolina at Chapel Hill, part-time instructor in Spanish and Portuguese, 1962-65, instructor in Spanish, 1965-66; Pennsylvania State University, University Park, assistant professor, 1966-70, associate professor, 1970-75, professor of Spanish, 1975—. *Member:* Modern Language Association of America, American Association of Teachers of Spanish and Portuguese, Instituto Internacional de Literatura Iberoamericana, Asociacion Internacional de Hispanistas, North East Modern Language Association, South Atlantic Modern Language Association, Phi Sigma Iota. *Awards, honors:* Fulbright fellow in Colombia, 1961-62; American Philosophical Society grant, 1969; Fulbright research grant in Brazil, 1976.

WRITINGS: (With Louis C. Perez) *Ancha es Castilla* (cultural reader adapted from the book by Eduardo Caballero Calderon), Van Nostrand, 1971; (contributor) John B. Means, editor, *Essays on Brazilian Literature,* Simon & Schuster, 1971; (with Frank Dauster) *En un acto: Nueve piezas hispanoamericas,* Van Nostrand, 1974; (with George Woodyard) *Dramatists in Revolt: The Contemporary Latin American Theatre,* University of Texas Press, 1975; (with Woodyard) *A Bibliography of Studies on the Latin American Theatre, 1940-1974,* Center for Latin American Studies, University of Texas, 1976.

Contributor of articles and reviews to *Bollettino de Ca'Foscari, Luso-Brazilian Review, Romance Notes, Hispania, Boletin Cultural y Bibliografico* (Bogota), *Latin American Theatre Review, Theatre Documentation, Inter-American Review of Bibliography, Topic, Modern Language Journal, South Atlantic Bulletin,* and *Modern International Drama.* Editorial associate, *Modern International Drama,* 1967—; member of editorial board, *Latin American Theatre Review,* 1969—; associate editor, *Hispania,* 1972-74.

WORK IN PROGRESS: Editing with Frank Dauster, an anthology of plays from Latin America; articles on the contemporary Spanish American theatre and the theatre of Alfredo Dias Gomes.

* * *

LYON, Melvin (Ernest) 1927-

PERSONAL: Born December 24, 1927, in Escondido, Calif.; son of Horace Todd (a businessman) and Louise (Arndt) Lyon; married Rosemary Primbs, November 21, 1953; children: Catherine, David, Thomas, Susan. *Education:* University of California, Berkeley, A.B., 1949; University of California, Los Angeles, M.A., 1954; University of Wisconsin, Ph.D., 1960. *Politics:* Liberal independent. *Religion:* None. *Home:* 511 Eastridge Dr., Lincoln, Neb. 68510. *Office:* Department of English, University of Nebraska, Lincoln, Neb. 68508.

CAREER: University of North Dakota, Grand Forks, instructor, 1958-59, assistant professor of English, 1959-61; George Washington University, Washington, D.C., assistant professor of English, 1961-64; University of Nebraska, Lincoln, assistant professor, 1964-67, associate professor, 1967-73, professor of English, 1973—. *Military service:* U.S. Army, 1950-52. *Member:* Modern Language Association of America, Phi Beta Kappa.

WRITINGS: Symbol and Idea in Henry Adams, University of Nebraska Press, 1970; *The Centrality of Hart Crane's "The Broken Tower"* (pamphlet), University of Nebraska Press, 1972. Contributor to language journals.

WORK IN PROGRESS: Research on American autobiographies, especially of the twentieth century; research on Edward Dahlberg.

BIOGRAPHICAL/CRITICAL SOURCES: Virginia Quarterly Review, autumn, 1970.

*   *   *

LYONS, David (Barry) 1935-

PERSONAL: Born February 6, 1935, in New York, N.Y.; son of Joseph (a garment worker) and Betty (a bookkeeper; maiden name, Janower) Lyons; married Sandra Yetta Nemiroff (a social worker), December 18, 1955; children: Matthew, Emily, Jeremy. *Education:* Attended Cooper Union School of Engineering, 1952-54, 1956-57; Brooklyn College (now Brooklyn College of the City University of New York), B.A., 1960; Harvard University, M.A., 1963, Ph.D., 1963. *Home:* 309 Mitchell St., Ithaca, N.Y. 14850. *Office:* Department of Philosophy, Cornell University, Ithaca, N.Y. 14850.

CAREER: Has worked as a skilled mechinist and a designer draftsman; Cornell University, Ithaca, N.Y., assistant professor, 1964-67, associate professor, 1967-71, professor of philosophy, 1971—. Visiting associate professor, University of Michigan, summer, 1968. *Member:* American Philosophical Association, American Society for Political and Legal Philosophy, Society for Philosophy and Public Affairs, Aristotelian Society, American Association of University Professors. *Awards, honors:* Guggenheim fellow, University of London, 1970-71; Society for the Humanities fellow, Cornell University, 1972-73; Clark Distinguished Teaching Award, Cornell University, 1976; National Endowment for the Humanities fellow, 1977-78.

WRITINGS: Forms and Limits of Utilitarianism, Clarendon Press, 1965; *In the Interest of the Governed: A Study in Bentham's Philosophy of Utility and Law*, Clarendon Press, 1973. Contributor to philosophy journals. Co-editor, *Philosophical Review*, 1968-70, 1973-76.

WORK IN PROGRESS: Rights, Liberty and the General Welfare: A Study of Utilitarian, Moral, and Political Theory; Ethics and the Rule of Law: An Introduction to Legal and Political Philosophy.

*   *   *

LYTTLE, Richard B(ard) 1927-

PERSONAL: Surname is pronounced "*lit*-il"; born June 9, 1927, in Los Angeles, Calif.; son of Herbert George (a businessman) and Florence (Burleson) Lyttle; married Jean Haldeman (a teacher), December 17, 1949; children: Herbert G. (deceased), Matthew H., Jenny G. *Education:* University of California, Berkeley, B.A., 1950. *Home and office address:* Box 403, Point Reyes Station, Calif. 94956. *Agent:* Barthold Fles, 507 Fifth Ave., New York, N.Y. 10017.

CAREER: Rancho Dos Rios, Ojai, Calif., cowboy and ranch hand, 1950-54; *Oxnard Press-Courier,* Oxnard, Calif., reporter and editor, 1954-62; *Independent-Journal,* San Rafael, Calif., reporter and editor, 1962-67; College of Marin, Kentfield, Calif., adult education instructor, 1972—. *Military service:* U.S. Navy, 1945-46. *Member:* Inverness Yacht Club (commodore, 1969). *Awards, honors:* Matrix award, Los Angeles Alumnae chapter of Theta Sigma Phi, for best news story in a community daily, 1957.

WRITINGS: Challenged by Handicap, Reilly & Lee, 1971; *Polar Frontiers,* Parents' Magazine Press, 1972; *Paints, Inks, and Dyes,* Holiday House, 1974; *How to Beat the High Cost of Sailing,* Regnery, 1976; *Getting into Pro Basketball,* F. Watts, 1978.

All published by Doubleday: *The Complete Beginner's Guide to Bicycling,* 1974; *A Year in the Minors* (Junior Literary Club selection), 1975; *The Complete Beginner's Guide to Backpacking,* 1975; *Basic Hockey Strategy,* 1976; *Soccer Fever,* 1977; *The Complete Beginner's Guide to Physical Fitness,* 1978; *The Complete Beginner's Guide to Skiing,* 1978.

With Edward F. Dolan, Jr.; all published by Doubleday: *Martina Navratilova,* 1977; *Bobby Clarke,* 1977; *Archie Griffin,* 1977; *Fred Lynn,* 1978; *Janet Guthrie,* 1978; *Scott May,* 1978.

*   *   *

MABERLY, Norman C(harles) 1926-

PERSONAL: Born March 16, 1926; married Phyllis Moselen, October 21, 1951; children: Linda Ellen. *Education:* Walla Walla College, B.Th., 1952; Andrews University, M.A., 1953; University of Southern California, Ed.D., 1962. *Religion:* Seventh-day Adventist. *Home:* 11314 Laverne Dr., Riverside, Calif. 92505. *Office:* Department of Education, Loma Linda University, Riverside, Calif. 92354.

CAREER: Harcourt, Brace, Jovanovich, Inc., New York, N.Y., senior editor, 1963-66; Walla Walla College, College Place, Wash., associate professor, 1966-68, professor of education psychology, 1968-76; Loma Linda University, Riverside, Calif., professor of foundations of education, 1976—. *Member:* American Educational Research Association, National Council on Measurement in Education.

WRITINGS: The Standard Score Scale for Tests in the Evaluation and Adjustment Series, Harcourt, 1966; *Dynamic Speed Reading,* New American Library, 1966, published as *Mastering Speed Reading,* 1969, revised edition, 1973.

WORK IN PROGRESS: A book, *Assigning Letter-Grades,* completed and awaiting publication.

*   *   *

MACCOBY, Michael 1933-

PERSONAL: Surname is pronounced *Mack*-oby; born March 5, 1933, in Mount Vernon, N.Y.; son of Max (a rabbi) and Dora (Steinberg) Maccoby; married Sandylee Weille (a portrait painter), December 19, 1959; children: Anne Alexandra, Maria Izett, Nora Harriet, Max Francis. *Education:* Harvard University, B.A., 1954, Ph.D., 1960; studied at New College, Oxford, 1954-55, University of Chicago, 1955-56, and Mexican Institute of Psychoanalysis, 1960-64. *Home:* 4825 Linnaean Ave. N.W., Washington, D.C. 20008.

CAREER: University of Chicago, Chicago, Ill., instructor in social science, 1955-56; Harvard University, Cambridge, Mass., secretary of committee on educational policy, 1956-60; research fellow, U.S. Public Health Service, 1960-63; psychoanalyst in private practice in Mexico City, Mexico, and Washington, D.C., 1962—. Visiting and resident fellow, Institute for Policy Studies, Washington, D.C., 1969-77. Visiting professor of social psychology, Universidad Nacional Autonoma de Mexico, Mexico City, 1960-61; lecturer in psychology, University of California, Santa Cruz, 1967-68; fellow, Center for Advanced Study in the Behavioral

Sciences, Stanford, Calif., 1968-69. Member of board of directors, Centro Intercultural de Documentacion, Cuernavaca, Mexico, 1966-69; research associate for program on technology and society, Harvard University, 1970—. *Member:* American Psychological Association, American Anthropological Association, International Council for the Quality of Working Life, Sociedad Mexicana de Psicoanalisis. *Awards, honors:* Woodrow Wilson fellowship, Oxford University, 1954-55.

WRITINGS: (Author of introduction) Barbara O'Brien, *Operators and Things: The Inner Life of a Schizophrenic,* Arlington Press, 1959; (with Erich Fromm) *Social Character in a Mexican Village,* Prentice-Hall, 1970; (author of introduction) David C. H. Sheppard and Neal Q. Herrick, *Where Have All the Robots Gone?,* Macmillan, 1972; (author of introduction) Herrick, *The Quality of Work and Its Outcomes,* Academy for Contemporary Problems, 1975; *The Gamesman: The New Corporate Leaders,* Simon & Schuster, 1976.

Contributor: J. Roosevelt, editor, *The Liberal Papers,* Doubleday, 1961; J. M. Potter and others, editors, *Peasant Society: A Reader,* Little, Brown, 1967; Jerome S. Bruner and others, editors, *Studies in Cognitive Growth,* Wiley, 1967; Ralph Stavins, editor, *Television Today: The End of Communication and the Death of Community,* Institute for Policy Studies, 1969; J. H. Skolnick and others, editors, *Crisis in American Institutions,* Little, Brown, 1970; David C. McClelland and others, editors, *The Drinking Man,* Free Press, 1972; Phillip Brenner, Robert Borosage, and Bethany Weidner, editors, *Exploring Contradictions: Papers from the Congressional Staff Seminars on Political Economy,* McKay, 1974; R. Fairfield, editor, *Humanizing the Workplace,* Prometheus Books, 1974. Also contributor to many psychiatry and social science journals in United States and Mexico.

WORK IN PROGRESS: Research project on technology, work, and character; a study of economic and human development.

* * *

MACIEL, Judi(th Anne) 1942-
(Judith Anne Stewart)

PERSONAL: Born September 17, 1942, in Oklahoma City, Okla.; daughter of Arthur Monroe (an IBM manager) and Helen Ruth (Truitt) Cox; married Manuel Maciel, January 27, 1963 (divorced June 2, 1971); married Ronald E. Stewart (a salesman), February 11, 1972; children: (first marriage) Belinda Mandi (deceased) and Billye Marguerite (twins), Miguel Timoteo. *Education:* Attended Oklahoma Baptist University, 1961-63; Southwestern State College, B.S., 1967. *Religion:* Baptist-Church of Christ. *Office:* Fairview School, 2431 Southwest 89th, Oklahoma City, Okla. 73159.

CAREER: Elementary school teacher in Watonga, Loyal, and Moore, Oklahoma, 1967-72; Fairview School, Oklahoma City, Okla., elementary school teacher, 1972—. *Member:* Oklahoma Education Association.

WRITINGS: Martin's Important Day (juvenile), illustrations by Michael Hampshire, Harvey House, 1972.

AVOCATIONAL INTERESTS: Sewing, water color, leather tooling, sculpture, copper and aluminum tooling, basket weaving, candle-making.†

* * *

MacKELLAR, William 1914-

PERSONAL: Born February 20, 1914, in Glasgow, Scot-

land; brought to United States when he was eleven; son of John (a blacksmith) and Mary (Justice) MacKellar; married Helen Mulcahy, April 10, 1954; children: John, Laurie, David. *Education:* Studied at New York University for three years and at University of Geneva. *Home:* 40 Mountain Rd., West Hartford, Conn. 06107. *Agent:* McIntosh & Otis, Inc., 475 Fifth Ave., New York, N.Y. 10017. *Office:* Royal Typewriter Co., Hartford, Conn. 06106.

CAREER: Royal Typewriter Company, New York City, assistant credit manager, 1942, International Division advertising manager, 1954, Geneva, Switzerland, International Division sales promotion manager, 1958, New York City, assistant to president of International Division, 1962, Hartford, Conn., export manager, 1965—. Writer for children and teen-agers. *Military service:* U.S. Army, Signal Corps, 1942-45; served in North Africa and Europe. *Awards, honors:* Citation in Child Study Association of America Children's Book Awards, 1957, for *Wee Joseph.*

WRITINGS: The Mystery of the Ruined Abbey, McGraw, 1954; *Kickoff,* McGraw, 1955; *Danger in the Mist,* McGraw, 1956; *The Team That Wouldn't Quit,* McGraw, 1957; *Wee Joseph,* McGraw, 1957; *Two for the Fair,* McGraw, 1958; *A Goal for Greg,* McKay, 1958; *Ghost in the Castle,* McKay, 1960; *A Dog Like No Other,* McKay, 1965; *A Place by the Fire,* McKay, 1966; *The Secret of the Dark Tower,* McKay, 1967; *Score: A Baker's Dozen Sports Stories,* McKay, 1967; *A Very Small Miracle,* Crown, 1969; *Mound Menace,* Follett, 1969; *The Smallest Monster in the World,* McKay, 1969; *Secret of the Sacred Stone,* McKay, 1970; *A Ghost around the House,* McKay, 1970; *The Mystery of Mordach Castle,* Follett, 1970; *The Ghost of Grannoch Moor,* Dodd, 1973; *Alfie and Me and the Ghost of Peter Stuyvesant,* Dodd, 1974; *The Cat that Never Died,* Dodd, 1976; *The Kid Who Owned Manhattan Island,* Dodd, 1976. Stories included in anthologies and school readers, and published in *Boys' Life* and other magazines.

SIDELIGHTS: William MacKellar told *CA:* "I have always felt that the chief end of the fiction writer is to entertain. This should be particularly true when one is writing for young people. I have never felt it was my special mission on earth to motivate and inspire young readers. Others can do that much more effectively than I can. My purpose, as I see it, is to write books that are amusing and interesting and which leave the reader with a fresh insight into the world around him." MacKellar continues: "It seems to me that a writer should use his background and interests in his stories. A number of my sheep dog stories are set in Scotland and I have utilized my Swiss experience in several of my teen age mysteries. Other books reflect the years I spent in New York and Connecticut. It is of course the characters who bring a story alive but a strong and colorful background helps."

BIOGRAPHICAL/CRITICAL SOURCES: Hartford Times, September 26, 1971; *Hartford Courant,* April 12, 1976.

* * *

MACKEY, Louis H(enry) 1926-

PERSONAL: Born September 24, 1926, in Sidney, Ohio; son of Louis Henry (a laborer) and Clara Emma (Maurer) Mackey; married Caroll D. Brandt, June, 1948; married Linda K. Barabas, July 8, 1968; children: Stephen Louis, Thomas Adam, Jacob Louis, Eva Maria. *Education:* Capital University, B.A., 1948; Duke University, graduate study, 1948-50; Yale University, M.A., 1953, Ph.D., 1954. *Home:*

3001 Dancy St., Austin, Tex. 78722. *Office:* Department of Philosophy, University of Texas, 316 Waggener Hall, Austin, Tex. 78712.

CAREER: Yale University, New Haven, Conn., instructor, 1953-55, assistant professor of philosophy, 1955-59; Rice University, Houston, Tex., associate professor, 1959-65, professor of philosophy, 1965-67; University of Texas at Austin, professor of philosophy, 1967—. *Awards, honors:* National Endowment for the Humanities fellowship for independent study and research, 1976-77.

WRITINGS: Kierkegaard: A Kind of Poet, University of Pennsylvania Press, 1971. Contributor to *Review of Metaphysics, Thought, Arion, Southwestern Journal of Philosophy,* and *Franciscan Studies.*

WORK IN PROGRESS: A book of essays on problems in medieval philosophy, focusing on the relations of faith, reason, and language in the Augustinian tradition.

* * *

MACKIN, John H(oward) 1921-

PERSONAL: Born May 8, 1921, in Boardman, Wis.; son of John Howard (a farmer) and Marene (Rushenberg) Mackin; married Martha Howard (a professor of chemistry), June 26, 1947; children: Joanna Lee, Lynne Marene, Ross Howard, Scott Allen. *Education:* University of Wisconsin, A.B., 1943; University of Chicago, A.M., 1947, Ph.D., 1962. *Religion:* "Protestant Christian." *Home:* 1007 Maple Ave., Evanston, Ill. 60202. *Office:* Department of English, University of Illinois at Chicago Circle, Box 4348, Chicago, Ill. 60680.

CAREER: Chicago City College, Chicago, Ill., instructor in English at Woodrow Wilson campus, 1947-48, Wright campus, 1950-51; University of Illinois at Chicago Circle, assistant professor, 1962-67, associate professor of English, 1967—, assistant dean of College of Liberal Arts and Sciences, 1962-68. *Military service:* U.S. Navy Construction Battalion, 1943-46; became lieutenant junior grade. *Member:* Modern Language Association of America, National Council for Teachers of English. *Awards, honors:* Danforth associate, 1971—.

WRITINGS: Classical Rhetoric for Modern Discourse, Free Press, 1969.

WORK IN PROGRESS: The Teaching—Death and Catastasis in Elizabethan Plot Structure; The Function of Comedy in Shakespeare's "King John"; St. Augustine and Socratic Rhetoric; fiction based on rural life in Wisconsin in 1930's.

* * *

MacLEAN, Janet Rockwood 1917-

PERSONAL: Born March 8, 1917, in Bennington, Vt.; daughter of Frederick Herman and Mary (Hunter) Rockwood; married John Richard Phillips, Jr., March 28, 1938; married second husband, William F. MacLean (a superintendent of construction), December 28, 1952; children: (first marriage) Patricia Kaye (Mrs. Ira Christian Smith), John Richard. *Education:* University of Vermont, B.S. (magna cum laude), 1938; Indiana University, M.S., 1953, Ph.D., 1959. *Religion:* Methodist. *Home:* 630 West Sylvan Lane, Bloomington, Ind. 47401. *Office:* Department of Recreation and Park Administration, Indiana University, Bloomington, Ind. 47401.

CAREER: High school teacher of French and English in North Troy, Vt., 1938-39; with private nursery school in Detroit, Mich., 1940-44; with federal child care center in Bennington, Vt., 1945-47; high school teacher of speech and theater in Bennington, 1947-51; City of Bennington, municipal playground supervisor, 1947, community center director, 1947, superintendent of recreation, 1948-51; Indiana University at Bloomington, campus recreation director, 1951-53, instructor, 1951-58, assistant professor, 1958-62, associate professor, 1963-65, professor of recreation, 1965—. Conductor of municipal playground leadership institutes, youth leadership workshops, and workshops for nursing home administrators. Consultant to White House Conference on Aging, 1961, 1971; member of committee on leisure, Indiana Commission on Aged and Aging, 1959—.

MEMBER: National Recreation and Park Association (chairman of board on professional education), National Council on Aging, Federation of National Professional Recreation Associations, American Association for Health, Physical Education and Recreation (Midwest vice-president for recreation), American Recreation Society, National Recreation Association (member of board of trustees), Society of Park and Recreation Educators (past president), Indiana Park and Recreation Association, Phi Beta Kappa. *Awards, honors:* Golden Reel International Award; Charles Brightbill Award from University of Illinois, 1975; National Society of Park and Recreation Educators distinguished fellow award, 1976; National Recreation and Park Association distinguished service award, 1976.

WRITINGS: (With R. E. Carlson and T. R. Deppe) *Recreation in American Life,* Wadsworth, 1963; (with Deppe and H. L. Frye) *Forceful Communications through Visual Resources,* National Recreation Association, 1963; (contributor) W. Morris and H. L. Jacobs, editors, *Nursing and Retirement Homes,* Iowa State University Press, 1965. Writer of various monographs and instructional films. Contributor to *Aging in Indiana,* 1960, *Education for Aging,* 1973, and *Recreation in American Life.* Also contributor of articles to *International Encyclopedia of Sports Medicine, Grolier's Encyclopedia,* and recreation journals.

SIDELIGHTS: Janet MacLean told *CA:* "The medical profession is often said to be a 'matter of life and death.' My profession, serving the leisure needs of people, is a matter of *life* itself. In a world of increased leisure for more people, the opportunity to write and talk about the emerging leisure ethic is most challenging. In my judgment, how we as individuals use or misuse our leisure may not only condition the quality of our lives but may relate to survival itself in terms of psychological balance, physical well being and the preservation of the environments in which we or future generations may move."

* * *

MacLEAN, Katherine 1925-
(Charles Dye)

PERSONAL: Born January 22, 1925, in Montclair, N.J.; daughter of Gordon (a chemical engineer) and Ruth (Crawford) MacLean; married Charles Dye (a writer), 1951 (divorced); married David Mason (a writer), February 15, 1956 (divorced); children: (second marriage) Christopher Dennis. *Education:* Barnard College, B.A., 1950; attended University of Connecticut, 1961-64 and University of Maine, 1965-66; Goddard College, M.A., 1976. *Politics:* "Pacifist, civil rights liberal, economic conservative." *Religion:* "Open—still investigating religious history, experimental evidence." *Home:* 30 Day St., South Portland, Me. 04106. *Agent:* Virginia Kidd, Box 278, Milford, Pa. 18337.

CAREER: Worked as an antibiotics laboratory assistant, 1944-45, and as a food manufacturing quality control laboratory technician, 1945-46; Hi-Pro Animal Feed, Frankfort, Del., office manager, 1952-53; Memorial Hospital and Knickerbocker Hospital, New York, N.Y., technician, 1954-56; writer of science fiction since 1949. Lecturer, University of Connecticut, 1962-64, University of Maine, 1966-67, Free University of Marin County and Free University of Berkeley, 1968, at University of Maine, 1972, and at an experimental high school in Orange City, Fla., 1969-70. Member: Science Fiction Writers of America, Science Fiction Research Association, Society for General Systems Research, Mensa, Neighborhood Environmental Improvement Council, Audubon Society. Awards, honors: Nebula Award, Science Fiction Writers of America, 1971.

WRITINGS—Science fiction: (With Harry Harrison) Web of the Worlds, Ace Books, 1955; (with Charles V. DeVet) Cosmic Checkmate, Ace Books, 1962; The Diploids, Avon, 1962; The Man in the Bird Cage, Ace Books, 1971; Missing Man, Putnam, 1975. Contributor of over thirty short stories to magazines, two under the name Charles Dye, some of them reprinted in science fiction anthologies.

SIDELIGHTS: "H. G. Wells, warning 'the twentieth century will be a race between education and disaster' has molded my life," Katherine MacLean writes. "As a supreme method of popular education science fiction stories display all possible disasters resulting from logically expected events.... For me, the work of writing science fiction is an integration of lifetime studies of psychology, biology, and history. It is a way to think."

BIOGRAPHICAL/CRITICAL SOURCES: Kingsley Amis, New Maps of Hell: A Survey of Science Fiction, Harcourt, 1960.

* * *

Mac MASTER, Robert E(llsworth) 1919-

PERSONAL: Born October 10, 1919, in Winthrop, Mass.; son of Joseph O. (a painter) and Ruby M. (Slocomb) Mac Master; married Ann E. Lynch, April 28, 1942; children: Angus M., Martha A., David J. Education: Harvard University, A.B., 1941, A.M., 1948, Ph.D., 1952. Home: 461 Main St., Hingham, Mass. 02043. Office: Department of History, Massachusetts Institute of Technology, Cambridge, Mass. 02139.

CAREER: Massachusetts Institute of Technology, Cambridge, instructor, 1952-53, assistant professor, 1953-60, associate professor of history, 1960-67, professor of history and literature, 1967—, chairman of history section, 1970-72. Military service: U.S. Army, Field Artillery, 1941-46. U.S. Army Reserve, 1946-69. Member: American Association for the Advancement of Slavic Studies.

WRITINGS: Danilevsky: A Russian Totalitarian Philosopher, Harvard University Press, 1967. Contributor of articles to history journals.

WORK IN PROGRESS: Tolstoi at the Time of the Emancipation.

* * *

MACMILLAN, Mona 1908-

PERSONAL: Born March 26, 1908, in London, England; daughter of Sir Hugh Justin (an admiral) and Constance Marion (Crossman) Tweedie; married William Miller Macmillan (a professor and author), 1934 (died October 1, 1974); children: Lindsay (Mrs. Alexander Dow), Duncan, Hugh,

Catriona (Mrs. Alestair Miller; died October 23, 1976). Education: Attended University of Cape Town, one year, and London School of Economics and Political Science, one year. Politics: Socialist. Religion: Roman Catholic. Home: Yew Tree Cottage, Long Wittenham, Abingdon, Berkshire, England.

CAREER: Workers' Educational Association lecturer, 1960-63; writer. Member: Royal Commonwealth Society, African Studies Association of Great Britain, Catholic Institute of International Relations, Union of Catholic Mothers (president of Oxford section, 1968-70), St. Andrews Overseas Society, Queen Elizabeth House (Oxford), Wittenham Women's Institute.

WRITINGS: Smoking Flax (play), International Missionary Council, 1945; Introducing East Africa, Faber, 1953, revised edition, 1955; The Land of Look Behind: A Study of Jamaica, Faber, 1958; Henry Barkly: Mediator and Moderator, A. A. Balkema, 1967, Verry, 1968. Writer of scripts for British Broadcasting Corp., 1939-45. Contributor of articles on Africa to The Tablet.

SIDELIGHTS: Mona Macmillan completed her late husband's memoirs, My South Africa Years, which was published in 1975 by Philip. She told CA, she is "urged to write by conditions in South Africa."

* * *

MACNAB, P(eter) A(ngus) 1903-

PERSONAL: Born in 1903, in Portmahomack, Ross-shire, Scotland; son of Peter and Jeanie (Allan) Macnab; married Eugenie Alice Alexander, 1954; children: Peter Alexander, Wendy Alice. Education: Attended schools in Scotland. Politics: Conservative. Religion: Presbyterian. Home and office: Fairway, Summerlea Rd., West Kilbride, Ayrshire, Scotland.

CAREER: Clydesdale Bank Ltd., Glasgow, Scotland, manager of several branches, 1955-63. County councillor for West Kilbride District of Ayrshire, 1962-75. Professional guide in Scottish Tourist Guides Association; professional lecturer on Isle of Mull and Scottish highlands. Member: International P.E.N., West Kilbride Golf Club.

WRITINGS: The Isle of Mull, David & Charles, 1970, Fernhill, 1971. Contributor to radio programs, magazines, and newspapers (chiefly articles on Hebridean subjects); contributor to Lapidary Journal (San Diego).

WORK IN PROGRESS: Horse Island: Tall Tales from an Island.

SIDELIGHTS: P. A. Macnab told CA: "The art of writing gives the double satisfaction of fulfilling self-expression and at the same time interesting or entertaining other people. Basically my object is to preserve a record of an old way of life in the Highlands and Islands of Scotland, including folklore, superstition, history, personalities, topography, which would otherwise be lost for ever when an older generation passes on."

AVOCATIONAL INTERESTS: Golf, angling, photography, beekeeping, making ornamental crooks and sticks.

BIOGRAPHICAL/CRITICAL SOURCES: Listener, December 31, 1970.

* * *

MAC NAMARA, Donal E(oin) J(oseph) 1916-

PERSONAL: Born August 13, 1916, in New York, N.Y.; son of Daniel Patrick and Rita (Chambers) Mac Namara;

married Margaret Scott (a lawyer), June, 1953; children: Brian Scott. *Education:* Columbia University, B.Sc., 1939; New York University, M.P.A., 1946; Air Command and Staff College, U.S. Air Force, diploma, 1948. *Politics:* "Independent Liberal." *Religion:* Roman Catholic. *Home:* 206 Christie Hghts., Leonia, N.J. 07605. *Office:* 444 West 56th St., New York, N.Y. 10019.

CAREER: Rutgers University, New Brunswick, N.J., instructor in political science, 1948-49; University of Southern California, Los Angeles, assistant professor of police administration, 1949-50; New York Institute of Criminology, New York City, assistant dean, 1950-55, dean, 1955-65; City University of New York, New York City, professor of criminology at John Jay College of Criminal Justice, 1965—, and at Bernard M. Baruch College, 1966—. Managing partner, Flath, Weston & Mac Namara Associates, 1958-69. Assistant director, Delinquency Control Institute, 1949-50; director, Traffic Management Survey Fund, Inc., 1958-68; vice-president, Character Underwriters, Inc.; director, Crime Show Consultants. Visiting lecturer, University of Louisville, 1950—, State University of New York, 1950-56; visiting professor, Florida State University, 1959, University of Utah, 1961, 1962. Chairman of law enforcement institutes and lecturer in Graduate School of Public Administration, New York University, 1950-57; coordinator of police science program, Brooklyn College of the City University of New York, 1957-63. Senior instructor, Center for Correctional Training, 1963-65. Consultant, New York Housing Authority, 1955, New Jersey Law Enforcement Council, 1957-59, Commonwealth of Puerto Rico, 1960; educational consultant, Probation and Parole Officers Association. Executive vice-president, Bronx Real Estate Board. *Military service:* U.S. Army, Military Police and Intelligence, 1942-46; became major.

MEMBER: International Association of Chiefs of Police, Societe Internationale de Criminologie, Association Internationale de Droit Penal, American Association for the Advancement of Science (fellow), American Society of Criminology (fellow; secretary, 1949-51; vice-president, 1953-55, 1958-60; president, 1961), Association for the Psychiatric Treatment of Offenders, Institute of Social and Behavioral Science, Academy of Criminalistics (fellow; president, 1959-63), American League to Abolish Capital Punishment (president), American Sociological Association (fellow), National Council on Crime and Delinquency, American Correctional Association. *Awards, honors:* Herbert A. Bloch Award, American Society of Criminology, 1967.

WRITINGS: Problems of Sex Behavior, Crowell, 1969; *Perspectives on Correction,* Crowell, 1971; *Problems of Punishment and Rehabilitation,* Praeger, 1972; *Police: Problems and Prospects,* Praeger, 1974; *Criminal Justice,* Dushkin, 1976; *Sex, Crime and the Law,* Free Press, 1977. Editor-in-chief, *Criminology: An Interdisciplinary Journal,* 1976—; editor, *Journal of Corrective Psychiatry;* member of editorial boards, *Abstracts of Criminology and Penology* and *Abstracts of Police and Forensic Science.*

WORK IN PROGRESS: Crime and Delinquency in the U.S.S.R.; Social Pathology Among the Irish Tinkers.

SIDELIGHTS: Donal Mac Namara told *CA:* "I am a liberal, somewhat eclectic behavioral scientist with a strong bias against the punitive-repressive approach to those unable or unwilling to live by society's laws. I favor decriminalizing the penal code, eliminating criminal sanctions against consensual and/or victimless crimes (e.g., gambling, narcotics use, alcoholism, most sex offenses), humanizing our penal institutions, and adopting a much more tolerant and permissive attitude toward the eccentricities, idiosyncrasies, and even the peccadillos of our fellow men."

* * *

MACNEIL, Ian R(oderick) 1929-

PERSONAL: Born June 20, 1929, in New York, N.Y.; son of Robert L. (an architect) and Kathleen (Metcalf) Macneil; married Nancy Carol Wilson, March 29, 1952; children: Roderick, Jennifer, Duncan (deceased), Andrew. *Education:* University of Vermont, B.A. (magna cum laude), 1950; Harvard University, J.D. (magna cum laude), 1955. *Home:* 105 Devon Rd., Ithaca, N.Y. 14850. *Office:* School of Law, Cornell University, Ithaca, N.Y. 14853.

CAREER: Law clerk, Ropes, Gray, Best, Coolidge & Rugg, Boston, Mass., 1954-55, Smith & Yandell, Burlington, Vt., 1955, and for Hon. Peter Woodbury of the United States Court of Appeals for the First Circuit, Manchester, N.H., 1955-56; Sulloway Hollis Godfrey & Soden (law firm), Concord, N.H., associate, 1956-59; Cornell University, Ithaca, N.Y., assistant professor, 1959-62, associate professor, 1962-63, professor of law, 1963-72; University of Virginia, Charlottesville, professor of law and member of Institute for Advanced Studies, 1972-74; Cornell University, School of Law, professor of law, 1974—, Ingersoll Professor of Law, 1976—. Fulbright visiting professor of law, University of East Africa, Dar es Salaam, Tanzania, 1965-67; visiting professor of law, Duke University, 1971-72. Member of executive committee, Association of American Law Schools, 1970-71. Auditor, Town of Hopkinton, N.H., 1958-59; member of School Board Nominating Committee, Ithaca, 1969-70. *Military service:* U.S. Army, 1951-53, became lieutenant. U.S. Army Reserve, 1950-69, became major.

MEMBER: American Bar Association, African Law Association, New Hampshire Bar Association, Association of Canadian Law Teachers (associate), Standing Council of Scottish Chiefs, Phi Beta Kappa, Tau Kappa Alpha. *Awards, honors:* Emil Brown Preventive Law Award, 1971, for *Cases and Materials on Contracts: Exchange Transactions and Relationships.*

WRITINGS: Bankruptcy Law in East Africa, Oceana, 1966; *Contracts: Instruments for Social Co-operation: East Africa; Text, Cases, Materials,* Fred B. Rothman, 1968; (contributor) R. B. Schlesinger, editor, *Formation of Contracts: A Study of the Common Core of Legal Systems,* two volumes, Oceana, 1968; (with Robert Swain Morison) *Students and Decision Making,* Public Affairs Press, 1970; *Cases and Materials on Contracts: Exchange Transactions and Relationships,* Foundation Press, 1971, 2nd edition, 1978. Contributor of articles and reviews to *Cornell Law Quarterly, Foreign Exchange Bulletin, Journal of Legal Education, Harvard Law School Bulletin, East African Law Journal, Boston College Industrial and Commercial Law Review, New Hampshire Bar Journal, Southern California Law Review,* and other law journals.

WORK IN PROGRESS: A study of contracts in modern society.

SIDELIGHTS: Ian Macneil told *CA:* "Although my major subject area, contracts, is one viewed by most laymen, and indeed many professionals, as highly technical and inherently dry and dull, the fact is that we live in a society founded on contracts and dominated by economic exchange motivations and structures. This domination, coupled with mass populations, technological innovation, and economic growth, are the sources of many of our social and environmental problems. There is a relationship between contract legal doctrine and these problems, and my primary scholarly interest lies in exploring both this relationship and the broader subject of the interplay of economic exchange motivations and social structures, i.e., contracts, with social and environmental problems.''

*   *   *

MacVEAGH, Lincoln 1890-1972

October 1, 1890—January 15, 1972; American publisher and ambassador to foreign countries. *Obituaries: New York Times,* January 17, 1972; *Publishers Weekly,* February 28, 1972.

*   *   *

MACY, John W(illiams), Jr. 1917-

PERSONAL: Born April 6, 1917, in Chicago, Ill.; son of John Williams (an advertising executive) and Juliette (Shaw) Macy; married Joyce Hagen, February 12, 1944; children: Thomas Lawrence, Mary Derrick, Susan Bradford, Richard Hagen. *Education:* Wesleyan University, Middletown, Conn., B.A., 1938; further study at American University, 1938-39. *Politics:* Democrat. *Religion:* Episcopalian. *Home:* 1127 Langley Lane, McLean, Va. 22101. *Office:* Development and Resources Corp., 1629 K St. N.W., Washington, D.C. 20006.

CAREER: U.S. War Department, Washington, D.C., assistant director of civilian personnel, 1942-43, 1946-47; U.S. Atomic Energy Commission, Los Alamos, N.M., director of organization and personnel, 1947-51; U.S. Department of the Army, Washington, D.C., special assistant, 1951-53; Civil Service Commission, Washington, D.C., executive director, 1953-58, chairman, 1961-69; Wesleyan University, Middletown, Conn., executive vice-president, 1958-61; Corporation for Public Broadcasting, Washington, D.C., president, 1969-72; president, Council of Better Business Bureaus, 1973-74; Development and Resources Corp., Washington, D.C., president, 1975—. *Military service:* U.S. Army Air Forces, 1943-46; became captain. *Member:* American Society for Public Administration (president, 1958-59). *Awards, honors:* Ten honorary LL.D. degrees from colleges and universities; Presidential Medal of Freedom, 1969.

WRITINGS: Public Service: Human Side of Government, Harper, 1971; *To Irrigate a Wasteland,* University of California Press, 1974.

*   *   *

MADDOX, Robert James 1931-

PERSONAL: Born December 7, 1931, in Monroe, N.Y.; son of Robert Clarence and Alice (Lamey) Maddox; married Barbara J. Kressman, August 28, 1958; children: Quinn, Carol, Bourke. *Education:* Fairleigh Dickenson University, B.S., 1957; University of Wisconsin, M.S., 1958; Rutgers University, Ph.D., 1964. *Home:* 1633 Oxford Cir., State College, Pa. *Office:* Department of History, Pennsylvania State University, University Park, Pa. 16802.

CAREER: Paterson State College (now William Paterson College of New Jersey), Wayne, N.J., instructor in history, 1962-64; Michigan State University, East Lansing, assistant professor of history, 1964-66; Pennsylvania State University, University Park, assistant professor, 1966-68, associate professor, 1968-73, professor of history, 1973—. *Military*

service: U.S. Army, 1952-54; served in Infantry. *Member:* American Historical Association, Organization of American Historians, Society of Historians of American Foreign Relations.

WRITINGS: William E. Borah and American Foreign Policy, Louisiana State University Press, 1969; *The New Left and the Origins of the Cold War,* Princeton University Press, 1973; *The Unknown War with Russia,* Presidio Press, 1977; (editor) *Readings in American History,* Dushkin, 1977. Contributor of articles to *Journal of American History, Historian, Pacific Historical Review,* and *Mid-America.*

WORK IN PROGRESS: The Cold War Begins: 1945.

*   *   *

MADGETT, Naomi Long 1923-
(Naomi Cornelia Long, Naomi Long Witherspoon)

PERSONAL: Born July 5, 1923, in Norfolk, Va.; daughter of Clarence Marcellus (a clergyman) and Maude (a teacher; maiden name, Hilton) Long; married Julian F. Witherspoon, March 31, 1946 (divorced April 27, 1949); married William Harold Madgett, July 29, 1954 (divorced December 21, 1960); married Leonard Patton Andrews (an elementary school principal), March 31, 1972; children: (first marriage) Jill Witherspoon Boyer; stepchildren: William H., Gerald. *Education:* Virginia State College, B.A., 1945; New York University, additional study, 1945-46; Wayne State University, M.Ed., 1956, additional study, 1967-68; University of Detroit, additional study, 1961-62. *Politics:* Independent, but usually Democratic Party. *Religion:* Protestant (Congregational). *Home:* 16886 Inverness St., Detroit, Mich. 48221. *Office:* English Department, Eastern Michigan University, Ypsilanti, Mich. 48197.

CAREER: Michigan Chronicle, Detroit, Mich., reporter and copy reader, 1945-46; Michigan Bell Telephone Co., Detroit, service representative, 1948-54; English teacher in public high schools, Detroit, 1955-65, 1966-68; Oakland University, Rochester, Mich., research associate, 1965-66; Eastern Michigan University, Ypsilanti, Mich., associate professor, 1968-73, professor of English, 1973—. Visiting lecturer in English, University of Michigan, 1970-71; lecturer on Afro-American literature at colleges and universities. Editor, Lotus Press, 1974—. *Member:* National Council of Teachers of English, College Language Association, American Association of University Professors, National Association for the Advancement of Colored People, Poetry Society of Michigan, Detroit Women Writers, Delta Kappa Gamma, Alpha Kappa Alpha, Alpha Rho Omega. *Awards, honors:* Mott fellowship in English, 1965-66; Esther R. Beer poetry award, National Writers Club, 1957, for poem, "Native."

WRITINGS: (Under name Naomi Cornelia Long) *Songs to a Phantom Nightingale* (poems), Fortuny's, 1941; *One and the Many* (poems), Exposition, 1956; *Star by Star* (poems), Harlo, 1965, revised edition, 1970; (with Ethel Tincher and Henry B. Maloney) *Success in Language and Literature–B* (high school textbook), Follett, 1967; *Pink Ladies in the Afternoon* (poems), Lotus Press, 1972.

Poetry included in over seventy anthologies, including: *The Poetry of the Negro, 1746-1949,* edited by Langston Hughes and Arna Bontemps, Doubleday, 1949; *Beyond the Blues,* edited by Rosey E. Pool, Hand & Flower, 1962; *Kaleidoscope,* edited by Robert Hayden, Harcourt, 1967; *Soulscript,* edited by June Meyer Jordan, Doubleday, 1970; *Oral Interpretation,* edited by Charlotte I. Lee, Houghton, 1971;

New Black Voices, edited by Abraham Chapman, New American Library, 1972; *Within You, Without You,* edited by Betsy Ryan, Scholastic Book Services, 1973; *On Our Way,* edited by Lee Bennett Hopkins, Knopf, 1974; *Echoes from the Moon,* edited by Judith Goren, Elinor K. Rose, Gay Rubin, and Elaine Watson, Hot Apples Press, 1976. Contributor of poetry to various periodicals, including *Freedomways, Negro Digest, Negro History Bulletin, Phylon, Blue River Poetry Magazine, American Pen, Poetry Digest, Norwester,* and *Virginia Statesman.*

SIDELIGHTS: Naomi Madgett told *CA:* "As a child I was motivated by my father's library and the interests and inspiration of literary parents. I discovered Alfred Lord Tennyson and Langston Hughes at about the same time, sitting on the floor of my father's study when I was about seven or eight. I think my poetry represents something of the variety of interest and style that these two widely divergent poets represent. I would rather be a good poet than anything else I can imagine. It please me tremendously that my social-worker daughter is becoming a very good poet."

Madgett's papers are being collected in the Special Collections Library at Fisk University.

BIOGRAPHICAL/CRITICAL SOURCES: Phylon, winter, 1956; *English Journal,* April, 1957; *Michigan Chronicle,* January 15, 1966; *Negro Digest,* September, 1966; *Black Books Bulletin,* spring, 1974; *Black World,* September, 1974; *New Orleans Review,* September, 1976.

*   *   *

MADOW, Leo 1915-

PERSONAL: Surname is pronounced *May*-doe; born October 18, 1915, in Cleveland, Ohio; son of Solomon Martin (a building contractor) and Anna (Meyers) Madow; married Jean A. Weisman, April 16, 1942; children: Michael, Robert. *Education:* Western Reserve University (now Case Western Reserve University), B.A., 1937, M.D., 1942; Ohio State University, M.A., 1938. *Office:* Medical College of Pennsylvania, 3300 Henry Ave., Philadelphia, Pa. 19129.

CAREER: Jefferson Medical College of Pennsylvania, Philadelphia, instructor, 1948-52, assistant professor of neurology, 1952-56; Medical College of Pennsylvania (formerly Women's Medical College), Philadelphia, professor and chairman of department of neurology, 1956-71, professor of psychiatry, 1964-71, chairman of department of psychiatry, 1964—. *Military service:* U.S. Army, 1942-44; became captain. *Member:* American Psychoanalytic Association, American Psychiatric Association, American Neurological Association, American College of Physicians.

WRITINGS: (With Laurence H. Snow) *The Psychodynamic Implications of the Physiological Studies on Dreams,* C. C Thomas, 1970; (with Snow) *The Psychodynamic Implications of the Physiological Studies on Sensory Deprivation,* C. C Thomas, 1970; (with Snow) *The Psychodynamic Implications of the Physiological Studies on Psychomimetic Drugs,* C. C Thomas, 1971; *Anger: How to Recognize and Cope with It,* Scribner, 1971.

*   *   *

MAHONEY, John Leo 1928-

PERSONAL: Born February 4, 1928, in Somerville, Mass.; son of John Leo (a printer) and Margaret (Daly) Mahoney; married Ann Marie Dowd (a dental hygienist), September 1, 1956; children: John, Patricia, William. *Education:* Boston College, A.B., 1950, A.M., 1952; Harvard University,

Ph.D., 1957. *Politics:* Democrat. *Religion:* Roman Catholic. *Home:* 8 Sutherland Rd., Lexington, Mass. 02173. *Office:* Department of English, Boston College, Chestnut Hill, Mass. 02167.

CAREER: Boston College, Chestnut Hill, Mass., instructor, 1955-58, assistant professor, 1958-61, associate professor, 1961-65, professor of English, 1966—, chairman of department, 1962-67, 1969-70. Visiting professor, Harvard University, summers, 1963, 1965, 1969, 1971. *Military service:* U.S. Army, 1946-47. *Member:* Modern Language Association of America, Conference on British Studies, American Association of University Professors, Wordsworth-Coleridge Association, New England Modern Language Association.

WRITINGS: (Editor) *William Duff's Essay on Original Genius,* Scholars' Facsimiles & Reprints, 1963; (editor) *Dryden's Critical Essays,* Bobbs-Merrill, 1965. Contributor of articles to *English Studies, British Journal of Aesthetics, Drama Critique, Burke Newsletter, Wordsworth Circle,* and other publications.

WORK IN PROGRESS: A book on the literary criticism of William Hazlitt, and an anthology, *The English Romantic Poets.*

*   *   *

MAIMON, Morton A. 1931-

PERSONAL: Surname is pronounced "*May*-man"; born September 19, 1931, in Philadelphia, Pa.; son of Abram M. (a dentist) and Blanche (Apfelbaum) Maimon; married Elaine B. Plaskow (a professor of English), September 30, 1967; children: Gillian Blanche, Alan Marcus. *Education:* West Chester State College, B.S., 1953; University of Vermont, M.A., 1955; University of Pennsylvania, Ed.D., 1972. *Politics:* Independent. *Home:* 1701 Newbold Lane, Laverock, Pa. 19118.

CAREER: Board of Public Education, Philadelphia, Pa., head of English department, 1967—; Philadelphia High School for Girls, Philadelphia, head of English department, 1972—. Lecturer in education, University of Pennsylvania; lecturer in English, Rosemont College. Haverford Township School Board, member of board of directors, 1971-75, president, 1975—. *Member:* National Council of Teachers of English, Common Cause, Phi Delta Kappa.

WRITINGS: (With Benjamin Ashcom and William Reynolds) *Stories of the Inner City,* Globe Book, 1970.

WORK IN PROGRESS: Research on the "minischool" as a viable organizational alternative for urban elementary schools.

*   *   *

MAJUMDAR, R(amesh) C(handra) 1888-

PERSONAL: First name sometimes appears as Ramesal-Chandra; born December 4, 1888, in Kandarpara, East Pakistan (now part of Bangladesh); son of Haladhar (an advocate) and Bidhumukhi Majumdar; married Priyabala Sen, October, 1908 (deceased); children: Asok (son), Santi (Mrs. H. K. Sen; deceased), Sujata (Mrs. D. B. Sen; deceased), Sumitra (Mrs. H. Chaudhuri). *Education:* Presidency College, Calcutta, B.A., 1909, M.A., 1911; University of Calcutta, Ph.D., 1918. *Politics:* "Liberal, Democrat, not attached to a party." *Religion:* Hinduism. *Home:* 4 Bepin Pal Rd., P.O. Kalighat, Calcutta 26, India.

CAREER: University of Calcutta, Calcutta, India, lecturer

in history, 1914-21; University of Dacca, Ramna, East Pakistan (now Bangladesh), professor of history, 1921-37, vice-chancellor, 1937-42; Banaras Hindu University, Baranasi, India, principal of College of Indology, 1950-52; government-appointed director of board of editors compiling a history of the Freedom Movement in India, 1953-55; University of Nagpur, Nagpur, India, principal of College of Indology, 1955-57; visiting professor of Indian history at University of Chicago, Chicago, Ill., and University of Pennsylvania, Philadelphia, 1958. Distinguished lecturer at the major universities in India. Vice-president of UNESCO International Commission, responsible for publishing a history of mankind; member of bureau, International Council for Philosophy and Humanistic Studies. President of Indology Section, XXII International Congress of Orientalists, held in Istanbul.

MEMBER: Royal Asiatic Society of Great Britain and Ireland (honorary fellow), Asiatic Societies of Calcutta and Bombay (honorary fellow). *Awards, honors:* D.Litt. from University of Calcutta, Jadavpur University, and Rabindra Bharati University.

WRITINGS: Corporate Life in Ancient India (author's doctoral thesis at University of Calcutta), limited edition, S. N. Sen, 1918, revised and enlarged 2nd edition, University of Calcutta, 1922, 3rd edition, Verry, 1969; *The Early History of Bengal* (booklet), [London], 1925; *Ancient Indian Colonies in the Far East,* three volumes, privately printed, 1927; *Outline of Ancient Indian History and Civilisation,* Chuckervertty, Chatterjee, 1927, revised and enlarged edition published as *Ancient India,* Motilal Banarsidass, 1952, 6th revised edition, Verry, 1971; *Hindu Colonies in the Far East,* General Printers & Publishers (Calcutta), 1944, revised and enlarged 2nd edition, Verry, 1963; *Kambuja-Desa: Or, an Ancient Hindu Colony in Cambodia* (Sir William Meyer lectures, 1942-43), University of Madras, 1944; (with H. C. Raychaudhuri and Kalikinkar Datta) *An Advanced History of India,* Macmillan, 1946, 3rd edition, 1967; *Maharaja Rajballabh: A Critical Study Based on Contemporary Records,* University of Calcutta, 1947.

Inscriptions of Kambuja, Asiatic Society (Calcutta), 1953; *Ancient Indian Colonisation in South-east Asia* (Maharaja Sayajirao Gaekward honorarium lectures, 1953-54), G. H. Bhatt, 1955; *The Sepoy Mutiny and the Revolt of 1857,* Mukhopadhyay, 1957, 2nd edition, Verry, 1963; *Glimpses of Bengal in the Nineteenth Century* (three lectures), Verry, 1960; *Three Phases of India's Struggle for Freedom* (revision of first Birla Endowment lectures), Bharatiya Vidya Bhavan, 1961, 2nd edition, 1967; *History of the Freedom Movement in India,* three volumes, Mukhopadhyay, 1962-63, 2nd edition, 1971; *Svami Vivekananda: A Historical Review,* General Printers & Publishers, 1965; (contributor) *India at the Cross Roads,* Contemporary Publishers, 1965; *Expansion of Aryan Culture in Eastern India* (Pandita-Raja Atombapu Sharma memorial lectures), Atombapu Research Centre, 1968; *Historiography in Modern India* (Heras memorial lectures), Asia Publishing House, 1970; *On Rammohan Roy,* Asiatic Society, 1972; *History of Mediaeval Bengal,* G. Bharadwaj, 1973; *The Arab Invasion of India,* Sheikh Mubarak Ali, 1974; *Renascent India: First Phase,* G. Bharadwaj, 1976.

Editor: *The History of Bengal,* Volume I: *Hindu Period,* University of Dacca, 1943, edition in Bengali, 1949; (with Anant Sadashiv Altekar) *A New History of the Indian People,* Volume VI: *The Vakataka—Gupta Age,* Motilal Banarsi Dass, 1946, Verry, 1967; (with Swami Madhavananda) *Great Women of India,* Advaita Ashrama, 1953; *The Clas-*

sical Accounts of India, Mukhopadhyay, 1960; *Ancient India as Described by Megasthenes and Arrian,* revised 2nd edition, Chuckervertty, Chatterjee, 1960; *Swami Vivekananda Centenary Memorial Volume,* Centenary Publication Committee (Calcutta), 1963; *Bosons, Presented to Satyendra Nath Bose on the Occasion of His Seventieth Birthday,* Hindustan Publishing, 1964.

General editor, assisted by A. D. Pulsaker and A. K. Majumdar: *The History and Culture of the Indian People,* eleven volumes, Bharatiya Vidya Bhavan, 1951-69.

WORK IN PROGRESS: A history of ancient Bengal, in English; a history of modern Bengal, in Bengali; a history of the penal settlement of the Andamans, for the Government of India.

SIDELIGHTS: R. C. Majumdar has made extensive tours in the United States and Europe. His independent liberalism prompted him to write a "number of articles criticising the policy and achievements of the Government of India after independence, specially pointing out its wrong foreign and domestic policies."

BIOGRAPHICAL/CRITICAL SOURCES: H. B. Sarkar, editor, *R. C. Majumdar Felicitation Volume,* Mukhopadhyay, 1970.†

* * *

MAJUMDER, Sanat K(umer) 1929-

PERSONAL: Born November 1, 1929, in Khulna, Bengal, India (now in Bangladesh); naturalized U.S. citizen, 1966; son of Kalidas and Ranibala (Ghosh) Majumder; married Flora E. Clifford (a music supervisor), June 23, 1957; children: Protik (son), Shagarika (daughter). *Education:* University of Calcutta, B.Sc. (honors), 1949, M.Sc., 1951; University of New Hampshire, Ph.D., 1958. *Politics:* Liberal Democrat. *Home:* 190 Crescent St., Northampton, Mass., 01060. *Office:* Biology Department, Westfield State College, Westfield, Mass. 01085.

CAREER: Jute Agricultural Research Institute, West Bengal, India, research assistant in jute physiology, 1952-54; Brookhaven National Laboratory, Upton, N.Y., research associate, 1957, 1958-59; Central Rice Research Institute, Cuttack, India, plant physiologist, 1960-62; University of Hawaii, Honolulu, fellow in horticulture, 1962-64; St. Louis University, St. Louis, Mo., assistant professor of biology, 1964-67; Smith College, Northampton, Mass., associate professor of biological sciences, 1967-71; Westfield State College, Westfield, Mass., associate professor of biology, 1972—. Visiting summer professor, University of Massachusetts, 1968, 1970. *Member:* American Institute of Biological Sciences, American Society of Plant Physiologists, American Association of University Professors, Institute of Society, Ethics and the Life Sciences, Sigma Xi. *Awards, honors:* Indian Council for Agricultural Research grant, 1961-62.

WRITINGS: The Drama of Man and Nature, C. E. Merrill, 1971. Contributor of more than twenty articles to scientific journals in India, Canada, United States, and Germany.

WORK IN PROGRESS: Writing on the identity of man—both from biological and philosophical points of view; research on environmental and chemical control of plant growth, including effects of alternating electric fields.

* * *

MALERICH, Edward P. 1940-
(Edward Easton)

PERSONAL: Born October 21, 1940, in Moline, Ill.; son of

Edward Marion (in politics) and Virginia (House) Malerich; married Courtney Sherman (an actress), December 20, 1968 (divorced); children: Brooke. *Education:* Attended University of Illinois, 1958; Lincoln College, Lincoln, Ill., A.A., 1960; Pasadena Playhouse College of Theatre Art, student, 1960-62. *Home and office:* 400 West 43rd St., Apt. 38-P, New York, N.Y. 10036. *Agent:* Susan Ann Protter, 156 East 52nd St., New York, N.Y. 10022.

CAREER: Actor under name Edward Easton, appearing Off-Broadway in ''Party on Greenwich Ave.'' and ''The Caucasian Chalk Circle,'' in stock in ''The Lion in Winter,'' ''Cactus Flower,'' ''The Impossible Years,'' ''Barefoot in the Park,'' and other plays; television appearances include ''The Mike Douglas Show,'' ''Hallmark Hall of Fame,'' and ''Captain America.'' *Military service:* U.S. Army, 1963-66. *Member:* Screen Actors Guild, Actors' Equity Association, American Federation of Radio and Television Artists.

WRITINGS: The Wooden Sword (novel), Macfadden, 1970; *The Compleate Gentleman,* Manor, 1978.

WORK IN PROGRESS: Three books.

SIDELIGHTS: Edward Malerich told *CA:* ''This writer views a typewriter with a blank sheet of paper inserted with horror. He loathes writing. Why do it? Compulsion only. He considers himself an addict to his work. In some ways, it is worse than drugs. But a best seller *would* be nice.'' *Avocational interests:* Fencing, karate (holder of first degree black belt), horseback riding, swimming, scuba diving, playing flamenco and rock and roll guitar.

* * *

MALLY, E(mma) Louise 1908-

PERSONAL: Born January 18, 1908, in Dallas, Tex.; daughter of Maurice Henry (a merchant) and Fannie (Hernstadt) Mally. *Education:* Barnard College, B.A., 1930; Columbia University, graduate study, four years. *Politics:* ''Unaffiliated socialist.'' *Religion:* Atheist. *Home:* 54 West 16th St., New York, N.Y. 10011.

CAREER: Writer. *Member:* League of American Writers (finance secretary, 1939-41). *Awards, honors:* Breadloaf Writers Conference fellowship, 1945.

WRITINGS: The Mockingbird Is Singing, Holt, 1944; (editor) *A Treasury of Animal Stories,* Citadel, 1948; *The Tides of Dawn,* Sloane, 1949; *Abigail,* Appleton, 1956; (translator) Guenther Deicke, editor, *Immortal Lieder: 800 Years of German Poetry,* Seven-Seas Press, 1962; (contributing translator) Alan Bold, editor, *The Penguin Book of Socialist Verse,* Penguin, 1970.

WORK IN PROGRESS: Tall Boy Walking; a picaresque novel taking place in the 1830's; poetry.

SIDELIGHTS: E. Louise Mally told *CA:* ''For the last several years, I have been very active in my community . . . in anti-war activities. . . . Vital, in this country, is peace—specifically, total withdrawal from the Vietnam invasion, the rights of Blacks . . . and for the world, the protection of the environment. Eventually, we are going to have to learn, if we survive, to control man's desire for power over man . . . the answer may lie in psychology as well as [in] legal restraints.''

* * *

MALMBERG, Carl 1904-
(Timothy Trent)

PERSONAL: First syllable of surname rhymes with ''calm''; born June 26, 1904, in Oshkosh, Wis.; son of Anton Martin (superintendent of a mining plant) and Kirsten Marie (Jensen) Malmberg; married Elizabeth Newhall, January 10, 1940. *Education.* Studied at Lawrence College (now University), Appleton, Wis., 1921-23, and Columbia University, 1924-27. *Address:* Route 1, Warner, N.H. 03278. *Agent:* Barthold Fles Literary Agency, 507 Fifth Ave., New York, N.Y. 10017.

CAREER: American Telephone & Telegraph Co., New York City, writer, 1928-29; New York Telephone Co., New York City, clerk in accounting department, 1930-32; free-lance work, 1933-36; H. & H. Publishing Co., New York City, editor of *Health & Hygiene* (monthly magazine), 1936-38; Works Progress Administration Writers' Project, New York City, supervisor, later managing supervisor, 1938-39; American Optometric Association, New York City, writer in public health bureau, 1940-41; U.S. Public Health Service, Washington, D.C., writer, 1941-45, assigned as chief investigator to Subcommittee on Wartime Health and Education of U.S. Senate Committee on Education and Labor, 1944-45; Democratic National Committee, Washington, D.C., writer (of speeches and other campaign materials), 1945-46; free-lance writer, 1947-48; Will, Folsom & Smith, Inc. (public relations and fund-raising firm serving nonprofit hospitals), New York City, writer, 1948-69. Free-lance writer, translator from the Danish, Norwegian, and Swedish, and reader for publishers. *Member:* New Hampshire Historical Society, Warner (N.H.) Historical Society.

WRITINGS—Nonfiction: *Diet and Die,* Hillman-Curl, 1935; *140 Million Patients,* Reynal & Hitchcock, 1947; *America Is Also Scandinavian* (juvenile), Putnam, 1970; (editor) *Warner, New Hampshire, 1880-1974,* Warner Historical Society, 1974.

Fiction under pseudonym Timothy Trent: *Night Boat,* Godwin, 1934; *All Dames Are Dynamite,* Godwin, 1935; *Fall Guy,* Godwin, 1936.

Translations from the Danish: Leif Panduro, *Kick Me in the Traditions (Rend mig i tradtionerne),* Eriksson, 1961; Carl Erik Soya, *Seventeen (Sytten),* Eriksson, 1961, reprinted as *The Rites of Spring,* Pyramid Publications, 1962, and as *17,* Pyramid Publications, 1967; Jacob Paludan, *Joergen Stein,* University of Wisconsin Press, 1966; Leif Panduro, *One of Our Millionaires Is Missing (Vejen til Jylland),* Grove, 1967; Tom Kristensen, *Havoc (Haervaerk),* University of Wisconsin Press, 1968; Jens Kruuse, *War for an Afternoon (Som vanvid),* Pantheon, 1968; Jens August Schade, *People Meet (Mennesker moedes),* Dell, 1967. Also translator of short story for *View from Another Shore,* edited by Franz Rottensteiner, Seabury, 1973. Translator of many short stories and articles for *American-Scandinavian Review.*

Writer of radio scripts. Contributor of more than one hundred articles to magazines, including *Woman, New Republic, Reader's Digest, Cunarder, Parents' Magazine, Equality, Health and Hygiene, Consumer Union Reports,* and *Popular Psychology Guide.*

WORK IN PROGRESS: Research in American and Scandinavian history and in Scandinavian literature.

AVOCATIONAL INTERESTS: Maintaining and improving about sixty acres of woodland and field that once were a New Hampshire farm.

* * *

MALO, John W. 1911-

PERSONAL: Born April 11, 1911, in Ringo, Kan.; son of

John (a farmer) and Helen (Kocol) Malo; married Renee B. Mier (a free-lance artist), November 24, 1935; children: Kenneth, Marcia. *Education:* Northwestern University, B.S. in Ed., 1934; DePaul University, M.A. in Ed., 1947; also studied at University of Warsaw, 1935, and University of Chicago. *Home:* 9633 Surrey Rd., Castle Rock, Colo. 80104.

CAREER: Foreman High School, Chicago, Ill., teacher and coach, 1941-56, counsellor, 1956-60, assistant principal, 1960-71. Canoeing guide in hinterland of Canada. *Member:* Outdoor Writers Association of America, American Snowmobile Association, Association of Great Lakes Outdoor Writers, Rocky Mountain Outdoor Writers (member of board). *Awards, honors:* Coach of the Year Award of Chicagoland Prep Writers, 1953; Ford Foundation fellowship for study and travel, 1953-54; citation in annual competition sponsored by Evinrude Motors and Outdoor Writers Association of America, 1970, for *Canoeing;* Thermos Award, 1972, for "excellence in writing and personal endeavor on outdoor recreation."

WRITINGS: Canoeing (youth book), Follett, 1969; *Malo's Complete Guide to Canoeing and Canoe-Camping,* Quadrangle, 1969; *Wilderness Canoeing,* Macmillan, 1971; *Snowmobiling: The Guide,* Macmillan, 1971; *All-Terrain Adventure Vehicles,* Macmillan, 1972; *Complete Guide to Housebeating,* Macmillan, 1974; *Motor-Camping around Europe,* Stackpole, 1974; *Tranquil Trails,* Greatlakes Living Press, 1977. Writer of magazine and newspaper articles on canoeing and snowmobiling.

WORK IN PROGRESS: A book on the canoe trails of the Midwest.

SIDELIGHTS: John Malo first became interested in canoeing as a teen-ager and has been exploring stateside and Canadian wilderness streams and introducing young people to outdoor life ever since. Praising Malo's work in this field, the Outdoor Writers Association of America, cited Malo for " . . . creating an awareness of the recreational potential of the nation's waterways, and the need for preservation of the natural beauty of these waters." He has traveled by canoe in unmapped areas of Canada, kayaked in the Dnieper River in the Carpathians, and paddled a dugout canoe in British Honduras and Guatemala. He also has tried gold panning and uranium prospecting in the American West and fished in both fresh and salt water.

*   *   *

MALOFF, Saul 1922-

PERSONAL: Born September 6, 1922, in New York, N.Y.; son of David and Yetta (Friedman) Maloff; children: Jadis Karla Lorca (Mrs. Michael Norman). *Education:* City College (now City College of the City University of New York), B.A., 1943; University of Iowa, M.A., 1947, Ph.D., 1952. *Politics:* Independent. *Home:* Painter Hill, Roxbury, Conn. 06783. *Agent:* Helen Brann Agency, 14 Sutton Pl. S., New York, N.Y. 10022.

CAREER: Writer; former books editor of *Newsweek.* Member of faculties of literature, University of Iowa, 1946-49, University of Michigan, 1949-51, Indiana University, 1951-55, College of the City of New York (now City College of the City University of New York), 1955-56, Pratt Institute, 1956-59, University of Puerto Rico, 1959-60, New York University and New School for Social Research, 1960-62, Bennington College, 1962-64, and Hunter College of the City University of New York, 1968-71. Member of faculty, Suffield Writers Conference. Editor-in-chief, Ken Pub-

lishing Co., 1957-59. Consultant, Guggenheim Foundation, National Humanities Faculty, and George Polk Memorial Awards. *Military service:* U.S. Army, 1943-46. *Member:* P.E.N. (member of executive board), American Association of University Professors. *Awards, honors:* George Polk Memorial Award for literary criticism, Long Island University, 1967; Guggenheim fellowship, 1968-69.

WRITINGS: (Editor with the editors of *Esquire*) *All about Women,* Harper, 1963; (editor) *The Young Readers' Treasury of British and American Verse,* Avon, 1963; (with others) *The Modern British Novel,* Southern Illinois University Press, 1965; (editor and author of introduction) *The Avon Treasury of Poetry,* Avon, 1965; *Happy Families* (novel), Scribner, 1968; *Heartland* (novel), Scribner, 1974. Contributor to *Commonweal, New Republic, New York Times Book Review, Nation, Saturday Review, Texas Quarterly, Critique,* and other publications. Literary editor, *Newsweek,* 1964-69.

WORK IN PROGRESS—All novels: *Shickses; The Price of a Carabao; Generations; For Such a Time as This.*

SIDELIGHTS: Reviewing *Happy Families,* Clara Siggins writes: "With the closest possible eye for detail and with perceptions that are sharpened to razor-edge, we are introduced to the American Family as a moribund institution. . . . There is superb craftsmanship here as ideas come and go, that are fragmentary and elusive. Mr. Maloff has the ability to bring us into direct contact with the minutiae of life, its feel, and color, and smell, its nuance and humor." Frederic Raphael feels that "where the old-fashioned [family] novelist used to delight in pursuing his characters down the byways of plot, Mr. Maloff, like his distinguished peers, tracks every inner twinge and rhapsodizes on every metaphysical analogy. Any one page of *Happy Families* is likely to contain enough verbal acrobatics to astonish the mind and challenge the wit, but I am bound to say that Maloff has written what I think is at times a dirty and rather twisted book." Lucy Rosenthal believes that the novel's serious flaw, if it has one, "is the frantic overwriting, the flip side of Maloff's love of language. And the ending, a daydream, is unworthy of this swinging and energetic book."

J. R. Frakes calls *Heartland* "a richly satisfying, rip-roaring, wheel-spinning phenomenon of a book which recklessly mixes one-dimensional figures with four-dimensional pain, heartburn with fear-and-trembling, Rabelaisian catalogues with Levi-Straussian structures, Winnie-the-Pooh with the Talmud." Jonathan Yardley writes: "The principal difficulty with Saul Maloff's intelligent and entertaining new novel is that the ground it explores has already been rather thoroughly plowed. Its central theme—that of the vaguely intellectual New York Jew set uncomfortably down on a corn-fed provincial campus—has been examined by, among others, Bernard Malamud in *A New Life* and John Updike in *Bech.* . . . Still Maloff is a novelist of skill and wit, and there is much to recommend in *Heartland.*"

Maloff told *CA:* "Aside from a stint in publishing and a longer one as books editor of *Newsweek* magazine, I've spent the larger part of my professional life teaching in universities; and now—prompted both by a weariness of the academic life and a wish to write without interruption—I've left that life to devote all my time to writing: novels principally and (as often as I must for immediate income) literary criticism for various periodicals."

BIOGRAPHICAL/CRITICAL SOURCES: New York Times, July 15, 1968, September 20, 1973; *Newsweek,* July 22, 1968; *New York Times Book Review,* July 28, 1968, September 16, 1973; *National Observer,* August 5, 1968; *Commonweal,* August 9, 1968, October 26, 1973; *Book World,* August 11, 1968; *Best Sellers,* August 15, 1968, October 15, 1973; *Washington Post,* August 17, 1968; *Publishers Weekly,* August 6, 1973; *National Review,* September 29, 1973; *Booklist,* November 1, 1973; *New York,* November 5, 1973; *Time,* November 19, 1973; *Contemporary Literary Criticism,* Volume V, Gale, 1976.

* * *

MANNE, Henry G. 1928-

PERSONAL: Surname rhymes with "uncanny"; born May 10, 1928, in New Orleans, La.; son of Geoffrey and Eva (Shainberg) Manne; married Bobbette Lee Taxer, August 19, 1968; children: Emily Kay, Geoffrey Adam. *Education:* Vanderbilt University, B.A. (cum laude), 1950; University of Chicago, J.D., 1952; Yale University, LL.M., 1953, J.S.D., 1966. *Office:* Law and Economics Center, University of Miami, 1541 Brescia, Coral Gables, Fla. 33124.

CAREER: Admitted to the Bar of the State of Illinois, and the Bar of the State of New York. In corporate law practice in Chicago, Ill., 1953-54; St. Louis University, St. Louis, Mo., assistant professor of law, 1956-57; University of Wisconsin—Madison, visiting assistant professor of law, 1957-59; St. Louis University, associate professor of law, 1959-62; George Washington University, Washington, D.C., associate professor, 1962-64, professor of law, 1964-68; University of Rochester, Rochester, N.Y., Kenan Professor of Law, 1968-74; University of Miami, Law and Economics Center, Coral Gables, Fla., director, 1974—. Visiting professor, Stanford University, 1971-72; visiting summer professor at University of California, Los Angeles, 1960, Hudson Institute, 1962, and University of Michigan, 1964; lecturer at University of Rome, University of Pisa, University of Strasbourg, and other universities, and for public and private associations. *Military service:* U.S. Air Force, 1954-56; became captain.

MEMBER: American Bar Association, American Economic Association, Association of American Law Schools (chairman of special committee on Supreme Court decisions, 1964-65), Phi Beta Kappa, Order of the Coif, Mont Pelerin Society (director).

WRITINGS: (Contributor) Grey Dorsey and John Dunsford, editors, *Constitutional Freedom and the Law,* McGraw, 1965; *Insider Trading and the Stock Market,* Free Press, 1966; *Supplementary Cases and Material for Business Association II,* Lerner Law Book Co., 1967; (editor) *Economic Policy and the Regulation of Corporate Securities,* American Enterprise Institute for Public Policy Research, 1969; (with Henry C. Wallich) *The Modern Corporation and Social Responsibility,* American Enterprise Institute for Public Policy Research, 1972; (with E. Solomon) *Wall Street in Transition: The Emerging System and Its Impact on the Economy,* New York University Press, 1974; *The Economics of Legal Relationships,* West Publishing, 1975; (with Roger L. Miller) *Gold, Money and the Law,* Aldine, 1975; (with Miller) *Auto Safety Regulation: The Cure or the Problem,* Thomas Horton, 1976; (editor with Miller) *Administrative Power and Economic Costs: The Auto Safety Illustration,* Aldine, 1976. Also contributor to *Conference on Comparative Law,* edited by Verrucoli, 1967. Contributor of more than one hundred articles and reviews to professional and scholarly journals. Associate editor, *University of Chicago Law Review.*

AVOCATIONAL INTERESTS: Collecting antique patent-medicine bottles.

BIOGRAPHICAL/CRITICAL SOURCES: New York Times, July 11, 1971; *Business Week,* July 24, 1971.

* * *

MANNELLO, George Jr. 1913-

PERSONAL: Born July 9, 1913, in New York, N.Y.; son of George Sr. and Jeanette (Stern) Mannello; married Jeannette Domres (a teacher), June 30, 1940; children: David, Donna, Peter, Donald. *Education:* City College of New York (now City College of the City University of New York), B.S., 1936; attended Columbia University, 1938; Duke University, M.S., 1942; New York University, Ph.D., 1952; attended Foreign Service Institute of U.S. State Department, 1952. *Home:* 908 Stanton Ave., Baldwin, N.Y. 11570. *Office:* Department of Elementary Education, Hofstra University, Hempstead, N.Y. 11550.

CAREER: Grade school teacher in public schools in Buffalo, N.Y., 1936-38, and Woodmere, N.Y., 1938-43; U.S. Army classification specialist at Georgetown University, Washington, D.C., and University of Maryland, College Park, 1943-45; Woodmere Junior High, Woodmere, social studies teacher, 1945-52; University of Rangoon, Rangoon, Burma, professor of educational psychology, 1953-54; Hofstra University, Hempstead, N.Y., assistant professor of secondary education, 1955-59, associate professor of elementary education, 1959-73, professor of elementary education, 1973-76, professor emeritus, 1976—, chairman of department, 1959-61. Adviser on teacher training, Point IV, Ministry of Education, Baghdad, Iraq, 1952; research consultant in education for U.S. Navy, Driver's Safety Service, New York, N.Y., 1959; adviser on teacher education, Ministry of Education, Ibadan, Nigeria, 1963-65.

MEMBER: United Nations Association, World Future Society, World Federalist Society, American Association of University Professors, National Society for the Study of Education, American Psychological Association, National Council for the Social Studies, National Geographic Society, Association for Higher Education, New Education Fellowship, New York State Teachers' Association, Phi Delta Kappa.

WRITINGS: Our Long Island, Noble, 1951, 3rd edition, 1964; *Educational Tests and Measurements,* University of Rangoon Press, 1954; (with Robert A. Davison) *Life in New York,* Holt, 1962; *Self Study Book: Life in New York,* Holt, 1963; *Americans All* (eleventh grade social studies text for slow learners), AMSCO School Publications, 1972; *Teaching Is Not for the Timid,* Vantage, 1975. Contributor of articles to *Instructor, Grade Teacher, School Executive, Exchange, New York State Education, Journal of Genetic Psychology, Phi Delta Kappan, Teachers' Monthly* (Nigeria), *Improving College and University Teaching, Educational Forum,* other educational journals, and periodicals on world government.

* * *

MANNERS, Robert A(lan) 1913-

PERSONAL: Born August 21, 1913, in New York, N.Y.; son of Abraham Rosen and Dora (Kniaz) Manners; married Margaret Hall, July 6, 1943 (divorced, July, 1955); married Jean Hall, September 12, 1955; children: (first marriage) Karen, John; (second marriage) Stephen, Katherine. *Education:* Columbia University, B.S., 1935, M.A., 1939, Ph.D., 1950. *Home:* 134 Sumner St., Newton, Mass. 02159. *Office:* Department of Anthropology, Brandeis University, Waltham, Mass. 02154.

CAREER: University of Rochester, Rochester, N.Y., instructor in anthropology, 1950-52; Brandeis University, Waltham, Mass., lecturer, 1952, assistant professor, 1952-56, associate professor, 1956-61, professor of anthropology, 1961—, chairman of department, 1963-68. Member of board of trustees, Research Institute for the Study of Man, 1966—. *Military service:* U.S. Army, 1942-46; became captain. *Member:* American Anthropological Association, African Studies Association, American Ethnological Society, Northeastern Anthropological Association (president, 1978—). *Awards, honors:* University of Illinois and Ford Foundation fellowship for research in Africa, 1957-58; National Science Foundation fellowship for research in Africa, 1961-62.

WRITINGS: (With others) *People of Puerto Rico,* University of Illinois Press, 1956; (editor with James Duffy) *Africa Speaks,* Van Nostrand, 1961; (editor) *Process and Pattern in Culture,* Aldine, 1964; (with others) *Contemporary Change in Traditional Societies,* University of Illinois Press, 1967; (editor with David Kaplan) *Theory in Anthropology: A Sourcebook,* Aldine, 1968; (with Kaplan) *Culture Theory,* Prentice-Hall, 1972; *Havasupai Indians: An Ethnohistorical Report,* Garland Publishing, 1974; *An Ethnological Report on the Hualapai Indians of Arizona,* Garland Publishing, 1974; *Southern Paiute and Chemehuevi: An Ethnohistorical Report,* Garland Publishing, 1974. Contributor of articles and reviews to professional and opinion journals. Editor-in-chief, *American Anthropologist,* 1973-75.

*   *   *

MAPP, Edward C(harles)

PERSONAL: Born in New York, N.Y.; son of Edward Cameron (a composer) and Estelle (Sampson) Mapp; children: Andrew. *Education:* City College (now City College of the City University of New York), B.A., 1953; Columbia University, M.S., 1956; New York University, Ph.D., 1970. *Politics:* Democrat. *Home:* 950 East 14th St., Brooklyn, N.Y. 11230. *Office:* New York City Community College of Applied Arts and Sciences of the City University of New York, 300 Jay St., Brooklyn, N.Y. 11201.

CAREER: New York Public Library, Research Libraries Information Division, New York, N.Y., library assistant, 1948-55; teacher of library and English in public schools in Brooklyn, N.Y., 1957-64; New York City Community College of Applied Arts and Sciences of the City University of New York, Brooklyn, professor of library and learning resources and chairman of department, 1964—. *Member:* American Association for Higher Education, American Association of University Professors, Committee for Public Higher Education, Volunteers of the Shelters, National Project Center for Film and the Humanities (member of advisory committee), One Hundred Black Men, National Conference of Christians and Jews (member of board of directors, Brooklyn region), New York Association of Junior Colleges, New York Library Club, United Nations Association of New York (member of board of directors), Education Alumni Association of New York University (member of board of directors), New York Interracial Colloquy.

WRITINGS: (Contributor) E. J. Josey, editor, *The Black Librarian in America,* Scarecrow, 1970; *Books for Occupational Education Programs: A List for Community Colleges, Technical Institutes and Vocational Schools,* Bowker, 1971; *Blacks in American Films: Today and Yesterday,* Scarecrow, 1972; (contributor) Josey, editor, *What Black Librarians Are Saying,* Scarecrow, 1972; *Puerto Rican Perspec-*

tives, Scarecrow, 1974; (contributor) Lindsay Patterson, editor, *Black Films and Film-Makers: A Comprehensive Anthology from Stereotype to Superhero,* Dodd, 1975; (contributor) Patricia Schuman, editor, *Social Responsibilities and Libraries,* Bowker, 1976; *Directory of Blacks in the Performing Arts,* Scarecrow, 1977. Author of column, "Mapp's Rap," for *New York Amsterdam News,* 1977. Contributor to education, library, Negro history, marketing, and film journals.

AVOCATIONAL INTERESTS: Travel, films, theatre, photography.

BIOGRAPHICAL/CRITICAL SOURCES: Film Library Quarterly, winter, 1972.

*   *   *

MARBUT, F(rederick) B(rowning)   1905-

PERSONAL: Born August 8, 1905, in Columbia, Mo.; son of Curtis Fletcher (a soil scientist) and Florence (Martin) Marbut; married Veronica Ann Dodd, August 18, 1934; children: Curtis Fletcher, Ann Bannon (Mrs. Alan J. Baker). *Education:* Attended University of Missouri, 1923-26; George Washington University, A.B., 1938; Harvard University, M.A., 1939; Ph.D., 1950. *Politics:* Democrat. *Home:* 1257 South Portofino Dr., Sarasota Fla. 33581.

CAREER: Started as reporter for *St. Louis Globe-Democrat,* St. Louis Mo., 1926-27, and then was reporter, sports editor, or copy reader for daily newspapers in Iowa, Montana, Canal Zone, and Washington, D.C., 1927-30; Associated Press, wire editor in New Haven, Conn., 1930-33, reporter in Washington (D.C.) Bureau, 1933-37; *Washington Times,* Washington, D.C., rewrite man, 1938; Kent State University, Kent, Ohio, 1941-44, began as instructor, became associate professor of journalism; Pennsylvania State University, University Park, associate professor, 1944-50, professor of journalism, 1950-66. Lecturer under auspices of U.S. Department of State in five South American countries, 1958; leader of special seminar at University College of the West Indies, 1960; visiting professor of journalism at National University of Nicaragua, 1962-63; lecturer in Quito, Ecuador, 1963. *Member:* Phi Kappa Psi. *Awards, honors:* Smith-Mundt scholar in Bolivia, 1957.

WRITINGS: News from the Capital: The Story of Washington Reporting, Southern Illinois University Press, 1971. Contributor of articles to *Dickinson Law Review* and journalism journals; has done book reviewing for a number of periodicals.

WORK IN PROGRESS: A history of the twentieth century stressing economics, science, and thought, tentatively entitled *The Twentieth Century: An Analytical History.*

*   *   *

MARCUSE, Ludwig   1894-1971

February 8, 1894—August 2, 1971; German biographer, philosopher, and educator. Obituaries: *Washington Post,* August 11, 1971.

*   *   *

MAREK, Kurt W(illi)   1915-1972
(C. W. Ceram)

January 20, 1915—April 12, 1972; German-born journalist and author of books on archaeology. Obituaries: *New York Times,* April 13, 1972; *Washington Post,* April 13, 1972; *L'Express,* April 17-23, 1972; *Newsweek,* April 24, 1972; *Time,* April 24, 1972. (See index for *CA* sketch)

MARGETSON, Stella   1912-

PERSONAL: Born March 6, 1912, in London, England; daughter of Laurence (a business executive) and Florence (an actress; stage name, Collingbourne) Margetson. *Education:* Educated privately. *Home:* 15 Hamilton Ter., London, England. *Agent:* A. P. Watt, 26/28 Bedford Row, London WC1R 4HL, England; and Collins-Knowlton-Wing, 575 Madison Ave., New York, N.Y. 10022.

CAREER: Writer.

WRITINGS: Flood Tide, and Other Stories, J. Crowther, 1943; *Peter's Wife* (fiction), Heinemann, 1948; *The Prisoners* (novel), Heinemann, 1949; *Journey by Stages: An Account of Travelling by Stage Coach and Mail between 1660 and 1840,* Cassell, 1967; *Leisure and Pleasure in the Nineteenth Century,* Coward, 1969; *Victorian London: An Illustrated Survey,* Hastings House, 1969 (published in England as *Fifty Years of Victorian London,* Macdonald & Co., 1969); *Leisure and Pleasure in the Eighteenth Century,* Cassell, 1970; *Regency London,* Praeger, 1971; *The Long Party: High Society in the Twenties and Thirties,* Saxon House, 1974.

Radio plays, all broadcast by British Broadcasting Corp.: "The Prisoners" (adapted from her novel), 1952; "Lucertola," 1953; "Leading Lady," 1954; "These Quickening Years," 1954; "Village in the Stars," 1955; "Seven Stages," 1955. Contributor of fiction and historical features to *Homes and Gardens, Country Life,* and other publications.

WORK IN PROGRESS: Research into nineteenth-century social history.

AVOCATIONAL INTERESTS: Conservation of the environment.

BIOGRAPHICAL/CRITICAL SOURCES: Books and Bookmen, July, 1967; *Punch,* April 16, 1969; *Canadian Forum,* August, 1969.

*   *   *

MARIQUE, Joseph M(arie-) F(elix)   1899-

PERSONAL: Born June 3, 1899, in Brussels, Belgium; son of Pierre J. and Miriam (Jalhay) Marique. *Education:* Fordham University, A.B., 1918; Woodstock College, M.A., 1924; Ignatiuskolleg, Valkenburg, Netherlands, S.T.D., 1931; Johns Hopkins University, Ph.D., 1941. *Politics:* "Not registered." *Home and office:* College of the Holy Cross, Worcester, Mass. 01610.

CAREER: Priest of Society of Jesus (Jesuits); Fordham University, Bronx, N.Y., associate professor of classics, 1939-51; College of the Holy Cross, Worcester, Mass., director of Institute for Early Christian Iberian Studies and of Hellenic Tradition Seminar, 1954—. Has done field work in archaeology on Mallorca and in Cadiz Province. *Member:* American Philological Association, American Catholic Historical Association, American Society of Church History, Classical Association of New England.

WRITINGS: (With others) *Fathers of the Church,* Volume I, Cima Publishing, 1947; (editor) *Leaders of Iberian Christianity (50-750),* Daughters of St. Paul, 1962; (editor of English edition) *Inscriptions of Balearic Islands Up to Arab Conquest,* translation by Louis Cavell, Institute for Early Christian Iberian Studies, College of the Holy Cross, 1972. Editor, *Classical Folia,* 1945—.

WORK IN PROGRESS: Research concerned with Roman and Visigothic Hispania.

MARKOVIC, Vida E.   1916-

PERSONAL: Born December 16, 1916, in Zagreb, Yugoslavia; daughter of Edward M. (an economist; killed by the Gestapo, 1939) and Marija (Vall) Markovic; married Dusan J. Milankovic (an international lawyer), October 14, 1946; children: Marija, Vera. *Education:* Attended University of Belgrade, 1935-39; University of Leeds, Ph.D., 1954. *Politics:* Socialist. *Home:* 29 Laze Simica, Belgrade, Yugoslavia. *Office:* English Seminar, University of Belgrade, 34 Takovska, Belgrade, Yugoslavia.

CAREER: School teacher in Belgrade, Yugoslavia, 1940; spent several periods in prison during the German occupation, 1941-44; took up journalistm, 1944-47, then changed over to university work; lived and studied in England, 1951-54; University of Belgrade, Faculty of Philology, Belgrade, associate professor of English and head of department, 1960-70, professor of modern literature, 1971—; University of Nis, Philosophical Faculty, Nis, Yugoslavia, founder and first chairman of English department, 1971—. Visiting professor in department of English at various universities in Yugoslavia for short periods, 1961-71, and at University of Novi Sad, 1963-65; visiting fellow at Princeton University, 1965-66; lecturer at Bryn Mawr College and Simon Frazer University, 1966; visiting professor at University of Oregon, summers, 1967-69; research fellow, Folger Shakespeare Library, 1973. Visited seventeen American universities as guest of U.S. Department of State, 1962. *Member:* International Association of University Professors of English (member of consultative committee, 1974—), International Federation of Modern Languages and Literatures.

WRITINGS: Engleski roman XX veka, Naucna Knjiga, Volume I, 1963, revised edition, 1968, Volume II, 1965, revised edition, 1977; *The Changing Face: Disintegration of Personality in the Twentieth-Century British Novel, 1900-1950,* Southern Illinois University Press, 1970; *Prilog epistemologiji knjizevnosti* (title means "Towards an Epistemology of Literature"), [Yugoslavia], 1978. Contributor to *Texas Studies in Literature and Language* and of more than ninety essays and studies to other periodicals, mainly in Yugoslavia. Advisory editor, *New Literary History.*

WORK IN PROGRESS: Volume III of *Engleski roman XX veka,* covering postwar British and American fiction; *Raskol izmedju reci i igre: Sukob dve estetike* (title means "Rift between the Word and the Play: Two Aesthetics at War"); literary portraits of leading writers and outstanding humanists; notes on her life and experience for memoirs.

SIDELIGHTS: As a journalist, Vida Markovic attended the Paris Peace Conference in the summer of 1946 and the first session of the United Nations in New York later that same year. During her years as head of the English department at the University of Belgrade she initiated and carried out modernization and reforms in English studies. Since 1971 she has been experimenting with new teaching methods at the University of Nis, where she has a young staff numbering about twenty. Markovic intends her memoirs to "serve as a bridge between my prewar and the present postwar generation, to contribute to cultural and actual continuity in Yugoslavia, a country that has gone through a revolution and continues building its future through revolutionary changes."

*   *   *

MARKOVITZ, Irving Leonard   1934-

PERSONAL: Born August 9, 1934, in Mckeesport, Pa.; son of Adolf and Kate Markovitz; married Ruth Helen Feinberg (a sociologist), June 29, 1958; children: Amy Miriam, Jonathan Paul. *Education:* Brandeis University, B.A., 1956; Boston University, M.A., 1958; University of California, Berkeley, Ph.D., 1967. *Office:* Department of Political Science, Queens College of the City University of New York, Flushing, N.Y. 11367.

CAREER: New York University, New York, N.Y., visiting assistant professor of political science, 1962-63; Social Science Research Council-American Council of Learned Societies Foreign Area Program fellow, doing research in Paris, France, Senegal, West Africa, and the United States, 1964-66; Queens College of the City University of New York, Flushing, N.Y., lecturer, 1966-67, assistant professor, 1967-70, associate professor, 1970-71, professor of political science, 1972—. Research scholar, University of Ghana, 1968, 1973. *Member:* African Studies Association (fellow), American Political Science Association. *Awards, honors:* Ford Foundation grant, 1964-66; National Endowment for the Humanities grant, 1969; City University of New York faculty research award, 1973.

WRITINGS: Leopold Sedar Senghor and the Politics of Negritude, Atheneum, 1969; (editor) *African Politics and Society: Basic Issues and Problems of Government and Development,* Free Press, 1970; *Power and Class in Africa,* Prentice-Hall, 1977. Contributor to *Jefferson Encyclopedia, McGraw-Hill Encyclopedia of World Biography,* and *Americana Annual;* contributor of about sixty articles and translations to journals of politics and African studies.

WORK IN PROGRESS: Kwame Nkrumah and the Modernization of Ghana: A Political History; a comparative study of the ideology and political role of middle-level civil servants in selected cities in Senegal and Ghana.

*   *   *

MARKS, Geoffrey 1906-

PERSONAL: Born May 20, 1906, in Melbourne, Australia; son of Sir Henry and Lady Marks of Suva, Fiji Islands; married Beatrice Terry (an actress), 1932 (died, 1970). *Education:* Trinity College, Oxford, B.A., 1928, M.A., 1940. *Home:* Apt. J-1, 1765 East 55th St., Chicago, Ill. 60615. *Agent:* Barthold Fles Literary Agency, 507 Fifth Ave., New York, N.Y. 10017.

CAREER: Admitted to the Bar, Honorable Society of the Inner Temple, 1929; writer in Chicago, Ill. and New York City, 1930-32; in practice of law in London, England and the Fiji Islands, 1933-35; Grace Morse (literary agent), New York City, associate, 1935-36; Farkasch Organization, New York City, teacher of dental practice administration, 1936-39; American Humidaire Corp., Grand Rapids, Mich., executive vice-president, 1940-41; New Organization School, New York City, dean, 1947-49; headed own firm of professional management consultants, Seattle, Wash., 1950-61; American Society of Reconstructive Surgeons, Chicago, executive secretary, 1962; professional management consultant in Chicago, 1963-65; *Physician's Management,* Chicago, associate editor, 1965-72. *Military service:* U.S. Army, 1942-46; became captain.

WRITINGS: (With Harold Donaldson Eberlin and Frank A. Wallis) *Down the Tiber and Up to Rome,* Lippincott, 1930; (with Alan E. Nourse) *The Management of a Medical Practice,* Lippincott, 1963; *How to Practice Successful Dentistry,* Lippincott, 1963; *The Medieval Plague,* Doubleday, 1971; *The Amazing Stethoscope,* Messner, 1971.

With William K. Beatty; all published by Scribner's: *The*

Medical Garden, 1971; *Women in White,* 1972; *The Story of Medicine in America,* 1973; *The Precious Metals of Medicine,* 1975; *Epidemics,* 1976. Contributor to medical and management journals.

*   *   *

MARR, David G. 1937-

PERSONAL: Born September 22, 1937, in Macon, Ga.; son of Henry George (an auditor) and Louise M. (a teacher; maiden name, Brown) Marr; married Phan Thi Ai, April 15, 1963; children: Daniel G., Aileen T. *Education:* Dartmouth College, B.A. (magna cum laude), 1959; University of California, Berkeley, M.A., 1966, Ph.D., 1968.

CAREER: University of California, Berkeley, lecturer in history, 1968-69, assistant professor of Vietnamese studies, 1969-72; Cornell University, Ithaca, N.Y., co-director of Indochina Resource Center, 1971-72. *Military service:* U.S. Marine Corps, 1959-64; became captain. *Member:* Committee of Concerned Asian Scholars, Vietnam Studies Coordinating Group, Phi Beta Kappa. *Awards, honors:* Woodrow Wilson fellowship, 1964; Fulbright-Hays grant, 1968; National Endowment for the Humanities grant, 1971-72.

WRITINGS: (Contributor) Donald Emmerson, editor, *Students and Politics in Emerging Nations,* Praeger, 1969; *Vietnamese Anticolonialism: 1885-1925,* University of California Press, 1971; (contributor) Noam Chomsky and Howard Zinn, editors, *Critical Essays on the Pentagon Papers,* Beacon, 1972; (editor) Phan Boi Chau and Ho Chi Minh, *Reflections from Captivity: Phan Boi Chau's "Prison Notes" and Ho Chi Minh's "Prison Diary,"* translated by Christopher Jenkins, Ohio University Press, 1977. Also author of *Tradition and Revolution in Vietnam,* 1974. Contributor to professional journals.

WORK IN PROGRESS: Vietnamese Anticolonialism: 1925-1945; Revolutionary Consciousness and the Dissemination of Quoc-Ngu in Vietnam.

AVOCATIONAL INTERESTS: Tennis, hiking.†

*   *   *

MARRUS, Michael Robert 1941-

PERSONAL: Born February 3, 1941, in Toronto, Ontario, Canada; son of Elliott Lloyd and Lillian (Brenzel) Marrus; married Carol Randi Greenstein (a teacher), May 13, 1971; children: two. *Education:* University of Toronto, B.A., 1963; University of California, Berkeley, M.A., 1964, Ph.D., 1968. *Office:* Department of History, University of Toronto, Toronto, Ontario, Canada M5S 1A1.

CAREER: University of Toronto, Toronto, Ontario, assistant professor, 1968-73, associate professor, 1973-77, professor of history, 1978—.

WRITINGS: The Politics of Assimilation: A Study of the French Jewish Community at the Time of the Dreyfus Affair, Clarendon Press, 1971; (editor) *The Emergence of Leisure,* Harper, 1974. Contributor of articles on French and Jewish history to journals.

WORK IN PROGRESS: Research on Vichy France and the Jews.

*   *   *

MARSH, Peter T(imothy) 1935-

PERSONAL: Born December 8, 1935, in Toronto, Ontario, Canada; son of Henry Hooper (a bishop in the Anglican

Church) and Margaret (Heakes) Marsh; married Margaret Elizabeth Watts, December 29, 1962; children: Stephen, Andrea, Susan. *Education:* University of Toronto, B.A. (honors), 1958; Cambridge University, Ph.D., 1962. *Home:* 110 Berkeley Dr., Syracuse, N.Y. 13210. *Office:* Department of History, Syracuse University, Syracuse, N.Y. 13210.

CAREER: University of Saskatchewan, Saskatoon, instructor, 1962-63, assistant professor of history, 1963-67; Syracuse University, Syracuse, N.Y., associate professor of history, 1967—, chairman of department, 1968-70. Visiting tutor, University of Sussex, 1966; visiting fellow at All Souls College, Oxford University, 1966-67, and Emmanuel College, Cambridge University, 1974; visiting professor of Victorian studies, University of Leicester, 1970. *Member:* American Historical Association, Conference on British Studies (national chairman, 1975-77), Association for Canadian Studies in the United States, American Association of University Professors. *Awards, honors:* Canada Council senior fellowship, 1966-67; Earhart Foundation research grants, 1971, 1972, and 1973; American Council of Learned Societies grant-in-aid, 1973; Academy of Political Science research grant, 1974.

WRITINGS: The Victorian Church in Decline: Archbishop Tait and the Church of England, 1868-1882, University of Pittsburgh Press, 1969; *The Discipline of Popular Government: Lord Salisbury's Domestic Statecraft, 1881-1902,* Harvester Press, 1978. Contributor of articles and reviews to *Victorian Studies, Canadian Journal of Theology, Journal of British Studies, Political Science Quarterly,* and history journals.

WORK IN PROGRESS: Comparative studies of conservative politics in Britain, the United States, and Canada during the nineteenth and twentieth centuries.

SIDELIGHTS: Peter Marsh's *The Victorian Church in Decline* "is scholarly, learned, well written, and marked by that insight and judgment which come from true expertise in an intricate subject," writes Robert Blake.

BIOGRAPHICAL/CRITICAL SOURCES: Spectator, February 28, 1969.

*   *   *

MARSHALL, Byron K. 1936-

PERSONAL: Born May 11, 1936, in San Francisco, Calif.; son of William Hanlay (a businessman) and Bessie (Milton) Marshall; married Sally M. Clair, June 21, 1959 (divorced, 1972); married Vera Munkberg Fant, April 4, 1974; children: (first marriage) Jessica Brooks, Byron Hanlay; stepchildren: Michele Fant, Lara Fant. *Education:* Stanford University, B.A., 1959, M.A, 1961, Ph.D., 1966; additional study at Keio University, Tokyo, 1957-58, and Center for Japanese Studies, Tokyo, 1961-63. *Home:* 2021 Franklin St. S.E., Minneapolis, Minn. 55414. *Office:* Department of History, University of Minnesota, Minneapolis, Minn. 55455.

CAREER: University of Minnesota, Minneapolis, assistant professor, 1966-68, associate professor of history, 1968—. Visiting professor of history, Center for Oriental Studies, College of Mexico, Mexico City, 1969. *Member:* American Historical Association, Association for Asian Studies (member of Northeast Asian council, 1976-79), American Association for Asian Studies, American Association of University Professors, American Civil Liberties Union, Midwest Conference on Asian Affairs (president, 1975-76). *Awards, honors:* American Council of Learned Societies-

Social Science Research Council fellowship, 1969-70; Fulbright-Hays fellow.

WRITINGS: Capitalism and Nationalism in Prewar Japan: The Ideology of the Business Elite, 1868-1941, Stanford University Press, 1967; *Nihon no Shihonshugi to nashonarizumu,* Daiyamondasha (Tokyo), 1968; (with Edward Farmer and others) *A Comparative History of Civilizations in Asia,* Addison-Wesley, 1977. Contributor to political science and history journals.

WORK IN PROGRESS: The Academic Elite and Social Change in Japan, completion expected in 1980.

*   *   *

MARSHALL, Lenore Guinzburg 1899-1971

September 7, 1899—September 23, 1971; American poet and novelist. Obituaries: *New York Times,* September 25, 1971; *Washington Post,* September 26, 1971. (See index for *CA* sketch)

*   *   *

MARTI-IBANEZ, Felix 1912(?)-1972

1912(?)—May 24, 1972; Spanish-born American psychiatrist, novelist, essayist, and short story writer. Obituaries: *New York Times,* May 25, 1972; *Time,* June 5, 1972.

*   *   *

MARTIN, F(rancis) David 1920-

PERSONAL: Born March 29, 1920, in Johnstown, Pa.; son of Francis C. (a banker) and Agnes (Stover) Martin; married Doris Georg, June 26, 1942; children: Marilyn Suzanne (Mrs. William Gale Reish), Timothy, Amy, Janice. *Education:* University of Chicago, A.B., 1942, Ph.D. (with honors), 1949. *Politics:* Independent. *Home:* R.D. 1, Lewisburg, Pa. 17837. *Office:* Department of Philosophy, Bucknell University, Lewisburg, Pa. 17837.

CAREER: University of Chicago, Chicago, Ill., instructor in humanities, 1947-49; Bucknell University, Lewisburg, Pa., assistant professor, 1949-50, associate professor, 1950-56, professor of philosophy, 1956—. *Military service:* U.S. Army, 1942-46; became first lieutenant. *Member:* American Philosophical Association, American Society for Aesthetics, Metaphysical Society of America, Renaissance Society of America, American Association of University Professors (vice-president of Pennsylvania Division), Phi Beta Kappa (honorary member), Phi Sigma Tau. *Awards, honors:* Bucknell University research grants, 1956, 1961, 1964, 1967; Fulbright research scholar in Italy, 1957-59; Lilly Foundation fellowship, 1966-67; Christian Lindback Award for distinguished teaching, 1967.

WRITINGS: Art and the Religious Experience, Bucknell University Press, 1972; (with Lee Jacobus) *Art and the Humanities,* McGraw, 1975. Contributor of articles to journals of philosophy and aesthetics.

WORK IN PROGRESS: The Aesthetics of Sculpture.

AVOCATIONAL INTERESTS: Nature, music, golf, and Italy.

*   *   *

MARTIN, Roscoe C(olman) 1903-1972

November 18, 1903—May 12, 1972; American political scientist and author. Obituaries: *New York Times,* May 14, 1972. (See index for *CA* sketch)

MASON, Paul T(aylor) 1937-

PERSONAL: Born October 30, 1937, in St. Louis, Mo.; son of Paul Taylor (a pharmacist) and Zelma (De Lassus) Mason; married Carolyn Ann McDermott, June 13, 1959; children: Ann Marie, Kathryn A. *Education:* St. Louis University, B.S., 1959, A.M., 1961, Ph.D., 1964. *Home:* 1015 Lindsay Rd., Carnegie, Pa. 15106. *Office:* Department of History, Duquesne University, Pittsburgh, Pa. 15219.

CAREER: Duquesne University, Pittsburgh, Pa., assistant professor, 1963-65, associate professor, 1966-69, professor of history, 1969—, director of history forum, 1973-75. *Member:* American Historical Association, American Association of University Professors, Group for the Use of Psychology in History.

WRITINGS: (With Thomas P. Neill) *The Life of Christ in His Church,* Daniel Reardon, 1963; (editor) *Totalitarianism,* Heath, 1967. Contributor of articles and reviews to *American Catholic Historical Review, Duquesne Review,* and *Clio.*

WORK IN PROGRESS: The Agony of European Modernization.†

*   *   *

MASTNY, Vojtech 1936-

PERSONAL: Given name is pronounced Voytekh; born February 26, 1936, in Prague, Czechoslovakia; son of Antonin and Jindriska (Rybakova) Mastny; married Catherine Louise Kacmarynski (an editor), July 25, 1964; children: Catherine Paula, John Adalbert, Elizabeth A. *Education:* Charles University of Prague, Promovany Historik, 1962; Columbia University, Ph.D., 1968. *Politics:* Democrat. *Religion:* Roman Catholic. *Home:* 2306 Briar Hill Dr., Champaign, Ill. 61820. *Office:* Department of History, 309 Gregory Hall, University of Illinois, Urbana, Ill. 61801

CAREER: California State College (now University), Long Beach, assistant professor of history, 1967-68; Columbia University, New York, N.Y., assistant professor of history, 1968-74, acting director, Institute on East Central Europe, 1970-71; University of Illinois at Urbana-Champaign, associate professor of history, 1974—. Senior visiting member, St. Antony's College, Oxford University, 1972; visiting associate professor of Soviet studies, Johns Hopkins University, 1977-78. *Member:* American Historical Association, American Association for the Advancement of Slavic Studies, American Committee on the History of the Second World War. *Awards, honors:* Clarke F. Ansley Award, 1968, for manuscript of *The Czechs under Nazi Rule;* Alexander von Humboldt faculty fellow, 1972; Lehram Institute research fellow, 1974-75; Guggenheim fellow and fellow of the Institute for the study of World Politics, 1977-78.

WRITINGS: (Editor) *Disarmament and Nuclear Tests, 1964-69,* Facts on File, 1970; *The Czechs under Nazi Rule: The Failure of National Resistance, 1939-1942,* Columbia University Press, 1971; (editor) *Czechoslovakia: Crisis in World Communism,* Facts on File, 1972; (editor) *East European Dissent,* Facts on File, 1972, Volume I: *1953-1964,* Volume II: *1965-1970; Russia's Road to the Cold War: Diplomacy, Warfare, and Communism, 1941-45,* Columbia University Press, 1978. Contributor to *Foreign Affairs, American Historical Review, Journal of Modern History, Problems of Communism, New Leader,* and other journals. Book review editor, *Slavic Review.*

SIDELIGHTS: Vojtech Mastny has traveled extensively in Europe and keeps a summer home in England. He can speak or read German, French, Russian, Polish, Spanish, and Italian, as well as Czech and English.

*   *   *

MATLAW, Myron 1924-

PERSONAL: Born May 21, 1924, in Berlin, Germany; married Julia Moody, 1950; children: Laura, John. *Education:* Hofstra University, B.A., 1949; University of Chicago, M.A., 1950, Ph.D., 1953. *Office:* Department of English, Queens College of the City University of New York, Flushing, N.Y. 11367.

CAREER: University of Illinois at Chicago Circle, instructor in English, 1953-55; Auburn University, Auburn, Ala., assistant professor of English, 1955-56; Hunter College (now Hunter College of the City University of New York), New York, N.Y., instructor in English, 1957-60; Queens College of the City University of New York, Flushing, N.Y., professor of English, 1960—. Visiting professor of English and drama, University of Hawaii, 1967-68. *Military service:* U.S. Army, Military Intelligence, 1943-46; became second lieutenant. *Member:* Modern Language Association of America, American Society for Theatre Research. *Awards, honors:* American Council of Learned Societies award, 1959.

WRITINGS: (With James B. Stronks) *Pro and Con,* Houghton, 1960; (editor) *Story and Critic,* Harper, 1963; (editor) *The Black Crook and Other 19th-Century Plays,* Dutton, 1967; *Modern World Drama: An Encyclopedia,* Dutton 1972. Contributor to *Encyclopedia Americana;* contributor to popular and scholarly journals.

WORK IN PROGRESS: A biography of James O'Neill.

*   *   *

MATSON, Virginia (Mae) Freeberg 1914-

PERSONAL: Born August 25, 1914, in Chicago, Ill.; daughter of Axel George (a sales manager) and Mae (Dalrymple) Freeberg; married Edward John Matson (a corporation vice-president), October 18, 1941; children: Karin (Mrs. Rudolf A. Renfer, Jr.), Sara (Mrs. Carl B. Drake III), E. Robert, Laurence D., David O. *Education:* Chicago Teachers College (now Northeastern Illinois University), elementary certificate, 1933, graduate study, 1962; University of Kentucky, B.A., 1934; Northwestern University, M.A., 1941, graduate study, 1960-61, 1962. *Politics:* Democrat. *Religion:* Society of Friends. *Home:* 950 North St. Mary's Rd., Libertyville, Ill. 60048. *Office:* The Grove School, 40 East Old Mill Rd., Lake Forest, Ill. 60045.

CAREER: Chicago Public Schools, Chicago, Ill., high school science teacher, 1934-41; Ridge Farm School, Lake Forest, Ill., teacher, 1945-46; Lake County Schools, Lake County, Ill., teacher, 1956-58; Grove School, Lake Forest, Ill., founder and executive director, 1959—. *Member:* Friends of Literature, Illinois Council of Exceptional Children (treasurer), Lake County Health Care Association, Society of Midland Authors. *Awards, honors:* Chicago "100" I Will award, 1971; Friends of Literature fiction award, 1972, for *Abba, Father.*

WRITINGS: Shadow of the Lost Rock, Scripture Press, 1956, reprinted as *Buried Alive,* Moody, 1970; *Abba, Father,* Moody, 1971; *A School for Peter,* Creation House, 1974. Contributor of over 250 articles to periodicals, including *Chicago Tribune, Waukegan News-Sun,* and *Libertyville Independent Register.*

WORK IN PROGRESS: Saul, the King; The Mummy

That Came Alive; The Inheritance, a book on Abraham; a mystery, *The Last Battle.*

AVOCATIONAL INTERESTS: Travel, gardening, and photography.

* * *

MATT, Paul R(obert) 1926-

PERSONAL: Born March 27, 1926, in Cincinnati, Ohio; son of Oscar J. and Loretta C. (Fink) Matt; married Joan M. Woeste (her husband's assistant in publishing *Historical Aviation Album*), June 18, 1949. *Education:* Attended parochial schools in Cincinnati, Ohio, and completed high school courses while in U.S. Navy. *Home:* 5220 Camellia Ave., Temple City, Calif. 91780. *Office:* Historical Aviation Album, Box 33, Temple City, Calif. 91780.

CAREER: After World War II was a commercial and industrial photographer; head model builder for engineering firm in El Monte, Calif., 1959-65; editor and publisher of *Historical Aviation Album,* Temple City, Calif., 1965—. *Military service:* U.S. Navy, aerial photographer, 1944-46; became photographer's mate first class. *Member:* American Aviation Historical Society.

WRITINGS: U.S. Navy and Marine Corps Fighters, 1918-1962, Harleyford Publications (London), 1962. Editor with Peter M. Bowers, *Aviation Photo Album,* 1968—. Contributor to *Air Progress, American Aircraft Modeler,* and *Journal of the AAHS.*

WORK IN PROGRESS: Research and writing for further volumes of *Historical Aviation Album* ("there's no end to the series") and other titles under the *Album* name.

* * *

MATTHEWS, Jacklyn Meek 1933-

PERSONAL: Born December 5, 1933, in Sacramento, Calif.; daughter of Bert Bookam (an engineer) and Laura (Hanlon) Meek; married Roger Towne, July 30, 1948; married second husband, F. Leslie Matthews (an artist and filmmaker), January 30, 1965; children: (first marriage) Margaret (Mrs. Tom Bortolazzo), Stephen Clifford, Anne, Cathy; (second marriage) John. *Education:* Attended Sarah Dix Hamlin School. *Home:* 1814 Anacopa St., Santa Barbara, Calif. 93101.

AWARDS, HONORS: Third prize of Santa Barbara Adult Education Center children's story contest, for *Edward and the Night Horses.*

WRITINGS: (Juvenile) *Edward and the Night Horses,* illustrated by Don Freeman, Golden Gate, 1971.

WORK IN PROGRESS: Three books, *The First Starfish, Tale of Rahi,* and *The Door;* a short story.

AVOCATIONAL INTERESTS: Haiku poetry, painting watercolors for children.†

* * *

MATTHEWS, John H(arold) 1925-
(Jack Matthews)

PERSONAL: Born July 22, 1925, in Columbus, Ohio; son of John Harold (an attorney) and Lulu (Grover) Matthews; married Barbara Reese, September 16, 1947; children: Cynthia Ann (Mrs. Wyman Warnock), Barbara Ellen (Mrs. Craig Platt), John H. III. *Education:* Ohio State University, B.A., 1949, M.A., 1954. *Home:* 24 Briarwood Dr., Athens, Ohio 45701. *Agent:* Ann Elmo Agency, Inc., 52 Vanderbilt

Ave., New York, N.Y. 10017. *Office:* Department of English, Ellis Hall, 209-E, Ohio University, Athens, Ohio 45701.

CAREER: Urbana College, Urbana, Ohio, associate professor, 1959-62, professor of English, 1962-64; Ohio University, Athens, professor, 1964—, distinguished professor of English, 1977—. Distinguished writer-in-residence, Wichita State University, 1970-71. *Military service:* U.S. Coast Guard, 1943-45. *Awards, honors:* Vanderwater Poetry Prize, Ohio State University, 1953, 1954; Borestone Mountain Poetry Award, 1959, for "From the Uncertainty for Our Dire Predictions," and 1965, for "Summer Dances"; Ohioana Fiction Award, 1965, for *Bitter Knowledge;* Quill Award, 1967, for "The Hotel"; Florence Roberts Head Award, 1968, for *Hanger Stout, Awake!;* Guggenheim Foundation grant in creative writing, 1974-75.

WRITINGS—Under name Jack Matthews: *Bitter Knowledge* (short stories), Scribner, 1964; *An Almanac for Twilight* (poems), University of North Carolina Press, 1966; *Hanger Stout, Awake!* (novel), Harcourt, 1967; *Beyond the Bridge* (novel), Harcourt, 1970; *The Tale of Asa Bean* (novel), Harcourt, 1971; *The Charisma Campaigns* (novel), Harcourt, 1972; (editor with Elaine Hemley) *The Writer's Signature* (textbook), Scott, Foresman, 1972; (editor and contributor) *Archetypal Themes in the Modern Story,* St. Martin's, 1973; *Pictures of the Journey Back* (novel), Harcourt, 1973; (author of introduction) James S. Brisbin, editor, *Belden, the White Chief,* Ohio University Press, 1974; *Collecting Rare Books for Pleasure and Profit,* Putnam, 1977. Work represented in anthologies, including *Best Poems of 1965,* Pacific Books, 1966, *Short Stories from the Little Magazines,* Scott, Foresman, 1970, *The Best American Short Stories,* 1970, 1975, and *Prize Stories 1972: The O. Henry Awards,* Doubleday, 1972.

Chapbooks: *In a Theatre of Buildings,* Ox Head, 1970; *Book Collecting and the Search for Reality,* privately printed by Library Associates of Wichita State University, 1972; *Private Landscapes* (poems), Duane Schneider Press, 1975. Contributor of nearly 200 articles, reviews, poems, and short stories to *Northern Review, Contemporary Fiction, Epoch, Today, College English, Commonweal, Tamesis, Southern Humanities Review, Nation,* and numerous other periodicals.

SIDELIGHTS: John Matthews' interests include the culture of the American Indian and classical studies. He writes: "I have many interests that merge with my professional interests in some ways, but which also possess some of the qualities of recreation. I like to travel, drive my car for inspiration and relaxation, walk, hunt, fish, read, jog, and collect first editions and other rare books."

* * *

MATTHEWS, Roy A(nthony) 1927-

PERSONAL: Born July 1, 1927, in London, England; son of Harold Marten and Hilda (Heaney) Matthews; married Rosemary Brunsdon, November 26, 1955; children: Paul Duncan, Ian Guy, Claire Fiona, Alexander Noel. *Education:* St. John's College, Cambridge, B.A., 1951, M.A., 1953. *Politics:* Liberal. *Home:* 280 Second Ave., Ottawa, Ontario, Canada K1S 2H9. *Office:* Economic Council of Canada, Ottawa, Ontario, Canada.

CAREER: Migrated to Canada from England, 1954; Philips Electronics Industries Ltd., Toronto, Ontario, market research analyst, 1954-56; Canadian Industries Ltd., Montreal, Quebec, economist, 1956-60; National Industrial Conference Board, Canadian Office, Montreal, economist, 1960-64; Private Planning Association of Canada, Montreal, director of research, Canadian-American Committee, 1964-68, acting executive director of Association, 1969-71, director of research, Canadian Economic Policy Committee, 1971; associate director of research, Atlantic Economic Studies Program, 1966-71; International Development Research Centre assignment at Centre de Recherches en Developpement Economique, Universite de Montreal, Montreal, research on the role of the multinational corporation in economic development, 1972; Economic Council of Canada, Ottawa, senior staff economist, 1973—. Canadian Institute of International Affairs, former member of executive committee, Montreal branch, honorary secretary, 1962-64, consultant, 1970—; consultant to Canadian International Development Agency, Ottawa, 1969. Member of board of directors, Foster Parents Plan of Canada and Canadian Council for International Co-operation. *Military service:* Royal Air Force, 1945-48.

MEMBER: Canadian Economics Association, Canadian Political Science Association, Society for International Development. *Awards, honors:* Ford Foundation travel and study award for research in Europe, 1969.

WRITINGS: (Editor) *Business Outlook in Canada, 1964,* National Industrial Conference Board (Montreal), 1963; (editor) *Problems and Policies in Canadian Manufacturing,* National Industrial Conference Board, 1964; (co-author) *A New Trade Strategy for Canada and the United States,* Canadian-American Committee, 1966; *Britain and the Common Market: A Contemporary Canadian View/La Grande-Bretagne et Le Marche Commun: Opinion Canadienne Actuelle* (booklet), bilingual edition, Canadian Institute of International Affairs, 1968; (with Stuart Proudfoot) *Ways of Increasing the Involvement of Canadian Private Interests in the Developing Countries,* Canadian International Development Agency (Ottawa), 1969; (with G. Doxey, R. Wonnacott, and others) *The Implications for Canada of a Canada-Commonwealth Caribbean Free Trade Arrangement,* Private Planning Association of Canada, 1969; *Industrial Viability in a Free Trade Economy: A Program of Adjustment Policies for Canada,* University of Toronto Press, 1971. Author of various unpublished government reports.

Contributor: *Canadian-American Planning: The 7th Annual Conference, 1965,* University of Toronto Press, 1966; *La Grande-Bretagne Rejoint l'Europe,* Librairie Plon (Paris), 1967; *From Commonwealth to Common Market,* Penguin, 1968; *Dix Ans d'Integration Europeenne/Ten Years of European Integration,* Les Presses de l'Ecole des Hautes Etudes Commerciales (Montreal), 1968; *Writings on Canadian-American Studies,* Michigan State University, 1968; I.-D. Pal, editor, *Canadian Economic Issues,* Macmillan, 1971; *The Multinational Firm and the Nation State,* Collier, 1972. Contributor of articles to *Foreign Affairs, International Journal* (Toronto), *The World Today* (London), *Queen's Quarterly* (Kingston), *Harvard Business Review, Weltwirtschaftliches Archiv* (Kiel), *Agenor* (Brussels), *L'Actualite Economique* (Montreal), *Round Table* (London), *Canadian Forum* (Toronto), *L'Action Nationale* (Montreal), *Financial Times* (London), *Business Management Record, Globe and Mail* (Toronto), *Columbia Journal of World Business, New York Times, Financial Times of Canada,* and other economics journals and periodicals.

MATTHIAS, John (Edward) 1941-

PERSONAL: Born September 5, 1941, in Columbus, Ohio; son of John Marshall (a judge) and Lois (Kirkpatrick) Matthias; married Diana Adams, December 29, 1967; children: Cynouai, Laura. *Education:* Ohio State University, B.A., 1963; Stanford University, M.A., 1966; University of London, additional graduate study, 1966-67. *Home:* 17700 Ireland Rd., South Bend, Ind. 46614. *Office:* Department of English, University of Notre Dame, Notre Dame, Ind. 46556.

CAREER: University of Notre Dame, Notre Dame, Ind., assistant professor of English, 1967—. Has given poetry readings at Stanford University, Ohio State University, University of London, and other universities. *Member:* American Association of University Professors, Greater London Arts Association, New York State Council on the Arts, Illinois Arts Council. *Awards, honors:* Woodrow Wilson fellow, 1963-64; Fulbright grant at University of London, 1966-67; O'Brien Award, Center for the Study of Man, 1975; visiting fellowship at Clare College, Cambridge University, 1975-76.

WRITINGS: Bucyrus (poems), Swallow Press, 1971; (editor) *Twenty-three Modern British Poets,* Swallow Press, 1971; *Other Poems,* John Jacobs, 1971; *Turns* (poems), Swallow Press, 1976; *Herman's Poems* (pamphlet), Sceptre Press, 1973; *Double Derivation Association and Cliché: From the Great Tournament Roll of Westminster* (pamphlet), Wine Press, 1975; *Two Poems* (pamphlet), Sceptre Press, 1976; *Crossing* (poems), Swallow Press, in press; (translator with Goran Printz-Pahlson) *Contemporary Swedish Poetry,* Anvil Press, in press.

Contributor to anthologies, including: *Experiments in Prose,* edited by Eugene Wildman, Swallow Press, 1969; *New Poetry Anthology II,* edited by Michael Anania, Swallow Press, 1972; *Heartland II,* edited by Lucian Stryk, Northern Illinois University Press, 1975; *A Tumult for John Berryman,* edited by Marguerite Harris, Dryad Press, 1976; *The Indiana Experience,* edited by A.L. Lazarus, Indiana University Press, 1977. Also author with David Isele of oratorio, "Cognition Prefix." Contributor of about thirty poems and reviews to *Nation, Tri-Quarterly, Literary Review, Prairie Schooner, Prism-International, Poetry, Encounter, New York Quarterly, Second Aeon, Antioch Review,* and other periodicals. Advisory editor, *Purple Sage,* 1969-70, and *Indiana Writes.*

WORK IN PROGRESS: Selected Writings of David Jones, for Faber, and *Letters of David Jones to H. S. Ede,* for Anvil Press.

*   *   *

MAUERMANN, Mary Anne 1927-

PERSONAL: Born April 15, 1927, in Seattle, Wash.; daughter of Glenn Arthur (a teacher and writer) and Babette (Plechner) Hughes; married William Gordon Mauermann (a teacher), August 16, 1946; children: Wendy Ann (Mrs. Daniel A. Roberts), Scott Gordon. *Education:* Attended Stanford University, summer, 1945, University of Pennsylvania, 1945-46, and University of Washington, Seattle at various intervals. *Religion:* Episcopalian. *Home:* 16123 41st Ave. N.E., Seattle, Wash. 98155. *Agent:* Ann Elmo Agency, Inc., 52 Vanderbilt Ave., New York, N.Y. 10017.

CAREER: Teacher of adult education courses in creative writing in Seattle, Wash., 1966—; Writing Shop (professional writing school), Seattle, founder with husband and teacher, 1969—; currently teacher of writing at Shoreline Community College, Seattle. *Member:* Free Lances.

WRITINGS—All juveniles: *Spotlight Summer,* Washburn, 1964; *The Magic Tower,* Washburn, 1965; *Strangers into Friends,* Washburn, 1969. Contributor to *Redbook.*

WORK IN PROGRESS: A romance-suspense novel for adults.

* * *

MAUNDER, W(illiam) J(ohn) 1932-

PERSONAL: Born August 3, 1932, in Nelson, New Zealand; son of George William (a banker) and Merle (Fabian) Maunder; married Melva Dawn Mills, October 10, 1959; children: Denise Robyn, Philip John. *Education:* University of New Zealand, B.Sc., 1954, M.Sc. (honors), 1956; University of Otago, Ph.D., 1966. *Religion:* Presbyterian. *Home:* 56 Rangoon St., Wellington 4, New Zealand. *Office address:* New Zealand Meteorological Service, Box 722, Wellington, New Zealand.

CAREER: New Zealand Meteorological Service, Wellington, meteorologist, 1955-57, 1959-61; Canadian Meteorological Service, Toronto, Ontario, meteorological officer, 1957; Royal Canadian Air Force Station, Clareshom, Alberta, meteorological instructor, 1958; University of Otago, Dunedin, New Zealand, lecturer in geography, 1961-66; University of Victoria, Victoria, British Columbia, assistant professor of geography, 1966-69; New Zealand Meteorological Service, meteorologist, 1970—. Visiting assistant professor of geography, Waterloo Lutheran University, 1967, University of Delaware, 1968; visiting lecturer in atmospheric sciences, University of Missouri, 1969-70. Participant, National Science Foundation Task Group on the Human Dimensions of the Atmosphere, 1966-67. *Member:* American Meteorological Society, New Zealand Geographical Society (Otago branch; secretary, 1962-64; chairman, 1965-66; member of editorial board, 1972—).

WRITINGS: (Editor and contributor) *Pollution . . . What It Is, What It Does, What Can Be Done about It,* Evening Division, University of Victoria, 1969; *The Value of the Weather,* Barnes & Noble, 1970.

Contributor: R. G. Lister and R. P. Hargreaves, editors, *Central Otago,* New Zealand Geographical Society, 1965; W. R. D. Sewell, editor, *Human Dimensions of the Atmosphere,* National Science Foundation, 1968; J. G. Nelson and M. J. Chambers, editors, *Process and Method in Canadian Geography—Climate,* Methuen, 1970; Sewell and H. D. Foster, editors, *The Geographer and Society,* University of Victoria, 1970; H. Landsberg, editor, *World Survey of Climatology,* Volume XIII, Elsevier, 1971. Contributor of articles and reviews to journals.

WORK IN PROGRESS: Research into the social and economic aspects of the atmospheric sciences.

SIDELIGHTS: W. J. Maunder has traveled in North and South America, Europe, Asia, and Australia.

BIOGRAPHICAL/CRITICAL SOURCES: Geographical Review, April, 1971.†

* * *

MAURER, Charles Benes 1933-

PERSONAL: Born January 17, 1933, in Oak Park, Ill.; son of Charles Walter (a machinist) and Blanche (Benes) Maurer; married Marjorie Merz, June 11, 1954; children: James Charles. *Education:* University of Michigan, B.A.,

1954, A.M.L.S., 1970; Northwestern University, M.A., 1958, Ph.D., 1965. *Home:* 157 Edgewood Dr., Granville, Ohio 43023. *Office:* W. H. Doane Library, Denison University, Granville, Ohio 43023.

CAREER: University of Illinois at Chicago Circle, assistant instructor in German, 1961-62; Lawrence University, Appleton, Wis., instructor in German, 1962-65; University of Michigan, Ann Arbor, assistant professor of German, 1965-71, acting coordinator of foreign languages residential college, 1968-69, coordinator, 1969-71; Denison University, Granville, Ohio, library director, 1971—. *Military service:* U.S. Navy, 1954-57; became lieutenant junior grade. *Member:* American Library Association, American Association of University Professors, American Library Association of Ohio.

WRITINGS: Call to Revolution: The Mystical Anarchism of Gustav Landauer, Wayne State University Press, 1971.

* * *

MAXWELL, D(esmond) E(rnest) S(tewart) 1925-

PERSONAL: Born July 6, 1925, in Londonderry, Northern Ireland; son of Ernest Victor (a businessman) and Rose (Stewart) Maxwell; married Joy Eakin, August 6, 1955; children: Amanda Rosemary Gillian. *Education:* Trinity College, Dublin, Ireland, B.A., 1947, Ph.D., 1950. *Home:* 79 Royal Orchard Blvd., Thornhill, Ontario, Canada. *Office:* Department of English, York University, Toronto, Ontario, Canada M3J 1P3.

CAREER: University of Ghana, Accra, lecturer in English, 1956-61; Civil Service Commission, London, England, assistant director of examinations, 1961-63; University of Ibadan, Ibadan, Nigeria, professor of English and head of department, 1963-67, dean of Faculty of Arts, 1966-67; York University, Toronto, Ontario, professor of English, 1967—, director of graduate program in English, 1967-70, master of Winters College, 1969—. *Member:* International Association of University Professors of English, Modern Humanities Research Association, Canadian Association for Irish Studies (chairman, 1973-74; president, 1977-80), National Liberal Club (London, England), University Club (Dublin, Ireland).

WRITINGS: The Poetry of T. S. Eliot, Routledge & Kegan Paul, 1952, Barnes & Noble, 1961; *American Fiction: The Intellectual Background,* Columbia University Press, 1963; *Cozzens,* Oliver & Boyd, 1964; (editor with S. B. Bushrui) *W. B. Yeats, 1865-1965: Centenary Essays on the Art of W. B. Yeats,* Ibadan University Press, 1965; (with Thomas A. Dunn) *Introducing Poetry: An Anthology of Poems in English,* Pergamon, 1966; *Herman Melville,* Humanities, 1968; *Poets of the Thirties,* Routledge & Kegan Paul, 1969, Barnes & Noble, 1970; *Brian Friel,* Bucknell University Press, 1973. Contributor to *Encyclopaedia Britannica.*

WORK IN PROGRESS: Writing on contemporary Irish theatre; research for *The Making of "Borstal Boy."*

AVOCATIONAL INTERESTS: Convivial living.

* * *

MAYER, Bernadette 1945-

PERSONAL: Born May 12, 1945, in Brooklyn, N.Y.; daughter of Theodore A. (an electrician) and Marie (Stumpf) Mayer. *Education:* New School for Social Research, B.A., 1967; also attended Barnard College, Columbia University, and College of New Rochelle. *Home:* 100 Main St., Lenox, Mass. 01240.

CAREER: Poet. Awards, honors: Poets Foundation grant, 1967; National Institute of Arts and Letters grant, 1971; Creative Artists Public Service Program (CAPS) grant in fiction, 1976.

WRITINGS: Story, 0 to 9 Press, 1968; Moving, Angel Hair Press, 1971; Memory, North Atlantic Books, 1976; Studying Hunger, Big Sky, 1976; Poetry, Kulchur Foundation, 1976.

Anthologized in Anthology of New York Poets, edited by Ron Padgett and David Shapiro, Random House, 1970, Another World, edited by Anne Waldman, Bobbs-Merrill, 1971, Young American Poets 2, edited by Paul Carroll, Follett, 1972, Individuals, edited by Alan Sondheim Dutton, 1975, and None of the Above, edited by Michael Lally, Crossing Press, 1976. Contributor of poetry to Ice, Tzarad, 0 to 9, Lines, and other publications. Poetry transmitted through John Giorno's "Dial-a-Poem." Editor with Vito Acconci, 0 to 9 magazine and books, 1968, with Ed Friedman, Unnatural Acts, 1972, and with Lewis Warsh, United Artists, 1977.

WORK IN PROGRESS: The Golden Book of Words, poems; Quarantine, the Studying Hunger journals, for North Atlantic Books.

*   *   *

MAYER, Herbert T. 1922-

PERSONAL: Born August 25, 1922, in St. Louis, Mo.; son of Frederick E. (a professor) and Martha (Luehrmann) Mayer; married Arline E. Knepper (a secretary), June 8, 1949; children; Thomas, Tedra, Virginia. Education: Attended Concordia College, Milwaukee, Wis., 1939-42; Concordia Seminary, St. Louis, Mo., B.D., 1948, S.T.M., 1957; Washington University, St. Louis, Mo., M.A., 1949, Ph.D., 1973. Home: 7136 Washington, University City, Mo. 63130. Office: Seminex, 607 North Grand Ave., St. Louis, Mo. 63103.

CAREER: Ordained a Lutheran minister; Concordia Teachers College, Seward, Neb., instructor, 1949-51; Mt. Calvary Lutheran Church, Janesville, Wis., pastor, 1952-57; Concordia College, Milwaukee, Wis., assistant professor of history, 1957-59; Concordia Seminary, St. Louis, Mo., associate professor, 1959-64, professor of historical theology, 1964-74; Seminex, St. Louis, professor, 1974—. Visiting scholar, Ecumenical Institute for Advanced Theological Studies, Jerusalem, 1975. Member: American Historical Association, Church History Society, Concordia Historical Institute, Society of Biblical Literature. Awards, honors: D.Litt., Concordia College, St. Paul, Minn., 1971; John W. Behnken post-doctoral fellow, 1974-75.

WRITINGS—All published by Concordia: (Contributor) Carl S. Meyer, editor, Moving Frontiers: Readings in the History of the Lutheran Church and the Missouri Synod, 1965; (editor) Interpreting the Holy Scriptures: Principles for the Proper Study of the Bible, 1967; The Books of the New Testament, 1969; (contributor) Oscar E. Feucht, editor, Family Authority in the Church, 1970; (co-editor) Providence of God, 1972. Contributor of articles to Concordia Theological Monthly, and church periodicals. Managing editor, Currents in Theology and Mission, 1974, and Concordia Theological Monthly.

*   *   *

MAYNARD, Richard Allen 1942-

PERSONAL: Born August 30, 1942, in Philadelphia, Pa.; son of Gene and Sue (Kauffman) Maynard; married Lorraine Edelsohn (a teacher), June 20, 1965; children: Jeffrey, Kevin. Education: Temple University, B.S. (with honors), 1964, M.A., 1965; graduate study at Temple University, University of Pennsylvania, Princeton University and Haverford College, 1965-69. Home: 9807 Haldeman Ave., Apt. B-203, Philadelphia, Pa. 19115. Office: Scholastic Magazines, 50 West 44th St., New York, N.Y. 10036.

CAREER: Simon Gratz High School, Philadelphia, Pa., teacher of social studies and Afro-American history, 1965-72; Great Lakes Colleges Association, Philadelphia, teacher of Afro-American history and consultant in teacher training, 1968-72; Community College of Philadelphia, Philadelphia, instructor in American and Afro-American history, 1969-72; Scholastic Magazines, New York City, special editor and teacher-in-residence, 1972—. Free-lance writer, particularly of film guides for motion picture distributors. Consultant-lecturer on teacher training in Afro-American studies and on film study for various school districts and education associations, including Delaware Council on the Social Studies, Center for Understanding Media, New York City, Hope College (Holland, Mich.), National Council of Teachers of English, Kansas Language Arts Association, New Jersey Council of Teachers of English, University of Florida, and Virginia Commonwealth University.

WRITINGS: The Celluloid Curriculum: How to Use Movies in the Classroom, Hayden, 1971; The Black Man on Film: Racial Stereotyping, Hayden, 1972; Images of Africa on Film, Hayden, 1972; The Film as Propaganda: A Nation at War, Hayden, 1972; The West on Film: Myth and Reality, Hayden, 1972; (editor) "Literature of the Screen" series, four volumes, Scholastic Book Services, 1973; Mass Communications Arts, two volumes, Scholastic Book Services, 1974; Classroom Cinema, Teachers College Press, 1977. Educational films reviewer and films editor, Scholastic Teacher, 1970—. Contributor of articles to Media and Methods, About Education, Social Studies, Scholastic Teacher, Independent Schools Bulletin, Virginal English Bulletin, and Kansas Journal of Language Arts.

BIOGRAPHICAL/CRITICAL SOURCES: Philadelphia English Club Newsletter, January, 1972; Scholastic Teacher, March 1972; Texas Outlook, April, 1972; Catholic Newsletter, May 15, 1972.

*   *   *

MAZZARO, Jerome 1934-

PERSONAL: Surname is pronounced Motts-are-oh; born November 25, 1934, in Detroit, Mich.; son of Emmacolato (a laborer) and Carmela Maria (Pedalino) Mazzaro. Education: Wayne University (now Wayne State University), A.B., 1954; University of Iowa, M.A., 1956; Wayne State University, Ph.D., 1963. Home: 147 Capen Blvd., Buffalo, N.Y. 14226. Office: Department of Modern Languages, State University of New York, Buffalo, N.Y. 14260.

CAREER: General Motors Corp., Detroit, Mich., technical and procedures writer, 1955-56; University of Detroit, Detroit, instructor in English, 1958-61; State University of New York College at Cortland, assistant professor of English, 1962-64; State University of New York at Buffalo, professor of English and comparative literature, 1964—. Military service: U.S. Army Reserve, 1957-64. Member: Dante Society of America, Mark Twain Society. Awards, honors: Guggenheim fellowship in poetry, 1964.

WRITINGS: The Achievement of Robert Lowell: 1939-1959, University of Detroit Press, 1960; (translator) Juvenal, Satires, University of Michigan Press, 1965; The Poetic

Themes of Robert Lowell, University of Michigan Press, 1965; *Changing the Windows* (verse), Ohio State University Press, 1966; (editor) *Modern American Poetry,* McKay, 1970; *Transformations in the Renaissance English Lyric,* Cornell University Press, 1970; (editor) *Profile of Robert Lowell,* C. E. Merrill, 1971; (editor) *Profile of William Carlos Williams,* C. E. Merrill, 1971; *William Carlos Williams: The Later Poetry,* Cornell University Press, 1973. Contributor to *Britannica Junior Encyclopaedia* and to *Compton's Year Book,* 1962—. Editor, *Fresco,* 1960-61 and *Modern Poetry Studies,* 1970—; assistant editor, *North American Review,* 1963-65 and *Noetics,* 1964-65; contributing editor, *Salmagundi,* 1967—, *American Poetry Review,* 1972—, and *Italian-Americana,* 1974—; poetry editor, *Helios,* 1977—.

WORK IN PROGRESS: A volume of poems; a book on Robert Lowell; essays on contemporary poetry.

SIDELIGHTS: Regarding *Changing the Windows,* Joseph Bennett writes in the *New York Times Book Review:* "Jerome Mazzaro's first volume of verse utilizes what is by now a settled convention in American poetry: the presentation, in woeful flashes, of painful scenes, preferably from the life of the poet's parents—scenes which tend to terminate in psychiatric wards.... The fact that his subject matter and approach are by now almost cliches should not hinder us from appreciating Mazzaro's abilities.... [He] has an anachronistic and, in context, completely disloyal and heretical longing for the made, the achieved poem. 'Always the Threshold of a Horse' displays a playful ingenuity and ingratiating verbal expectancy.... 'Brother to Mars' presents a formal, restrained elegy, without the cute autobiographical tricks and synthetic shocks in which his tradition revels. The elegy is dignified, elegant, meaningful, and manly. Jerome Mazzaro is a poet who should be recognized outside the school from which he derives."

In *American Literature,* Donald Hill writes of *The Poetic Themes of Robert Lowell:* "Mr. Mazzaro gives us a number of hitherto unidentified sources for Lowell's ideas, allusions, and quotations.... What holds his book together and gives it special interest is his attempt to trace in Lowell's poems the dramatic outline of a highly significant spiritual career or destiny.... Many of Mr. Mazzaro's proposals deserve consideration and argument, but his verbal clumsiness and imprecision will, I am afraid, limit the full use of his book to an audience of unusually patient readers."

Modern American Poetry "... is a highly sophisticated collection, designed, most probably, to accompany a college level course of readings in poetry," writes Victor Howes in the *Christian Science Monitor.* "... Mr. Mazzaro has opted to represent a variety of schools: new critical, phenomenological, stylistic, mythic, and impressionistic."

BIOGRAPHICAL/CRITICAL SOURCES: American Literature, January, 1967; *New York Times Book Review,* January 8, 1967; *Christian Science Monitor,* July 16, 1970.

*   *   *

McALLASTER, Elva   1922-

PERSONAL: Born August 30, 1922, near Marienthal, Kan.; daughter of Rollin Marquis and Edna Pearl (Stahley) McAllaster. *Education:* Attended Garden City Junior College (now Community College), 1938-40; Greenville College, A.B., 1944; University of Illinois, A.M., 1945, Ph.D., 1948; postdoctoral study at University of London, 1948, Institut auf dem Rosenberg, Switzerland, 1962, and British Museum Library, 1963-64. *Religion:* Free Methodist. *Home:* 312 East

Beaumont, Greenville, Ill. 62246. *Office:* Department of English, Greenville College, Greenville, Ill. 62246.

CAREER: Seattle Pacific College, Seattle, Wash., associate professor, 1948-50, professor of English, 1950-56; Greenville College, Greenville, Ill., professor of English, 1956—. Poet-in-residence, Westmont College, 1971-72. *Member:* Modern Language Association of America, National Council of Teachers of English, Milton Society of America, National Audubon Society, National Cathedral Association, Conference on Christianity and Literature (co-founder; secretary, 1956-58), Sierra Club, Phi Beta Kappa.

WRITINGS: My Heart Hears Heaven's Reville (poetry), Light & Life Press, 1954; *Echoes from Intercession* (poetry), Moody, 1966; *Here and Now* (poetry), 1968; *Strettam* (fiction), Zondervan, 1972. Contributor of articles, short stories, and poems to newspapers and magazines.

WORK IN PROGRESS: A book of poems about Israel; a volume of her collected essays from periodicals; other poetry.

SIDELIGHTS: Elva McAllaster has been influenced by the works of Gerard Manley Hopkins, John Milton, Robert Browning, and C. S. Lewis.

AVOCATIONAL INTERESTS: Outdoors, photography, travel.

*   *   *

McALLISTER, Bruce (Hugh)   1946-

PERSONAL: Born October 17, 1946, in Baltimore, Md.; son of James Addams and Bernice (Lyons) McAllister; married Caroline Reid (an early childhood teacher), September 5, 1970. *Education:* Claremont Men's College, B.A., 1969; University of California, Irvine, M.F.A., 1971. *Residence:* Redlands, Calif. *Office:* Department of English, University of Redlands, Redlands, Calif. 92373.

CAREER: University of Redlands, Redlands, Calif., part-time visiting instructor in writing, 1971-72, assistant professor of English and director of writing program, 1974—. Rewriter for United Press International (UPI), 1967, and Doubleday Multimedia, 1969—; associate editor, WCPR Press, 1972—. *Member:* Science Fiction Writers of America, Coordinating Council of Literary Magazines. *Awards, honors:* Bread Loaf Writer's Conference scholar, 1972; Squaw Valley Community of Writers fellow, 1973.

WRITINGS: Humanity Prime, Ace, 1971; (contributor) Michael Malone and Myron Roberts, editors, *From Pop to Culture,* Holt, 1971; (contributor) Willis E. McNelly and Leon Stover, editors, *Above the Human Landscape,* Goodyear Publishing, 1972.

Work is represented in anthologies, including: *Ninth Annual of the Year's Best Science Fiction,* Simon & Schuster, 1963; *The Year's Best Science Fiction: 1969,* Putnam, 1971; *World's Best Science Fiction: 1970,* Ace, 1971; *Twenty Years of Fantasy and Science Fiction,* Putnam, 1971; *Mars: We Love You,* Doubleday, 1971; *Showcase,* Harper, 1973; *New Worlds #10,* Corgi Books, 1977; *Science Fiction and Fantasy,* Barron's, 1978; *100 Science Fiction Short Shorts,* Doubleday, 1978; *The Year's Best Science Fiction: 1977,* Thomas Nelson, 1978.

Contributor to science fiction magazines, including *Fantasy and Science Fiction, Galaxy, If,* and *Fantastic;* contributor of poetry and fiction to literary journals. Managing editor, "Best Science Fiction" series, Harrison & Aldiss, 1973-75.

WORK IN PROGRESS: Novel, poetry, short fiction.

AVOCATIONAL INTERESTS: Languages, archaeology, oceanography, the social sciences and natural sciences, painting and art history, literature, travel (has lived in Italy and traveled throughout Europe, with archaeological emphasis in England, France, and Italy).

* * *

McCALL, Robert B(ooth) 1940-

PERSONAL: Born June 21, 1940, in Milwaukee, Wis.; son of John I. (a metallurgist) and Blanche (Booth) McCall; married Rozanne Allison (a remedial reading specialist), June 13, 1962; children: Darin, Stacey. *Education:* DePauw University, A.B., 1962; University of Illinois, M.A., 1964, Ph.D., 1965. *Office:* Boys Town Center for the Study of Youth Development, Boys Town, Neb. 68010.

CAREER: University of North Carolina at Chapel Hill, assistant professor of psychology, 1966-68; Antioch College, Yellow Springs, Ohio, associate professor of psychology, 1968-77; Fels Research Institute, Yellow Springs, senior scientist and chairman of department of psychology, 1968-71, chief of section on perceptual cognitive development, 1971-77; Boys Town Center for the Study of Youth Development, Boys Town, Neb., fellow, 1977—. *Member:* American Association for the Advancement of Science, American Psychological Association (fellow), Society for Research in Child Development, Midwest Psychological Association, Phi Beta Kappa. *Awards, honors:* National Science Foundation post-doctoral fellow, Harvard University, 1965-66.

WRITINGS: Fundamental Statistics for Psychology, Harcourt, 1970, 2nd edition, with student guide, 1975; (with Jerome Kagan) *Change and Continuity in Infancy,* Wiley, 1971; *Intelligence and Heredity,* Learning Systems Co., 1975. Also author, with L. K. Conn, of student guide to *Psychology: An Introduction,* by Kagan and E. Havemann, Harcourt, 1968, 3rd edition with Havemann, 1976.

Contributor: P. Mussen, editor, *Manual of Child Psychology,* Wiley, 1970; Dwain N. Walcher and Donald L. Peters, editors, *Early Childhood: The Development of Self-regulatory Mechanisms,* Academic Press, 1971; U. Lehr and F. E. Weinert, editors, *Entwicklung und PersoenlichKelt,* Kohlhammer, 1975; M. Lewis, editor, *Origins of Intelligence,* Plenum, 1976; I. C. Uzgiris and F. Weizmann, editors, *The Structuring of Experience,* Plenum, in press; J. D. Osofsky, editor, *Handbook of Infant Development,* Wiley, in press; M. H. Bornstein and W. Kessen, editors, *Psychological Development from Infancy,* Erlbaum, in press. Contributor to *International Encyclopedia of Neurology, Psychiatry, Psychoanalysis, and Psychology* and *Monographs of the Society of Research in Child Development.* Contributor of articles and reviews to *Journal of Experimental Child Psychology, Child Development, Developmental Psychology, Science, American Psychologist, Journal of Comparative and Physiological Psychology* and other publications. Member of editorial board, *Child Development Journal, Journal of Experimental Child Psychology,* and *Intelligence.*

* * *

McCASLIN, Nellie 1914-

PERSONAL: Born August 20, 1914, in Cleveland, Ohio; daughter of Paul G. and Nellie McCaslin. *Education:* Western Reserve University (now Case Western Reserve University), B.A., 1936, M.A., 1937; New York University, Ph.D., 1957. *Politics:* Democrat. *Religion:* Presbyterian. *Home:* 40 East Tenth St., New York, N.Y. 10003. *Office:*

Program in Educational Theatre, New York University, Washington Square, New York, N.Y. 10003.

CAREER: Tudor Hall, Indianapolis, Ind., teacher of dramatic arts, 1937-44; National College of Education, Evanston, Ill., instructor in drama and English, 1944-56; Mills College of Education, New York City, drama instructor and dean of students, 1957-72; New York University, Program in Educational Theatre, New York City, member of faculty, 1972—. Instructor, Columbia University, part-time, 1961-67. *Member:* American Theatre Association (fellow), American Association of University Professors, Children's Theatre Association of America (former regional governor; national president). *Awards, honors:* Jennie Heiden Award, 1968, for excellence in theatre for children.

WRITINGS: Legends in Action, Row-Peterson, 1945; *More Legends in Action,* Row-Peterson, 1950; *Tall Tales and Tall Men,* Macrae, 1956; *Pioneers in Petticoats,* Row-Peterson, 1961; *Little Snow Girl,* Coach House Press, 1963; *The Rabbit Who Wanted Red Wings,* Coach House Press, 1963; *Creative Dramatics in the Classroom,* McKay, 1968, 2nd edition, 1974; *Theatre for Children: A History,* University of Oklahoma Press, 1971; *Act Now!,* S. G. Phillips, 1975; *Children and Drama,* McKay, 1975; *Theatre for Young Audiences,* McKay, 1977; *Puppet Fun,* McKay, 1977.

* * *

McCLELLAN, Robert F., Jr. 1934-

PERSONAL: Born June 6, 1934, in Chicago, Ill.; son of Robert F. and Katherine (Shaw) McClellan; married Sara A. Greer (a department head in speech pathology), June 23, 1959; children: Mary, Karen, Sara, Martha. *Education:* Attended Miami University, Oxford, Ohio; Michigan State University, B.A., 1956, Ph.D., 1964; Church Divinity School of the Pacific, B.D., 1959. *Home:* 424 Cedar St., Marquette, Mich. 49855. *Office:* Department of History, Northern Michigan University, Marquette, Mich. 49855.

CAREER: Clergyman of Episcopal Church, serving in Cordova, Alaska, 1959-60, as Episcopal chaplain of Michigan State University, East Lansing, 1961-62, and in DeWitt, Mich., 1962-64; Ohio State University, Columbus, instructor in history, 1964-65; Northern Michigan University, Marquette, associate professor of history, 1965—. Visiting summer professor, Michigan State University, 1968. *Member:* American Historical Association, Organization of American Historians, American Association of University Professors, American Civil Liberties Union. *Awards, honors:* National Endowment for the Humanities grant, summer, 1970.

WRITINGS: The Heathen Chinee: The American Image of China, 1890-1905, Ohio State University Press, 1971. Contributor to historical journals.

WORK IN PROGRESS: Two books, *For Whites Only: The Racial Factor in American Foreign Policy* and *Anti-Japanese Attitudes in American History.*

* * *

McCLELLAND, Charles E(dgar III) 1940-

PERSONAL: Born July 29, 1940, in San Antonio, Tex.; son of Charles Edgar, Jr. and Frances (Hobbs) McClelland. *Education:* Princeton University, A.B., 1962; attended University of Munich, 1960-61; Yale University, M.A., 1963, Ph.D., 1967. *Home:* 1002 Richmond Dr. N.E., Albuquerque, N.M. 87106. *Office:* Department of History, University of New Mexico, Albuquerque, N.M. 87131.

CAREER: Princeton University, Princeton, N.J., instructor in history, 1966-68; University of Pennsylvania, Philadelphia, assistant professor of European history, 1968-74; University of New Mexico, Albuquerque, associate professor of history, 1974—. Member: American Historical Association, Phi Beta Kappa. Awards, honors: Woodrow Wilson fellowship, 1962.

WRITINGS: The German Historians and England: A Study in 19th-Century Views, Cambridge University Press, 1971; (with S. P. Scher) Postwar German Culture, Dutton, 1974.

WORK IN PROGRESS: State, Society and University in Germany, 1700-1914.

*   *   *

McCLINTOCK, Theodore 1902-1971

1902—November 21, 1971; American editor, author, and translator of books in German. Obituaries: New York Times, November 22, 1971; Publishers Weekly, December 20, 1971.

*   *   *

McCLOSKEY, Maxine E(laine) 1927-

PERSONAL: Born April 26, 1927, in Portland, Ore.; daughter of Leslie Z. (a businessman) and Lydia (Sarajarvi) Mugg; married Clyde R. Johnson (died March 4, 1964); married J. Michael McCloskey (executive director of Sierra Club), June 17, 1965; children: (first marriage) Claire, Laura, James, Rosemary. Education: University of California, Berkeley, A.A., 1948; Portland State College (now University), B.S., 1962; Reed College, M.A., 1963. Politics: Democrat. Religion: Unitarian Universalist. Home: 93 Florada Ave., Piedmont, Calif. 94610.

CAREER: St. Helen's Hall, Portland, Ore., instructor in social studies, 1963-64; Portland State College (now University), Portland, instructor in history, 1964-65; College of Marin, Kentfield, Calif., instructor in history, 1965-66; Sierra Club, San Francisco, Calif., executive secretary for Tenth and Eleventh Biennial Wilderness Conferences, 1967, 1969; Merritt College, Oakland, Calif., instructor in history and political science, 1968-77. Oregon secretary to U.S. Senator Richard L. Neuberger, 1955-56, 1959; campaign assistant to U.S. Senator Maurine B. Neuberger, 1960; alternate delegate and member of platform committee, Democratic National Convention, 1964; Project Jonah (for conservation of whales, porpoises and dolphins), secretary of board of directors, 1973, president, 1977—; organizer of symposium on endangered species, American Association for the Advancement of Science, 1974; chairman, Citizens Nongame Advisory Committee of California Department of Fish and Game, 1975—; delegate, International Union for Conservation of Nature and Natural Resources, 1977. Member: American Historical Association, Sierra Club, Oregon Historical Society.

WRITINGS: (Editor with James P. Gilligan) Wilderness and the Quality of Life, Sierra Club, 1969; (editor) Wilderness, the Edge of Knowledge, Sierra Club, 1970. Contributor to New Book of Knowledge. Editor of publications, Federation of Western Outdoor Clubs, 1973-75; editor of annual reports, California Citizen Non-game Advisory Committee, 1976, 1977.

*   *   *

McCONICA, James Kelsey 1930-

PERSONAL: Born April 24, 1930, in Luseland, Saskatche-wan, Canada; son of Thomas Henry and Edith Wilma (Crates) McConica. Education: University of Saskatchewan, B.A. (first class honors), 1951; Oxford University, B.A. (first class honors, history), 1954, M.A., 1957, D.Phil., 1963; University of Toronto, M.A. (philosophy), 1964. Home: 59 Queen's Park Crescent, Toronto, Ontario, Canada. Office: Pontifical Institute of Mediaeval Studies, Toronto, Ontario, Canada.

CAREER: Roman Catholic priest; ordained in Congregation of St. Basil, 1968. University of Saskatchewan, Saskatoon, instructor, 1956-57, assistant professor of history, 1957-62; Pontifical Institute of Mediaeval Studies, Toronto, Ontario, associate professor, 1967-70, professor of history, 1971—; University of Toronto, Centre of Medieval Studies, Toronto, professor, 1972—, associate director, 1973-76. Oxford University, visiting fellow, All Souls College, 1969-71, 1977, special Ford lecturer, 1977; fellow, Davis Center for Historical Studies, Princeton University, 1971. Canadian representative to International Commission for the History of Universities, International Congress of Historical Sciences, 1976—. Member: Royal Historical Society (England; fellow, 1964—), British Records Association, Oxford Historical Society, American Historical Association, Renaissance Society of America, American Society for Reformation Research, Canadian Association of Rhodes Scholars, Exeter College Association (Oxford). Awards, honors: Rhodes scholar, 1951; Guggenheim fellow, 1969-70; Killam senior research scholar, 1976-77.

WRITINGS: English Humanists and Reformation Politics under Henry VIII and Edward VI, Clarendon Press, 1965; (contributor) J. J. Coppen, editor, Scrinium Erasmianum, Volume II, E. J. Brill, 1969; (contributor) George Watson, editor, New Cambridge Bibliography of English Literature, Volume I, Cambridge University Press, 1972; (contributor) Charles Trinkaus, editor, The Pursuit of Holiness in Late Medieval and Renaissance Religion, E. J. Brill, 1974; (contributor) Lawrence Stone, editor, The University in Society, Volume I, Princeton University Press, 1974; (editor) The Correspondence of Erasmus, Letters 298 to 445 (1515-1516), University of Toronto Press, 1976; (editor) The Correspondence of Erasmus, Letters 446 to 593 (1516-1517), University of Toronto Press, 1977. Historical editor and chairman of editorial board, "Collected Works of Erasmus" series, University of Toronto Press, 1969—. Member of editorial board, History of Education (History of Education Society, England).

WORK IN PROGRESS: Tudor Oxford, Volume III of "The History of the University of Oxford," for Clarendon Press; Henry VIII and the Reformation, for English Universities Press (London).

*   *   *

McCORISON, Marcus Allen 1926-

PERSONAL: Born July 17, 1926, in Lancaster, Wis.; son of Joseph Lyle, Jr. (a Congregational minister) and Ruth (Mink) McCorison; married Janet Knop (an architectural preservationist), June 10, 1950; children: Marcus, Judith, Andrew, Mary, James, Peter. Education: Ripon College, A.B., 1950; University of Vermont, M.A., 1951; Columbia University, M.S. in L.S., 1954. Politics: Democrat. Religion: Christian (Congregationalist). Home: 43 Laconia Rd., Worcester, Mass. 01609. Office: American Antiquarian Society, 185 Salisbury St., Worcester, Mass. 01609.

CAREER: Kellogg-Hubbard Library, Montpelier, Vt., librarian, 1954-55; Dartmouth College, Hanover, N.H., chief of Rare Books Department, 1955-59; University of Iowa libraries, Iowa City, head of Special Collections, 1959-60; American Antiquarian Society, Worcester, Mass., librarian, 1960—, director, 1967—. Consultant, Free Public Library Commission, state of Vermont, 1957-59; overseer, Old Sturbridge Village, 1968—; member of advisory committee, Elutherian Mills-Hagley Foundation, 1971-74. *Military service:* U.S. Naval Reserve, 1944-46; U.S. Army, 1951-52; became first lieutenant. *Member:* American Library Association, Association of College and Research Libraries (chairman, rare books section, 1965-66), American Antiquarian Society, Bibliographical Society of America (second vice-president, 1976—), Independent Research Libraries Association (chairman, 1972-73), Organization of American Historians, Massachusetts Historical Society, Vermont Historical Society (trustee, 1956-66), New Hampshire Library Association (president, 1959), Beta Phi Mu, Grolier Club, Club of Odd Volumes.

WRITINGS: Vermont Imprints, 1778-1820, American Antiquarian Society, 1963, additions and corrections, 1968, additions and corrections, 1973; (editor) *Catalogue of the Redwood Library Company of Newport, Rhode Island, 1764,* Yale University Press, 1965; *A Society's Chief Joys,* American Antiquarian Society, 1969; (editor and author of introduction) Isaiah Thomas, *The History of Printing,* Imprint Society, 1970. Editor, *Proceedings* of the American Antiquarian Society, 1960-67.

WORK IN PROGRESS: Research on the history of printing and publishing.

AVOCATIONAL INTERESTS: Book collecting, amateur printing, hiking in small mountains.

*   *   *

McCRACKEN, Esther   1902-1971

June 25, 1902—August 11, 1971; British playwright and actress. Obituaries: *New York Times,* August 13, 1971; *Washington Post,* August 14, 1971.

*   *   *

McCRAW, Thomas Kincaid   1940-

PERSONAL: Born September 11, 1940, in Corinth, Miss.; son of John Carey (an engineer) and Olive (Kincaid) McCraw; married Susan Morehead, September 22, 1962; children: Elizabeth, Thomas. *Education:* University of Mississippi, B.A., 1962; University of Wisconsin, M.A., 1968, Ph.D., 1970. *Residence:* Austin, Tex. *Office:* Department of History, University of Texas, Austin, Texas. 78712.

CAREER: University of Texas at Austin, assistant professor, 1970-74, associate professor of history, 1974—. Visiting associate professor of business administration, Harvard Business School, Harvard University, 1976-78. *Military service:* U.S. Navy, 1962-66; became lieutenant. *Member:* American Historical Association, Organization of American Historians, State Historical Society of Wisconsin. *Awards, honors:* William P. Lyons Master's Essay Award from Loyola University of Chicago and Loyola University Press, 1969.

WRITINGS: Morgan vs. Lilienthal: The Feud within the TVA, Loyola University Press, 1970; *TVA and the Power Fight, 1933-1939,* Lippincott, 1971; (contributor) Lewis L. Gould, editor, *The Progressive Era,* Syracuse University Press, 1974. Contributor to *American Heritage* and *History Review.*

WORK IN PROGRESS: Research on government regulation of business in twentieth-century America.

McDONALD, Pauline   1907-

PERSONAL: Born April 20, 1907, in Remson, N.Y.; daughter of Orson (a businessman) and Edith (Hughes) Williams; married Dennis Anthony McDonald (owner of a nursery school), October 12, 1935; children: Patricia Ann (Mrs. James Fountain), Kay Roberta (Mrs. Richard Heineman). *Education:* Oneonta State Normal School (now State University of New York College at Oneonta), State Kindergarten-Elementary Teaching Credential, 1928; graduate study at Columbia University, University of California, Los Angeles, and University of Southern California. *Politics:* Republican. *Religion:* Methodist. *Home:* 5243 Shenandoah Ave., Los Angeles, Calif. 90056. *Office:* Palms Tiny Tot Nursery School, 3614 Motor Ave., Los Angeles, Calif. 90034.

CAREER: Former public school kindergarten teacher in New York and California; Palms Tiny Tot Nursery School, Los Angeles, Calif., director, 1949—. First vice-president, Culver City (Calif.) Guidance Clinic, 1971; member of board of Didi Hirsch Mental Health Center (Culver City), 1973—. *Member:* Southern California Association for the Education of Young Children (treasurer, 1971).

WRITINGS: (With Doris V. Brown) *Creative Art for Home and School,* Lawrence Publishing (Los Angeles), 1969, revised edition, Borden Publishing, 1975; (with Brown) *Learning Begins at Home: A Stimulus for a Child's I.Q.,* Lawrence Publishing, 1969. Contributor of articles to *Home Life* and other magazines.

SIDELIGHTS: Pauline McDonald told *CA:* "The reason that I spend my spare moments writing magazine articles is because parents learn everything else in life but about 'parenthood.' Through my years of experience in the field of early childhood education, I find joy and self-worth in sharing these experiences with parents who are seeking simple answers."

*   *   *

McDONNELL, Helen M(argaret)   1923-

PERSONAL: Born July 31, 1923, in Bogota, N.J.; daughter of Maurice Martin (a civil servant) and Helen (Vollmer) McDonnell. *Education:* Monmouth College, West Long Branch, N.J., A.A., 1956, A.B., 1958; Seton Hall University, M.A., 1959; Rutgers University, Ph.D., 1970. *Religion:* Roman Catholic. *Home:* 2927 Bangs Ave., Neptune, N.J. 07753. *Office:* Ocean Township High School, West Park Ave., Oakhurst, N.J. 07755.

CAREER: Civil servant, Fort Monmouth, N.J., 1942-58; high school English teacher in Asury Park, N.J., 1958-59; Wall High School, Belmar, N.J., chairman of English department, 1959-64; Ocean Township High School, Oakhurst, N.J., English supervisor, 1965—. Instructor in English, Monmouth College, 1960-62. *Member:* National Council of Teachers of English (chairman of committee on comparative and world literature, 1974—), National Education Association, National Conference of Secondary School English Department Chairmen, New Jersey Association of Teachers of English, Delta Kappa Gamma. *Awards, honors:* Ford Foundation grant, summer, 1959; English-Speaking Union scholarship, Oxford University, summer, 1964; Woodrow Wilson fellowship, 1964-65.

WRITINGS: (Compiler) *Nobel Parade: Selections by Winners of the Award for Literature,* Scott, Foresman, 1975.

"Man in Literature" series; compiler with James E. Miller and Robert O'Neal, except as indicated; published by Scott,

Foresman in 1970, except as indicated: *Man in Literature; Teutonic Literature in English Translation; Literature from Greek and Roman Antiquity; Italian Literature in Translation; Russian and Eastern European Literature; Black African Voices; Translations from the French; Literature of the Eastern World; Literature from Spain and the Americas;* (compiler with Miller and Myrtle Jones) *England in Literature,* revised edition (McDonnell was not associated with earlier edition), 1973. Contributor of articles and reviews to *Scholastic Teacher.*

WORK IN PROGRESS: Revisions of *England in Literature* and *Counterpoint in Literature,* for Scott, Foresman.

SIDELIGHTS: Helen McDonnell told *CA:* "Finding material to suit the grade level and scope of an anthology is a fascinating research task; writing the 'frame' is an absorbing creative task in that what emerges must be greater than the sum of its parts. In short, editing anthologies has been for me an intensely satisfying experience."

* * *

McDONNELL, Kilian (Perry) 1921-

PERSONAL: Born September 16, 1921, in Great Falls, Mont.; son of Joseph P. and Anna Dorothea (Auerbach) McDonnell. *Education:* St. John's University, Collegeville, Minn., B.A., 1947; University of Ottawa, S.T.L., 1960; graduate study in theology at University of Tuebingen, 1962-63, University of Muenster, 1963, and University of Heidelberg, 1964; Theological Faculty Trier, Trier, Germany, Ph.D., 1964. *Politics:* Democrat. *Home:* St. John's Abbey, Collegeville, Minn. 56321. *Office:* Institute for Ecumenical and Cultural Research, St. John's University, Collegeville, Minn. 56321.

CAREER: Roman Catholic priest of Benedictine Order; spent four years in parish work, three years in Hastings, Minn., and one year in Detroit Lakes, Minn.; St. John's University, Collegeville, Minn., instructor, 1955-60, associate professor, 1965-76, professor of theology, 1976—, founder of Institute for Ecumenical and Cultural Research, 1967, executive director, 1968-73, president, 1973—. Consultor and participant in Uniting Council of World Alliance of Reformed Churches and World Congregational Fellowship in Nairobi, 1970; chairman of Vatican delegation, Vatican consultation with International Alliance of Reformed Churches (Presbyterian-Congregationalist), 1970—; chairman of Vatican delegation, International Vatican-Pentecostal Churches dialog, 1971—; liason between the Vatican and the Catholic Charismatic Renewal, 1973—; secretary of national Presbyterian-Roman Catholic consultation; member of national Luther-Roman Catholic consultation. *Member:* Catholic Theological Society, Society for the Scientific Study of Religion.

WRITINGS: Nothing but Christ, Liturgical Press, 1954; *The Restless Christian,* Sheed, 1958; *John Calvin, the Church and the Eucharist,* Princeton University Press, 1967; (editor) *The Holy Spirit and Power,* Doubleday, 1975; *The Charismatic Renewal and the Churches,* Seabury, 1976.

Contributor: *Research in Religions,* Lumen Vitae Press, 1957; Daniel Callahan, editor *Symposium on God: Father, Son and Holy Spirit,* Sheed, 1969. Contributor to theological journals and to lay-oriented religious periodicals including *Lumen Vitae.* Columnist, *Sign,* 1954-61; scripture editor, *Worship,* 1958-60; editor, *Sponsa Regis,* 1958-64; associate editor, *Worship,* 1969—, and *One in Christ,* 1971—; contributing editor, *New Covenant,* 1973—.

WORK IN PROGRESS: The Charismatic Renewal and Ecumenism.

* * *

McFEELY, William S(hield) 1930-

PERSONAL: Born September 25, 1930, in New York, N.Y.; son of William C. and Marguerite (Shield) McFeely; married Mary Drake (a librarian), September 13, 1952; children: W. Drake, Eliza, Jennifer. *Education:* Amherst College, B.A., 1952; Yale University, M.A., 1962, Ph.D., 1966. *Home:* 23 Ashfield Lane, South Hadley, Mass. 01075. *Office:* Department of History, Mount Holyoke College, South Hadley, Mass. 01075.

CAREER: First National City Bank, New York, N.Y., assistant cashier, 1952-61; Yale University, New Haven, Conn., assistant professor, 1966-69, associate professor of history, 1969-70; Mount Holyoke College, South Hadley, Mass., professor of history, 1970—, dean of faculty, 1970-73. *Member:* American Historical Association, Association for the Study of Negro Life and History, Organization of American Historians.

WRITINGS: Yankee Stepfather: General O. O. Howard and the Freedmen, Yale University Press, 1968; (with Thomas J. Ladenburg) *The Black Man in the Land of Equality,* Hayden, 1969; (contributor) J. C. Curtis and C. C. Gould, editors, *The Black Experience in America,* University of Texas Press, 1970; (contributor) N. I. Huggins and M. Kilson, editors, *Key Issues in the Afro-American Experience,* Harcourt, 1971.

WORK IN PROGRESS: Research in the Grant administration, in Black urban communities, and in the 1786 rebellion in western Massachusetts.

BIOGRAPHICAL/CRITICAL SOURCES: New York Review of Books, February 27, 1969; *New York Times,* April 9, 1972.

* * *

McGEEHAN, Robert 1933-

PERSONAL: Born July 3, 1933. *Education:* Washington and Lee University, A.B., 1954; Fordham University Law School, J.D., 1957; Columbia University, Ph.D., 1969. *Office:* Department of Political Science, City College of the City University of New York, Convent Ave. and 138th St., New York, N.Y. 10031.

CAREER: Admitted to Bar of the State of New Jersey, 1958; Columbia University, New York City, research assistant, 1962-67, teaching assistant, 1963-64, instructor in government, 1967-69; Kingsborough Community College of the City University of New York, Brooklyn, N.Y., instructor in political science, 1965-66; City College of the City University of New York, New York City, lecturer, 1967-70, assistant professor of political science, 1970—; Graduate School and University Center of the City University of New York, New York City, research associate in European studies, 1971—. *Military service:* U.S. Army, Intelligence Corps, 1958-60. *Member:* International Studies Association, International Institute for Strategic Studies, American Political Science Association, American Society of International Law, American Association of University Professors, Conference Group on German Politics, New Jersey Bar Association.

WRITINGS: The German Rearmament Question: American Diplomacy and European Defense after World War II, University of Illinois Press, 1971. Contributor to *War/Peace*

Report, Journal of International Affairs, and *American Political Science Review.*†

*   *   *

McGILVERY, Laurence 1932-
(Mercury E. C. L. Van Geil)

PERSONAL: Born May 21, 1932 in Los Angeles, Calif.; son of Neil Lee and Joan (Girard) McGilvery; married Geraldine Malloy (a rare book dealer), July 5, 1955; children: Lynette, Lise, Erin, Justin. *Education:* Attended Los Angeles City College, 1949-51; Pomona College, B.A., 1954. *Politics:* "Registered Democrat." *Address:* P.O. Box 852, La Jolla, Calif. 92038.

CAREER: Walter Dorwin Teague Associates (engineering consultants), Pomona and Sunnyvale, Calif., engineer, 1955-60; The Nexus (paperback bookshop), La Jolla, Calif., owner and manager with wife, 1960-66; Laurence McGilvery, La Jolla, owner and manager with wife of mail order business selling rare and out-of-print books on fine arts, and editing and publishing books on the fine arts, 1965—. *Member:* Antiquarian Booksellers Association of America, Art Libraries Society of North America, American Civil Liberties Union.

WRITINGS: (Editor) *Artforum, 1962-1968: A Cumulative Index to the First Six Volumes,* Laurence McGilvery, 1970; (contributor) George Dowden, compiler, *A Bibliography of Works by Allen Ginsberg: October, 1943 to July 1, 1967,* City Lights, 1971; (editor with Diane di Prima) *The Floating Bear, Numbers 1-37, 1961-68: A Complete, Annotated, Facsimile Edition,* Laurence McGilvery, 1972; (contributor) Richard Kempton, compiler, *Art Nouveau: An Annotated Bibliography,* Hennessey & Ingalls, 1977.

WORK IN PROGRESS: Writing in the fields of art reference and bibliography.

*   *   *

McGINN, John T. 1900(?)-1972

1900(?)—May 28, 1972; American Roman Catholic Paulist priest and author. Obituaries: *New York Times,* May 29, 1972; *Washington Post,* May 30, 1972.

*   *   *

McGLOIN, John Bernard 1912-

PERSONAL: Born March 8, 1912, in San Francisco, Calif.; son of Daniel J. (a civil servant) and Mary Loreta (Kelly) McGloin. *Education:* University of Santa Clara, A.B., 1935; Gonzaga University, M.A., 1936; St. Louis University, Ph.D., 1948. *Politics:* Democrat. *Home and office:* Department of History, University of San Francisco, Golden Gate at Parker Ave., San Francisco, Calif. 94117.

CAREER: Roman Catholic priest of Society of Jesus (Jesuits); University of San Francisco, San Francisco, Calif., assistant professor, 1948-52, associate professor, 1952-63, professor of western and California history, 1963—. Former member of San Francisco Landmarks Preservation Advisory Board. *Member:* American Catholic Historical Association, Western History Association, California Historical Society. *Awards, honors:* Award of Merit, California Historical Society; Distinguished Teaching Award, University of San Francisco, 1972.

WRITINGS: Eloquent Indian: The Life of James Bouchard, California Jesuit, Stanford University Press, 1949; *California's First Archbishop: The Life of Joseph S. Ale-*

many, *O.P.,* Herder & Herder, 1966; *Jesuits by the Golden Gate: The Society of Jesus in San Francisco, 1849-1969,* University of San Francisco Press, 1972. Contributor of more than twenty-five articles on early California Catholic history to journals. Former member of board of editors, *Pacific Historical Review.*

WORK IN PROGRESS: Continuing research for a textbook, *San Francisco: The Story of a City.*

*   *   *

McINNIS, Noel F. 1936-

PERSONAL: Born October 29, 1936, in Freeport, Ill.; son of Frederick (a musician) and Carol (Thompson) McInnis; married June Knudsen, December 21, 1958 (divorced, 1975); children: Holly, Scott. *Education:* Kendall College, A.A., 1956; Northwestern University, B.S., 1958, M.A., 1962. *Home address:* P.O. Box 3178, Aspen, Colo. 81611.

CAREER: Kendall College, Evanston, Ill., director of admissions, 1959-60, chairman of social science department, 1965-67, director of educational advancement, 1965-70; Center for Curriculum Design (non-profit educational foundation), Evanston, director, 1970-74; free-lance writer and educational consultant in Aspen, Colo., 1974—. *Military service:* U.S. Army Reserve, 1960-66.

WRITINGS: (Editor with others) Robert Theobald, *An Alternative Future for America* (speeches and essays), Swallow Press, 1968, revised and enlarged edition published as *An Alternative Future for America Two,* 1970; (editor with Richard L. Heiss) *Can Man Care for the Earth?,* Abingdon, 1971; *You Are an Environment: Teaching/Learning Environmental Values,* Center for Curriculum Design, 1972, 2nd edition, Museum and Science Center, 1977; (editor with others) *Somewhere Else: A Living/Learning Catalog,* Swallow Press, 1973; (editor with Don Albrecht) *What Makes Education Environmental,* Data Courier, 1975; (co-author) *The Whole Earth Happens as You Do: The Balance of Lifekind,* Environments for Learning, 1975; *How One-derful To Be,* Supper-Money Press, 1977; *Everywhere I Go, There I Am,* Supper-Money Press, 1977.

WORK IN PROGRESS: A book of poetry and prose entitled *Living and Loving on the Tao.*

*   *   *

McINTOSH, Christopher 1943-

PERSONAL: Born September 21, 1943, in Tunbridge Wells, Kent, England; son of Angus (a university professor) and Barbara (Bainbridge) McIntosh; married Robina Court, July 31, 1965; children: Angus James, Jason Stuart. *Education:* Christ Church, Oxford, M.A. (with honors), 1965. *Home:* 13 North Rd., Berkhamsted, Hertfordshire, England.

CAREER: Country Life (magazine), London, England, editorial administrator and writer of feature articles on archaeology and folklore, 1967—.

WRITINGS: The Astrologers and Their Creed: An Historical Outline, foreword by Agehananda Bharati, Hutchinson, 1969, Praeger, 1970; *Astrology,* Macdonald & Co., 1970; *Eliphas Levi and the French Occult Revival,* Rider & Co., 1972.

AVOCATIONAL INTERESTS: Painting, walking.

McKAY, Don(ald) 1932-

PERSONAL: Born August 13, 1932, in Kearny, N.J.; son of Alexander (a decorator) and Ruth (Barker) McKay; married Jo Ann Aust (a nursery school teacher), July 13, 1957; children: Robert, James, Donna. *Education:* New Jersey State Teachers College (now Jersey City State College), B.A., 1954; Teachers College, Columbia University, further study, 1957-59; Paterson State College (now William Paterson College of New Jersey), M.A., 1966; Montclair State College, further study, 1975-78. *Politics:* Independent. *Home:* 8 Fairway, Maywood, N.J. 07607. *Office:* Nanuet Public Schools, Nanuet, N.Y. 10954.

CAREER: Teacher in elementary schools in New York and New Jersey, 1954-64; Emerson Junior-Senior High School, Emerson, N.J., reading specialist, 1964-68; Nanuet Public Schools, Nanuet, N.Y., reading consultant, 1968—. Instructor in Reading Clinic, Fairleigh Dickinson University, 1962-66; instructor in adult education courses, 1964-66; adjunct instructor, graduate school, College of New Rochelle, 1972—. Maywood Board of Education, elected member, 1969-75, president, 1972. *Military service:* U.S. Army, 1955-57. *Member:* International Reading Association (president of North Jersey Council, 1968-69).

WRITINGS: (Editor) *Wild Wheels,* Dell 1969; (editor) *On Two Wheels,* Dell, 1971. Member of selection board, *Weekly Reader* Children's Book Club, Xerox Education Publications, 1970—.

WORK IN PROGRESS: Studying children's literature and psycholinguistic learning theories.

SIDELIGHTS: Don McKay told *CA,* "One of the joys of teaching is watching kids read—a beautiful sight often missed by those attempting to teach without providing time for kids to learn."

*   *   *

McKEAN, John Richard 1939-

PERSONAL: Born January 15, 1939, in Centralia, Wis.; son of John B. (a newspaper publisher) and Helen M. (Welch) McKean. *Education:* University of Washington, Seattle, B.A., 1960, M.A., 1964, Ph.D., 1967. *Home address:* Route 5, Box 269-A, Fort Collins, Colo. 80521. *Office:* Department of Economics, Colorado State University, Fort Collins, Colo. 80521.

CAREER: University of Alberta, Edmonton, assistant professor of economics, 1965-66; University of Washington, Seattle, lecturer in business administration, 1966-68; University of Idaho, Moscow, assistant professor of economics, 1968-69; Colorado State University, Fort Collins, associate professor, 1969-74, professor of economics, 1974—. Contracting and consulting researcher for various organizations, including Bureau of Land Management, Economic Research Service, and the state of Colorado. *Member:* American Economic Association, Econometric Society, Western Regional Science Association, Western Economic Association, Omicron Delta Epsilon.

WRITINGS: (Contributor) John Lindauer, editor, *Macroeconomic Readings,* Free Press, 1968; (editor with Ronald Wykstra) *Readings in Economics,* Harper, 1971; (with Wykstra) *Study Guide* to accompany *Introductory Economics,* Harper, 1971; *An Economic Analysis of Water Use in Colorado's Economy,* Environmental Resource Center, 1975; (with S. L. Gray and others) *Economic Analysis of Water Use in Boulder, Larimer, and Weld Counties, Colorado,* Colorado State Experiment Station, 1976. Contributor

to journals, including *American Economist, Journal of Business,* and *Journal of Water Resources Research.*

WORK IN PROGRESS: Analysis of Water and Energy Shortages in Colorado; Regional Coal Demands in the United States: An Econometric Study; A Benefits Analysis of Yosemite National Park.

*   *   *

McKEAN, Roland N(eely) 1917-

PERSONAL: Born October 30, 1917, in Mulberry Grove, Ill.; married Anne Webster (an occupational therapy aid), March 28, 1944; children: Margaret A. (Mrs. John P. Peraza), John V. *Education:* University of Chicago, A.B., 1939, A.M. and Ph.D., 1948. *Office:* Department of Economics, University of Virginia, Charlottesville, Va. 22903.

CAREER: Vanderbilt University, Nashville, Tenn., assistant professor of economics, 1948-51; RAND Corp., Santa Monica, Calif., research economist, 1951-63; University of California, Los Angeles, professor of public finance, 1964-68; University of Virginia, Charlottesville, professor of public finance, 1968—. *Military service:* U.S. Army Air Forces, 1941-45; became first lieutenant; received Distinguished Flying Cross with cluster. *Member:* American Economic Association, Southern Economic Association (president, 1972). *Awards, honors:* Social Science Research Council grant, 1961-62; Fulbright research scholar in Glasgow, 1962.

WRITINGS: Efficiency in Government through Systems Analysis, Wiley, 1958; (with Charles J. Hitch) *Economics of Defense in the Nuclear Age,* Harvard University, 1960; (with Joseph A. Kershaw) *Teacher Shortages and Salary Schedules,* McGraw, 1962; (editor) *Issues in Defense Economics,* National Bureau of Economic Research, 1967; *Public Spending,* McGraw, 1968. Contributor to professional journals. Member of board of editors, *American Economic Review,* 1962-64.

WORK IN PROGRESS: Research in implications of different resource or property rights, especially resource rights of officials in government.

*   *   *

McKINNEY, Eleanor Ruth 1918-

PERSONAL: Born August 6, 1918, in Comstock, Neb.; daughter of Chester Arthur (a teacher) and Elsie (Gaddis) McKinney. *Education:* New Jersey State Teachers College (now Trenton State College), B.S., 1939; Columbia University, B.L.S., 1949; Western Michigan University, Ed.S., 1967. *Politics:* Republican. *Religion:* Methodist. *Home:* 3226 Tamsin Ave., Kalamazoo, Mich. 49008. *Office:* School of Librarianship, Western Michigan University, Kalamazoo, Mich. 49001.

CAREER: Junior high school teacher and librarian in Oaklyn, N.J., 1939-41; high school librarian in Ocean Grove, N.J., 1941-46; elementary school librarian in East Orange, N.J., 1946-49, South Orange-Maplewood, N.J., 1949-54, and Montclair, N.J., 1956-66; Western Michigan University, Kalamazoo, visiting summer professor, 1966, assistant professor, 1967-71, associate professor of librarianship, 1971—. Field services instructor, Newark State College (now Keane College of New Jersey), 1964-65; visiting summer professor, Rutgers University, 1964, 1965. *Member:* American Association of School Librarians, American Library Association, Michigan Association of School Librarians, Beta Phi Mu.

WRITINGS: (With Valerie Noble) *The Good Seed,*

Western Michigan University Press, 1970. Contributor to library and education journals. Columnist for *Library Journal,* 1963-65.

* * *

McLAUGHLIN, Terence (Patrick) 1928-

PERSONAL: Born December 21, 1928, in Essex, England; son of Robert Sidney (a company director) and Emily (Gardner) McLaughlin; married Eve Pearson (a genealogist), July 15, 1950; children: Nicholas Moray, Carey Sheridan, Lindsay Claire (daughter), Antony Roger. *Education:* University of Southampton, B.Sc., 1950. *Home and office:* "Varneys," 18 Rudds Lane, Haddenham, Buckinghamshire, England. *Agent:* Laurence Pollinger Ltd., 18 Maddox St., London W1R OEU, England.

CAREER: Unilever Ltd., London, England, research manager, 1954-60; Lever Industrial, London, technical director, 1960-67; self-employed technical consultant in Twickenham, England, 1968—. Director, Quadriga Products Ltd. (chemical manufacturing company); consultant to Consumers' Association. *Member:* International Solar Energy Society, Royal Institute of Chemistry (London; associate member).

WRITINGS: (With J. B. Wilkinson) *Modern Cosmeticology,* Hill, 1962; *The Cleaning, Hygiene, and Maintenance Handbook,* Business Publications, 1969, Prentice-Hall, 1972; *Music and Communication,* St. Martin's, 1970; *Dirt: A History of the Western World as Seen through the Uses and Abuses of Dirt,* Stein & Day, 1971 (published in England as *Coprophilia,* Cassell, 1971); *The Gilded Lily,* Cassell, 1972; *A House for the Future,* Independent Television Books, 1976; *Make Your Own Electricity,* David & Charles, 1977. Contributor of articles to *Daily Telegraph* (London); contributor to television and radio broadcasts on pollution and music.

WORK IN PROGRESS: Extension of the psychological/neurophysiological theory of aesthetics outlined in *Music and Communication* into a larger book, *The Human Equations of Music;* research on variations in human modes of thinking.

SIDELIGHTS: Terence McLaughlin told *CA* that his writing falls into three "almost mutually exclusive groups: (a) technical books (detergency, pollution, factory methods, etc.), (b) music, aesthetics, psychology of thought, and (c) historically based sociology, oddities of human customs and habits. I see all these as 'useful' kinds of writing, but personally regard (b) as the most important. I was trained as a scientist, and earn part of my living as such, but have always had a great interest in, and detailed knowledge of the arts, particularly music (competent pianist, knowledge of composition methods, etc., though no time to compose)."

AVOCATIONAL INTERESTS: "Almost everything except sport," especially book collecting, drawing, woodworking, and house remodeling.

* * *

McLELLAN, David 1940-

PERSONAL: Born February 10, 1940, in Hertfordshire, England; son of Robert (a university teacher) and Olive (Bush) McLellan; married Annie Brassart (a translator), July 1, 1967; children: Gabrielle, Stephanie. *Education:* St. Johns College, Oxford, M.A., 1962, D.Phil., 1968. *Politics:* Labour. *Religion:* Roman Catholic. *Home:* 13 Ivy Lane, Canterbury, Kent, England. *Agent:* Harold Matson Co., Inc., 22 East 40th St., New York, N.Y. 10016. *Office:* Department of Politics, University of Kent, Kent, England.

CAREER: University of Kent, Kent, England, lecturer, 1966-71, senior lecturer in politics, 1971, reader, 1972-76, professor of political theory, 1976—.

WRITINGS: The Young Hegelians and Karl Marx, Praeger, 1969; *Marx Before Marxism,* Harper, 1970; *Karl Marx: Early Texts,* Barnes & Noble, 1971; (editor and translator) Karl Marx, *The Grundrisse,* Harper, 1971; *The Thought of Karl Marx,* Harper, 1972; *Karl Marx: His Life and Thought,* Harper, 1974; *Marx,* Fontana Books, 1975.

WORK IN PROGRESS: Engels; History of Marxism, for Harper.

BIOGRAPHICAL/CRITICAL SOURCES: Saturday Review, August 7, 1971; *Washington Post,* February 13, 1974.

* * *

McLEOD, Emilie Warren 1926-

PERSONAL: Born December 2, 1926, in Boston, Mass.; daughter of Shields (a physician) and Alice (Springfield) Warren; married Guy Collingwood McLeod (a research biologist), June, 1950; children: Sara, Susan, Stuart. *Education:* Mount Holyoke College, B.A., 1948. *Home:* 60 Carlton Rd., Waban, Mass. 02168. *Office:* Atlantic Monthly Press, 8 Arlington St., Boston, Mass. 02168.

CAREER: Reporter, Falmouth Enterprises, 1947-48; *Ladies' Home Journal,* New York, N.Y., editorial assistant, 1948-49; Houghton Mifflin Co., Boston, Mass., assistant children's book editor, 1950-52; Atlantic Monthly Press, Boston, children's book editor, 1956-76, associate director, 1976—. *Member:* American Library Association, Mount Holyoke Alumnae Association, Mount Holyoke Club of Boston (member of board of directors, 1961-73; president, 1970-72).

*WRITINGS—*For children; published by Little, Brown, except as indicated: *The Seven Remarkable Bears,* Houghton, 1954; *Clancy's Witch,* 1959; *One Snail and Me,* 1961; *The Bear's Bicycle,* 1975.

WORK IN PROGRESS: "Finding, encouraging, and editing the work of authors and artists who believe that children deserve the best of books."

* * *

McMAHON, Thomas (Arthur) 1943-

PERSONAL: Born April 21, 1943, in Dayton, Ohio; son of Howard Oldford (a physicist) and Lucille (Nelson) McMahon; married Carol Ehlers, June 20, 1965; children: James Robert, Elizabeth Kirsten. *Education:* Cornell University, S.B., 1965; Massachusetts Institute of Technology, Ph.D., 1970. *Office:* Division of Applied Sciences, Harvard University, Cambridge, Mass. 02138.

CAREER: Harvard University, Cambridge, Mass., research fellow, 1970-71, assistant professor, 1971-74, associate professor, 1974-77, Gordon McKay Professor of Applied Mechanics and professor of biology, 1977—.

WRITINGS: Principles of American Nuclear Chemistry: A Novel, Little, Brown, 1970. Contributor to *Science, Scientific American,* and other scientific journals.

WORK IN PROGRESS: A second novel; research on the applications of physics to medicine and biology.

BIOGRAPHICAL/CRITICAL SOURCES: Nature, April 2, 1970; *Life,* July 24, 1970; *Time,* August 24, 1970; *New York Times,* August 29, 1970; *Christian Science Monitor,* October 1, 1970; *New Yorker,* November 7, 1970.

McMILLEN, Neil R(aymond) 1939-

PERSONAL: Born January 2, 1939, in Lake Odessa, Mich.; son of Reo F. (an engineer) and Bessie (Aukland) McMillen; married Beverly Smith (a librarian), March 18, 1960; children: Caroline Leslie, Hunter Neil. *Education:* University of Southern Mississippi, B.A., 1961, M.A., 1963; Vanderbilt University, Ph.D., 1969. *Home:* 509 Bay St., Hattiesburg, Miss. 39401. *Office:* Department of History, University of Southern Mississippi, Hardy St., Hattiesburg, Miss. 39401.

CAREER: Ball State University, Muncie, Ind., assistant professor of history, 1967-69; University of Southern Mississippi, Hattiesburg, assistant professor, 1969-70, dean of the Basic College, 1970-71, associate professor of history, 1971—. *Military service:* U.S. Marine Corps, 1957. *Member:* Southern Historical Association, Organization of American Historians. *Awards, honors:* Woodrow Wilson fellowships, 1963-64, 1966-67.

WRITINGS: The Citizens' Council: Organized Resistance to the Second Reconstruction, 1954-1964, University of Illinois Press, 1971; *Thomas Jefferson: Philosopher of Freedom,* Rand McNally, 1973; (with Charles Sellers and Henry May) *A Synopsis of American History,* 4th edition (McMillen was not associated with earlier editions), Rand McNally, 1977. Also contributor to Richard A. McLemore, editor, *Mississippi: A History,* University and College Press of Mississippi. Contributor to *Arkansas Historical Quarterly, Tennessee Historical Quarterly, Southern Quarterly, Ball State Film Forum, Michigan History, Journal of Mississippi History, Journal of Negro History, History Teacher, Choice,* and other journals.

WORK IN PROGRESS: History of the Negro in Mississippi, 1890-1945.

* * *

McMILLEN, Wheeler 1893-

PERSONAL: Born January 27, 1893, near Ada, Ohio; son of Lewis Dodd (a farmer) and Ella (Wheeler) McMillen; married Dorothy Doane, May 28, 1915 (died March 29, 1974); children: Robert Doane. *Education:* Attended Ohio Northern University, 1911-12. *Politics:* Conservative. *Home:* 3001 Veazey Ter. N.W., Washington, D.C. 10008.

CAREER: Reporter and desk editor on newspapers in Ohio, Indiana, and Illinois, 1911-14; *Covington Republican* (weekly), Covington, Ind., owner and publisher, 1914-18; operated family farm near Ada, Ohio, 1918-22; *Farm and Fireside* (later *Country Home*), New York, N.Y., associate editor, 1922-34, editor, 1934-37, editorial director, 1937-39; Farm Journal, Inc., Philadelphia, Pa., editor-in-chief of *Farm Journal,* 1939-55, vice-president of company, 1955-63; *Pathfinder,* Washington, D.C., editor-in-chief, 1946-52. Member of board of directors, New Jersey Bell Telephone Co., 1949-65, and Bankers National Life Insurance Co., 1954-71. Organizer, with aid of Henry Ford and others, of Farm Chemurgic Council, 1935, and president or chairman, 1937-62; executive director, President's Commission on Increased Industrial Use of Agricultural Products, 1956-57; member, President's Advisory Committee on Youth Fitness, 1957-58. Boy Scouts of America, member of national board, 1939-68, vice-president of national council, 1959-63, member of advisory council, 1968—. Director, New Jersey State Chamber of Commerce, 1943-51; chairman, New Jersey Public Health Council, 1947-49. Trustee of Rutgers University, 1943-52, and of Farm Foundation.

MEMBER: American Agricultural Editors' Association (president, 1934-38), National Audubon Society (member of board of directors, 1949-55), Philadelphia Society for Promoting Agriculture (president, 1959-60), Cosmos Club (Washington, D.C.). *Awards, honors:* LL.D., Ohio Northern University, 1940; D.Litt., Parsons College, 1952; Louis Bromfield Malabar Farm Foundation Gold Medal for services to conservation; Silver Antelope and Silver Buffalo of Boy Scouts of America for services to youth; several Freedoms Foundations and other awards for editorials and speeches.

WRITINGS: The Farming Fever, Appleton, 1924; *The Young Collector,* Appleton, 1926; *Too Many Farmers,* Morrow, 1929; *New Riches from the Soil,* Van Nostrand, 1946; *Land of Plenty,* Holt, 1961; *Why America Is Rich,* Caxton, 1963; (editor) *Harvest: An Anthology of Farm Writing,* Appleton, 1963; *Possums, Politicians and People,* Countryside Press (Philadelphia), 1964; *Bugs or People?,* Appleton, 1965; *Fifty Useful Americans,* Putnam, 1965; *The Farmer,* Potomac, 1966; *The Green Frontier,* Putnam, 1969; *Weekly on the Wabash,* Southern Illinois University Press, 1969; *Ohio Farm,* Ohio State University Press, 1974.

WORK IN PROGRESS: Feeding the Multitudes: The Epic of American Farmers.

SIDELIGHTS: Many of Wheeler McMillen's books have been translated into French, Spanish, Portuguese, Arabic, Burmese, and Japanese.

* * *

McMILLIN, (Joseph) Laurence (Jr.) 1923-

PERSONAL: Born June 7, 1923, in Atlanta, Ga.; son of Joseph Lawrence and Margaret (Pool) McMillin; married Marguerite Gainey (a secretary), July, 1950. *Education:* Princeton University, A.B. (summa cum laude), 1948; Claremont Graduate School, M.A., 1960. *Office:* 1175 West Base Line Rd., Claremont, Calif. 91711.

CAREER: Memphis Press-Scimitar, Memphis, Tenn., copy editor and reporter, 1948-55; Webb School of California, Claremont, teacher, 1955—, head of English department, 1963-66, director of studies, 1966-68, assistant to headmaster, 1969-72, academic dean, 1972—, holder of Libaw Chair in Individual Humanities, 1974—. *Military service:* U.S. Army, Field Artillery, and U.S. Army Air Forces, 1943-46. *Member:* National Association of Independent Schools, Western Association of Schools and Colleges, Phi Beta Kappa.

WRITINGS: The Schoolmaker: Sawney Webb and the Bell Buckle Story, University of North Carolina Press, 1971. Also author of *The Disciples of Love.* Contributor of articles to *Independent School Bulletin* and *Alumni Bulletin* (Webb School of California). Editor, *Alumni Bulletin* of Webb School, 1961-74.

WORK IN PROGRESS: The Education of Albert Einstein: Adventures in Holy Curiosity; a biography, tentatively entitled *The Water Titan; The Promise of Our Individual Humanity: The Unfinished American Testament;* editing an anthology, *Readings in Individual Humanity*

SIDELIGHTS: Laurence McMillin told *CA:* "I aim to make biography 'read like fiction,' to use fictional techniques without fictionalizing, to raise biography to the level of the literary art that captures the highest—and most certain—realities of human experience. As artistic practice, it is what Solzhenitsyn has called 'literary investigation.' As individual experience, it is what Einstein celebrated in his own life as 'release from the painful commonplace and the chains of our own desires.'"

He adds: "My big aim is to find in the remarkable 'American Experience' the 'Human Experience,' to explore the widely discredited 'American Dream.' As outdated individualism distorted it, modern groupthink oppresses it. Our plight is reflected in what Saul Bellow has called the failure of modern writing 'to represent mankind adequately.' Yet this dream keeps leading us to unexpected 'rich' realities, lost to humanity in the mass at all socioeconomic levels, but achieved by individual persons who have, especially through their inner life, emerged from the commonplace afflictions of boredom and mechanical routine. There is inspiration as well as challenge in Bellow's promise that characters pre-exist and have to be found; one's unique, developing human life has the greatest value of anything on earth. In both my writing and spirited dialogue with promising and gifted members of the younger generation, I mentally fight for the principle, ignored at our civilization's peril, that 'all the valuable achievements we receive from society have been brought about in the course of countless generations by creative individuals.' Without this wisdom, articulated here by Albert Einstein, science grows mechanical monsters and art drifts into mass-producing idiot-tales."

BIOGRAPHICAL/CRITICAL SOURCES: Los Angeles Herald Examiner, July 11, 1971; *Choice,* October, 1971; *Journal of American History,* March, 1972.

* * *

McQUILKIN, Frank 1936-

PERSONAL: Born September 17, 1936, in Philadelphia, Pa.; son of George (a laborer) and Adelaide (O'Malley) McQuilkin. *Education:* St. Norbert College, A.B., 1959; San Francisco State College (now University), M.A., 1969. *Office:* Department of English, Rutgers University, Camden, N.J. 08102.

CAREER: Rutgers University, Camden Campus, Camden, N.J., instructor, 1970-73, assistant professor of English, 1973—. Member of board of directors, Philadelphia Writers' Conference.

WRITINGS: Think Black: An Introduction to Black Political Power, introduction by Yosef ben Jochannan, Bruce, 1970. Contributor of about twenty poems to periodicals, including *Epos, Descant, America, Forum,* and *Catholic World.*

WORK IN PROGRESS: The Puppet Game, a novel; a second novel.†

* * *

McROBERTS, R(obert) Lewis 1944-

PERSONAL: Born March 23, 1944, in Janesville, Wis.; son of Irvin Udell and Opal (Crecelius) McRoberts; married Michele Martin (a high school art teacher), August 21, 1965. *Education:* Wisconsin State University—Oshkosh (now University of Wisconsin—Oshkosh), B.A., 1966; University of Iowa, M.F.A., 1968. *Office:* Department of Fine Arts, Roger Williams College, Bristol, R.I. 02809.

CAREER: Wisconsin State University—Superior (now University of Wisconsin—Superior), instructor in English, 1968-69; Roger Williams College, Bristol, R.I., instructor in English and creative writing and coordinator of fine arts, 1969—. Member, Associated Writing Programs. *Member:* Academy of American Poets, Psi Chi.

WRITINGS: (Editor with Robert T. Crotty and Geoffrey Clark) *Workshop: A Spontaneous Approach to Literature,* Cummings, 1971; *Lip Service,* Ithaca House, 1976. Contributor of poems to literary journals.

WORK IN PROGRESS: Poems; another anthology, with Geoffrey Clark.

AVOCATIONAL INTERESTS: Writing poetry, reading, sailing, tennis, gardening, music.

* * *

MEANS, Gordon P(aul) 1927-

PERSONAL: Born May 9, 1927, in Spokane, Wash.; son of Paul Banwell and Nathalie (Toms) Means; married Ingunn Norderval (a professor), June 9, 1956; children: Kristin, Norval, Erik, Kaia. *Education:* Attended University of Oregon, 1946-47, and Grinnell College, 1947-48; Reed College, B.A., 1950; University of Washington, Seattle, M.A., 1952, Ph.D., 1960. *Home:* 1271 King St. W., Hamilton, Ontario, Canada. *Office:* Department of Political Science, McMaster University, Hamilton, Ontario, Canada.

CAREER: Willamette University, Salem, Ore., assistant professor of political science, 1958-60; Gustavus Adolphus College, St. Peter, Minn., assistant professor of political science, 1960-65; University of Iowa, Iowa City, assistant professor of political science, 1965-66; University of Washington, Seattle, associate professor of political science, 1966-67; McMaster University, Hamilton, Ontario, associate professor, 1967-73, professor of political science, 1973—. Smith-Mundt Visiting Professor, University of Malaya, 1962-63; visiting lecturer, University of Singapore, 1963; researcher in India for Himalayan Border Countries Project, University of California, Berkeley, 1968-69. *Military service:* U.S. Navy, 1945-46.

MEMBER: American Political Science Association, Association for Asian Studies, Royal Asiatic Society, Western Political Science Association, Canadian Council for Southeast Asian Studies, Canadian Society for Asian Studies. *Awards, honors:* Ford Foundation grants, 1954-55, 1974-75; Canada Council research grants, 1969-70, 1974-75.

WRITINGS: (Contributor) M. M. Thomas and M. Abel, editors, *Religion, State, and Ideologies in East Asia,* East Asia Christian Conference, 1965; *Malaysian Politics,* New York University Press, 1970, 2nd revised edition, Hodder & Stoughton, 1976; (contributor) Roman Serbyn, editor, *Federalisme et Nations,* Presses de l'Universite du Quebec, 1971; (contributor) Robert Kearney, editor, *Politics and Modernization in South and Southeast Asia,* Wiley, 1975. Contributor to political science journals.

WORK IN PROGRESS: Social change and elite development among tribal people in Southeast Asia; the role of religion in politics in Southeast Asia.

* * *

MEANS, John Barkley 1939-

PERSONAL: Born January 2, 1939, in Cincinnati, Ohio; son of Walker Wilson (a civil engineer) and Rosetta (Miller) Means. *Education:* University of Illinois, B.A. (with honors and high distinction), 1960, M.A., 1963, Ph.D., 1968. *Politics:* Independent. *Religion:* Protestant. *Office:* Center for Critical Languages, Temple University, Philadelphia, Pa. 19122.

CAREER: U.S. Department of State, Washington, D.C., intelligence analyst, 1962-64; University of Illinois, Urbana, instructor in Portuguese, 1964-68; Temple University, Philadelphia, Pa., assistant professor, 1968-72, associate professor of Portuguese, 1972—, co-chairman, department of Spanish and Portuguese, 1971-75, director of Center for Critical Languages, 1975—. Consultant, U.S. Peace Corps.

Military service: U.S. Army, 1960-61; became first lieutenant.

MEMBER: Modern Language Association of America, English Association of Great Britain, American Association of Teachers of Spanish and Portuguese, American Council on the Teaching of Foreign Languages, American Association of University Professors, Latin American Studies Association, National Association of Self-Instructional Language Programs (member of national board of directors), Associacao Brasileira de Linguistica, Instituto Brasil-Estados Unidos (Rio de Janeiro), Sigma Delta Pi, Phi Lambda Beta (founding president, Illinois chapter).

WRITINGS: (Editor) *Essays on Brazilian Literature,* Simon & Schuster, 1971. Contributor of articles to *North American Review, Portugues* (Sao Paulo), *Books Abroad,* and other journals.

WORK IN PROGRESS: Research on self-instructional foreign language learning in contemporary American higher education, on the life and works of J. M. Machado de Assis, and on contemporary Brazilian civilization and culture; comparative Anglo-American/Luso-Brazilian literary studies.

SIDELIGHTS: John Means is interested in the language and literature of Portugal and Brazil, the social and political evolution of modern Brazil, trends in self-instructional foreign language education at the secondary and college levels, and the development of curricula in the "less commonly taught foreign languages in U.S. higher education."

* * *

MECH, L(ucyan) David 1937-
(Dave Mech)

PERSONAL: Surname rhymes with "peach"; born January 18, 1937, in Auburn, N.Y.; son of Lucyan Frank (foreman laborer in a chemical plant) and Margaret C. (Nade) Mech; married Betty Ann Smith, August 30, 1958; children: Sharon E., Stephen D., Nicholas E., Christopher A. *Education:* Cornell University, B.S., 1958; Purdue University, Ph.D., 1962; University of Minnesota, postdoctoral study, 1962-63. *Politics:* Independent. *Religion:* "No organized religion." *Home:* 1315 66th Ave. N.E., Minneapolis, Minn. 55432. *Office:* U.S. Fish and Wildlife Service, North Central Forest Equipment Station, Folwell Ave., St. Paul, Minn. 55108.

CAREER: University of Minnesota, Museum of Natural History, Minneapolis, research associate, 1963-66; Macalester College, St. Paul, Minn., assistant professor of biology and research associate, 1966-69; U.S. Bureau of Sport Fisheries and Wildlife, Minneapolis, Minn., wildlife research biologist, beginning 1969; currently wildlife research biologist with U.S. Fish and Wildlife Service, North Central Forest Experiment station, St. Paul, Minn. Has spoken widely on wolf ecology and research and on animal-tracking (more than ninety engagements since 1968), including lectures at Serengeti Research Institute in Tanzania, 1970; also has appeared on network television in the National Broadcasting Co. specials, "The Wolf Men" and "Our Endangered Wildlife," and on the "Dick Cavett Show."

MEMBER: Ecological Society of America, American Society of Mammalogists, Wildlife Society, Minnesota Zoological Society (member of board of directors). *Awards, honors:* National Institutes of Health fellowship, 1963-64; Special Achievement Award of U.S. Bureau of Sport Fisheries and Wildlife, 1970; Special Achievement Award from U.S. Fish and Wildlife Service, 1970; Terrestial Wildlife Publication Award from Wildlife Society, 1972, and Best Wildlife Book award from Symposium on Threatened and Endangered Wildlife, 1974, both for *The Wolf;* Civil Servant of the Year award from U.S. Fish and Wildlife Service, 1973.

WRITINGS: The Wolves of Isle Royale, U.S. Government Printing Office, 1966; *The Wolf: The Ecology and Behavior of an Endangered Species,* Natural History Press, 1970; (editor with L. D. Frenzel, Jr., and contributor) *Ecological Studies of the Timber Wolf in Northeastern Minnesota,* North Central Forest Experiment Station (St. Paul), 1971; (with D. G. Schneider and J. R. Tester) *Movements of Female Raccoons and Their Young as Determined by Radio-Tracking,* Animal Behavior Monographs, 1971. Contributor of over fifty articles and reviews, some under name Dave Mech, to scientific publications, and about seventy articles to more popular periodicals and newspapers, including *Reader's Digest, Naturalist, Sports Afield, Outdoor Life, Animal Kingdom,* and *National Geographic.*

WORK IN PROGRESS: Further ecological and behavioral research on timber wolves in northern Minnesota.

AVOCATIONAL INTERESTS: Wildlife photography, music.

BIOGRAPHICAL/CRITICAL SOURCES: New York Times Book Review, June 14, 1970.

* * *

MECKIER, Jerome (Thomas) 1941-

PERSONAL: Born September 16, 1941, in Jersey City, N.J.; married Nancy Winter, December 28, 1968; children: Alison. *Education:* Le Moyne College, Syracuse, N.Y., A.B. (summa cum laude), 1963; Harvard University, M.A., 1964, Ph.D., 1968. *Politics:* None. *Religion:* Roman Catholic. *Home:* 209 Taylor Dr., Lexington, Ky. 40505. *Office:* Department of English, University of Kentucky, Lexington, Ky. 40506.

CAREER: University of Massachusetts—Amherst, assistant professor of English, 1967-70; University of Kentucky, Lexington, associate professor, 1970-75, professor of English, 1975—. *Member:* Modern Language Association of America, Dickens Society (trustee), South Atlantic Modern Language Association, Dickens Fellowship. *Awards, honors:* Woodrow Wilson fellow, 1963; Huntington Library fellow, 1971, 1973; National Endowment for the Humanities younger humanist fellow, 1974.

WRITINGS: Aldous Huxley: Satire and Structure, Barnes & Noble, 1969. Contributor to scholarly journals. Member of board of editors, *Dickens Studies Annual.*

WORK IN PROGRESS: Further studies on Huxley and Dickens.

AVOCATIONAL INTERESTS: Horse racing.

* * *

MECKLIN, John Marin 1918-1971

January 29, 1918—October 29, 1971; American editor, journalist, and author. Obituaries: *New York Times,* October 31, 1971; *Time,* November 8, 1971.

* * *

MEEKS, John E.

PERSONAL: Born in Pine Bluff, Ark.; son of John T. (a farmer) and Edna (Goacher) Meeks; married Anita Copeland, June 20, 1954; children: Ann Catherine, Julia Copeland, Melinda. *Education:* Attended Vanderbilt University; Hendrix College, B.A. (with highest honors), 1954; University of Tennessee, M.D., 1957. *Office:* 4460 MacArthur Blvd., Washington, D.C. 20007.

CAREER: Intern at Memphis city hospitals; University of Cincinnati, Cincinnati, Ohio, resident in psychiatry, 1958-60, fellow in child psychiatry, 1960-62; University of Texas, Southwestern Medical School, Dallas, instructor, 1964-65, assistant professor, 1965-69, associate professor of psychiatry, 1969-70, clinical associate professor of psychiatry, 1970-73, director of children's division, department of psychiatry, 1965-70; private practice of psychiatry, Dallas, Tex., 1970-73; Psychiatric Institute of Washington, Washington, D.C., director of child and adolescent services, 1973—. Certified in psychiatry by American Board of Neurology and Psychiatry, 1963, and in child psychiatry, 1966. Member of staff at Parkland Memorial Hospital, Children's Medical Center, and Presbyterian Hospital, Dallas. *Military service:* U.S. Air Force, Medical Corps, 1962-64; became captain.

MEMBER: American Academy of Child Psychiatry, American Medical Association, American Psychiatric Association, American Orthopsychiatric Association, American Association of Psychiatric Clinics for Children, Texas Society of Child Psychiatry, Dallas County Medical Association, Dallas Neuropsychiatric Society.

WRITINGS: The Fragile Alliance: An Orientation to the Outpatient Psychotherapy of Adolescents, Williams & Wilkins, 1971. Contributor to psychiatry journals and *Hospital Medicine.*

WORK IN PROGRESS: What to Do until the Adult Comes: A Guide for Parents of Adolescents; chapters for textbooks.

AVOCATIONAL INTERESTS: Music (especially jazz), pool, tennis, and (light) gardening.

*   *   *

MEETER, Glenn 1934-

PERSONAL: Born May 5, 1934, in Hammond, Ind.; son of John Arthur and Joan (Hoekman) Meeter; married Marlene Meyerink, August 10, 1955; children: Barbara Ann, Nancy Lynn, Joel Arthur, Alison Joan. *Education:* Calvin College, A.B., 1955; Vanderbilt University and George Peabody College for Teachers, M.A.T. (joint degree), 1956; University of Iowa, Ph.D., 1966. *Politics:* Democrat. *Religion:* Congregationalist. *Home:* 140 Tilton Park Dr., DeKalb, Ill. 60115. *Office:* Department of English, Northern Illinois University, DeKalb, Ill. 60115.

CAREER: High school English teacher in Lansing, Ill., 1956-60; University of Southern California, Los Angeles, assistant professor, 1964-69, associate professor of English, 1969; Northern Illinois University, DeKalb, associate professor of English, 1969—, director of undergraduate English studies. *Member:* Modern Language Association of America, Midwest Modern Language Association. *Awards, honors:* Breadloaf scholarship, 1970, for short story, "Waiting for Daddy"; Graves Award from Pomona College and American Council of Learned Societies, 1968-69, for study.

WRITINGS: Bernard Malamud and Philip Roth, Eerdmans, 1968; (contributor) Frank N. Magill, editor, *Magill's Literary Annual,* Salem Press, 1972; (contributor) Jerome K. Klinkowitz and J. L. Somer, editors, *The Vonnegut Statement,* Delacorte, 1973. Short stories anthologized in *Innovative Fiction,* edited by Klinkowitz and Somer, Dell, 1972,

and *Redbook's Famous Fiction,* edited by Anne Mollegen Smith, Redbook Books, 1977. Contributor of stories to literary journals such as *Chicago Review, South Dakota Review, Ohio Review,* and *Epoch,* and to national magazines, including *Atlantic* and *Redbook.*

WORK IN PROGRESS: Short fiction; a book-length study of contemporary American novels; with Robert Detweiler, *Faith in Fiction,* an anthology of short stories; a novel, *Letters to Barbara.*

*   *   *

MEGGYESY, David M. 1941-
(Dave Meggyesy)

PERSONAL: Surname is pronounced Meg-a-*see;* born November 1, 1941, in Cleveland, Ohio; son of Joseph Meggyesy; married Nancy Ann Elizabeth Kennedy, August 19, 1961; children: Christopher, Jennifer. *Education:* Syracuse University, B.A., 1963; Washington University, St. Louis, Mo., Ph.D. candidate.

CAREER: Linebacker with St. Louis Cardinals of National Football League, 1963-70.

WRITINGS: (Under name Dave Meggyesy) *Out of Their League,* Ramparts, 1970.

WORK IN PROGRESS: Football: The All-American Myth.

SIDELIGHTS: David Meggyesy, known to his Cardinal teammates as "Super-Psych," dropped out of football in 1970 to write his book for the Institute for the Study of Sport and Society. In the book he rips pro football as "one of the most dehumanizing experiences a person can face."

BIOGRAPHICAL/CRITICAL SOURCES: New York Times, January 11, 1971; *Washington Post,* January 11, 1971; *Best Sellers,* February 1, 1971; *Life,* March 5, 1971.†

*   *   *

MEHRABIAN, Albert 1939-

PERSONAL: Born November 17, 1939, in Tabriz, Iran; naturalized U.S. citizen. *Education:* Massachusetts Institute of Technology, B.S. and M.S., 1961; Clark University, Ph.D., 1964. *Office:* Department of Psychology, University of California, 405 Hilgard, Los Angeles, Calif. 90024.

CAREER: University of California, Los Angeles, assistant professor, 1964-70, associate professor, 1970-76, professor of psychology, 1976—. *Member:* American Psychological Association (fellow), Sigma Xi.

WRITINGS: (With Morton Wiener) *Language Within Language: Immediacy, a Channel in Verbal Communication,* Appleton, 1968; *An Analysis of Personality Theories,* Prentice-Hall, 1968; *Tactics of Social Influence,* Prentice-Hall, 1970; *Silent Messages,* Wadsworth, 1971; *Nonverbal Communication,* Aldine-Atherton, 1972; *Public Places and Private Spaces,* Basic Books, 1976.

Contributor of numerous articles to psychology journals, including *Journal of Personality and Social Psychology, Psychological Reports, Journal of Verbal Learning and Verbal Behavior, Psychology Today, Educational and Psychological Measurement, Sociometry, Journal of Consulting Psychology,* and *Acta Psychologica.* Consulting editor and contributor, *Journal of Psycholinguistic Research;* divisional editor, *Proceedings* of American Psychological Association, 1969.

WORK IN PROGRESS: Research on personality models and personality measurement.

MEISCH, Richard A(lden) 1943-

PERSONAL: Born October 5, 1943, in Minneapolis, Minn. *Education:* University of Minnesota, B.A., 1964, Ph.D. and M.D., 1970. *Home:* 436 Woodlawn Ave., St. Paul, Minn. 55105. *Office address:* Mayo Box 392, University of Minnesota, Minneapolis, Minn. 55455.

CAREER: Assistant professor of psychiatry and pharmacology, University of Minnesota, Minneapolis. *Member:* Phi Beta Kappa.

WRITINGS: (Editor with Travis Thompson and Roy Pickens) *Readings in Behavioral Pharmacology,* Appleton, 1970.

*   *   *

MEISSNER, W(illiam) W. 1931-

PERSONAL: Born February 13, 1931, in Buffalo, N.Y.; son of William Walter (a surgeon) and Mary (Glauber) Meissner. *Education:* St. Louis University, B.A., 1957, M.A. and Ph.L., 1958; Woodstock College, S.T.L., 1962; Harvard University, M.D., 1967. *Home:* 6 Sumner Rd., Cambridge, Mass. 02138. *Office:* Department of Psychiatry, Medical School, Harvard University, Cambridge, Mass.

CAREER: Roman Catholic priest of Society of Jesus (Jesuits); Mount Auburn Hospital, Cambridge, Mass., medical intern, 1967-68; Massachusetts Mental Health Center, Boston, clinical fellow in psychiatry, 1968-71, staff psychiatrist, 1971—; Cambridge Hospital, Cambridge, staff psychiatrist, 1972—; Boston Psychoanalytic Institute, Boston, chairman of faculty, 1975—; Harvard University, Medical School, Cambridge, associate clinical professor of psychiatry, 1976—. *Member:* American Psychiatric Association, Northern New England Psychiatric Society, Boston Psychoanalytic Society, Sigma Xi. *Awards, honors:* Deutsch Prize of Boston Psychoanalytic Institute, 1968.

WRITINGS: Annotated Bibliography in Religion and Psychology, Academy of Religion and Mental Health, 1961; *Group Dynamics in the Religious Life,* University of Notre Dame Press, 1965; *Foundations for a Psychology of Grace,* Paulist Press, 1965; *The Assault on Authority: Dialogue or Dilemma?,* Orbis Books, 1971; (with Elizabeth R. Zetzel) *Basic Concepts in Psychoanalytic Psychiatry,* Basic Books, 1972. Also author of *The Paranoid Process.*

*   *   *

MELCHER, Daniel 1912-

PERSONAL: Born July 10, 1912, in Newton Center, Mass.; son of Frederic Gershon (president, R. R. Bowker Co. and editor of *Publishers' Weekly*) and Marguerite (a writer, playwright and poet; maiden name, Fellows) Melcher; married Peggy Zimmerman, March 3, 1937 (died March, 1967); married Margaret Saul, October 3, 1967; children: Frederic G. II. *Education:* Harvard University, A.B., 1934. *Religion:* Unitarian-Universalist. *Home:* Glen Echo Farm, RFD 4, Charlottesville, Va. 22901.

CAREER: Allen & Unwin, London, England, publicity assistant, 1934; student of publishing methods in London and Leipzig, Germany, 1935; Henry Holt & Co., New York City, editorial and sales work, 1936; Oxford University Press, New York City, direct mail and advertising manager, 1937-39; Alliance Book Corporation, New York City, production manager, 1939-40; Viking Press, New York City, worked on children's books promotion, 1940-42; U.S. Treasury Department, War Finance Division, Education Section, Washington, D.C., national director, 1942-45; National Committee on Atomic Information, Washington, D.C., director, 1946; R. R. Bowker Company, New York City, promotion manager, 1947-58, publisher of *Library Journal,* 1947-68, vice-president, 1959-63, division president (Jaques Cattell Press), 1961-67, president, 1963-68, chairman of the board, 1968-69; publishing consultant, with assignments, among others, from American Book Publishers' Council and W. R. Grace & Co.; Institutes for the Achievement of Human Potential, Philadelphia, Pa., member of board of directors, 1970; Gale Research Company, Detroit, Mich., chairman of the board, 1971-73. Succeeded his father as donor of the Newbery and Caldecott Medals, awarded annually by the Children's Services Division of the American Library Association to the most distinguished children's books of the year; sponsor of annual Frederic G. Melcher Award by the Unitarian-Universalist Association for the most distinguished contribution to the literature of liberal religion. *Member:* American Library Association, Harvard Club of New York City.

WRITINGS: Young Mr. Stone, Book Publisher (juvenile career book), Dodd, 1939, special printing, Court Book Co., 1941; (with Nancy Larrick) *The Printing and Promotion Handbook: How to Plan, Produce, and Use Printing, Advertising, and Direct Mail,* McGraw, 1949, 3rd edition, 1966; *So You Want to Get into Book Publishing: The Jobs, the Pay, and How to Start* (pamphlet), Publishers' Weekly, 1956, revised edition, 1967; (with wife, Margaret Saul Melcher) *Melcher on Acquisition,* American Library Association, 1971; (contributor) Sigfred Taubert, editor, *Book Trade of the World,* Volume II: *Americas, Australia, New Zealand,* Bowker, 1976. Contributor to *Encyclopedia of Library and Information Science,* edited by Allen Kent, Dekker, 1977. Contributor to *Library Journal, Publishers' Weekly, Bookseller* (London), and *American Libraries.*

SIDELIGHTS: It is hard for older people in the world of books to remember that *Books in Print* has not always existed, or for younger users to imagine that libraries, book shops, or publishing firms could ever get along without it. It was not, however, until 1949 that *Books in Print* first appeared, the product of Daniel Melcher's publishing imagination and mechanical ingenuity. (He invented both the camera and mounting equipment which made speedy, economical production of *BIP* possible.)

During his career at Bowker, he also created *Subject Guide to Books in Print, Paperbound Books in Print, American Book Publishing Record, Forthcoming Books, School Library Journal,* the *Bowker Annual,* and *Libros en Venta* (a "books-in-print" of the Spanish world, in preparation for which he learned Spanish by playing tapes while shaving, driving, working in his shop, and so on).

Colleague Nancy Larrick once wrote of Melcher: "Quiet, somewhat retiring in a large group, Dan Melcher has a knack of forging deeply loyal friendships in some quarters while raising antagonism in others.... Anyone who has worked with Melcher is soon aware that his mind simply operates in a higher gear than anyone else's, a fact he has never fully accepted," and a fact which sometimes leads to tensions and misunderstandings on the job. "But," Larrick continued, "As one devoted friend of 25 years standing put it, 'Dan apologizes so beautifully that it's worth the price.' 'Maybe I've had more practice than anyone,'" was Melcher's rejoinder.

Melcher's sharp-focus approach to problems and his wide grasp of publishing technology and economics perhaps contributed to his resignation from Bowker after Xerox entered the picture. At any rate, in a typically direct statement which was widely quoted by delighted conglomerate-watchers, Melcher said in a front-page *New York Times* interview about his resignation: "It was a communications problem. The planning group within the Xerox Education Division has no background in education or publishing, and I had no background in oil, plastics, chemicals or business machine sales [as did the planning group], and we just weren't on the same wave length."

All is not mechanics and economics in Melcher's world, however. As Larrick pointed out: "Each of the Melcher miracles is basic to a great dream of universal education and world understanding.... He does these things as a poet sharpens his pencil before writing a sonnet. The big objective is that more books will be read by more people."

A logical aspect of this objective is concern with the ability—or inability—to read, and it was an interest in dyslexia which caused him to familiarize himself with the work of building function in brain-damaged children being carried on by Glenn Doman and Carl Delacato and their associates at the Institutes for the Achievement of Human Potential in Philadelphia.

Melcher told *CA:* "Out of their twenty years' work, and 6,000 case histories, emerges what I find to be convincing evidence that a child—any child—can and will learn to read as early as he learns to talk, granted equal opportunity. The two processes are, after all, neurologically equivalent. Understanding words in print in no way asks more of the brain than understanding words of speech. (Sensing the difference between two words in print may actually be easier than sensing the difference between two human faces.)

"All infants have an inborn 'rage to learn,' blunted though it will be by years of 'don't' 'not now,' 'can't you see mother is busy,' 'do be quiet,' and 'why don't you go and play with your toys.' Consider the vast relief to child, mother, and teacher alike if a child, unutterably bored with his 'toys,' could, at will, replace the all-too-exhaustible resources of mother or teacher with the inexhaustible resources of the printed page.

"Consider the gain to all if a child could be introduced to 'Look, Jane, look,' at an age when he was still excited over discovering the very existence of language—instead of four years later when the let-down from TV to reading primer is almost enough to put him off reading for life."

AVOCATIONAL INTERESTS: Metal working, optics, electronics, scuba diving (he has explored the coasts off Puerto Rico, Majorca, Mexico, and the Galapagos Islands, in addition to many areas of the United States), skiing, flying, gliding, forestry (650 acres in New Hampshire and Virginia), wines, photography, sailing, silk screen printing, and languages.

BIOGRAPHICAL/CRITICAL SOURCES: Bulletin of Bibliography, May-August, 1966; *New York Times,* December 20, 1967; *Publishers' Weekly,* June 10, 1968; *New York Times,* January 31, 1969.

*   *   *

MELLANDER, Gustavo Adolfo 1935-

PERSONAL: Born January 30, 1935, in Los Angeles, Calif.; son of Harold J. (a businessman) and Adela M. (Navarro) Mellander. *Education:* Canal Zone College, A.A., 1957; George Washington University, A.B., 1959, M.A., 1960, Ph.D., 1965. *Home:* 599 Broadway, Apt. 9J, Paterson, N.J. 07514. *Office:* Passaic County Community College, Paterson, N.J. 07505.

CAREER: George Washington University, Washington, D.C., instructor in history, 1961-64; American University, Washington, D.C., research associate, 1964-65; Pembroke State University, Pembroke, N.C., associate professor of history and chairman of social science division, 1965-66; Inter-American University, San Juan, P.R., professor of history and academic dean, 1966-69; York College of Pennsylvania, York, professor of Latin American history and government and dean of academic affairs, 1969-72; Office of the Chancellor of Higher Education, Trenton, N.J., director of the Office for Private Colleges and Universities, 1972-75; Passaic County Community College, Paterson, N.J., president, 1975—. Participant, Institute for Academic Deans, 1969—. Member of board of directors, San Juan Tubercular Association, 1968-69; member of City of Paterson Board of Education, 1977—. Vice-chairman, Bergen-Passaic Health System Agency; member of board of directors, Saint Joseph's Hospital and Medical Center. Member of board of trustees, Don Bosco College; member of advisory board, Assumption College. *Member:* American Association of University Administrators, American Studies Association, American Historical Association, Southern Historical Association, Pi Gamma Mu.

WRITINGS: (With Clifford Barnett) *Area Handbook for Cuba,* U.S. Government Printing Office, 1961; (with Lyman Legters) *Area Handbook for Panama,* U.S. Government Printing Office, 1962; (with Bela Maday) *Area Handbook for Malaysia and Singapore,* U.S. Government Printing Office, 1966; (with Carl E. Hatch) *The York Dispatch Index: The Depression 1930's,* Strine, 1971; *The United States in Panamanian Politics,* Interstate, 1971; (with Hatch) *York County's Presidential Elections,* Strine, 1972. Also author of *The York Dispatch Index: The 1940's.*

WORK IN PROGRESS: Confessions of an Academic Administrator.

SIDELIGHTS: Gustavo Mellander told *CA:* "I divide my time these days between two major interests, the Panama Canal question and the very pressing crisis of standards in higher education. I think the new treaty represents a major breakthrough, a coming-of-age for United States foreign policy with regard to our rights and responsibilities in Latin America. The days are long gone when we can 'send the Marines in.' But I think, nevertheless, we should make certain that the United States retains ready and open access to the Canal.

"Because I am now a college president, most of my time is spent in issues of education. I am extremely disturbed by the results of education's experiments with social promotion, life adjustment, and all the other excess baggage of a permissive culture. If we do not reverse ourselves, and begin stressing the basics in education, we are destroying ourselves, our children, and our civilization. We must demand that children learn and that teachers teach. Realistic but rigorous academic standards at every level of education will salvage our schools and whole generations of children yet to come."

*   *   *

MELLOR, John W(illiams) 1928-

PERSONAL: Born December 28, 1928, in Paris, France; brought to United States in 1929, naturalized in 1940; son of Desmond Williams and Katherine (Beardsley) Mellor; married Arlene Gladys Patton, June 11, 1950 (divorced, 1971); married Uma J. Lele, February 11, 1972; children: (first marriage) Michael John Williams, Brian Ashby Williams,

Mark Allan Williams. *Education:* Cornell University, B.Sc., 1950, M.Sc., 1951, Ph.D., 1954; Oxford University, Diploma, 1952. *Religion:* None. *Home:* 511 Cameron Pt., Alexandria, Va. 22314. *Office:* International Food Policy Research Institute, 1776 Massachusetts Ave., Washington, D.C. 20036.

CAREER: Cornell University, Ithaca, N.Y., instructor, 1952-54, assistant professor, 1954-58, associate professor, 1958-61, professor of agricultural economics, 1961-77, Center for International Studies, associate director, 1961-65, director, 1965; International Food Policy Research Institute, Washington, D.C., director, 1977—. Did teaching and research for Agricultural Development Council in Agra, India, 1959-60, and for Rockefeller Foundation in New Delhi, India, 1963-64; researcher in New Delhi, 1967-68. Consultant to World Bank, Food and Agriculture Organization of the United Nations, and Rockefeller Foundation.

MEMBER: American Agricultural Economics Association, American Economic Association, American Academy of Arts and Sciences (fellow). *Awards, honors:* Fulbright scholar at Oxford University, 1951-52; Council of Economic and Cultural Affairs fellow at Balwant Rajput College, 1959-60; American Agricultural Economics Association Award for best published research, 1968, for "Towards a Theory of Agricultural Development" published as chapter in *Agricultural Development and Economic Growth.*

WRITINGS: The Economics of Agricultural Development, Cornell University Press, 1966; (with Thomas F. Weaver, Uma J. Lele, and Sheldon R. Simon) *Developing Rural India: Plan and Practice,* Cornell University Press, 1968; *The New Economics of Growth: A Strategy for India and the Developing World,* Twentieth Century Fund, 1976.

Contributor: E. O. Heady, editor, *Food: A Tool in International Development,* Iowa State University Press, 1962; Irwin T. Sanders, editor, *The Professional Education of Students from Other Lands,* Council on Social Work Education, 1963; Herman M. Southworth and Bruce F. Johnston, editors, *Agricultural Development and Economic Growth,* Cornell University Press, 1967; Kurt R. Anschel, Russell H. Brannon, and Eldon D. Smith, editors, *Agricultural Cooperatives and Markets in Developing Countries,* Praeger, 1969; Clifton R. Wharton, Jr., editor, *Subsistence Agriculture and Economic Development,* Aldine, 1969; Karl A. Fox and D. Gale Johnson, editors, *A.E.A. Readings in the Economics of Agriculture,* Volume XIII, Irwin, 1969; Kenneth L. Turk, editor, *Some Issues Emerging from Recent Breakthroughs in Food Production,* New York State College of Agriculture, 1971.

Author of monographs and research reports on agricultural development and pricing. Contributor to *International Encyclopedia of the Social Sciences, Encyclopaedia Britannica,* and *Land, the Yearbook of Agriculture.* Contributor of about thirty articles and reviews to farming and farm economics journals in United States and India.

WORK IN PROGRESS: Research on food policy.

* * *

MENDELSOHN, Martin 1935-

PERSONAL: Born November 6, 1935, in London, England; son of Arthur and Rebecca (Caplin) Mendelsohn; married Phyllis Linda Sobell, September 20, 1959; children: Paul Arthur, David Edward. *Education:* Law Society School of Law, London, England, qualified as solicitor (honors), 1959. *Home:* 110 Woodcock Hill, Kenton Harrow, Middlesex,

England. *Office:* Adlers & Aberstones, 9 St. Clare St., Minories, London E.C.3, England.

CAREER: Adlers & Aberstones, London, England, lawyer, 1959—. *Member:* Law Society.

WRITINGS: The Guide to Franchising, Pergamon, 1970; *Obtaining a Franchise,* Department of Trade and Industry, 1973, revised edition, 1975.

* * *

MENDELSON, Lee 1933-

PERSONAL: Born March 24, 1933; son of Palmer (a grower) and Jeanette Mendelson; married Debbie Mendelson, December 20, 1953; children: Glenn, Linda. *Education:* Stanford University, B.A., 1954. *Home and office:* 1408 Chapin Ave., Burlingame, Calif. 94040.

CAREER: Lee Mendelson Film Productions, Inc., Burlingame, Calif., president, 1963—. Writer, producer, and director of television specials, including the animated "Charlie Brown" series, "America and Americans" and "Travels with Charley" (both John Steinbeck specials), "It Couldn't Be Done," "The Record Makers," and the program commemorating the 100th anniversary of the national parks. Member of board of directors, KQED (San Francisco educational station). *Military service:* U.S. Air Force, navigator, 1954-57; became first lieutenant; received Commendation Ribbon. *Member:* Writers Guild of America. *Awards, honors:* Two Emmy Awards from Academy of Television Arts and Sciences and three George Foster Peabody Awards, all for television specials.

WRITINGS: Charlie Brown and Charlie Shulz, World Publishing, 1970.

* * *

MENDENHALL, George E(mery) 1916-

PERSONAL: Born August 13, 1916, in Muscatine, Iowa; son of George Newton (a professor) and Mary Christine (Johnson) Mendenhall; married Eathel Louise Tidrick, December 6, 1943; children: George David, Lauri Philip, Stanley Theodore, Gordon Louis, Stephen Robert. *Education:* Midland College, Fremont, Neb., B.A., 1936; Gettysburg Seminary, B.D., 1938; Johns Hopkins University, Ph.D., 1947. *Politics:* Independent. *Home:* 1510 Cedar Bend Dr., Ann Arbor, Mich. 48105. *Office:* Department of Near Eastern Studies, University of Michigan, Ann Arbor, Mich. 48109.

CAREER: Ordained a Lutheran minister, 1942; Trinity Lutheran Church, Laramie, Wyo., pastor, 1942-43; Hamma Divinity School, Springfield, Ohio, assistant professor, 1947-50, associate professor of Old Testament, 1950-52; University of Michigan, Ann Arbor, associate professor, 1952-58, professor of Near Eastern languages and literature, 1958—, Henry Russell Lecturer, 1972-73. American School of Oriental Research, Jerusalem, Jordan, annual professor, 1955-56, director, 1965-66; field supervisor, British School of Archaeology in Jerusalem, in escavation of Jericho, 1956; A. O. Lovejoy Lecturer, Johns Hopkins University, 1967; director, American Center of Oriental Research, Amman, Jordan, 1975. President, Lutheran Student Foundation, University of Michigan, 1962-65. *Military service:* U.S. Naval Reserve, 1943-46; became lieutenant junior grade. *Member:* American Oriental Society (president, Middle West Branch, 1951), Society of Biblical Literature (president, Midwest Section, 1960), Archaeological Institute of America, American Schools of Oriental Research, Biblical

Colloquium (president, 1963-65). *Awards, honors:* Litt. D., Midland College, Fremont, Neb., 1963; National Endowment for the Humanities senior fellow, 1971.

WRITINGS: Law and Covenant in Israel and the Ancient Near East, Biblical Colloquium, 1956; (consulting editor and contributor) *The Interpreter's Dictionary of the Bible,* Abingdon, 1962; *The Tenth Generation: The Origins of the Biblical Tradition,* Johns Hopkins Press, 1973. Contributor of articles to *Journal of Biblical Literature, Biblical Archaeologist, Bulletin* of American Schools of Oriental Research, *Journal of Near Eastern Studies,* and to *Encyclopaedia Britannica.* Associate editor, *Journal* of the American Oriental Society, 1954-59.

WORK IN PROGRESS: Decipherment of the Byblos Syllabic Inscriptions for *Berytus* monograph series, published by American University of Beirut; with William H. Brownlee, publication of the "Philistine" documents from Hebron, including photographs, transcription, and computer-programmed analysis of the language by Mendenhall's son, Stanley T. Mendenhall; several journal articles on biblical and archaeological subjects; *The Book of Numbers,* for Doubleday-Anchor; research on unknown new scripts, from Cyprus to Yemen in origin, from 1750 B.C. to 1192 A.D. in date.

SIDELIGHTS: George E. Mendenhall has traveled extensively throughout the Near East, frequently in connection with excavations of archaeological sites. He uses German, French, Italian, Turkish, Arabic, Greek, Latin, Hebrew, Aramaic, Assyrian, Syriac Egyptian, Old South Arabic, Luwian, Hittite, Phoenician, and Ugaritic, and is "very much involved in comparative Semitic languages because of the Byblos Syllabic Texts that push back our knowledge of Canaanite languages by about 500 years—to about 2000 B.C. The languages and writing systems of the ancient world are far more diverse and complex than we have any inkling of, in my judgment."

Mendenhall told *CA* he considers most important "the concern to understand the Bible in its own historical context in the ancient Near East. . . . Ancient pagan religion is the deification of the state and the economy, and such religion has always led to calamity, for it inevitably dehumanizes both the dominators and those subjected, and has often in the past resulted in the destruction of civilization. Power is intrinsically evil, for it excludes the possibility of an ethically responsible moral choice, and inevitably polarizes society to an extent that seriously endangers its viability. That is why there are so many dead civilizations and languages for the archaeologist to dig up. . . . The first half of recorded human history, from about 3000 B.C. to 500 B.C., is only slowly emerging from obscurity and presents a most exciting challenge for the foreseeable future. Enormous progress has been made particularly in the past two decades, but very little of this has become available to the general educated public, and all sorts of misconceptions based upon 19th century ideologies are still very dominant, both regarding the ancient pre-Greek civilizations and the Bible itself. But the whole field is still very much in its infancy; there are whole Empires in the ancient world about which we know next to nothing from excavations waiting to be discovered and placed into historical context."

AVOCATIONAL INTERESTS: Gardening, photography (including aerial photography of archaeological sites), leatherworking.

MENDENHALL, James Edgar 1903-1971

1903—December 24, 1971; American author of textbooks on consumer education. Obituaries: *New York Times,* December 25, 1971; *Washington Post,* December 25, 1971.

*   *   *

MERCHANT, Jane (Hess) 1919-1972

1919—January 3, 1972; American author and poet. Obituaries: *Publishers Weekly,* January 24, 1972. (See index for *CA* sketch)

*   *   *

MERLIS, George 1940-

PERSONAL: Born February 7, 1940, in New York, N.Y.; son of Martin Richard (a physician) and Ethel (Pollack) Merlis; married Susan Crane, November 20, 1961; children: James Duncan, Andrew Richard. *Education:* University of Pennsylvania, A.B., 1960; Columbia University, M.S., 1961. *Home:* 140 Cadman Plaza W., Brooklyn, N.Y. 11201. *Agent:* Charles Neighbors, 240 Waverly Pl., New York, N.Y. 10014. *Office:* ABC News, 7 West 66th St., New York, N.Y. 10023.

CAREER: Rome Daily American, Rome, Italy, sports editor, 1961; *World Telegram & Sun,* New York City, reporter, assistant city editor, 1961-66; *World Journal Tribune,* New York City, day city editor, 1966-67; *New York News,* New York City, metropolitan desk supervisor, 1967; American Broadcasting Corp., New York City, director of public relations for television and radio news, 1967—. *Military service:* U.S. Army Reserve, 1962-69; became sergeant. *Member:* Authors Guild, National Academy of Television Arts and Sciences, Radio-Television News Directors Association, Newspaper Reporters Association of New York, New York Newspaper Guild.

WRITINGS: V.P.: A Novel of Vice Presidential Politics, Morrow, 1971. Contributor to *New Republic, National Review, Columbia Journalism Review, Signature,* and *New York Times.*

WORK IN PROGRESS: Myths, a novel; a non-fiction baseball book; various television projects.

SIDELIGHTS: George Merlis told *CA:* "My greatest interests are journalism, writing and reading—not necessarily in that order. My major concerns are the decline of the American language—which, with its 'inputs,' 'outputs,' 'incursions,' and 'escalations,' is losing its flavor and becoming computer-talk—and American politics and society—which are succumbing to mechanized mendacity from charisma merchandisers."

AVOCATIONAL INTERESTS: Photography.

*   *   *

MERRITT, Dixon Lanier 1879-1972

1879—January 9, 1972; American editor, historian, and poet. Obituaries: *New York Times,* January 11, 1972; *Washington Post,* January 13, 1972.

*   *   *

MERRITT, James D. 1934-

PERSONAL: Born September 13, 1934, in Lebanon, N.H.; son of L. Morse and Eva (Van Buskirk) Merritt; divorced. *Education:* University of New Hampshire, B.A., 1955; University of Rhode Island, M.A., 1958; University of Wisconsin, Ph.D., 1964. *Residence:* New York, N.Y. *Office:* Department of English, Brooklyn College of the City University of New York, Brooklyn, N.Y. 11210.

CAREER: University of Pittsburgh, Pittsburgh, Pa., assistant professor of English, 1963-66; Brooklyn College of the City University of New York, Brooklyn, N.Y., assistant professor, 1966-71, associate professor, 1972-75, professor of English, 1975—. *Member:* Victorian Society of America, Society of Architectural Historians, Friends of Cast Iron Architecture, American Civil Liberties Union.

WRITINGS: (Editor) *The Pre-Raphaelite Poem,* Dutton, 1966; *Ronald Firbank,* Twayne, 1969; (editor with Thomas Boyle) *The Urban Adventurers,* McGraw, 1972. Also author of more than a dozen *World Book* entries on nineteenth-century writers. Contributor of essays to critical collections and articles to *Opera News* and Victorian studies journals.

WORK IN PROGRESS: Editing with Thomas Boyle, *The Victorian Sensation Novel;* writing *Learothamco,* an architectural guide to an imaginary city; a critical biography of H. P. Lovecraft.

AVOCATIONAL INTERESTS: Opera, rock music, architecture (has served as a guide for architectural tours), science fiction.

* * *

METZGER, Erika A(lma) 1933-

PERSONAL: Born April 8, 1933, in Berlin, Germany; daughter of Otto A. and Alma (Nitschke) Hirt; married Michael M. Metzger (a professor), August 30, 1958. *Education:* Received teaching certificate from College in Goettingen, Germany, 1954; Free University, West Berlin, Germany, diploma, 1958; Cornell University, M.A., 1961; State University of New York at Buffalo, Ph.D., 1967. *Office:* Clemens Hall, State University of New York at Buffalo, Buffalo, N.Y. 14260.

CAREER: University of Illinois, Urbana, instructor in German, 1961-63; State University of New York at Buffalo, part-time instructor, 1963-67, assistant professor, 1967-72, associate professor of German, 1972—. *Member:* International Association of Scholars in German, Modern Language Association of America, American Association of Teachers of German.

WRITINGS: (With husband, Michael M. Metzger) *Clara und Robert Schumann,* Houghton, 1967; (with M. M. Metzger) *Paul Klee,* Houghton, 1967; (editor with A. George de Capua) *Hoffmannswaldau,* Volumes III and IV, Niemeyer (Tuebingen), 1970; (editor) Hans Assmann von Abschatz, *Poetische Uebersetzungen und Gedichte,* H. Lang (Bern), 1970; (with M. M. Metzger) *Stefan George,* Twayne, 1972. Also author of *Gedichte/Poems,* 1977. Contributor of articles and reviews to *Publication of the Modern Language Association, Monatshefte, Modern Language Journal,* and *Journal of English and German Philology.* Editor of literary journals, *Lyrik und Prosa* and *Klingsor.*

WORK IN PROGRESS: Editing baroque poetry; research on Stefan George and Hermann Hesse.

* * *

MEYEN, Edward L. 1937-

PERSONAL: Born May 19, 1937, in North Platte, Neb.; son of Edward C. (employed by railroad) and Evelyn (Anderson) Meyen Moses; married E. Marie Magruder; children: Bradley, Brett, Joy, Blake, Janelle. *Education:* Colo-

rado State College (now University of Northern Colorado), B.A., 1958, M.A., 1959; attended Western State College of Colorado, 1957-58, and Iowa State University, 1962-63; State University of Iowa, Ph.D., 1968. *Office:* Department of Special Education, University of Kansas, Lawrence, Kan. 66044.

CAREER: Teacher of mentally retarded in Rocky Ford, Colo., 1957-58; Colorado State College (now University of Northern Colorado), Greeley, supervising teacher at laboratory school, 1958-60; Iowa State Department of Public Instruction, Des Moines, consultant for the mentally retarded, 1960-64; Iowa State Board of Control, Des Moines, director of Iowa Comprehensive Plan to Combat Mental Retardation, 1964-65; University of Iowa, Des Moines, lecturer, 1965-66, instructor and project director at Special Education Curriculum Development Center, 1966-68, assistant professor, 1968-70, director of Special Education Curriculum Development Center, 1968-69, associate professor of special education, 1970-73; University of Kansas, Lawrence, professor of special education and chairman of department, 1973—. Field reader, Bureau for Education for the Handicapped. *Member:* American Association on Mental Deficiency, Council for Exceptional Children, Phi Delta Kappa.

WRITINGS: (Contributor) William R. Gearhart, editor, *Handbook on the Administration of Special Education,* C. C Thomas, 1967; *Planning Community Services for the Mentally Retarded,* International Textbook Co., 1967; (with Donald L. Carr) *An Investigation of Teacher Perceived Instructional Problems: Indicators of In-Service Training Needs for Teachers of the Educable Mentally Retarded,* Office of Education, Bureau for Education for the Handicapped, 1968; *The Missouri Conference on the Categorical/Non-Categorical Issue in Special Education,* University of Missouri, 1971; *Developing Units of Instruction: For the Mentally Retarded and Other Children with Learning Problems,* W. C. Brown, 1972, 2nd edition, 1976; (with Glenn A. Verguson and Richard J. Whelan) *Strategies for Teaching Exceptional Children,* Love Publishing Co., 1972; (compiler with Verguson and Whelan) *Alternatives for Teaching Exceptional Children,* Love Publishing Co., 1975. Contributor to *Journal of Special Education, Mental Retardation, Training School Bulletin, Exceptional Children, Midland Schools,* and other journals. Editor, *Focus on Exceptional Children;* field editor, *Teaching Exceptional Children.*

WORK IN PROGRESS: Research on performanced-based teacher training.

AVOCATIONAL INTERESTS: Landscaping, outdoor sports, and antiques.†

* * *

MEYER, Charles R. 1920-

PERSONAL: Born September 30, 1920, in Chicago, Ill.; son of Francis A. (a salesman) and Elizabeth (Teuchert) Meyer. *Education:* St. Mary of the Lake Seminary, M.A., 1945, S.T.D., 1952; Rosary College, B.S.L.S., 1948; post-doctoral study at Gregorian University, Rome, 1948-49. *Home and office:* St. Mary of the Lake Seminary, Mundelein, Ill. 60060.

CAREER: Roman Catholic priest; St. Mary of the Lake Seminary, Mundelein, Ill., assistant professor, 1949-67, associate professor, 1967-69, professor of historical and systematic theology, 1969—, librarian, 1949-68, dean of students, 1956-67, dean of School of Theology, 1976—. *Member:* Catholic Theological Society of America, American Catholic Historical Association, American Society for Church History.

WRITINGS: The Thomistic Concept of Justifying Contrition, St. Mary of the Lake Seminary, 1949; *A Contemporary Theology of Grace,* Alba, 1971; *The Touch of God: A Theological Analysis of Religious Experience,* Alba, 1972; *Man of God: A Study of the Priesthood,* Doubleday, 1974; *What a Modern Catholic Believes about the Holy Spirit,* Thomas More Association, 1974. Contributor to *New Catholic Encyclopedia;* contributor to theology journals.

WORK IN PROGRESS: Research on the religious experience.

SIDELIGHTS: Charles Meyer is competent in Latin, Greek, French, German, Spanish, Italian, and Hebrew. *Avocational interests:* Electronics.

* * *

MEYER, Frank S(traus) 1909-1972

May 9, 1909—April 2, 1972; American editor and political writer. Obituaries: *New York Times,* April 3, 1972. (See index for *CA* sketch)

* * *

MICHAEL, Henry N(athaniel) 1913-

PERSONAL: Born July 14, 1913, in Pittsburgh, Pa.; son of Anthony N. and Albina (Dubska) Michael; married Ida Nemez, June 8, 1943; children: Susan Shelly, Richard Carleton, Andrew Paul. *Education:* University of Pennsylvania, B.A., 1948, M.A., 1951, Ph.D., 1954. *Home:* 2712 Pine Valley Lane, Ardmore, Pa. 19003. *Office:* MASCA, University Museum, 33rd and Spruce Sts., Philadelphia, Pa. 19104.

CAREER: University of Pennsylvania, Philadelphia, instructor in geography, 1948-54; Smith, Kline & French, Philadelphia, editor, 1954-56; J. B. Lippincott, Philadelphia, editor, 1956-58; Temple University, Philadelphia, assistant professor, 1959-62, associate professor, 1962-65, professor of geography and anthropology and chairman of the department, 1965—; University Museum, Philadelphia, research associate, 1960—. Research associate in radiocarbon laboratory, University of Pennsylvania, 1960—. Has done field work in U.S. Southwest, Alaska, California, Nevada, Czechoslovakia, Lebanon, Egypt, and Greece. *Military service:* U.S. Army, 1942-45; became first lieutenant.

MEMBER: Arctic Institute of North America, Association of American Geographers (fellow), American Anthropological Association, Royal Geographical Society, American Association for the Advancement of Science, American Association for the Advancement of Slavic Studies, Association of Delaware Valley Geographers (council member), Philadelphia Anthropological Society, Sigma Xi. *Awards, honors:* American Philosophical Society grant-in-aid, 1952-53.

WRITINGS—Editor, ''Anthropology of the North: Translations from Russian Sources'' series, published by University of Toronto Press, except as indicated: S. I. Rudenko, *The Ancient Culture of the Bering Sea and the Eskimo Problem,* 1961; *Studies in Siberian Ethnogenesis,* 1962; M. G. Levin, *Ethnic Origins of the Peoples of Northeastern Asia,* 1963; *Studies in Siberian Shamanism,* 1963; *The Archeology and Geomorphology of Northern Asia: Selected Works,* 1964; A. P. Okladnikov, *The Soviet Far East in Antiquity,* 1965; *Lieutenant Zagoskin's Travels in Russian America, 1842-1844: The First Ethnographic and Geographic Investi-*

gations in the Yukon and Kuskokwin Valleys of Alaska, 1967; A. P. Okladnikov, *Yakutia before Its Incorporation into the Russian State,* McGill-Queen's University Press, 1970; (and annotator) V. N. Chernetsov and W. Moszynska, *The Archaeology of Western Siberia,* McGill-Queen's University Press, 1972.

Contributor: *Races of Mankind, Lands and Peoples,* Grolier Society, 1953; I. U. Olsson, editor, *Radiocarbon Variations and Absolute Chronology,* Wiley, 1970; (and editor with E. K. Ralph) *Dating Techniques for the Archaeologist,* M.I.T. Press, 1971. General editor, ''Anthropology of the North'' series, 1959—. Contributor to *American Anthropologist, American Antiquity, Radiocarbon, Arctic, Archaeometry,* and other publications. Member of publications committee, Arctic Institute, 1967-70.

WORK IN PROGRESS: Comparative articles on dendrochronological and radiocarbon dating in the eastern Mediterranean and dynastic Egypt.

* * *

MICHAEL, Thomas A. 1933-
(Tom Michael)

PERSONAL: Born April 1, 1933, in South Whitely, Ind.; son of Samuel Elden (a barber) and Edna (Smith) Michael; married Bonnie Jo Bohnstedt, June 10, 1955; children: Ann E., Judith E., John S. *Education:* Wabash College, A.B., 1955; Union Theological Seminary, New York, N.Y., M.Div., 1959; Drexel University, doctoral candidate, 1969—. *Home:* 6925 Collins Ave., Pennsauken, N.J. 08109. *Office:* Drexel University, philadelphia, Pa. 19104.

CAREER: Ordained United Presbyterian minister, 1959; pastor of Presbyterian churches in Campbell Hall and Yonkers, New York, 1959-66; United Presbyterian Church, Interboard Office of Personnel, Philadelphia, Pa., researcher in personnel development, 1966-69; Drexel University, Philadelphia, research assistant, 1969—. Co-founder Yonkers Day Care Organization; director, Auburn Theological Seminary, 1965-69; director and organizational consultant, Organizational Renewal Associates, Inc.; also conducts sensitivity training groups. *Member:* Phi Beta Kappa. *Awards, honors:* Fulbright fellowship, Phillips University, Marburg, Germany, 1955-56.

WRITINGS—Under name Tom Michael: (With David Ng) *How to Cope in the Computer Age without Pulling the Plug,* Friendship, 1971. Contributor to *Christian Century.*

WORK IN PROGRESS: Research on use of organization development interventions in local government; analyzing organizations using categories from ethology.†

* * *

MICHELSON, William M. 1940-

PERSONAL: Born January 26, 1940, in Trenton, N.J.; son of Harry Robert (a teacher) and Mildred (Schwartz) Michelson; married Ellen-Rachel Brause, June 17, 1962; children: Louisa, Daniel, Ethan, Jeremy. *Education:* Princeton University, A.B. (magna cum laude), 1961; Harvard University, M.A., 1963, Ph.D., 1965. *Office:* Department of Sociology, University of Toronto, Toronto, Ontario, Canada.

CAREER: Princeton University, Princeton, N.J., instructor, 1964-65, assistant professor of sociology, 1965-66; Ontario Institute for Studies in Education, Toronto, assistant professor, 1966-68, associate professor of sociology and educational planning, 1968-69; University of Toronto, Toronto, assistant professor, 1966-68, associate professor of sociology, 1968-69, associate professor of sociology and urban studies, 1969-72, professor of sociology, 1972—, Centre for Urban and Community Studies, acting director, 1972-73, associate director, 1973—, director of The Child in the City Programme, 1976—. Senior researcher, Canadian Ministry of State for Urban Affairs, Ottawa, 1971-72. Visiting professor at University of California, Berkeley, summer, 1966, and University of Lund, Lund, Sweden, spring, 1971, 1975-76. Member of committee of examiners for Graduate Record Examination in Advanced Sociology, Educational Testing Service, 1968-73.

MEMBER: International Sociological Association, American Sociological Association, Canadian Sociology and Anthropology Association, World Society for Ekistics, Environmental Design Research Association, Working Group on Time-Budgets and Social Activity, European Centre for Documentation and Coordination in the Social Sciences (chairman, 1974—), Phi Beta Kappa. *Awards, honors:* Woodrow Wilson fellowship, 1961-62; National Science Foundation fellowship, 1962-64; Bobbs-Merrill and Free Press Book Awards, 1963, for work on general and special Ph.D. examinations in sociology; Canada Council leave fellowship, 1975-76.

WRITINGS: Man and His Urban Environment: A Sociological Approach, Addison-Wesley, 1970, 2nd edition, 1976; *Behavioral Research Methods in Environmental Design,* Dowden, 1975; (with Kent P. Schwirian and others) *Contemporary Topics in Urban Sociology,* General Learning Press, 1977.

Contributor: L. S. Bourne and others, editors, *The Form of Cities in Central Canada,* University of Toronto Press, 1973; Marcia P. Effrat, editor, *The Community,* Free Press, 1974; Christopher Beattie and Stewart Crysdale, editors, *Sociology Canada: Readings,* Butterworth, 1974; *Science for Better Environment,* Science Council of Japan, 1976; Daniel Stokols, editor, *Perspectives on Environment and Behavior: Theory, Research and Application,* Plenum, 1976. Contributor to sociology journals in Canada and the United States. Member of editorial advisory board, *Environmental Behavior;* consulting editor, *American Journal of Sociology.*

WORK IN PROGRESS: Interdisciplinary research on the child in the city.

*   *   *

MILES, Michael W.   1945-

PERSONAL: Born May 11, 1945, in Portsmouth, Va.; son of Wade M., Jr. (a businessman) and Amelia (Davis) Miles; married Donalda Buchanan (a student counselor), November 27, 1969 (divorced March, 1976). *Education:* Princeton University, B.A. (with high honors), 1967; University of California, Berkeley, M.A., 1968. *Home:* 606 Joyner St., Greensboro, N.C. *Agent:* John Cushman Associates, Inc., 25 West 43rd St., New York, N.Y. 10016.

CAREER: Goddard College, Plainfield, Vt., member of history faculty, 1969-74; *Greensboro Daily News,* Greensboro, N.C., member of staff, 1976—. *Member:* Phi Beta Kappa.

WRITINGS: The Radical Probe: The Logic of Student Rebellion, Atheneum, 1971. Contributor to national magazines and newspapers, including *New Republic* and *Baltimore Sun.* Editor, *Change* (magazine).

WORK IN PROGRESS: A book on right-wing Republicanism, for Oxford University Press.

MILLER, Barry   1946-

PERSONAL: Born December 4, 1946, in Brooklyn, N.Y.; son of Sidney and Anne (Lipshitz) Miller. *Education:* Parson's School of Design, Certificate in Graphic Design, 1967; New School for Social Research, B.F.A., 1971; additional study at Brooklyn College of the City University of New York, 1970-71, and Hofstra University, 1973-77. *Home and office:* 57 The Boulevard, Sea Cliff, N.Y. 11579.

CAREER: Clairol, Inc., New York City, boardman, 1967—; Chalek & Dreyer (advertising agency), New York City, assistant art director, 1967-68; Siegel Design Associates, New York City, junior art director, 1968-69; M. & J. Levine (advertising agency), New York City, assistant art director, 1969-70; Loews Corp., New York City, assistant art director, 1970-72; Woodward Mental Health Center, Rehabilitation Division, Freeport, N.Y., supervisor of photography, graphic arts, silk screening, and arts and crafts, 1972-77; self-employed leather designer and craftsman, 1977—.

WRITINGS: Alphabet World (juvenile), photographs by author, Macmillan, 1971.

AVOCATIONAL INTERESTS: Photography, painting, poetry, music, song-writing.

*   *   *

MILLER, Charles E.   1929-

PERSONAL: Born December 11, 1929, in New Orleans, La.; son of Oscar S. (a salesman) and Charlotte (Hug) Miller. *Education:* St. Mary's Seminary, Perryville, Mo., B.A., 1952, graduate study, 1952-56; University of Southern California, M.A., 1962. *Home:* 5012 East Seminary Rd., Camarillo, Calif. 93010. *Office:* St. John's Seminary, Camarillo, Calif. 93010.

CAREER: Roman Catholic priest of Vincentian Order (C.M.); St. John's Seminary, Camarillo, Calif., professor of homilectics, 1956—, dean of studies, 1965—. Has made television appearances on "Life with Linkletter," "Virginia Graham Show," and other programs.

WRITINGS: Pius XII Mass Hymnal, Gregorian Institute of America, 1959, revised and enlarged edition published as *Praying the Mass in Song,* 1965; (with Oscar J. Miller) *To Sow the Seed,* Joseph F. Wagner, 1967; *A Sense of Celebration,* Joseph F. Wagner, 1969; (with Miller) *Communicating Christ,* Joseph F. Wagner, 1970; (with John A. Grindel) *Repentance and Renewal,* Alba, 1971; (with Miller and Michael M. Roebert) *Announcing the Good News,* Alba, 1971; (with Miller and Roebert) *Breaking the Bread,* Alba, 1972; (with Grindel) *Until He Comes,* Alba, 1972; *Living in Christ,* Alba, 1974; *Making Holy the Day,* Catholic Book Publishing, 1975; *Love in the Language of Penance,* Alba, 1976. Wrote words and music of song, "The Christmas Star," Walt Disney Music, 1969. Contributor to *Catholic Digest, Homiletic and Pastoral Review, Pastoral Life, Tidings,* and other periodicals.

*   *   *

MILLER, George H(all)   1919-

PERSONAL: Born August 5, 1919, in Evanston, Ill.; son of Donald C. (a banker) and Janet (Hall) Miller. *Education:* University of Michigan, A.B., 1941, Ph.D., 1951; Harvard University, M.A., 1949. *Home:* 511 Union St., Ripon, Wis. 54971. *Office:* Department of History, Ripon College, Ripon, Wis. 54971.

CAREER: University of Michigan, Ann Arbor, instructor in history, 1951-54; Ripon College, Ripon, Wis., assistant professor, 1954-59, associate professor, 1959-65, professor of history, 1965—. *Military service:* U.S. Army, 1941-45; received Bronze Star Medal and Purple Heart. *Member:* American Historical Association, Organization of American Historians, Economic History Association, American Association of University Professors, State Historical Society of Wisconsin.

WRITINGS: (With S. M. Pedrick) *A History of Ripon, Wisconsin,* Ripon Historical Society, 1964; *Railroads and the Granger Laws,* University of Wisconsin Press, 1972.

*   *   *

MILLER, Hugh Milton 1908-

PERSONAL: Born March 29, 1908, in St. Paul, Minn.; son of James Milton (a dentist) and Elsie (Tilley) Miller; married Jeanne Vical (a teacher), June 25, 1934; children: Louise (Mrs. Guy Lewis), Marilyn, Mary Margaret. *Education:* University of Oregon, B.A., 1930; Columbia University, graduate study, 1938; Harvard University, M.A., 1939, Ph.D., 1941. *Home:* 3304 Wilway Ave. N.E., Albuquerque, N.M. 87106.

CAREER: Music teacher in public schools in Glendale and Eugene, Ore., 1931-36; Monticello Junior College, Alton, Ill., assistant professor of music, 1940-41; North Texas State College (now University), Denton, associate professor of music, 1941-47; University of New Mexico, Albuquerque, professor of music, 1947-73, professor emeritus, 1973—, head of the department, 1947-57. Visiting professor, University of Oregon, 1955-56; lecturer, University of Auckland, 1958; exchange professor, University of Hawaii, 1966-67. *Member:* Phi Kappa Phi, Phi Mu Alpha, Phi Kappa Psi.

WRITINGS: History of Music, Barnes & Noble, 1947, 4th edition, Harper, 1972; *Introduction to Music,* Barnes & Noble, 1958, 2nd edition, 1978. Contributor to *Musical Quarterly, Music and Letters, Journal of the American Musicological Society,* and other publications. Editor, *Program Notes,* Albuquerque Civic Symphony, 1947-53.

WORK IN PROGRESS: Humor in Music; Texture in Music.

SIDELIGHTS: Hugh M. Miller told *CA:* "My writing has been almost entirely in the field of music; more specifically, in areas related to musicology. My aspirations have been to contribute something to the world's knowledge about music, its literature or its compositional techniques. Also, my books have been academically oriented to provide motivation and guidance to the student of music history or music appreciation."

AVOCATIONAL INTERESTS: Photography, woodwork, swimming, bicycling, gardening, and carving.

*   *   *

MILLER, John N. 1933-

PERSONAL: Born July 20, 1933, in Van Wert, Ohio; son of Stephen Arthur (an educator) and Marion (Neely) Miller; married Louise Spoerri, August 25, 1956; children: Eric, Mark. *Education:* Denison University, A.B., 1955; Stanford University, A.M., 1960, Ph.D., 1964. *Politics:* Democrat. *Home:* 428 West College St., Granville, Ohio 43023. *Office:* Department of English, Denison University, Granville, Ohio 43023.

CAREER: Whitman College, Walla Walla, Wash., in-

structor in English, 1960-62; Denison University, Granville, Ohio, 1962—, currently professor of English. Trustee, Denison Commons Club, Inc.

WRITINGS: A World of Her Own: Writers and the Feminist Controversy, C. E. Merrill, 1971. Contributor of poems to literary magazines.

WORK IN PROGRESS: A series of essays on contemporary British and American poets; a volume of poems.

SIDELIGHTS: John Miller told *CA,* "I believe in writing and maintaining an unfashionably traditional poetry—often rhymed and somewhat metrical, narrative and discorsive at times, with full-fledged people projecting existences apart from the psychic depths of the author."

*   *   *

MILLER, K(eith) Bruce 1927-

PERSONAL: Born August 12, 1927, in Washington, D.C.; son of Paul Richard (an engineer) and Laurence (Broussard) Miller; married Aiko Suzuki, July 24, 1965; children: Christopher Arlen, Roland Timothy. *Education:* Baylor University, B.A., 1950, M.A., 1952; Princeton Theological Seminary, graduate study, 1952-53; University of Southern California, Ph.D., 1963; also took advanced studies in violin under Robert Pollack for five years. *Home:* 4525 Roberts Rd., Fairfax, Va. 22032. *Office:* Office of the President, Luther Rice College, Alexandria, Va. 22310.

CAREER: Los Angeles Music and Art School, Los Angeles, Calif., teacher of violin, 1955-60; University of Southern California, Los Angeles, American Baptist campus chaplain, 1958-76, part-time instructor in history of ideas, 1959-62, part-time lecturer in philosophy, 1964-71; Luther Rice College, Alexandria, Va., president, 1976—. Post-doctoral research fellow, Yale University, 1970-71. *Member:* American Academy of Religion, American Philosophical Association.

WRITINGS: Ideology and Moral Philosophy: The Relation of Moral Ideology to Dynamic Moral Philosophy, Humanities, 1971.

WORK IN PROGRESS: A book on philosophical ethics; a book on philosophy of mind.

AVOCATIONAL INTERESTS: Chamber music, bicycling.

*   *   *

MILLER, Robert A(llen) 1932-

PERSONAL: Born February 17, 1932, in Wheeling, W. Va.; son of Fred J. Miller and Rose (Kovash) Miller; married Helen Hedges (an artist), June 20, 1953; children: Tara Lee, Burke Allen, Robert Nathan, Keith Carroll. *Education:* Duke University, A.B., 1952; George Washington University, M.D., 1956. *Religion:* Episcopal. *Office:* Naples Medical Center, 831 4th Ave. N., Naples, Fla. 33940.

CAREER: Naples Medical Center, Naples, Fla., practice of internal medicine and cardiology, 1962—; Naples Community Hospital, Naples, director, Coronary Care Unit, 1965—, chief of staff, 1967—. President, Naples Medical and Professional Center, 1976—. Organizer and director, Peoples National Bank, Naples. *Military service:* U.S. Army, 1958-61; served in Medical Corps; became captain. *Member:* Florida Heart Association.

WRITINGS: How to Live with a Heart Attack, Chilton, 1971, revised edition, 1973.

WORK IN PROGRESS: A layman's guide to venereal disease.

MILLER, Robert H(enry) 1889-

PERSONAL: Born February 9, 1889, in North Manchester, Ind.; son of Robert H. (a minister) and Emma (Norris) Miller; married Maude E. Reiff, June 6, 1916; children: Robert, John, Mary Emma (Mrs. Gene Coe). *Education:* Manchester College, A.B., 1916; Garrett Theological Seminary, B.D., 1931; Northwestern University, M.A., 1931. *Politics:* Republican. *Home:* Timbercrest Home, North Manchester, Ind. 46962.

CAREER: Ordained a minister of Church of the Brethren; pastor of churches in Los Angeles and LaVerne, Calif. and North Manchester, Ind., 1917-29; Manchester College, North Manchester, instructor in religion and philosophy, 1929-59; interim pastor in eight churches throughout United States, 1959-68. *Member:* American Philosophical Association, American Academy of Religion, Midwest Philosophical Association. *Awards, honors:* D.D., Manchester College, 1922.

WRITINGS: The Lord's Prayer, Brethren Press, 1929; *The Life Portrayed in the Sermon on the Mount,* W. A. Wilde, 1934; *The Hunger of the Heart* (book of prayers), Brethren Press, 1972.

WORK IN PROGRESS: A book of children's stories, completed and awaiting publication; comments on the Gospel of John.

SIDELIGHTS: Robert H. Miller told *CA:* "My interest has always been a strongly but not solely rational approach to religion which is accentuated with years. While it is important for scholars to write for scholars, many people do not read and would find it difficult to read this scholarly dialogue. Because of my training and experience I entertain the hope that I may be able to speak to some of these who seem to be left outside the auditorium."†

* * *

MILLER, Stephen J(ohn) 1936-

PERSONAL: Born September 11, 1936, in Secaucus, N.J.; son of George W. and Constance (Adamowicz) Miller; married Roberta M. Brahm, September 17, 1960; children: Andrew S., Rodney J., Jessica A. *Education:* St. Peter's College, Jersey City, N.J., B.S., 1958; St. Louis University, Ph.D., 1962. *Politics:* Democrat. *Religion:* Roman Catholic.

CAREER: Washington University and Jewish Hospital, both St. Louis, Mo., research associate, 1960-62; Community Studies, Inc., Kansas City, Mo., resident sociologist, 1962-64, consultant, 1964-65; Brandeis University, Waltham, Mass., assistant professor, 1964-67, associate professor of sociology, 1967-72; Center for Community Health and Medical Care, Boston, Mass., assistant director, 1968—; Harvard University, Medical School, Boston, associate dean, beginning 1969, assistant professor of preventive and social medicine, beginning 1973. Visiting assistant professor, Washington University, summers, 1965-66. Member, Massachusetts Governor's Commission on Elderly Affairs, 1970—; Peter Bent Brigham Hospital, member of advisory committee, 1970-71, chairman of advisory committee, 1971-72. Consultant, Association of American Medical Colleges, 1966-67, Rhode Island Department of Public Assistance, 1967-68.

MEMBER: American Sociological Association (fellow), Society for the Study of Social Problems (chairman of committee on new projects, 1966-67), Association of American Medical Colleges, Midwest Sociological Society, Eastern Sociological Society. *Awards, honors:* Greater Boston Junior Chamber of Commerce award for community service, 1969.

WRITINGS: (With W. D. Bryant) *A Division of Nursing Labor,* Community Studies, Inc., 1965; (contributor) Arnold M. Rose, editor, *Older People and Their Social World,* F. A. Davis, 1965; (contributor) Bernice L. Neugarten, editor, *Middle Age and Aging,* University of Chicago Press, 1968; (contributor) Irwin Deutscher and Elizabeth Thompson, editors, *Among the People: Studies of the Urban Poor,* Basic Books, 1969; *Prescription for Leadership: Training for the Medical Elite,* Aldine, 1970; (contributor) Donald Kent and others, editors, *Research Planning and Action for the Elderly,* Behavioral Publications, 1972; (contributor) *Handbook of Medical Sociology,* Prentice-Hall, 1972; (contributor) Eliot Freidson, editor, *The Professions and Their Prospects,* Sage Publications, 1972.

Contributor of articles to *Encyclopedia of Social Work* and to journals, including *Sociological Quarterly, Training for New Trends, Working with Older People,* and *Social Problems.* Deputy editor, *Journal of Health and Social Behavior,* 1969—.

WORK IN PROGRESS: Research on social organization of institutions and professions; studying the organization of professional education.†

* * *

MILLER, Stuart Creighton 1927-

PERSONAL: Born June 2, 1927, in New York, N.Y.; son of Stewart Gillespie (a policeman) and Suzanne Morrow (Dunleavy) Miller; married Naomi Esterowitz (an interior decorator), June 11, 1955; children: Sarah Fanny, Peter Isaac. *Education:* Colgate University, B.A., 1950; Sorbonne, University of Paris, further study, 1949-50; Columbia University, M.A., 1955, Ph.D., 1966. *Home:* 181 San Carlos Ave., Sausalito, Calif. 94965. *Office:* Department of Social Sciences, San Francisco State University, San Francisco, Calif. 94132.

CAREER: High school social studies teacher in Garden City, N.Y., 1955-59; Columbia University, New York, N.Y., instructor in history, 1959-62; San Francisco State University, San Francisco, Calif., assistant professor, 1962-66, associate professor, 1966-71, professor of social sciences, 1971—. *Military service:* U.S. Navy, 1945-47, 1951-53; became lieutenant. U.S. Naval Reserve, 1953-62; became lieutenant commander. *Member:* American Historical Association, Organization of American Historians, Association for Asian Studies, Chinese Historical Society of America.

WRITINGS: The Unwelcome Immigrant: The American Image of the Chinese, University of California Press, 1969; (contributor) John King Fairbank, editor, *The Missionary Enterprise in China and America,* Harvard University Press, 1974; *Benevolent Assimilation: The American Conquest of the Philippines,* Braziller, in press. Contributor to history journals.

AVOCATIONAL INTERESTS: Sports, surfing, tennis, skiing.

* * *

MILLER, Wilma H(ildruth) 1936-

PERSONAL: Born March 8, 1936, in Dixon, Ill.; daughter of William A. (an electrician) and Ruth (Hanson) Miller. *Education:* Northern Illinois University, B.S., 1958, M.S.,

1961; University of Arizona, Ed. D., 1967. *Religion:* Protestant. *Home:* 302 North Coolidge, Normal, Ill. 61761. *Office:* Department of Education, Illinois State University, Normal, Ill. 61761.

CAREER: Elementary school teacher in Dixon, Ill., 1958-63, and Tucson, Ariz., 1963-64; Wisconsin State University (now University of Wisconsin), Whitewater, assistant professor of reading, 1965-68; Illinois State University, Normal, associate professor, 1968-72, professor of education, 1972—. Visiting professor, Western Washington State College (now Western Washington University), 1970. *Member:* International Reading Association, American Educational Research Association, Illinois Association for Higher Education, Kappa Delta Pi, Pi Lambda Theta. *Awards, honors:* Citation of merit, International Reading Association, 1968, for doctoral dissertation; Illinois State University summer fellowship, 1970.

WRITINGS—Published by Center for Applied Research in Education, except as indicated: *Identifying and Correcting Reading Difficulties in Children,* 1971; (editor) *Elementary Reading Today: Selected Articles,* Holt, 1972; *The First R: Elementary Reading Today,* Holt, 1972, 2nd edition, 1977; *Diagnosis and Correction of Reading Difficulties in Secondary School Students,* 1973; *Reading Diagnosis Kit,* 1974; *Reading Correction Kit,* 1975. Editor, *The Reading Clinic,* Center for Applied Research in Education, 1975-77. Contributor to *Reading Teacher, Elementary English, Elementary School Journal, Clearinghouse, Illinois School Research,* and other publications.

*   *   *

MILLGRAM, Abraham E(zra)   1901-

PERSONAL: Born February 1, 1901, in Russia; came to United States in 1913, naturalized citizen; son of Israel M. and Mollie (Kraus) Millgram; married Ida E. Tulchinsky, July 6, 1930 (died, 1973); children: Hillel I. *Education:* City College of New York (now City College of the City University of New York), B.S., 1924; Columbia University, M.A., 1927; Jewish Theological Seminary of America, Rabbi, 1927; Dropsie College for Hebrew and Cognate Learning (now Dropsie University), Ph.D., 1942. *Home:* 12 Ben-Maimon Ave., Jerusalem, Israel, 92262.

CAREER: Temple Beth Israel, Philadelphia, Pa., rabbi, 1930-40; University of Minnesota, Hillel Foundation, Minneapolis, director, 1940-45; United Synagogue Commission on Jewish Education, New York, N.Y., educational director, 1945-61. *Awards, honors:* D.H.L., Jewish Theological Seminary, 1959.

WRITINGS: Sabbath: Day of Delight, Jewish Publication Society, 1944; *Handbook for the Congregational School Board Member,* United Synagogue Commission on Jewish Education, 1953; (editor) *An Anthology of Medieval Hebrew Literature,* Abelard, 1961; *Great Jewish Ideas,* B'nai B'rith Hillel Foundations, 1964; *Jewish Worship,* Jewish Publication Society, 1971.

WORK IN PROGRESS: Two books tentatively entitled *Jerusalem the Faithful City,* a history of Jerusalem, its inhabitants, shrines and institutions, and *The Holy City in Christian Literature.*

SIDELIGHTS: Abraham Millgram told *CA:* "Living in Jerusalem is responsible for the writing of my work *Jewish Worship.* One needs only a little sensitivity to feel the holiness of this ancient city and to experience a powerful urge to express this feeling. Man's relationship with God, especially

that of a Jew, becomes a reality and this enabled me to write on the difficult subject of Jewish worship, its history and content."

*   *   *

MILLS, William Donald   1925-

PERSONAL: Born February 17, 1925, in Long Beach, Calif.; son of Thomas Cullom (an oil field worker) and Louise (McCoy) Mills; married Roberta Fogg, June 27, 1948; children: Thomas, Timothy, Terrand, Kimberley Cushnie. *Education:* University of California, Berkeley, B.A., 1949; University of Southern California, M.A., 1950; University of Madrid, Ph.D., 1964. *Office:* Department of Spanish, Long Beach City College, 4901 East Caron St., Long Beach, Calif. 90808.

CAREER: Long Beach City College, Long Beach, Calif., instructor, 1952-66, professor of Spanish and head of department, 1967—. *Military service:* U.S. Army Air Forces, 1943-45; became sergeant. *Member:* Modern Language Association of America, Teachers of English to Speakers of Other Languages. *Awards, honors:* Del Amo Foundation grant, 1963-64.

WRITINGS: (Translator with Vicente Gaos) *Los Toros: Bullfighting,* Indice, 1964; *Developing Sentence Habits,* American Book Co., 1966; *Generating the Paragraph and Short Essay,* Appleton, 1969.

WORK IN PROGRESS: Research on language development in children and remedial reading, cures.

*   *   *

MILNE, Lorus J.

PERSONAL: Born in Toronto, Ontario, Canada; son of Charles S. (a businessman) and Edna S. (Johnson) Milne; married Margery Greene (a writer, lecturer, and teacher). *Education:* University of Toronto, B.A. (honors), 1933; Harvard University, M.A., 1934, Ph.D., 1936. *Politics:* Republican. *Home:* 1 Garden Lane, Durham, N.H. 03824. *Office:* Spaulding Life Sciences Building, University of New Hampshire, Durham, N.H. 03824.

CAREER: Associate professor and professor at universities and colleges in Texas, New York, Virginia, Pennsylvania, and Vermont; University of New Hampshire, Durham, professor of zoology, 1948—. Visiting professor of environmental technology, Florida International University, 1974. Consultant-writer for American Institute of Biological Sciences; consultant-leader under UNESCO to New Zealand Department of Education; exchangee to South Africa under United States-South Africa Leader Exchange Program. Jointly appointed with wife as "Keepers of the Swans," 1968—, by town of Durham, N.H. *Member:* American Association for the Advancement of Science, Animal Behavior Society, American Society of Zoologists, Woods Hole Marine Biological Laboratory Corporation, Sigma Xi, Explorers Club.

WRITINGS: Machine Shop Methods, Prentice-Hall, 1950.

With wife, Margery Milne: *A Multitude of Living Things,* Dodd, 1947; *The Biotic World and Man,* Prentice-Hall, 1952, 3rd edition, 1965; *The Mating Instinct,* Little, Brown, 1954; *The World of Night,* Harper, 1956; *Paths across the Earth,* Harper, 1958; *Animal Life,* Prentice-Hall, 1959; *Plant Life,* Prentice-Hall, 1959; (with Ralph Buchsbaum and Mildred Buchsbaum) *The Lower Animals: Living Invertebrates of the World,* Doubleday, 1960; *The Balance of Nature,* Knopf, 1960; (with the editors of *Life*) *The Mountains,*

Time-Life Books, 1962; *The Senses of Animals and Men*, Atheneum, 1962; *The Valley: Meadow, Grove, and Stream*, Harper, 1963; *Water and Life*, Atheneum, 1964; *Living Plants of the World*, Random House, 1967, 2nd edition, 1975; *Patterns of Survival*, Prentice-Hall, 1967; *The Ages of Life: A New Look at the Effects of Time on Mankind and Other Living Things*, Harcourt, 1968; *North American Birds*, Prentice-Hall, 1969; *The Nature of Life: Earth, Plants, Animals, Man, and Their Effect on Each Other*, Crown, 1970; *The Cougar Doesn't Live Here Any More: Does the World Still Have Room for Wildlife?*, Prentice-Hall, 1971; *The Arena of Life: The Dynamics of Ecology*, Doubleday, 1972; *Invertebrates of North America*, Doubleday, 1972; *The Animal in Man*, McGraw-Hill, 1972; (with Franklin Russell) *The Secret Life of Animals*, Dutton, 1975; *A World Alive*, New Hampshire Publishing, 1977; *Ecology out of Joint*, Scribner's, 1977.

Books for young people, all with Margery Milne: *Famous Naturalists*, Dodd, 1952; *Because of a Tree*, Atheneum, 1963; *The Crab That Crawled Out of the Past*, Atheneum, 1965; *Gift from the Sky*, Atheneum, 1967; *The Phoenix Forest*, Atheneum, 1968; *The Nature of Animals*, Lippincott, 1969; *When the Tide Goes Far Out*, Atheneum, 1970; *The Nature of Plants*, Lippincott, 1971; *The How and Why of Growing*, Atheneum, 1972; (contributor) *Because of a Flower*, Atheneum, 1975. Contributor to *Encyclopaedia Britannica*, *Time*, *National Geographic*, and other publications. Associate editor, *Fauna*.

SIDELIGHTS: About seventeen of Lorus Milne's books have been issued in foreign editions.

BIOGRAPHICAL/CRITICAL SOURCES: Books and Bookmen, December 4, 1967; *Book World*, January 14, 1968; *New York Times Book Review*, June 30, 1968; *Children's Book World*, November 3, 1968; *Best Sellers*, June 1, 1969; *New Yorker*, December 20, 1969.

* * *

MILNE, Margery

PERSONAL: Born in New York, N.Y.; daughter of S. Harrison (a businessman) and Beatrice (Gutman) Greene; married Lorus J. Milne (a professor of zoology, writer, and lecturer). *Education:* Hunter College (now Hunter College of the City University of New York), B.A., 1933; Columbia University, M.A., 1934; Radcliffe College, M.A., 1936, Ph.D., 1939. *Politics:* Republican. *Home:* 1 Garden Lane, Durham, N.H. 03824.

CAREER: Instructor, assistant professor, or lecturer at colleges and universities in Maine, Virginia, Pennsylvania, Massachusetts, Vermont, and New Hampshire. Consultant-writer for American Institute of Biological Sciences; consultant, Department of Education, Wellington, New Zealand. Jointly appointed with husband as "Keepers of the Swans," 1968—, by town of Durham, N.H. *Member:* Conservation Foundation, Nature Conservancy, Society of Women Geographers, Phi Beta Kappa, Phi Sigma, Sigma Xi.

WRITINGS—All with husband, Lorus J. Milne: *A Multitude of Living Things*, Dodd, 1947; *The Biotic World and Man*, Prentice-Hall, 1952, 3rd edition, 1965; *The Mating Instinct*, Little, Brown, 1954; *The World of Night*, Harper, 1956; *Paths across the Earth*, Harper, 1958; *Animal Life*, Prentice-Hall, 1959; *Plant Life*, Prentice-Hall, 1959; (with Ralph Buchsbaum and Mildred Buchsbaum) *The Lower Animals: Living Invertebrates of the World*, Doubleday, 1960; *The Balance of Nature*, Knopf, 1960; (with the editors of *Life*) *The Mountains*, Time-Life Books, 1962; *The Senses*

of Animals and Men, Atheneum, 1962; *The Valley: Meadow, Grove, and Stream*, Harper, 1963; *Water and Life*, Atheneum, 1964; *Living Plants of the World*, Random House, 1967, 2nd edition, 1975; *Patterns of Survival*, Prentice-Hall, 1967; *The Ages of Life: A New Look at the Effects of Time on Mankind and Other Living Things*, Harcourt, 1968; *North American Birds*, Prentice-Hall, 1969; *The Nature of Life: Earth, Plants, Animals, Man, and Their Effect on Each Other*, Crown, 1970; *The Cougar Doesn't Live Here Any More: Does the World Still Have Room for Wildlife?*, Prentice-Hall, 1971; *The Arena of Life: The Dynamics of Ecology*, Doubleday, 1972; *Invertebrates of North America*, Doubleday, 1972; *The Animalia Man*, McGraw, 1972; (with Franklin Russell) *The Secret Life of Animals*, Dutton, 1975; *A World Alive*, New Hampshire Publishing, 1977; *Ecology Out of Joint*, Scribner, 1977.

Books for young people, all with Lorus J. Milne: *Famous Naturalists*, Dodd, 1952; *Because of a Tree*, Atheneum, 1963; *The Crab That Crawled Out of the Past*, Atheneum, 1965; *Gift from the Sky*, Atheneum, 1967; *The Phoenix Forest*, Atheneum, 1968; *The Nature of Animals*, Lippincott, 1969; *When the Tide Goes Far Out*, Atheneum, 1970; *The Nature of Plants*, Lippincott, 1971; *The How and Why of Growing*, Atheneum, 1972; (contributor) *Because of a Flower*, Atheneum, 1975.

Contributor of natural history articles to *Audubon Magazine*, *American Scholar*, *Natural History Magazine*, *New York Times Magazine*, *Scientific American*, and other periodicals, and of research reports to biological journals.

BIOGRAPHICAL/CRITICAL SOURCES: Books and Bookmen, December, 1967; *Book World*, January 14, 1968; *New York Times Book Review*, June 30, 1968; *Children's Book World*, November 3, 1968; *New Yorker*, December 20, 1969.

* * *

MILNS, R(obert) D(avid) 1938-

PERSONAL: Born November 26, 1938, in Doncaster, Yorkshire, England; son of James (a company director) and Dorothy Maude (Midgeley) Milns; married Diana Margaret Cooper, July 1, 1961 (divorced); married Lynette Victoria Burton, 1977; children: (first marriage) Alexander Philip, Nicholas Robert, Helen Cecilia. *Education:* University of Leeds, B.A. (first class honors), 1960; Cambridge University, B.A. (first class honors), 1962. *Home:* 3-117 Macquarie St., Saint Lucia, Queensland 4067, Australia. *Office:* Department of Classics, University of Queensland, Brisbane, Queensland 4069, Australia.

CAREER: Queen Elizabeth Grammar School, Wakefield, England, assistant classics master, 1962-64; University of New England, Armidale, New South Wales, Australia, lecturer in classics, 1964-66, senior lecturer in classics, 1967-68, associate professor in classics, 1969-70; University of Queensland, Brisbane, Australia, professor of classics, 1970—, dean, Faculty of Arts, 1974-76. Member of governing council, North Brisbane College of Advanced Education. *Member:* Australian Society of Classical Studies, Australian Universities Language and Literary Association, Queensland History Teachers Association (joint patron), Dante Alighieri Society (Brisbane; president).

WRITINGS: Alexander the Great, R. Hale, 1968, Pegasus, 1969; (with J. R. Ellis) *The Spectre of Philip*, Sydney University Press, 1970. Contributor to classical journals.

WORK IN PROGRESS: A book on the uses of documentary evidence in the study of Roman history.

SIDELIGHTS: A *New Yorker* reviewer writes of *Alexander the Great:* "[R. D. Milns] makes no attempt to deny the greatness of Alexander of Macedon. He warmly celebrates his subject's military genius . . . , and he acknowledges that in linking the East and the West he literally changed the course of history. He perceives and demonstrates that Alexander was an unstable personality (given to homicidal rages), a megalomaniac (as witnessed by his deification of himself), a conqueror rather than a statesman, a philistine, and spiteful, cruel, ungrateful, alcoholic, and probably homosexual. The result is an excellent portrait in the human round of a usually shadowy figure . . .".

In addition to the classical languages, R. D. Milns is competent in German, Italian, and French.

AVOCATIONAL INTERESTS: Listening to music, films, the promotion of the languages and cultures of minority groups.

BIOGRAPHICAL/CRITICAL SOURCES: New Yorker, April 25, 1970.

*   *   *

MILTON, John R(onald) 1924-

PERSONAL: Born May 24, 1924, in Anoka, Minn.; son of John Peterson (a professor of theology) and Euphemia (Swanson) Milton; married Leonharda Hinderlie (an artist), August 3, 1946; children: Nanci Lynn. *Education:* University of Minnesota, B.A., 1948, M.A., 1951; University of Denver, Ph.D., 1961. *Politics:* Independent. *Religion:* Lutheran. *Home:* 630 Thomas St., Vermillion, S.D. 57069. *Office:* Department of English, University of South Dakota, Vermillion, S.D. 57069.

CAREER: Augsburg College, Minneapolis, Minn., instructor in English and philosophy, 1949-56; Jamestown College, Jamestown, N.D., professor of English and chairman of department, 1957-63, chairman of Humanities Division, 1962-63; University of South Dakota, Vermillion, professor of English, 1963—, director of creative writing, 1965—, chairman of English department, 1963-65. Lecturer or visiting professor at other universities, including Indiana State University and North Dakota State University, 1966. *Military service:* U.S. Army, 1943-46; served in Pacific. *Member:* Western Literature Association (president, 1970-71), Western History Association, American Studies Association of Minnesota and the Dakotas, Delta Phi Lambda. *Awards, honors:* Helene Wurlitzer Foundation fellow, 1965; National Endowment for the Arts writing fellow, 1976-77.

WRITINGS: The Loving Hawk (poems), North Dakota State University Press, 1962; *The Tree of Bones* (poems), Verb Publications (Denver), 1965; *This Lonely House* (poems), James D. Thueson, 1969.

(Editor) *The American Indian Speaks,* University of South Dakota Press, Volume I, 1970, Volume II, 1971; *Three West: Conversations with Vardis Fisher, Max Evans, and Michael Straight,* University of South Dakota Press, 1970; *Oscar Howe: An American Indian Artist,* Dillon, 1972; *Conversations with Frank Waters,* Swallow Press, 1972; *The Tree of Bones and Other Poems,* Dakota Press, 1973; *Crazy Horse,* Dillon, 1974; *Conversations with Frederick Manfred,* University of Utah Press, 1974; *The Blue Belly of the World* (poems), Spirit Mound Press, 1974.

(Editor) *The Literature of South Dakota,* Dakota Press, 1976; *Notes to a Bald Buffalo* (novel), Spirit Mound Press, 1976; *South Dakota: A Bicentennial History,* Norton, 1977. Contributor to literature journals. Editor, *South Dakota Review,* 1963—.

WORK IN PROGRESS: Green Rain, a novel.

SIDELIGHTS: John R. Milton told *CA:* "Writing is an obsession, sometimes mild and sometimes strong. It is an urge to understand myself and the people around me through giving shape to miscellaneous experiences. It is an urge to communicate. And, let no one try to fool himself, it is also a desire to leave something behind, to say to future generations 'I was here.' The obsession co-exists with procrastination, which makes writing very difficult. I have an intense love-hate relationship with my typewriter. I do almost nothing in longhand because my fingers will not move fast enough; and yet I am slow and careful on the typewriter, feeling for the right word or phrase, not wanting to revise more than I absolutely have to. I think, stew, fidget, go through mental torture before I begin writing, and then I try to make the first draft the only draft. It is a painful method but I cannot seem to use any other.

"In poetry, I suppose that I have been influenced largely by William Carlos Williams and Wallace Stevens; in fiction, by Gertrude Stein, Hemingway, Steinbeck, and Walter Van Tilburg Clark. The techniques of poetry tend to carry over into the fiction, which means that my style is rhythmic and imagistic but that the stories—especially the longer ones—can be weak in plot. That does not bother me; I was not a born story-teller. I mean to evoke, to lull and tease the reader into a subtle understanding of something he may not have been aware of before. Subject matter can be called regional because I believe firmly that the best writing is grounded or rooted to a place from which it then opens out to the rest of the world.

"In my present environment—the prairie and plains—the culture of the Dakota Indians is important and it finds its way into much of my writings. I seem to be working toward some kind of fusion of Scandinavian and white and Jungian values with the myths and ceremonies of the Western American Indian. A few kind readers think that I am getting close, as in *The Blue Belly of the World,* but I want to explore the possibilities further in a long novel. A short story, 'The Inheritance of Emmy One Horse,' was translated into Chinese and Dutch and also reprinted in England, indicating a wide interest in the mind and soul of the American Indian; but, a novel with the same title and same chief characters has been called by every publisher it has visited, 'not a potential bestseller.' Which brings me to advice for the young (or old) writer: write for yourself. It is nice to be published, but it is much more important to write in order to please yourself. Commercialism has replaced literature to a large extent in our time. That is deplorable, of course, and frustrating to the serious writer. Even so, it is important that writers keep on working to the best of their abilities, for the sake of the writing itself. Laziness and prostitution of one's craft are the two cardinal sins for any artist."

AVOCATIONAL INTERESTS: Photography.

BIOGRAPHICAL/CRITICAL SOURCES: Minneapolis Sunday Tribune, December 21, 1969, December 9, 1973, June 27, 1976; *American West,* November, 1972; *Western American Literature,* November, 1975; *Pacific Historical Review,* August, 1976.

*   *   *

MINEAR, Richard H(offman) 1938-

PERSONAL: Surname is pronounced "My-near"; born December 31, 1938, in Evanston, Ill.; son of Paul S. (a teacher) and Gladys (Hoffman) Minear; married Edith Christian, August 18, 1962; children: Robert C., Edward L.

Education: Yale University, A.B., 1960; Harvard University, M.A., 1962, Ph.D., 1968. *Office:* Department of History, University of Massachusetts, Amherst, Mass. 01002.

CAREER: Ohio State University, Columbus, assistant professor of history, 1967-70; University of Massachusetts—Amherst, associate professor, 1970-76, professor of history, 1976—. *Awards, honors:* Fulbright senior research grant, 1970-71.

WRITINGS: Japanese Tradition and Western Law, Harvard University Press, 1970; *Victors' Justice: The Tokyo War Crimes Trial,* Princeton University Press, 1971; (editor) *Through Japanese Eyes,* Praeger, 1974.

WORK IN PROGRESS: Japanese Confucian Thought; Japanese-American Relations 1930-1960.

SIDELIGHTS: Reviewing *Victors' Justice: The Tokyo War Crimes Trial* in *Best Sellers,* Bernard Williams states that Richard H. Minear ''. . . challenges the 'credibility of the Tokyo trial and its verdict.'" He continues, ''. . . Political and emotional factors at the immediate conclusion of World War II unfortunately played a key role in the holding of the war trials, trials based on a sincere hope that they would prevent the outbreak of any future wars. The verdict reached by the Justices of the Tokyo trial was indeed a 'victors' justice.''

BIOGRAPHICAL/CRITICAL SOURCES: Best Sellers, December 15, 1971.

*   *   *

MINTZ, Max M. 1919-

PERSONAL: Born August 21, 1919, in London, England; son of Samuel and Janie (Stein) Mintz; married Mildred Patricia O'Rourke (an artist), January 11, 1944; children: Kenneth Andrew. *Education:* City College (now City College of the City University of New York), B.S.S., 1941; New York University, A.M., 1947, Ph.D., 1957. *Religion:* Unitarian Universalist. *Home:* 104 Norman Rd., Hamden, Conn. 06514. *Office:* Department of History, Southern Connecticut State College, 501 Crescent St., New Haven, Conn. 06515.

CAREER: State Teachers College (now State University of New York College at Plattsburgh), assistant professor of history, 1948-51; International Business Machines Corp., Poughkeepsie, N.Y., associate engineer, 1951-63; Southern Connecticut State College, New Haven, assistant professor, 1963-66, associate professor, 1966-70, professor of history, 1970—. *Military service:* U.S. Army, 1944-46; served in Europe. *Member:* Organization of American Historians, New York Historical Society.

WRITINGS: Gouverneur Morris and the American Revolution, University of Oklahoma Press, 1970. Contributor of articles to *New York History, Pennsylvania Magazine of History and Biography,* and *History Today,* and book reviews to *New Republic, New York Times Book Review,* and *Saturday Review.*

*   *   *

MIRACLE, Gordon E. 1930-

PERSONAL: Born May 28, 1930, in Olympia, Wash.; son of Gordon T. and Corine (Orlebeke) Miracle; married Christa Stoeter, June 29, 1957; children: Gary, Gregory, Glenn. *Education:* Attended Oshkosh State College, 1948-50; University of Wisconsin, B.B.A., 1952, M.B.A., 1958, Ph.D., 1962. *Home:* 1461 Cheboygan Rd., Okemos, Mich.

48864. *Office:* Department of Advertising, College of Communication Arts and Sciences, Michigan State University, East Lansing, Mich. 48823.

CAREER: U.S. Army, civilian employee in Germany, 1955-57; University of Wisconsin—Madison, instructor in commerce, 1959-60; University of Michigan, Ann Arbor, instructor, 1960-61, assistant professor of marketing, 1961-66; Michigan State University, East Lansing, associate professor, 1966-70, professor of advertising, 1970—, chairman of department, 1974—. Consultant and business researcher, 1959—. Visiting professor, North European Management Institute, Oslo, Norway, 1972-73. Chairman, Citizens for Meridian Park, 1971. *Military service:* U.S. Army, 1952-55. *Member:* American Marketing Association, American Economic Association, Society for International Development, Association for Education in International Business, American Association for International Business (chairman of Midwest region, 1970-72; national secretary, 1973-75), American Academy of Advertising., Alpha Kappa Psi. *Awards, honors:* Ford Foundation fellow, 1961-62, and summer, 1964.

WRITINGS: (Editor) *Marketing Decision Making: Strategy and Payoff,* Bureau of Business Research, Graduate School of Business Administration, University of Michigan, 1965; *Management of International Advertising,* Bureau of Business Research, Graduate School of Business Administration, University of Michigan, 1966; (with Gerald Albaum) *International Marketing Management,* Irwin, 1970, instructor's manual, 1971.

Contributor to numerous books, including: Jerome B. Kernanan and Montrose Sommers, editors, *Perspectives in Marketing Theory,* Appleton, 1968; C. Robert Patty and Louis H. Vrederberg, editors, *Readings in Global Marketing Management,* Appleton, 1969; Rewoldt, Scott, and Warshaw, *Introduction to Marketing Management,* Irwin, 1969; Chester R. Wasson, *Cases in Buying Behavior and Marketing Decisions,* Challenge Books, 1969; Roger Barton, editor, *Handbook of Advertising Management,* McGraw, 1970; Heinz-Dietrich Fischer and John C. Merrill, editors, *International Communication: Media, Channels, Functions,* Hastings House, 1970; John L. Kraushaar and Louis H. Vorzimer, editors, *Essentials of an Effective Marketing Program: Readings,* D. H. Mark, 1970; William R. Darden and Rudolph P. Lamone, editors, *Marketing Management and the Decision Sciences: Theory and Applications,* Allyn & Bacon, 1971; John K. Ryans, Jr. and James C. Baker, editors, *World Marketing: A Multinational Approach,* Wiley, 1971; Sturdivant and others, editors, *Perspectives in Marketing Management Readings,* Scott, Foresman, 1971; Martin L. Bell, editor, *Marketing Concepts and Strategy,* 2nd edition, Houghton, 1972; Stuart H. Britt, editor, *Marketing Handbook,* Dartnell, 1972; Ashok Kapoor and Phillip D. Grub, editors, *The Multinational Enterprise in Transition,* Darwin Press, 1972.

Writer of business case studies; contributor of about twenty articles and reviews to scholarly journals.

WORK IN PROGRESS: A book on the economics of advertising; research on advertising and government.

*   *   *

MISH, Charles C(arroll) 1913-

PERSONAL: Born June 27, 1913, in Williamsport, Pa.; son of Charles Carroll and Elizabeth Reeves (Rex) Mish; married Mary Frances Faulkner, January 19, 1945. *Education:* University of Pennsylvania, B.A., 1936, M.A., 1946, Ph.D.,

1950. *Home:* 3925 Legation St. N.W., Washington, D.C. 20015. *Office:* English Department, University of Maryland, College Park, Md. 20740.

CAREER: University of Maryland, College Park, instructor, 1948-55, assistant professor, 1955-58, associate professor, 1958-61, professor of seventeenth-century literature, 1961—.

WRITINGS: (Editor) *Short Fiction of the Seventeenth Century,* New York University Press, 1963, published as *Anchor Anthology of Short Fiction of the Seventeenth Century,* Doubleday-Anchor, 1963; (editor) *English Prose Fiction, 1600-1700: A Chronological Checklist,* University Press of Virginia, 1967; (editor) *Restoration Prose Fiction, 1666-1700: An Anthology of Representative Pieces,* University of Nebraska Press, 1970.

*   *   *

MITCHELL, Adrian   1932-
(Volcano Jones, Apeman Mudgeon)

PERSONAL: Born October 24, 1932, in London, England; son of James Gibb (a scientist) and Kathleen (a teacher; maiden name, Fabian) Mitchell; married Celia Hewitt (an actress). *Education:* Attended Oxford University, 1952-55. *Politics:* "My brain socialist/My heart anarchist/My eyes pacifist/My blood revolutionary." *Religion:* "Everything that lives is Holy." *Home:* 33 South Hill Park, London N.W.3, England. *Agent:* Timothy Corrie, Fraser & Dunlop Scripts Ltd., 91 Regent St., London W1R 8RU, England.

CAREER: Writer, poet, and playwright; *Oxford Mail,* Oxford, England, reporter, 1955-57; *Evening Standard,* London, England, reporter, 1957-59; State University of Iowa, Iowa City, instructor at writers workshop, 1963-64; University of Lancaster, Lancaster, England, Granada fellow in the arts, 1967-69; Wesleyan University, Middletown, Conn., fellow at Center for Humanities, 1971. *Military service:* Royal Air Force, 1951-52. *Member:* Writers Guild of Great Britain, Society of Authors, Poets Conference, National Union of Journalists. *Awards, honors:* Gregory Award for Poetry, 1961; co-recipient, translation award, P.E.N., 1966, for *Marat/Sade;* Tokyo Festival Television Film Award, 1971.

WRITINGS: If You See Me Comin' (novel), Macmillan, 1962; *Poems,* J. Cape, 1964; *Out Loud* (poems), Grossman, 1968; *The Bodyguard* (novel), J. Cape, 1970, Doubleday, 1971; (editor) Tim Daly, *Jump, My Brothers, Jump: Poems from Prison,* Freedom Press, 1970; *Ride the Nightmare: Verse and Prose,* J. Cape, 1971; (editor with Brian Elliott) *Bard in the Wilderness,* Thomas Nelson (Melbourne), 1971; *Wartime* (novel), J. Cape, 1973; (with John Fuller and Peter Levi) *Penguin Modern Poets,* Book 22, Penguin, 1973; *The Apeman Cometh* (poems), J. Cape, 1976; (with Joan Jana) *Victor Jana: His Life and Songs,* Hamish Hamilton, 1976.

Plays: "Animals Can't Laugh," produced on Granada TV, 1961; (author of libretto) Richard Rodney Bennett, "The Ledge," first produced in London at Sadlers Wells Theatre, 1962; (author of verse adaptation) Peter Weiss, *The Persecution and Assassination of Jean-Paul Marat as Performed by the Inmates of the Asylum of Charenton under the Direction of the Marquis de Sade* (two-act; first produced on West End at Aldwych Theatre, August 20, 1964; produced on Broadway at Martin Beck Theatre, December 27, 1965; production filmed by United Artists, 1967), J. Calder, 1965, Atheneum, 1966; (adapter of libretto) Emanuel Schikaneder and Carl L. Giesecke, "The Magic Flute," first produced in London, 1966; (adapter) Jose Triana, "The Criminals," first

produced in London, 1967; (author of lyrics) Peter Brook, *Tell Me Lies: The Book of the Royal Shakespeare Production US/Vietnam/US/Experiments/Politics* (first produced as "US" on West End at Aldwych Theatre, 1966), Bobbs-Merrill, 1968 (published in England as *US: The Book of the Royal Shakespeare Production US/Vietnam/US/Experiments/Politics,* Calder & Boyers, 1968).

Tyger: A Celebration of the Life and Work of William Blake (first produced as "Tyger" on West End at the New Theatre, July 20, 1971), J. Cape, 1971; "Tamburlane the Mad Hen," first produced in Devonshire, 1971; *Man Friday* [and] *Mind Your Head* (contains "Man Friday," first produced on television by British Broadcasting Corp., October 30, 1972, and "Mind Your Head," first produced in Liverpool, 1975), Eyre Methuen, 1974; (adapter) Nikolai Gogol, "The Inspector General," first produced in Nottingham, 1974. Also author of libretto for radio play, "The Island," 1963; author of screenplay, "Tell Me Lies," 1968, and of film commentary for "The Body," produced by Kestrel Films, 1969; author of television documentary, "William Blake," 1971. Other plays include "A Seventh Man" and "White Suit Blues"; other television plays include "Daft as a Brush" and "Glad Day." Recorded, with Stevie Smith, "Poems," produced by Argo, 1974. Has written "daft poems" under the pseudonyms Volcano Jones and Apeman Mudgeon.

SIDELIGHTS: In a review of *Out Loud,* Anthony Thwaite says that the book "proclaims itself through its title. These are poems for speaking. They are also poems that presuppose a youngish, leftish, protest-prone audience, and one that is very much there in a public place: not a diffused scatter of isolated radio-listeners or solitary readers but a pop crowd wanting to be entertained.... Adrian Mitchell's poems have most of the virtues and some of the vices that one would expect, given such an audience. They are clear, direct, funny, warm-hearted, and eloquent. They are also sometimes obvious, banal, whimsical, and too genially sure of a welcome: the Queen, the bourgeois, the term 'critics' and the word 'peace' invite responses which can too easily be satisfied. It will be a pity if Mitchell's real talent for making poetry public is crudified and dissipated by an audience that too readily sits there waiting for him to hit old targets." Peter Bland agrees that "public causes sometimes get the better of him but his heart's in the right place . . . on the page that is and not on his sleeve. Just one quibble. It's about Mitchell's constant habit of repeating himself. Only Hindu prophets, pop singers or the anonymous authors of nursery-rhymes can get away with seven- or eight-line refrains."

Adrian Mitchell's ability to reach the "pop audience" is further evidenced by reaction to his drama. Mary Holland feels that in *Tyger* "Mr. Mitchell's politics often seem confused and simplistic. But his commitment and his chief talent as a writer is in communicating in the market place, using his vivid tumbling gift with words to put across ideas of change to people who are not in these days much accustomed to the power of poetry. His natural audience are the young, the disaffected, those who seek, in however stumbling and incoherent a fashion, to bring about quite basic changes in our society. To reach them, to communicate Blake's rage and his humanity, Mr. Mitchell has drawn a play in poster colours with poster thoughts. Much of *Tyger* is strong, crude, unsubtle. It reaches out to an audience sated with television, pop music, the gutter press." A reviewer for *Variety* says that the play "reportedly was four years in gestation, and that kind of preparation time should have produced something sharper. But if Adrian Mitchell's book is uneven and Mike Westbrook's score only serviceable, *Tyger* still manages to be fairly engrossing, impressively produced with strong sight values. Its major achievement may be in the way it stretches English musicals and not the least of the show's virtues is the courage of its innovating.''

BIOGRAPHICAL/CRITICAL SOURCES: Observer Review, March 3, 1968; *New Statesman,* March 22, 1968, July 30, 1971; *London Magazine,* June, 1968, August, 1968; *Book World,* July 28, 1968; *Observer,* August 30, 1970; *Variety,* August 11, 1971; *Plays & Players,* September, 1971; *Stage,* November 2, 1972.

* * *

MITCHELL, Don(ald Earl) 1947-

PERSONAL: Born October 15, 1947, in Chicago, Ill.; son of Wayne Treleven (an electrical engineer) and Elizabeth (Bowker) Mitchell; married Cheryl Warfield, November 29, 1969; children: Ethan. *Education:* Swarthmore College, A.B., 1969. *Politics:* Democrat. *Religion:* Protestant. *Home:* R.D. 2, Vergennes, Vt. 05491. *Agent:* Blanche C. Gregory, Inc., 2 Tudor City Pl., New York, N.Y. 10017.

CAREER: American Baptist Board of Education and Publication, Valley Forge, Pa., staff member, 1971; The New School, Wayne, Pa., high school teacher, 1972; writer, and sheep breeder at Treleven Farm in Vermont, 1973—.

WRITINGS—All novels: *Thumb Tripping,* Little, Brown, 1970; *Four-Stroke,* Little, Brown, 1973. Also author of *Heretical Passions;* author of screenplay for film "Thumb Tripping" based on his novel of the same title, for Avco Embassy Pictures Corp., 1969-70; contributor to *Best Short Stories of 1971,* Houghton. Contributor to *Harper's, Atlantic, Esquire, Shenandoah, Viva,* and *Country Journal.*

WORK IN PROGRESS: An anti-pastoral novel of winter and madness.

SIDELIGHTS: Don Mitchell told *CA:* "Our cultural climate consistently offers the novelist a Faustian bargain: acclaim, in exchange for spilling the guts of one's personal life to the reading public. In this climate nearly all serious fiction is assumed to be personal history held at arm's—or forearm's, or wrist's—length. Small wonder that the day's themes are self-doubt, betrayal, endemic schizophrenia and the difficulty of authentic interaction with other people. In the last few years I've decided to opt for mental health. Farming and carpentry have helped, and the discipline of living somewhat in the middle of nowhere. No more do I view my personal life as a laboratory or seed-ground for creating fiction. Rather, I write to go someplace else, to live other lives, to get out of my skin. It remains to be seen whether this will be rewarded in the marketplace.''

BIOGRAPHICAL/CRITICAL SOURCES: New York Times Book Review, August 2, 1970; *Best Sellers,* August 15, 1970.

* * *

MITCHELL, Jerry 1905(?)-1972

1905(?)—May 22, 1972; American sportswriter. Obituaries: *New York Times,* May 24, 1972.

* * *

MITCHELL, Ruth K.

PERSONAL: Born in Wauwatosa, Wis.; daughter of Albert and Ruth P. (Weber) Schulke; married Richard H. Mitchell,

February 18, 1957 (died, 1959); children: Beth Kay. *Education:* University of Wisconsin, B.S., 1957, M.S., 1966; University of Pittsburgh, Advanced Certificate, 1968, doctoral candidate, 1968—.

CAREER: Librarian; has worked at Milwaukee School of Engineering, Milwaukee, Wis., and Library Office, Oregon State System of Higher Education, Eugene. *Member:* American Library Association, American Society for Information Science, Association for Computing Machinery, American Association of University Professors.

WRITINGS: Information Science and Computer Basics: An Introduction, Linnet Books, 1971. Contributor to library journals; writer of science fiction and mystery stories under an undisclosed pseudonym.

WORK IN PROGRESS: A mystery novel.†

* * *

MITCHISON, Rosalind (Mary) 1919-

PERSONAL: Born April 11, 1919, in Manchester, England; daughter of Edward Murray (a university lecturer) and Rosalind (Smith) Wrong; married John Murdoch Mitchison (a professor of zoology at University of Edinburgh), June 21, 1947; children: Sally, Neil, Harriet, Amanda. *Education:* Oxford University, M.A. (honors), 1942. *Religion:* None. *Home:* Great Yew, Ormiston, East Lothiar, Scotland. *Office:* Department of Economic History, University of Edinburgh, Edinburgh, Scotland.

CAREER: University of Manchester, Manchester, England, assistant lecturer in history, 1943-46; Oxford University, Oxford, England, tutor in modern history, 1946-47; University of Edinburgh, Edinburgh, Scotland, assistant in history, 1954-57; University of Glasgow, Glasgow, Scotland, assistant, 1962-63, part-time lecturer in Scottish history, 1966-67; University of Edinburgh, 1967-76, reader in economic history, 1976—.

WRITINGS: Agricultural Sir John: The Life of Sir John Sinclair of Ulbster, Bles, 1962; *A History of Scotland,* Barnes & Noble, 1970; (editor with N. T. Phillipson) *Scotland in the Age of Improvement,* Aldine, 1970; *British Population Change since 1860,* Macmillan, 1977; (contributor) M. W. Flinn, editor, *Scottish Population History from the Seventeenth Century to the 1930s,* Cambridge University Press, 1977.

WORK IN PROGRESS: Research on Scottish social history.

* * *

MOAT, John 1936-

PERSONAL: Born September 11, 1936, in India; married Antoinette Galletti; children: Elsbeth Merlin, Ben John. *Education:* Oxford University, M.A., 1960. *Agent:* A. D. Peters & Co., 10 Buckingham St., London WC2N 6BU, England.

WRITINGS: 6d. per annum (poems), Phoenix Press, 1966; (self-illustrated) *Heorot* (novel), Cresset, 1968; *A Standard of Verse: With Nine Poems (by others),* Phoenix Press, 1969; *Thunder of Grass* (poems), Cresset, 1970; *The Tugen and the Toot* (novel), Barrie & Jenkins, 1973; *The Ballad of the Leat* (verse), Arc Publications, 1974.

* * *

MOCKLER, Robert J. 1932-

PERSONAL: Born May 23, 1932, in St. Louis, Mo.; son of

Colman M. (a business executive) and Veronica (McKenna) Mockler. *Education:* Attended Fordham University, 1949-51, and University of Paris, 1951-52; Harvard University, A.B. (with honors), 1954, M.B.A., 1959; Columbia University, M.A. (with honors), 1957, Ph.D., 1971; summer study at University of Grenoble, 1951, and University of Bonn, 1954. *Home:* 213 East 89th St., New York, N.Y. 10028. *Office:* Department of Management, St. John's University, Jamaica, N.Y. 11432.

CAREER: International Paper Co., New York City, treasurer's assistant, 1959-61; *Time,* New York City, circulation development manager, 1961-62; *National Observer,* New York City, circulation sales manager, 1962-64; Famous Photographers School, New York City, advertising and market research manager, 1964-66; Columbia Broadcasting System, New York City, marketing director for installment sales, Direct Marketing Services Division, 1966-68. St. John's University, Jamaica, N.Y., professor of business administration, 1962—. *Military service:* U.S. Army, 1955-57.

WRITINGS: (Editor and contributor) *Putting Computers to Work More Effectively in Business Publishing,* American Business Press, 1969; (contributor) *The Management of Forecasting,* St. John's University Press, 1969; (editor and contributor) *Readings in Management Control,* Prentice-Hall, 1970; (editor and contributor) *New Profit Opportunities in Business Publishing,* American Business Press, 1970; (editor and contributor) *Readings in Business Planning and Policy Formulation,* Prentice-Hall, 1972; *The Management Control Process,* Prentice-Hall, 1972; *Business Planning and Policy Formulation,* Prentice-Hall, 1972, 2nd edition, 1978; *Management Decision Making in Behavioral Situations,* Austin Press, 1973; *The Business Management Process,* Austin Press, 1973; *Management Information Systems,* C. E. Merrill, 1974; *Business and Society,* Harper, 1975. Contributor of twenty articles to management journals.

*   *   *

MOELLEKEN, Wolfgang W. 1934-

PERSONAL: Born January 14, 1934; son of August and Emmi Moelleken; married Melita Hildebrandt, 1957; children: Brent, Alan, Sonja. *Education:* University of British Columbia, B.Ed., 1961; University of Washington, Seattle, M.A., 1962, Ph.D., 1965. *Office:* Department of Foreign Languages and Literatures, Purdue University, Lafayette, Ind. 47907.

CAREER: University of California, Riverside, acting assistant professor, 1964-65, assistant professor of German, 1965-67; University of Virginia, Charlottesville, associate professor of German, 1967-68; State University of New York at Stony Brook, associate professor of German, 1968-69; University of California, Davis, associate professor, 1969-72, professor of German, 1972-77; Purdue University, Lafayette, Ind., professor of German and head of department of foreign languages and literatures, 1977—. Visiting instructor in German, University of Colorado, Boulder, 1964. *Awards, honors:* Grants-in-aid from American Council of Learned Societies, 1966, and American Philosophical Society, 1972, 1975; California Humanities Institute fellowship, 1966, 1970; Regents fellowships, 1972, 1973, 1975.

WRITINGS: (With John T. Brewer) *Deutsche Perspektiven,* Heath, 1968; *Liebe und Ehe: Lehrgedichte von dem Stricker,* University of North Carolina Press, 1970; *Der Stricker: Von Uebelen wiben,* H. Lang & Cie (Bern), 1970; *Niederdeutsch der Molotschna- und Chortitzamennoniten*

in British Columbia, Kanada, Max Niemeyer (Tuebingen), 1972; (with G. Agler and Robert E. Lewis) *Die Kleindichtung des Strickers,* Kuemmerle (Goeppingen), five volumes, 1973-78; (with D. Karch) *Siedlungs-Pfaelzisch im Kreis Waterloo, Ontario, Kanada,* Max Niemeyer, 1977. Contributor to *German Quarterly, Journal of Germanic Studies, Publications of the American Dialect Society, Zeitschrift fuer Mundartforschung, Zeitschrift fuer deutsche Philologie,* and other journals.

*   *   *

MOHL, Raymond A(llen) 1939-

PERSONAL: Born October 8, 1939, in Tarrytown, N.Y.; son of Raymond and Eileen (Mcfadden) Mohl; married Nancy Engle (a teacher), December 24, 1960; children: Raymond J., Nancy A. *Education:* Hamilton College, B.A., 1961; Yale University, M.A.T., 1962; New York University, M.A., 1965, Ph.D., 1967. *Home:* 2519 North Ocean Blvd., No. 404, Boca Raton, Fla. 33431. *Office:* History Department, Florida Atlantic University, Boca Raton, Fla. 33431.

CAREER: Valhalla High School, Valhalla, N.Y., social studies teacher, 1962-64; New York University, New York, N.Y., instructor in history, 1966; Indiana University Northwest, Gary, assistant professor, 1967-70, associate professor of history, 1970; Florida Atlantic University, Boca Raton, assistant professor, 1970-71, associate professor, 1970-74, professor of history, 1974—. Lecturer in American urban history at Public Service Institute, Chicago, 1967, and at N.D.E.A. Institute for Advanced Study in History, Indiana University, Indianapolis, 1968. Has presented papers at meetings of professional organizations.

MEMBER: American Historical Association, Organization of American Historians, American Studies Association, Labor Historians, Urban History Group, Immigration History Group, Social Welfare History Group, American Federation of Teachers, Southern Historical Association, Phi Alpha Theta. *Awards, honors:* Grant-in-aid for research, Indiana University, 1968, 1970; graduate faculty fellowship, Indiana University, 1968, 1969, 1970; Council on Research in Economic History research grant, 1968; American Philosophical Society research grant, 1969; second prize, Binkley-Stephenson competition, *Journal of American History,* 1970, for article "Humanitarianism in the Preindustrial City: The New York Society for the Prevention of Pauperism, 1817-1823"; Danforth associate award, 1970; Florida Atlantic University summer research grant, 1971, 1973, 1975; Younger Humanist fellowship, National Endowment for the Humanities, 1972-73; grant-in-aid from Immigration Research Center, University of Minnesota, 1975; faculty career development grant from Florida Atlantic University, 1976-77.

WRITINGS: (Editor with Neil Betten) *Urban America in Historical Perspective,* Weybright, 1970; *Poverty in New York, 1783-1825,* Oxford University Press, 1971; (editor with James F. Richardson, and contributor) *The Urban Experience,* Wadsworth, 1972; (contributor) Richard L. Watson, Jr. and William H. Cartwright, editors, *American History and Culture,* National Council for the Social Studies, 1972; (contributor) James B. Lane and David Goldfield, editors, *The Enduring Ghetto,* Lippincott, 1973; (contributor) Norris Hundley, Jr., editor, *The Chicano,* American Bibliographic Center-Clio Press, 1975.

Abstractor for *Historical Abstracts* and *America: History and Life;* general editor of "American Urban Studies" series, Kennikat, 1972—. Contributor of articles to *Journalism Quarterly, New York History, History Today, Mid-America, Labor History, Social Science Quarterly, Journal of the American Institute of Planners*, and other publications; contributor of reviews to *American Quarterly, New-York Historical Society Quarterly, American Historical Review*, and other publications. Editor, *Journal of Urban History*, 1973—.

WORK IN PROGRESS: Progressive Education and Social Order: The Gary Plan and Urban Schooling, 1900-1940, for Kennikat; monographs on the ethnic history of Gary, Indiana; *Cultural Pluralism and the International Institute Movement; The Urban Missionary Movement, 1800-1860.*

* * *

MOLDENHAUER, Joseph J(ohn) 1934-

PERSONAL: Born February 9, 1934, in Rastatt, Germany; came to United States in 1938, naturalized in 1945; son of Hans Walter (a musicologist) and Margot (Kuhn) Moldenhauer; married Joanne McConnell, June 17, 1957; children: David, Margo. *Education:* Amherst College, B.A., 1956; Columbia University, M.A., 1957, Ph.D., 1964. *Residence:* Austin, Tex. *Office:* Department of English, University of Texas, Austin, Tex. 78712.

CAREER: University of Texas at Austin, special instructor, 1957-62, instructor, 1962-64, assistant professor, 1964-68, associate professor, 1968-72, professor of English, 1972—. *Member:* Modern Language Association of America, Thoreau Society, Phi Beta Kappa. *Awards, honors:* Guggenheim fellowship, 1968-69.

WRITINGS: (Editor) *The Merrill Studies in "Walden,"* C. E. Merrill, 1971; (editor) Henry David Thoreau, *The Maine Woods*, Princeton University Press, 1972; (editor) Thoreau, *Early Essays and Miscellanies*, Princeton University Press, 1975. Contributor of essays to anthologies and professional journals.

WORK IN PROGRESS: Editing Thoreau's *Cape Cod* and volumes of Thoreau's *Journal*, for Princeton University Press; continuing critical work on Poe, Thoreau, and other mid-nineteenth century American writers.

* * *

MOLLENKOTT, Virginia R(amey) 1932-

PERSONAL: Surname is accented on first syllable, which rhymes with "doll"; born January 28, 1932, in Philadelphia, Pa.; daughter of Robert Franklin (a chiropractor) and May (Lotz) Ramey; married Friedrich H. Mollenkott (a teacher), June 17, 1954 (divorced); children: Paul F. *Education:* Bob Jones University, B.A., 1953; Temple University, M.A., 1955; New York University, Ph.D., 1964. *Politics:* Independent. *Religion:* Episcopal. *Home:* 11 Yearling Trail, Mt. Laurel Lakes, Hewitt, N.J. 07421. *Office:* Department of English, William Paterson College, 300 Pompton Rd., Wayne, N.J. 07470.

CAREER: Temple University, Philadelphia, Pa., instructor in English, 1954-55; Shelton College, Ringwood, N.J., instructor, 1955-56, associate professor of English and chairperson of department, 1956-63; Nyack Missionary College, Nyack, N.Y., chairperson of English department, 1963-67; William Paterson College, Wayne, N.J., associate professor, 1967-74, professor of English, 1974—, chairperson of department, 1972-76. *Member:* Modern Language Association of America (assembly delegate, 1975-78; member of executive committee, Division on Religion and Literature,

1977-81), Milton Society of America (member of executive committee, 1975-78), National Council of Teachers of English, Conference on Christianity and Literature (member of board of directors, 1974-77), English Graduate Association (New York University; member of steering committee, 1963—; president, 1967-68).

WRITINGS: Adamant and Stone Chips: A Christian Humanist Approach to Knowledge, Word Books, 1967; *In Search of Balance*, Word Books, 1969; (editor) *Adam among the Television Trees: An Anthology of Verse by Contemporary Christian Poets*, Word Books, 1971; (contributor) Ted Hipple, editor, *Readings for Teaching in Secondary Schools*, Macmillan, 1973; (contributor) James D. Simmonds, editor, *Milton Studies VI*, University of Pittsburgh Press, 1975; (contributor) Paul Jewett, editor, *Man as Male and Female*, Eerdmans, 1975; *Women, Men and the Bible*, Abingdon, 1977. Contributor to *The Christian Ministry in a World of Crisis*, 1970, and *Guide to Life on Campus*, 1973; stylistic consultant, New International Version Bible Translation Committee, 1970—. Contributor to journals, including *Christianity Today, Studies in Philology*, and *Today's Education*. Assistant editor, *Seventeenth-Century News;* chief bibliographer, Conference on Christianity and Literature *Newsletter*, 1967—.

WORK IN PROGRESS: A series of articles for *The Milton Encyclopedia* to be published by Bucknell University Press; an article for *Trust to Good Verses: Essays in Honor of Robert Herrick*, edited by J. Max Patrick and Roger B. Rollin for University of Pittsburgh Press; an article for *Milton Tercentenary Volume*, edited by Patrick for University of Wisconsin Press; a book with Letha Scanzoni, *New Times, New Issues, New Visions.*

* * *

MONHEIM, Leonard M. 1911-1971

June 7, 1911—October 18, 1971; American educator and author of medical textbooks. Obituaries: *New York Times*, October 21, 1971.

* * *

MONSMA, Stephen V(os) 1936-

PERSONAL: Born September 22, 1936, in Pella, Iowa; son of Martin (a clergyman and educator) and Marie (Vos) Monsma; married Mary Carlisle, December 19, 1964; children: Martin Stephen, Kristin Joy. *Education:* Calvin College, A.B., 1958; Georgetown University, M.A., 1961; Michigan State University, Ph.D., 1965. *Politics:* Democrat. *Religion:* Christian Reformed. *Home:* 829 North Kentview Dr. N.E., Grand Rapids, Mich. 49505. *Office:* Michigan House of Representatives, The Capitol, Lansing, Mich. 48909.

CAREER: State University of New York College at Plattsburgh, assistant professor of political science, 1964-67; Calvin College, Grand Rapids, Mich., associate professor, 1967-73, professor of political science, 1973-74, chairman of department, 1969-74; member of Michigan House of Representatives, 1975—. *Member:* American Political Science Association, Kent County Democratic Committee (member of executive committee), Grand Rapids Urban League, Evangelicals for Social Action (member of board, 1977—), Churches' Center for Theology and Public Policy (member of board, 1976—). *Awards, honors:* Institute for Advanced Christian Studies scholar, 1972-73.

WRITINGS: American Politics: A Systems Approach,

Holt, 1969, 3rd edition, 1976; (editor with Jack Van Der Slik) *American Politics: Research and Readings,* Holt, 1970; (with Paul Henry) *The Dynamics of the American Political System,* Dryden, 1972; *The Unraveling of America,* Inter-Varsity, 1974. Contributor to political science journals.

* * *

MOODY, J. Carroll 1934-

PERSONAL: Born January 3, 1934, in Abilene, Tex.; son of Jesse Carroll and Louise (Fryar) Moody; married Carolyn Van Meter, May 1, 1953; children: Lou Ann, Debra Sue, Elaine, David Charles, Melissa Carol. *Education:* University of Corpus Christi (now Texas A & I University at Corpus Christi), B.A., 1956; Texas College of Arts and Industries (now Texas A & I University), M.A., 1960; University of Oklahoma, Ph.D., 1963. *Home:* 1533 Huntington Rd., DeKalb, Ill. 60115. *Office:* Department of History, Northern Illinois University, DeKalb, Ill. 60115.

CAREER: Teacher of history in public schools in Corpus Christi, Tex., 1956-60; University of Toledo, Toledo, Ohio, assistant professor of history, 1963-68, assistant dean of College of Arts and Sciences, 1966-68; Northern Illinois University, DeKalb, associate professor of history, 1968—, chairman of department, 1974—. *Military service:* U.S. Naval Reserve, active duty, 1950-55. *Member:* Organization of American Historians, Labor Historians, American Association of University Professors, American Federation of Teachers, Southern Labor History Association, Illinois Labor History Society, Phi Alpha Theta.

WRITINGS: (With Gilbert C. Fite) *The Credit Union Movement: Origins and Development, 1850-1970,* University of Nebraska Press, 1971; (contributor) William H. Cartwright and Richard L. Watson, Jr., editors, *The Reinterpretation of American History and Culture,* National Council for the Social Studies, 1973.

WORK IN PROGRESS: Steelworkers and the Great Depression: 1929-1936.

* * *

MOODY, Richard 1911-

PERSONAL: Born September 30, 1911, in Des Moines, Iowa; son of Carl Eric and Josephine (Peterson) Moody; married Esther Carol Martin (a television producer), February 26, 1937; children: Pamela (Mrs. Gilbert C. Powers), Eric Craig. *Education:* Drake University, B.A., 1932, M.A., 1934; attended Yale University, 1932-33, 1934-35; Cornell University, Ph.D., 1942. *Home address:* Red Ridge, R.R. 1, Bloomington, Ind. 47401. *Office:* Department of Theatre and Drama, Indiana University, Bloomington, Ind. 47401.

CAREER: Actor and announcer in New York, N.Y., 1935-36; University of Illinois at Urbana-Champaign, Urbana, instructor in speech and theatre, 1936-40; Indiana University at Bloomington, assistant professor, 1942-43, associate professor, 1946-55, professor of speech and theatre, 1955—, director of Indiana University Theatre, 1958-70. Visiting assistant professor of speech and theatre, Northwestern University, 1946; visiting associate professor, University of Hawaii, 1952. Member, Committee on International Exchange of Persons, Theatre Advisory Committee, 1966. *Military service:* U.S. Naval Reserve, Communications Officer, 1943-46; became lieutenant. *Member:* American Educational Theatre Association, Speech Association of

America, American Society for Theatre Research, British Society for Theatre Research, Theatre Communications Group, University Resident Theatre Association (member of board of directors, 1968-70), National Theatre Conference (member of board of directors, 1970-73). *Awards, honors:* Guggenheim fellow, 1959-60; Distinguished Alumni award, Drake University, 1961; National Endowment for the Humanities senior fellow, 1973-74.

WRITINGS: America Takes the Stage, Indiana University Press, 1955; *The Astor Place Riot,* Indiana University Press, 1958; *Edwin Forrest: First Star of the American Stage,* Knopf, 1960; (contributor) Clyde W. Dow, editor, *An Introduction to Graduate Study in Speech and Theatre,* Michigan State University Press, 1961; (editor) Noah Ludlow, *Dramatic Life as I Found It,* Benjamin Blom, 1965; (editor) *Dramas from the American Theatre, 1762-1909,* World Publishing, 1966; *Lillian Hellman: Playwright,* Bobbs-Merrill, 1972. Contributor to *Quarterly Journal of Speech, American Heritage Magazine, Educational Theatre Journal, Compton's Encyclopedia, World Book Encyclopedia,* and other publications.

WORK IN PROGRESS: An article for *A History of Drama in the English Language,* for Methuen, and a book-length biography of Edward Harrigan.

BIOGRAPHICAL/CRITICAL SOURCES: Detroit News, June 25, 1972.

* * *

MOORE, Archie Lee 1916-

PERSONAL: Born December 13, 1916, in Benoit, Miss.; son of Thomas and Lorena Wright; married Joan Hardy, 1955; children: Billy, Rena, Joanie, Hardy, D'Angelo, Anthony. *Address:* P.O. Box 13333, San Diego, Calif. 92113. *Agent:* C. M. Vandeburg, 29229 Heathercliff Rd., Malibu Beach, Calif. 90265.

CAREER: World light-heavyweight boxing champion, 1952-62; Any Boy Can Clubs, Inc., San Diego, Calif., founder, 1965—. Lecturer throughout the United States to Boy Scouts and other groups. Youth consultant to State of California. Athletic director, Buenaventura Academy, Ventura, Calif. *Awards, honors:* Mr. San Diego-1968.

WRITINGS: The Archie Moore Story, McGraw, 1960; (with Leonard Pearl) *Any Boy Can,* Prentice-Hall, 1971.

SIDELIGHTS: Known as one of the most philosophical members of the boxing community, Archie Moore has combined a highly successful fighting career with writing and acting. His autobiography, *The Archie Moore Story,* was called "... an intriguing bit of Americana ..." by reviewer William Hogan. Moore made his motion picture debut in the 1959 production of Metro-Goldwyn-Mayer's "The Adventures of Huckleberry Finn."

Moore told *CA,* "My principal work now is working to help underprivileged youths of all races and religions; to end discrimination and make equality, life, liberty, and the pursuit of happiness a reality for all people."

BIOGRAPHICAL/CRITICAL SOURCES: Archie Moore, *The Archie Moore Story,* McGraw, 1960; *San Francisco Chronicle,* July 13, 1960; *New Yorker,* September 10, 1960.

* * *

MOORE, Bidwell 1917-

PERSONAL: Born December 22, 1917, in Chattanooga,

Tenn.; son of Orville Monroe (an army officer) and Willa (Rippard) Moore; married Clarissa DeBost Downing (a school librarian), March 15, 1942; children: Bidwell DeBost, Peter Rippard, Clarissa Elizabeth, Christopher Downing. *Education:* U.S. Military Academy, B.S., 1940. *Politics:* Republican. *Religion:* Episcopalian. *Home:* 8008 Birnam Wood Dr., McLean, Va. 22101. *Agent:* Bertha Klausner International Literary Agency, Inc., 71 Park Ave., New York, N.Y. 10016.

CAREER: U.S. Army, artillery and intelligence officer and teacher in military schools, 1940-65, retired as colonel; manufacturers' representative, 1966—. Served with First Infantry Division, 1940-45; assistant military attache, Bern, Switzerland, 1948-49; later General Staff officer in United States and overseas posts. *Member:* Army-Navy Country Club. *Awards, honors*—Military: Silver Star, Bronze Star (three), Combat Infantryman's Badge, and Legion of Merit, all during World War II; General Staff Citation.

WRITINGS: As Long as Tommorow (novel), Luce, 1971. Contributor to *Combat Forces Journal.*

WORK IN PROGRESS: Another novel.

AVOCATIONAL INTERESTS: Golf, tennis, horseback riding.

* * *

MOORE, Harold A. 1913-

PERSONAL: Born October 4, 1913, in Champaign, Ill.; son of Oscar O. and Margaret (Parker) Moore; married Berenice Ann, July 2, 1938 (died March, 1975); married Mildred Magers, March 8, 1976; children: (first marriage) Margaret Ann, Lynn Ellen. *Education:* University of Illinois, B.S., 1937, M.S., 1939, further study, 1949-52, 1953-57. *Politics:* Republican. *Religion:* Methodist. *Home:* 711 West Osage St., Normal, Ill. 61761.

CAREER: High school science teacher in Mounds, Ill., 1939-41, and Lawrenceville, Ill., 1941-46; high school teacher of biology and audiovisual director, La Salle, Ill., 1946-47; Illinois State University, Normal, instructor, 1947-53, assistant professor, 1953-69, associate professor of biological sciences, 1969-76, biology supervisory teacher at Laboratory School, 1947-76. *Member:* National Association of Biology Teachers, National Education Association, Association of Midwestern College Biology Teachers, Illinois State Academy of Science, Northern Illinois Association of Biology Teachers, Illinois Education Association, Beta Beta Beta, Phi Sigma.

WRITINGS: (With Blanche McAvoy) *A Study Guide for Biology,* Burgess, 1953; (with John R. Carlock) *The Spectrum of Life,* with laboratory guide, Harper, 1969.

WORK IN PROGRESS: Revising *The Spectrum of Life,* and accompanying laboratory guide.

AVOCATIONAL INTERESTS: Rock hunting, travel, fishing.

* * *

MOORE, Jack B(ailey) 1933-

PERSONAL: Born October 23, 1933, in Newark, N.J.; son of Raymond John and Clara (Jones) Moore; married Judith Bowker (a social worker), August 18, 1956; children: Sean, Brendan, Devin, Deirdre, Tamsin. *Education:* Drew University, B.A., 1955; Columbia University, M.A., 1956; University of North Carolina, Ph.D., 1962. *Politics:* Independent. *Home address:* Route 5, Box 133, Lutz, Fla.

33549. *Office:* University of South Florida, Tampa, Fla. 33620.

CAREER: West Virginia University, Morgantown, instructor in English, 1956-58; University of North Carolina, Chapel Hill, assistant fellow in English, 1958-60; Washington and Lee University, Lexington, Va., instructor in English, 1960-62; University of South Florida, Tampa, professor of humanities, 1962—. Visiting professor of English, Fourah Bay College, 1968-69. *Member:* American Association of University Professors, American Civil Liberties Union (member of executive board, 1969—), South Atlantic Modern Language Association of America. *Awards, honors:* Bread Loaf fellow in fiction, 1962; American Philosophic Society grants, 1966, 1971; Fulbright scholar, 1967-68; Faculty Lecturer award, 1968; Danforth associate, 1969; Florida Endowment for the Humanities grant, 1975, 1976.

WRITINGS: (Editor with Rex James Burbank) *The Literature of Early America,* C. E. Merrill, 1967; *Idylls of the King—Tennyson* (study guide), Barnes & Noble, 1968; *James Fenimore Cooper: "The Last of the Mohicans"* (study guide), Barnes & Noble, 1969; (editor with Burbank) *The Literature of the American Renaissance,* C. E. Merrill, 1969; *Maxwell Bodenheim,* Twayne, 1969; (editor with Burbank) *The Literature of the American Realistic Period,* C. E. Merrill, 1970. Contributor of fiction to *New Mexico Quarterly* and *Esquire,* of articles to *Studies in Short Fiction, Colorado Quarterly,* and *African Literature Today.*

WORK IN PROGRESS: W.E.B. Du Bois, for Twayne; a book on the impact of Africa upon Afro-American writers and artists.

AVOCATIONAL INTERESTS: American and black American and African culture; inversigating social issues through humanities' techniques.

* * *

MOORE, John Rees 1918-

PERSONAL: Born October 15, 1918, in Washington, D.C.; son of John Brooks (a professor) and Florence (Rees) Moore; married Betty Drawbaugh (a college professor), July 16, 1954; children: Steven Abel, Sarah Brooks. *Education:* Reed College, B.A., 1940; Harvard University, M.A., 1942; Columbia University, Ph.D., 1957. *Home:* 7038 Goff Rd., Hollins, Va. 24019. *Office:* Department of English, Hollins College, Hollins, Va. 24020.

CAREER: University of Georgia, Athens, assistant professor of English, 1946; Carnegie Institute (now Carnegie-Mellon University), Pittsburgh, Pa., instructor in English, 1947; Lehigh University, Bethlehem, Pa., instructor in English, 1947-50; Hollins College, Hollins, Va., assistant professor, 1957-60, associate professor, 1961-67, professor of English, 1968—, chairman of department, 1971-74. American representative to International Kahlil Gibran Festival, Beirut, 1970. *Military service:* U.S. Army Air Forces, 1942-45; became sergeant. *Member:* Modern Language Association of America, American Committee for Irish Studies (vice-chairman, 1968-72; chairman-elect, 1972-75), South Atlantic Modern Language Association.

WRITINGS: (Editor with Louis D. Rubin, Jr.) *The Idea of an American Novel,* Crowell, 1961; (contributor) D.E.S. Maxwell and S. B. Bushrui, editors, *W. B. Yeats: Centenary Essays,* Ibadan University Press, 1965; *Masks of Love and Death: Yeats as Dramatist,* Cornell University Press, 1971; (editor with R.H.W. Dillard and George Garrett) *The Sounder Few,* University of Georgia Press, 1971; (contributor) Bushrui, editor, *Sunshine and the Moon's Delight: Centenary Tribute to J. M. Synge*, Harper, 1972. *Hollins Critic*, co-editor, 1964-67, editor, 1971—.

WORK IN PROGRESS: An anthology of short fiction illustrating cultural conflict between the old and the new; a book relating certain works of older authors to current issues.

SIDELIGHTS: John Moore told *CA:* "Right now it is vital to try to hold what seems to be breaking in pieces together. As a humanist, the past seems to me an essential area of knowledge if the future is to have any intelligible meaning. Yet a mere holding action, resistance to change, might be even worse than a reckless plunge into the unknown future. As teachers our job is to build bridges by convincing ourselves by exposure to the 'new' (if we can) that mutual adaptation is possible between generations. We must listen and learn from students and have the confidence and will to persuade them to listen and learn from us.

"I am interested in trying to explore the literary imagination as exemplified in fiction unfamiliar to most Americans—in Africa, Asia, and especially the smaller nations of Europe—as a stimulus to our thinking about cultural conflict. From another perspective, I want to examine some of the great authors in English tradition in the light of our present needs to see what light they have to offer. The year I spent in Ireland and the year I spent in Greece both suggested in different but overlapping ways the limitations of a too provincial American view of the world."

AVOCATIONAL INTERESTS: Tennis, music, travel.

* * *

MOORE, Lester L(ee) 1924-

PERSONAL: Born July 14, 1924, in Blackshear, Ga.; son of Lester Lee (an optometrist) and Grace (Patterson) Moore. *Education:* University of Miami, Coral Gables, Fla., A.B., 1948; Columbia University, A.M., 1949, Ed.D., 1966. *Home:* Moorcroft, R.D. 2, LeRaysville, Pa. 18829. *Office:* Department of Theatre Art and Speech, Rutgers University, Newark, N.J. 07102.

CAREER: Florida State University, Tallahassee, instructor in English and humanities, 1949-52; Rutgers University, Newark Campus, Newark, N.J., instructor, 1952-56, assistant professor, 1956-66, associate professor, 1966-69, professor of theater art and speech, 1969—, founder and chairman of department, 1952-66, 1969—. Associate director, Parkway Playhouse and Art Center, Burnsville, N.C., summers, 1952, 1956-65; director of North Carolina Tercentennial Pageant, 1963, of segment of New Jersey Tercentennial Pageant, 1964; has directed more than 150 plays; lecturer and recitalist on folk music and on classic theaters of the Orient. *Military service:* U.S. Army, 1943-46. *Member:* Japan Society, Speech Association of the Eastern States. *Awards, honors:* Grant to study classic Hindu theatre, principally in London, 1975.

WRITINGS: Outside Broadway: A History of the Professional Theatre in Newark, N.J. from the Beginning to 1867, Scarecrow, 1970. Had several original plays produced as undergraduate; writer of children's stories. Contributor to *Journal of the New Jersey Speech Association*. Editor, *Parkway Playbill*, 1961-65.

WORK IN PROGRESS: A monograph on classic Hindu theatre; articles on cinema; a novel.

AVOCATIONAL INTERESTS: Redecorating his early nineteenth-century farm house, growing roses.

MOORE, Marianne Craig 1887-1972

November 15, 1887—February 5, 1972; American poet and baseball fan. Obituaries: *Detroit News*, February 6, 1972; *New York Times*, February 6, 1972; *Washington Post*, February 7, 1972; *Newsweek*, February 14, 1972; *Publishers Weekly*, February 14, 1972; *Time*, February 14, 1972; *Current Biography*, March, 1972; *National Review*, March 3, 1972. (See index for *CA* sketch)

* * *

MOORE, Marie Drury 1926-

PERSONAL: Born January 4, 1926, in South Orange, N.J.; daughter of Peter James and Dorothy A. (Cashin) Drury; children: Peter, James. *Education:* Attended Seton Hall University. *Religion:* Roman Catholic.

CAREER: Newark News, Newark, N.J., reporter, 1943-51; Goodway Publications, Fort Lauderdale, Fla., editor and writer, 1969-70; *Florida Profile* (magazine), Fort Lauderdale, editor, 1971. Free-lance feature writer for newspapers, 1967—; distributor for Amway Corp. *Member:* Theta Sigma Phi (historian of Florida Atlantic chapter, 1971).

WRITINGS: Two Princes, A Witch and Miss Katie O'Flynn (juvenile), illustrations by Sean Morrison, Prentice-Hall, 1970. Formerly wrote "Chippy Chipmunk and His Friends," a weekly column in *Ramsey Journal*, Ramsey, N.J.

WORK IN PROGRESS: Two juvenile books, *The Zero Who Was Nothing* and *God Made Color*.†

* * *

MOORE, Richard 1927-

PERSONAL: Born September 25, 1927, in Greenwich, Conn.; son of James Howard and Gertrude (Ehrhardt) Moore; married Janet Elizabeth Packer, May 12, 1961; children: Stephanie, Tania, Claudia. *Education:* Yale University, B.A., 1950; Trinity College, Hartford, Conn., M.A., 1956; Boston University, doctoral studies, 1955-57. *Home:* 81 Clark St., Belmont, Mass. 02178. *Office:* New England Conservatory of Music, Boston, Mass. 02115.

CAREER: Berlitz School, Paris, France, teacher of English, 1950; with Hartford Fire Insurance Co., Hartford, Conn., 1953-54; Boston University, Boston, Mass., teacher of English, 1956-57; Trinity College, Burlington, Vt., instructor in English, 1962-65; New England Conservatory of Music, Boston, member of English faculty, 1965—. Fanny Hurst Visiting Professor of English, Brandeis University, fall, 1976. *Military service:* U.S. Air Force, 1950-53; became second lieutenant. *Awards, honors:* Bread Loaf Writer's Conference fellowship in poetry, 1957; Fulbright scholar in Freiburg, Germany, 1958-59.

WRITINGS: A Question of Survival (poems), University of Georgia Press, 1971; *Word from the Hills* (poems), University of Georgia Press, 1972; *The Autobiography of a Mouse* (epic poem), Seagull Publications, in press. Contributor of more than one hundred poems to *New Yorker, Atlantic, Harper's, Saturday Review, Nation, Listener, American Scholar, Mademoiselle, Modern Occasions, Transatlantic Review, Poetry, Poetry Northwest, Perspective, Southern Review, Denver Quarterly*, and other publications; contributor of essays and reviews to *Poetry, Nation*, and other periodicals.

WORK IN PROGRESS: Poetry, prose.

SIDELIGHTS: Richard Moore told *CA*, "I try for poems

that are passionate, clear, classic in form, and darkly humorous.''

AVOCATIONAL INTERESTS: Mathematics, music.

BIOGRAPHICAL/CRITICAL SOURCES: Mademoiselle, November, 1964; *American Scholar,* summer, 1968; *Roanoke Times,* July 25, 1971.

*　　*　　*

MOOTE, A(lanson) Lloyd 1931-

PERSONAL: Born March 22, 1931, in Hamilton, Ontario, Canada; son of Stanley A. (a clergyman) and Grace (Wood) Moote; married Barbara Brown; children: Karen, Peter, Daphne, Robert. *Education:* University of Toronto, B.A., 1954; University of Minnesota, M.A., 1956, Ph.D., 1958. *Religion:* Episcopalian. *Home:* 1078 South Hayworth Ave., Los Angeles, Calif. 90035. *Office:* Department of History, University of Southern California, Los Angeles, Calif. 90007.

CAREER: University of Toronto, Toronto, Ontario, lecturer in history, 1958-61; University of Cincinnati, Cincinnati, Ohio, assistant professor of history, 1961-62; University of Southern California, Los Angeles, assistant professor, 1962-65, associate professor, 1965-71, professor of history, 1971—. *Member:* American Historical Association, Society for French Historical Studies, Past and Present Society. *Awards honors:* Koren Prize, Society for French Historical Studies, 1962, for article in *French Historical Studies;* American Philosophical Society research grant, 1962; National Endowment for the Humanities grant, 1969-70; Guggenheim fellowship, 1977.

WRITINGS: The Seventeenth Century: Europe in Ferment, Heath, 1970; (contributor) John C. Rule, editor, *Louis XIV and the Craft of Kingship,* Ohio State University Press, 1970; *The Revolt of the Judges: The Parlement of Paris and the Fronde, 1643-1652,* Princeton University Press, 1971. Contributor to *Journal of Modern History, Past and Present, American Historical Review, Canadian Historical Review, Canadian Journal of History, Personalist,* and *Queen's Quarterly.* Member of editorial board, *French Historical Studies,* 1971-73.

WORK IN PROGRESS: A biography of Louis XIII, 1601-1643.

AVOCATIONAL INTERESTS: Classical music, spectator sports, playing tennis.

*　　*　　*

MOQUIN, Wayne (Francis) 1930-

PERSONAL: Born October 24, 1930, in Chicago, Ill.; son of William F. (a landscape gardener) and Clara (Gilbertson) Moquin. *Education:* Augustana College, Rock Island, Ill., B.A., 1952; attended Lutheran School of Theology at Chicago, 1954-55; Luther Theological Seminary, St. Paul, Minn., G.Th., 1957. *Politics:* Independent. *Home:* 3225 Home Ave., Berwyn, Ill. 60402. *Office: Encyclopaedia Britannica,* 425 North Michigan Ave., Chicago, Ill. 60611.

CAREER: Pastor of Lutheran church in Proctor, Minn., 1957-59; assistant pastor in Cedar Rapids, Iowa, 1959-60; Sacred Design Associates, Minneapolis, Minn., writer, 1961-62; San Francisco Productions, Chicago, Ill., member of staff, 1964-73; member of staff, *Encyclopaedia Britannica,* 1973—. *Member:* Organization of American Historians, Norwegian-American Historical Association, Minnesota Historical Society, Phi Beta Kappa.

WRITINGS: (Editor with George Ducas and Thomas Stauffer, under the direction of Mortimer Adler and Charles Van Doren) *Annals of America,* twenty volumes, Encyclopaedia Britannica, 1968; (editor) *Makers of America,* ten volumes, Encyclopaedia Britannica, 1971; (editor) *Documentary History of the Mexican-Americans,* Praeger, 1971; (editor) *Great Documents in American Indian History,* Praeger, 1973; (co-editor) *Documentary History of Italian Americans,* Praeger, 1974; (with Van Doren) *The American Way of Crime,* Praeger, 1976; (associate editor) *Great Treasury of Western Thought,* Bowker, 1977. Contributor to *Webster's American Biographies,* Merriam, 1974.

AVOCATIONAL INTERESTS: Playing bridge, travel.

*　　*　　*

MORENO, Antonio Elosegui 1918-

PERSONAL: Born March 1, 1918, in San Sebastian, Spain; son of Jose Luis Luque (employed in industry) and Concepcion (Elosegui) Moreno. *Education:* University of Madrid, D.Arch., 1945; University of California, Berkeley, B.S., 1955, M.S., 1958; St. Thomas Aquinas College, River Forest, Ill., Ph.D., 1960. *Home:* 5890 Birch Court, Oakland, Calif. 94618. *Office:* Graduate Theological Union, 2465 Le Conte Ave., Berkeley, Calif. 94709.

CAREER: Ordained Roman Catholic priest, 1951; University of Notre Dame, Notre Dame, Ind., 1958-60, 1964-66, began as instructor, became professor of philosophy; Graduate Theological Union, Berkeley, Calif., professor of philosophy, 1966—.

WRITINGS: Jung, Gods, and Modern Man, University of Notre Dame Press, 1970. Contributor of over thirty articles to journals in the United States, Canada, Spain, and Italy.

WORK IN PROGRESS: A book on the philosophy of mathematics.

*　　*　　*

MORGAN, Robert 1944-

PERSONAL: Born October 3, 1944, in Hendersonville, N.C.; son of Clyde R. (a farmer) and Fannie (Levi) Morgan; married Nancy Bullock, August 6, 1965; children: Benjamin Ray, Laurel Keith. *Education:* University of North Carolina at Chapel Hill, B.A., 1965; University of North Carolina at Greensboro, M.F.A., 1968. *Home:* 105 North Wood Rd., Freeville, N.Y. 13068. *Office:* Department of English, Cornell University, Ithaca, N.Y. 14850.

CAREER: Cornell University, Ithaca, N.Y., lecturer, 1971-73, assistant professor of English, 1973—. *Awards, honors:* National Endowment for the Arts grant, 1968, and 1974.

WRITINGS: Zirconia Poems, Lillabulero Press, 1969; *Red Owl* (poems), Norton, 1972; *Land Diving* (poems), Louisiana State University Press, 1976.

WORK IN PROGRESS: An autobiographical poem about the southern mountains.

SIDELIGHTS: Robert Morgan told *CA:* ''Though I passed through college mostly as a math student, and have since worked at many kinds of jobs, writing has always given me a center and continuity. At times it has held me on course when nothing else seemed to work. The poets I have read most are probably Whitman and Dickinson, in that order. I was attracted to Whitman early for his ability to combine the grand scheme and voice with accurate humble details, and to Dickinson for, among other things, her explosive concentrations of distance in mythic particulars.''

BIOGRAPHICAL/CRITICAL SOURCES: Choice, March, 1973; *The Small Farm,* March, 1975; *Ironwood,* Number 6, 1975; *Epoch,* Volume XXVIII, number 1, 1977.

*　　*　　*

MORRILL, George Percival   1920-

PERSONAL: Born May 14, 1920, in Montclair, N.J.; son of George Pillsbury (a civil engineer) and Alice Maud (Gray) Morrill; married Phyllis Christensen (a teacher), July 5, 1945; children: George Peter, Michael Lee, Christopher, Timothy Alan. *Education:* Wesleyan University, Middletown, Conn., B.A., 1942, M.A., 1957. *Politics:* Independent. *Religion:* Congregationalist. *Home:* Thayer Rd., Higganum, Conn. 06441. *Agent:* Brandt & Brandt, 101 Park Ave., New York, N.Y. 10017. *Office:* American Education Publications, Inc., 245 Long Hill Rd., Middletown, Conn. 06457.

CAREER: After college worked as foundryman, well digger, jackhammer operator, and longshoreman in Bermuda; seaman and deck officer in U.S. Merchant Marine, 1944-46, riding convoys in North Atlantic and Middle East; University of Connecticut, New London Branch, instructor in English, 1947-50; Readex Microprint, Chester, Vt., plant manager, 1950-55; American Education Publications, Inc., Middletown, Conn., editor-writer, 1957—. Member, board of directors, Brainerd Memorial Library, 1960—. *Member:* Socratic Literary Society.

WRITINGS: Dark Sea Running (novel), McGraw, 1959; *The Multimillionaire Straphanger: A Life of John Emory Andrus,* Wesleyan University Press, 1971; *Snow, Stars and Wild Honey* (memoir), Lippincott, 1976. Contributor of sea stories and articles to *Collier's, Saturday Evening Post, Cosmopolitan, Argosy, Farm Journal, Bluebook, Holiday, Reader's Digest,* and other magazines.

WORK IN PROGRESS: A novel; articles.

AVOCATIONAL INTERESTS: Reading, hiking, building, swimming, and playing touch football with his sons.

*　　*　　*

MORRIS, John N(elson)   1931-

PERSONAL: Born June 18, 1931, in Oxford, England; son of Charles and Charlotte (Maurice) Morris; married Anne de La Chapelle, May 27, 1966; children: Julia, John George, Richard. *Education:* Hamilton College, A.B., 1953; Columbia University, M.A., 1956, Ph.D., 1964. *Office:* Department of English, Washington University, St. Louis, Mo. 63130.

CAREER: University of Delaware, Newark, instructor in English, 1957-58; Columbia University, New York, N.Y., lecturer, 1958-60, instructor in English, 1960-61; San Francisco State College (now University), San Francisco, Calif., lecturer in English, 1961-62; Columbia University, instructor, 1962-64, assistant professor of English, 1964-67; Washington University, St. Louis, Mo., associate professor, 1967-71, professor of English, 1971—. *Military service:* U.S. Marine Corps, 1953-55; became first lieutenant. *Member:* Modern Language Association of America, Phi Beta Kappa.

WRITINGS: (With M. X. Lesser) *Modern Short Stories: The Fiction of Experience,* McGraw, 1962; *Versions of the Self: Studies in English Autobiography,* Basic Books, 1966; *Green Business: Poems,* Atheneum, 1970; *The Life beside This One: Poems,* Atheneum, 1975. Contributor to literature journals.

WORK IN PROGRESS: Poems; research on eighteenth-century English literature.

*　　*　　*

MORRIS, Norman S.   1931-

PERSONAL: Born April 28, 1931, in Philadelphia, Pa.; son of Benjamin Mitchell and Reba (Goldberg) Morris; married Sandra Toll, May 7, 1961; children: Kenneth, Gregory, Benjamin. *Education:* Temple University, A.B., 1952; Northwestern University, M.A., 1955. *Office:* CBS News, 524 West 57th St., New York, N.Y.

CAREER: Voice of America, Washington, D.C., news producer-writer, 1965-67; Columbia Broadcasting System (CBS), New York, N.Y., news writer, 1967-69, producer-writer, 1969-72, acting executive producer, 1972—. *Military service:* U.S. Marine Corps, 1952-54; received letter of commendation. *Member:* Sigma Delta Chi. *Awards, honors:* Writers Guild of America Award, 1973, for "American Woman," 1976, for "American Inheritance"; Silver Gavel Award from American Bar Association, 1976, for "Hearing for American Justice"; American Medical Association Award, Ohio State University Award, both 1976, for "Progress American Medicine"; Ohio State University Awards, 1976, for "Bicential Broadcasts," and "America: This I Believe"; Overseas Press Club Award, 1977, for "World Looks at America."

WRITINGS: Television's Guild, Little, Brown, 1971. Contributor of articles to national periodicals, including *Esquire* and *Atlantic.*

BIOGRAPHICAL/CRITICAL SOURCES: Variety, October 6, 1971.

*　　*　　*

MORRIS, Robert Kerwin   1933-

PERSONAL: Born April 28, 1933, in Greenwich, Conn.; son of Julian L. Morris and Lilian S. Berger; married Penny Wilson, August 5, 1960; children: Antony, Theodore. *Education:* Cornell University, B.A., 1954, M.A., 1958; University of Wisconsin, Ph.D., 1963. *Home:* South Rd., Denmark, Me. 04022. *Office:* Department of English, City College of the City University of New York, New York, N.Y. 10031.

CAREER: City College of the City University of New York, New York, N.Y., professor of English, 1963—. *Military service:* U.S. Army, 1956-58.

WRITINGS: The Novels of Anthony Powell, University of Pittsburgh Press, 1968; *The Consolations of Ambiguity: An Essay on the Novels of Anthony Burgess,* University of Missouri Press, 1971; *Continuance and Change: The Contemporary British Novel Sequence,* Southern Illinois University Press, 1972; *Paradoxes of Order,* University of Missouri Press, 1975; (co-editor) *The Achievement of William Styron,* University of Georgia Press, 1976; (editor) *Old Lines, New Faces,* Fairleigh Dickinson University Press, 1977.

WORK IN PROGRESS: A novel; a critical biography of Kenneth Roberts.

SIDELIGHTS: In reviewing *The Novels of Anthony Powell,* W. D. Quesenbery states: "[It] is useful in several ways. First it is not so esoteric that it cannot serve as an introduction for those just beginning to read Powell.... Morris, much to his credit, is able to write simply and clearly of [Powell's] complex relationships without oversimplification."

Robert Morris told *CA*: "I am not an anglophile, but, unabashedly, a student and devotee of Anglo-Saxon culture. I always have been since the day I first read D. H. Lawrence. I still feel that British literature is the most overwhelming body of literature ever produced, and the finest, if not, really, the greatest.

"Next to reading and writing, I put all my energies into working the land. Maybe a book of mine will survive, but certainly the land will."

BIOGRAPHICAL/CRITICAL SOURCES: Contemporary Literature, Volume X, number 1, winter, 1969; *Criticism*, Volume XI, number 1, winter, 1969.

*   *   *

MORRISH, (Ernest) Ivor (James) 1914-

PERSONAL: Born February 8, 1914, in London, England; son of Reginald (an author) and Clara (Masey) Morrish; married Thelma Whitton, January 7, 1939; children: Marlene, Keith, Julian, Carl, Terence, Clare. *Education:* University of Bristol, B.A., 1938; St. Catherine's College, Oxford, graduate study, 1938-39; University of London, B.A., 1946, B.D., 1949, Academic Diploma in Education, 1955. *Home:* 128 Croydon Rd., Caterham, Surrey, England. *Office:* Allen & Unwin Ltd., 40 Museum St., London WC1A 1LU, England.

CAREER: Head of divinity department, Sir George Monoux Grammar School, 1947-49; head of divinity and social science department, Purley Grammar School, 1949-61; senior lecturer in divinity and tutor librarian, Bognor Regis College of Education, 1961-67; La Sainte Union College of Education, Southampton, Hampshire, England, principal lecturer in education, 1967-74; Allen & Unwin Ltd., London, England, editor of Unwin Education Books, 1970—. Former adviser to Wolsey Hall, Oxford University. *Military service:* British Army, Infantry, Royal Electrical and Mechanical Engineers, Royal Army Ordnance Corps, 1939-46; became technical sergeant; received Pacific Star, France and Germany Star, and 1939-45 Star. *Member:* British Sociological Association, Royal Anthropological Institute, Society of Authors, Royal Society of Arts (fellow), Oxford Society.

WRITINGS: Disciplines of Education, Allen & Unwin, 1967, Barnes & Noble, 1968; *Education since 1800,* Barnes & Noble, 1970, revised edition, Allen & Unwin, in press; *The Background of Immigrant Children,* Verry, 1971; *Introduction to the Sociology of Education,* Allen & Unwin, 1972; *Aspects of Educational Change,* Allen & Unwin, 1976; *Obeah, Christ and Rastaman: Jamaica and Its Religion,* James Clark, in press.

AVOCATIONAL INTERESTS: Sociology of language, anthropology, mysticism, education, philosophy, racial problems, and study of religions.

*   *   *

MORROW, William L(ockhart) 1935-

PERSONAL: Born October 15, 1935, in Oskaloosa, Iowa; son of Harold M. and Helen (Turner) Morrow; divorced; children: Gregory William. *Education:* Southwest Missouri State College (now University), B.A., 1957; University of Iowa, M.A., 1959, Ph.D., 1961. *Politics:* Democrat. *Religion:* Methodist. *Home:* 106 Thomas Nelson Lane, Williamsburg, Va. 23185. *Office:* Department of Government, College of William and Mary, Williamsburg, Va. 23185.

CAREER: DePauw University, Greencastle, Ind., assis-

tant professor, 1961-65, associate professor of political science, 1965-71; College of William and Mary, Williamsburg, Va., professor of government, 1971—. Visiting associate professor of political science, Indiana University, 1970. *Military service:* U.S. Army, 1957. U.S. Army Reserve, 1958-65; retired as captain. *Member:* American Political Science Association, American Society for Public Administration, Southern Political Science Association. *Awards, honors:* Congressional fellowship, American Political Science Association, 1965-66; selected an "Outstanding Young Man of America," 1970; Public Administration fellowship, National Association of Schools of Public Affairs and Administration, 1973-74.

WRITINGS: Congressional Committees, Scribner, 1969; *Public Administration: Politics and the Political System,* Random House, 1975. Contributor to *Journal of Politics, American Political Science Review, Public Administration Review, Public Personnel Review,* and *Improving College and University Teaching.*

WORK IN PROGRESS: Public Policy and Administration; Public Administration and the Presidency.

AVOCATIONAL INTERESTS: High fidelity records, classical music, spectator sports, tape recording.

BIOGRAPHICAL/CRITICAL SOURCES: Book World, September 9, 1969.

*   *   *

MOSELY, Philip Edward 1905-1972

September 21, 1905—January 13, 1972; American author of books on international relations. Obituaries: *New York Times,* January 14, 1972; *Washington Post,* January 15, 1972.

*   *   *

MOSER, Lawrence E. 1939-

PERSONAL: Born March 25, 1939, in Jersey City, N.J.; son of Ferdinand T. and Helen (Bauer) Moser. *Education:* Fordham University, A.B., 1963, M.A. and Ph.L., 1967; Woodstock College, B.D., 1970, S.T.M., 1971; Brown University, graduate study.

CAREER: Entered Society of Jesus (Jesuits), 1957, and was ordained to Roman Catholic priesthood, 1970.

WRITINGS: Home Celebrations: Studies in American Pastoral Liturgy, Paulist/Newman, 1970.

AVOCATIONAL INTERESTS: Photography (has exhibited abstract black and white photographs at de Saisset Gallery of University of Santa Clara and a number of his prints are in private collections).†

*   *   *

MOSS, James A(llen) 1920-

PERSONAL: Born March 27, 1920, in Newark, N.J.; son of William Henry and Marion T. (Wright) Moss; married Juanita Wright, January 15, 1942; children: Jay Allen, Alison Wright. *Education:* Attended Fordham University, 1942-43; New School for Social Research, B.A., 1948, graduate study, 1950-51; Columbia University, M.A., 1949, Ph.D., 1957. *Home:* 222 East 80th St., New York, N.Y. 10021. *Office:* African-American Studies Department, Adelphi University, Garden City, N.Y. 11530.

CAREER: Union College and University, Schenectady, N.Y., assistant professor of sociology, 1957-61; Southern Regional Council, Atlanta, Ga., director of research, 1961-

62; U.S. Department of State, Washington, D.C., special assistant for behavioral research, 1962-67; State University of New York at Buffalo, professor of sociology, 1967-77, associate dean, 1968-70, acting dean of international studies, 1970-71; Adelphi University, Garden City, N.Y., professor of social sciences and director of Afro-American studies program, 1977—. Lecturer at Howard University, 1966-67; visiting professor at Vassar College, 1969-70; visiting lecturer and vice-president for academic affairs at Medgar Evers College of the City University of New York, 1971-72. Chairman, Select Committee on Equal Opportunity, 1968-70. Consultant to United Planning Organization, 1967-68, Ford Foundation, 1971-72, Phelps-Stokes Foundation, 1972, Howard University, 1974, and Urban Family Center, 1974-75. *Military service:* U.S. Army, 1942-46; became sergeant. *Member:* American Sociological Association, Eastern Sociological Association. *Awards, honors:* U.S. Specialist grant, 1961-62; Woodrow Wilson fellowship, Smithsonian Institute, 1972-73; Ford Foundation travel fellowship, 1973—.

WRITINGS: The Black Man in America: Integration and Separation, Dell, 1971. Contributor of about sixty articles to journals. Contributing editor, *Journal of Human Relations,* 1964-67.

WORK IN PROGRESS: Co-authoring *Race Relations in a World Perspective.*

* * *

MOTHERSHEAD, Harmon Ross 1931-

PERSONAL: Born June 17, 1931, in Taylor County, Iowa; son of Harold T. (a farmer) and Mable (Stickleman) Mothershead; married Ellen Hall (a college financial aids coordinator), June 1, 1952; children: Kelly Ross, Kimbal Hall. *Education:* Northwest Missouri State College (now University), B.S.Ed., 1953; University of Colorado, M.A., 1959, Ph.D., 1969. *Politics:* Democrat. *Religion:* Methodist. *Home:* 624 West Third, Maryville, Mo. 64468. *Office:* Department of History, Northwest Missouri State University, Maryville, Mo. 64468.

CAREER: Teacher in public schools in Lakewood, Colo., 1955-65; Northwest Missouri State University, Maryville, assistant professor, 1965-69, associate professor, 1969-75, professor of history, 1975—. Staff member, Defense Education Act Institute, Kansas State University, Manhattan, summer, 1965. *Military service:* U.S. Army, 1953-55; served in Korea. *Member:* Organization of American Historians, Western History Association.

WRITINGS: Swan Land and Cattle Company Ltd., University of Oklahoma Press, 1971. Contributor to *Chronicles of Oklahoma, Northwest Missouri State University Studies, Annals of Wyoming,* and to other magazines in Colorado and Wyoming.

WORK IN PROGRESS: Studies of the Cattlemen's Association, cattle companies, and the entire cattle industry; research into the stockyards in St. Joseph, Mo.

* * *

MOTTO, Carmine J. 1914-

PERSONAL: Born November 20, 1914, in New York, N.Y.; son of Joseph A. (a government worker) and Mary (Santare) Motto; married Flora Buschini, January 30, 1943; children: Paul, Irene. *Education:* Attended Columbia University, 1933-34. *Politics:* None. *Religion:* Roman Catholic. *Residence:* White Plains, N.Y.

CAREER: State Police, New York City, trooper, 1936-41;

U.S. Secret Service, Washington, D.C., worked as agent to protect U.S. Presidents and their families (from Roosevelt to Johnson), 1941-62, special agent in charge of New York Special Counterfeit Detail, New York City, 1962-70; U.S. Department of the Treasury, New York City, deputy director, Office of Law Enforcement, beginning 1970. Technical adviser to Jack Webb for "O'Hara" television series. Lecturer at law enforcement centers throughout the United States. *Military service:* U.S. Marine Corps, 1942-46; became captain. *Awards, honors:* U.S. Department of the Treasury Superior Performance Awards for supervision of counterfeiting investigation, 1962, 1964, 1970; U.S. Secret Service Albert Gallatin Award, 1970.

WRITINGS: Undercover, C. C Thomas, 1971.

WORK IN PROGRESS: An autobiography, tentatively entitled *Special Agent.*††

* * *

MOUZELIS, Nicos P. 1939-

PERSONAL: Born January 22, 1939, in Athens, Greece; son of Panayiotis (an industrialist) and Zaira (Xirov) Mouzelis; married Lilea Hadjigeorgiou (a student), 1967; children: Zaira. *Education:* University of Geneva, Licence es Science Commerciale, 1961, Licence es Sociologie, 1962; London School of Economics and Political Science, Ph.D., 1967. *Home:* 35 Hollycroft Ave., London N.W.3, England. *Office:* London School of Economics and Political Science, University of London, Aldwych, London WC2A 2AE, England.

CAREER: University of Leicester, Leicester, England, lecturer in sociology, 1966-69; University of London, London School of Economics and Political Science, London, England, lecturer, 1970-76, senior lecturer in sociology, 1976—. *Military service:* Greek Navy, 1969-70.

WRITINGS: Organisation and Bureaucracy: An Analysis of Modern Theories, Routledge & Kegan Paul, 1967, Aldine, 1968, 2nd edition, 1975; *Greece: Aspects of Underdevelopment,* Macmillan, 1978. Contributor to sociological journals.

WORK IN PROGRESS: Capitalist Underdevelopment: A Theoretical Framework.

BIOGRAPHICAL/CRITICAL SOURCES: New Statesman, December 29, 1967.

* * *

MOYER, Kenneth E(van) 1919-

PERSONAL: Born November 19, 1919, in Chippewa Falls, Wis.; son of J. Evan and Margaret E. (Lashway) Moyer; married Doris Virginia Johnson, 1943; children: Robert S., Cathy L. *Education:* Park College, A.B. (with honors), 1943; Washington University, St. Louis, Mo., M.A., 1948, Ph.D., 1951. *Home:* 252 Gates Dr., Munhall, Pa. 15120. *Office:* Department of Psychology, Carnegie-Mellon University, Pittsburgh, Pa. 15213.

CAREER: Pearl River Junior College, Poplarville, Miss., instructor in psychology and physical education, 1946-47; Washington University, St. Louis, Mo., veteran's counselor and part-time instructor in psychology, 1947-49; Carnegie-Mellon University (formerly Carnegie Institute of Technology), Pittsburgh, Pa., instructor, 1949-50, assistant professor, 1950-54, associate professor, 1954-61, professor of psychology, 1961—, acting head of department, 1971—. Consultant on higher education, Government of Norway,

1954; visiting scientist, American Psychological Association and National Science Foundation, 1963, 1965, 1972. Member of research advisory committee, Pennsylvania Commonwealth Mental Health Foundation; consultant in executive development, Psychological Service of Pittsburgh. *Military service:* U.S. Marine Corps, Ordnance, 1943-46; served on Saipan, Okinawa, and in China; became first lieutenant.

MEMBER: American Psychological Association (fellow), American Association for the Advancement of Science (fellow), Psychonomic Society, Midwestern Psychological Association, Southern Society of Philosophy and Psychology, Pittsburgh Psychological Association (member of board of directors), Sigma Xi, Theta Kappa Theta. *Awards, honors:* Carnegie Foundation Award for excellence in teaching, 1954; Wisdom Award of Honor, 1970.

WRITINGS: The Physiology of Hostility, Markham, 1971; *You and Your Child—A Primer for Parents,* Nelson-Hall, 1974; *The Physiology of Aggression and Implications for Control,* Raven Press, 1976; *The Psychobiology of Aggression,* Harper, 1976; *A Readers Guide to Aggressive Behavior,* Alan Liss, in press.

Contributor: J. H. Sandberg, editor, *Introduction to the Behavioral Sciences,* Holt, 1969; B. E. Eleftheriou and J. P. Scott, editors, *The Physiology of Aggression and Defeat,* Plenum, 1971; J. L. Singer, editor, *The Control of Aggression and Violence: Cognitive and Physiological Factors,* Academic Press, 1971; Amelie Schmidt-Mummendey and H. D. Schmidt, editors, *Aggressives Verhalten,* Juventa-Verlag, 1971; J. F. Knutson, editor, *Control of Aggression: Implications from Basic Research,* Aldine, 1973; R. L. Van de Wiele, R. M. Richart, and R. C. Friedman, editors, *Sex Differences in Behavior,* Wiley, 1974; W. Fields and W. Sweet, editors, *Houston Neurological Symposium on Neural Bases of Violence and Aggression,* Warren Green, 1975; A. Cohen, G. Cole, and B. Bailey, editors, *Prison Violence,* Lexington Books, 1976. Contributor of more than fifty articles to psychology and mental health journals.

WORK IN PROGRESS: Neuroanatomy: Text and Diagrams, for Harper.

AVOCATIONAL INTERESTS: Sculpture, electronics, cooking.

* * *

MRAZEK, James E(dward) 1914-

PERSONAL: Surname is pronounced Ma-*rah*-zek; born June 18, 1914, in Chicago, Ill.; son of Charles Joseph (a druggist) and Rose (Polka) Mrazek; married Smilax Lexa, June 14, 1940; married second wife, Thelma Stevens (an editor), November 28, 1971; children: (first marriage) Joanne (Mrs. Alfred G. Clarke), James Edward, Jr. *Education:* U.S. Military Academy, B.S., 1938; U.S. Army Command and General Staff College, graduate, 1948; Georgetown University, M.A., 1952, additional graduate study, 1958-61. *Home:* 5500 Friendship Blvd., Chevy Chase, Md. 20015.

CAREER: U.S. Army, regular officer, 1938-58, retired as colonel; University of Pittsburgh, Pittsburgh, Pa., research associate in Washington, D.C., 1961-66; Radio Corp. of America, technical writer for Goddard Space Flight Center, Beltsville, Md., 1966-68. During World War II trained all U.S. airborn divisions in glider tactics, commanded a glider infantry battalion in 13th Airborne Division and later a glider regiment in 82nd Airborne Division; after the war served on Army staffs in Germany and Korea, and in Washington,

D.C.; Army attache in Prague, Czechoslovakia, 1949-50, supervisor of allied personnel attending Command and General Staff College, Fort Leavenworth, Kan., 1957-58. *Awards, honors*—Military: Legion of Merit.

WRITINGS: Arlington National Cemetery (guidebook), privately printed, 1968; *Prelude to Dunkerque,* Luce, 1968; *The Art of Winning Wars,* Walker & Co., 1968; *The Fall of Eben Emael,* Luce, 1970; (with wife, Thelma Mrazek) *Vieques, Puerto Rico,* privately printed, 1971; *Sailplanes and Soaring,* Stackpole, 1973; *The Glider War,* St. Martin's, 1976; *Hang Gliding and Soaring,* St. Martin's, 1976; *Fighting Gliders of World War II,* St. Martin's, 1977. Contributor to *Reader's Digest* and to military journals in United States and abroad, sometimes under an undisclosed pseudonym.

WORK IN PROGRESS: Olympics at a Glance.

SIDELIGHTS: James Mrazek told *CA* that in *The Art of Winning Wars* he "used ideas on creativity to bring some sense to the real meaning of leadership in war. The implications of the book's message to the conduct of war have yet to be thoroughly understood by the U.S. military establishment. This is not so in other nations. In my glider books, I promote the importance in World War II of the historically neglected transport glider pilots' and glider troopers' valiant achievements as well as the performance of battle gliders which served so effectively in combat and transformed war forever. This transformation started when German glider forces landed on the surface of Belgium's 'impregnable' fort Eben Emael at dawn, May 11, 1940, and forced its capitulation in a day."

Mrazek describes himself as "a skier, skin diver, mushroom hunter, a poker into the world's nooks and corners, and a lover of the full life." Many of his books have been translated into German.

* * *

MULLIGAN, John Joseph 1918-

PERSONAL: Born July 30, 1918, in Dorchester, Mass.; married Mary Blinstrub, 1948 (divorced, 1973); children: Kathleen, John J., Jr., Kevin, Marybeth. *Education:* Boston College, A.B. (cum laude), 1940; Rutgers University, M.A., 1942; Boston University, Ph.D., 1957. *Office:* Department of Modern Languages, Villanova University, Villanova, Pa. 19085.

CAREER: Cranwell Preparatory School, Lenox, Mass., German, history, and civics teacher, 1946-48; Boston College, Chestnut Hill, Mass., instructor, 1948-51, assistant professor of German language and literature, 1951-58; Long Beach State College (now California State University, Long Beach), assistant professor of German language and literature, and Latin, 1958-61; Villanova University, Villanova, Pa., associate professor, 1961-65, professor of German language and literature, 1966—, co-director, Language Laboratory, 1961-63. Consultant, foreign language program, U.S. Marine Corps Schools, Quantico, Va., 1962-63; U.S. Marine Corps Command and Staff College, member of adjunct faculty, 1969-71, advisor to director, 1971-73. *Military service:* U.S. Marine Corps Reserve, 1942—, served on active duty in World War II, 1942-46, and Korean War, 1953-54; received Presidential Unit Citation and Navy Letter of Commendation; currently colonel.

MEMBER: Modern Language Association of America, American Council on the Teaching of Foreign Languages, American Association of Teachers of German (vice-president, Boston chapter, 1956-57), American Association of University Professors, American Lessing Society, Marine Corps Reserve Officers Association (member of board of governors, Philadelphia chapter, 1963-66), Philological Association of the Pacific Coast, German Society of Pennsylvania.

WRITINGS: Jetzt lesen wir! (intermediate German grammar with tapes), Scott, Foresman, 1965, revised edition, 1970; (compiler and editor) *Gestern, heute und morgen: Prosa aus unserem Jahrhundert* (intermediate college text), Scribner, 1968; (editor) *Von Stufe zu Stufe: Deutsche Erzaehlungen unserer Zeit* (German reader), Harper, 1969; (with Adolph Wegener and Theodore L. Lowe) *Modern College German* (elementary German grammar), Harper, 1971; (compiler and editor with Hans Thomas Aretz) *Junge Deutsche Autoren* (intermediate college reader), D. Van Nostrand, 1973. Also author of "German Pattern Drills," Series I (50 tapes for language laboratory use), and accompanying teacher's guide, Electronic Teaching Laboratories, 1963, and advisor to Series II, 1963. Contributor to *German Quarterly.* Contributing editor, *Pennsylvania State Modern Language Association Bulletin,* 1965-68.

WORK IN PROGRESS: An article on Kleist's *Prinz Friedrich von Homburg;* editing an anthology of German literature.

AVOCATIONAL INTERESTS: Golf, hiking, photography.

*   *   *

MULLINS, Nicholas C(reed) 1939-

PERSONAL: Born June 2, 1939, in Boise, Idaho; son of Robert Wilson (a professor and naval officer) and Eleanor (Callahan) Mullins; married Carolyn Johns (a free-lance editor), June 21, 1962; children: Nicholas Johns, Robert Corydon, Nancy Carolyn. *Education:* Attended Deep Springs College, 1957-59; Cornell University, B.S., 1962, M.A., 1963; Harvard University, Ph.D., 1967. *Religion:* Protestant. *Office:* Department of Sociology, Ballantine Hall, Indiana University, Bloomington, Ind. 47401.

CAREER: Vanderbilt University, Nashville, Tenn., assistant professor of sociology, 1966-68; Dartmouth College, Hanover, N.H., assistant professor of sociology, 1968-71, chairman of mathematics and social science program, 1969-71; Indiana University at Bloomington, associate professor, 1971-77, professor of sociology, 1977—. Member, Institute for Advanced Study, 1976-77. *Member:* American Sociological Association, American Association for the Advancement of Science, Science and Public Policy Studies Group.

WRITINGS: The Art of Theory: Construction and Use, Harper, 1971; *Theories and Theory Groups in Contemporary American Sociology,* Harper, 1973; *Science: Some Sociological Perspectives,* Bobbs-Merrill, 1973; (contributor) Karin D. Knorr, Herman Strasser, and H. G. Zillian, editors, *Determinants and Controls of Scientific Development,* D. Reidel, 1975; (contributor) Strasser and Knorr, editors, *Wissenschaftssteuerung: Soziale Prozesse de Wissenschaftsentwicklung,* Campus Verlag, 1976; (contributor) S. Leinhardt and P. Holland, editors, *Social Networks,* Academic Press, 1978. Contributor to sociology journals.

WORK IN PROGRESS: Power, Social Structure and Advice in American Science: The United States National Science Advisory System, 1950-1972; Elites of Mind, expected completion in 1979.

SIDELIGHTS: Nicholas Mullins writes: "I am a writer of books and articles which add to our knowledge of the way in which science works. I am working to write my esoteric and academic investigations so that they can be read by any educated person."

*   *   *

MUNRO, Alice 1931-

PERSONAL: Born July 10, 1931, in Wingham, Ontario, Canada; daughter of Robert Eric (a farmer) and Ann (Chamney) Laidlaw; married James Munro (a bookseller), December 29, 1951 (divorced, 1976); married Gerald Fremlin (a geographer), 1976; children: (first marriage) Sheila, Jenny, Andrea. *Education:* Attended University of Western Ontario, 1949-51. *Politics:* New Democratic Party. *Religion:* Unitarian Universalist. *Residence:* Clinton, Ontario, Canada.

CAREER: Writer. *Awards, honors:* Governor General's Literary Award, 1969, for *Dance of the Happy Shades;* Canadian Bookseller's Award, 1972, for *Lives of Girls and Women.*

WRITINGS: Dance of the Happy Shades (short stories), Ryerson, 1968; *Lives of Girls and Women* (novel), McGraw, 1971; *Something I've Been Meaning to Tell You* (short stories), McGraw, 1974. Two stories included in *Canadian Short Stories, Second Series,* Oxford University Press, 1968.

SIDELIGHTS: In a review of *Dance of the Happy Shades,* Martin Levin writes that "the short story is alive and well in Canada, where most of the fifteen tales originate like fresh winds from the North. Alice Munro," he continues, "creates a solid habitat for her fiction—southwestern Ontario, a generation or more in the past—and is in sympathetic vibration with the farmers and townspeople who live there." Peter Prince calls the stories in this collection "beautifully controlled and precise. And always this precision appears unstrained. The proportions so exactly fit the writer's thematic aims that in almost every case it seems that really no other words *could* have been used, certainly no more or less." Ronald Blythe believes that "the stories are all to do with discovering personal freedom within an accepted curtailment. There is no intentional nostalgia although, strangely enough, one frequently finds oneself rather wistfully caught up in some of the scenes so perfectly evoked; and there is no distortion in the characterisation."

Reviewing *Something I've Been Meaning to Tell You,* Kildare Dobbs writes: "Readers who enjoyed the earlier books because they confirmed the reality of the Canadian small town experience for a certain generation, or because they seemed to reinforce some of the ideology of the women's movement, will find more of the same. But they will find something else, too. There is a hint at hermetic concerns in the first story, ironic suggestions of a quest for the grail. . . . All the stories are told with the skill which the author has perfected over the years, narrated with meticulous precision in a voice that is unmistakeably Ontarian in its lack of emphasis, its sly humour and willingness to live with a mystery." Joyce Carol Oates finds that the reader will be "most impressed by the feeling behind [Alice Munro's] stories—the evocation of emotions, ranging from bitter hatred to love, from bewilderment and resentment to awe. In all her work . . . there is an effortless, almost conversational tone, and we know we are in the presence of an art that works to conceal itself, in order to celebrate its subject."

BIOGRAPHICAL/CRITICAL SOURCES: Canadian

Forum, February, 1969; *Time,* January 15, 1973; *New York Times Book Review,* September 23, 1973; *New Statesman,* May 3, 1974; *Listener,* June 13, 1974; *Saturday Night,* July, 1974; *Ontario Review,* fall, 1974; *Contemporary Literary Criticism,* Volume VI, Gale, 1976.

* * *

MUNSON, Amelia H. (?)-1972

(?)—January 21, 1972; American librarian and author. Obituaries: *New York Times,* January 26, 1972; *Publishers Weekly,* February 7, 1972.

* * *

MUNSON, Fred C(aleb) 1928-

PERSONAL: Born August 19, 1928, in Groton, N.Y.; son of J. Paul (a teacher) and Johanna (Huffnagel) Munson; married Mary Thorp, August 6, 1953; children: Marguerite, F. Caleb, Jonathan, Nathan. *Education:* Attended Michigan State University, 1947-48; Cornell University, B.S., 1952; Massachusetts Institute of Technology, Ph.D., 1959. *Politics:* Democrat. *Religion:* Protestant. *Home:* 9981 Bethel Church Rd., Manchester, Mich. 48158. *Office:* University of Michigan, SPH II, 109 Observatory, Ann Arbor, Mich. 48104.

CAREER: Standard Vacuum Oil Co., India, employee relations officer, 1952-55; University of Michigan, Ann Arbor, assistant professor, 1959-64, associate professor, 1964-71, currently professor of hospital administration. Ford Foundation consultant to Shri Ram Center for Industrial Relations, New Delhi, India, 1965-66. *Member:* Population Association of America, American Public Health Association.

WRITINGS: Labor Relations in the Lithographic Industry, Harvard University Press, 1963; *History of the Lithographers Union,* Wertheim Committee, 1963; (with C. P. Thakur) *Industrial Relations System in Printing Industry,* Shri Ram Centre for Industrial Relations, 1969; *Indian Trade Unions: Structure and Function,* Institute of International Commerce and Bureau of Industrial Relations, University of Michigan, 1970; (with Richard Jelinek and Robert Smith) *Service Unit Management: An Organizational Approach to Improved Patient Care,* W. K. Kellogg Foundation, 1971; (with J. R. Griffith and W. M. Hancock) *Cost Control in Hospitals,* Health Administration Press, 1976.

* * *

MURDOCK, Eugene C(onverse) 1921-

PERSONAL: Born April 30, 1921, in Lakewood, Ohio; son of Stanley Howard and Elizabeth (Carter) Murdock; married Margaret Bowes McColl, October 7, 1950; children: Gordon Graham, Kathryn Carter. *Education:* College of Wooster, A.B., 1943; Columbia University, M.A., 1948, Ph.D., 1951. *Politics:* Democrat. *Home:* 415 Columbia Ave., Williamstown, W.Va. 26187. *Office:* Department of History, Marietta College, Marietta, Ohio 45750.

CAREER: Rio Grande College, Rio Grande, Ohio, professor of history, 1952-56; Marietta College, Marietta, Ohio, assistant professor, 1956-60, associate professor, 1960-63, professor of history, 1963—, chairman of department, 1972—. *Military service:* U.S. Army, 1943-46; served in European theater. *Member:* American Historical Association, Organization of American Historians, Southern Historical Association, Ohio Academy of History (member of executive council, 1970-73).

WRITINGS: Ohio's Bounty System in the Civil War, Ohio State University Press, 1963; *Patriotism Limited: 1862-1865,* Kent State University Press, 1967; *One Million Men,* Society Press, 1971. Contributor of articles, abstracts, and reviews to professional journals. Author of a series of radio scripts for ''The Ohio Story,'' 1950.

* * *

MURDY, Louise Baughan 1935-

PERSONAL: Born September 28, 1935, in Dover, N.H.; daughter of Denver Ewing (a professor of English) and Thelma (Ramsey) Baughan; married William George Murdy, Jr. (a professor of psychology), August 23, 1958; children: William Ewing, Anne Elizabeth. *Education:* University of Florida, B.A., 1957, Ph.D., 1962; University of North Carolina, M.A., 1958. *Religion:* Presbyterian. *Home:* 659 Guilford Rd., Rock Hill, S.C. 29730. *Office:* Department of English, Winthrop College, Rock Hill, S.C. 29730.

CAREER: Florida State University, Tallahassee, instructor in humanities and English, 1962-63; Winthrop College, Rock Hill, S.C., part-time assistant professor, 1963-70, part-time associate professor, 1970-74, associate professor of English, 1974—, Danforth associate, 1969—. *Member:* Phi Beta Kappa, Pi Sigma Alpha, Phi Kappa Phi (secretary of Winthrop College chapter, 1964-65), Sigma Tau Delta.

WRITINGS: Sound and Sense in Dylan Thomas's Poetry, Mouton & Co., 1966. Contributor to *Encyclopedia Americana.*

WORK IN PROGRESS: Co-author of *Hemingway's "A Clean, Well-Lighted Place": Experiment in Allegory.*

AVOCATIONAL INTERESTS: Family, study of art history, crafts (especially petitpoint), travel.

* * *

MURO, James J(oseph) 1934-

PERSONAL: Born March 13, 1934, in Central City, Pa.; son of James J. and Mary (Kuna) Muro; married Patricia Hart; children: Joel. *Education:* Lock Haven State College, B.S., 1956; Rutgers University, M.Ed., 1961; University of Georgia, Ed.D., 1965. *Religion:* Catholic. *Office:* College of Education, North Texas State University, Denton, Tex. 76203.

CAREER: Hackettstown School Department, Hackettstown, N.J., teacher and counselor, 1958-60; Sparta School Department, Sparta, N.J., counselor, 1960-63; University of Maine at Orono, associate professor of education, beginning 1965; North Texas State University, Denton, dean, College of Education, 1977—. Consultant to Title III projects in Camden and Unity, Me., and National Association of Independent Schools. Regional coordinator, Educator Training Center. Chairman, Building Committee, Veazie, Me., 1969—. *Military service:* U.S. Army, 1957-58; served in Europe. *Member:* Student Personnel Association for Teacher Education (member of executive board), New England Personnel and Guidance Association (member of executive committee). *Awards, honors:* U.S. Office of Education grants, 1967-72; selected ''Educator of the Year,'' 1971.

WRITINGS: (With Stanley Freeman) *Readings in Group Counseling: Elementary School Guidance,* International Textbook Co., 1968; *Elementary School Guidance: What It Should Be,* University of Maine Press, 1969; (with George Prescott) *The Counselor's Work in the Elementary School,* International Textbook Co., 1970; (with Don Dinkmeyer) *Group Counseling: Theory and Practice,* F. E. Peacock, 1971; (contributor) W. H. Van Hoose, J. J. Pietrofesa, and

J. Carlson, editors, *The Elementary School Counselor: A Composite View,* Houghton, 1973; *Youth: Time, Leisure, Spirit* (monograph), edited by Herman Peters, C. E. Merrill, 1975; *Counseling in the Elementary and Middle Schools,* W. C. Brown, 1977. Contributor to *Georgia Education Journal, Reading Improvement, Clearing House, Journal of the Association of College Admissions Counselors, Counselor Education and Supervision Journal, School Counselor,* and other publications. Member of editorial board, *E.S.G.C. Journal,* 1969—; editor, *Humanist Educator,* 1977—.

AVOCATIONAL INTERESTS: Outdoor activities, travel, gourmet cooking.

* * *

MURPHEY, Rhoads 1919-

PERSONAL: Born August 13, 1919, in Philadelphia, Pa.; son of William Rhoads and Emily (Hawkins) Murphey; married Eleanor Albertson, January 12, 1952; children: Katherine, Rhoads, David, Ellen. *Education:* Harvard University, A.B. (magna cum laude), 1941, M.A. (history), 1942, M.A. (international and regional studies: China), 1948, Ph.D., 1950. *Home:* 2012 Washtenaw, Ann Arbor, Mich. 48104. *Office:* Department of Geography, University of Michigan, Ann Arbor, Mich. 48104.

CAREER: University of Washington, Seattle, assistant professor, 1952-55, associate professor, 1955-60, professor of geography, 1960-64; University of Michigan, Ann Arbor, professor of geography, 1964—, director of Center for Chinese Studies, 1969-76. Visiting professor, University of Pennsylvania, 1957-58. Director of conferences for diplomats in Asia, American Friends Service Committee, 1954-56. Founder and director, Citizens to Change U.S. China Policy, 1970-72. *Wartime service:* Friends Ambulance Unit, Chinese National Health Administration, and War Prisoners' Aid, 1942-46; served in Kunming, Chengtu, Shanghai, Chungking, and other Chinese cities. *Member:* Association for Asian Studies (director, 1959-65, 1967-70; executive secretary-treasurer, 1976—), Association of American Geographers (councillor, 1963-66). *Awards, honors:* Ford Foundation fellow, 1955-56; Guggenheim fellow and fellow of St. John's College, Cambridge University, 1966-67.

WRITINGS: Shanghai: Key to Modern China, Harvard University Press, 1953; *An Introduction to Geography,* Rand McNally, 1961, 4th edition, 1978; (with others) *A New China Policy,* Yale University Press, 1965; (editor with Albert Feuerwerker and M. Wright) *Approaches to Modern Chinese History,* University of California Press, 1967; *The Scope of Geography,* Rand McNally, 1969, 2nd edition, 1973; (contributor) P. F. Griffin, editor, *Geography of Population,* Stanford University Press, 1969.

The Treaty Ports and China's Modernization: What Went Wrong?, Center for Chinese Studies, University of Michigan, 1970; *The Treaty Ports,* Macmillan, 1972; (with Maurice Meisner) *The Mozartian Historian,* University of California Press, 1976; *The Outsiders: Westerners in India and China,* University of Michigan Press, 1977. Contributor of over thirty articles to professional journals, including *Geographical Review, Geographic Journal, Asian Survey,* and *Journal of Asian Studies.* Editor, *Journal of Asian Studies,* 1956-65; regional editor for Asia, *Encyclopaedia Britannica,* 1952-62; editor, *Michigan Papers in Chinese Studies,* 1967-76.

MURPHY, James J. 1923-

PERSONAL: Born September 9, 1923, in San Jose, Calif.; son of James Joseph (a clerk) and Marie Therese (Utzerath) Murphy; married Kathleen Woods, February 7, 1948; children: Sheila Maureen, Brian Robert. *Education:* Saint Mary's College of California, B.A., 1947; Stanford University, M.A., 1950, Ph.D., 1957. *Religion:* Roman Catholic. *Home:* 915 Villanova Dr., Davis, Calif. 95616. *Office:* Department of Rhetoric, University of California, Davis, Calif. 95616.

CAREER: United Press International (UPI), San Francisco, Calif., newsman, 1947-48; Stanford University, Stanford, Calif., assistant professor of speech, 1954-59; Princeton University, Princeton, N.J., assistant professor of speech, 1959-65; University of California, Davis, associate professor, 1965-68, professor of rhetoric, 1968—, vice-chancellor, 1968-69, associate dean, College of Letters and Science, 1972—. *Military service:* U.S. Army Air Forces, 1943-45. U.S. Air Force Reserve, 1945-69; retired as major. *Member:* Modern Language Association of America, Speech Communication Association, International Society for the History of Rhetoric, Mediaeval Academy of America, Medieval Association of the Pacific (president, 1966-70), Pacific Philological Association. *Awards, honors:* Anniversary Award for Distinguished Scholars, Speech Association of America, 1965; American Council of Learned Societies fellow, 1971-72; annual book award, Speech Communication Association, 1975, for *Rhetoric in the Middle Ages.*

WRITINGS: (With Jon M. Ericson) *The Debaters Guide,* Bobbs-Merrill, 1961; (editor) *Quintilian on the Early Education of the Citizen-Orator,* Library of Liberal Arts, 1966; (editor with Peter Kontos) *Teaching Urban Youth,* Wiley, 1967; (editor) *Demosthenes on the Crown,* Random House, 1967; (editor and translator) *Three Medieval Rhetorical Arts,* University of California Press, 1971; (editor) *Medieval Rhetoric: A Select Bibliography,* University of Toronto Press, 1971; (editor) *A Synoptic History of Classical Rhetoric,* Random House, 1972; *Rhetoric in the Middle Ages: A History of Rhetorical Theory from Saint Augustine to the Renaissance,* University of California Press, 1974; (editor and contributor) *Medieval Eloquence: Studies in the Theory and Practice of Medieval Rhetoric,* University of California Press, 1977. Contributor of over twenty articles to periodicals, including *Medieval Studies, Speech Monographs, Philological Quarterly,* and *Journal of the American Forensic Association.* Editor, *Chronica;* member of editorial boards, *Speech Monographs, Philosophy and Rhetoric,* and *Quarterly Journal of Speech.*

WORK IN PROGRESS: Renaissance Rhetoric: A Short-Title Catalogue and Bibliography.

SIDELIGHTS: James Murphy told *CA:* "There is an ancient Greek saying that 'he who does not know rhetoric will be a victim of it.' Since human communication has always been a dominant force in our civilization, I've long been interested in tracing its history to see how its future can be shaped. I always tell students they must study the history of rhetoric so they won't spend their time re-inventing the wheel—that is, redoing what someone else has already done. When you look at it that way, the history of rhetoric is a fascinating subject that tells us a good deal about every stage of our civilization.''

MURPHY, Reg 1934-

PERSONAL: Born January 7, 1934, in Hoschton, Pa.; son of John Lee (a grocer) and Mae (Ward) Murphy; married Virginia Rawls, December 23, 1954; children: Karen Leigh, Susan Virginia. *Education:* Attended Mercer University and Harvard University. *Office:* San Francisco Examiner, 110 Fifth St., San Francisco, Calif. 94119.

CAREER: Macon Telegraphy, Macon, Ga., political editor, 1955-65; *Atlanta Constitution,* Atlanta, Ga., political editor, 1961-65, editor, 1968-75; *San Francisco Examiner,* San Francisco, Calif., editor and publisher, 1975—. Host of daily television news show in Atlanta. *Member:* Atlanta Press Club, Sigma Delta Chi. *Awards, honors:* American Press award; Sigma Delta Chi public service award; Nieman fellowship, Harvard University.

WRITINGS: (With Hal Gulliver) *The Southern Strategy,* Scribner, 1971. Contributor to national periodicals, including *Harper's* and *New York Times Magazine.*

WORK IN PROGRESS: The Vanishing South.

SIDELIGHTS: In 1974, Reg Murphy was kidnapped and held for ransom by persons claiming to be members of the American Revolutionary Army, an ultra-right organization which had apparently been incensed by what they referred to as the "leftist" and "liberal" American media. Originally Murphy was told that their demands for his release included the resignation of "all government officials" and immediate "free elections." However they eventually decided to free him in exchange for a $700,000 ransom to be paid by the *Atlanta Constitution.* After confirming that Murphy was still alive, *Constitution* managing editor Jim Minter dropped the money at a place designated by the kidnappers, and Murphy was released forty-nine hours after his abduction. Murphy later wrote his account of the ordeal for publication in the *Constitution.*

AVOCATIONAL INTERESTS: Photography, golf.

BIOGRAPHICAL/CRITICAL SOURCES: Newsweek, March 4, 1974.

* * *

MURPHY, Warren B. 1933-

PERSONAL: Born September 13, 1933, in Jersey City, N.J.; married Dawn Walters, June 25, 1955 (divorced, 1973); children: Deirdre, Megan, Brian, Ardath. *Education:* Attended St. Peter's College, 1968-69. *Religion:* None. *Home:* 53 Duncan Ave., Jersey City, N.J. 07304. *Agent:* Jed Mattes, International Creative Management, 40 West 57th St., New York, N.Y. 10019.

CAREER: Reporter and editor; presently public relations counselor and speechwriter in New Jersey. Acting director of community affairs, Jersey City, N.J., 1971; member of Hackensack Meadowlands Development Commission. *Military service:* U.S. Air Force, Alaskan Air Command, 1952-56; became sergeant. *Member:* American Newspaper Guild. *Awards, honors:* Freedoms Foundation award, 1955; public relations award from National League of Cities, 1963.

WRITINGS—All published by Pinnacle: *Created the Destroyer,* 1971; *Death Check,* 1972; *China Puzzle,* 1972; *Mafia Fix,* 1972; *Dead End Street,* 1973; *Down and Dirty,* 1974; *Lynch Town,* 1974. Also author of *City in Heat* and *One Night Stand;* author, with Hal Dresner and Rod Whitaker, of screenplay "The Eiger Sanction," for Universal Pictures, 1975. Editor, *Road to Anarchy,* riot commission report of New Jersey Patrolmen's Benevolent Association, 1968.

WORK IN PROGRESS: A political novel.

AVOCATIONAL INTERESTS: Anthropology, chess, golf, politics.

* * *

MURRAY, Jerome T(homas) 1928-

PERSONAL: Born November 13, 1928, in Chicago, Ill.; son of Thomas C. (a merchant) and Ruth (Goldsberry) Murray; married Magdalene Kalodimos, June 20, 1953 (divorced, 1976); children: Therese Marie, Rosanne, Margaret Anne Marie. *Education:* Loyola University of Chicago, B.S., 1950; attended Illinois Institute of Technology, 1961-62, 1964-66, and Bogan Junior College, 1962-64; Chicago State University, candidate for M.A., 1977—. *Home and office:* 453 Raintree Dr., Glen Ellyn, Ill. 60137. *Agent:* Porter, Gould & Dierks, 1236 Sherman Ave., Evanston, Ill. 60202.

CAREER: Reuben H. Donnelley Corp. (advertising agency), Chicago, Ill., account executive, 1957-67; International Business Machines Corp. (IBM), Chicago, marketing representative, 1967-69; Honeywell Institute of Information Science, Chicago, manager of Institute, 1969-70; Roosevelt University, Chicago, director of Computer Center, 1970-71. *Military service:* U.S. Army, Medical Service Corps, Psychiatric Cold Injury Study, First Combined Forces Research Team, 1950-52; served in Korea. *Member:* Mensa, Lawn Aqua Club (Oak Lawn, Ill.; charter member).

WRITINGS: The Student and the New Math, Regnery, Volume I, 1965, Volume II, 1966; *An Introduction to Computing: IBM System/3,* McGraw, 1971; *Programming in RPG II: IBM System/3,* McGraw, 1971; *Systems Analysis and Design: In an IBM Environment,* McGraw, 1973.

SIDELIGHTS: Jerome Murray told *CA:* "Technical writing is a cold, ruthless business that I have tried to humanize. Progress is a relentless task master though, and has little place for humanizing. Between a rock and a hard place the search for softness is often thankless. Yet, technology is our single hope for survival and at this point the realities are technically grim.... The technical explosion goes on and the last chapter has yet to be written. We obey but one rule—change."

* * *

MURRAY, John MacDougall 1910-

PERSONAL: Born May 28, 1910, in Jersey City, N.J.; son of James Campbell (a contractor) and Mary MacIntyre (MacDougall) Murray; married Gladys Marie Fleming, May 28, 1938 (deceased); married Justine Huntley Ulp, July 3, 1954; children: (first marriage) Margot Elena (Mrs. William A. Gordon); (second marriage) Mary Ruth. *Education:* Attended Columbia University, 1928-31, and Rochester Institute of Technology, 1937-39. *Politics:* Republican. *Religion:* Protestant. *Home:* 91 Pomona Dr., Rochester, N.Y. 14616.

CAREER: Newspaper reporter in New York, N.Y. and New Jersey, 1932-39; Rochester Gas and Electric Co., Rochester, N.Y., sales representative, 1939-41; Boise Cascade—Rochester Division, Rochester, supervisor of technical training, beginning 1941. *Member:* Fraternal Order of Eagles, Rochester Writer's Club.

WRITINGS: Trial at Topha, Lenox Hill, 1971; *Good Guys Wear Black,* Lenox Hill, 1971; *Coffin for McCullough,* Lenox Hill, 1971; *Justice Rides a Bay,* Lenox Hill, 1972; *Retribution in Lead,* Lenox Hill, 1972. Contributor of articles and short stories to popular journals and men's magazines. Author of "In This Corner," a newspaper column.

WORK IN PROGRESS: Dialogues with Gabriel; Council of Pumpkin Butte.

AVOCATIONAL INTERESTS: History, beauty, the occult, man.

*   *   *

MUTCHLER, David E(dward) 1941-

PERSONAL: Born June 21, 1941, in Lexington, Ky.; son of John Robert and Mary Louise (McNicol) Mutchler; married Sheila McPhelin, July 22, 1967 (divorced, 1976); children: Mamie, Meghan. Education: Xavier University, Cincinnati, Ohio, Litt.B., 1963; St. Louis University, A.B., 1965; Washington University, St. Louis, Mo., M.A., 1966, Ph.D., 1970. Religion: Roman Catholic. Home: 3226 Quesada St. N.W., Washington, D.C. 20015. Office: Department of State AID/PHA/POP, Washington, D.C. 20523.

CAREER: Federal City College, Washington, D.C., assistant professor of sociology, 1969—; U.S. Department of State, Agency for International Development, Washington, D.C., sociologist, 1971—. Member: American Sociological Association, International Union for Scientific Study of Population, Population Association of America.

WRITINGS: The Church as a Political Factor in Latin America, Praeger, 1971. Contributor to Studies in Comparative International Development and Social Research.

WORK IN PROGRESS: Writing on research organization, policy research, politics of research, and bureaucratic ethics.

*   *   *

MYERS, J(ohn) William 1919-

PERSONAL: Born December 1, 1919, in Huntington, W.Va.; son of Condon William (an engraver) and Mary Olive (Fox) Myers: married Nancy Hortense Paxton, July 6, 1942 (died 1954); children: Martha Ann (Mrs. Philip L. Parks), Lenora Ellen (Mrs. James Johns), Nancy Louise (Mrs. Gerald D. Smith), John Charles. Education: Ohio Wesleyan University, B.A., 1951; Bowling Green State University, M.A., 1952. Politics: Liberal Democrat. Address: East Morenci St., Lyons, Ohio 43533.

CAREER: Ordained a Methodist minister in 1948; minister, Ohio Annual Conference of the Methodist Church, 1944-54; transferred to the Unitarian Church, 1956; currently employed by Unitarian Universalist Church, Lyons, Ohio. Journeyman letterpress and lithographic printer, editor, publisher, book designer, and free-lance writer, 1954—. Lecturer on poetry and religion. Member: American Academy of Poets, Poetry Society of America, Catholic Poetry Society of America, American Translators Association, Ohio Poetry Society, Poetry Society of Virginia. Awards, honors: Nomination for Pulitzer Prize in Poetry, 1964, for Green Are My Words; London Literary Circle award, 1967, for poem, "Prayer for a House I Never Had."

WRITINGS—Poetry: Evening Exercises, Humanist Education Press, 1956; These Mown Dandelions, Ohio Poetry Review Press, 1959; My Mind's Poor Birds, Elgeuera Press, 1963; Alley to an Island, New Merrymount Press, 1963; Green Are My Words, New Merrymount Press, 1964; Sun Bands and Other Poems, Georgetown Press, 1964; Anatomy of a Feeling, New Merrymount Press, 1966; Variations on a Nightingale, New Merrymount Press, 1968; A Greene County Ballad, New Merrymount Press, 1972; The Sky Is Forever, New Merrymount Press, 1974; Something Will Be Mine, New Merrymount Press, 1976; Annotations

1951, New Merrymount Press, 1977. Translator from the German of poetry of Johann W. Von Goethe, Friedrich Hoelderlin, Joseph von Eichendorff, Friedrich Rueckert, Edward Moerike, Reiner Kunze, Gottfried Keller, Friedrich Nietzsche, Richard Dehmel, Stefan Anton George, Hermann Hesse, Franz Werfel, and Karl Krolow. Contributor of poems to over sixty journals and newspapers, including American Weave, Bitterroot, Cardinal Poetry Quarterly, Descant, Free Lance, Hartford Courant, Laurel Review, Meanjin Quarterly, New York Herald Tribune, South and West, and Spirit; contributor of bibliographies to Twentieth Century Literature and Dasein: The Quarterly Review. Reviewer for Chicago Sun-Times. Editor, Mid-Lakes Humanist (American Humanist Association publication), 1956-59, Ohio Poetry Review, 1957-59, Anthropos, the Quarterly of Humanist Poetry, 1958-59, Ohio Poetry Society Bulletin, 1958-59, and Poetry Dial, 1959-61; poetry editor, Humanist, 1961-62; advisory and contributing editor, Dasein: The Quarterly Review, 1962—.

WORK IN PROGRESS: Stones of Promise, a new collection of poetry; The Climate Within: Readings for the Liberal Church; the selected poems of Stefan Anton George in a new translation; a new translation of the passages from Nietzsche's Zarathustra which form the text of A Mass of Life by Frederick Delius.

SIDELIGHTS: J. William Myers told CA, "I care for nothing as deeply as poetry." He cites as major influences on his life and work George Santayana and Stefan Anton George, who shows "uncompromising opposition to the spirit of this present age with its materialistic greed, its craze for enjoyment, and its mental and moral distraction." Avocational interests: Cooking, baking, making wines.

BIOGRAPHICAL/CRITICAL SOURCES: Columbus Dispatch, May 22, 1969; Observer-Reporter (Washington, Pa.), June 23, 1969; Record-Outlook (McDonald, Pa.), November 18, 1971; Newark Advocate, May 1, 1978.

*   *   *

MYERS, Walter Dean 1937-

PERSONAL: Born August 12, 1937, in Martinsburg, W.Va.; children: Karen, Michael. Education: Attended City College of the City University of New York. Office: Bobbs-Merrill Co., Inc., 4 West 58th St., New York, N.Y. 10019.

CAREER: New York State Department of Labor, Brooklyn, employment supervisor, 1966-69; Bobbs-Merrill Co., Inc. (publisher), New York, N.Y., senior trade editor, 1970—. Military service: U.S. Army, 1954-57. Awards, honors: Interracial Council Award for Children's Books, 1968, for Where Does the Day Go?.

WRITINGS—Juveniles: Where Does the Day Go?, illustrations by Leo Carty, Parents' Magazine Press, 1969; The Dragon Takes a Wife, illustrations by Ann Grifalconi, Bobbs-Merrill, 1972; The Dancers, illustrations by Anne Rockwell, Parents' Magazine Press, 1972; Fly, Jimmy, Fly!, illustrations by Moneta Barnett, Putnam, 1974; The World of Work: A Guide to Choosing a Career, Bobbs-Merrill, 1975; Fast Sam, Cool Clyde, and Stuff, Viking, 1975; Social Welfare, F. Watts, 1976; Brainstorm, photographs by Chuck Freedman, F. Watts, 1977; Mojo and the Russians, Viking, 1977.

Short stories represented in anthologies, including What We Must See: Young Black Storytellers, edited by Orde Coombs, Dodd, 1971, and We Be Word Sorcerers: 25 Sto-

ries by Black Americans, edited by Sonia Sanchez, Bantam, 1973. Contributor of articles and fiction to periodicals, including *Black Creation* and *Black World.*†

* * *

MYRES, Sandra Lynn 1933-

PERSONAL: Born May 17, 1933, in Columbus, Ohio; daughter of George Y. (a physician) and Lucille (Stockdale) Swickard; married Charles E. Myres (a chemist), July 2, 1953 (divorced, 1973). *Education:* Attended Rice University, 1950-51; Texas Technological College (now Texas Tech University), B.A., 1957, M.A., 1960; Texas Christian University, Ph.D., 1967. *Home:* 2019 Terlingua, No. 148, Arlington, Tex. 76010. *Office:* Department of History, University of Texas, Arlington, Tex. 76019.

CAREER: Schreiner Institute (now College), Kerrville, Tex., instructor in history, 1960-61; University of Texas at Arlington, assistant professor, 1967-71, associate professor of history, 1971—. Executive director, Texas Committee for the Humanities and Public Policy, 1973-75. Editorial consultant in history, American Continental Publishing Co. *Member:* Organization of American Historians, American Association for State and Local History, Western History Association, Southwest Council for Latin American Studies, Western Writers of America Society for Historical Archaeology, Texas State Historical Association, Fort Worth Westerners.

WRITINGS: S. D. Myres: Saddlemaker, privately printed, 1961; (editor) *Force without Fanfare,* Texas Christian University Press, 1968; *The Ranch in Spanish Texas: 1690-1800,* Texas Western Press, 1969; (editor with Harold M. Hollingsworth) *Essays on the American West,* University of Texas Press, 1969; *One Man, One Vote: Gerrymandering vs. Reapportionment,* Steck, 1970; (contributor) *Indian Tribes of Texas,* Texian Press, 1971; (editor with Margaret F. Morris) *Essays On U.S. Foreign Relations,* University of Texas Press, 1974; (contributor) *Broken Treaties and Forked Tongues,* Caxton, 1976; (author of introduction) *Cavalry Wife: The Diary of Eveline Alexander, 1866-67,* Texas A&M University Press, 1977. Contributor to *McGraw-Hill Encyclopedia of World Biography* and *Readers Encyclopedia of the American West;* contributor to history journals.

WORK IN PROGRESS: A book on Indians of Texas, for a series, and a volume of women's overland journals, 1849-1870.

SIDELIGHTS: Sandra Myres told *CA:* "As both teacher and author, I believe one activity enhances the other. I find my research adds to my classroom activities and enables me to bring new material to the attention of my students, and frequently my students contribute new ideas or directions for research. For me, writing is an avocation which melds with my teaching career."

AVOCATIONAL INTERESTS: Raising and exhibiting Pembroke Welsh corgis.

* * *

NADEL, Mark V(ictor) 1943-

PERSONAL: Born October 30, 1943, in New York, N.Y.; son of Henry and Brenda (Glassman) Nadel; married Beverly Camras, December 23, 1967; children: Matthew Henry, Daniel Camras. *Education:* University of California, Berkeley, B.A., 1965; Johns Hopkins University, M.A., 1967, Ph.D., 1970. *Office:* Government Research Corp., 1730 M St. N.W., Washington, D.C. 20036.

CAREER: Cornell University, Ithaca, N.Y., assistant professor of government, 1969-75; professional staff member, Government Operations Committee, U.S. Senate, 1976-77; Government Research Corp., Washington, D.C., senior regulatory analyst, 1977—. *Member:* American Political Science Association. *Awards, honors:* Brookings Institution research fellowship, 1968-69; National Endowment for the Humanities junior humanist fellowship, 1972-73.

WRITINGS: The Politics of Consumer Protection, Bobbs-Merrill, 1971; (editor with Robert Weissberg) *American Democracy: Theory and Reality,* Wiley, 1972; *Corporations and Political Accountability,* Heath, 1976.

WORK IN PROGRESS: Research on federal regulatory policies.

* * *

NAGEL, Stuart S(amuel) 1934-

PERSONAL: Born August 29, 1934, in Chicago, Ill.; son of Leo I. (a store owner) and Florence (Pritikin) Nagel; married Joyce Golub, September 1, 1957; children: Brenda Ellen, Robert Franklin. *Education:* Attended University of Chicago, 1955; Northwestern University, B.S., 1957, J.D., 1958, Ph.D., 1961. *Politics:* Democratic Party. *Religion:* Jewish. *Home:* 1720 Park Haven, Champaign, Ill. 61820. *Office:* Department of Political Science, University of Illinois at Urbana-Champaign, Urbana, Ill. 61801.

CAREER: Pennsylvania State University, University Park, instructor in political science, 1960-61; University of Arizona, Tucson, assistant professor of political science, 1961-62; University of Illinois at Urbana-Champaign, assistant professor, 1962-64, associate professor, 1965-67, professor of political science, 1968—, member of University Research Board, 1962—. Visiting fellow, National Institute of Law Enforcement and Criminal Justice, U.S. Department of Justice, 1974-75. Occasional part-time general legal practice, 1958—; assistant counsel, U.S. Senate Subcommittee on Administrative Practice, Washington, D.C., 1966; trial attorney, National Labor Relations Board, Chicago, Ill., 1966; attorney and director, Office of Economic Opportunity Legal Services Agency, Champaign, Ill., 1966-70. Consultant to government agencies, commercial research firms, and university research bureaus.

MEMBER: International Association for Philosophy of Law and Social Philosophy, Policy Studies Organization (secretary-treasurer), Law and Society Association, American Bar Association, American Political Science Association, International Academy of Forensic Psychology (member of board of governors, 1971—), Midwest Political Science Association. *Awards, honors:* Research grants from Illinois Center for Education in Politics, 1963, American Council of Learned Societies, 1964-65, Center for Advanced Study in the Behavioral Sciences, Palo Alto, Calif., 1964-65, East-West Center of Hawaii, 1965, National Science Foundation, 1970-73, and Ford Foundation, 1975-79; Russell Sage research fellow, Yale Law School, 1970-71.

WRITINGS: (Editor) *Evaluation Charts on Delay in Administrative Proceedings,* U.S. Government Printing Office, 1966; (editor) *Questionnaire Survey on Delay in Administrative Proceedings,* U.S. Government Printing Office, 1966; *The Legal Process from a Behavioral Perspective,* Dorsey, 1969; (editor) *Law and Social Change,* Sage Publications, 1970; (editor) *New Trends in Law and Politics Research,* Law & Society Association, 1971; (editor) *The Rights of the Accused in Law and Action,* Sage Publications, 1972; (editor) *Law and Social Change,* Sage Publications,

1973; *Comparing Elected and Appointed Judicial Systems*, Sage Publications, 1973; *Minimizing Costs and Maximizing Benefits in Providing Legal Services to the Poor*, Sage Publications, 1973; *Policy Studies Directory*, Policy Studies Organization, 1973, revised edition, 1976; (editor) *Environmental Politics*, Praeger, 1974.

(Editor) *Policy Studies and the Social Sciences*, Heath, 1975; (editor) *Policy Studies in America and Elsewhere*, Heath, 1975; *Improving the Legal Process*, Heath, 1975; (editor) *Political Science Utilization Directory*, Policy Studies Organization, 1975; *Operations Research Methods*, Sage Publications, 1976; *The Applications of Mixed Strategies: Civil Rights and Other Multi-Activity Policies*, Sage Publications, 1976; (editor) *Modeling the Criminal Justice System*, Sage Publications, 1977; *Legal Policy Analysis*, Heath, 1977; *Legal Process Modeling*, Sage Publications, 1977; (editor) *Policy Studies Review Annual*, Sage Publications, 1977; (editor) *Policy Studies Grants Directory*, Policy Studies Organization, 1977; *Too Much or Too Little Policy: The Example of Pretrial Release*, Sage Publications, 1977; *Decision Theory and the Legal Process*, Heath, 1978.

Contributor: Glendon Austin Schubert, editor, *Judicial Decision-Making*, Free Press, 1963; Schubert, editor, *Judicial Behavior: A Reader in Theory and Research*, Rand McNally, 1964; *Should Law Enforcement Agencies in the U.S. Be Given Greater Freedom in the Investigation and Prosecution of Crime?*, U.S. Government Printing Office, 1965; Simon Dinitz and Walter C. Reckless, editors, *Critical Issues in the Study of Crime*, Little, Brown, 1968; Raymond W. Mack and Kimball Young, editors, *Principles of Sociology*, 4th edition, Van Nostrand, 1968; Frederick Wirt and Willis Hawley, editors, *New Dimensions of Freedom in America*, Chandler Publishing, 1969; Theodore L. Becker, editor, *The Impact of Supreme Court Decisions: Empirical Studies*, Oxford University Press, 1969; Richard Quinney, *Crime and Justice in Society*, Little, Brown, 1969.

Robert I. Mendelsohn and James R. Klonoski, *The Politics of Local Justice*, Little, Brown, 1970; Abraham S. Blumberg, editor, *Law and Order: The Scales of Justice*, Aldine, 1970; *Political and Legal Obligation: Nomos XII*, Atherton, 1970; Norman Johnston and others, editors, *Sociology of Punishment and Correction*, 2nd edition, Wiley, 1970; Irving L. Horwitz and Mary S. Strong, *Sociological Realities*, Harper, 1971; Thomas R. Dye, *The Measurement of Policy Impact*, Florida State University Press, 1971; Theodore L. Becker and Vernon Murray, editors, *Government Lawlessness in America*, Oxford University Press, 1971; Fred W. Grupp Jr. and Marvin Maurer, editors, *Political Behavior in the United States*, Appleton, 1972; Gresham M. Sykes and others, editors, *Law and Social Science Research*, University of Denver Law School, 1972; Gary T. Marx, editor, *Muckraking Sociology: Research as Social Criticism*, Dutton, 1972; Joseph R. Fiszman and Gene S. Poschman, editors, *The American Political Arena*, Little, Brown, 1972; Robert Weissberg and Mark Nadel, editors, *Democracy and the American Political System*, Wiley, 1972; Theodore Becker and Malcolm Feeley, editors, *The Impact of Supreme Court Decisions*, Oxford University Press, 1973; Walter D. Burnham, editor, *Politics/America*, Van Nostrand, 1973; Abraham S. Blumberg, editor, *Law and Order: The Scales of Justice*, Dutton, 1973; L. Papayanopoulous, editor, *Democratic Representation and Apportionment*, New York Academy of Sciences, 1973.

Matthew Holden and Dennis Dresang, editors, *What Government Does*, Sage Publications, 1974; Irving Horowitz and Charles Nanry, editors, *Sociological Realities II*, Har-

per, 1975; Tom Cook and Frank Scioli, editors, *Methodologies for Analyzing Public Policies*, Lexington Books, 1975; Lester Milbrath, editor, *Environmental Policy*, Sage Publications, 1975; Dorothy James, editor, *Analyzing Poverty Policy*, Heath, 1975; Gordon Tullock, editor, *Frontiers of Economics*, University Publications, 1975; Charles Jones and Robert Thomas, editors, *Public Policy-Making in a Federal System*, Sage Publications, 1976; G. Dorsey and G. Doyle, editors, *Freedom and Equality*, Oceana, 1977; John Gardiner, editor, *Public Law and Public Policy*, Praeger, 1977; Rita Simon, editor, *Research in Law and Sociology*, Jai Press, 1977; William Starbuck, editor, *Handbook of Organizational Design*, Elsevier, 1977.

Contributor of articles to law and social science journals, including *Rutgers Journal of Law and Computers, American Bar Association Journal, Chicago Daily Law Bulletin, U.C.L.A. Law Review, Wisconsin Law Review, Stanford Law Review, Jurimetrics Journal, Journal of Criminal Law, Stanford Law Review, Transaction: Social Science and Modern Society, Polity, Current History, American Behavioral Scientist, Public Opinion Quarterly, Western Political Quarterly, Public Administration Review, Justice System Journal, Human Behavior, Policy Analysis, Political Methodology, Judicature, American Behavioral Scientist*, and *Urban Law Review*; contributor of reviews to *American Political Science Review, Modern Uses of Logic in Law, American Sociological Review*, and other journals. Editor, *Policy Studies Journal*; member of editorial board, *Law and Society Review*, 1966—; member of editorial advisory board, *Sage Criminal Justice System Annuals*, 1971—; member of editorial board, *Journal of Politics*, 1972—.

WORK IN PROGRESS: A series of books dealing with the applications of optimizing methods to various policy problems, particularly those in the criminal justice field; *Methodological Controversies in Social Science Research; Testing Criminal Justice Models*.

SIDELIGHTS: Stuart Nagel told *CA:* "My work as a political scientist is directed toward research, teaching, and administrative work designed to develop and communicate knowledge about what causes legal policies and decisions to be what they are, and especially what effects alternative legal policies and decisions are likely to have. Hopefully, this work will contribute to both scholarly theories of the legal process, and to practical improvements in making the process more effective and objective in achieving given goals."

*   *   *

NAGI, Mostafa H. 1934-

PERSONAL: Born June 15, 1934, in Samalig, Egypt; son of Faried A. (a mayor) and Hamida (Shenishen) Nagi. *Education:* Cairo University, B.Sc., 1958; Bowling Green State University, M.A., 1967; University of Connecticut, Ph.D., 1970. *Home:* 1451 Clough St., Apt. 207A, Bowling Green, Ohio 43402. *Office:* Department of Sociology, Bowling Green State University, Bowling Green, Ohio 43402.

CAREER: Higher Institute of Public Services, Cairo, Egypt, coordinator and social specialist, 1958-60; Ministry of Agriculture, Lataqua, Syria, agricultural specialist, 1960-62; Ministry of Agriculture, Cairo, agricultural specialist, 1962-64; Bowling Green State University, Bowling Green, Ohio, instructor, 1969-70, assistant professor of sociology, 1970—. Member of Task Force on Research and Development, White House Conference on Aging, State of Ohio, 1971; member of Needs Meeting Task Force for the Aged,

State of Ohio, 1972. *Military service:* Egyptian Army, 1956-57. *Member:* Population Association of America, American Sociological Association, Gerontological Society, Indian Society of Labor Economists, Gamma Sigma Delta.

WRITINGS: Labor Force and Employment in Egypt: A Demographic and Socioeconomic Analysis, Praeger, 1971. Also editor of and contributor to *Language and Societies in Comparative Perspectives: A Reader in the Sociology of Development.* Contributor to sociological journals.

WORK IN PROGRESS: With William Jackson, *Academia and Environment; Language and Modernization;* editing with Edward G. Stockwell, *Urbanization in the Middle East: A Reader in Urban Demography;* research on job satisfaction and retirement plans among United Auto Workers members.

*   *   *

NAGY-TALAVERA, Nicholas M(anuel) 1929-

PERSONAL: Born February 14, 1929, in Budapest, Hungary; son of Sandor (an industrialist and merchant) and Hermina (Rebhuhn-Abarbanel) Nagy. *Education:* Attended University of Vienna one year; University of California, Berkeley, B.A., 1959, M.A. and M.L.S., 1961, Ph.D., 1966. *Office:* Department of History, California State University, Chico, Calif. 95926.

CAREER: Idaho State University, Pocatello, assistant professor of history, 1965-66; University of Portland, Portland, Ore., assistant professor of history, 1966-67; California State University, Chico, 1967—, began as assistant professor, currently associate professor of history. *Member:* American Historical Association. *Awards, honors:* Hoover Institution research grant.

WRITINGS: The Green Shirts and the Others: A History of Fascism in Hungary and Rumania, Hoover Institution, 1970; *Recollections of Soviet Labor Camps 1949-55,* University of California Bancroft Library (Berkeley), 1971.

WORK IN PROGRESS: The Historian-Politician of East Central Europe, completion expected in 1979; *Autobiographical Notes.*

SIDELIGHTS: In addition to his native tongue, Nicholas Nagy-Talavera speaks, reads, and writes Spanish, Portuguese, French, German, Russian, and Rumanian; he speaks and reads Serbo-Croatian, Polish, Czech, Slovak, Yiddish, and Ladino. He has some knowledge of Arabic and all Slavonic or Latin tongues.

*   *   *

NAIDIS, Mark 1918-

PERSONAL: Born August 5, 1918, in New York, N.Y.; son of Benjamin (a physician) and Fanny (Sherman) Naidis; married Jacquelyne June Schulze (a school teacher), June 10, 1948; children: Margaret Ruth. *Education:* University of California, Los Angeles, B.A., 1938, M.A., 1941; Stanford University, Ph.D., 1951. *Home:* 10847 Canby Ave., Northridge, Calif. 91326. *Office:* Department of History, Los Angeles Valley College, Van Nuys, Calif. 91401.

CAREER: Institute of International Education, New York, N.Y., senior researcher, 1951-52; Los Angeles Valley College, Van Nuys, Calif., associate professor, 1955-62, professor of history, 1962—. Part-time professor of history, San Fernando Valley State College (now California State University, Northridge), 1960-71. Visiting lecturer, University of California, Los Angeles, 1961-62; visiting professor at San

Francisco State College (now University), 1962, Rutgers University, 1964, University of Alberta, 1965, California State College, Dominquez Hills, 1966-67, University of Hawaii, 1968, University of British Columbia, 1970, and University of Newcastle, New South Wales, Australia, 1971. Researcher at India Office Library, Commonwealth Relations Office, London, 1960-61, and in India, 1967. *Military service:* U.S. Army Air Forces, served in India-Burma Theatre, 1941-46; became captain. *Member:* American Historical Association, Royal Historical Society, Association for Asian Studies, Conference on British History. *Awards, honors:* National Endowment for the Humanities fellow, London, summer, 1974.

WRITINGS: Notes on the Relationship between Economic Development and Education in India, Institute of International Education, 1952; *India: A Short Introductory History,* Macmillan, 1966; *The Second British Empire, 1783-1965,* Addison-Wesley, 1970; *The Western Tradition,* Dryden Press, 1972. Contributor to *Pacific Historical Review, American Historical Review, Historian, South Atlantic Quarterly,* and other publications.

*   *   *

NAKANO, Hirotaka 1942-

PERSONAL: Born November 29, 1942, in Aomori, Japan. *Education:* Kuwazawa Design School, graduate, 1964. *Home:* 4-3-1-Nishi-Ekebukuro, Toshimaku, Tokyo, Japan.

CAREER: Worked at Visual Animation Studio for three years before becoming writer and illustrator of books for children.

WRITINGS—Self-illustrated; all published by Fukuinkan-Shoten: *A Fish and the Moon,* 1966; *The Elephant Happy,* 1968, translation published as *Elephant Blue,* Bobbs-Merrill, 1970; *The Curious Zoo,* 1971; *The Red Apple,* 1971.

Books illustrated: Keiko Murayama, *The Doctor in the Big Wood,* Akane-Shobo, 1970; Shigeo Watanabe, *She Is a Witch,* Gakken, 1971.††

*   *   *

NAROLL, Raoul 1920-

PERSONAL: Born September 10, 1920, in Canada; married Frada Kaufman, 1941; children: Maud Margaret. *Education:* University of California, Los Angeles, A.B., 1950, M.A., 1952, Ph.D., 1953. *Home:* 4695 Main St., Snyder, N.Y. 14226. *Office:* Department of Anthropology, State University of New York at Buffalo, Buffalo, N.Y. 14214.

CAREER: Human Relations Area Files, Washington, D.C., research associate, 1955-57; San Fernando Valley State College (now California State University, Northridge), assistant professor, 1957-60, associate professor of anthropology, 1960-62; Northwestern University, Evanston, Ill., associate professor, 1962-65, professor of anthropology, sociology, and political science, 1965-67, acting chairman of department of anthropology, 1964-65; State University of New York at Buffalo, professor of anthropology, 1967—. President, Human Relations Area Files, 1973—. Field work in Germany, 1945, Austria, 1956, Greece, 1965-66, and Switzerland, 1966. *Military service:* U.S. Army, 1939-45; became captain.

MEMBER: American Anthropological Association (fellow), American Association for the Advancement of Science, American Ethnological Society. *Awards, honors:* Center for Advanced Study in the Behavioral Sciences fellow, 1954-55; four grants from National Institute of Mental

Health, 1957-63; three grants from National Science Foundation, 1960-71.

WRITINGS: Data Quality Control, Free Press, 1962; (editor with Ronald Cohen, and contributor) *A Handbook of Method in Cultural Anthropology,* Natural History Press, 1970; (with wife, Frada Naroll) *Main Currents in Cultural Anthropology,* Appleton, 1973; (with Frada Naroll and Vern L. Bullough) *Military Deterrence in History,* State University of New York Press, 1974.

Contributor: H. H. Freeland, *Iran,* Human Relations Area File Press, 1957; Frank Moore, editor, *Readings in Cross-Cultural Methodology,* Human Relations Area File Press, 1961; Barry Farrell, editor, *Approaches to Comparative and International Politics,* Northwestern University Press, 1966; H. M. Blalock and Ann B. Blalock, editors, *Methodology in Social Research,* McGraw, 1968; Stanley C. Plog and Robert F. Edgerton, editors, *Changing Perspectives in Mental Illness,* Holt, 1969; Davis B. Bobrow, editor, *Weapons Systems Effectiveness: Political and Psychological Perspectives on Continental Defense,* Praeger, 1969; Dean G. Pruitt and Richard C. Snyder, editors, *Theory and Research on the Causes of War,* Prentice-Hall, 1969; I. L. Horowitz and Mary Strong, editors, *Sociological Realities,* Harper, 1971; Francis L. K. Hsu, editor, *Psychological Anthropology: Approaches to Culture and Personality,* 2nd edition, Schenkman, 1972.

Contributor to *Southwestern Journal of Anthropology, American Journal of Obstetrics and Gynecology, Man, American Anthropologist, Current Anthropology, Ciencias Politicas y Sociales* (Mexico City), *Social Research,* and other professional journals. Editor, *Behaviour Science Research* and *American Behavioral Scientist;* associate editor, *Journal of Conflict Resolution* and *Journal of Cross-Cultural Psychology.*

WORK IN PROGRESS: The Human Situation, Volume I: *The Moral Order,* Volume II: *Human Progress,* Volume III: *Travail.*

* * *

NASSAR, Eugene Paul 1935-

PERSONAL: Born June 20, 1935, in Utica, N.Y.; son of Michael Joseph and Mintaha (Kassouf) Nassar; married Karen Nocian, December 30, 1969; children: Anne, Laura, Paul. *Education:* Kenyon College, B.A., 1957; Worcester College, Oxford, M.A., 1960; Cornell University, Ph.D., 1962. *Religion:* Maronite Catholic. *Home:* 704 Lansing St., Utica, N.Y. 13501. *Office:* Department of English, Utica College of Syracuse University, Utica, N.Y. 13502.

CAREER: Hamilton College, Clinton, N.Y., instructor in English, 1962-64; Utica College of Syracuse University, Utica, N.Y., assistant professor, 1964-66, associate professor, 1966-71, professor of English, 1971—. *Member:* Phi Beta Kappa. *Awards, honors:* Rhodes scholarship; Woodrow Wilson fellowship; Cornell graduate fellowship; National Foundation on the Arts and Humanities, grant, 1967, fellowship, 1972.

WRITINGS: Wallace Stevens: An Anatomy of Figuration, University of Pennsylvania Press, 1965; *The Rape of Cinderella: Essays in Literary Continuity,* Indiana University Press, 1970; *East Utica* (fiction), Munson William Proctor Institute, 1971; *"The Cantos" of Ezra Pound: The Lyric Mode,* Johns Hopkins University Press, 1975. Contributor of articles to *Essays in Criticism, Renascence, College English, Paideuma,* and *Mosaic.*

WORK IN PROGRESS: Essays: Critical and Metacritical.

NAZAROFF, Alexander I. 1898-

PERSONAL: Born February 21, 1898, in Kiev, Russia; son of Ivan S. (a physician) and Ludmilla (Tripolitoff) Nazaroff; married Barbara De Carriere, September 12, 1918. *Education:* University of Odessa, law student, 1916-19. *Religion:* Russian Orthodox Church. *Home:* 12 East 97th St., New York, N.Y. 10029.

CAREER: In earlier years was free-lance writer, chiefly on Russian literature, history, and politics, for various publications, including *New York Times Book Review,* 1923-35, and *New York Herald-Tribune Magazine* (later *This Week*), 1929-35; free-lance researcher, chiefly on Russia, for *Time, Fortune,* and other publications, 1935-47; U.S. Information Agency, New York City, author and broadcaster of reviews on American cultural life to the Soviet Union, 1947-54; United Nations Secretariat, New York City, translator, 1954-65. *Member:* Association of Former International Civil Servants (New York), United Nations Association.

WRITINGS: (Editor and translator) Nicholas Evreinoff, *The Theatre in Life,* Brentano, 1927; *Tolstoy: The Inconstant Genius* (biography), Stokes, 1929, reprinted, Books for Libraries, 1972; *The Land of the Russian People* (teen book), Lippincott, 1944, later editions published as *The Land and People of Russia,* 5th revised edition, 1972; *Picture Map Geography of the USSR* (teen book), Lippincott, 1969.

WORK IN PROGRESS: A biography of Peter the Great of Russia.

SIDELIGHTS: Before coming to the United States, Alexander Nazaroff spent more than two years in Turkey, and has done a great deal of traveling since. He visits Europe a few weeks almost every year—chiefly England, France, and Spain.

* * *

NEALON, Thomas E. 1933-

PERSONAL: Born April 16, 1933, in Cleveland, Ohio; son of Michael H. (a travel agent) and M. Stella (Babin) Nealon; married Carol Ann Anthony, June 25, 1960; children: Mary Ellen, Michael, Paul, Peter, Mark, Christopher. *Education:* John Carroll University, A.B., 1957; Fordham University, M.A., 1960, P.D., 1972; Hofstra University, P.D., 1968. *Religion:* Roman Catholic. *Home:* 55 Ball Park Lane, Hicksville, N.Y. 11801. *Office:* Department of Reading, Nassau Community College, Garden City, N.Y. 11530.

CAREER: Nassau Community College, Garden City, N.Y., assistant professor, 1965-67, associate professor, 1968-71, professor of reading, 1971—, chairman of department, 1967—. *Member:* International Reading Association, College Reading Association, American Association of University Professors, New York State Association of Junior Colleges, Two-Year College Reading Association (president, 1970-71).

WRITINGS: (With Frederick J. Sieger) *Vocabulary: A Key to Better College Reading,* Prentice-Hall, 1970; (editor) *Selected Proceedings of "Reading Issues in the Two Year Colleges,"* Nassau Community College, 1972. Contributor to *Journal of Reading.*

WORK IN PROGRESS: Research on placement of disadvantaged students in college programs without the requirement of preparatory study.

NECKER, Claire (Kral) 1917-

PERSONAL: Born October 16, 1917, in Chicago, Ill.; daughter of Joseph James (in publishing) and Josephine (Kral) Nemec; married Walter L. Necker (a librarian), August 21, 1939 (divorced, 1968). *Education:* Northwestern University, M.S., 1938; non-academic training in librarianship. *Politics:* Liberal. *Religion:* Pantheist. *Home:* 10 Country Rd., Westport, Conn. 06880.

CAREER: Has worked as museum curator, physics lab technician, chemistry lab technician, and partner in antiquarian book business specializing in natural history; Lake County Public Library, Independence Hill, Ind., book cataloger, 1969-75.

WRITINGS: Cats and Dogs, A. S. Barnes, 1969; *The Natural History of Cats,* A. S. Barnes, 1970; *Four Centuries of Cat Books,* Scarecrow, 1972; *Supernatural Cats,* Doubleday, 1972; *The Cat's Got Our Tongue,* Scarecrow, 1973; (contributor) Judy Fireman, editor, *Cat Catalog,* Workman Publishing, 1976. Contributor of nature articles to periodicals.

WORK IN PROGRESS: Editing an anthology, *CATalysts,* for Thomas Nelson; a book on the cat in music, *Pussyfooting through Music,* for Stein & Day; *Dunel and Dingoes;* further books about cats.

SIDELIGHTS: Claire Necker has researched her books in the libraries and art galleries of the United States, Mexico, Great Britain, and France. She told *CA:* "A reverence for all nature has governed my entire life.... My M.S. was in animal ecology and I took all the zoology courses the university offered.... Living in dune country, then on a small farm, and now in a semi-rural area, has kept me in close contact with the outdoors.... Cruelty to any life form and the continual disregard and destruction of our natural heritage distress me more than anything else and I do what I can to alleviate both. My hope is that my writing will aid in this by creating a better understanding of living things.... I continue to write principally about cats for two reasons. First, they're my favorite animal, and second, a definitive history about cats is needed. Hopefully, my contributions will be this history."

*   *   *

NEELY, Bill 1930-

PERSONAL: Born August 18, 1930, in Jane Lew, W.Va.; son of Walter (a merchant) and Madge (Bush) Neely; married Martina Winemiller (a model), November 27, 1965; children: Michael, Jodi, Annamaria, Susan, Walter III. *Education:* West Virginia Wesleyan College, A.B., 1952; West Virginia University, graduate study, 1952-53. *Politics:* Republican. *Religion:* Methodist. *Home and office address:* P.O. Box 500, Jane Lew, W. Va. 26378.

CAREER: Goodyear Tire & Rubber Co., Akron, Ohio, manager of racing public relations, 1961-66; Humble Oil Corp., Houston, Tex., public relations manager of central region, 1966-70. *Member:* Public Relations Society of America, Sigma Delta Chi.

WRITINGS—Published by Regnery, except as indicated: *Spirit of America,* 1971; *Grand National,* 1971; *A Closer Walk,* 1972; *Country Gentleman,* 1973; *Stand on It,* Little, Brown, 1974; *Drag Racing,* 1974; *Cars to Remember,* 1975. Contributor to *Playboy* and *Sports Illustrated.*

WORK IN PROGRESS: A novel.

NEFF, H(arry) Richard 1933-

PERSONAL: Born January 22, 1933, in Lancaster, Pa.; son of Harry Myer (a florist) and Ada (Baxter) Neff; married Gertrude Simmons, August 20, 1955; children: David Harry, Anne Elizabeth, Stephen Harvey, Susan Blanche, John Richard. *Education:* Franklin and Marshall College, A.B., 1954; Princeton Theological Seminary, B.D., 1957; San Francisco Theological Seminary, S.T.M., 1970. *Politics:* Independent. *Home:* 12905 Cherrywood Lane, Bowie, Md. 20715.

CAREER: Ordained to Presbyterian ministry, 1957; minister in Nottingham, Pa., 1957-61, and Middletown, Pa., 1961-69; Christian Community Presbyterian Church, Bowie, Md., minister, 1969—. *Member:* Council of Churches of Greater Washington, Bowie Clergy Association, Phi Beta Kappa.

WRITINGS: Psychic Phenomena and Religion: ESP, Prayer, Healing, Survival, Westminster, 1971.

WORK IN PROGRESS: Dissertation for doctorate at San Francisco Theological Seminary.

AVOCATIONAL INTERESTS: Camping with his family (they have camped all across the United States and Canada).

*   *   *

NEGANDHI, A(nant) R(anchoddas) 1933-

PERSONAL: Born December 24, 1933, in Bombay, India; came to United States in 1959; son of Ranchhoddas G. and R. (Prabhan) Negandhi; married Erna A. Adeline, June 3, 1966; children: Amin, Pia. *Education:* University of Bombay, B.A., 1958, B.Com., 1959; Texas Christian University, M.B.A. in management, 1960, M.B.A. in personnel administration, 1961; Michigan State University, Ph.D., 1964. *Home:* 1380 Mockingbird Dr., Kent, Ohio 44240. *Office:* Comparative Administration Research Institute, Kent State University, Kent, Ohio 44242.

CAREER: Khatau Textile Mills, Bombay, India, research analyst, 1952-59; Montgomery Ward & Co., Fort Worth, Tex., market research analyst trainee, 1960-61; Michigan State University, East Lansing, research associate, 1961-64; University of California, Los Angeles, assistant professor of business administration, 1964-67; Kent State University, Kent, Ohio, professor of organizational theory and behavior and director of Center for Business and Economic Research, 1967-75, professor of organizational theory and international business and director of Comparative Administration Research Institute, 1975—. Currently visiting research fellow of International Institute of Management in Berlin, Germany. Summer resident fellow in India and Taiwan, 1967-72. Consulting editor, Vora & Co. Publishing (India). *Member:* Academy of Management (program chairman, international and comparative management division), Society of Applied Anthropology. *Awards, honors:* Ford Foundation grant for comparative management studies, 1966-69; Council of Economic Cooperation and Development grant in Taiwan, 1968-69; selected as "Outstanding Educator of America," 1971.

WRITINGS: Private Foreign Investment Climate in India, Bureau of Business and Economic Research, Michigan State University, 1965; *The Foreign Private Investment Climate in India,* Vora, 1966; (with Richard Florentz Gonzalez) *The United States Overseas Executive: His Orientations and Career Patterns,* Bureau of Business and Economic Research, Michigan State University, 1967; (with S. B. Prasad) *Managerialism for Economic Development,* Nijhoff, 1968; (editor with A. J. Melcher and J. P. Schwitter) *Comparative*

Administration and Management: Conceptual Schemes and Research Findings, Bureau of Economic and Business Research, Kent State University, 1969; *Organizational Behavior Models,* Bureau of Economic and Business Research, Kent State University, 1970; *Modern Organizational Theory: Contextual Environmental and Socio-Cultural Variables,* Kent State University Press, 1970; *Environmental Settings in Organizational Functioning,* Center for Business and Economic Research, Kent State University, 1971; *Organization Theory in an Interorganizational Perspective,* Center for Business and Economic Research, Kent State University, 1971; *Comparative Management,* Appleton, 1971; *Management and Economic Development: The Case of Taiwan,* Nijhoff, 1973; *Interorganization Theory,* Comparative Administration Research Institute, Kent State University, 1975; *The Frightening Angels: A Study of U.S. Multinationals in Developing Nations,* Kent State University Press, 1975; *Organization Theory in an Open System: A Study of Transferring Advanced Management Practices to Developing Nations,* Dunellen, 1975.

Contributor to *Journal of Business, Economic Weekly, California Management Review, International Dimension in Business, Economic Record, Academy of Management Journal, Economic Studies, Management International,* and other journals. Editor, *Organization and Administrative Sciences.*

WORK IN PROGRESS: A comprehensive study of multinational corporations.

SIDELIGHTS: A. R. Negandhi told *CA* that he is "professionally interested in studying complex organizations in cross-cultural settings. [I] am enrolled in [a] large-scale study to ascertain the transferability of advanced management practices to developing countries." He speaks and writes nine languages and has traveled around the world four times.

*   *   *

NEIDERMAN, Andrew 1940-

PERSONAL: Surname is pronounced *Ny*-der-man; born October 26, 1940, in Brooklyn, N.Y.; son of George and Anne (Malisoff) Neiderman; married Diane Wilson, February 8, 1964; children: Melissa Gay, Erik Richard. *Education:* Attended Hunter College of the City University of New York, Bronx Campus, (now Herbert H. Lehman College of the City University of New York), 1958-60; State University of New York at Albany, B.A., 1962, M.A., 1964. *Politics:* Liberal Democrat. *Religion:* Hebrew. *Home:* Wildwood Dr., South Fallsburgh, N.Y. 12779. *Agent:* James Brown Associates, 25 West 43rd St., New York, N.Y. 10036. *Office:* Fallsburgh Central School, Fallsburgh, N.Y. 12733.

CAREER: Fallsburgh Central School, Fallsburgh, N.Y., English teacher, 1964—, audio-visual director. Town historian, Fallsburgh, 1977. *Member:* New York State Teachers Association, Sullivan County Teachers Council (president, 1971-72), Fallsburgh Teachers Association (president, 1969).

WRITINGS: Sisters (novel), Stein & Day, 1971. Also author of *The Sesquicentennial of Fallsburg Township,* 1976. Contributor of short stories to *The Young Judean, English Record, Interaction,* and other periodicals, of poetry to *Prairie Schooner, University Review, Cimarron Review,* and other periodicals, of short plays to *Scholastic Magazine's Voice,* and of articles to *Media and Methods* and *Campaign Insight.*

WORK IN PROGRESS: Two novels, *Beyond the Front Lines* and *The Vigilante.*

SIDELIGHTS: Andrew Neiderman told *CA* that he has been most influenced by Kurt Vonnegut. He added: "Mainly, today, I am concerned with the theme of violence. I am concerned with how we are driven to acts of violence by an imposing society and [an] entrapping environment."

*   *   *

NEIL, J. Meredith 1937-

PERSONAL: Born June 2, 1937, in Boise, Idaho; son of Carl Hurst (a truck driver) and Ellen (Hurt) Neil; married Virginia Mary Bivens, August 16, 1958; children: John-Marcus Moore. *Education:* Yale University, B.A., 1959; University of Wisconsin, M.S., 1963; Washington State University, Ph.D., 1966. *Home and office:* 1410 Wilcomb St., Boise, Idaho 83705.

CAREER: Teacher in public school in Boise, Idaho, 1959-61; Sam Houston State College (now University), Huntsville, Tex., assistant professor of history, 1966-67; University of Hawaii, Honolulu, assistant professor, 1967-71, associate professor, 1971-74 (on leave, 1972-74); Idaho Bicentennial Commission, Boise, executive director, 1972-76; University of Victoria, Victoria, British Columbia, visiting lecturer, 1976-77; free-lance writer in Boise, 1977—. *Member:* American Studies Association, Organization of American Historians, Popular Culture Association, Society of Architectural Historians, Institute for the Study of Universal History, American Institute of Architects (historian of Hawaii chapter, 1971-72). *Awards, honors:* Summer research stipend, National Endowment for the Humanities, 1968.

WRITINGS: Paradise Improved: Environmental Design in Hawaii, University Press of Virginia, 1972; (editor with Marshall Fishwick) *Popular Architecture,* Bowling Green State University Popular Press, 1974; *Toward a National Taste: America's Quest for Aesthetic Independence,* University Press of Hawaii, 1975; *Saints and Oddfellows: A Bicentennial Sample of Idaho Architecture,* Boise Gallery of Art, 1976. Contributor to *Idaho Yesterdays, Historian, Southern Humanities Review, Journal of American History,* and other publications.

WORK IN PROGRESS: The Dream Denied: Artists and Popular Taste in Modern America.

*   *   *

NETTL, Paul 1889-1972

January 10, 1889—January 8, 1972; Bohemian-born educator and author of books on music and musicians. Obituaries: *New York Times,* January 9, 1972. (See index for *CA* sketch)

*   *   *

NETTLER, Gwynn 1913-

PERSONAL: Born July 7, 1913, in New York, N.Y. *Education:* University of California, Los Angeles, A.B., 1934; Claremont Colleges (now Claremont Graduate School), M.A., 1936; Stanford University, Ph.D., 1946. *Office:* Department of Sociology, University of Alberta, Edmonton, Alberta, Canada.

CAREER: Stanford University, Stanford, Calif., instructor in sociology, 1941-44; Reed College, Portland, Ore., instructor in sociology, 1944-45; University of Washington, Seattle, assistant professor of sociology, 1945-46; University of California, Santa Barbara, associate professor of sociology, 1946-51; private practice of clinical psychology, Beverly Hills, Calif., 1952-54, and San Francisco, Calif., 1954-57; Community Council of Houston, Houston, Tex., director of child welfare study, 1957-59; Dando, S.A., Mexico City, Mexico, associate in industrial psychology, 1959-61; Nevada State Department of Health, Reno Mental Health Center, senior clinical psychologist, 1961-63; University of Alberta, Edmonton, associate professor, 1963-66, professor of sociology, 1966—. Visiting summer professor at University of California, Los Angeles, 1947, 1966, and University of California, Berkeley, 1950; lecturer at Monterey Peninsula College, 1955-57, and University of Houston, 1957-59; visiting professor at Illinois Institute of Technology, 1967.

MEMBER: American Psychological Association, American Sociological Association, American Association for the Advancement of Science, American Association for Public Opinion Research, Society for the Study of Social Problems, Mind Association, Society for the Study of Social Biology, Western Psychological Association, Pacific Sociological Association.

WRITINGS: Explanations (philosophy of science textbook), McGraw, 1970; *Explaining Crime* (criminology textbook), McGraw, 1974, 2nd edition, 1977; *Social Concerns* (textbook), McGraw, 1976.

Contributor: D. N. Jackson and S. Messick, editors, *Problems in Human Assessment,* McGraw, 1967; L. T. Wilkins, editor, *Readings in Deviance,* Prentice-Hall, 1969; Clarizio and others, editors, *Contemporary Issues in Educational Psychology,* Allyn & Bacon, 1969; T. Ellwein, editor, *The Alienation of Man in a Sane Society,* Juventa Verlag, 1970; Martin Wolfgang, Leonard Savitz, and Norman Johnston, editors, *The Sociology of Crime and Delinquency,* Wiley, 1970; J. W. Petras and J. E. Curtis, editors, *The Sociology of Knowledge,* Praeger, 1970; Kassinove, Meier, and Vane, editors, *Selected Academic Readings,* Associated Educational Services, 1971; P. E. Converse, editor, *Measures of Social Psychological Attitudes,* University of Michigan Press, 1971; F. G. Scott and K. R. Thomas, editors, *Confrontations of Death: A Teaching Method and Selected Readings,* Appleton, 1971; L. D. Goodstein and R. I. Lanyon, editors, *Readings in Personality Assessment,* Wiley, 1971. Contributor of more than sixty articles and reviews to journals.

WORK IN PROGRESS: Textbooks in social psychology and criminology.

*   *   *

NEUBURG, Victor E.   1924-

PERSONAL: Born March 8, 1924, in Steyning, England; son of Victor B. (a writer) and K. R. (Goddard) Neuburg; married Anne Hilsum (a teacher), October 11, 1944; children: Caroline. *Education:* Studied at Goldsmiths' College and Institute of Education, London; University of Leicester, M.Ed., 1967. *Politics:* Socialist. *Religion:* Atheist. *Home:* Widdershins, 13 Linden Rd., London N.10, England. *Office:* Polytechnic of North London, Holloway, London N7 8DB, England.

CAREER: Schoolmaster before moving to higher education; Polytechnic of North London, London, England, senior lecturer in history and bibliography, 1968—. *Military service:* British Army, 1942-47; became sergeant. *Member:* Bibliographical Society, Society for Folklife Studies, Society for the Study of Labour History, Past and Present Society, Society for Army Historical Research, Agricultural History Society.

WRITINGS: Chapbooks: A Bibliography of References to English and American Chapbook Literature of the Eighteenth and Nineteenth Centuries, Vine Press, 1964, 2nd edition, Woburn Press, 1972; *Points and Pitfalls: A First Notebook in French Composition,* University Tutorial Press, 1965; *Points and Pitfalls: A First Notebook in German Composition,* University Tutorial Press, 1965; (co-editor) *Henry IV,* Part 1, University Tutorial Press, 1965; *The Penny Histories: A Study of Chapbooks for Young Readers Over Two Centuries,* Oxford University Press, 1968, Harcourt, 1969.

Popular Education in 18th Century England, Woburn Press, 1972; *The Past We See Today,* Oxford University Press, 1972; *Popular Literature: A History and Guide,* Pelican, 1977; *Thomas Frognal Dibdin: A Selection from His Writings,* Scarecrow, in press. Regular contributor to *Times Literary Supplement* and reviewer for other publications. General editor, Woburn Press.

WORK IN PROGRESS: A study of radicalism in England; ongoing work in popular literature.

SIDELIGHTS: Victor Neuburg's father operated a private press, the Vine Press, in Sussex during the 1920's. He was responsible for the first publication of work by Dylan Thomas—in the *Sunday Referee,* a London newspaper. *Avocational interests:* ''Compulsive collector of books—regret the passing of the old style second-hand bookshop.''

BIOGRAPHICAL/CRITICAL SOURCES: Saturday Review, May 10, 1969.

*   *   *

NEUHAUS, Richard (John)   1936-

PERSONAL: Born May 14, 1936, in Pembroke, Ontario, Canada; son of Clemens H. (a clergyman) and Ella (Prange) Neuhaus. *Education:* Lutheran Concordia College (now Concordia Lutheran College), Austin, Tex., B.A., 1957, M.Div., 1960; graduate study at Concordia Seminary, St. Louis, Mo., Wayne State University, and Washington University, St. Louis. *Home and office:* 195 Maujer St., Brooklyn, N.Y. 11206.

CAREER: Lutheran pastor, Church of St. John the Evangelist, Brooklyn, N.Y., 1961—. Clergy and Laymen Concerned about Vietnam, founder, 1966, affiliate, 1966-75; Congressional candidate, 14th District (Brooklyn, N.Y.), 1970; delegate to Democratic Convention, Chicago, 1968, and Miami, 1972; member of board of directors of SANE and Liturgical Conference. *Awards, honors:* Catholic Press Association award, 1968.

WRITINGS: (Editor) *Theology and the Kingdom of God,* Westminster, 1969; (with Peter Berger) *Movement and Revolution,* Doubleday, 1970; *In Defense of People,* Macmillan, 1971; *Time toward Home: The American Experiment as Revelation,* Seabury, 1975; (with Berger) *Against the World for the World,* Seabury, 1976; *Christian Faith and Public Policy,* Augsburg, 1977. Regular contributor to *Commonweal, National Catholic Reporter, Harper's, New York Review of Books, Christian Century,* and *Worldview.* Editor, *Una Sancta,* 1963-68; senior editor, *Worldview.*

WORK IN PROGRESS: The Gospel of Vindication, for Basic Books.

BIOGRAPHICAL/CRITICAL SOURCES: James Finn,

Protest, Politics and Pacifism, Random House, 1968; Francine Gray, *Divine Disobedience,* Christian Classics, 1970; *National Review,* April 7, 1970; *Lutheran Forum,* spring, 1972.

* * *

NEUMAN, Betty Mavine 1924-

PERSONAL: Born September 11, 1924, in Lowell, Ohio; daughter of Jerry Lewis (a farmer) and Zelpha (Peters) Reynolds; married Richard Neuman (a doctor), July 10, 1954 (divorced, 1962); children: Nancy Monet. *Education:* Peoples Hospital School of Nursing, Akron, Ohio, R.N., 1947; University of California, Los Angeles, B.S. (with honors), 1957, M.S., 1966. *Home:* 1136 West Sixth St., Los Angeles, Calif. 90017.

CAREER: University of California, Los Angeles, lecturer and chairman of Community Mental Health Nursing program, beginning 1967. Consultant, Thompson-Ramo Woolridge Co. *Member:* California Nurses Association, California League for Nurses, California Marriage-Family Counseling Association, California Real Estate Association, UCLA Nurses Alumni Association.

WRITINGS: (Contributor) *Communicating Research in Nursing,* Western Interstate Commission for Higher Education, 1970; (with G. W. Deloughery and Kristine Gebbie) *Consultation and Community Organization in Community Mental Health Nursing,* Williams & Wilkins, 1971. Contributor of articles to *Journal of Psychiatric Nursing, Public Personnel Review, Comparative Group Studies,* and *Nursing Research.*

WORK IN PROGRESS: A book on refinement of group dynamics aspect of mental health consultation.

AVOCATIONAL INTERESTS: Real estate, marriage and family counseling.†

* * *

NEUMANN, William Louis 1915-1971

March 4, 1915—September 30, 1971; American educator and historian. Obituaries: *New York Times,* October 2, 1971; *Washington Post,* October 2, 1971. (See index for *CA* sketch)

* * *

NEUMEYER, Peter F(lorian) 1929-

PERSONAL: Born August 4, 1929, in Munich, Germany; son of Alfred and Eva M. (Kirchheim) Neumeyer; married Helen Snell (a textbook editor, summer teacher at nature center, and music professor), December 27, 1952; children: Zachary Thomas, Christopher Muir, Daniel Patrick. *Education:* University of California, Berkeley, B.A., 1951, M.A., 1955, Ph.D., 1963. *Home:* 665 Lashley St., Morgantown, W.Va. 26505. *Office:* Department of English, West Virginia University, Morgantown, W.Va. 26505.

CAREER: Worked while attending school as dishwasher, lifeguard, swimming teacher, camp counselor, and truck driver; teacher in California public schools, 1957-58, 1960-61; University of California, Berkeley, instructor in English, 1962-63; Harvard University, Cambridge, Mass., assistant professor of education, 1963-69; State University of New York at Stony Brook, associate professor of English, 1969-73; West Virginia University, Morgantown, chairman of English department, 1973—. Former president, Medford (Mass.) Educational Council; representative for Project

Plan, Three Village Schools, Setauket, N.Y. *Member:* Modern Language Association of America, National Council of Teachers of English. *Awards, honors:* First prize for poem "Gulls" in *Rebel* (magazine), 1964.

WRITINGS: (Editor) *Twentieth Century Interpretations of "The Castle"* (by Franz Kafka), Prentice-Hall, 1969.

Juvenile books: *Donald and the . . . ,* Addison-Wesley, 1969; (with Edward Gorey) *Donald Has a Difficulty,* Fantod Press, 1970; (with Gorey) *Why We Have Day and Night,* Young Scott Books, 1970; *The Faithful Fish,* Young Scott Books, 1971. Contributor of more than twenty articles to professional journals, and poems and essays to magazines and journals.

WORK IN PROGRESS: Research on children and literature, on the work of Franz Kafka, and on contemporary poetry.

SIDELIGHTS: "*Tristram Shandy* is the book that first suggested to me the possibilities in literature," Peter Neumeyer writes. "I read the book in an otherwise dull sophomore survey course in English literature. I several times veered to other majors. . . . tried anthropology and Law School. I was mighty happy to return to Chaucer, and to people who wanted to talk about books. Probably a long history of back ailments, laying me up for great stretches of time, forced me to write—for had I never been flat on my back, I would have spent absolutely all my time doing what I love still above all other things: hiking, fishing, swimming, and best of all, riding great ocean rollers in to shore. What is important? Probably to listen. Listen. Listen. Observe. That way you come close to understanding, perhaps loving, surely forgiving. . . .''

Neumeyer says that his books "were written really because they had to get out of me—so, written for me—and people who have as peculiar a sense of humor or of what is important as I do, may find them entertaining. They certainly weren't written specifically with children in mind. In fact, I personally, don't think *Donald and the . . . ,* or *Donald Has a Difficulty,* or *Why We Have Day and Night* are children's books at all. They're books without too many words, beautifully illustrated by Edward Gorey. Somebody other than the author decided to give them card catalogue numbers that classified them as children's books. *Why We Have Day and Night* is much influenced by the writing of Franz Kafka, on whom I do research. The last page of that book is very important, and is misprinted. It is all white. It was intended to be all black. That was pretty much the point of the book. Librarians who get it should write on the last page of the book, 'Color me black,' and let some child do it."

BIOGRAPHICAL/CRITICAL SOURCES: New York Review of Books, April 10, 1969; *Saturday Review,* April 17, 1971.

* * *

NEWCOMB, Theodore Mead 1903-

PERSONAL: Born in 1903, in Rock Creek, Ohio; married Mary E. Shiperd, August 27, 1931; children: Esther, Suzanne, Theodore Mead, Jr. *Education:* Oberlin College, A.B.; Columbia University, Ph.D., 1929. *Home:* 1045 Cedar Bend Dr., Ann Arbor, Mich. 48105. *Office:* Department of Psychology, University of Michigan, Ann Arbor, Mich. 48104.

CAREER: Assistant professor of psychology at Lehigh University, Bethlehem, Pa., 1929-30, and Western Reserve University (now Case Western Reserve University), Cleveland, Ohio, 1930-34; Bennington College, Bennington, Vt., teacher of psychology, 1934-41; University of Michigan, Ann Arbor, associate professor, 1941-46, professor of sociology and psychology, 1946—, chairman, Doctoral Program in Social Psychology, 1947-63, associate director, Residential College, 1964—, Mary Ann and Charles R. Walgreen, Jr. Professor for the Study of Human Understanding, 1969—. Fulbright scholar, Tavistock Institute of Human Relations, London, England, 1951-52; fellow, Center for Advanced Study in the Behavioral Sciences, 1956-57; visiting fellow, Western Behavioral Sciences Institute, 1961-66. Antioch College, trustee, 1959-65, chairman, 1966. *Military service:* U.S. Army, 1942-45; served with Foreign Broadcast Intelligence Service.

MEMBER: American Academy of Arts and Sciences (fellow), American Sociological Society (member of council, 1951-54), American Psychological Association (president, Division of Personality and Social Psychology, 1948-49; president, 1955-56; chairman, Social Psychology Section, 1966-67), Society for the Psychological Study of Social Issues (president, 1945-46), National Academy of Sciences. *Awards, honors:* Distinguished Scientific Contribution Award, American Psychological Association, 1976.

WRITINGS: The Consistency of Certain Extrovert-Introvert Behavior Patterns in 51 Problem Boys, Teachers College, Columbia University, 1929; (with Gardner and Lois Barclay Murphy) *Experimental Social Psychology,* revised edition (Newcomb was not associated with earlier editions), Harper, 1937; (editor and contributor with W. I. Newstetter and M. J. Feldstein) *Group Adjustment: A Study in Experimental Sociology,* Western Reserve University, 1938; (editor and contributor with George W. Hartmann) *Industrial Conflict: A Psychological Interpretation* (first yearbook of Society for the Psychological Study of Social Issues), Cordon, 1939; *Personality and Social Change: Attitude Formation in a Student Community,* Dryden, 1943; (editor and contributor with E. L. Hartley) *Readings in Social Psychology,* Holt, 1947, 2nd edition (with Hartley and G. E. Swanson), 1952, 3rd edition (with Hartley and Eleanor Maccoby), 1958.

Social Psychology, Dryden, 1950; (editor with others and contributor) *Current Theory and Research in Motivation,* University of Nebraska Press, 1952; *The Acquaintance Process,* Holt, 1961; (with Richard Flacks) *Deviant Subcultures on a College Campus,* University of Michigan, c.1964; (with Ralph H. Turner and Philip E. Converse) *Social Psychology: The Study of Human Interaction* (partial, preliminary version published under same title by Ann Arbor Publishers, 1961), Holt, 1965, 2nd edition, Tavistock Publications, 1966; (editor with Everett K. Wilson) *College Peer Groups: Problems and Prospects for Research,* Aldine, 1966; (with K. Koenig, Richard Flacks, and D. Warwick) *Persistence and Change: Bennington College and Its Students after 25 Years,* Wiley, 1967; (editor and contributor with others) *Theories of Cognitive Consistency,* Rand McNally, 1968; (with Kenneth Feldman) *The Impact of College on Students,* two volumes, Jossey-Bass, 1969.

Contributor: Goodwin Watson, editor, *Civilian Morale,* Houghton, 1942; T. G. Andrews, editor, *Methods of Psychology,* Wiley, 1948; John H. Rohrer and Muzafer Sherif, editors, *Social Psychology at the Crossroads,* Harper, 1951; James Edward Hulett, Jr. and Ross Stagner, editors, *Problems in Social Psychology: An Interdisciplinary Inquiry,* University of Illinois Press, 1952; Leon Festinger and Daniel Katz, editors, *Research Methods in the Behavioral Sciences,* Dryden, 1953; John Gillin, editor, *For a Science*

of Social Man, Macmillan, 1954; Roland Young, editor, *Approaches to the Study of Politics,* Northwestern University Press, 1958; Renato Tagiuri and Luigi Petrullo, editors, *Person Perception and Interpersonal Behavior,* Stanford University Press, 1958; Sigmund Koch, editor, *Psychology: A Study of a Science,* Volume III, McGraw, 1959; Robert King Merton, L. Broom, and L. Cottrell, Jr., editors, *Sociology Today: Problems and Prospects,* Volume II, Basic Books, 1959; Dorwin Cartwright and A. F. Zander, editors, *Group Dynamics: Research and Theory,* 2nd edition, Row, Peterson, 1960; J. C. Pealman and E. L. Harley, editors, *Festschrift for Gardner Murphy,* Harper, 1960; R. L. Sutherland and others, editors, *Personality Factors on the College Campus,* Hogg Foundation, University of Texas, 1961; Nevitt Sanford, editor, *The American College,* Wiley, 1962; *The Student in Higher Education,* American Council on Education, 1965; Otto Klineberg and Richard Christie, editors, *Perspectives in Social Psychology,* Holt, 1965; Jerry Gaff, editor, *The Cluster College,* Jossey-Bass, 1970; *The New Colleges: Toward an Appraisal,* American College Testing Program, 1971; Bernard I. Murstein, editor, *Theories of Attraction and Love,* Springer Publishing, 1971.

Contributor of articles to various psychology and sociology journals, including *Mental Hygiene, Teachers College Record, Journal of Educational Psychology, American Sociological Review, Sociometry, Public Opinion Quarterly, Annals of American Academy of Political and Social Sciences, Journal of Abnormal and Social Psychology, Journal of Human Relations, American Psychologist, Journal of Personality, Journal of Social Issues,* and *Political Science Quarterly.* Editor, *Psychological Review,* 1954-59.

* * *

NEWMAN, Louis Israel 1893-1972

December 20, 1893—March 9, 1972; American rabbi and religious writer. Obituaries: *New York Times,* March 10, 1972. (See index for *CA* sketch)

* * *

NEWMAN, P(aul) B(aker) 1919-

PERSONAL: Born May 12, 1919, in Chicago, Ill.; son of Paul Jones (a publisher's representative) and Virginia Evelyn (Murray) Newman; married Anne Royall (a college teacher), February 27, 1945; children: Betsy, Paula Anne, William. *Education:* Attended Antioch College, 1936-38; University of Chicago, B.S., 1940, Ph.D., 1958; University of Iowa, M.F.A., 1951. *Politics:* Independent. *Religion:* Society of Friends (Quaker). *Home:* 2215 Hassell Pl., Charlotte, N.C. 28209. *Office:* Department of English, Queens College, Charlotte, N.C. 28274.

CAREER: University of Puerto Rico, Mayaguez, lecturer in English, 1956-58; Kansas State University, Manhattan, assistant professor of English, 1959-62; Queens College, Charlotte, N.C., associate professor, 1963-67, professor of English, 1967—. Visiting poet and teacher of creative writing for Poetry in the Schools program of North Carolina Arts Council and South Carolina Arts Commission; conductor of poetry workshop at Erskine College, 1972. Member of board of directors, Charlotte English-speaking Union, 1969—. *Military service:* U.S. Army Air Forces, weather forecaster, 1940-45; served in North Africa, Italy, Ireland, and England; became captain.

MEMBER: National Council of Teachers of English, Modern Language Association of America, American Association of University Professors, South Atlantic Modern

Language Association. *Awards, honors:* William Billings Fiske Award for poetry, University of Chicago, 1955; Charlotte English-Speaking Union scholar at Exeter College, Oxford University, 1967; Roanoke-Chowan Poetry Cup, North Carolina Literary and Historical Association, 1968, for *The Cheetah and the Fountain,* and 1971, for *The Ladder of Love;* Crucible Award for poetry, 1970.

WRITINGS—Poetry: *The Cheetah and the Fountain,* South & West, 1968; *Dust of the Sun,* South & West, 1969; *The Ladder of Love,* Smith-Horizon Press, 1970; *Paula: A Narrative Poem,* Dragons Teeth Press, 1975; *House on the Saco,* Bauhan William, 1977. Contributor of poems and articles to literary reviews. Has adapted his poems for poetry-films, "Paula," "The Washington Trail," and "On the Coast."

SIDELIGHTS: P. B. Newman wrote *CA:* "I am interested in making poetry-films. I have made three, so far: "Paula," "The Washington Trail," and "On the Coast," using my own poems and appropriate music. The idea behind these films is to give poetry to the listener in a way that is slightly more dramatic—that is, somewhat closer to the stage. Poetry when read aloud and combined with other forms, such as film and music (or dance or pantomime), may help people to like dramatic poetry. I think the interest in hearing poetry read aloud is indicative of this. So much of poetry begins with a willingness to listen to the moods and tones within the poetry. My films (and their accompanying music) direct the watcher toward these moods. . . ."

A dramatic production of P. B. Newman's poems, entitled "The Sea Flight," was presented by the Laboratory Theater at the University of North Carolina at Chapel Hill in 1971. He has sailed to the Bahamas and traveled through Spain, Italy, and Greece, collecting material for his poems.

BIOGRAPHICAL/CRITICAL SOURCES: Charlotte Observer, December 12, 1971.

*   *   *

NEWPORT, John P(aul)   1917-

PERSONAL: Born June 16, 1917, in Buffalo, Mo.; son of Marvin Jackson and Mildred (Morrow) Newport; married Eddie Belle Leavell; children: Martha Ellen, Frank Marvin, John Paul, Jr. *Education:* William Jewell College, B.A., 1938; Southern Baptist Theological Seminary, Louisville, Ky., Th.M., 1941, Th.D., 1946; University of Edinburgh, Ph.D., 1953; Texas Christian University, M.A., 1963; also attended Tulsa University, 1948-49, Tulane University, 1951-52, Harvard University, 1958-59, Union Theological Seminary, 1965, University of Basel, and University of Zurich. *Office:* Department of Religious Studies, Rice University, Houston, Tex. 77701.

CAREER: Baylor University, Waco, Tex., associate professor of religion and director of graduate studies in religion, 1949-51; New Orleans Baptist Theological Seminary, New Orleans, La., associate professor of philosophy of religion and New Testament, 1951-52; Southwestern Baptist Theological Seminary, Fort Worth, Tex., professor of philosophy of religion and chairman of the department, 1952-76; Rice University, Houston, Tex., Chavanne Professor of Religious Studies, 1976—. Field work director, Boston University School of Theology, 1958-59; visiting scholar, Union Theological Seminary, 1965; visiting professor, Rice University, 1971, 1972-73. Lecturer and speaker at colleges and universities in United States and Asia. *Member:* American Academy of Religion (president of Southwestern division, 1967-68), Society of Biblical Literature and Exegesis, South-

western Philosophical Association. *Awards, honors:* Rockefeller Foundation grant, Harvard University, 1958-59; D.Lett., William Jewell College, 1967.

WRITINGS: (Contributor) Norman Wade Cox, editor, *Encyclopedia of Southern Baptists,* Broadman, 1958; *Theology and Contemporary Art Forms,* Word Books, 1971; (contributor) Clifton D. Allen, editor, *Broadman Commentary,* Volume I, Broadman, 1971; *Demons, Demons, Demons,* Broadman, 1972; *Why Christians Fight over the Bible,* Thomas Nelson, 1974; (contributor) John W. Montgomery, editor, *Demon Possession,* Bethany Fellowship, 1976; *The New Consciousness Revolution and the Bible,* Broadman, 1977; *Paul Tillich,* Word Books, 1977. Contributor to *Review and Expositor, Southwestern Journal of Theology, Baptist Student,* and other publications.

*   *   *

NEWTH, Rebecca   1940-

PERSONAL: Born September 21, 1940, in Lansing, Mich.; daughter of William Arthur and Catherine (Messenger) Newth; married John Harrison (a librarian), December 16, 1961; children: Gloria, John, Olivia. *Education:* Michigan State University, B.A., 1962. *Politics:* Democrat. *Religion:* Christian. *Home:* 60 Boston Post Rd., Guilford, Conn. 06437.

CAREER: Poet. Participant, "Pacifica Poetry Series," WBAI radio, 1977, and Poets at City Hall, Boston, 1977. *Awards, honors:* National Endowment for the Arts award, 1971, for a poem, "Hannibal over the Mountains . . . ," published in *Sumac* magazine.

WRITINGS: Xeme (poems), Sumac Press, 1971; *A Journey Whose Bones Are Mine* (poems), Truck Press, 1978. Poem anthologized in *The American Literary Anthology Three,* edited by George Plimpton and Peter Ardery, Viking, 1970. Contributor of poetry to *Stony Brook, Sumac, Hearse, Truck, Hanging Loose, Essence,* and other journals.

WORK IN PROGRESS: A new book of poems.

*   *   *

NICHELSON, F(loyd) Patrick   1942-

PERSONAL: Born March 23, 1942, in Long Beach, Calif.; son of Arthur F. (an aerospace technician) and Shirley (Bennett) Nichelson; married Maureen O'Hara, January 30, 1965; married second wife, Karen H. Sviridoff, October 9, 1970; children: (first marriage) Monica; (second marriage) Raina, Christopher. *Education:* St. John's College, Camarillo, Calif., B.A., 1963; additional study at St. John's Seminary, Camarillo, 1963-64, and California State College at Long Beach (now California State University, Long Beach), 1965; Immaculate Heart College, Los Angeles, M.A., 1968; University of Southern California, additional graduate study. *Religion:* Roman Catholic. *Home:* 234 San Vincente, No. 20, Santa Monica, Calif. 90402. *Office:* Department of Religious Studies, California State University, 18111 Nordhoff St., Northridge, Calif. 91324.

CAREER: Teacher and dean of students at a private high school, Los Angeles, Calif., 1966-68; University of Southern Calif., Los Angeles, assistant to university chaplain, 1968-70; California State University, Northridge, 1970—, began as instructor, currently associate professor of religious studies and director of Institute for the Advancement of Teaching and Learning. Technical writer, Watts Labor Community Action Committee, Los Angeles, 1970. *Member:* American Academy of Religion.

WRITINGS: (With John Orr) *The Radical Suburb: Soundings in Changing American Character,* Westminster, 1970.

WORK IN PROGRESS: A study of the significance of Samuel T. Coleridge on imagination and social ethics.

*   *   *

NICHOLS, J(ohn) G(ordon)   1930-

PERSONAL: Born July 24, 1930, in Liverpool, England; son of Albert Henry and Dorothy (Worrall) Nichols; married Eileen Kennedy (a lecturer), April 2, 1956; children: Alice and Elaine (twins), Rachel. *Education:* University of Liverpool, B.A. (honors), 1951, diploma in education, 1952, M.A., 1966, Ph.D., 1970. *Politics:* None. *Religion:* Roman Catholic. *Home:* 43 Warren Dr., Wallasey, Merseyside, England. *Office:* Department of English, Notre Dame College of Education, Mount Pleasant, Liverpool, England.

CAREER: Teacher of English, Liverpool, England, 1954-62; Edge Hill College of Education, Ormskirk, England, lecturer, 1962-64; Notre Dame College of Education, Liverpool, senior lecturer, 1964-66, principal lecturer, 1966, head of English department, 1970—. *Military service:* National Service, 1952-54; became sergeant. *Member:* National Association for the Teaching of English, National Association of Teachers in Further and Higher Education.

WRITINGS: The Flighty Horse (poems), Liverpool University Press, 1968; *The Poetry of Ben Jonson* (criticism), Barnes & Noble, 1969; (editor with T. Pey) *The Poet's Purpose* (poetry anthology), Cassell, 1969; (contributor) Thomas Kabdebo and Paul Tabori, editors, *A Tribute to Gyula Illyes,* Occidental Press, 1968; (contributor) Kabdebo and Tabori, editors, *Gyula Illyes' Poems,* Chatto & Windus, 1971; *The Poetry of Sir Philip Sidney* (criticism), Liverpool University Press, 1974; (contributor) Kabdebo, editor, *100 Hungarian Poems,* Manchester Albion Editions, 1976. Contributor of poems to *English, Anglo-Welsh Review, Review of English Literature,* and *Times Literary Supplement.*

WORK IN PROGRESS: Translation of Hungarian poetry for an anthology by Kabdebo and Tabori, for Mouton & Co.

*   *   *

NIEWYK, Donald L.   1940-

PERSONAL: Surname rhymes with "*see*-like"; born December 21, 1940, in Grand Rapids, Mich.; son of Albert and Henrietta (Streelman) Niewyk. *Education:* Western Michigan University, B.A., 1962; Tulane University of Louisiana, M.A., 1964, Ph.D., 1968; Free University of Berlin, graduate fellow, 1966-67. *Office:* Department of History, Southern Methodist University, Dallas, Tex. 75275.

CAREER: Xavier University of Louisiana, New Orleans, instructor in history, 1967-68; Ithaca College, Ithaca, N.Y., assistant professor of history, 1968-72; Southern Methodist University, Dallas, Tex., associate professor of history, 1972—. *Member:* American Historical Association, Conference Group for Central European History, Phi Alpha Theta. *Awards, honors:* College Center of the Finger Lakes research grant, 1969; American Philosophical Society research grant, 1974.

WRITINGS: Socialist, Anti-Semite, and Jew: German Social Democracy Confronts the Problem of Anti-Semitism, 1918-1933, Louisiana State University Press, 1971. Contributor of articles and reviews to *Internationale Wissenschaftliche Korrespondenz, Societas, Historical Abstracts, Leo Baeck Institute Yearbook, 1971,* and *Jewish Social Studies.*

WORK IN PROGRESS: A history of the Jews in Weimar Germany.

*   *   *

NISSEN, Lowell A(llen)   1932-

PERSONAL: Born January 10, 1932, in Fergus Falls, Minn.; son of Nanning Henry (a farmer) and Marie (Chell) Nissen; married Beverly Chloupek, July 31, 1960. *Education:* Attended Gustavus Adolphus College, 1949-50; University of Minnesota, B.A., 1954, M.A., 1958; University of Nebraska, Wolfe fellow, 1958-59, Regent's fellow, 1959-60, Ph.D., 1962. *Religion:* Lutheran. *Home address:* Route 3, Fayetteville, Ark. 72701. *Office:* Department of Philosophy, University of Arkansas, Fayetteville, Ark. 72701.

CAREER: University of Arkansas, Fayetteville, instructor in philosophy, 1963—. *Military service:* U.S. Army, 1954-56. *Member:* American Philosophical Association, Philosophy of Science Association, Phi Beta Kappa.

WRITINGS: John Dewey's Theory of Inquiry and Truth, Humanities, 1966; (with Thomas S. Vernon) *Reflective Thinking: The Fundamentals of Logic,* Wadsworth, 1968. Contributor of articles to *Philosophy of Science, British Journal for the Philosophy of Science, Personalist,* and *Mind.*

WORK IN PROGRESS: Research on teleological and functional explanations in the life sciences.††

*   *   *

NOAH, Harold J(ulius)   1925-

PERSONAL: Born January 21, 1925, in London, England; son of Abraham and Sophia (Cohen) Noah; married Norma Mestel, October 20, 1945; married second wife, Helen Claire Chisnell, October 14, 1966; children: Deborah Ann Susan, Carolyn Anne Elizabeth, Adam Pierre Michael, David Harold Michael. *Education:* London School of Economics and Political Science, B.Sc., 1946, graduate study, 1959-60; King's College, London, Teacher's Diploma, 1949, Academic Diploma, 1954; Columbia University, Ph.D., 1964. *Home:* 560 Riverside Dr., New York, N.Y. 10027. *Office:* Teachers College, Columbia University, New York, N.Y. 10027.

CAREER: Southwest London College of Commerce, London, England, instructor in economics, 1948-49; Henry Thornton School, London, assistant master, later head of economics department, 1949-60; Fairleigh Dickinson University, Madison, N.J., assistant professor of economics, 1960-61; Columbia University, New York, N.Y., instructor, 1962-64, assistant professor, 1964-66, associate professor of comparative education, 1966-69, professor of economics and education, 1969—, Institute of Philosophy and Politics of Education, Teachers College, director, 1974—, dean of Teachers College, 1976—. Consultant, Organization for Economic Cooperation and Development, Paris, France, 1971—. *Member:* Royal Economic Society, American Economic Association, American Association for the Advancement of Slavic Studies, Comparative and International Education Society (president, 1973-74), Comparative Education Society in Europe.

WRITINGS: Financing Soviet Schools, Teachers College Press, 1967; (translator and editor) *The Economics of Education in the U.S.S.R.,* Praeger, 1969; (with Max A. Eckstein) *Toward a Science of Comparative Education,* Macmillan, 1969; (with Eckstein) *Scientific Investigations in Comparative Education,* Macmillan, 1969; *Germany: Re-*

view of National Policies, Organization for Economic Cooperation and Development, 1972; (with Eckstein) *Metropolitanism and Education: A Comparative Study* (monograph), Institute of Philosophy and Politics of Education, Teachers College, Columbia University, 1973; *Canada: Review of National Policies,* Organization for Economic Cooperation and Development, 1976; (with A. H., Passow and others) *The National Case Study: An Empirical Comparative Study of Twenty-One Educational Systems,* Almqvist & Wiksell, 1976. Editor of *Comparative Education Review,* 1966-71, of *Soviet Education,* 1971—.

SIDELIGHTS: Scientific Investigations in Comparative Education has been published in a Spanish translation.

BIOGRAPHICAL/CRITICAL SOURCES: Saturday Review, August 16, 1969.

*   *   *

NOLTE, William H(enry) 1928-

PERSONAL: Born May 2, 1928, in Tulia, Tex.; son of Eugene Arch and Myrtle (Burns) Nolte; married Alice Froehling (a librarian), June 12, 1954; children: Katherine Ann. *Education:* Attended Texas Technical College (now Texas Tech University), 1947-49; University of Missouri, A.B., 1951; University of Texas, M.A., 1952; University of Illinois, Ph.D., 1959. *Politics:* Independent. *Religion:* None. *Home:* 4502 Storkland Dr., Columbia, S.C. 29206. *Office:* Department of English, University of South Carolina, Columbia, S.C. 29208.

CAREER: University of Oregon, Eugene, instructor, 1959-61, assistant professor of English, 1961-65; University of Missouri at St. Louis, associate professor of English, 1965-67; University of South Carolina, Columbia, professor of English, 1967—, chairman of department, 1974—. *Military service:* U.S. Army Air Forces, 1946-47.

WRITINGS: H. L. Mencken: Literary Critic, Wesleyan University Press, 1966; (editor) *H. L. Mencken's Smart Set Criticism,* Cornell University Press, 1968; *Guide to H. L. Mencken,* C. E. Merrill, 1969; *Checklist of H. L. Mencken,* C. E. Merrill, 1969; *Guide to Robinson Jeffers,* C. E. Merrill, 1970; *Checklist of Robinson Jeffers,* C. E. Merrill, 1970; *Rock and Hawk: Robinson Jeffers and the Romantic Agony,* University of Georgia Press, 1978.

WORK IN PROGRESS: Contributing to *The Alternative: An American Spectator.*

BIOGRAPHICAL/CRITICAL SOURCES: New Republic, September 14, 1968; *National Review,* September 24, 1968; *Comparative Literature,* winter, 1968; *New Yorker,* May 31, 1969; *Western Humanities Review,* spring, 1969.

*   *   *

NOONAN, Julia 1946-

PERSONAL: Born October 25, 1946, in Brooklyn, N.Y.; daughter of Francis M. (an engineer) and Mary (Richardson) Noonan. *Education:* Pratt Institute, graduate in graphic arts (with honors), 1968. *Address:* 205 East 78th St., Apt. 11F, New York, N.Y. 10021.

CAREER: Free-lance illustrator, 1968—. Illustrations have appeared in *Seventeen, Ladies' Home Journal, Town and Country, Redbook, New York Magazine,* and other magazines; also has done posters, calendars, and book work for Scholastic Book Services.

WRITINGS—Author and illustrator: *The Best Thing to Be* (juvenile), Doubleday, 1971.

Illustrator: Charles Perrault, *Puss in Boots* (adapted by Arthur Luce Klein from *Les Contes de fees*), Doubleday, 1970; John Langstaff, *Gather My Gold Together: Accumulative Songs for Four Seasons,* Doubleday, 1971; *The Pied Piper of Hamlin,* Scholastic Book Services, 1972; Patricia A. McKillip, *The Throme of the Errill of Sherill,* Atheneum, 1973; Laurence Yep, *Sweetwater,* Harper, 1973; (Ellin Green, editor) Laurence Housman, *The Rat-catcher's Daughter,* Atheneum, 1974; Judith Barrett, *Peter's Pocket,* Atheneum, 1974; Jane H. Yolen, *The Magic Three of Solatia,* Crowell, 1974; Clyde R. Bulla, *Marco Moonlight,* Crowell, 1976.

WORK IN PROGRESS: Illustrations for a series of children's "readers," for Heath.

SIDELIGHTS: Julia Noonan told *CA:* "After my brief exposure to publishing, I've become discouraged by the unwillingness of publishers to invest in higher quality production. There is a definite absence of four color process printing which limits the artist and cheats the child of the beauty that better reproduction affords." *Avocational interests:* Animals; "would also enjoy hearing from children if any wish to write."

*   *   *

NORMAN, Barbara (Barbara Makanowitzky)

PERSONAL: Born in Highland Park, Ill.; daughter of Harold William (a lawyer) and Vera (an illustrator; maiden name, Stone) Norman; married Paul Makanowitzky (a musician), October 29, 1955. *Education:* Attended Mills College, 1945, 1946; Stanford University, B.A., 1947. *Home:* 510 Huntington Dr., Ann Arbor, Mich. 48104. *Agent:* Robert P. Mills Ltd., 156 East 52nd St., New York, N.Y. 10022.

CAREER: U.S. Government, Washington, D.C., Munich, Germany, and Paris, France, researcher and reports writer, 1949-57; Ecole National des Sciences Politiques, Paris, historical researcher, 1961-62; free-lance reader and translator for publishers, institutions, and magazines in New York, N.Y. and Paris, 1959-64.

WRITINGS: (Translator under name Barbara Makanowitzky) Ivan Turgenev, *Fathers and Sons,* Bantam, 1959; (translator under name Barbara Makanowitzky) Leo Tolstoi, *The Short Stories of Leo Tolstoi,* Bantam, 1960; (translator under name Barbara Makanowitzky) Anton Chekhov, *The Short Novels of Chekhov,* Bantam, 1963; *The Spanish Cookbook,* Atheneum, 1966; *The Russian Cookbook,* Atheneum, 1967; *Tales of the Table,* Prentice-Hall, 1972; *Requiem for a Spanish Village,* Stein & Day, 1972; *Napoleon and Tallyrand: The Last Two Weeks,* Stein & Day, 1976. Contributor to magazines.

WORK IN PROGRESS: A history.

AVOCATIONAL INTERESTS: Travel, swimming, tennis, riding.

*   *   *

NORRIS, Kathleen 1947-

PERSONAL: Born July 27, 1947, in Washington, D.C.; daughter of John Heyward (a musician) and Lois (Totten) Norris. *Education:* Bennington College, B.A., 1969. *Residence:* Lemmon, S.D.

CAREER: Academy of American Poets, New York, N.Y., program secretary, 1969-73; affiliated with Leaves of Grass, Inc., Lemmon, S.D., 1973—. *Awards, honors:* Provincetown Fine Arts Center fellowship, 1972; Creative Artists Public Service grant, New York State, 1972-73.

WRITINGS: Falling Off, Big Table Publishing, 1971. Contributor to anthologies, *Another World,* Bobbs-Merrill, 1970, and *I Hear My Sisters Saying,* edited by C. Konek and D. Walters, Crowell, 1976. Contributor to *Dragonfly, Lillabulero, Sumac, Tennessee Poetry Journal,* and other periodicals.

WORK IN PROGRESS: A second book of poems.

* * *

NORTHEN, Helen 1914-

PERSONAL: Born June 5, 1914, in Butte, Mont.; daughter of John Alfred and Amelia (Anderson) Northen. *Education:* University of Washington, A.B., 1937; University of Pittsburgh, M.S., 1944; University of Pennsylvania, further graduate study, 1949-50; Bryn Mawr College, Ph.D., 1953; London School of Economics and Political Science, postdoctoral study, 1961. *Politics:* Democrat. *Religion:* Protestant. *Home:* 1707 Micheltorena St., Los Angeles, Calif. 90026. *Office:* School of Social Work, University of Southern California, Los Angeles, Calif. 90007.

CAREER: Young Women's Christian Association, Pittsburgh, Pa., program director and camp director, 1944-49; University of Pittsburgh, Pittsburgh, field instructor in social work, 1945-49; University of Hawaii, Honolulu, associate professor of social work, 1951-53; University of Southern California, Los Angeles, associate professor, 1953-59, professor of social work, 1959—. Teacher of short courses and institutes at University of Wisconsin, Portland State University, University of Houston, and other universities. Member of national board, Camp Fire Girls, Inc., 1961-69; member of board of Los Angeles branch, All Nations Foundation, 1963—. *Member:* National Association of Social Workers (chairman of national group work commission; board member of Los Angeles chapter), Council on Social Work Education, National Conference on Social Welfare, Society for Clinical Social Work, Group for the Advancement of Social Work Practice.

WRITINGS: Social Work with Groups, Columbia University Press, 1969; (editor with R. W. Roberts and contributor) *Theories of Social Work with Groups,* Columbia University Press, 1976. Contributor to social work, public welfare, and sociology journals. Member of editorial board, *Small Group Behavior, Social Work with Groups,* and *Abstracts for Social Workers.*

SIDELIGHTS: Helen Northen's first book has been translated into German, Dutch, and Portuguese.

* * *

NORTON, Alice 1926-

PERSONAL: Born April 20, 1926, in Columbus, Ohio; daughter of Kenneth Bain and Marion (Hayes) Norton. *Education:* Wellesley College, B.A., 1947; University of Illinois, M.S., 1962. *Address:* P.O. Box 516, Ridgefield, Conn. 06877.

CAREER: Reader's Digest, Pleasantville, N.Y., editorial assistant, 1947-51; Protestant Episcopal Church, National Council, Greenwich, Conn., editorial assistant, 1952-53; KLZ-Television, Denver, Colo., continuity director, 1953-54; Eastman Oil Well Survey Co., Denver, assistant to director of public relations, 1954-55; Denver Public Library, Denver, public relations officer, 1955-61; Westchester Library System, Mount Vernon, N.Y., public relations direc-

tor, 1962-66; Alice Norton Public Relations (firm serving cultural and educational agencies), Ridgefield, Conn., owner and operator, 1968—.

MEMBER: Public Relations Society of America, American Library Association (chairman of public relations section, 1963-64; chairman of National Library Week committee, 1975-77), Library Public Relations Council (president, 1969-70), New York Library Club (member of board of directors, 1971-75), Southwestern Connecticut Library Association (member of board of directors, 1974-77), New York Wellesley Club, Adirondack Mountain Club. *Awards, honors:* Wellesley College Stevens traveling fellowship, 1966-67.

WRITINGS: Public Relations: A Guide to Information Sources, Gale, 1970. Also author of a pamphlet, "Evaluating Performance," National Communication Council for Human Services. Contributor of articles to periodicals.

SIDELIGHTS: Alice Norton told *CA:* "Writing gives me the opportunity to describe for librarians the benefits that sound public relations practices can bring to their libraries. Through my consulting services I can communicate with only a small number of libraries. Through articles and my book I have been able to communicate with thousands."

* * *

NOURSE, Mary Augusta 1880(?)-1971

1880(?)—October 23, 1971; American history teacher and author. Obituaries: *Washington Post,* October 27, 1971.

* * *

NOVAK, Bogdan C(yril) 1919-

PERSONAL: Born October 9, 1919, in Ljubljana, Slovenia, Yugoslavia; came to U.S. in 1951, naturalized in 1958; son of Cyril and Slava (Lendovsek) Novak; married Maria Bolha, September 5, 1964. *Education:* University of Ljubljana, Diploma in Law, 1944; Loyola University, Chicago, Ill., M.A., 1955; Los Angeles State College (now California State University, Los Angeles), graduate student, 1955-56; University of Chicago, Ph.D., 1961. *Office:* Department of History, University of Toledo, Toledo, Ohio 43606.

CAREER: Teacher in elementary and secondary schools in Free Territory of Trieste, 1947-51; St. Augustine High School, San Diego, Calif., teacher, 1956-57; Indiana University, Gary Extension (now Indiana University Northwest), part-time instructor in history, 1960-61; Roosevelt University, Chicago, Ill., lecturer in history, 1961; University of Toledo, Toledo, Ohio, assistant professor, 1961-65, associate professor, 1965-69, professor of history, 1969—. *Member:* Conference Group of Central European History, American Association for the Advancement of Slavic Studies, Conference on Slavic and East European History, Society for Slovene Studies, American Association for Southeast European Studies, Association for the Study of the Nationalities (U.S.S.R. and East Europe), Ohio Academy of History, Phi Alpha Theta (honorary member). *Awards, honors:* American Philosophical Society grant for research in Italy, 1968.

WRITINGS: Trieste, 1941-1954: The Ethnic, Political, and Ideological Struggle, University of Chicago Press, 1970; (contributor) Rado L. Lencek, editor, *Papers in Slovene Studies,* Columbia University Press, 1975; (contributor) Wayne S. Vucinich, editor, *History of Historical Writing in Eastern Europe,* Columbia University Press, in press. Contributor of articles and reviews to *Slovenska drzava, Zbornik*

Svobodne Slovenije, Most, Balkan Studies, Journal of Modern History, Zaliv, and other journals.

SIDELIGHTS: Bogdan Novak's *Trieste, 1941-1954* has been published in Italian.

* * *

NOVAK, Maximillian E(rwin)   1930-

PERSONAL: Born March 26, 1930, in New York, N.Y.; son of George and Elsie (Loewy) Novak; married Demetra Palamari, June 13, 1954 (divorced, 1963); married Estelle Gershgoren (an assistant professor of English), August 21, 1966; children: (second marriage) Ralph, Daniel, Rachel. *Education:* University of California, Los Angeles, B.A., 1952, M.A., 1954, Ph.D., 1958; St. John's College, Oxford, D.Phil., 1961. *Religion:* Jewish. *Home:* 10380 Dunleer Dr., Los Angeles, Calif. 90064. *Office:* Department of English, University of California, 405 Hilgard Ave., Los Angeles, Calif. 90024.

CAREER: University of California, Los Angeles, professor of English, 1962—, Clark Library Professor, 1973-74. *Member:* International Association of University Professors of English, Modern Language Association of America, American Society for Eighteenth Century Studies, Oxford Society. *Awards, honors:* Fulbright-Hays fellow, 1955-57; Guggenheim fellowship, 1965-66.

WRITINGS: *Economics and the Fiction of Daniel Defoe,* University of California Press, 1962; *Defoe and the Nature of Man,* Clarendon Press, 1963; (with Herbert Davis) *The Uses of Irony* (pamphlet), Clark Library, 1966; (editor with G. Guffey) Dryden, *Works,* Volume X, University of California Press, 1970; *Congreve,* Twayne, 1971; (with Aubrey Williams) *Congreve Consider'd* (pamphlet), Clark Library, 1971; (with Edward Dudley) *The Wildman Within,* Pittsburgh University Press, 1972; (editor with David Rodes) Thomas Southerne, *Oroonoko,* Regents Drama Series, 1976; (editor) *English Literature in the Age of Disguise,* University of California Press, 1977. Editor, University of Southern Illinois "Defoe" series; editor, Augustan Reprint Society.

WORK IN PROGRESS: *The Continuity of Fictional Forms;* Volume XIII of Dryden's *Works;* a critical study of I. J. Singer, with wife, Estelle Novak.

SIDELIGHTS: Maximillian Novak's special areas of interest are the novel in general, eighteenth-century literature, and restoration and eighteenth-century drama.

* * *

NOVICK, David   1906-

PERSONAL: Born September 19, 1906, in Easton, Pa.; son of Samuel Novick (a banker); married Mildred Hartshough, June 14, 1935 (died, 1939); married Mary Bateman, December 18, 1940. *Education:* Brown University, Ph.B., 1929; Lafayette College, M.A., 1930; New York University, graduate study, 1930-34. *Home:* 1032 Second St., Santa Monica, Calif. 90403.

CAREER: New York University, New York, N.Y., instructor in economics, 1930-34; U.S. Tariff Commission, Washington, D.C., economist, 1934-41; War Production Board, Washington, D.C., controller, 1941-44, director of programming and statistics bureau, 1945-46, director of demobilization bureau, 1946-47; RAND Corp., Santa Monica, Calif., head of cost analysis, 1949-68, member of research council, 1968-70; David Novick Associates, Santa Monica, president, 1961—. Visiting professor of economics,

University of Puerto Rico, 1947-49. Member of advisory council on federal reports, 1962—; member of panel of experts, Project to Develop a Program Planning-Budgeting Evaluation System Design for Local Schools, Research Corp. of the Association of School Business Officials, 1968-71; director, program budget panel, North Atlantic Council Seminar on Advanced Management, College of Europe, 1969. Member of board of directors, Roosevelt Raceway, 1962-68, Westbury Electronics, 1963-67, CapTech, Inc., 1967-76, Southwestern Research and General Investment Co., 1968-69, 1971-73, and Vector Management, Inc. Special advisor and consultant to U.S. House Ways and Means Committee, 1937-40, U.S. Department of Defense, 1947-48, and other government agencies. Member of board of governors, Los Angeles Mental Health Association, 1968-73. *Member:* American Economics Association, American Statistical Society, American Arbitration Association, Cosmos Club. *Awards, honors:* Social Science Research Council grant-in-aid, 1947.

WRITINGS: (With Melvin Anshen and W. C. Truppner) *Wartime Production Controls,* Columbia University Press, 1949; (with G. A. Steiner) *Wartime Industrial Statistics,* University of Illinois Press, 1950; *Efficiency and Economy in Government through New Budgeting and Accounting Procedures,* RAND Corp., 1953.

System and Total Force Cost Analysis, RAND Corp., 1961; *An Economic Study of Harness Horse Racing,* Modern Printing Co., 1962; (editor and contributor) *Program Budgeting: Program Analysis and the Federal Budget,* abridged edition, U.S. Government Printing Office, 1965, Harvard University Press, 1966, 2nd edition, Harvard University Press, 1968; *Eficiencia y economia en el gobierno mediante procedimientos presupuestarios y contables,* Central Regional de Ayuda Tecnica, Agencia Para El Desarrollo Internacional, 1967.

(Editor and contributor) *Current Practice in Program Budgeting,* Crane, Russak, 1973; (with Kurt Bleicken, W. E. Depuy, and J. W. Noah) *A World of Scarcities,* Halsted, 1976.

Contributor: G. A. Steiner, editor, *Economic Problems of War,* Wiley, 1942; Steiner, editor, *Managerial Long-Range Planning,* McGraw, 1963; Erich Jantsch, editor, *Perspectives of Planning,* Organization for Economic Co-operation and Development, 1968; Horst Claus Recktenwald, editor, *Nutzen-Kosten-Analyse und Programmbudget,* J.D.B. Mohr, 1970.

* * *

NUDELMAN, Jerrold   1942-

PERSONAL: Born June 4, 1942, in Brooklyn, N.Y.; son of Henry David (a knitwear manufacturer) and Frances (Cohen) Nudelman. *Education:* Queens College of the City University of New York, B.A., 1964; New York University, M.A., 1965, additional graduate study, 1965—. *Home:* 226-26 Union Turnpike, Flushing, N.Y. 11364. *Office:* Department of Basic Educational Skills, Queensborough Community College of the City University of New York, Bayside, N.Y. 11364.

CAREER: Queensborough Community College of the City University of New York, Bayside, N.Y., assistant professor of basic educational skills, 1967—, supervisor of writing skills program in Evening Division, 1970-75. *Member:* Modern Language Association of America, National Council of Teachers of English, Conference on College Composition and Communications, English in the Two Year College (Northeast region).

WRITINGS: (With Lynn Quitman Troyka) *Steps in Composition,* Prentice-Hall, 1970, alternate 2nd edition, in press; *Taking Action: Writing, Reading, Speaking, and Listening Through Simulation Games,* Prentice-Hall, 1975. Contributor to *English in the Two-Year College.*

* * *

NUNN, Frederick M. 1937-

PERSONAL: Born October 29, 1937, in Portland, Ore.; son of Leslie L. (a physician) and Marion (Gillis) Nunn; married Tey Diana Rebolledo (a language instructor), September 10, 1960 (divorced, 1973); married Susan Karant Boles (a historian), February 8, 1974; children: (first marriage) Tey Marianna; (second marriage) Jessica. *Education:* University of Oregon, B.A., 1959; graduate study at University of Mexico, 1958, and University of California, Berkeley, 1960; University of New Mexico, M.A., 1963, Ph.D., 1963. *Home:* 3055 Northwest Vaughn, Portland, Ore. 97210. *Office:* Department of History, Portland State University, Portland, Ore. 97207.

CAREER: Portland State University, Portland, Ore., assistant professor, 1965-67, associate professor, 1967-72, professor of history, 1972—. *Member:* American Historical Association, Latin American Studies Association.

WRITINGS: Chilean Politics, 1920-1931: The Honorable Mission of the Armed Forces, University of New Mexico Press, 1970; *The Military in Chilean History: Essays on Civil-Military Relations,* University of New Mexico Press, 1976. Contributor to *Hispanic American Historical Review, The Americas, Journal of Latin American Studies, Inter-American Economic Affairs, Luso-Brazilian Review, Phylon,* and others.

WORK IN PROGRESS: Studying facets of civil-military relations in Latin American countries, with several publications expected to result.

SIDELIGHTS: Frederick Nunn has traveled and studied extensively in Latin America since 1958.

* * *

NUNN, G(odfrey) Raymond 1918-

PERSONAL: Born May 18, 1918, in Pirbright, England; son of A.G.C. (a physiotherapist) and Sybil (Bolton) Nunn; married E. Margaret Brown, September 20, 1948; children: Pamela Elizabeth, Michael David, Lesley Margaret. *Education:* University of London, London School of Economics, student, 1937-40, 1947-48, School of Oriental and African Studies, B.A. (honors), 1950, School of Librarianship and Archives, diploma, 1951; University of Michigan, M.A., 1954, Ph.D., 1957. *Religion:* Episcopal. *Home:* 2631 Ferdinand Ave., Honolulu, Hawaii 96822. *Office:* Asian Studies Program, University of Hawaii, Honolulu, Hawaii 96822.

CAREER: University of Michigan, Ann Arbor, head of Asia library, 1951-61, lecturer in history, 1959-61; University of Hawaii, Honolulu, director of East-West Center Library, 1961-64, professor of history, 1961—, professor of Asian studies, 1964—. *Military service:* Indian Army, 1940-47; became major. *Member:* International Association of Orientalist Librarians (president), Association for Asian Studies. *Awards, honors:* Ford Foundation special fellowship, 1956.

WRITINGS: Michigan Library Resources on Asia, University Library, University of Michigan, 1958; *Chinese Publishing Statistics, 1949-1959,* Association for Asian Studies, 1960; *Chinese Periodicals, International Holdings, 1949-*

1960, Association for Asian Studies, 1961; *Resources for Research on Asia,* East-West Center Library, 1965; *Publishing in Mainland China,* M.I.T. Press, 1966; *South and Southeast Asia, a Bibliography of Bibliographies,* East-West Center Library, 1966; *East Asia, a Bibliography of Bibliographies,* East-West Center Library, 1967; *Asia, Selected and Annotated Guide to Reference Works,* M.I.T. Press, 1971; *Indonesian Newspapers, an International Union List,* Chinese Materials and Reference Aids Service Center (Taipei), 1972; (with Do Van-Anh) *Vietnamese, Cambodian and Laotian Newspapers, an International Union List,* Chinese Materials and Reference Aids Service Center, 1972; *Burmese and Thai Newspapers, an International Union List,* Chinese Materials and Reference Aids Service Center, 1972; *Asian Libraries and Librarianship,* Scarecrow, 1973; *Asia, a Core Collection,* University Microfilm, 1973; *Southeast Asian Periodicals, an International Union List,* Mansell, 1977.

WORK IN PROGRESS: Japanese and Korean Periodicals and Newspapers in Western Languages, an International Union List.

SIDELIGHTS: G. Raymond Nunn told *CA,* "My primary interest is to establish data, and develop a historical account of the forms in which communication has taken place in Asia, with an emphasis on the modern and contemporary period."

* * *

NURGE, Ethel 1920-

PERSONAL: Born August 21, 1920, in Brooklyn, N.Y.; daughter of Albert and Matilda (Rosebrock) Nurge. *Education:* University of New Mexico, B.A., 1950; University of Chicago, M.A., 1951; Cornell University, Ph.D., 1955. *Politics:* None. *Religion:* None. *Office:* Department of Community Health, University of Kansas Medical Center, 39th and Rainbow, Kansas City, Kan. 66103.

CAREER: South Dakota State University, Brookings, assistant professor of anthropology, 1963-65; Frobenius Institut, Frankfort, Germany, research associate, 1965-66; McMaster University, Hamilton, Ontario, associate professor, 1966-68; University of Kansas Medical Center, Kansas City, associate professor in department of community health, 1968—. *Military service:* U.S. Navy, WAVES, 1941-44; served as radio operator. *Member:* American Anthropological Association, American Ethnological Society, Current Anthropology (associate), Society of Medical Anthropologists. *Awards, honors:* Fulbright grant, Silliman University, Philippines, 1955-56.

WRITINGS: Life in a Leyte Village, University of Washington Press, 1965; *The Modern Sioux: Social Systems and Reservation Culture,* University of Nebraska Press, 1970; (contributor) Dana Raphael, editor, *Female: Reproduction, Power and Change,* Mouton, 1975; *Blue Light in the Village,* University of Nebraska Press, 1977. Contributor of articles to journals, including *Philippines Sociological Review, Silliman Journal, Eugenics Quarterly, Journal of Tropical Pediatrics, American Anthropologist, Proceedings of the Rip Van Winkle Clinic, Hessische Blaetter fuer Volksbildung,* and *Anthropos.* Associate editor, *Current Anthropology,* 1962-65.

WORK IN PROGRESS: Analyzing field notes on a Philippine village.

SIDELIGHTS: Ethel Nurge told *CA:* "Although I am by training a medical anthropologist and thus a teacher and researcher as well as an author, I sometimes think that I should have followed a literary career. This was urged on me in college but due to the belated endurance of adolescent rebellion, I resisted the advice! Writing remains a first pleasure for me and perhaps someday I shall let the rest fall away like dross.''

* * *

NYE, Robert 1939-

PERSONAL: Born March 15, 1939, in London, England; son of Oswald William and Frances Dorothy (Weller) Nye; married Judith Pratt, 1959; married second wife, Aileen Campbell (an artist), 1968; children: (first marriage) Jack, Taliesin, Malory; (second marriage) Owen, Sharon, Rebecca. *Education:* Attended schools in England. *Residence:* Kinsale, County Cork, Ireland. *Agent:* Anthony Sheil Associates, Ltd., 52 Floral St., Covent Garden, London WC2E 9DA, England; and Wallace, Aitken & Sheil, Inc., 118 East 61st St., New York, N.Y. 10021.

CAREER: Writer. *Awards, honors: Guardian* fiction prize, 1976, for *Falstaff.*

WRITINGS: Juvenilia 1 (verse), Scorpion Press, 1961; *Juvenilia 2* (verse), Scorpion Press, 1963; *Taliesin* (children's novel), Faber, 1966, Hill & Wang, 1967; *March Has Horse's Ears* (children's stories), Faber, 1966, Hill & Wang, 1967; *Doubtfire* (novel), Calder & Boyars, 1967, Hill & Wang, 1968; *Beowulf* (children's novel), Hill & Wang, 1968; *Darker Ends* (verse), Hill & Wang, 1969; *Tales I Told My Mother* (short stories), Hill & Wang, 1969.

Wishing Gold (children's novel), Macmillan, 1970, Hill & Wang, 1971; (with William Watson) *Sawney Bean* (play), Calder & Boyars, 1970; *Poor Pumpkin* (children's stories), Macmillan, 1971, Hill & Wang, 1972; (editor) *A Choice of Sir Walter Raleigh's Verse,* Faber, 1972; *Cricket* (children's stories), Bobbs-Merrill, 1973; (editor) *William Barnes of Dorset: A Selection of His Poems,* Carcanet Press, 1973; (editor) *A Choice of Swinburne's Verse,* Faber, 1973; "Penthesilea," "Fugue," "Sisters" (plays), Calder & Boyars, 1975; (editor) *The Book of Sonnets,* Oxford University Press (New York), 1976 (published in England as *The Faber Book of Sonnets,* Faber, 1976); *Divisions on a Ground* (verse), Carcanet Press, 1976; *Falstaff* (novel), Little, Brown, 1976.

WORK IN PROGRESS: A novel about Merlin, for Hamilton.

BIOGRAPHICAL/CRITICAL SOURCES: Statesman, February 9, 1968; *Books & Bookmen,* August, 1970; *Times Literary Supplement,* September 3, 1976; *Manchester Guardian,* November 25, 1976; *New York Review of Books,* January 20, 1977.

* * *

NYLANDER, Carl 1932-

PERSONAL: Born March 3, 1932, in Stockholm, Sweden; son of Lennart (a diplomat) and Margareta (Fjellander) Nylander; married Christina Leczinsky, February 28, 1965 (divorced, 1977); children: Nike Elisabeth, Peter Thomas. *Education:* University of Uppsala, B.A., 1955, M.A., 1965, Ph.D., 1970. *Home:* Islands Brygge 15, 2300 Copenhagen S, Denmark. *Office:* Institute of Classical and Near Eastern Archaeology, Vandkunsten 5, 1467 Copenhagen K, Denmark.

CAREER: Swedish Institute for Classical Studies, Athens, Greece, secretary, 1956-57; Bryn Mawr College, Bryn Mawr, Pa., associate professor of classical and Near Eastern archaeology, 1970-77; University of Copenhagen, Copenhagen, Denmark, professor of classical and Near Eastern archaeology, 1977—. Has done field work on excavations in Iran, Greece, and Italy. Lecturer on Swedish radio.

WRITINGS: Den Djupa Brunnen (essays), Wahlstrom & Widstrand, 1965, translation by Joan Tate published as *The Deep Well,* St. Martin's, 1970; *Ionians in Pasargadae: Studies in Old Persian Architecture,* University of Uppsala Press, 1970. Contributor of scholarly and popular articles, literary criticism, and poems to periodicals.

WORK IN PROGRESS: Research on problems in Persian, Near Eastern, Greek, and Etruscan archaeology.

SIDELIGHTS: Carl Nylander's *The Deep Well* was selected by archaeologist Jacquetta Hawkes as one of the best books of 1969. She writes: "Few archaeologists have Nylander's breadth of understanding, sensibility or style. At the same time, his thinking is critical and exact."

Nylander speaks German, French, Italian, Greek, and some Persian, in addition to his native language and English.

BIOGRAPHICAL/CRITICAL SOURCES: Observer Review, December 21, 1969.

* * *

OAKES, Vanya 1909-

PERSONAL: Given name originally Virginia; born September 13, 1909, in Nutley, N.J.; daughter of Herbert Henry (a banker) and Emma (Armstrong) Oakes. *Education:* University of California, Berkeley, B.A., 1932; University of Southern California, M.L.S., 1959. *Home:* 1153 North Vista, Los Angeles, Calif. 90046.

CAREER: Free-lance writer in China and Southeast Asia for magazines and newspapers, 1932-41; public lecturer, 1941-44; Los Angeles City College, Los Angeles, Calif., instructor in journalism and world affairs, 1945-57; Los Angeles (Calif.) Public Library, Los Angeles, reference and young adult librarian, 1959-75. *Member:* American Library Association, Common Cause, California Library Association, California Council on Children's Literature, Friends of the Hollywood Library, Los Angeles United Nations Association.

WRITINGS—Juvenile fiction, except as noted: *White Man's Folly* (adult nonfiction), Houghton, 1943; *The Bamboo Gate* (short stories), Macmillan, 1946; *By Sun and Star,* Macmillan, 1948; *Footprints of the Dragon,* V. H. Winston, 1949; *Willy Wong, American,* Messner, 1951; *Desert Harvest,* V. H. Winston, 1953; *Roy Sato,* Messner, 1955; *Hawaiian Treasure,* Messner, 1957; *Island of Flame,* John Day, 1960; *Challenging Careers in the Library World* (young adult nonfiction), Messner, 1970.

WORK IN PROGRESS: A nonfiction book about resources and services of libraries; adult non-fiction about southeast Asia and southern India.

SIDELIGHTS: Vanya Oakes told *CA:* "At any writer's workshop some speaker will advise 'find a void and fill it.' There are two voids I would like to fill, now that in retirement I have returned to writing. Fifteen years as a public librarian convinced me that many, maybe most, Americans are not aware that the public library is the 'information place' available to everyone; that they do not realize the extent of the resources and services, nor how to use them. Void 2 is our ignorance about the Far East—ignorance about which contributed to the Viet Nam disaster. In 1975 I spent several months on a return trip to southeast Asia and beyond, to Sri Lanka and southern India. Two problems: masses of material and am a painfully slow writer.''

* * *

O'BANION, Terry 1936-

PERSONAL: Born August 19, 1936, in La Belle, Fla.; son of Terry Hugh and Olney (Blount) O'Banion; married Rebecca Welch (a teacher), December 31, 1970; children: Michael Kerry, Erin Katherine. *Education:* University of Florida, B.A. (cum laude), 1958, M.Ed., 1961; Florida State University, Ph.D., 1966. *Home:* 1414 Greenfield, Los Angeles, Calif. 90025. *Office:* League for Innovation in the Community College, 1100 Glendon Ave., Suite 925, Los Angeles, Calif. 90024.

CAREER: High school teacher of English and psychology in La Belle, Fla., 1958-60; Central Florida Junior College, Ocala, dean of students, 1961-64; Santa Fe Junior College, Gainesville, Fla., dean of student affairs, 1966-67; University of Illinois, Urbana, professor of higher education, 1967-75; currently executive director of League for Innovation in the Community College, Los Angeles, Calif. Visiting professor at National Defense Education Act summer institutes for junior college counselors at University of Florida, 1965-66, and University of Hawaii, 1968. College Entrance Examination Board, former junior college representative on committee on college information and former member of national advisory committee on junior college testing.

MEMBER: American Personnel and Guidance Association, American College Personnel Association, American Association of Community and Junior Colleges, National Association of Student Personnel Administrators, American Association for Higher Education, Kappa Delta Pi, Phi Delta Kappa. *Awards, honors: Teachers for Tomorrow* was selected by U.S. Information Agency as part of American Education Book Exhibit to be displayed in twenty-six countries and was also selected in 1973 as one of the Outstanding Books in Education.

WRITINGS: (With April O'Connell) *The Shared Journey: An Introduction to Encounter,* Prentice-Hall, 1970; *New Directions in Community College Student Personnel Programs,* American College Personnel Association, 1971; (with Alice Thurston) *Student Development Programs in Community Junior Colleges,* Prentice-Hall, 1972; *Teachers for Tomorrow: Staff Development in the Community Junior College,* University of Arizona Press, 1972; *The People Who Staff the People's College: A Report to the National Advisory Council for Education Professions Development,* Educational Professional Development Assistance, Office of Education, 1972; (editor) *Student Development Programs in Illinois Community Colleges,* Illinois Junior College Board, 1972.

Contributor: James Harvey, editor, *Student Personnel Work in the 70's,* Harper College, 1968; Patricia Graham, editor, *Student Participation in Governance,* U.S. National Student Association, 1969; *Community College Governance: The Local Board,* Center for Development of Community College Education, University of Washington, 1969; Walter Johnson, editor, *College Student Personnel: Readings and Bibliographies,* Houghton, 1970; John H. Brennecke and Robert C. Amick, editors, *The Shared Journey Significance: The Struggle We Share,* Glencoe Press, 1971; Joseph W. Fordyce, *A Day at Santa Fe,* Santa Fe Junior College, 1971; (with Fordyce) William Ogilvie and Max Raines, editors, *Perspectives on the Community Junior College,* Appleton, 1971; *Proceedings of the Two Year, Post Secondary Education Institute,* University of Minnesota, 1972; Wilga M. Rivers, editor, *Changing Patterns in Foreign Language Programs,* Newbury House, 1972; Robert R. Reilley, editor, *The Bicultural Student Personnel Specialist in the Community Junior College,* Texas A&M University, 1973; *Education for Transition: Search for a New Balance,* Fourth Annual Institute on the Community College (Sarnia, Ontario), 1973; Roger Yarrington, editor, *Educational Opportunity for All: New Staff for New Students,* American Association of Community and Junior Colleges, 1974.

Contributor to *Junior College Journal, Adult Leadership, American Vocational Journal, Journal of College Student Personnel, Junior College Research Review, College and University, Journal of Higher Education,* and other education publications and periodicals.

* * *

O'CONNOR, Daniel William 1925-

PERSONAL: Born March 17, 1925, in Jersey City, N.J.; son of Daniel William (a salesman) and Emma P. (Ritz) O'Connor; married Carolyn Lockwood, June 26, 1954; children: Kathlyn Forssell, Daniel William III. *Education:* Dartmouth College, A.B., 1945; Union Theological Seminary, New York, B.D., 1950; Columbia University, M.A., 1956, Ph.D., 1960. *Home:* 3 Hillside Cir., Canton, N.Y. 13617. *Office:* Department of Religious Studies, St. Lawrence University, Canton, N.Y. 13617.

CAREER: Associate secretary, Student Christian Movement in New York State, 1947-48; Columbia University, New York, N.Y., executive secretary, Earl Hall, 1948-50; ordained to ministry of Congregational Christian Churches (now United Church of Christ), 1950; pastor in Paramus, N.J., 1950-55; St. Lawrence University, Canton, N.Y., assistant professor, 1959-63, associate professor, 1963-67, professor of religion, 1967—, Charles A. Dana Professor and chairman of department of religious studies, 1973—, associate dean of the college, 1967-68. Visiting scholar at Columbia University and Union Theological Seminary, 1969-70. Assistant supervisor, joint archaeological expedition to Ai, 1969; supervisor, joint archaeological expedition to Khirbet Shema, 1971. *Military service:* U.S. Naval Reserve, 1943-45.

MEMBER: American Academy of Religion (secretary, Northeastern Region, 1968-70), Society of Biblical Literature, American Association of University Professors, U.S. Power Squadron (former member of board of directors of St. Lawrence Squadron), Rotary Club of Canton (president, 1972-73).

WRITINGS: Peter in Rome: The Literary, Liturgical, and Archeological Evidence, Columbia University Press, 1969. Contributor to *Encyclopaedia Britannica* and religion journals.

* * *

O'CONNOR, Philip Francis 1932-

PERSONAL: Born December 3, 1932, in San Francisco, Calif.; son of John Joseph (an accountant) and Josephine (Browne) O'Connor; married Delores Doster; children: Dondi, John, Christopher, Erin, Justin. *Education:* University of San Francisco, B.S., 1954; San Francisco State College (now University), M.A., 1961; University of Iowa, M.F.A., 1963. *Home:* 221 Curtis Ave., Bowling Green,

Ohio 43402. *Office:* Department of English, Bowling Green University, Bowling Green, Ohio 43402.

CAREER: Clarkson College of Technology, Potsdam, N.Y., 1963-67, began as instructor, became assistant professor of humanities; Bowling Green University, Bowling Green, Ohio, 1967—, began as assistant professor, currently professor of English. *Awards, honors:* Iowa School of Letters Award in Short Fiction, 1971. *Military service:* U.S. Army; became lieutenant.

WRITINGS: Old Morals, Small Continents, Darker Times, University of Iowa Press, 1971; *A Season for Unnatural Causes,* University of Illinois Press, 1975.

WORK IN PROGRESS: A novel.

* * *

O'CONNOR, Thomas Henry 1922-

PERSONAL: Born December 9, 1922, in Boston, Mass.; son of John Francis (a postman) and Marie A. (Meany) O'Connor; married Mary C. MacDonald, June 11, 1949; children: Steven, Jeanne, Michael. *Education:* Boston College, A.B., 1949, M.A., 1950; Boston University, Ph.D., 1958. *Politics:* Democrat. *Religion:* Roman Catholic. *Home:* 1 Kew Rd., Braintree, Mass. 02184. *Office:* Department of History, Boston College, Carney Hall, Chestnut Hill, Mass. 02167.

CAREER: Boston College, Chestnut Hill, Mass., instructor, 1950-58, assistant professor, 1958-62, associate professor, 1962-69, professor of history, 1969—, chairman of department, 1962-70, vice-president of university academic senate, 1967-70. South Shore Association for Retarded Children, vice-president, 1970, 1971, president, 1972. *Military service:* U.S. Army, Signal Corps, 1943-46; served in India; became staff sergeant. *Member:* American Historical Association, American Catholic Historical Association, Organization of American Historians, American Association of University Professors, Lincoln Group of Boston, Civil War Round Table of Greater Boston.

WRITINGS: The Heritage of the American People, Allyn & Bacon, 1965; (editor) *Sources of the American Heritage: Readings,* Allyn & Bacon, 1965; *Lords of the Loom,* Scribner, 1968; *The Disunited States: The United States in the Era of Civil War and Reconstruction,* Dodd, 1972; *Religion and American Society,* Addison-Wesley, 1975; *Bibles, Brahmins, and Bosses,* Boston Public Library, 1976. Contributor to history and law journals.

WORK IN PROGRESS: Boston in the Age of Jackson, 1828-1845.

AVOCATIONAL INTERESTS: Playing piano, music, ice-skating, swimming, art (is an artist, illustrator, and cartoonist).

* * *

O'CONOR, John F(rancis) 1918-

PERSONAL: Born July 16, 1918, in Cincinnati, Ohio; son of Daniel J. (a manufacturer) and Ruth Katherine (Breuer) O'Conor; married Margaret Fortune, January 28, 1944; children: Margaret, John, Babara, Jane, James, Thomas, Dorothy. *Education:* Holy Cross College, A.B. (summa cum laude), 1939; Harvard University, J.D., 1942. *Politics:* "Registered as Republican." *Religion:* Roman Catholic.

CAREER: Admitted to the Bar of New York State, 1947; Root, Ballantine, Harlan, Bushby & Palmer (law firm), New York City, assistant attorney, 1946-51; American Smelting

& Refining Co., New York City, member of legal staff, 1952-55, assistant general counsel, 1955-56; currently full-time writer. Member of planning board, Mamaroneck, N.Y., 1956-58. Association for Help of Retarded Children, Westchester chapter, trustee, 1953-58, president, 1954-55; director, Greenwich Association for Retarded Children, 1959-60. Republican Club of Mamaroneck and Larchmont, New York, president, 1951-54, trustee, 1954-58. *Military service:* U.S. Army, infantry, 1942-46; became second lieutenant. *Member:* American Historical Association, American Bar Association, World Peace Through Law Center.

WRITINGS: Cold War and Liberation: A Challenge of Aid to the Subject Peoples, Vantage, 1961; (translator and commentator) E. Petrov-Skitaletz, *The Kronstadt Thesis for a Free Russian Government,* Speller, 1964; (translator and commentator) *The Sokolov Investigation into the Mysterious Disappearance of the Russian Imperial Family,* Speller, 1968. Contributor to *American Bar Association Journal, American Mercury, Catholic World,* and *Armenian Review.*

WORK IN PROGRESS: Research on the history of Russia and U.S.S.R. since 1900, for an historical novel; research on the investigation of the death of Tsar Nicholas II.

SIDELIGHTS: John F. O'Conor told *CA:* "My principal interest is to illuminate the plight of the people of Russia and Eastern Europe, in the hope that a fuller realization of their problems by other peoples will bring about an amelioration."††

* * *

ODEN, Marilyn Brown 1937-

PERSONAL: Born November 6, 1937, in Hollywood, Calif.; daughter of Harold David (a salesman) and Maxine (Miller) Brown; married William Bryant Oden (a minister), July 12, 1957; children: Danna Lee, Dirk, Valerie, Bryant. *Education:* Oklahoma State University, B.A., 1958; University of Oklahoma, M.Ed., 1970. *Politics:* Democrat. *Religion:* Methodist.

CAREER: Blanchard Memorial School, Boxborough, Mass., elementary teacher, 1959-61; University of Oklahoma, Norman, guidance counselor, beginning 1970. *Member:* League of Women Voters.

WRITINGS: The Minister's Wife: Person or Position, Abingdon, 1966; *Beyond Feminism: The Women of Faith in Action,* Abingdon, 1971.

WORK IN PROGRESS: A book on early adolescence.†

* * *

ODLE, Joe T(aft) 1908-

PERSONAL: Born August 19, 1908, in West Frankfort, Ill.; son of Harry Logan and Mary Winona (Dillon) Odle; married Clara Mabel Riley, July 17, 1930; children: Joe Thomas (deceased), Sara Ann (Mrs. Roland Maddox). *Education:* Union University, Jackson, Tenn., A.B., 1930; attended Southern Baptist Theological Seminary, 1934-35. *Home:* 1322 Robert Dr., Jackson, Miss. 39211.

CAREER: Baptist minister; pastor in churches in Orient, Ill., 1926, Gallaway and Rossville, Tenn., 1929-30, Barlow, Bandana, and Paducah, Ky., 1930-43; First Baptist Church, Crystal Springs, Miss., pastor, 1943-47; First Baptist Church, Gulfport, Miss., pastor, 1947-56; Mississippi Baptist Convention Board, Jackson, associate executive secretary, 1956-59, editor of *Baptist Record,* 1959-76. Member,

Southern Baptist Annuity Board, 1949-56; member of board, Baptist Joint Committee, 1961-68. *Member:* Associate Church Press, Evangelical Press Association, Southern Baptist Press Association (president, 1971), Rotary International.

WRITINGS: Church Member's Handbook, Broadman, 1941; *It's a Great Life,* Christ for World, 1967; *Is Christ Coming Soon?,* Broadman, 1971; *Why I Am a Baptist,* Broadman, 1972; *The King Is Coming,* Broadman, 1974.

WORK IN PROGRESS: The New Testament Church: The Greening of the Trees; New Testament Church Finance; Sermons in Great Stories; Revelation; an autobiography.

SIDELIGHTS: Joe Odle has traveled in Europe, South America, Central America, the Orient, and the Holy Land. His book, *Church Member's Handbook* has been published in Chinese and Spanish. *Avocational interests:* Collecting old typewriters, photography.

* * *

O'DWYER, James F. 1939-

PERSONAL: Born December 3, 1939, in Cashel, Ireland; naturalized U.S. citizen, December 18, 1970; son of James Joseph (a statesman) and Bridget (Atkins) O'Dwyer. *Education:* St. Patrick's Seminary, Thurles, Ireland, seminarian, 1959-65. *Office:* Cathedral of the Annunciation, 425 West Magnolia, Stockton, Calif. 95204.

CAREER: Roman Catholic priest, ordained in 1965; associate pastor of parishes in Stockton, Calif., 1965-67, and Angels Camp, Calif., 1967-69; Diocese of Stockton, director of Legion of Mary, 1967—, associate director of vocations, 1968—; Casa Manana Inn (housing project for elderly), member of board of directors, 1967—. Licensed by State of California as marriage, family, and child counselor. *Member:* California State Marriage Counseling Association (life member).

WRITINGS: St. Vincent Pallotti, Luceat, 1963; *Dreams of Destiny,* Willow House, 1970; *Face of Love,* Willow House, 1971; *Apollo,* Vantage, 1974. Also author of *To Live for Others,* 1971, and *Shine Up the Clock,* 1974.†

* * *

OFOSU-APPIAH, L(awrence) H(enry) 1920-

PERSONAL: Born March 18, 1920, in Ghana; married Victoria B. Addo (a teacher), September 15, 1925; children: Asantewa, Oseiwa, Asabea (all daughters). *Education:* Attended Achimota College, Accra, Ghana, 1932-41; Hertford College, Oxford, B.A., 1948, M.A., 1951; Jesus College, Cambridge, Diploma in Anthropology, 1949. *Politics:* Progress Party. *Religion:* Presbyterian. *Home:* 24 Obenesu Crescent, Accra, Ghana. *Office address:* Encyclopaedia Africana Secretariat, P.O. Box 2797, Accra, Ghana.

CAREER: University of Ghana, Legon, lecturer, 1949-59, senior lecturer, 1959-62, professor of classics, 1962-64; master, Akuafo Hall, Legon, 1962-64; Dartmouth College, Hanover, N.H., visiting professor, 1964-65; Dillard University, New Orleans, La., Edgar B. Stern Professor, 1965-66; Encyclopaedia Africana Secretariat, Accra, Ghana, director and editor-in-chief of *Encyclopaedia Africana* (biographical volumes), 1966—. Phelps-Stokes Visiting Professor, 1972. Director, Ghana Airways Corp., 1967-69. Chairman of Ghana Library Board, 1967-72, and Ghana Housing Corp., 1969-72. *Member:* Ghana Academy of Arts and Sciences (fellow; honorary secretary, 1969-70), Classical Association of Ghana (president, 1962-64), Classical Association of En-

gland and Wales, British School at Athens. *Awards, honors:* Fulbright fellowship, 1964-66.

WRITINGS: Slavery: A Brief Survey, Waterville Publishing House (Accra), 1969; (author of introduction) *The Courage and Foresight of Busia,* Waterville Publishing House, 1969; (editor and author of introduction) *A Journey to Independence and After* (J. B. Danquah's letters), Waterville Publishing House, Volume I, 1970, Volume II, 1971, Volume III, 1972; (editor and author of introduction) *People in Bondage,* Lerner, 1971; *The Life of Lt. General E. K. Kotoka,* Waterville Publishing House, 1972; *The Life and Times of J. B. Danquah,* Waterville Publishing House, 1974; *Dr. J.E.K. Aggrey* (biography), Waterville Publishing House, 1975; *Joseph Ephraim Casely Hayford: The Man of Vision and Faith,* Ghana Academy of Arts and Sciences, 1975; (editor) *Black Personalities in World Encyclopaedia of Black Peoples of the World,* Scholarly Press, 1975; (editor) *The Encyclopaedia Africana Dictionary of African Biography,* Volume I, Ethiopia-Ghana Reference Publications, 1977.

Translator: *The Odyssey of Homer,* Longmans, Green, 1957; *Odusseus: A Twi Translation of the Twenty-four Books of Homer's Odyssey,* Bureau of Ghana Languages, 1974; *Sophokles, Antigone: A Twi Translation,* Waterville Publishing House, 1976; *Sokrates Anoyi: A Twi Translation of Plato's Apology of Sokrates,* Waterville Publishing House, 1976.

WORK IN PROGRESS: An English-Twi dictionary; *Dictionary of African Biography,* Volume II.

* * *

OGG, Oscar (John) 1908-1971

December 13, 1908—August 10, 1971; American graphic artist and calligrapher. Obituaries: *New York Times,* August 11, 1971; *Publishers Weekly,* August 23, 1971. (See index for *CA* sketch)

* * *

OINAS, Felix Johannes 1911-

PERSONAL: Born March 6, 1911, in Tartu, Estonia; came to United States in 1949, naturalized in 1955; son of Ernst (a businessman) and Marie (Saarik) Oinas; married Lisbet Kove (a librarian), July 10, 1937; children: Helina (Mrs. Charles Anthony Piano), Valdar. *Education:* Attended Budapest University, 1935-36; Tartu State University, M.A., 1938; University of Heidelberg, additional study, 1946-48; Indiana University, Ph.D., 1952. *Religion:* Evangelical Lutheran. *Home:* 2513 East Eighth St., Bloomington, Ind. 47401. *Office:* Slavic Department, Indiana University, Bloomington, Ind. 47401.

CAREER: Budapest University, Budapest, Hungary, lecturer in Finno-Ugric languages, 1938-40; Baltic University, Hamburg, Germany, lecturer in Estonian language, 1946-48; Indiana University at Bloomington, lecturer, 1951-52, instructor, 1952-55, assistant professor, 1955-61, associate professor, 1961-65, professor of Slavic and Finno-Ugric languages, 1965—. *Member:* American Association of Teachers of Slavic and East European Languages, Linguistic Society of America, Modern Language Association of America, American Folklore Society, Finno-Ugrian Society (fellow), Finnish Academy of Sciences, Finnish Literary Society (fellow), Baltisches Forschungsinstitut (fellow), Finnish Folklore Society (fellow). *Awards, honors:* Fulbright grant, 1961-62; Guggenheim grants, 1961-62, 1966-

67; Ford International Studies grants, 1962, 1967; Fulbright-Hays grant, 1964-65; American Philosophical Society grant, 1965; American Council of Learned Societies travel grant 1973; National Endowment for the Humanities research grant, 1974.

WRITINGS: Petoefi, Estonian Literary Society, 1939; (editor with Karl Inno) *Eesti,* Eesti Rahvusfond, 1949; *The Karelians,* Human Relations Area Files Press, 1955; (editor) *Language Teaching Today,* Research Center, Indiana University, 1960; *The Development of Postpositional Cases in Balto-Finnic Languages,* Finno-Ugric Society, 1961; *Estonian General Reader,* Indiana University Publications, 1963, 2nd edition, 1972; *Basic Course in Estonian,* Indiana University Publications, 1966, 4th edition, 1975; *Studies in Finnic-Slavic Folklore Relations,* Finnish Academy, 1969; (editor) *The Study of Russian Folklore,* Mouton & Co., 1975; (co-editor) *Tractata Altaica: Denis Sinor sexagenario optime de rebus altaicis merito dedicata,* Otto Harrassowitz, 1976; (co-editor) *Folklore Today: Festschrift in Honor of Richard M. Dorson,* Indiana University Research Center, 1976; (editor) *The Heroic Epic and Saga,* Indiana University Press, 1978. Contributor of over seventy-five articles to *World, Journal of American Folklore, Slavic Review, General Linguistics, Studia Fennica,* and other publications. Review editor, *Slavic and East European Journal,* 1957-64.

WORK IN PROGRESS: Russian Heroic Epic; Slavic mythology.

SIDELIGHTS: Felix Oinas told *CA:* "My field of research is rather broad, and includes Slavic, Finno-Ugric, and Siberian folklore, mythology, literature, and languages. This breadth of interests is often a very positive thing, since it provides me with an abundance of fascinating research problems, frequently cross-cultural, which can then be viewed from a similar point of view. I am currently applying myself to intensive research in an effort to make up for the ten years lost during World War II."

* * *

OLBRICHT, Thomas H. 1929-

PERSONAL: Surname is pronounced like Albright; born November 3, 1929, in Thayer, Mo.; son of Benjamin Joseph (a rancher) and Agnes (Taylor) Olbricht; married Dorothy Jetta Kiel, June 8, 1951; children: Suzanne M., Eloise J., Joel C., Adele L., Erika M. *Education:* Northern Illinois University, B.S., 1951; University of Iowa, M.A., 1953, Ph.D., 1959; Harvard University, S.T.B., 1962. *Politics:* Democrat. *Religion:* Church of Christ. *Home:* 1400 Compere Blvd., Abilene, Tex. 79601. *Office:* Department of Philosophy, Abilene Christian College, Abilene, Tex. 79601.

CAREER: University of Dubuque, Dubuque, Iowa, assistant professor of speech and chairman of department, 1954-59; Pennsylvania State University, University Park, associate professor of speech, 1962-67; Abilene Christian College (now University), Abilene, Tex., professor of philosophy and religion, 1967—. *Member:* Society of Biblical Literature, American Academy of Religion (president, 1977-78), Speech Communication Association of America.

WRITINGS: Informative Speaking, Scott, Foresman, 1968. Associate editor, *Philosophy and Rhetoric, Southern Speech Communication Journal.* Editor, *Restoration Quarterly.*

WORK IN PROGRESS: Biblical Studies in America, completion expected in 1979; *The Encyclopedia of Biblical Studies,* completion expected in 1984.

OLDMAN, Oliver 1920-

PERSONAL: Born July 19, 1920, in New York, N.Y.; son of Max Alex and Rose (Mehlsack) Oldman; married Barbara Lublin, May 2, 1943; children: Andrew, Margaret (Mrs. Bruce Erman), Michele. *Education:* Harvard University, S.B., 1942, LL.B., 1953. *Home:* 15 Buckingham St., Cambridge, Mass. 02138. *Office:* Harvard Law School, F-306, Cambridge, Mass. 02138.

CAREER: Admitted to Bar of the State of New York, 1953, of the State of Massachusetts, 1958. Office of Price Administration, Washington, D.C., junior economist, 1942; University of Buffalo (now State University of New York at Buffalo), instructor in economics, 1946-50; Lublin Construction Co., Inc., Buffalo, vice-president, 1946-55; Hodgson, Russ, Andrews, Woods & Goodyear (law firm), Buffalo, associate, 1953-55; Harvard University, Law School, Cambridge, Mass., assistant professor, 1958-61, professor of tax law, 1961—, Learned Hand Professor of Law, 1976—, director of training for international tax program, 1955-65, director of program, 1965—. Consultant on taxation to governments of Venezuela, Chile, Colombia, Virgin Islands, Argentina, Ethiopia, Puerto Rico, and others. Member of advisory board, Inter-American Center of Tax Administration. *Military service:* U.S. Army, 1943-46; became first lieutenant. *Member:* American Bar Association, American Economic Association, National Tax Association (member of board of directors), International Fiscal Association.

WRITINGS: (With C. S. Shoup, S. S. Surrey, J. F. Due, and L. C. Fitch) *The Fiscal System of Venezuela,* Johns Hopkins Press, 1959; (editor with R. M. Bird) *Readings on Taxation in Developing Countries,* Johns Hopkins Press, 1964, 3rd edition, 1974; (with Aaron, Bird, and Kass) *Financing Urban Development in Mexico City,* Harvard University Press, 1967; (with P. Kelley) *Readings on Income Tax Administration,* Foundation Press, 1974; (with F. P. Schoettle) *State and Local Taxes and Finance,* Foundation Press, 1974; (with M. J. McIntyre) *Institutionalizing Tax Policy Planning,* International Bureau of Fiscal Documention, 1976. Contributor to tax journals.

WORK IN PROGRESS: Materials on Tax Policy, completion expected in 1979; *Valuation for Property Tax Purposes,* completion expected in 1981.

* * *

O'LEARY, Brian (Todd) 1940-

PERSONAL: Born January 27, 1940, in Boston, Mass.; son of Frederick A. and Mary Mabel (Todd) O'Leary; married Joyce Whitehead, June 20, 1964; children: Brian, Jr., Erin. *Education:* Williams College, B.A., 1961; Georgetown University, M.A., 1964; University of California, Berkeley, Ph.D., 1967. *Agent:* Lynn Nesbitt, International Creative Management, 40 West 57th St., New York, N.Y. 10019.

CAREER: National Aeronautics and Space Administration, Goddard Space Flight Center, Greenbelt, Md., physicist in Aeronomy and Meteorology Division, 1961-62; high school mathematics teacher in Washington, D.C., 1964; National Aeronautics and Space Administration, Manned Spacecraft Center, Houston, Tex., scientist-astronaut, 1967-68; University of Texas at Austin, assistant professor of astronomy, 1967-68; Cornell University, Ithaca, N.Y., research associate, 1968-69, assistant professor of astronomy, 1969-71; California State University, San Francisco (now San Francisco State University), associate professor of interdisciplinary sciences, 1971-72; Hampshire College, Amherst, Mass., assistant professor of astronomy and science policy assessment, 1972-75; U.S. House of Representatives, Interior Committee, Washington, D.C., special consultant to subcommittee on energy and environment, 1975—. Visiting associate, California Institute of Technology, Pasadena, 1971; lecturer, School of Law, University of California, Berkeley, 1971-72. Experimenter with Mariner Venus-Mercury Television Science Team, 1973.

MEMBER: International Astronomical Union, American Geophysical Union (secretary of planetology section, 1970-74), American Astronomical Society, American Association for the Advancement of Science (fellow), American Association of University Professors, Western Spectroscopy Association, Astronomical Society of the Pacific. *Awards, honors: The Making of an Ex-Astronaut* was chosen the best young adult book of 1970 by the American Library Association; research grants as principal investigator of Mariner Venus-Mercury Flyby, of observations of Mars, Venus, and the Galilean Satellites of Jupiter, 1971-72, and of other astronomical observations.

WRITINGS: The Making of an Ex-Astronaut, Houghton, 1970. Contributor of over thirty articles to scientific journals, and to *New York Times.*

WORK IN PROGRESS: Critiques of the space program with particular emphasis on NASA's proposed space shuttle system.

SIDELIGHTS: Brian O'Leary told *CA:* "I resigned as an astronaut in NASA's manned space program because of its overemphasis on test pilots and transportation systems rather than science.... The proposed space shuttle might become the nation's costliest boondoggle of all time—extremely wasteful, costing tens of billions of dollars. I have testified before U.S. Senate committees about this issue."

AVOCATIONAL INTERESTS: Hiking, tennis, skiing, jazz piano.

BIOGRAPHICAL/CRITICAL SOURCES: Nation, May 4, 1970; *New Yorker,* May 30, 1970.†

*   *   *

OLIVER, John Edward 1933-

PERSONAL: Born October 21, 1933, in Dover, Kent, England; son of Albert Edward and Florence (Allen) Oliver; married Sylvia Oberholzer, August 17, 1957; children: Frances Janine, Andrea Leigh. *Education:* University of London, B.Sc., 1956; University of Exeter, Postgraduate Certificate in Education, 1957; Columbia University, M.A., 1966, Ph.D., 1969. *Religion:* Episcopalian. *Home:* 8282 South 30th St., Terre Haute, Ind. 47802. *Office:* Department of Geography and Geology, Indiana State University, Terre Haute, Ind. 47809.

CAREER: Willesden Technical College, London, England, lecturer in geography and geology, 1957-58; Warwick Academy, Bermuda, senior master in geography and geology, 1958-65; Columbia University, New York, N.Y., lecturer, 1965-68, assistant professor of physical geography, 1968-73; Indiana State University, Terre Haute, associate professor of geography, 1973—. *Member:* American Geographical Society, Association of American Geographers, American Association for Advancement of Science, American Meteorological Society, Indiana Academy of Science.

WRITINGS: (With J. W. Watson and Catherine Foggo) *A Geography of Bermuda,* Collins, 1965; *What We Find When We Look at Maps* (juvenile), McGraw, 1970; *Climate and Man's Environment,* Wiley, 1973; *Perspectives on Applied*

Physical Geography, Duxbury, 1977. Contributor to *Cowles Comprehensive Encyclopedia, Encyclopedia of Earth Sciences, Saturday Review,* and geography journals. Assistant editor, *Journal of Human Ecology.*

WORK IN PROGRESS: Physical Geography in Context, for Duxbury.

*   *   *

OLSEN, Otto H(arald) 1925-

PERSONAL: Born October 2, 1925, in Bethlehem, Pa.; son of Oscar H. (an engineer) and Marcella (Tau) Olsen; married Corinne Mikkelsen (a teacher of the deaf), May 3, 1949; children: Stephen Tau, Amy Elizabeth. *Education:* Columbia University, A.B., 1952; Johns Hopkins University, Ph.D., 1959. *Politics:* Independent. *Religion:* None. *Home:* 155 Hollister Ave., DeKalb, Ill. 60115. *Office:* History Department, Northern Illinois University, DeKalb, Ill. 60115.

CAREER: University of North Carolina at Chapel Hill, instructor in World history, 1957-60; Old Dominion College (now University), Norfolk, Va., assistant professor of American history, 1960-64; Morgan State College, Baltimore, Md., associate professor of American history, 1964-67; Northern Illinois University, DeKalb, professor of American history, 1967—. Visiting professor at University of Wisconsin, 1966-67. *Military service:* U.S. Merchant Marine, 1943-49; served as navigation officer. *Member:* American Association of University Professors (Old Dominion College president, 1962-64; Virginia president, 1963-64), American Civil Liberties Union (DeKalb County chairman, 1969-70; chairman, Illinois Academic Freedom Committee, 1970-72), Organization of American Historians, American Historical Association, Association for the Study of Negro Life and History, North Carolina Literary and Historical Society. *Awards, honors:* R.D.W. Connor Award, North Carolina Historical Association, 1963, for an article, "The Ku Klux Klan: A Study in Reconstruction Politics and Propaganda."

WRITINGS: Carpetbagger's Crusade: The Life of Albion Winegar Tourgee, Johns Hopkins Press, 1965; (editor) *The Thin Disguise: Turning Point in Negro History—Plessy vs. Ferguson—Documentary Presentation, 1864-1896,* Humanities, 1967; (editor) Albion W. Tourgee, *Bricks without Straw,* Louisiana State University Press, 1969; (editor) *The Negro Question: From Slavery to Caste, 1863-1910,* Pitman, 1971. Contributor of articles to *Civil War History, North Carolina Historical Review, Science and Society,* and *Serif.*

WORK IN PROGRESS: A general history of Reconstruction in North Carolina, 1865-1876.

*   *   *

OLSON, David R(ichard) 1935-

PERSONAL: Born June 16, 1935, in Saskatoon, Saskatchewan, Canada; son of Walter Robert and Martha (Linder) Olson; married Frances M. Dunn, September 1, 1958; children: Joan, Bradley, Ellen, David, Kristen. *Education:* University of Saskatchewan, B.Ed., 1960; University of Alberta, M.Ed., 1962, Ph.D., 1963. *Home:* 12 Beachview Crescent, Toronto, Ontario, Canada. *Office:* Ontario Institute for Studies in Education, 252 Bloor St.W., Toronto, Ontario, Canada.

CAREER: Dalhousie University, Halifax, Nova Scotia, assistant professor of educational psychology, 1963-65; Harvard University, Cambridge, Mass., Center for Cognitive Studies, research fellow, 1965-66; Ontario Institute for

Studies in Education, Toronto, professor of applied psychology, 1966—. Fellow, Stanford Center for Research and Development in Teaching, Stanford, Calif. 1969-70; visiting fellow, Wolfson College, Oxford University, 1974-75, and fellow, Canadian Psychological Association, 1976—.

WRITINGS: Cognitive Development: The Child's Acquisition of Diagonality, Academic Press, 1970; *Media and Symbols: The Forms of Expression, Communication and Education*, University of Chicago Press, 1974. Also author, *Explorations In Inner Space: The Nature and Development of Spatial Cognition*.

*   *   *

OLSON, Eugene E. 1936-
(Brad Steiger)

PERSONAL: Born February 19, 1936, in Bode, Iowa; son of Erling E. (a farmer) and Hazel (Jensen) Olson; married Marilyn Gjefle (divorced, 1977); married Frances Paschall, 1977; children: (first marriage) Bryan, Steven, Kari, Julie. *Education:* Attended Luther College, 1953-57, and University of Iowa, 1963. *Home:* 5851 East Sharon Dr., Scottsdale, Ariz. 85254. *Agent:* Ruth H. Brod, 15 Park Ave., New York, N.Y. 10016.

CAREER: High school English teacher in Clinton, Iowa, 1957-63; Luther College, Decorah, Iowa, teacher of literature and creative writing, 1963-67; Other Dimensions, Inc., Decorah, president, 1970-74. Lecturer at colleges and for private groups. *Awards, honors:* Genie award for Metaphysical Writer of the Year, 1974.

*WRITINGS—*Under pseudonym Brad Steiger more than 60 books, including: *Strange Guests*, Ace Books, 1966; *The Unknown*, Popular Library, 1966; *ESP: Your Sixth Sense*, Award Books, 1966; (with Chaw Mank) *Valentino*, Macfadden, 1966, 2nd edition, 1975; *Strangers from the Skies*, Award Books, 1966; (with Joan Whritenour) *Flying Saucers Are Hostile*, Award Books, 1967; *The Mass Murderer*, Award Books, 1967; *The Enigma of Reincarnation*, Ace Books, 1967; *Real Ghosts, Restless Spirits and Haunted Minds*, Award Books, 1968; (with John Pendragon) *Pendragon: A Clairvoyant's Power of Prophecy*, Award Books, 1968; (editor) Pendragon, *The Occult World of John Pendragon*, Ace Books, 1968; *Voices from Beyond*, Award Books, 1968; *UFO Breakthrough*, Award Books, 1968; *In My Soul I Am Free*, Lancer Books, 1968; *Sex and the Supernatural*, Lancer Books, 1968; *The Mind Travellers*, Award Books, 1968; (with Pendragon) *Cupid and the Stars*, Ace Books, 1969; (with Ron Warmoth) *Tarot*, Award Books, 1969; *Sex and Satanism*, Ace Books, 1969; *Judy Garland*, Ace Books, 1969; (with Dorothy Spence Lauer) *How to Use ESP: The Hidden Powers of Your Mind*, Lancer Books, 1969; *The Weird, the Wild, and the Wicked*, Pyramid Publications, 1969; (with Loring G. Williams) *Other Lives*, Hawthorn, 1969.

(With Warren Smith) *What the Seers Predict in 1971*, Lancer Books, 1970; (with William Howard) *Handwriting Analysis*, Ace Books, 1970; *Know the Future Today: The Amazing Prophecies of Irene Hughes*, Paperback Library, 1970; *Aquarian Revelations*, Dell, 1971; (with Williams) *Minds Through Space and Time*, Award Books, 1971; *Secrets of Kuhuna Magic*, Award Books, 1971; *Haunted Lovers*, Dell, 1971; *The Psychic Feats of Olof Jonsson*, Prentice-Hall, 1971; *Strange Encounters with Ghosts*, Popular Library, 1972; *Irene Hughes on Psychic Safari*, Paperback Library, 1972; *Revelation: The Divine Fire*, Prentice-Hall, 1973; *Atlantis Rising*, Dell, 1973; *Mysteries of Time and Space*,

Prentice-Hall, 1974; *Medicine Power: The American Indian's Revival of His Spiritual Heritage and Its Relevance for Modern Man*, Doubleday, 1974; *Medicine Talk: A Guide to Walking in Balance and Surviving on the Earth Mother*, Doubleday, 1975; *Words from the Source*, Prentice-Hall, 1975; (editor with John W. White) *Other Worlds, Other Universes: Playing the Reality Game*, Doubleday, 1975; *A Roadmap of Time: How the Maxwell/Wheeler Energy Cycles Predict the History of the Next 25 Years*, Prentice-Hall, 1975; (editor with Hayden Hewes) *UFO Missionaries Extraordinary*, Pocket Books, 1976; *Psychic City–Chicago: Doorway to Another Dimension*, Doubleday, 1976; *Gods of Aquarius: UFOs and the Transformation of Man*, Harcourt, 1976; (editor) *Project Bluebook*, Ballantine, 1976; *Alien Meetings*, Ace Books, 1978; *You Will Live Again*, Dell, 1978; *Worlds Before Our Own*, Berkeley Publishing, in press.

Work represented in science-fiction anthologies, including *The Flying Saucer Reader*, New American Library, and *Ghosts, Witches, and Demons*, Scholastic Book Services. Contributor of articles and short stories to magazines, including *Fate, Family Weekly, Saga, Strange,* and *Occult*. Writer of syndicated newspaper column, "The Strange World of Brad Steiger."

WORK IN PROGRESS: A book tentatively entitled *Komar's Secrets of Pain Control*, for Berkeley Publishing; two novels, *Darmanian* and *The Chindi*.

BIOGRAPHICAL/CRITICAL SOURCES: Choice, July/August, 1973; *Kirkus Reviews*, December 1, 1973, September 1, 1974, December 1, 1974, January 15, 1975, April 1, 1975, September 15, 1975, December 15, 1975, November 1, 1976; *New Republic*, May 18, 1974.

*   *   *

OPPENHEIMER, Samuel P(hilip) 1903-

PERSONAL: Born March 18, 1903, in Baltimore, Md.; son of Max (a salesman) and Ray (Adler) Oppenheimer; married Mary Bamberger, October 9, 1934 (died June 17, 1938); married Lucille Sonn, August 5, 1948; children: (first marriage) Ruth Alice (Mrs. Jeffrey D. Oshlag; deceased). *Education:* Stevens Institute of Technology, M.E., 1924. *Religion:* Jewish. *Home and office:* 36 Yale Ter., West Orange, N.J. 07052.

CAREER: G.M. Weinstein Co., New York, N.Y., superintendent of construction, 1928-46; New Jersey Erectors, Newark, vice-president, 1947-50; Waverly Builders, Hillside, N.J., vice-president, 1957-68. *Member:* National Society of Professional Engineers (life member; secretary of Essex County, N.J. chapter, 1971-72).

WRITINGS: Erecting Structural Steel, McGraw, 1960; *Directing Construction for Profit: Business Aspects of Contracting*, McGraw, 1971.

WORK IN PROGRESS: A third book.

*   *   *

ORLANS, Harold 1921-

PERSONAL: Born July 29, 1921, in New York, N.Y.; son of Morris and Celia (Fudalowitz) Orlansky; married F. Barbara Hughes (a physiologist), July 18, 1959; children: Claire, Andrew, Nicholas. *Education:* City College (now City College of the City University of New York), B.SS., 1941; Yale University, Ph.D., 1949; London School of Economics and Political Science, research scholar, 1949-50. *Home:* 7035 Wilson Lane, Bethesda, Md. 20034. *Office:* National

Academy of Public Administration, Washington, D.C. 20036.

CAREER: San Francisco Call-Bulletin, San Francisco, Calif., reporter, 1941-42; University of Birmingham, Birmingham, England, visiting lecturer, 1950-51; Social Survey, London, England, senior information officer, 1951-52; Institute for Research in Human Relations, Philadelphia, Pa., research associate, 1952-54; National Science Foundation, Washington, D.C., program analyst and section chief of Office of Special Studies, 1954-59; White House Conference on Children and Youth, Washington, D.C., director of studies, 1959-60; Brookings Institution, Washington, D.C., senior fellow in governmental studies, 1960-73; National Academy of Public Administration, Washington, D.C., senior research associate, 1973—. Consultant to Research and Technical Programs Subcommittee of Committee on Government Operations, U.S. House of Representatives, 1966-67; visiting associate of Program of Technology and Society, Harvard University, 1970-71; preceptor, Nova University, 1976—. Member of Commission on the Year 2000. *Awards, honors:* Social Science Research Council fellow, 1948-49; Fulbright scholar in England, 1949-50.

WRITINGS: Stevenage: A Sociological Study of a New Town, Routledge & Kegan Paul, 1952, published as *Utopia Ltd.,* Yale University Press, 1953, new edition, Greenwood Press, 1971; *Opinion Polls on National Leaders,* Institute for Research in Human Relations, 1953; *Graduate Student Enrollment and Support in American Universities and Colleges, 1954,* National Science Foundation, 1957; *The Effects of Federal Programs on Higher Education: A Study of 36 Universities and Colleges,* Brookings Institution, 1962; (editor and contributor) Luther H. Evans and others, *Federal Departmental Libraries,* Brookings Institution, 1963; (editor) *The Use of Social Research in Federal Domestic Programs,* four volumes, Research and Technical Programs Subcommittee of Committee on Government Operations, U.S. House of Representatives, 1967; *Contracting for Atoms,* Brookings Institution, 1967; (contributor) Gideon Sjoberg, editor, *Ethics, Politics, and Social Research,* Schenkman, 1967; (editor) *Science Policy and the University,* Brookings Institution, 1968.

(Contributor) Harvey Perloff, editor, *The Future of the U.S. Government,* Braziller, 1971; (contributor) Albert Rosenthal, editor, *Public Science Policy,* University of New Mexico Press, 1972; *The Nonprofit Research Institute: Its Origin, Operation, Problems, and Prospects,* McGraw, 1972; *Contracting for Knowledge,* Jossey-Bass, 1973; *Private Accreditation and Public Eligibility,* Lexington Books, 1975; (contributor) Elisabeth Crawford and Norman Perry, editors, *Demand for Social Knowledge,* Sage Publications, 1976. Writer of monographs and research reports; contributor of about forty articles to *Encyclopedia of Education, Saturday Review, Encounter, Minerva,* and other publications.

* * *

O'ROURKE, John James Joseph 1926-

PERSONAL: Born February 1, 1926; son of John James (an accountant) and Marie (Mooney) O'Rourke. *Education:* St. Charles Borromeo Seminary, A.B., 1948; Pontifical Gregorian University, S.T.L., 1952; Pontifical Biblical Institute, L.S.S., 1954. *Home:* St. Charles Borromeo Seminary, Overbrook, Philadelphia, Pa. 19151. *Office:* 222 North 17th St., Philadelphia, Pa. 19103.

CAREER: Ordained Roman Catholic priest, 1951; St.

Charles Borromeo Seminary, Overbrook, Philadelphia, Pa., professor of New Testament and Biblical languages, 1954-74; archdiocesan theological consultant, 1974—. *Member:* Catholic Biblical Association of America, Catholic Theological Society of America, American Catholic Historical Society, Catholic Biblical Association of Great Britain, Studiorum Novi Testamenti Societas, Society of Biblical Literature, American Schools of Oriental Research, Philadelphia Seminar on Christian Origins. *Awards, honors:* Honorary Prelate of the Pope, 1976.

WRITINGS: (Editor with Stephen Benko) *The Catacombs and the Colosseum,* Judson, 1971. Contributor to religious periodicals. Contributing editor, *Religious and Theological Abstracts;* abstractor, *New Testament Abstracts.*

WORK IN PROGRESS: Research on Greek grammar, the Synoptic problem, and uses of computers for Biblical studies.

SIDELIGHTS: John O'Rourke's languages are Hellenistic Greek, Latin, French, Spanish, German, Biblical Hebrew, and Biblical Aramaic.

* * *

ORR, David 1929-

PERSONAL: Born July 19, 1929, in Montgomery, Ala.; son of Herman (an engineer) and Josie (Blackmon) Orr; married Christeen Nelson, September 21, 1951; married second wife, Darlene Cole (a music teacher), February 23, 1962; children: (first marriage) Pamela, Duncan; (second marriage) Jennifer, Vanessa. *Education:* University of North Carolina, B.A., 1951, M.A., 1954, Ph.D., 1960; University of Pittsburgh, M.B.A., 1975. *Home:* 9432 Highland Rd., Pittsburgh, Pa. 15237. *Office:* Orr Marketing Planning, Jenkins Arcade, Pittsburgh, Pa. 15222.

CAREER: Rollins College, Winter Park, Fla., instructor in English, 1957-58; University of North Carolina at Chapel Hill, instructor in English, 1958-59; Butler University, Indianapolis, Ind., instructor in English, 1959-62; Indiana University, Kokomo Campus (now Indiana University at Kokomo), assistant professor of English, 1962-66; Slippery Rock State College, Slippery Rock, Pa., professor of English and chairman of department, 1966-68; Point Park College, Pittsburgh, Pa., professor of English and chairman of department, 1968-75; director, National Market Analysis, 1975-76; Orr Marketing Planning, Pittsburgh, president, 1976—. Tenor soloist, Trinity Cathedral, Pittsburgh. Member of board of directors, Pittsburgh Oratorio Society and Allegheny Roundtable. *Military service:* U.S. Army, Medical Corps, 1951-53. *Member:* American Civil Liberties Union, Catch Society of America, American Marketing Association.

WRITINGS: Italian Renaissance Drama in England before 1625, University of North Carolina Press, 1970.

WORK IN PROGRESS: The World of Poetry.

* * *

ORR, Robert T. 1908-

PERSONAL: Born August 17, 1908, in San Francisco, Calif.; son of Robert Harris (a physician) and Agnes (Cockburn) Orr; married Dorothy Bowen (an author and mycologist), August 1, 1942; married second wife, Margaret Cunningham (a botanist), August 1, 1972; children: Nancy Jane (Mrs. Richard A. Davis). *Education:* University of San Francisco, B.S., 1929; University of California, Berkeley, M.A., 1931, Ph.D., 1937. *Home:* 30 Elm Ave., Lartspur,

Calif. 94939. *Office:* California Academy of Sciences, Golden Gate Park, San Francisco, Calif. 94118.

CAREER: U.S. National Park Service, wildlife technician, 1935-36; California Academy of Sciences, San Francisco, assistant curator, 1936-43, associate curator, 1944, curator of department of ornithology and mammalogy, 1945-75, associate director of academy, 1964-75, senior scientist, 1975—. University of San Francisco, San Francisco, Calif., assistant professor, 1942-48, associate professor, 1949-54, professor of biology, 1955-64. Acting instructor in natural history, Stanford University, summer, 1940; visiting professor of zoology, University of California, Berkeley, summer, 1962, spring, 1965. Member of advisory board, Belvedere Scientific Fund; associate member of board of directors, Audubon Canyon Ranch; member of advisory scientific committee, Charles Darwin Foundation for the Galapagos Islands.

MEMBER: American Association for the Advancement of Science (fellow; past president, Pacific Division), American Mycological Association, American Ornithologists' Union (fellow), American Society of Mammalogists (past president and honorary member), Society of Systematic Zoology (chairman of committee on endowments), Cooper Ornithological Society (past president of Northern Division and honorary member), Australian Mammal Society, National Audubon Society, Pacific Northwest Bird and Mammal Society, Save-the-Redwoods League, Wasmann Biological Society, California Academy of Sciences (fellow), Biological Society of Washington, Oregon Mycological Society, San Francisco Mycological Society (honorary member), San Francisco Zoological Society (vice-chairman of board of directors), Sigma Xi, Phi Sigma.

WRITINGS: Mammals of Lake Tahoe, California Academy of Sciences, 1949; *Vertebrate Biology,* Saunders, 1961, 3rd edition, 1971; (with Dorothy B. Orr) *Mushrooms and Other Common Fungi of the San Francisco Bay Region,* University of California Press, 1962; *The Animal Kingdom,* Macmillan, 1965; (with Dorothy B. Orr) *Mushrooms and Other Fungi of Southern California,* University of California Press, 1968; *Animals in Migration,* Macmillan, 1970; *The Mammals of North America,* Chanticleer, 1971; (with James Moffitt) *Birds of the Lake Tahoe Region,* California Academy of Sciences, 1971; *Marine Mammals of California,* University of California Press, 1972; (with wife, Margaret C. Orr) *Wildflowers of Western America,* Knopf, 1974; *The Little-Known Pika,* Macmillan, 1977; (with Dorothy B. Orr) *A Handbook of Western Mushrooms,* University of California Press, 1978.

WORK IN PROGRESS: Research on the behavior and taxonomy of seals, sea lions, and cetaceans along the coasts of California, Mexico, and the Galapagos Islands; studies on Mexican birds; research on the biology of bats.

AVOCATIONAL INTERESTS: Theater arts, photography.

*   *   *

ORTON, Vrest 1897-

PERSONAL: Born September 3, 1897, in Hardwick, Vt.; son of Gardner Lyman and Lelia (Teachout) Orton; married Rosita Lefkov, 1926 (divorced, 1932); married Mildred Ellen Wilcox, January 12, 1935; children: (first marriage) Geoffrey Dean Conrad; (second marriage) Lyman Kennerly, Jeremy Roderick. *Education:* Attended Harvard University. *Home and office:* Weston, Vt. 05161.

CAREER: Began as partner in an advertising agency in Los Angeles, Calif.; worked with U.S. Consular Service in Mexico, 1924-25; *American Mercury,* New York City, member of advertising and promotion staff, 1925-30; *Saturday Review of Literature,* New York City, advertising manager, 1927-28; *Colophon: Book Collectors' Quarterly,* New York City, founder and editor, 1930; Stephen Daye Press, Brattleboro, Vt., founder and general manager, 1931—; Countryman Press, Weston, Vt., founder and general manager, 1935; free-lance public relations counsel for Dartmouth College, Wesleyan University and other institutions, 1935-41; Vermont Guild Old-Time Crafts and Industries, Weston, co-founder, 1936, secretary-treasurer, 1936-38; Original Vermont Country Store (first revived store and national mail order business), Weston, founder and proprietor, 1945—. Chairman, Vermont Historical Sites Commission, 1951-59. Co-founder and director of public relations, Vermont for Eisenhower State Committee, 1952. *Military service:* U.S. Army, American Expeditionary Forces in France, 1918-19. U.S. War Department, deputy director, public relations readjustment division, general staff, Pentagon, 1942-45.

MEMBER: Vermont Historical Society (vice-president and member of board of curators, 1929-54), Players and Brook Club (both New York), Bentley Drivers' Club (England), Harvard Club of Vermont (vice-president, 1953—). *Awards, honors:* Cited as outstanding American retailer by New York University School of Retailing, 1952.

WRITINGS: Notes to Add to a Bibliography of Theodore Dreiser (booklet; supplementary notes to E. D. MacDonald's *A Bibliography of the Writings of Theodore Dreiser),* American Collector, 1928, expanded edition published as *Dreiserana: A Book about His Books,* Folcroft, 1929; *Proceedings of the Company of Amateur Brewers,* Stephen Daye Press, 1932, revised edition, Tuttle, 1972; *A Line of Men 100 Years Long,* Stephen Daye Press, 1936; (editor) *And So Goes Vermont,* Farrar & Rinehart, 1937; *Goudy, Master of Letters,* introduction by Frederic W. Goudy, Black Cat Press, 1939; *Mary Fletcher Comes Back,* privately printed, 1939.

Vermont Academic Way, privately printed, 1945; (with wife, Mildred Ellen Orton) *Cooking with Wholegrains,* Farrar, Straus, 1951, revised edition, 1971; *The Official Guide to Vermont's Historic Sites* (booklet), Vermont Historic Sites Commission, 1958; *Calvin Coolidge's Unique Vermont Inauguration: The Facts Winnowed from the Chaff,* Tuttle, 1960, revised edition, Calvin Coolidge Foundation, 1970; *The Famous Rogers Groups: A Complete Check-List and Collectors' Manual* (booklet), Vermont Country Store, 1960; *Observations on the Forgotten Art of Building a Good Fireplace,* Yankee Inc., 1969, revised edition, 1974; *Vermont Afternoons with Robert Frost,* Tuttle, 1971; *The American Cider Book,* Farrar, Straus, 1975. Also author of *The History of the Vermont Country Store,* 1975 and *Some Personal Observations on the Republic of Vermont,* 1977. Contributor to *A Treasury of Vermont Life,* 1956. Columnist, *Manchester Union-Leader,* Manchester, N.H., 1965—. Contributor to magazines. Co-founder, *Vermont Life;* editor and publisher, *The Voice of the Mountains.*

*   *   *

OSBORNE, J(ulius) K(enneth) 1941-

PERSONAL: Born June 11, 1941, in Mandan, N.D.; son of Martin Van Buren (a laborer) and Katherine (Bullinger) Osborne. *Education:* Regis College, B.A., 1964; Seattle University, M.A.T., 1970. *Office: Madrona,* 4730 Latona N.E., Seattle, Wash. 98105.

CAREER: North Dakota Department of Agriculture, surveyor, 1957-59; hospital orderly in Denver, Colo., 1961-64; teacher in secondary schools in Colorado and Seattle, Wash., 1964-65; University of Washington Medical Center, Seattle, medical librarian, beginning 1970; founder and operator of Gemini Press, Seattle, Wash.; also employed at various times as salesman, laborer, cook, dishwasher, lifeguard, counselor, office manager, and in other positions. *Military service:* Served four-year prison sentence for refusing induction. *Member:* Committee of Small Magazine Editors and Publishers.

WRITINGS: Leaving It All Behind: Early Poems, San Vito Press, 1970; *I Refuse,* Westminster, 1971; *Dream Sequence* (poems), Gemini Press, 1972. Contributor to *Seattle.* Coeditor and founder, *Madrona* (poetry quarterly), 1970—; editor, *Western Concept,* 1960.

WORK IN PROGRESS: Essays on Daniel Berrigan, Thomas Merton, and William Everson, for Westminister; a novel entitled *Jason Goody's Goodbye Book.*

SIDELIGHTS: J. K. Osborne has traveled in U.S., Canada, Mexico, Europe, Africa, and Australia. He describes himself as a "non-violent social activist, . . . one of the twelve original hippies in S.F. 1965-66, . . . active in draft resistance and 'The Movement'. . . ."†

* * *

OSBORNE, John W(alter) 1927-

PERSONAL: Born August 19, 1927, in Brooklyn, N.Y.; son of Douglas W. (an accountant) and Gertrude (Purcell) Osborne; married Frances Hannon (a secretary), August 2, 1958; children: David. *Education:* Rutgers University, B.A., 1957, M.A., 1959, Ph.D., 1961. *Home:* 24 Helen Ave., West Orange, N.J. 07052. *Office:* Department of History, Rutgers University, 84 College Ave., New Brunswick, N.J. 08903.

CAREER: Newark State College (now Kean College of New Jersey), Union, N.J., assistant professor of history, 1961-63; Newark College of Engineering (now New Jersey Institute of Technology), Newark, N.J., assistant professor of history, 1963-64; Rutgers University, New Brunswick, N.J., assistant professor, 1964-66, associate professor, 1966-69, professor of history, 1969—. Consulting editor, Irish University Press, 1969-71. *Member:* American Historical Association, Conference on British Studies.

WRITINGS: William Cobbett: His Thought and His Times, Rutgers University Press, 1966; *The Silent Revolution: The Industrial Revolution in England as a Source of Cultural Change,* Scribner, 1970; *John Cartwright,* Cambridge University Press, 1972. Contributor of articles to scholarly journals and encyclopedias. Editor, *Journal of the Rutgers University Libraries,* 1975—.

WORK IN PROGRESS: A history of conservative thought; a study of British radicalism in the early nineteenth century; a study of legal changes in England between 1750-1850.

AVOCATIONAL INTERESTS: Reading, travel, listening to classical music.

* * *

OSBURN, Charles B(enjamin) 1939-

PERSONAL: Born May 25, 1939, in Pittsburgh, Pa.; son of C. Benjamin (a podiatrist) and Lydia S. (Harmon) Osburn; married Margaret Anna Brimfield (an assistant manager of a bookstore), March 18, 1963; children: Christopher Bart. *Education:* Grove City College, B.A., 1961; Pennsylvania State University, M.A., 1963; University of North Carolina, M.S., 1971. *Home:* 1111 Church St., Evanston, Ill. 60201. *Office:* Northwestern University Library, 1935 Sheridan Rd., Evanston, Ill. 60201.

CAREER: Pennsylvania State University, University Park, instructor in French, 1963-66; Wisconsin State University (now University of Wisconsin), Whitewater, assistant professor of French, 1966-69; University of North Carolina at Chapel Hill, humanities bibliographer, 1969-74; State University of New York at Buffalo, Universities Libraries, assistant director for collection development, 1974-76; Northwestern University, Evanston, Ill., assistant university librarian for collection development, 1976—. Bibliographic consultant, Inter Documentation Co., Zug, Switzerland. *Member:* American Library Association, Modern Language Association of America (member of bibliographic staff), American Association of University Professors, Beta Phi Mu, Phi Sigma Iota.

WRITINGS: Research and Reference Guide to French Studies, Scarecrow, 1968; (editor) *The Present State of French Studies: A Collection of Research Reviews,* Scarecrow, 1971; (contributor) Franco Simone, editor, *Dizionario critico della letteratura francese,* Unione Tipografico-Editrice Torinese (Turin), 1972; *Guide to French Studies Supplement with Cumulative Indexes,* Scarecrow, 1972. Contributor to *Australian Journal of French Studies, Studi Francesi, Southeastern Librarian, French Studies, Revue des langues vivantes,* and *International Library Review.* Member of book review staff, *Library Journal;* American correspondent, *Repertoire Analytique de Litterature Francaise.*

WORK IN PROGRESS: National Patterns of Academic Research and the Provision of Library Resources.

AVOCATIONAL INTERESTS: Walking, bicycling, skating, beachcombing, wood-chopping, movies of the thirties and forties, big band jazz of the forties and fifties.

* * *

OSGOOD, Samuel M(aurice) 1920-1975

PERSONAL: Born March 2, 1920, in Middleboro, Mass.; son of Samuel P. (a Merchant Marine officer) and Henriette (Gufflet) Osgood; married Sara Ann Gordon (a reference librarian), May 22, 1948; children: Philip Gordon, Steven Gordon. *Education:* University of Nevada, B.A., 1949; Clark University, M.A., 1951, Ph.D., 1953. *Politics:* Democrat. *Religion:* Nondenominational. *Home:* 912 Crain Ave., Kent, Ohio 44240. *Office:* Department of History, Kent State University, Kent, Ohio 44242.

CAREER: Brown University, Prividence, R.I., instructor in history, 1954-58; Drexel Institute of Technology (now Drexel University), Philadelphia, Pa., assistant professor, 1958-61, associate professor, 1961-65, professor of history, 1965-66; State University of New York College at Geneseo, professor of history and chairman of department, 1966-68; Kent State University, Kent, Ohio, professor of modern European history, 1968-75. Fulbright lecturer in Bordeaux, Grenoble, Lyon, and Nice, France, 1964-65, in Paris-Nanterre and Nantes, France, 1965-66; visiting professor, University of Lyon, 1974-75. *Military service:* U.S. Naval Reserve, 1941-45; became petty officer first class. *Member:* American Historical Association, Society for French Historical Studies, Societe d'Histoire Moderne, Societe des Professeurs Francais en Amerique, Compagnon du Baillot

Bordelais, Ohio Academy of History, Phi Kappa Phi. *Awards, honors:* American Philosophical Society grants for research in France, 1956, 1957, 1961, 1963, 1968.

WRITINGS: French Royalism under the Third and Fourth Republics, Nijhoff, 1960, 2nd revised edition published as *French Royalism since 1870,* 1970; (editor) *Napoleon III: Buffoon, Modern Dictator, or Sphinx,* Heath, 1963, 2nd edition, 1973; (editor) *The Fall of France, 1940: Causes and Responsibilities,* Heath, 1965, 2nd edition, 1972; (contributor) Gerald N. Grob, editor, *Statesmen and Statescraft of the Modern West: Essays in Honor of Dwight E. Lee and H. Donaldson Jordon,* Barre, 1967. Contributor of about twenty articles and reviews to *Contemporary Review* (London), and other journals. Consultant and contributor to *Choice.*

WORK IN PROGRESS: Research for a book on Anglophobia in France since World War I.†

(Died August 6, 1975)

*   *   *

OSGOOD, William E(dward) 1926-

PERSONAL: Born March 24, 1926, in Nashua, N.H.; son of Horace E. (a contractor) and Ethel (Trow) Osgood; married Thelma Slabaugh (a librarian), June 18, 1949; children: Kathleen, Deborah. *Education:* University of New Hampshire, B.A., 1951; Simmons College, M.L.S., 1952. *Home:* Mill Hill, Northfield, Vt. 05663.

CAREER: Tuscarawas County Library, New Philadelphia, Ohio, county librarian, 1952-53; Dartmouth College, Hanover, N.H., reference assistant, 1953-55; Free Public Library Services, Montpelier, Vt., adult services librarian, 1955-56; Goddard College, Plainfield, Vt., librarian, 1957-72. Northfield observer for National Weather Service. Member, Vermont Governor's Advisory Panel on Scenery and Historic Sites, 1963. *Military service:* U.S. Army, 1944-46. *Member:* Center for Northern Studies (member of board of directors), American-Scandinavian Foundation (fellow), Vermont Academy of Arts and Sciences (incorporator and former trustee), Northfield Historical Society (incorporator; president, 1974-75).

WRITINGS: (With Leslie J. Hurley) *Ski Touring,* Tuttle, 1969, 2nd edition, 1974; (with Hurley) *The Snowshoe Book,* Stephen Greene Press, 1971, 2nd edition, 1975; *How to Earn a Living in the Country without Farming,* Garden Way Publishing, 1974; *Wintering in Snow Country,* Stephen Greene Press, 1977. Contributor to *Vermont Life.*

*   *   *

OSTWALD, Martin 1922-

PERSONAL: Born January 15, 1922, in Dortmund, Germany; came to United States in 1946, naturalized in 1956; son of Max (a lawyer) and Hedwig (Strauss) Ostwald; married Lore Weinberg (a social worker), December 27, 1948; children: Mark F., David H. *Education:* University of Toronto, B.A., 1946; University of Chicago, A.M., 1948; Columbia University, Ph.D., 1952. *Religion:* Jewish. *Home:* 2 Whittier Pl., Swarthmore, Pa. 19081. *Office:* Department of Classics, Swarthmore College, Swarthmore, Pa. 19081.

CAREER: Wesleyan University, Middletown, Conn., instructor in classics, 1950-51; Columbia University, New York, N.Y., 1951-58, began as lecturer, assistant professor of Greek and Latin, 1954-58; Swarthmore College, Swarthmore, Pa., associate professor, 1958-66, professor of classics, 1966—; University of Pennsylvania, Philadelphia, pro-

fessor of classical studies, 1968—. Member, Institute for Advanced Study, 1974-75. *Member:* American Philological Association, Archaeological Institute of America, Classical Association of Canada, Society for the Promotion of Hellenic Studies, Classical Association of the Atlantic States, Oriental Club of Philadelphia (president, 1969-70), Classical Club of Philadelphia (president, 1968-69), Phi Beta Kappa. *Awards, honors:* Fulbright research grant, 1961-62; American Council of Learned Societies fellowship, 1965-66; National Endowment for the Humanities senior fellowship, 1970-71; visiting fellow, Balliol College, Oxford University, 1970-71; Guggenheim fellowship, 1977-78.

WRITINGS—Published by Bobbs-Merrill, except as indicated: (Editor) Plato, *Protagoras,* 1956; (editor) Plato, *Statesman,* 1957; (translator and author of introduction and notes) Aristotle, *Nicomachean Ethics,* 1962; (with T. G. Rosenmeyer and J. W. Halporn) *The Meters of Greek and Latin Poetry,* 1963; *Nomos and the Beginnings of the Athenian Democracy,* Clarendon Press, 1969. Contributor to professional journals. Member of publications committee, American School of Classical Studies and *Monographs* of the American Philological Association.

WORK IN PROGRESS: Ancient Greek political thought.

*   *   *

OTTEN, C. Michael 1934-

PERSONAL: Born February 10, 1934, in Peoria, Ill.; son of John H. (a cabinetmaker) and Alice Otten; married Patrice Hester (a Montessori teacher), 1967. *Education:* St. Johns University, B.A., 1955; University of Vienna, graduate study; University of California, Berkeley, M.A., 1965, Ph.D., 1968. *Politics:* Liberal-radical. *Religion:* Roman Catholic. *Home:* 589 South 13th St., San Jose, Calif. 95112. *Office:* Department of Sociology, California State University, 125 South Seventh St., San Jose, Calif. 95192.

CAREER: California State University, San Jose, assistant professor, 1968-70, associate professor, 1970—. *Military service:* U.S. Army, counter intelligence, 1956-59. *Member:* American Sociological Association.

WRITINGS: University Authority and the Student: The Berkeley Experience, University of California Press, 1970. Contributor to professional journals.†

*   *   *

OTTENBERG, Simon 1923-

PERSONAL: Born June 6, 1923, in New York, N.Y.; son of Reuben (a physician) and Clarisse (Chene) Ottenberg; married Phoebe Vestal; married second wife, O. Nora J. Clarke, June 8, 1968 (died January, 1977). *Education:* University of Wisconsin, B.A., 1948; Northwestern University, Ph.D., 1957. *Home:* 2317 22nd Ave. E., Seattle, Wash. 98102. *Office:* Department of Anthropology, University of Washington, Seattle, Wash. 98105.

CAREER: University of Chicago, Chicago, Ill., instructor in anthropology, 1954; Washington State University, Pullman, acting instructor in anthropology, 1954-55; University of Washington, Seattle, instructor, 1955-57, assistant professor, 1957-63, associate professor, 1963-68, professor of anthropology, 1968—. Honorary visiting professor, University of Ghana, 1970-71. *Military service:* U.S. Army, Signal Corps, 1943-46; became technical sergeant. *Member:* African Studies Association (member of board of directors, 1966-69), American Anthropological Association, Royal Anthropological Institute, Nigerian Geographical Association, Historical Society of Nigeria. *Awards, honors:* P. A. Talbot book award for best social science book on West Africa, 1968, 1976; Guggenheim fellowship, 1970-71.

WRITINGS: (Editor with Phoebe V. Ottenberg) *Cultures and Societies of Africa,* Random House, 1960; *Double Descent in an African Society,* University of Washington Press, 1968; *Leadership and Authority in an African Society,* University of Washington Press, 1971; *The Masked Rituals of Afikpo: The Context of an African Art,* University of Washington Press, 1975. Contributor to professional journals.

* * *

OTTERSEN, (John) Ottar 1918-

PERSONAL: Born August 13, 1918, in Oslo, Norway; son of Petter O. and Sara (Lind) Ottersen; married Roennaug Mosse Jacobssen, 1950. *Education:* University of Oslo, Cand. theol., 1947, Practicum theol., 1948; University of Uppsala, Teol. kand., 1947. *Home:* Fredrikhovsgatan 3A, 115 22, Stockholm, Sweden. *Office:* SKS, Torsgatan 2, 111 23 Stockholm, Sweden.

CAREER: Clergyman of the Swedish National Church and clergyman of the Norwegian Sunday school secretary in Oslo, Norway, 1948-50; Swedish Church (Lutheran), diocesan curate in Straengnaes, 1950-55, curate and diocesan consultant in National Church, Stockholm, 1955-58; headmaster at Pedagogical Institute, Stockholm, and Christian Education Association of the Swedish Church, Stockholm, 1958-67; headmaster of Adult Education in the Churches of Sweden, 1967—.

WRITINGS: Dagens uppfostrings debatt, Studiebokfoerlaget, 1955; *De Viktigaste aaren,* Verbum, 1958, translation by Gene J. Lund published as *Those Most Important Years: Christian Training in Early Childhood,* Augsburg, 1966; *Det Gaeller vaara barn,* Verbum, 1960; *Fostran, Undervisning,* Verbum, 1970; *Aat vara foersamlingsfadder,* Verbum, 1970; *Foeraldra kunskap: De lyckliga aren,* Verbum, 1975; *Vaexa tar tid,* Verbum, 1977; *Magna tar tid,* Verbum, 1978.

* * *

OULAHAN, Richard 1918-

PERSONAL: Born August 8, 1918, in Washington, D.C.; son of Richard (a broker) and Mildred (Bacon) Oulahan; married Anne Regan, January 25, 1946; children: Carroll (Mrs. Thaddeus Sweet III), Richard, Molly (Mrs. Anthony Ventrella, Jr.), Dennis, Anthony, Joseph, Anne. *Education:* Attended University of North Carolina, 1937-38, and George Washington University, 1938-41. *Politics:* Democrat. *Religion:* Christian. *Agent:* Phyllis Jackson, International Creative Management, 40 West 57th St., New York, N.Y. 10019.

CAREER: Washington Post, Washington, D.C., reporter, 1938-42; Time, Inc., New York, N.Y., writer and correspondent for *Time,* 1947-62, writer for *Life,* 1962-68; freelance writer for magazines and stringer for Time-Life News Service in Madrid, Spain. *Military service:* U.S. Army, 1942-46; became captain.

WRITINGS: Life Guide to Mexico City, Time, Inc., 1967; *The Man Who: The Story of the Democratic National Convention of 1932,* Dial, 1971. Contributor to *Life Pictorial Atlas of the World,* Time, Inc., 1961; contributor to periodicals, including *Sports Illustrated, Saturday Review, Signature,* and *Reader's Digest.*

WORK IN PROGRESS: Political and travel reportage.

BIOGRAPHICAL/CRITICAL SOURCES: Best Sellers, March 1, 1971.†

* * *

OVARD, Glen F. 1928-

PERSONAL: Born July 24, 1928, in Henefer, Utah; married Beverly Bourne, December 27, 1948; children: Jacqueline, Kim, Ramona, David, Roxann, Kristi, Mailani. *Education:* Brigham Young University, B.S., 1949, M.Ed., 1954; Stanford University, Ed.D., 1959; additional graduate study at University of Utah, 1950, and Utah State University, 1951. *Office:* Department of Education, Brigham Young University, Provo, Utah 84601.

CAREER: Uintah School District, Vernal, Utah, high school counselor and teacher of social studies, 1949-52, principal, 1952-56; Brigham Young University, Provo, Utah, instructor in teacher education, 1956-57, assistant professor, 1959-61, associate professor, 1961-63, professor of education, 1963; curriculum consultant and senior high school supervisor for Alpine School District, American Fork, Utah, 1963-64; Brigham Young University, professor of education, 1964—, coordinator of education experimental programs, 1964-69. Program director, Rocky Mountain Educational Laboratory, 1966-67. President, Individualizing Instruction and Learning—World Wide Associates, 1969—. Summer professor at North Carolina College at Durham (now North Carolina Central University) and University of Missouri, 1967; summer workshop director and teacher in Hawaii for Pepperdine College (now University), 1969; director of conferences and workshops for Church College of Hawaii, 1970-71, and La Verne College, 1972. Consultant to Governor of Utah and Utah School Study Committee in Education and Economics, 1964, Kettering Foundation, 1967-70, and Hawaii State Department of Education, 1970-71.

WRITINGS: (Co-author) *Economic Education,* Utah State Department of Public Instruction, 1959; (editor) *On Planning Academic Classrooms: A Guide for Secondary School Planners,* Bruce, 1962; (editor) *Individualizing Instruction: The Administrator's Role,* Utah State Department of Public Instruction, 1965; (editor with Hugh Baird) *A Comprehensive Regional Approach to Small School Development,* Utah State Department of Public Instruction, 1966; *Administration of the Changing Secondary School,* Macmillan, 1966; (editor and contributor) *Change and Secondary School Administration: A Book of Readings,* Macmillan, 1968; (editor) *American Values in Conflict: In a Free Society and in Our Schools,* Utah Department of Public Instruction, 1969; (with J. Kenneth Davies) *Economics in the American System,* Lippincott, 1970, revised edition, 1976; (with Philip Kapfer) *Preparing and Using Individualized Learning Packages,* Educational Technology Publications, 1971; (with Patsy Salki) *Teachers Guide to Individualized Education,* Hawaii State Department of Education, 1972. Writer of monographs, research reports, and proposals; contributor of about fifteen articles to education journals.

WORK IN PROGRESS: Individualizing Instruction and Learning; writing on flexible scheduling, the continuous progress school, models for administration training.

* * *

OWEN, Jack 1929-
(Jack Dykes)

PERSONAL: Born June 21, 1929, in Yorkshire, England. *Home:* 46 Kingsway, Cottingham, North Humberside

HU16 5BB, England. *Agent:* Richard Gollner, Radala & Associates, 17 Avenue Mansions, Finchley Rd., London NW3 7AX, England.

CAREER: Commissioners of Customs and Excise, London, England, customs and excise officer, 1951—. *Military service:* British Army, 1947-49.

WRITINGS—Under pseudonym Jack Dykes; novels, except as indicated: *The Taste of Yesterday,* Dent, 1969; *Pig in the Middle,* Dent, 1971; *Harpoon to Kill,* Dent, 1972; *Smuggling on the Yorkshire Coast* (nonfiction), Dalesman Publishing, 1978.

WORK IN PROGRESS: The Whalers' Graveyard, a book about England's last Arctic whaler; *Roll, Alabama, Roll!,* a novel about the Confederacy's British gunboat.

SIDELIGHTS: Jack Owen told *CA:* "Writing is damned hard work. I wish I knew why I do it."

*   *   *

PADBERG, Daniel I(van) 1931-

PERSONAL: Born November 9, 1931, in Summersville, Mo.; son of Christopher Edward (a farmer) and Ruth (Badgely) Padberg; married Mildred True (an occupational therapist), August 5, 1956; children: Susan E., Jean E., Carol N. *Education:* University of Missouri, B.S., 1953, M.S., 1955; University of California, Berkeley, Ph.D., 1961. *Politics:* Independent. *Religion:* Protestant. *Home:* 1505 Alma Dr., Champaign, Ill. 61820. *Office:* College of Agriculture, University of Illinois, Urbana, Ill. 61801.

CAREER: Ohio State University, Columbus, assistant professor of agricultural economics, 1961-64; National Commission on Food Marketing, Washington, D.C. project leader in retailing, 1965-66; Cornell University, Itaca, N.Y., associate professor, 1966-71, professor of marketing, 1971-75; University of Illinois at Urbana-Champaign, head of department of agricultural economics, 1975—. Member, White House Task Force on farmer bargaining, 1967-68. Narrated a television documentary on food prices, 1972. *Military service:* U.S. Navy, 1955-58; became lieutenant junior grade, U.S. Naval Reserve, 1958-68; became lieutenant commander. *Member:* American Association for the Advancement of Science, American Agricultural Economics Association.

WRITINGS: Economics of Food Retailing, Food Distribution Program, Cornell University, 1968; *Today's Food Broker,* Chainstore Publishing Co., 1971. Also author of numerous papers on marketing and agricultural economics. Member of editorial council, *American Journal of Agricultural Economics,* 1971-74.

WORK IN PROGRESS: A study of nutritional labeling.

*   *   *

PAGE, Roch 1939-

PERSONAL: Born June 10, 1939, in Chicoutimi, Quebec, Canada; son of Jean-Joseph and Bella (Bouchard) Page. *Education:* Petit Seminaire, Chicoutimi, Quebec, B.A., 1960; Grand Seminaire St.-Thomas d'Aquin, B.Th., 1964; Gregorian University, Rome, Italy, B.D.C., 1966, L.D.C., 1967; St. Paul University, Ottawa, Ontario, D.D.C., 1968, Ph.D., 1968. *Home:* 223 Main, Ottawa, Ontario, Canada. *Office:* Faculty of Canon Law, St. Paul University, Ottawa, Ontario, Canada.

CAREER: Ordained Roman Catholic priest, 1964; Petit Seminaire, Chicoutimi, Quebec, professor of Catachese,

1964-65; Grand Seminaire St.-Thomas-d'Aquin, Chicoutimi, spiritual director, 1969-77; St. Paul University, Ottawa, Ontario, professor of Canon law, 1977—. Visiting professor, University of Three Rivers, 1971. Member of ecclesiastical tribunal of Chicoutimi and of Quebec. *Member:* Canadian Canon Law Society.

WRITINGS: Conseil diocesain de pastorale, Fides, 1969, translation by Bernard A. Prince published as *The Diocesan Pastoral Council,* Paulist/Newman, 1970; (co-author) *Secularite et engagement chretien,* Fides, 1976. Contributor to *Origins* and *Studia Canonica.*

BIOGRAPHICAL/CRITICAL SOURCES: Osservatore Romano (French edition), May 22, 1970; *Canadian Register,* November 7, 1970.

*   *   *

PAI, Young 1929-

PERSONAL: Born April 21, 1929, in Pyungyang, Korea; son of Minsoo (a minister) and Soonoak (Choi) Pai; married Sunok Chun (a physician), September 3, 1955; children: Jeannette, David, Loraine. *Education:* Macalester College, B.A., 1951, M.Ed., 1953; Rutgers University, Ed.D., 1959. *Home:* 5500 West 98th Pl., Overland Park, Kan. 66207. *Office:* School of Education, University of Missouri, Kansas City, Mo. 64110.

CAREER: Ewha Women's University, Seoul, Korea, assistant professor of education, 1954-55; New Jersey School Development Council, New Brunswick, N.J., research associate, 1956-59; Rutgers University, New Brunswick, instructor in philosophy and history of education, 1958-59; Park College, Parkville, Mo., assistant professor, 1959-62, associate professor, 1962-66, professor of education, 1966, director of English Language Institute, 1960-61, 1964-65, dean of men, 1960-62, associate dean of college, 1962-64, acting dean, 1962-63, chairman of Division of Social Sciences, 1965; University of Missouri—Kansas City, visiting associate professor, 1966-67, associate professor, 1967-70, professor of education, 1970—, Division of Social-Philosophical Foundations of Education, acting chairman, 1970-71, chairman, 1972—. Visiting lecturer at Yunseu University, 1955, and Pennsylvania State University, summer, 1960; visiting professor, Wayne State University, summer, 1962. Chairman, Kansas City (Mo.) Committee for International Visitors and Foreign Students, 1964-65.

MEMBER: Philosophy of Education Society (fellow; secretary-treasurer, 1972-74; president, 1977-78), American Educational Studies Association, Philosophy of Science Association, American Educational Research Association, Mind Association, American Association of University Professors, Kappa Delta Pi. *Awards, honors:* Danforth associate, 1970.

WRITINGS: (Editor with Joseph Myers, and contributor) *Philosophic Problems and Education,* Lippincott, 1967; *Teaching, Learning, and the Mind,* Houghton, 1973; (with Van Cleeve Morris) *Philosophy and the American School,* Houghton, 1976. Contributor to education journals.

WORK IN PROGRESS: Challenges to the American School.

AVOCATIONAL INTERESTS: Piano, vocal music, especially German lieder.

*   *   *

PAINE, Roberta M. 1925-

PERSONAL: Born October 2, 1925, in Los Angeles, Calif.;

daughter of Edward Harris (an engineer) and Josephine (Speakman) Paine. *Education:* Barnard College, A.B., 1947; Bryn Mawr College, M.A., 1953. *Politics:* Independent. *Religion:* Protestant. *Residence:* New York, N.Y. *Office:* Metropolitan Museum of Art, 5th Ave. and 82nd St., New York, N.Y. 10028.

CAREER: Metropolitan Museum of Art, New York, N.Y., senior lecturer, 1953-75, museum educator, 1975—.

WRITINGS—Published by Metropolitan Museum of Art, except as indicated: *How to Look at Paintings,* 1959; *The Renaissance,* 1960; *The Age of Exploration,* 1960; *India's Gods and Kings,* 1962; *Greek Mythology,* 1964; *Looking at Sculpture,* Lothrop, 1968; *The First Hundred Years,* 1971; *Looking at Architecture,* Lothrop, 1974.

WORK IN PROGRESS: A book on Egyptian mythology.

BIOGRAPHICAL/CRITICAL SOURCES: Best Sellers, November 1, 1968; *Children's Book World,* November 3, 1968; *New York Times Book Review,* November 3, 1968.

* * *

PAINTER, Helen W(elch) 1913-

PERSONAL: Born September 25, 1913, in Covington, Ind.; daughter of Charles V. (a farmer) and Rebecca Anne (Huffer) Welch; married William I. Painter (a former university professor), August 9, 1933 (died, 1972). *Education:* Indiana University, A.B., 1935, M.A., 1936, Ed.D., 1941. *Home:* 88 Monroe Ave., Cuyahoga Falls, Ohio 44221. *Office:* Satterfield Hall, Kent State University, Kent, Ohio 44242.

CAREER: Indiana University at Bloomington, psychologist, 1938-42; Shurtleff College, Alton, Ill., instructor in education and psychology, 1944-45; University of Akron, Akron, Ohio, professor of elementary education, 1945-67; Kent State University, Kent, Ohio, professor of elementary education and English, 1967—. Visiting professor at New Mexico Highlands University, 1938, Colorado College, 1963, and Ohio State University, 1965. Director, National Defense Education Act Institute, Kent State University, 1968. Consultant, Hawaii State Department of Education, 1968. Director, annual parent education workshop, Ohio Congress of Parents and Teachers, 1953-66. *Member:* International Reading Association, College English Association, National Council of Teachers of English, National Education Association, American Association of University Professors, Ohio Education Association, Ohio International Reading Association, Ohio Congress of Parents and Teachers (honorary), Delta Kappa Gamma, Pi Lambda Theta, Kappa Delta Pi, Eta Sigma Phi, Alpha Epsilon, Alpha Sigma Lambda.

WRITINGS: Mastering Your Language, grade seven, Lyons & Carnahan, 1966; *Mastering Your Language,* grade eight, Lyons & Carnahan, 1966; *Poetry and Children,* International Reading Association, 1970; (editor) *Reaching Children and Young People through Literature,* International Reading Association, 1971. Editor of column on children's literature, *Ohio Reading Teacher,* 1971-72; contributor to *Elementary English, Reading Teacher, Wilson Library Bulletin, Grade Teacher, English Journal,* and other professional journals.

SIDELIGHTS: Helen W. Painter has traveled to the Soviet Union, India, Iceland, Africa, South America, Guatemala, the South Pacific, the Orient, Mexico, Canada, and Western Europe.

PALEY, Morton D(avid) 1935-

PERSONAL: Born July 27, 1935, in New York, N.Y.; son of George and Augusta (Goldstein) Paley. *Education:* City College of New York (now City College of the City University of New York), B.A., 1957; attended Johns Hopkins University, spring, 1957; Brown University, M.A., 1958; Columbia University, Ph.D., 1964. *Office:* Department of English, University of California, Berkeley, Calif. 94720.

CAREER: Instructor in English at City College of the City University of New York, New York City, 1958-64, and New School for Social Research, New York City, 1962-64; University of California, Berkeley, 1964—, assistant professor, 1964-70, currently professor of English. *Member:* Poet's Workshop (London), Point Reyes Bird Observatory, Chelsea Arts Club (London). *Awards, honors:* San Francisco Browning Society Award; American Council of Learned Societies study fellowship, 1969-70; Guggenheim fellow, 1972-73.

WRITINGS: (Compiler) *20th Century Interpretations of "Songs of Innocence and of Experience,"* Prentice-Hall, 1969; *Energy and Imagination: A Study of the Development of Blake's Thought,* Clarendon Press, 1970; (co-editor) *William Blake: Essays in Honour of Sir Geoffrey Keynes,* Clarendon Press, 1973; *William Blake,* Phaidon Press, 1978. Contributor of numerous articles and reviews on Blake to learned journals, and of many poems to literary magazines. Co-editor, *Blake Newsletter.*

WORK IN PROGRESS: A book-length study of William Blake's *Jerusalem;* a book of poems, *The Tribute Money,* completed and awaiting publication; a long-range project, a book on the inter-relationships of poetry and painting in the 18th and early 19th centuries.

AVOCATIONAL INTERESTS: Birds, the cultures of the American Indian, drama, ballet, museum-going "for pleasure as well as for professional reasons," and travel in Europe, particularly England.

BIOGRAPHICAL/CRITICAL SOURCES: Modern Language Quarterly, September, 1971; *Times Literary Supplement,* December 10, 1971.

* * *

PALLAS, Dorothy Constance 1933-1971

1933—October 11, 1971; American ornithologist and author of nature books for children. Obituaries: *Publishers Weekly,* November 15, 1971.

* * *

PARENTE, Pascal P(rosper) 1890-1971

September 28, 1890—August 9, 1971; Italian-born American Roman Catholic theologian, priest, and educator. Obituaries: *New York Times,* August 11, 1971; *Washington Post,* August 11, 1971. (See index for *CA* sketch)

* * *

PARISH, James Robert 1944-

PERSONAL: Born April 21, 1944, in Cambridge, Mass.; son of Fred A. (an allergist) and Ann Lois (Magilavy) Parish. *Education:* University of Pennsylvania, B.A., 1964, LL.B., 1967. *Religion:* Jewish. *Home:* 225 East 70th St., No. 2F, New York, N.Y. 10021.

CAREER: Admitted to the bar of New York State, 1968; Cape Playhouse, Dennis, Mass., publicist and properties manager, 1961-64; Entertainment Copyright Research Co.,

Inc., New York City, director, 1967-68; *Variety*, New York City, reporter, 1968-69; *Motion Picture Daily*, New York City, reporter, 1969; Harold Rand & Co., Inc. (publicity firm), New York City, entertainment publicist, 1969-70; free-lance writer, 1970—. *Member:* Kate Smith U.S.A. Friends' Club, Phi Beta Kappa.

WRITINGS: (Associate editor with Paul Michael) *The American Movies Reference Book*, Prentice-Hall, 1969; (with Alan G. Barbour and Alvin H. Marill) *Errol Flynn: A Pictorial History*, Cinefax, 1969; (with Barbour and Marill) *Boris Karloff: A Pictorial History*, Cinefax, 1969; (associate editor with Leonard Maltin) *TV Movies*, New American Library, 1969.

(With Michael) *A Pictorial History of the Emmy Awards*, Crown, 1970; *The Fox Girls*, Arlington House, 1971; (editor) *The Great Movie Series*, A. S. Barnes, 1971; (with Marill) *The Cinema of Edward G. Robinson*, A. S. Barnes, 1972; *The Paramount Pretties*, Arlington House, 1972; *The Slapstick Queens*, Yoseloff, 1973; *Actors' Television Credits: 1950-1972*, Scarecrow, 1973, supplement, 1977; (with Ronald L. Bowers) *The MGM Stock Company*, Arlington House, 1973; (with Michael R. Pitts) *The Great Spy Pictures*, Scarecrow, 1974; *The RKO Gals*, Arlington House, 1974; (with Steven Whitney) *The George Raft File*, Drake, 1974; (with Whitney) *Vincent Price Unmasked*, Drake, 1974; *Hollywood's Great Love Teams*, Arlington House, 1974; (with Pitts) *Film Directors' Guide: The U.S.*, Scarecrow, 1974.

(With Don E. Stanke) *The Glamour Girls*, Arlington House, 1975; *The Elvis Presley Scrapbook*, Ballantine, 1975; (with Jack Ano) *Liza!*, Pocket Books, 1975; (with Pitts) *The Great Gangster Pictures*, Scarecrow, 1976; (with Pitts) *The Great Western Pictures*, Scarecrow, 1976; (with Leonard DeCarl) *Hollywood Players: The Forties*, Arlington House, 1976; (with William T. Leonard) *Hollywood Players: The Thirties*, Arlington House, 1976; *The Tough Guys*, Arlington House, 1976; *Great Child Stars*, Ace Books, 1976; *Great Western Stars*, Ace Books, 1976; (with Stanke) *The Swashbucklers*, Arlington House, 1976; *Great Movie Heroes*, Barnes & Noble, 1976; *The Jeanette MacDonald Story*, Mason/Charter, 1976; (with Pitts) *The Great Science Fiction Pictures*, Scarecrow, 1977; (with Stanke) *The All-Americans*, Arlington House, 1977; *The Complete Elvis Presley Scrapbook*, Ballantine, 1977; *Film Actors' Guide: Western Europe*, Scarecrow, 1977; (with Stanke) *The Leading Ladies*, Arlington House, 1977; *Hollywood Character Actors*, Arlington House, 1978; *Hollywood Beauties*, Arlington House, 1978; (with Leonard) *The Funsters*, Arlington House, 1978; (with Pitts) *Hollywood on Hollywood*, Scarecrow, 1978; *Hollywood Regulars*, Arlington House, 1978; (with Stanke) *The Forties Gals*, Arlington House, 1978; (with Greg W. Mank) *The Best of MGM*, Arlington House, 1978. Contributor to film magazines.

* * *

PARKER, Franklin 1921-

PERSONAL: Born June 2, 1921, in New York, N.Y.; married Betty June Persinger, June 12, 1950. *Education:* Berea College, B.A., 1949; University of Illinois, M.S., 1950; George Peabody College for Teachers, Ed.D., 1956. *Home:* 750 Amherst Rd., Morgantown, W.Va. 26505. *Office:* West Virginia University, 602-D Allen Hall, Morgantown, W.Va. 26506.

CAREER: Ferrum Junior College, Ferrum, Va., librarian, 1950-52; Belmont College, Nashville, Tenn., librarian and

teacher of library science, 1952-53; George Peabody College for Teachers, Nashville, circulation librarian, 1955-56; State Teachers College (now State University of New York College at New Paltz), associate professor of education, 1956-57; University of Texas, Main University (now University of Texas at Austin), associate professor of education, 1957-64; University of Oklahoma, Norman, professor of education, 1964-68; West Virginia University, Morgantown, Benedum Professor of Education, 1968—. Visiting summer professor at University of Calgary, 1969, University of Alberta, 1970, Northern Arizona University, 1971, University of Lethbridge, 1971, 1972, 1973, and Memorial University of Newfoundland, 1974. Consultant, U.S. Office of Education, 1966—. *Military service:* U.S. Army Air Forces, 1942-46.

MEMBER: African Studies Association (fellow), Philosophy of Education Society (fellow), History of Education Society (president, 1963-64), Comparative and International Education Society (vice-president, 1963-64; international secretary, 1965-68), Southwestern Philosophy of Education Society (president, 1960), Kappa Delta Pi, Phi Delta Kappa, Pi Gamma Mu, Phi Kappa Phi. *Awards, honors:* Harold R. W. Benjamin Fellow in International Education at University College of Rhodesia, 1957-58; Fulbright senior research scholar at Rhodes-Livingstone Institute, Zambia, 1961-62; Distinguished Alumnus Award, George Peabody College for Teachers, 1970.

WRITINGS: African Development and Education in Southern Rhodesia, Ohio State University Press, 1960; *Africa South of the Sahara*, Prentice-Hall, 1966; (with Brian Rose and others) *Education in Southern Africa*, Collier, 1970; *George Peabody: A Biography*, Vanderbilt University Press, 1971; (editor with wife, Betty June Parker) *American Dissertations on Foreign Education: A Bibliography with Abstracts*, Whitson Publishing, Volume I: *Canada*, 1971, Volume II: *India*, 1971, Volume III: *Japan*, 1972, Volume IV: *Africa*, 1973, Volume V: *Scandinavia*, 1974, Volume VI: *China*, two parts, 1974, Volume VII: *Korea*, 1976, Volume VIII: *Mexico*, 1976, Volume IX: *South America*, 1977, Volume X: *Central America*, 1977, Volume XI: *Pakistan and Bangladesh*, 1978, Volume XII: *Iran and Iraq*, 1978; *The Battle of the Books: Kanawha County*, Phi Delta Kappa, 1975; *What Can We Learn from the Schools of China?*, Phi Delta Kappa, 1977; (editor with Betty June Parker) *Women's Education: Annotated Bibliography of Books, Reports, and Dissertations*, Greenwood Press, in press.

Contributor: William W. Brickman and Stanley Lehrer, editors, *John Dewey: Master Educator*, Society for the Advancement of Education, 1961; Stewart Fraser, editor, *Government Policy and International Education*, Wiley, 1965; R. M. Thomas and others, editors, *Strategies for Curriculum Change: Cases from Thirteen Nations*, International Textbook Co., 1968; C. A. Bucher and Myra Goldman, editors, *Dimensions of Physical Education*, Mosby, 1969, 2nd edition, 1972; Fraser, editor, *International Understandings and Misunderstandings*, George Peabody College for Teachers, 1969; S. M. Holton, editor, *Understanding the American Public High School*, Allyn & Bacon, 1969; R. C. Waltmire, editor, *Readings for Secondary Education*, Central Michigan University Press, 1970; Raymond J. Agan and Joseph Hajda, editors, *Curriculum for Man in an International World*, Kansas State University, 1971; Harold R. W. Benjamin, editor, *The Saber-Tooth Curriculum*, memorial edition, McGraw, 1972; Brickman and Lehrer, editors, *Education and the New Faces of the Disadvantaged*, Wiley, 1972; John Barratt, editor, *Accelerated Development in*

Southern Africa, Macmillan, 1974; Francesco Cordasco and Brickman, editors, *A Bibliography of American Educational History: An Annotated and Classified Guide*, AMS Press, 1975; J. A. Johnston, editor, *Six Questions: Controversy and Conflict in Education*, Wiley, 1975; Glenn Smith and Charles R. Kniker, editors, *Myth and Reality: A Reader in Education*, 2nd edition, Allyn & Bacon, 1975.

Contributor of more than two hundred articles to encyclopedias and yearbooks, including *Americana Annual, Reader's Digest Almanac and Yearbook, Compton Yearbook, Encyclopedia of Education, Dictionary of Scientific Biography*, and *Collier's Yearbook;* contributor of more than 350 articles and reviews to journals. Member of editorial board, *Western Carolina University Journal of Education*, 1969-77, *Journal of Thought*, 1969—, *West Virginia University Magazine*, 1970—, *Vidya*, 1970-73, *Library College Journal Omnibus*, 1970-75, and *Core*. Book review editor, *Phi Delta Kappan*, 1976-77.

WORK IN PROGRESS: World Universities: Brief Histories, for Greenwood Press; further volumes of *American Dissertations on Foreign Education*.

SIDELIGHTS: Franklin Parker told *CA:* "My research, editing, and writing, have come mainly from my teaching fields and have allowed me to reach beyond the classroom to a larger audience. Luckily for over a quarter century I have had in my wife Betty June Parker an extraordinary collaborator. Normal irritations during work are soon forgotten, supplanted by satisfaction in the end product. The real joy is in conceiving and executing a writing project and, of course, in trying to make the next one more informative, creative, and aesthetically satisfying."

*   *   *

PARKER, Hershel 1935-
(Samuel Willis)

PERSONAL: Born November 26, 1935, in Comanche, Okla.; son of Lloyd (a botanist) and Martha (Costner) Parker; married Joanne Johnson (an English professor), June 29, 1963; children: Alison, Sabrina. *Education:* Lamar State College (now Lamar University), B.A., 1959; Northwestern University, M.A., 1960, Ph.D., 1963. *Religion:* None. *Office:* Department of English, University of Southern California, Los Angeles, Calif. 90007.

CAREER: Telegraph operator for Kansas City Southern Railway, 1952-59; University of Southern California, Los Angeles, professor of English, 1968—. *Member:* Modern Language Association of America (member of executive committee for American literature of the nineteenth century), Melville Society, Center for Editions of American Authors (member of executive committee, 1971-74). *Awards, honors:* Woodrow Wilson fellowship, 1959-60; Guggenheim fellowship, 1974-75; University of Southern California Creative Scholarship and Research Award, 1977.

WRITINGS—Editor: (Compiler with Tyrus Hillway) *Directory of Melville Dissertations*, Melville Society, 1962; *Gansevoort Melville's 1846 London Journal and Letters from England, 1845* (originally published in *Bulletin* of New York Public Library, December, 1965, and January, February, 1966), New York Public Library, 1966; *The Recognition of Herman Melville: Selected Criticism Since 1846*, University of Michigan Press, 1967; (with Harrison Hayford) Herman Melville, *Moby-Dick: An Authoritative Text* (includes reviews and letters by Melville, analogues and sources, and criticism), Norton, 1967; (and contributor with Hayford and G. Thomas Tanselle) *The Writings of Herman*

Melville, six volumes, Northwestern University Press and Newberry Library, Volume I: *Typee: A Peep at Polynesian Life*, 1968, Volume II: *Omoo: A Narrative of Adventures in the South Seas*, 1968, Volume III: *Redburn: His First Voyage; Being the Sailor-Boy Confessions and Reminiscences of the Son-of-a-Gentleman, in the Merchant Service*, 1969, Volume IV: *Mardi and a Voyage Thither*, 1970, Volume V: *White-Jacket; or, The World in a Man-of-War*, 1970, Volume VI: *Pierre*, 1971; (with Hayford) *Moby-Dick as Doubloon: Essays and Extracts, 1851-1970*, Norton, 1970; Herman Melville, *The Confidence-Man: His Masquerade; An Authoritative Text* (includes backgrounds and sources, reviews, criticism, and annotated bibliography), Norton, 1971; *Shorter Works of Hawthorne and Melville*, C. E. Merrill, 1972; (with Steven Mailloux) *Checklist of Melville Reviews*, Melville Society, 1975.

Also editor and author of introduction to Jonathan Macy's limited edition of Melville's *The Confidence-Man*, 1972. Contributor of articles, some under pseudonym Samuel Willis, to *American Literature, Studies in Short Fiction, New York Historical Society Quarterly, Modern Language Quarterly, Proof, Nineteenth-Century Fiction, Papers of the Bibliographical Society of America, Mississippi Quarterly, Studies in the Novel*, and other literary periodicals; also contributor of the Melville chapter to the annual volume of *American Literary Scholarship*, 1972—, and *Proof Yearbook of American Bibliographical and Textual Studies*, 1973.

WORK IN PROGRESS: Continuing work on *The Writings of Herman Melville* for Northwestern University Press and Newberry Library, especially *Moby-Dick, The Confidence-Man*, and *Clarel;* also engaged in various collaborative projects.

SIDELIGHTS: Hershel Parker told *CA:* "Much of my own writing in the last few years have in common the interpretive use of historical, biographical, and textual evidence. The Center for Editions of American Authors was in large part a failure but it established standards of scholarship that a good number of all-round scholar-critics are carrying on. I see my work as part of a 'New Scholarship,' the most significant movement in American literary study in several decades."

*   *   *

PARKER, W(illiam) H(enry) 1912-

PERSONAL: Born September 18, 1912, in Galt, Ontario, Canada; son of William Arthur (a builder) and Mabel (Peal) Parker; married Marjorie Dean, October 20, 1945; children: William Andrew, Richard. *Education:* Oxford University, B.A. (modern history; honors), 1934, B.A. (geography; honors), 1935, B.Sc., 1939, D.Phil., 1958. *Office:* Christ Church, Oxford University, Oxford OX1 1DP, England.

CAREER: Royal Military Academy, Sandhurst, England, senior lecturer in geography, 1947-52; McMaster University, Hamilton, Ontario, assistant professor of geography, 1952-56; University of Manitoba, Winnipeg, associate professor of geography, 1956-61; Oxford University, Oxford, England, lecturer in geography of the Soviet Union, 1964—. *Member:* Royal Geographical Society, Association of American Geographers, Canadian Association of Geographers, National Association for Soviet and East European Studies (Great Britain), Geographical Association (Great Britain).

WRITINGS: Canada, Nagel, 1955; *Anglo-America: The United States and Canada*, University of London Press, 1962, 2nd edition, 1971; *An Historical Geography of Russia*,

Aldine, 1969; *The Soviet Union,* Aldine, 1969; *The Superpowers: The United States and Soviet Union Compared,* Macmillan, 1972; *How They Live and Work: The Russians,* Praeger, 1973. Contributor to geographical journals.

WORK IN PROGRESS: Soviet Motor Transport and the Soviet Motor Industry.

SIDELIGHTS: W. H. Parker has traveled widely in the Soviet Union—by rail, plane, river boat, and car.

*   *   *

PARKES, Henry B. 1904-1972

November 2, 1904—January 7, 1972; British-born historian and educator. Obituaries: *New York Times,* January 8, 1972.

*   *   *

PARNAS, Raymond I. 1937-

PERSONAL: Born March 28, 1937, in St. Louis, Mo.; son of Milton and Evelyn (Barken) Parnas; married Joan Zeffren (a correctional counselor), June 10, 1962 (divorced); children: Andrew John, Daniel Seth. *Education:* Washington University, St. Louis, Mo., A.B., 1961, J.D., 1964; University of Wisconsin, LL.M., 1967, S.J.D., 1972. *Home:* 606 Sunset Ct., Davis, Calif. 95616. *Office:* School of Law, University of California, Davis, Calif. 95616.

CAREER: Goldstein & Price (law firm), St. Louis, Mo., associate, 1964-66; University of Arkansas, Fayetteville, assistant professor of law, 1967-69; University of California, Davis, professor of law, 1969—. Research lawyer, American Bar Foundation, 1970-71. Fellow of Social Science Methods in Legal Education Institute, University of Denver, 1968; fellow, National Endowment for the Humanities. Consultant, Arkansas Prison Project, 1967-69; senior consultant, California Senate Select Committee on Penal Institutions. *Military service:* U.S. Army, 1956-58. *Member:* Missouri Bar Association.

WRITINGS: (With Frank W. Miller, Robert O. Dawson, and George E. Dix) *Cases and Materials on the Administration of Criminal Justice and Related Processes,* Foundation Press, 1971, published as four books titled, *The Police Function,* 1971, *The Correctional Process,* 1971, *The Juvenile Justice Process,* 1971, and *The Mental Health Process,* 1971. Contributor to law journals.

WORK IN PROGRESS: I am, I cried: Memoirs of a Nobody, a novel; research on the relevance of the criminal law to spousal violence; an article proposing an alternative to plea bargaining.

SIDELIGHTS: Raymond I. Parnas was one of the primary draftsmen and negotiators of the Uniform Determinate Sentencing Act of 1976, signed into law in California in September, 1976. *Avocational interests:* Gardening, sports.

*   *   *

PASEWARK, William R(obert) 1924-

PERSONAL: Born September 9, 1924, in Mt. Vernon, N.Y.; son of William (a jeweler) and Barbara (Hermann) Pasewark; married M. Jean McHarg, March 17, 1956; children: William Robert, Lisabeth Jean, Jan Alison, Carolyn Ann, Scott Graham, Susan Gayle. *Education:* New York University, B.S., 1949, M.A., 1950, Ph.D., 1956. *Home:* 4403 West 11th St., Lubbock, Tex. 79416. *Office:* Box 4560, Texas Tech University, Lubbock, Tex. 79409.

CAREER: New York University, New York, N.Y., instructor in business education, 1949-51; Meredith College, Raleigh, N.C., associate professor of business education, 1951-52; Michigan State University, East Lansing, assistant professor of business education, 1952-56; Texas Tech University, Lubbock, professor of business education and chairman of the department, 1956—. Field reader, U.S. Office of Education. Consultant, Educational Testing Service, 1969; consultant to local and state educational systems and to two law firms. Member of administrative council, Presbytery of the Southwest; president, Lubbock Area Presbyterian Council, 1969-70. *Military service:* U.S. Marine Corps, 1943-46; became sergeant.

MEMBER: International Platform Association, National Education Association, National Business Education Association, American Vocational Association, Administrative Management Society, Mountain Plains Business Education Association, Texas Business Education Association, West Texas Museum Association, Pi Omega Pi, Kappa Phi Kappa, Phi Delta Kappa, Delta Pi Epsilon, Alpha Kappa Psi, Kappa Delta Pi, Lions International (director, 1968). *Awards, honors:* New York University Founders Day award for outstanding scholarship; selected an "Outstanding Educator of America," 1971; State of Texas Teacher of the Year from Texas Business Education Association; Certificate of Citation from Texas House of Representatives for contributions as a teacher and author.

WRITINGS: Teaching Typewriting through Television, Bureau of Business Research, Michigan State University, 1956; (with Peter L. Agnew) *Rotary Calculator Course,* 4th edition (Pasewark was not associated with earlier editions), South-Western, 1962; (with Agnew) *Key-Driven Calculator Course,* 4th edition (Pasewark was not associated with earlier editions), South-Western, 1962; (with Agnew and James B. Meehan) *Clerical Office Practice,* 3rd edition (Pasewark was not associated with earlier editions), South-Western, 1962, 5th edition, 1973; (with Agnew) *Full-Keyboard Adding-Listing Machine Course,* 3rd edition (Pasewark was not associated with earlier editions), South-Western, 1963; (with Agnew) *Ten-Key Adding-Listing Machine and Printing Calculator Course,* 3rd edition (Pasewark was not associated with earlier editions), South-Western, 1963, 4th edition (with Nicholas Cornelia), 1973; *Duplicating Machine Processes,* South-Western, 1971, 2nd edition, 1975; (with Cornelia and Agnew) *Office Machines Course,* 4th edition (Pasewark was not associated with earlier editions), South-Western, 1971; (with E. Dolores Kilchenstein) *Planning the Implementation of a Business Education Learning System,* Texas Education Agency, 1971; (with Meehan and Mary E. Oliverio) *Secretarial Office Procedures.* 8th edition (Pasewark was not associated with earlier editions), South-Western, 1972, 9th edition, 1977; (with Kilchenstein) *Individualized Instruction in Business and Office Education,* American Vocational Association, 1973; *Electronic and Mechanical Printing Calculator Course,* South-Western, 1974; *Electronic Display Calculator Course,* South-Western, 1975. Contributor to *Balance Sheet* and *Texas Techsan.* Associate editor, *American Business Education Yearbook,* 1953.

WORK IN PROGRESS: Research into improving college teaching, increasing office production, and efficient style for typewritten reports.

SIDELIGHTS: William R. Pasewark has traveled to Europe and many Pacific islands. His areas of vocational interest are developing educational learning systems and an institute to improve office production, and improving office production, college instruction, and vocational education. He told *CA:* "One of the most serious domestic, national problems is the devastating sequence of inappropriate education which contributes to unemployment, causing poverty and welfare that results in higher taxes. Major universities should accept their responsibility for helping to solve this serious domestic problem. Universities must start solving practical domestic problems if they expect to receive continued support from tax payers.''

* * *

PASSAGE, Charles Edward 1913-

PERSONAL: Born December 13, 1913, in Dansville, N.Y.; son of Willett Gideon (a railway conductor) and Catherine (Embser) Passage. *Education:* Attended University of Grenoble, 1933; University of Rochester, B.A., 1935; Harvard University, M.A., 1938, Ph.D., 1942. *Residence:* Dansville, N.Y.

CAREER: High school teacher of English and French in Orchard Park, N.Y., 1935-37; Harvard University, Cambridge, Mass., instructor in German and Slavic, 1946-49; Northwestern University, Evanston, Ill., assistant professor of German, 1949-50; Columbia University, New York City, assistant professor of German, 1950-53; John Hay Whitney Foundation, New York City, secretary of John Hay fellowships program, 1953-54; Brooklyn College of the City University of New York, Brooklyn, N.Y., assistant professor of German, 1954-56, assistant professor of comparative literature, 1956-60, associate professor, 1960-67, professor of comparative literature, 1967-71. *Military service:* U.S. Army, Signal Corps, cryptanalyst, 1942-45, instructor at Biarritz American University, 1945. *Member:* Phi Beta Kappa, Delta Phi Alpha. *Awards, honors:* Sheldon traveling fellowship, Harvard University, 1942.

WRITINGS: Dostoevski the Adapter, University of North Carolina Press, 1954; *The Russian Hoffmannists,* Mouton, 1963; (contributor) Werner Betz, Evelyn S. Coleman, and Kenneth Northcott, editors, *Taylor Starck Festschrift,* Mouton, 1963; *Friedrich Schiller,* Frederick Lingar Publishing, 1975; *Hillyear* (novel), Vantage, 1976.

Translator and author of introduction: Heinrich von Kleist, *The Prince of Homburg* (five-act play translated in verse), Bobbs-Merrill, 1956; Johann C. F. von Schiller, *Wallenstein* (includes *Wallenstein's Camp, The Piccolominis,* and *The Death of Wallenstein;* historical drama translated in verse), Ungar, 1958; Schiller, *Don Carlos* (five-act drama translated in verse), Ungar, 1959; Novalis, *Hymns to the Night and Other Selected Writings* (translated in verse and prose), Bobbs-Merrill, 1960; Schiller, *Mary Stuart* [and] *The Maid of Orleans* (two five-act plays translated in verse), Ungar, 1961; (with Helen M. Mustard) Wolfram von Eschenbach, *Parzival,* Random House, 1961; Schiller, *The Bride of Messina* [and] *William Tell* (also includes the fragment of *Demetrius;* translated in verse), Ungar, 1962; Johann Wolfgang von Goethe, *Iphigenia in Tauris* (five-act play translated in verse), Ungar, 1963; Goethe, *Faust,* Part I-II (translated in meters of the original, with notes), Bobbs-Merrill, 1965; Goethe, *Goetz von Berlichingen* (five-act play), Ungar, 1965; Goethe, *Torquato Tasso* (five-act play translated in verse), Ungar, 1966; Schiller, *Intrigue and Love,* Ungar, 1971; E.T.A. Hoffmann, *Three Maerchen of E.T.A. Hoffmann* (includes *Little Zaches, Surnamed Zinnober,* and *Princess Brambilla,* and *Master Flea*), University of South Carolina Press, 1971; (with James H. Mantinband) *Amphitryon: The Legend and Three Plays* (includes ''Plautus,'' ''Moliere,'' and ''Kleist''), University of North Carolina Press, 1974; von Eschenbach, *Willehalm,* Ungar, 1977.

Contributing translator: Angel Flores, editor, *An Anthology of German Poetry from Hoelderlin to Rilke in English Translation,* Doubleday-Anchor, 1960; Flores, editor, *Medieval Lyrics,* Random House, 1962; Alexander Gode and Frederick Ungar, editors, *An Anthology of German Poetry through the Nineteenth Century,* Ungar, 1964; Flores, editor, *Nineteenth Century German Tales,* Ungar, 1966.

Contributor of translations of poems by Catullus to *Signal* (quarterly review); contributor of his own poems to *Signal* and *Quest,* and articles and reviews to *American Slavic and East European Review, Germanic Review,* and other journals.

WORK IN PROGRESS: Seven plays of Goethe, translated in verse and prose; original works of fiction.

SIDELIGHTS: Charles Edward Passage told *CA:* ''My translations of German classics were undertaken in order to provide texts for courses in comparative literature. In my fiction I hope to explore new paths.'' In addition to French and German, Passage has varying degrees of competence in Latin, Greek, Dano-Norwegian, Italian, classical Arabic, and various older languages.

* * *

PATCHEN, Kenneth 1911-1972

December 13, 1911—January 8, 1972; American poet and graphic artist. Obituaries: *New York Times,* January 9, 1972; *Washington Post,* January 10, 1972; *Newsweek,* January 24, 1972; *Publishers Weekly,* January 24, 1972; *Time,* January 24, 1972. (See index for *CA* sketch)

* * *

PATERSON, Ann 1916-

PERSONAL: Born May 26, 1916, in Columbus, Ohio; daughter of Robert Gildersleeve (a tuberculosis association executive) and Alma (Wacker) Paterson. *Education:* Ohio State University, B.Sc., 1937, M.A., 1939; Columbia University, Ed.D., 1944. *Politics:* Democrat. *Religion:* Protestant. *Home:* 750 Gonzalez Dr., San Francisco, Calif. 94132. *Office:* Department of Physical Education, San Francisco State University, San Francisco, Calif. 94132.

CAREER: Ohio State University, Columbus, instructor, 1937-40, assistant professor, 1941-43, professor of physical education, 1937-56; San Francisco State University, San Francisco, Calif., professor and chairman of department of physical education for women, 1956-68, professor of physical education, 1968—. Member, Ohio Board of Education, Columbus, 1945-56. Member of women's board, U.S. Olympic Committee, 1958-68. *Member:* American Association for Health, Physical Education and Recreation, National Education Association, Association California State College Professors, California State Employees Association, Altrusa Club of San Francisco, San Francisco Hearing Society, California Association for Health, Physical Education and Recreation, California Teachers Association, California State Education Association, Kappa Kappa Gamma, P.E.O.

WRITINGS: (With Eula Lee West) *Team Sports for Girls,* Ronald, 1957, 2nd edition, 1972; (with Edmond C. Hallberg) *Background Readings for Physical Education,* Holt, 1967. Editor, ''New Designs in Health, Physical Education and Recreation'' series, nine volumes, published by C. E. Merrill; member of national editorial board, *The Encyclopedia of Education,* Macmillan, 1971.

PATERSON, R(onald) W(illiam) K(eith) 1933-

PERSONAL: Born September 20, 1933, in Arbroath, Scotland; son of Alfred William (a teacher) and Iris Mary (Guild) Paterson; married Angela Thackeray Marr (an adult education tutor), April 2, 1964. *Education:* University of St. Andrews, M.A., 1955, Dip.Ed., 1958, B.Phil., 1962. *Home:* 215 Boroughbridge Rd., York, England. *Office:* Department of Adult Education, University of Hull, Hull, England.

CAREER: Bromsgrove College of Further Education, Bromsgrove, England, assistant lecturer, 1958-59; University of Manchester, Manchester, England, staff tutor, Holly Royde College, 1959-61; University of Hull, Hull, England, lecturer in philosophy, department of adult education, 1962—. *Military service:* British Army, 1955-57; served in Royal Artillery. *Member:* Mind Association, British Society for Phenomenology, Society for Psychical Research. *Awards, honors:* Ph.D. from University of Hull, for published work, 1972.

WRITINGS: The Nihilistic Egoist: Max Stirner, published for University of Hull by Oxford University Press, 1971; *Values, Education, and the Adult,* Routledge & Kegan Paul, 1978. Contributor of articles and reviews to *Ratio, Philosophical Quarterly, Rewley House Papers, Adult Education,* and *Studies in Adult Education.*

WORK IN PROGRESS: Also engaged in research for a proposed book on consciousness and its objects, including sense-perception, memory, imagination, judgment, introspection, bodily sentience, and choice, "from a standpoint which might be described as that of 'radical realism.'"

SIDELIGHTS: R. W. K. Paterson told *CA:* "I have for a number of years been interested in those recent intellectual movements (e.g. existentialism, anarchism) which typify the disenchantment and sense of alienation so characteristic of Western culture at the present time. My study of the archetypal nihilism of Max Stirner arose from this interest. Contemporary nihilism seems to be rooted in philosophies which preach an extreme subjectivism, and I now find myself increasingly concerned to seek out and establish the objective basis, accessible to our common human consciousness, for our judgments about the world, ourselves, our conduct, and our society.... Thus in my book on the education of adults I have tried to show how the development of an individual as a full human person essentially involves developing his ability to grasp objective reality and to see and respond to its many different sides."

*   *   *

PATRICK, Clarence H(odges) 1907-

PERSONAL: Born December 25, 1907, in Winchester, Tenn.; son of C. Jesse (a livestock dealer) and Nettie (Hodges) Patrick; married Elizabeth Fleischmann, August 30, 1946; children: Adele. *Education:* Wake Forest College (now University), B.A., 1931; Andover Newton Theological School, B.D., 1934; Duke University, Ph.D., 1943; also attended Harvard University and Yale University. *Politics:* Democrat. *Religion:* Baptist. *Home:* 1880 Faculty Dr., Winston-Salem, N.C. 27106. *Office address:* Department of Sociology, Wake Forest University, Box 7808, Winston-Salem, N.C. 27109.

CAREER: Shorter College, Rome, Ga., professor of sociology, 1943-44; Meredith College, Raleigh, N.C., professor of sociology, 1944-47; Wake Forest University, Winston-Salem, N.C., professor of sociology, 1947—. North Carolina Board of Paroles, member of advisory board, 1949-53,

chairman, 1953-56; member and chairman, North Carolina Probation System, 1957-70; member, Inmate Grievance Commission.

WRITINGS: Alcohol, Culture, and Society, Duke University Press, 1952; *The North Carolina Parole System* (booklet), State of North Carolina, 1954; *Lunch-Counter Desegregation in Winston-Salem, N.C.,* Hanes Foundation, 1960; (contributor) Simon Dinitz and W. C. Reckless, editors, *Critical Issues in the Study of Crime,* Little, Brown, 1968; *The Police, Crime and Society,* C. C Thomas, 1972. Contributor to *Phylon, Pregled* (Yugoslavia), *Nichibei Forum* (Japan), *Journal of Criminal Law, Criminology and Police Science, Man in India,* and *Wake Forest Intramural Law Review.*

*   *   *

PATTERSON, L(yman) Ray 1929-

PERSONAL: Born February 18, 1929, in Macon, Ga.; son of Dallas DeVotie and Ida (Smith) Patterson; married Laura Davis, August 30, 1958; children: Laura Adelyn, Barbara Ida. *Education:* Mercer University, A.B., 1949, LL.B., 1957; Northwestern University, M.A., 1950; Harvard University, S.J.D., 1966. *Home:* 1039 Springdale Rd., Atlanta, Ga. 30306. *Office:* School of Law, Emory University, Atlanta, Ga. 30322.

CAREER: Mercer University, Macon, Ga., assistant professor of law, 1958-63; Vanderbilt University, Nashville, Tenn., associate professor, 1963-66, professor of law, 1966-73; Emory University, Atlanta, Ga., dean of School of Law, 1973—. *Military service:* U.S. Army, 1954.

WRITINGS: Copyright in Historical Perspective, Vanderbilt University Press, 1968; (with Elliott E. Cheatham) *The Profession of Law,* Foundation Press, 1971.

*   *   *

PAULSTON, Rolland G(lenn) 1929-

PERSONAL: Born June 10, 1929, in San Bernardino, Calif.; married Christina Bratt (a professor). *Education:* Attended University of Mexico, 1949; University of California, Los Angeles, A.B., 1952; University of Stockholm, M.S.Sc., 1963; Columbia University, Ed.D., 1966. *Office:* International and Development Education Program, University of Pittsburgh, Pittsburgh, Pa. 15260.

CAREER: Teacher of social studies at Los Angeles County (Calif.) public schools, 1956-59, and at American High School of Tangier, Tangier, Morocco, 1959-62; Columbia University, Teachers College, New York, N.Y., visiting assistant professor and research assistant at Center for Education in Latin America, 1966-68; University of Pittsburgh, School of Education, Pittsburgh, Pa., assistant professor, 1968-69, associate professor, 1969-72, professor, 1972—. Visiting professor and director, Institute for the Study of International Problems in Education, University of Stockholm, 1973. Consultant, 1969-76, to various organizations, including UNESCO and Peruvian Ministry of Education, Scandinavian Folk High School Council, World Bank, and AID and Venezuelan Ministry of Education.

MEMBER: Comparative and International Education Society (member of board of directors, 1973-74; vice-president, 1974; president, 1975-76), Society for Applied Anthropology (fellow). *Awards, honors:* Smith-Mundt grant, 1959-62; National Defense Education Act fellow in comparative and international education, 1964-66; National Endowment for the Humanities workshop grant, 1972; Scandinavian Folk High

School Council research grant, 1972; Scandinavian seminar research grant, 1973.

WRITINGS: Educacion y desarrollo socio economico de la selva peruana (booklet), Ministry of Education (Lima), 1967; *Investigaciones sobre la escuela y la comunidad peruana rural* (booklet), Ministry of Education (Lima), 1967; *La evolucion de la metodologia en estudios del cambio educativo* (booklet), [Lima], 1967; *Child Growth and Development in Peru* (written in Spanish), Center for Education in Latin America, Columbia University, 1968; (with Ernesto Estaban Achachau) *Desarrollo somatico y rendimiento fisico del escolar peruano*, [Lima], 1968; *Educational Change in Sweden: Planning and Accepting the Comprehensive School Reforms*, Teachers College Press, Columbia University, 1968; *Education and Community Development* (written in Spanish), AID Regional Technical Aids Center (Mexico City), 1969; *Educacion y el cambio dirigido de la comunidad*, Center for Studies in Education and Development, Harvard University, 1969; *Society, Schools and Progress in Peru*, Pergamon, 1971; *Non-Formal Education*, Praeger, 1972; *Folk Schools in Social Change*, Center for International Studies, University of Pittsburgh, 1974; *The Educational System of Cuba*, U.S. Department of Health, Education, and Welfare, 1975; *Conflicting Theories of Social and Educational Change*, World Bank, 1975; *Evaluating Educational Reform: An International Casebook*, World Bank, 1976; *Continuity and Change in Peruvian Education* (written in Spanish), Editorial Paidos, 1977; *Other Dreams, Other Schools: Folk Colleges and Popular Movements in Scandinavia and America*, Education Development Center, 1977; *Social and Educational Change in Socialist Cuba* (written in Spanish), Editorial Paidos, in press.

Contributor: *Educacion Universitaria Comparada*, Faculty of Education, San Marcos National University, 1967; Carmelo Mesa-Lago, editor, *Revolutionary Change in Cuba*, University of Pittsburgh Press, 1971; Marzio Barbagli, editor, *Scuola, potere e idologia*, Societa editrice il Mulino (Bologna), 1972; Cole S. Brembeck, editor, *New Strategies for Educational Development: The Search for Non-Formal Alternatives*, Heath, 1973; Donald Lemke and Richard Cummings, editors, *Educational Innovations in Latin America*, Scarecrow, 1973; David O'Shea, editor, *Education and Social Change in Latin America*, Center for Latin American Studies, University of California at Los Angeles, 1976; A. H. Halsey and J. Karabel, editors, *Power and Ideology in Education*, Oxford University Press, 1976; *Problemas de Desarrollo*, [Mexico], 1977. Contributor of articles to *International Review of Education, School and Society, Comparative Education Review, Journal of Developing Areas, Aportes, Estudios Andinos, America Indigena*, and other periodicals. Editorial board member, *Andean Studies, Cuban Studies*, and *Focus on Learning: A Journal of Educational Theory and Practice*.

WORK IN PROGRESS: Research on educational change processes in revolutionary and conservative societies, on non-formal alternatives to schooling, and on the political economy of education.

*   *   *

PAUTLER, Albert J., Jr. 1935-

PERSONAL: Born February 9, 1935, in Buffalo, N.Y.; son of Albert J. (a signalman) and Margaret (Philipps) Pautler; married Marilyn J. Stock, June 28, 1958; children: Mark, Ann, Mary, Michael. *Education:* State University of New York College at Buffalo, B.S., 1957, M.S., 1961; State University of New York at Buffalo, Ed.D., 1967. *Religion:* Roman Catholic. *Home:* 50 Bragg Ct., Williamsville, N.Y. 14221. *Office:* Faculty of Educational Studies, State University of New York at Buffalo, 410 Baldy Hall, Amherst, N.Y. 14260.

CAREER: Junior and senior high school teacher of industrial arts in Maryvale School System, Cheektowaga, N.Y., 1957-67, coordinator of·occupational skills, 1965-67; Rutgers University, New Brunswick, N.J., assistant professor in department of vocational-technical education of Graduate School of Education, 1967-69, associate professor and chairman of department of vocational education at University College, 1969-70; State University of New York at Buffalo, Amherst campus, 1970—, began as associate professor, currently professor in department of curriculum development and instructional media. *Member:* American Industrial Arts Association, National Education Association, American Vocational Association, American Vocational Education Research Association, Association for Supervision and Curriculum Development (member of commission on occupational preparation, 1970-72), National Association of Industrial and Technical Teacher Educators, Epsilon Pi Tau, Phi Delta Kappa.

WRITINGS: (With Carl J. Schaefer) *Review and Synthesis of Research in Trade and Industrial Education*, Ohio State University Press, 1970; *Teaching Shop and Laboratory Subjects*, C. E. Merrill, 1971; *Methods of Teaching Shop and Laboratory Subjects*, Allyn & Bacon, 1977. Writer of research reports; contributor of more than twenty articles to industrial education journals.

*   *   *

PAVLOWITCH, Stevan K. 1933-

PERSONAL: Born September 7, 1933, in Belgrade, Yugoslavia; son of Kosta (a diplomat) and Mara (Dyoukitch) St. Pavlowitch; married; one son. *Education:* University of Paris and University of Lille, licence es lettres, 1956; King's College, London, B.A., 1956, M.A., 1959; School of Slavonic and East European Studies, London, M.A., 1959. *Office:* Department of History, University of Southampton, Highfield, Southampton S09 5NH, England.

CAREER: Employed in field of public relations and as journalist in Brussels, Stockholm, Milan, and London, 1958-65; University of Southampton, Highfield, Southampton, England, 1965—, began as lecturer, currently senior lecturer in Balkan history.

WRITINGS: Anglo-Russian Rivalry in Serbia, 1837-1839: The Mission of Colonel Hodges, Mouton, 1961; *Yugoslavia*, Praeger, 1971; (contributor) B. Bond and I. Roy, editors, *War and Society*, Croom Helm, 1975. Contributor to *Slavonic and East European Review, La Revue d'Athenes, Slavic Review, Annales (Economies, Societes, Civilisations), Rassegna Storica del Risorgimento, Review of the Study Centre for Yugoslav Affairs, Eastern Churches Review, Armed Forces Society, European Studies Review*, and other journals. Member of board of trustees, *Eastern Churches Review*.

WORK IN PROGRESS: Research on Italian attitudes and policies towards Yugoslavia during World War II.

SIDELIGHTS: Stevan Pavlowitch wrote *CA* that he "enjoys studying the reverse of medals, unfashionable issues, people who have not won wars and come out on top, [and] being the devil's advocate in canonization proceedings." *Avocational interests:* Italy, eating, and the history of the Mascarene Islands.

PAYELLE, Raymond-Gerard   1898-1971
(Philippe Heriat)

September 15, 1898—October 10, 1971; French novelist, critic, and playwright. Obituaries: *New York Times*, October 11, 1971.

* * *

PAYNE, Jack   1926-

PERSONAL: Born January 15, 1926; son of Ernest (owner of a soda fountain syrup business) and Anna Payne; married, September 29, 1950; wife's name, Joan Natalie; children: David, Ronald, Jeffrey. *Education:* Attended University of Wisconsin, 1946, 1949, Kent State University, 1948-49, and Spencerian College, 1950-51. *Politics:* "Non-registered independent voter." *Religion:* Congregationalist. *Home:* 6409 Parkwood Way, Paradise, Calif. 95954.

CAREER: Business Opportunities Digest, Farmington, N.M., editor and publisher. Marketing director, Institute of Consulting Marketing Engineers, 1957-60. *Member:* National Writer's Club, Farmington Chamber of Commerce.

WRITINGS: Capital Sources: The Businessman's Source Manual of Finance, Business Opportunities Digest, 1963; *The Encyclopedia of Little-Known, Highly Profitable Business Opportunities,* Fell, 1971; *How to Make a Fortune in Finders' Fees,* Fell, 1973; *The New Encyclopedia of Little-Known Highly Profitable Business Opportunities,* Fell, 1974. Writer of more than two thousand items published in magazines, newsletters, and newspapers.

WORK IN PROGRESS: A book on business finance.

SIDELIGHTS: Jack Payne writes: "Like to rip and expose politicians and graft, every chance I get, and *help* the poor, 'silent majority', middle-class, small businessman who pays way more than his share of the tax freight to support all the nonsense coming regularly out of Congress."

* * *

PAYNE, James L.   1939-

PERSONAL: Born June 17, 1939, in New York, N.Y.; married, wife's name Suzanne E.; children: Ellen D., Rachel S. *Education:* Attended University of San Marcos, 1961; Oberlin College, B.A., 1962; University of California, Berkeley, M.A., 1963, Ph.D., 1967. *Office:* Department of Political Science, Texas A & M University, College Station, Tex. 77843.

CAREER: University of San Marcos, Lima, Peru, instructor in English, 1961; Wesleyan University, Middletown, Conn., assistant professor of political science, 1966-69; Johns Hopkins University, School of Advanced International Studies, Washington, D.C., associate professor of political science, 1970-72; Texas A & M University, College Station, professor of political science, 1972—. Guest lecturer, Yale University, 1967. *Awards, honors:* Woodrow Wilson fellow, 1962, 1965; Social Science Research Foundation grant, 1968.

WRITINGS: Labor and Politics in Peru: The System of Political Bargaining, Yale University Press, 1965; *Patterns of Conflict in Colombia,* Yale University Press, 1968; *The American Threat: The Fear of War as an Instrument of Foreign Policy,* Markham, 1970; *Incentive Theory and Political Process,* Heath, 1972; *Foundations of Empirical Political Analysis,* Rand McNally, 1973; *Principles of Social Science Measurement,* Lytton Circle, 1975. Contributor to political science journals.

PECH, Stanley Z.   1924-

PERSONAL: Born March 31, 1924, in Hradec Kralove, Czechoslovakia; became Canadian citizen; son of Jaromir (a salesman) and Irma (Szraga) Pech; married Vera Medlikova, September 12, 1949; children: Irene. *Education:* Attended Charles University of Prague, 1945-47; University of Alberta, M.A., 1950; University of Colorado, Ph.D., 1955. *Religion:* Protestant. *Home:* 4914 Queensland Rd., Vancouver, British Columbia, Canada. *Office:* Department of History, University of British Columbia, Vancouver, British Columbia, Canada.

CAREER: Western Montana College, Dillon, assistant professor of social studies, 1955-56; University of British Columbia, Vancouver, assistant professor, 1956-62, associate professor of Slavonic studies, 1962-67, associate professor of history, 1967-71, professor of history, 1971—. *Member:* Canadian Historical Association, Canadian Association of Slavists (president, 1966-67), Czechoslovak Society of Arts and Sciences in America.

WRITINGS: The Czech Revolution of 1848, University of North Carolina Press, 1969. Contributor to history journals.

WORK IN PROGRESS: A comparative study of the revolutionary movements among the Slavic nationalities of the Hapsburg monarchy, 1848-1849.

SIDELIGHTS: Stanley Pech reads French, Russian, Ukrainian, Slovak, German, Serbo-Croat, Slovene, Bulgarian, medieval Latin, Polish, and Belorussian.

* * *

PEDICORD, Harry William   1912-

PERSONAL: Born March 23, 1912, in Wheeling, W.Va.; son of Harry Lewis (an educator) and Alitha (Bell) Pedicord; married Adah Alison (a research scholar), August 23, 1939; children: Alison (Mrs. James T. Schleifer). *Education:* Washington and Jefferson College, A.B., 1933, M.A., 1934; Princeton Theological Seminary, Th.B., 1937; University of Pennsylvania, Ph.D., 1949. *Office:* Department of English and Speech, Thiel College, Greenville, Pa. 16125.

CAREER: Presbyterian minister. First Presbyterian Church, Bridgeport, Pa., assistant pastor, 1937-38, pastor, 1942-47; Church of the Covenant, Erie, Pa., executive minister, 1938-42; Hiland Presbyterian Church, Pittsburgh, Pa., pastor, 1947-63; Thiel College, Greenville, Pa., chairman, department of English and speech, 1963-77, professor emeritus, 1977—. *Member:* Modern Language Association of America, International Federation of Societies for Theatre Research (member of Plenary Committee, 1970—), American Society for Theatre Research (founder, 1956; chairman, 1962-70), Society for Theatre Research (Great Britain), Consular Law Society (fellow). *Awards, honors:* D.D. from Waynesburg College, 1949; D.Litt. from Washington and Jefferson College, 1961.

WRITINGS: The Theatrical Public in the Time of Garrick, King's Crown Press, 1954; (editor) *Course of Plays, 1740-2: An Early Diary of Richard Cross, Prompter to the Theatres,* John Rylands Library, University of Manchester, 1958; (editor) Nicholas Rowe, *The Tragedy of Jane Shore,* University of Nebraska Press, 1974. Editor, *Theatre Survey.*

WORK IN PROGRESS: The Plays of David Garrick; an index to the Burns Mantle *Best Plays Series, 1894-1964; The Promptbooks of David Garrick; Freemasonry and English Theatres of the Eighteenth Century.*

PEEL, J(ohn) D(avid) Y(eadon) 1941-

PERSONAL: Born November 13, 1941, in Dumfries, Scotland; son of Edwin Arthur (a professor of education) and Nora Kathleen (Yeadon) Peel; married Jennifer C. F. Pare, April 9, 1969; children: three sons. *Education:* Balliol College, Oxford, M.A. (first class honors), 1963; London School of Economics, Ph.D., 1966. *Religion:* Anglican. *Office:* Department of Sociology, University of Liverpool, Liverpool L69 3BX, England.

CAREER: University of Nottingham, Nottingham, England, assistant lecturer in sociology, 1966-70; University of London, London School of Economics and Political Science, London, England, lecturer in sociology, 1971-73; University of Ife, Ife, Nigeria, visiting reader in sociology, 1973-75; University of Liverpool, Liverpool, England, Charles Booth Professor of Sociology, 1975—. *Member:* African Studies Association of the United Kingdom, International African Institute.

WRITINGS: Aladura: A Religious Movement among the Yoruba, Oxford University Press, 1968; *Herbert Spencer: The Evolution of a Sociologist,* Basic Books, 1971.

WORK IN PROGRESS: Studying the integration of a local community in Nigeria into wider social ties; research on Christianization in Africa.

* * *

PEEL, John Donald 1908-

PERSONAL: Born December 5, 1908, in Geneva, N.Y.; son of Joseph Louis and Bertha (Roche) Peel; married Dolores Sampon, October 27, 1945; children: Robert L. *Education:* Hobart College, A.B. (with honors), 1933. *Home:* 608 Woodside Pl., Webster Groves, Mo. 63119.

CAREER: Free-lance writer employed in public relations, promotion, and industrial editing prior to 1965; Metropolitan Police Department, St. Louis, Mo., researcher in Planning and Development Division, 1965—. *Military service:* U.S. Army, 1942-45; became sergeant; served with Ninth Infantry Division from North Africa to Germany; received eight battle stars, Bronze Star, and distinguished unit citation.

WRITINGS—Published by C. C Thomas, except as indicated: *Anniversary Celebrations Made Easy,* Chilton, 1960; *Fundamentals of Training for Security Officers,* 1970; *The Story of Private Security,* 1971; *The Training, Licensing, and Guidance of Private Security Officers,* 1973.

* * *

PEGRUM, Dudley F(rank) 1898-

PERSONAL: Born May 28, 1898, in Romford, Essex, England; naturalized U.S. citizen; son of Frank and Elizabeth M. (Keen) Pegrum; married Marion Pheasey (died, January, 1966); children: Douglas Frank. *Education:* University of Alberta, B.A. (first class honors), 1922, M.A., 1924; University of California, Berkeley, Ph.D., 1927. *Religion:* Episcopalian. *Home:* 414 Denslow Ave., Los Angeles, Calif. 90049. *Office:* Department of Economics, University of California, Los Angeles, Calif. 90024.

CAREER: Canadian National Railways, Edmonton, Alberta, claims agent, 1918-19; high school teacher in Lethbridge, Alberta, 1923-25; University of California, Los Angeles, instructor, 1927-28, assistant professor, 1928-35, associate professor, 1935-44, professor of economics, 1944-65, professor emeritus, 1965—, chairman of department,

1938-44. Consultant to U.S. Government, and to transportation companies, public utilities, business firms, and trade associations. *Military service:* Royal Canadian Air Force, cadet, 1918.

MEMBER: American Economic Association, American Society of Traffic and Transportation, Transportation Research Forum, Western Economic Association (vice president, 1968), Southern California Economic Association, Alpha Kappa Psi, Pi Gamma Mu, Omicron Delta Epsilon, Delta Nu Epsilon. *Awards, honors:* Distinguished Award in Transportation, American Economic Association, 1966.

WRITINGS: Rate Theories and the California Railroad Commission, University of California Press, 1932, reprinted, Johnson Reprint, 1966; *Regulation of Public Utility Securities in California,* University of California Press, 1937; *The Regulation of Industry,* Irwin, 1949; *Public Regulation of Business,* Irwin, 1959, revised edition, 1965; *Transportation: Economics and Public Policy,* Irwin, 1963, 3rd edition, 1973. Contributor of more than a hundred articles to professional journals and trade publications.

WORK IN PROGRESS: Research on federal transportation policy and on public policy towards the business corporation.

AVOCATIONAL INTERESTS: Music, gardening, swimming, and other sports (in earlier years, wrestling; he was wrestling champion of Alberta in 1922).

* * *

PELAEZ, Jill 1924-

PERSONAL: Surname is pronounced Pel-*eye*-eth; born April 24, 1924, in Santurce, P.R.; daughter of Walter Keaton (a citrus grower) and Sybil Nice (Wende) Fletcher; married Emmanual Antonio Pelaez (executive director, Mental Health Assoc., Orange County), December 22, 1945; children: Jill (Mrs. Martin Baumgaertner), Gay Wende, David. *Education:* Attended Rollins College, 1944-45, B.A., 1973, M.A.T., 1976; attended University of Oklahoma, 1956-57; also studied art at Prado Museum, Madrid, Spain, 1962-64, and dance in Santurce, P.R., 1941, and at Chalif School of Ballet, New York, N.Y., 1943. *Home:* 3018 Westchester Ave., Orlando, Fla. 32803.

CAREER: Free-lance writer. Teacher at Lake Highland Preparatory School, Orlando, Fla., 1974-76; creative writing teacher at Rollins Summer Academy, 1977. *Member:* Authors Guild, National League of American Pen Women, Kappa Delta Pi.

WRITINGS: (Contributor) Johnson, Kress, and others, *Ideas and Images 32,* American Book Co., 1968; *Donkey Tales,* Abingdon, 1971. Contributor of short stories to *Humpty Dumpty* and *Highlights for Children,* of articles to *U.S. Lady,* and of poetry to *Stars and Stripes.* Fiction editor, *Flamingo* (Rollins College publication), 1944.

WORK IN PROGRESS: Poetic drama, *The Moonbell,* one act, and *The Golden Fox,* two act; a novel about early Florida.

SIDELIGHTS: Jill Pelaez, whose husband is a retired Air Force colonel, has lived in Puerto Rico, Spain, Germany, and ten of the fifty United States, and traveled in Mexico, England, France, Italy, Czechoslovakia, Poland, and Russia. She told *CA:* "As a volunteer and guest author in the local public schools as part of an educational supplemental program, I was drawn into teaching at a time when many of my contemporaries were retiring and settling down to a much quieter life. There was, necessarily, an absence of a few years from writing as I returned to college for my degrees in education. The ensuing years however, have been the most rewarding of my life and now as I return to writing, it is with new excitement and understanding of today's young people who are now very much a part of my everyday life.''

*   *   *

PELFREY, William   1947-

PERSONAL: Born March 10, 1947, in Detroit, Mich.; son of Warren Gayle (a bricklayer) and Helen (Gregory) Pelfrey. *Education:* Wayne State University, B.A., 1968; Ohio State University, graduate study, 1970-71. *Home address:* P.O. Box 391, Ashland, Ky. 41101.

CAREER: Writer; U.S. Department of State, foreign service officer serving in Pakistan and Venezuela, 1974-77; Ashland Oil, Inc., Ashland, Ky., senior writer, 1977—. *Military service:* U.S. Army, Infantry; received Bronze Star and Vietnamese Cross of Gallantry. *Member:* Phi Beta Kappa. *Awards, honors:* National Endowment for the Arts creative writing fellowship, 1973.

WRITINGS: The Big V, Liveright, 1972. Contributor to *New Republic, New York Times,* and *Atlantic.*

*   *   *

PELL, Eve   1937-

PERSONAL: Born April 9, 1937, in New York, N.Y.; daughter of Clarence C. and Eve (Mortimer) Pell; married Herbert McLaughlin; children: Daniel, Peter, John. *Education:* Bryn Mawr College, A.B., 1958. *Home:* 2315 Broadway, San Francisco, Calif. 94115. *Agent:* Mary Clemmey, Julian Bach Literary Agency, Inc., 3 East 48th St., New York. N.Y. 10017.

CAREER: Sarah Dix Hamlin School, San Francisco, Calif., English teacher, 1960-67.

WRITINGS: (With Paul Jacobs and Saul Landau) *To Serve the Devil,* Random House, 1971; (editor) *Maximum Security: Letters from Prison,* Dutton, 1972.†

*   *   *

PELLEGRENO, Ann Holtgren

PERSONAL: Married Don Pellegreno. *Education:* University of Michigan, B.M., 1958.

CAREER: Professional musician, 1954-60; English teacher in public schools in Saline, Mich., 1958-66; flight instructor and commercial pilot, 1966—. Author and lecturer, 1966—; member of advisory council, Iowa Board for Public Programs in the Humanities. Consultant to Des Moines Technical High School, Des Moines, Iowa. *Member:* Aviation-Space Writer's Association. *Awards, honors:* Aviation Space Writer's Association non-fiction book award, 1972.

WRITINGS: World Flight: The Earhart Trail, Iowa State University Press, 1971. Contributing editor, *Air Progress,* 1966-68. Midwest correspondent, *Air Trails,* 1969-71.

WORK IN PROGRESS: History of Iowa Aviation, 1856-1976.

*   *   *

PEMBERTON, John E(dward)   1930-

PERSONAL: Born May 27, 1930, in Manchester, England; son of James Frederick (a cycle maker) and Beatrice Alexandra (Heap) Pemberton; married Joyce Little, September

12, 1953; children: Martin John, Susan Joyce. *Education:* University of Manchester, B.A. (honors), 1951; University of Warwick, M.A. *Home:* "Rostherne," Hall Close, Maids Moreton, Buckingham MK18 1RH, England. *Office:* University College at Buckingham, Hunter St., Buckingham, MK18 1EG, England.

CAREER: Leicester Polytechnic, Leicester, England, deputy librarian, 1953-54; United States Information Service, Manchester, England, librarian, 1955-57; Normalair Ltd., Yeovil, Somerset, England, information officer, 1957-58; Liverpool City Library, Liverpool, England, technical documentation officer and librarian, 1958-59; Technical Information Co., Liverpool, senior documentation officer, 1959-61; English Electric Aviation Ltd., Wharton, Lancashire, England, indexing research project, 1961; International Library, Liverpool, librarian, 1961-66; University of Warwick Library, Coventry, England, politics and law librarian 1966-73; University College at Buckingham, Buckingham, England, librarian, 1973—. Consultant, Social Science Research Council, and Open University. *Member:* Aslib, Library Association (fellow), Royal Society of Arts (fellow).

WRITINGS: How to Find Out about France, Pergamon, 1966; *How to Find Out in Mathematics,* Pergamon, 1963, 2nd edition, 1969; *British Official Publications,* Pergamon, 1971, 2nd edition, 1973; *National Provision of Printed Ephemera in the Social Sciences,* University of Warwick Library, 1971; *European National Official Publications,* Aslib, 1974; *Literature Search and Compiling a Bibliography,* Open University Press, 1974; *Politics and Public Libraries in England and Wales, 1850-1970,* Library Association, 1977. Editor, "Student Literature Guides," Routledge & Kegan Paul, and "Guides to Official Publications," Pergamon. Contributor to *Aslib Proceedings, International Library Review, Journal of Librarianship, Library World,* and other periodicals. European and Commonwealth editor, *Government Publications Review;* member of editorial board, *Journal of Documentation.*

SIDELIGHTS: John Pemberton told *CA* that his "primary professional interest is in improving the provision of and access to primary materials in the social sciences, including official publications, both British and foreign.''

*   *   *

PENDLETON, Don(ald Eugene)   1927-
(Dan Britain, Stephan Gregory)

PERSONAL: Born December 12, 1927, in Little Rock, Ark.; son of Louis Thomas (a machinist) and Drucy (Valentine) Pendleton; married Marjorie Williamson, February 4, 1946; children: Stephen, Gregory, Rodney, Melinda, Jennifer, Derek. *Education:* Received GED certificate of high school equivalency, 1947. *Politics:* Independent. *Religion:* Independent. *Home and office address:* Route 11, Box 147, Bloomington, Ind. 47401.

CAREER: Novelist. Telegrapher for Southern Pacific Co. in California, 1948-58; controller for Federal Aviation Agency, 1958-61; worked in engineering management for Aerospace Systems Engineering in various locations in the U.S., 1961-67. *Military service:* U.S. Navy, 1942-47, 1952-54; served as radioman first class; received naval commendation medal. *Member:* International Platform Association, Authors Guild, Mystery Writers of America.

WRITINGS: Revolt, Olympia, 1968; *The Olympians,* Greenleaf Classics, 1968; *The Truth about Sex,* Phenix Publishers, 1969; *Cataclysm: The Day the World Died* (science fiction), Bee-Line Books, 1969; *The Guns of Terra 10,* Bee-Line Books, 1970; *Population Doomsday,* Bee-Line Books, 1970. Senior editor, *Orion,* 1967-68.

"The Executioner" series; published by Pinnacle Books, except as indicated: *The Executioner: War against the Mafia,* Bee-Line Books, 1969; ... *Death Squad,* Bee-Line Books, 1969; ... *Battle Mask,* Bee-Line Books, 1970; ... *Miami Massacre,* Bee-Line Books, 1970; ... *Continental Contract,* 1971; ... *Assault on Soho,* 1971; ... *Nightmare in New York,* 1971; ... *Chicago Wipe-Out,* 1971; ... *Vegas Vendetta,* 1971; ... *Caribbean Kill,* 1972; ... *California Hit,* 1972; ... *Boston Blitz,* 1972; ... *Washington IOU,* 1972; ... *San Diego Siege,* 1972; ... *Panic in Philly,* 1972; ... *Jersey Guns,* 1974; ... *Texas Storm,* 1974; ... *Detroit Deathwatch,* 1974; ... *New Orleans Knockout,* 1974; ... *Firebase Seattle,* 1975; ... *Hawaiian Hellground,* 1975; ... *St. Louis Showdown,* 1975; ... *Canadian Crisis,* 1975; ... *Colorado Killzone,* 1976; ... *Acapulco Rampage,* 1976; ... *Dixie Convoy,* 1976; ... *Savage Fire,* 1977; ... *Command Strike,* 1977; ... *Cleveland Pipeline,* 1977; *The Executioner's War Book,* 1977.

Under pseudonym Stephan Gregory: *Frame Up,* Vega Books, 1962; *All the Trimmings,* Midwood Books, 1965; *The Huntress,* Bee-Line Books, 1966; *The Insatiables,* Bee-Line Books, 1967; *The Sex Goddess,* Bee-Line Books, 1967; *Madame Murder,* Neva Books, 1967; *The Sexy Saints,* PEC Books, 1967; *The Hot One,* PEC Books, 1967; *Color Her Adulteress,* Brandon House, 1967; *All Lovers Accepted,* Phenix Publishers, 1968; *How to Achieve Sexual Ecstasy ... Every Time,* Medco Books, 1968; *The Sexually Insatiable Female,* Medco Books, 1968; *Hypnosis and the Sexual Life,* Phenix Publishers, 1968; *Religion and the Sexual Life,* Phenix Publishers, 1968; *Society and the Sexual Life,* Phenix Publishers, 1968; *Sex and the Supernatural,* Phenix Publishers, 1968; *ESP and the Sex Mystique,* Phenix Publishers, 1968; *Dialogues on Human Sexuality,* Phenix Publishers, 1968; *Secret Sex Desires,* Phenix Publishers, 1968; *The Sexuality Gap,* Phenix Publishers, 1968; *Hypnosis and the Free Female,* Phenix Publishers, 1969.

Under pseudonym Dan Britain: *The Godmakers,* Bee-Line Books, 1970; *Civil War II: The Day It Finally Happened,* Pinnacle Books, 1971.

SIDELIGHTS: Don Pendleton told *CA* he is "deeply interested in metaphysics and mysteries of existence—origin of man, destiny, etc. Went to sea at age of 14, ending formal education at that age; however, zest for learning and experiencing life has led the way through several career fields, culminating (I feel) in career as author. Wrote first book at age of 33, began full-time writing at age of 39, now have over fifty-seven published books and hundreds of shorter works. I regard writing as a self-revelation; this is perhaps my chief motivation.

"Although the 'Executioner' series is generally regarded as the prototype of the modern action-adventure sub-genre of American fiction, I did not begin the work with anything so grand in mind. I was, simply, investigating the metaphysics of violence and developing a central character to carry the theme. I was writing a novel—period. Looking back over a string of thirty successful sequels, I realize humbly that I am still writing the same novel. If and when I ever get it right, the work will be done and the series will end. Most satisfying to me is the thought that I have managed to touch a great many minds through my work. The series as a whole is being published in more than a dozen languages and in virtually every world market.

"I have now slowed down to a sane pace of four books per year. Research time very nearly equals typewriter time, and I take a month off just for play between books. Inside that loose framework, my work habits are chaotic. Often I will go through a marathon burst with upwards to seventy-two hours at the typewriter; some days I won't go near the damn thing. I work through emotion, creative crisis. If the crisis is not there then the work is flat and I cannot hope to involve my reader—and that, of course, is the name of the game: reader involvement in the writer's world."

* * *

PENICK, James (Lal), Jr. 1932-

PERSONAL: Born August 22, 1932, in Charleston, S.C.; son of James Lal, Sr. and Annie (Sheedy) Penick; married Barbara Perlmutter (a social worker), June 20, 1959; children: Michael Andrew, Katherine Leona. *Education:* College of William and Mary, B.A., 1957; University of California, Berkeley, M.A., 1959, Ph.D., 1962. *Residence:* Evanston, Ill. *Office:* Department of History, Loyola University, 820 North Michigan Ave., Chicago, Ill. 60611.

CAREER: California State Polytechnic College (now California Polytechnic State University), San Luis Obispo, assistant professor of history, 1963-65; Loyola University, Chicago, Ill., assistant professor, 1965-68, associate professor, 1968-72, professor of history, 1972—. *Military service:* U.S. Naval Reserve, 1950-54, active duty, 1951-54. *Member:* Organization of American Historians, American Society for Environmental History. *Awards, honors:* American Council of Learned Societies grant-in-aid, 1968.

WRITINGS: Progressive Politics and Conservation: The Ballinger-Pinchot Affair, University of Chicago Press, 1968; (editor with Carroll Pursell, Donald Swain, and Morgan Sherwood) *Politics of American Science: 1939 to the Present,* Rand McNally, 1965, revised edition, M.I.T. Press, 1972; *The New Madrid Earthquakes of 1811-1812,* University of Missouri Press, 1976. Contributor to history journals.

WORK IN PROGRESS: A history of crime in the Mississippi Valley before the Civil War.

* * *

PENNOCK, J(ames) Roland 1906-

PERSONAL: Born February 4, 1906, in Chatham, Pa.; son of James Levis and Alice Rakestraw (Carter) Pennock; married Helen B. Sharpless, January 24, 1931; children: Joan (Mrs. V. John Barnard), Judith Carter (Mrs. Albert F. Lilley). *Education:* Attended London School of Economics and Political Science, 1925-26; Swarthmore College, B.A., 1927; Harvard University, M.A., 1928, Ph.D., 1932. *Politics:* Democrat. *Religion:* Quaker. *Home:* 739 Harvard Ave., Swarthmore, Pa. 19081. *Office:* Department of Political Science, Swarthmore College, Swarthmore, Pa. 19081.

CAREER: Swarthmore College, Swarthmore, Pa., instructor, 1929-32, assistant professor, 1932-41, associate professor, 1941-45, professor of political science, 1945-62, Richter Professor of Political Science, 1962—, chairman of department, 1941-70. Administrative specialist, U.S. Social Security Board, 1936-37; principal divisional assistant, Office of Foreign Relief, U.S. Department of State, 1943; panel chairman, Regional War Labor Board, 1943-45. Social Science Research Council, chairman of Committee on Political Theory and Legal Philosophy Fellowships, 1954-60, member, board of directors, 1960-66. Visiting professor, Columbia University, 1950; visiting lecturer, Harvard University, 1953, and University of Pennsylvania, 1976; "visitor," Nuffield College, Oxford University, 1967.

MEMBER: International Political Science Association, American Political Science Association (member of council, 1953-55; vice president, 1963-64), American Society of Political and Legal Philosophy (editor, 1965—; president, 1968-70), Pennsylvania Association of Political Science and Public Administration, Phi Beta Kappa. *Awards, honors:* Guggenheim fellow, 1954-55.

WRITINGS: Administration and the Rule of Law, Farrar & Rinehart, 1941; *Liberal Democracy: Its Merits and Prospects,* Rinehart, 1950; (with others) *Democracy in the Mid-Twentieth Century: Problems and Prospects,* Department of Political Science, Washington University, 1960; (with David G. Smith) *Political Science: An Introduction,* Macmillan, 1964; (contributor) Oliver Garceau, editor, *Political Research and Political Theory,* Oxford University Press, 1968.

Editor: *Self-Government in Modernizing Nations,* Prentice-Hall, 1965; (and contributor with John W. Chapman) *Nomos* (yearbook of American Society for Political and Legal Philosophy), Atherton, Volume IX: *Equality,* 1967, Volume X: *Representation,* 1968, Volume XI: *Voluntary Associations,* 1969, Volume XII: *Political and Legal Obligation,* 1970, Volume XIII: *Privacy,* 1971, Volume XIV: *Coercion,* 1972, Volume XV: *The Limits of Law,* 1974, Volume XVI: *Participation in Politics,* 1974, Volume XVII: *Human Nature in Politics,* 1977, Volume XVIII: *Due Process,* 1977.

Contributor to *A Dictionary of the Social Sciences, International Encyclopedia of the Social Sciences, Encyclopaedia Britannica,* and other dictionaries and encyclopedias; contributor of articles to numerous professional journals, including *University of Pennsylvania Law Review, Georgetown Law Journal, Annals of the American Academy, Western Political Quarterly, Journal of Politics, Behavioral Science, World Politics,* and *Ethics.* Member of board of editors and contributor, *American Political Science Review,* 1965-68.

WORK IN PROGRESS: A book on democratic theory.

AVOCATIONAL INTERESTS: Political development in foreign countries, travel.

*   *   *

PEPPE, Rodney   1934-

PERSONAL: Surname is pronounced *Pep*py; born June 24, 1934, in Eastbourne, Sussex, England; son of Lionel Hill (a naval officer) and Vivienne (Parry) Peppe; married Tordis Tatjana Tekkel, July 16, 1960; children: Christen, Jonathan. *Education:* Attended Eastbourne School of Art, 1951-53, 1955-57, received National Diploma in Design; Central School of Art, London, Diploma in Illustration, 1959. *Religion:* Church of England. *Home and office:* Overdale, 19 Gong Hill Dr., Lower Bourne, Farnham, Surrey GU10 3HQ, England.

CAREER: S. H. Benson Ltd. (advertising agency), London, England, art director, 1959-64; J. Walter Thompson Company Ltd., London, art director for television, 1964-65; freelance graphic designer and consultant in London, 1965-74; illustrator of children's books, 1967—. Designer of corporate identity symbols for various companies; consultant designer to Ross Foods Ltd.; poster designer, Yvonne Arnaud Theatre; design consultant, Dee-Hill and Syon Park. *Military service:* British Army, Intelligence Corps, 1953-55; served in Malaya. *Awards, honors:* Royal Humane Society's testimonial for saving a life, 1952.

WRITINGS—All self-illustrated juveniles: *The Alphabet Book,* Four Winds, 1968; *Circus Numbers: A Counting Book,* Delacorte, 1969; *The House That Jack Built,* Delacorte, 1970; *Hey Riddle Diddle,* Holt, 1971; *Simple Simon,* Holt, 1972; *Cat and Mouse,* Holt, 1973; *Odd One Out,* Viking, 1974; *Humpty Dumpty,* Viking, 1975; *Picture Stories,* Puffin, 1976; *Rodney Peppe's Puzzle Book,* Viking, 1977.

"Henry" series; all published by Methuen: *Henry's Exercises,* 1975; *Henry's Garden,* 1975; *Henry's Present,* 1975; *Henry's Sunbathe,* 1975; *Henry Gets Out,* 1978; *Henry's Toy Cupboard,* 1978; *Henry's Aeroplane,* 1978.

Illustrator: Ralph and Jill Marchant, *The Little Painter,* Lerner, 1971.

WORK IN PROGRESS: A counting/tables book, for Methuen.

SIDELIGHTS: Rodney Peppe has made his own animated cartoons using a flat, cut-out technique. He told *CA:* "I enjoy drawing/talking to young children at book shows. They are a most useful feed-back for my work. I hope it's reciprocal! I plan to explore fields of children's television and character merchandising while retaining link with graphic design." In 1970 Peppe visited the U.S., hopes to return "to see more of America which I found very stimulating as regards to educational standards for young children."

Of his work as an illustrator, Peppe writes: "Picture book artists find themselves in rather a privileged position. They are the first communicators of still images to the very young, who as yet cannot read. Their pictures convey ideas which can stimulate the child's visual imagination and prepare him for the wonders to come. Unlike film images the pages can be studied, possessed and even eaten! As a picture book artist I like to think of my books being treated like favourite toys, and even eaten if that will increase sales. It's important too that an adult reading aloud to the child should not be bored or irritated by text and pictures. If, while satisfying these requirements I can foster aesthetic appreciation and encourage the child to make his own pictures, so much the better."

AVOCATIONAL INTERESTS: Collecting antique clocks, Japanese "netsuke," old children's books, and making new characters from wind-up toys.

*   *   *

PERCIVAL, John   1927-

PERSONAL: Born March 16, 1927; son of C. E. Percival (a railwayman); married Judith Cruickshank (a journalist). *Education:* St. Catherine's College Oxford, B.A., 1951, M.A., 1955. *Home:* 36 Great James St., London WC1N 3HB, England.

CAREER: Greater London Council, London, England, member of administrative staff of medical department, 1952—. Ballet critic, *Times* (London), 1965—. *Member:* Critics' Circle (chairman of ballet section).

WRITINGS: Antony Tudor, Dance Perspectives, 1963; *Modern Ballet,* Dutton, 1970; *The World of Diaghilev,* Dutton, 1971; *Experimental Dance,* Universe Books, 1971; *Nureyev: Aspects of the Dancer,* Putnam, 1975. Author of commentary of film on Rudolf Nureyev, "I Am a Dancer," 1972. London correspondent, *Dance Magazine* (New York), *Ballett* (Germany). Contributor to *Enciclopedia dello Spettacolo* (Rome), *Chambers's Yearbook,* and other publications. Association editor, *Dance and Dancers.*

WORK IN PROGRESS: A history of ballet in Britain; *John Cranko: The Man and His Heritage.*

* * *

PEREL, William M. 1927-

PERSONAL: Surname is pronounced Purr-*ell;* born October 17, 1927, in Chicago, Ill.; son of Charles Sumner (a lawyer) and Juanita (Darrah) Perel; married Irene Anne Hauptmann, November 13, 1946 (died May 1, 1947); married Eugenie Marie Anne Garic, December 21, 1962; children: (second marriage) Elizabeth Anne, Shirley Eugenie, Catherine Susan. *Education:* Indiana University, A.B., 1949, A.M., 1950, Ph.D., 1955. *Home:* 4400 East 25th St. N., Wichita, Kan. 67220. *Office:* Department of Mathematics, Wichita State University, Wichita, Kan. 67208.

CAREER: Georgia Institute of Technology, Atlanta, assistant professor of mathematics, 1954-56; Texas Technological College (now Texas Tech University), Lubbock, assistant professor of mathematics, 1956-59; Louisiana State University at New Orleans, associate professor of mathematics, 1959-62; University of North Carolina at Charlotte, professor of mathematics, 1963-66; Wichita State University, Wichita, Kan., professor of mathematics, 1966—, chairman of department, 1967—. Visiting professor at Stephen F. Austin State College (now University), summer, 1957, University of Detroit, summer, 1960, Randolph-Macon Woman's College, 1962-63, St. Augustine's College, summer, 1966, and Indiana University, summer, 1967. *Military service:* U.S. Army, 1946-47. *Member:* American Mathematical Society, Mathematical Association of America, American Association of University Professors, Edinburgh Mathematical Society, Wichita Urban League (member of housing committee), Sigma Xi.

WRITINGS: (With Philip D. Vairo) *Urban Education,* McKay, 1969; (contributor) Vairo, *How to Teach Disadvantaged Youth,* McKay, 1969; (contributor) Leonard H. Golubchik, *Urban, Social, and Educational Issues,* Kendall/Hunt, 1975.

WORK IN PROGRESS: Research on urban universities.

* * *

PERL, Arnold 1914-1971

April 14, 1914—December 11, 1971; American television producer and playwright. Obituaries: *New York Times,* December 12, 1971.

* * *

PERL, Lila

PERSONAL: Born in New York, N.Y.; daughter of Oscar and Fay (Rosenthal) Perl; married Charles Yerkow (a writer). *Education:* Brooklyn College (now Brooklyn College of the City University of New York), B.A.; additional study at Columbia University and New York University. *Residence:* Beechhurst, N.Y.

AWARDS, HONORS: American Library Association Notable Book Award, 1965, for *Red-Flannel Hash and Shoo-Fly Pie;* American Institute of Graphic Arts award, 1967, for *Rice, Spice, and Bitter Oranges;* National Science Teachers Association award, 1973, for *The Hamburger Book.*

WRITINGS: What Cooks in Suburbia, Dutton, 1961; *The Delights of Apple Cookery,* Coward, 1963; *The House You Want: How to Find It, How to Buy It,* McKay, 1965; *The Finishing Touch: A Book of Desserts,* New American Library, 1970.

Juvenile nonfiction: *Red-Flannel Hash and Shoo-Fly Pie: American Regional Foods and Festivals,* World Publishing, 1965; *Rice, Spice, and Bitter Oranges: Mediterranean Foods and Festivals,* World Publishing, 1967; *Foods and Festivals of the Danube Lands: Germany, Austria, Czechoslovakia, Hungary, Yugoslavia, Bulgaria, Romania, Russia,* World Publishing, 1969; *Yugoslavia, Romania, Bulgaria: New Era in the Balkans,* Thomas Nelson, 1970; *Living in Naples,* Thomas Nelson, 1970; *Living in Lisbon,* Thomas Nelson, 1971; *The Hamburger Book: All about Hamburgers and Hamburger Cookery,* Seabury, 1973; *Slumps, Grunts, and Snickerdoodles: What Colonial America Ate and Why,* Seabury, 1975; *Hunter's Stew and Hangtown Fry: What Pioneer America Ate and Why,* Seabury, 1977.

All published by Morrow: *Ethiopia: Land of the Lion,* 1972; *East Africa, Kenya, Tanzania, Uganda,* 1973; *America Goes to the Fair: All about State and County Fairs in the U.S.A.,* 1974; *Ghana and Ivory Coast: Spotlight on West Africa,* 1975; *The Global Food Shortage,* 1976; *Egypt: Rebirth on the Nile,* 1977; *Mexico: Crucible of the Americas,* 1978.

Juvenile fiction; published by Seabury, except as indicated: *No Tears for Rainey,* Lippincott, 1969; *Me and Fat Glenda* (Junior Literary Guild selection), 1972; *That Crazy April* (Junior Literary Guild selection), 1974; *The Telltale Summer of Tina C.,* 1975; *Dumb Like Me, Olivia Potts,* 1976.

SIDELIGHTS: Lila Perl told *CA:* "Writing is a learning experience for me—a never-ending source of intellectual and emotional stimulation. I love it with a passion and hope that the thrust of my own joy in the undertaking is conveyed in some measure to my readers. The feedback letters from readers of my young people's novels are an immense source of gratification. Every single letter is answered.

"With all due respect to fictional works based on history or personal reminiscence, and to fantasy, I feel that the times in which we are living are too complex, too challenging to be ignored, particularly by the writer of young people's literature. Contemporary settings and characters, situations and problems, in both fiction and non-fiction, lay claim to me. My concern is to sort out some of the turmoil, evoke, elucidate, and enrich the life of the imagination within that frame of reference."

* * *

PERLMAN, John N(iels) 1946-

PERSONAL: Born May 13, 1946, in Alexandria, Va.; son of Ellis S. (in congressional liaison work for Washington Metropolitan Area Transit Authority) and Bertha (Jessen) Perlman; married Janis Hadobas, May 26, 1967; children: Nicole Jeanne Kachina. *Education:* Ohio State University, B.A., 1969. *Home:* 1632 Mamaroneck Ave., Mamaroneck, N.Y. 10543.

CAREER: Teacher for Poetry-in-the-Schools programs in St. Paul, Minn., Georgia, California, and at Hommocks School, Larchmont, N.Y., 1971—. National Endowment for the Arts, Washington, D.C., poetry consultant, 1971—; Casper, Wyo., poet-in-residence for Wyoming Community Colleges, 1971-72. *Awards, honors:* Academy of American Poets awards, 1968, 1969; Vanderwater Prize, 1969.

WRITINGS—All poetry; published by Elizabeth Press, except as indicated: *Kachina,* Ohio State University Press, 1971; *Three Years Rings,* 1972; *Dinner 650 Warburton Ave.,*

1973; *Notes toward a Family*, 1975; *The Hudson: A Weave*, Jordan Davies Press, 1976; *Nicole*, 1976; *Self Portrait*, 1976; *Swath*, 1978. Contributor of poems to *Origin, Elizabeth, First Issue, Grosseteste Review*. Editor, *Shuttle* (literary magazine).

WORK IN PROGRESS: Homing, Powers, Letters, and *Corpus/Corpora,* all poetry.

* * *

PERRIGO, Lynn I(rwin) 1904-

PERSONAL: Born February 4, 1904, in Delphi, Ind.; son of Arnold J. (a teacher) and Rosa (Moyer) Perrigo; married Vera A. Bilby (a musician), August 17, 1929; children: Dwayne, Norma (Mrs. James Green), Byron. *Education:* Ball State University, B.A., 1933; University of Colorado, M.A., 1934, Ph.D., 1936. *Religion:* Protestant. *Home:* 1038 Fifth, Las Vegas, N.M. 87701. *Office:* Department of History, New Mexico Highlands University, Las Vegas, N.M. 87701.

CAREER: Teacher in schools in Muncie, Ind. and Gibson, Mont., 1921-26; Boy Scouts of America, Muncie, council executive, 1926-33; University of Kansas City (now University of Missouri—Kansas City), instructor, 1936-40, assistant professor, 1940-44, associate professor of history, 1944-45; University of Colorado, Boulder, assistant director of bureau of class instruction, 1946-47; New Mexico Highlands University, Las Vegas, professor of history and chairman of the department, 1947-71, professor emeritus, 1971—. Secretary, Governor's Commission on Historic Sites, 1964-68. President, United Fund, 1958; president, City Museum Board, 1961-70; board chairman, United Methodist Church, 1966-68; member, New Mexico Historical Records Advisory Board, 1975—. Consultant to Commission on Consolidation of West and East Las Vegas, 1966-70. *Member:* Organization of American Historians, Western Writers of America, Rio Grande Writers Association, Western Historical Association, Rocky Mountain Social Science Association, New Mexico Historical Association, Phi Kappa Phi, Pi Gamma Mu (national treasurer), Kiwanis International (president of local chapter, 1955).

WRITINGS: (With J. Fred Rippy) *Latin America: Its History and Culture,* Ginn, 1944; *Our Spanish Southwest,* Banks Upshaw, 1960; *Las Vegas and the Rough Riders,* City Museum, 1961; *The Rio Grande Adventure,* Lyons & Carnahan, 1965; *The American Southwest,* Holt, 1971; *La Reunion,* Yquado Press, 1975; *Gateway to Glorieta,* Yquado Press, 1977. Contributor of thirty articles to professional journals.

* * *

PERRY, David L. 1931-

PERSONAL: Born October 21, 1931, in Stockton, Calif.; son of Alfred Louis (an accountant) and Dytha (McIntyre) Perry; married Phyllis Penaluna (a teacher), February 8, 1953; children: Janet Marie, Jill Louise. *Education:* Attended Oregon State University, 1949-51; University of California, Berkeley, A.B., 1953, M.A., 1955, Ph.D., 1963. *Home:* 3190 Endicott Dr., Boulder, Colo. 80303. *Office:* Department of Philosophy, University of Colorado, Boulder, Colo. 80309.

CAREER: Long Beach State College (now California State University, Long Beach), assistant professor of philosophy, 1962-66; University of Colorado, Boulder, associate professor, 1966-74, professor of philosophy, 1974—. *Military ser-*

vice: U.S. Army, 1956-58. *Member:* American Philosophical Association, Wilderness Society, Colorado Mountain Club.

WRITINGS: The Concept of Pleasure, Mouton, 1967. Contributor to philosophy journals.

WORK IN PROGRESS: Research on ethics.

* * *

PETERFREUND, Stuart (Samuel) 1945-

PERSONAL: Born June 30, 1945, in Brooklyn, N.Y.; son of Harold (an automobile dealer) and Gloria (Doller) Peterfreund. *Education:* Cornell University, B.A., 1966; University of California, Irvine, M.F.A., 1968; University of Washington, Seattle, Ph.D., 1974. *Home:* 400 Springwood Rd., Little Rock, Ark. 72211.

CAREER: Wiltwyck School for Boys, Inc., Yorktown, N.Y., group care worker and psychological researcher, 1970-71 (period included in civilian public service, 1969-71, as conscientious objector to military duty); poet. Poet-in-residence, Southern Literary Festival, 1977. *Member:* Modern Language Association of America, Wordsworth-Coleridge Association, Byron Society, Keats-Shelley Society, Pi Delta Epsilon. *Awards, honors:* First prize in *Writer's Digest* Poetry Contest, 1970, for "Rainstorm in the Country"; Southern Federation of State Arts Agencies fellow, 1977; School of Criticism and Theory summer fellow, 1977.

WRITINGS: The Hanged Knife (poems), Ithaca House, 1970; *Harder than Rain* (poems), Ithaca House, 1977. Poetry included in *Quickly Aging Here: Some Poets of the 1970s,* edited by Geof Hewitt, Doubleday-Anchor, 1969, *A Government Job at Last: An Anthology of Work Poems, Mostly Canadian,* edited by Tom Wayman, McLeod, 1976, and *X-1: An Anthology of Experimental Fiction,* edited by Harry Smith, 1976. More than one hundred poems published in *Beloit Poetry Journal, Shenandoah,* and other literary magazines. Assistant editor, *Epoch,* 1964-66, 1969.

WORK IN PROGRESS: A third collection of poems; research on Keats, humor and comedy in Blake's poetry, and "theories of language as they relate to literature produced under their sway."

SIDELIGHTS: Stuart Peterfreund writes: "It seems to me that the best poets of the younger American School (40 and over, recent corpses allowed) such as Berryman, Logan, Merwin, Justice, Simpson and Roethke, are men, who having acknowledged the raw deal they got by being born (something Lowell has never gotten over), have made of the world a positive, though not necessarily optimistic vision, which they have justified by somehow withdrawing from the darkness and allowing themselves to be re-born into their own, visionary worlds. And when I speak of visionary I don't mean mystical, I mean metaphorical. And it is easier to live in the metaphor than in the darkness, as well as being far more productive. The projectivists, the New York poets, the *kayak* surrealists all fail for me because they never make the value judgement necessary in the creation of the metaphor for darkness. They show instead, how science can kill poetry: by recording process without questioning significance, by stressing the 'how' without questioning the 'why.'

"At any rate, in my own writing, I find it necessary to control reality. And the only reality I can control is the one I make for *me.* It's not the most exciting of all worlds. It's memories of my mother and grandfathers, the few girls I have loved, good friends I get drunk and riot with every time

I see them, the several times we ruled the world. It's sitting and drinking wine, listening to classical music on the radio very late at night in New York, knowing that I'm alive. It's stumbling through the dark and loving it for a minute, the way you love a city you've visited because you know your way around. And in the dark, if you can find your way, you're doing all right. There are many ways to do it, the best of them being to sing.''

He told *CA:* ''I am committed to the position that language has no absolute authority, but that language is the only authority there is. The position stresses the responsibility I take upon myself to read and write in as moral a way as possible. The position also stresses my commitment to a career based both in criticism and creative activity. I make no fundamental distinction between the need to read well and the need to write powerfully, nor do I make any fundamental distinction between the creative reading that leads to the literary text and the creative writing reading that leads to the critical text.''

BIOGRAPHICAL/CRITICAL SOURCES: Quickly Aging Here: Some Poets of the 1970s, edited by Geof Hewitt, Doubleday-Anchor, 1969; *Little Magazine,* winter, 1970-71; *Poetry Nippon,* summer, 1971; *Greenfield Review,* autumn, 1971.

*   *   *

PETERS, Maureen 1935-
(Veronica Black, Catherine Darby, Judith Rothman, Sharon Whitby)

PERSONAL: Born March 3, 1935, in Caernarvon, North Wales; daughter of Harry (a steward) and Vera (Knight) Peters; divorced; married second husband, George Ratcliffe, 1977; children: (first marriage) Vincent, Martin, Rachel, Emily. *Education:* University College of North Wales, B.A. and Dip. Ed., 1956. *Politics:* None. *Religion:* Roman Catholic. *Home:* 15 Dowhills Rd., Blundellsands, Crosby, Liverpool 23, England.

CAREER: Teacher of English to retarded children in Birmingham and Southend-on-Sea, England, 1956-58; author of novels. *Member:* Romantic Novelists Association (founder member, 1970—), Crosby Writers' Circle (member of committee, 1971—).

WRITINGS—All novels; all originally published by R. Hale: *Elizabeth the Beloved,* 1965, Beagle, 1971; *Katheryn, the Wanton Queen,* 1967, Beagle, 1971; *Mary, the Infamous Queen,* 1968, Beagle, 1971; *Bride for King James,* 1968; *Joan of the Lilies,* 1969; *The Rose of Hever,* 1969, published as *Anne, the Rose of Hever,* Beagle, 1971; *Flower of the Greys,* 1969.

Princess of Desire, 1970; *Struggle for a Crown,* 1970; *Shadow of a Tudor,* 1971; *Seven for St. Crispin's Day,* 1971; *The Cloistered Flame,* 1971; *The Woodville Wench,* 1972; *Henry VIII* (book of film), Beagle, 1972; *Curse of the Greys,* 1974; *The Queenmaker,* 1975; *Kate Alanna,* 1975; *A Child Called Freedom,* 1975; (under pseudonym Sharon Whitby) *The Last of the Greenwood,* Popular Library, 1975; (under pseudonym Sharon Whitby) *The Unforgotten Face,* 1975; (under pseudonym Judith Rothman) *With Murder in Mind,* 1975; *The Crystal and the Cloud,* 1977.

Under pseudonym Veronica Black: *Dangerous Inheritance,* 1969, Paperback Library, 1970; *Portrait of Sarah,* 1969, abridged edition, edited by Alice Sachs, Lenox Hill, 1970; *The Wayward Madonna,* Lenox Hill, 1970; *Footfall in the Mist,* Lenox Hill, 1971; *Master of Malcarew,* Lenox Hill,

1971; *The Enchanted Grotto,* 1972; *Moonflete,* 1972; *Fair Kilmeny,* 1972; *The House that Hated People,* 1974; *Tansy,* 1975; *Echo of Margaret,* in press. Also author of *The Willow Maid* and *Minstrel's Leap.*

Under pseudonym Catherine Darby; all published by Popular Library: *Falcon for a Witch,* 1975; *A Game of Falcons,* 1975; *Fortune for a Falcon,* 1975; *Season of the Falcon,* 1976; *A Pride of Falcons,* 1976; *Whisper Down the Moon,* 1976; *Frost on the Moon,* 1976; *The Flaunting Moon,* 1977; *The Falcon and the Moon,* 1977; *Falcon Rising,* 1977; *Falcon Sunset,* 1977; *Seed of the Falcon,* in press; *Falcon's Claw,* in press; *Falcon to the Lure,* in press; *Sing Me a Moon,* in press; *Cobweb across the Moon,* in press; *Moon in Pisces,* in press.

WORK IN PROGRESS: A Dream of Fair Serpents, under pseudonym Catherine Darby.

SIDELIGHTS: Maureen Peters told *CA* that she writes everything in longhand, working eight to ten hours a day. She is interested in the influence of the past over the present, and her main objective is "to tell a good story." *Avocational interests:* Hagiography, reading, the Tudor period, theatre, public speaking.

*   *   *

PETERSHAM, Maud 1889-1971

August 5, 1889—November 29, 1971; American author and illustrator of children's books. Obituaries: *New York Times,* November 30, 1971; *Washington Post,* December 3, 1971; *Publishers Weekly,* December 13, 1971.

*   *   *

PETERSON, Kenneth G(erard) 1927-

PERSONAL: Born May 30, 1927, in Brooklyn, N.Y.; son of Walter G. and Gertrude M. (Haberstock) Peterson; married Jane Elizabeth Shumaker, October 15, 1949; children: David S., Matthew E., Martha J., John G., Ruth A. *Education:* Drew University, B.A., 1946; Yale University, M.Div., 1949; Western Reserve University (now Case Western Reserve University), graduate study, 1951-53; University of California, Berkeley, M.L.S., 1963, Ph.D., 1968. *Politics:* Democrat. *Religion:* Presbyterian. *Home:* 911 Briarwood Dr., Carbondale, Ill. 62901. *Office:* Dean of Library Affairs, Southern Illinois University, Carbondale, Ill. 62901.

CAREER: Minister of Congregational churches in Burton, Ohio, 1949-55, and Chico, Calif., 1955-59; minister of United Church of Christ in Petaluma, Calif., 1959-62; Pacific Lutheran Theological Seminary, Berkeley, Calif., librarian, 1963-67; University of Virginia, Charlottesville, associate librarian, Alderman Library, 1968-76; Southern Illinois University at Carbondale, dean of library affairs, 1976—. Member of board of directors, Midwest Region Library Network. *Member:* American Library Association, Illinois Library Association, Ulysses S. Grant Association (member of board of directors), Beta Phi Mu, Pi Gamma Mu.

WRITINGS: An Introductory Bibliography for Theological Students, Pacific Lutheran Theological Seminary, 1964; *The University of California Library at Berkeley: 1900-1945,* University of California Press, 1970. Member of editorial board, Association of College and Research Libraries ''Publications in Librarianship.''

*   *   *

PETERSON, Robert W. 1925-

PERSONAL: Born December 19, 1925, in Warren, Pa.; son

of Oscar Albin (a railroader) and Allie (Anderson) Peterson; married Marguerite F. Laley, December 18, 1954; children: Thomas, Margaret. *Education:* Upsala College, B.A., 1950. *Home:* 18 Lincoln St., Ramsey, N.J. 07446.

CAREER: Titusville Herald, Titusville, Pa., city editor, 1952-54; *Chronicle-Telegram,* Elyria, Ohio, managing editor, 1954-61; *New York World-Telegram,* New York, N.Y., assistant news editor, 1961-66; *Scouting* (magazine), New Brunswick, N.J., reporter, 1971-74. *Military service:* U.S. Navy, torpedoman, 1944-46.

WRITINGS—Published by Facts on File, except as indicated: *Only the Ball Was White,* Prentice-Hall, 1970; (editor) *Rhodesian Independence,* 1971; (editor) *South African and Apartheid,* 1971, enlarged edition, 1975; (editor) *Agnew: The Coining of a Household Word,* 1972; (editor) *Space: From Gemini to the Moon and Beyond,* 1972; (editor) *Crime and the American Response,* 1973.

*   *   *

PETERSON, Russell Arthur 1922-

PERSONAL: Born July 11, 1922, in Minneapolis, Minn.; son of Oscar Arthur and Henrietta Peterson; married Thelma B. Renning, October 19, 1947; children: Anne Marie, Jan Arthur, Karen Louise, Barry Jacob. *Education:* Attended Augsburg College, 1940-42; Augustana College, Sioux Falls, S.D., B.A., 1944; Union Theological Seminary and Columbia University, graduate study, 1946; Luther Theological Seminary, C.T., 1947; University of Iowa, M.A., 1947; Oxford University, research student, 1958; University of North Dakota, Ph.D., 1959. *Home:* 802 Boyd Dr., Grand Forks, N.D. 58201. *Office:* Department of Education, University of North Dakota, Grand Forks, N.D. 58201.

CAREER: Lutheran clergyman, 1947—; pastor in Flandreau, S.D., 1947-50; Treatment Home for Emotionally Disturbed Boys, Fergus Falls, Minn., executive director, 1950-54; Dakota Lutheran Academy, Minot, N.D., president, 1954-57; University of North Dakota, Grand Forks, associate professor, 1960-67, professor of teacher education and philosophy of education, 1967—, chairman of department of education, 1971—. North Central Association of Colleges, examiner-consultant, 1962—. *Member:* National Education Association, Association for Higher Education, American Association of University Professors, Phi Delta Kappa. *Awards, honors:* Distinguished Service Award of U.S. Junior Chamber of Commerce, 1953, for work with mentally retarded.

WRITINGS: Luther for Today, privately printed, 1948; *Lutheranism and the Educational Ethic* (includes lectures published as *Luther for Today),* Meador, 1950; *How Love Will Help,* Meador, 1953; *God and I,* Meador, 1958; *Counseling Tips for the Beginning Teacher,* Kendall/Hunt, 1970; *Existentialism and the Creative Teacher,* Kendall/Hunt, 1970. Also author of *An Introduction to Theory of Knowledge, The Will in Human Learning,* and *A Dictionary of Philosophical Concepts,* all published by Graphic Publishing.

Translator: *The Modern Message of the Psalms: The Psalms in Basic English,* Meador, 1948; Christian Paulsen, *Children's Tales from Norway,* Meador, 1950; *The God that Job Had,* Colwell Press, 1951; *The Synoptic New Testament,* Meador, 1951. Contributor to education journals.

SIDELIGHTS: Russell Peterson has a working knowledge of Hebrew, Aramaic, German, Norwegian, French, and Latin.

PETTIGREW, Thomas Fraser 1931-

PERSONAL: Born March 14, 1931, in Richmond, Va.; son of Joseph Crane (a mechanical engineer) and Janet (Gibb) Pettigrew; married Ann Hallman (a medical doctor and public health specialist), February 25, 1956; children: Mark Fraser. *Education:* University of Virginia, A.B., 1952; Harvard University, M.A., 1955, Ph.D., 1956. *Politics:* "Ardent Democrat." *Religion:* Episcopalian. *Home:* 5 Follen St., Cambridge, Mass. 02138. *Office:* 1330 William James Hall, Harvard University, Cambridge, Mass. 02138.

CAREER: University of North Carolina at Chapel Hill, assistant professor of psychology, 1956-57; Harvard University, Cambridge, Mass., assistant professor, 1957-62, lecturer, 1962-64, associate professor, 1964-68, professor of social psychology, 1968-74, professor of psychology and sociology, 1974—. Member, Massachusetts Governor's Advisory Committee on Civil Rights, 1962-64; chairman, Episcopal Presiding Bishop's Advisory Committee on Race Relations, 1961-63; member, White House Task Force on Education, 1967; member of board, Race Relations Information Center, 1969-72; member of research advisory committee, Children's Television Workshop, 1970—. Consultant to U.S. Office of Education, 1965-68, U.S. Commission on Civil Rights, 1966-71, System Development Corp., Educational Testing Service, and to numerous public school systems. *Member:* Society for the Psychological Study of Social Issues (president, 1967-68), American Psychological Association (fellow), American Sociological Association (fellow), Phi Beta Kappa. *Awards, honors:* Guggenheim fellowship, 1967-68; National Science Foundation senior scientist fellowship, 1974; Center for Advanced Study in the Behavioral Sciences fellowship, 1975-76.

WRITINGS: (With E. Q. Campbell) Christians in Racial Crisis: A Study of the Little Rock Ministry, Public Affairs Press, 1959; *Negro American Intelligence,* Anti-Defamation League of B'nai B'rith, c.1964; (editor with Daniel C. Thompson) *Negro American Personality,* Society for the Psychological Study of Social Issues, 1964; *A Profile of the Negro American,* Van Nostrand, 1964; *Epitaph for Jim Crow,* Anti-Defamation League of B'nai B'rith, 1964; (with H. E. Freeman, H. M. Hughes, R. Morris, and L. G. Watts) *The Middle-Income Negro Family Faces Urban Renewal,* Brandeis University, 1964; *Racially Separate or Together?,* McGraw, 1971; (editor) *Racial Discrimination in the United States,* Harper, 1975; *The Social Psychology of Race,* Harcourt, 1978. Contributor to periodicals. Member of editorial boards, *Journal of Social Issues,* 1959-64, *Integrated Education,* 1963—, *Phylon,* 1965—, *Education and Urban Society,* 1968—, *Sociometry,* 1977-80, and *Political Behavior,* 1978—; associate editor, *American Sociological Review,* 1963-65.

WORK IN PROGRESS: With R. T. Riley and J. M. Ross, *Understanding Racial Change: Studies in American Race Relations.*

SIDELIGHTS: Thomas Pettigrew told *CA:* "As a native Southerner and a student of American race relations throughout my career, I feel strongly that racial justice will not come to the nation until Black Americans have open choice within the society free of discrimination. All of my writing is dedicated toward that end." *Avocational interests:* Chess.

*   *   *

PETTIT, Lawrence K. 1937-

PERSONAL: Born May 2, 1937, in Lewistown, Mont.; son

of George Edwin and Dorothy (Brown) Pettit; married Sharon Anderson, June 21, 1961 (divorced October 4, 1976); children: Jennifer Anna, Matthew Anderson, Allison Carol, Edward McLean. *Education:* University of Montana, B.A., 1959; Washington University, St. Louis, Mo., A.M., 1962; University of Wisconsin, Ph.D., 1965. *Politics:* Democrat. *Religion:* Lutheran. *Home:* 109 South Montana, Helena, Mont. 59601. *Office:* Montana University System, 33 South Last Chance Gulch, Helena, Mont. 59601.

CAREER: U.S. Senate, Washington, D.C., legislative assistant to James Murray, 1959-60, and to Lee Metcalf, 1962; Pennsylvania State University, University Park, 1964-67, began as assistant professor, became associate professor of political science; American Council on Education, Washington, D.C., member of administrative staff, 1967-69; Montana State University, Bozeman, chairman of department of political science, 1969-72; Montana University System, Helena, commissioner of higher education, 1972—. *Military service:* U.S. Army Reserve, 1955-63. *Member:* American Political Science Association, American Association for the Advancement of Science, American Association of University Professors (state president, 1970-72; member of national committee, 1970-73), State Higher Education Executive Officers Association, American Civil Liberties Union, Smithsonian Associates, Sigma Chi, Pi Sigma Alpha, Phi Alpha Theta, Tau Kappa Alpha, Montana Club, Masons Shrine.

WRITINGS: (Editor and contributor with H. S. Albinski) *European Political Processes,* Allyn & Bacon, 1968, 2nd edition, 1973; (editor and contributor with Edward Keynes) *Legislative Process in U.S. Senate,* Rand McNally, 1969; (editor and contributor with S. A. Kirkpatrick) *Social Psychology of Political Life,* Wadsworth, 1972; (contributor) George Angell, editor, *Handbook of Faculty Bargaining,* Jossey-Bass, 1977. Contributor to professional journals.

WORK IN PROGRESS: The Invasion of Canada, a novel, with Herbert C. Pace.

* * *

PHIBBS, Brendan (Pearse) 1916-

PERSONAL: Born December 3, 1916, in New York, N.Y.; son of Harry Clandillon and Teresa (Kelly) Phibbs; married Marie-Claire Harle, June 24, 1940; children: Susan, Henry, Judith, Hugh. *Education:* Northwestern University, B.S., 1938, M.D., 1941, M.Sc., 1946. *Politics:* Liberal. *Home:* 5845 North Piedra Seca, Tucson, Ariz.

CAREER: Member of clinical faculty, Northwestern University, Chicago, Ill.; private practice of cardiology in Casper, Wyo., 1952-71; University of Colorado, School of Medicine, Boulder, assistant clinical professor of cardiology, 1967-71; University of Arizona, College of Medicine, Tucson, associate professor of medicine (cardiology), 1971-73; Kino Community Hospital, Tucson, chairman of department of medicine and director of cardiology, 1973—. *Military service:* U.S. Army, Medical Corps, 1942-46; became major; received Bronze Star with oak-leaf cluster and V-device. *Member:* American College of Physicians (fellow), American College of Cardiology (fellow; governor for state of Arizona).

WRITINGS: The Cardiac Arrhythmias: A Guide for the General Practitioner, Mosby, 1961; *The Human Heart: The Layman's Guide to Heart Disease,* Mosby, 1967. Contributor of about forty articles to medical journals.

WORK IN PROGRESS: An autobiographical book about his career as a combat surgeon in World War II.

SIDELIGHTS: Brendan Phibbs told *CA* that his "goal in medical writing has been to clear away the mass of jargon, redundancy, and obfuscation which often makes relatively simple scientific facts obscure. Return to basic English with the use of the active tense, Anglo-Saxon stems, and simple declarative sentences. I am trying to shift to a different prose style for a book I am writing about my career as a combat command surgeon in the second World War and with this in mind, I am studying Joyce, Stendhel and A. J. Liebling, three of the greatest swordsmen in the syntactic arena."

* * *

PHILLIPS, Derek L(ee) 1934-

PERSONAL: Born January 22, 1934, in Corning, N.Y.; son of Charles John Phillips; married Patrice O'Malley, December 22, 1956; children: Kimberly, Bradford, Todd. *Education:* Rutgers University, A.B., 1959; University of Arizona, M.A., 1960; Yale University, Ph.D., 1962. *Home:* Hemonylaan 2, Amsterdam, Netherlands. *Office:* Sociologisch Instituut, Universiteit van Amsterdam, Korte Spinhuissteeg 3, Amsterdam, Netherlands.

CAREER: Wellesley College, Wellesley, Mass., instructor in sociology, 1962-63; Dartmouth College, Hanover, N.H., assistant professor of sociology, 1963-66; New York University, New York, N.Y., associate professor of sociology, 1966-71; Universiteit van Amsterdam, Amsterdam, Netherlands, professor of sociology, 1971—. Consultant to State of New Hampshire, Port Authority of New York, and Downtown Lower Manhattan Association. *Military service:* U.S. Army, 1954-56. *Member:* American Sociological Association.

WRITINGS: (Editor) *Studies in American Society,* Crowell, Volume I, 1965, Volume II, 1967; *Knowledge from What?,* Rand McNally, 1971; *Abandoning Method,* Jossey-Bass, 1973; *Wittgenstein and Scientific Knowledge,* Macmillan, 1977. Contributor to *American Sociological Review, American Journal of Sociology, Social Forces, Social Problems, Public Opinion Quarterly, Mens en Maatschappij,* and other publications.

WORK IN PROGRESS: A book on the problems of justice and equality in contemporary society.

* * *

PHILLIPS, Gerald M. 1928-

PERSONAL: Born December 1, 1928, in Cleveland, Ohio; son of Oskar (a laborer) and Henrietta (Szwimer) Philkofsky; married Nancy Faye Koslen, June 19, 1949; children: Dean Richard, Judith Miriam, Ellen Rose, Abigail Beth. *Education:* Case Western Reserve University, B.A., 1949, M.A., 1950, Ph.D., 1956. *Politics:* "Liberated Republican." *Religion:* Reformed Jewish. *Home:* 1212 South Pugh St., State College, Pa. 16802. *Office:* 225 Sparks Building, Pennsylvania State University, University Park, Pa. 16802.

CAREER: Pennsylvania State University, University Park, 1964—, currently professor of speech; ORCOMM (school and community communications firm), State College, Pa., owner, 1966—. *Member:* Speech Communication Association, Eastern Communication Association, Pennsylvania Speech Association.

WRITINGS: (With S. Crandell and J. Wigley) *Speech: A Course in Fundamentals,* Scott, Foresman, 1963; *Communication and the Small Group,* Bobbs-Merrill, 1966, 2nd edition, 1973; *Development of Oral Communication in the Classroom,* Bobbs-Merrill, 1969; (with E. Murray and D.

Truby) *Speech: Science-Art,* Bobbs-Merrill, 1970; (with E. Erickson) *Interpersonal Dynamics in the Small Group,* Random House, 1971; (with N. Metzger and D. Butt) *Communication and Education,* Holt, 1975; (with Metzger) *Intimate Communication,* Allyn & Bacon, 1976; (with J. Zolten) *Structuring Speech,* Bobbs-Merrill, 1976. Contributor of more than sixty articles to speech and education journals.

WORK IN PROGRESS: A book on overcoming shyness; research on individual coping in the bureaucracy.

*   *   *

PHILLIPS, James W. 1922-
(J. Philip Eblis, Bill McLaughlin)

PERSONAL: Born November 12, 1922, in Seattle, Wash.; son of Wendell and Goldie Nugget (McLaughlin) Phillips; married Elizabeth H. Shaw, December 10, 1943; children: James W., Jr., William R. *Education:* University of Washington, Seattle, B.A., 1949; attended Aspen Executive Institute, 1969. *Home:* 11302 Sand Point Way N.E., Seattle, Wash. 98125.

CAREER: Richland Villager (weekly newspaper), Richland, Wash., editor, 1949; *Columbia Basin News* (daily newspaper), Pasco, Wash., managing editor, 1950; *Pacific Northwest* (magazine), Seattle, Wash., associate editor, 1953; Bardahl International Oil Corp., Seattle, advertising manager, 1954-59; King Radio, Seattle, manager, 1960-70; Potlatch Advertising Agency, Seattle, general manager, 1972—. Northwest Writing Service, Seattle, owner, freelance writer, and public relations consultant, 1955—. Chairman, Seattle Youth Commission, 1965-67; member of board of directors, Northwest Artificial Kidney Center, 1969-72. *Military service:* U.S. Army; served in European theater, 1943-46; served in Korea, 1950-52; became second lieutenant; received Croix de Guerre and Silver Star. *Member:* American Names Society, British Names Society, Seattle Freelance Writers, Sigma Delta Chi Journalism Association.

WRITINGS: (With S. E. Mills) *Sourdough Sky,* Superior, 1969; *Washington State Place Names,* University of Washington Press, 1971; *Alaska-Yukon Place Names,* University of Washington Press, 1973. Author of TV, documentary, and industrial films. Contributor of more than three hundred articles to magazines in the United States, Canada, and England, sometimes under pseudonyms J. Philip Eblis and Bill McLaughlin. Founding editor, while in the service, of *The Ranger* (Fort Lewis, Wash., weekly newspaper); editorial consultant, *Pacific Search* (science journal); staff correspondent, *Alaska Industry;* editorial adviser, *Woodland Park Zoo Guide.*

*   *   *

PHILLIPS, John L(awrence), Jr. 1923-

PERSONAL: Born July 31, 1923, in Portland, Ore.; son of John Lawrence (a school principal) and Edith (Turner) Phillips; married Elaine Conrad, September 30, 1945; children: Greg and Jeff (twins). *Education:* Reed College, B.A., 1948, M.A., 1949; University of Utah, Ph.D., 1953. *Home:* 3233 Edson Dr., Boise, Idaho 83705. *Office:* Department of Psychology, Boise State University, Boise, Idaho 83707.

CAREER: Portland Public Schools, Portland, Ore., teacher, 1948-51; Carbon College (now College of Eastern Utah), Price, Utah, director of guidance and instructor in psychology, 1953-54; University of Utah, Salt Lake City,

instructor in educational psychology, 1954; Boise Junior College, Boise, Idaho, chairman of psychology department and director of student personnel services, 1954-57, dean of students, 1957-59, chairman of division of social sciences, 1959-68; Boise State University, Boise, professor of psychology and chairman of department, 1968—. State coordinator, American College Testing Program, 1959-66. Chairman, Board of Psychologist Examiners, State of Idaho, 1967-74. *Military service:* U.S. Army Air Forces, 1943-45; became second lieutenant. *Member:* American Association of University Professors (president of Boise Junior College Chapter, 1958-59), American Psychological Association Division on Teaching, American Association for the Advancement of Science, Rocky Mountain Psychological Association, Idaho Psychological Association (president, 1961-62), Idaho Academy of Science, Valley Personnel and Guidance Association (president, 1958-59).

WRITINGS: (Editor) *Counselor's Guide to Idaho Colleges,* Boise State College Press, 1965, 4th edition, 1971; *The Ontogenesis of Cognitive Structure,* Boise State College Press, 1966; (contributor) Frank W. Miller, editor, *Guidance Principles and Services,* C. E. Merrill, 1968; *Origins of Intellect: Piaget's Theory,* W. H. Freeman, 1969, 2nd edition, 1975; (contributor) Joseph M. Notterman, editor, *Readings in Behavior,* Random House, 1970; (contributor) Bruce Shertzer and Shelley C. Stone, editors, *Introduction to Guidance: Selected Readings,* Houghton, 1970; *Statistical Thinking: A Structural Approach,* W. H. Freeman, 1973. Contributor to *Journal of Educational Psychology, Clearing House, Rocky Mountain Psychologist, School Counselor,* and *Journal of Counseling Psychology.*

*   *   *

PHILMUS, Robert M. 1943-

PERSONAL: Born September 3, 1943, in New York, N.Y.; son of Herman (a designer) and Lillian (Jurmark) Philmus; married Maria Rita Rohr (a professor of English), June 12, 1967. *Education:* Brown University, B.A., 1964; University of California, San Diego, Ph.D., 1968. *Politics:* Democrat ("with a small 'd' as in ancient Greece"). *Religion:* Agnostic. *Home:* 4390 Coronation Ave., Montreal, Quebec, Canada. *Office:* Department of English, Concordia University, Loyola Campus, 7141 Sherbrooke St. W., Montreal, Quebec, Canada H4B 1R6.

CAREER: Carleton College, Northfield, Minn., instructor in English, 1967-68; Concordia University, Loyola Campus, Montreal, Quebec, assistant professor, 1968-72, associate professor, 1973-77, professor of English, 1977—. *Member:* Modern Language Association of America, Science Fiction Research Association, Phi Beta Kappa. *Awards, honors:* Academy of American Poets Prize, 1963.

WRITINGS: Into the Unknown: The Evolution of Science Fiction from Francis Godwin to H. G. Wells, University of California Press, 1970; (editor with David Y. Hughes) *H. G. Wells: Early Writings in Science and Science Fiction,* University of California Press, 1975; (editor) *H. G. Wells and Modern Science Fiction,* Bucknell University Press, 1977. Contributor of essays and reviews to literary journals. Member of editorial board, *Science Fiction Studies.*

WORK IN PROGRESS: Jonathan Swift and the Poetics of Indirection; The Literary Criticism of H. G. Wells.

*   *   *

PICKERING, James H(enry) 1937-

PERSONAL: Born July 11, 1937, in New York, N.Y.; son

of James Henry and Anita (Felber) Pickering; married Patricia Paterson, August 18, 1962; children: David Scott, Susan Elizabeth. *Education:* Williams College, B.A., 1959; Northwestern University, M.A., 1960, Ph.D., 1964. *Religion:* Protestant. *Home:* 1830 Bramble Dr., East Lansing, Mich. 48823. *Office:* The Honors College, Michigan State University, East Lansing, Mich. 48823.

CAREER: Michigan State University, East Lansing, assistant professor, 1965-68, associate professor, 1968-72, professor of English, 1972—, associate chairman of department and director of graduate study, 1968-75, director, Honors College, 1975—. *Member:* College English Association (director, 1976—), Midwest Modern Language Association, Phi Beta Kappa, Omicron Delta Kappa, Phi Kappa Phi.

WRITINGS: (Editor) Herman Melville, *Five Tales,* Dodd, 1967; (editor with E. Fred Carlisle) *The Harper Reader,* Harper, 1971; (editor) James Fenimore Cooper, *The Spy,* College & University Press, 1971; (compiler) *Fiction 100: An Anthology of Short Stories,* Macmillan, 1974; (editor) *The World Turned Upside Down: Poetry and Prose of the American Revolution,* Kennikat, 1975; (author of introduction) H. L. Barnum, *The Spy Unmasked,* Harbor Hill, 1975; (editor) *The City in American Literature,* Harper, 1977. Contributor to history and literature journals.

WORK IN PROGRESS: Research on colonial, revolutionary, and early nineteenth-century American literature.

* * *

PICKETT, Robert S. 1931-

PERSONAL: Born September 12, 1931, in Sanford, Me.; son of Max Edward and Edna (Phillips) Pickett; married Jane Niles (coordinator of honors council at Syracuse University), August 24, 1957; children: Elizabeth, Edward, Sarah. *Education:* University of Maine, B.S., 1953; Harvard University, A.M.T., 1957; Syracuse University, Ph.D., 1963. *Politics:* Democrat. *Religion:* Protestant. *Home:* 215 Stratford St., Syracuse, N.Y. 13210. *Office:* College for Human Development, Syracuse University, Syracuse, N.Y. 13210.

CAREER: Clarkson College of Technology, Potsdam, N.Y., assistant professor of liberal studies, 1962-64; Syracuse University, Syracuse, N.Y., assistant professor, 1964-70, associate professor, 1970-75, professor of child and family studies, 1975—, chairman of department, 1966-68, 1969-72, 1973-77, chairman of Syracuse University in the Netherlands, 1968-69, 1972-73. Visiting professor, University of Maine at Portland-Gorham, 1966, 1967. Associate, Danforth Foundation, 1968—. Metropolitan Commission of the United Methodist Church, Syracuse, chairman, 1967-68, member of board of directors, 1969—. *Military service:* U.S. Army, 1953-55. *Member:* American Historical Association, National Council on Family Relations, Organization of American Historians, Society for the Study of Social Problems, American Association of University Professors, Eastern Sociological Society, Tri-State Council on Family Relations.

WRITINGS: House of Refuge: Origins of Juvenile Reform in New York State, 1815-1857, Syracuse University Press, 1969. Contributor to religious and social science journals. Guest editor, *The Humanist,* May-June, 1975.

WORK IN PROGRESS: With Jeanne Davis, *Poverty Warriors at Bay: The Rise and Fall of the Community Action Training Center, 1964-1966;* an historical analysis of American family systems.

AVOCATIONAL INTERESTS: Art, coin-collecting, and drama.

* * *

PIERCE, Joe E. 1924-

PERSONAL: Born April 30, 1924, in Chickasha, Okla.; son of Velner Inez Pierce Campisi; married Gwendolyn Marie Harris (a school psychologist), April 29, 1944; children: Carol Jean (Mrs. Arthur Michael Colfer), David Brian. *Education:* Attended Bradley Polytechnic Institute (now Bradley University), 1943-44; University of Oklahoma, B.S., 1949; further study at University of Michigan, summer, 1952; Indiana University, M.A., 1952, Ph.D., 1955. *Politics:* Democrat. *Religion:* Congregationalist. *Home:* 512 Southwest Maplecrest Dr., Portland, Ore. 97219. *Agent:* Adele Bailey, 1000 Southern Artery, Quincy, Mass. 02169. *Office:* Department of Anthropology, Portland State University, Portland, Ore. 97207.

CAREER: Georgetown University, Washington, D.C., assistant professor of linguistics, 1955-61; Portland State University, Portland, Ore., associate professor, 1961-65, professor of anthropology, 1965—. Principal American representative for literacy project, Turkish Ministry of Defense, 1958-61; consultant to U.S. Peace Corps. *Military service:* U.S. Army, 1942-46, 1950-51; served in European theater. *Member:* American Oriental Society, American Anthropological Association, American Society of Political and Social Science, Linguistic Society of America, Middle East Studies Association, New York Academy of Science, Middle East Institute, Sigma Xi.

WRITINGS: Life in a Turkish Village, Holt, 1964; *A Linguistic Method of Teaching Second Languages,* Pageant, 1968; *Red Runs the Earth* (novel), Pageant, 1969; *Understanding the Middle East,* Tuttle, 1972; *The Sapien Homo* (poem), HaPi Press, 1972; *Languages and Linguistics,* Mouton, 1972. Also author of a Turkish word count, published by the Turkish Ministry of Education, in 1964. Contributor of more than seventy articles and monographs to professional journals.

WORK IN PROGRESS: The Bitter Winds, a novel; *Shades of Minos,* a novel; *Turks, Genii and ?,* a travel book; *Linguistic Analysis and English Grammar,* for Mouton; *The Hun,* an adventure novel; *Turkish Delight,* a novel.

SIDELIGHTS: Joe E. Pierce has lived and worked in Turkey and Japan, and speaks the languages of both countries.

* * *

PINCUS, Edward R. 1938-

PERSONAL: Born July 6, 1938, in New York, N.Y.; son of Jules and Anne (Schehr) Pincus; married Jane Kates (a craftswoman), June 20, 1960; children: Sami, Benjamin. *Education:* Brown University, A.B., 1960; further study at La Scola Normale Superiore di Pisa, 1960-61, and Harvard University, 1961-66. *Office:* Massachusetts Institute of Technology, E21-010, 77 Massachusetts Ave., Cambridge, Mass. 02139.

CAREER: Cambridgeport Film Corp., Cambridge, Mass., president, 1965—; Massachusetts Institute of Technology, Cambridge, lecturer, 1969-70, assistant professor, 1970-72, associate professor, 1972-76, adjunct professor of filmmaking, 1977—. *Member:* Society of Motion Picture and Television Engineers. *Awards, honors:* Fulbright fellow, 1960-61; Woodrow Wilson fellow, 1961-62; Guggenheim fellow, 1972-73.

WRITINGS: Guide to Filmmaking, New American Library, 1969, hardcover edition, Regnery, 1972.

WORK IN PROGRESS: Synchronous Sound Filmmaking; a five-year film diary.

BIOGRAPHICAL/CRITICAL SOURCES: Roy Levin, *Documentary Explorations,* Doubleday, 1971.

* * *

PINSKER, Sanford 1941-

PERSONAL: Born September 28, 1941, in Washington, Pa.; son of Morris David (a salesman) and Sonia (Molliver) Pinsker; married Ann Getson, January 28, 1968; children: Matthew, Beth. *Education:* Washington and Jefferson College, B.A., 1963; University of Washington, Seattle, Ph.D., 1967. *Religion:* Jewish. *Home:* 700 North Pine, Lancaster, Pa. 17604. *Office:* Department of English, Franklin and Marshall College, Lancaster, Pa. 17603.

CAREER: Franklin and Marshall College, Lancaster, Pa., assistant professor, 1967-75, associate professor of English, 1975—. *Member:* Modern Language Association of America, College English Association. *Awards, honors:* National Endowment for the Humanities fellowship, 1971; Graduate Institute for Modern Letters fellowship, 1971.

WRITINGS: Schlemiel as Metaphor: Studies in the Yiddish and American Jewish Novel, Southern Illinois University Press, 1971; *Still Life and Other Poems* (chapbook), Greenfield Review Press, 1975; *The Comedy That "Hoits": An Essay on the Fiction of Philip Roth,* University of Missouri Press, 1975; *The Languages of Joseph Conrad,* Editiones Rodopi, 1978; *Between Two Worlds: The American Novel in the 1960's,* Whitston Publishing, in press; *When Ozzie Nelson Died and Other Tragedies of Our Time* (poetry), Seagull, in press.

WORK IN PROGRESS: A book on Joyce Carol Oates; an anthology of American-Jewish poetry.

SIDELIGHTS: Sanford Pinsker told *CA:* "The important things to learn are how to laugh and how to pray. For me, poetry seems an ideal place to do both. It's a way of catching hold of a moment at a time when nearly everything threatens to slip by half-understood."

BIOGRAPHICAL/CRITICAL SOURCES: American Literature, November, 1971.

* * *

PITT, Peter (Clive Crawford) 1933-

PERSONAL: Born September 7, 1933, in London, England; son of Norman Ernest (a surgeon) and Emily Marjorie (Crawford) Pitt; married Anna Catherine Pratt, January 23, 1965; children: James, Rachel Louise, Daniel Crawford. *Education:* Guy's Hospital Medical School, London, M.B., B.S., M.R.C.S., and L.R.C.P., 1957, D.T.M.&H., 1960, M.R.C.P., 1961, F.R.C.S. (Ed.), 1963, F.R.C.S., 1964. *Politics:* Conservative. *Religion:* Church of England. *Home:* 3 Lake Rise, Romford, Essex, England. *Office:* 152 Harley St., London, England.

CAREER: British Army, Medical Corps, 1959-68; became major; surgeon at military hospitals in Kaduna, Northern Nigeria, 1961-63, Rinteln, Germany, 1965-66, and Dharan, Nepal, 1966-68; Redhill Hospital, Redhill, England, surgical registrar, 1968-70; Guy's Hospital, London, England, senior surgical registrar, 1970; Chase Farm Hospital, Enfield, Middlesex, England, senior surgical registrar, 1970—. Consultant surgeon, Old Church Hospital. Served as medical

officer to an expedition exploring central Iceland and observing winter warfare in Arctic Norway. *Member:* British Medical Association, P.E.N., Masons.

WRITINGS: Surgeon in Nepal, J. Murray, 1970. Contributor to medical journals.

WORK IN PROGRESS: Writing on medical topics.

AVOCATIONAL INTERESTS: Philately, skiing, photography.

BIOGRAPHICAL/CRITICAL SOURCES: Listener, December 31, 1970.

* * *

PLOWDEN, Alison 1931-

PERSONAL: Born December 18, 1931, in Simla, India; daughter of James Miles Chichele (an Army officer) and Margaret (Smith) Plowden. *Education:* Educated privately. *Residence:* Oxfordshire, England. *Agent:* John Johnson, Clerkenwell House, 45 Clerkenwell Green, London EC1R 0HT, England.

CAREER: British Broadcasting Corp. (BBC), London, England, secretary and scriptwriter, 1950-69.

WRITINGS: The Young Elizabeth, Macmillan, 1971; *As They Saw Them: Elizabeth I,* Harrap, 1971; *Mistress of Hardwick,* BBC Publications, 1972; *Danger to Elizabeth,* Macmillan, 1973; *The Case of Eliza Armstrong,* BBC Publications, 1974; *The House of Tudor,* Weidenfeld & Nicolson, 1976; *Marriage with My Kingdom,* Macmillan, 1977. Author of four radio plays, numerous radio historical feature scripts, and writer for BBC-Television series, "Mistress of Hardwick" and "The Case of Eliza Armstrong."

WORK IN PROGRESS: Tudor Women and Elizabeth Regina, 1588-1603.

* * *

PLOWDEN, David 1932-

PERSONAL: Born October 9, 1932, in Boston, Mass.; son of Roger Stanley and Mary (Butler) Plowden; married Pleasance Coggeshall, June 20, 1962 (divorced October, 1976); married Sandra Schoel-Kopf, July 8, 1977; children: (first marriage) John Stanley, Daniel Coggeshall. *Education:* Yale University, A.B., 1955. *Home:* 157 East 75th St., New York, N.Y. 10021.

CAREER: Great Northern Railway, Willmar, Minn., assistant to trainmaster, 1955-56; professional photographer, 1956—. *Awards, honors:* Guggenheim fellowship, 1968; Benjamin Barondess Award, 1970, for *Lincoln and His America;* Wilson Hicks Award, 1977.

WRITINGS—All with own photographs: *Farewell to Steam,* Greene, 1965; (editor) *Lincoln and His America: 1809-1865,* foreword by John Gunther, Viking, 1970; *The Hand of Man on America,* Smithsonian Institution Press, 1971; *The Floor of the Sky,* Sierra Club, 1972; *Commonplace,* Dutton, 1974; *Bridges: The Spans of North America,* Viking, 1974; *Tugboat,* Macmillan, 1976.

Photographer: Mab Wilson, *Gems,* Viking, 1967; Samuel Robinson Ogden, *America the Vanishing,* Greene, 1969; Patricia Coffin, *Nantucket,* Viking, 1971; Nelson P. Falorp, *Cape May to Montauk,* Viking, 1973; Berton Roueche, *Desert and Plain, the Mountains and the River,* Dutton, 1975. Contributor of articles with photographs to periodicals, including *American Heritage, Fortune, Horizon,* and *Architectural Forum.*

WORK IN PROGRESS: A book, *Industrial Landscape,* for Viking.

AVOCATIONAL INTERESTS: American history and environment.

* * *

PLUCKROSE, Henry (Arthur) 1931-
(Richard Cobbett)

PERSONAL: Born October 23, 1931, in London, England; son of Henry and Ethel Pluckrose; married Helen Fox, May 31, 1955; children: Patrick, Elspeth, Hilary. *Education:* Attended St. Mark and St. John College, 1952-54, and Institute of Education, London, part-time, 1958-60; College of Preceptors, F.C.P., 1976. *Home:* 3 Butts Lane, Danbury, Essex, England. *Office:* Evans Brothers Ltd., Montague House, Russell Sq., London WC1B 5BX, England.

CAREER: Teacher of elementary school-aged children in inner London, England, 1954-68; Prior Weston School, London, headteacher, 1968—; Evans Brothers Ltd., London, editor for art and craft in education, 1968—. *Military service:* British Army, Royal Army Education Corps, 1950-52.

WRITINGS: Let's Make Pictures, Mills & Boon, 1965, 2nd edition, 1972, Taplinger, 1967; *Creative Arts and Crafts: A Handbook for Teachers in Primary Schools,* Macdonald, 1966, 2nd edition, 1969, Roy, 1967; *Introducing Crayon Techniques,* Watson-Guptill, 1967; *Let's Work Large: A Handbook of Art Techniques for Teachers in Primary Schools,* Taplinger, 1967; *Introducing Acrylic Painting,* Watson-Guptill, 1968; (compiler) *The Art and Craft Book,* Evans Brothers, 1969; (editor with Frank Peacock) *A Dickens Anthology,* Mills & Boon, 1970; *Creative Themes,* Evans Brothers, 1969, International Publications Service, 1970; (editor) *A Book of Crafts,* Regnery, 1971; *Art & Craft Today,* Evans Brothers, 1971; *Art,* Citation Press, 1972; (compiler) *A Craft Collection,* Evans Brothers, 1973; *Open School, Open Society,* Evans Brothers, 1975; *Seen in Britain,* Mills & Boon, 1977; *A Sourcebook of Picture Making,* Evans Brothers, 1977.

All published by F. Watts: *Things to See,* 1971; *Things to Touch,* 1971; *Things to Hear,* 1973; *Things That Move,* 1973; *Things Big and Small,* 1974; *Things Have Shapes,* 1974; *Things That Pull,* 1974; *Things That Push,* 1974; *Things Light and Heavy,* 1975; *Things That Cut,* 1975; *Things Left and Right,* 1975; *Things That Grow,* 1975; *Things That Float,* 1975; *Things That Hold,* 1975; *Things Hard and Soft,* 1976; *Things Up and Down,* 1976.

Editor of "Starting Point" series; published by Mills & Boon, 1971: *Let's Use the Locality, Let's Paint, Let's Print, Let's Make a Picture, Let's Make a Puppet.* Editor of "On Location" series, sixteen books, published by Mills & Boon; author of the following books in the series: *Castles,* 1973; *Churches,* 1973; *Houses,* 1974; *Farms,* 1974; *Monasteries,* 1975.

WORK IN PROGRESS: More books in the "Starting Point" series of arts books for children five-to-eight and another series for the eight-to-thirteen.

BIOGRAPHICAL/CRITICAL SOURCES: Times Literary Supplement, April 16, 1970.

* * *

PLUNKETT, Thomas J. 1921-
PERSONAL: Born July 14, 1921, in Northern Ireland; son

of Emily Florence (Hunter) Plunkett; married Jean Mc-Murchie, September 20, 1947 (deceased); married Edith Mary Hodge, April 13, 1968; children: (first marriage) Linda Ann (Mrs. Daniel Wilcox). *Education:* Sir George Williams University, B.A., 1950; McGill University, M.A., 1952. *Home:* 78 Gore St., Kingston, Ontario, Canada. *Office:* School of Public Administration, Queens University, Kingston, Ontario, Canada.

CAREER: T. J. Plunkett Associates Ltd. (consulting and research service to governments), Montreal, Quebec, president, 1960-72; Queens University of Kingston, Kingston, Ontario, professor of public administration, 1972—, director of Institute of Local Government, 1972-77, director of School of Public Administration, 1977—. *Military service:* Royal Canadian Air Force, 1940-45; became sergeant. *Member:* Institute of Public Administration of Candad, Canadian Political Science Association, International City Managers' Association, Royal Institute of Public Administration (Great Britain), American Society of Planning Officials, Public Personnel Association.

WRITINGS: Municipal Organization in Canada, Canadian Federation of Municipalities, 1955, 3rd edition, 1958; *Urban Canada and Its Government: A Study of Municipal Organizations,* Macmillan, 1968. Also author of numerous reports on municipal and local government.

WORK IN PROGRESS: The Management of Canadian Urban Government, with G. M. Betts, for Institute of Local Government, Queens University.

BIOGRAPHICAL/CRITICAL SOURCES: Canadian Forum, December, 1968.

* * *

POERN, Ingmar 1935-
PERSONAL: Born August 19, 1935, in Vasa, Finland; son of Herman Hugo (a farmer) and Senni (Snickars) Poern. *Education:* Abo Academy, Fil. kand., 1960, Fil. lic., 1964; University of Birmingham, Ph.D., 1968. *Home:* 26 Chadbrook Crest, Brook Rd., Birmingham B15 3RL, England. *Office:* Department of Philosophy, University of Birmingham, P.O. Box 363, Birmingham B15 2TT, England.

CAREER: University of Birmingham, Birmingham, England, assistant lecturer, 1964-66, lecturer in philosophy, 1966—. Visiting lecturer, University of Uppsala, 1970-71. *Military service:* Finnish Army, 1960-61; became second lieutenant.

WRITINGS: Logic of Power, Barnes & Noble, 1970; *Elements of Social Analysis,* Institute of Philosophy, University of Uppsala, 1971; *Action Theory and Social Science,* D. Reidel, 1977. Contributor of poems to Finnish literary magazines.

AVOCATIONAL INTERESTS: Walking in Wales and Scotland.

* * *

POHLMAN, Edward 1933-
PERSONAL: Born January 30, 1933, in Chuchokee Malyan, India; came to United States in 1945; U.S. citizen; son of Edward W. and Edna (Kennedy) Pohlman; married Julia Mae Denlinger, September 2, 1956 (divorced, 1977); children: Douglas, Sharon. *Education:* La Sierra College, B.A., 1953; Andrews University, M.A., 1956; Ohio State University, M.A., 1958, Ph.D., 1960. *Office:* Birth Planning Research Center, University of the Pacific, Stockton, Calif. 95204.

CAREER: University of the Pacific, Stockton, Calif., assistant professor, 1961-64, associate professor, 1964-69, professor of psychology, 1969—, Birth Planning Research Center, director, 1972—. Visiting professor of psychology at Central Family Planning Institute, New Delhi, 1967-69, and University of California, Berkeley, 1972. Presented a series on population/birth planning on KCRA-TV, Sacramento, 1970. Consultant to World Health Organization and to National Institute of Child Health and Human Development. *Member:* American Psychological Association (member of task force on population and psychology, 1969-72). *Awards, honors:* Grants from Planned Parenthood/World Population, 1962-66 (series of grants), from Carolina Population Center, University of North Carolina for research in India, 1967-69, from U.S. Department of Health, Education, and Welfare for abortion counseling materials, 1971, and from National Institutes of Health for research on psychological effects of vasectomy, 1972-75.

WRITINGS: The Psychology of Birth Planning, Schenkman, 1969; *Children, Teachers and Parents View Birth Planning* (monograph), Central Family Planning Institute (New Delhi), 1970; *Incentives and Compensations in Population Programs* (monograph), Carolina Population Center, University of North Carolina, 1971; *How to Kill Population,* Westminster, 1971; *The God of Planet 607,* Westminster, 1972; (editor) *Population: A Clash of Prophets,* New American Library, 1973. Contributor of about fifty articles to professional journals.

*   *   *

POINTON, Marcia R(achel) 1943-

PERSONAL: Born August 8, 1943, in Newmarket, England; daughter of James R. V. (a schoolmaster) and Elsie (Richards) Collin; married Barry Simon Pointon (a children's author), August 1, 1964; children: Thomas Roland, Emily Martha. *Education:* University of Manchester, B.A. (first class honors), 1966, M.A., 1967, Ph.D., 1974. *Politics:* Socialist. *Religion:* Quaker. *Home:* 22 Freshfield Pl., Brighton BN2 2BN, Sussex, England. *Office:* Department of History and Theory of Art, University of Sussex, Brighton BN1 9RH, England.

CAREER: University of Sheffield, Sheffield, England, part-time lecturer and tutor in English and history of art in department of extramural studies, 1967; Open University, Bletchley, England, part-time tutor in English and history of art, 1970-73; University of Birmingham, Barber Institute of Fine Arts, Birmingham, England, research fellow, 1973-75; University of Sussex, Brighton, England, lecturer in history of art, 1975—.

WRITINGS: Milton and English Art, Manchester University Press, 1970; *William Dyce R.A., 1806-64: A Critical Biography,* Oxford University Press, in press.

WORK IN PROGRESS: A study of the art of William Mulready R.A., 1786-1863.

*   *   *

POPE, Robert H. 1925-

PERSONAL: Born October 15, 1925, in Bridgeport, Conn.; married Martha Jean Allen, September 6, 1947; children: Cynthia (Mrs. Delbert Liu), Robin, Jennifer. *Education:* University of Bridgeport, B.S. (mechanical engineering), 1951; Columbia University, M.S., 1954; New Brunswick Theological Seminary, B.S. (divinity), 1964. *Politics:* Liberal Democrat. *Home:* 39 Pascack Rd., Park Ridge, N.J.

07656. *Office:* Pascack Reformed Church, Park Ridge, N.J. 07656.

CAREER: Formerly rocket engineer designing and developing engine systems for air-to-ground missiles; Pascack Reformed Church, Park Ridge, N.J., pastor, 1972—. Member of board of directors of Park Ridge Public Library; president, Pascack Housing, Inc. *Military service:* U.S. Army, 1944-45.

WRITINGS: A Gift of Doubt, Prentice-Hall, 1971.

*   *   *

PORCARI, Constance Kwolek 1933-
(Constance Kwolek)

PERSONAL: Born June 20, 1933, in Schenectady, N.Y.; daughter of Stanley Constantant Kwolek and Marie (Simonds) Kwolek Preston; married Nicola Porcari, July 2, 1951 (separated, 1974); children: Nikki, Michael, Christopher, Lauren, Suzanne. *Education;* Attended public schools in Schenectady, N.Y. *Home:* 800 State St., Schenectady, N.Y. 12307.

CAREER: Has worked as a waitress, supermarket cashier, clerk, typist, laundry worker, house mother in a children's shelter, mailroom clerk, and concession attendant in an X-rated motion picture theater.

WRITINGS—Under name Constance Kwolek; *Loner* (novel), Doubleday, 1970. Contributor of short fiction to periodicals. Originator of drug information column in *Schenectady Gazette.* Editor, *Scene on Seventeen* (public television monthly magazine), 1969-70.

WORK IN PROGRESS: An erotic novel, *The Best Teacher;* a novel, *Under One Roof,* about societal hostility engendered by an adult female commune; *Journeywoman,* a novel about a hedonistic, nomadic cocktail pianist with a disturbing past.

*   *   *

PORTER, H(arry) C(ulverwell) 1927-

PERSONAL: Born November 9, 1927, in Bolton, Lancashire, England; son of Harry (a pharmacist) and Jessie (Hamilton) Porter. *Education:* Corpus Christi College, Cambridge, B.A., 1948, M.A., 1953, Ph.D., 1956. *Politics:* None. *Religion:* None. *Home:* 13 Warkworth St., Cambridge, England. *Office:* Faculty of History, Cambridge University, West Rd., Cambridge, Cambridgeshire, England.

CAREER: Princeton University, Princeton, N.J., Procter visiting fellow, 1956-57; University of Toronto, Toronto, Ontario, lecturer in history, 1957-59; University of California, Berkeley, visiting assistant professor of history, 1959-60; Cambridge University, Cambridge, England, fellow of Selwyn College, 1960-72, University lecturer in history, 1962—. *Military service:* British Army, 1948-50; became sergeant.

WRITINGS: Reformation and Reaction in Tudor Cambridge, Cambridge University Press, 1958; (with D. F. S. Thomson) *Erasmus and Cambridge,* University of Toronto Press, 1963; (contributor) George Bennett and John Walsh, editors, *Essays in Modern English Church History,* A. & C. Black, 1966; *Puritanism in Tudor England,* University of South Carolina Press, 1970; (contributor) *History of the English Speaking Peoples,* Volume XLVI, British Publishing, 1970. Author of operetta librettos (all first performed at Corpus Christi College, Cambridge), "Daisy Simpkins,"

1954, "The Literary Delinquent," 1955, and "The Dutch Uncle," 1956, and of British Broadcasting Corporation (BBC) television script, "Mary Stuart," televised in 1966. Contributor to history journals. *Cambridge Review,* editor, 1952-53, film editor, 1953-56.

WORK IN PROGRESS: England and the North American Indian, 1500-1700, for Duckworth.

* * *

PORTERFIELD, Nolan 1936-

PERSONAL: Born February 26, 1936, in Milliken, Colo.; son of Afton Arthur and Oneda (Beattie) Porterfield; married Peggy Pearce, December 22, 1956; children: Kelly Lynn. *Education:* Texas Technological College (now Texas Tech University), B.A., 1962, M.A., 1964; University of Iowa, Ph.D., 1970. *Home:* 402 North Sunset Blvd., Cape Girardeau, Mo. 63701. *Agent:* John W. Hawkins, Paul R. Reynolds, Inc., 599 Fifth Ave., New York, N.Y. 10017. *Office:* Department of English, Southeast Missouri State University, Cape Girardeau, Mo. 63701.

CAREER: Lamesa Daily Reporter, Lamesa, Tex., advertising manager and general manager, 1955-58; Southeast Missouri State University, Cape Girardeau, instructor, 1964-67, assistant professor, 1967-74, associate professor of English, 1974—. *Military service:* U.S. Army, 1958-60.

WRITINGS: (Contributor) Robert Shelton, editor, *The Country Music Story,* Bobbs-Merrill, 1966; (with Roy Swank) *Trail to Marked Tree,* Naylor, 1968; *A Way of Knowing,* Harper Magazine Press, 1971; (editor and author of introduction) *The Life of Jimmie Rodgers,* Country Music Foundation, 1975. Also author of a biography-discography of Jimmie Rodgers. Contributor to reviews and to *Harper's.*

WORK IN PROGRESS: A novel.

SIDELIGHTS: "Writing well is one of man's more truly pristine acts," Nolan Porterfield told *CA.* "Once having written well," he continued, "one achieves a state of grace, however temporarily. It may be the only thing that keeps me sane—or insane, as the need arises. With serious fiction in a state of flux, I'm looking for other ways—not really experimental ones (at least not so it shows)—to tell stories and write about people and affirm what few values I have."

* * *

POSTER, Mark 1941-

PERSONAL: Born July 6, 1941, in New York, N.Y.; son of Jacob H. (an accountant) and Rosalie (Greenstein) Poster; married Marianne Ross, July 24, 1965; children: Winifred, Jamie. *Education:* University of Pennsylvania, B.S., 1962; New York University, M.A., 1965, Ph.D., 1968. *Office:* Department of History, University of California, Irvine, Calif. 92664.

CAREER: University of California, Irvine, assistant professor, 1969-74, associate professor of European history of ideas, 1974—. *Military service:* U.S. Army, 1963-64; became first lieutenant.

WRITINGS: The Utopian Thought of Restif de la Bretonne, New York University Press, 1971; (editor) *Harmonian Man: Selected Writings of Charles Fourier,* Anchor, 1971; *Existential Marxism in Postwar France: From Sartre to Althusser,* Princeton University Press, 1975; (translator) Jean Baudrillard, *The Mirror of Production,* Telos Press, 1975; *The Family: A Critical Theory,* Seabury, in press.

POTEET, G(eorge) Howard 1935-

PERSONAL: Born March 31, 1935, in Baltimore, Md.; son of G. Howard (a computer operator) and Catherine (Aro) Poteet; married Hilda Klock, January 21, 1956 (divorced, 1961); married Frances Rosenthal (a teacher), October 3, 1961; children: Cynthia, Christopher, Jennifer. *Education:* Shippensburg State College, B.S., 1961; Columbia University, M.A., 1964, Prof. Dip., 1965, Ed.D., 1971. *Home:* 139 Sunrise Ter., Cedar Grove, N.J. 07009. *Office:* Department of English, Essex County College, 303 University Ave., Newark, N.J. 07102.

CAREER: English teacher in public schools in Pennsylvania and New Jersey, 1957-68; Essex County College, Newark, N.J., associate professor, 1968-74, professor of English, 1974—, head of department, 1968-75. President, G. Howard Poteet, Inc. (publishing firm). Film and linguistics consultant to schools and businesses. Member of town Committee on Narcotics and Drug Abuse, Cedar Grove. *Member:* National Council of Teachers of English (chairman of committee on film study), Modern Language Association of America, National Education Association. *Awards, honors:* Award of Excellence, Sixteenth Annual Exhibition of *Communications Arts* (magazine), 1975, for *Tom Swift and His Electric English Teacher.*

WRITINGS: Sentence Strategies: Writing for College, Harcourt, 1971; *The Compleat Guide to Film Study,* National Council of Teachers of English, 1972; *Tom Swift and His Electric English Teacher,* Pflaum-Standard, 1974; *Radio!,* Pflaum-Standard, 1975; *Death and Dying: A Bibliography,* Whitson Publishing, 1976; *How to Live in Your Van and Love It!,* Trail-R-Club of America, 1976; *Published Radio, TV, and Film Scripts: A Bibliography,* Whitson Publishing, 1976; *Workbench Guide to Tape Recorder Servicing,* Parker Publishing, 1976; *The Complete Guide to Making Money,* G. Howard Poteet, Inc., 1976; *Treasure Hunting in the City,* Ram Publishing, 1977; *Your Career in Chiropractic,* Richards Rosen, 1977.

Also author of tapes and text series, "The English Program," Williamsville Publishing, 1976. Contributor of poetry and short stories to periodicals and of articles to *English Journal, Media and Methods, Reading Instruction Journal,* and other professional and communications journals. Member of editorial board, *New Jersey Audio-Visual News;* contributing editor, *Film Journal Advertiser;* editor-in-chief, *How to Make Extra Money Newsletter.*

WORK IN PROGRESS: The Complete Guide to the Use and Maintenance of Hand and Power Tools; A Computer-Assisted Content Analysis of Film Criticism; A Critical History of Animated Cartoons; Film Criticism of Mordaunt Hall of the "New York Times"; The Film Star in Silent Films; The Flea-Market Wheeler-Dealer; Linguistic Analysis of Movie Ads; The RV Emergency Manual; Suicide: A Bibliography; Themes in Silent Films.

SIDELIGHTS: G. Howard Poteet told *CA:* "I have always wanted to write. When I was a young child, I took delight in writing stories. In the seventh grade I wrote a short story a week. My first published article, a description of winter in the country, was published during the summer between when I was in the eighth and ninth grades. I wrote for my high school papers in various schools that I attended and wrote for the newspaper and literary magazine while attending Shippensburg State College. However, I have always wanted to write for money and even today, I think that that is what proves a writer's worth. Even Shakespeare wrote for money, didn't he? Fame and all the trappings are less important than being paid cash for words. I know that most of my colleagues who are scholars will disagree (for after all, I have spent my life as a scholar—of sorts and I have the degree or union card, made it to become a full professor—tenured, of course and have been active in scholarly organizations). However, I fail to see why writers shouldn't be proud of the fact that someone is willing to pay to read what they've written.

"Of course, I have another interest in my writing. I believe that most writing is impossible. Absolutely impossible. I would like to write clearly. That is my goal—to say whatever I want to say so that it cannot possibly be misunderstood. Unfortunately, it seems that many scholars idolize obscurity and complexity. I think that the key to good writing is short sentences and simple words.

"If I have to have a purpose in writing, it is to show people how to do things—all sorts of things and to prove to them that almost anybody can do almost anything.... My advice to writers is to write and not to talk about writing or read about writing. Rather, they should read and find out what they like and then imitate it. Further, they should be as clear as possible.

"I have been influenced greatly by Hemingway and Steinbeck. However, I am fascinated by the writing of unknown or unsung copywriters who can turn interesting phrases and pack a world of meaning into a few concise well chosen words. I am not much interested in most contemporary writers of fiction at present but I enjoy reading non-fiction. It is very rare now days when I pick up a novel that holds my attention to the end. Very rare indeed. It's probably true that non-fiction is much more interesting than fiction at present and probably that will continue until fiction is a curiosity like much Victorian poetry."

After touring Auschwitz in the summer of 1974, Poteet wrote a poem, "For the Dead Children of Auschwitz." The poem was set to music and presented at a ceremony to the curator of Auschwitz by a group of American professors in Poland. The song is played before each group of people who tour the death camp.

AVOCATIONAL INTERESTS: Photography, bicycling, antiques, electronics.

*   *   *

POTOKER, Edward M(artin) 1931-

PERSONAL: Born June 13, 1931, in Newark, N.J.; son of Benjamin (a lawyer) and Bessie (Linn) Potoker; married Berit Arneberg, September 3, 1958; children: Eric Benjamin. *Education:* Dartmouth College, A.B. (magna cum laude), 1953; Columbia University, M.A., 1955, Ph.D., 1964. *Home:* 186 Riverside Dr., New York, N.Y. 10024. *Office:* Department of English, Bernard M. Baruch College of the City University of New York, New York, N.Y. 10010.

CAREER: New Yorker Magazine, New York City, member of editorial staff, 1957-58; University of Rochester, Rochester, N.Y., instructor in English, 1958-59; Hunter College of the City University of New York, New York City, lecturer in English, 1960; City College of the City University of New York, New York City, instructor, 1960-63, assistant professor of English, 1963-68; Bernard M. Baruch College of the City University of New York, New York City, assistant professor, 1969-70, associate professor of English and chairman of the department, 1971—. Member, legislative conference of the City University of New York. *Member:* Modern Language Association of America, American Asso-

ciation of University Professors, International Platform Association, Center for the Study of Democratic Institutions (Smithsonian Institution), Phi Beta Kappa, Andiron Club of New York. *Awards, honors:* Fulbright scholar at University of Munich, 1955-56.

WRITINGS: Ronald Firbank, Columbia University Press, 1969. Contributor to *Saturday Review, Nation, Encyclopedia International, New York Times Book Review, Phoenix,* and other publications. Founding member, *Journal of Critical Analysis.*

WORK IN PROGRESS: Post World War II German Literature; The Uncollected Stories and Plays of Ronald Firbank; a critical study of Ronald Firbank's novels, *Aesthetes' Yorick.*

*   *   *

POTTER, Dan (Scott) 1932-

PERSONAL: Born January 2, 1932; son of Horace and Wilmuth Lee (Skaggs) Potter. *Education:* University of Oklahoma, B.A., 1954; Yale University, M.F.A., 1965. *Politics:* Independent. *Religion:* Christian. *Agent:* Jane Wilson, John Cushman Associates, 25 West 43rd St., New York, N.Y. 10016.

CAREER: Writer. *Atlas* Magazine, New York, N.Y., editorial assistant, 1957-60; operator of a cabaret theatre in New Haven, Conn., 1960-62. *Military service:* U.S. Army. *Awards, honors:* Bread Loaf writing fellow, Middlebury College; runner-up, Delta Prize novel, 1965.

WRITINGS—Novels: The Town from the Treetop, Delacorte, 1965; *The Way of an Eagle,* Stein & Day, 1970; *The Age of Stoning,* Stein & Day, 1971.

Plays: "A Tango for Turtles," first produced in New Haven by Yale University Theatre; "The End of Mad Games," first produced in New Haven by Yale University Theatre; "The Enemy" (television), first produced by Canadian Broadcasting Corp. Also author of a screenplay, "The Way of an Eagle" (based on his novel). Contributor to *Redbook, McCall's, Cavalier,* and other publications.

WORK IN PROGRESS: A Candle for the Lord, a novel.

BIOGRAPHICAL/CRITICAL SOURCES: Best Sellers, March 1, 1970; *Times Literary Supplement,* December 25, 1970.††

*   *   *

POWELL, Adam Clayton 1908-1972

November 29, 1908—April 4, 1972; American congressman. Obituaries: *New York Times,* April 5, 1972; *Washington Post,* April 6, 1972; *L'Express,* April 10-16, 1972; *Time,* April 17, 1972.

*   *   *

POWELL, Peter John 1928-

PERSONAL: Born July 2, 1928, in Bryn Mawr, Pa.; son of William (a priest) and M. Helena (Teague) Powell; married Virginia Raisch (a caseworker), June 13, 1953; children: Katherine Anne, Christine Marie, John Christopher, Stephen Gregory. *Education:* Ripon College, B.A., 1950; Nashotah House Seminary, Nashotah, Wis., M.Div., 1953. *Politics:* Democrat. *Home:* 919 West Belden Ave., Chicago, Ill. 60614. *Office:* Newberry Library, 60 West Walton, Chicago, Ill. 60610.

CAREER: Ordained Anglo-Catholic priest, 1953; St. Timothy's Church, Chicago, Ill., priest-in-charge, 1953-60; St.

Augustine's Indian Center, Chicago, founder and director, 1961-70; Newberry Library, Chicago, scholar-in-residence, 1971—, research associate, 1975—. Founder and president, Foundation for the Preservation of American Indian Art and Culture, 1973—; member of advisory board, Center for the History of the American Indian. Consultant in Plains Indian ethnology, Southwest Museum, Los Angeles, Calif. *Member:* Western History Association, Phi Beta Kappa. *Awards, honors:* Rockefeller Foundation grant to study history and sacred ceremonies of Cheyenne Indians in Montana and Oklahoma, 1960-61; Bollingen Foundation fellowships, 1961, 1963; Chicago Commission on Human Relations annual award for work among American Indians, 1961; created Knight of the Kingdom of Yugoslavia by (deposed) King Peter II, 1968; Guggenheim fellowship, 1971; D.D., Nashotah House Seminary, 1971; National Endowment for the Humanities grants, 1973-74, for study of the role of chiefs and warrior societies in Cheyenne life, and 1975, to compile bibliography of books and manuscripts relating to the Cheyennes.

WRITINGS: (Contributor) Michael S. Kennedy, editor, *The Red Man's West,* Hastings House, 1965; *Sweet Medicine: The Continuing Role of the Sacred Arrows, the Sun Dance, and the Sacred Buffalo Hat in Northern Cheyenne History,* two volumes, University of Oklahoma Press, 1969; (author of introduction) Stanley Vestal, *Happy Hunting Grounds,* University of Oklahoma Press, 1975; (author of introduction) Maurice Frink, *Pine Ridge Medicine Man: The Biography of Doctor James R. Walker,* Colorado State Historical Society, in press. Contributor of articles on Indian history to journals. Member of editorial advisory board, *American Indian Art.*

WORK IN PROGRESS: Studying and recording the role of the chiefs and military societies in Northern Cheyenne history; also a study of Cheyenne military society art.

SIDELIGHTS: Peter John Powell has lived and worked among Indians since 1941. He is the first white man ever to have been elected to the Northern Cheyenne Chiefs' Society, and the first to have fasted with the Cheyenne on their sacred mountain for four days. He is a keeper of the Cheyenne sacred bundles.

BIOGRAPHICAL/CRITICAL SOURCES: Saturday Review, January 24, 1970, June 20, 1970; *New Yorker,* January 31, 1970; *Chicago Sun-Times,* March 8, 1970; *New York Times Book Review,* April 26, 1970.

*   *   *

PREEG, Ernest H.   1934-

PERSONAL: Born July 5, 1934, in Englewood, N.J.; son of Ernest W. (a port captain) and Claudia (Casper) Preeg; married Florence Tate, May 12, 1962. *Education:* New York Maritime College, B.S., 1956; New School for Social Research, M.A., 1962, Ph.D., 1964. *Home:* 2626 North Nelson St., Arlington, Va. 22207.

CAREER: American Export Lines Steamship Co., Hoboken, N.J., merchant marine officer, 1956-61; Brooklyn College of the City University of New York, Brooklyn, N.Y., lecturer in economics, 1962-63; U.S. Department of State, Foreign Service officer specializing in foreign economic policy, 1963—, with assignments as member of U.S. delegation to the Kennedy Round of Negotiations at Geneva, 1965-67, officer at American Embassy, London, 1968-69, member of planning staff, 1969-72, director of Organization for Economic Co-operation and Development and European Community Affairs, 1973-76, deputy assistant

secretary for international finance, 1976-77, and executive director of Economic Policy Group, 1977—. Foreign affairs fellow of Council on Foreign Relations and visiting scholar, Brookings Institution, 1967-68; research associate, National Planning Association, 1972-73. *Military service:* U.S. Naval Reserve, 1956-58; became lieutenant. *Member:* American Economic Association, American Foreign Service Association.

WRITINGS: Traders and Diplomats: An Analysis of the Kennedy Round of Negotiations under the General Agreement on Tariffs and Trade, Brookings Institution, 1970; *Economic Blocs and U.S. Foreign Policy,* National Planning Association, 1974. Contributor of articles and reviews to journals.

*   *   *

PREMINGER, Marion Mill   1913-1972

August 3, 1913—April 16, 1972; Viennese-born author, lecturer, and humanitarian. Obituaries: *New York Times,* April 18, 1972; *Newsweek,* May 1, 1972.

*   *   *

PREUS, Jacob A(all) O(ttesen)   1920-

PERSONAL: Born January 8, 1920, in St. Paul, Minn.; son of Jacob Aall Ottesen (a commissioner, state auditor, and Minnesota governor) and Idella Louise (Haugen) Preus; married Delpha Mae Holleque, June 12, 1943; children: Patricia (Mrs. Gerhard Bode), Delpha (Mrs. George Miller), Carolin (Mrs. Louis LaPrairie), Sarah (Mrs. Dennis Schwab), Idella (Mrs. Mark Moberg), Mary (Mrs. William Churchill), Jacob, Margaret (Mrs. Timothy Weible). *Education:* Luther College, Decorah, Iowa, B.A., 1941; Luther Seminary, St. Paul, Minn., B.D., 1945; University of Minnesota, M.A., 1946, Ph.D., 1951. *Office:* Lutheran Church-Missouri Synod, 500 North Broadway, St. Louis, Mo. 63102.

CAREER: Ordained Lutheran minister, 1945; Bethany College, Mankato, Minn., professor, 1947-50, 1956-58; Bethany Lutheran Church, Luverne, Minn., pastor, 1950-56; Concordia Seminary, Springfield, Ill., professor, 1958-62, president, 1962-69; Lutheran Church-Missouri Synod, St. Louis, Mo., president, 1969—. Member of Curriculum Commission of Board for Higher Education, Lutheran Church; Missouri Synod, member of Commission on Theology and Church Relations, observer at Helsinki; member of constituting commission of Lutheran Council in the U.S.A.

WRITINGS: (Contributor and translator) *Doctrine of Man in Chemnitz and Gerhardt,* Augsburg, 1954; (translator) Martin Chemnitz, *The Two Natures in Christ,* Concordia, 1970; *It Is Written,* Concordia, 1971.

WORK IN PROGRESS: Translating Martin Luther's *Commentary on Romans* and portions of John Gerhardt's *Dogmatics,* both to be published by Concordia.

*   *   *

PREUS, Robert   1924-

PERSONAL: Born October 16, 1924, in St. Paul, Minn.; son of Jacob Aall Ottesen (a commissioner, state auditor, and Minnesota governor) and Idella Louise (Haugen) Preus; married Donna Mae Rockman, May 29, 1948; children: Daniel, Klemet, Katherine, Rolf, Peter, Solveig, Christian, Karen, Ruth, Erik. *Education:* Luther College, B.A., 1944, B.D., 1947; University of Edinburgh, Ph.D., 1952; University of Strasbourg, D.Theol., 1968. *Politics:* Republican. *Home:* 1 Coverdale Pl., Fort Wayne, Ind. 46825.

CAREER: Ordained Lutheran minister, 1947; Concordia Seminary, St. Louis, Mo., assistant professor, 1957-60, associate professor, 1960-65, professor of systematic theology, 1965-74; Concordia Theological Seminary, Fort Wayne, Ind., president, 1974-77.

WRITINGS: The Inspiration of Scripture, Oliver & Boyd, 1955; *The Theology of Post-Reformation Lutheranism,* Concordia, Volume I, 1970, Volume II, 1972. Also author of *The Theology of the Book of Concord,* 1978. Contributor to *Concordia Theological Monthly, Springfielder, Lutherische Rundblick, Wisconsin Theological Quarterly, Scottish Journal of Theology, Lutheran Layman, Lutheran Witness, Affirm,* and other theological journals.

WORK IN PROGRESS: Volume III of *The Theology of Post-Reformation Lutheranism,* 1850 to around 1715.

*   *   *

PREVOST, Alain   1930(?)-1971
(d'Hugues Varnac)

1930(?)—December 19, 1971; French journalist and novelist. Obituaries: *L'Express,* December 27, 1971-January 2, 1972.

*   *   *

PRICE, Robert   1900-
(Morgan Drew)

PERSONAL: Born October 18, 1900, in New Radnor, Radnorshire, Wales; brought to United States in 1902, naturalized in 1906; son of James Edmond (a farmer) and Esther Ella (Thomas) Price; married Hazel Hanna Huston (a professor emeritus of home economics), September 5, 1938. *Education:* Denison University, Ph.B., 1928; Ohio State University, M.A., 1930, Ph.D., 1943. *Politics:* Independent. *Religion:* United Methodist. *Home:* Asbury Hall, Otterbein Home, Lebanon, Ohio 45036. *Agent:* Curtis Brown Ltd., 575 Madison Ave., New York, N.Y. 10022.

CAREER: Teacher in elementary schools in Licking County, Ohio, 1918-23; Ohio State University, Columbus, began as instructor, became assistant professor of English, 1928-44; Otterbein College, Westerville, Ohio, associate professor, 1945-46, professor of English, 1947-70, emeritus professor, 1970—, chairman of the department, 1954-65, archivist, 1968-70. *Member:* Midwest Studies Association, Ohio Folklore Society, Ohio Historical Society, Ohioana Library Association, Warren County (Ohio) Historical Society, Westerville (Ohio) Historical Society (archivist, 1960—), Phi Beta Kappa. *Awards, honors:* Fellowship in American studies, Library of Congress, 1945; citation in biography, Ohioana Library Association, 1955; citation, National Society for State and Local History, 1956; L.H.D., Otterbein College, 1973.

WRITINGS: (With S. A. Harbarger and A. B. Whitmer) *English for Engineers,* 4th edition (Price was not associated with earlier editions), McGraw, 1943; (with others) *Johnny Appleseed: A Voice in the Wilderness,* Swedenborg Foundation, 1943; *John Chapman: A Bibliography,* Swedenborg Foundation, 1944; *Johnny Appleseed: Man and Myth,* Indiana University Press, 1954; *Ben Hanby and Otterbein College: A Source Book,* Otterbein College, 1964; (editor) *The Road to Boston: 1860 Summer Correspondence of William Dean Howells,* Ohio Historical Society, 1971; *The Rabbit on the Lawn* (poems), Quiz and Quill Foundation, Otterbein College, 1975. Contributor to *Encyclopaedia Britannica, Collier's Encyclopedia, Indiana Authors and Their Books, English Journal, College English, New York Times,*

and other publications. Writer of poetry under pseudonym Morgan Drew. *Otterbein Miscellany,* founder, 1964, editor, 1966-70.

WORK IN PROGRESS: A work about Benjamin R. Hanby.

*   *   *

PRIEST, Christopher   1943-

PERSONAL: Born 1943 in England; divorced. *Residence:* London, England. *Address:* c/o Harper & Row Publishers, Inc., 597 Fifth Ave., New York, N.Y. 10017.

CAREER: Full-time writer, 1968—.

WRITINGS—Published by Harper, except as indicated: *Indoctrinaire,* 1970; *The Darkening Island,* 1972; *The Inverted World,* 1974; *Real-Time World,* New English Library, 1974; *The Space Machine,* 1976; *The Perfect Lover,* Scribner, 1978. Contributor of short stories and articles to British and American periodicals.

WORK IN PROGRESS: A novel tentatively entitled *The Affirmation.*

SIDELIGHTS: Christopher Priest told *CA:* "A writer discussing his own work is usually pompous or banal. A writer's private life is his own business. Yet somewhere between the fact of published work and the private life is the writer's only justification for existence; in this interface is the real work done. When I am working at the interface, I have not the least conception of what I am doing or why, although on either side of it I can be completely rational. All this is a vague way of saying that a writer can be modest or immodest about work he has finished, and try to analyse what he was attempting to do ... and before he undertakes a piece of work he can describe his ambitions for it, or his intentions with it. But while he is actually at work all he can do is write. It's very difficult to describe. I write because I enjoy writing, and that's as lucid as I can be."

*   *   *

PRIESTLEY, Barbara   1937-

PERSONAL: Born December 6, 1937, in London, England; daughter of George Gerrard and Anne (Peck) Wells; married Clive Priestley (in government service), August 4, 1961; children: Alison Virginia, Rebecca Janet. *Education:* University of Nottingham, B.A. (honors), 1959. *Politics:* "Left of centre." *Residence:* St. Johns Wood, London, England.

CAREER: Vocational counselor for Nottingham City, Nottingham, England, 1959-61, and for London County Council, London, England, 1961-64. Also has done primary teaching and market research on a temporary basis and occasional lecturing at University of Reading.

WRITINGS: (Compiler) *British Qualifications: A Comprehensive Guide to Educational, Technical, Professional and Academic Qualifications in Britain,* edited by Philip Kogan, Deutsch, 1966, 8th edition, Joseph Nicholas, 1977; *Your Career: In Retailing and the Distributive Trades,* Cornmarket Press/Daily Express, 1970; *Your Career: In Marketing, Sales and Market Research,* Cornmarket Press/Daily Express, 1970; *Your Career: In Teaching,* Cornmarket Press/Daily Express, 1970. Has written and broadcast scripts on motoring topics, humor, and personal reminiscences of United States for British Broadcasting Corp. radio.

WORK IN PROGRESS: A study of male attitudes to "women's lib."

SIDELIGHTS: In 1959 Barbara Priestley was the first woman ever to reach the finals of the National Student Debating Tournament for the *Observer* Mace. She says that she is interested in equality of work opportunity for women, but "otherwise uncommitted on 'women's lib'—so many of their grievances seem to be part of the *human* condition rather than peculiar to women."

AVOCATIONAL INTERESTS: Fencing, swimming.

BIOGRAPHICAL/CRITICAL SOURCES: Guardian, May 8, 1970.†

* * *

PROCHNAU, William W. 1937-

PERSONAL: Surname is pronounced *Prock*-now; born August 9, 1937, in Everett, Wash.; son of Emil W. (a businessman) and Florence (Foley) Prochnau; married Lani Gruger (a nurse), January 7, 1961 (divorced, 1978); children: Monica, Anna, Jennifer. *Education:* Attended Everett Junior College and Seattle University. *Home:* 2525 Minor E., Seattle, Wash. 98102. *Office: Post-Intelligencer,* Sixth and Wall Sts., Seattle, Wash. 98111.

CAREER: Everett Daily Herald, Everett, Wash., reporter, 1955-56; *Anchorage Daily News,* Anchorage, Alaska, sports editor, 1957; *Seattle Times,* Seattle, Wash., sports writer, 1958-62, Washington correspondent, 1963-73; manager of re-election campaign of Senator Warren G. Magnuson, 1974; free-lance writer, 1975; *Bellevue Daily Journal-American,* Bellevue, Wash., editor, 1975-76; *Post-Intelligencer,* Seattle, special projects reporter, 1977—. *Member:* National Press Club. *Awards, honors:* National Headliners Award for best domestic reporting of the first landing on the moon, 1969.

WRITINGS: (With Richard W. Larsen) *A Certain Democrat: Senator Henry M. Jackson,* Prentice-Hall, 1972. Author of several documentary films. Contributor to magazines.

* * *

PROKOFIEV, Aleksandr Andreyevich 1900-1971

December 2, 1900—September 18, 1971; Russian poet. Obituaries: *New York Times,* September 19, 1971; *Washington Post,* September 20, 1971.

* * *

PROKOFIEV, Camilla Gray 1938(?)-1971

1938(?)—December 17, 1971; British-born historian of Russian art. Obituaries: *New York Times,* January 26, 1972.

* * *

PROU, Suzanne 1920-

PERSONAL: Surname rhymes with "new"; born November 7, 1920, in Grimaud, France; daughter of Pierre (an army officer) and Marguerite Doreau; married Charles Prou (a professor of economics), April 20, 1944; children: Anne-Francoise Prou Paul. *Education:* Aix-en-Provence, Licence es Lettres, 1942. *Religion:* Roman Catholic. *Home:* 22 rue du Hameau, 75— Paris 15e, France.

CAREER: Novelist.

WRITINGS: Les Patapharis, Calmann-Levy, 1966, translation by Milton Stansbury published as *The Patapharis Affair,* Regnery, 1970; *Les Demoiselles sous les ebeniers,* Calmann-Levy, 1967; *L'Ete jaune,* Calmann-Levy, 1968; *La Ville sur la mer,* Calmann-Levy, 1970; *Merchamment, les*

oiseaux, Calmann-Levy, 1971, translation by Adrienne Foulke published as *The Paperhanger,* Harper, 1974; *La Petite boutique,* Mercure, 1973; *La terasse des Bernardini,* Calmann-Levy, 1973, translation by Joanna Kilmartin published as *The Bernardinis' Terrace,* Ellis, 1975, translation by Foulke published as *The Bernardini Terrace,* Harper, 1976; *Erika et le prince Grognon,* illustrations by Elisabeth Ivanovsky, Casterman, 1974; *Miroirs d'Edmee,* Calmann-Levy, 1976; *La Rapide Paris-Vintmille,* Mercure, 1977. Writer of radio plays: "La Fete," 1966; "Le the en mauve," 1968; "Une Oie, deux oies, trois oies," 1970. Contributor to *Le Monde.*

WORK IN PROGRESS: A book and a scenario.

SIDELIGHTS: Some of Suzanne Prou's books have been translated into as many as twenty languages, including Swedish and Spanish.

BIOGRAPHICAL/CRITICAL SOURCES: New York Times Book Review, June 14, 1970.

* * *

PUCKETT, (William) Ronald 1936-

PERSONAL: Born March 30, 1936, in Vansant, Va.; son of Burt and Ida (Baldwin) Puckett; married Edith L. Wood, July 17, 1957; children: Karen, Alan, Sheila. *Education:* Berea College, B.A., 1957; Florida State University, M.A., 1964. *Politics:* Democrat. *Religion:* Methodist. *Home:* 545 Carey Pl., Lakeland, Fla. 33803. *Office:* Department of English, Polk Community College, Winter Haven, Fla. 33880.

CAREER: Instructor in junior high and high schools in Lakeland, Fla. and Garden, Va., 1957-64; Polk Community College, Winter Haven, Fla., professor of English, 1964—. Radio announcer, WNRG, Grundy, Va., 1957-58. Tennis pro, Lakeland Bath and Racquet Club, 1970—, and Imperialakes Country Club, 1975—. *Member:* Florida Association of Public Junior Colleges. *Awards, honors:* Selected "Outstanding Young Teacher of the Year," Lakeland Junior Chamber of Commerce, 1962.

WRITINGS: (Compiler with M. L. Sutton and Henry Copps) *Now–Essays and Articles,* Glencoe Press, 1969; (with L. M. Sutton and M. L. Sutton) *College English: A Beginning,* Holbrook, 1969; (with L. M. Sutton) *A Simple Rhetoric,* Holbrook, 1969; (compiler with L. M. Sutton and O. K. Brown) *Journeys: An Introduction to Literature,* Holbrook, 1971.

SIDELIGHTS: Ronald Puckett has a strong interest in tennis, and is a ranked tennis player in Florida.

* * *

PULMAN, Michael Barraclough 1933-

PERSONAL: Middle name rhymes with "enough"; born April 20, 1933, in Liverpool, England; came to United States in 1950, naturalized in 1968; son of Maurice (a banker) and Beatrice Sara (Roberts) Pulman. *Education:* Attended Middlebury College, 1957-58; Princeton University, A.B. (cum laude), 1960; University of California, Berkeley, M.A., 1961, Ph.D., 1964; graduate study at University of London and Cambridge University, 1962-63. *Home:* 2620 South Fillmore, Denver, Colo. 80210. *Office:* Department of History, University of Denver, Denver, Colo. 80210.

CAREER: Duncan Ewing & Co. Ltd. (agents for lumber importers and shippers), trainee executive, 1954-57; Florida State University, Tallahassee, instructor, 1964-65, assistant professor, 1965-71, associate professor of history, 1971; University of Denver, Denver, Colo., associate professor of history, 1971—. Visiting assistant professor, University of California, Berkeley, summer, 1966. *Military service:* British Army, 1952-54; became lieutenant. British Army Reserve, 1954-57; became captain. *Member:* American Historical Association, Royal Historical Society (fellow), Historic Society of Lancashire and Cheshire.

WRITINGS: The Elizabethan Privy Council in the Fifteen Seventies, University of California Press, 1971. Contributor to *Journal of Library History, Journal of Politics, Albion, American Historical Review,* and *European History.*

WORK IN PROGRESS: Research on the life and work of Maud Diver; *The Essex Rebellion.*

* * *

PURCAL, John T(homas) 1931-

PERSONAL: Surname is pronounced Pur-*cal;* name legally changed, 1948; born September 20, 1931, in Kerala, India; son of Thomas John (a civil servant) and Anna (Kunchu) Puracal; married Nita K. Whale, December 12, 1964; children: Thomas Sachi, George Jamie. *Education:* University of Hull, B.Sc. (honors), 1959; Australian National University, Ph.D., 1964; Carlton University, Ottawa, Ontario, postdoctoral study, 1978. *Home:* 14 Colville St., Kings Langley, New South Wales 2147, Australia. *Office:* School of Economics, Macquarie University, North Ryde, New South Wales 2113, Australia.

CAREER: University of Singapore, Singapore, lecturer in economics, 1965-67; University of Calgary, Calgary, Alberta, assistant professor, 1967-69, associate professor of economics, 1969-74; Macquarie University, North Ryde, Australia, senior lecturer in economics, 1974—. Economist, International Bank for Reconstruction and Development, Washington, D.C., 1969-71. *Member:* Australian Economic Association, Australian Association for Asian Studies, Malayan Economic Society (life member; secretary, 1965-67). *Awards, honors:* Research grant from Agricultural Development Council, New York.

WRITINGS: (Editor) *The Monetary System of Malaysia and Singapore: Implications of the Split Currency,* University of Singapore, 1967; *Rice Economy: A Case Study of Four Villages in West Malaysia,* University of Malaya Press, 1971, published as *Rice Economy: Employment and Income in Malaysia,* East-West Center, 1972. Assistant editor, *Malayan Economic Review,* 1966-67.

WORK IN PROGRESS: Research on the role of health in economic development, and a comparative study of Australian and Canadian economic relationships with Japan.

* * *

PURDY, James 1923-

PERSONAL: Born July 17, 1923, in Ohio (Purdy has told an inquirer that the exact location of his birthplace is unknown); son of William and Vera Purdy. *Education:* Attended University of Chicago and University of Puebla, Mexico; additional study at University of Chicago. *Home:* 236 Henry St., Brooklyn, N.Y. 11201.

CAREER: Lawrence College (now University), Appleton, Wis., faculty member, 1949-53; for a time served as interpreter in Latin America, France, and Spain; began writing full time, 1953. *Awards, honors:* National Institute of Arts and Letters grant in literature ($2,000), 1958; Guggenheim fellow, 1958, 1962; Ford Foundation grant, 1961.

WRITINGS: (Self-illustrated) *63: Dream Palace* [and] *Don't Call Me By My Right Name, and Other Stories,* two volumes, privately printed, 1956, published separately in censored form as *Don't Call Me By My Right Name,* William-Fredericks 1956, and *63: Dream Palace,* Gollancz, 1957, *63: Dream Palace* published with additional stories as *Color of Darkness* (contains novella, "63: Dream Palace," and short stories, "Color of Darkness," "You May Safely Gaze," "Don't Call Me By My Right Name," "Eventide," "Why Can't They Tell You Why?," "Man and Wife," "You Reach for Your Hat," "A Good Woman," "Plan Now to Attend," "Sound of Talking," and "Cutting Edge,"), New Directions, 1957, *Color of Darkness* was published with an introduction by Edith Sitwell, Lippincott, 1961; *Malcolm* (novel), Farrar, Straus, 1959, reprinted with an introduction by David Daiches, Noonday, 1963; *The Nephew* (novel), Farrar, Straus, 1960; *Children Is All* (contains ten stories, including "Daddy Wolf," "Man and Wife," "Sound of Talking," "Why Can't They Tell You Why," "Everything Under the Sun," and "About Jessie Mae," and two plays, "Children Is All" and "Cracks"), New Directions, 1962; *Cabot Wright Begins* (novel), Farrar, Straus, 1964; (self-illustrated) *An Oyster Is a Wealthy Beast,* limited edition, Black Sparrow Press, 1967; *Eustace Chisholm and the Works,* Farrar, Straus, 1967; *Mr. Evening* (includes a story and nine poems), limited edition, Black Sparrow Press, 1968; (self-illustrated) *On the Rebound,* limited edition, Black Sparrow Press, 1970; *Sleepers in Moon-Crowned Valleys* (novel), Doubleday, Volume I: *Jeremy's Version,* 1970, Volume II: *The House of the Solitary Maggot,* 1974; *I Am Elijah Thrush,* Doubleday, 1972; *The Running Sun* (poems), Paul Warner Press, 1971; *Sunshine Is an Only Child,* Aloe Editions, 1973; *In a Shallow Grave,* Arbor House, 1977; *A Day after the Fair,* Five Trees Press, 1977; *Narrow Rooms,* Arbor House, 1978. Also author of two plays, "Mr. Cough Syrup and the Phantom Sex," 1960, and "Wedding Finger," 1974. Stories anthologized in *New Directions in Prose and Poetry 21,* edited by James Laughlin, New Directions, 1969, and other anthologies. Contributor to *Mademoiselle, Commentary,* and *New Yorker.*

WORK IN PROGRESS: Volume III of *Sleepers in Moon-Crowned Valleys.*

SIDELIGHTS: "So far as I'm aware," James Purdy once wrote, "I am against everything in America, everything publicized, and the eminent British and European writers who admire me, and have made my reputation, have praised my writing, not my membership in a club." Purdy, having been rejected by every first-line New York publisher, obtained funds for the private publication of *63: Dream Palace* [and] *Don't Call Me By My Right Name, and Other Stories,* and sent copies of the volumes to leading literary figures in London. Edith Sitwell (to whom he later dedicated *Color of Darkness)* was allegedly the first to find merit in the work. To her praises were joined those of Angus Wilson, Marianne Moore, Andre Maurois, and John Cowper Powys, who called him "the best kind of original genius of our day," and Dorothy Parker who remarked that Purdy's work was "of the highest rank in originality, insight, and power."

In spite of the acclaim he has won both here and abroad, Purdy still believes he is unread and unloved in America. Purdy told *CA:* "Reviewing in America is in a very bad state owing to the fact there are no serious book reviews, and reputations are made in America by political groups backed by money and power brokers who care nothing for original and distinguished writing, but are bent on forwarding the names of writers who are politically respectable. There are also almost no magazines today which will print original and distinguished fiction unless the author is a member of the 'New York literary establishment.' Reputations are made here, as in Russia, on political respectability, or by commerical acceptability. The worse the author, the more his is known." As a writer for *Book Week* noted, "Purdy's insistence that nobody reads him seems consistent with his bleak view of society. It is almost as though he believes the world is so bad it could not possibly accept him. If the world were to accept him, he would have to change his opinion of the world."

Many critics feel Purdy's world view, as expressed in his writings, is desolate at best. Gerald Weales expressed it this way: "The assumption is that all of us, in so far as Purdy really has the word on all of us, live in a house divided. For the most part the interior room, the 'real' one, the one where we *live,* is sealed off from the ones in which we meet other people, talk to them, desire them, marry them, kill them, construct them in our own image." Paul Herr writes that "James Purdy has created a world of his own. . . . His characters move on a stage as barren and starkly lighted as that of Samuel Beckett. . . . All man and woman relationships are presented as painful or absurd. . . . Upon occasion Purdy's people become angry, but they do not hate with passion. They call each other names. . . . It is a small, sad world, but it is also very close to an accurate image of life in America today." Many critics, including R.W.B. Lewis, have mentioned the "demonic originality" of Purdy's fiction. William Peden writes: "Purdy is as individualistic as a blue unicorn and at his best can do more with a whisper than most fiction writers do with a shout, as Dame Edith Sitwell has commented. Beneath the exterior of his stories, beneath the externally superficial conversations . . . the reader is afforded brief glimpses into a world in which the familiar suddenly becomes strange and terrible, as though one walking through a well-known terrain were suddenly to find himself at the edge of a void alive with sights and sounds only partly recognizable. Purdy's is a strange, unusual talent. His awareness of the murky depths of human cruelty or indifference is as startling as his recognition of their opposites."

Terry Southern mentions Purdy's "highly developed and often deceptive sense of the absurd." This sense is so unique and beguiling that Granville Hicks, in a review of *Malcolm* said: "What [Purdy] is up to . . . is not at all clear." Purdy's obscure vision may be due in part to his concern with human inscrutability, the inability to really understand human nature. "The more I read of Mr. Purdy the less I understand," T. F. Curley wrote for *Commonweal*. "[His] genius is at once so assured technically and so 'crazy' in its intuition that I wonder if he will ever come to grips with the familiar, the vulgar, the everyday." Herbert Gold has said of *The Nephew:* "Like Nabokov in *Lolita,* Purdy is pervaded by a hopeless, witty, intelligent nostalgia. He expects, but does not dare define just what it is he expects from life." Noting the dreamlike quality of Purdy's style, especially evident in his novel, *Jeremy's Version,* Guy Davenport of the *New York Times Book Review* writes: "All the characters . . . are trying to wake up and live, they tell themselves; their tragedy is that they do not know what this means, and remain as bewildered as children on a dull afternoon who want something, but do not know what they want."

Theodore Solotaroff, in a review of *Cabot Wright Begins,* states that Purdy, "a naturalist of unusual subtlety and a fantasist of unusual clarity," sometimes loses "the objectivity of his art" to the point where "characters and situations become inflated and pointless with exaggerations and the themes give way to a cackling and obscene rhetoric." W. T.

Scott wrote that "even in stories of real life, horror or terror are not, finally, enough. But the talent in *Color of Darkness* is so authoritative one expects it to do yet deeper things. It is a rich and passionate talent, already capable of memorable work, an excitement in new American writing." Peden believes that "nowhere does [Purdy] depict the morbid, the decadent and the sensational for their sake alone." Robert K. Morris agrees that "the end toward which he writes is a moral one."

Surprisingly enough, as Morris notes in his *Nation* review, in *Eustace Chisholm and the Works* "the quest turns out to be for love." Although he characteristically excluded, or perverted, love in his former work, in this novel "Purdy seems to have achieved a kind of self-liberation" in sounding "his first authentic note of love, hope, and compassion," according to a critic for *Book Week*. His previous novels having been a continuous "search for the proper expression of despair," in this novel "Purdy at last finds his theme, confronts despair, and surrenders to emotion, finding the proper balance between control and rage by giving up both, replacing the release of laughter with the release of compassion." Taken as a whole, Purdy's fiction can be regarded as one of the most powerful descriptions of "disassociation and human transgression to be found in American literature," in the words of Webster Schott. Schott believes Purdy's is a "personal torment of the kind that would drive a man to self-destruction if he couldn't write. 'I am not even writing novels,' Purdy says. 'I am writing *me.* I go on writing to tell myself at least what I have been through." In a letter to *CA* Purdy delivered a strong indictment of "our cigarette-beer-TV" culture, saying "I do not believe I am living in any Democracy but a plutocratic oligarchy run by Madison Avenue and vested interests." Since then he has written: "This is an age of exhibitionists, not souls. The press and the public primarily recognize only writers who give them 'doctored' current events as truth. . . . For me, the only 'engagement' or cause a 'called' writer can have (as opposed to a public writer) is his own vision and work. It is an irrevocable decision: he can march only in his own parade."

Dramatizations of several Purdy stories and his one-act play, *Children Is All,* were produced Off-Broadway, under that title, during the autumn, 1963 season. Edward Albee (who considers Purdy "a wonderfully cheerful, softspoken man") wrote a play based on *Malcolm,* first produced on Broadway at Shubert Theatre, January 11, 1966, and published by Atheneum in 1966. Merrick Gordon has written a television adaptation of *The Nephew,* scheduled for production by the British Broadcasting Corp.

Purdy has recorded "Eventide and Other Stories", released by Spoken Arts in 1968 and has recorded the entire text of his novella, *63: Dream Palace,* directed by Arthur Luce Klein and released by Spoken Arts in 1969. Purdy's work has been translated into 22 languages, including Chinese. The Modern Language Association of America devoted an entire seminar to Purdy's works at their San Francisco convention, 1975. A Purdy collection of manuscripts and critical letters is maintained at Yale University.

BIOGRAPHICAL/CRITICAL SOURCES:—Books: Joseph S. Waldmeir, editor, *Recent American Fiction: Some Critical Views,* Michigan State University, 1963; Richard Kostelanetz, editor, *On Contemporary Literature,* Avon, 1964; Harry T. Moore, editor, *Contemporary American Novelists,* Southern Illinois University Press, 1964; *The American Novel: Two Studies,* Kansas State Teachers College of Emporia, Graduate Division, 1965; Bettina Schwarzschild, *The Not-Right House: Essays on James*

Purdy, University of Missouri Press, 1969; *Contemporary Literary Criticism,* Gale, Volume II, 1974, Volume IV, 1975; Stephen D. Adams, *James Purdy,* Vision Press, 1976. Periodicals: *New York Times Book Review,* October 6, 1957, October 9, 1960, May 21, 1967, June 2, 1968, November 15, 1970; *Time,* December 9, 1957; *New York Times,* December 29, 1957, January 9, 1966; *Commonweal,* January 17, 1958, October 16, 1959; *Saturday Review,* January 25, 1958, September 26, 1959; *New York Herald Tribune Book Review,* December 29, 1957, October 11, 1959, November 18, 1962; *New Statesman,* May 7, 1960; *New Republic,* October 3, 1960; *Springfield Republican,* October 30, 1960; *Nation,* November 19, 1960, March 23, 1964, October 9, 1967, June 9, 1969; *Virginia Quarterly Review,* spring, 1963, autumn, 1967; *Wilson Library Bulletin,* March, 1964; *Book Week,* October 18, 1964, May 9, 1965, May 28, 1967; *New York Review of Books,* November 5, 1964; *Books,* February, 1967; *Life,* June 2, 1967; *Yale Review,* spring, 1968; *Twentieth Century Literature,* April, 1969; *Newsweek,* October 12, 1970; *Antioch Review,* spring, 1971; *Observer Review,* June 6, 1971; *Interview,* December, 1972; *Penthouse,* July, 1974; *Los Angeles Times,* December 18, 1977.

*   *   *

QUANDT, B. Jean   1932-

PERSONAL: Born August 30, 1932, in Cleveland, Ohio; daughter of John H. and Mary (Shepley) Briggs; married Richard E. Quandt (a professor), August 6, 1956; children: Stephen. *Education:* Connecticut College for Women (now Connecticut College), B.A., 1954; Radcliffe College, M.A., 1955; Rutgers University, Ph.D., 1970. *Home:* 162 Springdale Rd., Princeton, N.J. 08540.

CAREER: Rutgers University, New Brunswick, N.J., lecturer in history, 1970-71; Bryn Mawr College, Bryn Mawr, Pa., visiting lecturer in history, 1972-73; Rutgers University, visiting lecturer in history, spring, 1976; Princeton University, Princeton, N.J., visiting lecturer in history, spring, 1977.

WRITINGS: From the Small Town to the Great Community: The Social Thought of Progressive Intellectuals, Rutgers University Press, 1970. Contributor to education journals.

WORK IN PROGRESS: Research on feminism and reform in America.

*   *   *

QUINN, John Paul   1943-

PERSONAL: Born February 22, 1943, in New York, N.Y.; son of Paul Patrick (an advertising copywriter) and Catherine (Kenney) Quinn; married Zdenka Anezka Hodbodova (an author), July 10, 1968; children: Zdena Catherine. *Education:* Fordham University, B.A., 1964. *Home:* 88 Dean St., Stamford, Conn. 06902. *Office: Electrical Distributor,* 111 Prospect St., Stamford, Conn. 06901.

CAREER: Academy of Mount St. Michael, Bronx, N.Y., instructor in Latin and English, 1965-67; Buttenheim Publications, Inc. (business press), New York City, editor, 1967-69; Fairchild Publications, Inc. (business press), New York City, editor, 1969-76; *Electrical Distributor* (business magazine), Stamford, Conn., editor, 1976—.

WRITINGS: (Translator and adapter with wife, Zdenka Quinn) *The Water Sprite of the Golden Town* (from Bohemian folktales by Karel Erben and Bozena Nemcova), Macrae, 1971.

WORK IN PROGRESS: With wife, Zdenka Quinn, completing a novel based on the diaries of John Dee and on the life of Elizabeth Bathory, Countess of Cachtice; a children's book entitled *Rosalinda and the Basilisk.*

SIDELIGHTS: John Paul Quinn told *CA* he became aware through his wife, Zdenka, of "a mass of material—historical and literary—that has been relatively ignored by the English-speaking countries." *The Water Sprite of the Golden Town* is a children's book they have adapted from Czech tradition and literature. "Working as co-authors definitely has its advantages," Quinn told *CA,* in reference to writing with his wife. He continued: "Cross-fertilization of ideas and informed criticism are two of the obvious benefits. We also like to work on a few projects at a time, which we find is very good for keeping the imaginative juices flowing. For example, we found work on our fairy tale manuscript, *Rosalinda and the Basilisk,* moved along very quickly because it was something of a break between chapters and research on the serious historical novel about sixteenth-century Europe that we are now completing. And also, when your co-author happens to be your husband or wife, you can bet that a minimum of time will be wasted on formalities, rhetoric and the like. This contributes a healthy dose of practicality and pragmatism to the job. You either forgot your anniversary or you didn't; you either burned the roast or you didn't. You either wrote it the right way or you didn't. We can't imagine it any other way."

Concerning writing in general, Quinn said: "I consider what might be called the narrative element as the most essential quality of my work.... For a long while our works of letters continued to relate stories, telling them carefully and well. But in the past half-century there has been less of this and more and more posing, opinion-mongering and convoluted moralistic speculation contained between the covers of what it is considered to be fashionable to read. I should like to stay in the business of seanachie and skop, though regardless of fashion. It is, I think, the honest and the true way to write."

AVOCATIONAL INTERESTS: Travel.

BIOGRAPHICAL/CRITICAL SOURCES: Town and Village, January 20, 1972.

*   *   *

QUINN, Zdenka (Hodbodova)   1942-

PERSONAL: Born May 2, 1942, in Dobrovice, Czechoslovakia; came to United States in 1968; daughter of Miroslav (a design engineer) and Zdenka (Krejcikova) Hodbodova; married John Paul Quinn (an editor and author), July 10, 1968; children: Zdena Catherine. *Education:* Attended Antonin Zapotocky University of Economics, 1963-68. *Home:* 88 Dean St., Stamford, Conn. 06902.

CAREER: Writer and translator from the Czech.

WRITINGS: (Translator and adapter with husband, John Paul Quinn) *The Water Sprite of the Golden Town* (from Bohemian folktales by Karel Erben and Bozena Nemcova), Macrae, 1971.

WORK IN PROGRESS: With husband, John Paul Quinn, completing a novel based on the diaries of John Dee and on the life of Elizabeth Bathory, Countess of Cachtice; a children's book entitled *Rosalinda and the Basilisk.*

AVOCATIONAL INTERESTS: Skiing, Czech theatre, travel.

BIOGRAPHICAL/CRITICAL SOURCES: Town and Village, January 20, 1972.

RABKIN, Richard 1932-

PERSONAL: Born November 16, 1932; son of Jacob and Dorothy (Draper) Rabkin; married Judith Godwin (a research psychologist), June 8, 1961; children: Miriam, David, Jeffrey. *Education:* Harvard University, A.B., 1953; New York University, M.D., 1957. *Home:* 234 East 68th St., New York, N.Y. 10021.

CAREER: Private practice of psychiatry, New York, N.Y., 1963—. Assistant clinical professor, Medical Center, New York University. *Military service:* U.S. Air Force, 1961-63. *Member:* American Psychiatric Association, New York State Medical Society, New York County Medical Society.

WRITINGS: Inner and Outer Space: Introduction to a Theory of Social Psychiatry, Norton, 1970; (with Jacob Rabkin) *Fire Island: The Wonders of a Barrier Beach,* World Publishing, 1970; *Strategic Psychotherapy: Brief and Symptomatic Treatment,* Basic Books, 1977. Advisory editor, *Family Process* (a multidisciplinary journal of family research and treatment).

* * *

RADCLIFF-UMSTEAD, Douglas 1944-

PERSONAL: Born January 10, 1944, in Baltimore, Md.; married Countess Eleonora Della Fugata, September 7, 1964. *Education:* Johns Hopkins University, B.A., 1960; University of California, Berkeley, Ph.D., 1964. *Office:* Department of French and Italian, University of Pittsburgh, Pittsburgh, Pa. 15260.

CAREER: University of California, Santa Barbara, assistant professor of Italian and French, 1964-68; University of Pittsburgh, Pittsburgh, Pa., associate professor, 1968-77, professor of French and Italian, 1977—. Painter under initials DRU; member of Giovani Artisti Moderni in Florence, Italy, 1962-63; exhibitions in Italy, Maryland, California, and Pennsylvania. *Member:* Association of Teachers of French, Association of Teachers of Italian, Dante Society of America, Free World Academy. *Awards, honors:* National Endowment for the Humanities junior faculty fellowship, 1970; Guggenheim Foundation fellow, 1974.

WRITINGS: The Birth of Modern Comedy in Renaissance Italy, University of Chicago Press, 1969; *Ugo Foscolo: Biographical and Critical Study,* Twayne, 1970; (translator and author of introduction) Ugo Foscolo, *Last Letters of Jacopo Ortis* (novel), University of North Carolina Press, 1970; (with Patrizio Rossi) *Italiano oggi* (Italian review grammar and advanced reader), Appleton, 1971; (editor and contributor) *Innovation in Medieval Literature: Essays to the Memory of Alan Markman,* Medieval Studies Committee, University of Pittsburgh, 1971; *Death before Me Today* (prose poem), Free World Academy, 1971; (editor) *The University World: A Synoptic View of Higher Education in the Middle Ages and Renaissance,* University of Pittsburgh Press, 1975; (editor) *Roles and Images of Women,* University of Pittsburgh Press, 1976; *The Mirror of Our Anguish: A Study of Luigi Pirandello's Narrative Works,* Fairleigh Dickinson University Press, 1978. Contributor of articles to *Latin American Theatre Review, Philological Quarterly, Yale French Studies, Forum Italicum, Italica, Parola del Popolo, Mondo Libero,* and other journals. Member of editorial board, *Pirandello Newsletter.*

WORK IN PROGRESS: A study of the theme of lust in the *Divine Comedy.*

SIDELIGHTS: "Before I was a professor," Douglas Radcliff-Umstead told *CA,* "I believed I would have to 'publish or perish.' Now I know how a person can 'publish *and* perish.'"

* * *

RAGEN, Joseph E(dward) 1897-1971

November 22, 1897—September 22, 1971; American prison warden. Obituaries: *Washington Post,* September 27, 1971. (See index for *CA* sketch)

* * *

RAINE, Norman Reilly 1895-1971

June 23, 1895—July 19, 1971; American screen writer and creator of "Tugboat Annie." Obituaries: *New York Times,* July 29, 1971; *Time,* August 9, 1971.

* * *

RAJASEKHARAIAH, T(umkur) R(udraradhya) 1926-

PERSONAL: Born June 13, 1926, in Bangalore, Mysore State, India; son of T. R. (a state government officer) and Sulochana (Doddamani) Rudraradhya; married Vimala S. Doddamani, February 17, 1957; children: Rani Sulochana (daughter), Mallikarjuna and Harsha (sons). *Education:* University of Mysore, B.A., 1946; University of Nagpur, M.A., 1956. *Home:* Sivaprasada, Shivapuri Colony, Dharwar-1, Mysore State, India. *Office:* Karnatak University, Dharwar-3, Mysore State, India.

CAREER: University of Mysore, Mysore, India, lecturer, 1946-56, assistant professor of English literature, 1956-58; Karnatak University, Dharwar, India, reader, 1958-71, professor of English literature, 1971—. Member of American Studies Research Centre, Hyderabad. *Member:* All India English Teachers' Association. *Awards, honors:* Mysore State Academy Award for a book of short stories, 1960; senior Fulbright scholarship in United States, 1964-66; Knighthood of the Order of Mark Twain, *Mark Twain Journal,* 1974, for *The Roots of Whitman's Grass.*

WRITINGS: Swapanamangala and Other Stories (in Kannada), Sahajivana Prakashana (Dharwar), 1960; *Rudrakshi* (a book of poems in Kannada), Karnatak Sahitya Mandir (Dharwar), 1961; *The Roots of Whitman's Grass,* Fairleigh Dickinson University Press, 1970. Contributor of articles on English literature and Sanskrit drama to literature journals.

WORK IN PROGRESS: Walt Whitman: A Revaluation; research on the influence of Indian thought on English Romantic criticism.

* * *

RAJU, Poolla Tirupati 1904-
(Tirupati Raju Poolla)

PERSONAL: Born September 3, 1904, in Bapiraju Kohapalli, India; son of Narasimham and Satya (Narayana) Poolla; married P. Anna Purna; children: S. D. Poolla. *Education:* Benares Sanskrit College, Sampurna Madhyama in Nyaya, 1926, Sastri in Sanskrit literature, 1929; University of Allahabad, B.A., 1928; University of Calcutta, M.A., 1930, Ph.D., 1935. *Office:* Department of Philosophy, College of Wooster, Wooster, Ohio 44691.

CAREER: Andhra University, Waltair, India, lecturer and reader in philosophy, 1932-49; University of Rajasthan, Jaipur, India, professor of philosophy and psychology, 1949-62; College of Wooster, Wooster, Ohio, Gillespie Visiting Professor of Eastern Studies, 1962-64, professor of philosophy and Indian studies, 1964—. Tata Visiting Professor of Indian Philosophy, Asia Institute, 1949; visiting professor of philosophy, University of Hawaii, 1949, 1959, 1964, University of California, Berkeley, 1950, and University of Southern California, 1962; visiting professor of comparative philosophy, University of Illinois, 1952-53; Merton Guest Professor, University of Mainz, 1961-62. Lecturer at universities in India, United States, and Europe. Participant in conferences of professional organizations.

MEMBER: P.E.N., American Philosophical Association, Indian Philosophical Congress (sectional president, 1938, general president, 1960), All-India Oriental Conference (sectional president, 1943), All-India Philosophical Conference (general president, 1958), Committee on Gandhian Life and Philosophy, American Oriental Society, American Association for Asian Studies, Metaphysical Society of America, American Academy of Political and Social Science, American Association for the Advancement of Science, American Association of University Professors, Asia Society, Rotary International. *Awards, honors:* Certificate of Political Sufferers, Independent India, 1922; Order of Merit "Padma Bhushan" from president of India, 1958.

WRITINGS: Thought and Reality: Hegelianism and Advaita, Allen & Unwin, 1937; (editor with Dean Inge and others) *Comparative Studies in Philosophy,* Harper, 1951; *India's Culture and Her Problems,* University of Rajasthan, 1952; *Idealistic Thought of India,* Harvard University Press, 1953; *Telugu Literature,* International Book House (Bombay), 1954; *East and West in Philosophy,* University of Rajasthan, 1955; *Idealistic Approaches: Eastern and Western,* Baroda University, 1957; (editor and contributor with S. Radhakrishnan) *The Concept of Man: A Study in Comparative Philosophy,* Johnsen Publishing, 1960, 2nd edition, enlarged, 1966; *Indian Idealism and Modern Challenges,* Punjab University Publications Bureau, 1961; *Introduction to Comparative Philosophy,* University of Nebraska Press, 1962; (with W. T. Chan and others) *The Great Asian Religions: An Anthology,* Macmillan, 1962; (editor with Alburey Castell) *The Problem of the Self,* Nijhoff, 1969; *Lectures on Comparative Philosophy,* University of Poona, 1970; *The Philosophical Traditions of India,* Allen & Unwin, 1971, University of Pittsburgh Press, 1972. Contributor of over two hundred articles to philosophical journals and encyclopedias.

WORK IN PROGRESS: Prolegomena to Indian Philosophy; Phenomenological and Existential Consciousness; I-consciousness, Logos, and the Universal Spirit.

SIDELIGHTS: Many of Raju's books have been translated into Finnish, German, Spanish, Russian, and Japanese.

BIOGRAPHICAL/CRITICAL SOURCES: International Philosophical Quarterly, September, 1976.

* * *

RALPH, Elizabeth K(ennedy) 1921-

PERSONAL: Born February 5, 1921, in Trenton, N.J.; daughter of Paul Justus (a naval architect) and Margaret (Kennedy) Ralph. *Education:* Wellesley College, B.A., 1942; University of Pennsylvania, M.S., 1951, Ph.D., 1973. *Politics:* Republican. *Religion:* "Inactive." *Address:* Box 357, Woosamonsa Rd., Pennington, N.J. 08534. *Office:* University Museum, University of Pennsylvania, Philadelphia, Pa. 19104.

CAREER: Foote, Pierson & Co., Newark, N.J., junior electronics engineer, chemist, and assistant to chief radio

engineer, 1942-47; Kearfott Manufacturing Co., Newark, project engineer, 1947-49; University of Pennsylvania, Philadelphia, research assistant, 1951-55, associate in department of physics, 1955—, associate director of Applied Science Center for Archaeology, 1962—. Field work in Italy, Northern Ireland, Eire, United States, Canada, Greece, Mexico, Corsica, England, France, and Yugoslavia. *Member:* American Association for the Advancement of Science, Archaeological Institute of America, American Geophysical Union, Philadelphia Anthropological Society, Sigma Xi.

WRITINGS: (With others) *The Search for Sybaris, 1960-1965,* Lerici Editori (Rome), 1967; (contributor) D. J. McDougall, editor, *Thermoluminescence of Geological Materials,* Academic Press, 1968; (contributor) R. Berger, editor, *Scientific Methods in Medieval Archaeology,* University of California Press, 1970; (contributor) I. U. Olsson, editor, *Radiocarbon Variations and Absolute Chronology,* Wiley, 1970; (contributor) R. H. Brill, editor, *Science and Archaeology,* M.I.T. Press, 1971; (editor with H. N. Michael, and contributor) *Dating Techniques for the Archaeologist,* M.I.T. Press, 1971. Contributor to *Science, Pennsylvania Archaeologist, Wellesley Alumnae Magazine, American Antiquity, Expedition, American Journal of Science, Nature, American Journal of Archaeology, Archaeometry,* and other publications.

* * *

RAMSEY, Jarold 1937-

PERSONAL: Born September 1, 1937, in Bend, Ore.; son of A. S. (a rancher and a judge) and Wilma (Mendenhall) Ramsey; married Dorothy A. Quinn, August 16, 1959; children: Kate, Sophia, John. *Education:* University of Oregon, B.A. (with honors), 1959; University of Washington, Seattle, Ph.D., 1965. *Politics:* Democrat. *Religion:* Protestant. *Home:* 519 Wellington Ave., Rochester, N.Y. 14619. *Office:* English Department, University of Rochester, Rochester, N.Y. 14627.

CAREER: University of Rochester, Rochester, N.Y., instructor, 1965-66, assistant professor, 1966-70, associate professor of English, 1971—. Poetry director, Rochester Writers Workshop, 1971—; visiting professor of English, University of Victoria (British Columbia), 1974, 1976; consultant to various publishing companies. *Member:* Modern Language Association of America, American Folklore Society, Phi Beta Kappa. *Awards, honors:* Lillian Fairchild Award, 1973; National Endowment for the Humanities Librettist grant, 1974; Ingram Merrill Award, 1975; National Endowment for the Humanities creative writing fellowship, 1976.

WRITINGS: The Space between Us, Adam Books, 1970; *Love in an Earthquake,* University of Washington Press, 1973; (with Samuel Adler) *The Lodge of Shadows, a Cantata,* Fischer, 1976; *Coyote Was Going There: Indian Literature of the Oregon Country,* University of Washington Press, 1977. Poetry anthologized in *Shaking the Pumpkin,* edited by Jerome Rothenburg, Doubleday, 1972, and *Best Poems: Borestone Mountain Awards,* Pacific Books, 1973, 1975. Contributor to *Atlantic, Nation, Ohio Review, Poetry Northwest, Shenandoah, Quarterly Review of Literature, Northwest Review,* and other publications.

WORK IN PROGRESS: Telling the Fire, essays on American Indian literature; *At Home with Strangers,* a book of poems; *Mandy's Year,* a novel; a book on major modern British and American poets.

SIDELIGHTS: Jarold Ramsey told *CA:* "[I] grew up on a ranch in central Oregon, near an Indian reservation: the thrust of my poetry is to realize these influences (the forms of nature in a bleak, noble landscape, the imagination of the Indians who first possessed this landscape) as a way of coming to poetic terms with the qualities of life in our times. I'm much interested in so-called 'primitive' or 'folk' literature generally; I'd like to create a poetry of *ceremony*—conveying the sense that if you 'do it right,' something will happen.

"I rejoice in the reappearance of Regionalism in American writing: we very much need the sense of place. It may be that Art, like Charity its sponsor, should begin at home."

AVOCATIONAL INTERESTS: Fishing, mountain climbing, carpentry, woodcarving, and searching for Indian artifacts.

* * *

RANDALL, Julia (Sawyer) 1923-

PERSONAL: Born June 15, 1923, in Baltimore, Md.; divorced. *Education:* Bennington College, B.A., 1945; Johns Hopkins University, M.A., 1950. *Residence:* Baltimore County, Md.

CAREER: Harvard University, Cambridge, Mass., technician in biological laboratory, 1946-48; Johns Hopkins University, McCoy College, Baltimore, Md., instructor, 1949-52; University of Maryland Overseas Extension, Paris, France, instructor, 1952-53; Goucher College, Towson, Md., assistant in library, 1954-56; Peabody Conservatory, Baltimore, instructor, 1956-59; Towson State College (now University), Baltimore, 1958-62, began as instructor, became assistant professor of English; Hollins College, Hollins College, Va., assistant professor, 1962-66, associate professor of English, 1966-73. Has given poetry readings at Vanderbilt University, University of North Carolina, University of Tennessee, Library of Congress, Washington and Lee University, and other schools. *Awards, honors:* Sewanee *Review* fellowship in poetry, 1957-58; National Council on the Arts grant, 1966-67; National Institute of Arts and Letters Award in Literature, 1968-69.

WRITINGS—Poetry: The Solstice Tree, Contemporary Poetry, 1952; *Mimic August,* Contemporary Poetry, 1960; *Four Poems,* Tinker Press, 1964; *The Puritan Carpenter,* University of North Carolina Press, 1965; *Adam's Dream,* Tinker Press, 1966, published as *Adam's Dream: Poems,* Knopf, 1969. Contributor to *Botteghe Oscure, Poetry* (Chicago), *Kenyon Review, Sewanee Review,* and other literary magazines.

SIDELIGHTS: "Julia Randall writes the sort of canticle that only good sinners can write, a praise of created things that seems, because of its secularization, to rise more spontaneously and with a completely open lyricism," says a *Virginia Quarterly Review* critic. Dudley Fitts criticizes her as "too conscious of poetry as literature: it is as though she were haunted by seminars, distressed by dissections of poets greatly dead." Her poems are "wiry, wise, and astonishingly pure," writes Robert Wallace.

BIOGRAPHICAL/CRITICAL SOURCES: New York Times Book Review, April 17, 1966; *Saturday Review,* January 17, 1970; *Virginia Quarterly Review,* spring, 1970.

* * *

RAPER, J(ulius) R(owan) 1938-
(Jack Raper)

PERSONAL: Born March 12, 1938, in Raleigh, N.C.; son of Julius Rowan, Jr. (a social work administrator) and Emma (Hayes) Raper; married Anne Louise Browning (a research assistant, teacher, and author), December 22, 1962; children: Fern Rowanne, Keith Alexander. *Education:* University of North Carolina, A.B., 1960; Duke University, M.A., 1962; Northwestern University, Ph.D., 1966. *Politics:* "Independent: Jeffersonian-Liberal." *Religion:* "Independent: Neo-psycho-polytheist." *Home:* 1404 Wildwood Dr., Chapel Hill, N.C. 27514. *Office:* Department of English, University of North Carolina, Chapel Hill, N.C. 27514.

CAREER: U.S. Bureau of the Census, Washington, D.C., writer and editor, 1961; Chicago Northside Newspapers, Chicago, Ill., writer and editor, 1963; University of North Carolina at Chapel Hill, assistant professor, 1966-72, associate professor of American literature, 1972—. Fulbright lecturer in American literature, Aristotelian University of Salonika, Greece, 1972-74. *Member:* Modern Language Association of America, American Association of University Professors, South Atlantic Modern Language Association, Phi Beta Kappa. *Awards, honors:* Woodrow Wilson fellow, 1960; Council of Southern Universities fellowship, 1960-63.

WRITINGS: Without Shelter: The Early Career of Ellen Glasgow, Louisiana State University Press, 1971. Contributor of articles, poems, and stories to literary journals.

WORK IN PROGRESS: Taking Fire, a novel; continued research on American literature; *From the Sunken Garden: The Fiction of Ellen Glasgow, 1916-1945; A Reasonable Doubt: A Collection of Glasgow's Essays; Under the Byzantine Rainbow.*

SIDELIGHTS: "So many things happened during the two years I was in Greece," J. R. Raper wrote *CA,* "that I came back obsessed with traditional storytelling as opposed to psychological analysis in fiction. This obsession shows up in both my new fiction and my criticism. In the process I have developed a theory that fictions of action are themselves a psychology that turns people inside out."

* * *

RAPOPORT, Roger 1946-

PERSONAL: Born May 7, 1946, in Detroit, Mich.; son of Daniel B. and Shirley (Goodman) Rapoport; married Margot R. Lind, October 9, 1970. *Education:* University of Michigan, B.A., 1968. *Residence:* Berkeley, Calif. *Agent:* Sterling Lord Agency, 660 Madison Ave., New York, N.Y. 10021.

CAREER: Free-lance journalist, 1968—.

WRITINGS: (With L. J. Kirshbaum) *Is the Library Burning?,* Random House, 1969; *The Great American Bomb Machine,* Dutton, 1971; *The Superdoctors,* Playboy Press, 1975; (with Margot Lind) *The California Catalogue,* Dutton, 1977; (with Ken Uston) *The Big Player,* Holt, 1977. Contributor to magazines and newspapers, including *Esquire, New Republic, McCall's, Sports Illustrated, Atlantic, West, Ramparts, Wall Street Journal,* and *Washington Post.*

SIDELIGHTS: Roger Rapoport's special interest is investigative reporting—directed at finding ways to solve the various ecological, military, nuclear, and educational crises facing the country. "I'm not sure I've found answers but [I've] enjoyed looking for them," he writes.

RASKIN, Eugene 1909-

PERSONAL: Born September 5, 1909, in New York, N.Y.; son of Saul (an artist) and Raya (Rosenthal) Raskin; married Francesca Leonard (a singer), January 8, 1938; children: Michael, Jonathan. *Education:* Columbia University, B.A., 1930, M.Arch., 1932; University of Paris, C.I.A. et A., 1932. *Home:* 316 West 79th St., New York, N.Y. 10024. *Agent:* Curtis Brown Ltd., 575 Madison Ave., New York, N.Y. 10022.

CAREER: Principal, Phillips, Raskin & Volmer (architects), 1937-39; consultant and critic, 1939-42; Columbia University, New York, N.Y., professor of architecture, 1942-76. Playwright and composer. *Member:* American Institute of Architects, American Guild of Authors and Composers, American Federation of Musicians, Authors League of America, Dramatists Guild, American Society of Composers, Authors and Publishers. *Awards, honors:* Institute of International Education traveling fellow, 1932; Langley fellow of American Institute of Architects, 1952; first prize for documentary at American Film Festival, 1964, for "How to Look at a City"; Gold Record Award, 1969.

WRITINGS: Architecturally Speaking, Reinhold, 1954, 3rd edition, Bloch Publishing, 1970; *Sequel to Cities: The Post Urban Society,* Rebel Press (London), 1969, 3rd edition, Bloch Publishing, 1970; *Last Island* (play; first produced in Dallas, Tex., at Margo Jones Theater, 1954), Rebel Press, 1970; *Stranger in My Arms* (novel), Dell, 1971; *Architecture and People,* Prentice-Hall, 1975.

Unpublished plays: "One's a Crowd," first produced in New York at Greenwich Mews Theatre, 1951; "Amata," first produced Off-Broadway at Circle-in-the-Square Theatre, 1952; "Old Friend," produced on television, 1956. Published songs include an international hit, "Those Were the Days." Also author of scripts for films "How to Look at a City" and "How to Live in a City."

WORK IN PROGRESS: A novel; various articles.

SIDELIGHTS: Stranger in My Arms has been produced as a film. *Architecture and People* has been translated into Spanish.

*   *   *

RASKIN, Joseph 1897-

PERSONAL: Born April 14, 1897, in Russia; son of Naphthali (a merchant) and Lea (Vaniler) Raskin; married Edith Lefkowitz (a writer), October 30, 1936. *Education:* Attended National Academy of Design for seven years. *Politics:* Independent. *Home and office:* 59 West 71st St., New York, N.Y. 10023. *Agent:* Bertha Klausner International Literary Agency, Inc., 71 Park Ave., New York, N.Y. 10016.

CAREER: Painter and etcher; etchings of American universities exhibited in one-man show at New York Historical Society, 1975; work has been exhibited in galleries throughout the United States, including Carnegie Institute, Corcoran Gallery, and National Academy of Design, and in Paris and Berlin. *Member:* Audubon Artists Association. *Awards, honors:* Chalon Prize for painting, 1921; Mooney European scholarship in art, 1922; Tiffany Foundation fellowship, 1922-24.

WRITINGS: Portfolio of Harvard Etchings (self-illustrated), Rudge Publishing Co., 1935; (contributor) *Literature: Mythology and Folklore,* edited by James B. Hogins, Science Research Associates, 1975.

With wife, Edith Raskin; published by Lothrop, except as indicated: *Indian Tales,* Random House, 1969; *Tales Our Settlers Told,* 1971; *Ghosts and Witches Aplenty: More Tales Our Settlers Told,* 1973; *The Newcomers: Ten Tales of American Immigrants,* 1974; *Guilty or Not Guilty: Tales of Justice in Early America,* 1975; *Spies and Traitors: Tales of the Revolutionary and Civil Wars,* 1976; *Strange Shadows: Spirit Tales of Early America,* 1977.

WORK IN PROGRESS: Adventures on Land and Sea; Early American Tales.

SIDELIGHTS: Joseph Raskin told *CA:* "Ever since I can remember I liked to draw and paint. When I was twelve years old, impressed by an event that occurred in my little town of Nogaisk, I wrote a tragedy in five acts with an epilogue, which has remained a secret to this day. Also, I played the cornet in my high school band and tried to play any instrument I could lay my hands on. Believing that all the arts have basic principles in common, I tried to pursue them all. In time, however, painting and writing became my dominant interests.

"While studying abroad, I was impressed by the Rhine and the countryside along the Seine River. But returning home and seeing the Hudson River again, I was even more moved by the majesty of this waterway. Eventually its history prompted me, together with my wife, to write a group of tales about the Hudson which the Indians called the Shatemuc. Also the legends of New England where my wife and I spent many a summer inspired us to continue writing about early American life. At present my wife and I are engaged in writing still another book dealing with the same fascinating period."

AVOCATIONAL INTERESTS: Travel, music, sports, cooking.

*   *   *

RASMUSSEN, Wayne D(avid) 1915-

PERSONAL: Born February 5, 1915, in Ryegate, Mont.; son of Anton (a rancher) and Ethel (Bassett) Rasmussen; married Marion Hollingworth Fowler, December 27, 1939; children: Paul Wayne, Karen Ellen, Linda Marion. *Education:* Attended Eastern Montana College, 1932-33; University of Montana, B.A., 1937; George Washington University, M.A., 1939, Ph.D., 1950. *Home:* 3907 Ridge Rd., Annandale, Va. 22003. *Office:* U.S. Department of Agriculture, Washington, D.C. 20250.

CAREER: U.S. Department of Agriculture, Washington, D.C., records management, 1937-40, historian, 1940—, chief of agricultural history branch, 1961—. Lecturer, U.S. Department of Agriculture Graduate School, 1950; professor, University of Maryland, 1963—. *Military service:* U.S. Army, 1943-46. *Member:* Agricultural History Society (executive secretary, 1952-62, 1965; president, 1965), American Historical Association, Economic History Association, British Agricultural History Society, American Agricultural Economics Association, Organization of American Historians, Association for Living Historical Farms (president, 1977), Western Historical Association, Southern Historical Association, Cosmos Club.

WRITINGS: A History of the Emergency Farm Labor Supply Program, 1943-47, U.S. Government Printing Office, 1951; *Liberal Education and Agriculture,* Teachers College Press, 1957; (editor) *Readings in the History of American Agriculture,* University of Illinois Press, 1960; (editor) *Growth through Agricultural Progress* (lecture series), U.S. Department of Agriculture, 1961; (contributor) *Century of Service: The First One Hundred Years of the United States Department of Agriculture,* U.S. Government Printing Office, 1963; (contributor) *History of Technology,* Oxford University Press, 1963; (with Gladys L. Baker) *The United States Department of Agriculture,* Praeger, 1972; *Agricultural History in the United States: A Documentary History,* Random House, 1975; (contributor) Alan Fusonie and Leila Moran, editors, *Agricultural Literature: Proud Heritage—Future Promise,* Graduate School Press, U.S. Department of Agriculture, 1977. Editor, *Agricultural History,* 1952-53.

SIDELIGHTS: Wayne D. Rasmussen told *CA:* "Like most historians, I began writing to present the results of research. Today, I have another goal in mind—to make Americans aware of the importance of food and agriculture to this nation and the world. Maintaining a strong agriculture at home and making our farm technology available throughout the world is essential to peace."

*   *   *

RATNER, Rochelle 1948-

PERSONAL: Born December 2, 1948; daughter of Herman (a business executive) and Esther (Tischler) Ratner. *Education:* Studied at Bread Loaf Writers' Conference, 1968, and New School for Social Research, 1969. *Home:* 50 Spring St., New York, N.Y. 10012. *Office: Soho Weekly News,* 59 Spring St., New York, N.Y. 10012.

CAREER: East Village Other (newspaper), New York City, book review editor, 1970-71; *Soho Weekly News,* New York City, columnist, 1975—. Worked for Poetry-in-the-Schools programs in New York, New Hampshire, and South Carolina.

WRITINGS—Poems: A Birthday of Waters, New Rivers Press, 1971; *False Trees,* New Rivers Press, 1973; *Mysteries,* Ragnarok Press, 1976; *Pirates's Song,* Jordan Davies Press, 1976; *The Tightrope Walker,* Pennyworth Press, 1977; *Sea Air in a Grave Ground Hog Turns Toward,* Seagull Publications, 1977; *Graven Images,* illustrated by Bernard Solomon, Boxwood Press, 1977; *Quarry,* New Rivers Press, 1978. Contributor of poetry, articles, and fiction to numerous literary magazines and reviews, including *Nation, Sumac, Shenandoah, Far Point,* and *Cloud Marader.*

WORK IN PROGRESS: A novel, *Loving Kindness;* two books of poetry, *Harvest* and *Tellings;* a book on Delsarte with Niels Miller.

SIDELIGHTS: "I write from my experiences with myself," Rochelle Ratner says, "not from the landscape around me as much as I like to think I do. If I went to other places, my poems would most likely remain with the imagery I've been using all along—that of the sea, and my childhood."

*   *   *

RAVENAL, Earl C(edric) 1931-

PERSONAL: Born March 29, 1931, in New York, N.Y.; son of Alan M. (an executive) and Mildred (Sherman) Ravenal; married Carol Myers (a university professor), May 26, 1956; children: Cornelia Jane, John Brodhead, Rebecca Eliza. *Education:* Harvard University, B.A., 1952, Business School, graduate study, 1958; attended Cambridge University, 1952-53; Johns Hopkins School of Advanced International Studies, M.A., 1971, Ph.D., 1975. *Home:* 4439 Cathedral Ave. N.W., Washington, D.C. 20016. *Office:* School of

Advanced International Studies, Johns Hopkins University, Washington, D.C.

CAREER: Elbe File & Binder Co., Inc., Fall River, Mass., treasurer, 1955-65, president, 1965-67; U.S. Government, Washington, D.C., director of Asian Division, Systems Analysis, Department of Defense, 1967-69; Institute for Policy Studies, Washington, D.C., associate fellow, 1970-73; Johns Hopkins University, School of Advanced International Studies, Washington, D.C., professor of American foreign policy, 1973—; Georgetown University, School of Foreign Service, Washington, D.C., professor of international relations, 1975—. *Military service:* U.S. Army, 1953-55. *Member:* Council on Foreign Relations, American Political Science Association.

WRITINGS: (Editor and co-author) *Peace with China: U.S. Decisions for Asia,* Liveright, 1971; (co-editor and co-author) *Atlantis Lost: U.S.-European Relations after the Cold War,* New York University Press, 1976; *Foreign Policy in an Uncontrollable World,* Georgetown Center for Strategic and International Studies, 1977. Contributor of chapters to anthologies; contributor to journals, including *Foreign Affairs, Foreign Policy, Political Science Quarterly,* and *New Republic.*

WORK IN PROGRESS: Never Again: Learning from Our Foreign Policy Failures; Strategic Disengagement: The Case for a New American Foreign Policy; Beyond the Balance of Power: Foreign Policy and International Order.

AVOCATIONAL INTERESTS: Music; former professional violinist and chamber musician.

*   *   *

RAYNAL, Paul 1885(?)-1971

1885(?)—August 19, 1971; French playwright. Obituaries: *L'Express,* August 30-September 5, 1971.

*   *   *

READ, William M(erritt) 1901-

PERSONAL: Born June 24, 1901, in Dupont, Ind.; son of Parley Garfield (a contractor) and Ella (Smith) Read; married Arletta Otis, December 19, 1924 (died 1947); married Betty Jorgensen Delacy (a kindergarten teacher), April 30, 1948; children: (first marriage) Virginia (Mrs. Stephen Dunthorne), William M., Jr.; (second marriage) Elaine Marie (Mrs. Mark Buchanan), James Garfield. *Education:* DePauw University, B.A., 1923; University of Michigan, M.A., 1924, Ph.D., 1927. *Politics:* Democrat. *Religion:* Methodist. *Home:* 16619 74th Ave. N.E., Bothell, Wash. 98011. *Office:* DH-10, University of Washington, Seattle, Wash. 98195.

CAREER: Western Reserve University (now Case Western Reserve University), Cleveland, Ohio, instructor in classical languages, 1926-27; University of Washington, Seattle, assistant professor, 1927-36, associate professor, 1936-45, professor of classical languages, 1945-71, professor emeritus, 1971—, director, University of Washington Press, 1943-63. Democratic precinct committeeman. *Member:* American Philological Association, American Classical League, Pacific Northwest Conference on Foreign Languages, Classical Association of the Pacific Northwest (president, 1928; secretary-treasurer, 1972-75), Philological Association of Pacific Coast, Washington Association of Foreign Language Teachers, Phi Beta Kappa. *Awards, honors:* First Pro Lingua Award from Washington Association of Foreign Language Teachers, 1973.

WRITINGS: Michigan Manuscript 18 of the Gospels, University of Washington Press, 1942; *A Guide to Hans H. Oerberg, Lingua Latina Secundum Naturae Rationem Explicata*, privately printed, Volume I, 1971, Volume II, 1973. Also author of *A Manual for Teachers of Hans H. Oerberg, Lingua Latina Secundum Naturae Rationem Explicata*, Volumes I and II, 1973. Contributor of articles to *Classical Journal, Foreign Language Annals*, and *Classical Outlook*.

WORK IN PROGRESS: Editing Galen's *De Elementis*.

SIDELIGHTS: William M. Read learned linotype in order to set his own first book in the early 1940's, as a result of which he became director of the University of Washington Press, which published about 25 new titles per year when he left in 1963. He told *CA*, "Because Latin, when properly taught, can contribute more than any other language to the development of 'literacy,' i.e. the ability to read with understanding and to write with clarity, I am especially interested in trying to keep Latin in the schools and believe that the 'natural method,' as used by Oerberg, will help to do that."

*   *   *

REAVER, J(oseph) Russell   1915-

PERSONAL: Born August 4, 1915, in Phoenixville, Pa.; son of Joseph Russell (a business executive) and Ethel L. (Jester) Reaver; married Anna Grace Pavis, December 7, 1946; children: Rise (daughter). *Education:* Miami University, Oxford, Ohio, A.B. (magna cum laude), 1937; Ohio State University, M.A., 1938, Ph.D., 1942. *Home:* 1228 Cherokee Dr., Tallahassee, Fla. 32301. *Office:* Department of English, Florida State University, Tallahassee, Fla. 32306.

CAREER: Citadel, Charleston, S.C., assistant professor of English, 1942-44; University of Illinois, Urbana, instructor in English, 1944-47; Florida State University, Tallahassee, assistant professor, 1947-50, associate professor, 1950-63, professor of English, 1963—. Professor of American literature and chairman of faculty, Florida State Study Center, Florence, Italy, 1968-69.

MEMBER: International Society for Folk Narrative Research, Societe Internationale d'Ethnologie et de Folklore, International Comparative Literature Association, Modern Language Association of America, National Council of Teachers of English, American Folklore Society, American Dialect Society, College English Association, American Comparative Literature Association, Semiotic Society of America, Popular Culture Association, American Name Society, South Atlantic Modern Language Association (chairman of folklore section, 1955-56), Southeast Folklore Society, Northeast Folklore Society, Florida Council of Teachers of English (president, 1959-60), Emerson Society, Phi Beta Kappa, Phi Eta Sigma, Beta Pi Theta, Phi Sigma. *Awards, honors:* Florida State University Research Council grants for folklore research in Italy and Austria, 1967-68.

WRITINGS: Emerson as Mythmaker, University of Florida Press, 1954; (editor with Robert F. Davidson, Sarah Herndon, and William Ruff) *The Humanities in Contemporary Life*, Holt, 1960; (with George W. Boswell) *Fundamentals of Folk Literature*, Anthropological Publications, 1962; (editor with Davidson, Herndon, Ruff, and Nathan Starr) *The Humanistic Tradition*, Holt, 1964; (contributor) *Thomas Wolfe: Three Decades of Criticism*, New York University Press, 1968; *An O'Neill Concordance*, three volumes, Gale, 1969; (with Eric W. Carlson and J. Lasley Dameron) *Emerson's Relevance Today*, Transcendental, 1971; *Somewhere Safe to Sea*, Vantage, 1974. Contributor

to *Georgia Review, American Transcendental Quarterly*, and other journals.

WORK IN PROGRESS: Florida Folk Beliefs, for University of Nebraska Press; *Moments of Transition: A Reading of Emerson's Imagist Structure in "The Conduct of Life"; The Structure of the Zodiac in John Gardner's "Grendel"; Socio-psychic Levels of Oral Narration*.

*   *   *

REED, J(ames) D(onald)   1940-

PERSONAL: Born October 7, 1940, in Jackson, Mich.; son of Clair Samuel (a businessman) and Esther (Bryden) Reed; married Carol Berggren (a painter), June 16, 1962; married second wife, Christine Flowers (a physicist), June 14, 1968; children: (second marriage) Phoebe Christina. *Education:* Attended Albion College, 1958-60; Michigan State University, B.A., 1962; State University of New York at Stony Brook, graduate study, 1967-69; University of Montana, M.F.A., 1970. *Office: Sports Illustrated*, Time-Life Bldg., Rockefeller Center, New York, N.Y. 10020.

CAREER: Worked at a wide variety of jobs during the five years following the obtaining of his bachelor's degree; wrote poetry in Gloucester, Mass. on a Guggenheim fellowship, 1970-71; University of Massachusetts—Amherst, assistant professor of English, beginning 1971; currently member of staff, *Sports Illustrated*, New York, N.Y. *Awards, honors:* Discovery prize for new poets from Young Men's Hebrew Association/Poetry Center of New York, 1969.

WRITINGS: (With George Quasha, Jim Harrison, Charles Simic, and Dan Gerber) *Five Blind Men* (poems), Sumac Press, 1969; *Expressways* (poems), Simon & Shuster, 1969; *Whiskey Profiles* (poems), Baleen Press, 1971; *Fatback Odes* (long poems), Sumac Press, 1972. Contributor of poetry to anthologies, including *The "New Yorker" Book of Poems, Inside Outer Space*, and *Michigan Signatures*, and to magazines, including *McCall's, New Yorker, Stony Brook, Lillabulero*, and *Pony Tail*.

WORK IN PROGRESS: Rubber in All Four Gears, a novel.

BIOGRAPHICAL/CRITICAL SOURCES: New Leader, October 27, 1969.†

*   *   *

REED, Robert Rentoul, Jr.   1911-

PERSONAL: Born November 16, 1911, in New York, N.Y.; son of Robert R. (a lawyer) and Christine (Patten) Reed; married Julia Marshal, December 12, 1942; children: Rosalind R. (Mrs. James R. Bruno), Christine M. *Education:* Harvard University, student, 1930-32, 1933-34; Pomona College, A.B. (cum laude), 1937; Columbia University, M.A., 1946, Ph.D., 1950. *Home:* 621 East McCormick Ave., State College, Pa. 16801. *Office:* Department of English, Pennsylvania State University, University Park, Pa. 16802.

CAREER: Teacher in ranch schools in Arizona, 1936-39; Hudson River Naval Academy, Irvington-on-Hudson, N.Y., headmaster, 1945-46; Halsted School, Yonkers, N.Y., teacher of Latin and English, 1946-47; New York University, New York, N.Y., instructor in English, 1947-50; Pennsylvania State University, University Park, assistant professor, 1950-53, associate professor, 1953-75, professor of English, 1975—. Director of Boys' Clubs. *Military service:* U.S. Coast Guard, 1942-45; became lieutenant. *Member:* Renaissance Society of America, Shakespeare

Association of America, American Association of University Professors.

WRITINGS: Young April (poems), Elektra Press, 1937; *Bedlam on the Jacobean Stage,* Harvard University Press, 1952; *Occult on the Tudor and Stuart Stage,* Christopher, 1965; *Richard II: From Mask to Prophet,* Pennsylvania State University Press, 1968; *East of Hatteras* (poems), Christopher, 1969. Contributor of articles to *Anglia, Shakespeare Quarterly, Shaw Review,* and other journals; contributor of poetry to journals in United States and Canada.

WORK IN PROGRESS: Renaissance studies; *Man and God in Shakespeare;* poems.

AVOCATIONAL INTERESTS: Fishing, tennis, deep water sailing.

*   *   *

REED, Victor (Brenner)   1926-

PERSONAL: Born February 1, 1926, in Birmingham, Ala.; son of Leon and Sophie (Goldman) Reed; married Marcella Skarulis (a teacher), June 4, 1955; children: David, Jenny, Michael. *Education:* Harvard University, A.B., 1947, A.M., 1948; University of Paris, graduate study, 1955; Columbia University, Ph.D., 1964. *Religion:* Jewish. *Home:* 32 Martha Pl., Chappaqua, N.Y. 10514. *Office:* Department of English, Herbert H. Lehman College of the City University of New York, Bronx, N.Y. 10468.

CAREER: College of the City of New York (now City College of the City University of New York), New York, N.Y., lecturer in English, 1950-55; University of Helsinki, Helsinki, Finland, lektor in English, 1955-56; Fairleigh Dickinson University, Teaneck, N.J., instructor, 1958-60, assistant professor of English, 1960-63; Herbert H. Lehman College of the City University of New York, Bronx, N.Y., assistant professor, 1964-69, associate professor of English, 1970—. *Military service:* U.S. Navy, 1943-46; became ensign. *Member:* Modern Language Association of America.

WRITINGS: (With Clayton Andrews) *Handbook of Modern English,* Soederstroem, 1956; (editor with James Williams) *The Case of Aaron Burr,* Houghton, 1960; (editor with Gerald Willen) *A Casebook on Shakespeare's Sonnets,* Crowell, 1964. Contributor to journals, sometimes under undisclosed pseudonyms.

WORK IN PROGRESS: Research on modernist literature, Shakespeare, and the philosophy of literature.

*   *   *

REEP, Edward   1918-

PERSONAL: Born May 10, 1918, in Brooklyn, N.Y.; son of Joseph (an accountant) and Elsie (Abramson) Reep; married Karen Stevens, December 9, 1942; children: Susan (Mrs. Mark Smith), Cristine (Mrs. Rob Seidler), Janine, Mitchell. *Education:* Attended Art Center College of Design, five years. *Politics:* Democrat. *Religion:* "No religious preference." *Home:* 201 Poplar Dr., Greenville, N.C. 27834. *Office:* School of Art, East Carolina University, Greenville, N.C. 27834.

CAREER: Art Center College of Art and Design, Los Angeles, Calif., teacher of painting and drawing, 1946-50; Chouinard Art Institute, Los Angeles, teacher of painting and drawing and chairman of painting and foundation departments, 1950-70; Bisttram School of Fine Arts, Los Angeles, teacher of painting, 1950-51; East Carolina University, Greenville, N.C., artist-in-residence and professor of paint-

ing, 1970—. Visiting professor, Southern Illinois University, 1970. Consulting editor, Van Nostrand-Reinhold. War artist correspondent for *Life* and *United States Military History. Military service:* U.S. Army, 1941-46; became captain; received Bronze Star. *Member:* American Association of University Professors, National Watercolor Society (president and board member, 1955-57). *Awards, honors:* Guggenheim fellowship, 1945-46; recipient of numerous awards at national art exhibitions.

WRITINGS: The Content of Watercolor, Van Nostrand, 1969.

SIDELIGHTS: Edward Reep told *CA:* ". . . I am primarily an artist, teaching as most artists in America do, in order to supplement my income. The book *Content of Watercolor* was written at the request of the publishers who sought me out to fulfill a need. The area of watercolor painting was cluttered by the hobbyists, or how-to-do-it, and how-I-do-it approach. I believe my book to be the first in the field to treat watercolor, through the ages and to present trends, as a dignified and serious pursuit. Curiously, when I approached the book I hadn't painted much in watercolor for ten years, but had concentrated upon oil paintings, etc. Prior to that, the bulk of my work over a fifteen year period, was devoted to the medium. I felt obligated to do the book."

*   *   *

REEVES, Nancy   1913-

PERSONAL: Born December 9, 1913, in Philadelphia, Pa.; daughter of Koppel and Sadie (Finkler) Goldhaber; married Edward A. Reeves (a certified public accountant), March 3, 1944. *Education:* Hunter College (now Hunter College of the City University of New York), A.B., 1935; New York University, LL.B., 1938, J.D., 1974. *Home:* 2700 Neilson Way, Santa Monica, Calif. 90405.

CAREER: Admitted to the Bar of New York State, 1940, and the Bar of the State of California, 1946; private practice of law, New York, N.Y., 1941-42; State of California, Office of Attorney General at Sacramento, member of legal staff, 1945-47; private practice of law, Los Angeles, Calif., 1953-68. Visiting lecturer, University California, Los Angeles, 1969, 1971; lecturer at numerous universities, including University of Wisconsin, 1972, University of Massachusetts, 1973, University of Iowa, 1975, and University of Hawaii, 1978. Conductor of seminars at universities in England and the United States. Moderator of radio series, "A Woman's Place," sponsored by the Pacifica Foundation, and guest on television programs in the United States and Europe. Participant, U.S.-Soviet Women's Meeting on International Issues, 1964. Lecturer on the status of women in society in Denmark, Russia, the Netherlands, Poland, England, France, and the United States. Appointed "Feminist in Residence," under sponsorship of Pittsburgh Council of Higher Education, 1972. Official observer, International Women's Year Conference, Mexico City, 1975; participant in Round Table celebrating thirtieth anniversary of UNESCO, Paris, 1976. Member, California State Board of Education, 1976; member of advisory board, Women's Education Equity Communications Network, 1978.

MEMBER: National Organization for Women (member of national advisory board, 1975), International P.E.N., Women's International League for Peace and Freedom (president, Los Angeles branch; vice-president, California branch; member of national board), Federation Internationale des Femmes Juristes, Federation Internationale des Femmes des Carrieres Juridique. *Awards, honors:* Literary award, State Bar Convention of California, 1972, for *Womankind: Beyond the Stereotypes;* Mac Dowell Colony award, 1973, 1974, 1975.

WRITINGS: Womankind: Beyond the Stereotypes, Aldine-Atherton, 1971; (contributor) Rae Lee Siporin, editor, *Female Studies V,* Know, Inc., 1971; (contributor) Leo Kanowitz, editor, *Sex Roles in Law and Society,* University of New Mexico Press, 1973. Contributor to *Annals of New York Academy of Sciences, Nation, Women Speaking, Cultures, Los Angeles Times,* and other publications. Member of editorial board, annual on theory of women's status, University of Pittsburgh Press.

WORK IN PROGRESS: The Two Species, an evaluation of the codifications of reality internalized by the genders; "Ancient Law Suit," an educational television series related to in-service training for teachers; *The Death of Determinism,* a book of essays based on Reeves' recent talks that touch on the human condition.

SIDELIGHTS: Nancy Reeves speaks German, French, Swedish, some Russian, and a little Greek. She told *CA:* "[My] interest in the status of women in society began with the legal status of women. This led to research on the subject in various countries and ultimately to a study of the position of women in society with particular emphasis on the cultural patterns that obtain in systems very different from ours. In addition to visits to England, France, Italy, Greece, Mexico, Denmark, there was extended time spent in Sweden, Cuba, Israel, Poland, Russia (both European and Asian).... I have just returned from a study mission in China with the State Department of Education at the invitation of that government."

*   *   *

REEVES, Thomas Carl   1939-

PERSONAL: Born March 27, 1939, in Nashville, Tenn.; son of Thomas Carl (a supervisor with International Business Machines) and Vivian Emiline (Spinks) Reeves. *Education:* Birmingham-Southern College, B.A. (magna cum laude); Harvard University, S.T.B. (cum laude), 1962; American University, M.A.; additional graduate study at Free University of Berlin, 1964-65, and Humboldt University of Berlin, 1965-67. *Politics:* Radical independent. *Religion:* Episcopalian.

CAREER: Methodist clergyman, ordained in 1962; pastor in Wilsonville, Ala., 1958-60, in South Athol, Mass., 1962-64; Schiller College, Kleiningersheim, Germany, assistant professor of political science, 1967-68; Federal City College, Washington, D.C., assistant professor of political science, 1968-69; National Council to Repeal the Draft, Washington, D.C., national director, 1969-70; Mount St. Mary's College, Emmitsburg, Md., assistant professor of political science, 1970-71. Organized and led tours to Russia and East Europe, 1967, 1968, 1969; lecturer at universities in more than thirty states, and in Cuernavaca, Mexico, summer, 1971. Washington Runaway House, member of board, 1968-70.

MEMBER: American Political Science Association, Radical Caucus, American Friends Service Committee (registered lobbyist), National Council to Repeal the Draft (registered lobbyist), Fellowship of Reconciliation. *Awards, honors:* Fulbright fellow in Germany.

WRITINGS: (With Karl Hess; prefaces by Senators Mark O. Hatfield and George McGovern) *The End of the Draft,* Random House, 1970. Contributor to *Christian Century, Nation, Washington Free Press, New York Times,* and other publications.

WORK IN PROGRESS: Analyzing Strategies for Radical Change, on radical political and social change in the United States since 1960.

SIDELIGHTS: Thomas Reeves has visited the Soviet Union five times, including Siberia, Central Asia, and Caucasia, and traveled throughout eastern and western Europe and in North Africa.

BIOGRAPHICAL/CRITICAL SOURCES: Washington Post, November 27, 1970.†

*   *   *

REICHENBACH, Bruce R.   1943-

PERSONAL: Born December 13, 1943, in Staten Island, N.Y.; son of Robert C. (a minister) and Alberta (Snyder) Reichenbach; married Sharon L. Harvie (a teacher), August 14, 1965. *Education:* Wheaton College, Wheaton, Ill., B.A., 1965; Northwestern University, M.A., 1967, Ph.D., 1968. *Religion:* Presbyterian. *Home:* 707 West County Road B-2, Roseville, Minn. 55113. *Office:* Department of Philosophy, Augsburg College, Minneapolis, Minn. 55454.

CAREER: Augsburg College, Minneapolis, Minn., 1968—, began as assistant professor, currently professor of philosophy and chairman of department. Visiting faculty member, National University of Lesotho, Africa, 1976-77. *Member:* American Philosophical Association, Minnesota Philosophical Society (treasurer, 1969-71).

WRITINGS: The Cosmological Argument: A Reassessment, C. C Thomas, 1972; *Is Man the Phoenix?: A Study of Immortality,* Eerdmans, 1977. Contributor to philosophy and religion journals.

WORK IN PROGRESS: A book on the problem of evil.

SIDELIGHTS: Bruce Reichenbach told *CA:* "Writing in the area of philosophy of religion to some might seem to be a fruitless endeavor, considering that questions about the intelligibility and truth of statements which in one way or another involve the concept of God hardly ever seem to be resolved. Yet to immerse myself in this traditional quest presents for me a continuing and relevant intellectual challenge. I write not only that others might share my thoughts and discoveries, but more importantly to introduce order into my own set of beliefs. I find that having to put my ideas on paper forces me to greater clarity of thought, and indeed, at times brings me to positions which would have been only dimly glimpsed in advance, if at all. My goal is to create a satisfactory marriage between the truths of reason and the commitment of faith, a marriage which will stimulate my readers to the same end."

AVOCATIONAL INTERESTS: Archaeology, sports, camping, travel, photography.

*   *   *

REILLY, Esther H(untington)   1917-

PERSONAL: Born August 19, 1917, in Portland, Me.; daughter of Huntington Charles (a professor and writer) and Rachel (Foster) Whitman; married James Reilly (a teacher), May 18, 1943; children: Diane (Mrs. Joseph English), Rachel, Alison. *Education:* Douglass College, B.A., 1939; Parsons School of Design, Certificate in Interior Architecture and Design, 1943. *Politics:* Republican. *Religion:* Protestant. *Home and office:* 401 Marlowe St., Palo Alto, Calif. 94301. *Agent:* (Public relations) M. B. Sherry Baker, 2165 Jackson St., San Francisco, Calif. 94115.

CAREER: Lucille B. Chisholm, Interior Decorations,

Charlottesville, Va., associate, 1949-58; owner of interior design business in Palo Alto, Calif., 1958—. Teacher of interior design in Santa Clara Adult Education Program, 1959—, and at De Anza Junior College, 1969—. *Member:* American Society of Interior Designers, National Home Fashions League.

WRITINGS: At Home with Decorating, Chilton, 1971.

SIDELIGHTS: Esther Reilly wrote her book while living in Europe for a year; she spent one month each in twelve different countries.

* * *

REILLY, Mary Lonan 1926-

PERSONAL: Born February 8, 1926, in Alvord, Iowa; daughter of Bernard P. (a farmer) and Marie (O'Meara) Reilly. *Education:* Huron College, Huron, S.D., teacher training, 1944; College of St. Teresa, B.A., 1963; University of Notre Dame, M.A., 1965, Ph.D., 1970. *Home and office:* College of St. Teresa, Winona, Minn. 55987.

CAREER: Roman Catholic nun of Sisters of St. Francis; teacher and principal in elementary and junior high schools, 1949-64; College of St. Teresa, Winona, Minn., 1969—, began as assistant professor, currently associate professor of history. *Member:* American Historical Association, Organization of American Historians, American Catholic Historical Association, National Assembly of Women Religious, League of Women Voters, Women Historians of the Midwest, Minnesota Association of History Teachers, Winona Diocesan Sisters' Council, Winona County Historical Society. *Awards, honors:* Danforth associate, 1977.

WRITINGS: A History of the Catholic Press Association: 1911-1968, Scarecrow, 1971; (contributor) Robert Triso, editor, *Catholics in America, 1776-1976,* National Conference of Catholic Bishops, 1976.

* * *

REIMAN, Donald H(enry) 1934-

PERSONAL: Born May 17, 1934, in Erie, Pa.; son of Henry Ward (a teacher) and Mildred A. (a teacher; maiden name, Pearce) Reiman; married Mary Warner (a rare book restorer and conservator), September 21, 1958 (divorced); married Helene Dworzan (a writer and teacher), October 3, 1975; children: (first marriage) Laurel Elizabeth. *Education:* College of Wooster, B.A., 1956; University of Illinois, M.A., 1957, Ph.D., 1960. *Politics:* Democrat. *Religion:* Presbyterian. *Home:* 6495 Broadway, Bronx, N.Y. 10471. *Office:* Carl H. Pforzheimer Library, Room 815, 41 East 42nd St., New York, N.Y. 10017.

CAREER: Duke University, Durham, N.C., instructor, 1960-62, assistant professor of English, 1962-64; University of Wisconsin—Milwaukee, associate professor of English, 1964-65; Carl H. Pforzheimer Library, New York, N.Y., editor of *Shelley and his Circle,* 1965—. Adjunct professor of English, City University of New York, 1967-68; adjunct professor of English and senior research associate, Columbia University, 1969-74; visiting professor of English, St. Johns University, 1974-75. *Member:* Modern Humanities Research Association, Modern Language Association of America, Keats-Shelley Association of America (treasurer, 1973—), Byron Society, Wordsworth-Coleridge Association, English Institute, American Association of University Professors, Common Cause, Grolier Club, Phi Beta Kappa, Phi Kappa Phi. *Awards, honors:* American Council of Learned Societies grant, 1961-62, study fellow, 1963-64; as-

sociate fellow, Center for Advanced Study, Wesleyan University, 1963-64.

WRITINGS: Shelley's "Triumph of Life": A Critical Study, University of Illinois Press, 1965; *Percy Bysshe Shelley,* Twayne, 1968; (editor) *Shelley and his Circle,* Volumes V-VI, Harvard University Press, 1973; (editor) *The Romantics Reviewed,* nine volumes, Garland Publishing, 1972; (with Doucet Devin Fischer) *Byron on the Continent,* New York Public Library, 1974; (editor) *The Romantic Context: Poetry,* 128 volumes, Garland Publishing, 1976—; (with Sharon B. Powers) *Shelley's Poetry and Prose,* Norton, 1977.

Contributor: Frank Jordan, editor, *The English Romantic Poets: A Review of Research and Criticism,* 3rd revised edition (Reiman was not associated with earlier editions), Modern Language Association of America, 1972; John D. Baird, editor, *Editing Texts of the Romantic Period,* Hakkert (Toronto), 1972; *Norton Anthology of English Literature,* edited by M. H. Abrams, Norton, 1974. Also contributor to *The Reader's Encyclopedia of English Literature,* edited by William Godwin, Leigh Hunt, and Thomas Love.

Member of advisory board, *Milton and the Romantics,* 1975—, and *Studies in Romanticism,* 1977—. Contributor of over fifty articles and reviews on English and American literature to scholarly journals. Member of editorial board, *Keats-Shelley Journal,* 1968—.

WORK IN PROGRESS: The Poetry of History: Relationships among Historical and Biographical Events and Artistic Forms; editing with others, *The Evidence of the Imagination: Studies of Interactions between Life and Art in English Romantic Literature;* additional volumes of *The Romantic Context: Poetry* and *Shelley and his Circle.*

SIDELIGHTS: Donald Reiman told *CA:* "Beginning my scholarly career with a dissertation on one poem by Shelley, I have worked outward by employing the same techniques to literary works in other areas. I try to be eclectic in my approach, giving attention to textual problems, historical and biographical background, philosophical presuppositions underlying the work of art, and aesthetic problems of formal integrity, symbolism, and prosody. I hope ultimately to write studies of major British and American poets from Chaucer and Shakespeare (whom I have already treated in essays) through Yeats, Eliot, and Stevens."

* * *

REISMAN, Arnold 1934-

PERSONAL: Born August 2, 1934, in Lodz, Poland; naturalized U.S. citizen; son of Isidor and Rose (Yoskowitz) Reisman; married Judith Ann Gelernter (a composer, performer, and writer) March 12, 1955; children: Miriam, Ada, Deborah, Nina. *Education:* University of California, Los Angeles, B.S., 1955, M.S., 1957, Ph.D., 1963. *Religion:* Jewish. *Home:* 18428 Parkland Dr., Shaker Heights, Ohio 44122. *Office:* Department of Operations Research, Case Western Reserve University, Cleveland, Ohio 44106.

CAREER: City of Los Angeles, Calif., assistant mechanical engineer in department of water and power, 1955-57; California State College at Los Angeles (now California State University, Los Angeles), assistant professor, 1957-61, associate professor of engineering, 1961-66; University of Wisconsin—Milwaukee, visiting associate professor of engineering and business administration, 1966-67, visiting associate professor of engineering, 1967-68; Case Western Reserve University, Cleveland, Ohio, associate professor,

1968-71, professor of operations research, 1971—, director of interdisciplinary program in systems analysis. Visiting professor, Hebrew University of Jerusalem, 1975. Associate research engineer, Western Management Science Institute, 1964-65; vice-president, University Associates, Inc., Cleveland, 1968—. Consultant to federal departments, health service institutions, and to industry.

MEMBER: Operations Research Society of America, Institute of Management Sciences, American Society of Mechanical Engineers, American Association for the Advancement of Science (fellow; former member of council), American Society for Engineering Education, American Institute of Industrial Engineers (senior member), American Association of University Professors, Society for Advanced Medical Systems (fellow), New York Academy of Sciences, Phi Delta Kappa, Sigma Xi.

WRITINGS: (Editor and contributor) *Engineering: A Look Inward, a Reach Outward,* University of Wisconsin Press, 1967; *Engineering Economics: A Unified Approach,* Reinhold, 1970; *Managerial and Engineering Economics: A Unified Approach,* Allyn & Bacon, 1971; (with Burton V. Dean, Michael Salvador, and Muhittin Oral) *Industrial Inventory Control,* Gordon & Breach, 1972; (with Michael D. Mesarovic) *Systems Approach and the City,* North Holland, 1972; (with A. K. Rao) *Discounted Cash Flow Analysis: Stochastic Extensions,* American Institute of Industrial Engineers, 1973; (editor with M. L. Kiley, and contributor) *Health Care Delivery Planning,* Gordon & Breach, 1973.

Contributor: E. S. Buffa, editor, *Models for Production and Operations Management,* Wiley, 1963; E. S. Buffa, editor, *Readings in Production and Operations Management,* Wiley, 1966; Leslie Holliday, editor, *Integration of Technologies,* Hutchinson, 1966; Richard H. P. Kraft, editor, *Strategies of Educational Planning,* Florida State University Press, 1968; E. F. Schlifer, editor, *Library System Distribution Network Design,* Jerusalem Academic Press, 1973; J. W. Clark, editor, *Clinical Dentistry,* Harper, 1977.

Also contributor, J. R. Longstreet and W. G. Modrow, editors, *Readings in Finance,* D. M. Mark, H. Aly and D. M. Albanito, editors, *Models in Financial Management,* Holden-Day, R. L. Schultz and D. P. Slevin, editors, *Implementing Operations Research/Management Science,* American Elsevier, and *International Handbook on Data Processing,* 1977. Series editor, "Operations Management" series, Wiley, 1972—. Author of a number of research reports. Contributor of more than ninety articles to scholarly and professional journals.

* * *

REISS, James 1941-

PERSONAL: Surname is pronounced "Reece"; born July 11, 1941, in New York, N.Y.; son of Joseph and Cecile (Blocksberg) Reiss; married Barbara Eve Klevs (a poet and book reviewer), June 21, 1964; children: Heather Eve, Crystal Jo. *Education:* University of Chicago, B.A., 1963, M.A., 1964. *Office:* Department of English, Miami University, Oxford, Ohio 45056.

CAREER: Miami University, Oxford, Ohio, instructor, 1965-69, assistant professor, 1969-73, associate professor of English, 1973—. Visiting poet, Queens College of the City University of New York, 1975-76. *Member:* Poetry Society of America, Academy of American Poets. *Awards, honors:* Academy of American Poets first prizes, University of Chicago, 1960, 1962; Discovery Award from Poetry Center, Young Men's Hebrew Association, 1974; National Endow-

ment for the Humanities fellowship, 1974-75; Creative Artists Public Service Award, 1975-76; Big Apple Poetry Award, 1977.

WRITINGS: (Editor and author of introduction) *12 at Miami University,* Miami University, 1969; (editor with wife, Barbara Reiss) James Dickey, *Self-Interviews,* Doubleday, 1970; *The Breathers* (poems), Ecco Press, 1974. Contributor of poetry to numerous anthologies and to periodicals. Regular reviewer for Cleveland *Plain Dealer,* 1971-74.

WORK IN PROGRESS: A Candy Store in Washington Heights, a book of poems.

BIOGRAPHICAL/CRITICAL SOURCES: Antioch Review, fall, 1971; Alberta Turner, *Fifty Contemporary Poets,* McKay, 1977.

* * *

REMINGTON, Robin Alison 1938-

PERSONAL: Born January 15, 1938, in Boston, Mass.; daughter of Bradford Austin and Mabelle (Therrien) Remington; married Paul Wallace. *Education:* Southwest Texas State College (now University), A.B., 1958; Indiana University, M.A., 1961, Ph.D., 1966. *Residence:* Columbia, Mo. *Office:* Department of Political Science, University of Missouri, Columbia, Mo. 65201.

CAREER: Massachusetts Institute of Technology, Cambridge, research associate in communist studies, Center for International Studies, 1966-73, lecturer in humanities department, 1970; University of Missouri—Columbia, associate professor of political science, 1974—. Visiting lecturer, Boston University, 1972-73, and Yale University, 1973-74. Exchange scholar to Belgrade, Yugoslavia, Institute of International Politics and Economics, 1970-71. *Member:* American Political Science Association, American Association for Southeast European Studies (member of executive council, 1976-77).

WRITINGS: (Editor) *Winter in Prague: Documents on Czechoslovak Communism in Crisis,* M.I.T. Press, 1969; *The Warsaw Pact: Case Studies in Communist Conflict Resolution,* M.I.T. Press, 1971.

Contributor: John Wells and Maria Wilhelm, editors, *The People vs. Presidential War,* Dunellen Publishing, 1970; Catherine McArdle Kelleher, editor, *Political-Military Systems: Comparative Perspectives,* Sage Publications, Inc., 1974; Frank B. Horton III and others, editors, *Comparative Defense Policy,* Johns Hopkins Press, 1974; William E. Griffiths, editor, *The Soviet Empire: Expansion and Detente,* Lexington Books, 1976; Charles Gati, editor, *The International Politics of Eastern Europe,* Praeger, 1976; Gary K. Bertsch and Thomas W. Ganschow, editors, *Comparative Communism: The Soviet, Chinese, and Yugoslav Models,* W. H. Freeman, 1976; Judy Bertelsen, editor, *Nonstate Nations in International Politics: Comparative System Analyses,* Praeger, 1977. Contributor to professional journals, including *East European Quarterly, Survey, Orbis, Current History,* and *Survival and Balkanistica: Occasional Papers in Southeast European Studies.*

WORK IN PROGRESS: A comparative analysis of civil-military relations in Yugoslavia, Albania, and Rumania with special attention to the impact of popular militias on the professional armed forces.

SIDELIGHTS: Robin Alison Remington speaks Russian, French, and Serbo-Croatian. She has traveled to U.S.S.R., Poland, Czechoslovakia, and Yugoslavia.

RENAY, Liz 1926-

PERSONAL: Surname is pronounced Ren-*ay;* born April 14, 1926, in Chandler, Ariz.; daughter of William Andrew (a construction worker) and Ada Mae (Phillips) Dobbins; married previously to Ricky Romano, Paul McLain, Lou O'Lear, Bill Forrest, Reed Morgan, and Thomas W. Freeman; married seventh husband, Jerry Heidebrink (manager of the Silver Slipper casino in Las Vegas); children: (second marriage) John, Brenda. *Education:* Attended high school in Mesa, Ariz. *Religion:* Agnostic. *Home:* 3858 Pima Lane, Las Vegas, Nev. 89109. *Agent:* Irwin Zucker, 714 North Crescent Dr., Beverly Hills, Calif. *Office:* 6565 Sunset Blvd., Hollywood, Calif.

CAREER: Actress, entertainer, painter, and writer; has starred in four stage plays and twenty motion pictures, and appeared in twelve other pictures; also does a night club act. Has conducted her own radio and television shows, and taught oil painting classes and charm courses. *Member:* Screen Actors Guild, Actors' Equity Association, American Federation of Television and Radio Artists. *Awards, honors:* Winner of beauty contests, including Twentieth Century-Fox Marilyn Monroe Look-Alike Contest, 1955; first prize for oil paintings at National Arts Festival, New York, 1963, and Los Angeles Arts Fair, 1965; Most Versatile Artist Award, Las Vegas Art Fair, 1968.

WRITINGS: How to Attract Men, Playlark Publishing, 1966; *My Face for the World to See* (autobiography), Lyle Stuart, 1971. Formerly author of a regular column for *National Insider;* currently staff writer and author of a regular column for *Las Vegas Sun.* Contributor to *Saturday Evening Post, National Insider,* and other magazines.

WORK IN PROGRESS: A motion picture script on the life of Christ, "King of the Jews"; *Hang onto Your Youth,* for Bantam; preparing her own television talk-show for production in Las Vegas.

SIDELIGHTS: My Face for the World to See was translated and appeared in a French edition in 1975. *Avocational interests:* Swimming, tennis, horseback riding, singing, and dancing.

BIOGRAPHICAL/CRITICAL SOURCES: Variety, December 9, 1970, October 6, 1971; *Best Sellers,* August 1, 1971; Liz Renay, *My Face for the World to See,* Lyle Stuart, 1971.

*   *   *

RENNER, Bruce 1944-

PERSONAL: Born in 1944, in Los Angeles, Calif.; son of Stanley and Catherine (Wendt) Renner; married Julie Doos (divorced); children: Ona. *Education:* University of Wisconsin, B.S., 1970; Columbia University, M.F.A., 1972. *Residence:* Wisconsin.

CAREER: Poet. Teacher in Poetry-in-the-Schools program in Indiana, 1972-73; lecturer in department of English, University of Wisconsin, 1974; lecturer in English department, Marquette University, 1977-78. *Awards, honors:* Selected one of two midwest regional winners, Book-of-the-Month Club Writing Fellowship Competition, 1968; creative writing grant, Ariadne Foundation, 1971.

WRITINGS: (With Dan Rose) *Poetry,* University of Wisconsin Press, 1967; *Six Poems,* Union Pearl Press, 1972. Also author of a pamphlet, *13 Songs for Ona,* 1976. Contributor to *Choice, Esquire, Shenandoah, Arts in Society, Tempest, Milwaukee Journal, Prairie Schooner, Minnesota Review,* and other publications. Editor, *Cheshire,* 1967-68.

WORK IN PROGRESS: Book of Figures; a book of stories; poems.

*   *   *

RENWICK, Fred B(lackwell) 1930-

PERSONAL: Born February 1, 1930, in Union, S.C.; son of Freddie Choice (an undertaker) and Annie-Belle (Blackwell) Renwick; divorced; children: Michelle Ann, Scott Blackwell and Leslie Francis (twins), F. Leopold Alexander. *Education:* Morehouse College, B.S. (with honors), 1950; Harvard University, S.M., 1956; New York University, M.B.A. (with distinction), 1965, Ph.D., 1966. *Address:* P.O. Box 65, Teaneck, N.J. 07666. *Office:* Graduate School of Business Administration, New York University, New York, N.Y. 10006.

CAREER: General Electric Co., Utica, N.Y., electronics engineer, 1953-54; National Security Agency, U.S. Department of Defense, Washington, D.C., electronics engineer, 1955-57; American Bosch Arma Corp., Garden City, N.Y., electronics engineer, 1957-59; International Telephone & Telegraph Corp., Paramus, N.Y., electronics engineer, 1959-64; New York University, Graduate School of Business Administration, New York, N.Y., instructor, 1966-67, assistant professor, 1967-69, associate professor, 1969-71, professor of finance, 1971—, finance area chairman, 1972—. Visiting scholar, Littauer Center, Harvard University, 1971-72. Member of Economic Advisory Council, U.S. Department of Commerce. Member of Investments and Finance and Budget Committees, board of trustees, Spelman College. Consultant, Conference Board, Inc. *Member:* American Statistical Association, Institute of Electrical and Electronics Engineers, American Finance Association, American Economic Association.

WRITINGS: Introduction to Investments and Finance: Theory and Analysis, Macmillan, 1971. Contributor to *Management Sciences, Industrial Management Review,* and *Journal of Finance.*

*   *   *

REPLANSKY, Naomi 1918-

PERSONAL: Born May 23, 1918, in New York, N.Y.; daughter of Sol and Fannie (Ginsberg) Replansky. *Education:* University of California, Los Angeles, B.A., 1956. *Home:* 146 West 76th St., New York, N.Y. 10023.

MEMBER: P.E.N. American Center, Phi Beta Kappa.

WRITINGS: Ring Song (poems), Scribner, 1952. Contributor of poems and translations to American and European magazines and anthologies.

WORK IN PROGRESS: A second volume of poems.

*   *   *

REUTHER, Ruth E. 1917-

PERSONAL: Born February 27, 1917, in Gainesville, Tex.; daughter of Edwin Jerry (a railroad clerk) and Grace (Patrick) Huffaker; married James Richard Reuther (an optometrist), January 26, 1941; children: Alma Grace (Mrs. B. E. Richardson). *Education:* Cooke County Junior College, A.A., 1936; North Texas State Teachers College (now North Texas State University), B.S., 1938; further study at Midwestern University and Oklahoma University. *Politics:* Democrat. *Religion:* Baptist. *Home:* 4450 Phillips, Wichita Falls, Tex. 76308. *Agent:* A. L. Fierst, 630 Ninth Ave., New York, N.Y. 10036.

CAREER: Teacher in Wichita Falls, Tex., 1958-73. Free-lance writer. Former member of Gainesville Community Circus. Member: National Education Association, International Reading Association, Texas State Teacher's Association, Texas Parents and Teachers (life member), Poetry Society of Texas (past vice-president), Wichita Falls Poetry Society (past president), Order of the Eastern Star, Kappa Delta Pi, Delta Kappa Gamma. Awards, honors: Cokesbury Award runner-up, 1971.

WRITINGS: Wife of Four Hobbies, Pageant, 1957; Gray C: Circus Horse (juvenile), Houghton, 1970. Contributor of short stories and articles on meditation to numerous magazines.

WORK IN PROGRESS: A religious novel; a children's book.

SIDELIGHTS: Ruth Reuther told CA: "I prefer to write children's books because it is my belief that if you write a good one, you are 'writing a memory.' Each of us has one book we remember best from childhood. I hope that Gray C: Circus Horse will be that book for some child." Avocational interests: Gardening, photography.

*   *   *

REVANKAR, Ratna G.   1937-

PERSONAL: Born March 23, 1937, in Bangalore, Mysore State, India; daughter of K. V. (a jeweller) and Krishnabai Rao; married Ganapathi R. Revankar (a scientist), April 28, 1966. Education: University of Mysore, B.A., 1957; Karnatak University, D.P.A., 1962, Ph.D., 1968; Banaras Hindu University, M.A., 1963. Religion: Hindu. Home: 20312 Santa Ana Ave., #8, Santa Ana, Calif. 92707. Office: Department of Political Science, Karnatak University, Dharwar-3, Mysore State, India.

CAREER: University of Utah, Salt Lake City, teaching associate, 1968-69; Karnatak University, Dharwar, Mysore State, India, pool officer, 1970—.

WRITINGS: Indiana Constitution: A Case Study of Backward Classes, Fairleigh Dickinson University Press, 1970.

WORK IN PROGRESS: Research on Indo-American relations, 1960-72.††

*   *   *

REYNOLDS, Donald E.   1931-

PERSONAL: Born July 20, 1931, in Munday, Tex.; son of William Erwin (an accountant) and Abbigail (Norman) Reynolds; married Martha Ann Sawyer, April 17, 1960; children: William Norman, Donald Wayne. Education: North Texas State College (now University), B.A. (with high honors), 1957, M.A., 1958; Tulane University, Ph.D., 1966. Politics: Democrat. Religion: Baptist. Home: 2805 Rix St., Commerce, Tex. 75428. Office: Department of History, East Texas State University, East Texas Station, Commerce, Tex. 75428.

CAREER: East Texas State University, Commerce, assistant professor, 1965-68, associate professor of history, 1968—. Military service: U.S. Navy, 1951-55; became petty officer third class. Member: Southern Historical Association, Southwestern Social Science Association, Texas State Historical Association, Lions Club.

WRITINGS: Editors Make War: Southern Newspapers in the Secession Crisis, Vanderbilt University Press, 1970. Contributor to historical journals.

WORK IN PROGRESS: The Texas Slave Insurrection Panic of 1860.

AVOCATIONAL INTERESTS: Travel, painting, singing (has sung in opera and oratorio, but not professionally).

*   *   *

REYNOLDS, Paul Davidson   1938-

PERSONAL: Born March 5, 1938, in Mattoon, Ill.; son of John Tom (a petroleum engineer) and Barbara (Barteldes) Reynolds; married Anne-Marie Therese Lair (a college professor), 1965; children: Christopher Mosdale, Nicole. Education: University of Kansas, B.S., 1960; Stanford University, M.B.A., 1964, M.A., 1966, Ph.D., 1969. Home: 4222 Grimes Ave. S., Minneapolis, Minn. 55416. Office: Department of Sociology, University of Minnesota, Minneapolis, Minn. 55455.

CAREER: San Francisco State College (now University), San Francisco, Calif., lecturer in sociology, 1967-68; University of California, Riverside, acting assistant professor, 1968-69, assistant professor of sociology, 1969-70; University of Minnesota, Minneapolis, assistant professor, 1970-72, associate professor of sociology, 1972—. Consultant to American Psychological Association, 1971 and UNESCO, 1975-76. Military service: U.S. Army, Ordnance Corps, 1960-61, 1962; became first lieutenant. U.S. Army Reserve, 1962-68. Member: American Sociological Association, American Association of University Professors. Awards, honors: Summer faculty fellowship, University of California, Riverside, 1969.

WRITINGS: A Primer in Theory Construction, Bobbs-Merrill, 1971. Contributor to International Social Science Journal, Behavioral Science, American Sociological Review, and other publications.

WORK IN PROGRESS: Value Dilemmas: Ethics in Social Research, for Allyn & Bacon.

*   *   *

RHOADS, Edward J(ohn) M(ichael)   1938-

PERSONAL: Born January 7, 1938, in Canton, China; son of Howard G. (a teacher) and Chi Kit (Ngan) Rhoads; married Suzanne Kain, December 20, 1969; children: Jennifer. Education: Yale University, A.B., 1960; Harvard University, A.M., 1961, Ph.D., 1970. Office: History Department, University of Texas, Austin, Tex. 78712.

CAREER: University of Texas at Austin, assistant professor, 1967-74, associate professor of history, 1974—. Member: Association for Asian Studies, Society for Ch'ing Studies, Committee of Concerned Asian Scholars.

WRITINGS: The Chinese Red Army, 1927-1963: An Annotated Bibliography, East Asian Research Center, Harvard University, 1964; China's Republican Revolution: The Case of Kwangtung, 1895-1913, Harvard University Press, 1975.

WORK IN PROGRESS: A book on Manchu-Chinese relations at the end of the Ch'ing dynasty, 1895-1912.

*   *   *

RIBEIRO, Darcy   1922-

PERSONAL: Born October 26, 1922, in Montes Claros, Minas Gerais, Brazil; son of Reginaldo (an industrialist) and Josefina (an elementary school teacher; maiden name, Silveira) Ribeiro; married Berta Gleizer (an anthropologist), May 15, 1948. Education: University of Sao Paulo, graduate in social sciences, specializing in cultural anthropology, 1946. Politics: Socialist. Religion: "Catholic formation, agnostic." Address: c/o Clifford Evans, Department of Anthropology, Smithsonian Institution, Washington, D.C. 20560.

CAREER: Professional researcher in Brazilian ethnology and Indian affairs, Rio de Janeiro, Brazil, 1947-57; Universidade do Brasil, Rio de Janeiro, professor, 1955-61; Universidade de Brasilia, Brasilia, Brazil, organizer and first rector, 1962-63; Brazilian Government, under President Joao Goulart, Minister of Education and Culture, 1963, Minister Chief of the Civil House of the Presidency of the Republic of Brazil, 1963-64; forced to leave Brazil after overthrow of Goulart government, 1964; Universidad de la Republica Oriental del Uruguay, Montevideo, professor of anthropology, 1964-68; cleared of charges by a Brazilian military court, allowed to return to Brazil in September, 1968; arrested for investigation after new coup in December, 1968, imprisoned for nine months before being acquitted and again exiled from country, 1969; Universidad Central de Venezuela, Caracas, coordinator, Interdisciplinary Seminar of Human Sciences, and assistant to rector, 1969-70, also assistant to rector of Universidad de los Andes, Merida, Venezuela, 1969-70; Universidad de Chile, Instituto de Estudios Internacionales, research professor, 1970-72; Center of Studies of Popular Participation, Peru, director, 1973-76; Center of Studies of the Third World, Mexico City, Mexico, co-creator, 1976. Researcher and planner of national university system of Peru for Consejo Nacional de la Universidad Peruana, and member of planning commission for University of the Human Sciences, to be established in Alger, Algeria, 1971-72; symposium organizer, XLII International Congress of Americanists, Paris, 1976. *Military service:* Brazilian Army, 1940-41.

MEMBER: Brazilian Anthropological Society, American Anthropological Association, Chilean Anthropological Association. *Awards, honors:* Fabio Prado award for essays, Sao Paulo Writers Association, 1950, for *Religiao e mitologia Kadiweu;* Joao Ribeiro award, Brazilian Academy of Letters, 1957, for *Arte plumaria dos indios Kaapor;* received highest medals of Brazilian Army, Navy, and Air Force for service to Goulart Government, 1962-63; Doctor Honoris Causa, Universidad de la Republica Oriental del Uruguay, 1968.

WRITINGS: Religiao e mitologia Kadiweu, Conselho Nacional de Protecao aos Indios (Rio de Janeiro), 1950, published in *Kadiweu* (see below); *Arte Kadiweu,* Ministerio da Educacao e Cultura (Rio de Janeiro), 1954, published in *Kadiweu* (see below); *Culturas e linguas indigenas do Brasil,* Centro Brasileiro de Pesquisas Educacionais, 1957; (with wife, Berta G. Ribeiro) *Arte plumaria dos indios Kaapor* (includes summary in English), Editora Civilizacao Brasileira (Rio de Janeiro), 1957; *O Indigenista rondon,* Ministerio da Educacao e Cultura, 1958.

A Universidade de Brasilia, Ministerio da Educacao e Cultura, 1960; *Plano orientador da Universidade de Brasilia,* Editora Universidade de Brasilia, 1962; *A Universidade e a Nacao,* Ministerio da Educacao e Cultura, 1962; *A Politica indigenista brasileira,* Ministerio da Agricultura, 1962; (contributor) Aldo Solari and S. M. Lipset, editors, *Elites in Latin America,* Oxford University Press, 1967; (contributor) J. H. Hopper, editor, *Indians of Brazil in the XXth Century,* Institute of Cross-Cultural Research (Washington), 1967; *O Processo civilizatorio: Etapas da evolucao socio-cultural,* Editora Civilizacao Brasileira, 1968, 3rd edition, 1975, translation by Betty J. Meggers published as *The Civilizational Process,* foreword by Meggers, Smithsonian Institution Press, 1968; *La Universidad necesaria,* Editorial Galerna, 1967, 3rd edition, 1971, expanded edition published as *La*

Universidad latinoamericana, Universidad de la Republica Oriental del Uruguay (Montevideo), 1968, 3rd edition, Editorial Universitaria (Santiago), 1971; *Las Americas y la civilizacion: Proceso de formacion y causas del Desarrollo desigual de los pueblos americanos,* three volumes, Centro Editor de America Latina (Buenos Aires), 1969, original Portuguese version published as *As Americas e a civilizacao,* Editora Civilizacao Brasileira, 1970, translation by Linton Lomas Barrett and Marie McDavid Barrett published as *The Americas and Civilization,* Dutton, 1971; *Propuestas acerca del subdesarrollo: El Brasil como problema,* Editorial Arca (Montevideo), 1969, original Portuguese version published as *Teoria do Brasil,* Editora Paz e Terra, 1971, 2nd edition, 1975.

Os Indios e a civilizacao: O Processo de integracao das populacoes indigenas no Brasil moderno, Editora Civilizacao Brasileira, 1970, 2nd edition, Editora Vozes, 1977; *Universidad Central de Venezuela: Propuestas acerca de la renovacion,* Ediciones del Rectorado, Universidad Central de Venezuela, 1970, published as *Estructura y renovacion universitaria,* Ediciones W. R. (Caracas), 1970; *El Dilema de America Latina* (originally written in Portuguese but published in Spanish), Siglo XXI (Mexico), 1971, 5th edition, 1976; *Configuraciones Historico-Culturales Americanas,* Centro de Estudios Latinoamericanos, 1972; *La Universidad nueva: Un proyecto,* Editorial Ciencia Nueva (Buenos Aires), 1973; *Uira sai a procura de Deus,* Editora Paz e Terra, 1974, 2nd edition, 1976; (contributor) Patricia J. Lyon, editor, *Native South Americans,* Little, Brown, 1974; (contributor) P. B. Hammond, editor, *Physical Anthropology and Archaeology: Introductory Readings,* 2nd edition, Macmillan, 1976; *Maira* (novel), Editora Civilizacao Brasileira, 1976. Also author of *La Universidad Peruana,* Centro de Estudios de Participacion Popular (Lima), *Kadiweu: Ensaios etnologicos sobre o azar, o saber e a beleza* (includes *Religiao e mitologia Kadiweu* and *Arte Kadiweu*), Editora Vozes (Petropolis), and of introductory material for several anthropology books. Contributor to *Museum* (Paris), *Americas, Sociologia* (Sao Paulo), *Anhembi* (Sao Paulo), *Revista Civilizacao Brasileira* (Rio de Janeiro), *Current Anthropology, Revista Mexicana de Sociologia, Estudios Internacionales* (Santiago), and *Revista de la Universidad* (Mexico).

WORK IN PROGRESS: A textbook "intended to revise and fuse both anthropological conceptual scheme and historic materialism," entitled *Critic Theory of Culture: An Introduction to Dialectical Anthropology;* the last two volumes of "Anthropology of Civilization" series, *O Brasil Rustico* and *O Brasil Emergente,* for Editora Civilizacao Brasileira.

SIDELIGHTS: Darcy Ribeiro is an "expert in university structural reforms in Brazil, Uruguay, Venezuela, Chile and Peru." He told *CA* that four kinds of experiences have influenced his personality and work: "First, my professional anthropological field work of over ten years among indigenous and peasant populations in Brazil; second, my experience as educator and university planner . . . [third] that of left politician, militantly interested not only in the study but also in the accomplishment of the social revolution in Latin America; and finally, my experience as political exile, eager to understand my country (and return to it) and the world trends today."

Ribeiro's books have been translated into German, Italian, Spanish, and English. Chapters of *Uira sai a procura de Deus* have been adapted for the filmscripts of "Os Indios Urubus-Kaapor" and "Uira."

BIOGRAPHICAL/CRITICAL SOURCES: Foreword by Betty J. Meggers, *The Civilizational Process,* Smithsonian Institution Press, 1968; *Natural History,* June-July, 1969; *Current Anthropology,* Numbers 4-5, 1970; *American Anthropologist,* Number 4, 1970; epilogue by Heinz Rudolf Sonntag, *Der Zivilisatorische Prozess* (German translation of Ribeiro's *O Processo civilizatorio: Etapas da evolucao socio-cultural*), Suhrkamp Verlag, 1971; *New York Review of Books,* January 31, 1971; foreword by Alberto Filippi, *El Dilema de America Latina,* Il Saggitore II, 1972.

*   *   *

RICE, Cy 1905-1971

May 22, 1905—August 23, 1971; American newsman and author. Obituaries: *Washington Post,* August 27, 1971. (See index for *CA* sketch)

*   *   *

RICE, Lawrence D. 1929-

PERSONAL: Born May 21, 1929, in Brownfield, Tex.; son of Charles Lawrence and Mary (Houck) Rice; married Norma Davis, November 10, 1946; children: Brenda (Mrs. Richard Romaire), Paula D., Lezlee D. *Education:* Eastern New Mexico University, B.A. (with honors), 1959, M.A., 1960; Texas Technological College (now Texas Tech University), Ph.D., 1967. *Home:* 5 Brentwood Cir., Lafayette, La. 70503. *Office:* Department of History, University of Southwestern Louisiana, Lafayette, La. 70504.

CAREER: Rice Construction Co., Lovington, N.M., general superintendent, 1946-54; Navarro Junior College, Corsicana, Tex., head of department of history, 1960-63; University of Southwestern Louisiana, Lafayette, instructor, 1965-67, assistant professor, 1967-69, associate professor of history, 1969—, head of department, 1971—. *Member:* Southern Historical Association, Southwestern Social Science Association, Phi Alpha Theta. *Awards, honors:* National Foundation for the Humanities fellow, 1969-70.

WRITINGS: The Negro in Texas, 1874-1900, Louisiana State University Press, 1971.

WORK IN PROGRESS: A book on contemporary black periodicals.

*   *   *

RICHARDS, Jack W(esley) 1933-

PERSONAL: Born October 2, 1933, in Bartlesville, Okla.; son of Charles W. and Elizabeth (Hall) Richards; married Linda A. Carter, April 9, 1960; children: Laurie, Karen, Grant. *Education:* San Jose State College (now San Jose State University), B.A., 1956, M.A., 1957. *Politics:* Democrat. *Home:* 8535 Burchell Rd., Gilroy, Calif. 95020. *Office:* Department of Physical Education, Gavilan College, Gilroy, Calif. 95020.

CAREER: Teacher at Abraham Lincoln High School, San Jose, Calif., 1958-70; Gavilan College, Gilroy, Calif., teacher of English and basketball coach, 1970—, athletic director, 1976—. *Military service:* California National Guard, 1957-62. *Member:* Athletic Motivation Research Association, California Coaches Association.

WRITINGS: The Scramble Attack for Winning Basketball, Parker Publishing, 1969; *Psychology of Coaching,* Allyn & Bacon, 1970; (editor) *Treasury of Basketball Drills from Top Coaches,* Parker Publishing, 1971; *Coach's Practical Guide*

to Athletic Motivation, Allyn & Bacon, 1972; *Complete Guide to Sports Scoring and Record Keeping,* Parker Publishing, 1975; *Attacking Zone Defenses in Basketball,* Parker & Sons, 1977. Co-originator of "Plays for Reading," a reading program for grades 4, 5, and 6, consisting of 24 plays, with 10 scripts for each play.

WORK IN PROGRESS: Dynamics of Coaching, for Allyn & Bacon.

*   *   *

RICHARDS, Jane 1934-

PERSONAL: Born January 26, 1934, in Southsea, Hampshire, England; daughter of Kenneth Abbot and Ida (Fletcher-Porter) Gray; married Roy Richards (director of a breakfast cereal company), December 22, 1956 (divorced); married Richard George; children: (first marriage) Mark Jonathan, Julius Edward, Daniel James. *Education:* Educated in Sussex, England. *Religion:* Protestant. *Home:* St. Peters Cottage, Aldwincle, Kettering, Northamptonshire, England.

CAREER: Worked as fashion model in London, England, 1953-56; ran interior design and traveling picture dealing business in London, 1966-68.

WRITINGS: A Horse Grows Up, Walker & Co., 1972.

WORK IN PROGRESS: A novel; a children's book on handwriting; a dictionary of terminology used in horse world.

AVOCATIONAL INTERESTS: "Everything to do with horses," literature, art, interior design, antiques, calligraphy, yoga, and showing weimaraner dogs.

*   *   *

RICHARDSON, John Martin, Jr. 1938-

PERSONAL: Born March 12, 1938, in New York, N.Y.; son of John Martin and Marguerite (Pentz) Richardson; married Janice Bartlett (a fashion designer), December 30, 1960; children: Heather Bradford. *Education:* Dartmouth College, B.A., 1960; University of Minnesota, Ph.D., 1968. *Politics:* Democrat. *Religion:* Society of Friends. *Office:* Center for Technology and Administration, American University, Washington, D.C. 20016.

CAREER: Case Western Reserve University, Cleveland, Ohio, assistant professor of political science, 1969-75; American University, Washington, D.C., associate professor and director of Center for Technology and Administration, 1975—. *Military service:* U.S. Navy, 1960-65; became lieutenant. *Member:* American Political Science Association, Royal African Society. *Awards, honors:* Social Science Research Council postdoctoral research training fellowship, 1969.

WRITINGS: Partners in Development, Michigan State University Press, 1968.

Contributor: R. T. Holt and J. E. Turner, editors, *The Methodology of Comparative Research,* Free Press, 1970; (with Thomas Pelsoci) Kan Chen, editor, *Urban Dynamics: Extensions and Reflections,* San Francisco Press, 1971; (with Pelsoci) M. D. Mesarovic and A. Reisman, editors, *Systems Approach and the City,* North-Holland Publishing, 1972; *Water, 1973,* American Institute of Chemical Engineers, 1973; R. L. Chartrand, editor, *Information Technology Serving Society,* Pergamon, in press. Contributor of numerous scholarly papers to conferences and seminars. Also contributor to journals.

WORK IN PROGRESS: Development of the *World Population Society Composite Index,* intended to express changing data on population in relation to food, energy, health, housing, land, environment, and economy.

SIDELIGHTS: John Richardson told *CA:* "I believe that writing is an essential step in analyzing an issue, putting our thoughts in systematic order, offering opportunity for our ideas to be challenged and therefore improved and sharpened, and providing means to stimulate interest or at least awareness from other people in the issues we think important to the community. However, we have to always bear in mind that words have their own limits in conveying ideas and feelings of the writer; words being concrete and static means used to express abstract and rapidly changeable agents such as ideas and feelings."

*   *   *

RICHARDSON, Midge Turk   1930-
(Midge Turk)

PERSONAL: Born March 26, 1930, in Los Angeles, Calif.; daughter of Charles A. (in law and contract division of Los Angeles city school system) and Marie (Lindekin) Turk; married Hamilton F. Richardson (in investments), February 8, 1974. *Education:* Immaculate Heart College, B.A., 1952, M.A., 1957; additional study at University of Pittsburgh, Duquesne University, and University of California, Santa Barbara. *Politics:* Democrat. *Religion:* Roman Catholic. *Home:* 920 Park Ave., PH-B, New York, N.Y. 10028. *Agent:* Sterling Lord Agency, 660 Madison Ave., New York, N.Y. 10021. *Office: Seventeen,* 850 Third Ave., New York, N.Y. 10022.

CAREER: Former nun of the Sisters of the Immaculate Heart of Mary; high school principal in Los Angeles, Calif., 1959-66; New York University, New York City, assistant dean, School of the Arts, 1966-67; *Glamour* (magazine), New York City, college editor, 1967-74; *CO-ED* (magazine), New York City, editor-in-chief and editorial director, 1974-75; *Seventeen* (magazine), New York City, executive editor, 1975—. Member of board of Sloane House, Young Men's Christian Association, New York City, 1970-71. *Member:* Fashion Group.

WRITINGS—Under name Midge Turk: *The Buried Life: A Nun's Journey,* World Publishing, 1971; *Gordon Parks: A Biography* (juvenile), Crowell, 1971. Author of film, "Our Young People," for NBC-TV. Editorial director, *Forecast,* 1974-75.

BIOGRAPHICAL/CRITICAL SOURCES: New York Times, February 5, 1970; *New Republic,* June 12, 1971; *Best Sellers,* July 1, 1971; *New York Times Book Review,* July 11, 1971; *New York Post,* July 29, 1972; *New York News,* June 2, 1974.

*   *   *

RICHARDSON, Miles (Edward)   1932-

PERSONAL: Born January 22, 1932, in Palestine, Tex.; son of Mark Carl (a machinist) and Florence (Adams) Richardson; married Valerie Woodger, December 19, 1959; children: Victoria, Penn, Stanley. *Education:* Stephen F. Austin State College (now University), B.Sc., 1957; Louisiana State University, graduate study, 1957-58; Tulane University, Ph.D., 1965. *Politics:* Democrat. *Religion:* None. *Home:* 1352 Aberdeen, Baton Rouge, La. 70808. *Office:* Department of Geography and Anthropology, Louisiana State University, Baton Rouge, La. 70803.

CAREER: Indiana State College (now Indiana University of Pennsylvania), Indiana, Pa., assistant professor, 1963-64, associate professor of anthropology, 1964-65; Louisiana State University, Baton Rouge, assistant professor, 1965-69, associate professor, 1969-71, professor of anthropology, 1971—, chairman of department, 1969-72. Did anthropological field work in Colombia, 1962-63, in Costa Rica, summer, 1967. *Military service:* U.S. Air Force, 1950-54; became staff sergeant. *Member:* American Anthropological Association, Association of American Geographers, Southern Anthropological Society (secretary-treasurer, 1970-73; president, 1975-76).

WRITINGS: San Pedro, Colombia: Small Town in a Developing Society, Holt, 1970; *The Human Mirror: Material and Spatial Images of Man,* Louisiana State University Press, 1974. Contributor of about twenty articles and reviews to anthropology journals.

WORK IN PROGRESS: Articles on the communicative function of material culture, the meaning of the Spanish American Christ, and humans as heroes; short fiction on human loneliness.

*   *   *

RICHARDSON, Mozelle Groner   1914-

PERSONAL: Born January 26, 1914; daughter of Grover Cleveland and Jessie (Head) Groner; married William T. Richardson (owner of an automobile agency), August 25, 1939; children: William T., Jr., Judy (Mrs. David Markley), Susie (Mrs. Ted Gumerson), Rock Grover. *Education:* Student at several colleges since 1931, including the University of Oklahoma. *Politics:* Registered Democrat but voting Independent. *Religion:* Protestant. *Home:* 1611 Guilford, Oklahoma City, Okla. 73120. *Agent:* Curtis Brown, Ltd., 575 Madison Ave., New York, N.Y. 10022.

CAREER: Author. Has held various positions including secretary, newspaper reporter, and mystery writer. *Member:* P.E.N., Mystery Writers of America, Authors Guild. *Awards, honors:* University of Oklahoma writer's award, 1973.

WRITINGS: Portrait of Fear, Warner Paperback, 1971; *The Curse of Kalispoint,* Warner Paperback, 1971; *The Masks of Thespis,* Warner Paperback, 1973; *Candle in the Wind,* Morrow, 1973; *A Song of India,* Morrow, 1975; *Daughter of the Sacred Mountain,* Morrow, 1977.

SIDELIGHTS: Several of Mozelle Groner Richardson's books have been published in French and German.

*   *   *

RIDGEWAY, Marian E(lizabeth)   1913-

PERSONAL: Born September 20, 1913, in Kansas City, Mo.; daughter of William Jefferson (a county official) and Esther L. (Crooks) Ridgeway. *Education:* University of Missouri, B.J., 1935, A.M., 1946; University of Illinois, Ph.D., 1952. *Politics:* Democrat. *Religion:* Christian Church (Disciples of Christ). *Home:* 1211 West Schwartz, Apt. 6, Carbondale, Ill. 62901. *Office:* Department of Government, Southern Illinois University, Carbondale, Ill. 62901.

CAREER: Employed by Resettlement Administration, Indianapolis, Ind., 1935-36, and by U.S. Farm Security Administration, Indianapolis, 1936-40; U.S. Civil Service Commission, Washington, D.C., junior clerical examiner and junior administrative examiner, 1940-42, 1942-44; U.S. Department of Agriculture, Bureau of Agricultural Economics, Washington, D.C., survey quantifier, 1942; State College of Washington (now Washington State University), Pullman, instructor in government, 1946-47; University of Kansas, Lawrence, instructor in government, 1947-49; Southern Illinois University, Carbondale, lecturer, 1952-53, assistant professor, 1953-56, associate professor, 1956-70, professor of government, 1970-73, professor emeritus, 1973—. Instructor in government, University of Missouri, summers, 1946-48. Research consultant, Illinois State Government, 1966-67. *Member:* American Political Science Association, National Municipal League, American Association of University Women (local vice-president), Midwest Political Science Association, Illinois League of Women Voters (president of local chapter, 1961-63).

WRITINGS: The Missouri Basin's Pick-Sloan Plan, University of Illinois Press, 1955; *Interstate Compacts: A Question of Federalism,* Southern Illinois University Press, 1971. Contributor of articles to journals in her field. Associate editor, *The University Woman,* American Association of University Women, 1961-63.

WORK IN PROGRESS: Research on environmental politics and administration.

AVOCATIONAL INTERESTS: Travel, local history, genealogy, gardening.

* * *

RIGG, Robinson P(eter) 1918-

PERSONAL: Born January 13, 1918, in Blackpool, England; son of Robinson Patrick (an officer in colonial service) and Lilian Mary (Clough) Rigg; married Jane Lane Dorothy Senior (an audiovisual consultant), April, 1958; children: Richard John, Alan James. *Education:* Attended Mount St. Mary's College in England, 1928-36; University of Liverpool, A.B., 1939. *Home:* 1234 Isabella St., Evanston, Ill. 60201; and 139 A Bedford Court Mansions, London W.C.1, England. *Office:* Combined Insurance Co. of America, 5050 Broadway, Chicago, Ill. 60640.

CAREER: Foreign Office, German Section, London, England, vice-chairman of Whitley Council, 1947-52; *Industrial Screen,* London, publisher and editor, 1957-62; *Financial Times,* London, industrial film correspondent, 1958-63; Robinson P. Rigg Associates (communications consultants), London, partner, 1963—; Combined Insurance Co. of America, Chicago, Ill., communications consultant, European Division, 1966-69, public relations associate, 1969-72, director of public relations and advertising, 1972-74, vice-president of public relations and advertising, 1974—. Chairman, Industrial Film Correspondents Group, London, 1966-69. Director, Robin Publications Ltd., London. Examiner, Institute of Public Relations, 1960-69; member of national publicity committee, Royal Society for the Prevention of Accidents, 1967-69. Trustee, Illinois Council on Economic Education, 1977—. *Military service:* British Army, Royal Artillery, 1939-42.

MEMBER: Royal Photographic Society (fellow), Institute of Directors (fellow), Public Relations Society of America, Health Insurance Association of America (member of consumer relations committee, 1974—; chairman, 1975-77), British Kinematograph, Sound and Television Society, Institute of Journalism, National Union of Journalists, British Industrial and Scientific Film Association, Society of Authors, Michigan Shores Club, Chicago Press Club.

WRITINGS: (Contributor) George A. Bull, editor, *Director's Handbook,* McGraw, 1969; *Audiovisual Aids and*

Techniques in Managerial and Supervisory Training, Hamish Hamilton, 1969, Olympic Film Service (New York), 1970. Contributor to *Industrial Advertising Manager's Handbook* and to periodicals and newspapers, including *Film User, Business Screen, Handelsblatt, Times,* and *Director.*

WORK IN PROGRESS: A book on visual communication in the twentieth century.

* * *

RIGGS, James (Lear) 1929-

PERSONAL: Born September 23, 1929, in Webster City, Iowa; son of Max E. (an administrator) and Ann (Wykoff) Riggs; married Doris Jean Miller, December 23, 1951; children: James Randall, Robin Lee. *Education:* Oregon State University, B.S., 1951, M.S., 1958, Ph.D., 1962. *Religion:* Protestant. *Home:* 1210 South West Timian, Corvallis, Ore. 97330. *Office:* Industrial Engineering Department, Oregon State University, Corvallis, Ore. 97331.

CAREER: Oregon State University, Corvallis, instructor, 1957-62, associate professor, 1962-66, professor of industrial engineering, 1966—, head of department, 1968—. Member of affiliate faculty, Japan-American Institute of Management Science, Hawaii, 1973—. Consultant to business institutions and government agencies. *Military service:* U.S. Marine Corps, 1951-56; became captain. *Member:* American Society of Engineering Education, American Institute of Industrial Engineering, Institute of Management Science, Sigma Xi. *Awards, honors:* Carter Award for outstanding teaching, 1967; Fulbright Distinguished Professor to Yugoslavia, 1975.

WRITINGS: (With C. O. Heath) *Guide to Cost Reduction through Critical Path Scheduling,* Prentice-Hall, 1966; *Economic Decision Models,* McGraw, 1968; *Production Systems: Planning, Analysis and Control,* Wiley, 1970, 2nd edition, 1976; (with others) *Industrial Organization and Management,* McGraw, 1971; *The Art of Management,* McGraw, 1974; (with M. S. Inoue) *Introduction to Operations Research and Management Science,* McGraw, 1975; *Engineering Economics,* McGraw, 1977. Contributor to professional journals. Reviewer for several textbook companies, Asian Productivity Organization, and professional journals. Consulting editor, McGraw series in Industrial Engineering and Management Science.

WORK IN PROGRESS: Revisions of two textbooks; a popular tradebook, *Riggs' Unrulies.*

* * *

RIPLEY, (William Young) Warren 1921-

PERSONAL: Born April 13, 1921, in Samarcand, N.C.; son of Clements (a writer) and Katharine (a writer; maiden name, Ball) Ripley; married Quintillia Shuler, December 30, 1943; children: William Young Warren, Jr., Clements. *Education:* Yale University, B.A., 1943. *Politics:* Conservative ("not a party member"). *Religion:* Episcopalian. *Home:* 8 Orange St., Charleston, S.C. 29401. *Office:* Charleston *Evening Post,* 134 Columbus St., Charleston, S.C. 29402.

CAREER: State (newspaper), Columbia, S.C., reporter, 1946-47; *Charleston Evening Post,* Charleston, S.C., reporter, 1947-50, state editor, 1950—. *Military service:* U.S. Army, 1943-45; became first lieutenant. U.S. Army Reserve, 1945-63; became major. *Member:* Company of Military Historians, South Carolina Historical Society (fellow; vice-president, 1964), Charleston Library Society (secretary, 1971-75; president, 1975—). *Awards, honors:* Founders Award of Museum of the Confederacy, 1970, for *Artillery and Ammunition of the Civil War.*

WRITINGS: Artillery and Ammunition of the Civil War, Van Nostrand, 1970. Editor of three local history newspaper tabloids (paperbacks), *The Civil War at Charleston,* which he co-authored, 1961, *50 Famous Houses of Charleston,* 1969, and *Charles Towne—Birth of a City,* which he wrote, 1970. Contributor to *Liberty, Civil War Times Illustrated,* and *American History Illustrated.*

AVOCATIONAL INTERESTS: Collecting Civil War artillery projectiles, collecting rocks and minerals and doing lapidary work, making scale reproductions of weapons, making mahogany furniture.

* * *

RIPPLE, Richard E. 1931-

PERSONAL: Born July 30, 1931; son of Edward Ripple; children: Lynne. *Education:* University of Wisconsin—Milwaukee, B.A., 1952; University of Wisconsin—Madison, M.S., 1956, Ph.D., 1960. *Office:* School of Education, Cornell University, Ithaca, N.Y. 14850.

CAREER: Teacher in public and military schools, 1952-60; Cornell University, Ithaca, N.Y., assistant professor, 1961-64, associate professor, 1964-69, professor of educational psychology, 1969—. Member, New York State College Proficiency Examination Committee in Educational Psychology. *Member:* American Psychological Association (fellow), American Educational Research Association, Association for Supervision and Curriculum Development, Eastern Psychological Association, Northeastern Educational Research Association of New York State (president, 1968-69), Phi Delta Kappa. *Awards, honors:* Senior Fulbright scholar at University of Exeter, 1967-68.

WRITINGS: Programmed Instruction: A New Approach to Teaching and Learning, Cornell University, 1962; (editor) *Readings in Learning and Human Abilities: Educational Psychology,* Harper, 1964, 2nd edition, 1971; (editor with Verne Rockcastle, and contributor) *Piaget Rediscovered,* Cornell University, 1964; (with Robert P. O'Reilly) *The Relationship of Anxiety, Creativity, and Intelligence to Success in Learning from Programmed Instruction,* Cornell University, 1966; (with Marvin D. Glock and Jason Millman) *Learner Characteristics and Instructional Mode: The Relationship of Anxiety, Compulsivity, Creativity and Exhibitionism to Success in Learning from Programmed and Conventional Instruction,* Cornell University, 1967; (contributor) *Aspects of Educational Technology,* Volume II, Methuen, 1968; (with H. J. Klausmeier) *Learning and Human Abilities: Educational Psychology,* 3rd edition (Ripple was not associated with earlier editions), Harper, 1971; (editor with J. Kent Davis and Donald J. Treffinger) *Handbook on Teaching Educational Psychology,* Academic Press, 1977. Author of manuals, study courses, and reports on pilot projects. Contributor to yearbooks and education journals. Advisory editor for educational psychology, J. B. Lippincott Co.; editor, *Educational Psychologist* (newsletter).

* * *

RIPPLEY, La Vern J. 1935-

PERSONAL: Born March 2, 1935; son of Louis G. and Johanna (Rucinski) Rippley; married Barbara Jean Brickner, August 20, 1960; children: John Francis, Larissa Jean. *Edu-*

cation: Kent State University, M.A., 1961; Ohio State University, Ph.D., 1965. *Politics:* Democratic. *Religion:* Catholic. *Home:* 909 Ivanhoe Dr., Northfield, Minn. 55057. *Office:* Department of German, St. Olaf College, Northfield, Minn. 55057.

CAREER: Ohio Wesleyan University, Delaware, instructor, 1964-65, assistant professor of German, 1965-67; St. Olaf College, Northfield, Minn., associate professor, 1967-71, professor of German, 1971—, chairman of department, 1967-74. *Military service:* U.S. Army Reserve, 1958-64; served on active duty, 1958-60; became sergeant. *Member:* Modern Language Association of America, American Association of Teachers of German, Norwegian-American Historical Society, American Society for the History of Germans from Russia. *Awards, honors:* Fulbright fellowship, 1963-64.

WRITINGS: The Columbus Germans, Society for the History of Germans in Maryland, 1968; *Of German Ways,* Dillon, 1970; (translator and editor) Nicolaus Mohr, *Excursion through America,* R. H. Donnelley, 1973; (translator and editor with Armand Bauer) *Russian-German Settlements in the United States,* Institute for Regional Studies, 1974; *The German-Americans,* Twayne, 1976. Contributor of over seventy articles and seventy-five reviews to periodicals.

WORK IN PROGRESS: Studies on local history, immigration, settlement patterns, ethnic architecture and folk ways, mapping ethnic rural communities.

* * *

RISSOVER, Fredric 1940-

PERSONAL: Born October 5, 1940, in Cincinnati, Ohio; son of Meyer and Esther (Marmer) Rissover. *Education:* University of Cincinnati, B.A., 1962, M.A., 1965; University of Iowa, additional study, 1972-73. *Politics:* Liberal. *Religion:* Jewish/Humanist. *Home:* 6514 Chamberlain, University City, Mo. 63130. *Office:* Department of English, St. Louis Community College at Meramec, 11333 Big Bend Blvd., Kirkwood, Mo. 63122.

CAREER: St. Louis Community College at Meramec, Kirkwood, Mo., assistant professor of English, 1965—. Sponsor, Save the Children Federation; director of drama, City Players of St. Louis. *Awards, honors:* Ford Foundation teaching fellowship, 1961-63.

WRITINGS: (Editor with David C. Birch) *Mass Media and the Popular Arts,* McGraw, 1971, 2nd edition, 1977. Author of scripts for local educational television programs and college theatre. Contributor to *Speech Teacher.*

SIDELIGHTS: Fredric Rissover has traveled in Europe and has worked in Head Start and recreation programs with Indian children in New Mexico.

* * *

RIVKIN, Ellis 1918-

PERSONAL: Born September 7, 1918, in Baltimore, Md.; son of Moses Isaachar and Beatrice (Leibowitz) Rivkin; married Zelda Zafren, June 29, 1941; children: Roslyn (Mrs. Charles Weinberger), Sharon (Mrs. Keith Kilburn). *Education:* Johns Hopkins University, B.A. (with honors), 1941, Ph.D., 1946; Baltimore Hebrew College, B.H.L., 1944. *Religion:* Jewish. *Home:* 7610 Reading Rd., Cincinnati, Ohio 45237. *Office:* Hebrew Union College—Jewish Institute of Religion, 3101 Clifton Ave., Cincinnati, Ohio 45220.

CAREER: Dropsie College for Hebrew and Cognate

Learning (now Dropsie University), Philadelphia, Pa., Cyrus Adler postdoctoral research fellow, 1946-48; Gratz College, Philadelphia, instructor in Jewish history, 1946-49; Hebrew Union College—Jewish Institute of Religion, Cincinnati, Ohio, assistant professor, 1949-51, associate professor, 1951-53, professor of Jewish history, 1953-65, Adolph S. Ochs Professor of Jewish History, 1965—. Visiting professor of religion and philosophy, Antioch College, 1963, Dropsie University, 1970, and Southern Methodist University, 1977; Joseph Rosenblatt Lecturer in Judaica, University of Utah, 1967. *Member:* International Platform Association, American Historical Society, Academy of Political Science, American Academy of Political and Social Science, Center for Study of Presidency, Economic History Association, Mediaeval Academy of America, Society of Biblical Literature, Association of Jewish Studies, American Association for the Advancement of Science (fellow), Central Conference of American Rabbis, Phi Beta Kappa. *Awards, honors:* Simon Guggenheim fellowship, 1962-63; American Philosophical Society grant, 1965; American Council of Learned Societies grant, 1965; D.H.L., 1975.

WRITINGS: Leon da Modena and the Kol Sakhal, Hebrew Union College-Jewish Institute of Religion, 1952; *The Dynamics of Jewish History,* New College, 1970; *The Shaping of Jewish History: A Radical New Interpretation,* Scribner, 1971.

Contributor: Jacob R. Marcus, editor, *Essays in American Jewish History,* American Jewish Archives, 1955; Joseph Kitagawa, editor, *Modern Trends in World Religions,* Open Court, 1959; Meir Ben Horin, editor, *Studies and Essays in Honor of Abraham A. Neuman,* Ktav, 1962; Daniel J. Silver, editor, *In the Time of Harvest,* Macmillan, 1963; Max Kreutzberger, editor, *Studies of the Leo Baeck Institute,* Ungar, 1967; Moses A. Shulvass, editor, *Perspectives in Jewish Learning,* College of Jewish Studies, 1966; (author of prolegomenon) W. O. Oesterly and Erwin Rosenthal, editors, *Judaism and Christianity,* Ktav, 1969. Also contributor, Ronald Sobel, editor, *When Yesterday Becomes Tomorrow,* Congregation Emanuel of the City of New York, Bertram W. Korn, editor, *A Bicentennial Festschrift for Jacob Rader Marcus,* and *Eretz-Israel-Nelson Glueck Memorial Volume,* 1975.

Contributor to *Encyclopaedia Britannica, New International Encyclopedia, World Book Encyclopedia;* contributor to journals and periodicals, including *Journal of Modern History, American Historical Review, Journal of Economic History, Civilisations, Jewish Quarterly Review, Jewish Heritage, Reconstructionist, Jewish Teacher, Judaism, Commentary,* and *Saturday Review,* among other publications. Member of editorial boards, *Hebrew Union College Annual* and *Jewish Quarterly Review;* member of publication committee, Jewish Publication Society.

WORK IN PROGRESS: The Hidden Revolution: An Analysis of Pharisaism as an Historical Phenomenon; A Developmental History of Jews and Judaism for Christian Seminaries; and a book tentatively entitled *Globalism: The Highest Stage of Capitalism,* for Scribner.

*   *   *

RIVLIN, Alice M(itchell) 1931-

PERSONAL: Born March 4, 1931, in Philadelphia, Pa.; daughter of Allan C. G. and Georgianna (Fales) Mitchell; married, 1955 (divorced, 1977); children: Catherine Amy, Allan Mitchell, Douglas Gray. *Education:* Bryn Mawr College, B.A., 1952; Radcliffe College, M.A., 1955, Ph.D.,

1958. *Home:* 2842 Chesterfield Pl. N.W., Washington, D.C. 20008. *Office:* Congressional Budget Office, U.S. Congress, Washington, D.C. 20515.

CAREER: Brookings Institution, Washington, D.C., research fellow, 1957-58, staff member of Economic Studies Division, 1958-66, senior staff economist, 1963-66; U.S. Department of Health, Education, and Welfare, Washington, D.C., deputy assistant secretary for program coordination, 1966-68, assistant secretary for planning and evaluation, 1968-69; Brookings Institution, senior fellow, 1969-75; U.S. Congress, Washington, D.C., director of Congressional Budget Office, 1975—. Consultant to U.S. House Committee on Education and Labor, 1961-62, to U.S. Secretary of Treasury, 1964-66. Chairman, National Academy of Sciences-National Research Council Committee on Federal Agency Evaluation Research, 1971—; director at large, National Bureau of Economic Research, 1971—. Trustee of Institute for Educational Development, 1969-71, Negro Student Fund, 1969—, National Assembly for Social Policy and Development, 1970—, and Washington Center for Metropolitan Studies, 1970. *MemberG* American Economic Association. *Awards, honors:* LL.D., Hood College, 1970; Founders Award, Radcliffe College, 1970.

WRITINGS: The Role of the Federal Government in Financing Higher Education, Brookings Institution, 1961; (with Guy Orcutt and others) *Microanalysis of Socioeconomic Systems: A Simulation Study,* Harper, 1961; (with Selma Mushkin) *Measures of State and Local Fiscal Capacity and Tax Effort,* U.S. Advisory Commission on Intergovernmental Relations, 1962; (with Walter Salant and others) *The U.S. Balance of Payments in 1968,* Brookings Institution, 1963; *Systematic Thinking for Social Action* (H. Rowan Gaither lectures at University of California, Berkeley), Brookings Institution, 1971; (with Charles L. Schultze, Edward R. Fried, and Nancy Teeters) *Setting National Priorities: The 1972 Budget,* Brookings Institution, 1971; (with Schultze, Fried, and Teeters) *Setting National Priorities: The 1973 Budget,* Brookings Institution, 1972.

Contributor: Selma J. Mushkin, editor, *Economics of Higher Education,* U.S. Office of Education, 1962; William G. Bowen and Frederick G. Harbison, editors, *Unemployment in a Prosperous Economy,* Princeton University Press, 1965; F. X. Quinn, editor, *Population Ethics,* Corpus Publications, 1968; *Compendium of Papers on the Economics of Higher Education in the United States,* U.S. Joint Economic Committee, 1969; *Needs of Elementary and Secondary Education for the Seventies,* U.S. House Committee on Education and Labor, 1970. Supervisor for books published by U.S. Department of Health, Education, and Welfare.

Contributor to *Progressive, New York Times Sunday Magazine,* and to economics and political science journals. Editorial writer for *Washington Post,* July-October, 1971 (on leave from Brookings Institution); member of editorial board of *Journal of Law and Education,* 1971—; member of advisory editorial board of *Journal of Human Resources.*

*   *   *

ROBERTS, David S(tuart) 1943-

PERSONAL: Born May 29, 1943, in Denver, Colo.; son of Walter Orr (an astrophysicist) and Janet (Smock) Roberts; married Sharon Morris, October 29, 1967. *Education:* Harvard University, B.A., 1965; University of Denver, M.A., Ph.D., 1970. *Office:* Department of Literature, Hampshire College, Amherst, Mass. 01002.

CAREER: Hampshire College, Amherst, Mass., 1970—, began as assistant professor, currently associate professor of literature and mountaineering. *Member:* American Alpine Club.

WRITINGS: *Mountain of My Fear,* Vanguard, 1968; *Deborah: A Wilderness Narrative,* Vanguard, 1970; (contributor) *Earth and the Great Weather,* Friends of the Earth, 1971; (contributor) Franklin Russell, editor, *The Mountains of America,* Abrams, 1975. Contributor of articles and reviews to mountaineering journals and national periodicals, including *Saturday Evening Post* and *New York Times Book Review.*

WORK IN PROGRESS: A novel and a memoir.

AVOCATIONAL INTERESTS: Mountaineering (has made fourteen trips to Alaska).

BIOGRAPHICAL/CRITICAL SOURCES: *Publisher's Weekly,* April 1, 1968; *Appalachia,* December, 1974.

* * *

ROBERTS, James Deotis 1927-

PERSONAL: Born July 12, 1927, in Spindale, N.C.; married Elizabeth Caldwell (an elementary teacher), June 5, 1953; children: Edin Charmaine, James Deotis, Jr., Carlita Rose, Kristina LaFerne. *Education:* Johnson C. Smith University, A.B. (magna cum laude), 1947; Shaw University, B.D., 1950; Hartford Seminary Foundation, B.D., 1951, S.T.M., 1952; University of Edinburgh, Ph.D., 1957; also studied at Cambridge University, 1956, Duke University, 1960, University of Wisconsin, 1962, University of Michigan, 1967. *Residence:* Silver Spring, Md. *Office:* School of Religion, Howard University, Washington, D.C. 20001.

CAREER: Pastor of Baptist church in Tarboro, N.C., 1948-50, and assistant pastor in Hartford, Conn., 1950-52; Georgia Baptist College, Macon, dean of religion, 1952-53; Shaw University, Raleigh, N.C., assistant professor of philosophy and religion, 1953-55; interim pastor of Congregational church in Glasgow, Scotland, 1956-57; Shaw University, associate professor of philosophy and religion, and college minister, 1957-58; Howard University, School of Religion, Washington, D.C., 1958—, began as instructor, professor of the history and philosophy of religion and Christian theology, 1967—. Visiting professor at Catholic University of America, 1968-69, 1970-72, Swarthmore College, 1969-70, Wesley Theological Seminary, 1970-71, and University of Virginia, 1971-72; lecturer at American Baptist Seminary, Princeton University, and Vanderbilt University. Honorary regent, International Sociological Research Institute; member of Theological Commission, National Committee of Black Churchmen.

MEMBER: American Academy of Religion, Biblical Theologians. *Awards, honors:* Ford Foundation faculty fellowships, summers, 1963-66; Society for Religion in Higher Education traveling fellowship, 1964-65; American Association of Theological Schools fellowship at Harvard University, spring, 1965; Howard University study-travel research grant, 1971.

WRITINGS: *Faith and Reason in Pascal, Bergson and James,* Christopher, 1962; *From Puritanism to Platonism in Seventeenth Century England,* Nijhoff, 1968; (contributor) J. S. Roucek and T. P. Kiernan, editors, *The Negro Impact on Western Civilization,* Philosophical Library, 1970; *Liberation and Reconciliation: A Black Theology,* Westminster, 1971; (editor with James Gardiner) *Quest for a Black Theology,* Pilgrim Press, 1971; *A Black Political Theology,* West-

minster, 1974; *Oppression and Liberation in World History,* Orbis, 1978. Also author of *Extending Redemption and Reconciliation,* Christian Board of Publication (St. Louis). Contributor of articles and reviews to professional journals. Editor, *Journal of Religious Thought,* 1974—.

* * *

ROBERTS, John R. 1934-

PERSONAL: Born March 7, 1934, in Indiana; son of Paul D. and Irene (McMurray) Roberts; married Lorraine Bielski (a teacher), August 5, 1955; children: Stephanie, Mary, Claire, Milissa, Lisa, John. *Education:* Indiana State University, B.A. (magna cum laude), 1955; University of Illinois, M.A., 1957, Ph.D., 1962. *Politics:* Independent. *Religion:* Roman Catholic. *Home:* 407 Longfellow, Columbia, Mo. 65201. *Office:* Department of English, University of Missouri, Columbia, Mo. 65201.

CAREER: University of Wisconsin—Madison, assistant professor of English, 1962-66; University of Detroit, Detroit, Mich., associate professor of English, 1966-68; University of Missouri—Columbia, associate professor, 1968-72, professor of English, 1972—, chairman of department, 1974—. *Member:* Modern Language Association of America, Milton Society of America, Central Renaissance Conference, Midwest Modern Language Association.

WRITINGS: *A Critical Anthology of English Recusant Devotional Prose: 1558-1603,* Duquesne University Press, 1966; *An Annotated Bibliography of the Criticism of John Donne: 1912-1967,* University of Missouri Press, 1973; *George Herbert: An Annotated Bibliography of Modern Criticism, 1905-1974,* University of Missouri Press, in press. Contributor to literature journals.

* * *

ROBERTS, Kenneth H(arris) 1930-

PERSONAL: Born November 16, 1930, in Radford, Va.; son of Henry Harris and Wanda (Holmes) Roberts; married Sandra Willey (a teacher), August 20, 1955; children: Kevin David, Kenneth Jeffrey. *Education:* Denison University, B.A., 1957; Ohio State University, M.A., 1958, Ph.D., 1966. *Home:* 800 West End Ave., New York, N.Y. 10025. *Office:* Department of Theater and Cinema, Hunter College of the City University of New York, 695 Park Ave., New York, N.Y. 10021.

CAREER: Independent film director and producer; professional stage actor and director; Hunter College of the City University of New York, New York, N.Y., director of cinema, 1964—. *Military service:* U.S. Air Force, 1950-54. *Member:* University Film Association, The Players (member of board of directors), Actors' Equity Association.

WRITINGS: (With Win Sharples, Jr.) *A Primer for Film-Making: A Complete Guide to 16mm and 35mm Film Production,* Pegasus, 1971.

WORK IN PROGRESS: *O.I.L.,* a novel; two screenplays.

AVOCATIONAL INTERESTS: Travel, scuba diving.

* * *

ROBERTS, Leonard W(ard) 1912-

PERSONAL: Born January 28, 1912, in Osborn, Ky.; son of Louis J. (a minister) and Rhoda (a postmistress; maiden name, Osborn) Roberts; married Edith Reynolds (a teacher); children: Sue Roberts Adkins, Margaret Roberts Biller, Rita Roberts Kelley, Lynneda Roberts Denny. *Edu-*

cation: Berea College, A.B., 1939; University of Iowa, M.A., 1943; Indiana University, further graduate study, summer, 1948; University of Kentucky, Ph.D., 1954. *Religion:* Christian. *Home address:* Box 266, Stanville, Ky. 41659. *Office:* Appalachian Studies Center, Pikeville College, Pikeville, Ky. 41501.

CAREER: Brevard College, Brevard, N.C., instructor in health education and music, 1940-42; University of North Carolina at Chapel Hill, teaching fellow, 1943-45; Berea College, Berea, Ky., instructor in English, 1945-50; Piedmont College, Demorest, Ga., professor of English, 1953-54; Union College, Barbourville, Ky., professor of English and chairman of department of English and Division of Languages, 1954-58; Morehead State University, Morehead, Ky., professor of English and chairman of department, 1958-61; West Virginia Wesleyan College, Buckhannon, professor of English and chairman of department, 1961-68; Pikeville College, Pikeville, Ky., chairman of Division of Humanities, 1968—. Folklore consultant; teacher corps consultant. *Military service:* U.S. Army, 1930-33.

MEMBER: Modern Language Association of America, National Council of Teachers of English, American Association of University Professors (secretary), American Folklore Society, National Folk Festival Association (president, 1970-72), Kentucky Folklore Society, Tennessee Folklore Society, Pike County Historical Society (president), Preservation Council of Pike County, Big Sandy Valley Historical Society (secretary).

WRITINGS—All folklore: (Compiler) *I Bought Me a Dog and Other Folktales from the Southern Mountains,* Council of Southern Mountains, 1954; (compiler) *South from Hell-fer-Sartin,* University of Kentucky Press, 1955; (compiler) *Nippy and theYankee Doodle,* Council of Southern Mountains, 1958; *Up Cut Shin and Down Greasy,* University of Kentucky Press, 1959; *Folk Stories and Songs of the Couch Family,* University of Kentucky Press, 1959; (contributor) Tristram P. Coffin, editor, *Our Living Traditions: An Introduction to American Folklore,* Basic Books, 1968; *Old Greasybeard: Tales from the Cumberland Gap,* Folklore Associates, 1969; *Sang Branch Settlers: Folksongs and Tales of a Kentucky Mountain Family,* University of Texas Press, 1974. Editor, *Laurel Review,* 1964-68, and *Twigs,* 1969—.

WORK IN PROGRESS: In the Pine, a book of folk songs of Kentucky, for University of Kentucky Press; *Kentucky Superstitions,* three volumes.

SIDELIGHTS: "Having grown up in Appalachia," Leonard Roberts told *CA,* "I found myself drawn back to it from afar. Then I began to study the people, their history, ethnic origins, traditions, and way of life. This accounts for a great mass of folklore, traditions, [and] local history that I have in my archives and that I am endeavoring to put in order and to publish as time permits."

AVOCATIONAL INTERESTS: Folk singing and dancing; folklore telling and collecting.

*   *   *

ROBERTS, Paul Craig   1939-

PERSONAL: Born April 3, 1939, in Atlanta, Ga.; son of Paul Craig, Jr. (a businessman) and Lamar (Dryman) Roberts; married Linda Jane Fisher, July 3, 1969. *Education:* Georgia Institute of Technology, B.S., 1961; University of Virginia, graduate study, 1961-62, 1963-64, Ph.D., 1967; University of California, Berkeley, graduate study, 1962-63;

Merton College, Oxford, Relm fellow, 1964-65; also studied at Goethe Institute in Germany, summer, 1964. *Home:* 505 South Fairfax St., Alexandria, Va. 22314.

CAREER: Virginia Polytechnic Institute, Blacksburg, assistant professor of economics, 1965-69; University of New Mexico, Albuquerque, visiting associate professor of economics, 1969-71; Hoover Institution on War, Revolution and Peace, Stanford, Calif., national fellow, 1971-72, research fellow, 1972-77, senior research fellow, 1978—. Visiting associate professor, Tulane University, 1969; visiting professor, Georgetown University, summer, 1972; adjunct professor of economics, George Mason University, 1976—. U.S. House of Representatives, staff associate, Committee on Appropriations and economic counsel to Representative Jack Kemp, 1975-76, chief economist, minority staff, Committee on the Budget, 1976-77; economic counsel to Senator Orrin Hatch, U.S. Senate, 1977—. *Member:* American Economic Association, American Association for the Advancement of Slavic Studies, Public Choice Society. *Awards, honors:* Exchange student to Soviet Union, summer, 1961; research grants from American Philosophical Society and Relm Foundation, 1968.

WRITINGS: Alienation and the Soviet Economy, University of New Mexico Press, 1971; *Marx's Theory of Exchange, Alienation, and Crisis,* Hoover Institution, 1973. Contributor to *Vedecke Informace* (Czechoslovakia), *Classica et Mediaevalia, Slavic Review, Soviet Studies, Modern Age,* and to finance and economic journals.

SIDELIGHTS: Paul Roberts told *CA:* "Good writing is like freedom and discipline. Like freedom, it is an achievement that must be renewed daily. Like discipline, it is a struggle. We are all by now familiar with the modern alienated intellectual whose alienation amounts to a moral hatred of existing society. He has a passion for moral improvement of his society, but he has worked out the doctrine of doubt to its logical conclusion. Since he cannot find moral motives safe from the suspicion of mere conformity, self-interest, or hypocrisy, he can find no safe grounds for moral affirmation. His moral passions, being thus denied legitimate expression, are satisfied by turning his skepticism against his own society. He denounces its institutions and policies as masks for the material profit of vested interests. Michael Polanyi has shown that this inconsistent combination of moral skepticism with moral indignation is held together by their joint attack on existing society. For too long Western writers have been victims of this syndrome. Western civilization has relied for so long on a self-critical posture as its means of achieving improvement that there is nothing left to unmask and denounce. The challenge that writers face today is to restore affirmation as a tenable mode of expression."

*   *   *

ROBERTS, Ron E.   1939-

PERSONAL: Born July 31, 1939, in Chariton, Iowa; son of William E. (a salesman) and Mae (Blue) Roberts; married Patricia Sprague, June 5, 1960 (divorced, 1973); children: Niccolo, Alan. *Education:* Attended Graceland College, 1957-59; Drake University, B.A., 1961; Louisiana State University, M.A., 1964, Ph.D., 1969. *Politics:* Social Democrat. *Religion:* Druid. *Home:* 2115 Olive, Cedar Falls, Iowa 50613. *Office:* Department of Sociology, University of Northern Iowa, Cedar Falls, Iowa 50613.

CAREER: Memphis State University, Memphis, Tenn., instructor in sociology, 1964-66; Graceland College, Lamoni, Iowa, assistant professor of sociology, 1966-67; Louisiana State University, Baton Rouge, special lecturer, 1967-69; University of Northern Iowa, Cedar Falls, 1969—, began as assistant professor, professor of sociology, 1976—. *Member:* American Sociological Association.

WRITINGS: The New Communes: Coming Together in America, Prentice-Hall, 1971; *Social Movements: Between the Balcony and the Barricades,* Mosby, 1974; *Sociology with a Human Face,* Mosby, 1976; *Critical Social Problems,* Mosby, in press.

* * *

ROBINSON, A(rthur) N(apoleon) R(aymond) 1926-

PERSONAL: Born December 16, 1926, in Tobago, Trinidad and Tobago; son of James Andrew (a headmaster) and Isabella (Muir) Robinson; married Patricia Jean Rawlins (director of research at Central Bank), July 1, 1961; children: David Arthur Andrew, Ann-Margaret Muir. *Education:* University of London, LL.B., 1949; Inner Temple, London, Barrister-at-Law, 1951; St. John's College, Oxford, B.A. (honors), 1954. *Home:* Robinson St., Scarborough, Trinidad and Tobago. *Office:* 34 Abercromby, Port-of-Spain, Trinidad and Tobago.

CAREER: In private practice of law, Port-of-Spain, Trinidad and Tobago, 1955—. Member of Parliament; Minister of Finance of Trinidad and Tobago, 1961-67, of External Affairs, 1967-70, Deputy Prime Minister, 1967-70. Visiting scholar, Law School, Harvard University, 1967; executive director, Foundation for the Establishment of an International Criminal Court. *Awards, honors:* Distinguished International Criminal Lawyer Award, International Law Commission, 1977.

WRITINGS: The New Frontier and the New Africa, Caribbean Printers, 1964; *Fiscal Reform in Trinidad and Tobago,* P.N.M. Publishing, 1966; *The Mechanics of Independence: A Study in Political and Economic Transformation,* M.I.T. Press, 1971. Contributor to *Encyclopaedia Britannica.*

WORK IN PROGRESS: Development and Human Dignity.

AVOCATIONAL INTERESTS: Travel, swimming.

* * *

ROBINSON, Daniel N. 1937-

PERSONAL: Born March 9, 1937, in Monticello, N.Y.; son of Henry Stoddard (an executive) and Margaret (Kimbizis) Robinson; married Francine Malasko, September 18, 1967. *Education:* Colgate University, B.A., 1958; Hofstra University, M.A., 1960; City University of New York, Ph.D., 1965. *Home:* 1237 37th St. N.W., Washington, D.C. 20007. *Office:* Department of Psychology, Georgetown University, Washington, D.C. 20007.

CAREER: Columbia University, New York, N.Y., senior research psychologist, Electronic Research Laboratories, 1960-68; Amherst College, Amherst, Mass., assistant professor, 1968-69, associate professor of psychology, 1969-71; Georgetown University, Washington, D.C., associate professor, 1970-73, professor of psychology, 1973—. Visiting lecturer in psychology, Princeton University, 1965-68. Consulting psychologist to National Institutes of Mental Health and National Science Foundation. *Member:* American Psychological Association (fellow), British Psychological Association (fellow), American Association of University Professors, American Association for the Advancement of Science, New York Academy of Science, Sigma Xi.

WRITINGS: (Editor) *Heredity and Achievement,* Oxford University Press, 1970; (editor) *Readings in the Origins and Principles of Psychology,* Dickenson, 1972; *Psychology: A Study of Its Origins and Principles,* Dickenson, 1972; *The Enlightened Machine: An Introduction to Neuropsychology,* Dickenson, 1973; *An Intellectual History of Psychology,* Macmillan, 1976; *Psychology: Traditions and Perspectives,* Van Nostrand, 1976. Contributor to psychology journals.

WORK IN PROGRESS: Editing *Significant Contributions to the History of Psychology,* twenty-eight volumes, for University Publications of America.

* * *

ROBINSON, Janet O(live) 1939-

PERSONAL: Born October 31, 1939, in Ripley, Derbyshire, England; daughter of John William (an accountant) and Gladys (Leadbeter) Robinson; married David Ernest Howard (an engineer), October 3, 1970. *Education:* University of Reading, B.A. (honors), 1962. *Home:* 76 Darvell Dr., Chesham, Buckinghamshire, England. *Office:* British Council, 10 Spring Gardens, London SW1A 2BN, England.

CAREER: British Council, London, England, librarian, English-Teaching Information Centre, 1964-76, Medical Information Service, 1977—. *Member:* Library Association.

WRITINGS: An Annotated Bibliography of Modern Language Teaching: Books and Articles, 1946-67, Oxford University Press, 1969.

* * *

ROBINSON, Thomas W. 1935-

PERSONAL: Born February 9, 1935, in Milwaukee, Wis.; married, 1962; children: two. *Education:* Carleton College, B.A., 1957; Columbia University, M.I.A., 1959, Ph.D., 1969.

CAREER: Columbia University, New York City, instructor in international organization, 1964; Dartmouth College, Hanover, N.H., instructor in political science, 1964-65; Rand Corp., Santa Monica, Calif., researcher, 1965-71; Council on Foreign Relations, New York City, visiting fellow, 1971—. Has also taught at University of Southern California, 1967, University of California, Los Angeles, 1968-71, and Princeton University, 1972. *Military service:* U.S. Army, 1965. *Member:* Association for Asian Studies, American Political Science Association, American Association for the Advancement of International Law, International Studies Association, American Association for the Advancement of Slavic Studies, Peace Research Society, Los Angeles Committee on Foreign Relations. *Awards, honors:* Fulbright fellowship.

WRITINGS: Game Theory and Politics, Rand Corp., 1970; *China Data Retrieval,* Rand Corp., 1970; *A Politico-Military Biography of Lin Piao, Part I: 1907-1949,* Rand Corp., 1971; (editor and contributor) *The Cultural Revolution in China,* University of California Press, 1971; (contributor) Robert Scalapino, *Elites in the People's Republic of China,* University of Washington Press, 1972. Contributor of about thirty articles to political science journals.

WORK IN PROGRESS: Part II of the Lin Piao biography; projects on new theories and methods in international forecasting, and on Chinese strategic doctrine in the context of Chinese foreign policy and domestic politics.†

ROCKE, Russell 1945-

PERSONAL: Born February 8, 1945, in New York, N.Y.; son of Sande (in advertising) and Mary (Cuozz) Rocke. *Education:* Tulane University, B.A., 1967, J.D., 1968. *Politics:* "Quien sabe?" *Religion:* "Quien sabe?"

CAREER: VISTA, Washington, D.C., and New York City, lawyer, 1969-70; Sales Ammunition, Inc. (advertising and sales promotion agency), New York City, president, beginning 1970. Chairman of board of directors, Southern Press, 1973—.

WRITINGS: The Grandiloquent Dictionary, Prentice-Hall, 1972. Editor, *Barataria Review* and *Books: A New Orleans Review,* 1973—.

WORK IN PROGRESS: A book about the innate poetry of pidgin English; an adventure trilogy concerning expeditions in Africa and Nepal; a sequel to *The Grandiloquent Dictionary;* a play entitled "Twenty-four Hours in Figuig."†

*　*　*

RODNICK, David 1908-

PERSONAL: Born May 10, 1908, in New Haven, Conn.; married Elizabeth Wright Amis (an editor), March 24, 1945; children: Amie Bowman. *Education:* New York University, B.S., 1931; Yale University, M.A., 1933; University of Pennsylvania, Ph.D., 1936. *Home:* 4806 17th St., Lubbock, Tex. 79416.

CAREER: Consulting sociologist and cultural historian, 1936-49; social scientist with U.S. Office of War Information, 1942-43, with Office of Strategic Services in England and Germany, 1944-45, with Office of Military Government in Germany, 1945-46; Columbia University, New York, N.Y., member of staff of research project on contemporary cultures, 1947; University of Oslo, Oslo, Norway, Fulbright professor, 1949-50; consultant to Economic Cooperation Administration and Mutual Security Agency, Washington, D.C., 1951-52; sociologist with Human Resources Research Institute, U.S. Air Force, France, 1952-54, with Institute of International Social Research, Princeton, N.J., 1955-59; Inter-American University of Puerto Rico, San German, chairman of Social Science Division, 1959-61; Iowa Wesleyan College, Mount Pleasant, professor of sociology and anthropology, 1961-63; Army War College, Carlisle, Pa., professor of sociology, 1963-65; Midwestern University, Wichita Falls, Tex., professor of sociology and anthropology, 1965-67; Texas Tech University, Lubbock, professor of sociology, 1967-77; University of Hamburg, Hamburg, Germany, Fulbright professor and visiting professor, 1975-77; Furman University, Greenville, S.C., visiting professor of sociology and cultural anthropology, 1977-78. Visiting professor at Pennsylvania State University, 1962, University of Iowa, 1963, University of Saskatchewan, 1967, University of Manitoba, 1968, and Lakehead University, 1969.

MEMBER: American Sociological Association (fellow), American Anthropological Association (fellow), Society for Applied Anthropology (fellow), American Association for the Advancement of Science (fellow). *Awards, honors:* Postdoctoral honors fellow, Yale University, 1936-38; Social Science Research Council fellow in Czechoslovakia, 1948-49; Social Science Research Council grant, University of Stockholm, 1950.

WRITINGS: The Fort Belknap Assiniboine of Montana: A Study in Culture Change (doctoral thesis, 1936; a study for U.S. Indian Service), privately printed, 1938; *Spanish-Indian Contacts in Texas, 1718-1818* (monograph), National

Park Service, 1942; *St. Louis and the Growth of the West, 1764-1890* (monograph), National Park Service, 1942; *Postwar Germans: An Anthropologist's Account,* Yale University Press, 1948; *An Operational Outline of Czechoslovakian Cultures* (monograph), Human Resources Research Institute, 1953; *An Interim Report on French Culture* (monograph), Human Resources Research Institute, 1954; *Report on the French People* (monograph), Human Resources Research Institute, 1954; *The Norwegians: A Study in National Culture,* Public Affairs Press, 1955; *British Foreign Policy Patterns* (monograph), Institute for International Social Research, 1956; (with Herbert Luethy) *French Motivations in the Suez Crisis* (monograph), Institute for International Social Research, 1956; (with Hadley Cantril) *On Understanding the French Left* (monograph), Institute for International Social Research, 1956; (with Cantril) *Politics of Despair,* Basic Books, 1958; (with Lloyd Free) *Six Allies and a Neutral,* Free Press, 1959; *Germany Revisited* (monograph), Institute for International Social Research, 1959; *Aspects of American Culture* (monograph), Fund for Human Ecology, 1959; *Some Notes on Japanese Culture* (monograph), Fund for Human Ecology, 1959; *Some Universals in Human Behavior* (monograph), Fund for Human Ecology, 1959.

(With Verne Ray) *Primitive Pragmatists,* University of Washington Press, 1964; *An Introduction to Man and His Development,* Appleton, 1966; *The Strangled Democracy: Czechoslovakia 1948-1969,* Caprock Press, 1970; *Essays on an America in Transition,* Caprock Press, 1972; *Man's Quest for Autonomy: A Background for Modernization,* Caprock Press, 1974. Writer of other monographs on Asia, Africa, Latin America, and Europe. Also author of *Personal Odyssey: Field Notes on a Changing Europe 1944-1958, The Politics of Powerlessness: A Study of French Communism 1955-56,* and *Louis Juchereau de St. Denis 1676-1744.* Contributor to professional journals and to encyclopedias.

WORK IN PROGRESS: A book of essays, *Germany in Transition,* for Caprock Press; a study of demography and background of Hamburg, for Caprock Press; a book on contemporary Europe.

SIDELIGHTS: David Rodnick speaks French, German, Norwegian, and Czech; he reads Swedish, Italian, Spanish, and Danish.

*　*　*

ROEBURT, John 1909(?)-1972

1909(?)—May 22, 1972; American author of detective novels and radio and television dramas. Obituaries: *New York Times,* May 24, 1972.

*　*　*

ROGERS, Augustus James III 1929-

PERSONAL: Born February 20, 1929, in Benzonia, Mich.; son of Augustus James II and Agnes (Challoner) Rogers; married Esther Hagen (a pianist), August 27, 1949; children: Augustus James IV, Sally Jane, Lisa Anne. *Education:* Michigan State University, B.S., 1951, M.A., 1966, Ph.D., 1969. *Religion:* Episcopalian. *Home:* Hilltop, Beulah, Mich. 49617. *Office:* Department of Economics, University of Wisconsin—Milwaukee, Milwaukee, Wis. 53201.

CAREER: University of Wisconsin—Milwaukee, assistant professor, 1968-72, associate professor of economics, 1972—.

WRITINGS: Choice: An Introduction to Economics,

Prentice-Hall, 1971, 2nd edition, 1974; (with T. D. Crocker) *Environmental Economics,* Dryden, 1971; *Macro-economic Principles,* Dryden, 1972; *Goods and Not-So-Goods,* Dryden, 1972; *The Economics of Crime,* Dryden, 1973. Editor of ''Principles of Economics'' series, nine volumes, Dryden, 1972.

WORK IN PROGRESS: Contemporary Economics.†

* * *

ROGERS, Robert 1928-

PERSONAL: Born October 3, 1928, in Milwaukee, Wis.; son of Ralph Waldo and Lura (Messner) Rogers; married Joanne Edenborg; children: Crane Francis; stepchildren: Kristian Paul Solem. *Education:* University of Michigan, A.B., 1950; Columbia University, A.M., 1954, Ph.D., 1961. *Office:* Department of English, State University of New York College at Buffalo, Buffalo, N.Y. 14222.

CAREER: Worcester Polytechnic Institute, Worcester, Mass., instructor in English, 1957-60; Rutgers University, Douglass College, New Brunswick, N.J., instructor in English, 1960-62; State University of New York College at Buffalo, lecturer, 1962-63, assistant professor, 1963-66, associate professor, 1966-71, professor of English, 1971—. *Military service:* U.S. Navy, 1950-53. *Member:* Modern Language Association of America.

WRITINGS: (Contributor) Walter K. Gordon, editor, *Literature in Critical Perspectives,* Appleton, 1968; *A Psychoanalytical Study of the Double in Literature,* Wayne State University Press, 1970. Contributor to literature journals.

WORK IN PROGRESS: A book on the psycho-dynamics of metaphor.

* * *

ROGO, D. Scott 1950-

PERSONAL: Born February 1, 1950, in Los Angeles, Calif.; son of Jack (an accountant) and Winifred (Jacobs) Rogo. *Education:* Attended University of Cincinnati, 1967-68; San Fernando Valley State College (now California State University, Northridge), B.A., 1971. *Politics:* Democrat (conservative). *Home:* 6544 Hesperia Ave., Resada, Calif. 91335.

CAREER: Parapsychologist. *Member:* American Society for Psychical Research, Society for Psychical Research (London), Parapsychological Association.

WRITINGS: NAD: A Study of Some Unusual ''Other-World'' Experiences, University Books, 1970; *A Psychic Study of the ''Music of the Spheres,''* University Books, 1972; *The Welcoming Silence,* University Books, 1973; *An Experience of Phantoms,* Taplinger, 1974; *Parapsychology: A Century of Inquiry,* Taplinger, 1975; *In Search of the Unknown,* Taplinger, 1976; *Exploring Psychic Phenomena,* Quest Books, 1976; *The Haunted Universe,* New American Library, 1977; *Exploring the Out-of-Body Experience,* Viking, 1977; *PK: The Psychic Force of the Will,* Taplinger, 1977. Contributor to parapsychology and paraphysics journals. Regular reviewer, *Fate.*

* * *

ROGOFF, Harry 1882-1971

December 11, 1882—November 30, 1971; Russian-born American editor, journalist, and author of works in Yiddish. Obituaries: *New York Times,* December 1, 1971; *Time,* December 13, 1971.

ROHR, John A. 1934-

PERSONAL: Born July 31, 1934, in Evanston, Ill.; son of John W. and Agnes (Madden) Rohr; married Kathleen Lehman, May 6, 1972; children: Paul Lehman, Mark Adam. *Education:* Loyola University, Chicago, Ill., A.B., 1957; Georgetown University, M.A., 1964; Woodstock College, S.T.L., 1966; University of Chicago, Ph.D., 1970. *Home:* 1028 Monterey Ct., Park Forest, Ill. 60466. *Office:* Department of Public Service, Governors State University, Park Forest, Ill. 60466.

CAREER: Former Roman Catholic priest of Society of Jesus (Jesuits); Georgetown University, Washington, D.C., instructor in theology, 1965; Loyola University, Chicago, Ill., assistant professor of political science, 1969-71; Governors State University, Park Forest, Ill., professor of government, 1971—. *Military service:* U.S. Naval Reserve, 1965—; current rank, lieutenant commander. *Member:* American Political Science Association, American Society for Public Administration.

WRITINGS: Prophets without Honor: Public Policy and the Selective Conscientious Objector, Abingdon, 1971; *Ethics for Bureaucrats: An Essay on Law and Values,* Dekker, 1978.

AVOCATIONAL INTERESTS: Tennis, bridge.

* * *

ROHRER, Daniel M(organ) 1941-

PERSONAL: Born October 27, 1941; son of Albert Elton and Marietta (Morgan) Rohrer. *Education:* Western Michigan University, B.A., 1964; University of Wisconsin, M.A., 1969; Boston College, J.D. candidate, 1979. *Office:* Department of Communications, Boston College, Chestnut Hill, Mass. 02167.

CAREER: Walston & Co., Inc. (stock brokerage firm), Grand Rapids, Mich., trader, 1959-63; Waukegan Township High School, Waukegan, Ill., teacher, 1965-66; Oberlin College, Oberlin, Ohio, instructor, 1966-70; Boston College, Chestnut Hill, Mass., 1970—, began as instructor in communications, currently director of forensics.

WRITINGS: (With others) *By Weight of Arms,* National Textbook Co., 1969; (with others) *Environment Crisis,* National Textbook Co., 1970; (with others) *Modern Debate Case Techniques,* National Textbook Co., 1970; *Justice before the Law,* National Textbook Co., 1971.

WORK IN PROGRESS: With Allan Lichtman and Jerome R. Corsi, a book which will attempt to synthesize argumentation and decision theory, *The New Argumentation.*

AVOCATIONAL INTERESTS: Photography, writing, public speaking, travel.

* * *

ROLLS, Eric C(harles) 1923-

PERSONAL: Born April 25, 1923, in Grenfell, New South Wales, Australia; son of William Charles (a farmer) and Lilian (Mitchell) Rolls; married Joan Stephenson (a pharmacist), February 27, 1953; children: Kim Stephen, Kerry Jane, Andrew Mitchell. *Education:* Studied through Blackfriars' Correspondence School, 1929-34, and then attended high school in Sydney, 1935-39. *Politics:* ''Varies.'' *Religion:* Church of England. *Home:* Cumberdeen, Baradine, New South Wales 2858, Australia.

CAREER: Farmer and grazier in Baradine and Boggabri, New South Wales, Australia, 1948—; writer. *Military ser-*

vice: Australian Imperial Forces, Signals, 1941-46; served on New Guinea. *Member:* Australian Society of Authors. *Awards, honors:* David Myer Trust Award for poetry, 1968, for *Sheaf Tosser;* two Commonwealth Literary Fund grants to write the human history of Chinese in Australia, 1969-70; first prize for nonfiction in Cook Bi-Centenary Competition, 1970, for *They All Ran Wild;* first prize for children's book in John Franklin Competition, 1974; for *Running Wild;* Braille Book of the Year award, 1975, for *The River;* Literature Board fellowship, 1975-77.

WRITINGS: Sheaf Tosser, and Other Poems, Angus & Robertson, 1967; *They All Ran Wild: The Story of Pests on the Land in Australia,* Angus & Robertson, 1969, children's version published as *Running Wild,* Angus & Robertson, 1972; *The River* (nonfiction), Angus & Robertson, 1974; *The Green Mosaic* (poems), Thomas Nelson, in press. Poetry has been published in literary magazines and newspapers and reprinted in a number of anthologies.

WORK IN PROGRESS: Pilliga, the nonfiction story of the growth of a huge self-regenerating commercial forest on land occupied only one hundred years ago by sheep and cattle runs; a human history of the Chinese in Australia, for Angus & Robertson.

SIDELIGHTS: Eric Rolls told *CA:* "Poetry is a compulsion and usually thrusts itself upon me at inconvenient times. The aim of my prose is to make history literature. Facts are a fine discipline to the imagination. They function like the formalities of poetry and force one to stretch for the right language. Australian history has a particular fascination because so much of it took place outside the law. There was more attempt to hide it than to record it."

*   *   *

ROME, Florence   1910-

PERSONAL: Born September 24, 1910, in Chicago, Ill.; daughter of Maurice David (an insurance broker) and Rose (Brish) Miles; married Harold Rome (a composer and lyricist), February 3, 1939; children: Joshua, Rachel. *Education:* Attended University of Illinois, 1928-29. *Home:* 1035 Fifth Ave., New York, N.Y. 10028. *Agent:* Gloria Safier, Inc., 667 Madison Ave., New York, N.Y. 10021.

CAREER: Ruthrauff & Ryan (advertising agency), New York City, copy writer, 1938-46; Young & Rubicam (advertising agency), New York City, copy writer, 1948-53. *Member:* Authors Guild.

WRITINGS: The Scarlett Letters, Random House, 1971; *The Tattooed Men,* Delacorte, 1975. Contributor of articles and short fiction to national magazines, including *McCall's, Cosmopolitan,* and *Stage.*

WORK IN PROGRESS: With Arlene Francis, an autobiography of Arlene Francis.

*   *   *

ROMM, Ethel Grodzins   1925-

PERSONAL: Surname is pronounced Rome; born March 3, 1925, in Lowell, Mass.; daughter of David Melvin and Taube (Bialoblotka) Grodzins; married Al Romm (a newspaper editor), July 10, 1954; children: David, Daniel, Joseph. *Religion:* Jewish. *Home:* 17 Highland Ave., Middletown, N.Y. 10940.

CAREER: Westover Army Air Base, Chicopee, Mass., civilian supervisor in engineering department, 1943-45; Associated Engineers, Springfield, Mass., project supervisor,

1946-54. Lecturer in interior design, Orange County Community College. *Awards, honors:* Winner of Dorothy Dawe Cup three times, for newspaper column on home furnishings.

WRITINGS: Open Conspiracy: What America's Angry Generation Is Saying, Stackpole, 1970; *Throw Out Wednesday,* Holt, 1973; *Marvelous Machines,* Holt, 1973. Writes weekly newspaper column, "The House You Live In." Contributor to *New York, Esquire,* and other magazines.

WORK IN PROGRESS: A book on cults in America; a series of English textbooks for elementary and junior high school students, for Harcourt.

*   *   *

RONAN, William W.   1917-

PERSONAL: Born April 22, 1917, in Rochester, Pa.; son of Redmond L. and Augusta (Whipple) Ronan; married Elizabeth Stahl, December 5, 1941; children: Patrick W., Elizabeth M. *Education:* Geneva College, A.B., 1938; University of Pittsburgh, M.S., 1948, Ph.D., 1952. *Home:* x224 Beechaven Rd., Atlanta, Ga. 30324. *Office:* Department of Psychology, Georgia Institute of Technology, Atlanta, Ga. 30332.

CAREER: Jones & Laughlin Steel Corp., Pittsburgh, Pa., trainee in metallurgy, 1938-42; Blaw-Knox Co., Pittsburgh, research metallurgist, 1942-46; U.S. Steel Corp., Pittsburgh, training engineer, 1946-50; University of Massachusetts—Amherst, faculty member, 1950-52; American Institutes for Research, Pittsburgh, project director, 1952-54; Ketchum, McLeod & Grove, Pittsburgh, manager of opinion research, 1954-56; Mesta Machine Co., West Homestead, Pa., director of training, 1956-65; Georgia Institute of Technology, Atlanta, associate professor of psychology, 1965—. Certified psychologist in state of Pennsylvania; licensed psychologist in state of Georgia. *Military service:* U.S. Army Air Corps, 1942-45; became second lieutenant. *Member:* American Psychological Association, Georgia Psychological Association, Sigma Xi.

WRITINGS: (Contributor) R. B. Cattell and H. J. Butcher, editors, *The Prediction of Achievement and Creativity,* Bobbs-Merrill, 1968; (with E. P. Prien) *Perspectives on the Measurement of Human Performance,* Appleton, 1971; *Development of an Instrument to Evaluate College Classroom Teaching Effectiveness,* U.S. Department of Health, Education and Welfare, 1971. Writer of about twenty research reports; contributor to psychology journals.

WORK IN PROGRESS: A book on psychology.

*   *   *

ROOS, Leslie L(eon), Jr.   1940-

PERSONAL: Born July 20, 1940, in San Francisco, Calif.; son of Leslie Leon (an attorney) and Susan (Clarke) Roos; married Noralou Preston (a university professor), June 17, 1963; children: Christopher. *Education:* Stanford University, A.B. (with distinction), 1962; Massachusetts Institute of Technology, Ph.D., 1967. *Home:* 208 Dromore, Winnipeg, Manitoba, Canada R3M 0J3. *Office:* Faculty of Administrative Studies, University of Manitoba, Winnipeg, Manitoba, Canada R3T 2N2.

CAREER: Brandeis University, Waltham, Mass., assistant professor of politics, 1967-69; Northwestern University, Evanston, Ill., assistant professor of political science, 1969-72; University of Manitoba, Faculty of Administrative Studies, Winnipeg, 1973—, began as associate professor, currently professor. *Military service:* U.S. Army, 1962. U.S. Army Reserve, 1962-68. *Member:* Phi Beta Kappa. *Awards, honors:* Ford Foundation faculty research fellowship, 1969; National Health Research Scholar, 1977—.

WRITINGS: (With wife, Noralou P. Roos) *Managers of Modernization: Organization and Elites in Turkey, 1950-1969,* Harvard University Press, 1971; (editor and contributor) *The Politics of Ecosuicide,* Holt, 1971; (editor with James A. Caporaso and contributor) *Quasi-Experimental Approaches,* Northwestern University Press, 1973. Contributor to *Administrative Science Quarterly, Public Opinion Quarterly, Behavioral Science, Policy Analysis, New England Journal of Medicine, Medical Care,* and other publications.

WORK IN PROGRESS: With Noralou P. Roos, *Controversial Surgery: Evaluating the Impact of Tonsillectomy.*

* * *

ROOS, Noralou P(reston) 1942-

PERSONAL: Born April 21, 1942, in Pomona, Calif.; daughter of Willard (a printer) and Elizabeth (Palmer) Preston; married Leslie L. Roos, Jr. (a university professor), June 17, 1963; children: Christopher. *Education:* Stanford University, A.B., 1963; Massachusetts Institute of Technology, Ph.D., 1968. *Home:* 208 Dromore, Winnipeg, Manitoba, Canada R3M 0J3. *Office:* Faculty of Administrative Studies, University of Manitoba, Winnipeg, Manitoba, Canada R3T 2N2.

CAREER: Massachusetts Institute of Technology, Cambridge, Mass., assistant professor of political science, 1968-69; Northwestern University, Evanston, Ill., assistant professor of organizational behavior, 1969-72; University of Manitoba, Faculty of Administrative Studies, Winnipeg, 1973—, began as associate professor, currently professor. Research associate, Hospital Research and Educational Trust, 1971-72. *Awards, honors:* American Association of Collegiate Schools of Business—Sears Faculty Fellowship, 1972; National Health Research Scientist, 1973—.

WRITINGS: (With husband, Leslie L. Roos) *Managers of Modernization: Organization and Elites in Turkey, 1950-1969,* Harvard University Press, 1971; (contributor) James A. Caporaso and Leslie L. Roos, editors, *Quasi-Experimental Approaches,* Northwestern University Press, 1973. Contributor to *Public Opinion Quarterly, Administrative Science Quarterly, Daedalus, Public Policy, New England Journal of Medicine, Medical Care, Inquiry,* and other publications.

WORK IN PROGRESS: With Leslie L. Roos, *Controversial Surgery: Evaluating the Impact of Tonsillectomy.*

* * *

ROPER, William L(eon) 1897-
(David Fry, William Sparkman)

PERSONAL: Born May 6, 1897, near Republic, Mo.; son of William Fry (a farmer and electrician) and Minerva Jane (Sparkman) Roper; married Violet May Corwin (a musician and author), August 15, 1923 (died, 1967); married Zenith Armstrong Westbrook (a teacher and organist), May 24, 1969 (died, 1975); children: (first marriage) Rosemary Ellen (Mrs. Anthony H. Ivins). *Education:* Attended Drury College 1916-17; took correspondence courses in writing after returning from war. *Politics:* Independent. *Religion:* Unity Church. *Home:* 11843 Monte Vista Ave., Chino, Calif. 91710.

CAREER: Worked briefly as commercial artist in St. Louis, Mo., before getting into newspaper work; worked on newspapers in Missouri, Kansas, Texas, Washington, and California, 1923-29; *Los Angeles Examiner,* Los Angeles, Calif., reporter and rewrite man, 1929-35; public relations representative of fifty Superior Court judges of Los Angeles County, editor of *Los Angeles Bar Journal,* and publicity director for ten branches of Los Angeles Young Men's Christian Association (Y.M.C.A.), 1935-38; *Los Angeles Times,* Los Angeles, member of news staff, 1942-45; *San Antonio (Texas) Evening News,* member of news staff, 1947-48; *Texas City Sun,* Texas City, Tex., executive editor, 1949-50; free-lance writer, 1953—. Publicity director for political campaigns of Lieutenant Governor George Hatfield, Calif., 1938, Governor Dan Moody, Tex., 1942, U.S. Senator William F. Knowland, 1946, and Lieutenant Governor Goodwin J. Knight, Calif., 1950. *Military service:* U.S. Army, 1917-19; served in France; received Purple Heart. *Member:* Forney Historical Society of Anniston, Ala. (Calif. representative; honorary member of board of trustees).

WRITINGS: (Contributor) *A Treasury of Success Unlimited* (anthology), Hawthorn, 1967; (with Bob Crane) *Golden Chronicle* (history of California Highway Patrol, 1920-70), Association of California Highway Patrolmen (Sacramento), 1970; *Roy Rogers, King of the Cowboys* (biography), Denison, 1971; (with Leonard J. Arrington) *William Spry: Man of Firmness, Governor of Utah,* Utah State Historical Society and University of Utah Press, 1971; *Sequoyah and His Miracle,* Montana Reading Clinic, 1972; (with Treesa Drury) *Consumer Power,* Nash Publishing, 1974; *How to Win in Politics,* Chilton, 1978. Author of a series of articles on self-made millionaires for *Success Unlimited,* and of a series on heroes of religious liberty for *Liberty;* contributor of articles to *Coronet, American Weekly, Empire Magazine, Marine Corps Gazette, Writer's Digest, Campaign Insight, Western Publications, New York Times, American Legion Magazine, Yachting,* and many other periodicals; contributor to *California Highway Patrolman* under own name and formerly under pseudonyms David Fry and William Sparkman.

WORK IN PROGRESS: Life in the Ozarks, an autobiographical work.

SIDELIGHTS: William L. Roper told *CA:* "Now that I've authored or co-authored six published books and sold hundreds of articles to a wide variety of publications, after years of newspaper editorial work, I think I may have a few words of advice for would-be writers. My first suggestion would be: read widely, not just the books recommended by the book clubs, but biographies, the classics, and what Edna Ferber, Mary Roberts Rinehart, W. Somerset Maugham, Edgar Wallace, James Thurber and others have written about their own experiences as writers. Especially read everything, you can find, in the field of your special interests.

"Reared in an Ozark community that had no public library, I was fortunate in having teachers and friends who loaned me books. I read everything I could get. And I've spent much of my adult life in public libraries, reading and doing research. So I am to a large extent self-educated through library reading. Consequently, I regard libraries as one of my greatest benefactors. God bless Andrew Carnegie, the patron saint of our public libraries."

Roper is fascinated by the "old Horatio Alger theme," and has based numerous articles and books on the lives of "poor boys who had won fame and fortune," including Henry Kaiser, Orison Swett Marden, Edwin Wendell Pauley, John S.

Armstrong, Eddie Rickenbacker, Steve McQueen, and Walt Disney. During the late 1930's Roper's occupation as public relations representative for Los Angeles judges took him into the political arena as publicity director for several election campaigns. While working in William F. Knowland's first senatorial campaign, Roper met Richard M. Nixon and helped launch him on his political career by finding him a good publicity man, Bill Arnold.

BIOGRAPHICAL/CRITICAL SOURCES: Progress-Bulletin (Pomona, Calif.), May 15, 1971.

*   *   *

ROSE, Daniel M.   1940-

PERSONAL: Born November 16, 1940, in Oskaloosa, Iowa; son of D. R. and Nina Dorothy (Walter) Rose; married Karen Johnson, December 22, 1962. *Education:* Attended Asbury College, 1958-60; University of Wisconsin, B.A., 1965, M.A., 1968, Ph.D. candidate, 1968; University of Pennsylvania, postgraduate study, 1969-71.

CAREER: University of Kentucky, Medical School, Lexington, medical illustrator, 1960-61; Villard Avenue Neighborhood Center, Milwaukee, Wis., boys' group worker, 1961-62; University of Pennsylvania, Philadelphia, research fellow of Center for Urban Ethnography, 1969-71, research associate, 1972-73. Visiting summer lecturer, University of Wisconsin—Milwaukee, 1969. *Member:* American Academy of Political and Social Science, American Anthropological Association, American Ethnological Society, American Society for Aesthetics and Art Criticism, American Sociological Association, Midwest Sociological Society. *Awards, honors:* Ford Foundation fellow, 1969.

WRITINGS: (With Bruce Renner) *Poetry 1967,* University of Wisconsin—Milwaukee Press, 1967; *The Abyss* (poetry), University of Wisconsin, Department of Art, 1970. Contributor of articles and reviews to *Poetry, Quixote,* and to sociological and anthropological journals.

WORK IN PROGRESS: Become Another Son, Enter the World at a New Place, a book of poems; a history of the influence of non-European languages on British ideas of language in the nineteenth and early twentieth centuries; doctoral dissertation based on twenty-four months of fieldwork with an Afro-American population in a North American city; short stories.††

*   *   *

ROSE, Jerry D.   1933-

PERSONAL: Born July 20, 1933, in Norman, Okla.; son of J. C. (an oil field worker) and Ruth (Brock) Rose; married LoVetra A. Schwartz (a nurse), June 5, 1965; children: Christopher Robin, Kara Jeanine, Keilly Rachele. *Education:* University of Oklahoma, B.S., 1954, Ed.M., 1954; University of Wisconsin, Ph.D., 1966. *Home:* 161 Central Ave., Fredonia, N.Y. 14063. *Office:* Department of Sociology, State University of New York College, Fredonia, N.Y. 14063.

CAREER: Southwestern State College, Weatherford, Okla., assistant professor of sociology, 1958-61; New York University, New York, N.Y., assistant professor of sociology, 1964-67; State University of New York College at Fredonia, associate professor, 1967-71, professor of sociology, 1971—. *Military service:* U.S. Army, 1955-57; became first lieutenant. *Member:* American Sociological Association, Eastern Sociological Society.

WRITINGS: Introduction to Sociology, Rand McNally,

1971, 3rd edition, 1976; *Peoples: The Ethnic Dimension in Human Relations,* Rand McNally, 1976; *Outbreaks and Movements: The Sociology of Collective Behavior,* Free Press, in press.

*   *   *

ROSE, Marilyn Gaddis   1930-

PERSONAL: Born April 2, 1930, in Fayette, Mo.; daughter of Merrill Elmer (a college teacher) and Florence (a teacher; maiden name Lyon) Gaddis; married James Leo Rose, December 23, 1956 (divorced, 1966); married Stephen David Ross (a college professor), November 16, 1968; children: (second marriage) David Gaddis. *Education:* Central Methodist College, Fayette, Mo., B.A. (summa cum laude), 1952; Universite de Lyon, Fulbright scholar, 1952-53; University of South Carolina, M.A., 1955; University of Missouri, Ph.D., 1958. *Politics:* Independent. *Religion:* Protestant. *Home:* 4 Johnson Ave., Binghamton, N.Y. 13905. *Office:* Comparative Literature Department, State University of New York, Binghamton, N.Y. 13901.

CAREER: Stephens College, Columbia, Mo., teacher of comparative literature, 1958-68; State University of New York at Binghamton, associate professor, 1968-73, professor of comparative literature, 1973—, chairman of department, 1971-74, 1975—, director, Translator Training Program. Associate professor of comparative literature, Indiana University, summer, 1968; visiting fellow, Humanities Research Centre, Australian National University. *Member:* American Association of University Professors (vice-president of New York conference, 1972-73), American Committee for Irish Studies, Modern Language Association of America, American Association of Teachers of French, Association for Dada and Surrealism, North East Modern Language Association, Phi Beta Kappa. *Awards, honors:* Stephens research grants, 1964-66; State University of New York fellowships, 1969, 1974.

WRITINGS: (Translator) Villiers de l'Isle-Adam, *Axel,* Dolmen Press, 1970; *Julian Green, Gallic-American Novelist,* Herbert Lang, 1971; *Jack B. Yeats, Painter and Poet,* Herbert Lang, 1972; *Katharine Tynan,* Bucknell University Press, 1973. Contributor of articles to academic journals.

*   *   *

ROSE, Thomas   1938-

PERSONAL: Born August 10, 1938, in St. Paul, Minn.; son of Edward H. and Margaret (Simon) Rose. *Education:* San Francisco State College (now University), B.A., 1963; University of Wisconsin—Milwaukee, M.A., 1966; Antioch College, Ph.D., 1972. *Residence:* Garrett Park, Md. 20766. *Office:* Department of Sociology, Montgomery College, Rockville, Md. 20850.

CAREER: Federal City College, Washington, D.C., assistant professor of sociology, 1967-70; Hood College, Frederick, Md., assistant professor of sociology, 1970-71; Montgomery College, Rockville, Md., 1971—, began as assistant professor, currently associate professor of sociology. *Military service:* U.S. Navy, 1956-58.

WRITINGS: (Author of introduction with James Rodgers) J. T. Headley, *Great Riots of New York,* text edition, Bobbs-Merrill, 1969; (editor) *Violence in America: A Historical and Contemporary Reader,* Random House, 1970; (with Charles S. Martin) *History of Myersville, Md.,* Myersville Volunteer Fire Co., 1971.

WORK IN PROGRESS: A history of Wolfsville, Md.; a study of changing rural America.

ROSEN, Gerald 1938-

PERSONAL: Born December 24, 1938, in New York, N.Y.; son of Sol (a retail liquor dealer) and Eve (Berger) Rosen; married Charlotte Mayer (a typesetter), March 27, 1962 (divorced, 1976). *Education:* Rensselaer Polytechnic Institute, B.E.E., 1960; Wharton School, M.B.A., 1962; University of Pennsylvania, A.M., 1966, Ph.D., 1969. *Politics:* "Cranky American individualist." *Religion:* "American comic Buddhist." *Office:* California State College, Sonoma, Rohnert Park, Calif. 94928.

CAREER: Magid Liquor Store, New York, N.Y., manager, 1967-71; California State College, Sonoma, Rohnert Park, Calif., instructor in writing and literature, 1971—. *Military service:* U.S. Army, 1962-65; became first lieutenant. *Member:* Beta Gamma Sigma.

WRITINGS: Blues for a Dying Nation (novel), Dial, 1972; *The Carmen Miranda Memorial Flagpole* (novel), Presidio Press, 1977; *Zen in the Art of J. D. Salinger* (nonfiction), Creative Arts Books, 1977. Contributor to *Partisan Review, American Quarterly, San Francisco Review of Books,* and other journals.

WORK IN PROGRESS: Two novels.

SIDELIGHTS: Gerald Rosen told *CA* he is interested in "rock music, dancing, Zen, humor, sports, jazz and classical music. My writing has been influenced by artists like Jean Luc Godard, Janis Joplin, Jimi Hendrix, Charlie Parker, J. S. Bach and Sakyamuni. The purpose of my writing is to destroy the way the reader has been taught to see the world. My jokes are armed and should be considered dangerous."

BIOGRAPHICAL/CRITICAL SOURCES: Pacific Sun (San Rafael), March 1, 1972.

*   *   *

ROSEN, Norma (Gangel) 1925-

PERSONAL: Born August 11, 1925, in New York; daughter of Louis (a businessman) and Rose (Miller) Gangel; married Robert S. Rosen (a teacher), August 30, 1960; children: Anne Beth, Jonathan Aaron. *Education:* Mount Holyoke College, B.A. (cum laude), 1946; Columbia University, M.A., 1953. *Religion:* Jewish. *Home:* 11 Mereland Rd., New Rochelle, N.Y. 10804. *Agent:* Gloria Loomis, A. Watkins Agency, 77 Park Ave., New York, N.Y. 10016. *Office:* Department of English, College of New Rochelle, New Rochelle, N.Y. 10801.

CAREER: Harper & Row Publishers, Inc., New York City, book designer, 1955-59; New School for Social Research, New York City, teacher of creative writing workshops, 1966-69; Harvard University, Cambridge, Mass., teacher of essay writing, 1971; Herbert H. Lehman College of the City University of New York, New York City, teacher of writing, 1975-76; College of New Rochelle, New Rochelle, N.Y., teacher of writing, 1977—. Visiting professor of writing, University of Pennsylvania, 1970. *Member:* International P.E.N., Phi Beta Kappa. *Awards, honors:* Eugene F. Saxton grant, 1960; Radcliffe Institute fellowship, 1971-73; New York State Creative Artist Public Service grant, 1975-76.

WRITINGS: Joy to Levine! (novel), Knopf, 1962; *Green* (novella and short stories), Harcourt, 1967; *Touching Evil* (novel), Harcourt, 1969. Contributor of stories, articles, and reviews to national periodicals, including *New Yorker, Commentary, New York Times,* and *Ms.*

WORK IN PROGRESS: Several novels.

SIDELIGHTS: Norma Rosen "writes beautifully, with unusual style," says a *Newsday* critic in a review of *Touching Evil.* James R. Frakes praises the "remarkably firm characterizations" of *Green* but adds, "the style, usually tight and lucid, is too often marred by painfully self-conscious imagery." Several critics classify Rosen as a "woman's writer" because of her concern with the emotional life of her characters. Don Crinklaw, reviewing *Green* for *Commonweal,* laments: "All the spokesmen for the Other Side are parodies in a stacked deck. . . . I wonder at the author's tendency to cradle [her woman protagonists] in a sympathy she does not extend the males in such generous measure."

BIOGRAPHICAL/CRITICAL SOURCES: New Yorker, April 7, 1962; *New Republic,* May 6, 1967; *New York Times Book Review,* June 18, 1967; *Commonweal,* October 13, 1967; *Book World,* August 31, 1969; *Newsday,* September 13, 1969; *Publisher's Weekly,* September 16, 1969.

*   *   *

ROSEN, Seymour Michael 1924-

PERSONAL: Born July 29, 1924, in New York, N.Y.; son of Harry Francis (stepfather) and Sonia (Sarakowska) Dwyer; married Elisabeth Meyer, June 6, 1950; children: Edith Vivion (Mrs. George Curtis Rogers), Kenneth Adlai, Julie Ann. *Education:* Brown University, A.B., 1950; Columbia University, M.A. and Certificate of Russian Institute, 1952; also attended Georgetown University, 1957-58. *Home:* 3724 Jenifer St. N.W., Washington, D.C. 20015. *Office:* Office of Education, U.S. Department of Health, Education, and Welfare, 7th and D St. S.W., Washington, D.C. 20202.

CAREER: U.S. Department of State, research analyst, Soviet area, 1953-56; Library of Congress, Washington, D.C., senior social science research analyst, 1956-58; propaganda analyst for U.S. Government, 1958-60; U.S. Department of Health, Education, and Welfare, Office of Education, Washington, D.C., specialist in comparative education for U.S.S.R. and Eastern Europe, 1960—. Visiting lecturer on Soviet education and culture, U.S. Department of State, 1963-65, American University (Washington, D.C.), 1963, Loyola College (Baltimore, Md.), 1963, U.S. Defense Department, and various colleges and professional groups. Chairman, U.S. delegation to study Soviet education system, 1963. *Military service:* U.S. Naval Reserve, 1942-46; served with Fleet Marine Force; received Presidential Unit Citation and Purple Heart. *Member:* American Association for Advancement of Slavic Studies, Comparative and International Education Society.

WRITINGS: Higher Education in the U.S.S.R., U.S. Government Printing Office, 1963; (with Nellie Apanasewicz) *Higher Education in Poland,* U.S. Government Printing Office, 1964; *Part-Time Education in the U.S.S.R.,* U.S. Government Printing Office, 1965; *Soviet Programs in International Education,* U.S. Government Printing Office, 1971; *Education and Modernization in the U.S.S.R.,* Addison-Wesley, 1971. Contributor of articles to *Comparative Education Review, Higher Education, Phi Delta Kappan, School and Society, Annual Economic Indicators for the U.S.S.R.,* and *American Bibliography of Russian and East European Studies.* Editor, *Soviet Education,* 1968-69.

WORK IN PROGRESS: Research and writing on various aspects of education in U.S.S.R. and Eastern Europe; *Education in the U.S.S.R.: Research and Innovation,* for U.S. Government Printing Office.

SIDELIGHTS: Seymour Rosen told *CA* that foreign travel is his "major motivating force, and vocational and avocational interest." He has traveled in the Pacific Islands, China, U.S.S.R., Yugoslavia, Poland, Greece, Israel, Great Britain, Western Europe, and Mexico. He equates foreign travel with "the stimulus and study of other peoples and cultures, which began at the age of three with an infant's observation of a Polish-Jewish Irish-Catholic marriage."

*   *   *

ROSENWALD, Henry M(artin)   1905-

PERSONAL: Born December 20, 1905, in Nuremberg, Germany; son of Charles Alfred (a judge) and Alice (Rosenfeld) Rosenwald. *Education:* Erlangen University, Germany, LL.D., 1930; Catholic University of the Sacred Heart, Milan, Italy, Jur.D., 1934; Fordham University, LL.B., 1943. *Religion:* Catholic. *Home:* 60 Broadway, Apt. 1008, Providence, R.I. 02903. *Office:* Providence College, Providence, R.I. 02918.

CAREER: Attorney at law, Nuremberg, Germany, 1929-33; consultant in law and instruction, Milan, Italy, 1934-39; instructor in German, Schools of Commerce, Milan, 1933-37; U.S. Army Specialized Training instructor in German, University of Alabama, University, and Georgetown University, Washington, D.C., 1943; counsel with U.S. War Department, Legal Division, U.S. Military Government in Germany, 1946-47; Providence College, Providence, R.I., professor of German language and literature, 1957-71, professor emeritus, 1971—. *Military service:* U.S. Army, served with Intelligence in Europe, 1943-45, and Korea, 1950-51. *Member:* American Association of Teachers of German (president, R.I. branch, 1959-61), Modern Language Association of America, American Association of University Professors, Goethe Society of New England (charter member), Delta Epsilon Sigma, Delta Phi Alpha.

WRITINGS: (Editor) *The Age of Romanticism,* Ungar, 1959; *Jahrhundertwende,* Harcourt, 1968; (with George E. Boyd) *Der Tod in Venedig,* Oxford University Press, 1972. Contributor to *Delta Epsilon Sigma Bulletin.*

*   *   *

ROSS, Davis R. B.   1934-

PERSONAL: Born January 23, 1934, in Albany, N.Y.; son of George G. (an accountant) and Noel (Davis) Ross; married Esther M. Haerle, April 26, 1958; children: Christopher, Timothy, Bruce. *Education:* Attended Harvard University, 1951-54; New York University, B.A., 1960, M.A., 1961; Columbia University, Ph.D., 1967. *Home:* 367 High St., Closter, N.J. 07624. *Office:* Department of History, Herbert H. Lehman College of the City University of New York, New York, N.Y. 10468.

CAREER: Hunter College of the City University of New York, Bronx, N.Y., lecturer in history, 1962-65; Columbia University, New York City, instructor, 1965-67, assistant professor of history, 1967-71; Herbert H. Lehman College of the City University of New York, New York City, associate professor of history, 1971—. *Military service:* U.S. Army, 1954-56. *Member:* American Historical Association, Organization of American Historians.

WRITINGS: Preparing for Ulysses: Politics and Veterans during World War II, Columbia University Press, 1969; (editor with Alden T. Vaughan and John Duff) *The Structure of American History,* six volumes, Crowell, 1970-71; (contributor) Arthur Schlesinger, Jr., editor, *History of U.S. Political Parties,* four volumes, Bowker, 1973.

WORK IN PROGRESS: The Political Industry, 1937-1955.

*   *   *

ROSSITER, John   1916-
(Jonathan Ross)

PERSONAL: Born March 2, 1916, in Devonshire, England; son of William Ronald (a soldier) and Emily Irene (Adams) Rossiter; married Joan Gaisford, February 21, 1942; children: Sally (Mrs. Gordon Neil Pike). *Education:* Attended preparatory and military schools in Woolwich and Bulford, 1924-32. *Politics:* Conservative. *Religion:* "Still searching." *Home:* 33 Milford Hill, Shady Bower, Salisbury, Wiltshire SP1 2QL, England. *Agent:* Murray Pollinger, 4 Garrick St., London WC2E 9BH, England.

CAREER: British Police Service, Wiltshire, England, detective chief superintendent, 1936-69. *Military service:* Royal Air Force and Army, 1942-45; served in glider pilot regiment; became flight lieutenant.

WRITINGS: The Murder Makers, Cassell, 1970; *The Deadly Green,* Cassell, 1970, Walker & Co., 1971; *The Victims,* Cassell, 1971; *A Rope for General Dietz,* Constable, 1972; *The Manipulators,* Cassell, 1973, Simon & Schuster, 1974; *The Villains,* Cassell, 1974, Walker & Co., 1976; *The Golden Virgin,* Constable, 1975, published as *The Deadly Gold,* Walker & Co., 1975. Contributor of drawings and articles on entomology to periodicals; contributor of cartoons to *Punch, Aeroplane,* and other magazines.

Under pseudonym Jonathan Ross: *The Blood Running Cold,* Cassell, 1968; *Diminished by Death,* Cassell, 1968; *Dead at First Hand,* Cassell, 1969; *The Deadest Thing You Ever Saw,* Cassell, 1969, McCall, 1970; *Here Lies Nancy Frail,* Saturday Review Press, 1972; *The Burning of Billy Toober,* Constable, 1972, Walker & Co., 1976; *I Know What It's Like to Die,* Constable, 1976.

WORK IN PROGRESS: And Yet, the Earth Lies Over Her; an untitled crime novel.

SIDELIGHTS: John Rossiter told *CA:* "The majority of my crime books are based on my experiences as a detective officer investigating murder and other serious crimes. My pilot training in Arizona was the background for the novel *The Murder Makers.* My residence in Spain was used to provide the background for the novels *A Rope for General Dietz* and *The Golden Virgin.*

"I believe that most successful writers have inside them a Walter Mitty-ish character trying to get out. Where they have not, they possess an arrogance requiring them to tell the world how it should be. Either defect (to which I own) will be a catalyst for the addictive compulsion a writer must have to sit out what is virtually a solitary exercise in his workshop for breast-beating. Children learn to speak their language by listening, invariably before attending school. A writer must have read copiously to be able to write. I am firmly of the opinion that he cannot be taught it. He should never allow the nonsensical intricacies of academic grammar and syntax to worry him into not writing; or, into writing with a strangulated concern for grammatical exactitude. These two bogies never yet sold a book on their own. Their repair and correction, if necessary, gives publishers' editors their *raison d'etre* and, we trust, a commensurate salary. The road for an aspiring writer is usually long and stony, all too often lined with the debris of rejections. He should never ask advice other than from a published writer; never an opinion from a relative or friend. Therein waits a self-dug black pit from which it is difficult to climb." Eight of Rossiter's novels have been translated into German.

BIOGRAPHICAL/CRITICAL SOURCES: Punch, February 14, 1968; *Times Literary Supplement,* September 26, 1968, December 11, 1969, May 26, 1972, July 7, 1972; *Observer,* September 13, 1970; *Best Sellers,* November 1, 1970, March 1, 1971, October 1, 1972; *New York Times Book Review,* November 29, 1970, April 18, 1971, October 1, 1972, October 8, 1972; *National Review,* April 20, 1971; *Books and Bookmen,* September, 1971, August, 1972; *Economist,* November 6, 1971.

*   *   *

ROTHBERG, Abraham   1922-

PERSONAL: Born January 14, 1922, in New York, N.Y.; son of Louis and Lottie (Drimmer) Rothberg; married Esther Conwell (a physicist), September 30, 1945; children: Lewis. *Education:* Brooklyn College (now Brooklyn College of the City University of New York), B.A., 1942; University of Iowa, M.A., 1947; Columbia University, Ph.D., 1952. *Politics:* Independent. *Religion:* Jewish. *Office:* 340 Pelham Rd., Rochester, N.Y. 14610.

CAREER: Worked at many jobs, including professional singer, waiter, and with an electronics firm while completing his education; Hofstra College (now University), Hempstead, N.Y., instructor in English and humanities, 1947-51; Columbia University, New York City, instructor in creative writing, 1948; Free Europe Press (publications division of Radio Free Europe), New York City, editor-in-chief of press and of *East Europe* (magazine), and senior political counselor to Free Europe Committee, 1952-59; George Braziller, Inc. (publishers), New York City, managing editor, 1959; *New Leader,* New York City, managing editor, 1960-61; roving correspondent in Europe for *National Observer* and *Guardian,* 1962-63; Bantam Books, Inc., New York City, senior editor, 1966-67; full-time writer, 1967-73; St. John Fisher College, Rochester, N.Y., professor of English, 1973—. *Military service:* U.S. Army, 1943-45; became sergeant. *Member:* Authors League, P.E.N. *Awards, honors:* Ford Foundation fellow, 1951-52; John H. McGinnis Award for short story, 1969, for essay, 1974.

WRITINGS: Abraham (juvenile), Behrman, 1952; *An Eyewitness History of World War II,* four volumes, Bantam, 1962; *The Thousand Doors* (novel), Holt, 1965; *The Heirs of Cain* (novel), Putnam, 1966; *The Song of David Freed* (novel), Putnam, 1968; *The Boy and the Dolphin* (juvenile), Norton, 1969; *The Other Man's Shoes* (novel), Simon & Schuster, 1969; *The Sword of the Golem* (novel), McCall, 1971; *Aleksandr Solzhenitsyn: The Major Novels,* Cornell University Press, 1971; *Heirs of Stalin: Dissidence and the Soviet Regime, 1953-1970,* Cornell University Press, 1972; *The Stalking Horse* (novel), Saturday Review Press, 1972.

Editor: (With Martha Foley) *U.S. Stories: Stories of the 48 States,* Farrar, Straus, 1949; *Flashes in the Night: Contemporary Hungarian Short Stories,* Random House, 1958; *The Bar-Mitzvah Companion,* Behrman, 1959; *Anatomy of a Moral: The Political Essays of Milovan Djilas,* Praeger, 1959; *Call of the Wild and White Fang,* Bantam, 1963; *Dr. Jekyll and Mr. Hyde,* Bantam, 1967; *Great Adventure Stories of Jack London,* Bantam, 1967. Also editor, with Solomon Simon and Morrison Bial, of *The Rabbi's Bible,* three volumes, Behrman, 1969-74. Contributor of short stories, essays, poems, articles, and reviews to magazines; his magazine writing has been included in a number of anthologies. Chairman of editorial board, *Stateside,* 1947-49.

SIDELIGHTS: Abraham Rothberg has received praise for his novels as well as his journalism. K. G. Jackson called

The Thousand Doors "a thrilling 'novel of international intrigue.' . . . The danger is electric and ever-threatening; the young woman . . . is lovely and sad; the country and cities are theatrically beautiful; and Mr. Rothberg makes the best of all of it." M. K. Grant called the book "top drawer international intrigue, concerned with real people, real problems, and real responsibilities. . . . This is a remarkably well-written first novel. . . ." *The Heirs of Cain* continues in much the same vein. Jane Oppenheim wrote: "[This] is more than an espionage novel. . . . Rothberg has engaged upon an introspective study of man and the human condition. . . . [His] people and his scenes are very real. . . . He has handled what could have been a run-of-the-mill spy-thriller in a disturbingly thought-provoking fashion. [This] is a frightening novel of our times."

In *The Song of David Freed* Rothberg turns his attention to the time of his youth. Saul Maloff wrote: "The novel is suffused with nostalgia—the attempt of a novelist to re-immerse himself in the springs of his beginnings . . . in the book's charged emotional atmosphere, there is sometimes a tendency to melodrama. But in the main, this is a sweet, unabashedly sentimental, memory-washed 'song' of a boy's journey from green to blasted fields." Meyer Levin said of the book: "It sings . . . of a touching and trying time in Jewish life in America."

The Other Man's Shoes is a very complex book. Peter Wolfe says that Rothberg's "powerful imagination, intellectual depth, and driving style bring to life the dizzying experience of American city life in the late 1960s." He believes, though, that the book "has a hard, knowing tone that tends to bully not only the characters and the reader but also the language." With *The Sword of the Golem* Rothberg goes off in still another direction. R. J. Milch writes: "Rothberg's profoundly contemporary version of the Golem legend is rich in paradox, in awareness of the mythic dimensions of the Golem idea, and in Jewish color and religious content." Rothberg's work has taken him to many parts of the world, and he has used his varied experiences to good advantage in his novels, as well as his non-fiction works.

BIOGRAPHICAL/CRITICAL SOURCES: Harper's, May, 1965; *Best Sellers,* December 1, 1966, January 15, 1968, February 15, 1969, February 1, 1971; *Nation,* December 5, 1966; *New York Times Book Review,* January 14, 1968, February 9, 1969, February 14, 1971; *Newsweek,* February 12, 1968; *Hudson Review,* autumn, 1968; *Saturday Review,* March 8, 1961, January 31, 1971.

*   *   *

ROTHMAN, David J.   1937-

PERSONAL: Born April 30, 1937, in New York, N.Y.; married; wife's name Sheila; children: Matthew. *Education:* Columbia University, B.A., 1958; Harvard University, M.A., 1959, Ph.D., 1964. *Office:* 715 Hamilton Hall, Columbia University, New York, N.Y. 10027.

CAREER: Columbia University, New York, N.Y., assistant professor, 1964-67, associate professor, 1967-70, professor of history, 1971—. Fulbright professor, Hebrew University, Jerusalem, 1968-69. Fellow of Center for the Study of History of Liberty in America, Harvard University, 1965-66; member of Committee to Study Incarceration, sponsored by Field Foundation, 1971-72. *Awards, honors:* Grants from American Philosophical Society, 1967, and U.S. Department of Health, Education and Welfare, 1968-69; fellowships from Social Science Research Council, 1968, National Endowment for the Humanities, 1971-72, and National Science Foundation, 1972-73; Albert J. Beveridge Prize, American Historical Association, 1971, for *Discovery of the Asylum: Social Order and Disorder in the Young Republic.*

WRITINGS: Politics and Power: The United States Senate, 1869-1901, Harvard University Press, 1966; (with Neil Harris and Stephan Thernstrom) *The History of the United States: Source Readings,* two volumes, Holt, 1968; *Discovery of the Asylum: Social Order and Disorder in the Young Republic,* Little, Brown, 1971; (editor with wife, Sheila M. Rothman) *On Their Own: The Poor in Modern America,* Addison-Wesley, 1972; (with Willard Gaylin, Ira Glasser, and Steven Marcus) *Doing Good: The Limits of Benevolence,* Pantheon, 1978. Also editor of *The Sources of American Society.* Advisory editor of Arno's *Poverty in America: The Historical Record,* 1971, and *The Family in America,* 1972. Contributor to history journals.

*   *   *

ROTHWELL, Kenneth S(prague)   1921-

PERSONAL: Born May 26, 1921, in Bay Shore, N.Y.; son of Clarence A. (a realtor) and Benita (Buckel) Rothwell; married Marilyn Mae Gregg (a nurse practitioner), June 26, 1954; children: Kenneth, Jr., Mary Carroll, Elizabeth Gregg, Anne Gregg. *Education:* University of North Carolina at Chapel Hill, B.A., 1948; Columbia University, M.A., 1949, Ph.D., 1956. *Religion:* Episcopalian. *Home:* 425 South Willard St., Burlington, Vt. 05401. *Office:* Department of English, University of Vermont, Burlington, Vt. 05401.

CAREER: University of Kansas, Lawrence, instructor in English, 1949-50; University of Rochester, Rochester, N.Y., instructor in English, 1952-55; University of Cincinnati, Cincinnati, Ohio, instructor in English, 1955-57; University of Kansas, assistant professor, 1957-62, associate professor, 1962-66, professor of English, 1966-70; University of Vermont, Burlington, professor of English, 1970—. *Military service:* U.S. Army, Infantry, 1942-46; became first lieutenant. *Member:* Modern Language Association of America (chairman of college section, 1973-75), National Council of Teachers of English, Renaissance Society of America (president of central Renaissance conference, 1968-69), Shakespeare Association of America, Malone Society. *Awards, honors:* Watkins faculty scholarship, University of Kansas, 1959; grants-in-aid, American Philosophical Society, 1964, 1968.

WRITINGS: Questions of Rhetoric and Usage, Little, Brown, 1971, 2nd edition, 1974. Contributor to *College English, Renaissance News, Modern Philology, Comparative Literature Studies,* and other publications. Co-editor of *Shakespeare on Film Newsletter.*

WORK IN PROGRESS: Romeo and Juliet on Film; Shakespeare's Epistolary Interests.

AVOCATIONAL INTERESTS: Tennis, cross-country skiing.

*   *   *

ROTTER, Julian B(ernard)   1916-

PERSONAL: Born October 22, 1916, in New York, N.Y.; son of Abraham and Bessie (Goldstein) Rotter; married Clara E. Barnes, April 2, 1941; children: Jean, Richard. *Education:* Brooklyn College (now Brooklyn College of the City University of New York), B.A., 1937; University of Iowa, M.A., 1938; Indiana University, Ph.D., 1941. *Office:*

Department of Psychology, University of Connecticut, Storrs, Conn. 06268.

CAREER: Worcester State Hospital, Worcester, Mass., intern, 1938-39; Norwich State Hospital, Norwich, Conn., psychologist, 1941-42; Ohio State University, Columbus, associate professor, 1946-49, professor of clinical psychology, 1949-63, director of psychology clinic, 1951-63; University of Connecticut, Storrs, professor of clinical psychology and director of clinical psychology training program, 1963—. *Military service:* U.S. Army and U.S. Army Air Forces, 1942-46; became first lieutenant. *Member:* American Psychological Association (fellow; president of Division of Personality and Social Psychology, 1969-70; president of Division of Clinical Psychology, 1970-71), Eastern Psychological Association (president, 1976-77). *Awards, honors:* Award for distinguished contribution to clinical psychology, American Psychological Association, 1968.

WRITINGS: (With Janet Rafferty) *Manual for the Rotter Incomplete Sentences Test,* Psychological Corp., 1950; *Social Learning and Clinical Psychology,* Prentice-Hall, 1954; *Clinical Psychology,* Prentice-Hall, 1964, revised edition, 1971; (with June Chance and E. Jerry Phares) *Applications of Social Learning Theory,* Holt, 1972; (with Dorothy Hochreich) *Personality,* Scott, Foresman, 1975. Contributor of nearly a hundred articles and reviews to psychology journals.

*   *   *

ROWELL, John W(illiam)   1914-

PERSONAL: Born April 17, 1914, in Akron, Ohio; son of William Edward and Grace (Baker) Rowell; married Helen Hilliard, June 29, 1940. *Education:* Purdue University, B.S., 1936. *Politics:* Republican. *Religion:* Presbyterian. *Home address:* Box 14, Columbus, Ind. 47201. *Office:* Cummins Engine Co., Inc., 1000 Fifth St., Columbus, Ind. 47201.

CAREER: Engineer, 1936-41; Cummins Engine Co., Inc., Columbus, Ind., engineer, 1941-45, technical editor, 1945-55, supervisor of sales literature, 1955—. Republican precinct committeeman and delegate to state convention, 1964—. *Member:* Bartholomew County Historical Society, Columbus Civil War Round Table (president, 1965—).

WRITINGS: Yankee Cavalrymen: Through the Civil War with the Ninth Pennsylvania Cavalry, University of Tennessee Press, 1971; *Yankee Artillerymen: Through the Civil War with Eli Lilly's Indiana Battery,* University of Tennessee Press, 1975. Contributor to Civil War journals.

AVOCATIONAL INTERESTS: Reading history and science, gardening.

*   *   *

ROWEN, Ruth Halle   1918-

PERSONAL: Born April 5, 1918, in New York, N.Y.; daughter of Louis (a lawyer) and Ethel (Fried) Halle; married Seymour M. Rowen (a lawyer), October 13, 1940 (died October 7, 1976); children: Mary Helen (Mrs. David Obelkevich), Louis Halle. *Education:* Barnard College, B.A., 1939; Columbia University, M.A., 1941, Ph.D., 1948. *Home:* 115 Central Park W., New York, N.Y. 10023. *Office:* Department of Music, City College of the City University of New York, 138th St. and Convent Ave., New York, N.Y. 10031.

CAREER: Carl Fischer, Inc. (music publisher), New York City, manager of educational department, 1954-63; City College of the City University of New York, New York City, lecturer, 1963-64, assistant professor, 1963-67, associate professor, 1967-72, professor of musicology, 1972—. Professor of musicology, Graduate School and University Center of the City University of New York, 1967—. *Member:* American Musicological Society, American Society of Composers, Authors and Publishers, Music Library Association, College Music Society, National Federation of Music Clubs, International Musicological Society.

WRITINGS: Early Chamber Music, Kings Crown Press, 1949, Da Capo Press, 1972; (with Bill Simon) *Jolly Come Sing and Play,* Carl Fischer, 1956; (with Adele T. Katz) *Hearing: Gateway to Music,* Summy-Birchard, 1959; *Music through Sources and Documents,* Prentice-Hall, 1978. Contributor to music and music library publications.

AVOCATIONAL INTERESTS: Bridge (life master in American Contract Bridge League), tennis, swimming.

*   *   *

ROZENTAL, Alek A(ron)   1920-

PERSONAL: Born August 21, 1920, in Warsaw, Poland; naturalized U.S. citizen; married Caryl June Stewart, September, 1950 (divorced, 1968); children: Gail, Lynn. *Education:* Attended University of Warsaw, 1937-38, and Sorbonne, University of Paris, 1938-39; University of London, B.Sc. (high honors), 1948; University of Minnesota, M.A., 1950, Ph.D., 1955; London School of Economics and Political Science, post-doctoral study, 1957-58. *Office address:* United Nations Development Program, Box 30218, Nairobi, Kenya.

CAREER: British Ministry of Town and Country Planning, London, England, research officer, 1948-49; University of Minnesota, Minneapolis, instructor, 1950-55, lecturer in economics, 1955-56; St. Louis University, St. Louis, Mo., assistant professor, 1956-59, associate professor of economics, 1959-60; U.S. Agency for International Development, financial adviser in Laos, 1960-63, chief economist of U.S. Mission to Vietnam, 1963-65; National Planning Association, Washington, D.C., chief of party of research team in Thailand, 1965-67, senior economist, 1967-68; United Nations, New York, N.Y., financial consultant to development program in Taipei, Taiwan, 1968-71, chief economist of urban study in Nairobi, Kenya, 1971—. Teacher in National Center of Administration, Vientiane, Laos, 1961-62, at Thammasat University, 1965-67, at University of Maryland Bangkok Program, 1966; lecturer at University of the Philippines, 1966-67, and Tung-hai University, 1968-70. Consultant to U.S. Office of Education, 1960, and other government groups, and to private industry. *Military service:* Served with Polish Armed Forces in France and England, 1940-45.

MEMBER: Society for Economic Development, Royal Economic Society (fellow). *Awards, honors:* Social Science Foundation fellow, 1957; Ford Foundation fellow in international relations at University of London, 1957-58; Committee on Economic Development of the South research fellow, 1959.

WRITINGS: Investment Policy of Minnesota's Trust Funds, University of Minnesota, 1956; (co-author) *Governor's Tax Study Committee Report,* Colwell Press, 1957; (contributor) *Crisis in Medicine,* Harper, 1961; (editor and contributor) *Studies in Vietnamese Economy,* Agency for International Development, 1964; *Finance and Development in Thailand,* Praeger, 1970. Writer of research monographs; contributor of more than forty articles and reviews to economic journals in the United States and abroad.

WORK IN PROGRESS: Financial Aspects of Urban and Regional Development.

SIDELIGHTS: Alek Rozental is fluent in French, as well as English and his native Polish; he speaks some German, Thai, and Chinese.††

*   *   *

RUANO, Argimiro   1924-
(Nazario Ruano)

PERSONAL: Born October 3, 1924, in Salamanca, Spain; son of Sebastian (a farmer) and Maria Luisa (Laiglesia) Ruano; married Christiane Fischer (a nurse), 1966; children: Sebastian, Maria Teresa. *Education:* Attended Universidad de Salamanca, 1948, and Universite de Louvain, 1954; Universidad de Santo Domingo, Licenciatura en Filosofia, 1955, Doctor en Filosofia, 1956; Universidad Central de Madrid, Licenciatura en Filosofia y Letras, 1966; Universidad de Navarra, Doctor en Filosofia y Letras, 1967. *Office:* Departamento de Humanidades, Recinto Universitario de Mayaguez, Puerto Rico 00708.

CAREER: Monk, 1940-47, and Catholic priest, 1947-65. Colegio Mayor de Filosofia "La Santa," Avila, Spain, professor of philosophy and psychology, 1949-53; Instituto de Cultura Religiosa Superior, Avila, professor of philosophy, 1950-52; University of Santo Domingo, Santo Domingo, Dominican Republic, professor of medical deontology, 1959; counselor of "Agrupacion Cultural Abside"; counselor of cinema censorship under Bishop of Santo Domingo; University of the State of Mexico, Toluca, Mexico, professor of logic and psychology, 1961-62; Catholic University of Puerto Rico, Ponce, Puerto Rico, professor of mental hygiene and ethics, Phi Delta Gamma counselor, 1962-63; University of Puerto Rico, professor of humanities at Rio Piedras extension and Mayaguez campus, 1963—, associate director of *Atenea* (faculty review) and professor of graduate Hispanic Studies, Mayaguez campus, 1969—. *Military service:* Aviacion militar dominicana, 1957; Hospital Militar Marion, Dominican Republic, chaplain, 1957-58; became first lieutenant.

WRITINGS: La psicologia de Santa Teresa, Estudios del Colegio Filosofico "La Santa" (Avila), 1950, 2nd edition, Editorial Jus (Mexico), 1955; *Filosofia de la mistica,* Ediciones Studium (Madrid/Buenos Aires), 1953; *Quien es ella,* Impresora Arte y Cine (Santo Domingo), 1956; *Lo que cabe en un verso,* Ediciones del Instituto Domincano de Cultura Hispanica, 1957; *Matrimonio,* Coleccion Arquero (Santo Domingo), 1957; *Que es una mujer?,* Ediciones Studium, 1961; *Solo Dios basta,* Ediciones Mundo Mejor (Mexico), 1961; *La esposa de un crucifijo,* Editorial Herrero (Mexico), 1961; *Esperanza,* Editorial Unitas (Mexico), 1966; *Logica y mistica,* Cuadernos de Artes y Ciencias, Recinto Universitario de Mayaguez, 1970; *La mistica clasica,* Editorial Edil (Rio Piedras), 1971; *San Juan de la Cruz clasico,* Editorial Edil, 1971; *Teresa de Avila clasica,* Editorial Edil, 1972; *Biblia universitaria: El origen de este universo,* Artes Graficas Benzal (Madrid), 1975; *El diario de un sacerdote casado,* Artes Graficas Benzal, 1975.

Under name Nazario Ruano: *La musica callada: Teologia del silencio,* Editorial de Espiritualidad (Avila), 1953, 2nd edition, Editorial Unitas, 1960; *Carmelita,* Impresora Arte y Cine, 1956, 2nd edition, Editorial Herrero, 1961; *Desnudez: Lo mistico y lo literario en San Juan de la Cruz,* Editorial Polis (Mexico), 1961; *Muerte de amor: Don Juan Tenorio y San Juan de la Cruz,* Editorial Frumentum (Mexico), 1962.

Editor: (And author of prologue) Crisogono, *Compendio de*

ascetica y mistica, 3rd edition, Revista de Espiritualidad (Madrid), 1949; St. Teresa de Avila, *Exclamaciones y meditaciones sobre los cantares,* Editorial de Espiritualidad, 1952; (with Guillermo Diaz Plaja) *Antologia mayor de la literatura espanola,* Editorial Labor (Barcelona), 1958.

Translator into Spanish: (And author of introduction) St. Therese de Lisieux, *Historia de un alma,* Editorial de Espiritualidad, 1954, 3rd edition, 1959; (and author of introduction) Francesco Evola, *Pastor,* Impresora Arte y Cine, 1958; (and author of introduction) St. Therese de Lisieux, *Manuscritos autobiograficos,* Editorial Herrero, 1962; (with Leonor de Paiz) Samivel, *Le Soleil se leve en Grece,* Editorial Herrero, 1962.

Contributor of articles to *El Diario de Avila,* 1947-52, *Aromas del Carmelo* (Camaguey, Cuba), 1958, *Mundo Mejor* (Mexico), 1959-62, and *El Debate* (Ponce), 1962-63. Contributor to *La Ciudad de Dios* (El Escorial), *Revista de Espiritualidad* (Madrid), *Revista Dominicana de Filosofia* (Dominican Republic), *Espiritualidad* (Mexico), *Horizontes* (Ponce), *Revista de Letras* (Mayaguez), *Isla Literaria* (San Juan), and *Atenea* (Mayaguez).

WORK IN PROGRESS: Historia del misticismo occidental.†

* * *

RUARK, Gibbons 1941-

PERSONAL: Born December 10, 1941, in Raleigh, N.C.; son of Henry Gibbons (a minister) and Sarah (Jenkins) Ruark; married Kay Stinson, October 5, 1963; children: Jennifer Kay, Emily Westbrook. *Education:* University of North Carolina at Chapel Hill, A.B., 1963; University of Massachusetts, M.A., 1965. *Office:* Department of English, University of Delaware, Newark, Del. 19711.

CAREER: University of North Carolina at Greensboro, instructor in English, 1965-68; University of Delaware, Newark, assistant professor, 1968-73, associate professor of English, 1973—. *Awards, honors:* National Arts Council awards for poetry, 1968, and 1971, for *A Program for Survival.*

WRITINGS: (Editor with Robert Watson) *The Greensboro Reader,* University of North Carolina Press, 1968; *A Program for Survival* (poems), University Press of Virginia, 1971; *Reeds* (poems), Texas Tech Press, 1977. Poems included in *American Literary Anthology #1,* Farrar, Strauss, 1968, *Best Poems of 1968,* edited by Lionel Stevenson and others, Pacific Books, 1969, and *Best Poems of 1974,* edited by Stevenson and others, Pacific Books, 1975.

WORK IN PROGRESS: Poems.

SIDELIGHTS: James Whitehead finds Gibbons Ruark "quiet, reflective; in fact nostalgia is his vision, particularly in memories of his dead father.... Ruark accepts and loves the family that raised him, and he accepts and loves the family he is raising in turn. Affirming family and friends, he makes marvelous poetry in the process."

The poems in *A Program for Survival* are, according to Michael Heffernan, "of a high and difficult sort, not easily achieved and less easily contrived. These poems took a long time: nothing here was slapped down unrevised, nothing here depends for its effects on cryptic, half-digested talk to obfuscate some basic vacancy.... There is an emotional authenticity about all these poems that makes them almost overpowering with a kind of uncanny, unrelenting force. They stay in the mind because they have been, many of them, driven there so deeply they will not pry loose."

A tape recording of Ruark's poems has been placed in the archives of the Library of Congress.

BIOGRAPHICAL/CRITICAL SOURCES: Midwest Quarterly, Volume XII, 1971; *Virginia Quarterly Review,* autumn, 1971; *Saturday Review,* December 18, 1971; *Contemporary Literary Criticism,* Volume III, Gale, 1975.

* * *

RUBIN, Frederick 1926-

PERSONAL: Born June 6, 1926, in Budapest, Hungary; son of Albert and Aranka (Klein) Rubin. *Education:* Budapest University, B.A., 1953, B.Sc. (with honors), 1953. *Home and office:* 55 Belsize Park, London N.W.3, England.

CAREER: Sleep-Learning Association, London, England, research officer, 1965-68; Chorley College of Education, Chorley, Lancastershire, England, part-time senior lecturer, 1968-69. Free-lance consultant to medical companies. Adviser and consultant on East European Communism and Soviet bloc affairs to research institutes.

WRITINGS: (Editor and contributor) *Current Research in Hypnopaedia,* American Elsevier, 1968; *Learning and Sleep: Theory and Practice of Hypnopaedia,* John Wright, 1971. Also author of research reports and papers dealing with Soviet countries. Contributor to *General Practitioner, London Times, New Scientist, Nature, East West Digest, Soviet Analyst,* and *Journal* of the Royal United Services Institute for Defence Studies.

SIDELIGHTS: Frederick Rubin travelled in the U.S.S.R. to study hypnopaedia, and is interested in the application of this "sleep-learning" tutorial system to the individual and to groups, through the use of electronic audio aids, tape recorders, etc., as an aid in the acquisition of languages and other subjects. Since 1971, Rubin has been primarily interested in East-West relations, current Hungarian military matters and training, and in the possibilities of approaching the scholarly study of the social, political, and military intelligence as an academic discipline.

BIOGRAPHICAL/CRITICAL SOURCES: Nature, September 24, 1971.

* * *

RUDOLPH, Donna Keyse 1934-

PERSONAL: Born November 3, 1934, in Scott City, Kan.; daughter of Delmar C. (a farmer) and Iva (Crist) Keyse; married G. A. Rudolph (a librarian), September 15, 1962; children: Anne Keyse, William Keyse. *Education:* Stephens College, A.A., 1954; Stanford University, A.B., 1956; Western Reserve University (now Case Western Reserve University), M.S.L.S., 1961. *Politics:* Democrat. *Religion:* Christian. *Home:* Route 1, Hickman, Neb. 68372.

CAREER: Garden City Junior College, Garden City, Kan., instructor in Spanish, 1958-60; Harvard University, Cambridge, Mass., gifts and exchange librarian, 1961-62; Ohio University, Athens, assistant education librarian, 1962-63; Kansas State University, Manhattan, instructor in Spanish, 1964-65; University of San Marcos, Lima, Peru, librarian, 1965-66; Kansas State University, instructor in Spanish, 1967-68. *Member:* American Library Association, League of Women Voters.

WRITINGS: (With husband, G. A. Rudolph) *Historical Dictionary of Venezuela,* Scarecrow, 1971.

AVOCATIONAL INTERESTS: Breeding and raising American quarter horses.

RUDOLPH, Erwin Paul 1916-

PERSONAL: Born April 30, 1916, in Keyesport, Ill.; son of Selden P. and Mattie (Carroll) Rudolph; married June Johnson (an elementary teacher), August 20, 1938; children: James Thomas, Erwin P. (deceased). *Education:* Greenville College, A.B., 1938; Ohio State University, M.A., 1944; University of Illinois, Ph.D., 1962. *Religion:* Protestant. *Home:* 111 Thompson Dr., Wheaton, Ill. 60187. *Office:* Department of English, Wheaton College, Wheaton, Ill. 60187.

CAREER: Ordained minister in Free Methodist Church of North America; pastor of churches in Columbus, Ohio, 1941-44, and Toledo, Ohio, 1944-48; Greenville College, Greenville, Ill., instructor in English, 1948-49; Wheaton College, Wheaton, Ill., instructor, 1950-55, assistant professor, 1955-60, associate professor, 1960-66, professor of English, 1966—, chairman of Division of Languages and Literature, 1966-75. *Member:* Modern Language Association of America, Conference on Christianity and Literature, National Council of Teachers of English.

WRITINGS: Goodby, My Son, Zondervan, 1971; (editor) William Law, *Christian Perfection,* Creation House, 1975; *John Bunyan and "Pilgrim's Progress,"* Victor Books, 1977; *The John Donne Sampler,* Victor Books, 1978. Contributor to *The New International Dictionary of the Christian Church* and to *Eternity.*

WORK IN PROGRESS: A critical work on William Law, for Twayne.

*   *   *

RUDOLPH, Marguerita 1908-

PERSONAL: Born March 14, 1908, in Chernigov, Russia; came to United States in 1924, naturalized in 1935; daughter of Khaim J. (a farmer and merchant) and Sopfia (Beliavskaya) Gurvich; married Joseph Rudolph, July 3, 1930; children: Alicia (Mrs. John Kaufmann). *Education:* University of Kansas, B.A., 1929; University of Minnesota, additional study, 1929-30; Bank Street College of Education, M.S., 1954. *Politics:* Independent. *Religion:* Eclectic. *Home and office:* 192-20B 64th Cir., Fresh Meadows, N.Y. 11365.

CAREER: Department of Welfare, New York City, director of child care centers, 1946-49; Fresh Meadows Nursery School, New York City, head teacher, 1949-57; Great Neck Community School, Great Neck, N.Y., director, 1957-70; educational consultant and author, 1970—. Teacher of writing and juvenile literature, Art and Writing Center, Instituto Allende, San Miguel, Mexico, winter sessions, 1973—. Instructor in preschool education for summer sessions or extension courses at Adelphi University, Long Island University, and Hampton Institute. Consultant to Head Start Program, Nassau-Suffolk counties, N.Y., 1966-69. *Member:* National Association for the Education of Young Children, Writers Guild, United Nations Association, National Audubon Society.

*WRITINGS—*Juvenile, except as noted: *Masha: The Little Goose Girl,* Macmillan, 1939; *The Great Hope,* introduction by Pearl S. Buck, John Day, 1948; *Look At Me,* Mc-Graw, 1967; *I Like a Whole One,* McGraw, 1968; *A Present for You,* McGraw, 1971; *Sharp and Shiny,* McGraw, 1971; *Today Is Not My Birthday,* McGraw, 1973; *The Sneaky Machine,* McGraw, 1974.

Other: (With Dorothy H. Cohen) *Kindergarten and Early School,* Appleton, 1964, revised edition, Prentice-Hall, 1977; *You Can Learn Russian,* Little, Brown, 1964; *The*

Magic Sack (Lithuanian folktale retold), McGraw, 1967; *I Am Your Misfortune* (Latvian folktale retold), Seabury, 1968; *Brave Soldier and a Dozen Devils* (Latvian folktale retold), Seabury, 1970; *Magic Egg and Other Rumanian Folk Stories,* Little, Brown, 1971; *From Hand To Hand,* McGraw, 1973; *Should the Children Know?,* Schocken, 1978.

Translator from the Russian: Evgenli I. Charushin, *Baby Bears,* Macmillan, 1944; Charushin, *Little Grey Wolf,* Macmillan, 1963; Vsevolod Garshin, *The Traveling Frog,* McGraw, 1966; K. Ushinsky, *How a Shirt Grew in the Field,* McGraw, 1967; Boris V. Zakhoder, *Star Bright,* Lothrop, 1969; Zakhoder, *Rosachok,* Lothrop, 1970; Zakhoder, *How a Piglet Crashed the Christmas Party,* Lothrop, 1971; Kornei Chukovsky, *Telephone,* Bobbs-Merrill, 1971; Zakhoder, *The Crocodile's Toothbrush,* McGraw, 1973.

Stories included in a number of anthologies for children including: *Forward,* Scott, Foresman, 1943; *Under the Christmas Tree,* Macmillan, 1948; *Open Roads,* American Book Co., 1957; *Jack and Jill Round the Year,* Little, Brown, 1958. Contributor of stories and verses to children's magazines; contributor of adult nonfiction to professional journals and popular magazines.

SIDELIGHTS: Marguerita Rudolph told *CA:* "Being a teen-age immigrant in Kansas, with no knowledge of English rendered me a deaf-mute illiterate, a condition forcing me to learn the language, and do it well. I then determined to become a writer. I was then and am now thrilled with the English language. A significant influence on my writing was early acquaintance with great Russian literature; this also affected my retention of Russian language and subsequently successful translation of literary works for children."

*   *   *

RUIZ-FORNELLS, Enrique 1925-

PERSONAL: Born December 6, 1925, in Madrid, Spain; son of Camilio and Terese (Silverde) Ruiz-Fornells; married Cynthia Young (a professor of Spanish), March 21, 1959. *Education:* University of Seville, Bachillerato, 1944; attended International University Menendez Pelayo, 1950; Official School of Journalism, Madrid, M.A., 1951; University of Madrid, M.A., 1953, Ph.D., 1958; also attended University of Paris, 1952, and Northwestern University, 1953-54. *Home:* 222 Highlands, Tuscaloosa, Ala. 35401. *Office:* Department of Romance Languages, University of Alabama, University, Ala. 35486.

CAREER: University of Madrid, Madrid, Spain, assistant professor, 1950-55, associate professor of Spanish-American history, 1955-57; McGill University, Montreal, Quebec, lecturer in Spanish, 1959-61; University of South Carolina, Columbia, assistant professor of Romance languages, 1961-63; University of Alabama, University, associate professor, 1963-66, professor of Romance languages, 1966—, director of summer program in Spain, 1971-73. Professor of Spanish, American Embassy, Madrid, 1955-57; visiting professor, Washington University, St. Louis, Mo., 1967-68; part-time visiting professor, Mississippi State University, 1968-75; University of Madrid, representative in United States, 1967-75, teacher and secretary of summer courses for North American students. *Military service:* Spanish Army, 1949-51; became second lieutenant.

MEMBER: American Association of Teachers of Spanish and Portuguese (member of travel committee, 1964-67; president of Alabama chapter, 1967, 1976; member of national executive council, 1970-72), Asociacion Internacional de

Hispanistas, Modern Language Association of America, American Association of University Professors, Oficina de Informacion y Vigilancia del Espanol, Asociacion Cultural Iberoamericana (Madrid), Asociacion Cultural Hispano-Norteamericana (Madrid), South Atlantic Modern Language Association (secretary of Spanish section II, 1965, chairman, 1966), Sigma Delta Pi. *Awards, honors:* Medalla al Merito Turistico (Spain), 1968; Encomienda al Merito Civil (Spain), 1972.

WRITINGS: Estudiantes espanoles en los Estados Unidos: Diez anos de intercambio, Asociacion Cultural Hispano-Norteamericana, 1956; (editor with Robina E. Henry) Joaquin Calvo Sotelo, *La Muralla,* Appleton, 1962; (editor with James R. Chatham) *Doctoral Dissertations in Hispanic Languages and Literature, 1876-1966: The United States, Canada and Puerto Rico,* University of Kentucky Press, 1970; (compiler) *A Concordance to the Poetry of Gustavo Adolfo Becquer* (in English and Spanish), University of Alabama Press, 1970; (compiler) *Las Concordancias del Ingenioso Hidalgo Don Quijote de la Mancha,* Ediciones Cultura Hispanica, 1976. Author of seven occasional papers for various organizations. Contributor of more than sixty articles and reviews to journals. Assistant editor, *Mundo Hispanico* (Madrid), 1954-55, *Cuadernos Hispanoamericanos* (Madrid), 1958-59, and ''Ediciones Cultura Hispanica'' (Madrid), 1958-59; editor, *Revista de Estudios Hispanicos* (University of Alabama), 1966—.

WORK IN PROGRESS: A critical edition of Lope de Vega's *La Discoridia en los casados;* a concordance to the poetry of Leopoldo Panero; an anthology of the Don Juan plays in the twentieth-century Spanish theater.

SIDELIGHTS: Enrique Ruiz-Fornells has lived in Morocco, France, Italy, Canada, and England, as well as his native country, Spain.

* * *

RUNYON, John H(arold) 1945-

PERSONAL: Born June 30, 1945, in Reading, Pa.; son of James Hilliard (a chemical engineer) and Ruth Emma (Kantner) Runyon; married Sally Sutphen, July 8, 1967; children: Erica Lyn. *Education:* Drew University, B.A., 1967; Union Theological Seminary, New York, N.Y., further study, 1967-68; Rutgers University, M.A., 1969, doctoral candidate, 1969-73. *Religion:* Methodist. *Home:* 36 South Dr., East Brunswick, N.J. 08816. *Office:* Township of East Brunswick, 1 Jean Walling Civic Center, East Brunswick, N.J. 08816.

CAREER: Rutgers University, New Brunswick, N.J., instructor in political science, Eagleton Institute of Politics, 1969-71, instructor in political science and staff assistant to president, 1971-73; Township of East Brunswick, East Brunswick, N.J., assistant to mayor, 1973-74, administrator, 1974—, acting mayor, 1975. Political consultant to American Broadcasting Company on New Jersey elections, 1970, 1972, 1974, 1976; political analyst, New Jersey public television, 1971; tabulation coordinator, New Jersey Election Service, 1970; member of many civic groups in East Brunswick, including Planning Board, 1974—, executive board of Chamber of Commerce, 1974—, Arts Council, and museum and library committees. Member of board of trustees, Drew University, 1971-76. *Member:* International City Managers Association, American Political Science Association, American Academy of Political and Social Science, National Municipal League, American Society of Public Administration, National League of Cities, National Council

for Urban Economic Development, National Trust for Historic Preservation, New Jersey Municipal Management Association, New Jersey League of Municipalities, Middlesex County Managers Association.

WRITINGS: (With Jennifer Verdini Plotkin and wife, Sally S. Runyon) *Source Book of American Presidential Campaign and Election Statistics, 1948-1968,* Ungar, 1971.

WORK IN PROGRESS: Continuing research on American presidential campaigns and elections.

AVOCATIONAL INTERESTS: Instrumental music (plays organ, piano, and tuba), collecting political memorabilia.

* * *

RUSSELL, Conrad 1937-

PERSONAL: Born April 15, 1937, in Sussex, England; son of Lord Bertrand Arthur William (the philosopher) and Patricia (Spence) Russell; married Elizabeth Sanders, August 11, 1962; children: Nicholas Lyulph, John Francis. *Education:* Attended Eton College; Oxford University, B.A., 1958, M.A., 1962. *Politics:* Liberal. *Religion:* None. *Office:* Bedford College, University of London, London N.W.1, England.

CAREER: University of London, London, England, reader, 1960-74, lecturer in history, 1974—. *Member:* Royal Historical Society.

WRITINGS: The Crisis of Parliaments: English History, 1509-1660, Oxford University Press, 1971, 3rd revised edition, 1977; (editor) *The Origins of the English Civil War,* Macmillan, 1972. Contributor to history journals.

WORK IN PROGRESS: Parliament and English Politics, 1621-1629; research toward a biography of John Pym.

* * *

RUSSELL, Helen Ross 1915-

PERSONAL: Born February 21, 1915, in Myerstown, Pa.; daughter of George Smith and Helen (Boyd) Ross; married Robert S. Russell (an art professor), September 24, 1960. *Education:* West Chester State College, teaching certificate, 1934; Lebanon Valley College, B.A., 1943; Cornell University, M.A., 1947, Ph.D., 1949. *Politics:* Independent Mugwump. *Religion:* Christian. *Home:* 44 College Dr., Jersey City, N.J. 07305. *Agent:* Curtis Brown, Ltd., 575 Madison Ave., New York, N.Y. 10022.

CAREER: Teacher, in one-room rural school, Lebanon County, Pa., 1934-35, of 3rd grade, Bethel Township, Pa., 1935-42, of art and science, Lebanon City Schools, Lebanon, Pa., 1943-46; Massachusetts State College at Fitchburg (now Fitchburg State College), professor of biology, 1949-66, chairman of science department, 1951-56, dean of studies, 1956-66; part-time science consultant to Wave Hill Center for Environmental Studies, New York City, 1966-70, and to Manhattan Country School, New York City, 1970—. *Member:* American Association for the Advancement of Science (fellow), American Nature Study Society (secretary, 1954-58; president, 1974), Conservation Education Association (life member), New York Academy of Sciences, Women's Society of Christ United Methodist Church (Jersey City; president, 1972-76), Citizens Advisory Council (Jersey City).

*WRITINGS—*All juveniles, except as indicated: *City Critters,* Hawthorn, 1969, revised edition, American Nature Study Society, 1976; *The True Book of Buds,* Childrens Press, 1970; *Clarion, the Killdeer,* Hawthorn, 1970; *Winter*

Search Party: A Guide to Insects and Other Invertebrates, Thomas Nelson, 1971; *The True Book of Springtime Tree Seeds,* Childrens Press, 1972; *Winter: A Field Trip Guide,* Little, Brown, 1972; *Soil: A Field Trip Guide,* Little, Brown, 1972; *Small Worlds: A Field Trip Guide,* Little, Brown, 1972; *Ten Minute Field Trips: Using the School Grounds for Environmental Studies* (adult book), J. G. Ferguson, 1972; *Water: A Field Trip Guide,* Little, Brown, 1973; *Earth, the Great Recycler,* Thomas Nelson, 1973; *Foraging for Dinner,* Thomas Nelson, 1975.

Contributor of more than 60 articles to *Junior Encyclopaedia Britannica.* Author of 15 video tapes and one filmstrip; science editor, *Junior Encyclopaedia Britannica,* 1955-70. Author of a syndicated weekly food feature, "In the Kitchen with Helen Ross Russell." Contributor of over 80 articles to periodicals.

WORK IN PROGRESS: An adult book on dandelions.

SIDELIGHTS: Helen Ross Russell writes: "My husband sometimes points to our plastic kitchen waste basket with a round hole melted in the center of one side and explains that this kind of situation is an occupational hazard that goes with being married to an author who always tests everything before it goes into her books even if the testing involves putting a candle in a waste basket to create a dark work area for the study of a demonstration of eclipses in the middle of a sunny day.

"There are other hazards too. Like travelling with a cage of bagworms for six weeks, eating everything described in *Foraging for Dinner,* and being served five Bavarian creams in one week until the recipe for Bavarian cream made with yogurt was standardized. Anyone who didn't know the Russells might think that his life was indeed difficult, but the truth of the matter is that while I am the person who pushes the pencil, we are a team and Robert Russell contributes ideas and evaluations and helps with observations while he adapts to vacations planned around the dates when dandelion will be blooming or directed geographically by the need to be at a certain spot at a given time in order to see a once-a-year event just as I adapt to his study of Pre-Columbian art.

"In fact, it is he who has freed me in the last ten years to write on a full-time basis. For though I have written 'for publication' ever since I started producing books for my dolls and a weekly newspaper for my grandmother and other relatives when I was eight years old, I never had time to write as much as I wanted. I still don't—but if I can just find a way to invent a 25 hour day, a 10 day week, and a 60 week year I might make it someday!

"Of course, I could write a great deal more if I didn't take time out to teach children, to conduct workshops on wild food or on using the urban areas to teach about the environment and if I weren't deeply involved in social and environmental issues. But in reality these things are also a part of my writing for I write about the things that I believe in and enjoy for people whom I believe in and enjoy."

AVOCATIONAL INTERESTS: Young people, the natural world, social justice and responsibility, writing, wild foods, cooking, skiing, "travelling with my husband to learn about Pre-Columbian art at original sites."

* * *

RUTHERFORD, Margaret 1882-1972

May 11, 1882—May 22, 1972; British actress and comedienne. Obituaries: *New York Times,* May 23, 1972; *Washington Post,* May 23, 1972; *L'Express,* May 29-June 4, 1972; *Newsweek,* June 5, 1972; *Time,* June 5, 1972.

RUTLEDGE, Albert J(ohn) 1934-

PERSONAL: Born December 29, 1934, in New Haven, Conn.; son of John Joseph and Constance (Yesmentes) Rutledge; married Catherine Dougherty, June 21, 1958; children: Eileen, Marianne, John, Steven. *Education:* New York State College of Forestry, B.S., 1956; University of Illinois, M.L.A., 1964. *Residence:* Urbana, Ill. *Office:* Department of Landscape Architecture, University of Illinois at Urbana-Champaign, Urbana, Ill. 61801.

CAREER: National Park Service, Washington, D.C., landscape architect, 1956-62; University of Illinois at Urbana-Champaign, associate professor of landscape architecture, 1962—. Member of board of directors, Champaign County Development Council Foundation, 1964-68; vice-president, Champaign-Urbana Board of Catholic Education, 1968-71. *Military service:* National Guard, 1957-63. *Member:* American Society of Landscape Architects.

WRITINGS: Anatomy of a Park: The Essentials of Recreation Area Planning and Design, McGraw, 1971. Contributor to *Landscape Architecture.*

WORK IN PROGRESS: Research on effects of design upon behavior as it relates to park properties.†

* * *

RUTSTEIN, David D(avis) 1909-

PERSONAL: Born February 5, 1909, in Wilkes-Barre, Pa.; son of Harry and Nellie (Davis) Rutstein; married Mazie Weissman, February 22, 1935; married second wife, Ruth E. Rickel, August 11, 1951; children: (first marriage) Catherine (Mrs. Robert B. Meyer), David D., Jr. *Education:* Harvard University, S.B. (cum laude), 1930, M.D. (cum laude), 1934. *Politics:* Independent. *Religion:* None. *Home:* 98 Winthrop St., Cambridge, Mass. 02138. *Office:* 10 Shattuck St., Boston, Mass. 02115.

CAREER: Wilkes-Barre General Hospital, Wilkes-Barre, Pa., intern, 1934-35; Boston City Hospital, Boston, Mass., house officer, 1935-36; Harvard Medical School, Boston, research fellow in pediatrics at Children's Hospital, 1936-37, assistant in bacteriology, 1936-37; Albany Medical College, Albany, N.Y., assistant in medicine, 1937-38, instructor, 1938-40, assistant professor of medicine, 1940-43; Columbia University, College of Physicians and Surgeons, New York, N.Y., instructor in medicine, 1943-47; Harvard Medical School, professor of preventive medicine, 1947-65, Ridley Watts Professor of Preventive Medicine, 1966-75, Ridley Watts Professor of Preventive Medicine, emeritus, 1975—, head of department, 1947-69. Distinguished physician, Veterans Administration, 1976—. Visiting professor at Syracuse University, 1952, at University of Vermont, 1970; visiting institute lecturer at Massachusetts Institute of Technology, 1970-71. Diplomate of National Board of Medical Examiners, 1937, of American Board of Internal Medicine, 1941, of American Board of Preventive Medicine and Public Health, 1951. Associate visiting physician, Bellevue Hospital, 1943-47; physician, House of Good Samaritan and Children's Hospital Medical Center, 1947-75; associate physician, Massachusetts General Hospital, 1949-61. Consultant to Peter Brent Brigham Hospital, 1947—, Massachusetts General Hospital, 1961—, Beth Israel Hospital, 1964—, and other hospitals. New York State Department of Health, medical consultant on pneumonia, 1937-40, chief of Cardiac Bureau, 1940-42; New York City Department of Health, deputy commander, 1943-46, director of Bureau laboratories, 1943-45; national director of Gas Protection Section, U.S. Office of Civilian Defense, 1942-43; U.S. chairman,

United Kingdom-United States Cooperative Rheumatic Fever Study, 1950-65; World Health Organization, chairman of expert committee on rheumatic diseases, 1956, chairman of expert committee on prevention of rheumatic fever, 1966; chairman of research advisory council, United Cerebral Palsy Foundation, 1963-66; member of national advisory council, Peace Corps, 1968-69, and special medical advisory group, Veterans Administration, 1968-73; chairman, subcommittee on technology and systems transfer, National Academy of Engineering, 1970-73; member of governing board, Action Thematique Programee "Sante," Centre National de le Recherche Scientifique (Paris), 1975—. Consultant to National Institutes of Health and various bureaus of U.S. Public Health Service, 1948—, Worcester Foundation for Experimental Biology, 1961-68. *Military service:* U.S. Public Health Service Reserve, commissioned medical director, 1951—.

MEMBER: American Academy of Arts and Sciences (councilor, 1973-77), American Association for the Advancement of Science (fellow), American Epidemiological Society (president, 1966-67), American Federation for Clinical Research, American Public Health Association (member of governing council, 1962-65), American Heart Association (vice-president, 1954-57), American Rheumatism Association, International Epidemiological Association, American Society for Clinical Investigation, Biomedical Engineering Society, Royal Society of Medicine (London), New York Academy of Medicine, New York Academy of Sciences (fellow), Harvey Society, Academie Nationale de Medicine (Paris; foreign correspondent), Boylston Medical Society (president, 1960-61), Sigma Xi, Alpha Omega Alpha, Delta Omega.

AWARDS, HONORS: Benjamin Franklin Magazine Award in science, 1958, for "The Influenza Epidemic" in *Harper's;* Gold Heart Award of American Heart Association, 1959; Jubilee Metal of Swedish Medical Society, 1966; Chevalier of Legion of Honor (France).

WRITINGS: Lifetime Health Record, Harvard University Press, 1958; *The Coming Revolution in Medicine,* M.I.T. Press, 1967; (with Murray Eden) *Engineering and Living Systems,* M.I.T. Press, 1970; *Blueprint for Medical Care,* M.I.T. Press, 1974.

Contributor: J. R. Paul, editor, *The Epidemiology of Rheumatic Fever and Some of Its Public Health Aspects,* 2nd edition, American Heart Association, 1943; Franklin H. Top, editor, *Communicable Diseases,* 2nd edition, Mosby, 1947, 3rd edition, 1955; H. M. Marvin and others, *You and Your Heart: A Clinic for Laymen on the Heart and Circulation,* Random House, 1950; Haven Emerson, editor, *Administrative Medicine,* 2nd edition, Thomas Nelson, 1951; John H. Knowles, editor, *Hospitals, Doctors and the Public Interest,* Harvard University Press, 1965; *Mainstreams of Medicine,* University of Texas Press, 1970; Paul A. Freund, editor, *Experimentation with Human Subjects,* Braziller, 1970.

Contributor of more than ninety articles to medical journals, magazines, and newspapers, including *Atlantic, Harper's,* and *Reader's Digest.* Member of editorial board, *Circulation,* 1949-57, *American Review of Tuberculosis and Pulmonary Disease,* 1955-58, *Medical Care,* 1963-69, and *Methods of Information in Science,* 1965-77.

WORK IN PROGRESS: Papers on measurement of the quality of medical care, regionalization of medical care, and genetic aspects of alcoholism.

SIDELIGHTS: In her review of David D. Rutstein's *Blueprint for Medical Care,* Anne R. Somers notes: "Blue-

printing of social institutions in a society as dynamic as ours is a tricky business. On the one hand, the model can provide a useful definition of the goal we seek and a benchmark against which to measure progress. On the other hand, if overdone, it can become a static, authoritarian roadblock to continued progress. Dr. Rutstein's heroic effort to provide a single blueprint for our future health care illustrates both sides of the coin. Despite the fact that few will agree with all aspects of the Rutstein blueprint, it is an important book. It deserves to be widely read—and widely argued about."

Rutstein is a professional wine taster for importers and a member of the Confrerie des Chevaliers du Tastevin-Nuits-St.-George.

BIOGRAPHICAL/CRITICAL SOURCES: New York Times Book Review, November 10, 1968; *New England Journal of Medicine,* May 16, 1974; *Annals of the American Academy of Political and Social Science,* September, 1974; *Choice,* October, 1974.

*   *   *

RUTTENBERG, Stanley H(arvey)   1917-

PERSONAL: Born March 19, 1917, in St. Paul, Minn.; son of Charles and Fannie (Weinstein) Ruttenberg; married Gertrude Bernstein, November 28, 1940; children: Joel, Ruth, Charles. *Education:* University of Pittsburgh, B.S., 1937. *Home:* 6310 Maiden Lane, Bethesda, Md. 20034. *Office:* 1211 Connecticut Ave. N.W., Washington, D.C. 20036.

CAREER: Hull House, Chicago, Ill., assistant to the director, 1938; Congress of Industrial Organizations (CIO), Washington, D.C., organizer and field representative in Ohio Valley, 1937-38, associate director of research, 1939-43, 1946-48, director of department of education and research, 1948-55; American Federation of Labor and Congress of Industrial Organizations (AFL-CIO), Washington, D.C., director of department of research, 1955-63; U.S. Department of Labor, Washington, D.C., special assistant to the secretary, 1963-65, assistant secretary of labor for manpower and manpower administrator, 1966-69; Stanley H. Ruttenberg & Associates, Inc. (economic consultants), Washington, D.C., president, 1969—. Director, National Bureau of Economic Research, 1940-41, 1948-62; UNESCO, member of executive committee, 1948-53, vice-chairman of executive committee, 1952, special adviser to American delegation at international conferences, 1949, 1950; public member, Foreign Service Selection Board, 1950; public adviser, General Agreement on Tariffs and Trade Negotiation (GATT), Geneva, 1956, 1958; member, U.S. Commission on Money and Credit, 1958-61; labor specialist, U.S. Department of State Educational Exchange Program, 1959; member of board of directors, Resources for the Future. *Military service:* U.S. Army, Quartermaster Corps, 1943-46; became first lieutenant. *Member:* American Economic Association, Industrial Relations Research Association (member of executive board, 1953), National Planning Association.

WRITINGS: (Senior author, assisted by Jocelyn Gutchess) *Manpower Challenge of the 1970's: Institutions and Social Change,* Johns Hopkins Press, 1970; (with Gutchess) *The Federal-State Employment Service: A Critique,* Johns Hopkins Press, 1970.

*   *   *

RYAN, Jessica Cadwalader   1915(?)-1972

1915(?)—May 22, 1972; American actress and author. Obituaries: *New York Times,* May 24, 1972.

RYAN, Pat M(artin) 1928-

PERSONAL: Born February 13, 1928, in Lexington, Ky.; son of Pat M. (a life insurance executive) and Juanita (Wagner) Ryan; married Jamice E. Robinson, December 25, 1955; children: Deirdre Diane, Sean Philip, Siobhan Moira. *Education:* Attended University of Missouri, 1946-48; University of California, Berkeley, B.A., 1949, graduate study, 1954-55; Stanford University, M.A., 1950; Yale University, Ph.D., 1959; postdoctoral study at University of London, 1966, Purdue University and University of Arizona, 1967, State University of New York at Buffalo, 1968, and University of North Carolina at Greensboro, 1974-76. *Home address:* P.O. Box 662, Clarkson, N.Y. 14430.

CAREER: Washington Post, Washington, D.C., copy boy and book reviewer, 1952-53; Colorado School of Mines, Golden, instructor in English, 1955-56; *Milford Citizen,* Milford, Conn., theatre and music reviewer, 1957-59; University of Arizona, Tucson, associate professor of drama, 1959-62; California State Polytechnic College (now California Polytechnic State University), San Luis Obispo, assistant professor of English, 1962-63; Wayne State College, Wayne, Neb., professor of English and languages division chairman, 1963-64; Eastern Montana College, Billings, professor of English and language/literature division chairman, 1964-65; Indiana University, Fort Wayne, associate professor of English, 1965-67; State University of New York College at Brockport, professor of English, 1967-70, director of sponsored research, 1970-72; Fulbright lecturer in American literature, University of Turku, Turku, Finland, and Abo Akademie, Domkyrkotorget, Finland, 1972-73; visiting lecturer in English, University of North Carolina at Greensboro, and North Carolina Central University, Durham, 1973-74; visiting lecturer in U.S. history, University of North Carolina at Greensboro, and Appalachian State University, Boone, N.C., 1974-76. Project director, U.S. Office of Education grant, State University of New York College at Brockport, 1970-72. Nation and federation officer, Y.M.C.A. Indian Guides, Monroe County, N.Y., 1969-71. Consultant to U.S. Peace Corps Training Program, 1962, Urban Problems Institute, State University of New York College at Brockport, 1969, Learning Institute of North Carolina, 1974-75, and to Greensboro (N.C.) Public Schools, 1975-76. *Military service:* U.S. Army, Medical Corps, 1951-53. *Member:* American Society for Theatre Research, Modern Language Association of America, Organization of American Historians. *Awards, honors:* Indiana University foundation grant, 1966; senior Fulbright-Hays scholar, 1972-73.

WRITINGS: (Editor) Aristotle, *Rhetoric: An Abstract of Principles of Public Speaking,* Colorado School of Mines, 1956; *Thomas Lodge, Gentleman,* Shoe String, 1958; (compiler) *History of the Modern Theatre: A Selective Bibliography,* University of Arizona, 1960; (editor) Thomas Wolfe, *The Mountains,* University of North Carolina Press, 1970; *Tombstone Theatre Tonight!: A Chronicle of Entertainment on the Southwestern Mining Frontier,* The Westerners, 1966; (compiler) *American Drama Bibliography: A Checklist of Publications in English,* Fort Wayne Public Library, 1969; (compiler) *Black Writing in the U.S.A.: A Bibliographic Guide,* Drake Memorial Library, 1969; *Social Science* (verse), Vietnam Moratorium (Brockport, N.Y.), 1969; *Blue-grass* (verse; pamphlet), Writers' Forum, 1972. Also author of *John Brougham,* published by Twayne.

Contributor to *Amex-Canada, Journal of American History, Shenandoah, Quarterly Journal of Speech, Arizona Quarterly, Enciclopedia dello Spettacolo, Evergreen Review, Notable American Women, 1607-1950, Dictionary of American Biography,* and other publications. Assistant editor, *Arizona and the West,* 1960-62; associate editor, *Speech Monographs,* 1961-62; editorial advisor, Twayne Publishers, 1966-67.

SIDELIGHTS: Pat Ryan told *CA:* "Most of my writing is about American authors and theatrical performers, whom I have hoped to present as self-aware artists, not just colorful celebrities.... I am fascinated by both Fanny Brice and David Warfield's Jewishness and their classic comedy; curious about Langston Hughes and Richard Wright's contrasting psychic and literary responses to Africa; and amazed at John Brougham and Eugene O'Neill's imbued Irishism. Finding out about Americans' pluralistic cultural past has meant going back to grad school, twice travelling to Europe, and teaching U.S. history. I am still learning how to write."

* * *

RYAN, William M(artin) 1918-

PERSONAL: Born June 22, 1918, in Clinton, Iowa; son of William T. (a salesman) and Vada (Hoover) Ryan; married Fay S., April 2, 1944 (divorced, 1965); married Hilda P., September 29, 1972. *Education:* St. Ambrose College, A.B., 1940; University of Colorado, additional study, summer, 1947; University of Michigan, M.A., 1950; University of Texas, Ph.D., 1955. *Politics:* Democrat. *Religion:* Roman Catholic. *Home:* 8825 Fairway, Leawood, Kan. 66206. *Office:* Department of English, University of Missouri, Kansas City, Mo. 64110.

CAREER: St. Ambrose College, Davenport, Iowa, instructor, 1946-50, assistant professor of English, 1950-52; University of Missouri—Kansas City, 1955—, began as instructor, currently professor of English. Member of United Nations Speakers Service, 1959-64. *Military service:* U.S. Naval Reserve, amphibious task group, active duty, 1943-46; served in South Pacific theater; became lieutenant junior grade. *Member:* Modern Language Association of America, Mediaeval Academy of America, American Association of University Professors, National Association for the Advancement of Colored People.

WRITINGS: William Langland, Twayne, 1968; (contributor) Archibald A. Hill, editor, *Studies in Languages, Literature, and Culture of the Middle Ages and Later,* University of Texas Press, 1969; (editor) *The Linguists and the Literature,* University of Missouri—Kansas City, 1971. Contributor of about twenty articles to scholarly journals.

WORK IN PROGRESS: A Poet for Sundry Folk, a book on Chaucer's storytelling; *Bella Medievalia to Go to Bed With,* an anthology of medieval writings.

* * *

RYBKA, Edward F(rank) 1928-

PERSONAL: Born April 14, 1928, in Cleveland, Ohio; son of Jan (a machine operator) and Lottie (Antoszewski) Rybka; married Irene R. Kubisiak, September 26, 1953; children: Edward William, Robert Stephen, Michelle Renee. *Education:* Attended Wilcox Business College, 1950; Cleveland State University, B.A., 1962. *Politics:* Conservative. *Religion:* Catholic. *Home:* 38 Pepper Creek Dr., Cleveland, Ohio 44124. *Office:* Rybka Realty Inc., 5085 Turney Rd., Garfield Heights, Ohio 44125.

CAREER: Rybka Realty Inc., Garfield Heights, Ohio,

owner and president, 1956—. Instructor in real estate sales at John Carroll University and Cleveland Community College. Chairman, School Board Levies, Cleveland, Ohio; member of advisory board, Jennings Home for Aged, trustee, member of board of directors, Marymount Hospital, member of advisory board, St. Anthony Home for Boys, and member of executive committee board, Notre Dame College, all Cleveland, Ohio. *Military service:* U.S. Navy, 1946-48; served as pharmacist 3rd class. *Member:* National Association of Real Estate Boards, Ohio Association of Real Estate Boards, Joint Veterans Commission of Cuyahoga County (Ohio; president), Cleveland Area Board of Realtors, Cleveland Society of Poles (recording secretary), Lions Club.

WRITINGS: The Number One Success System to Boost Your Earnings in Real Estate, Prentice-Hall, 1971. Contributor of articles to *Real Estate Today.*

BIOGRAPHICAL/CRITICAL SOURCES: Properties Magazines, July, 1968, May, 1976.

*   *   *

RYDELL, Wendy
(Wendell Rydell)

PERSONAL: Born in Perth Amboy, N.J.; daughter of Abraham and Sadie (Gottesman) Wilner; married Chester Rydell (president of Noble-Rydell, Inc.), April 6, 1952; children: Susan, David. *Education:* Ohio State University, B.A., 1947; Mexico City College, M.A., 1949. *Home:* 51 Wintercress Lane, East Northport, N.Y. 11731.

CAREER: Former beat reporter for *Newark Evening News,* Newark, N.J., and copywriter for several department stores in New York, N.Y.; occasional columnist for small New Jersey weeklies. Member of board of trustees, East Northport Library. *Member:* Theta Sigma Phi, Chi Delta Phi, Alpha Lambda Delta.

WRITINGS—Filmstrips; published by Avna, except as indicated: "Image Makers," Eye-Gate House, 1969; "Black Image Makers," Eye-Gate House, 1969; "Afro-American Heritage," Eye-Gate House, 1970; "Families in Action," Eye-Gate House, 1971; "They Came to America," 1971; "Poverty: Living in the Other America," 1971; "Indians: Strangers in Their Own Land," 1972; "It's Up to You," Eye-Gate House, 1972; "The City: How America Lives," 1972; "Suburbia: How America Lives," 1972; "The Power of the Presidency," 1973; "Corporate America: The Power Brokers," 1973; "The Populist Movement," 1973; "Consumerism: Revolution in the Marketplace," 1973; "V.D.: The Silent Epidemic," 1974; "The Women's Movement," 1974; "Challenge and Change: Growing Up in America," 1974; "Coping: Strategies for Growth," 1974; "Alcohol: America's Drug of Choice," 1974; "Marijuana Update," 1974; "Rape: The Savage Crime," 1975; "The Youth-Killers," 1975; "Human Ecology: The Inner Battle," 1975; "Sex Roles: Redefining the Difference," 1975; "You and the World of Work," 1975; "How to Buy a Doctor," 1976; "The Smoking Habit: How to Kill It," 1976; "You Have the Right: Underage in America," 1976.

Textbooks: Book 5, and units in books 4 and 6, in "Triple I" collateral reading series for multi-ethnic elementary students, American Book Co., 1970; contributor of more than 250 short storie to various other reading series. Also author of forty cassettes on science and social studies at the elementary level.

Other: (With Stephen Schepp) *Pot, Pills and Powders: The Truth about Drugs,* Western Publishing, 1973; *The Instant Home Fashion Sewing Encyclopedia,* Career Institute, 1973; (with George Gilbert) *The Great Book of Magic,* Abrams, 1976.

Juveniles; under pseudonym Wendell Rydell: *Abelard Sports Books: Basketball,* Abelard, 1971; *Abelard Sports Books: Football,* Abelard, 1971; *Abelard Sports Books: Baseball,* Abelard, 1972; *The Name of the Game: Basketball,* Interlyth, Ltd., 1972; *The Name of the Game: Football,* Interlyth, Ltd., 1972; *The Name of the Game: Baseball,* Interlyth, Ltd., 1972.

WORK IN PROGRESS: Several filmstrip sets on human emotions; a filmstrip set on friendship.

AVOCATIONAL INTERESTS: Painting and sculpture ("with great enthusiasm and little talent"), sewing and decorating, sports of all kinds ("mostly as a spectator").

*   *   *

RYDEN, Hope

PERSONAL: Born in St. Paul, Minn.; daughter of Ernest E. (a minister) and Agnes (Johnson) Ryden. *Education:* Attended Augustana College, Rock Island, Ill.; University of Iowa, B.A. *Home:* 345 East 81st St., New York, N.Y. 10028.

CAREER: Drew Associates (affiliate of Time-Life Broadcast), New York City, film producer, 1960-64; Hope Ryden Productions, New York City, film producer, writer, and director, 1965; American Broadcasting Corp., New York City, feature producer for ABC-TV evening news, 1966-68; free-lance documentary film producer, 1968—. Free-lance still photographer. *Awards, honors:* "Oppie" award for best book in Americana category, 1970, and *Library Journal* citation as one of 100 best sci-tech titles, 1970, for *America's Last Wild Horses;* Screen Writers Guild nomination for best film documentary, 1970, for "Missing in Randolph"; New York Public Library citations for *God's Dog* and *America's Last Wild Horses;* Cine Golden Eagle award for "The Wellsprings."

WRITINGS: America's Last Wild Horses, Dutton, 1970; *The Wild Colt,* Coward, 1972; *Mustangs: A Return to the Wild,* Viking, 1972; *God's Dog,* Coward, 1975; *The Wild Pups,* Putnam, 1975.

Documentary films: "Susan Starr," produced by Drew Associates/Time-Life Films, 1962; "Jane," produced by Drew Associates/Time-Life Films, 1963; "Mission to Malaya," produced by Drew Associates/ABC-TV Network News, 1964; "Operation Gwamba," produced by Hope Ryden Productions and CBS-TV, 1965; "To Love A Child," produced by ABC-TV News, 1969; "Missing in Randolph," produced by ABC-TV News, 1970; "Strangers in Their Own Land: The Chicanos," produced by ABC-TV News, 1971; "The Wellsprings," produced by PBS-TV, 1976; "Beginning Again at Fifty," produced by CBS-TV, 1977; "The Forties: A Crossroad," produced by CBS-TV, 1977.

Contributor of articles to *Look, Children's Day, National Geographic, Reader's Digest, National Parks,* and *Conservation Magazine;* contributor of photographs to *National Geographic, Time, New York Times, Reader's Digest, Children's Day,* and other periodicals.

WORK IN PROGRESS: A book on deer, for Putnam.

SIDELIGHTS: Hope Ryden told *CA:* "I feel very little attention has been paid to North American wildlife. Most people are more concerned with animals on other continents whose fate is beyond our control. Our own animals are exploited by commercial interests or removed if they have little or no commercial value and stand in the way of fuller exploitation of some other facet of nature. Though many people are enlightened regarding the balance of nature, the concept is not practised in wildlife management. I wish to make this understood.''

*   *   *

SABLE, Martin Howard 1924-

PERSONAL: Born September 24, 1924, in Haverhill, Mass.; son of Benjamin (a distributor) and Ida (Saberlinsky) Sable; married Minna Gibbs, February 5, 1950; children: James S., Charles D. *Education:* Boston University, A.B., 1946, M.A., 1952; Universidad Nacional Autonoma de Mexico, Doctorate, 1952; Simmons College, M.S., 1959. *Home:* 4518 North Larkin St., Milwaukee, Wis. 53211. *Office:* School of Library and Information Science, University of Wisconsin, Milwaukee, Wis.

CAREER: Northeastern University, Boston, Mass., staff librarian and bibliographer, 1959-63; California State College at Los Angeles (now California State University, Los Angeles), language librarian, 1963-64; Los Angeles County Library, Hawthorne, Calif., reference librarian, 1964-65; University of California, Los Angeles, assistant research professor at Latin American Center, 1965-68; University of Wisconsin—Milwaukee, School of Library and Information Science, associate professor, 1968—. Bibliographer, Office of Latin American Studies, Harvard University, 1962-63. *Member:* Institute of International Education, Library Association of Colombia (honorary member), American Library Association, Conference on Latin American History, Association of American Library Schools, Latin American Studies Association, American Association of University Professors, North Central Council of Latin Americanists.

WRITINGS: A Selective Bibliography in Science and Engineering, G. K. Hall, 1964; *Master Directory for Latin America,* Latin American Center, University of California (Los Angeles), 1965; *Periodicals for Latin American Economic Development, Trade and Finance: An Annotated Bibliography,* Latin American Center, University of California, 1965; (contributor) Jose Rubia Barcia and M. A. Zeitlin, editors, Unamuno, *Creator and Creation,* University of California Press, 1967; *A Guide to Latin American Studies,* two volumes, Latin American Center, University of California, 1967; *UFO Guide: 1947-1967,* Rainbow Press, 1967; *Communism in Latin America, an International Bibliography: 1900-1945,* Latin American Center, University of California, 1968; *A Bio-Bibliography of the Kennedy Family,* Scarecrow, 1969; *Urbanization Research, with Special Reference to Latin America: An Inventory,* Center for Latin American Studies, University of Wisconsin—Milwaukee, 1969; *Latin American Agriculture: A Bibliography,* Center for Latin American Studies, University of Wisconsin—Milwaukee, 1970; *Latin American Studies in the Non-Western World and Eastern Europe,* Scarecrow, 1970; *Latin American Urbanization: A Guide to the Literature, Organizations and Personnel,* Scarecrow, 1971; *International and Area Studies Librarianship: Case Studies,* Scarecrow, 1973; *The Guerrilla Movement in Latin America,* University of Wisconsin—Milwaukee, 1977. Also author of *Latin American Jewry: A Research Guide,* 1977. Contributor to *New England Modern Language Association Bulletin, Current History, American Documentation, International Library Re-*

view, *RQ,* and *International Educational and Cultural Exchange.*

WORK IN PROGRESS: Latin American Research Resources.

SIDELIGHTS: Martin Sable speaks fluent Spanish and French, and is competent in Portuguese, German, Italian, Latin, and Hebrew. *Avocational interests:* Folklore.

*   *   *

SAERCHINGER, Cesar 1884-1971

October 23, 1884—October 10, 1971; French-born American radio broadcaster, foreign correspondent, and musicologist. Obituaries: *New York Times,* October 11, 1971; *Washington Post,* October 12, 1971.

*   *   *

SAINSBURY, Eric (Edward) 1925-

PERSONAL: Born December 16, 1925, in London, England; married, 1956; children: one son. *Education:* Balliol College, Oxford, B.A., 1950, M.A., 1954; University of Sheffield, postgraduate diploma in social studies, 1955; London School of Economics and Political Science, certificate in applied social studies, 1956. *Residence:* Sheffield, England. *Office:* Department of Sociological Studies, University of Sheffield, Sheffield, England.

CAREER: Probation officer in various locations in England, 1956—; University of Sheffield, Sheffield, England, tutor in casework, 1961-66, lecturer and senior lecturer, 1966-77, professor of social administration, 1977—. *Member:* Association of Social Work Teachers, Association of University Teachers, British Association of Social Workers, Association of Teachers in Social Work Education, Sheffield City Probation Committee, Joint University Council for Social and Public Administration (chairman, social work education committee).

WRITINGS: (Editor) *Field Work in Social Administration Courses,* National Council of Social Service, 1966; (contributor) *Supervision of Community Work Students,* National Council of Social Service, 1969; (contributor) *Field Work for Community Work,* National Council of Social Service, 1970; *Social Diagnosis in Casework,* Routledge & Kegan Paul, 1970; (contributor) *Field Work Training for Social Work,* H.M.S.O., 1971; *Social Work with Families,* Routledge & Kegan Paul, 1975; *The Personal Social Services,* Pitman, 1977. Contributor to *International Social Work, Indian Journal of Social Work, Crucible,* and *Case Conference;* book reviewer in *Social Work Today, British Journal of Social Work, Journal of Social Policy,* and other professional journals. Member of editorial board, *British Journal of Social Work.*

WORK IN PROGRESS: Organizational influences on the perceptions of social work practices; social factors contributing to infant deaths.

*   *   *

St. CLAIR, David 1932-

PERSONAL: Born October 2, 1932, in Newton Falls, Ohio; son of Lee (a millwright) and Ruth (Sutton) St. Clair. *Education:* Attended Columbia University and New School for Social Research. *Agent:* James Brown Associates, Inc., 22 East 60th St., New York, N.Y. 10022.

CAREER: St. Clair spent five years as a professional actor; in 1956 he went to Mexico and then started by land to travel into Central and South America; he reached Brazil, where he worked full-time for *Time* and *Life* until 1965; currently a free-lance writer, and lecturer on the occult. Psychic consultant for national television series, "You Asked For It." *Member:* Screen Writers Guild, Authors Guild, International Platform Association, American Society for Psychical Research, California Society for Psychical Research (past president), London Society for Psychical Research.

WRITINGS: (Translator) Carolina Maria de Jesus, *Child of the Dark,* Dutton, 1962 (published in England as *Beyond All Pity,* Souvenir Press, 1962); *The Mighty, Mighty Amazon,* Funk, 1968; (with Charles A. Cabell) *Safari: Pan Am's Guide to Hunting with Gun and Camera,* Pan American Airways, 1968; *Drum and Candle,* Doubleday, 1971; *The Psychic World of California,* Doubleday, 1972; *Psychic Healers,* Doubleday, 1973; *How Your Psychic Powers Can Make You Rich,* Bantam, 1975; *Pagans, Priests and Prophets,* Prentice-Hall, 1976; *Watseka,* Playboy Press, 1977; *Instant ESP,* Prentice-Hall, 1978. Contributor to many magazines, "from London to Johannesburg and from *Playboy* to *Catholic Digest.*" Also author of syndicated column, "The Occult," published in *San Francisco Chronicle* and other newspapers.

WORK IN PROGRESS: The St. Patrick Brigade, for Fawcett; a psychic novel trilogy, for Souvenir Press.

SIDELIGHTS: David St. Clair told *CA:* "I made many expeditions into the Amazon and Mato Grosso jungles. I've lived with naked Indians, dined on gold plates with presidents, and have been initiated into voodoo temples. . . . I've talked to spirits, communicated with and even photographed a ghost, but the living still interest me more than the dead. I believe in the spirit world, in reincarnation, and in spirit intervention in our lives. I've seen too much of it *not* to believe." St. Clair continues: "Now I'm branching out into other lines, mostly historical fiction where I can mix facts with paranormal happenings. I'm quite excited about the new direction."

*   *   *

SAINT-DENIS, Michel   1897-1971

September 13, 1897—July 31, 1971; French-born British stage director and producer. Obituaries: *New York Times,* August 1, 1971, August 2, 1971; *Washington Post,* August 3, 1971. (See index for *CA* sketch)

*   *   *

SALADINO, Salvatore   1922-

PERSONAL: Born September 5, 1922, in Italy; son of Giuseppe (a civil servant) and Francesca (Calcara) Saladino; married Zina Mannone, June 21, 1953; children: Joseph Francis, Casper Christopher. *Education:* College of the City of New York (now City College of the City University of New York), B.S.S., 1947; Columbia University, A.M., 1948, Ph.D., 1955. *Home:* 27 Poppy Dr., Massapequa Park, N.Y. 11762. *Office:* Department of History, Queens College of the City University of New York, Flushing, N.Y. 11367

CAREER: Queens College of the City University of New York, Flushing, N.Y., 1955—, began as instructor, professor of history, 1970—. Visiting Fulbright lecturer, Universities of Pavia, Naples, Florence, 1956-57; visiting lecturer, Cooper Union, 1962; visiting professor, Columbia University, 1967. Presented radio programs on contemporary civilization on WNYC-Radio, 1961-62, and WHN-Ra-

dio, 1962-64. *Military service:* U.S. Army, Military Intelligence, 1943-46; became sergeant. U.S. Army Reserve, 1946-64; became first lieutenant. *Member:* Society for Italian Historical Studies, American Historical Association, American Catholic Historical Association. *Awards, honors:* Fulbright research award, Italy, 1949-50; Fulbright lecture award, Italy, 1956-57.

WRITINGS: (Contributor) Hans Rogger and Eugen Weber, editors, *The European Right,* University of California Press, 1965; (with Shepard B. Clough) *A History of Modern Italy,* Columbia University Press, 1968; *Italy from Unification to 1919,* Crowell, 1970; (contributor) Edward R. Tannenbaum and Emiliana P. Noether, editors, *Modern Italy,* New York University Press, 1974. Contributor to history journals.

WORK IN PROGRESS: The Italian Parliament at War: 1914-1919.

AVOCATIONAL INTERESTS: Modern and contemporary symphonic music, Italian opera.

*   *   *

SALEH, Dennis   1942-

PERSONAL: Surname is pronounced *Say*-luh; born December 8, 1942, in Chicago, Ill.; son of William (a businessman) and Kathryn (McKoy) Saleh; married Michele Johnson, September 13, 1969; children: Brandon Michael, Bree Danelle. *Education:* Fresno State College (now California State University, Fresno), B.A. (psychology), 1964; University of Arizona, graduate study, 1965-66; University of California, Irvine, M.F.A. (creative writing), 1968. *Home:* 1996 Grandview, Seaside, Calif. 93955.

CAREER: University of California, Riverside, lecturer in English, 1968-69; lecturer in creative writing at University of California, Santa Cruz, 1969-71, and California State University, San Diego (now San Diego State University), 1972-73; California State University, Fresno, lecturer in English, 1973-74.

WRITINGS: (Editor with James McMichael) *Just What the Country Needs, Another Poetry Anthology,* Wadsworth, 1971; *A Guide to Familiar American Incest* (poems), Triskelion Press, 1972; *Palmway* (poems), Ithaca House, 1976; *100 Chameleons* (poems), New Rivers Press, 1978.

WORK IN PROGRESS: Two collections of poems, *Very Funny* and *Says Who; Rock Art,* an anthology of record album covers.

*   *   *

SALLIS, James   1944-

PERSONAL: Born December 21, 1944, in Helena, Ark.; son of Chappelle H. (a clerk) and Mildred (Liming) Sallis; married Jane Rose (an artist), February 21, 1964; children: Dylan Anthony. *Education:* Attended Tulane University, 1962-64. *Politics:* None. *Religion:* None.

CAREER: Free-lance writer; previously employed as college instructor, publisher's reader, and magazine editor.

WRITINGS: A Few Last Words, Hart-Davis, 1969, Macmillan, 1970; (editor) *The War Book,* Dell, 1971; (editor) *The Shores Beneath,* Avon, 1971; *Down Home: Country-Western,* Macmillan, 1971. Editor, *New Worlds,* London, 1969-70.††

*   *   *

SALTONSTALL, Richard, Jr.   1937-

PERSONAL: Born March 14, 1937, in Boston, Mass.; son

of Richard, Sr. and Mary Bowditch (Rogers) Saltonstall; married Emily Lincoln Davis, June 13, 1959; children: Richard III, Mary Rogers, Patrick Gurdon, Andrew Cunningham. *Education:* Harvard University, B.A., 1959. *Politics:* Independent. *Religion:* Episcopalian. *Home and office:* 9310 Georgetown Pike, Great Falls, Va. 22066. *Agent:* Mitchell Hamilburg Agency, 292 South La Cienega Blvd., Suite 212, Beverly Hills, Calif. 90211.

CAREER: Seattle Times, Seattle, Wash., reporter, 1961-64; free-lance reporter, Seattle, 1964-65; *Time* (magazine), correspondent from San Francisco, Calif., 1965-67, correspondent from Washington, D.C., 1967-71; free-lance journalist, 1971—. President, Wilderness Public Rights Fund, and Blackfly Furniture Co. Member of State of Virginia Commission on Solid Waste Disposal, and Piedmont Environmental Council. *Military service:* U.S. Navy, 1959-61; became lieutenant.

MEMBER: Conservation Foundation, Sierra Club, National Audubon Society, Smithsonian Institution, National History Museum, National Trust for Historic Preservation, National Parks Association, International Oceanography Foundation, American Rivers Conservation Council (member of steering committee), American Canoe Association, Canoe Cruisers Association, Appalachian Mountain Club, California Tomorrow, Maine Nature Conservancy (vice-chairman), Maine Natural Resources Council, Mystic Seaport.

WRITINGS: Your Environment and What You Can Do about It, Walker & Co., 1971; (with James K. Page, Jr.) *Brownout and Slowdown,* Walker & Co., 1972; *Maine Pilgrimage,* Little, Brown, 1974. Contributing editor, *Living Wilderness.*

WORK IN PROGRESS: Articles on Maine and environmental topics and on historical biography.

SIDELIGHTS: Richard Saltonstall told *CA:* "Writing is a day to day proposition, like any other job. You can't write in inspirational spurts or moves. You keep plugging, even if the stuff is drivel. You can't get sidetracked, as I have, into 'causes'."

* * *

SAMUEL, Maurice 1895-1972

February 8, 1895—May 4, 1972; American author, critic, and lecturer on Jewish themes. Obituaries: *New York Times,* May 5, 1972; *Washington Post,* May 6, 1972.

* * *

SANCHEZ, Sonia 1934-

PERSONAL: Born September 9, 1934, in Birmingham, Ala.; daughter of Wilson L. and Lena (Jones) Driver; children: Anita, Morani, Mungu. *Education:* Hunter College (now Hunter College of the City University of New York), B.A., 1955. *Politics:* "Blackness."

CAREER: Staff member, Downtown Community School, San Francisco, Calif., 1965-67; San Francisco State College (now University), San Francisco, instructor, 1966-68; University of Pittsburgh, Pittsburgh, Pa., assistant professor, 1969-70; Rutgers University, New Brunswick, N.J., assistant professor, 1970-71; Manhattan Community College of the City University of New York, New York, N.Y., assistant professor of Black literature and creative writing, 1971-73. Teacher of creative writing, City College of the City University of New York, 1972; associate professor, University of Massachusetts—Amherst, 1972-73. *Awards, honors:*

P.E.N. Writing Award, 1969; National Institute of Arts and Letters grant, 1970; Ph.D., Wilberforce University.

WRITINGS: Homecoming (poetry), Broadside Press, 1969; *We a BaddDDD People* (poetry), Broadside Press, 1970; *It's a New Day: Poems for Young Brothas and Sistuhs,* Broadside Press, 1971; (editor) *Three Hundred and Sixty Degrees of Blackness Comin' at You* (poems), 5x Publishing Co., 1971; *Love Poems,* Third Press, 1973; *A Blues Book for Blue Magical Women* (poems), Broadside Press, 1973; *The Adventures of Fat Head and Square Head* (juvenile), Third Press, 1973; (editor) *We Be Word Sorcerers: 25 Stories by Black Americans* (anthology), Bantam, 1973; *The Afternoon of Small Head, Fat Head and Square Head* (juvenile), Third Press, 1974.

Contributor of poetry to numerous anthologies, including *Potero Negro* ("Black Power"), edited by Roberto Giammanco, Giu. Laterza & Figli, 1968, *BlackFire,* edited by LeRoi Jones and Roy Neal, Morrow, 1968, *For Malcolm: Poems on the Life and Death of Malcolm X,* edited by Dudley Randall and Margaret G. Burroughs, Broadside, 1968, *The Writing on the Wall: One Hundred Eight American Poems of Protest,* edited by Walter Lowenfels, Doubleday, 1969, *In a Time of Revolution: Poems from Our Third World,* edited by Lowenfels, Random House, 1970, *Soulscript,* edited by June M. Jordan, Doubleday, 1970, *Broadside Treasury,* edited by Gwendolyn Brooks, Broadside, 1971, *Black Poets,* edited by Dudley Randall, Bantam, 1971, *We Speak as Liberators: Young Black Poets,* edited by Orde Coombs, Dodd, 1971. Poems also included in *Night Comes Softly* and *Black and Loud.*

Plays: "The Bronx Is Next," first produced in New York at Theatre Black, October 3, 1970; "Sister Son/ji," first produced with "Cop and Blow" and "Players Inn" by Neil Harris and "Gettin' It Together" by Richard Wesley as "Black Visions," Off-Broadway at New York Shakespeare Festival Public Theatre, 1972 (included in *New Plays from Black Theatre*). Also author of plays, "Dirty Hearts," 1972, "Malcolm/Man Don't Live Here No More," 1972, and "Uh Huh, But How Do It Free Us," 1973. Contributor to periodicals, including *Black Scholar, Journal of Black Poetry, Negro Digest,* and *Nickel Review.*

BIOGRAPHICAL/CRITICAL SOURCES: Black World, June, 1971; *Newsweek,* April 17, 1972; *Time,* May 1, 1972; *Black Creation,* fall, 1973; *Contemporary Literary Criticism,* Volume V, Gale, 1976.†

* * *

SAND, Richard E(ugene) 1924-

PERSONAL: Born January 16, 1924, in Cleveland, Ohio; son of Nathan Joseph and Ida E. (Pearlman) Sand; married Morleen Snider, April 7, 1944; children: Lauren Joy, Terry Ellen. *Education:* Ohio State University, B.A., 1946, M.D., 1950. *Agent:* Arthur Pine Associates, Inc., 1780 Broadway, New York, N.Y. 10019. *Office:* 5400 Balboa Blvd., Encino, Calif. 91316.

CAREER: Fitzsimons General Hospital, Denver, Colo., intern, 1950-51; general medical practice, Akron, Ohio, 1951-57; Hollywood Presbyterian Hospital, Los Angeles, Calif., resident in obstetrics and gynecology, 1957-60; private practice of obstetrics and gynecology in Encino, Calif., 1960—. Diplomate, American Board of Obstetrics and Gynecology. *Military service:* U.S. Army Air Forces, 1941-45; became captain; received Distinguished Flying Cross, Air Medal with oak leaf cluster, and Presidential Citation. *Awards, honors:* Fellow, American College of Obstetricians and Gynecologists.

WRITINGS: Things Your Mother Never Told You, Nash Publishing, 1971; *Just for Women,* Wilshire,. 1976. Contributor of articles to *Cosmopolitan, Modern Girl, Woman's Magazine,* and *Physician's Management.*

WORK IN PROGRESS: A book, *Expectant Fatherhood.*

*   *   *

SANDERS, Dorothy Lucie   1917-
(Lucy Walker)

PERSONAL: Born May 4, 1917, in Boulder Gold Fields, Western Australia; daughter of William Joseph (a clergyman and founder of Christ Church Grammar School, Western Australia) and Ada Lucy (Walker) McClemans; married Colsell Sanders (an emeritus professor and former chairman of Tertiary Education Commission in Western Australia), September 5, 1936; children: Jonathan William, Colin Creeth and Lucyann (twins). *Education:* Attended Perth College for ten years and University of Western Australia as part-time student for four years; Claremont Teachers' College, Teachers' Certificate, 1938. *Politics:* "No fixed attitudes but tend to Liberal." *Religion:* Church of England. *Home:* 20 Jukes Way, Wembley Gardens, Western Australia 6016, Australia. *Agent:* Paul R. Reynolds, Inc., 12 East 41st St., New York, N.Y. 10017.

CAREER: Former teacher in Australia; writer and lecturer. Member of State Library Board, Western Australia; former member, State Advisory Board to Australian Broadcasting Commission, and Children's Court, Perth. *Member:* Society of Women Writers and Journalists (London), Australian Society of Authors, Fellowship of Australian Writers, Royal Perth Yacht Club (associate member). `

WRITINGS: Fairies on the Doorstep, Australasian Publishing Co., 1948; *Six for Heaven,* Hodder & Stoughton, 1953, reprinted under pseudonym Lucy Walker, Collins, 1969; *Shining River,* Hodder & Stoughton, 1954, reprinted under pseudonym Lucy Walker, Collins, 1969; *Waterfall,* Hodder & Stoughton, 1956; *Ribbons in Her Hair,* Hodder & Stoughton, 1957; *Pepper Tree Bay,* Hodder & Stoughton, 1959; *Monday in Summer,* Hodder & Stoughton, 1961.

Under pseudonym Lucy Walker; published by Collins, except as indicated: *Sweet and Faraway,* 1954, Arcadia House, 1957; *One Who Kisses,* 1954; *Come Home, Dear,* 1956; *Heaven Is Here,* Arcadia House, 1957; *Master of Ransome,* Arcadia House, 1958; *Orchard Hill,* Arcadia House, 1958; *Stranger from the North,* 1959; *Kingdom of the Heart,* 1959; *Love in a Cloud,* 1960; *Loving Heart,* 1960; *The Moonshiner,* 1961, published as *Cupboard Love,* Arcadia House, 1963; *Wife to Order,* 1961, Arcadia House, 1962; *The Distant Hills,* 1962; *Down in the Forest,* 1962; *The Call of the Pines,* 1963, Arcadia House, 1966; *Follow Your Star,* 1963; *A Man Called Masters,* 1963; *Reaching for the Stars,* 1964; *The Man from Outback,* 1964; *The Other Girl,* 1965, Arcadia House, 1967; *The Ranger in the Hills,* 1966; *Reaching for the Stars,* 1966; *The River Is Down,* 1967; *Home at Sundown,* 1968; *The Gone-Away Man,* 1969; *The Bell Branch,* 1970; *Joyday for Jodi,* 1971; *The Mountain that Went to the Sea,* 1972; *Girl Alone,* 1973; *The Run Away Girl,* 1975; *Gamma's Girl,* 1977. Contributor of short stories and articles to magazines in Australia and the United Kingdom.

SIDELIGHTS: Dorothy Sanders told *CA* she "began writing for school magazines and has 'never stopped.'" Sanders regularly visits the Australian outback, the locale of many of her books. *Avocational interests:* Collecting the work of Australian writers and painters and early colonial furniture; golf, yachting.

*   *   *

SANDERS, Marion K.   1905-1977

PERSONAL: Born August 14, 1905; married Theodore M. Sanders, 1926 (died, 1965); children: Mary Von Euler, Michael. *Education:* Wellesley College, B.A., 1925. *Home:* 200 East 33rd St., New York, N.Y. 10016. *Office: Atlas World Press Review,* 230 Park Ave., New York, N.Y. 10017.

CAREER: Port of New York Authority, New York City, assistant director of public relations, 1939-44; U.S. Office of War Information, Washington, D.C., news editor, 1944-46; U.S. Department of State, Washington, D.C., editor-in-chief of *Amerika* (Russian-language magazine) and chief of magazine branch of overseas publications, 1946-52; free-lance writer, 1952-58; *Harper's,* New York City, senior editor, 1958-70, contributing editor, 1970-77; *Atlas World Press Review,* New York City, managing editor, 1973-77. Adjunct assistant professor of writing, School of Continuing Education, New York University, 1967-68; free-lance writer and editor, 1970-77. New York correspondent, "Regional Report," National Educational Television, 1965-66. *Member:* Society of American Historians (fellow), American Civil Liberties Union (member of national board, 1967-68; member of mass communications committee, 1969-77), Citizens Committee for Children of New York (member of board of directors, 1972-77). *Awards, honors:* Distinguished Alumna Award, Wellesley College, 1973; Kappa Tau Alpha Award for research in journalism, 1974; Front Page Award, Newswomen's Club of New York, 1974.

WRITINGS: The Lady and the Vote, Houghton, 1956; (editor) *The Crisis in American Medicine,* Harper, 1961; *The Professional Radical: Conversations with Saul Alinsky,* Harper, 1970; *Dorothy Thompson: Legend in Her Time,* Houghton, 1973. Contributor of articles to *Harper's, Columbia Journalism Review,* and *New York Times Magazine.*

(Died September 16, 1977)

*   *   *

SANDERSON, Peter (Crawshaw)   1929-

PERSONAL: Born May 8, 1929, in Dewsbury, England; son of Sydney Auty (a clerk) and Marianne (Crawshaw) Sanderson; married Eileen Orr, December 22, 1956; children: Julia Alison. *Education:* Hertford College, Oxford, M.A., 1950. *Home:* 5 Clyde Rd., Wallington, Surrey, England. *Office:* LAMSAC, 35 Belgrave Sq., London S.W.1, England.

CAREER: National Cash Register Ltd., London, England, programmer, 1961-64; Atlas Computing Service, London, England, training officer, 1964-66; Wandsworth Technical College, London, England, senior lecturer, 1966-70; LAMSAC (management services), London, England, advisory officer, 1970—. Consultant on local government computer applications.

WRITINGS: Computers for Management, Pan Books, 1969; *Computer Languages,* Butterworth & Co., 1970; *Interactive Computing in BASIC: An Introduction to Interactive Computing and a Practical Course in the BASIC Language,* Petrocelli, 1973; *Management Information Systems and the Computer,* Pan Books, 1975; *Minicomputers,* Butterworth & Co., 1976.

AVOCATIONAL INTERESTS: The music of Elgar, computer applications in the arts, medieval history, genealogy.†

* * *

SANDVED, Arthur O. 1931-

PERSONAL: Born February 2, 1931, in New York, N.Y.; son of Ole and Ane (Aarsland) Sandved; married Ruth Oegaard, August 22, 1953; children: Kristin Elisabeth, Anne Reidun, Margrete. *Education:* University of Oslo, Candidatus Philologiae, 1959, Ph.D., 1968. *Politics:* Conservative. *Religion:* Christian. *Home:* Nordengveien 3, Billingstad, Norway. *Office:* British Institute, University of Oslo, P.O. Box 1003, Blindern, Oslo 3, Norway.

CAREER: University of Trondheim, Trondheim, Norway, lecturer in English, 1959-62; University of Oslo, Oslo, Norway, lecturer, 1963-70, reader in English philology, 1971-74, professor of English language, 1974—.

WRITINGS: (With Paul Christophersen) *Notes on English Grammar,* Universitetsforlaget (Oslo), 1967; *Studies in the Language of Caxton's Malory and That of the Winchester Manuscript,* Humanities, 1968; (with Christophersen) *An Advanced English Grammar,* Macmillan (London), 1969, Humanities, 1970; *Exercises in English Grammar,* Norwegian Universities Press, 1971.

WORK IN PROGRESS: Studying the genesis of Abbot Aelfric's rhythmical prose.

* * *

SANJIAN, Avedis K(rikor) 1921-

PERSONAL: Born February 24, 1921, in Marash, Turkey; naturalized U.S. citizen; son of Krikor (a coppersmith) and Nazle (Kalayan) Sanjian; married Helen Karaghuzian, 1950; children: Gregory. *Education:* American University of Beirut, B.A., 1949; University of Michigan, M.A., 1950, Ph.D., 1956. *Religion:* Armenian Apostolic. *Home:* 545 Muskingum Pl., Pacific Palisades, Calif. 90272. *Office:* Department of Near Eastern Languages and Cultures, University of California, Los Angeles, Calif. 90024.

CAREER: Harvard University, Cambridge, Mass., research fellow, 1957-61, assistant professor of Armenian, 1961-65; University of California, Los Angeles, associate professor, 1965-68, professor of Armenian, 1968—, director of Armenian studies program, 1969—. *Member:* American Oriental Society, Middle East Institute, Middle East Studies Association.

WRITINGS: The Armenian Communities in Syria under Ottoman Dominion, Harvard University Press, 1965; *Colophons of Armenian Manuscripts, 1301-1480: A Source for Middle Eastern History,* Harvard University Press, 1969; *A Catalogue of Medieval Armenian Manuscripts in the United States,* University of California Press, 1976. Contributor to professional journals.

WORK IN PROGRESS: Editing, with Andreas Tietze, Eremya Chelebi Komurjan's *The Jewish Bride; The Armenian School of Miniature Painting at Gladzor,* with Thomas Mathews; *Vahan Tekryan: An Armenian Poet Laureate.*

* * *

SAPORI, Armando 1892-

PERSONAL: Born July 11, 1892, in Siena, Italy; son of Giuseppe and Zuleika (Lenzi) Sapori; married Cadira Nervegna, February 11, 1920 (deceased); children: Giuliana. *Education:* University of Siena, Laureato in giurisprudenza (Doctor of Jurisprudence), 1919. *Politics:* Independent (on the left). *Religion:* Roman Catholic. *Home:* Via Sabbatini 8, Milan, Italy 20136.

CAREER: Providence of Firenze (Florence), Italy, archivist, 1921-32; University of Ferrara, Ferrara, Italy, professor extraordinary of economic and financial history, 1932-35; Commercial University Luigi Bocconi, Milan, Italy, head of economic history, 1932-65, rector, 1952-67; Institute of Social Science Cesare Alfieri, Florence, Italy, head of political history, 1933-35; University of Florence, Faculty of Economics and Commerce, Florence, Italy, ordinary professor of economics, 1935-62. Counselor, Municipality of Florence, 1946-51; member of Italian Senate, 1948-53 (first legislative body elected after the country became a republic).

MEMBER: International Institute of Communication (honorary member), Societa europea di cultura, Accademia nazionale dei Lincei (fellow), Accademia di scienze e lettere la Colombaria, Societa italiana per l'organizzazione internazionale, Societa italiana degli economisti, Istituto lombardo di scienze e lettere, Societa italiana di storia del diritto, Accademia delle scienze dell'Istituto di Bologna (corresponding member), Economic History Association (United States; honorary member), Serbian Academy of Sciences and Letters (foreign member), Mediaeval Academy of America (corresponding member), Royal Historical Society (corresponding member), Association Marc Bloch (member of executive committee), Rotary Club (Milan; honorary member).

AWARDS, HONORS: Honorary degrees from Faculty of Letters, University of Poitiers, 1950, and Faculty of Letters and Science, University of Paris, 1960; Premio nazionale generale della classe di scienze morali storiche e filologiche dell'Accademia nazionale dei Lincei, 1953; Medaglia d'oro dei benemeriti della scuola, della cultura e dell'arte, 1956; Medaglia d'oro di benemerenza del Commune di Milano, 1958; Knight of Legion of Honor (France), 1958; gold medal from Province of Milan, 1960; Grand Officer of Order of Merit of Italian Republic, 1965; gold medal from City of Siena, Italy, 1967; Premio Biancamano, 1968; Premio la Madonnina, 1969.

WRITINGS: (With others) *Studi su Dante e rassegna bibliografica delle pubblicazioni del secentenario* (includes studies by various authors and a review by Sapori), Deputazione Toscana di Storia Patria (Florence), 1921; *La Crisi delle compagnie mercantili dei Bardi e dei Peruzzi,* Olschki (Florence), 1926.

Una Compagnia de Calimala ai primi del Trecento, Olschki, 1932; (editor) *I Libri di commercio dei Peruzzi,* Fratelli Treves (Milan), 1934.

Studi di storia economica medievale, Sansoni (Florence), 1940, 3rd edition published as *Studi di storia economica: Secoli XIII, XIV, XV,* Volumes I-II, 1955, Volume III, 1967; *Mercatores,* Garzanti (Milan), 1941; (editor) *I Libri della ragione bancaria dei Gianfigliazzi,* Garzanti, 1943; *Il Mercante italiano nel Medio Evo* (text), Universitaria Editrice (Florence), 1945; *Mondo finito* (autobiography), Edizioni Leonardo (Rome), 1946, 2nd edition published with *Cose che capitano* (see below); *La Compagnia dei Frecobaldi in Inghilterra,* Olschki, 1947.

Lezioni di storia economica, Goliardica (Milan), 1951, enlarged edition, 1955; *Le Marchand italien au Moyen Age* (lectures and bibliography), A. Colin (Paris), 1952, translation by Patricia Ann Kennen published as *The Italian Merchant in the Middle Ages,* Norton, 1970; (editor) *I Libri degli Alberti del Giudice,* Garzanti, 1952; *Compagnie e mercanti di Firenze antica,* Barbera (Florence), 1956, translation published as *Merchants and Companies in Ancient Florence,* Barbera, 1956; *L'Eta della Rinascita: Secoli XIII-XVI,* Goliardica, 1958; *Attivita manifatturiera in Lombardia dal 1600 al 1914,* Associazione Industriale Lombarda (Milan), 1959.

Un Secolo di economia italiana: Ragioni di orgoglio e di fiducia, Cisalpino, 1966; *Come uno storico vede gli uomini* (collection of 36 of Sapori's drawings), Pizzi (Milan), 1966, 2nd edition, 1967.

(Editor) *Libro giallo della compagnia dei Covoni,* Cisalpino, 1970; *Mondo finito* [and] *Cose che capitano* (memoirs), Cisalpino, 1971; *Armando Sapori ricorda,* Cisalpino, 1971.

SIDELIGHTS: Sapori, the dean of Italian economic historians, was a journalist in his youth, writing for the daily newspaper, *Vedetta Senese.* The first volume of his memoirs, *Mondo finito,* covers the rise of the middle class in Italy, fascism, and the second World War. The second, *Cose che capitano,* deals with his political experiences under the Republic and academic life. He is a violinist, philatelist (specializing in the postage of earlier Italy), and an artist. He has, he says, traded his drawing board for clay (sculpture), working on human figures and animals of fantasy.

BIOGRAPHICAL/CRITICAL SOURCES: Giuliana Sapori, *Elenco degli scritti di Armando Sapori,* [Florence], 1952; *Studi in onore di Armando Sapori,* two volumes, Cisalpino, 1957 (contains ''Profil d' Armando Sapori,'' by Lucien Febvre and ''Armando Sapori storico'' by Gino Luzzatto); *Notizie sull'attivita: La Vita e le opere di Armando Sapori,* University of Florence, 1962; *Belfagor,* number 6, 1962; *Nuova Rivista Storica,* Volume XLVII, 1963; *Armando Sapori ricorda,* Cisalpino, 1971.†

*   *   *

SARNOFF, Dorothy 1917-

PERSONAL: Born May 25, 1917, in New York, N.Y.; daughter of Jacob (a surgeon) and Belle (Roosin) Sarnoff; married Milton Raymond (a stockbroker), March 15, 1957. *Education:* Cornell University, B.A., 1935. *Home:* 40 Central Park S., New York, N.Y. 10019. *Office:* Dorothy Sarnoff Speech Dynamics, Inc., 111 West 57th St., New York, N.Y. 10019.

CAREER: Singer-actress, appearing on Broadway in ''The King and I,'' ''Magdalena,'' ''Rosalinda,'' and ''My Darling Aida,'' and with New York City Center Opera, Philadelphia Opera, and Los Angeles Civic Light Opera; vocal soloist with New York Philharmonic and San Francisco, Los Angeles, and Philadelphia Symphony Orchestras; speech consultant to industry, politicians, and television personalities; chairman of Dorothy Sarnoff Speech Dynamics, Inc., New York City. Lecturer, currently giving seminars for business executives in England, France, Austria, Denmark, Sweden, and the United States.

WRITINGS: Speech Can Change Your Life: Tips on Speech, Conversation, and Speech Making, Doubleday, 1970.

WORK IN PROGRESS: A second book.

SIDELIGHTS: Dorothy Sarnoff told *CA:* ''I write out of my experiences in consulting and teaching courses . . . in how to present yourself to others through alternatives of behavior—whether on the dais, on TV, at congressional meetings. . . . All my work is done with closed-circuit TV. It gives the best evidence about yourself.''

BIOGRAPHICAL/CRITICAL SOURCES: Variety, December 2, 1970.

SATTLER, Helen Roney 1921-

PERSONAL: Born March 2, 1921, in Newton, Iowa; daughter of Louie Earl (a farmer) and Hazel (Cure) Roney; married Robert E. Sattler (a chemical engineer), September 30, 1950; children: Richard, Kathryn. *Education:* Southwest Missouri State College (now University), B.S., 1946; Famous Artist's School, Certificate in Commercial Art, 1960. *Politics:* Democrat. *Religion:* Christian. *Residence:* Bartlesville, Okla. 74003.

CAREER: Elementary teacher in Aldrich, Mo., 1941-42, Norwood, Mo., 1942-45, and Marshfield, Mo., 1945-48; Kansas City Public Library, Kansas City, Mo., children's librarian, 1948-49; Standard Oil of New Jersey, elementary teacher at company school on Aruba (Dutch island off Venezuelan coast), 1949-50. *Member:* Society of Children's Book Writers, Oklahoma Writers Federation, Bartlesville Artist's Association (treasurer, 1960), Bartlesville Writer's Association (chairman, 1967-68).

WRITINGS: Kitchen Carton Crafts, Lothrop, 1970; *A Beginning to Read Book of Puzzles,* Denison, 1971; *Holiday Gifts, Favors and Decorations,* Lothrop, 1971; *The Eggless Cookbook,* A. S. Barnes, 1972; *Sockcraft,* Lothrop, 1972; *Jewelry from Junk,* Lothrop, 1973; *Recipes for Art and Craft Materials,* Lothrop, 1973; *Jar and Bottle Craft,* Lothrop, 1974; *Train Whistles,* Lothrop, 1977; *Bible Puzzle Collection,* Baker Book, 1977; *Bible Puzzle Pack,* Baker Book, 1977. Contributor of puzzles, how-to articles, stories, and verse to more than forty magazines, including *Child Life, Junior Discoveries, Jack and Jill, Boys' Life, Wee Wisdom, Instructor, Cricket, Trails,* and *Highlights for Children.*

WORK IN PROGRESS: A nature book, a puzzle book, and a craft book.

SIDELIGHTS: Helen Sattler writes: ''Many years of experience working with children as a teacher, mother, and Scout leader led to my creating crafts and puzzles, first for magazine publication then in books. I believe that puzzles stimulate their minds and that most children can be taught to work with their hands and be creative if shown a few basic designs to get them started. A toy or gift made by themselves is more valuable than an expensive one bought in a store. Creative work need not be expensive. This is what I try to show in my craft books.'' Sattler has visited most of the fifty states, Canada, Mexico, Haiti, Cuba, and Aruba.

AVOCATIONAL INTERESTS: Painting, drawing, cooking, crafts, and puzzle solving.

*   *   *

SAULS, Roger 1944-

PERSONAL: Born November 7, 1944, in Hahira, Ga. *Politics:* None. *Religion:* ''All.'' *Home:* 36-C Stratford Hills, Chapel Hill, N.C. 27514.

CAREER: Manager of a bookstore in Chapel Hill, N.C., 1968—. *Awards, honors:* Discovery grant, National Endowment for the Arts, 1970.

WRITINGS: The Gun Child, Grande Ronde, 1968; *Swarm,* Poetry Review Press, 1970; *Light,* Loom Press, 1975. Editor, *New Lazarus Review.*

*   *   *

SAVAGE, Leonard J(immie) 1917-1971

November 20, 1917—November 3, 1971; American mathematician and educator. Obituaries: *New York Times,* November 4, 1971. (See index for *CA* sketch)

SAVITT, Ronald 1939-

PERSONAL: Born September 3, 1939, in Reno, Nev.; son of Sol (a businessman) and Ella (Levin) Savitt. *Education:* University of California, Berkeley, A.B., 1961, M.B.A., 1963; University of Pennsylvania, Ph.D., 1967. *Office:* Faculty of Business Administration and Commerce, University of Alberta, Edmonton, Alberta, Canada T6G 2G1.

CAREER: Boston University, Boston, Mass., associate professor of marketing, 1966-72; University of Alberta, Faculty of Business Administration and Commerce, Edmonton, professor, 1973—, chairman of department of marketing and economic analysis, 1976. *Member:* American Economic Association, Academy of Political and Social Scientists, Canadian Economics Association, American Marketing Association. *Awards, honors:* Hays-Fulbright fellow to Turkey, 1972-73.

WRITINGS: (With J. C. Narver) *The Marketing Economy: An Analytical Approach,* Holt, 1971; (editor with Narver) *Analytical Readings in the Marketing Economy,* Holt, 1971; *Marketing and Economic Development: The Case of Turkey,* Bagazici University, 1973; (with S. A. Braun and M. J. Dunn) *Analysis for Marketing Strategies: A Canadian Perspective,* University of Alberta, 1974; *A Survey of Methodologies for Evaluating the Effectiveness of Consumer Programmes,* Consumer Research Council (Canada), 1975.

*   *   *

SAX, Joseph L. 1936-

PERSONAL: Born February 3, 1936, in Chicago, Ill.; son of Benjamin H. and Mary (Silverman) Sax; married Eleanor C. Gettes, June 18, 1958; children: Katherine Elaine, Valerie Beth, Anne-Marie. *Education:* Harvard University, A.B., 1957; University of Chicago, J.D., 1959. *Office:* Law School, University of Michigan, Ann Arbor, Mich. 48104.

CAREER: Attorney in Washington, D.C., 1959-62; University of Colorado, Boulder, 1962-66, began as assistant professor, became associate professor of law; University of Michigan, Ann Arbor, professor of law, 1966—. Member of environmental studies board, National Academy of Sciences. *Military service:* U.S. Air Force Reserve, 1960-66. *Member:* American Bar Association, Michigan Bar Association. *Awards, honors:* Environmental Quality Award, U.S. Environmental Protection Agency, 1975; American Motors Conservation Award, 1976.

WRITINGS: (Contributor) Robert E. Clark, editor, *Waters and Water Rights,* Allen Smith, 1967; *Water Law: Planning and Policy,* Bobbs-Merrill, 1968; *Defending the Environment: A Strategy for Citizen Action,* introduction by George McGovern, Knopf, 1971. Contributor to law journals and to *Esquire, Saturday Review, American Heritage, New Republic, Natural History,* and other magazines.

BIOGRAPHICAL/CRITICAL SOURCES: Washington Post, April 14, 1971.

*   *   *

SAYLOR, Irene 1932-

PERSONAL: Born March 13, 1932, in Elizabethtown, Pa.; daughter of Guy R. and Evelyn (Bell) Saylor. *Education:* Albright College, B.A., 1953; Syracuse University, M.S., 1955. *Home:* 109 West King St., Lancaster, Pa. 17603. *Office:* Pennsylvania State Library, Harrisburg, Pa.

CAREER: Orange Public Library, Orange, N.J., reference librarian, 1955-58, 1964; Elizabethtown College, Elizabeth-

town, Pa., library cataloger, 1964-68; Pennsylvania State Library, Harrisburg, library cataloger, 1968—. *Awards, honors:* Philadelphia Regional Writers Conference first prize for novel, 1965.

WRITINGS: The Lilac Ghost, Crown, 1970. Also author of television plays.

WORK IN PROGRESS: A second Gothic novel.

AVOCATIONAL INTERESTS: Travel, painting in oil.

*   *   *

SAYRE, Wallace S. 1905-1972

June 24, 1905—May 18, 1972; American authority on city government. Obituaries: *New York Times,* May 19, 1972; *Washington Post,* May 20, 1972; *Publishers Weekly,* May 29, 1972; *Time,* May 29, 1972.

*   *   *

SCAER, David P(aul) 1936-

PERSONAL: Born March 13, 1936, in Brooklyn, N.Y.; son of Paul Henry (a Lutheran pastor) and Victoria (Zimmermann) Scaer; married Dorothy Hronetz (a registered nurse and instructor), June 18, 1960; children: David Paul, Jr., Stephen Charles, Peter James. *Education:* Concordia College, Bronxville, N.Y., A.A., 1955; Concordia Theological Seminary, St. Louis, Mo., B.A., 1957, M.Div., 1960, Th.D., 1963; graduate study at Kansas State University, 1958-59, and University of Muenster, 1960-62; postdoctoral study at University of Heidelberg. *Politics:* Republican. *Religion:* Lutheran. *Home:* 1211 Westwind Pl., Fort Wayne, Ind. 46825; and Pocono Pines, Pa. 18350. *Office:* Concordia Theological Seminary, Fort Wayne, Ind.

CAREER: Ordained Lutheran clergyman, 1962; University of Illinois, Champaign, part-time instructor in Bible and ethics, 1966-76; Concordia Theological Seminary, Fort Wayne, Ind. (formerly in Springfield, Ill.), assistant professor, 1966-69, associate professor, 1969-77, professor of systematic theology, 1977—. Member of Illinois Right to Life, 1973-76. *Member:* Society of Biblical Literature, Evangelical Theological Society, Concordia Historical Society. *Awards, honors:* John W. Behnken postdoctoral fellowship for study in Europe, 1969.

WRITINGS: The Lutheran World Federation Today, Concordia, 1971; *The Apostolic Scriptures,* Concordia, 1971; *What Do You Think of Jesus?,* Concordia, 1973; *Getting into the Story of the Book of Concord,* in press. Contributor to *Christianity Today, Cresset,* and *Lutheran Witness.* Editor, *Concordia Theological Quarterly.*

*   *   *

SCHAEFER, Claude 1913-

PERSONAL: Born August 11, 1913, in Breslau, Germany; son of Paul and Selma (Sulke) Schaefer; married Denise Hazera (a translator); children: Brigitte Alexandre, Marianne Alexandre Sinclair. *Education:* University of Paris, Docteur de l'Universite, 1947, Docteur es lettres d'Etat, 1971. *Home:* 23 rue Campagne Premiere, Apt. 12, 75014 Paris, France. *Office:* Institut d'Histoire de l'Art, University of Tours, 37000 Tours, France.

CAREER: Professor of art history in South America, 1942-60; University of Montreal, Montreal, Quebec, associate professor of history of art, 1963-73; University of Tours, Tours, France, professor of art history, 1973—. Visiting professor of history of art, Brandeis University, 1961, Chatham

College, 1962-63. *Member:* College Art Association of America, Societe Nationale des Antiquaires de France, Comite Francais d'Histoire de l'Art. *Awards, honors:* Carriere Award, Institut de France, 1955, for *La Sculpture en ronde-bosse au XIVe siecle dans le Duche de Bourgogne.*

WRITINGS: Joaquin Torres Garcia, Poseidon (Buenos Aires), 1947; *La Sculpture en ronde-bosse au XIVe siecle dans le Duche de Bourgogne,* Librairie Clavier (Paris), 1954; (editor) Jean Fouquet, *Les Heures d'Etienne Chevalier,* preface by Charles Sterling, Imprimeurs Draeger Freres and Editions Vilo, 1971, translation by Marianne Sinclair published as *The Hours of Etienne Chevalier,* Braziller, 1971. Contributor of articles to *Gazette des Beaux-Arts, Art Bulletin* (New York), *Bulletin* of the Societe Nationale des Antiquaires de France, and to *Encyclopaedia Universalis.*

WORK IN PROGRESS: Research on late mediaeval French art and Jean Fouquet; a catalogue of the miniatures of Jean Colombe.

AVOCATIONAL INTERESTS: South American contemporary art, pre-Colombian art of Mexico, esthetics and history of the eighteenth century.

*   *   *

SCHAFF, David 1943-

PERSONAL: Born February 16, 1943, in Bryn Mawr, Pa.; son of David Schley (an investment broker) and Dorothea (Heckscher) Schaff. *Education:* Yale University, B.A., 1965; University of California, Berkeley, M.A., 1969, Ph.D., 1974. *Home:* 1862 California St. N.W., Washington, D.C. 20009.

CAREER: University of California, Berkeley and Davis campuses, associate and instructor in art history, 1966-71; University of California, Santa Cruz, associate professor, 1973-74; University of Delaware, Newark, associate professor, 1974-76; coordinator of traveling exhibitions service, Association of Science and Technology Centers, 1976-78; museum programs and art research consultant, 1978—. *Awards, honors:* National Endowment for the Arts awards for editing first issue of *Cassiopeia,* 1968, and second issue of *Ephemeris,* 1970; Mabelle MacLeod Lewis grant for research in art history, 1970-71; Kress Fellowship, National Gallery of Art, 1972-73; University of Delaware research grant, 1975.

WRITINGS—Poems, except as indicated: *Tables,* Sun Press Leo, 1967; *The Ladder,* Dariel Press, 1968; *The Moon by Day,* Four Seasons Foundation, 1971; *Bay Articulation in Early Christian Architecture* (nonfiction), University of California Press, 1974. Contributor to small literary magazines. Contributor of articles and reviews to *Art International, Medieval and Renaissance Manuscripts from the Lessing J. Rosenwald Collection* (National Gallery of Art catalog), and other periodicals. Editor, *Cassiopeia* and *Ephemeris,* 1968-70.

WORK IN PROGRESS: Periferal Vision (prose); *An Album of Mirrors; Imaginary Guest;* prose articles on twentieth-century art and architecture.

*   *   *

SCHALK, Adolph F(rancis) 1923-

PERSONAL: Born January 17, 1923, in St. Louis, Mo.; son of Konstantin (a carpenter) and Louise (Chanitz) Schalk. *Education:* Attended St. Louis University, 1946-48, University of Notre Dame, 1953, and Marquette University, 1954.

Politics: "Democratic socialism (Democratic party)." *Religion:* Roman Catholic. *Home:* Casa Arlecchino, CH 6579 Indemini, Ticino, Switzerland.

CAREER: Queen's Work Publishers, St. Louis, Mo., editorial assistant, 1946-48; *Sun-Herald* (Roman Catholic daily newspaper), Kansas City, Mo., founding co-editor, 1949-51; *Today* Magazine, Chicago, Ill., editor, 1952-55; *The Bridge,* Hamburg, Germany, editor, 1956-62; free-lance writer and translator. Makes frequent appearances on West German television. *Member:* Swiss Foreign Press Association. *Awards, honors:* First prize, Catholic Press Association, 1949, 1964, for outstanding reporting.

WRITINGS: (With Daniel Callahan) *Federal Aid and Catholic Schools,* Helicon, 1964; (with John G. Deedy, Jr.) *Eyes on the Modern World,* Kenedy, 1965; *The Germans,* Prentice-Hall, 1971; *The Germans in America,* Claretian Publications, 1973. Author of radio scripts for West German and Swiss broadcasting studios. Contributor of numerous articles to U.S. and European publications, including *Saturday Review, Neue Zuercher Zeitung, Weltwoche,* and *Commonweal.*

WORK IN PROGRESS: Research in international humor; short stories.

SIDELIGHTS: Adolph Schalk told *CA:* "To me life is a Mount Everest and writing is like climbing it because it is there! I write for many reasons, to work off my aggressions, to get rid of pent up emotions, to drive reality into a corner, to isolate that one grain of sand on the beach that is different from all the others, and above all not to answer questions but to underline them, to emphasize the obvious and catalyze a lost sense of wonder for nature and the simple values of life. Arrogant or not, I want to be one more voice pleading and fighting for human rights, for the elimination of hunger and destitution, and, not least, to get others to share with me experiences, insights, joys of life.

"I have no illusions about reaching millions, my aim is always toward that one individual who just may happen to pick up an article or book of mine or listen to me on radio or TV. I always try to picture one person in my audience, at times of the older generation, at other times a child, and I write for that one person. If there is a spin-off reaching others, so much the better. But I don't count on it. I write essentially for the individual. In an age of growing mass regimentation individualism is increasingly important.

"My basic approach in writing is first of all to do intense research and never, never approach any topic or problem with preconceived notions of how it should be. I always let the facts tell their own story and am constantly alert to any new fact that may change or even totally upset conclusions drawn on the basis of prior facts. An extremely important principle to me also is to make a point always of seeking out the opinions of those diametrically opposed to my own conviction, to give the opposition a chance. In cases of doubt I try to state the conflicting points of view as clearly as I can and let the reader draw his (her) own conclusions. . . .

"My advice to aspiring writers is to keep writing courses to a minimum, spend at least one year driving a taxi, or as waiters, ditchdiggers, construction workers, miners, and write notes at least two hours a day. Then a year on a small town daily or weekly works wonders. Finally, they should keep in mind the famous injunction of Mark Twain, 'The difference between the right word and an almost right word is the difference between lightning and a lightning bug.' "

AVOCATIONAL INTERESTS: Hiking, music, watching

people, books, theatre, cultivated humor, swimming, boating, sightseeing.

*   *   *

SCHANG, Frederick C. 1893-

PERSONAL: Born December 15, 1893, in New York, N.Y.; son of Frederick C. (a manufacturer) and Blanche E. (Mock) Schang; married Emily Sterz, 1920; children: Frederick III (deceased), Rosalind (Mrs. Philip Swanson). *Education:* Columbia University, B.Lit., 1915. *Politics:* Independent. *Home:* 405 Seagate Tower North, 200 Mac Farlane Dr., Delray Beach, Fla. 33444; and 62 Oneck Rd., Westhampton Beach, N.Y. 11978.

CAREER: New York Tribune, New York City, dramatic reporter, 1914-17; press agent for U.S. tours, Diaghileff Ballet Russe, 1917-18; Metropolitan Musical Bureau (concert managers with clients including Caruso and Chaliapin), New York City, secretary and director, 1920-29; Columbia Artists Management, Inc., New York City, member of firm, 1930-65, president, 1955-63. Partner, Coppicus & Schang (later Schang, Doulens, & Wright; managers for Robert Shaw Chorale, Virtuosi di Roma, Trapp Family Singers, DePaur Infantry Chorus, Pro Musica, and others), New York City; has managed Lily Pons, Dorothy Kirsten, Harold Bauer, Vronsky and Babin, and introduced La Argentina, Jooss Ballet, Dancers of Bali, Royal Danish Ballet, and many others; other artists under his aegis have included Anna Case, Rosa Ponselle, Grace Moore, Jussi Bjoerling, Lotte Lehmann, Licia Albanese, Robert Merrill, Pablo Casals, Albert Spalding, Ossip Gabrilowitsch, and David Oistrakh. *Military service:* U.S. Army Air Forces, 1942-44; became major. *Awards, honors:* Ritter of Danebrog, first class, from King of Denmark, and Royal Order of Vasa, first class, from King of Sweden, both for musical achievements.

WRITINGS: Visiting Cards of Celebrities, Gale, 1971; *Visiting Cards of Prima Donnas,* Vantage Press, 1977. Also author of *Visiting Cards of Violinists,* 1975. Contributor to *The Dance Encyclopedia,* A. S. Barnes, 1949, and to music trade journals.

SIDELIGHTS: Frederick Schang has long been an ardent collector. At one time he owned an important collection of the works of the Swiss artist Paul Klee. He has also collected stamps and autographs. Since his retirement he has written books based on his collection of visiting cards. In order to avoid dispersing this collection of more than 850 cards, he gave 800 of them to the Columbia University Library in 1977. The remaining cards, on painters and sculptors, were given to the Metropolitan Museum of Art.

*   *   *

SCHECHTER, Ruth Lisa 1927-

PERSONAL: Born January 2, 1927, in Boston, Mass.; married; husband's name, Jerry. *Education:* Attended New York University, 1960-62, New School for Social Research, 1962-64, and professional writing workshops. *Religion:* Humanist. *Home:* 9 Van Cordland Pl., Croton-on-Hudson, N.Y. 10520.

CAREER: Holds New York Board of Education certification as teacher of creative writing; certified poetry therapist. Poetry therapist at Alfred Adler Mental Hygiene Clinic, 1968; poet-in-residence, Mundelein College, 1969; counsellor and poetry therapist, Odyssey House, New York, N.Y., 1971-77. Teacher of poetry workshops in Harlem, for adult education groups, and privately for special students

and ex-addicts. Has given poetry readings in coffee houses, at New York public libraries, and at colleges and universities, including Colgate University, Syracuse University, Marymount College, Hunter College of the City University of New York, University of Connecticut, Marist College, South Dakota State University, and University of Maine. Chairman of poetry/literature program, Bronx Council of the Arts, 1969; director, Croton Council on the Arts, 1977. *Member:* Poetry Society of America, Poetry Forum, American Poetry Therapists, Vermont Writers' League. *Awards, honors:* Mac Dowell Colony fellowships, 1963, 1970; Cecil Hemley Award, Poetry Society of America, 1975.

WRITINGS: Near the Wall of Lion Shadows (poems), Salt Mount Press, 1969, 2nd edition, 1970; *Movable Parts* (narrative poem), Folder Editions, 1970; *Suddenly Thunder* (poems), Barlenmir House, 1972; *Offshore* (poems), Barlenmir House, 1974. Author of two-act play, "Alan, Carlos, Theresa," produced Off-Broadway, 1969. A long-play recording of Schechter reading her poems with commentary was produced at Lamont Poetry Library of Harvard University, 1969. Work included in poetry anthologies, including *From the Belly of the Shark, The Writing on the Wall, Eidelons,* and *For Neruda: For Chile.* Contributor of poetry to periodicals, including *Prairie Schooner, Occidental Review, Forum, Southwest Review, New York Quarterly, Beloit Poetry Journal, International Quarterly, Chicago Tribune, Up from Under, American Dialog,* and *Rising Tides.*

WORK IN PROGRESS: Moving Closer, for Catalyst Press; *Clockworks,* for Barlenmir House; *Double Exposure; Snapshots,* for Catalyst Press.

SIDELIGHTS: Ruth Lisa Schechter told *CA:* "A bird flies, a fish swims and a writer writes—a natural and inevitable compulsion to express thoughts and feelings in words, despite the low remuneration offered for daily living, the adoration of the long dead writer, the acceptance and rejection which is merged with the writer's lifestyle. As e. e. cummings said: 'Does this sound dismal? It isn't. It's the most wonderful life on earth. Or so I feel.'

"For me, the making of a poem creates some order in its demands for definitions that change relative to love, life, birth, death and loneliness ... those large, universal emotions in which we are all involved, no matter what age, color or creed. The craft of poetry is a constant challenge and never dull ... an adventure much like mountain climbing, an act of curiosity, skill and exhilaration akin to the joy of being and staying alive. With it, quite naturally, is the pain of struggling with a poem that refuses to get born at a particular time.

"I've been influenced by other writers, American, Indian, Japanese, Chinese and European. Amongst many have been and still are: Seferis, Neruda, Bogan, Millay, Dickenson, Muir, Levertov, Sexton, Lorca, Ginsberg, Whitman, Rich. Their perceptivity, passion and originality, fidelity to 'the word' and respect for their craft have inspired and encouraged me.

"The current literary scene is not too different for poets than other former scenes, except for the changes in language and more government grant support for some writers. Publishing has changed. It is an industry of mergers and corporation structure and the 'big sale' is not necessarily equated with literary quality. Few editors have the time to form the kind of relationship that Perkins had with Thomas Wolfe. Our libraries are still not stocked with enough books of poetry that are representative of the active and energetic contemporary poetry scene. On the positive side, more people are writing poetry and more women are participating as teachers, authors and poets.''

*   *   *

SCHEIMANN, Eugene 1897-

PERSONAL: Born February 19, 1897; son of Morris (a tailor) and Anna (Grunwald) Scheimann; married first wife, Lillian, 1930 (divorced); married June Davis (a secretary), November 11, 1951; children: (first marriage) Barbara Cummings, Elizabeth Dimond. Education: University of Budapest, M.D., 1922. Politics: ''Brotherhood of Men.'' Religion: Jewish. Home: 4170 North Marine Dr., Chicago, Ill. 60613. Office: 854 North Clark St., Chicago, Ill. 60610.

CAREER: Private practice of medicine, Chicago, Ill., 1926—. Served as physician for the Illinois Central Railroad; former attending physician for Salvation Army; former lodge physician for German-Hungarian Sick Benefit Society; emergency physician for Chicago Medical Society; former member, local Selective Service Board. Lecturer; makes frequent radio and television appearances. Member: American Medical Association, American Association of Railway Surgeons, American Federation of Astrologers.

WRITINGS: (With G. Marikin) A Doctor's Approach to Sensible Dieting and Weight Control, Budlong, 1968; A Doctor's Guide to Better Health through Palmistry, Prentice-Hall, 1969; (with Paul G. Neimark) A Doctor's Approach to Alcohol and Alcoholism, Budlong, 1969; (with Neimark) Sex and the Overweight Woman, New American Library, 1970; Key to Better Health, Dodd, 1971; Sex Can Save Your Heart and Life, Crown, 1973. Author of columns, ''Let's Stay Well'' and ''Bedside Manner.'' Contributor to Journal of the American Medical Association, Journal of Mental and Nervous Diseases, Psychoanalytic Review, Sexology, Family Weekly, Cosmopolitan, and other publications. Contributing editor, Forum.

WORK IN PROGRESS: Love, Loneliness and Liquor.

*   *   *

SCHENKER, Alexander M(arian) 1924-

PERSONAL: Born December 20, 1924, in Cracow, Poland; naturalized U.S. citizen; son of Oskar (a lawyer) and Gizela (Szaminski) Schenker; married Eliane Reinhold, August 31, 1958; married second wife, Krystyna Czajka, October 15, 1970; children: (first marriage) Alfred R., Michael J.; (second marriage) Catherine I. Education: Yale University, M.A., 1951, Ph.D., 1953. Home: 145 Deepwood Dr., Hamden, Conn. 06517. Office: Department of Slavic Languages and Literatures, Yale University, New Haven, Conn. 06520.

CAREER: Yale University, New Haven, Conn., instructor, 1951-56, assistant professor of Russian and Polish, 1956-62, associate professor of Slavic linguistics, 1962-67, professor of Slavic linguistics, 1967—. Member: Modern Language Association of America, American Association of Teachers of Slavic and East European Languages, International Linguistics Association, Polish Institute of Arts and Sciences in America, Linguistic Society of America, Connecticut Academy of Arts and Sciences.

WRITINGS: Polish Declension, Mouton & Co., 1964; Beginning Polish, Yale University Press, Volume I, 1966, Volume II, 1968; (editor) Fifteen Modern Polish Short Stories: An Annotated Reader, Yale University Press, 1970. Contributor to professional journals.

SCHEPS, Clarence 1915-

PERSONAL: Born January 16, 1915, in Houston, Tex.; son of Benjamin and Libbie (Solman) Scheps; married Mary Esther Brown, August 19, 1939; children: Philip, Edward. Education: Rice University, B.A., 1935; Columbia University, M.S., 1936; Louisiana State University, Ph.D., 1941. Home: 6321 Freret St., New Orleans, La. 70118. Office: Tulane University, 6823 St. Charles, New Orleans, La. 70118.

CAREER: Louisiana State University, Baton Rouge, instructor in accounting, 1937-41; Louisiana State Department of Education, Baton Rouge, state supervisor of finance, 1941-46; University of Mississippi, University, comptroller, 1946-47; Tulane University, New Orleans, La., executive assistant to president, 1947-48, comptroller, 1948-52, vice-president and comptroller, 1952-65, executive vice-president, 1965—. Member of board of directors, I.C.B. Corp. and International City Bank, New Orleans. American Council on Education committee on taxation, member, 1959-65, chairman, 1962; National Institutes of Health, member of research centers committee, 1959-62, and child health and human development committee, 1962-65. American Red Cross, chairman of New Orleans chapter, 1966-68, member of chapter board of directors, 1950—; member of board of directors, United Fund for Greater New Orleans, 1958-62, and currently, of New Orleans chapter, National Conference of Christians and Jews.

MEMBER: National Association of College and University Business Officers (president, 1965-67; chairman of professional development committee, 1969—), Southern Association of College and University Business Officers (president, 1959-60), Phi Beta Kappa, Beta Gamma Sigma, Omicron Delta Kappa.

WRITINGS: Accounting for Colleges and Universities, Louisiana State University Press, 1949, revised edition (with E. E. Davidson), 1971.

*   *   *

SCHEUERLE, William H(oward) 1930-

PERSONAL: Born March 12, 1930, in Irwin, Pa.; son of Lewis Jacob and Alice (Ramsey) Scheuerle; married Jane Walker (a speech clinician), June 21, 1958; children: Angela Elizabeth, Ramsey William. Education: Muskingum College, B.A., 1952; University of Pennsylvania, M.A., 1954; Syracuse University, Ph.D., 1964. Home: 813 Bellemeade Cir., Temple Terrace, Fla. 33617. Office: Department of English, University of South Florida, Tampa, Fla. 33620.

CAREER: University of South Florida, Tampa, assistant professor, 1964, associate professor, 1967-72, professor of English, 1972—, assistant vice-president for academic affairs, 1972-74, associate vice-president for academic affairs, 1974—. Coordinator of humanities and fine arts, State University System of Florida, Tallahassee, 1969-71. Military service: U.S. Army, 1954-56. Member: Modern Language Association of America, Dickens Society, Milton Society of America, Research Society for Victorian Periodicals (president of board of trustees, 1975-77). Awards, honors: American Philosophical Society grant, 1966; National Endowment for the Humanities summer stipend, 1967.

WRITINGS: (Editor and author of introduction) Henry Kingsley, Ravenshoe, University of Nebraska Press, 1967; The Neglected Brother, Florida State University Press, 1971. Contributor to Studies in Short Fiction, Victorian Poetry, Australian Literary Studies, Studies in English Litera-

ture, and other publications. Consultant and researcher, *Wellesley Index to Victorian Periodicals;* coordinator, *Victorian Periodicals Newsletter Project Number 3.*

WORK IN PROGRESS: A chapter on Victorian periodicals; a book on John Forster.

AVOCATIONAL INTERESTS: Collecting first editions, needlepoint, and making miniatures.

* * *

SCHMIDT, Steven (Thomas) 1927-

PERSONAL: Born July 7, 1927, in Chicago, Ill.; son of Emil J. (an engineer) and Elizabeth (Bolin) Schmidt; married Jean Moore, July, 1952; married second wife, Muriel Clusky, July, 1955; married third wife, Mary (Mitzi) Verduce (a painter and poet), June 20, 1959; children: Teri Lynne Meltcher and Sherwood Meltcher (stepchildren). *Education:* Attended Wright Junior College, 1948-49, and Milton College, 1949-51; Mexico City College, B.A., 1957. *Agent:* Howard Moorepark, 444 East 82nd St., New York, N.Y. 10028.

CAREER: Technical editor and writer, Los Angeles, Calif., 1957-70. *Military service:* U.S. Navy, 1945-48, 1951-55. *Member:* C. G. Jung Foundation for Analytical Psychology. *Awards, honors:* Creative writing award from *Leprechaun Review* for "The Fire-Sower" (poem) and "The Chosen" (short story), 1968.

WRITINGS: Astrology 14: Your New Sun Sign, Bobbs-Merrill, 1970; *The Astrology 14 Horoscope: How to Cast and Interpret It,* illustrated by wife, Mitzi Schmidt, Bobbs-Merrill, 1974; (with Ken Kayatta) *Successful Terrariums: A Step-by-Step Guide,* Houghton, 1975. Also author of film scripts, "Island of Death" and "The Ringleader," for Compass Films, Rome, 1964-65.

WORK IN PROGRESS: Research on *Wednesday,* an experimental novel-poem; poems; *Astropsychology;* "Simon Magus," a play.

AVOCATIONAL INTERESTS: Gnosticism, history, all attempts to enlarge and extend the human mind and spirit.

BIOGRAPHICAL/CRITICAL SOURCES: Time, November 23, 1970; *Flightime,* August, 1971; *Southland Sunday,* January 9, 1972.†

* * *

SCHNEIDER, Harold K(enneth) 1925-

PERSONAL: Born August 24, 1925, in Aberdeen, S.D.; son of Frank X. and Bernice (Anderson) Schneider; married Carol Snyder, September 11, 1948; children: Ann, Amy, Carrie, David. *Education:* Macalester College, B.A., 1946; attended Seabury-Western Theological Seminary, 1946-48; Northwestern University, Ph.D., 1953. *Home address:* R.R. 13, Bloomington, Ind. 47401. *Office:* Department of Anthropology, Rawles Hall, Indiana University, Bloomington, Ind. 47401.

CAREER: Lawrence University, Appleton, Wis., instructor, 1953-57, assistant professor, 1957-62, associate professor, 1962-66, professor of anthropology, 1966-70, chairman of department, 1961-70; Indiana University at Bloomington, professor of anthropology, 1970—. Visiting summer professor at Fordham University, 1957, Indiana University, 1964, and Hamline University, 1965, 1970. Did field work in Kenya, 1951-52, Tanganyika, 1959-60, and studied economy and society in Africa, 1966-67. Visited Ethiopia in 1975, and Botswana in 1976-77, to assess research possibilities. Visited universities in Liberia, Nigeria, Uganda, Tanganyika, Kenya, and Ethiopia in 1962 as consultant to Associated Colleges of the Midwest.

MEMBER: American Anthropological Association, American Association for the Advancement of Science, International African Institute, African Studies Association, Current Anthropology (fellow), Central States Anthropological Society (president, 1965). *Awards, honors:* Fulbright and Social Science Research Council study grant, 1951-52; National Science Foundation research grants, 1959-60, 1966-67.

WRITINGS: (Contributor) William Bascon and M. J. Herskovits, editors, *Continuity and Change in African Cultures,* University of Chicago, 1959; (contributor) Herskovits and Michael Harwitz, editors, *Economic Transition in Africa,* Northwestern University Press, 1964; (with E. E. LeClair, Jr.) *Economic Anthropology: Readings in Theory and Analysis,* Holt, 1968; (contributor) Gwendolen Carter and Ann Paden, editors, *Expanding Horizons in African Studies,* Northwestern University Press, 1969; (contributor) Donald Marshall and Robert Suggs, editors, *Human Sexual Behavior,* Basic Books, 1970; *The Wahi Wanyaturu: Economics in an African Society,* Aldine, 1970; *Economic Man,* Heath, 1974. Contributor of about twenty articles to anthropology journals.

WORK IN PROGRESS: The Peoples of Africa, for Prentice-Hall; *Livestock and Equality: Culture, Society and Economy in East Africa.*

SIDELIGHTS: Harold Schneider told *CA:* "I write books for various reasons, as do we all I'm sure. A major reason is my wish to participate in the scholarly community by presenting my ideas to the community. And I hope thereby also to benefit from the respect of my colleagues. But I also write because I like to do so. To me formulating an idea and shaping it up for publication is intellectually the most stimulating (but also painful) kind of experience."

AVOCATIONAL INTERESTS: Sailing on the Great Lakes, horseback riding on his ranch in rural Indiana.

* * *

SCHOENFELD, Maxwell Philip 1936-

PERSONAL: Born June 15, 1936, in Erie, Pa.; son of Maxwell Theodore (a businessman) and Mary Ruth (Hannon) Schoenfeld. *Education:* Allegheny College, B.A., 1957; Cornell University, M.A., 1959, Ph.D., 1962. *Office:* Department of History, University of Wisconsin, Eau Claire, Wis. 54701.

CAREER: Northland College, Ashland, Wis., assistant professor of history, 1962-64; University of Wisconsin—Eau Claire, assistant professor, 1964-66, associate professor, 1966-72, professor of history, 1972—. *Member:* American Historical Association, Conference of British Studies, Historical Association (Great Britain), Navy Records Society (Great Britain). *Awards, honors:* Johnson Foundation award for distinguished teaching, 1970.

WRITINGS: The Restored House of Lords, Mouton, 1967; *The War Ministry of Winston Churchill,* Iowa State University Press, 1972; *Sir Winston Churchill: His Life and Times,* Dryden, 1973. Contributor to *American Neptune.*†

* * *

SCHOEPFER, Virginia B. 1934-

PERSONAL: Born March 17, 1934, in Queens, New York, N.Y.; daughter of Joseph G. and Georgianna (Dickason)

Schoepfer; married J. D. McDowell, August 20, 1976; children: (previous marriage) Edith Ann. *Education:* Studied at New York University and Pace College (now University). *Politics:* Republican. *Religion:* Lutheran. *Home:* 128-8 Birch Dr., Bricktown, N.J. 08723.

CAREER: Legal secretary and law office manager for eighteen years. Taught legal secretarial courses and yoga-ballet (she trained as a ballet dancer) in adult education classes.

WRITINGS: Legal Dictation Book, Speedwriting, 1967; *Desk Companion for the Legal Secretary,* W. H. Anderson, 1970; *Stenospeed for the Legal Secretary,* Career Institute, 1973; *Legal Secretarial Typewriting and Dictation,* Educational Research Associates, 1974.

WORK IN PROGRESS: A handbook for legal secretaries.

*   *   *

SCHROLL, Herman T(heodore III) 1946-

PERSONAL: Born January 24, 1946, in Lansing, Mich.; son of Herman Theodore (a businessman) and Charlotte J. (McAuley) Schroll, Jr.; married R. Michelle Harrold (a librarian), June 12, 1968. *Education:* Michigan State University, B.A., 1968; University of Maryland, M.A., 1971.

CAREER: Teacher of English in high school in Carsonville, Mich., 1968-69; Hillcrest Children's Center, Washington, D.C., preschool teachers' aide (civilian public service as conscientious objector to military duty), beginning 1971. *Member:* Phi Beta Kappa, Phi Kappa Phi, Omicron Delta Kappa.

WRITINGS: Harold Pinter: A Study of His Reputation (1958-1969) and a Checklist, Scarecrow, 1971.

WORK IN PROGRESS: Research on William Faulkner; research on contemporary theater.

AVOCATIONAL INTERESTS: Chess, woodcarving, candlemaking.††

*   *   *

SCHUETTINGER, Robert Lindsay 1936-

PERSONAL: Born September 12, 1936, in New York, N.Y.; son of Edward Andrew (a farmer) and Mildred (McKenna) Schuettinger. *Education:* Queens College (now Queens College of the City University of New York), Flushing, N.Y., B.A., 1959; graduate study at Columbia University, 1959-60, and at Oxford University and Inns of Court, London, 1962-64; University of Chicago, M.A., 1968, A.B.D., 1970. *Politics:* Republican. *Religion:* Episcopalian. *Home:* 2805 Olive St. N.W., Washington, D.C. 20007.

CAREER: Catholic University of America, Washington, D.C., assistant professor of political science, 1965-68; University of St. Andrews, St. Andrews, Scotland, visiting professor of political science, 1968-70; Lynchburg College, Lynchburg, Va., assistant professor of political science, 1970-73; U.S. House of Representatives, Republican Steering Committee, Washington, D.C., senior research associate, 1973—. Lecturer, New School for Social Research, 1966; visiting lecturer, Davenport College, Grand Rapids, Mich., and Yale University, New Haven, Conn., 1974—. Director of political science summer study tours in Europe, 1968, 1969, 1971. *Military service:* U.S. Naval Reserve, 1957-65. *Member:* University Professors for Academic Order, Mont Pelerin Society, Carlton Dining Club of Oxford University, Reform Club, Oxford and Cambridge Universities Club.

WRITINGS: (Editor) *The Conservative Tradition in European Thought,* Putnam, 1970; (contributor) *Toward Liberty: Essays in Honor of Ludwig von Mises,* Institute of Humane Studies (Menlo Park, Calif.), 1971; *Lord Acton: Historian of Liberty,* Arlington House, 1974; *A Brief Survey of Price and Wage Controls from 2800 B.C. to A.D. 1952,* Heritage Foundation, 1974. Also author of *South Africa: The Vital Link.* Contributor to *New Leader, National Review,* and other publications.

WORK IN PROGRESS: Two books, *The Political Economy of Dugald Stewart* and *The Development of Diplomacy.*†

*   *   *

SCHULMAN, L(ester) M(artin) 1934-

PERSONAL: Born September 3, 1934, in Brooklyn, N.Y.; son of David and Rose (Tirnauer) Schulman; married Janet Schuetz (a writer of juvenile books), May 19, 1957; children: Nicole. *Education:* Antioch College, B.A., 1955. *Politics:* "Alienated." *Religion:* None. *Home and office:* 290 Riverside Dr., Apt. 7B, New York, N.Y. 10025. *Agent:* Harriet Wasserman, Russell & Volkening, Inc., 551 Fifth Ave., New York, N.Y. 10017.

CAREER: Popular Library, Inc., New York City, editor, 1963-65; Bantam Books, Inc., New York City, editor, 1966-67; Dell Publishing Co., New York City, editor, 1967-69. *Military service:* U.S. Army, 1957-59.

WRITINGS—Editor; all juvenile anthologies except as indicated: *Come Out of the Wilderness* (Black anthology), Popular Library, 1965; *Winners and Losers,* Macmillan, 1968; *The Loners: Short Stories about the Young and Alienated,* Macmillan, 1970; *The Cracked Looking Glass: Stories of Other Realities,* Macmillan, 1971; *Travelers,* Macmillan, 1972; *A Woman's Place,* Macmillan, 1974.

WORK IN PROGRESS: A novel for young adults; captions for a juvenile picture book; a detective novel.

*   *   *

SCHUMAN, Patricia Glass 1943-

PERSONAL: Born March 15, 1943, in New York, N.Y.; daughter of Milton and Shirley (Goodman) Glass; married Alan B. Schuman, August 30, 1964 (divorced, 1973). *Education:* University of Cincinnati, A.B., 1963; Columbia University, M.L.S., 1966. *Religion:* Jewish. *Home:* 77 Fulton St., New York, N.Y. 10038. *Office address:* Neal-Schuman Publishers, P.O. Box 1687, FDR Station, New York, N.Y. 10022.

CAREER: Brooklyn Public Library, Brooklyn, N.Y., librarian trainee, 1963-65; teacher of library in high school in New York City, 1966; New York City Community College of the City University of New York, New York City, assistant professor and acquisitions librarian, 1967-70; R. R. Bowker Co., New York City, associate editor of *School Library Journal,* 1970-73, senior acquisitions editor in book editorial department, 1973-76; Neal-Schuman Publishers, New York City, president, 1976—. *Member:* American Library Association (member of council, 1972-80), Social Responsibilities Round Table (coordinator, 1971), Women's National Book Association.

WRITINGS: Materials for Occupational Education: An Annotated Source Guide, Bowker, 1971; *Social Responsibility and Libraries,* Bowker, 1976. Contributor to library journals.

SCHWARTZ, Barry N. 1942-

PERSONAL: Born October 15, 1942, in Brooklyn, N.Y.; son of Emanuel and Tillie (Kirsch) Schwartz; married, June, 1963; wife's name, Elizabeth (divorced); children: Juliet Eve. *Education:* Pratt Institute, B.Ch.E., 1964; New York University, M.A., 1965, Ph.D. candidate, 1965-67; Antioch College, Ph.D. candidate, 1971. *Politics:* "Life-affirming."

CAREER: Pratt Institute, Brooklyn, N.Y., instructor in humanities, 1965-69, part-time lecturer in graphic art and design, 1966-69, in social science, 1967-69; New York City Community College of Applied Arts and Sciences, Brooklyn, assistant professor in Division of Continuing Education, 1969-70, adjunct lecturer, beginning 1970, assistant professor in communication arts and skills department, beginning 1970. Director of educational planning, Central Brooklyn Neighborhood College, 1967-69; associate director, Center for the Study of Social Change, beginning 1970. Programmer, Station WBAI (FM radio), 1966-67, and creator and producer of "The Examined Life"; research coordinator, Archives of American Art, 1970-71. *Member:* American Association of Museums, Museums Collaborative, Architectural League of New York.

WRITINGS: (With R. E. L. Masters, Jean Houston, and Stanley Krippner) *Psychedelic Art,* Grove, 1968; (editor with Robert Disch) *Hard Rains: Conflict and Conscience in America,* Prentice-Hall, 1970; (editor with Disch, and contributor) *White Racism: Its History, Pathology, Practice,* Dell, 1970; (editor with Disch) *Killing Time: A Guide to Life in the Happy Valley,* Prentice-Hall, 1972; *Affirmative Education,* Prentice-Hall, 1972; *America/America* (poetry), Barlenmir House, 1972; (editor) *Human Connection and the New Media,* Prentice-Hall, 1973; *The New Humanism: Art in a Time of Change,* Praeger, 1974; *The Voyeur of Our Time* (poetry), Barlenmir, 1974.

Articles, originally published in literary and arts journals, have been included in *Art and Anti-Art, Living Lyrics,* and other collections; contributor of poetry to four anthologies and about twenty little literary periodicals, including *Discourse, Trace, Poetry Parade, Fireflower,* and *Encore.* Contributing editor, *Arts in Society* and *Etcetera;* editor, *Readers and Writers,* 1967-68, and *New Writer;* columnist, *Today's Filmaker,* 1973—.

WORK IN PROGRESS: Orientation for the Visual Experience, for Praeger; *The Radical Students College Handbook,* for Gordon & Breach.

AVOCATIONAL INTERESTS: Collecting tropical fish, dogs, birds, and other living things.

BIOGRAPHICAL/CRITICAL SOURCES: Midwest Quarterly, spring, 1969, October, 1970; *Nation,* summer, 1970.†

*   *   *

SCHWARTZ, Israel J(acob) 1885-1971

1885—September 18, 1971; American poet and translator in Yiddish. Obituaries: *New York Times,* September 19, 1971.

*   *   *

SCHWARTZ, Joseph 1925-

PERSONAL: Born April 9, 1925, in Milwaukee, Wis.; son of Alfred George and Mary (Wutchek) Schwartz; married Joan Marie Jackson, August 28, 1954; children: Adam. *Education:* Marquette University, B.A., 1946, M.A., 1947; University of Wisconsin, Ph.D., 1952. *Politics:* Republican.

Religion: Roman Catholic. *Home:* 8516 West Mequon Rd., 112N, Mequon, Wis. 53092. *Office:* Department of English, Marquette University, Milwaukee, Wis. 53233.

CAREER: Marquette University, Milwaukee, Wis., instructor, 1950-54, assistant professor, 1954-59, associate professor, 1959-64, professor of English, 1964—, chairman of department, 1963—. Chairman of Region X, Woodrow Wilson National Fellowship Foundation. Vice-president, Board of Education of Catholic Archdiocese of Milwaukee, 1976-77. Member of sponsoring committee, Ad Hoc Committee in Defense of Life. *Member:* Modern Language Association of America, American Association of University Professors, National Council of Teachers of English (member of board of directors, 1965-68), Catholic Renascence Society (member of board of directors, 1968—; president, 1976—), Rhetoric Society of America, Midwest Modern Language Association (member of executive committee, 1974-77), Alpha Sigma Nu, Sigma Tau Delta, Delta Sigma Rho. *Awards, honors:* Ford Foundation grant, 1956-58; Marquette University, distinguished alumni award, School of Speech, 1967, faculty award for teaching excellence, 1974.

WRITINGS: (With Jerome Archer) *A Reader for Writers,* McGraw, 1962, 3rd edition, 1971; (with John Rycenga) *Perspectives of Language,* Ronald, 1963; (with Rycenga) *The Province of Rhetoric,* Ronald, 1965; (with Archer) *Exposition,* McGraw, 1966, 2nd edition, 1970; (with R. C. Roby) *Poetry: Meaning and Form,* McGraw, 1969; *Hart Crane: An Annotated Critical Bibliography,* David Lewis, 1970; (with R. G. Schweik) *Hart Crane: A Descriptive Bibliography,* University of Pittsburgh Press, 1972. Contributor of articles and reviews to literary and professional journals. Member of editorial board, *Renascence.*

WORK IN PROGRESS: Hart Crane: A Portrait of the Artist in His Time, 1916-1933.

AVOCATIONAL INTERESTS: European travel, gardening, tennis.

*   *   *

SCHWARTZ, Lois C. 1935-

PERSONAL: Born August 15, 1935, in New York, N.Y.; daughter of Arthur H. (an attorney) and Dorothy (Blaine) Schwartz. *Education:* University of Michigan, A.B. (with distinction), 1957 (spent junior year, 1955-56, at London School of Economics and Political Science). *Residence:* New York, N.Y. *Office:* Esprit Consulting Corp., 299 West 12th St., New York, N.Y. 10014.

CAREER: Harry N. Abrams, Inc., New York City, editorial assistant, 1957-59; Jewish Theological Seminary of America, New York City, associate producer of radio/television programs, 1959-62; Grolier, Inc., New York City, managing editor, *Book of Knowledge,* 1962-65; Center for Urban Education, New York City, consultant, 1965-66; Harcourt, Brace & Jovanovich, New York City, audiovisual editor, 1966-67; Innovative Instruction, Inc. (subsidiary of Sterling Institute), New York City, co-founder and vice-president, 1967-72; Esprit Consulting Corp., New York City, president, 1972—. *Member:* International Industrial Television Association, National Society for Performance and Instruction, American Society for Training and Development.

WRITINGS: (With Sande Friedman) *No Experience Necessary,* Dell, 1971.

SIDELIGHTS: Lois Schwartz has lived in Greece as well as in London.

SCHWARTZ, Pepper 1945-

PERSONAL: Born May 11, 1945, in Chicago, Ill.; daughter of Julius J. (an attorney) and Gertrude (Puris) Schwartz; divorced. Education: Washington University, B.A. (magna cum laude), 1967, M.A. (magna cum laude), 1968; Yale University, M.Phil., 1970, Ph.D., 1973. Home: 612 36th, Seattle, Washington. Office: Department of Sociology, University of Washington, Seattle, Wash. 98105.

CAREER: University of Washington, Seattle, member of faculty, 1972—. Member of Washington State Government Commission on Venereal Disease, 1974-77, and of National Institute of Mental Health review committee. Member: National Assembly for Policy Research and Development (trustee), National Woman's Resource Center, Council for Woman's Equality (vice-chairwoman), American Sociological Association (member of council on sex roles, 1975-76; member of committee on the status of women, 1977-80), Pacific Sociological Association, Sociologists for Women in Society, YWCA (national board member), Phi Beta Kappa. Awards, honors: Russell Sage Foundation grant, 1975; National Science Foundation grant, 1977-80.

WRITINGS: (Editor with Richard Feller and Elaine Fox, and contributor) A Student's Guide to Sex on Campus, New American Library, 1971; (with Janet Lever) Women at Yale, Bobbs-Merrill, 1971; (with Judith Long Laws) Sociological Perspectives on Female Sexuality, Dryden, 1977. Contributor to Yale Law Journal, Sexual Behavior, Ms., and New Woman.

WORK IN PROGRESS: Bisexuality, with Philip Blumstein and Jane Adams; a book on couples, with Blumstein; a book on relationships, with Janet Lever.

*   *   *

SCOALES, William 1933-

PERSONAL: Born February 4, 1933, in St. Paul, Minn.; son of William Alexander and Georgia (Hecht) Scoales; married Patricia Moore, June 6, 1958; children: Nicholas. Education: University of California, Los Angeles, B.A., 1960. Residence: Los Angeles, Calif.

CAREER: Writer. Military service: U.S. Naval Reserve, 1955-57.

WRITINGS: Duckfoot, Bobbs-Merrill, 1971. Author of television scripts produced in Australia, 1962.

WORK IN PROGRESS: A novel entitled Wildlife.

SIDELIGHTS: William Scoales told CA: "The needless, reckless killing of animals has motivated the book I'm working on. Something can be done about it." Avocational interests: Drums, surfing, animals, good writers, and great thinkers.††

*   *   *

SCOBY, Donald R(ay) 1931-

PERSONAL: Born March 18, 1931, in Fargo, N.D.; son of Otis C. (a farmer) and Stella (McClanahan) Scoby; married Glenna J. Norrie (an educational diagnostician), June 19, 1956; children: Melodye Jean. Education: Kansas State College of Agriculture and Applied Science (now Kansas State University), B.S., 1957; Nebraska State Teachers College at Peru (now Peru State College), M.S., 1960; University of Texas, graduate study, 1960-61; North Dakota State University of Agriculture and Applied Science, Ph.D., 1968. Politics: Democrat. Religion: Methodist. Residence: Sabetha, Kan. Office: Department of Biology, North Dakota State University of Agriculture and Applied Science, Fargo, N.D. 58102.

CAREER: Farmer in Sabetha, Kan., 1955-60; Sabetha High School, Sabetha, science teacher, 1957-60, assistant principal, 1957-58; science teacher and science department chairman in high schools of Colorado Springs, Colo., 1961-65; North Dakota State University of Agriculture and Applied Science, Fargo, environmental biologist, 1967—, instructor, 1967-68, assistant professor, 1968-71, associate professor of biology, 1971—. Environmental education consultant, Southeastern North Dakota Community Action Program. Military service: U.S. Air Force, 1951-54; served as aerial gunner; became sergeant. Member: Ecological Society of America, American Institute of Biological Sciences, National Association of Biology Teachers, Zero Population Growth (Chapter 71, Fargo, N.D.; president and organizer, 1968-70), Sigma Xi, Phi Delta Kappa. Awards, honors: Named North Dakota Conservationist of the Year by North Dakota Wildlife Federation, 1971.

WRITINGS: (Editor) Environmental Ethics, Burgess, 1971. Contributor of articles to science periodicals.

WORK IN PROGRESS: Revising curriculum materials for beginning and environmental biology; articles for education journals.

SIDELIGHTS: Donald Scoby told CA that he has "strongly advocated that population and life style interact to cause pollution problems. Nothing can be solved on a long term basis until we get at the source of the problems, population and life style." He says that he has devoted the last ten years to "development of a more self-sufficient life-style. As such my non-renewable energy consumption has decreased at least seventy-five percent, the cost of living has decreased, while quality of life has increased. This involves organic gardening, canning, solar heating, wood heating, efficient car transportation, site analysis and construction techniques within conventional house types, etc."

*   *   *

SCOTLAND, James 1917-
(Ronald Emerson, Kenneth Little)

PERSONAL: Born September 8, 1917, in Glasgow, Scotland; son of Duncan Anderson (a clerk) and Mary (Emmerson) Scotland; married Jean Cowan, March 21, 1944; children: Colin George Emmerson, Alastair Duncan. Education: University of Glasgow, M.A., 1939, B.L., 1940, LL.B., 1943, M.Ed., 1949. Religion: Church of Scotland (Presbyterian). Home: 67 Forest Rd., Aberdeen, Scotland. Office: Aberdeen College of Education, Hilton Pl., Aberdeen, Scotland.

CAREER: Allan Glen's School, Glasgow, Scotland, teacher of English and history, 1947-49; Jordanhill College of Education, Glasgow, lecturer in history, 1949-50, principal lecturer in education, 1950-61; Aberdeen College of Education, Aberdeen, Scotland, principal, 1961—. Playwright and writer for radio and television. Visiting professor at Acadia University, Wolfville, Nova Scotia, 1963, and Stranmillis College, Belfast, Northern Ireland, 1965. Member, Police Advisory Board for Scotland. Chairman, Scottish Community Drama Association, 1965-70; chairman, General Teaching Council for Scotland, 1976—; secretary, Standing Conference of Studies in Education. Military service: British Army, Royal Artillery and Royal Army Educational Corps, 1940-46; became major.

WRITINGS: Modern Scotland: A Short History from 1707

to the Present Day, G. Bell, 1953; *Our Law,* Scottish Television Ltd., 1955; *The History of Scottish Education,* two volumes, University of London Press, 1969; (contributor) John D. Nisbet and Gordon Kirk, editors, *Scottish Education Looks Ahead,* W. & R. Chambers, 1969; (with David Thomas) *Management of Innovation in Education,* Organization for Economic Cooperation and Development, 1970; (contributor) D. E. Lomax, editor, *Education of Teachers in Britain,* Wiley, 1973.

Plays, largely in Scots dialect, have been published in script (acting) form by St. Giles Press; all have been performed in Scotland and some in England as well; all the full-length plays have been presented at the Edinburgh Festival, *The Honours of Drumlie* was also performed on radio and television, and seven of the one-act plays have been on radio. Three-act: *The Honours of Drumlie,* 1955; (with Arthur Blake) *A Surgeon for Lucinda* (musical play), 1958; *Whisky Galore* (by arrangement with Compton Mackenzie), 1966; *The Sorcerer's Tale,* 1968; *Wild Geese at Midnight,* 1970; *Cambusdonald Royal,* 1973. One-act: (Sole author) *A Surgeon for Lucinda* (short version), 1954; *We'll Go No More A'Reivin,* 1957; *Union Riots,* 1961; *Himself When Young,* 1964; *The Dark Assize,* 1965; *The Friends of the People,* 1966; *Hallowe'en,* 1967; *A Shilling for the Beadle,* 1968; *O Whistle and I'll Come to You, My Lad,* 1969; *The Rape of the Mace,* 1971; *The Highlander,* 1971; *Grand Finale,* 1972; *Baptie's Lass,* 1972; *The Burning Question,* 1974; *The Girl of the Golden City,* 1974.

Also author of about two hundred radio programs, mainly under the pseudonym Kenneth Little, for British Broadcasting Corp., principally between 1955-61, but some up to the present. Writer of revues, under the pseudonym Ronald Emerson, for the Citizens Theatre, Glasgow, 1955-60. Has also written about twenty television programs, mostly plays and entertainment, for B.B.C., Scottish Television, and Grampian Television since 1957. Contributor to journals.

* * *

SCOTT, Anne Firor 1921-

PERSONAL: Born April 24, 1921, in Montezuma, Ga.; daughter of John William (a college professor) and Mary (Moss) Firor; married Andrew MacKay Scott (a college professor), June 2, 1947; children: Rebecca Jarvis, David MacKay, Donald MacKay. *Education:* University of Georgia, A.B., 1941; Northwestern University, M.A., 1944; Radcliffe College, Ph.D., 1949. *Politics:* Democrat. *Home:* 1028 Highland Woods, Chapel Hill, N.C. 27514. *Office:* Department of History, 230 Allen Bldg., Duke University, Durham, N.C. 27706.

CAREER: International Business Machines Corp. (IBM), Atlanta, Ga., private secretary, 1941-42; League of Women Voters of the United States, Washington, D.C., program associate, 1944-47, congressional representative and editor of *National Voter,* 1951-53; Haverford College, Haverford, Pa., lecturer in history, 1957-58; University of North Carolina at Chapel Hill, lecturer in history, 1959-60; Duke University, Durham, N.C., assistant professor, 1962-65, associate professor, 1965-70, professor of history, 1971—. Occasional lecturer, Johns Hopkins Center, University of Bologna, 1960-61. Chairperson, North Carolina Governor's Commission on the Status of Women, 1963-64; member of federal Citizens Advisory Council on Status of Women, 1964-68. *Member:* American Historical Association, Organization of American Historians, Southern Historical Association, Phi Beta Kappa. *Awards, honors:* American Asso-

ciation of University Women national fellow, 1956-57; National Endowment for the Humanities senior fellow, 1967-68, 1976-77.

WRITINGS: (Editor) *Jane Addams: Democracy and Social Ethics,* Harvard University Press, 1964; (contributor) Wayne Booth, editor, *The Knowledge Most Worth Having,* University of Chicago Press, 1967; (contributor) Kenneth Underwood, editor, *The Church, the University and Social Policy,* Volume II, Wesleyan University Press, 1969; *The Southern Lady,* University of Chicago Press, 1970; *The American Woman: Who Was She?,* Prentice-Hall, 1970; *Women in American Life,* Houghton, 1970; (editor) *What Is Happening to American Women?,* South Atlantic Newspaper Publishers Association, 1970; (with Andrew M. Scott) *One-Half the People,* Lippincott, 1976. Contributor to literary journals and popular magazines, including *American Heritage.*

WORK IN PROGRESS: Studies on women as institution builders in the nineteenth and twentieth centuries.

AVOCATIONAL INTERESTS: Tennis, travel, wilderness camping.

* * *

SCOTT, Edward M. 1919-

PERSONAL: Born August 31, 1919, in Green Bay, Wis.; son of James M. (a cook) and Lilian (Plouff) Scott; married Kathryn L. Hague (a registered nurse), February 20, 1954; children: Kathleen Marie, Mike J., Maureen V., Tim A., Molly K. *Education:* University of Notre Dame, B.A., 1946; University of Portland, M.S., 1951, Ph.D., 1953. *Politics:* Democrat. *Religion:* Roman Catholic. *Home:* 15345 Southwest Bull Mountain Rd., Tigard, Ore. 97223.

CAREER: Eastern Oregon State Hospital, Pendleton, chief clinical psychologist, 1953-56; State of Oregon, Portland, consultant psychologist in Mental Health Division, 1956-60, clinic director, Alcohol and Drug Section, 1960—. Associate clinical professor of psychology, University of Oregon Medical School, 1970—. *Member:* American Psychological Association, American Society of Clinical Hypnosis, Academy of Religion and Mental Health, Portland Academy of Hypnosis (president, 1970), Notre Dame Club of Oregon (president).

WRITINGS—All published by C. C Thomas: *Struggles in an Alcoholic Family,* 1970; *An Area for Happiness,* 1971; *The Adolescent Gap: Research Findings of Drug-Using and Non-Drug-Using Teens,* 1972; (editor with wife, Kathryn L. Scott) *Criminal Rehabilitation within and without the Walls,* 1973. Contributor of over forty articles to professional journals. Associate editor, *International Journal of Offender Therapy and Comparative Criminology;* editorial consultant, *Psychotherapy.*

WORK IN PROGRESS: Editing a book on convicts.

* * *

SCOTT, Johnie Harold 1946-

PERSONAL: Born May 8, 1946, in Cheyenne, Wyo.; son of Johnie (a laborer) and Mattie Lee (Livingston) Scott; married Joyce LaVerne Hurdle (a music teacher), November 21, 1967; children: Tadd Onomowale. *Education:* Attended Harvard University, 1964-65, and East Los Angeles Junior College, 1965-66; Stanford University, B.A., 1970, M.A., 1972. *Politics:* Independent Democrat. *Religion:* Baptist. *Residence:* Inglewood, Calif.

CAREER: Frederick Douglass House Foundation, Los Angeles, Calif., national coordinator of project development, 1966; Stanford University, Stanford, Calif., teacher in Cinema Arts Workshop, Department of Afro-American Studies, 1967-72, artistic director and producer, Black Theatre Productions, 1967-70; *Newsweek,* San Francisco, Calif., editorial intern, 1969-70; *Time,* San Francisco, correspondent, 1972-73; currently director of affairs, Afro-West: Theatre of the Black Arts. Filmmaker for Midpeninsula Urban Coalition, Fair Housing Campaign, 1970-71; film director and member of board of directors, Human Perspectives, Inc., Woodside, Calif., 1971—. Program coordinator, Watts Writers Workshop Career Academy, Los Angeles, 1970—; member of board of directors, University of the Streets (educational program for residents of Lower East Side), New York, N.Y., 1971—. Member of arts committee, Urban Arts Foundation, Palo Alto, Calif., 1970—; special assistant, Watts Community Housing Corp.; administrative assistant to Assemblyman Leon Ralph, California State Legislature. Consultant on minority group history, Opportunities Industrialization Center West, Menlo Park, Calif.

MEMBER: American Film Institute (charter member), Alpha Phi Alpha. *Awards, honors:* "Emmy" award nomination from Academy of Television Arts and Sciences, 1966, for "The Angry Voices of Watts"; scholarship to intern as director of film, "Across 110th Street," Academy of Motion Picture Arts and Sciences, 1971-72.

WRITINGS: "The Angry Voices of Watts" (television documentary), produced by National Broadcasting Company in 1966; "The New Voices of Watts" (television documentary), produced by National Broadcasting Company in 1968; "David" (3-act play), commissioned by Los Angeles Festival of Performing Arts, 1969.

Contributor: Budd Schulberg, editor, *From the Ashes: Voices of Watts,* New American Library, 1966; J. Anthony Lukas, *Don't Shoot! We Are Your Children,* Random House, 1971. Poetry anthologized in *The New Black Poetry,* edited by Clarence Major, International Publishers, 1967, *We Speak as Liberators: Young Black Poets,* edited by Orde Coombs, Dial, 1969, *Brilliant Corners,* edited by Bob O'-Meally and Richard Grant, Stanford University Press, 1967-71, and *A Rock against the Wind,* edited by Lindsay Patterson, Dodd, 1973. Contributor of poems to *Time, Los Angeles Magazine, Antioch Review, Black on Black* (Stanford University), and *Stanford Alumni Almanac;* contributor of essays to *Harper's, Pageant, Western Review* (University of New Mexico), *New Lady,* and *Stanford Alumni Almanac.*

WORK IN PROGRESS: Diary of personal experiences as young black writer-filmmaker in Harlem, for New American Library.

BIOGRAPHICAL/CRITICAL SOURCES: New Yorker, August, 1966; *New York Times,* December 11, 1966, December 12, 1966; J. Anthony Lukas, *Don't Shoot! We Are Your Children,* Random House, 1971.†

* * *

SCROGGINS, Daniel C(oy) 1937-

PERSONAL: Born June 19, 1937, in Compton, Ark.; son of Coy (a farmer) and Mary (Petree) Scroggins; married Jeanne Colonna, February 11, 1960. *Education:* University of Arkansas, B.A., 1958, M.A., 1960; Universidad de Buenos Aires, graduate study, 1958-59; University of Michigan, Ph.D., 1967. *Home:* 1211 Frances Dr., Columbia, Mo. 65201. *Office:* Department of Romance Languages, University of Missouri, Columbia, Mo. 65201.

CAREER: University of Miami, Miami, Fla., assistant professor of Spanish, 1963-66; Indiana University at Bloomington, assistant professor of Spanish, 1967-69; University of Missouri—Columbia, assistant professor, 1969-71, associate professor of Spanish, 1971—. *Member:* Modern Language Association of America, American Association of University Professors, Latin American Studies Association, American Association of Teachers of Spanish and Portuguese, Missouri State Historical Society, Phi Beta Kappa, Phi Eta Sigma. *Awards, honors:* Nichols Romance Language Award, 1958; Fulbright grants, 1958, 1975; American Council of Learned Societies grant, 1958.

WRITINGS: A Concordance of Jose Hernandez' Martin Fierro, University of Missouri Press, 1971. Contributor to *American Hispanist.*

WORK IN PROGRESS: Research in Argentine and colonial Spanish-American literatures.

* * *

SEALEY, Danguole 1931-

PERSONAL: Born November 18, 1931, in Kaunas, Lithuania; daughter of Juozas and Adele (Vaitaitis) Sadunas; married Raphael Sealey (a historian), August 13, 1957 (divorced). *Education:* Attended University College of North Wales. *Religion:* Roman Catholic. *Address:* Immaculate Conception Convent, Putnam, Conn. 06260.

WRITINGS: To Regions of No Admittance, Manyland Books, 1968; *Recollections of a Childhood,* Manyland Books, 1971.

In Lithuanian: *Kai tu arti manes (Close to Me),* [Los Angeles], 1965; *Tu esi mano zeme (You Are My Earth),* [Boston], 1967; *Laiskai Dievui (Letters to God),* Ateitis, 1970; *Pakeliui i Emmaus (On the Road to Emmaus),* [Putnam, Conn.], 1974.

* * *

SEARS, Stephen W. 1932-

PERSONAL: Born July 27, 1932, in Lakewood, Ohio; son of John F. (a chemist) and Josephine (Ward) Sears; married second wife, Sally Tyson, September 26, 1970; children: (first marriage) Jeffrey Alan, Kathryn Grace. *Education:* Oberlin College, B.A., 1954. *Home:* 9 South Huckleberry Dr., Norwalk, Conn. 06850. *Office:* American Heritage Publishing Co., 10 Rockefeller Plaza, New York, N.Y. 10020.

CAREER: American Heritage Publishing Co., New York, N.Y., assistant editor, *American Heritage* (magazine), 1954-57, assistant editor, Major Books Division, 1957-61, editor, American Heritage Junior Library, 1961-64, executive editor, Education Division, 1964-71, senior editor, Book Division, 1971—.

WRITINGS—Youth books; all published by American Heritage Press: (With Marvin W. McFarland as consultant) *Air War against Hitler's Germany,* 1964; (with E. M. Eller as consultant) *Carrier War in the Pacific,* 1966; (with I.S.O. Playfair as consultant) *Desert War in North Africa,* 1967; (with S.L.A. Marshall as consultant) *The Battle of the Bulge,* 1969.

Adult books; all published by American Heritage Press: *The Century Collection of Civil War Art,* 1974; *Hometown U.S.A.,* 1975; *The Automobile in America,* 1977.

SEASHORE, Stanley E. 1915-

PERSONAL: Born September 4, 1915, in Wahoo, Neb.; son of August Theodore and Jennie Rose Seashore; married Eva Danielson, August 29, 1940; children: Karen Seashore Louis, Christine Sigrid. *Education:* University of Iowa, B.A., 1937; University of Minnesota, M.A., 1939; University of Michigan, Ph.D., 1954. *Home:* 2270 Manchester Rd., Ann Arbor, Mich. 48104. *Office:* Institute for Social Research, University of Michigan, Box 1248, Ann Arbor, Mich. 48106.

CAREER: Personnel manager, U.S. Steel Corp., 1939-45; A. T. Kearney & Co., Chicago, Ill., staff consultant, 1945-50; University of Michigan, Ann Arbor, assistant professor, 1956-60, associate professor, 1960-64, professor of psychology, 1964—, program director, Institute for Social Research, 1950—. Chairman, Commission for Certification of Psychologists, State of Michigan. *Member:* American Psychological Association (fellow; president of Division of Organizational and Industrial Psychology, 1968-69), American Sociological Association, Association for Applied Anthropology, American Board of Professional Psychologists, Sigma Xi. *Awards, honors:* Fulbright fellow, 1956-57; Guggenheim fellow, 1965-66; NIAS fellow, 1972-73.

WRITINGS: Group Cohesiveness in the Industrial Work Group, Institute for Social Research, University of Michigan, 1954; (with David Bowers) *Changing the Structure and Functioning of an Organization,* Institute for Social Research, University of Michigan, 1963; (with Alfred Marrow and Bowers) *Management by Participation,* Harper, 1967; (with Robert McNeill) *Management of the Urban Crisis,* Free Press, 1971. Contributor of about thirty articles to social science journals.

* * *

SEBENTHALL, R(oberta) E(lizabeth) 1917-
(Paul Kruger)

PERSONAL: Born January 6, 1917, in Eau Claire, Wis.; daughter of Robert G. and Laura R. (Cote) Sebenthall. *Home and office:* 104 Thompson St., Mount Horeb, Wis. 53572.

AWARDS, HONORS: National Endowment for the Arts award, 1970, for *Acquainted with a Chance of Bobcats.*

WRITINGS—Mystery novels under pseudonym Paul Kruger; all published by Simon & Schuster: *Weep for Willow Green,* 1966; *Weave a Wicked Web,* 1967; *The Finish Line,* 1968; *If the Shroud Fits,* 1969; *The Bronze Claws,* 1972; *The Cold Ones,* 1972.

Under name R. E. Sebenthall: *Acquainted with a Chance of Bobcats* (poems), Rutgers University Press, 1969; (contributor) John Judson, editor, *Voyages to an Inland Sea,* University of Wisconsin—La Crosse, 1972; (contributor) *Heartland II: Poets of the Midwest,* edited by Lucien Stryk, Northern Illinois University Press, 1975.

WORK IN PROGRESS: Several other collections of poetry.

SIDELIGHTS: R. E. Sebenthall told *CA:* "In my poetry (which I regard as my serious work) I have not wanted to express my personal feelings and thoughts directly—that is, as so-called confessional poetry. I wanted, rather, to see myself and my personal experience as part of the larger life around me, to explore the extent to which I and others shared basic experience. At the same time, I did want to convey my own particular vision of life—a vision that has seemed bleak and even tragic to some people, but which I

feel has never been a despairing one. I wanted to affirm that fact that life held much good, while not blinking the fact that it held much evil. I wanted to puncture some of the pretensions, hypocrisies and evasions we all tend to resort to, often quite unconsciously. On another level, I have been very concerned with metaphysics, with the various myths, religions and philosophical beliefs that (in my opinion) we human beings devise for shelter in what I see as a huge, indifferent and often terrifying universe."

* * *

SECHER, Bjorn 1929-

PERSONAL: Born September 4, 1929, in Copenhagen, Denmark; naturalized U.S. citizen, 1957; son of Mathias and Sigrid (Rosenkrands) Secher. *Education:* Studied advanced mathematics at Johannesburg College, Denmark. *Office:* B. Secher Associates, 3300 Northeast 16th Ct., Ft. Lauderdale, Fla. 33305.

CAREER: Businessman in Denmark, Germany, England, and Spain before coming to U.S. in 1954; president of a textile machinery import company in South Carolina, 1960-63; B. Secher Associates, Ft. Lauderdale, Fla., director and lecturer, 1963—. Former president, Bjorn Secher Foundation and Institute for Professional Development. Originator of personal development motivational and self-discovery programs. *Military service:* Royal Danish Guard, 1949-50. *Awards, honors:* Several national sales awards.

WRITINGS: Appointment with Success, Fell, 1971. Also author of *Success Is Luck . . . Ask Any Failure* and a set of "12 Rules for Success," Bjorn Secher Foundation, 1969.

WORK IN PROGRESS: Six half-hour cassette tapes on human motivation and behavior pattern.

SIDELIGHTS: Bjorn Secher is interested in "the reason (rules) for individual expansion." He told *CA:* "Attitude is the thought behind the things we do. . . . Man's chance lies in his changing . . . of Habit Pattern, the everyday automatic action and reaction."

* * *

SEFERIADES, Giorgos Stylianou 1900-1971
(George Seferis)

February 22, 1900—September 20, 1971; Greek diplomat and poet. Obituaries: *New York Times,* September 21, 1971; *Washington Post,* September 21, 1971; *Publishers Weekly,* October 4, 1971; *Time,* October 4, 1971; *Current Biography,* November, 1971. (See index for *CA* sketch)

* * *

SEGRE, Emilio (Gino) 1905-

PERSONAL: Surname is pronounced Say-*gray;* born February 1, 1905, in Tivoli, Italy; naturalized U.S. citizen, 1944; son of Giuseppe (an industrialist) and Amelia (Treves) Segre; married Elfriede Spiro, 1936 (died, 1970); married Rosa Mines, 1972; children: (first marriage) Claudio, Amelia Segre Terkel, Fausta; (second marriage) Segre Walsby. *Education:* University of Rome, Ph.D., 1928. *Home:* 36 Crest Rd., Lafayette, Calif. 94549. *Office:* Department of Physics, University of California, Berkeley, Calif. 94720.

CAREER: University of Rome, Rome, Italy, assistant professor of physics, 1932-36; University of Palermo, Palermo, Italy, professor and director of physics laboratory, 1936-38; University of California, Berkeley, research associate and lecturer, 1938-43; Los Alamos Scientific Laboratory, Los

Alamos, N.M., physicist and group leader, 1943-46; University of California, Berkeley, professor of physics, 1946-72, professor emeritus, 1972—. Visiting professor, University of Illinois, 1951-52; visiting professor at other institutions, including Columbia University, University of Rome, and University of Rio de Janeiro. Co-discoverer of slow neutrons, the antiproton, and of the elements technetium, astatine, and plutonium-239. *Military service:* Italian Army, 1928-29; became lieutenant.

MEMBER: National Academy of Sciences, American Physical Society (fellow), American Philosophical Society, American Academy of Arts and Sciences, Accademia Nazionale dei Lincei, Academy of Sciences of Peru, Society for the Progress of Science (Uruguay), Academy of Science of Heidelberg, Indian Academy of Sciences (Bangalore), Societa Italiana di fisica, Societa Italiana Progresso Science (honorary member). *Awards, honors:* Rockefeller Foundation fellow in Germany and Holland, 1930-32; Guggenheim fellow; Fulbright fellow; Hofmann Medal of German Chemical Society, 1954; honorary professor at University of San Marcos, 1955; Cannizzaro Medal of Accademia Nazionale dei Lincei, 1956; co-winner with Owen Chamberlain of Nobel Prize in physics, 1959, for discovery of the antiproton; honorary doctorates from University of Palermo, 1959, Hebrew Union College—Jewish Institute of Religion, 1960, Gustavus Adolphus College, 1967, and Tel Aviv University, 1972.

WRITINGS: Nuclei and Particles, Benjamin Co., 1953, 2nd edition, 1977; (editor) *Experimental Nuclear Physics,* Wiley, 1953; *Enrico Fermi, Physicist,* University of Chicago Press, 1970. Also author of *Personaggi e Scoperte nella Fisica Contemporanea.* Contributor of many articles to physics journals. Editor, *Annual Review of Nuclear Science.*

SIDELIGHTS: Emilio Segre's books have been published in Italian, Russian, Japanese, and Spanish.

* * *

SEIFERT, Shirley L(ouise) 1888-1971

May 22, 1888—September 1, 1971; American author of historical novels. Obituaries: *New York Times,* September 4, 1971; *Washington Post,* September 4, 1971; *Publishers Weekly,* October 4, 1971. (See index for *CA* sketch)

* * *

SEJIMA, Yoshimasa 1913-

PERSONAL: Born August 29, 1913, in Hokkaido, Japan; son of Shimpei (headman of his town) and Yana Sejima; married Yae Shimoda, December 14, 1943; children: Yoshie, Momoko. *Education:* Attended Rikkyo University. *Home:* 5-6-12 Tsujido-Motomachi, Fujisawa-shi, Kanagawa-ken, Japan. *Office:* Tama Art University, 3-15-34 Kaminoge-cho, Setagaya-ku, Tokyo, Japan.

CAREER: Tama Art University, Tokyo, Japan, professor of oil painting, 1953—.

WRITINGS—Illustrator: Yasoo Takeichi, *Okorinbo No Tonosama,* Shikosha, 1970, published in the United States as *The Mighty Prince,* Crown, 1971.†

* * *

SELIGSON, Tom 1946-

PERSONAL: Born January 16, 1946, in New York, N.Y.; son of Julius (an insurance salesman) and Gertrude

(Goodman) Seligson. *Education:* Columbia University, B.A., 1968. *Politics:* Radical. *Religion:* Humanist. *Home:* 325 Riverside Dr., New York, N.Y. 10025. *Agent:* Writers and Artists, 162 West 56th St., New York, N.Y. 10019.

CAREER: Teacher in elementary schools in New York, N.Y., 1968-70. *Member:* Peoples Coalition for Peace and Justice.

WRITINGS: (Editor with Marc Libarle) *The High School Revolutionaries,* Random House, 1970; *To Be Young in Babylon,* Paperback Library, 1971; *Stalking* (novel), New American Library, 1978. Contributor to magazines and newspapers, including *Evergreen Review, Look, New York Times, Glamour, Penthouse, Viva, Genesis, Gallery, Crawdaddy,* and *Village Voice.* Associate editor, *Defiance;* entertainment editor, *Mystery Monthly;* contributing editor, *Gallery.*

BIOGRAPHICAL/CRITICAL SOURCES: Westport News, October 2, 1970; *Westport Fair Press,* December 16, 1971.

* * *

SELTZER, Leon F(rancis) 1940-

PERSONAL: Born August 9, 1940, in Philadelphia, Pa.; son of Joseph (a butcher) and Rose (Kushnir) Seltzer; married Maxine Wolfson. *Education:* Temple University, B.A., 1962; University of Illinois, M.A., 1964; State University of New York at Buffalo, Ph.D., 1968. *Home:* 2838 Hampshire Rd., Cleveland Heights, Ohio 44118. *Office:* Department of English, Cleveland State University, Cleveland, Ohio 44115.

CAREER: Queens College of the City University of New York, Flushing, N.Y., assistant professor of English, 1967-70; Cleveland State University, Cleveland, Ohio, associate professor of English, 1970—. Judge, National Council of Teachers of English Annual Achievement Awards, 1973—. *Member:* National Council of Teachers of English, Modern Language Association of America, College English Association, National Association for Psychoanalytic Criticism. *Awards, honors:* Third prize in *College English* Rhetoric Contest, 1967; Cleveland State University research initiation award, 1972, and senior research award, 1977.

WRITINGS: The Vision of Melville and Conrad: A Comparative Study, Ohio University Press, 1970. Contributor of numerous articles to literature journals.

WORK IN PROGRESS: A book on values in contemporary American fiction.

SIDELIGHTS: Leon Seltzer told *CA:* "I have come, retrospectively, to see myself as a moral-psychological critic, in that virtually all of my articles (on Melville, Conrad, Dreiser, Hemingway, Faulkner, Heller, and Vonnegut), as well as my one published book to date, tend to focus on the psychological dynamics and moral implications of fictive behavior. My present interest—determining and assessing the values implicit in some of our most representative novelists—hopes to put to worthwhile critical use the psychological-moral theories of modern humanistic psychology."

* * *

SEN, Sudhir 1906-

PERSONAL: Born December 29, 1906, in Comilla, Bengal, India; son of Haradas (a lawyer) and Swarnamoyee (Neogy) Sen; married Kamala Gupta, December 14, 1940; children:

Shankar (son), Sheila (Mrs. Jay Jassanof), Shyamoli (daughter). *Education:* University of Calcutta, B.A. (honors), 1928; London School of Economics and Political Science, B.Sc. (honors), 1931; University of Bonn, Dr. rer. pol., 1933. *Office:* 307 East 44th St., Apt. 1707, New York, N.Y. 10017.

CAREER: International Thrift Institute, Milan, Italy, economic adviser, 1937-38; Tagore Institute of Rural Reconstruction, Bengal, India, director of rural development work, 1939-42; Viceroy's Executive Council, New Delhi, India, private secretary to Commerce and Food Member, 1942-43; Government of Bengal, Bengal, economic statistician in Civil Supplies Department, 1943-44, agricultural adviser in Agriculture Department, 1944-45; Government of India, Ministry of Finance, provincial national savings officer in Bengal, 1945-46; Damodar Valley Project (multipurpose development of Damodar River basin), secretary, 1946-47; Embassy of India, Moscow, Soviet Union, economic adviser, 1947-48; Damodar Valley Corp., chief executive, 1948-54 (spent four months, 1948, with Tennessee Valley Authority, Knoxville, Tenn., studying its program and methods); Great Eastern Shipping Co. Ltd., Bombay, India, general manager and adviser to managing agents, 1954-56; United Nations Technical Assistance Board, New York, N.Y., director of Programme Division, 1956-61, resident representative and director of special fund programs, Ghana, 1961-62, deputy administrator of U.N. Temporary Executive Authority in West New Guinea/West Irian, Indonesia, 1962-63, representative of development programs in Yugoslavia, 1963-66. Visiting professor of sociology, Brown University, 1967-68. Fellow, Alexander von Humboldt-Stiftung, Berlin, 1931-33, and Deutsch-Akademischier Austauschdienst, Munich, 1934-35. Secretary of sub-committee on rural marketing and finance, National Planning Committee of India, 1939-42; lecturer, University of Calcutta, 1939-42. *Member:* Society for International Development. *Awards, honors:* National Science Foundation fellow at Brown University, 1967-68.

WRITINGS: Die Goldbewegungen nach Frankreich in den letzten Jahren: Ursachen und Wirkungen (title means "Gold Movements into France in Recent Years—Causes and Effects"), Bonn, 1933; *Deutchland und die indische Wirtschaft* (title means "Germany and the Indian Economy"), Ferdinand Enke Verlag, 1937; *Conflict of Economic Ideologies in India: An Attempt at Reconciliation,* Viswa-Bharati, 1941; *Land and Its Problems,* Viswa-Bharati, 1943; *Rabindranath Tagore on Rural Reconstruction,* Viswa-Bharati, 1943; (contributor) Julian Huxley, editor, *The Humanist Frame,* Allen & Unwin, 1961, Harper, 1962; *United Nations in Economic Development: Need for a New Strategy,* Oceana, 1969; *A Richer Harvest: New Horizons for Developing Countries,* Orbis, 1974; *Reaping the Green Revolution: Food and Jobs for All,* Orbis, 1975; *Turning the Tide,* Macmillan, 1978. Contributor to *Economist, Capital* (Calcutta), *Commerce and Times of India* (Bombay), and other economic and financial journals in Germany, England, and India.

WORK IN PROGRESS: Obligations of Affluence, for Orbis.

SIDELIGHTS: Sudhir Sen told *CA:* "There are several reasons why I write. First, it is a kind of addiction—for some at least it is not hard to become pen-alcoholics. This incipient tendency, rooted in my early teenage, hardened over the years and grew into a kind of inner imperative. Second, a quarter century of intense bureaucratic life clashed with this imperative. Even when the monthly cheque filled the pocket

fairly well, only too often it left a sense of void within. I had to do an enormous amount of writing—letters, documents, reports. . . . How I longed for the day when I would be free to write on subjects that I could choose, in a style that suited my taste, and to publish the works in my own name! The three freedoms proved extremely hard to combine. Third, crowning it all was a deepening conviction: As economists we have made a travesty of our vocation. In particular, our performance in third-world development has been stunningly mediocre. Yet, what could be more important for an economist worth his salt than to try and, if not overcome, at least alleviate the problems of poverty, population and hunger that are exploding in today's world? So I was impelled to delve deep into these problems, sort them out as best I could, and press my own solutions in an effort to halt the accelerating drift towards a global disaster. Finally, as pressures built up within, I had no real choice but to bow and take up the pen. Yes, writing is a drudgery, and the pen is the toughest task master I have known. But it also offers some rare bonus. For one thing, it helps keep my diastolic low; and for another, I am now my own slave, something I had long yearned for. The magic of this voluntary slavery turns drudgery into fun.''

Sudhir Sen speaks German, French, Italian, and some Russian.

* * *

SENN, Peter R(ichard) 1923-

PERSONAL: Born November 22, 1923, in Milwaukee, Wis.; son of Paul and Dorothie (Severens) Senn; married Mary Stone, August 30, 1947; children: Martha, Paul. *Education:* Studied at Oregon State College (now University), 1941-43, and Syracuse University, 1943-44; University of Chicago, M.A., 1947; University of Paris, Diplome d'Etudes Superieures de Sciences Economiques (with honors), 1949, Docteur en droit (with honors), 1951. *Home:* 1121 Hinman Ave., Evanston, Ill. 60202. *Office:* Department of Economics, Wright College, Chicago City College, 3400 North Austin Ave., Chicago, Ill. 60634.

CAREER: Pennsylvania State University, University Park, assistant professor of economics, 1950-52; Chicago City College, Wright Branch (now Chicago City College, Wright College), Chicago, Ill., associate professor of economics, 1952-59; National Institute of Labor Education, Chicago, assistant director of Ethical and Moral Standards Project, 1960-61; Chicago Board of Education, Chicago, television coordinator, 1962; Roosevelt University, Chicago, professor of economics, 1963-64; Chicago City College, Wright College, professor of economics, 1964—. Instructor at schools and institutes at various universities. Holds directorships on several boards of companies. Consultant to universities, business, and professional organizations. Participant in seminars and conferences for various academic, professional, business, state, local, and federal bodies. *Military service:* U.S. Army, World War II. *Member:* American Economic Association, American Association of University Professors, Illinois Education Association. *Awards, honors*—Military: American Theater Medal, Asiatic-Pacific Theater Medal, Philippine Liberation Medal with Bronze Star, Battle Stars for New Guinea, Southern Philippines, and Luzon.

WRITINGS: Eighteen Years of Social Security, Research Council for Economic Security, 1954; *Problems of State and Local Finance in Illinois,* School of Business, Northwestern University, 1958; *Liberal Education for Trade Union*

Leaders: Problems and Prospects for a University Level Program, University College, University of Chicago, 1958; *Instructor's Manual for The Use of Case Material in Labor Education,* National Institute of Labor Education, 1961; *Cases for Use in Labor Education,* National Institute of Labor Education, 1961; (with Wayne Leys) *Fifty Ways to Evaluate Your Teaching,* National Institute of Labor Education, 1961; (with R. Isaacs and J. Dyckman) *Capital Requirements for Urban Development and Renewal,* McGraw, 1961; (with Wayne Leys) *Teaching Ethics in Labor Education,* National Institute of Labor Education, 1962; (contributor) *Our Working World,* grade 2, Science Research Associates, 1965; *Economics and the Idea of Mankind,* Council for the Study of Mankind, 1968; (with wife, Mary Senn) *A Short Guide to Literature of the Social Sciences,* Social Science Education Consortium, 1968; (with Joanne L. Binkley) *Consumer Education: Questions and Resources,* E.R.I.C. Clearinghouse for Social Studies and Social Science Education Consortium, 1971; *Social Science and Its Methods,* Holbrook, 1971; *Urban Economics,* C. E. Merrill, 1977; *Important Economic Issues in Recent American History,* C. E. Merrill, 1978. Contributor of articles and book reviews to *Pennsylvania Business Survey, Journal of Finance, Social Studies, Journal of the History of Ideas, Social Education, Social Economics,* and other publications.

* * *

SENNETT, Ted 1928-

PERSONAL: Surname originally Sinitsky; legally changed, 1955; born March 20, 1928, in Brooklyn, N.Y.; son of Benjamin and Fannie (Friedman) Sinitsky; married Roxane Gerber, February 14, 1954; children: Robert, David, Karen. *Education:* Brooklyn College (now Brooklyn College of the City University of New York), B.A., 1948; Columbia University, M.A., 1949; further study at New York University, 1951-53. *Home:* 31 Patton Lane, Closter, N.J. 07624.

CAREER: Charles Scribner's Sons, New York City, director of advertising, 1967-69; Praeger Publishing, New York City, director of promotion, advertising, and publicity, 1969-70; *New York Times,* New York City, promotion manager in Book Division, 1970-71; Crowell-Collier and Macmillan, Inc., New York City, marketing manager in Library Division, 1971-74. *Military service:* U.S. Army, 1953-55. *Member:* Publisher's Advertising Club.

WRITINGS: (With Martin Gross) *Are You Sure You're Kosher?,* Ericsson, 1964; *Warner Brothers Presents,* Arlington House, 1971; *Lunatics and Lovers,* Arlington House, 1974; (editor) *The Movie Buff's Book,* Harcourt, 1975; (editor) *The Old-Time Radio Book,* Harcourt, 1976; *The Movie Buff's Book 2,* Harcourt, 1977; *Your Show of Shows,* Macmillan, 1977.

* * *

SEXTON, Virgil Wesley 1918-

PERSONAL: Born May 26, 1918, in Spartansburg, Pa.; son of Harvey M. (a farmer) and Emma (Martin) Sexton; married Catherine Cobb (a home economist), June 25, 1941; children: Linda (Mrs. Keith Patrick), John, Judi (Mrs. Ross Faris). *Education:* Asbury College, B.A. (cum laude), 1941; Garrett Theological Seminary, B.D. (with honors), 1944; also attended Boston University and University of Michigan. *Politics:* Democrat. *Home:* 1322 Thompson St., Key West, Fla. 33040. *Office:* Ley Memorial United Methodist Church, 1304 Truman Ave., Key West, Fla. 33040.

CAREER: Ordained minister of United Methodist Church; pastor of churches in southern Indiana, 1944-76, and in Key West, Fla., 1976— . United Methodist Church, New York, N.Y., assistant general secretary of cultivation, Board of Missions, 1966-68; United Methodist Church, Dayton, Ohio, assistant general secretary for planning, General Program Council, 1968-76. *Military service:* U.S. Navy, chaplain, 1946-47, 1952-54; became commander; served in Korea. *Member:* American Institute of Planners (affiliate), Association for Clinical Pastoral Education, Inc., National Planning Association, Masonic Lodge, Scottish Rite. *Awards, honors:* D.D., University of Evansville, 1966.

WRITINGS: Listening to the Church: A Realistic Profile of Grassroots Opinion, Abingdon, 1971. Contributor to religion journals.

WORK IN PROGRESS: Research on opinions and attitudes of church men and women; research on process planning; studying values in decision-making.

AVOCATIONAL INTERESTS: Travel, hunting, fishing, conservation.†

* * *

SHAFER, Neil 1933-

PERSONAL: Born April 24, 1933, in Chicago, Ill.; son of Joseph (a dentist) and Gertrude (Gerstein) Shafer; married Edith Oelsner, June 7, 1964; children: Joel, Daniel, Deborah. *Education:* Arizona State College (now University), B.A., 1955; Catholic University of America, M.Music, 1959. *Office:* Western Publishing Co., Inc., Racine, Wis. 53404.

CAREER: Music teacher in elementary schools in Montgomery County, Md., 1959-62; Western Publishing Co., Inc., Racine, Wis., numismatic editor, 1962-75, senior editor, 1976— . Assistant conductor, Racine Symphony Orchestra, 1963-72; music director and coordinator, Kiwanis Youth Symphony of Racine, 1966— . Ex-officio member, Racine Symphony board of directors. *Military service:* U.S. Air Force, 1955-59; played with Air Force Band; became staff sergeant. *Member:* International Bank Note Society (member of board of directors), Organization of International Numismatists (former second vice-president; former member of board of directors), American Numismatic Association (life member), Society of Paper Money Collectors, Numismatic Literary Guild, Token and Medal Society, and many others. *Awards, honors:* Nathan Gold Memorial Award, 1967; certificate of award, Society of Paper Money Collectors, 1968; literary award, Paper Money Collectors of Michigan, 1970.

WRITINGS: U.S. Territorial Coinage for the Philippine Islands, Whitman Publishing, 1961; *A Guide Book of Philippine Paper Money,* Whitman Publishing, 1964; *A Guide Book of Modern U.S. Currency,* Western Publishing, 1965, 7th edition, 1975; *Philippine Emergency and Guerrilla Currency of World War II,* Western Publishing, 1974; *Let's Collect Paper Money!,* Western Publishing, 1976. Contributor to many paper money catalogs. Coordinating editor, *Current Coins of the World,* Western Publishing, 7th edition, 1976. *Whitman Numismatic Journal,* contributor, 1964-68, associate editor, 1968— .

WORK IN PROGRESS: A revision of *U.S. Territorial Coinage for the Philippine Islands;* a listing of all U.S.D.A. food stamps and coupons from 1939 to date; a listing of store issued food coupon change scrip, tokens for Food Stamp Program.

SIDELIGHTS: Neil Shafer told *CA:* "To begin with, I do not consider myself an author in the true sense, just a researcher and compiler of data I believe will be useful to collectors entering or already in a particular area of interest. I am concentrating my research efforts in paper money of the world because until recent years there had been very little done to gather and present the kind of information vitally needed by those potentially interested in the field. Examining literally thousands of notes over the years has taught me a great deal, and has given me a basis upon which to pursue serious research into a number of relatively unknown areas of paper money. As far as work habits in producing a new book are concerned, I find that it takes me a long time just 'living' with the project, thinking about it, looking around at related items, and then all of a sudden it can burst forth and I will have a basic outline of what I wish to include in the finished product. But as with any creative endeavor, it is as Brahms is supposed to have said: 'Composition is 5% inspiration and 95% perspiration.' I fully agree."

BIOGRAPHICAL/CRITICAL SOURCES: Racine Journal-Times, December 6, 1964.

*   *   *

SHAPIRO, Joan Hatch   1928-

PERSONAL: Born August 20, 1928, in Oslo, Norway; American citizen; daughter of Robert Lenox and Gertrude (MacDermott) Roessle; married Daniel Shapiro (a physician), 1952; children: Judy, Ellen, Mark. *Education:* Middlebury College, A.B. (cum laude), 1948; Oxford University, graduate study, 1948-50; Columbia University, M.S.S.W., 1953, postgraduate study, 1964, 1966, 1969. *Residence:* Wilmington, Vt.

CAREER: Travelers Aid Society, New York City, case worker, 1950-51; Manhattan State Hospital, New York City, psychiatric social worker, 1951-52; St. Luke's Hospital Center, New York City, psychiatric social worker, 1962-63, chief psychiatric social worker and chief consultant for community resources, 1964-69; Columbia University, School of Social Work, New York City, field supervisor, 1965-69; New York City Planning Commission, New York City, principal social planner, 1969—. Guest lecturer, Barnard College, 1968; guest lecturer and consultant, University of Florida, Tallahassee, 1968-70; associate professor, Division of Community Psychiatry, Columbia University, 1970-72; associate professor, School of Social Work and department of social anthropology, Smith College, 1972—. Chairman of section of community group work, National Conference on Social Welfare, 1969.

WRITINGS: (Contributor) Katherine Spencer, editor, *Socio-Cultural Elements in Casework: A Case Book of Seven Ethnic Case Studies,* Council on Social Work Education, 1955; *Transcending Fear of the Stranger* (monograph), United Neighborhood Houses, 1968; (with Barbara Hoffberg) *S.R.O.: A Service-Research Study,* Columbia University Urban Center and St. Luke's Hospital Center, 1969; *Communities of the Alone,* Association Press, 1971. Contributor to *Social Work, Social Work Practice,* and *American Journal of Orthopsychiatry.*

*   *   *

SHARKEY, Bernarda   1934-

PERSONAL: Born March 24, 1934, in Pond Creek, Okla.; daughter of Anthony Joseph and Catherine (Isaacs) Sharkey. *Education:* Earned B.A., Oklahoma, 1956; St. Mary's College, Notre Dame, Ind., M.A., 1969; Catholic University of America, M.A., 1971. *Religion:* Roman Catholic.

CAREER: Teacher in junior high schools in Oklahoma, 1952-68; Office of Religious Education, Diocese of Oklahoma City, Okla., staff member, 1969-71; Team Ministry at St. Joseph's, Norman, Okla., staff member, 1972-74; Archdiocese of San Francisco, Office of Religious Education, San Francisco, Calif., staff member, 1975—.

WRITINGS: Growing to Wonder, Paulist/Newman, 1972; (contributor) *Parish and Family,* Liturgical Conference, 1972; *A Case for Worship,* Silver Burdett, 1975; (contributor) *The New Rite of Penance,* Liturgical Conference, 1976. Also author of *Between,* published by Oklahoma Office of Religious Education. Contributor of articles and poetry to numerous periodicals, including *Catechist, Today,* and *Catholic School Journal.*

AVOCATIONAL INTERESTS: "Anything creative," especially the arts, writing poetry, and working with people.

*   *   *

SHAW, Henry I(var), Jr.   1926-

PERSONAL: Born June 29, 1926, in Yonkers, N.Y.; son of Henry I. (a dentist) and Virginia (Hernandez) Shaw; married Juanita Hubble, August 27, 1949; children: Marc, Brooke, Drake, Pierce. *Education:* Attended The Citadel, 1943-44; Hope College, B.A. (cum laude), 1949; Columbia University, M.A., 1950. *Politics:* Independent. *Religion:* Unitarian. *Home:* 8514 Oakford Dr., Springfield, Va. 22152. *Office:* History and Museums Division, U.S. Marine Corps Headquarters, Washington, D.C. 20380.

CAREER: U.S. Marine Corps, History and Museums Division, Washington, D.C., historian, 1951-62, chief historian, 1962—. Member of Inter-University seminar on armed forces and society. *Military service:* U.S. Marine Corps Reserve, 1944-46, 1950-51; became sergeant. *Member:* American Historical Association, Organization of American Historians, Royal Marine Historical Society, Military Historical Society, American Military Institute (trustee, 1977—), American Committee on the History of the Second World War, Society for Army Historical Research, Marine Corps Association, Naval Historical Foundation, Company of Military Historians (editor-in-chief, 1958-71), First Marine Division Association (secretary, 1970—), Rolling Hills Swim Club, Inc. *Awards, honors:* Marine Corps Meritorious Civilian Service award, 1954; Navy Department Superior Civilian Service Medal, 1963, 1967.

WRITINGS—All published by U.S. Government Printing Office, except as indicated: (With C. S. Nichols) *Okinawa: Victory in the Pacific,* 1955; (with F. O. Hough and V. E. Ludwig) *Pearl Harbor to Guadalcanal,* 1958; (with D. T. Kane) *Isolation of Rabaul,* 1963; (with B. A. Nalty and E. T. Turnbladh) *Central Pacific Drive,* 1966; (with B. M. Frank) *Victory and Occupation,* 1968; *Tarawa: A Legend Is Born,* Ballantine, 1969; (with R. W. Donnelly) *Blacks in the Marine Corps,* 1976. Contributor to *Military Affairs, Marine Corps Gazette, World War II,* and *History of the Second World War.* Managing editor, *Military Collector and Historian,* 1954-58.

WORK IN PROGRESS: Research into eighteenth- and nineteenth-century British military history, loyalists in the American Revolution, and U.S. Marine Corps and the Royal Marines.

SHAW, Ray

PERSONAL: Daughter of David and Lillian (Levinson) Shaw; married Eugene O. Rappaport (a medical doctor; deceased); children: Lee, Faith. *Education:* Attended New York University and Northwestern University. *Home:* 255 West 90th St., New York, N.Y. 10024. *Agent:* Ruth Aley, 145 East 35th St., New York, N.Y. 10016.

CAREER: Free-lance sculptor, photographer, and writer; has sculpted the hands of many celebrities, including those of Bernard Baruch, Lauren Bacall, Irving Berlin, Margaret Bourke-White, Jack Dempsey, General James Doolittle, Albert Einstein, Mischa Elman, Helen Hayes, Joe Louis, Clare Booth Luce, President Prado of Peru, Franklin D. Roosevelt, Bishop Fulton J. Sheen, Lowell Thomas, Margaret Truman, Sir Ernest McMillan, Fritz Reiner, and George Szell; has exhibited sculpture and photographs in numerous cities throughout United States, and covered photo assignments and lectured in many foreign countries for UNICEF, the World Bank, International Business Machines Corp., and others. *Member:* Overseas Press Club, Authors Guild, Authors League of America, Women's Press Club of New York.

WRITINGS: Cat Nips, Essandess, 1970; (with Charlotte Zolotow) *A Week in Lateef's World: India,* Crowell Collier, 1971; *The Nutcracker* (photo-story of the ballet), Prentice-Hall, 1971; *New York for Children,* Outerbridge & Lazard, 1971; *Work and Play around the World,* Award Books, 1971; *How to Find Those Great Overseas Jobs,* Award Books, 1972; *Candle Art,* Morrow, 1973; *Washington for Children,* Scribner, 1975. Contributor of articles to *Musical America, Family Circle, Maclean's* (Canada), *American Magazine, Charm,* and other periodicals.

WORK IN PROGRESS: A Week in Tooran's World: Iran, and *A Week in a Zuni Indian Child's World,* both for Crowell Collier; research on a book on Tibet; compiling photos to illustrate Walt Whitman's poetry.

SIDELIGHTS: Ray Shaw has traveled in Algeria, Denmark, England, Iceland, Ireland, India, Iran, Morocco, Switzerland, Tunisia, Turkey, Mexico and other countries on photo-journalistic assignments; she is presently awaiting word on a trip to China to execute book assignments. Shaw's sculpture of the hands of President F. D. Roosevelt is on permanent exhibit at the Hyde Park Library.

AVOCATIONAL INTERESTS: The dance, cooking.

*   *   *

SHAWN, Edwin Meyers   1891-1972
(Ted Shawn)

October 21, 1891—January 9, 1972; American father of modern dance. Obituaries: *New York Times,* January 10, 1972; *Washington Post,* January 11, 1972; *L'Express,* January 17-23, 1972; *Newsweek,* January 24, 1972; *Time,* January 24, 1972.

*   *   *

SHAY, Arthur   1922-

PERSONAL: Born March 31, 1922, in New York, N.Y.; son of Hyman and Mollie (Schesten) Shay; married Florence Gerson, November 30, 1944; children: Jane (Mrs. Jay Lynch), Harmon, Richard, Lauren, Steven. *Education:* Attended Brooklyn College, 1939-42. *Home:* 618 Indian Hill Rd., Deerfield, Ill. 60015.

CAREER: Time, Inc., New York, N.Y., reporter and bu-

reau chief for *Life* and *Time,* 1947-50; free-lance photographer and writer in Chicago, Ill., and vicinity, 1951—. Public relations director, Deerfield Citizens for Human Rights, 1959-78. Photographic consultant tt Blue Cross Association and to *Handball and Racquetball* (magazine). *Military service:* U.S. Army Air Forces, 1942-47; served in European and Pacific theaters; became first lieutenant; received Distinguished Flying Cross and Air Medal (five). *Member:* American Society of Magazine Photographers (secretary, 1968-72). *Awards, honors:* Over ninety-five photographic awards.

WRITINGS—Self-illustrated with photographs: "What Happens" series, published by Reilly & Lee: *What Happens When You Put Money in the Bank,* 1967; ... *When You Mail a Letter,* 1967; ... *When You Travel by Plane,* 1968; ... *When You Make a Telephone Call,* 1968; ... *When You Go to the Hospital,* 1969; ... *in a Car Factory,* 1969; ... *at a Television Station,* 1969; ... *When You Build a House,* 1970; ... *When You Spend Money,* 1970; ... *at the Zoo,* 1971; ... *When You Turn on the Light,* 1972; ... *at a Gas Station,* 1972; ... *at a Newspaper,* 1972; ... *at an Animal Hospital,* 1972; ... *at the Circus,* 1972; ... *in a Skyscraper,* 1972; ... *at a State Fair,* 1973; ... *at a Weather Station,* 1973; ... *When You Turn on the Gas,* 1975.

"What It's Like" series, published by Reilly & Lee: *What It's Like to be a Doctor,* 1971; ... *to be a Fireman,* 1971; ... *to be a Pilot,* 1971; ... *to be a Policeman,* 1971; ... *to be a Nurse,* 1972; ... *to be a Teacher,* 1972; ... *to be a Dentist,* 1972; ... *to be a Musician,* 1972; ... *to be a TV Producer,* 1973.

Other: *How a Family Grows* (sex education book; introductory notes by Morris Fishbein and Ner Littner), Reilly & Lee, 1968; (with Paul Haber) *Inside Handball,* Reilly & Lee, 1970; (with Chuck Leve) *Winning Raquetball,* Contemporary Books, 1976; (with Jean Sauser) *Inside Raquetball for Women,* Contemporary Books, 1977; (with Sauser) *Teaching Your Child Raquetball,* Contemporary Books, 1978; *Forty Common Errors in Golf and How to Correct Them,* Contemporary Books, 1978; *Forty Common Errors in Tennis and How to Correct Them,* Contemporary Books, 1978; (with Terry Fancher) *Forty Common Errors in Racquetball and How to Correct Them,* Contemporary Books, 1978.

Also author, with Marty Hogan and Charles Brumfield, of *Power Racquetball.* Author of play, "A Clock for Nikita," produced in Chicago at Stagelight Theater, 1964. More than 16,000 photographs have been published in *Time, Life, Fortune, Sports Illustrated,* and in books, brochures, and annual reports he has prepared or helped prepare for business and industrial firms.

*   *   *

SHEEHAN, Paul V(incent)   1904-

PERSONAL: Born August 7, 1904, in Everett, Wash.; son of Thomas Francis (a contractor) and Mary Anna (Winninghoff) Sheehan; married Mary Ann Hemenway, August 19, 1932; children: Pamela Ann (Mrs. Edgar Arnold Kaiser). *Education:* University of Washington, Seattle, A.B., 1926, A.M., 1930; University of Southern California, Ph.D., 1942. *Home:* 76 East Cortland, Fresno, Calif. 93704. *Office:* 311 North Fulton, Fresno, Calif. 93701.

CAREER: High school teacher in Kirkland, Wash., 1927-30; Fresno State College (now California State University, Fresno), Fresno, Calif., instructor, 1930-36, assistant professor, 1938-43, associate professor, 1943-46, professor of journalism, 1946-69, coordinator of public information, 1943-57, chairman of department of journalism, 1951-69, professor emeritus, 1969—. Visiting lecturer in journalism, Syracuse University, 1936-67; interim staff member of West Coast newspapers. California Department of Education, chairman of state curriculum committee on journalism, 1951, special assistant to state director of education and coordinator of state informational program on needs of California institutions, 1958. Former member of board of directors of American Cancer Society and Fresno County Tuberculosis Association.

MEMBER: Association for Education in Journalism, Fresno Press Club (president, 1967-68), Sigma Delta Chi, Alpha Phi Gamma (president, 1952-53). *Awards, honors:* Awards for service to journalism from California Intercollegiate Press Association and California Press Women, 1969.

WRITINGS: Better Business Letters, Benjamin H. Sanborn & Co., 1939; *Reportorial Writing,* Chilton, 1972. Contributor of articles to professional publications.

*   *   *

SHELDON, Richard (Robert) 1932-

PERSONAL: Born July 12, 1932, in Kansas City, Kan.; son of Richard Robert (a surgeon) and Helen (Zerzan) Sheldon; married Karen Ryden Sears, February 8, 1964; children: Katherine Palmer, John Ryden, Robert Charles. *Education:* University of Kansas, B.A., 1954; University of Michigan, L.L.B., 1960, Ph.D., 1966. *Home:* 86 South Main, Hanover, N.H. 03755. *Office:* Department of Russian Language and Literature, Dartmouth College, Hanover, N.H. 03755.

CAREER: Grinnell College, Grinnell, Iowa, assistant professor of Russian and head of department, 1965-66; Dartmouth College, Hanover, N.H., assistant professor, 1966-70, associate professor of Russian and chairman of department of Russian language and literature, 1970—. Visiting assistant professor, University of California, Berkeley, summer, 1968; visiting professor, Stanford University, spring, 1974. *Military service:* U.S. Army, 1955-57. *Member:* American Association of University Professors, American Association of Teachers of Slavic and East European Languages, American Association for the Advancement of Slavic Studies. *Awards, honors:* American Council of Learned Societies grant, 1970; fellow, Center for Advanced Study, University of Illinois, 1969-70.

WRITINGS: (Editor and translator) Viktor Shklovsky, *A Sentimental Journey,* Cornell University Press, 1970; (editor and translator) Shklovsky, *Zoo, or Letters Not about Love,* Cornell University Press, 1971; (editor and translator) Shklovsky, *Third Factory,* Ardis, 1977; (compiler) *Viktor Shklovsky: An International Bibliography of Works by and about Him,* Ardis, 1977. Contributor to Slavic language journals.

WORK IN PROGRESS: A monograph on the life and work of Viktor Shklovsky.

*   *   *

SHELTON, Richard 1933-

PERSONAL: Born June 24, 1933, in Boise, Idaho; son of Leonard P. and Hazel (Ashlock) Shelton; married Lois Bruce (a director of a poetry center), December 24, 1956; children: Brad Scott. *Education:* Attended Harding College, 1951-53; Abilene Christian College (now University), B.A., 1958; University of Arizona, M.A., 1961. *Home:* 1548 West Plaza DeLirios, Tucson, Ariz. 85705. *Office:* Department of English, University of Arizona, Tucson, Ariz. 85721.

CAREER: Teacher in public schools of Bisbee, Ariz., 1958-60; University of Arizona, Tucson, instructor, 1960-70, assistant professor of English, 1970—. Director of writers workshop at Arizona State Prison, Arizona Commission on the Arts and Humanities, 1974—. *Military service:* U.S. Army, 1956-58. *Member:* P.E.N., Rocky Mountain Modern Language Association, Arizona Commission on the Arts and Humanities (member of literary selection panel). *Awards, honors:* International Poetry Forum's United States award, 1970; Borestone Mountain Poetry Award, 1972, for "Requiem for Sonora"; National Endowment for the Arts writers fellowship, 1977.

WRITINGS—Poetry: Journal of Return, Kayak, 1969; *The Tattooed Desert,* University of Pittsburgh Press, 1971; *Calendar,* Baleen Press, 1972; *The Heroes of Our Time,* Best Cellar Press, 1972; *Of All the Dirty Words,* University of Pittsburgh Press, 1972; *Among the Stones,* Monument Press, 1972; *You Can't Have Everything,* University of Pittsburgh Press, 1975; *Chosen Place,* Best Cellar Press, 1975; (editor) *The Unfinished Man: The Poems of Paul David Ashley,* Baleen Press, 1977. Contributor of poems to literary and popular journals, including *New Yorker.*

*   *   *

SHEPARD, Martin 1934-

PERSONAL: Born November 9, 1934, in New York, N.Y.; son of Mac and Marcia Shepard; married second wife, Judith (an actress), February, 1971; children: (first marriage) Marc, Richard, Yan Alan. *Education:* New York University, A.B., 1956, M.D., 1960. *Politics:* Radical/Conservative. *Religion:* Mystical. *Home address:* Box 43, Sagaponack, N.Y. 11962.

CAREER: Private practice as psychiatrist in New York City, 1964-70; Anthos, New York City, co-director, 1969-72; writer; designer and home builder in East Hampton, N.Y. Consulting psychiatrist, New York City Department of Corrections, Rikers Island, 1968-70.

WRITINGS: (With Marjorie Lee) *Games Analysts Play,* Putnam, 1970; (with Lee) *Marathon 16,* Putnam, 1970; *The Love Treatment,* Peter H. Wyden, 1971; *A Psychiatrist's Head,* Peter H. Wyden, 1972; (with Lee) *Sexual Marathon,* Pinnacle, 1972; *The Do-It-Yourself Psychotherapy Book,* Peter H. Wyden, 1973; *Beyond Sex Therapy,* Penthouse, 1974; *Fritz,* Dutton, 1975; *Someone You Love Is Dying,* Harmony, 1975; *A Question of Values,* Dutton, 1976, published as *The Couch,* Bantam, 1977. Contributing editor, *Annual Survey of Psychoanalysis,* 1958-59.

WORK IN PROGRESS: "Top Secret."

SIDELIGHTS: Martin Shepard told *CA,* "A successful writer needs a measure of talent, a bit of diligence, luck with reviewers, and the favor of God."

BIOGRAPHICAL/CRITICAL SOURCES: New York Times, June 1, 1970.

*   *   *

SHEPHERD, Elizabeth

PERSONAL: Born in Boston, Mass.; daughter of Donald F. (a manufacturer) and Emma (a botanist; maiden name, Couch) Cameron; married Peter Shepherd (a literary agent), 1960; children: Ann, Adam. *Education:* Bryn Mawr College, B.A., 1948; Columbia University, M.A., 1977; also attended University of Bordeaux and Harvard University. *Residence:* New York, N.Y.

CAREER: Dalton Schools, New York City, teacher of English, 1954-55; Oxford University Press, New York City, assistant trade editor, 1955-60; Dell Publishing Co., New York City, trade editor, 1960-63; Grolier Publications, New York City, science editor, 1963-66; educational therapist; writer for children. Member: Authors Guild.

WRITINGS—Juvenile; published by Lothrop, except as indicated: Jellyfishes, 1969; In a Pygmy Camp, 1969; The Discoveries of Esteban the Black, Dodd, 1970; In Our Carib Indian Village, 1971; Tracks between the Tides, 1972; Arms of the Sea: Our Vital Estuaries, 1973; Minnows, 1974. Contributor of articles on subjects concerned with children's welfare to magazines.

WORK IN PROGRESS: Tuna; Hypnosis.

SIDELIGHTS: Elizabeth Shepherd told CA: "[I] read much anthropology and natural science. [I] try to write on subjects that expand my own knowledge about the way men live together and use their surroundings. [My] intense dislike of waste—whether human or material—motivates much of what I do. [I] seek to share with children life-affirming values."

AVOCATIONAL INTERESTS: Hiking, sailing.

*   *   *

SHERBURNE, James (Robert) 1925-

PERSONAL: Born May 22, 1925, in East Lansing, Mich.; son of Thomas Lilley and Ida May (Mead) Sherburne; married Margaret McDowell (a lawyer), October 17, 1947; married second wife, Nancy Garner (an actress), April 19, 1952; children: (second marriage) James R., Jr., Nancy Lee, Jenny Louise. Education: Attended Berea College, 1943-44; University of Kentucky, B.A., 1947. Politics: Left Independent. Religion: Agnostic. Home: Midway, Ky. 40347. Agent: William Morris Agency, 1350 Avenue of the Americas, New York, N.Y. 10019.

CAREER: Henri, Hurst & McDonald, Inc. (advertising agency), Chicago, Ill., copy writer, 1947-54; Foote, Cone & Belding, Inc. (advertising agency), Chicago, copy writer, 1954-57; Edward H. Weiss, Inc. (advertising agency), Chicago, senior copy writer, 1957-59; Campbell-Mithun, Inc. (advertising agency), Chicago, senior copy writer, 1959-60; Needham, Louis & Brorby, Inc. (advertising agency), Chicago, copy supervisor, 1960-62; Arthur Meyerhoff & Associates (advertising agency), Chicago, associate creative director, 1962-68; Columbia College, Chicago, instructor in English and advertising, 1969-70. Instructor and lecturer in creative writing at Berea College, Eastern Kentucky University, Bellarmine College, and in the Louisville Public School System. Military service: U.S. Naval Reserve, active duty, 1943-46; became lieutenant junior grade; commanded a patrol craft. Member: Authors Guild. Awards, honors: Friends of Literature award, 1971, for Hacey Miller.

WRITINGS—All published by Houghton: Hacey Miller, 1971; The Way to Fort Pillow, 1972; Stand like Men, 1973; Rivers Run Together, 1974.

WORK IN PROGRESS: On Both Your Houses; The Buffalo Soldiers; a novel, as yet untitled.

*   *   *

SHERMAN, Arnold 1932-

PERSONAL: Born May 27, 1932, in New York, N.Y.; son of Joseph (a button salesman) and Gladys Sherman; married Mary Lucille Harris, 1952; children: Michele, Jonathan, Laura. Education: Attended Brooklyn College (now Brooklyn College of the City University of New York). Religion: Jewish. Home: Moshav Michmoret, Israel.

CAREER: Aviation Week, New York, N.Y., news editor, 1957-63; Israel Aircraft Industries, Lod, Israel, public relations director, 1963-65; El Al-Israel Airlines, Lod, public relations director, 1965—. Military service: U.S. Army, 1951-52. Israeli Army, 1967—.

WRITINGS: Impaled on a Cactus Bush: An American Family in Israel, Sabra Books, 1970; In the Bunkers of Sinai, Sabra Books, 1971; El Al: The Story of an Airline, Vallentine, Mitchell, 1973; Lightning in the Skies, Bitan, 1973; When God Judged and Men Died, Bantam, 1973; The Druse, Bazak, 1974; The Pomeranz Connection, Stone, 1976; Israel on Ten to Fifteen Dollars a Day, Frommer, 1976; Blue Sky, Red Sea, Edanim, 1977; Dream of Rohamim, Bitan, 1977. Also author of Impaled on a Rhino's Horn, Bitan. Contributor to American and Israeli periodicals.

WORK IN PROGRESS: History of Illegal Immigration into Palestine.

SIDELIGHTS: Arnold Sherman lived in Paris for one year and in Mallorca for a year. In 1971 he went on safari in East Africa.

*   *   *

SHERMAN, Ray W(esley) 1884-1971

1884—October 24, 1971; American author and automotive editor. Obituaries: New York Times, October 27, 1971.

*   *   *

SHESTACK, Alan 1938-

PERSONAL: Born June 23, 1938, in New York, N.Y.; son of David (a wholesaler) and Sylvia (Saffran) Shestack; married Nancy Jane Davidson (a teacher of Asian history), September, 1967. Education: Wesleyan University, Middletown, Conn., B.A., 1961; Harvard University, M.A., 1963. Politics: Democrat. Religion: Jewish. Home: 191 Bishop St., New Haven, Conn. 06511. Office: Department of Art History, Yale University, New Haven, Conn. 06520.

CAREER: National Gallery of Art, Washington, D.C., curator of prints, 1964-67; Yale University, New Haven, Conn., curator of prints and drawings, Art Gallery, 1967-71; director of Art Gallery and adjunct professor of art history, 1971—. Member: College Art Association of America, Print Council of America (vice-president, 1970-71), Phi Beta Kappa. Awards, honors: Woodrow Wilson fellow, 1962-63; David E. Finley fellow of National Gallery of Art, 1963-65.

WRITINGS: Master E. S. (catalogue), Philadelphia Museum of Art, 1967; Fifteenth Century Engravings of Northern Europe (catalogue), National Gallery of Art, 1967; (editor) The Complete Engravings of Martin Schongauer, Dover, 1970; Master LCz and Master WB, Collectors Editions, 1971.

WORK IN PROGRESS: Prints: Styles and Media, for Penguin; research on history of graphic art, German art of the fifteenth and sixteenth centuries, and contemporary American art.

SIDELIGHTS: Alan Shestack spent a year in Austria and Germany studying the holdings of the great print collections.

*   *   *

SHEWMAKER, Kenneth E. 1936-

PERSONAL: Born June 26, 1936, in Los Angeles, Calif.;

son of James V. and Jeanette (Martin) Shewmaker; married Elisabeth Spalteholz, June 12, 1960; children: Richard Glenn, Nancy Jeanette. *Education:* Concordia Teachers College, River Forest, Ill., B.S., 1960; University of California, Berkeley, M.A., 1961; Northwestern University, Ph.D., 1966. *Politics:* Independent. *Religion:* Lutheran. *Home address:* Greensboro Rd., R.F.D., Lebanon, N.H. 03766. *Office:* Department of History, Dartmouth College, Hanover, N.H. 03755.

CAREER: Northwestern University, Evanston, Ill., instructor in history, 1965-66; College of William and Mary, Williamsburg, Va., assistant professor of history, 1966-67; Dartmouth College, Hanover, N.H., assistant professor, 1967-72, associate professor of history, 1972—. Member of board of control, New England district, Lutheran Church—Missouri Synod, 1972—. *Member:* American Historical Association, Organization of American Historians, Society for Historians of American Foreign Relations, New Hampshire Historical Society. *Awards, honors:* Joint Committee on Contemporary China of Social Science Research Council and American Council of Learned Societies research grant, 1967-68; Stuart L. Bernath Prize for best first or second book on U.S. diplomatic history, Society for Historians of American Foreign Relations, 1972; National Historical Publications Commission research grant, 1972-73.

WRITINGS: Americans and Chinese Communists, 1927-1945: A Persuading Encounter, Cornell University Press, 1971; (contributor) Richard Lowitt and Joseph F. Wall, editors, *Interpreting Twentieth-Century America: A Reader,* Crowell, 1973. Contributor to *Dictionary of American Biography.* Contributor to professional journals. Associate editor, "The Papers of Daniel Webster."

WORK IN PROGRESS: Editing the diplomatic papers of Daniel Webster.

* * *

SHIGA, Naoya 1883-1971

1883—October, 1971; Japanese writer of short stories and essays. Obituaries: *Time,* November 1, 1971.

* * *

SHILOH, Ailon 1924-

PERSONAL: Born September 5, 1924, in Toledo, Ohio; married Cynthia Amias (a teacher), August 31, 1952; children: Michael, Gabriel, Dina. *Education:* University of New Mexico, B.A. (with honors), 1949; University of Michigan, M.A., 1950; Dropsie College for Hebrew and Cognate Learning (now Dropsie University), Ph.D., 1958. *Politics:* Independent. *Religion:* Jewish. *Home:* 7 Hechalutz, Jerusalem, Israel. *Office:* Department of Anthropology, University of South Florida, Tampa, Fla. 33620.

CAREER: Research associate, Hadassah Medical Organization, 1954-65; University of Pittsburgh, Graduate School of Public Health, Pittsburgh, Pa., professor of anthropology in public health, 1966-73; University of South Florida, Tampa, director of graduate studies, 1973—.

WRITINGS: Peoples and Cultures of the Middle East, Random House, 1969; *Studies in Human Sexual Behavior: The American Scene,* C. C Thomas, 1970; *Alternatives to Doomsday,* Berger Press, 1971; *By Myself I'm a Book: An Oral History of the Early Jewish Experience in Pittsburgh,* American Jewish Historical Society, 1972; *Ethnic Groups of America: Their Morbidity, Mortality and Behavior Disorders,* C. C Thomas, Volume I: *The Jews,* 1973, Volume II:

The Blacks, 1974. Also author of *Christianity against Jesus* and *Primitive Christianity.*

* * *

SHIVERS, Jay S(anford) 1930-

PERSONAL: Born July 7, 1930, in New York, N.Y.; son of Ted M. and Mabel (Sinkoff) Shivers; married Rhoda Goldstein (a teacher), February 14, 1951; children: Jed Mark. *Education:* Indiana University, B.S., 1952; New York University, M.A., 1953, additional study, 1953-55; University of Wisconsin, Ph.D., 1958. *Politics:* Independent. *Home:* South Eagleville Rd., Storrs, Conn. 06268. *Office:* U-34, University of Connecticut, Storrs, Conn. 06268.

CAREER: Hillside Psychiatric Hospital, Glen Oaks, N.Y., recreational leader, 1952-53; Goldwater Memorial Hospital, Welfare Island, N.Y., director of recreational rehabilitation, 1953; University of Wisconsin—Madison, instructor in education, 1955-57; U.S. Veterans Administration Hospital, Madison, Wis., recreational supervisor, 1957-58; Mississippi Southern College (now University of Southern Mississippi), Hattiesburg, professor of recreational service education and chairman of department, 1958-62; University of Connecticut, Storrs, assistant professor, 1962-66, associate professor, 1967-69, professor of recreational service education, 1970—. Visiting summer professor at Eastern Washington State College (now Eastern Washington University), 1963, and California State College at Hayward (now California State University, Hayward), 1967. Chairman of Mansfield (Conn.) Recreational Services Commission, 1965—, and Mansfield Park Planning Committee, 1962—. Member of scientific committee, Van Cle Foundation, 1976. *Military service:* U.S. Army, Counter-Intelligence Corps, special agent, 1953-55.

MEMBER: International Recreation Association, World Leisure and Recreation Association, International Playground Association, International Rehabilitation Association, National Recreation and Park Association, Society of Professional Recreation Educators, National Therapeutic Recreational Society, American Association for Health, Physical Education and Recreation, American Association of University Professors, United World Federalists, Connecticut Recreation and Park Association, Sierra Club, Phi Delta Kappa. *Awards, honors:* Certificate of Achievement from Hospital Section, American Recreation Society, 1965; Honor Award of Connecticut Recreation Society, 1968.

WRITINGS: Horizons Unlimited: The Organization of Recreational Services in the State of Mississippi, Mississippi Recreation Association, 1959; (with George Hjelte) *Public Administration of Park and Recreational Services,* Macmillan, 1962; *Leadership in Recreational Service,* Macmillan, 1963; *Principles and Practices of Recreational Service,* Macmillan, 1967; *Camping: Management, Counselling, Program,* Appleton, 1971; *Planning Recreational Places,* A. S. Barnes, 1971; (with Hjelte) *Public Administration of Recreational Services,* Lea & Febiger, 1972; (with C. R. Calder) *Recreational Crafts for School and Community,* McGraw, 1974; (with Hollis F. Fait) *Therapeutic Recreational Service,* Lea & Febiger, 1975; *Essentials of Recreational Service,* Lea & Febiger, 1978; *Perceptions of Recreation and Leisure,* Holbrook, 1978; *Recreational Leadership: Group Dynamics and Interpersonal Relations,* Holt, 1978.

Also author of master plans for recreational service in various towns. Contributor of more than thirty articles to recreation and rehabilitation journals. Member of editorial board,

Recreation in Treatment Centers (annual publication), 1962-69, editor, 1964-66.

WORK IN PROGRESS: Problems in Recreational Service: A Case Method Approach; with Hollis F. Fait, *Recreational Service for the Aging,* for Saunders; with George Hjelte, *Public Administration of Recreational Service,* for Lea & Febiger.

*   *   *

SHOBERG, Lore   1949-

PERSONAL: Born January 25, 1949, in San Diego, Calif.; son of Clifford A. (a truck driver) and Beverly (Canfield) Shoberg; married Patricia Fitzgerald, March 23, 1968; children: Lore Christian. *Education:* Attended public schools. *Politics:* "Not interested." *Religion:* "Not interested."

CAREER: Free-lance cartoonist and illustrator for D.C. Comics, Inc., *National Lampoon* (magazine), and others.

WRITINGS—All juvenile: *Morgan and Things,* McGraw, 1972; *Machine,* McGraw, 1973; *Willy!,* McGraw, 1974. Coauthor of horror stories for "House of Mystery" series, D. C. Comics, Inc.

AVOCATIONAL INTERESTS: Making films, music (plays guitar), silk screening, making children's posters.†

*   *   *

SHRYOCK, Richard Harrison   1893-1972

March 29, 1893—January 30, 1972; American medical historian and educator. Obituaries: *New York Times,* February 1, 1972; *Washington Post,* February 2, 1972; *Publishers Weekly,* February 14, 1972. (See index for *CA* sketch)

*   *   *

SIEGEL, Martin   1933-

PERSONAL: Born May 27, 1933, in Brooklyn, N.Y.; son of Samuel G. (an accountant) and Helen (Berger) Siegel; married Judith Tobias; children: Sally Hortense. *Education:* Cornell University, B.S., 1955; Hebrew Union College, B.H.L., 1960, M.A.H.L., 1960.

CAREER: Rabbi of congregation in Wheeling, W. Va., 1962-67; Wheeling College, Wheeling, professor of Jewish studies, 1965-67; Temple Sinai, Lawrence, N.Y., rabbi, 1967-72; Woodmere Academy, Woodmere, N.Y., teacher of comparative religion, beginning 1967; State University of New York at Stony Brook, professor of theology, beginning 1971. Chairman, West Virginia Council on the Arts and Humanities, 1964-67. *Military service:* U.S. Navy, chaplain, 1960-62; became captain. *Member:* American Academy of Religion, Central Conference of American Rabbis.

WRITINGS: Amen: The Diary of Rabbi Martin Siegel, edited by Melvin Ziegler, World Publishing, 1971; (editor with Michael Zeik) *Root and Branch: The Jewish/Christian Dialogue,* Charles N. Roth, 1973. Contributor to *Military Chaplain.*

WORK IN PROGRESS: A book on the Judaization of Christianity; and *The Next Stage: Sexual Religion.*

BIOGRAPHICAL/CRITICAL SOURCES: New York Magazine, January 18, 1971; *Time,* March 15, 1971; *Newsday,* May 8, 1971.†

*   *   *

SIFTON, Paul F.   1893(?)-1972

1893(?)—April 4, 1972; American newsman, labor lobbyist, and author. Obituaries: *Washington Post,* April 8, 1972.

SILEN, Juan Angel   1938-

PERSONAL: Born May 20, 1938, in San Juan, P.R.; son of Juan and Armida T. (Acevedo) Silen; married Nancy A. Zayas (a translator and member of Environmental Quality Board of Puerto Rico), November 16, 1962 (divorced February, 1971); married Milagros A. Ortiz, July 23, 1974; children: (first marriage) Juan Angel, Yenan, Carlos Ivan; (second marriage) Omar Ahmed. *Education:* University of Puerto Rico, B.A. (social science), 1959, B.A. (education), 1960, M.A., 1969, Ph.D., 1978. *Politics:* Nationalist. *Religion:* None. *Office:* Editorial de la Libreria Internacional, Rio Piedras, P.R.

CAREER: Department of Labor, San Juan, P.R., research interviewer, Minimum Wage Board, 1961; San Jose School District, San Juan, teacher, Central High School, 1962, history and geography teacher, Dr. Jose N. Gandara School, 1962-69; City University of New York, New York, N.Y., instructor in history and culture of Puerto Rico, Queens College, 1969-71, Brooklyn College, 1970, SEEK Program, Queens College, assistant director, 1969-70, associate director, director of faculty and of tutorial services, 1970-71; Editorial de la Libreria Internacional, Rio Piedras, P.R., chief editor, 1972— . Lecturer, Bernard M. Baruch College of the City University of New York, 1969, Casa Las Americas, New York, 1970, Hunter College of the City University of New York, 1970, and State University of New York at Buffalo, 1970; instructor, Graduate School of Social Work, New York University, 1970-71; Puerto Rican studies department, State University of New York at Albany, visiting associate professor, 1975-77, acting chairman of department, 1977. Consultant, African-Hispanic Institute, New York, 1969-70, Puerto Rican Forum, New York, 1970-71.

MEMBER: Ateneo Puertorriqueno, Asociacion de Maestros de Puerto Rico, Asociacion de Empleados del Estado Libre Asociado de Puerto Rico. *Awards, honors:* Medal from Association for Historical Museum of Puerto Rico, 1955; first prize in short stories, General Studies Faculty, University of Puerto Rico, 1955-56; honorary award from Puerto Rican Literary Institute, 1977, for *Hacia una vision positiva del puertorriqueno.*

WRITINGS: La Abuelona (short story), Primera Iglesia Bautista de Santurce, 1957; *La Guerrilla Civica,* Rojo y Negro (Rio Piedras), 1967; *Lares: Apuntes para una historia,* Talleres Graficos Interamericanos (San Juan), 1968; *Comentarios en torno a una filosofia educativa para Puerto Rico,* Universidad de Puerto Rico, 1969; *Hacia una vision positiva del puertorriqueno,* Editorial Edil (Rio Piedras), 1970, 4th edition, 1976, translation by Cedric Belfrage published as *We, the Puerto Rican People: A Story of Oppression and Resistance,* Monthly Review Press, 1971; *Historia del Grito de Lares,* Ediciones KIKIRIKI, 1972; *La mujer en la lucha hoy,* Ediciones KIKIRIKI, 1973; *La nueva lucha de Independencia,* Editorial Edil, 1973; *Historia de la nacion puertorriquena,* Editorial Edil, 1973; *De la guerrilla civica a la nacion dividia,* Editorial Puerto, 1974; *Pedro Albizu Campos,* Editorial Cultural, 1976; *Lelolay* (short novel), Editorial Cultural, in press; *Obuao Moin* (short stories), Editorial Cultural, in press; *La generacion de escritores de 1970,* Editorial Cultural, in press.

Regular contributor to *Claridad* and *El Imparcial;* contributor of short stories, verse, and biographies to *Alma Latina, Presente,* and to University of Puerto Rico publications, *Campus* and *Universidad.* Director, *Universidad* (newspaper), 1960-61, *Claridad* (newspaper), 1962-63, *Rojo y Negro* (magazine), 1967.

WORK IN PROGRESS: La duz derramada, El humo era negro, and *La carta en el camino,* all novels; *Las ninas hambrientas.*

* * *

SILLS, David Lawrence 1920-

PERSONAL: Born August 24, 1920, in New York, N.Y.; married Yole Granata, 1948; children: Gregory L. *Education:* Dartmouth College, B.A., 1942; Yale University, M.A., 1948; Columbia University, Ph.D., 1956. *Home:* 95 Circle Dr., Hastings-on-Hudson, N.Y. *Office:* Social Science Research Council, 605 Third Ave., New York, N.Y. 10016.

CAREER: Headquarters, Supreme Commander of Allied Powers in Japan, research analyst with Public Opinion and Sociological Research Division, 1947-50; Columbia University, New York City, research associate, Bureau of Applied Social Research, 1952-61, lecturer in sociology, School of General Studies, 1959-61, adjunct research associate, Bureau of Applied Social Research, 1962-68; United Nations Technical Assistance Organization, expert at Demographic Training and Research Centre, Bombay, India, 1960-61; Crowell Collier & Macmillan, Inc., New York City, editor of *International Encyclopedia of the Social Sciences,* 1962-67; Center for Advanced Study in the Behavioral Sciences, Stanford, Calif., fellow, 1967-68; Population Council, New York City, associate director of Demographic Division, 1968-69, director of Demographic Division, 1969-72; Social Science Research Council, New York City, executive associate, 1973—. Visiting scholar, Russell Sage Foundation, 1973. *Military service:* U.S. Army, 1942-46; became first lieutenant. *Member:* American Sociological Association (fellow), American Association for Public Opinion Research.

WRITINGS: (With others) *The Japanese Village in Transition,* Natural Resources Section, Supreme Commander of Allied Powers in Japan, 1950; *The Volunteers: Means and End in a National Organization,* Free Press, 1957; (contributor) Daniel Lerner, editor, *The Passing of Traditional Society,* Free Press, 1958; (contributor) Nathan E. Cohen, editor, *The Citizen Volunteer,* Harper, 1960; (contributor) Harvey S. Perloff and Henry Cohen, editors, *Urban Research and Education in the New York Metropolitan Region,* Volume II, New York Regional Plan Association, 1965; (editor with William A. Glaser) *The Government of Associations: Selections from the Behavioral Sciences,* Bedminster, 1966; (editor and contributor) *International Encyclopedia of the Social Sciences,* seventeen volumes, Macmillan, 1968; (contributor) C. S. Wallia, editor, *Toward Century 21,* Basic Books, 1970. Contributor to *New York Times* and professional journals.

BIOGRAPHICAL/CRITICAL SOURCES: Christian Century, September 25, 1968; *New York Review of Books,* February 27, 1969.

* * *

SILVER, Gerald A(lbert) 1932-

PERSONAL: Born June 5, 1932, in Omaha, Neb.; son of Harry and Rose (Albert) Silver; children: Steven, Barbara, Richard, Larry. *Education:* Los Angeles City College, A.A., 1953; Los Angeles State College of Applied Arts and Sciences (now California State University, Los Angeles), B.A., 1955; California State College at Los Angeles (now California State University, Los Angeles), M.A., 1965; University of California, Los Angeles, Ed.D., 1969. *Resi-*

dence: North Hollywood, Calif. *Office:* Literary Graphics, 12444 Victory Blvd., Suite 405A, North Hollywood, Calif. 91606.

CAREER: Silver Star Printing Co., Los Angeles, Calif., owner, 1950-61; Los Angeles City College, Los Angeles, assistant professor of business administration, 1961—; writer and photographer, 1962—. Instructor of technical writing seminars in Los Angeles. Has appeared on television and has had speaking engagements at professional meetings and at various educational institutions.

WRITINGS: Printing Estimating, American Technical Society, 1970; *Modern Graphic Arts Paste-up,* American Technical Society, 1973; *Simplified BASIC Programming,* McGraw, 1974; *Computer Algorithms and Flowcharting,* McGraw, 1975; *Professional Printing Estimating,* North American Publishing, 1975; *Simplified ANSI Fortran IV Programming,* Harcourt, 1976; *Introduction to Systems Analysis,* Prentice-Hall, 1976; *Data Processing for Business,* Harcourt, 1977; *Small Computers Systems for Business,* McGraw, 1978; *Introduction to Modern Business,* McGraw, 1978. Contributor to professional journals.

WORK IN PROGRESS: Social Impact of Computers, for Harcourt.

AVOCATIONAL INTERESTS: Electronics, foreign travel.

* * *

SILVERMAN, Morris 1894-1972

November 19, 1894—March 4, 1972; American rabbi and author of books on Judaica. Obituaries: *Publishers Weekly,* April 17, 1972.

* * *

SIMON, Arthur 1930-

PERSONAL: Born July 28, 1930, in Eugene, Ore.; son of Martin P. and Ruth (Troemel) Simon; married Carol Schoonmaker, July 28, 1968; children: Nathan Paul, Peter Martin. *Education:* Attended Dana College, 1948-51; Concordia Seminary, St. Louis, Mo., M.Div., 1956, M.S.T., 1957. *Home:* 411 East Tenth St., New York, N.Y. 10009. *Office:* 207 East 16th St., New York, N.Y. 10003.

CAREER: Trinity Lutheran Church, New York City, pastor, 1961-73; Bread for the World, New York City, executive director, 1974—. *Awards, honors:* National Religious Book Award from Religious Press Associations, 1976, for *Bread for the World.*

WRITINGS: Faces of Poverty, Concordia, 1966; *Stuyvesant Town, U.S.A.: Pattern for Two Americas,* New York University Press, 1970; *Breaking Bread with the Hungry,* Augsburg, 1971; (with brother, Paul Simon) *The Politics of World Hunger,* Harper Magazine Press, 1973; *Bread for the World,* Paulist/Newman, 1975. Contributor to national and religious magazines, including *Atlantic Monthly, New Republic, Commonweal,* and *Christian Century.*

BIOGRAPHICAL/CRITICAL SOURCES: Commonweal, January 22, 1971; *Christian Century,* March 17, 1971.

* * *

SIMON, Boris-Jean 1913(?)-1972

1913(?)—April 14, 1972; French painter and art historian. Obituaries: *L'Express,* April 24-30, 1972.

SIMON, Howard 1903-

PERSONAL: Born July 22, 1903, in New York, N.Y.; son of Samuel and Bertha (Seide) Simon; married Charlie May Hogue (an author; divorced, 1936); married Mina Lewiton (an author), January 20, 1936 (died, 1969); married Pony M. Bouche, June 18, 1971; children: (second marriage) Bettina (Mrs. James Niederer). *Education:* Studied at National Academy of Art, New York, 1920-21, and Julien Academy, Paris, 1922-23. *Home and studio:* Lilac Hill, Stanfordville, N.Y. 12581.

CAREER: Artist; author, illustrator, and designer of books; adjunct professor of art at New York University, New York, N.Y., 1946-64. Paintings, drawings, woodcuts and lithographs have been shown in a number of exhibits in America and at Victoria and Albert Museum, London; has had one-man shows at Art Center, New York, at Smithsonian Institution, and at Three Arts Gallery, Poughkeepsie, N.Y.; work included in collections of Metropolitan Museum, New York Public Library, New York University Gallery of Portraits, and other galleries. *Member:* American Institute of Graphic Arts, Dutchess County Art Association.

WRITINGS: 500 Years of Art and Illustration, from Albrecht Duerer to Rockwell Kent, World Publishing, 1942, 2nd edition published as *500 Years of Art in Illustration, from Albrecht Duerer to Rockwell Kent,* 1945, and 3rd edition, revised, under same title, 1949; (editor) George B. Bridgman, *Complete Guide to Drawing from Life,* Sterling, 1952 (published in England as *Bridgman's Complete Guide to Drawing from Life,* Foulsham, 1955); *Primer of Drawing for Adults,* Sterling, 1953, revised edition published as *Primer of Drawing,* 1958, reprinted as *Techniques of Drawing,* 1963, revised edition, under same title, Dover, 1972; *Watercolor,* Pitman, 1963; (with wife, Mina Lewiton) *If You Were an Eel, How Would You Feel?,* Follett, 1963; (with Mina Lewiton) *Who Knows Where Winter Goes?,* Follett, 1966; *Cabin on a Ridge* (autobiographical), Follett, 1970. Also author of *The Creation According to Genesis* (portfolio of wood engravings), 1977.

Illustrator: Eliot H. Paul, *La Rive Gauche,* McMullen (Paris), 1925; Voltaire, *Candide,* Washburn, 1929; Theophile Gautier, *Mademoiselle de Maupin,* Washburn, 1929.

Michael Gold, *Jews without Money,* Liveright, 1930; Harry E. Burroughs, *Tale of a Vanished Land,* Houghton, 1930; Samuel Butler, *The Way of All Flesh,* Diehl, 1930; Francois Rabelais, *Gargantua and Pantagruel,* Washburn, 1930; Herman Melville, *Moby Dick,* A. & C. Boni, 1931; Wayman Hogue, *Back Yonder: An Ozark Chronicle,* Minton, Balch, 1932; Francois Villon, *Lyrics,* Spiral Press, 1933; Charlie May Hogue Simon, *Robin on the Mountain,* Dutton, 1934; Charlie May Hogue Simon, *Teeny Gay,* Dutton, 1936; John Ise, *Sod and Stubble . . . ,* Wilson-Erickson, 1936; Maurice S. Sullivan, *Jedediah Smith: Trader and Trail Breaker,* Press of the Pioneers, 1936; Anton P. Chekhov, *Plays,* Diehl, 1936, also published as *The Cherry Orchard and Other Plays,* Grosset, 1936; Marjorie Knight, *Alexander's Christmas Eve,* Dutton, 1938; Hayyim Nahman Bialik, *And It Came to Pass: Legends and Stories about King David and King Solomon,* Hebrew Publishing, 1938; Charlie May Hogue Simon, *Bright Morning,* Dutton, 1939; Bob Barton, *Old Covered Wagon Days,* Dutton, 1939; Lorraine Beim and Jerrold Beim, *The Burro That Had a Name,* Harcourt, 1939.

Marjorie Knight, *Alexander's Birthday,* Dutton, 1940; May Justus, *Mr. Songcatcher and Company,* Doubleday, 1940;

Ada Claire Darby, *Columbine Susan,* Stokes, 1940; Harry Levy, *The Dog That Wanted to Whistle,* Lothrop, 1940; Dorothy Cottrell, *Wilderness Orphan,* Messner, 1940; Lorraine Beim and Jerrold Beim, *Lucky Pierre,* Harcourt, 1940; Charlie May Hogue Simon, *Roundabout,* Dutton, 1941; Effie Louise Power, *Osceola Buddy,* Dutton, 1941; Lorraine Beim and Jerrold Beim, *The Little Igloo,* Harcourt, 1941; Harry Levy, *The Burro That Learned to Dance,* Knopf, 1942; Abraham Burstein, *West of the Nile: A Story of Saadia Gaon,* Hebrew Publishing, 1942; Charlie May Hogue Simon, *Younger Brother: A Cherokee Indian Tale,* Dutton, 1942; Harry Levy, *The Bombero: Tales from Latin America,* Knopf, 1943; Marjorie Knight, *Alexander's Vacation,* Dutton, 1943; David A. Boehm, *Stampography,* Printed Arts Co., 1945, revised edition, Sterling, 1951; Deborah Pessin, *The Aleph-bet Story Book,* Jewish Publication Society, 1946; Charles Dickens, *Christmas Stories,* World Publishing, 1946; Mark Twain, *The Prince and the Pauper,* World Publishing, 1948; Moritz Jagendorf, *The Marvelous Adventures of Johnny Caesar Cicero Darling,* Vanguard, 1949; Moritz Jagendorf, *Upstate, Downstate: Folk Stories of the Middle Atlantic States,* Vanguard, 1949.

Vera M. Graham, *Treasure in the Covered Wagon,* Lippincott, 1952; David A. Boehm and Fred Reinfeld, *Blazer the Bear,* Sterling, 1953; Sofie Schieker, *House at the City Wall,* Follett, 1955; William Wise, *Jonathan Blake* (poems), Knopf, 1956; Eula M. Phillips, *Chucko: The Boy with the Good Name,* Follett, 1957.

Clarice Maizel, *Son of Condor,* Criterion, 1964; Elaine M. Ward, *A Big Book,* Abingdon, 1965; Betty Morrow, *A Great Miracle: The Story of Hanukkah,* Harvey House, 1968.

Bonnie Nims, *Always at Home: The Story of Sea Shells,* E. M. Hale, 1970; William E. Keyser, *Day of the Week,* E. M. Hale, 1976.

Illustrator of Mina Lewiton's juvenile books: *The March King,* Didier, 1944; *Beasts of Burden,* Lothrop, 1954; *Rachel,* F. Watts, 1954; *Rachel and Herman,* F. Watts, 1957; *Candita's Choice,* Harper, 1959; *Faces Looking Up,* Harper, 1960; *Animals of the Field and Forest,* Whitman Publishing, 1961; *Lighthouses of America,* Follett, 1963; *That Bad Carlos,* Harper, 1964; *Beasts of Burden,* Lothrop, 1965; Samuel Taylor Coleridge, *The Rime of the Ancient Mariner,* edited by Mina Lewiton, Duell, Sloan & Pearce, 1966; Henry Wadsworth Longfellow, *Evangeline* and *The Song of Hiawatha,* both edited by Mina Lewiton, Duell, Sloan & Pearce, 1966; *Especially Humphrey,* Delacorte, 1967; *Is Anyone Here?,* Atheneum, 1967.

WORK IN PROGRESS: An autobiographical book on Paris in the 1920's.

*   *   *

SIMON, Julian L. 1932-

PERSONAL: Born February 12, 1932, in Newark, N.J.; son of Philip M. and Mae (Goodstein) Simon; married Rita Mintz (a sociologist), June 25, 1961; children: David, Judith, Daniel. *Education:* Harvard University, B.A., 1953; University of Chicago, M.B.A., 1959, Ph.D., 1961. *Religion:* Jewish. *Home:* 1105 South Busey Ave., Urbana, Ill. *Office:* Departments of Economics and of Business Administration, University of Illinois, Urbana, Ill. 61801.

CAREER: Ziff-Davis Publishing Co., New York City, assistant promotion manager, 1956; William Douglas MacAdams, Inc., New York City, advertising copywriter, 1956-57; University of Chicago, Chicago, Ill., associate director of library use study, 1959-61; Julian Simon Associates (mail-order firm and advertising agency), Newark, N.J., owner, 1961-63; University of Illinois at Urbana-Champaign, assistant professor of advertising, 1963-66, assistant and associate professor of marketing, 1966-69, professor of economics and of marketing, 1969—. Hebrew University of Jerusalem, visiting senior lecturer, 1968, first Lipson visiting professor of international marketing and faculty member in department of demography, 1970-71, visiting professor, 1974-75. *Military service:* U.S. Navy, 1953-56; became lieutenant, junior grade.

WRITINGS: How to Start and Operate a Mail-Order Business, McGraw, 1965; *Basic Research Methods in Social Science,* Random House, 1969; (with Herman H. Fussler) *Patterns of Use of Books in Large Research Libraries,* University of Chicago Press, 1969; *Issues in the Economics of Advertising,* University of Illinois Press, 1970; *The Management of Advertising,* Prentice-Hall, 1971; *The Effects of Income on Fertility,* Carolina Population Center, 1974; *Applied Managerial Economics,* Prentice-Hall, 1975; *The Economics of Population Growth,* Princeton University Press, 1977. Contributor of more than eighty articles to economics, management, marketing, and other journals; contributor of short stories to *Cavalier, December,* and *Brooklyn Jewish Review.*

* * *

SIMON, Michael A(rthur) 1936-

PERSONAL: Born December 20, 1936, in Glen Ridge, N.J.; son of Israel W. (a businessman) and Helen (Rose) Simon; married Shannon Slon (a teacher), February 23, 1964; children: Jason Charles, Jennifer Elizabeth. *Education:* Amherst College, B.A., 1958; Harvard University, M.A., 1960, Ph.D., 1967. *Home:* Stonemill Rd., Storrs, Conn. 06268. *Office:* Department of Philosophy, University of Connecticut, Storrs, Conn. 06268.

CAREER: Hamilton College, Clinton, N.Y., instructor in philosophy, 1964-66; University of Connecticut, Storrs, assistant professor, 1966-71, associate professor of philosophy, 1971—. Member of Mansfield (Conn.) volunteer fire department, 1971—. *Member:* American Philosophical Association, Society for Philosophy and Public Affairs, Sigma Xi.

WRITINGS: The Matter of Life: Philosophical Problems of Biology, Yale University Press, 1971. Contributor to professional journals, including *American Philosophical Quarterly, Mind,* and *Philosophy and Phenomenological Research.*

WORK IN PROGRESS: A book on the nature of explanation of human action and explanation in the social sciences.

* * *

SIMONS, Hans 1893-1972

July 1, 1893—March 28, 1972; German-born American political scientist and educator. Obituaries: *New York Times,* March 29, 1972; *Current Biography,* May, 1972.

* * *

SIMONSON, Harold P(eter) 1926-

PERSONAL: Born December 27, 1926, in Tacoma, Wash.; son of Peter Hans (a carpenter) and Hilma (Mork) Simonson; married Carolyn Ady (an English teacher at Tacoma Community College), November 20, 1951; children: Eric, Greta, Peter. *Education:* University of Puget Sound,

B.A., 1950, B.Ed., 1951; Northwestern University, M.A., 1951, Ph.D., 1958; additional graduate study at University of Edinburgh, 1954, and Princeton Theological Seminary, 1964; University of St. Andrews, B.Phil. in Divinity, 1972. *Home:* 4104 North Waterview, Tacoma, Wash. 98407. *Office:* Department of English, University of Washington, Seattle, Wash. 98195.

CAREER: Thessalonika Agricultural and Industrial Institute, Thessalonika, Greece, instructor in English, 1953-54; University of Puget Sound, Tacoma, Wash., 1955-68, began as instructor, became professor of English; University of Washington, Seattle, professor of English, 1968—. *Military service:* U.S. Army, 1946-48. *Member:* Modern Language Association of America, National Council of Teachers of English, American Studies Association. *Awards, honors:* Fulbright grant, 1953.

WRITINGS: (Editor) *Cross Currents: A Collection of Essays from Contemporary Magazines,* Harper, 1959; *Zona Gale,* Twayne, 1962; (editor) *Trio: A Book of Stories, Plays, and Poems,* Harper, 1962, 3rd edition, 1970; (editor with Philip E. Hager) *Salinger's "Catcher in the Rye": Clamor vs. Criticism,* Heath, 1963; (editor and author of introduction) Frederick J. Turner, *Significance of the Frontier in American History,* Ungar, 1963; *Francis Grierson,* Twayne, 1966; *Writing Essays,* Harper, 1966; (editor) *American Perspective* (essays), McGraw, 1968; *The Closed Frontier: Studies in American Literary Tragedy,* Holt, 1970; *Quartet: A Book of Stories, Plays, Poems and Critical Essays,* Harper, 1970, second edition, 1973; (editor) Francis Grierson, *The Valley of Shadows,* College and University Press, 1970; (editor and author of introduction) *Jonathan Edwards: Selected Writings,* Ungar, 1970; *Strategies in Criticism,* Holt, 1971; (editor with John Magee) *Dimensions of Man,* Harper, 1973; *Jonathan Edwards: Theologian of the Heart,* Eerdmans, 1974.

* * *

SIMPSON, Dick 1940-

PERSONAL: Born November 8, 1940, in Houston, Tex.; son of Warren Weldon and Ola Ela (Felts) Simpson; married Mary Scott Head, September 8, 1965. *Education:* Attended Agricultural and Mechanical College of Texas (now Texas A&M University), 1959-60; University of Texas, B.A., 1963; Indiana University, M.A., 1964, Ph.D., 1968. *Politics:* Independent. *Home:* 849 West Wolfram, Chicago, Ill. 60657. *Office:* Department of Political Science, University of Illinois at Chicago Circle, Box 4348, Chicago, Ill. 60680.

CAREER: University of Illinois at Chicago Circle, assistant professor, 1967-72, associate professor of political science, 1972—; City of Chicago (Ill.), alderman of 44th ward, 1971—. Founder and executive director, Independent Precinct Organization. Illinois state campaign manager for Eugene McCarthy, 1968. *Member:* American Political Science Association, National Association of Neighborhoods (member of national board), Lakeview Citizens Council, Campaign Against Pollution (member of steering committee). *Awards, honors:* Foreign Area fellowship for research in Africa, 1966-67; Silver Circle Award for excellence in teaching from University of Illinois, 1971.

WRITINGS: Who Rules? An Introduction to the Study of Politics, Swallow Press, 1970; (contributor) Victor Olorunsola, editor, *The Politics of Cultural Sub-Nationalism in Africa,* Doubleday, 1972; *Winning Elections: A Handbook in Participatory Politics,* Swallow Press, 1972; *Chicago's Future: An Anthology of Reports, Speeches, and Scholar-*

ship *Providing an Agenda for Change,* Stipes, 1976; (with George Beam) *Strategies for Change: How to Make the American Political Dream Work,* Swallow Press, 1976. Producer of films, "By the People," 1970, and "Give Us This Day," 1972.

WORK IN PROGRESS: Reinventing Democracy.

SIDELIGHTS: Dick Simpson told *CA:* "I believe that study, teaching and political action should inform each other, that reflection should govern both the practice of politics and the study of politics. After the fashion of Plato's philosopher-kings I have thought that knowledge and ruling are best developed together. Thus, I merge three full-time jobs into a single career—I am a full-time student of politics, a full-time professor and a full-time politician. Each experience adds depth and substance to the other. Thus my writing is focused on the real world of politics but as seen in the perspective of political theory."

*　　　*　　　*

SIMPSON, Elizabeth Leonie

PERSONAL: Born in Pasadena, Calif.; children: Martha, Garth, Bethany. *Education:* University of Michigan, B.A., 1951, M.A., 1953; University of California, Berkeley, Ph.D., 1970; University of Southern California, postdoctoral study, 1971-72. *Home:* 850 Second St., Santa Monica, Calif. 90403. *Office:* Waite Phillips Hall, University of Southern California, Los Angeles, Calif. 90007.

CAREER: University of Michigan, Ann Arbor, technical writer and editor at Willow Run Laboratories, 1955-57; high school teacher in Ypsilanti, Mich., 1960, Whittier, Calif., 1960-61, and Los Altos, Calif., 1962-63; free-lance writer, 1963-66; Center for the Study of Instruction, San Francisco, Calif., project editor, deputy director, and research associate, 1966-68; University of Southern California, Los Angeles, assistant professor of education and associate director of Center for International Education, 1970-72, adjunct professor, 1972—. Visiting associate professor of social ecology, University of California, Irvine, 1974, Simon Fraser University, 1976, and University of Victoria, 1977. Member of board of trustees, Humanistic Psychology Institute, 1976-77.

MEMBER: American Political Science Association, American Orthopsychiatric Association, Society for the Psychological Study of Social Issues, American Educational Research Association, Association for Humanistic Psychology, California Humanities Association (charter member), Pi Lambda Theta. *Awards, honors:* National distinguished research award from Pi Lambda Theta, 1970.

WRITINGS: Tramontane: A Novella, Smith/Horizon Press, 1968; (co-author) *The Social Sciences: Concepts and Values* (series for K-9 grades), eight volumes, Harcourt, 1970-72; *Five Poems,* P'Nye Press, 1970; *Democracy's Stepchildren: A Study of Need and Belief,* Jossey-Bass, 1971; (editor with Thelma Gomez) *Independent Activities for Learning Centers,* Mss Information, 1971; (with Mary A. Gray) *Humanistic Education: An Interpretation,* Ballinger, 1976.

Contributor: T. Lickona, editor, *Moral Development and Behavior: Theory, Research and Social Issues,* Holt, 1976; L. M. Berman and J. A. Roderick, editors, *Feelings, Valuing, and the Art of Growing,* Association for Supervision and Curriculum Development, 1977; L. Rubin, editor, *Handbook of Curriculum: Administration and Theory,* Allyn & Bacon, 1977; S. Renshon, editor, *Handbook of Po-*

litical Socialization: Theory and Research, Free Press, 1977. Also author, with Page Smith and Bramwell Fletcher, of *The American Revolution Experience, 1776-1976,* 1974. Contributor of short stories and poems to *Satire, North American Review, Ave Maria, Prairie Schooner,* and other journals; contributor of about a dozen articles to professional journals.

WORK IN PROGRESS: River Run Deep, River Run Strong: Confluence in Humanistic Education, for Winston Press.

*　　　*　　　*

SIXSMITH, Eric Keir Gilborne 1904-

PERSONAL: Born October 15, 1904, in Barry, Glamorganshire, Wales; son of Charles Frederick Gilborne (a doctor) and Muriel Marion (Dudley) Sixsmith; married Rosemary Aileen Godden, March 22, 1941; children: Joanna Margaret, Angus John Godden, Edmund Charles Dudley. *Education:* Attended Harrow School, 1919-22, Royal Military College, Sandhurst, 1922-24, Staff College, Quetta, 1935-36, and Imperial Defence College, 1951. *Politics:* No party allegiance. *Home:* Riversleigh, Langport, Somerset, England. *Agent:* Herbert van Thal, London Authors Representation Ltd., Regent House, London W1A 2JT, England.

CAREER: British Army, 1924-61; commissioned in The Cameronians (Scottish Rifles), 1924; served with 2nd Infantry Brigade, 1939-40, 51st Highland Division, 1941-42, Royal Scots Fusiliers in Italy (wounded), 1944; commanded 2nd Battalion Cameronians, 1944; British War Office, deputy director, staff duties, 1945-46; brigade commander in India, 1946-47; War Office, deputy director of personnel administration, 1947-50; chief of staff in Hong Kong, 1952; chief of staff of Far East Land Forces, 1952-54; commanded 43rd Infantry Division, 1954-57; Supreme Headquarters of Allied Powers Europe, assistant chief of staff (organization and training), 1957-61; retired in 1961, with rank of major-general. *Awards, honors:* Commander of Order of the British Empire, 1946; Companion of the Bath, 1951.

WRITINGS: British Generalship in the Twentieth Century, Arms & Armour Press, 1970; *Eisenhower as Military Commander,* Batsford, 1973; *Douglas Haig,* Weidenfeld & Nicolson, 1976. Regular contributor to *Army Quarterly.*

AVOCATIONAL INTERESTS: Gardening, music.

*　　　*　　　*

SIZER, Theodore Ryland 1932-

PERSONAL: Born June 23, 1932, in New Haven, Conn.; son of Theodore (a professor of art history) and Caroline (Foster) Sizer; married Nancy Faust (a teacher), July 2, 1955; children: Theodore II, Judith Ryland, Harold Faust, Lydia Ellen. *Education:* Yale University, A.B., 1953; Harvard University, M.A.T., 1957, Ph.D., 1961. *Home:* 189 Main St., Andover, Mass. 01810. *Office:* Phillips Academy, Andover, Mass. 01810.

CAREER: Roxbury Latin School, West Roxbury, Mass., teacher, 1955-56; Melbourne Grammar School, Melbourne, Victoria, Australia, teacher, 1958; Harvard University, Cambridge, Mass., assistant professor of education, 1961-64, dean of Faculty of Education, 1964-72; Phillips Academy, Andover, Mass., headmaster, 1972—. Visiting professor, University of Bristol, England, 1971. Member of visiting committee, Yale College and Harvard College. *Military service:* U.S. Army, Field Artillery, 1953-55. *Member:* American Historical Association, American Asso-

ciation of School Administrators, National Association of Secondary School Principals, Union Club (Boston), Century Association (New York). *Awards, honors:* Ped.D., Lawrence University, 1969; Guggenheim fellowship, 1971; Litt.D., Union College, 1972.

WRITINGS: Secondary Schools at the Turn of the Century, Yale University Press, 1964; *The Age of the Academies,* Teachers College Press, 1964; (editor) *Religion and Public Education,* Houghton, 1967; (author of introduction) J. M. Gustafson and others, editors, *Moral Education: Five Lectures,* Harvard University Press, 1970; *Places for Learning, Places for Joy,* Harvard University Press, 1972. Contributor to *Saturday Review, Psychology Today,* and other journals.

*   *   *

SKURZYNSKI, Gloria (Joan) 1930-

PERSONAL: Born July 6, 1930, in Duquesne, Pa.; daughter of Aylmer Kearney and Serena (Decker) Flister; married Edward Joseph Skurzynski (an aerospace engineer), December 1, 1951; children: Serena, Janine, Joan, Alane, Lauren. *Education:* Attended Mt. Mercy College, Pittsburgh, Pa., 1948-50. *Religion:* Roman Catholic. *Home:* 2559 Spring Haven Dr., Salt Lake City, Utah 84109.

CAREER: U.S. Steel Corp., Pittsburgh, Pa., statistical clerk, 1950-52.

WRITINGS—All juvenile: *The Magic Pumpkin,* Four Winds, 1971; *The Remarkable Journey of Gustavus Bell,* Abingdon, 1973; *The Poltergeist of Jason Morey,* Dodd, 1975; *In a Bottle with a Cork on Top,* Dodd, 1976; *Two Fools and a Faker,* Lothrop, 1977; *Artificial Parts for People,* Four Winds, 1978. Contributor of over three dozen short stories and articles to magazines. Children's book reviewer, *Marriage and Family Living.*

SIDELIGHTS: Gloria Skurzynski told *CA:* "One of the most rewarding fringe benefits of writing is the opportunity to interview, for research purposes, experts in various fields. Almost all knowledgeable people are more than willing—they're eager—to share information about their work. And since these are the people who really make the world move, conversing with them is bound to stimulate a writer's imagination."

*   *   *

SKUTCH, Alexander F(rank) 1904-

PERSONAL: Born May 20, 1904, in Baltimore, Md.; son of Robert Frank (an antiquarian) and Rachel (Frank) Skutch; married Pamela Lankester, April 27, 1950; children: Edwin (adopted). *Education:* Johns Hopkins University, A.B., 1925, Ph.D., 1928. *Politics:* None. *Religion:* "Not affiliated with any church." *Home:* El Quizarra, San Isidro del General, Costa Rica.

CAREER: After receiving doctorate went to Panama and Honduras on research fellowships from Johns Hopkins University, 1928-30; continued research as National Research Council fellow, 1930-31; Johns Hopkins University, Baltimore, Md., instructor in botany, 1931-32; Museo Nacional de Costa Rica, San Jose, curator of plants, 1940; U.S. Department of Agriculture, botanist on rubber survey in Peru, Ecuador, and Colombia, 1940-41; University of Costa Rica, San Jose, professor of ornithology, 1964; naturalist working independently in Guatemala, 1932-34, Panama, 1935, and Costa Rica, 1935—. Member of El Quizarra School Board, 1962.

MEMBER: American Ornithologists' Union (life fellow), British Ornithologists' Union (honorary member), Cooper Ornithological Society (honorary member), Wilson Ornithological Society, Audubon Society of Costa Rica (honorary president). *Awards, honors:* Guggenheim fellowships, 1946-47, 1952; Brewster Medal of American Ornithologists' Union for writings in ornithology, 1950.

WRITINGS: Life Histories of Central American Birds, illustrated with drawings by Don R. Eckelberry, Cooper Ornithological Society, Volume I, 1954, Volume II, 1960, Volume III, 1969; *The Quest of the Divine: An Inquiry into the Source and Goal of Morality and Religion,* Meador, 1956; *Life Histories of Central American Highland Birds,* Nuttall Ornithological Club (Cambridge, Mass.), 1967; *The Golden Core of Religion,* Holt, 1970; *A Naturalist in Costa Rica,* University of Florida Press, 1971; *Studies of Tropical American Birds,* Nuttall Ornithological Club, 1972; *The Life of the Hummingbird,* illustrated by Arthur B. Singer, Crown, 1973; *Parent Birds and Their Young,* University of Texas Press, 1976. A study of the quetzal was included in *Smithsonian Institution Annual Report,* 1947. Contributor to *Auk, Ibis, Condor,* and *Wilson Bulletin* (publications of ornithological societies), and to magazines, including *Animal Kingdom, Nature,* and *Scientific Monthly.*

WORK IN PROGRESS: A Bird Watcher in Tropical America, for University of Texas Press; *The Imperative Call,* for University of Florida Press; *Aves de Costa Rica,* for Editorial Costa Rica; continuing study of tropical American birds.

SIDELIGHTS: Alexander Skutch became deeply interested in tropical birds while doing research in Central America, 1928-30 and, since no support for studying them was available in the depression years, he paid his own way, largely by collecting and selling botanical specimens. After doing this for about eight years he bought a farm in a Costa Rican valley, then easily accessible only by air, and settled there in 1941 to continue his studies. He and his wife, daughter of a Costa Rican naturalist, whom he married after living alone on the farm for nine years, now live with their son close by a rushing river and a large tract of tropical forest.

Philosophy and religion have been Skutch's chief interests outside of ornithology and botany. "My philosophical writings remain largely unpublished," he writes. "I am greatly concerned about man's destruction of nature, and believe that the only sound approach to conservation is through the stabilization of population. I believe that religion's chief contribution to humanity has been teaching people to care—about their own souls or characters, their neighbors, and the world in which they live. To know, appreciate, and preserve all the beautiful and wonderful things our planet contains is, in my opinion, the proper end of man."

*   *   *

SLADE, Tony 1936-

PERSONAL: Born September 24, 1936, in Gosport, England; son of Frederick W. A. (a teacher) and Dora (Baker) Slade; married Jean Roberts (a teacher), August 25, 1961; children: Elisabeth Sarah, Sean Tristan. *Education:* University of Bristol, M.A., 1960. *Politics:* "Plenty; Leftish." *Religion:* None. *Office:* Department of English, University of Adelaide, Adelaide, South Australia.

CAREER: University of Adelaide, Adelaide, South Australia, senior lecturer in English, 1966—, deputy chairman of department, 1977—.

WRITINGS: D. H. Lawrence, Evans Brothers, 1969, Arco, 1970; (contributor) J. J. Anderson, editor, *Chaucer: The Canterbury Tales, a Casebook,* Macmillan, 1974. Contributor to professional journals and local film magazines. Editor, *Southern Review* (Adelaide), 1967-69.

WORK IN PROGRESS: Research on Chaucer, Hardy, western films, and popular culture in the 1960's.

AVOCATIONAL INTERESTS: Soccer, folk music.

*   *   *

SLESINGER, Warren 1933-

PERSONAL: Born July 20, 1933, in Neptune, N.J.; son of Allan (a hotel manager) and Edna (Trudel) Slesinger; married Betty Ann Raders (an English teacher), September 29, 1956; children: Kurt and Kris (twins), Hugh. *Education:* Bowdoin College, B.A., 1956; University of Iowa, M.F.A., 1961; graduate study at University of Wisconsin—Milwaukee, 1963, and School of Irish Studies, Dublin, 1972. *Home:* 408 Haverford Pl., Swarthmore, Pa. 19081. *Office:* University of Pennsylvania Press, 3933 Walnut St., Philadelphia, Pa. 19104.

CAREER: Macmillan Co., New York City, member of sales staff, 1961-64; Holt, Rinehart & Winston, New York City, manager, 1961-68; D. C. Heath & Co., Lexington, Mass., history and political science editor, 1969; College of Wooster, Wooster, Ohio, assistant professor of English, 1969-74; University of Pennsylvania Press, Philadelphia, marketing manager, 1975—. Part-time instructor at Olivet College, 1963-67, and at University of Wisconsin—Milwaukee, 1964-68. Worked in Poetry-in-the-Schools programs in Indiana, Ohio, and Pennsylvania. Member of board of consultants, National Student Book Club. *Military service:* U.S. Army, 1957-59; became first lieutenant. *Member:* Poetry Society of America, Ohio Poetry Association. *Awards, honors:* Finalist, Lamont Poetry Contest, 1970; Ingram Merrill grant-in-aid, 1974.

WRITINGS: Field with Figurations (poems), Cummington, 1970; (editor) *The Individual Voice* (poetry anthology), Indiana Arts Commission, 1974; (contributor) *Heartland II: Poets of the Midwest,* edited by Lucien Stryk, Northern Illinois University Press, 1975. Contributor of poetry to periodicals.

WORK IN PROGRESS: A second collection of original poems.

SIDELIGHTS: Warren Slesinger has traveled in England, France, Germany, Austria, Canada, Mexico. He described himself to CA as "a late liberal with a disposition toward the French existentialist and the German Jew; a poet who hopes an emotion unique in degree, depth and difference from all other emotions is poetry; a poet who believes the voice is the register of emotion in the poem, its sense of a human presence, its living instrument."

*   *   *

SLIDE, Anthony 1944-

PERSONAL: Born November 7, 1944, in Birmingham, England; son of Clifford Frederick and Mary (Eaton) Slide. *Education:* Attended grammar school in Birmingham, England. *Politics:* None. *Religion:* None. *Office:* National Film Information Service, Academy of Motion Picture Arts and Sciences, 8949 Wilshire Blvd., Beverly Hills, Calif. 90211.

CAREER: Silent Picture (quarterly devoted to the art and

history of silent film), London, England, founder and editor, 1968-74; American Film Institute, Washington, D.C., associate archivist, 1972-75; Academy of Motion Picture Arts and Sciences, Beverly Hills, Calif., coordinator of National Film Information Service, 1975—. American Film Institute, research associate, 1971-72. National Film Theatre, London, consultant on silent film programming; organizer of first silent film festival ever held in England, 1970.

WRITINGS: Sir Michael Balcon (monograph), British Film Institute, 1969; *Lillian Gish* (monograph), British Film Institute, 1969; (with Paul O'Dell) *Griffith and the Rise of Hollywood,* A. S. Barnes, 1970; (with O'Dell) *Early American Cinema,* A. S. Barnes, 1971; *The Griffith Actresses,* A. S. Barnes, 1973; (with Edward Wagenknecht) *The Films of D. W. Griffith,* Crown, 1975; *The Idols of Silenc,* A. S. Barnes, 1976; *The Big V: A History of the Vitagraph Company,* Scarecrow, 1976; *Early Women Directors,* A. S. Barnes, 1977; *Aspects of American Film History Prior to 1920,* Scarecrow, 1978. Contributor of articles on the history of the cinema to various periodicals. Member of editorial board, *Quarterly Review of Film Studies.*

*   *   *

SLOAN, Stephen 1936-

PERSONAL: Name legally changed; born June 24, 1936, in New York, N.Y.; son of George H. and Lolly (Berger) Solomon; children: Christopher, Gregory. *Education:* Attended St. Lawrence University, 1954-56; New York University, B.A., 1958, M.A., 1962, Ph.D., 1967. *Office:* Department of Political Science, University of Oklahoma, Norman, Okla. 73069.

CAREER: University of Oklahoma, Norman, assistant professor, 1966-70, associate professor, 1970-77, professor of political science, 1977—. *Military service:* U.S. Naval Reserve, 1954-62. *Member:* International Institute for Strategic Studies, Association for Asian Studies, International Studies Association, Midwest Political Science Association. *Awards, honors:* Fulbright appointment to Tribhuvan University, Nepal, 1972.

WRITINGS: A Study in Political Violence: The Indonesian Experience, Rand McNally, 1971. Contributor of reviews to political science journals.

WORK IN PROGRESS: Research, articles, and specialized projects on international terrorism.

*   *   *

SLOANE, Arthur A(llan) 1931-

PERSONAL: Born June 17, 1931, in Boston, Mass.; son of Alvin (a professor) and Florence (Goldberg) Sloane; married Louise Susan Perlmutter, July 2, 1963; children: Amy Jennifer, Laura Ellen. *Education:* Harvard University, A.B., 1953, D.B.A., 1963; Columbia University, M.B.A., 1958. *Home:* 302 Old Oak Rd., Newark, Del. 19711. *Office:* Department of Business Administration, University of Delaware, Newark, Del. 19711.

CAREER: Sylvania Electric Products, Inc., Boston, Mass., personnel administrator, 1959-60; Indiana University at Bloomington, assistant professor of personnel, 1963-66; University of Delaware, Newark, associate professor, 1966-70, professor of industrial relations, 1970—. Member of national roster of labor arbitrators, Federal Mediation and Conciliation Service. *Military service:* U.S. Army, 1954-56. *Member:* Industrial Relations Research Association, American Arbitration Association (member of National Labor Panel), Beta Gamma Sigma.

WRITINGS: (With Fred Witney) *Labor Relations,* Prentice-Hall, 1967, 2nd edition, 1972. Contributor to business and industrial relations journals.

WORK IN PROGRESS: "The Unionization of College Professors," a series of articles.

AVOCATIONAL INTERESTS: Tennis, walking, reading.

* * *

SLUSSER, Dorothy M. 1922-

PERSONAL: Born May 26, 1922, in Wichita, Kan.; daughter of George M. and Mildred (Pieffer) Mallett; married Gerald H. Slusser (a seminary professor), November 24, 1943; children: Peter, Andrew. *Education:* Attended University of Kansas, 1940-41, University of Arizona, 1941-42, and University of Texas, 1958-60; Webster College, M.A. (psychology), 1973. *Politics:* Democrat. *Religion:* Presbyterian. *Home:* 1122 Glenway Dr., St. Louis, Mo. 63122. *Office:* Regional Manager, Marketing Support System, Computer Sales International, Inc., St. Louis, Mo.

CAREER: Howard & Stofft, Tucson, Ariz., head of book department, 1941-42; Braniff Airways, Dallas, Tex., instructor in celestial navigation, radio and dead reckoning navigation instructor on Braniff contract with Air Transport Command, Brownsville, Tex., 1942-43; secretary in Dallas, 1956-58; *American Journal of Psychology,* Austin, Tex., business manager, 1958-60; Computer Sales International, Inc., St. Louis, Mo., regional manager, marketing support system, 1977—. *Member:* Environmental and Social Action Committee (chairman, 1970-71), Coalition for the Environment (St. Louis; member of board of directors), Jefferson Township Democrats for Responsible Politics, Jefferson Township Democratic Club.

WRITINGS: Bible Stories Retold for Adults, Westminster, 1960; *At the Foot of the Mountain,* Westminster, 1961; (with husband, Gerald H. Slusser) *The Jesus of Mark's Gospel,* Westminster, 1967; (with Gerald H. Slusser) *Technology: The God that Failed,* Westminster, 1971; *People and the Earth's Resources,* Milliken Press, 1976. Contributor to religious periodicals.

WORK IN PROGRESS: A study of Jungian psychology.

SIDELIGHTS: Dorothy M. Slusser told *CA:* "I first started writing on our kitchen table, and I sent the manuscript to the publisher to get if off the kitchen table. That was many years ago, and since then, all books have been commissioned, which is good news and bad news—good because you know they will be published, but sometimes confining as to subject matter. Writing is a solitary affair, and since all my writing has been non-fiction, it has been rewarding to plunge into many fields of interest, as with the environmental concern, which has resulted in two books so far."

AVOCATIONAL INTERESTS: European travel (lived in Scotland), camping.

* * *

SMITH, Betty (Wehner) 1896-1972

December 15, 1896—January 17, 1972; American novelist and playwright. Obituaries: *New York Times,* January 18, 1972; *Washington Post,* January 19, 1972; *Newsweek,* January 31, 1972; *Publishers Weekly,* January 31, 1972; *Time,* January 31, 1972; *Current Biography,* March, 1972. (See index for *CA* sketch)

SMITH, C(hristopher) U(pham) M(urray) 1930-

PERSONAL: Born December 27, 1930, in Brixham, Devonshire, England; son of Murray James (a schoolmaster) and Mary (Upham) Smith; married Rosemary Edmonds (an adult literacy coordinator), March 25, 1961. *Education:* University of Birmingham, B.Sc., 1954; University of London, B.Sc., 1960; University of Edinburgh, Diploma in Biophysics, 1963. *Home:* 104 Moorcroft Rd., Birmingham B13 8LU, England. *Office:* University of Aston in Birmingham, Gosta Green, Birmingham B4 7ET, England.

CAREER: Bolton Institute of Technology, Bolton, England, assistant lecturer, 1955-59; University of Aston in Birmingham, England, lecturer, 1959-73, senior lecturer in biological sciences, 1973—. *Member:* Institute of Biology, British Biophysical Society, Royal Microscopical Society, National Brain Research Association.

WRITINGS: The Architecture of the Body, Faber, 1964; *Molecular Biology: A Structural Approach,* M.I.T. Press, 1968; *The Brain: Towards an Understanding,* Putnam, 1970; *The Problem of Life: An Essay in the Origins of Biological Thought,* Halsted, 1976. Contributor to *Nature, Adult Education,* and other journals.

WORK IN PROGRESS: The Matter of Mankind: A Modern Exploration of Man's Place in Nature.

AVOCATIONAL INTERESTS: Foreign travel.

* * *

SMITH, Dodie
(C. L. Anthony, Charles Henry Percy)

PERSONAL: Formal name, Dorothy Gladys; born in Whitefield, Lancashire, England; daughter of Ernest Walter and Ella (Furber) Smith; married Alec Macbeth Beesley, 1939. *Education:* Attended Royal Academy of Dramatic Art, London. *Home:* The Barretts, Finchingfield, Essex, England.

CAREER: Wrote a screenplay, "Schoolgirl Rebels," under the pseudonym Charles Henry Percy while a student at Royal Academy of Dramatic Art; actress, 1915-22, appearing first at Tottenham Palace in "Playgoers," then mainly touring and playing with repertory companies; left the stage to become a buyer at Heal & Son, London, England; gave up business after the success of her first professionally produced play, "Autumn Crocus," 1931; playwright using the pseudonym C. L. Anthony up to 1935; since then has been writing under her own name.

WRITINGS—Novels, except as indicated: *I Capture the Castle* (Literary Guild selection), Little, Brown, 1948; *The New Moon with the Old,* Little, Brown, 1963; *The Town in Bloom,* Little, Brown, 1965; *It Ends with Revelations,* Little, Brown, 1967; *A Tale of Two Families,* Walker & Co., 1970; *Look Back with Love* (autobiography), Heinemann, 1974; *The Girl from the Candlelit Bath,* W. H. Allen, 1978; *Look Back with Mixed Feelings* (autobiography), W. H. Allen, 1978.

Juvenile books: *The Hundred and One Dalmatians,* Heinemann, 1956, Viking, 1957; *The Starlight Barking: More about the Hundred and One Dalmations,* Heinemann, 1967, Simon & Schuster, 1968; *The Midnight Kittens,* W. H. Allen, 1978.

Plays: *Call It a Day* (three-act comedy; first produced in London at Globe Theatre, 1935; produced on Broadway at Morosco Theatre, 1936), Gollancz, 1936, acting edition, Samuel French, 1937; *Bonnet over the Windmill* (three-act comedy; first produced in London at New Theatre, 1937), Heinemann, 1937; *Dear Octopus* (three-act comedy; first produced in London at Queen's Theatre, 1938; produced on Broadway at Broadhurst Theatre, 1939; revived in London at Theatre Royal, Haymarket, 1967), Heinemann, 1938, acting edition, Samuel French, 1939; *Three Plays: Autumn Crocus, Service, Touch Wood,* Heinemann, 1939; *Lovers and Friends* (three-act comedy; first produced on Broadway at Plymouth Theatre, 1943), Samuel French, 1944; *Letter from Paris* (three-act comedy adapted from Henry James' novel, *The Reverberator;* first produced in London at Aldwych Theatre, 1952), Heinemann, 1954; *I Capture the Castle* (two-act romantic comedy adapted by the author from her novel of the same title; first produced in London at Aldwych Theatre, 1953), Samuel French, 1953; "These People, Those Books," three-act comedy, first produced in Leeds at Grand Theatre, 1958; *Amateur Means Lover* (three-act comedy, first produced in Liverpool at Liverpool Playhouse, 1961), Samuel French, 1962. Also co-author of screenplays "The Uninvited," 1944 and "Darling, How Could You!," 1951.

Plays under pseudonym C. L. Anthony: "British Talent," first produced in London at Three Arts Club, 1924; *Autumn Crocus* (three-act comedy; first produced in London at Lyric Theatre, April, 1931; produced on Broadway, at Morosco Theatre, November, 1932), Samuel French, 1931; *Service* (three-act comedy; first produced in London at Wyndham's Theatre, 1932), Gollancz, 1932, acting edition, Samuel French, 1937; *Touch Wood* (three-act comedy; first produced in London at Theatre Royal, Haymarket, 1934), Samuel French, 1934.

WORK IN PROGRESS: Volume III of Smith's autobiography.

SIDELIGHTS: Describing her early playwriting experience, Dodie Smith wrote: "When I was eighteen months old my father died, and after that my mother and I lived with her family—my grandparents, three uncles and two aunts—in an old house with a garden sloping towards the Manchester Ship Canal. It was a stimulating household. Both my mother and grandmother wrote and composed. Almost everyone sang and played some musical instrument (we owned three pianos, a violin, a mandolin, a guitar and a banjo) and one uncle, an admirable amateur actor, was often to be heard rehearsing, preferably with me on hand to give him his cues. Although I had been taken to theatres long before I could read, it was this hearing of my uncle's parts which really aroused my interest in acting and in playwriting; the cues I gave got longer and longer and, by the age of nine, I had written a forty-page play. When I read this aloud to my mother she fell asleep—to awake and say apologetically, 'But, darling, it was so dull.'" Smith continued with her thoughts on writing: "I have come to enjoy writing novels better than writing plays (which is just as well, in view of the vastly changed modern theatre). I find I can live right inside a novel; while working on a play, I can merely sit in front of it. Not that I fully enjoy writing anything. I am unhappy when not working and I do, at least, enjoy planning work. But once I start, nothing I achieve seems as good as I hoped it would be. I revise and revise and revise. I consider myself a lightweight author, but God knows I approach my work with as much seriousness as if it were Holy Writ."

The Hundred and One Dalmatians was filmed as Walt Disney's "101 Dalmatians," and both that book and its sequel, *The Starlight Barking,* have also been issued in paperback editions in England and America and altogether have been published in 12 countries. *Autumn Crocus* was filmed in England, 1934, *Call It a Day* was made into a movie by Warner Brothers, 1937, *Service* was filmed by MGM in 1944 as "Looking Forward," and *Dear Octopus* was filmed in England, 1945. Although Smith's first novel, *I Capture the Castle,* was written for adults, she says that it has "largely been taken over by teen-agers." She and her husband spent fifteen years in America (1939-53), but returned to England in the early 1950's to live in a three-hundred-year-old country house where their current menage consists of two dalmatians, two donkeys, fantail pigeons, and wild ducks on the pond.

*   *   *

SMITH, Dwight L.   1918-

PERSONAL: Born April 11, 1918, in West Elkton, Ohio; son of Clarence S. (a minister) and Mary (Barnhart) Smith; married Jane DeLeon, May 5, 1955; children: Gregory B. *Education:* Indiana Central College, A.B., 1940; Indiana University, A.B., 1941, Ph.D., 1949. *Religion:* Presbyterian. *Home:* 409 Emerald Woods Dr., Oxford, Ohio 45056. *Office:* Department of History, Miami University, Oxford, Ohio 45056.

CAREER: Indiana Central College, Indianapolis, instructor in history, 1942-43; Ohio State University, Columbus, instructor in history, 1949-53; Miami University, Oxford, Ohio, assistant professor, 1953-56, associate professor, 1956-60, professor of history, 1960—. Visiting instructor in history, Centre College of Kentucky, 1952; Carnegie Visiting Assistant Professor of History, Columbia University, 1954-55; visiting professor of history, Indiana University, 1962-63, University of Alberta, 1964, Colorado College, 1965, University of British Columbia, 1967, and University of New Mexico, 1968. Presbyterian Church, deacon, 1957-60, elder, 1961-66, church historian, 1966—. *Military service:* U.S. Army Air Corps, 1943-46; became staff sergeant.

MEMBER: American Historical Association, Association for Canadian Studies, Canadian Historical Association, Organization of American Historians, American-Indian Ethnohistoric Conference (president, 1955-56), Western History Association, Ohio Academy of History, Ohio Historical Society (research historian, 1950-51), Indiana Central College Alumni Association (member of board of directors, 1964-70; president, 1968-69), Oxford Museum Association (member of board of trustees, 1956-60; president, 1957-58). *Awards, honors:* Newberry Library fellow, 1952, 1964; Miami University research fellow, 1957, 1959; Lilly Endowment fellow, 1962.

WRITINGS: From Greene Ville to Fallen Timbers, Indiana Historical Society, 1952; (editor) *The Western Journals of John May,* Historical and Philosophical Society of Ohio, 1961; (editor with C. Gregory Crampton) *The Hoskaninni Papers,* University of Utah Press, 1961; *Down the Colorado,* University of Oklahoma Press, 1965; *Western Life in the Stirrups,* Caxton Club, 1965; *The Photographer and the River,* Stagecoach Press, 1967; (editor) *John D. Young and the Colorado Gold Rush,* Lakeside Press, 1969; (editor with Lloyd W. Garrison) *The American Political Process,* American Bibliographical Center, 1972; *Afro-American History: A Bibliography,* American Bibliographical Center, 1974; *Indians of the United States and Canada: A Bibliography,* American Bibliographical Center, 1975; *Era of the American Revolution,* American Bibliographical Center, 1975.

Contributor: *The Governors of Ohio,* The Ohio Historical Society, 1954; K. Ross Toole and others, editors, *Probing the American West,* Museum of New Mexico Press, 1962; John F. Mc Dermott, editor, *Travelers on the Western Frontier,* University of Illinois Press, 1970; *The French, the Indians, and George Rogers Clark in the Illinois Country,* Indiana Historical Society, 1977. Contributor to many professional journals, including *Historical Abstracts* and *America: History and Life.* Editor, *The Old Northwest,* 1974—.

*   *   *

SMITH, Grover C(leveland) 1923-

PERSONAL: Born September 6, 1923, in Atlanta, Ga.; son of Grover C. (a retail-credit executive) and Lillian Julia (Mc Daniel) Smith; married Phyllis Jean Snyder, June 19, 1948 (divorced, 1965); married Dulcie Barbara Soper, December 29, 1965; children: (first marriage) Alice Elizabeth, Charles Grover; (second marriage) Stephen Kenneth, Julia Margaret. *Education:* Columbia University, A.B., 1944, M.A., 1945, Ph.D., 1950. *Politics:* Independent. *Office:* Department of English, Duke University, Durham, N.C. 27706.

CAREER: Rutgers University, New Brunswick, N.J., instructor in English, 1946-48; Yale University, New Haven, Conn., instructor in English, 1948-52; Duke University, Durham, N.C., instructor, 1952-55, assistant professor, 1955-61, associate professor, 1961-66, professor of English, 1966—. Visiting summer lecturer at College of the City of New York (now City College of the City University of New York), 1946-48, New York University, 1963, Columbia University, 1963-64, and Wake Forest College (now University), 1966. *Military service:* U.S. Army, 1943. *Awards, honors:* Poetry Chap-Book Award of Poetry Society of America, 1957, for *T. S. Eliot's Poetry and Plays;* Guggenheim fellowship, 1958; American Council of Learned Societies research grant, 1965; American Philosophical Society research grant, 1965.

WRITINGS: T. S. Eliot's Poetry and Plays: A Study in Sources and Meaning, University of Chicago Press, 1956, 2nd edition, 1974; (editor) *Josiah Royce's Seminar 1913-1914,* Rutgers University Press, 1963; (editor) *Letters of Aldous Huxley,* Chatto & Windus, 1969, Harper, 1970; *Archibald MacLeish,* University of Minnesota Press, 1971; (contributor) R. J. Porter and J. D. Brophy, editors, *Modern Irish Literature: Essays in Honor of William York Tindall,* Iona College Press, 1972; *Ford Madox Ford,* Columbia University Press, 1972. Contributor to professional journals. Advisory editor, *T. S. Eliot Review,* 1974—.

WORK IN PROGRESS: A book-length study of T. S. Eliot's *The Waste Land.*

BIOGRAPHICAL/CRITICAL SOURCES: Spectator, November 29, 1969; *New Republic,* May 16, 1970; *Esquire,* September, 1970.

*   *   *

SMITH, Ken(neth John) 1938-

PERSONAL: Born December 4, 1938, in Rudston, Yorkshire, England; son of John and Millicent (Sitch) Smith; married Ann Minnis, August 1, 1960; children: Nicole, Danny, Kate. *Education:* University of Leeds, B.A., 1963. *Politics:* "Scepticism." *Religion:* "Scepticism." *Home and office:* 21 Nelson Rd., Exeter, Devon, United Kingdom.

CAREER: Teacher in elementary school, Dewsbury, England, 1963-64; lecturer in English and social studies at technical college, Batley, England, 1964-65; lecturer in poetry

and writing at Exeter College of Arts, Exeter, England, 1965-69; Slippery Rock State College, Slippery Rock, Pa., instructor in poetry and writing, 1969-72; visiting writer at Clark University and College of the Holy Cross, Worcester, Mass., 1972-73; University of Leeds, Leeds, England creative writing fellow, 1976-78. *Military service:* Royal Air Force, 1958-60. *Awards, honors:* Commendation in Cheltenham Festival, 1964; Gregory Award, 1967, for *The Pity;* Arts Council Great Britain bursary, 1975.

WRITINGS—Poetry: *Eleven Poems,* Northern House, 1963; *The Pity,* J. Cape, 1967; *Academic Board,* Peeks Press, 1969; *Work, Distances,* Swallow Press, 1972; *Frontwards in a Backwards Movie,* Arc Books, 1973; *The Wild Rose,* Stinktree, 1973; *Hawk Wolf,* Sceptre, 1975; *Anus Mundi,* Four Zoas, 1976; *Blue's Rocket,* Warts & All, 1976; *Island Called Henry the Navigator,* Cat's Pyjamas, 1976.

WORK IN PROGRESS: The Poet's Guide to the City of Exeter, a history; *Little Snapshots of the Rain,* a book of poems; prose.

SIDELIGHTS: Ken Smith says that his current interests lie "in the division between visionary man and political animal; between the constancy of desire and its failure; between the want to speak and the failure of language to communicate."

*   *   *

SMITH, Ralph (Bernard) 1939-

PERSONAL: Born May 9, 1939, in Bingley, Yorkshire, England. *Education:* University of Leeds, B.A., 1959, Ph.D., 1963. *Office:* School of Oriental and African Studies, University of London, London, W.C.1, England.

CAREER: University of London, School of Oriental and African Studies, London, England, lecturer, 1962-71, reader in history of Southeast Asia, 1971—.

WRITINGS: Viet-Nam and the West, Heinemann, 1968, Cornell University Press, 1970; *Land and Politics in the England of Henry VIII,* Oxford University Press, 1970. Contributor of articles on Vietnamese history to learned journals.

WORK IN PROGRESS: A history of Vietnamese communism from 1930 to the present.

*   *   *

SMITH, Vincent E(dward) 1915-1972

August 20, 1915—May 16, 1972; American philosopher and educator. Obituaries: *New York Times,* May 17, 1972.

*   *   *

SMITHSON, Norman 1931-

PERSONAL: Born September 6, 1931, in Leeds, Yorkshire, England; son of Harold (a teacher) and E. Louise (Eastwood) Smithson. *Education:* Attended elementary and secondary schools in England. *Home:* 55 Woodslry Rd., Leeds LS6 1SB, Yorkshire, England. *Agent:* Harvey Unna & Stephen Durbridge Ltd., 14 Beaumont Mews, Marylebone High St., London W1N 4HE, England.

CAREER: Journalist and writer with local and national press, beginning at age fourteen; currently playwright, short story and feature writer, as free-lancer and for British Broadcasting Corp. radio and television. *Military service:* British Army, Royal Signals, 1950-52. *Member:* National Union of Journalists, Writers' Guild of Great Britain. *Awards, honors:* Award from Writers' Guild of Great Britain, 1967, for best British radio drama; Yorkshire Arts Association award.

WRITINGS: The World of Little Foxy, Gollancz, 1969. Contributor to anthologies, including *Living Expression,* Ginn, 1968, *In a Few Words,* E. J. Arnold, 1968, *Best Movie Stories,* Faber, 1969, and *Fifth Windmill Book of One-Act Plays,* Heinemann, 1970. Founder and editor, *North.*

WORK IN PROGRESS: Fishermen, Feasts, and Other Northern Customs and Characters; a collection of short stories and a novel; autobiographical stories.

SIDELIGHTS: Norman Smithson likes novels by American authors of the thirties and British surveys of literature, also collections of short stories and essays on their origination and development. *Avocational interests:* Theater and cinema; sporting activities.

* * *

SNELL, John Leslie, Jr. 1923-1972

June 2, 1923—May 27, 1972; American historian, author, and educator. Obituaries: *New York Times,* May 29, 1972. (See index for *CA* sketch)

* * *

SNIDERMAN, Florence (Lama) 1915-

PERSONAL: Born June 21, 1915, in Grand Rapids, Mich.; daughter of William Edgar and Florence (Little) Lama; married Henry Sniderman (an accountant), January 19, 1935; children: Michael David, Jon Henry. *Education:* Attended Oberlin College, 1932-33; Wayne State University, B.A., 1959; University of Michigan, M.A.L.S., 1960, M.A., 1966. *Residence:* San Jose, Costa Rica.

CAREER: Wayne State University, Detroit, Mich., reference librarian, 1960-71. *Member:* Theatre Library Association, Phi Beta Kappa.

WRITINGS: (Editor with Paul Breed) *Dramatic Criticism Index: Bibliography of Commentaries on Playwrights from Ibsen to the Avant-Garde,* Gale, 1972.

* * *

SNOW, Edgar Parks 1905-1972

July 19, 1905—February 15, 1972; American journalist and writer on China. Obituaries: *New York Times,* February 16, 1972; *Washington Post,* February 16, 1972; *Nation,* February 28, 1972; *Time,* February 28, 1972; *Current Biography,* April, 1972.

* * *

SPECTORSKY, A(uguste) C(omte) 1910-1972

August 13, 1910—January 17, 1972; American editor, publisher and author. Obituaries: *New York Times,* January 18, 1972; *Washington Post,* January 18, 1972; *Newsweek,* January 31, 1972; *Time,* January 31, 1972; *Publishers Weekly,* February 7, 1972; *Current Biography,* March, 1972. (See index for *CA* sketch)

* * *

SPEWACK, Samuel 1899-1971

September 16, 1899—October 14, 1971; Russian-born American author of stage and screen comedies and novels. Obituaries: *New York Times,* October 15, 1971; *Washington Post,* October 16, 1971; *Time,* October 25, 1971.

STANLEY-BROWN, Katherine (Oliver) 1893(?)-1972

1893(?)—April 15, 1972; American writer of books and articles for literary magazines. Obituaries: *Washington Post,* April 22, 1972.

* * *

STAPP, Arthur D(onald) 1906-1972

December 26, 1906—January 10, 1972; American newsman and author of juvenile novels. Obituaries: *Publishers Weekly,* February 7, 1972. (See index for *CA* sketch)

* * *

STASIO, Marilyn L(ouise) 1940-

PERSONAL: Born August 20, 1940, in Boston, Mass.; daughter of Joseph and Margaret (Crivello) Stasio; married Richard J. Hummler (an associate theater producer), April 24, 1971. *Education:* Regis College, Weston, Mass., B.A. (cum laude), 1960; Columbia University, M.A., 1961. *Home:* 164 West 79th St., Apt. 6B, New York, N.Y. 10024; and Lake Shore Dr., Preston, Conn. *Agent:* Harold Ober Associates, Inc., 40 East 49th St., New York, N.Y. 10017.

CAREER: Cue, New York, N.Y., theater critic, 1968-78. Lecturer, New School for Social Research, 1967. Member of nominating committee, Antoinette Perry Awards, 1969-70, 1971-72; member of play selection committee, Eugene O'Neill Playwrights Conference. *Member:* Drama Critics Circle, Drama Desk.

WRITINGS: (Compiler) *Broadway's Beautiful Losers,* Delacorte, 1972. Entertainment editor, *Ingenue,* 1969-70; theater critic, *Grolier's New Book of Knowledge Annual,* 1970—. Contributor to *Playbill, Playfare, Ms., Harper's Bazaar,* and other magazines.

WORK IN PROGRESS: A novel, *The Lily Room;* a screenplay, "Comeback."

AVOCATIONAL INTERESTS: Politics, Italian, anthropology, Renaissance art and literature.

BIOGRAPHICAL/CRITICAL SOURCES: Choice, March, 1973.†

* * *

STEKERT, Ellen J(ane) 1935-

PERSONAL: Born May 26, 1935, in New York, N.Y.; daughter of Martin Michael (a businessman) and Rita (Waintrob) Stekert. *Education:* Cornell University, B.A., 1957; Indiana University, M.A., 1961; University of Pennsylvania, Ph.D., 1965. *Office:* English Department, University of Minnesota, Minneapolis, Minn. 55455.

CAREER: Wayne State University, Detroit, Mich., assistant professor, 1963-68, associate professor, 1968-72, professor of folklore, 1972-73, director of Folklore Archives, 1966-73; University of Minnesota, Minneapolis, professor of folklore, 1973—; Minnesota state folklorist and director of Minnesota Folklife Center, 1976—. Visiting professor of folklore, University of California, Berkeley, 1972-73. Art commissioner, City of Minneapolis, 1975-77. Consultant for Public Health grants on child and infant health. Has read papers, given lectures and concerts to numerous universities and seminar groups throughout the U.S. *Member:* American Folklore Society (member of various committees, 1966-75; executive board member-at-large, 1970-78; recording secretary, 1972-76; president, 1976-78), Modern Language Association of America, American Anthropological Association,

Society of American Archivists, Society of Ethnomusicology, American Association of University Professors, American Federation of Teachers, American Federation of Musicians (Local 802, New York branch). *Awards, honors:* Newport Folk Foundation grant, 1965; Wayne State University grants-in-aid, 1965-66, 1966-67, 1967-68; Indiana University grants for field work, 1967, 1968; research recognition award, Wayne State University Alumni Association, 1968, to study folkways of Southern mountaineers living in Detroit; American Council of Learned Societies travel grant, 1969; National Endowment for the Arts grant, 1976.

WRITINGS: (Editor with Americo Paredes, and contributor) *The Urban Experience and Folk Tradition,* University of Texas Press, 1971.

Contributor: Bruce Jackson, editor, *Folklore and Society: Essays in Honor of Benjamin A. Botkin,* Folklore Associates, 1966; Kenneth S. Goldstein and Robert M. Byington, editors, *Two Penny Ballads and Four Dollar Whiskey: A Pennsylvania Folklore Miscellany,* published for Pennsylvania Folklore Society by Folklore Associates, 1966; Austin E. Fife and Alta Fife, *Cowboy and Western Songs,* C. N. Potter, 1969; Otto Feinstein, editor, *Ethnic Groups in the City: Culture, Institutions, and Power,* Heath, 1971; Wayland D. Hand, editor, *Folklore of Mountain and Plain: Studies in Honor of Austin E. Fife,* privately printed, 1972. Contributor of numerous articles on folklore and folk music and reviews of recordings and concerts to *Keystone Folklore Quarterly, Folklore and Folk Music Archivist, Kentucky Folklore Record, Midwest Folklore, Detroit Free Press, Historical Society of Michigan Chronicle, Western Historical Quarterly, Ethnomusicology, Southern Folklore Quarterly,* and other folklore journals; contributor to *Proceedings* of Fourth (1968) and Fifth (1969) Annual Southeastern Michigan Junior Science and Humanities Symposium. Writer of monthly column, "Views and Reviews," *Tune Up,* published by Philadelphia Folksong Society, 1962-63. *Journal of American Folklore,* assistant to editor, 1958-59, associate editor, 1968-73, special editor of April-June, 1970 issue; editor, *Annual Report* of Wayne State University Folklore Archive, 1967-70, and *Annual Report* of American Folklore Society, 1972-76; member of editorial board, *Minneapolis Review of the Arts,* 1975-76.

WORK IN PROGRESS: Continuing research on Southern Appalachian adaptive behavior in urban environments analyzed in terms of traditional behavior and beliefs and lore; writings on medical beliefs and comparative aesthetics of folk literature, especially folk song; study of the influence of individuals upon tradition.

SIDELIGHTS: Ellen Stekert, one of the country's leading authorities on folklore, is herself a professional folksinger, with six long playing records to her credit. She often performs at universities, has given concerts and concert lectures throughout the United States, and is a personal friend of many of the best known folk performers in the country. Whether back packing in the mountains or researching ethnic, deviate, or transplanted cultural groups in urban societies, she often carries her guitar and tape recorder. One of her continuing projects is documentation and analysis of the folksong enthusiast interest of the 1960's. Michael Owen Jones, a reviewer for *Journal of American Folklore,* was "especially impressed with Ellen Stekert's tracing of the urban folksong movement" in her essay, "Cents and Nonsense in the Urban Folksong Movement: 1930-1966" (published in *Folklore and Society: Essays in Honor of Benjamin A. Botkin).* Jones noted her "breakdown of the present situation into the four directions of traditional singers, imitators

of traditional style, utilizers (urban pop and urban art), and the new esthetic; and her analysis of the movement's role in creating a new idiom of popular entertainment. Miss Stekert's well-written essay epitomizes the volume's theme and provides a good conclusion to the volume."

Stekert regards folklore as traditional material and often substitutes the word "tradition" for "folklore" in her lectures and writings. She believes "folklorists today are doing exciting and innovative work that other fields of social science have long ignored. . . . Culture provides the tradition which is then used by the individual as an expressive vocabulary. Thus on one hand folklore is a conservative force, while on the other it gives the individual within culture the building blocks of tradition with which to build his own structures."

Early in 1972 the U.S. Department of Housing and Urban Development named *The Urban Experience and Folk Tradition* "book of the week." In one of the essays in the book, entitled "Focus for Conflict: Southern Mountain Medical Beliefs in Detroit," Stekert points out that mountain people, used to being part of a close-knit community, have a difficult time adjusting to the alienation and impersonality of the urban environment. One of her strong beliefs is that folklore is a prime resource and expressive device used in times of crisis; e.g., "during the racial unrest in the United States in the late 1960's, rumors of mutilations of children spread throughout the country, rumors which in actuality were extensions of traditional legends told as long ago as the fifth century A.D." As Stekert told an interviewer for the *Detroit News:* "Oral literature reflects the values of the times. . . . What people read as 'literature' now is really a mixture of folklore that has been passed down. If there had been folklore study in Shakespeare's time, we could better understand him today."

BIOGRAPHICAL/CRITICAL SOURCES: Journal of American Folklore, April-June, 1967, July-September, 1967; *Detroit News,* February, 1972.

* * *

STEVENS, James F. 1892-1971

1892—December 30, 1971; American lumberman and author of children's books. Obituaries: *New York Times,* January 1, 1972; *Washington Post,* January 2, 1972.

* * *

STEWARD, Julian H. 1902-1972

January 31, 1902—February 6, 1972; American social anthropologist. Obituaries: *New York Times,* February 8, 1972; *Washington Post,* February 11, 1972.

* * *

STEWART, George 1892-1972

February 11, 1892—February 21, 1972; American soldier, author, and Presbyterian minister. Obituaries: *New York Times,* February 22, 1972; *Publishers Weekly,* March 13, 1972.

* * *

STEWART, John (William) 1920-
(Jack Cole)

PERSONAL: Born October 1, 1920, in Chicago, Ill.; son of Ray Hiram Stewart and Mary Ethel (Holby) Stewart Cole; married Rose Elton Day, October 1, 1941 (divorced, 1945);

children: Rosanne Margaret (Mrs. Alan Dean Wood), John William Dean. *Education:* Attended public schools in Gary, Ind., Alhambra and Huntington Park, Calif.; extension courses at University of California, Los Angeles. *Politics:* "Registered Democrat, but vote for man, not party." *Religion:* Presbyterian. *Home:* 629 Darfield Ave., Covina, Calif. 91724.

CAREER: Employed in brokerage firm, as private secretary, and by U.S. Government, prior to 1962; adult education teacher, San Gabriel Valley, Calif., 1962-72; now full-time writer and lecturer. Co-founder and former president, San Gabriel Little Theatre, 1954; co-founder and president, Masque Players of Alhambra, 1962—. *Member:* Authors Guild, American Film Institute.

WRITINGS—For young people: *The Key to the Kitchen,* Lothrop, 1970; *Frederic Remington: Artist of the Western Frontier,* Lothrop, 1971; *Secret of the Bats: Exploration of the Carlsbad Caverns,* Westminster, 1972; *The Circus Is Coming,* Westminster, 1973; *Winds in the Woods,* Westminster, 1975.

Plays: "Leonora's Lost Love," first produced in San Gabriel, Calif. at San Gabriel Little Theatre, May, 1954; "Nobody's Perfect," first produced in Alhambra, Calif. at Masque Players Theatre, June, 1970; "The Waiting Room," first produced in Alhambra, Calif., at Masque Players Theatre, March, 1972. Also author of "Damnation" (screenplay), 1969.

Other: (Compiler) *Filmarama,* Scarecrow, Volume I: *The Formidable Years 1892-1919,* 1975, Volume II: *The Flaming Years 1920-1929,* 1977, Volume III: *The Golden Years 1930-1939,* in press.

Contributor to *Alhambra Free Press and Post Advocate* and many other periodicals. Field editor, *Offbeat,* 1959-60. Writer under name Jack Cole of column, "The Cole Shute," in *Offbeat.*

WORK IN PROGRESS: Murder-Go-Round, a comedy-mystery play; a dialect book for writers; *Night Hawk,* a fictionalized account of the Fetterman Massacre at Fort Phil Kearny; Volumes IV, V, and VI of *Filmarama; Booth,* a historical novel about John Wilkes Booth.

SIDELIGHTS: John Stewart told *CA:* "There are three things a writer must have: a maniacal desire to write, self-discipline (a writer must MAKE the time to write, he will never FIND it), and self confidence. Young people today have a greater opportunity to begin writing as most schools now have creative writing courses; unfortunately on the lower levels, it is taught by English teachers rather than professional writers." Stewart continues: "As a professional writer, I am often asked by various schools to talk to the students from the second grade up through high school; I find the lower grades much more receptive and open minded on the subject. After a brief talk, there is a question and answer period, then I put a word on the board and ask the youngsters to write whatever comes to mind. The results are fantastic! Teachers later tell me interest in both reading and writing improve. That is more rewarding than a check—well, almost!"

BIOGRAPHICAL/CRITICAL SOURCES: San Gabriel Valley Tribune Sunday Magazine, October 11, 1970.

*   *   *

STOREY, Victoria Carolyn 1945-
(Vicky Martin)

PERSONAL: Born May 22, 1945, in Windsor, Berkshire, England; daughter of Lancelot Arthur (a banker) and Jean (Slocock) Martin; married Thomas Michael Storey (a chartered accountant), July 28, 1969; children: Eleanor Caroline, Susannah Jemima, Harriet Tamsin. *Education:* Winkfield Place, cordon bleu, 1962; also attended Byam Shaw School of Art, 1962-65. *Politics:* Conservative. *Religion:* Church of England. *Home:* Newells Farm House, Lower Beeding, Horsham, Sussex, England. *Agent:* John Farquharson Ltd., 8 Bell Yard, Bellhouse, London WC2A 2JR, England.

CAREER: Has worked as a cook, 1965-66, a receptionist, 1966-67, and a dealer in antiques, 1967-68; writer, 1968—.

WRITINGS: (Under name Vicky Martin) *September Song,* Macmillan, 1969, Thomas Nelson, 1971; *The Windmill Years,* St. Martin's, 1978. Author of over seventy short stories and about six serials.

WORK IN PROGRESS: Another novel.

AVOCATIONAL INTERESTS: Fashion, cooking, house decoration, antiques, travel.

*   *   *

STOUT, Ruth 1884-

PERSONAL: Born June 14, 1884, in Girard, Kan.; daughter of John Wallace (a county superintendent) and Lucetta Todhunter Stout; married Fred Rossiter, June 25, 1939 (died, 1960). *Education:* "Couldn't waste my time on college." *Politics:* "None, really. I always vote a protest vote." *Religion:* "Born a Quaker. No religion now." *Home:* Poverty Hollow Road, Redding Ridge, Conn. 06896.

CAREER: Employed at various times before marriage as baby nurse, telephone operator, store clerk, bookkeeper, office manager, secretary, lecturer and arranger of lectures and debates, and owned a tea-room in Greenwich Village. Participated in famine relief work with Quakers in Russia. Professional gardener and writer.

WRITINGS: How to Have a Green Thumb without an Aching Back: A New Method of Mulch Gardening, Exposition Press, 1955; *Company Coming: Six Decades of Hospitality, Do It Yourself and Otherwise,* Exposition Press, 1958; *It's a Woman's World,* Doubleday, 1960; *Gardening without Work: For the Aging, the Busy, and the Indolent,* Devin-Adair, 1961; *If You Would Be Happy,* Doubleday, 1962; *The Ruth Stout No Work Garden Book,* Rodale Press, 1971; *I've Always Done It My Way,* Exposition Press, 1976; *As We Remember Mother,* Exposition Press, 1976. Writer of column for three local papers, and articles for numerous periodicals, including *Organic Gardening.*

SIDELIGHTS: Ruth Stout told *CA:* "I've always been a 100% non-conformist. I've always hated to travel and still do. Never learned to drive a car because I didn't want to go anywhere. I have never paid the slightest attention to etiquette, but didn't know I was 'out of step' until I got married . . . and my husband pointed it out to me. He enjoyed it. Discharged from a job once because I didn't wear a hat (30 years before it was 'done'). Had my hair bobbed before anybody. I never was a joiner. Given many lectures to garden clubs but never joined one. No gift for foreign languages, but learned Russian because I simply had to read Dostoevski in the original. On subjects I consider vital: I have never had an ounce of patriotism. I don't believe in murder—maybe, possibly, in self-defense. Also, I think everyone has a right to kill himself if he wants to. And I do believe in mercy killing. Politics—an awful, awful mess."

When asked by an interviewer what she considers her biggest success, Ms. Stout said: "It's so obvious. At the age of

87 I grow vegetables for two people the year-round, doing all the work myself and freezing the surplus. I tend several flower beds, write a column every week, answer an awful lot of mail, do the housework and cooking,—and never do any of these things after 11 o'clock in the morning! But that is my one real success, because I have had over 3000 people from every state and from Canada come to see my easy method and I have received thousands of letters, thanking me for making gardening easy for them. Or possible. And I feel that if you really *help* people you've done something worthwhile.'' An unorthodox, organic gardener, Ruth Stout arrived at her ''no work'' methods after many years of ''following the rules.'' Her books and articles were written in order to share her methods and philosophy of gardening.

BIOGRAPHICAL/CRITICAL SOURCES: Organic Gardening, October, 1971.

* * *

STRICKLAND, Cowles   1903(?)-1971

1903(?)—October 20, 1971; American stage director and educator. Obituaries: *Washington Post,* October 22, 1971; *New York Times,* October 23, 1971.

* * *

SWEZEY, Kenneth M.   1905(?)-1972

1905(?)—February 25, 1972; American author of books on popular science. Obituaries: *New York Times,* February 28, 1972.

* * *

TAIT, Dorothy   1902(?)-1972
(Ann Fairbairn, Jay Allison Stuart)

1902(?)—February 8, 1972; American newswoman and novelist. Obituaries: *New York Times,* February 11, 1972; *Publishers Weekly,* February 28, 1972.

* * *

TAYLOR, Arnold H.   1929-

PERSONAL: Born November 29, 1929, in Regina, Va.; son of Isaiah (a farmer) and Tina (Layton) Taylor; children: Arnold Bradford. *Education:* Virginia Union University, B.A. (cum laude), 1951; Howard University, M.A., 1952; Catholic University of America, Ph.D., 1963. *Office:* Department of History, Howard University, Washington, D.C. 20059.

CAREER: Benedict College, Columbia, S.C., instructor, 1955-57, assistant professor, 1957-59, associate professor, 1959-62, professor of history, 1963-64; Southern University, New Orleans Center, New Orleans, La., professor of history and chairman of department, 1964-65; North Carolina College at Durham (now North Carolina Central University), professor of history, 1965-70; University of Connecticut, Storrs, professor of history, 1970-72; Howard University, Washington, D.C., professor of history, 1972—. Fulbright professor of American history at Jadavpur University, Calcutta, 1967-68, and American Studies Research Centre, Hyderabad, spring, 1968; visiting professor at University of North Carolina at Greensboro, 1969-70. *Military service:* U.S. Army, 1953-54.

MEMBER: American Historical Association, Organization of American Historians, Association for the Study of Negro Life and History, Society for Historians of American Foreign Relations, American Association of University Professors, Phi Alpha Theta. *Awards, honors:* American Council of Learned Societies grant, 1968; Ford Foundation faculty fellowship, 1969-70.

WRITINGS: American Diplomacy and the Narcotics Traffic, 1900-1939, Duke University Press, 1969; *Travail and Triumph: Black Life and Culture in the South since the Civil War,* Greenwood Press, 1976. Contributor to history journals.

WORK IN PROGRESS: American Diplomacy and Humanitarian Reform Movements, 1870-1940; The Black Response to American Foreign Policy.

* * *

TAYLOR, Bob L(eslie)   1923-

PERSONAL: Born May 19, 1923, in Martinsburg, W.Va.; son of Leslie Owen and Mer aline (Peterson) Taylor; married Eleanor D. Sorensen, May 13, 1952; children: Ann Eleanor, Nancy Jane. *Education:* University of Nebraska, B.S., 1948; Northwestern University, M.A., 1951; Indiana University, Ed.D., 1957. *Home:* 214 Seminole Dr., Boulder, Colo. 80303. *Office:* School of Education, University of Colorado, Boulder, Colo. 80302.

CAREER: Science teacher in high schools in Iowa, 1948-51; history teacher in high school in Omaha, Neb., 1953-55; San Francisco State College (now University), San Francisco, Calif., assistant professor, 1957-61, associate professor of secondary education, 1961-63; University of Colorado, Boulder, associate professor, 1963-67, professor of secondary education, 1967—. Summer lecturer, Indiana University, 1958-63. *Military service:* U.S. Army, 1944-46, 1951-53; became first lieutenant. *Member:* American Educational Research Association, National Council for the Social Studies (member of national board of directors, 1973-75), Association for Supervision and Curriculum Development (chairman of social studies committee, 1969-72), Association of Teacher Educators (member of national executive board, 1968-71), National Education Association, Phi Delta Kappa.

WRITINGS: (With L. O. Taylor and Don McMahill) *The American Secondary School,* Appleton, 1960; (with Robert C. McKean) *The Teacher in Colorado,* Pruett, 1965, revised edition, 1966; (writing chairman) *Mental Health and Teacher Education,* Association for Student Teaching, 1967; (editor) *Trends in Secondary Education,* University of Colorado Press, 1969; (compiler with Tom L. Groom) *ASCD Index of Social Studies Projects,* Association for Supervision and Curriculum Development, 1971.

* * *

TAYLOR, Charlene M(ae)   1938-

PERSONAL: Born November 26, 1938, in Liberal, Kan.; daughter of Charles David (a businessman) and Lola Mae (Wood) Taylor. *Education:* University of Wichita (now Wichita State University), B.A. (cum laude), 1960; University of Illinois, A.M., 1962, Ph.D., 1965; University of Edinburgh, Diploma in English Studies, 1963; Georgetown University, J.D., 1976. *Politics:* Democrat. *Religion:* Episcopalian. *Home:* 6437 Calle de San Alberto, Tucson, Ariz. 85710. *Office:* Suite 602, Transamerica Bldg., Tucson, Ariz. 85710.

CAREER: University of California, Riverside, lecturer in English, 1965-66; University of Arizona, Tucson, assistant professor of English, 1966-72; private practice of law in Tucson. Administrative assistant to director of Joint Legislative Task Force on Organized Crime. *Member:* American

Bar Association, Arizona Bar Association, Pima County Bar Association.

WRITINGS: (Editor with William· H. McBurney) *English Prose Fiction, 1700-1800, in the University of Illinois Library,* University of Illinois Press, 1965; (editor) George Etherege, *She Would if She Could,* University of Nebraska Press, 1971. Also editor of Stuart Herzog's *Impact Study of the Equal Rights Amendment; Subject: Arizona Constitution and Statutes,* 1973.

*   *   *

TAYLOR, Henry (Splawn)   1942-

PERSONAL: Born June 21, 1942, in Loudon County, Va.; son of Thomas Edward (a farmer) and Mary (Splawn) Taylor; married Sarah Bean, June 12, 1965 (divorced, January 12, 1967); married Frances Carney, June 29, 1968; children: (second marriage) Thomas Edward, Richard Carney. *Education:* University of Virginia, B.A., 1965; Hollins College, M.A., 1966. *Religion:* Society of Friends. *Address:* Box 51, Lincoln, Va. 22078. *Office:* Literature Department, American University, Massachusetts and Nebraska Aves. N.W., Washington, D.C. 20016.

CAREER: Roanoke College, Salem, Va., instructor in English, 1966-68; University of Utah, Salt Lake City, assistant professor of English, 1968-71; American University, Washington, D.C., associate professor of literature, 1971—. Director, University of Utah Writers' Conference, 1969-72. *Member:* Modern Language Association of America, Society for the Study of Southern Literature, South Atlantic Modern Language Association. *Awards, honors:* Academy of American Poets prize, University of Virginia, 1962, 1964; Utah State Institute of Fine Arts poetry prize, 1969, 1971.

WRITINGS: The Horse Show at Midnight (poems), Louisiana State University Press, 1966; *Breakings* (poems), Solo Press, 1971; *Poetry: Points of Departure* (textbook), Winthrop Publishing, 1974; *An Afternoon of Pocket Billiards* (poems), University of Utah Press, 1975; *The Water of Light: A Miscellany in Honor of Brewster Ghiselin,* University of Utah Press, 1976. Anthologized in several publications, including *The Girl in the Black Raincoat,* edited by George Garrett, Duell, Sloan & Pearce, 1966, *University and College Poetry Prizes, 1960-66,* edited by William Meredith, Academy of American Poets, 1967, and *Introduction to Poetry,* edited by X. J. Kennedy, Little, Brown, 1971. Taylor's translations are included in *Poems from France,* edited by William Jay Smith, Crowell, 1967, and *Poems from Italy,* edited by William Jay Smith, Crowell. Contributor to *Plume and Sword, Shenandoah, Encounter, Nation, Beloit Poetry Journal, Georgia Review, Book Week, Western Humanities Review,* and other periodicals. *Magill's (Masterplots) Literary Annual,* Salem Press, contributor, 1967-76, associate editor, 1971—. Contributing editor, *Hollins Critic,* 1970—.

WORK IN PROGRESS: The Children of Herakles, a translation from Euripides in collaboration with Robert A. Brooks; *The Flying Change,* a book of poems; a collection of critical writings.

SIDELIGHTS: The Virginia Quarterly Review critic called Henry Taylor "a new young poet of distinctive voice and sure craftsmanship.... His poems, refreshingly unpretentious, honest, and direct, are the product of an imagination disciplined in life and art, inspired and strengthened by reality. Whether working in intimate short lyrics, parodies, or longer reflective poems, Mr. Taylor maintains precise control over his feeling and his medium, writing poetry for those who care about truth and artistry."

BIOGRAPHICAL/CRITICAL SOURCES: Virginia Quarterly Review, summer, 1966; *Times Literary Supplement,* August 18, 1966.

*   *   *

TAYLOR, Vernon L.   1922-

PERSONAL: Born February 26, 1922, in Gilman, Ill.; son of John W. (an electrical engineer) and Harriet (Crouch) Taylor; married Juanita Barton (a teacher), November 18, 1943; children: Kimberly, Rosanna, Lucinda, Scott. *Education:* Illinois Wesleyan University, B.A., 1944; Boston University, S.T.B., 1948; Northwestern University, Ph.D., 1959. *Residence:* Middletown, Ill. 62666. *Office:* Evening College, Lincoln Land Community College, Springfield, Ill. 62708.

CAREER: National College, Kansas City, Mo., associate professor of speech and chairman of Humanities Division, 1959-61; Central Missouri State College (now University), Warrensburg, professor of speech and chairman of department, 1961-68; Platte College, Columbus, Neb., dean of faculty, 1968-73; Lincoln Land Community College, Springfield, Ill., dean of evening college, 1973—. *Member:* Speech Communication Association.

WRITINGS: The Art of Argument, Scarecrow, 1971. Also author of *Teaching Tips,* 1974, *Day of Camel,* 1975, and *Rest Stop,* 1977.

WORK IN PROGRESS: The Art of Illustration; Truman Speaking; The Profit Loser.

*   *   *

TEAL, G. Donn   1932-

PERSONAL: Born October 26, 1932, in Columbus, Ohio; son of Gerald D. (a Western Electric supervisor) and Helen (Hileman) Teal. *Education:* Florida State University, B.A. (magna cum laude), 1955; University of Pennsylvania, M.A. (cum laude), 1956. *Office:* Ballantine Books, 201 East 50th St., New York, N.Y. 10022.

CAREER: Abington Senior High School, Abington, Pa., French teacher, 1957-64; Girard College, Philadelphia, Pa., chairman, French department, 1964-65; Prentice-Hall, Inc., Englewood Cliffs, N.J., assistant editor, 1966-68; Rio Grande College, Rio Grande, Ohio, assistant professor of sociology, 1967; Alfred A. Knopf, Inc., New York City, copy editor, 1968-74; Ballantine Books, Inc., New York City, senior copy editor, 1975—. Free-lance writer and critic. *Military service:* U.S. Air Force, 1956; became second lieutenant. *Member:* Phi Beta Kappa, Omicron Delta Kappa, Phi Kappa Phi.

WRITINGS: The Gay Militants, Stein & Day, 1971. Contributor of articles to *New York Times, Advocate,* and *Gay.*

SIDELIGHTS: An article by G. Donn Teal published in the *New York Times* in February, 1969, was, according to him, "the first by an admitted homosexual to speak out against society's stereotype of 'gay people'—as reflected in theater, on screen, and in literature." He also told *CA* that *The Gay Militants,* a complete history/anthology of the American Gay Liberation Movement issued in 1971, was the first published book on the homosexual liberation movement.

*   *   *

TEETERS, Negley K(ing)   1896-1971

November 16, 1896—October 30, 1971; American criminologist and author. Obituaries: *New York Times*, October 31, 1971. (See index for *CA* sketch)

* * *

TELLER, Judd L. 1912-1972

1912—May 3, 1972; Austrian-born American writer on Jewish-Americans. Obituaries: *New York Times*, May 5, 1972; *Washington Post*, May 7, 1972.

* * *

TELSER, Lester G(reenspan) 1931-

PERSONAL: Born January 3, 1931, in Chicago, Ill.; son of Asher and Edith (Greenspan) Telser; married Sylvia R. Trossman (a social worker), June 24, 1956; children: Joshua, Tamar. *Education:* Roosevelt University, A.B., 1951; Harvard University, additional study, 1951-52; University of Chicago, A.M., 1953, Ph.D., 1956. *Residence:* Chicago, Ill. *Office:* Department of Economics, University of Chicago, Chicago, Ill. 60637.

CAREER: University of Chicago, Cowles Commission for Research in Economics, Chicago, Ill., research assistant, 1952-54; U.S. Department of Agriculture, Agricultural Marketing Service, and University of Chicago, Chicago, cooperative agent, 1954-55; Iowa State College (now Iowa State University of Science and Technology), Ames, assistant professor of economics, 1955-56; University of Chicago, assistant professor, 1958-60, associate professor, 1960-63, professor of economics, 1963—. Visiting research fellow, Cowles Foundation for Research in Economics, Yale University, 1964-65. Consultant to Arthur D. Little, 1961-62, 1967, and to Rand Corp., 1964-67. *Military service:* U.S. Army, 1956-58. *Member:* American Economic Association, Econometric Society (fellow), American Statistical Association (fellow). *Awards, honors:* Ford Foundation faculty research fellow, 1969-70.

WRITINGS: (Contributor) Don Patinkin, editor, *Essays in Econometrics and Mathematical Economics*, Stanford University Press, 1963; *Competition, Collusion and Game Theory*, Aldine-Atherton, 1972; (with R. L. Graves) *Functional Analysis in Mathematical Economics*, University of Chicago Press, 1972; *Economic Theory and the Core*, University of Chicago Press, 1978. Contributor to *Review of Economic Studies, Journal of Farm Economics, Journal of Political Economy, Review of Economics and Statistics, Journal of Business, Journal of Law and Economics, American Economic Review, Law and Contemporary Problems*, and other publications. Associate editor, *Journal of American Statistical Association*, 1966-69, and *Review of Economics and Statistics*, 1972—.

* * *

THEROUX, Paul 1941-

PERSONAL: Born April 10, 1941, in Medford, Mass.; son of Albert Eugene and Anne (Dittami) Theroux; married Anne Castle (a broadcaster), December 4, 1967; children: Marcel Raymond, Louis Sebastian. *Education:* Attended University of Maine, 1959-60; University of Massachusetts, B.A., 1963; Syracuse University, further study, 1963. *Politics:* Socialist. *Agent:* Blanche C. Gregory, Inc., 2 Tudor City Pl., New York, N.Y. 10017.

CAREER: Soche Hill College, Limbe, Malawi, lecturer in English, 1963-65; Makerere University, Kampala, Uganda, lecturer in English, 1965-68; University of Singapore, Singapore, lecturer in English, 1968-71; professional writer,

1971—. Visiting lecturer, University of Virginia, 1972-73. *Awards, honors:* Robert Hamlet one-act play award, 1960; *Playboy* Editorial Award, 1971, 1976; Literature Award, American Academy of Arts and Letters, 1977.

WRITINGS—Novels; published by Houghton, except as indicated: *Waldo*, 1967; *Fong and the Indians*, 1968; *Girls at Play*, 1969; *Murder in Mount Holly*, Alan Ross, 1969; *Jungle Lovers*, 1971; *Saint Jack*, 1973; *The Black House*, 1974; *The Family Arsenal* (Book-of-the-Month Club selection), 1976; *Picture Palace*, 1978.

Other books; published by Houghton, except as indicated: *V. S. Naipaul: An Introduction to His Work*, Africana Publishing Corp., 1972; *Sinning with Annie and Other Stories* (collection of stories), 1972; *The Great Railway Bazaar: By Train through Asia* (travel), 1975; *The Consul's File* (collection of stories), 1977.

Contributor of fiction and poetry to *Encounter, Atlantic Monthly, Commentary, Playboy*, London *Times, Harper's Bazaar*, and other periodicals; contributor of reviews to *New York Times, New Statesman*, London *Times*, and other periodicals in the United States and England.

SIDELIGHTS: Paul Theroux, who served as a Peace Corps volunteer in Africa, told *CA* that he has lived a good portion of his adult life "outside the United States, mainly in equatorial places . . . ; I did not plan to be away so long but that is the way it has worked out and, as it happens, expatriation is often my fictional subject. I am not an exile, simply a person who enjoys travelling in temptingly named places (Burma, Java, Singapore, The Congo, Central Africa, the Cotswolds)."

Whether or not he himself is an exile or an expatriot, many of Theroux's characters are indeed in this position, strangers in exotic lands, and Theroux's clashes of culture are fitting backgrounds for his biting humor and occasional dark moods. Reviewing *Fong and the Indians*, set in a newly independent East African nation, Geoffrey Godsett writes that "the situations . . . are outrageous. So are most of the characters. But they manage at the same time to be outrageously funny, with a funniness that comes so close to the frequent tragedy of the human condition that this reader found himself wincing. . . . Theroux's East Africans and East African Asians will probably cause offense to the more sensitive inhabitants of the territories about which he writes. But his Americans are just as ruthlessly drawn." Constance Wagner finds that the book "cuts so close to the bone of truth that anyone familiar with the 'developing nations' must regard it as selective and hilarious reportage. . . . There is no flagging of interest from beginning to end. The wildly assorted personae move in and out, figures in an absurd dance of rapacity, racism, and misconception. All are equally preposterous—and fully believable: Africans, Asians, whites, cheating, despising, mistrusting one another."

Girls at Play is set in Kenya and is a darker tale than *Fong*, but again the scenery is an important backdrop for the novel. A reviewer for the *Times Literary Supplement* writes that "the country is every bit as important as the characters. Its effect is pernicious; its principal weapon, dilapidation—both physical and spiritual. . . . Even in its smaller aspects, the novel is unremittingly depressing. . . . The book's power lies in Mr. Theroux's ability to instil an aura of seediness and decay, and a resultant tension, in which violence is a constant possibility." Lawrence Lafore also mentions the indifferent violence, writing that Theroux "tells his terror and cruelty with cold detachment dressed in wit and irony, and his cold-bloodedness is so relentless that it becomes in itself a sort of cruelty inflicted on the readers. He is out to instruct us in the ways that life and death can be horrible, and he does so with such persuasiveness that quite trivial details become nightmares.''

L. J. Davis writes of the *Jungle Lovers*, which is set in Malawi, a small central African country in which Theroux has lived: ''Theroux has chosen to measure himself against a very tall ghost indeed: Joseph Conrad. *Jungle Lovers* is an audacious attempt to tell the other half of *The Heart of Darkness*.... His portrait of modern Malawi is as good as one could want, and the book deserves a wide readership on the basis of his insights alone. Throughout the book one seems to hear the echoes of Conrad's voice.'' *The Black House*, in which an English anthropologist and his wife, Alfred and Emma Munday, return to their native Dorset after ten years of studying an isolated African tribe, is described by Roger Sale as ''a reverse *Heart of Darkness*.'' Munday finds in Dorset ''the same village as the one he left, an isolated tribal world of suspicion, acrimony, and suppressed violence.'' Although Sale finds that ''the total effect is indeed murky and unsatisfactory,'' he concludes that ''Paul Theroux, whatever the tangles he has gotten himself into here, is a real writer, full of achievement even in this unachieved novel, full of promise.''

Clashes of cultures also dominate Theroux's work in genres other than the novel. Geoffrey Wagner found the stories in *Sinning with Annie* ''strained and heavy-breathing. Each is an encounter between some American and a culture-representing character—Russian, Czech, Indian, Malayan.... But there is little to differentiate these efficient anecdotes from run-of-the-mill 'creative writing' assignments.'' Conversely, the reviewer for *Choice* writes: ''In the remarkably diverse stories of this collection Theroux quickly and deftly creates worlds for his readers to lose themselves in. His episodes take place in Asia, Africa, eastern Europe, Russia, and other far-flung spots, yet each seems thoroughly convincing, filled with the detail and nuance of local color.'' The reviewer continues with the comment that Theroux ''has been likened to Conrad, Joyce Cary, and Evelyn Waugh; one might also sense a bit of Kafka in these tales. One of Theroux's character comments, 'I promised to be ingenious'—a comment equally appropriate to his author.''

The central character of Theroux's latest book, *Picture Palace*, is the fictitious famed and aging photographer, Maude Coffin Pratt. Christopher Willcox calls Maude ''a wonderful creation—raffish, bawdy, eccentric in the authentic way that some artists have.... She is also embittered, rightfully, over the assumptions made about the old and the daily tyranny inflicted upon them. Finally, she is evidence that old people have the same need to change and grow that younger folks reserve for themselves.'' Willcox believes the book has a ''peculiar English flavor'' reminiscent of Graham Greene in ''the strong narrative quality of Theroux's work. He knows how to tell a story while he is making his point, a rare quality in serious American fiction. *Picture Palace* is a thoughtful novel that entertains mightily while it discusses art, reality, mortality, and fame.''

BIOGRAPHICAL/CRITICAL SOURCES: Harper's, May, 1967; *Kenyon Review*, September, 1967; *New Yorker*, November 11, 1967, November 8, 1969; *Time*, August 23, 1968; *Christian Science Monitor*, September 5, 1968; *Saturday Review*, September 28, 1968; *New York Times Book Review*, November 3, 1968, September 28, 1969, November 5, 1972, September 8, 1974, August 24, 1975, July 11, 1976; *Times Literary Supplement*, June 12, 1969, November 17, 1972, April 27, 1973, March 26, 1976; *Books Abroad*, summer, 1969, winter, 1971; *National Observer*, October 6, 1969; *Virginia Quarterly Review*, winter, 1969, winter, 1970; *New Republic*, November 29, 1969; *Punch*, December 10, 1969; *London Magazine*, January, 1970; *Life*, May 21, 1971; *New York Times*, May 29, 1971, August 23, 1977, May 31, 1978; *National Review*, June 29, 1971, November 10, 1972; *Book World*, August 8, 1971, September 15, 1974; *Choice*, July, 1973; *Encounter*, July, 1973; *New Statesman*, October 4, 1974, October 17, 1975; *Spectator*, October 12, 1974; *Hudson Review*, winter, 1974; *Contemporary Literary Criticism*, Gale, Volume V, 1976, Volume VIII, 1978; *Detroit News*, June 4, 1978.

*   *   *

THOMAS, Ross (Elmore)   1926-
(Oliver Bleeck)

PERSONAL: Born February 19, 1926, in Oklahoma City, Okla.; son of J. Edwin (a contractor) and Laura (Dean) Thomas. *Education:* University of Oklahoma, B.A., 1949. *Politics:* ''Occasionally.'' *Religion:* ''Seldom.'' *Agent:* Warren Bayless, 551 Fifth Ave., New York, N.Y. 10017.

CAREER: Daily Oklahoman, Oklahoma City, Okla., reporter, 1943-44; public relations director, National Farmers Union, 1952-56; Stapp, Thomas & Wade, Inc., Denver, Colo., president, 1956-57; reporter in Bonn, Germany, 1958-59; Patrick Dolan & Associates Ltd., Ibadan, Nigeria, representative, 1959-61; consultant to U.S. Government, 1964-66. *Military service:* U.S. Army, 1944-46. *Awards, honors:* Edgar Allan Poe Award, Mystery Writers of America, 1967, for *The Cold War Swap*.

WRITINGS—All published by Morrow, except as indicated: *The Cold War Swap*, 1966; *The Spy in the Vodka*, Hodder & Stoughton, 1967; *The Seersucker Whipsaw*, 1967; *Cast a Yellow Shadow*, 1967; *The Singapore Wink*, 1968; (with William H. Crook) *The Story of VISTA: Volunteers in Service to America*, 1969; *The Fools in Town Are on Our Side*, 1970; *The Backup Men*, 1971; *The Thief Who Painted Sunlight*, Hodder & Stoughton, 1971; *The Porkchoppers*, 1972; *If You Can't Be Good*, 1973; *The Money Harvest*, 1975; *Yellow Dog Contract*, 1976.

Under pseudonym Oliver Bleeck; all published by Morrow: *The Brass Go-Between*, 1969; *Protocol for a Kidnapping*, 1970; *The Procane Chronicle*, 1972; *The Highbinders*, 1974; *No Questions Asked*, 1976.

WORK IN PROGRESS: Film script for *The Brass Go-Between*.

SIDELIGHTS: A *New Yorker* reviewer states: ''Mr. Thomas has proved that he has the skill and the ingenuity and the humor and the information that are necessary to the construction of a good suspense story, and he has special gifts of his own—a quick, flexible style and the ability to build his characters fast....'' Sarah Booth Conroy finds Thomas' ability with dialogue especially noteworthy. ''Thomas has a forked tongue which curls around exactly the sort of speech in time and space for each character....''

BIOGRAPHICAL/CRITICAL SOURCES: Books, March, 1970; *Washington Post*, January 8, 1971; *New Yorker*, February 27, 1971; *Best Sellers*, January 15, 1971, July 1, 1971.†

*   *   *

THOMSON, William A.   1879-1971

1879—October 2, 1971; American newspaper writer, publisher, and advertiser. Obituaries: *New York Times*, October 5, 1971.

TIMOSHENKO, Stephen P.   1878-1972

December 22, 1878—May 29, 1972; Russian-born American educator and author in theoretical and applied mechanics. Obituaries: *Washington Post,* June 1, 1972.

* * *

TOWBER, Chaim   1902(?)-1972

1902(?)—February 26, 1972; American playwright, lyricist, and actor. Obituaries: *New York Times,* February 28, 1972.

* * *

TRAVERS, P(amela) L(yndon)   1906-

PERSONAL: Born in 1906, in Queensland, Australia. *Education:* Privately educated. *Home:* Chelsea, London, England.

CAREER: Writer, journalist, dancer, and actress in Australia and England; full-time writer in England, 1930—. Writer-in-residence, Radcliffe College, Cambridge, Mass., 1965-66, Smith College, Northampton, Mass., 1966-67, and Scripps College, Claremont, Calif., 1970.

WRITINGS: Mary Poppins, Reynal & Hitchcock, 1934, Harcourt, 1962; *Mary Poppins Comes Back,* Reynal & Hitchcock, 1935 (previous two titles appeared in one volume, *Mary Poppins and Mary Poppins Comes Back,* Reynal & Hitchcock, 1937, Harcourt, 1963); *Moscow Excursion,* Reynal & Hitchcock, 1935; *Happy Ever After,* Reynal & Hitchcock, 1940; *I Go by Sea, I Go by Land,* Harper, 1941, new edition, Norton, 1964; *Mary Poppins Opens the Door,* Reynal & Hitchcock, 1943, Harcourt, 1962; *Mary Poppins in the Park,* Harcourt, 1952; *The Fox at the Manger,* Norton, 1962; *Mary Poppins from A to Z,* Harcourt, 1962; *Friend Monkey,* Harcourt, 1971; *Mary Poppins in the Kitchen,* Harcourt, 1976; *About the Sleeping Beauty,* McGraw, 1976.

Stories taken from *Mary Poppins*; all published by Simon & Schuster: *The Gingerbread Shop,* 1952; *Mr. Wiggs Birthday Party,* 1952; *Stories from Mary Poppins,* 1952; *The Magic Compass,* 1953.

SIDELIGHTS: P. L. Travers prefers not to be photographed, believing these likenesses to be too inaccurate, although she told *CA* she does "like the bronze head by Gertrude Herries, famous English sculptor . . . and the pen drawing by the English artist, Agar." She said: "I am a writer who likes anonymity, believing that all that concerns the general public is the books themselves which are, in the truest sense, any author's biography," and has been quoted as saying: "It doesn't matter if an author exists. It matters only if the work lives."

Travers began to write before she was seven years old. When she arrived in Ireland, while still very young, George Russell, writing under the famed pseudonym "AE," published Travers' poetry in his paper, the *Irish Statesman,* and continued his interest in her work until his death. The writing of *Mary Poppins* began as an amusement for the author while she was recovering from an illness, and a friend's interest in the sketches convinced her to allow them to grow into a book.

To commemorate Travers' delightful character, Mary Poppins, Mortimer Browning wrote "Mary Poppins Suite for Orchestra," and a dramatization of *Mary Poppins,* written by Sara Spencer, was published by Children's Theater Press, c. 1940. The horticultural world, too, has responded to *Mary Poppins'* appeal by bringing out two different

"Mary Poppins" roses, and one rose has been named "Pamela Travers." *Mary Poppins* has been translated into more than twenty languages, and sales of the book have run into the millions.

Travers told an interviewer for *Publishers Weekly:* "I was brought up on fairy tales and I have been intensely interested and enchanted by myths, legends, and folklore all my life. I feel strongly that this is what underlies everything—all our so-called real life is based on this so-called unreal world—but it is infinitely more real than anything that happens externally."

The author once lived in a 900 year-old, small, thatched manor house which is mentioned in the Doomsday Book, and is of interest to archeological scholars. She now has a late Georgian house in Chelsea and a house in Dublin, Ireland. Travers has traveled to the United States and Russia, and made her home in this country during World War II.

BIOGRAPHICAL/CRITICAL SOURCES: New York Times, October 4, 1966, October 15, 1966; *Publishers Weekly,* December 13, 1971; *Children's Literature Review,* Volume II, Gale, 1976.

* * *

TVARDOVSKY, Alexandr Trifonovich   1910-1971

June 21, 1910—December 18, 1971; Russian poet and editor. Obituaries: *Detroit News,* December 19, 1971; *New York Times,* December 19, 1971; *Washington Post,* December 19, 1971; *Newsweek,* December 27, 1971; *L'Express,* December 27, 1971-January 2, 1972.

* * *

UDRY, J(oe) Richard   1928-

PERSONAL: Born October 12, 1928, in Covington, Ky.; married Janice Louise May; children: Leslie, Susan. *Education:* Northwestern University, B.S., 1950; Long Beach State College (now California State University, Long Beach), B.A., 1956; University of Southern California, Ph.D., 1960. *Office:* Department of Sociology, University of North Carolina, Chapel Hill, N.C. 27541.

CAREER: Chaffey College, Alta Loma, Calif., instructor in sociology, 1960-62; California State Polytechnic College (now California Polytechnic State University), San Luis Obispo, assistant professor of sociology, 1962-65; University of North Carolina at Chapel Hill, associate professor, 1965-69, professor of maternal and child health and sociology, 1969—. Associate director, Carolina Population Center, 1967—. Principal investigator, research evaluation of HEW Family Planning Programs. Advisor to National Institute of Child Health and Human Development. *Member:* American Sociological Association, American Public Health Association, National Council on Family Relations, Population Association of America.

WRITINGS: The Social Context of Marriage, Lippincott, 1966, 2nd edition, 1971. Contributor to *Journal of Educational Sociology, Social Forces, Sociology and Social Research, American Journal of Sociology, Demography, Nature, Encyclopedia Americana,* and other publications. Associate editor, *Social Forces* and *Journal of Marriage and Family.*

* * *

ULLMAN, Pierre L(ioni)   1929-

PERSONAL: Born October 31, 1929, in Nice, France (U.S.

citizen by birth); son of Eugene Paul (an artist) and Suzanne (Lioni) Ullman; married Mary Meade McDowell, June 9, 1956; children: Katherine Meade, Susan Randolph. *Education:* Yale University, B.A., 1952; attended University of Salamanca, Spain, 1954-55; Columbia University, M.A., 1956; Princeton University, Ph.D., 1962. *Religion:* Episcopalian. *Home:* 749 East Beaumont Ave., Milwaukee, Wis. 53217. *Office:* Department of Spanish and Portuguese, University of Wisconsin, Milwaukee, Wis. 53201.

CAREER: Spanish, French, and Latin teacher at Choate School, Wallingford, Conn., 1956-57, and St. Bernard's School, Gladstone, N.J., 1957-58; Rutgers University, New Brunswick, N.J., instructor in Romance languages, 1961-63; University of California, Davis, assistant professor of Spanish, 1963-65; University of Wisconsin—Milwaukee, associate professor, 1965-69, professor of Spanish, 1969—, chairman of department, 1966-67. Visiting professor of Spanish, University of Minnesota, 1970-71. *Military service:* U.S. Army, 1952-54. *Member:* Modern Language Association of America, American Association of Teachers of Spanish and Portuguese, American Association of Teachers of Esperanto, Universal Esperanto Association, Esperanto League for North America, American Association of University Professors, Midwest Modern Language Association.

WRITINGS: Mariano de Larra and Spanish Political Rhetoric, University of Wisconsin Press, 1971.

Contributor: Melvin J. Friedman, editor, *The Vision Obscured: Perceptions of Some Twentieth-Century Catholic Novelists,* Fordham University Press, 1970; Manuel Criado de Val, editor, *El arcipreste de Hita,* SERESA (Barcelona), 1973; Sola-Sole, Crisafulli, and Damiani, editors, *Estudios Literarios de hispanistas norteamericanos dedicados a Helmut Hatzfeld,* Hispam (Barcelona), 1974. Contributor of articles on Spanish literature from the Middle Ages to the present to journals, including *PMLA, MLN, Romance Notes, Hispanofila, Forum for Modern Language Studies, Anales Cervantinos, Revista de Estudios Hispanicos, Romanic Review, Insula,* and of book reviews to *Hispania* and *Revista Hispanica Moderna.* Advisory editor, *Papers in Language and Literature,* and *Ibero-Americanos.*

WORK IN PROGRESS: Articles on Lope de Vega, Galdos, Clarin, Cervantes, Larra, and Palacio Valdes.

AVOCATIONAL INTERESTS: Esperanto movement, contemporary Esperanto poetry.

*   *   *

UNTHANK, Luisa-Teresa
(Tessa Brown Unthank)

PERSONAL: Born in Wakefield, Yorkshire, England; married Kenneth Nelson Brown, June 1, 1957 (died July 5, 1962); married Cecil Herman Unthank (a professor of biology), September 26, 1963. *Education:* University of London, B.A.; University of North Carolina at Greenville, M.A., 1965; University of Liverpool, Ph.D., 1973. *Politics:* Fabian. *Home:* York Cottage, Williamsburg, Ky. 40769. *Office:* Department of English, Cumberland College, Williamsburg, Ky. 40769.

CAREER: Windsor College, Buenos Aires, Argentina, director of English studies, 1957-58; Elmore Green School, Walsall, Staffordshire, England, head of English department, 1958-60; University of New Mexico, Carlsbad Branch, instructor in English literature, 1960-63; Cumberland College, Williamsburg, Ky., associate professor of English literature, 1964—. *Member:* American Association of

University Professors, Bronte Society, Society of Authors, Society of Women Writers and Journalists, Society of Yorkshire Bookmen, Mensa Society, Vegetarian Society. *Awards, honors:* Fulbright grant to teach in United States, 1955-56; Danforth fellowship for Shakespeare study, 1965; awarded prize for short story "Wait Awhile, Wait Awhile" from Society of Women Writers and Journalists, 1976.

WRITINGS: Bibliography of Maria Edgeworth, AMS Press, 1972. Regular monthly columnist, *New Vegetarian,* 1973—. Contributor of articles, short stories, and poems to periodicals, including *Women Speaking, Southern Folklore Quarterly, Cats Magazine, National Humanitarian, The Dalesman,* and *Michigan Quarterly Review.*

WORK IN PROGRESS: A biography of Letitia Elizabeth Landon; a collection of children's stories; short stories and articles.

SIDELIGHTS: Luisa-Teresa Unthank told *CA:* "My career has been motivated by inspiring English teachers and a couple of inspiring professors (the latter all too rare!). I am still excited about literature and try to convey to my own students a sense of this excitement. As I see it, there is no excuse for dull, lazy, sloppy teachers—of anything! I began my writing career as a journalist but switched to teaching when I realised that women were not going far in journalism (things are better, but still have a long way to go). I now write when I can, which is not often enough, but I feel my students must come first and college teaching is, anyway, my bread and butter. I live under terrible guilt at not writing more—mostly do my writing at week-ends and late in the night. Although I have lived in the U.S.A. for several years now, I am still 'possessed' by my Yorkshire background which, honestly, was straight out of a house that looked like Wuthering Heights. Naturally I have been very much influenced by the Brontes, Dr. Phyllis Bentley, Storm Jameson, John Braine and other Yorkshire writers and I go back whenever I can. As I look back I am delighted to see, as one of those inspiring professors told me long ago, that I have, indeed, been ahead of my time—especially in such matters as careers for women, childlessness from choice, ZPG, vegetarianism, and other things once considered far out. Like Brigid Brophy, who is also a writer/vegetarian, I am dedicated to this cause and delighted to see the shift towards this way of life. I am also involved in animal welfare work, ecology, etc. Advice to aspiring writers? Only that which I constantly try to take myself: Apply seat of pants to seat of chair daily (or nightly), study the markets, refuse to accept rejection and keep on making trips to the Post Office with 'stuff.' Hard, lonely work—but eminently worthwhile."

*   *   *

VALDES, Nelson P. 1945-
(Ricardo Leyva)

PERSONAL: Born May 19, 1945, in Havana, Cuba; came to U.S. in 1961, became U.S. citizen; married Maxine Conant (a poet); children: Ricardo Alberto, Alisa Lynn. *Education:* University of New Mexico, B.A., 1970, Ph.D., 1972. *Politics:* Socialist, anti-bureaucratic. *Religion:* None. *Mailing address:* General Delivery, Bosque, N.M. 87006. *Office:* Department of Sociology, University of New Mexico, Albuquerque, N.M. 87106.

CAREER: Formerly history instructor, University of New Orleans, New Orleans, Louisiana; University of New Mexico, Albuquerque, researcher, 1965-70, instructor, 1970-76, assistant professor of sociology, 1976—. *Member:* Latin American Studies Association, American Historical Association. *Awards, honors:* Ford Foundation, National Defense Education Act, and Woodrow Wilson fellowships.

WRITINGS—Editor: (With Rolando Bonachea) *Che: The Selected Works of Ernesto Guevara,* M.I.T. Press, 1969; (with Edwin Lieuwen) *The Cuban Revolution: A Research Study Guide,* University of New Mexico Press, 1971; (with Bonachea, and contributor under pseudonym Ricardo Leyva) *Cuba in Revolution,* Doubleday-Anchor, 1972; (with Bonachea) *Revolutionary Struggle: The Selected Works of Fidel Castro,* Volume I, M.I.T. Press, 1972. Contributor of articles on Cuba to *Aportes* (Paris), *Latin American Research Review, Dissent, Science and Society, New Politics,* and *Workers' Power.*

WORK IN PROGRESS: Women in Cuba: A History; Anarchism in Cuba.

SIDELIGHTS: Nelson P. Valdes is interested in democratization of Communist regimes, labor movements, anarchism and underdevelopment, and social revolution in Latin America. He told *CA:* "The writer Leszek Kolakowski and some of Trotsky's works have influenced my thinking. Exile has had its effects also." *Avocational interests:* Classical music.

*   *   *

VANCE, Bruce 1931-

PERSONAL: Born June 23, 1931, in Chesley, Ontario, Canada; son of Clarence and Hazel (Thompson) Vance; married Patricia Humphreys, 1960; children: Kevin Christopher, James Geoffrey. *Education:* University of Toronto, B.A., 1953, M.A., 1956; additional study at Ontario College of Education, 1955, and Ontario Institute for Studies in Education, 1972. *Office:* Language Study Centre, Toronto Board of Education, 155 College St., Toronto 2B, Ontario, Canada.

CAREER: New Liberty Magazine, Toronto, Ontario, fiction editor, 1953-54; Ridley College, St. Catherines, Ontario, master in lower school, 1954-55; Board of Education, Collingwood, Ontario, head of English department, 1956-59; Toronto Board of Education, Toronto, teacher, 1959—, assistant head of English department, 1963, head of English department, 1964—, coordinating consultant for Language Study Centre, 1967—.

WRITINGS: (Adapter for junior high school students) Edith Hamilton, *Mythology,* published as *The Age of Heroes,* McClelland & Stewart (Toronto), 1959; (editor) Geoffrey Household, *Watcher in the Shadows,* McClelland & Stewart (Toronto), 1962; (editor) Farley Mowat, *Lost in the Barrens,* McClelland & Stewart (Toronto), 1962; (editor) *Narrative and Rhythm: An Introduction to Poetry,* McClelland & Stewart (Toronto), 1964; (editor) Agatha Christie, *The Murder of Roger Ackroyd,* Science Research Associates (Toronto), 1968; (editor) *Moonrise* (anthology), Thomas Nelson (Toronto), 1969; (editor) *The Fullness of Noon* (anthology), Thomas Nelson (Toronto), 1969; (editor) *The Eye of the Beholder* (anthology), Thomas Nelson (Toronto), 1970; (editor) *Microcosm* (anthology), Thomas Nelson (Toronto), 1970; (editor) *Short Plays for Reading and Acting,* Clarke, Irwin (Toronto), 1970; (editor) *Being Born and Growing Older* (anthology), Van Nostrand, 1971; (editor) *In and Out of Love,* (anthology), Van Nostrand, 1971.

"Folios for Writers" series, published by Clarke, Irwin (Toronto): *Description,* 1969; *Narration,* 1969; *Exposition,* 1969; *Poetry,* 1970; *Advertising,* 1973.

VANDER HILL, C(harles) Warren 1937-

PERSONAL: Born September 20, 1937, in Nyack, N.Y.; son of Lavern John (a minister) and Jeannette (Fisher) Vander Hill; married Joy Philip (an elementary teacher), August 13, 1960; children: Jon Charles, Sara Lynn. *Education:* Hope College, A.B., 1960; University of Denver, M.A., 1961, Ph.D., 1967. *Religion:* Protestant. *Home:* 306 Normandy, Muncie, Ind. 47304. *Office:* Department of History, Ball State University, Muncie, Ind. 47306.

CAREER: Grand Rapids Junior College, Grand Rapids, Mich., instructor in history, 1962-65; Ball State University, Muncie, Ind., assistant professor of history, 1965-66; Hope College, Holland, Mich., assistant professor of American history, 1966-68; Ball State University, associate professor, 1968-72, professor of history, 1974—, director of university honors program, 1972—, director of Whitinger scholars program, 1974. Consultant on state-based humanities programs, National Endowment for the Humanities, 1976. *Member:* American Historical Association, Organization of American Historians, Popular Culture Association, Historical Society of Michigan, Delta Tau Kappa. *Awards, honors:* Henry Rowe Schoolcraft Award of Historical Society of Michigan for research on Michigan history, 1970; National Endowment for the Humanities media grant, 1977.

WRITINGS: Gerrit J. Diekema, Eerdmans, 1970; *Settling the Great Lakes Frontier,* Michigan Historical Commission, 1970; (editor with Dwight W. Hoover) *American Society in the Twentieth Century* (readings), Wiley, 1972; (editor with Robert Warner) *A Michigan Reader, 1865-Present,* Eerdmans, 1974. Editor, "Great Men of Michigan" series published by Eerdmans. Contributor to *Westerners Brand Book,* 1962, and to *Michigan History* and other periodicals.

WORK IN PROGRESS: Research on Dutch immigration to America, especially to the Midwest.

SIDELIGHTS: C. Warren Vander Hill told *CA,* "In recent years I have become more and more interested in the quality (or lack of it) of trout fishing as one way to understand more fully environmental and ecological problems." *Avocational interests:* Sports (played basketball to the regional professional level and is Ball State University's faculty representative to the Midwestern Athletic Conference).

*   *   *

Van der VEER, Judy 1912-

PERSONAL: Born October 17, 1912, in Oil City, Pa.; daughter of Tunis Herbert and Alice (Case) Van der Veer. *Education:* "I am a high school drop-out." *Home:* Star Route, Ramona, Calif. *Agent:* Ruth Aley, Maxwell Aley Associates, 145 East 35th St., New York, N.Y. 10016.

CAREER: Grew up in San Diego but "escaped from schools and cities at an early age" to live in the country; writer.

WRITINGS: River Pasture, Longmans, Green, 1936; *Brown Hills,* Longmans, Green, 1938; *November Grass,* Longmans, Green, 1940, reprinted, Comstock Editions, 1972; *A Few Happy Ones,* Appleton, 1943; (contributor) J. H. Jackson, editor, *Continent's End,* Whittlesey House, 1944; (contributor) Roderick Peattie, editor, *Pacific Coast Ranges,* Vanguard, 1946; *My Valley in the Sky,* Messner, 1959; *Hold the Rein Free,* Golden Gate, 1966; *Wallace the Wandering Pig,* Harcourt, 1967; *Higher than the Arrow,* Golden Gate, 1969; *To the Rescue,* Harcourt, 1969; *The Gray Mare's Colts,* Golden Gate, 1971; *Long Trail for Francisco,* Childrens Press, 1974.

Stories, articles, and poems have been published in magazines and included in anthologies. Contributor to various periodicals.

WORK IN PROGRESS: More books based on "the ideas I receive from knowing animals and people."

SIDELIGHTS: Judy Van der Veer told *CA:* "I live in the country with lots of animals and see lots of people. I hate to travel but have done some. I have more fun at home. I also hate all hunters, trappers and poisoners. I am interested in things like the importance of the individual, whether animal or human and like all races and/or colors of people, but hate people who destroy land and animals."

* * *

VAN ERMENGEM, Frederic 1881-1972

1881—January 20, 1972; Belgian poet, essayist, and novelist. Obituaries: *L'Express,* January 31-February 6, 1972.

* * *

VARA, Albert C. 1931-

PERSONAL: Born January 1, 1931, in Philadelphia, Pa.; son of Frank and Tersilla (Viano) Vara. *Education:* St. Joseph's College, Philadelphia, B.S., 1958; Villanova University, M.S.L.S., 1963; additional study at University of Pennsylvania, 1958-60, Drexel University, 1961, and Temple University, 1969—. *Religion:* Roman Catholic. *Residence:* Philadelphia, Pa. *Office:* Paley Library, Temple University, Philadelphia, Pa. 19122.

CAREER: Redstone Arsenal Branch Library, Huntsville, Ala., library clerk, 1953-54; University of Pennsylvania Main Library, Philadelphia, clerk-typist in acquisition department, 1959-60; Free Library of Philadelphia, Philadelphia, trainee, 1960-61; St. Joseph's College, Philadelphia, founder and manager of library, Academy of Food Marketing, 1961-68, instructor in food bibliography, 1963-67; Raphael Landivar University, Guatemala City, Guatemala, founder of food and beverage library, Guatemalan Institute of Food Marketing, 1968; Temple University, Paley Library, Philadelphia, senior assistant librarian in business section, 1969—. Chairman of Social Science Division, Special Libraries Council of Philadelphia and Vicinity, 1965-66. *Military service:* U.S. Army, 1952-54. *Member:* Xavier-Damians (president, 1971).

WRITINGS: Food and Beverage Industries: A Bibliography and Guidebook, Gale, 1970. Contributor to library journals. Co-compiler, *Philadelphia Magazine: Subject Index,* 1973; compiler of several information sources guides, 1973.

WORK IN PROGRESS: University and College Business Libraries: A Network System of Information; research on evaluative criteria for food marketing facilities in developing nations; *Basic Library Resources in Business: A Bibliography.*

* * *

VENDROVSKII, David Efimovich 1879-1971
(David Vendrovsky, Zalman Wendroff, Zalman Wendrowsky)

1879—October (?), 1971; Russian short story writer and translator into Yiddish. Obituaries: *New York Times,* October 6, 1971; *Washington Post,* October 7, 1971.

WADDELL, Jack O('Brien) 1933-

PERSONAL: Born March 23, 1933, in Council Bluffs, Iowa; son of George Earl (a laborer) and Olivetta (Salisbury) Waddell; married Carol Norris, March 22, 1959; children: Larry, Michael, Ramona. *Education:* University of Kansas, B.A., 1955; University of Texas, M.A., 1962; University of Arizona, Ph.D., 1966. *Politics:* "Usually democratic." *Religion:* "Nonaffiliated-humanist." *Home:* 3921 Old Romney Rd., Lafayette, Ind. 47905. *Office:* Department of Sociology and Anthropology, Purdue University, West Lafayette, Ind. 47907.

CAREER: Senior parole officer with welfare department, Kansas City, Mo., 1957-59; Travis County Adult Probation Office, Austin, Tex., adult probation officer, 1960-62; Southeast Missouri State College (now University), Cape Girardeau, instructor in anthropology, 1962-63; Purdue University, West Lafayette, Ind., assistant professor, 1966-70, associate professor of anthropology, 1970—. *Military service:* U.S. Navy, Hospital Corps, 1956-57. *Member:* American Anthropological Association (fellow), Society for Applied Anthropology, American Ethnological Society, American Society for Ethnohistory.

WRITINGS: Papago Indians at Work, University of Arizona Press, 1969; (editor with O. Michael Watson) *The American Indian in Urban Society,* Little, Brown, 1971; *Cross-Cultural Approaches to the Study of Alcohol,* Mouton, 1976; (editor with Michael Everett) *Native American Drinking in the Southwest,* University of Arizona Press, in press. Contributor of articles and book reviews to journals.

WORK IN PROGRESS: An ethnography of Papago Indian drinking; a book on comparative religion; journal articles.

SIDELIGHTS: Jack Waddell told *CA* that he is "interested in environmental problems . . . [and] in cultural and social alternative ethics besides progress and technological overdevelopment."

* * *

WADE, L(arry) L(ee) 1935-

PERSONAL: Born June 22, 1935, in Enterprise, Ore.; son of Russel W. and Marie (Murphy) Wade; married Joyce Ahrens, August, 1963; children: Gregory Robert. *Education:* University of Oregon, B.S., 1960, M.A., 1962, Ph.D., 1965. *Home:* 409 Cabrillo Ave., Davis, Calif. 95616. *Office:* Department of Political Science, University of California, Davis, Calif. 95616.

CAREER: U.S. Bureau of the Budget, Washington, D.C., budget examiner, 1963-64; University of North Carolina at Charlotte, assistant professor of political science, 1964-65; San Fernando Valley State College (now California State University, Northridge), Los Angeles, Calif., assistant professor of political science, 1965-66; Purdue University, Lafayette, Ind., assistant professor of political science, 1966-68; University of California, Davis, associate professor of political science, 1968—. *Military service:* U.S. Army, Medical Corps, 1954-56. *Member:* American Political Science Association. *Awards, honors:* National Science Foundation science faculty fellow, 1971-72.

WRITINGS: (With D. A. Strickland and R. E. Johnston) *A Primer of Political Analysis,* Markham, 1968; (with R. L. Curry) *A Theory of Political Exchange,* Prentice-Hall, 1968; (with Curry) *A Logic of Public Policy,* Wadsworth, 1970; *The Elements of Public Policy,* C. E. Merrill, 1972; (with R. L. Meek) *Politics in America,* Duxbury, 1976; (with B. S. Kim) *The Political Economy of Success,* Kyung Hee University Press (Seoul), 1977.

WADLINGTON, Walter 1931-

PERSONAL: Born January 17, 1931, in Biloxi, Miss.; son of Walter J., Jr. (an attorney) and Bernice (Taylor) Wadlington; married Ruth Hardie, August, 1955; children: Claire, Charlotte, Susan, Derek. *Education:* Duke University, A.B., 1951; Tulane University, LL.B., 1954. *Home:* 1620 Keith Valley Rd., Charlottesville, Va. 22901. *Office:* School of Law, University of Virginia, Charlottesville, Va. 22901.

CAREER: Newspaper reporter and photographer, Biloxi, Miss., 1951; private law practice, New Orleans, La., 1954-55, 1958-59; Tulane University, New Orleans, assistant professor of law, 1960-62; University of Virginia, Charlottesville, associate professor, 1962-64, professor of law, 1964-70, James Madison Professor of Law, 1970—. Visiting professor of law at Louisiana State University, summer, 1966, University of North Carolina at Chapel Hill, summer, 1967, Brown University, summer, 1969, and Southern Methodist University, summer, 1970. *Military service:* U.S. Army, Judge Advocate Corps, 1955-58; became captain. *Member:* Louisiana Bar Association, Virginia Bar Association. *Awards, honors:* Fulbright scholar, University of Edinburgh, 1959-60; sesquicentennial scholar, University of Virginia, 1969.

WRITINGS: (With Monrad Paulsen and Julius Goebel) *Domestic Relations Cases and Materials,* Foundation Press, 1970, 2nd edition, 1974; (with Paulsen) *Statutory Materials on Family Law,* Foundation Press, 1971, 2nd edition, 1974. Contributor to legal, medical, and other journals.

WORK IN PROGRESS: Research on marriage and divorce law reform and on legal impact of biomedical developments.

* * *

WALDMAN, Diane 1936-

PERSONAL: Born February 24, 1936, in New York, N.Y.; daughter of Robert and Beatrice Rose (Albert) Deleson; married Paul Waldman (an artist), 1957. *Education:* Hunter College (now Hunter College of the City University of New York), B.F.A., 1956; New York University, M.A., 1965; Institute of Fine Arts, Certificate in Museum Training, 1965. *Office:* Guggenheim Museum, 1071 Fifth Ave., New York, N.Y. 10028.

CAREER: Guggenheim Museum, New York, N.Y., staff member, 1965-71, curator of exhibitions, 1971—.

WRITINGS: Roy Lichtenstein: Drawings and Prints, Chelsea House, 1970; *Ellsworth Kelly: Drawings, Collages, and Prints,* New York Graphic Society, 1971; *Roy Lichtenstein,* Abrams, 1971; *Joseph Cornell,* Braziller, 1977.

* * *

WALKER, Barbara K(erlin) 1921-
(Beth Kilreon)

PERSONAL: Born October 13, 1921, in Ann Arbor, Mich.; daughter of Oscar Fahnestock (a school administrator) and Mildred M. (Baldwin) Kerlin; married Warren Stanley Walker (Horn Professor of English at Texas Tech University), December 9, 1943; children: Brian, Theresa Sue. *Education:* New York College for Teachers (now State University of New York at Albany), B.A., 1943, M.A., 1947; Cornell University, graduate courses in folklore. *Religion:* Disciples of Christ. *Home and office:* 3703 66th St., Lubbock, Tex. 79413.

CAREER: Junior high school teacher in Cornwall, N.Y., 1943-45, and Ithaca, N.Y., 1948-49; Albany Academy for

Girls, Albany, N.Y., teacher, 1947-48; Cornell University Press, Ithaca, associate editor and first reader, 1949-51; Blackburn College, Carlinville, Ill., professor of English and education, 1952-59; Parsons College, Fairfield, Iowa, instructor in English and education, 1959-61; teacher of English as a foreign language at elementary school in Ankara, Turkey, 1961-62; Parsons College, professor in English and education and college editor, 1962-64. Half-time lecturer in undergraduate and graduate children's literature courses, Texas Tech University, spring, 1973. Member of board of directors, Project Impact, government-sponsored program at Library-Learning Center, Lubbock. Initiated and led first Internationalism in Children's Literature European graduate seminar program, summer, 1973.

MEMBER: African Literature Association, Children's Literature Association, Friends of the International Youth Library (Munich), National Book League (London), National Retired Teachers Association, Turkish-American Association, American Folklore Society, Authors Guild, American Friends of Turkey, American Library Association, Texas Institute of Letters, Texas Folklore Society, Texas Cultural Alliance (member of advisory board), Texas Library Association, Phi Kappa Phi, Delta Zeta, Alpha Beta Alpha, Lubbock City Panhellenic. *Awards, honors:* Cited by Turkish Ministry of Education for acquainting American children with Turkish culture, 1967; named Texas' most distinguished Delta Zeta alumna, 1970; awarded bronze medal, Institute of Pedagogy, University of Padua, 1973, for international service to children and literature; commissioned by UNICEF to compile an international children's joke book, 1973; subject of two "Voice of America" broadcasts, 1977, for work with Turkish materials for non-Turkish children; Caldecott award nominations for *How the Hare Told the Truth about His Horse* and *New Patches for Old.*

WRITINGS—Adult: (Editor with husband, Warren S. Walker) *Nigerian Folk Tales,* Rutgers University Press, 1961; (editor with Warren S. Walker) *The Erie Canal: Gateway to Empire,* Heath, 1963.

Juvenile: *Just Say Hic!* Follett, 1965; *Hilili and Dilili,* Follett, 1965; (with Mine Sumer) *Stargazer to the Sultan,* Parents' Magazine Press, 1967; *Watermelons, Walnuts, and the Wisdom of Allah, and Other Tales of the Hoca,* Parents' Magazine Press, 1967; *Once There Was and Twice There Wasn't,* Follett, 1968; *The Dancing Palm Tree and Other Nigerian Folktales,* Parents' Magazine Press, 1968; *I Packed My Trunk,* Follett, 1969; (with Naki Tezel) *The Mouse and the Elephant,* Parents' Magazine Press, 1969; *Pigs and Pirates: A Greek Tale* (Junior Literary Guild selection), David White, 1969.

The Round Sultan and the Straight Answer, Parents' Magazine Press, 1970; *Korolu, the Singing Bandit,* Crowell, 1970; *The Courage of Kazan,* Crowell, 1971; *The Ifrit and the Magic Gifts,* Follett, 1972; *How the Hare Told the Truth about His Horse,* Parents' Magazine Press, 1972; *New Patches for Old,* Parents' Magazine Press, 1974; *Teeny-Tiny and the Witch-Woman,* Pantheon, 1975; *Laughing Together: Giggles and Grins from around the Globe,* Four Winds Press, 1977; (with Mabel Ross) *"On Another Day . . .": Tales Told among the Nkundo of Zaire,* Archon Books, 1978; *Pazes and Muzzles and More,* Four Winds Press, 1978; *Three Foxy Tales,* Parents' Magazine Press, 1978.

Contributor of more than 300 stories, poems, plays, and articles to folklore, education, and children's periodicals, including *Child Life, Journal of American Folklore, Horn*

Book, Children's Digest, Cricket, Elementary English, Grade Teacher, and Instructor; the pseudonym, Beth Kilreon, has been used chiefly in Humpty Dumpty's Magazine, for which she supplied the "At Home with the Humpty Dumpty Family" page each month, 1958-70. Member of editorial board, New York Folklore Quarterly, 1948-52; yearbook editor, Lubbock City Panhellenic, 1969-73.

WORK IN PROGRESS: To Set Them Free: The Story of Mustapha Kemal Ataturk.

SIDELIGHTS: Barbara Walker has been working with her husband since 1961 on the Uysal-Walker Archive of Turkish Oral Narrative to be housed in the Texas Tech University Library and is curator of the collection. The collection includes more than two thousand Turkish folktales in Turkish (of which one-third have been translated into English), recorded from field collecting in Turkey, 1961-77. They began collecting the folktales, children's games, rhymes, and riddles in rural Turkey in 1961-62 when Warren Walker was Fulbright lecturer in American literature at University of Ankara and plan to continue collecting "as long as we live." Walker spent the summer of 1966 in Turkey gathering materials on Ataturk, worked there again in 1974, and plans additional field-collecting visits as opportunity allows.

Barbara Walker told CA that international understanding is her "primary interest, pursued through [my] writing, through travel in behalf of the International Youth Library (1974, 1976), and through the continuation of the Internationalism in Children's Literature European study program. Work on the UNICEF-commissioned children's joke book (1973-1976) was exciting and productive, with a harvest of 'funnies' from 98 countries in 56 languages. The work with Mabel Ross on Nkundo folktales (1971-1977) has been full of surprises and satisfactions." Because her husband shares her enthusiasm for internationalism, their house has been "home away from home" for visitors from all parts of the world, including Botswana, China, Czechoslovakia, England, India, Japan, Malaysia, Nigeria, Switzerland, West Germany, Yugoslavia, and Zaire. "And coming at all hours of the day are children, who regard [me] as both live-in storyteller and branch librarian."

Pigs and Pirates and New Patches for Old have been filmed by Weston Woods Studios, Just Say Hic! by Bailey-Film Associates, and The Mouse and the Elephant, by Parents' Magazine Enterprises. I Packed My Trunk was used on "Sesame Street." Teeny-Tiny and the Witch-Woman is being produced as a filmstrip by Random House and as a motion picture by Weston Woods Studios.

Manuscript and production materials of five of Barbara Walker's books have been placed on permanent loan to the University of Minnesota Library. All of her juveniles and all working materials, including artwork for How the Hare Told the Truth about His Horse and New Patches for Old, are included in the International Youth Library in Munich.

AVOCATIONAL INTERESTS: Fishing and boating off an island in Georgian Bay, Ontario, where the Walkers homesteaded in 1954 and built their own cottage; storytelling and speaking to children and adults.

BIOGRAPHICAL/CRITICAL SOURCES: Lamp (Delta Zeta publication), summer, 1970, summer, 1973.

* * *

WALKER, Kenneth Francis 1924-
(W. Gifford-Jones)

PERSONAL: Born February 28, 1924, in Croydon, England; son of Walter Francis and Annie (Harrison) Walker; married Susan Diana Turner, February 8, 1956; children: Robert, John, Brett, Diana. Education: University of Toronto, B.A., 1946; Harvard University, M.D., 1950, postgraduate training in gynecology and obstetrics, 1950-56. Home: 9237 Niagara Parkway, R.R.3, Niagara Falls, Ontario, Canada. Agent: Collins-Knowlton-Wing, Inc., 575 Madison, New York, N.Y. 10022. Office: Medical Arts Building, 6150 Valley Way, Niagara Falls, Ontario, Canada.

CAREER: Douglas Memorial Hospital, Fort Erie, Ontario, consulting gynecologist, 1956—; Greater Niagara General Hospital, Niagara Falls, Ontario, gynecologist, 1956—; Niagara Hospital, Niagara-on-the-Lake, Ontario, consulting gynecologist, 1972—. Member of board of directors, Lincoln Trust and Savings Co. Member: Ontario Medical Association, Buffalo Gynecological Society, Niagara Falls Club.

WRITINGS—All under pseudonym W. Gifford-Jones: Hysterectomy: A Book for the Patient, University of Toronto Press, 1961; On Being a Woman: The Modern Woman's Guide to Gynecology, McClelland & Stewart, 1969, Macmillan, 1971; The Doctor Game, McClelland & Stewart, 1975; What Every Woman Should Know about Hysterectomy, Fitzhenry & Whiteside, 1977. Author of weekly syndicated column, "The Doctor Game."

* * *

WALLACE, Alexander Fielding 1918-
(A. W. Fielding, Xan Fielding)

PERSONAL: Born November 26, 1918, in Ootacamund, India; son of Alexander Lumsden (a Royal Army officer) and Mary (Fielding) Wallace; married Daphne Vivian (an author), July 7, 1953. Education: Attended universities in Germany, 1936-37 and New College, Oxford, 1947-48.

CAREER: Writer and translator; observer on Allied Mission for observing Greek Plebiscite, 1946; observer on United Nations Special Committee on Balkans, 1948. Military service: British Army, 1940-46; served in Intelligence Corps; became lieutenant-colonel. Member: Travellers Club (London), Society of Authors (London), Special Forces Club (London).

WRITINGS—All under name Xan Fielding: Five Poems, privately printed, 1946; The Stronghold: An Account of the Four Seasons in the White Mountains of Crete, Secker & Warburg, 1953; Hide and Seek: The Story of a Wartime Agent, Secker & Warburg, 1954; (editor and author of notes) George Psychoundakis, Cretan Runner: His Story of the German Occupation, Transatlantic, 1955; Corsair Country: The Diary of a Journey along the Barbary Coast, Dufour, 1958; (contributor) Sacheverell Sitwell, editor, Great Houses of Europe, Putnam, 1961; (contributor) Great Palaces of Europe, introduction by Sacheverell Sitwell, Putnam, 1964; The Money Spinner: Monte Carlo Casino, Little, Brown, 1977.

Translator from the French, under name Xan Fielding: Pierre Boulle, The Bridge over the River Kwai, Vanguard, 1954, new edition, Science Research Associates, 1968 (published in England as The Bridge on the River Kwai, Secker & Warburg, 1954); Pierre Boulle, Not the Glory, Vanguard, 1955 (published in England as William Conrad, Secker & Warburg, 1955, reissued as Spy Converted, Collins, 1960); Pierre Boulle, Face of a Hero, Vanguard, 1956 (published in England as Saving Face, Secker & Warburg, 1956); Pierre Boulle, Test, Vanguard, 1957 (published in England as White Man's Test, Secker & Warburg, 1957); Jean Hougron, Reap the Whirlwind, Hutchinson, 1958; Pierre Boulle,

S.O.P.H.I.A., Vanguard, 1959 (published in England as *Sacrilege in Malaya*, Secker & Warburg, 1959).

Pierre Boulle, *A Noble Profession*, Vanguard, 1960 (published in England as *For a Noble Cause*, Secker & Warburg, 1961); Michel Mohrt, *Mariners' Prison*, Weidenfeld & Nicolson, 1961; Viking, 1963; Jean Larteguy, *The Centurions*, Avon, 1961 (published in England as *Lost Command*, Arrow Books, 1966); Pierre Boulle, *The Executioner*, Vanguard, 1962 (published in England as *The Chinese Executioner*, Secker & Warburg, 1962); Pierre Boulle, *Planet of the Apes*, Vanguard, 1963 (published in England as *Monkey Planet*, Secker & Warburg, 1964); Jean Larteguy, *The Praetorians*, Dutton, 1963; Gabriel Chevallier, *Clochemerle les Bains*, Secker & Warburg, 1964; Jean Larteguy, *Yellow Fever*, Dutton, 1965; Pierre Boulle, *The Garden on the Moon*, Vanguard, 1965; (with Elisabeth Abbott) Pierre Boulle, *Time Out of Mind, and Other Stories*, Vanguard, 1966; Jean Larteguy, *The Hounds of Hell*, Dutton, 1966; Pierre Boulle, *My Own River Kwai*, Vanguard, 1967; Pierre Boulle, *The Source of the River Kwai*, Secker & Warburg, 1967; Jean Larteguy, *The Bronze Drums*, Knopf, 1967; Pierre Boulle, *The Photographer*, Vanguard, 1968 (published in England as *An Impartial Eye*, Secker & Warburg, 1968); Jean Larteguy, *Sauveterre*, W. H. Allen, 1968.

Pierre Schoendoerffer, *Farewell to the King*, Stein & Day, 1970; Bernard Clavel, *Victory at Le Mans*, Delacorte, 1971; Jean Larteguy, *No Peace on Earth*, W. H. Allen, 1971; Jean Larteguy, *The Freedom Fighters*, W. H. Allen, 1972; Gerard Nery, *Julie Crevecoeur*, Collins, 1972; Fernand Fournier-Aubry, *Don Fernando: The Story of Fernand Fournier-Aubry*, Franklin Talmy, 1974; Jean Larteguy, *Presumed Dead*, W. H. Allen, 1974.

Translator from the French, under name A. W. Fielding: Andre Malraux, *The Walnut Trees of Altenburg*, Lehmann, 1952; Michel Mourre, *In Spite of Blasphemy*, Lehmann, 1953.

WORK IN PROGRESS: Additional translations.

AVOCATIONAL INTERESTS: Travelling in the Balkans and Near East, gardening, reading.

BIOGRAPHICAL/CRITICAL SOURCES: W. Stanley Moss, *Ill Met by Moonlight*, Harrap, 1950; A. M. Rendel, *Appointment in Crete*, Wingate, 1953; George Psychoundakis, *Cretan Runner*, Murray, 1955; Bickham Sweet-Escott, *Baker Street Irregular*, Methuen, 1965; E. H. Cookridge, *They Came from the Sky*, Heinemann, 1965; Cookridge, *Inside S.O.E.*, Barker, 1966; M.R.D. Foot, *SOE in France*, H.M.S.O., 1966; Lawrence Durrell and Henry Miller, *A Private Correspondence*, Faber, 1966.†

* * *

WALLERSTEIN, Robert S(olomon) 1921-

PERSONAL: Born January 28, 1921, in Berlin, Germany; came to United States in 1923, naturalized in 1928; son of Lazar (a physician) and Sara (Guensberg) Wallerstein; married Judith Saretsky (a university instructor), January 26, 1947; children: Michael, Nina, Amy. *Education:* Columbia University, B.A., 1941, M.D., 1944. *Home:* 290 Beach Rd., Belvedere, Calif. 94920. *Office:* Langley-Porter Neuropsychiatric Institute, University of California, 401 Parnassus, San Francisco, Calif. 94143.

CAREER: Certified by American Board of Psychiatry and Neurology, 1953, and by Topeka Institute for Psychoanalysis, 1958; Mount Sinai Hospital, New York, N.Y., intern, 1944-45, assistant resident, 1945-46, resident, 1948-49; Winter VA Hospital, Topeka, Kan., resident, 1949-51, chief of psychosomatic section and staff psychiatrist, 1951-53; Menninger Foundation, Topeka, senior psychiatrist and associate director of department of research, 1954-65, director of department of research, 1965-66; Topeka Institute for Psychoanalysis, Topeka, training and supervising analyst, 1965-66; Mount Zion Hospital, San Francisco, Calif., chief of psychiatry, 1966—; San Francisco Psychoanalytic Institute, San Francisco, training and supervising analyst, 1966—; University of California, San Francisco, clinical professor, 1967-75, professor of psychiatry, chairman of department, and director of Langley-Porter Neuropsychiatric Institute, 1975—. Lecturer at Menninger School of Psychiatry, 1951-66, and Topeka Institute of Psychoanalysis, 1959-66; fellow, Center for Advanced Study in the Behavioral Sciences, 1964-65. Research Scientist Career Development Committee, National Institute of Mental Health, member, 1966-70, chairman, 1968-70. Consultant to psychosomatic section, Winter VA Hospital, 1954-66, and to psychiatric staff, Topeka State Hospital, 1957-66. *Military service:* U.S. Army, medical officer, 1946-48; became captain.

MEMBER: International Psychoanalytic Association, American Psychoanalytic Association (member of executive committee, 1970-72; president, 1971-72), American Psychiatric Association (fellow), American College of Physicians (fellow), American Orthopsychiatric Association (fellow), American Medical Association, American Association for the Advancement of Science, Center for Advanced Psychoanalytic Studies, Group for the Advancement of Psychiatry (chairman of committee on research, 1960-66), California Medical Association, San Francisco Psychoanalytic Society, San Francisco Medical Society. *Awards, honors:* Heinz Hartmann Award, New York Psychoanalytic Institute, 1968; Arthur Marshall Distinguished Alumnus Award, Menninger Foundation, 1972; J. Elliott Royer Award, University of California, San Francisco, 1973.

WRITINGS: (With others) *Hospital Treatment of Alcoholism: A Comparative, Experimental Study*, Basic Books, 1957; (with Rudolf Ekstein) *The Teaching and Learning of Psychotherapy*, Basic Books, 1958; (with others) *Prediction in Psychotherapy Research: A Method for the Transformation of Clinical Judgments in Testable Hypotheses*, International Universities Press, 1968; *Psychotherapy and Psychoanalysis: Theory, Practice, Research*, International Universities Press, 1975.

Contributor: Eli A. Rubinstein and Morris B. Parloff, editors, *Research in Psychotherapy*, American Psychological Association, 1959; Mary R. Haworth, editor, *Child Psychotherapy*, Basic Books, 1964; Louis A. Gottschalk and Arthur H. Auerbach, editors, *Methods of Research in Psychotherapy*, Appleton, 1966; John M. Schlien, editor, *Research in Psychotherapy*, Volume III, American Psychological Association, 1968; Irwin M. Marcus, editor, *Currents in Psychoanalysis*, International Universities Press, 1971; Robert R. Holt, editor, *New Horizon for Psychotherapy*, International Universities Press, 1971; Louise Diamant, editor, *Case Studies in Psychopathology*, C. E. Merrill, 1971; Daniel Offer and Daniel Freedman, editors, *Modern Psychiatry and Clinical Research: Essays in Honor of Roy R. Grinker, Sr.*, Basic Books, 1972; Jack Citrin and Paul M. Sniderman, editors, *Handbook of Research on Personality and Politics*, Aldine, 1972; Albert Cain, editor, *Survivors of Suicide*, C. C Thomas, 1972.

Contributor to many professional journals, including *American Journal of Tropical Medicine*, *Journal* of Mount Sinai Hospital, *American Practitioner*, *American Journal of Med-*

icine, Psychiatry, Psychosomatic Medicine, Journal of the American Psychoanalytic Association, *Psychoanalytic Study of the Child,* and *International Journal of Psychoanalysis.* Member of editorial boards, *Psychological Issues,* 1959—, *Journal of Psychiatric Research,* 1963-64, *Journal* of the American Psychoanalytic Association, 1965-67, 1969-71, *Archives of General Psychiatry,* 1966-75, *Journal of Nervous and Mental Diseases,* 1966-72, and *Psychoanalysis and Contemporary Science,* 1970—; editor for North America, *International Journal of Psycho-Analysis,* 1967—; consulting editor, *Bulletin* of Menninger Clinic, 1970—.

WORK IN PROGRESS: Perspectives on Psychoanalytic Supervision, a monograph.

* * *

WALT, Lewis W(illiam) 1913-

PERSONAL: Born February 16, 1913, in Waubaunsee County, Kan.; son of Albert Miller and Estella May (Shields) Walt; married Nancy Mary Sheehan, June 10, 1944 (divorced); married June B. Jacobsen, August 27, 1971; children: (first marriage) Lewis William, Jr., Lawrence Cecil, Mary Katherine. *Education:* Colorado State University, B.A. (chemistry), 1936; graduate of Marine Corps Command and Staff College, 1950, and National War College, 1960. *Politics:* Republican. *Religion:* Methodist. *Home:* 2242 O'Hara Ct., Orlando, Fla. 32806.

CAREER: U.S. Marine Corps officer, 1936-71, rising to brigadier general, 1961, major general, 1965, lieutenant general, 1966, and, during his tour as assistant commandant of the Marine Corps, 1968-71, to the rank of four-star general; retired, 1971; U.S. Marines Youth Foundation, Colorado Springs, Colo., executive director, 1971. Commissioned second lieutenant in the Marines, 1936; first saw combat as platoon leader in China, 1937-38; served on Guam, 1939-41; fought in the Tulagi, Florida, and Guadalcanal campaigns in the Solomon Islands, 1942 (wounded in action on Guadalcanal), in New Britain, 1943-44, at Peleliu, 1944, and in Korea, 1952-53; after serving as a regimental commander and chief of staff of 1st Marine Division in Korea, he had stateside assignments, 1953-65, including assistant director of personnel at Marine Corps Headquarters, Washington, D.C., 1957-59, Marine Corps representative on joint advanced study group, Joint Chiefs of Staff, 1960-61, assistant division commander, 2nd Marine Division, Camp Lejeune, 1961-62, and director of Marine Corps Landing Force Development Center, Quantico, 1962-65; commanding general of III Marine Amphibious Force in Vietnam, 1965-67, and also commanding general of 3rd Marine Division, 1965-66, and senior adviser, I Corps, Republic of Vietnam, 1966-67; prior to his appointment as assistant commandant of the Marine Corps, he was deputy chief of staff for manpower and director of personnel at Corps Headquarters, Washington, D.C., 1967-68. Head of U.S. Senate investigation of international drug traffic, 1972; senior military member of Presidential Clemency Board, 1974-75. Consultant, U.S. Army, 1972-77, and U.S. Navy, 1977.

AWARDS, HONORS—Military: Silver Star Medal, Purple Heart, and Navy Cross and Gold Star in lieu of second Navy Cross, in World War II; Legion of Merit and Bronze Star Medal, both with combat "v," in Korean War; Distinguished Service Medal in Vietnam War, and Distinguished Service Medal as assistant commandant of the Marine Corps; foreign decorations include Chinese Order of Cloud and Banner, Korean Presidential Unit Citation, and four other awards from Republic of Korea, and Vietnamese National Order, 3rd class, Vietnamese National Order, 4th class, Gallantry Cross with palm, and three other decorations from South Vietnam. Academic: LL.D. from Barry College, 1967, and Colorado State University, 1970; Golden Plate Award from National Academy of Achievements, 1973.

WRITINGS: Strange War, Strange Strategy: A General's Report on Vietnam, Funk, introduction by Lyndon B. Johnson, 1970; *America Faces Defeat,* Apollo, 1972. Contributor to *Reader's Digest* and to military publications.

SIDELIGHTS: Lewis Walt told *CA:* "I wrote *Strange War, Strange Strategy* in an effort to explain the nature of the Vietnam war after serving two and a half years as a commander of over 100,000 U.S. troops in that war. *America Faces Defeat,* I wrote because I felt a deep responsibility to the American people to warn them of the great build-up of the Soviet offensive war capabilities which are today becoming more and more apparent."

* * *

WAMBAUGH, Joseph (Aloysius, Jr.) 1937-

PERSONAL: Born January 22, 1937, in East Pittsburgh, Pa.; son of Joseph A. (a police officer) and Anne (Malloy) Wambaugh; married Dee Allsup, November 26, 1955; children: Mark, David. *Education:* Chaffey College, A.A., 1958; California State College (now University), Los Angeles, B.A., 1960, M.A., 1968. *Religion:* Roman Catholic. *Home address:* P.O. Box 8657, San Marino, Calif. 91108.

CAREER: Los Angeles (Calif.) Police Department, 1960-74, became detective sergeant; writer. Creator and consultant, "Police Story" series for National Broadcasting Co. and "The Blue Knight" series for Columbia Broadcasting System. *Military service:* U.S. Marine Corps, 1954-57.

WRITINGS—All novels: *The New Centurions,* Atlantic-Little, Brown, 1971; *The Blue Knight,* Atlantic-Little Brown, 1972; *The Onion Field,* Delacorte, 1973; *The Choirboys,* Delacorte, 1975; *The Black Marble,* Delacorte, 1978.

SIDELIGHTS: Thomas Fleming feels that *The New Centurions,* Wambaugh's first book, "performs one of those essential and enduring functions the novel—and the novel alone—can perform. It takes us into the minds and hearts, into the nerves and (sometimes literally) into the guts of other human beings—and, in the hands of a good writer, it achieves a mixture of empathy and objectivity that creates genuine understanding. . . . [Wambaugh] stands outside it all, seemingly as indifferent as the ideal Joycean novelist, calmly letting his characters tell their stories. One can see, to some extent, where his sympathies lie. But he achieves more than enough objectivity to give the reader a picture of everyday police work more revealing than a thousand hours of 'Dragnet' or 'The Mod Squad.'" After describing some of the violent scenes depicted in *The New Centurions,* Jose M. Ferrer III states: "Such incidents have been written about before as well as dramatized for TV audiences. In such cases they are usually presented for thrills, or to sharpen the pace of a story. In *Centurions,* they are encountered as a policeman would encounter them, matter-of-factly, almost at random, and all the more real for it." Ferrer makes the point that Wambaugh "has been admonished by L.A. Police Chief Edward M. Davis, officially, because he failed to get permission to publish *The New Centurions.* Presumably, though, the department also was not pleased by Wambaugh's literary lapse of organizational loyalty. Of course, it is those very displays of unblurred vision that keep Wambaugh's book unpreachy, believable, and out of trouble with the reader."

John J. Fried, however, finds that the book "is not without flaws, the most conspicuous of which is its style.... [Wambaugh's] writing is frequently awkward, a kind of low-grade Irving Wallace, especially when he tries to teach the reader a lesson or two in Constitutional Law. He is at his best when writing about the everyday life of the cop on the beat, and this is the real strength of the novel."

Eric Pace found *The Blue Knight* to be "fascinating reading for anyone whose curiosity was whetted by what the Knapp Commission showed of the dark side of police life. Once again, the author gives a cop's-eye-view of police brutality and free-loading as well as police courage and compassion." But he feels that Bumper Morgan, police officer and main character in the novel, "has attributes that seem unlikely in a man his age. He digs hard rock. He dates a black chick. He gets involved with a 19-year-old belly dancer. Perhaps things are different on the Coast. Or it could be argued that these are particularizing details meant to keep Bumper from being a stock figure. This reader was left with the impression that Bumper's character was incomplete in the young author's mind—and has been fleshed out with bits and pieces of Wambaugh's own experiences and tastes." Pace concludes: "*The Blue Knight* abounds in vivid vignettes of police life and the Los Angeles streets. It effectively conveys the loneliness of an aging man who puts too much of himself into his work. Its warty portrayal of the police will make it controversial in some quarters." A reviewer for *Publishers Weekly* calls the book a "hard-hitting, tough talking, utterly realistic novel about an average cop on the beat.... If this particular 'blue knight' is no cardboard hero, he is very real, occasionally pitiable, and Wambaugh understands him inside out and makes us do so, too."

In a review of *The Onion Field,* Frank Paul Le Veness says that the book "presents an extremely skillful portrayal of one of California's most notorious crimes and its 'longest, most intricate court case.' ... [Wambaugh] has not merely presented a disturbing crime story and dramatic court case, but has undertaken a psychological study of the major characters: two convicted killers, their policeman victim, and the latter's partner.... [The book] offers a penetrating character study, delving into the backgrounds that helped bring all four men to that onion field. It is a study of poverty, broken homes and criminality, as well as of dedication, strength and sincerity. The style is suspenseful and should hold the reader in its grip from start to finish." A *Publishers Weekly* writer calls *The Onion Field* "powerful reading—precisely what one anticipates from this smashing storyteller.... Wambaugh's spare, vivid documentary style draws the marrow out of police, court and psychiatric records while shaping a strong case for the reform of American criminal justice." James Conaway writes: "Wambaugh is obviously indebted to Truman Capote—who, in 1965, demonstrated his skill in applying a novelist's techniques to a true-crime narrative. Both *In Cold Blood* and *The Onion Field* involved a prodigious amount of research, and are equally compelling. Wambaugh takes greater liberties with his characters and he lacks Capote's neatness. But in terms of scope, revealed depth of character, and dramatic coherence, this is the more ambitious book.... Wambaugh convincingly demonstrates that he belongs to the tradition of Dreiser and Farrell—constructing from a glut of well-observed detail, unspectacular and often squalid lives lived among the concrete freeways, the bright, tawdry strips, the transience, brutality and beleaguered decency of a society set on the edge of America."

John Leonard believes that "very little in Wambaugh's first

two novels prepares one for the scabrous humor and ferocity of *The Choirboys. The New Centurions* and *The Blue Knight* were bittersweet slices of naturalism, unlikely Hamlets on wry crisp, as if to elaborate the extenuating circumstance that cops, too, have feelings and may often be the victims of their particularity. In *The Choirboys* Wambaugh comes on like a Celine derailed along the laugh-track. His characters are a brutalized 'M.A.S.H.' unit.... Wambaugh proposes an anarchy that lusts for accidents to happen and assigns blame randomly; a uniformed proletariat to mop up our bloody mess—a kind of Drano for dissolving sludge in society's clogged plumbing—which, at the same time, is unable to save itself from being wasted; a necessary alienation, an 'ordinary' brutishness, a lethal banality, an imponderable ... what? We aren't dignified enough to be evil.... Wambaugh is as specific, as visceral, as the strangled child who happens to be one's own son. His is a funny book that makes one gag. He is on his way to rediscovering original sin." According to a reviewer for *Atlantic Monthly* "Mr. Wambaugh appears to have thrown into this novel everything that loyalty and discretion deleted from his work while he remained a member of the Los Angeles Police Department. The action is constant and the dialogue is tough. The writing has a careless barbarity that may be deliberate, for Mr. Wambaugh is explaining that police work is a one-way ticket to hell."

Reviewing *The Black Marble,* Jerome Charyn says: "Joseph Wambaugh, a former policeman who writes about cops on the planet of Los Angeles has created a detective, Andrei Mikhailovich Valnikov, who is almost as touching, variable, and bravely idiotic as Nabokov's Professor Pnin.... As the misadventures of a sad, unlikely cop, *The Black Marble* is a very funny book. The problem with the novel is that it strays from Valnikov much too often. Joseph Wambaugh hasn't found a story that can contain his fat, haunted detective. The plot seems silly next to Valnikov's 'sad runny eyes.' ... The characters around Valnikov are a pile of weak grotesques. Most of them ... seem to come out of a simpler and much blunter novel. It's as if all of Wambaugh's *energy* and *love* have gone into the creation of Detective Sergeant Valnikov." John Leonard declares: "Somebody should get a grip on Joseph Wambaugh with one hand, and slap him back into shape with the other. He ought not to be allowed to be cute. In *The Choirboys* he looked as though he had lapped Celine and might even be gaining on the young Dostoyevsky: human beings were the pits, and Los Angeles cops had pitched their tent in a septic tank—'The Big Sewer,' he now calls it—and everybody was either going to drown or 'eat his gun.' After too many battered children and severed heads, the soul itself became a mean street. There was nothing cute about *The Choirboys.* ... *The Black Marble* is, in part, both sentimental and cute.... There are many, many good things about [the book] because Mr. Wambaugh is too talented to be cute full-time. The opening scene, with Valnikov drunk at a Russian Christmas vesper service, having lost his handcuffs, is splendid.... Equally good are the depictions of shabby gentility in Pasadena, big-time dog show lunacy in the Los Angeles Memorial Sports Arena, sniper fire, life in the kennels and in the station house. Nobody handles such material as well as Mr. Wambaugh."

Joseph Wambaugh told an interviewer: "Cops want people to like them, and that's why a lot of them don't like [*The New Centurions*]. They want people to have that stereotyped TV image of a cop—which is awfully wholesome and terribly tiresome. The cops in my book have been called brutal, racist, cheating, fornicating bastards. . . . All they are, in the end, is people. What the hell does anybody expect?''

Two of Wambaugh's novels have been made into films: ''The New Centurions,'' directed by Richard Fleischer, and ''The Choirboys,'' directed by Robert Aldrich. *The Blue Knight* was produced as a ''mini series'' which starred William Holden, and then as a regular series with George Kennedy in the title role; both versions were networked by the National Broadcasting Company.

BIOGRAPHICAL/CRITICAL SOURCES: Best Sellers, January 15, 1971, February 15, 1972, October 15, 1973, February, 1976; *New York Times,* January 22, 1971, September 7, 1973, January 8, 1978; *New York Times Book Review,* January 31, 1971, February 13, 1972, September 2, 1973, December 3, 1973, November 2, 1975, January 11, 1978; *Time,* February 15, 1971, February 28, 1972, September 24, 1973; *National Review,* March 9, 1971, April 2, 1976; *New Republic,* March 13, 1971; *Publishers Weekly,* January 3, 1972, July 23, 1973, September 1, 1975, July 12, 1976; *Book World,* March 5, 1972, September 2, 1973, October 20, 1974, January 24, 1978; *New York,* April 1, 1972; *Times Literary Supplement,* March 16, 1973, November 1, 1974, April 9, 1976; *Atlantic Monthly,* October, 1973, November, 1975; *America,* January 19, 1974; *Contemporary Literary Criticism,* Volume III, Gale, 1975; *Bookviews,* January, 1978.

* * *

WANG, Hui-Ming 1922-
(H.M.W.)

PERSONAL: Born February 25, 1922, in China; son of Shi Kai and Ming Chi Wang; married Anna Look (a sculptor), October 1, 1951; children: Dennis, James, Kathleen. *Education:* University of Missouri, Columbia, B.S., 1949; New York University, M.A., 1953. *Home:* Greenfield Rd., Montague, Mass. 01351. *Office:* Department of Art, University of Massachusetts, Amherst, Mass. 01002.

CAREER: Yale University, New Haven, Conn., faculty member, 1951-61; University of Massachusetts—Amherst, professor of art, 1964—. Artist and woodcutter.

WRITINGS: Epoh Studio Woodcuts (folio), Epoh Studio, 1968; *Birds and Animals* (folio of wood engravings), Gehenna Press, 1969; *The Boat Untied and Other Poems* (Chinese calligraphy, translations of T'ang poems, and woodcuts), Barre, 1971; *The Land on the Tip of a Hair* (poems in wood), Barre, 1972; (illustrator) Robert Bly, *Jumping Out of Bed,* Barre, 1972; (translator from the Chinese and illustrator) Mao Tse-Tung, *Ten Poems and Lyrics,* University of Massachusetts Press, 1975.

WORK IN PROGRESS: Wang Hui-Ming's Paintings, Watercolors and Woodcuts; more T'ang poems, translations, and calligraphy.

* * *

WANG, Leonard J(udah) 1926-

PERSONAL: Born March 9, 1926, in New York, N.Y.; son of Leopold (an attorney) and Gertrude (Lewis) Wang; married Sabine Eisenberg (a teacher), September 11, 1949; children: Sharon Brenda, Anne Beverly, Ruth Deborah. *Education:* City College (now City College of the City University of New York), B.A., 1947; Columbia University, M.A., 1948, Ph.D., 1955. *Home:* 1064 East 27th St., Brooklyn, N.Y. 11210. *Office:* Department of Foreign Languages and Literatures, Newark Campus, Rutgers University, Newark, N.J.

CAREER: Columbia University, New York, N.Y., lecturer in French, 1948-55; Queens College (now Queens College of the City University of New York), Flushing, N.Y., instructor in French, 1955-57; Columbia University, instructor in French, 1957-58; Rutgers University, Newark Campus, Newark, N.J., instructor in French, 1958-59, assistant professor, 1959-63, associate professor, 1963-70, professor of Romance languages, 1970—, chairman of department of foreign languages and literatures, 1969-72. *Military service:* U.S. Marine Corps, 1944. *Member:* Modern Language Association of America, Mediaeval Academy of America, Renaissance Society of America, Societe d'etude du XVIIe Siecle (Paris), Phi Beta Kappa.

WRITINGS: (With wife, Sabine E. Wang) *Le Voyage Imaginaire,* Macmillan, 1970. Contributor to French, American, and German journals.

WORK IN PROGRESS: The ''Classical Doctrine'' of the Troubadours; The Curious Success of Failure: The Fortunes of Corneille's ''Pertharite.''

* * *

WARD, Charles D(uane) 1935-

PERSONAL: Born December 31, 1935, in Stillwater, Okla.; son of Troy J. (a businessman) and Alice (McAlister) Ward; married Karen Monahan, June 25, 1966. *Education:* Pomona College, B.A., 1958; University of North Carolina, M.A., 1962, Ph.D., 1963. *Office:* Department of Psychology, California State University, Fullerton, Calif. 92634.

CAREER: University of Maryland, College Park, assistant professor, 1963-67, associate professor of psychology, 1967-75; currently affiliated with department of psychology, California State University, Fullerton. *Member:* American Psychological Association. *Awards, honors:* Fellowships from National Science Foundation, 1962, and National Institute of Mental Health, 1962-63; grants from Social Science Research Council, 1963, and Office of Naval Research, 1967-71; Research and Publication Award, Far East Division, University of Maryland, 1972.

WRITINGS: Laboratory Manual in Experimental Social Psychology, Holt, 1970. Contributor of more than a dozen articles to psychology journals.

* * *

WARE, Clyde 1932-

PERSONAL: Born December 22, 1932, in Clarksburg, W.Va.; son of Clyde Coster (an attorney) and Mary Dorothy (Scott) Ware; married Kay Doubleday (an actress), June 1, 1959; married second wife, Davey Davison (an actress), April 30, 1963; married third wife, Charley Young (a model), September 22, 1974 (divorced October 10, 1975); children: (first marriage) Jud Scott; (second marriage) Lee Ashby. *Education:* Attended high school in West Virginia. *Home:* 1252 North Laurel Ave., Los Angeles, Calif. 90046. *Agent:* Ben Conway & Associates, 999 North Doheny Dr., Los Angeles, Calif. 90069.

CAREER: Jud-Lee Productions, Inc. (motion picture company), Hollywood, Calif., president, 1970—. Writer and director for motion pictures and television.

WRITINGS: The Innocents (novel), Norton, 1969; *The Eden Tree* (novel), Touchstone, 1971. Writer of twenty-five scripts for ''Gunsmoke,'' and various episodes for ''Rawhide,'' ''The Man from U.N.C.L.E.,'' ''Hitchcock Hour,'' ''Bracken's World,'' ''Daniel Boone,'' ''Doctor Kildare,'' and other television programs; writer of television movies,

"Pretty Boy Floyd," produced by Universal and ABC-TV, "Hatfields and McCoys," produced by ABC-TV, "All the Kind Strangers," and "The Silent Gun"; writer, producer, and director of feature films, "No Drums, No Bugles," produced by Cinerama, and "When the Line Goes Through," produced by Wargay (Canada).

WORK IN PROGRESS: A novel, *Jill;* a television pilot, "Cadet," for Metro-Goldwyn-Mayer and NBC-TV; "Clyde," a feature film for United Artists; "Lydia," a feature film for Colony Four Productions; "The Candy Killing," a two-hour NBC-TV special, with host F. Lee Bailey; "Lewis and Clark," a two-hour television special for Universal; "Men to Match the Mountains," a mini-series.

AVOCATIONAL INTERESTS: Travel, playing basketball.

BIOGRAPHICAL/CRITICAL SOURCES: Best Sellers, October 15, 1969; *New York Times,* February 24, 1972.

* * *

WARK, David M(ayer) 1934-

PERSONAL: Born August 8, 1934, in Los Angeles, Calif.; son of Jack L. and Julia (Mayer) Wark; married Marianne Heimann, September 8, 1957 (died, 1972); married Mary Ann Barrows, February 20, 1977; children: (first marriage) Kathleen, Jeffrey. *Education:* Pomona College, B.A., 1956; University of Minnesota, Ph.D., 1961. *Home:* 1588 Northrop, St. Paul, Minn. 55108. *Office:* Department of Psychology, 190 Coffey Hall, University of Minnesota, St. Paul, Minn. 55101.

CAREER: University of Minnesota, St. Paul, assistant professor, 1963-66, associate professor, 1966-71, professor of psychology, 1971—. Visiting scholar, University of London, 1976. Consultant, Bureau of Criminal Apprehension, State of Minnesota. *Military service:* U.S. Army, Medical Service Corps, 1961-63; became captain. *Member:* American Association for the Advancement of Science, American Psychological Association, International Reading Association, National Reading Association, National Reading Conference, College Reading Association, National Society for Programmed Instruction (founding office; member of board of directors, 1961-64), North Central Reading Association (treasurer), Minnesota Reading Association.

WRITINGS: (Contributor) Edward Fry, editor, *Pros and Cons of Rewards,* Rutgers University Press, 1969; (contributor) Fry, editor, *Speed Reading?,* Rutgers University Press, 1970; (with Monica Mogen) *Read, Underline, Review,* McGraw, 1970; (with Alton Raygor) *Systems for Study,* McGraw, 1970; (contributor) Raygor and James Wallace, editors, *Guide to McGraw-Hill Basic Skills System,* McGraw, 1970. Writer of television tapes on adult study skills, Telstar Productions (St. Paul), 1976. Editor of or contributor to yearbooks of National Reading Conference, 1962—, and of North Central Reading Association, 1965—. Contributor of about fifty articles to education journals.

WORK IN PROGRESS: A revision of *Systems for Study* incorporating newest research findings; research in the effect of anxiety on comprehension of college-level texts.

* * *

WATERMAN, Leroy 1875-1972

July 4, 1875—May 9, 1972; American biblical scholar and educator. Obituaries: *Washington Post,* May 10, 1972. (See index for *CA* sketch)

WATSON, O(scar) Michael 1936-
(Billie Shears)

PERSONAL: Born June 7, 1936, in Knoxville, Tenn.; son of Oscar Mauldin (a physician) and Helen (Lay) Watson; married Mary Jo Moriconi (a weaver), August 11, 1962; children: Katherine Lynn, Julia Ann. *Education:* University of Colorado, B.A., 1964, M.A., 1966, Ph.D., 1968. *Politics:* "Longhaired hippy freak radical." *Religion:* "Shamanism." *Office:* Department of Sociology and Anthropology, Purdue University, Lafayette, Ind. 47907.

CAREER: Purdue University, Lafayette, Ind., assistant professor, 1967-70, associate professor of anthropology, 1971—. Visiting assistant professor of anthropology, University of California, Los Angeles, 1970-71. Consultant to National Institute of Mental Health. Part-time tap dance instructor, Art Linkletter Personality Center. *Military service:* U.S. Marine Corps, 1957-60. *Member:* American Anthropological Association, Sigma Xi.

WRITINGS: Proxemic Behavior: A Cross-Cultural Study, Mouton, 1970; (editor with Jack O. Waddell) *The American Indian in Urban Society,* Little, Brown, 1971; *Symbolic and Expressive Uses of Space: An Introduction to Proxemic Behavior,* Addison-Wesley, 1972; (with Waddell) *American Indian Urbanization,* Princeton University Press, 1973; *Cultural Anthropology in an Evolutionary Perspective: Manual for Anthropology,* Collegiate Publishing, 1974. Miscellaneous works, as yet unpublished, written under name Billie Shears.

AVOCATIONAL INTERESTS: Woodworking, photography.†

* * *

WATTERSON, Joseph 1900-1972

August 7, 1900—May 30, 1972; American architect and author. Obituaries: *Washington Post,* June 3, 1972. (See index for *CA* sketch)

* * *

WEINSTOCK, Herbert 1905-1971

November 16, 1905—October 21, 1971; American editor, translator and biographer of composers. Obituaries: *New York Times,* October 23, 1971; *Saturday Review,* November 27, 1971. (See index for *CA* sketch)

* * *

WEINWURM, George F(elix) 1935-

PERSONAL: Born May 13, 1935, in Vienna, Austria; son of Ernest Herman and Carla (Winternitz) Weinwurm; married Diane Nystrom, June 10, 1961; children: Danny, Krista. *Education:* New York University, B.M.E., 1955; University of Southern California, M.B.A., 1966. *Office:* 16642 Morrison St., Encino, Calif. 91436.

CAREER: Lockheed Aircraft Corp., Burbank, Calif., design engineer, 1955-56; System Development Corp., Santa Monica, Calif., unit head, 1959-60, assistant to branch head, 1961-66, technical advisor to management and member of corporate planning staff, 1966-70; Security Pacific National Bank, Los Angeles, Calif., vice-president of Corporate Planning Division, beginning 1970; currently president, G. F. Weinwurm, Inc. (management advisers), Encino, Calif. Presented papers at and chaired sessions of meetings of professional management organizations. *Military service:* U.S. Air Force, 1956-59; became captain. *Member:* Association for Computing Machinery, American Association for the Advancement of Science, Operations Research Society of America, Society for Management Information Systems, Institute of Management Sciences, Philosophy of Science Association.

WRITINGS: (Contributor) A. B. Frielink, editor, *Economics of Automatic Data Processing,* North-Holland Publishing, 1965; (contributor) Martin Kenneth Starr, editor, *Executive Readings in Management Science,* Macmillan, 1965; Peter Paul Schoderbeck, editor, *Readings in Management Systems,* Wiley, 1967; (editor and contributor) *On the Management of Computer Programming,* Auerbach Publishers, 1970; (with Ernest H. Weinwurm) *Long-Term Profit Planning,* American Management Association, 1971. Contributor to *California Management Review,* and other publications.

WORK IN PROGRESS: Why Planning Fails.

* * *

WEISBERG, Barry

PERSONAL: Son of Laurence and Sarah Weisberg; married Gail Rubin; children: one. *Education:* University of California, Berkeley, B.A., 1966. *Home:* 1018 Austin Blvd., Oak Park, Ill. 60302.

CAREER: San Jose State College (now University), San Jose, Calif., part-time instructor in politics of ecology, 1967-68; Bay Area Institute, San Francisco, Calif., co-director, 1969-71. Associate fellow, Institute for Policy Studies, Washington, D.C. Contributor to Pacifica radio stations.

WRITINGS: (Editor) *Ecocide in Indochina: The Ecology of War,* Harper, 1970; *Beyond Repair: The Ecology of Capitalism,* Beacon Press, 1971. Also author of *The Politics of Ecology,* 1970, and *Our Lives at Stake: Shell Strike, 1973,* 1973. Contributor to magazines and newspapers, including *Ramparts, Nation,* and *Guardian.*

WORK IN PROGRESS: Editing *The Re-Unification of Korea; The Power of Petroleum: The Political Economy of Oil in Capitalist Society; The Ecology of Socialism.*†

* * *

WEISMANN, Donald L(eroy) 1914-

PERSONAL: Born October 12, 1914, in Milwaukee, Wis.; son of Fred Othello and Stella (Custer) Weismann; married Elizabeth Wilder (an art historian and writer), September 12, 1949; children: Anne Weismann Verge, Christopher Thomas. *Education:* University of Wisconsin—Milwaukee, B.S., 1935; University of Wisconsin—Madison, Ph.M., 1940; Ohio State University, Ph.D., 1950; graduate study at University of Minnesota, University of St. Louis, and Harvard University. *Home:* 405 Buckeye Trail, Austin, Tex. 78746. *Office:* Department of Comparative Studies, University of Texas, Austin, Tex. 78712.

CAREER: North Texas State Teachers College (now North Texas State University), Denton, associate professor of art, 1940; Illinois State Normal University (now Illinois State University), Normal, assistant professor of art, 1940-42, 1946-48; Wayne University (now Wayne State University), Detroit, Mich., assistant professor of art, 1949-51; University of Kentucky, Lexington, professor of art and chairman of the department, 1951-54; University of Texas at Austin, professor of art, 1954—, chairman of art department, 1954-58, university professor in the arts, 1964—, chairman of department of comparative studies, 1967-72. Member, National Council on the Arts, 1966-72, National Advisory

Council, Danforth Foundation Graduate Fellowship Program, 1969-72, and Committee of the National Endowment for the Arts, 1969-72, Consultant, Ford Foundation Program in Humanities and the Arts (New York City), Southwestern University, Rice University, U.S. Information Service, Harvard University, U.S. National Commission for U.N.E.S.C.O., and National Council on the Arts. Member of board of acquisitions, McNay Art Institute. *Military service:* U.S. Navy, communications and security officer, 1943-45; became lieutenant junior grade.

MEMBER: American Association of University Professors, National Humanities Faculty, American Council of Learned Societies (member of fellowship selection committee, 1973-76), Texas Commission on the Arts and Humanities (member of education advisory panel, 1974-76), Illinois State Art Education Association (president). *Awards, honors:* University of Texas Research Institute grants, 1961-62, 1971; Bromberg Award for excellence in teaching, 1965; *Cactus* Award for excellence in teaching, 1970; recipient of prizes and awards for paintings at Milwaukee Art Institute, Butler Institute of American Art, Dallas Museum of Fine Arts, Houston Museum of Fine Arts, Art Institute of Chicago, Oklahoma Art Center, and at other institutions.

WRITINGS: Some Folks Went West, Steck, 1960; *Jelly Was the Word,* Pemberton, 1965; *Language and Visual Form: The Personal Record of a Dual Creative Process,* University of Texas Press, 1968; *The Visual Arts as Human Experience,* Prentice-Hall. 1970; *Why Draw?,* Chandler & Sharp, 1974; *The Twelve Cadavers of Joseph Mariner,* Pemberton, 1977. Also author of filmscripts, "Terlingua," 1972, "Station X," 1974, and "Azimuth," 1976.

* * *

WEISSMAN, Philip 1911(?)-1972

1911(?)—February 27, 1972; American psychoanalyst and writer on the theatre. Obituaries: *New York Times,* February 28, 1972.

* * *

WHALEY, Donald L. 1934-

PERSONAL: Born August 17, 1934, in Bloomington, Ind.; son of Walter Joseph and Hazel (Pardue) Whaley; married Betty McGregor, June 18, 1960; children: Angella, Shannon, Laura. *Education:* Monterey Peninsula College, A.A., 1954; Indiana University, B.A., 1961; Florida State University, M.S., 1963, Ph.D., 1966. *Office address:* Department of Psychology, North Texas State University, Box 13707, North Texas, Tex. 76203.

CAREER: North Texas State University, North Texas, Tex., assistant professor of psychology, 1969—, director of Center of Behavioral Studies, 1972—. Licensed and certified clinical psychologist by Texas State Board of Examiners of Psychologists. *Member:* American Association for the Advancement of Science, Southwestern Psychological Association, Sigma Xi.

WRITINGS: (With Richard W. Malott and Roger E. Ulrich) *Analysis of Behavior: Principles and Applications,* W. C. Brown, 1967; *Attitudes of Science: A Program for a Student-Centered Seminar,* W. C. Brown, 1967; *A Manual for Developmental Stages in Retardation,* Michigan Department of Mental Health, 1969; (with Malott) *Elementary Principles of Behavior,* Appleton, 1971; (with Malott) *Psychology,* Behaviordelia, 1976. Contributor of articles to professional journals.

WORK IN PROGRESS: For Those Who Would Measure the Mind, Statistics for People Who Don't Like Statistics, The Hope Salesman, all for Behaviordelia.†

* * *

WHEELER, Lora Jeanne 1923-

PERSONAL: Born June 28, 1923, in Rockland, Idaho; daughter of Jesse K. (a machinery distributor) and Mary (Miller) Wheeler. *Education:* University of Utah, B.A., 1944; Columbia University, B.S. in L.S., 1945. *Politics:* Republican. *Religion:* Church of Jesus Christ of Latter-day Saints. *Home:* Thunderbird Campus, Glendale, Ariz. 85301. *Office:* American Graduate School of International Management, Thunderbird Campus, Glendale, Ariz. 85301.

CAREER: University of Utah, Salt Lake City, circulation librarian, 1945-48, reference librarian, 1948-53; American Graduate School of International Management, Glendale, Ariz., librarian, 1953—. *Member:* American Library Association, Arizona State Library Association (secretary, 1960-61), Soroptimist Club.

WRITINGS: International Business and Foreign Trade: A Management Guide, Gale, 1968.

* * *

WHEELER, Penny Estes 1943-

PERSONAL: Born March 31, 1943, in Dallas, Tex.; daughter of James W. (an accountant) and Pauline (Neff) Estes; married Gerald William Wheeler (a book editor), June 18, 1968; children: Robin, Noelle, Bronwen, James. *Education:* Southwestern Union College, A.A., 1964; Andrews University, B.S., 1967. *Home:* Route 2, Valley View Rd., Goodlettsville, Tenn. 37072.

CAREER: Teacher of second grade, Nashville, Tenn., 1967-68.

WRITINGS: Your Career in Elementary Education, Southern Publishing, 1970; *A Time of Tears and Laughter,* Southern Publishing, 1971; *Three for the Show,* Southern Publishing, 1973. Writer of television scripts for religious programs and two series of church youth lessons. Contributor to education and juvenile church magazines.

WORK IN PROGRESS: A collection of stories for juveniles, for Southern Publishing; three additional books for young people.

SIDELIGHTS: Penny Wheeler told CA, "Religious writing for young people—my main field—tends to lack craftsmanship, but I feel that to properly represent its subject [one] should pay even greater attention to quality writing." A number of Wheeler's articles have been published overseas, including some translations into Afrikaans.

* * *

WHEELWRIGHT, Richard 1936-

PERSONAL: Born September 2, 1936, in Covington, Ky.; son of Richard Palmer (a bond cashier) and Edith (Spurlock) Wheelwright; married Carolyn Kelley, September 2, 1961. *Education:* Attended Illinois Institute of Technology, 1954-57; University of Iowa, B.A., 1960, M.F.A., 1969, additional graduate study; also attended graduate courses at University of Cincinnati, summers, 1962-67. *Agent:* Paul R. Reynolds, Inc., 12 East 41st St., New York, N.Y. 10017.

CAREER: Math and English teacher at Dixie Heights High School, Fort Mitchell, Ky., 1960-63, Holly Lodge Grammar School, Smethwick, England, 1963-64, and Verde Valley

School, Sedona, Ariz., 1964-67; University of Iowa, Iowa City, member of Writers' Workshop, 1968—, instructor in television and film and film adviser, 1974—. Screenwriter, The Cannon Group, Inc. (producer of theatrical films), New York, N.Y., 1970—. *Awards, honors:* Academy of Motion Picture Arts and Sciences film writing fellowship, 1972.

WRITINGS: Jump (novel), Paperback Library, 1971. Also author of *Steppingstone,* 1971, and, with W. P. Fox, of *The Great Southern Amusement Company,* 1972; author of screenplays, "Jump," Cannon Group, 1971, and "The Man Who Fell to Earth," Cannon Group, 1972. Contributor of short stories to literary magazines.

WORK IN PROGRESS: A novel and screenplay, *Vigilantes.*

SIDELIGHTS: Richard Wheelwright has lived and traveled widely in Europe, is competent in French and Old English. While teaching at the Verde Valley School in Arizona, a private college prep school with an anthropology-centered curriculum, he conducted anthropological study trips to Mexico and to Hopi and Navajo reservations. He is "very interested in the math of probabilities," and the sciences.†

* * *

WHITBURN, Joel Carver 1939-

PERSONAL: Born November 29, 1939, in Wauwatosa, Wis.; son of Russell and Ruth (Bird) Whitburn; married Frances Mudgett, April 25, 1964; children: Kim Marie. *Education:* Attended Elmhurst College, 1957-58, and University of Wisconsin—Milwaukee, 1958-60. *Religion:* Protestant. *Home and office address:* P.O. Box 200, Menomonee Falls, Wis. 53051.

CAREER: Carnation-Miller Brewing Can Co., Milwaukee, Wis., office manager, 1964-68; Taylor Electric Co., Milwaukee, member of sales and record promotion staff, 1968-70.

*WRITINGS—*Published by Record Research, except as indicated: *Record Research, 1955-1969,* 1970, supplement, 1971, published as *Top Pop Records, 1955-1970,* Gale, 1972, annual supplements, 1973—; *Top Country & Western Records, 1949-1971,* 1972, annual supplements, 1973—; *Top Pop Records, 1940-1955,* 1973; *Top Rhythm & Blues Records, 1949-1971,* 1973, annual supplements, 1973—; *Joel Whitburn's Top LP's, 1945-1972,* 1973, annual supplements, 1973—; *Joel Whitburn's Top Easy Listening Records, 1961-1974,* 1975, annual supplements, 1975—.

WORK IN PROGRESS: Revised editions of *Top Pop Records, 1955-1970, Top Country & Western Records, 1949-1971,* and *Top Rhythm & Blues Records, 1949-1971.*

SIDELIGHTS: Joel Whitburn collects all records listed in his books and has over 12,000 in his personal collection.

* * *

WILLEFORD, Charles (Ray III) 1919-
(Will Charles)

PERSONAL: Born January 2, 1919, in Little Rock, Ark.; son of Charles Ray II and Aileen (Lowey) Willeford; married Mary Jo Norton (an English professor), July 1, 1951 (divorced, October, 1976). *Education:* Palm Beach Junior College, A.A., 1960; University of Miami, A.B. (magna cum laude), 1962, M.A., 1964. *Office:* Department of English, Miami-Dade Junior College, 1101 104th St. S.W., Miami, Fla. 33157.

CAREER: U.S. Army, 1936-56, retiring as master sergeant; University of Miami, Coral Gables, Fla., instructor in humanities, 1964-67; Miami-Dade Junior College, Miami, Fla., assistant professor, 1967-68, chairman of departments of English and philosophy, 1968-70, associate professor of English, 1970—. *Member:* Authors League of America, Mystery Writers of America, Vorpal Blades. *Awards, honors*—Military: Silver Star; Bronze Star; Purple Heart; Luxembourg Croix de Guerre. Civilian: Beacon Fiction award, 1956, for *Pick-Up;* Mark Twain Award, Mark Twain Society of America, 1973, for *Cockfighter.*

WRITINGS: Proletarian Laughter (poems), Alicat Bookshop Press, 1948; ''The Saga of Mary Miller'' (radio serial), broadcast by WLKH and AKAH, Armed Forces Radio Service, 1948; *High Priest of California,* Beacon Publication Corp., 1953; *Until I Am Dead,* Beacon Publication Corp., 1954; *Pick-Up,* Beacon Publication Corp., 1955; *Lust Is a Woman,* Beacon Publication Corp., 1956; ''The Basic Approach'' (television play), networked by Canadian Broadcasting Corp., 1956; *The Black Mass of Brother Springer,* Beacon Publication Corp., 1958; *The Director,* N-L Publishers, 1960; *Understudy,* N-L Publishers, 1961; *The Machine in Ward Eleven,* Belmont Books, 1963; *Poontang and Other Poems,* New Athenean Press, 1967; (under pseudonym Will Charles) *The Hombre from Sonora,* Lenox Hill, 1971; *The Burnt Orange Heresy,* Crown, 1971; *Cockfighter,* Crown, 1972; *A Guide for the Undehemorrhoided* (autobiography), Star Publishing, 1977. Also author of ''Born to Kill'' (screenplay), 1974. Columnist for *Village Post* and *Miami Herald;* contributor of fiction and nonfiction to *Books Abroad, Saturday Review, Playboy, Writer's Digest, Pageant, Sports Illustrated, Gent, Nugget, Air Force,* and other publications. Associate editor, *Alfred Hitchcock Mystery Magazine,* 1964.

WORK IN PROGRESS: A biography, *Jim Tully: The Underworld Years;* a novel, *The Shark–Infested Custard.*

SIDELIGHTS: Charles Willeford writes to *CA:* ''The turning point in my career occurred in October, 1959, when my long short story, 'The Machine in Ward Eleven,' was published in *Playboy.* Prior to that time I had been advised by editors, writing teachers, and by other writers that it was impossible to have an insane person as a sympathetic hero. I did not believe them, because I had a hunch that madness was a predominant theme and a normal condition for Americans living in the second half of this century. The publication of 'The Machine in Ward Eleven' and its reception by readers confirmed what I had only heretofore suspected. Since then, of course, it has been reconfirmed for me many times, and by many contemporary writers and films and plays; but the acceptance of this condition does not mean that I am overjoyed by it. Happiness as a writer is still hard to come by in a nation where tranquilizers like valium outsell aspirin. At any rate, it was the understanding and the acceptance of the madness of our times that enabled me to write my best novel to date, *The Burnt Orange Heresy.*''

BIOGRAPHICAL/CRITICAL SOURCES: Harper's, October, 1971.

*   *   *

WINCHELL, Walter   1897-1972

April 7, 1897—February 20, 1972; American journalist, radio commentator, and gossip columnist. Obituaries: *New York Times,* February 21, 1972; *Washington Post,* February 22, 1972; *Variety,* February 23, 1972; *Newsweek,* March 6, 1972; *Time,* March 6, 1972; *Current Biography,* April, 1972.

WITTKOWER, Rudolf   1901-1971

June 22, 1901—October 11, 1971; German-born educator and art historian. Obituaries: *New York Times,* October 12, 1971.

*   *   *

WOLFSON, Victor   1910-
(Langdon Dodge)

PERSONAL: Born March 8, 1910, in New York, N.Y.; son of Adolph (a newspaper and candy store proprietor and boarding house operator) and Rebecca (a seamstress; maiden name, Hochstein) Wolfson; married Alice L. Dodge (an administrative assistant), March 21, 1942; children: Martin, Nicholas, John (deceased), Thomas. *Education:* University of Wisconsin, B.A., 1931. *Home:* 549 East 86th St., New York, N.Y. 10028.

CAREER: Novelist and playwright; began theatre career as assistant stage manager on Broadway for Elmer Rice's play, ''Counsellor-at-Law,'' 1932; followed this with other writing, directing, and producing jobs. Instructor in playwrighting at New York University, New York, N.Y., 1941-42. Member of executive board of Theatre Union, 1933-36. *Member:* Dramatists Guild (member of council, 1941-56; secretary, 1943-46), Authors League of America (representative to council, 1947—), P.E.N., Writers Guild of America, East. *Awards, honors:* Emmy Award, National Academy of Television Arts and Sciences, 1961, for television documentary, ''Winston Churchill—The Valiant Years.''

WRITINGS: The Lonely Steeple (novel), Simon & Schuster, 1945; *The Eagle on the Plain* (novel), Simon & Schuster, 1947; (under pseudonym Langdon Dodge) *Midsummer Madness* (mystery novel), published for the Crime Club by Doubleday, 1950; *My Prince! My King!,* P. Davies, 1962; *The Man Who Cared: A Life of Harry S. Truman* (juvenile), Farrar, Straus, 1966; *The Mayerling Murder: The Assassination of Crown Prince Rudolph of Austria,* Prentice-Hall, 1969; *Cabral* (novel), Avon, 1972.

Plays: (With Victor Trivas) ''Crime and Punishment'' (adapted from the work by Fedor Dostoevskii), first produced on Broadway at Biltmore Theatre, January 22, 1935; ''Bitter Stream'' (adapted from the novel *Fontamara* by Ignazio Silone), first produced in New York at Civic Repertory Theatre, March 30, 1936; *Excursion* (three-act comedy; first produced in New York at Vanderbilt Theatre, April 9, 1937), Random House, 1937; *Pastoral* (three-act comedy; first produced on Broadway at Henry Miller's Theatre, November 1, 1939), Dramatists Play Service, 1940; ''The Family'' (adapted from the novel by Nina Fedorova), first produced on Broadway at Windsor Theatre, March 30, 1943; ''Love in the City,'' first produced in Cleveland, Ohio, at Cleveland Play House, February, 1947; ''Pride's Crossing,'' first produced on Broadway at Biltmore Theatre, November 20, 1950; ''Murder in the Family,'' first produced in Stockbridge, Mass., at Berkshire Playhouse, July, 1952; ''American Gothic'' (dramatization of his novel, *The Lonely Steeple*), first produced Off-Broadway at Circle in the Square, November 10, 1953; (author of book with Stella Unger) ''Seventh Heaven'' (musical), first produced on Broadway at ANTA Theatre, May 26, 1955; ''Boston Love Story,'' first produced in New Hope, Pa., at Bucks County Playhouse, August, 1958; ''All in the Family'' (adapted from the novel by Marc-Gilbert Sauvejon), first produced on West End at Strand Theatre, June 17, 1959.

Author of television scripts for "Alfred Hitchcock Presents," and "Five Star Matinee," produced by National Broadcasting Co. (NBC), of scripts for "Suspense," "Climax," "The Invisible Man," "Solitaire," "Janet Dean," "Registered Nurse," and "Lineup," produced by Columbia Broadcasting System (CBS), the "FDR" series for American Broadcasting Co. (ABC) and the "Truman" series for WNEW-TV. Author of television documentary, "Winston Churchill—The Valiant Years," produced by ABC in 1960. Also author of radio plays and film scripts. Contributor of short stories to *New Yorker*, *Harper's*, and *McCall's*.

SIDELIGHTS: Victor Wolfson's first novel, *The Lonely Steeple*, a psychological melodrama set in New England, put him "at the top among writers of psychological horror stories," according to T. S. Winslow of *Book Week*. Lewis Funke calls the book "an unpretentious debut and within its scope a commendable one." In a review for *Saturday Review of Literature*, Grace Frank writes: "The author, heretofore known chiefly as a dramatist, has brought to this story some of the qualities especially associated with the theatre: suspense, moving situations, and a problem not finally resolved until the last act. But his mastery of his material, his creation of character and atmosphere, the tightness of his whole design, these belong to the best traditions of the novel as well as the play, and they show him to be an accomplished and distinguished craftsman in the art of fiction."

A village in the Catskills is the setting for Wolfson's second novel, *The Eagle on the Plain*, described by Diana Trilling of *Nation* as both "a folk story of life in a poor little backroads community" and "a fable of freedom . . . at once truly touching and uncomfortably inflated." B. R. Redman writes that "Wolfson leads us by enticing ways from broad comedy to matters not at all comical, from humorous realism to something very like allegory. He does this with much skill, and with notable success."

AVOCATIONAL INTERESTS: Walking, painting.

BIOGRAPHICAL/CRITICAL SOURCES: Book Week, September 16, 1945; *New York Times*, September 23, 1945; *Saturday Review of Literature*, October 20, 1945, July 26, 1947; *New Yorker*, July 26, 1947; *Nation*, August 23, 1947; *New York Times Book Review*, May 8, 1966.

*   *   *

WRIGHT, Irene Aloha   1879-1972

December 19, 1879—April 6, 1972; American historian on Spain and the Caribbean. Obituaries: *New York Times*, April 8, 1972; *Washington Post*, April 8, 1972.

*   *   *

WYLIE, Philip (Gordon)   1902-1971

May 12, 1902—October 25, 1971; American novelist, essayist, and short story writer. Obituaries: *Detroit Free Press*, October 26, 1971; *New York Times*, October 26, 1971; *Washington Post*, October 26, 1971; *Publishers Weekly*, November 1, 1971; *Time*, November 8, 1971. (See index for *CA* sketch)

*   *   *

YEHOSHUA, Abraham B.   1936-

PERSONAL: Given name sometimes is spelled Avraham; born December 9, 1936, in Jerusalem; son of Yakov (an Orientalist) and Malka (Rosilio) Yehoshua; married Rivka Kirsninski (a clinical psychologist at Haifa-Clinic for Mental Health), June 14, 1960; children: Sivan, Gideon, Naum.

Education: Hebrew University of Jerusalem, B.A., 1961, graduate of Teachers College, 1962. *Politics:* Labor. *Religion:* Jewish. *Home:* 102A Sea Rd., Haifa, Israel. *Office:* Department of Literature, Haifa University, Haifa, Israel.

CAREER: Hebrew University of Jerusalem High School, Jerusalem, Israel, teacher, 1961-63; Israeli School, Paris, France, director, 1963-64; World Union of Jewish Students, Paris, secretary-general, 1964-67; Haifa University, Haifa, Israel, dean of students, 1967-71, senior lecturer, 1971-77, professor of literature, 1977—. Lecturer on tour of American college and university campuses, 1969; visiting fellow, St. gcross College, Oxford, 1975-76. Member of board of art, Haifa Municipal Theatre. Adviser to drama editorial board, Israeli Television Network. *Military service:* Israel Army, paratrooper in Nachtal unit, 1954-57. *Awards, honors:* Akum Prize, 1961; second prize in Kol-Yisrael Competition, 1964, for radio script, "The Professor's Secret"; Municipality of Ramat-Gan Prize, 1968, for short story collection, *Mul ha-ye'arot;* University of Iowa fellowship in international literature program, 1969; Prime Minister Prize, 1972.

WRITINGS: Mot ha-zaken (short story collection; title means "The Death of an Old Man"), [Tel Aviv], 1962; *Mul ha-ye'arot* (short story collection; title means "Over Against the Woods"), [Israel], 1968; *Three Days and a Child* (short stories), translated by Miriam Arad, Doubleday, 1970; *Early in the Summer of 1970* (novella), Schocken, 1972, Doubleday, 1977; *Two Plays: A Night in May and Last Treatment* ("A Night in May" first produced in Tel-Aviv by "Bimot" Theatre, 1969), Schocken, 1974; *Until Winter* (short story collection), Hakibbutz, 1974; *The Lover* (novel), Schocken, 1977.

His short stories, which have been appearing in journals and newspapers since 1957, have been included in anthologies published in Hebrew, French, English, Danish, Spanish, and Norwegian. Member of editorial board, *Keshet* (literary magazine), 1967—, and *Siman Kria*.

SIDELIGHTS: Reviewing *Three Days and a Child*, Eisig Silberschlag writes that Abraham Yehoshua is "a surrealist with an admiration for realists . . . a new, authentic voice in Israeli literature—a representative voice of the injured and insulted in an alien world." Gila Ramras-Rauch says that in this collection of short stories "Yehoshua eliminates the setting of specific time and place, so that the individual is set against a surreal background. The influence of Kafka and Agnon is apparent here; it was felt especially in his first stories. Like those teachers of his, he writes modern fables which take place in no-place and no-time. This serves a double purpose: to avoid the complexities of modern pluralistic existence, and to display the abyss between man and time."

In a review of *Early in the Summer of 1970* Anatole Broyard calls Yehoshua's stories "a brilliant evocation of one face of life in Israel. An orderly disorder, an emergency accepted almost casually in a life of emergencies, a generation pushed by history beyond surprise—and behind them, another generation, upset by everything, burdened with ideas and emotions like refugees fleeing with as much of their belongings as they can carry. In the no-man's-land between these two generations, between Israel's past and its future, Mr. Yehoshua finds the tension that informs his remarkable work."

Abraham Yehoshua's works have been translated into numerous languages, including Korean, Japanese, and Swedish. *Three Days and a Child* and *Early in the Summer of 1970* have been produced as films ("Three Days and a Child" was chosen to represent Israel at the Cannes Film Festival).

BIOGRAPHICAL/CRITICAL SOURCES: Books Abroad, spring, 1971; New York Times, February 4, 1977.

* * *

YIP, Wai-lim 1937-
(Wei-lien Yeh)

PERSONAL: Born June 20, 1937, in Kwangtung, China; son of Yuk-man and Chi-hing (Leung) Yip; married Tzu-mei Liao, September 7, 1961; children: June, Jonas. Education: National Taiwan University, B.A., 1959; Taiwan Normal University, M.A., 1961; University of Iowa, M.F.A., 1964; Princeton University, Ph.D., 1967. Religion: None. Office: Department of Literature, University of California at San Diego, La Jolla, Calif. 92038.

CAREER: University of California, San Diego, La Jolla, assistant professor of Chinese and comparative literature, 1967—. Member: Modern Literature and Arts Association (Hong Kong). Awards, honors: Poetry award from Ch'uang-shih-chi, 1965, for ''Chiang-lin'' (English version of poem appeared as ''Descending'' in Trace, 1953); literary prize from Taiwan Ministry of Education, 1971, for Order's Growth, a book of critical essays.

WRITINGS: Fu-ke (title means ''Fugue''; poems), Modern Literature Press (Taiwan), 1964; Ezra Pound's ''Cathay'', Princeton University Press, 1969; Hsien-hsiang Ching-yen Piao-hsien (title means ''Phenomenon, Experience, Expression''), Culture House (Hong Kong), 1969, published in Taiwan as Essays on Modern Chinese Fiction, Morning Bell Press, 1970; Ch'ou-tu (title means ''Grief: Crossing''; poems), Cactus (Taiwan), 1969; Modern Chinese Poetry: Poets from the Republic of China, University of Iowa Press, 1970; Chih-hsu ti Sheng-chang (title means ''Order's Growth''; critical essays), Chih-wen Press, 1971; Hiding the Universe: Poems of Wang Wei, Mushinsha-Grossman (New York), 1972; Hsing-chih-pien-yuan (title means ''Edge of Waking''; poems, paintings, mixed-media with record), Universe (Taiwan), 1972; Yeh-Wei-lein Tzu-hsuan-chi (poems), Li Ming Press, 1974; Yeh-hua ti ku-ssu (title means ''The Wild Flower Story''), Chung-wai wen-hsueh Press, 1974; Chung-shy Ke-ch'ang, Li Ming Press, 1976; Chinese Poetry: Major Modes and Genres, VC Press, 1976.

WORK IN PROGRESS: A study of Chinese poetics which may merge with modern poetics.

SIDELIGHTS: Wai-lim Yip (Yeh is an alternate version of his name in Chinese) has ''been very much involved in the making of modern, and particularly avant-garde, Chinese poetry.'' He says that he became a bilingual poet by chance, and remains a bilingual poet. He has been translating the work of T. S. Eliot, St. John Perse, and others into Chinese, modern Chinese poets into English, and formulating a theory of translation. Yip told CA he ''is responsible for a new articulation of the aesthetic of mixed-media in Taiwan.''

* * *

YOUNG, Chesley Virginia 1919-
(Chesley Virginia Barnes)

PERSONAL: Born September 7, 1919, in Hamburg, Ark.; daughter of Lewis Chesley (a physician) and Winifred Elimer (Massey) Barnes; married Morris N. Young (a physician and author), 1948; children: Cheryl Lesley Viling, Charles Chesley. Education: University of Arkansas, B.A., 1947; Columbia University, M.A., 1951. Religion: Methodist. Home: 270 Riverside Dr., New York, N.Y. 10025. Office: 2 Fifth Ave., New York, N.Y. 10011.

CAREER: Statistician for U.S. Civil Service in Washington, D.C. and Cincinnati, Ohio, 1941-42; New York City Board of Education, New York, N.Y., teacher in childhood education, 1954-67. President, Denton & Haskins Corp. (music company); vice-president, Intercollegiate Syndicate, Inc. (music company); secretary, Gem Music Corp. Military service: U.S. Army, Women's Army Corps, 1942-45; became captain; received WAAC medal, American Campaign medal, World War II Victory Medal, EAME Campaign Medal with one battle star, Unit Meritorious service placque. Member: American Society of Composers, Authors and Publishers, National Women's Party, Daughters of the American Revolution (regent, New York City), Horticultural Society, Manhattan Business and Professional Women's Club (president, 1949-51), Washington Square Business and Professional Women's Club, Friends of Joan of Arc (president, 1965-68), Women's Auxiliary of New York Polyclinic Hospital and Medical School (president, 1970-71), Women's Auxiliary of Beekman Downtown Hospital, Chester County (Pa.) Historical Society, D. & H. Canal Historical Society, Zeta Tau Alpha, Kappa Delta Pi (honorary), Pi Kappa.

WRITINGS: (With husband, Morris N. Young) How to Read Faster and Remember More, Parker Publishing, 1965; The Magic of a Mighty Memory, Parker Publishing, 1971. Composer of songs, ''Have You'' (with Barnard A. Young), 1949, and ''Come On, Come to the Fair'' (with son and daughter, Charles and Cheryl Young), 1963.

Editor, under name Chesley Virginia Barnes: Wilfred Jonson, Card Tricks, Dover, 1952; Wilfred Jonson, Magic Tricks, Dover, 1952.

WORK IN PROGRESS: Research on the genealogy of several families and on the American Revolution; assembling, with husband, Morris N. Young, their memory and mnemonics collection; an American historical novel.

SIDELIGHTS: Chesley Virginia Young told CA she has assembled, with her husband, ''the world's largest collection of illusion practices,'' which has been donated in part to the Library of Congress and the libraries of the University of Texas and University of California, Berkeley.

AVOCATIONAL INTERESTS: Music.

* * *

YOUNG, Morris N. 1909-

PERSONAL: Born July 20, 1909, in Lawrence, Mass.; son of Charles Michael (a merchant) and Ida (Davis) Young; married Chesley Virginia Barnes (an author and educator), 1948; children: Cheryl Lesley Viling, Charles Chesley. Education: Massachusetts Institute of Technology, B.S., 1930; Harvard University, M.A., 1931; Columbia University, M.D., 1935. Home: 270 Riverside Dr., New York, N.Y. 10025. Office: 170 Broadway, New York, N.Y. 10038.

CAREER: Queens General Hospital, Long Island, N.Y., intern, 1935-37; Harlem Eye and Ear Hospital, New York City, resident in ophthalmology, 1938-40; ophthalmologist in private practice in New York City, 1940—; University Hospital, New York City, assistant attending in ophthalmology, 1947-61; French & Polyclinic Medical School and Health Center, New York City, attending and professor in ophthalmology, 1958—; Beekman Downtown Hospital, New York City, chief ophthalmologist. 1970—. Consultant in ophthalmology, Beth Israel Medical Center, 1972—. Diplomate of American Board of Ophthalmology. Medical adviser to Director of Selective Service, New York City, 1956—. Mili-

tary service: U.S. Army Reserve, 1930-69; served on active duty, 1941-45; became colonel in Medical Corps; received EAME Campaign Medal, World War II Victory Medal, two battle stars, American Defense Service Medal, American Campaign Medal, Meritorious Service Medal, Army Reserve Medal.

MEMBER—Professional societies: American Medical Association, Society of Eye Surgeons, American Academy of Compensation Medicine, American Academy of Ophthalmology and Otolaryngology, American Association of Ophthalmology, Association for Research in Vision and Ophthalmology, Association of Military Surgeons of the United States (Manhattan Executive Council), National Society for the Prevention of Blindness, New York State Association of the Professions, New York State Medical Society, New York State Ophthalmological Society, New York Society of Surgeons, Inc., New York County Medical Society, Pan American Ophthalmological Foundation, Pan American Medical Association, Reserve Officers Association, Retired Officers Association, Society of Military Ophthalmologists, Contact Lens Association of Ophthalmologists, Association of Harvard Chemists, Clinical Society of New York Polyclinic Hospital, Queens General Hospital Alumni Association.

Nonprofessional societies: Memory Research Center, Society of American Magicians, International Brotherhood of Magicians, Magic Collectors Association (founder), Magic Circle (London; associate, Inner Magic Circle), Grecian Lodge (Mass.), National Sojourners (Manhattan; former president), Heroes of '76 Martyrs Camp (former commander), D & H Canal Historical Society, Order of Lafayette. *Awards, honors:* New York State Military Masonic Veteran of the year, 1968; Sovereign Order of St. John of Jerusalem (Knight of Malta).

WRITINGS: Hobby Magic, Trilon Press, 1950; (editor with Walter B. Gibson) *Houdini on Magic,* Dover, 1954; *Bibliography of Memory,* Chilton, 1961; (with Gibson) *Houdini's Fabulous Magic,* Chilton, 1961; (with Gibson) *How to Develop an Exceptional Memory,* Chilton, 1962; (with wife, Chesley Virginia Young) *How to Read Faster and Remember More,* Parker Publishing, 1965; (with John Stolfus) *The Complete Guide to Science Fair Competition,* Hawthorn, 1972. Author of Columbia University song, with Arnold P. Guerriero and Carlton Bates, "The Lion's Loose Again." Contributor of numerous articles to *Military Surgeon, Bulletin* of the U.S.A. Medical Department, *Archives of Otolaryngology,* and to magic publications. Editor, *Magicol* (magic collectors magazine), 1949-52; editor, *Nyamsus* newsletter, 1968-70.

Also author of text, "The Story of Blackstone's Party Magic on Records," Life Music Corp., 1950.

WORK IN PROGRESS: Assembling, with wife, Chesley Virginia Young, memory and mnemonics collection; a book on popular music.

AVOCATIONAL INTERESTS: Music.

* * *

YOUNGS, Betty F(errell) 1928-

PERSONAL: Born February 15, 1928, in Durham, N.C.; daughter of Rufus F. (a barber shop owner) and Ora Ethel (Walker) Ferrell; married Paul A. Youngs (a college physics teacher), August 23, 1966; children: Douglas Lee (stepson). *Education:* Mars Hill College, A.A., 1949; George Peabody College for Teachers, B.S., 1952; Columbia University, ad-

ditional study, 1961; Arizona State University, Tempe, M.A., 1971. *Religion:* Baptist. *Home:* 6310 West Fairmount Ave., Phoenix, Ariz. 85033.

CAREER: Baptist Board, Nashville, Tenn., editorial assistant, 1950-54, style editor, vocational guidance consultant, and editor of vocational guidance materials, 1958-66; First Baptist Church, Durham, N.C., pastor's assistant, 1954-57; State Baptist Board, Raleigh, N.C., assistant to state missions director, 1957-58. *Member:* National Religious Public Relations Associations, American Personnel and Guidance Association (associate), Tennessee Guidance Association, Theta Sigma Phi.

WRITINGS: Let's Explore Jobs (juvenile), Broadman, 1971; *What's Bugging You?,* Broadman, 1973. Contributor of articles to national publications.

WORK IN PROGRESS: A book on career guidance for teenagers.

AVOCATIONAL INTERESTS: Music, reading, golf, homemaking.

* * *

ZARRO, Richard A(llen) 1946-

PERSONAL: Born September 18, 1946; son of Eugene (a sales engineer) and Vita (Monterroso) Zarro. *Education:* Attended Miami University, Oxford, Ohio, for two years; Columbia University, creative writing fellow, 1971-72.

CAREER: Has worked as a journalist, *Newark Evening News,* Newark, N.J., a creative director, Promotion Center, New York City, an associate editor, Photographic Trade News Publishing Co., New York City, and a writer for "Knowledge Mod Style," a syndicated radio show produced by Jennings Radio Corp., New York City. Photographer, poet, and artist. Has had exhibitions of artwork at Montclair Community Art Show, N.J., 1969, International Visual Poetry Exhibit in Paris and London, 1969, Brooklyn Museum Art School (graphics), 1970, Walcott-Fields Gallery, New York City, 1970, Oppegard Gallery, New York City, 1970 and 1971, and other shows. Has read poetry and performed at churches, universities, cafes, theatres, and on radio in New York City. *Military service:* Conscientious objector. *Awards, honors:* Brooklyn Museum Art School study grant, 1970-71; Doubleday/Columbia Creative Writing Award, 1971, for novel "A Time for Silence: Between the Coming In and the Coming Out."

WRITINGS: The King of Numbers (fable for adults & children), Jarrow Press, 1971; *Cosmic Telegram # 777 and Ode to Madame Joy* (poetry, photos, etchings), Mother & Child Reunion Press, 1971; (contributor) John Price, editor, *Life Show* (photographic anthology), Bantam, 1971; (editor with Hugh Seidman) *Westbeth Poetry Anthology,* IF Press, 1971. Editor of *Aquarian Angel* ("a new age primer and catalogue"), Harper; also author of screenplay based on his novel, "A Time for Silence: Between the Coming In and the Coming Out," produced by Togg Films in 1972; author of dialogue for film, "Another America."

Author of several unpublished volumes of poetry, including: "Fractured Passiontunes and Other Scenes of Desolation Approaching a Near Illusion," "Nothing New under the Sun-Memoirs of a Black Circus," "That's That or the Coming Attractions of the Third Order," "Songs of Debeve," "Enough Is Enough or Another Invitation to a Journey," "Sounds of Light or Remembering That I Had to Learn to Sleep." Author of an unpublished novel, "A Time for Silence: Between the Coming In and the Coming Out," and two children/adult fables, "A Town without Sound" and "Jairus and the Golden Flame." Contributor of photographs to *Stereo Review* and to photographic trade news publications; contributor to *New Philosophy, Corduroy,* and other journals. Poetry editor, *Woodstock Aquarian;* book reviewer, *Newark Evening News,* 1969.

WORK IN PROGRESS: A novel, *Transit Zero;* an epic poem, *The Great Procession; Transit Zero* research on the Apocalypse, tarot cards, Second Coming, Spiritual Awareness, Cosmic Consciousness, paraphysics.

SIDELIGHTS: Richard Zarro told *CA:* "I have started a foundation designed to handle the problems of world growth outlined in the Potomac Association Book *Limits to Growth.* The Transformation Foundation is dedicated to the education of our society from Self-consciousness to World or Cosmic consciousness. Spiritual awareness and evolutionary growth are both the interests of my art and its guiding force." Zarro has acted in two films: he plays the role of a revolutionary in "Another America," produced in 1972, and is a priest in "The Sacrifice," released by Togg Films in 1972.††

*   *   *

ZIM, Sonia Bleeker   1909-1971
(Sonia Bleeker)

November 28, 1909—November 13, 1971; Russian-born American author of youth books on Indians. Obituaries: *Publishers Weekly,* December 20, 1971. (See index for *CA* sketch)

*   *   *

ZWERENZ, Gerhard   1925-
(Peer Tarrok)

PERSONAL: Born June 3, 1925, in Crimmitschau, Saxony; son of Rudolf and Liesbeth (Wiedl) Zwerenz; married Ingrid Hoffmann, January 22, 1957; children: Catharina. *Education:* Studied at University of Leipzig, 1952-56, mainly in the department of philosophy under Ernst Bloch. *Politics:* "No party." *Religion:* "Without religion."

CAREER: Trained as a coppersmith; soldier in German Army and then Soviet prisoner, 1942-48; policeman, 1948-50; teacher, 1950-51; full-time writer, 1956—. Speaker at universities in Germany and participant in conferences. *Member:* International P.E.N.

WRITINGS: Aristotelische und Brechtsche Dramatik, Greifenverlag, 1956; *Magie, Sternenglaube, Spiritismus: Streifzuege durch den Aberglauben* (on occult sciences), Urania-Verlag, 1956; *Aufs Rad geflochten* (novel), Kiepenheuer & Witsch, 1959; *Die Liebe der toten Maenner* (novel), Kiepenheuer & Witsch, 1959.

Aergernisse: Von der Maas bis an die Memel (political diary), Kiepenheuer & Witsch, 1961; *Wider die deutschen Tabus* (on the Allied occupation), P. List, 1962; *Gesaenge auf dem Markt: Phantastische Geschichten und Liebeslieder,* Kiepenheuer & Witsch, 1962; *Heldengedenktag: Dreizehn Versuche in Prosa, eine ehrerbietige Haltung einzunehmen,* Scherz, 1964, translation by Eric Mosbacher

published as *Remembrance Day: Thirteen Attempts in Prose to Adopt an Attitude of Respect,* Dutton, 1966; *Casanova, oder der Kleine Herr in Krieg und Frieden* (novel), Scherz, 1966, translation by William Whitman published as *Casanova, Or Little Peter in War and Peace,* Grove Press, 1970; *Walter Ulbricht* (biography), Scherz, 1966; *Vom Nutzen des dicken Fells und andere Geschichten* (stories), Goldmann, 1968; *Erbarmen mit den Maennern* (novel), Scherz, 1968; *Kupfer* (comedy), Scherz, 1968; *Die Lust am Sozialismus* (on student political activity), H. Heine, 1969.

(Under pseudonym Peer Tarrok) *Rasputin* (novel), Melzer Verlag, 1970; *Kopf und Bauch: Die Geschichte eines Arbeiters der unter die Intellektuellen gefallen ist,* S. Fischer, 1971; *Buegertum und Pornographie,* Normalverlag, 1971; *Bericht aus dem Landesinneren: City, Strecke, Siedlung,* S. Fischer, 1972; *Nicht alles gefallen lassen,* S. Fischer, 1972; *Der plebejische Intellektuelle* (essays), S. Fischer, 1972; *Die Erde is unbewohnbar wie der Mond* (novel), S. Fischer, 1973; *Der Widerspruch: Autobiographischer Bericht* (autobiography), S. Fischer, 1974; *Vorbereitungen zur Hochzeit: Erzahlungen,* S. Fischer, 1975; *Die Quadrigs des Mischa Wolf* (novel), S. Fischer, 1975; *Lasst Kinder ran!,* illustrated by Heinz Edelmann, C. Bertelsmann, 1976. His writings are included in a number of anthologies and collections. Occasional contributor to journals and newspapers.†

*   *   *

ZWINGER, Ann   1925-

PERSONAL: Born March 12, 1925, in Muncie, Ind.; daughter of William Thomas (an attorney) and Helen (Glass) Haymond; married Herman H. Zwinger (a photographer and pilot), June 18, 1952; children: Susan, Jane, Sara. *Education:* Wellesley College, B.A., 1946; Indiana University, M.A., 1950; Radcliffe College, further graduate study, 1951-52. *Residence:* Colorado Springs, Colo. *Agent:* Marie Rodell-Fran Collin Agency, 141 East 55th St., New York, N.Y. 10022.

CAREER: Smith College, Northampton, Mass., instructor in art history, 1950-51; Benet Hill Academy, Colorado Springs, Colo., instructor in art 1963-66; currently director, American Electric Power Company. Member of board of trustees, Colorado Springs School; member of board of directors, Firends of the Library, Penrose Public Library, Colorado Springs. *Awards, honors:* Indiana Authors' Day Award, 1971, for nature and ecology writings; John Burroughs Memorial Association Award and Award for Nonfiction, Friends of American Writers, 1976, for *Run, River, Run;* D.H.L., Colorado College, 1976; Alumnae Achievement Award, Wellesley College, 1977; Sara Chapman Francis Medal, Garden Club of America, 1977.

WRITINGS: (Self-illustrated) *Beyond the Aspen Grove,* Random House, 1970; *Land above the Trees,* Harper, 1972; *Run, River, Run,* Harper, 1975.

WORK IN PROGRESS: Wind in the Rock, for Harper.

BIOGRAPHICAL/CRITICAL SOURCES: New York Times Book Review, July 12, 1970; *Harvard,* September, 1975.